~~Wright Studio~~
~~1000~~ 1000 Pembroke St.
Victoria, B.C.

The Norton Anthology
of English Literature
THIRD EDITION

VOLUME 1

The Norton Anthology of English Literature
THIRD EDITION

M. H. Abrams, *General Editor*
Professor of English, Cornell University

E. Talbot Donaldson
Professor of English, Yale University

Hallett Smith
Professor of English, California Institute of Technology

Robert M. Adams
Professor of English, University of California at Los Angeles

Samuel Holt Monk
Professor Emeritus, University of Minnesota

Lawrence Lipking
Professor of English, Princeton University

George H. Ford
Professor of English, University of Rochester

David Daiches
Professor of English, University of Sussex

VOLUME 1

W · W · NORTON & COMPANY · INC · New York

Brief Lives by John Aubrey, edited by Andrew Clark, 1898. Selection reprinted by permission of the Clarendon Press.
Beowulf, a new prose translation by E. Talbot Donaldson. Copyright © 1966 by W. W. Norton & Company, Inc. Reprinted by permission of the publisher.
From *The New English Bible*. © The Delegates of the Oxford University Press and The Syndics of the Cambridge University Press 1970. Selection reprinted by permission.
The Book of Beasts, by T. H. White. Copyright © 1954 by T. H. White. Selection reprinted by permission of G. P. Putnam's Sons.
Boswell on the Grand Tour: Germany and Switzerland, 1764, edited by Frederick A. Pottle. Copyright © 1928, 1953, by Yale University. Selection reprinted by permission of McGraw-Hill Book Company, Inc.
Chaucer's Poetry: An Anthology for the Modern Reader, edited by E. T. Donaldson. Copyright © 1958 by The Ronald Press Company. Selections reprinted by permission of the publishers.
Utopia, by Thomas More. Translated and edited by H. V. S. Ogden. Copyright © 1949 by AHM Publishing Corporation. Selections reprinted by permission of AHM Publishing Corporation.
The Diary of Samuel Pepys, originally published by University of California Press; selections reprinted by permission of The Regents of the University of California and G. Bell & Sons, Ltd.
"My Cat Jeoffry" from Christopher Smart's poem "Jubilate Agno." Reprinted by permission of Rupert Hart-Davis.
The Poems of Sir Philip Sidney, edited by William A. Ringler, Jr. Copyright © 1962 by Oxford University Press. Selections reprinted by permission of the Clarendon Press, Oxford.
Sir Gawain and the Green Knight, a new verse translation by Marie Borroff. Copyright © 1967 by W. W. Norton & Company, Inc. Reprinted by permission of the publisher.

o 393 09301 8 (Cloth Edition)
o 393 09304 2 (Paper Edition)

All Rights Reserved

Library of Congress Cataloging in Publication Data

Abrams, Meyer Howard, ed.
    The Norton anthology of English literature.
    1. English literature (Collections) I. Title.
PR1109.A22   1974   820'.8   73–19982

Published simultaneously in Canada
by George J. McLeod Limited, Toronto

Book design by John Woodlock

PRINTED IN THE UNITED STATES OF AMERICA

3 4 5 6 7 8 9 0

Contents

v

The Sixteenth Century (1485–1603)   475

Contents · ix

xvi · *Contents*

The Restoration and the
Eighteenth Century (1660–1798)

The Table of Contents for Volume 2 will be found on page 2483.

Preface
to the Third Edition

The Norton Anthology was invented for use in the indispensable course designed to introduce students to the greatness, continuity, and variety of British literature. Its strength is that it is grounded, not on a priori views of what might be taught in such a course, but on long experience in actually teaching it. The first edition of the anthology in 1962 was the product of more than a decade of experimentation with the introductory course by several of the editors, who then proceeded to test the book in their continued teaching. Ever since its publication, we have received a steady stream of suggestions—some of them solicited, but most volunteered—from hundreds of users, who view the anthology with a loyal but critical eye. This third edition is thus the product of a sustained collaboration between editors, teachers, and their students.

The changes in this edition are in line with recent scholarly discoveries and important shifts in critical interests. All of the changes, however, are guided by the principles that were established for the original edition. These are: (1) that the selection make possible a study in depth of the major British writers in verse and prose (now including novelists), in the context of the chief literary modes and traditions of their age; (2) that the representation be copious enough to allow each instructor to select the works that he prefers to teach; (3) that the student be given the most accurate possible texts, edited so as to make them immediately accessible and printed in a format that is easy to the hand and inviting to the eye; (4) that the editorial introductions and glosses be adequate to make an understanding of the texts independent of dictionaries and reference books, so that the book can be read anywhere—in the student's room, in a coffee lounge, or under a tree; and (5) that it be light and comfortably portable, on the ground that if students won't carry their anthology to class, lectures and discussions lose a major part of their value.

A scattering of selections, which a canvass of teachers revealed to be assigned infrequently or not at all, have been omitted; a very much greater number have been added. Among the medieval additions are Chaucer's early *Parliament of Fowls* and two more of his *Canterbury Tales*, as well as a third drama (*Abraham and Isaac*) and a second medieval romance, *Sir Orfeo*, shorter and less sophisticated than *Sir Gawain and the Green Knight,* which we retain. There are important additions to Spenser and to a number of 16th- and 17th-century poets. We have added a number of new prose writers for the same periods, and reviewed those that we have retained; more importantly, we have organized them according to their major concerns, so that for the first time a student is enabled to see a development both in style and in content for writers who are generally given short shrift in anthologies. Four Books of *Paradise Lost* (I, II, III, and IX) are reprinted in their totality, together with an increased representation of the other Books; while *Gulliver's Travels*, with the addition to Parts II and IV of Part I and the central passages of Part III, is now virtually complete. Other additions in the 18th century are Pope's *Eloisa to Abelard* and the Fourth Book of his *Dunciad,* as well as selections from John Gay, from Anne Finch (Countess of Winchilsea), from the Earl of Rochester, from the long poems of Christopher Smart, and from the prose writings of Johnson and Burke. There are several new poems (including parts of *Jerusalem*) and two important letters by William Blake. In accordance with our policy to include newly discovered masterpieces (our second edition made available Wordsworth's hitherto unpublished *Ruined Cottage*), we introduce, from manuscript, the whole of Wordsworth's earliest version of *The Prelude*, which he wrote in two parts in 1798–99—a work that can be read either as a very great independent poem or in comparison with our expanded selections from *The Prelude* of 1850, to which the passages in the *Two-Part Prelude* are keyed by footnote references. The anthology now includes substantial selections from Dorothy Wordsworth's great *Journals* and from De Quincey's *Confessions of an English Opium-Eater,* and new items from the prose writings of Hazlitt, Mill, Ruskin, and Carlyle, as well as a number of additional poems by Coleridge (including *This Lime-Tree Bower, The Pains of Sleep, Limbo*), Shelley (including the complete *Alastor*), Byron (the whole of an English Canto of *Don Juan,* the last that Byron wrote), Keats (all five of his great *Odes* are now reprinted), Tennyson (two complete *Idylls of the King*), Browning (an added dramatic monologue), Swinburne, and D. H. Lawrence. The representation of contemporary poetry has also been expanded; it now contains substantial selections from two poets who have attained a

major status—Hugh MacDiarmid and David Jones—and a new section of ten poets who have done their most important work since
the mid-20th century.

The addition of a number of new plays provides a comprehensive
overview of English drama, from *Everyman* to *Endgame*. There are
now three medieval plays (*Everyman*, *The Second Shepherds' Play*,
and *Abraham and Isaac*) and four Elizabethan and Jacobean
plays; in addition to Marlowe's *Doctor Faustus* and Shakespeare's
Henry IV, Part 1, which we have offered since the first edition, we
now have Shakespeare's *King Lear* and Webster's *Duchess of Malfi*
(to the best of our knowledge, no other anthology of this nature
provides a choice between two Shakespeare plays or the opportunity
to study a masterpiece of the Jacobean period). There are also two
masques (Johnson's *Pleasure Reconciled to Virtue* and Milton's
Comus), a Restoration comedy (*The Way of the World*), selections from two Romantic closet dramas (Shelley's *Prometheus
Unbound* and Byron's *Manfred*), Shaw's *Major Barbara*, and the
concluding scene of Beckett's *Endgame*.

Another notable innovation in this edition stems from our conviction that it is not possible to represent justly the literature of the
Victorian age without exemplifying its major and most distinctive
genre, the novel. Consequently, Dickens and George Eliot are now
given their due status as major writers by self-sufficient excerpts,
chosen in a way adapted to the characteristic procedure of each novelist: Dickens is represented by selections that display his creative
abundance and variety in self-contained dramatic scenes, and
George Eliot is represented by coherent selections from *The Mill
on the Floss* that show, from within the character's own mind,
Maggie Tulliver in the process of growing up from childhood
through adolescence to young womanhood. Other additions, long
and short, now make it possible to study, from materials in the
anthology, the development of prose fiction, from Bunyan's *Pilgrim's
Progress* through Defoe's *Mrs. Veal*, Swift's *Gulliver's Travels*,
the narrative *Spectator Papers*, Johnson's *Rasselas*, and the novels
of Dickens and George Eliot, to a variety of novelists in our
own century. In this last category, two complete short novels have
been added, Conrad's *Heart of Darkness* and Lawrence's *The Fox*
(supplementing two of Lawrence's short stories and a chapter from
The Rainbow); there are short stories by E. M. Forster and Virginia Woolf; a second story, *Clay*, has been included from Joyce's
Dubliners, in addition to the previous excerpts from all three of
Joyce's novels; while new selections from two novels by Samuel
Beckett, together with the scene from *Endgame*, acknowledge Beckett's importance as the most influential of living writers. And by a

triumph of the papermaker's and bookmaker's art, these and other additions have been achieved without materially affecting the essential feature of a Norton anthology—its comfortable size and easy portability.

It should be noted that the new materials greatly enhance the possibilities for using the anthology to study topical, as well as historical and generic, developments in English literature. To cite only a few examples: The visionary mode in literature is now represented by Chaucer's dream-vision, *The Parliament of Fowls*; a new selection from Passus XXI (the "Harrowing of Hell") of *Piers Plowman*; Spenser's "Mutabilitie Cantos"; visionary poems by Crashaw, Vaughan, and Traherne; a new "Topic" on 18th-century theories of genius and the creative imagination; the poetry of Christopher Smart; William Blake's discussions of imaginative vision in prose and his exemplification of such vision in two new poems (*The Mental Traveller* and the opening and apocalyptic conclusion of his greatest "prophecy," *Jerusalem*); Coleridge's *Kubla Khan, The Pains of Sleep*, and *Limbo*; De Quincey's dream visions and dream fugues; Shelley's *Alastor*; Browning's *Childe Roland*; and the poems of Swinburne, Francis Thompson, and Yeats. A central literary form, the spiritual autobiography of crisis and the quest for identity, can now be studied in its major instances, religious and secular, such as Bunyan's *Grace Abounding*, Wordsworth's *Prelude*, Blake's *Jerusalem* (in one dimension of its reference), De Quincey's *Confessions*, Shelley's *Alastor*, Carlyle's *Sartor Resartus*, Mill's *Autobiography*, Tennyson's *In Memoriam*, and T. S. Eliot's *Little Gidding*. And the literature by and about women has been substantially supplemented so that it now includes, among other items, three of "the marriage group" of *The Canterbury Tales*, the Countess of Winchelsea, Anne Radcliffe, Dorothy Wordsworth, George Eliot (an essay on feminist writers of her time, as well as the chapters about Maggie Tulliver growing up in a man's world), selections from John Stuart Mill's *The Subjection of Women* and Tennyson's *Princess*, Elizabeth Barrett Browning, Emily Brontë, Christina Rossetti, Virginia Woolf, Elizabeth Jennings, and Doris Lessing.

Other features of the earlier editions have been retained, and in many instances improved. The Topics in the literary, critical, or intellectual ambience of a period have proved their usefulness as added reading, as illustrations in a lecture, or as starting places for assigned essays. In response to a canvass of teachers, some of the Topics have been dropped, others altered or supplemented, and a new one added. In accordance with our principle that texts for undergraduates should be no less scrupulously accurate than those for scholars, all of the Shelley texts, notoriously unreliable in all the inclusive editions of that poet, have been newly edited from manuscripts and earlier editions by Dr. Donald H. Reiman, and Jonathan

Wordsworth and Stephen Gill have prepared the text of Wordsworth's *Two-Part Prelude* of 1799 from a manuscript that, except for fragments, has never before been published.

All texts are printed in the form which makes them most immediately available to their particular audience. In accordance with this principle, we have normalized spelling and capitalization (and, very sparingly, punctuation) according to modern American usage, but only in cases where the change does not alter semantic, phonological, or metric qualities, nor affect distinctive features of the author's original publication. Thus the verse of Spenser, Burns, Shelley, Hopkins, MacDiarmid, and David Jones, as well as the prose of Dorothy Wordsworth's *Journals*, of Keats's letters, and of the writings of Carlyle, Joyce, and Shaw have been reproduced exactly; and only minor changes necessary for ready intelligibility (mainly in punctuation) have been made in the poems etched by William Blake. The works of Chaucer, as well as other writings in Middle English that are not too difficult for the novice, have also been left in the original language; each word, however, is consistently spelled in that variant of its scribal forms which is closest to modern English.

Each editor has reconsidered and rewritten his introductory essays and has revised his footnotes to take advantage of recent scholarship and also to make them as simple and lucid as possible. In selected instances, editorial headnotes or footnotes briefly indicate possible interpretations of a difficult work or passage. The reason for this procedure is a practical one. The anthology includes some of the most complex and problematic writings in the language, and the normal procedure in teaching the course is to assign a number of texts which there is no time to discuss adequately—or, often, to discuss at all—in the classroom. Our endeavor is to provide a necessary modicum of guidance to the student, but in a fashion that simply opens out possibilities for his independent judgment and that provides, not definitive readings, but points of departure for dialogue in the classroom.

We continue other editorial procedures which have proved their usefulness in the earlier editions. The historical and biographical introductions, although succinct, are sufficiently informative to eliminate the need for supplementary books on the lives of authors and on the literary, social, and cultural history of England. In each introduction we identify at the beginning a few dates which are of crucial importance for orienting the student. After each text, we cite (when known) the date of composition on the left and the date of first publication in book form on the right; in some instances, the latter is preceded by the date of first printing in a periodical. Writings which include a large proportion of unfamiliar words are glossed in the margin, in order that the reader may assimilate the translation without interrupting the flow of his reading. In the limited instances when part of a text has been omitted, that fact is indicated by the word *From* before the title, and the place of the omission in the text is indicated by three asterisks.

The bibliographical guides at the end of each volume, keyed to periods and to the individual authors, are designed to encourage students to read further on their own, and also to serve as points of departure for assigned essays. All the bibliographies have been brought up to date for this third edition. As a convenience to the student who wants to build his own library of literary biography, history, and criticism, the symbol of a dagger indicates all titles currently available in paperback. The glossary of terms has now been considerably expanded under the title "Poetic Forms and Literary Terminology."

To the hundreds of teachers throughout the United States and Canada who have helped us to design and improve these volumes, the editors express their deep gratitude; they are too numerous to list here, but each will recognize the changes that he has suggested. We wish especially to acknowledge the advice of Scott Elledge (Cornell University); Jerome Beaty and J. Paul Hunter (Emory University); Marilyn Gaull (Temple University); Ronald Gottesman (University of Wisconsin at Parkside); Donald Gray (Indiana University); David Kalstone (Rutgers, The State University); Juliet McGrath (University of Rochester); and Hugh Maclean (The State University of New York at Albany). Our greatest debt is to George P. Brockway and John Benedict of W. W. Norton & Company, Inc., as well as to John Francis and Carol Schwab; to Norton's copyediting staff, especially Emily Garlin and Calvin K. Towle; and to James L. Mairs and Roy Tedoff of Norton's production department. All have helped greatly to mitigate the chronic dilemmas in the attempt to represent, justly and accurately, the immense scope of English literature within a single text.

M. H. ABRAMS

The Norton Anthology
of English Literature
THIRD EDITION

VOLUME 1

The Middle Ages

(To 1485)

ca. 450:   Anglo-Saxon Conquest.
597:          St. Augustine arrives in Kent; beginning of Anglo-Saxon conversion to Christianity.
871–899:   Reign of King Alfred.
1066:   Norman Conquest.
ca. 1200:   Beginnings of Middle English literature.
1360–1400:   The summit of Middle English literature: Geoffrey Chaucer; *Piers Plowman*; *Sir Gawain and the Green Knight*.
1485:   William Caxton's printing of Sir Thomas Malory's *Morte Darthur*, one of the first books printed in England.

The medieval period in English literature extends for more than 800 years, from Cædmon's *Hymn* at the end of the 7th century to *Everyman* at the end of the 15th. Historians used to divide this period into two parts, calling the earlier centuries the Dark Ages in order to distinguish their quality from that of the later centuries, when European culture attained one of the summits of its history. Though this distinction is misleading—for the Dark Ages were only relatively dark—it is nevertheless true that the English Middle Ages embraced two quite different periods of literary history, the Old English (or Anglo-Saxon) and the Middle English, sharply divided from each other by the Norman duke William's conquest of the island in 1066. Both English culture and the English language changed radically in the years following this event, and English literature was given a new spirit.

Because it is impossible to read the Old English language without a great deal of study, Old English texts printed in this book are given in translation. Middle English texts such as Chaucer's, written in a dialect which is the ancestor of Modern Standard English, appear in the original, but have been spelled in a way that it is hoped will aid the reader. Middle English texts written in the more difficult regional dialects are given in translation. Analyses of the sounds and grammar of Middle English, and of Old and Middle English prosody, appear at the end of this introduction.

1

THE ANGLO-SAXONS AND THE HEROIC IDEAL

The Anglo-Saxon invasion of the island of Britain which began in the first half of the 5th century was a phase of a great folk migration that had started some centuries earlier and was to continue for several more—the movement of the Germanic tribes from the northeast of Europe into the areas of the Roman Empire to the west, south, and southeast. The so-called Anglo-Saxon invaders of Britain actually consisted of three tribes, the Angles, the Saxons, and the Jutes. Although each was independent, through their common Germanic heritage these tribes were closely allied with one another and with the many other tribes that already had or would in the future overrun much of the old Roman Empire. They shared the same pre-historic ancestors: even in historical times their individual tongues amounted to little other than variant dialects of a common language, while the customs of one tribe differed little from those of another.

In its earliest period Germanic society had been organized by families: the head of the family was the chief of his close kinsmen, and the family formed an independent political entity. With the passing of time, the unit of society tended to grow larger as a number of families united under a single superior chieftain or "king," to use the word derived from the Old Germanic name for chief. But the unit grew to be very large only rarely, when some particularly successful king attracted others to him in order to perform some specific exploit; and such larger unions rarely endured long after the completion of the venture for which they had been formed. The normal order of society was made up of a number of small bands, which, while they did not always live at peace with one another, still shared a sense of community and kinship, especially in the face of a common enemy such as the people whose lands they were invading; but when they had con-quered, their natural political divisiveness reasserted itself. Thus long after the Anglo-Saxons had become settled in Britain, the island was still broken up into a bewildering number of kingdoms, some of them very short-lived, and a coherent union of all Englishmen was not achieved until after the Norman conquest.

The same general organization of many kings coexisting within a common culture had been characteristic of that other migratory people, the Greeks (or, more accurately, Achaeans), who centuries earlier had overrun the region of the eastern Mediterranean. And both to the Achaeans and to the Germanic peoples the ideal of kingly behavior was enormously impor-tant—indeed, it was perhaps the chief spiritual force behind the civiliza-tions they both developed, the creative power that, in their earliest periods, shaped their history and their literature. It is generally called the heroic ideal; and put most simply, the heroic ideal was excellence. The hero-king strove to do better than anyone else the things that an essentially migratory life demanded: to sail a ship through a storm, to swim a river or a bay, to tame a horse, to choose a campsite and set firm defenses, in times of peace even to plow a field or build a hall, but always and above all, to fight. Skill and courage were the primary qualities of a king who should successfully lead his people in battle and sustain them during peace.

In its oldest form, the ideal was appropriate only to kings, but because society was so closely knit, all the more important male members of the tribe tended to imitate it. (Germanic society was wholly dominated by males: women are rarely mentioned in the surviving records of it, and only if they are the wives or daughters of kings.) In general, of course, the heroic ideal of conduct was aristocratic, restricted to the king and his immediate retainers, though without that quality of unreality and remoteness from daily life that we associate with later medieval aristocracy. The king was the active leader of a small number of fellow warriors who, as members of his household, beheld all that he did. A successful king won from his retainers complete loyalty. It was their duty to defend him in battle, to give up their own lives while defending or avenging his. In return the king gave his retainers gifts from the spoil that had been accumulated in warfare. Royal generosity was one of the most important aspects of heroic behavior, for it symbolized the excellence of the king's rule, implying on the one hand that the retainers deserved what they were given because of their loyalty to him, and, on the other, showing that he himself was worthy of such loyalty. The heroic ideal had a very practical bearing on the life of the people whom the king ruled.

While the heroic ideal would win practical success for a king, it had also another, perhaps more important end—enduring fame. In cultures whose religion, unlike Christianity, offers no promise of an afterlife, a name that will live on after one's death serves as the closest substitute for immortality. From this arises the heroic paradox, still latent in our own civilization, that by dying gloriously one may achieve immortality. The poet who could sing the story of his heroic life was, of course, the agent upon whom the hero depended for his fame, and a good poet—or bard, to use the customary term for the poet of heroic life—was a valued member of a primitive court. Alexander is said to have expressed envy of Achilles because he had had a Homer to celebrate his deeds. The poetic form which primitive bards evolved for their heroic narratives is called "epic"; it is characterized by a solemn dignity of tone and elevation of style. Their poems were not written down, but recited aloud from memory, and hence most of them have been lost: in Greek there have survived Homer's two epics, the *Iliad* and the *Odyssey*, while from Germanic culture the chief survivor is the Old English *Beowulf*. But enough has been preserved to show the enduring popularity of heroic stories throughout the migratory phase of the two peoples, who never tired of hearing the deeds of their folk heroes. Thus the immortality that the old heroes had sought was achieved through poetry, and poetry in turn gave inspiration to later men in leading their own lives.

CHRISTIANITY AND OLD ENGLISH CULTURE

Whatever literary materials the Anglo-Saxons brought with them when they came to Britain existed only in their memories, for the making of written records was something they learned only when they were converted to Christianity. The Celtic inhabitants whose land they were seizing were Christians, as had been the Romans whose forces had occupied the island since the 1st century and whose withdrawal at the beginning of the 5th had opened the way to the Anglo-Saxons; but for 150 years after the beginning of the invasion Christianity was maintained only in the remoter regions where the Anglo-Saxons failed to penetrate. In the year 597, however, St. Augustine was sent by Pope Gregory as a missionary to King Ethelbert of Kent, one of the most southerly of the kingdoms into which England was divided, and about the same time missionaries from Ireland began to preach

Christianity in the north. Within 75 years the island was once more predominantly Christian. Ethelbert himself was one of the first Englishmen to be converted, and it is indicative of the relationship between Christianity and writing that the first written specimen of the Old English (Anglo-Saxon) language is a code of laws promulgated by the first English Christian king.

In the centuries that followed up till the Norman Conquest England produced a large number of distinguished, highly literate churchmen. One of the earliest of these was Bede, whose *Ecclesiastical History of the English People*, written in Latin, was completed in 731; this remains our most important source of knowledge about the Anglo-Saxon period. In the next generation Alcuin, a man of wide culture, became the friend and advisor of the Frankish Emperor Charlemagne, whom he assisted in making the Frankish court a great center of learning: thus by the year 800 English culture had developed so richly that it overflowed its insular boundaries. But the greatest impetus on English culture came from a man who was not of the clergy: Alfred, king of the West Saxons from 871 to 899, who for a time united all the kingdoms of southern England and beat off those new Germanic invaders, the Vikings. This most active king was an enthusiastic patron of literature. He himself translated various works from Latin, the most important of which was Boethius' *Consolation of Philosophy*, the early 6th-century Roman work whose heroic stoicism has proved continuingly congenial to the English temperament. Under Alfred's direction Bede's *History* was also translated into Old English, and the *Anglo-Saxon Chronicle* was begun: this year-by-year record of important events in England was maintained until the middle of the 12th century. Furthermore, the preservation of many of the surviving earlier English works, including *Beowulf*, is due to the fact that copies of them were made in the West Saxon dialect because of the impetus Alfred gave to literary studies. Though the political stability that Alfred achieved was not long-lived, the culture he nourished so lovingly was maintained at a high level until the very end of the Old English period.

OLD ENGLISH POETRY

The genius for heroic poetry the Anglo-Saxons brought with them when they came to Britain, as they probably also brought with them the alliterative form (see the section on "Old and Middle English Prosody") in which all the Old English poetry that has survived was composed. Since they wrote nothing down until they had become Christianized, and since in many respects Christian ideals and heroic ideals are antipathetic, it is natural that very little poetry has survived that is surely pre-Christian in composition. But much of *Beowulf*, the greatest of Germanic epics, is evidently pre-Christian, even though the author of the particular form of the poem that has come down to us was a Christian who refers to events of the Old (but not of the New) Testament. Several other short pieces or fragments also seem to reflect the pagan period without Christian coloring. Yet the vast bulk of Old English poetry is specifically Christian, devoted to religious subjects. Interestingly enough, however, it is almost all in the heroic mode: while the Anglo-Saxons adapted themselves readily to the ideals of Christianity, they did not do so without adapting Christianity to their own heroic ideal. In order to make the alien world of the Bible intelligible to their hearers, Old English poets (almost all of whom are nameless) infused it with many of the values that they had inherited from their own history. Thus Moses and St. Andrew, Christ and God the Father share the attributes of a *Beowulf*, are represented as heroes who performed famous deeds. In the *Dream of the Rood*, the Cross speaks of Christ as "the young hero, ... strong and stouthearted," whose crucifixion is less a passion than an heroic action. In *Cædmon's Hymn* the creation of heaven and earth is seen as a mighty deed, an "establishment of wonders" not altogether unlike Hrothgar's building of the hall Heorot in *Beowulf*. The sad consciousness of the transience of all earthly good combined with the compulsion to go on striving—so characteristic of the heroic spirit—appears most poignantly in two Christian laments, the *Wanderer*. and the *Seafarer*. That the heroic ideal held its value down to the end of the Old English period is shown by the *Battle of Maldon*, in which the defeat of English defenders by a band of marauding Vikings is described in the highest tradition of Germanic heroism. Against doom, there is only courage.

The world of Old English poetry is a dark one, and to a modern reader it may also seem a narrow one with narrow laws that exclude all but sardonic laughter. Men in the mead-hall are said to be cheerful, but even there they think of struggle in war, of possible triumph but more possible failure. Romantic love—one of the principal topics of later literature—appears hardly at all. Men seem seldom to relax: clothed in their armor, they are always preparing to test their courage against fate. (They are, indeed, so habitually seen as warriors that in the earlier poetry the words for "man" and "warrior" are often interchangeable.) Depressing as this world may seem, it is recreated in Old English poetry with extraordinary intensity, with high spiritual excitement. This excitement is achieved in part by the frequent use of ironic understatement. Actions and things are spoken of as less than they really are because, apparently, the speaker wishes to suggest that they are more—or perhaps other—than they are. "They cared not for battle," says the author of the *Battle of Maldon* about those cowardly Englishmen who fled the fight. Even the "kenning," that highly formalized compound metaphor common to Old Germanic poetry, often seems to suggest potentials ironically—"whale's road" or "swan's path" for a sea so perilous for men lacking the physical equipment of whales and swans. The dignity the Anglo-Saxons assigned to poetry—which was the repository of the ancient traditions by which they lived—apparently prevented the humor latent in ironic understatement from reaching any expression more overt than a grim smile. Yet despite its somberness, Old English poetry goes about its business of depicting harsh reality with an extraordinary subtlety and intensity.

THE NORMAN CONQUEST AND ITS EFFECTS

In the year 1066 England was once more invaded and conquered by a Germanic people, though one whose culture was widely different from the Anglo-Saxons. The Normans—the name is actually a form of "Norsemen" —were the descendants of Scandinavian adventurers who at the beginning of the 10th century had seized a wide part of northern France. A highly adaptable nation, they had adopted the language of the land they had settled in and had set up a powerful state; while its ruler was technically a duke subject to the king of France, Normandy was actually an independent political entity. The invasion of England was led by the energetic Duke William. The English were divided and irresolute; at the decisive Battle of Hastings they were defeated by the Normans and their leader Harold was killed. Thereafter William's forces overran much of England, and the Norman duke became its king and insured the succession to his descendants. But, kings of England though they were, he and his followers were not as much interested in the country he had won (though they were constantly fighting the Welsh, the Scots, and their own barons for control of parts or the whole of it) as they were in their continental possessions. The first seven English kings were mostly absentee rulers—and their presence within the kingdom was seldom less troublesome for it than their absence from it. It was not, indeed, until the 13th century, with the reign of Henry III (1216–72) that England became the principal concern of its kings. And it was not until the very end of the Middle Ages that English monarchs finally gave up trying to make good their continental claims and became, perforce, purely English.

The immediate effect of the Norman Conquest upon English literature was to remove it from the care of the aristocracy—the spiritual if not actual descendants of the Anglo-Saxon kings and their retainers—and to deprive it of that cohesive spirit that it had previously possessed. The great aristocratic households, which were the centers of pre-Conquest cultural activity, were broken up or parceled out to the Conqueror's Norman barons, and the English aristocracy was either displaced or forced into service with the invaders. For a considerable time, even the English language seems to have fallen into disuse as a vehicle for written literature, for very little survives of English between the Conquest and the year 1200. Initially, men of education who continued to produce literary works wrote either in Latin or in Anglo-Norman, the dialect of French that was spoken by the new rulers of England. But since the practical Normans were less preoccupied with culture than the English, the literature in Anglo-Norman was not very distinguished and was not very long-enduring, hardly surviving the reign of Edward I (1272–1307). Latin, which had always been and continued to be the language of the international church, produced a fairly rich literature in England during this period—especially in the 12th century. But throughout the Middle Ages, Latin literature remained essentially conservative and remote, not much dealing with the subjects that are of importance in the development of vernacular literature. Thus for more than a century the twin snobberies—social on the part of Anglo-Norman, intellectual on the part of Latin—probably pre-empted the energies of educated men who might at an earlier or a later time have written in English.

But even if the educated were writing literature in other languages, the uneducated were undoubtedly continuing to compose—if not to write—in English. When written English literature begins to reappear at the end of the 12th century, the larger part of it carries the stamp of popular or at least semi-popular origin; indeed, considered in its bulk, Middle English literature is a popular literature. Its origin in the orders of society below the top provides its most striking contrast with Old English literature: most of the latter seems to be uttered by a single aristocratic voice, grave, decorous, responsible, speaking in terms of high communal aspirations. Middle English literature, on the other hand, is uttered by a medley of different voices, dealing with a wide range of topics in a great diversity of styles and tones and genres. Originality of thought, to be sure, is a rare feature of this literature, for no matter how diverse the voices may be, they often seem to be saying precisely the same things as each other. Yet Middle English literature has virtues not found in Old English. Because its writers addressed themselves to a popular audience, they achieved a greater immediacy, a greater recognizability; a modern reader experiences little difficulty in understanding the world they are talking about. The change is perhaps most obvious in the narrative of adventure, where the idealized hero of Old English yields place to the more sympathetic if less admirable man who not only fights and fights again, but also laughs and cries, plays games, and, above all, falls in and out of love—the non-aristocratic man was the readier to supplant the epic hero because a mature Christianity places as much value on a plain man's soul as it does on an epic hero's. In dealing with this new kind of hero the writer's imaginative perspective was broadened as much, perhaps, as his ability to see deeply was decreased. And the perspective now included women, who became, finally, recognized as half of the human race. True, they appear ordinarily as stereotypes, whether in romance and love lyric or in anti-feminist satire—that enormous body of literature that had its foundation in the monastic culture that dominated so much of European thought in the Middle Ages. But woman's place in society was, in any case, recognized in literature, and this recognition undoubtedly reflects a changing attitude in history itself. There are no arch-feminists in literature before Chaucer's Wife of Bath, but she could never have been invented, even by a Chaucer, unless she had had recognizable forebears, with independent minds and incomes, in Bath and elsewhere before Chaucer's time.

While the portrayal of life in Middle English literature is often shallow, it is nevertheless a life in which we find much that evokes our sympathy. Sometimes, when it is portrayed as lively and gay, colorful, full of surprise, its attractiveness earns our active appreciation, and even when some austere moralist reduces human experience to mere wretchedness we may experience amid the overlying gloom the sudden charm of poignancy. Lack of profound vision does not prevent an accurate presentation of the details of life from being pleasing and sometimes moving. And humor—the chief virtue of Middle English literature—is apt to flash anywhere, even in the most solemn and foreboding of moralizations.

The lack of originality in Middle English literature is partly due to the attempt by many writers, both religious and secular, to make their works reflect the unchanging principles of medieval Christian doctrine. Until almost the end of the 14th century Christian teaching was primarily concerned with the issue of personal salvation, putting more emphasis on the moral and spiritual responsibilities of the individual than it did on his ethical or social responsibilites. Medieval religious idealism characteristically looked to the world to come for the only answer to men's troubles and considered the reformation of this world neither possible nor especially desirable. So constant is the attitude that life in this world is only a waiting period before we enter something better (or worse) that the modern reader is apt to get the impression that the Middle Ages was a period of intellectual and social stasis, a period in which time was standing still. And the fact is that not only in specifically moral and doctrinal literature, whose premises are timeless, but also in ephemeral literature designed merely to provide entertainment one senses this unchangingness: a romance written at the beginning of the 13th century differs little from one written in the 15th (with which it shares its plot), and at the very end of the period Malory is still peopling with his knights a never-never land of chivalry that had its origin in 12th-century France.

It is clear enough that between 1066 and 1485 England underwent large political and social changes—in the developments in feudalism, the gradual evolution of Parliament, the growth of cities and of the middle class along with the increase in foreign trade, and in many other similar phenomena. But apparently the changes occurred too slowly to produce much intellectual awareness of them on the part of writers. The great exception—to this and to all other generalizations—is Chaucer, whose pages are informed, especially in his handling of the bourgeois, by an excited sense of the novelty of social life in his own times. Langland's *Piers Plowman* also possesses something of this quality—though without Chaucer's tone of approval. But in an age where most people were born in the same village where their grandparents had been born and lived virtually the same lives, doing the same work with the same tools, enjoying the same sports and the same festivals, large slow-moving change is probably bound to be imperceptible to all but the most acute observers—imperceptible and, if perceived, disapproved.

But if in a broad historical sense change was imperceptible, in the daily lives of medieval men it was all too visible. Indeed, the inevitability of change—for the worse, even in the lives of people already apparently wholly wretched—is one of the most insistently repetitive themes of Middle English literature. Nor is this theme to be thought of merely as another expression of the world-hating doctrine. Rather, the theme and the world-hating doctrine itself are both results of the violence of life in the Middle Ages, a violence not matched again in western history until our own times. Famine, war, pestilence, and death—these are the riders who passed through the streets of medieval cities and villages by night and by day. The fact that eight of the eighteen kings who ruled England between 1066 and 1485 died deaths of violence or deaths resulting from violent activity is characteristic of the times. Men hardly less august were also constantly meeting death in battles, or by murder, or by accident, or, not infrequently, on the scaffold before a fascinated populace. The chroniclers who record these events say little of the lower orders of society, but constant warfare against enemies at home and abroad, the depredations of the powerful in supplying themselves from the fruits of the toil of the poor, the fearful severity of the laws combined with the failure to enforce them against the strong, and, especially after the middle of the 14th century, recurrent pestilence compounded by famine—all these explain why change for the worse seems to have been the unchanging expectation of medieval people. And, even in the temporary absence of these events, the coldness and darkness of an English winter for people living in badly insulated dwellings with only minimal heat and light might well seem to make life a bleak perpetual twilight.

In view of the violence prevalent during most of the period, it is perhaps extraordinary that so much literature was produced. But even in the worst of times things are not always and everywhere at their worst; spring does come, and some people get through life almost untouched by disasters that seem historically to be omnipresent. And the fact is that, except in its most ruthlessly world-hating forms, Middle English literature is often permeated by a curious normality, and is, indeed, less preoccupied with its age's violence than we are with ours, probably because people then never conceived of a time when violence was not a fact of life. Despite being constantly warned to expect change for the worse, people in the Middle Ages seem, in their daily lives, to have pursued the same pleasures that we pursue today —pursued them with rather more relish because they were rarer: this is clear from the accounts both of those who approved of the pursuit and of those who did not. As the general atmosphere of violence suggests, medieval society was in some ways more primitive than our own—or more frankly primitive—and may thus seem to us more childlike. People took tremendous pleasure in color, in dress, in ritual, in parades, in spectacles, in elaborate food and drink (when they could get them), in all those aspects of life that children especially love, and most adults do not scorn. Like children, medieval people were subject to emotional extremes—they wept more quickly than we do, went more quickly from weeping to laughter and back again, were headstrong and hasty, quick to sin zestily and to repent heartily and then to sin and repent again. Yet is is a mistake to overemphasize this childishness: their life was physically more limited than ours, without our comforts, our mobility, our communications; it was even more precarious, more uncertain; but as it is reflected in the best writers, they lived their life very richly and perhaps with greater awareness and greater savor than we do ours.

MIDDLE ENGLISH LITERATURE

It has been said earlier that from the century and a half after the Conquest very little English literature has survived, and it is probable that in that period very little was written. But that literature was still being composed, if not written down, during the period is suggested by the first considerable Middle English poem to have come down to us: this is Layamon's *Brut*, written about 1205 in an alliterative prosody that is clearly directly descended from the Old English poetic measure, though the subleties of the older measure have disappeared. Apparently, at least for oral purposes, alliterative poetry never ceased to be composed, as is further suggested by its reappearance later in written form in the so-called "alliterative revival" of the 14th century, which culminated in *Piers Plowman* and *Sir Gawain and the Green Knight*. Layamon's *Brut* is also interesting because it contains the first treatment in English of the Arthurian legend, the story that was to catch the imagination of so many English writers of later times. Layamon's source was a Norman work by the poet Wace, which was in turn based on the Englishman Geoffrey of Monmouth's Latin *History of the Kings of Britain*. According to the old tradition, England had been founded by one Brutus who was a descendant of the Trojan Aeneas, the founder of Rome, and after whom *Brit*ain was named (hence the title *Brut*). Of Brutus' descendants the most distinguished was Arthur, who according to the legend freed Britain from the Roman yoke and successfully defended it from the Anglo-Saxon invaders. It is a double curiosity about the Arthurian legend that not only did the British (Celtic) Arthur become in later centuries the great legendary hero of Englishmen—whose ancestors he was presumably successful in beating off the island—but also that the Arthurian legend itself reached its fullest development in France, whither it may have been brought by Celts crossing the channel to Brittany—some of them perhaps fleeing from the Anglo-Saxons. In any case, after Geoffrey and Layamon, England produced no original writers on Arthur—as opposed to translators from the French—until the poet of *Gawain* (whom some critics suspect of translating) and Malory—also a translator, but on so grand a scale as to rank as truly original.

Both Layamon and the poet of *Beowulf* dealt with legendary materials which they thought of as history. Layamon's treatment, however, is different from (and far less impressive than) the epic mode of *Beowulf*: it moves toward the genre, so characteristic of the later Middle Ages, known as "romance." The romance has certain typical features: it generally concerns knights and involves a large amount of fighting as well as a number of miscellaneous adventures; it makes liberal use of the improbable, often of the supernatural; it is often—though not always—involved with romantic love; characterization is standardized, so that heroes, heroines, and wicked stewards could easily move from one romance to another without causing any disturbance in the narrative; the plots generally consist of a great number of events, and the same event is apt to occur several times within the same romance; and the style is apt to be easy and colloquial—not infrequently loose and repetitious.

Although it was enormously popular in medieval England—it makes up a large fraction of the total of preserved Middle English literature—Middle English romance is apt to disappoint the modern reader. Unfortunately, very few accomplished poets—the *Gawain*-poet and Chaucer are two of the principal exceptions—turned their hand to romance; it was apparently left largely to minstrels and other uncultivated versifiers addressing a semi-literate audience, often in dog-trot verse full of windy clichés. The great age of medieval romance had been the 12th and early 13th centuries, and its chief breeding ground had been aristocratic society in France, where such poets as Chrétien de Troyes spun their marvelously sophisticated tales. The Middle English purveyors of romance, functioning before non-aristocratic audiences in the second half of the 13th and in the 14th century, introduced the French romances into English (the majority of the surviving English romances are either proved or suspected adaptations from the French). The result of the lag in time and change in audience is artistically unfortunate, though often unintentionally amusing. Aristocratic ideals of behavior of a different era and an alien society were replaced by patterns of behavior that could be easily comprehended by bourgeois and lower-class Englishmen. Heroes who have all the accouterments of the most chivalrous of knights are apt to behave in the crudest fashion, whether they are fighting, eating, or making love: they act as a petty bourgeois might if suddenly given an opportunity to enjoy the high scale of living of chivalric aristocracy with no education in how such a life should be conducted. Nevertheless, it is often agreeable to watch the blunt Englishman who replaced the aristocratic hero react with practical common sense to the extravagant situations in which the poem has placed him. And there is one very charming exception to the rule that translation brings deterioration: *Sir Orfeo*, apparently based on a lost French poem recasting the classical legend of Orpheus and Eurydice, transmits much of that delicacy and magic which the reader who first approaches medieval romance expects to find in it.

By far the larger proportion of surviving Middle English literature is religious, though it is not necessarily true that an equal proportion of the literature actually composed in Middle English was religious. The church had a virtual monopoly on literacy during much of the Middle Ages, for the average person who had learned to read and write probably had done so because he had signified his intention (not always fulfilled) of becoming a cleric—that is, an ecclesiast, performing one of the many functions of the church: otherwise, he would probably not have received any but the most elementary kind of education. Furthermore, the church not only had this direct claim upon the services of the majority of literate men but also was itself a large producer of books in the physical sense (books were actually handwritten manuscripts) as well as a maintainer (especially in monasteries) of libraries. Therefore it is quite natural that religious literature should bulk large. But the literature that has been lost probably contained a very large number of secular items. Professional storytellers such as minstrels committed to memory tales that they had heard others recite or had composed themselves and did not trouble to write them down—if, indeed, they could write. Their stories depended for survival on some literate hearer who thought them worth recording—and perhaps few clerics would take the trouble. And even secular literature that had been recorded might sometimes be lost because of the low esteem in which it was held by austere churchmen who would enforce St. Paul's precept that everything that is written ought to express specific Christian doctrine: when library shelves became crowded, it was probably the secular works that were removed to make room for books more beneficial to the spirit.

Unfortunately, good doctrine is not necessarily good literature, and the larger part of Middle English religious writing is literature at all only in the broadest sense of that word: sermons, homilies, saints' lives, penitential tracts, manuals for priests, mystical writings, lyric poems, moral allegories, stories of miracles—all the possible genres of religious writing are represented profusely, though not, in quality, richly. An occasional individual work distinguishes itself strikingly from the surrounding drabness—for instance, the very early *Ancrene Riwle*, or "Rule for Anchoresses" (female religious recluses), or a late lyric like *I Sing of a Maiden*. But the brilliant exceptions are few and far between: few minds were able to sustain originality amid the oppressive conventionality of doctrine and response to doctrine. Since virtually all those who were capable of writing had been trained by and for the church, there was, apart from the romances, very little secular literature, though it is possible that some secular literature has failed to survive because it was disapproved of for being secular. But probably few educated men before the time of Chaucer had the temerity to venture into the secular. We are fortunate that the work of one such person, the author of the early *Owl and the Nightingale*, has survived, for this humorous debate between birds is the most original and Chaucer-like poem before Chaucer himself.

During the last quarter of the 14th century Middle English literature flowered suddenly and inexplicably in three great poets, writing at almost the same time and giving supreme artistic expression to almost all the characteristic genres of Middle English. The author of *Sir Gawain and the Green Knight* not only produced the best romance of the entire period, but also wrote some of its best religious poetry; his Biblical narrative in alliterative verse, *Patience*, the story of Jonah, is rivaled only by certain Old English poems. In the *Pearl* he combined elegy with theology to produce the most moving religious poem—and the most finely wrought poem—of the English later Middle Ages. William Langland's achievement in *Piers Plowman* is important both in literature and in history, since he faced squarely the great religious and social issues of his day—and these became the great issues of the following century and a half: imitations of *Piers Plowman* which borrow both Piers himself and Langland's anti-ecclesiastical satire played an important part in bringing on the reformation of the church which Langland prophesied but would have deplored. Needless to say, no imitator approaches Langland in the extraordinary originality of his weaving together of all sorts of genres of religious literature, from the most menacing sermon to the most dazzling lyric. Geoffrey Chaucer's achievement was greatest of all. The new perspective which English literature after the Conquest had attained had revealed broader horizons, but they were too broad and too clouded with distractions to enable the average writer to bring everything into clear focus. It takes a powerfully disciplined mind to comprehend infinite variety in a single artistic vision. Such a mind was Chaucer's. While he was entirely rooted in the soil of the Middle Ages and tried his hand at a large number of medieval genres, his art is so fully realized as to carry him out of the Middle Ages and make him one of the two or three greatest poets in English.

This sudden florescence in the *Gawain*-poet, Langland, and Chaucer may have been partly due to patronage of literature by the well-to-do. Chaucer was a "court" poet who seems to have been encouraged not only by John of Gaunt but perhaps also by Gaunt's father, Edward III (died 1377), as well as by his nephew Richard II (deposed 1399), and, in the last year of the poet's life, by Gaunt's son, Henry IV. The *Gawain*-poet probably wrote for a provincial aristocratic court, remote from London but no less interested in literary art. Even William Langland seems to have enjoyed patronage, but from what source it is hard to be sure; it is probable that at one time or another he was sheltered by monasteries, and it is not unlikely that he ended his life in one. In any case English literature is fortunate that these three great contemporary poets all found encouragement from one source or another.

But patronage does not assure great poetry. Chaucer's friend, the poet John Gower, also enjoyed royal patronage, but he has not proved much of a threat to Chaucer's reputation. He seems a far more typically medieval writer than Chaucer: he wrote three works which, linguistically at least, summarized the English Middle Ages: one in Latin, one in Norman French, and one, *Confessio Amantis* ("The Lover's Confession"), in English. Were it not for its proximity to Chaucer, this last would probably be rated somewhat higher than it has been, for it is a work of considerable skill and interest. And it is certainly infinitely superior to anything produced by the English poets of the next century, some of whom enjoyed patronage but all of whom seem, after Chaucer, to represent regression into the worst vices of medieval literature. The most Chaucerian of Chaucer's followers are, indeed, Scotsmen, and the best of them, Robert Henryson and William Dunbar, who often reflect Chaucer's satirical spirit and his liveliness, belong not to the medieval period but to the Renaissance.

Yet if the 15th century in England lacks great names (Thomas Malory alone enjoys a high reputation as a literary artist), it is nevertheless a period in which popular literature flourished. Some of the best lyrics, religious and secular, date from this time; and this was also the century in which many of the ballads were composed. It was also the period of much activity in drama. The mystery plays, which had probably become established in the previous century, continued to be performed widely, and the cycles of these religious dramas that have been preserved from York, Chester, and Wakefield date from the 15th century. The same century saw the development of the morality play, culminating in *Everyman*. The authors of the plays, ballads, and lyrics of the century are nameless; aside from the plays, manuscripts of which were kept only by the towns in which the performances were given, these anonymous works were probably transmitted orally and only haphazardly written down. Fortunately for the future history of English literature, Malory's *Morte Darthur*, written during its author's long sojourn in prison, did not have to depend on the chance survival of a manuscript; it was printed in 1485 by William Caxton, who had introduced printing by movable type to England less than ten years earlier. Malory's is the last great medieval work of literature. Using mostly French sources, Malory put together a history of King Arthur and his knights which, while wholly fictional, has received much the same honor from later Englishmen that earlier Englishmen accorded *Beowulf*.

MEDIEVAL ENGLISH

The medieval works in this book were composed in two different states of our language: Old English, the language which took shape among the Germanic settlers of England and preserved its integrity until the Norman Conquest radically altered English civilization; and Middle English, the earliest records of which date from the early 12th century and which gave way to Modern English shortly after the introduction of printing at the end of the 15th century. Old English is a very heavily inflected language (that is, the words change form, to indicate changes in usage, such as person, number, tense, case, mood, etc. Most languages have some inflection—for example, the personal pronouns in Modern English have different forms when used as objects—but a "heavily inflected" language is one in which almost all classes of words undergo elaborate patterns of change). Its vocabulary is almost entirely Germanic. In Middle English, the inflectional system is weakened; and a large number of words were introduced into it from France, so that many of the older native words disappeared. Because of the difficulty of Old English, all selections from it in this book have been given in translation. In order that the reader may see an example of the language, *Cædmon's Hymn* has been printed in the original, together with an interlinear translation. The present discussion, then, is concerned only with Middle English.

The chief difficulty with Middle English for the modern reader is caused not by its inflections so much as by its spelling, which may be described as a rough-and-ready phonetic system, and by the fact that it is not a single standardized language, but consists of a number of regional dialects each with its own peculiarities of sound and its own systems for representing sounds in writing. The Midland dialect—the dialect of London and of Chaucer, and the ancestor of our own standard speech—

differs greatly from the dialect spoken in the west of England (the original dialect of *Piers Plowman*), and from that of the northwest (*Sir Gawain and the Green Knight*), and from that of the north (*The Second Shepherd's Play*), and these dialects differ from one another. In this book, the long texts composed in the more difficult dialects have been translated or modernized; and those which, like Chaucer, *Everyman*, the lyrics, and the ballads, appear in the original, have been respelled in a way that it is hoped will aid the reader. The remarks which follow apply chiefly to Chaucer's Midland English, though certain non-Midland dialectal variations are noted if they occur in some of the other selections.

I. THE SOUNDS OF MIDDLE ENGLISH: GENERAL RULES

The following general analysis of the sounds of Middle English will enable the reader who has not time for detailed study to read Middle English aloud so as to preserve some of its most essential characteristics, without, however, giving heed to many important details. Section II, Detailed Analysis, is designed for the reader who wishes to go more deeply into the pronunciation of Middle English.

Middle English differs from Modern English in three principal respects: 1. the pronunciation of the long vowels *a, e, i* (or *y*), *o*, and *u* (spelled *ou, ow*); 2. the fact that Middle English final *e* is often sounded; 3. the fact that all Middle English consonants are sounded.

1. *Long Vowels*

Middle English vowels are long when they are doubled (*aa, ee, oo*) or when they are terminal (*he, to, holy*); *a, e,* and *o* are long when followed by a single consonant plus a vowel (*name, mete, note*). Middle English vowels are short when they are followed by two consonants.

Long *a* is sounded like the *a* in Modern English "father": *maken, maad*.

Long *e* may be sounded like the *a* in Modern English "name" (ignoring the distinction between the close and open vowel): *be, sweete*.

Long *i* (or *y*) is sounded like the *i* in Modern English "machine": *lif, whit; myn, holy*.

Long *o* may be sounded like the *o* in Modern English "note" (again ignoring the distinction between the close and open vowel): *do, soone*.

Long *u* (spelled *ou, ow*) is sounded like the *oo* in Modern English "goose": *hous, flowr*.

Note that in general Middle English long vowels are pronounced like long vowels in modern languages other than English. Short vowels and diphthongs, however, may be pronounced as in Modern English.

2. *Final e*

In Middle English syllabic verse, final *e* is sounded like the *a* in "sofa" to provide a needed unstressed syllable: *Another Nonnë with hire haddë she*. But (cf. *hire* in the example) final *e* is suppressed when not needed for the meter. It is commonly silent before words beginning with a vowel or *h*.

3. *Consonants*

Middle English consonants are pronounced separately in all combinations—*gnat: g-nat; knave: k-nave; write: w-rite; folk: fol-k*. In a simplified system of pronunciation the combination *gh* as in *night* or *thought* may be treated as if it were silent.

II. THE SOUNDS OF MIDDLE ENGLISH: DETAILED ANALYSIS

1. *Simple Vowels*

Sound	Pronunciation	Example
long *a* (spelled *a, aa*)	*a* in "father"	*maken, maad*
short *a*	*o* in "hot"	*cappe*
long *e* close (spelled *e, ee*)	*a* in "name"	*be, sweete*
long *e* open (spelled *e, ee*)	*e* in "there"	*mete, heeth*
short *e*	*e* in "set"	*setten*
final *e*	*a* in "sofa"	*large*
long *i* (spelled *i, y*)	*i* in "machine"	*lif, myn*
short *i*	*i* in "wit"	*wit*
long *o* close (spelled *o, oo*)	*o* in "note"	*do, soone*
long *o* open (spelled *o, oo*)	*oa* in "broad"	*go, goon*
short *o*	*o* in "oft"	*pot*
long *u* when spelled *ou, ow*	*oo* in "goose"	*hous, flowr*
long *u* when spelled *u*	*u* in "pure"	*vertu*
short *u* (spelled *u, o*)	*u* in "full"	*ful, love*

Doubled vowels and terminal vowels are always long, while single vowels before two consonants other than *th, ch* are always short. The vowels *a, e,* and *o* are long before a single consonant followed by a vowel: *nāmë, sēkë* (sick), *hōly*. In general, words that have descended into Modern English reflect their original Middle English quantity: *līven* (to live), but *līf* (life).

The close and open sounds of long *e* and long *o* may often be identified by the Modern English spellings of the words in which they appear. Original long close *e* is generally represented in Modern English by *ee*: "sweet," "knee," "teeth," "see" have close *e* in Middle English, but so does "be"; original long open *e* is generally represented in Modern English by *ea*: "meat," "heath," "sea," "great," "breath" have open *e* in Middle English. Similarly, original long close *o* is now generally represented by *oo*: "soon," "food," "good," but also "do," "to"; original long open *o* is represented either by *oa* or by *o*: "coat," "boat," "moan," but also "go," "bone," "foe," "home." Notice that original close *o* is now almost always pronounced like the *oo* in "goose," but that original open *o* is almost never so pronounced; thus it is often possible to identify the Middle English vowels through Modern English sounds.

The nonphonetic Middle English spelling of *o* for short *u* has been preserved in a number of Modern English words ("love," "son," "come"), but in others *u* has been restored: "sun" (*sonne*), "run" (*ronne*).

For the treatment of final *e*, see above, General Rules, section 2.

2. *Diphthongs*

Sound	Pronunciation	Example
ai, ay, ei, ay	between *ai* in "aisle" and *ay* in "day"	*saide, day, veine, preye*
au, aw	*ou* in "out"	*chaunge, bawdy*
eu, ew	*ew* in "few"	*newe*

oi, oy	oy in "joy"	*joye, point*
ou, ow	ou in "thought"	*thought, lowe*

Note that in words with *ou, ow* which in Modern English are sounded with the *ou* of "about," the combination indicates not the diphthong but the simple vowel long *u* (see above, Simple Vowels).

3. Consonants

In general, all consonants except *h* were always sounded in Middle English, including consonants that have become silent in Modern English, such as the *g* in *gnaw*, the *k* in *knight*, the *l* in *folk*, and the *w* in *write*. In noninitial *gn*, however, the *g* was silent as in Modern English "sign." Initial *h* was silent in short common English words and in words borrowed from French, and may have been almost silent in all words. The combination *gh* as in *night* or *thought* was sounded like the *ch* of German *ich* or *nach*. Note that Middle English *gg* represents both the hard sound of "dagger" and the soft sound of "bridge."

III. PARTS OF SPEECH AND GRAMMAR

1. Nouns

The plural and possessive of nouns end in *es*, formed by adding *s* or *es* to the singular: *knight, knightes; roote, rootes;* a final consonant is frequently doubled before *es: bed, beddes*. A common irregular plural is *yën*, from *yë*, eye.

2. Pronouns

The chief differences from Modern English are as follows:

Modern English	Middle English
I	I, *ich* (*ik* is a northern form)
you (singular)	*thou* (subjective); *thee* (objective)
her	*hir(e), her(e)*
its	*his*
you (plural)	*ye* (subjective); *you* (objective)
their	*hir*
them	*hem*

In formal speech, the second person plural is often used for the singular. The possessive adjectives *my, thy* take *n* before a word beginning with a vowel or *h: thyn yë, myn host*.

3. Adjectives

Adjectives ending in a consonant add final *e* when they stand before the noun they modify and after another modifying word such as *the, this, that*, or nouns or pronouns in the possessive: *a good hors*, but *the* (*this, my, the kinges*) *goode hors*. They also generally add *e* when standing before and modifying a plural noun, a noun in the vocative, or any proper noun: *goode men, oh goode man, faire Venus*.

Adjectives are compared by adding *er(e)* for the comparative, *est(e)* for the superlative. Sometimes the stem vowel is shortened or altered in the process: *sweete, swettere, swettest; long, lenger, lengest*.

4. Adverbs

Adverbs are formed from adjectives by adding *e, ly*, or *liche*; the adjective *fair* thus yields *faire, fairly, fairliche*.

5. Verbs

Middle English verbs, like Modern English verbs, are either "weak" or "strong." Weak verbs form their preterites and past participles with a *t* or *d* suffix and preserve the same stem vowel throughout their systems, though it is sometimes shortened in the preterite and past participle: *love, loved; bend, bent; hear, heard; meet, met.* Strong verbs do not use the *t* or *d* suffix, but vary their stem vowel in the preterite and past participle: *take, took, taken; begin, began, begun; find, found, found.*

The inflectional endings are the same for Middle English strong verbs and weak verbs except in the preterite singular and the imperative singular. In the following paradigms, the weak verbs *loven* (to love) and *heeren* (to hear), and the strong verbs *taken* (to take) and *ginnen* (to begin) serve as models.

	Present Indicative	Preterite Indicative
I	*love, heere*	*loved(e), herde*
	take, ginne	*took, gan*
thou	*lovest, heerest*	*lovedest, herdest*
	takest, ginnest	*tooke, gonne*
he, she, it	*loveth, heereth*	*loved(e), herde*
	taketh, ginneth	*took, gan*
we, ye, they	*love(n) (th), heere(n) (th)*	*loved(e) (en), herde(n)*
	take(n) (th), ginne(n) (th)	*tooke(n), gonne(n)*

The present plural ending *eth* is southern, while the *e(n)* ending is Midland and characteristic of Chaucer. In the north, *s* may appear as the ending of all persons of the present. In the weak preterite, when the ending *e* gave a verb three or more syllables, it was frequently dropped. Note that in certain strong verbs like *ginnen* there are two distinct stem vowels in the preterite: even in Chaucer's time, however, one of these had begun to replace the other, and Chaucer occasionally writes *gan* for all persons of the preterite.

	Present Subjunctive	Preterite Subjunctive
Singular	*love, heere*	*lovede, herde*
	take, ginne	*tooke, gonne*
Plural	*love(n), heere(n)*	*lovede(n), herde(n)*
	take(n), ginne(n)	*tooke(n), gonne(n)*

In verbs like *ginnen,* which have two stem vowels in the indicative preterite, it is the vowel of the plural and of the second person singular that is used for the preterite subjunctive.

The imperative singular of most weak verbs is *e:* (*thou*) *love,* but of some weak verbs and all strong verbs, the imperative singular is without termination: (*thou*) *heer, taak, gin.* The imperative plural of all verbs is either *e* or *eth:* (*ye*) *love(th), heere(th), take(th), ginne(th).*

The infinitive of verbs is *e* or *en: love(n), heere(n), take(n), ginne(n).*

The past participle of weak verbs is the same as the preterite without inflectional ending: *loved, herd.* In strong verbs the ending is either *e* or *en: take(n), gonne(n).* The prefix *y* often appears on past participles: *yloved, yherd, ytake(n).*

OLD AND MIDDLE ENGLISH PROSODY

All the poetry of Old English is in the same verse form. The verse unit is the single line, since rhyme was not used to link one line to another, except very occasionally in late Old English. The organizing device of the line is alliteration, the beginning of several words with the same sound ("Foemen fled"). The Old English alliterative line contains four principal stresses, and is divided into two half-lines of two stresses each by a strong medial caesura, or pause. These two half-lines are linked to each other by the alliteration: at least one of the two stressed words in the first half-line, and usually both of them, begin with the same sound as the first stressed word of the second half-line (the second stressed word is generally non-alliterative). The fourth line of *Beowulf* is an example:

Oft Scyld Scefing   sceaþena þreatum.

For further examples, see *Cædmon's Hymn*, printed below. It will be noticed that any vowel alliterates with any other vowel. In addition to the alliteration, the length of the unstressed syllables and their number and pattern is governed by a highly complex set of rules. When sung or intoned—as it was—to the rhythmic strumming of a harp, Old English poetry must have been wonderfully impressive in the dignified, highly formalized way which aptly fits both its subject matter and tone.

The majority of Middle English verse is either in alternately stressed rhyming verse, adapted from French after the Conquest, or in alliterative verse that is descended from Old English. The latter preserves the caesura of Old English and in its purest form the same alliterative system, the two stressed words of the first half-line (or at least one of them) alliterating with the first stressed word in the second half-line. But most of the alliterative poets allowed themselves a number of deviations from the norm. All four stressed words may alliterate, as in the first line of *Piers Plowman:*

In a summer season   when soft was the sun.

Or the line may contain five, six, or even more stressed words, of which all or only the basic minimum may alliterate:

A fair field full of folk   found I therebetween.

There is no rule determining the number of unstressed syllables, and at times some poets are apt to ignore alliteration entirely. As in Old English, any vowel may alliterate with any other vowel; furthermore, since initial *h* was silent or lightly pronounced in Middle English, words beginning with *h* are treated as though they began with the following vowel.

There are two general types of stressed verse with rhyme. In the more common, stressed and unstressed syllables alternate regularly: x X x X x X; or, with two unstressed syllables intervening: x x X x x X x x X; or a combination of the two: x x X x X x x x X (of the reverse patterns, only X x X x X x is common in English). There is also a line which can only be defined as containing a predetermined number of stressed syllables but an irregular number and pattern of unstressed syllables. Much Middle English verse has to be read without expectation of regularity: some of this was evidently composed in the irregular meter, but some was probably originally composed according to a strict metrical system which has been obliterated by scribes careless of fine points. One receives the impression that many of the lyrics—as well as the *Second Shepherd's Play*—were at least composed with regular syllabic alternation. In the ballads, on the other hand, and in the play *Everyman*, only the number of stresses is predetermined (and perhaps not even this in *Everyman*), but not the number or placement of unstressed syllables.

In pre-Chaucerian verse the number of stresses, whether regularly or irregularly alternated, was most often four, though sometimes the number was three, and rose in some poems to seven. Rhyme in Middle English as in Modern English may be either between adjacent or alternate lines, or may occur in more complex patterns. The *Canterbury Tales* are in rhymed couplets, the line containing five stresses with regular alternation —technically known as iambic pentameter, the standard English poetic line, perhaps introduced into English by Chaucer. In reading Chaucer and much pre-Chaucerian verse one must remember that the final *e*, which is silent in Modern English, was pronounced at any time in order to provide a needed unstressed syllable. Evidence seems to indicate that it was also pronounced at the end of the line, even though it thus produced a line with eleven syllables. Although he was a very regular metricist, Chaucer used various conventional devices which are apt to make the reader stumble until he understands them. Final *e* is often not pronounced before a word beginning with a vowel or *h*, and may be suppressed whenever metrically convenient. The same medial and terminal syllables that are slurred in Modern English are apt to be suppressed in Chaucer's English: *Canter-b'ry* for *Canterbury*; *ev'r* (perhaps *e'er*) for *evere*. The plural in *es* may either be syllabic or reduced to *s* as in Modern English. Despite these seeming irregularities, Chaucer's verse is not difficult to read if one constantly bears in mind the basic pattern of the iambic pentameter line.

Old English Poetry

CÆDMON'S HYMN

Cædmon's *Hymn* is one of the oldest of preserved English poems, having been written between 658 and 680. Bede, the great cleric of Old English times, tells the story of its composition in his *Ecclesiastical History of the English People* (completed in 731). Cædmon, a Northumbrian layman, had all his life felt himself incompetent in the art of verse, and when, according to the custom that was used at feasts, the harp was passed around the table so that each guest might entertain the others with a song, Cædmon always found a pretext to take himself from the table before the harp reached him. One night when he had thus avoided singing, he fell asleep in the stable where he had gone to tend the animals. He dreamed that someone came to him and said, "Cædmon, sing me something," and when Cædmon excused himself, the other insisted that he sing, directing him to celebrate the beginning of created things. Cædmon at once sang the *Hymn*. On waking, he remembered his verses; and thereafter, Bede tells us, he was able to express any given sacred topic in excellent poetry after only a few hours of work. He became a monk and devoted his life to the composition of Christian verse, but none of the religious poetry in Old English that has been preserved may surely be ascribed to him except his first short work.

The poem is given here in a West Saxon form with a literal interlinear translation. In Old English spelling, æ (as in Cædmon's name and line 3) is a vowel symbol that has not survived; it represented both a short *a* sound and a long open *e* sound. þ (line 2) and ð both represented the sound *th*. The large space in the middle of the line indicates the caesura.

Cædmon's Hymn

Nu sculon   herigean   heofonrices   Weard
Now we must praise   heaven-kingdom's Guardian,

Meotodes   meahte   and his modgeþanc
the Creator's might   and his mind-plans,

weorc   Wuldor-Fæder   swa   he wundra   gehwæs
the work of the Glory-Father,   when he of wonders of every one,

ece Drihten	or onstealde
eternal Lord.	the beginning established.[1]
He ærest sceop	ielda[2] bearnum
He first created	for men's sons
heofon to hrofe	halig Scyppend
heaven as a roof,	holy Creator;
ða middangeard	moncynnes Weard
then middle-earth	mankind's Guardian,
ece Drihten	æfter teode
eternal Lord,	afterwards made—
firum foldan	Frea aelmihtig
for men earth,	Master almighty.

THE DREAM OF THE ROOD

The *Dream of the Rood* (i.e., of the Cross) is the finest of a rather large number of religious poems in Old English. Neither its author nor its date of composition is known. It appears in a late 10th-century manuscript located in Vercelli in northern Italy, a manuscript made up of Old English religious poems and sermons. The poet Cynewulf, about whom nothing is surely known except that he wrote four Old English homiletic poems (two of them found in the Vercelli manuscript), has sometimes been credited with the *Dream*, but on no very convincing evidence. The poem may antedate its manuscript by almost three centuries, for some passages from the Rood's speech were carved, with some variations, in runes on a stone cross early in the 8th century: this is the famous Ruthwell Cross, which is preserved near Dumfries in southern Scotland. The precise relation of the poem to this cross is, however, uncertain.

The homiletic tone of the Dreamer's meditation may seem anticlimactic after the intensity, so terse and exciting, of the Rood's address to him, but the former is nevertheless an admirable frame for the latter. The experience of the Cross—its humiliation at the hands of those who changed it from tree to instrument of punishment for criminals, its humility when the young hero Christ mounts upon it, and its pride as the restored "tree of glory"—has a suggestive relevance to the condition of the sad, lonely, sin-stained Dreamer. In the Cross's experience, hope has replaced torment; when, at the end of the poem, the Dreamer describes Christ's triumphant

---

1. I.e., "established the beginning of every one of wonders."
2. The later manuscript copies read *eorþan*, "earth," for *ælda* (West Saxon *ielda*), "men's."

progress from hell to heaven, the verse recaptures some of the excitement of the Cross's address, reflecting the Dreamer's response to the hope that has been brought him.

The Dream of the Rood[1]

Behold, I shall tell of a most marvelous dream—what I dreamed at midnight, when men and their voices were at rest. It seemed to me that I saw a tree, more wonderful than any other, reach high aloft, bathed in light, brightest of wood. All that beacon[2] was covered with gold. Four gems were set where it met the earth, and five more stood on it high about the crosspiece. There looked upon it many hosts of angels, fair in the form God gave them of old. This was surely no felon's gallows, for holy spirits beheld it, men upon earth, and all this glorious creation. Wonderful was the triumphant tree, and I stained with sin, wounded with wrongdoing. I saw the tree of wonder, adorned with clothes, shine brilliantly, decked with gold; splendidly had jewels covered the Lord's tree. But through that gold I might see wretches' ancient agony, for now it began to bleed upon the right side. I was sadly troubled, afraid of that fair sight. I saw that beacon, changeable, alter in clothes and in color: now was it wet with moisture, drenched with blood's flowing, now adorned with treasure. But I lay there a long while looking upon the Saviour's tree, troubled in mind, until I heard it give voice; the noblest of trees began to speak.

"It was long ago—still I remember it—that I was hewn down at the wood's edge, taken from my stump. Fierce foes seized me, shaped me into the spectacle that they wished, bade me lift their felons. Men carried me on their shoulders to a hill where they set me down; foes enough fastened me there. Then I saw the Master of Mankind hasten with all his heart because he wished to climb upon me. I did not dare against God's word bow or break, though I saw earth's surface tremble. All foemen I might have felled, but I stood fast. The young hero stripped himself—he who was God almighty—strong and stouthearted. He climbed upon the high gallows, valiant, in the sight of many, for he would redeem mankind. I shook when the warrior embraced me, yet I dared not bow to earth, fall to the ground's surface: I must stand fast. A cross was I raised; I lifted up the Mighty King, Lord of the Heavens; I dared not bend. They pierced me with dark nails—on me are the wounds seen, open hateful gashes. Nor did I dare do harm to any of them. They mocked

1. This prose translation, by the present editor, has been based in general on the edition of the poem by J. C. Pope, *Seven Old English Poems* (1966).

2. The Old English word *beacen* means also "token" or "sign" and "battle standard."

us both together. I was all wet with blood shed from the sides of that man by the time that he had sent forth his spirit. Many bitter things I had endured on the hill. I saw the God of Hosts cruelly racked. Darkness had covered with its mists the Ruler's body, the bright splendor. Shadow came forth, dark under the clouds. All creation wept, bewailed the King's fall: Christ was on Cross.

"Yet from afar, ready and willing, there came some to the Lord.[3] I saw all this. Sore was I troubled, yet I bent to the hands of the men, with all my heart humble. They took Almighty God, lifted him from his great torment. The warriors let me stand, stained with blood. I was all wounded with arrows. They laid him down, limb-weary, stood at his body's head, gazed upon Heaven's Lord; and he rested him there a while, exhausted after the great struggle. In the sight of his slayer[4] warriors began to build him an earth-home, carved it out of bright stone, set therein the Wielder of Triumphs. Then they began to sing for him a song of lament, sad in the evening. Then would they depart, tired, from the great Lord. He rested with small host; yet we[5] stood in our places a good while, weeping. The song of the men rose up. The body grew cold, the spirit's fair dwelling. Then they began to fell us to the earth—that was a fearful fate. They buried us in a deep pit. Yet thanes[6] of the Lord, friends, heard of me there[7] . . . decked me with gold and silver.

"Thou might now understand, man beloved of me, that I had endured suffering of evils, of grievous sorrows. Now is the happy time come that far and wide men upon earth adore me, and all this glorious creation prays to this beacon. On me the Son of God suffered for a while; therefore now I tower glorious under the heavens, and I may heal every one of those that hold me in awe. Once I was made the hardest of torments, most loathsome to men, before I made open the true road to life for all who have voices. Lo, the Lord of Glory honored me above all the trees of the wood, the Ruler of Heaven, just as his mother also, Mary herself, Almighty God for the sake of all men honored above all woman's kind.

"Now I bid thee, man beloved of me, that thou tell this vision to men. Reveal with thy words that it is the tree of glory on which Almighty God suffered for mankind's many sins and for the deeds done by Adam long ago. Death he tasted there; yet the Lord rose again in his great might to help mankind. Then he ascended into Heaven; but he will come again hither to seek mankind on doomsday, the Lord himself, Almighty God, and his angels with him, that at that time he who has the power to judge may judge each one as in

---

3. According to John xix.38–39, it was Joseph of Arimathaea and Nicodemus who received Christ's body from the Cross.
4. I.e., the Cross.
5. I.e., Christ's Cross and those on which the two thieves were crucified.
6. Members of the King's body of warriors.
7. A number of lines describing the finding of the Cross have apparently been lost here.

this transitory life he deserves. Nor may any be unafraid of the word that the Ruler will speak. Before his multitude he will ask where the man is who in the name of the Lord would taste bitter death as he did on the Cross. But then they will be afraid and will little know what they may begin to answer to Christ. Yet there need not any be afraid who bears on his breast the best of beacons. For through the Cross shall every soul who thinks to dwell with the Lord seek his kingdom[8] in his earthly journey."

Then blithe-hearted, confident, I prayed to the Cross, there where I was alone, without company. My heart was drawn away from earth's paths. Often I endured weariness of spirit. Now is there hope of life, that I may seek the tree of triumph, honor it more often than other men, since I am alone. Great is the desire of my heart for the Cross, and my hope of protection rests in it. I have not many powerful friends on earth, for they have gone from the joys of the world, sought for themselves the King of Glory; now they live in Heaven with the High Father, dwell in glory. And every day I expect the time when the Lord's Cross that I beheld here on earth shall fetch me in this transitory life and bring me where bliss is great, joy in Heaven, where the Lord's folk are set at the feast, where bliss is eternal. And may it place me where I may thereafter dwell in glory, enjoy with the saints their delight. May the Lord be my friend, who here on earth suffered for man's sins on the gallows tree. He redeemed us and granted us life, a heavenly home. Hope was restored, with glory and bliss, to those who suffered in fire.[9] The Son was victorious in that foray, mighty and successful. Then he came with many, a host of spirits, into God's kingdom, the All-Powerful Ruler, and the angels and all the saints who then dwelt in Heaven rejoiced when their Ruler, Almighty God, came where his home was.

8. I.e., the Lord's.
9. This and the following sentences refer to the Harrowing (i.e., pillaging) of Hell: after His death upon the Cross, Christ descended into hell, from which He released the souls of certain of the patriarchs and prophets, conducting them triumphantly to heaven.

BEOWULF

Beowulf, the oldest of the great long poems written in English, was probably composed more than twelve hundred years ago, in the first half of the eighth century. Its author may have been a native of what was then West Mercia, the West Midlands of England today, though the late tenth-century manuscript, which alone preserves the poem, originated in the south in the kingdom of the West Saxons. In 1731, before any modern transcription of the text had been made, the manuscript was seriously damaged in the fire that destroyed the building in London which housed the extraordinary collection of medieval English manuscripts made by Sir Robert Bruce Cotton (1571–1631). As a result of the fire and of subsequent deterioration of the manuscript, a number of lines and words have been lost from the poem, but even if the manuscript had not been damaged, the poem would still have been difficult, because the poetic Old English (or Anglo-Saxon) in which it was written is itself hard, the style is allusive, the ideas often seem remote and strange to modern perceptions, and because the text was inevitably corrupted during the many transcriptions which must have intervened in the two and a half centuries between the poem's composition and the copying of the extant manuscript. Yet despite its difficulty, the somber grandeur of *Beowulf* is still capable of stirring the hearts of readers, and because of its excellence as well as its antiquity, the poem merits the high position that it is generally assigned in the study of English poetry.

While the poem itself is English in language and origin, it deals not with native Englishmen, but with their Germanic forebears, especially with two south Scandinavian tribes, the Danes and the Geats, who lived on the Danish island of Zealand and in southern Sweden, respectively. Thus, the historical period it concerns—insofar as it may be said to refer to history at all —is some two centuries before the poem was written; that is, it concerns a time following the initial invasion of England by Germanic tribes in 449, but before the Anglo-Saxon migration was completed, and perhaps before the arrival of the ancestors of the audience to whom the poem was sung: this audience may have considered itself to be of the same Geatish stock as the hero, Beowulf. The one datable fact of history mentioned in the poem is a raid on the Franks made by Hygelac, the king of the Geats at the time Beowulf was a young man, and this raid occurred in the year 520. Yet despite their antiquity, the poet's materials must have been very much alive to his audience, for the elliptical way in which he alludes to events not directly concerned with his plot demands of the listener a wide knowledge of traditional Germanic history. This knowledge was probably kept alive by other heroic poetry, of which little has been preserved in English, though much must once have existed. As it stands, *Beowulf* is not only unique as an example of the Old English epic, but is also the greatest of the surviving epics composed by the Germanic peoples.

It is generally agreed that the poet who put the old materials into their present form was a Christian, and that his poem reflects a Christian tradition: the conversion of the Germanic settlers in England had largely been completed during the century preceding the one in which the poet wrote. But there is little general agreement as to how clearly *Beowulf* reflects a Christian tradition or, conversely, the actual nature of the Christian tradition that it is held to reflect. Many specifically Christian references occur, especially to the Old Testament: God is said to be the Creator of all things and His will seems recognized (sporadically if not systematically) as being identical with Fate (*wyrd*); Grendel is described as a descendant of Cain, and the sword that Beowulf finds in Grendel's mother's lair has engraved on it the story of the race of giants and their destruction by flood; the dead await God's judgment, and Hell and the Devil are ready to receive the souls of Grendel and his mother, while believers will find the Father's embrace; Hrothgar's speech of advice to Beowulf (section XXV) seems to reflect patristic doctrine in its emphasis on conscience and the Devil's lying in wait for the unwary. Yet there is no reference to the New Testament—to Christ and His Sacrifice which are the real bases of Christianity in any intelligible sense of the term. Furthermore, readers may well feel that the poem achieves rather little of its emotional power through invocation of Christian values or of values that are consonant with Christian doctrine as we know it. Perhaps the sense of tragic waste which pervades the Finnsburg episode (section XVI) springs from a Christian perception of the insane futility of the primitive Germanic thirst for vengeance; and the facts that Beowulf's chief adversaries are not men but monsters and that before his death he is able to boast that as king of the Geats he did not seek wars with neighboring tribes may reflect a Christian's appreciation for peace among men. But while admitting such values, the poet also invokes many others of a very different order, values that seem to belong to an ancient, pagan, warrior society of the kind described by the Roman historian Tacitus at the end of the first century. It should be noted that even Hrothgar's speech about conscience is directed more toward making Beowulf a good Germanic leader of men than a good Christian. One must, indeed, draw the conclusion from the poem itself that while Christian is a correct term for the religion of the poet and of his audience, it was a Christianity that had not yet by any means succeeded in obliterating an older pagan tradition, which still called forth powerful responses from men's hearts, despite the fact that many aspects of this tradition must be abhorrent to a sophisticated Christian. In this connection it is well to recall that the missionaries from Rome who initiated the conversion of the English proceeded in a conciliatory manner, not so much uprooting paganism in order to plant Christianity as planting Christianity in the faith that it would ultimately choke out the weeds of paganism. And the English clung long to some of their ancient traditions: for instance, the legal principle of the payment of *wergild* (defined below) remained in force until the Norman Conquest, four centuries after the conversion of the English.

In the warrior society whose values the poem constantly invokes, the most important of human relationships was that which existed between the warrior—the thane—and his lord, a relationship based less on subordination of one man's will to another's than on mutual trust and respect. When a warrior vowed loyalty to his lord, he became not so much his servant as his voluntary companion, one who would take pride in defending him and fighting in his wars. In return, the lord was expected to take affectionate care of his thanes and to reward them richly for their valor: a good king, one like Hrothgar or Beowulf, is referred to by such poetic epithets as "protector of warriors" and "dispenser of treasure" or "ring-giver," and the failure of bad kings is ascribed to their ill-temper and avarice, both of which alienate them from their retainers. The material benefit of this arrangement between lord and thane is obvious, yet under a good king the relationship seems to have had a significance more spiritual than material. Thus the treasure that an ideal Germanic king seizes from his enemies and rewards his retainers with is regarded as something more than mere wealth that will serve the well-being of its possessor; rather, it is a kind of visible proof that all parties are realizing themselves to the full in a spiritual sense—that the men of this band are congenially and successfully united with one another. The symbolic importance of treasure is illustrated by the poet's remark that the gift Beowulf gave the Danish coast-guard brought the latter honor among his companions, and even more by the fact that although Beowulf dies while obtaining a great treasure for his people, such objects as are removed from the dragon's hoard are actually buried with him as a fitting sign of his ultimate achievement.

The relationship between kinsmen was also of deep significance to this society and provides another emotional value for Old English heroic poetry. If one of his kinsmen had been slain, a man had the special duty of either killing the slayer or exacting from him the payment of *wergild* ("man-price"): each rank of society was evaluated at a definite price, which had to be paid to the dead man's kinsmen by the killer who wished to avoid their vengeance—even if the killing had been accidental. Again, the money itself had less significance as wealth than as a proof that the kinsmen had done what was right. Relatives who failed either to exact *wergild* or to take vengeance could never be happy, having found no practical way of satisfying their grief for their kinsmen's death. "It is better for a man to avenge his friend than much mourn," Beowulf says to the old Hrothgar, who is bewailing Aeschere's killing by Grendel's mother. And one of the most poignant passages in the poem describes the sorrow of King Hrethel after one of his sons had accidentally killed another: by the code of kinship Hrethel was forbidden to kill or to exact compensation from a kinsman, yet by the same code he was required to do one or the other in order to avenge the dead. Caught in this curious dilemma, Hrethel became so disconsolate that he could no longer face life.

It is evident that the need to take vengeance would create never-ending feuds, which the practice of marrying royal princesses to the kings or princes of hostile tribes did little to mitigate, though the purpose of such marriages was to replace hostility by alliance. Hrothgar wishes to make peace with the Heatho-Bards by marrying his daughter to their king, Ingeld, whose father was killed by the Danes; but as Beowulf predicts, sooner or later the Heatho-Bards' desire for vengeance on the Danes will erupt, and there will be more bloodshed. And the Danish princess Hildeburh, married to Finn of the Jutes, will see her son and her brother both killed while fighting on opposite sides in a battle at her own home, and ultimately will see her husband killed by the Danes in revenge for her brother's death. Beowulf himself is, for a Germanic hero, curiously free of involvement in feuds of this sort, though he does boast that he avenged the death of his king, Heardred, on his slayer Onela. Yet the potentiality—or inevitability—of sudden attack, sudden change, swift death is omnipresent in *Beowulf*: men seem to be caught in a vast web of reprisals and counterreprisals from which there is little hope of escape. This is the aspect of the poem which is apt to make the most powerful impression on the reader—its strong sense of doom.

Beowulf himself is chiefly concerned not with tribal feuds but with fatal evil both less and more complex. Grendel and the dragon are threats to the security of the lands they infest just as human enemies would be, but they are not part of the social order and presumably have no one to avenge their deaths (that Grendel's mother appeared as an avenger seems to have been a surprise both to Beowulf and to the Danes). On the other hand, because they are outside the normal order of things, they require of their conqueror something greater than normal warfare requires. In each case, it is the clear duty of the king and his companions to put down the evil. But the Danish Hrothgar is old and his companions unenterprising, and excellent though Hrothgar has been in the kingship, he nevertheless lacks the quality that later impels the old Beowulf to fight the dragon that threatens his people. The poem makes no criticism of Hrothgar for this lack; he merely seems not to be the kind of man—one might almost say he was not fated—to develop his human potential to the fullest extent that Fate would permit: that is Beowulf's role. In undertaking to slay Grendel, and later Grendel's mother, Beowulf is testing his relationship with unknowable destiny. At any time, as he is fully aware, his luck may abandon him and he may be killed, as, indeed, he is in the otherwise successful encounter with the dragon. But whether he lives or dies, he will have done all that any man could do to develop his character heroically. It is this consciousness of testing Fate that probably explains the boasting that modern readers of heroic poetry often find offensive. When he boasts, Beowulf is not only demonstrating that he has chosen the heroic way of life, but is also choosing it, for when he invokes his former courage as pledge of his future courage, his boast becomes a vow; the hero has put himself in a position from which he cannot withdraw.

Courage is the instrument by which the hero realizes himself. "Fate often saves an undoomed man when his courage is good," says Beowulf in his account of his swimming match: that is, if Fate has not entirely doomed a man in advance, courage is the quality that can perhaps influence Fate against its natural tendency to doom him now. It is this complex statement (in which it is hard to read the will of God for Fate) that Beowulf's life explores: he will use his great strength in the most courageous way by going alone, even unarmed, against monsters. Doom, of course, ultimately claims him, but not until he has fulfilled to its limits the pagan ideal of a heroic life. And despite the desire he often shows to Christianize pagan virtues, the Christian poet remains true to the older tradition when, at the end of his poem, he leaves us with the impression that Beowulf's chief reward is pagan immortality: the memory in the minds of later men of a hero's heroic actions. The poem itself is, indeed, a noble expression of that immortality

We offer a prose translation of *Beowulf* because we believe that only a prose translation, made with no other end in mind than fidelity to the original, can transmit to the reader a real sense of its meaning. To make it a modern poem is, inevitably, to make it a different poem. The author of one of the best verse translations of *Beowulf* emphasizes that "a creative recreation [i.e., a poetic translation] is a creation"; no two creative artists can create the same thing. If, on the other hand, a verse translation does not try to be a poem in its own right, then it can only be versification, a literal rendering constantly distracted from literalism by the need to versify, as a more creative translation is constantly distracted from literalism by the translator's creativity.

There are, moreover, linguistic reasons why Old English poetry is impossible to translate in such a way as to reproduce the extraordinary tone of the original. First, the great force of Old English poetry depends on the prominence of its nouns and compound nouns, which form the backbone of the majority of its lines. Second, the nouns and other important words— verbs and, less commonly than in modern English, adjectives—stand relatively free of the "little" words such as articles and prepositions that are necessary to modern English syntax. Since it is an inflectional language, Old English dispenses with many prepositions, and by its very nature it dispenses with articles. What is important to the primary sense stands out strongly without linguistic distraction, and the powerful effect is one that modern English poetry cannot achieve.

There are thirteen words in the first three lines of *Beowulf*:

> Hwæt, wē Gārdena in gēardagum
> Yes, we (of the) Spear-Danes in (the) old days

> þēodcyninga þrym gefrūnon
> (Of the) kings (of the) people (the) might (have) heard (of)

> hū þā æþelingas ellen fremedon
> How those princes brave action performed

Six of the thirteen words are nouns: *Gārdena*, *gēardagum*, *þēodcyninga*, *þrym*, *æþelingas*, and *ellen*, and three of these are compound: *Gār-dena*, "Spear-Danes"; *gēar-dagum*, "year-days"; and *þēod-cyninga*, "people-kings." There are two verbs, *gefrūnon* and *fremedon*, and an interjection, *Hwæt*, and only four "little" words. On the other hand, a literal translation,

> Yes, we have heard of the might of the kings of the people of the Spear-Danes in the old days, how those princes performed brave action,

has twenty-six words: seven nouns, only one of which is a compound, two verbs, two adjectives, the interjection, and the rest—more than half of the total—"little words." Obviously, a good translator can get around using some of the "little" words, but he cannot eliminate them all: a survey of translations, both prose and poetry, finds that the lowest number of words achieved in these lines is twenty. The presence of little words impairs the forcefulness of the original, almost half of whose words are substantives: indeed, if one counts the compounds as double nouns, then more than half of the total of the original's words are substantives.

Furthermore, all six of the Old English nouns are in the alliterative position where they receive the full weight of the metrical emphasis. Not surprisingly, a modern English literal translation of these nouns produces almost no natural alliterative pairs. A good poet will, of course, use his ingenuity to find alliterative synonyms, but this task, hard at best, is made harder by the fact that many of the important nouns of Anglo-Saxon culture had many synonyms, but today have none: there are many words for *sword* in Old English, but hardly more than one in idiomatic modern English. The search for alliteration, moreover, often results in a change in the sense or emphasis of the original. To begin a poem with the line

> Lo! we have listened to many a lay

is not unattractive. But to begin *Beowulf* with it is not satisfactory: the line alliterates, but only at the cost of making our having listened to a lay (there is no lay in the original) more important than the Spear-Danes in the old days, which is what the poem is about.

> Hear me! We've heard of Danish heroes

is a good deal more forceful, and hence Old English, in spirit; but the alliterative emphasis on *Hear* and *heard* causes a tautological malfunction: one might suppose that since we've heard of Danish heroes, we are now going to hear about something else. The search for alliteration has destroyed the subtlety with which the Old English poet introduced his own poem on the old heroic days.

Rather than try to create a new and lesser poem for the reader, it seems better to offer him in prose the literal materials from which he can recreate the poem.

TRIBES AND GENEALOGIES

I. The Danes (Bright-, Half-, Ring-, Spear-, North-, East-, South-, West-Danes; Scyldings, Honor-, Victor-, War-Scyldings; Ing's friends).

II. The Geats (Sea-, War-, Weather-Geats)

III. The Swedes.

IV. Miscellaneous.

A. The Half-Danes (also called Scyldings) involved in the fight at Finnsburg may represent a different tribe from the Danes of paragraph I, above. Their king Hoc had a son, Hnaef, who succeeded him, and a daughter Hildeburh, who married Finn, king of the Jutes.

B. The Jutes or Frisians are represented as enemies of the Danes in the fight at Finnsburg and as allies of the Franks or Hugas at the time Hygelac the Geat made the attack in which he lost his life and from which Beowulf swam home. Also allied with the Franks at this time were the Hetware.

C. The Heatho-Bards (i.e., "Battle-Bards") are represented as inveterate enemies of the Danes. Their king Froda had been killed in an attack on the Danes, and Hrothgar's attempt to make peace with them by marrying his daughter Freawaru to Froda's son Ingeld failed when the latter attacked Heorot. The attack was repulsed, though Heorot was burned.

---

† The daughter of Hygelac who was given to Eofor may have been born to him by a former wife, older than Hygd.

Beowulf [1]

[Prologue: The Earlier History of the Danes]

Yes, we have heard of the glory of the Spear-Danes' kings in the old days—how the princes of that people did brave deeds.

Often Scyld Scefing [2] took mead-benches away from enemy bands, from many tribes, terrified their nobles—after the time that he was first found helpless.[3] He lived to find comfort for that, became great under the skies, prospered in honors until every one of those who lived about him, across the whale-road, had to obey him, pay him tribute. That was a good king.

Afterwards a son was born to him, a young boy in his house, whom God sent to comfort the people: He had seen the sore need they had suffered during the long time they lacked a king. Therefore the Lord of Life, the Ruler of Heaven, gave him honor in the world: Beow [4] was famous, the glory of the son of Scyld spread widely in the Northlands. In this way a young man ought by his good deeds, by giving splendid gifts while still in his father's house, to make sure that later in life beloved companions will stand by him, that people will serve him when war comes. Through deeds that bring praise, a man shall prosper in every country.

Then at the fated time Scyld the courageous went away into the protection of the Lord. His dear companions carried him down to the sea-currents, just as he himself had bidden them do when, as protector of the Scyldings,[5] he had ruled them with his words —long had the beloved prince governed the land. There in the harbor stood the ring-prowed ship, ice-covered and ready to sail, a prince's vessel. Then they laid down the ruler they had loved, the ring-giver, in the hollow of the ship, the glorious man beside the mast. There was brought great store of treasure, wealth from lands far away. I have not heard of a ship more splendidly furnished with war-weapons and battle-dress, swords and mail-shirts. On his breast lay a great many treasures that should voyage with him far out into the sea's possession. They provided him with no lesser gifts, treasure of the people, than those had done who at his beginning first sent him forth on the waves, a

---

1. The translation into modern English, by the editor (1966), is based on F. Klaeber's third edition of the poem (1950); in general, the emendations suggested by J. C. Pope, *The Rhythm of Beowulf,* second edition (1966), have been adopted. The division into sections headed by roman numerals is that of the manuscript, which makes, however, no provision for Section XXX.
2. The meaning is probably "son of

Sceaf," although Scyld's origins are mysterious.
3. As is made clear shortly below, Scyld arrived in Denmark as a child alone in a ship loaded with treasures.
4. Although the manuscript reads "Beowulf," most scholars now agree that it should read "Beow." Beow was the grandfather of the Danish king Hrothgar.
5. I.e., the Danes ("descendants of Scyld").

child alone. Then also they set a golden standard high over his head, let the water take him, gave him to the sea. Sad was their spirit, mournful their mind. Men cannot truthfully say who received that cargo, neither counsellors in the hall nor warriors under the skies.

(I) Then in the cities was Beow of the Scyldings beloved king of the people, long famous among nations (his father had gone elsewhere, the king from his land), until later great Healfdene was born to him. As long as he lived, old and fierce in battle, he upheld the glorious Scyldings. To him all told were four children born into the world, to the leader of the armies: Heorogar and Hrothgar and the good Halga. I have heard tell that [. . . was On]ela's queen,[6] beloved bed-companion of the Battle-Scylfing.

[Beowulf and Grendel]

[THE HALL HEOROT IS ATTACKED BY GRENDEL]

Then Hrothgar was given success in warfare, glory in battle, so that his retainers gladly obeyed him and their company grew into a great band of warriors. It came to his mind that he would command men to construct a hall, a mead-building large[r] than the children of men had ever heard of, and therein he would give to young and old all that God had given him, except for common land and men's bodies.[7] Then I have heard that the work was laid upon many nations, wide through this middle-earth, that they should adorn the folk-hall. In time it came to pass—quickly, as men count it—that it was finished, the largest of hall-dwellings. He gave it the name of Heorot,[8] he who ruled wide with his words. He did not forget his promise: at the feast he gave out rings, treasure. The hall stood tall, high and wide-gabled: it would wait for the fierce flames of vengeful fire;[9] the time was not yet at hand for sword-hate between son-in-law and father-in-law to awaken after murderous rage.

Then the fierce spirit[1] painfully endured hardship for a time, he who dwelt in the darkness, for every day he heard loud mirth in the hall; there was the sound of the harp, the clear song of the scop.[2] There he spoke who could relate the beginning of men far back in time, said that the Almighty made

6. The text is faulty, so that the name of Healfdene's daughter has been lost; her husband Onela was a Swedish (Scylfing) king.
7. Or "men's lives." Apparently slaves, along with public land, were not in the king's power to give away.
8. I.e., "Hart."
9. The destruction by fire of Heorot occurred at a later time than that of

the poem's action, probably during the otherwise unsuccessful attack of the Heatho-Bard Ingeld on his father-in-law Hrothgar, mentioned in the next clause.
1. I.e., Grendel.
2. The "scop" was the Anglo-Saxon minstrel, who recited poetic stories to the accompaniment of a harp.

earth, a bright field fair in the water that surrounds it, set up in triumph the lights of the sun and the moon to lighten land-dwellers, and adorned the surfaces of the earth with branches and leaves, created also life for each of the kinds that move and breathe.—Thus these warriors lived in joy, blessed, until one began to do evil deeds, a hellish enemy. The grim spirit was called Grendel, known as a rover of the borders, one who held the moors, fen and fastness. Unhappy creature, he lived for a time in the home of the monsters' race, after God had condemned them as kin of Cain. The Eternal Lord avenged the murder in which he slew Abel. Cain had no pleasure in that feud, but He banished him far from mankind, the Ruler, for that misdeed. From him sprang all bad breeds, trolls and elves and monsters—likewise the giants who for a long time strove with God: He paid them their reward for that.

(II.) Then, after night came, Grendel went to survey the tall house—how, after their beer-drinking, the Ring-Danes had disposed themselves in it. Then he found therein a band of nobles asleep after the feast: they felt no sorrow, no misery of men. The creature of evil, grim and fierce, was quickly ready, savage and cruel, and seized from their rest thirty thanes. From there he turned to go back to his home, proud of his plunder, sought his dwelling with that store of slaughter.

Then in the first light of dawning day Grendel's war-strength was revealed to men: then after the feast weeping arose, great cry in the morning. The famous king, hero of old days, sat joyless; the mighty one suffered, felt sorrow for his thanes, when they saw the track of the foe, of the cursed spirit: that hardship was too strong, too loathsome and long-lasting. Nor was there a longer interval, but after one night Grendel again did greater slaughter—and had no remorse for it—vengeful acts and wicked: he was too intent on them. Thereafter it was easy to find the man who sought rest for himself elsewhere, farther away, a bed among the outlying buildings—after it was made clear to him, told by clear proof, the hatred of him who now controlled the hall.[3] Whoever escaped the foe held himself afterwards farther off and more safely. Thus Grendel held sway and fought against right, one against all, until the best of houses stood empty. It was a long time, the length of twelve winters, that the lord of the Scyldings suffered grief, all woes, great sorrows. Therefore, sadly in songs, it became well-known to the children of men that Grendel had fought a long time with Hrothgar, for many half-years maintained mortal spite, feud, and enmity—constant war. He wanted no peace with any of the men of the Danish host, would not withdraw his deadly rancor, or pay compensation: no

3. I.e., Grendel.

counselor there had any reason to expect splendid repayment at the hands of the slayer.[4] For the monster was relentless, the dark death-shadow, against warriors old and young, lay in wait and ambushed them. In the perpetual darkness he held to the misty moors: men do not know where hell-demons direct their footsteps.

Thus many crimes the enemy of mankind committed, the terrible walker-alone, cruel injuries one after another. In the dark nights he dwelt in Heorot, the richly adorned hall. He might not approach the throne, [receive] treasure, because of the Lord; He had no love for him.[5]

This was great misery to the lord of the Scyldings, a breaking of spirit. Many a noble sat often in council, sought a plan, what would be best for strong-hearted men to do against the awful attacks. At times they vowed sacrifices at heathen temples, with their words prayed that the soul-slayer [6] would give help for the distress of the people. Such was their custom, the hope of heathens; in their spirits they thought of Hell, they knew not the Ruler, the Judge of Deeds, they recognized not the Lord God, nor indeed did they know how to praise the Protector of Heaven, the glorious King. Woe is him who in terrible trouble must thrust his soul into the fire's embrace, hope for no comfort, not expect change. Well is the man who after his death-day may seek the Lord and find peace in the embrace of the Father.

[THE COMING OF BEOWULF TO HEOROT]

(III.) So in the cares of his times the son of Healfdene constantly brooded, nor might the wise warrior set aside his woe. Too harsh, hateful and long-lasting was the hardship that had come upon the people, distress dire and inexorable, worst of night-horrors.

A thane of Hygelac,[7] a good man among the Geats, heard in his homeland of Grendel's deeds: of mankind he was the strongest of might in the time of this life, noble and great. He bade that a good ship be made ready for him, said he would seek the war-king over the swan's road, the famous prince, since he had need of men. Very little did wise men blame him for that adventure, though he was dear to them; they urged the brave one on, examined the omens. From the folk of the Geats the good man had chosen warriors of the bravest that he could

---

4. According to old Germanic law, a slayer could achieve peace with his victim's kinsmen only by paying them *wergild*, i.e., compensation for the life of the slain man.
5. Behind this obscure passage seems to lie the idea that Grendel, unlike Hrothgar's thanes, could not approach the throne to receive gifts from the king, having been condemned by God as an outlaw.
6. I.e., the Devil. Despite this assertion that the Danes were heathen, their king, Hrothgar, speaks consistently as a Christian.
7. I.e., Beowulf the Geat, whose king was Hygelac.

find; one of fifteen he led the way, the warrior sought the wooden ship, the sea-skilled one the land's edge. The time had come: the ship was on the waves, the boat under the cliff. The warriors eagerly climbed on the prow—the sea-currents eddied, sea against sand; men bore bright weapons into the ship's bosom, splendid armor. Men pushed the well-braced ship from shore, warriors on a well-wished voyage. Then over the sea-waves, blown by the wind, the foam-necked boat traveled, most like a bird, until at good time on the second day the curved prow had come to where the seafarers could see land, the sea-cliffs shine, towering hills, great headlands. Then was the sea crossed, the journey at end. Then quickly the men of the Geats climbed upon the shore, moored the wooden ship; mail-shirts rattled, dress for battle. They thanked God that the wave-way had been easy for them.

Then from the wall the Scyldings' guard who should watch over the sea-cliffs saw bright shields borne over the gangway, armor ready for battle; strong desire stirred him in mind to learn what the men were. He went riding on his horse to the shore, thane of Hrothgar, forcefully brandished a great spear in his hands, with formal words questioned them: "What are you, bearers of armor, dressed in mail-coats, who thus have come bringing a tall ship over the sea-road, over the water to this place? Lo, for a long time I have been guard of the coast, held watch by the sea so that no foe with a force of ships might work harm on the Danes' land: never have shield-bearers more openly undertaken to come ashore here; nor did you know for sure of a word of leave from our warriors, consent from my kinsmen. I have never seen a mightier warrior on earth than is one of you, a man in battle-dress. That is no retainer made to seem good by his weapons—unless his appearance belies him, his unequalled form. Now I must learn your lineage before you go any farther from here, spies on the Danes' land. Now you far-dwellers, sea-voyagers, hear what I think: you must straightway say where you have come from."

(IV.) To him replied the leader, the chief of the band unlocked his word-hoard: "We are men of the Geatish nation and Hygelac's hearth-companions. My father was well-known among the tribes, a noble leader named Ecgtheow. He lived many winters before he went on his way, an old man, from men's dwellings. Every wise man wide over the earth readily remembers him. Through friendly heart we have come to seek your lord, the son of Healfdene, protector of the people. Be good to us and tell us what to do: we have a great errand to the famous one, the king of the Danes. And I too do not think that anything ought to be kept secret: you know whether it is so, as we have indeed heard, that among the Scyldings I know not what foe, what dark doer of hateful deeds in the black nights, shows in terrible manner strange malice, injury and slaughter. In openness of heart I may teach Hrothgar remedy for that, how he, wise and good, shall overpower the foe—if change is ever to come to him, relief from evil's distress—and how his surging cares may be made to cool. Or else ever after he will suffer tribulations, constraint, while the best of houses remains there on its high place."

The guard spoke from where he sat on his horse, brave officer: "A sharp-witted shield-warrior who thinks well must be able to judge each of the two things, words and works. I understand this: that here is a troop friendly to the Scyldings' king. Go forward, bearing weapons and war-gear. I will show you the way; I shall also bid my fellow-thanes honorably to hold your boat against all enemies, your new-tarred ship on the sand, until again over the sea-streams it bears its beloved men to the Geatish shore, the wooden vessel with curved prow. May it be granted by fate that one who behaves so bravely pass whole through the battle-storm."

Then they set off. The boat lay fixed, rested on the rope, the deep-bosomed ship, fast at anchor. Boar-images [8] shone over cheek-guards gold-adorned, gleaming and fire-hardened—the war-minded boar held guard over fierce men. The warriors hastened, marched together until they might see the timbered hall, stately and shining with gold; for earth-dwellers under the skies that was the most famous of buildings in which the mighty one waited—its light gleamed over many lands. The battle-brave guide pointed out to them the shining house of the brave ones so that they might go straight to it. Warrior-like he turned his horse, then spoke words: "It is time for me to go back. The All-Wielding Father in His grace keep you safe in your undertakings. I shall go back to the sea to keep watch against hostile hosts."

(V.) The road was stone-paved, the path showed the way to the men in ranks. War-corselet shone, hard and hand-wrought, bright iron rings sang on their armor when they first came walking to the hall in their grim gear. Sea-weary they set down their broad shields, marvelously strong protections, against the wall of the building. Then they sat down on the bench—mail-shirts, warrior's clothing, rang out. Spears stood together, sea-men's weapons, ash steel-gray at the top. The armed band was worthy of its weapons.

Then a proud-spirited man [9] asked the warriors there about their lineage: "Where do you bring those gold-covered shields

8. Carved images of boars (sometimes represented as clothed like human warriors) were placed on helmets in the belief that they would protect the wearer in battle.
9. Identified below as Wulfgar.

from, gray mail-shirts and visored helmets, this multitude of battle-shafts? I am Hrothgar's herald and officer. I have not seen strangers—so many men—more bold. I think that it is for daring—not for refuge, but for greatness of heart—that you have sought Hrothgar." The man known for his courage replied to him; the proud man of the Geats, hardy under helmet, spoke words in return: "We are Hygelac's table-companions. Beowulf is my name. I will tell my errand to Healfdene's son, the great prince your lord, if, good as he is, he will grant that we might address him." Wulfgar spoke—he was a man of the Wendels, his bold spirit known to many, his valor and wisdom: "I will ask the lord of the Danes about this, the Scyldings' king, the ring-giver, just as you request—will ask the glorious ruler about your voyage, and will quickly make known to you the answer the good man thinks best to give me."

He returned at once to where Hrothgar sat, old and hoary, with his company of earls. The man known for his valor went forward till he stood squarely before the Danes' king: he knew the custom of tried retainers. Wulfgar spoke to his lord and friend: "Here have journeyed men of the Geats, come far over the sea's expanse. The warriors call their chief Beowulf. They ask that they, my prince, might exchange words with you. Do not refuse them your answer, gracious Hrothgar. From their war-gear they seem worthy of earls' esteem. Strong indeed is the chief who has led the warriors here."

(VI.) Hrothgar spoke, protector of the Scyldings: "I knew him when he was a boy. His father was called Ecgtheow: Hrethel of the Geats [1] gave him his only daughter for his home. Now has his hardy offspring come here, sought a fast friend. Then, too, seafarers who took gifts there to please the Geats used to say that he has in his handgrip the strength of thirty men, a man famous in battle. Holy God of His grace has sent him to us West-Danes, as I hope, against the terror of Grendel. I shall offer the good man treasures for his daring. Now make haste, bid them come in together to see my company of kinsmen. In your speech say to them also that they are welcome to the Danish people."

Then Wulfgar went to the hall's door, gave the message from within: "The lord of the East-Danes, my victorious prince, has bidden me say to you that he knows your noble ancestry, and that you brave-hearted men are welcome to him over the sea-swells. Now you may come in your war-dress, under your battle helmets, to see Hrothgar. Let your war-shields, your wooden spears, await here the outcome of the talk."

Then the mighty one rose, many a warrior about him, a company of strong thanes. Some waited there, kept watch over the

---

1. Hrethel was the father of Hygelac and Beowulf's grandfather and guardian.

weapons as the brave one bade them. Together they hastened, as the warrior directed them, under Heorot's roof. The war-leader, hardy under helmet, advanced till he stood on the hearth. Beowulf spoke, his mail-shirt glistened, armor-net woven by the blacksmith's skill: "Hail, Hrothgar! I am kinsman and thane of Hygelac. In my youth I have set about many brave deeds. The affair of Grendel was made known to me on my native soil: sea-travelers say that this hall, best of buildings, stands empty and useless to all warriors after the evening-light becomes hidden beneath the cover of the sky. Therefore my people, the best wise earls, advised me thus, lord Hrothgar, that I should seek you because they know what my strength can accomplish. They themselves looked on when, bloody from my foes, I came from the fight where I had bound five, destroyed a family of giants, and at night in the waves slain water-monsters, suffered great pain, avenged an affliction of the Weather-Geats on those who had asked for trouble—ground enemies to bits. And now alone I shall settle affairs with Grendel, the monster, the demon. Therefore, lord of the Bright-Danes, protector of the Scyldings, I will make a request of you, refuge of warriors, fair friend of nations, that you refuse me not, now that I have come so far, that alone with my company of earls, this band of hardy men, I may cleanse Heorot. I have also heard say that the monster in his recklessness cares not for weapons. Therefore, so that my liege lord Hygelac may be glad of me in his heart, I scorn to bear sword or broad shield, yellow wood, to the battle, but with my grasp I shall grapple with the enemy and fight for life, foe against foe. The one whom death takes can trust the Lord's judgment. I think that if he may accomplish it, unafraid he will feed on the folk of the Geats in the war-hall as he has often done on the flower of men. You will not need to hide my head [2] if death takes me, for he will have me blood-smeared; he will bear away my bloody flesh meaning to savor it, he will eat ruthlessly, the walker alone, will stain his retreat in the moor; no longer will you need trouble yourself to take care of my body. If battle takes me, send to Hygelac the best of war-clothes that protects my breast, finest of mail-shirts. It is a legacy of Hrethel, the work of Weland.[3] Fate always goes as it must."

(VII.) Hrothgar spoke, protector of the Scyldings: "For deeds done, my friend Beowulf, and for past favors you have sought us. A fight of your father's brought on the greatest of feuds. With his own hands he became the slayer of Heatholaf among the Wylfings. After that the country of the Weather-Geats might not keep him, for fear of war. From there he sought the folk of the South-Danes, the Honor-Scyldings, over the sea-swell. At that time I was first ruling the Danish people and, still in my youth,

2. I.e., "bury my body."   3. The blacksmith of the Norse gods.

held the wide kingdom, hoard-city of heroes. Heorogar had died then, gone from life, my older brother, son of Healfdene—he was better than I. Afterwards I paid blood-money to end the feud; over the sea's back I sent to the Wylfings old treasures; he[4] swore oaths to me.

"It is a sorrow to me in spirit to say to any man what Grendel has brought me with his hatred—humiliation in Heorot, terrible violence. My hall-troop, warrior-band, has shrunk; fate has swept them away into Grendel's horror. (God may easily put an end to the wild ravager's deeds!) Full often over the ale-cups warriors made bold with beer have boasted that they would await with grim swords Grendel's attack in the beer-hall. Then in the morning this mead-hall was a hall shining with blood, when the day lightened, all the bench-floor blood-wet, a gore-hall. I had fewer faithful men, beloved retainers, for death had destroyed them. Now sit down to the feast and unbind your thoughts, your famous victories, as heart inclines."

[THE FEAST AT HEOROT]

Then was a bench cleared in the beer-hall for the men of the Geats all together. Then the stout-hearted ones went to sit down, proud in their might. A thane did his work who bore in his hands an embellished ale-cup, poured the bright drink. At times a scop sang, clear-voiced in Heorot. There was joy of brave men, no little company of Danes and Weather-Geats.

(VIII.) Unferth spoke, son of Ecglaf, who sat at the feet of the king of the Scyldings, unbound words of contention—to him was Beowulf's undertaking, the brave seafarer, a great vexation, for he would not allow that any other man of middle-earth should ever achieve more glory under the heavens than himself: "Are you that Beowulf who contended with Breca, competed in swimming on the broad sea, where for pride you explored the water, and for foolish boast ventured your lives in the deep? Nor might any man, friend nor enemy, keep you from the perilous venture of swimming in the sea. There you embraced the sea-streams with your arms, measured the sea-ways, flung forward your hands, glided over the ocean; the sea boiled with waves, with winter's swell. Seven nights you toiled in the water's power. He overcame you at swimming, had more strength. Then in the morning the sea bore him up among the Heathoraemas; from there he sought his own home, dear to his people, the land of the Brondings, the fair stronghold, where he had folk, castle, and treasures. All his boast against you the son of Beanstan carried out in deed. Therefore I expect the worse results for you—though you have prevailed everywhere in battles, in grim war—if you

---

4. Ecgtheow, whose feud with the Wylfings Hrothgar had settled.

dare wait near Grendel a night-long space."

Beowulf spoke, the son of Ecgtheow: "Well, my friend Unferth, drunk with beer you have spoken a great many things
about Breca—told about his adventures. I maintain the truth that
I had more strength in the sea, hardship on the waves, than
any other man. Like boys we agreed together and boasted—we
were both in our first youth—that we would risk our lives in the
salt sea, and that we did even so. We had naked swords, strong
in our hands, when we went swimming; we thought to guard
ourselves against whale-fishes. He could not swim at all far from
me in the flood-waves, be quicker in the water, nor would I move
away from him. Thus we were together on the sea for the time
of five nights until the flood drove us apart, the swelling sea,
coldest of weathers, darkening night, and the north wind battle-
grim turned against us: rough were the waves. The anger of the
sea-fishes was roused. Then my body-mail, hard and hand-linked,
gave me help against my foes; the woven war-garment, gold-
adorned, covered my breast. A fierce cruel attacker dragged me
to the bottom, held me grim in his grasp, but it was granted
me to reach the monster with my sword-point, my battle-blade.
The war-stroke destroyed the mighty sea-beast—through my hand.

(IX.) "Thus often loathsome assailants pressed me hard. I
served them with my good sword, as the right was. They had
no joy at all of the feast, the malice-workers, that they should
eat me, sit around a banquet near the sea-bottom. But in the
morning, sword-wounded they lay on the shore, left behind by
the waves, put to sleep by the blade, so that thereafter they
would never hinder the passage of sea-voyagers over the deep
water. Light came from the east, bright signal of God, the sea
became still so that I might see the headlands, the windy walls
of the sea. Fate often saves an undoomed man when his courage
is good. In any case it befell me that I slew with my sword
nine sea-monsters. I have not heard tell of a harder fight by
night under heaven's arch, nor of a man more hard-pressed in
the sea-streams. Yet I came out of the enemies' grasp alive, weary
of my adventure. Then the sea bore me onto the lands of the
Finns, the flood with its current, the surging waters.

"I have not heard say of you any such hard matching of
might, such sword-terror. Breca never yet in the games of war—
neither he nor you—achieved so bold a deed with bright swords
(I do not much boast of it), though you became your brothers'
slayer, your close kin; for that you will suffer punishment in hell,
even though your wit is keen. I tell you truly, son of Ecglaf, that
Grendel, awful monster, would never have performed so many
terrible deeds against your chief, humiliation in Heorot, if your
spirit, your heart, were so fierce in fight as you claim. But he has

noticed that he need not much fear the hostility, not much dread
the terrible sword-storm of your people, the Victory-Scyldings.
He exacts forced levy, shows mercy to none of the Danish
people; but he is glad, kills, carves for feasting, expects no
fight from the Spear-Danes. But I shall show him soon now the
strength and courage of the Geats, their warfare. Afterwards he
will walk who may, glad to the mead, when the morning light
of another day, the bright-clothed sun, shines from the south on the
children of men."

Then was the giver of treasure in gladness, gray-haired and
battle-brave. The lord of the Bright-Danes could count on help.
The folk's guardian had heard from Beowulf a fast-resolved
thought.

There was laughter of warriors, voices rang pleasant, words
were cheerful. Wealhtheow came forth, Hrothgar's queen, mindful
of customs, gold-adorned, greeted the men in the hall; and the
noble woman offered the cup first to the keeper of the land of
the East-Danes, bade him be glad at the beer-drinking, beloved
of the people. In joy he partook of feast and hall-cup, king
famous for victories. Then the woman of the Helmings went
about to each one of the retainers, young and old, offered them
the costly cup, until the time came that she brought the mead-
bowl to Beowulf, the ring-adorned queen, mature of mind. Sure
of speech she greeted the man of the Geats, thanked God that
her wish was fulfilled, that she might trust in some man for help
against deadly deeds. He took the cup, the warrior fierce in
battle, from Wealhtheow, and then spoke, one ready for fight—
Beowulf spoke, the son of Ecgtheow: "I resolved, when I set out
on the sea, sat down in the sea-boat with my band of men, that
I should altogether fulfill the will of your people or else fall
in slaughter, fast in the foe's grasp. I shall achieve a deed of
manly courage or else have lived to see in this mead-hall my
ending day." These words were well-pleasing to the woman, the
boast of the Geat. Gold-adorned, the noble folk-queen went to
sit by her lord.

Then there were again as at first strong words spoken in the
hall, the people in gladness, the sound of a victorious folk, until,
in a little while, the son of Healfdene wished to seek his evening
rest. He knew of the battle in the high hall that had been plotted
by the monster, plotted from the time that they might see the
light of the sun until the night, growing dark over all things, the
shadowy shapes of darkness, should come gliding, black under
the clouds. The company all arose. Then they saluted each other,
Hrothgar and Beowulf, and Hrothgar wished him good luck,
control of the wine-hall, and spoke these words: "Never before,
since I could raise hand and shield, have I entrusted to any

man the great hall of the Danes, except now to you. Hold now and guard the best of houses: remember your fame, show your great courage, keep watch against the fierce foe. You will not lack what you wish if you survive that deed of valor."

(X.) Then Hrothgar went out of the hall with his company of warriors, the protector of the Scyldings. The war-chief would seek the bed of Wealhtheow the queen. The King of Glory— as men had learned—had appointed a hall-guard against Grendel; he had a special mission to the prince of the Danes: he kept watch against monsters.

And the man of the Geats had sure trust in his great might, the favor of the Ruler. Then he took off his shirt of armor, the helmet from his head, handed his embellished sword, best of irons, to an attendant, bade him keep guard over his war-gear. Then the good warrior spoke some boast-words before he went to his bed, Beowulf of the Geats: "I claim myself no poorer in war-strength, war works, than Grendel claims himself. Therefore I will not put him to sleep with a sword, so take away his life, though surely I might. He knows no good tools with which he might strike against me, cut my shield in pieces, though he is strong in fight. But we shall forgo the sword in the night—if he dare seek war without weapon—and then may wise God, Holy Lord, assign glory on whichever hand seems good to Him."

The battle-brave one laid himself down, the pillow received the earl's head, and about him many a brave seaman lay down to hall-rest. None of them thought that he would ever again seek from there his dear home, people or town where he had been brought up; for they knew that bloody death had carried off far too many men in the wine-hall, folk of the Danes. But the Lord granted to weave for them good fortune in war, for the folk of the Weather-Geats, comfort and help that they should quite overcome their foe through the might of one man, through his sole strength: the truth has been made known that mighty God has always ruled mankind.

There came gliding in the black night the walker in darkness. The warriors slept who should hold the horned house—all but one. It was known to men that when the Ruler did not wish it the hostile creature might not drag them away beneath the shadows. But he, lying awake for the fierce foe, with heart swollen in anger awaited the outcome of the fight.

(XI.) Then from the moor under the mist-hills Grendel came walking, wearing God's anger. The foul ravager thought to catch some one of mankind there in the high hall. Under the clouds he moved until he could see most clearly the wine-hall, treasure-house of men, shining with gold. That was not the first time that he had sought Hrothgar's home. Never before or since in his life-days did he find harder luck, hardier hall-thanes. The creature deprived of joy came walking to the hall. Quickly the door gave way, fastened with fire-forged bands, when he touched it with his hands. Driven by evil desire, swollen with rage, he tore it open, the hall's mouth. After that the foe at once stepped onto the shining floor, advanced angrily. From his eyes came a light not fair, most like a flame. He saw many men in the hall, a band of kinsmen all asleep together, a company of war-men. Then his heart laughed: dreadful monster, he thought that before the day came he would divide the life from the body of every one of them, for there had come to him a hope of full-feasting. It was not his fate that when that night was over he should feast on more of mankind.

The kinsman of Hygelac, mighty man, watched how the evil-doer would make his quick onslaught. Nor did the monster mean to delay it, but, starting his work, he suddenly seized a sleeping man, tore at him ravenously, bit into his bone-locks, drank the blood from his veins, swallowed huge morsels; quickly he had eaten all of the lifeless one, feet and hands. He stepped closer, then felt with his arm for the brave-hearted man on the bed, reached out towards him, the foe with his hand; at once in fierce response Beowulf seized it and sat up, leaning on his own arm. Straightway the fosterer of crimes knew that he had not en-countered on middle-earth, anywhere in this world, a harder hand-grip from another man. In mind he became frightened, in his spirit: not for that might he escape the sooner. His heart was eager to get away, he would flee to his hiding-place, seek his rabble of devils. What he met there was not such as he had ever before met in the days of his life. Then the kinsman of Hygelac, the good man, thought of his evening's speech, stood upright and laid firm hold on him: his fingers cracked. The giant was pulling away, the earl stepped forward. The notorious one thought to move farther away, wherever he could, and flee his way from there to his fen-retreat; he knew his fingers' power to be in a hateful grip. That was a painful journey that the loathsome de-spoiler had made to Heorot. The retainers' hall rang with the noise—terrible drink [5] for all the Danes, the house-dwellers, every brave man, the earls. Both were enraged, fury-filled, the two who meant to control the hall. The building resounded. Then was it much wonder that the wine-hall withstood them joined in fierce

5. The metaphor reflects the idea that the chief purpose of a hall such as Heorot was as a place for men to feast in.

fight, that it did not fall to the ground, the fair earth-dwelling; but it was so firmly made fast with iron bands, both inside and outside, joined by skillful smith-craft. There started from the floor—as I have heard say—many a mead-bench, gold-adorned, when the furious ones fought. No wise men of the Scyldings ever before thought that any men in any manner might break it down, splendid with bright horns, have skill to destroy it, unless flame should embrace it, swallow it in fire. Noise rose up, sound strange enough. Horrible fear came upon the North-Danes, upon every one of those who heard the weeping from the wall, God's enemy sing his terrible song, song without triumph—the hell-slave bewail his pain. There held him fast he who of men was strongest of might in the days of this life.

(XII.) Not for anything would the protector of warriors let the murderous guest go off alive: he did not consider his life-days of use to any of the nations. There more than enough of Beowulf's earls drew swords, old heirlooms, wished to protect the life of their dear lord, famous prince, however they might. They did not know when they entered the fight, hardy-spirited warriors, and when they thought to hew him on every side, to seek his soul, that not any of the best of irons on earth, no war-sword, would touch the evil-doer: for with a charm he had made victory-weapons useless, every sword-edge. His departure to death from the time of this life was to be wretched; and the alien spirit was to travel far off into the power of fiends. Then he who before had brought trouble of heart to mankind, committed many crimes—he was at war with God—found that his body would do him no good, for the great-hearted kinsman of Hygelac had him by the hand. Each was hateful to the other alive. The awful monster had lived to feel pain in his body, a huge wound in his shoulder was exposed, his sinews sprang apart, his bone-locks broke. Glory in battle was given to Beowulf. Grendel must flee from there, mortally sick, seek his joyless home in the fen-slopes. He knew the more surely that his life's end had come, the full number of his days. For all the Danes was their wish fulfilled after the bloody fight. Thus he who had lately come from far off, wise and stout-hearted, had purged Heorot, saved Hrothgar's house from afflliction. He rejoiced in his night's work, a deed to make famous his courage. The man of the Geats had fulfilled his boast to the East-Danes; so too he had remedied all the grief, the malice-caused sorrow that they had endured before, and had had to suffer from harsh necessity, no small distress. That was clearly proved when the battle-brave man set the hand up under the curved roof—the arm and the shoulder: there all together was Grendel's grasp.

[CELEBRATION AT HEOROT]

(XIII.) Then in the morning, as I have heard, there was many a warrior about the gift-hall. Folk-chiefs came from far and near over the wide-stretching ways to look on the wonder, the footprints of the foe. Nor did his going from life seem sad to any of the men who saw the tracks of the one without glory—how, weary-hearted, overcome with injuries, he moved on his way from there to the mere [6] of the water-monsters with life-failing footsteps, death-doomed and in flight. There the water was boiling with blood, the horrid surge of waves swirling, all mixed with hot gore, sword-blood. Doomed to die he had hidden, then, bereft of joys, had laid down his life in his fen-refuge, his heathen soul: there hell took him.

From there old retainers—and many a young man, too—turned back in their glad journey to ride from the mere, high-spirited on horseback, warriors on steeds. There was Beowulf's fame spoken of; many a man said—and not only once—that, south nor north, between the seas, over the wide earth, no other man under the sky's expanse was better of those who bear shields, more worthy of ruling. Yet they found no fault with their own dear lord, gracious Hrothgar, for he was a good king. At times battle-famed men let their brown horses gallop, let them race where the paths seemed fair, known for their excellence. At times a thane of the king, a man skilled at telling adventures, songs stored in his memory, who could recall many of the stories of the old days, wrought a new tale in well-joined words; this man undertook with his art to recite in turn Beowulf's exploit, and skillfully to tell an apt tale, to lend words to it.

He spoke everything that he had heard tell of Sigemund's valorous deeds, many a strange thing, the strife of Waels's son,[7] his far journeys, feuds and crimes, of which the children of men knew nothing—except for Fitela with him, to whom he would tell everything, the uncle to his nephew, for they were always friends in need in every fight. Many were the tribes of giants that they had laid low with their swords. For Sigemund there sprang up after his death-day no little glory—after he, hardy in war, had killed the dragon, keeper of the treasure-hoard: under the hoary stone the prince's son had ventured alone, a daring deed, nor was Fitela with him. Yet it turned out well for him, so that his sword went through the gleaming worm and stood fixed in the wall, splendid weapon: the dragon lay dead of the murdering stroke. Through his courage the great warrior had brought it about that he might at his own wish enjoy the ring-hoard. He

6. Lake. 7. Waels was Sigemund's father.

loaded the sea-boat, bore into the ship's bosom the bright treasure, offspring of Waels. The hot dragon melted.

He was adventurer most famous, far and wide through the nations, for deeds of courage—he had prospered from that before, the protector of warriors—after the war-making of Heremod had come to an end, his strength and his courage.[8] Among the Jutes Heremod came into the power of his enemies, was betrayed, quickly dispatched. Surging sorrows had oppressed him too long: he had become a great care to his people, to all his princes; for many a wise man in former times had bewailed the journey of the fierce-hearted one—people who had counted on him as a relief from affliction—that that king's son should prosper, take the rank of his father, keep guard over the folk, the treasure and stronghold, the kindgom of heroes, the home of the Scyldings. The kinsman of Hygelac became dearer to his friends, to all mankind: crime took possession of Heremod.

Sometimes racing their horses they passed over the sand-covered ways. By then the morning light was far advanced, hastening on. Many a stout-hearted warrior went to the high hall to see the strange wonder. The king himself walked forth from the women's apartment, the guardian of the ring-hoards, secure in his fame, known for his excellence, with much company; and his queen with him passed over the path to the mead-hall with a troop of attendant women.

(XIV.) Hrothgar spoke—he had gone to the hall, taken his stand on the steps, looked at the high roof shining with gold, and at Grendel's hand: "For this sight may thanks be made quickly to the Almighty: I endured much from the foe, many griefs from Grendel: God may always work wonder upon wonder, the Guardian of Heaven. It was not long ago that I did not expect ever to live to see relief from any of my woes—when the best of houses stood shining with blood, stained with slaughter, a far-reaching woe for each of my counselors, for every one, since none thought he could ever defend the people's stronghold from its enemies, from demons and evil spirits. Now through the Lord's might a warrior has accomplished the deed that all of us with our skill could not perform. Yes, she may say, whatever woman brought forth this son among mankind—if she still lives —that the God of Old was kind to her in her child-bearing. Now, Beowulf, best of men, in my heart I will love you as a son: keep well this new kinship. To you will there be no lack

---

8. Heremod was an unsuccessful king of the Danes, one who began brilliantly but became cruel and avaricious, ultimately having to take refuge among the Jutes, who put him to death. His reputation was thus overshadowed by that of Sigemund.

of the good things of the world that I have in my possession. Full often I have made reward for less, done honor with gifts to a lesser warrior, weaker in fighting. With your deeds you yourself have made sure that your glory will be ever alive. May the Almighty reward you with good—as just now he has done."

Beowulf spoke, the son of Ecgtheow: "With much good will we have achieved this work of courage, that fight, have ventured boldly against the strength of the unknown one. I should have wished rather that you might have seen him, your enemy brought low among your furnishings. I thought quickly to bind him on his deathbed with hard grasp, so that because of my hand-grip he should lie struggling for life—unless his body should escape. I could not stop his going, since the Lord did not wish it, nor did I hold him firmly enough for that, my life-enemy: he was too strong, the foe in his going. Yet to save his life he has left his hand behind to show that he was here—his arm and shoulder; nor by that has the wretched creature bought any comfort; none the longer will the loathsome ravager live, hard-pressed by his crimes, for a wound has clutched him hard in its strong grip, in deadly bonds. There, like a man outlawed for guilt, he shall await the great judgment, how the bright Lord will decree for him."

Then was the warrior more silent in boasting speech of warlike deeds, the son of Ecglaf,[9] after the nobles had looked at the hand, now high on the roof through the strength of a man, the foe's fingers. The end of each one, each of the nail-places, was most like steel; the hand-spurs of the heathen warrior were monstrous spikes. Everyone said that no hard thing would hurt him, no iron good from old times would harm the bloody battle-hand of the monster.

(XV.) Then was it ordered that Heorot be within quickly adorned by hands. Many there were, both men and women, who made ready the wine-hall, the guest-building. The hangings on the walls shone with gold, many a wondrous sight for each man who looks on such things. That bright building was much damaged, though made fast within by iron bonds, and its door-hinges sprung; the roof alone came through unharmed when the monster, outlawed for his crimes, turned in flight, in despair of his life. That is not easy to flee from—let him try it who will—but driven by need one must seek the place prepared for earth-dwellers, soul-bearers, the sons of men, the place where, after its feasting, one's body will sleep fast in its death-bed.

Then had the proper time come that Healfdene's son should go to the hall; the king himself would share in the feast. I have

---

9. I.e., Unferth, who had taunted Beowulf the night before.

never heard that a people in a larger company bore themselves better about their treasure-giver. Men who were known for courage sat at the benches, rejoiced in the feast. Their kinsmen, stout-hearted Hrothgar and Hrothulf, partook fairly of many a mead-cup in the high hall. Heorot within was filled with friends: the Scylding-people had not then known treason's web.[1]

Then the son of Healfdene gave Beowulf a golden standard to reward his victory—a decorated battle-banner—a helmet and mail-shirt: many saw the glorious, costly sword borne before the warrior. Beowulf drank of the cup in the mead-hall. He had no need to be ashamed before fighting men of those rich gifts. I have not heard of many men who gave four precious, gold-adorned things to another on the ale-bench in a more friendly way. The rim around the helmet's crown had a head-protection, wound of wire, so that no battle-hard sharp sword might badly hurt him when the shield-warrior should go against his foe. Then the people's protector commanded eight horses with golden bridles to be led into the hall, within the walls. The saddle of one of them stood shining with hand-ornaments, adorned with jewels: that had been the war-seat of the high king when the son of Healfdene would join sword-play: never did the warfare of the wide-known one fail when men died in battle. And then the prince of Ing's friends [2] yielded possession of both, horses and weapons, to Beowulf: he bade him use them well. So generously the famous prince, guardian of the hoard, repaid the warrior's battle-deeds with horses and treasure that no man will ever find fault with them—not he that will speak truth according to what is right.

(XVI.) Then further the lord gave treasure to each of the men on the mead-bench who had made the sea-voyage with Beowulf, gave heirlooms; and he commanded that gold be paid for the one whom in his malice Grendel had killed—as he would have killed more if wise God and the man's courage had not forestalled that fate. The Lord guided all the race of men then, as he does now. Yet is discernment everywhere best, forethought of mind. Many a thing dear and loath he shall live to see who here in the days of trouble long makes use of the world.

There was song and music together before Healfdene's battle-leader, the wooden harp touched, tale oft told, when Hrothgar's scop should speak hall-pastime among the mead-benches . . . [of] Finn's retainers when the sudden disaster fell upon them. . . .[3]

1. A reference to the later history of the Danes, when, after Hrothgar's death, his nephew Hrothulf apparently drove his son and successor Hrethric from the throne.
2. Ing was a legendary Danish king, and his "friends" are the Danes.
3. The lines introducing the scop's song seem faulty. The story itself is recounted in a highly allusive way, and many of its details are obscure, though some help is offered by an independent version of the story given in a fragmentary Old English lay called *The Fight at Finnsburg*.

The hero of the Half-Danes, Hnaef of the Scyldings, was fated to fall on Frisian battlefield. And no need had Hildeburh [4] to praise the good faith of the Jutes: blameless she was deprived of her dear ones at the shield-play, of son and brother; wounded by spears they fell to their fate. That was a mournful woman. Not without cause did Hoc's daughter lament the decree of destiny when morning came and she might see, under the sky, the slaughter of kinsmen—where before she had the greatest of world's joy. The fight took away all Finn's thanes except for only a few, so that he could in no way continue the battle on the field against Hengest, nor protect the survivors by fighting against the prince's thane. But they offered them peace-terms,[5] that they should clear another building for them, hall and high seat, that they might have control of half of it with the sons of the Jutes; and at givings of treasure the son of Folcwalda [6] should honor the Danes each day, should give Hengest's company rings, such gold-plated treasure as that with which he would cheer the Frisians' kin in the high hall. Then on both sides they confirmed the fast peace-compact. Finn declared to Hengest, with oaths deep-sworn, unfeigned, that he would hold those who were left from the battle in honor in accordance with the judgment of his counselors, so that by words or by works no man should break the treaty nor because of malice should ever mention that, princeless, the Danes followed the slayer of their own ring-giver, since necessity forced them. If with rash speech any of the Frisians should insist upon calling to mind the cause of murderous hate, then the sword's edge should settle it.

The funeral pyre was made ready and gold brought up from the hoard. The best of the warriors of the War-Scyldings [7] was ready on the pyre. At the fire it was easy to see many a blood-stained battle-shirt, boar-image all golden—iron-hard swine—many a noble destroyed by wounds: more than one had died in battle. Then Hildeburh bade give her own son to the flames on Hnaef's pyre, burn his blood vessels, put him in the fire at the shoulder of

---

4. Hildeburh, daughter of the former Danish king Hoc and sister of the ruling Danish king Hnaef, was married to Finn, king of the Jutes (Frisians). Hnaef with a party of Danes made what was presumably a friendly visit to Hildeburh and Finn at their home Finnsburg, but during a feast a quarrel broke out between the Jutes and the Danes (since the scop's sympathies are with the Danes, he ascribes the cause to the bad faith of the Jutes), and in the ensuing fight Hnaef and his nephew, the son of Finn and Hildeburh, were killed, along with many other Danes and Jutes.

5. It is not clear who proposed the peace terms, but in view of the teller's Danish sympathies, it was probably the Jutes that sought the uneasy truce from Hengest, who became the Danes' leader after Hnaef's death. The truce imposed upon Hengest and the Danes the intolerable condition of having to dwell in peace with the Jutish king who was responsible for the death of their own king.

6. I.e., Finn.

7. I.e., Hnaef.

his uncle. The woman mourned, sang her lament. The warrior took his place.[8] The greatest of death-fires wound to the skies, roared before the barrow. Heads melted as blood sprang out—wounds opened wide, hate-bites of the body. Fire swallowed them—greediest of spirits—all of those whom war had taken away from both peoples: their strength had departed.

(XVII.) Then warriors went to seek their dwellings, bereft of friends, to behold Friesland, their homes and high city.[9] Yet Hengest stayed on with Finn for a winter darkened with the thought of slaughter, all desolate. He thought of his land, though he might not drive his ring-prowed ship over the water—the sea boiled with storms, strove with the wind, winter locked the waves in ice-bonds—until another year came to men's dwellings, just as it does still, glorious bright weather always watching for its time. Then winter was gone, earth's lap fair, the exile was eager to go, the guest from the dwelling: [yet] more he thought of revenge for his wrongs than of the sea-journey—if he might bring about a fight where he could take account of the sons of the Jutes with his iron. So he made no refusal of the world's custom when the son of Hunlaf[1] placed on his lap Battle-Bright, best of swords: its edges were known to the Jutes. Thus also to war-minded Finn in his turn cruel sword-evil came in his own home, after Guthlaf and Oslaf complained of the grim attack, the injury after the sea-journey, assigned blame for their lot of woes: breast might not contain the restless heart. Then was the hall reddened from foes' bodies, and thus Finn slain, the king in his company, and the queen taken. The warriors of the Scyldings bore to ship all the hall-furnishings of the land's king, whatever of necklaces, skillfully wrought treasures, they might find at Finn's home. They brought the noble woman on the sea-journey to the Danes, led her to her people.

The lay was sung to the end, the song of the scop. Joy mounted again, bench-noise brightened, cup-bearers poured wine from wonderful vessels. Then Wealhtheow came forth to walk under gold crown to where the good men sat, nephew and uncle: their friendship was then still unbroken, each true to the other.[2] There too Unferth the spokesman sat at the feet of the prince

8. The line is obscure, but it perhaps means that the body of Hildeburh's son was placed on the pyre.
9. This seems to refer to the few survivors on the Jutish side.
1. The text is open to various interpretations. The one adopted here assumes that the Dane Hunlaf, brother of Guthlaf and Oslaf, had been killed in the fight, and that ultimately Hunlaf's son demanded vengeance by the sym-bolical act of placing his father's sword in Hengest's lap, while at the same time Guthlaf and Oslaf reminded Hengest of the Jutes' treachery. It is not clear whether the subsequent fight in which Finn was killed was waged by the Danish survivors alone, or whether the party first went back to Denmark and then returned to Finnsburg with reinforcements.
2. See section XV, note 1, above.

of the Scyldings: each of them trusted his spirit, that he had much courage, though he was not honorable to his kinsmen at sword-play. Then the woman of the Scyldings spoke:

"Take this cup my noble lord, giver of treasure. Be glad, gold-friend of warriors, and speak to the Geats with mild words, as a man ought to do. Be gracious to the Geats, mindful of gifts [which] [3] you now have from near and far. They have told me that you would have the warrior for your son. Heorot is purged, the bright ring-hall. Enjoy while you may many rewards, and leave to your kinsmen folk and kingdom when you must go forth to look on the Ruler's decree. I know my gracious Hrothulf, that he will hold the young warriors in honor if you, friend of the Scyldings, leave the world before him. I think he will repay our sons with good if he remembers all the favors we did to his pleasure and honor when he was a child."

Then she turned to the bench where her sons were, Hrethric and Hrothmund, and the sons of the warriors, young men together. There sat the good man Beowulf of the Geats beside the two brothers.

(XVIII.) The cup was borne to him and welcome offered in friendly words to him, and twisted gold courteously bestowed on him, two arm-ornaments, a mail-shirt and rings, the largest of necklaces of those that I have heard spoken of on earth. I have heard of no better hoard-treasure under the heavens since Hama carried away to his bright city the necklace of the Brosings,[4] chain and rich setting: he fled the treacherous hatred of Eormenric, got eternal favor. This ring Hygelac of the Geats,[5] grandson of Swerting, had on his last venture, when beneath his battle-banner he defended his treasure, protected the spoils of war: fate took him when for pride he sought trouble, feud with the Frisians. Over the cup of the waves the mighty prince wore that treasure, precious stone. He fell beneath his shield; the body of the king came into the grasp of the Franks, his breast-armor and the neck-ring together. Lesser warriors plundered the fallen after the war-harvest: people of the Geats held the place of corpses.

The hall was filled with noise. Wealhtheow spoke, before the company she said to him: "Wear this ring, beloved Beowulf, young man, with good luck, and make use of this mail-shirt from

3. The text seems corrupt.
4. The Brisings' (Brosings') necklace had been worn by the goddess Freya. Nothing more is known of this story of Hama, who seems to have stolen the necklace from the famous Gothic king Eormenric.

5. Beowulf is later said to have presented the necklace to Hygelac's queen, Hygd, though here Hygelac is said to have been wearing it on his ill-fated expedition against the Franks and Frisians, into whose hands it fell at his death.

the people's treasure, and prosper well; make yourself known with your might, and be kind of counsel to these boys: I shall remember to reward you for that. You have brought it about that, far and near, for a long time all men shall praise you, as wide as the sea surrounds the shores, home of the winds. While you live, prince, be prosperous. I wish you well of your treasure. Much favored one, be kind of deeds to my son. Here is each earl true to other, mild of heart, loyal to his lord; the thanes are at one, the people obedient, the retainers cheered with drink do as I bid."

Then she walked to her seat. There was the best of feasts, men drank wine. They did not know the fate, the grim decree made long before, as it came to pass to many of the earls after evening had come and Hrothgar had gone to his chambers, the noble one to his rest. A great number of men remained in the hall, just as they had often done before. They cleared the benches from the floor. It was spread over with beds and pillows. One of the beer-drinkers, ripe and fated to die, lay down to his hall-rest. They set at their heads their battle-shields, bright wood; there on the bench it was easy to see above each man his helmet that towered in battle, his ringed mail-shirt, his great spear-wood. It was their custom to be always ready for war whether at home or in the field, in any case at any time that need should befall their liege lord: that was a good nation.

[GRENDEL'S MOTHER'S ATTACK]

(XIX.) Then they sank to sleep. One paid sorely for his evening rest, just as had often befallen them when Grendel guarded the gold-hall, wrought wrong until the end came, death after misdeeds. It came to be seen, wide-known to men, that after the bitter battle an avenger still lived for an evil space: Grendel's mother, woman, monster-wife, was mindful of her misery, she who had to dwell in the terrible water, the cold currents, after Cain became sword-slayer of his only brother, his own father's son. Then Cain went as an outlaw to flee the cheerful life of men, marked for his murder, held to the wasteland. From him sprang many a devil sent by fate. Grendel was one of them, hateful outcast who at Heorot found a waking man waiting his warfare. There the monster had laid hold upon him, but he was mindful of the great strength, the large gift God had given him, and relied on the Almighty for favor, comfort and help. By that he overcame the foe, subdued the hell-spirit. Then he went off wretched, bereft of joy, to seek his dying-place, enemy of mankind. And his mother, still greedy and gallows-grim, would go on a sorrowful venture, avenge her son's death.

Then she came to Heorot where the Ring-Danes slept throughout the hall. Then change came quickly to the earls there, when Grendel's mother made her way in. The attack was the less terrible by just so much as is the strength of women, the war-terror of a wife, less than an armed man's when a hard blade, forge-hammered, a sword shining with blood, good of its edges, cuts the stout boar on a helmet opposite. Then in the hall was hard-edged sword raised from the seat, many a broad shield lifted firmly in hand: none thought of helmet, of wide mail-shirt, when the terror seized him. She was in haste, would be gone out from there, protect her life after she was discovered. Swiftly she had taken fast hold on one of the nobles, then she went to the fen. He was one of the men between the seas most beloved of Hrothgar in the rank of retainer, a noble shield-warrior whom she destroyed at his rest, a man of great repute. Beowulf was not there, for earlier, after the treasure-giving, another lodging had been appointed for the renowned Geat. Outcry arose in Heorot: she had taken, in its gore, the famed hand. Care was renewed, come again on the dwelling. That was not a good bargain, that on both sides they had to pay with the lives of friends.

Then was the old king, the hoary warrior, of bitter mind when he learned that his chief thane was lifeless, his dearest man dead. Quickly Beowulf was fetched to the bed-chamber, man happy in victory. At daybreak together with his earls he went, the noble champion himself with his retainers, to where the wise one was, waiting to know whether after tidings of woe the All-Wielder would ever bring about change for him. The worthy warrior walked over the floor with his retainers—hall-wood resounded—that he might address words to the wise prince of Ing's friends, asked if the night had been pleasant according to his desires.

(XX.) Hrothgar spoke, protector of the Scyldings: "Ask not about pleasure. Sorrow is renewed to the people of the Danes: Aeschere is dead, Yrmenlaf's elder brother, my speaker of wisdom and my bearer of counsel, my shoulder-companion when we used to defend our heads in battle, when troops clashed, beat on boar-images. Whatever an earl should be, a man good from old times, such was Aeschere. Now a wandering murderous spirit has slain him with its hands in Heorot. I do not know by what way the awful creature, glorying in its prey, has made its retreat, gladdened by its feast. She has avenged the feud—that last night you killed Grendel with hard hand-grips, savagely, because too long he had diminished and destroyed my people. He fell in the fight, his life forfeited, and now the other has come, a mighty worker of wrong, would avenge her kinsman, and has carried far her revenge—as many a thane may think who weeps in his spirit for his treasure-giver, bitter sorrow in heart. Now the hand lies lifeless that was strong in support of all your desires.

"I have heard landsmen, my people, hall-counselors, say this, that they have seen two such huge walkers in the wasteland holding to the moors, alien spirits. One of them, so far as they could clearly discern, was the likeness of a woman. The other wretched shape trod the tracks of exile in the form of a man, except that he was bigger than any other man. Land-dwellers in the old days named him Grendel. They know of no father, whether in earlier times any was begotten for them among the dark spirits. They hold to the secret land, the wolf-slopes, the windy headlands, the dangerous fen-paths where the mountain stream goes down under the darkness of the hills, the flood under the earth. It is not far from here, measured in miles, that the mere stands; over it hang frost-covered woods, trees fast of root close over the water. There each night may be seen fire on the flood, a fearful wonder. Of the sons of men there lives none, old of wisdom, who knows the bottom. Though the heath-stalker, the strong-horned hart, harassed by hounds makes for the forest after long flight, rather will he give his life, his being, on the bank than save his head by entering. That is no pleasant place. From it the surging waves rise up black to the heavens when the wind stirs up awful storms, until the air becomes gloomy, the skies weep. Now once again is the cure in you alone. You do not yet know the land, the perilous place, where you might find the seldom-seen creature: seek if you dare. I will give you wealth for the feud, old treasure, as I did before, twisted gold—if you come away."

(XXI.) Beowulf spoke, the son of Ecgtheow: "Sorrow not, wise warrior. It is better for a man to avenge his friend than much mourn. Each of us must await his end of the world's life. Let him who may get glory before death: that is best for the warrior after he has gone from life. Arise, guardian of the kingdom, let us go at once to look on the track of Grendel's kin. I promise you this: she will not be lost under cover, not in the earth's bosom nor in the mountain woods nor at the bottom of the sea, go where she will. This day have patience in every woe—as I expect you to."

Then the old man leapt up, thanked God, the mighty Lord, that the man had so spoken. Then was a horse bridled for Hrothgar, a curly-maned mount. The wise king moved in state; the band of shield-bearers marched on foot. The tracks were seen wide over the wood-paths where she had gone on the ground, made her way forward over the dark moor, borne lifeless the best of retainers of those who watched over their home with Hrothgar. The son of noble forebears [6] moved over the steep

---

6. I.e., **Hrothgar**.

rocky slopes, narrow paths where only one could go at a time, an unfamiliar trail, steep hills many a lair of water-monsters. He went before with a few wise men to spy out the country, until suddenly he found mountain trees leaning out over hoary stone, a joyless wood: water lay beneath, bloody and troubled. It was pain of heart for all the Danes to suffer, for the friends of the Scyldings, for many a thane, grief to each earl when on the cliff over the water they came upon Aeschere's head. The flood boiled with blood—the men looked upon it—with hot gore. Again and again the horn sang its urgent war-song. The whole troop sat down to rest. Then they saw on the water many a snake-shape, strong sea-serpents exploring the mere, and water-monsters lying on the slopes of the shore such as those that in the morning often attend a perilous journey on the paths of the sea, serpents and wild beasts.

These fell away from the shore, fierce and rage-swollen: they had heard the bright sound, the war-horn sing. One of them a man of the Geats with his bow cut off from his life, his water-warring, after the hard war-arrow stuck in his heart: he was weaker in swimming the lake when death took him. Straightway he was hard beset on the waves with barbed boar-spears, strongly surrounded, pulled up on the shore, strange spawn of the waves. The men looked on the terrible alien thing.

Beowulf put on his warrior's dress, had no fear for his life. His war-shirt, hand-fashioned, broad and well-worked, was to explore the mere: it knew how to cover his body-cave so that foe's grip might not harm his heart, or grasp of angry enemy his life. But the bright helmet guarded his head, one which was to stir up the lake-bottom, seek out the troubled water—made rich with gold, surrounded with splendid bands, as the weapon-smith had made it in far-off days, fashioned it wonderfully, set it about with boar-images so that thereafter no sword or battle-blade might bite into it. And of his strong supports that was not the least which Hrothgar's spokesman [7] lent to his need: Hrunting was the name of the hilted sword; it was one of the oldest of ancient treasures; its edge was iron, decorated with poison-stripes, hardened with battle-sweat. Never had it failed in war any man of those who grasped it in their hands, who dared enter on danger-ous enterprises, onto the common meeting place of foes: this was not the first time that it should do work of courage. Surely the son of Ecglaf, great of strength, did not have in mind what, drunk with wine, he had spoken, when he lent that weapon to a better sword-fighter. He did not himself dare to risk his life under the warring waves, to engage his courage: there he lost his glory,

7. I.e., Unferth.

his name for valor. It was not so with the other when he had armed himself for battle.

[BEOWULF ATTACKS GRENDEL'S MOTHER]

(XXII.) Beowulf spoke, the son of Ecgtheow: "Think now, renowned son of Healfdene, wise king, now that I am ready for the venture, gold-friend of warriors, of what we said before, that, if at your need I should go from life, you would always be in a father's place for me when I am gone: be guardian of my young retainers, my companions, if battle should take me. The treasure you gave me, beloved Hrothgar, send to Hygelac. The lord of the Geats may know from the gold, the son of Hrethel may see when he looks on that wealth, that I found a ring-giver good in his gifts, enjoyed him while I might. And let Unferth have the old heirloom, the wide-known man my splendid-waved sword, hard-edged: with Hrunting I shall get glory, or death will take me."

After these words the man of the Weather-Geats turned away boldly, would wait for no answer: the surging water took the warrior. Then was it a part of a day before he might see the bottom's floor. Straightway that which had held the flood's tract a hundred half-years, ravenous for prey, grim and greedy, saw that some man from above was exploring the dwelling of monsters. Then she groped toward him, took the warrior in her awful grip. Yet not the more for that did she hurt his hale body within: his ring-armor shielded him about on the outside so that she could not pierce the war-dress, the linked body-mail, with hateful fingers. Then as she came to the bottom the sea-wolf bore the ring-prince to her house so that—no matter how brave he was —he might not wield weapons; but many monsters attacked him in the water, many a sea-beast tore at his mail-shirt with war-tusks, strange creatures afflicted him. Then the earl saw that he was in some hostile hall where no water harmed him at all, and the flood's onrush might not touch him because of the hall-roof. He saw firelight, a clear blaze shine bright.

Then the good man saw the accursed dweller in the deep, the mighty mere-woman. He gave a great thrust to his sword—his hand did not withhold the stroke—so that the etched blade sang at her head a fierce war-song. Then the stranger found that the battle-lightning would not bite, harm her life, but the edge failed the prince in his need: many a hand-battle had it endured before, often sheared helmet, war-coat of man fated to die: this was the first time for the rare treasure that its glory had failed.

But still he was resolute, not slow of his courage, mindful of fame, the kinsman of Hygelac. Then, angry warrior, he threw away the sword, wavy-patterned, bound with ornaments, so that it lay on the ground, hard and steel-edged: he trusted in his strength, his mighty hand-grip. So ought a man to do when he thinks to get long-lasting praise in battle: he cares not for his life. Then he seized by the hair Grendel's mother—the man of the War-Geats did not shrink from the fight. Battle-hardened, now swollen with rage, he pulled his deadly foe so that she fell to the floor. Quickly in her turn she repaid him his gift with her grim claws and clutched at him: then weary-hearted, the strongest of warriors, of foot-soldiers, stumbled so that he fell. Then she sat upon the hall-guest and drew her knife, broad and bright-edged. She would avenge her child, her only son. The woven breast-armor lay on his shoulder: that protected his life, withstood entry of point or of edge. Then the son of Ecgtheow would have fared amiss under the wide ground, the champion of the Geats, if the battle-shirt had not brought help, the hard war-net—and holy God brought about victory in war; the wise Lord, Ruler of the Heavens, decided it with right, easily, when Beowulf had stood up again.

XXIII. Then he saw among the armor a victory-blessed blade, an old sword made by the giants, strong of its edges, glory of warriors: it was the best of weapons, except that it was larger than any other man might bear to war-sport, good and adorned, the work of giants. He seized the linked hilt, he who fought for the Scyldings, savage and slaughter-bent, drew the patterned-blade; desperate of life, he struck angrily so that it bit her hard on the neck, broke the bone-rings. The blade went through all the doomed body. She fell to the floor, the sword was sweating, the man rejoiced in his work.

The blaze brightened, light shone within, just as from the sky heaven's candle shines clear. He looked about the building; then he moved along the wall, raised his weapon hard by the hilt, Hygelac's thane, angry and resolute: the edge was not useless to the warrior, for he would quickly repay Grendel for the many attacks he had made on the West-Danes—many more than the one time when he slew in their sleep fifteen hearth-companions of Hrothgar, devoured men of the Danish people while they slept, and another such number bore away, a hateful prey. He had paid him his reward for that, the fierce champion, for there he saw Grendel, weary of war, lying at rest, lifeless with the wounds he had got in the fight at Heorot. The body bounded wide when it suffered the blow after death, the hard sword-swing; and thus he cut off his head.

At once the wise men who were watching the water with Hrothgar saw that the surging waves were troubled, the lake stained with blood. Gray-haired, old, they spoke together of the good warrior, that they did not again expect of the chief that he would come victorious to seek their great king; for many agreed on it, that the sea-wolf had destroyed him.

Then came the ninth hour of the day. The brave Scyldings left the hill. The gold-friend of warriors went back to his home. The strangers sat sick at heart and stared at the mere. They wished—and did not expect—that they would see their beloved lord himself.

Then the blade began to waste away from the battle-sweat, the war-sword into battle-icicles. That was a wondrous thing, that it should all melt, most like the ice when the Father loosens the frost's fetters, undoes the water-bonds—He Who has power over seasons and times: He is the true Ruler. Beowulf did not take from the dwelling, the man of the Weather-Geats, more treasures —though he saw many there—but only the head and the hilt, bright with jewels. The sword itself had already melted, its patterned blade burned away: the blood was too hot for it, the spirit that had died there too poisonous. Quickly he was swimming, he who had lived to see the fall of his foes; he plunged up through the water. The currents were all cleansed, the great tracts of the water, when the dire spirit left her life-days and this loaned world.

Then the protector of seafarers came toward the land, swimming stout-hearted; he had joy of his sea-booty, the great burden he had with him. They went to meet him, thanked God, the strong band of thanes, rejoiced in their chief that they might see him again sound. Then the helmet and war-shirt of the mighty one were quickly loosened. The lake drowsed, the water beneath the skies, stained with blood. They went forth on the foot-tracks, glad in their hearts, measured the path back, the known ways, men bold as kings. They bore the head from the mere's cliff, toilsomely for each of the great-hearted ones: four of them had trouble in carrying Grendel's head on spear-shafts to the gold-hall —until at last they came striding to the hall, fourteen bold warriors of the Geats; their lord, high-spirited, walked in their company over the fields to the mead-hall.

Then the chief of the thanes, man daring in deeds, enriched by new glory, warrior dear to battle, came in to greet Hrothgar. Then Grendel's head was dragged by the hair over the floor to where men drank, a terrible thing to the earls and the woman with them, an awful sight: the men looked upon it.

[FURTHER CELEBRATION AT HEOROT]

(XXIV.) Beowulf spoke, the son of Ecgtheow: "Yes, we have brought you this sea-booty, son of Healfdene, man of the Scyldings, gladly, as evidence of glory—what you look on here. Not easily did I come through it with my life, the war under water, not without trouble carried out the task. The fight would have been ended straightway if God had not guarded me. With Hrunting I might not do anything in the fight, though that is a good weapon. But the Wielder of Men granted me that I should see hanging on the wall a fair, ancient great-sword—most often He has guided the man without friends—that I should wield the weapon. Then in the fight when the time became right for me I hewed the house-guardians. Then that war-sword, wavy-patterned, burnt away as their blood sprang forth, hottest of battle-sweats. I have brought the hilt away from the foes. I have avenged the evil deeds, the slaughter of Danes, as it was right to do. I promise you that you may sleep in Heorot without care with your band of retainers, and that for none of the thanes of your people, old or young, need you have fear, prince of the Scyldings—for no life-injury to your men on that account, as you did before."

Then the golden hilt was given into the hand of the old man, the hoary war-chief—the ancient work of giants. There came into the possession of the prince of the Danes, after the fall of devils, the work of wonder-smiths. And when the hostile-hearted creature, God's enemy, guilty of murder, gave up this world, and his mother too, it passed into the control of the best of worldly kings between the seas, of those who gave treasure in the Northlands.

Hrothgar spoke—he looked on the hilt, the old heirloom, on which was written the origin of ancient strife, when the flood, rushing water, slew the race of giants—they suffered terribly: that was a people alien to the Everlasting Lord. The Ruler made them a last payment through water's welling. On the sword-guard of bright gold there was also rightly marked through rune-staves, set down and told, for whom that sword, best of irons, had first been made, its hilt twisted and ornamented with snakes. Then the wise man spoke, the son of Healfdene—all were silent: "Lo, this may one say who works truth and right for the folk, recalls all things far distant, an old guardian of the land: that this earl was born the better man. Glory is raised up over the far ways—your glory over every people, Beowulf my friend. All of it, all your strength, you govern steadily in the wisdom of your heart. I shall fulfill my friendship to you, just as we spoke before. You shall become a comfort, whole and long-lasting, to your people, a help to warriors.

"So was not Heremod to the sons of Ecgwela, the Honor-Scyldings. He grew great not for their joy, but for their slaughter, for the destruction of Danish people. With swollen heart he killed his table-companions, shoulder-comrades, until he turned

away from the joys of men, alone, notorious king, although mighty
God had raised him in power, in the joys of strength, had set
him up over all men. Yet in his breast his heart's thought grew
blood-thirsty: no rings did he give to the Danes for glory.
He lived joyless to suffer the pain of that strife, the long-lasting
harm of the people. Teach yourself by him, be mindful of mu-
nificence. Old of winters, I tell this tale for you.

"It is a wonder to say how in His great spirit mighty God gives
wisdom to mankind, land and earlship—He possesses power over all
things. At times He lets the thought of a man of high lineage
move in delight, gives him joy of earth in his homeland, a stronghold of men to rule over, makes regions of the world so subject
to him, wide kingdoms, that in his unwisdom he may not himself have mind of his end. He lives in plenty; illness and age in
no way grieve him, neither does dread care darken his heart, nor
does enmity bare sword-hate, for the whole world turns to his
will—he knows nothing worse—(XXV.) until his portion of pride
increases and flourishes within him; then the watcher sleeps, the
soul's guardian; that sleep is too sound, bound in its own cares,
and the slayer most near whose bow shoots treacherously. Then
is he hit in the heart, beneath his armor, with the bitter arrow—
he cannot protect himself—with the crooked dark commands of
the accursed spirit. What he has long held seems to him too little,
angry-hearted he covets, no plated rings does he give in men's
honor, and then he forgets and regards not his destiny because
of what God, Wielder of Heaven, has given him before, his
portion of glories. In the end it happens in turn that the loaned
body weakens, falls doomed; another takes the earl's ancient treasure, one who recklessly gives precious gifts, does not fearfully
guard them.

"Keep yourself against that wickedness, beloved Beowulf, best
of men, and choose better—eternal gains. Have no care for pride,
great warrior. Now for a time there is glory in your might: yet
soon it shall be that sickness or sword will diminish your strength,
or fire's fangs, or flood's surge, or sword's swing, or spear's flight,
or appalling age; brightness of eyes will fail and grow dark; then
it shall be that death will overcome you, warrior.

"Thus I ruled the Ring-Danes for a hundred half-years under
the skies, and protected them in war with spear and sword against
many nations over middle-earth, so that I counted no one as
my adversary underneath the sky's expanse. Well, disproof of
that came to me in my own land, grief after my joys, when Grendel,
ancient adversary, came to invade my home. Great sorrow of heart I
have always suffered for his persecution. Thanks be to the Ruler,
the Eternal Lord, that after old strife I have come to see in my life-

time, with my own eyes, his blood-stained head. Go now to your seat, have joy of the glad feast, made famous in battle. Many of our treasures will be shared when morning comes."

The Geat was glad at heart, went at once to seek his seat as the wise one bade. Then was a feast fairly served again, for a second time, just as before, for those famed for courage, sitting about the hall.

Night's cover lowered, dark over the warriors. The retainers all arose. The gray-haired one would seek his bed, the old Scylding. It pleased the Geat, the brave shield-warrior, immensely that he should have rest. Straightway a hall-thane led the way on for the weary one, come from far country, and showed every courtesy to the thane's need, such as in those days seafarers might expect as their due.

Then the great-hearted one rested; the hall stood high, vaulted and gold-adorned; the guest slept within until the black raven, blithe-hearted, announced heaven's joy. Then the bright light came passing over the shadows. The warriors hastened, the nobles were eager to set out again for their people. Bold of spirit, the visitor would seek his ship far thence.

Then the hardy one bade that Hrunting be brought to the son of Ecglaf,[8] that he take back his sword, precious iron. He spoke thanks for that loan, said that he accounted it a good war-friend, strong in battle; in his words he found no fault at all with the sword's edge. he was a thoughtful man. And then they were eager to depart, the warriors ready in their armor. The prince who had earned honor of the Danes went to the high seat where the other was: the man dear to war greeted Hrothgar.

[Beowulf Returns Home]

(XXVI.) Beowulf spoke, the son of Ecgtheow: "Now we sea-travelers come from afar wish to say that we desire to seek Hygelac. Here we have been entertained splendidly according to our desire: you have dealt well with us. If on earth I might in any way earn more of your heart's love, prince of warriors, than I have done before with warlike deeds, I should be ready at once. If beyond the sea's expanse I hear that men dwelling near threaten you with terrors, as those who hated you did before, I shall bring you a thousand thanes, warriors to your aid. I know of Hygelac, lord of the Geats, though he is young as a guardian of the people, that he will further me with words and works so that I may do you honor and bring spears to help you, strong support where you have need of men. If Hrethric, king's son, decides to come to the court of the Geats, he can find many friends there;

8. I.e., Unferth.

far countries are well sought by him who is himself strong."

Hrothgar spoke to him in answer: "The All-Knowing Lord sent those words into your mind: I have not heard a man of so young age speak more wisely. You are great of strength, mature of mind, wise of words. I think it likely if the spear, sword-grim war, takes the son of Hrethel, sickness or weapon your prince, the people's ruler, and you have your life, that the Sea-Geats will not have a better to choose as their king, as guardian of their treasure, if you wish to hold the kingdom of your kinsmen. So well your heart's temper has long pleased me, beloved Beowulf. You have brought it about that peace shall be shared by the peoples, the folk of the Geats and the Spear-Danes, and enmity shall sleep, acts of malice which they practiced before; and there shall be, as long as I rule the wide kingdom, sharing of treasures, many a man shall greet his fellow with good gifts over the sea-bird's baths; the ring-prowed ship will bring gifts and tokens of friendship over the sea. I know your people, blameless in every respect, set firm after the old way both as to foe and to friend."

Then the protector of earls, the kinsman of Healfdene, gave him there in the hall twelve precious things; he bade him with these gifts seek his own dear people in safety, quickly come back. Then the king noble of race, the prince of the Scyldings, kissed the best of thanes and took him by his neck: tears fell from the gray-haired one. He had two thoughts of the future, the old and wise man, one more strongly than the other—that they would not see each other again, bold men at council. The man was so dear to him that he might not restrain his breast's welling, for fixed in his heartstrings a deep-felt longing for the beloved man burned in his blood. Away from him Beowulf, warrior glorious with gold, walked over the grassy ground, proud of his treasure. The sea-goer awaited its owner, riding at anchor. Then on the journey the gift of Hrothgar was oft-praised: that was a king blameless in all things until age took from him the joys of his strength—old age that has often harmed many.

(XXVII.) There came to the flood the band of brave-hearted ones, of young men. They wore mail-coats, locked limb-shirts. The guard of the coast saw the coming of the earls, just as he had done before. He did not greet the guests with taunts from the cliff's top, but rode to meet them, said that the return of the warriors in bright armor in their ship would be welcome to the people of the Weather-Geats. There on the sand the broad sea-boat was loaded with armor, the ring-prowed ship with horses and rich things. The mast stood high over Hrothgar's hoard-gifts. He gave the boat-guard a sword wound with gold, so that thereafter on the mead-bench he was held the worthier for the treasure, the heirloom. The boat moved out to furrow the deep water, left the land of the Danes. Then on the mast a sea-cloth, a sail, was made fast by a rope. The boat's beams creaked: wind did not keep the sea-floater from its way over the waves. The sea-goer moved, foamy-necked floated forth over the swell, the ship with bound prow over the sea-currents until they might see the cliffs of the Geats, the well-known headlands. The ship pressed ahead, borne by the wind, stood still at the land. Quickly the harbor-guard was at the sea-side, he who had gazed for a long time far out over the currents, eager to see the beloved men. He [9] moored the deep ship in the sand, fast by its anchor ropes, lest the force of the waves should drive away the fair wooden vessel. Then he bade that the prince's wealth be borne ashore, armor and plated gold. It was not far for them to seek the giver of treasure, Hygelac son of Hrethel, where he dwelt at home near the sea-wall, himself with his retainers.

The building was splendid, its king most valiant, set high in the hall, Hygd [1] most youthful, wise and well-taught, though she had lived within the castle walls few winters, daughter of Hae-reth. For she was not niggardly, nor too sparing of gifts to the men of the Geats, of treasures. Modthryth,[2] good folk-queen, did dreadful deeds [in her youth]: no bold one among her retainers dared venture—except her great lord—to set his eyes on her in daylight, but [if he did] he should reckon deadly bonds pre-pared for him, arresting hands: that straightway after his seizure the sword awaited him, that the patterned blade must settle it, make known its death-evil. Such is no queenly custom for a woman to practice, though she is peerless—that one who weaves peace [3] should take away the life of a beloved man after pretended injury. However the kinsman of Hemming stopped that:[4] ale-drinkers gave another account, said that she did less harm to the people, fewer injuries, after she was given, gold-adorned, to the young warrior, the beloved noble, when by her father's teach-ing she sought Offa's hall in a voyage over the pale sea. There on the throne she was afterwards famous for generosity, while living made use of her life, held high love toward the lord of

9. Beowulf.
1. Hygd is Hygelac's young queen. The suddenness of her introduction here is perhaps due to a faulty text.
2. A transitional passage introducing the contrast between Hygd's good be-havior and Modthryth's bad behavior as young women of royal blood seems to have been lost. Modthryth's practice of having those who looked into her face put to death may reflect the folk-motif of the princess whose unsuccessful suitors are executed, though the text

does not say that Modthryth's victims were suitors. Modthryth's "great lord" was probably her father.
3. Daughters of kings were frequently given in marriage to the king of a hostile nation in order to bring about peace; hence Modthryth may be called "one who weaves peace."
4. Offa, an Angle king who according to legend ruled Mercia in England; who Hemming was—besides being Offa's forebear—is not known.

warriors, [who was] of all mankind the best, as I have heard, between the seas of the races of men. Since Offa was a man brave of wars and gifts, wide-honored, he held his native land in wisdom. From him sprang Eomer to the help of warriors, kinsman of Hemming, grandson of Garmund, strong in battle.[5]

(XXVIII.) Then the hardy one came walking with his troop over the sand on the sea-plain, the wide shores. The world-candle shone, the sun moved quickly from the south. They made their way, strode swiftly to where they heard that the protector of earls, the slayer of Ongentheow,[6] the good young war-king, was dispensing rings in the stronghold. The coming of Beowulf was straightway made known to Hygelac, that there in his home the defender of warriors, his comrade in battle, came walking alive to the court, sound from the battle-play. Quickly the way within was made clear for the foot-guests, as the mighty one bade.

Then he sat down with him, he who had come safe through the fight, kinsman with kinsman, after he had greeted his liege lord with formal speech, loyal, with vigorous words. Haereth's daughter moved through the hall-building with mead-cups, cared lovingly for the people, bore the cup of strong drink to the hands of the warriors. Hygelac began fairly to question his companion in the high hall, curiosity pressed him, what the adventures of the Sea-Geats had been. "How did you fare on your journey, beloved Beowulf, when you suddenly resolved to seek distant combat over the salt water, battle in Heorot? Did you at all help the wide-known woes of Hrothgar, the famous prince? Because of you I burned with seething sorrows, care of heart—had no trust in the venture of my beloved man. I entreated you long that you should in no way approach the murderous spirit, should let the South-Danes themselves settle the war with Grendel. I say thanks to God that I may see you sound."

Beowulf spoke, the son of Ecgtheow: "To many among men it is not hidden, lord Hygelac, the great encounter—what a fight we had, Grendel and I, in the place where he made many sorrows for the Victory-Scyldings, constant misery. All that I avenged, so that none of Grendel's kin over the earth need boast of that clash at night—whoever lives longest of the loathsome kind, wrapped in malice. There I went forth to the ring-hall to greet Hrothgar. At once the famous son of Healfdene, when he knew my purpose, gave me a seat with his own sons. The company was in joy:

5. Offa, the only person that may be identified as English in this English poem, receives high praise; apparently the names of his father Garmund and son Eomer would strike a responsive chord in the poet's audience.

6. Ongentheow was a Scylfing (Swedish) king, whose story is fully told below, sections XL and XLI. In fact Hygelac was not his slayer, but is called so because he led the attack on the Scylfings in which Ongentheow was killed.

I have not seen in the time of my life under heaven's arch more mead-mirth of hall-sitters. At times the famous queen, peace-pledge of the people, went through all the hall, cheered the young men; often she would give a man a ring-band before she went to her seat. At times Hrothgar's daughter bore the ale-cup to the retainers, to the earls throughout the hall. I heard hall-sitters name her Freawaru when she offered the studded cup to warriors. Young and gold-adorned, she is promised to the fair son of Froda.[7] That has seemed good to the lord of the Scyldings, the guardian of the kingdom, and he believes of this plan that he may, with this woman, settle their portion of deadly feuds, of quarrels.[8] Yet most often after the fall of a prince in any nation the deadly spear rests but a little while, even though the bride is good.

"It may displease the lord of the Heatho-Bards and each thane of that people when he goes in the hall with the woman, [that while] the noble sons of the Danes, her retainers, [are] feasted,[9] the heirlooms of their ancestors will be shining on them [1]—the hard and wave-adorned treasure of the Heatho-Bards, [which was theirs] so long as they might wield those weapons, (XXIX.) until they led to the shield-play, to destruction, their dear companions and their own lives. Then at the beer he [2] who sees the treasure, an old ash-warrior who remembers it all, the spear-death of warriors—grim is his heart—begins, sad of mind, to tempt a young fighter in the thoughts of his spirit, to awaken war-evil, and speaks this word:

" 'Can you, my friend, recognize that sword, the rare iron-blade, that your father, beloved man, bore to battle his last time in armor, where the Danes slew him, the fierce Scyldings, got possession of the battle-field, when Withergeld [3] lay dead, after the fall of warriors? Now here some son of his murderers walks in the hall, proud of the weapon, boasts of the murder, and wears the treasure that you should rightly possess.' So he will provoke and remind at every chance with wounding words until that moment comes that the woman's thane,[4] forfeiting life, shall lie dead, blood-smeared from the sword-bite, for his father's deeds. The other escapes with his life, knows the land well. Then on both sides the oath of the earls will be broken;

---

7. I.e., Ingeld, who succeeded his father a king of the Heatho-Bards.
8. I.e., the feud between the Danes and Heatho-Bards.
9. The text is faulty here.
1. I.e., the weapons and armor which had once belonged to the Heatho-Bards and were captured by the Danes will be worn by the Danish attendants of Hrothgar's daughter Freawaru when she

goes to the Heatho-Bards to marry king Ingeld.
2. I.e., some old Heatho-Bard warrior.
3. Apparently a leader of the Heatho-Bards in their unsuccessful war with the Danes.
4. I.e., the Danish attendant of Freawaru who is wearing the sword of his Heatho-Bard attacker's father.

then deadly hate will well up in Ingeld, and his wife-love after the surging of sorrows will become cooler. Therefore I do not think the loyalty of the Heatho-Bards, their part in the alliance with the Danes, to be without deceit—do not think their friendship fast.

"I shall speak still more of Grendel, that you may readily know, giver of treasure, what the hand-fight of warriors came to in the end. After heaven's jewel had glided over the earth, the angry spirit came, awful in the evening, to visit us where, unharmed, we watched over the hall. There the fight was fatal to Hondscioh, deadly to one who was doomed. He was dead first of all, armed warrior. Grendel came to devour him, good young retainer, swallowed all the body of the beloved men. Yet not for this would the bloody-toothed slayer, bent on destruction, go from the gold-hall empty-handed; but, strong of might, he made trial of me, grasped me with eager hand. His glove [5] hung huge and wonderful, made fast with cunning clasps: it had been made all with craft, with devil's devices and dragon's skins. The fell doer of evils would put me therein, guiltless, one of many. He might not do so after I had stood up in anger. It is too long to tell how I repaid the people's foe his due for every crime. My prince, there with my deeds I did honor to your people. He slipped away, for a little while had use of life's joy. Yet his right hand remained as his spoor in Heorot, and he went from there abject, mournful of heart sank to the mere's bottom.

"The lord of the Scyldings repaid me for that bloody combat with much plated gold, many treasures, after morning came and we sat down to the feast. There was song and mirth. The old Scylding, who has learned many things, spoke of times far-off. At times a brave one in battle touched the glad wood, the harp's joy; at times he told tales, true and sad; at times he related strange stories according to right custom; at times, again, the great-hearted king, bound with age, the old warrior, would begin to speak of his youth, his battle-strength. His heart welled within when, old and wise, he thought of his many winters. Thus we took pleasure there the livelong day until another night came to men.

"Then in her turn Grendel's mother swiftly made ready to take revenge for his injuries, made a sorrowful journey. Death had taken her son, war-hate of the Weather-Geats. The direful woman avenged her son, fiercely killed a warrior: there the life of Aeschere departed, a wise old counselor. And when morning came the folk of the Danes might not burn him, death-weary, in the fire, nor place him on the pyre, beloved man: she had borne

---

5. Apparently a large glove that could be used as a pouch.

his body away in fiend's embrace beneath the mountain stream. That was the bitterest of Hrothgar's sorrows, of those that had long come upon the people's prince. Then the king, sore-hearted, implored me by your life [6] that I should do a man's work in the tumult of the waters, venture my life, finish a glorious deed. He promised me reward. Then I found the guardian of the deep pool, the grim horror, as is now known wide. For a time there we were locked hand in hand. Then the flood boiled with blood, and in the war-hall I cut off the head of Grendel's mother with a mighty sword. Not without trouble I came from there with my life. I was not fated to die then, but the protector of earls again gave me many treasures, the son of Healfdene.

(XXXI.) "Thus the king of that people lived with good customs. I had lost none of the rewards, the meed of my might, but he gave me treasures, the son of Healfdene, at my own choice. I will bring these to you, great king, show my good will. On your kindnesses all still depends: I have few close kinsmen besides you, Hygelac."

Then he bade bring in the boar-banner—the head-sign—the helmet towering in battle, the gray battle-shirt, the splendid sword—afterwards spoke words: "Hrothgar, wise king, gave me this armor; in his words he bade that I should first tell you about his gift: he said that king Heorogar,[7] lord of the Scyldings, had had it for a long time; not for that would he give it, the breast-armor, to his son, bold Heoroweard, though he was loyal to him. Use it all well!"

I have heard that four horses, swift and alike, followed that treasure, fallow as apples. He gave him the gift of both horses and treasure. So ought kinsmen do, not weave malice-nets for each other with secret craft, prepare death for comrades. To Hygelac his nephew was most true in hard fights, and each one mindful of helping the other. I have heard that he gave Hygd the neck-ring, the wonderfully wrought treasure, that Wealhtheow had given him—gave to the king's daughter as well three horses, supple and saddle-bright. After the gift of the necklace, her breast was adorned with it.

Thus Beowulf showed himself brave, a man known in battles, of good deeds, bore himself according to discretion. Drunk, he slew no hearth-companions. His heart was not savage, but he held the great gift that God had given him, the most strength of all mankind, like one brave in battle. He had long been despised,[8] so that the sons of the Geats did not reckon him brave, nor

---

6. I.e., "in your name."
7. Hrothgar's elder brother, whom Hrothgar succeeded as king.

8. Beowulf's poor reputation as a young man is mentioned only here.

would the lord of the Weather-Geats do him much gift-honor on the mead-bench. They strongly suspected that he was slack, a young man unbold. Change came to the famous man for each of his troubles.

Then the protector of earls bade fetch in the heirloom of Hrethel,[9] king famed in battle, adorned with gold. There was not then among the Geats a better treasure in sword's kind. He laid that in Beowulf's lap, and gave him seven thousand [hides of land], a hall and a throne. To both of them alike land had been left in the nation, home and native soil: to the other more especially wide was the realm, to him who was higher in rank.

[Beowulf and the Dragon]

Afterwards it happened, in later days, in the crashes of battle, when Hygelac lay dead and war-swords came to slay Heardred [1] behind the shield-cover, when the Battle-Scylfings, hard fighters, sought him among his victorious nation, attacked bitterly the nephew of Hereric—then the broad kingdom came into Beowulf's hand. He held it well fifty winters—he was a wise king, an old guardian of the land—until in the dark nights a certain one, a dragon, began to hold sway, which on the high heath kept watch over a hoard, a steep stone-barrow. Beneath lay a path unknown to men. By this there went inside a certain man [who made his way near to the heathen hoard; his hand took a cup, large, a shining treasure. The dragon did not afterwards conceal it though in his sleep he was tricked by the craft of the thief. That the people discovered, the neighboring folk—that he was swollen with rage].[2]

(XXXII.) Not of his own accord did he who had sorely harmed him [3] break into the worm's hoard, not by his own desire, but for hard constraint; the slave of some son of men fled hostile blows, lacking a shelter, and came there, a man guilty of wrong-doing. As soon as he saw him,[4] great horror arose in the stranger; [yet the wretched fugitive escaped the terrible worm . . . When the sudden shock came upon him, he carried off a precious cup.][5] There were many such ancient treasures in the earth-house, as in the old days some one of mankind had prudently hidden there the huge legacy of a noble race, rare treasures. Death had taken them all in earlier times, and the only one of the nation of people who still survived, who walked

9. Hygelac's father.
1. Hygelac's son Heardred, who succeeded Hygelac as king, was killed by the Swedes (Heatho-Scylfings) in his own land, as is explained more fully below, section XXXIII. His uncle Hereric was perhaps Hygd's brother.

2. This part of the manuscript is badly damaged, and the text within brackets is highly conjectural.
3. The dragon.
4. The dragon.
5. Several lines of the text have been lost.

there longest, a guardian mourning his friends, supposed the same of himself as of them—that he might little while enjoy the long-got treasure. A barrow stood all ready on the shore near the sea-waves, newly placed on the headland, made fast by having its entrances skillfully hidden. The keeper of the rings carried in the part of his riches worthy of hoarding, plated gold; he spoke few words:

"Hold now, you earth, now that men may not, the possession of earls. What, from you good men got it first! War-death has taken each man of my people, evil dreadful and deadly, each of those who has given up this life, the hall-joys of men. I have none who wears sword or cleans the plated cup, rich drinking vessel. The company of retainers has gone elsewhere. The hard helmet must be stripped of its fair-wrought gold, of its plating. The polishers are asleep who should make the war-mask shine. And even so the coat of mail, which withstood the bite of swords after the crashing of the shields, decays like its warrior. Nor may the ring-mail travel wide on the war-chief beside his warriors. There is no harp-delight, no mirth of the singing wood, no good hawk flies through the hall, no swift horse stamps in the castle court. Baleful death has sent away many races of men."

So, sad of mind, he spoke his sorrow, alone of them all, moved joyless through day and night until death's flood reached his heart. The ancient night-ravager found the hoard-joy standing open, he who burning seeks barrows, the smooth hateful dragon who flies at night wrapped in flame. Earth-dwellers much dread him. He it is who must seek a hoard in the earth where he will guard heathen gold, wise for his winters: he is none the better for it.

So for three hundred winters the harmer of folk held in the earth one of its treasure-houses, huge and mighty, until one man angered his heart. He bore to his master a plated cup, asked his lord for a compact of peace: thus was the hoard searched, the store of treasures diminished. His requests were granted the wretched man: the lord for the first time looked on the ancient work of men. Then the worm woke; cause of strife was renewed: for then he moved over the stones, hard-hearted beheld his foe's footprints—with secret stealth he had stepped forth too near the dragon's head. (So may an undoomed man who holds favor from the Ruler easily come through his woes and misery.) The hoard-guard sought him eagerly over the ground, would find the man who had done him injury while he slept. Hot and fierce-hearted, often he moved all about the outside of the barrow. No man at all was in the emptiness. Yet he took joy in the thought of war, in the work of fighting. At times he turned back into the barrow, sought his rich cup. Straightway he found that some man had tampered with his gold, his splendid treasure. The hoard-guard waited restless until evening came; then the barrow-keeper was in rage: he would requite that precious drinking cup with vengeful fire. Then the day was gone—to the joy of the worm. He would not wait long on the sea-wall, but set out with fire, ready with flame. The beginning was terrible to the folk on the land, as the ending was soon to be sore to their giver of treasure.

(XXXIII.) Then the evil spirit began to vomit flames, burn bright dwellings; blaze of fire rose, to the horror of men; there the deadly flying thing would leave nothing alive. The worm's warfare was wide-seen, his cruel malice, near and far—how the destroyer hated and hurt the people of the Geats. He winged back to the hoard, his hidden hall, before the time of day. He had circled the land-dwellers with flame, with fire and burning. He had trust in his barrow, in his war and his wall: his expectation deceived him.

Then the terror was made known to Beowulf, quickly in its truth, that his own home, best of buildings, had melted in surging flames, the throne-seat of the Geats. That was anguish of spirit to the good man, the greatest of heart-sorrows. The wise one supposed that he had bitterly offended the Ruler, the Eternal Lord, against old law. His breast within boiled with dark thoughts—as was not for him customary. The fiery dragon with his flames had destroyed the people's stronghold, the land along the sea, the heart of the country. Because of that the war-king, the lord of the Weather-Geats, devised punishment for him. The protector of fighting men, lord of earls, commanded that a wonderful battle-shield be made all of iron. Well he knew that the wood of the forest might not help him—linden against flame. The prince good from old times was to come to the end of the days that had been lent him, life in the world, and the worm with him, though he had long held the hoarded wealth. Then the ring-prince scorned to seek the far-flier with a troop, a large army. He had no fear for himself of the combat, nor did he think the worm's war-power anything great, his strength and his courage, because he himself had come through many battles before, dared perilous straits, clashes of war, after he had purged Hrothgar's hall, victorious warrior, and in combat crushed to death Grendel's kin, loathsome race.

Nor was that the least of his hand-combats where Hygelac was slain, when the king of the Geats, the noble lord of the people, the son of Hrethel, died of sword-strokes in the war-storm among the Frisians, laid low by the blade. From there Beowulf came away by means of his own strength, performed a feat of swimming; he had on his arm the armor of thirty earls when he turned back to the sea. There was no need for the Hetware [6] to exult in the foot-battle when they bore their shields against him: few came again from that warrior to seek their homes. Then the son of Ecgtheow swam over the water's expanse, forlorn and alone, back to his people. There Hygd offered him hoard and kingdom, rings and a prince's throne. She had no trust in her son, that he could hold his native throne against foreigners now that Hygelac was dead. By no means the sooner might the lordless ones get consent from the noble that he would become lord of Heardred or that he would accept royal power.[7] Yet he held him up among the people by friendly counsel, kindly with honor, until he became older,[8] ruled the Weather-Geats.

Outcasts from over the sea sought him, sons of Ohthere.[9] They had rebelled against the protector of the Scylfings, the best of the sea-kings of those who gave treasure in Sweden, a famous lord. For Heardred that became his life's limit: because of his hospitality there the son of Hygelac got his life's wound from the strokes of a sword. And the son of Ongentheow went back to seek his home after Heardred lay dead, let Beowulf hold the royal throne, rule the Geats: that was a good king.

(XXXIV.) In later days he was mindful of repaying the prince's fall, became the friend of the destitute Eadgils;[1] with folk he supported the son of Ohthere over the wide sea, with warriors and weapons. Afterwards he got vengeance by forays that brought with them cold care: he took the king's life.

Thus he had survived every combat, every dangerous battle, every deed of courage, the son of Ecgtheow, until that one day when he should fight with the worm. Then, one of twelve, the lord of the Geats, swollen with anger, went to look on the dragon. He had learned then from what the feud arose, the fierce malice to men: the glorious cup had come to his possession from the hand of the finder: he was the thirteenth of that company, the man who had brought on the beginning of the war, the sad-hearted slave—wretched, he must direct them to the place. Against his will he went to where he knew of an earth-hall, a barrow beneath the ground close to the sea-surge, to the strug-

6. I.e., a tribe, with whom the Frisians were allied.
7. I.e., Beowulf refused to take the throne from the rightful heir Heardred.
8. I.e., Beowulf supported the young Heardred.
9. Ohthere succeeded his father Ongentheow as king of the Scylfings (Swedes), but after his death his brother Onela seized the throne, driving out Ohthere's sons Eanmund and Eadgils. They were given refuge at the Geatish court by Heardred, whom Onela attacked for this act of hospitality. In the fight Eanmund and Heardred were killed, and Onela left the kingdom in Beowulf's charge.
1. The surviving son of Ohthere was befriended by Beowulf, who supported him in his successful attempt to gain the Swedish throne and who killed the usurper Onela.

gling waves: within, it was full of ornaments and gold chains. The terrible guardian, ready for combat, held the gold treasure, old under the earth. It was no easy bargain for any man to obtain. Then the king, hardy in fight, sat down on the headland; there he saluted his hearth-companions, gold-friend of the Geats. His mind was mournful, restless and ripe for death: very close was the fate which should come to the old man, seek his soul's hoard, divide life from his body; not for long then was the life of the noble one wound in his flesh.

Beowulf spoke, the son of Ecgtheow: "In youth I lived through many battle-storms, times of war. I remember all that. I was seven winters old when the lord of treasure, the beloved king of the folk, received me from my father: King Hrethel had me and kept me, gave me treasure and feast, mindful of kinship. During his life I was no more hated by him as a man in his castle than any of his own sons, Herebeald and Haethcyn, or my own Hygelac. For the eldest a murder-bed was wrongfully spread through the deed of a kinsman, when Haethcyn struck him down with an arrow from his horned bow—his friend and his lord—missed the mark and shot his kinsman dead, one brother the other, with the bloody arrowhead. That was a fatal fight, without hope of recompense, a deed wrongly done, baffling to the heart; yet it had happened that a prince had to lose life unavenged.

"So it is sad for an old man to endure that his son should ride young on the gallows. Then he may speak a story, a sorrowful song, when his son hangs for the joy of the raven, and, old in years and knowing, he can find no help for him. Always with every morning he is reminded of his son's journey elsewhere. He cares not to wait for another heir in his hall, when the first through death's force has come to the end of his deeds. Sorrowful he sees in his son's dwelling the empty wine-hall, the windy resting place without joy—the riders sleep, the warriors in the grave. There is no sound of the harp, no joy in the dwelling, as there was of old. (XXXV.) Then he goes to his couch, sings a song of sorrow, one alone for one gone. To him all too wide has seemed the land and the dwelling.

"So the protector of the Weather-Geats bore in his heart swelling sorrow for Herebeald. In no way could he settle his feud with the life-slayer; not the sooner could he wound the warrior with deeds of hatred, though he was not dear to him. Then for the sorrow that had too bitterly befallen him he gave up the joys of men, chose God's light. To his sons he left—as a happy man does—his land and his town when he went from life.

"Then there was battle and strife of Swedes and Geats, over

the wide water a quarrel shared, hatred between hardy ones, after Hrethel died. And the sons of Ongentheow [2] were bold and active in war, wanted to have no peace over the seas, but about Hreosnabeorh often devised awful slaughter. That my friends and kinsmen avenged, both the feud and the crime, as is well-known, though one of them bought it with his life, a hard bargain: the war was mortal to Haethcyn, lord of the Geats.[3] Then in the morning, I have heard, one kinsman avenged the other on his slayer with the sword's edge, when Ongentheow attacked Eofor: the war-helm split, the old Scylfing fell mortally wounded: his hand remembered feuds enough, did not withstand the life-blow.

"I repaid in war the treasures that he [4] gave me—with my bright sword, as was granted me by fate: he had given me land, a pleasant dwelling. There was not any need for him, any reason, that he should have to seek among the Gifthas or the Spear-Danes or in Sweden in order to buy with treasure a worse warrior. I would always go before him in the troop, alone in the front. And so all my life I shall wage battle while this sword endures that has served me early and late ever since I became Daeghrefn's slayer in the press—the warrior of the Hugas.[5] He could not bring armor to the king of the Frisians, breast ornament, but fell in the fight, keeper of the standard, a noble man. Nor was my sword's edge his slayer, but my warlike grip broke open his heart-streams, his bone-house. Now shall the sword's edge, the hand and hard blade, fight for the hoard."

[BEOWULF ATTACKS THE DRAGON]

Beowulf spoke, for the last time spoke words in boast: "In my youth I engaged in many wars. Old guardian of the people, I shall still seek battle, perform a deed of fame, if the evil-doer will come to me out of the earth-hall."

Then he saluted each of the warriors, the bold helmet-bearers, for the last time—his own dear companions. "I would not bear sword, weapon, to the worm, if I knew how else according to my boast I might grapple with the monster, as I did of old with Grendel. But I expect here hot battle-fire, steam and poison. Therefore I have on me shield and mail-shirt. I will not flee a foot-step from the barrow-ward, but it shall be with us at the wall as fate allots, the ruler of every man. I am confident in

2. I.e., the Swedes Onela and Ohthere: the reference is, of course, to a time earlier than that referred to in section XXXIII, note 9.
3. Haethcyn had succeeded his father Hrethel as king of the Geats after his accidental killing of his brother Herebeald. When Haethcyn was killed while attacking the Swedes, he was succeeded by Hygelac, who, as the next sentence relates, avenged Haethcyn's death on Ongentheow. The death of Ongentheow is described below, sections XL and XLI.
4. Hygelac.
5. I.e., the Franks.

heart, so I forgo help against the war-flier. Wait on the barrow, safe in your mail-shirts, men in armor—which of us two may better bear wounds after our bloody meeting. This is not your venture, nor is it right for any man except me alone that he should spend his strength against the monster, do this man's deed. By my courage I shall get gold, or war will take your king, dire life-evil."

Then the brave warrior arose by his shield; hardy under helmet he went in his mail-shirt beneath the stone-cliffs, had trust in his strength—that of one man: such is not the way of the cowardly. Then he saw by the wall—he who had come through many wars, good in his great-heartedness, many clashes in battle when troops meet together—a stone arch standing, through it a stream bursting out of the barrow: there was welling of a current hot with killing fires, and he might not endure any while unburnt by the dragon's flame the hollow near the hoard. Then the man of the Weather-Geats, enraged as he was, let a word break from his breast. Stout-hearted he shouted; his voice went roaring, clear in battle, in under the gray stone. Hate was stirred up, the hoard's guard knew the voice of a man. No more time was there to ask for peace. First the monster's breath came out of the stone, the hot war-steam. The earth resounded. The man below the barrow, the lord of the Geats, swung his shield against the dreadful visitor. Then the heart of the coiled thing was aroused to seek combat. The good war-king had drawn his sword, the old heirloom, not blunt of edge. To each of them as they threatened destruction there was terror of the other. Firm-hearted he stood with his shield high, the lord of friends, while quickly the worm coiled itself; he waited in his armor. Then, coiling in flames, he came gliding on, hastening to his fate. The good shield protected the life and body of the famous prince, but for a shorter while than his wish was. There for the first time, the first day in his life, he might not prevail, since fate did not assign him such glory in battle. The lord of the Geats raised his hand, struck the shining horror so with his forged blade that the edge failed, bright on the bone, bit less surely than its folk-king had need, hard-pressed in perils. Then because of the battle-stroke the barrow-ward's heart was savage, he exhaled death-fire—the war-flames sprang wide. The gold-friend of the Geats boasted of no great victories: the war blade had failed, naked at need, as it ought not to have done, iron good from old times. That was no pleasant journey, not one on which the famous son of Ecgtheow would wish to leave his land; against his will he must take up a dwelling-place elsewhere—as every man must give up the days that are lent him.

It was not long until they came together again, dreadful foes. The hoard-guard took heart, once more his breast swelled with his breathing. Encircled with flames, he who before had ruled a folk felt harsh pain. Nor did his companions, sons of nobles, take up their stand in a troop about him with the courage of fighting men, but they crept to the wood, protected their lives. In only one of them the heart surged with sorrows: nothing can ever set aside kinship in him who means well.

(XXXVI.) He was called Wiglaf, son of Weohstan, a rare shield-warrior, a man of the Scylfings,[6] kinsman of Aelfhere. He saw his liege lord under his war-mask suffer the heat. Then he was mindful of the honors he had given him before, the rich dwelling-place of the Waegmundings, every folk-right such as his father possessed. He might not then hold back, his hand seized his shield, the yellow linden-wood; he drew his ancient sword. Among men it was the heirloom of Eanmund, the son of Ohthere: [7] Weohstan had become his slayer in battle with sword's edge—an exile without friends; and he bore off to his kin the bright-shining helmet, the ringed mail-armor, the old sword made by giants that Onela had given him,[8] his kinsman's war-armor, ready battle-gear: he did not speak of the feud, though he had killed his brother's son.[9] He [1] held the armor many half-years, the blade and the battle-dress, until his son might do manly deeds like his old father. Then he gave him among the Geats war-armor of every kind, numberless, when, old, he went forth on the way from life. For the young warrior this was the first time that he should enter the war-storm with his dear lord. His heart's courage did not slacken, nor did the heirloom of his kinsman fail in the battle. That the worm found when they had come together.

Wiglaf spoke, said many fit words to his companions—his mind was mournful: "I remember that time we drank mead, when we

---

6. Though in the next sentence Wiglaf is said to belong to the family of the Waegmundings, the Geatish family to which Beowulf belonged, he is here called a Scylfing (Swede), and immediately below his father Weohstan is represented as having fought for the Swede Onela in his attack on the Geats. But for a man to change his nation was not unusual, and Weohstan, who may have had both Swedish and Geatish blood, had evidently become a Geat long enough before to have brought up his son Wiglaf as one. The identity of Aelfhere is not known.

7. See above, section XXXIII, note 9. Not only did Weohstan support Onela's attack on the Geat king Heardred, but

actually killed Eanmund whom Heardred was supporting, and it is Eanmund's sword that Wiglaf is now wielding.

8. The spoils of war belonged to the victorious king, who apportioned them among his fighters: thus Onela gave Weohstan the armor of Eanmund, whom Weohstan had killed.

9. This ironic remark points out that Onela did not claim *wergild* or seek vengeance from Weohstan, as in other circumstances he ought to have done inasmuch as Weohstan had killed Onela's close kinsman, his nephew Eanmund: but Onela was himself trying to kill Eanmund.

1. Weohstan.

promised our lord in the beer-hall—him who gave us these rings—
that we would repay him for the war-arms if a need like this
befell him—the helmets and the hard swords. Of his own will
he chose us among the host for this venture, thought us worthy
of fame—and gave me these treasures—because he counted us
good war-makers, brave helm-bearers, though our lord intended
to do this work of courage alone, as keeper of the folk, because
among men he had performed the greatest deeds of glory, daring
actions. Now the day has come that our liege lord has need of
the strength of good fighters. Let us go to him, help our war-
chief while the grim terrible fire persists. God knows of me that
I should rather that the flame enfold my body with my gold-
giver. It does not seem right to me for us to bear our shields
home again unless we can first fell the foe, defend the life of
the prince of the Weather-Geats. I know well that it would be
no recompense for past deeds that he alone of the company of
the Geats should suffer pain, fall in the fight. For us both shall
there be a part in the work of sword and helmet, of battle-shirt
and war-clothing."

Then he waded through the deadly smoke, bore his war-helmet
to the aid of his king, spoke in few words: "Beloved Beowulf,
do all well, for, long since in your youth, you said that you
would not let your glory fail while you lived. Now, great-
spirited noble, brave of deeds, you must protect your life with
all your might. I shall help you."

After these words, the worm came on, angry, the terrible
malice-filled foe, shining with surging flames, to seek for the second
time his enemies, hated men. Fire advanced in waves; shield burned
to the boss; mail-shirt might give no help to the young spear-warrior;
but the young man went quickly under his kinsman's shield when
his own was consumed with flames. Then the war-king was again
mindful of fame, struck with his war-sword with great strength so
that it stuck in the head-bone, driven with force: Naegling broke,
the sword of Beowulf failed in the fight, old and steel-gray. It was
not ordained for him that iron edges might help in the combat. Too
strong was the hand that I have heard strained every sword with its
stroke, when he bore wound-hardened weapon to battle: he was
none the better for it.

Then for the third time the folk-harmer, the fearful fire-
dragon, was mindful of feuds, set upon the brave one when the
chance came, hot and battle-grim seized all his neck with his
sharp fangs: he was smeared with life-blood, gore welled out
in waves.

(XXXVII.) Then, I have heard, at the need of the folk-king
the earl at his side made his courage known, his might and his

keenness—as was natural to him. He took no heed for that head,[2] but the hand of the brave man was burned as he helped his kinsman, as the man in armor struck the hateful foe a little lower down, so that the sword sank in, shining and engraved; and then the fire began to subside. The king himself then still controlled his senses, drew the battle-knife, biting and war-sharp, that he wore on his mail-shirt: the protector of the Weather-Geats cut the worm through the middle. They felled the foe, courage drove his life out, and they had destroyed him together, the two noble kinsmen. So ought a man be, a thane at need. To the prince that was the last moment of victory for his own deeds, of work in the world.

Then the wound that the earth-dragon had caused began to burn and to swell; at once he felt dire evil boil in his breast, poison within him. Then the prince, wise of thought, went to where he might sit on a seat near the wall. He looked on the work of giants, how the timeless earth-hall held within it stone-arches fast on pillars. Then with his hands the thane, good without limit, washed him with water, blood-besmeared, the famous prince, his beloved lord, sated with battle; and he unfastened his helmet.

Beowulf spoke—despite his wounds spoke, his mortal hurts. He knew well he had lived out his days' time, joy on earth; all passed was the number of his days, death very near. "Now I would wish to give my son my war-clothing, if any heir after me, part of my flesh, were granted. I held this people fifty winters. There was no folk-king of those dwelling about who dared approach me with swords, threaten me with fears. In my land I awaited what fate brought me, held my own well, sought no treacherous quarrels, nor did I swear many oaths unrightfully. Sick with life-wounds, I may have joy of all this, for the Ruler of Men need not blame me for the slaughter of kinsmen when life goes from my body. Now quickly go to look at the hoard under the gray stone, beloved Wiglaf, now that the worm lies sleeping from sore wounds, bereft of his treasure. Be quick now, so that I may see the ancient wealth, the golden things, may clearly look on the bright curious gems, so that for that, because of the treasure's richness, I may the more easily leave life and nation I have long held."

(XXXVIII.) Then I have heard that the son of Weohstan straightway obeyed his lord, sick with battle-wounds, according to the words he had spoken, went wearing his ring-armor, woven battle-shirt, under the barrow's roof. Then he saw, as he went

---

2. I.e., the dragon's flame-breathing head.

by the seat, the brave young retainer, triumphant in heart, many precious jewels, glittering gold lying on the ground, wonders on the wall, and the worm's lair, the old night-flier's—cups standing there, vessels of men of old, with none to polish them, stripped of their ornaments. There was many a helmet old and rusty, many an arm-ring skillfully twisted. (Easily may treasure, gold in the ground, betray each one of the race of men, hide it who will.) Also he saw a standard all gold hang high over the hoard, the greatest of hand-wonders, linked with fingers' skill. From it came a light so that he might see the ground, look on the works of craft. There was no trace of the worm, for the blade had taken him. Then I have heard that one man in the mound pillaged the hoard, the old work of giants, loaded in his bosom cups and plates at his own desire. He took also the standard, brightest of banners. The sword of the old lord—its edge was iron—had already wounded the one who for a long time had been guardian of the treasure, waged his fire-terror, hot for the hoard, rising up fiercely at midnight, till he died in the slaughter.

The messenger was in haste, eager to return, urged on by the treasures. Curiosity tormented him, whether eagerly seeking he should find the lord of the Weather-Geats, strength gone, alive in the place where he had left him before. Then with the treasures he found the great prince, his lord, bleeding, at the end of his life. Again he began to sprinkle him with water until this word's point broke through his breast-hoard—he spoke, the king, old man in sorrow, looked on the gold: "I speak with my words thanks to the Lord of All for these treasures, to the King of Glory, Eternal Prince, for what I gaze on here, that I might get such for my people before my death-day. Now that I have bought the hoard of treasures with my old life, you attend to the people's needs hereafter: I can be here no longer. Bid the battle-renowned make a mound, bright after the funeral fire, on the sea's cape. It shall stand high on Hronesness as a reminder to my people, so that sea-travelers later will call it Beowulf's barrow, when they drive their ships far over the darkness of the seas."

He took off his neck the golden necklace, bold-hearted prince, gave it to the thane, to the young spear-warrior—gold-gleaming helmet, ring, and mail-shirt, bade him use them well. "You are the last left of our race, of the Waegmundings. Fate has swept away all my kinsmen, earls in their strength, to destined death. I have to go after." That was the last word of the old man, of the thoughts of his heart, before he should taste the funeral pyre, hot hostile flames. The soul went from his breast to seek the doom of those fast in truth.

[Beowulf's Funeral]

(XXXIX.) Then sorrow came to the young man that he saw him whom he most loved on the earth, at the end of his life, suffering piteously. His slayer likewise lay dead, the awful earth-dragon bereft of life, overtaken by evil. No longer should the coiled worm rule the ring-hoard, for iron edges had taken him, hard and battle-sharp work of the hammers, so that the wide-flier, stilled by wounds, had fallen on the earth near the treasure-house. He did not go flying through the air at midnight, proud of his property, showing his aspect, but he fell to earth through the work of the chief's hands. Yet I have heard of no man of might on land, though he was bold of every deed, whom it should prosper to rush against the breath of the venomous foe or disturb with hands the ring-hall, if he found the guard awake who lived in the barrow. The share of the rich treasures became Beowulf's, paid for by death: each of the two had journeyed to the end of life's loan.

Then it was not long before the battle-slack ones left the woods, ten weak troth-breakers together, who had not dared fight with their spears in their liege lord's great need. But they bore their shields, ashamed, their war-clothes, to where the old man lay, looked on Wiglaf. He sat wearied, the foot-soldier near the shoulders of his lord, would waken him with water: it gained him nothing. He might not, though he much wished it, hold life in his chieftain on earth nor change anything of the Ruler's: the judgment of God would control the deeds of every man, just as it still does now. Then it was easy to get from the young man a grim answer to him who before had lost courage. Wiglaf spoke, the son of Weohstan, a man sad at heart, looked on the unloved ones:

"Yes, he who will speak truth may say that the liege lord who gave you treasure, the war-gear that you stand in there, when he used often to hand out to hall-sitters on the ale-benches, a prince to his thanes, helmets and war-shirts such as he could find mightiest anywhere, both far and near—that he quite threw away the war-gear, to his distress when war came upon him. The folk-king had no need to boast of his war-comrades. Yet God, Ruler of Victories, granted him that he might avenge himself, alone with his sword, when there was need for his courage. I was able to give him little life-protection in the fight, and yet beyond my power I did begin to help my kinsman. The deadly foe was ever the weaker after I struck him with my sword, fire poured less strongly from his head. Too few defenders thronged about the prince when the hard time came upon him. Now there shall cease for your race the receiving of treasure and the giving of swords, all enjoyment of pleasant homes, comfort. Each man of your kindred must go deprived of his land-right when nobles from afar learn of your flight, your inglorious deed. Death is better for any earl than a life of blame."

(XL.) Then he bade that the battle-deed be announced in the city, up over the cliff-edge, where the band of warriors sat the whole morning of the day, sad-hearted, shield-bearers in doubt whether it was the beloved man's last day or whether he would come again. Little did he fail to speak of new tidings, he who rode up the hill, but spoke to them all truthfully: "Now the joy-giver of the people of the Weathers, the lord of the Geats, is fast on his death-bed, lies on his slaughter-couch through deeds of the worm. Beside him lies his life-enemy, struck down with dagger-wounds—with his sword he might not work wounds of any kind on the monster. Wiglaf son of Weohstan sits over Beowulf, one earl by the lifeless other, in weariness of heart holds death-watch over the loved and the hated.

"Now may the people expect a time of war, when the king's fall becomes wide-known to the Franks and the Frisians. A harsh quarrel was begun with the Hugas when Hygelac came traveling with his sea-army to the land of the Frisians, where the Hetware assailed him in battle, quickly, with stronger forces, made the mailed warrior bow; he fell in the ranks: that chief gave no treasure to his retainers. Ever since then the good will of the Merewioing king has been denied us.

"Nor do I expect any peace or trust from the Swedish people, for it is wide-known that Ongentheow took the life of Haethcyn, Hrethel's son, near Ravenswood when in their over-pride the people of the Geats first went against the War-Scylfings. Straightway the wary father of Ohthere,[3] old and terrible, gave a blow in return, cut down the sea-king,[4] rescued his wife, old woman of times past, bereft of her gold, mother of Onela and Ohthere, and then he followed his life-foes until they escaped, lordless, painfully, to Ravenswood. Then with a great army he besieged those whom the sword had left, weary with wounds, often vowed woes to the wretched band the livelong night, said that in the morning he would cut them apart with sword-blades, [hang] some on gallows-trees as sport for birds. Relief came in turn to the sorry-hearted together with dawn when they heard Hygelac's horn and trumpet, his sound as the good man came on their track with a body of retainers. (XLI.) Wide-seen was the bloody track of Swedes and

3. I.e., Ongentheow.
4. I.e., Haethcyn, king of the Geats. Haethcyn's brother Hygelac, who succeeded him, was not present at this battle, but arrived after the death of Haethcyn with reinforcements to relieve the survivors and to pursue Ongentheow in his retreat to his city.

Geats, the slaughter-strife of men, how the peoples stirred up the feud between them. Then the good man went with his kinsmen, old and much-mourning, to seek his stronghold: the earl Ongentheow moved further away. He had heard of the warring of Hygelac, of the war-power of the proud one. He did not trust in resistance, that he might fight off the sea-men, defend his hoard against the war-sailors, his children and wife. Instead he drew back, the old man behind his earth-wall.

"Then pursuit was offered to the people of the Swedes, the standards of Hygelac overran the stronghold as Hrethel's people pressed forward to the citadel. There Ongentheow the gray-haired was brought to bay by sword-blades, and the people's king had to submit to the judgment of Eofor alone. Wulf [5] son of Wonred had struck him angrily with his weapon so that for the blow the blood sprang forth in streams beneath his hair. Yet not for that was he afraid, the old Scylfing, but he quickly repaid the assault with worse exchange, the folk-king, when he turned toward him. The strong son of Wonred could not give the old man a return blow, for Ongentheow had first cut through the helmet of his head so that he had to sink down, smeared with blood—fell on the earth: he was not yet doomed, for he recovered, though the wound hurt him. The hardy thane of Hygelac,[6] when his brother lay low, let his broad sword, old blade made by giants, break the great helmet across the shield-wall; then the king bowed, the keeper of the folk was hit to the quick.

"Then there were many who bound up the brother, quickly raised him up after it was granted them to control the battle-field. Then one warrior stripped the other, took from Ongentheow his iron-mail, hard-hilted sword, and his helmet, too; he bore the arms of the hoary one to Hygelac. He accepted that treasure and fairly promised him rewards among the people, and he stood by it thus: the lord of the Geats, the son of Hrethel, when he came home, repaid Wulf and Eofor for their battle-assault with much treasure, gave each of them a hundred thousand [units] of land and linked rings: there was no need for any man on middle-earth to blame him for the rewards, since they had performed great deeds. And then he gave Eofor his only daughter as a pledge of friendship—a fair thing for his home.

"That is the feud and the enmity, the death-hatred of men, for which I expect that the people of the Swedes, bold shield-warriors after the fall of princes, will set upon us after they learn that our prince has gone from life, he who before held hoard and

5. The two sons of Wonred, Wulf and Eofor, attacked Ongentheow in turn. Wulf was struck down but not killed by the old Swedish king, who was then slain by Eofor.
6. I.e., Eofor.

kingdom against our enemies, did good to the people, and further still, did what a man should. Now haste is best, that we look on the people's king there and bring him who gave us rings on his way to the funeral pyre. Nor shall only a small share melt with the great-hearted one, but there is a hoard of treasure, gold uncounted, grimly purchased, and rings bought at the last now with his own life. These shall the fire devour, flames enfold—no earl to wear ornament in remembrance, nor any bright maiden add to her beauty with neck-ring; but mournful-hearted, stripped of gold, they shall walk, often, not once, in strange countries— now that the army-leader has laid aside laughter, his game and his mirth. Therefore many a spear, cold in the morning, shall be grasped with fingers, raised by hands; no sound of harp shall waken the warriors, but the dark raven, low over the doomed, shall tell many tales, say to the eagle how he fared at the feast when with the wolf he spoiled the slain bodies."

Thus the bold man was a speaker of hateful news, nor did he much lie in his words or his prophecies. The company all arose. Without joy they went below Earnaness [7] to look on the wonder with welling tears. Then they found on the sand, soulless, keeping his bed of rest, him who in former times had given them rings. Then the last day of the good man had come, when the war-king, prince of the Weather-Geats, died a wonderful death. First they saw the stranger creature, the worm lying loathsome, opposite him in the place. The fire-dragon was grimly terrible with his many colors, burned by the flames; he was fifty feet long in the place where he lay. Once he had joy of the air at night, came back down to seek his den. Then he was made fast by death, had made use of the last of his earth-caves. Beside him stood cups and pitchers, plates and rich swords lay eaten through by rust, just as they had been there in the bosom of the earth for a thousand winters. Then that huge heritage, gold of men of old, was wound in a spell, so that no one of men must touch the ring-hall unless God himself, the True King of Victories—He is men's protection—should grant to whom He wished to open the hoard—whatever man seemed fit to Him.

(XLII.) Then it was seen that the act did not profit him who wrongly kept hidden the handiworks under the wall. The keeper had first slain a man like few others, then the feud had been fiercely avenged. It is a wonder where an earl famed for courage may reach the end of his allotted life—then may dwell no longer in the mead-hall, man with his kin. So it was with Beowulf when he sought quarrels, the barrow's ward: he himself did not then know in what way his parting with the world should come. The

7. The headland near where Beowulf had fought the dragon.

great princes who had put it [8] there had laid on it so deep a curse until doomsday that the man who should plunder the place should be guilty of sins, imprisoned in idol-shrines, fixed with hell-bonds, punished with evils—unless the Possessor's favor were first shown the more clearly to him who desired the gold.

Wiglaf spoke, the son of Weohstan: "Often many a man must suffer distress for the will of one man, as has happened to us. We might by no counsel persuade our dear prince, keeper of the kingdom, not to approach the gold-guardian, let him lie where he long was, live in his dwelling to the world's end. He held to his high destiny. The hoard has been made visible, grimly got. What drove the folk-king thither was too powerfully fated. I have been therein and looked at it all, the rare things of the chamber, when it was granted me—not at all friendly was the journey that I was permitted beneath the earth-wall. In haste I seized with my hands a huge burden of hoard-treasures, of great size, bore it out here to my king. He was then still alive, sound-minded and aware. He spoke many things, old man in sorrow, and bade greet you, commanded that for your lord's deeds you make a high barrow in the place of his pyre, large and conspicuous, since he was of men the worthiest warrior through the wide earth, while he might enjoy wealth in his castle.

"Let us now hasten to see and visit for the second time the heap of precious jewels, the wonder under the walls. I shall direct you so that you may look on enough of them from near at hand—rings and broad gold. Let the bier be made ready, speedily prepared, when we come out, and then let us carry our prince, beloved man, where he shall long dwell in the Ruler's protection."

Then the son of Weohstan, man brave in battle, bade command many warriors, men who owned houses, leaders of the people, that they carry wood from afar for the pyre for the good man. "Now shall flame eat the chief of warriors—the fire shall grow dark—who often survived the iron-shower when the storm of arrows driven from bow-strings passed over the shield-wall— the shaft did its task, made eager by feather-gear served the arrowhead."

And then the wise son of Weohstan summoned from the host thanes of the king, seven together, the best; one of eight warriors, he went beneath the evil roof. One who walked before bore a torch in his hands. Then there was no lot to decide who should plunder that hoard, since the men could see that every part of it rested in the hall without guardian, lay wasting. Little did any man mourn that hastily they should bear out the rare treasure.

8. The treasure.

Also they pushed the dragon, the worm, over the cliff-wall, let the wave take him, the flood enfold the keeper of the treasure. Then twisted gold was loaded on a wagon, an uncounted number of things, and the prince, hoary warrior, borne to Hronesness.

(XLIII.) Then the people of the Geats made ready for him a funeral pyre on the earth, no small one, hung with helmets, battle-shields, bright mail-shirts, just as he had asked. Then in the midst they laid the great prince, lamenting their hero, their beloved lord. Then warriors began to awaken on the barrow the greatest of funeral-fires; the wood-smoke climbed, black over the fire; the roaring flame mixed with weeping—the wind-surge died down—until it had broken the bone-house, hot at its heart. Sad in spirit they lamented their heart-care, the death of their liege lord. [And the Geatish woman, wavy-haired, sang a sorrowful song about Beowulf, said] [9] again and again that she sorely feared for herself invasions of armies, many slaughters, terror of troops, humiliation, and captivity. Heaven swallowed the smoke.

Then the people of the Weather-Geats built a mound on the promontory, one that was high and broad, wide-seen by seafarers, and in ten days completed a monument for the bold in battle, surrounded the remains of the fire with a wall, the most splendid that men most skilled might devise. In the barrow they placed rings and jewels, all such ornaments as troubled men had earlier taken from the hoard. They let the earth hold the wealth of earls, gold in the ground, where now it still dwells, as useless to men as it was before. Then the brave in battle rode round the mound, children of nobles, twelve in all, would bewail their sorrow and mourn their king, recite dirges and speak of the man. They praised his great deeds and his acts of courage, judged well of his prowess. So it is fitting that man honor his liege lord with words, love him in heart when he must be led forth from the body. Thus the people of the Geats, his hearth-companions, lamented the death of their lord. They said that he was of world-kings the mildest of men and the gentlest, kindest to his people, and most eager for fame.

9. The manuscript is badly damaged and the interpretation conjectural.

THE WANDERER

The lament of *The Wanderer* is an excellent example of the elegiac mood so common in Old English poetry. The loss of a lord, of companions in arms, of a mead-hall (in which Anglo-Saxon life realized itself to the full) are themes that enhance the melancholy tone of *Beowulf* as they are the emotional basis for such a poem as the present one. But nowhere more poignantly expressed than in *The Wanderer* is the loneliness of the exile in search of a new lord and hall: this is what Beowulf's father, Ecgtheow, would have suffered, had it not been for Hrothgar's hospitality. To the wretched seeker all weather is wintry, for nature seems to conspire to match a man's mood as he moves over the water from one land to another, yearning for a home and kin to replace those vanished ones that still fill his thoughts.

As is true of most Old English elegiac laments, both the language and the structure of *The Wanderer* are difficult. The poem begins with a speaker who voices hope of finding comfort after many tribulations, one who is identified as an "earth-walker." After the interruption, this wanderer continues to speak—to himself—of his long search for a new home, describing how he must keep his thoughts locked within him while he makes his search. But these thoughts form the most vivid and moving part of his soliloquy—how, floating upon the sea, dazed with sorrow and fatigue, he imagines that he sees his old companions, and how, as he wakens to reality, they vanish over the water like sea-birds.

The second part of the poem, beginning with the seventh paragraph ("Therefore I cannot think why * * * "), expands the theme from one man to all men in a world wasted by war and time. It is probable that the speaker of this part of the poem is the same as that of the earlier part, but it is at least possible, as a scholar has recently argued, that the poet meant the second part to be assigned to a different speaker, one of a more thoughtful turn of mind who draws philosophical implications from the experience of the first. The later speaker derives such cold comfort as he can from asking the old question, *Ubi sunt?*—where are they who were once so glad to live? And he concludes with the thought that this "resting place of earth" shall be emptied of mankind. This man, "wise in heart," sits apart at the council, apparently as an indication of his detachment from life. The poem concludes with a characteristic Old English injunction to practice restraint on earth, place hope only in heaven.

The Wanderer is preserved only in the Exeter Book, a manuscript copied about 975, which contains the largest surviving collection of Old English poetry.

The Wanderer[1]

"Often the lone-dweller lives to find favor, mildness of the Lord, though long over the water-way, troubled in heart, he has had to stir with his arms the frost-cold sea, tread the tracks of exile. Fully fixed is his fate."

So spoke the earth-walker, mindful of hardships, of cruel war-slaughters—and the fall of dear kinsmen.

1. The translation by the editor is based on the text edited by J. C. Pope in *Seven Old English Poems* (1966); the indication of a new speaker at the beginning of the seventh paragraph is also adopted from Pope.

"Often before the dawn of each day, alone, I have had to speak my cares: there is now none of the living to whom I dare clearly say my heart's thought. I know for truth that it is an excellent custom in a man that he lock fast his heart's coffer, keep his mind's hoard-case closed, purpose what he will. The weary-hearted may not withstand fate, nor the torn spirit bring help. Therefore those eager for fame often bind sorrowful thought fast in their breast-coffer.

"So I, often wretched with care, deprived of my homeland, far from dear kinsmen, had to fasten my heart's thought with fetters—after the time, in years long past, that I covered my gold-friend in the darkness of earth; and thence downcast I crossed over the woven waves, winter-sad, yearning for a hall, sought a giver of treasure—where, far or near, I might find one who should know of my people or would comfort me friendless, receive me with gladness. He who has felt it knows how cruel a companion is sorrow to him who has no beloved protectors. The path of exile attends him, not twisted gold—frozen are the thoughts in his heart-case, no joy of earth. He remembers the hall-warriors and the taking of treasure—how in his youth his gold-friend made him accustomed to feasting. All delight ends.

"Indeed, he who must long forgo the counsel-words of a beloved lord knows how it will seem to him in his mind, when together sorrow and sleep often bind the poor lone-dweller, that he is embracing and kissing his liege lord and laying his hands and head on his knee, as in the old days when sometimes he shared in the gift-giving. Then the lordless man wakens again, sees before him the yellow waves, the sea-birds bathe, spread their feathers, frost and snow fall, mingled with hail.

"Then the wounds of his heart are deeper, sore for want of his dear one. Sorrow is made new as memory of kinsmen moves through his mind: he greets them with glad words, eagerly looks on them, a company of warriors. They fade again, moving away over the water: such fleeting ones' spirit brings there no well-known voices. Care is renewed in him who many and often times must send his weary heart over the woven waves."

"Therefore I cannot think why my heart's thought should not grow dark when through this world I consider all the life of men—with what terrible swiftness they forgo the hall-floor, bold young retainers. So each day this middle-earth fails and falls. Indeed, no man may become wise before he has had a share of winters in the kingdom of this world. The wise must be patient, must never be too hot-hearted, nor too hasty of speech, nor too weak of wars, nor too wanting of thought, nor too fearful, nor too glad, nor too greedy for wealth, nor ever too eager of boast before he has clear knowing.

A man must wait, when he speaks boast, until, sure-minded, he knows clearly whither the thought of hearts will turn.

"The wise warrior must observe how ghostly it will be when all the wealth of this world stands waste, as now here and there through this middle-earth walls stand blown by the wind, covered with frost-fall, the dwellings storm-beaten. The wine-halls totter, the lord lies bereft of joy, all the company has fallen, bold men beside the wall. Some war took away, bore them on their way forth; one a bird carried off over the deep sea, one the gray wolf shared with death, another a man with sad face hid in an earth-pit.

"So the Creator of men's generations laid waste this dwelling-ground until the old works of giants stood idle, empty of the sound of the stronghold's keepers. Therefore the wise in heart thinks deeply on this wall-place and this dark life, remembers the great number of deadly combats long ago, and speaks these words: 'Where has the horse gone? Where the young warrior? Where is the giver of treasure? What has become of the seats for the feasts? Where are the joys of the hall? Alas, the bright cup! Alas, the mailed warrior! Alas, the prince's glory! How has that time gone, vanished beneath night's cover, just as if it had never been! The wall, wonderfully high, adorned with snake-images, stands now over the old traces of the beloved company. Might of the ash-spears has carried away the earls, weapons greedy for slaughter—Fate the mighty, and storms beat on the stone walls, thick-falling snow binds the earth; winter's roar, when darkness comes, the night-shadow falls, sends from the north harsh hailstones in hatred of men. All the kingdom of earth is wretched, work of the fates changes the world under the skies. Here wealth is fleeting, here friend is fleeting, here man is fleeting, here woman is fleeting—all this resting place of earth shall be emptied.' "

So spoke the wise in heart, sat apart at the council. Good is he who keeps his pledge, must never man utter too quickly the passion of his breast, unless he knows first how to achieve remedy, an earl with his valor. Well will it be with him who seeks favor, support from the Father in heaven, where for us the only stronghold stands.

THE BATTLE OF MALDON

The *Battle of Maldon* celebrates an event of the year 991, when a large party of Scandinavian raiders met the English defense forces on the estuary of the Blackwater River (the Pant of the poem), near Maldon in Essex. The Vikings had made a number of successful raids on seaports in the vicinity, after which they had encamped on an island near the mouth of the river. The island, since it was accessible from the mainland by a causeway that might be used only at low tide, provided a natural base from which the Vikings could continue their hit-and-run depredations on the countryside. Birhtnoth, the Earl of Essex, who was leader of the English militia, took up his position at the end of the causeway and from there was able to prevent the enemy from crossing to the mainland. As the poem relates, however, in his "overconfidence" he allowed them free passage so that a battle might take place. As a result, he was himself killed, and many of the defenders took to their heels; but the earl's retinue —his close associates and retainers—continued to fight bravely until they were overwhelmed. In the incomplete form in which the poem has come down to us we do not hear of the ultimate defeat of the English, though the grim tone and in particular the famous speech of Birhtwold prepare us for the disaster.

The unknown poet of late Anglo-Saxon times was apparently well versed in heroic English poetry of the type of *Beowulf*, and he does a brilliant job of adapting traditional epic mannerisms to his description of a local battle of no particular historical importance, which involved people with whom he was acquainted. The defense forces were actually no more than a home guard: inexperienced farmers and laborers conscripted for the local defense, together with a small group of aristocrats who were acquainted with heroic martial tradition but had not before had the opportunity to behave heroically. Since the defeat of the Scandinavians at Brunanburg in 937, the kingdom had enjoyed a long, peaceful respite from attack; the present Viking raid was, indeed, the beginning of a new and bloody era during which the realm that Alfred had consolidated weakened badly under Ethelred "the Unready." Godric and his brothers, who, according to the poem, fled from the battle, are representative of those Englishmen who preferred to pay tribute rather than to fight. But Birhtnoth and his retinue are of the traditional tough fiber, and it is especially in their speeches and single combats that the poet uses the epic style, contenting himself elsewhere with a forceful but generally realistic narrative of what occurred. Birhtnoth's decision to let the Vikings cross the river is treated in the epic manner as an instance of heroic overconfidence, like Beowulf's refusal to use his sword against the unarmed Grendel —but in this case it is a gesture that leads to tragic doom. Probably Birhtnoth had a practical motive for his rashness: if the Vikings were prevented from raiding here, they would simply sail along the coast to a less well-defended spot in order to continue their depredations. Only their destruction would insure general peace; but from the local point of view, Birhtnoth's permitting the enemy to come where he could fight with them might well appear as the rashly noble act of a traditional hero.

The poem was written down in a manuscript that was reduced to charred fragments in the same fire that damaged the *Beowulf* manuscript. Fortunately, a transcript had been made of it before the fire, and on this modern editions depend. Even before the manuscript was burned the poem must have lacked a number of lines at its beginning and end, though most scholars feel that nothing very substantial has been lost.

The Battle of Maldon[1]

Then he[2] commanded each of his warriors to leave his horse, drive it far away, and walk forward, trusting in his hands and in his good courage. When Offa's kinsman[3] understood that the earl would not put up with cowardice, he let his beloved hawk fly from his hand toward the woods and advanced to the battle: by this men might know that the youth would not weaken in the fight once he had taken up his weapons. Eadric wished also to serve his lord the earl in the battle; he carried his spear forward to the conflict. He was of good heart as long as he might hold shield and broadsword in his hands; he carried out the vow that he had made, now that he was to fight before his lord.

Then Birhtnoth began to place his men at their stations; he rode about and advised them, taught the troops how they should stand and hold the place and bade them grasp their shields aright, firm in their hands, and have no fear. When he had arranged his folk properly, he alighted among them where it seemed best to him, where he knew his retainers to be most loyal.

Then the Vikings' herald stood on the river bank, cried out loudly, spoke words, boastfully proclaimed the seafarers' message to the earl where he stood on the shore: "Bold seamen have sent me to thee, have commanded me to say to thee that thou must quickly send treasure in order to protect thyself; and it is better for you to buy off this spear-assault with tribute than to have us give you harsh war. There is no need for us to destroy one another, if you are rich enough to pay. With the gold we will confirm truce. If thou that art highest here decide upon this, that thou wilt ransom thy people, and in return for peace give the seamen money in the amount they request, and receive peace from us, we will go to ship with the tribute, set sail on the sea, and keep peace with you."

Birhtnoth spoke, raised his shield, his slender ash-spear, uttered words, angry and resolute gave him answer: "Dost thou hear, seafarer, what this folk says? They will give you spears for tribute, poisoned point and old sword, heriot[4] that avails you not in battle. Sea-wanderers' herald, take back our answer, speak to thy people a message far more hateful, that here stands with his host an undis-

---

1. In this prose translation by the present editor, a few liberties have been taken with the text in order to make clear the references of some of the loosely used Old English terms for "warrior." The translation is in general based on the text in J. C. Pope's *Seven Old English Poems* (1966).
2. Earl Birhtnoth, commander of the English defense forces.
3. Offa is mentioned later in the poem as one of Birhtnoth's principal retainers; his young kinsman is not otherwise identified.
4. The weapons a tenant received from his lord; they were returned to the lord upon the tenant's death.

graced earl who will defend this country, my lord Æthelred's[5] homeland, folk and land. Heathen shall fall in the battle. It seems to me too shameful that you should go to ship with our tribute unfought, now that you have come thus far into our land. Not so easily shall you get treasure: point and edge shall first reconcile us, grim battle-play, before we give tribute."

Then he ordered the men to bear their shields, go forward so that they all stood on the river bank. Because of the water neither band could come to the other: after the ebb, the floodtide came flowing in; currents met and crossed. It seemed to them too long a time before they might bear their spears together. On the river Pant they stood in proud array, the battle-line of the East Saxons and the men from the ash-ships. Nor might any of them injure another, unless one should receive death from the flight of an arrow.

The tide went out. The seamen stood ready, many Vikings eager for war. The earl, protector of men, bade a war-hard warrior—he was named Wulfstan, of bold lineage—to hold the bridge:[6] he was Ceola's son, who with his spear pierced the first man bold enough to step upon the bridge. There stood with Wulfstan fearless fighters, Ælfhere and Maccus, bold men both who would not take flight from the ford, but defended themselves stoutly against the enemy as long as they might wield weapons.

When the loathed strangers saw that, and understood clearly that they would face bitter bridge-defenders there, they began to prefer words to deeds,[7] prayed that they might have access to the bank, pass over the ford and lead their forces across. Then in his overconfidence the earl began to yield ground—too much ground— to the hateful people: Birhthelm's son began to call over the cold water while warriors listened: "Now the way is laid open for you. Come straightway to us, as men to battle. God alone knows which of us may be master of the field."

The slaughter-wolves advanced, minded not the water, a host of Vikings westward over the Pant, over the bright water bore their shields: sailors to land brought shields of linden. Opposite stood Birhtnoth with his warriors, ready for the fierce invaders. He ordered his men to form a war-hedge[8] with their shields and to hold the formation fast against the enemy. Now was combat near, glory in battle. The time had come when doomed men should fall. Shouts were raised; ravens circled, the eagle eager for food. On earth there was uproar.

They let the file-hard spears fly from their hands, grim-ground

5. King Ethelred "the Unready," who reigned from 978 to 1016.
6. Not a bridge in the modern sense, but probably a stone causeway, under water even at low tide; immediately below, it is called a ford.

7. Literally, "to practice deception"— an overstatement due to the poet's scorn for fighters who refused to do things the hard heroic way.
8. A wall of shields (a common defensive formation).

javelins. Bows were busy, shield felt point. Bitter was the battle-rush. On either side warriors fell, young men lay dead. Wulfmær was wounded, chose the slaughter-bed: kinsman of Birhtnoth—his sister's son—he was cruelly hewn down with swords. Then requital was made to the Vikings: I have heard that Eadweard struck one fiercely with his sword, withheld not the stroke, so that the warrior fell doomed at his feet; for this his lord gave the chamberlain[9] thanks when he had opportunity. Thus men stood firm in the battle, stern of purpose. Eagerly all these armed fighters contended with one another to see who could be the first with his weapon's point to take life from doomed man. The slain fell, carrion, to the earth. The defenders stood fast; Birhtnoth urged them on, bade each man who would win glory from the Danes to give his whole heart to the battle.

A war-hard Viking advanced, raised up his weapon, his shield to defend himself, moved against Birhtnoth. As resolute as the churl,[1] the earl advanced toward him. Each of them meant harm to the other. Then the seaman threw his southern-made[2] spear so that the fighters' chief was wounded. But he thrust the spear with his shield so that the shaft split and the spearhead broke off and sprang away.[3] The war-chief was maddened; with his spear he stabbed the proud Viking that had given him the wound. Wise in war was the host's leader: he let his spear go through the man's neck, guided his hand so that he mortally wounded the raider. Then he quickly stabbed another, breaking through the mail-shirt: in the breast, quite through the corselet, was this one wounded; at his heart stood the poisoned point. The earl was the blither; the bold man laughed, gave thanks to God that the Lord had given him this day's work.

One of the Vikings loosed a javelin from his hand, let it fly from his fist, and it sped its way through Æthelred's noble thane. By the earl's side stood a lad not yet grown, a boy in the battle, son of Wulfstan, Wulfmær the young, who plucked full boldly the bloody spear from the warrior. He sent the hard spear flying back again: its point went in, and on the earth lay the man who had sorely wounded his lord. Then an armed Viking stepped toward the earl. He wished to seize the earl's war-gear, make booty of rings and ornamented sword. Then Birhtnoth took his sword from its sheath, broad and bright-edged, and struck at his assailant's coat of mail. Too soon one of the seafarers hindered him, wounded the earl in his arm. Then the gold-hilted sword fell to the earth: he might not hold the hard blade, wield his weapon. Yet he spoke

9. I.e., Eadweard.
1. Here "churl" means something like "villain."
2. Apparently the Vikings preferred weapons made in England or France—

the "south."
3. The maneuver described frees the spear from the wounded man's body and enables him to take retaliatory action.

words, the hoar battle-leader, encouraged his men, bade them go forward stoutly together. He might no longer stand firm on his feet. He looked toward Heaven and spoke: "I thank thee, Ruler of Nations, for all the joys that I have had in the world. Now, gentle Lord, I have most need that thou grant my spirit grace, that my soul may travel to thee—under thy protection, Prince of Angels, depart in peace. I beseech thee that fiends of hell harm it not." Then the heathen warriors slew him and both the men who stood by him; Ælfnoth and Wulfmær both were laid low; close by their lord they gave up their lives.

Then there retired from the battle those who did not wish to be there. The son of Odda was the first to flee: Godric went from the fight and left the good man that had given him many a steed. He leaped upon the horse that his lord had owned, upon trappings that he had no right to, and both his brothers galloped with him, Godwine and Godwig cared not for battle, but went from the war and sought the wood, fled to its fastness and saved their lives—and more men than was in any way right, if they remembered all the favors he had done for their benefit. So Offa had said to him that day at the meeting he had held in the place, that many there spoke boldly who would not remain firm at need.

The folk's leader had fallen, Æthelred's earl: all his hearth-companions saw that their lord lay dead. Then the proud thanes advanced; men without fear pressed eagerly on. They all desired either of two things, to leave life or avenge the man they loved. Thus Ælfric's son urged them on; the warrior young of winters spoke words; Ælfwine it was who spoke, and spoke boldly: "Remember the speeches we have spoken so often over our mead,[4] when we raised boast on the bench, heroes in the hall, about hard fighting. Now may the man who is bold prove that he is. I will make my noble birth known to all, that I was of great kin in Mercia. My grandfather was named Ealhelm, a wise earl, worldly-prosperous. Thanes among that people shall not have reason to reproach me that I would go from this band of defenders, seek my home, now that my lord lies hewn down in battle. To me that is greatest of griefs: he was both my kinsman and my lord." Then he went forward, bent on revenge, and with the point of his spear pierced one of the pirate band, so that he lay on the earth, destroyed by the weapon. Then Ælfwine began to encourage his comrades, friends and companions, to go forward.

Offa spoke, shook his ash-spear: "Lo, thou, Ælfwine, hast encouraged us all, thanes in need. Now that our lord the earl lies on the earth, there is need for us all that each one of us encourage

4. Boasting of prowess while drinking is a common element in Old English poetry.

the other, warriors to battle, as long as he may have and hold weapon, hard sword, spear and good blade. The coward son of Odda, Godric, has betrayed us all; when he rode off on that horse, on that proud steed, many a man thought that he was our lord. Therefore here on the field folk were dispersed, the shield-wall broken. Curses on his action, by which he caused so many men here to flee."

Leofsunu spoke, raised the linden buckler, his shield to defend himself; he answered the warrior: "I promise that I will not flee a footstep hence, but I will go forward, avenge my dear lord in the fight. Steadfast warriors about Sturmer[5] need not reproach me with their words that now that my patron is dead I would go lordless home, abandon the battle. But weapon, point and iron, shall take me." Full wrathful he went forward, fought fiercely; flight he despised.

Then Dunnere spoke, shook his spear; humble churl,[6] he cried over all, bade each warrior avenge Birhtnoth: "He who intends to avenge his lord on the folk may not hesitate nor care for life." Then they advanced: they cared not for life. The retainers began to fight hardily, fierce spear-bearers, and prayed God that they might avenge their patron and bring destruction to their enemies.

The hostage[7] began to help them eagerly. He was of bold kin among the Northumbrians, the son of Ecglaf: his name was Æscferth. He did not flinch at the war-play, but threw spears without pause. Now he hit shield, now he pierced man: each moment he caused some wound, as long as he might wield weapons.

Eadweard the Long still stood in the line, ready and eager, spoke boasting words, how he would not flee a footstep nor turn back, now that his chief lay dead. He broke the shield-wall and fought against the foe until he had worthily avenged his treasure-giver on the sea-men—before he himself lay on the slaughter-bed.

So also did Æthelric, noble companion, eager and impetuous; he fought most resolutely, this brother of Sibirht, as did many another: they split the hollow shield and defended themselves boldly [8]. . . . The shield's rim broke and the mail-shirt sang one of horror's songs. Then in the battle Offa struck the seafarer so that he fell on the earth, and there Gadd's kinsman himself sought the ground: Offa was quickly hewn down in the fight. He had, however, performed what he had promised his lord, what he had vowed before to his ring-giver, that they should either both ride to the town, hale to their home, or fall among the host, die of wounds in the slaughter-

5. The Essex village where the speaker lived.
6. I.e., freeman of the lowest rank.
7. Among Germanic peoples, hostages of high rank generally fought on the side of the warriors who held them in hostage.
8. Apparently a description of a Viking's attack on Offa has been lost.

place. He lay as a thane should, near his lord.

Then there was a crash of shields. The seamen advanced, enraged by the fight. Spear oft pierced life-house of doomed man. Then Wistan advanced: Thurstan's son fought against the men. He was the slayer of three of them in the throng before the son of Wigelm [9] lay dead in the carnage. There was stubborn conflict. Warriors stood fast in the fight. Fighting men fell, worn out with wounds: slain fell among slain.

All the while Oswold and Eadwold, brothers both, encouraged the men, with their words bade their dear kinsmen that they should stand firm at need, wield their weapons without weakness.

Birhtwold spoke, raised his shield—he was an old retainer—shook his ash-spear; full boldly he exhorted the men: "Purpose shall be the firmer, heart the keener, courage shall be the more, as our might lessens.[1] Here lies our lord all hewn down, good man on ground. Ever may he lament who now thinks to turn from war-play. I am old of life; from here I will not turn, but by my lord's side, by the man I loved, I intend to lie."

So also the son of Æthelgar encouraged them all to the battle: this Godric oft let spear go, slaughter-shaft fly on the Vikings; thus he advanced foremost among the folk, hewed and laid low until he died in the fighting: he was not that Godric who fled the battle.

---

9. Identification uncertain: perhaps Offa was the son of Wigelm.

1. These famous lines appear thus in the original: "Hige sceal þe heardra, heorte þe cenre, / mod sceal þe mare, þe ure mægen lytlaþ."

GEOFFREY CHAUCER

(ca. 1343–1400)

1370: The *Book of the Duchess* (first important extant poem).
1372: First Italian journey: contact with Italian literature.
1385: *Troilus and Criseide*.
1386: *Canterbury Tales* begun.

Social thought in the Middle Ages lagged far behind social realities. Medieval England did not recognize the existence of any class between the aristocracy, a relatively small group that attained its position by birth alone, and the commons, which included everyone not of high birth. There was, theoretically, no way by which one might advance from the commons to the aristocracy. But in actual fact there existed a large and increasingly important middle class that was constantly infiltrating the aristocracy, and it was into this middle class that Chaucer was born. He was the son of a well-to-do wine merchant, and probably spent his boyhood in the down-to-earth atmosphere of London's Vintry, the wine-merchandising area; here, despite the privileges, especially in the way of education, that his father's wealth secured for him, he must have mixed daily with other commoners of all sorts. He might well have passed his whole life there, counting casks and money; but in his early teens he was sent to serve as a page in one of the great aristocratic households of England, that of Lionel of Antwerp, a son of the reigning monarch, Edward III. The rest of his life Chaucer spent in close association with the ruling nobility of the kingdom, not only with Lionel, but with his more powerful brother John of Gaunt; with their father King Edward; with their nephew Richard II, who succeeded to the throne in 1377; and finally with John's son Henry IV, who deposed his cousin and became king in 1399. Chaucer's wife Philippa was a member of the households of Edward's queen and of John of Gaunt's second wife, Constance of Castile, and she was doubtless of higher birth than the poet. A Thomas Chaucer, who was probably their son, was an eminent man in the next generation, and an Alice Chaucer, quite possibly Chaucer's granddaughter, was sufficiently important in her day to have been married successively to the Earl of Salisbury and the Duke of Norfolk. The theoretically unbridgeable gap between the commons and the aristocracy was thus ably bridged by the poet.

In order to accomplish this, Chaucer must have been able in other ways than as a poet, though doubtless his extraordinary poetic ability was of great service to his advancement. Yet if one were to rely merely on the preserved historical records, one would have little reason to suspect that the Geoffrey Chaucer they keep mentioning ever wrote a line of verse. We catch glimpses of him serving as a page in Lionel's household (1357); as a soldier getting himself captured by the French in one of Edward III's many sallies to the continent (1359); of his being the well-beloved *vallectus* of Edward III (1367)—despite the term, which means "valet." Chaucer's duties were hardly menial—and the well-beloved servant of John of Gaunt (1374), and of receiving substantial rewards for his services; of his being sent to Italy to assist in arranging a trade agreement with the Genoese (1372), and to France, perhaps to assist in getting a royal bride for young Prince Richard (1377); of his receiving a rent-free house on the city wall of London (1374); of his keeping, "in his own hand," the accounts for which he was responsible as Controller of the Customs and Subsidies on Wool for the port of London (1374–86)—and the wool trade was England's largest trade; of other trips abroad on official business; of his becoming Justice of the Peace and Knight of the Shire (Member of Parliament) for the county of Kent (1385–86); of his erecting grandstands, inventorying pots and pans, and getting himself robbed as Clerk of the King's Works (1389–91); of his being appointed deputy forester of one of the royal preserves in Somerset (1391); and—throughout his life—of his receiving grants and annuities, or having them confirmed by royal act when a new king took the throne, or asking that butts of wine given him by the crown be transformed into cash, or merely asking for money or more money. We last glimpse him, in the final months of his life, renting a house in the garden of Westminster Abbey, within a stone's throw of Westminster Hall, the ancient seat of English government.

CHAUCER'S LITERARY CAREER

It might seem that a man so busy would have had little time to write poetry, but Chaucer seems to have been an assiduous versifier all his adult life. Unfortunately, few of his poems can be precisely dated, and some have not been preserved. Probably among his earliest works was a translation of the *Roman de la Rose*, a 13th-century French poem that exercised a profound influence on Chaucer's work. The first part of the *Roman* is an allegory, written by Guillaume de Lorris, which tells, in the form of a dream, the progress of a youthful love affair. Guillaume left the poem unfinished, but an enormous sequel was added to it after Guillaume's death by Jean de Meun: in this sequel the young courtier finally wins his lady (the rose), but not until Jean has discussed at great length many of the issues considered important by medieval intellectuals. The poem is a mixture of highly diverse elements, and it is characteristic of Chaucer's love of variety that he was able to assimilate into his own work both the courtly emotionalism of Guillaume and the philosophical, often satiric, detachment of Jean. Of a 14th-century English translation of the French poem only a fragment has come down to us, and that without any mention of the translator's name; scholars are generally agreed that the first 1700 lines of this fragment are Chaucer's.

Chaucer's work on the *Roman* is thought to have been done during the 60's. During this decade he probably made other translations from the French, and kept on sharpening his rhetorical tools. At the end of the decade he produced his first major work (and the only one of his poems that can be accurately dated): the *Book of the Duchess*, probably completed in early 1370, an elegy for John of Gaunt's first wife, the lovely Blanche of Lancaster, who died in 1369. This is at once one of Chaucer's most derivative and most original poems: many of its octosyllabic lines are translated directly from various works by Jean Froissart, a French poet contemporary with Chaucer, and from his countryman Guillaume de Machaut as well as from other Frenchmen; yet the plan of the work is imaginative and daring, and as a whole the elegy is on a level of excellence never attained by the poets from whom Chaucer is borrowing. It is also interesting to observe how that tact which was later to earn Chaucer his status as a minor diplomat controls the direction of the poem and gives it artistic form.

In the first period of his literary activity Chaucer's specific poetic models were French, but a knowledge of writings in Latin lies behind virtually everything he wrote—although the Latin writers Chaucer read were not the same as those which we should study today. He probably had a more than adequate knowledge of the *Aeneid* and of Ovid in the original, but it is likely that he knew the other classical authors mostly through French translations and paraphrases. He was directly familiar with a number of (to us) cumbersome medieval Latin poems. Certainly his favorite Latin writer was Boethius, the 6th-century Roman whose *Consolation of Philosophy*, written while its author was in prison awaiting his execution, became one of the most valued of books for the whole Middle Ages, which never failed to find inspiration and comfort in its nobly stoic doctrine. Chaucer's own philosophical attitude, that of living wholeheartedly in the world while remaining spiritually detached from it, is at least partially a legacy from Boethius. His wooden but painstaking prose translation of the *Consolation*, probably made during the 70's, is only one of innumerable indications of Chaucer's reverence for the Roman writer.

The journey that Chaucer made to Italy in 1372 was in all likelihood a milestone in his literary development. Hitherto the influences upon him had been largely French and Latin, and while he may have read Italian before, it is likely that it was his Italian journey that immersed him in the works of Dante, Petrarch, and Boccaccio—the last two still alive at the time of Chaucer's visit, though he probably did not meet them. Between Chaucer and the greatest of the Italian writers, Dante, there was a large dissimilarity of temperament; yet if Chaucer could not assimilate *The Divine Comedy*, he nevertheless appreciated its austere moral grandeur, and his work shows its influences in subtle, oblique ways. Moreover, one of his funniest poems, the *House of Fame*, written sometime while he was in the customs (1374–86), may be read as a light-hearted imitation of the *Comedy*, though not a wholly successful one. From the works of Petrarch, also a writer of alien temperament, Chaucer obtained less, though he accords him respect on the several occasions when he mentions him. It was Boccaccio, whose cast of mind was far more congenial to Chaucer than the more sober Dante and Petrarch, who was to provide the source for some of Chaucer's finest poems— though his name is never mentioned in Chaucer's works. Many of the *Canterbury Tales* are indebted to one or another of Boccaccio's works, as is his lovely, cryptic love vision, the *Parliament of Fowls* (between 1375 and 1385). And his longest poem, *Troilus and Criseide*, probably completed about 1385, is an adaptation of Boccaccio's *Il Filostrato* ("The

Love-Stricken"). The Italian work is one of considerable stature, which Chaucer reworked into one of the greatest love poems in any language. Even if he had never written the *Canterbury Tales*, *Troilus* would have secured Chaucer a place among the great English poets.

Chaucer probably began work on the *Canterbury Tales* in 1386, and this was his chief literary interest until his death. The old tripartite division of Chaucer's literary career which assigns him a French period (to 1372), and an Italian period (1372–85), calls this last period of his life "English." But it was not English in the same sense as the earlier periods were French and Italian (i.e., dominated by French and Italian models), for the fact is that Chaucer from the beginning to the end stands apart from the mainstream of English literature. In the Rhyme of Sir Thopas, which he assigns himself in the *Canterbury Tales*, the wonderful fun he makes of popular Middle English romances shows his intimate knowledge of them; and undoubtedly he had read much English writing of all kinds. Yet his notion of literary art seems to have excluded many of the common characteristics—and the characteristic vices—of what had been and was being written in English, so that it is difficult to relate his work to that of his fellow English writers. His friend John Gower is a case in point: like Chaucer, he wrote a collection of English narrative poems in his *Confessio Amantis* ("The Lover's Confession"), and Chaucer tells some of the same stories in the *Canterbury Tales* and in the *Legend of Good Women*. The last, which may have interrupted Chaucer's work on the *Canterbury Tales* in the late 80's, was apparently assigned him by some eminent person; in order to make amends for his portrait of the unfaithful Criseide, he had to write a series of short poems celebrating famous faithful women. To make each story prove exactly the same point and nothing more is something that the conventional Gower had no trouble in doing. Yet Chaucer was able to complete the tales of only nine solemnly steadfast ladies before giving up in something like despair, and the most amusing thing about his narratives is his evident exasperation with having to make everything accord to a single formula. He could not bring himself to use the simple moralistic technique of conventional English poetry, and what Gower treats seriously appears in Chaucer often to be bordering on burlesque. Every comparison between Chaucer and run-of-the-mill English poetry either so exalts him as to make the act of comparison ludicrous or else, when Chaucer is trying to behave conventionally, shows him writing with his left hand. Chaucer had no really "English" period; English poetry had little to teach the first great English poet.

CHAUCER'S ART

The extraordinary variety of the *Canterbury Tales* as well as their number might well have demanded their author's full energy and attention during the last fourteen years of his life, but while he was at work on them he continued, almost to the end, to perform what seem to have been full-time jobs having nothing to do with literature. Doubtless this practical business prevented him from achieving more than the 22 tales he finished; and it probably made him search his old papers for tales that he could work in without substantial revision. Yet if it reduced his literary output—which, even so, is enormous—this lifelong involvement with the practical is one of the chief reasons for his greatness as a poet. From his birth to his death he dealt continually with all sorts of people, the highest and the lowest, and his wonderfully observant mind made the most of this ever-present opportunity. His wide reading gave him plots and ideas, but his experience gave him people. As a commoner himself he had a sympathy with and understanding of the lower classes that few men who attained his ultimate station might boast of—and the lower classes must have accepted him. Similarly, he seems to have won full acceptance from the proud and important personages with whom he associated at court, and this he could not have won if he had not understood them perfectly. He understands both the high and the low, but he remains curiously detached from both, and it is detachment, perfectly balanced in his poetry by sympathy, which distinguishes Chaucer's art. Although he was born a commoner, he did not live as a commoner; and although he was accepted by the aristocracy, he must always have been conscious of the fact that he did not really belong to that society of which birth alone could make one a true member. Medieval aristocratic society arrogated to itself all idealism, and Chaucer characteristically regards life in terms of aristocratic ideals; but he never lost the ability, which for the poorer class was also a positive necessity, of regarding life as a purely practical matter. The art of being at once involved in and detached from a given situation is peculiarly Chaucer's.

In the physical realm, double vision results in a blurred image, but not so in Chaucer's poetic world, where images have often an extraordinary clarity, as if reality itself were made more real. His Prioress in the *Canterbury Tales* is an example of the basic human paradox which places what people are in opposition to what they think they are or pretend to be: Chaucer shows us clearly her inability to be what she professes to be, a nun; shows also the inadequacy of what she thinks a nun ought to be, a lady; and shows the great human charm of what she is, a woman. The elements of the portrait are divided between the critical and the admiring: a heavily satiric poet might well enhance the critical comment, so that our ultimate impression would be of the Prioress' weakness, while a sentimental one might enhance her amiable side so as to make that the aspect which we should remember. But in Chaucer's handling the reality comprehends both sides of the Prioress, expresses the paradox without attempting to resolve it. He appears to have been a man who had no illusions about the world or its inhabitants, but was nevertheless deeply fond of them both, and thought it worth while to keep the world spinning as well as possible, either by telling stories of high artistic truth or by counting pots and pans.

The text given here is from the present editor's *Chaucer's Poetry: An Anthology for the Modern Reader* (1958). For the *Canterbury Tales* the Hengwrt Manuscript has provided the textual basis. The spelling has been altered to improve consistency, and has been modernized in so far as is possible without distorting the phonological values of the Middle English. Discussions of Middle English pronunciation, grammar, and prosody will be found in the introduction to the period.

The Canterbury Tales

Chaucer's original plan for the *Canterbury Tales* projected about 120 stories, two for each pilgrim to tell on the way to Canterbury and two more on the way back. Chaucer actually completed only 22, though two more exist in fragments; a modification of the original plan is seen in the assignment of one of the completed tales to a pilgrim who was not a member of the group that assembled at Southwark. The work was probably first conceived in 1386, when Chaucer was living in Greenwich, some miles east of London. From his house he might have been able to see the pilgrim road that led toward the shrine of the famous English saint, Thomas à Becket, the Archbishop of Canterbury who was murdered in his cathedral in 1170. Medieval pilgrims were notorious tale-tellers (liars, according to the austere Langland), and the sight and sound of the bands riding toward Canterbury may well have suggested to Chaucer the idea of using a fictitious pilgrimage as a "framing" device for a number of stories. Collections of stories linked by such a device were common in the later Middle Ages. Chaucer's contemporary John Gower had used one in his *Confessio Amantis*; earlier in the century Boccaccio had placed the hundred tales of his *Decameron* in the mouths of ten characters, each of whom told a tale a day for ten days; and another Italian, Giovanni Sercambi, had placed a series of stories in the mouth of the leader of a group of persons journeying on horseback. Even if, as seems likely, Chaucer was unaware of the Italian precedents, the device of the framing fiction was in the air.

Chaucer's artistic exploitation of the device is, however, altogether his own. In Gower and Sercambi, one speaker relates all the stories; and in Boccaccio, the relationship between any one of the ten speakers and the story he tells is haphazard, so that reassignment of all the stories to different speakers would not materially change the effect. But in the best of the *Canterbury Tales* there is a fascinating accord between the narrator and his story, so that the story takes on rich overtones from what we have learned of its teller in the General Prologue and elsewhere, and the character himself grows and is revealed by his story. Chaucer conducts two fictions simultaneously—that of the individual tale and that of the pilgrim to whom he has assigned it. He develops the second fiction not only through the General Prologue but also through the "links," the interchanges among the pilgrims between stories. These interchanges sometimes lead to animosities. Thus the Miller's Tale offends the Reeve, who, formerly a carpenter, sees himself slandered in the figure of the Miller's silly, cuckolded carpenter; and the Reeve replies with a story that scores a miller who seems very like the pilgrim Miller. Similarly the Friar and the Summoner quarrel at the end of the Wife of Bath's Prologue, so that when the Friar is called upon he tells a tale most offensive to the Summoner, who in turn retaliates with an even more offensive story about a friar. The effect of each of these tales is enhanced by the animus of its teller, while the description of the animus in the links is exciting in itself: we are given at once a story and a drama. Furthermore, the Wife of Bath's monstrous feminism sets up resonances that are felt through all the succeeding tales. Indeed, so powerful are these resonances that some see in them a thematic unifying device: the question of marriage that the Wife introduces is further treated from two opposing points of view by the Clerk and the Merchant, and is finally settled by the common sense of the Franklin. In addition to such artistic stratagems as these, the personality and mind of the reporter—a half-burlesque version of Chaucer himself—permeates the poem and enriches its meaning.

The composition of none of the tales can be accurately dated; most of them were written during the last fourteen years of Chaucer's life, though some which fail to fit their tellers may be much earlier. The popularity of the poem in late medieval England is attested by the number of surviving manuscripts: more than 80, mostly from the 15th century. It was also twice printed by Caxton, and often reprinted by Caxton's early successors. The manuscripts reflect the unfinished state of the poem—the fact that when he died Chaucer had not made up his mind about a number of details, and hence left many inconsistencies. The poem appears in the manuscripts as nine or ten "fragments" or blocks of tales; the order of the poems within each fragment is generally the same, but the order of the fragments themselves varies widely. The fragment containing the General Prologue, the Knight's, Miller's and Reeve's Tales, and the Cook's unfinished tale, always comes first, and the fragment consisting of the Parson's Tale and the Retraction always comes last; but the others, such as that containing the Wife of Bath, the Friar, and the Summoner, or that consisting of the Physician and Pardoner, or the longest fragment consisting of six tales concluding with the Nun's Priest's, are by no means stable in relation to one another. The order followed here is one of the two that seems most nearly satisfactory.

This volume contains three of the four tales which constitute the so-called "marriage group": according to the eminent scholar George Lyman Kittredge, Chaucer gave a kind of organization to the *Canterbury Tales* by including within it a continuing debate on marriage and the role of partners in marriage. The Wife of Bath begins the debate by putting forth her highly unorthodox opinion that the woman should have sovereignty in marriage, exacting obedience from her husband. Such a theory naturally offends the orthodox Clerk, who counters with the story of Griselda (not printed here), who is meekly obedient to her monstrously cruel husband and who by her patient suffering finally overcomes his monstrousness. This tale in turn offends the Merchant, who while agreeing with the Clerk that wives should be obedient to their husbands endeavors to prove that wives are as a class faithless and treacherous to their husbands, pretending obedience to them but deceiving them behind their backs. The debate is finally settled by the Franklin's description of the marriage of Arveragus and Dorigen, in which each member surrenders sovereignty to the other, obedient to each other's will, and loving one another truly but with patience. The first three of the debaters recommend or depict extreme positions: the Franklin recognizes that mutual tolerance alone is a realistic solution to the problems of marriage.

THE GENERAL PROLOGUE

Chaucer did not need to make a pilgrimage himself in order to meet the types of people that his fictitious pilgrimage includes, for most of them had long inhabited literature as well as life: the ideal Knight, who had fought against the pagans in all the great battles of the last half-century;

his son the Squire, a lover out of any love poem; the Prioress without a vocation but with the dogs and jewelry that satirical literature was always condemning nuns for; the hunting Monk and flattering Friar, chief butts of medieval satirists; the too-busy and too-rich lawyer; the prosperous Franklin; the fraudulent Doctor; the Wife—or Archwife—of Bath; the austere Parson; and so on down through the lower orders to that flamboyant hypocrite, the Pardoner, a living vice. One meets all these types in medieval literature, and, since literature imitates life, one might have met them also in medieval society, as Chaucer, with his wide experience, undoubtedly did. Indeed, it has been argued that in some of his portraits he is drawing real people; but the appearance of doing so is actually a function of his art, which is able to endow types with a reality we generally associate only with people we know. Chaucer achieves this effect largely by persuading us that his own interest lies only in the visible, in what actually met his eye on the pilgrimage. He pretends to let the salient features of each pilgrim leap out directly at the reader, and does not seem to mind if some of his descriptions are from top to toe, others all toe and no top. This imitation of the way our minds actually perceive reality may make us fail to notice the care with which Chaucer has selected his details in order to give an integrated sketch of the person being described. While they are generally not full-blown literary symbols, most of these details give something more than mere verisimilitude to the description; actually, they mediate between the world of types and the world of real people. Independent bourgeois women of the time were often makers of cloth, so that the Wife of Bath's proficiency at the trade is, in one way, merely part of her historical reality; yet the first weaver of cloth was the unparadised Eve, and her descendant is an unregenerate member of the distaff side. The Franklin's red face and white beard are in the same way merely individualizing factors in the portrait; yet the red face and white beard seem always to associate themselves with a man of good will who likes good living, and since Chaucer's time they have become the distinguishing marks of a kind of mythic Franklin, Santa Claus.

The rich suggestiveness of the details is what makes the portraits worth reading again and again. One may begin by enjoying the bright if flat photographic image of reality that the reporter creates, but one will find that the initial appearance of flatness is deceptive, and that the more one rereads the more complex and significant the portraits become. Here, as elsewhere in his work, Chaucer shows himself to be a rival to Shakespeare in the art of providing entertainment on the most primitive level, and at the same time, of significantly increasing the reader's ability to comprehend reality.

From The Canterbury Tales
The General Prologue

Whan that April with his° showres soote°	*its / sweet*
The droughte of March hath perced to the roote,	
And bathed every veine[1] in swich° licour,°	*such / liquid*

1. I.e., in plants.

Of which vertu² engendred is the flowr;
5 Whan Zephyrus³ eek° with his sweete breeth   *also*
Inspired hath in every holt° and heeth°   *grove / field*
The tendre croppes,° and the yonge sonne⁴   *shoots*
Hath in the Ram his halve cours yronne,
And smale fowles maken melodye
10 That sleepen al the night with open yë°—   *eye*
So priketh hem° Nature in hir corages⁵—   *them*
Thanne longen folk to goon° on pilgrimages,   *go*
And palmeres⁶ for to seeken straunge strondes
To ferne halwes, couthe° in sondry londes;   *known*
15 And specially from every shires ende
Of Engelond to Canterbury they wende,
The holy blisful martyr⁷ for to seeke
That hem hath holpen° whan that they were seke.° *helped / sick*
    Bifel that in that seson on a day,
20 In Southwerk⁸ at the Tabard as I lay,
Redy to wenden on my pilgrimage
To Canterbury with ful° devout corage,   *very*
At night was come into that hostelrye
Wel nine and twenty in a compaignye
25 Of sondry folk, by aventure° yfalle   *chance*
In felaweshipe, and pilgrimes were they alle
That toward Canterbury wolden° ride.   *would*
The chambres and the stables weren wide,
And wel we weren esed° at the beste.⁹   *accommodated*
30 And shortly, whan the sonne was to reste,¹
So hadde I spoken with hem everichoon°   *every one*
That I was of hir felaweshipe anoon,°   *at once*
And made forward² erly for to rise,
To take oure way ther as³ I you devise.°   *describe*
35   But nathelees,° whil I have time and space,⁴ *nevertheless*
Er° that I ferther in this tale pace,°   *before / pass*
Me thinketh it accordant to resoun⁵
To telle you al the condicioun
Of eech of hem, so as it seemed me,
40 And whiche they were, and of what degree,
And eek in what array that they were inne:
And at a knight thanne° wol I first biginne.   *then*
    A Knight ther was, and that a worthy man,
That fro the time that he first bigan
45 To riden out, he loved chivalrye,

---

2. By the power of which.
3. The west wind.
4. The sun is young because it has run only halfway through its course in Aries, the Ram—the first sign of the zodiac in the solar year.
5. Their hearts.
6. Palmers, wide-ranging pilgrims—especially those who sought out the "straunge strondes" (foreign shores) of the Holy Land. "Ferne halwes": far-off shrines.

7. St. Thomas à Becket, murdered in Canterbury Cathedral in 1170.
8. Southwark, site of the Tabard Inn, was then a suburb of London, south of the Thames River.
9. In the best possible way.
1. Had set.
2. I.e., (we) made an agreement.
3. "Ther as": where.
4. I.e., opportunity.
5. It seems to me according to reason.

Trouthe[6] and honour, freedom and curteisye.
Ful worthy was he in his lordes werre,°   *war*
And therto hadde he riden, no man ferre,°   *further*
As wel in Cristendom as hethenesse,°   *heathen lands*
50 And[7] evere honoured for his worthinesse.
    At Alisandre[8] he was whan it was wonne;
Ful ofte time he hadde the boord bigonne[9]
Aboven alle nacions in Pruce;
In Lettou had he reised,° and in Ruce,   *campaigned*
55 No Cristen man so ofte of his degree;
In Gernade at the sege eek hadde he be
Of Algezir, and riden in Belmarye;
At Lyeis was he, and at Satalye,
Whan they were wonne; and in the Grete See[1]
60 At many a noble armee° hadde he be.   *assembly of forces*
    At mortal batailes[2] hadde he been fifteene,
And foughten for oure faith at Tramissene
In listes[3] thries,° and ay° slain his fo.   *thrice / always*
This ilke° worthy Knight hadde been also   *same*
65 Somtime with the lord of Palatye[4]
Again° another hethen in Turkye;   *against*
And everemore he hadde a soverein pris.°   *reputation*
And though that he were worthy,[5] he was wis,
And of his port° as meeke as is a maide.   *demeanor*
70 He nevere yit no vilainye° ne saide   *rudeness*
In al his lif unto no manere wight:[6]
He was a verray,° parfit,° gentil knight.   *true / perfect*
But for to tellen you of his array,
His hors° were goode, but he was nat gay.   *horses*
75 Of fustian° he wered° a gipoun[7]   *thick cloth / wore*
Al bismotered with his haubergeoun,[8]
For he was late come from his viage,°   *expedition*
And wente for to doon his pilgrimage.
    With him ther was his sone, a yong Squier,[9]
80 A lovere and a lusty bacheler,
With lokkes crulle° as they were laid in presse.   *curly*
Of twenty yeer of age he was, I gesse.

---

6. Integrity. "Freedom" is here generosity of spirit, while "curteisye" is courtesy.
7. I.e., and he was.
8. The Knight has taken part in campaigns fought against all three groups of pagans who threatened Europe during the 14th century: the Moslems in the Near East, from whom Alexandria was seized after a famous siege; the northern barbarians in Prussia, Lithuania, and Russia; and the Moors in North Africa. The place names in the following lines refer to battlegrounds in these continuing wars.
9. Sat in the seat of honor at military feasts.
1. The Mediterranean.
2. Tournaments fought to the death.

3. Lists, tournament grounds.
4. "The lord of Palatye" was a pagan: alliances of convenience were often made during the Crusades between Christians and pagans.
5. I.e., a valiant knight.
6. "No manere wight": any sort of person. In Middle English, negatives are multiplied for emphasis, as in these two lines: "nevere," "no," "ne," "no."
7. Tunic worn underneath the coat of mail.
8. All rust-stained from his hauberk (coat of mail).
9. The vague term "Squier" (Squire) here seems to be the equivalent of "bacheler," a young knight still in the service of an older one.

Of his stature he was of evene° lengthe,   *moderate*
And wonderly delivere,° and of greet° strengthe.   *agile / great*
85 And he hadde been som time in chivachye[1]
In Flandres, in Artois, and Picardye,
And born him wel as of so litel space,[2]
In hope to stonden in his lady° grace.   *lady's*
Embrouded° was he as it were a mede,[3]   *embroidered*
90 Al ful of fresshe flowres, white and rede;°   *red*
Singing he was, or floiting,° al the day: *whistling*
He was as fressh as is the month of May.
Short was his gowne, with sleeves longe and wide.
Wel coude he sitte on hors, and faire ride;
95 He coude songes make, and wel endite,°   *compose verse*
Juste[4] and eek daunce, and wel portraye° and write.   *sketch*
So hote° he loved that by nightertale[5]   *hotly*
He slepte namore than dooth a nightingale.
Curteis he was, lowely,° and servisable,   *humble*
100 And carf biforn his fader at the table.[6]
A Yeman[7] hadde he and servants namo°   *no more*
At that time, for him liste[8] ride so;
And he[9] was clad in cote and hood of greene.
A sheef of pecok arwes,° bright and keene,   *arrows*
105 Under his belt he bar° ful thriftily;°   *bore / properly*
Wel coude he dresse° his takel° yemanly:[1]   *tend to / gear*
His arwes drouped nought with fetheres lowe.
And in his hand he bar a mighty bowe.
A not-heed° hadde he with a brown visage.   *close-cut head*
110 Of wodecraft wel coude° he al the usage.   *knew*
Upon his arm he bar a gay bracer,[2]
And by his side a swerd° and a bokeler,[3]   *sword*
And on that other side a gay daggere,
Harneised° wel and sharp as point of spere;   *mounted*
115 A Cristophre[4] on his brest of silver sheene;°   *bright*
An horn he bar, the baudrik[5] was of greene.
A forster° was he soothly,° as I gesse.   *forester / truly*
Ther was also a Nonne, a Prioresse,[6]
That of hir smiling was ful simple and coy.
120 Hir gretteste ooth was but by sainte Loy!°   *Eloi*
And she was cleped° Madame Eglantine.   *named*
Ful wel she soong° the service divine,   *sang*
Entuned° in hir nose ful semely;[7]   *chanted*

1. On cavalry expeditions. The places in the next line are sites of skirmishes in the constant warfare between the English and the French.
2. I.e., considering the little time he had been in service.
3. Mead, meadow.
4. Joust, fight in a tournament.
5. At night.
6. It was a squire's duty to carve his lord's meat.
7. The "Yeman" (Yeoman) is an independent commoner who acts as the Knight's military servant; "he" is the Knight.
8. "Him liste": it pleased him to.
9. I.e., the Yeoman.
1. In a workmanlike way.
2. Wristguard for archers.
3. Buckler (a small shield).
4. St. Christopher medal.
5. Baldric (a supporting strap).
6. The Prioress is the mother superior of her nunnery. "Simple and coy": sincere and mild.
7. In a seemly manner.

And Frenssh she spak ful faire and fetisly,°   *elegantly*
125 After the scole° of Stratford at the Bowe⁸—   *school*
    For Frenssh of Paris was to hire unknowe.
    At mete° wel ytaught was she withalle:°   *meals / besides*
    She leet° no morsel from hir lippes falle,   *let*
    Ne wette hir fingres in hir sauce deepe;
130 Wel coude she carve a morsel, and wel keepe°   *take care*
    That no drope ne fille° upon hir brest.   *should fall*
    In curteisye was set ful muchel hir lest.⁹
    Hir over-lippe wiped she so clene
    That in hir coppe° ther was no ferthing° seene   *cup / bit*
135 Of grece,° whan she dronken hadde hir draughte;   *grease*
    Ful semely after hir mete she raughte.°   *reached*
    And sikerly° she was of greet disport,¹   *certainly*
    And ful plesant, and amiable of port,°   *mien*
    And pained hire to countrefete cheere²
140 Of court, and to been statlich° of manere,   *dignified*
    And to been holden digne³ of reverence.
    But, for to speken of hir conscience,
    She was so charitable and so pitous°   *merciful*
    She wolde weepe if that she saw a mous
145 Caught in a trappe, if it were deed° or bledde.   *dead*
    Of⁴ smale houndes hadde she that she fedde
    With rosted flessh, or milk and wastelbreed;°   *fine white bread*
    But sore wepte she if oon of hem were deed,
    Or if men smoot it with a yerde smerte;⁵
150 And al was conscience and tendre herte.
    Ful semely hir wimpel° pinched° was,   *headdress / pleated*
    Hir nose tretis,° hir yën° greye as glas,   *well-formed / eyes*
    Hir mouth ful smal, and therto° softe and reed,°   *moreover / red*
    But sikerly° she hadde a fair forheed: *certainly*
155 It was almost a spanne brood,⁶ I trowe,°   *believe*
    For hardily,° she was nat undergrowe.   *assuredly*
    Ful fetis° was hir cloke, as I was war;°   *becoming / aware*
    Of smal° coral aboute hir arm she bar   *dainty*
    A paire⁷ of bedes, gauded al with greene,
160 And theron heeng° a brooch of gold ful sheene,°   *hung / bright*
    On which ther was first writen a crowned A,⁸
    And after, *Amor vincit omnia.*⁹
      Another Nonne with hire hadde she
    That was hir chapelaine,° and preestes three.¹   *secretary*

---

8. The French learned in a convent school in Stratford-at-the-Bow, a suburb of London, was evidently not up to the Parisian standard.
9. I.e., her chief delight lay in good manners.
1. Of great good cheer.
2. And took pains to imitate the behavior.
3. And to be considered worthy.
4. I.e., some.
5. If someone struck it with a rod sharply.
6. A handsbreadth wide.
7. String (i.e., a rosary); "gauded al with greene": provided with green beads to mark certain prayers.
8. An *A* with an ornamental crown on it.
9. A Latin motto meaning "Love conquers all."
1. Although he here awards this charming lady three priests, Chaucer later reduces the number to one.

165   A Monk ther was, a fair for the maistrye,[2]
       An outridere[3] that loved venerye,°   hunting
       A manly man, to been an abbot able.°   worthy
       Ful many a daintee° hors hadde he in stable,   fine
       And whan he rood,° men mighte his bridel heere   rode
170   Ginglen° in a whistling wind as clere   jingle
       And eek as loude as dooth the chapel belle
       Ther as this lord was kepere of the celle.[4]
       The rule of Saint Maure or of Saint Beneit,[5]
       By cause that it was old and somdeel strait—
175   This ilke Monk leet olde thinges pace,°   pass away
       And heeld° after the newe world the space.[6]   held
       He yaf nought of that text a pulled hen[7]
       That saith that hunteres been° nought holy men,   are
       Ne that a monk, whan he is recchelees,[8]
180   Is likned til° a fissh that is waterlees—   to
       This is to sayn, a monk out of his cloistre;
       But thilke° text heeld he nat worth an oystre.   that same
       And I saide his opinion was good:
       What° sholde he studye and make himselven wood° why / crazy
185   Upon a book in cloistre alway to poure,
       Or swinke° with his handes and laboure,   work
       As Austin bit?[9] How shal the world be served?
       Lat Austin have his swink to him reserved!
       Therfore he was a prikasour° aright.   hard rider
190   Grehoundes he hadde as swift as fowl in flight.
       Of priking° and of hunting for the hare   riding
       Was al his lust,° for no cost wolde he spare.   pleasure
       I sawgh his sleeves purfiled° at the hand   fur-lined
       With gris,° and that the fineste of a land;   gray fur
195   And for to festne his hood under his chin
       He hadde of gold wrought a ful curious[1] pin:
       A love-knotte in the grettere° ende ther was.   greater
       His heed was balled,° that shoon as any glas,   bald
       And eek his face, as he hadde been anoint:
200   He was a lord ful fat and in good point;[2]
       His yën steepe,° and rolling in his heed,   protruding
       That stemed as a furnais of a leed,[3]
       His bootes souple,° his hors in greet estat°— supple / condition
       Now certainly he was a fair prelat.[4]
205   He was nat pale as a forpined° gost: wasted away
       A fat swan loved he best of any rost.
       His palfrey° was as brown as is a berye.   saddle horse

---

2. I.e., a superlatively fine one.
3. A monk charged with supervising property distant from the monastery.
4. Keeper of an outlying cell (branch) of the monastery.
5. St. Maurus and St. Benedict, authors of monastic rules. "Somdeel strait": somewhat strict.
6. I.e., in his own lifetime (?).
7. He didn't give a plucked hen for that text.
8. Reckless, careless of rule.
9. I.e., as St. Augustine bids. St. Augustine had written that monks should perform manual labor.
1. Of careful workmanship.
2. In good shape, plump.
3. That glowed like a furnace with a pot in it.
4. Prelate (an important churchman).

A Frere[5] ther was, a wantoune and a merye,
A limitour, a ful solempne° man.   *pompous*
210 In alle the ordres foure is noon that can°   *knows*
So muche of daliaunce° and fair langage: *flirtation*
He hadde maad ful many a mariage
Of yonge wommen at his owene cost;   *married off women*
Unto his ordre he was a noble post.[6]   *he had gotten in troub.*
215 Ful wel biloved and familier was he
With frankelains over al[7] in his contree,
And with worthy wommen of the town—
For he hadde power of confessioun,
As saide himself, more than a curat,°   *parish priest*
220 For of° his ordre he was licenciat.[8]   *by*
Ful swetely herde he confessioun,
And plesant was his absolucioun.
He was an esy man to yive penaunce
Ther as he wiste to have[9] a good pitaunce;°   *donation*
225 For unto a poore ordre for to yive
Is signe that a man is wel yshrive;[1]
For if he yaf, he dorste make avaunt°   *boast*
He wiste that a man was repentaunt;
For many a man so hard is of his herte
230 He may nat weepe though him sore smerte:[2]
Therfore, in stede of weeping and prayeres, *shows greed/avarice*
Men mote° yive silver to the poore freres.[3] *of F.*   *may*
His tipet° was ay farsed° ful of knives)   *scarf / packed*
And pinnes, for to yiven faire wives;   *HE was a LADY'S MAN*
235 And certainly he hadde a merye note;
Wel coude he singe and playen on a rote;°   *fiddle*
Of yeddinges he bar outrely the pris.[4]
His nekke whit was as the flowr-de-lis;°   *lily*
Therto he strong was as a champioun.
240 He knew the tavernes wel in every town,
And every hostiler° and tappestere,°   *innkeeper / barmaid*
Bet° than a lazar[5] or a beggestere.   *better*
For unto swich a worthy man as he   SATIRE!
Accorded nat, as by his facultee,[6]
245 To have with sike° lazars aquaintaunce: *sick*
It is nat honeste,° it may nought avaunce,°   *dignified / profit*
For to delen with no swich poraile.[7]   HYPOCRITE; AVOIDS POOR PEOP.

---

5. The "Frere" (Friar) is a member of one of the four religious orders whose members live by begging; as a "limitour" (line 209) he has been granted exclusive begging rights within a certain limited area.
6. I.e., pillar.
7. I.e., with franklins everywhere. Franklins were well-to-do country men.
8. I.e., licensed to hear confessions.
9. Where he knew he would have.
1. Shriven, absolved.
2. Though he is sorely grieved.
3. Before granting absolution, the confessor must be sure the sinner is con-

trite; moreover, the absolution is contingent upon the sinner's performance of an act of satisfaction. In the case of Chaucer's Friar, a liberal contribution served both as proof of contrition and as satisfaction.
4. He absolutely took the prize for ballads.
5. Leper; "beggestere": female beggar.
6. It was not suitable because of his position.
7. I.e., poor people. The oldest order of friars had been founded by St. Francis to administer to the spiritual needs of precisely those classes the Friar avoids.

But al with riche, and selleres of vitaile;°   *foodstuffs*
And over al ther as profit sholde arise,
250 Curteis he was, and lowely of servise.
Ther was no man nowher so vertuous:°   *efficient*
He was the beste beggere in his hous.°   *friary*
And yaf a certain ferme for the graunt:[8]
Noon of his bretheren cam ther in his haunt.[9]
255 For though a widwe° hadde nought a sho,°   *widow / shoe*
So plesant was his *In principio*[1]
Yit wolde he have a ferthing° er he wente;   *small coin*
His purchas was wel bettre than his rente.[2] *he got more th. r. income*
And rage he coude as it were right a whelpe;[3]
260 In love-dayes[4] ther coude he muchel° helpe,   *much*
For ther he was nat lik a cloisterer,
With a thredbare cope, as is a poore scoler,
But he was lik a maister[5] or a pope.
Of double worstede was his semicope,°   *short robe*
265 And rounded as a belle out of the presse.°   *bell-mold*
Somwhat he lipsed° for his wantounesse° *lisped / affectation*
To make his Englissh sweete upon his tonge;
And in his harping, whan he hadde songe,°   *sung*
His yën twinkled in his heed aright
270 As doon the sterres° in the frosty night.   *stars*
This worthy limitour was cleped Huberd.
    A Marchant was ther with a forked beerd,
In motelee,[6] and hye on hors he sat,
Upon his heed a Flandrissh° bevere hat,   *Flemish*
275 His bootes clasped faire and fetisly.°   *elegantly*
His resons° he spak ful solempnely,   *opinions*
Souning° alway th'encrees of his winning.   *sounding*
He wolde the see were kept for any thing[7]
Bitwixen Middelburgh and Orewelle.
280 Wel coude he in eschaunge sheeldes[8] selle.
This worthy man ful wel his wit bisette:°   *employed*
Ther wiste° no wight that he was in dette,   *knew*
So statly° was he of his governaunce,[9]   *dignified*
With his bargaines,[1] and with his chevissaunce.
285 Forsoothe he was a worthy man withalle;
But, sooth to sayn, I noot° how men him calle. *don't know*

8. And he paid a certain rent for the privilege of begging.
9. Assigned territory.
1. A friar's usual salutation (John i.1): "In the beginning (was the Word)."
2. I.e., the money he got through such activity was more than his regular income.
3. And he could flirt wantonly, as if he were a puppy.
4. Days appointed for the settlement of lawsuits out of court.
5. A man of recognized learning.

6. Motley, a cloth of mixed color.
7. I.e., he wished the sea to be guarded at all costs. The sea route between Middelburgh (in the Netherlands) and Orwell (in Suffolk) was vital to the Merchant's export and import of wool—the basis of England's chief trade at the time.
8. Shields, *ecus* (French coins): he could speculate profitably (if illegally) in foreign exchange.
9. The management of his affairs.
1. Bargainings; "chevissaunce": borrowing.

A Clerk[2] ther was of Oxenforde also
That unto logik hadde longe ygo.[3]
As lene was his hors as is a rake,
290 And he was nought right fat, I undertake,
But looked holwe,° and therto sobrely.   *hollow*
Ful thredbare was his overeste courtepy,[4]
For he hadde geten him yit no benefice,
Ne was so worldly for to have office.°   *secular employment*
295 For him was levere[5] have at his beddes heed
Twenty bookes, clad in blak or reed,
Of Aristotle and his philosophye,
Than robes riche, or fithele,° or gay sautrye.[6]   *fiddle*
But al be that he was a philosophre[7]
300 Yit hadde he but litel gold in cofre;°   *coffer*
But al that he mighte of his freendes hente,°   *take*
On bookes and on lerning he it spente,
And bisily gan for the soules praye
Of hem that yaf him wherwith to scoleye.°   *study*
305 Of studye took he most cure° and most heede.   *care*
Nought oo° word spak he more than was neede,   *one*
And that was said in forme[8] and reverence,
And short and quik,° and ful of heigh sentence:[9]   *lively*
Souning° in moral vertu was his speeche,   *resounding*
310 And gladly wolde he lerne, and gladly teche.

        A Sergeant of the Lawe,[1] war and wis,
That often hadde been at the Parvis[2]
Ther was also, ful riche of excellence.
Discreet he was, and of greet reverence—
315 He seemed swich, his wordes weren so wise.
Justice he was ful often in assise°   *circuit courts*
By patente[3] and by plein° commissioun.   *full*
For his science° and for his heigh renown   *knowledge*
Of fees and robes hadde he many oon.
320 So greet a purchasour° was nowher noon;   *speculator in land*
Al was fee simple[4] to him in effect—
His purchasing mighte nat been infect.[5]
Nowher so bisy a man as he ther nas;°   *was not*
And yit he seemed bisier than he was.
325 In termes[6] hadde he caas and doomes alle

2. The Clerk is a student at Oxford; in order to become a student, he would have had to signify his intention of becoming a cleric, but he was not bound to proceed to a position of responsibility in the church.
3. Who had long since matriculated in philosophy.
4. Outer cloak. "Benefice": ecclesiastical living.
5. He would rather.
6. Psaltery (a kind of harp).
7. The word may also mean "alchemist."

8. With decorum.
9. Elevated thought.
1. The Sergeant is not only a practicing lawyer, but one of the high justices of the nation. "War and wis": wary and wise.
2. The "Paradise," a meeting place for lawyers and their clients.
3. Royal warrant.
4. "Fee simple": owned outright without legal impediments.
5. Invalidated on a legal technicality.
6. I.e., by heart. "Caas and doomes": lawcases and decisions.

That from the time of King William[7] were falle.
Therto he coude endite and make a thing,[8]
Ther coude no wight pinchen° at his writing;   *cavil*
And every statut coude° he plein° by rote.[9]   *knew / entire*
330 He rood but hoomly ° in a medlee cote,[1]   *unpretentiously*
Girt with a ceint of silk, with barres smale.
Of his array telle I no lenger tale.

A Frankelain[2] was in his compaignye:
Whit was his beerd as is the dayesye;°   *LIKE SANTA*   *daisy*
335 Of his complexion he was sanguin.[3]
Wel loved he by the morwe a sop in win.[4]
To liven in delit° was evere his wone,°   *sensual delight / wont*
For he was Epicurus[5] owene sone,
That heeld opinion that plein° delit   *full*
340 Was verray felicitee parfit.
An housholdere and that a greet was he:
Saint Julian[6] he was in his contree.
His breed, his ale, was always after oon;[7]
A bettre envined° man was nevere noon.   *wine-stocked*
345 Withouten bake mete was nevere his hous,
Of fissh and flessh, and that so plentevous°   *plenteous*
It snewed° in his hous of mete and drinke,   *snowed*
Of alle daintees that men coude thinke.
After° the sondry sesons of the yeer   *according to*
350 So chaunged he his mete[8] and his soper.
Ful many a fat partrich hadde he in mewe,°   *cage*
And many a breem,° and many a luce° in stewe.[9]   *carp / pike*
Wo was his cook but if his sauce were
Poinant° and sharp, and redy all his gere.   *pungent*
355 His table dormant in his halle alway
Stood redy covered all the longe day.[1]
At sessions[2] ther was he lord and sire.
Ful ofte time he was Knight of the Shire.
An anlaas° and a gipser° al of silk   *dagger / purse*
360 Heeng at his girdel,[3] whit as morne° milk.   *morning*
A shirreve° hadde he been, and countour.[4]   *sheriff*
Was nowher swich a worthy vavasour.[5]

7. I.e., the Conqueror (reigned 1066–87).
8. Compose and draw up a deed.
9. By heart.
1. A coat of mixed color. "Ceint": belt; "barres": transverse stripes.
2. The "Frankelain" (Franklin) is a prosperous country man, whose lower-class ancestry is no impediment to the importance he has attained in his county.
3. A reference to the fact that the Franklin s temperament is dominated by blood as well as to his red face.
4. I.e., in the morning he was very fond of a piece of bread soaked in wine.
5. The Greek philosopher whose teaching is popularly believed to make pleasure the chief goal of life.
6. The patron saint of hospitality.
7. Always of the same high quality.
8. Dinner; "soper": supper.
9. Fishpond.
1. Tables were usually dismounted when not in use, but the Franklin kept his mounted and set ("covered"), hence "dormant."
2. I.e., sessions of the justices of the peace. "Knight of the Shire": county representative in Parliament.
3. Hung at his belt.
4. Auditor of county finances.
5. Member of an upper, but not an aristocratic, feudal class.

An Haberdasshere and a Carpenter,
A Webbe,° a Dyere, and a Tapicer°—   *weaver / tapestry-maker*
365 And they were clothed alle in oo liveree[6]
Of a solempne and greet fraternitee.
Ful fresshe and newe hir gere apiked° was;   *polished*
Hir knives were chaped° nought with bras,   *mounted*
But al with silver; wrought ful clene and weel
370 Hir girdles and hir pouches everydeel.°   *altogether*
Wel seemed eech of hem a fair burgeis°   *burgher*
To sitten in a yeldehalle° on a dais.   *guildhall*
Everich, for the wisdom that he can,[7]
Was shaply° for to been an alderman.   *suitable*
375 For catel° hadde they ynough and rente,°   *property / income*
And eek hir wives wolde it wel assente—
And elles certain were they to blame:
It is ful fair to been ycleped "Madame,"
And goon to vigilies[8] all bifore,
380 And have a mantel royalliche ybore.[9]
A Cook they hadde with hem for the nones,[1]
To boile the chiknes with the marybones,°   *marrowbones*
And powdre-marchant tart and galingale.[2]
Wel coude he knowe° a draughte of London ale.   *recognize*
385 He coude roste, and seethe,° and broile, and frye,   *boil*
Maken mortreux,° and wel bake a pie.   *stews*
But greet harm was it, as it thoughte° me,   *seemed to*
That on his shine a mormal° hadde he.   *ulcer*
For blankmanger,[3] that made he with the beste.
390 A Shipman was ther, woning° fer by weste—   *dwelling*
For ought I woot,° he was of Dertemouthe.[4]   *know*
He rood upon a rouncy° as he couthe,[5]   *large nag*
In a gowne of falding° to the knee.   *heavy wool*
A daggere hanging on a laas° hadde he   *strap*
395 Aboute his nekke, under his arm adown.
The hote somer hadde maad his hewe° al brown;   *color*
And certainly he was a good felawe.
Ful many a draughte of win hadde he drawe[6]
Fro Burdeuxward,[7] whil that the chapman sleep:
400 Of nice° conscience took he no keep;°   *fastidious / heed*
If that he faught and hadde the hyer hand,
By water he sente hem hoom to every land.
But of his craft, to rekene wel his tides,

6. In one livery, i.e., the uniform of
their "fraternitee" or guild, a partly religious, partly social organization.
7. Was capable of.
8. Feasts held on the eve of saints'
days. "Al bifore": i.e., at the head of
the procession.
9. Royally carried.
1. For the occasion.
2. "Powdre-marchant" and "galingale"
are flavoring materials.
3. An elaborate stew.
4. Dartmouth, a port in the southwest
of England.
5. As best he could.
6. Drawn, i.e., stolen.
7. From Bordeaux; i.e., while carrying
wine from Bordeaux (the wine center
of France). "Chapman sleep": merchant
slept.

His stremes° and his daungers° him bisides,[8]   *currents / hazards*
405 His herberwe° and his moone, his lodemenage,[9]   *anchorage*
There was noon swich from Hulle to Cartage.[1]
Hardy he was and wis to undertake;
With many a tempest hadde his beerd been shake;
He knew alle the havenes° as they were   *harbors*
410 Fro Gotland to the Cape of Finistere,[2]
And every crike° in Britaine° and in Spaine.   *inlet / Brittany*
His barge ycleped was the Maudelaine.°   *Magdalene*

With us ther was a Doctour of Physik:°   *medicine*
In al this world ne was ther noon him lik
415 To speken of physik and of surgerye.
For° he was grounded in astronomye,°   *because / astrology*
He kepte° his pacient a ful greet deel[3]   *tended to*
In houres[4] by his magik naturel.
Wel coude he fortunen the ascendent
420 Of his images[5] for his pacient.
He knew the cause of every maladye,
Were it of hoot or cold or moiste or drye,
And where engendred and of what humour:[6]
He was a verray parfit praktisour.[7]
425 The cause yknowe,° and of his harm the roote,   *known*
Anoon he yaf the sike man his boote.°   *remedy*
Ful redy hadde he his apothecaries
To senden him drogges° and his letuaries,°   *drugs / medicines*
For eech of hem made other for to winne:
430 Hir frendshipe was nought newe to biginne.
Wel knew he the olde Esculapius,[8]
And Deiscorides and eek Rufus,
Olde Ipocras, Hali, and Galien,
Serapion, Razis, and Avicen,

8. Around him.
9. Pilotage.
1. From Hull (in northern England) to Cartagena (in Spain).
2. From Gotland (an island in the Baltic) to Finisterre (the westernmost point in Spain).
3. Closely.
4. I.e., the astrologically important hours (when conjunctions of the planets might help his recovery). "Magik naturel": natural—as opposed to black—magic.
5. Assign the propitious time, according to the position of stars, for using talismanic images. Such images, representing either the patient himself or points in the zodiac, were thought to be influential on the course of the disease.
6. Diseases were thought to be caused by a disturbance of one or another of the four bodily "humors," each of which, like the four elements, was a compound of two of the elementary

qualities mentioned in line 422: the melancholy humor, seated in the black bile was cold and dry (like earth); the sanguine, seated in the blood, hot and moist (like air); the choleric, seated in the yellow bile, hot and dry (like fire); the phlegmatic, seated in the phlegm, cold and moist (like water).
7. True perfect practitioner.
8. The Doctor is familiar with the treatises that the Middle Ages attributed to the "great names" of medical history, whom Chaucer names in lines 431–36: the purely legendary Greek demigod Aesculapius; the Greeks Dioscorides, Rufus, Hippocrates, Galen, and Serapion; the Persians Hali and Rhazes; the Arabians Avicenna and Averroës; the early Christians John (?) of Damascus and Constantine Afer; the Scotsman Bernard Gordon; the Englishmen John of Gatesden and Gilbert, the former an early contemporary of Chaucer.

435 Averrois, Damascien, and Constantin,
Bernard, and Gatesden, and Gilbertin.
Of his diete mesurable° was he,   *moderate*
For it was of no superfluitee,
But of greet norissing° and digestible.   *nourishment*
440 His studye was but litel on the Bible.
In sanguin° and in pers° he clad was al,   *blood-red / blue*
Lined with taffata and with sendal;°   *silk*
And yit he was but esy of dispence;°   *expenditure*
He kepte that he wan in pestilence.⁹
445 For° gold in physik is a cordial,¹   *because*
Therfore he loved gold in special.
    A good Wif was ther of biside Bathe,
But she was somdeel deef, and that was scathe.°   *a pity*
Of cloth-making she hadde swich an haunt,°   *practice*
450 She passed° hem of Ypres and of Gaunt.²   *surpassed*
In al the parissh wif ne was ther noon
That to the offring³ bifore hire sholde goon,
And if ther dide, certain so wroth° was she   *angry*
That she was out of alle charitee.
455 Hir coverchiefs ful fine were of ground°—   *texture*
I dorste° swere they weyeden° ten pound   *dare / weighed*
That on a Sonday weren° upon hir heed.   *were*
Hir hosen weren of fin scarlet reed,°   *red*
Ful straite yteyd,⁴ and shoes ful moiste° and newe. *unworn*
460 Bold was hir face and fair and reed of hewe.
She was a worthy womman al hir live:
Housbondes at chirche dore⁵ she hadde five,
Withouten other compaignye in youthe—
But therof needeth nought to speke as nouthe.°   *now*
465 And thries hadde she been at Jerusalem;
She hadde passed many a straunge° streem;   *foreign*
At Rome she hadde been, and at Boloigne,
In Galice at Saint Jame, and at Coloigne:⁶
She coude° muchel of wandring by the waye.   *knew*
470 Gat-toothed° was she, soothly for to saye.   *gap-toothed*
Upon an amblere⁷ esily she sat,
Ywimpled° wel, and on hir heed an hat   *veiled*
As brood as is a bokeler or a targe,⁸
A foot-mantel° aboute hir hipes large,   *riding skirt*
475 And on hir feet a paire of spores° sharpe.   *spurs*
In felaweshipe wel coude she laughe and carpe:°   *talk*

9. He saved the money he made during the plague time.
1. A stimulant. Gold was thought to have some medicinal properties.
2. Ypres and Ghent ("Gaunt") were Flemish cloth-making centers.
3. The offering in church, when the congregation brought its gifts forward.
4. Tightly laced.
5. In medieval times, weddings were performed at the church door.
6. Rome; Boulogne (in France); St. James (of Compostella) in Galicia (Spain); Cologne (in Germany): all sites of shrines much visited by pilgrims.
7. Horse with an easy gait.
8. "Bokeler" and "targe": small shields.

Of remedies of love she knew parchaunce,°   *as it happened*
For she coude of that art the olde daunce.[9]
    A good man was ther of religioun,
480 And was a poore Person° of a town,   *parson*
But riche he was of holy thought and werk.
He was also a lerned man, a clerk,
That Cristes gospel trewely° wolde preche;   *faithfully*
His parisshens° devoutly wolde he teche.   *parishioners*
485 Benigne he was, and wonder° diligent,   *wonderfully*
And in adversitee ful pacient,
And swich he was preved° ofte sithes.°   *proved / times*
Ful loth were him to cursen for his tithes,[1]
But rather wolde he yiven, out of doute,[2]
490 Unto his poore parisshens aboute
Of his offring[3] and eek of his substaunce:°   *property*
He coude in litel thing have suffisaunce.°   *sufficiency*
Wid was his parissh, and houses fer asonder,
But he ne lafte° nought for rain ne thonder,   *neglected*
495 In siknesse nor in meschief,° to visite   *misfortune*
The ferreste° in his parissh, muche and lite,[4]   *farthest*
Upon his feet, and in his hand a staf.
This noble ensample° to his sheep he yaf   *example*
That first he wroughte,[5] and afterward he taughte.
500 Out of the Gospel he tho° wordes caughte,°   *those / took*
And this figure he added eek therto:
That if gold ruste, what shal iren do?
For if a preest be foul, on whom we truste,
No wonder is a lewed° man to ruste.   *uneducated*
505 And shame it is, if a preest take keep,°   *heed*
A shiten° shepherde and a clene sheep.   *befouled*
Wel oughte a preest ensample for to yive
By his clennesse how that his sheep sholde live.
He sette nought his benefice[6] to hire
510 And leet his sheep encombred in the mire
And ran to London, unto Sainte Poules,[7]
To seeken him a chaunterye[8] for soules,
Or with a bretherhede to been withholde,[9]
But dwelte at hoom and kepte wel his folde,
515 So that the wolf ne made it nought miscarye:
He was a shepherde and nought a mercenarye.

9. I.e., she knew all the tricks of that trade.
1. He would be most reluctant to invoke excommunication in order to collect his tithes.
2. Without doubt.
3. The offering made by the congregation of his church was at the Parson's disposal.
4. Great and small.
5. I.e., he practiced what he preached.
6. I.e., his parish. A priest might rent his parish to another and take a more profitable position. "Leet": i.e., he did not leave.
7. St. Paul's Cathedral.
8. Chantry, i.e., a foundation that employed priests for the sole duty of saying masses for the souls of certain persons. St. Paul's had many of them.
9. Or to be employed by a brotherhood; i.e., to take a lucrative and fairly easy position as chaplain with a parish guild.

And though he holy were and vertuous,
He was to sinful men nought despitous,°   *scornful*
Ne of his speeche daungerous° ne digne,° *disdainful / haughty*
520 But in his teching discreet and benigne,
To drawen folk to hevene by fairnesse
By good ensample—this was his bisinesse.
But it° were any persone obstinat,   *if there*
What so he were, of heigh or lowe estat,
525 Him wolde he snibben° sharply for the nones:[1] *scold*
A bettre preest I trowe° ther nowher noon is. *believe*
He waited after[2] no pompe and reverence,
Ne maked him a spiced conscience,[3]
But Cristes lore° and his Apostles twelve *teaching*
530 He taughte, but first he folwed it himselve.
  With him ther was a Plowman, was his brother,
That hadde ylad° of dong° ful many a fother.[4] *carried / dung*
A trewe swinkere° and a good was he,   *worker*
Living in pees° and parfit charitee.   *peace*
535 God loved he best with al his hoole° herte *whole*
At alle times, though him gamed or smerte,[5]
And thanne his neighebor right as himselve.
He wolde thresshe, and therto dike° and delve, *dig ditches*
For Cristes sake, for every poore wight,
540 Withouten hire, if it laye in his might.
His tithes payed he ful faire and wel,
Bothe of his propre swink[6] and his catel.° *property*
In a tabard° he rood upon a mere.° *short coat / mare*
  Ther was also a Reeve° and a Millere, *estate manager*
545 A Somnour, and a Pardoner[7] also,
A Manciple,° and myself—ther were namo. *steward*
  The Millere was a stout carl° for the nones. *fellow*
Ful big he was of brawn° and eek of bones— *muscle*
That preved[8] wel, for overal ther he cam
550 At wrastling he wolde have alway the ram.[9]
He was short-shuldred, brood,° a thikke knarre.° *broad / bully*
Ther was no dore that he nolde heve of harre,[1]
Or breke it at a renning° with his heed.° *running / head*
His beerd as any sowe or fox was reed,°   *red*
555 And therto brood, as though it were a spade;
Upon the cop° right of his nose he hade   *ridge*
A werte,° and theron stood a tuft of heres, *wart*
Rede as the bristles of a sowes eres;
His nosethirles° blake were and wide.   *nostrils*

1. On any occasion.
2. I.e., expected.
3. Nor did he assume an overfastidious conscience.
4. Load.
5. Whether he was pleased or grieved.
6. His own work.
7. "Somnour" (Summoner): server of summonses to the ecclesiastical court; Pardoner: dispenser of papal pardons. See lines 625 and 671, and notes, below.
8. Proved, i.e., was evident.
9. A ram was frequently offered as the prize in wrestling.
1. He would not heave off (its) hinge.

560 A swerd and a bokeler° bar° he by his side. *shield / bore*
His mouth as greet was as a greet furnais.° *furnace*
He was a janglere° and a Goliardais,[2] *chatterer*
And that was most of sinne and harlotries.° *obscenities*
Wel coude he stelen corn and tollen thries[3]—
565 And yit he hadde a thombe[4] of gold, pardee.° *by heaven*
A whit cote and a blew hood wered° he. *wore*
A baggepipe wel coude he blowe and soune,° *sound*
And therwithal° he broughte us out of towne. *therewith*
    A gentil Manciple[5] was ther of a temple,
570 Of which achatours° mighte take exemple *buyers of food*
For to been wise in bying of vitaile;° *victuals*
For wheither that he paide or took by taile,[6]
Algate he waited so in his achat[7]
That he was ay biforn[8] and in good stat.
575   Now is nat that of God a ful fair grace
That swich a lewed° mannes wit shal pace° *ignorant / surpass*
The wisdom of an heep of lerned men?
Of maistres° hadde he mo than thries ten *masters*
That weren of lawe expert and curious,° *cunning*
580 Of whiche ther were a dozeine in that hous
Worthy to been stiwardes of rente° and lond *income*
Of any lord that is in Engelond,
To make him live by his propre good[9]
In honour dettelees but if[1] he were wood,° *insane*
585 Or live as scarsly° as him list° desire, *sparely / it pleases*
And able for to helpen al a shire
In any caas° that mighte falle° or happe, *event / befall*
And yit this Manciple sette hir aller cappe![2]
    The Reeve[3] was a sclendre° colerik man; *slender*
590 His beerd was shave as neigh° as evere he can; *close*
His heer was by his eres ful round yshorn;
His top was dokked[4] lik a preest biforn;
Ful longe were his legges and ful lene,
Ylik a staf, ther was no calf yseene.° *visible*
595 Wel coude he keepe° a gerner° and a binne— *guard / granary*
Ther was noon auditour coude on him winne.[5]
Wel wiste° he by the droughte and by the rain *knew*
The yeelding of his seed and of his grain.

2. Goliard, teller of ribald stories.
3. Take toll thrice—i.e., deduct from the grain far more than the lawful percentage.
4. Thumb. The narrator seems to be questioning the validity of the adage that (only) an honest miller has a golden thumb.
5. The Manciple is the steward of a community of lawyers in London (a "temple").
6. By talley, i.e., on credit.
7. Always he was on the watch in his purchasing.
8. I.e., ahead of the game. "Stat": financial condition.
9. His own money.
1. Out of debt unless.
2. This Manciple made fools of them all.
3. The Reeve is the superintendent of a large farming estate; "colerik" (choleric) describes a man whose dominant humor is yellow bile (choler)—i.e., a hot-tempered man.
4. Cut short: the clergy wore the head partially shaved.
5. I.e., find him in default.

His lordes sheep, his neet,° his dayerye,   *cattle*
600 His swin, his hors, his stoor,° and his pultrye   *stock*
Was hoolly° in this Reeves governinge,   *wholly*
And by his covenant yaf⁶ the rekeninge,
Sin° that his lord was twenty-yeer of age.   *since*
There coude no man bringe him in arrerage.⁷
605 Ther nas baillif, hierde, nor other hine,
That he ne knew his sleighte and his covine⁸—
They were adrad° of him as of the deeth.°   *afraid / plague*
His woning° was ful faire upon an heeth;°   *dwelling / meadow*
With greene trees shadwed was his place.
610 He coude bettre than his lord purchace.°   *acquire goods*
Ful riche he was astored° prively.°   *stocked / secretly*
His lord wel coude he plesen subtilly,
To yive and lene° him of his owene good,°   *lend / property*
And have a thank, and yit a cote and hood.
615 In youthe he hadde lerned a good mister:°   *occupation*
He was a wel good wrighte, a carpenter.
This Reeve sat upon a ful good stot°   *stallion*
That was a pomely° grey and highte° Scot. *dapple / was named*
A long surcote° of pers° upon he hade,⁹   *overcoat / blue*
620 And by his side he bar° a rusty blade.   *bore*
Of Northfolk was this Reeve of which I telle,
Biside a town men clepen Baldeswelle.°   *Bawdswell*
Tukked¹ he was as is a frere aboute,
And evere he rood the hindreste of oure route.²
625   A Somnour³ was ther with us in that place
That hadde a fir-reed° cherubinnes⁴ face,   *fire-red*
For saucefleem° he was, with yën narwe,   *pimply*
And hoot° he was, and lecherous as a sparwe,°   *hot / sparrow*
With scaled° browes blake and piled⁵ beerd: *scabby*
630 Of his visage children were aferd.°   *afraid*
Ther nas quiksilver, litarge, ne brimstoon,
Boras, ceruce, ne oile of tartre noon,⁶
Ne oinement that wolde clense and bite,
That him mighte helpen of his whelkes° white,   *blotches*
635 Nor of the knobbes° sitting on his cheekes.   *lumps*
Wel loved he garlek, oinons, and eek leekes,
And for to drinke strong win reed as blood.
Thanne wolde he speke and crye as he were wood;°   *mad*

6. And according to his contract he gave.
7. Convict him of being in arrears financially.
8. There was no bailiff (i.e., foreman), shepherd, nor other farm laborer whose craftiness and plots he didn't know.
9. "Upon he hade": he had on.
1. With clothing tucked up.
2. Hindmost of our group.
3. The "Somnour" (Summoner) is an employee of the ecclesiastical court, whose defined duty is to bring to court persons whom the archdeacon—the justice of the court—suspects of offenses against canon law. By this time, however, summoners had generally transformed themselves into corrupt detectives who spied out offenders and blackmailed them by threats of summonses.
4. Cherub's, often depicted in art with a red face.
5. Uneven, partly hairless.
6. These are all ointments for diseases affecting the skin, probably diseases of venereal origin.

And whan that he wel dronken hadde the win,
640 Thanne wolde he speke no word but Latin:
A fewe termes hadde he, two or three,
That he hadde lerned out of som decree;
No wonder is—he herde it al the day,
And eek ye knowe wel how that a jay°   parrot
645 Can clepen "Watte"[7] as wel as can the Pope—
But whoso coude in other thing him grope,°   examine
Thanne hadde he spent all his philosophye;[8]
Ay *Questio quid juris*[9] wolde he crye.
      He was a gentil harlot° and a kinde;   rascal
650 A bettre felawe sholde men nought finde:
He wolde suffre,° for a quart of win,   permit
A good felawe to have his concubin
A twelfmonth, and excusen him at the fulle;[1]
Ful prively a finch eek coude he pulle.[2]
655 And if he foond° owher° a good felawe   found / anywhere
He wolde techen him to have noon awe
In swich caas of the Ercedekenes curs,[3]
But if[4] a mannes soule were in his purs,
For in his purs he sholde ypunisshed be.
660 "Purs is the Ercedekenes helle," saide he.
      But wel I woot he lied right in deede:
Of cursing° oughte eech gilty man drede,   excommunication
For curs wol slee° right as assoiling° savith— slay / absolution
And also war him of a *significavit*.[5]
665   In daunger[6] hadde he at his owene gise° disposal
The yonge girles of the diocise,
And knew hir conseil,° and was al hir reed.[7]   secrets
A gerland hadde he set upon his heed
As greet as it were for an ale-stake;[8]
670 A bokeler hadde he maad him of a cake.
      With him ther rood a gentil Pardoner[9]
Of Rouncival, his freend and his compeer,°   comrade
That straight was comen fro the Court of Rome.
Ful loude he soong,° "Com hider, love, to me." sang
675 This Somnour bar to him a stif burdoun:[1]

7. Call out: "Walter"—like modern parrots' "Polly."
8. I.e., learning.
9. "What point of law does this investigation involve?": a phrase frequently used in ecclesiastical courts.
1. "At the fulle": fully. Ecclesiastical courts had jurisdiction over many offenses which today would come under civil law, including sexual offenses.
2. "To pull a finch" is to have carnal dealings with a woman.
3. Archdeacon's sentence of excommunication.
4. "But if": unless.
5. And also one should be careful of a *significavit* (the writ which transferred the guilty offender from the ecclesiastical to the civil arm for punishment).
6. Under his domination.
7. Was their chief source of advice.
8. A tavern was signalized by a pole ("ale-stake"), rather like a modern flagpole, projecting from its front wall; on this hung a garland, or "bush."
9. A Pardoner dispensed papal pardon for sins to those who contributed to the charitable institution that he was licensed to represent; this Pardoner purported to be collecting for the hospital of Roncesvalles ("Rouncival") in Spain, which had a London branch.
1. I.e., provided him with a strong vocal accompaniment.

Was nevere trompe° of half so greet a soun.   *trumpet*
    This Pardoner hadde heer as yelow as wex,
But smoothe it heeng° as dooth a strike° of
      flex;°   *hung / hank / flax*
    By ounces² heenge his lokkes that he hadde,
680 And therwith he his shuldres overspradde,°   *overspread*
But thinne it lay, by colpons,° oon by oon;   *strands*
But hood for jolitee° wered° he noon,   *nonchalance / wore*
For it was trussed up in his walet:°   *pack*
Him thoughte he rood al of the newe jet.°   *fashion*
685 Dischevelee° save his cappe he rood al bare.   *with hair down*
Swiche glaring yën hadde he as an hare.
A vernicle³ hadde he sowed upon his cappe,
His walet biforn him in his lappe,
Bretful° of pardon, comen from Rome al hoot.°   *brimful / hot*
690 A vois he hadde as smal° as hath a goot;°   *fine / goat*
No beerd hadde he, ne nevere sholde have;
As smoothe it was as it were late yshave:
I trowe° he were a gelding or a mare.   *believe*
    But of his craft, fro Berwik into Ware,⁴
695 Ne was ther swich another pardoner;
For in his male° he hadde a pilwe-beer°   *bag / pillowcase*
Which that he saide was Oure Lady veil;
He saide he hadde a gobet° of the sail   *piece*
That Sainte Peter hadde whan that he wente
700 Upon the see, til Jesu Crist him hente.°   *seized*
He hadde a crois° of laton,° ful of stones,   *cross / brassy metal*
And in a glas he hadde pigges bones,
But with thise relikes⁵ whan that he foond°   *found*
A poore person° dwelling upon lond,⁶   *parson*
705 Upon° a day he gat° him more moneye   *in / got*
Than that the person gat in monthes twaye;
And thus with feined° flaterye and japes°   *false / tricks*
He made the person and the peple his apes.°   *dupes*
But trewely to tellen at the laste,
710 He was in chirche a noble ecclesiaste;
Wel coude he rede a lesson and a storye,°   *liturgical narrative*
But alderbest° he soong an offertorye,   *best of all*
For wel he wiste° whan that song was songe,   *knew*
He moste° preche and wel affile° his tonge   *must / sharpen*
715 To winne silver, as he ful wel coude—
    Therfore he soong the merierly° and loude.   *more merrily*
      Now have I told you soothly in a clause⁷
Th'estaat, th'array, the nombre, and eek the cause

---

2. I.e., thin strands.
3. Portrait of Christ's face as it was said to have been impressed on St. Veronica's handkerchief.
4. Probably towns south and north of London.

5. Relics—i.e., the pigs' bones which the Pardoner represented as saints' bones.
6. "Upon lond": upcountry.
7. I.e., in a short space.

Why that assembled was this compaignye
720 In Southwerk at this gentil hostelrye
That highte the Tabard, faste° by the Belle;[8]   *close*
But now is time to you for to telle
How that we baren us[9] that ilke° night   *same*
Whan we were in that hostelrye alight;
725 And after wol I telle of oure viage,°   *trip*
And al the remenant of oure pilgrimage.
But first I praye you of youre curtcisye
That ye n'arette it nought my vilainye[1]
Though that I plainly speke in this matere
730 To telle you hir wordes and hir cheere,°   *behavior*
Ne though I speke hir wordes proprely;°   *accurately*
For this ye knowen also wel as I:
Who so shal telle a tale after a man
He moot° reherce,° as neigh as evere he can,   *must / repeat*
735 Everich a word, if it be in his charge,°   *responsibility*
Al speke he[2] nevere so rudeliche and large,°   *broadly*
Or elles he moot telle his tale untrewe,
Or feine° thing, or finde° wordes newe;   *falsify / devise*
He may nought spare[3] although he were his brother:
740 He moot as wel saye oo word as another.
Crist spak himself ful brode° in Holy Writ,   *broadly*
And wel ye woot no vilainye is it;
Eek Plato saith, who so can him rede,
The wordes mote be cosin to the deede.
745 Also I praye you to foryive it me
Al° have I nat set folk in hir degree   *although*
Here in this tale as that they sholde stonde:
My wit is short, ye may wel understonde.
Greet cheere made oure Host[4] us everichoon,
750 And to the soper sette he us anoon.°   *at once*
He served us with vitaile° at the beste.   *food*
Strong was the win, and wel to drinke us leste.°   *it pleased*
A semely man oure Hoste was withalle
For to been a marchal[5] in an halle;
755 A large man he was, with yën steepe,°   *prominent*
A fairer burgeis° was ther noon in Chepe[6]—   *burgher*
Bold of his speeche, and wis, and wel ytaught,
And of manhood him lakkede right naught.
Eek therto he was right a merye man,
760 And after soper playen he bigan,
And spak of mirthe amonges othere thinges—

---

8. Another tavern in Southwark.
9. Bore ourselves.
1. That you do not charge it to my
lack of decorum.
2. Although he speak.
3. I.e., spare anyone.

4. The Host is the landlord of the
Tabard Inn.
5. Marshal, one who was in charge of
feasts.
6. Cheapside, bourgeois center of London.

Whan that we hadde maad oure rekeninges[7]—
And saide thus, "Now, lordinges, trewely,
Ye been to me right welcome, hertely.°   *heartily*
765 For by my trouthe, if that I shal nat lie,
I sawgh nat this yeer so merye a compaignye
At ones in this herberwe° as is now.   *inn*
Fain° wolde I doon you mirthe, wiste I[8] how.   *gladly*
And of a mirthe I am right now bithought,
770 To doon you ese, and it shal coste nought.
        "Ye goon to Canterbury—God you speede;
The blisful martyr quite you youre meede.[9]
And wel I woot as ye goon by the waye
Ye shapen you[1] to talen° and to playe,   *converse*
775 For trewely, confort ne mirthe is noon
To ride by the waye domb as stoon;°   *stone*
And therfore wol I maken you disport
As I saide erst,° and doon you som confort;   *before*
And if you liketh alle, by oon assent,
780 For to stonden at[2] my juggement,
And for to werken as I shal you saye,
Tomorwe whan ye riden by the waye—
Now by my fader° soule that is deed,   *father's*
But° ye be merye I wol yive you myn heed!°   *unless / head*
785 Holde up youre handes withouten more speeche."
        Oure counseil was nat longe for to seeche;°   *seek*
Us thoughte it was nat worth to make it wis,[3]
And graunted him withouten more avis,°   *deliberation*
And bade him saye his voirdit° as him leste.[4]   *verdict*
790 "Lordinges," quod he, "now herkneth for the beste;
But taketh it nought, I praye you, in desdain.
This is the point, to speken short and plain,
That eech of you, to shorte with oure waye
In this viage, shal tellen tales twaye°—   *two*
795 To Canterburyward, I mene it so,
And hoomward he shal tellen othere two,
Of aventures that whilom° have bifalle;   *once upon a time*
And which of you that bereth him best of alle—
That is to sayn, that telleth in this cas
800 Tales of best sentence° and most solas°—   *purport / delight*
Shal have a soper at oure aller cost,[5]
Here in this place, sitting by this post,
Whan that we come again fro Canterbury.
And for to make you the more mury°   *merry*
805 I wol myself goodly° with you ride—   *kindly*
Right at myn owene cost—and be youre gide.

7. Had paid our bills.
8. If I knew.
9. Pay you your reward.
1. "Shapen you": intend.
2. Abide by.

3. We didn't think it worthwhile to make it an issue of it.
4. It pleased.
5. At the cost of us all.

And who so wol my juggement withsaye°   *contradict*
Shal paye al that we spende by the waye.
And if ye vouche sauf that it be so,
810 Telle me anoon, withouten wordes mo,°   *more*
And I wol erly shape me⁶ therfore."
 This thing was graunted and oure othes swore
With ful glad herte, and prayden⁷ him also
That he wolde vouche sauf for to do so,
815 And that he wolde been oure governour,
And of oure tales juge and reportour,°   *accountant*
And sette a soper at a certain pris,°   *price*
And we wol ruled been at his devis,°   *disposal*
In heigh and lowe; and thus by oon assent
820 We been accorded to his juggement.
And therupon the win was fet° anoon;   *fetched*
We dronken and to reste wente eechoon
Withouten any lenger° taryinge.   *longer*
 Amorwe° whan that day bigan to springe *in the morning*
825 Up roos oure Host and was oure aller cok,⁸
And gadred us togidres in a flok,
And forth we riden, a litel more than pas,°   *a step*
Unto the watering of Saint Thomas;⁹
And ther oure Host bigan his hors arreste,°   *halt*
830 And saide, "Lordes, herkneth if you leste:°   *it please*
 Ye woot youre forward° and it you recorde:¹ *agreement*
If evensong and morwesong° accorde,° *morningsong / agree*
Lat see now who shal telle the firste tale.
As evere mote I drinken win or ale,
835 Who so be rebel to my juggement
Shal paye for al that by the way is spent.
Now draweth cut² er that we ferrer twinne:
He which that hath the shorteste shal biginne.
 "Sire Knight," quod he, "my maister and my lord,
840 Now draweth cut, for that is myn accord.°   *will*
Cometh neer," quod he, "my lady Prioresse,
And ye, sire Clerk, lat be youre shamefastnesse°— *modesty*
Ne studieth nought. Lay hand to, every man!"
 Anoon to drawen every wight bigan,
845 And shortly for to tellen as it was,
Were it by aventure, or sort, or cas,³
The soothe° is this, the cut fil° to the Knight; *truth / fell*
Of which ful blithe and glad was every wight,
And telle he moste° his tale, as was resoun,   *must*
850 By forward and by composicioun,⁴

---

6. Prepare myself.
7. I.e., we prayed.
8. Was rooster for us all.
9. A watering place near Southwark.
1. You recall it.

2. I.e., draw lots; "ferrer twinne": go farther.
3. Whether it was luck, fate, or chance.
4. By agreement and compact.

As ye han herd. What needeth wordes mo?
And whan this goode man sawgh that it was so,
As he that wis was and obedient
To keepe his forward by his free assent,
855 He saide, "Sin I shal biginne the game,
What, welcome be the cut, in Goddes name!
Now lat us ride, and herkneth what I saye."
And with that word we riden forth oure waye,
And he bigan with right a merye cheere°   *countenance*
860 His tale anoon, and saide as ye may heere.

The Miller's Tale[1]

The Introduction

Whan that the Knight hadde thus his tale ytold,[2]
In al the route° nas ther yong ne old   *group*
That he ne saide it was a noble storye,
And worthy for to drawen° to memorye,   *recall*
5 And namely° the gentils everichoon.   *especially*
    Oure Hoste lough° and swoor, "So mote I goon,[3]   *laughed*
This gooth aright: unbokeled is the male.°   *pouch*
Lat see now who shal telle another tale.
For trewely the game is wel bigonne.
10 Now telleth ye, sire Monk, if that ye conne,°   *can*
Somwhat to quite° with the Knightes tale."   *repay*
    The Millere, that for dronken[4] was al pale,
So that unnethe° upon his hors he sat,   *with difficulty*
He nolde avalen° neither hood ne hat,   *doff*
15 Ne abiden no man for his curteisye,
But in Pilates vois[5] he gan to crye,

---

1. The Miller's Tale belongs to the literary genre known as the "fabliau," a short story in verse that generally involves bourgeois or lower-class characters in an outrageous, often obscene plot, which is, however, realistically handled by the narrator. The fabliau is peculiarly French, and aside from the three or four examples in Chaucer there are few representatives of it in English. Yet Chaucer was supreme in this kind of tale as in many others, and the Miller's Tale is generally considered the best-told fabliau in any language.
    Two originally separate plots are the basis of the Miller's Tale, both of them probably already old in Chaucer's time. In the first, a student—students are often the heroes of fabliaux and were probably often their authors—creates an opportunity to sleep with a woman by persuading her husband that Noah's flood is about to be repeated; and in the second, a lover who has been tricked into a humiliatingly misdirected kiss takes a dreadful vengeance on his tormentor. Whether or not Chaucer first united these traditional plots is not clear, but in any case their union, culminating in the scorched student's cry of "Water!" is a brilliant stroke, and brilliantly handled by Chaucer.
2. The Knight's Tale is actually the first one told on the Canterbury pilgrimage, immediately following the General Prologue.
3. So might I walk.
4. I.e., drunkenness.
5. The harsh voice usually associated with the character of Pontius Pilate in the mystery plays.

And swoor, "By armes[6] and by blood and bones,
I can° a noble tale for the nones,   *know*
With which I wol now quite the Knightes tale."
20   Oure Hoste sawgh that he was dronke of ale,
And saide, "Abide, Robin, leve° brother,   *dear*
Som bettre man shal telle us first another.
Abide, and lat us werken thriftily."°   *with propriety*
   "By Goddes soule," quod he, "that wol nat I,
25 For I wol speke or elles go my way."
   Oure Host answerde, "Tel on, a devele way![7]
Thou art a fool; thy wit is overcome."
   "Now herkneth," quod the Millere, "alle and some.[8]
But first I make a protestacioun°   *public affirmation*
30 That I am dronke: I knowe it by my soun.°   *tone of voice*
And therfore if that I mis° speke or saye,   *amiss*
Wite it[9] the ale of Southwerk, I you praye;
For I wol telle a legende and a lif
Bothe of a carpenter and of his wif,
35 How that a clerk hath set the wrightes cappe."[1]
   The Reeve answerde and saide, "Stint thy clappe![2]
Lat be thy lewed° dronken harlotrye.°   *ignorant / obscenity*
It is a sinne and eek° a greet folye   *also*
To apairen° any man or him defame,   *injure*
40 And eek to bringen wives in swich fame.°   *report*
Thou maist ynough of othere thinges sayn."
   This dronken Millere spak ful soone again,
And saide, "Leve° brother Osewold,   *dear*
Who hath no wif, he is no cokewold.°   *cuckold*
45 But I saye nat therfore that thou art oon.
Ther ben ful goode wives many oon,°   *a one*
And evere a thousand goode ayains oon badde.
That knowestou wel thyself but if thou madde.°   *rave*
Why artou angry with my tale now?
50 I have a wif, pardee, as wel as thou,
Yit nolde° I, for the oxen in my plough,   *would not*
Take upon me more than ynough
As deemen of myself that I were oon:
I wol bileve wel that I am noon.
55 An housbonde shal nought been inquisitif
Of Goddes privetee,° nor of his wif.   *secrets*
So[3] he may finde Goddes foison° there,   *plenty*
Of the remenant° needeth nought enquere."°   *rest / inquire*
   What sholde I more sayn but this Millere
60 He nolde his wordes for no man forbere,
But tolde his cherles tale in his manere.
M'athinketh° that I shal reherce° it here,   *I regret / repeat*

6. I.e., by God's arms.
7. I.e., in the devil's name.
8. Each and every one.
9. Blame it on.

1. I.e., how a clerk made a fool of a carpenter.
2. Stop your chatter.
3. Provided that.

And therfore every gentil wight I praye,
Deemeth nought, for Goddes love, that I saye
65 Of yvel entente, but for° I moot reherse   *because*
Hir tales alle, be they bet° or werse,   *better*
Or elles falsen° som of my matere.   *falsify*
And therfore, whoso list it nought yheere
Turne over the leef, and chese° another tale,   *choose*
70 For he shal finde ynowe,° grete and smale,   *enough*
Of storial⁴ thing that toucheth gentilesse,°   *gentility*
And eek moralitee and holinesse:
Blameth nought me if that ye chese amis.
The Millere is a cherl, ye knowe wel this,
75 So was the Reeve eek, and othere mo,
And harlotrye° they tolden bothe two.   *ribaldry*
Aviseth you,⁵ and putte me out of blame:
And eek men shal nought maken ernest of game.

The Tale

Whilom° ther was dwelling at Oxenforde   *once upon a time*
80 A riche gnof° that gestes heeld to boorde,⁶   *boor*
And of his craft he was a carpenter.
With him ther was dwelling a poore scoler,
Hadde lerned art,⁷ but al his fantasye°   *interest*
Was turned for to lere° astrologye,   *learn*
85 And coude a certain of conclusiouns,
To deemen by interrogaciouns,⁸
If that men axed° him in certain houres   *asked*
Whan that men sholde have droughte or elles showres,
Or if men axed him what shal bifalle
90 Of every thing—I may nat rekene hem alle.
This clerk was cleped° hende⁹ Nicholas.   *called*
Of derne love he coude, and of solas,¹
And therto he was sly and ful privee,°   *secretive*
And lik a maide meeke for to see.
95 A chambre hadde he in that hostelrye
Allone, withouten any compaignye,
Ful fetisly ydight² with herbes swoote,°   *sweet*
And he himself as sweete as is the roote
Of licoris or any setewale.³
100 His *Almageste*⁴ and bookes grete and smale,
His astrelabye,⁵ longing for his art,
His augrim stones,⁶ layen faire apart

4. Historical, i.e., true.
5. Take heed.
6. I.e., took in boarders.
7. Who had completed the first stage of university education (the trivium).
8. I.e., and he knew a number of propositions on which to base astrological analyses (which would reveal the matters in ll. 87–90).
9. Handy, sly, attractive.

1. I.e., he knew about secret love and pleasurable practices.
2. Elegantly furnished.
3. Setwall, a spice.
4. 2nd-century treatise by Ptolemy, still the standard astronomy textbook.
5. Astrolabe, an astronomical instrument. "Longing for": belonging to.
6. Counters used in arithmetic.

On shelves couched° at his beddes heed;   *set*
His presse° ycovered with a falding reed;[7]   *storage chest*
105 And al above ther lay a gay sautrye,°   *psaltery*
On which he made a-nightes melodye
So swetely that al the chambre roong,°   *rang*
And *Angelus ad Virginem*[8] he soong,
And after that he soong the *Kinges Note:*
110 Ful often blessed was his merye throte.
And thus this sweete clerk his time spente
After his freendes finding and his rente.[9]
        This carpenter hadde wedded newe° a wif   *lately*
Which that he loved more than his lif.
115 Of eighteteene yeer she was of age;
Jalous he was, and heeld hire narwe in cage,
For she was wilde and yong, and he was old,
And deemed himself been lik a cokewold.[1]
He knew nat Caton,[2] for his wit was rude,
120 That bad men sholde wedde his similitude:[3]
Men sholde wedden after hir estat,[4]
For youthe and elde° is often at debat.   *age*
But sith that he was fallen in the snare,
He moste endure, as other folk, his care.
125   Fair was this yonge wif, and therwithal
As any wesele° hir body gent and smal.[5]   *weasel*
A ceint she wered, barred[6] al of silk;
A barmcloth° as whit as morne milk   *apron*
Upon hir lendes,° ful of many a gore;°   *loins / strip of cloth*
130 Whit was hir smok,° and broiden[7] al bifore   *undergarment*
And eek bihinde, on hir coler° aboute,   *collar*
Of° col-blak silk, withinne and eek withoute;   *with*
The tapes° of hir white voluper°   *ribbons / cap*
Were of the same suite of[8] hir coler;
135 Hir filet° brood° of silk and set ful hye;   *headband / broad*
And sikerly° she hadde a likerous° yë;   *certainly / wanton*
Ful smale ypulled[9] were hir browes two,
And tho were bent,° and blake as any slo.°   *arching / sloeberry*
She was ful more blisful on to see
140 Than is the newe perejonette° tree,   *pear*
And softer than the wolle° is of a wether;°   *wool / ram*
And by hir girdel° heeng° a purs of lether,   *belt / hung*
Tasseled with silk and perled with latoun.[1]

---

7. Red coarse wool.
8. "The Angel's Address to the Virgin,"
a hymn; *"Kinges Note"*: probably a
popular song of the time.
9. In accordance with his friends' provision and his own income.
1. I.e., suspected of himself that he was
like a cuckold.
2. Dionysius Cato, the supposed author
of a book of maxims used in elementary
education.

3. Commanded that one should wed his
equal.
4. Men should marry according to their
condition.
5. Slender and delicate.
6. A belt she wore, with transverse
stripes.
7. Embroidered.
8. I.e., the same pattern as.
9. Delicately plucked.
1. I.e., with brassy spangles on it.

In al this world, to seeken up and down,
145 Ther nis no man so wis that coude thenche°   *imagine*
So gay a popelote° or swich° a wenche.   *doll / such*
Ful brighter was the shining of hir hewe
Than in the Towr² the noble° yforged newe.   *gold coin*
But of hir song, it was as loud and yerne°   *lively*
150 As any swalwe sitting on a berne.°   *barn*
Therto she coude skippe and make game³
As any kide or calf folwing his dame.°   *mother*
Hir mouth was sweete as bragot or the meeth,⁴
Or hoord of apples laid in hay or heeth.°   *heather*
155 Winsing° she was as is a joly° colt,   *skittish / high-spirited*
Long as a mast, and upright° as a bolt.°   *straight / arrow*
A brooch she bar upon hir lowe coler
As brood as is the boos° of a bokeler;°   *boss / shield*
Hir shoes were laced on hir legges hye.
160 She was a primerole,° a piggesnye,°   *cowslip / pig's eye*
For any lord to leggen° in his bedde,   *lay*
Or yit for any good yeman to wedde.
      Now sire, and eft° sire, so bifel the cas   *again*
That on a day this hende Nicholas
165 Fil° with this yonge wif to rage° and playe,   *happened / flirt*
Whil that hir housbonde was at Oseneye⁵
(As clerkes been ful subtil and ful quainte),°   *clever*
And prively he caughte hire by the queinte,°   *pudendum*
And saide, "Ywis, but if ich° have my wille,   *I*
170 For derne° love of thee, lemman, I spille,"°   *secret / die*
And heeld hire harde by the haunche-bones,
And saide, "Lemman,° love me al atones,⁶   *mistress*
Or I wol dien, also° God me save."   *so*
And she sproong° as a colt dooth in a trave,⁷   *sprang*
175 And with hir heed she wried° faste away;   *twisted*
She saide, "I wol nat kisse thee, by my fay.°   *faith*
Why, lat be," quod she, "lat be, Nicholas!
Or I wol crye 'Out, harrow,° and allas!'   *help*
Do way youre handes, for youre curteisye!"
180 This Nicholas gan mercy for to crye,
And spak so faire, and profred him so faste,⁸
That she hir love him graunted atte laste,
And swoor hir ooth by Saint Thomas of Kent⁹
That she wolde been at his comandement,
185 Whan that she may hir leiser¹ wel espye.
"Myn housbonde is so ful of jalousye
That but ye waite° wel and been privee,   *be on guard*
I woot right wel I nam but deed," quod she.

---

2. The Tower of London.
3. Play.
4. "Bragot" and "meeth" are honey
drinks.
5. A town near Oxford.

6. Right now.
7. Frame for a restive horse.
8. I.e., pushed himself so vigorously.
9. Thomas à Becket.
1. I.e., opportunity.

"Ye moste been ful derne as in this cas."
190 "Nay, therof care thee nought," quod Nicholas.
"A clerk hadde litherly biset his while,[2]
But if he coude a carpenter bigile."
And thus they been accorded and ysworn
To waite° a time, as I have told biforn.   *watch for*
195 Whan Nicholas hadde doon this everydeel,
And thakked° hire upon the lendes° weel,   *patted / loins*
He kiste hire sweete, and taketh his sautrye,
And playeth faste, and maketh melodye.

Thanne fil° it thus, that to the parissh chirche,   *befell*
200 Cristes owene werkes for to wirche,°   *perform*
This goode wif wente on an haliday:°   *holy day*
Hir forheed shoon as bright as any day,
So was it wasshen whan she leet° hir werk.   *left*

Now was ther of that chirche a parissh clerk,
205 The which that was ycleped° Absolon: *called*
Crul° was his heer, and as the gold it shoon,   *curly*
And strouted° as a fanne[3] large and brode;   *spread out*
Ful straight and evene lay his joly shode.[4]
His rode° was reed, his yën greye as goos.°   *complexion / goose*
210 With Poules window corven[5] on his shoos,
In hoses° rede he wente fetisly.°   *stockings / elegantly*
Yclad he was ful smale° and proprely,   *finely*
Al in a kirtel° of a light waget°—   *tunic / blue*
Ful faire and thikke been the pointes[6] set—
215 And therupon he hadde a gay surplis,°   *surplice*
As whit as is the blosme upon the ris.°   *bough*
A merye child° he was, so God me save.   *lad*
Wel coude he laten° blood, and clippe, and shave,   *let*
And maken a chartre of land, or acquitaunce;[7]
220 In twenty manere° coude he trippe and daunce   *ways*
After the scole of Oxenforde tho,
And with his legges casten° to and fro,   *prance*
And playen songes on a smal rubible;°   *fiddle*
Therto he soong somtime a loud quinible,[8]
225 And as wel coude he playe on a giterne:°   *guitar*
In al the town nas brewhous ne taverne
That he ne visited with his solas,°   *entertainment*
Ther any gailard tappestere[9] was.

But sooth to sayn, he was somdeel squaimous°   *squeamish*
230 Of farting, and of speeche daungerous.°   *fastidious*
This Absolon, that joly° was and gay,   *pretty, amorous*
Gooth with a cencer° on the haliday,   *incense-burner*

2. Poorly employed his time.
3. Wide-mouthed basket for separating grain from chaff.
4. Parting of the hair.
5. Carved with intricate designs, like the tracery in the windows of St. Paul's.
6. Laces for fastening the tunic and holding up the hose.
7. Legal release.
8. Part requiring a very high voice.
9. Gay barmaid.

Cencing the wives of the parissh faste,
And many a lovely look on hem he caste,
235 And namely° on this carpenteres wif: *especially*
To looke on hire him thoughte a merye lif.
She was so propre° and sweete and likerous,[1]   *neat*
I dar wel sayn, if she hadde been a mous,
And he a cat, he wolde hire hente° anoon.   *pounce on*
240 This parissh clerk, this joly Absolon,
Hath in his herte swich a love-longinge°   *lovesickness*
That of no wif ne took he noon offringe—
For curteisye he saide he wolde noon.
The moone, whan it was night, ful brighte shoon,°   *shone*
245 And Absolon his giterne° hath ytake—   *guitar*
For paramours° he thoughte for to wake—   *love*
And forth he gooth, jolif° and amorous,   *pretty*
Til he cam to the carpenteres hous,
A litel after cokkes hadde ycrowe,
250 And dressed him up by a shot-windowe[2]
That was upon the carpenteres wal.
He singeth in his vois gentil and smal,°   *dainty*
"Now dere lady, if thy wille be,
I praye you that ye wol rewe° on me,"   *have pity*
255 Ful wel accordant to his giterninge.[3]
This carpenter awook and herde him singe,
And spak unto his wif, and saide anoon,
"What, Alison, heerestou nought Absolon
That chaunteth thus under oure bowres° wal?"   *bedroom's*
260 And she answerde hir housbonde therwithal,
"Yis, God woot, John, I heere it everydeel."
This passeth forth. What wol ye bet than weel?[4]
Fro day to day this joly Absolon
So woweth° hire that him is wo-bigoon: *woos*
265 He waketh° al the night and al the day;   *stays awake*
He kembed° his lokkes brode[5] and made him gay;   *combed*
He woweth by menes and brocage,[6]
And swoor he wolde been hir owene page;°   *personal servant*
He singeth, brokking° as a nightingale;   *trilling*
270 He sente hire piment,[7] meeth, and spiced ale,
And wafres° piping hoot out of the gleede;°   *pastries / coals*
And for she was of towne,[8] he profred meede°—   *bribe*
For som folk wol be wonnen for richesse,
And som for strokes,° and som for gentilesse.   *blows*
275 Somtime to shewe his lightnesse and maistrye,[9]
He playeth Herodes[1] upon a scaffold° hye.   *platform, stage*

1. Wanton, appetizing.
2. Took his position by a hinged window.
3. In harmony with his guitar-playing.
4. Better than well.
5. I.e., wide-spreading.

6. By intermediaries and mediation.
7. Spiced wine; "meeth": mead.
8. Since she was a town woman.
9. Facility and virtuosity.
1. Herod, a role traditionally played as
a bully in the mystery plays.

But what availeth him as in this cas?
She loveth so this hende Nicholas
That Absolon may blowe the bukkes horn;[2]
280 He ne hadde for his labour but a scorn.
And thus she maketh Absolon hir ape,[3]
And al his ernest turneth til a jape.°   *joke*
Ful sooth is this proverbe, it is no lie;
Men saith right thus: "Alway the nye slye
285 Maketh the ferre leve to be loth."[4]
For though that Absolon be wood° or wroth,   *furious*
By cause that he fer was from hir sighte,
This nye° Nicholas stood in his lighte.   *nearby*
    Now beer° thee wel, thou hende Nicholas,   *bear*
290 For Absolon may waile and singe allas.
    And so bifel it on a Saterday
This carpenter was goon til Oseney,
And hende Nicholas and Alisoun
Accorded been to this conclusioun,
295 That Nicholas shal shapen° hem a wile°   *arrange / trick*
This sely[5] jalous housbonde to bigile,
And if so be this game wente aright,
She sholden sleepen in his arm al night—
For this was his desir and hire° also.   *hers*
300 And right anoon, withouten wordes mo,
This Nicholas no lenger wolde tarye,
But dooth ful softe unto his chambre carye
Bothe mete and drinke for a day or twaye,
And to hir housbonde bad hire for to saye,
305 If that he axed after Nicholas,
She sholde saye she niste° wher he was—   *didn't know*
Of al that day she sawgh him nought with yë:
She trowed° that he was in maladye,   *believed*
For for no cry hir maide coude him calle,
310 He nolde answere for no thing that mighte falle.°   *happen*
    This passeth forth al thilke° Saterday   *this*
That Nicholas stille in his chambre lay,
And eet,° and sleep,° or dide what him leste,[6]   *ate / slept*
Til Sonday that the sonne gooth to reste.
315   This sely carpenter hath greet mervaile
Of Nicholas, or what thing mighte him aile,
And saide, "I am adrad,° by Saint Thomas,   *afraid*
It stondeth nat aright with Nicholas.
God shilde° that he deide sodeinly!   *forbid*
320 This world is now ful tikel,° sikerly: *changeable*
I sawgh today a corps yborn to chirche
That now a° Monday last I sawgh him wirche.°   *on / work*

2. Blow the buck's horn, i.e., go without reward.
3. I.e., thus she makes a fool of Absolon.
4. Always the sly man at hand makes
the distant dear one hated.
5. "Poor innocent."
6. He wanted.

Go up," quod he unto his knave° anoon,   *manservant*
"Clepe° at his dore or knokke with a stoon.°   *call / stone*
325 Looke how it is and tel me boldely."
    This knave gooth him up ful sturdily,
And at the chambre dore whil that he stood
He cride and knokked as that he were wood,°   *mad*
"What? How? What do ye, maister Nicholay?
330 How may ye sleepen al the longe day?"
But al for nought: he herde nat a word.
An hole he foond ful lowe upon a boord,
Ther as the cat was wont in for to creepe,
And at that hole he looked in ful deepe,
335 And atte laste he hadde of him a sighte.
    This Nicholas sat evere caping° uprighte   *gaping*
As he hadde kiked° on the newe moone.   *gazed*
Adown he gooth and tolde his maister soone
In what array° he saw this ilke° man.   *condition / same*
340   This carpenter to blessen him[7] bigan,
And saide, "Help us, Sainte Frideswide!
A man woot litel what him shal bitide.
This man is falle, with his astromye,[8]
In som woodnesse° or in som agonye.   *madness*
345 I thoughte ay° wel how that it sholde be: *always*
Men sholde nought knowe of Goddes privetee.
Ye, blessed be alway a lewed° man   *ignorant*
That nought but only his bileve° can.°   *creed / knows*
So ferde° another clerk with astromye: *fared*
350 He walked in the feeldes for to prye
Upon the sterres,° what ther sholde bifalle,   *stars*
Til he was in a marle-pit[9] yfalle—
He saw nat that. But yit, by Saint Thomas,
Me reweth sore[1] for hende Nicholas.
355 He shal be rated of[2] his studying,
If that I may, by Jesus, hevene king!
Get me a staf that I may underspore,°   *pry up*
Whil that thou, Robin, hevest° up the dore.   *heave*
He shal[3] out of his studying, as I gesse."
360 And to the chambre dore he gan him dresse.[4]
His knave was a strong carl° for the nones,°   *fellow / purpose*
And by the haspe he haaf° it up atones: *heaved*
Into° the floor the dore fil° anoon.   *on / fell*
This Nicholas sat ay as stille as stoon,
365 And evere caped up into the air.
This carpenter wende° he were in despair,   *thought*
And hente° him by the shuldres mightily,   *seized*
And shook him harde, and cride spitously,°   *roughly*

7. Cross himself.
8. Illiterate form of "astronomye."
9. Pit from which a fertilizing clay is dug.
1. I sorely pity.
2. Scolded for.
3. I.e., shall come.
4. Took his stand.

"What, Nicholay, what, how! What! Looke adown!
370 Awaak and thenk on Cristes passioun!⁵
I crouche⁶ thee from elves and fro wightes."
Therwith the nightspel saide he anoonrightes⁷
On foure halves° of the hous aboute,   *sides*
And on the threshfold° on the dore withoute: *threshold*
375 "Jesu Crist and Sainte Benedight,°   *Benedict*
Blesse this hous from every wikked wight!
For nightes nerye the White Pater Noster.⁸
Where wentestou, Sainte Petres soster?"°   *sister*
And at the laste this hende Nicholas
380 Gan for to sike° sore, and saide, "Allas,   *sigh*
Shal al the world be lost eftsoones° now?"   *again*
    This carpenter answerde, "What saistou?
What, thenk on God as we doon, men that swinke."⁹
    This Nicholas answerde, "Fecche me drinke,
385 And after wol I speke in privetee
Of certain thing that toucheth me and thee.
I wol telle it noon other man, certain."
    This carpenter gooth down and comth again,
And broughte of mighty ale a large quart,
390 And when that eech of hem hadde dronke his part,
This Nicholas his dore faste shette,°   *shut*
And down the carpenter by him he sette,
And saide, "John, myn hoste lief° and dere,   *beloved*
Thou shalt upon thy trouthe° swere me here   *word of honor*
395 That to no wight thou shalt this conseil° wraye;°   *secret / disclose*
For it is Cristes conseil that I saye,
And if thou telle it man,¹ thou art forlore,°   *lost*
For this vengeance thou shalt have therfore,
That if thou wraye me, thou shalt be wood." ²
400   "Nay, Crist forbede it, for his holy blood,"
Quod tho this sely° man. "I nam no labbe,³   *innocent*
And though I saye, I nam nat lief to gabbe.⁴
Say what thou wilt, I shal it nevere telle
To child ne wif, by him that harwed helle."⁵
405   "Now John," quod Nicholas, "I wol nought lie.
I have yfounde in myn astrologye,
As I have looked in the moone bright,
That now a Monday next, at quarter night,⁶
Shal falle a rain, and that so wilde and wood,°   *furious*
410 That half so greet was nevere Noees° flood.   *Noah's*
This world," he saide, "in lasse° than an hour   *less*

---

5. I.e., the Crucifixion.
6. Make the sign of the cross on;
"wightes": wicked creatures.
7. The night-charm he said right away.
8. I.e., the White Lord's Prayer defend
(us). This personification was considered a powerful beneficent spirit.
9. Work.

1. To anyone.
2. Go mad.
3. Blabbermouth.
4. And though I say it myself, I don't
like to gossip.
5. By Him that despoiled hell—i.e.,
Christ.
6. I.e., shortly before dawn.

Shal al be dreint,° so hidous is the showr.   *drowned*
Thus shal mankinde drenche° and lese° hir lif."   *drown / lose*
  This carpenter answerde, "Allas, my wif!
415 And shal she drenche? Allas, myn Alisoun!"
For sorwe of this he fil almost[7] adown,
And saide, "Is there no remedye in this cas?"
  "Why yis, for[8] Gode," quod hende Nicholas,
"If thou wolt werken after lore and reed[9]—
420 Thou maist nought werken after thyn owene heed;°   *head*
For thus saith Salomon that was ful trewe,
'Werk al by conseil and thou shalt nought rewe.'°   *be sorry*
And if thou werken wolt by good conseil,
I undertake, withouten mast or sail,
425 Yit shal I save hire and thee and me.
Hastou nat herd how saved was Noee
Whan that oure Lord hadde warned him biforn
That al the world with water sholde be lorn?"°   *lost*
  "Yis," quod this carpenter, "ful yore ago."
430 "Hastou nat herd," quod Nicholas, "also
The sorwe of Noee with his felaweshipe?
Er that he mighte gete his wif to shipe,
Him hadde levere,[1] I dar wel undertake,
At thilke time than alle his wetheres blake
435 That she hadde had a ship hirself allone.[2]
And therfore woostou° what is best to doone?   *do you know*
This axeth° haste, and of an hastif° thing   *requires / urgent*
Men may nought preche or maken tarying.
Anoon go gete us faste into this in°   *lodging*
440 A kneeding trough or elles a kimelin°   *brewing tub*
For eech of us, but looke that they be large,°   *wide*
In whiche we mowen swimme as in a barge,[3]
And han therinne vitaile suffisaunt[4]
But for a day—fy° on the remenaunt!   *fie*
445 The water shal aslake° and goon away   *diminish*
Aboute prime[5] upon the nexte day.
But Robin may nat wite° of this, thy knave,   *know*
Ne eek thy maide Gille I may nat save.
Axe nought why, for though thou axe me,
450 I wol nought tellen Goddes privetee.°   *secrets*
Suffiseth thee, but if thy wittes madde,°   *go mad*
To han° as greet a grace as Noee hadde.   *have*
Thy wif shal I wel saven, out of doute.
Go now thy way, and speed thee heraboute.
455 But whan thou hast for hire° and thee and me   *her*

7. Almost fell.
8. I.e., by.
9. Act according to learning and advice.
1. He had rather. "Wetheres": rams. I.e., he'd have given all the rams he had.

2. The reluctance of Noah's wife to board the ark is a traditional comic theme in the mystery plays.
3. In which we can float as in a vessel.
4. Sufficient food.
5. 9 A.M.

Ygeten us thise kneeding-tubbes three,
Thanne shaltou hangen hem in the roof ful hye,
That no man of oure purveyance° espye.   *foresight*
And whan thou thus hast doon as I have said,
460 And hast oure vitaile faire in hem ylaid,
And eek an ax to smite the corde atwo,
Whan that the water comth that we may go,
And broke an hole an heigh[6] upon the gable
Unto the gardinward,[7] over the stable,
465 That we may freely passen forth oure way,
Whan that the grete showr is goon away,
Thanne shaltou swimme as merye, I undertake,
As dooth the white doke° after hir drake.   *duck*
Thanne wol I clepe,° 'How, Alison? How, John?   *call*
470 Be merye, for the flood wol passe anoon.'
And thou wolt sayn, 'Hail, maister Nicholay!
Good morwe, I see thee wel, for it is day!'
And thanne shal we be lordes al oure lif
Of al the world, as Noee and his wif.
475 But of oo thing I warne thee ful right:
Be wel avised on that ilke night
That we been entred into shippes boord
That noon of us ne speke nought a word,
Ne clepe, ne crye, but been in his prayere,
480 For it is Goddes owene heeste dere.[8]
Thy wif and thou mote hange fer atwinne,[9]
For that bitwixe you shal be no sinne—
Namore in looking than ther shal in deede.
This ordinance is said: go, God thee speede.
485 Tomorwe at night whan men been alle asleepe,
Into oure kneeding-tubbes wol we creepe,
And sitten there, abiding Goddes grace.
Go now thy way, I have no lenger space°   *time*
To make of this no lenger sermoning.
490 Men sayn thus: 'Send the wise and say no thing.'
Thou art so wis it needeth thee nat teche:
Go save oure lif, and that I thee biseeche."
    This sely carpenter gooth forth his way:
Ful ofte he saide allas and wailaway,
495 And to his wif he tolde his privetee,
And she was war,° and knew it bet° than he,   *aware / better*
What al this quainte cast° was for to saye.°   *trick / mean*
But nathelees she ferde° as she wolde deye,   *acted*
And saide, "Allas, go forth thy way anoon.
500 Help us to scape,° or we been dede eechoon.   *escape*
I am thy trewe verray wedded wif:
Go, dere spouse, and help to save oure lif."
    Lo, which a greet thing is affeccioun!°   *emotion*

6. On high.   8. Precious commandment.
7. Toward the garden.   9. Far apart.

Men may dien of imaginacioun,
505 So deepe° may impression be take.   *deeply*
This sely carpenter biginneth quake;
Him thinketh verrailiche° that he may see   *truly*
Noees flood come walwing° as the see   *rolling*
To drenchen° Alison, his hony dere.   *drown*
510 He weepeth, waileth, maketh sory cheere;
He siketh° with ful many a sory swough,°   *sighs / breath*
And gooth and geteth him a kneeding-trough,
And after a tubbe and a kimelin,
And prively he sente hem to his in,°   *dwelling*
515 And heeng° hem in the roof in privetee;   *hung*
His owene hand he made laddres three,
To climben by the ronges° and the stalkes° *rungs / uprights*
Unto the tubbes hanging in the balkes,°   *rafters*
And hem vitailed,° bothe trough and tubbe,   *victualed*
520 With breed and cheese and good ale in a jubbe,°   *jug*
Suffising right ynough as for a day.
But er that he hadde maad al this array,
He sente his knave, and eek his wenche also,
Upon his neede[1] to London for to go.
525 And on the Monday whan it drow to[2] nighte,
He shette° his dore withouten candel-lighte,   *shut*
And dressed° alle thing as it sholde be,   *arranged*
And shortly up they clomben° alle three.   *climbed*
They seten° stille wel a furlong way.[3]   *sat*
530 "Now, Pater Noster, clum,"[4] saide Nicholay,
And "Clum" quod John, and "Clum" saide Alisoun.
This carpenter saide his devocioun,
And stille he sit° and biddeth his prayere,   *sits*
Awaiting on the rain, if he it heere.°   *might hear*
535 The dede sleep, for wery bisinesse,
Fil° on this carpenter right as I gesse   *fell*
Aboute corfew time,[5] or litel more.
For travailing of his gost[6] he groneth sore,
And eft° he routeth,° for his heed mislay.[7] *then / snores*
540 Down of the laddre stalketh Nicholay,
And Alison ful softe adown she spedde:
Withouten wordes mo they goon to bedde
Ther as the carpenter is wont to lie.
Ther was the revel and the melodye,
545 And thus lith° Alison and Nicholas   *lies*
In bisinesse of mirthe and of solas,°   *pleasure*
Til that the belle of Laudes[8] gan to ringe,
And freres in the chauncel° gonne singe.   *chancel*
This parissh clerk, this amorous Absolon,
550 That is for love alway so wo-bigoon,

1. On an errand for him.
2. Drew toward.
3. The time it takes to go a furlong (i.e., a few minutes).
4. Hush (?).
5. Probably about 8 P.M.
6. Affliction of his spirit.
7. Lay in the wrong position.
8. The first church service of the day.

Upon the Monday was at Oseneye,
With compaignye him to disporte and playe,
And axed upon caas⁹ a cloisterer
Ful prively after John the carpenter;
555 And he drow him apart out of the chirche,
And saide, "I noot:¹ I sawgh him here nought wirche
Sith Saterday. I trowe that he be went
For timber ther oure abbot hath him sent.
For he is wont for timber for to go,
560 And dwellen atte grange² a day or two.
Or elles he is at his hous, certain.
Where that he be I can nought soothly sayn."
    This Absolon ful jolif was and light,³
And thoughte, "Now is time to wake al night,
565 For sikerly,° I sawgh him nought stiringe   *certainly*
Aboute his dore sin day bigan to springe.
So mote° I thrive, I shal at cokkes crowe   *may*
Ful prively knokken at his windowe
That stant° ful lowe upon his bowres⁴ wal.   *stands*
570 To Alison now wol I tellen al
My love-longing,° for yet I shal nat misse   *lovesickness*
That at the leeste way⁵ I shal hire kisse.
Som manere confort shal I have, parfay.°   *in faith*
My mouth hath icched al this longe day:
575 That is a signe of kissing at the leeste.
Al night me mette⁶ eek I was at a feeste.
Therfore I wol go sleepe an hour or twaye,
And al the night thanne wol I wake and playe."
    Whan that the firste cok hath crowe, anoon
580 Up rist° this joly lovere Absolon,   *rises*
And him arrayeth gay at point devis.⁷
But first he cheweth grain⁸ and licoris,
To smellen sweete, er he hadde kembd° his heer.   *combed*
Under his tonge a trewe-love⁹ he beer,°   *bore*
585 For therby wende° he to be gracious.°   *supposed / pleasing*
He rometh° to the carpenteres hous,   *strolls*
And stille he stant° under the shot-windowe—   *stands*
Unto his brest it raughte,° it was so lowe—   *reached*
And ofte he cougheth with a semisoun.°   *small sound*
590 "What do ye, hony-comb, sweete Alisoun,
My faire brid,¹ my sweete cinamome?
Awaketh, lemman° myn, and speketh to me.   *mistress*
Wel litel thinken ye upon my wo
That for your love I swete° ther I go.   *sweat*
595 No wonder is though that I swelte° and swete: *melt*
I moorne as doth a lamb after the tete.°   *tit*

---

9. By chance; "cloisterer": here, a member of the religious order of Osney Abbey.
1. Don't know; "wirche": work.
2. The outlying farm belonging to the abbey.
3. Was very amorous and gay.
4. Bower's, bedroom's.
5. I.e., at least.
6. I dreamed.
7. To perfection.
8. Grain of paradise (a spice).
9. Sprig of a clover-like plant.
1. Bird or bride.

Ywis, lemman, I have swich love-longinge,
That lik a turtle° trewe is my moorninge: *dove*
I may nat ete namore than a maide."
600   "Go fro the windowe, Jakke fool," she saide.
"As help me God, it wol nat be com-pa-me.° *come-kiss-me*
I love another, and elles I were to blame,
Wel bet° than thee, by Jesu, Absolon. *better*
Go forth thy way or I wol caste a stoon,
605 And lat me sleepe, a twenty devele way."[2]
    "Allas," quod Absolon, "and wailaway,
That trewe love was evere so yvele biset.[3]
Thanne kis me, sin that it may be no bet,
For Jesus love and for the love of me."
610   "Woltou thanne go thy way therwith?" quod she.
"Ye, certes, lemman," quod this Absolon.
"Thanne maak thee redy," quod she. "I come anoon."
And unto Nicholas she saide stille,° *quietly*
"Now hust,° and thou shalt laughen al thy fille." *hush*
615 This Absolon down sette him on his knees,
And said, "I am a lord at alle degrees,[4]
For after this I hope ther cometh more.
Lemman, thy grace, and sweete brid, thyn ore!"° *mercy*
    The windowe she undooth, and that in haste.
620 "Have do," quod she, "come of and speed thee faste,
Lest that oure neighebores thee espye."
    This Absolon gan wipe his mouth ful drye:
Derk was the night as pich or as the cole,
And at the windowe out she putte hir hole,
625 And Absolon, him fil no bet ne wers,[5]
But with his mouth he kiste hir naked ers,
Ful savourly,° er he were war of this. *with relish*
Abak he sterte,° and thoughte it was amis, *started*
For wel he wiste a womman hath no beerd.
630 He felte a thing al rough and longe yherd,° *haired*
And saide, "Fy, allas, what have I do?"
    "Teehee," quod she, and clapte the windowe to.
And Absolon gooth forth a sory pas.[6]
    "A beerd, a beerd!" quod hende Nicholas,
635 "By Goddes corpus,° this gooth faire and weel." *body*
    This sely Absolon herde everydeel,
And on his lippe he gan for anger bite,
And to himself he saide, "I shal thee quite."° *repay*
    Who rubbeth now, who froteth° now his lippes *wipes*
640 With dust, with sond,[7] with straw, with cloth, with chippes,
But Absolon, that saith ful ofte allas?
"My soule bitake° I unto Satanas,° *commit / Satan*
But me were levere[8] than all this town," quod he,
"Of this despit° awroken° for to be. *insult / avenged*

2. In the name of twenty devils.
3. Ill-used.
4. In every way.
5. It befell him neither better nor worse.
6. I.e., walking sadly.
7. Sand.
8. I had rather.

645 Allas," quod he, "allas I ne hadde ybleint!"°   *turned aside*
His hote love was cold and al yqueint,°   *quenched*
For fro that time that he hadde kist hir ers
Of paramours he sette nought a kers,⁹
For he was heled° of his maladye.   *cured*
650 Ful ofte paramours he gan defye,°   *renounce*
And weep° as dooth a child that is ybete.   *wept*
A softe paas¹ he wente over the streete
Until° a smith men clepen daun Gervais,²   *to*
That in his forge smithed plough harneis:°   *equipment*
655 He sharpeth shaar and cultour³ bisily.
This Absolon knokketh al esily,°   *quietly*
And saide, "Undo, Gervais, and that anoon."°   *at once*
    "What, who artou?" "It am I, Absolon."
"What, Absolon? What, Cristes sweete tree!
660 Why rise ye so rathe?° Ey, benedicite,°   *early / bless me*
What aileth you? Som gay girl, God it woot,
Hath brought you thus upon the viritoot.⁴
By Sainte Note, ye woot wel what I mene."
    This Absolon ne roughte nat a bene⁵
665 Of al his play. No word again he yaf:
He hadde more tow on his distaf⁶
Than Gervais knew, and saide, "Freend so dere,
This hote cultour in the chimenee° here,   *fireplace*
As lene⁷ it me: I have therwith to doone.
670 I wol bringe it thee again ful soone."
    Gervais answerde, "Certes, werc it gold,
Or in a poke nobles alle untold,⁸
Thou sholdest have, as I am trewe smith.
Ey, Cristes fo,⁹ what wol ye do therwith?"
675   "Therof," quod Absolon, "be as be may.
I shal wel telle it thee another day,"
And caughte the cultour by the colde stele.°   *handle*
Ful softe out at the dore he gan to stele,
And wente unto the carpenteres wal:
680 He cougheth first and knokketh therwithal
Upon the windowe, right as he dide er.°   *before*
    This Alison answerde, "Who is ther
That knokketh so? I warante¹ it a thief."
    "Why, nay," quod he, "God woot, my sweete lief,°   *dear*
685 I am thyn Absolon, my dereling.
Of gold," quod he, "I have thee brought a ring—
My moder yaf it me, so God me save;
Ful fin it is and therto wel ygrave:°   *engraved*
This wol I yiven thee if thou me kisse."
690   This Nicholas was risen for to pisse,

9. He didn't care a piece of cress for woman's love.
1. I.e., quiet walk.
2. Master Gervais.
3. He sharpens plowshare and coulter (the turf-cutter on a plow).
4. I.e., on the prowl.

5. Didn't care a bean.
6. I.e., more on his mind.
7. I.e., please lend.
8. Or gold coins all uncounted in a bag.
9. Foe, i.e., Satan.
1. I.e., wager.

And thoughte he wolde amenden[2] al the jape:°   *joke*
He sholde kisse his ers er that he scape.
And up the windowe dide he hastily,
And out his ers he putteth prively,
695 Over the buttok to the haunche-boon.
    And therwith spak this clerk, this Absolon,
"Speek, sweete brid, I noot nought wher thou art."
This Nicholas anoon leet flee[3] a fart
As greet as it hadde been a thonder-dent°   *thunderbolt*
700 That with the strook he was almost yblent,°   *blinded*
And he was redy with his iren hoot,°   *hot*
And Nicholas amidde the ers he smoot:°   *smote*
Of gooth the skin an hande-brede° aboute;   *handsbreadth*
The hote cultour brende so his toute°   *buttocks*
705 That for the smert he wende for to[4] die;
As he were wood° for wo he gan to crye,   *crazy*
"Help! Water! Water! Help, for Goddes herte!"
    This carpenter out of his slomber sterte,
And herde oon cryen "Water!" as he were wood,
710 And thoughte, "Allas, now cometh Noweles[5] flood!"
He sette him up withoute wordes mo,
And with his ax he smoot the corde atwo,
And down gooth al: he foond neither to selle
Ne breed ne ale til he cam to the celle,[6]
715 Upon the floor, and ther aswoune° he lay.   *in a faint*
    Up sterte hire[7] Alison and Nicholay,
And criden "Out" and "Harrow" in the streete.
The neighebores, bothe smale and grete,
In ronnen for to gauren° on this man   *gape*
720 That aswoune lay bothe pale and wan,
For with the fal he brosten° hadde his arm;   *broken*
But stonde he moste° unto his owene harm,   *must*
For whan he spak he was anoon bore down[8]
With° hende Nicholas and Alisoun: *by*
725 They tolden every man that he was wood—
He was agast so of Noweles flood,
Thurgh fantasye, that of his vanitee°   *folly*
He hadde ybought him kneeding-tubbes three,
And hadde hem hanged in the roof above,
730 And that he prayed hem, for Goddes love,
To sitten in the roof, *par compaignye*.[9]
    The folk gan laughen at his fantasye.
Into the roof they kiken° and they cape,°   *peer / gape*
And turned al his harm unto a jape,°   *joke*
735 For what so that this carpenter answerde,
It was for nought: no man his reson° herde;   *argument*
With othes grete he was so sworn adown,

2. Improve on.
3. Let fly.
4. Thought he would.
5. The carpenter is confusing Noah and Noel (Christmas).
6. He found time to sell neither bread nor ale until he arrived at the foundation.
7. Started.
8. Refuted.
9. For company's sake.

That he was holden° wood in al the town,   *considered*
For every clerk anoonright heeld with other:
740 They saide, "The man was wood, my leve brother,"
And every wight gan laughen at this strif.°   *fuss*
Thus swived° was the carpenteres wif   *slept with*
For al his keeping° and his jalousye,   *guarding*
And Absolon hath kist hir nether° yë,   *lower*
745 And Nicholas is scalded in the toute:
This tale is doon, and God save al the route!°   *company*

The Wife of Bath's Prologue and Tale

The Prologue [1]

Experience, though noon auctoritee
Were in this world, is right ynough for me
To speke of wo that is in mariage:
For lordinges,° sith I twelf yeer was of age—   *gentlemen*
5 Thanked be God that is eterne on live—
Housbondes at chirche dore[2] I have had five
(If I so ofte mighte han wedded be),
And alle were worthy men in hir degree.

1. The Wife of Bath is the remarkable culmination of many centuries of an antifeminism that was particularly nurtured by the medieval church. In their eagerness to exalt the spiritual ideal of chastity, certain theologians developed an idea of womankind that was nothing less than monstrous. According to these, insatiable lecherousness and indomitable shrewishness (plus a host of attendant vices) were characteristic of women. This notion was given most eloquent expression by St. Jerome in his attack (written about A.D. 400) on the monk Jovinian, who had uttered some good words for matrimony, and it is Jerome that the Wife of Bath comes forward not, curiously enough, to refute, but to confirm. The first part of her Prologue is a mass of quotations from that part of Jerome's tract where he is appealing to St. Paul's Epistle (I Corinthians vii) for antimatrimonial authority. On the narrow issue of her right to remarry, to be sure, the Wife finds fault—rather mildly—with Jerome, but on the more central issue of why she wishes to marry and remarry she expresses no disagreement with him. Yet in the failure to defend herself and refute the saint, she somehow manages to make the latter's point of view look a good deal sillier than she looks herself; and instead of embodying the satire on womanhood that one would expect because of her origins in antifeminist literature, she becomes instead a satirist of the grotesquely woman-hating men who had first defined her personality.

More important, because of the extraordinary vitality that Chaucer has imparted to her, the Wife of Bath by the end of her Prologue comes to bear a less significant relation to satire than she does to reality itself. Making the best of the world in which they have arbitrarily been placed is the occupation of both the Wife of Bath and the reader, and it is in doing this that the Wife ceases to be a monstrosity of fiction and becomes alive—wonderfully alive, both to the potentialities of which she and her world are capable and to the limitations that even in her world time and age place upon her. It is especially in the attitude with which she regards these limitations that her fiction becomes most true to life, since they are also the limitations imposed by the real world. Despite the loss of youth and beauty, her best weapons, she faces her future not only with a woman's ability to endure and enjoy what she cannot reshape, but also with a zest for life on its own terms that is almost more than human.

2. The actual wedding ceremony was celebrated at the church door, not in the chancel.

But me was told, certain, nat longe agoon is,
10 That sith that Crist ne wente nevere but ones
To wedding in the Cane[3] of Galilee,
That by the same ensample° taughte he me   *example*
That I ne sholde wedded be but ones.
Herke eek,° lo, which° a sharp word for the nones,[4]   *also / what*
15 Biside a welle, Jesus, God and man,
Spak in repreve° of the Samaritan: *reproof*
"Thou hast yhad five housbondes," quod he,
"And that ilke° man that now hath thee   *same*
Is nat thyn housbonde." Thus saide he certain.
20 What that he mente therby I can nat sayn,
But that I axe° why the fifthe man   *ask*
Was noon housbonde to the Samaritan?[5]
How manye mighte she han in mariage?
Yit herde I nevere tellen in myn age
25 Upon this nombre diffinicioun.°   *definition*
Men may divine° and glosen° up and down,   *guess / interpret*
But wel I woot,° expres,° withouten lie,   *know / expressly*
God bad us for to wexe[6] and multiplye:
That gentil text can I wel understonde.
30 Eek wel I woot° he saide that myn housbonde   *know*
Sholde lete° fader and moder and take to me,[7]   *leave*
But of no nombre mencion made he—
Of bigamye or of octogamye:[8]
Why sholde men thanne speke of it vilainye?
35 Lo, here the wise king daun° Salomon: *master*
I trowe° he hadde wives many oon,[9]   *believe*
As wolde God it leveful° were to me   *permissible*
To be refresshed half so ofte as he.
Which yifte[1] of God hadde he for alle his wives!
40 No man hath swich that in this world alive is.
God woot this noble king, as to my wit,°   *knowledge*
The firste night hadde many a merye fit°   *bout*
With eech of hem, so wel was him on live.[2]
Blessed be God that I have wedded five,
45 Of whiche I have piked out the beste,[3]
Bothe of hir nether° purs and of hir cheste.°   *lower / moneybox*
Diverse scoles maken parfit° clerkes,   *perfect*
And diverse practikes[4] in sondry werkes
Maken the werkman parfit sikerly:°   *certainly*
50 Of five housbondes scoleying° am I.   *schooling*
Welcome the sixte whan that evere he shal![5]

3. Cana (see John ii.1).
4. To the purpose.
5. Christ was actually referring to a sixth man who was not married to the Samaritan woman (cf. John iv.6 ff.).
6. I.e., increase. See Genesis i.28.
7. See Matthew xix.5.
8. I.e., of two or even eight marriages. The Wife is referring to successive, rather than simultaneous marriages.
9. Solomon had 700 wives and 300 concubines (I Kings xi.3).
1. What a gift.
2. I.e., so pleasant a life he had.
3. Whom I have cleaned out of everything worthwhile.
4. Practical experiences.
5. I.e., shall come along.

For sith I wol nat kepe me chast in al,
Whan my housbonde is fro the world agoon,
Som Cristen man shal wedde me anoon.°   right away
55 For thanne th'Apostle[6] saith that I am free
To wedde, a Goddes half,[7] where it liketh me.
He said that to be wedded is no sinne:
Bet° is to be wedded than to brinne.°   better / burn
What rekketh me[8] though folk saye vilainye
60 Of shrewed° Lamech[9] and his bigamye?   cursed
I woot wel Abraham was an holy man,
And Jacob eek, as fer as evere I can,°   know
And eech of hem hadde wives mo than two,
And many another holy man also.
65 Where can ye saye in any manere age
That hye God defended° mariage   prohibited
By expres word? I praye you, telleth me.
Or where comanded he virginitee?
I woot as wel as ye, it is no drede,°   doubt
70 Th'Apostle, whan he speketh of maidenhede,°   maidenhood
He saide that precept therof hadde he noon:
Men may conseile a womman to be oon,°   single
But conseiling nis no comandement.
He putte it in oure owene juggement.
75 For hadde God comanded maidenhede,
Thanne hadde he dampned° wedding with the
            deede;[1]   condemned
And certes, if there were no seed ysowe,
Virginitee, thanne wherof sholde it growe?
Paul dorste nat comanden at the leeste
80 A thing of which his maister yaf° no heeste.°   gave / command
The dart[2] is set up for virginitee:
Cacche whoso may, who renneth° best lat see.   runs
But this word is nought take of[3] every wight,
But ther as[4] God list° yive it of his might.   it pleases
85 I woot wel that th'Apostle was a maide,°   virgin
But nathelees, though that he wroot and saide
He wolde that every wight were swich° as he,   such
Al nis but conseil to virginitee;
And for to been a wif he yaf me leve
90 Of indulgence; so nis it no repreve°   disgrace
To wedde me[5] if that my make° die,   mate
Withouten excepcion of bigamye[6]—

6. St. Paul.
7. On God's behalf; "it liketh me": I
please.
8. What do I care.
9. The first man whom the Bible mentions as having two wives (Genesis
iv.19–24).

1. I.e., at the same time.
2. I.e., prize in a race.
3. Understood for, i.e., applicable to.
4. Where.
5. For me to marry.
6. I.e., without there being any legal objection on the score of remarriage.

Al° were it good no womman for to touche   *although*
(He mente as in his bed or in his couche,
95 For peril is bothe fir° and tow° t'assemble—   *fire / flax*
Ye knowe what this ensample may resemble).[7]
This al and som,[8] he heeld virginitee
More parfit than wedding in freletee.°   *frailty*
(Freletee clepe I but if[9] that he and she
100 Wolde leden al hir lif in chastitee.)
I graunte it wel, I have noon envye
Though maidenhede preferre° bigamye:°   *excel / remarriage*
It liketh hem to be clene in body and gost.°   *spirit*
Of myn estaat ne wol I make no boost;
105 For wel ye knowe, a lord in his houshold
Ne hath nat every vessel al of gold:
Some been of tree,° and doon hir lord servise.   *wood*
God clepeth folk to him in sondry wise,
And everich hath of God a propre[1] yifte,
110 Som this, som that, as him liketh shifte.°   *ordain*
Virginitee is greet perfeccioun,
And continence eek with devocioun,
But Crist, that of perfeccion is welle,°   *source*
Bad nat every wight he sholde go selle
115 Al that he hadde and yive it to the poore,
And in swich wise folwe him and his fore:[2]
He spak to hem that wolde live parfitly°—   *perfectly*
And lordinges, by youre leve, that am nat I.
I wol bistowe the flour of al myn age
120 In th'actes and in fruit of mariage.
    Telle me also, to what conclusioun°   *end*
Were membres maad of generacioun
And of so parfit wis a wrighte ywrought?[3]
Trusteth right wel, they were nat maad for nought.
125 Glose° whoso wol, and saye bothe up and down   *interpret*
That they were maked for purgacioun
Of urine, and oure bothe thinges smale
Was eek to knowe a femele from a male,
And for noon other cause—saye ye no?
130 Th'experience woot it is nought so.
So that the clerkes be nat with me wrothe,
I saye this, that they been maad for bothe—
That is to sayn, for office° and for ese   *excretion*
Of engendrure, ther we nat God displese.
135 Why sholde men elles in hir bookes sette
That man shal yeelde[4] to his wif hir dette?

---

7. I.e., what this metaphor may apply to.
8. This is all there is to it.
9. Frailty I call it unless.
1. I.e., his own.

2. Matthew xix.21: "Fore": footsteps.
3. And wrought by so perfectly wise a maker.
4. I.e., pay.

Now wherwith sholde he make his payement
If he ne used his sely° instrument?   innocent
Thanne were they maad upon a creature
140 To purge urine, and eek for engendrure.
      But I saye nought that every wight is holde,°   bound
That hath swich harneis° as I to you tolde,   equipment
To goon and usen hem in engendrure:
Thanne sholde men take of chastitee no cure.°   heed
145 Crist was a maide° and shapen as a man,   virgin
And many a saint sith that the world bigan,
Yit lived they evere in parfit chastitee.
I nil envye no virginitee:
Lat hem be breed° of pured° whete seed,   bread / refined
150 And lat us wives hote° barly breed—   be called
And yit with barly breed, Mark telle can,
Oure Lord Jesu refresshed many a man.[5]
In swich estaat as God hath cleped us
I wol persevere: I nam nat precious.°   fastidious
155 In wifhood wol I use myn instrument
As freely° as my Makere hath it sent.   generously
If I be daungerous,° God yive me sorwe: stand-offish
Myn housbonde shal it han bothe eve and morwe,°   morning
Whan that him list[6] come forth and paye his dette.
160 An housbonde wol I have, I wol nat lette,[7]
Which shal be bothe my dettour° and my thral,°   debtor / slave
And have his tribulacion withal
Upon his flessh whil that I am his wif.
I have the power during al my lif
165 Upon his propre° body, and nat he: own
Right thus th'Apostle tolde it unto me,
And bad oure housbondes for to love us weel.
Al this sentence° me liketh everydeel.°   purport / entirely

                    [AN INTERLUDE]

      Up sterte° the Pardoner and that anoon: started
"Now dame," quod he, "by God and by Saint John,
170 Ye been a noble prechour in this cas.
I was aboute to wedde a wif: allas,
What° sholde I bye° it on my flessh so dere?   why / purchase
Yit hadde I levere wedde no wif to-yere."°   this year
175 "Abid," quod she, "my tale is nat bigonne.
Nay, thou shalt drinken of another tonne,°   tun
Er that I go, shal savoure wors than ale.
And whan that I have told thee forth my tale
Of tribulacion in mariage,
180 Of which I am expert in al myn age—

5. In the descriptions of the miracle of the loaves and fishes, it is actually John, not Mark, who mentions barley bread (vi.9).
6. When he wishes to.
7. I will make no difficulty.

This is to saye, myself hath been the whippe—
Thanne maistou chese° wheither thou wolt sippe   *choose*
Of thilke° tonne that I shal abroche:°   *this same / broach*
Be war of it, er thou too neigh approche,
185 For I shal telle ensamples mo than ten.
'Whoso that nile° be war by othere men,   *would not*
By him shal othere men corrected be.'
Thise same wordes writeth Ptolomee:
Rede in his *Almageste* and take it there."[8]
190   "Dame, I wolde praye you if youre wil it were,"
Saide this Pardoner, "as ye bigan,
Telle forth youre tale; spareth for no man,
And teche us yonge men of youre practike."°   *mode of operation*
"Gladly," quod she, "sith it may you like;°   *please*
195 But that I praye to al this compaignye,
If that I speke after my fantasye,[9]
As taketh nat agrief° of that I saye,   *amiss*
For myn entente nis but for to playe."

[THE WIFE CONTINUES]

Now sire, thanne wol I telle you forth my tale.
200 As evere mote I drinke win or ale,
I shal saye sooth: tho° housbondes that I hadde,   *those*
As three of hem were goode, and two were badde.
The three men were goode, and riche, and olde;
Unnethe° mighte they the statut holde   *with difficulty*
205 In which they were bounden unto me—
Ye woot wel what I mene of this, pardee.
As help me God, I laughe whan I thinke
How pitously anight I made hem swinke;°   *work*
And by my fay,° I tolde of it no stoor:[1]   *faith*
210 They hadde me yiven hir land and hir tresor;
Me needed nat do lenger diligence
To winne hir love or doon hem reverence.
They loved me so wel, by God above,
That I ne tolde no daintee of[2] hir love.
215 A wis womman wol bisye hire evere in oon[3]
To gete hire love, ye, ther as she hath noon.
But sith I hadde hem hoolly in myn hand,
And sith that they hadde yiven me al hir land,
What° sholde I take keep° hem for to plese,   *why / care*
220 But it were for my profit and myn ese?
I sette hem so awerke,° by my fay,°   *awork / faith*
That many a night they songen° wailaway.   *sang*

---

8. The *Almagest*, an astronomical work by the Greek astronomer and mathematician Ptolemy (second century A.D.), contains no such aphorism. The aphorism does, however, appear in a collection ascribed to him.
9. If I speak according to my whim.
1. I set no store by it.
2. Set no value on.
3. Busy herself constantly.

The bacon was nat fet° for hem, I trowe,   *brought back*
That some men han in Essexe at Dunmowe.[4]
225 I governed hem so wel after° my lawe   *according to*
That eech of hem ful blisful was and fawe°   *glad*
To bringe me gaye thinges fro the faire;
They were ful glade whan I spak hem faire,
For God it woot, I chidde° hem spitously.°   *chided / cruelly*
230   Now herkneth how I bar me[5] proprely:
Ye wise wives, that conne understonde,
Thus sholde ye speke and bere him wrong on honde[6]—
For half so boldely can ther no man
Swere and lie as a woman can.
235 I saye nat this by wives that been wise,
But if it be whan they hem misavise.[7]
A wis wif, if that she can hir good,[8]
Shal bere him on hande the cow is wood,[9]
And take witnesse of hir owene maide
240 Of hir assent.[1] But herkneth how I saide:
"Sire olde cainard,° is this thyn array?[2]   *sluggard*
Why is my neighebores wif so gay?
She is honoured overal ther she gooth:
I sitte at hoom; I have no thrifty° cloth.   *decent*
245 What doostou at my neighebores hous?
Is she so fair? Artou so amorous?
What roune° ye with oure maide, benedicite?[3]   *whisper*
Sire olde lechour, lat thy japes° be.   *tricks, intrigues*
And if I have a gossib° or a freend,   *confidant*
250 Withouten gilt ye chiden as a feend,
If that I walke or playe unto his hous.
Thou comest hoom as dronken as a mous,
And prechest on thy bench, with yvel preef.[4]
Thou saist to me, it is a greet meschief°   *misfortune*
255 To wedde a poore womman for costage.[5]
And if that she be riche, of heigh parage,°   *descent*
Thanne saistou that it is a tormentrye
To suffre hir pride and hir malencolye.
And if that she be fair, thou verray knave,
260 Thou saist that every holour° wol hire have: *whoremonger*
She may no while in chastitee abide
That is assailed upon eech a side.
   "Thou saist som folk desiren us for richesse,

4. The Dunmow flitch was awarded to the couple who after a year of marriage could claim no quarrels, no regrets, and the desire, if freed, to remarry one another.
5. Bore myself, behaved.
6. Accuse him falsely.
7. When they make a mistake.
8. If she knows what's good for her.
9. Shall persuade him the chough has gone crazy. The chough, or jackdaw, was popularly supposed to tell husbands of their wives' infidelity.
1. And call as a witness her maid, who is on her side.
2. I.e., is this how you behave?
3. Bless me.
4. I.e., (may you have) bad luck.
5. Because of the expense.

Som[6] for oure shap, and som for oure fairnesse,
265 And som for she can outher° singe or daunce, *either*
And som for gentilesse and daliaunce,° *flirtatiousness*
Som for hir handes and hir armes smale°— *slender*
Thus gooth al to the devel by thy tale![7]
Thou saist men may nat keepe[8] a castel wal,
270 It may so longe assailed been overal.° *everywhere*
And if that she be foul, thou saist that she
Coveiteth° every man that she may see; *desires*
For as a spaniel she wol on him lepe,
Til that she finde som man hire to chepe.° *buy*
275 Ne noon so grey goos gooth ther in the lake,
As, saistou, wol be withoute make;° *mate*
And saist it is an hard thing for to weelde° *possess*
A thing that no man wol, his thankes, heelde.[9]
Thus saistou, lorel,° whan thou goost to bedde, *loafer*
280 And that no wis man needeth for to wedde,
Ne no man that entendeth° unto hevene— *aims*
With wilde thonder-dint[1] and firy levene
Mote thy welked nekke be tobroke![2]
Thou saist that dropping° houses and eek smoke *leaking*
285 And chiding wives maken men to flee
Out of hir owene hous: a, benedicite,
What aileth swich an old man for to chide?
Thou saist we wives wil oure vices hide
Til we be fast,[3] and thanne we wol hem shewe—
290 Wel may that be a proverbe of a shrewe!° *villain*
Thou saist that oxen, asses, hors,° and houndes, *horses*
They been assayed at diverse stoundes;° *times*
Bacins, lavours,° er that men hem bye, *washbowls*
Spoones, stooles, and al swich housbondrye,° *household goods*
295 And so be° pottes, clothes, and array°— *are / clothing*
But folk of wives maken noon assay
Til they be wedded—olde dotard shrewe!
And thanne, saistou, we wil oure vices shewe.
Thou saist also that it displeseth me
300 But if that thou wolt praise my beautee,
And but thou poure alway upon my face,
And clepe me 'Faire Dame' in every place,
And but thou make a feeste on thilke day
That I was born, and make me fressh and gay,
305 And but thou do to my norice° honour, *nurse*
And to my chamberere within my bowr,[4]
And to my fadres folk, and his allies[5]—

6. "Som," in this and the following
lines, means "one."
7. I.e., according to your story.
8. I.e., keep safe.
9. No man would willingly hold.
1. Thunderbolt; "levene": lightning.

2. May thy withered neck be broken!
3. I.e., married.
4. And to my chambermaid within my
bedroom.
5. Relatives by marriage.

Thus saistou, olde barel-ful of lies.
And yit of our apprentice Janekin,
310 For his crispe° heer, shining as gold so fin,   *curly*
And for he squiereth me bothe up and down,
Yit hastou caught a fals suspecioun;
I wil° him nat though thou were deed° tomorwe.   *want / dead*
  "But tel me this, why hidestou with sorwe[6]
315 The keyes of thy cheste away fro me?
It is my good° as wel as thyn, pardee.   *property*
What, weenestou° make an idiot of oure dame? *do you think to*
Now by that lord that called is Saint Jame,
Thou shalt nought bothe, though thou were wood,°   *furious*
320 Be maister of my body and of my good:
That oon thou shalt forgo, maugree thine yën.[7]
  "What helpeth it of me enquere° and spyen?   *inquire*
I trowe thou woldest loke° me in thy cheste.   *lock*
Thou sholdest saye, 'Wif, go wher thee leste.° *it may please*
325 Taak youre disport. I nil leve° no tales: *believe*
I knowe you for a trewe wif, dame Alis.'
We love no man that taketh keep or charge[8]
Wher that we goon: we wol been at oure large.[9]
Of alle men yblessed mote he be
330 The wise astrologen° daun Ptolomee,   *astronomer*
That saith this proverbe in his *Almageste*:
'Of alle men his wisdom is the hyeste
That rekketh° nat who hath the world in honde.'   *cares*
By this proverbe thou shalt understonde,
335 Have thou[1] ynough, what thar° thee rekke or care *need*
How merily that othere folkes fare?
For certes, olde dotard, by youre leve,
Ye shal han queinte° right ynough at eve: *pudendum*
He is too greet a nigard that wil werne°   *refuse*
340 A man to lighte a candle at his lanterne;
He shal han nevere the lasse° lighte, pardee.   *less*
Have thou ynough, thee thar nat plaine thee.[2]
  "Thou saist also that if we make us gay
With clothing and with precious array,
345 That it is peril of oure chastitee,
And yit with sorwe thou moste enforce thee,[3]
And saye thise wordes in th'Apostles name:
'In habit° maad with chastitee and shame   *clothing*
Ye wommen shal apparaile you,' quod he,
350 'And nat in tressed heer[4] and gay perree,°   *jewelry*
As perles ne with gold ne clothes riche.'[5]

---

6. I.e., with sorrow to you.
7. Despite your eyes—i.e., despite anything you can do about it.
8. Notice or interest.
9. I.e., liberty.

1. If you have.
2. I.e., you need not complain.
3. Strengthen your position.
4. I.e., elaborate hairdo.
5. See I Timothy ii.9.

After thy text, ne after thy rubriche,[6]
I wol nat werke as muchel as a gnat.
Thou saidest this, that I was lik a cat:
355 For whoso wolde senge° a cattes skin,   *singe*
Thanne wolde the cat wel dwellen in his in;°   *lodging*
And if the cattes skin be slik° and gay,   *sleek*
She wol nat dwelle in house half a day,
But forth she wol, er any day be dawed,[7]
360 To shewe her skin and goon a-caterwawed.°   *caterwauling*
This is to saye, if I be gay, sire shrewe,
I wol renne° out, my borel° for to shewe.   *run / clothing*
Sire olde fool, what helpeth[8] thee t'espyen?
Though thou praye Argus with his hundred yën
365 To be my wardecors,° as he can best,   *bodyguard*
In faith, he shal nat keepe° me but me lest:[9]   *guard*
Yit coude I make his beerd,[1] so mote I thee.°   *thrive*
"Thou saidest eek that ther been thinges three,
The whiche thinges troublen al this erthe,
370 And that no wight may endure the ferthe.°   *fourth*
O leve° sire shrewe, Jesu shorte° thy lif!   *dear / shorten*
Yit prechestou and saist an hateful wif
Yrekened is for oon of thise meschaunces.
Been ther nat none othere resemblaunces
375 That ye may likne youre parables to,[2]
But if[3] a sely° wif be oon of tho?   *innocent*
"Thou liknest eek wommanes love to helle,
To bareine° land ther water may nat dwelle;   *barren*
Thou liknest it also to wilde fir—
380 The more it brenneth,° the more it hath desir   *burns*
To consumen every thing that brent° wol be;   *burned*
Thou saist right° as wormes shende° a tree,   *just / destroy*
Right so a wif destroyeth hir housbonde—
This knowen they that been to wives bonde."°   *bound*
385 Lordinges, right thus, as ye han understonde,
Bar I stifly mine olde housbondes on honde[4]
That thus they saiden in hir dronkenesse—
And al was fals, but that I took witnesse
On Janekin and on my nece also.
390 O Lord, the paine I dide hem and the wo,
Ful giltelees, by Goddes sweete pine!°   *suffering*
For as an hors I coude bite and whine;°   *whinny*
I coude plaine° and° I was in the gilt,   *complain / if*
Or elles often time I hadde been spilt.°   *ruined*
395 Whoso that first to mille comth first grint.°   *grinds*

6. Rubric, i.e., direction.
7. Has dawned.
8. What does it help.
9. Unless I please.
1. I.e., deceive him.
2. Isn't there something else appropriate that you can apply your metaphors to?
3. Unless.
4. I rigorously accused my old husbands.

I plained first: so was oure werre stint.[5]
They were ful glade to excusen hem ful blive°   *quickly*
Of thing of which they nevere agilte hir live.[6]
Of wenches wolde I beren hem on honde,
400 Whan that for sik[7] they mighte unnethe° stonde,   *scarcely*
Yit tikled I his herte for that he
Wende° I hadde had of him so greet cheertee.[8]   *thought*
I swoor that al my walking out by nighte
Was for to espye wenches that he dighte.[9]
405 Under that colour[1] hadde I many a mirthe.
For al swich wit is yiven us in oure birthe:
Deceite, weeping, spinning God hath yive
To wommen kindely° whil they may live.   *naturally*
And thus of oo thing I avaunte me:[2]
410 At ende I hadde the bet° in eech degree,   *better*
By sleighte or force, or by som manere thing,
As by continuel murmur° or grucching;°   *complaint / grumbling*
Namely° abedde hadden they meschaunce: *especially*
Ther wolde I chide and do hem no plesaunce;[3]
415 I wolde no lenger in the bed abide
If that I felte his arm over my side,
Til he hadde maad his raunson° unto me;   *ransom*
Thanne wolde I suffre him do his nicetee.°   *lust*
And therfore every man this tale I telle:
420 Winne whoso may, for al is for to selle;
With empty hand men may no hawkes lure.
For winning° wolde I al his lust endure,   *profit*
And make me a feined appetit—
And yit in bacon[4] hadde I nevere delit.
425 That made me that evere I wolde hem chide;
For though the Pope hadde seten° hem biside,   *sat*
I wolde nought spare hem at hir owene boord.
For by my trouthe, I quitte° hem word for word.   *repaid*
As help me verray God omnipotent,
430 Though I right now sholde make my testament,
I ne owe hem nat a word that it nis quit.
I broughte it so aboute by my wit
That they moste yive it up as for the beste,
Or elles hadde we nevere been in reste;
435 For though he looked as a wood° leoun,   *furious*
Yit sholde he faile of his conclusioun.°   *object*
　　Thanne wolde I saye, "Goodelief, taak keep,[5]
How mekely looketh Wilekin, oure sheep!

---

5. Our war brought to an end.
6. Of a thing in which they never offended in their lives.
7. I.e., sickness.
8. Affection.
9. Had intercourse with.

1. I.e., excuse.
2. Boast.
3. Show them no affection.
4. I.e., old meat.
5. Good friend, take notice.

Com neer my spouse, lat me ba° thy cheeke—   *kiss*
440 Ye sholden be al pacient and meeke,
And han a sweete-spiced[6] conscience,
Sith ye so preche of Jobes pacience;
Suffreth alway, sin ye so wel can preche;
And but ye do, certain, we shal you teche
445 That it is fair to han a wif in pees.
Oon of us two moste bowen, doutelees,
And sith a man is more resonable
Than womman is, ye mosten been suffrable.°   *patient*
What aileth you to grucche° thus and grone?   *grumble*
450 Is it for ye wolde have my queinte° allone?   *pudendum*
Why, taak it al—lo, have it everydeel.°   *altogether*
Peter, I shrewe° you but ye love it weel.   *curse*
For if I wolde selle my bele chose,[7]
I coude walke as fressh as is a rose;
455 But I wol keepe it for youre owene tooth.°   *taste*
Ye be to blame. By God, I saye you sooth!"
Swiche manere° wordes hadde we on honde.   *kind of*
Now wol I speke of my ferthe° housbonde.   *fourth*
   My ferthe housbonde was a revelour—
460 This is to sayn, he hadde a paramour°—   *mistress*
And I was yong and ful of ragerye,°   *wantonness*
Stibourne° and strong and joly as a pie:°   *untamable / magpie*
How coude I daunce to an harpe smale,°   *gracefully*
And singe, ywis,° as any nightingale,   *indeed*
465 Whan I hadde dronke a draughte of sweete win.
Metellius, the foule cherl, the swin,
That with a staf birafte° his wif hir lif   *deprived*
For° she drank win, though I hadde been his wif,   *because*
Ne sholde nat han daunted me fro drinke;
470 And after win on Venus moste° I thinke,   *must*
For also siker° as cold engendreth hail,   *sure*
A likerous° mouth moste han a likerous° tail: *greedy / lecherous*
In womman vinolent° is no defence—   *bibulous*
This knowen lechours by experience.
475   But Lord Crist, whan that it remembreth me[8]
Upon my youthe and on my jolitee,
It tikleth me aboute myn herte roote—
Unto this day it dooth myn herte boote°   *good*
That I have had my world as in my time.
480 But age, allas, that al wol envenime,°   *poison*
Hath me biraft[9] my beautee and my pith—
Lat go, farewel, the devel go therwith!
The flour is goon, ther is namore to telle:
The bren° as I best can now moste I selle;   *bran*
485 But yit to be right merye wol I fonde.°   *strive*

6. I.e., delicate.   8. When I look back.
7. Fair thing.   9. Has taken away from me.

Now wol I tellen of my ferthe housbonde.
    I saye I hadde in herte greet despit
That he of any other hadde delit,
But he was quit,° by God and by Saint Joce: *paid back*
490 I made him of the same wode a croce[1]—
Nat of my body in no foul manere—
But, certainly, I made folk swich cheere
That in his owene grece I made him frye,
For angre and for verray jalousye.
495 By God, in erthe I was his purgatorye,
For which I hope his soule be in glorye.
For God it woot, he sat ful ofte and soong°   *sang*
Whan that his sho ful bitterly him wroong.°   *pinched*
Ther was no wight save God and he that wiste°   *knew*
500 In many wise how sore I him twiste.
He deide whan I cam fro Jerusalem,
And lith ygrave under the roode-beem,[2]
Al° is his tombe nought so curious[3]   *although*
As was the sepulcre of him Darius,
505 Which that Apelles wroughte subtilly:[4]
It nis but wast to burye him preciously.°   *expensively*
Lat him fare wel, God yive his soule reste;
He is now in his grave and in his cheste.
    Now of my fifthe housbonde wol I telle—
510 God lete his soule nevere come in helle—
And yit he was to me the moste shrewe:[5]
That feele I on my ribbes al by rewe,[6]
And evere shal unto myn ending day.
But in oure bed he was so fressh and gay,
515 And therwithal so wel coulde he me glose°   *wheedle*
Whan that he wolde han my bele chose,
That though he hadde me bet° on every boon,° *beaten / bone*
He coude winne again my love anoon.°   *immediately*
I trowe I loved him best for that he
520 Was of his love daungerous[7] to me.
We wommen han, if that I shal nat lie,
In this matere a quainte fantasye:
Waite what[8] thing we may nat lightly° have,   *easily*
Therafter wol we crye al day and crave;
525 Forbede us thing, and that desiren we;
Preesse on us faste, and thanne wol we flee.
With daunger oute we al oure chaffare:[9]
Greet prees° at market maketh dere° ware, *crowd / expensive*

1. I made him a cross of the same wood. The proverb has much the same sense as the one quoted in line 493.
2. And lies buried under the rood beam (the crucifix beam running between nave and chancel).
3. Carefully wrought.
4. According to medieval legend, the artist Apelles decorated the tomb of Darius, king of the Persians.
5. Worst rascal.
6. In a row.
7. I.e., he played hard to get.
8. "Waite what": whatever.
9. With coyness, we spread out our merchandise.

And too greet chepe is holden at litel pris.[1]
530 This knoweth every womman that is wis.
    My fifthe housbonde—God his soule blesse!—
Which that I took for love and no richesse,
He somtime was a clerk at Oxenforde,
And hadde laft° scole and wente at hoom to boorde   *left*
535 With my gossib,° dwelling in oure town—   *confidante*
God have hir soule!—hir name was Alisoun;
She knew myn herte and eek my privetee°   *secrets*
Bet° than oure parissh preest, as mote I thee.°   *better / thrive*
To hire biwrayed° I my conseil° al,   *disclosed / secrets*
540 For hadde myn housbonde pissed on a wal,
Or doon a thing that sholde han cost his lif,
To hire,° and to another worthy wif,   *her*
And to my nece which I loved weel,
I wolde han told his conseil everydeel;°   *entirely*
545 And so I dide ful often, God it woot,
That made his face often reed° and hoot°   *red / hot*
For verray shame, and blamed himself for he
Hadde told to me so greet a privetee.
    And so bifel that ones in a Lente—
550 So often times I to my gossib wente,
For evere yit I loved to be gay,
And for to walke in March, Averil, and May,
From hous to hous, to heere sondry tales—
That Janekin clerk and my gossib dame Alis
555 And I myself into the feeldes wente.
Myn housbonde was at London al that Lente:
I hadde the better leiser for to playe,
And for to see, and eek for to be seye°   *seen*
Of lusty folk—what wiste I wher my grace°   *luck*
560 Was shapen° for to be, or in what place?   *destined*
Therfore I made my visitaciouns
To vigilies[2] and to processiouns,
To preching eek, and to thise pilgrimages,
To playes of miracles and to mariages,
565 And wered upon[3] my gaye scarlet gites°—   *dress*
Thise wormes ne thise motthes ne thise mites,
Upon my peril, frete° hem neveradeel: *ate*
And woostou why? For they were used weel.
    Now wol I tellen forth what happed me.
570 I saye that in the feeldes walked we,
Til trewely we hadde swich daliaunce,°   *flirtation*
This clerk and I, that of my purveyaunce°   *foresight*
I spak to him and saide him how that he,
If I were widwe, sholde wedde me.

---

1. Too good a bargain is held at little   2. Feasts preceding a saint's day.
value.   3. Wore.

575 For certainly, I saye for no bobaunce,°   *boast*
    Yit was I nevere withouten purveyaunce
    Of mariage n'of othere thinges eek:
    I holde a mouses herte nought worth a leek
    That hath but oon hole for to sterte° to,   *run*
580 And if that faile thanne is al ydo.[4]
    I bar him on hand[5] he hadde enchaunted me
    (My dame taughte me that subtiltee);
    And eek I saide I mette° of him al night: *dreamed*
    He wolde han slain me as I lay upright,°   *supine*
585 And al my bed was ful of verray blood—
    "But yit I hope that ye shul do me good;
    For blood bitokeneth gold, as me was taught."
    And al was fals, I dremed of it right naught,
    But as I folwed ay my dames° lore°   *mother's / teaching*
590 As wel of that as othere thinges more.
    But now sire—lat me see, what shal I sayn?
    Aha, by God, I have my tale again.
        Whan that my ferthe housbonde was on beere,°   *bier*
    I weep° algate,° and made sory cheere,   *wept / anyhow*
595 As wives moten,° for it is usage,°   *must / custom*
    And with my coverchief covered my visage;
    But for I was purveyed° of a make.°   *provided / mate*
    I wepte but smale, and that I undertake.°   *guarantee*
        To chirche was myn housbonde born amorwe[6]
600 With neighebores that for him maden sorwe,
    And Janekin oure clerk was oon of tho.
    As help me God, whan that I saw him go
    After the beere, me thoughte he hadde a paire
    Of legges and of feet so clene[7] and faire,
605 That al myn herte I yaf unto his hold.°   *possession*
    He was, I trowe,° twenty winter old,   *believe*
    And I was fourty, if I shal saye sooth—
    But yit I hadde alway a coltes tooth:[8]
    Gat-toothed° was I, and that bicam me weel;   *gap-toothed*
610 I hadde the prente[9] of Sainte Venus seel.
    As help me God, I was a lusty oon,
    And fair and riche and yong and wel-bigoon,°   *well-situated*
    And trewely, as mine housbondes tolde me,
    I hadde the beste quoniam° mighte be.   *pudendum*
615 For certes I am al Venerien[1]
    In feeling, and myn herte is Marcien:
    Venus me yaf my lust, my likerousnesse,°   *lecherousness*
    And Mars yaf me my sturdy hardinesse.

4. I.e., the game is up.
5. I pretended to him.
6. In the morning.
7. I.e., neat.
8. I.e., youthful appetites.
9. Print, i.e., a birthmark; "seel": seal.
1. Astrologically influenced by Venus;
"Marcien": influenced by Mars.

Myn ascendent was Taur[2] and Mars therinne—
620 Allas, allas, that evere love was sinne!
 I folwed ay° my inclinacioun   *ever*
 By vertu of my constellacioun;[3]
 That made me I coude nought withdrawe
 My chambre of Venus from a good felawe.
625 Yit have I Martes° merk upon my face,   *Mars'*
 And also in another privee place.
 For God so wis° be my savacioun,° *surely / salvation*
 I loved nevere by no discrecioun,
 But evere folwede myn appetit,
630 Al were he short or long or blak or whit;
 I took no keep,° so that he liked° me, *heed / pleased*
 How poore he was, ne eek of what degree.
  What sholde I saye but at the monthes ende
 This joly clerk Janekin that was so hende°   *nice*
635 Hath wedded me with greet solempnitee,° *splendor*
 And to him yaf I al the land and fee°   *property*
 That evere was me yiven therbifore—
 But afterward repented me ful sore:
 He nolde suffre no thing of my list.°   *pleasure*
640 By God, he smoot° me ones on the list° *struck / ear*
 For that I rente° out of his book a leef,   *tore*
 That of the strook° myn ere weex° al deef. *blow / grew*
 Stibourne° I was as is a leonesse,   *stubborn*
 And of my tonge a verray jangleresse,° *blabbermouth*
645 And walke I wolde, as I hadde doon biforn,
 From hous to hous, although he hadde it[4] sworn;
 For which he often times wolde preche,
 And me of olde Romain geestes° teche,   *stories*
 How he Simplicius Gallus lafte° his wif,   *left*
650 And hire forsook for terme of al his lif,
 Nought but for open-heveded he hire sey[5]
 Looking out at his dore upon a day.
  Another Romain tolde he me by name
 That, for his wif was at a someres° game *summer's*
655 Withouten his witing,° he forsook hire eke; *knowledge*
 And thanne wolde he upon his Bible seeke
 That ilke proverbe of Ecclesiaste[6]
 Where he comandeth and forbedeth faste° *strictly*
 Man shal nat suffre his wif go roule° aboute; *roam*
660 Thanne wolde he saye right thus withouten doute:
 "Whoso that buildeth his hous al of salwes,° *willow sticks*
 And priketh° his blinde hors over the falwes,[7] *rides*

---

2. My birth sign was the constellation Taurus.
3. I.e., horoscope.
4. I.e., the contrary.
5. Just because he saw her bareheaded.
6. Ecclesiasticus (xxv.25).
7. Plowed land.

And suffreth his wif to go seeken halwes,°   *shrines*
Is worthy to be hanged on the galwes."°   *gallows*
665 But al for nought—I sette nought an hawe[8]
Of his proverbes n'of his olde sawe;
N'I wolde nat of him corrected be:
I hate him that my vices telleth me,
And so doon mo, God woot, of us than I.
670 This made him with me wood al outrely:[9]
I nolde nought forbere° him in no cas.   *submit to*
    Now wol I saye you sooth, by Saint Thomas,
Why that I rente° out of his book a leef,   *tore*
For which he smoot me so that I was deef.
675 He hadde a book that gladly night and day
For his disport he wolde rede alway.
He cleped it *Valerie*[1] *and Theofraste*,
At which book he lough° alway ful faste;   *laughed*
And eek ther was somtime a clerk at Rome,
680 A cardinal, that highte Saint Jerome,
That made a book[2] again Jovinian;
In which book eek ther was Tertulan,[3]
Crysippus, Trotula, and Helouis,
That was abbesse nat fer fro Paris;
685 And eek the Parables of Salomon,[4]
Ovides *Art*, and bookes many oon—
And alle thise were bounden in oo volume.
And every night and day was his custume,
Whan he hadde leiser and vacacioun
690 From other worldly occupacioun,
To reden in this book of wikked wives.
He knew of hem mo legendes and lives
Than been of goode wives in the Bible.
For trusteth wel, it is an impossible°   *impossibility*
695 That any clerk wol speke good of wives,
But if it be of holy saintes lives,
N'of noon other womman nevere the mo—
Who painted the leon, tel me who?[5]
By God, if wommen hadden writen stories,
700 As clerkes han within hir oratories,

8. I did not rate at the value of a haw-thorn berry.
9. Entirely.
1. I.e., the *Letter of Valerius Concern-ing Not Marrying*, by Walter Map; "*Theofraste*": Theophrastus' *Book Concerning Marriage.* Medieval manu-scripts often contained a number of different works, sometimes, as here, dealing with the same subject.
2. St. Jerome's antifeminist *Reply to Jovinian*; "again": against.
3. Tertullian, author of treatises on sexual modesty. Crysippus (or Chrysip-pus), in the next line, is mentioned by Jerome as an antifeminist; Trotula was a female doctor whose presence here is unexplained; "Helouis" is Eloise, whose love affair with the great scholar Abe-lard was a medieval scandal.
4. The Biblical Book of Proverbs; "Ovides *Art*": Ovid's *Art of Love.*
5. In one of Aesop's fables, the lion, shown a picture of a man killing a lion, asked who painted the picture. Had a lion been the artist, of course, the roles would have been reversed.

They wolde han writen of men more wikkednesse
Than al the merk[6] of Adam may redresse.
The children of Mercurye and Venus[7]
Been in hir werking° ful contrarious:°   *operation / opposed*
705 Mercurye loveth wisdom and science,
And Venus loveth riot° and dispence;°   *parties / expenditures*
And for hir diverse disposicioun
Each falleth in otheres exaltacioun,[8]
And thus, God woot, Mercurye is desolat
710 In Pisces wher Venus is exaltat,[9]
And Venus falleth ther Mercurye is raised:
Therfore no womman of no clerk is praised.
The clerk, whan he is old and may nought do
Of Venus werkes worth his olde sho,°   *shoe*
715 Thanne sit° he down and writ° in his dotage   *sits / writes*
That wommen can nat keepe hir mariage.
    But now to purpose why I tolde thee
That I was beten for a book, pardee:
Upon a night Janekin, that was oure sire,[1]
720 Redde on his book as he sat by the fire
Of Eva first, that for hir wikkednesse
Was al mankinde brought to wrecchednesse,
For which that Jesu Crist himself was slain
That boughte° us with his herte blood again—   *redeemed*
725 Lo, heer expres of wommen may ye finde
That womman was the los° of al mankinde.[2]   *ruin*
    Tho° redde he me how Sampson loste his heres: *then*
Sleeping his lemman° kitte° it with hir sheres,   *mistress / cut*
Thurgh which treson loste he both his yën.
730   Tho redde he me, if that I shal nat lien,
Of Ercules and of his Dianire,[3]
That caused him to sette himself afire.
    No thing forgat he the sorwe and wo
That Socrates hadde with his wives two—
735 How Xantippa caste pisse upon his heed:
This sely° man sat stille as he were deed;   *silly*
He wiped his heed, namore dorste he sayn
But "Er that thonder stinte,° comth a rain."   *stops*
    Of Pasipha[4] that was the queene of Crete—
740 For shrewednesse° him thoughte the tale sweete—   *malice*

---

6. Mark, sex.
7. I.e., clerks and women, astrologically ruled by Mercury and Venus respectively.
8. Because of their contrary positions (as planets), each one descends (in the belt of the zodiac) as the other rises; hence one loses its power as the other becomes dominant.
9. I.e., Mercury is deprived of power in Pisces (the sign of the Fish), where Venus is most powerful.
1. My husband.
2. The stories of wicked women Chaucer drew mainly from St. Jerome and Walter Map.
3. Dejanira unwittingly gave Hercules a poisoned shirt, which hurt him so much that he committed suicide by fire.
4. Pasiphaë, who fell in love with a bull.

Fy, speek namore, it is a grisly thing
Of hir horrible lust and hir liking.°   *pleasure*
    Of Clytermistra⁵ for hir lecherye
That falsly made hir housbonde for to die,
745 He redde it with ful good devocioun.
    He tolde me eek for what occasioun
Amphiorax⁶ at Thebes loste his lif:
Myn housbonde hadde a legende of his wif
Eriphylem, that for an ouche° of gold   *trinket*
750 Hath prively unto the Greekes told
Wher that hir housbonde hidde him in a place,
For which he hadde at Thebes sory grace.
Of Livia⁷ tolde he me and of Lucie:
They bothe made hir housbondes for to die,
755 That oon for love, that other was for hate;
Livia hir housbonde on an even late
Empoisoned hath for that she was his fo;
Lucia likerous° loved hir housbonde so   *lecherous*
That for° he sholde alway upon hire thinke,   *in order that*
760 She yaf him swich a manere love-drinke
That he was deed er it were by the morwe.⁸
And thus algates° housbondes han sorwe.   *constantly*
    Thanne tolde he me how oon Latumius
Complained unto his felawe Arrius
765 That in his gardin growed swich a tree,
On which he saide how that his wives three
Hanged hemself for herte despitous.⁹
    "O leve° brother," quod this Arrius,   *dear*
"Yif me a plante of thilke blessed tree,
770 And in my gardin planted shal it be."
    Of latter date of wives hath he red
That some han slain hir housbondes in hir bed
And lete hir lechour dighte¹ hire al the night,
Whan that the cors° lay in the floor upright;°   *corpse / supine*
775 And some han driven nailes in hir brain
Whil that they sleepe, and thus they han hem slain;
Some han hem yiven poison in hir drinke.
He spak more harm than herte may bithinke,°   *imagine*
And therwithal he knew of mo proverbes
780 Than in this world ther growen gras or herbes:
"Bet is," quod he, "thyn habitacioun
Be with a leon or a foul dragoun

5. Clytemnestra, who, with her lover Aegisthus, slew her husband Agamemnon.
6. Amphiaraus, betrayed by his wife Eriphyle and forced to go to the war against Thebes.
7. Livia murdered her husband in behalf of her lover Sejanus. "Lucie": Lucilla, who was said to have poisoned her husband, the poet Lucretius, with a potion designed to keep him faithful.
8. He was dead before it was near morning.
9. For malice of heart.
1. Have intercourse with.

Than with a womman using° for to chide."   *accustomed*
"Bet is," quod he, "hye in the roof abide
785 Than with an angry wif down in the hous:
They been so wikked° and contrarious,   *perverse*
They haten that hir housbondes loveth ay."
He saide, "A womman cast° hir shame away   *casts*
Whan she cast of° hir smok,"² and ferthermo,   *off*
790 "A fair womman, but she be chast also,
Is like a gold ring in a sowes nose."
Who wolde weene,° or who wolde suppose   *think*
The wo that in myn herte was and pine?°   *suffering*
    And whan I sawgh he wolde nevere fine°   *end*
795 To reden on this cursed book al night,
Al sodeinly three leves have I plight°   *snatched*
Out of his book right as he redde, and eke
I with my fist so took³ him on the cheeke
That in oure fir he fil° bakward adown.   *fell*
800 And up he sterte as dooth a wood° leoun,   *raging*
And with his fist he smoot me on the heed°   *head*
That in the floor I lay as I were deed.
And whan he sawgh how stille that I lay,
He was agast, and wolde have fled his way,
805 Til atte laste out of my swough° I braide:°   *swoon / started*
"O hastou slain me, false thief?" I saide,
"And for my land thus hastou mordred° me?   *murdered*
Er I be deed° yit wol I kisse thee."   *dead*
And neer he cam and kneeled faire adown,
810 And saide, "Dere suster Alisoun,
As help me God, I shal thee nevere smite.
That I have doon, it is thyself to wite.°   *blame*
Foryif it me, and that I thee biseeke."
And yit eftsoones° I hitte him on the cheeke,   *again*
815 And saide, "Thief, thus muchel am I wreke.°   *avenged*
Now wol I die: I may no lenger speke."
    But at the laste with muchel care and wo
We fille⁴ accorded by us selven two.
He yaf me al the bridel° in myn hand,   *bridle*
820 To han the governance of hous and land,
And of his tonge and his hand also;
And made⁵ him brenne° his book anoonright tho.   *burn*
And whan that I hadde geten unto me
By maistrye° al the sovereinetee,°   *skill / dominion*
825 And that he saide, "Myn owene trewe wif,
Do as thee lust° the terme of al thy lif;   *it pleases*
Keep thyn honour, and keep eek myn estat,"
After that day we hadde nevere debat.

2. Undergarment.   4. I.e., became.
3. I.e., hit.   5. I.e., I made.

God help me so, I was to him as kinde
830 As any wif from Denmark unto Inde,
And also trewe, and so was he to me.
I praye to God that sit° in majestee,   *sits*
So blesse his soule for his mercy dere.
Now wol I saye my tale if ye wol heere.

[ANOTHER INTERRUPTION]

835   The Frere lough° whan he hadde herd al this: *laughed*
"Now dame," quod he, "so have I joye or blis,
This is a long preamble of a tale."
And whan the Somnour herde the Frere gale,°   *exclaim*
"Lo," quod the Somnour, "Goddes armes two,
840 A frere wol entremette him[6] everemo!
Lo, goode men, a flye and eek a frere
Wol falle in every dissh and eek matere.
What spekestou of preambulacioun?
What, amble or trotte or pisse or go sitte down!
845 Thou lettest° oure disport in this manere."   *hinder*
    "Ye, woltou so, sire Somnour?" quod the Frere.
"Now by my faith, I shal er that I go
Telle of a somnour swich a tale or two
That al the folk shal laughen in this place."
850   "Now elles, Frere, I wol bishrewe° thy face,"   *curse*
Quod this Somnour, "and I bishrewe me,
But if I telle tales two or three
Of freres, er I come to Sidingborne,[7]
That I shal make thyn herte for to moorne—
855 For wel I woot thy pacience is goon."
    Oure Hoste cride, "Pees, and that anoon!"
And saide, "Lat the womman telle hir tale:
Ye fare as folk that dronken been of ale.
Do, dame, tel forth youre tale, and that is best."
860   "Al redy, sire," quod she, "right as you lest°—   *it pleases*
If I have licence of this worthy Frere."
"Yis, dame," quod he, "tel forth and I wol heere."

6. Intrude himself.
7. Sittingbourne (a town forty miles from London).

The Tale[1]

In th'olde dayes of the King Arthour,
Of which that Britouns° speken greet honour,   *Bretons*
865 Al was this land fulfild of faïrye:[2]
The elf-queene with hir joly compaignye
Daunced ful ofte in many a greene mede°—   *meadow*
This was the olde opinion as I rede;
I speke of many hundred yeres ago.
870 But now can no man see none elves mo,
For now the grete charitee and prayeres
Of limitours,[3] and othere holy freres,
That serchen every land and every streem,
As thikke as motes in the sonne-beem,
875 Blessing halles, chambres, kichenes, bowres,
Citees, burghes,° castels, hye towres,   *townships*
Thropes, bernes, shipnes,[4] dayeries—
This maketh that ther been no faïries.
For ther as wont to walken was an elf
880 Ther walketh now the limitour himself,
In undermeles° and in morweninges,°   *afternoons / mornings*
And saith his Matins and his holy thinges,
As he gooth in his limitacioun.[5]
Wommen may go saufly° up and down: *safely*
885 In every bussh or under every tree
Ther is noon other incubus[6] but he,
And he ne wol doon hem but dishonour.
    And so bifel it that this King Arthour
Hadde in his hous a lusty bacheler,
890 That on a day cam riding fro river,[7]
And happed° that, allone as he was born,   *it happened*

1. The story of the knight who fully realizes what women most desire only after having been told it in a number of ways was popular in Chaucer's time and a natural one for him to assign to the Wife of Bath, whose well-loved fifth husband had also been slow to learn. But Chaucer reshaped the tale in such a way as to make it fit the Wife and her thesis even more closely. In the other medieval versions of the story the knight is guiltless of any offense to womanhood, and in several of them he is Sir Gawain, traditional model of chivalric courtesy, who weds the hideous hag to save not his own life but that of his lord, King Arthur. Chaucer has made the knight a most ill-behaved and ill-mannered man who needs to learn what women most desire as much in order to redeem his disagreeably virile character as to save his neck. Because within her story he is the sole male in a world of women, Dame Alice is able not only to prove conclusively the value of woman's sovereignty, but also to pay her respects to a world of men that had preached antifeminism, a world here represented by a single rapist.

The story is suited to the Wife's own character psychologically as well as dramatically, for she, like the old hag, had wedded a young man—though unlike the hag she could not restore her former beauty. But if there is a touch of melancholy in the incompleteness of this similarity, it is sharply dispelled by the Wife's final comments, which reassert the sturdy fighting spirit that permeates her Prologue.
2. I.e., filled full of supernatural creatures.
3. Friars licenced to beg in a certain territory.
4. Thorps (villages), barns, stables.
5. I.e., the friar's assigned area. His "holy thinges" are prayers.
6. A spirit that lies with mortal women. "Ne * * * but" in the next line means "only."
7. Hawking, usually carried out on the banks of a stream.

He sawgh a maide walking him biforn;
Of which maide anoon, maugree hir heed,[8]
By verray force he rafte° hir maidenheed;   *deprived her of*
895 For which oppression° was swich clamour,   *rape*
And swich pursuite° unto the King Arthour,   *petitioning*
That dampned was this knight for to be deed[9]
By cours of lawe, and sholde han lost his heed—
Paraventure° swich was the statut tho—   *perhaps*
900 But that the queene and othere ladies mo
So longe prayeden the king of grace,
Til he his lif him graunted in the place,
And yaf him to the queene, al at hir wille,
To chese° wheither she wolde him save or spille.[1]   *choose*
905 The queene thanked the king with al hir might,
And after this thus spak she to the knight,
Whan that she saw hir time upon a day:
"Thou standest yit," quod she, "in swich array°   *condition*
That of thy lif yit hastou no suretee.°   *guarantee*
910 I graunte thee lif if thou canst tellen me
What thing it is that wommen most desiren:
Be war and keep thy nekke boon° from iren.   *bone*
And if thou canst nat tellen me anoon,
Yit wol I yive thee leve for to goon
915 A twelfmonth and a day to seeche° and lere°   *search / learn*
An answere suffisant° in this matere,   *satisfactory*
And suretee wol I han er that thou pace,°   *pass*
Thy body for to yeelden in this place."
    Wo was this knight, and sorwefully he siketh.°   *sighs*
920 But what, he may nat doon al as him liketh,
And atte laste he chees° him for to wende,   *chose*
And come again right at the yeres ende,
With swich answere as God wolde him purveye,°   *provide*
And taketh his leve and wendeth forth his waye.
925 He seeketh every hous and every place
Wher as he hopeth for to finde grace,
To lerne what thing wommen love most.
But he ne coude arriven in no coost[2]
Wher as he mighte finde in this matere
930 Two creatures according in fere.[3]
    Some saiden wommen loven best richesse;
Some saide honour, some saide jolinesse;°   *wantonness*
Some riche array, some saiden lust° abedde,   *pleasure*
And ofte time to be widwe and wedde.
935 Some saide that oure herte is most esed
Whan that we been yflatered and yplesed—
He gooth ful neigh the soothe, I wol nat lie:
A man shal winne us best with flaterye,

8. Despite her head, i.e., despite any-   1. Put to death.
thing she could do.   2. I.e., country.
9. This knight was condemned to death.   3. Agreeing together.

And with attendance and with bisinesse°   *assiduousness*
940 Been we ylimed,° bothe more and lesse.   *ensnared*
    And some sayen that we loven best
For to be free, and do right as us lest,°   *it pleases*
And that no man repreve° us of oure vice,   *reprove*
But saye that we be wise and no thing nice.°   *foolish*
945 For trewely, ther is noon of us alle,
If any wight wol clawe us on the galle,°   *sore spot*
That we nil kike° for° he saith us sooth: *kick / because*
Assaye and he shal finde it that so dooth.
For be we·nevere so vicious withinne,
950 We wol be holden° wise and clene of sinne.   *considered*
    And some sayn that greet delit han we
For to be holden stable and eek secree,[4]
And in oo purpos stedefastly to dwelle,
And nat biwraye° thing that men us telle—   *disclose*
955 But that tale is nat worth a rake-stele.°   *rake handle*
Pardee, we wommen conne no thing hele:°   *conceal*
Witnesse on Mida.° Wol ye heere the tale?   *Midas*
    Ovide, amonges othere thinges smale,
Saide Mida hadde under his longe heres,
960 Growing upon his heed, two asses eres,
The whiche vice° he hidde as he best mighte   *defect*
Ful subtilly from every mannes sighte,
That save his wif ther wiste° of it namo.   *knew*
He loved hire most and trusted hire also.
965 He prayed hire that to no creature
She sholde tellen of his disfigure.°   *deformity*
    She swoor him nay, for al this world to winne,
She nolde do that vilainye or sinne
To make hir housbonde han so foul a name:
970 She nolde nat telle it for hir owene shame.
But nathelees, hir thoughte that she dyde°   *would die*
That she so longe sholde a conseil° hide;   *secret*
Hire thoughte it swal° so sore aboute hir herte   *swelled*
That nedely som word hire moste asterte,[5]
975 And sith she dorste nat telle it to no man,
Down to a mareis° faste° by she ran—   *marsh / close*
Til she cam there hir herte was afire—
And as a bitore[6] bombleth in the mire,
She laide hir mouth unto the water down:
980 "Biwray° me nat, thou water, with thy soun,"°   *betray / sound*
Quod she. "To thee I telle it and namo:°   *to no one else*
Myn housbonde hath longe asses eres two.
Now is myn herte al hool,[7] now is it oute.
I mighte no lenger keepe it, out of doute."
985 Here may ye see, though we a time abide,

---

4. Reliable and also close-mouthed.
5. Of necessity some word must escape her.

6. Bittern, a heron. "Bombleth": makes a booming noise.
7. I.e., sound.

Yit oute it moot:° we can no conseil hide.   *must*
The remenant of the tale if ye wol heere,
Redeth Ovide, and ther ye may it lere.[8]
    This knight of which my tale is specially,
990 Whan that he sawgh he mighte nat come therby—
This is to saye what wommen loven most—
Within his brest ful sorweful was his gost,°   *spirit*
But hoom he gooth, he mighte nat sojurne:°   *delay*
The day was come that hoomward moste° he turne.   *must*
995 And in his way it happed him to ride
In al this care under a forest side,
Wher as he sawgh upon a daunce go
Of ladies foure and twenty and yit mo;
Toward the whiche daunce he drow ful yerne,[9]
1000 In hope that som wisdom sholde he lerne.
But certainly, er he cam fully there,
Vanisshed was this daunce, he niste° where.   *knew not*
No creature sawgh he that bar° lif,   *bore*
Save on the greene he sawgh sitting a wif—
1005 A fouler wight ther may no man devise.°   *imagine*
Again[1] the knight this olde wif gan rise,
And saide, "Sire knight, heer forth lith° no way.°   *lies / road*
Telle me what ye seeken, by youre fay.°   *faith*
Paraventure it may the better be:
1010 Thise olde folk conne° muchel thing," quod she.   *know*
    "My leve moder,"° quod this knight, "certain,   *mother*
I nam but deed but if that I can sayn
What thing it is that wommen most desire.
Coude ye me wisse,° I wolde wel quite youre hire."[2]   *teach*
1015   "Plight me thy trouthe here in myn hand," quod she,
"The nexte thing that I requere° thee,   *require of*
Thou shalt it do, if it lie in thy might,
And I wol telle it you er it be night."
    "Have heer my trouthe," quod the knight. "I graunte."
1020   "Thanne," quod she, "I dar me wel avaunte°   *boast*
Thy lif is sauf,° for I wol stande therby.   *safe*
Upon my lif the queene wol saye as I.
Lat see which is the pruddeste° of hem alle   *proudest*
That wereth on[3] a coverchief or a calle°   *headdress*
1025 That dar saye nay of that I shal thee teche.
Lat us go forth withouten lenger speeche."
Tho rouned° she a pistel° in his ere,   *whispered / sentence*
And bad him to be glad and have no fere.
    Whan they be comen to the court, this knight
1030 Saide he hadde holde his day as he hadde hight,°   *promised*
And redy was his answere, as he saide.
Ful many a noble wif, and many a maide,

---

8. Learn. The reeds disclosed the secret by whispering *"aures asinelli"* (asses' ears).
9. Drew very quickly.

1. I.e., to meet.
2. Repay your trouble.
3. That wears.

And many a widwe—for that they been wise—
The queene hirself sitting as justise,
1035 Assembled been this answere for to heere,
And afterward this knight was bode° appere.   *bidden to*
To every wight comanded was silence,
And that the knight sholde telle in audience°   *pen hearing*
What thing that worldly wommen loven best.
1040 This knight ne stood nat stille as dooth a best,° *beast*
But to his question anoon answerde
With manly vois that al the court it herde.
   "My lige° lady, generally," quod he,   *liege*
"Wommen desire to have sovereinetee°   *dominion*
1045 As wel over hir housbonde as hir love,
And for to been in maistrye him above.
This is youre moste desir though ye me kille.
Dooth as you list:° I am here at youre wille."   *please*
   In al the court ne was ther wif ne maide
1050 Ne widwe that contraried° that he saide,   *contradicted*
But saiden he was worthy han° his lif.   *to have*
   And with that word up sterte° that olde wif,   *started*
Which that the knight sawgh sitting on the greene;
"Mercy," quod she, "my soverein lady queene,
1055 Er that youre court departe, do me right.
I taughte this answere unto the knight,
For which he plighte me his trouthe there
The firste thing I wolde him requere°   *require*
He wolde it do, if it laye in his might.
1060 Bifore the court thanne praye I thee, sire knight,"
Quod she, "that thou me take unto thy wif,
For wel thou woost that I have kept° thy lif.   *saved*
If I saye fals, say nay, upon thy fay."
   This knight answerde, "Allas and wailaway,
1065 I woot right wel that swich was my biheeste.°   *promise*
For Goddes love, as chees° a newe requeste: *choose*
Taak al my good and lat my body go."
   "Nay thanne," quod she, "I shrewe° us bothe two. *curse*
For though that I be foul and old and poore,
1070 I nolde for al the metal ne for ore
That under erthe is grave° or lith° above,   *buried / lies*
But if thy wif I were and eek thy love."
   "My love," quod he. "Nay, my dampnacioun!°   *damnation*
Allas, that any of my nacioun[4]
1075 Sholde evere so foule disparaged° be."   *disgraced*
But al for nought, th'ende is this, that he
Constrained was: he needes moste hire wedde,
And taketh his olde wif and gooth to bedde.
   Now wolden some men saye, paraventure,
1080 That for my necligence I do no cure[5]
To tellen you the joy and al th'array

4. I.e., family.   5. I do not take the trouble.

That at the feeste was that ilke day.
To which thing shortly answere I shal:
I saye ther nas no joye ne feeste at al;
1085 Ther nas but hevinesse and muche sorwe.
For prively he wedded hire on morwe,[6]
And al day after hidde him as an owle,
So wo was him, his wif looked so foule.
     Greet was the wo the knight hadde in his thought:
1090 Whan he was with his wif abedde brought,
He walweth° and he turneth to and fro.   *tosses*
His olde wif lay smiling everemo,
And saide, "O dere housbonde, benedicite,°   *bless me*
Fareth° every knight thus with his wif as ye?   *behaves*
1095 Is this the lawe of King Arthures hous?
Is every knight of his thus daungerous?°   *stand-offish*
I am youre owene love and youre wif;
I am she which that saved hath youre lif;
And certes yit ne dide I you nevere unright.
1100 Why fare ye thus with me this firste night?
Ye faren like a man hadde lost his wit.
What is my gilt? For Goddes love, telle it,
And it shal been amended if I may."
     "Amended!" quod this knight. "Allas, nay, nay,
1105 It wol nat been amended neveremo.
Thou art so lothly° and so old also,   *loathsome*
And therto comen of so lowe a kinde,°   *race*
That litel wonder is though I walwe and winde.°   *turn*
So wolde God myn herte wolde breste!"°   *break*
1110 "Is this," quod she, "the cause of youre unreste?"
"Ye, certainly," quod he. "No wonder is."
     "Now sire," quod she, "I coude amende al this,
If that me liste, er it were dayes three,
So° wel ye mighte bere you[7] unto me.   *provided that*
1115 "But for ye speken of swich gentilesse
As is descended out of old richesse—
That therfore sholden ye be gentilmen—
Swich arrogance is nat worth an hen.
Looke who that is most vertuous alway,
1120 Privee and apert,[8] and most entendeth ay
To do the gentil deedes that he can,
Taak him for the gretteste° gentilman.   *greatest*
Crist wol° we claime of him oure gentilesse,   *desires that*
Nat of oure eldres for hir 'old richesse.'[9]
1125 For though they yive us al hir heritage,
For which we claime to been of heigh parage,°   *descent*
Yit may they nat biquethe for no thing
To noon of us hir vertuous living,
That made hem gentilmen ycalled be,

---

6. In the morning.   8. Privately and publicly.
7. Behave.   9. See Chaucer's *Gentilesse*, line 16.

1130 And bad[1] us folwen hem in swich degree.
    "Wel can the wise poete of Florence,
That highte Dant,[2] speken in this sentence;°   *topic*
Lo, in swich manere rym is Dantes tale:
'Ful selde° up riseth by his braunches[3] smale   *seldom*
1135 Prowesse° of man, for God of his prowesse   *excellence*
Wol that of him we claime oure gentilesse.'
For of oure eldres may we no thing claime
But temporel thing that man may hurte and maime.
Eek every wight woot this as wel as I,
1140 If gentilesse were planted natureelly
Unto a certain linage down the line,
Privee and apert, thanne wolde they nevere fine°   *cease*
To doon of gentilesse the faire office°—   *function*
They mighte do no vilainye or vice.
1145   "Taak fir and beer° it in the derkeste hous   *bear*
Bitwixe this and the Mount of Caucasus,
And lat men shette° the dores and go thenne,° *shut / thence*
Yit wol the fir as faire lie[4] and brenne°   *burn*
As twenty thousand men mighte it biholde:
1150 His° office natureel ay wol it holde,   *its*
Up° peril of my lif, til that it die.   *upon*
Heer may ye see wel how that genterye°   *gentility*
Is nat annexed° to possessioun,[5]   *related*
Sith folk ne doon hir operacioun
1155 Alway, as dooth the fir, lo, in his kinde.°   *nature*
For God it woot, men may wel often finde
A lordes sone do shame and vilainye;
And he that wol han pris of his gentrye,[6]
For he was boren° of a gentil hous,   *born*
1160 And hadde his eldres noble and vertuous,
And nil himselven do no gentil deedes,
Ne folwen his gentil auncestre that deed° is,   *dead*
He nis nat gentil, be he duc or erl—
For vilaines sinful deedes maken a cherl.
1165 Thy gentilesse[7] nis but renomee°   *renown*
Of thine auncestres for hir heigh bountee,°   *magnanimity*
Which is a straunge° thing for thy persone.   *alien*
For gentilesse[8] cometh fro God allone.
Thanne comth oure verray gentilesse of grace:
1170 It was no thing biquethe us with oure place.
Thenketh how noble, as saith Valerius,[9]
Was thilke Tullius Hostilius
That out of poverte° roos to heigh noblesse.   *poverty*
Redeth Senek,° and redeth eek Boece:° *Seneca / Boethius*
1175 Ther shul ye seen expres that no drede° is   *doubt*

1. I.e., they bade.
2. Dante; see his *Convivio*.
3. I.e., by its own efforts.
4. I.e., remain.
5. I.e., inheritable property.

6. Have credit for his noble birth.
7. I.e., the gentility you claim.
8. I.e., true gentility.
9. A Roman historian.

That he is gentil that dooth gentil deedes.
And therfore, leve housbonde, I thus conclude:
Al were it that mine auncestres weren rude,[1]
Yit may the hye God—and so hope I—
1180 Graunte me grace to liven vertuously.
Thanne am I gentil whan that I biginne
To liven vertuously and waive° sinne.   avoid
    "And ther as ye of poverte me repreve,°   reprove
The hye God, on whom that we bileve,
1185 In wilful° poverte chees° to live his lif;   voluntary / chose
And certes every man, maiden, or wif
May understonde that Jesus, hevene king,
Ne wolde nat chese° a vicious living.   choose
Glad poverte is an honeste° thing, certain;   honorable
1190 This wol Senek and othere clerkes sayn.
Whoso that halt him paid of[2] his poverte,
I holde him riche al hadde he nat a sherte.°   shirt
He that coveiteth[3] is a poore wight,
For he wolde han that is nat in his might;
1195 But he that nought hath, ne coveiteth° have,   desires to
Is riche, although we holde him but a knave.
Verray poverte it singeth proprely.°   appropriately
Juvenal saith of poverte, 'Merily
The poore man, whan he gooth by the waye,
1200 Biforn the theves he may singe and playe.'
Poverte is hateful good, and as I gesse,
A ful greet bringere out of bisinesse;[4]
A greet amendere eek of sapience
To him that taketh it in pacience;
1205 Poverte is thing, although it seeme elenge,°   wretched
Possession that no wight wol chalenge;[5]
Poverte ful often, whan a man is lowe,
Maketh[6] his God and eek himself to knowe;
Poverte a spectacle° is, as thinketh me,   pair of spectacles
1210 Thurgh which he may his verray freendes see.
And therfore, sire, sin that I nought you greve,
Of my poverte namore ye me repreve.°   reproach
    "Now sire, of elde° ye repreve me: old age
And certes sire, though noon auctoritee
1215 Were in no book, ye gentils of honour
Sayn that men sholde an old wight doon favour,
And clepe him fader for youre gentilesse—
And auctours[7] shal I finden, as I gesse.
    "Now ther ye saye that I am foul and old:
1220 Thanne drede you nought to been a cokewold,°   cuckold
For filthe and elde, also mote I thee,[8]
Been grete wardeins° upon chastitee.   guardians

1. I.e., low born.
2. Considers himself satisfied with.
3. I.e., suffers desires.
4. I.e., cares.
5. Claim as his property.
6. I.e., makes him.
7. I.e., authorities.
8. So may I thrive.

But nathelees, sin I knowe your delit,
I shal fulfille youre worldly appetit.
1225 "Chees now," quod she, "oon of thise thinges twaye:
To han me foul and old til that I deye
And be to you a trewe humble wif,
And nevere you displese in al my lif,
Or elles ye wol han me yong and fair,
1230 And take youre aventure° of the repair⁹   chance
That shal be to youre hous by cause of me—
Or in som other place, wel may be.
Now chees youreselven wheither° that you liketh."   whichever
    This knight aviseth him¹ and sore siketh;°   sighs
1235 But atte laste he saide in this manere:
"My lady and my love, and wif so dere,
I putte me in youre wise governaunce:
Cheseth° youreself which may be most plesaunce²   choose
And most honour to you and me also.
1240 I do no fors the wheither³ of the two,
For as you liketh it suffiseth° me."   satisfies
    "Thanne have I gete° of you maistrye," quod she,   got
"Sin I may chese and governe as me lest?"°   it pleases
    "Ye, certes, wif," quod he. "I holde it best."
1245 "Kisse me," quod she. "We be no lenger wrothe.
For by my trouthe, I wol be to you bothe—
This is to sayn, ye, bothe fair and good.
I praye to God that I mote sterven wood,⁴
But° I to you be al so good and trewe   unless
1250 As evere was wif sin that the world was newe.
And but I be tomorn° as fair to seene   tomorrow morning
As any lady, emperisse, or queene,
That is bitwixe the eest and eek the west,
Do with my lif and deeth right as you lest:
1255 Caste up the curtin, looke how that it is."
    And whan the knight sawgh verraily al this,
That she so fair was and so yong therto,
For joye he hente° hire in his armes two;   took
His herte bathed in a bath of blisse;
1260 A thousand time arewe° he gan hire kisse,   in a row
And she obeyed him in every thing
That mighte do him plesance or liking.°   pleasure
And thus they live unto hir lives ende
In parfit° joye. And Jesu Crist us sende   perfect
1265 Housbondes meeke, yonge, and fresshe abedde—
And grace t'overbide° hem that we wedde.   outlive
And eek I praye Jesu shorte° hir lives   shorten
That nought wol be governed by hir wives,
And olde and angry nigardes of dispence°—   expenditure
1270 God sende hem soone a verray° pestilence!   veritable

9. I.e., visits.   3. I do not care whichever.
1. Considers.   4. Die mad.
2. Pleasure.

The Merchant's Tale[1]

The Introduction

"Weeping and wailing, care and other sorwe
I knowe ynough, on even and amorwe,"[2]
Quod the Marchant, "and so doon othere mo[3]
That wedded been. I trowe° that it be so,   believe
5   For wel I woot° it fareth so with me.   know
I have a wif, the worste that may be:
For though the feend to hire ycoupled were,
She wolde him overmacche, I dar wel swere.
What sholde I you reherce in special
10   Hir heigh malice? She is a shrewe at al.[4]
Ther is a long and large difference
Bitwixe Grisildis grete pacience[5]
And of my wif the passing° crueltee.   surpassing
Were I unbounden, also moote I thee,[6]
15   I wolde nevere eft° comen in the snare.   again
We wedded men live in sorwe and care—
Assaye° whoso wole and he shal finde   try
I saye sooth, by Saint Thomas of Inde,
As for the more° part—I saye nat alle: larger
20   God shilde° that it sholde so bifalle.   forbid
A, goode sire Host, I have ywedded be

1. The last incident of the Merchant's Tale is a common fabliau (see the Miller's Tale, above, note 1), but in preparing for the brief scene in which a wife climbs upon the shoulders of her blind husband into a pear tree in order to copulate with her lover there, Chaucer has shown a most un-fabliau-like expansiveness with his description of the old husband and how he got and treated his young wife: he thus turns a simple bawdy joke into an ample consideration of marriage and wives and of the narrator's very masculine but un-understanding attitude toward them. The Merchant himself has recently been married to what he considers a dreadful shrew, and the Clerk's just-finished story of Griselda, who suffered with extraordinary patience all sorts of abuse from her husband, has made the Merchant most indignant. Since he does not believe in Griselda, he tries to set the record straight by telling of the treachery of young May to old January. But if his intent is misogynistic, in his narrative he is so manipulated by Chaucer that one's sympathies are, if anywhere, as much with the cheating wife as the deceived husband. January is the type of the senile lecher of whom May is the unwilling victim, and if her behavior does nothing to disprove a woman-hater's prejudices, January's behavior provides her with a good excuse for acting as she does.
   The tale is a wonderfully—indeed, outrageously—funny one, and many readers will be content to accept it as such; but other readers may be struck by Chaucer's profound exploration of the teller, whose disappointment with marriage seems to stem from a puerile notion of what a woman is, and who consequently blames women rather than himself for the disappointment. In his assessment of women there is no middle term: women, he finds, are not docile beasts ever ready to serve their husbands' whims; *therefore* they are deceitful adulterers like May. There is nothing between Griselda and May. In his disillusionment the Merchant spews forth hatred—on May for her treachery, on January for his senile folly in believing what the Merchant himself once believed, and, perhaps most of all, on himself.
2. Evening and morning.
3. I.e., so do others too.
4. In every respect.
5. For Griselda see note 1, above. The Clerk has concluded his tale with the humorous advice to wives not to be patient in marriage as Griselda was, but to make their husbands "weep and wail" (see line 1, above).
6. If I were freed, so might I thrive.

Thise monthes two, and more nat, pardee,⁷
And yit I trowe he that al his live
Wiflees hath been, though that men wolde him rive°   *pierce*
25 Unto the herte, ne coude in no manere
Tellen so muchel sorwe as I now here
Coude tellen of my wives cursednesse."°   *wickedness*
    "Now," quod oure Host, 'Marchant, so God you blesse,
Sin° ye so muchel knowen of that art,   *since*
30 Ful hertely I praye you telle us part."
    "Gladly," quod he, "but of myn owene sore
For sory herte I telle may namore."

The Tale

Whilom⁸ ther was dwelling in Lumbardye°   *Lombardy*
A worthy knight that born was of Pavie,°   *Pavia*
35 In which he lived in greet prosperitee;
And sixty yeer a wiflees man was he,
And folwed ay° his bodily delit   *always*
On wommen ther as was his appetit,
As doon thise fooles that been seculer.⁹
40 And whan that he was passed sixty yeer—
Were it for holinesse or for dotage
I can nat saye—but swich a greet corage°   *desire*
Hadde this knight to been a wedded man,
That day and night he dooth al that he can
45 T' espyen where he mighte wedded be,
Praying oure Lord to graunten him that he
Mighte ones° knowe of thilke° blisful lif   *once / that*
That is bitwixe an housbonde and his wif,
And for to live under that holy bond
50 With which that first God man and womman boond.°   *bound*
"Noon other lif," saide he, "is worth a bene,°   *bean*
For wedlok is so esy and so clene
That in this world it is a Paradis."
Thus saide this olde knight that was so wis.
55   And certainly, as sooth as God is king,
To take a wif, it is a glorious thing,
And namely° whan a man is old and hoor:°   *especially / gray*
Thanne is a wif the fruit° of his tresor;°   *best part / treasure*
Thanne sholde he take a yong wif and a fair,
60 On which he mighte engendren him an heir,
And lede his lif in joye and in solas,°   *delight*
Wher as thise bacheleres singe allas,
Whan that they finde any adversitee
In love, which nis but childissh vanitee.
65 And trewely, it sit° wel to be so   *suits*
That bacheleres have ofte paine and wo:
On brotel° ground they builde, and brotelnesse   *brittle*

---

7. From French *par Dieu*, "by God."   9. I.e., not in clerical orders.
8. Once upon a time.

They finde whan they weene° sikernese;°	*expect / security*
They live but as a brid° or as a beest	*bird*
70 In libertee and under noon arrest,°	*control*
Ther as a wedded man in his estat	
Liveth a lif blisful and ordinat°	*regulated*
Under this yok of marriage ybounde:	
Wel may his herte in joye and blisse habounde.°	*abound*
75 For who can be so buxom° as a wif?	*obedient*
Who is so trewe and eek so ententif°	*attentive*
To keepe him, sik and hool, as is his make?[1]	
For wele° or wo she wol him nat forsake.	*happiness*
She nis nat wery him to love and serve,	
80 Though that he lie bedrede° til he sterve.°	*bedridden / die*
And yit some clerkes sayn it is nat so,	
Of whiche he Theofraste[2] is oon of tho°—	*those*
What fors° though Theofraste liste° lie?	*matter / it pleases*
"Ne taak no wif," quod he, "for housbondrye°	*economy*
85 As for to spare in houshold thy dispence.°	*expenses*
A trewe servant dooth more diligence	
Thy good to keepe than thyn owene wif,	
For she wol claime half part al hir lif.	
And if thou be sik, so God me save,	
90 Thy verray° freendes or a trewe knave°	*true / servant*
Wol keepe thee bet° than she that waiteth ay[3]	*better*
After thy good, and hath do many a day.	
And if thou take a wif unto thyn hold,	
Ful lightly° maistou been a cokewold."°	*easily / cuckold*
95 This sentence° and an hundred thinges worse	*sentiment*
Writeth this man, ther[4] God his bones curse!	
But take no keep° of al swich vanitee:	*heed*
Defye Theofraste and herke me.	
A wif is Goddes yifte verraily;	
100 Alle othere manere yiftes hardily,°	*certainly*
As landes, rentes,° pasture, or commune,[5]	*income*
Or moebles,° alle been yiftes of Fortune,	*furniture*
That passen as a shadwe upon a wal.	
But drede nat, if plainly speke I shal,	
105 A wif wol laste and in thyn hous endure	
Wel lenger than thee list,° paraventure.	*please*
Mariage is a ful greet sacrament.	
He which that hath no wif I holde him shent.°	*ruined*
He liveth helplees and al desolat—	
110 I speke of folk in seculer estat.	
And herke why I saye nat this for nought	
That womman is for mannes help ywrought:	

---

1. To watch over him, sick and healthy, as is his mate.
2. Theophrastus, author of an anti-feminist argument preserved in St. Jerome's invective against Jovinian: see note to line 681 of the Wife of Bath's Prologue, above.
3. Lies in wait constantly.
4. I.e., may.
5. Pasturage rights.

The hye God, whan he hadde Adam maked
And sawgh him allone, bely-naked,
115 God of his grete goodnesse saide than,
"Lat us now make an help unto this man
Lik to himself." And thanne he made him Eve.
Heer may ye see, and heerby may ye preve°   *prove*
That wif is mannes help and his confort,
120 His Paradis terrestre° and his disport.   *terrestrial*
So buxom° and so vertuous is she   *obedient*
They moste° needes live in unitee: *must*
Oo° flessh they been, and oo flessh, as I gesse,   *one*
Hath but oon herte in wele° and in distresse.   *happiness*
125   A wif, a, Sainte Marye, benedicite,°   *bless me*
How mighte a man han any adversitee
That hath a wif? Certes, I can nat saye.
The blisse which that is bitwixe hem twaye,
Ther may no tonge telle or herte thinke.
130 If he be poore, she helpeth him to swinke.°   *work*
She keepeth his good and wasteth neveradeel.°   *nothing*
Al that hir housbonde lust° hire liketh° weel.   *desires / pleases*
She saith nat ones "Nay" whan he saith "Ye."
"Do this," saith he. "Al redy, sire," saith she.
135   O blisful ordre of wedlok precious,
Thou art so merye and eek° so vertuous,   *also*
And so commended and approved° eek,   *approved*
That any man that halt him worth a leek[6]
Upon his bare knees oughte al his lif
140 Thanken his God that him hath sent a wif,
Or elles praye to God him for to sende
A wif to laste unto his lives ende:
For thanne his lif is set in sikernesse.°   *security*
He may nat be deceived, as I gesse,
145 So that he werke after his wives reed;°   *advice*
Thanne may be boldely keepen up his heed,°   *head*
They been so trewe and therwithal so wise;
For which, if thou wolt werken as the wise,
Do alway so as wommen wol thee rede.°   *advise*
150 Lo how that Jacob, as thise clerkes rede,[7]
By good conseil of his moder Rebekke
Boond° the kides° skin aboute his nekke,   *bound / kid's*
For which his fadres benison° he wan.°   *blessing / won*
   Lo Judith, as the storye eek telle can,
155 By good conseil she Goddes peple kepte,[8]
And slow° him Olofernus° whil he slepte.   *slew / Holofernes*

6. Considers himself worth a leek.
7. See Genesis xxv, which tells how Jacob won from his father the blessing that was properly his brother Esau's when, following his mother Rebecca's suggestion, he used a goatskin to simulate Esau's hairiness, thus deceiving the blind Isaac.
8. The Book of Judith tells how she saved her people by decapitating the general of an attacking army, Holofernes, while he was in a drunken sleep.

Lo Abigail by good conseil how she[9]
Saved her housbonde Nabal whan that he
Sholde han been slain. And looke Ester[1] also
160 By good conseil delivered out of wo
The peple of God, and made him Mardochee°   Mordecai
Of Assuere° enhaunced° for to be.   Ahasuerus / exalted
    Ther is nothing in gree° superlatif,   degree
As saith Senek,[2] above an humble wif.
165 Suffre thy wives tonge, as Caton[3] bit.°   bids
She shal comande and thou shalt suffren it,
And yit she wol obeye of curteisye.
    A wif is kepere° of thyn housbondrye:°   guardian / household
Wel may the sike man biwaile and weepe
170 Theras° ther is no wif the hous to keepe.   where
I warne thee, if wisely thou wolt wirche,°   work
Love wel thy wif as Crist loved his chirche;
If thou lovest thyself thou lovest thy wif:
No man hateth his flessh, but in his lif
175 He fostreth it, and therfore bidde I thee,
Cherisse thy wif or thou shalt nevere thee.°   prosper
Housbonde and wif, what so men jape° or playe,   joke
Of worldly folk holden the siker° waye.   sure
They been so knit[4] ther may noon harm bitide,
180 And namely° upon the wives side.—   especially
    For which this Januarye of whom I tolde
Considered hath inwith° his dayes olde   within
The lusty lif, the vertuous quiete
That is in mariage hony sweete,
185 And for his freendes on a day he sente
To tellen hem th'effect of his entente.
    With face sad° this tale he hath hem told: sober
He saide, "Freendes, I am hoor° and old,   gray
And almost, God woot, on my pittes brinke:[5]
190 Upon my soule somwhat moste° I thinke.   must
I have my body folily° dispended°—   foolishly / expended
Blessed be God that it shal been amended.
For I wol be, certain, a wedded man,
And that anoon, in al the haste I can,
195 Unto som maide fair and tendre of age.

9. See I Samuel xxv, which tells how Abigail persuaded David not to kill her husband Nabal, who had offended him; her action, however, was motivated less by a desire to spare Nabal than by a desire to prevent David from unnecessarily shedding blood: after Abigail told Nabal what she had done, he died, and Abigail became one of David's wives.
1. The Book of Esther tells how she saved her kinsman Mordecai and all her people by charming King Ahasuerus, whose concubine she had been forced to become. She persuaded the king to put to death Haman, the chief enemy of the Jews; his ten sons; and hundreds of Haman's supporters.
2. Seneca, the Roman philosopher, who was often cited as the author of pieces of sententious wisdom even though, as here, the remark is not to be found in his works.
3. I.e., the Cato Book, a school primer.
4. Joined together.
5. Grave's edge.

I praye you shapeth° for my mariage   *arrange*
Al sodeinly,° for I wol nat abide;°   *quickly / wait*
And I wol fonde° t'espyen on my side   *try*
To whom I may be wedded hastily.
200 But for as muche as ye been mo° than I,   *more*
Ye shullen rather° swich a thing espyen *sooner*
Than I, and wher me best were to allyen.
  But oo thing warne I you, my freendes dere:
I wol noon old wif han in no manere;
205 She shal nat passe twenty yeer certain—
Old fissh and young flessh wol I have fain.° *gladly*
Bet° is," quod he, "a pik[6] than a pikerel, *better*
And bet than old boef° is the tendre veel:° *beef / veal*
I wol° no womman thritty yeer of age— *wish*
210 It is but bene-straw and greet forage.[7]
And eek thise olde widwes, God it woot,° *knows*
They conne so muche craft on Wades boot,[8]
So muchel broken harm whan that hem leste,[9]
That with hem sholde I nevere live in reste.
215 For sondry scoles maketh subtile clerkes:
Womman of manye scoles half a clerk is.[1]
But certainly a yong thing may men gie,° *guide*
Right as men may warm wex° with handes plye.° *wax / mold*
Wherfore I saye you plainly in a clause,
220 I wol noon old wif han right for this cause:
For if so were I hadde swich meschaunce
That I in hire ne coude han no plesaunce,
Thanne sholde I lede my lif in avoutrye,° *adultery*
And go straight to the devel whan I die;
225 Ne children sholde I none upon hire geten,
Yit me were levere houndes hadde me eten
Than that myn heritage sholde falle
In straunge[2] hand; and this I telle you alle:
I dote nat, I woot° the cause why   *know*
230 Men sholde wedde, and ferthermore woot I
Ther speketh many a man of mariage
That woot namore of it than woot my page
For whiche causes man sholde take a wif:
If he ne may nat live chast his lif,
235 Take him a wif with greet devocioun,
By cause of leveful° procreacioun   *lawful*
Of children, to th'honour of God above,
And nat only for paramour[3] or love;

---

6. A pike was considered to be an old pickerel.
7. I.e., a thirty-year-old woman is only bean-straw (dried bean-stems) and coarse winter fodder.
8. They have so much skill in Wade's boat: Wade was a legendary hero, but his relevance here is not clear.
9. I.e., (they can) traffic so much in injuries when they feel like it.
1. Women are part-time students in many schools.
2. I.e., unlineal.
3. Bodily love.

And for they sholde lecherye eschue,°   *eschew*
240 And yeelde[4] hir dette whan that it is due;
Or for that eech of hem sholde helpen other
In meschief, as a suster shal the brother,
And live in chastitee ful holily—
But sires, by youre leve, that am nat I.
245 For God be thanked, I dar make avaunt,°   *boast*
I feele my limes° stark° and suffisaunt° *limbs / strong / competent*
To do al that a man bilongeth to.
I woot myself best what I may do.
    Though I be hoor, I fare as dooth a tree
250 That blosmeth er the fruit ywoxen° be,   *grown*
And blosmy tree nis neither drye ne deed:°   *dead*
I feele me nowher hoor but on myn heed;
Myn herte and alle my limes° been as greene   *limbs*
As laurer° thurgh° the yeer is for to seene. *laurel / through*
255 And sin that ye han herd al myn entente,
I praye you to my wil ye wol assente."
    Diverse men diversely him tolde
Of mariage manye ensamples[5] olde:
Some blamed it, some praised it, certain;
260 But at the laste, shortly for to sayn,
As alday° falleth altercacioun   *constantly*
Bitwixe freendes in disputisoun,°   *argument*
Ther fil° a strif bitwixe his bretheren two,   *occurred*
Of whiche that oon was cleped Placebo;[6]
265 Justinus soothly called was that other.
    Placebo saide, "O Januarye brother,
Ful litel neede hadde ye, my lord so dere,
Conseil to axe° of any that is here,   *ask*
But° that ye been so ful of sapience° *except / wisdom*
270 That you ne liketh, for youre heigh prudence,
To waiven° fro the word of Salomon;   *depart*
This word saide he unto us everichoon:
'Werk alle thing by conseil,' thus saide he,
'And thanne shaltou nat repenten thee.'[7]
275 But though that Salomon spak swich a word,
Myn owene dere brother and my lord,
So wisly° God my soule bringe at reste,   *surely*
I holde youre owene conseil is the beste.
For brother myn, of me take this motif.°   *proposition*
280 I have now been a court-man al my lif,
And God it woot, though I unworthy be,
I have stonden in ful greet degree
Abouten lordes in ful greet estat,

4. I.e., pay.
5. Illustrative stories.
6. Placebo takes his name from the first word of the Latin of Psalm cxiv.9 (Vulgate), "I shall please (the Lord in the land of the living)." Justinus in the next line suggests a just man.
7. The quotation is not from any of the works of Solomon but from Ecclesiasticus xxxii.19. Like Seneca, Solomon was often given credit for bits of sententious wisdom.

Yit hadde I nevere with noon of hem debat;
285 I nevere hem contraried,° trewely;   contradicted
I woot wel that my lord can° more than I;   knows
What that he saith, I hold it ferm° and stable;   firm
I saye the same or elles thing semblable.°   similar
A ful greet fool is any conseilour
290 That serveth any lord of heigh honour
That dar presume or elles thenken° it   imagine
That his conseil sholde passe[8] his lordes wit.
Nay, lordes be no fooles, by my fay.°   faith
Ye han yourselven shewed heer today
295 So heigh sentence° so holily and weel,   sentiments
That I consente and conferme everydeel
Youre wordes alle and your opinioun.
By God, ther nis no man in al this town,
Ne in Itaile,° coude bet° han ysaid.   Italy / better
300 Crist halt him[9] of this conseil wel apaid.°   pleased
And trewely it is an heigh corage°   spirit
Of any man that stapen° is in age   advanced
To take a yong wif! By my fader kin,
Youre herte hangeth on a joly pin!
305 Dooth now in this matere right as you leste,°   please
For finally, I holde it for the beste."
        Justinus that ay° stille sat and herde,   always
Right in this wise he to Placebo answerde:
"Now, brother myn, be pacient I praye,
310 Sin° ye han said, and herkneth what I saye: since
Senek[1] amonges othere wordes wise
Saith that a man oughte him right wel avise
To whom he yiveth his land or his catel;°   property
And sin I oughte avisen me right wel
315 To whom I yive my good away fro me,
Wel muchel more I oughte avised be
To whom I yive my body for alway.
I warne you wel, it is no childes play
To taken a wif withouten avisement.°   deliberation
320 Men moste enquere°—this is myn assent°—   inquire / opinion
Wher° she be wis, or sobre, or dronkelewe,[2]   whether
Or proud, or elles otherways a shrewe,
A chidestere,° or wastour of thy good,   chider
Or riche, or poore, or elles mannissh wood[3]—
325 Al be it so that no man finden shal
Noon in this world that trotteth[4] hool° in al,   whole
Ne man ne beest swich as men coude devise.°   imagine
But nathelees, it oughte ynough suffise
With any wif, if so were that she hadde

---

8. Be superior to.   2. Given to drunkenness.
9. Considers himself.   3. Unfemininely inclined to rage.
1. For Seneca, see note to line 164, 4. Trots, i.e., appears.
above.

330 Mo° goode thewes° than hir vices badde.   *more / characteristics*
   And al this axeth° leiser for t'enquere.   *requires*
   For God it woot, I have wept many a tere
   Ful prively sin° that I hadde a wif: *since*
   Praise whoso wol a wedded mannes lif,
335 Certain I finde in it but cost and care,
   And observances° of alle blisses bare.   *duties*
   And yit, God woot, my neighebores aboute,
   And namely° of wommen many a route,°   *especially / group*
   Sayn that I have the moste stedefast wif,
340 And eek the mekeste° oon that bereth lif—   *meekest*
   But I woot best where wringeth° me my sho.°   *pinches / shoe*
   Ye mowe° for me right as you liketh do.   *may*
   Aviseth you—ye been a man of age—
   How that ye entren into mariage,
345 And namely° with a yong wif and a fair.   *especially*
   By him that made water, erthe, and air,
   The youngeste man that is in al this route
   Is bisy ynough to bringen it aboute
   To han his wif allone. Trusteth me,
350 Ye shul nat plesen hire fully yeres three—
   This is to sayn, to doon hire ful plesaunce:
   A wif axeth ful many an observaunce.[5]
   I praye you that ye be nat yvele apaid."[6]
     "Wel," quod this Januarye, "and hastou said?
355 Straw for thy Senek and for thy proverbes!
   I counte° nat a panier° ful of herbes   *value / basket*
   Of scole-termes.[7] Wiser men than thou,
   As thou hast herd, assenteden right now
   To my purpos. Placebo, what saye ye?"
360   "I saye it is a cursed man," quod he
  "That letteth° matrimoigne,°
      sikerly."°   *hinders / matrimony / certainly*
   And with that word they risen sodeinly,
   And been assented fully that he sholde
   Be wedded whan him liste and wher[8] he wolde.
365   Heigh fantasye° and curious°
      bisinesse°   *imagining / careful / attentiveness*
   Fro day to day gan in the soule impresse[9]
   Of Januarye aboute his mariage:
   Many fair shap and many a fair visage
   Ther passeth thurgh his herte night by night;
370 As whoso tooke a mirour polisshed bright,
   And sette it in a commune market-place,
   Thanne sholde he see ful many a figure pace°   *pass*
   By his mirour; and in the same wise
   Gan Januarye inwith° his thought devise   *within*

---

5. Little ritual.
6. Ill-pleased.
7. School terms, i.e., subtle arguments.
8. I.e., to whom.
9. I.e., took hold upon the spirit.

375 Of maidens whiche that dwelten him biside.
    He wiste° nat wher that he mighte abide:°   *knew / settle*
    For if that oon have beautee in hir face,
    Another stant° so in the peples grace   *stands*
    For hir sadnesse° and hir benignitee,   *constancy*
380 That of the peple grettest vois[1] hath she;
    And some were riche and hadden badde name.
    But nathelees, bitwixe ernest and game,
    He atte laste appointed him on[2] oon,
    And leet° alle othere° from his herte goon,   *let / others*
385 And chees° hire of his owene auctoritee°—   *chose / authority*
    For Love is blind alday° and may nat see.   *always*
    And whan that he was in his bed ybrought,
    He portrayde in his herte and in his thought
    Hir fresshe beautee and hir age tendre,
390 Hir middel smal, hir armes longe and sclendre,
    Hir wise governance,° hir gentilesse,°   *behavior / gentility*
    Hir wommanly bering and hir sadnesse.°   *constancy*
    And whan that he on hire was condescended,°   *settled*
    Him thoughte his chois mighte nat been amended;[3]
395 For whan that he himself concluded[4] hadde,
    Him thoughte eech other mannes wit so badde,
    That impossible it were to replye[5]
    Again his chois: this was his fantasye.
       His freendes sente he to at his instaunce,
400 And prayed hem to doon him that plesaunce
    That hastily they wolden to him come:
    He wolde abregge° hir labour alle and some;[6]   *shorten*
    Needeth namore for him to go ne ride;
    He was appointed° ther he wolde abide.   *determined*
405   Placebo cam and eek his freendes soone,
    And alderfirst[7] he bad° hem alle a boone,   *prayed*
    That noon of hem none argumentes make
    Again the purpos which that he hath take,
    Which purpos was plesant to God, saide he,
410 And verray° ground of his prosperitee.   *true*
       He saide ther was a maiden in the town
    Which that of beautee hadde greet renown;
    Al° were it so she were of smal degree,[8]   *although*
    Suffiseth him hir youthe and hir beautee;
415 Which maide he saide he wolde han to his wif,
    To lede in ese and holinesse his lif,
    And thanked God that he mighte han hire al,[9]
    That no wight his blisse parten° shal;   *share*
    And prayde hem to labouren in this neede,
420 And shapen° that he faile not to speede.[1]   *arrange*

---

1. I.e., loudest acclaim.
2. Determined upon.
3. Improved upon.
4. Come to a decision.
5. I.e., to object.
6. Each and every one of them.

7. First of all.
8. Low social rank.
9. Her youth and beauty are enough for him.
1. Attain his end.

For thanne he saide his spirit was at ese.
"Thanne is," quod he, "no thing may me displese.
Save oo thing priketh in my conscience,
The which I wol reherce in youre presence.

425 I have," quod he, "herd said ful yore[2] ago
Ther may no man han parfite° blisses two—   *perfect*
This is to saye, in erthe and eek in hevene.
For though he keepe him fro the sinnes sevene,
And eek from every braunche[3] of thilke° tree,   *that*

430 Yit is ther so parfit° felicitee   *perfect*
And so greet ese and lust° in mariage,   *pleasure*
That evere I am agast now in myn age
That I shal lede now so merye a lif,
So delicat,° withouten wo and strif,   *delightful*

435 That I shal han myn hevene in erthe here.
For sith° that verray hevene is bought so dere   *since*
With tribulaciouns and greet penaunce,
How sholde I thanne, that live in swich plesaunce
As alle wedded men doon with hir wives,

440 Come to the blisse ther Crist eterne on live is?
This is my drede, and ye, my bretheren twaye,
Assoileth° me this question, I praye."   *resolve*
    Justinus, which that hated his folye,
Answerde anoonright° in his japerye;°   *straightway / joking*

445 And for he wolde his longe tale abregge.°   *shorten*
He wolde noon auctoritee allegge,°   *adduce*
But saide, "Sire, so there be noon obstacle
Other than this, God of his heigh miracle
And of his mercy may so for you wirche,°   *work*

450 That er ye have youre right[4] of holy chirche,
Ye may repente of wedded mannes lif,
In which ye sayn ther is no wo ne strif.
And elles God forbede but° he sente   *unless*
A wedded man him grace to repente

455 Wel ofte rather° than a sengle° man.   *sooner / single*
And therfore, sire, the beste reed° I can:[5]   *advice*
Despaire you nought, but have in youre memorye
Paraunter° she may be youre purgatorye;   *perhaps*
She may be Goddes mene[6] and Goddes whippe!

460 Thanne shal youre soule up to hevene skippe
Swifter than dooth an arwe out of a bowe.
I hope to God heerafter shul ye knowe
That ther nis noon so greet felicitee
In marriage, ne nevere mo° shall be,   *more*

465 That you shal lette° of youre savacioun,   *hinder*
So that ye use, as skile° is and resoun,   *reason*

---

2. I.e., long.
3. The seven deadly sins were divided into branches and sub-branches, so that the total number of sins one was in danger of committing was very high.
4. Due, i.e., burial.
5. Am capable of.
6. Means, i.e., agent.

The lustes° of youre wif attemprely,°   *pleasures / moderately*
And that ye plese hire nat too amorously,
And that ye keepe you eek from other sinne.
470 My tale is doon, for my wit is thinne.
Beeth nat agast heerof, my brother dere,
But lat us waden° out of this matere.   *move*
The Wif of Bathe, if ye han understonde,
Of mariage which ye han on honde
475 Declared hath ful wel in litel space.
Fareth now wel. God have you in his grace."
    And with that word this Justin and his brother
Han take hir leve and eech of hem of other,
For whan they saw that it moste° needes be   *must*
480 They wroughten so by sly° and wis tretee°   *clever / negotiation*
That she, this maiden which that Mayus highte,° *was named*
As hastily as evere that she mighte,
Shal wedded be unto this Januarye.
    I trowe it were too longe you to tarye
485 If I you tolde of every scrit° and bond   *writ*
By which that she was feffed in[7] his lond,
Or for to herknen of hir riche array;
But finally ycomen is that day
That to the chirche bothe be they went
490 For to receive the holy sacrament.
    Forth comth the preest with stole aboute his nekke,
And bad hire be lik Sarra and Rebekke[8]
In wisdom and in trouthe° of mariage,   *fidelity*
And saide his orisons as is usage,
495 And croucheth[9] hem, and bad God sholde hem blesse,
And made al siker° ynough with holinesse.   *secure*
    Thus been they wedded with solempnitee,
And at the laste sitteth he and she
With other worthy folk upon the dais.
500 Al ful of joye and blisse is the palais,
And ful of instruments[1] and of vitaile,°   *foodstuffs*
The moste daintevous° of al Itaile.   *tasty*
Biforn hem stoode instruments of swich soun,°   *sound*
That Orpheus n'of Thebes Amphioun[2]
505 Ne maden nevere swich a melodye.
At every cours thanne cam loud minstralcye,
That nevere tromped Joab[3] for to heere,
Ne he Theodamas[4] yit half so clere
At Thebes whan the citee was in doute.

---

7. Endowed with.
8. In the medieval marriage ceremony, the priest enjoined the bride to imitate Sarah and Rebecca. Sarah was Abraham's wife, the mother of Isaac; for Rebecca, see note to line 150, above.
9. Signs with the cross.
1. I.e., provisions.

2. Orpheus and Amphioun were legendary musicians of ancient Greece.
3. Joab, King David's officer, on several occasions controlled the people with the sound of his trumpet.
4. Theodamas was a Theban seer whose auguries were announced with a trumpet.

510 Bacus° the win hem shenketh° al aboute,   *Bacchus / pours*
    And Venus laugheth upon every wight,
    For Januarye was bicome hir knight,
    And wolde bothe assayen his corage
    In libertee and eek in mariage;
515 And with hir firbrand in hir hand aboute
    Daunceth bifore the bride and al the route.°   *company*
    And certainly, I dar right wel saye this:
    Ymeneus° that God of Wedding is   *Hymen*
    Sawgh nevere his lif so merye a wedded man.
520 Hold thou thy pees, thou poete Marcian,[5]
    That writest us that ilke wedding murye°   *merry*
    Of hire Philologye and him Mercurye,
    And of the songes that the Muses songe°—   *sang*
    Too smal is bothe thy penne and eek thy tonge
525 For to descriven° of this mariage.   *describe*
    Whan tendre youthe hath wedded stouping° age,   *stooping*
    Ther is swich mirthe that it may nat be writen;
    Assayeth it yourself, thanne may ye witen°   *learn*
    If that I lie or noon in this matere.
530   Mayus, that sit° with so benigne a cheere° *sits / expression*
    Hire to biholde it seemed faïrye°—   *magic*
    Queene Ester[6] looked nevere with swich an yë
    On Assuer, so meeke a look hath she—
    I may you nat devise al hir beautee,
535 But thus muche of hir beautee telle I may,
    That she was lik the brighte morwe of May,
    Fulfild[7] of alle beautee and plesaunce.
        This Januarye is ravisshed in a traunce
    At every time he looked on hir face,
540 But in his herte he gan hire to manace°   *menace*
    That he that night in armes wolde hire straine° *constrain*
    Harder than evere Paris dide Elaine.[8]
    But nathelees yit hadde he greet pitee
    That thilke night offenden hire moste° he,   *must*
545 And thoughte, "Allas, O tendre creature,
    Now wolde God ye mighte wel endure
    Al my corage,[9] it is so sharp and keene:
    I am agast ye shul it nat sustene°—   *sustain*
    But God forbede that I dide al my might!
550 Now wolde God that it were woxen° night,   *grown*
    And that the night wolde lasten everemo.
    I wolde that al this peple were ago."
    And finally he dooth al his labour,
    As he best mighte, saving his honour,

5. Martianus Capella, author of a medieval Latin poem which describes the wedding of Philology and Mercury.
6. For Esther and Ahasuerus, see note to line 159, above.
7. Filled full.
8. Helen of Troy.
9. Spirit, but with the added sense of sexual prowess.

555 To haste hem fro the mete in subtil wise.
The time cam that reson was to rise,
And after that men daunce and drinken faste,
And spices al aboute the hous they caste.
And ful of joye and blis is every man—
560 Al but a squier highte° Damian,   called
Which carf° biforn the knight ful many a day: carved
He was so ravisshed on his lady May
That for the verray paine he was neigh wood;°   mad
Almost he swelte° and swouned° ther he stood,   fainted / swooned
565 So sore hath Venus hurt him with hir brand,
As that she bar it dauncing in hir hand.
And to his bed he wente him hastily.
Namore of him at this time speke I,
But ther I lete him weepe ynough and plaine,°   complain
570 Til fresshe May wol rewen[1] on his paine.
    O perilous fir that in the bedstraw breedeth![2]
O familier fo that his service bedeth!°   offers
O servant traitour, false hoomly° hewe,°   domestic / servant
Lik to the naddre° in bosom, sly, untrewe!°   adder / treacherous
575 God shilde° us alle from youre aquaintaunce!   defend
O Januarye, dronken in plesaunce
In mariage, see how thy Damian,
Thyn owene squier and thy boren° man,   born
Entendeth for to do thee vilainye!°   harm
580 God graunte thee thyn hoomly fo espye,
For in this world nis worse pestilence
Than hoomly fo alday° in thy presence.   always
    Parfourned° hath the sonne his ark diurne:[3]   performed
No lenger may the body of him sojurne
585 On th'orisonte° as in that latitude;   horizon
Night with his mantel that is derk and rude
Gan oversprede th' hemisperye° aboute,   hemisphere
For which departed is this lusty route,°   company
For Januarye with thank on every side.
590 Hoom to hir houses lustily they ride,
Wher as they doon hir thinges as hem leste,°   please
And whan they sawgh hir time go to reste.
    Soone after that this hastif° Januarye   impatient
Wol go to bedde—he wol no lenger tarye.
595 He drinketh ipocras, clarree and vernage[4]
Of spices hote t'encreessen° his corage,   increase
And many a letuarye° hadde he ful fin,°   medicine / pure
Swich as the cursed monk daun Constantin[5]
Hath writen in his book *De Coitu:*

1. Have pity.
2. I.e., starts.
3. Diurnal arc.
4. The beverages mentioned here were
thought to be aphrodisiac.
5. Constantinus Afer, author of a treatise on copulation.

600 To eten hem alle he nas no thing eschu.°   *averse*
And to his privee freendes thus saide he:
"For Goddes love, as soone as it may be,
Lat voiden° al this hous in curteis wise."   *empty*
And they han doon right as he wol devise.

605 Men drinken and the travers° drawe anoon.   *curtains*
The bride was brought abedde as stille as stoon.
And whan the bed was with° the preest yblessed,   *by*
Out of the chambre hath every wight him dressed.°   *turned*
And Januarye hath faste in armes take

610 His fresshe May, his Paradis, his make;°   *mate*
He lulleth hire, he kisseth hire ful ofte—
With thikke bristles of his beerd unsofte,
Lik to the skin of houndfissh,° sharpe as brere,°   *dogfish / briar*
For he was shave al newe in his manere—

615 He rubbeth hire aboute hir tendre face,
And saide thus, "Allas, I moot trespace[6]
To you, my spouse, and you greetly offende
Er time come that I wol down descende.
But nathelees, considereth this," quod he,

620 "Ther nis no werkman, whatsoevere he be,
That may bothe werke wel and hastily.
This wol be doon at leiser parfitly.°   *perfectly*
It is no fors° how longe that we playe: *matter*
In trewe wedlok coupled be we twaye,

625 And blessed be the yok that we been inne,
For in oure actes we mowe° do no sinne;   *may*
A man may do no sinne with his wif,
Ne hurte himselven with his owene knif;
For we han leve to playe us by the lawe."

630 Thus laboureth he til that the day gan dawe,°   *dawn*
And thanne he taketh a sop in fin clarree,[7]
And upright in his bed thanne sitteth he;
And after that he soong° ful loude and clere,   *sang*
And kiste his wif and made wantoune cheere:

635 He was al coltissh,° ful of ragerye,°   *frisky / flirtatiousness*
And ful of jargon as a flekked pie.°   *magpie*
The slakke skin aboute his nekke shaketh
Whil that he soong, so chaunteth he and craketh.°   *caws*
But God woot what that May thoughte in hir herte

640 Whan she him saw up sitting in his sherte,°   *shirt*
In his night-cappe and with his nekke lene—
She praiseth nat his playing worth a bene.°   *bean*
Thanne saide he thus, "My reste wol I take.
Now day is come I may no lenger wake."

645 And down he laide his heed and sleep° til prime,[8]   *slept*
And afterward whan that he saw his time

6. Must do injury.   8. 9 A.M.
7. Bread soaked in fine wine.

Up riseth Januarye. But fresshe May
Heeld hir chambre unto the fourthe day,
As usage is of wives for the beste,
650 For every labour som time moot° han reste,   *must*
Or elles longe may he nat endure—
This is to sayn, no lives° creature,   *living*
Be it fissh or brid° or beest or man.   *bird*
    Now wol I speke of woful Damian
655 That languissheth for love, as ye shal heere.
Therfore I speke to him in this manere:
    I saye, "O sely° Damian, allas,   *silly*
Answere to my demande as in this cas:
How shaltou to thy lady fresshe May
660 Telle thy wo? She wol away saye nay.
Eek if thou speke, she wol thy wo biwraye.°   *disclose*
God be thyn help I can no bettre saye."
    This sike Damian in Venus fir
So brenneth° that he dieth for desir,   *burns*
665 For which he putte his life in aventure:[9]
No lenger mighte he in this wise endure,
But prively a penner° gan he borwe,   *pen-case*
And in a lettre wroot he al his sorwe,
In manere of a complainte or a lay,
670 Unto his faire fresshe lady May;
And in a purs of silk heeng[1] on his sherte
He hath it put and laid it at his herte.
    The moone, that at noon was thilke° day   *that*
That Januarye hath wedded fresshe May
675 In two of Taur, was into Cancre gliden,[2]
So longe hath Mayus in hir chambre abiden,
As custume is unto thise nobles alle:
A bride shal nat eten in the halle
Til dayes foure, or three dayes atte leeste,
680 Ypassed been—thanne lat hire go to feeste.
    The fourthe day compleet fro noon to noon,
Whan that the hye masse was ydoon,
In halle sit° this Januarye and May,   *sits*
As fressh as is the brighte someres day.
685 And so bifel how that this goode man
Remembred him upon this Damian,
And saide, "Sainte Marye, how may it be
That Damian entendeth° nat to me?   *attends*
Is he ay sik, or how may this bitide?"
690   His squiers whiche that stooden ther biside
Excused him by cause of his siknesse,
Which letted° him to doon his bisinesse: *prevented*
Noon other cause mighte make him tarye.

9. Risked his life.
1. That hung.
2. In two degrees of Taurus (the sign of the Bull) had moved into Cancer (the sign of the Crab).

"That me forthinketh,³" quod this Januarye.
695 "He is a gentil squier, by my trouthe.
If that he deide, it were harm and routhe.°   *pity*
He is as wis, discreet, and eek secree,
As any man I woot of his degree,
And therto manly and eek servisable,
700 And for to be a thrifty° man right able.   *proper*
But after mete as soone as evere I may,
I wol myself visite him, and eek May,
To do him al the confort that I can."
And for that word him blessed every man
705 That of his bountee° and his gentilesse°   *goodness / courtesy*
He wolde so conforten in siknesse
His squier—for it was a gentil deede.
    "Dame," quod this Januarye, "take good heede:
At after-mete⁴ ye with your wommen alle,
710 Whan ye han been in chambre out of this halle,
That alle ye go to this Damian.
Dooth him disport°—he is a gentil man—   *cheer*
And telleth him that I wol him visite,
Have I no thing but rested me a lite.⁵
715 And speede you faste, for I wol abide
Til that ye sleepe faste by my side."
And with that word he gan to him to calle
A squier that was marchal⁶ of his halle,
And tolde him certain thinges what he wolde.
720   This fresshe May hath straight hir way yholde
With alle hir wommen unto Damian:
Down by his beddes side sit° she than,   *sits*
Conforting him as goodly as she may.
    This Damian, whan that his time he sey,°   *saw*
725 In secree wise his purs and eek his bille,°   *letter*
In which that he ywriten hadde his wille,
Hath put into hir hand withoute more,
Save that he siketh° wonder deepe and sore,   *sighs*
And softely to hire right thus saide he:
730 "Mercy, and that ye nat discovere° me,   *betray*
For I am deed if that this thing be kid."⁷
The purs hath she inwith° hir bosom hid,   *within*
And wente hir way—ye gete namore of me.
But unto Januarye ycomen is she,
735 That on his beddes side sit ful softe,
And taketh hire and kisseth hire ful ofte,
And laide him down to sleepe and that anoon.
She feined hire⁸ as that she moste° goon   *must*
Ther as ye woot that every wight moot° neede,   *must*
740 And whan she of this bille hath taken heede,

3. I regret.   6. Marshal, major-domo.
4. After dinner.   7. Made known.
5. After I've rested just a little.   8. Pretended.

She rente° it al to cloutes° at the laste,   *tore / shreds*
And in the privee softely it caste.
    Who studieth now but faire fresshe May?
Adown by olde Januarye she lay,
745 That sleep° til that the coughe hath him awaked.   *slept*
Anoon he prayde hire strepen° hire al naked;   *strip*
He wolde of hire, he saide, han som plesaunce;
He saide hir clothes dide him encombraunce.
And she obeyeth, be hire lief° or loth.   *agreeable*
750 But lest that precious° folk be with me wroth,   *fastidious*
How that he wroughte I dar nat to you telle—
Or wheither hire thoughte[9] Paradis or helle.
But here I lete hem werken in hir wise
Til evensong roong° and that they moste arise.   *rang*
755   Were it by destinee or aventure,°   *accident*
Were it by influence[1] or by nature,
Or constellacion that in swich estat
The hevene stood that time fortunat
As for to putte a bille of Venus werkes[2]—
760 For alle thing hath time, as sayn thise clerkes—
To any womman for to gete hir love,
I can nat saye, but grete God above,
That knoweth that noon act is causelees.
He deeme[3] of al, for I wol holde my pees.
765   But sooth is this: how that this fresshe May
Hath taken swich impression that day
Of pitee on this sike Damian,
That from hir herte she ne drive can
The remembrance° for to doon him ese.   *memorandum*
770 "Certain," thoughte she, "whom that this thing displese
I rekke° nat. For here I him assure   *care*
To love him best of any creature,
Though he namore hadde than his sherte."°   *shirt*
Lo, pitee renneth° soone in gentil herte!   *runs*
775   Here may ye see how excellent franchise°   *generosity*
In wommen is whan they hem narwe avise.[4]
Som tyrant is, as ther be many oon,
That hath an herte as hard as is a stoon,
Which wolde han lete him sterven° in the place,   *die*
780 Wel rather than han graunted him hir grace,
And hem rejoisen in hir cruel pride,
And rekke nat[5] to been an homicide.
    This gentil May, fulfilled[6] of pitee,
Right of hir[7] hand a lettre maked she,
785 In which she graunteth him hir verray grace:
Ther lakketh nought only but day and place

---

9. It seemed.   4. Consider closely.
1. I.e., occult interference.   5. Do not scruple.
2. Present a petition for Venus' works.   6. Filled full.
3. Let him judge.   7. In her own.

Wher that she mighte unto his lust suffise;°   *satisfy*
For it shal be right as he wol devise.
And when she saw hir time upon a day
790 To visite this Damian gooth May,
And subtilly this lettre down she threste°   *thrust*
Under his pilwe: rede it if him leste.
She taketh him by the hand and harde him twiste,°   *twisted*
So secrely that no wight of it wiste,°   *knew*
795 And bad him be al hool,[8] and forth she wente
To Januarye whan that he for hire sente.
    Up riseth Damian the nexte morwe:°   *morning*
Al passed was his siknesse and his sorwe.
He kembeth° him, he preineth° him and
      piketh,°   *combs / preens / cleans*
800 He dooth al that his lady lust° and liketh.   *pleases*
And eek to Januarye he gooth as lowe°   *humbly*
As evere dide a dogge for the bowe.[9]
He is so plesant unto every man—
For craft is al, whoso that do it can—
805 That every wight is fain° to speke him good.   *glad*
And fully in his lady grace he stood.
Thus lete° I Damian aboute his neede,   *leave*
And in my tale forth I wol proceede.
    Some clerkes holden that felicitee
810 Stant° in delit,[1] and therfore certain he,   *stands*
This noble Januarye, with al his might
In honeste° wise as longeth° to a knight,   *honorable / befits*
Shoop° him to live ful deliciously: *arranged*
His housing, his array as honestly
815 To his degree was maked as a kinges.
Amonges othere of his honeste thinges,
He made a gardin walled al of stoon—
So fair a gardin woot I nowher noon,
For out of doute I verraily suppose
820 That he that wroot the *Romance of the Rose*[2]
Ne coude of it the beautee wel devise;
Ne Priapus[3] ne mighte nat suffise—
Though he be god of gardins—for to telle
The beautee of the gardin, and the welle°   *spring*
825 That stood under a laurer° alway greene.   *laurel*
Ful ofte time he Pluto[4] and his queene
Proserpina and al hir fairye°   *fairies*
Disporten hem and maken melodye

---

8. I.e., get well.
9. The image is of a well-trained hunting dog.
1. Material delight.
2. Guillaume de Lorris' French allegory, set in the garden of love.
3. A fertility god associated with the male sexual organ.

4. Pluto was the god of the underworld who kidnaped the young girl Proserpina and made her his mate. In this tale the two have lost their great mythic stature —though not their history—and have become king and queen of the medieval otherworld—"fairye."

Aboute that welle, and daunced, as men tolde.
830 This noble knight, this Januarye the olde,
Swich daintee° hath in it to walke and playe,   *delight*
That he wol no wight suffre bere the keye,
Save he himself; for of the smale wiket°   *wicket-gate*
He bar alway of silver a cliket,°   *latch-key*
835 With which whan that him leste he it unshette.°   *unlocked*
And whan he wolde paye his wif hir dette
In somer seson, thider wolde he go,
And May his wif, and no wight but they two.
And thinges whiche that were nat doon abedde,
840 He in the gardin parfourned° hem and spedde.   *performed*
And in this wise many a merye day
Lived this Januarye and fresshe May.
But worldly joye may nat alway dure°   *continue*
To Januarye, ne to no creature.
845   O sodein° hap,° O thou Fortune
             unstable,   *unanticipated / change*
Lik to the scorpion so deceivable,°   *deceitful*
That flaterest with thyn heed° whan thou wolt stinge,   *head*
Thy tail is deeth thurgh thyn enveniminge![5]
O brotel° joye, O sweete venim°
             quainte!°   *brittle / poison / curious*
850 O monstre, that so subtilly canst painte
Thy yiftes under hewe of stedfastnesse,
That thou deceivest bothe more and lesse,
Why hastou Januarye thus deceived,
That haddest him for thy fulle freend received?
855 And now thou hast biraft[6] him bothe his yën,
For sorwe of which desireth he to dien.
Allas, this noble Januarye free,°   *generous*
Amidde his lust[7] and his prosperitee,
Is woxen° blind, and that al sodeinly.   *grown*
860 He weepeth and he waileth pitously,
And therwithal the fir of jalousye,
Lest that his wife sholde falle in som folye,
So brente° his herte that he wolde fain°   *burned / gladly*
That som man bothe hire and him hadde slain;
865 For neither after his deeth ne in his lif,
Ne wolde he that she were love ne wif,
But evere live as widwe in clothes blake,
Soul° as the turtle[8] that hath lost hir make.°   *sole / mate*
But atte laste, after a month or twaye,
870 His sorwe gan assuage, sooth to saye,
For whan he wiste° it may noon other be,   *knew*
He paciently took his adversitee—

5. Poisoning; the scorpion was popularly supposed to charm its victim by the innocent appearance of its head before stinging with its tail.
6. Deprived of.
7. Heart's desire.
8. Turtle-dove.

Save out of doute he may nat forgoon
That he nas jalous everemore in oon.[9]
875 Which jalousye it was so outrageous
That neither in halle ne in noon other hous,
Ne in noon other place neverthemo,
He nolde suffre hire for to ride or go,
But if that he hadde hand on hire alway:
880 For which ful ofte weepeth fresshe May,
That loveth Damian so benignely
That she moot° outher° dien sodeinly,   *must / either*
Or elles she moot han him as hire leste.
She waiteth[1] whan hir herte wolde breste.
885   Upon that other side Damian
Bicomen is the sorwefulleste man
That evere was, for neither night ne day
Ne mighte he speke a word to fresshe May,
As to his purpos of no swich matere,
890 But if that Januarye moste° it heere,   *must*
That hadde an hand upon hire evermo;
But nathelees, by writing to and fro,
And privee signes, wiste[2] what she mente,
And she knew eek the fin° of his entente.   *end*
895 O Januarye, what mighte it thee availe
Though thou mightest see as fer as shippes saile?
For as good is blind deceived be,
As be deceived whan a man may see.
Lo Argus, which that hadde an hundred yën,
900 For al that evere be coude poure° or pryen,   *gaze*
Yit was he blent,[3] and God woot so been mo°   *others*
That weenen° wisly° that it be nat so.   *think / surely*
Passe over is an ese,° and saye namore.   *relief*
    This fresshe May that I spak of so yore,[4]
905 In warm wex° hath emprinted the cliket°   *wax / key*
That Januarye bar of that smale wiket,
By which into his gardin ofte he wente;
And Damian that knew al hir entente
The cliket countrefeted[5] prively—
910 Ther nis namore to saye, but hastily
Som wonder by this cliket shal bitide,
Which ye shal heeren if ye wol abide.
    O noble Ovide, sooth saistou, God woot,
What sleighte° it is, though it be long and hoot,[6]   *trick*
915 That he[7] nil finde it out in som manere!
By Pyramus and Thisbee may men lere:°   *learn*
Though they were kept ful longe straite° overal, *strictly*
They been accorded rouning[8] thurgh a wal,

---

9. Constantly.
1. I.e., anticipates the time.
2. I.e., he knew.
3. Blinded, deceived.
4. Long ago.

5. I.e., duplicated.
6. Hot, i.e., perilous.
7. I.e, Love.
8. Whispering: the story of Pyramus and Thisbe is in Ovid's *Metamorphoses*.

Ther no wight coude han founde out swich a sleighte.
920 But now to purpos: er that dayes eighte
Were passed, er the month of Juin,° bifil   *June*
That Januarye hath caught so greet a wil—
Thurgh egging of his wif—him for to playe
In his gardin, and no wight but they twaye,
925 That in a morwe unto his May saith he,
"Ris up, my wif, my love, my lady free;
The turtles° vois is herd, my douve° sweete;   *turtle-dove's / dove*
The winter is goon with alle his raines wete.
Com forth now with thine yën columbin.°   *dove-like*
930 How fairer been thy brestes than is win!
The garden is enclosed al aboute:
Com forth, my white spouse! out of doute,
Thou hast me wounded in myn herte. O wif,
No spot of thee ne knew I al my lif.
935 Com forth and lat us taken oure disport—
I chees° thee for my wif and my confort."   *chose*
    Swiche olde lewed⁹ wordes used he.
On Damian a signe made she
940 That he sholde go biforn with his cliket.
This Damian thanne hath opened the wiket,
And in he sterte,° and that in swich manere   *went*
That no wight mighte it see neither yheere,
And stille he sit° under a bussh anoon.   *sits*
    This Januarye, as blind as is a stoon,
945 With Mayus in his hand and no wight mo,
Into his fresshe gardin is ago,¹
And clapte to² the wiket sodeinly.
"Now wif," quod he, "here nis but thou and I,
That art the creature that I best love,
950 For by that Lord that sit in hevene above,
Levere ich hadde to dien on a knif
Than thee offende, trewe dere wif.
For Goddes sake, thenk how I thee chees,°   *chose*
Nought for no coveitise,° doutelees,   *avarice*
955 But only for the love I hadde to thee.
And though that I be old and may nat see,
Beeth to me trewe, and I wol telle why.
Three thinges, certes, shal ye winne therby:
First, love of Crist, and to yourself honour,
960 And al myn heritage, town and towr³—
I yive it you: maketh chartres as you leste.
This shal be doon tomorwe er sonne reste,
So wisly° God my soule bringe in blisse.   *surely*
I praye you first in covenant ye me kisse,
965 And though that I be jalous, wite° me nought: *blame*

9. Unskillful: the words are a paraphrase of several passages in the Song of
Solomon.

1. Has gone.
2. Slammed shut.
3. I.e., castle.

Ye been so deepe emprinted in my thought,
That whan that I considere youre beautee,
And therwithal the unlikly elde[4] of me,
I may nought, certes, though I sholde die,
970 Forbere to been out of youre compaignye
For verray° love. This is withouten doute.   *true*
Now kis me, wif, and lat us rome aboute."
    This fresshe May, whan she thise wordes herde,
Benignely to Januarye answerde,
975 But first and forward° she bigan to weepe.   *foremost*
"I have," quod she, "a soule for to keepe°   *save*
As wel as ye, and also myn honour,
And of my wifhood thilke tendre flowr,
Which that I have assured° in youre hond,   *pledged*
980 Whan that the preest to you my body boond;°   *bound*
Wherfore I wol answere in this manere,
By the leve of you, my lord so dere:
I praye to God that nevere dawe° the day   *dawn*
That I ne sterve° as foule° as womman may,   *die / shamefully*
985 If evere I do unto my kin that shame,
Or elles I empaire° so my name   *impair*
That I be fals; and if I do that lak,°   *crime*
Do strepe me,[5] and putte me in a sak,
And in the nexte° river do me drenche:[6]   *nearest*
990 I am a gentil womman and no wenche.
Why speke ye thus? But men been evere untrewe,
And wommen have repreve° of you ay newe.   *reproof*
Ye han noon other countenance,[7] I leve,°   *believe*
But speke to us of untrust and repreve."
995   And with that word she saw wher Damian
Sat in the bussh, and coughen she bigan,
And with hir finger signes made she
That Damian sholde climbe upon a tree
That charged° was with fruit; and up he wente,   *loaded*
1000 For verraily he knew al hir entente,
And every signe that she coude make,
Wel bet° than Januarye, hir owene make,°   *better / mate*
For in a lettre she haddle told him al
Of this matere how he werken shal.
1005 And thus I lete him sitte on the pirye,°   *pear tree*
And Januarye and May roming mirye.
    Bright was the day and blew° the firmament.   *blue*
Phebus hath of gold his stremes° down sent   *beams*
To gladen every flowr with his warmnesse.
1010 He was that time in Geminis,[8] as I gesse,
But litel fro his declinacioun[9]

4. Unsuitable old age.
5. Have me stripped.
6. Have me drowned.
7. I.e., way of covering your own fault.
8. The Sign of the Twins.
9. I.e., position upon entering.

Of Cancer, Joves exaltacioun.[1]
And so bifel that brighte morwetide°   *morning-time*
That in that gardin in the ferther side
1015 Pluto, that is king of fairye,
And many a lady in his compaignye,
Folwing his wif, the queene Proserpina
Which that he ravisshed out of Etna
Whil that she gadred flowres in the mede—
1020 In Claudian[2] ye may the stories rede
How in his grisly carte he hire fette°—   *fetched*
This king of fairye thanne adown him sette
Upon a bench of turves fressh and greene,
And right anoon thus saide he to his queene.
1025   "My wif," quod he, "ther may no wight saye nay:
Th' experience so preveth° every day   *proves*
The treson which that womman dooth to man.
Ten hundred thousand tales tellen I can
Notable of youre untrouthe° and
        brotelnesse.°   *infidelity / fickleness*
1030 O Salomon, wis and richest of richesse,
Fulfild of sapience° and of worldly glorye,   *wisdom*
Ful worthy been thy wordes to memorye
To every wight that wit and reson can°—   *recognizes*
Thus praiseth he yit the bountee of man:
1035 'Amonges a thousand men yit foond° I oon,   *found*
But of wommen alle foond I noon.'[3]
Thus saith the king that knoweth youre wikkednesse.
And Jesus filius Syrak[4] as I gesse,
Ne speketh of you but selde° reverence—   *seldom*
1040 A wilde fir and corrupt pestilence
So falle upon youre bodies yit tonight!
Ne see ye nought this honourable knight?
By cause, allas, that he is blind and old,
His owene man shal make him cokewold.°   *cuckold*
1045 Lo wher he sit,° the lechour in the tree!   *sits*
     Now wol I graunten of my majestee
Unto this olde, blinde, worthy knight
That he shal have ayain his yën-sight,
Whan that his wif wolde doon him vilainye.
1050 Thanne shall he knowen al hir harlotrye,
Bothe in repreve° of hire and othere mo."   *reproof*
   "Ye shal?" quod Proserpine. "Wol ye so?
Now by my modres sires[5] soule I swere
That I shal yiven hire suffisant° answere,   *satisfactory*

---

1. Of Cancer, the Sign of the Crab, which is Jupiter's exaltation, or position of dominant influence.
2. Claudian was the author of the late Latin poem *The Rape of Proserpine*, which describes Pluto's seizure of Pro-serpina in Aetna, in Sicily.
3. Ecclesiastes vii.28.
4. Jesus, son of Sirak, supposed author of the Book of Ecclesiasticus.
5. Mother's father's.

1055 And alle wommen after for hir sake,
That though they be in any gilt ytake,
With face bold they shul hemself excuse,
And bere hem down that wolde hem accuse:
For lak of answere noon of hem shal dien.

1060 Al° hadde men seen a thing with bothe his yën,   *although*
Yit shal we wommen visagen[6] it hardily,°   *confidently*
And weepe and swere and chide subtilly,
So that ye men shul been as lewed° as gees—   *stupid*
What rekketh me[7] of youre auctoritees?°   *authorities*

1065 I woot wel that this Jew, this Salomon,
Foond° of us wommen folies many oon,   *found*
But though that he ne foond no good womman,
Yit hath ther founde many another man
Wommen ful trewe, ful goode and vertuous.

1070 Witnesse on hem that dwelte in Cristes hous:
With martyrdom they preved hir constaunce.°   *constancy*
The Romain geestes[8] eek maken remembraunce
Of many a verray, trewe wif also.
But sire, ne be nat wroth, al be it so,

1075 Though that he saide he foond no good womman,
I praye you, take the sentence° of the man: *meaning*
He mente thus, that in soverein bountee[9]
Nis noon but God, but neither he ne she.
Ey, for verray God that nis but oon,

1080 What make ye so muche of Salomon?
What though he made a temple, Goddes hous?
What though he were riche and glorious?
So made he eek a temple of false goddes:
How mighte he do a thing that more forbode° is?   *forbidden*

1085 Pardee, as faire as ye his name emplastre,°   *whitewash*
He was a lechour and an idolastre,°   *idolator*
And in his elde° he verray God forsook.   *old age*
And if God ne hadde, as saith the book,
Yspared him for his fadres sake, he sholde

1090 Have lost his regne rather° than he wolde.°   *sooner / wanted*
I sette[1] right nought of al the vilainye
That ye of wommen write a boterflye.°   *butterfly*
I am a womman, needes moot° I speke,   *must*
Or elles swelle til myn herte breke.

1095 For sithen° he saide that we been jangleresses,[2]   *since*
As evere hool[3] I moote brouke° my tresses,   *enjoy*
I shal nat spare for no curteisye
To speke him harm that wolde[4] us vilainye."

6. Face out.
7. Do I care.
8. Stories, i.e., the *Gesta Romanorum*, a collection of pious tales.
9. Paramount excellence.

1. I.e., care.
2. Idle talkers.
3. I.e., in health.
4. I.e., wished on.

"Dame," quod this Pluto, "be no lenger° wroth.   *longer*
1100 I yive it up. But sith° I swoor myn ooth   *since*
That I wolde graunten him his sighte ayain,
My word shal stonde, I warne you certain.
I am a king: it sit° me nought to lie."   *suits*
"And I," quod she, "a queene of fairye:
1105 Hir answere shal she have, I undertake.
Lat us namore wordes heerof make.
Forsoothe, I wol no lenger you contrarye."°   *contradict*
Now lat us turne again to Januarye
That in the gardin with his faire May
1110 Singeth ful merier than the papenjay,°   *parrot*
"You love I best, and shal, and other noon."
So longe aboute the aleyes⁵ is he goon
Til he was come ayains thilke⁶ pirye,°   *pear tree*
Wher as this Damian sitteth ful mirye
1115 On heigh among the fresshe leves greene.
This fresshe May, that is so bright and sheene,°   *shining*
Gan for to sike° and saide, "Allas, my side!   *sigh*
Now sire," quod she, "for ought that may bitide,
I moste° han of the peres° that I see,   *must / pears*
1120 Or I moot die, so sore longeth me⁷
To eten of the smale peres greene.
Help for hir love that is of hevene queene!
I telle you wel, a womman in my plit°   *condition*
May han to fruit so greet an appetit
1125 That she may dien but° she of it have."   *unless*
"Allas," quod he, "that I ne hadde heer a knave°   *servant*
That coude climbe! Allas, allas," quod he,
"For I am blind!" "Ye, sire, no fors,"° quod she.   *matter*
"But wolde ye vouche sauf, for Goddes sake,
1130 The pirye inwith° youre armes for to take—   *within*
For wel I woot that ye mistruste me—
Thanne sholde I climbe wel ynough," quod she,
"So I my foot mighte sette upon youre bak."
"Certes," quod he, "theron shal be no lak,°   *fault*
1135 Mighte I you helpen with myn herte blood."
He stoupeth° down, and on his bak she stood,   *stoops*
And caughte hire by a twiste,° and up she gooth.   *twig*
Ladies, I praye you that ye be nat wroth:
I can nat glose,⁸ I am a rude man.
1140 And sodeinly anoon this Damian
Gan pullen up the smok and in he throong.°   *pressed*
And whan that Pluto sawgh this grete wrong,
To Januarye he yaf again his sighte,
And made him see as wel as evere he mighte;

5. Garden paths.   7. I long.
6. That same.   8. Speak circumspectly.

₁₁₄₅ And whan that he hadde caught his sighte again,
Ne was ther nevere man of thing so fain.°   *glad*
But on his wif his thought was everemo:
Unto the tree he caste his yën two,
And sawgh that Damian his wif had dressed°   *placed*
₁₁₅₀ In swich manere it may nat been expressed,
But if⁹ I wolde speken uncurteisly,
And up he yaf a roring and a cry,
As dooth the moder whan the child shal die.
"Out! Help! Allas! Harrow!"° he gan to crye.   *alarm*
₁₁₅₅ "O stronge° lady store,° what doostou?"   *flagrant / crude*
    And she answerde, "Sire, what aileth you?
Have pacience and reson in youre minde.
I have you holpe° on bothe youre yën blinde.   *helped*
Up° peril of my soule, I shal nat lien,   *upon*
₁₁₆₀ As me was taught, to hele° with youre yën   *heal*
Was no thing bet° to make you to see   *better*
Than strugle with a man upon a tree:
God woot I dide it in ful good entente."
    "Strugle!" quod he. "Ye, algate¹ in it wente!
₁₁₆₅ God yive you bothe on shames deeth to dien!
He swived² thee: I saw it with mine yën,
And elles be I hanged by the hals."°   *neck*
    "Thanne is," quod she, "my medicine al fals.
For certainly if that ye mighte see,
₁₁₇₀ Ye wolde nat sayn thise wordes unto me.
Ye han som glimsing° and no parfit° sighte."   *glimpsing / perfect*
    "I see," quod he, "as wel as evere I mighte,
Thanked be God, with bothe mine yën two,
And by my trouthe, me thoughte he dide thee so."
₁₁₇₅   "Ye maze,³ maze, goode sire," quod she.
"This thank have I for I have maad you see.
Allas," quod she, "that evere I was so kinde!"
    "Now dame," quod he, "lat al passe out of minde.
Com down, my lief,° and if I have missaid,   *dear*
₁₁₈₀ God help me so as I am yvele apaid.⁴
But by my fader soule, I wende have sein⁵
How that this Damian hadde by thee lain,
And that thy smok hadde lain upon thy brest."
    "Ye, sire," quod she, "ye may weene° as you lest.   *think*
₁₁₈₅ But sire, a man that waketh out of his sleep
He may nat sodeinly wel taken keep°   *notice*
Upon a thing, ne seen it parfitly,
Til that he be adawed° verraily;   *wakened*

---

9. Unless.   3. Are dazed.
1. At any rate.   4. Ill-pleased.
2. Copulated with.   5. Thought I saw.

Right so a man that longe hath blind ybe
1190 Ne may nat sodeinly so wel ysee,
First whan his sighte is newe come again,
As he that hath a day or two ysein.°   *seen*
Til that youre sighte ysatled° be a while,   *settled*
Ther may ful many a sighte you bigile.
1195 Beeth war,° I praye you, for, by hevene king,   *were*
Ful many a man weeneth to see a thing
And it is al another than it seemeth:
He that misconceiveth, he misdeemeth."°   *misjudges*
And with that word she leep° down fro the tree.   *leapt*
1200   This Januarye, who is glad but he?
He kisseth hire and clippeth° hire ful ofte,   *hugs*
And on hir wombe he stroketh hire ful softe,
And to his palais hoom he hath hire lad.°   *led*
Now goode men, I praye you to be glad.
1205 Thus endeth here my tale of Januarye.
God blesse us and moder, Sainte Marye.
                    Amen

The Epilogue

"Ey, Goddes mercy," saide oure Hoste tho,
"Now swich a wif I praye God keepe me fro.°   *from*
1210 Lo whiche° sleightes° and subtilitees   *what / tricks*
In wommen been, for ay as bisy as bees
Been they us sely° men for to deceive,   *innocent*
And from a sooth evere wol they waive.°   *depart*
By this Marchantes tale it preveth[6] weel.
1215 But, doutelees, as trewe as any steel
I have a wif, though that she poore be;
But of hir tonge a labbing° shrewe is she,   *blabbing*
And yit she hath an heep of vices mo—
Therof no fors,° lat alle swiche thinges go.   *matter*
1220 But wite° ye what? In conseil° be it said,   *know / secrecy*
Me reweth[7] sore I am unto hire teyd°—   *tied*
For and° I sholde rekenen every vice   *if*
Which that she hath, ywis, I were too nice.°   *foolish*
And cause why? it sholde reported be,
1225 And told to hire of some of this meinee.°   *group*
Of whom? it needeth nat for to declare,
Sin wommen connen oute swich chaffare.[8]
And eek my wit suffiseth nat therto
To tellen al; wherfore my tale is do."

---

6. I.e., is proved.   8. I.e., since women know how to bring
7. I regret.   into the open matters of this sort.

The Franklin's Tale[1]

The Introduction[2]

"In faith, Squier, thou hast thee wel yquit°   *acquitted*
And gentilly. I praise wel thy wit,"
Quod the Frankelain. "Considering thy youthe,
So feelingly thou spekest, sire, I allowe° thee: *praise*
5 As to my doom° ther is noon that is heer   *judgment*
Of eloquence that shal be thy peer,
If that thou live. God yive thee good chaunce,
And in vertu sende thee continuaunce,
For of thy speeche I have greet daintee.°   *delight*
10 I have a sone, and by the Trinitee,
I hadde levere than twenty pound worth land,
Though it right now were fallen[3] in myn hand,
He were a man of swich discrecioun
As that ye been. Fy on possessioun
15 But if[4] a man be vertuous withal!
I have my sone snibbed° and yit shal   *scolded*
For he to vertu listeth nat entende,°   *attend*
But for to playe at dees° and to dispende,[5]   *dice*
And lese° al that he hath is his usage.   *lose*
20 And he hath levere talken with a page

1. The Franklin says that his tale is a Breton lay, a sub-genre of romance of which *Sir Orfeo* is the best English representative. Indeed, the Franklin's definition of the Breton lay resembles the definition at the beginning of *Sir Orfeo* so closely that it has led to suspicions that the latter was not only the Franklin's source but the chief source of Chaucer's own knowledge of the genre. The source of the Franklin's Tale itself is probably not a lost Breton lay but an old story told by, among others, Boccaccio. But in any case, features found in Breton lays also occur in the Franklin's Tale: a rash promise that must be kept; a supernatural intervention in a plot containing a love situation; stylistic simplicity; and a generally optimistic spirit.
The Franklin is a fine type of the man of humble origins who has risen to the middle class and has adopted the aspirations of the aristocracy while accumulating wealth. His tale shows a nice blend of unselfconscious interest in the value of money and a self-conscious one in *gentilesse*, the gentle behavior which should distinguish not only the nobly born but (as the Wife of Bath's old hag tells her husband) any free-born man. In this tale *gentilesse* embraces the virtues of patience (which Dorigen has to learn the hard way) and, more significantly, of *trouthe* and *freedom*, "integrity" and "generosity." Though the Franklin shows no awareness of the Biblical text, "Ye shall know the truth and the truth shall make you free" (John viii.32), his tale exemplifies it almost in the manner of a parable. The characters concerned resolve to maintain their *trouthe*—their pledged word—and this sets up a chain reaction of *freedom* which releases them from the dire consequences that keeping their word would entail: when the old law of the covenant is honored, it brings into being the new law of forgiveness. The word *franklin* means "freeman," a meaning Chaucer seems to be playing on when in the last lines of the tale he has the Franklin ask about the three men in the story, "Which was the most free?"

2. The Squire has been speaking for more than 650 lines but has not made much narrative progress in his enormously over-plotted Oriental tale of Cambyuskan and his three children when the Franklin speaks, apparently interrupting the story. It is uncertain, however, whether the Franklin's words represent an intentional interruption or whether they were written to be spoken at the end of the Squire's Tale, which Chaucer intended sometime to complete.
3. I.e., delivered.
4. Unless.
5. Spend money.

Than to commune with any gentil wight,
Where he mighte lerne gentilesse° aright."   *gentility*
   "Straw for thy gentilesse!" Quod oure Host.
"What, Frankelain, pardee sire, wel thou woost°   *know*
25 That eech of you moot° tellen atte leeste   *must*
A tale or two, or breken his biheeste."°   *promise*
   "That knowe I wel, sire," quod the Frankelain.
"I praye you, haveth me nat in desdain,
Though to this man I speke a word or two."
30   "Tel on thy tale withouten wordes mo."
   "Gladly, sire Host," quod he, "I wol obeye
Unto youre wil. Now herkneth what I saye.
I wol you nat contrarien[6] in no wise
As fer as that my wittes wol suffise.
35 I praye to God that it may plesen you:
Thanne woot I wel that it is good ynow."°   *enough*

The Prologue

Thise olde gentil Britons° in hir dayes   *Bretons*
Of diverse adventures maden layes,
Rymeyed[7] in hir firste Briton tonge;
40 Whiche layes with hir instruments they songe,°   *sung*
Or elles redden° hem for hir plesaunce;   *read*
And oon of hem have I in remembraunce,
Which I shal sayn with good wil as I can.
   But sires, by cause I am a burel° man,   *ignorant*
45 At my biginning first I you biseeche
Have me excused of my rude speeche.
I lerned nevere retorike,° certain: *rhetoric*
Thing that I speke it moot° be bare and plain;   *must*
I sleep° nevere in the Mount of Parnaso,[8]   *slept*
50 Ne lerned Marcus Tullius Scithero;°   *Cicero*
Colours[9] ne knowe I noon, withouten drede,°   *doubt*
But swiche colours as growen in the mede,°   *meadow*
Or elles swiche as men dye or painte;
Colours of retorike been too quainte:°   *unfamiliar*
55 My spirit feeleth nat of swich matere.
But if you list, my tale shul ye heere.

The Tale

In Armorik,° that called is Britaine,°   *Armorica / Brittany*
Ther was a knight that loved and dide his paine[1]
To serve a lady in his beste wise;
60 And many a labour, many a greet emprise°   *enterprise*

---

6. Act contrary to.   9. I.e., rhetorical figures.
7. Composed in rhyme.   1. I.e., made every effort.
8. Parnassus, home of the Muses.

He for his lady wroughte er she were wonne,
For she was oon[2] the faireste under sonne,
And eek therto come of so heigh kinrede°   *kindred*
That wel unnethes[3] dorste this knight for drede
65 Telle hire his wo, his paine, and his distresse.
But atte laste she for his worthinesse,
And namely° for his meeke obeisaunce,°   *especially / obedience*
Hath swich a pitee caught of his penaunce°   *suffering*
That prively she fil of[4] his accord
70 To taken him for hir housbonde and hir lord,
Of swich lordshipe as men han over hir wives.
And for to lede the more in blisse hir lives,
Of his free wil he swoor hire as a knight
That nevere in al his lif he day ne night
75 Ne sholde upon him take no maistrye°   *dominion*
Again hir wil, ne kithe° hire jalousye,   *show*
But hire obeye and folwe hir wil in al,
As any lovere to his lady shal°—   *ought*
Save that the name of sovereinete,°   *sovereignty*
80 That wolde he have, for shame of[5] his degree.
    She thanked him, and with ful greet humblesse
She saide, "Sire, sith of youre gentilesse
Ye profre me to have so large[6] a reine.
Ne wolde nevere God bitwixe us twaine.
85 As in[7] my gilt, were outher° werre° or strif. *either / war*
Sire, I wol be your humble, trewe wif—
Have heer my trouthe[8]—til that myn herte breste."° *break*
Thus been they bothe in quiete and in reste.
    For oo thing, sires, saufly° dar I saye: *safely*
90 That freendes° everich° other moot° obeye, *lovers / each / must*
If they wol longe holden compaignye.
Love wol nat be constrained by maistrye:°   *force*
Whan maistrye comth, the God of Love anoon
Beteth his winges and farewel, he is goon!
95 Love is a thing as any spirit free;
Wommen of kinde[9] desiren libertee,
And nat to been constrained as a thral°—   *slave*
And so doon men, if I sooth sayen shal.
Looke who that is most pacient in love,
100 He is at his avantage al above.
Pacience is an heigh vertu, certain,
For it venquissheth,° as thise clerkes sayn,   *vanquishes*
Thinges that rigour sholde nevere attaine.[1]
For° every word men may nat chide or plaine:° *at / complain*
105 Lerneth to suffre, or elles, so mote I goon,[2]

2. I.e., one of.
3. With difficulty.
4. I.e., fell in.
5. Out of respect for.
6. I.e., free.

7. As a result of.
8. Troth, word of honor.
9. By nature.
1. I.e., overcome.
2. So may I walk.

Ye shul it lerne, wherso° ye wol or noon.   *whether*
For in this world, certain, ther no wight is
That he ne dooth or saith somtime amis:
Ire, siknesse, or constellacioun,[3]
110 Win, wo, or chaunging of complexioun[4]
Causeth ful ofte to doon amis or speken.
On every wrong a man may nat be wreken:°   *avenged*
After the time moste° be temperaunce   *must*
To every wight that can on governaunce.[5]
115 And therfore hath this wise worthy knight
To live in ese suffrance° hire bihight,°   *toleration / promised*
And she to him ful wisly° gan to swere   *surely*
That nevere sholde ther be defaute° in here.   *defect*
    Here may men seen an humble wis accord:
120 Thus hath she take hir servant and hir lord—
Servant in love and lord in marriage.
Thanne was he bothe in lordshipe and servage.[6]
Servage? Nay, but in lordshipe above,
Sith° he hath bothe his lady and his love;   *since*
125 His lady, certes, and his wif also,
The which that[7] lawe of love accordeth to.
And whan he was in this prosperitee,
Hoom with his wif he gooth to his contree,
Nat fer fro Pedmark[8] ther his dwelling was,
130 Wher as he liveth in blisse and in solas.°   *delight*
    Who coude telle but he hadde wedded be
The joye, the ese, and the prosperitee
That is bitwixe an housbonde and his wif?
A yeer and more lasted this blisful lif,
135 Til that the knight of which I speke of thus,
That of Kairrud[9] was cleped° Arveragus,   *called*
Shoop him[1] to goon and dwelle a yeer or twaine
In Engelond, that cleped was eek° Britaine,   *also*
To seeke in armes worshipe and honour—
140 For al his lust° he sette in swich labour—   *pleasure*
And dwelled ther two yeer, the book saith thus.
    Now wol I stinte° of this Arveragus,   *cease*
And speke I wol of Dorigen his wif,
That loveth hir housbonde as hir hertes lif.
145 For his absence weepeth she and siketh,°   *sighs*
As doon thise noble wives whan hem liketh.[2]
She moorneth, waketh, waileth, fasteth, plaineth;°   *complains*
Desir of his presence hire so distraineth°   *afflicts*
That al this wide world she sette[3] at nought.
150 Hir freendes, whiche that knewe hir hevy thought,

---

3. I.e., planetary influences.
4. The balance of humors in the body.
5. Is capable of self-control.
6. Position of a servant.
7. As.

8. Penmarch, in Brittany.
9. Kerru, a town in Brittany.
1. Prepared.
2. It pleases.
3. I.e., valued.

Conforten hire in al that evere they may:
They prechen hire, they telle hire night and day
That causelees she sleeth° hirself, allas;   *slays*
And every confort possible in this cas
155 They doon to hire with al hir bisinesse,°   *assiduousness*
Al for to make hire leve° hir hevinesse.   *abandon*
    By proces,[4] as ye knowen everichoon,
Men may so longe graven° in a stoon   *engrave*
Til som figure therinne emprinted be:
160 So longe han they conforted hire til she
Received hath, by hope and by resoun,
The emprinting of hir consolacioun,
Thurgh which hir grete sorwe gan assuage:
She may nat alway duren° in swich rage.°   *remain / passion*
165   And eek Arveragus in al this care
Hath sent hir lettres hoom of his welfare,
And that he wol come hastily again—
Or elles hadde this sorwe hir herte slain.
Hir freendes sawe hir sorwe gan to slake,°   *diminish*
170 And prayed hire on knees, for Goddes sake,
To come and romen hire in compaignye,
Away to drive hir derke fantasye,
And finally she graunted that requeste:
For wel she saw that it was for the beste.
175   Now stood hir castel faste by the see,
And often with hir freendes walketh she,
Hire to disporte upon the bank an heigh,
Wher as she many a ship and barge° seigh,°   *vessel / saw*
Sailing hir cours wher as hem liste go—
180 But thanne was that a parcel° of hir wo,   *component*
For of hirself ful ofte, "Allas!" saith she,
"Is ther no ship of so manye as I see
Wol bringen hoom my lord? Thanne were myn herte
Al warisshed° of his bittre paines smerte."   *recovered*
185   Another time ther wolde she sitte and thinke,
And caste hir yën downward fro the brinke;
But whan she sawgh the grisly rokkes blake,
For verray° fere so wolde hir herte quake   *real*
That on hir feet she mighte hire nat sustene:°   *sustain*
190 Thanne wolde she sitte adown upon the greene
And pitously into the see biholde,
And sayn right thus, with sorweful sikes° colde:[5]   *sighs*
    "Eterne God that thurgh thy purveyaunce°   *providence*
Ledest the world by certain governaunce,
195 In idel,[6] as men sayn, ye nothing make:
But Lord, thise grisly feendly° rokkes blake,   *hostile*
That seemen rather a foul confusioun

4. Course of time.   6. I.e., without purpose.
5. I.e., grievous.

Of werk, than any fair creacioun

Of swich a parfit° wis God and a stable,   *perfect*

200 Why han ye wrought this werk unresonable?

For by this werk south, north, ne west ne eest,

Ther nis yfostred man ne brid[7] ne beest:

It dooth no good, to my wit, but anoyeth.

See ye nat, Lord, how mankinde it destroyeth?

205 An hundred thousand bodies of mankinde

Han rokkes slain, al° be they nat in minde: *although*

Which mankinde is so fair part of thy werk

That thou it madest lik to thyn owene merk:[8]

Thanne seemed it ye hadde a greet cheertee°   *affection*

210 Toward mankinde. But how thanne may it be

That ye swiche menes° make it to destroyen?—   *means*

Whiche menes do no good, but evere anoyen.

I woot wel clerkes wol sayn as hem leste,[9]

By arguments, that al is for the beste,

215 Though I ne can the causes nat yknowe.

But thilke° God that made wind to blowe,   *that*

As keepe my lord! This[1] my conclusioun.

To clerkes lete° I al disputisoun,°   *leave / disputation*

But wolde God that alle thise rokkes blake

220 Were sonken° into helle for his sake!   *sunken*

Thise rokkes slain myn herte for the fere."

Thus wolde she sayn with many a pitous tere.

    Hir freendes sawe that it was no disport

To romen by the see, but disconfort,

225 And shopen° for to playen somwher elles: *arranged*

They leden hire by rivers and by welles,°   *springs*

And eek in othere places delitables;°   *delightful*

They dauncen and they playen at ches and tables.°   *backgammon*

    So on a day, right in the morwetide,°   *morning*

230 Unto a gardin that was ther biside,

In which that they hadde maad hir ordinaunce°   *arrangements*

Of vitaile° and of other purveyaunce,°   *food / provisions*

They goon and playe hem al the longe day.

And this was on the sixte morwe° of May,   *morning*

235 Which May had painted with his softe showres

This gardin ful of leves and of flowres;

And craft of mannes hand so curiously°   *skillfully*

Arrayed hadde this gardin trewely

That nevere was ther gardin of swich pris,°   *excellence*

240 But if[2] it were the verray Paradis.

The odour of flowres and the fresshe sighte

Wolde han maked any herte lighte

That evere was born, but if too greet siknesse,

---

7. Bird; "yfostred": fed.   1. I.e., this is.
8. Mark, i.e., image.   2. Unless.
9. May please.

Or too greet sorwe heeld it in distresse,
245 So ful it was of beautee with plesaunce.
At after-diner gonne they to daunce,
And singe also, save Dorigen allone,
Which made alway hir complainte and hir mone,°   *moan*
For she ne sawgh him on the daunce go
250 That was hir housbonde and hir love also.
But nathelees she moste° a time abide,   *must*
And with good hope lete° hir sorwe slide.   *make*
    Upon this daunce, amonges othere men,
Daunced a squier bifore Dorigen
255 That fressher was and jolier° of array,   *gayer*
As to my doom,° than is the month of May.   *judgment*
He singeth, daunceth, passing° any man   *surpassing*
That is or was sith° that the world bigan.   *since*
Therwith he was, if men him sholde descrive,°   *describe*
260 Oon of the beste-faring° man on live: *handsomest*
Yong, strong, right vertuous, and riche and wis,
And wel-biloved, and holden in greet pris.°   *repute*
And shortly, if the soothe I tellen shal,
Unwiting of[3] this Dorigen at al,
265 This lusty squier, servant to Venus,
Which that ycleped° was Aurelius,   *called*
Hadde loved hire best of any creature
Two yeer and more, as was his aventure.
But nevere dorste he tellen hire his grevaunce:
270 Withouten coppe° he drank al his penaunce.[4]   *cup*
He was despaired, no thing dorste he saye—
Save in his songes somwhat wolde he wraye°   *disclose*
His wo, as in a general complaining:
He saide he loved and was biloved no thing;[5]
275 Of which matere made he manye layes,
Songes, complaintes, roundels, virelayes.[6]
How that he dorste nat his sorwe telle,
But languissheth as a furye dooth in helle;
And die he moste,° he saide, as dide Ekko   *must*
280 For Narcisus that dorste nat telle hir wo.[7]
In other manere than ye heere me saye
Ne dorste he nat to hire his wo biwraye,°   *disclose*
Save that paraventure° som time at daunces,   *perchance*
Ther yonge folk keepen hir observaunces,[8]
285 It may wel be he looked on hir face
In swich a wise as man that asketh grace;
But no thing wiste° she of his entente.   *knew*

3. Unknown to.
4. Suffering; i.e., he suffered in silence.
5. Not at all.
6. The lover unable to declare his love conventionally expressed his frustration by writing verse: Aurelius produced five kinds of verse, but only rondels and virelays are strictly defined forms.
7. Echo was unable to communicate her love for Narcissus and eventually died in despair.
8. Carry on their rituals.

Nathelees° it happed, er they thennes°
    wente,   *nevertheless / thence*
By cause that he was hir neighebour,
290 And was a man of worshipe and honour,
And hadde⁹ yknowen him of time yore,¹
They fille° in speeche, and forth more and more   *fell*
Unto his purpos drow° Aurelius,   *drew*
And whan he sawgh his time, he saide thus:
295   "Madame," quod he, "by God that this world made,
So that I wiste° it mighte youre herte glade,°   *knew / gladden*
I wolde that day that youre Arveragus
Wente over the see that I, Aurelius,
Hadde went ther nevere I sholde have come again.
300 For wel I woot my service is in vain:
My gerdon° is but bresting° of myn herte.   *reward / breaking*
Madame, reweth² upon my paines smerte,
For with a word ye may me slee° or save.   *slay*
Here at youre feet God wolde that I were grave!°   *buried*
305 I ne have as now no leiser more to saye:
Have mercy, sweete, or ye wol do° me deye."   *make*
    She gan to looke upon Aurelius:
"Is this youre wil?" quod she, "and saye ye thus?
Nevere erst,"° quod she, "ne wiste I what ye mente.   *before*
310 But now, Aurelie, I knowe youre entente,
By thilke° God that yaf me soule and lif,   *that*
Ne shal I nevere been untrewe wif,
In word ne werk, as fer as I have wit.
I wol be his to whom that I am knit:°   *joined*
315 Take this for final answere as of me."
But after that in play thus saide she:
    "Aurelie," quod she, "by hye God above,
Yit wolde I graunte you to been youre love,
Sin° I you see so pitously complaine,   *since*
320 Looke what day that endelong° Britaine   *along*
Ye remeve° alle the rokkes, stoon by stoon,   *remove*
That they ne lette° ship ne boot° to goon.   *hinder / boat*
I saye, whan ye han maad the coost° so clene   *coast*
Of rokkes that there nis no stoon yseene,
325 Thanne wol I love you best of any man—
Have heer my trouthe°—in al that evere I can.   *word*
For wel I woot that it shal nevere bitide.
Lat swiche folies out of youre herte slide!
What daintee° sholde a man han by his lif   *delight*
330 For to love another mannes wif,
That hath hir body whan so that him liketh?"³
    Aurelius ful ofte sore siketh:°   *sighs*

9. I.e., she had.   2. Have pity on.
1. Long past.   3. It pleases.

"Is ther noon other grace in you?" quod he.
"No, by that Lord," quod she, "that maked me."
335 Wo was Aurelie whan that he this herde,
And with a sorweful herte he thus answerde.
"Madame," quod he, "this were an impossible.
Thanne moot° I die of sodein deeth horrible."   *must*
And with that word he turned him anoon.
340 Tho° come hir othere freendes many oon,   *then*
And in the aleyes° romeden up and down,   *paths*
And no thing wiste of this conclusioun,
But sodeinly bigonne revel newe,
Til that the brighte sonne loste his hewe,
345 For th' orisonte° hath reft[4] the sonne his light—   *horizon*
This is as muche to saye as it was night.
And hoom they goon in joye and in solas,°   *delight*
Save only wrecche° Aurelius, allas.   *wretched*
He to his hous is goon with sorweful herte;
350 He seeth he may nat from his deeth asterte;°   *escape*
Him seemed that he felte his herte colde;
Up to the hevene his handes he gan holde,
And on his knees bare he sette him down,
And in his raving saide his orisoun.
355 For verray wo out of his wit he braide;°   *went*
He niste[5] what he spak, but thus he saide;
With pitous herte his plainte° hath he bigonne   *lament*
Unto the goddes, and first unto the sonne:
He saide, "Appollo, god and governour
360 Of every plaunte, herbe, tree and flowr,
That yivest after thy declinacioun[6]
To eech of hem his time and his sesoun,
As thyn herberwe[7] chaungeth, lowe or hye;
Lord Phebus, cast thy merciable° yë   *merciful*
365 On wrecche Aurelie which that am but lorn.°   *lost*
Lo, lord, my lady hath my deeth ysworn
Withouten gilt, but° thy benignitee   *unless*
Upon my deedly herte have som pitee;
For wel I woot, lord Phebus, if you lest,[8]
370 Ye may me helpen, save my lady, best.[9]
Now voucheth sauf that I may you devise°   *describe*
How that I may been holpe,° and in what wise: *helped*
Youre blisful suster, Lucina[1] the sheene,°   *bright*
That of the see is chief goddesse and queene—
375 Though Neptunus have deitee in the see,
Yit emperisse° aboven him is she—   *empress*
Ye knowen wel, lord, that right as hir desir

4. Deprived of.
5. Knew not.
6. Who give, according to your position in the sky.
7. Lodging, i.e., one of the astrological houses in which the planets reside in alternation.
8. It pleases.
9. Except for my lady, you may help me best.
1. I.,e., Diana, the Moon.

Is to be quiked° and lighted of youre fir,   quickened
For which she folweth you ful bisily,°   constantly
380 Right so the see desireth naturelly
To folwen hire, as she that is goddesse
Bothe in the see and rivers more and lesse;
Wherfore, lord Phebus, this is my requeste:
Do this miracle—or do° myn herte breste°—   make / break
385 That now next at this opposicioun,[2]
Which in the signe shal be of the Leoun,
As prayeth hire so greet a flood to bringe.
That five fadme° at the leeste it overspringe°   fathoms / overrun
The hyeste rok in Armorik Britaine;
390 And lat this flood endure yeres twaine:
Thanne certes to my lady may I saye,
'Holdeth youre heeste,° the rokkes been awaye.'   promise
    Lord Phebus, dooth this miracle for me!
Praye hire she go no faster cours than ye—
395 I saye this, prayeth youre suster that she go
No faster cours than ye thise yeres two:
Thanne shal she been evene at the fulle alway,
And spring-flood lasten bothe night and day.
And but° she vouche sauf in swich manere   unless
400 To graunte me my soverein lady dere,
Praye hire[3] to sinken every rok adown
Into hir owene derke regioun
Under the ground ther Pluto dwelleth inne,
Or nevere mo° shal I my lady winne.   more
405 Thy temple in Delphos° wol I barefoot seeke.   Delphi
    Lord Phebus, see the teres on my cheeke,
And of my paine have som compassioun."
And with that word in swoune° he fil° adown,   swoon / fell
And longe time he lay forth in a traunce.
410 His brother, which that knew of his penaunce,°   pain
Up caughte him, and to bedde he hath him brought.
Despaired in this torment and this thought
Lete° I this woful creature lie—   leave
Chese[4] he for me wher° he wol live or die.   whether
415 Arveragus with hele° and greet honour,   prosperity
As he that was of chivalrye the flowr,
Is comen hoom, and othere worthy men:
O, blisful artou now, thou Dorigen,
That hast thy lusty housbonde in thine armes,
420 The fresshe knight, the worthy man of armes,
That loveth thee as his owene hertes lif.
No thing list[5] him to been imaginatif
If any wight hadde spoke whil he was oute

2. The position of the sun and moon   3. I.e., Diana in her capacity as goddess
when they are at a 180-degree angle   of the underworld.
from one another as seen from the   4. Let him choose.
earth.   5. It pleases.

To hire of love; he ne hadde of it no doute:
425 He nought entendeth[6] to swich matere,
But daunceth, justeth,° maketh hire good cheere.   *jousts*
And thus in joye and blisse I lete hem dwelle,
And of the sike Aurelius wol I telle.
    In langour and in torment furious
430 Two yeer and more lay wrecche Aurelius,
Er any foot he mighte on erthe goon,
Ne confort in this hadde he noon,
Save of his brother, which that was a clerk:
He knew of al this wo and al this werk,
435 For to noon other creature, certain,
Of this matere he dorste no word sayn.
Under his brest he bar it more secree°   *secret*
Than evere dide Pamphilus for Galathee.[7]
His brest was hool° withoute° for to seene,   *whole / outwardly*
440 But in his herte ay° was the arwe keene;   *ever*
And wel ye knowe that of a sursanure[8]
In surgerye is perilous the cure,
But° men mighte touche the arwe or come therby.   *unless*
His brother weep° and wailed prively,   *wept*
445 Til at the laste him fil in remembrance[9]
That whiles he was at Orliens° in France,   *Orleans*
As yonge clerkes that been likerous°   *desirous*
To reden artes[1] that been curious,°   *occult*
Seeken in every halke and every herne[2]
450 Particuler[3] sciences for to lerne,
He him remembred that, upon a day,
At Orliens in studye a book he sey°   *saw*
Of magik naturel,[4] which his felawe,
That was that time a bacheler of lawe—
455 Al were he[5] ther to lerne another craft—
Hadde prively upon his desk ylaft:°   *left*
Which book spak muchel of the operaciouns
Touching the eighte and twenty mansiouns[6]
That longen° to the moone—and swich folye   *belong*
460 As in oure dayes is nat worth a flye,
For holy chirches faith in oure bileve°   *creed*
Ne suffreth noon illusion us to greve.
And whan this book was in his remembraunce,
Anoon for joye his herte gan to daunce,
465 And to himself he saide prively,
"My brother shal be warisshed° hastily,   *cured*
For I am siker° that ther be sciences   *sure*

---

6. Pays attention.
7. Pamphilus and Galataea are the lovers in the medieval Latin *Pamphilus de Amore.*
8. Superficially healed wound.
9. I.e., he happened to remember.
1. Study subjects.

2. Every nook and cranny.
3. Out of the way.
4. Natural magic employs astrological knowledge rather than spirits.
5. Although he was.
6. I.e., daily positions.

By whiche men make diverse apparences,°   *apparitions*
Swiche as thise subtile tregettoures° playe;   *magicians*
470 For ofte at feestes have I wel herd saye
That tregettours withinne an halle large
Have maad come in a water and a barge,°   *ship*
And in the halle rowen up and down;
Som time hath seemed come a grim leoun;
475 Som time flowres springe° as in a mede;   *grow*
Som time a vine and grapes white and rede;
Som time a castel al of lim° and stoon—   *lime*
And whan hem liked voided⁷ it anoon:
Thus seemed it to every mannes sighte.
480   Now thanne conclude I thus: that if I mighte
At Orliens som old felawe yfinde
That hadde thise moones mansions in minde,
Or other magik naturel above,
He sholde wel make my brother han his love.
485 For with an apparence a clerk may make
To mannes sighte that alle the rokkes blake
Of Britaine were yvoided everichoon,
And shippes by the brinke comen and goon,
And in swich forme enduren a day or two:
490 Thanne were my brother warisshed° of his wo;   *cured*
Thanne moste° she needes holden hir biheeste,°   *must / promise*
Or elles he shal shame hire at the leeste."
    What sholde I make a lenger° tale of this?   *longer*
Unto his brothers bed he comen is,
495 And swich confort he yaf him for to goon
To Orliens, that up he sterte° anoon,   *started*
And on his way forthward thanne is he fare,
In hope for to been lissed° of his care.   *assuaged*
    Whan they were come almost to that citee,
500 But if it were a two furlong or three,
A yong clerk roming by himself they mette,
Which that in Latin thriftily° hem grette,°   *properly / greeted*
And after that he saide a wonder thing:
"I knowe," quod he, "the cause of your coming."
505 And er they ferther any foote wente,
He tolde hem al that was in hir entente.
    This Briton clerk him axed° of felawes,   *asked*
The whiche that he hadde knowe in olde dawes,°   *days*
And he answerde him that they dede° were;   *dead*
510 For which he weep° ful ofte many a tere.   *wept*
    Down of his hors Aurelius lighte anoon,
And with this magicien forth is he goon
Hoom to his hous, and maden hem wel at ese:
Hem lakked no vitaile that mighte hem plese;
515 So wel arrayed hous as ther was oon
Aurelius in his lif saw nevere noon.

7. Caused to disappear.

He shewed him er he wente to soper°   *supper*
Forestes, parkes ful of wilde deer:
Ther saw he hertes° with hir hornes hye,   *harts*
520 The gretteste° that evere were seen with yë;   *greatest*
He sawgh of hem an hundred slain with houndes,
And some with arwes bledde of bittre woundes.
   He saw, when voided[8] were thise wilde deer,
Thise fauconers° upon a fair river,   *falconers*
525 That with hir hawkes han the heron slain.
Tho sawgh he knightes justing° in a plain.   *jousting*
And after this he dide him this plesaunce,
That he him shewed his lady on a daunce—
On which himself he daunced, as him thoughte.
530 And whan this maister that this magik wroughte
Sawgh it was time, he clapte his handes two,
And farewel, al oure revel was ago.
And yit remeved° they nevere out of the hous   *moved*
Whil they sawe al this sighte merveilous,
535 But in his studye, ther as his bookes be,
They sitten stille, and no wight but they three.
   To him this maister called his squier
And saide him thus, "Is redy oure soper?
Almost an houre it is, I undertake,
540 Sith I you bad oure soper for to make,
Whan that thise worthy men wenten with me
Into my studye, ther as my bookes be."
   "Sire," quod this squier, "whan it liketh you,
It is al redy, though ye wol right now."
545 "Go we thanne soupe," quod he, "as for the beste:
This amorous folk som time mote° han hir reste."   *must*
   At after-soper fille° they in tretee°   *fell / negotiation*
What somme° sholde this maistres gerdon° be   *sum / reward*
To remeven° alle the rokkes of Britaine,   *remove*
550 And eek from Gerounde[9] to the mouth of Seine:
He made it straunge,[1] and swoor, so God him save,
Lasse° than a thousand pound he wolde nat have,   *less*
Ne gladly for that somme he wolde nat goon.
   Aurelius with blisful herte anoon
555 Answerde thus, "Fy on a thousand pound!
This wide world, which that men saye is round,
I wolde it yive, if I were lord of it.
This bargain is ful drive, for we been knit.[2]
Ye shal be payed trewely, by my trouthe.
560 But looketh now, for no necligence or slouthe,°   *sloth*
Ye tarye us heer no lenger than tomorwe."
   "Nay," quod this clerk, "have heer my faith to borwe."[3]
   To bedde is goon Aurelius whan him leste,°   *pleased*

---

8. Made to disappear.
9. The Gironde river.
1. I.e., difficulties.

2. I.e., this bargain is fully made, for we are in accord.
3. As a pledge.

And wel neigh al that night he hadde his reste:
565 What for his labour and his hope of blisse,
His woful herte of penance° hadde a lisse.°   *suffering / alleviation*
    Upon the morwe, whan that it was day,
To Britaine tooke they the righte° way,   *direct*
Aurelius and this magicien biside,
570 And been descended ther they wolde abide;
And this was, as thise bookes me remembre,[4]
The colde frosty seson of Decembre.
    Phebus wax° old, and hewed° lik
        latoun,°   *grew / colored / brass*
That in his hote declinacioun[5]
575 Shoon as the burned° gold with stremes°
        brighte;   *burnished / beams*
But now in Capricorn[6] adown he lighte,
Wher as he shoon ful pale, I dar wel sayn:
The bittre frostes with the sleet and rain
Destroyed hath the greene in every yeerd.°   *yard*
580 Janus[7] sit° by the fir with double beerd,   *sits*
And drinketh of his bugle horn[8] the win;
Biforn him stant° brawn° of the tusked swin,   *stands / flesh*
And "Nowel!" crieth every lusty man.
    Aurelius in al that evere he can
585 Dooth to this maister cheere and reverence,
And prayeth him to doon his diligence
To bringen him out of his paines smerte,
Or with a swerd that he wolde slitte his herte.[9]
This subtil clerk swich routhe° hadde of this man   *pity*
590 That night and day he spedde him[1] that he can
To waiten a time of his conclusioun[2]—
This is to sayn, to make illusioun
By swich an apparence° or jogelrye[3]   *apparition*
(I ne can° no termes of astrologye)   *know*
595 That she and every wight sholde weene° and saye   *think*
That of Britaine the rokkes were awaye,
Or elles they were sonken° under grounde.   *sunk*
So at the laste he hath his time yfounde
To maken his japes° and his wrecchednesse[4]   *tricks*
600 Of swich a supersticious cursednesse.°   *wickedness*
His tables tolletanes[5] forth hath he brought,
Ful wel corrected; ne ther lakked nought,
Neither his collect ne his expans yeres,[6]

4. Recall to me.
5. I.e., celestial position.
6. The House of the Goat.
7. The god with two faces who knew both past and future, perpetuated in the name "January."
8. Wild ox horn.
9. I.e., stab his own heart.
1. Hurried.
2. To watch for a time for his astrologi-

cal operation.
3. Optical illusion.
4. Miserable performance.
5. Astronomical tables based on the latitude of Toledo, in Spain.
6. Neither his table of collect years nor his table of expanse years: the former recorded planetary movements for long periods such as twenty years, the latter for short periods of a year.

Ne his rootes,[7] ne his othere geres,°   *paraphernalia*
605 As been his centres and his arguments,[8]
And his proporcionels convenients,[9]
For his equacions in every thing;
And by his eighte spere[1] in his werking°   *operation*
He knew ful wel how fer Alnath was shove[2]
610 Fro the heed of thilke fixe Aries above
That in the ninte spere considered is:[3]
Ful subtilly he calculed° al this.   *calculated*
    When he hadde founde his firste mansioun,[4]
He knew the remenant by proporcioun,[5]
615 And knew the arising of his moone weel,
And in whos face and terme[6] and every deel,°   *part*
And knew ful wel the moones mansioun
Accordant[7] to his operacioun,
And knew also his othere observaunces°   *rules*
620 For swiche illusions and swiche meschaunces
As hethen folk useden in thilke° dayes;   *those*
For which no lenger maked he delayes,
But, thurgh his magik, for a wike° or twaye   *week*
It seemed that alle the rokkes were awaye.
625   Aurelius, which that yit despaired is
Wher° he shall han his love or fare amis,   *whether*
Awaiteth night and day on this miracle;
And whan he knew that there was noon obstacle,
That voided were thise rokkes everichoon,
630 Down to his maistres feet he fil° anoon,   *fell*
And saide, "I, woful wrecche Aurelius,
Thanke you, lord, and lady myn Venus,
That me han holpen° fro my cares colde."   *helped*
And to the temple his way forth hath he holde,
635 Wher as he knew he sholde his lady see.
And whan he saw his time, anoon right he,
With dredful° herte and with ful humble cheere,   *fear-struck*
Salued° hath his soverein lady dere.   *greeted*
    "My right[8] lady," quod this woful man,
640 "Whom I most drede and love as best I can,
And lothest were of al this world displese,
Nere it[9] that I for you have swich disese
That I moste° dien heer at youre foot anoon,   *must*

---

7. Tables for making astrological propositions concerning planetary position, degrees of influence, etc.
8. Centers and arguments are astronomical instruments for determining the positions of planets in relation to fixed stars.
9. Fitting proportionals, i.e., special tables for scaling down more general planetary motions to the most particular.
1. Sphere: i.e., the sphere of the fixed stars.
2. He knew full well how far Alnath (the star Aries) had moved.
3. From the head of that fixed star Aries which is considered to be above, in the ninth sphere.
4. I.e., the first position of the moon.
5. He knew the remnant (rest of the positions) by the use of proportion.
6. Face and term are sectors of the signs of the zodiac.
7. I.e., to be comfortable.
8. Own true.
9. Were it not.

Nought wolde I telle how me is wo-bigoon.
645 But certes, outher° moste I die or plaine:°   *either / complain*
Ye sleen° me giltelees for verray paine;   *slay*
But of my deeth though that ye have no routhe,°   *pity*
Aviseth you[1] er that ye breke youre trouthe.
Repenteth you, for thilke God above,
650 Er ye me sleen° by cause that I you love.   *slay*
For Madame, wel ye woot what ye han hight°—   *promised*
Not that I chalenge any thing of right
Of you, my soverein lady, but youre grace:
But in a gardin yond at swich a place,
655 Ye woot right wel what ye bihighten° me,   *promised*
And in myn hand youre trouthe plighten ye
To love me best. God woot ye saiden so,
Al° be that I unworthy am therto.   *although*
Madame, I speke it for the honour of you
660 More than to save myn hertes lif right now.
I have do so as ye comanded me,
And if ye vouche sauf, ye may go see.
Dooth as you list, have youre biheeste° in minde,   *promise*
For quik° or deed° right ther ye shal me finde.   *living / dead*
665 In you lith° al to do° me live or deye: *lies / cause*
But wel I woot the rokkes been awaye."
    He taketh his leve and she astoned° stood: *astonished*
In al hir face nas a drope of blood;
She wende° nevere have come in swich a trappe.   *thought*
670 "Allas," quod she, "that evere this sholde happe!
For wende I nevere by possibilitee
That swich a monstre° or merveile mighte be;   *wonder*
It is agains the proces[2] of nature."
And hoom she gooth a sorweful creature.
675 For verray fere unnethe° may she go.°   *scarcely / walk*
She weepeth, waileth al a day or two,
And swouneth° that it routhe° was to see.   *swoons / pity*
But why it was to no wight tolde she,
For out of town was goon Arveragus.
680 But to hirself she spak and saide thus,
With face pale and with ful sorweful cheere,°   *countenance*
In hir complainte, as ye shal after heere:
    "Allas," quod she, "on thee, Fortune, I plaine,°   *complain*
That unwar° wrapped hast me in thy chaine,   *unawares*
685 For which t' escape woot I no socour°—   *help*
Save only deeth or dishonour:
Oon of thise two bihoveth me to chese.°   *choose*
But nathelees yit have I levere to lese°   *lose*
My lif, than of my body to have a shame,
690 Or knowen myselven fals or lese my name,

---

1. Consider.   2. Due course.

And with my deeth I may be quit,[3] ywis.
Hath ther nat many a noble wif er this,
And many a maide, yslain hirself, allas,
Rather than with hir body doon trespas?°   *sin*
695   Yis, certes, lo, thise stories beren witnesse:
Whan thritty tyrants ful of cursednesse°   *wickedness*
Hadde slain Phidon[4] in Atthenes atte feeste,
They comanded his doughtren for t'arreste,
And bringen hem biforn hem in despit°   *scorn*
700   Al naked, to fulfille hir foule delit,
And in hir fadres blood they made hem daunce
Upon the pavement—God yive hem meschaunce!
For which thise woful maidens, ful of drede,
Rather than they wolde lese° hir maidenhede,   *lose*
705   They prively been stert[5] into a welle,
And dreinte° hemselven, as the bookes telle.   *drowned*
They of Messene lete enquere and seeke[6]
Of Lacedomye° fifty maidens eke,   *Lacedaemonia*
On whiche they wolden doon hir lecherye;
710   But ther was noon of al that compaignye
That she nas slain, and with a good entente
Chees° rather for to die than assente   *chose*
To been oppressed° of hir maidenhede: *ravished*
Why sholde I thanne to die been in drede?
715   Lo, eek, the tyrant Aristoclides
That loved a maiden highte Stymphalides,°   *Stymphalis*
Whan that hir fader slain was on a night,
Unto Dianes temple gooth she aright,
And hente° the image in hir handes two;   *seized*
720   Fro which image wolde she nevere go:
No wight ne mighte hir handes of it arace,°   *tear*
Til she was slain right in the selve° place.   *same*
Now sith° that maidens hadden swich despit°   *since / indignation*
To been defouled with mannes foul delit,
725   Wel ought a wif rather hirselven slee°   *slay*
Than be defouled, as it thinketh me.
What shal I sayn of Hasdrubales wif
That at Cartage birafte[7] hirself hir lif?
For whan she saw that Romains wan° the town,   *won*
730   She took hir children alle and skipte adown
Into the fir, and chees rather to die
Than any Romain dide hire vilainye.
Hath nat Lucrece yslain hirself, allas,

---

3. Freed from dilemma.
4. The story of Phidon's daughters and the thirty tyrants, as well as all the following stories about virtuous women, are from St. Jerome's tract against Jovinian.
5. Have jumped.
6. Had inquiries and searches made.
7. Deprived; Hasdrubal was King of Carthage when it was destroyed by the Romans.

At Rome whan that she oppressed° was   *raped*
735 Of° Tarquin, for hire thoughte it was a shame   *by*
To liven whan that she hadde lost hir name?
     The sevene maidens of Milesie° also   *Miletus*
Han slain hemself for verray drede and wo
Rather than folk of Gaule hem sholde oppresse:
740 Mo° than a thousand stories, as I gesse,   *more*
Coude I now telle as touching this matere.
     Whan Habradate° was slain, his wif so dere   *Abradates*
Hirselven slow,° and leet hir blood to glide   *slew*
In Habradates woundes deepe and wide,
745 And saide, 'My body at the leeste way
Ther shal no wight defoulen, if I may.'[8]
     What sholde I mo ensamples° herof sayn?   *examples*
Sith° that so manye han hemselven slain   *since*
Wel rather than they wolde defouled be,
750 I wol conclude that it is bet° for me   *better*
To sleen° myself than been defouled thus: *slay*
I wol be trewe unto Arveragus,
Or rather slee myself in som manere—
As dide Demociones° doughter dere,   *Demotion's*
755 By cause that she wolde nat defouled be.
     O Cedasus,° it is ful greet pitee   *Scedasus*
To reden how thy doughtren deide, allas,
That slowe hemself for[9] swich manere cas.
     As greet a pitee was it, or wel moor,
760 The Theban maiden that for Nichanor°   *Nicanor*
Hirselven slow right for swich manere wo.
Another Theban maiden dide right so:
For oon of Macedonie hadde hire oppressed,
She with hir deeth hir maidenhede redressed.[1]
765   What shal I sayn of Nicerates wif
That for swich caas birafte hirself hir lif?
     How trewe eek was to Alcebiades[2]
His love, that rather for to dien chees°   *chose*
Than for to suffre his body unburied be.
770   Lo, which a wif was Alceste,"[3] quod she.
     "What saith Omer[4] of goode Penolopee?
Al Greece knoweth of hir chastitee.
     Pardee, of Laodomia[5] is writen thus,
That whan at Troye was slain Protheselaus,

---

8. If I can help it.
9. I.e., for fear of.
1. Made amends for.
2. Alcibiades' mistress risked death by burying his body after he had been decapitated by the Spartan Lysander; she did not, however, lose her life as a result.

3. Alcestis, the proposed heroine of Chaucer's *Legend of Good Women*, died in her husband's place.
4. Homer relates Odysseus' return from Troy to his faithful wife Penelope.
5. Lacodamia followed her dead husband Proteslaus to the underworld.

775 No lenger wolde she live after his day.
    The same of noble Porcia[6] telle I may:
Withoute Brutus coude she nat live,
To whom she hadde al hool° hir herte yive.   *whole*
    The parfit wifhood of Arthemesie[7]
780 Honoured is thurgh al the Barbarye.
    O Teuta[8] queen, thy wifly chastitee
To alle wives may a mirour be!
    The same thing I saye of Biliea,
Of Rodogone, and eek Valeria."[9]
785 Thus plained° Dorigen a day or twaye,   *lamented*
Purposing evere that she wolde deye.
    But nathelees upon the thridde night
Hoom cam Arveragus, this worthy knight,
And axed° hire why that she weep° so sore,   *asked / wept*
790 And she gan weepen evere lenger the more.[1]
    "Allas," quod she, "that evere I was born:
Thus have I said," quod she; "thus have I sworn—"
And tolde him al as ye han herd bifore:
It needeth nat reherce it you namore.
795   This housbonde with glad cheer° in freendly wise   *manner*
Answerde and saide as I shal you devise:
    "Is there ought elles, Dorigen, but this?"
    "Nay, nay," quod she, "God help me so as wis,°   *surely*
This is too muche, and° it were Goddes wille."   *if*
800   "Ye, wif," quod he, "lat sleepen that° is stille.   *what*
It may be wel paraunter° yit today.   *perhaps*
Ye shul youre trouthe[2] holden, by my fay,°   *faith*
For God so wisly° have mercy upon me,   *surely*
I hadde wel levere ystiked° for to be,   *stabbed*
805 For verray love which that I to you have,
But if[3] ye sholde youre trouthe keepe and save:
Trouthe is the hyeste thing[4] that man may keepe."
    But with that word he brast° anoon to weepe,   *burst*
And saide, "I you forbede, up° paine of deeth,   *upon*
810 That nevere whil thee lasteth lif ne breeth,
To no wight tel thou of this aventure.
As I may best I wol my wo endure,
Ne make no countenance° of hevinesse,   *appearance*
That folk of you may deemen° harm or gesse."   *suspect*

---

6. Portia swallowed burning coals on learning of Brutus' death at the battle of Philippi.
7. Artemesia built for her husband King Mausolus the famed tomb called the Mausoleum.
8. Teuta, Queen of Illyria, was unmarried: Dorigen seems to be stretching a point.
9. Bilia's prowess seems to have consisted in enduring her husband's bad breath in uncomplaining silence; Rhodogune slew her nurse, who suggested that she remarry; Valeria refused to marry again.
1. Always more and more.
2. Pledged word.
3. Unless.
4. Legal bond.

815   And forth he cleped° a squier and a maide: *called*
    "Go forth anoon with Dorigen," he saide,
    "And bringeth hire to swich a place anoon."
    They tooke hir leve and on hir way they goon,
    But they ne wiste° why they thider wente: *knew*
820 He nolde no wight tellen his entente.
    Paraventure an heep of you, ywis,°   *indeed*
    Wol holden him a lewed° man in this,   *stupid*
    That he wol putte his wif in jupartye.°   *jeopardy*
    Herkneth the tale er ye upon hire crye:
825 She may have better fortune than you seemeth,[5]
    And whan that ye han herd the tale, deemeth.°   *judge*
    This squier which that highte Aurelius,
    On Dorigen that was so amorous,
    Of aventure[6] happed° hire to meete   *happened*
830 Amidde the town, right in the quikkest° streete,   *busiest*
    As she was boun° to goon the way forth right°   *prepared / direct*
    Toward the gardin ther as she hadde hight;°   *promised*
    And he was to the gardinward also,
    For wel he spied whan she wolde go
835 Out of hir hous to any manere place.
    But thus they meete of aventure or grace,
    And he salueth° hire with glad entente,   *greets*
    And axed° of hire whiderward she wente.   *asked*
    And she answerde half as she were mad,
840 "Unto the gardin as myn housbonde bad,°   *bade*
    My trouthe for to holde, allas, allas!"
    Aurelius gan wondren on this cas,
    And in his herte hadde greet compassioun
    Of hire and of hir lamentacioun,
845 And of Arveragus, the worthy knight,
    That bad hire holden al that she hadde hight,
    So loth him was his wif sholde breke hir trouthe;
    And in his herte he caughte of this greet routhe,°   *pity*
    Considering the beste on every side
850 That fro his lust° yit were him levere abide[7]   *pleasure*
    Than doon so heigh a cherlissh wrecchednesse[8]
    Agains franchise° and alle gentilesse;   *generosity*
    For which in fewe wordes saide he thus:
    "Madame, sayeth to youre lord Arveragus
855 That sith° I see his grete gentilesse   *since*
    To you, and eek I see wel youre distresse,
    That him were levere han shame—and that were routhe—
    Than ye to me sholde breke thus youre trouthe,
    I have wel levere[9] evere to suffre wo

5. It seems.
6. By chance.
7. I.e., abstain.

8. I.e., low-born, miserable act.
9. Had much rather.

860	Than I departe° the love bitwixe you two. — *divide*
	I you releesse, Madame, into youre hond,
	Quit every serement° and every bond — *oath*
	That ye han maad to me as herbiforn,
	Sith° thilke time which that ye were born. — *since*
865	My trouthe I plighte, I shal you nevere repreve° — *reproach*
	Of no biheeste.° And here I take my leve, — *promise*
	As of the treweste and the beste wif
	That evere yit I knew in al my lif.
	But every wif be war of hir biheeste:
870	On Dorigen remembreth at the leeste.
	Thus can a squier doon a gentil deede
	As wel as can a knight, withouten drede."° — *doubt*
	She thanketh him upon hir knees al bare,
	And hoom unto hir housbonde is she fare,
875	And tolde him al as ye han herd me said.
	And be ye siker,° he was so wel apaid° — *sure / pleased*
	That it were impossible me to write.
	What sholde I lenger of this caas endite?
	Arveragus and Dorigen his wif
880	In soverein blisse leden forth hir lif.
	Never eft° ne was ther angre hem bitweene: — *again*
	He cherisseth hire as though she were a queene,
	And she was to him trewe of everemore.
	Of thise two folk ye gete of me namore.
885	Aurelius, that his cost hath al forlorn,° — *lost*
	Curseth the time that evere he was born.
	"Allas," quod he, "allas that I bihighte° — *promised*
	Of pured° gold a thousand pound of wighte° — *refined / weight*
	Unto this philosophre. How shall I do?
890	I see namore but that I am fordo.° — *ruined*
	Myn heritage moot° I needes selle — *must*
	And been a beggere. Here may I nat dwelle,
	And shamen al my kinrede° in this place, — *kindred*
	But° I of him may gete bettre grace. — *unless*
895	But nathelees I wol of him assaye
	At certain dayes yeer by yere to paye,
	And thanke him of his grete curteisye:
	My trouthe wol I keepe, I nil nat lie."
	With herte soor he gooth unto his cofre,
900	And broughte gold unto this philosophre
	The value of five hundred pound, I gesse,
	And him biseecheth of his gentilesse
	To graunten him dayes[1] of the remenaunt,° — *remainder*
	And saide, "Maister, I dar wel make avaunt° — *boast*
905	I failed nevere of my trouthe as yit,
	For sikerly° my dette shal be quit — *surely*

---

1. I.e., extended terms.

Towardes you, how evere that I fare,
To goon abegged° in my kirtel° bare.   *abegging / undergarment*
But wolde ye vouche sauf upon suretee°   *security*
910 Two yeer or three for to respiten² me,
Thanne were I wel, for elles moot° I selle   *must*
Myn heritage: ther is namore to telle."
    This philosophre sobrely answerde,
And saide thus, whan he thise wordes herde,
915 "Have I nat holden covenant unto thee?"
    "Yis, certes, wel and trewely," quod he.
    "Hastou nat had thy lady as thee liketh?"³
    "No, no," quod he and sorwefully he siketh.°   *sighs*
    "What was the cause? Tel me if thou can."
920 Aurelius his tale anoon bigan,
And tolde him al as ye han herd bifore:
It needeth nat to you reherce it more.
He saide, "Arveragus, of gentilesse,
Hadde levere die in sorwe and in distresse
925 Than that his wif were on hir trouthe fals."
The sorwe of Dorigen he tolde him als,°   *also*
How loth hire was to been a wikked wif,
And that she levere hadde lost that day hir lif,
And that hir trouthe she swoor thurgh innocence:
930 She nevere erst° hadde herd speke of apparence.°   *before / illusion*
"That made me han of hire so greet pitee;
And right as freely° as he sente hire me,   *generously*
As freely sente I hire to him again:
This al and som,⁴ ther is namore to sayn."
935   This philosophre answerde, "Leve° brother,   *dear*
Everich of you dide gentilly to other.
Thou art a squier, and he is a knight:
But God forbede, for his blisful might,
But if a clerk coude doon a gentil deede
940 As wel as any of you, it is no drede.°   *doubt*
    Sire, I releesse thee thy thousand pound,
As thou right now were cropen out of the ground,⁵
Ne nevere er° now ne haddest knowen me.   *before*
For sire, I wol nat take a peny of thee,
945 For al my craft° ne nought for my travaile.°   *art / labor*
Thou hast ypayed wel for my vitaile:°   *food*
It is ynough. And farewel, have good day."
And took his hors and forth he gooth his way.
    Lordinges, this question thanne wol I axe now:
950 Which was the moste free,° as thinketh you?   *generous*
Now telleth me, er that ye ferther wende.
I can namore: my tale is at an ende.

---

2. Give respite.   4. This is all there is to it.
3. It pleases.   5. Had crept.

The Pardoner's Prologue and Tale[1]

The Introduction

Oure Hoste gan to swere as he were wood;°   *insane*
"Harrow,"° quod he, "by nailes[2] and by blood,   *help*

1. The Pardoner is the chief actor in a grim comedy which shows how a clever hypocrite exploits Christian principles in order to enrich himself—and which, in the Epilogue, suggests that the exploiter of Christian principles is not immune to their operation. The medieval pardoner's function was to collect money for charitable enterprises supported by branches of the church and to act as the Pope's agent in rewarding donors with some temporal remission of their sins. According to theological doctrine, St. Peter—and through him his papal successors—received from Christ the power to make a gift of mercy from God's infinite treasury to those of the faithful that had earned special favor, such as contributors to charity. The charitable enterprises themselves—generally hospitals—hired pardoners to raise money, but the pardoners had also to be licensed by the Pope to pass on to contributors the papal indulgence. By canon law pardoners were permitted to work only in a prescribed area; within that area they might visit churches during Sunday service, briefly explain their mission, receive contributions, and, in the Pope's name, issue indulgence, which was considered not a sale, but a free gift made in return for a free gift. In actual fact pardoners seem seldom to have behaved as the law required them. Since a parish priest was forbidden to exclude properly licensed pardoners, they made their way into churches at will, and once there did not confine themselves to a mere statement of their business, but rather, in order to make the congregation free of its gifts, preached highly emotive sermons and boasted of the extraordinary efficacy of their own particular pardon, claiming for it powers that not even the Pope could have invested it with. An honest pardoner, if such existed, was entitled to a percentage of his collections; dishonest pardoners took more than their share, and some took everything; indeed, some were complete frauds, bearing forged credentials which, in an age when even clerical illiteracy was common, were no less impressive than if they had been real.

While Chaucer's Pardoner belongs, as he boastfully tells us, to the most dishonest class of fund-gatherers, he is an extremely able one. His text is always the same: *Radix malorum est cupiditas*, "The love of money is the root of all evil," and he uses it most effectively in order to frighten his hearers into a generosity that will fulfill his own cupidity. The Pardoner's audacious description of his behavior in a parish church is followed by a sample sermon on his invariable text. Aware that his audience is more interested in narrative than in the moralization one expects of a sermon he first introduces the three dissolute young men of his *exemplum*, that is, of the story which is to illustrate concretely the sermon's point. Having titillated his hearers with the promise of a lurid story, he proceeds to the moralization; curiously enough, this does not concern the sin of avarice, but drunkenness, gluttony, lechery, gambling, and cursing. Yet the apparent lack of logic serves the Pardoner's deeper purpose, for these are the sins people find it exciting to hear about. When his audience has thus been emotionally prepared by a discussion of the debauchees' more flamboyant sins, the Pardoner tells his *exemplum* of the destructiveness of avarice, shutting it off at the moment of highest interest, and concluding with a demand to the congregation for money in return for his pardon.

The story of the young men who seek Death only to find him in a treasure that had made them forget him is a masterpiece of irony, and indeed the Pardoner is in all ways a master ironist. So highly developed is his own sense of irony that it enables him to feel superior not only to other men but to God, for he dares to exempt himself from the effect of his Christian text. Yet the brief Epilogue seems to show that God's irony, like His other attributes, is supreme. The one fact that the Pardoner's candid confession has concealed—that it was perhaps spoken in order to conceal—is that he is a eunuch. When in the Epilogue his proud avarice leads him to see if he can get money from the pilgrims to whom he has revealed his hypocrisy, the Pardoner's secret is revealed by the Host's coarse response, and the verbal facility by which he maintains his superiority fails him.

2. I.e., God's nails.

This was a fals cherl and a fals justise.[3]
As shameful deeth as herte may devise
5 Come to thise juges and hir advocats.
Algate° this sely° maide is slain, allas!   *at any rate / innocent*
Allas, too dere boughte she beautee!
Wherfore I saye alday° that men may see   *always*
The yiftes of Fortune and of Nature
10 Been cause of deeth to many a creature.
As bothe yiftes that I speke of now,
Men han ful ofte more for harm than prow.°   *benefit*
"But trewely, myn owene maister dere,
This is a pitous tale for to heere.
15 But nathelees, passe over, is no fors:[4]
I praye to God so save thy gentil cors,°   *body*
And eek thine urinals and thy jurdones,[5]
Thyn ipocras[6] and eek thy galiones,
And every boiste° ful of thy letuarye°—   *box / medicine*
20 God blesse hem, and oure lady Sainte Marye.
So mote I theen,[7] thou art a propre man,
And lik a prelat, by Saint Ronian![8]
Saide I nat wel? I can nat speke in terme.[9]
But wel I woot, thou doost° myn herte to erme°   *make / grieve*
25 That I almost have caught a cardinacle.[1]
By corpus bones,[2] but if I have triacle,°   *medicine*
Or elles a draughte of moiste° and corny° ale,   *fresh / malty*
Or but I heere anoon° a merye tale,   *at once*
Myn herte is lost for pitee of this maide.
30 "Thou bel ami,[3] thou Pardoner," he saide,
"Tel us som mirthe or japes° right anoon."   *joke*
"It shal be doon," quod he, "by Saint Ronion.
But first," quod he, "here at this ale-stake[4]
I wol bothe drinke and eten of a cake."
35 And right anoon thise gentils gan to crye,
"Nay, lat him telle us of no ribaudye.°   *ribaldry*
Tel us som moral thing that we may lere,°   *learn*
Som wit,[5] and thanne wol we gladly heere."
"I graunte, ywis," quod he, "but I moot thinke
40 Upon som honeste° thing whil that I drinke."   *decent*

3. The Host has been affected by the Physician's sad tale of the Roman maiden Virginia, whose great beauty caused a judge to attempt to obtain her person by means of a trumped-up lawsuit in which he connived with a "churl" who claimed her as his slave; in order to preserve her chastity, her father killed her.
4. I.e., never mind.
5. Jordans (chamber pots): the Host is somewhat confused in his endeavor to use technical medical terms.
6. A medicinal drink named after Hippocrates; "galiones": a medicine, prob-ably invented on the spot by the Host, named after Galen.
7. So might I thrive.
8. St. Ronan or St. Ninian, with a pos-sible play on "runnion" (sexual organ).
9. Speak in technical idiom.
1. Apparently a cardiac condition, con-fused in the Host's mind with a car-dinal.
2. An illiterate oath, mixing "God's bones" with *corpus dei*. "But if": un-less.
3. Fair friend.
4. Sign of a tavern.
5. I.e., something with significance.

The Prologue

Lordinges—quod he—in chirches whan I preche,
I paine me[6] to han an hautein° speeche,　　　　　　　*loud*
And ringe it out as round as gooth a belle,
For I can al by rote[7] that I telle.
45　My theme is alway oon,[8] and evere was:
Radix malorum est cupiditas.[9]
First I pronounce whennes° that I come,　　　　　　*whence*
And thanne my bulles[1] shewe I alle and some:
Oure lige lordes seel on my patente,[2]
50　That shewe I first, my body to warente,°　　　　*keep safe*
That no man be so bold, ne preest ne clerk,
Me to destourbe of Cristes holy werk.
And after that thanne telle I forth my tales[3]—
Bulles of popes and of cardinales,
55　Of patriarkes and bisshopes I shewe,
And in Latin I speke a wordes fewe,
To saffron with[4] my predicacioun,°　　　　　　　*preaching*
And for to stire hem to devocioun.
　　　Thanne shewe I forth my longe crystal stones,°　　*jars*
60　Ycrammed ful of cloutes° and of bones—　　　　　*rags*
Relikes been they, as weenen° they eechoon.　　　*suppose*
Thanne have I in laton° a shulder-boon　　　　　　*zinc*
Which that was of an holy Jewes sheep.
"Goode men," I saye, "take of my wordes keep:°　　*notice*
65　If that this boon be wasshe in any welle,
If cow, or calf, or sheep, or oxe swelle,
That any worm hath ete or worm ystonge,[5]
Take water of that welle and wassh his tonge,
And it is hool[6] anoon. And ferthermoor,
70　Of pokkes° and of scabbe and every soor°　　　*pox / sore*
Shal every sheep be hool that of this welle
Drinketh a draughte. Take keep eek° that I telle:　*also*
If that the goode man that the beestes oweth°　　*owns*
Wol every wike,° er that the cok him croweth,　　*week*
75　Fasting drinken of this welle a draughte—
As thilke° holy Jew oure eldres taughte—　　　*that same*
His beestes and his stoor° shal multiplye.　　　*stock*
　　　"And sire, also it heleth jalousye:
For though a man be falle in jalous rage,
80　Lat maken with this water his potage,°　　　　　*soup*
And nevere shal he more his wif mistriste,°　　*mistrust*

---

6. Take pains.
7. I know all by heart.
8. I.e., the same.
9. Avarice is the root of evil (I Timothy vi.10).
1. Episcopal mandates; "alle and some": each and every one.

2. I.e., the Pope's seal on my papal license.
3. I go on with my yarn.
4. To add spice to.
5. That has eaten or been bitten by any worm.
6. I.e., sound.

Though he the soothe of hir defaute wiste,[7]
Al hadde she[8] taken preestes two or three.
  "Here is a mitein° eek that ye may see: *mitten*
85 He that his hand wol putte in this mitein
He shal have multiplying of his grain,
Whan he hath sowen, be it whete or otes—
So that he offre pens or elles grotes.[9]
  "Goode men and wommen, oo thing warne I you:
90 If any wight be in this chirche now
That hath doon sinne horrible, that he
Dar nat for shame of it yshriven° be,   *absolved*
Or any womman, be she yong or old,
That hath ymaked hir housbonde cokewold,°   *cuckold*
95 Swich folk shal have no power ne no grace
To offren to[1] my relikes in this place;
And whoso findeth him out of swich blame,
He wol come up and offre in Goddes name,
And I assoile° him by the auctoritee   *absolve*
100 Which that by bulle ygraunted was to me."
  By this gaude° have I wonne, yeer by yeer,   *trick*
An hundred mark[2] sith° I was pardoner.   *since*
I stonde lik a clerk in my pulpet,
And whan the lewed° peple is down yset,   *ignorant*
105 I preche so as ye han herd bifore,
And telle an hundred false japes° more.   *tricks*
Thanne paine I me[3] to strecche forth the nekke,
And eest and west upon the peple I bekke[4]
As dooth a douve,° sitting on a berne;°   *dove / barn*
110 Mine handes and my tonge goon so yerne°   *fast*
That it is joye to see my bisinesse.
Of avarice and of swich cursednesse°   *sin*
Is al my preching, for to make hem free°   *generous*
To yiven hir pens, and namely° unto me,   *especially*
115 For myn entente is nat but for to winne,[5]
And no thing for correccion of sinne:
I rekke° nevere whan that they been beried°   *care / buried*
Though that hir soules goon a-blakeberied.[6]
For certes, many a predicacioun°   *sermon*
120 Comth ofte time of yvel entencioun:
Som for plesance of folk and flaterye,
To been avaunced° by ypocrisye,   *promoted*
And som for vaine glorye, and som for hate;
For whan I dar noon otherways debate,°   *fight*
125 Thanne wol I stinge him with my tonge smerte
In preching, so that he shal nat asterte°   *escape*

7. Knew the truth of her infidelity.
8. Even if she had.
9. Pennies, groats, coins.
1. To make gifts in reverence of.
2. Marks (pecuniary units).
3. I take pains.
4. I.e., I shake my head.
5. Only to gain.
6. Go blackberrying, i.e., go to hell.

To been defamed falsly, if that he
Hath trespassed to[7] my bretheren or to me.
For though I telle nought his propre name,
130 Men shal wel knowe that it is the same
By signes and by othere circumstaunces.
Thus quite° I folk that doon us displesaunces;[8]   *pay back*
Thus spete° I out my venim under hewe°   *spit / color*
Of holinesse, to seeme holy and trewe.
135 But shortly myn entente I wol devise:°   *describe*
I preche of no thing but for coveitise;
Therfore my theme is yit and evere was
Radix malorum est cupiditas.
    Thus can I preche again that same vice
140 Which that I use, and that is avarice.
But though myself be gilty in that sinne,
Yit can I make other folk to twinne°   *separate*
From avarice, and sore to repente—
But that is nat my principal entente:
145 I preche no thing but for coveitise.
Of this matere it oughte ynough suffise.
    Thanne telle I hem ensamples[9] many oon
Of olde stories longe time agoon,
For lewed° peple loven tales olde—   *ignorant*
150 Swiche thinges can they wel reporte and holde.[1]
What, trowe° ye that whiles I may preche,   *believe*
And winne gold and silver for° I teche,   *because*
That I wol live in poverte wilfully?
Nay, nay, I thoughte° it nevere, trewely,   *intended*
155 For I wol preche and begge in sondry landes;
I wol nat do no labour with mine handes,
Ne make baskettes and live therby,
By cause I wol nat beggen idelly.[2]
I wol none of the Apostles countrefete:°   *imitate*
160 I wol have moneye, wolle,° cheese, and whete,   *wool*
Al were it[3] yiven of the pooreste page,
Or of the pooreste widwe in a village—
Al sholde hir children sterve[4] for famine.
Nay, I wol drinke licour of the vine
165 And have a joly wenche in every town.
But herkneth, lordinges, in conclusioun,
Youre liking° is that I shal telle a tale: *pleasure*
Now have I dronke a draughte of corny ale,
By God, I hope I shal you telle a thing
170 That shal by reson been at youre liking;
For though myself be a ful vicious man,
A moral tale yit I you telle can,

---

7. Injured.
8. Do us discourtesies.
9. *Exempla* (stories illustrating moral principles).

1. Repeat and remember.
2. I.e., without profit.
3. Even though it were.
4. Even though her children should die.

Which I am wont to preche for to winne.
Now holde youre pees, my tale I wol biginne.

The Tale

175   In Flandres whilom° was a compaignye   *once*
    Of yonge folk that haunteden° folye—   *practiced*
    As riot, hasard, stewes,[5] and tavernes,
    Wher as with harpes, lutes, and giternes°   *guitars*
    They daunce and playen at dees° bothe day and night,   *dice*
180 And ete also and drinke over hir might,[6]
    Thurgh which they doon the devel sacrifise
    Within that develes temple in cursed wise
    By superfluitee° abhominable.   *overindulgence*
    Hir othes been so grete and so dampnable
185 That it is grisly for to heere hem swere:
    Oure blessed Lordes body they totere[7]—
    Hem thoughte that Jewes rente° him nought ynough.   *tore*
    And eech of hem at otheres sinne lough.°   *laughed*
    And right anoon thanne comen tombesteres,°   *dancing girls*
190 Fetis° and smale,° and yonge frutesteres,[8]   *shapely / neat*
    Singeres with harpes, bawdes,° wafereres[9]—   *pimps*
    Whiche been the verray develes officeres,
    To kindle and blowe the fir of lecherye
    That is annexed unto glotonye:[1]
195 The Holy Writ take I to my witnesse
    That luxure° is in win and dronkenesse.   *lechery*
    Lo, how that dronken Lot[2] unkindely°   *unnaturally*
    Lay by his doughtres two unwitingly:
    So dronke he was he niste° what he wroughte.   *didn't know*
200 Herodes, who so wel the stories soughte,[3]
    Whan he of win was repleet at his feeste,
    Right at his owene table he yaf his heeste°   *command*
    To sleen° the Baptist John, ful giltelees.   *slay*
    Senek[4] saith a good word doutelees:
205 He saith he can no difference finde
    Bitwixe a man that is out of his minde
    And a man which that is dronkelewe,°   *drunken*
    But that woodnesse, yfallen in a shrewe,[5]
    Persevereth lenger than dooth dronkenesse.
210 O glotonye, ful of cursednesse!°   *wickedness*
    O cause first of oure confusioun!°   *downfall*
    O original of oure dampnacioun,°   *damnation*
    Til Crist hadde bought° us with his blood again!   *redeemed*

5. Wild parties, gambling, brothels.
6. Beyond their capacity.
7. Tear apart (a reference to oaths sworn by parts of His body, such as "God's bones!" or "God's teeth!").
8. Fruit-selling girls.
9. Girl cake-vendors.
1. I.e., closely related to gluttony.

2. For Lot, see Genesis xix.30–36.
3. For the story of Herod and St. John the Baptist, see Mark vi.17–29. "Who so * * * soughte": i.e., whoever looked it up in the Gospel would find.
4. Seneca, the Roman Stoic philosopher.
5. But that madness, occurring in a wicked man.

Lo, how dere, shortly for to sayn,
215 Abought° was thilke° cursed vilainye;   *paid for / that same*
Corrupt was al this world for glotonye:
Adam oure fader and his wif also
Fro Paradis to labour and to wo
Were driven for that vice, it is no drede.°   *doubt*
220 For whil that Adam fasted, as I rede,
He was in Paradis; and whan that he
Eet° of the fruit defended° on a tree,   *ate / forbidden*
Anoon he was out cast to wo and paine.
O glotonye, on thee wel oughte us plaine!°   *complain*
225   O, wiste a man[6] how manye maladies
Folwen of excesse and of glotonies,
He wolde been the more mesurable°   *moderate*
Of his diete, sitting at his table.
Allas, the shorte throte, the tendre mouth,
230 Maketh that eest and west and north and south,
In erthe, in air, in water, men to swinke,°   *work*
To gete a gloton daintee mete and drinke.
Of this matere, O Paul, wel canstou trete:
"Mete unto wombe,° and wombe eek unto mete,   *belly*
235 Shal God destroyen bothe," as Paulus saith.[7]
Allas, a foul thing is it, by my faith,
To saye this word, and fouler is the deede
Whan man so drinketh of the white and rede[8]
That of his throte he maketh his privee°   *privy*
240 Thurgh thilke cursed superfluitee.°   *overindulgence*
   The Apostle[9] weeping saith ful pitously,
"Ther walken manye of which you told have I—
I saye it now weeping with pitous vois—
They been enemies of Cristes crois,°   *cross*
245 Of whiche the ende is deeth—wombe is hir god!"[1]
O wombe, O bely, O stinking cod,°   *bag*
Fulfilled° of dong° and of corrupcioun!   *filled full / dung*
At either ende of thee foul is the soun.°   *sound*
How greet labour and cost is thee to finde!°   *provide for*
250 Thise cookes, how they stampe[2] and straine and grinde,
And turnen substance into accident[3]
To fulfillen al thy likerous° talent!°   *dainty / appetite*
Out of the harde bones knokke they
The mary,° for they caste nought away   *marrow*
255 That may go thurgh the golet[4] softe and soote.°   *sweetly*
Of spicerye° of leef and bark and roote   *spices*
Shal been his sauce ymaked by delit,

---

6. If a man knew.
7. See I Corinthians vi.13.
8. I.e., white and red wines.
9. I.e., St. Paul.
1. See Philippians iii.18.
2. Pound.

3. A philosophic joke, depending on the distinction between inner reality (substance) and outward appearance (accident).
4. Through the gullet.

To make him yit a newer appetit.
But certes, he that haunteth swiche delices°   *pleasures*
260 Is deed° whil that he liveth in tho° vices.   *dead / those*
    A lecherous thing is win, and dronkenesse
Is ful of striving° and of wrecchednesse.   *quarreling*
O dronke man, disfigured is thy face!
Sour is thy breeth, foul artou to embrace!
265 And thurgh thy dronke nose seemeth the soun
As though thou saidest ay,° "Sampsoun, Sampsoun."   *always*
And yit, God woot,° Sampson drank nevere win.[5]   *knows*
Thou fallest as it were a stiked swin;[6]
Thy tonge is lost, and al thyn honeste cure,
270 For dronkenesse is verray sepulture°   *burial*
Of mannes wit° and his discrecioun.   *intelligence*
In whom that drinke hath dominacioun
He can no conseil° keepe, it is no drede.°   *secrets / doubt*
Now keepe you fro the white and fro the rede—
275 And namely° fro the white win of Lepe[7]   *particularly*
That is to selle in Fisshstreete or in Chepe:[8]
The win of Spaine creepeth subtilly
In othere wines growing faste° by,   *close*
Of which ther riseth swich fumositee°   *heady fumes*
280 That whan a man hath dronken draughtes three
And weeneth° that he be at hoom in Chepe,   *supposes*
He is in Spaine, right at the town of Lepe,
Nat at The Rochele ne at Burdeux town;[9]
And thanne wol he sayn, "Sampsoun, Sampsoun."
285   But herkneth, lordinges, oo° word I you praye,   *one*
That alle the soverein actes,[1] dar I saye,
Of victories in the Olde Testament,
Thurgh verray God that is omnipotent,
Were doon in abstinence and in prayere:
290 Looketh° the Bible and ther ye may it lere.°   *behold / learn*
    Looke Attila, the grete conquerour,[2]
Deide° in his sleep with shame and dishonour,   *died*
Bleeding at his nose in dronkenesse:
A capitain sholde live in sobrenesse.
295   And overal this, aviseth you[3] right wel
What was comanded unto Lamuel[4]—
Nat Samuel, but Lamuel, saye I—
Redeth the Bible and finde it expresly,
Of win-yiving° to hem that han[5] justise: *wine-serving*

5. Before Samson's birth an angel told his mother that he would be a Nazarite throughout his life; members of this sect took no strong drink.
6. Stuck pig. "Honeste cure": care for self-respect.
7. A town in Spain.
8. Fishstreet and Cheapside in the London market district.
9. The Pardoner is joking about the illegal custom of adulterating fine wines of Bordeaux and La Rochelle with strong Spanish wine.
1. Distinguished deeds.
2. Attila was the leader of the Huns who captured Rome in the 5th century.
3. Consider.
4. Lemuel's mother told him that kings should not drink (Proverbs xxxi.4–5).
5. I.e., administer.

300 Namore of this, for it may wel suffise.
    And now that I have spoken of glotonye,
    Now wol I you defende° hasardrye:°   *prohibit / gambling*
    Hasard is verray moder° of lesinges,°   *mother / lies*
    And of deceite and cursed forsweringes,
305 Blaspheme of Crist, manslaughtre, and wast° also   *waste*
    Of catel° and of time; and ferthermo,   *property*
    It is repreve° and contrarye of honour   *disgrace*
    For to been holden a commune hasardour,°   *gambler*
    And evere the hyer he is of estat
310 The more is he holden desolat.[6]
    If that a prince useth hasardrye,
    In alle governance and policye
    He is, as by commune opinioun,
    Yholde the lasse° in reputacioun.   *less*
315 Stilbon, that was a wis embassadour,
    Was sent to Corinthe in ful greet honour
    Fro Lacedomye° to make hir alliaunce,   *Sparta*
    And whan he cam him happede° parchaunce   *it happened*
    That alle the gretteste° that were of that lond   *greatest*
320 Playing at the hasard he hem foond,   *found*
    For which as soone as it mighte be
    He stal him[7] hoom again to his contree,
    And saide, "Ther wol I nat lese° my name,   *lose*
    N'I wol nat take on me so greet defame°   *dishonor*
325 You to allye unto none hasardours:
    Sendeth othere wise embassadours,
    For by my trouthe, me were levere[8] die
    Than I you sholde to hasardours allye.
    For ye that been so glorious in honours
330 Shal nat allye you with hasardours
    As by my wil, ne as by my tretee."°   *treaty*
    This wise philosophre, thus saide he.
    Looke eek that to the king Demetrius
    The King of Parthes,° as the book[9] saith us,   *Parthians*
335 Sente him a paire of dees° of gold in scorn,   *dice*
    For he hadde used hasard therbiforn,
    For which he heeld his glorye or his renown
    At no value or reputacioun.
    Lordes may finden other manere play
340 Honeste° ynough to drive the day away.   *honorable*
    Now wol I speke of othes false and grete
    A word or two, as olde bookes trete:
    Greet swering is a thing abhominable,
    And fals swering is yit more reprevable.°   *reprehensible*
345 The hye God forbad swering at al—

6. I.e., dissolute.
7. He stole away.
8. I had rather.
9. The book that relates this and the previous incident is the *Policraticus* of the 12th-century Latin writer, John of Salisbury.

Witnesse on Mathew.[1] But in special
Of swering saith the holy Jeremie,[2]
"Thou shalt swere sooth thine othes and nat lie,
And swere in doom[3] and eek in rightwisnesse,
350 But idel swering is a cursednesse."°   *wickedness*
   Biholde and see that in the firste Table[4]
Of hye Goddes heestes° honorable   *commandments*
How that the seconde heeste of him is this:
"Take nat my name in idel or amis."
355 Lo, rather° he forbedeth swich swering   *sooner*
Than homicide, or many a cursed thing.
I saye that as by ordre thus it stondeth—
This knoweth that[5] his heestes understondeth
How that the seconde heeste of God is that.
360 And fertherover,° I wol thee telle al plat°   *moreover / flat*
That vengeance shal nat parten° from his hous   *depart*
That of his othes is too outrageous.
"By Goddes precious herte!" and "By his nailes!"°   *fingernails*
And "By the blood of Crist that is in Hailes,[6]
365 Sevene is my chaunce, and thyn is cink and traye!"[7]
"By Goddes armes, if thou falsly playe
This daggere shal thurghout thyn herte go!"
This fruit cometh of the bicche bones[8] two—
Forswering, ire, falsnesse, homicide.
370 Now for the love of Crist that for us dyde,
Lete° youre othes bothe grete and smale.   *leave*
But sires, now wol I telle forth my tale.
   Thise riotoures° three of whiche I telle,   *revelers*
Longe erst er prime[9] ronge of any belle,
375 Were set hem in a taverne to drinke,
And as they sat they herde a belle clinke
Biforn a cors° was caried to his grave.   *corpse*
That oon of hem gan callen to his knave:°   *servant*
"Go bet,"[1] quod he, "and axe° redily°   *ask / promptly*
380 What cors is this that passeth heer forby,
And looke° that thou reporte his name weel."°   *be sure / well*
   "Sire," quod this boy, "it needeth neveradeel:[2]
It was me told er ye cam heer two houres.
He was, pardee, an old felawe of youres,
385 And sodeinly he was yslain tonight,°   *last night*
Fordronke° as he sat on his bench upright;   *very drunk*
Ther cam a privee° thief men clepeth° Deeth,   *stealthy / call*
That in this contree al the peple sleeth,°   *slays*

1. "But I say unto you, Swear not at all" (Matthew v.34).
2. Jeremiah (iv.2).
3. Equity; "rightwisnesse": righteousness.
4. I.e., the first four of the Ten Commandments.
5. I.e., he that.
6. An abbey in Gloucestershire supposed to possess some of Christ's blood.
7. Five and three.
8. I.e., damned dice.
9. Long before 9 A.M.
1. Better, i.e., quick.
2. It isn't a bit necessary.

And with his spere he smoot his herte atwo,
390 And wente his way withouten wordes mo.
He hath a thousand slain this° pestilence.   *during this*
And maister, er ye come in his presence,
Me thinketh that it were necessarye
For to be war of swich an adversarye;
395 Beeth redy for to meete him everemore:
Thus taughte me my dame.° I saye namore."   *mother*
   "By Sainte Marye," saide this taverner,
"The child saith sooth, for he hath slain this yeer,
Henne° over a mile, within a greet village,   *hence*
400 Bothe man and womman, child and hinc³ and page.
I trowe° his habitacion be there.   *believe*
To been avised° greet wisdom it were   *wary*
Er that he dide a man a dishonour."
   "Ye, Goddes armes," quod this riotour,
405 "Is it swich peril with him for to meete?
I shal him seeke by way and eek by streete,⁴
I make avow to Goddes digne° bones.   *worthy*
Herkneth, felawes, we three been alle ones:°   *of one mind*
Lat eech of us holde up his hand to other
410 And eech of us bicome otheres brother,
And we wol sleen this false traitour Deeth.
He shal be slain, he that so manye sleeth,
By Goddes dignitee, er it be night."
   Togidres han thise three hir trouthes plight⁵
415 To live and dien eech of hem with other,
As though he were his owene ybore° brother.   *born*
And up they sterte,° al dronken in this rage,   *started*
And forth they goon towardes that village
Of which the taverner hadde spoke biforn.
420 And many a grisly ooth thanne han they sworn,
And Cristes blessed body they torente:°   *tore apart*
Deeth shal be deed° if that they may him hente.°   *dead / catch*
   Whan they han goon nat fully half a mile,
Right as they wolde han treden° over a stile,   *stepped*
425 An old man and a poore with hem mette;
This olde man ful mekely hem grette,°   *greeted*
And saide thus, "Now lordes, God you see."⁶
   The pruddeste° of thise riotoures three   *proudest*
Answerde again, "What, carl° with sory grace,   *churl*
430 Why artou al forwrapped save thy face?
Why livestou so longe in so greet age?"
   This olde man gan looke in his visage,
And saide thus, "For° I ne can nat finde   *because*
A man, though that I walked into Inde,
435 Neither in citee ne in no village,

3. Farm laborer.   5. Pledged their words of honor.
4. By highway and byway.   6. May God protect you.

That wolde chaunge his youthe for myn age;
And therfore moot I han myn age stille,
As longe time as it is Goddes wille.
"Ne Deeth, allas, ne wol nat have my lif.
440 Thus walke I lik a restelees caitif,°   *captive*
And on the ground which is my modres° gate *mother's*
I knokke with my staf bothe erly and late,
And saye, 'Leve° moder, leet me in: *dear*
Lo, how I vanisshe, flessh and blood and skin.
445 Allas, whan shal my bones been at reste?
Moder, with you wolde I chaunge° my cheste⁷ *exchange*
That in my chambre longe time hath be,
Ye, for an haire-clout⁸ to wrappe me.'
But yit to me she wol nat do that grace,
450 For which ful pale and welked° is my face. *withered*
But sires, to you it is no curteisye
To speken to an old man vilainye,°   *rudeness*
But° he trespasse° in word or elles in deede. *unless / offend*
In Holy Writ ye may yourself wel rede,
455 'Agains⁹ an old man, hoor° upon his heed, *hoar*
Ye shal arise.'¹ Wherfore I yive you reed,° *advice*
Ne dooth unto an old man noon harm now,
Namore than that ye wolde men dide to you
In age, if that ye so longe abide.
460 And God be with you wher ye go° or ride: *walk*
I moot go thider as I have to go."
  "Nay, olde cherl, by God thou shalt nat so,"
Saide this other hasardour anoon.
"Thou partest nat so lightly,° by Saint John! *easily*
465 Thou speke° right now of thilke traitour Deeth, *spoke*
That in this contree alle oure freendes sleeth:
Have here my trouthe, as thou art his espye,
Tel wher he is, or thou shalt it abye,°   *pay for*
By God and by the holy sacrament!
470 For soothly thou art oon of his assent²
To sleen us yonge folk, thou false thief."
  "Now sires," quod he, "if that ye be so lief° *anxious*
To finde Deeth, turne up this crooked way,
For in that grove I lafte° him, by my fay,° *left / faith*
475 Under a tree, and ther he wol abide:
Nat for youre boost° he wol him no thing hide. *boast*
See ye that ook?° Right ther ye shal him finde. *oak*
God save you, that boughte again³ mankinde,
And you amende." Thus saide this olde man.
480 And everich of thise riotoures ran
Til he cam to that tree, and ther they founde

---

7. Chest for one's belongings, used here as the symbol for life—or perhaps a coffin.
8. Haircloth, for a winding sheet.
9. In the presence of.
1. Cf. Leviticus xix.32.
2. I.e., one of his party.
3. Redeemed.

Of florins° fine of gold ycoined rounde   *coins*
Wel neigh an eighte busshels as hem thoughte—
Ne lenger thanne after Deeth they soughte,
485 But eech of hem so glad was of the sighte,
For that the florins been so faire and brighte,
That down they sette hem by this precious hoord.
The worste of hem he spak the firste word:
    "Bretheren," quod he, "take keep° what that I saye: *heed*
490 My wit is greet though that I bourde° and playe.   *joke*
This tresor hath Fortune unto us yiven
In mirthe and jolitee oure lif to liven,
And lightly° as it cometh so wol we spende.   *easily*
Ey, Goddes precious dignitee, who wende[4]
495 Today that we sholde han so fair a grace?
But mighte this gold be caried fro this place
Hoom to myn hous—or elles unto youres—
For wel ye woot that al this gold is oures—
Thanne were we in heigh felicitee.
500 But trewely, by daye it mighte nat be:
Men wolde sayn that we were theves stronge,°   *flagrant*
And for oure owene tresor doon us honge.[5]
This tresor moste ycaried be by nighte,
As wisely and as slyly as it mighte.
505 Therfore I rede° that cut° amonges us alle   *advise / lots*
Be drawe, and lat see wher the cut wol falle;
And he that hath the cut with herte blithe
Shal renne° to the town, and that ful swithe,°   *run / quickly*
And bringe us breed and win ful prively;
510 And two of us shal keepen° subtilly   *guard*
This tresor wel, and if he wol nat tarye,
Whan it is night we wol this tresor carye
By oon assent wher as us thinketh best."
That oon of hem the cut broughte in his fest°   *fist*
515 And bad hem drawe and looke wher it wol falle;
And it fil° on the yongeste of hem alle,   *fell*
And forth toward the town he wente anoon.
And also° soone as that he was agoon,°   *as / gone away*
That oon of hem spak thus unto that other:
520 "Thou knowest wel thou art my sworen brother;
Thy profit wol I telle thee anoon:
Thou woost wel that oure felawe is agoon,
And here is gold, and that ful greet plentee,
That shal departed° been among us three.   *divided*
525 But nathelees, if I can shape° it so   *arrange*
That it departed were among us two,
Hadde I nat doon a freendes turn to thee?"
    That other answerde, "I noot[6] how that may be:

---

4. Who would have supposed.   6. Don't know.
5. Have us hanged.

He woot that the gold is with us twaye.
530 What shal we doon? What shal we to him saye?"
    "Shal it be conseil?"[7] saide the firste shrewe.°   *villain*
"And I shal telle in a wordes fewe
What we shul doon, and bringe it wel aboute."
    "I graunte," quod that other, "out of doute,
535 That by my trouthe I wol thee nat biwraye."°   *expose*
    "Now," quod the firste, "thou woost wel we be twaye,
And two of us shal strenger° be than oon: *stronger*
Looke whan that he is set that right anoon
Aris as though thou woldest with him playe,
540 And I shal rive° him thurgh the sides twaye,   *pierce*
Whil that thou struglest with him as in game,
And with thy daggere looke thou do the same;
And thanne shal al this gold departed be,
My dere freend, bitwixe thee and me.
545 Thanne we may bothe oure lustes° al fulfille,   *desires*
And playe at dees° right at oure owene wille."   *dice*
And thus accorded been thise shrewes twaye
To sleen the thridde, as ye han herd me saye.
    This yongeste, which that wente to the town,
550 Ful ofte in herte he rolleth up and down
The beautee of thise florins newe and brighte.
"O Lord," quod he, "if so were that I mighte
Have al this tresor to myself allone,
Ther is no man that liveth under the trone°   *throne*
555 Of God that sholde live so merye as I."
And at the laste the feend oure enemy
Putte in his thought that he sholde poison beye,°   *buy*
With which he mighte sleen his felawes twaye—
Forwhy° the feend foond him in swich livinge   *because*
560 That he hadde leve° him to sorwe bringe:[8]   *permission*
For this was outrely° his fulle entente,   *plainly*
To sleen hem bothe, and nevere to repente.
    And forth he gooth—no lenger wolde he tarye—
Into the town unto a pothecarye,°   *apothecary*
565 And prayed him that he him wolde selle
Som poison that he mighte his rattes quelle,°   *kill*
And eek ther was a polcat[9] in his hawe°   *yard*
That, as he saide, his capons hadde yslawe,°   *slain*
And fain he wolde wreke him[1] if he mighte
570 On vermin that destroyed him[2] by nighte.
    The pothecarye answerde, "And thou shalt have
A thing that, also° God my soule save,   *as*
In al this world ther is no creature
That ete or dronke hath of this confiture°—   *mixture*

---

7. A secret.
8. Christian doctrine teaches that the devil may not tempt men except with God's permission.
9. A weasel-like animal.
1. He would gladly avenge himself.
2. I.e., were ruining his farming.

575 Nat but the mountance° of a corn° of whete—   *amount / grain*
       That he ne shal his lif anoon forlete.°   *lose*
       Ye, sterve° he shal, and that in lasse° while   *die / less*
       Than thou wolt goon a paas[3] nat but a mile,
       The poison is so strong and violent."
580 This cursed man hath in his hand yhent°   *taken*
       This poison in a box and sith° he ran   *then*
       Into the nexte streete unto a man
       And borwed of him large botels three,
       And in the two his poison poured he—
585 The thridde he kepte clene for his drinke,
       For al the night he shoop him[4] for to swinke°   *work*
       In carying of the gold out of that place.
       And whan this riotour with sory grace
       Hadde filled with win his grete botels three,
590 To his felawes again repaireth he.
          What needeth it to sermone of it more?
       For right as they had cast° his deeth bifore,   *plotted*
       Right so they han him slain, and that anoon.
       And whan that this was doon, thus spak that oon:
595 "Now lat us sitte and drinke and make us merye,
       And afterward we wol his body berye."°   *bury*
       And with that word it happed him par cas[5]
       To take the botel ther the poison was,
       And drank, and yaf his felawe drinke also,
600 For which anoon they storven° bothe two.   *died*
          But certes I suppose that Avicen
       Wroot nevere in no canon ne in no *fen*[6]
       Mo wonder signes[7] of empoisoning
       Than hadde thise wrecches two er hir ending:
605 Thus ended been thise homicides two,
       And eek the false empoisonere also.
          O cursed sinne of alle cursednesse!
       O traitours homicide, O wikkednesse!
       O glotonye, luxure,° and hasardrye!   *lechery*
610 Thou blasphemour of Crist with vilainye
       And othes grete of usage° and of pride!   *habit*
       Allas, mankinde, how may it bitide
       That to thy Creatour which that thee wroughte,
       And with his precious herte blood thee boughte,°   *redeemed*
615 Thou art so fals and so unkinde,° allas?   *unnatural*
          Now goode men, God foryive you youre trespas,
       And ware° you fro the sinne of avarice: *guard*
       Myn holy pardon may you alle warice°—   *save*
       So that ye offre nobles or sterlinges,[8]

---

3. Take a walk.
4. He was preparing.
5. By chance.
6. The *Canon of Medicine,* by Avicenna,
an 11th-century Arabic philosopher,

was divided into sections called *"fens."*
7. More wonderful symptoms.
8. "Nobles" and "sterlinges" were valuable coins.

620 Or elles silver brooches, spoones, ringes.
    Boweth your heed under this holy bulle!
    Cometh up, ye wives, offreth of youre wolle!°   *wool*
    Youre name I entre here in my rolle: anoon
    Into the blisse of hevene shul ye goon.
625 I you assoile° by myn heigh power—   *absolve*
    Ye that wol offre—as clene and eek as cleer
    As ye were born.—And lo, sires, thus I preche.
    And Jesu Crist that is oure soules leeche°   *physician*
    So graunte you his pardon to receive,
630 For that is best—I wol you nat deceive.

The Epilogue

    "But sires, oo word forgat I in my tale:
    I have relikes and pardon in my male°   *bag*
    As faire as any man in Engelond,
    Whiche were me yiven by the Popes hond.
635 If any of you wol of devocioun
    Offren and han myn absolucioun,
    Come forth anoon, and kneeleth here adown,
    And mekely receiveth my pardoun,
    Or elles taketh pardon as ye wende,
640 Al newe and fressh at every miles ende—
    So that ye offre alway newe and newe⁹
    Nobles or pens whiche that be goode and trewe.
    It is an honour to everich that is heer
    That ye have a suffisant° pardoner   *competent*
645 T'assoile you in contrees as ye ride,
    For aventures whiche that may bitide:
    Paraventure ther may falle oon or two
    Down of his hors and breke his nekke atwo;
    Looke which a suretee° is it to you alle   *safeguard*
650 That I am in youre felaweshipe yfalle
    That may assoile you, bothe more and lasse,¹
    Whan that the soule shal fro the body passe.
    I rede° that oure Hoste shal biginne,   *advise*
    For he is most envoluped° in sinne.   *involved*
655 Com forth, sire Host, and offre first anoon,
    And thou shalt kisse the relikes everichoon,°   *each one*
    Ye, for a grote: unbokele° anoon thy purs."   *unbuckle*
    "Nay, nay," quod he, "thanne have I Cristes curs!
    Lat be," quod he, "it shal nat be, so theech!°   *may I thrive*
660 Thou woldest make me kisse thyn olde breech°   *breeches*
    And swere it were a relik of a saint,
    Though it were with thy fundament depeint.°   *stained*
    But, by the crois which that Sainte Elaine foond,²

9. Over and over.
1. Both high and low (i.e., everybody).
2. I.e., by the cross that St. Helena found. Helena, mother of Constantine the Great, was reputed to have found the True Cross.

I wolde I hadde thy coilons° in myn hond, testicles
665 In stede of relikes or of saintuarye.° relic-box
Lat cutte hem of: I wol thee helpe hem carve.
They shal be shrined in an hogges tord."° turd
This Pardoner answerde nat a word:
So wroth he was no word ne wolde he saye.
670 "Now," quod oure Host, "I wol no lenger playe
With thee, ne with noon other angry man."
But right anoon the worthy Knight bigan,
Whan that he sawgh that al the peple lough,° laughed
"Namore of this, for it is right ynough.
675 Sire Pardoner, be glad and merye of cheere,
And ye, sire Host that been to me so dere,
I praye you that ye kisse the Pardoner,
And Pardoner, I praye thee, draw thee neer,
And as we diden lat us laughe and playe."
680 Anoon they kiste and riden forth hir waye.

The Nun's Priest's Tale[1]

A poore widwe somdeel stape° in age advanced
Was whilom° dwelling in a narwe[2] cotage, once upon a time
Biside a grove, stonding in a dale:
This widwe of which I telle you my tale,
5 Sin thilke° day that she was last a wif, that same
In pacience ladde° a ful simple lif. led

1. The Nun's Priest's Tale is an example of the literary genre known as the "beast fable," in which animals behave like human beings. The beast fable is inevitably injurious to man's dignity, since to pretend that animals behave like men is to suggest that men behave like animals, for a pig cannot look like a man unless a man in some way looks like a pig. In the Nun's Priest's Tale, as in its French source, the history of Reynard the Fox, the beast fable is combined with the mock heroic, and the result is doubly injurious to man's dignity. The elevated language of true heroic poetry means to enhance the splendid deeds of men of great stature, while the elevated language of mock heroic, by treating the trivial as if it were sublime, reveals man's lack of dignity in the awful gulf that separates the idealized language from the petty action it describes; and when the petty action is carried on not even by men, but by animals masquerading as men (that is, by men reduced to the status of animals), the loss of human dignity is even greater.
The nominal hero of the Tale is Chauntecleer, a fowl of courtly bearing, profound learning, and superior crowing. This rooster is, like Achilles or Aeneas, made the center of a "great" action—which, however, takes up a relatively small portion of the total number of lines in the poem. The hero of the larger portion, and the real hero of the poem, is rhetoric, which is responsible for all Chauntecleer's importance, though it almost drowns his story in its vast tumid flow. Rhetoric as employed by the Nun's Priest includes not only elevated speech, but proverbs, saws, conventional similes—all the clichés of formal language and thought. Epic mannerisms abound; proverbs fly thick and fast and contradict one another with impunity; sententious generalizations about the tragic inevitability of certain events, the bad counsel given by women, and the folly of heeding flattery are successively used to account for Chauntecleer's near-fall; and throughout the tale learned pedantry invokes rhetorical tradition to footnote the least original of ideas. All rhetoric's ordering devices achieve a fine disorder.
2. I.e., small.

For litel was hir catel° and hir rente,°   *property / income*
By housbondrye° of swich as God hire sente   *economy*
She foond° hirself and eek hir doughtren two.   *provided for*
10 Three large sowes hadde she and namo,
 Three kin,° and eek a sheep that highte Malle.   *cows*
Ful sooty was hir bowr° and eek hir halle,   *bedroom*
In which she eet ful many a sclendre° meel;   *scanty*
Of poinant° sauce hire needed neveradeel: *pungent*
15 No daintee morsel passed thurgh hir throte—
Hir diete was accordant to hir cote.°   *cottage*
Repleccioun° ne made hire nevere sik: *overeating*
Attempre° diete was al hir physik,°   *moderate / medicine*
And exercise and hertes suffisaunce.°   *contentment*
20 The goute lette hire nothing for to daunce,[3]
N'apoplexye shente° nat hir heed.°   *hurt / head*
No win ne drank she, neither whit ne reed:°   *red*
Hir boord° was served most with whit and blak,[4]   *table*
Milk and brown breed, in which she foond no lak;[5]
25 Seind bacon, and somtime an ey° or twaye,   *egg*
For she was as it were a manere daye.[6]
A yeerd° she hadde, enclosed al withoute   *yard*
With stikkes, and a drye dich aboute,
In which she hadde a cok heet° Chauntecleer: *named*
30 In al the land of crowing nas° his peer.   *was not*
His vois was merier than the merye orgon
On massedayes that in the chirche goon;[7]
Wel sikerer[8] was his crowing in his logge°   *dwelling*
Than is a clok or an abbeye orlogge;°   *timepiece*
35 By nature he knew eech ascensioun
Of th'equinoxial[9] in thilke town:
For whan degrees fifteene were ascended,
Thanne crew[1] he that it mighte nat been amended
His comb was redder than the fin coral,
40 And batailed° as it were a castel wal;   *battlemented*
His bile° was blak, and as the jeet° it shoon;   *bill / jet*
Like asure[2] were his legges and his toon;°   *toes*
His nailes whitter° than the lilye flowr,   *whiter*
And lik the burned° gold was his colour.   *burnished*
45 This gentil cok hadde in his governaunce
Sevene hennes for to doon al his plesaunce,°   *pleasure*
Whiche were his sustres and his paramours,[3]
And wonder like to him as of colours;

3. The gout didn't hinder her at all from dancing.
4. I.e., milk and bread.
5. Found no fault. "Seind": scorched (i.e., broiled).
6. I.e., a kind of dairymaid.
7. I.e., is played.
8. More reliable.
9. I.e., he knew by instinct each step in the progression of the celestial equator. The celestial equator was thought to make a 360-degree rotation around the earth every 24 hours; therefore a progression of 15 degrees would be equal to the passage of an hour (line 37).
1. Crowed; "amended": improved.
2. Lapis lazuli.
3. His sisters and his mistresses.

Of whiche the faireste hewed° on hir throte   *colored*
50 Was cleped faire damoisele Pertelote:
Curteis she was, discreet, and debonaire,°   *meek*
And compaignable,[4] and bar° hirself so faire,   *bore*
Sin thilke day that she was seven night old,
That trewely she hath the herte in hold
55 Of Chauntecleer, loken° in every lith.°   *locked / limb*
He loved hire so that wel was him therwith.[5]
But swich a joye was it to heere hem singe,
Whan that the brighte sonne gan to springe,
In sweete accord *My Lief is Faren in Londe*[6]—
60 For thilke time, as I have understonde,
Beestes and briddes couden speke and singe.
    And so bifel that in a daweninge,
As Chauntecleer among his wives alle
Sat on his perche that was in the halle,
65 And next him sat this faire Pertelote,
This Chauntecleer gan gronen in his throte,
As man that in his dreem is drecched° sore.   *troubled*
    And whan that Pertelote thus herde him rore,
She was agast, and saide, "Herte dere,
70 What aileth you to grone in this manere?
Ye been a verray slepere,[7] fy, for shame!"
    And he answerde and saide thus, "Madame,
I praye you that ye take it nat agrief.°   *amiss*
By God, me mette I was in swich meschief[8]
75 Right now, that yit myn herte is sore afright.
Now God," quod he, "my swevene recche aright,[9]
And keepe my body out of foul prisoun!
Me mette how that I romed up and down
Within oure yeerd, wher as I sawgh a beest,
80 Was lik an hound and wolde han maad arrest[1]
Upon my body, and han had me deed.[2]
His colour was bitwixe yelow and reed,
And tipped was his tail and bothe his eres
With blak, unlik the remenant° of his heres;°   *rest / hairs*
85 His snoute smal, with glowing yën twaye.
Yit of his look for fere almost I deye:°   *die*
This caused me my groning, doutelees."
    "Avoi,"° quod she, "fy on you, hertelees!°   *fie / coward*
Allas," quod she, "for by that God above,
90 Now han ye lost myn herte and al my love!
I can nat love a coward, by my faith.
For certes, what so any womman saith,
We alle desiren, if it mighte be,

4. Companionable.
5. That he was well contented.
6. A popular song of the time.
7. Sound sleeper.
8. I dreamed that I was in such misfortune.
9. Interpret my dream correctly (i.e., in an auspicious manner).
1. Would have laid hold.
2. I.e., killed me.

To han housbondes hardy, wise, and free,°   *generous*
95 And secree,° and no nigard, ne no fool,   *discreet*
Ne him that is agast of every tool,°   *weapon*
Ne noon avauntour.° By that God above,   *boaster*
How dorste ye sayn for shame unto youre love
That any thing mighte make you aferd?
100 Have ye no mannes herte and han a beerd?
Allas, and conne° ye been agast of swevenes?°   *can / dreams*
No thing, God woot, but vanitee³ in swevene is!
Swevenes engendren of replexiouns,⁴
And ofte of fume° and of complexiouns,°   *gas / bodily humors*
105 Whan humours been too habundant in a wight.⁵
Certes, this dreem which ye han met° tonight   *dreamed*
Comth of the grete superfluitee
Of youre rede colera,⁶ pardee,
Which causeth folk to dreden° in hir dremes   *fear*
110 Of arwes,° and of fir with rede lemes,°   *arrows / flames*
Of rede beestes, that they wol hem bite,
Of contek,° and of whelpes grete and lite⁷—   *strife*
Right° as the humour of malencolye⁸   *just*
Causeth ful many a man in sleep to crye
115 For fere of blake beres° or boles° blake,   *bears / bulls*
Or elles blake develes wol hem take.
Of othere humours coude I tell also
That werken many a man in sleep ful wo,
But I wol passe as lightly° as I can.   *quickly*
120 Lo, Caton,⁹ which that was so wis a man,
Saide he nat thus? 'Ne do no fors of¹ dremes.'
Now, sire," quod she, "whan we flee fro the bemes,²
For Goddes love, as take som laxatif.
Up° peril of my soule and of my lif,   *upon*
125 I conseile you the beste, I wol nat lie,
That bothe of colere and of malencolye
Ye purge you; and for° ye shal nat tarye,   *in order that*
Though in this town is noon apothecarye,
I'shal myself to herbes techen you,
130 That shal been for youre hele³ and for youre prow,
And in oure yeerd tho herbes shal I finde,
The whiche han of hir propretee by kinde°   *nature*
To purge you binethe and eek above.
Foryet° nat this, for Goddes owene love.   *forget*
135 Ye been ful colerik° of complexioun;   *bilious*

---

3. I.e., empty illusion.
4. Dreams have their origin in over-eating.
5. I.e., when humors are too abundant in a person. Pertelote's diagnosis is based on the familiar concept that an overabundance of one of the bodily humors in a person affected his temperament.

6. Red bile.
7. And of big and little dogs.
8. I.e., black bile.
9. Dionysius Cato, supposed author of a book of maxims used in elementary education.
1. Pay no attention to.
2. Fly down from the rafters.
3. Health; "prow": benefit.

Ware° the sonne in his ascencioun   *beware that*
Ne finde you nat repleet° of humours hote;°   *filled / hot*
And if it do, I dar wel laye° a grote   *bet*
That ye shul have a fevere terciane,[4]
140 Or an agu that may be youre bane.°   *death*
A day or two ye shul han digestives
Of wormes, er ye take youre laxatives
Of lauriol, centaure, and fumetere,[5]
Or elles of ellebor° that groweth there,   *hellebore*
145 Of catapuce, or of gaitres beries,[6]
Of herbe-ive° growing in oure yeerd ther merye is.[7] *herb ivy*
Pekke hem right up as they growe and ete hem in.
Be merye, housbonde, for youre fader kin!
Dredeth no dreem: I can saye you namore."
150   "Madame," quod he, "graunt mercy of youre lore.[8]
But nathelees, as touching daun° Catoun,   *master*
That hath of wisdom swich a greet renown,
Though that he bad no dremes for to drede,
By God, men may in olde bookes rede
155 Of many a man more of auctoritee°   *authority*
Than evere Caton was, so mote I thee,°   *thrive*
That al the revers sayn of his sentence,°   *opinion*
And han wel founden by experience
That dremes been significaciouns
160 As wel of joye as tribulaciouns
That folk enduren in this lif present.
Ther needeth make of this noon argument:
The verray preve[9] sheweth it in deede.
   "Oon of the gretteste auctour[1] that men rede
165 Saith thus, that whilom two felawes wente
On pilgrimage in a ful good entente,
And happed so they comen in a town,
Wher as ther was swich congregacioun
Of peple, and eek so strait of herbergage,[2]
170 That they ne founde as muche as oo cotage
In which they bothe mighte ylogged° be;   *lodged*
Wherfore they mosten° of necessitee   *must*
As for that night departe° compaignye.   *part*
And eech of hem gooth to his hostelrye,
175 And took his logging as it wolde falle.°   *befall*
That oon of hem was logged in a stalle,
Fer° in a yeerd, with oxen of the plough;   *far away*
That other man was logged wel ynough,
As was his aventure° or his fortune,   *lot*

---

4. Tertian (recurring every other day).
5. Of laureole, centaury, and fumitory.
These, and the herbs mentioned in the
next lines, were all common medieval
medicines used as cathartics.
6. Of caper berry or of gaiter berry.

7. Where it is pleasant.
8. Many thanks for your instruction.
9. Actual experience.
1. I.e., one of the greatest authors (perhaps Cicero).
2. And also such a shortage of lodging.

180 That us governeth alle as in commune.
And so bifel that longe er it were day,
This man mette° in his bed, ther as he lay,   *dreamed*
How that his felawe gan upon him calle,
And saide, 'Allas, for in an oxes stalle
185 This night I shal be mordred° ther I lie!   *murdered*
Now help me, dere brother, or I die!
In alle haste com to me,' he saide.
    "This man out of his sleep for fere abraide,ᶜ   *started up*
But whan that he was wakened of his sleep,
190 He turned him and took of this no keep:°   *heed*
Him thoughte his dreem nas but a vanitee.
Thus twies in his sleeping dremed he,
And atte thridde time yit his felawe
Cam, as him thoughte, and saide, 'I am now slawe:°   *slain*
195 Bihold my bloody woundes deepe and wide.
Aris up erly in the morwe tide³
And atte west gate of the town,' quod he,
'A carte ful of dong° ther shaltou see,   *dung*
In which my body is hid ful prively:
200 Do thilke carte arresten boldely.⁴
My gold caused my mordre, sooth to sayn'—
And tolde him every point how he was slain,
With a ful pitous face, pale of hewe.
And truste wel, his dreem he foond° ful trewe,   *found*
205 For on the morwe° as soone as it was day,   *morning*
To his felawes in° he took the way,   *lodging*
And whan that he cam to this oxes stalle,
After his felawe he bigan to calle.
    "The hostiler° answerde him anoon,   *innkeeper*
210 And saide, 'Sire, youre felawe is agoon:°   *gone away*
As soone as day he wente out of the town.'
    "This man gan fallen in suspecioun,
Remembring on his dremes that he mette;°   *dreamed*
And forth he gooth, no lenger wolde he lette,°   *tarry*
215 Unto the west gate of the town, and foond
A dong carte, wente as it were to donge° lond,   *put manure on*
That was arrayed in that same wise
As ye han herd the dede° man devise;   *dead*
And with an hardy herte he gan to crye,
220 'Vengeance and justice of this felonye!
My felawe mordred is this same night,
And in this carte he lith° gaping upright!°   *lies / supine*
I crye out on the ministres,' quod he,
'That sholde keepe and rulen this citee.
225 Harrow,° allas, here lith my felawe slain!'   *help*
What sholde I more unto this tale sayn?
The peple up sterte° and caste the carte to grounde,   *started*

---

3. In the morning.   4. Boldly have this same cart stopped.

And in the middel of the dong they founde
The dede man that mordred was al newe.[5]

230 "O blisful God that art so just and trewe,
Lo, how that thou biwrayest° mordre alway!   *disclose*
Mordre wol out, that see we day by day:
Mordre is so wlatsom° and abhominable   *loathsome*
To God that is so just and resonable,
235 That he ne wol nat suffre it heled° be,   *concealed*
Though it abide a yeer or two or three.
Mordre wol out: this my conclusioun.
And right anoon ministres of that town
Han hent° the cartere and so sore him pined,[6] *seized*
240 And eek the hostiler so sore engined,°   *racked*
That they biknewe° hir wikkednesse anoon, *confessed*
And were anhanged° by the nekke boon.   *hanged*
Here may men seen that dremes been to drede.[7]

"And certes, in the same book I rede—
245 Right in the nexte chapitre after this—
I gabbe° nat, so have I joye or blis—   *lie*
Two men that wolde han passed over see
For certain cause into a fer contree,
If that the wind ne hadde been contrarye
250 That made hem in a citee for to tarye,
That stood ful merye upon an haven° side— *harbor's*
But on a day again° the even tide   *toward*
The wind gan chaunge, and blewe right as hem leste:[8]
Jolif° and glad they wenten unto reste,   *merry*
255 And casten hem[9] ful erly for to saile.

"But to that oo man fil° a greet mervaile;   *befell*
That oon of hem, in sleeping as he lay,
Him mette[1] a wonder dreem again the day:
Him thoughte a man stood by his beddes side,
260 And him comanded that he sholde abide,
And saide him thus, 'If thou tomorwe wende,
Thou shalt be dreint:° my tale is at an ende.' *drowned*
"He wook and tolde his felawe what he mette,
And prayed him his viage° to lette;°   *voyage / delay*
265 As for that day he prayed him to bide.
"His felawe that lay by his beddes side
Gan for to laughe, and scorned him ful faste.° *hard*
'No dreem,' quod he, 'may so myn herte agaste° *terrify*
That I wol lette° for to do my thinges.° *delay / business*
270 I sette nat a straw by thy dreminges,[2]
For swevenes been but vanitees and japes:[3]
Men dreme alday° of owles or of apes,[4]   *constantly*

5. Recently.
6. Tortured.
7. Worthy of being feared.
8. Just as they wished.
9. Determined.

1. He dreamed.
2. I don't care a straw for your dream-
ings.
3. Dreams are but illusions and frauds.
4. I.e., of absurdities.

And of many a maze° therwithal—   delusion
Men dreme of thing that nevere was ne shal.[5]
275 But sith I see that thou wolt here abide,
And thus forsleuthen° wilfully thy tide,°   waste / time
Good woot, it reweth me;[6] and have good day.'
And thus he took his leve and wente his way.
But er that he hadde half his cours ysailed—
280 Noot I nat why ne what meschaunce it ailed—
But casuelly the shippes botme rente,[7]
And ship and man under the water wente,
In sighte of othere shippes it biside,
That with hem sailed at the same tide.
285 And therfore, faire Pertelote so dere,
By swiche ensamples olde maistou lere°   learn
That no man sholde been too recchelees°   careless
Of dremes, for I saye thee doutelees
That many a dreem ful sore is for to drede.
290   "Lo, in the lif of Saint Kenelm[8] I rede—
That was Kenulphus sone, the noble king
Of Mercenrike°—how Kenelm mette a thing   Mercia
A lite° er he was mordred on a day.   little
His mordre in his avision° he sey.°   dream / saw
295 His norice° him expounded everydeel°   nurse / entirely
His swevene, and bad him for to keepe him[9] weel
For traison, but he nas but seven yeer old,
And therfore litel tale hath he told
Of any dreem,[1] so holy was his herte.
300 By God, I hadde levere than my sherte[2]
That ye hadde rad° his legende as have I.   read
   "Dame Pertelote, I saye you trewely,
Macrobeus,[3] that writ the *Avisioun*
In Affrike of the worthy Scipioun,
305 Affermeth° dremes, and saith that they been   confirms
Warning of thinges that men after seen.
   "And ferthermore, I praye you looketh wel
In the Olde Testament of Daniel,
If he heeld° dremes any vanitee.[4]   considered
310 "Rede eek of Joseph[5] and ther shul ye see
Wher° dremes be somtime—I saye nat alle—   whether
Warning of thinges that shul after falle.
   "Looke of Egypte the king daun Pharao,
His bakere and his botelere° also,   butler

5. I.e., shall be.
6. I'm sorry.
7. I don't know why nor what was the trouble with it—but accidentally the ship's bottom split.
8. Kenelm succeeded his father as king of Mercia at the age of 7, but was slain by his aunt (in 821).
9. Guard himself.
1. Therefore he has set little store by any dream.
2. I.e., I'd give my shirt.
3. Macrobius wrote a famous commentary on Cicero's account in *De Republica* of the dream of Scipio Africanus Minor; the commentary came to be regarded as a standard authority on dream lore.
4. See Daniel vii.
5. See Genesis xxxvii.

315 Wher they ne felte noon effect in dremes.[6]
Whoso wol seeke actes of sondry remes°   *realms*
May rede of dremes many a wonder thing.
"Lo Cresus, which that was of Lyde° king,   *Lydia*
Mette° he nat that he sat upon a tree,   *dreamed*
320 Which signified he sholde anhanged° be?   *hanged*
"Lo here Andromacha, Ectores° wif,   *Hector's*
That day that Ector sholde lese° his lif,   *lose*
She dremed on the same night biforn
How that the lif of Ector sholde be lorn,°   *lost*
325 If thilke° day he wente into bataile;   *that same*
She warned him, but it mighte nat availe:°   *do any good*
He wente for to fighte nathelees,
But he was slain anoon° of Achilles.   *right away*
But thilke tale is al too long to telle,
330 And eek it is neigh day, I may nat dwelle.
Shortly I saye, as for conclusioun,
That I shal han of this avisioun[7]
Adversitee, and I saye ferthermoor
That I ne telle of[8] laxatives no stoor,
335 For they been venimes,° I woot it weel: *poisons*
I hem defye, I love hem neveradeel.°   *not a bit*
"Now lat us speke of mirthe and stinte° al this.   *stop*
Madame Pertelote, so have I blis,
Of oo thing God hath sente me large grace:
340 For whan I see the beautee of youre face—
Ye been so scarlet reed° aboute youre yën—   *red*
It maketh al my drede for to dien.
For also siker° as *In principio*,[9]   *certain*
Mulier est hominis confusio.[1]
345 Madame, the sentence° of this Latin is,   *meaning*
'Womman is mannes joye and al his blis.'
For whan I feele anight youre softe side—
Al be it that I may nat on you ride,
For that oure perche is maad so narwe, allas—
350 I am so ful of joye and of solas°   *delight*
That I defye bothe swevene and dreem."
And with that word he fleigh° down fro the beem,   *flew*
For it was day, and eek his hennes alle,
And with a "chuk" he gan hem for to calle,
355 For he hadde founde a corn lay in the yeerd.
Real° he was, he was namore aferd:°   *regal / afraid*
He fethered[2] Pertelote twenty time,
And trad[3] hire as ofte er it was prime.

---

6. See Genesis xxxix–xli.
7. Divinely inspired dream (as opposed to the more ordinary "swevene" or "dreem").
8. Set by.
9. A tag from the Gospel of St. John which gives the essential premises of

Christianity: "In the beginning was the Word."
1. Woman is man's ruination.
2. I.e., embraced.
3. Trod, copulated with; "prime": 9 A.M.

He looketh as it were a grim leoun,
360 And on his toes he rometh up and down:
Him deined[4] nat to sette his foot to grounde.
He chukketh whan he hath a corn yfounde,
And to him rennen° thanne his wives alle.   run
Thus royal, as a prince is in his halle,
365 Leve I this Chauntecleer in his pasture,
And after wol I telle his aventure.
      Whan that the month in which the world bigan,
That highte March, whan God first maked man,
Was compleet, and passed were also,
370 Sin March bigan, thritty dayes and two,[5]
Bifel that Chauntecleer in al his pride,
His sevene wives walking him biside,
Caste up his yën to the brighte sonne,
That in the signe of Taurus hadde yronne
375 Twenty degrees and oon and somwhat more,
And knew by kinde,° and by noon other lore,   nature
That it was prime, and crew with blisful stevene.°   voice
"The sonne," he saide, "is clomben[6] up on hevene
Fourty degrees and oon and more, ywis.
380 Madame Pertelote, my worldes blis,
Herkneth thise blisful briddes° how they singe,   birds
And see the fresshe flowres how they springe:
Ful is myn herte of revel and solas."
But sodeinly him fil° a sorweful cas,°   befell / chance
385 For evere the latter ende of joye is wo—
God woot that worldly joye is soone ago,
And if a rethor° coude faire endite,   rhetorician
He in a cronicle saufly° mighte it write,   safely
As for a soverein notabilitee.[7]
390 Now every wis man lat him herkne me:
This storye is also° trewe, I undertake,   as
As is the book of *Launcelot de Lake*,[8]
That wommen holde in ful greet reverence.
Now wol I turne again to my sentence.°   main point
395   A colfox[9] ful of sly iniquitee,
That in the grove hadde woned° yeres three,   dwelled
By heigh imaginacion forncast,[1]
The same night thurghout the hegges° brast°   hedges / burst
Into the yeerd ther Chauntecleer the faire
400 Was wont, and eek his wives, to repaire;

4. He deigned.
5. The rhetorical time-telling is perhaps burlesque; it can be read as yielding the date April 3, though May 3 seems intended from lines 374–75: on May 3 the sun would have passed some twenty degrees through Taurus (the Bull), the second sign of the zodiac; the sun would be forty degrees from the horizon at 9 o'clock in the morning.
6. Has climbed.
7. Indisputable fact.
8. Romances of the courteous knight Lancelot of the Lake were very popular.
9. Fox with black markings.
1. Predestined by divine planning.

And in a bed of wortes° stille he lay   *cabbages*
Til it was passed undren° of the day,   *midmorning*
Waiting his time on Chauntecleer to falle,
As gladly doon thise homicides alle,
405 That in await liggen to mordre[2] men.
O false mordrour, lurking in thy den!
O newe Scariot![3] Newe Geniloun!
False dissimilour!° O Greek Sinoun,[4]   *dissembler*
That broughtest Troye al outrely° to sorwe!   *utterly*
410 O Chauntecleer, accursed be that morwe°   *morning*
That thou into the yeerd flaugh° fro the bemes!   *flew*
Thou were ful wel ywarned by thy dremes
That thilke day was perilous to thee;
But what that God forwoot° moot° needes be,   *foreknows / must*
415 After° the opinion of certain clerkes: *according to*
Witnesse on him that any parfit° clerk is   *perfect*
That in scole is greet altercacioun
In this matere, and greet disputisoun,°   *disputation*
And hath been of an hundred thousand men.
420 But I ne can nat bulte° it to the bren,°   *sift / husks*
As can the holy doctour Augustin,
Or Boece, or the bisshop Bradwardin[5]—
Wheither that Goddes worthy forwiting°   *foreknowledge*
Straineth me nedely[6] for to doon a thing
425 ("Nedely" clepe I simple necessitee),
Or elles if free chois be graunted me
To do that same thing or do it nought,
Though God forwoot° it er that I was wrought;   *foreknew*
Or if his witing° straineth neveradeel,   *knowledge*
430 But by necessitee condicionel[7]—
I wol nat han to do of swich matere:
My tale is of a cok, as ye may heere,
That took his conseil of his wif with sorwe,
To walken in the yeerd upon that morwe
435 That he hadde met° the dreem that I you tolde.   *dreamed*
Wommenes conseils been ful ofte colde,[8]
Wommanes conseil broughte us first to wo,
And made Adam fro Paradis to go,
Ther as he was ful merye and wel at ese.
440 But for I noot° to whom it mighte displese   *don't know*
If I conseil of wommen wolde blame,

---

2. That lie in ambush to murder.
3. Judas Iscariot. "Geniloun" is Ganelon, who betrayed Roland to the Saracens (in the medieval French epic *The Song of Roland*).
4. Sinon, who persuaded the Trojans to take the Greeks' wooden horse into their city—with, of course, the result that the city was destroyed.
5. St. Augustine, Boethius (6th-century Roman philosopher, whose *Consolation*

of Philosophy was translated by Chaucer), and Thomas Bradwardine (Archbishop of Canterbury, d. 1349) were all concerned with the interrelationship between man's free will and God's foreknowledge.
6. Constrains me necessarily.
7. Boethius' "conditional necessity" permitted a large measure of free will.
8. I.e., baneful.

Passe over, for I saide it in my game°—   *sport*
Rede auctours where they trete of swich matere,
And what they sayn of wommen ye may heere—
445 Thise been the cokkes wordes and nat mine:
I can noon harm of no womman divine.°   *guess*
    Faire in the sond° to bathe hire merily   *sand*
Lith° Pertelote, and alle hir sustres by,   *lies*
Again° the sonne, and Chauntecleer so free°   *in / noble*
450 Soong° merier than the mermaide in the see—   *sang*
For Physiologus[9] saith sikerly
How that they singen wel and merily.
    And so bifel that as he caste his yë
Among the wortes on a boterflye,°   *butterfly*
455 He was war of this fox that lay ful lowe.
No thing ne liste him[1] thanne for to crowe,
But cride anoon "Cok cok!" and up he sterte,°   *started*
As man that[2] was affrayed in his herte—
For naturelly a beest desireth flee
460 Fro his contrarye[3] if he may it see,
Though he nevere erst° hadde seen it with his yë.   *before*
This Chauntecleer, whan he gan him espye,
He wolde han fled, but that the fox anoon
Saide, "Gentil sire, allas, wher wol ye goon?
465 Be ye afraid of me that am youre freend?
Now certes, I were worse than a feend
If I to you wolde° harm or vilainye.   *meant*
I am nat come youre conseil° for t'espye,   *secrets*
But trewely the cause of my cominge
470 Was only for to herkne how that ye singe:
For trewely, ye han as merye a stevene°   *voice*
As any angel hath that is in hevene.
Therwith ye han in musik more feelinge
Than hadde Boece,[4] or any that can singe.
475 My lord your fader—God his soule blesse!—
And eek youre moder, of hir gentilesse,°   *gentility*
Han in myn hous ybeen, to my grete ese.
And certes sire, ful fain° wolde I you plese.   *gladly*
    "But for men speke of singing, I wol saye,
480 So mote I brouke[5] wel mine yën twaye,
Save ye, I herde nevere man so singe
As dide youre fader in the morweninge.
Certes, it was of herte[6] al that he soong.°   *sang*
And for to make his vois the more strong,
485 He wolde so paine him[7] that with bothe his yën

9. Supposed author of a bestiary, a book of moralized zoology describing both natural and supernatural animals (including mermaids).
1. He wished.
2. Like one who.
3. I.e., his natural enemy.
4. Boethius also wrote a treatise on music.
5. So might I enjoy the use of.
6. Heartfelt.
7. Take pains.

He moste winke,[8] so loude wolde he cryen;
And stonden on his tiptoon therwithal,
And strecche forth his nekke long and smal;
And eek he was of swich discrecioun
490 That ther nas no man in no regioun
That him in song or wisdom mighte passe.
I have wel rad° in *Daun Burnel the Asse*[9]   read
Among his vers how that ther was a cok,
For a preestes sone yaf him a knok[1]
495 Upon his leg whil he was yong and nice,°   foolish
He made him for to lese° his benefice.[2]   lose
But certain, ther nis no comparisoun
Bitwixe the wisdom and discrecioun
Of youre fader and of his subtiltee.
500 Now singeth, sire, for sainte° charitee!   holy
Lat see, conne° ye youre fader countrefete?"°   can / imitate
   This Chauntecleer his winges gan to bete,
As man that coude his traison nat espye,
So was he ravisshed with his flaterye.
505   Allas, ye lordes, many a fals flatour°   flatterer
Is in youre court, and many a losengeour,°   deceiver
That plesen you wel more, by my faith,
Than he that soothfastnesse° unto you saith!   truth
Redeth Ecclesiaste[3] of flaterye.
510 Beeth war, ye lordes, of hir trecherye.
   This Chauntecleer stood hye upon his toos,
Strecching his nekke, and heeld his yën cloos,
And gan to crowe loude for the nones;°   occasion
And daun Russel the fox sterte° up atones,   jumped
515 And by the gargat° hente° Chauntecleer,   throat / seized
And on his bak toward the wode him beer,°   bore
For yit ne was ther no man that him sued.°   followed
   O destinee that maist nat been eschued!°   eschewed
Allas that Chauntecleer fleigh° fro the bemes!   flew
520 Allas his wif ne roughte nat of[4] dremes!
And on a Friday fil° al this meschaunce!   befell
   O Venus that art goddesse of plesaunce,
Sin that thy servant was this Chauntecleer,
And in thy service dide al his power—
525 More for delit than world[5] to multiplye—
Why woldestou suffre him on thy day[6] to die?
   O Gaufred,[7] dere maister soverein,

8. He had to shut his eyes.
9. Master Brunellus, a discontented
donkey, was the hero of a 12th-century
satirical poem by Nigel Wireker.
1. Because a priest's son gave him a
knock.
2. The offended cock neglected to crow
so that his master, now grown to manhood, overslept, missing his ordination

and losing his benefice.
3. The Book of Ecclesiasticus, in the
Apocrypha.
4. Didn't care for.
5. I.e., population.
6. Friday is Venus' day.
7. Geoffrey of Vinsauf, a famous medieval rhetorician, who wrote a lament on
the death of Richard I in which he

That, whan thy worthy king Richard was slain
With shot,[8] complainedest his deeth so sore,
530 Why ne hadde I now thy sentence and thy lore,[9]
The Friday for to chide as diden ye?
For on a Friday soothly slain was he.
Thanne wolde I shewe you how that I coude plaine[1]
For Chauntecleres drede and for his paine.
535 Certes, swich cry ne lamentacioun
Was nevere of ladies maad whan Ilioun°   *Ilium, Troy*
Was wonne, and Pyrrus[2] with his straite swerd,
Whan he hadde hent° King Priam by the beerd   *seized*
And slain him, as saith us *Eneidos*,[3]
540 As maden alle the hennes in the cloos,°   *yard*
Whan they hadde seen of Chauntecleer the sighte.
But sovereinly[4] Dame Pertelote shrighte°   *shrieked*
Ful louder than dide Hasdrubales[5] wif
Whan that hir housbonde hadde lost his lif,
545 And that the Romains hadden brend° Cartage: *burned*
She was so ful of torment and of rage°   *madness*
That wilfully unto the fir she sterte,°   *jumped*
And brende hirselven with a stedefast herte.
O woful hennes, right so criden ye
550 As, whan that Nero brende the citee
Of Rome, criden senatoures wives
For that hir housbondes losten alle hir lives:[6]
Withouten gilt this Nero hath hem slain.
Now wol I turne to my tale again.
555 The sely° widwe and eek hir doughtres two   *innocent*
Herden thise hennes crye and maken wo,
And out at dores sterten° they anoon,   *leaped*
And sien° the fox toward the grove goon,   *saw*
And bar upon his bak the cok away,
560 And criden, "Out, harrow,° and wailaway,   *help*
Ha, ha, the fox," and after him they ran,
And eek with staves many another man:
Ran Colle oure dogge, and Talbot and Gerland,[7]
And Malkin with a distaf in hir hand,
565 Ran cow and calf, and eek the verray hogges,
Sore aferd° for berking of the dogges   *frightened*
And shouting of the men and wommen eke.
They ronne° so hem thoughte hir herte breke;[8]   *ran*
They yelleden as feendes doon in helle;

scolded Friday, the day on which the
king died.
8. I.e., a missile.
9. Thy wisdom and thy learning.
1. Lament.
2. Pyrrhus was the Greek who slew
Priam, king of Troy. "Straite": rigorous, unsparing.
3. As the *Aeneid* tells us.

4. Splendidly.
5. Hasdrubal was king of Carthage
when it was destroyed by the Romans.
6. According to the legend, Nero not
only set fire to Rome (in A.D. 64) but
also put many senators to death.
7. Two other dogs.
8. Would break.

570 The dokes° criden as men wolde hem quelle;°   *ducks / kill*
    The gees for fere flowen° over the trees;   *flew*
    Out of the hive cam the swarm of bees;
    So hidous was the noise, a, benedicite,°   *bless me*
    Certes, he Jakke Straw[9] and his meinee°   *company*
575 Ne made nevere shoutes half so shrille
    Whan that they wolden any Fleming kille,
    As thilke day was maad upon the fox:
    Of bras they broughten bemes° and of box,°   *trumpets / boxwood*
    Of horn, of boon,° in whiche they blewe and pouped,[1]   *bone*
580 And therwithal they skriked[2] and they houped—
    It seemed as that hevene sholde falle.
       Now goode men, I praye you herkneth alle:
    Lo, how Fortune turneth° sodeinly   *reverses, overturns*
    The hope and pride eek of hir enemy.
585 This cok that lay upon the foxes bak,
    In al his drede unto the fox he spak,
    And saide, "Sire, if that I were as ye,
    Yit sholde I sayn, as wis° God helpe me,   *surely*
    'Turneth ayain, ye proude cherles alle!
590 A verray pestilence upon you falle!
    Now am I come unto this wodes side,
    Maugree your heed,[3] the cok shal here abide.
    I wol him ete, in faith, and that anoon.' "
       The fox answerde, "In faith, it shal be doon."
595 And as he spak that word, al sodeinly
    The cok brak from his mouth deliverly,°   *nimbly*
    And hye upon a tree he fleigh° anoon.   *flew*
       And whan the fox sawgh that he was agoon,
    "Allas," quod he, "O Chauntecleer, allas!
600 I have to you," quod he, "ydoon trespas,
    In as muche as I maked you aferd
    Whan I you hente° and broughte out of the yeerd.   *seized*
    But sire, I dide it in no wikke° entente: *wicked*
    Come down, and I shal telle you what I mente.
605 I shal saye sooth to you, God help me so."
       "Nay thanne," quod he, "I shrewe° us bothe two: *curse*
    But first I shrewe myself, bothe blood and bones,
    If thou bigile me ofter than ones;
    Thou shalt namore thurgh thy flaterye
610 Do° me to singe and winken with myn yë.   *cause*
    For he that winketh whan he sholde see,
    Al wilfully, God lat him nevere thee."°   *thrive*
       "Nay," quod the fox, "but God yive him meschaunce
    That is so undiscreet of governaunce°   *self-control*
615 That jangleth° whan he sholde holde his pees."   *chatters*

9. One of the leaders of the Peasant's Revolt in 1381, which was partially directed against the Flemings living in London.

1. Tooted.
2. Shrieked; "houped": whooped.
3. Despite your head—i.e., despite anything you can do.

Lo, swich it is for to be recchelees°   *careless*
And necligent and truste on flaterye.
But ye that holden this tale a folye
As of a fox, or of a cok and hen,
620 Taketh the moralitee, goode men.
For Saint Paul saith that al that writen is
To oure doctrine it is ywrit, ywis:[4]
Taketh the fruit, and lat the chaf be stille.
Now goode God, if that it be thy wille,
625 As saith my lord, so make us alle goode men,
And bringe us to his hye blisse. Amen.

From The Parson's Tale[1]
The Introduction

By that[2] the Maniciple hadde his tale al ended,
The sonne fro the south line[3] was decended
So lowe, that he nas nat to my sighte
Degrees nine and twenty as in highte.

4. See Romans xv.4.

1. Among the moral writers of the later Middle Ages the pilgrimage was so commonly treated as an allegory of man's life that Chaucer's audience must have been surprised to find the *Canterbury Tales* so little allegorical. At the end of his life, however, and at the end of his work, Chaucer seems to have been caught up in the venerable allegory. Some ten months before his death he rented a house in the garden of Westminster Abbey, and it is possible that during these months—perhaps when he felt his death approaching—he fell under the influence of the monks of Westminster. In any case, in the Parson's Tale, and in its short Introduction and in the Retraction that follows it, Chaucer seems to be making an end for two pilgrimages that had become one, that of his fiction and that of his life.

In the Introduction to the tale we find the 29 pilgrims moving through a nameless little village as the sun sinks to within 29 degrees of the horizon. The atmosphere contains something of both the chill and the urgency of a late autumn afternoon, and we are surprised to find that the pilgrimage is almost over, that there is need for haste in order to make that "good end" that every medieval Christian hoped for. This delicately suggestive passage, rich with allegorical overtones, introduces an extremely long sermon on penitence and the seven deadly sins, probably translated by Chaucer from French or Latin some years earlier, before he had begun the *Canterbury Tales*.

The sermon is at times not without animation, but in general Chaucer provides no exception to the statement that Middle English prose is inferior to Middle English verse. But then the intent of the sermon is didactic, not artistic, and according to the more rigorous theologians of the time, didactic intent is infinitely more important than artistic expression.

It is to this doctrine that Chaucer yielded at the end of his life. The Retraction which follows and concludes the Parson's Tale offers Chaucer's apology for having written all the works on which his reputation as a great poet depends, not only such stories as the Miller's Tale, but also his loveliest and seemingly most harmless poems. Yet a readiness to deny his own reality before the reality of his God is implicit in many of Chaucer's works, and the placement of the Retraction within the artistic structure of the *Canterbury Tales* suggests that while Chaucer denied his art, he seems to have recognized that he and it were inseparable.

2. By the time that.

3. I.e., the line that runs some 28 degrees to the south of the celestial equator and parallel to it.

⁵ Four of the clokke it was, so as I gesse,
For elevene foot, or litel more or lesse,
My shadwe was at thilke time as there,
Of swich feet as° my lengthe parted° were   *as if / divided*
In sixe feet equal of proporcioun.⁴
¹⁰ Therwith the moones exaltacioun⁵—
I mene Libra—alway gan ascende,
As we were entring at a thropes° ende.   *village's*
For which oure Host, as he was wont to gie°   *lead*
As in this caas oure joly compaignye,
¹⁵ Saide in this wise, "Lordinges everichoon,
Now lakketh us no tales mo than oon:
Fulfild is my sentence° and my decree;   *purpose*
I trowe° that we han herd of eech degree;   *believe*
Almost fulfild is al myn ordinaunce.
²⁰ I praye to God, so yive him right good chaunce
That telleth this tale to us lustily.
Sire preest," quod he, "artou a vicary,°   *vicar*
Or arte a Person? Say sooth, by thy fay.°   *faith*
Be what thou be, ne breek° thou nat oure play,   *break*
²⁵ For every man save thou hath told his tale.
Unbokele and shew us what is in thy male!°   *bag*
For trewely, me thinketh by thy cheere°   *expression*
Thou sholdest knitte up wel a greet matere.
Tel us a fable anoon, for cokkes bones!"
³⁰   This Person answerde al atones,⁶
"Thou getest fable noon ytold for me,
For Paul, that writeth unto Timothee,
Repreveth° hem that waiven soothfastnesse,⁷   *reproves*
And tellen fables and swich wrecchednesse.
³⁵ Why sholde I sowen draf° out of my fest,°   *chaff / fist*
Whan I may sowen whete if that me lest?⁸
For which I saye that if you list to heere
Moralitee and vertuous matere,
And thanne that ye wol yive me audience,
⁴⁰ I wol ful fain,° at Cristes reverence,   *gladly*
Do you plesance leveful° as I can.   *lawful*
But trusteth wel, I am a southren man:
I can nat geeste Rum-Ram-Ruf by lettre⁹—
Ne, God woot, rym holde° I but litel bettre.   *consider*
⁴⁵ And therfore, if you list, I wol nat glose;¹
I wol you telle a merye tale in prose,
To knitte up al this feeste and make an ende.
And Jesu for his grace wit me sende

·4. This detailed analysis merely says
that the shadows are lengthening.
5. I.e., the astrological sign in which
the moon's influence was dominant.
"Libra": the constellation of the
Scales.
6. Immediately.
7. Depart from truth. See I Timothy
i.4.
8. It pleases me.
9. I.e., I cannot tell stories in the
alliterative measure (without rhyme):
this form of poetry was not common
in southeastern England.
1. I.e., speak in order to please.

To shewe you the way in this viage°   *journey*
50 Of thilke parfit glorious pilgrimage
    That highte Jerusalem celestial.
    And if ye vouche sauf, anoon I shal
    Biginne upon my tale, for which I praye
    Telle youre avis:° I can no bettre saye.   *opinion*
55 But nathelees, this meditacioun
    I putte it ay under correccioun
    Of clerkes, for I am nat textuel:[2]
    I take but the sentence,° trusteth wel.   *meaning*
    Therfore I make protestacioun°   *public acknowledgment*
60 That I wol stonde to correccioun."
        Upon this word we han assented soone,
    For, as it seemed, it was for to doone
    To enden in som vertuous sentence,°   *doctrine*
    And for to yive him space and audience;
65 And bede[3] oure Host he sholde to him saye
    That alle we to telle his tale him praye.
        Oure. Hoste hadde the wordes for us alle:
    "Sire preest," quod he, "now faire you bifalle:
    Telleth," quod he, "youre meditacioun.
70 But hasteth you; the sonne wol adown.
    Beeth fructuous,° and that in litel space,°   *fruitful / time*
    And to do wel God sende you his grace.
    Saye what you list, and we wol gladly heere."
    And with that word he saide in this manere.

Chaucer's Retraction

Now praye I to hem alle that herkne this litel tretis[8] or rede,
that if ther be any thing in it that liketh[9] hem, that therof they
thanken oure Lord Jesu Crist, of whom proceedeth al wit[1] and al
goodnesse. And if ther be any thing that displese him, I praye hem
also that they arrette it to the defaute of myn unconning,[2] and nat
to my wil, that wolde ful fain have said bettre if I hadde had conning. For oure book saith, "Al that is writen is writen for oure doctrine,"[3] and that is myn entente. Wherfore I biseeke[4] you mekely,
for the mercy of God, that ye praye for me that Crist have mercy
on me and foryive me my giltes, and namely[5] of my translacions
and enditinges of worldly vanitees, the whiche I revoke in my
retraccions: as is the *Book of Troilus;* the *Book* also *of Fame;* the
Book of the Five and Twenty Ladies;[6] the *Book of the Duchesse;*
the *Book of Saint Valentines Day of the Parlement of Briddes;* the

2. Literal, faithful to the letter.
3. I.e., we bade.
8. Hear this little treatise.
9. Pleases.
1. Understanding.
2. Ascribe it to the defect of my lack of

skill.
3. Romans xv.4.
4. Beseech.
5. Especially. "Enditinges": compositions.
6. I.e., the *Legend of Good Women.*

Tales of Canterbury, thilke that sounen into[7] sinne; the *Book of the Leon*;[8] and many another book, if they were in my remembrance, and many a song and many a leccherous lay: that Crist for his grete mercy foryive me the sinne. But of the translacion of Boece[9] *De Consolatione*, and othere bookes of legendes of saintes, and omelies,[1] and moralitee, and devocion, that thanke I oure Lord Jesu Crist and his blisful Moder and alle the saintes of hevene, biseeking hem that they from hennes[2] forth unto my lives ende sende me grace to biwaile my giltes and to studye to the salvacion of my soule, and graunte me grace of verray penitence, confession, and satisfaccion to doon in this present lif, thurgh the benigne grace of him that is king of kinges and preest over alle preestes, that boughte[3] us with the precious blood of his herte, so that I may been oon of hem at the day of doom that shulle be saved. *Qui cum patre et Spiritu Sancto vivis et regnas Deus per omnia saecula.*[4] Amen.

1386–1400

The Parliament of Fowls[1]

The lif so short, the craft so long to lerne,
Th'assay° so sharp, so hard the conqueringe,
The dredful joye alway that slit[2] so yerne,°
Al this mene I by Love, that my feelinge
5 Astonieth[3] with his wonderful werkinge
So sore, ywis, that whan I on him thinke,
Nat woot° I wel wher° that I flete° or
      sinke.

attempt
quickly

know / whether / float

7. Those that tend toward.
8. The *Book of the Lion* has not been preserved.
9. Boethius.
1. Homilies.
2. Hence.
3. Redeemed.
4. Who with the Father and the Holy Spirit livest and reignest God forever.
1. *The Parliament of Fowls* is one of Chaucer's loveliest but most elusive poems. The form is that of a dream vision, in which the narrator is usually someone in search of love who dreams that he wakes into a May morning during which he has some kind of love experience. The narrator of the *Parliament* seems to be in search of love, but he is apparently disqualified in advance from ever attaining it. His poetic valentine is written, therefore, from the point of view of one who is a stranger to the very thing that a valentine is supposed to celebrate. Though hardly an enthusiastic tourist, he is granted a visit to a highly erotic temple of love, and then—with somewhat more enthusiasm—watches the process of the birds choosing their mates under the supervision of the goddess Nature. This incident promises to afford a more constructive idea of love than the stasis of the vision of the temple; but the fact is that the choosing of mates is held up most of the day by the argument of three male eagles asserting their right to obtain the same female. Only in the very last lines of the poem do the birds receive their mates, and the three eagles get none. The frustration which seems a part of the dreamer's nature and which makes itself felt in the lovely paralysis of the temple of love infects in a different way the lively business of the birds' parliament. Love remains a mystery to the frustrated narrator, but a mystery with its own manifold frustrations.
2. Slides, slips away.
3. Is astonished.

For al be that I knowe nat Love in deede,
Ne woot how that he quiteth° folk hir hire,°   *pays / wages*
10   Yit happeth me ful ofte in bookes rede
Of his miracles and his cruel ire;
That rede I wel, he wol be lord and sire:
I dar nat sayn—his strokes been so sore—
But[4] "God save swich a lord!"—I saye namore.

15   Of usage,° what for lust° and what
       for lore,°   *habit / pleasure / instruction*
On bookes rede I ofte, as I you tolde;
But wherfore that I speke al this: nat yore°   *long*
Agoon it happed me for to biholde
Upon a book, was write with lettres olde;
20   And therupon, a certain thing to lerne,
The longe day ful faste I redde and yerne.°   *eagerly*

For out of olde feeldes, as men saith,
Cometh al this newe corn° from yeer to yere;   *grain*
And out of olde bookes, in good faith,
25   Cometh al this newe science that men lere.°   *learn*
But now to purpos as of this matere:
To rede forth so gan me to delite
That al that day me thoughte but a lite.[5]

This book of which I make of mencioun
30   Entitled was al thus, as I shal telle:
"Tullius of the Dreem of Scipioun."[6]
Chapitres sevene it hadde, of hevene and helle
And erthe, and soules that therinne dwelle;
Of which as shortly as I can it trete,
35   Of his sentence[7] I wol you sayn the grete:°   *substance*

First telleth it when Scipion was come
In Affrike, how he meeteth Massinisse,°   *Masinissa*
That him for joye in armes hath ynome;°   *taken*
Thanne telleth he hir speeche, and of the blisse
40   That was bitwixe hem til that day gan misse;[8]
And how his auncestre Affrican, so dere
Gan in his sleep that night to him appere.

Thanne telleth it that from a sterry° place   *starry*
How Affrican[9] hath him Cartage° shewed,   *Carthage*
45   And warned him biforn of al his grace,
And saide what man, lered° other°
       lewed,°   *learned / or / uneducated*
That loved commune° profit, wel ythewed,°   *common / behaved*

---

4. I.e., anything but.
5. I.e., little while.
6. I.e., (Macrobius' edition of) Marcus Tullius Cicero on the dream of Scipio: Macrobius' commentary on Cicero's work was the great source of medieval dream lore.
7. Its story.
8. Come to an end.
9. Scipio Africanus Major, the famous antagonist of Hannibal.

He sholde into a blisful place wende,
Ther as joye is that last° withouten ende.   *lasts*

50   Thanne axed° he if folk that now been dede°   *asked / dead*
Han lif and dwelling in another place;
And African saide, "Ye, withouten drede,°   *doubt*
And that oure present worldes lives space
Nis but a manere deeth, what way we trace.[1]
55   And rightful folk shul goon after they die
To hevene"; and shewed him the Galaxye.

Thanne shewed he him the litel erthe that here is,
At regard of[2] the hevenes quantitee;°   *size*
And after shewed he him the nine speres;°   *spheres*
60   And after that the melodye herde he
That cometh of thilke[3] speres thries three,
That welle° is of musik and melodye   *source*
In this world here, and cause of armonye.°   *harmony*

Thanne bad he him, sin erthe was so lite,°   *little*
65   And deceivable,° and ful of harde grace,   *deceitful*
That he ne sholde him in the world delite.
Thanne tolde he him in certain yeres space
That every sterre sholde come into his place,
Ther it was first, and al sholde out of minde
70   That in this world is doon of al mankinde.

Thanne prayed him Scipion to telle him al
The way to come into that hevene blisse;
And he saide, "Know thyself first immortal,
And looke ay bisily thou werke and wisse°   *teach*
75   To commune profit, and thou shalt nat misse
To comen swiftly to this place dere,
That ful of blisse is, and of soules clere.

But brekeres of the lawe, sooth to sayne,
And likerous° folk, after that they been dede°   *lecherous / dead*
80   Shul whirle aboute th'erthe alway in paine,
Til many a world be passed, out of drede,°   *doubt*
And that[4] foryiven is hir wikked deede:°   *deed*
Thanne shal they comen into this blisful place,
To which to comen, God sende thee his grace."

85   The day gan folwen and the derke night,
That reveth[5] beestes from hir bisinesse,°   *anxiety*
Birafte me my book for lak of light,
And to my bed I gan me for to dresse,°   *prepare*

1. Is nothing but a kind of death, what-   3. Those same.
ever path we follow.   4. I.e., until.
2. In comparison to.   5. Takes away.

Fulfild° of thought and bisy° hevinesse: *filled / anxious*
90 For bothe I hadde thing which that I nolde,[6]
And eek I nadde[7] that thing that I wolde.

But finally my spirit at the laste,
Forwery[8] of my labour al the day,
Took reste, that made me to sleepe faste;
95 And in my sleep I mette,° as that I lay,   *dreamed*
How Affrican, right in the same array
That Scipion him saw bifore that tide,°   *time*
Was come, and stood right at my beddes side.

The wery hunter, sleeping in his bed,
100 To wode° ayain his minde gooth anoon;   *wood*
The juge dremeth how his plees been sped;
The cartere dremeth how his carte is goon;
The riche, of gold; the knight fight° with his foon;° *fights / foes*
The sike met° he drinketh of the tonne;[9]   *dreams*
105 The lovere met he hath his lady wonne.

Can I nat sayn if that the cause were
For I hadde red of Affrican biforn,
That made me to mete° that he stood there: *dream*
But thus saide he: "Thou hast thee so wel born° *behaved*
110 In looking of myn olde book totorn,°   *tattered*
Of which Macrobie[1] roughte° nat a lite,°   *cared / little*
That somdeel° of thy labour wolde I quite.""° *somewhat / repay*

Cytherea,° thou blisful lady sweete,   *Venus*
That with thy firbrand dauntest whom thee lest,[2]
115 And madest me this swevene° for to mete,   *dream*
Be thou myn help in this, for thou maist best;
As wisly° as I sawgh thee north-north-west   *surely*
Whan I bigan my swevene for to write,
So yif° me might to ryme and eek t'endite.   *give*

120 This forsaide Affrican me hente° anoon,   *took*
And forth with him unto a gate broughte,
Right of a park walled with greene stoon,
And over the gates with lettres large ywroughte
Ther were vers ywriten, as me thoughte,
125 On either side, of ful greet difference,
Of which I shal now sayn the plein° sentence:° *full / meaning*

"Thurgh me men goon into that blisful place
Of hertes hele° and deedly° woundes cure;   *healing / deadly*
Thurgh me men goon unto the welle° of grace,   *spring*

---

6. Didn't want.
7. Didn't have.
8. Tired out.

9. Tun, i.e., vessel of medicinal liquid.
1. See note to line 31, above.
2. It pleases.

130 Ther greene and lusty May shal evere endure:
This is the way to al good aventure;
Be glad, thou redere,° and thy sorwe of-caste;³   *reader*
Al open am I: passe in, and speed thee faste."

"Thurgh me men goon," thanne spak that other side,
135 "Unto the mortal strokes of the spere
Of which Desdain and Daunger° is the gide,   *haughtiness*
That nevere yit shal fruit ne leves bere;
This streem you ledeth to the sorweful were°   *dam*
Ther as the fissh in prison is al drye:
140 Th'eschewing° is only the remedye."   *avoidance*

Thise vers° of gold and blak ywriten were,   *verses*
Of whiche I gan astonied° to biholde,   *astonished*
Forwhy° that oon encreessed ay my fere,   *because*
And with that other gan myn herte bolde.⁴
145 That oon me hette,° that other dide me colde:⁵   *inflamed*
No wit⁶ hadde I, for errour,° for to chese° *bewilderment / choose*
To entre or fleen, or me to save or lese.⁷

Right as bitwixen adamantes° two   *magnets*
Of evene might, a pece of iren set
150 Ne hath no might to meve° to ne fro—   *move*
For what that oon may hale,° that other let°— *pull / prevents*
Ferde° I, that niste⁸ whether me was bet° *fared / better*
To entre or leve, til African my gide
Me hente,° and shoof° in at the gates wide, *seized / shoved*

155 And saide, "It stant° writen in thy face   *stands*
Thyn errour, though thou telle it nat to me;
But dreed thee nat to come into this place,
For this writing nis no thing ment by thee.
Ne by noon but° he Loves servant be;   *unless*
160 For thou of love hast lost thy tast, I gesse,
As sik man hath of sweete and bitternesse.

But nathelees, although that thou be dul,
Yit that thou canst nat do, yit maist thou see;
For many a man that may nat stonde a pul,⁹
165 It liketh him at wrastling for to be,
And deemen° yit wher° he do bet or he.   *judge / whether*
And ther, if thou haddest conning for t'endite,
I shal thee shewe matere for to write."

---

3. Cast off.   7. Bring to ruin.
4. Become bold.   8. Knew not.
5. Caused me to cool.   9. I.e., engage in wrestling.
6. I.e., power to come to a decision.

With that myn hand he took in his anoon,
170 Of which I confort caughte, and that as faste;
But Lord, so I was glad and wel bigoon,[1]
For overal wher that I mine yën caste
Were trees clad with leves that ay° shal laste,   *ever*
Eech in his kinde, of colour fressh and greene
175 As emeraude, that joye was to seene.

The bildere[2] ook, and eek the hardy assh;
The pilere elm, the cofre° unto caraine;   *box*
The boxtree pipere; holm to whippes lassh;
The sailing firre; the cypres, deeth° to plaine;°   *death / complain*
180 The shetere ew; the asp for shaftes plaine;°   *smooth*
The olive of pees; and eek the dronke vine;
The victour palm; the laurer to divine.

A gardin saw I ful of blosmy boughes
Upon a river in a greene mede,°   *meadow*
185 Ther as the swetnesse everemore ynough is,
With flowres white, blewe, and yelowe, and rede,
And colde welle-stremes no thing dede,[3]
That swimmen ful of smale fisshes lighte,
With finnes rede, and scales silver-brighte.

190 On every bough the briddes° herde I singe   *birds*
With vois of angel in hir armonye;°   *harmony*
Some bisied hem hir briddes forth to bringe.
The litel conies° to hir play gonne hie;°   *rabbits / hasten*
And ferther al aboute I gan espye
195 The dredful° ro, the buk, the hert, the hinde,   *frightened*
Squireles, and beestes smale of gentil kinde.

Of instruments of stringes in accord
Herde I so playe a ravisshing swetnesse
That God, that Makere is of al and Lord,
200 Ne herde nevere bettre, as I gesse.
Therwith a wind, unnethe° it mighte be lesse,   *scarcely*
Made in the leves greene a noise softe
Accordant to[4] the briddes song alofte.

The air of that place so attempre° was   *temperate*
205 That nevere was grevance of hoot° ne cold;   *hot*

---

1. Joyous.
2. The trees in this stanza are characterized by their traditional functions, real or symbolic: the oak for building; the ash wherever hardwood is required; the elm used both for posts and coffins; the boxtree from which musical pipes are made; the holm for whips; the fir for masts; the cypress, associated with death; the yew for bows; the aspen for arrow-shafts; the olive, associated with peace; the vine with drunkenness; the palm with victory; and the laurel, used in augury.
3. I.e., stagnant
4. In tune with.

Ther weex° eek every hoolsom spice and gras: *grew*
No man may there waxe sik ne old.
Yit was ther joye more than a thousandfold
Than man can telle; ne nevere wolde it nighte,[5]
210 But ay cleer day to any mannes sighte.

Under a tree biside a welle° I sey°   *spring / saw*
Cupide oure lord his arwes forge and file;
And at his feet his bowe al redy lay,
And Wil his doughter tempered al this while
215 The hevedes[6] in the welle, and with hir wile°   *skill*
She couched hem after they sholde serve,[7]
Some for to slee,° and some to wounde and kerve.°   *slay / cut*

Tho was I war of Plesance anoonright,
And of Array, and Lust,° and Curteisye,   *desire*
220 And of the Craft that can and hath the might
To doon° by force a wight to doon° folye: *cause*
Disfigurat was she, I nil nat lie.
And by hemself under an ook, I gesse,
Saw I Delit that stood by Gentilesse.

225 I saw Beautee withouten any attir,
And Youthe ful of game and jolitee,
Foolhardinesse, and Flaterye, and Desir,
Messagerye, and Meede, and other three—[8]
Hir names shal nat here be told for° me;   *by*
230 And upon pileres grete of jasper longe
I saw a temple of bras yfounded stronge.

Aboute that temple daunceden alway
Wommen ynowe,° of whiche some ther were   *enough*
Faire of hemself, and some of hem were gay;
235 In kirteles al dischevele[9] wente they there:
That was hir office° alway, yeer by yere.   *duty*
And on the temple of douves° white and faire   *doves*
Saw I sittinge many an hundred paire.

Bifore the temple-dore ful sobrely
240 Dame Pees sat with a curtin° in hir hond,   *curtain*
And by hir side, wonder discreetly,
Dame Pacience sitting ther I foond,°   *found*
With face pale, upon an hil of sond;°   *sand*
And aldernext[1] withinne and eek withoute
245 Biheeste and Art, and of hir folk a route.[2]

---

5. Become night.
6. Arrowheads.
7. I.e., she laid them down in order according to how they should serve.
8. I.e., Messagery (the allegorical figure which represents go-betweens), Meed

(cash payment), and a number of others.
9. With hair loose.
1. Next of all.
2. Promise and Subtlety, and of their people a number.

Within the temple of sikes° hote as fir — *sighs*
I herde a swough³ that gan aboute renne,° — *run*
Whiche sikes were engendred with desir,
That maden every auter° for to brenne° — *altar / burn*
250 Of newe flaumbe;° and wel espied I thenne — *flame*
That al the cause of sorwes that they drie° — *endure*
Cometh of the bittre goddesse Jalousye.

The god Priapus⁴ saw I, as I wente,
Within the temple in soverein place stonde,
255 In swich array as whan the asse him shente⁵
With cry by night, and with his sceptre in honde;
Ful bisily men gonne assaye and fonde⁶
Upon his heed° to sette, of sondry hewe, — *head*
Gerlandes ful of flowres fresshe and newe.

260 And in a privee corner in disport
Foond° I Venus and hir porter Richesse, — *found*
That was ful noble and hautain° of hir
    port;° — *haughty / bearing*
Derk was the place, but afterward lightnesse
I saw a lite°—unnethe° it mighte be lesse; — *little / scarcely*
265 And on a bed of gold she lay to reste,
Til that the hote sonne gan to weste.⁷

Hire gilte heres with a golden threed° — *unbraided*
Ybounden were, untressed° as she lay; — *thread*
And naked from the brest up to the heed
270 Men mighte hire seen; and soothly for to say,
The remenant was wel covered to my pay° — *pleasure*
Right with a subtil coverchief of Valence:
Ther nas no thikker cloth of no defence.⁸

The place yaf a thousand savours soote,° — *sweet*
275 And Bacus,° god of win, sat hire biside, — *Bacchus*
And Ceres next that dooth of hunger boote,⁹
And as I saide, amiddes lay Cypride,° — *Venus*
To whom on knees two yonge folk ther cride
To been hir° help; but thus I leet hire lie, — *their*
280 And ferther in the temple I gan espye,

That, in despit of Diane the chaste,¹
Ful many a bowe ybroke heeng° on the wal, — *hung*

---

3. Murmuring sound.
4. A fertility god depicted with a large sexual organ: see line 256, below.
5. Abashed: Priapus' assault on the chastity of a certain nymph was frustrated when she was awakened by the cry of an ass.
6. Endeavor and strive.

7. Go west.
8. I.e., there was no thicker cloth (than the thin kerchief made in Valence) to defend her from sight.
9. Allays hunger: Ceres was the goddess of vegetation.
1. Diana was goddess of chastity.

Of maidenes swiche as gonne° hir times waste   *did*
In hir service; and painted overal
285 Ful many a storye, of which I touche shal
A fewe, as of Caliste and Atalante,[2]
And many a maide of which the name I wante.°   *lack*

Semiramis, Candace, and Ercules,°   *Hercules*
Biblis, Dido, Thisbe, and Pyramus,
290 Tristam, Isoude,° Paris, and Achilles,   *Isolde*
Elaine,[3] Cleopatre, and Troilus,
Sylla,° and eek the moder[4] of Romulus: *Scylla*
Alle thise were painted on that other side,
And al hir love, and in what plit° they dyde.   *circumstances*

295 Whan I was come ayain unto the place
That I of spak, that was so soote° and greene,   *sweet*
Forth welk° I tho° myselven to solace;   *walked / then*
Tho was I war° wher that ther sat a queene,   *aware*
That as of light the someres sonne sheene°   *bright*
300 Passeth° the sterre,° right so over°
  mesure   *surpasses / star / beyond*
She fairer was than any creature.

And in a launde° upon an hil of flowres   *meadow*
Was set this noble goddesse Nature;
Of braunches were hir halles and hir bowres,
305 Ywrought after hir cast° and hir mesure;°   *contrivance / design*
Ne was ther fowl that cometh of engendrure°   *engendering*
That they ne were alle prest° in hir presence   *ready*
To take hir doom,° and yive hire audience.   *judgment*

For this was on Saint Valentines day,
310 Whan every brid° cometh ther to chese° his
  make,°   *bird / choose / mate*
Of every kinde that men thinke may;
And that so huge a noise gan they make,
That erthe and air and tree and every lake
So ful was that unnethe° was ther space   *hardly*
315 For me to stonde, so ful was al the place.

And right as Alain[5] in the "Plainte of Kinde"
Deviseth° Nature in array and face,   *describes*
In swich array men mighte hire there finde.
This noble emperesse,° ful of grace,   *empress*

---

2. Callisto, Atalanta, and the others named in the following stanza were famous lovers.
3. Helen of Troy.
4. Mother, i.e., Rhea Sylvia.

5. Alanus de Insulis, whose medieval Latin poem the *Complaint of Nature* personifies Nature much as Chaucer does.

320 Bad every fowl to take his owene place,
As they were wont alway, from yeer to yere,
Saint Valentines Day, to stonden there.

That is to sayn, the fowles of ravine°   *prey*
Were hyest set, and thanne the fowles smale
325 That eten as hem Nature wolde encline.
As worm, or thing of which I telle no tale;
And waterfowl sat lowest in the dale;
But fowl that liveth by seed sat on the greene,
And that so fele° that wonder was to seene.   *many*

330 Ther mighte men the royal egle finde,
That with his sharpe look perceth° the sonne;   *pierces*
And othere egles of a lower kinde
Of whiche that clerkes wel devise° conne;   *discourse*
Ther was the tyrant with his fetheres donne°   *dun*
335 And greye—I mene the goshawk—that dooth pine°   *hurt*
To briddes for his outrageous ravine.°   *voracity*

The gentil faucon that with his feet distraineth[6]
The kinges hand; the hardy sperhawk° eke,   *sparrow hawk*
The quailes fo; the merlion° that paineth°   *merlin / takes pains*
340 Himself ful ofte the larke for to seeke;
Ther was the douve° with hir yën meeke;   *dove*
The jalous swan, ayains[7] his deeth that singeth;
The owle eek that of deeth the bode° bringeth;   *warning*

The crane, geant° with his trompes° soun;   *giant / trumpet's*
345 The theef, the chough[8] and eek the jangling°   *chattering*
  pie;°   *magpie*
The scorning jay; the eeles fo, heroun;
The false lapwing, ful of trecherye;
The starling that the conseil° can biwrye;°   *secret / disclose*
The tame rodok,[9] and the coward kite;
350 The cok, that orlogge° is of thropes lite;[1]   *timepiece*

The sparwe,° Venus sone; the nightingale,   *sparrow*
That clepeth° forth the greene leves newe;   *calls*
The swalme,° mortherere° of the fowles
  smale[2]   *swallow / murderer*
That maken hony of flowres fresshe of hewe;
355 The wedded turtel,° with hir herte trewe;   *turtle-dove*

---

6. Takes hold on; falcons, being royal birds, are often pictured perched on the hands of kings. The qualities and behavior assigned to this and the other birds in these four stanzas are evidently traditional, but in some cases the appropri- ateness of the assignment is obscure.
7. At the coming of.
8. A kind of crow.
9. Ruddock, European robin.
1. Little villages.
2. I.e., bees.

The pecok, with his angeles clothes brighte;
The fesant, scornere of the cok by nighte;[3]

The wakere[4] goos; the cokkou evere unkinde;
The popinjay ful of delicasye;°   *daintiness*
360 The drake, stroyere[5] of his owene kinde;
The stork, the wrekere of avouterye;[6]
The hote[7] cormerant of glotonye;
The raven wis; the crowe with vois of care;
The throstel° old; the frosty feeldefare.[8]   *thrush*

365 What sholde I sayn? Of fowles every kinde
That in this world hath fetheres and stature,°   *standing*
Men mighten in that place assembled finde,
Bifore the noble goddesse Nature;
And everich of hem dide his bisy cure[9]
370 Benignely to chese° or for to take,   *choose*
By hir accord, his formel[1] or his make.°   *mate*

But to the point: Nature heeld on hir hond
A formel egle, of shap the gentileste
That evere she among hir werkes foond,°   *found*
375 The most benigne and the goodlieste:
In hire was every vertu at his reste,[2]
So ferforth[3] that Nature hirself hadde blisse
To looke on hire, and ofte hir beek to kisse.

Nature, vicarye° of the Almighty Lord   *vicar*
380 That hoot, cold, hevy, light, and moist and dreye°   *dry*
Hath knit° with evene nombres of accord,   *joined*
In esy vois gan for to speke and saye,
"Fowles, take heede of my sentence, I praye;
And for youre ese, in fothering of youre neede,
385 As faste as I may speke, I wol you speede.

Ye knowe wel how, Saint Valentines Day,
By my statut and thurgh my governaunce,
Ye come for to chese—and flee° youre way—   *fly*
Youre makes° as I prike[4] you with plesaunce.   *mates*
390 But nathelees, my rightful ordinaunce

3. The pheasant scorns the rooster perhaps because the pheasant is supposed to be capable of mating with domestic hens.
4. Wakener: geese are reputed to have awakened Rome against a stealthy barbarian attack. The cuckoo is unkind—unnatural—because it deposits its eggs in the nests of other birds.
5. Destroyer: drakes sometimes kill their young.
6. Avenger of adultery: storks were supposed to kill their adulterous mates.
7. Hot: the ravenous cormorant is thought of as burning from its own gluttony.
8. Fieldfare, another kind of thrush.
9. Acted with anxious care.
1. Female eagle or hawk.
2. I.e., at home.
3. To such an extent.
4. Prick, inspire.

May I nat breke, for al this world to winne,
That he that most is worthy shal biginne.

The tercelet° egle, as that ye knowe ful weel,   *male*
The fowl royal aboven every degree,
395 The wise and worthy, secree, trewe as steel,
Which I have formed, as ye may wel see,
In every part as it best liketh me—
It needeth nat his shap you to devise—
He shal first chese° and speken in his gise.°   *choose / manner*

400 And after him by ordre shul ye chese,
After youre kinde, everich as you liketh,
And as youre hap is shul ye winne or lese°—   *lose*
But which of you that love most entriketh,°   *entraps*
God sende him hire that sorest for him siketh.""°   *sighs*
405 And therwithal the tercel⁵ gan she calle,
And saide, "My sone, the chois is to you falle.

But nathelees, in this condicioun
Moot° be the chois of everich that is here: *must*
That she agree to his eleccioun,
410 What so he be that sholde be hir fere.°   *mate*
This is oure usage alway, from yeer to yere:
And who so may at this time have his grace,
In blisful time he cam into this place."

With heed enclined and with humble cheere
415 This royal tercel spak and taried nought:
"Unto my soverein lady, and nat my fere,
I chese, and chese with wil and herte and thought,
The formel on your hand, so wel ywrought,
Whos I am al, and evere wil hire serve,
420 Do what hire list to do° me live or sterve;°   *cause / die*

Biseeking hire of mercy and of grace,
As she that is my lady sovereine—
Or lat me die present in this place:
For certes, longe I may nat live in paine,
425 For in myn herte is corven° every veine;   *cut*
And having reward° only to my trouthe,   *regard*
My dere herte, have of my wo som routhe.°   *pity*

And if that I to hire be founde untrewe,
Disobeisant,° or wilful necligent,   *disobedient*
430 Avauntour,° or in proces° love a newe,   *boaster / time*
I praye to you, this by my juggement:

5. Male eagle.

That with thise fowles be I al torent[6]
That ilke° day that evere she me finde   *same*
To hire untrewe, or in my gilt° unkinde.   *guilt*

435 And sin° that hire loveth noon so wel as I—   *since*
Al be that she me nevere of love bihette°—   *promised*
Thanne oughte she be myn thurgh hir mercy,
For other bond can I noon on hire knette;°   *fasten*
Ne nevere for no wo ne shal I lette°   *stop*
440 To serven hire, how fer° so that she wende;   *far*
Saye what you list: my tale is at an ende."

Right as the fresshe, rede rose newe
Ayain[7] the somer sonne coloured is,
Right so for shame al waxen° gan the hewe   *increase*
445 Of this formel, whan she herde al this.
She neither answerde wel, ne saide amis,
So sore abasshed was she, til that Nature
Saide, "Doughter, drede you nought, I you assure."

Another tercel egle spak anoon,
450 Of lower kinde, and saide, "That shal nat be!
I love hire bet° than ye doon, by saint John,   *better*
Or at the leeste I love as wel as ye,
And lenger° have served hire in my degree: *longer*
And if she sholde have loved for long loving,
455 To me ful longe[8] hadde be the guerdoning.°   *reward*

I dar eek sayn, if she me finde fals,
Unkinde, or janglere,° or rebel in any wise,   *blabber-mouth*
Or jalous, do me hangen by the hals;[9]
And but° I bere me in hir servise   *unless*
460 As wel as that my wit can me suffise,
From point to point, hir honour for to save,
Take ye my lif, and al the good I have."

The thridde° tercel egle answerde tho:°   *third / then*
"Now, sires, ye seen the litel leiser° here,   *leisure*
465 For every fowl crieth out to been ago
Forth with his make,° or with his lady dere;   *mate*
And eek Nature hirself ne wol nat heere,
For tarying here, nat half that I wolde saye;
And but° I speke, I moot° for sorwe deye: *unless / must*

470 Of long service avaunte° I me no thing—   *boast*
But as possible is me to die today

6. Torn apart.
7. I.e., in the light of.
8. I.e., long ago.
9. Have me hanged by the neck.

For wo, as he that hath been languisshing
This twenty yeer; and as wel happen may
A man may serven bet,° and more to pay[1]   better
475 In half a yeer, although it were no more,
Than som man dooth that hath served ful yore.°   long

I saye nat this by me, for I ne can
Doon no service that may my lady plese;
But I dar sayn I am hir trewest man,
480 As to my doom,° and fainest[2] wolde hire ese;°   judgment / please
At shorte wordes, til that deeth me sese,°   seize
I wil been hires, whether I wake or winke,
And trewe in al that herte may bithinke."

Of al my lif, sin° that day I was born,   since
485 So gentil plee in love or other thing
Ne herde nevere no man me biforn,
Who that hadde leiser and conning
For to reherce hir cheere° and hir speking: behavior
And from the morwe° gan this speeche laste,   morning
490 Til downward drow° the sonne wonder faste.   drew

The noise of fowles for to been delivered
So loude roong:° "Have doon, and lat us wende!"   rang
That wel wende° I the wode hadde al toslivered.[3]   thought
"Come of!" they criden, "allas, ye wole us shende.°   ruin
495 Whan shal youre cursed pleting° have an ende?   pleading
How sholde a juge either partye leve,°   believe
For ye or nay, withouten other preve?"°   proof

The goos, the cokkou, and the doke° also   duck
So cride, "Kek kek, cokkou, quek quek," hye
500 That thurgh mine eres the noise wente tho.°   then
The goos saide, "Al this nis nat worth a flye!
But I can shape° herof a remedye: quickly
And I wol saye my verdit faire and swithe°   arrange
For waterfowl, who so be wroth or blithe."

505 "And I for wormfowl," quod the fool cokkou.
"And I wol of myn owene auctoritee,
For commune speed,° take on me the charge°
   now: profit / responsibility
For to delivere us is greet charitee."
"Ye may abide a while yit, pardee,"
510 Quod the turtel,° "if it be youre wille: turtle-dove
A wight may speke him were as fair been stille.[4]

1. To greater pleasure.
2. Most gladly.
3. Fallen to pieces.
4. A person may speak who had better have remained quiet (?).

I am a seedfowl, oon[5] the unworthieste,
That woot° I wel, and litel of conninge;   *know*
But bet° is that a wightes tonge reste[6]   *better*
515 Than entremetten him of[7] swich doinge
Of which he neither rede° can ne singe.   *advise*
And who so dooth, ful foule himself accloyeth:°   *overloads*
For office uncommitted[8] ofte anoyeth."

Nature, which that alway hadde an ere
520 To murmur of the lewednesse[9] bihinde,
With facound° vois saide, "Holde youre tonges there,   *eloquent*
And I shal soone, I hope, a conseil finde
You to delivere, and from this noise unbinde;
I jugge of every folk men shul oon calle
525 To sayn the verdit for you fowles alle."

Assented was to this conclusioun
The briddes alle; and fowles of ravine°   *prey*
Han chosen first, by plain° eleccioun,   *open*
The tercelet of the faucon to diffine[1]
530 Al hir sentence, as hem liste[2] to termine;°   *decide*
And to Nature him gonne to presente,
And she accepteth him with glad entente.

The tercelet saide thanne, "In this manere
Ful hard were it to preve° by resoun   *prove*
535 Who loveth best this gentil formel here,
For everich hath swich replicacioun,[3]
That noon by skiles° may been brought adown.   *reasons*
I can nat see that arguments availe:
Thanne seemeth it ther moste° be bataile."   *must*

540 "Al redy," quod thise egles tercels tho.°   *then*
"Nay, sires," quod he, "if that I dorste it saye,
Ye doon me wrong, my tale is nat ydo.
For sires, ne taketh nat agrief,° I praye,   *amiss*
It may nat goon as ye wolde in this waye:
545 Oure° is the vois that han the charge° on
                    honde,   *ours / responsibility*
And to the juges doom° ye moten° stonde.   *judgment / must*

And therfore, pees; I saye, as to my wit,
Me wolde thinke[4] how that the worthieste
Of knighthood, and lengest hath used it,[5]
550 Most° of estaat, of blood the gentileste,   *greatest*

5. I.e., one of.
6. Be quiet.
7. Interfere in.
9. I.e., to the complaining of the unsophisticated birds in the distance.
1. Present.

2. All their opinion as it pleased them
to decide.
3. Ability to reply.
4. It would seem to me.
5. And the one who longest has practiced it.

Were sittingest[6] for hire, if that hire leste;
And of thise three she woot hirself, I trowe,
Which that he be, for hire is light[7] to knowe."

The waterfowles han hir hedes laid
555 Togidre; and of a short avisement,°   *deliberation*
Whan everich hadde his large golee° said,   *mouthful*
They saiden soothly, alle by oon assent,
How that the goos, with hir facounde gent,[8]
"That so desireth to pronounce oure neede
560 Shal telle oure tale," and prayed God hire speede.

As for thise waterfowles tho bigan
The goos to speke, and in hir cakelinge
She saide, "Pees, now take keep,° every man,   *heed*
And herkneth which° a reson I shal bringe: *what*
565 My wit is sharp, I love no taryinge.
I saye, I rede° him, though he were my brother,   *advise*
But° she wil love him, lat him take another."   *unless*

"Lo, here a parfit° reson of a goos,"   *perfect*
Quod the sperhawk. "Nevere mote° she thee!°   *may / thrive*
570 Lo, swich it is to have a tonge loos!
Now pardee, fool, now were it bet° for thee   *better*
Han holde thy pees than shewe thy nicetee.°   *foolishness*
It lith° nat in his might ne in his wille,   *lies*
But sooth is said, a fool can nat be stille."

575 The laughtre aroos of gentil fowles alle,
And right anoon the seedfowl chosen hadde
The turtel trewe, and gonne hire to hem calle,
And prayed hire for to sayn the soothe sadde°   *earnestly*
Of this matere, and axed° what she radde:°   *asked / advised*
580 And she answerde that plainly hir entente
She wolde it shewe, and soothly what she mente.

"Nay, God forbede a lovere sholde chaunge,"
The turtel saide, and weex° for shame al reed.   *grew*
"Though that his lady everemore be straunge,°   *hostile*
585 Yit lat him serve hire til that he be deed.°   *dead*
Forsoothe, I praise nat the gooses reed.°   *advice*
'For though she dyde, I wolde[9] noon other make:°   *mate*
I wil been hires° til that the deeth me take.'"   *hers*

"Wel bourded,"° quod the doke, "by myn hat!   *joked*
590 That men shal loven alway causelees—

---

6. Most suitable.
7. For it is easy for her.
8. Gentle eloquence.

9. Would want: the turtle-dove, a female, is apparently quoting a sentimental bit of verse appropriate for a male.

Who can a reson finde or wit in that?
Daunceth he merye that is mirthelees?
What sholde I rekke° of him that is recchelees?[1]   care
595 Ye, queke,"° yit said the doke, ful wel and faire: quack
"Ther been mo sterres,° God woot, than a paire."   stars

"Now fy, cherl," quod the gentil tercelet:
"Out of the donghil cam that word ful right.
Thou canst nat seen what thing is wel biset;[2]
Thou farest° by love as owles doon by light: behave
600 The day hem blent,° but wel they seen by night.   blinds
Thy kinde is of so lowe a wrecchednesse
That what love is thou canst nat seen ne gesse."

Tho gan the cokkou putte him forth in prees°   public
For fowl that eteth worm, and saide blive,°   straightaway
605 "So I," quod he, "may have my make in pees,
I recche° nat how longe that ye strive.   care
Lat eech of him be solein° al hir live,   single
This is my reed,° sin° they may nat accorde: advice / since
This shorte lesson needeth nat recorde."[3]

610 "Ye, have the gloton fild ynough his paunche,
Thanne are we wel," saide thanne a merlioun.°   merlin
"Thou mortherere° of the haysoge° on
            the braunche   murderer / hedge-sparrow
That broughte thee forth,[4] thou reweful° glotoun,   pitiful
Live thou solein,° wormes corrupcioun,   single
615 For no fors is of lak of thy nature:[5]
Go, lewed° be thou whil that the world may
            dure."°   ignorant / endure

"Now pees," quod Nature, "I comande heer,
For I have herd al youre opinioun,
And in effect yit be we nevere the neer.°   nearer
620 But finally, this is my conclusioun:
That she hirself shal han the eleccioun
Of whom hire list; and who be wroth or blithe,
Him that she cheseth° he shal hire have as swithe.[6]   chooses

For sin° it may nat here discussed be   since
625 Who loveth hire best, as saith the tercelet,
Thanne wol I doon hire this favour, that she
Shal have right him on whom hir herte is set,
And he hire that his herte hath on hire knet.°   fastened

---

1. Doesn't care.
2. I.e., in good condition.
3. I.e., to be recorded.
4. The hedge-sparrow has reared (brought forth) the cuckoo because the
egg from which the cuckoo was hatched was placed in the hedge-sparrow's nest.
5. I.e., for it doesn't matter if your line dies out.
6. At once.

Thus jugge I, Nature, for I may nat lie:
630 To noon estaat have I noon other yë.[7]

But as for conseil° for to chese a make,   *advice*
If I were Reson, certes thanne wolde I
Conseile you the royal tercel take—
As saide the tercelet ful skilfully—
635 As for the gentileste and most worthy,
Which I have wrought so wel to my plesaunce
That to you oughte it been a suffisaunce."[8]

With dredful vois the formel tho° answerde,   *then*
"Myn rightful lady, goddesse of Nature,
640 Sooth is that I am evere under youre yerde,°   *rod*
As is another lives[9] creature,
And moot° been youre° whil that my lif may
        dure;°   *must / yours / last*
And therfore, graunteth me my first boone,°   *prayer*
And myn entente you wol I sayn wel soone."

645 "I graunte it you," quod she. And right anoon
This formel egle spak in this degree:
"Almighty queene, unto° this yeer be goon,   *until*
I axe° respit for to avise me,[1]   *ask*
And after that to have my chois al free:
650 This al and som that I wol speke and saye:
Yet gete namore although ye do me deye.[2]

I wol nat serve Venus ne Cupide
Forsoothe, as yit, by no manere waye."
"Now, sin° it may noon otherwise bitide,"   *since*
655 Quod tho Nature, "here is namore to saye.
Thanne wolde I that thise fowles were awaye,
Eech with his make,° for tarying lenger here,"   *mate*
And saide hem thus, as ye shul after heere.

"To you speke I, you tercelets," quod Nature.
660 "Beeth of good herte, and serveth alle three:
A yeer is nat so longe to endure,
And eech of you paine him[3] in his degree
For to do wel; for God woot, quit° is she   *delivered*
Fro you this yeer, what after so bifalle:
665 This entremes° is dressed° for you alle."   *intermission / ordained*

And whan this werk al brought was to an ende,
To every fowl Nature yaf his make

---

7. I.e., I take no other consideration into account.
8. I.e., that it ought to be enough for you.
9. I.e., any other living.
1. Think it over.
2. Put me to death.
3. Take pains.

By evene accord, and on hir way they wende.
But Lord, the blisse and joye that they make,
For eech gan other in his winges take,
And with hir nekkes eech gan other winde,
Thanking alway the noble queen of Kinde.°   *Nature*

But first were chosen fowles for to singe—
As yeer by yere was alway the usaunce°   *custom*
To singe a roundel at hir departinge,
To doon to Nature honour and plesaunce.
The note,° I trowe, ymaked was in Fraunce;   *music*
The wordes were swiche as ye may here finde
The nexte vers, as I now have in minde.

"Now welcome, somer, with thy sonne softe,
That hast thise wintres wedres° overshake,°   *storms / dispelled*
And driven away the large nightes blake.
Saint Valentin, that art ful heigh on lofte,
Thus singen smale fowles for thy sake:
Now welcome, somer, with thy sonne softe,
That hast thise wintres wedres overshake,
And driven away the large nightes blake.

Wel han they cause for to gladen ofte,
Sith° eech of hem recovered hath his make;   *since*
Ful blisful mowe° they singe whan they wake: *may*
Now welcome, somer, with thy sonne softe,
That hast thise wintres wedres overshake,
And driven away the large nightes blake."

And with the shouting, whan the song was do,
That fowles maden at hir flight away,
I wook, and othere bookes took me to
To rede upon; and yit I rede alway,
In hope, ywis° to rede so somday,   *indeed*
That I shal mete° somthing for to fare   *dream*
The bet;° and thus to rede I nil nat spare.   *better*
ca. 1380

LYRICS AND OCCASIONAL VERSE[1]
To Rosamond[2]

Madame, ye been of alle beautee shrine
As fer as cercled is the mapemounde:[3]
For as the crystal glorious ye shine,
And like ruby been youre cheekes rounde.
5 Therwith ye been so merye and so jocounde
That at a revel whan that I see you daunce
It is an oinement unto my wounde,
Though ye to me ne do no daliaunce.[4]

For though I weepe of teres ful a tine,°   *tub*
10 Yit may that wo myn herte nat confounde;
Youre semy° vois, that ye so smale outtwine,[5]   *small*
Maketh my thought in joye and blis habounde:°   *abound*
So curteisly I go with love bounde
That to myself I saye in my penaunce,[6]
15 "Suffiseth me to love you, Rosemounde,
Though ye to me ne do no daliaunce."

Was nevere pik walwed in galauntine[7]
As I in love am walwed and ywounde,
For which ful ofte I of myself divine
20 That I am trewe Tristam[8] the secounde;
My love may not refreide nor affounde;[9]
I brenne° ay in amorous plesaunce: *burn*
Do what you list, I wol youre thral° be founde, *slave*
Though ye to me ne do no daliaunce.

1. As a man of accomplishments who was often at court, Chaucer must, like other courtiers, have been called upon to write both occasional verses and lyrics. Of the handful of these shorter poems that have survived, several of the best are included here: they reveal the ways in which Chaucer handled some of the poetic modes and attitudes of his time. These modes—particularly the lyric strain, which seeks expression in a brief form—seem to have been uncongenial to his temperament. Some, in fact, might well be termed "anti-lyrics"; these are the poems where the extreme conventions of the courtly-love lyric become a framework in which Chaucer's irony and indirection may be brought into immediate play. Chaucer's best work, however, is in his longer poems, for irony and indirection are qualities which can be given proper development only if the poet has ample room to work in.

2. This lyric extends the extravagant images of the stylized courtly-love lyric to outrageous lengths: a lover might well weep a flood of tears but would hardly measure them by the tubful (line 9), and he might be overwhelmed with love—but not like a fish buried in sauce (line 17). The general imperturbability of tone contrasts ironically with the grotesque metaphors.

3. I.e., to the farthest circumference of the map of the world.

4. I.e., show me no encouragement.

5. That you so delicately spin out.

6. I.e., pangs of unrequited love.

7. Pike rolled in galantine sauce.

8. The famous lover of Isolt (Iseult, Isolde) in medieval legend, renowned for his constancy.

9. Cool nor chill.

To His Scribe Adam[1]

Adam scrivain,° if evere it thee bifalle   *scribe*
Boece[2] or *Troilus* for to writen newe,
Under thy longe lokkes thou moste[3] have the scalle,° *scurf*
But after my making thou write more trewe,[4]
5 So ofte a day I moot° thy werk renewe,   *must*
It to correcte, and eek to rubbe and scrape:
And al is thurgh thy necligence and rape.°   *haste*

Complaint to His Purse[5]

To you. my purs, and to noon other wight,
Complaine I, for ye be my lady dere.
I am so sory, now that ye be light,
For certes, but if[6] ye make me hevy cheere,
5 Me were as lief[7] be laid upon my beere;°   *bier*
For which unto youre mercy thus I crye:
Beeth hevy again, or elles moot° I die.   *must*

Now voucheth sauf this day er it be night
That I of you the blisful soun may heere,
10 Or see youre colour, lik the sonne bright,
That of yelownesse hadde nevere peere.
Ye be my life, ye be myn hertes steere,°   *rudder, guide*
Queene of confort and of good compaignye:
Beeth hevy again, or elles moot I die.

15 Ye purs, that been to me my lives light
And saviour, as in this world down here,
Out of this tonne[8] helpe me thurgh your might,
Sith that ye wol nat be my tresorere;°   *disburser*
For I am shave as neigh° as any frere.°   *close / friar*
20 But yit I praye unto youre curteisye:
Beeth hevy again, or elles moot I die.

1. This *jeu d'esprit*, called forth by the inefficiency of his amanuensis, is written in the verse form of Chaucer's great poem *Troilus and Criseide*.
2. I.e., Chaucer's translation of Boethius' *De Consolatione*. "*Troilus*": *Troilus and Criseide*.
3. I.e., may you.
4. Unless you write more accurately what I've composed.
5. In this variation on the courtly-love lyric the conventional language of love is both used and misused to express love of cash. Ladies, like coins, should be golden, and like purses they should not be "light" (i.e., fickle). On the other hand, they should not be heavy, as purses should be. The poem is in the characteristic three-stanza *ballade* form, with the usual "envoy" addressed to a noble patron. In this case the patron apparently heard the complaint, for, three days after his accession (in 1399), King Henry IV renewed and increased the pension Chaucer had received from Richard II.
6. Unless.
7. I'd just as soon.
8. Tun, meaning "predicament."

Envoy to Henry IV

O conquerour of Brutus Albioun,[9]
Which that by line and free eleccioun
Been verray king, this song to you I sende:
25 And ye, that mowen° alle oure harmes amende,   *may*
Have minde upon my supplicacioun.

Merciless Beauty[1]

1

Youre yën two wol slee° me sodeinly: *slay*
I may the beautee of hem nat sustene,°   *withstand*
So woundeth it thurghout myn herte keene.°   *keenly*

And but° youre word wol helen hastily   *unless*
5 Myn hertes wounde, whil that it is greene,[2]
  Youre yën two wol slee me sodeinly:
  I may the beautee of hem nat sustene.

Upon my trouthe, I saye you faithfully
That ye been of my lif and deeth the queene,
10 For with my deeth the trouthe shal be scene.
  Youre yën two wol slee me sodeinly:
  I may the beautee of hem nat sustene,
  So woundeth it thurghout myn herte keene.

2

So hath youre beautee fro youre herte chaced
15 Pitee, that me ne availeth nought to plaine:°   *complain*
For Daunger halt[3] youre mercy in his chaine.

Giltelees my deeth thus han ye me purchaced;°   *procured*
I saye you sooth, me needeth nought to feine:°   *dissemble*
  So hath youre beautee fro youre herte chaced
20   Pitee, that me ne availeth nought to plaine.

Allas, that nature hath in you compaced°   *enclosed*
So greet beautee that no man may attaine
To mercy, though he sterve° for the paine.   *die*
  So hath youre beautee fro youre herte chaced

9. Britain (Albion) was supposed to have been founded by Brutus, the grandson of Aeneas, the founder of Rome.
1. The first two sections of this poem employ the typical imagery and extravagant emotion of courtly-love lyrics—the power of the lady's eyes to slay the lover, for instance, and the struggle between her native pity and her "daunger" (haughtiness). But it ends where a real lyric could never end: the poet's self-congratulation, at the failure of his affair, on his unimpaired health.
2. I.e., fresh.
3. Haughtiness holds.

25   Pitee, that me ne availeth nought to plaine:
    For Daunger halt youre mercy in his chaine.

3

    Sin I fro Love escaped am so fat,
    I nevere thenke° to been in his prison lene: *intend*
    Sin I am free, I counte him nat a bene.[4]

30 He may answere and saye right this and that;
    I do no fors,[5] I speke right as I mene:
    Sin I fro Love escaped am so fat,
    I nevere thenke to been in his prison lene.

    Love hath my name ystrike° out of his sclat,°   *struck / slate*
35 And he is strike out of my bookes clene
    For everemo; ther is noon other mene.°   *solution*
    Sin I fro Love escaped am so fat,
    I nevere thenke to been in his prison lene:
    Sin I am free, I counte him nat a bene.

Gentilesse[6]

    The firste fader and findere° of gentilesse,   *founder*
    What° man desireth gentil for to be   *whatever*
    Moste folwe his traas,° and alle his wittes dresse[7]   *path*
    Vertu to sue,° and vices for to flee: *follow*
5 For unto vertu longeth° dignitee,   *belongs*
    And nought the revers, saufly° dar I deeme,   *safely*
    Al were he[8] mitre, crowne, or diademe.

    This firste stok was ground of rightwisnesse,°   *righteousness*
    Trewe of his word, sobre, pietous,[9] and free,
10 Clene of his gost,° and loved bisinesse   *spirit*
    Against the vice of slouthe,° in honestee;   *sloth*
    And but his heir love vertu as dide he,
    He is nat gentil, though he riche° seeme,   *noble*
    Al were he mitre, crowne, or diademe.

15 Vice may wel be heir to old richesse,
    But ther may no man, as ye may wel see,
    Biquethe his heir his vertuous noblesse:
    That is appropred° unto no degree   *exclusively assigned*

---

4. I don't consider him worth a bean.
5. I don't care.
6. The virtue of "gentilesse" combined a courtesy of manner with a courtesy of mind. That it is not the inevitable adjunct of aristocratic birth (though most appropriate to it) was a medieval commonplace, to which Chaucer here gives succinct—if conventional—expression. It is important to observe, however,

that the moral democracy implied by this doctrine was never transferred by the Middle Ages to the political or even the social realm.
7. I.e., must follow his (the first father's) path and dispose all his (own) wits.
8. Even if he wear.
9. Merciful; "free": generous.

But to the firste fader in majestee,
20 That maketh his heir him that wol him queme,° *please*
Al were he mitre, crowne, or diademe.

Truth[1]

Flee fro the prees° and dwelle with soothfastnesse; *crowd*
Suffise unto° thy thing, though it be smal; *to be content with*
For hoord hath[2] hate, and climbing tikelnesse;° *insecurity*
Prees hath envye, and wele° blent° overal. *prosperity / blinds*
5 Savoure° no more than thee bihoove shal; *relish*
Rule wel thyself that other folk canst rede:° *advise*
And Trouthe shal delivere,[3] it is no drede.° *doubt*

Tempest thee nought al crooked to redresse[4]
In trust of hire[5] that turneth as a bal;
10 Muche wele stant in litel bisinesse;[6]
Be war therfore to spurne ayains an al.[7]
Strive nat as dooth the crokke° with the wal. *pot*
Daunte° thyself that dauntest otheres deede: *master*
And Trouthe shal delivere, it is no drede.

15 That thee is sent, receive in buxomnesse;° *obedience*
The wrastling for the world axeth° a fal; *asks for*
Here is noon hoom, here nis but wildernesse:
Forth, pilgrim, forth! Forth, beest, out of thy stal!
Know thy countree, looke up, thank God of al.
20 Hold the heigh way and lat thy gost° thee lede: *spirit*
And Trouthe shal delivere, it is no drede.

Therfore, thou Vache,[8] leve thyn olde wrecchednesse
Unto the world; leve[9] now to be thral.
Crye him mercy that of his heigh goodnesse
25 Made thee of nought, and in especial
Draw unto him, and pray in general,
For thee and eek for othere, hevenelich meede:° *reward*
And Trouthe shal delivere, it is no drede.

1. Taking as his theme Christ's words to his disciples (in John viii.32), "And ye shall know the truth, and the truth shall make you free," Chaucer plays upon the triple meaning that the Middle English word "trouthe" seems to have had for him: the religious truth of Christianity, the moral virtue of integrity, and the philosophical idea of reality. By maintaining one's faith and one's integrity, one rises superior to the vicissitudes of this world and comes eventually to know reality—which is not, however, of this world.
2. Hoarding causes.
3. I.e., truth shall make you free.
4. Do not disturb yourself to straighten all that's crooked.
5. Fortune, who turns like a ball in that she is always presenting a different aspect to men.
6. Peace of mind stands in little anxiety.
7. I.e. to kick against the pricks.
8. Probably Sir Philip de la Vache, with a pun on the French for "cow."
9. I.e. cease.

SIR ORFEO

(ca. 1300)

Sir Orfeo is a reworking of the classical myth of the great musician Orpheus and his wife Eurydice. According to Ovid's *Metamorphoses*, Eurydice died of a snake-bite at her wedding and went to Hades, the place of the dead. Orpheus undertook to follow her there, and having come before Pluto and Proserpina, the king and queen of Hades, he so pleased them with his music that they granted Eurydice's release—on the condition, however, that she should follow behind Orpheus as they left Hades and that he should not look back at her. But Orpheus did look back, and Eurydice disappeared into Hades. Ovid's stories were told and retold during the Middle Ages, and frequently the teller altered the plot to suit his own purposes—in her tale the Wife of Bath (lines 958ff.) substitutes Midas' wife for his barber as the discoverer of his asses' ears. The poet of *Sir Orfeo* has given the story a happy ending and has replaced its alien classical elements with familiar elements of medieval folklore. Hades has become the land of *Fairye*, the medieval otherworld, inhabited by supernatural creatures who seem human in most respects but who exist under laws incomprehensible to ordinary human beings. There is no rational explanation of why the king of Fairye should seize Dame Heurodis (Eurydice), except that by going to sleep under an *impe-tree* (a grafted fruit-tree), she unwittingly violated a taboo and put herself in his power. In folklore trees are, of course, often given sinister properties: in lines 885 ff. of her tale the Wife of Bath comments that incubi once resided under trees, and in *The Faerie Queene* I.ii.30 the Redcross Knight has a frightening experience with a tree he is sitting under. In the Otherworld Dame Heurodis continues to sleep under a tree—apparently a replica of the one in her own garden.

That the poem was the product of a minstrel seems certain because of the emphasis laid upon the value of music. Orfeo is an excellent harper who welcomes all good harpers to his court. When he becomes a hermit, he keeps his harp near him and plays on it to solace himself. The animals and birds crowd around him in delight—as they did with Orpheus—and like the original Orpheus he frees his wife by his music. When he returns to his own kingdom it is by his harp and his harping that he is identified. Even Orfeo's steward appreciates music: in most medieval romances stewards are pictured as wicked, for they were the court officers responsible for offering or withholding hospitality for minstrels, and apparently they often withheld it. With unusual tact, the poet depicts a good steward who, partly because of his courtesy to harpers, becomes king after Orfeo's death.

The poem was probably translated from a French romance of the kind called a Breton lay. As the name implies, this genre of romance had its origin in Brittany, a place noted for its minstrelsy. Other surviving lays share with *Sir Orfeo* a plot involving the supernatural, wedded or romantic love, and a rash promise; they also share the poem's stylistic simplicity, brevity, and a generally optimistic spirit. Chaucer's Franklin's Tale imitates the form, and it is probable that his model was *Sir Orfeo*, whose opening lines the Franklin seems to be echoing in his own story. The English translation was probably made before 1300, but it has survived in only three manuscripts of later date. Some scholars believe that the best of these, the Auchinleck manuscript, may once have been read by Chaucer. Only the Auchinleck manuscript makes the interesting identification of *Traciens* (Thrace) with Winchester: some English minstrel poet obviously adapted the poem to a performance at Winchester, which had, indeed, in Old English times been the seat of a kingdom. (It was probably the same poet who, fractionally learned, names King Pluto and King Juno among Orfeo's ancestors.)

The text presented here is based on the Auchinleck manuscript, though the spelling has been normalized and readings from the other manuscripts adopted where they seem better than Auchinleck's. In view of the large amount of evident corruption in all three manuscripts, the editor has made a number of conjectural emendations. The original metrical form was probably octosyllabic couplets with alternating stress, but what has come down to us are loose four-stressed couplets. As in Chaucer, there are many "headless" lines, where the stress falls on the first syllable of the line, even though the syllable is not a rhetorically important one; and also as in Chaucer, while final *e* is frequently used to achieve an unstressed syllable, it is equally often ignored.

Sir Orfeo

    We reden ofte and finden ywrite—
    As thise clerkes doon° us wite°—   *cause / to learn*
    The layes that been of harping[1]
    Been yfounde° of freely° thing.   *composed / pleasant*
5   Some been of werre° and some of wo,   *war*
    And some of joye and mirthe also,
    And some of trecherye and of gile;
    And some of happes° that fellen° while,° *events / occurred / once*
    And some of bourdes° and ribaudye,°   *jokes / ribaldry*
10   And manye been of faïrye.[2]
    Of alle thing that men may see,
    Most of love forsoothe they be.
    In Britain° thise layes been wrought,   *Brittany*
    First yfounde° and forth ybrought.   *composed*
15   Of aventures that felle° by dayes[3]   *occurred*
    The Britons° therof maden layes: *Bretons*
    Whan they mighte owher° yheere°   *anywhere / hear*
    Of any merveiles that ther were,
    They tooken hem hir harpes with game,°   *pleasure*
20   Maden layes and yaf° hem name.   *gave*
    Of aventures that han bifalle
    I can some telle, but nought alle.
    Herkneth, lordinges° that been trewe,   *gentlemen*
    I wol you telle of Sir Orfewe.
25   Orfeo was a riche° king,   *noble*

1. I.e., composed to be sung to the harp.
2. Fairyland, and, more commonly, the other-world and its supernatural inhabitants.
3. Once.

In Engelond an heigh lording,
A stalworth° man and hardy bo,°   *valiant / both*
Large° and curteis° he was also.   *generous / courteous*
His fader was come of King Pluto,
30 And his moder of King Juno,
That sometime were as goddes yholde°   *considered*
For aventures that they dide and tolde.
    This king sojourned in Traciens°   *Thrace*
That is a citee of noble defens°   *fortification*
35 (For Winchester was cleped° tho°   *called / then*
Traciens withouten no°).   *denial*
Orfeo most of any thing
Loved the glee° of harping: *music*
Siker° was every good harpour   *certain*
40 Of him to have muche honour.
Himself he lerned for to harpe,
And laide° theron his wittes sharpe;°   *applied / keenly*
He lerned so ther nothing was
A bettre harpour in no plas.°   *place*
45 In al the world was no man bore°   *born*
That ones° Orfeo sat bifore,   *once*
And° he mighte of his harping heere,   *if*
But he sholde thinke that he were
In oon of the joyes of Paradis,
50 Swich melodye in his harping is.
    Orfeo hadde a queene of pris°   *excellence*
That was ycleped° Dame Heurodis,   *named*
The fairest lady for the° nones°   *that / matter*
That mighte goon° on body and bones,   *walk*
55 Ful of love and of goodnesse—
But no man may telle hir fairnesse.
    Bifel so, the comsing° of May,   *beginning*
When merye and hot is the day,
And away been winter showres,
60 And every feeld is ful of flowres,
And blosme breme° on every bough   *glorious*
Overal° wexeth° merye ynough,   *everywhere / grows*
This eeche° queene Dame Heurodis   *same*
Took with hire two maides of pris°   *excellence*
65 And wente in the undertide°   *forenoon*
To playe in an orchard-side,
To see the flowres sprede° and springe   *open*
And to heere the fowles singe.
    They setten hem down alle three
70 Faire° under an impe-tree;°   *fairly / grafted fruit tree*
And wel soon this faire queene
Fel on sleepe upon the greene.
The maidens durste hire not awake,
But lete hire lie and reste take.
75 So she slepte til afternoon
That undertide was al ydoon.°   *passed*

But as soone as she gan wake
She cried and loothly bere° gan make: *outcry*
She frotte° hir hondes and hir feet   *tore at*
80 And cracched° hir visage—it bledde weet;° *scratched / wet*
Hir riche robe she al torit,°   *tears apart*
And was ravised° out of her wit.   *ravished*
The two maidenes hire biside
Ne durste with hire no leng° abide,   *longer*
85 But runne to the palais right
And tolde bothe squier and knight
That hir queene awede° wolde,   *go mad*
And bad hem go and hire atholde.°   *restrain*
Knightes runne and ladies also,
90 Damiseles sixty and mo,°   *more*
In th' orchard to the queene they come,
And hire up in armes nome,°   *took*
And broughte hire to bed at laste,
And heelde hire there fine° faste.   *very*
95 But evere she heeld° in oo° cry,   *continued / one*
And wolde uppe° and awy.°   *get up / go away*
  Whan the king herde that tiding
Nevere him nas worse for no thing:
Orfeo cam with knightes tene°   *ten*
100 To chambre right bifore the queene,
And looked and saide with greet° pitee,   *great*
"O leve° lif, what aileth thee?—   *dear*
That evere yit hast been so stille,
And now thou gredest° wonder shille.° *cry out / shrilly*
105 Thy body that was so whit ycore°   *excellent*
With thine nailes is all totore.°   *torn*
Allas, thy rode° that was so reed° *complexion / red*
Is as wan as thou were deed.°   *dead*
And also thy fingres smale
110 Been al bloody and al pale.
Allas, thy lovesome yën two
Looketh so° man dooth on his fo.   *as*
A, dame, ich° biseeche mercy—   *I*
Lete been al this reweful° cry,   *pitiful*
115 And tel me what° thee is and how, *what the matter with*
And what thing may thee helpe now."
  Tho° lay she stille at the laste,   *then*
And gan to weepe swithe° faste,°   *very / hard*
And saide thus the king unto:
120 "Allas, my lord Sir Orfeo,
Sitthen° we first togider were   *since*
Ones wrothe° nevere we nere,   *angry*
But evere ich have yloved thee
As my lif, and so thou me.
125 But now we mote° deele° atwo— *must / separate*
Do thy best, for I moot° go."   *must*
  "Allas," quath he, "forlorn ich am!

Whider wilt thou go and to wham?°   *whom*
Whider thou goost ich wil with thee,
130 And whider I go thou shalt with me."
"Nay, nay, sire, that nought nis.[4]
Ich wil thee telle al how it is:
As ich lay this undertide°   *forenoon*
And slepte under oure orchard-side,
135 Ther come to me two faire knightes,
Wel y-armed al to rightes,
And bad me comen on hying°   *in haste*
And speke with hir lord the king;
And ich answerede at° wordes bolde   *in*
140 That I ne durste nought ne I nolde.°   *would not*
They prikked again as they mighte drive.[5]
Tho° cam hir king also blive°   *then / straightway*
With an hundred knightes and mo,
And damiseles an hundred also,
145 Alle on snow-white steedes;
As white as milk were hir weedes:°   *clothes*
I ne seigh° nevere yit bifore   *saw*
So faire creatures ycore.°   *splendid*
The king hadde a crown on his heed:°   *head*
150 It nas of silver n'of gold reed,°   *red*
But it was of a precious stoon;
As brighte as the sonne it shoon.
And as soone as he to me cam,
Wolde ich, nolde ich, he me nam°   *took*
155 And made me with him to ride
Upon a palfrey him biside,
And broughte me to his palais
Wel attired° in eech a ways,°   *equipped / way*
And shewed me castels and towrs,
160 Riveres, foreestes, frith° with flowres,   *meadow*
And his riche steedes eechoon,
And sitthen° broughte me again hoom   *afterwards*
Into oure owene orche-yard,°   *orchard*
And saide to me thus afterward,
165 'Looke tomorwe that thou be
Right here under this impe-tree,
And thanne thou shalt with us go,
And live with us everemo.°   *evermore*
And if thou makest us ylet,°   *resistance*
170 Where° thou be, thou worst° yfet.°   *wherever / shall be / fetched*
And al totore° thy limes al   *torn apart*
That no thing thee helpe shal.
And though thou beest so totorn,
Yit thou worst° with us yborn.' "°   *shall be / carried off*

---

4. I.e., that's no use.   5. I.e., they rode as fast as they could.

175   When king Orfeo herde this cas,°   *circumstance*
O, wee!"° quath he, "allas, allas!   *woe*
Lever me were to lete° my lif   *leave*
Than thus to lese° the queene my wif."   *lose*
He asked conseil at° eech a man,   *from*
180   But no man him helpe can.
     Amorwe° the undertide is come,   *next day*
And Orfeo hath his armes ynome,°   *taken*
And wel ten hundred knightes with him,
Eech y-armed, stout and grim.
185   And with the queene wenten he   *they*
Right unto that impe-tree.
They made sheltrom° in eech a side,   *military formation*
And saide they wolde ther abide
And die there everichoon,
190   Er the queene sholde from hem goon.
And yit amiddes hem ful right
The queene was away ytwight,°   *snatched*
With° faïrye forth ynome:°   *by / taken*
Men wiste nevere wher she was bicome.[6]
195   Tho° was ther crying, weep and wo;   *then*
The king into his chambre is go
And ofte swooned upon the stoon,°   *floor*
And made swich dool and swich moon[7]
That nye° his lif was yspent°—   *nearly / finished*
200   Ther was noon amendement.°   *remedy*
     He clepte° togider his barouns,   *called*
Eerles, lordes of renouns,°   *great names*
And whan they alle ycomen were,
"Lordinges," he saide, "bifor you here
205   Ich ordaine myn heigh steward
To wite° my kingdom afterward;   *keep*
In my stede been he shal
To keepe my londes overal.°   *everywhere*
For now I have my queene ylore,°   *lost*
210   The faireste lady that evere was bore,°   *born*
Nevere eft° I nil° no womman see;   *again / will not*
In wildernesse now wil ich tee°   *go*
And live ther for everemore,
With wilde beestes in holtes° hore.°   *woods / gray*
215   And whan ye wite° that I be spent,°   *learn / dead*
Make you than a parlement
And chese° you° a newe king: *choose / for yourselves*
Now dooth youre best with al my thing."
Tho° was ther weeping in the halle,   *then*
220   And greet° cry among hem alle;   *great*
Unnethe° mighte olde or yong   *scarcely*

---

6. No one knew what had become of her.
7. And made such lamentation and such complaint.

For weeping speke a word with tonge.
They kneeled alle adown in fere°   together
And prayede him if his wille were,
225 That he ne sholde from hem go.
"Do way," quath he, "it shal be so."
    Al his kingdom he forsook;
But° a sclavin° on him he took: only / pilgrim's cloak
He hadde no kirtel° ne noon hood,   short coat
230 Shert ne yit noon other good.
But his harp he took algate,°   at any rate
And dide him barefoot out at yate:°   gate
No man moste° with him go.   must
    O way,° what° ther was weep and wo,   alas / how
235 Whan he that hadde been king with crown
Wente so poorelich out of town.
Thrugh the wode° and over heeth   wood
Into the wildernesse he geeth.°   goes
Nothing he fint° that him is aise,°   finds / easy
240 But evere he liveth in greet malaise.
He that hadde wered° the fowe and gris,[8]   worn
And on bed the purper° bis,°   purple / linen
Now on harde heeth he lith,°   lies
With leves and grasse he him writh.°   covers
245 He that hadde had castels and towres,
Rivere, foreest, frith° with flowres,   meadow
Now though it ginne snowe and freese,
This king moot° make his bed in meese.°   must / moss
He that hadde had knightes of pris,°   renown
250 Bifore him kneeling and ladis,
Now seeth he nothing that him liketh,°   pleases
But wilde wormes° by him striketh.°   snakes / glide
He that hadde yhad plentee
Of mete and drinke, of eech daintee,
255 Now may he alday° digge and wrote°   constantly / scrounge
Er he finde his fille of roote.
In somer he liveth by wilde fruit
And berien° but goode lite;[9]   berries
In winter may he nothing finde
260 But roote, grasses, and the rinde.°   bark
Al his body away was dwined°   wasted
For misaise, and al tochined.°   scarred
Lord, who may telle of the sore
This king suffered ten yeer and more?
265 His heer of his beerd, blak and rowe,°   rugged
To his girdel-stede° was growe.   waist
His harp wheron was al his glee
He hidde in an holwe tree,
And whan the weder was cleer and bright,

8. White and gray fur; i.e., royal ermine.   9. Little good.

270 He took his harp to him wel right,
    And harped at his owene wille:°   *pleasure*
    In al the woode the soun gan shille,°   *resound*
    That wilde beestes that ther beeth
    For joy abouten him they teeth;°   *draw*
275 And alle the fowles that ther were
    Come and sete on eech a brere°   *briar*
    To here his harping afine,°   *to the end*
    So muche melodye was therine.
    When he his harping lete° wolde,   *leave off*
280 No beest by him abide nolde.
      Ofte he mighte see him bisides
    In the hote undertides°   *mornings*
    The king of fairy with his route°   *company*
    Come to hunte him al aboute
285 With dinne, cry, and with blowing,
    And houndes also with him berking.
    But no beeste they ne nome°   *took*
    No nevere he niste wher they bicome.[1]
    And otherwhile he mighte see,
290 As a greet oost° by him tee,°   *host / passed*
    Wel atourned° ten hundred knightes,   *equipped*
    Eech y-armed to his rightes,°   *fittingly*
    Of countenance stout and fiers,°   *fierce*
    With manye displayed° baners,   *unfurled*
295 And eech his swerd ydrawe holde,
    But nevere he niste° wher they wolde,   *knew not*
    And somwhile he seigh° other thing: *saw*
    Knightes and ladies come dauncing,
    In quainte° atir, degisely,°   *elegant / wonderfully*
300 Quainte pas° and softely.   *step*
    Tabours° and trumpes yede° him by,   *drums / went*
    And al manere mïnstracy.°   *minstrelsy*
      And on a day he seigh° biside   *saw*
    Sixty ladies on horse ride,
305 Gentil and jolif° as brid° on ris°—   *pretty / bird / bough*
    Nought oo man amonges hem nis.
    And eech a faucon on hond beer,°   *bore*
    And riden on hawking by river.
    Of game they founde wel good haunt,°   *plenty*
310 Maulardes,° hairoun,° and cormeraunt.   *mallards / herons*
    The fowles of° the water ariseth;   *from*
    The faucons hem wel deviseth:°   *descry*
    Eech faucon his preye slough.°   *slew*
    That seigh° Orfeo and lough:°   *saw / laughed*
315 "Parfay!"° quath he, "ther is fair game!   *by faith*
    Thider ich wil,° by Goddes name.   *will go*
    Ich was ywon° swich° werk to see."   *accustomed / such*

---

1. Nor did he ever learn what happened to them.

He aroos and thider gan tee.°   *draw*
To a lady he was ycome,
320 Biheeld, and hath wel undernome,°   *understood*
And seeth by al thing that it is
His owene queene Dame Heurodis,
Yerne° biheeld hire and she him eke,°   *eagerly / also*
But neither to other a word ne speke.
325 For misaise that she on him seigh°   *saw*
That hadde been so riche and heigh,
The teres felle out of hir yë.
The othere ladies this ysye°   *saw*
And maked hire away to ride:
330 She moste° with him no lenger° abide.   *must / longer*
     "Allas," quath he, "now me is wo.
Why nil° deeth now me nought slo?°   *will not / slay*
Allas, wrecche,° that I ne mighte   *wretched one*
Die now after this sighte.
335 Allas, too longe last° my lif   *lasts*
Whan I ne dar nought to my wif—
Ne she to me—oo word ne speke.
Allas, why nil myn herte breke?
Parfay,"° quath he, "tide what bitide,   *by faith*
340 Whider so thise ladies ride
The selve° waye ich wil strecche:°   *same / go*
Of lif ne deeth me nothing recche."°   *care*
     His sclavin° he dide on also spak°   *cloak / at once*
And heeng° his harp upon his bak,   *hung*
345 And hadde wel good wil to goon:
He ne spared neither stub ne stoon.[2]
In at a roche° the ladies rideth   *rock, cave*
And he after and nought abideth.
     Whan he was in the roche ago
350 Wel three mile other° mo,   *or*
He cam into a fair countrey,
As bright so° sonne on somers day,   *as*
Smoothe and plain° and alle greene: *flat*
Hil ne dale nas ther noon seene.
355 Amidde the lond a castel he seigh,°   *saw*
Riche and real° and wonder heigh.   *royal*
Al the utemoste° wal   *outmost*
Was cleer° and shined as crystal.   *bright*
An hundred towres ther were aboute,
360 Degiseliche,° and batailed[3] stoute.   *wonderful*
The butres° cam out of the diche   *buttress*
Of reed gold y-arched riche.[4]
The vousour° was anourned° al   *vaulting / adorned*

2. I.e., neither stump nor stone pre-   4. I.e., made of red gold that arched
vented him.   splendidly: gold was commonly described
3. I.e., furnished with battlements.   as red in Middle English.

Of eech manere divers aumal.°   *enamel*
365 Within ther were wide wones,°   *halls*
And alle were fulle of precious stones.
The worste pilar on to biholde
Al it was of burnist golde.
Al that lond was evere light,
370 For when it sholde be therk° and night   *dark*
The riche stones lighte gonne[5]
As brighte as dooth at noon the sonne.
No man may telle ne thinke in thought
The riche werk that ther was wrought.
375 By alle thing him thinkth it is
The proude court of Paradis.
    In this castel the ladies alighte:
He wolde in after, if he mighte.
Orfeo knokketh at the yate:°   *gate*
380 The porter was redy therate
And asked what he wolde have ydo.°   *done*
"Parfay,° ich am a minstrel, lo,   *by faith*
To solace° thy lord with my glee   *delight*
If[6] his sweete wille be."
385 The porter undide the gate anoon
And lete him into the castel goon.
    Than he gan looke aboute al
And seigh,° lying within the wal,   *saw*
Of folk that ther were thider ybrought,
390 And thoughte° dede,° and nere nought:[7]   *seemed / dead*
Some stoode withouten hade,°   *head*
And some none armes hade,
And some thurgh the body hadde wounde,
And some laye woode° ybounde;   *mad*
395 And some armed on horse sete,
And some astrangled as they ete,
And some were in watre adreint,°   *drowned*
And some with fire al forshreint,°   *shriveled*
Wives ther laye on child-bedde,
400 Some dede and some awedde.°   *driven mad*
And wonder fele° ther laye bisides   *many*
Right as they slepte hir undertides.°   *forenoons*
Each was thus in this world ynome,°   *taken*
With° faïrye thider ycome.   *by force of*
405 Ther he seigh his owene wif,
Dame Heurodis, his leve° lif,   *dear*
Sleepe under an impe-tree:
By hir clothes he knew it was she.
    Whan he hadde seen thise mervailes alle
410 He wente into the kinges halle.

5. Did light it.   7. Were not.
6. If it.   8. I.e., an alcove.

Than seigh he ther a seemly sighte:
A tabernacle[8] wel ydight°—   *arrayed*
Hir maister king therinne sete,
And hir queene fair and sweete.
415 Hir crownes, hir clothes shoon so brighte
That unnethe° he biholde hem mighte.   *with difficulty*
   Whan he hadde seen al this thing,
He kneeled adoun bifor the king:
"O lord," he saide, "if thy wil were,
420 My minstracye thou sholdest yheere."°   *hear*
The king answerede, "What man art thou
That art hider ycomen now?
Ich, ne noon that is with me,
Ne sente never after thee.
425 Sith° that ich here regne° gan   *since / reign*
I ne foond° nevere so hardy man   *found*
That hider to us durste wende
But° that ich him wolde ofsende."°   *unless / send for*
"Lord," quath he, "ye trowe° wel   *may believe*
430 I nam but a poore minstrel,
And, sire, it is the maner of us
To seeche many a lordes hous.
And theigh° we not welcome be,   *though*
Yit we mote° profere forth oure glee."°   *must / music*
435   Bifor the king he sat adown
And took his harp so merye of soun,
And tempreth° it as he wel can.   *tunes*
And blisful notes he ther gan
That alle that in the palais were
440 Come to him for to heere,
And lieth adoun to his feete,
Hem thinkth his melodye so sweete.
The king herkneth and sit° ful stille: *sits*
To heere his glee he hath good wille.
445 Good bourde° he hadde of his glee: *entertainment*
The riche queene also hadde she.
   Whan he hadde stint° of his harping,   *ceased*
Then saide to him the riche king,
"Minstrel, me liketh wel thy glee.
450 Now aske of me what it may be—
Largeliche° ich wil thee paye.   *generously*
Now speke and thou might it assaye."
"Sire," he saide, "ich praye thee
That thou woldest yive me
455 The eeche° lady, bright on blee,°   *very / of hue*
That sleepeth under the impe-tree."
"Nay," quath the king, "that nought nere:[9]
A sory couple of you it were;

9. I.e., that wouldn't do.

For thou art lene,° rowe,° and blak, *lean / rough*
460 And she is lovesom, withoute lak.° *blemish*
A loothly thing it were forthy° *therefore*
To seen hire in thy compaigny."
        "O sire," he saide, "gentil king,
Yit were it a wel fouler thing
465 To heere a lesing° of the mouthe. *lie*
So, sire, as ye saide nouthe° *now*
What ich wolde aske, have I wolde,
A kinges word moot° needes be holde." *must*
"Thou sayest sooth," the king saide than,
470 "And sith° I am a trewe man, *since*
I wol wel that it be so:
Taak hire by the hond and go.
Of hire ich wol that thou be blithe."
        He kneeled adown and thanked him swithe;° *quickly*
475 His wif he took by the hond
And dide him swithe out of that lond,
And wente° him out of that thede:° *turned / country*
Right as he cam the way he yede.° *went*
        So longe he hath the way ynome° *taken*
480 To Winchester he is ycome,
That somtime was his owene citee,
But no man knew that it was he.
No forther than the townes ende
For knoweleche[1] he durste wende.
485 But in a beggeres bild° ful narwe° *house / small*
Ther he hath take his herbarwe° *lodging*
(To him and to his owene wife),
As a minstrel of poore lif,
And asked tidinges of that lond,
490 And who the kingdom heeld in hond.
The poore begger in his cote° *hovel*
Tolde him everich° a grote°— *every / bit*
How hir queene was stole awy,° *away*
Ten yeer goon, with° faïry. *by*
495 And how hir king in exile yede° *went*
But no man wiste° in which thede;° *knew / country*
And how the steward the lond gan holde,
And othere many thinges him tolde.
        Amorwe ayain the noon-tide[2]
500 He maked his wif ther abide,
And beggeres clothes he borwed anoon,° *straightaway*
And heeng° his harp his rigge° upon, *hung / back*
And wente him into that citee,
That men mighte him biholde and see.
505 Bothe eerles and barouns bolde,
Burgeis° and ladies him gan biholde: *burgesses*

---

1. I.e., for fear of being recognized.   2. In the morning towards noontime.

"Lord," they saide, "swich° a man!   such
How longe the heer° him hangeth upon!   hair
Lo, how his beerd hangeth to his knee!
510 He is yclungen° also° a tree!"   withered / as
        And as he yede° in the streete,   walked
With his steward he gan meete.
And loude he sette him on a cry,
"Sir steward," he saide, "grant mercy!
515 Ich am an harpour of hethenesse:°   heathen country
Help me now in this distresse."
The steward saide, "Com with me, com:
Of that I have thou shalt have som.
Eech harpour is welcome me to
520 For my lordes love, Sir Orfeo."
        Anoon they wente into the halle,
The steward and the lordes alle.
The steward wessh° and wente to mete,   washed
And manye lordes by him sete.
525 Ther were trumpours° and tabourers,°   trumpeters / drummers
Harpours fele,° and crouders:°   many / fiddlers
Muche melodye they maked alle.
And Orfeo sat stille in halle.
And herkneth; whan they been al stille,
530 He took his harp and tempered° shille°—   played / loudly
The blisfullest notes he harped there
That evere man yherde with ere.
Eech man liked wel his glee.
        The steward looked and gan ysee,
535 And the harp knew also blive.°   right away
"Minstrel," he saide, "so mote° thou thrive,   may
Where haddest thou this harp and how?
I praye that thou me telle now."
        "Lord," quath he, "in uncouthe° thede,°   strange / country
540 Thurgh a foreest as I yede,°   walked
I foond° lying in a dale   found
A man with° lions totorn° smale,   by / torn to bits
And wolves him frette° with teeth so sharp.   bit
By him I foond this eeche° harp   very
545 Wel ten yeer it is ago."
        "O," quath the steward, "now me is wo!
That was my lord Sir Orfeo.
Allas, wrecche, what shal I do
That have swich° a lord ylore?°   such / lost
550 A, way,° that evere ich was ybore°   woe / born
That him was so harde grace y-yarked,°   ordained
And so vile deeth ymarked."°   appointed
Adown he fel aswoone to grounde.
His barouns him tooke up that stounde°   time
555 And telleth him how that it geeth:°   goes

It is no boote° of mannes deeth. — *remedy*
   King Orfeo knew wel by than° — *that*
His steward was a trewe man
And loved him as him oughte to do,
560 And stondeth up and saith thus, "Lo,
Steward, herkne now this thing:
If ich were Orfeo the king
And hadde ysuffered ful yore° — *long*
In wildernesse muche sore,
565 And hadde ywonne my queene awey° — *away*
Out of the lond of faïry,
And hadde ybrought the lady hende° — *gracious*
Right here to the townes ende,
And with a begger hir in°ynome,° — *lodging / taken*
570 And were myselve hider ycome
Poorelich to thee thus stille,° — *secretly*
For to assaye° thy goode wille, — *test*
And° ich founde thee thus trewe, — *if*
Thou ne sholdest it nevere rewe:° — *regret*
575 Sikerliche,° for love or ay,° — *surely / dread*
Thou sholdest be king after my day.
If thou of my deeth haddest been blithe,
Thou sholdest have voided° also swithe." — *been dismissed*
   Tho° alle tho° that therinne sete — *then / those*
580 That is was Orfeo underyete,° — *understood*
And the steward wel him knew:
Over and over the boord° he threw — *table*
And fel adown to his feete.
So dide eech lord that ther sete,
585 And alle they saide at oo° crying, — *one*
"Ye beeth oure lord, sire, and oure king."
Glade they were of his live:
To chambre they ladde him as blive,° — *at once*
And bathed him and shaved his beard,
590 And tired° him as a king apert.° — *dressed / openly*
And sith° with greet processioun — *after*
They broughte the queene into the town,
With alle manere minstracye.
Lord, ther was greet melodye:
595 For joye they wepte with hir yë
That hem so sound° ycomen sye.° — *healthy / saw*
   Now Orfeo newe corouned° is, — *crowned*
And his queene Dame Heurodis,
And lived longe afterward,
600 And sitthen° king was the steward. — *afterward*
   Harpours in Britain after than° — *that*
Herde how this merveile bigan
And made a lay of good liking,° — *well-pleasing*
And nempned° it after the king. — *named*

605 That lay is "Orfeo" yhote:°   °called
    Good is the lay, sweete is the note.
      Thus cam Sir Orfeo out of his care:
    God grante us alle wel to fare.

SIR GAWAIN AND THE GREEN KNIGHT
(ca. 1375–1400)

Nothing is known about the author of *Sir Gawain and the Green Knight* except that he probably wrote the three religious poems (*Patience, Purity,* and *Pearl*) preserved in the same manuscript as *Sir Gawain* (no other copies of any of the poems have come to light); and he may also have written a fifth poem, which, like the others, is alliterative, but is preserved in a different manuscript—a charming legend of St. Erkenwald. The dialect of *Sir Gawain* points to an origin in provincial England, about 150 miles northwest of the capital: thus of the three great poets of late medieval England, two, the authors of *Sir Gawain* and *Piers Plowman,* were representatives of cultural centers remote from the royal court at London where Chaucer spent his life. We know almost nothing about these provincial centers, but the works that emanated from them demonstrate a high level of culture. The poet of *Sir Gawain,* indeed, was a most sophisticated and urbane writer, and even though his language (a dialect most difficult for us today and probably difficult for London men in his own time) and his alliterative measure would have been considered barbaric by Chaucer's London audience, the subtlety of his perceptions and the delicacy with which he handles his narrative is not unworthy of Chaucer himself. And although it is impossible to date the poem with any accuracy, its author must have been an almost exact contemporary of Chaucer.

It is possible that the plot of *Sir Gawain* came ready-made to the poet, who may have found it in some lost French poem or have heard it recited in English—perhaps even in Welsh—in his own country. The motif of the green man's decapitation originates in very ancient folklore, probably in a vegetation myth in which the beheading would have been a ritual death that insured the return of spring to the earth and the regrowth of the crops. But this primitive theme has been entirely rationalized by the late medieval poet, who sees in his inherited plot an opportunity to study how successfully Gawain, as a man wholly dedicated to Christian ideals, maintains those ideals when he is subjected to unusual pressures. The poem is a rare combination: at once a comedy—even a satire—of manners and a profoundly Christian view of man's character and his destiny. The court of King Arthur is presented, in the most grandiose and laudatory of language, as the place where the ideal of chivalry has reached its zenith, where all is courtesy and martial prowess in defense of the right. The praise bestowed by the poet upon this court may seem excessive, and indeed the sequel suggests that the author made it so intentionally. For when the court is invaded by the Green Knight, arrogant, monstrous, and yet exasperatingly reasonable, it suddenly seems to become slightly unreal, as if, the Green Knight insultingly implies, its reputation were founded more on fiction than on fact—as if the poets that celebrated it had been working harder to enhance its glory than the knights themselves. In any case, the court is to receive a testing, which is naturally entrusted to the most courteous and valiant knight of the Round Table (in this most English of Arthurian romances Gawain has not been replaced as the best of knights by the continental-born Lancelot).

Once Gawain has set out to keep his promise to the Green Knight, his humiliation—and by inference that of the court—begins: in describing Gawain's adventures the poet, for all his epic enhancement and overt praise for the hero, actually tells a tale of his increasing helplessness. First of all Gawain's courtesy fails him—not, to be sure, in the sense that he relinquishes it, but in the sense that it involves him in a profoundly embarrassing and dangerous situation with the lady: it results in trouble instead of the serenity that courtesy, as the diplomat's virtue, is supposed to procure. Then the second of his great virtues, his martial prowess, is denied to him by the promise he has made not to defend himself against the Green Knight's return stroke. Thus betrayed by or cut off from the two qualities that he supposes to have made him the splendid knight people think him to be, he also, with very human lack of logic, momentarily cuts himself off from the power that has actually permitted those qualities to flourish in him. For when the pressures increase, St. Mary's knight, no longer able to rely on himself, relies not on St. Mary but on a belt of supposed magical powers, which he must accept from the lady with ignominy and hide from her lord with dishonesty. When the Green Knight spares his life there is revealed to Gawain his own real impoverishment, the complete incapacity of the greatest of Arthur's knights to help himself. He has found that without God's grace the virtues which he has made particularly his own are of no use to him—that, indeed, he no longer possesses them. The poem ends happily; but the baldric that the courtiers wear in honor of Gawain's adventure is a reminder that what God asks of men is not primarily courtly or martial prowess, but a humble and a contrite heart.

This didactic point is made with a most Chaucer-like indirection, a fine irony that strips Gawain of his pretensions but leaves him his charm and shows him sympathy for the really quite unfair nature of his predicament—and which also enjoys, and makes the reader enjoy, the embarrassment the hero is made to suffer. *Sir Gawain* is one of the latest and certainly the best of the Middle English romances; yet its greatness lies in the fact that, without ever ceasing to be a romance, a fiction full of the most exquisite comic touches, it is something much larger, one of the really significant literary achievements of the Middle Ages.

Sir Gawain and the Green Knight [1]

Part I

Since the siege and the assault was ceased at Troy,
The walls breached and burnt down to brands and ashes,
The knight that had knotted the nets of deceit
Was impeached for his perfidy, proven most true, [2]
It was high-born Aeneas and his haughty race   5
That since prevailed over provinces, and proudly reigned
Over well-nigh all the wealth of the West Isles. [3]
Great Romulus [4] to Rome repairs in haste;
With boast and with bravery builds he that city
And names it with his own name, that it now bears.   10
Ticius [5] to Tuscany, and towers raises,
Langobard in Lombardy lays out homes,
And far over the French Sea, Felix Brutus [6]
On many broad hills and high Britain he sets,
           most fair.   15
      Where war and wrack and wonder
      By shifts have sojourned there,
      And bliss by turns with blunder
      In that land's lot had share.

And since this Britain was built by this baron great,   20
Bold boys bred there, in broils delighting,
That did in their day many a deed most dire.
More marvels have happened in this merry land
Than in any other I know, since that olden time,
But of those that here built, of British kings,   25
King Arthur was counted most courteous of all,
Wherefore an adventure I aim to unfold,
That a marvel of might some men think it,
And one unmatched among Arthur's wonders.
If you will listen to my lay but a little while,   30
As I heard it in hall, I shall hasten to tell
           anew.
      As it was fashioned featly
      In tale of derring-do,
      And linked in measures meetly   35
      By letters tried and true.

1. The Modern English translation is by Marie Borroff (1967), who has reproduced the alliterative meter of the original as well as the "bob and wheel," the five-line rhyming group that concludes each of the long irregular stanzas. 2. The treacherous knight is either Aeneas himself or Antenor, both of whom were, according to medieval tradition, traitors to their city Troy; but Aeneas was actually tried ("impeached") by the Greeks for his refusal to hand over to them his sister Polyxena. 3. Perhaps western Europe. 4. The legendary founder of Rome is here given Trojan ancestry, like Aeneas. 5. Not otherwise known. "Langobard" was the reputed founder of Lombardy. 6. Great-grandson of Aeneas and legendary founder of Britain; not elsewhere given the name Felix (Latin "happy").

This king lay at Camelot [7] at Christmastide;
Many good knights and gay his guests were there,
Arrayed of the Round Table [8] rightful brothers,
With feasting and fellowship and carefree mirth.   40
There true men contended in tournaments many,
Joined there in jousting these gentle knights,
Then came to the court for carol-dancing,
For the feast was in force full fifteen days,
With all the meat and the mirth that men could devise,   45
Such gaiety and glee, glorious to hear,
Brave din by day, dancing by night.
High were their hearts in halls and chambers,
These lords and these ladies, for life was sweet.
In peerless pleasures passed they their days,   50
The most noble knights known under Christ,
And the loveliest ladies that lived on earth ever,
And he the comeliest king, that that court holds,
For all this fair folk in their first age
          were still.   55
        Happiest of mortal kind,
        King noblest famed of will;
        You would now go far to find
        So hardy a host on hill.

While the New Year was new, but yesternight come,   60
This fair folk at feast two-fold was served,
When the king and his company were come in together,
The chanting in chapel achieved and ended.
Clerics and all the court acclaimed the glad season,
Cried Noel anew, good news to men;   65
Then gallants gather gaily, hand-gifts to make,
Called them out clearly, claimed them by hand,
Bickered long and busily about those gifts.
Ladies laughed aloud, though losers they were,
And he that won was not angered, as well you will know. [9]   70
All this mirth they made until meat was served;
When they had washed them worthily, they went to their seats,
The best seated above, as best it beseemed,
Guenevere the goodly queen gay in the midst
On a dais well-decked and duly arrayed   75
With costly silk curtains, a canopy over,
Of Toulouse and Turkestan tapestries rich,
All broidered and bordered with the best gems
Ever brought into Britain, with bright pennies
        to pay.   80

7. Capital of Arthur's kingdom, presumably located in southwest England or southern Wales.
8. According to legend, Merlin made the Round Table after a dispute broke out among Arthur's knights about precedence: it seated 100 knights. The table described in the poem is not round.
9. The dispensing of New Year's gifts seems to have involved kissing.

Fair queen, without a flaw,
She glanced with eyes of grey.
A seemlier that once he saw,
In truth, no man could say.

But Arthur would not eat till all were served;   85
So light was his lordly heart, and a little boyish;
His life he liked lively—the less he cared
To be lying for long, or long to sit,
So busy his young blood, his brain so wild.
And also a point of pride pricked him in heart,   90
For he nobly had willed, he would never eat
On so high a holiday, till he had heard first
Of some fair feat or fray some far-borne tale,
Of some marvel of might, that he might trust,
By champions of chivalry achieved in arms,   95
Or some suppliant came seeking some single knight
To join with him in jousting, in jeopardy each
To lay life for life, and leave it to fortune
To afford him on field fair hap or other.
Such is the king's custom, when his court he holds   100
At each far-famed feast amid his fair host
              so dear.
       The stout king stands in state
       Till a wonder shall appear;
       He leads, with heart elate,   105
       High mirth in the New Year.

So he stands there in state, the stout young king,
Talking before the high table [1] of trifles fair.
There Gawain the good knight by Guenevere sits,
With Agravain à la dure main on her other side,   110
Both knights of renown, and nephews of the king.
Bishop Baldwin above begins the table,
And Yvain, son of Urien, ate with him there.
These few with the fair queen were fittingly served;
At the side-tables sat many stalwart knights.   115
Then the first course comes, with clamor of trumpets
That were bravely bedecked with bannerets bright,
With noise of new drums and the noble pipes.
Wild were the warbles that wakened that day
In strains that stirred many strong men's hearts.   120
There dainties were dealt out, dishes rare,
Choice fare to choose, on chargers so many
That scarce was there space to set before the people
The service of silver, with sundry meats,
              on cloth.   125
       Each fair guest freely there
       Partakes, and nothing loth;

1. The high table is on a dais; the side   and run along the walls at a right angle
tables (line 115) are on the main floor   with the high table.

Twelve dishes before each pair;
Good beer and bright wine both.

Of the service itself I need say no more,   130
For well you will know no tittle was wanting.
Another noise and a new was well-nigh at hand,
That the lord might have leave his life to nourish;
For scarce were the sweet strains still in the hall,
And the first course come to that company fair,   135
There hurtles in at the hall-door an unknown rider,
One the greatest on ground in growth of his frame:
From broad neck to buttocks so bulky and thick,
And his loins and his legs so long and so great,
Half a giant on earth I hold him to be,   140
But believe him no less than the largest of men,
And that the seemliest in his stature to see, as he rides,
For in back and in breast though his body was grim,
His waist in its width was worthily small,
And formed with every feature in fair accord   145
             was he.
        Great wonder grew in hall
        At his hue most strange to see,
        For man and gear and all
        Were green as green could be.   150

And in guise all of green, the gear and the man:
A coat cut close, that clung to his sides,
And a mantle to match, made with a lining
Of furs cut and fitted—the fabric was noble,
Embellished all with ermine, and his hood beside,   155
That was loosed from his locks, and laid on his shoulders.
With trim hose and tight, the same tint of green,
His great calves were girt, and gold spurs under
He bore on silk bands that embellished his heels,
And footgear well-fashioned, for riding most fit.   160
And all his vesture verily was verdant green;
Both the bosses on his belt and other bright gems
That were richly ranged on his raiment noble
About himself and his saddle, set upon silk,
That to tell half the trifles would tax my wits,   165
The butterflies and birds embroidered thereon
In green of the gayest, with many a gold thread.
The pendants of the breast-band, the princely crupper,
And the bars of the bit were brightly enameled;
The stout stirrups were green, that steadied his feet,   170
And the bows of the saddle and the side-panels both,
That gleamed all and glinted with green gems about.
The steed he bestrides of that same green
             so bright.
        A green horse great and thick;   175
        A headstrong steed of might;

> In broidered bridle quick,
> Mount matched man aright.

Gay was this goodly man in guise all of green,
And the hair of his head to his horse suited;   180
Fair flowing tresses enfold his shoulders;
A beard big as a bush on his breast hangs,
That with his heavy hair, that from his head falls,
Was evened all about above both his elbows,
That half his arms thereunder were hid in the fashion   185
Of a king's cap-à-dos,[2] that covers his throat.
The mane of that mighty horse much to it like,
Well curled and becombed, and cunningly knotted
With filaments of fine gold amid the fair green,
Here a strand of the hair, here one of gold;   190
His tail and his foretop twin in their hue,
And bound both with a band of a bright green
That was decked adown the dock with dazzling stones
And tied tight at the top with a triple knot
Where many bells well burnished rang bright and clear.   195
Such a mount in his might, nor man on him riding,
None had seen, I dare swear, with sight in that hall
> so grand.
>> As lightning quick and light
>> He looked to all at hand;   200
>> It seemed that no man might
>> His deadly dints withstand.

Yet had he no helm, nor hauberk neither,
Nor plate, nor appurtenance appending to arms,
Nor shaft pointed sharp, nor shield for defense,   205
But in his one hand he had a holly bob
That is goodliest in green when groves are bare,
And an ax in his other, a huge and immense,
A wicked piece of work in words to expound:
The head on its haft was an ell long;   210
The spike of green steel, resplendent with gold;
The blade burnished bright, with a broad edge,
As well shaped to shear as a sharp razor;
'Stout was the stave in the strong man's gripe,
That was wound all with iron to the weapon's end,   215
With engravings in green of goodliest work.
A lace lightly about, that led to a knot,
Was looped in by lengths along the fair haft,
And tassels thereto attached in a row,
With buttons of bright green, brave to behold.   220
This horseman hurtles in, and the hall enters;

---

2. The word *capados* occurs in this form in Middle English only in *Gawain*, here and in line 572. The translator has interpreted it, as the poet apparently did also, as *cap-à-dos*—i.e., a garment covering its wearer "from head to back," on the model of *cap-à-pie*, "from head to foot," referring to armor.

Riding to the high dais, recked he no danger;
Not a greeting he gave as the guests he o'erlooked,
Nor wasted his words, but "Where is," he said,
"The captain of this crowd? Keenly I wish   225
To see that sire with sight, and to himself say
                    my say."
                He swaggered all about
                To scan the host so gay;
                He halted, as if in doubt   230
                Who in that hall held sway.

There were stares on all sides as the stranger spoke,
For much did they marvel what it might mean
That a horseman and a horse should have such a hue,
Grow green as the grass, and greener, it seemed,   235
Than green fused on gold more glorious by far.
All the onlookers eyed him, and edged nearer,
And awaited in wonder what he would do,
For many sights had they seen, but such a one never,
So that phantom and faerie the folk there deemed it,   240
Therefore chary of answer was many a champion bold,
And stunned at his strong words stone-still they sat
In a swooning silence in the stately hall.
As all were slipped into sleep, so slackened their speech
                    apace.   245
                Not all, I think, for dread,
                But some of courteous grace
                Let him who was their head
                Be spokesman in that place.

Then Arthur before the high dais that entrance beholds,   250
And hailed him, as behooved, for he had no fear,
And said "Fellow, in faith you have found fair welcome;
The head of this hostelry Arthur am I;
Leap lightly down, and linger, I pray,
And the tale of your intent you shall tell us after."   255
"Nay, so help me," said the other, "He that on high sits,
To tarry here any time, 'twas not mine errand;
But as the praise of you, prince, is puffed up so high,
And your court and your company are counted the best,
Stoutest under steel-gear on steeds to ride,   260
Worthiest of their works the wide world over,
And peerless to prove in passages of arms,
And courtesy here is carried to its height,
And so at this season I have sought you out.
You may be certain by the branch that I bear in hand   265
That I pass here in peace, and would part friends,
For had I come to this court on combat bent,
I have a hauberk at home, and a helm beside,
A shield and a sharp spear, shining bright,

And other weapons to wield, I ween well, to boot,   270
But as I willed no war, I wore no metal.
But if you be so bold as all men believe,
You will graciously grant the game that I ask
               by right."
           Arthur answer gave   275
           And said, "Sir courteous knight,
           If contest here you crave,
           You shall not fail to fight."

"Nay, to fight, in good faith, is far from my thought;
There are about on these benches but beardless children,   280
Were I here in full arms on a haughty steed,
For measured against mine, their might is puny.
And so I call in this court for a Christmas game,
For 'tis Yule and New Year, and many young bloods about;
If any in this house such hardihood claims,   285
Be so bold in his blood, his brain so wild,
As stoutly to strike one stroke for another,
I shall give him as my gift this gisarme noble,
This ax, that is heavy enough, to handle as he likes,
And I shall bide the first blow, as bare as I sit.   290
If there be one so wilful my words to assay,
Let him leap hither lightly, lay hold of this weapon;
I quitclaim it forever, keep it as his own,
And I shall stand him a stroke, steady on this floor,
So you grant me the guerdon to give him another,   295
               sans blame.
           In a twelvemonth and a day
           He shall have of me the same;
           Now be it seen straightway
           Who dares take up the game."   300

If he astonished them at first, stiller were then
All that household in hall, the high and the low;
The stranger on his green steed stirred in the saddle,
And roisterously his red eyes he rolled all about,
Bent his bristling brows, that were bright green,   305
Wagged his beard as he watched who would arise.
When the court kept its counsel he coughed aloud,
And cleared his throat coolly, the clearer to speak:
"What, is this Arthur's house," said that horseman then,
"Whose fame is so fair in far realms and wide?   310
Where is now your arrogance and your awesome deeds,
Your valor and your victories and your vaunting words?
Now are the revel and renown of the Round Table
Overwhelmed with a word of one man's speech,
For all cower and quake, and no cut felt!"   315
With this he laughs so loud that the lord grieved;
The blood for sheer shame shot to his face,
               and pride.

With rage his face flushed red,
And so did all beside.
Then the king as bold man bred
Toward the stranger took a stride.   320

And said "Sir, now we see you will say but folly,
Which whoso has sought, it suits that he find.
No guest here is aghast of your great words.   325
Give to me your gisarme, in God's own name,
And the boon you have begged shall straight be granted."
He leaps to him lightly, lays hold of his weapon;
The green fellow on foot fiercely alights.
Now has Arthur his ax, and the haft grips,   330
And sternly stirs it about, on striking bent.
The stranger before him stood there erect,
Higher than any in the house by a head and more;
With stern look as he stood, he stroked his beard,
And with undaunted countenance drew down his coat,   335
No more moved nor dismayed for his mighty dints
Than any bold man on bench had brought him a drink
                    of wine.
            Gawain by Guenevere
            Toward the king doth now incline: 340
            "I beseech, before all here,
            That this melee may be mine."

"Would you grant me the grace," said Gawain to the king,
"To be gone from this bench and stand by you there,
If I without discourtesy might quit this board,   345
And if my liege lady misliked it not,
I would come to your counsel before your court noble.
For I find it not fit, as in faith it is known,
When such a boon is begged before all these knights,
Though you be tempted thereto, to take it on yourself 350
While so bold men about upon benches sit,
That no host under heaven is hardier of will,
Nor better brothers-in-arms where battle is joined;
I am the weakest, well I know, and of wit feeblest;
And the loss of my life would be least of any;   355
That I have you for uncle is my only praise;
My body, but for your blood, is barren of worth;
And for that this folly befits not a king,
And 'tis I that have asked it, it ought to be mine,
And if my claim be not comely let all this court judge, 360
                    in sight."
                The court assays the claim,
                And in counsel all unite
                To give Gawain the game
                And release the king outright.   365

Then the king called the knight to come to his side,

And he rose up readily, and reached him with speed,
Bows low to his lord, lays hold of the weapon,
And he releases it lightly, and lifts up his hand,
And gives him God's blessing, and graciously prays   370
That his heart and his hand may be hardy both.
"Keep, cousin," said the king, "what you cut with this day,
And if you rule it aright, then readily, I know,
You shall stand the stroke it will strike after."
Gawain goes to the guest with gisarme in hand,   375
And boldly he bides there, abashed not a whit.
Then hails he Sir Gawain, the horseman in green:
"Recount we our contract, ere you come further.
First I ask and adjure you, how you are called
That you tell me true, so that trust it I may."   380
"In good faith," said the good knight, "Gawain am I
Whose buffet befalls you, whate'er betide after,
And at this time twelvemonth take from you another
With what weapon you will, and with no man else
         alive."   385
      The other nods assent:
      "Sir Gawain, as I may thrive,
      I am wondrous well content
      That you this dint shall drive."

"Sir Gawain," said the Green Knight, "By God, I rejoice   390
That your fist shall fetch this favor I seek,
And you have readily rehearsed, and in right terms,
Each clause of my covenant with the king your lord,
Save that you shall assure me, sir, upon oath,
That you shall seek me yourself, wheresoever you deem   395
My lodgings may lie, and look for such wages
As you have offered me here before all this host."
"What is the way there?" said Gawain, "Where do you dwell?
I heard never of your house, by Him that made me,
Nor I know you not, knight, your name nor your court.   400
But tell me truly thereof, and teach me your name,
And I shall fare forth to find you, so far as I may,
And this I say in good certain, and swear upon oath."
"That is enough in New Year, you need say no more,"
Said the knight in the green to Gawain the noble,   405
"If I tell you true, when I have taken your knock,
And if you handily have hit, you shall hear straightway
Of my house and my home and my own name;
Then follow in my footsteps by faithful accord.
And if I spend no speech, you shall speed the better: 410
You can feast with your friends, nor further trace
        my tracks.
      Now hold your grim tool steady
      And show us how it hacks."
      "Gladly, sir; all ready,"   415
      Says Gawain; he strokes the ax.

The Green Knight upon ground girds him with care:
Bows a bit with his head, and bares his flesh:
His long lovely locks he laid over his crown,
Let the naked nape for the need be shown.   420
Gawain grips to his ax and gathers it aloft—
The left foot on the floor before him he set—
Brought it down deftly upon the bare neck,
That the shock of the sharp blow shivered the bones
And cut the flesh cleanly and clove it in twain,   425
That the blade of bright steel bit into the ground.
The head was hewn off and fell to the floor;
Many found it at their feet, as forth it rolled;
The blood gushed from the body, bright on the green,
Yet fell not the fellow, nor faltered a whit,   430
But stoutly he starts forth upon stiff shanks,
And as all stood staring he stretched forth his hand,
Laid hold of his head and heaved it aloft,
Then goes to the green steed, grasps the bridle,
Steps into the stirrup, bestrides his mount,   435
And his head by the hair in his hand holds,
And as steady he sits in the stately saddle
As he had met with no mishap, nor missing were
                    his head.
          His bulk about he haled,   440
          That fearsome body that bled;
          There were many in the court that quailed
          Before all his say was said.

For the head in his hand he holds right up;
Toward the first on the dais directs he the face,   445
And it lifted up its lids, and looked with wide eyes,
And said as much with its mouth as now you may hear:
"Sir Gawain, forget not to go as agreed,
And cease not to seek till me, sir, you find,
As you promised in the presence of these proud knights.   450
To the Green Chapel come, I charge you, to take
Such a dint as you have dealt—you have well deserved
That your neck should have a knock on New Year's morn.
The Knight of the Green Chapel I am well-known to many,
Wherefore you cannot fail to find me at last;   455
Therefore come, or be counted a recreant knight."
With a roisterous rush he flings round the reins,
Hurtles out at the hall-door, his head in his hand,
That the flint-fire flew from the flashing hooves.
Which way he went, not one of them knew   460
Nor whence he was come in the wide world
                    so fair.
          The king and Gawain gay
          Make game of the Green Knight there,
          Yet all who saw it say   465
          'Twas a wonder past compare.

Though high-born Arthur at heart had wonder,
He let no sign be seen, but said aloud
To the comely queen, with courteous speech,
"Dear dame, on this day dismay you no whit;   470
Such crafts are becoming at Christmastide,
Laughing at interludes, light songs and mirth,
Amid dancing of damsels with doughty knights.
Nevertheless of my meat now let me partake,
For I have met with a marvel, I may not deny."   475
He glanced at Sir Gawain, and gaily he said,
"Now, sir, hang up your ax, that has hewn enough,"
And over the high dais it was hung on the wall
That men in amazement might on it look,
And tell in true terms the tale of the wonder.   480
Then they turned toward the table, these two together,
The good king and Gawain, and made great feast,
With all dainties double, dishes rare,
With all manner of meat and minstrelsy both,
Such happiness wholly had they that day   485
                    in hold.
          Now take care, Sir Gawain,
          That your courage wax not cold
          When you must turn again
          To your enterprise foretold.   490

Part II

This adventure had Arthur of handsels first
When young was the year, for he yearned to hear tales;
Though they wanted for words when they went to sup,
Now are fierce deeds to follow, their fists stuffed full.
Gawain was glad to begin those games in hall,   495
But if the end be harsher, hold it no wonder,
For though men are merry in mind after much drink,
A year passes apace, and proves ever new:
First things and final conform but seldom.
And so this Yule to the young year yielded place,   500
And each season ensued at its set time;
After Christmas there came the cold cheer of Lent,
When with fish and plainer fare our flesh we reprove;
But then the world's weather with winter contends:
The keen cold lessens, the low clouds lift;   505
Fresh falls the rain in fostering showers
On the face of the fields; flowers appear.
The ground and the groves wear gowns of green;
Birds build their nests, and blithely sing
That solace of all sorrow with summer comes   510
                    ere long.
          And blossoms day by day

Bloom rich and rife in throng;
Then every grove so gay
Of the greenwood rings with song.   515

And then the season of summer with the soft winds,
When Zephyr sighs low over seeds and shoots;
Glad is the green plant growing abroad,
When the dew at dawn drops from the leaves,
To get a gracious glance from the golden sun.   520
But harvest with harsher winds follows hard after,
Warns him to ripen well ere winter comes;
Drives forth the dust in the droughty season,
From the face of the fields to fly high in air.
Wroth winds in the welkin wrestle with the sun,   525
The leaves launch from the linden and light on the ground,
And the grass turns to gray, that once grew green.
Then all ripens and rots that rose up at first,
And so the year moves on in yesterdays many,
And winter once more, by the world's law,   530
                    draws nigh.
                At Michaelmas [3] the moon
                Hangs wintry pale in sky;
                Sir Gawain girds him soon
                For travails yet to try.   535

Till All-Hallows' Day [4] with Arthur he dwells,
And he held a high feast to honor that knight
With great revels and rich, of the Round Table.
Then ladies lovely and lords debonair
With sorrow for Sir Gawain were sore at heart;   540
Yet they covered their care with countenance glad:
Many a mournful man made mirth for his sake.
So after supper soberly he speaks to his uncle
Of the hard hour at hand, and openly says,
"Now, liege lord of my life, my leave I take;   545
The terms of this task too well you know—
To count the cost over concerns me nothing.
But I am bound forth betimes to bear a stroke
From the grim man in green, as God may direct."
Then the first and foremost came forth in throng: 550
Yvain and Eric and others of note,
Sir Dodinal le Sauvage, the Duke of Clarence,
Lionel and Lancelot and Lucan the good,
Sir Bors and Sir Bedivere, big men both,
And many manly knights more, with Mador de la Porte.   555
All this courtly company comes to the king
To counsel their comrade, with care in their hearts;
There was much secret sorrow suffered that day
That one so good as Gawain must go in such wise

3. September 29.   4. All Saints' Day, November 1.

To bear a bitter blow, and his bright sword   560
                              lay by.
              He said, "Why should I tarry?"
              And smiled with tranquil eye;
              "In destinies sad or merry,
              True men can but try."   565

He dwelt there all that day, and dressed in the morning;
Asked early for his arms, and all were brought.
First a carpet of rare cost was cast on the floor
Where much goodly gear gleamed golden bright;
He takes his place promptly and picks up the steel,   570
Attired in a tight coat of Turkestan silk
And a kingly cap-à-dos, closed at the throat,
That was lavishly lined with a lustrous fur.
Then they set the steel shoes on his sturdy feet
And clad his calves about with comely greaves,   575
And plate well-polished protected his knees,
Affixed with fastenings of the finest gold.
Fair cuisses enclosed, that were cunningly wrought,
His thick-thewed thighs, with thongs bound fast,
And massy chain-mail of many a steel ring   580
He bore on his body, above the best cloth,
With brace burnished bright upon both his arms,
Good couters and gay, and gloves of plate,
And all the goodly gear to grace him well
                              that tide.   585
              His surcoat blazoned bold;
              Sharp spurs to prick with pride;
              And a brave silk band to hold
              The broadsword at his side.

When he had on his arms, his harness was rich,   590
The least latchet or loop laden with gold;
So armored as he was, he heard a mass,
Honored God humbly at the high altar.
Then he comes to the king and his comrades-in-arms,
Takes his leave at last of lords and ladies,   595
And they clasped and kissed him, commending him to Christ.
By then Gringolet was girt with a great saddle
That was gaily agleam with fine gilt fringe,
New-furbished for the need with nail-heads bright;
The bridle and the bars bedecked all with gold;   600
The breast-plate, the saddlebow, the side-panels both,
The caparison and the crupper accorded in hue,
And all ranged on the red the resplendent studs
That glittered and glowed like the glorious sun.
His helm now he holds up and hastily kisses,   605
Well-closed with iron clinches, and cushioned within;

It was high on his head, with a hasp behind,
And a covering of cloth to encase the visor,
All bound and embroidered with the best gems
On broad bands of silk, and bordered with birds, 610
Parrots and popinjays preening their wings,
Lovebirds and love-knots as lavishly wrought
As many women had worked seven winters thereon,
           entire.
      The diadem costlier yet 615
      That crowned that comely sire,
      With diamonds richly set,
      That flashed as if on fire.

Then they showed forth the shield, that shone all red,
With the pentangle [5] portrayed in purest gold. 620
About his broad neck by the baldric he casts it,
That was meet for the man, and matched him well.
And why the pentangle is proper to that peerless prince
I intend now to tell, though detain me it must.
It is a sign by Solomon sagely devised 625
To be a token of truth, by its title of old,
For it is a figure formed of five points,
And each line is linked and locked with the next
For ever and ever, and hence it is called
In all England, as I hear, the endless knot. 630
And well may he wear it on his worthy arms,
For ever faithful five-fold in five-fold fashion
Was Gawain in good works, as gold unalloyed,
Devoid of all villainy, with virtues adorned
           in sight. 635
      On shield and coat in view
      He bore that emblem bright,
      As to his word most true
      And in speech most courteous knight.

And first, he was faultless in his five senses, 640
Nor found ever to fail in his five fingers,
And all his fealty was fixed upon the five wounds
That Christ got on the cross, as the creed tells;
And wherever this man in melee took part,
His one thought was of this, past all things else, 645
That all his force was founded on the five joys [6]
That the high Queen of heaven had in her child.
And therefore, as I find, he fittingly had
On the inner part of his shield her image portrayed,
That when his look on it lighted, he never lost heart. 650
The fifth of the five fives followed by this knight

5. A five-pointed star, formed by five
lines which are drawn without lifting
the pencil from the paper, supposed to
have mystical significance; as Solomon's
sign (line 625) it was enclosed in a
circle.
6. The Annunciation, Nativity, Resurrection, Ascension, and Assumption.

Were beneficence boundless and brotherly love
And pure mind and manners, that none might impeach,
And compassion most precious—these peerless five
Were forged and made fast in him, foremost of men. 655
Now all these five fives were confirmed in this knight,
And each linked in other, that end there was none,
And fixed to five points, whose force never failed,
Nor assembled all on a side, nor asunder either,
Nor anywhere at an end, but whole and entire 660
However the pattern proceeded or played out its course.
And so on his shining shield shaped was the knot
Royally in <u>red gold</u> against <u>red gules</u>,
That is the peerless pentangle, <u>prized of old</u>
<u>in lore</u>. 665

        Now armed is Gawain gay,
        And bears his lance before,
        And soberly said good day,
        He thought forevermore.

He struck his steed with the spurs and sped on his way 670
So fast that the flint-fire flashed from the stones.
When they saw him set forth they were sore aggrieved,
And all sighed softly, and said to each other,
Fearing for their fellow, "Ill fortune it is
That you, man, must be marred, that most are worthy! 675
His equal on this earth can hardly be found;
To have dealt more discreetly had done less harm,
And have dubbed him a duke, with all due honor.
A great leader of lords he was like to become,
And better so to have been than battered to bits, 680
Beheaded by an elf-man,[7] for empty pride!
Who would credit that a king could be counseled so,
And caught in a cavil in a Christmas game?"
Many were the warm tears they wept from their eyes
When goodly Sir Gawain was gone from the court 685
        that day.
        No longer he abode,
        But speedily went his way
        Over many a wandering road,
        As I heard my author say. 690

Now he rides in his array through the realm of Logres,[8]
Sir Gawain, God knows, though it gave him small joy!
All alone must he lodge through many a long night
Where the food that he fancied was far from his plate;
He had no mate but his mount, over mountain and plain, 695
Nor man to say his mind to but almighty God,
Till he had wandered well-nigh into North Wales.
All the islands of Anglesey he holds on his left,

---

7. Supernatural being.
8. One of the names for Arthur's kingdom.

And follows, as he fares, the fords by the coast,
Comes over at Holy Head, and enters next   700
The Wilderness of Wirral 9—few were within
That had great good will toward God or man.
And earnestly he asked of each mortal he met
If he had ever heard aught of a knight all green,
Or of a Green Chapel, on ground thereabouts,   705
And all said the same, and solemnly swore
They saw no such knight all solely green
               in hue.
       Over country wild and strange
       The knight sets off anew;   710
       Often his course must change
       Ere the Chapel comes in view.

Many a cliff must he climb in country wild;
Far off from all his friends, forlorn must he ride;
At each strand or stream where the stalwart passed   715
'Twere a marvel if he met not some monstrous foe,
And that so fierce and forbidding that fight he must.
So many were the wonders he wandered among
That to tell but the tenth part would tax my wits.
Now with serpents he wars, now with savage wolves,   720
Now with wild men of the woods, that watched from the rocks,
Both with bulls and with bears, and with boars besides,
And giants that came gibbering from the jagged steeps.
Had he not borne himself bravely, and been on God's side,
He had met with many mishaps and mortal harms.   725
And if the wars were unwelcome, the winter was worse,
When the cold clear rains rushed from the clouds
And froze before they could fall to the frosty earth.
Near slain by the sleet he sleeps in his irons
More nights than enough, among naked rocks,   730
Where clattering from the crest the cold stream ran
And hung in hard icicles high overhead.
Thus in peril and pain and predicaments dire
He rides across country till Christmas Eve,
             our knight.   735
       And at that holy tide
       He prays with all his might
       That Mary may be his guide
       Till a dwelling comes in sight.

By a mountain next morning he makes his way   740
Into a forest fastness, fearsome and wild;
High hills on either hand, with hoar woods below,
Oaks old and huge by the hundred together.
The hazel and the hawthorn were all intertwined

---

9. Gawain went from Camelot north to
the northern coast of Wales, opposite
the islands of Anglesey; there he turned
east across the Dee to the forest of
Wirral in Chesire.

With rough raveled moss, that raggedly hung,   745
With many birds unblithe upon bare twigs
That peeped most piteously for pain of the cold.
The good knight on Gringolet glides thereunder
Through many a marsh and mire, a man all alone;
He feared for his default, should he fail to see   750
The service of that Sire that on that same night
Was born of a bright maid, to bring us His peace.
And therefore sighing he said, "I beseech of Thee, Lord,
And Mary, thou mildest mother so dear,
Some harborage where haply I might hear mass   755
And Thy matins tomorrow—meekly I ask it,
And thereto proffer and pray my pater and ave
                    and creed."
                    He said his prayer with sighs,
                    Lamenting his misdeed;   760
                    He crosses himself, and cries
                    On Christ in his great need.

No sooner had Sir Gawain signed himself thrice
Than he was ware, in the wood, of a wondrous dwelling,
Within a moat, on a mound, bright amid boughs   765
Of many a tree great of girth that grew by the water—
A castle as comely as a knight could own,
On grounds fair and green, in a goodly park
With a palisade of palings planted about
For two miles and more, round many a fair tree.   770
The stout knight stared at that stronghold great
As it shimmered and shone amid shining leaves,
Then with helmet in hand he offers his thanks
To Jesus and Saint Julian,[1] that are gentle both,
That in courteous accord had inclined to his prayer;   775
"Now fair harbor," said he, "I humbly beseech!"
Then he pricks his proud steed with the plated spurs,
And by chance he has chosen the chief path
That brought the bold knight to the bridge's end
                    in haste.   780
                    The bridge hung high in air;
                    The gates were bolted fast;
                    The walls well-framed to bear
                    The fury of the blast.

The man on his mount remained on the bank   785
Of the deep double moat that defended the place.
The wall went in the water wondrous deep,
And a long way aloft it loomed overhead.
It was built of stone blocks to the battlements' height,
With corbels under cornices in comeliest style;   790
Watch-towers trusty protected the gate,

1. Patron saint of hospitality.

With many a lean loophole, to look from within:
A better-made barbican the knight beheld never.
And behind it there hoved a great hall and fair:
Turrets rising in tiers, with tines [2] at their tops,   795
Spires set beside them, splendidly long,
With finials [3] well-fashioned, as filigree fine.
Chalk-white chimneys over chambers high
Gleamed in gay array upon gables and roofs;
The pinnacles in panoply, pointing in air,   800
So vied there for his view that verily it seemed
A castle cut of paper for a king's feast.
The good knight on Gringolet thought it great luck
If he could but contrive to come there within
To keep the Christmas feast in that castle fair   805
     and bright.
    There answered to his call
    A porter most polite;
    From his station on the wall
    He greets the errant knight.   810

"Good sir," said Gawain, "Wouldst go to inquire
If your lord would allow me to lodge here a space?"
"Peter!" said the porter, "For my part, I think
So noble a knight will not want for a welcome!"
Then he bustles off briskly, and comes back straight,   815
And many servants beside, to receive him the better.
They let down the drawbridge and duly went forth
And kneeled down on their knees on the naked earth
To welcome this warrior as best they were able.
They proffered him passage—the portals stood wide—   820
And he beckoned them to rise, and rode over the bridge.
Men steadied his saddle as he stepped to the ground,
And there stabled his steed many stalwart folk.
Now come the knights and the noble squires
To bring him with bliss into the bright hall.   825
When his high helm was off, there hied forth a throng
Of attendants to take it, and see to its care;
They bore away his brand and his blazoned shield;
Then graciously he greeted those gallants each one,
And many a noble drew near, to do the knight honor.   830
All in his armor into hall he was led,
Where fire on a fair hearth fiercely blazed.
And soon the lord himself descends from his chamber
To meet with good manners the man on his floor.
He said, "To this house you are heartily welcome: 835
What is here is wholly yours, to have in your power
     and sway."
    "Many thanks," said Sir Gawain;
    "May Christ your pains repay!"

---

2. Spikes.   3. Gable ornaments.

> The two embrace amain   840
> As men well met that day.

Gawain gazed on the host that greeted him there,
And a lusty fellow he looked, the lord of that place:
A man of massive mold, and of middle age;
Broad, bright was his beard, of a beaver's hue,   845
Strong, steady his stance, upon stalwart shanks,
His face fierce as fire, fair-spoken withal,
And well-suited he seemed in Sir Gawain's sight
To be a master of men in a mighty keep.
They pass into a parlor, where promptly the host   850
Has a servant assigned him to see to his needs,
And there came upon his call many courteous folk
That brought him to a bower where bedding was noble,
With heavy silk hangings hemmed all in gold,
Coverlets and counterpanes curiously wrought,   855
A canopy over the couch, clad all with fur,
Curtains running on cords, caught to gold rings,
Woven rugs on the walls of eastern work,
And the floor, under foot, well-furnished with the same.
With light talk and laughter they loosed from him then   860
His war-dress of weight and his worthy clothes.
Robes richly wrought they brought him right soon,
To change there in chamber and choose what he would.
When he had found one he fancied, and flung it about,
Well-fashioned for his frame, with flowing skirts,   865
His face fair and fresh as the flowers of spring,
All the good folk agreed, that gazed on him then,
His limbs arrayed royally in radiant hues,
That so comely a mortal never Christ made
> as he.   870
> Whatever his place of birth,
> It seemed he well might be
> Without a peer on earth
> In martial rivalry.

A couch before the fire, where fresh coals burned,   875
They spread for Sir Gawain splendidly now
With quilts quaintly stitched, and cushions beside,
And then a costly cloak they cast on his shoulders
Of bright silk, embroidered on borders and hems,
With furs of the finest well-furnished within,   880
And bound about with ermine, both mantle and hood;
And he sat at that fireside in sumptuous estate
And warmed himself well, and soon he waxed merry.
Then attendants set a table upon trestles broad,
And lustrous white linen they laid thereupon,   885
A saltcellar of silver, spoons of the same.
He washed himself well and went to his place,
Men set his fare before him in fashion most fit.

There were soups of all sorts, seasoned with skill,
Double-sized servings, and sundry fish,   890
Some baked, some breaded, some broiled on the coals,
Some simmered, some in stews, steaming with spice,
And with sauces to sup that suited his taste.
He confesses it a feast with free words and fair;
They requite him as kindly with courteous jests,   895
               well-sped.
          "Tonight you fast [4] and pray;
          Tomorrow we'll see you fed."
          The knight grows wondrous gay
          As the wine goes to his head.   900

Then at times and by turns, as at table he sat,
They questioned him quietly, with queries discreet,
And he courteously confessed that he comes from the court,
And owns him of the brotherhood of high-famed Arthur,
The right royal ruler of the Round Table,   905
And the guest by their fireside is Gawain himself,
Who has happened on their house at that holy feast.
When the name of the knight was made known to the lord,
Then loudly he laughed, so elated he was,
And the men in that household made haste with joy   910
To appear in his presence promptly that day,
That of courage ever-constant, and customs pure,
Is pattern and paragon, and praised without end:
Of all knights on earth most honored is he.
Each said solemnly aside to his brother,   915
"Now displays of deportment shall dazzle our eyes
And the polished pearls of impeccable speech;
The high art of eloquence is ours to pursue
Since the father of fine manners is found in our midst.
Great is God's grace, and goodly indeed,   920
That a guest such as Gawain he guides to us here
When men sit and sing of their Savior's birth
               in view.
          With command of manners pure
          He shall each heart imbue;   925
          Who shares his converse, sure,
          Shall learn love's language true."

When the knight had done dining and duly arose,
The dark was drawing on; the day nigh ended.
Chaplains in chapels and churches about   930
Rang the bells aright, reminding all men
Of the holy evensong of the high feast.
The lord attends alone; his fair lady sits
In a comely closet, secluded from sight.
Gawain in gay attire goes thither soon;   935

---

4. Gawain is said to be "fasting" because the meal, though elaborate, consisted only of fish dishes, appropriate to a fasting day.

The lord catches his coat, and calls him by name,
And has him sit beside him, and says in good faith
No guest on God's earth would he gladlier greet.
For that Gawain thanked him; the two then embraced
And sat together soberly the service through.   940
Then the lady, that longed to look on the knight,
Came forth from her closet with her comely maids.
The fair hues of her flesh, her face and her hair
And her body and her bearing were beyond praise,
And excelled the queen herself, as Sir Gawain thought.   945
He goes forth to greet her with gracious intent;
Another lady led her by the left hand
That was older than she—an ancient, it seemed,
And held in high honor by all men about.
But unlike to look upon, those ladies were,   950
For if the one was fresh, the other was faded:
Bedecked in bright red was the body of one;
Flesh hung in folds on the face of the other;
On one a high headdress, hung all with pearls;
Her bright throat and bosom fair to behold,   955
Fresh as the first snow fallen upon hills;
A wimple the other one wore round her throat;
Her swart chin well swaddled, swathed all in white;
Her forehead enfolded in flounces of silk
That framed a fair fillet, of fashion ornate,   960
And nothing bare beneath save the black brows,
The two eyes and the nose, the naked lips,
And they unsightly to see, and sorrily bleared.
A beldame, by God, she may well be deemed,
                    of pride!   965
            She was short and thick of waist,
                Her buttocks round and wide;
            More toothsome, to his taste,
                Was the beauty by her side.

When Gawain had gazed on that gay lady,   970
With leave of her lord, he politely approached;
To the elder in homage he humbly bows;
The lovelier he salutes with a light embrace.
He claims a comely kiss, and courteously he speaks;
They welcome him warmly, and straightway he asks   975
To be received as their servant, if they so desire.
They take him between them; with talking they bring him
Beside a bright fire; bade then that spices
Be freely fetched forth, to refresh them the better,
And the good wine therewith, to warm their hearts.   980
The lord leaps about in light-hearted mood;
Contrives entertainments and timely sports;
Takes his hood from his head and hangs it on a spear,
And offers him openly the honor thereof
Who should promote the most mirth at that Christmas feast;   985

"And I shall try for it, trust me—contend with the best,
Ere I go without my headgear by grace of my friends!"
Thus with light talk and laughter the lord makes merry
To gladden the guest he had greeted in hall
                    that day.   990
        At the last he called for light
        The company to convey;
        Gawain says goodnight
        And retires to bed straightway.

On the morn when each man is mindful in heart   995
That God's son was sent down to suffer our death,
No household but is blithe for His blessed sake;
So was it there on that day, with many delights.
Both at larger meals and less they were lavishly served
By doughty lads on dais, with delicate fare;   1000
The old ancient lady, highest she sits;
The lord at her left hand leaned, as I hear;
Sir Gawain in the center, beside the gay lady,
Where the food was brought first to that festive board,
And thence throughout the hall, as they held most fit,   1005
To each man was offered in order of rank.
There was meat, there was mirth, there was much joy,
That to tell all the tale would tax my wits,
Though I pained me, perchance, to paint it with care;
But yet I know that our knight and the noble lady   1010
Were accorded so closely in company there,
With the seemly solace of their secret words,
With speeches well-sped, spotless and pure,
That each prince's pastime their pleasures far
                    outshone.   1015
        Sweet pipes beguile their cares,
        And the trumpet of martial tone;
        Each tends his affairs
        And those two tend their own.

That day and all the next, their disport was noble,   1020
And the third day, I think, pleased them no less;
The joys of St. John's Day [5] were justly praised,
And were the last of their like for those lords and ladies;
Then guests were to go in the gray morning,
Wherefore they whiled the night away with wine and
    with mirth,   1025
Moved to the measures of many a blithe carol;
At last, when it was late, took leave of each other,
Each one of those worthies, to wend his way.
Gawain bids goodbye to his goodly host
Who brings him to his chamber, the chimney beside,   1030
And detains him in talk, and tenders his thanks
And holds it an honor to him and his people

5. December 27.

That he has harbored in his house at that holy time
And embellished his abode with his inborn grace.
"As long as I may live, my luck is the better   1035
That Gawain was my guest at God's own feast!"
"Noble sir," said the knight, "I cannot but think
All the honor is your own—may heaven requite it!
And your man to command I account myself here
As I am bound and beholden, and shall be, come   1040
                    what may."
                The lord with all his might
                Entreats his guest to stay;
                Brief answer makes the knight:
                Next morning he must away.   1045

Then the lord of that land politely inquired
What dire affair had forced him, at that festive time,
So far from the king's court to fare forth alone
Ere the holidays wholly had ended in hall.
"In good faith," said Gawain, "you have guessed the truth: 1050
On a high errand and urgent I hastened away,
For I am summoned by myself to seek for a place—
I would I knew whither, or where it might be!
Far rather would I find it before the New Year
Than own the land of Logres, so help me our Lord!   1055
Wherefore, sir, in friendship this favor I ask,
That you say in sober earnest, if something you know
Of the Green Chapel, on ground far or near,
Or the lone knight that lives there, of like hue of green.
A certain day was set by assent of us both   1060
To meet at that landmark, if I might last,
And from now to the New Year is nothing too long,
And I would greet the Green Knight there, would God but allow,
More gladly, by God's Son, than gain the world's wealth!
And I must set forth to search, as soon as I may;   1065
To be about the business I have but three days
And would as soon sink down dead as desist from my errand."
Then smiling said the lord, "Your search, sir, is done,
For we shall see you to that site by the set time.
Let Gawain grieve no more over the Green Chapel;   1070
You shall be in your own bed, in blissful ease,
All the forenoon, and fare forth the first of the year,
And make the goal by midmorn, to mind your affairs,
                    no fear!
                Tarry till the fourth day   1075
                And ride on the first of the year.
                We shall set you on your way;
                It is not two miles from here."

Then Gawain was glad, and gleefully he laughed:

"Now I thank you for this, past all things else!   1080
Now my goal is here at hand! With a glad heart I shall
Both tarry, and undertake any task you devise."
Then the host seized his arm and seated him there;
Let the ladies be brought, to delight them the better,
And in fellowship fair by the fireside they sit;   1085
So gay waxed the good host, so giddy his words,
All waited in wonder what next he would say.
Then he stares on the stout knight, and sternly he speaks:
"You have bound yourself boldly my bidding to do—
Will you stand by that boast, and obey me this once?"   1090
"I shall do so indeed," said the doughty knight;
"While I lie in your lodging, your laws will I follow."
"As you have had," said the host, "many hardships abroad
And little sleep of late, you are lacking, I judge,
Both in nourishment needful and nightly rest;   1095
You shall lie abed late in your lofty chamber
Tomorrow until mass, and meet then to dine
When you will, with my wife, who will sit by your side
And talk with you at table, the better to cheer
               our guest.   1100
         A-hunting I will go
         While you lie late and rest."
         The knight, inclining low,
         Assents to each behest.

"And Gawain," said the good host, "agree now to this: 1105
Whatever I win in the woods I will give you at eve,
And all you have earned you must offer to me;
Swear now, sweet friend, to swap as I say,
Whether hands, in the end, be empty or better."
"By God," said Sir Gawain, "I grant it forthwith!   1110
If you find the game good, I shall gladly take part."
"Let the bright wine be brought, and our bargain is done,"
Said the lord of that land—the two laughed together.
Then they drank and they dallied and doffed all constraint,
These lords and these ladies, as late as they chose,   1115
And then with gaiety and gallantries and graceful adieux
They talked in low tones, and tarried at parting.
With compliments comely they kiss at the last;
There were brisk lads about with blazing torches
To see them safe to bed, for soft repose   1120
               long due.
      Their covenants, yet awhile,
      They repeat, and pledge anew;
      That lord could well beguile
      Men's hearts, with mirth in view.   1125

Part III

Long before daylight they left their beds;
Guests that wished to go gave word to their grooms,
And they set about briskly to bind on saddles,
Tend to their tackle, tie up trunks.
The proud lords appear, appareled to ride,   1130
Leap lightly astride, lay hold of their bridles,
Each one on his way to his worthy house.
The liege lord of the land was not the last
Arrayed there to ride, with retainers many;
He had a bite to eat when he had heard mass;   1135
With horn to the hills he hastens amain.
By the dawn of that day over the dim earth,
Master and men were mounted and ready.
Then they harnessed in couples the keen-scented hounds,
Cast wide the kennel-door and called them forth,   1140
Blew upon their bugles bold blasts three;
The dogs began to bay with a deafening din,
And they quieted them quickly and called them to heel,
A hundred brave huntsmen, as I have heard tell,
together.   1145
    Men at stations meet;
    From the hounds they slip the tether;
    The echoing horns repeat,
    Clear in the merry weather.

At the clamor of the quest, the quarry trembled;   1150
Deer dashed through the dale, dazed with dread;
Hastened to the high ground, only to be
Turned back by the beaters, who boldly shouted.
They harmed not the harts, with their high heads,
Let the bucks go by, with their broad antlers,   1155
For it was counted a crime, in the close season,
If a man of that demesne should molest the male deer.
The hinds were headed up, with "Hey!" and "Ware!"
The does with great din were driven to the valleys.
Then you were ware, as they went, of the whistling of arrows; 1160
At each bend under boughs the bright shafts flew
That tore the tawny hide with their tapered heads.
Ah! they bray and they bleed, on banks they die,
And ever the pack pell-mell comes panting behind;
Hunters with shrill horns hot on their heels—   1165
Like the cracking of cliffs their cries resounded.
What game got away from the gallant archers
Was promptly picked off at the posts below
When they were harried on the heights and herded to the streams:
The watchers were so wary at the waiting-stations,   1170
And the greyhounds so huge, that eagerly snatched,
And finished them off as fast as folk could see
with sight.
    The lord, now here, now there,

Spurs forth in sheer delight.   1175
And drives, with pleasures rare,
The day to the dark night.

So the lord in the linden-wood leads the hunt
And Gawain the good knight in gay bed lies,
Lingered late alone, till daylight gleamed,   1180
Under coverlet costly, curtained about.
And as he slips into slumber, slyly there comes
A little din at his door, and the latch lifted,
And he holds up his heavy head out of the clothes;
A corner of the curtain he caught back a little   1185
And waited there warily, to see what befell.
Lo! it was the lady, loveliest to behold,
That drew the door behind her deftly and still
And was bound for his bed—abashed was the knight,
And laid his head low again in likeness of sleep;   1190
And she stepped stealthily, and stole to his bed,
Cast aside the curtain and came within,
And set herself softly on the bedside there,
And lingered at her leisure, to look on his waking.
The fair knight lay feigning for a long while,   1195
Conning in his conscience what his case might
Mean or amount to—a marvel he thought it.
But yet he said within himself, "More seemly it were
To try her intent by talking a little."
So he started and stretched, as startled from sleep,   1200
Lifts wide his lids in likeness of wonder,
And signs himself swiftly, as safer to be,
                        with art.
            Sweetly does she speak
            And kindling glances dart,   1205
            Blent white and red on cheek
            And laughing lips apart.

"Good morning, Sir Gawain," said that gay lady,
"A slack sleeper you are, to let one slip in!
Now you are taken in a trice—a truce we must make,   1210
Or I shall bind you in your bed, of that be assured."
Thus laughing lightly that lady jested.
"Good morning, good lady," said Gawain the blithe,
"Be it with me as you will; I am well content!
For I surrender myself, and sue for your grace,   1215
And that is best, I believe, and behooves me now."
Thus jested in answer that gentle knight.
"But if, lovely lady, you misliked it not,
And were pleased to permit your prisoner to rise,
I should quit this couch and accoutre me better,   1220
And be clad in more comfort for converse here."
"Nay, not so, sweet sir," said the smiling lady;
"You shall not rise from your bed; I direct you better:
I shall hem and hold you on either hand,

And keep company awhile with my captive knight.   1225
For as certain as I sit here, Sir Gawain you are,
Whom all the world worships, whereso you ride;
Your honor, your courtesy are highest acclaimed
By lords and by ladies, by all living men;
And lo! we are alone here, and left to ourselves: 1230
My lord and his liegemen are long departed,
The household asleep, my handmaids too,
The door drawn, and held by a well-driven bolt,
And since I have in this house him whom all love,
I shall while the time away with mirthful speech   1235
                at will.

1st temptation

        My body is here at hand,
        Your each wish to fulfill;
        Your servant to command
        I am, and shall be still."   1240

"In good faith," said Gawain, "my gain is the greater,
Though I am not he of whom you have heard;
To arrive at such reverence as you recount here
I am one all unworthy, and well do I know it.
By heaven, I would hold me the happiest of men   1245
If by word or by work I once might aspire
To the prize of your praise—'twere a pure joy!"
"In good faith, Sir Gawain," said that gay lady,
"The well-proven prowess that pleases all others,
Did I scant or scout it, 'twere scarce becoming.   1250
But there are ladies, believe me, that had liefer far
Have thee here in their hold, as I have today,
To pass an hour in pastime with pleasant words,
Assuage all their sorrows and solace their hearts,
Than much of the goodly gems and gold they possess.   1255
But laud be to the Lord of the lofty skies,
For here in my hands all hearts' desire
                doth lie."
        Great welcome got he there
        From the lady who sat him by;   1260
        With fitting speech and fair
        The good knight makes reply.

"Madame," said the merry man, "Mary reward you!
For in good faith, I find your beneficence noble.
And the fame of fair deeds runs far and wide,   1265
But the praise you report pertains not to me,
But comes of your courtesy and kindness of heart."
"By the high Queen of heaven" (said she) "I count it not so,
For were I worth all the women in this world alive,
And all wealth and all worship were in my hands,   1270
And I should hunt high and low, a husband to take,
For the nurture I have noted in thee, knight, here,
The comeliness and courtesies and courtly mirth—
And so I had ever heard, and now hold it true—

No other on this earth should have me for wife."   1275
"You are bound to a better man," the bold knight said,
"Yet I prize the praise you have proffered me here,
And soberly your servant, my sovereign I hold you,
And acknowledge me your knight, in the name of Christ."
So they talked of this and that until 'twas nigh noon,   1280
And ever the lady languishing in likeness of love.
With feat words and fair he framed his defense,
For were she never so winsome, the warrior had
The less will to woo, for the wound that his bane
               must be.   1285
        He must bear the blinding blow,
        For such is fate's decree;
        The lady asks leave to go;
        He grants it full and free.

Then she gaily said goodbye, and glanced at him, laughing,   1290
And as she stood, she astonished him with a stern speech:
"Now may the Giver of all good words these glad hours repay!
But our guest is not Gawain—forgot is that thought."
"How so?" said the other, and asks in some haste,
For he feared he had been at fault in the forms of his speech.   1295
But she held up her hand, and made answer thus:
"So good a knight as Gawain is given out to be,
And the model of fair demeanor and manners pure,
Had he lain so long at a lady's side,
Would have claimed a kiss, by his courtesy,   1300
Through some touch or trick of phrase at some tale's end."
Said Gawain, "Good lady, I grant it at once!
I shall kiss at your command, as becomes a knight,
And more, lest you mislike, so let be, I pray."
With that she turns toward him, takes him in her arms,   1305
Leans down her lovely head, and lo! he is kissed.
They commend each other to Christ with comely words,
He sees her forth safely, in silence they part,
And then he lies no later in his lofty bed,
But calls to his chamberlain, chooses his clothes,   1310
Goes in those garments gladly to mass,
Then takes his way to table, where attendants wait,
And made merry all day, till the moon rose
               in view
        Was never knight beset   1315
        'Twixt worthier ladies two:
        The crone and the coquette;
        Fair pastimes they pursue.

And the lord of the land rides late and long,
Hunting the barren hind over the broad heath.   1320
He had slain such a sum, when the sun sank low,
Of does and other deer, as would dizzy one's wits.
Then they trooped in together in triumph at last,
And the count of the quarry quickly they take.

The lords lent a hand with their liegemen many,   1325
Picked out the plumpest and put them together
And duly dressed the deer, as the deed requires.
Some were assigned the assay of the fat:
Two fingers'-width fully they found on the leanest.
Then they slit the slot open and searched out the paunch,   1330
Trimmed it with trencher-knives and tied it up tight.
They flayed the fair hide from the legs and trunk,
Then broke open the belly and laid bare the bowels,
Deftly detaching and drawing them forth.
And next at the neck they neatly parted   1335
The weasand [6] from the windpipe, and cast away the guts.
At the shoulders with sharp blades they showed their skill,
Boning them from beneath, lest the sides be marred;
They breached the broad breast and broke it in twain,
And again at the gullet they begin with their knives,   1340
Cleave down the carcass clear to the breach;
Two tender morsels they take from the throat,
Then round the inner ribs they rid off a layer
And carve out the kidney-fat, close to the spine,
Hewing down to the haunch, that all hung together,   1345
And held it up whole, and hacked it free,
And this they named the numbles,[7] that knew such terms
                              of art.
                    They divide the crotch in two,
                    And straightway then they start
                    To cut the backbone through   1350
                    And cleave the trunk apart.

With hard strokes they hewed off the head and the neck,
Then swiftly from the sides they severed the chine,
And the corbie's bone [8] they cast on a branch.
Then they pierced the plump sides, impaled either one   1355
With the hock of the hind foot, and hung it aloft,
To each person his portion most proper and fit.
On a hide of a hind the hounds they fed
With the liver and the lights,[9] the leathery paunches,
And bread soaked in blood well blended therewith.   1360
High horns and shrill set hounds a-baying,
Then merrily with their meat they make their way home,
Blowing on their bugles many a brave blast.
Ere dark had descended, that doughty band   1365
Was come within the walls where Gawain waits
                              at leisure.
                    Bliss and hearth-fire bright
                    Await the master's pleasure;
                    When the two men met that night,   1370
                    Joy surpassed all measure.

6. Esophagus.   ("corbies").
7. The other internal organs.   9. Lungs.
8. A bit of gristle assigned to the ravens

Then the host in the hall his household assembles,
With the dames of high degree and their damsels fair.
In the presence of the people, a party he sends
To convey him his venison in view of the knight.   1375
And in high good-humor he hails him then,
Counts over the kill, the cuts on the tallies,
Holds high the hewn ribs, heavy with fat.
"What think you, sir, of this? Have I thriven well?
Have I won with my woodcraft a worthy prize?"   1380
"In good earnest," said Gawain, "this game is the finest
I have seen in seven years in the season of winter."
"And I give it to you, Gawain," said the goodly host,
"For according to our covenant, you claim it as your own."
"That is so," said Sir Gawain, "the same say I: 1385
What I worthily have won within these fair walls,
Herewith I as willingly award it to you."
He embraces his broad neck with both his arms,
And confers on him a kiss in the comeliest style.
"Have here my profit, it proved no better;   1390
Ungrudging do I grant it, were it greater far."
"Such a gift," said the good host, "I gladly accept—
Yet it might be all the better, would you but say
Where you won this same award, by your wits alone."
"That was no part of the pact; press me no further,   1395
For you have had what behooves; all other claims
                    forbear."
          With jest and compliment
          They conversed, and cast off care;
          To the table soon they went;
          Fresh dainties wait them there.   1400

And then by the chimney-side they chat at their ease;
The best wine was brought them, and bounteously served;
And after in their jesting they jointly accord
To do on the second day the deeds of the first: 1405
That the two men should trade, betide as it may,
What each had taken in, at eve when they met.
They seal the pact solemnly in sight of the court;
Their cups were filled afresh to confirm the jest;
Then at last they took their leave, for late was the hour,   1410
Each to his own bed hastening away.
Before the barnyard cock had crowed but thrice
The lord had leapt from his rest, his liegemen as well.
Both of mass and their meal they made short work:
By the dim light of dawn they were deep in the woods   1415
                    away.
          With huntsmen and with horns
          Over plains they pass that day;
          They release, amid the thorns,
          Swift hounds that run and bay.   1420

Soon some were on a scent by the side of a marsh;
When the hounds opened cry, the head of the hunt
Rallied them with rough words, raised a great noise.
The hounds that had heard it came hurrying straight
And followed along with their fellows, forty together.   1425
Then such a clamor and cry of coursing hounds
Arose, that the rocks resounded again.
Hunters exhorted them with horn and with voice;
Then all in a body bore off together
Between a mere in the marsh and a menacing crag,   1430
To a rise where the rock stood rugged and steep,
And boulders lay about, that blocked their approach.
Then the company in consort closed on their prey:
They surrounded the rise and the rocks both,
For well they were aware that it waited within,   1435
The beast that the bloodhounds boldly proclaimed.
Then they beat on the bushes and bade him appear,
And he made a murderous rush in the midst of them all;
The best of all boars broke from his cover,
That had ranged long unrivaled, a renegade old,   1440
For of tough-brawned boars he was biggest far,
Most grim when he grunted—then grieved were many,
For three at the first thrust he threw to the earth,
And dashed away at once without more damage.
With "Hi!" "Hi!" and "Hey!" "Hey!" the others followed,   1445
Had horns at their lips, blew high and clear.
Merry was the music of men and of hounds
That were bound after this boar, his bloodthirsty heart
                          to quell.
              Often he stands at bay,   1450
              Then scatters the pack pell-mell;
              He hurts the hounds, and they
              Most dolefully yowl and yell.

Men then with mighty bows moved in to shoot,
Aimed at him with their arrows and often hit,   1455
But the points had no power to pierce through his hide,
And the barbs were brushed aside by his bristly brow;
Though the shank of the shaft shivered in pieces,
The head hopped away, wheresoever it struck.
But when their stubborn strokes had stung him at last,   1460
Then, foaming in his frenzy, fiercely he charges,
Hies at them headlong that hindered his flight,
And many feared for their lives, and fell back a little.
But the lord on a lively horse leads the chase;
As a high-mettled huntsman his horn he blows;   1465
He sounds the assembly and sweeps through the brush,
Pursuing this wild swine till the sunlight slanted.
All day with this deed they drive forth the time
While our lone knight so lovesome lies in his bed,

Sir Gawain safe at home, in silken bower   1470
        so gay.
      The lady, with guile in heart,
      Came early where he lay;
      She was at him with all her art
      To turn his mind her way.   1475

She comes to the curtain and coyly peeps in;
Gawain thought it good to greet her at once,
And she richly repays him with her ready words,
Settles softly at his side, and suddenly she laughs,
And with a gracious glance, she begins on him thus: 1480
"Sir, if you be Gawain, it seems a great wonder—
A man so well-meaning, and mannerly disposed,
And cannot act in company as courtesy bids,
And if one takes the trouble to teach him, 'tis all in vain.
That lesson learned lately is lightly forgot,   1485
Though I painted it as plain as my poor wit allowed."
"What lesson, dear lady?" he asked all alarmed;
"I have been much to blame, if your story be true."
"Yet my counsel was of kissing," came her answer then,
"Where favor has been found, freely to claim   1490
As accords with the conduct of courteous knights."
"My dear," said the doughty man, "dismiss that thought;
Such freedom, I fear, might offend you much;
It were rude to request if the right were denied."
"But none can deny you," said the noble dame,   1495
"You are stout enough to constrain with strength, if you choose,
Were any so ungracious as to grudge you aught."
"By heaven," said he, "you have answered well,
But threats never throve among those of my land,
Nor any gift not freely given, good though it be.   1500
I am yours to command, to kiss when you please;
You may lay on as you like, and leave off at will."
        With this,
      The lady lightly bends
      And graciously gives him a kiss;   1505
      The two converse as friends
      Of true love's trials and bliss.

"I should like, by your leave," said the lovely lady,
"If it did not annoy you, to know for what cause
So brisk and so bold a young blood as you,   1510
And acclaimed for all courtesies becoming a knight—
And name what knight you will, they are noblest esteemed
For loyal faith in love, in life as in story;
For to tell the tribulations of these true hearts,
Why, 'tis the very title and text of their deeds,   1515
How bold knights for beauty have braved many a foe,
Suffered heavy sorrows out of secret love,
And then valorously avenged them on villainous churls

And made happy ever after the hearts of their ladies.
And you are the noblest knight known in your time;   1520
No household under heaven but has heard of your fame,
And here by your side I have sat for two days
Yet never has a fair phrase fallen from your lips
Of the language of love, not one little word!
And you, that with sweet vows sway women's hearts,   1525
Should show your winsome ways, and woo a young thing,
And teach by some tokens the craft of true love.
How! are you artless, whom all men praise?
Or do you deem me so dull, or deaf to such words?
                    Fie! Fie!   1530
          In hope of pastimes new
          I have come where none can spy;
          Instruct me a little, do,
          While my husband is not nearby."

"God love you, gracious lady!" said Gawain then;   1535
"It is a pleasure surpassing, and a peerless joy,
That one so worthy as you would willingly come
And take the time and trouble to talk with your knight
And content you with his company—it comforts my heart.
But to take to myself the task of telling of love,   1540
And touch upon its texts, and treat of its themes
To one that, I know well, wields more power
In that art, by a half, than a hundred such
As I am where I live, or am like to become,
It were folly, fair dame, in the first degree!   1545
In all that I am able, my aim is to please,
As in honor behooves me, and am evermore
Your servant heart and soul, so save me our Lord!"
Thus she tested his temper and tried many a time,
Whatever her true intent, to entice him to sin,   1550
But so fair was his defense that no fault appeared,
Nor evil on either hand, but only bliss
                    they knew.
          They linger and laugh awhile;
          She kisses the knight so true,   1555
          Takes leave in comeliest style
          And departs without more ado.

Then he rose from his rest and made ready for mass,
And then a meal was set and served, in sumptuous style;
He dallied at home all day with the dear ladies,   1560
But the lord lingered late at his lusty sport;
Pursued his sorry swine, that swerved as he fled,
And bit asunder the backs of the best of his hounds
When they brought him to bay, till the bowmen appeared
And soon forced him forth, though he fought for dear life,   1565
So sharp were the shafts they shot at him there.
But yet the boldest drew back from his battering head,

Till at last he was so tired he could travel no more,
But in as much haste as he might, he makes his retreat
To a rise on rocky ground, by a rushing stream.   1570
With the bank at his back he scrapes the bare earth,
The froth foams at his jaws, frightful to see.
He whets his white tusks—then weary were all
Those hunters so hardy that hoved round about
Of aiming from afar, but ever they mistrust   1575
             his mood.
        He had hurt so many by then
        That none had hardihood
        To be torn by his tusks again,
        That was brainsick, and out for blood.   1580

Till the lord came at last on his lofty steed,
Beheld him there at bay before all his folk;
Lightly he leaps down, leaves his courser,
Bares his bright sword, and boldly advances;
Straight into the stream he strides towards his foe.   1585
The wild thing was wary of weapon and man;
His hackles rose high; so hotly he snorts
That many watched with alarm, lest the worst befall.
The boar makes for the man with a mighty bound
So that he and his hunter came headlong together   1590
Where the water ran wildest—the worse for the beast,
For the man, when they first met, marked him with care,
Sights well the slot, slips in the blade,
Shoves it home to the hilt, and the heart shattered,
And he falls in his fury and floats down the water,   1595
            ill-sped.
        Hounds hasten by the score
        To maul him, hide and head;
        Men drag him in to shore
        And dogs pronounce him dead.   1600

With many a brave blast they boast of their prize,
All hallooed in high glee, that had their wind;
The hounds bayed their best, as the bold men bade
That were charged with chief rank in that chase of renown.
Then one wise in woodcraft, and worthily skilled,   1605
Began to dress the boar in becoming style:
He severs the savage head and sets it aloft,
Then rends the body roughly right down the spine;
Takes the bowels from the belly, broils them on coals,
Blends them well with bread to bestow on the hounds.   1610
Then he breaks out the brawn in fair broad flitches,
And the innards to be eaten in order he takes.
The two sides, attached to each other all whole,
He suspended from a spar that was springy and tough;
And so with this swine they set out for home;   1615
The boar's head was borne before the same man

That had stabbed him in the stream with his strong arm,
                    right through.
            He thought it long indeed
            Till he had the knight in view;   1620
            At his call, he comes with speed
            To claim his payment due.

The lord laughed aloud, with many a light word,
When he greeted Sir Gawain—with good cheer he speaks.
They fetch the fair dames and the folk of the house;   1625
He brings forth the brawn, and begins the tale
Of the great length and girth, the grim rage as well,
Of the battle of the boar they beset in the wood.
The other man meetly commended his deeds
And praised well the prize of his princely sport,   1630
For the brawn of that boar, the bold knight said,
And the sides of that swine surpassed all others.
Then they handled the huge head; he owns it a wonder,
And eyes it with abhorrence, to heighten his praise.
"Now, Gawain," said the good man, "this game becomes yours   1635
By those fair terms we fixed, as you know full well."
"That is true," returned the knight, "and trust me, fair friend,
All my gains, as agreed, I shall give you forthwith."
He clasps him and kisses him in courteous style,
Then serves him with the same fare a second time.   1640
"Now we are even," said he, "at this evening feast,
And clear is every claim incurred here to date,
                    and debt."
            "By Saint Giles!" the host replies,
            "You're the best I ever met!   1645
            If your profits are all this size,
            We'll see you wealthy yet!"

Then attendants set tables on trestles about,
And laid them with linen; light shone forth,
Wakened along the walls in waxen torches.   1650
The service was set and the supper brought;
Royal were the revels that rose then in hall
At that feast by the fire, with many fair sports:
Amid the meal and after, melody sweet,
Carol-dances comely and Christmas songs,   1655
With all the mannerly mirth my tongue may describe.
And ever our gallant knight beside the gay lady;
So uncommonly kind and complaisant was she,
With sweet stolen glances, that stirred his stout heart,
That he was at his wits' end, and wondrous vexed;   1660
But he could not in conscience her courtship repay,
Yet took pains to please her, though the plan might
                    go wrong.
            When they to heart's delight
            Had reveled there in throng,   1665

To his chamber he calls the knight,
And thither they go along.

And there they dallied and drank, and deemed it good sport
To enact their play anew on New Year's Eve,
But Gawain asked again to go on the morrow,   1670
For the time until his tryst was not two days.
The host hindered that, and urged him to stay,
And said, "On my honor, my oath here I take
That you shall get to the Green Chapel to begin your chores
By dawn on New Year's Day, if you so desire.   1675
Wherefore lie at your leisure in your lofty bed,
And I shall hunt hereabouts, and hold to our terms,
And we shall trade winnings when once more we meet,
For I have tested you twice, and true have I found you;
Now think this tomorrow: the third pays for all;   1680
Be we merry while we may, and mindful of joy,
For heaviness of heart can be had for the asking."
This is gravely agreed on and Gawain will stay.
They drink a last draught and with torches depart
                    to rest.   1685
          To bed Sir Gawain went;
          His sleep was of the best;
          The lord, on his craft intent,
          Was early up and dressed.

After mass, with his men, a morsel he takes;   1690
Clear and crisp the morning; he calls for his mount;
The folk that were to follow him afield that day
Were high astride their horses before the hall gates.
Wondrous fair were the fields, for the frost was light;
The sun rises red amid radiant clouds,   1695
Sails into the sky, and sends forth his beams.
They let loose the hounds by a leafy wood;
The rocks all around re-echo to their horns;
Soon some have set off in pursuit of the fox,
Cast about with craft for a clearer scent;   1700
A young dog yaps, and is yelled at in turn;
His fellows fall to sniffing, and follow his lead,
Running in a rabble on the right track,
And he scampers all before; they discover him soon,
And when they see him with sight they pursue him the faster,   1705
Railing at him rudely with a wrathful din.
Often he reverses over rough terrain,
Or loops back to listen in the lee of a hedge;
At last, by a little ditch, he leaps over the brush,
Comes into a clearing at a cautious pace,   1710
Then he thought through his wiles to have thrown off the hounds
Till he was ware, as he went, of a waiting-station
Where three athwart his path threatened him at once,
                    all gray.

Quick as a flash he wheels   1715
And darts off in dismay;
With hard luck at his heels
He is off to the wood away.

Then it was heaven on earth to hark to the hounds
When they had come on their quarry, coursing together!   1720
Such harsh cries and howls they hurled at his head
As all the cliffs with a crash had come down at once.
Here he was hailed, when huntsmen met him;
Yonder they yelled at him, yapping and snarling;
There they cried "Thief!" and threatened his life,   1725
And ever the harriers at his heels, that he had no rest.
Often he was menaced when he made for the open,
And often rushed in again, for Reynard was wily;
And so he leads them a merry chase, the lord and his men,
In this manner on the mountains, till midday or near,   1740
While our hero lies at home in wholesome sleep
Within the comely curtains on the cold morning.
But the lady, as love would allow her no rest,
And pursuing ever the purpose that pricked her heart,
Was awake with the dawn, and went to his chamber   1735
In a fair flowing mantle that fell to the earth,
All edged and embellished with ermines fine;
No hood on her head, but heavy with gems
Were her fillet and the fret [1] that confined her tresses;
Her face and her fair throat freely displayed;   1730
Her bosom all but bare, and her back as well.
She comes in at the chamber-door, and closes it with care,
Throws wide a window—then waits no longer,
But hails him thus airily with her artful words,
                              with cheer: 1745
          "Ah, man, how can you sleep?
          The morning is so clear!"
          Though dreams have drowned him deep,
          He cannot choose but hear.

Deep in his dreams he darkly mutters   1750
As a man may that mourns, with many grim thoughts
Of that day when destiny shall deal him his doom
When he greets his grim host at the Green Chapel
And must bow to his buffet, bating all strife.
But when he sees her at his side he summons his wits,   1755
Breaks from the black dreams, and blithely answers.
That lovely lady comes laughing sweet,
Sinks down at his side, and salutes him with a kiss.
He accords her fair welcome in courtliest style;
He sees her so glorious, so gaily attired,   1760
So faultless her features, so fair and so bright,

---

1. Ornamental net.

His heart swelled swiftly with surging joys.
They melt into mirth with many a fond smile,
And there was bliss beyond telling between those two,
at height. 1765
Good were their words of greeting;
Each joyed in other's sight;
Great peril attends that meeting
Should Mary forget her knight.

For that high-born beauty so hemmed him about, 1770
Made so plain her meaning, the man must needs
Either take her tendered love or distastefully refuse.
His courtesy concerned him, lest crass he appear,
But more his soul's mischief, should he commit sin
And belie his loyal oath to the lord of that house. 1775
"God forbid!" said the bold knight, "That shall not befall!"
With a little fond laughter he lightly let pass
All the words of special weight that were sped his way;
"I find you much at fault," the fair one said,
"Who can be cold toward a creature so close by your side, 1780
Of all women in this world most wounded in heart,
Unless you have a sweetheart, one you hold dearer,
And allegiance to that lady so loyally knit
That you will never love another, as now I believe.
And, sir, if it be so, then say it, I beg you; 1785
By all your heart holds dear, hide it no longer
with guile."
"Lady, by Saint John,"
He answers with a smile,
"Lover have I none, 1790
Nor will have, yet awhile."

"Those words," said the woman, "are the worst of all,
But I have had my answer, and hard do I find it!
Kiss me now kindly: I can but go hence
To lament my life long like a maid lovelorn." 1795
She inclines her head quickly and kisses the knight,
Then straightens with a sigh, and says as she stands,
"Now, dear, ere I depart, do me this pleasure:
Give me some little gift, your glove or the like,
That I may think on you, man, and mourn the less." 1800
"Now by heaven," said he, "I wish I had here
My most precious possession, to put it in your hands,
For your deeds, beyond doubt, have often deserved
A repayment far passing my power to bestow.
But a love-token, lady, were of little avail; 1805
It is not to your honor to have at this time
A glove as a guerdon from Gawain's hand,
And I am here on an errand in unknown realms
And have no bearers with baggage with becoming gifts,
Which distresses me, madame, for your dear sake. 1810

A man must keep within his compass: account it neither grief
nor slight."

"Nay, noblest knight alive,"
Said that beauty of body white,
"Though you be loath to give,   1815
Yet you shall take, by right."

She reached out a rich ring, wrought all of gold,
With a splendid stone displayed on the band
That flashed before his eyes like a fiery sun;
It was worth a king's wealth, you may well believe.   1820
But he waved it away with these ready words:
"Before God, good lady, I forego all gifts;
None have I to offer, nor any will I take."
And she urged it on him eagerly, and ever he refused,
And vowed in very earnest, prevail she would not.   1825
And she sad to find it so, and said to him then,
"If my ring is refused for its rich cost—
You would not be my debtor for so dear a thing—
I shall give you my girdle; you gain less thereby."
She released a knot lightly, and loosened a belt   1830
That was caught about her kirtle, the bright cloak beneath,
Of a gay green silk, with gold overwrought,
And the borders all bound with embroidery fine,
And this she presses upon him, and pleads with a smile,
Unworthy though it were, that it would not be scorned.   1835
But the man still maintains that he means to accept
Neither gold nor any gift, till by God's grace
The fate that lay before him was fully achieved.
"And be not offended, fair lady, I beg,
And give over your offer, for ever I must   1840
decline.

I am grateful for favor shown
Past all deserts of mine,
And ever shall be your own
True servant, rain or shine."   1845

"Now does my present displease you," she promptly inquired,
"Because it seems in your sight so simple a thing?
And belike, as it is little, it is less to praise,
But if the virtue that invests it were verily known,
It would be held, I hope, in higher esteem.   1850
For the man that possesses this piece of silk,
If he bore it on his body, belted about,
There is no hand under heaven that could hew him down,
For he could not be killed by any craft on earth."
Then the man began to muse, and mainly he thought   1855
It was a pearl for his plight, the peril to come
When he gains the Green Chapel to get his reward:
Could he escape unscathed, the scheme were noble!
Then he bore with her words and withstood them no more,

And she repeated her petition and pleaded anew,   1860
And he granted it, and gladly she gave him the belt,
And besought him for her sake to conceal it well,
Lest the noble lord should know—and the knight agrees
That not a soul save themselves shall see it thenceforth
                              with sight.   1865
          He thanked her with fervent heart,
          As often as ever he might;
          Three times, before they part,
          She has kissed the stalwart knight.

Then the lady took her leave, and left him there,   1870
For more mirth with that man she might not have.
When she was gone, Sir Gawain got from his bed,
Arose and arrayed him in his rich attire;
Tucked away the token the temptress had left,
Laid it reliably where he looked for it after.   1875
And then with good cheer to the chapel he goes,
Approached a priest in private, and prayed to be taught
To lead a better life and lift up his mind,
Lest he be among the lost when he must leave this world.
And shamefaced at shrift he showed his misdeeds   1880
From the largest to the least, and asked the Lord's mercy,
And called on his confessor to cleanse his soul,
And he absolved him of his sins as safe and as clean
As if the dread Day of Judgment should dawn on the morrow.
And then he made merry amid the fine ladies   1885
With deft-footed dances and dalliance light,
As never until now, while the afternoon wore
                              away.
          He delighted all around him,
          And all agreed, that day,   1890
          They never before had found him
          So gracious and so gay.

Now peaceful be his pasture, and love play him fair!
The host is on horseback, hunting afield;
He has finished off this fox that he followed so long: 1895
As he leapt a low hedge to look for the villain
Where he heard all the hounds in hot pursuit,
Reynard comes racing out of a rough thicket,
And all the rabble in a rush, right at his heels.
The man beholds the beast, and bides his time,   1900
And bares his bright sword, and brings it down hard,
And he blenches from the blade, and backward he starts;
A hound hurries up and hinders that move,
And before the horse's feet they fell on him at once
And ripped the rascal's throat with a wrathful din.   1905
The lord soon alighted and lifted him free,
Swiftly snatched him up from the snapping jaws,
Holds him over his head, halloos with a will,

And the dogs bayed the dirge, that had done him to death.
Hunters hastened thither with horns at their lips,   1910
Sounding the assembly till they saw him at last.
When that comely company was come in together,
All that bore bugles blew them at once,
And the others all hallooed, that had no horns.
It was the merriest medley that ever a man heard,   1915
The racket that they raised for Sir Reynard's soul
                       that died.
          Their hounds they praised and fed,
          Fondling their heads with pride,
          And they took Reynard the Red   1920
          And stripped away his hide.

And then they headed homeward, for evening had come,
Blowing many a blast on their bugles bright.
The lord at long last alights at his house,
Finds fire on the hearth where the fair knight waits,   1925
Sir Gawain the good, that was glad in heart.
With the ladies, that loved him, he lingered at ease;
He wore a rich robe of blue, that reached to the earth
And a surcoat lined softly with sumptuous furs;
A hood of the same hue hung on his shoulders;   1930
With bands of bright ermine embellished were both.
He comes to meet the man amid all the folk,
And greets him good-humoredly, and gaily he says,
"I shall follow forthwith the form of our pledge
That we framed to good effect amid fresh-filled cups."   1935
He clasps him accordingly and kisses him thrice,
As amiably and as earnestly as ever he could.
"By heaven," said the host, "you have had some luck
Since you took up this trade, if the terms were good."
"Never trouble about the terms," he returned at once,   1940
"Since all that I owe here is openly paid."
"Marry!" said the other man, "mine is much less,
For I have hunted all day, and nought have I got
But this foul fox pelt, the fiend take the goods!
Which but poorly repays those precious things   1945
That you have cordially conferred, those kisses three
                   so good."
          "Enough!" said Sir Gawain;
          "I thank you, by the rood!"
          And how the fox was slain   1950
          He told him, as they stood.

With minstrelsy and mirth, with all manner of meats,
They made as much merriment as any men might
(Amid laughing of ladies and light hearted girls;
So gay grew Sir Gawain and the goodly host)   1955
Unless they had been besotted, or brainless fools.
The knight joined in jesting with that joyous folk,

Until at last it was late; ere long they must part,
And be off to their beds, as behooved them each one.
Then politely his leave of the lord of the house   1960
Our noble knight takes, and renews his thanks:
"The courtesies countless accorded me here,
Your kindness at this Christmas, may heaven's King repay!
Henceforth, if you will have me, I hold you my liege,
And so, as I have said, I must set forth tomorrow,   1965
If I may take some trusty man to teach, as you promised,
The way to the Green Chapel, that as God allows
I shall see my fate fulfilled on the first of the year."
"In good faith," said the good man, "with a good will
Every promise on my part shall be fully performed."   1970
He assigns him a servant to set him on the path,
To see him safe and sound over the snowy hills,
To follow the fastest way through forest green
                and grove.
          Gawain thanks him again,   1975
          So kind his favors prove,
          And of the ladies then
          He takes his leave, with love.

Courteously he kissed them, with care in his heart,
And often wished them well, with warmest thanks,   1980
Which they for their part were prompt to repay.
They commend him to Christ with disconsolate sighs;
And then in that hall with the household he parts—
Each man that he met, he remembered to thank
For his deeds of devotion and diligent pains,   1985
And the trouble he had taken to tend to his needs;
And each one as woeful, that watched him depart,
As he had lived with him loyally all his life long.
By lads bearing lights he was led to his chamber
And blithely brought to his bed, to be at his rest.   1990
How soundly he slept, I presume not to say,
For there were matters of moment his thoughts might well
                pursue.
          Let him lie and wait;
          He has little more to do,   1995
          Then listen, while I relate
          How they kept their rendezvous.

Part IV

Now the New Year draws near, and the night passes,
The day dispels the dark, by the Lord's decree;
But wild weather awoke in the world without: 2000
The clouds in the cold sky cast down their snow
With great gusts from the north, grievous to bear.
Sleet showered aslant upon shivering beasts;

The wind warbled wild as it whipped from aloft,
And drove the drifts deep in the dales below. 2005
Long and well he listens, that lies in his bed;
Though he lifts not his eyelids, little he sleeps;
Each crow of the cock he counts without fail.
Readily from his rest he rose before dawn,
For a lamp had been left him, that lighted his chamber. 2010
He called to his chamberlain, who quickly appeared,
And bade him get him his gear, and gird his good steed,
And he sets about briskly to bring in his arms,
And makes ready his master in manner most fit.
First he clad him in his clothes, to keep out the cold, 2015
And then his other harness, made handsome anew,
His plate-armor of proof, polished with pains,
The rings of his rich mail rid of their rust,
And all was fresh as at first, and for this he gave thanks
           indeed. 2020
           With pride he wears each piece,
           New-furbished for his need:
           No gayer from here to Greece;
           He bids them bring his steed.

In his richest raiment he robed himself then: 2025
His crested coat-armor, close-stitched with craft,
With stones of strange virtue on silk velvet set;
All bound with embroidery on borders and seams
And lined warmly and well with furs of the best.
Yet he left not his love-gift, the lady's girdle; 2030
Gawain, for his own good, forgot not that:
When the bright sword was belted and bound on his haunches,
Then twice with that token he twined him about.
Sweetly did he swathe him in that swatch of silk,
That girdle of green so goodly to see, 2035
That against the gay red showed gorgeous bright.
Yet he wore not for its wealth that wondrous girdle,
Nor pride in its pendants, though polished they were,
Though glittering gold gleamed at the tips,
But to keep himself safe when consent he must 2040
To endure a deadly dint, and all defense
           denied.
           And now the bold knight came
           Into the courtyard wide;
           That folk of worthy fame 2045
           He thanks on every side.

Then was Gringolet girt, that was great and huge,
And had sojourned safe and sound, and savored his fare;
He pawed the earth in his pride, that princely steed.
The good knight draws near him and notes well his look, 2050
And says sagely to himself, and soberly swears,
"Here is a household in hall that upholds the right!"

The man that maintains it, may happiness be his!
Likewise the dear lady, may love betide her!
If thus they in charity cherish a guest   2055
That are honored here on earth, may they have His reward
That reigns high in heaven—and also you all;
And were I to live in this land but a little while,
I should willingly reward you, and well, if I might."
Then he steps into the stirrup and bestrides his mount;   2060
His shield is shown forth; on his shoulder he casts it;
Strikes the side of his steed with his steel spurs,
And he starts across the stones, nor stands any longer
     to prance.
    On horseback was the swain   2065
    That bore his spear and lance;
    "May Christ this house maintain
    And guard it from mischance!"

The bridge was brought down, and the broad gates
Unbarred and carried back upon both sides;   2070
He commended him to Christ, and crossed over the planks;
Praised the noble porter, who prayed on his knees
That God save Sir Gawain, and bade him good day,
And went on his way alone with the man
That was to lead him ere long to that luckless place   2075
Where the dolorous dint must be dealt him at last.
Under bare boughs they ride, where steep banks rise,
Over high cliffs they climb, where cold snow clings;
The heavens held aloof, but heavy thereunder
Mist mantled the moors, moved on the slopes.   2080
Each hill had a hat, a huge cape of cloud;
Brooks bubbled and broke over broken rocks,
Flashing in freshets that waterfalls fed.
Roundabout was the road that ran through the wood
Till the sun at that season was soon to rise,   2085
     that day.
    They were on a hilltop high;
    The white snow round them lay;
    The man that rode nearby
    Now bade his master stay.   2090

"For I have seen you here safe at the set time,
And now you are not far from that notable place
That you have sought for so long with such special pains.
But this I say for certain, since I know you, sir knight,
And have your good at heart, and hold you dear—   2095
Would you heed well my words, it were worth your while—
You are rushing into risks that you reck not of:
There is a villain in yon valley, the veriest on earth,
For he is rugged and rude, and ready with his fists,
And most immense in his mold of mortals alive,   2100
And his body bigger than the best four

That are in Arthur's house, Hector [2] or any.
He gets his grim way at the Green Chapel;
None passes by that place so proud in his arms
That he does not dash him down with his deadly blows,   2105
For he is heartless wholly, and heedless of right,
For be it chaplain or churl that by the Chapel rides,
Monk or mass-priest or any man else,
He would as soon strike him dead as stand on two feet.
Wherefore I say, just as certain as you sit there astride,   2110
You cannot but be killed, if his counsel holds,
For he would trounce you in a trice, had you twenty lives
       for sale.
    He has lived long in this land
    And dealt out deadly bale;   2115
    Against his heavy hand
    Your power cannot prevail.

"And so, good Sir Gawain, let the grim man be;
Go off by some other road, in God's own name!
Leave by some other land, for the love of Christ,   2120
And I shall get me home again, and give you my word
That I shall swear by God's self and the saints above,
By heaven and by my halidom [3] and other oaths more,
To conceal this day's deed, nor say to a soul
That ever you fled for fear from any that I knew."   2125
"Many thanks!" said the other man—and demurring he speaks—
"Fair fortune befall you for your friendly words!
And conceal this day's deed I doubt not you would,
But though you never told the tale, if I turned back now,
Forsook this place for fear, and fled, as you say,   2130
I were a caitiff coward; I could not be excused.
But I must to the Chapel to chance my luck
And say to that same man such words as I please,
Befall what may befall through Fortune's will
       or whim.   2135
    Though he be a quarrelsome knave
    With a cudgel great and grim,
    The Lord is strong to save:
    His servants trust in Him."

"Marry," said the man, "since you tell me so much,   2140
And I see you are set to seek your own harm,
If you crave a quick death, let me keep you no longer!
Put your helm on your head, your hand on your lance,
And ride the narrow road down yon rocky slope
Till it brings you to the bottom of the broad valley.   2145
Then look a little ahead, on your left hand,
And you will soon see before you that self-same Chapel,
And the man of great might that is master there.

2. Either the Trojan hero or one of   3. Holiness or, more likely, patron
Arthur's knights.   saints.

Now goodbye in God's name, Gawain the noble!
For all the world's wealth I would not stay here,
Or go with you in this wood one footstep further!"   2150
He tarried no more to talk, but turned his bridle,
Hit his horse with his heels as hard as he might,
Leaves the knight alone, and off like the wind
                goes leaping.   2155
      "By God," said Gawain then,
      "I shall not give way to weeping;
      God's will be done, amen!   *FAITH*
      I commend me to His keeping."

He puts his heels to his horse, and picks up the path;   2160
Goes in beside a grove where the ground is steep,
Rides down the rough slope right to the valley;
And then he looked a little about him—the landscape was wild,
And not a soul to be seen, nor sign of a dwelling,
But high banks on either hand hemmed it about,   2165
With many a ragged rock and rough-hewn crag;
The skies seemed scored by the scowling peaks.
Then he halted his horse, and hoved there a space,
And sought on every side for a sight of the Chapel,
But no such place appeared, which puzzled him sore,   2170
Yet he saw some way off what seemed like a mound,
A hillock high and broad, hard by the water,
Where the stream fell in foam down the face of the steep
And bubbled as if it boiled on its bed below.
The knight urges his horse, and heads for the knoll;   2175
Leaps lightly to earth; loops well the rein
Of his steed to a stout branch, and stations him there.
He strides straight to the mound, and strolls all about,
Much wondering what it was, but no whit the wiser;
It had a hole at one end, and on either side,   2180
And was covered with coarse grass in clumps all without,
And hollow all within, like some old cave,
Or a crevice of an old crag—he could not discern
                aright.
      "Can this be the Chapel Green?   2185
      Alack!" said the man, "Here might
      The devil himself be seen
      Saying matins at black midnight!"

"Now by heaven," said he, "it is bleak hereabouts;
This prayer-house is hideous, half-covered with grass!   2190
Well may the grim man mantled in green
Hold here his orisons, in hell's own style!
Now I feel it is the Fiend, in my five wits,
That has tempted me to this tryst, to take my life;
This is a Chapel of mischance, may the mischief take it!   2195
As accursed a country church as I came upon ever!"

With his helm on his head, his lance in his hand,
He stalks toward the steep wall of that strange house.
Then he heard, on the hill, behind a hard rock,
Beyond the brook, from the bank, a most barbarous din: 2200
Lord! it clattered in the cliff fit to cleave it in two,
As one upon a grindstone ground a great scythe!
Lord! it whirred like a mill-wheel whirling about!
Lord! it echoed loud and long, lamentable to hear!
Then "By heaven," said the bold knight, "That business
          up there   2205
Is arranged for my arrival, or else I am much
                    misled.
          Let God work! Ah me!
          All hope of help has fled!
          Forfeit my life may be   2210
          But noise I do not dread."

Then he listened no longer, but loudly he called,
"Who has power in this place, high parley to hold?
For none greets Sir Gawain, or gives him good day;
If any would a word with him, let him walk forth   2215
And speak now or never, to speed his affairs."
"Abide," said one on the bank above over his head,
"And what I promised you once shall straightway be given."
Yet he stayed not his grindstone, nor stinted its noise,
But worked awhile at his whetting before he would rest,   2220
And then he comes around a crag, from a cave in the rocks,
Hurtling out of hiding with a hateful weapon,
A Danish [4] ax devised for that day's deed,
With a broad blade and bright, bent in a curve,
Filed to a fine edge—four feet it measured   2225
By the length of the lace that was looped round the haft.
And in form as at first, the fellow all green,
His lordly face and his legs, his locks and his beard,
Save that firm upon two feet forward he strides,
Sets a hand on the ax-head, the haft to the earth;   2230
When he came to the cold stream, and cared not to wade,
He vaults over on his ax, and advances amain
On a broad bank of snow, overbearing and brisk
                    of mood.
          Little did the knight incline   2235
          When face to face they stood;
          Said the other man, "Friend mine,
          It seems your word holds good!"

"God love you, Sir Gawain!" said the Green Knight then,
"And well met this morning, man, at my place!   2240
And you have followed me faithfully and found me betimes,
And on the business between us we both are agreed:

4. I.e., long-bladed.

Twelve months ago today you took what was yours,
And you at this New Year must yield me the same.
And we have met in these mountains, remote from all eyes: 2245
There is none here to halt us or hinder our sport;
Unhasp your high helm, and have here your wages;
Make no more demur than I did myself
When you hacked off my head with one hard blow."
"No, by God," said Sir Gawain, "that granted me life,   2250
I shall grudge not the guerdon, grim though it prove;
Bestow but one stroke, and I shall stand still,
And you may lay on as you like till the last of my part
                    be paid."
                He proffered, with good grace,   2255
                His bare neck to the blade,
                And feigned a cheerful face:
                He scorned to seem afraid.

Then the grim man in green gathers his strength,
Heaves high the heavy ax to hit him the blow.   2260
With all the force in his frame he fetches it aloft,
With a grimace as grim as he would grind him to bits;
Had the blow he bestowed been as big as he threatened,
A good knight and gallant had gone to his grave.
But Gawain at the great ax glanced up aside   2265
As down it descended with death-dealing force,
And his shoulders shrank a little from the sharp iron.
Abruptly the brawny man breaks off the stroke,
And then reproved with proud words that prince among knights.
"You are not Gawain the glorious," the green man said,   2270
"That never fell back on field in the face of the foe,
And now you flee for fear, and have felt no harm:
Such news of that knight I never heard yet!
I moved not a muscle when you made to strike,
Nor caviled at the cut in King Arthur's house;   2275
My head fell to my feet, yet steadfast I stood,
And you, all unharmed, are wholly dismayed—
Wherefore the better man I, by all odds,
                    must be."
                Said Gawain, "Strike once more;   2280
                I shall neither flinch nor flee;
                But if my head falls to the floor
                There is no mending me!"

"But go on, man, in God's name, and get to the point!
Deliver me my destiny, and do it out of hand,   2285
For I shall stand to the stroke and stir not an inch
Till your ax has hit home—on my honor I swear it!"
"Have at thee then!" said the other, and heaves it aloft,
And glares down as grimly as he had gone mad.
He made a mighty feint, but marred not his hide;   2290

Withdrew the ax adroitly before it did damage.
Gawain gave no ground, nor glanced up aside,
But stood still as a stone, or else a stout stump
That is held in hard earth by a hundred roots.
Then merrily does he mock him, the man all in green: 2295
"So now you have your nerve again, I needs must strike;
Uphold the high knighthood that Arthur bestowed,
And keep your neck-bone clear, if this cut allows!"
Then was Gawain gripped with rage, and grimly he said,
"Why, thrash away, tyrant, I tire of your threats;   2300
You make such a scene, you must frighten yourself.
Said the green fellow, "In faith, so fiercely you speak
That I shall finish this affair, nor further grace
        allow."
      He stands prepared to strike   2305
      And scowls with both lip and brow;
      No marvel if the man mislike
      Who can hope no rescue now.

He gathered up the grim ax and guided it well:
Let the barb at the blade's end brush the bare throat;   2310
He hammered down hard, yet harmed him no whit
Save a scratch on one side, that severed the skin;
The end of the hooked edge entered the flesh,
And a little blood lightly leapt to the earth.
And when the man beheld his own blood bright on the snow,   2315
He sprang a spear's length with feet spread wide,
Seized his high helm, and set it on his head,
Shoved before his shoulders the shield at his back,
Bares his trusty blade, and boldly he speaks—
Not since he was a babe born of his mother   2320
Was he once in this world one-half so blithe—
"Have done with your hacking—harry me no more!
I have borne, as behooved, one blow in this place;
If you make another move I shall meet it midway
And promptly, I promise you, pay back each blow   2325
        with brand.
      One stroke acquits me here;
      So did our covenant stand
      In Arthur's court last year—
      Wherefore, sir, hold your hand!"   2330

He lowers the long ax and leans on it there,
Sets his arms on the head, the haft on the earth,
And beholds the bold knight that bides there afoot,
How he faces him fearless, fierce in full arms,
And plies him with proud words—it pleases him well.   2335
Then once again gaily to Gawain he calls,
And in a loud voice and lusty, delivers these words:
"Bold fellow, on this field your anger forbear!

No man has made demands here in manner uncouth,
Nor done, save as duly determined at court.   2340
I owed you a hit and you have it; be happy therewith!
The rest of my rights here I freely resign.
Had I been a bit busier, a buffet, perhaps,
I could have dealt more directly, and done you some harm.
First I flourished with a feint, in frolicsome mood,   2345
And left your hide unhurt—and here I did well
By the fair terms we fixed on the first night;
And fully and faithfully you followed accord:
Gave over all your gains as a good man should.
A second feint, sir, I assigned for the morning   2350
You kissed my comely wife—each kiss you restored.
For both of these there behooved but two feigned blows
                    by right.
          True men pay what they owe;
          No danger then in sight.   2355
          You failed at the third throw,
          So take my tap, sir knight.

"For that is my belt about you, that same braided girdle,
My wife it was that wore it; I know well the tale,
And the count of your kisses and your conduct too,   2360
And the wooing of my wife—it was all my scheme!
She made trial of a man most faultless by far
Of all that ever walked over the wide earth;
As pearls to white peas, more precious and prized,
So is Gawain, in good faith, to other gay knights.   2365
Yet you lacked, sir, a little in loyalty there,
But the cause was not cunning, nor courtship either,
But that you loved your own life; the less, then, to blame."
The other stout knight in a study stood a long while,
So gripped with grim rage that his great heart shook.   2370
All the blood of his body burned in his face
As he shrank back in shame from the man's sharp speech.
The first words that fell from the fair knight's lips:
"Accursed be a cowardly and covetous heart!
In you is villainy and vice, and virtue laid low!"   2375
Then he grasps the green girdle and lets go the knot,
Hands it over in haste, and hotly he says:
"Behold there my falsehood, ill hap betide it!
Your cut taught me cowardice, care for my life,
And coveting came after, contrary both   2380
To largesse and loyalty belonging to knights.
Now am I faulty and false, that fearful was ever
Of disloyalty and lies, bad luck to them both!
                    and greed.
          I confess, knight, in this place,   2385
          Most dire is my misdeed;
          Let me gain back your good grace,
          And thereafter I shall take heed."

Then the other laughed aloud, and lightly he said,
"Such harm as I have had, I hold it quite healed.   2390
You are so fully confessed, your failings made known,
And bear the plain penance of the point of my blade,
I hold you polished as a pearl, as pure and as bright
As you had lived free of fault since first you were born.
And I give you, sir, this girdle that is gold-hemmed   2395
And green as my garments, that, Gawain, you may
Be mindful of this meeting when you mingle in throng
With nobles of renown—and known by this token
How it chanced at the Green Chapel, to chivalrous knights.
And you shall in this New Year come yet again   2400
And we shall finish out our feast in my fair hall,
     with cheer."
    He urged the knight to stay,
    And said, "With my wife so dear
    We shall see you friends this day,   2405
    Whose enmity touched you near."

"Indeed," said the doughty knight, and doffed his high helm,
And held it in his hands as he offered his thanks,
"I have lingered long enough—may good luck be yours,
And He reward you well that all worship bestows!   2410
And commend me to that comely one, your courteous wife,
Both herself and that other, my honoured ladies,
That have trapped their true knight in their trammels so quaint.
But if a dullard should dote, deem it no wonder,
And through the wiles of a woman be wooed into sorrow,   2415
For so was Adam by one, when the world began,
And Solomon by many more, and Samson the mighty—
Delilah was his doom, and David thereafter
Was beguiled by Bathsheba, and bore much distress;
Now these were vexed by their devices—'twere a very joy   2420
Could one but learn to love, and believe them not.
For these were proud princes, most prosperous of old,
Past all lovers lucky, that languished under heaven,
     bemused.
    And one and all fell prey   2425
    To women that they had used;
    If I be led astray,
    Methinks I may be excused.

"But your girdle, God love you! I gladly shall take
And be pleased to possess, not for the pure gold,   2430
Nor the bright belt itself, nor the beauteous pendants,
Nor for wealth, nor worldly state, nor workmanship fine,
But a sign of excess it shall seem oftentimes
When I ride in renown, and remember with shame
The faults and the frailty of the flesh perverse,   2435
How its tenderness entices the foul taint of sin;
And so when praise and high prowess have pleased my heart,
A look at this love-lace will lower my pride.

But one thing would I learn, if you were not loath,
Since you are lord of yonder land where I have long sojourned   2440
With honor in your house—may you have His reward
That upholds all the heavens, highest on throne!
How runs your right name?—and let the rest go."
"That shall I give you gladly," said the Green Knight then;
"Bercilak de Hautdesert this barony I hold,   2445
Through the might of Morgan le Faye,[5] that lodges at my house,
By subtleties of science and sorcerers' arts,
The mistress of Merlin,[6] she has caught many a man,
For sweet love in secret she shared sometime
With that wizard, that knows well each one of your knights   2450
                    and you.
          Morgan the Goddess, she,
          So styled by title true;
          None holds so high degree
          That her arts cannot subdue.   2455

"She guided me in this guise to your glorious hall,
To assay, if such it were, the surfeit of pride
That is rumored of the retinue of the Round Table.
She put this shape upon me to puzzle your wits,
To afflict the fair queen, and frighten her to death   2460
With awe of that elvish man that eerily spoke
With his head in his hand before the high table.
She was with my wife at home, that old withered lady,
Your own aunt [7] is she, Arthur's half-sister,
The Duchess' daughter of Tintagel, that dear King Uther   2465
Got Arthur on after, that honored is now.
And therefore, good friend, come feast with your aunt;
Make merry in my house; my men hold you dear,
And I wish you as well, sir, with all my heart,
As any mortal man, for your matchless faith."   2470
But the knight said him nay, that he might by no means.
They clasped then and kissed, and commended each other
To the Prince of Paradise, and parted with one
                    assent.
          Gawain sets out anew;   2475
          Toward the court his course is bent;
          And the knight all green in hue,
          Wheresoever he wished, he went.

Wild ways in the world our worthy knight rides
On Gringolet, that by grace had been granted his life.   2480
He harbored often in houses, and often abroad,
And with many valiant adventures verily he met
That I shall not take time to tell in this story.

---

5. Arthur's half-sister, an enchantress who sometimes abetted him, sometimes made trouble for him.
6. The wise magician who had helped Arthur become king.
7. Morgan was the daughter of Igraine, Duchess of Tintagel, and her husband the Duke; Igraine conceived Arthur when his father Uther lay with her through one of Merlin's trickeries.

The hurt was whole that he had had in his neck,
And the bright green belt on his body he bore,   2485
Oblique, like a baldric, bound at his side,
Below his left shoulder, laced in a knot,
In betokening of the blame he had borne for his fault;
And so to court in due course he comes safe and sound.
Bliss abounded in hall when the high-born heard   2490
That good Gawain was come; glad tidings they thought it.
The king kisses the knight, and the queen as well,
And many a comrade came to clasp him in arms,
And eagerly they asked, and awesomely he told,
Confessed all his cares and discomfitures many,   2495
How it chanced at the Chapel, what cheer made the knight,
The love of the lady, the green lace at last.
The nick on his neck he naked displayed
That he got in his disgrace at the Green Knight's hands,
                                    alone.   2500
                    With rage in heart he speaks,
                    And grieves with many a groan;
                    The blood burns in his cheeks
                    For shame at what must be shown.

"Behold, sir," said he, and handles the belt,   2505
"This is the blazon of the blemish that I bear on my neck;
This is the sign of sore loss that I have suffered there
For the cowardice and coveting that I came to there;
This is the badge of false faith that I was found in there,
And I must bear it on my body till I breathe my last.   2510
For one may keep a deed dark, but undo it no whit,
For where a fault is made fast, it is fixed evermore."
The king comforts the knight, and the court all together
Agree with gay laughter and gracious intent
That the lords and the ladies belonging to the Table,   2515
Each brother of that band, a baldric should have,
A belt borne oblique, of a bright green,
To be worn with one accord for that worthy's sake.
So that was taken as a token by the Table Round,
And he honored that had it, evermore after,   2520
As the best book of knighthood bids it be known.
In the old days of Arthur this happening befell;
The books of Brutus' deeds bear witness thereto
Since Brutus, the bold knight, embarked for this land
After the siege ceased at Troy and the city fared   2525
                                    amiss.
                    Many such, ere we were born,
                    Have befallen here, ere this.
                    May He that was crowned with thorn
                    Bring all men to His bliss! Amen.   2530

Hony Soyt Qui Mal Pense [8]

8. "Shame be to the man who has evil in his mind." This is the motto of the Order of the Garter, founded ca. 1350: apparently a copyist of the poem associated this order with the one founded to honor Gawain.

PIERS PLOWMAN
(ca. 1372–1386)

The large number of manuscripts in which the *Vision of Piers Plowman* has been preserved indicates its wide popularity from the end of the 14th century up to the reign of Elizabeth I. Yet celebrated as the poem was, we know little about its origin. It exists in three versions, which scholars refer to as the A, B, and C Texts. The first, about 2,400 lines long, stops at a rather inconclusive point in the action; the second is a revision of the first plus an extension of more than 4,000 lines; and the third is a revision of the second. The name frequently associated with the poem is William Langland, but who he was and whether he wrote all three versions is not known. The little that can be inferred about him suggests that he came from the west of England and was probably a native of the Malvern Hills area in which the poem is set and where many of the surviving manuscripts were copied. If he wrote all three versions, then his interests and opinions must have changed while he was at work, for the versions differ from one another in many respects; but if more than one poet was involved, then it is extraordinary that all three versions share the same highly individual style and reflect the same curious and interesting poetic personality. Whatever its origin, the poem was avidly read and studied by a great many people. Within four years of the writing of the second version—which scholars have good evidence to date 1377, the year of Edward III's death and Richard II's accession to the throne—it had become so well known that the leaders of the Peasants' Revolt of 1381 used phrases borrowed from it as part of the rhetoric of the rebellion. The poem must therefore have managed to catch the imagination of a number of readers.

Piers Plowman has the form of a dream vision, a common medieval type in which the author presents his story under the guise of having dreamed it. Most dream visions concern romantic love; *Piers Plowman* also concerns love, but in this instance the love is theological. The dream vision generally involves allegory, not only because one expects from a dream the unrealistic, the fanciful, but also because men have always suspected that dreams relate the truth in a disguised form—that they are natural allegories. *Piers Plowman* is perhaps the greatest of English allegories, though the reader who expects to find in it the kind of definite and clear statement that allegory makes in the morality *Everyman* will be disappointed; allegory here is used not so much in order to define the known, as the character "Good Deeds" does in that play, as to explore the unknown, in particular the great spiritual mysteries of Christianity. When handling these the poet's imagination (for convenience let us assume a single poet, Langland) is apt to soar into a mode of expression that stimulates and excites the reader's imagination while, perhaps, bewildering his intellect. Langland's theme is nothing less than the history of Christianity as it unfolds both in the world of the Old and New Testaments and in the life and heart of an individual 14th-century Christian—two seemingly distinct realms between which the poet's allegory moves with dizzying rapidity.

Expanding the genre of dream-vision, *Piers Plowman* takes the form of a whole series of visions, separated by brief intervals when the narrator is awake. The first passage chosen for translation—the Prologue to the poem —introduces the famous first vision of the Field of Folk. The poet thought of Christianity as properly informing—and reforming—society, and he describes 14th-century English society in terms of its failure to represent an ideal society living in accord with Christian principles: hence the satirical poetry for which Langland is generally noted. Society's failure, of course, is attributable in part to the corruption of the church and churchmen, and whenever he considers clerical and ecclesiastical corruption, he pours out savagely indignant satire. But he is equally angry with the failure of the wealthy laity—untaught by the church to practice charity—to alleviate the sufferings of the poor, and it was probably his preoccupation with the poor that made his poem popular with the rebels of 1381; these, though confused in their motives, were eager to obtain correction of certain social abuses that Langland touches upon. This use of his poem must have horrified him, for despite his interest in social reform, he remains a fundamentally conservative and orthodox thinker: yet his passionate sympathy for the common man—idealized in his titular hero Piers the Plowman—made him seem a radical who felt that true religion was best represented not by the church but by the humblest orders of society. Many persons reading his poem more than a century and a half after it was written (it was first printed in 1550) saw in its Prologue strong historical reasons for the reformation of the church that had been carried out in the intervening years.

The second selection represents a wholly different side of Langland's art. It is a description of the central event of Christianity, Christ's crucifixion, followed by an account of his descent into Hell. In this passage Langland's hero Piers is partially identified with Christ: Piers first appears in the poem as a simple, honest farmer, but later assumes aspects of Adam and Moses. With this development his farm produce becomes not simple foodstuffs but the souls of the patriarchs and prophets, and of all mankind, which must be redeemed from Satan's power by Christ's sacrifice on the cross. In lines 19 and 33 these souls are referred to as the "fruit" of Piers Plowman which Christ, having assumed Piers's human nature, will win back from Hell. The crucifixion Langland describes as a literal, historical event—yet he also talks of it as if it were a medieval jousting between the Christ-knight and an opponent. With Christ's death on the cross, the dreamer descends to the gates of Hell, outside of which Christ's soul appears as a great light. The dreamer then hears the debate of the Four Daughters of God, Truth (adherence to the letter of the law), Righteousness, Peace, and Mercy. These highly traditional allegorical figures argue the effectiveness of the Old Law in relation to the New: the first two insist that Adam and Eve and their followers are unredeemably damned for their sin in Eden; the last two uphold the possibility that a New Law may bring them forgiveness. The dreamer then hears the debate that is going on inside of Hell among the devils, who wonder how and whether they can defend themselves from the great light outside the gate (this scene is based on the apocryphal Gospel of Nicodemus, an enormously popular and influential text for the Middle Ages). While the devils are speaking, Hell's gates are broken and Christ enters. He justifies despoiling (or "harrowing," the old word) Hell of the souls of the patriarchs and prophets by showing how the New Law he is bringing fulfills rather than breaks the Old. Lucifer is bound, the Four Daughters of God are reconciled, and the Dreamer wakes to celebrate Easter.

From The Vision of Piers Plowman

From *The Prologue*: [*The Field of Folk*][1]

In a summer season, whan soft was the sun,
I rigged myself up in a long robe, rough like a sheep's,
With skirts hanging like a hermit's, unholy of works,
Went wide in this world, wonders to hear.
But on a May morning, on Malvern Hills,   5
A marvel befell me—magic it seemed.
I was weary of wandering, and went for a rest
Under a broad bank, by a brook's side;
And as I lay lolling, looking at the water,
I slid into a sleep, it sounded so pleasant.   10
Then there met me a marvelous dream,
That I was in a wilderness—where, I'd no notion.
As I looked into the east, up high toward the sun,
I saw a tower on a hill-top, trimly built;
A deep dale beneath, a dungeon-tower in it,   15
With deep dark ditches, dreadful to see.
A fair field full of folk found I there between,
Of all manner of men, the mean and the rich,
Working and wandering, as the world asks.
Some put themselves to plowing, played very seldom,   20
In setting plants and sowing seeds sweated hard,
Winning what wasters use up in gluttony.
And some put themselves to pride, wore proud garments,
Came all costumed in costly clothes.
To prayers and penance put themselves many,   25
All for love of our Lord lived hard lives,
In hope they might have heaven-kingdom's bliss—
Such as anchorites and hermits that hold to their cells,
Care not through the country to cavort about,
With some lush livelihood their limbs to please.   30
And some made themselves merchants—they managed better—
At least it seems to our sight that such men prosper.
And some make mirth, as minstrels can,
And get gold with their games—blameless, I believe;
But jokers and jabbers, Judas' children,   35
Invent fantasies to tell about, make fools of themselves,
And have what wit they need to work if they wanted.
What Paul preaches of them, I'll not put it here:

1. The editor has followed the readings of the B text in his translation of the Prologue of the poem, but has followed the structure of the A text in omitting a long, rather technical passage added by

B. Readings of B are preferred because in some cases they seem superior to A. The text is based on a new edition of B now in preparation.

Qui loquitur turpiloquium[2] is Lucifer's helper.
Beggars and bead-sayers[3] fast about went   40
With their bellies and their bags brimful crammed,
Staged flyting-matches[4] for their food, fought over ale:
In gluttony, God knows, they go to bed,
And rise with ribaldry, those Robert's boys.[5]
Sleepiness and slothfulness follow such always.   45
Pilgrims and palmers[6] made pacts with each other
To seek Saint James[7] and saints at Rome:
They went on their way with lots of wise tales,
And got leave to tell lies all their lives after.
A whole heap of hermits with hookéd staffs   50
Went off to Walsingham[8]—with their wenches behind them.
Great long lubbers that didn't like to work
Clothed themselves in copes[9] to keep distinct from others,
And held forth as hermits to have their ease.
I found there friars, all the four orders,   55
Preaching to the people for profit of their guts,
Glozing the Gospel any way good for them,
For craving for copes construed it as they pleased:
Many of these Masters[1] may buy expensive clothes,
For their money and their merchandise march hand in hand.[2] 60
For since Charity[3] has proved a peddler, principally to shrive
         lords,
Many marvels have been meted out within a few years.
Unless Holy Church and all friars hold together better
The worst trouble in the world will well up soon.
There preached a pardoner[4] as if he a priest were,   65
Brought forth a bull with bishop's seals,
Said that he himself could absolve them all
Of falseness in fasting of vows they'd broken.
Unlearned men believed him, and liked well his words,
Came up cowering to kiss his bulls;   70
He banged them with his brevet[5] and bleared their eyes,
And raked in with his ragman[6] rings and brooches.
Thus they give their gold for gluttons' feeding,
And scatter it to scoundrels schooled in lechery.
If the bishop were blessed and worth both his ears   75
His seal should not be sent to deceive the people.

---

2. "Who speaks slander": the text is not St. Paul's, but a reason for not quoting something from St. Paul that would be slanderous.
3. Prayer-sayers, i.e., people who offered to pray for the souls of those who gave them alms.
4. Contests in which the participants took turns insulting each other, preferably in verse.
5. I.e., robbers.
6. Professional pilgrims.
7. I.e., his shrine in Compostela, Spain.
8. English town possessing a famous shrine to the Virgin Mary.
9. Hermits' or friars' capes.

1. I.e., Masters of Divinity.
2. I.e., the money they make consists entirely of the proceeds from their sales (of shrift).
3. The ideal of the friars—as stated by St. Francis, founder of the Franciscans —was simply charity.
4. An official empowered to pass on from the pope temporal indulgence for their sins to people who contributed to charitable enterprises; pardoners often abused their office: see Chaucer's Pardoner, General Prologue, lines 671ff. "Bull": papal license.
5. Pardoner's license.
6. Rolled-up documents.

But it's not by the bishop's leave that the boy preaches,
For the parish priest and the pardoner split the silver
That the poor of the parish should be paid otherwise.
Parsons and parish priests complained to the bishop   80
That their parishes were poor since the pestilence time,[7]
To have a license and a leave at London to dwell,
And sing[8] there for simony—for silver is sweet.[9]

* * *

Yet stood there scores of men in scarves of silk[1]—
Law-sergeants[2] they seemed who served in court,   85
Pleaded cases for pennies,[3] and impounded[4] the law,
And not for love of our Lord unloosed their lips once:
You might better measure mist on Malvern Hills
Than get a "mum" from their mouths till money is showed.
Barons and burgesses and bondmen also   90
I saw in this assembly, as you shall hear later;
Bakers and brewers and butchers many,
Woolen-websters [5] and weavers of linen,
Tailors and tinkers, tax-collectors of markets,
Masons and miners and many other trades;   95
Of all kinds of living laborers there leapt forth some,
Such as diggers of ditches that do their work badly,
And drive away the day with "Dieu save Dame Emme."[6]
Cooks and their kitchen-boys cried, "Hot pies, hot!
Pork and good goose—go dine quickly."   100
Tavern-keepers to them told the same tale;
"White wine of Alsace and wine of Gascony,
Of the Rhine and La Rochelle, to wash the roast down."
All this I saw sleeping, and seven times more.

Passus XXI: [*The Harrowing of Hell*][7]

Wool-clad and wet-shoed went I forth after
As a mindless mortal that minds no sorrow,
And trudged forth like a tramp, time of all my life,
Till I grew weary of the world and wished again to sleep,

7. Since 1349, England had suffered a number of epidemics of the plague, which had produced famines and depopulated the countryside.
8. I.e., sing masses. Wealthy persons, especially in London, set up foundations to pay priests to sing masses for their own souls and those of their relatives. "Simony": abuse of ecclesiastical office; a priest who had charge of a parish was canonically prohibited from exercising any other salaried function in the church.
9. Here the B text adds 125 lines to the A text.
1. A silk scarf was a lawyer's badge of office.
2. Important lawyers: see the Prologue to the *Canterbury Tales*, lines 311ff.

3. Pennies were fairly valuable coins in medieval England.
4. Held in legal custody.
5. Weavers of wool.
6. "God save Dame Emma": apparently a popular song.
7. The translation by the editor is based on Passus XXI of the C text which parallels Passus XVIII of B. The two texts differ little in this section of the poem, but the later version seems on artistic grounds slightly preferable to the earlier. A few readings have been introduced from B where C appears to be corrupt, and several short digressive passages have been omitted. The translator has taken the liberty of altering several disheartening expressions of medieval prejudice.

And lay down till Lent, and long time I slept.   5
Of children and of cheers of "*Gloria, laus!*"[8] chiefly I dreamed,
And how "Hosanna!" to an organ old folk sang.
One resembling the Samaritan[9] and somewhat Piers Plowman[1]
Barefoot on an ass's back bootless came riding
Without spurs or spear—sprightly he looked,   10
As is the nature of a knight that draws near to be dubbed,
To get himself gilt spurs and engraved jousting shoes.
Then was Faith watching from a window and cried, "A *fili David!*"
As does a herald-of-arms when armed men come to jousts.
Old Jews of Jerusalem for joy they sang,   15
"*Benedictus qui venit in nomine Domini.*"
Then I asked Faith what all that affair meant
And who should joust in Jerusalem. "Jesus," he said,
"And fetch what the Fiend claims, the fruit of Piers Plowman."
"Is Piers Plowman in this place?" said I, and he winked at me: 20
"*Liberum arbitrium Dei*[2] for love has undertaken
That this Jesus for his gentleness shall joust in Piers's arms,
In his helmet and in his hauberk, *humana natura*,[3]
That Christ not be known here for *consummatus Deus*.[4]
In the plate armor of Piers Plowman this jouster shall ride,   25
For no hard blow shall hurt him as *in deitate Patris*."[5]
"Who shall joust with Jesus?" said I, "Jews or scribes?"
"Nay," said Faith, "but the Fiend and False-Doom-to-Die.
Death says he will undo and down bring
All that live or look on land or on water.   30
Life says that he lies and has laid his life in pledge
That for all that Death can do, in three days he'll walk
And fetch from the Fiend the fruit of Piers Plowman,
And lay it where he likes, and Lucifer bind,
And beat and bring down bale-death forever.   35
    O mors, ero mors tua."[6]
Then came Pilate with many people *sedens pro tribunali*[7]
To see how doughtily Death should do and judge both their rights.
The judge and the justicers against Jesus they were
And all the court cried "*Crucifige!*"[8] loud.   40

8. The first words of an anthem, "Glory, praise, and honor," which was sung by children in Palm Sunday processions during the Middle Ages. The background of the beginning of this part of the poem is the Biblical account of Christ's entry into Jerusalem on Palm Sunday, when the crowds greeted him crying, "Hosanna (line 7) to the son of David (line 13); Blessed is he that comes in the name of the Lord (line 16); Hosanna in the highest": see Matthew xxi.9. The poet moves without transition from Palm Sunday to Good Friday.
9. In the previous vision, the dreamer has encountered Abraham or Faith (mentioned in lines 13, 17, 28, and 98 below), Moses or Hope, and the Good Samaritan or Charity, who was riding toward a "jousting in Jerusalem," and who now appears as an aspect of Christ. For the Good Samaritan, see Luke x.
1. For Piers Plowman, see the introductory note.
2. The free will of God.
3. Human nature.
4. The perfect (three-personed) God.
5. In the godhead of the Father.
6. "O death, I will be thy death" (Hosea xiii.14). In the preceding line "bale-death" means fire-death, or hell.
7. "Sitting as a judge" (echoing Matthew xxvii.19).
8. "Crucify him" (John xix.6).

Then a plaintiff appeared before Pilate and said,
"This Jesus has made jokes about Jerusalem's temple,
That he would have it down in one day and in three days after
Put it up again all new—here he stands that said it—
And yet build it every bit as big in all dimensions, 45
As long and as broad both, above and below,
And as wide as it ever was—this we all witness."
"*Crucifige!*" said a sergeant, "sure, he's a witch."
"*Tolle, tolle!*"9 said another, and took keen thorns
And began of green thorn a garland to make, 50
And set it sore on his head, and said then in envy,
"*Ave, rabbi,*"1 said that wretch, and shot reeds at his eyes.
And they nailed him with three nails naked on a cross,
And with a pole a potion put up to his lips
And bade him drink to delay his death and his days lengthen, 55
And said, "If he is subtle, himself now will he help.
If you are Christ and a king's son, come down from the cross,
Then we'll believe that Life loves you and will not let you die."
"*Consummatum est*"2 said Christ and commenced to swoon,
Piteously and pale like a prisoner dying. 60
The Lord of Light and of Life laid his eyes together;
The day for dread withdrew and dark became the sun;
The temple's wall tottered and split in two pieces;3
The hard rock was rent apart and right dark night it seemed;
The earth quaked and quivered as if it were a quick thing, 65
And dead men for that din came out of deep graves
And told why that tempest so long a time lasted:
"For a bitter battle," the dead body said;
"Life and Death in this darkness, one destroys the other:
But no one will know surely which shall have the victory 70
Before Sunday about sunrise"—and sank with that to earth.
Some said he was God's son that so fair died:
    "*Vere filius Dei erat iste*";4
And some said he was a sorcerer: "We should see first
Whether he's dead or not dead, down before he's taken." 75
Two thieves were there that suffered death that time
Upon crosses beside Christ—such was the common law.
A constable came forth and cracked their legs in two
And their arms afterward of either of those thieves.
But there was no bastard so bold God's body to touch: 80
Since Christ was a knight and a king's son, Nature decreed
        that time
That no one should have the hardiness to touch him in his
        dying.
But there came close a blind knight with a keen-ground spear

9. "Away with him, away with him" (John xix.15).
1. "Hail, master" (Matthew xxvi.49). These are actually Judas' words when he kissed Christ in order to identify him to the arresting officers.
2. "It is finished" (John xix.30).
3. According to the Biblical accounts (Matthew xxvii.51, Luke xxiii.45), it was the veil (*velum*) not the wall (*vallum*) of the temple which was split in two. The account Langland knew substituted one word for the other: he probably did not know the Bible at first hand.
4. "Truly this was the Son of God" (Matthew xxvii.54).

Called Longinus[5] as the letter tells, who long had lost his sight;
Before Pilate and the other people in the place he waited.   85
Although he was unwilling, he was made that time
To joust with Jesus, this blind Jew Longinus.
For all that watched there were unwilling, mounted or on foot,
To touch him or tamper with him or take him down and bury
        him,
Except this blind bachelor[6] that bore him through the heart: 90
The blood sprang down along the spear and unsparred[7] the
        knight's eyes.
Then the knight fell upon his knees and cried, "Now, Jesu,
        mercy!
Against my will it was, Lord, that such a wound I gave you."
He sighed and said, "Sore I repent it:
For the deed that I have done, my doom lies in your grace;   95
My possessions and my person both, at your pleasure take them,
And have ruth on me rightful Jesu"—and right with that he
        wept.
Then did Faith fiercely the false justices despise
"Who made the blind beat the dead—it was a bully's deed;
Cursed cowards, no kind of knighthood was it ever   100
To beat a bound body with any bright weapon.
The guerdon yet has he gotten for all his great wounds,
For your champion chevalier, the chief knight of you all,
Yields himself as a coward crying quick to Jesus' will.
For once this darkness is done Death shall be vanquished,   105
And you lawless lords have lost, for Life shall have the victory."

* * *

What for fear of this affair and of false men
I withdrew in that darkness to *descendit ad inferna,*[8]
And there I saw soothly, *secundum scripturas,*[9]
Out of the west as it were a wench as I thought   110
Came walking in the way—toward hell she looked.
Mercy was that maid's name, a mild thing withal,
A most gracious girl and goodly of speech.
Her sister as it seemed came softly walking
Out of the east, opposite, and westward she moved   115
A comely creature and clean—Truth was her name.
Because of the virtue that followed her afraid was she never.
When these maidens met, Mercy and Truth,
Each asked the other of this great wonder,
Of the din and the darkness and how the day lowered,   120
And what a gleam and a great light glowed before hell.
"I wonder at this strange stir, in faith," said Truth,
And have fared forth to find what this marvel means."

---

5. Longinus is named in the apocryphal Gospel of Nicodemus, which provided Langland with the material for much of this portion of his poem.
6. Knight.
7. Opened; in the original there is a play on words with "spear."
8. "He descended into hell" (from the Creed).
9. According to the Scriptures.

"Do not marvel," said Mercy, "mirth is its meaning:
A maid named Mary, mother without touching   125
By any kind of creature, conceived through speech
And grace of the Holy Ghost, grew great with child—
Without woman's stain into this world she brought him.
And that my tale is true I take God to witness:
Since that baby was born thirty winters been passed,   130
Who died and suffered death this day about midday.
And that is the cause of this eclipse that now covers the sun,
In meaning that man shall from murk be drawn
While the glare of this great light goes to blind Lucifer.
For patriarchs and prophets have preached of this often: 135
What through a tree was taken a tree shall restore,[1]
And what Death brought down a death shall raise."
"What you tell," said Truth, "is a tale of nonsense,
For Adam and Eve and Abraham and the rest,
Patriarchs and prophets that in pain lie,   140
Never believe that yonder light aloft shall bring them
Or have them out of hell—hold your tongue, Mercy.
It's but trifling that you talk of: I, Truth, know the truth,
That whatever is once in hell, out comes it never.
Job the perfect patriarch disproves what you say: 145
   Quia in inferno nulla est redemptio."[2]
Then Mercy full mildly mouthed these words:
"From experience," she said, "I suppose they shall be saved.
Venom destroys venom, and from that I find evidence
That Adam and Eve shall have cure: 150
For of all vexing venoms the vilest is the scorpion's—
May no medicine amend the place where he stings
Till dead he is dabbed thereon; then he undoes it,
The previous poisoning, through the power of himself.
So shall this death destroy—I dare bet my life—   155
All that Death and the Devil did first to Eve.
And just as the beguiler through guile beguiled man first,
So shall grace that began everything make a good end
And beguile the beguiler—and that's a good trick:
   Ars ut artem falleret."[3]   160
"Now let's stop," said Truth, "I see as I think
Out of the nip of the north, not far away,
Righteousness come running—let's rest a while,
For she knows far more than we: she was here before us both."
   "That is sooth," said Mercy, "and I see toward the south   165
Where Peace comes playing in patience clothed.
Love has desired her long—I believe it may be
That Love has sent her some letter, what this light means

1. The first tree bore the fruit which Adam and Eve ate, thereby damning mankind; the second tree is the cross on which Christ was crucified, thereby redeeming mankind.
2. "Since in hell there is no redemption" (the idea occurs in Job vii.9).
3. "A trick by which to trick a trickster" (from a medieval Latin hymn).

That hovers over hell thus: she will us tell."
When Peace in patience clothed approached near them both,170
Righteousness reverenced her in her rich clothing,
And prayed Peace to tell her to what place she was going,
And in her gay garments whom to gladden she thought.
"My will is to wend," said she, "and welcome them all
That many a day I might not see for murk of sin.   175
Adam and Eve and others too in hell,
Moses and many more merry shall sing,
And I shall dance thereto—do you so, sister.
Because Jesus jousted well joy begins to dawn:
   Ad vesperum demorabitur fletus et ad matutinum laetitia.[4]180
Love that is my lover such letters sent me
That Mercy my sister and I mankind shall save,
And that God has fully given and granted me, Peace, and Mercy
To be man's bondsmen for evermore after.
Lo, here's the patent," said Peace: "*In pace in idipsum;*   185
And that this deed shall endure, *Dormiam et requiescam.*"[5]
"What, are you raving?" said Righteousness. "Or are you
            really drunk?
Do you believe that yonder light might unlock hell
And save man's soul? Sister, don't believe it.
At the beginning God gave the doom himself   190
That Adam and Eve and every one that followed them
Should die downright and dwell in pain after
If they touched a tree and the tree's fruit ate.
Adam afterward against his forbidding
Fed of the fruit and forsook as it were   195
The love of our Lord and his lore both,
And followed what the Fiend taught and his flesh's will
Against reason. I, Righteousness, record this with truth
That their pain shall be perpetual and no prayer help them.
So let them chew as they chose, and let us not chide, sisters, 200
For it's misery without amends, the morsel they ate."
"And I shall prove," said Peace, "that their pain may have end,
And trouble into time of joy turn at the last.
For if they had not known of woe, no joy would they have felt,
For no one knows what well-being is who woe knew never,   205
Nor what is hot hunger who never had need.
Who could correctly white color describe
If all the world were white—swan-white all things?
If no night were, no one, I believe,
Should be well aware what day means.   210
If God had not suffered something from outside himself

4. "Weeping will endure for a night but joy comes in the morning" (Psalm xxix.6 Vulgate).
5. The patent, or document conferring authority, consists of phrases from Psalm iv.9–10 Vulgate: "I will both lay me down in peace and sleep: for thou, Lord, only hast placed me in hope."

He would never have known well whether death was sour or
    sweet.
Nor should a right rich man that lives in rest and ease
Know what woe is if it weren't for Nature's death.
So God that began everything of his good will   215
Became man of a maid mankind to save,
And suffered himself to be sold to see the sorrow of dying,
And this cures all care and cause is of rest.
For till a plague comes upon us—I dare proclaim it—
No man knows, I think, what 'enough' really means.   220
Therefore God of his great goodness the first man Adam
Placed in pleasance and in perfect joy.
And afterward he suffered him to sin, sorrow to feel,
To see what well-being was—truly to know it.
And afterward God offered himself and took Adam's nature   225
To see what he had suffered, in three sundry places—
In heaven and on earth, and now to hell he goes
To learn what all woe is that knows well all joy.
    Omnia probate; quod bonum est tenete.[6]
So shall it fare with these folk, by their folly and their sin   230
They shall learn what love is and relief without end.
No one knows what war is where peace prevails,
Nor what is true well-being till 'Woe, alas!' teaches him."
Then was there a wight with two broad eyes:
Book was that beaupere's[7] name, a bold man of speech.   235
"By God's body," said this Book, "I will bear witness
That when this boy was born there blazed a star,
That all the wise men of the world with one wit agreed
That such a baby was born in Bethlehem city
That should save man's soul and sin destroy.   240
And all the elements," said the Book, "hereof bore witness:
That he was God who wrought the world the welkin first
    showed;
All those who were in heaven took *stella comata*[8]
And tended her like a torch to reverence his birth
The light followed the Lord into the low earth;   245
The water witnesses that he was God for he walked on him dry.
Peter the Apostle perceived his walking,
And as he went on the water knew him well and said,
    '*Domine, iube me venire ad te super aquas.*'[9]
And lo how the sun did lock her light in herself   250
When she saw him suffer that sun and sea made.
The earth for heavy heart that he would suffer
Quaked like a quick thing, and all the rock crashed down.

---

6. "Prove all things; hold fast that
which is good" (I Thessalonians v.21).
7. Fine fellow's: Book's two broad eyes
suggest the Old and New Testaments.

8. Hairy star, i.e., comet.
9. "Lord, bid me come to thee on the
waters" (Matthew xiv.28).

Lo, hell might not hold but opened when God suffered,
And let out Simeon's sons to see him hang on cross.   255
  Non visurum se mortem.[1]
And now shall Lucifer believe it, loath though he is,
For Jesus like a giant[2] with an engine comes yonder
To break and to beat down all that be against him,
And to have out of hell all that he pleases.   260
And yet I, Book, will be burnt unless he rises to life
And comforts all his kin and out of care brings them."
"Let us cease," said Truth, "I hear and see both
A spirit speaks to hell and bids unspar the gates":
  "*Attolite portas, principes, vestras, Et elevamini, portae
    aeternales, Et introibit Rex gloriae,*"[3]   265
A voice loud in that light to Lucifer[4] said,
"Princes of this place, quick unpin the gates,
For here comes with crown the King of all glory."
Then sighed Satan and said to hell,
"Such a light against our leave Lazarus[5] it fetched: 270
Care and cumbrance has come to us all;
If this king comes in mankind will he fetch
And have it where Lazarus is, and easily bind me.
Patriarchs and prophets have prated of this long,
That such a lord and a light should lead them all hence.   275
But rise up, Ragamuffin, and reach me all the bars
That Belial your belsire[6] used to beat your dame,
And I shall make this lord delay and his light stop;
Before we're blinded by brightness let's go bar the gates,
Check them and chain them and every chink block   280
So that no light may leap in at louver or at loophole.
Ashtaroth, hoot out and have out our boys,
Colting and all his kin to keep our goods safe.
Boiling brimstone burning cast it out
All hot on their heads that enter near the walls.   285
Aim bows of brake[7] and brazen guns
And shoot out shot enough to shatter his ranks.
Put Mahoud at the mangonel[8] and millstones hurl,

1. Simeon, who was present at the presentation of the infant Jesus in the temple, had been told by the Holy Ghost
that "he should not see death" (Luke
ii.26) before he had seen the "Lord's
Christ." The apocryphal Gospel of Nicodemus says that Simeon's sons were
raised from the dead at the time of
Jesus' death.
2. I.e., like Samson, who carried off the
gates of Gaza; see Judges xvi.3.
3. "Lift up your gates, O princes, and
be ye lifted up, everlasting doors, and
the King of glory shall come in" (Psalm
xxiii.7 Vulgate).

4. Langland, following an old tradition
also reflected in Milton's *Paradise Lost*,
pictures hell as populated by a number
of devils: Lucifer, who began the war in
heaven and tempted Eve in Eden; Satan
(line 269); Ragamuffin (line 276); Belial
(line 277); Ashtaroth (line 282); Colting
(line 283); Mahoud (line 288); and
Goblin (line 319) are all named as
"fiends."
5. For the raising of Lazarus from the
dead, see John xi.
6. Grandfather.
7. Large crossbows operated by a winch.
8. Catapult.

With crooks and caltrops[9] let's crush them all."
"Listen," said Lucifer, "for I this lord know—   290
Both this lord and this light, it's long ago I've known him.
May no death do harm to this lord, nor any devil's tricks,
But he walks where he will; yet beware him of the perils:
If he bereaves me of my right he robs me by force,
For by right and by reason the race that is here   295
Body and soul be mine, both good and evil.
For he himself said it that sire is of heaven
That Adam and Eve and all their issue
Should die dolefully and dwell here forever
If they touched a tree or took an apple from it.   300
Thus this lord of light such a law made,
And since he's a lawful lord, I don't believe he will
Rob us of our right, since reason damned them.
And since we've possessed them seven thousand winters,
And he never denied our right, and now would begin,   305
Then he would be worse than his word that is witness of truth."
"That is true," said Satan, "but I'm sore afraid
Because you got them by guile and his garden violated,
Against his love and his leave on his land trespassed—
Not in form of a fiend but in form of an adder—   310
And enticed Eve to eat by herself:
        Vae soli![1]
And promised her and him after to know
As two gods with God both good and evil:
Thus with treason and treachery you tricked them both,   315
And made them break their obedience by blabbing lies to them,
And so you had them out and hither at the last.
It is not goodly gotten where guile is the cause."
"And God will not be beguiled," said Goblin, "nor be tricked.
We have no true title to them, for your treason caused it."   320
"Certainly, I'm afraid," said the Fiend,[2] "that Truth will
        fetch them out.
And as you beguiled God's image by going like an adder,
So God has beguiled us all by going like a man."
"For God has gone," said Goblin, "in a man's likeness
These thirty winters, as I think—gone about and preached.   325
I've assailed him with sin, and sometimes I asked
Whether he was God or God's son—he gave me short answer.
Thus he's been tricked out like a tidy man these two and
        thirty winters.
And when I saw it was so I sought how I might

9. Devices equipped with prongs that were placed on the ground to impede cavalry attacks; "crooks" were hooked sticks used by the defenders of a castle against besiegers trying to scale the walls.
1. "Woe to one that is alone" (Ecclesiastes iv.10).
2. Here and in line 339 it is assumed that "the Fiend" is Lucifer's most articulate critic Satan, but it may be that the poet is referring to Goblin when he writes "fiend."

Hinder them that hated him lest they should him martyr: 330
I would have lengthened his life, for I believed if he died,
That if his soul should come hither, it would shame us all.
For the body while it walked on its bones busy was it ever
To teach men to be true and to love each other,
And this life and law, if it's long followed,   335
It shall undo us devils, and down bring us all.
And now I see where a soul comes sailing hitherward
With glory and great light—God it is, I know."
"I say we should flee," said the Fiend, "all fast away,
For it were better for us not to be than abide in his sight.   340
For your lies, Lucifer, we first lost our joy,
And out of heaven hither your pride made us fall.
Because we believed your lies there, we lost our bliss,
And now for a later lie that you lied to Eve
We have lost our lordship on land and in hell: 345
   Nunc princeps huius mundi eiicietur foras."[3]
Again the light bade unlock and Lucifer answered,
"What lord are you?" said Lucifer. A voice aloud said,
"The lord of might and of main that made all things.
Dukes of this dim place, quick undo these gates,   350
That Christ may come in, the king's son of heaven."
And with that breath hell broke with all Belial's bars,
For any warrior or watchman wide opened the gates.
Patriarchs and prophets, *populus in tenebris*,[4]
Sang Saint John's song, *Ecce agnus Dei*.[5]   355
Lucifer might not look, so light blinded him,
And those that our Lord loved forth with that light flew.
"Behold me here," said our Lord, "both in body and in soul,
For all sinful souls to save the right of us both.
Although reason recorded and right of myself   360
That if they ate the apple, all should die,
I ordered not that they be held here in hell forever.
For the deadly sin that they did, your deceit caused it:
With guile you got them out against all reason.
For in my palace Paradise in the person of an adder   365
Falsely you fetched there what befell me to guard,
Closed them and beguiled them and my garden profaned
Against my love and my leave. The Old Law teaches
That beguilers be beguiled and in their guile fall.
And whoever hits out a man's eye or else his front teeth   370
Or any manner of member maims or hurts,
The same sore shall he have that any one smites so:
   Dentem pro dente et oculum pro oculo.[6]

3. "Now shall the prince of this world be cast out" (John xii.31): "prince of this world" is a title for the Devil.
4. "People in the shades": the phrase is from the Gospel of Nicodemus.
5. "Behold the Lamb of God" (John i.36).
6. "A tooth for a tooth and an eye for an eye" (Exodus xxi.24, Matthew v.38).

So life shall lose life where life has taken life;
So that life should requite life the Old Law requires: 375
Ergo[7] soul shall requite soul and sin to sin turn,
And all that man misdid I, man, amend it;
And what Death undid my death shall restore,
And both quicken and requite what was quenched through sin.
And guile is beguiled through grace at the last: 380
    Ars ut artem falleret.[8]
So believe it not, Lucifer, against the law I fetch
Here any sinful soul solely by force,
But through right and through reason ransom here my liege-
    men.
    Non veni solvere legem sed adimplere.[9] 385
So what was gotten with guile through grace is now won back,
And as Adam and Eve through a tree died,
Adam and all through a tree shall turn to life.
And now begins your guile against you to turn,
And my grace to grow ever greater and wider. 390
The bitterness that you have brewed, imbibe it yourself
Who are doctor of Death—drink that you made.
For I that am lord of Life, love is my drink,
And for that drink today I died upon earth.
But I will drink from no ditch nor from deep clergy,[1] 395
But only from common cups—all Christian souls.
But your drink will be death, and deep hell your bowl.
I fought so I feel thirsty still for man's soul's sake:
    Sitio.[2]
May no drink moisten me nor my thirst slake 400
Till vintage-time fall in the vale of Jehoshaphat[3]
Where I will drink right ripe wine, *Resurrectio mortuorum.*[4]
And then shall I come as a king crowned with angels
And have out of hell all men's souls.
Fiends and fiendkins before me shall stand 405
And be at my bidding, wherever I best please.
But to be merciful to men then my nature requires,
For we are brothers of one blood, though not in baptism all;
But all that are my whole brothers, in blood and in baptism,
Shall never again come into hell, be they once out: 410
    Tibi soli peccavi et malum coram te feci.[5]

---

7. "Therefore": the Latin conjunction was used in formal debate to introduce the conclusion derived from a number of propositions.
8. "A trick by which to trick a trickster."
9. "I have not come to destroy the law but to fulfill it" (Matthew v.17).
1. Apparently Christ is saying that his love is not limited to the priestly class.
2. "I thirst" (John xix.28).
3. On the evidence of Joel iii.2, 12, it is

possible to locate the site of the Last Judgment as the Vale of Jehoshaphat.
4. "The resurrection of the dead" (from the Creed).
5. "Against thee only have I sinned and done this evil in thy face"; the remainder of the verse (Psalm i.6 Vulgate), "that thou mightest be justified when thou speakest, and be clear when thou judgest," assigns the sole power of judging the sinner to God, since it is only against God that the sinner has acted.

It is not the use on earth to hang any felon
Oftener than once, though he were a traitor;
And if the king of the kingdom come at that time
Where a thief should suffer death or such punishment,   415
Law grants he should give him life if he looked upon him.
And I that am king over kings shall come at such a time
Where doom to death damns all wicked,
And if law wills I look on them, it lies in my grace
Whether they die or not die, did they never so evil,   420
If it be any bit paid for, the boldness of their sin.
I may do mercy in accord with my righteousness and all my
　　　true words;
Though Holy Writ wishes that I be avenged on all that worked
　　　evil—
　　Nullum malum impunitum et nullum bonum irremunera-
　　　　tum[6]—
They shall be cleansed clearly and cured of their sins   425
In my prison purgatory till *Parce*[7] says "Stop!"
And my mercy shall be shown to many of my half-brothers,
For blood-kin may see blood-kin both hungry and cold,
But blood-kin may not see blood-kin bleed without his pity.
　　Audivi arcana verba quae non licet homini loqui.[8]   430
But my righteousness and right shall reign in hell,
And mercy rule all mankind before me in heaven.
For I would be an unkind king unless I my kin helped
And especially at such a need where help is surely needed:
　　Non intres in iudicium cum servo tuo.[9]   435
Thus by law," said our Lord, "lead I will from hence
All those that I loved who believed in my coming.
But for the lie that you lied, Lucifer, to Eve,
You shall buy it back bitterly"—and bound him with chains.
Ashtaroth and all the others hid themselves in corners: 440
They dared not look at our Lord, the least of them all,
But let him lead forth whomever he liked and leave
　　　whom he pleased.
Many hundreds of angels harped then and sang,
　　"Culpat caro, purgat caro, regnat Deus Dei caro."[1]   445
Then piped Peace of poets a note:
　　"Clarior est solito post maxima nebula phoebus;
　　　Post inimicitias clarior est amor."[2]

6. "[He is a just judge who leaves] no
evil unpunished and no good unrewarded": not from the Bible, but from
Pope Innocent III's *Concerning Contempt for the Word.*
7. "Spare."
8. "I heard secret words which it is not
lawful for a man to utter" (II Corinthians xii.4). The relevance of the verse is
not clear: perhaps the poet is claiming
a mystical authority for putting into
Christ's mouth a promise to save many

of his "half-brothers"—i.e., the unbap-
tized, who were often considered unredeemably damned.
9. "Enter not into judgment with thy
servant" (Psalm clxii.2 Vulgate).
1. "Flesh sins, flesh redeems, flesh reigns
as God of God" (from a medieval
hymn).
2. "Brighter is ordinarily the sun after
biggest clouds; after hostilities brighter is
love" (source unknown).

"After sharpest showers," said Peace, "most bright shines the
sun;
No weather is warmer than after watery clouds,
Nor any love lovelier or more loving friends   450
Than after war and weeping when Love and Peace are masters.
Was never war in this world nor wickeder envy
That Love if he liked to laughing might not bring,
And Peace through patience might all perils stop."
"Truce!" said Truth. "You tell us true, by Jesus.   455
Let's kiss in covenant and each of us clasp other."
"And let no people," said Peace, "perceive that we argued,
For nothing is impossible to him that is almighty."
"You say sooth," said Righteousness, and reverently she kissed
Peace, and Peace her, *per saecula saeculorum.*[3]   460
     Misericordia et veritas obviaverunt sibi; iustitia et pax os-
         culatae sunt.[4]
Truth blew a trumpet then and sang *"Te Deum Laudamus,"*[5]
And then Love strummed a lute with a loud note,
     "Ecce quam bonum et quam iocundum habitare
         fratres in unum."[6]
Till the day dawned these damsels caroled,   465
When bells rang to the Resurrection, and right with that I
waked
And called Kit my wife and Calote my daughter:
"Arise and go reverence God's resurrection,
And creep to the cross on knees and kiss it for a jewel,
And a most rightful relic, none richer on earth,   470
For God's blessed body it bore for our cure,
And it frightens the Fiend, for such is its might
May no grisly ghost glide in its shadow."

3. "For ever and ever": the liturgical
formula.
4. "Mercy and truth have met together:
righteousness and peace have kissed each
other" (Pslam lxxxiv.11 Vulgate).

5. "We praise thee, O Lord."
6. "Behold how good and how pleasant
it is for brothers to dwell together in
unity" (Psalm cxxxii.1 Vulgate).

MIDDLE ENGLISH LYRICS

The best of the Middle English lyrics, both religious and secular, seem remarkably fresh despite the fact that in both theme and form they are extremely conventional—at times almost stylized. The song of spring (the
French *reverdie*), the love lyric and love complaint, the celebration of the
Virgin Mary, the witty satire of women, the meditation upon Calvary—
even the rollicking verse in praise of good food, good drink, and good living—are members of ancient genres, most of which had developed in France
(some of the poems here printed closely parallel French lyrics). The poet's
love in *Alison* is conventional even in her name, which is that of the Wife
of Bath and of the heroine of the Miller's Tale, and the poet could have

written her praise without ever having loved anything more feminine than books, which contained hundreds of ladies with Alison's charms. The fact that most of them would have been blue-eyed blondes might make love for a black-eyed brunette seem daringly realistic, but conventions set up anti-conventions which become as rigid as their older antitheses. Yet those who feel that such a lyric as *Alison* is the genuine complaint of a 13th-century English lad are right in their reactions as readers if wrong in fact, for the poem re-creates excellently the excitement of young love—and the time must have been full of young men yearning for black-eyed Alisons.

It is the same with the spring songs. Spring returns in much the same literary terms in poem after poem, year after year, century after century, but the best medieval spring songs also vigorously reproduce the actual excite-ment of its natural return every March and April. For while every good poet brings something of his own observing to the tradition he is following, the writers of medieval lyrics are especially distinguished for their unself-consciousness and immediacy. Just as there was no consciousness on the part of the medieval man of anachronism—historical differences in time or place—there seems to have been no self-consciousness about his attempts to express himself in poetic terms: convention apparently liberated him, instead of oppressing him in the way it is often supposed to do. It is with perfect naturalness that the poet of *Sunset on Calvary* relives the scene, standing with the mother Mary beside the cross on which her Son hangs; or the poet of *I Sing of a Maiden* visualizes the mystery of the Virgin Birth in terms of the most natural of mysteries, the falling dew; or the poet of *Adam Lay Bound* cheerfully regards Adam's sin and its dire consequences as a kind of childish naughtiness and punishment that had the tremendous effect of bringing Christ to earth. The very simplicity of the poet's attitude achieves the most striking artistic results.

Several of the poems printed here depend on traditions that are no longer alive. The *Corpus Christi Carol* relies upon the ancient fertility myth of the Fisher King which had been caught up and Christianized in Ar-thurian legend. *I Have a Young Sister* is a riddling poem that is reminiscent of the Old English riddles, though its clues, highly suggestive sexual sym-bols, are of a fully developed sophistication.

It is impossible to date the individual lyrics with any certainty. Perhaps the oldest is the *Cuckoo Song*, which is probably of the 12th century, and one may guess that the other spring songs are of the late 13th or early 14th; but some of the best of the lyrics (*I Sing of a Maiden*, *Adam Lay Bound*) may be of the 15th century. In general, we know only that the poems must be earlier than the manuscripts in which they appear, but because of the fact that an early lyric might have been reworded by a late scribe in such a way as to make it appear late, we can rarely tell by how many years any given lyric preceded the manuscript that records it. The sources of the texts printed here are too diverse to be listed. Spelling has been normalized as in the selections from Chaucer.

Fowls in the Frith

Fowles° in the frith,°   *birds / woods*
The fisshes in the flood,
And I mon waxe wood:[1]
Much sorwe° I walke with   *sorrow*
5 For beste[2] of boon° and blood.   *bone*

Alison

Bitweene° Merch and Averil,   *in the seasons of*
When spray biginneth to springe,
The litel fowl hath hire wil°   *pleasure*
On hire leod[3] to singe.
5 Ich° libbe° in love-longinge   *I / live*
For semlokest° of alle thinge. *seemliest, fairest*
Heo° may me blisse bringe: *she*
 Ich am in hire baundoun.°   *power*
 An hendy hap ich habbe yhent,[4]
10 Ichoot° from hevene it is me sent: *I know*
From alle[5] wommen my love is lent,° *removed*
 And light° on Alisoun.   *alights*

On hew° hire heer° is fair ynough, *hue / hair*
Hire browe browne, hire yë° blake; *eye*
15 With lossum cheere heo on me lough;[6]
With middel smal and wel ymake;
But° heo me wolle to hire take *Unless*
For to been hire owen make,°   *mate*
Longe to liven ichulle° forsake, *I will*
20 And feye° fallen adown.   *dead*
 An hendy hap, etc.

Nightes when I wende° and wake, *turn*
Forthy° mine wonges° waxeth wan: *therefore / cheeks*
Levedy,° al for thine sake   *lady*
25 Longinge is ylent me on.[7]
In world nis noon so witer° man *clever*
That al hire bountee° telle can; *excellence*
Hire swire° is whittere° than the swan, *neck / whiter*
 And fairest may° in town.   *maid*
30 An hendy, etc.

Ich am for wowing° al forwake,° *wooing / worn out from waking*
Wery so water in wore.[8]
Lest any reve me[9] my make
Ich habbe y-yerned yore.[1]
35 Bettere is tholien° while° sore *endure / for a time*
Than mournen evermore.

1. Must go mad.
2. Probably "the best," i.e., his lady.
The meaning "beast" is, however, not
impossible.
3. In her language.
4. A gracious chance I have received.
5. I.e., all other.
6. With lovely face she on me smiled.
7. Longing has come upon me.
8. Perhaps "millpond."
9. Deprive me.
1. I have been worrying long since.

Geinest under gore,²
    Herkne to my roun:°   *song*
    An hendy, etc.

My Lief Is Faren in Londe

My lief is faren in londe³—
Allas, why is she so?
And I am so sore bonde°   *bound*
I may nat come her to.
5 She hath myn herte in holde
Wherever she ride or go°—   *walk*
With trewe love a thousand folde.

Western Wind

Westron wind, when will thou blow?
The small rain down can rain.
Christ, that my love were in my arms,
And I in my bed again.

I Have a Young Sister

I have a yong suster
    Fer° biyonde the see;   *far*
Manye be the druries°   *gifts*
    That she sente me.

5 She sente me the cherye
    Withouten any stoon,°   *stone*
And so she dide the dove
    Withouten any boon.°   *bone*

She sente me the brere°   *briar*
10   Withouten any rinde;°   *bark*
She bad me love my lemman°   *mistress*
    Withoute longinge.

How sholde any cherye
    Be withoute stoon?
15 And how sholde any dove
    Be withoute boon?

How sholde any brere
    Be withoute rinde?
How sholde I love my lemman
20   Withoute longinge?

2. Fairest beneath clothing.   3. My beloved has gone away.

Whan the cherye was a flowr,
  Thanne hadde it no stoon;
Whan the dove was an ey,°   *egg*
  Thanne hadde it no boon.

25 Whan the brere was unbred,°   *ungrown*
  Thanne hadde it no rinde;
Whan the maiden hath that° she loveth,   *what*
  She is withoute longinge.

A Bitter Lullaby

Lullay, lullay, litel child, why weepestou so sore?
Needes most° thou weepe, it was y-yarked° thee
    yore[4]   *must / destined*
Evere to live in sorwe, and siken° everemore,   *sigh*
As thine eldren dide er this, whil they alives° wore.° *alive / were*
5   Lullay, lullay, litel child, child, lullay, lullow,
    Into uncouth° world ycomen so art thou.   *strange*

Beestes and thise fowles, the fisshes in the flood,
And eech sheef° alives, ymaked of boon and blood,   *creature*
Whan they cometh to the world they dooth hemself som
    good—
10 Al but the wrecche° brol° that is of Adames
    blood.   *wretched / brat*
    Lullay, lullay, litel child, to care art thou bimet:° *destined*
    Thou noost nat this worldes wilde bifore thee is yset.[5]

Child, if it bitideth that thou shalt thrive and thee,° *prosper*
Thenk° thou were yfostered up thy moder°
    knee;   *remember / mother's*
15 Evere have minde° in thyn herte of thise thinges three: *thought*
Whennes thou comest, what thou art, and what shal come of
    thee.
    Lullay, lullay, litel child, child, lullay, lullay:
    With sorwe thou come into this world, with sorwe thou
      shalt away.

Ne tristou[6] to this world, it is thy fulle° fo: *entire*
20 The riche it maketh poore, the poore riche also;
It turneth wo to wele° and eek wele to wo: *well-being*
Ne triste° no man to this world whil it turneth so.   *trust*
    Lullay, lullay, litel child, the foot is in the wheele:[7]
    Thou noost[8] whether it wol turne to wo other to wele.

---

4. Long since.
5. You don't know that the wild beasts of this world are set before you (i.e., preferred to you).
6. Don't trust.
7. I.e., Fortune's foot is turning the wheel on which all people must ride.
8. Don't know.

25 Child, thou art a pilgrim in wikkednesse ybore;°   *born*
   Thou wandrest in this false world—thou looke thee bifore:
   Deeth shal come with a blast out of a wel dim bore°   *cranny*
   Adames kinne down to caste—himself hath do bifore.⁹
      Lullay, lullay, litel child, so wo thee warp° Adam   *wove*
30   In the land of Paradis through wikkenesse° of
       Satan.   *wickedness*

   Child, thou nart¹ a pilgrim, but an uncouth° gest: *unknown*
   Thy dayes beeth ytold,° thy journeys
       beeth ycest°   *numbered / determined*
   Whider thou shalt wenden, north other° est,°   *or / east*
   Deeth thee shal bitide with bitter bale° in brest.   *pain*
35   Lullay, lullay, litel child, this wo Adam thee wroughte
      Whan he the apple eet, And Eve it him bitoughte.²

The Cuckoo Song

   Sumer is ycomen in,
   Loude sing cuckou!
   Groweth seed and bloweth meed,³
   And springth the wode° now.   *wood*
5 Sing cuckou!

   Ewe bleteth after lamb,
   Loweth after calve cow,
   Bulloc sterteth,° bucke verteth,°   *leaps / breaks wind*
   Merye sing cuckou!
10 Cuckou, cuckou,
   Wel singest thou cuckou:
   Ne swik° thou never now!   *cease*

Tell Me, Wight in the Broom

   "Say me, wight in the broom,°   *shrub*
   What is me for to doon?
   Ich° have the werste bonde°   *I / husband*
   That is in any londe."

5   "If thy bonde is ille,°   *bad*
   Hold thy tonge stille."

9. ? To cast down Adam's kin as Adam himself has previously caused that it should be cast down.
1. Are not.
2. Gave it to him.
3. The meadow blossoms.

I Am of Ireland

Ich am of Irlonde,
And of the holy londe
   Of Irlonde.
Goode sire, praye ich thee,
5 For of° sainte charitee,   *sake of*
Com and dance with me
   In Irlonde.

Sunset on Calvary

Now gooth sunne under wode:[4]
Me reweth,[5] Marye, thy faire rode.°   *face*
Now gooth sunne under tree:
Me reweth, Marye, thy sone and thee.

I Sing of a Maiden

I sing of a maiden
   That is makelees:°   *matchless*
King of alle kinges
   To° her sone she chees.°   *as / chose*

                                as
5 He cam also° stille
   Ther° his moder° was   *where / mother*
As dewe in Aprille
   That falleth on the gras.

He cam also stille
10   To his modres bowr
As dewe in Aprille
   That falleth on the flowr.

He cam also stille
   Ther his moder lay
15 As dewe in Aprille
   That falleth on the spray.

Moder and maiden
   Was nevere noon but she:
Wel may swich° a lady   *such*
20   Godes moder be.

4. Wood, i.e., the Cross.   5. I pity.

Adam Lay Bound

Adam lay ybounden, bounden in a bond,
Four thousand winter thoughte he not too long;
And al was for an apple, an apple that he took,
As clerkes finden writen, writen in hire book.
5 Ne hadde[6] the apple taken been, the apple taken been,
Ne hadde nevere Oure Lady have been hevene Queen.
Blessed be the time that apple taken was:
Therfore we mown° singen *Deo Gratias*.[7]   *may*

The Corpus Christi Carol

Lully, lullay, lully, lullay,
The faucon° hath borne my make° away.   *falcon / mate*

He bare him up, he bare him down,
He bare him into an orchard brown.

5 In that orchard ther was an hall
That was hanged with purple and pall.°   *black velvet*

And in that hall ther was a bed:
It was hanged with gold so red.

And in that bed ther lith° a knight,   *lies*
10 His woundes bleeding by day and night.

By that beddes side ther kneeleth a may,°   *maid*
And she weepeth both night and day.

And by that beddes side ther standeth a stoon:°   *stone*
Corpus Christi[8] writen theron.

6. Had not.   8. Body of Christ.
7. Thanks be to God.

THE SECOND SHEPHERDS' PLAY
(ca. 1385)

The *Second Shepherds' Play* is the finest example in English of a medieval mystery play. The word "mystery" in this context refers to the spiritual mystery of Christ's redemption of mankind, and mystery plays are dramatizations of incidents of the Old Testament, which foretells that redemption, and of the New, which recounts it. In England the mysteries were generally composed in cycles containing as many as 48 individual plays; a typical cycle would begin with the Creation, continue with the Fall of Man, and proceed through the most significant events of the Old Testament, such as the Flood, to the New Testament, which provided plays on the Nativity, the chief events of Christ's life, the Crucifixion, the Harrowing of Hell (based on sources now deemed apocryphal), and the Last Judgment. This kind of drama had its origin within the very walls of the medieval church, in the liturgical dialogue that had long been a characteristic feature of formal Christian worship. The exchanges between priest and congregation in the celebration of the Mass are essentially dramatic, as are also the exchanges between several sections of the choir in the singing of an anthem. By a natural elaboration of these dialogues, the texts of which are based on Biblical or Apocryphal sources, a church drama came into being—indeed, it ultimately developed so fully that there was no longer room for it within the liturgy; it then had to be presented separately. In England it was given a home in the churchyard, but as it became increasingly secularized and increasingly pervaded by the rough popular humor of medieval minstrelsy, it lost its place even in the churchyard. By the time of their fullest development, the mysteries were acted in the streets of the town.

Despite secularization and separation from the church proper, mystery plays never lost their religious impulse. They were generally performed at the time of one of two great church festivals—Whitsuntide, the week following the seventh Sunday after Easter, or Corpus Christi, a week later—and their performance was one of the important ways in which the unlearned layman of the Middle Ages participated directly in the celebration of his religion. Every trade in urban society had its guild, an organization combining the functions of a modern club, trade union, and religious society, and each of these guilds had its traditional play to perform on the days when the cycles were presented. In certain of the towns each company had a wagon which served as a stage. The wagon would proceed from one strategic point in the town to another, and the play would be performed a number of times on the same day: the spectators gathered at any one strategic point would never be without a play before them, and might see the whole cycle without moving. In other towns, however, the plays were probably acted out in sequence at a single place—an innyard or some other such natural theater.

The *Second Shepherds' Play*, which was probably played at Wakefield in Yorkshire, is a member of one of the four great cycles of English mysteries that have been preserved in their entirety; from what must have originally been a great number of other cycles we possess only a few individual pieces. The Wakefield cycle has two plays for shepherds; it is the second which is reprinted below. The artistic level of most of the Middle English mysteries is not high: a kind of rough piety, at times mixed with a crude humor, is characteristic of most of them, though there are happy exceptions. The happiest of these are certain of the Wakefield plays, which display a sophisticated artistic intelligence at work beneath the apparent naïveté. This intelligence belonged undoubtedly to one individual, who probably revised traditional plays. His identity is not known, but because of his achievement scholars refer to him as the Wakefield Master. He was probably a highly educated cleric stationed in the vicinity of Wakefield, perhaps a friar of a nearby priory. He appreciated the rough humor and rough piety of the traditional plays, but he also knew how to refine both qualities without appearing to do so, and, more important, he knew how to combine the humorous and the religious so that the former serves the latter rather than detracting from it. In the *Second Shepherds' Play*, by linking the comic subplot of Mak and Gill with the solemn story of Christ's nativity, the Wakefield Master has produced a dramatic parable of what the Nativity means in Christian history and in Christian hearts. No one will fail to observe the parallelism between the stolen sheep, ludicrously disguised as Mak's latest heir, lying in the cradle, and the real Lamb of God, born in the stable among beasts. A complex of relationships based upon this relationship suggests itself. But perhaps the most important point is that the charity twice shown by the shepherds—in the first instance to the supposed son of Mak and in the second instance to Mak and Gill when they decide to let them off with only the mildest of punishments—is rewarded when they are invited to visit the Christ Child, the embodiment of charity. The bleak beginning of the play, with its series of individual complaints, is ultimately balanced by the optimistic ending, which sees the shepherds once again singing together in harmony.

Characterization in the mystery plays is usually rather slight, except in the case of stereotypes like Noah's stubborn wife or the ranting Herod (both mentioned in Chaucer's Miller's Tale). Mak therefore stands high above the generality and is perhaps the best humorous character outside of Chaucer's works in this period. A braggart of the worst kind, he has something of Falstaff's charm; and he resembles Falstaff also in his grotesque attempts to maintain the last shreds of his dignity when he is caught in a lie. Most readers will be glad that the shepherds do not carry out their threat to have the death penalty invoked for his crime.

The Second Shepherds' Play[1]

Dramatis Personae

COLL	GILL
GIB	ANGEL
DAW	MARY
MAK	

[*A moor.*]

[*Enter* COLL.]

COLL. Lord, what[2] these weathers are cold, and I am ill happed;
    I am nearhand dold,° so long have I napped;   *numb*
    My legs they fold,° my fingers are chapped.   *give way*
    It is not as I would, for I am all lapped°   *wrapped*
5   In sorrow:
        In storms and tempest,
        Now in the east, now in the west,
        Woe is him has never rest
          Midday nor morrow.

10   But we silly° husbands° that walks on the
        moor,   *poor / farmers*
    In faith we are nearhands out of the door.[3]
    No wonder, as it stands, if we be poor,
    For the tilth° of our lands lies fallow as the
        floor,   *arable part*
        As ye ken.°   *know*
15   We are so hammed,
        Fortaxed, and rammed,
        We are made hand-tamed
          With these gentlery-men.[4]

    Thus they reave us[5] our rest—Our Lady them wary!° *curse*
20   These men that are lord-fest,[6] they cause the plow tarry.
    That men say is for the best, we find it contrary.
    Thus are husbands oppressed in point to miscarry.[7]
        On live

1. The text is based on that given by A. W. Pollard in *The Towneley Plays* (1897), but has been freely edited. Spelling has been normalized except where rhyme makes changes impossible. Since the original text has no indications of scenes and only four stage directions, written in Latin, appropriate scenes of action and additional stage directions have been added; the four original stage directions are identified in the footnotes.

2. How; "ill happed": badly covered.
3. I.e., homeless.
4. We are so hamstrung, overtaxed, and beaten down (that) we are made slaves by these highborn men. Coll is complaining of the peasant's hard lot, at the mercy of the agents of the Crown and of the wealthy landholders.
5. Deprive us of.
6. Attached to lords.
7. To the point of ruin. "On live": in life.

Thus hold they us under,
25   Thus they bring us in blunder,°   *trouble*
It were a great wonder
    And° ever should we thrive.   *if*

There shall come a swain as proud as a po:°   *peacock*
He must borrow my wain,° my plow also;   *wagon*
30   Then I am full fain° to grant ere he go.   *glad*
Thus live we in pain, anger, and woe,
    By night and by day.
He must have if he lang° it,   *wants*
If I should forgang it:[8]
35   I were better be hanged
    Than once say him nay.[9]

For may he get a paint-sleeve[1] or a brooch nowadays,
Woe is him that him grieve or once again-says.°   *gainsays*
Dare no man him reprieve, what mastery he maes.[2]
40   And yet may no man lieve° one word that he says,   *believe*
    No letter.
He can make purveyance[3]
    With boast and bragance,°   *bragging*
And all is through maintenance°   *protection*
45   Of men that are greater.

It does me good, as I walk thus by mine one,°   *self*
Of this world for to talk in manner of moan.
To my sheep will I stalk, and hearken anon,
There abide on a balk,° or sit on a stone,   *grassy mound*
50   Full soon;
    For I trow,° pardie,°   *think / by God*
True men if they be,
    We get more company
    Ere it be noon.

    [*Enter* GIB, *who at first does not see* COLL.]
55 GIB.   Benste and Dominus,[4] what may this bemean?°   *mean*
Why fares this world thus? Such have we not seen.
Lord, these winds are spiteous° and the weathers full
    keen   *cruel*
And the frosts so hideous they water mine een,°   *eyes*
    No lie.
60   Now in dry, now in wet,
    Now in snow, now in sleet,
    When my shoon° freeze to my feet   *shoes*
    It is not all easy.

---

8. Even if I have to do without it.
9. In the manuscript, this stanza follows the next.
1. Embroidered sleeve (i.e., sign of authority).

2. No one dares to reprove him, no matter what force he uses.
3. Requisition (of private property).
4. Bless us and Lord.

But as far as I ken,° or yet as I go,°   *see / walk*
65 We silly wedmen dree mickle woe;[5]
We have sorrow then and then[6]—it falls oft so.
Silly Capple,[7] our hen, both to and fro
  She cackles;
 But begin she to croak,
70 To groan or to cluck,
 Woe is him our cock,
  For he is in the shackles.

These men that are wed have not all their will:
When they are full hard stead[8] they sigh full still;
75 God wot° they are led full hard and full ill; *knows*
In bower nor in bed they say nought theretill.° *thereagainst*
  This tide°   *time*
 My part have I fun;°   *found, learned*
 I know my lesson:
80 Woe is him that is bun,°   *bound*
  For he must abide.

But now late in our lives—a marvel to me,
That I think my heart rives° such wonders to see; *splits*
What that destiny drives it should so be[9]—
85 Some men will have two wives, and some men three
  In store.
 Some are woe[1] that has any,
 But so far can° I,   *know*
 Woe is him that has many,
90   For he feels sore.

But young men a-wooing, for God that you
  bought,°   *redeemed*
Be well ware of wedding and think in your thought:
"Had I wist"° is a thing, it serves of nought. *known*
Mickle° still° mourning has wedding home
  brought,   *much / continual*
95 And griefs
 With many a sharp shower,°   *fight*
 For thou may catch in an hour
 That° shall savor° full sour *what / taste*
  As long as thou lives.

100 For as ever read I 'pistle,° I have one to my fere[2] *Epistle*
As sharp as a thistle, as rough as a brere;° *briar*
She is browed like a bristle, with a sour-loten cheer;[3]
Had she once wet her whistle she could sing full clear
  Her Pater Noster.

5. We poor married men suffer much
woe.
6. Constantly.
7. I.e., one's wife.
8. Beset; "still": constantly.

9. What destiny causes must occur.
1. I.e., wretched.
2. As my mate.
3. She has brows like pig's bristles **and**
a sour-looking face.

105   She is great as a whale;
         She has a gallon of gall:
         By Him that died for us all,
             I would I had run to° I had lost her.   *until*

COLL. Gib, look over the raw!° Full deafly ye stand!   *hedge*
110 GIB. Yea, the devil in thy maw, so tariand![4]
         Saw thou awhere° of Daw?   *anywhere*
COLL.   Yea, on a
             lea-land°   *pasture land*
         Heard I him blaw.[5] He comes here at hand,
             Not far.
             Stand still.
GIB.   Why?
115 COLL. For he comes, hope° I.   *think*
GIB.   He will make us both a lie
             But if[6] we be ware.

         [*Enter* DAW, *who does not see the others.*]
DAW.   Christ's cross me speed, and Saint Nicholas!
         Thereof had I need: it is worse than it was.
120   Whoso could take heed and let the world pass,
         It is ever in dread° and brickle° as glass,   *doubt / brittle*
             And slithes.°   *slips away*
         This world foor° never so,   *behaved*
         With marvels mo° and mo,   *more*
125   Now in weal, now in woe,
             And all thing writhes.°   *changes*

         Was never sin° Noah's flood such floods seen,   *since*
         Winds and rains so rude and storms so keen:
         Some stammered, some stood in doubt,[7] as I
             ween.°   *suppose*
130   Now God turn all to good! I say as I mean.
             For ponder:
             These floods so they drown
             Both in fields and in town,
             And bears all down,
135   And that is a wonder.

         We that walk on the nights, our cattle to keep,
         We see sudden° sights when other men sleep.   *unexpected*
         Yet methink my heart lights: I see shrews peep.[8]
         [*He sees the others, but does not hail them.*]
         Ye are two tall wights.° I will give my sheep   *creatures*
140   A turn.
             But full ill have I meant:[9]

---

4. Yes, the devil take thy guts for being so late.
5. Blow (his horn).
6. Unless.

7. The line apparently refers to men's
behavior at the time of Noah's flood.
8. I see rascals are watching.
9. But that is a poor idea.

As I walk on this bent°	*field*
I may lightly° repent,	*quickly*
My toes if I spurn.°	*stub*

145 Ah, sir, God you save, and master mine!
A drink fain would I have, and somewhat to dine.

COLL. Christ's curse, my knave, thou art a lither hine![1]

GIB. What, the boy list° rave! Abide unto sine.[2]   *wants to*
We have made it.[3]

150 Ill thrift on thy pate!
Though the shrew° came late   *rascal*
Yet is he in state
To dine, if he had it.

DAW. Such servants as I, that sweats and swinks,°   *toil*
155 Eats our bread full dry, and that me forthinks.°   *angers*
We are oft wet and weary when master-men winks,°   *sleep*
Yet comes full lately° both dinners and drinks.   *tardily*
But nately°   *profitably*
Both our dame and our sire,
160 When we have run in the mire,
They can nip at our hire,[4]
And pay us full lately.

But here my troth, master, for the fare° that ye
make°   *food / provide*
I shall do thereafter: work as I take.[5]
165 I shall do a little, sir, and among° ever
lake,°   *meanwhile / play*
For yet lay my supper never on my stomach
In fields.
Whereto should I threap?°   *haggle*
With my staff can I leap,[6]
170 And men say, "Light cheap
Litherly foryields."[7]

COLL. Thou were an ill lad to ride a-wooing
With a man that had but little of spending.[8]

GIB. Peace, boy, I bade—no more jangling,
175 Or I shall make thee full rad,° by the heaven's
King,   *quickly*
With thy gauds.°   *tricks*
Where are our sheep, boy? We scorn.[9]

DAW. Sir, this same day at morn
I them left in the corn
180 When they rang Lauds.[1]

1. Thou art a worthless servant.
2. Wait till later.
3. I.e., had dinner.
4. They can deduct from our wages
5. I.e., work in the same way as I am paid.
6. I.e., run away.
7. A cheap bargain repays badly (a proverb).
8. You would be a bad servant for a poor man to take wooing with him.
9. I.e., waste time.
1. Rang the bells for the church service held at dawn.

	They have pasture good, they cannot go wrong.	
COLL.	That is right. By the rood,° these nights are long!	cross
	Yet I would, ere we yode,° one gave us a song.	went
GIB.	So I thought as I stood, to mirth° us among.°	cheer / meanwhile
185 DAW.	I grant.	
COLL.	Let me sing the tenory.°	tenor
GIB.	And I the treble so hee.°	high
DAW.	Then the mean° falls to me.	middle part
	Let see how you chant.	

[They sing.—Enter MAK *with a cloak over his clothes.[2]]*

190 MAK.	Now, Lord, for thy names seven, that made both moon and starns[3]	
	Well mo than I can neven, thy will, Lord, of me tharns.[4]	
	I am all uneven°—that moves oft my harns.[5]	at odds
	Now would God I were in heaven, for there weep no barns°	children
	So still.°	continually
195 COLL.	Who is that pipes so poor?	
MAK.	[aside] Would God ye wist° how I foor!°	knew / fared
	[aloud] Lo, a man that walks on the moor	
	And has not all his will.	
GIB.	Mak, where has thou gane?° Tell us tiding.	gone
200 DAW.	Is he come? Then ilkane[6] take heed to his thing.	
	[Snatches a cloak from him.]	
MAK.	What! Ich[7] be a yeoman, I tell you, of the king,	
	The self and the same, sond° from a great lording	messenger
	And sich.°	suchlike
	Fie on you! Goth hence	
205	Out of my presence:	
	I must have reverence.	
	Why, who be ich?	
COLL.	Why make ye it so quaint? Mak, ye do wrang.[8]	
GIB.	But, Mak, list ye saint? I trow that ye lang.[9]	
210 DAW.	I trow the shrew can paint[1]—the devil might him hang!	
MAK.	Ich shall make complaint and make you all to thwang°	be flogged
	At a word,	
	And tell even° how ye doth.	exactly

---

2. Mak's entrance is a stage direction in the original MS.
3. Stars.
4. Well more than I can name, thy will, Lord, falls short in regard to me.
5. That often disturbs my brains.
6. Each one; "thing": possessions. The stage direction here is in the MS.

7. I (the southern form): Mak is pretending to be an important person from the south.
8. Why do you behave in such an unfriendly manner? Mak, you do wrong.
9. But, Mak, do you want to act as if you were a saint? I guess you do.
1. I think the shrew can play tricks.

COLL. But Mak, is that sooth?
215   Now take out that southern tooth,[2]
         And set in a turd!

GIB. Mak, the devil in your ee![3] A stroke would I lean you!
DAW. Mak, know ye not me? By God, I could teen° you.   *vex*
MAK. God look° you all three: Methought I had seen you. *guard*
220 Ye are a fair company.

COLL.   Can ye now mean you?[4]

GIB.   Shrew, peep![5]
       Thus late as thou goes,
       What will men suppose?
       Thou has an ill nose[6]
225   Of stealing of sheep.

MAK. And I am true as steel, all men wate.°   *know*
    But a sickness I feel that holds me full hate:° *hot, feverish*
    My belly fares not weel, it is out of estate.
DAW. Seldom lies the devil dead by the gate.[7]
230 MAK.   Therefore
       Full sore am I and ill
       If I stand stone-still:
       I eat not a needill[8]
       This month and more.

235 COLL. How fares thy wife? By my hood, how fares sho?° *she*
MAK. Lies waltering,° by the rood, by the fire, lo! *lounging*
    And a house full of brood.° She drinks well, too: *children*
    Ill speed other good that she will do![9]
       But sho
240   Eats as fast as she can;
       And ilk° year that comes to man   *every*
       She brings forth a lakan,°   *baby*
       And some years two.

    But were I now more gracious° and richer by
       far,   *prosperous*
245 I were eaten out of house and of harbar.°   *home*
    Yet is she a foul douce,° if ye come nar:[1] *sweetheart*
    There is none that trows° nor knows a
       war°   *imagines / worse*
       Than ken° I.   *know*
       Now will ye see what I proffer:
250   To give all in my coffer
       Tomorn at next[2] to offer
       Her head-masspenny.[3]

---

2. Now stop speaking like a southerner.
3. Eye; "lean": lend.
4. Remember.
5. Rascal, watch out.
6. Noise, i.e., reputation.
7. Road (i.e., the devil is always on the move).
8. Needle, i.e., a little bit.
9. I.e., that's the only good thing she does.
1. I.e., near the truth.
2. "Tomorn at next": tomorrow.
3. The penny paid for a mass for her departed spirit.

GIB. I wot° so forwaked° is none in this shire.   *know / sleepless*
       I would sleep if° I taked less to my hire.   *even if*

255 DAW. I am cold and naked and would have a fire.
       I am weary forraked° and run in the mire.   *from walking*
         Wake thou.[4]

GIB.   Nay, I will lie down by,
        For I must sleep, truly.

260 DAW.   As good a man's son was I
        As any of you.

       But Mak, come hither, between shall thou lie down.

MAK. Then might I let you bedeen of that ye would rown,[5]
        No dread.°   *doubt*

265   From my top to my toe,
       [*Saying his prayers.*]
        Manus tuas commendo
        Pontio Pilato.[6]
        Christ's cross me speed!

       [*He gets up as the others sleep and speaks.*][7]
       Now were time for a man that lacks what he would

270   To stalk privily than° unto a fold,   *then*
       And nimbly to work than, and be not too bold,
       For he might abuy° the bargain if it were told *pay for*
         At the ending.
       Now were time for to reel:°   *move spryly*

275   But he needs good counseel
        That fain would fare weel°   *well*
        And has but little spending.

       [*He casts a spell.*]
       But about you a circill,° as round as a moon,   *circle*
       To° I have done that° I will, till that it be
         noon,   *until / what*

280   That ye lie stone-still to that I have done;
       And I shall say theretill° of good words a
         foon:°   *moreover / few*
        "On height,
       Over your heads my hand I lift.
       Out go your eyes! Fordo your sight!"[8]

285   But yet I must make better shift
        And it be right.[9]

       Lord, what° they sleep hard—that may ye all hear. *how*
       Was I never a shephard, but now will I lear.°   *learn*
       If the flock be scar'd, yet shall I nip near.

290   How! Draws hitherward! Now mends our cheer

---

4. You stay awake.
5. Then I might hinder you if you
wanted to whisper together.
6. Mak's prayer means, "Thy hands I
commend to Pontius Pilate."

7. One of the original stage directions.
8. May your sight be rendered powerless.
9. If it is to be all right.

From sorrow.
A fat sheep, I dare say!
A good fleece, dare I lay!°   *bet*
Eft-quit° when I may,   *repay*
    But this will I borrow.
295
    [*Exit with sheep.*]

[MAK'S *house.* MAK *speaks outside the door.*]

MAK. How, Gill, art thou in? Get us some light.
GILL. [*within*] Who makes such a din this time of the night?
I am set for to spin; I hope not I might[1]
Rise a penny to win—I shrew° them on height!   *curse*
300
    So fares
    A housewife that has been
    To be raised thus between:[2]
    Here may no note° be seen   *completed work*
    For such small chares.°   *chores*

305 MAK. Good wife, open the heck!° Sees thou not what I   *door*
      bring?
GILL. I may thole thee draw the sneck.[3] Ah, come in, my
      sweeting.
MAK. Yea, thou thar not reck of[4] my long standing.
    [*She opens the door.*]
GILL. By the naked neck art thou like for to hing.°   *hang*
MAK.   Do way!
310
    I am worthy° my meat,   *worthy of*
    For in a strait° can I get   *pinch*
    More than they that swink° and sweat   *work*
    All the long day.

Thus it fell to my lot, Gill, I had such grace.
315 GILL. It were a foul blot to be hanged for the case.
MAK. I have 'scaped,° Jelot,[5] oft as hard a glase.°   *escaped / blow*
GILL. But "So long goes the pot to the water," men says,
      "At last
    Comes it home broken."
320 MAK.   Well know I the token,
    But let it never be spoken!
    But come and help fast.

I would he were flain,° I list° well eat: *skinned / wish*
This twelvemonth was I not so fain of one sheep-meat.
325 GILL. Come they ere he be slain, and hear the sheep bleat—
MAK. Then might I be taen°—that were a cold sweat!   *taken*
    Go spar°   *fasten*
    The gate° door.   *street*

1. I don't think I could.
2. This is what happens to anyone who's been a housewife—to be got up all the time.
3. I may let you draw the latch.
4. You need not care about.
5. I.e., Gill.

GILL.   Yes, Mak,
       For and° they come at thy back—   *if*
330 MAK.   Then might I buy,° for all the pack,   *have to pay*
       The devil of the war.°   *worse*

GILL. A good bourd have I spied, sin thou can none:[6]
       Here shall we him hide, to° they be gone,   *until*
       In my cradle. Abide, let me alone,
335   And I shall lie beside in childbed and groan.
MAK.   Thou red,°   *get ready*
         And I shall say thou was light°   *delivered*
         Of a knave-child° this night.   *boy child*
GILL.   Now well is me day bright
340   That ever was I bred.[7]

       This is a good guise° and a fair cast:°   *method / trick*
       Yet a woman's advise helps at the last.
       I wot° never who spies: again go thou fast.   *know*
MAK. But° I come ere they rise, else blows a cold blast.   *unless*
345   I will go sleep.
         Yet sleeps all this meny,°   *company*
         And I shall go stalk privily,
         As it had never been I
           That carried their sheep.

     [*The moor. The shepherds are waking.*]

350 COLL. *Resurrex a mortruus!*[8] Have hold my hand!
       Judas carnas dominus![9] I may not well stand.
       My foot sleeps, by Jesus, and I walter°
          fastand.°   *lie / fasting*
       I thought that we laid us full near England.
GIB.   Ah, yea?
355   Lord, what° I have slept weel!°   *how / well*
         As fresh as an eel,
         As light I me feel
           As leaf on a tree.

DAW. Benste° be herein! So my body quakes,   *blessing*
360   My heart is out of skin, what-so° it
          makes.°   *whatever / causes*
       Who makes all this din? So my brows blakes,[1]
       To the door will I win. Hark, fellows, wakes!
         We were four:
         See ye awhere of Mak now?
365 COLL. We were up ere thou.

6. A good trick have I found, since you know none.
7. Now it was a good day that I was born.
8. An illiterate oath referring, apparently, to Christ's Resurrection from the dead.
9. Judas, (in?)carnate lord.
1. The meaning is probably "my eyes are dim." Daw's head may be under a blanket.

GIB.   Man, I give God avow
       Yet yede he naw're.[2]

DAW. Methought he was lapped° in a wolfskin.   *covered*
COLL. So are many happed° now, namely°
       within.   *clad / especially*
370 DAW. When we had long napped, methought with a gin°   *snare*
       A fat sheep he trapped, but he made no din.
GIB.   Be still:
       Thy dream makes thee wood.°   *mad*
       It is but phantom, by the rood.°   *cross*
375 COLL. Now God turn all to good,
       If it be his will.

GIB.   Rise, Mak, for shame! Thou lies right lang.°   *long*
MAK. Now Christ's holy name be us amang!°   *among*
       What is this? For Saint Jame, I may not well gang.°   *walk*
380   I trow° I be the same. Ah, my neck has lain
       wrang.°   *think / wrong*
       [*One of them twists his neck.*]
       Enough!
       Mickle thank! Sin yestereven
       Now, by Saint Strephen,[3]
       I was flayed with a sweven[4]—
385   My heart out of slough.°   *skin*

     I thought Gill began to croak and travail full sad,°   *hard*
     Well-near at the first cock, of a young lad,
     For to mend° our flock—then be I never glad: *increase*
     I have tow on my rock[5] more than ever I had.
390   Ah, my head!
       A house full of young tharms!°   *guts*
       The devil knock out their harns!°   *brains*
       Woe is him has many barns,°   *children*
       And thereto little bread.

395   I must go home, by your leave, to Gill, as I thought.
     I pray you look° my sleeve, that I steal nought.   *examine*
     I am loath you to grieve or from you take aught.
DAW. Go forth! Ill might thou chieve!° Now would I we
       sought[6]   *prosper*
       This morn
400   That we had all our store.
COLL. But I will go before.
       Let us meet.
GIB.   Whore?°   *where*
DAW. At the crooked thorn.

---

2. He's gone nowhere yet.   5. Flax on my distaff (i.e., trouble).
3. Probably St. Stephen.   6. I want us to seek.
4. I was terrified by a dream.

[MAK'S *house.* MAK *at the door.*]

MAK. Undo this door! Who is here? How long shall I stand?
405 GILL. Who makes such a bere?° Now walk in the
        weniand!⁷   *clamor*
MAK. Ah, Gill, what cheer? It is I, Mak, your husband.
GILL. Then may we see here the devil in a band,⁸
        Sir Guile!
        Lo, he comes with a lote°   *noise*
410   As he were holden in the throat:
        I may not sit at my note°   *work*
        A hand-long° while.   *short*

MAK. Will ye here what fare⁹ she makes to get her a glose?
     And does nought but lakes° and claws her toes?   *plays*
415 GILL. Why, who wanders? Who wakes? Who comes? Who
        goes?
     Who brews? Who bakes? What makes me thus
        hose?°   *hoarse*
        And than°   *then*
        It is ruth° to behold,   *pity*
        Now in hot, now in cold,
420   Full woeful is the household
        That wants° a woman.   *lacks*

     But what end has thou made with the herds,°
        Mak?   *shepherds*
MAK. The last word that they said when I turned my back,
     They would look that they had their sheep all the pack.
425   I hope¹ they will not be well paid when they their sheep
        lack.
        Pardie!°   *by God*
     But how-so the game goes,
     To me they will suppose,°   *suspect*
     And make a foul nose,°   *noise*
430   And cry out upon me.

     But thou must do as thou hight.°   *promised*
GILL.   I accord me theretill.²
     I shall swaddle him right in my cradill.
     If it were a greater sleight, yet could I help till.³
     I will lie down straight.° Come, hap°
        me.   *straightway / cover*
MAK.   I will.
435 GILL.   **Behind**
     Come Coll and his marrow;°   *mate*
     They will nip us full narrow.

7. **Waning of** the moon (an unlucky   1. Expect; "paid": pleased.
time).   2. I agree to it.
8. **On a leash.**   3. I.e., with it.
9. **Fuss;** "glose": excuse.

MAK.	But I may cry "Out, harrow,"°	*help*
	The sheep if they find.	

440 GILL. Hearken ay when they call—they will come anon.
      Come and make ready all, and sing by thine one.°   *self*
      Sing "lullay"° thou shall, for I must groan,   *lullaby*
      And cry out by the wall on Mary and John
          For sore.°   *pain*
445   Sing "lullay" on fast
          When thou hears at the last,
          And but I play a false cast,[4]
          Trust me no more.

[*The moor.*]

DAW. Ah, Coll, good morn. Why sleeps thou not?
450 COLL. Alas that ever I was born! We have a foul blot:
      A fat wether° have we lorn.°   *ram / lost*
DAW.   Marry, God's forbot![5]
GIB. Who should do us that scorn? That were a foul spot!
COLL.   Some shrew.°   *rascal*
      I have sought with my dogs
455   All Horbury shrogs,°   *thickets*
      And of fifteen hogs
      Found I but one ewe.[6]

DAW. Now trow me,° if ye will, by Saint Thomas of
          Kent,   *believe*
      Either Mak or Gill was at that assent.°   *conspiracy*
460 COLL. Peace, man, be still! I saw when he went.
      Thou slanders him ill, thou ought to repent
          Good speed.
GIB.   Now as ever might I thee,°   *thrive*
      If I should even here dee,°   *die*
465   I would say it were he
          That did that same deed.

DAW. Go we thither, I read,° and run on our feet.   *advise*
      Shall I never eat bread the sooth to I weet.[7]
COLL. Nor drink in my head, with him till I meet.
470 GIB. I will rest in no stead° till that I him greet,   *place*
          My brother.
          One I will hight:[8]
          Till I see him in sight
          Shall I never sleep one night
475   There° I do another.   *where*

4. Unless I play a false trick.
5. God forbid.
6. And with fifteen young sheep I found only a ewe (i.e., the wether was missing).
7. Until I know the truth.
8. One thing will I promise.

[MAK's *house.* MAK *and* GILL *within, she in bed groaning, he singing a lullaby; the shepherds enter outside the door.*]

DAW. Will ye hear how they hack?[9] Our sire list croon.

COLL. Heard I never none crack° so clear out of tune.   *song*
    Call on him.

GIB.   Mak, undo your door soon!°   *at once*

MAK. Who is that spake, as° it were noon,   *as if*
480   On loft?[1]
    Who is that, I say?

DAW. Good fellows, were it day.[2]

MAK. As far as ye may,
      [*opening*] Good,° speaks soft   *good men*

485 Over a sick woman's head, that is at malease.[3]
    I had liefer° be dead ere she had any
        disease.°   *rather / distress*

GILL. Go to another stead, I may not well wheeze:°   *breathe*
    Each foot that ye tread goes through my nese.°   *nose*
    So, hee!°   *scat*

490 COLL. Tell us, Mak, if you may,
    How fare ye, I say?

MAK. But are ye in this town today?
    Now how fare ye?

Ye have run in the mire and are wet yit.
495 I shall make you a fire if you will sit.
    A nurse would I hire—Think ye one[4] yit?
    Well quit is my hire—my dream, this is it
      A season.[5]
    I have barns,° if ye knew,   *children*
500   Well mo° than enew:°   *more / enough*
    But we must drink as we brew,
      And that is but reason.

I would ye dined ere ye yode.° Methink that ye
      sweat.   *went*

GIB. Nay, neither mends our mood[6] drink nor meat.

505 MAK. Why, sir, ails you aught but good?[7]

DAW.   Yea, our sheep that we get
    Are stolen as they yode:° our loss is great.   *walked*

MAK.   Sirs, drinks!
    Had I been thore°   *there*
    Some should have bought° it full sore.   *paid for*

510 COLL. Marry, some men trows° that ye wore,°   *think / were*
    And that us forthinks.°   *disturbs*

---

9. Bellow. "List": wants to.
1. Loudly.
2. Good companions, if it were daytime.
3. That feels badly.
4. Can you think of one?

5. Right on time.
6. Appeases our anger.
7. Is there anything wrong with you? "Get": tend.

GIB. Mak, some men trows that it should be ye.

DAW. Either ye or your spouse, so say we.

MAK. Now if you have suspouse° to Gill or to me,   *suspicion*

515　　Come and ripe° the house, and then may ye see   *search*

　　　　　Who had her[8]—

　　　　　If I any sheep fot,°   *fetched*

　　　　　Either cow or stot[9]—

　　　　　And Gill my wife rose not

520　　　　　Here sin she laid her.

　　As I am true and leal,° to God here I pray   *just*

　　That this be the first meal that I shall eat this day.

COLL. Mak, as I have sele,[1] advise thee, I say:

　　　　　[*They begin the search.*]

　　He learned timely to steal that could not say nay.

525 GILL.　　I swelt!°   *die*

　　　　　Out, thieves, from my wones!°   *dwelling*

　　　　　Ye come to rob us for the nones.[2]

MAK.　　Hear ye not how she groans?

　　　　　Your hearts should melt.

530 GILL. Out, thieves, from my barn!° Nigh him not thore![3]   *child*

MAK. Wist ye how she had farn,[4] your hearts would be sore.

　　You do wrong, I you warn, that thus comes before

　　To a womman that has farn°—but I say no

　　　　　more.   *been in labor*

GILL.　　Ah, my middill!

535　　　　I pray to God so mild,

　　　　　If ever I you beguiled,

　　　　　That I eat this child

　　　　　　That lies in this cradill.

MAK. Peace, woman, for God's pain, and cry not so!

540　　Thou spills° thy brain and makes me full woe.   *spoil*

GIB. I trow our sheep be slain. What find ye two?

DAW. All work we in vain; as well may we go.

　　　　　But hatters,[5]

　　　　　I can find no flesh,

545　　　　Hard nor nesh,°   *soft*

　　　　　Salt nor fresh,

　　　　　　But two tome° platters.   *empty*

　　Quick cattle[6] but this, tame nor wild,

　　None, as have I bliss, as loud as he smiled.[7]

　　　　　[*Approaches the cradle.*]

550 GILL. No, so God me bliss,° and give me joy of my child!   *bless*

---

8. I.e., the sheep.
9. Either female or male.
1. Happiness; "advise thee": take thought.
2. You come for the purpose of robbing us.

3. Approach him not there.
4. If you knew how she had fared.
5. Except for clothing.
6. Livestock.
7. Smelled as badly as he (the baby).

COLL. We have marked° amiss—I hold us beguiled.   *aimed*
GIB.   Sir, don!°   *thoroughly*
               Sir—Our Lady him save—
               Is your child a knave?[8]
555 MAK.   Any lord might him have,
                    This child, to his son.

               When he wakens he kips,° that joy is to see.   *kicks*
DAW. In good time to his hips, and in sely.[9]
               But who were his gossips,° so soon ready?   *godparents*
560 MAK. So fair fall their lips—
COLL.   Hark, now, a lee.°   *lie*
MAK.   So God them thank,
               Perkin, and Gibbon Waller, I say,
               And gentle John Horne, in good fay°—   *faith*
               He made all the garray
565   With the great shank.[1]

GIB.   Mak, friends will we be, for we are all one.°   *in accord*
MAK. We? Now I hold for me, for mends get I none.[2]
               Farewell all three, all glad[3] were ye gone.
DAW. Fair words may there be, but love is there none
570   This year.
               [*They go out the door.*]
COLL. Gave ye the child anything?
GIB.   I trow not one farthing.
DAW. Fast again will I fling.°   *dash*
               Abide ye me there.

575   Mak, take it to no grief if I come to thy barn.°   *child*
MAK. Nay, thou does me great reprief,[4] and foul has thou farn.
DAW. Thy child it will not grief, that little day-starn°   *day star*
               Mak, with your leaf,° let me give your barn   *leave*
               But sixpence.
580 MAK. Nay, do way, he sleeps.
DAW. Methinks he peeps.°   *opens his eyes*
MAK. When he wakens he weeps.
               I pray you go hence.

DAW. Give me leave him to kiss, and lift up the clout.[5]
               [*Lifts the cover.*]
585   What the devil is this? He has a long snout.
               [*The others re-enter.*]
COLL. He is marked[6] amiss. We wot ill about.
GIB.   Ill-spun weft, ywis, ay comes foul out.[7]

8. Boy (although Mak takes the word in its alternate meaning of "rascal").
9. Perhaps "that's the best thing for him."
1. He made all the trouble with his long legs (the reference is obscure).
2. Now I'll remain apart, for I get no apology.
3. I.e., I would be glad.
4. Shame; "farn": behaved.
5. Cover.
6. Fashioned. "We wot ill about": we know mischief has been at work.
7. An ill-spun web, indeed, always comes out badly.

Aye, so!
He is like to our sheep.

590 DAW. How, Gib, may I peep?
COLL. I trow kind will creep
Where it may not go.[8]

GIB. This was quaint gaud and a fair cast.[9]
It was a high fraud.

DAW. Yea, sirs, was't.

595 Let burn this bawd and bind her fast.
A false scaud° hang at the last: *scold*
So shall thou.
Will you see how they swaddle
His four feet in the middle?

600 Saw I never in cradle
A horned lad ere now.

MAK. Peace bid I! What, let be your fare!°   *fuss*
I am he that him gat,° and yond woman him bare.   *begot*
COLL. What devil shall he hat?° Mak? Lo, Gib, Mak's
heir!   *be named*

605 GIB. Let be all that: now God give him care°—   *sorrow*
I sawgh.[1]

GILL. A pretty child is he
As sits on a woman's knee,
A dillydown, pardie,

610 To gar° a man laugh.   *make*

DAW. I know him by the earmark—that is a good token.
MAK. I tell you, sirs, hark, his nose was broken.
Sithen° told me a clark that he was
forspoken.°   *later / bewitched*
COLL. This is a false wark.° I would fain be
wroken.°   *work / avenged*

615 Get wapen.°   *weapon*
GILL. He was taken with° an elf—   *by*
I saw it myself—
When the clock struck twelf
He was forshapen.°   *transformed*

620 GIB. Ye two are well feft sam in a stead.[2]
DAW. Sin[3] they maintain their theft, let do them to dead.
MAK. If I trespass eft,° gird° off my head.   *again / cut*
With you will I be left.[4]

COLL.   Sirs, do my read:°   *advice*
For this trespass

625 We will neither ban° ne flite,°   *curse / wrangle*

8. I think kinship will creep where it
can't walk (i.e., only a parent could
love this child).
9. This was a strange trick and a fine
dodge.

1. Probably "I saw it."
2. I.e., you two birds of a feather properly flock together.
3. Since; "dead": death.
4. I put myself in your mercy.

Fight nor chite,°   *chide*
But have done as tite,°   *quickly*
And cast him in canvas.
[*They toss* MAK *in a blanket.*]

[*The moor.*]

COLL. Lord, what° I am sore, in point for to brist!°   *how / burst*
630   In faith, I may no more—therefore will I rist.°   *rest*
GIB. As a sheep of seven score[5] he weighed in my fist:
        For to sleep aywhore° methink that I list.° *anywhere / want*
DAW.   Now I pray you
           Lie down on this green.
635 COLL.   On these thieves yit I mean.°   *think*
DAW.   Whereto should ye teen?°   *worry*
           Do as I say you.

[*An* ANGEL *sings* Gloria in Excelsis *and then speaks.*][6]
ANGEL. Rise, herdmen hend,° for now is he born   *gentle*
        That shall take fro the fiend that Adam had lorn;[7]
640   That warlock° to shend,° this night is he
                born.   *devil / confound*
        God is made your friend now at this morn
              He beheests.°   *promises*
           At Bedlem° go see: *Bethlehem*
           There lies that free,°   *noble one*
645   In a crib full poorly,
           Betwixt two beasts.
           [*Exit.*]

COLL. This was a quaint steven[8] that ever yet I hard.°   *heard*
        It is a marvel to neven° thus to be scar'd.° *tell of / scared*
GIB. Of God's Son of heaven he spake upward.°   *on high*
650   All the wood on a leven methought that he gard
              Appear.[9]
DAW.   He spake of a barn°   *child*
           In Bedlem, I you warn.
COLL.   That betokens yond starn.[1]
655   Let us seek him there.

GIB. Say, what was his song? Heard ye not how he cracked it,[2]
        Three breves[3] to a long?
DAW.   Yea, marry, he hacked it.
        Was no crochet° wrong, nor nothing that lacked it.[4] *note*
COLL. For to sing us among, right as he knacked° it,   *trilled*
660   I can.°   *know how*
GIB. Let see how ye croon!

5. 140 pounds.   seem full of light.
6. One of the original stage directions.   1. That's what yonder star means.
7. What Adam had brought to ruin.   2. Sang it out.
8. Fine voice.   3. Short notes; "hacked": sang loud.
9. I thought he made the whole wood   4. It lacked.

Can ye bark at the moon?

DAW. Hold your tongues! Have done!

COLL. Hark after, than!

665 GIB. To Bedlem he bade that we should gang:°   *go*
    I am full rad° that we tarry too lang.°   *afraid / long*

DAW. Be merry and not sad; of mirth is our sang:
    Everlasting glad to meed may we fang.[5]

COLL.   Without nose°   *noise*
670   Hie we thither forthy°   *therefore*
    To that child and that lady;
    If° we be wet and weary,   *though*
      We have it not to lose.[6]

GIB. We find by the prophecy—let be your din!—
675 Of David and Isay, and mo than I min,[7]
    That prophesied by clergy° that in a virgin   *learning*
    Should he light° and lie, to sloken° our sin *alight / quench*
      And slake° it,   *relieve*
     Our kind,[8] from woe,
680   For Isay said so:
    Ecce virgo
     Concipiet[9] a child that is naked.

DAW. Full glad may we be and° we abide that day   *if*
    That lovely to see, that all mights may.[1]
685 Lord, well were me for once and for ay
    Might I kneel on my knee, some word for to say
      To that child.
     But the angel said
     In a crib was he laid,
690   He was poorly arrayed,
      Both mean° and mild.   *lowly*

COLL. Patriarchs that has been, and prophets beforn,
    That desired to have seen this child that is born,
    They are gone full clean—that have they lorn.[2]
695 We shall see him, I ween,° ere it be morn,   *think*
      To token.[3]
     When I see him and feel,
     Then wot I full weel[4]
     It is true as steel
700   That prophets have spoken:

   To so poor as we are that he would appear,
   First find, and declare by his messenger.

5. Eternal joy as our reward may we receive.
6. We must not neglect it.
7. Of David and Isaiah and more than I remember.
8. I.e., mankind.
9. Behold, a virgin shall conceive (Isaiah vii.14).
1. I.e., when we see that lovely one who is all-powerful.
2. That (sight) have they lost.
3. As a sign.
4. Then know I full well.

GIB. Go we now, let us fare, the place is us near.

DAW. I am ready and yare,° go we in fere[5]   *prepared*

705   To that bright.°   *glorious one*

          Lord, if thy wills be—

          We are lewd° all three—   *ignorant*

          Thou grant us some kins glee[6]

          To comfort thy wight.°   *creature*

[A *stable in Bethlehem.*]

710 COLL. Hail, comely and clean! Hail, young child!

          Hail Maker, as I mean, of° a maiden so mild!   *born of*

          Thou has waried,° I ween, the warlock° so

             wild.   *put a curse on / devil*

          The false guiler of teen,[7] now goes he beguiled.

             Lo, he merries!

715   Lo, he laughs, my sweeting!

          A well fair meeting!

          I have holden my heting:°   *promise*

          Have a bob° of cherries.   *bunch*

GIB. Hail, sovereign Saviour, for thou has us sought!

720   Hail freely food[8] and flower, that all thing has wrought!

          Hail, full of favor, that made all of nought!

          Hail! I kneel and I cower.° A bird have I brought *crouch*

             To my barn.°   *child*

          Hail, little tiny mop!°   *baby*

725   Of our creed thou art crop.°   *head*

          I would drink on thy cup,

             Little day-starn.

DAW. Hail, darling dear, full of Godhead!

          I pray thee be near when that I have need.

730   Hail, sweet is thy cheer°—my heart would bleed   *face*

          To see thee sit here in so poor weed,°   *clothing*

             With no pennies.

          Hail! Put forth thy dall!°   *hand*

          I bring thee but a ball:

735   Have and play thee withal,

          And go to the tennis.

MARY. The Father of heaven, God omnipotent,

          That set all on seven,[9] his Son has he sent.

          My name could he neven, and light ere he went.[1]

740   I conceived him full even through might as he meant.[2]

             And now is he born.

             He[3] keep you from woe!

---

5. Together.
6. Some kind of cheer.
7. The false grievous deceiver.
8. Noble child.
9. Who created everything perfectly.

1. My name did he name, and alighted ere he went.
2. I conceived him through his power, just as he intended.
3. May he.

I shall pray him so.
Tell forth as ye go,
745 And min on[4] this morn.

COLL. Farewell, lady, so fair to behold,
With thy child on thy knee.
GIB. But he lies full cold.
Lord, well is me. Now we go, thou behold.
DAW. Forsooth, already it seems to be told
750 Full oft.
COLL. What grace we have fun!°   *received*
GIB. Come forth, now are we won!°   *redeemed*
DAW. To sing are we bun:°   *bound*
Let take on loft.[5]
[*They sing.*]

4. Remember.   5. Let's raise our voices.

THE BROME PLAY OF ABRAHAM AND ISAAC

(ca. 1400–1425)

The story of Abraham and Isaac as told in Genesis xxii is a very spare account of an incident that appealed greatly to the medieval imagination, which was always stimulated by a situation in which an ideal is upheld at the expense of all normal human values. This all-or-nothing attitude may also be seen in Chaucer's Franklin's Tale, where Arveragus delivers his wife to an adulterer in order that she should not be guilty of breaking her word, one's pledged word being, according to him, the most demanding of human contracts. In the story of Abraham and Isaac, it is obedience to God's command that a father sacrifice his son that must be carried out. The audience is, of course, aware that the awful consequences of upholding the ideal will at the last minute be canceled. Meanwhile, however, the mind luxuriates in a realistic depiction of the people involved in the threatening action. Medieval sentimentality appears in the play at its most intense as Abraham discusses, first with himself and then with his beloved son, the consequences of obeying God, and as Isaac expresses at once his natural desire not to die and his willingness to do so through obedience to his father—whom, indeed, he rebukes for delaying, which only increases the agony of them both. The play, like *Everyman*, closes with the explanation of a Doctor (a learned man) of the moral the audience should draw from the play; but the play itself not only makes its moral point about the importance of obeying the divine will, but also prefigures the sacrifice in later Biblical history of Jesus, the Lamb of God, for whom there could be no last-minute substitute of the kind that saves Isaac.

The Brome play of *Abraham and Isaac* is one of six English mystery plays on this subject that have survived. (For a discussion of the mystery plays, see the introduction to the *Second Shepherds' Play*, above.) It is preserved in a single manuscript of the late 15th century (Brome is the name of its 19th-century owner), a miscellany containing items of Middle English verse, legal deeds, accounts, etc. It is not known how the original compiler of the manuscript received a copy of the play. Presumably it was derived from an otherwise lost mystery cycle, and part of it closely resembles the play of *Abraham and Isaac* in the Chester cycle, though whether the Brome play draws on the Chester play or the Chester play on it is not clear. Nor is it possible to assign a firmer date to it than the first quarter of the 15th century.

The present text, based on the manuscript in the Beinecke Library of Yale University, has been modernized. The edition of the play in Norman Davis, *Non-Cycle Plays and Fragments* (1970), has provided the editor with much help.

The Brome Play of Abraham and Isaac

Dramatis Personae

ABRAHAM	ISAAC
GOD	DOCTOR
ANGEL	

[A Field.]

ABR. Father of heaven omnipotent,
    With all my heart to thee I call.
  Thou hast give me both land and rent,°   *money*
  And my lifelode° thou hast me sent: *livelihood*
5   I thank thee highly evermore of° all.   *for*

  First of the earth thou madest Adam,
    And Eve also to be his wife:
  All other creatures of them two cam;
  And now thou hast granted me, Abraham,
10   Here in this land to lead my life.

  In my age thou has granted me this,
    That this young child with me shall won.°   *dwell*
  I love no thing so much, ywis,°   *indeed*
  Except thine own self, dear Father of bliss,
15   As Isaac here, my own sweet son.

  I have divers° children mo°   *various / more*
    The which I love not half so weel.°   *well*
  This fair sweet child, he cheers me so
  In every place where that I go
20   That no disease° here may I feel.   *disquiet*

And therefore, Father of heaven, I pray
    For his health and for his grace:
Now, Lord, keep him both night and day
    That never no disease nor fray°   *terror*
25   Come to my child in no place.

Now come on, Isaac, my own sweet child,
    Go we home and take our rest.
ISA. Abraham, my father so mild,
    To follow you I am full prest,°   *ready*
30   Both early and late.
ABR. Come, on, sweet child, I love thee best
    Of all the children that ever I begate.

[Heaven.]

GOD. Mine angel, fast hie° thee thy way,   *hasten*
    And unto middle-earth anon° thou go.   *straightaway*
35 Abraham's heart now will I assay°   *test*
    Whether that he be steadfast or no.

Say I command him for to take
    Isaac his son that he loveth so weel,°   *well*
And sacrifice with his blood he make
40   If of° my friendship he will feel.   *any part of*

Show him the way unto the hill
    Where that his sacrifice shall be.
I shall assay now his good will,
    Whether he loveth better his child or me.
45   All men shall take example him be°   *by*
My commandëments how they shall fulfill.

[The Field.]

ABR. Now, Father of heaven that formed all thing,
    My prayers I make to thee again.
For this day my tender offering
50   Here I must give to thee, certain.
A, Lord God, almighty king,
    What manner beast will make thee most fain?°   *glad*
If I had thereof very° knowing   *true*
    It should be done with all my main
55   Full soon anon.
To do thy pleasing on an hill
Verily it is my will,
    Dear Father, God alone.
        [*Enter* ANGEL.]
ANG. Abraham, Abraham, will thou rest?

60   Our Lord commandeth thee to take
   Isaac thy young son that thou lovest best,
    And sacrifice with his blood thou make.

   Into the land of Moriah thou go
   And offer thy child unto thy lord:
65   I shall thee lead and show also.
     Unto God's heast,° Abraham, accord,°   *command / obey*
      And follow me upon this green.°   *ground*
ABR. Welcome to me be my Lordes sand,°   *message*
    And I will not his heast withstand.
70   Yet Isaac my young son in land
     A full dear child to me hath been.

   I had liefer,° if God had be pleased,   *rather*
    For to 'a° forbore° all the good I have *have / forgone*
   Than Isaac my son should 'a be deceased,°   *dead*
75   So God in heaven my soul moot° save.   *may*

   I loved never thing so much in eard,°   *earth*
    And now I must the child go kill.
   A, Lord God, my conscience is strongly steard,° *moved*
   And yet, my dear Lord, I am sore afeard
80   To grouch° anything against your will.   *grudge*

   I love my child as I do my life,
    But yet I love my God much more,
   For though my heart would make any strife,
   Yet will I not spare for child nor wife,
85   But do after my Lordës lore.°   *teaching*

   Though I love my son never so weel,
    Yet smite off his head soon I shall.
   A, Father of heaven, to thee I kneel:
   An hard death my son shall feel
90   For to honour thee, Lord, withal.

ANG. Abraham, Abraham, this is well said,
    And all these commandements look thou save.°   *keep*
   But in thy heart be nothing dismayed.
ABR. Nay, nay, forsooth, I hold me well paid,°   *pleased*
95   To please my God with the best I have.

   For though my heart be heavily set
    To see the blood of my own dear son,
   Yet for all this I will not let,°   *refrain*
   But Isaac my son I will go fet,°   *fetch*
100   And come as fast as ever we con.°   *can*

Now, Isaac, my own dear son,
    Where art thou, child? Speak to me.
      [*Enter* ISAAC.]
ISA. My fair sweet father, I am here,
    And make my prayers to the Trinity.

105 ABR. Rise up, my child, and fast come hither,
    My gentle barn° that art so wise,   *child*
For we two, child, must go togither,
    And unto my Lord make sacrifice.

ISA. I am full ready, my father, lo!
110   Even at your hands I stand right here.
And whatsoever ye bid me do,
    It shall be done with glad cheer,
      Full well and fine.
ABR.   A, Isaac, my own son so dear,
115   God's blessing I give thee, and mine.

Hold this faggot upon thy back,
    And here myself shall fire bring.
ISA. Father, all this gear will I pack:
    I am full fain° to do your bidding.   *glad*
120 ABR. A, Lord of heaven, my hands I wring;
    This childës words my heart all wrack.°   *ruin*

Now, Isaac son, go we our way
    Unto yon mount with all our main.°   *strength*
ISA. Go we, father, as fast as we may:
125   To follow you I am full fain,
      Although I be slender.
      [*They climb a hill.*]
ABR.   A, Lord, my heart it breaketh on twain,°   *in two*
    This childës words, they be so tender.

A, Isaac, my son, anon lay it down:
130   No longer upon thy back it bear.
For I must make me ready boun°   *quickly*
    To honor my Lord God so dear.

ISA. Lo,° my father, where it is: *look*
    To cheer you alway I draw me near.
135 But father, I marvel sore of this,
    Why that ye make this heavy° cheer,°   *gloomy / face*
And also, father, evermore dread I:
    Where is your quick° beast that ye should kill?   *living*
Both fire and wood we have ready,
140   But quick beast have we none on this hill.

      A quick beast, I woot° well, must be dead   *know*
        Your sacrifice that ye should make.
ABR. Dread thee not, my child, I thee read,°   *advise*
      Our Lord will send me unto this stead°   *place*
145   Some manner of beast for me to take,
        Through his sweet sand.°   *message*
ISA. Ye, father, by my heart ginneth° quake   *begins*
       To see that sharp sword in your hand.

       Why bear ye your sword drawen so?
150   Of your countenance I have much wonder.
ABR. A, Father of heaven, as I am woe!
       This child here breaketh my heart asunder.

ISA. Tell me, dear father, ere that ye cease,
       Bear ye your sword drawen for me?
155 ABR. A, Isaac, my sweet son, peace, peace!
       For ywis° thou break my heart on three.   *indeed*

ISA. Now truly, somewhat, father, methink
       That ye mourn thus more and more.
ABR. A, Lord of heaven, thy grace let sink,°   *descend*
160   For my heart was never half so sore.

ISA. I pray you, father, let me wit°   *know*
       Whether I shall have any harm or no?
ABR. Ywis, sweet son. I may not tell thee yit°   *yet*
      My heart is now so full of woe.
165 ISA. Dear father, I pray, hideth nought from me
       But some of your thought that he tell on.°   *forth*
ABR. A, Isaac, I must kill thee.
ISA.   Kill me, father? Alas, what have I done?

       If I have trespassed against you ought
170   With a yard° ye make me full mild.   *rod*
       And with your sharp sword kill me nought,
       For ywis, father, I am but a child.

ABR. I am full sorry, son, thy blood to spill,
       But truly my child I may not chees.°   *choose*
175 ISA. Now I would my mother were here on this hill:
       She would kneel for me on both her knees
         To save my life.
       And sithen° my mother is not here   *since*
       I pray you, father, change your cheer,[1]
180   And kill me not with your knife.

ABR. Forsooth, son, but if° I thee kill,   *unless*
       I should grieve God right sore, I dread.

1. I.e., mind.

It is his commandment and also his will
 That I should do this same deed.

185 He commanded me, son, certain,
 To make my sacrifice with thy blood.
ISA. And is it God's will that I should be slain?
ABR. Yea, truly, Isaac my son so good,

And therefore my hands I wring.
190 ISA. Now, father, against my Lordës will
  I will never grouch,° loud or still: *complain*
 He might 'a sent me a better ending
  If it had 'a been his will.
ABR. Forsooth, son, but° I did this deed,   *unless*
195 Grievously displeased our Lord will be.
ISA. Nay, nay, father, God forbede
  That ever ye should grieve him for me.

Ye have other children, one or two,
 The which ye should love well by kind.°   *nature*
200 I pray you, father, make ye no woe,
For be I once dead and fro you go,
 I shall be so on out of your mind.

Therefore do our Lord's bidding,
 And when I am dead, pray for me.
205 But, father, tell ye my mother no thing:
 Say I am in another country dwelling.
ABR. A, Isaac, Isaac, blessed may thou be.

My heart beginneth strongly to rise
 To see the blood of thy blessed body.
210 ISA. Father,° sin it may be no other wise   *since*
  Let it pass over as well as I.

But, father, ere I go unto my death
 I pray ye bless me with your hand.
ABR. Now, Isaac, with all my breath
215 My blessing I give thee upon this land.
  And God's also thereto, ywis.
 A, Isaac, Isaac, son, up thou stand,
  Thy fair sweet mouth that I may kiss.

ISA. Now farewell, my own father so fine,
220 And greet well my mother in eard.[2]
 But I pray you, father, to hide mine eyn°   *eyes*
  That I see not the stroke of your sharp swerd° *sword*
   That my flesh shall defile.
ABR. Son, thy words make me weep full sore.

2. On earth.

225   Now, dear son Isaac, speak no more.
ISA. A, my own dear father, wherefore?
       We shall speak together here but a while.

       And sithen° that I must needs be dead,   *since*
       Yet, my dear father, to you I pray:
230   Smite but few strokes at my head,
       And make an end as soon as ye may,
       And tarry not too long.
ABR. Thy meek words, child, make me affray°   *fear*
       So "wailaway"° may be my song,   *alas*

235   Except all-only Goddës will.
       A, Isaac, mine own sweet child,
       Yet kiss me again upon this hill.
       In all this world is none so mild.

ISA. Now truly, father, all this tarrying
240   It nought doth but my heart harm.
       I pray you, father, make an ending.
ABR.   Come up, sweet son, into my arm.

       I must bind thy handës two,
       Although thou be never so mild.
245 ISA. A, mercy, father, why should ye so do?
ABR.   That thou shouldest not let° me, child.   *hinder*

ISA. Nay, ywis, father, I will not let you:
       Do on, for me, all your will,
       And on the purpose that ye have set you,
250   For Goddës love, keep it forth still.
       I am full sorry this day to die,
       But yet I keep° not my God to grieve.   *care*
       Do on your list,° for me, hardily,°   *pleasure / confidently*
       My fair sweet father, I give you leave.

255   But, father, I pray you evermore
       Tell ye my mother of this no deal:°   *bit*
       If she wist° it, she would weep full sore.   *knew*
       For father, she loveth me full weel:°   *well*
       Goddës blessing have mote° she.   *may*
260   Now farewell, my mother so sweet:
       We two be like° no more to meet.   *likely*
ABR. A, Isaac, son, thou makest me greet°   *weep*
       And with thy words distemperest° me.   *distress*

ISA. Ywis, sweet father, I am sorry to grieve you:
265   I cry you mercy of that° I have done.   *what*
       And of all trespass that ever I did meve° you,   *cause*
       Now, father, forgive me ere ye have done.

God of heaven be with me!

ABR. A, dear child, leave off thy moans.
270   In all thy life thou grieved me never ones.°   *once*
    Now blessed be thou, body and bones,
        That thou were bred and born to me.

Thou hast be to me child full good;
        But child, though I mourn never so fast,
275   Yet must I needs here at the last
    In this place shed all thy blood.

Therefore, my son, here shall thou lie:
        Unto my work I must me stede.°   *set*
    Ywis, I had as lief myself to die,
280   If God will be pleased with my dead,°   *death*
        And mine own body for to offer.

ISA. A, mercy, father, mourn ye no more.
    Your weeping maketh my heart sore
        As my own death that I shall suffer.

285   Your kerch,° father, about my eyes ye wind.   *handkerchief*
ABR.   So I shall, my sweetest child in eard.°   *earth*
ISA. Now yet, good father, have this in mind,
        And smite me not often with your sharp swerd,°   *sword*
        But hastily that it be sped.
290 ABR. Now farewell, my child so full of grace.
ISA. A, father, father, turn downward my face
        For of your sword I am ever adread.

ABR. To do this deed I am full sorry,
        But, Lord, thine heast° I will not withstand.   *command*
295 ISA. A, Father of heaven, to thee I cry:
        Lord, receive me into thy hand.

ABR. Lo, now is the time come, certain,
        That my sword in his neck shall bite.
    A, Lord, my heart riseth thereagain:
300   I find it not in my heart to smite.
        My heart will now thereto.
    Yet fain I would work my Lordës will.
    But this young innocent lies so still
    I find it not in my heart him to kill.
305   O Father of heaven, what shall I do?

ISA. A, mercy, father, why tarry ye so?
        And let me lie thus long on this heath?
    Now I would to God the stroke were do.
    Father, I pray you, short° my woe,   *shorten*
310   And let me not look³ thus after my death.

3. I.e., wait for.

ABR. Now, heart, why wouldest thou not break on three?
   Yet shall thou not make me to God unmild.° *disobedient*
I will no longer let° for thee, *delay*
For that my God aggrieved would be.
315 Now hold° the stroke, my own dear child. *receive*
   [As ABRAHAM *raises the sword, enter the* ANGEL,
   who snatches it from him.]
ANG. I am an angel, thou mayst be blithe,
   That from heaven to thee is sent.
Our Lord thanketh thee an hundred sithe° *times*
For the keeping of his commandëment.

320 He knoweth thy will and also thy heart,
   That thou dreadest him above all thing,
And some of thy heaviness for to depart,° *remove*
   A fair ram yonder I gan° bring. *did*

He standeth tied, lo, among the breris.° *briars*
325   Now, Abraham, amend thy mood,
For Isaac thy young son that here is
   This day shall not shed his blood.

Go make thy sacrifice with yon ram,
   For unto heaven I go now home.
330 Now farewell, blessed Abraham,
   The way is full gain° that I must gone. *straight*
   Take up thy son so free.° *gentle*
ABR.   A, Lord, I thank thee of thy great pity
Now I am eathed° in divers wise. *comforted*
335 Arise up, Isaac, my dear son, arise,
   Arise up, sweet child, and come to me.

ISA. A, mercy, father, why smite ye nought?
   A, smite on, father, once with your knife.
ABR. Peace, my sweet son, and take no thought,
340   For our Lord of heaven hath granted thy life,
   By his angel now, that thou shalt nought

Die this day, son, truëly.
ISA. A, father, full glad then were I—
   Ywis,° father, I say ywis— *yes*
345 Full glad were I if this tale were true.
ABR. An hundred times, my son fair of hue.
   For joy thy mouth now will I kiss.

ISA. A, my dear father Abraham,
   Will not God be wroth° that we do thus? *angry*
350 No, no, hardily,° my sweet son, *assuredly*
For he hath sent us yon same ram
   Hither down on this hill to us.

Yon beast shall die here in thy stead
In the worship of our Lord alone.
355 Go fet° him hither, my child, indeed,   *fetch*
ISA. Father, I will go hent° him by the head.   *seize*
    And bring yon beast with me anon.
        [ISAAC *brings him the sheep.*]
    A, sheep, sheep, blessed mote° thou be   *may*
    That ever thou were sent down hither.
360 Thou shall this day die for me
    In the worship of the Holy Trinity:
       Now come fast and go we togither
        To my father in hie.°   *haste*
    Though thou be never so gentle and good,
365 Yet had I liefer thou sheddest thy blood,
       Ywis,° sheep, than I.   *indeed*

Lo, father, I have brought here full smart
    This gentle sheep, and him you I give.
    But Lord, I thank thee with all my heart;
370 For I am glad that I shall live
       And kiss once my dear mother.
ABR. Now be right merry, my sweet child,
    For this quick beast that is so mild
    Here I shall present before all other.

375 ISA. And I shall fast begin to blow:
    This fire shall burn a full good speed.
    But father, while I stoop down low,
    Ye will not kill me with thy sword, I trow?°   *trust*
ABR. No, hardily,° sweet son, have no dread: *assuredly*
380 My mourning is past.
ISA. Yea, but I would that sword were sheathed.
    For father, it maketh me full ill aghast.
       [ABRAHAM *makes his offering, kneeling.*]
ABR. Now Lord God of heaven in Trinity,
    Almighty God omnipotent,
385 Mine offering I make in the worship of thee,
    And with this quick beast I thee present.
    Lord, receive thou mine intent,
    As thou art God and ground of our gree.°   *favor*
       [*Enter* GOD.]
GOD. Abraham, Abraham, well mote° thou speed,°   *may / prosper*
390 And Isaac thy young son thee by.
    Truly, Abraham, for this deed
    I shall multiply your bothers° seed   *of you both*
       As thick as stars be in the sky,
        Both more and less;
395 And as thick as gravel° in the sea   *pebbles*
    So thick multiplied your seed shall be:
       This grant I you for your goodness.

Of you shall come fruit great won°   *supply*
And ever be in bliss without end;
400   For ye dread me as God alone
And keep my commandëments every one,
    My blessing I give wheresoever ye wend.
      [*Exit.*]

ABR. Lo, Isaac my son, how thinketh ye
    By this work that we have wrought?
405   Full glad and blithe may we be
    Against God's will that we grouched° nought,   *resisted*
      Upon this fair heath.
ISA. A, father, I thank our Lord every deal°   *bit*
    That my wit served me so weel
410   For to dread God more than my death.

ABR. Why, dearworthy son,° were thou adread?   *beloved*
    Hardily,° child, tell me thy lore.   *confidently / mind*
ISA. Yea, by my faith, father, now have I read,[4]
    I was never so afraid before
415   As I have been at yon hill.
    But by my faith, father, I swear
    I will nevermore come there
      But° it be against my will.   *unless*
ABR. Yea, come on with me, my own sweet son,
420   And homeward fast now let us gone.
ISA. By my faith, father, thereto I un;°   *consent*
    I had never so good will to go home,
    And to speak with my good mother.
ABR. A, Lord of heaven, I thank thee,
425   For now I may lead home with me
    Isaac my young son so free,°   *gentle*
      The gentlest child above all other.

    Now go we forth, my blessed son.
ISA. I grant, father, and let us gone,
430   For by my truth, were I at home
      I would never go out under that form,[5]
      This may I well avow.
    I pray God give us grace evermo,°   *evermore*
    And all tho° that we be holding° to.   *those / obliged*
      [*Exit. Enter* DOCTOR.]
435 DOC. Lo, sovereigns and sirs, now have we shewed
    This solemn story to great and small,
    It is good learning to learned and lewd,°   *ignorant*
    And to the wisest of us all,
      Withouten any barring.°   *denial*
440   For this story showeth you here
    How we should keep, to our powére,°   *ability*
      God's commandments without grouching.°   *complaint*

4. I.e., that I think.
5. Guise, i.e., as the victim of a blood-sacrifice (?).

Trow° ye, sirs, and° God sent an angel   *think / if*
   And commanded you your child to slain,°   *slay*
445 By your truth, is there any of you
   That either would grouch or strive theragain?

How think ye now, sirs, thereby?
   I trow there be three or four or mo;°   *more*
And these women that weep so sorrowfully
450   When that their children die them for.°   *from*
   As nature will, and kind.°   *nature*
   It is but folly, I may well avow,
To grouch against God or to grieve yow,°   *yourselves*
For ye shall never see him mischieved,° well I
   know,   *discomforted*
455   By land nor water, have this in mind.

And grouch not against our Lord God,
   In wealth or woe, whether° that he you send,   *whichever*
Though ye be never so hard bestead,°   *put*
   For when he will he may it amend.

460 His commandments truly if ye keep with good heart,
   As this story hath now showed you beforn,
And faithfully serve him while ye be quart,°   *healthy*
   Than° ye may please God both even and morn.   *then*
   Now Jesu that weareth the crown of thorn,
465   Bring us all to heaven-bliss.

EVERYMAN

(ca. 1485)

Everyman is the best surviving example of that kind of medieval drama
which is known as the morality play. Moralities apparently evolved side by
side with the mysteries and in England were, like them, acted by trade
guilds, though they were composed individually and not in cycles. They
too have a primarily religious purpose, though their method of attaining
it is different. The mysteries endeavored to make the Christian religion
more real to the unlearned by dramatizing significant events in Biblical
history and by showing what these events meant in terms of human experience. The moralities, on the other hand, employed allegory to dramatize the moral struggle that Christianity envisions as present in every man:
the actors are every man and the qualities within him, good or bad, and
the plot consists of his various reactions to these qualities as they push
and pull him one way or another—that is, in Christian terms, toward
heaven or toward hell. The intent of the morality is more overtly didactic
than the mystery, but most of the moralities share with the mysteries a
good deal of rough humor. This is perhaps more evident in other plays
of the genre than in *Everyman*, where the chief humor lies in the undue

haste with which the hero's friends abandon him when he calls on them for help.

Everyman inculcates its austere lesson by the simplicity and directness of its language and of its approach. A fine sense of inevitability is built up as Everyman is stripped, one by one, of those apparent goods on which he had relied. First he is deserted by his patently false friends: his casual companions, his kinsmen, and his wealth. Receiving some comfort from his enfeebled good deeds, he falls back on them and on his other resources—his strength, his beauty, his intelligence, and his knowledge—qualities which, when properly used, help to make an integrated man. These assist him through the crisis in which he must make up his book of accounts, but at the end, when he must go to the grave, all desert him save his good deeds alone. While the play contains rather too much direct sermonizing, it makes most effectively its grim point that man can take with him from this world nothing that he has received, only what he has given.

In *Everyman* allegory appears in its most meticulously worked-out form. Each actor has his allegorical significance defined by his name and behaves entirely within the limits of that definition. The onlooker takes a good deal of intellectual satisfaction in watching the nice operation of the allegorical equations. On the other hand, one might object that allegory, when so neatly handled, sacrifices for a kind of mathematical regularity the suggestiveness that inheres in the far looser allegory of such a work as *Piers Plowman*, which stimulates the imagination more than it satisfies the intellect. Nevertheless, when it is well staged and well acted, *Everyman*, despite its uncompromising didacticism, is a powerful drama.

The play was written near the end of the 15th century. It is probably a translation of a Flemish play, though it is not impossible that the Flemish play is the translation and the English *Everyman* the original.

Everyman[1]

Dramatis Personae

MESSENGER	KNOWLEDGE
GOD	CONFESSION
DEATH	BEAUTY
EVERYMAN	STRENGTH
FELLOWSHIP	DISCRETION
KINDRED	FIVE-WITS
COUSIN	ANGEL
GOODS	DOCTOR
GOOD DEEDS	

HERE BEGINNETH A TREATISE HOW THE HIGH FATHER OF HEAVEN SENDETH DEATH TO SUMMON EVERY CREATURE

1. The text is based upon the earliest printing of the play (no manuscript is known) by John Skot about 1530, as reproduced by W. W. Greg (Louvain, 1904). The spelling has been modernized except where modernization would spoil the rhyme, and modern punctuation has been added. The stage directions have been amplified.

TO COME AND GIVE ACCOUNT OF THEIR LIVES IN THIS
WORLD, AND IS IN MANNER OF A MORAL PLAY

[*Enter* MESSENGER.]

MESSENGER. I pray you all give your audience,
And hear this matter with reverence,
By figure² a moral play,
The Summoning of Everyman called it is,
5 That of our lives and ending shows
How transitory we be all day.³
The matter is wonder precious,
But the intent of it is more gracious
And sweet to bear away.
10 The story saith: Man, in the beginning
Look well, and take good heed to the ending,
Be you never so gay.
You think sin in the beginning full sweet,
Which in the end causeth the soul to weep,
15 When the body lieth in clay.
Here shall you see how fellowship and jollity,
Both strength, pleasure, and beauty,
Will fade from thee as flower in May.
For ye shall hear how our Heaven-King
20 Calleth Everyman to a general reckoning.
Give audience and hear what he doth say.

[*Exit* MESSENGER.—*Enter* GOD.]

GOD. I perceive, here in my majesty,
How that all creatures be to me unkind,°   *thoughtless*
Living without dread in worldly prosperity.
25 Of ghostly° sight the people be so blind,   *spiritual*
Drowned in sin, they know me not for their God.
In worldly riches is all their mind:
They fear not of my righteousness the sharp rod;
My law that I showed when I for them died
30 They forget clean, and shedding of my blood red.
I hanged between two,⁴ it cannot be denied:
To get them life I suffered to be dead.
I healed their feet, with thorns hurt was my head.
I could do no more than I did, truly—
35 And now I see the people do clean forsake me.
They use the seven deadly sins damnable,
As pride, coveitise,° wrath, and lechery⁵   *avarice*
Now in the world be made commendable.
And thus they leave of angels the heavenly company.
40 Every man liveth so after his own pleasure,
And yet of their life they be nothing sure,
I see the more that I them forbear,
The worse they be from year to year:
All that liveth appaireth° fast.   *degenerates*

---

2. In form.
3. Always.
4. I.e., the two thieves between whom

Christ was crucified.
5. The other three deadly sins are envy, gluttony, and sloth.

45 Therefore I will, in all the haste,
Have a reckoning of every man's person.
For, and° I leave the people thus alone   *if*
In their life and wicked tempests,
Verily they will become much worse than beasts;
50 For now one would by envy another up eat.
Charity do they all clean forgeet.
I hoped well that every man
In my glory should make his mansion,
And thereto I had them all elect.°   *chosen*
55 But now I see, like traitors deject,°   *abased*
They thank me not for the pleasure that I to° them   *for*
    meant,
Nor yet for their being that I them have lent.
I proffered the people great multitude of mercy,
And few there be that asketh it heartily.°   *sincerely*
60 They be so cumbered° with worldly riches   *encumbered*
That needs on them I must do justice—
On every man living without fear.
Where art thou, Death, thou mighty messenger?
        [*Enter* DEATH.]
DEATH. Almighty God, I am here at your will,
65 Your commandment to fulfill.
GOD. Go thou to Everyman,
    And show him, in my name,
    A pilgrimage he must on him take,
    Which he in no wise may escape;
70 And that he bring with him a sure reckoning
    Without delay or any tarrying.
DEATH. Lord, I will in the world go run over all,[6]
    And cruelly out-search both great and small.
        [*Exit* GOD.]
    Everyman will I beset that liveth beastly
75 Out of God's laws, and dreadeth not folly.
    He that loveth riches I will strike with my dart,
    His sight to blind, and from heaven to depart°—   *separate*
    Except that Almsdeeds be his good friend—
    In hell for to dwell, world without end
80 Lo, yonder I see Everyman walking:
    Full little he thinketh on my coming;
    His mind is on fleshly lusts and his treasure,
    And great pain it shall cause him to endure
    Before the Lord, Heaven-King.
        [*Enter* EVERYMAN.]
85 Everyman, stand still! Whither art thou going
    Thus gaily? Hast thou thy Maker forgeet?°   *forgotten*
EVERYMAN. Why askest thou?
    Why wouldest thou weet?°   *know*
DEATH. Yea, sir, I will show you:
90 In great haste I am sent to thee

6. Everywhere.

From God out of his majesty.

EVERYMAN. What! sent to me?

DEATH. Yea, certainly.

Though thou have forgot him here,

95 He thinketh on thee in the heavenly sphere,

As, ere we depart, thou shalt know.

EVERYMAN. What desireth God of me?

DEATH. That shall I show thee:

A reckoning he will needs have

100 Without any longer respite.

EVERYMAN. To give a reckoning longer leisure I crave.

This blind° matter troubleth my wit.   *unexpected*

DEATH. On thee thou must take a long journey:

Therefore thy book of count° with thee thou bring, *accounts*

105 For turn again thou cannot by no way.

And look thou be sure of thy reckoning,

For before God thou shalt answer and shew

Thy many bad deeds and good but a few—

How thou hast spent thy life and in what wise,

110 Before the Chief Lord of Paradise.

Have ado that we were in that way,[7]

For weet thou well thou shalt make none attornay.[8]

EVERYMAN. Full unready I am such reckoning to give.

I know thee not. What messenger art thou?

115 DEATH. I am Death that no man dreadeth,[9]

For every man I 'rest,° and no man spareth;   *arrest*

For it is God's commandment

That all to me should be obedient.

EVERYMAN. O Death, thou comest when I had thee least in

mind.

120 In thy power it lieth me to save:

Yet of my good° will I give thee, if thou will be kind, *goods*

Yea, a thousand pound shalt thou have—

And defer this matter till another day.

DEATH. Everyman, it may not be, by no way.

125 I set nought by[1] gold, silver, nor riches,

Nor by pope, emperor, king, duke, nor princes,

For, and° I would receive gifts great,   *if*

All the world I might get.

But my custom is clean contrary:

130 I give thee no respite. Come hence and not tarry!

EVERYMAN. Alas, shall I have no longer respite?

I may say Death giveth no warning.

To think on thee it maketh my heart sick,

For all unready is my book of reckoning.

135 But twelve year and I might have a biding,[2]

My counting-book I would make so clear

That my reckoning I should not need to fear.

---

7. I.e., let's get started at once.
8. I.e., none to appear in your stead.
9. That fears nobody.

1. I care nothing for.
2. If I might have a delay for just
   twelve years.

Wherefore, Death, I pray thee, for God's mercy,
Spare me till I be provided of remedy.
140 DEATH. Thee availeth not to cry, weep, and pray;
But haste thee lightly° that thou were gone that   *quickly*
    journay,
And prove° thy friends, if thou can.   *test*
For weet° thou well the tide° abideth no man,   *know / time*
And in the world each living creature
145 For Adam's sin must die of nature.[3]
EVERYMAN. Death, if I should this pilgrimage take
And my reckoning surely make,
Show me, for saint° charity,   *holy*
Should I not come again shortly?
150 DEATH. No, Everyman. And thou be once there,
Thou mayst never more come here,
Trust me verily.
EVERYMAN. O gracious God in the high seat celestial,
Have mercy on me in this most need!
155 Shall I have no company from this vale terrestrial
Of mine acquaintance that way me to lead?
DEATH. Yea, if any be so hardy
That would go with thee and bear thee company.
Hie° thee that thou were gone to God's magnificence, *hasten*
160 Thy reckoning to give before his presence.
What, weenest° thou thy life is given thee,   *suppose*
And thy worldly goods also?
EVERYMAN. I had weened so, verily.
DEATH. Nay, nay, it was but lent thee.
165 For as soon as thou art go,
Another a while shall have it and then go therefro,
Even as thou hast done.
Everyman, thou art mad! Thou hast thy wits° five,   *senses*
And here on earth will not amend thy live![4]
170 For suddenly I do come.
EVERYMAN. O wretched caitiff! Whither shall I flee
That I might 'scape this endless sorrow?
Now, gentle Death, spare me till tomorrow,
That I may amend me
175 With good advisement.°   *preparation*
DEATH. Nay, thereto I will not consent,
Nor no man will I respite,
But to the heart suddenly I shall smite,
Without any advisement.
180 And now out of thy sight I will me hie:
See thou make thee ready shortly,
For thou mayst say this is the day
That no man living may 'scape away.
    [*Exit* DEATH.]

3. Naturally.   4. In thy life.

EVERYMAN. Alas, I may well weep with sighs deep:
185 Now have I no manner of company
     To help me in my journey and me to keep.°   guard
     And also my writing⁵ is full unready—
     How shall I do now for to excuse me?
     I would to God I had never be geet!⁶
190 To my soul a full great profit it had be.
     For now I fear pains huge and great.
     The time passeth: Lord, help, that all wrought!
     For though I mourn, it availeth nought.
     The day passeth and is almost ago:°   gone by
195 I wot° not well what for to do.   know
     To whom were I best my complaint to make?
     What and I to Fellowship thereof spake,
     And showed him of this sudden chance?
     For in him is all mine affiance,°   trust
200 We have in the world so many a day
     Be good friends in sport and play.
     I see him yonder, certainly.
     I trust that he will bear me company.
     Therefore to him will I speak to ease my sorrow.
          [*Enter* FELLOWSHIP.]
205 Well met, good Fellowship, and good morrow!
     FELLOWSHIP. Everyman, good morrow, by this day!
     Sir, why lookest thou so piteously?
     If anything be amiss, I pray thee me say,
     That I may help to remedy.
210 EVERYMAN. Yea, good Fellowship, yea:
     I am in great jeopardy.
     FELLOWSHIP. My true friend, show to me your mind.
     I will not forsake thee to my life's end
     In the way of good company.
215 EVERYMAN. That was well spoken, and lovingly!
     FELLOWSHIP. Sir, I must needs know your heaviness.°   sorrow
     I have pity to see you in any distress.
     If any have you wronged, ye shall revenged be,
     Though I on the ground be slain for thee,
220 Though that I know before that I should die.
     EVERYMAN. Verily, Fellowship, gramercy.°   many thanks
     FELLOWSHIP. Tush! by thy thanks I set not a stree.°   straw
     Show me your grief and say no more.
     EVERYMAN. If I my heart should to you break,°   disclose
225 And then you to turn your mind fro me,
     And would not me comfort when ye hear me speak,
     Then should I ten times sorrier be.
     FELLOWSHIP. Sir, I say as I will do, indeed.
     EVERYMAN. Then be you a good friend at need.
230 I have found you true herebefore.

5. I.e., ledger.   6. Been begotten.

FELLOWSHIP. And so ye shall evermore.
    For, in faith, and thou go to hell,
    I will not forsake thee by the way.
EVERYMAN. Ye speak like a good friend. I believe you well.
235   I shall deserve° it, and° I may.   *repay / if*
FELLOWSHIP. I speak of no deserving, by this day!
    For he that will say and nothing do
    Is not worthy with good company to go.
    Therefore show me the grief of your mind,
240   As to your friend most loving and kind.
EVERYMAN. I shall show you how it is:
    Commanded I am to go a journay,
    A long way, hard and dangerous,
    And give a strait° count,° without delay,   *strict / accounting*
245   Before the high judge Adonai.[7]
    Wherefore I pray you bear me company,
    As ye have promised, in this journay.
FELLOWSHIP. This is matter indeed! Promise is duty—
    But, and I should take such a voyage on me,
250   I know it well, it should be to my pain.
    Also it maketh me afeard, certain.
    But let us take counsel here, as well as we can—
    For your words would fear° a strong man.   *frighten*
EVERYMAN. Why, ye said if I had need,
255   Ye would me never forsake, quick ne dead,
    Though it were to hell, truly.
FELLOWSHIP. So I said, certainly.
    But such pleasures° be set aside, the sooth to say.   *jokes*
    And also, if we took such a journay,
260   When should we again come?
EVERYMAN. Nay, never again, till the day of doom.
FELLOWSHIP. In faith, then will not I come there!
    Who hath you these tidings brought?
EVERYMAN. Indeed, Death was with me here.
265 FELLOWSHIP. Now by God that all hath bought,°   *redeemed*
    If Death were the messenger,
    For no man that is living today
    I will not go that loath° journay—   *loathsome*
    Not for the father that begat me!
270 EVERYMAN. Ye promised otherwise, pardie.°   *by God*
FELLOWSHIP. I wot well I said so, truly.
    And yet, if thou wilt eat and drink and make good cheer,
    Or haunt to women the lusty company,[8]
    I would not forsake you while the day is clear,
275   Trust me verily!
EVERYMAN. Yea, thereto ye would be ready—
    To go to mirth, solace,° and play: *pleasure*

7. I.e., God.
8. Or frequent the lusty company of women.

Your mind to folly will sooner apply°   *attend*
Than to bear me company in my long journay.
280 FELLOWSHIP. Now in good faith, I will not that way.
But, and thou will murder or any man kill,
In that I will help thee with a good will.
EVERYMAN. O that is simple° advice, indeed!   *foolish*
Gentle fellow, help me in my necessity:
285 We have loved long, and now I need—
And now, gentle Fellowship, remember me!
FELLOWSHIP. Whether ye have loved me or no,
By Saint John, I will not with thee go!
EVERYMAN. Yet I pray thee take the labor and do so much for
me,
290 To bring me forward,⁹ for saint charity,
And comfort me till I come without the town.
FELLOWSHIP. Nay, and thou would give me a new gown,
I will not a foot with thee go.
But, and thou had tarried, I would not have left thee so.
295 And as now, God speed thee in thy journey!
For from thee I will depart as fast as I may.
EVERYMAN. Whither away, Fellowship? Will thou forsake me?
FELLOWSHIP. Yea, by my fay!° To God I betake°
thee.   *faith / commend*
EVERYMAN. Farewell, good Fellowship! For thee my heart is
sore.
300 Adieu forever—I shall see thee no more.
FELLOWSHIP. In faith, Everyman, farewell now at the ending:
For you I will remember that parting is mourning.
[*Exit* FELLOWSHIP.]
EVERYMAN. Alack, shall we thus depart° indeed—   *part*
Ah, Lady, help!—without any more comfort?
305 Lo, Fellowship forsaketh me in my most need!
For help in this world whither shall I resort?
Fellowship herebefore with me would merry make,
And now little sorrow for me doth he take.
It is said, "In prosperity men friends may find
310 Which in adversity be full unkind."
Now whither for succor shall I flee,
Sith° that Fellowship hath forsaken me?   *since*
To my kinsmen I will, truly,
Praying them to help me in my necessity.
315 I believe that they will do so,
For kind will creep where it may not go.¹
I will go 'say°—for yonder I see them—   *assay*
Where° be ye now my friends and kinsmen.   *whether*
[*Enter* KINDRED *and* COUSIN.]
KINDRED. Here be we now at your commandment:

---

9. Escort me.
1. For kinship will creep where it can-

not walk (i.e., kinsmen will suffer hardship for one another).

₃₂₀ Cousin, I pray you show us your intent
In any wise, and not spare.
COUSIN. Yea, Everyman, and to us declare
If ye be disposed to go anywhither.
For, weet° you well, we will live and die togither.   *know*
₃₂₅ KINDRED. In wealth and woe we will with you hold,
For over his kin a man may be bold.[2]
EVERYMAN. Gramercy,° my friends and kinsmen
   kind.   *much thanks*
Now shall I show you the grief of my mind.
I was commanded by a messenger
₃₃₀ That is a high king's chief officer:
He bade me go a pilgrimage, to my pain—
And I know well I shall never come again.
Also I must give a reckoning strait,°   *strict*
For I have a great enemy that hath me in wait,[3]
₃₃₅ Which intendeth me to hinder.
KINDRED. What account is that which ye must render?
That would I know.
EVERYMAN. Of all my works I must show
How I have lived and my days spent;
₃₄₀ Also of ill deeds that I have used
In my time sith life was me lent,
And of all virtues that I have refused.
Therefore I pray you go thither with me
To help me make mine account, for saint charity.
₃₄₅ COUSIN. What, to go thither? Is that the matter?
Nay, Everyman, I had liefer fast[4] bread and water
All this five year and more!
EVERYMAN. Alas, that ever I was bore!°   *born*
For now shall I never be merry
₃₅₀ If that you forsake me.
KINDRED. Ah, sir, what? Ye be a merry man:
Take good heart to you and make no moan.
But one thing I warn you, by Saint Anne,
As for me, ye shall go alone.
₃₅₅ EVERYMAN. My Cousin, will you not with me go?
COUSIN. No, by Our Lady! I have the cramp in my toe:
Trust not to me. For, so God me speed,
I will deceive you in your most need.
KINDRED. It availeth you not us to 'tice.°   *entice*
₃₆₀ Ye shall have my maid with all my heart:
She loveth to go to feasts, there to be nice,°   *wanton*
And to dance, and abroad to start.[5]
I will give her leave to help you in that journey,
If that you and she may agree.

---

2. I.e., for a man may make demands   4. I.e., rather fast on.
of his kinsmen.   5. To go gadding about.
3. I.e., Satan lies in ambush for me.

365 EVERYMAN. Now show me the very effect° of your mind: *bent*
  Will you go with me or abide behind?
 KINDRED. Abide behind? Yea, that will I and I may!
  Therefore farewell till another day.
   [*Exit* KINDRED.]
 EVERYMAN. How should I be merry or glad?
370 For fair promises men to me make,
  But when I have most need they me forsake.
  I am deceived. That maketh me sad.
 COUSIN. Cousin Everyman, farewell now,
  For verily I will not go with you;
375 Also of mine own an unready reckoning
  I have to account—therefore I make tarrying.
  Now God keep thee, for now I go.
   [*Exit* COUSIN.]
 EVERYMAN. Ah, Jesus, is all come hereto?° *to this*
  Lo, fair words maketh fools fain:° *glad*
380 They promise and nothing will do, certain.
  My kinsmen promised me faithfully
  For to abide with me steadfastly,
  And now fast away do they flee.
  Even so Fellowship promised me.
385 What friend were best me of to provide?
  I lose my time here longer to abide.
  Yet in my mind a thing there is:
  All my life I have loved riches;
  If that my Good° now help me might, *Goods*
390 He would make my heart full light.
  I will speak to him in this distress.
  Where art thou, my Goods and riches?
 GOODS. [*within*] Who calleth me? Everyman? What, hast thou
  haste?
  I lie here in corners, trussed and piled so high,
395 And in chests I am locked so fast—
  Also sacked in bags—thou mayst see with thine eye
  I cannot stir, in packs low where I lie.
  What would ye have? Lightly° me say. *quickly*
 EVERYMAN. Come hither, Good, in all the haste thou may,
400 For of counsel I must desire thee.
   [*Enter* GOODS.]
 GOODS. Sir, and° ye in the world have sorrow or adversity, *if*
  That can I help you to remedy shortly.
 EVERYMAN. It is another disease° that grieveth me: *distress*
  In this world it is not, I tell thee so.
405 I am sent for another way to go,
  To give a strait count general
  Before the highest Jupiter[6] of all.
  And all my life I have had joy and pleasure in thee:

6. I.e., God.

Therefore I pray thee go with me,

410 For, peradventure, thou mayst before God Almighty

My reckoning help to clean and purify.

For it is said ever among[7]

That money maketh all right that is wrong.

GOODS. Nay, Everyman, I sing another song:

415 I follow no man in such voyages.

For, and I went with thee,

Thou shouldest fare much the worse for me;

For because on me thou did set thy mind,

Thy reckoning I have made blotted and blind,°   *illegible*

420 That thine account thou cannot make truly—

And that hast thou for the love of me.

EVERYMAN. That would grieve me full sore,

When I should come to that fearful answer.

Up, let us go thither together.

425 GOODS. Nay, not so, I am too brittle, I may not endure.

I will follow no man one foot, be ye sure.

EVERYMAN. Alas, I have thee loved and had great pleasure

All my life-days on good and treasure.

GOODS. That is to thy damnation, without leasing,°   *lie*

430 For my love is contrary to the love everlasting.

But if thou had me loved moderately

during,°   *in the meanwhile*

As to the poor to give part of me,

Then shouldest thou not in this dolor be,

Nor in this great sorrow and care.

435 EVERYMAN. Lo, now was I deceived ere I was ware,

And all I may wite° misspending of time.   *blame on*

GOODS. What, weenest° thou that I am thine?   *suppose*

EVERYMAN. I had weened so.

GOODS. Nay, Everyman, I say no.

440 As for a while I was lent thee;

A season thou hast had me in prosperity.

My condition° is man's soul to kill;   *disposition*

If I save one, a thousand I do spill.°   *ruin*

Weenest thou that I will follow thee?

445 Nay, from this world, not verily.

EVERYMAN. I had weened otherwise.

GOODS. Therefore to thy soul Good is a thief;

For when thou art dead, this is my guise°—   *custom*

Another to deceive in the same wise

450 As I have done thee, and all to his soul's repreef.°   *shame*

EVERYMAN. O false Good, cursed thou be,

Thou traitor to God, that hast deceived me

And caught me in thy snare!

GOODS. Marry, thou brought thyself in care,°   *sorrow*

455 Whereof I am glad:

7. Now and then.

I must needs laugh, I cannot be sad.

EVERYMAN. Ah, Good, thou hast had long my heartly°   *sincere*
    love;
I gave thee that which should be the Lord's above.
But wilt thou not go with me, indeed?
460   I pray thee truth to say.
GOODS. No, so God me speed!
    Therefore farewell and have good day.
        [*Exit* GOODS.]
EVERYMAN. Oh, to whom shall I make my moan
    For to go with me in that heavy° journay?   *sorrowful*
465   First Fellowship said he would with me gone:°   *go*
His words were very pleasant and gay,
But afterward he left me alone.
Then spake I to my kinsmen, all in despair,
And also they gave me words fair—
470   They lacked no fair speaking,
But all forsake me in the ending.
Then went I to my Goods that I loved best,
In hope to have comfort; but there had I least,
For my Goods sharply did me tell
475   That he bringeth many into hell.
Then of myself I was ashamed,
And so I am worthy to be blamed:
Thus may I well myself hate.
Of whom shall I now counsel take?
480   I think that I shall never speed
Till that I go to my Good Deed.
But alas, she is so weak
That she can neither go° nor speak.   *walk*
Yet will I venture° on her now.   *gamble*
485   My Good Deeds, where be you?
GOOD DEEDS. [*speaking from the ground*] Here I lie, cold in the
    ground:
Thy sins hath me sore bound
That I cannot stear.°   *stir*
EVERYMAN. O Good Deeds, I stand in fear:
490   I must you pray of counsel,
For help now should come right well.
GOOD DEEDS. Everyman, I have understanding
That ye be summoned, account to make,
Before Messiah of Jer'salem King.
495   And you do by me,[8] that journey with you will I take.
EVERYMAN. Therefore I come to you my moan to make.
I pray you that ye will go with me.
GOOD DEEDS. I would full fain, but I cannot stand, verily.
EVERYMAN. Why, is there anything on you fall?°   *fallen*
500 GOOD DEEDS. Yea, sir, I may thank you of all:

8. I.e., if you do what I say.

If ye had perfectly cheered me,
Your book of count full ready had be.
    [GOOD DEEDS *shows him the account book*.]
Look, the books of your works and deeds eke,°   *also*
As how they lie under the feet,
505 To your soul's heaviness.°   *distress*
EVERYMAN. Our Lord Jesus help me!
  For one letter here I cannot see.
GOOD DEEDS. There is a blind° reckoning in time of
    distress!   *illegible*
EVERYMAN. Good Deeds, I pray you help me in this need,
510 Or else I am forever damned indeed.
  Therefore help me to make reckoning
  Before the Redeemer of all thing
  That King is and was and ever shall.
GOOD DEEDS. Everyman, I am sorry of° your fall   *for*
515 And fain would help you and I were able.
EVERYMAN. Good Deeds, your counsel I pray you give me.
GOOD DEEDS. That shall I do verily,
  Though that on my feet I may not go;
  I have a sister that shall with you also,
520 Called Knowledge, which shall with you abide
  To help you to make that dreadful reckoning.
    [*Enter* KNOWLEDGE.]
KNOWLEDGE. Everyman, I will go with thee and be thy guide,
  In thy most need to go by thy side.
EVERYMAN. In good condition I am now in everything,
525 And am whole content with this good thing,
  Thanked be God my Creator.
GOOD DEEDS. And when he hath brought you there
  Where thou shalt heal thee of thy smart,°   *pain*
  Then go you with your reckoning and your Good Deeds to-
    gether
530 For to make you joyful at heart
  Before the blessed Trinity.
EVERYMAN. My Good Deeds, gramercy!
  I am well content, certainly,
  With your words sweet.
535 KNOWLEDGE. Now go we together lovingly
  To Confession, that cleansing river.
EVERYMAN. For joy I weep—I would we were there!
  But I pray you give me cognition,°   *knowledge*
  Where dwelleth that holy man Confession?
540 KNOWLEDGE. In the House of Salvation:
  We shall find him in that place
  That shall us comfort, by God's grace.
    [KNOWLEDGE *leads* EVERYMAN *to* CONFESSION.]
  Lo, this is Confession: kneel down and ask mercy,
  For he is in good conceit° with God Almighty.   *esteem*

545 EVERYMAN. [*kneeling*] O glorious fountain that all uncleanness
     doth clarify,⁹
 Wash from me the spots of vice unclean,
 That on me no sin may be seen.
 I come with Knowledge for my redemption,
 Redempt° with heart and full contrition,   *redeemed*
550 For I am commanded a pilgrimage to take
 And great accounts before God to make.
 Now I pray you, Shrift, mother of Salvation,
 Help my Good Deeds for my piteous exclamation.
 CONFESSION. I know your sorrow well, Everyman:
555 Because with Knowledge ye come to me,
 I will you comfort as well as I can,
 And a precious jewel I will give thee,
 Called Penance, voider° of adversity.   *expeller*
 Therewith shall your body chastised be—
560 With abstinence and perseverance in God's service.
 Here shall you receive that scourge of me,
 Which is penance strong° that ye must endure,   *harsh*
 To remember thy Saviour was scourged for thee
 With sharp scourges, and suffered it patiently.
565 So must thou ere thou 'scape that painful pilgrimage.
 Knowledge, keep° him in this voyage,   *guard*
 And by that time Good Deeds will be with thee.
 But in any wise be secure° of mercy—   *certain*
 For your time draweth fast—and ye will saved be.
570 Ask God mercy and he will grant, truly.
 When with the scourge of penance man doth him°   *himself*
  bind,
 The oil of forgiveness then shall he find.
 EVERYMAN. Thanked be God for his gracious work,
 For now I will my penance begin.
575 This hath rejoiced and lighted my heart,
 Though the knots¹ be painful and hard within.
 KNOWLEDGE. Everyman, look your penance that ye fulfill,
 What pain that ever it to you be;
 And Knowledge shall give you counsel at will
580 How your account ye shall make clearly.
 EVERYMAN. O eternal God, O heavenly figure,
 O way of righteousness, O goodly vision,
 Which descended down in a virgin pure
 Because he would every man redeem,
585 Which Adam forfeited by his disobedience;
 O blessed Godhead, elect and high Divine,°   *divinity*
 Forgive my grievous offense!
 Here I cry thee mercy in this presence:
 O ghostly Treasure, O Ransomer and Redeemer,

9. Purify.
1. I.e., the knots on the scourge (whip) of penance. "Within": i.e., to my senses.

590 Of all the world Hope and Conduiter,°   *guide*
　　Mirror of joy, Foundator° of mercy,   *Founder*
　　Which enlumineth° heaven and earth thereby,   *lights up*
　　Hear my clamorous complaint, though it late be;
　　Receive my prayers, of thy benignity.
595 Though I be a sinner most abominable,
　　Yet let my name be written in Moses' table.[2]
　　O Mary, pray to the Maker of all thing
　　Me for to help at my ending,
　　And save me from the power of my enemy,
600 For Death assaileth me strongly.
　　And Lady, that I may by mean of thy prayer
　　Of your Son's glory to be partner—
　　By the means of his passion I it crave.
　　I beseech you help my soul to save.
605 Knowledge, give me the scourge of penance:
　　My flesh therewith shall give acquittance.°   *satisfaction for sins*
　　I will now begin, if God give me grace.
　　KNOWLEDGE. Everyman, God give you time and
　　　　　space!°   *opportunity*
　　Thus I bequeath you in the hands of our Saviour:
610 Now may you make your reckoning sure.
　　EVERYMAN. In the name of the Holy Trinity
　　My body sore punished shall be:
　　Take this, body, for the sin of the flesh!
　　Also° thou delightest to go gay and fresh,   *as*
615 And in the way of damnation thou did me bring,
　　Therefore suffer now strokes of punishing!
　　Now of penance I will wade the water clear,
　　To save me from purgatory, that sharp fire.
　　GOOD DEEDS. I thank God, now can I walk and go,
620 And am delivered of my sickness and woe.
　　Therefore with Everyman I will go, and not spare:
　　His good works I will help him to declare.
　　KNOWLEDGE. Now, Everyman, be merry and glad:
　　Your Good Deeds cometh now, ye may not be sad.
625 Now is your Good Deeds whole and sound,
　　Going° upright upon the ground.   *walking*
　　EVERYMAN. My heart is light, and shall be evermore.
　　Now will I smite faster than I did before.
　　GOOD DEEDS. Everyman, pilgrim, my special friend,
630 Blessed be thou without end!
　　For thee is preparate° the eternal glory.   *prepared*
　　Ye have me made whole and sound·
　　Therefore I will bide by thee in every stound.°   *trial*
　　EVERYMAN. Welcome, my Good Deeds! Now I hear thy voice,
635 I weep for very sweetness of love.

2. "Moses' table" is here the tablet on which are recorded those who have been
baptized and have done penance.

KNOWLEDGE. Be no more sad, but ever rejoice:
 God seeth thy living in his throne above.
 Put on this garment to thy behove,°   *advantage*
 Which is wet with your tears—
640 Or else before God you may it miss
 When ye to your journey's end come shall.
EVERYMAN. Gentle Knowledge, what do ye it call?
KNOWLEDGE. It is a garment of sorrow;
 From pain it will you borrow:°   *redeem*
645 Contrition it is
 That getteth forgiveness;
 It pleaseth God passing° well.   *surpassingly*
GOOD DEEDS. Everyman, will you wear it for your heal?° *welfare*
EVERYMAN. Now blessed be Jesu, Mary's son,
650 For now have I on true contrition.
 And let us go now without tarrying.
 Good Deeds, have we clear our reckoning?
GOOD DEEDS. Yea, indeed, I have it here.
EVERYMAN. Then I trust we need not fear.
655 Now friends, let us not part in twain.
KNOWLEDGE. Nay, Everyman, that will we not, certain.
GOOD DEEDS. Yet must thou lead with thee
 Three persons of great might.
EVERYMAN. Who should they be?
660 GOOD DEEDS. Discretion and Strength they hight,° *are called*
 And thy Beauty may not abide behind.
KNOWLEDGE. Also ye must call to mind
 Your Five-Wits° as for your counselors.   *senses*
GOOD DEEDS. You must have have them ready at all hours.
665 EVERYMAN. How shall I get them hither?
KNOWLEDGE. You must call them all togither,
 And they will be here incontinent.°   *at once*
EVERYMAN. My friends, come hither and be present,
 Discretion, Strength, my Five-Wits, and Beauty!
  [*They enter.*]
670 BEAUTY. Here at your will we be all ready.
 What will ye that we should do?
GOOD DEEDS. That ye would with Everyman go
 And help him in his pilgrimage.
 Advise you:³ will ye with him or not in that voyage?
675 STRENGTH. We will bring him all thither,
 To his help and comfort, ye may believe me.
DISCRETION. So will we go with him all togither.
EVERYMAN. Almighty God, loved° might thou be!   *praised*
 I give thee laud that I have hither brought
680 Strength, Discretion, Beauty, and Five-Wits—lack I
   nought—
 And my Good Deeds, with Knowledge clear,

3. Take thought.

All be in my company at my will here:
I desire no more to my business.

STRENGTH. And I, Strength, will by you stand in distress,
685   Though thou would in battle fight on the ground.

FIVE-WITS. And though it were through the world round,
We will not depart for sweet ne sour.

BEAUTY. No more will I, until death's hour,
Whatsoever thereof befall.

690 DISCRETION. Everyman, advise you first of all:
Go with a good advisement° and deliberation.   *preparation*
We all give you virtuous° monition°   *confident / prediction*
That all shall be well.

EVERYMAN. My friends, hearken what I will tell;
695   I pray God reward you in his heaven-sphere;
Now hearken all that be here,
For I will make my testament,
Here before you all present:
In alms half my good° I will give with my hands twain,   *goods*
700   In the way of charity with good intent;
And the other half, still[4] shall remain,
I 'queath° to be returned there it ought to be.   *bequeath*
This I do in despite of the fiend of hell,
To go quit out of his perel,[5]
705   Ever after and this day.

KNOWLEDGE. Everyman, hearken what I say:
Go to Priesthood, I you advise,
And receive of him, in any wise,[6]
The holy sacrament and ointment° togither;   *extreme unction*
710   Then shortly see ye turn again hither:
We will all abide you here.

FIVE-WITS. Yea, Everyman, hie you that ye ready were.
There is no emperor, king, duke, ne baron,
That of God hath commission
715   As hath the least priest in the world being:
For of the blessed sacraments pure and bening°   *benign*
He beareth the keys, and thereof hath the cure°   *care*
For man's redemption—it is ever sure—
Which God for our souls' medicine
720   Gave us out of his heart with great pine,°   *torment*
Here in this transitory life for thee and me.
The blessed sacraments seven there be:
Baptism, confirmation, with priesthood° good,   *ordination*
And the sacrament of God's precious flesh and blood,
725   Marriage, the holy extreme unction, and penance:
These seven be good to have in remembrance,
Gracious sacraments of high divinity.

EVERYMAN. Fain° would I receive that holy body,   *gladly*

4. I.e., which still.
5. In order to go free of danger from

him.
6. At all costs.

And meekly to my ghostly° father I will go.   *spiritual*

730 FIVE-WITS. Everyman, that is the best that ye can do:
    God will you to salvation bring.
    For priesthood exceedeth all other thing:
    To us Holy Scripture they do teach,
    And converteth man from sin, heaven to reach;
735   God hath to them more power given
    Than to any angel that is in heaven.
    With five words[7] he may consecrate
    God's body in flesh and blood to make,
    And handleth his Maker between his hands.
740   The priest bindeth and unbindeth all bands,[8]
    Both in earth and in heaven.
    Thou ministers° all the sacraments seven;   *administer*
    Though we kiss thy feet, thou were worthy;
    Thou art surgeon that cureth sin deadly;
745   No remedy we find under God
    But all only priesthood.[9]
    Everyman, God gave priests that dignity
    And setteth them in his stead among us to be.
    Thus be they above angels in degree.
       [*Exit* EVERYMAN.]
750 KNOWLEDGE. If priests be good, it is so, surely.
    But when Jesu hanged on the cross with great smart,°   *pain*
    There he gave out of his blessed heart
    The same sacrament in great torment,
    He sold them not to us, that Lord omnipotent:
755   Therefore Saint Peter the Apostle doth say
    That Jesus's curse hath all they
    Which God their Saviour do buy or sell,[1]
    Or they for any money do take or tell.[2]
    Sinful priests giveth the sinners example bad:
760   Their children sitteth by other men's fires, I have heard;
    And some haunteth women's company
    With unclean life, as lusts of lechery.
    These be with sin made blind.
   FIVE-WITS. I trust to God no such may we find.
765   Therefore let us priesthood honor,
    And follow their doctrine for our souls' succor.
    We be their sheep and they shepherds be
    By whom we all be kept in surety.
    Peace, for yonder I see Everyman come,
770   Which hath made true satisfaction.

---

7. The five words ("For this is my body") spoken by the priest when he offers the wafer at communion.
8. A reference to the power of the keys, inherited by the priesthood from St. Peter, who received it from Christ (Matthew xvi.19) with the promise that whatever St. Peter bound or loosed on earth would be bound or loosed in heaven.
9. Except from priesthood alone.
1. To give or receive money for the sacraments is simony, named after Simon, who wished to buy the gift of the Holy Ghost and was cursed by St. Peter.
2. Or who, for any sacrament, take or count out money.

GOOD DEEDS. Methink it is he indeed.
    [*Re-enter* EVERYMAN.]
EVERYMAN. Now Jesu be your alder speed![3]
    I have received the sacrament for my redemption,
    And then mine extreme unction.
775   Blessed be all they that counseled me to take it!
    And now, friends, let us go without longer respite.
    I thank God that ye have tarried so long.
    Now set each of you on this rood° your hond   *cross*
780   I go before there° I would be. God be our guide!   *where*
STRENGTH. Everyman, we will not from you go
    Till ye have done this voyage long.
DISCRETION. I, Discretion, will bide by you also.
KNOWLEDGE. And though this pilgrimage be never so
        strong,°   *harsh*
785   I will never part you fro.
STRENGTH. Everyman, I will be as sure by thee
    As ever I did by Judas Maccabee.[4]
EVERYMAN. Alas, I am so faint I may not stand—
    My limbs under me doth fold!
790   Friends, let us not turn again to this land,
    Not for all the world's gold.
    For into this cave must I creep
    And turn to earth, and there to sleep.
BEAUTY. What, into this grave, alas?
795 EVERYMAN. Yea, there shall ye consume,° more and lass.[5] *decay*
BEAUTY. And what, should I smother here?
EVERYMAN. Yea, by my faith, and nevermore appear.
    In this world live no more we shall,
    But in heaven before the highest Lord of all.
800 BEAUTY. I cross out all this! Adieu, by Saint John—
    I take my tape in my lap and am gone.[6]
EVERYMAN. What, Beauty, whither will ye?
BEAUTY. Peace, I am deaf—I look not behind me,
    Not and thou wouldest give me all the gold in thy chest.
    [*Exit* BEAUTY.]
805 EVERYMAN. Alas, whereto may I trust?
    Beauty goeth fast away fro me—
    She promised with me to live and die!
STRENGTH. Everyman, I will thee also forsake and deny.
    Thy game liketh° me not at all.   *pleases*
810 EVERYMAN. Why then, ye will forsake me all?
    Sweet Strength, tarry a little space.
STRENGTH. Nay, sir, by the rood of grace,
    I will hie me from thee fast,

3. The prosperer of you all.
4. Judas Maccabaeus was an enormously powerful warrior in the defense of Israel against the Syrians in late Old Testament times.
5. More and less (i.e., all of you).
6. I tuck my skirts in my belt and am off.

Though thou weep till thy heart tobrast.°   break
815 EVERYMAN. Ye would ever bide by me, ye said.
    STRENGTH. Yea, I have you far enough conveyed!°   escorted
        Ye be old enough, I understand,
        Your pilgrimage to take on hand:
        I repent me that I hither came.
820 EVERYMAN. Strength, you to displease I am to blame,[7]
        Yet promise is debt, this ye well wot.°   know
    STRENGTH. In faith, I care not:
        Thou art but a fool to complain;
        You spend your speech and waste your brain.
825   Go, thrust thee into the ground.
            [*Exit* STRENGTH.]
    EVERYMAN. I had weened° surer I should you have
            found.   supposed
        He that trusteth in his Strength
        She him deceiveth at the length.
        Both Strength and Beauty forsaketh me—
830   Yet they promised me fair and lovingly.
    DISCRETION. Everyman, I will after Strength be gone:
        As for me, I will leave you alone.
    EVERYMAN. Why Discretion, will ye forsake me?
    DISCRETION. Yea, in faith, I will go from thee.
835   For when Strength goeth before,
        I follow after evermore.
    EVERYMAN. Yet I pray thee, for the love of the Trinity,
        Look in my grave once piteously.
    DISCRETION. Nay, so nigh will I not come.
840   Farewell everyone!
            [*Exit* DISCRETION.]
    EVERYMAN. O all thing faileth save God alone—
        Beauty, Strength, and Discretion.
        For when Death bloweth his blast
        They all run fro me full fast.
845 FIVE-WITS. Everyman, my leave now of thee I take.
        I will follow the other, for here I thee forsake.
    EVERYMAN. Alas, then may I wail and weep,
        For I took you for my best friend.
    FIVE-WITS. I will no longer thee keep.°   watch over
850   Now farewell, and there an end!
            [*Exit* FIVE-WITS.]
    EVERYMAN. O Jesu, help, all hath forsaken me!
    GOOD DEEDS. Nay, Everyman, I will bide with thee:
        I will not forsake thee indeed;
        Thou shalt find me a good friend at need.
855 EVERYMAN. Gramercy, Good Deeds! Now may I true friends
        see.
        They have forsaken me every one—

7. I'm to blame for displeasing you.

I loved them better than my Good Deeds alone.
Knowledge, will ye forsake me also?

KNOWLEDGE. Yea, Everyman, when ye to Death shall go,
860   But not yet, for no manner of danger.

EVERYMAN. Gramercy, Knowledge, with all my heart!

KNOWLEDGE. Nay, yet will I not from hence depart
Till I see where ye shall become.[8]

EVERYMAN. Methink, alas, that I must be gone
865   To make my reckoning and my debts pay,
For I see my time is nigh spent away.
Take example, all ye that this do hear or see,
How they that I best loved do forsake me,
Except my Good Deeds that bideth truly.

870 GOOD DEEDS. All earthly things is but vanity.
Beauty, Strength, and Discretion do man forsake,
Foolish friends and kinsmen that fair spake—
All fleeth save Good Deeds, and that am I.

EVERYMAN. Have mercy on me, God most mighty,
875   And stand by me, thou mother and maid, holy Mary!

GOOD DEEDS. Fear not: I will speak for thee.

EVERYMAN. Here I cry God mercy!

GOOD DEEDS. Short our end, and 'minish our pain.[9]
Let us go, and never come again.

880 EVERYMAN. Into thy hands, Lord, my soul I commend:
Receive it, Lord, that it be not lost.
As thou me boughtest,° so me defend,   *redeemed*
And save me from the fiend's boast,
That I may appear with that blessed host
885   That shall be saved at the day of doom.
In manus tuas, of mights most,
Forever *commendo spiritum meum*.[1]

      [EVERYMAN *and* GOOD DEEDS *descend into the grave.*]

KNOWLEDGE. Now hath he suffered that we all shall endure,
The Good Deeds shall make all sure.
890   Now hath he made ending,
Methinketh that I hear angels sing
And make great joy and melody
Where Everyman's soul received shall be.

ANGEL. [*within*] Come, excellent elect° spouse to Jesu![2] *chosen*
895   Here above thou shalt go
Because of thy singular virtue.
Now the soul is taken the body fro,
Thy reckoning is crystal clear:
Now shalt thou into the heavenly sphere—
900   Unto the which all ye shall come
That liveth well before the day of doom.

---

8. Till I see what shall become of you.
9. I.e., make our dying quick and diminish our pain.
1. "Into thy hands, O greatest of powers, I commend my spirit forever."
2. Man's soul is often referred to as the bride of Jesus.

[*Enter* DOCTOR.³]

DOCTOR. This memorial° men may have in mind: *reminder*
    Ye hearers, take it of worth,⁴ old and young,
    And forsake Pride, for he deceiveth you in the end.
905 And remember Beauty, Five-Wits, Strength, and Discretion,
    They all at the last do Everyman forsake,
    Save his Good Deeds there doth he take—
    But beware, for and they be small,
    Before God he hath no help at all—
9:0 None excuse may be there for Everyman.
    Alas, how shall he do than?°   *then*
    For after death amends may no man make,
    For then mercy and pity doth him forsake.
    If his reckoning be not clear when he doth come,
915 God will say, *"Ite, maledicti, in ignem eternum!"*⁵
    And he that hath his account whole and sound,
    High in heaven he shall be crowned,
    Unto which place God bring us all thither,
    That we may live body and soul together.
920 Thereto help, the Trinity!
    Amen say ye, for saint charity.

3. The Doctor is the learned theologian   5. "Depart, ye cursed, into everlasting
who explains the meaning of the play.   fire."
4. Prize it.

POPULAR BALLADS

Ballads are anonymous narrative songs that have been preserved by oral transmission. Although any stage of a given culture may produce ballads, they are most characteristic of primitive societies such as that of the American frontier in the 18th and 19th centuries or that of the English-Scottish border region in the later Middle Ages. These northern English songs, even divorced from the tunes to which they were once sung, are narrative poems of great literary interest.

    The origins of the popular (or folk) ballad are much disputed. The theory that they were first composed by communal effort, taking shape as the songs with which primitive people accompanied ritual dances, no longer seems plausible. On the other hand, the forms in which the ballads have come down to us show that they have been subjected to a continuing process of revision, both conscious and unconscious, by those through whose lips and memories they passed. Though the English ballads were probably composed during the 500 year period from 1200 to 1700, few of them were printed before the 18th century and some not until the 19th. Bishop Thomas Percy (1729–1811) was among the first to take a literary interest in ballads, stimulated by his chance discovery of a 17th-century manuscript in which a number of them had been copied down among a great welter of Middle English verse. Percy's publication of this material in his *Reliques of Ancient English Poetry* inspired others, notably

Sir Walter Scott, to go to the living source of the ballads and to set them down on paper at the dictation of the border people among whom the old songs were still being sung. These collectors often found that one ballad was remembered differently by different people: for instance, when one speaks of *Sir Patrick Spens* one is actually speaking of a number of poems that tell the same story in slightly or widely different words. If a single original form by a single author lies behind this diversity, it is too far back in the mists of time to be recovered.

A work that is the product of a consciously artistic mind will not ordinarily be improved by the revision that most ballads have been subjected to, but some of the ballads are probably better in their revised form than they were in their original form. The distinctive quality that popular ballads share is spareness: they are apt to deal only with the culminating incident or climax of a plot, to describe that event with intense compression, to put the burden of narration on allusive monologue or dialogue, and to avoid editorial comment. This concentration upon the bare essential is precisely that quality that the fallible human memory is likely not only to preserve but also to enhance, for the effort of remembering causes a sloughing-off of what is not strictly relevant. Some of the best of the ballads may have thus been refined in their transmission through men's minds, gaining rather than losing artistic stature.

The fact that ballads were originally songs is important to their development. The simplicity of the tunes to which they were sung not only influenced the distinctive verse form—normally a quatrain with four stresses per line—but also encouraged a corresponding simplicity in the narrative itself, and made individualizing flourishes impossible. Furthermore, the choral practice of using refrains and other kinds of repetitions probably lent the ballad one of its most impressive qualities, for while the actual narratives are tightly compressed, ballads rarely develop in an unbroken line. The reader—originally, the hearer—is constantly made to pause by a repeated phrase, or even by nonsense syllables, which provide suspense in a very primitive and effective form. The progress to a foreknown, foredoomed conclusion is paradoxically made to seem more inevitable, more urgent, by such relaxations of narrative tension. The use of repetition and refrain also imparts to the ballads something of the quality of incantation, of ritual, of liturgy—all of which are, of course, themselves closely allied with music.

Most of the best ballads have as their subject a tragic incident, often a murder or accidental death, generally involving supernatural elements. These motifs are a part of the common legacy of European folklore, and many of the English ballads have counterparts in other languages. To this class belong, among the selections chosen for inclusion here, *Lord Randall, Edward, Barbara Allan*, the *Wife of Usher's Well*, the *Three Ravens*, and—though not in its present form—*Sir Patrick Spens*. Not all the ballads with folklore motifs are tragic, however, for *Thomas Rhymer* has a happy ending. This ballad has gone through an added stage of evolution, for it is a shortening—a reduction to ballad form—of a romance which is preserved in a longer and more sophistication form; but the romance itself had its origin in some ancient folk tale, and there may have been an earlier ballad on the same theme, with, perhaps, a less happy conclusion.

Some ballads have as their subject actual historical incidents. Two late songs, the *Bonny Earl of Murray* and *Bonny George Campbell*, lament the political murders of two popular 16th-century Scots nobles. The presumably much older ballad *Sir Patrick Spens* may be based on a historical incident of the end of the 13th century. Yet all three of these achieve that mood of sadness that is characteristic of the best of the tragic stories derived from ancient folklore. The quasi-historical Robin Hood ballads, which form a large class by themselves, are less impressive. Most of them seem to have been composed relatively late and hence not to have gone through many stages of oral transmission; they lack the better ballads' intensity, often exhibiting an expansive development that is not free from chattiness. They are probably the work of minstrels who exploited the old folklore figure of Robin Hood by making him a symbol of that rebellion against authority that their own hearers perhaps longed for but did not dare to undertake. In the ballads Robin Hood is placed in a kind of never-never land of English history, where he can strike down tyrants with impunity, but often with far too much gloating: the attractive folklore figure of a natural, freedom-loving man has been burdened with too many political and social implications.

St. Steven and King Herod is hardly a ballad in the same sense as the other poems discussed here. It was probably not transmitted orally, for it contains Latin, and it shows none of the characteristic signs of having passed through more than a single stage of composition. Its author was probably a learned cleric who was exploiting the ballad form for religious purposes—an exploitation so successful as to earn the poem classification as a true ballad despite its evident artificiality.

The great collection of English ballads is that of F. J. Child, *The English and Scottish Popular Ballads*, first published in 1882. The numbers under which Child lists the various versions of each of the ballads printed here are given in footnotes to the individual titles. The versions chosen for this anthology are those which the editor considers the most effective as poetry. Spelling has been modernized; the majority of the northernisms in the originals have been retained.

Lord Randall¹

"Oh where ha'e ye been, Lord Randall my son?
O where ha'e ye been, my handsome young man?"
  "I ha'e been to the wild wood: mother, make my bed soon,
  For I'm weary wi' hunting, and fain° wald° lie
      down."   *gladly / would*

5 "Where gat ye your dinner, Lord Randall my son?
Where gat ye your dinner, my handsome young man?"
  "I dined wi' my true love; mother, make my bed soon,
  For I'm weary wi' hunting, and fain wald lie down."

"What gat ye to your dinner, Lord Randall my son?
10 What gat ye to your dinner, my handsome young man?"
  "I gat eels boiled in broo:° mother, make my bed
      soon,   *broth*
  For I'm weary wi' hunting and fain wald lie down."

"What became of your bloodhounds, Lord Randall my son?
What became of your bloodhounds, my handsome young man?"
15 "O they swelled and they died: mother, make my bed soon,
  For I'm weary wi' hunting and fain wald lie down."

"O I fear ye are poisoned, Lord Randall my son!
O I fear ye are poisoned, my handsome young man!"
  "O yes, I am poisoned: mother, make my bed soon,
20 For I'm sick at the heart, and I fain wald lie down."

Edward²

"Why does your brand sae drap wi' bluid,³
      Edward, Edward?
Why does your brand sae drap wi' bluid,
      And why sae sad gang° ye, O?"   *go*
5 "O I ha'e killed my hawk sae guid,
      Mither, mither,
O I ha'e killed my hawk sae guid,
      And I had nae mair° but he, O."   *more*

"Your hawkes bluid was never sae reid,°   *red*
10   Edward, Edward.
Your hawkes bluid was never sae reid,
      My dear son I tell thee, O."

---

1. Child, No. 12.
2. Child, No. 13.

3. I.e., why does your sword so drip
with blood?

"O I ha'e killed my reid-roan° steed,   *chestnut*
      Mither, mither,
15 O I ha'e killed my reid-roan steed,
    That erst° was sae fair and free, O."   *before*

"Your steed was auld° and ye ha'e gat mair,   *old*
      Edward, Edward.
Your steed was auld and ye ha'e gat mair:
20   Som other dule° ye dree,° O."   *grief / suffer*
"O I ha'e killed my fader dear,
      Mither, mither,
O I ha'e killed my fader dear,
    Alas and wae° is me, O!"   *woe*

25 "And whatten° penance wul ye dree for that,   *what sort of*
      Edward, Edward?
And whatten penance wul ye dree for that,
    My dear son, now tell me, O?"
"I'll set my feet in yonder boat,
30   Mither, mither,
I'll set my feet in yonder boat,
    And I'll fare over the sea, O."

"And what wul ye do wi' your towers and your ha',
      Edward, Edward?
35 And what wul ye do wi' your towers and your ha',
    That were sae fair to see, O?"
"I'll let thame stand til they down fa',
      Mither, mither,
I'll let thame stand til they down fa',
40   For here never mair maun° I be, O."   *must*

"And what wul ye leave to your bairns° and your wife,   *children*
      Edward, Edward,
And what wul ye leave to your bairns and your wife,
    Whan ye gang over the sea, O?"
45 "The warldes room⁴ late° them beg thrae° life,   *let / through*
      Mither, mither,
The warldes room late them beg thrae life,
    For thame never mair wul I see, O."

"And what wul ye leave to your ain° mither dear,   *own*
50   Edward, Edward?
And what wul ye leave to your ain mither dear,
    My dear son, now tell me, O?"
"The curse of hell frae° me sal° ye bear,   *from / shall*
      Mither, mither,
55 The curse of hell frae me sal ye bear,
    Sic° counseils ye gave to me, O."   *such*

---

4. The world's space.

Barbara Allan[1]

It was in and about the Martinmas[2] time,
 When the green leaves were a-fallin',
That Sir John Graeme in the West Country
 Fell in love with Barbara Allan.

5 He sent his man down through the town
 To the place where she was dwellin':
"O haste and come to my master dear,
 Gin° ye be Barbara Allan."   *if*

O slowly, slowly rase° she up,   *rose*
10 To the place where he was lyin',
And when she drew the curtain by:
 "Young man, I think you're dyin'."

"O it's I'm sick, and very, very sick,
 And 'tis a' for Barbara Allan."
15 "O the better for me ye sal° never be,   *shall*
 Though your heart's blood were a-spillin'.

"O dinna ye mind,[3] young man," said she,
 "When ye the cups were fillin',
That ye made the healths gae° round and round, *go*
20 And slighted Barbara Allan?"

He turned his face unto the wall,
 And death with him was dealin':
"Adieu, adieu, my dear friends all,
 And be kind to Barbara Allan."

25 And slowly, slowly, rase she up,
 And slowly, slowly left him;
And sighing said she could not stay,
 Since death of life had reft° him.   *deprived*

She had not gane° a mile but twa,°   *gone / two*
30 When she heard the dead-bell knellin',
And every jow° that the dead-bell ga'ed[4]   *stroke*
 It cried, "Woe to Barbara Allan!"

"O mother, mother, make my bed,
 O make it soft and narrow:
35 Since my love died for me today,
 I'll die for him tomorrow."

---

1. Child, No. 84.
2. November 11.

3. Don't you remember.
4. I.e., made.

The Wife of Usher's Well[1]

There lived a wife at Usher's Well,
    And a wealthy wife was she;
She had three stout and stalwart sons,
    And sent them o'er the sea.

5 They hadna' been a week from her,
    A week but barely ane,°   *one*
When word came to the carlin° wife   *old*
    That her three sons were gane.°   *gone*

They hadna' been a week from her,
10   A week but barely three,
When word came to the carlin wife
    That her sons she'd never see.

"I wish the wind may never cease,
    Nor fashes° in the flood,   *disturbances*
15 Till my three sons come hame° to me,   *home*
    In earthly flesh and blood."

It fell about the Martinmas,[2]
    When nights are lang and mirk,°   *dark*
The carlin wife's three sons came hame,
20 And their hats were o' the birk.[3]

It neither grew in sike° nor ditch,   *field*
    Nor yet in ony sheugh,°   *furrow*
But at the gates o' Paradise
    That birk grew fair eneugh.

25 "Blow up the fire, my maidens,
    Bring water from the well:
For a' my house shall feast this night,
    Since my three sons are well."

And she has made to them a bed,
30 She's made it large and wide,
And she's ta'en her mantle her about,
    Sat down at the bedside.

Up then crew the red, red cock,
    And up and crew the gray.
35 The eldest to the youngest said,
    " 'Tis time we were away."[4]

1. Child, No. 79.
2. November 11.
3. Birch: those returning from the dead were thought to wear vegetation on their heads.
4. Dead men must return to their graves at cockcrow.

The cock he hadna' crawed but once,
 And clapped his wings at a',
When the youngest to the eldest said,
40 "Brother, we must awa'.°   *away*

"The cock doth craw, the day doth daw,°   *dawn*
 The channerin'° worm doth chide: *fretting*
Gin° we be missed out o' our place,   *if*
 A sair pain we maun bide.[5]

45 "Fare ye weel,° my mother dear,   *well*
 Fareweel to barn and byre.°   *cow house*
And fare ye weel, the bonny lass
 That kindles my mother's fire."

The Three Ravens[1]

There were three ravens sat on a tree,
 Down a down, hay down, hay down,
There were three ravens sat on a tree,
 With a down,
5 There were three ravens sat on a tree,
They were as black as they might be,
 With a down, derry, derry, derry, down, down.

The one of them said to his mate,
"Where shall we our breakfast take?"

10 "Down in yonder green field
There lies a knight slain under his shield.

"His hounds they lie down at his feet,
So well they can their master keep.

"His hawks they fly so eagerly,°   *fiercely*
15 There's no fowl° dare him come nigh."   *bird*

Down there comes a fallow° doe,   *red-brown*
As great with young as she might go.°   *walk*

She lifted up his bloody head,
And kissed his wounds that were so red.

20 She got him up upon her back,
And carried him to earthen lake.°   *pit*

She buried him before the prime;[2]
She was dead herself ere evensong time.

5. A sore pain we must abide.   2. The first hour of the morning.
1. Child, No. 26.

God send every gentleman
25 Such hawks, such hounds, and such a lemman.°   *mistress*

Bonny George Campbell[3]

High upon Highlands
 And low upon Tay,
Bonny George Campbell
 Rade° out on a day.   *rode*

5 Saddled and bridled
 And gallant rade he:
Hame° cam his guid horse,   *home*
 But never cam he.

Out cam his auld mither,
10 Greeting fu' sair,[4]
And out cam his bonny bride,
 Riving° her hair.   *tearing*

Saddled and bridled
 And booted rade he:
15 Toom° hame cam the saddle,   *empty*
 But never cam he.

"My meadow lies green,
 And my corn is unshorn,
My barn is to build,
20 And my babe is unborn."

Saddled and bridled
 And booted rade he;
Toom hame cam the saddle,
 But never cam he.

Sir Patrick Spens[1]

The king sits in Dumferline town,
 Drinking the blude-reid° wine: *blood-red*
"O whar will I get a guid sailor
 To sail this ship of mine?"

3. Child, No. 210. The form printed
here is a composite, made up from
several variant versions by the ballad-
collector Motherwell.
4. Weeping full sore.
1. Child, No. 58.

5 Up and spak an eldern° knicht,   *ancient*
    Sat at the king's richt knee:
"Sir Patrick Spens is the best sailor
    That sails upon the sea."

The king has written a braid° letter   *broad*
10   And signed it wi' his hand,
And sent it to Sir Patrick Spens,
    Was walking on the sand.

The first line that Sir Patrick read,
    A loud lauch° lauched he;   *laugh*
15 The next line that Sir Patrick read,
    The tear blinded his ee.°   *eye*

"O wha° is this has done this deed,   *who*
    This ill deed done to me,
To send me out this time o' the year,
20   To sail upon the sea?

"Make haste, make haste, my mirry men all,
    Our guid ship sails the morn."
"O say na° sae,° my master dear,   *not / so*
    For I fear a deadly storm.

25 "Late late yestre'en I saw the new moon
    Wi' the auld° moon in her arm,   *old*
And I fear, I fear, my dear master,
    That we will come to harm."

O our Scots nobles were richt laith°   *loath*
30   To weet° their cork-heeled shoon,°   *wet / shoes*
But lang owre° a' the play were played   *ere*
    Their hats they swam aboon.°   *above*

O lang, lang may their ladies sit,
    Wi' their fans into their hand,
35 Or e'er they see Sir Patrick Spens
    Come sailing to the land.

O lang, lang may the ladies stand,
    Wi' their gold kembs° in their hair,   *combs*
Waiting for their ain° dear lords,   *own*
40   For they'll see thame na mair.°   *more*

Half o'er,[2] half o'er to Aberdour
    It's fifty fadom° deep,   *fathoms*
And there lies guid Sir Patrick Spens,
    Wi' the Scots lords at his feet.

2. Halfway over.

The Bonny Earl of Murray[1]

Ye Highlands and ye Lawlands,°   *Lowlands*
    O where have you been?
They have slain the Earl of Murray,
    And they laid him on the green.

5 "Now wae° be to thee, Huntly,[2]   *woe*
    And wherefore did you sae?°   *so*
I bade you bring him wi' you,
    But forbade you him to slay."

He was a braw° gallant,   *brave*
10   And he rid[3] at the ring;
And the bonny Earl of Murray,
    O he might have been a king.

He was a braw gallant,
    And he played at the ba';°   *ball*
15 And the bonny Earl of Murray
    Was the flower amang them a'.

He was a braw gallant,
    And he played at the glove;[4]
And the bonny Earl of Murray,
20   O he was the queen's love.

O lang will his lady
    Look o'er the Castle Down,
Ere she see the Earl of Murray
    Come sounding[5] through the town.

Thomas Rhymer[1]

True Thomas lay on Huntly bank;
    A ferly° he spied wi' his ee;°   *wonder / eye*
And there he saw a lady bright
    Come riding down by the Eildon Tree.[2]

5 Her shirt was o' the grass-green silk,
    Her mantle o' the velvet fine;
At ilka° tett° of her horse's mane   *every / braid*
    Hung fifty sil'er bells and nine.

---

1. Child, No. 181.
2. Huntly, who slew Murray in 1592, had been ordered by King James VI of Scotland (the speaker of this stanza) to arrest the earl.
3. Rode. "The ring" was a hanging ring which mounted knights tried to impale on their spears.

4. Either the goal in a race or else a lady's favor.
5. Blowing horns.
1. I.e., Thomas the Minstrel. Child, No. 37.
2. Trees in folklore are often frequented by supernatural beings.

True Thomas he pulled off his cap
10   And louted° low down to his knee: *bowed*
"All hail, thou mighty Queen of Heaven!
    For thy peer on earth I never did see."

"O no, O no, Thomas," she said,
    "That name does not belang to me;
15 I am but the Queen of fair Elfland,
    That am hither come to visit thee.

"Harp° and carp,° Thomas," she said,   *play / speak*
    "Harp and carp along wi' me;
And if ye dare to kiss my lips,
20   Sure of your body I will be."

"Betide me weal, betide me woe,
    That weird° shall never daunten me."   *fate*
Sine° he has kissed her rosy lips,   *then*
    All underneath the Eildon Tree.

25 "Now ye maun° go wi' me," she said,   *must*
    "True Thomas, ye maun go wi' me;
And ye maun serve me seven years
    Through weal or woe, as may chance to be."

She mounted on her milk-white steed;
30   She's ta'en True Thomas up behind;
And ay whene'er her bridle rung,
    The steed flew swifter than the wind.

O they rade° on and farther on;   *rode*
    The steed gaed° swifter than the wind,   *went*
35 Until they reached a desert wide,
    And living land was left behind.

"Light down, light down now, True Thomas,
    And lean your head upon my knee.
Abide and rest a little space,
40   And I will show you ferlies three.

"O see ye not yon narrow road,
    So thick beset with thorns and briars?
That is the path of righteousness,
    Though after it but few inquires.

45 "And see ye not that braid,° braid road   *broad*
    That lies across that lily leven?[3]
That is the path of wickedness,
    Though some call it the road to heaven.

"And see not ye that bonny road
50   That winds about the ferny brae?°   *hillside*

3. Probably "lawn."

That is the road to fair Elfland,
    Where thou and I this night maun gae.°   *go*

"But Thomas, ye maun hold your tongue,
    Whatever ye may hear or see;
55 For if you speak word in Elfenland,
    Ye'll ne'er get back to your ain° country."   *own*

O they rade on and farther on,
    And they waded through rivers aboon° the knee,   *above*
And they saw neither sun nor moon,
60   But they heard the roaring of the sea.

It was mirk,° mirk night, and there was nae stern-light,[4] *dark*
    And they waded through red blude to the knee,
For a' the blude that's shed on earth
    Rins° through the springs o' that country.   *runs*

65 Sine they came onto a garden green,
    And she pulled an apple frae° a tree.   *from*
"Take this for thy wages, True Thomas,
    It will give thee the tongue that never can lee."°   *lie*

"My tongue is mine ain," True Thomas said;
70   "A gudely° gift ye wad° gi'e to me!   *goodly / would*
I neither dought° to buy nor sell   *feared*
    At fair or tryst° where I may be.   *meeting place*

"I dought neither speak to prince or peer,
    Nor ask of grace frae fair lady."
75 "Now hold thy peace," the lady said,
    "For as I say, so must it be."

He has gotten a coat of the even° cloth,   *smooth*
    And a pair of shoes of velvet green;
And till seven years were gane and past,
80   True Thomas on earth was never seen.

Robin Hood and the Three Squires[1]

There are twelve months in all the year,
    As I hear many men say,
But the merriest month in all the year
    Is the merry month of May.

5 Now Robin Hood is to Nottingham gone,
    With a link-a-down and a-day,
And there he met a silly° old woman,   *poor, innocent*
    Was weeping on the way.

---

4. No starlight.   1. Child, No. 140.

"What news? what news, thou silly old woman?
10   What news hast thou for me?"
Said she, "There's three squires in Nottingham town,
    Today is condemned to dee."°   *die*

"O have they parishes burnt?" he said,
    "Or have they ministers slain?
15 Or have they robbed any virgin,
    Or with other men's wives have lain?"

"They have no parishes burnt, good sir,
    Nor yet have ministers slain,
Nor have they robbed any virgin,
20   Nor with other men's wives have lain."

"O what have they done?" said bold Robin Hood,
    "I pray thee tell to me."
"It's for slaying of the king's fallow° deer,   *brown-red*
    Bearing their longbows with thee."

25 "Dost thou not mind,° old woman," he said,   *remember*
    "Since thou made me sup and dine?
By the truth of my body," quoth bold Robin Hood,
    "You could not tell it in better time."

Now Robin Hood is to Nottingham gone,
30   *With a link-a-down and a-day,*
And there he met with a silly old palmer,[2]
    Was walking along the highway.

"What news? what news, thou silly old man?
    What news, I do thee pray?"
35 Said he, "Three squires in Nottingham town
    Are condemned to die this day."

"Come change thine apparel with me, old man,
    Come change thine apparel for mine.
Here is forty shillings in good silver,
40   Go drink it in beer or wine."

"O thine apparel is good," he said,
    "And mine is ragged and torn.
Wherever you go, wherever you ride,
    Laugh ne'er an old man to scorn."

45 "Come change thine apparel with me, old churl,
    Come change thine apparel with mine:
Here are twenty pieces of good broad gold,
    Go feast thy brethren with wine."

Then he put on the old man's hat,
50   It stood full high on the crown:
"The first bold bargain that I come at,
    It shall make thee come down."

2. A poor old palmer: a palmer was one who had made the pilgrimage to the Holy Land.

Then he put on the old man's cloak,
    Was patched black, blue, and red:
55 He thought it no shame all the day long
    To wear the bags of bread.

Then he put on the old man's breeks,°   *underbreeches*
    Was patched from ballup³ to side:
"By the truth of my body," bold Robin can° say,   *did*
60   "This man loved little pride."

Then he put on the old man's hose,°   *tights*
    Were patched from knee to wrist:
"By the truth of my body," said bold Robin Hood,
    "I'd laugh if I had any list."°   *desire*

65 Then he put on the old man's shoes,
    Were patched both beneath and aboon:°   *above*
Then Robin Hood swore a solemn oath,
    "It's good habit° that makes a man."   *clothing*

Now Robin Hood is to Nottingham gone,
70   *With a link-a-down and a-down,*
And there he met with the proud sheriff,
    Was walking along the town.

"O Christ you save, O sheriff," he said,
    "O Christ you save and see:
75 And what will you give to a silly old man
    Today will your hangman be?"

"Some suits, some suits," the sheriff he said,
    "Some suits I'll give to thee;
Some suits, some suits, and pence thirteen,
80   Today's a hangman's fee."

Then Robin he turns him round about,
    And jumps from stock° to stone: *stump*
"By the truth of my body," the sheriff he said,
    "That's well jumped, thou nimble old man."

85 "I was ne'er a hangman in all my life,
    Nor yet intends to trade.
But cursed be he," said bold Robin,
    "That first a hangman was made.

"I've a bag for meal, and a bag for malt,
90   And a bag for barley and corn,
A bag for bread, and a bag for beef,
    And a bag for my little small horn.

"I have a horn in my pocket:
    I got it from Robin Hood:
95 And still when I set it to my mouth,
    For thee it blows little good."

3. I.e., center.

"O wind° thy horn, thou proud fellow: *blow*
    Of thee I have no doubt;°   *fear*
I wish that thou give such a blast
100   Till both thy eyes fall out."

The first loud blast that he did blow,
    He blew both loud and shrill,
A hundred and fifty of Robin Hood's men
    Came riding over the hill.

105 The next loud blast that he did give,
    He blew both loud and amain,
And quickly sixty of Robin Hood's men
    Came shining⁴ over the plain.

"O who are those," the sheriff he said,
110   "Come tripping over the lea?"°   *meadow*
"They're my attendants," brave Robin did say,
    "They'll pay a visit to thee."
They took the gallows from the slack,°   *hollow*
    They set it in the glen;
115 They hanged the proud sheriff on that,
    Released their own three men.

St. Steven and King Herod¹

Saint Steven was a clerk
    In King Herodes hall,
And served him of bread and cloth
    As every king befall.²

5 Steven out of kitchen came
    With boar's head on hand;
He saw a star was fair and bright
    Over Bedlem° stand.   *Bethlehem*

He cast adown the boar's head
10   And went into the hall:
"I forsake thee, King Herodes,
    And thy works all.

"I forsake thee, King Herodes,
    And thy works all:
15 There is a child in Bedlem born
    Is better than we all."

"What aileth thee, Steven?
    What is thee befall?
Lacketh thee either meat or drink
20   In King Herodes hall?"

---

4. I.e., making a brave show.   2. As is appropriate to every king.
1. Child, No. 22.

"Lacketh me neither meat ne drink
    In King Herodes hall:
There is a child in Bedlem born
    Is better than we all."

25 "What aileth thee, Steven?
    Art thou wood, or ginnest weede?[3]
Lacketh thee either gold or fee°   *property*
    Or any rich weed?"°   *clothing*

"Lacketh me neither gold ne fee
30   Ne none rich weed:
There is a child in Bedlem born
    Shall help us at our need."

"That is also° sooth,° Steven,   *as / true*
    Also sooth, ywis,°   *indeed*
35 As this capon crow shal
    That lith° here in my dish."   *lies*

That word was not so soon said,
    That word in that hall,
The capon crew *Christus natus est*[4]
40   Among the lords all.

"Riseth up, my tormentors,
    By two and all by one,
And leadeth Steven out of this town,
    And stoneth him with stone."

45 Tooken they Steven,
    And stoned him in the way;
And therefore is his even[5]
    Christ's own day.

3. Art thou insane or beginning to go   4. Christ is born.
mad?   5. Eve: the day before his feast day.

SIR THOMAS MALORY
(ca. 1405–1471)

1451:   First of a long series of arrests and imprison-
                ments.
ca. 1469–70: *Morte Darthur* completed in prison.
1485:   *Morte Darthur* printed by William Caxton.

The little that we know of Malory (and that the Malory discussed here was indeed the Malory who wrote the *Morte Darthur* is an assumption that has recently been challenged severely though by no means fatally) suggests a man of violent temperament much given to lawless action. He seems to have been a respectable enough person in his youth, but in 1451 he got into difficulties with the law that lasted the rest of his life. In that year he was arrested in order to prevent his doing injury—presumably further injury—to a priory in Lincolnshire, and shortly thereafter he was accused of a number of criminal acts. These included escaping from prison after his first arrest, twice breaking into and plundering the Abbey of Coombe, extorting money from various persons, and committing rape. Malory pleaded innocent of all charges, and it is indeed possible that he was less guilty of (or had more provocation for) the crimes than the records make it appear. The years of the Wars of the Roses were violent ones, when a supporter of the party out of power was apt to be subjected to much persecution by the ruling group; such a man might at times feel himself justified in taking the law into his own hands in order to recover what had wrongfully been taken from him. But one suspects that Malory took the law into his own hands with unnecessary enthusiasm.

How much time Malory passed in prison is not known, but he was surely a prisoner in 1468 after he had supported an unsuccessful Lancastrian revolt against the Yorkist king, Edward IV, who specifically excluded Malory from two amnesties granted to the Lancastrians. It was probably in prison that he became engaged on the *Morte Darthur;* he was still in prison when he completed it, and may have died there. The book was printed (and edited) in 1485 by William Caxton, the first English printer. A manuscript of it that has recently come to light helps us to a better text than Caxton's.

Arthurian romance, of which Malory's book is a compilation, is a body of highly diverse narrative materials which originated at various times among various peoples and which only gradually became associated with the name of Arthur. Arthur himself was probably a British or Roman-British king who resisted the Anglo-Saxon invasions of England in the 6th century, but his historical reality is less important than the legendary role he played as the great figure around whom the medieval ideal of chivalry flourished. At its simplest, chivalry is the code that governs the actions of the knight-adventurer who rides out in search of wrongs that he may right—typically in search of ladies whom he may rescue from monsters, churls, and wicked (non-Arthurian) knights. The ideal was invented and given a local habitation in the brilliantly imaginative and idealistic 12th century. History had, of course, never witnessed such knights, such ladies, nor such a landscape as that on which their adventures took place, and when chivalry was first invented it was already placed in the past. Man's urge to devise an idealized past seems to be recurrent, for the Camelot of Arthur has its counterpart in the Sherwood Forest of Robin Hood and in the American West. All three of these fictions have the same ideal: that of maintaining order in an essentially lawless land by the efforts of the individual, who fights for the right against seemingly overwhelming odds. Naïve as the practice of this ideal may seem in the Arthurian fiction, the ideal itself has made an important contribution to civilization—though if one imitates literally the Arthurian practice of enforcing the right by violence, as Malory's life suggests that he did, one will find oneself not maintaining order, but disrupting it.

The Arthurian milieu attracted to itself all sorts of diverse motifs, such as the remnants of primitive pagan religious rites, heavily moralized Christianity, an elaborate and in general flagrantly immoral code of romantic love, and others equally miscellaneous. In 13th-century France the amorphous Arthurian material was given a kind of order in a series of prose narratives. Long and often rather vaguely told, these formed the chief material which Malory further edited and ordered while translating it into English.

His book is attractive, however, not only because it is the best and most complete treatment of the story of Arthur and his knights, but also because it is one of the greatest pieces of prose in English. Malory was the first English writer to make prose as sensitive an instrument of narrative as English poetry had always been. One has only to turn from a page of Chaucer's prose to a page of Malory's to be struck by the naturalness and lack of self-consciousness of the later writer. Indeed, Malory achieves in his prose that wonderful impression of simplicity that Chaucer achieves only in his poetry. No matter how extravagant the adventure Malory is recounting, he always manages to give it a hard base of realism. He is in particular a master of naturalistic dialogue, with which he keeps his narrative close to earth. And both he and the majority of his characters are masters of understatement who express themselves, in moments of great emotional tension, with a bare minimum of words. The result is highly provocative to the reader's imagination, which is made, in a sense, to do the writer's work for him. This appeal to the reader's creative imagination probably explains why the *Morte Darthur* brings forth such widely differing responses from its readers, who agree, perhaps, only in their affection for the work.

"The Death of Arthur"—the incident that gives the book its title, though the book itself concerns the whole life of Arthur—is one of Malory's finest passages, and the one on which Tennyson based a famous *Idyll.* Largely at the insistence of his nephew Gawain, Arthur has been in France, futilely besieging his friend Lancelot in a halfhearted attempt to punish him for having been Queen Guinevere's lover. Word comes to the King that his bastard son Mordred has seized the kingdom, and Arthur leads his forces back to England. Mordred attacks them upon their landing, and Gawain is mortally wounded and dies, though not before he has repented for having insisted that Arthur fight Lancelot and has written Lancelot to come to the aid of his former lord.

From Morte Darthur[1]
[*The Death of Arthur*]

So upon Trinity Sunday at night King Arthur dreamed a wonderful dream, and in his dream him seemed[2] that he saw upon a chafflet a chair, and the chair was fast to a wheel, and thereupon sat King Arthur in the richest cloth of gold that might be made.

1. The selection here given is from the section of the book that Caxton called Book XXI, Chaps. 3–7, with omissions. The text has been based on the Winchester MS., with some readings introduced from the Caxton edition; spelling has been modernized and modern punctuation added.
2. It seemed to him. "Chafflet": scaffold.

And the King thought there was under him, far from him, an hideous deep black water, and therein was all manner of serpents, and worms, and wild beasts, foul and horrible. And suddenly the King thought that the wheel turned upside down, and he fell among the serpents, and every beast took him by a limb. And then the King cried as he lay in his bed, "Help, help!"

And then knights, squires, and yeomen awaked the king, and then he was so amazed that he wist[3] not where he was. And then so he awaked[4] until it was nigh day, and then he fell on slumbering again, not sleeping nor thoroughly waking. So the King seemed[5] verily that there came Sir Gawain unto him with a number of fair ladies with him. So when King Arthur saw him, he said, "Welcome, my sister's son. I weened ye had been dead. And now I see thee on-live, much am I beholden unto Almighty Jesu. Ah, fair nephew and my sister's son, what been these ladies that hither be come with you?"

"Sir," said Sir Gawain, "all these be ladies for whom I have foughten for when I was man living. And all these are tho[6] that I did battle for in righteous quarrels, and God hath given them that grace, at their great prayer, because I did battle for them for their right, that they should bring me hither unto you. Thus much hath given me leave God, for to warn you of your death. For and ye fight as tomorn[7] with Sir Mordred, as ye both have assigned,[8] doubt ye not ye must be slain, and the most party of your people on both parties. And for the great grace and goodness that Almighty Jesu hath unto you, and for pity of you and many mo[9] other good men there shall be slain, God hath sent me to you of his special grace to give you warning that in no wise ye do battle as tomorn, but that ye take a treatise[1] for a month-day. And proffer you largely,[2] so that tomorn ye put in a delay. For within a month shall come Sir Lancelot with all his noble knights and rescue you worshipfully and slay Sir Mordred and all that ever will hold with him."

Then Sir Gawain and all the ladies vanished. And anon the King called upon his knights, squires, and yeomen, and charged them wightly[3] to fetch his noble lords and wise bishops unto him. And when they were come the King told them of his avision,[4] that Sir Gawain had told him and warned him that, and he fought on the morn, he should be slain. Then the King commanded Sir Lucan the Butler[5] and his brother Sir Bedivere the Bold, with two bish-

---

3. Knew.
4. Lay awake.
5. It seemed to the King.
6. Those.
7. If you fight tomorrow.
8. Decided.
9. More. "There": i.e., who there.
1. Treaty, truce. "For a month-day":

for a month from today.
2. Make generous offers.
3. Quickly.
4. Dream.
5. "Butler" here is probably only a title of high rank, although it was originally used to designate the officer who had charge of wine for the king's table.

ops with them, and charged them in any wise to take a treatise for a month-day with Sir Mordred. "And spare not: proffer him lands and goods as much as ye think reasonable."

So then they departed and came to Sir Mordred where he had a grim host of an hundred thousand, and there they entreated[6] Sir Mordred long time. And at the last Sir Mordred was agreed for to have Cornwall and Kent by King Arthur's days,[7] and after that, all England, after the days of King Arthur.

Then were they condescended[8] that King Arthur and Sir Mordred should meet betwixt both their hosts, and everich[9] of them should bring fourteen persons. And so they came with this word unto Arthur. Then said he, "I am glad that this is done," and so he went into the field.

And when King Arthur should depart, he warned all his host that, and they see any sword drawn, "Look ye come on fiercely and slay that traitor Sir Mordred, for I in no wise trust him." In like wise Sir Mordred warned his host that "And ye see any manner of sword drawn, look that ye come on fiercely, and so slay all that ever before you standeth, for in no wise I will not trust for this treatise." And in the same wise said Sir Mordred unto his host, "For I know well my father will be avenged upon me."

And so they met as their pointment[1] was and were agreed and accorded thoroughly. And wine was fetched and they drank together. Right so came an adder out of a little heath-bush, and it stung a knight in the foot. And so when the knight felt him so stung, he looked down and saw the adder. And anon he drew his sword to slay the adder, and thought[2] none other harm. And when the host on both parties saw that sword drawn, then they blew beams,[3] trumpets, and horns, and shouted grimly. And so both hosts dressed them[4] together. And King Arthur took his horse and said, "Alas, this unhappy day!" and so rode to his party, and Sir Mordred in like wise.

And never since was there never seen a more dolefuller battle in no Christian land, for there was but rushing and riding, foining[5] and striking; and many a grim word was there spoken of either to other, and many a deadly stroke. But ever King Arthur rode throughout the battle[6] of Sir Mordred many times and did full nobly, as a noble king should do, and at all times he fainted never. And Sir Mordred did his devoir[7] that day and put himself in great peril.

And thus they fought all the long day, and never stinted[8] till the noble knights were laid to the cold earth. And ever they fought still

6. Dealt with.
7. During King Arthur's lifetime.
8. Agreed.
9. Each.
1. Arrangement.
2. Meant.

3. Trumpets.
4. Prepared to come.
5. Lunging.
6. Battalion.
7. Knightly duty.
8. Stopped.

till it was near night, and by then was there an hundred thousand laid dead upon the down. Then was King Arthur wood-wroth[9] out of measure when he saw his people so slain from him. And so he looked about him and could see no mo[1] of all his host, and good knights left no mo on-live, but two knights: the t'one[2] was Sir Lucan the Butler and [the other] his brother Sir Bedivere. And yet they were full sore wounded.

"Jesu, mercy," said the King, "where are all my noble knights become?[3] Alas that ever I should see this doleful day! For now," said King Arthur, "I am come to mine end. But would to God," said he, "that I wist[4] now where were that traitor Sir Mordred that has caused all this mischief."

Then King Arthur looked about and was ware where stood Sir Mordred leaning upon his sword among a great heap of dead men.

"Now give me my spear," said King Arthur unto Sir Lucan, "for yonder I have espied the traitor that all this woe hath wrought."

"Sir, let him be," said Sir Lucan, "for he is unhappy.[5] And if ye pass this unhappy day ye shall be right well revenged upon him. And, good lord, remember ye of your night's dream, and what the spirit of Sir Gawain told you tonight, and yet God of his great goodness hath preserved you hitherto. And for God's sake, my lord, leave off by this,[6] for, blessed be God, ye have won the field: for yet we been here three on-live, and with Sir Mordred is not one on-live. And therefore if ye leave off now, this wicked day of destiny is past."

"Now, tide[7] me death, tide me life," said the King, "now I see him yonder alone, he shall never escape mine hands. For at a better avail[8] shall I never have him."

"God speed you well!" said Sir Bedivere.

Then the King got his spear in both his hands and ran toward Sir Mordred, crying and saying, "Traitor, now is thy deathday come!"

And when Sir Mordred saw King Arthur he ran until him with his sword drawn in his hand, and there King Arthur smote Sir Mordred under the shield, with a foin[9] of his spear, throughout the body more than a fathom.[1] And when Sir Mordred felt that he had his death's wound, he thrust himself with the might that he had up to the burr[2] of King Arthur's spear, and right so he smote his father King Arthur with his sword holden in both his hands, upon the side of the head, that the sword pierced the helmet and

9. Mad with rage.
1. Others.
2. That one, i.e., the first.
3. What has become of all my noble knights?
4. Knew.
5. I.e., unlucky for you.

6. I.e., with this much accomplished.
7. Betide.
8. Advantage.
9. Thrust.
1. Six feet.
2. Hand guard.

the tay[3] of the brain. And therewith Sir Mordred dashed down stark dead to the earth.

And noble King Arthur fell in a swough[4] to the earth, and there he swooned oftentimes, and Sir Lucan and Sir Bedivere ofttimes heaved him up. And so, weakly betwixt them, they led him to a little chapel not far from the seaside, and when the King was there, him thought him reasonably eased. Then heard they people cry in the field. "Now go thou, Sir Lucan," said the King, "and do me to wit[5] what betokens that noise in the field."

So Sir Lucan departed, for he was grievously wounded in many places. And so as he yede[6] he saw and harkened by the moonlight how that pillers[7] and robbers were come into the field to pill and to rob many a full noble knight of brooches and bees[8] and of many a good ring and many a rich jewel. And who that were not dead all out[9] there they slew them for their harness and their riches. When Sir Lucan understood this work, he came to the King as soon as he might and told him all what he had heard and seen. "Therefore by my read,"[1] said Sir Lucan, "it is best that we bring you to some town."

"I would it were so," said the King, "but I may not stand, my head works[2] so. Ah, Sir Lancelot," said King Arthur, "this day have I sore missed thee. And alas that ever I was against thee, for now have I my death, whereof Sir Gawain me warned in my dream."

Then Sir Lucan took up the King the t'one party[3] and Sir Bedivere the other party; and in the lifting up the King swooned and in the lifting Sir Lucan fell in a swoon that part of his guts fell out of his body, and therewith the noble knight's heart burst. And when the King awoke he beheld Sir Lucan how he lay foaming at the mouth and part of his guts lay at his feet.

"Alas," said the King, "this is to me a full heavy[4] sight to see this noble duke so die for my sake, for he would have holpen[5] me that had more need of help than I. Alas that he would not complain him for[6] his heart was so set to help me. Now Jesu have mercy upon his soul."

Then Sir Bedivere wept for the death of his brother.

"Now leave this mourning and weeping, gentle knight," said the King, "for all this will not avail me. For wit thou well, and[7] I might live myself, the death of Sir Lucan would grieve me evermore. But my time passeth on fast," said the King. "Therefore," said King

---

3. Edge.
4. Swoon.
5. Let me know.
6. Walked.
7. Plunderers.
8. Bracelets.
9. Entirely. "Harness": armor.

1. Advice.
2. Aches.
3. On one side.
4. Sorrowful.
5. Helped.
6. Because.
7. If.

Arthur unto Sir Bedivere, "take thou here Excalibur[8] my good sword and go with it to yonder water's side; and when thou comest there I charge thee throw my sword in that water and come again and tell me what thou sawest there."

"My lord," said Sir Bedivere, "your commandment shall be done, and [I shall] lightly[9] bring you word again."

So Sir Bedivere departed. And by the way he beheld that noble sword, that the pommel[1] and the haft was all precious stones. And then he said to himself, "If I throw this rich sword in the water, thereof shall never come good, but harm and loss." And then Sir Bedivere hid Excalibur under a tree. And so, as soon as he might, he came again unto the King and said he had been at the water and had thrown the sword into the water.

"What saw thou there?" said the King.

"Sir," he said, "I saw nothing but waves and winds."

"That is untruly said of thee," said the King. "And therefore go thou lightly again and do my commandment; as thou art to me lief[2] and dear, spare not, but throw it in."

Then Sir Bedivere returned again and took the sword in his hand. And yet him thought[3] sin and shame to throw away that noble sword. And so eft[4] he hid the sword and returned again and told the King that he had been at the water and done his commandment.

"What sawest thou there?" said the King.

"Sir," he said, "I saw nothing but waters wap and waves wan."[5]

"Ah, traitor unto me and untrue," said King Arthur, "now hast thou betrayed me twice. Who would have weened that thou that hast been to me so lief and dear, and thou art named a noble knight, and would betray me for the riches of this sword. But now go again lightly, for thy long tarrying putteth me in great jeopardy of my life, for I have taken cold. And but if thou do now as I bid thee, if ever I may see thee I shall slay thee mine[6] own hands, for thou wouldest for my rich sword see me dead."

Then Sir Bedivere departed and went to the sword and lightly took it up, and so he went to the water's side; and there he bound the girdle[7] about the hilts, and threw the sword as far into the water as he might. And there came an arm and an hand above the water and took it and clutched it, and shook it thrice and brandished; and then vanished away the hand with the sword into the

---

8. The sword which Arthur had received as a young man from the Lady of the Lake; it is presumably she who catches it when Bedivere finally throws it into the water.
9. Quickly.
1. Rounded knob on the hilt; "haft": handle.
2. Beloved.
3. It seemed to him.
4. Again.
5. The phrase seems to mean "waters wash the shore and waves grow dark."
6. I.e., with mine.
7. Sword belt.

water. So Sir Bedivere came again to the King and told him what he saw.

"Alas," said the King, "help me hence, for I dread me I have tarried overlong."

Then Sir Bedivere took the King upon his back and so went with him to that water's side. And when they were at the water's side, even fast[8] by the bank hoved[9] a little barge with many fair ladies in it; and among them all was a queen; and all they had black hoods, and all they wept and shrieked when they saw King Arthur.

"Now put me into that barge," said the King; and so he did softly. And there received him three ladies with great mourning, and so they set them[1] down. And in one of their laps King Arthur laid his head, and then the queen said, "Ah, my dear brother, why have ye tarried so long from me? Alas, this wound on your head hath caught overmuch cold." And anon they rowed fromward the land, and Sir Bedivere beheld all tho ladies go froward him.

Then Sir Bedivere cried and said, "Ah, my lord Arthur, what shall become of me, now ye go from me and leave me here alone among mine enemies?"

"Comfort thyself," said the King, "and do as well as thou mayest, for in me is no trust for to trust in. For I must into the vale of Avilion[2] to heal me of my grievous wound. And if thou hear nevermore of me, pray for my soul."

But ever the queen and ladies wept and shrieked that it was pity to hear. And as soon as Sir Bedivere had lost the sight of the barge he wept and wailed and so took[3] the forest, and went all that night. And in the morning he was ware betwixt two holts hoar[4] of a chapel and an hermitage.[5] * * *

Thus of Arthur I find no more written in books that been authorized,[6] neither more of the very certainty of his death heard I never read,[7] but thus was he led away in a ship wherein were three queens: that one was King Arthur's sister, Queen Morgan la Fée, the t'other[8] was the Queen of North Wales, and the third was the Queen of the Waste Lands. * * *

Now more of the death of King Arthur could I never find but that these ladies brought him to his burials,[9] and such one was buried there that the hermit bore witness that sometime was Bishop

8. Close.
9. Waited.
1. I.e., they sat.
2. A legendary island, sometimes identified with the earthly paradise.
3. Took to. "Went": walked.
4. Ancient copses.
5. In the passage here omitted, Sir Bedivere meets the former Bishop of Canterbury, now a hermit, who describes how on the previous night a company of ladies had brought to the chapel a dead body, asking that it be buried. Sir Bedivere exclaims that the dead man must have been King Arthur, and vows to spend the rest of his life there in the chapel as a hermit.
6. That have authority.
7. Tell.
8. The second.
9. Grave.

of Canterbury.[1] But yet the hermit knew not in certain that he was verily the body of King Arthur, for this tale Sir Bedivere, a Knight of the Table Round, made it to be written. Yet some men say in many parts of England that King Arthur is not dead, but had by the will of our Lord Jesu into another place. And men say that he shall come again and he shall win the Holy Cross. Yet I will not say that it shall be so, but rather I will say, Here in this world he changed his life. And many men say that there is written upon his tomb this verse: *Hic iacet Arthurus, rex quondam, rexque futurus.*[2]

1469–70   1485

1. Of whom the hermit, who was for-   2. "Here lies Arthur, who was once king
merly Bishop of Canterbury, bore wit- and king will be again."
ness.

WILLIAM CAXTON

(ca. 1422–1491)

In his early years Caxton was a prosperous merchant who traded mostly in the low countries. In 1470, at the command of his patroness, Margaret of Burgundy, he completed a translation into English of the French *Recueil des Histoires de Troie* (i.e., collection of the stories of Troy), which he had begun earlier in his leisure time. This work, circulated in manuscript, became so popular that the demand for it exceeded the number of copies that could be readily produced by scribes. Caxton thereupon went to Cologne, where he studied the newly developed art of printing, and subsequently set up a press at Bruges in Belgium. In 1475 he printed his translation of the Troy book (the first book printed in English), and in the next year returned to England, where he established England's first printing press, in London. Among his first publications were Chaucer's *Canterbury Tales* (1478; second edition about 1484). In 1485 he printed Malory's work, with the Preface reproduced here.

A shrewd publisher and practiced writer, as well as a pioneer printer, Caxton gives a most astute and inviting account of Malory's work and the personage after whom it was named. Caxton himself evidently put small credence in the historicity of Arthur, but by appearing—in all modesty—to have been overwhelmed by the faith that eminent people had in Arthur's existence, as well as by the survival of certain relics that seemed to support such faith, he encourages the reader to lay aside his own skepticism (although the warning remains: "ye are at your liberty" to accept or reject the truth of Malory's narrative). In describing the work itself, Caxton is careful to emphasize its exemplary qualities, "the noble acts of chivalry" that knights performed in the old days, from which one may learn virtuous conduct; but he is also careful not to suppress the fact—though he presents it in tantalizing subordination—that the book contains much that is exemplary only in the negative sense: "cowardice, murder, hate, * * * and sin," which for some might, perhaps, enhance the book's appeal.

Preface to *Morte Darthur*

After that I had accomplished and finished divers histories as well of contemplation as of other historial and worldly acts of great conquerors and princes, and also certain books of ensamples [1] and doctrine, many noble and divers gentlemen of this royalme of England camen and demanded me many and ofttimes wherefore that I have not do [2] made and imprint the noble history of the Saint Grail and of the most renommed [3] Christian king, first and chief of the three best Christian, and worthy,[4] king Arthur, which ought most to be remembered among us Englishmen tofore all other Christian kings.

For it is notoirly [5] known through the universal world that there been nine worthy and the best that ever were, that is to wit, three Paynims,[6] three Jews, and three Christian men. As for the Paynims, they were tofore the Incarnation of Christ, which were named, the first Hector of Troy, of whom th'istory is common both in ballad and in prose, the second Alexander the Great, and the third Julius Caesar, Emperor of Rome, of whom th'istories been well known and had.[7] And as for the three which also were tofore th'Incarnation of our Lord, of whom the first was Duke Joshua which brought the children of Israel into the land of behest,[8] the second David, king of Jerusalem, and the third Judas Maccabeus, of these three the Bible rehearseth all their noble histories and acts. And sith [9] the said Incarnation have been three noble Christian men stalled [1] and admitted through the universal world into the number of the nine best and worthy, of whom was first the noble Arthur, whose noble acts I purpose to write in this present book here following. The second was Charlemagne, or Charles the Great, of whom th'istory is had in many places, both in French and English; and the third and last was Godefroy of Bouillon, of whose acts and life I made a book unto th'excellent prince and king of noble memory, King Edward the Fourth.

The said noble gentlemen instantly required [2] me t'imprint th'istory of the said noble king and conqueror king Arthur and of his knights, with th'istory of the Saint Grail and of the death and end-

1. Exemplary stories.
2. Caused to be.
3. Renowned.
4. I.e., one of the Nine Worthies
5. Notoriously.
6. Pagans.

7. Available.
8. Promised Land.
9. Since.
1. Assigned.
2. Urgently requested.

ing of the said Arthur, affirming that I ought rather t'imprint his acts and noble feats than of Godefroy of Bouillon or any of the other eight, considering that he was a man born within this royalme and king and emperor of the same, and that there been in French divers and many noble volumes of his acts, and also of his knights.

To whom I answered that divers men hold opinion that there was no such Arthur and that all such books as been made of him been but feigned and fables, because that some chronicles make of him no mention ne remember him nothing, ne of his knights.

Whereto they answered, and one in special said, that in him that should say or think that there was never such a king called Arthur might well be aretted [3] great folly and blindness, for he said that there were many evidences of the contrary. First, ye may see his sepulture [4] in the monastery of Glastonbury; and also in *Polychronicon*,[5] in the fifth book, the sixth chapter, and in the seventh book, the twenty-third chapter, where his body was buried, and after founden and translated [6] into the said monastery. Ye shall see also in th'istory of Bochas,[7] in his book *De Casu Principum*, part of his noble acts, and also of his fall. Also Galfridus, in his British book,[8] recounteth his life. And in divers places of England many remembrances been yet of him and shall remain perpetually, and also of his knights: first, in the abbey of Westminster, at Saint Edward's shrine, remaineth the print of his seal in red wax, closed in beryl, in which is written PATRICIUS ARTHURUS BRITANNIE GALLIE GERMANIE DACIE IMPERATOR;[9] item, in the castle of Dover ye may see Gawain's skull and Cradok's mantle; at Winchester, the Round Table; in other places Lancelot's sword and many other things.

Then, all these things considered, there can no man reasonably gainsay but there was a king of this land named Arthur. For in all places, Christian and heathen, he is reputed and taken for one of the nine worthy, and the first of the three Christian men. And also he is more spoken of beyond the sea, mo [1] books made of his noble acts, than there be in England; as well in Dutch, Italian, Spanish, and Greekish, as in French. And yet of record remain in witness of him in Wales, in the town of Camelot, the great stones and marvelous works of iron lying under the ground, and royal vaults, which divers now living hath seen. Wherefore it is a marvel why he is no

3. Imputed.
4. Burial place.
5. A Latin history by Ranulph Higden (d. 1364), an English translation of which was printed by Caxton in 1482.
6. Carried
7. The Italian Giovanni Boccaccio (d. 1375), whose book *Concerning the Falls of Illustrious Men* ("Concerning the Fall of Princes," according to Caxton) was a favorite of the later Middle Ages.

8. Geoffrey of Monmouth, whose *History of the Kings of Britain* (ca. 1136), begins with the story of the founding of Britain by Brutus, Aeneas' great-grandson, who was believed to have given his name to Britain: hence Caxton's "Brutish."
9. The Noble Arthur, Emperor of Britain, Gaul, Germany, and Dacia.
1. More.

more renowned in his own country, save only it accordeth to the word of God, which saith that no man is accept for a prophet in his own country.

Then, all these things foresaid alleged,[2] I could not well deny but that there was such a noble king named Arthur, and reputed one of the nine worthy, and first and chief of the Christian men. And many noble volumes be made of him and of his noble knights in French, which I have seen and read beyond the sea, which been not had in our maternal tongue. But in Welsh been many, and also in French, and some in English, but nowhere nigh all. Wherefore, such as have late been drawn out briefly into English, I have, after the simple cunning that God hath sent to me, under the favor and correction of all noble lords and gentlemen, emprised [3] to imprint a book of the noble histories of the said king Arthur and of certain of his knights, after a copy unto me delivered, which copy sir Thomas Malory did take out of certain books of French and reduced it into English.

And I, according to my copy, have done set it [4] in imprint to the intent that noble men may see and learn the noble acts of chivalry, the gentle and virtuous deeds that some knights used in tho [5] days, by which they came to honor, and how they that were vicious were punished and oft put to shame and rebuke; humbly beseeching all noble lords and ladies with all other estates, of what estate or degree they been of, that shall see and read in this said book and work, that they take the good and honest acts in their remembrance, and to follow the same; wherein they shall find many joyous and pleasant histories and noble and renomed acts of humanity, gentleness, and chivalries. For herein may be seen noble chivalry, courtesy, humanity, friendliness, hardiness, love, friendship, cowardice, murder, hate, virtue, and sin. Do after the good and leave the evil, and it shall bring you to good fame and renommee.[6]

And for to pass the time this book shall be pleasant to read in, but for to give faith and belief that all is true that is contained herein, ye be at your liberty. But all is written for our doctrine, and for to beware that we fall not to vice ne sin, but t'exercise and follow virtue, by which we may come and attain to good fame and renommee in this life, and after this short and transitory life to come unto everlasting bliss in heaven; the which He grant us that reigneth in heaven, the Blessed Trinity. AMEN.

Then, to proceed forth in this said book, which I direct unto all noble princes, lords and ladies, gentlemen or gentlewomen, that desire to read or hear read of the noble and joyous history of the great conqueror and excellent king, king Arthur, sometime king of this

---

2. Having been cited.
3. Undertaken.
4. Have caused it to be set.

5. Those.
6. Renown.

noble royalme then called Britain, I, William Caxton, simple person, present this book following which I have emprised t'imprint: and treateth of the noble acts, feats of arms of chivalry, prowess, hardiness, humanity, love, courtesy, and very [7] gentleness, with many wonderful histories and adventures.

1485

7. True.

Topic in Medieval Literature

MEDIEVAL ATTITUDES TOWARD
LIFE ON EARTH

> Unto the woman he said, I will greatly multiply thy sorrow
> and thy conception; in sorrow thou shalt bring forth children; and thy
> desire shall be to thy husband, and he shall rule over thee.
>
> And unto Adam he said, Because thou hast hearkened unto the
> voice of thy wife, and hast eaten of the tree, of which I commanded
> thee, saying, Thou shalt not eat of it: cursed is the ground for thy sake;
> in sorrow shalt thou eat of it all the days of thy life;
>
> Thorns also and thistles shall it bring forth to thee; and thou shalt
> eat the herb of the field:
>
> In the sweat of thy face shalt thou eat bread, till thou return unto the
> ground; for out of it wast thou taken: for dust thou art, and unto dust
> shalt thou return.
>
> Genesis iii.16–19

The words with which the Lord God cursed Adam and Eve after their
transgression formed, for many articulate men in the Middle Ages, an
accurate image of human life: something which was wretched because the
Creator had made it so. Such thinkers believed that man had to acknowledge the wretchedness of his life and feel contempt for the world in which
he lived in order to attain spiritual salvation. Christianity, by teaching that
eternal life in heaven is the reward for right behavior on earth, exalts the
values of the future life over those of the present. Many medieval men, characteristically extremist, tended to make of the relative an absolute: if the
life to come is perfectly good, then it seemed logical to suppose that the
present life must be perfectly bad, so that even what seems good about it
must, in fact, be evil. Had not Christ promised the Kingdom of Heaven
to those who were most wretched on earth, and warned that a rich man
would have great difficulty getting into heaven? Therefore it seemed to many
a fair inference that those who were not miserable forfeited the Kingdom of Heaven. Thus by the Old Testament and the New, wretchedness
seemed confirmed as the inevitable and proper condition for mankind.

But even in an era when life was—from the modern point of view—
wretched for most men in fact as well as in theory, the average man was
reluctant to stop pursuing whatever apparent goods life had to offer. It

thus became the responsibility of his spiritual and moral mentors to try to persuade him to scorn the present while making sure of the future. The title of a late 12th-century tract by Pope Innocent III—*Contempt for the World; or, The Wretchedness of the Human Condition*—would serve to describe a very large amount of medieval writing designed to give the reader a correct set of values. Characteristic literary expressions of this doctrine, as well as modifications and contradictions of it, are given in the selections below.

Contempt for the World   The noblest statement of the proposition that life's goods are unreal fails to invoke the Christian doctrine of a life to come in order to validate its argument, although its author seems to have been a Christian: this is Boethius' *Consolation of Philosophy*, composed about 523 while the writer, an eminent Roman citizen, was in prison awaiting execution for "crimes against the state"—actually for having upheld older Roman political ideals against the reigning emperor, Theodoric the Ostrogoth. According to Boethius' stoic teaching, the man who refuses to commit himself to life's seeming goods makes himself spiritually invulnerable to its ills. Although this triumph over the world is a spiritual one, it takes place while man is alive and in the world. Boethius envisages neither future reward nor future punishment. More orthodox Christian writers could, of course, stress the surpassing importance of the world to come in their disparagement of this world. Yet a surprising number of them chose not to do so, but instead took a gloomy satisfaction in reminding the reader that he is dust, that all his pleasures are dusty, and that he will return to dust. If there is any mention of a life to come, it is apt to take the form of a threat of eternal damnation. The very frequent expression of such obstinate defeatism probably helped to popularize Boethius, who does offer positive aid to the suffering spirit. Thus in literature Boethius' ideas are often restated as a kind of general consolation for the ills of life: by reminding us that all men must suffer woe and must die, the writer hopes to comfort us for our specific griefs and losses. Even in this watered-down Boethianism there is a wholesome perspective that is lacking to those monitory poems which can see only man's earthiness.

BOETHIUS: *From* The Consolation of Philosophy[1]

[Triumph over the World]

Whoever is unstained of virtue, constant and well-ordered of life, who has put proud chance under foot and looks upright upon either kind of Fortune, may keep his countenance undisturbed. Neither the rage of the sea nor its threats, as it stirs upward the swell from its depths, shall move that man. Neither the unstable mountain that is called Vesuvius, which writhes out smoking fires through its broken

---

1. Based on Chaucer's Middle English rendering (Book I, Meter 4).

chimneys, nor the track of the thunderbolt that is wont to smite high towers shall move that man. Wherefore then, O wretches, do you dread tyrants who, villainous and mad, are without any strength? Hope for no thing, and dread nought; and so shall you disarm the wrath of the impotent tyrant. But whoever quaking dreads or desires a thing that is not constant in its own right, that man has cast away his shield and is moved from his place, and entangles himself in the chain with which he may be dragged.

Earth Took of Earth [2]

Erthe took of erthe erthe with wogh;°	harm
Erthe other erthe to the erthe drogh;°	drew
Erthe laide erthe in erthen throgh:°	coffin
Thanne hadde erthe of erthe erthe ynogh.°	enough

The Last Journey [3]

	If man him bithoughte,	
	Innerliche° and ofte,	deeply
	How hard is the fore°	journey
	Fro bedde to floore,	
5	How rueful is the flitte°	passage
	Fro floore to pitte,°	grave
	Fro pitte to pine°	torment
	That nevere shal fine,°	end
	I weene° that no sinne	think
10	Sholde his herte winne.	

A Change in Perspective

	Whan the turf is thy towr,	
	And thy pit° is thy bowr,°	grave / bedroom
	Thy weel° and thy white throte	welfare
	Shulen wormes to note:[4]	
5	What helpeth thee thenne	
	Al the worldes wenne?°	pleasure

2. The earliest of a great number of English "earth" poems (early 13th century).

3. This and the next poem are of the 13th century.

4. I.e., shall become business for worms.

GEOFFREY CHAUCER: [A Thoroughfare Full of Woe]⁵

No man myghte gladen Theseus
Savyng his olde fader Egeus
That knew this worldes transmutacioun,
As he hadde seyn° it chaungen up and down,   seen
5 Joye after wo, and wo after gladnesse,
And shewed hem ensample and lyknesse:
"Right as ther deyed° nevere man," quod he,   died
"That he ne lyved in erthe in som degree,
Right so ther lyved nevere man," he seyde,
10 "In al this world that som tyme he ne deyde.
This world nys but a thurghfare ful of wo,
And we been pilgrymes passynge to and fro:
Deeth is an ende of every worldly soore."

5. From the Knight's Tale, A2837-49 (in complete editions). Theseus, lord of
Athens, is grieving at the death of his knight Arcite.

The Goddess Fortune   The image of the goddess Fortune is one
of the Middle Age's chief literary devices for persuading the reader that
this world is a sorry one. Fortune is a legacy from pagan Rome who was
used to good effect by Boethius in his *Consolation* and to less good effect
by hundreds of writers following Boethius. She is generally imagined as
constantly turning a vertical wheel that has chairs fastened on its rim; in
one of these chairs man rides, sometimes on the ascendant or at the apex
of the wheel's orbit, but always in the end dashed down to its lowest point,
where he ends his life in misery. (For one vivid description of Fortune, see
King Arthur's dream, as told by Malory). In the *Consolation* Fortune
is made the means by which Boethius persuades the reader to put no trust
in the seeming goods of life and to accept its ills without complaint. Ultimately, Boethius tells us, Fortune is merely the agent of the benevolent
Prime Mover who governs the universe. Translated into specifically Christian terms, Fortune should become the agent of God, exercising his inscru-
table will on earth, as she appears in Dante. But once again the full and
mature vision proved beyond the capability of the majority of medieval
writers, in whom Fortune becomes a purely malevolent power whose function is to make life miserable. Writers, the piety of whose motives it is
impossible to doubt, interpreted all history as proving nothing more than
that Fortune holds all men in her malicious sway. Works such as Boccaccio's *Falls of Illustrious Men*, Chaucer's Monk's Tale, and Lydgate's *Falls
of Princes* consist of a series of biographies of eminent men betrayed by
Fortune—"tragedies," according to the medieval definition. Though these
writers thought that they were serving Christianity and mankind, in their
enthusiasm for railing at Fortune they often seal themselves up within a

moral vacuum: a man becomes a "tragic" figure merely by falling from high to low, and it does not matter that he might richly deserve his fall, so that Nero's life is as tragic as that of the worthiest of heroes. In the general disparagement of life's values, even those values which lie at the heart of Christianity tended to disappear.

BOETHIUS: *From* The Consolation of Philosophy [1]

[*Fortune Defends Herself*]

O man, wherefore do you recriminate me with your daily complaints? What wrong have I done you? What goods have I bereft you of that were yours? Strive or argue with me concerning the possession of riches or of dignities before whatever judge you will, and if you may show me that any mortal man has ever received any of those things as his and his alone, then will I grant freely that those same things were yours which you now seek.

When nature brought you forth out of your mother's womb I received you naked and wanting all things, and I nourished you with my riches, and was ready and eager to sustain you through my favor: and now that makes you impatient with me. And I surrounded you with all the abundance of all the goods that are in my control. Now it pleases me to withdraw my hand. You have had grace such as one has who has made use of someone else's goods: you have no right to complain as if you had really lost all your possessions. Why do you complain then? I have done you no wrong. Riches, honors, and other such things are of my right. They are my servants and recognize me as their mistress. They come with me, and depart when I turn away. I can confidently say that if those things whose loss you complain of had been yours, you would not have lost them.

Shall I alone, then, be forbidden to exercise my right? Surely it is permissible for the sky to bring bright day and after that to cover the day with dark night. The year too has leave to apparel the face of the earth now with fruit, now with flowers, and sometimes to destroy them with rain and cold. And the sea has a right sometimes to be calm and blandishing with smooth water, and sometimes to be horrible with waves and winds. But the desire of man, which cannot be quenched—shall it force me to be steadfast, although steadfastness is strange to my ways? Such is my nature, and this game I play continually: I turn the whirling wheel and the circle spins. I am glad to change the lowest to the highest, and the highest to the lowest. Mount up if you will, provided you do so under this condition, that you will not maintain that I do you wrong though you descend down when the rules of my game require it.

1. Based on Chaucer's Middle English rendition (Book II, Prose 2).

DANTE: [Fortune an Agent of God's Will][2]

"Master," said I to him, "now tell me further, this Fortune, on which thou touchest to me, what is it, which has the goods of the world so in its clutches?"

And he to me: "O foolish creatures, how great is that ignorance which harms you! I would have thee now receive my opinion concerning her. He whose wisdom transcends all, made the heavens, and gave them their guides, so that every part shines on every part, distributing equally the light. In like wise for the splendors of the world, He ordained a general ministress and guide, who should from time to time transfer the vain goods from race to race, and from one blood to another, beyond the resistance of human wit. Wherefore one race rules, and another languishes, pursuant to her judgment, which is hidden like the snake in the grass. Your wisdom has no withstanding of her: she foresees, judges, and pursues her reign, as theirs the other gods. Her permutations have no truce; necessity compels her to be swift, so often comes he who obtains a turn. This is she who is so set upon the cross, even by those who ought to give her praise, giving her blame amiss and ill report. But she is blessed and hears this not: with the other Primal Creatures she turns her sphere, and blessed she rejoices."

GEOFFREY CHAUCER: [The Monk's Definition of Tragedy][3]

	I wol biwaille in manere of tragedie	
	The harm of hem that stoode in heigh degree	
	And fillen° so that ther nas no remedie	*fell*
	To brynge hem out of hire adversitee.	
5	For certeyn, whan that Fortune list° to flee,	*desires*
	Ther may no man the cours of hire withholde:	
	Lat no man triste° on blynde prosperitee;	*trust*
	Beth war by this ensamples trewe and olde.	

2. From *Inferno* VII.48 ff., in Charles Eliot Norton's translation. Dante is discussing Fortune with Virgil, his guide through Hell.
3. From the Monk's Tale, B[2] 3181-88.

GEOFFREY CHAUCER: [The Tragedy
of Pierre de Lusignan] [4]

O worthy Petro, kyng of Cipre°, also	*Cyprus*
That Alisaundre wan by heigh maistrie,[5]	
Ful many an hethen wroghtestow ful wo,	
Of which thyne owene liges° hadde envie,	*lieges*
5 And for no thyng but for thy chivalrie	
They in thy bed han slayn thee by the morwe: [6]	
Thus kan Fortune hire wheel governe and gye°,	*guide*
And out of joye bryngen men to sorwe.	

4. King of Cyprus, whose recapture of Alexandria from the Saracens in 1365 was considered one of the great feats of Christendom; he was ultimately murdered by one of his followers. His life thus provides an apt demonstration of the turn of Fortune's wheel. The Monk's Tale, B[2] 3581-8.
5. That won Alexandria by great force.
6. In the morning.

"Life is Sweet"   Disgust for the world, no matter how pious the motives of those who express it, must to some extent deny the Bible's statement that the work of the Creator is good, a fact that will be at least occasionally evident to all men's senses. That earth's beauty continued to inspire joy in medieval hearts is attested by such lyrics as *Spring Has Come* (p. 286), which occur in profusion in all the vernaculars. On a more exalted plane, William Langland in *Piers Plowman* pays reverence to the divine Creator's ordering of nature, and in so doing brings the reader a comforting sense of the closeness of God to His handiwork on earth. But while earth's beauty is one proof of life's potential goodness, a far more powerful one is young love. Such lyrics as *Alison* (p. 284), of which there are a number, suggest that to try to teach hatred of the world to a lover is a lost cause; and the hero of the French romance *Aucassin and Nicolete* says that he will gladly pay for his earthly love with an eternity of hell. Other poets rebut the moralists with rollicking poems in praise of good eating and good drinking, and one—probably a monk—takes refuge from the austerities of life in splendid fantasy, in which he pictures an earthly paradise, the *Land of Cockaigne*, where all life's forbidden pleasures are freely and joyously practiced.

[A Vision of Nature in *Piers Plowman*] [1]

And sleeping I saw all this, and soon came Kind [2]
And named me by name, and bade me note well,
And through the wonders of this world wise to become.

1. From the B Text: XI.312-21, 336-46, 354-59. The translation is the present editor's.
2. Nature.

And on a mountain called Middle-earth, as it seemed to me then,
I was fetched forth through natural forms to learn   5
Of every creature, Kind, my Creator to love.
I saw the sun and the sea and the sand after,
And where birds and beasts by their mates were moving:
Wild worms in woods, and wonderful fowls,
With flecked feathers and of varied colors.   10

* * *

Birds I beheld that in bushes made nests—
Had never man the mastery to make the smallest.
I wondered from whom or where the magpie
Learned to lay the sticks in which she lays and broods:
Has no carpenter the craft to construct her nest so well;   15
If any mason could make a mold for it, it would be much wonder.
And yet I marveled more how many other birds
Covered and concealed full craftily their eggs
In marshes and in moors, in mires and waters,
For fear of other fowls and for wild beasts,   20
And for men should not find them when they from them went.

* * *

And soon I looked upon the sea, and so forth on the stars:
I saw many marvels which may not be told now.
I saw flowers in the field and their fair colors,
And how among the green grass grew so many hues,   25
And some sour and some sweet—wonder strange I thought it;
On their kind and their color to comment would take long.

From Aucassin and Nicolete[3]

[Aucassin Renounces Paradise]

In Paradise what have I to win? Therein I seek not to enter, but
only to have Nicolete, my sweet lady that I love so well. For into
Paradise go none but such folk as I shall tell thee now: Thither go
these same old priests, and halt old men and maimed, who all day
and night cower continually before the altars, and in the crypts; and
such folk as wear old amices [4] and old clouted frocks, and naked folk
and shoeless, and covered with sores, perishing of hunger and thirst,
and of cold, and of little ease. These be they that go into Paradise,
with them have I naught to make. But into Hell would I fain go;
for into Hell fare the goodly clerks, and goodly knights that fall in
tourneys and great wars, and stout men at arms, and all men noble.
With these would I liefly go. And thither pass the sweet ladies and
courteous that have two lovers or three, and their lords also thereto.
Thither goes the gold, and the silver, and cloth of vair, and cloth

3. From Andrew Lang's translation. Aucassin makes this reply to someone who
has warned him that if he finds his lost
lady he will run the risk of sinning with
her and thus of losing Paradise.
4. Cloaks worn by the clergy.

of gris,[5] and harpers, and makers, and the prince of this world. With these I would gladly go, let me but have with me Nicolete, my sweetest lady.

The Land of Cockaigne [6]

Far out in the ocean west of Spain
There is a land that's called Cockaigne.
There is no land beneath the air
With Cockaigne's excellence can compare.
Though Paradise is merry and bright,   5
Cockaigne is the fairer site.
What has Paradise got to show,
Where only fruit and green trees grow?
Though it has joy and pleasure sweet,
There's only apples for you to eat;   10
It has no hall, no bower, no bench,
And only water your thirst to quench;
There's little company there for you:
Elijah and Enoch are the only two; [7]
And well you know that men no more   15
Than a pair can be a dreadful bore.

In Cockaigne is food and drink
Got without trouble or sweat or swink.[8]
The food is choice, the drink is fine,
At lunch, at tea time, or when you dine.   20
There is no doubt, I make it clear,
There is no land on earth its peer;
Beneath the sky such joy and bliss
No land can show to compare with this.

There is many a lovely sight: 25
It's always day, there is no night;
There is no ill will, grudge, or strife;
There is no death, but only life;
There is no lack of food or cloth;
No man is there with woman wroth.   30

There is no serpent, wolf, nor fox,
Horse nor sheep, cow nor ox;
No pigs or goats does it enclose:
There's no need there to hold your nose.

---

5. Gray and gray-and-white fur, probably of squirrels.
6. The translation is the present editor's, based on the text given in R. H. Robbins' *Historical Poems of the XIVth and XVth Centuries* (1959).

7. On Biblical evidence, they were the only mortals to have been "translated" alive to Paradise (Genesis v.24, II Kings xi.11-12, Hebrews xi.5).
8. Labor.

Of stable or stud there is no trace: 35
This is a wholly pleasant place.
There is no fly, no flea, no louse,
In clothes, in town, in bed, in house.
There is no thunder, sleet, nor hail,
No ugly worm or slimy snail.   40
There is no storm, no rain, no wind;
There is no man or woman blind;
But all is pleasure, joy, and glee:
Well is the man that there may be.

There are rivers great and fine,   45
Of oil, of milk, of honey and wine.
Water is used there for no thing
Except to look at, and washing.
There're fruits for every appetite,
For all is comfort and delight.   50

Also there is an abbey fair:
White and gray monks both live there.
It has many bowers and halls—
All of pastry are the walls,
Of flesh, of fish, of choicest meat,
The tastiest that man could eat.   55
Of sugar cakes are the shingles all,
Of church, of cloister, bower and hall;
The pinnacles are fat puddings,
Fit to be served to princes or kings.   60
You may eat whatever you will:
It is your right to take your fill,
For all is common to young or old,
To strong, to fierce, to meek, to bold.

There is a cloister fair and bright,   65
Wide and long, a lovely sight.
The pillars of that cloister wall
Are each a single crystal tall:
Of jasper green and coral red
Is each one's bottom, and its head.   70
In the meadow is a tree
Very nice for you to see:
Of ginger and galingale[9] its root,
Of zedoary every shoot;
Its flowers are mace, the choicest kind,   75
Sweet-smelling cinnamon is its rind;
Its fruit is clove of pleasant smack;
Of cubebs,[1] too, there is no lack.
There are roses red of hue,
And lilies pleasing to the view: 80
They never fade by day or night.

9. "Galingale" and "zedoary" are varieties of ginger.

1. "Mace" and "cubeb" are spices.

This surely is a most sweet sight.
Four springs there are come from that ground:
Of water that will make you sound,
Of balm,[2] of treacle, and of wine   85
Spiced, and flowing without decline.
The streams that flow out of these springs
Are paved with gold and precious things:
Pearl as big as onion grown,
Sapphire, ruby, and star-stone;   90
Emerald, jacinth, and prasine,
Beryl, onyx, topaz fine,
Amethyst and chrysolite,
Chalcedony and hepatite.

So many and various are the birds,   95
To name them all I lack the words—
Throstle, thrush, and nightingale,
Woodpecker, partridge, lark, and quail,
That are always singing with all their might—
They keep it up both day and night.   100
And another thing I mustn't omit:
The geese, fresh roasted from the spit,
Fly to the abbey—God it wot—
And cry out, "Geese all hot, all hot!"
They bring of stuffing a great supply,   105
The best prepared that you could buy.

The tender larks, as is well known,
Fly to a watering mouth on their own,
All fixed up in an elegant stew,
With a sauce designed to titillate you.   110
There is no need to order drink:
Just take enough without more swink.

When the monks have gone to Mass,
All the windows that are of glass
Turn themselves into crystal bright   115
To give the monks a better light.
And when the Mass has all been said
And the prayers have all been read,
The crystal turns back into glass,
Of the same sort that it earlier was.   120

The younger monks, day upon day,
After dinner go out to play:
There is no hawk or bird so fast,
Nor that better flies in the airy vast,
Than the young monks, high of mood,   125
Sailing on wings of sleeves and hood.

When the Abbot sees them soar,
It always makes his pleasure more.

2. A soothing fluid; "treacle" is a medicinal fluid that cures all ailments.

But when the monks their flight prolong,
He summons them to evensong.   130
Yet still the monks come not to ground,
But keep on flying round and round.

When the Abbot thus does learn
That flying monks his summons spurn,
He takes what maiden he can find   135
And upward turns her white behind,
And beats the tabors with his hand,
To make his monks alight on land.

When his monks that sight espy,
Down to the maiden quick they fly,   140
And to the wench they too attend,
And spank her on her white rear end.
And after all their thirsty swink,
Meekly the monks go home to drink,
And in an orderly formation   145
Parade toward their night's collation.

Another abbey's near at hand,
A nunnery that's fair and grand,
Upon a river of sweet milk,
Wherein is great supply of silk.   150
When sun shines hot through summer's air,
The young nuns will their boat prepare,
And sail forth from the river's shore,
Pushing their skiff with pole and oar.
When from their abbey they're away,   155
They take their habits off to play,
And down into the water leap,
And skillfully they swim the deep.
The young monks, when they this espy,
They take right off and thither fly,   160
And when they to the nuns have won,
Then each monk for his own takes one,
And quickly carries forth his prey
To the abbey vast and gray,
Where each one teaches to his nun   165
An upsy downsy orison.

A monk who will be stallion good
And knows how best to set his hood,
Shall have—and no man interfere—
Twelve wives for each and every year.   170
And not through grace, but all through right,
With which to make himself delight.

And of these monks who can sleep best,
And give his body greatest rest,

Has cause to hope, with God's good aid,   175
Soon Father Abbot to be made.

Whoso will come that land unto,
Full great penance must he do.
Seven whole years in hogs' manure
He must wade—of that I'm sure—   180
And all that time up to the chin:
And thus he shall to that land win.

Lordings good and kind and true,
May you to earth not say adieu
Before you've had a proper chance   185
To undergo all that penance,
So that you may that land attain,
And nevermore come here again.
Let's pray to God it may so be;
Amen, for holy charity.   190

"Beauty That Must Die"   Some of the most poignant poetry of
the Middle Ages results from a combination of two extreme attitudes toward life, expressing at once appreciation for the beauty of the world and
acknowledgment that this beauty is so transitory that, viewed against the
background of eternity, it is scarcely more than an illusion. In poetry of
this sort, an important part is often played by the *ubi sunt* device, which
takes its name from the first two words of the Latin sentence, *Ubi sunt qui
ante nos fuerunt?* ("Where are they who before us were?"). In asking the
question the poet evokes for a moment the splendor of life, symbolized by
famous persons of the past, and then, by his inevitably grim answer, condemns it to death. The tone of such poems will vary from the austerely
monitory to the hauntingly sad, depending upon how the poet describes the
"they" of the question, and how he phrases his answer: whether he sides
with death or with life or tries to balance delicately between them.

[Ubi Sunt Qui ante Nos Fuerunt?]

Where beeth they biforen us weren,
Houndes ledden and hawkes beren,°   *bore*
   And hadden feeld and wode?
The riche ladies in hir bowr,
5 That wereden ° gold in hir tressour,°   *wore / hair*
   With hir brighte rode,°   *faces*

Eten and drunken and maden hem glad;
Hir lif was al with gamen ylad; [1]

---

1. With pleasure led.

Men kneeleden hem biforen:
They beren hem wel swithe hye.[2]
And in a twinkling of an ye
Hir soules weren forloren.

10

FRANÇOIS VILLON: The Ballad of Dead Ladies[3]

Tell me now in what hidden way is
Lady Flora the lovely Roman?[4]
Where's Hipparchia, and where is Thaïs,[5]
Neither of them the fairer woman?
Where is Echo, beheld of no man,
Only heard on river and mere—
She whose beauty was more than human?[6] . . .
But where are the snows of yesteryear?

5

Where's Héloïse, the learned nun,
For whose sake Abeillard, I ween,
Lost manhood and put priesthood on?[7]
(From Love he won such dule and teen!)
And where, I pray you, is the queen[8]
Who willed that Buridan should steer
Sewed in a sack's mouth down the Seine?
But where are the snows of yesteryear?

10

15

White Queen Blanche, like a queen of lilies,
With a voice like any mermaidén[9]—
Bertha Broadfoot, Beatrice, Alice,
And Ermengarde, the lady of Maine[1]—
And that good Joan whom Englishmen

20

2. Very proudly.
3. Villon (b. 1431), a French poet and vagabond, regarded as the first and one of the greatest of French lyrists. This translation of his *Ballade du Temps Jadis* is by Dante Gabriel Rossetti.
4. Probably the Roman goddess of flowers and spring, later thought of as a wealthy and beautiful woman.
5. Hipparchia was the wife of Crates, Greek Cynic philosopher (3rd century B.C.). Thaïs is either the courtesan who accompanied Alexander the Great on his Asian expedition or the Egyptian courtesan who became a saint.
6. Echo was the nymph who pined away for Narcissus until nothing was left of her except her voice.
7. Héloïse fell in love with her teacher, Pierre Abelard (1079-1142), scholastic philosopher and theologian; they were

secretly married in order not to hinder Abelard's advancement in the church. Héloïse's uncle, in revenge, had Abelard emasculated in order to make him canonically incapable of ecclesiastical preferment. Abelard became a monk and Héloïse a nun. "Dule and teen": grief and pain.
8. Marguerite de Bourgogne, heroine of the legend of the Tour de Nesle, according to which she had her numerous lovers killed and thrown into the Seine; Jean Buridan, rector of the University of Paris, escaped.
9. Perhaps Blanche of Castille, mother of Louis IX of France (1226-70).
1. Names of famous medieval ladies; Bertha Broadfoot was mother of Charlemagne, king of the Franks and emperor of the West (742-814).

At Rouen doomed and burned her there [2]—
    Mother of God, where are they then? . . .
But where are the snows of yesteryear?

Nay, never ask this week, fair lord,   25
    Where they are gone, nor yet this year,
Except with this for an overword—
    "But where are the snows of yesteryear?"

GEOFFREY CHAUCER: [This Worlde That Passeth
Soone as Floures Faire][3]

O yonge fresshe folkes, he or she,
In which that love up groweth with youre age,
Repeyreth home fro worldly vanitee,
And of youre herte up casteth the visage
5 To thilke God that after his ymage
Yow made, and thynketh al nys but a faire,
This worlde that passeth soone as floures faire;

 And loveth hym the which that right for love
Upon a crois oure soules for to beye
10 First starf and roos and sit in hevene above:
For he nyl° falsen no wight, dar I leye,°   *will not / wager*
That wol his herte al holly on hym leye—
And syn° he best to love is and most meke,   *since*
What nedeth feynede loves for to seke?

2. Joan of Arc; she saved France from conquest but was later imprisoned and burned at the stake for heresy and witchcraft in 1431.
3. From *Troilus and Criseide*, V.1835-48.

The Sixteenth Century

(1485-1603)

1485: Accession of Henry VII inaugurates age of the Tudor sovereigns.
1509: Accession of Henry VIII.
1517: Martin Luther's Wittenberg Theses; beginning of the Reformation.
1535: Henry VIII acknowledged "Supreme Head on Earth" of the English church.
1557: Publication of *Tottel's Miscellany*, containing poems by Sir Thomas Wyatt, Henry Howard Earl of Surrey, and others.
1558: Accession of Queen Elizabeth I.
1576: The Theatre, the first permanent structure in England for the presentation of plays, is built.
1588: Defeat of the Spanish Armada.
1603: Death of Elizabeth I; accession of James I, first of the Stuart line.

ENGLAND UNDER HENRY VII

The 16th century in England is the age of the Tudor sovereigns. There were three generations of them; they ruled England from 1485 to 1603. Before the first Tudor, the Earl of Richmond who became Henry VII, won his crown by defeating Richard III at Bosworth field, the country had for more than thirty years been torn by a dynastic strife between the houses of York and Lancaster. Henry VII was Lancastrian, but he married Elizabeth of the house of York, sister of Edward V and neice of the Yorkist king he defeated, Richard III. The barons, impoverished and divided by the dynastic wars, could not effectively oppose the power of the crown, and the church, the other great force in society, was closer to alliance with royal power than to opposition. So Tudor government meant, in comparison with what had gone before and with other conceivable alternatives, a government of strong central authority, of order, and of practical solutions to problems.

About a decade before Henry VII won his throne, the art of printing from movable type, a German invention, had been introduced into England by William Caxton (ca. 1422–91), who had learned and practiced it in the Low Countries. Literacy had been increasing during the 15th century, so that many more people could read than in Chaucer's time. It is estimated that some 30 per cent of the people could read English in the early 15th century and some 60 per cent by 1530. Printing of course made books cheaper and more plentiful, and accordingly there were more opportunities to read and more incentive to learn to read.

Seven years after Henry VII became king, Columbus discovered America, and a few years later Vasco da Gama reached the Orient by sailing around the Cape of Good Hope. The English were not pioneers in the discovery and exploration of the western hemisphere, but the consequences of new discoveries were to affect their place in the world profoundly, for in the next century they became great colonizers and merchant-adventurers.

Significant changes in trade and in the arts of war also marked the early years of the Tudor regime. Henry VII made commercial treaties with European countries; England, which had always been a sheep-raising country, began to manufacture and export significant amounts of cloth. As lands were enclosed to permit grazing on a larger scale, people were driven off the land to the cities, London grew into a metropolitan market, and business in the modern sense began to develop. At the same time the old feudal structure began to break down, partly because the introduction of firearms had made obsolete the old armored knight on horseback, as well as the English bowman who had won such famous victories in France under King Henry V. The "new men" who supported the Tudors and profited from their favor could adapt themselves more easily to a changed society than could the survivors of the great families of the feudal 15th century.

Yet it would be a mistake to visualize these changes as sudden and dramatic. Although Caxton introduced printed books, and was an author and translator as well as a printer, his publications consisted of long prose romances translated from the French, collections of moral sayings, and other works—such as Malory's *Morte Darthur*—that were medieval rather than modern. And even though the armored knight was obsolete, for a century jousts and tournaments took place at court and the approved code of behavior was the traditional code of chivalry. As often in an age of spectacular novelty, full of significance for the future, men's minds looked back instead of forward. Confronted with innovation, they dreamed of an idealized past instead of looking forward to an uncertain future. The best writers of the time of Henry VII were imitators of Chaucer, who had died about a century before. They were Scottish rather than English: William Dunbar (ca. 1460–ca. 1520), Gavin Douglas (1475–1522), and Sir David Lindsay (1485–1555). Even the English writers looked back; a typical one is Stephen Hawes (1474–1523), who imitated not Chaucer but John Lydgate, monk of Bury.

HUMANISM

During the 15th century a few English clerics and government officials had journeyed to Italy and had seen something of the extraordinary cultural and intellectual movement flourishing in the city-states there. But it was only near the end of the century that Italian influence came to be important, and it was not until the accession of Henry VIII to the throne in 1509 that a notable renaissance took place in England.

A great leader of the intellectual movement known as humanism was Sir Thomas More, Henry's Lord Chancellor, who gave up his life rather than bow to Henry as head of the English church. More's masterpiece, *Utopia*, was written in Latin, and was an appeal to all of Europe to reconsider social institutions in the light of reason and to achieve economic equality and peace. His English writings were largely on controversial subjects; his most ambitious one was a history of Richard III. In it More justified the Tudor dynasty by blackening its predecessor. More's friend Erasmus of Rotterdam spent some time in England, and his influence was strong, especially in the field of education. In the humanists' view, education was based upon the classics and the Bible, was to be liberal in the modern sense, yet extremely practical. It was designed to prepare able people for the duties of government. Queen Elizabeth herself, with her command of languages and her practical sense of the problems of diplomacy, was a fine example of the humanistically educated ruler.

Elizabethan education was based upon the medieval *trivium* (grammar, logic, and rhetoric) and *quadrivium* (arithmetic, geometry, astronomy, and music). Grammar was of course Latin grammar, and the rhetoric that went with it was a rigorous discipline in all the stylistic devices used by classical authors. The purpose was a utilitarian one—to train the student to speak and write good Latin, the language of diplomacy, of the professions, and of all higher learning. But the books read and studied rhetorically were not considered mere exhibitions of literary style; from the *Sententiae Pueriles* for beginners, on up through Terence, Virgil, Horace, and Cicero's *De Officiis*, the works were studied for the moral, political, and philosophical content they offered. Elizabethan schoolmasters might use the system of double translation, from English into Latin and then from Latin back into English, to develop facility and rhetorical elegance, but they well knew that the rapid development from child into man (so much more rapid than we consider either feasible or desirable) required moral instruction, and this was to be found in the Latin classics. It was a mission of the English humanists like Colet, Elyot, and Ascham to persuade the English gentry that their sons should be bred to this kind of learning as the most suitable preparation for public service.

Although Sir Thomas More had turned naturally to Latin in writing his *Utopia*, the choice was not as easy for succeeding generations. In fact, the question of whether to write in English or in Latin became a question of great seriousness. The vernaculars seemed relatively new and unstable to learned men, and with their great desire for eternal fame it was natural that they should concern themselves about the durability of their medium. Furthermore, the age of the humanists had emphasized the value of the classical languages; Cicero and the other masters of rhetoric were imitated in their own tongues. But in Italy, France, and England alike, there came to be a revolt against this sterile and slavish imitation of the classics. It is the contention of Joachim Du Bellay's *Défense et Illustration de la Langue Française* (1549) that the value of a language is not inherent in the language itself, but depends upon what great and fine works are written in that language; furthermore, and this is even more important, the feeling of nationality itself dictates that the vernacular should be used. If the tongue of the people is not so refined and polished as the Greek or Latin, all the more reason why men of learning should improve it by study- ing it and writing their most ambitious works in it. Roger Ascham (1515– 68), tutor to Princess Elizabeth, included in his book on archery called *Toxophilus* (1545) a defense of writing in English, though he said it would be easier for him to write in Latin or Greek. He dedicated the book to King Henry, and his patriotic motives are expressed in verses addressed to England:

> Stick to the truth, and evermore thou shall
> Through Christ, King Henry, the book and the bow,
> All manner of enemies quite overthrow.

Richard Mulcaster (ca. 1530–1611), principal of the Merchant Taylors' School and teacher of Edmund Spenser, said:

I do write in my natural English tongue, because though I make the learned my judges, which understand Latin, yet I mean good to the un- learned, which understand but English. * * * For is it not indeed a mar- velous bondage, to become servants to one tongue for learning's sake the most of our time, with loss of most time, whereas we may have the very same treasure in our own tongue, with the gain of most time? our own bearing the joyful title of our liberty and freedom, the Latin tongue remembering us of our thralldom and bondage? I love Rome, but London better; I favor Italy, but England more; I honor the Latin, but I worship the English.

THE REFORMATION—HENRY VIII, EDWARD VI, AND MARY

Humanists like Erasmus advocated and practiced a scholarly and critical study of the Scriptures; humanists like More were opposed to corrupt and ignorant clergy and such abuses as the sale of papal indulgences and par- dons. But when, after Martin Luther nailed his famous Theses to the church door in Wittenberg in 1517, the Reformation itself gathered force, Erasmus and More drew back. Humanism and Reformation for a while seemed to be hostile forces.

What was the Reformation? From the point of view of those who sup- ported it, it was a return to pure Christianity—cleansing the church of all the filth and idolatry that had accumulated over the centuries. From a less partisan point of view it was the break-up of western Christendom, the secularization of society, the establishment of princely ascendancy over the church, and consequently the identification of religious feelings with patri- otic, nationalistic ones. From the point of view of the Catholic Church it was, of course, damnable heresy.

In England, one cannot say that the Reformation had an ideological basis. There had been John Wycliffe and the Lollard movement, a pop- ular protest in the time of Chaucer, but little of this survived in the sec- ond decade of the 16th century. The split with the Church of Rome was caused by a man who considered himself a Catholic champion against Luther and his opinions: Henry VIII, who for writing a book against

Luther had been given the title "Defender of the Faith" by Pope Leo X. Henry's motives were dynastic, not religious; he needed a legitimate son and he could not get one without the divorce which Rome refused him. He insisted upon being Supreme Head of the English church and requiring oaths of allegiance to him in that role; Sir Thomas More, his Lord Chancellor, resigned and finally gave up his life rather than sign such an oath. More's successor, Thomas Cromwell, dissolved the monasteries and distributed the property to a group of people who thereafter would not side with Rome. And though under Henry the great English translator of the Bible, William Tyndale, was persecuted, driven out of England, and finally martyred in 1536, it was also in Henry's reign that the Scriptures in English were made available in The Great Bible of 1539 to anyone who could read.

Under Henry's son, the child king Edward VI (b. 1537; reigned 1547–53), the English Reformation, which had taken place for political reasons, acquired a strong religious and spiritual force. Protestant theologians from the Continent swarmed to England, the Book of Common Prayer was published in 1549 and 1552, and by 1553, the year of the boy king's death, the 42 Articles which officially defined the beliefs of the English church were thoroughly Protestant.

The successor to the young Protestant king was his older sister Mary, half-Spanish and devoutly Catholic, who married her cousin, Philip II of Spain. The leading Protestants either fled to the Continent or were burned at the stake as heretics; ideologically the Reformation could be reversed, but some of its practical consequences, like the distribution of monastery lands, could not. A Spaniard on the throne of England was not popular, and Mary, whose accession had been opposed by the Council which had proclaimed Lady Jane Grey queen, and whose throne was challenged by a rebellion led by Sir Thomas Wyatt the Younger, son of the poet, dared not press her people too far. She could herself return to Roman allegiance but she could not undo the work of her father and brother. The most necessary thing to do was something she could not do—produce an heir. (Had she done so, England and the United States would probably be Catholic countries today.) Her reign was short, and the Protestant exiles swarmed back at her death to be a potent force in English society during the long reign of Mary's half sister, Elizabeth.

NATIONALISM—ELIZABETH I

Elizabeth Tudor, who ascended the throne in 1558 and ruled until 1603, was one of the most remarkable political geniuses ever produced by a people which has not been barren of political geniuses. Vain, difficult, and headstrong, she nevertheless had a very shrewd instinct about her country's strengths and weaknesses, and she identified herself with her country as no previous ruler had done. Although she was susceptible to the flattery of her courtiers and favorites, she nevertheless entrusted power to such solid men as William Cecil and Francis Walsingham. Cecil (1520–98) was her chief and most trusted Secretary. He devoted his great talents with unswerving loyalty to preserving a balance of forces in England, maintaining the queen's supremacy over ambitious nobles, and extracting money from the Commons to run the government. Walsingham (ca. 1530–90), a gifted diplomat and administrator, was her principal architect of foreign policy.

England's strength lay in its middle position in the balance of power in Europe—it could throw its weight either way in the power contest between Spain and France; it could support or fail to support the Protestant uprising in the Low Countries. Moreover the queen was unmarried, and the general assumption was that of course she would marry, since as her father had undoubtedly taught her, one of a monarch's major duties is to provide an unquestioned, strong, legitimate heir to the throne. As long as she was capable of bearing children, Elizabeth's possible marriage was an important factor in European diplomacy. By the time it was too late to marry, England was strong and united, capable of shaking off (in 1588) the attempt of the Spanish king, Philip II, to invade the country. What unified England more than anything else was the papal bull of 1570, excommunicating Elizabeth and relieving her subjects of their loyalty to her. This bull, had it taken effect, would have brought to the throne Mary Queen of Scots, Catholic by faith and French by culture—an insupportable thought; Englishmen rallied to their queen and she became a symbol of Englishness and nationalism. The adulation of her, in the face of trouble on the Scottish border, near-chaos in Ireland, and varying threats from the Continent, grew to almost religious heights; her beauty (which was exaggerated), her wisdom (which generally did not need exaggeration), and her divine mission to guide England became articles of faith. In 1588 the defeat of the great Spanish Armada, the mightiest invasion fleet ever mounted against England, seemed to justify that faith.

England's weakness was its politico-religious division. The Catholics, who had never been reformed and who adhered to the pro-Spanish faction of the previous reign, and the Protestant exiles, whose sojourn on the Continent had only sharpened their zeal for the eradication of papistry everywhere in Europe, were the extremes. Between them were the majority of Englishmen whose main desire was for order (remembering the civil conflicts of the previous century), and for these Englishmen Elizabeth, in her person and her policy, became the symbol and the cause.

In matters of religion Elizabeth chose a middle way which satisfied neither the Catholics nor the Puritans. She imposed a form of service, compelled her subjects to attend it, and left their consciences to themselves. The effect was again nationalistic; in the settled and established Elizabethan church, Christians looked toward neither Rome nor Geneva as the prime source of authority, but to the throne of their own sovereign.

The desire for commercial profit also strengthened nationalistic feelings. In 1493 the Pope had divided the new world between the Spanish and the Portuguese by drawing a line from pole to pole (hence Brazil speaks Portuguese today and the rest of Latin America speaks Spanish): the English were not in the picture. But by the end of Edward VI's reign the Company of Merchant Adventurers was founded and Englishmen had become interested in Asia and North America. As Protestantism progressed, many fishing fleets lacked work, for the sale of fish depended in great part upon the Catholic practice of eating no meat on Fridays and other fast days. So they turned to piracy, preying on Spanish ships which were returning laden with wealth from the New World. This business soon became a private undeclared war, with the queen and her courtiers investing in these raids privately but accepting no responsibility for them. The greatest of many dazzling exploits was the voyage of Francis Drake in 1577–80: he sailed through the Straits of Magellan, pillaged Spanish towns on the Pacific, reached as far north as San Francisco, crossed to the Philippines and returned around the Cape of Good Hope; he came back with £1,000,000 in treasure, and his investors earned a dividend of 5,000 per cent. Queen Elizabeth knighted him on the deck of his ship, *The Golden Hind*.

More than anything else, the mere survival of Elizabeth for so long provided the opportunity for nationalistic consciousness and feeling to become established. When she came to the throne in 1558 she was 25 years old; her sister had reigned only five years and her brother only six, but she would remain queen for almost 45 years. The second half of the 16th century is very appropriately called the Elizabethan age.

DRAMATIC LITERATURE

If the morality play *Everyman* at the end of the 15th century marks the end of the Middle Ages, we must look for the beginnings of modern drama to the household of John Morton, Archbishop of Canterbury and Chancellor of England under Henry VII, where young Thomas More served as a page. There at Christmastime plays or revels were put on, and the story goes that young More would sometimes improvise a part and step in with the players. Cardinal Morton even maintained a chaplain on his staff, Henry Medwall, to write plays for his princely entertainment; two of them have survived, called *Nature* and *Fulgens and Lucrece*. These plays were short, given in the great hall at Lambeth Palace, and were called "interludes." Some of these interludes, especially those by John Heywood, are heavily dependent upon French farce.

Interludes and morality plays continued to be popular down to Shakespeare's lifetime, but the development of the drama into a sophisticated art form required another influence—the classics. In the middle of the century we find a schoolmaster, Nicholas Udall, writing a classical comedy in English, based upon the Latin comedies his students had been reading. He called it *Ralph Roister Doister*. About the same time another comedy, classical in form but English in content, was amusing the students at Cambridge. It was called *Gammar Gurton's Needle*. Lively, vivid, native English material put into the regular form of the Latin comedies of Plautus and Terence: this is the fortunate combination that looked forward to the comedies of Shakespeare. *Ralph Roister Doister* contains a classical *miles gloriosus* (cowardly braggart soldier) who is the remote ancestor of Shakespeare's Sir John Falstaff in *I Henry IV*.

The Latin tragedies of Seneca had a similar influence. They were constructed in five acts and had violent and bloody plots, resounding rhetorical speeches, and ghosts among the cast of characters. Moreover Seneca is full of references to Fortune, a Roman goddess who turned her wheel and brought those who had reached the top down to the bottom. The precarious position of men in high estate formed a basis for Elizabethan tragedy, as it had for medieval. The mid-16th century contribution to the type of literature represented by Boccaccio's *Falls of Illustrious Men*, Chaucer's *Monk's Tale*, and Lydgate's *Falls of Princes* was a collection of verse complaints called *The Mirror for Magistrates*. A "mirror" in the old sense was a warning, and a "magistrate" was anyone in a position of power or authority. The first regular English tragedy was called *Gorboduc or Ferrex and Porrex*; it was written by two lawyers, Thomas Sackville and

Thomas Norton. It was first produced at the Inner Temple (a law school) in 1561 and later acted before the queen. The play is set in the legendary very early period of English history shared by Shakespeare's *King Lear*, and, like Lear, its hero divides his kingdom among his children with disastrous results. It is important also that *Gorboduc* is in blank verse rather than in one of the awkward verse forms characteristic of much midcentury writing.

The fusion of classical form with English content brought about the possibility of a mature and artistic drama. But such drama must have an audience, a theater, and professional actors. The earliest English drama had been acted by members of the clergy in the church; medieval miracle and mystery plays had been acted by amateurs—members of the local trade guilds—ordinarily on wagons in the streets of the towns. Moralities and interludes were produced by semi-amateur groups who traveled about, or by the servants of a lord in the hall of his castle. Much dramatic activity took place at winter and midsummer festivals, and it should be remembered that before the Reformation there were many more holidays than there were later. The drama of the Elizabethan age retained much of the festive atmosphere of its infancy.

The actors who traveled about giving their performances wherever they could were not men of respectable status; they tended to be classified with jugglers, acrobats, mountebanks, and other persons of dubious character. In 1545 they were classified by statute as idle rogues and vagabonds; as such, they were subject to arrest. Some noblemen maintained a company of actors as their personal servants, wearing livery and the badge of their masters. They could travel and practice their craft when not needed by their lords, and they were of course exempt from the statute. So it came about that the professional acting companies of Shakespeare's time, including Shakespeare's own, attached themselves to a nobleman and were technically his servants, even though virtually all of their time was devoted to, and their income came from, the public. The rise in social status of actors during Shakespeare's lifetime is illustrated by the fact that he and his fellows were made officers of the royal household when James came to the throne and were sworn as Grooms of the Chamber in ordinary without fee.

The earliest successful acting companies, if success is measured by acceptance at court, were companies of boys. Richard Edwards, Master of the Children of the Chapel Royal in the 1560s, wrote plays for them, and for almost twenty years the rival company, the Children of Paul's (the choir school of St. Paul's cathedral) regularly presented plays at court.

The adult actors played in various places—great houses, the hall of an Inn of Court, on makeshift stages, or in London inn-yards. In 1576 James Burbage, one of the Earl of Leicester's players, built a structure to house their performances and called it The Theatre. It was in Shoreditch, outside the limits of the City of London and accordingly beyond the jurisdiction of the city authorities, who were generally hostile to dramatic spectacles. Other public theaters were erected, and before long enclosed private theaters were secured, under conditions which would allow them freedom from municipal control.

The public theaters were usually oval in shape, with an unroofed yard in the center where the groundlings stood, covered seats in three rising tiers around the yard, and a platform stage jutting out into the yard and surrounded on three sides by spectators. Plays were given in the afternoon and of course were dependent on fair weather. The private theaters were indoors, artificially lighted, and patronized by a more select audience. After 1608 Shakespeare's company had its regular public theater, the Globe, and a private theater, the Blackfriars.

The companies were what would now be called "repertory companies"—that is, they filled the roles of each play from members of their own group, not employing outsiders, and they performed a number of different plays on consecutive days, not continuing a single play for a "run." The principal actors were shareholders in the profits of the company. Boys were apprenticed to actors just as they had been apprenticed to master craftsmen in the guilds; they took the women's parts in plays until their voices changed. The plays might be bought for the company from hack writers; or, as in Shakespeare's company, the group might include an actor-playwright who could supply it with some (but by no means all) of its plays. The text remained the property of the company, but a popular play was eagerly sought by the printers, and the company sometimes had trouble achieving effective control over its rights to the play. The editors of the first collected edition of Shakespeare's plays, the First Folio (1623) said that up until then the readers had been "abused with divers stolen and surreptitious copies, maimed and deformed by the frauds and stealths of injurious impostors." This is true of the so-called "bad quartos," such as the first quarto of *Hamlet* (1603) but the second quarto of that play (1604) was probably printed from Shakespeare's manuscript.

POET, PATRON, AND PUBLISHER

In the court the greatest opportunities existed, but there also were the greatest disappointments to be found. "It was overrun with place-seekers," writes M. St. Clare Byrne in *Elizabethan Life in Town and Country*, "but it was also undeniably the focus of the national life. It drew to it the clever mountebanks, but also the real vigor and talent. It captured and stimulated men's imaginations, even if eventually it disheartened and disgusted them." Men like Sir Christopher Hatton and Sir Walter Ralegh leaped from obscurity to great power and prominence as a result of their success as courtiers, but it must not be forgotten that they had other abilities than the gallantry and dancing which have made them famous in anecdote. The security of the courtier was always precarious, and there was scarcely one of Queen Elizabeth's courtiers who did not know, at some time or other, the harshness of the sovereign's disapproval. The great guide and conduct book for the courtier was Castiglione's *Il Cortegiano* (1528, translated into English by Sir Thomas Hoby in 1561), and according to its theses the function of the courtier was to give good and honest advice to the prince. But, as Sir Philip Sidney found out when he tried to advise the queen against a French marriage, advice is not always relished by a monarch whose powers over any individual subject are almost absolute. As a result there was a long tradition of literature against court life, comparing it unfavorably to the country life of the retired and obscure man. Sir Thomas Wyatt's verse epistles to Sir Francis Bryan and John Poins are early examples of this attitude, and it runs all through the period. Of course the fact that there was a "tradition" means that everything unfavorable said about the court should not be taken at its face value. But enough evidence exists to show that there was a definite feeling that court life was too precarious, too superficial, too corrupt, too hypocritical. From the time of Wyatt to the time of Ralegh the bitter tone is consistent.

For literary men like Edmund Spenser and Lyly, men who by birth were not in a position to be real courtiers, the court offered a faint hope of livelihood, notice, and encouragement. But for these two, at any rate, it was a source of bitter disappointment. Lyly's long wait for the office of the Revels and Spenser's disillusionment after hoping for court favor (reflected in *Mother Hubberds Tale* and *Colin Clouts Come Home Againe*) tell the story. Much of the satire of the period is directed against the superficiality and treachery of the court atmosphere. "A thousand hopes, but all nothing," wailed Lyly, "a hundred promises, but yet nothing."

Although most of the literature which is still considered worth reading shows the predominant influences of the court, it would be a mistake to underestimate the influence of the City of London on the literary taste and production of the period. London had grown tremendously since the time of Chaucer. Instead of a population of about 50,000 it had 93,276 in 1563 and 224,275 in 1605. It was by far the most important city in the realm, and the political history of the 17th century is understandable only if one recognizes the great power the City had, even as against the Crown. The printing presses were located in London, the publishers were located in London, and the mass of the middle-class population which set the style for literature written for the ordinary man lived in London. The middle class found among the university men some writers who catered to them: Thomas Heywood is a good example. And although Thomas Nashe scornfully rejects the claim of the bourgeois to have any literary taste at all or to have any ability at producing literature, still the class had its own writers, like Thomas Deloney, and it knew what it liked—books of instruction, romances, religious tracts, and sensational ballads. Whether the aristocrats admitted it or not, the standards and tastes of the middle class affected all writing, all publishing, and all literary success. For finally the writer saw his work exhibited on the stalls of St. Paul's churchyard, and the customers who frequented that center of the book trade were more often members of the middle class than of the court circle. Louis B. Wright has shown (in his *Middle-Class Culture in Elizabethan England*) how extensive and profound was the influence of the citizenry upon the writing and publication of books, and how bourgeois standards of edification and utility dictated to most of the authors of the time.

Next to the court and the City, the most important sources of literature were of course the two universities. In Elizabeth's reign they were old-fashioned in their curriculum, poor in discipline, and undistinguished in learning, in comparison with what they had been a generation before. There was a great shortage of ministers in the country, partly because of the poor living standard provided for members of the clergy and partly because of the loss of ministers through the religious changes of the middle of the century. Hence the universities were attempting to train ministers exclusively. The university man had either to get a fellowship and remain in academic life (which almost always meant taking holy orders), to enter the church and get a poor living, or to go into law or medicine. The career of a professional man of letters as such did not exist: literature was regarded as an adjunct, not a primary occupation.

The university graduate who came to London to make a literary career for himself faced a very difficult situation. It is best pictured, perhaps, in the Cambridge trilogy of *Parnassus* plays, performed at the end of the century but fairly faithfully reflecting conditions which held good during the whole period. It was the university wits, to be sure, who gave to the drama some of the classical form it needed, and who inaugurated the great literary vogue of the 90's. But the lives of Nashe and Marlowe, of Robert Greene and George Peele, do not suggest that the path was easy. The diary of Philip Henslowe, a leading theatrical manager, has entry after entry showing university graduates in prison or in debt or even at best miserably eking out an existence patching plays.

Financial rewards for writing and publishing prose or poetry came mostly in the form of gifts from patrons—in reality the old system of master and servant which had come down from the Middle Ages and had not changed much with the invention of printing. The writer by a dedication hoped for a suitable reward, and in an age when honor and vanity were motives much more sharply defined or observed than they are today, this procedure sometimes worked. Yet the patron whose vanity was amply satisfied by his own conceit and would not reward an author for a dedication remained a constant irritation to the writers of the time, and we hear many complaints that the age is degenerate because patrons are not more munificent. There were some generous and literary-minded patrons, notably Sir Philip Sidney and his sister Mary, the Countess of Pembroke. Shakespeare's relations with his patron, the Earl of Southampton, little as we know about them, were apparently satisfactory, as the dedication to *The Rape of Lucrece* (1594) is much warmer and more personal than the earlier one, to *Venus and Adonis* (1593). But the experience of Robert Greene is perhaps more typical than that of Shakespeare in this respect. He had sixteen different patrons for seventeen books; this suggests that he was not fortunate in finding favor or support from any one. A fraudulent practice grew up of printing the book and then printing off separate dedications, so that an impecunious author could deceive several patrons each into thinking that he was the one to be honored by the volume. Two or three pounds seems to have been the usual reward for the dedication of a pamphlet or small volume of verse. Ben Jonson, who fared much better than most of his contemporaries, sums up the matter, for poets at least, when he says: "Poetry in this latter age hath proved but a mean mistress to such as have wholly addicted themselves to her, or given their names up to her family. Those who have but saluted her on the way, and now and then tendered their visits, she hath done much for, and advanced in the way of their own professions (both the law and the gospel) beyond all they could have hoped or done for themselves without her favor."

The other possible source of reward, besides the patron, was the publisher. And rewards from the publisher in the 16th century were nothing at all like the rewards from that source now. In the first place there was no such thing as copyright, and no such thing, in the ordinary way, as royalties paid according to the sale of the book. An author sold his manuscript to the publisher outright, for what seems now like a ridiculously low price—for a pamphlet or small book of poetry, usually forty shillings.

The writer's troubles were not over when he had written his book, gone through the difficulty of finding a publisher, and finally come to terms with him for the sale of it. He still had to face the many and stringent regulations of the press by political and ecclesiastical authorities, and the fact that he had sold the manuscript did not exempt him from responsibility for what was in it. The authorities were, first, the Privy Council and the Court of Star Chamber, the highest political authority in the realm below the queen; then the Court of High Commission, the supreme ecclesiastical authority, which sometimes supervised matters which had only the slightest connection with religion; then the Stationers' Company, with whom a book had to be registered but who supervised and protected the publisher and printer rather than the author.

The principal rules governing the publication of books were that the number of printers (not publishers) was strictly limited; that nothing could be printed except in the City of London and the Universities of Oxford and Cambridge; that everything printed must receive the imprimatur of the Archbishop of Canterbury and the Bishop of London or their representatives; and that everything published in London must be entered in the registers of the Stationers' Company, if any kind of property protection were desired for it. An example of the regulation which reached back of the publisher to the author himself can be seen in the history of John Stubbs, who protested against Elizabeth's projected French marriage in a pamphlet called *The Discovery of a Gaping Gulf* (1579). For writing this pamphlet, Stubbs was condemned to have his right hand cut off with one stroke of a butcher's cleaver. When the execution had taken place, Stubbs took off his hat with his left hand and cried "God save the queen!"

Almost every writer of the period got into some sort of trouble for publishing a book. It might be prison, it might be merely a reprimand, it might be an investigation by the Star Chamber. It was dangerous to put pen to paper, and it was so unprofitable that it is a wonder that any original writing was published at all. Yet the Elizabethan age is an extremely prolific one in writing and publishing. The *Short Title Catalogue* of the Bibliographical Society, which lists works and editions published between 1475 and 1640, includes over 26,000 items, and it does not include all that were published.

To suppose that poetry, or even prose, circulated only in printed form would be a mistake. The 16th century was the first century of the printed book, and the older way, of circulating in manuscript, lingered on into the 17th century. This was particularly true of poets of gentle or noble rank. Sidney is the most prominent example. Sir John Harington, in his translation of Ariosto's *Orlando Furioso* in 1591, mentions a sonnet of Sidney's "which many I am sure have read"; that particular sonnet was not published until seven years later. Many people kept commonplace books in which they would copy down poems from borrowed manuscript copies. Professional scribes made a living by copying manuscripts, for authors or for readers. There are even complaints by printers of the hoarding of literary manuscripts by "their grand possessors." There is a difference, which has not always been appreciated, between the poetry of the professional poets who wrote for print and the gentle or noble poets who wrote for circulation in manuscript among their cultivated friends.

ART, NATURE, AND POETRY

Elizabethan taste had some very definite and particular characteristics of its own, and the student who wishes to read Elizabethan literature in the spirit of its own time must adjust his mind to the differences between the aesthetic principles of the 16th century and those of our own day. In the 16th century there still remained much of the medieval awareness of the arts as *crafts*, and every writer of the period shows an amazing knowledge of the techniques of many crafts or "mysteries" now unfamiliar. Shakespeare is not an isolated example, and it has been often noticed that his works show an intimate knowledge of such matters as gardening, hawking, dressmaking, archery, building, and so on. Managing the great horse in the tournament was an art. Sailing was an art. Planting a kitchen garden was an art. What they had in common was that they all used the materials of nature but exploited the ingenuity of man's mind. The same fundamental characteristic was thought to apply to the art or craft of writing.

We have been taught by the Romantic movement to glorify nature and to regard the works of art as attempts, usually unsuccessful, to emulate nature. This conception would have seemed strange indeed to the Elizabethans. They recognized, of course, that nature was the cause and basis of all; but that seemed to them no reason why the ingenuity of man should not be used in enabling nature to outdo herself. In *The Winter's Tale* Polixenes is amused at the naïveté of Perdita, who protests that she will have no streaked carnations or gillyflowers in her garden because

> I have heard it said
> There is an art which in their piedness shares
> With great creating nature.

"Say there be," replies Polixenes,

> Yet nature is made better by no mean
> But nature makes that mean. So, over that art
> Which you say adds to nature, is an art
> That nature makes. You see, sweet maid, we marry
> A gentler scion to the wildest stock
> And make conceive a bark of baser kind
> By bud of nobler race. This is an art
> Which does mend nature—change it rather; but
> The art itself is nature.

There was no uneasiness in the Elizabethan mind about a possible conflict between art and nature, for the reason that Polixenes gives. And the improvement by device, by arrangement, by art, of something naturally beautiful extended to all aspects of life, so that there was felt to be no great gulf between literature and the sports of the field or the arts of the kitchen.

The Elizabethan garden was designed as a square, filled with elaborate and intricate, but perfectly regular, design. Francis Bacon protests at gardens which include plots of different colored earths, so arranged as to form a design even without the flowers planted in them; he says he sees enough of this kind of thing in confections and tarts. Yet the very protest shows that his taste was perhaps not typical, and a contemporary might well have asked him why a garden should not look like a confection from the baker's—they were both samples of the art of design. Some Elizabethans had their houses built in the shape of an E, out of honor to the queen, and one man, John Thorpe, designed his house in the form of his own initials. These instances were extreme, of course, but they show the tendency.

Contrapuntal music (composed of several independent melodies joined together), which was sung by the Elizabethans in an accomplished amateur manner, was an intricate kind of music, with elaborate patterns and complex harmonies. The composer Thomas Morley (ca. 1557–1603) says of the madrigal:

As for the music, it is, next unto the motet, the most artificial and to men of understanding most delightful. If therefore you will compose in this kind you must possess yourself with an amorous humor * * * so that you must in your music be wavering like the wind, sometime wanton, sometime grave and staid, otherwhile effeminate; you may maintain points and revert them, use triplaes and show the very uttermost of your variety, and the more variety you show the better shall you please.

But a rigid form was to control all of this extravagance, just as the square border of a garden and the regularity of the pattern controlled the exuberance of the curves in the "knot" or design.

The verse forms used by the Elizabethans range from the extremely simple four-line ballad stanza through the rather complicated form of the sonnet to the elaborate and beautiful 18-line stanza of Spenser's *Epithalamion*. A stanza such as

> The man of life upright
> Whose guileless heart is free
> From all dishonest deeds
> Or thought of vanity

might have been written by any one of many poets at almost any time in the 16th century; it happened to have been written by a fine craftsman, Thomas Campion, near the end of it. Henry Howard, Earl of Surrey, who introduced blank verse into English and helped introduce the sonnet in the reign of Henry VIII, was also a practitioner of a form of iambic couplet in which the first line had twelve syllables and the second fourteen:

> The young man eke that feels his bones with pains oppressed,
> How he would be a rich old man, to live and lie at rest.

This verse form, called "poulter's measure" (because a poulter's dozen was supposed to be sometimes twelve and sometimes fourteen), was the most common verse form in the 60's and 70's. Its dreary monotony in long stretches is matched only by the "fourteener" couplet of fourteen syllables in a line. We still have examples of these forms in our hymnbooks; when each line of poulter's measure is printed as two lines, the hymnbooks call it "short meter"; when they so divide fourteeners they call it "common meter."

Sonnets, which the Elizabethans often called "quatorzains," using the term "sonnet" loosely for any short poem, are fourteen-line poems in iambic pentameter with elaborate rhyme schemes. The most common Italian form, which Wyatt, Sidney, and others imitated, was divided structurally into the octave (first eight lines) and the sestet (last six). A typical rhyme scheme was *abba abba cdc dee*. The so-called English sonnet, introduced by Surrey and practiced by Shakespeare, is structurally three quatrains and a couplet: *abab cdcd efef gg*. Spenser, the most experimental and the most gifted prosodist of the century, preferred a form that is harder to write and richer in rhymes: *abab bcbc cdcd ee*.

The six-line "Troilus stanza" and the seven-line rhyme royal stanza, both practiced by Chaucer, survived into the 16th century. Shakespeare used the former in *Venus and Adonis* and the latter in *The Rape of Lucrece;* that popular collection of historical poems, *The Mirror for Magistrates,* features rhyme royal.

An innovation was Spenser's nine-line stanza, called after him the "Spenserian stanza," which added to the Italian ottava rima (*abab bc bc*) an additional line of twelve syllables, an Alexandrine, rhyming with the preceding line. This is the stanza form which serves so well the large descriptive and narrative requirements of *The Faerie Queene.* The elaborate scheme of the stanza Spenser devised for his *Epithalamion* perhaps illustrates the height of Elizabethan craftsmanship in verse. Its eighteen lines rhyme *ababcc*, then various combinations in the second six, and finally three couplets. Lines 6, 11, and 16 are short, having only six syllables contrasted to the pentameter's ten, and the last line is an Alexandrine, as in the Spenserian stanza.

GENRES AND CONVENTIONS IN POETRY

A literary convention is a pattern that has become habitual and arouses certain expectations in the reader. For the Elizabethan poet available conventions enabled him to assume particular responses from his audience and to show his learning by his exploitation of these well-known patterns and his virtuosity by his ingenious elaborations of them. It must not be supposed that these conventions were lifeless forms, so stale with use that they no longer carried meaning or conviction. They were charged with values, with associations. They related writer and reader to other times, other languages, other cultures.

The pastoral convention presented a simple and idealized world, inhabited by shepherds and shepherdesses, concerned not at all with war or politics or commerce. Its business consisted of tending the flocks, friendly poetic contests among shepherds, love, and the pursuit of contentment rather than fame or fortune.

Pastoral lyrics expressed the joys of pastoral life or disappointment in love. Pastoral eclogues were dialogues between shepherds in which a poetic contest was staged, or there was serious, satirical comment on abuses in the great world concealed in the disguise of the homely local concerns of country folk. There were also, of course, pastoral dramas and pastoral romances (prose fiction) which embodied the same values of *otium* (leisure), freedom from pride and ambition, and the pursuit of humble contentment.

Another popular convention was that of the mythological-erotic poem, derived from Ovid mainly but influenced by Italian imitations of him. In the middle ages Ovid's poetry had been allegorized and interpreted morally —the same process that has overtaken the love songs in the Song of Solomon in the Old Testament. This process continued on into the 17th century, but a newer treatment of the convention returned to the frank sensuality of the Latin amatory poets and allowed for elaborate mythological decoration of the narrative without worrying about moral propriety or allegorical interpretation. Such poems appealed to a courtly taste; they validated the senses and they asserted the primacy of physical beauty and the imagination. Shakespeare in *Venus and Adonis* and Marlowe in *Hero and Leander* were among the poets who practiced in this convention.

Sometimes related to the Ovidian tradition but separate from it in origin was the convention of the complaint poem. This goes back to a medieval genre represented by works of the Italian Boccaccio and his English imitators, Lydgate and the authors of *The Mirror for Magistrates*. The complaint poem is essentially tragic and moral. In it the ghost of someone who fell from high place bemoans his fate and warns others. If the ghost is a woman, like Daniel's Rosamund, her fall was caused by the frailty of her sex and the poem may be related to the Ovidian tradition. Another kind of poem, which came both from Ovid and the *Mirror for Magistrates* tradition, was the heroical epistle, practised notably by Drayton.

The Elizabethan sonnet, which reached the height of its vogue in the last decade of the 16th century, depended upon a convention established by Petrarch and followed by his many imitators in Italy and France. In this tradition the poet complains of his lady's coldness; he describes the contrary states of feeling the lover experiences; and he writes sonnets on the conventional themes of sleep, absence, originality, renunciation, and others. The purposes of the love sonneteers differed, of course, but what they had in common might be described as an ambition to give dignity and power to the theme of love by the elaborate rhetorical and stylistic devices available in the Petrarchan tradition. Lesser poets often produced nothing but standard conceits served up in fourteen-line helpings, but major poets such as Sidney, Spenser, and Shakespeare wrote sonnets of power and originality that stand out as major poetic products of the Elizabethan Age.

The conventional forms for satire were less well fixed in the 16th century than in some later periods, though there is a good deal of Elizabethan satirical verse. Some examples belong to a medieval tradition coming down from *Piers Plowman*, which was believed to be the only English masterpiece in satire until satires by the "university wits" in the tradition of the Latin satirists Persius and Juvenal began to appear, and some were written by young John Donne and circulated only in manuscript until after the poet's death in 1631. The epigram was a form that flourished, both in the classical tradition of Martial and in the lyric form of words for a madrigal; the famous *The Silver Swan* is an example.

Poetry for music also followed some conventions: the dance song of course had its definite rhythms and refrains, and many well-known tunes provided the formula by which poet after poet composed new words. In the polyphonic madrigal, the same phrases tend to be repeated again and again, while the words often get lost in the music because various voices sing different words at the same time. As a result, the poem written as a madrigal is usually short and simple both in language and ideas. The "ayre," however, is a song written for a single voice to a lute accompaniment and is usually sung straight through. Since the words are much more intelligible, the thought can be more complex. While the poem is often a good deal longer than the madrigal (since the same melody is repeated over and over), the poem is divided into repetitive stanzas.

There were conventions as well for the heroic poem, of which Spenser's *Faerie Queene* is the prime example. The classical epics of Homer and Virgil had their influence, but so did the romantic Italian epics of Ariosto and Tasso. Chapman's Homer and Harington's Ariosto were regarded by contemporaries as something more than translation, having much of the interest and significance of original poems.

The major conventions in poetry did not stifle originality; they served as both an ordering device and a challenge that stimulated the poet to something fresh and new. When these conventions were alive for writers and readers, they had significance in themselves, which was an essential part of the total significance of the poem. Knowledge of the more important Elizabethan conventions is not simply of scholarly interest; it is essential to the experience of the poem as a poem.

ELIZABETHAN MOODS AND ATTITUDES

The English Renaissance was no sharp break with the past. Attitudes and feelings which had been characteristic of the 15th or 14th centuries persisted well down into the era of humanism and Reformation. George Gascoigne, the leading writer of the 1570's, has in many ways a medieval point of view, and the popular collection of verse tales of the fall of princes called *The Mirror for Magistrates* (first published in 1559, and reprinted with additions in 1563, 1587, and 1610) derives from Lydgate and Boccaccio. Even a lyric by that flamboyant and "modern" Elizabethan, Sir Walter Ralegh, may embody a sentiment of the vanity and transitoriness of all earthly ambitions and achievements. The Dance of Death and related images were still living symbols to the Elizabethan imagination; witness Shakespeare's *Richard II* (III.ii.152–70):

> And nothing can we call our own but death
> And that small model of the barren earth
> Which serves as paste and cover to our bones.
> For God's sake let us sit upon the ground
> And tell sad stories of the death of kings!
> How some have been deposed; some slain in war;
> Some haunted by the ghosts they have deposed;
> Some poisoned by their wives; some sleeping killed—
> All murthered; for within the hollow crown
> That rounds the mortal temples of a king
> Keeps Death his court, and there the antic sits,
> Scoffing his state and grinning at his pomp;
> Allowing him a breath, a little scene,
> To monarchize, be feared, and kill with looks;
> Infusing him with self and vain conceit,
> As if this flesh which walls about our life
> Were brass impregnable: and humored thus,
> Comes at the last, and with a little pin
> Bores through the castle wall, and farewell king!

Yet there was at the same time a spirit of joy and gaiety, of innocence and lightheartedness, that future ages were to look back on as "merry England." This spirit is popular, it comes from the folk and from the persistent love of Englishmen for their countryside; it is spontaneous, yet it seems somehow stable and permanent. Perhaps its best expression is in the songs of Shakespeare's plays:

> When daffodils begin to peer,
> With heigh! the doxy over the dale,
> Why, then comes in the sweet o' the year;
> For the red blood reigns in the winter's pale.

or

> When daisies pied and violets blue
> And ladysmocks all silver-white
> And cuckoobuds of yellow hue
> Do paint the meadows with delight.

The mood of pastoral, as we have already seen in our notice of that convention, is generally one of quiet contentment, of reflective leisure, of the enjoyment of a simple, idealized world. Marlowe's *Passionate Shepherd to His Love* beautifully invokes this world.

There was of course also among the Elizabethans the opposite mood: the burning desire for conquest, for achievement, for surmounting all obstacles. The Elizabethans called it "the aspiring mind." The great projector of this mood is Christopher Marlowe, who has his heroes fling themselves into the pursuit of power—

> Is it not passing brave to be a king
> And ride in triumph through Persepolis?—

or into the lust for gold—

> Infinite riches in a little room—

or into the search for knowledge—

> All things that move between the quiet poles
> Shall be at my command; emperors and kings
> Are but obeyed in their several provinces,
> Nor can they raise the wind or rend the clouds;
> But his dominion that excels in this
> Stretcheth as far as doth the mind of man.

Marlowe's heroes are defeated finally, all of them, but their fiery spirit in assaulting the limits of the possible echoes after they are gone.

The Elizabethan spirit has been described as "sensuous, comprehensive, extravagant, disorderly, thirsty for beauty, abounding in the zest for life." This is part of the truth, but not all of it. Fundamentally, the thought and feeling of Shakespeare's contemporaries was far more deeply affected by Christian humanism than by the extravagances of Marlowe. We need to remember Ben Jonson, with his classical principles of structure and decorum and his ideal of the balanced man. Jonson was in every respect more typical of his age than Shakespeare. His emphasis upon learning, his reconciliation of ancient models and English content, and his critical responsibility truly represent the ideal English poet of his time, as Sidney would have visualized him. Because his major work was done after 1603, he is represented in the 17th-century section of this anthology.

The second generation of English humanists—men like Roger Ascham (1515–68, tutor to Queen Elizabeth), Sir John Cheke (1514–57, professor of Greek at Cambridge), and Thomas Wilson (1525–81, rhetorician and translator)—combined an earnest Protestant Christianity with their classical learning, and Ascham vigorously opposed the more secular, pagan humanism that was coming out of Italy. These men shaped the University of Cambridge, which in turn shaped many men. It was an Oxford man, however—Richard Hooker—who provided in his great work, *The Laws of Ecclesiastical Polity* (1593 and later), the supreme masterpiece of English Christian humanism. In so far as his doctrine is concerned, Spenser is a Christian humanist, and the label can justly be applied to John Milton, both in content and in form.

If the beginning of the Tudor era showed more links with the past than with the future, it is equally true that the end of Elizabeth's reign prefigured some of the conflict and uncertainty of the time to come. "The disenchantment of the Elizabethans" is a phrase that has been used to describe it. In 1599, the year of Spenser's death, occurred the abortive revolt of the Earl of Essex. Elizabeth was old, a peaceful succession was by no means assured, and the rifts in society which were to mean civil war in the midcentury were already present. An outbreak of satire and epigrams had to be stopped by the authorities. Some of the cynical undercurrent in Shakespeare's *Hamlet* and *Troilus and Cressida* reflects the spirit of the time. John Donne was already writing his poems, and a very different age, the 17th century, was in the offing. In 1603 Elizabeth, the last of the Tudors, died, and to the immense relief of anxious Englishmen, the succession took place peacefully. The new monarch was the Protestant James VI of Scotland, who became James I of England.

SIR THOMAS WYATT THE ELDER
(1503–1542)

Wyatt was born at Allington Castle in Kent, and educated at St. John's College, Cambridge. He spent most of his life as a courtier and diplomat, serving King Henry VIII as Clerk of the King's Jewels and as ambassador to Spain and to the Emperor Charles V. He was also a member of various missions to France and Italy. He spent much of his adult life abroad; his interest in foreign literature, especially Italian, is evident from his translations and imitations of poems by the Italian sonneteers Petrarch, Sannazaro, Alamanni, and others. The life of a courtier under Henry VIII was not a calm life: Wyatt was twice arrested and imprisoned, once in 1536, after a quarrel with the Duke of Suffolk, and again in 1541, when he was charged with treason, lodged in the Tower of London, and stripped of all his property. On both occasions he was fortunate enough to regain the king's favor and receive a pardon. His praise of quiet retired life in the country and the cynical comments about foreign courts in his verse epistle to John Poins derive from his own experience.

For all his travel abroad, Wyatt remained essentially an Englishman. His poetry includes not only the sonnets, based upon Italian models, but also many delightful lyrics with short stanzas and refrains in the manner of the native English "ballet" (pronounced to rhyme with *mallet*) or dance-song. Wyatt's own temperament and disposition show more clearly in these English poems than in the sonnets. The lover in the Petrarchan sonnet is usually in a mood of doleful despair; the typical poem is essentially a complaint, though the interest lies in following the elaborately worked out "conceits" or comparisons. The lover is abject, he is the lady's slave; her coldness is a perpetual torture to him. In the ballets, however, a rather gay, manly independence is the characteristic note.

The sonnet, a 14-line poem with a complicated rhyme scheme, was introduced into English by Wyatt. He took his subject matter from Petrarch's sonnets, for the most part, but his rhyme schemes came from other Italian models. The most common rhyme scheme in Wyatt's sonnets is *abba abba cddc ee*; the usual Italian structure of an octave (first eight lines) followed after a turn in the sense by a sestet (last six lines) was already beginning to break down into the "English" structure for the sonnet, three quatrains and a couplet.

Although Wyatt intended to publish a collection of his poems, he never did so. In fact, very little of his verse was published until after his death. In aristocratic circles poems circulated in manuscript and were copied by hand; the general public usually saw courtiers' poems only when some enterprising publisher acquired manuscripts, perhaps already formed into a collection, and printed them as a miscellany. An early volume of this sort, called *The Court of Venus*, published a few Wyatt poems before 1540. A dozen such collections were published during the second half of the 16th century, with titles like *A Paradise of Dainty Devices*, *A Handful of*

Pleasant Delights, and *A Gorgeous Gallery of Gallant Inventions.* By far the most important of these miscellanies was issued by the printer Richard Tottel in 1557 (15 years after Wyatt's death) with the title *Songs and Sonnets written by the Right Honorable Lord Henry Howard late Earl of Surrey and other.* Until modern times it was always called simply *Songs and Sonnets* (Shakespeare has his Master Slender in *The Merry Wives of Windsor* say "I had rather than forty shillings I had my book of Songs and Sonnets here"); but now it is always referred to as *Tottel's Miscellany.* The printer, Richard Tottel, addressed the reader in an interesting epistle:

That to have well written in verse, yea and in small parcels, deserveth great praise, the works of divers Latins, Italians and other do prove sufficiently. That our tongue is able in that kind to do as praiseworthily as the rest, the honorable style of the noble Earl of Surrey and the weightiness of the deep-witted Sir Thomas Wyatt the Elder's verse, with several graces in sundry good English writers, do show abundantly. It resteth now, gentle reader, that thou think it not ill done to publish, to the honor of the English tongue, and for profit of the studious of English eloquence, those works which the ungentle hoarders up of such treasure have heretofore envied thee. And for this point, good reader, thine own profit and pleasure in these presently, and moe hereafter, shall answer for my defence. If perhaps some mislike the stateliness of style, removed from the rude skill of common ears, I ask help of the learned to defend their learned friends, the authors of this work. And I exhort the unlearned, by reading to be more skilfull, and to purge that swinelike grossness that maketh the sweet marjoram not to smell to their delight.

The anthology includes 271 poems—97 attributed to Wyatt, 40 to Surrey, 40 to Nicholas Grimald, and 94 to "Uncertain Authors." It is surely one of the most important books in the history of English literature, for it was the channel through which the main currents of European Renaissance poetry flowed into the British Isles. In it the sonnet, blank verse, *terza rima,* ottava rima, rondeau, and other forms were naturalized into English, and suddenly the ragged, undisciplined, pedestrian verse of the first part of the century became antiquated. When Wyatt was a boy it was possible for Alexander Barclay, an ambitious and by no means uneducated poet, to write verse like this:

> The famous poets with the muses nine
> With wit inspired, fresh, pregnant and divine,
> Say boldly endite in style substantial;
> Some in poems high and historical,
> Some them delight in heavy tragedies
> And some in wanton or merry comedies.

Wyatt was not primarily concerned with regularity of accent and smoothness of rhythm. By the time *Tottel's Miscellany* was published, Wyatt's rather rough and vigorous metrical practice was felt to be crude, and Tottel's editor smoothed out the versification. We reprint *They Flee from Me* in the versions of the Egerton manuscript and of Tottel. The Egerton manuscript (E. MS.) contains poems in Wyatt's own hand and corrections in his hand of scribal texts. The Devonshire manuscript (D. MS.) was not apparently in the poet's possession, but some of its texts seem earlier than Egerton's and it furnishes additional poems.

The Long Love That in My Thought Doth Harbor[1]

The long love that in my thought doth harbor,
And in my heart doth keep his residence,
Into my face presseth with bold pretense
And therein campeth, spreading his banner.[2]
She that me learns to love and suffer   5
And wills that my trust and lust's negligence[3]
Be reined by reason, shame, and reverence
With his hardiness taketh displeasure.
Wherewithal unto the heart's forest he fleeth,
Leaving his enterprise with pain and cry,   10
And there him hideth, and not appeareth.
What may I do, when my master feareth,
But in the field with him to live and die?
For good is the life ending faithfully.

E. MS.

Farewell, Love

Farewell, Love, and all thy laws forever,
Thy baited hooks shall tangle me no more;
Senec and Plato call me from thy lore,
To perfect wealth my wit for to endeavor.[4]
In blind error when I did persever,   5
Thy sharp repulse, that pricketh ay so sore,
Hath taught me to set in trifles no store
And 'scape forth since liberty is lever.[5]
Therefore farewell, go trouble younger hearts,
And in me claim no more authority;   10
With idle youth go use thy property,
And thereon spend thy many brittle darts.
For hitherto though I have lost all my time,
Me lusteth[6] no longer rotten boughs to climb.

E. MS.

1. Wyatt's version of Petrarch's *Sonnetto in Vita* 91; his younger friend, the Earl of Surrey, also translated it (see *Love, That Doth Reign and Live Within My Thought*).
2. I.e., the poet's blush. The first four lines of this sonnet contain the "conceit" (or elaborately sustained metaphor) of love as a kind of warrior who "harbors" in the speaker's thought, lives in his heart, and occasionally invades his face "with bold pretense" (i.e., making bold claim). He flaunts his warlike presence by means of the "banner." Elaborate metaphors of this kind are found often in Elizabethan love poetry; sometimes an entire sonnet will turn on one conceit. "Learns": teaches.
3. I.e., my open and careless revelation of my love. "Shame": modesty, shamefastness.
4. I.e., "Senec" (Seneca, the Roman moral philosopher and tragedian) and Plato call him to educate his mind to perfect well-being ("wealth").
5. More pleasing, dearer.
6. I care.

I Find No Peace[7]

I find no peace and all my war is done,
I fear and hope, I burn and freeze like ice,
I fly above the wind, yet can I not arise,
And naught I have and all the world I scize on;
That looseth nor locketh holdeth me in prison,[8]   5
And holdeth me not; yet can I 'scape nowise;
Nor letteth me live nor die at my devise,[9]
And yet of death it giveth none occasion.
Without eyen[1] I see; and without tongue I plain;
I desire to perish, and yet I ask health;   10
I love another, and thus I hate myself;
I feed me in sorrow, and laugh in all my pain.
Likewise displeaseth me both death and life,
And my delight is causer of this strife.

                                       E. MS.

Madam, Withouten Many Words

Madam, withouten many words,
Once [2] I am sure ye will or no,
And if ye will, then leave your bordes,[3]
And use your wit and show it so.

And with a beck ye shall me call,   5
And if of one that burneth alway
Ye have any pity at all,
Answer him fair with yea or nay.

If it be yea I shall be fain,
If it be nay, friends as before;   10
Ye shall another man obtain
And I mine own and yours no more.

                                       E. MS.

---

7. In the opening lines of this sonnet, translated from Petrarch, *Sonnetto in Vita* 90, Wyatt reveals the early 16th-century preference for one-syllable words in poetry, which George Gascoigne justified by remarking that "the more monosyllables that you use, the truer Englishman you shall seem."

8. I.e., love that keeps no jail but yet imprisons me. The whole sonnet is a series of paradoxes; it represents a popular Petrarchan convention.
9. Wish.
1. Eyes; "plain": complain.
2. Sometime.
3. Jests.

Whoso List to Hunt[1]

Whoso list [2] to hunt, I know where is an hind,
But as for me, alas, I may no more.
The vain travail hath wearied me so sore
I am of them that farthest cometh behind.
Yet may I, by no means, my wearied mind   5
Draw from the deer, but as she fleeth afore,
Fainting I follow. I leave off therefore,
Since in a net I seek to hold the wind.
Whoso list her hunt, I put him out of doubt,
As well as I, may spend his time in vain.   10
And graven with diamonds in letters plain
There is written, her fair neck round about,
"Noli me tangere, for Caesar's I am,
And wild for to hold, though I seem tame."

                                     E. MS.

My Lute, Awake!

My lute, awake! Perform the last
Labor that thou and I shall waste,
And end that I have now begun;
For when this song is sung and past,
My lute, be still, for I have done.   5

As to be heard where ear is none,
As lead to grave in marble stone [3]
My song may pierce her heart as soon.
Should we then sigh or sing or moan?
No, no, my lute, for I have done.   10

The rocks do not so cruelly
Repulse the waves continually
As she my suit and affection.
So that I am past remedy,
Whereby my lute and I have done.   15

Proud of the spoil that thou hast got
Of simple hearts, thorough love's shot;
By whom, unkind, thou hast them won,
Think not he hath his bow forgot,
Although my lute and I have done.   20

1. An adaptation of Petrarch, *Rime* 190, perhaps influenced by commentators on Petrarch, who said that *Noli me tangere quia Caesaris sum* ("Touch me not, for I am Caesar's") was inscribed on the collars of Caesar's hinds which were then set free and were presumably safe from hunters. Wyatt's sonnet is usually supposed to refer to Anne Boleyn, in whom Henry VIII became interested in 1526.
2. Cares.
3. I.e., when sound may be heard with no ear to hear it, or when soft lead is able to carve ("grave") hard marble.

Vengeance shall fall on thy disdain
That makest but game on earnest pain.
Think not alone under the sun
Unquit [4] to cause thy lovers plain,
Although my lute and I have done.   25

Perchance thee lie withered and old
The winter nights that are so cold,
Plaining in vain unto the moon.
Thy wishes then dare not be told.
Care then who list,[5] for I have done.   30

And then may chance thee to repent
The time that thou hast lost and spent
To cause thy lovers sigh and swoon.
Then shalt thou know beauty but lent,
And wish and want as I have done.   35

Now cease, my lute. This is the last
Labor that thou and I shall waste,
And ended is that we begun.
Now is this song both sung and past;
My lute, be still, for I have done.   40

E. MS.

They Flee from Me

They flee from me, that sometime did me seek,
With naked foot stalking in my chamber.
I have seen them, gentle, tame, and meek,
That now are wild, and do not remember
That sometime they put themselves in danger   5
To take bread at my hand; and now they range,
Busily seeking with a continual change.

Thankéd be fortune it hath been otherwise,
Twenty times better; but once in special,
In thin array, after a pleasant guise,   10
When her loose gown from her shoulders did fall,
And she me caught in her arms long and small,[1]
And therewithall sweetly did me kiss
And softly said, "Dear heart, how like you this?"

It was no dream, I lay broad waking.   15
But all is turned, thorough my gentleness,
Into a strange fashion of forsaking;
And I have leave to go, of her goodness,

4. Unrevenged. "Plain": to complain.   1. Slender.
5. Likes.

And she also to use newfangleness.[2]
But since that I so kindely[3] am servéd,   20
I fain would know what she hath deservéd.

E. MS.

The Lover Showeth How He Is Forsaken
of Such as He Sometime Enjoyed

They flee from me, that sometime did me seek
With naked foot stalking within my chamber.
Once have I seen them gentle, tame, and meek
That now are wild, and do not once remember
That sometime they have put themselves in danger   5
To take bread at my hand, and now they range,
Busily seeking in continual change.

Thankéd be fortune, it hath been otherwise,
Twenty times better; but once especial,
In thin array, after a pleasant guise,   10
When her loose gown did from her shoulders fall,
And she me caught in her arms long and small,
And therewithal, so sweetly did me kiss
And softly said, "Dear heart, how like you this?"

It was no dream, for I lay broad awaking.   15
But all is turned now, through my gentleness,
Into a bitter fashion of forsaking.
And I have leave to go, of her goodness,
An she also to use newfangleness.
But since that I unkindly so am servéd,
How like you this, what hath she now deservéd?   20

Tottel, 1557

Divers Doth Use

Divers doth use, as I have heard and know,
When that to change their ladies do begin,
To mourne and wail, and never for to lin,[4]
Hoping thereby to pease[5] their painful woe.
And some there be, that when it chanceth so   5
That women change and hate where love hath been,
They call them false and think with words to win

2. Fickleness.
3. Naturally, but with an ironic sug-   "kindly."
gestion of the modern meaning of   4. Cease.
                                    5. Appease, relieve.

The hearts of them which otherwhere doth grow.
But as for me, though that by chance indeed
Change hath outworn the favor that I had,   10
I will not wail, lament, nor yet be sad,
Nor call her false that falsely did me feed,
But let it pass, and think it is of kind [6]
That often change doth please a woman's mind.

D. MS.

Tangled I Was in Love's Snare

Tangled I was in love's snare,
Oppressed with pain, torment with care,
Of grief right sure, of joy full bare,
Clean in despair by cruelty—
But ha! ha! ha! full well is me,   5
For I am now at liberty.

The woeful day so full of pain,
The weary night all spent in vain,
The labor lost for so small gain,
To write them all it will not be.   10
But ha! ha! ha! full well is me,
For I am now at liberty.

Everything that fair doth show,
When proof is made it proveth not so,
But turneth mirth to bitter woe;   15
Which in this case full well I see.
But ha! ha! ha! full well is me,
For I am now at liberty.

Too great desire was my guide
And wanton will went by my side;   20
Hope ruléd still, and made me bide
Of love's craft th' extremity.
But ha! ha! ha! full well is me,
For I am now at liberty.

With feignéd words which were but wind   25
To long delays I was assigned;
Her wily looks my wits did blind;
Thus as she would I did agree.
But ha! ha! ha! full well is me,
For I am now at liberty.   30

Was never bird tangled in lime [7]
That brake away in better time

6. Nature.   bark, used to catch small birds.
7. A sticky substance made from holly

Than I, that rotten boughs did climb,
And had no hurt, but 'scapéd free.
Now ha! ha! ha! full well is me,   35
For I am now at liberty.

1557

Lux, My Fair Falcon[8]

Lux, my fair falcon, and your fellows all,
  How well pleasant it were your liberty!
Ye not forsake me that fair might ye befall.
  But they that sometime liked my company,
Like lice away from dead bodies they crawl;   5
  Lo, what a proof in light adversity!
But ye, my birds, I swear by all your bells,
Ye be my friends, and so be but few else.

1557

Mine Own John Poins[1]

Mine own John Poins, since ye delight to know
The cause why that homeward I me draw,
And flee the press of courts, whereso they go,
Rather than to live thrall, under the awe
Of lordly looks, wrapped within my cloak,   5
To will and lust[2] learning to set a law;
It is not for because I scorn and mock
The power of them to whom Fortune hath lent
Charge over us, of right to strike the stroke.[3]
But true it is that I have always meant   10
Less to esteem them than the common sort,
Of outward things that judge in their intent
Without regard what doth inward resort.
I grant sometime that of glory the fire
Doth touch my heart; me list not to report   15
Blame by honor, and honor to desire.[4]
But how may I this honor now attain

That cannot dye the color black a liar?
My Poins, I cannot frame me tune to feign,
To cloak the truth, for praise without desert, 20
Of them that list all vice for to retain.
I cannot honor them that sets their part
With Venus and Bacchus all their life long;[5]
Nor hold my peace of them, although I smart.
I cannot crouch nor kneel to do so great a wrong, 25
To worship them like God on earth alone,
That are as wolves these sely[6] lambs among.
I cannot with my words complain and moan
Nor suffer naught, nor smart without complaint,
Nor turn the word that from my mouth is gone; 30
I cannot speak and look like a saint,

Use wiles for wit, or make deceit a pleasure;
And call craft counsel, for profit still to paint;
I cannot wrest the law to fill the coffer,
With innocent blood to feed myself fat, 35
And do most hurt where most help I offer.
I am not he that can allow the state
Of high Caesar, and damn Cato[7] to die,
That with his death did 'scape out of the gate
From Caesar's hands, if Livy[8] do not lie, 40
And would not live where liberty was lost,
So did his heart the common weal[9] apply.
I am not he, such eloquence to boast
To make the crow in singing as the swan,
Nor call the lion of coward beasts the most, 45
That cannot take a mouse as the cat can;
And he that dieth of hunger of the gold,
Call him Alexander,[1] and say that Pan
Passeth Apollo in music manifold;[2]
Praise Sir Thopas for a noble tale, 50
And scorn the story that the Knight told;[3]
Praise him for counsel that is drunk of ale;
Grin when he laugheth that beareth all the sway,
Frown when he frowneth, and groan when he is pale;
On others' lust to hang both night and day— 55
None of these points would ever frame in me;
My wit is naught: I cannot learn the way;
And much the less of things that greater be
That asken help of colors of device[4]

---

5. I.e., I cannot honor those who devote themselves to Venus (goddess of love-making) and Bacchus (god of drinking).
6. Innocent.
7. Cato the Younger, the famous Roman patriot who committed suicide rather than submit to Caesar.
8. Titus Livius (59 B.C.–A.D. 17), the great Roman historian.
9. The common good, or the state.

1. Alexander yearned for more worlds to conquer.
2. Pan's music was simple and rustic, played on "Pan's pipes."
3. The silly tale of Sir Thopas, in Chaucer's *Canterbury Tales*, is told by Chaucer himself, until the Host forces him to stop. The Knight's Tale is the most courtly and dignified of the tales.
4. Tricks of rhetoric.

To join the mean with each extremity.   60
With nearest virtue to cloak alway the vice,
And as to purpose, likewise it shall fall
To press the virtue that it may not rise;
As drunkenness, good fellowship to call;
The friendly foe, with his double face,   65
Say he is gentle and courteous therewithal;
And say that favel[5] hath a goodly grace
In eloquence; and cruelty to name
Zeal of justice, and change in time and place;
And he that suff'reth offense without blame,   70
Call him pitiful, and him true and plain
That raileth reckless to every man's shame,
Say he is rude that cannot lie and feign,
The lecher a lover, and tyranny
To be the right of a prince's reign.   75
I cannot, I: no, no, it will not be.
This is the cause that I could never yet
Hang on their sleeves, that weigh, as thou mayst see,
A chip of chance more than a pound of wit.
This maketh me at home to hunt and hawk,   80
And in foul weather at my book to sit,
In frost and snow then with my bow to stalk.
No man doth mark whereso I ride or go.
In lusty leas[6] at liberty I walk,
And of these news I feel nor weal nor woe,   85
Save that a clog doth hang yet at my heel.[7]
No force for that, for it is ordered so
That I may leap both hedge and dike full well;
I am not now in France, to judge the wine,
With sav'ry sauce those delicates[8] to feel;   90
Nor yet in Spain, where one must him incline,
Rather than to be, outwardly to seem.
I meddle not with wits that be so fine;
Nor Flanders' cheer[9] letteth not my sight to deem
Of black and white, nor taketh my wit away   95
With beastliness, they beasts do so esteem.
Nor am I not where Christ is given in prey
For money, poison, and treason—at Rome[1]
A common practice, uséd night and day.
But here I am in Kent and Christendom,   100
Among the Muses, where I read and rhyme;
Where, if thou list, my Poins, for to come,
Thou shalt be judge how I do spend my time.

E. MS.

5. Flattery.
6. Pleasant fields.
7. "I feel neither happiness nor un-happiness about current political af-fairs, except that a 'clog' (i.e., his confinement on parole to his estate) keeps me from traveling far." Note that "news" is a plural in Elizabethan English. "No force": no matter.

8. Delicacies.
9. I.e., the drinking for which Flemings were notorious in the 16th century; "letteth": hinders, prevents.
1. In *Tottel's Miscellany*, published in the reign of the Catholic Queen Mary, these lines were altered as follows: "where *truth* is given in prey / For money, poison and treason; *of some*."

HENRY HOWARD, EARL OF SURREY
(1517–1547)

Surrey was the eldest son of the Duke of Norfolk, who was the premier English nobleman and the chief bulwark of the old aristocracy against the rising tide of "new men" and the Reformed religion. Surrey was descended from kings on both sides of his family; he was brought up with Henry VIII's illegitimate son, the Duke of Richmond, who married Surrey's sister. Some stories indicate that Surrey was a proud, high-spirited youth, not above wandering about the streets at night, in the company of Sir Thomas Wyatt's son, using stone-bows to break the windows of sober sleeping citizens. Surrey, like his father and grandfather, was an able soldier, and the Howards were called upon whenever military brilliance was needed. But their fortunes at court depended upon Henry's queens; the Howards were in high favor when Surrey's cousin, Catherine Howard, was queen, but they were low on Fortune's wheel when the queen was Jane Seymour, the mother of the future king.

Surrey's importance as a poet rests upon his continuing the practice of the sonnet in English as instituted by Wyatt and establishing a form for it which was used by Shakespeare and has become known as the "English" sonnet form: three quatrains and a couplet, rhyming *abab cdcd efef gg*. Even more significantly, he was the first English poet to publish in blank verse—unrhymed iambic pentameter—a verse form that has so flourished in the succeeding four centuries that it seems almost indigenous and inevitable to the language. The work in which he used this "strange meter," as the publisher called it, was a translation of part of Virgil's *Aeneid*. Book IV was published in 1554 and Book II in 1557. Surrey was of course a courtier poet, interested in circulating his poems in manuscript rather than in printing them, but he did publish a poetic tribute to Wyatt. The bulk of his poetry first appeared in *Tottel's Miscellany*.

Surrey shows a more regular maintenance of normal accent than Wyatt, and he is often more fluent and musical. His poetic diction is clear and consistent, and in many ways Surrey indicates the direction in which the main stream of English verse will flow. Yet he often seems less vivid and vigorous than Wyatt, and he perhaps takes the figurative language he uses less seriously.

Love, That Doth Reign and Live Within My Thought[1]

Love, that doth reign and live within my thought,
And built his seat within my captive breast,
Clad in the arms wherein with me he fought,
Oft in my face he doth his banner rest.

---

1. Compare this version of Petrarch's *Sonnetto in Vita* 91 with Wyatt's translation of the same original (*The Long* *Love That in My Thought Doth Harbor*, printed earlier in this anthology).

But she that taught me love and suffer pain,   5
My doubtful hope and eke[2] my hot desire
With shamefast look to shadow and refrain,
Her smiling grace converteth straight to ire.
And coward Love, then, to the heart apace
Taketh his flight, where he doth lurk and plain,[3]   10
His purpose lost, and dare not show his face.
For my lord's guilt thus faultless bide I pain,
Yet from my lord shall not my foot remove:
Sweet is the death that taketh end by love.

1557

The Soote Season[4]

The soote season, that bud and bloom forth brings,
With green hath clad the hill and eke the vale;
The nightingale with feathers new she sings;
The turtle to her make[5] hath told her tale.
Summer is come, for every spray now springs;   5
The hart hath hung his old head on the pale;
The buck in brake his winter coat he flings,
The fishes float with new repairéd scale;
The adder all her slough away she slings,
The swift swallow pursueth the fliés small;   10
The busy bee her honey now she mings.[6]
Winter is worn, that was the flowers' bale.[7]
And thus I see among these pleasant things,
Each care decays, and yet my sorrow springs.

1557

Alas! So All Things Now Do Hold Their Peace[7a]

Alas! so all things now do hold their peace,
Heaven and earth disturbéd in no thing;
The beasts, the air, the birds their song do cease,
The nightés chare[8] the stars about doth bring.
Calm is the sea, the waves work less and less;   5
So am not I, whom love, alas, doth wring,
Bringing before my face the great increase
Of my desires, whereat I weep and sing,
In joy and woe, as in a doubtful ease.

2. Also; "shamefast": modest.
3. Complain.
4. In this adaptation from Petrarch's *Sonnetto in Morte* 42, Surrey has changed the details of nature from Italian to English. Note that the sonnet has only two rhymes. "Soote":

sweet. fragrant.
5. Turtledove to her mate.
6. Mingles.
7. Harm.
7a. Translated from Petrarch's *Sonnetto in Vita* 113.
8. From Italian *carro* (the Great Bear).

For my sweet thoughts sometime do pleasure bring,   10
But by and by the cause of my disease[9]
Gives me a pang that inwardly doth sting,
When that I think what grief it is again
To live and lack the thing should rid my pain.

1557

Give Place, Ye Lovers, Here Before

Give place, ye lovers, here before
That spent your boasts and brags in vain;
My lady's beauty passeth more
The best of yours, I dare well sayn [1]
Than doth the sun the candlelight,   5
Or brightest day the darkest night,

And thereto hath a troth as just [2]
As had Penelope the fair,
For what she saith, ye may it trust
As it by writing sealéd were,   10
And virtues hath she many moe
Than I with pen have skill to show.

I could rehearse, if that I wold,[3]
The whole effect of Nature's plaint,
When she had lost the perfect mold   15
The like to whom she could not paint;
With wringing hands how she did cry
And what she said, I know it, I.

I know she swore, with raging mind,
Her kingdom only set apart,   20
There was no loss, by law of kind,[4]
That could have gone so near her heart;
And this was chiefly all her pain:
She could not make the like again.

Sith [5] nature thus gave her the praise   25
To be the chiefest work she wrought,
In faith, methinks some better ways
On your behalf might well be sought
Than to compare, as ye have done,
To match the candle with the sun.   30

1557

---

9. Dis-ease, i.e., discomfort.   3. Would.
1. Say.   4. Nature.
2. Constancy as firm.   5. Since.

My Friend, the Things That Do Attain[6]

My friend, the things that do attain
The happy life be these, I find:
The riches left, not got with pain;
The fruitful ground; the quiet mind;

The equal friend; no grudge, no strife;   5
No charge of rule, nor governance;
Without disease, the healthy life;
The household of continuance;

The mean diet, no dainty fare;
Wisdom joined with simpleness;   10
The night dischargéd of all care,
Where wine the wit may not oppress:

The faithful wife, without debate;
Such sleeps as may beguile the night;
Content thyself with thine estate,   15
Neither wish death, nor fear his might.

1547

6. A translation of an epigram by the Latin poet Martial (X.47). The theme, a glorification of "the mean estate," is very common in Elizabethan literature.

From The Fourth Book of Virgil[1]

ENTREATING OF THE LOVE BETWEEN AENEAS AND DIDO, TRANSLATED
INTO ENGLISH AND DRAWN INTO A STRANGE METER BY HENRY LATE
EARL OF SURREY, WORTHY TO BE EMBRACED

[The Hunt]

Then from the seas the dawning gan arise.
The sun once up, the chosen youth gan throng
Unto the gates; the hayes[2] so rarely knit,
The hunting staves with their broad heads of steel,
And of Massile[3] the horsemen, forth they brake;   5
Of scenting hounds a kennel huge likewise.
And at the threshold of her chamber door
The Carthage lords did there the queen await;
The trampling steed, with gold and purple decked,
Chawing the foamy bit, there fiercely stood.   10
Then issued she, backed with a great rout,[4]

1. These are lines 129–68 in Virgil.
2. Nets.
3. Massilia (Marseilles).
4. Band, troop.

Clad in a cloak of Tyre embroidered rich.
Her quiver hung behind her back, her tresses
Wound up with gold, her purple vestures eke
Buttoned with gold. The Troyans of her train   15
Before her go, with gladsome Iulus.[5]
Aeneas eke, the goodliest of the rout,
Makes one of them and joineth close the throngs;
Like when Apollo leaveth Lycia,
His wintering place, and Xanthus' floods likewise,[6]   20
To visit Delos, his mother's mansion,
For to repair and furnish new her choir,
The Candians and folk of Driopis,
And painted Agathyrsies shout and cry,[7]
Environing the altars round about,   25
When he walks upon Mount Cynthus' top,[8]
His sparkled tresses he pressed with garlands soft
Of tender leaves, and trusséd up in gold,
His quivering darts clattering behind his back—
So fresh and lusty did Aeneas seem,   30
Such lordly port in countenance present.
     But to the hills and wild holts[9] when they came,
From the rock's top then driven, savage roes
Avail[1] the hill, above to the other side,
Through the wide lands, whereas their course,   35
The harts likewise, in troops taking their flight,
Raising the dust, the mountains fast forsake.
The child Iulus, blithe of his swift steed,
Amidst the plain now pricks by them, now these,
And to encounter wisheth oft in mind   40
The foaming boar, instead of timorous beasts,
Or lion brown might from the hill descend.
     In the meanwhile the heavens gan rumble sore;
In tail thereof, a mingled shower with hail.
The Tyrian folk and eke the Troyan youth   45
And Venus' nephew the cottages for fear
Sought round about; the floods fell from the hills.
Dido, a den, the Troyan prince likewise
Chanced upon. Our mother then, the Earth,
And Juno that hath charge of marriage,   50
First tokens gave with burning gledes[2] of flame,
And, privy to the wedlock, lightning skies,
And the nymphs wailed from the mountain's top.

                                                           1554

---

5. Son of Aeneas.
6. Lycia is a country on the south coast of Asia Minor; Xanthus, the chief river of Lycia. Delos, an island, was Apollo's birthplace.
7. "Candians": Cretans. "Driopis" is Doris, in Greece; the "Agathyrsies" were tattooed people from Transylvania.
8. A mountain in Delos, where both Apollo and Artemis were born.
9. Woods.
1. Gain.
2. Coals, embers.

SIR PHILIP SIDNEY
(1554–1586)

Sir Philip Sidney—courtier, soldier, scholar, poet, friend, and patron—seemed to the Elizabethans to embody all the traits of character and personality they admired: he was Castiglione's *Il Cortegiano* come to life. When he was killed in battle in the Low Countries at the age of 32, all England mourned.

He was the son of Sir Henry Sidney, thrice Lord Deputy of Ireland, and of a sister of Robert Dudley, Earl of Leicester, the most spectacular and powerful of all the queen's subjects. He entered Shrewsbury School in 1564, at the age of 10, on the same day as Fulke Greville, who became his lifelong friend and biographer. Greville said of Sidney, "though I lived with him and knew him from a child, yet I never knew him other than a man—with such staidness of mind, lovely and familiar gravity, as carried grace and reverence above greater years." Although he attended Oxford, he left without taking a degree. His education was completed by extended travels on the Continent, where he had opportunities to meet the most important men of the time and to be witness to such crucial events as the Massacre of St. Bartholomew's Day, August 23, 1572. Sidney's family background and education were Protestant, but this slaughter of the French Huguenots undoubtedly strengthened his Protestant sympathies. Another important influence was his friendship with the scholar-diplomat Hubert Languet.

On his return to England he lived the life of a prominent courtier, serving occasionally on diplomatic missions and actively encouraging literary men such as Edward Dyer, Fulke Greville, and, most importantly, the young Edmund Spenser, who dedicated *The Shepheardes Calender* to him as "the president of noblesse and of chevalree." So strong were Sidney's Protestant convictions that he incurred the queen's displeasure by opposing her projected marriage to the Duke of Anjou; this led to his dismissal from court for a time. He retired to Wilton, the estate of his beloved sister Mary, Countess of Pembroke, and there he wrote, at her request and for her entertainment, a pastoral romance called *Arcadia*.

Sidney's romance exists in two forms, called the "Old Arcadia" and the "New Arcadia." The "New Arcadia" was published in fragmentary form, almost three books, in 1590. In 1593 the Countess of Pembroke republished it with slight changes and added the last three books of the "Old Arcadia," but the first three books of the earlier version remained in manuscript until the 20th century. As William Ringler says, "The *Arcadia*, in both its old and new forms, is the most important original work of English prose fiction produced before the 18th century." The romance's complicated plot is full of oracles, disguisings, mistaken identity, melodramatic incidents and tangled love situations. Some episodes are of political interest, and Sidney clearly put more of his serious thought on statecraft into it than he pretends when he describes the book as mere entertainment. The *Arcadia* also contains many poems—eclogues and songs which are interspersed throughout the narrative; they represent Sidney's experimental and exploratory ventures into verse. A good example is the double sestina, "Ye Goatherd Gods."

In 1579, the same year in which he dedicated *The Shepheardes Calender* to Sidney, Spenser wrote to his friend Gabriel Harvey, "New books I hear of none but only of one that writing a certain book called *The School of Abuse*, and dedicating it to Master Sidney, was for his labor scorned, if at least it be in the goodness of that nature to scorn." The book referred to was by Stephen Gosson; it was an attack upon poets and players from a narrowly Puritan point of view. Sidney did not specifically answer Gosson's attack, but he must have had it in mind when he composed, at some uncertain date, a major piece of critical prose which was published after his death under the titles *The Defense of Poesy* and *An Apology for Poetry*. In this long essay Sidney systematically defends poetry (indeed all imaginative literature) against its attackers. He points out the antiquity of poetry, and its prestige in the ancient world. He establishes its universality. He cites the names given to poets by the Romans (*vates* or prophet) and the Greeks (*poietes* or maker) to indicate their ancient dignity. But, he says, the real defense of the poet depends not upon what he has been but upon what he does. All arts depend upon works of nature, but the poet, supreme among artists, can make another nature, new and more beautiful. "Nature never set forth the earth in so rich tapestry as divers poets have done, neither with pleasant rivers, fruitful trees, sweet-smelling flowers, nor whatsoever else may make the too much loved earth more lovely." Moreover, the poet presents virtues and vices in a more lively and telling way than nature does; his function is to teach and delight at the same time. He is superior to the philosopher and the historian, because he is more concrete than the one and more universal than the other. Sidney shows himself to be a thorough student of Aristotle when he explains poetry as an art of imitation in which the artist imitates not merely what is, but also what might be. He refutes the charge that poets are liars by stating that "the poet nothing affirmeth," and he maintains that poetry does not abuse man's wits by arousing base desires but that man's wits abuse poetry. Then Sidney surveys the English literary scene as it looked to him. He found little to praise: Surrey's lyrics, the *Mirror for Magistrates*, Spenser's *Shepheardes Calender* (though he disliked Spenser's use of antique language). The drama was generally bad (he was writing before the great achievements of the Elizabethans), and its failure to observe the classical unities of time and place was, for Sidney, a particular weakness. He concludes by a general defense of English as a language suitable for poetry and a humorous defiance of those who will not be converted by his defense. Despite the seriousness and logical rigor of Sidney's essay, it has many delightful personal touches. His manner is graceful and easy; it exhibits that *sprezzatura*, or casualness in doing something difficult perfectly, which Castiglione had held up as an ideal in *The Courtier*.

Sidney's *Astrophel and Stella* ("Starlover and Star") is the first of the great Elizabethan sonnet cycles. These collections, imitative of Petrarch or of his French imitators, were based upon a well-understood convention. The poet undertook to display all the contrary feelings of a lover—hope and despair, tenderness and bitterness, exultation and modesty, by the use of "conceits" or ingenious comparisons. Many of these became traditional, and eventually, stale: the poet who complained that in love he both burned and froze, or that his sighs were the winds driving his ship on a tossing sea, was echoing many an earlier poet. So Sidney protests, in the role of Astrophel, that he uses no standard conventional phrases; his verse is original and comes from the heart. (This pretense is also conventional.) But what gives Sidney's sonnets their extraordinary vigor and freshness is Sidney's ability to dramatize. He uses dialogue, is often colloquial, and he heightens the situation as much as he can within the fourteen lines.

The sonnet cycle has a framework of plot, but it does not tell a story. Yet there is a rather mysterious story hinted at in Sidney's cycle, and some of these hints point to what may be an actual episode in the poet's life. Penelope Devereux, Lady Rich, is supposed to be the original of Stella, and some of the sonnets contain puns on the name "Rich." On the other hand, Stella is virtuous in the sonnets, and refuses Astrophel anything more than a kiss, whereas the historical Penelope Devereux was apparently a different kind of woman. But there is little profit in speculating on the events behind an Elizabethan sonnet cycle; as Sidney said in his *Apology,* "the poet nothing affirmeth."

Sidney called poetry his "unelected vocation," and he did not publish it himself. His view of himself was probably more that of patron than of artist. Yet his achievement as the author of the most important work of prose fiction in his age, the most important piece of literary criticism, and the most important sonnet cycle surely qualify him as a major author. The texts here printed have been reviewed against those in William Ringler's newly authoritative edition, *The Poems of Sir Philip Sidney* (1962).

Ye Goatherd Gods[1]

STREPHON. Ye goatherd gods, that love the grassy mountains,
Ye nymphs which haunt the springs in pleasant valleys,
Ye satyrs joyed with free and quiet forests,
Vouchsafe your silent ears to plaining music,
Which to my woes gives still an early morning, 5
And draws the dolor on till weary evening.

KLAIUS. O Mercury,[2] foregoer to the evening,
O heavenly huntress of the savage mountains,
O lovely star, entitled of the morning,
While that my voice doth fill these woeful valleys, 10

1. From Sidney's pastoral-heroic romance, the *Arcadia.* The poem is a dialogue between two shepherds, Strephon and Klaius, both of whom are in love with the absent Urania. Sidney, of course, knew no shepherds like this: the figures and the landscape in the poem belong to the pastoral tradition of an elegant idealized country life—usually Greek.

The form of the poem is basically that of the sestina, which has six-line stanzas and a final triplet of three lines; the terminal words of each stanza are the same, but rearranged according to a definite pattern, and all six terminal words must appear in the final triplet. Sestinas usually have six stanzas, but Sidney has here created a double sestina, of twelve stanzas. The *Arcadia* has about eighty interpolated poems, some of them ingenious metrical experiments like this one.

2. The evening star. The "huntress" is Diana, the moon; the "lovely star" is Lucifer, the morning star.

Vouchsafe your silent ears to plaining music,
Which oft hath Echo tired in secret forests.

STREPHON. I, that was once free burgess[3] of the forests,
Where shade from sun, and sport I sought in evening,
I, that was once esteemed for pleasant music, 15
Am banished now among the monstrous mountains
Of huge despair, and foul affliction's valleys,
Am grown a screech owl to myself each morning.

KLAIUS. I, that was once delighted every morning,
Hunting the wild inhabiters of forests, 20
I, that was once the music of these valleys,
So darkened am that all my day is evening,
Heartbroken so that molehills seem high mountains
And fill the vales with cries instead of music.

STREPHON. Long since, alas, my deadly swannish[4] music 25
Hath made itself a crier of the morning,
And hath with wailing strength climbed highest mountains;
Long since my thoughts more desert be than forests,
Long since I see my joys come to their evening,
And state[5] thrown down to overtrodden valleys. 30

KLAIUS. Long since the happy dwellers of these valleys
Have prayed me leave my strange exclaiming music
Which troubles their day's work and joys of evening;
Long since I hate the night, more hate the morning;
Long since my thoughts chase me like beasts in forests 35
And make me wish myself laid under mountains.

STREPHON. Meseems I see the high and stately mountains
Transform themselves to low dejected valleys;
Meseems I hear in these ill-changéd forests
The nightingales do learn of owls their music; 40
Meseems I feel the comfort of the morning
Turned to the mortal serene[6] of an evening.

KLAIUS. Meseems I see a filthy cloudy evening
As soon as sun begins to climb the mountains;
Meseems I feel a noisome[7] scent, the morning 45
When I do smell the flowers of these valleys;
Meseems I hear, when I do hear sweet music,
The dreadful cries of murdered men in forests.

STREPHON. I wish to fire the trees of all those forests;
I give the sun a last farewell each evening; 50
I curse the fiddling finders-out of music;

3. Citizen.
4. Doleful, like the song supposedly sung by the swan just before its death.
5. High position.
6. Deadly dew.
7. Stinking. "The morning": i.e., in the morning.

With envy I do hate the lofty mountains
And with despite despise the humble valleys;
I do detest night, evening, day, and morning.

KLAIUS.   Curse to myself my prayer is, the morning;   55
My fire is more than can be made with forests,
My state more base than are the basest valleys.
I wish no evenings more to see, each evening;
Shaméd, I hate myself in sight of mountains
And stop mine ears, lest I grow mad with music.   60

STREPHON.   For she whose parts maintained a perfect music,
Whose beauties shined more than the blushing morning,
Who much did pass[8] in state the stately mountains,
In straightness passed the cedars of the forests,
Hath cast me, wretch, into eternal evening   65
By taking her two suns from these dark valleys.

KLAIUS.   For she, to whom compared, the Alps are valleys,
She, whose least word brings from the spheres their music,
At whose approach the sun rose in the evening,
Who where she went bare[9] in her forehead morning,   70
Is gone, is gone, from these our spoiléd forests,
Turning to deserts our best pastured mountains.

STREPHON.   These mountains witness shall, so shall these valleys,
These forests eke, made wretched by our music,

KLAIUS.   Our morning hymn is this, and song at evening.   75
1577–1580   1593

Thou Blind Man's Mark

Thou blind man's mark,[1] thou fool's self-chosen snare,
Fond fancy's scum, and dregs of scattered thought;
Band [2] of all evils, cradle of causeless care;
Thou web of will, whose end is never wrought;
Desire, desire! I have too dearly bought,   5
With price of mangled mind, thy worthless ware;
Too long, too long, asleep thou hast me brought,
Who should my mind to higher things prepare.
But yet in vain thou hast my ruin sought;
In vain thou madest me to vain things aspire;   10
In vain thou kindlest all thy smoky fire;
For virtue hath this better lesson taught—
Within myself to seek my only hire,
Desiring naught but how to kill desire.

1581   1598

8. Surpass.   1. Target.
9. Bore.   2. Swaddling band.

Leave Me, O Love

Leave me, O love which reachest but to dust;
And thou, my mind, aspire to higher things;
Grow rich in that which never taketh rust,
Whatever fades but fading pleasure brings.
Draw in thy beams, and humble all thy might   5
To that sweet yoke where lasting freedoms be;
Which breaks the clouds and opens forth the light,
That doth both shine and give us sight to see.
O take fast hold; let that light be thy guide
In this small course which birth draws out to death,   10
And think how evil becometh him to slide,
Who seeketh heav'n, and comes of heav'nly breath.[3]
Then farewell, world; thy uttermost I see;
Eternal Love, maintain thy life in me.

1581   1598

The Nightingale

The nightingale, as soon as April bringeth[1]
Unto her rested sense a perfect waking,
(While late bare earth, proud of new clothing, springeth),
Sings out her woes, a thorn her song-book making,
And mournfully bewailing,   5
Her throat in tunes expresseth
What grief her breast oppresseth
For Tereus' force on her chaste will prevailing.
O Philomela fair, O take some gladness,
That here is juster cause of plaintful sadness: 10
Thine earth now springs, mine fadeth;
Thy thorn without, my thorn my heart invadeth.

Alas, she hath no other cause of anguish
But Tereus' love, on her by strong hand wroken,[2]
Wherein she suffering, all her spirits languish;   15
Full womanlike complains her will was broken.
But I, who daily craving,
Cannot have to content me,
Have more cause to lament me,
Since wanting is more woe than too much having.   20
O Philomela fair, O take some gladness,

---

3. I.e., and think how evil it is for one who is seeking heaven and has a divine spirit or soul in him to descend to earthly things.
1. The nightingale sings in England for only a few weeks after its return from winter quarters in the south. Mythology has it that while singing "she" presses her breast against a thorn, to remind her of the bitter pain suffered when, as Philomela, she was raped by her brother-in-law King Tereus, and had her tongue torn out.
2. Inflicted.

That here is juster cause of plaintful sadness:
Thine earth now springs, mine fadeth;
Thy thorn without, my thorn my heart invadeth.

1581   1598

Ring Out Your Bells

Ring out your bells, let mourning shows be spread;
For Love is dead—
All Love is dead, infected
With plague of deep disdain;
Worth, as naught worth, rejected,   5
And Faith fair scorn doth gain.
From so ungrateful fancy,
From such a female franzy,
From them that use men thus,
Good Lord, deliver us![1]   10

Weep, neighbors, weep; do you not hear it said
That Love is dead?
His deathbed, peacock's folly;
His winding sheet is shame;
His will, false-seeming holy;   15
His sole exec'tor, blame.
From so ungrateful, &c.

Let dirge be sung and trentals[2] rightly read,
For Love is dead;
Sir Wrong his tomb ordaineth   20
My mistress Marble-heart,
Which epitaph containeth,
"Her eyes were once his dart."
From so ungrateful, &c.

Alas, I lie, rage[3] hath this error bred;   25
Love is not dead;
Love is not dead, but sleepeth
In her unmatchéd mind,
Where she his counsel keepeth,
Till due desert she find.   30
Therefore from so vile fancy,
To call such wit a franzy,
Who Love can temper thus,
Good Lord, deliver us!

1598

1. The funeral of Love is celebrated with a tolling of bells, a hanging of black crape "shows," and a refrain from Litany. "Franzy": frenzy.

2. A service for the dead consisting of thirty masses.
3. Madness.

From Astrophel and Stella[1]

1

Loving in truth, and fain [2] in verse my love to show,
That the dear she might take some pleasure of my pain,
Pleasure might cause her read, reading might make her know,
Knowledge might pity win, and pity grace obtain,
I sought fit words to paint the blackest face of woe: 5
Studying inventions fine, her wits to entertain,
Oft turning others' leaves, to see if thence would flow
Some fresh and fruitful showers upon my sunburnt brain.
But words came halting[3] forth, wanting Invention's stay;
Invention, Nature's child, fled stepdame Study's blows;   10
And others' feet still seemed but strangers in my way.
Thus, great with child to speak, and helpless in my throes,
Biting my truant pen, beating myself for spite:
"Fool," said my Muse to me, "look in thy heart, and write!"

5

It is most true that eyes are formed to serve
The inward light,[4] and that the heavenly part
Ought to be king, from whose rules who do swerve,
Rebels to nature, strive for their own smart.
It is most true, what we call Cupid's dart   5
An image is, which for ourelves we carve,
And, fools, adore in temple of our heart,
Till that good god make church and churchman starve.
True, that true beauty virtue is indeed,
Whereof this beauty can be but a shade,   10
Which elements with mortal mixture breed.[5]
True, that on earth we are but pilgrims made,
And should in soul up to our country move.
True, and yet true that I must Stella love.

6

Some lovers speak, when they their Muses entertain,
Of hopes begot by fear, of wot[6] not what desires,
Of force of heavenly beams infusing hellish pain,
Of living deaths, dear wounds, fair storms, and freezing fires;
Someone his song in Jove and Jove's strange tales attires,   5
Bordered with bulls and swans, powdered with golden rain;[7]

1. The first sonnet is one of six in the cycle that are written in hexameters.
2. Desirous.
3. Limping. "Stay": crutch, support.
4. I.e., the soul. The concessions made in the argument of this sonnet are to Platonic and Christian doctrines as opposed to romantic love.
5. This beauty is a mixture of the four elements (earth, air, water, fire) and as such is mortal. According to Platonic doctrine the only true beauty (identical with virtue) is a divine idea or essence and is immortal.
6. Know.
7. In classical mythology Jove courted Europa in the shape of a bull, Leda as a swan, and Danaë as a golden shower.

Another humbler wit to shepherd's pipe[8] retires,
Yet hiding royal blood full oft in rural vein.
To some a sweetest plaint a sweetest style affords,
While tears pour out his ink, and sighs breathe out his words, 10
His paper pale despair, and pain his pen doth move.
I can speak what I feel, and feel as much as they,[9]
But think that all the map of my state I display
When trembling voice brings forth, that I do Stella love.

10

Reason, in faith thou art well served, that still
Wouldst brabbling [1] be with sense and love in me;
I rather wished thee climb the Muses' hill,
Or reach the fruit of nature's choicest tree,
Or seek heaven's course, or heaven's inside to see.   5
Why shouldst thou toil our thorny soil to till?
Leave sense, and those which sense's objects be;
Deal thou with powers of thoughts; leave love to will.
But thou wouldst needs fight both with love and sense,
With sword of wit, giving wounds of dispraise,   10
Till downright blows did foil thy cunning fence; [2]
For soon as they strake thee with Stella's rays,
Reason, thou kneel'dst, and offeredst straight to prove
By reason good, good reason her to love.

18

With what sharp checks I in myself am shent,[3]
When into Reason's audit I do go,
And by just counts myself a banckrout [4] know
Of all those goods, which heaven to me hath lent;
Unable quite to pay even Nature's rent,   5
Which unto it by birthright I do owe;
And which is worse, no good excuse can show,
But that my wealth I have most idly spent.
My youth doth waste, my knowledge brings forth toys,[5]
My wit doth strive those passions to defend,   10
Which for reward spoil it with vain annoys.
I see my course to lose myself doth bend:
I see and yet no greater sorrow take,
Then that I lose no more for Stella's sake.

21

Your words, my friend, right healthful caustics, blame
My young mind marred, whom Love doth windlass [6] so,

That mine own writings like bad servants show
My wits, quick in vain thoughts, in virtue lame;
That Plato I read for nought, but if he tame   5
Such coltish gyres,[7] that to my birth I owe
Nobler desires, lest else that friendly foe,
Great expectation, wear a train of shame.
For since mad March great promise made of me,
If now the May of my years much decline,   10
What can be hoped my harvest time will be?
Sure you say well; your wisdom's golden mine
Dig deep with learning's spade; now tell me this,
Hath this world ought so fair as Stella is?

31

With how sad steps, Oh Moon, thou climb'st the skies!
How silently, and with how wan a face!
What, may it be that even in heavenly place
That busy archer [8] his sharp arrows tries?
Sure, if that long-with-love-acquainted eyes   5
Can judge of love, thou feel'st a lover's case,
I read it in thy looks; thy languished grace,
To me, that feel the like, thy state descries.
Then, even of fellowship, Oh Moon, tell me,
Is constant love deemed there but want of wit?   10
Are beauties there as proud as here they be?
Do they above love to be loved, and yet
Those lovers scorn whom that love doth possess?
Do they call virtue there ungratefulness? [9]

39

Come sleep! Oh sleep, the certain knot of peace,
The baiting place [1] of wit, the balm of woe,
The poor man's wealth, the prisoner's release,
The indifferent judge between the high and low;
With shield of proof [2] shield me from out the prease   5
Of those fierce darts Despair at me doth throw;
Oh make in me those civil wars to cease;
I will good tribute pay, if thou do so.
Take thou of me smooth pillows, sweetest bed,
A chamber deaf to noise and blind to light,   10
A rosy garland and a weary head;
And if these things, as being thine by right,
Move not thy heavy grace, thou shalt in me,
Livelier than elsewhere, Stella's image see.

41

Having this day my horse, my hand, my lance
Guided so well that I obtained the prize,[3]

---

7. Youthful gyrations.
8. Cupid.
9. I.e., do they call ungratefulness virtue there (as they do here)?
1. A place for refreshment on a journey.

2. Proven strength. "Prease": press, crowd.
3. At an actual tournament in the summer of 1581.

Both by the judgment of the English eyes
And of some sent from that sweet enemy, France,
Horsemen my skill in horsemanship advance,   5
Town-folks my strength; a daintier judge applies
His praise to sleight which from good use [4] doth rise;
Some lucky wits impute it but to chance;
Others, because of both sides I do take
My blood from them who did excel in this,[5]   10
Think nature me a man-at-arms did make.
How far they shoot awry! The true cause is,
Stella looked on, and from her heavenly face
Sent forth the beams which made so fair my race.

64

No more, my dear, no more these counsels try;
Oh, give my passions leave to run their race;
Let Fortune lay on me her worst disgrace;
Let folk o'ercharged with brain against me cry;
Let clouds bedim my face, break in mine eye;   5
Let me no steps but of lost labor trace;
Let all the earth with scorn recount my case;
But do not will me from my Love to flie.
I do not envy Aristotle's wit,[6]
Nor do aspire to Caesar's bleeding fame,   10
Nor ought do care, though some above me sit,
Nor hope nor wish another course to frame,
But that which once may win thy cruel heart:
Thou art my wit, and thou my virtue art.

71

Who will in fairest book of Nature know,
How Virtue may best lodged in beauty be,
Let him but learn of Love to read in thee,
Stella, whose fair lines, which true goodness show.
There shall he find all vices' overthrow,   5
Not by rude force, but sweetest sovereignty
Of reason, from whose light those night birds [7] fly;
That inward sun in thine eyes shineth so.
And not content to be Perfection's heir
Thyself, dost strive all minds that way to move,   10
Who mark in thee what is in thee most fair.
So while thy beauty draws the heart to love,
As fast thy Virtue bends that love to good:
"But ah," desire still cries, "give me some food."

74

I never drank of Aganippe well,
Nor ever did in shade of Tempe sit,[8]

4. Cleverness which from experience.
5. I.e., because my ancestors on both sides were distinguished in the tournament.
6. Wisdom.
7. Night birds, like owls, conventionally symbolized vices.
8. Aganippe: a well at the foot of Mt. Helicon in Greece, sacred to the Muses; Tempe: a valley beside Mt. Olympus, sacred to Apollo, the god of song.

And Muses scorn with vulgar brains to dwell;
Poor layman I, for sacred rites unfit.
Some do I hear of poets' fury tell,   5
But, God wot, wot not what they mean by it;
And this I swear by blackest brook of hell,[9]
I am no pick-purse of another's wit.
How falls it then that with so smooth an ease
My thoughts I speak; and what I speak doth flow   10
In verse, and that my verse best wits doth please?
Guess we the cause. What, is it thus? Fie, no.
Or so? Much less. How then? Sure thus it is:
My lips are sweet, inspired with Stella's kiss.

1582   1591

Fourth Song[1]

Only joy, now here you are,
Fit to hear and ease my care;
Let my whispering voice obtain
Sweet reward for sharpest pain;
Take me to thee, and thee to me.   5
"No, no, no, no, my dear, let be."

Night hath closed all in her cloak,
Twinkling stars love-thoughts pro-
            voke,
Danger hence good care doth keep,
Jealousy itself doth sleep;   10
Take me to thee, and thee to me.
"No, no, no, no, my dear, let be."

Better place no wit can find,
Cupid's yoke to loose or bind;
These sweet flowers on fine bed too,   15
Us in their best language woo;
Take me to thee, and thee to me.
"No, no, no, no, my dear, let be."

This small light the moon bestows
Serves thy beams but to disclose;   20
So to raise my hap more high,
Fear not else, none can us spy;
Take me to thee, and thee to me.
"No, no, no, no, my dear, let be."

That you heard was but a mouse,   25
Dumb sleep holdeth all the house;
Yet asleep, methinks they say,

---

9. The river Styx.
1. One of a number of songs that appear among *Astrophel and Stella* sonnets in the Folio edition of 1598; this one comes between Sonnets 85 and 86.

Young folks, take time while you
    may;
Take me to thee, and thee to me.
"No, no, no, no, my dear, let be."   30

Niggard time threats, if we miss
This large offer of our bliss,
Long stay ere he grant the same;
Sweet, then, while each thing doth
    frame,
Take me to thee, and thee to me.   35
"No, no, no, no, my dear, let be."

Your fair mother is abed,
Candles out and curtains spread;
She thinks you do letters write;
Write, but let me first endite;   40
Take me to thee, and thee to me.
"No, no, no, no, my dear, let be."

Sweet, alas, why strive you thus?
Concord better fitteth us;
Leave to Mars the force of hands,   45
Your power in your beauty stands;
Take me to thee, and thee to me.
"No, no, no, no, my dear, let be."

Woe to me, and do you swear
Me to hate? but I forbear;   50
Cursed be my destines all,
That brought me so high to fall;
Soon with my death I will please
    thee.
"No, no, no, no, my dear, let be."

1591, 1598

From An Apology for Poetry

* * * There is no art delivered to mankind that hath not the works of nature for his principal object, without which they could not consist, and on which they so depend, as they become actors and players, as it were, of what nature will have set forth. So doth the astronomer look upon the stars, and, by that he seeth, setteth down what order nature hath taken therein.[1] So do the geometrician and arithmetician in their diverse sorts of quantities. So doth the musician in times tell you which by nature agree,[2] which not. The

1. I.e., according to that which he sees, he sets down what arrangements nature has made.   2. Which musical measures fit together naturally.

natural philosopher thereon[3] hath his name, and the moral philosopher standeth upon the natural virtues, vices, and passions of man; and "follow nature," saith he, "therein, and thou shalt not err." The lawyer saith what men have determined; the historian what men have done. The grammarian speaketh only of the rules of speech; and the rhetorician and logician, considering what in nature will soonest prove and persuade, thereon give artificial rules, which still are compassed within the circle of a question according to the proposed matter.[4] The physician weigheth the nature of a man's body, and the nature of things helpful or hurtful unto it. And the metaphysic, though it be in the second and abstract notions, and therefore be counted supernatural, yet doth he indeed build upon the depth of nature. Only the poet, disdaining to be tied to any such subjection, lifted up with the vigor of his own invention, doth grow in effect another nature, in making things either better than nature bringeth forth, or, quite anew, forms such as never were in nature, as the Heroes,[5] Demigods, Cyclops, Chimeras, Furies, and such like: so as he goeth hand in hand with nature, not enclosed within the narrow warrant of her gifts, but freely ranging only within the zodiac of his own wit.

Nature never set forth the earth in so rich tapestry as divers poets have done—neither with pleasant rivers, fruitful trees, sweet-smelling flowers, nor whatsoever else may make the too much loved earth more lovely. Her[6] world is brazen, the poets only deliver a golden. But let those things alone, and go to man—for whom as the other things are, so it seemeth in him her uttermost cunning is employed—and know whether she have brought forth so true a lover as Theagenes, so constant a friend as Pylades, so valiant a man as Orlando, so right a prince as Xenophon's Cyrus,[7] so excellent a man every way as Virgil's Aeneas. Neither let this be jestingly conceived, because the works of the one be essential, the other in imitation or fiction; for any understanding knoweth the skill of the artificer standeth in that idea or foreconceit of the work, and not in the work itself. And that the poet hath that idea is manifest, by delivering them forth in such excellency as he hath imagined them. Which delivering forth also is not wholly imaginative, as we are wont to say by them that build castles in the air: but so far

3. I.e., from studying nature; the "natural philosopher" is what we would call a scientist. "Standeth upon": takes as his subject matter.

4. I.e., which apply only to the particular situation for which the rule was devised. "Weigheth": studies, considers.

5. Sidney uses the word in its Greek sense, meaning a deified man; "Cyclops": one-eyed giants in Homer's *Odyssey*; "Chimeras": fire-breathing monsters, with lion's head, goat's body, and serpent's tail.

6. I.e., nature's. "Brazen": a reference to the traditional idea that the first age of man was the Golden Age, and that deterioration then followed through the Silver Age and the Brazen Age down to the present Iron Age.

7. Theagenes: hero of Heliodorus' Greek romance *Aethiopica;* Pylades was the constant friend of the Greek hero Orestes; Orlando: hero of Ariosto's *Orlando Furioso;* Cyrus: hero of Xenophon's *Cyropaedia.*

substantially it worketh, not only to make a Cyrus, which had been but a particular excellency, as nature might have done, but to bestow a Cyrus upon the world, to make many Cyruses, if they will learn aright why and how that maker made him.

Neither let it be deemed too saucy a comparison to balance the highest point of man's wit with the efficacy of nature; but rather give right honor to the heavenly Maker of that maker,[8] who, having made man to his own likeness, set him beyond and over all the works of that second nature: which in nothing he showeth so much as in poetry, when with the force of a divine breath he bringeth things forth far surpassing her doings, with no small argument to the incredulous of that first accursed fall of Adam, since our erected wit[9] maketh us know what perfection is, and yet our infected will keepeth us from reaching unto it.[1] But these arguments will by few be understood, and by fewer granted. Thus much (I hope) will be given me, that the Greeks with some probability of reason gave him the name above all names of learning. Now let us go to a more ordinary opening[2] of him, that the truth may be more palpable: and so I hope, though we get not so unmatched a praise as the etymology of his names will grant, yet his very description, which no man will deny, shall not justly be barred from a principal commendation.

Poesy therefore is an art of imitation, for so Aristotle termeth it [3] in his word *mimesis,* that is to say, a representing, counterfeiting, or figuring forth—to speak metaphorically, a speaking picture; with this end, to teach and delight. Of this have been three several kinds.

The chief, both in antiquity and excellency, were they that did imitate the inconceivable excellencies of God. Such were David in his Psalms; Solomon in his Song of Songs, in his Ecclesiastes, and Proverbs; Moses and Deborah in their Hymns; and the writer of Job, which, beside other, the learned Emanuel Tremellius and Franciscus Junius [4] do entitle the poetical part of the Scripture. Against these none will speak that hath the Holy Ghost in due holy reverence. In this kind, though in a full wrong divinity, were Orpheus, Amphion, Homer in his Hymns, and many other, both Greeks and Romans, and this poesy must be used by whosoever

8. Sidney had earlier explained that the word "poet" comes from the Greek word for "maker." The "maker" is then in a role like that of God, but on a lower level—an anticipation of the idea of the poet as creator.

9. I.e., our elevated, undebased intelligence.

1. The "will" is "infected" because corrupted and weakened by original sin in the Fall.

2. Analysis or explanation. Sidney goes on to explain poetry as an art of imitation, following Aristotle. There are three

kinds: divine poetry, which imitates the excellencies of God; philosophical poetry, which imitates learning; and a third kind, which we generally call simple "poetry," and which imitates life as it might be and should be, for the purpose of conveying instruction and delight.

3. In the *Poetics* 1.2, but Sidney is probably drawing here on Scaliger's *Poetice* I.i.

4. Two 16th-century Protestant scholars who published a Latin translation of the Bible in 1575–80.

will follow St. James's counsel in singing psalms when they are merry, and I know is used with the fruit of comfort by some, when, in sorrowful pangs of their death-bringing sins, they find the consolation of the never-leaving goodness.

The second kind is of them that deal with matters philosophical: either moral, as Tyrtaeus, Phocylides, and Cato;[5] or natural, as Lucretius and Virgil's *Georgics*; or astronomical, as Manilius and Pontanus; or historical, as Lucan; which who mislike, the fault is in their judgments quite out of taste, and not in the sweet food of sweetly uttered knowledge.

But because this second sort is wrapped within the fold of the proposed subject, and takes not the course of his own invention, whether they properly be poets or no let grammarians dispute; and go to the third, indeed right[6] poets, of whom chiefly this question ariseth, betwixt whom and these second is such a kind of difference as betwixt the meaner sort of painters, who counterfeit only such faces as are set before them, and the more excellent, who, having no law but wit, bestow that in colors upon you which is fittest for the eye to see, as the constant though lamenting look of Lucretia, when she punished in herself another's fault[7] (wherein he painteth not Lucretia whom he never saw, but painteth the outward beauty of such a virtue). For these third be they which most properly do imitate to teach and delight, and to imitate borrow nothing of what is, hath been, or shall be; but range, only reined with learned discretion, into the divine consideration of what may be, and should be. These be they that, as the first and most noble sort may justly be termed *vates*,[8] so these are waited on in the excellentest languages and best understandings, with the foredescribed name of poets; for these indeed do merely make to imitate, and imitate both to delight and teach, and delight to move men to take that goodness in hand, which without delight they would fly as from a stranger, and teach, to make them know that goodness whereunto they are moved: which being the noblest scope to which ever any learning was directed, yet want there not idle tongues to bark at them.

These be subdivided into sundry more special denominations. The most notable be the heroic, lyric, tragic, comic, satiric, iambic, elegiac, pastoral, and certain others, some of these being termed according to the matter they deal with, some by the sorts of verses they liked best to write in; for indeed the greatest part of poets have appareled their poetical inventions in that numbrous[9] kind

---

5. Dionysius Cato was the reputed author of *Disticha de moribus,* four books of epigrammatic moral precepts in Latin hexameters used as a textbook in Elizabethan schools.

6. Real.

7. Lucretia was the wife of L. Tarquinius Colatinus, outraged by Sextus, son of Tarquinius Superbus. See Shakespeare *The Rape of Lucrece.*

8. A *vates* was originally a prophet or oracle; later the term was used for a poet.

9. Not "numerous," but in "numbers" or metrical lines.

of writing which is called verse—indeed but appareled, verse being but an ornament and no cause to poetry, since there have been many most excellent poets that never versified, and now swarm many versifiers that need never answer to the name of poets. For Xenophon,[1] who did imitate so excellently as to give us *effigiem iusti imperii*, "the portraiture of a just Empire," under name of Cyrus (as Cicero saith of him), made therein an absolute heroical poem. So did Heliodorus in his sugared invention of that picture of love in Theagenes and Chariclea;[2] and yet both these writ in prose: which I speak to show that it is not rhyming and versing that maketh a poet—no more than a long gown maketh an advocate, who though he pleaded in armor should be an advocate and no soldier. But it is that feigning notable images of virtues, vices, or what else, with that delightful teaching, which must be the right describing note to know a poet by, although indeed the Senate of Poets hath chosen verse as their fittest raiment, meaning, as in matter they passed all in all, so in manner to go beyond them—not speaking (table-talk fashion or like men in a dream) words as they chanceably fall from the mouth, but peizing[3] each syllable of each word by just proportion according to the dignity of the subject.

Now therefore it shall not be amiss first to weigh this latter sort of poetry by his works, and then by his parts, and, if in neither of these anatomies[4] he be condemnable, I hope we shall obtain a more favorable sentence. This purifying of wit, this enriching of memory, enabling of judgment, and enlarging of conceit, which commonly we call learning, under what name soever it come forth, or to what immediate end soever it be directed, the final end is to lead and draw us to as high a perfection as our degenerate souls, made worse by their clayey lodgings, can be capable of. This, according to the inclination of the man, bred many formed impressions. For some that thought this felicity principally to be gotten by knowledge and no knowledge to be so high and heavenly as acquaintance with the stars, gave themselves to astronomy; others, persuading themselves to be demigods if they knew the causes of things, became natural and supernatural philosophers; some an admirable delight drew to music; and some the certainty of demonstration to the mathematics. But all, one and other, having this scope—to know, and by knowledge to lift up the mind from the dungeon of the body to the enjoying his own divine essence. But when by the balance of experience it was found that the astronomer looking to the stars might fall into a ditch, that the inquiring philosopher might be blind in himself, and the mathematician might draw forth a straight line with a crooked heart, then, lo, did proof, the overruler of opinions, make manifest that all these are but serving

---

1. Xenophon's *Cyropaedia* is an idealized and romanticized biography, in prose, of Cyrus the Great.

2. See note 7, page 478.
3. Weighing.
4. Analyses.

sciences, which, as they have each a private end in themselves, so yet are they all directed to the highest end of the mistress-knowledge, by the Greeks called *architectonike*, which stands (as I think) in the knowledge of a man's self, in the ethic and politic consideration, with the end of well doing and not of well knowing only:— even as the saddler's next end is to make a good saddle, but his farther end to serve a nobler faculty, which is horsemanship; so the horseman's to soldiery, and the soldier not only to have the skill, but to perform the practice of a soldier. So that, the ending end of all earthly learning being virtuous action, those skills, that most serve to bring forth that, have a most just title to be princes over all the rest.[5] * * *

But since I have run so long a career in this matter, methinks, before I give my pen a full stop, it shall be but a little more lost time to inquire why England (the mother of excellent minds) should be grown so hard a stepmother to poets, who certainly in wit ought to pass all other, since all only proceedeth from their wit, being indeed makers of themselves, not takers of others. How can I but exclaim,

Musa, mihi causas memora, quo numine laeso![8]

Sweet poesy, that hath anciently had kings, emperors, senators, great captains, such as, besides a thousand others, David, Adrian, Sophocles, Germanicus,[9] not only to favor poets, but to be poets; and of our nearer times can present for her patrons a Robert, King of Sicily, the great King Francis of France, King James of Scotland;[1] such cardinals as Bembus and Bibiena; such famous preachers and teachers as Beza and Melancthon; so learned philosophers as Fracastorius and Scaliger; so great orators as Pontanus and Muretus; so piercing wits as George Buchanan;[2] so grave counselors as, be-

5. In the omitted portion Sidney compares the poet with the moral philosopher, who gives precepts, and the historian, who gives examples; the poet is their superior because he gives both. The poet can invent, but the historian is "captived to the truth of a foolish world." The moral philosopher may teach more systematically, but the poet affects the feelings and therefore influences action. The poet is the monarch of the human sciences. Sidney defends the various kinds of literature and refutes the traditional complaints that poets tell lies, that poetry is effeminate, that poetry abuses man's wit, and that Plato banished poets from his commonwealth. He calls for laurels for poets instead of abuse of their art.

8. "O Muse, call to mind the causes: what divinity was injured?" (*Acneid* I.8).

9. Adrian is the Emperor Hadrian; Sophocles, the great Greek dramatist,

was also a general; Germanicus, 1st-century Roman emperor, translated poetry.

1. Robert d'Anjou, King of Naples, friend of Petrarch and Boccaccio; Francis I of France was a great patron of arts and letters; King James I of Scotland was author of the *King's Quair*.

2 Pietro Cardinal Bembo, a stylist and man of letters (he also appears in Castiglione's *Courtier*); Bernardo da Bibbiena, a writer of comedy and private secretary to Lorenzo de Medici. Theodore Beza and Philip Melancthon were prominent European Protestant theologians. Fracastorius and Julius Caesar Scaliger were famous Italian scholars. John Jovius Pontanus was an Italian medieval poet; Muretus was the Latinized name of Marc Antoine Muret, French scholar and writer. George Buchanan was the foremost Scottish writer of the 16th century.

sides many, but before all, that Hospital of France,[3] than whom (I think) that realm never brought forth a more accomplished judgment, more firmly builded upon virtue—I say these, with numbers of others, not only to read others' poesies, but to poetize for others' reading—that poesy, thus embraced in all other places, should only find in our time a hard welcome in England, I think the very earth lamenteth it, and therefore decketh our soil with fewer laurels than it was accustomed. For heretofore poets have in England also flourished, and, which is to be noted, even in those times when the trumpet of Mars did sound loudest. And now that an overfaint quietness should seem to strew the house for poets,[4] they are almost in as good reputation as the mountebanks at Venice. Truly even that, as of the one side it giveth great praise to poesy, which like Venus (but to better purpose) hath rather be troubled in the net with Mars than enjoy the homely quiet of Vulcan;[5] so serves it for a piece of a reason why they are less grateful to idle England, which now can scarce endure the pain of a pen. Upon this necessarily followeth, that base men with servile wits undertake it, who think it enough if they can be rewarded of the printer. And so as Epaminondas is said, with the honor of his virtue, to have made an office, by his exercising it, which before was contemptible, to become highly respected,[6] so these, no more but setting their names to it, by their own disgracefulness disgrace the most graceful poesy. For now, as if all the Muses were got with child, to bring forth bastard poets, without any commission they do post over the banks of Helicon, till they make the readers more weary than posthorses, while, in the meantime, they,

Queis meliore luto finxit praecordia Titan,[7]

are better content to suppress the outflowing of their wit than, by publishing them, to be accounted knights of the same order. But I that, before ever I durst aspire unto the dignity, am admitted into the company of the paper-blurrers, do find the very true cause of our wanting estimation is want of desert, taking upon us to be poets in despite of Pallas. Now, wherein we want desert were a thankworthy labor to express: but if I knew, I should have mended myself. But I, as I never desired the title, so have I neglected the means to come by it. Only, overmastered by some thoughts, I yielded an inky tribute unto them. Marry, they that delight in poesy itself should seek to know what they do, and how they do, and, especially,

---

3. Michel de l'Hospital, Chancellor of France and defender of the Huguenots.
4. I.e., now that peace has strewn rushes on the floor to make poets comfortable. "Mountebanks": vendors of quack medicines.
5. Vulcan discovered his wife Venus in bed with Mars; he entrapped them in a net and called the other gods to see them, expecting the lovers to suffer ridicule and shame, but he was the victim of their laughter himself.
6. He was sewer commissioner in Thebes.
7. "Whose hearts Titan [Prometheus] had formed of better clay" (Juvenal, *Satires* XIV.34–35).

look themselves in an unflattering glass of reason, if they be inclinable unto it. For poesy must not be drawn by the ears; it must be gently led, or rather it must lead; which was partly the cause that made the ancient-learned affirm it was a divine gift, and no human skill: since all other knowledges lie ready for any that hath strength of wit; a poet no industry can make, if his own genius be not carried unto it; and therefore is it an old proverb, *Orator fit, Poeta nascitur.*[8] Yet confess I always that as the fertilest ground must be manured, so must the highest-flying wit have a Daedalus[9] to guide him. That Daedalus, they say, both in this and in other, hath three wings to bear itself up into the air of due commendation: that is, Art, Imitation, and Exercise. But these, neither artificial rules nor imitative patterns, we much cumber ourselves withal. Exercise indeed we do, but that very fore-backwardly: for where we should exercise to know, we exercise as having known: and so is our brain delivered of much matter which never was begotten by knowledge. For, there being two principal parts—matter to be expressed by words and words to express the matter—in neither we use Art or Imitation rightly. Our matter is *Quodlibet*[1] indeed, though wrongly performing Ovid's verse,

> *Quicquid conabar dicere, versus erit:*

never marshaling it into an assured rank, that almost the readers cannot tell where to find themselves.

Chaucer, undoubtedly, did excellently in his *Troilus and Cressida;* of whom, truly, I know not whether to marvel more, either that he in that misty time could see so clearly, or that we in this clear age walk so stumblingly after him. Yet had he great wants, fit to be forgiven in so reverent antiquity. I account the *Mirror of Magistrates*[2] meetly furnished of beautiful parts, and in the Earl of Surrey's *Lyrics* many things tasting of a noble birth, and worthy of a noble mind. The *Shepherd's Calendar* hath much poetry in his Eclogues, indeed worthy the reading, if I be not deceived. That same framing of his style to an old rustic language I dare not allow, since neither Theocritus in Greek, Virgil in Latin, nor Sannazaro in Italian[3] did affect it. Besides these, do I not remember to have seen but few (to speak boldly) printed, that have poetical sinews in them: for proof whereof, let but most of the verses be put in prose, and then ask the meaning; and it will be found that one verse did but beget another, without ordering at the first what should be at the last; which becomes a confused mass of words,

---

8. "An orator is made, but a poet must be born one."
9. The legendary craftsman who invented wings for himself and his son Icarus. Icarus did not follow his father's instructions and fell into the sea.
1. "Anything you please." The phrase following may be translated, "Whatever I try to write will become verse."
2. A large collection of Elizabethan poems on the downfall of princes and men of power. The "beautiful parts" were probably in Sackville's Induction to it.
3. Three models for pastoral poetry.

with a tingling sound of rhyme, barely accompanied with reason.

Our tragedies and comedies (not without cause cried out against), observing rules neither of honest civility nor of skillful poetry, excepting *Gorboduc*[4] (again, I say, of those that I have seen), which notwithstanding, as it is full of stately speeches and well-sounding phrases, climbing to the height of Seneca's style, and as full of notable morality, which it doth most delightfully teach, and so obtain the very end of poesy, yet in truth it is very defectious in the circumstances, which grieveth me, because it might not remain as an exact model of all tragedies. For it is faulty both in place and time, the two necessary companions of all corporal actions. For where the stage should always represent but one place, and the uttermost time presupposed in it should be, both by Aristotle's precept and common reason, but one day, there is both many days, and many places, inartificially imagined. But if it be so in *Gorboduc*, how much more in all the rest, where you shall have Asia of the one side, and Afric of the other, and so many other under-kingdoms, that the player, when he cometh in, must ever begin with telling where he is, or else the tale will not be conceived? Now ye shall have three ladies walk to gather flowers, and then we must believe the stage to be a garden. By and by we hear news of shipwreck in the same place, and then we are to blame if we accept it not for a rock. Upon the back of that comes out a hideous monster, with fire and smoke, and then the miserable beholders are bound to take it for a cave. While in the meantime two armies fly in, represented with four swords and bucklers,[5] and then what hard heart will not receive it for a pitched field? Now, of time they are much more liberal, for ordinary it is that two young princes fall in love. After many traverses,[6] she is got with child, delivered of a fair boy; he is lost, groweth a man, falls in love, and is ready to get another child; and all this in two hours' space: which, how absurd it is in sense, even sense may imagine, and art hath taught, and all ancient examples justified, and, at this day, the ordinary players in Italy will not err in. Yet will some bring in an example of *Eunuchus* in Terence,[7] that containeth matter of two days, yet far short of twenty years. True it is, and so was it to be played in two days, and so fitted to the time it set forth. And though Plautus hath in one place done amiss, let us hit with him, and not miss with him. But they will say, How then shall we set forth a story, which containeth both many places and many times? And do they not know that a tragedy is tied to the laws of poesy, and not of history; not bound to follow the story, but, having liberty, either to feign a quite new

4. A Senecan play by Thomas Sackville and Thomas Norton, published in 1565 and called the first regular English tragedy. The tragedies of the Roman dramatist Seneca (5 B.C.–A.D. 65) are written in a highly rhetorical, declamatory style.
5. Shields.
6. Difficulties, mishaps.
7. Terence (195–159 B.C.) and Plautus (251–184 B.C.) were the chief Latin writers of comedy.

matter, or to frame the history to the most tragical conveniency? Again, many things may be told which cannot be showed, if they know the difference betwixt reporting and representing. As, for example, I may speak (though I am here) of Peru, and in speech digress from that to the description of Calicut; but in action I cannot represent it without Pacolet's horse.[8] And so was the manner the ancients took, by some Nuncius[9] to recount things done in former time or other place. Lastly, if they will represent an history, they must not (as Horace saith) begin *ab ovo*,[1] but they must come to the principal point of that one action which they will represent. By example this will be best expressed. I have a story of young Polydorus,[2] delivered for safety's sake, with great riches, by his father Priam to Polymnestor, king of Thrace, in the Trojan war time. He, after some years, hearing the overthrow of Priam, for to make the treasure his own, murdereth the child. The body of the child is taken up by Hecuba. She, the same day, findeth a sleight to be revenged most cruelly of the tyrant. Where now would one of our tragedy writers begin, but with the delivery of the child? Then should he sail over into Thrace, and so spend I know not how many years, and travel numbers of places. But where doth Euripides? Even with the finding of the body, leaving the rest to be told by the spirit of Polydorus. This need no further to be enlarged; the dullest wit may conceive it.

But besides these gross absurdities, how all their plays be neither right tragedies, nor right comedies, mingling kings and clowns, not because the matter so carrieth it, but thrust in clowns by head and shoulders, to play a part in majestical matters, with neither decency nor discretion,[3] so as neither the admiration and commiseration, nor the right sportfulness, is by their mongrel tragicomedy obtained. I know Apuleius[4] did somewhat so, but that is a thing recounted with space of time, not represented in one moment: and I know the ancients have one or two examples of tragicomedies, as Plautus hath *Amphitruo*.[5] But, if we mark them well, we shall find, that they never, or very daintily, match hornpipes[6] and funerals. So falleth it out that, having indeed no right comedy, in that comical part of our tragedy we have nothing but scurrility, unworthy of any chaste ears, or some extreme show of doltishness, indeed fit to lift up a loud laughter, and nothing else: where the whole tract of a comedy should be full of delight, as the tragedy should be still maintained in a well-raised admiration. But our comedians

---

8. A magic horse in the French romance *Valentine and Orson.* "Calicut": Calcutta.
9. Messenger.
1. From the beginning (literally, "from the egg").
2. In Euripides' *Hecuba.*
3. Mingling of social levels (kings and clowns) was thought to be a violation of the principle of decorum.
4. Not a dramatist, but the 2nd-century Roman author of the popular satirical novel, *The Golden Ass.*
5. *Amphitruo* is tragicomic only in that it contains gods and heroes; otherwise it is pure comedy.
6. Merry tunes for country dances.

think there is no delight without laughter; which is very wrong, for though laughter may come with delight, yet cometh it not of delight, as though delight should be the cause of laughter; but well may one thing breed both together. Nay, rather in themselves they have, as it were, a kind of contrariety: for delight we scarcely do but in things that have a conveniency to ourselves or to the general nature: laughter almost ever cometh of things most disproportioned to ourselves and nature. Delight hath a joy in it, either permanent or present. Laughter hath only a scornful tickling. For example, we are ravished with delight to see a fair woman, and yet are far from being moved to laughter. We laugh at deformed creatures, wherein certainly we cannot delight. We delight in good chances, we laugh at mischances; we delight to hear the happiness of our friends, or country, at which he were worthy to be laughed at that would laugh. We shall, contrarily, laugh sometimes to find a matter quite mistaken and go down the hill against the bias, in the mouth of some such men, as for the respect of them one shall be heartily sorry, yet he cannot choose but laugh; and so is rather pained than delighted with laughter. Yet deny I not but that they may go well together. For as in Alexander's picture well set out we delight without laughter, and in twenty mad antics we laugh without delight, so in Hercules, painted with his great beard and furious countenance, in woman's attire, spinning at Omphale's commandment,[7] it breedeth both delight and laughter. For the representing of so strange a power in love procureth delight: and the scornfulness of the action stirreth laughter. But I speak to this purpose, that all the end of the comical part be not upon such scornful matters as stirreth laughter only, but, mixed with it, that delightful teaching which is the end of poesy. And the great fault even in that point of laughter, and forbidden plainly by Aristotle, is that they stir laughter in sinful things, which are rather execrable than ridiculous; or in miserable, which are rather to be pitied than scorned. For what is it to make folks gape at a wretched beggar, or a beggarly clown; or, against law of hospitality, to jest at strangers, because they speak not English so well as we do? What do we learn? Since it is certain

> *Nil habet infelix paupertas durius in se,*
> *Quam quod ridiculos homines facit.*[8]

But rather a busy loving courtier, a heartless threatening Thraso, a self-wise-seeming schoolmaster, an awry-transformed traveler—these if we saw walk in stage names, which we play naturally, therein were delightful laughter, and teaching delightfulness: as in the

---

7. Hercules was so infatuated with Omphale, queen of Lydia, that he submitted to being dressed as a female slave and forced to spin wool.

8. "Unfortunate poverty has in itself nothing harder to bear than that it makes men ridiculous" (Juvenal, *Satires* III.152–53).

other, the tragedies of Buchanan do justly bring forth a divine admiration. But I have lavished out too many words of this play matter. I do it because, as they are excelling parts of poesy, so is there none so much used in England, and none can be more pitifully abused; which, like an unmannerly daughter showing a bad education, causeth her mother Poesy's honesty to be called in question.

Other sorts of poetry almost have we none, but that lyrical kind of songs and sonnets: which, Lord, if He gave us so good minds, how well it might be employed, and with how heavenly fruit, both private and public, in singing the praises of the immortal beauty, the immortal goodness of that God who giveth us hands to write and wits to conceive; of which we might well want words, but never matter; of which we could turn our eyes to nothing, but we should ever have new budding occasions. But truly many of such writings as come under the banner of unresistible love, if I were a mistress, would never persuade me they were in love; so coldly they apply fiery speeches, as men that had rather read lovers' writings, and so caught up certain swelling phrases (which hang together like a man which once told me the wind was at northwest, and by south, because he would be sure to name winds enough), than that in truth they feel those passions, which easily (as I think) may be betrayed by that same forcibleness, or *energia* (as the Greeks call it) of the writer. But let this be a sufficient though short note, that we miss the right use of the material point of poesy.

Now, for the outside of it, which is words, or (as I may term it) diction, it is even well worse. So is that honey-flowing matron Eloquence appareled, or rather disguised, in a courtesan-like painted affectation: one time with so farfetched words, they may seem monsters, but must seem strangers, to any poor Englishman; another time, with coursing of a letter,[9] as if they were bound to follow the method of a dictionary; another time, with figures and flowers,[1] extremely winter-starved. But I would this fault were only peculiar to versifiers, and had not as large possession among prose-printers, and (which is to be marveled) among many scholars, and (which is to be pitied) among some preachers. Truly I could wish, if at least I might be so bold to wish in a thing beyond the reach of my capacity, the diligent imitators of Tully [2] and Demosthenes (most worthy to be imitated) did not so much keep Nizolian paperbooks [3] of their figures and phrases, as by attentive translation (as it were) devour them whole, and make them wholly theirs. For now

9. Alliteration.
1. Of rhetoric.
2. Cicero.
3. Marius Nizolius or Nizzoli (1498?–1576), Italian rhetorician and lexicographer, published a collection of Ciceronian phrases in 1535. Ascham mentions the keeping of similar books in *The Scholemaster*.

they cast sugar and spice upon every dish that is served to the table, like those Indians, not content to wear earrings at the fit and natural place of the ears, but they will thrust jewels through their nose and lips, because they will be sure to be fine. Tully, when he was to drive out Catiline, as it were with a thunderbolt of eloquence, often used that figure of repetition, *Vivit. Vivit? Immo in Senatum venit*,[4] etc. Indeed, inflamed with a well-grounded rage, he would have his words (as it were) double out of his mouth, and so do that artificially which we see men do in choler naturally. And we, having noted the grace of those words, hale them in sometime to a familiar epistle, when it were too much choler to be choleric.

Now for similitudes in certain printed discourses, I think all Herbarists,[5] all stories of beasts, fowls, and fishes are rifled up, that they come in multitudes to wait upon any of our conceits; which certainly is as absurd a surfeit to the ears as is possible: for the force of a similitude not being to prove anything to a contrary disputer, but only to explain to a willing hearer; when that is done, the rest is a most tedious prattling, rather over-swaying the memory from the purpose whereto they were applied, than any whit informing the judgment, already either satisfied, or by similitudes not to be satisfied. For my part, I do not doubt, when Antonius and Crassus, the great forefathers of Cicero in eloquence, the one (as Cicero testifieth of them) pretended not to know art, the other not to set by it, because with a plain sensibleness they might win credit of popular ears; which credit is the nearest step to persuasion; which persuasion is the chief mark of oratory—I do not doubt (I say) but that they used these knacks very sparingly; which, who doth generally use, any man may see doth dance to his own music; and so be noted by the audience more careful to speak curiously than to speak truly.

Undoubtedly (at least to my opinion undoubtedly) I have found in divers small-learned courtiers a more sound style than in some professors of learning: of which I can guess no other cause, but that the courtier, following that which by practice he findeth fittest to nature, therein (though he know it not) doth according to art, though not by art: where the other, using art to show art, and not to hide art (as in these cases he should do), flieth from nature, and indeed abuseth art.

But what? Methinks I deserve to be pounded for straying from poetry to oratory: but both have such an affinity in this wordish consideration, that I think this digression will make my meaning receive the fuller understanding—which is not to take upon me to teach poets how they should do, but only, finding myself sick among the rest, to show some one or two spots of the common in-

---

4. Sidney quotes rather freely from memory a line from Cicero (*Catiline*, 1, 2): "He lives, nay more, he comes into the Senate."

5. Writers who, like Lyly, introduce botanical and zoological analogies into their writing.

fection grown among the most part of writers: that, acknowledging ourselves somewhat awry, we may bend to the right use both of matter and manner; whereto our language giveth us great occasion, being indeed capable of any excellent exercising of it. I know some will say it is a mingled language. And why not so much the better, taking the best of both the other? Another will say it wanteth grammar. Nay truly, it hath that praise, that it wanteth not grammar: for grammar it might have, but it needs it not; being so easy of itself, and so void of those cumbersome differences of cases, genders, moods, and tenses, which I think was a piece of the Tower of Babylon's curse, that a man should be put to school to learn his mother tongue. But for the uttering sweetly and properly the conceits of the mind, which is the end of speech, that hath it equally with any other tongue in the world: and is particularly happy in compositions of two or three words together, near the Greek, far beyond the Latin: which is one of the greatest beauties can be in a language.

Now, of versifying there are two sorts, the one ancient, the other modern: the ancient marked the quantity of each syllable, and according to that framed his verse; the modern observing only number [6] (with some regard of the accent), the chief life of it standeth in that like sounding of the words, which we call rhyme. Whether of these be the most excellent, would bear many speeches. The ancient, no doubt, more fit for music, both words and tune observing quantity, and more fit lively to express divers passions, by the low and lofty sound of the well-weighed syllable. The latter likewise, with his rhyme, striketh a certain music to the ear: and, in fine, since it doth delight, though by another way, it obtains the same purpose: there being in either sweetness, and wanting in neither majesty. Truly the English, before any other vulgar language I know, is fit for both sorts: for, for the ancient, the Italian is so full of vowels that it must ever be cumbered with elisions; the Dutch so, of the other side, with consonants, that they cannot yield the sweet sliding fit for a verse; the French, in his whole language, hath not one word that hath his accent in the last syllable saving two, called *antepenultima*; and little more hath the Spanish: and, therefore, very gracelessly may they use dactyls. The English is subject to none of these defects.

Now, for the rhyme, though we do not observe quantity, yet we observe the accent very precisely: which other languages either cannot do, or will not do so absolutely. That *caesura*, or breathing place in the midst of the verse, neither Italian nor Spanish have, the French, and we, never almost fail of. Lastly, even the very

---

6. "Quantity" meant length or duration of a syllable; by "number" Sidney means merely counting the syllables.

rhyme itself the Italian cannot put in the last syllable, by the French named the "masculine rhyme," but still in the next to the last, which the French call the "female," or the next before that, which the Italians term *sdrucciola*. The example of the former is *buono: suono*, of the *sdrucciola, femina: semina*. The French, of the other side, hath both the male, as *bon: son*, and the female, as *plaise: taise*, but the *sdrucciola* he hath not: where the English hath all three, as *due: true; father: rather; motion: potion*;[1] with much more which might be said, but that I find already the triflingness of this discourse is much too much enlarged.

So that since the ever-praiseworthy poesy is full of virtue-breeding delightfulness, and void of no gift that ought to be in the noble name of learning; since the blames laid against it are either false or feeble; since the cause why it is not esteemed in England is the fault of poet-apes, not poets; since, lastly, our tongue is most fit to honor poesy, and to be honored by poesy; I conjure you all that have had the evil luck to read this ink-wasting toy of mine, even in the name of the Nine Muses, no more to scorn the sacred mysteries of poesy, no more to laugh at the name of "poets," as though they were next inheritors to fools, no more to jest at the reverent title of a "rhymer"; but to believe, with Aristotle, that they were the ancient treasurers of the Grecians' divinity; to believe, with Bembus, that they were first bringers-in of all civility; to believe, with Scaliger, that no philosopher's precepts can sooner make you an honest man than the reading of Virgil; to believe, with Clauserus,[2] the translator of Cornutus, that it pleased the heavenly Deity, by Hesiod and Homer, under the veil of fables, to give us all knowledge, logic, rhetoric, philosophy, natural and moral, and *Quid non?*;[3] to believe, with me, that there are many mysteries contained in poetry, which of purpose were written darkly, lest by profane wits it should be abused; to believe, with Landin,[4] that they are so beloved of the gods that whatsoever they write proceeds of a divine fury; lastly, to believe themselves, when they tell you they will make you immortal by their verses.

Thus doing, your name shall flourish in the printers' shops; thus doing, you shall be of kin to many a poetical preface; thus doing, you shall be most fair, most rich, most wise, most all; you shall dwell upon superlatives. Thus doing, though you be *libertino patre natus*,[5] you shall suddenly grow *Herculea proles*,[6]

---

1. These were three-syllable words in Elizabethan pronunciation.
2. Conrad Clauser (ca. 1520–1611), a German scholar; he translated a Greek treatise by Cornutus, who was a contemporary of Nero's.
3. What not.

4. Cristofero Landino, 15th-century Italian scholar and onetime tutor to Lorenzo de Medici.
5. "Born of a freed slave father."
6. I.e., a descendent of Hercules. The next phrase means "if my songs are of any avail" (*Aeneid* IX.446).

Si quid mea carmina possunt.

Thus doing, your soul shall be placed with Dante's Beatrix, or Virgil's Anchises. But if (fie of such a but) you be born so near the dull-making cataract of Nilus[7] that you cannot hear the planet-like music of poetry, if you have so earth-creeping a mind that it cannot lift itself up to look to the sky of poetry, or rather, by a certain rustical disdain, will become such a mome[8] as to be a Momus of poetry; then, though I will not wish unto you the ass's ears of Midas,[9] nor to be driven by a poet's verses (as Bubonax[1] was) to hang himself, nor to be rhymed to death, as is said to be done in Ireland;[2] yet thus much curse I must send you, in the behalf of all poets, that while you live, you live in love, and never get favor for lacking skill of a sonnet, and, when you die, your memory die from the earth for want of an epitaph.

1595

7. According to Cicero, people living near the cataracts of the Nile became deaf from the noise. "Planet-like music": the music of the spheres was supposed to be the most beautiful of all music.
8. A stupid person; "Momus": a critic.
9. He was given ass's ears because he preferred Pan's playing to Apollo's.
1. Bupalus, a sculptor, was so ashamed when his works were satirized by the poet Hipponax that he hanged himself. Sidney fuses the two names.
2. There was a popular tradition that Irish bards could cause death by their incantations.

EDMUND SPENSER
(1552–1599)

1579: Publication of *The Shepheardes Calender.*
1580: In Ireland, where he remains for the rest of his life.
1590: First three books of *The Faerie Queene* published.

The greatest nondramatic poet of the English Renaissance, Edmund Spenser, was born in London, probably in 1552, and attended the Merchant Taylors' School under its famous headmaster Richard Mulcaster. In 1569 he went to Cambridge as a "sizar" or poor scholar. His Cambridge experience strongly colored the rest of his life; it was at the university that Spenser began as a poet by translating some poems for a volume of anti-Catholic propaganda. His work, then and later, reflects the strong Puritanical environment of Cambridge where the popular preacher Thomas Cartwright was beginning to make the authorities uneasy. Spenser's friendship with Gabriel Harvey, a Cambridge don, humanist, pamphleteer, and eccentric, also began at the university. Some correspondence between Harvey and Spenser, published in 1580, shows that they were interested in theories of poetry and in experiments in quantitative versification in English; it also shows that Spenser had ambitious plans as a poet.

He proceeded through the university, receiving the degree of B.A. in
1573 and M.A. in 1576. He then entered upon a series of positions in the
retinues of prominent men, including Dr. John Young, Bishop of Rochester; the Earl of Leicester, the queen's favorite; and finally, Lord Grey of
Wilton, Lord Deputy of Ireland. During his employment in Leicester's
household he came to know Sir Philip Sidney and his friend Sir Edward
Dyer, courtiers who were interested in promoting a new English poetry.
Spenser's own contribution to the movement is *The Shepheardes Calender,*
published in 1579 and dedicated to Sidney in the verses:

> To His Booke
> Goe little booke: thy selfe present,
> As child whose parent is unkent,
> To him that is the president
> Of noblesse and of chevalree.
> And if that Envie barke at thee,
> As sure it will, for succoure flee
> Under the shadow of his wing
> And, asked who thee forth did bring,
> A shepheardes swaine saye did thee sing,
> All as his straying flocke he fedde;
> And when his honor has thee redde,
> Crave pardon for my hardy hedde.
> But if that any aske thy name,
> Say thou wert base begot with blame,
> For thy thereof thou takest shame.
> And when thou art past jeopardee,
> Come tell me what was said of mee
> And I will send more after thee.
>
> Immerito [Unworthy].

The *Calender* consists of twelve pastoral eclogues, one for each month of
the year. Each is prefaced by an illustrative woodcut representing the characters or theme of the poem and picturing the appropriate sign of the zodiac
for that month in the clouds above. The eclogue was a classical form, practiced by Virgil and others; it presents, usually in dialogue between shepherds,
the moods and feelings and attitudes of the simple life. But often the
pastoral eclogue criticizes the world as it is by reflection from the world as
it might be, and in Spenser, as in other Renaissance poets, the eclogue at
times becomes didactic or satirical. Though it pretends to represent simple
shepherds, it is really commenting on contemporary affairs. The eclogues of
the *Calender* are divided by its commentator, "E. K.," into three groups—
plaintive, recreative, and moral. Of the moral eclogues, the final and
climactic one is *October*, which deals with the problem of poetry in modern
life and the responsibility of the poet in time—in an important way, the
theme of the whole *Calender*. It looks forward to related themes in Milton's
Lycidas.

Spenser used a deliberately archaic language, partly out of homage to
Chaucer, whom he refers to as Tityrus, the god of shepherds, "who taught
me, homely as I can, to make." But Spenser also used this language to get
a rustic effect. The patron to whom the *Calender* is dedicated did not

approve; Sidney wrote in his *Apology for Poetry*, "The Shepheardes Calender hath much poetry in his Eclogues, indeed worthy the reading, if I be not deceived. That same framing of his style to an old rustic language I dare not allow, since neither Theocritus in Greek, Virgil in Latin, nor Sannazaro in Italian did affect it." Another classical purist, Ben Jonson, growled that Spenser "writ no language," but that he would have him read for his matter. It would be a pity to follow Jonson's advice too literally, for Spenser's skillful use of many verse forms and his extraordinary musical effects indicate that here indeed is a poet to inaugurate the "new poetry" of the Elizabethan age.

There are thirteen different meters in *The Shepheardes Calender:* three kinds of couplet; three kinds of four-line stanza; three kinds of six-line stanza; stanzas of eight, nine, and ten lines; and a sestina. Some of these Spenser invented, some he adapted, but most of them were novel: only three or four were at all common in 1579. Spenser was a prolific experimenter: of the thirteen different meters in the *Calender* he used only three in his later poems. He went on to make further innovations—the special rhyme scheme of the Spenserian sonnet, richer than any other; the remarkably beautiful adaptation of Italian *canzone* forms for the *Epithalamion* and *Prothalamion*, and the nine-line stanza of *The Faerie Queene*, with its extraordinary six-foot line at the end, are only the most famous. Spenser is sometimes called the "poet's poet" because so many later English poets have learned the art of versification from him. In the 19th century alone his influence may be seen in Shelley's *Revolt of Islam*, Byron's *Childe Harold's Pilgrimage*, Keats's *Eve of St. Agnes*, and Tennyson's *The Lotos Eaters*.

The year after the publication of *The Shepheardes Calender* Spenser went to Ireland to serve Lord Grey; he spent the rest of his life there, except for two visits to England. He was at work on his great romantic epic, *The Faerie Queene*, when Sir Walter Ralegh visited him at Kilcolman Castle; the result was a trip to England and the publication, in 1590, of the first three books of *The Faerie Queene*. After that there was no question that Edmund Spenser was "the prince of poets in his time." He published a volume of poems called *Complaints*; a pastoral sequel to some of the eclogues in *The Shepheardes Calender* called *Colin Clouts Come Home Againe* (1595), which gave his views of the English court on his visit there in 1590; a sonnet cycle, *Amoretti*, and two marriage poems, *Epithalamion* and *Prothalamion*, but he completed only six of his projected twelve books of *The Faerie Queene*: in 1596 the first three books appeared again, with alterations, together with Books IV, V, and VI; the so-called "Mutability Cantos" first appeared in the edition of 1609.

In the second half of the decade, Ireland was torn by revolt and civil war; Spenser's castle was destroyed, and the poet was sent to England with messages from the besieged garrison in Ireland. He died in Westminster on January 13, 1599, and was buried near his beloved Chaucer in what is now called the Poets' Corner of Westminster Abbey.

Spenser is a complex genius who cannot be put into neatly labeled categories. He is, for instance, strongly influenced by Renaissance Neoplatonism, but remains always firmly grounded in earthiness and practicality. In *The Faerie Queene* he reaches toward the highest ideals of the Renaissance but knows, at the same time, what it is to want to remain an animal. He is a lover and celebrator of physical beauty, and he is sternly moral. His "morality" is, however, not of the repressive sort; it arises from his understanding of right action and of the temptations that entrap men as they try to achieve such action. Spenser was strongly influenced by Puritanism in his early days; he always remained a thoroughgoing Protestant; the Roman Catholic Church is made a villain in *The Faerie Queene*—and yet his understanding of faith and of sin has its roots in the great Catholic thinkers. He is profoundly English and patriotic; in him nationality and religion were inextricably joined. In the Proem to Book V of *The Faerie Queene* he characteristically looks back to the antique world and compares his own time with it most unfavorably. Yet his strongest links are not with the past, despite his love of Chaucer and his deliberately antique language: his closest affinity is with Milton, who was born nine years after Spenser's death. Milton called Spenser a better teacher than Scotus or Aquinas. He recognized Spenser, his great predecessor, as, like himself, a Christian humanist and British poet-prophet.

Spenser's poetry is always printed in the original spelling and punctuation (although a few of the most confusing punctuation marks have been altered in the present text), since it was a deliberate choice on Spenser's part that his language should seem antique. (A modern reader who read Shakespeare or the King James version of the Bible in the original spelling would not find as much difference in Spenser, but he would find some.) Furthermore, Spenser uses his spelling to suggest rhymes to the eye, sometimes to suggest etymologies, often incorrectly. The fact that Spenser's spelling is inconsistent is simply typical of his time; in the 16th century a man varied the spelling of even his name to suit convenience or a whim.

From THE SHEPHEARDES CALENDER[1]
October
Argument

In Cuddie[2] is set out the perfecte paterne of a Poete, whiche finding no maintenaunce of his state and studies, complayneth of

1. When *The Shepheardes Calender* was published in 1579, each of the twelve eclogues was followed by a "Glosse," which contained explications of difficult or archaic words, together with learned discussions of—and disagreements with—Spenser's ideas, imagery, and poetics. The Glosses are by one "E. K.," whose identity has never been satisfactorily ascertained. Although certain scholars have suggested that E. K. was Spenser himself, it is equally possible that he was a friend.

E. K.'s editorial apparatus is usually printed along with the poems from the *Calender*. In the text that follows, the present editor has incorporated the glosses into the footnotes, abridging only some of E. K.'s longer exegeses, anecdotes, and tags from classical and contemporary authors; the original spelling has also been retained. E. K. first discusses the poem's sources: "This Aeglogue is made in imitation of Theocritus his xvi. Idilion, wherein hee reproved the Tyranne Hiero of Syracuse for his nigardise towarde Poetes, in whome is the power to make men immortal for theyr good dedes, or shameful for their naughty lyfe. And the lyke also is in Mantuane. The style hereof as also that in Theocritus, is more loftye then the rest, and applyed to the heighte of Poeticall witte." Actually Spenser's eclogue owes very little to Theocritus, but it does draw heavily upon the fifth eclogue of Baptista Spagnuoli, called Mantuan.

2. "I doubt whether by Cuddie be specified the authour selfe, or some

the contempte of Poetrie, and the causes thereof: Specially having bene in all ages, and even amongst the most barbarous alwayes of singular accounpt[3] and honor, and being indede so worthy and commendable an arte: or rather no arte, but a divine gift and heavenly instinct not to bee gotten by laboure and learning, but adorned with both: and poured into the witte by a certaine ἐνθουσιασμὸς[4] and celestiall inspiration, as the Author hereof els where at large discourseth, in his booke called the *English Poete*, which booke being lately come to my hands, I mynde also by Gods grace upon further advisement to publish.

PIERS

Cuddie, for shame hold up thy heavye head,
And let us cast with what delight to chace,
And weary thys long lingring Phoebus race.[5]
Whilome° thou wont the shepheards laddes to leade,   *formerly*
5 In rymes, in ridles, and in bydding base:[6]
Now they in thee, and thou in sleepe art dead.

CUDDIE

Piers, I have pyped erst° so long with payne,   *up to now*
That all mine Oten reedes[7] bene rent and wore:
And my poore Muse hath spent her spared store,
10 Yet little good hath got, and much lesse gayne.
Such pleasaunce makes the Grashopper so poore,
And ligge so layd,[8] when Winter doth her straine:

The dapper[9] ditties, that I wont devise,
To feede youthes fancie, and the flocking fry,[1]
15 Delighten much: what I the bett forthy?
They han the pleasure, I a sclender prise.
I beate the bush, the byrds to them doe flye:
What good thereof to Cuddie can arise?

PIERS

Cuddie, the prayse is better, then the price,
20 The glory eke much greater then the gayne:
O what an honor is it, to restraine
The lust of lawlesse youth with good advice:[2]

---

other. For in the eyght Aeglogue the same person was brought in, singing a Cantion of Colins making, as he sayth. So that some doubt, that the persons be different" [E. K.'s Glosse].
3. Account, reputation.
4. The Greek word from which "enthusiasm" derives; it means inspiration. The *"English Poete"* is a lost work by Spenser, apparently never published.
5. I.e., let us see how we may pass the day pleasantly.
6. A popular game, here probably a poetry contest.
7. "Avena" [E. K.'s Glosse]. Avena means "stalks" and was used by Virgil (*Ecloques* I.2) to signify the shepherd's pipe. E. K. thinks Spenser's "oten

reeds" translates Avena.
8. "Lye so faynt and unlustie" [E. K.'s Glosse]. The reference is to the fable of the industrious ant and the carefree grasshopper.
9. "Pretye" [E. K.'s Glosse].
1. "Frye is a bold Metaphore, forced from the spawning fishes. For the multitude of young fish be called the frye" [E. K.'s Glosse]. In the next line, "what * * * for thy?" means, "what better am I for this reason?"
2. "This place seemeth to conspyre with Plato, who in his first booke *de Legibus* sayth, that the first invention of Poetry was of very vertuous intent * * *" [E. K.'s Glosse].

Or pricke° them forth with pleasaunce of thy vaine,   *stimulate*
Whereto thou list their traynéd° willes entice.   *ensnared*

25 Soone as thou gynst to sette thy notes in frame,
O how the rurall routes° to thee doe cleave: *crowds*
Seemeth thou dost their soule of sence bereave,[3]
All as the shepheard, that did fetch his dame
From Plutoes balefull bowre withouten leave:
30 His musicks might the hellish hound did tame.

CUDDIE

So praysen babes the Peacoks spotted traine,
And wondren at bright Argus blazing eye:[4]
But who rewards him ere the more forthy?
Or feedes him once the fuller by a graine?
35 Sike° prayse is smoke, that sheddeth in the skye,   *such*
Sike words bene wynd, and wasten soone in vayne.

PIERS

Abandon then the base and viler clowne,°   *rustic*
Lyft up thy selfe out of the lowly dust:
And sing of bloody Mars, of wars, of giusts,°   *jousts*
40 Turne thee to those, that weld° the awful crowne.   *wield*
To doubted[5] Knights, whose woundlesse armour rusts,
And helmes unbruzéd wexen dayly browne.

There may thy Muse display her fluttryng wing,[6]
And stretch herselfe at large from East to West:
45 Whither thou list in fayre Elisa rest,
Or if thee please in bigger notes to sing,
Advaunce the worthy whome shee loveth best,
That first the white beare to the stake did bring.[7]

3. "What the secrete working of Musick is in the myndes of men, as well appeareth, hereby, that some of the auncient Philosophers, and those the moste wise, as Plato and Pythagoras held for opinion, that the mynd was made of a certaine harmonie and musicall nombers, for the great compassion and likenes of affection in thone and in the other * * * So that it is not incredible which the Poete here sayth, that Musick can bereave the soule of sence" [E. K.'s Glosse]. The "shepheard" in the next line is "Orpheus: of whom is sayd, that by his excellent skil in Musick and Poetry, he recovered his wife Eurydice from hell" [E. K.'s Glosse].
4. "Of Argus is before said, that Juno to him committed hir husband Jupiter his Paragon Iô, bicause he had an hundred eyes: but afterwarde Mercury wyth hys Musick lulling Argus aslepe, slew him and brought Iô away, whose eyes it is sayd that Juno for his eternall memory placed in her byrd the Pea-cocks tayle. For those coloured spots indeede resemble eyes" [E. K.'s Glosse].
5. Redoubted, dreaded. The knights' "armour" is "woundlesse" because "un-wounded in warre, [they] doe rust through long peace" [E. K.'s Glosse].
6. "A poeticall metaphore: whereof the meaning is, that if the Poet list showe his skill in matter of more dignitie, then is the homely Aeglogue, good occasion is him offered of higher veyne and more Heroicall argument, in the person of our most gratious soveraign, whom (as before) he calleth Elisa. Or if mater of knighthoode and chevalrie please him better, that there be many Noble and valiaunt men, that are both worthy of his payne in theyr deserved prayses, and also favourers of hys skil and faculty" [E. K.'s Glosse].
7. "He meaneth (as I guesse) the most honorable and renowmed the Erle of Leycester * * * " [E. K.'s Glosse]. Leicester's device was the bear and ragged staff.

And when the stubborne stroke of stronger stounds,°   *efforts*
50 Has somewhat slackt the tenor of thy string:[8]
Of love and lustihead tho mayst thou sing,
And carrol lowde, and leade the Myllers rownde,[9]
All° were Elisa one of thilke same ring.   *although*
So mought our Cuddies name to Heaven sownde.

CUDDIE

55 Indeede the Romish Tityrus,[1] I heare,
Through his Mecaenas left his Oaten reede,
Whereon he earst° had taught his flocks to feede,   *before*
And laboured lands to yield the timely eare,
And eft did sing of warres and deadly drede,[2]
60 So as the Heavens did quake his verse to here.

But ah Mecaenas is yclad in claye,
And great Augustus long ygoe is dead:
And all the worthies liggen wrapt in leade,
That matter made for Poets on to play:
65 For ever, who in derring doe[3] were dreade,
The loftie verse of hem was lovéd aye.[4]

But after vertue gan for age to stoupe,
And mighty manhode brought a bedde of ease:[5]
The vaunting Poets found nought worth a pease,
70 To put in preace[6] among the learned troupe.
Tho gan the streames of flowing wittes to cease,
And sonnebright honour pend in shamefull coupe.[7]

And if that any buddes of Poesie,
Yet of the old stocke gan to shoote agayne:

8. "That is when thou chaungest thy verse from stately discourse, to matter of more pleasaunce and delight" [E. K.'s Glosse].
9. "A kind of daunce" [E. K.'s Glosse]. "Ring," in the next line, E. K. explains as a "company of dauncers."
1. "Well knowen to be Virgile, who by Mecaenas means was brought into the favour of the Emperor Augustus, and by him moved to write in loftier kinde, then he erst had doen" [E. K.'s Glosse].
2. "In these three verses are the three severall workes of Virgile intended. For in teaching his flocks to feede, is meant his Aeglogues. In labouring of lands, is hys Bucoliques. In singing of wars and deadly dreade, is his divine Aeneis figured" [E. K.'s Glosse].
3. "In manhoode and chevalrie" [E. K.'s Glosse].
4. "He sheweth the cause, why Poetes were wont be had in such honor of noble men; that is, that by them their worthines and valor shold through

theyr famous Posies be commended to al posterities. Wherefore it is sayd, that Achilles had never bene so famous, as he is, but for Homeres immortal verses. Which is the only advantage, which he had of Hector. * * * As also that Alexander destroying Thebes, when he was enformed that the famous Lyrick Poet Pindarus was borne in that citie, not onely commaunded streightly, that no man should upon payne of death do any violence to that house by fire or otherwise: but also specially spared most, and some highly rewarded, that were of hys kinne. * * * Such honor have Poetes alwayes found in the sight of princes and noble men. Which this author here very well sheweth, as els where more notably" [E. K.'s Glosse].
5. "He sheweth the cause of contempt of Poetry to be idlenesse and basenesse of mynd" [E. K.'s Glosse].
6. Put in press, crowd in among.
7. Coop. E. K. explains the phrase as "shut up in slouth, as in a coope or cage."

75 Or it mens follies mote be forst to fayne,
And rolle with rest in rymes of rybaudrye:
Or as it sprong, it wither must agayne:
Tom Piper makes us better melodie.[8]

PIERS

O pierlesse Poesye, where is then thy place?
80 If nor in Princes pallace thou doe sitt:
(And yet is Princes pallace the most fitt)
Ne brest of baser birth[9] doth thee embrace.
Then make thee winges of thine aspyring wit,
And, whence thou camst, flye backe to heaven apace.

CUDDIE

85 Ah Percy it is all to weake and wanne,
So high to sore, and make so large a flight:
Her peecéd pyneons[1] bene not so in plight,
For Colin fittes such famous flight to scanne:
He, were he not with love so ill bedight,
90 Would mount as high, and sing as soote as Swanne.[2]

PIERS

Ah fon,° for love does teach him climbe so hie,   *fool*
And lyftes him up out of the loathsome myre:
Such immortall mirrhor,[3] as he doth admire,
Would rayse ones mynd above the starry skie.
95 And cause a caytive corage[4] to aspire,
For lofty love doth loath a lowly eye.

CUDDIE

All otherwise the state of Poet stands,
For lordly love is such a Tyranne fell:
That where he rules, all power he doth expell.
100 The vaunted verse a vacant head demaundes,
Ne wont with crabbéd care the Muses dwell.
Unwisely weaves, that takes two webbes in hand.

Who ever casts to compasse weightye prise,
And thinks to throwe out thondring words of threate:
105 Let powre in lavish cups and thriftie bitts of meate,[5]
For Bacchus fruite is frend to Phoebus wise.

---

8. "An Ironicall Sarcasmus, spoken in derision of these rude wits, whych make more account of a ryming rybaud, then of skill grounded upon learning and judgment" [E. K.'s Glosse].
9. "The meaner sort of men" [E. K.'s Glosse].
1. Patched-up wings. "Unperfect skil. Spoken wyth humble modestie" [E. K.'s Glosse]. "Colin fittes": it is appropriate for Colin (Spenser).
2. "The comparison seemeth to be strange: for the swanne hath ever wonne small commendation for her swete singing: but it is sayd of the learned that the swan a little before hir death, singeth most pleasantly, as prophecying by a secrete instinct her neere destinie * * *" [E. K.'s Glosse].
3. "Beauty, which is an excellent object of Poeticall spirites * * *" [E. K.'s Glosse].
4. "A base and abject minde" [E. K.'s Glosse].
5. I.e., let him pour lavish drink and nourishing ("thrifty") food.

And when with Wine the braine begins to sweate,
The nombers flowe as fast as spring doth ryse.

Thou kenst not Percie howe the ryme should rage.
110 O if my temples were distaind° with wine,[6]   *distended*
And girt in girlonds of wild Yvie twine,
How I could reare the Muse on stately stage,
And teache her tread aloft in bus-kin[7] fine,
With queınt Bellona[8] in her equipage.

115 But ah my corage cooles ere it be warme,
For thy, content us in thys humble shade:
Where no such troublous tydes° han us assayde,   *seasons*
Here we our slender pipes may safely charme.[9]

PIERS

And when my Gates shall han their bellies layd:[1]
120 Cuddie shall have a Kidde to store his farme.

Cuddies Embleme.[2]
Agitante calescimus illo &c.

1579

6. "He seemeth here to be ravished with a Poetical furie. For (if one rightly mark) the numbers rise so ful, and the verse groweth so big, that it seemeth he hath forgot the meanenesse of shepheards state and stile" [E. K.'s Glosse]. E. K. adds an explanation of "wild Yvie" in the next line: "For it is dedicated to Bacchus and therefore it is sayd that the Maenades (that is Bacchus franticke priestes) used in theyr sacrifice to carry *Thyrsos*, which were pointed staves or Javelins, wrapped about with yvie."
7. "It was the maner of Poetes and plaiers in tragedies to were buskins, as also in Comedies to use stockes and light shoes. So that the buskin in Poetry is used for tragical matter * * * " [E. K.'s Glosse].
8. "Strange Bellona; the goddesse of battaile, that is Pallas, which may therefore wel be called queint for that (as Lucian saith) when Jupiter hir father was in traveile of her, he caused his sonne Vulcane with his axe to hew his head. Out of which leaped forth lustely a valiant damsell armed at all poyntes, whom seeing Vulcane so faire and comely, lightly leaping to her, preferred her some cortesie, which the Lady disdeigning, shaked her speare at him, and threatned his saucinesse. Therefore such straungenesse is well applyed to her" [E. K.'s Glosse]. E. K. also glosses "equipage": order.
9. "Temper and order. For Charmes were wont to be made by verses as Ovid sayth, *Aut si carminibus*" [E. K.'s Glosse]. E. K. had a slip of memory: the fragment is not in Ovid.
1. I.e., when my goats bear their young.
2. An "embleme" is a motto or relevant quotation. The Latin line, of which Spenser gives the first three words here, is from Ovid, *Fasti* vi.5: "There is a god within us; it is from his stirring that we feel warm." E. K. comments on the quotation: "Hereby is meant, as also in the whole course of this Aeglogue, that Poetry is a divine instinct and unnatural rage passing the reache of comen reason. Whom Piers answereth *Epiphonematicos* [by way of summary] as admiring the excellencye of the skyll whereof in Cuddie hee hadde alreadye hadde a taste."

The Faerie Queene
Spenser's masterpiece is a poem peculiarly characteristic of its age. It is a "courtesy book," like Castiglione's *Courtier*, intended to "fashion a gentleman or noble person" by exhibiting the traits such a person should have. Only six of the twelve projected books were finished. These exhibit the virtues of Holiness, Temperance, Chastity, Friendship, Justice, and Courtesy. A fragment of another book, the cantos

on Mutability, also survives. But whereas the ordinary courtesy book was a piece of explanation and exhortation, *The Faerie Queene* is also a poem, and, as Elizabethans all believed, a poem teaches by delighting. Spenser's great work is full of adventures and marvels, dragons, witches, enchanted trees, giants, jousting knights, and castles; a romantic epic, like Ariosto's *Orlando Furioso* (1516). But it is also an allegory, like Tasso's *Gerusalemme Liberata* (1575); the heroes of the several books represent the virtues portrayed in those books. The Redcrosse Knight in Book I is of course St. George, the patron saint of England, but he also represents Holiness, as Sir Guyon in Book II represents Temperance (not simply abstinence in drinking but self-control under all the temptations of the senses). The heroes do not have the virtues they represent at the beginning of their adventures—they acquire them in the course of the book. Spenser explains his allegorical method in a preliminary letter to Sir Walter Ralegh; however he does not explain what would be obvious to every contemporary reader, the many conventional symbols and attributes which would identify his characters. For example, when a woman appears who has a miter, wears scarlet clothes, and comes from the river Tiber, the reader is supposed to know immediately that she represents the Roman Catholic Church, which had been so often identified by Protestant preachers with the Whore of Babylon in the Book of Revelation.

Book I of *The Faerie Queene* is in a way an epitome of the whole poem, or the part of it Spenser completed. It is almost entirely self-contained; it has been called a miniature epic in itself. It consists of twelve cantos, as Virgil's *Aeneid* consists of twelve books. The introductory lines are intended to remind the reader of Virgil, who began with pastoral poetry and moved on to the epic, as Spenser is now doing.

The theme is not arms and the man, however, but something more romantic—"Fierce warres and faithfull loves." The scenery, too, is not classical but romantic. There are plains and forests and caves and castles and magical trees and springs; one meets dwarfs and giants and lions and pilgrims and magicians and Saracens or "paynims" (with French names). An accurate map of Faerie Land is impossible but unnecessary; if you are going somewhere you just start out and, after many adventures, get there. A clear, pleasant stream may be dangerous to drink because it produces loss of strength. Any stranger you meet is more than likely to be a villain and to be in disguise.

The good people are subject to the Faerie Queene and are called Faeries or Elves. They are human beings, though not much individualized. They undergo the trials and tribulations men undergo in the ordinary world, but these events are told in a romantic, fantastic way in order to arouse wonder. The bad creatures, people and monsters, are various vices, evils, and temptations, often revealed to the reader by their names or by the short verse summaries at the beginning of each canto but not revealed to the hero until he has conquered them. Houses, castles, and animals also stand for abstract virtues or vices. The world of Faerie Land is a visual world in which the meaning of something is made fully evident by its appearance when stripped of all disguise.

Read as romantic narrative, the plot of Book I is a series of chivalric adventures undertaken by the Redcrosse Knight culminating in his killing the dragon, rescuing Una's parents, and winning her as his bride. Read as spiritual allegory, the book tells the story of the Christian's struggle for salvation—his wandering between the evil extremes of pride and despair, his encounter with the seven deadly sins, his separation from and reunion with the one true faith, the purgation of his sinfulness, and his final salvation by divine grace added to heroic effort.

The poem can be enjoyed on many levels, and it may, in fact, work on several of these levels at a time. In addition to being—most especially—a heroic poem and a spiritual allegory, it also embodies many religious and political aspects of Spenser's own England; a "political allegory" runs all through Book I. This is a romantic, "medieval," heroic, religious, political, magical world, and the reader entering it must be prepared to move as the story moves, taking the meanings on whatever level seems most viable at the moment. Spenser is not a great explainer; more usually, he gives the reader a scene or a surface, and lets the full allegorical import work its way out.

Moreover, that scene or surface may draw on the riches of literary and pictorial traditions. Entire episodes may be adopted from the Italian romantic epics of Ariosto and Tasso and, either through them or independently, from Homer, Virgil, or Ovid (this was an age when borrowing and reworking earlier materials was praiseworthy in a poet). Places, such as Lucifera's castle; individual attributes, such as Una's lamb or Speranza's anchor; even names or colors came to Spenser from the classics, from theologians, from liturgical tradition, from the village pulpit, from folk tales and pageants, from tapestries, paintings, and emblem books. In our notes we have attempted to show what some of the sources were—but more important is the understanding that these traditions had a life for Spenser and his readers; they could flow together, separate, recombine.

The strangeness of *The Faerie Queene* becomes, on closer acquaintance, a source of delight. No work of the English Renaissance is more exuberant, more fertile, more full.

From THE FAERIE QUEENE
A Letter of the Authors

EXPOUNDING HIS WHOLE INTENTION IN THE COURSE OF THIS WORKE:
WHICH FOR THAT IT GIVETH GREAT LIGHT TO THE READER, FOR THE
BETTER UNDERSTANDING IS HEREUNTO ANNEXED

*To the Right noble, and Valorous, Sir Walter Raleigh knight,
Lo. Wardein of the Stanneryes, and her Majesties liefetenaunt
of the County of Cornewayll*

Sir knowing how doubtfully all Allegories may be construed, and
this booke of mine, which I have entituled the *Faery Queene*, being a continued Allegory, or darke conceit, I have thought good as
well for avoyding of gealous opinions and misconstructions, as also
for your better light in reading thereof, (being so by you commanded,) to discover unto you the general intention and meaning,
which in the whole course thereof I have fashioned, without expressing of any particular purposes or by-accidents [1] therein occasioned. The generall end therefore of all the booke is to fashion [2] a
gentleman or noble person in vertuous and gentle discipline:
Which for that I conceived shoulde be most plausible and pleasing,
being coloured with an historicall fiction, the which the most part
of men delight to read, rather for variety of matter, then for profite
of the ensample: I chose the historye of King Arthure, as most fitte
for the excellency of his person, being made famous by many mens
former workes, and also furthest from the daunger of envy, and
suspition of present time.[3] In which I have followed all the antique
Poets historicall, first Homere, who in the Persons of Agamemnon
and Ulysses hath ensampled a good governour and a vertuous man,
the one in his *Ilias*, the other in his *Odysseis*: then Virgil, whose
like intention was to doe in the person of Aeneas: after him Ariosto
comprised them both in his Orlando: and lately Tasso dissevered
them againe, and formed both parts in two persons, namely that
part which they in Philosophy call Ethice, or vertues of a private
man, coloured in his Rinaldo: The other named Politice in his
Godfredo.[4] By ensample of which excellente Poets, I labour to
pourtraict in Arthure, before he was king, the image of a brave
knight, perfected in the twelve private morall vertues, as Aristotle

---

1. Secondary matters.
2. I.e., to represent (secondarily, to educate).
3. I.e., free from current political controversy.
4. Lodovico Ariosto (1474–1533) was
author of the epic-romance *Orlando Fu-*
rioso, first published in complete form
in 1532; Torquato Tasso (1544–95)
published his chivalric romance *Rinaldo*
in 1562 and the epic *Gerusalemme Lib-*
erata (centered on the heroic figure of
Count Godfredo) in 1581.

hath devised,[5] the which is the purpose of these first twelve bookes: which if I finde to be well accepted, I may be perhaps encouraged, to frame the other part of polliticke vertues in his person, after that hee came to be king. To some I know this Methode will seeme displeasaunt, which had rather have good discipline delivered plainly in way of precepts, or sermoned at large, as they use, then thus clowdily enwrapped in Allegoricall devises. But such, me seeme, should be satisfide with the use of these dayes, seeing all things accounted by their showes, and nothing esteemed of, that is not delightfull and pleasing to commune sence. For this cause is Xenophon preferred before Plato, for that the one in the exquisite depth of his judgment, formed a Commune welth [6] such as it should be, but the other in the person of Cyrus and the Persians fashioned a governement such as might best be: So much more profitable and gratious is doctrine by ensample, then by rule. So have I laboured to doe in the person of Arthure: whome I conceive after his long education by Timon, to whom he was by Merlin delivered to be brought up, so soone as he was borne of the Lady Igrayne, to have seene in a dream or vision the Faery Queen, with whose excellent beauty ravished, he awaking resolved to seeke her out, and so being by Merlin armed, and by Timon throughly instructed, he went to seeke her forth in Faerye land. In that Faery Queene I meane glory in my generall intention, but in my particular I conceive the most excellent and glorious person of our soveraine the Queene, and her kingdome in Faery land. And yet in some places els, I doe otherwise shadow [7] her. For considering she beareth two persons, the one of a most royall Queene or Empresse, the other of a most vertuous and beautifull Lady, this latter part in some places I doe express in Belphoebe, fashioning her name according to your owne excellent conceipt of Cynthia,[8] (Phoebe and Cynthia being both names of Diana.) So in the person of Prince Arthure I sette forth magnificence in particular, which vertue for that (according to Aristotle and the rest) it is the perfection of all the rest, and conteineth in it them all, therefore in the whole course I mention the deedes of Arthure applyable to that vertue, which I write of in that booke. But of the xii. other vertues, I make xii. other knights the patrones, for the more variety of the history. Of which these three bookes contayn three, The first of the knight of the Redcrosse, in whome I expresse Holynes: The seconde of Sir Guyon, in whome I sette forth Temperaunce: The third of Brito-

5. Aristotle did not devise twelve private moral virtues: Spenser was in fact relying upon more modern philosophers— his friend Lodowick Bryskett and the Italian Piccolomini. That Spenser actually planned a poem four times as long as the six books we now have rather staggers the imagination, but his language is plain.
6. The allusion is to Plato's *Republic* and Xenophon's *Cyropaedia*.
7. Picture, portray.
8. Ralegh's poem *Cynthia* praised Queen Elizabeth.

martis a Lady knight, in whome I picture Chastity. But because the beginning of the whole worke seemeth abrupte and as depending upon other antecedents, it needs that ye know the occasion of these three knights severall adventures. For the Methode of a Poet historicall is not such, as of an Historiographer. For an Historiographer discourseth of affayres orderly as they were donne, accounting as well the times as the actions; but a Poet thrusteth into the middest, even where it most concerneth him, and there recoursing to the thinges forepaste, and divining of thinges to come, maketh a pleasing Analysis of all. The beginning therefore of my history, if it were to be told by an Historiographer, should be the twelfth booke, which is the last, where I devise that the Faery Queene kept her Annuall feaste xii. dayes, uppon which xii. severall dayes, the occasions of the xii. severall adventures hapned, which being undertaken by xii. severall knights, are in these xii books severally handled and discoursed. The first was this. In the beginning of the feaste, there presented him selfe a tall clownishe [9] younge man, who falling before the Queen of Faeries desired a boone (as the manner then was) which during that feast she might not refuse: which was that hee might have the atchievement of any adventure, which during that feaste should happen, that being graunted, he rested him on the floore, unfitte through his rusticity for a better place. Soone after entred a faire Ladye in mourning weedes, riding on a white Asse, with a dwarfe behind her leading a warlike steed, that bore the Armes of a knight, and his speare in the dwarfes hand. Shee falling before the Queene of Faeries, complayned that her father and mother an ancient King and Queene, had bene by an huge dragon many years shut up in a brasen Castle, who thence suffred them not to yssew: and therefore besought the Faery Queene to assygne her some one of her knights to take on him that exployt. Presently that clownish person upstarting, desired that adventure: whereat the Queene much wondering, and the Lady much gainesaying, yet he earnestly importuned his desire. In the end the Lady told him that unlesse that armour which she brought, would serve him (that is the armour of a Christian man specified by Saint Paul v. Ephes.) that he could not succeed in that enterprise, which being forthwith put upon him with dewe furnitures [1] thereunto, he seemed the goodliest man in al that company, and was well liked of the Lady. And eftesoones taking on him knighthood, and mounting on that straunge Courser, he went forth with her on that adventure: where beginneth the first booke, vz.

A gentle knight was pricking on the playne. &c.

The second day ther came in a Palmer bearing an Infant with

9. Rustic-looking.   1. Suitable equipment.

bloody hands, whose Parents he complained to have bene slayn by an Enchaunteresse called Acrasia: and therfore craved of the Faery Queene, to appoint him some knight, to performe that adventure, which being assigned to Sir Guyon, he presently went forth with that same Palmer: which is the beginning of the second booke and the whole subject thereof. The third day there came in, a Groome who complained before the Faery Queene, that a vile Enchaunter called Busirane had in hand a most faire Lady called Amoretta, whom he kept in most grievous torment, because she would not yield him the pleasure of her body. Whereupon Sir Scudamour the lover of that Lady presently tooke on him that adventure. But being unable to performe it by reason of the hard Enchauntments, after long sorrow, in the end met with Britomartis, who succoured him, and reskewed his love.

But by occasion hereof, many other adventures are intermedled, but rather as Accidents, then intendments.[2] As the love of Britomart, the overthrow of Marinell, the misery of Florimell, the vertuousnes of Belphoebe, the lasciviousnes of Hellenora, and many the like.

Thus much Sir, I have briefly overronne to direct your understanding to the wel-head of the History, that from thence gathering the whole intention of the conceit, ye may as in a handfull gripe al the discourse, which otherwise may happily[3] seeme tedious and confused. So humbly craving the continuaunce of your honorable favour towards me, and th'eternall establishment of your happines, I humbly take leave.

23. January, 1589
Yours most humbly affectionate.
ED. SPENSER.

The First Booke of the Faerie Queene

CONTAYNING
*The Legende of the
Knight of the Red Crosse,*
OR
OF HOLINESSE

1

Lo I the man, whose Muse whilome did maske,
    As time her taught, in lowly Shepheards weeds,[4]

2. That is, there are episodes that are merely romantic and not specifically allegorical. Characters are often types, not symbols.
3. By chance.
4. I.e., behold me, the poet who ap-

propriately appeared before ("whilome") as a writer of humble pastoral (i.e., *The Shepheardes Calender*). These lines are imitated from the verses prefixed to Virgil's *Aeneid*.

Am now enforst a far unfitter taske,
For trumpets sterne to chaunge mine Oaten reeds,[5]
5　And sing of Knights and Ladies gentle deeds;
Whose prayses having slept in silence long,[6]
Me, all too meane, the sacred Muse areeds °　　　　　　*appoints*
To blazon broad emongst her learned throng:
Fierce warres and faithfull loves shall moralize my song.

2

10　Helpe then, O holy Virgin chiefe of nine,[7]
Thy weaker Novice to performe thy will,
Lay forth out of thine everlasting scryne [8]
The antique rolles, which there lye hidden still,
Of Faerie knights and fairest Tanaquill,[9]
15　Whom that most noble Briton Prince [1] so long
Sought through the world, and suffered so much ill,
That I must rue his undeservéd wrong:
O helpe thou my weake wit, and sharpen my dull tong.

3

And thou most dreaded impe [2] of highest Jove,
20　Faire Venus sonne, that with thy cruell dart
At that good knight so cunningly didst rove,°　　　　　　*shoot*
That glorious fire it kindled in his hart,
Lay now thy deadly Heben ° bow apart,　　　　　　*ebony*
And with thy mother milde come to mine ayde:
25　Come both, and with you bring triumphant Mart,[3]
In loves and gentle jollities arrayd,
After his murdrous spoiles and bloudy rage allayd.

4

And with them eke,° O Goddesse heavenly bright,　　　　　　*also*
Mirrour of grace and Majestie divine,
30　Great Lady of the greatest Isle, whose light
Like Phoebus lampe throughout the world doth shine,
Shed thy faire beames into my feeble eyne,
And raise my thoughts too humble and too vile,°　　　　　　*lowly*
To thinke of that true glorious type ° of thine,　　　　　　*pattern*
35　The argument of mine afflicted stile:
The which to heare, vouchsafe, O dearest dred [4] a-while.

Canto I

The Patron of true Holinesse,
Foule Errour doth defeate:
Hypocrisie him to entrappe,
Doth to his home entreate.

5. To write heroic poetry, of which the trumpet is a symbol, instead of pastoral poetry like *The Shepheardes Calender*, symbolized by the humble shepherd's pipe ("Oaten reeds").
6. Lines 5 and 6 are imitated from the opening lines of Ariosto's *Orlando Furioso*.
7. Clio, the Muse of history; "weaker": too weak.
8. A chest for papers.
9. I.e., Gloriana.
1. I.e., Arthur.
2. Child, i.e., Cupid.
3. Mars, god of war and lover of Venus.
4. Object of awe.

1

A Gentle Knight was pricking ° on the plaine,   *cantering*
  Ycladd in mightie armes and silver shielde,
  Wherein old dints of deepe wounds did remaine,
  The cruell markes of many a bloudy fielde;
5 Yet armes till that time did he never wield: [5]
  His angry steede did chide his foming bitt,
  As much disdayning to the curbe to yield:
  Full jolly ° knight he seemd, and faire did sitt,   *courageous*
As one for knightly giusts ° and fierce encounters   *tourneys, jousts*
    fitt.

2

10 But on his brest a bloudie Crosse he bore,
  The deare remembrance of his dying Lord,
  For whose sweete sake that glorious badge he wore,
  And dead as living ever him adored:
  Upon his shield the like was also scored,
15 For soveraine hope, which in his helpe he had:
  Right faithfull true he was in deede and word,
  But of his cheere [6] did seeme too solemne sad; °   *serious*
Yet nothing did he dread, but ever was ydrad.°   *dreaded, feared*

3

Upon a great adventure he was bond,
20 That greatest Gloriana to him gave,
  That greatest Glorious Queene of Faerie Lond,
  To winne him worship, and her grace to have,
  Which of all earthly things he most did crave;
  And ever as he rode, his hart did earne °   *yearn*
25 To prove his puissance in battell brave
  Upon his foe, and his new force to learne;
Upon his foe, a Dragon horrible and stearne.

4

A lovely Ladie rode him faire beside,
  Upon a lowly Asse more white then snow,
30 Yet she much whiter, but the same did hide
  Under a vele, that wimpled ° was full low,   *folded*
  And over all a blacke stole she did throw,
  As one that inly mournd: so was she sad,
  And heavie sat upon her palfrey slow:
35 Seeméd in heart some hidden care she had,
And by her in a line a milke white lambe she lad.[7]

---

5. Redcrosse wears the armor of the Christian man, as Spenser explained in the letter to Ralegh: "put on the whole armor of God, that ye may be able to stand against the wiles of the devil" (Ephesians vi.10–22). The armor bears the dents of every Christian's fight against evil; Redcrosse himself is as yet untried.
6. Facial expression.

7. The lady will be called by name in line 405; she is Una, short for *Una Vera Fides,* "The One True Faith" (if it is true it can only be *one*). But, like other figures, she may bear other roles and attributes. Therefore she may also be the Church of England, with whom Redcrosse, in his role as Britain (St. George) will be united. Her parents typify all mankind—originally lords of

5

So pure an innocent, as that same lambe,
  She was in life and every vertuous lore,
  And by descent from Royall lynage came
40 Of ancient Kings and Queenes, that had of yore
  Their scepters stretcht from East to Westerne shore,
  And all the world in their subjection held;
  Till that infernall feend with foule uprore
  Forwasted all their land, and them expeld:
45 Whom to avenge, she had this Knight from far compeld.°   *summoned*

6

Behind her farre away a Dwarfe did lag,
  That lasie seemd in being ever last,
  Or wearied with bearing of her bag
  Of needments at his backe.[8] Thus as they past,
50 The day with cloudes was suddeine overcast,
  And angry Jove an hideous storme of raine
  Did poure into his Lemans[9] lap so fast,
  That every wight° to shrowd° it did constrain,   *creature/cover*
And this faire couple eke ° to shroud themselves were fain.   *also*

7

55 Enforst to seeke some covert nigh at hand,
  A shadie grove not far away they spide,
  That promist ayde the tempest to withstand:
  Whose loftie trees yclad with sommers pride,
  Did spred so broad, that heavens light did hide,
60 Not perceable with power of any starre:
  And all within were pathes and alleies wide,
  With footing worne, and leading inward farre:
Faire harbour that them seemes; so in they entred arre.

8

And foorth they passe, with pleasure forward led,
65 Joying to heare the birdes sweete harmony,
  Which therein shrouded from the tempest dred,
  Seemd in their song to scorne the cruell sky.
  Much can° they prayse the trees, so straight and hy,   *did*
  The sayling Pine, the Cedar proud and tall,

Eden, now fallen. She is veiled because fallen man cannot see the one truth but only fragments thereof, and she is sad because man is fallen. It is a characteristic Spenserian subtlety that Una enters the poem under a veil and only appears to the Redcrosse Knight, unveiled and radiant, in Canto vii. The "lowly Asse" she rides (line 29) is a figure of humility (cf. Christ's entry into Jerusalem), and the "lambe" is that of innocence. Having filled its symbolic function, the lamb does not appear in the poem again. C. S. Lewis, in *The Allegory of Love* (pp. 310–11) discusses another aspect of Spenser's alle-gorical imagination that this passage reveals: "the lady was commonly represented leading her lamb in the pageants [local religious dramas] of St. George and the dragon." That is, many of the associations evoked in *The Faerie Queene* are not merely literary but "popular, homely, patriotic."

8. The Dwarfe is sometimes taken as Redcrosse's conscience—useful in emergencies, otherwise forgotten or lost. In addition, or alternatively, the Dwarfe may represent common sense or common prudence.

9. His lover, i.e., the earth.

70   The vine-prop Elme, the Poplar never dry,
        The builder Oake, sole king of forrests all,
The Aspine good for staves, the Cypresse funerall.

9

The Laurell, meed° of mightie Conquerours   *reward*
    And Poets sage, the Firre that weepeth still,
75   The Willow worne of forlorne Paramours,
    The Eugh obedient to the benders will,
    The Birch for shafts, the Sallow for the mill,
    The Mirrhe sweete bleeding in the bitter wound,
    The warlike Beech, the Ash for nothing ill,
80   The fruitfull Olive, and the Platane round,
The carver Holme, the Maple seeldom inward sound.[1]

10

Led with delight, they thus beguile the way,
    Untill the blustring storme is overblowne;
    When weening° to returne, whence they did stray,   *supposing*
85   They cannot finde that path, which first was showne,
    But wander too and fro in wayes unknowne,
    Furthest from end then, when they neerest weene,
    That makes them doubt, their wits be not their owne:
    So many pathes, so many turnings seene,
90 That which of them to take, in diverse doubt they been.

11

At last resolving forward still to fare,
    Till that some end they finde or° in or out,   *either*
    That path they take, that beaten seemd most bare,
    Which when by tract[2] they hunted had throughout,
95   And like to lead the labyrinth about;°   *out of*
    At length it brought them to a hollow cave,
    Amid the thickest woods. The Champion stout
    Eftsoones° dismounted from his courser brave,   *forthwith*
And to the Dwarfe a while his needlesse spere he gave.

12

100 "Be well aware," quoth then that Ladie milde,
    "Least suddaine mischiefe ye too rash provoke:
    The danger hid, the place unknowne and wilde,
    Breedes dreadfull doubts: Oft fire is without smoke,
    And perill without show: therefore your stroke
105   Sir knight with-hold, till further triall made."
    "Ah Ladie," said he, "shame were to revoke
    The forward footing for° an hidden shade: *because of*
Vertue gives her selfe light, through darkenesse for to wade."

13

"Yea but," quoth she, "the perill of this place
110   I better wot then you, though now too late

---

1. In these lines, Spenser has been imitating Chaucer's catalogue of trees in the *Parliament of Fowls;* the convention goes back to Ovid.
2. By following the track.

To wish you backe returne with foule disgrace,
Yet wisedome warnes, whilest foot is in the gate,
To stay the steepe, ere forcéd to retrate.
This is the wandring wood, this Errours den,
115 A monster vile, whom God and man does hate:
Therefore I read° beware." "Fly fly," quoth then   *advise*
The fearefull Dwarfe: "this is no place for living men."

14

But full of fire and greedy hardiment,°   *boldness*
The youthfull knight could not for ought be staide,
120 But forth unto the darksome hole he went,
And lookéd in: his glistring armor made
A litle glooming light, much like a shade,
By which he saw the ugly monster plaine,
Halfe like a serpent horribly displaide,[3]
125 But th' other halfe did womans shape retaine,
Most lothsom, filthie, foule, and full of vile disdaine.

15

And as she lay upon the durtie ground,
Her huge long taile her den all overspred,
Yet was in knots and many boughtes° upwound,   *coils*
130 Pointed with mortall sting. Of her there bred
A thousand yong ones, which she dayly fed,
Sucking upon her poisonous dugs, eachone
Of sundry shapes, yet all ill favoréd:
Soone as that uncouth° light upon them shone,   *unfamiliar*
135 Into her mouth they crept, and suddain all were gone.

16

Their dam upstart, out of her den effraide,
And rushéd forth, hurling her hideous taile
About her curséd head, whose folds displaid
Were stretcht now forth at length without
140   entraile.°   *winding, coiling*
She lookt about, and seeing one in mayle
Arméd to point, sought backe to turne againe;
For light she hated as the deadly bale,°   *evil*
Ay wont in desert darknesse to remaine,
145 Where plaine none might her see, nor she see any plaine.

17

Which when the valiant Elfe[4] pereived, he lept
As Lyon fierce upon the flying pray,
And with his trenchand° blade her boldly kept   *cutting*
From turning backe, and forcéd her to stay:
150 Therewith enraged she loudly gan to bray,

3. That Errour (or theological, doctrinal heresy) is half serpent reminds us of the primal error in Eden, which the serpent instigated. "Errour," at first glance, may not seem an important demon; here Lewis is helpful in reminding us that "Spenser is writing in an age of religious doubt and controversy when the avoid-ance of error is a problem as pressing as, and in a sense prior to, the conquest of sin" (*Allegory of Love*, p. 334). The description echoes both classical and Biblical monsters (cf. Revelation ix.7–10).
4. Knight of Faerie Land.

150 And turning fierce, her speckled taile advaunst,
Threatning her angry sting, him to dismay:
Who nough aghast, his mightie hand enhaunst:°   *lifted up*
The stroke down from her head unto her shoulder glaunst.

18

Much daunted with that dint, her sence was dazd,
155 Yet kindling rage, her selfe she gathered round,
And all attonce her beastly body raizd
With doubled forces high above the ground:
Tho° wrapping up her wrethéd sterne arownd,   *then*
Lept fierce upon his shield, and her huge traine°   *tail*
160 All suddenly about his body wound,
That hand or foot to stirre he strove in vaine:
God helpe the man so wrapt in Errours endlesse traine.

19

His Lady sad to see his sore constraint,
Cride out, "Now now Sir knight, shew what ye bee,
165 Add faith unto your force, and be not faint:
Strangle her, else she sure will strangle thee."
That when he heard, in great perplexitie,
His gall did grate for griefe° and high disdaine,   *wrath*
And knitting all his force got one hand free,
170 Wherewith he grypt her gorge° with so great paine,   *neck*
That soone to loose her wicked bands did her constraine.

20

Therewith she spewd out of her filthy maw
A floud of poyson horrible and blacke,
Full of great lumpes of flesh and gobbets raw,
175 Which stunck so vildly, that it forst him slacke
His grasping hold, and from her turne him backe:
Her vomit full of bookes and papers[5] was,
With loathly frogs and toades, which eyes did lacke,
And creeping sought way in the weedy gras:
180 Her filthy parbreake° all the place deféd has.[6]   *vomit*

21

As when old father Nilus gins to swell
With timely pride above the Aegyptian vale,
His fattie° waves do fertile slime outwell,   *rich*
And overflow each plaine and lowly dale:
185 But when his later spring gins to avale,°   *subside*
Huge heapes of mudd he leaves, wherein there breed
Ten thousand kindes of creatures, partly male
And partly female of his fruitfull seed;
Such ugly monstrous shapes elswhere may no man reed.°   *see*

---

5. The reference is to books and pamphlets of Catholic propaganda, particularly attacks on Queen Elizabeth in 1588—and, indeed, to violent religious controversy of any kind.

6. Revelation xvi.13: "And I saw three unclean spirits like frogs come out of the mouth of the dragon, and out of the mouth of the beast, and out of the mouth of the false prophet."

22

190 The same so sore annoyéd has the knight,
    That welnigh chokéd with the deadly stinke,
    His forces faile, ne can no longer fight.
    Whose corage when the feend perceived to shrinke,
    She pouréd forth out of her hellish sinke
195   Her fruitfull curséd spawne of serpents small,
    Deforméd monsters, fowle, and blacke as inke,
    Which swarming all about his legs did crall,
And him encombred sore, but could not hurt at all.

23

    As gentle Shepheard in sweete even-tide,
200   When ruddy Phoebus gins to welke° in west,   *sink*
    High on an hill, his flocke to vewen wide,
    Markes which do byte their hasty supper best;
    A cloud of combrous gnattes do him molest,
    All striving to infixe their feeble stings,
205   That from their noyance he no where can rest,
    But with his clownish° hands their tender wings   *rustic*
He brusheth oft, and oft doth mar their murmurings.

24

    Thus ill bestedd,° and fearfull more of shame,   *situated*
    Then of the certaine perill he stood in,
210   Halfe furious unto his foe he came,
    Resolved in minde all suddenly to win,
    Or soone to lose, before he once would lin;°   *cease, stop*
    And strooke at her with more then manly force,
    That from her body full of filthie sin
215   He raft° her hatefull head without remorse;   *cut away*
A streame of cole black bloud forth gushéd from her corse.

25

    Her scattred brood, soone as their Parent deare
    They saw so rudely falling to the ground,
    Groning full deadly, all with troublous feare,
220   Gathred themselves about her body round,
    Weening their wonted entrance to have found
    At her wide mouth: but being there withstood
    They flockéd all about her bleeding wound,
    And suckéd up their dying mothers blood,
225 Making her death their life, and eke° her hurt their good.   *also*

26

    That detestable sight him much amazde,
    To see th' unkindly Impes of heaven accurst,
    Devoure their dam; on whom while so he gazd,
    Having all satisfide their bloudy thurst,
230   Their bellies swolne he saw with fulnesse burst,
    And bowels gushing forth: well worthy end
    Of such as drunke her life, the which them nurst;
    Now needeth him no lenger labour spend,
His foes have slaine themselves, with whom he should contend.

27

235   His Ladie seeing all, that chaunst, from farre
          Approcht in hast to greet his victorie,
          And said, "Faire knight, borne under happy starre,
          Who see your vanquisht foes before you lye;
          Well worthy be you of that Armorie,[7]
240   Wherein ye have great glory wonne this day,
          And prooved your strength on a strong enimie,
          Your first adventure: many such I pray,
      And henceforth ever wish, that like succeed it may."

28

      Then mounted he upon his Steede againe,
245   And with the Lady backward sought to wend;
          That path he kept, which beaten was most plaine,
          Ne ever would to any by-way bend,
          But still did follow one unto the end,
          The which at last out of the wood them brought.
250   So forward on his way (with God to frend[8])
          He passéd forth, and new adventure sought;
      Long way he travelléd, before he heard of ought.

29

      At length they chaunst to meet upon the way
          An aged Sire, in long blacke weedes yclad,[9]
255   His feete all bare, his beard all hoarie gray,
          And by his belt his booke he hanging had;
          Sober he seemde, and very sagely sad,°   *pensive*
          And to the ground his eyes were lowly bent,
          Simple in shew, and voyde of malice bad,
260   And all the way he prayéd, as he went,
      And often knockt his brest, as one that did repent.[1]

30

      He faire the knight saluted, louting° low,   *bowing*
          Who faire him quited,° as that courteous was: *answered*
          And after askéd him, if he did know
265   Of straunge adventures, which abroad did pas.
          "Ah my deare Sonne," quoth he, "how should, alas,
          Silly° old man, that lives in hidden cell,   *innocent*
          Bidding° his beades all day for his trespas,   *telling*
          Tydings of warre and worldly trouble tell?
270   With holy father sits not with such things to mell.°   *meddle*

7. I.e., Christian armor.
8. With God as friend.
9. Dressed in long black garments.
1. The Sire is in reality Archimago (arch, or head, magician)—i.e., hypocrisy, the archdeceiver, Satan, idolatry of the Roman Catholic Church. He is disguised as a holy man, as evil is so often under the guise of good in Christian thought and legend. Note (especially in lines 312–15) that his "holiness" is in talking, not in doing, and that he is far too reminiscent of the Catholic monasteries to be trustworthy. The black magician in hermit's disguise often appears in medieval romance and in Italian romance epics.

31

"But if of daunger which hereby doth dwell,
  And homebred evill ye desire to heare,
  Of a straunge man I can you tidings tell,
  That wasteth all this countrey farre and neare."
275 "Of such," said he, "I chiefly do inquere,
  And shall you well reward to shew the place,
  In which that wicked wight his dayes doth weare:
  For to all knighthood it is foule disgrace,
That such a cursed creature lives so long a space."

32

280 "Far hence," quoth he, "in wastfull° wildernesse   *desolate*
  His dwelling is, by which no living wight
  May ever passe, but thorough great distresse."
  "Now," sayd the Lady, "draweth toward night,
  And well I wote, that of your later° fight   *recent*
285 Ye all forwearied be: for what so strong,
  But wanting rest will also want of might?
  The Sunne that measures heaven all day long,
At night doth baite° his steedes the Ocean waves emong. *feed, refresh*

33

"Then with the Sunne take Sir, your timely rest,
290 And with new day new worke at once begin:
  Untroubled night they say gives counsell best."
  "Right well Sir knight ye have advised bin,"
  Quoth then that aged man; "the way to win
  Is wisely to advise: now day is spent;
295 Therefore with me ye may take up your In°   *lodging*
  For this same night." The knight was well content:
So with that godly father to his home they went.

34

A little lowly Hermitage it was,
  Downe in a dale, hard by a forests side,
300 Far from resort of people, that did pas
  In travell to and froe: a little wyde°   *apart*
  There was an holy Chappell edifyde,°   *built*
  Wherein the Hermite dewly wont° to say   *was wont*
  His holy things each morne and eventyde:
305 Thereby a Christall streame did gently play,
Which from a sacred fountaine welléd forth alway.

35

Arrivéd there, the little house they fill,
  Ne looke for entertainement, where none was:
  Rest is their feast, and all things at their will;
310 The noblest mind the best contentment has.
  With faire discourse the evening so they pas:
  For that old man of pleasing wordes had store,
  And well could file his tongue as smooth as glas;
  He told of Saintes and Popes, and evermore
315 He strowd an *Ave-Mary* after and before.

36

The drouping Night thus creepeth on them fast,
    And the sad humour[2] loading their eye liddes,
    As messenger of Morpheus[3] on them cast
    Sweet slombring deaw, the which to sleepe them biddes.
320   Unto their lodgings then his guestes he riddes:°   *leads*
    Where when all drownd in deadly sleepe he findes,
    He to his study goes, and there amiddes
    His Magick bookes and artes of sundry kindes,
He seekes out mighty charmes, to trouble sleepy mindes.

37

325 Then choosing out few wordes most horrible
    (Let none them read), thereof did verses frame,
    With which and other spelles like terrible,
    He bade awake blacke Plutoes griesly Dame,[4]
    And curséd heaven, and spake reprochfull shame
330   Of highest God, the Lord of life and light;
    A bold bad man, that dared to call by name
    Great Gorgon, Prince of darknesse and dead night,
At which Cocytus quakes, and Styx[5] is put to flight.

38

And forth he cald out of deepe darknesse dred
335   Legions of Sprights, the which like little flyes
    Fluttring about his ever damnéd hed,
    A-waite whereto their service he applyes,
    To aide his friends, or fray° his enimies: *frighten*
    Of those he chose out two, the falsest twoo,
340   And fittest for to forge true-seeming lyes;
    The one of them he gave a message too,
The other by him selfe staide other worke to doo.

39
                                          dispersed

He making speedy way through sperséd° ayre,
    And through the world of waters wide and deepe,
    To Morpheus house doth hastily repaire.
345   Amid the bowels of the earth full steepe,
    And low, where dawning day doth never peepe,
    His dwelling is; there Tethys[6] his wet bed
    Doth ever wash, and Cynthia[7] still doth steepe
350   In silver deaw his ever-drouping hed,
Whiles sad Night over him her mantle black doth spred.

40

Whose double gates he findeth lockéd fast,
    The one faire framed of burnisht Yvory,
    The other all with silver overcast;
355   And wakefull dogges before them farre do lye,

---

2. Heavy moisture.
3. The god of sleep.
4. I.e., Proserpine.

5. Rivers of hell.
6. The wife of Ocean.
7. I.e., Diana, the goddess of the moon.

Watching to banish Care their enimy,
Who oft is wont to trouble gentle Sleepe.
By them the Sprite doth passe in quietly,
And unto Morpheus comes, whom drownéd deepe
360 In drowsie fit he findes: of nothing he takes keepe.° *notice*

41

And more, to lulle him in his slumber soft,
 A trickling streame from high rocke tumbling downe
And ever-drizling raine upon the loft,
 Mixt with a murmuring winde, much like the sowne
365 Of swarming Bees, did cast him in a swowne:° *faint*
 No other noyse, nor peoples troublous cryes,
As still° are wont t'annoy the walléd towne, *always*
 Might there be heard: but carelesse Quiet lyes,
Wrapt in eternall silence farre from enemyes.[8]

42

370 The messenger approching to him spake,
 But his wast° wordes returnd to him in vaine: *wasted*
So sound he slept, that nought mought him awake.
 Then rudely he him thrust, and pusht with paine,
 Whereat he gan to stretch: but he againe
375 Shooke him so hard, that forced him to speake.
 As one then in a dreame, whose dryer braine[9]
Is tost with troubled sights and fancies weake,
He mumbled soft, but would not all his silence breake.

43

The Sprite then gan more boldly him to wake,
380 And threatned unto him the dreaded name
Of Hecate:[1] whereat he gan to quake,
 And lifting up his lumpish head, with blame
 Halfe angry askéd him, for what he came.
"Hither," quoth he, "me Archimago sent,
385 He that the stubborne Sprites can wisely tame,
He bids thee to him send for his intent
A fit false dreame, that can delude the sleepers sent."° *senses*

44

The God obayde, and calling forth straight way
 A diverse° dreame out of his prison darke, *misleading*
390 Delivered it to him, and downe did lay
 His heavie head, devoide of carefull carke,[2]
 Whose sences all were straight benumbd and starke.
He backe returning by the Yvorie dore,[3]

---

8. Spenser is imitating descriptions of the house of Morpheus in Chaucer, Ovid, and other ancient writers, but he achieves originality, particularly by means of the sound effects in stanza 41.
9. According to the old physiology, old people and other light sleepers had too little moisture in the brain.
1. Queen of Hades.
2. Anxious concerns.
3. False dreams came through the ivory door, true dreams through the gate of horn (Homer, *Odyssey* XIX.562–67; Virgil, *Aeneid* VI.893–96).

Remounted up as light as chearefull Larke,
395   And on his litle winges the dreame he bore
In hast unto his Lord, where he him left afore.

45

Who all this while with charmes and hidden artes,
    Had made a Lady of that other Spright,
    And framed of liquid ayre her tender partes
400   So lively,° and so like in all mens sight,   *lifelike*
    That weaker° sence it could have ravisht quight   *too weak*
    The maker selfe for all his wondrous witt,
    Was nigh beguiléd with so goodly sight:
    Her all in white he clad, and over it
405 Cast a blacke stole, most like to seeme for Una[4] fit.

46

Now when that ydle dreame was to him brought
    Unto that Elfin knight he bad him fly,
    Where he slept soundly void of evill thought
    And with false shewes abuse his fantasy,°   *imagination*
410   In sort as[5] he him schooléd privily:
    And that new creature borne without her dew[6]
    Full of the makers guile, with usage sly
    He taught to imitate that Lady trew,
Whose semblance she did carrie under feignéd hew.°   *form*

47

415 Thus well instructed, to their worke they hast
    And comming where the knight in slomber lay
    The one upon his hardy head him plast,
    And made him dreame of loves and lustfull play
    That nigh his manly hart did melt away,
420   Bathéd in wanton blis and wicked joy:
    Then seeméd him his Lady by him lay,
    And to him playnd,° how that false wingéd boy   *complained*
Her chast hart had subdewd, to learne Dame pleasures toy.

48

And she her selfe of beautie soveraigne Queene
425   Faire Venus seemde unto his bed to bring
    Her, whom he waking evermore did weene
    To be the chastest flowre, that ay° did spring   *ever*
    On earthly braunch, the daughter of a king,
    Now a loose Leman° to vile service bound: *paramour*
430   And eke the Graces seeméd all to sing,
    Hymen iô Hymen, dauncing all around,
Whilst freshest Flora her with Yvie girlond crownd.[7]

---

4. The lady is now given her name.
5. In the way.
6. Unnaturally.
7. The three graces of classical mythology were personifications of grace and beauty, yet here they sing a call to the pleasures of the marriage bed (Hymen was god of marriage). On Flora, cf. E.K.'s Glosse to the March eclogue: "the Goddesse of flowres, but indede (as saith Tacitus) a famous harlot."

49

In this great passion of unwonted lust,
 Or wonted feare of doing ought amis,
435 He started up, as seeming to mistrust
  Some secret ill, or hidden foe of his:
  Lo there before his face his Lady is,
  Under blake stole hyding her bayted hooke,
  And as halfe blushing offred him to kis,
440 With gentle blandishment and lovely looke,
Most like that virgin true, which for her knight him took.

50

All cleane dismayd to see so uncouth sight,
 And halfe enragéd at her shamelesse guise,
 He thought have slaine her in his fierce despight:°   *indignation*
445 But hasty heat tempring with sufferance wise,
  He stayde his hand, and gan himselfe advise
  To prove his sense, and tempt her faignéd truth.
  Wringing her hands in wemens pitteous wise,
  Tho can she[8] weepe, to stirre up gentle ruth,°   *pity*
450 Both for her noble bloud, and for her tender youth.

51

And said, "Ah Sir, my liege Lord and my love,
 Shall I accuse the hidden cruell fate,
 And mightie causes wrought in heaven above,
 Or the blind God, that doth me thus amate,°   *dismay*
455 For° hopéd love to winne me certaine hate?   *instead of*
  Yet thus perforce he bids me do, or die.
  Die is my dew: yet rew my wretched state
  You, whom my hard avenging destinie
Hath made judge of my life or death indifferently.

52

460 "Your owne deare sake forst me at first to leave
 My Fathers kingdome," There she stopt with teares;
 Her swollen hart her speach seemd to bereave,
  And then againe begun, "My weaker yeares
  Captived to fortune and frayle worldly feares,
465 Fly to your faith for succour and sure ayde:
  Let me not dye in languor and long teares.
  "Why Dame," quoth he, "what hath ye thus dismayd?
What frayes ye, that were wont to comfort me affrayd?"

53

"Love of your selfe," she said, "and deare° constraint   *dire*
470 Lets me not sleepe, but wast the wearie night
 In secret anguish and unpittied plaint,
  Whiles you in carelesse sleepe are drownéd quight."
  Her doubtfull words made that redoubted knight
  Suspect her truth: yet since no untruth he knew,

8. Then she began to.

475 Her fawning love with foule disdainefull spight
 He would not shend,° but said, "Deare dame I rew,   *reject*
That for my sake unknowne such griefe unto you grew.

54

"Assure your selfe, it fell not all to ground;
 For all so deare as life is to my hart,
480 I deeme your love, and hold me to you bound;
 Ne let vaine feares procure your needlesse smart,
 Where cause is none, but to your rest depart."
 Not all content, yet seemd she to appease°   *cease*
 Her mournefull plaintes, beguiléd of her art,
485 And fed with words, that could not chuse but please,
So slyding softly forth, she turnd as to her ease.

55

Long after lay he musing at her mood,
 Much grieved to thinke that gentle Dame so light,
 For whose defence he was to shed his blood.
490 At last dull wearinesse of former fight
 Having yrockt a sleepe his irkesome spright,°   *spirit*
 That troublous dreame gan freshly tosse his braine,
 With bowres, and beds, and Ladies deare delight:⁹
 But when he saw his labour all was vaine,
495 With that misforméd spright he backe returnd againe.

Canto II

*The guilefull great Enchaunter parts
The Redcrosse Knight from Truth:
Into whose stead faire falshood steps,
And workes him wofull ruth.*

1

By this the Northerne wagoner had set
 His seven fold teame behind the stedfast starre,¹
 That was in Ocean waves yet never wet,
 But firme is fixt, and sendeth light from farre
5 To all, that in the wide deepe wandring arre.
 And chearefull Chaunticlere with his note shrill
 Had warnéd once, that Phoebus fiery carre²
 In hast was climbing up the Easterne hill,
Full envious that night so long his roome did fill.

2

10 When those accurséd messengers of hell,
 That feigning dreame, and that faire-forgéd Spright
 Came to their wicked maister, and gan tell
 Their bootelesse° paines, and ill succeeding night: *useless*
 Who all in rage to see his skilfull might

---

9. Redcrosse has been unable to distinguish the false Una from the true because his reason has been clouded by desire (see I.ii.6).

1. I.e., by this time the Big Dipper had set behind the North Star.
2. The chariot of the sun.

15 Deluded so, gan threaten hellish paine
     And sad Prosérpines wrath, them to affright.
     But when he saw his threatning was but vaine,
   He cast about, and searcht his balefull° bookes againe.   *deadly*

                              3
   Eftsoones he tooke that miscreated faire,
20   And that false other Spright, on whom he spred
       A seeming body of the subtile aire,
       Like a young Squire, in loves and lusty-hed
       His wanton dayes that ever loosely led,
       Without regard of armes and dreaded fight:
25   Those two he tooke, and in a secret bed,
       Covered with darknesse and misdeeming° night,   *misleading*
   Them both together laid, to joy in vaine delight.

                              4
   Forthwith he runnes with feignéd faithfull hast
     Unto his guest, who after troublous sights
30   And dreames, gan now to take more sound repast,°   *rest*
       Whom suddenly he wakes with fearefull frights,
       As one aghast with feends or damnéd sprights,
       And to him cals, "Rise rise unhappy Swaine,
       That here wex old in sleepe, whiles wicked wights
35   Have knit themselves in Venus shamefull chaine;
   Come see, where your false Lady doth her honour staine."

                              5
   All in amaze he suddenly up start
     With sword in hand, and with the old man went;
     Who soone him brought into a secret part,
40   Where that false couple were full closely ment°   *mingled*
       In wanton lust and lewd embracément:
       Which when he saw, he burnt with gealous fire,
       The eye of reason was with rage yblent,°   *blinded*
       And would have slaine them in his furious ire,
45 But hardly was restreinéd of that aged sire.

                              6
   Returning to his bed in torment great,
     And bitter anguish of his guiltie sight,
     He could not rest, but did his stout heart eat,
     And wast his inward gall with deepe despight,
50   Yrkesome of life, and too long lingring night.
       At last faire Hesperus[3] in highest skie
       Had spent his lampe, and brought forth dawning light
       Then up he rose, and clad him hastily;
   The Dwarfe him brought his steed: so both away do fly.[4]

                              7
55 Now when the rosy-fingred Morning faire,
     Weary of aged Tithones[5] saffron bed,

3. The evening star.
4. Reason and discrimination are defeated, and so "Holiness" is separated
from the one true faith.
5. The husband of Aurora, goddess of
the dawn.

Had spred her purple robe through deawy aire,
And the high hils Titan° discoveréd,   *the sun*
The royall virgin shooke off drowsy-hed,
60 And rising forth out of her baser° bowre,   *humbler*
Lookt for her knight, who far away was fled,
And for her Dwarfe, that wont to wait each houre;
Then gan she waile and weepe, to see that woefull stowre.°   *affliction*

8

And after him she rode with so much speede
65 As her slow beast could make; but all in vaine:
For him so far had borne his light-foot steede,
Prickéd with wrath and fiery fierce disdaine,
That him to follow was but fruitlesse paine;
Yet she her weary limbes would never rest,
70 But every hill and dale, each wood and plaine
Did search, sore grievéd in her gentle brest,
He so ungently left her, whom she lovéd best.

9

But subtill Archimago, when his guests
He saw divided into double parts,
75 And Una wandring in woods and forrests,
Th' end of his drift, he praisd his divelish arts
That had such might over true meaning harts;
Yet rests not so, but other meanes doth make,
How he may worke unto her further smarts:
80 For her he hated as the hissing snake,
And in her many troubles did most pleasure take.

10

He then devisde himselfe how to disguise;
For by his mightie science° he could take   *knowledge*
As many formes and shapes in seeming wise,
85 As ever Proteus to himselfe could make:
Sometime a fowle, sometime a fish in lake,
Now like a foxe, now like a dragon fell,°   *fierce*
That of himselfe he oft for feare would quake,
And oft would flie away. O who can tell
90 The hidden power of herbes, and might of Magicke spell?

11

But now seemde best, the person to put on
Of that good knight, his late beguiléd guest:
In mighty armes he was yclad anon,
And silver shield: upon his coward brest
95 A bloudy crosse, and on his craven crest
A bounch of haires discolourd diversly:
Full jolly knight he seemde, and well addrest,
And when he sate upon his courser free,
Saint George himself ye would have deeméd him to be.[6]

6. Archimago, in disguising himself as Holiness, takes on the role of the Anti-Christ.

12

100 But he the knight, whose semblaunt° he did beare,   *likeness*
　　　The true Saint George was wandred far away,
　　　Still flying from his thoughts and gealous feare;
　　　Will was his guide,[7] and griefe led him astray.
　　　At last him chaunst to meete upon the way
105 A faithlesse Sarazin° all armed to point,   *Saracen*
　　　In whose great shield was writ with letters gay
　　　Sans foy:[8] full large of limbe and every joint
He was, and caréd not for God or man a point.

13

He had a faire companion of his way,
110 A goodly Lady clad in scarlot red,
　　　Purfled° with gold and pearle of rich assay,   *decorated*
　　　And like a Persian mitre on her hed
　　　She wore, with crownes and owches° garnishéd,   *brooches*
　　　The which her lavish lovers to her gave;
115 Her wanton palfrey all was overspred
　　　With tinsell trappings, woven like a wave,
Whose bridle rung with golden bels and bosses brave.

14

With faire disport° and courting dalliaunce   *diversion*
　　　She intertainde her lover all the way:
120 But when she saw the knight his speare advaunce,
　　　She soone left off her mirth and wanton play,
　　　And bad her knight addresse him to the fray:
　　　His foe was nigh at hand. He prickt° with pride   *pranced*
　　　And hope to winne his Ladies heart that day,
125 Forth spurréd fast: adowne his coursers side
The red bloud trickling staind the way, as he did ride.

15

The knight of the Redcrosse when him he spide,
　　　Spurring so hote with rage dispiteous,
　　　Gan fairely couch° his speare, and towards ride: *lower*
130 Soone meete they both, both fell and furious,
　　　That daunted with their forces hideous,
　　　Their steeds do stagger, and amazéd stand,
　　　And eke themselves too rudely rigorous,
　　　Astonied° with the stroke of their owne hand,   *stunned*
135 Do backe rebut,° and each to other yeeldeth land.   *recoil*

16

As when two rams stird with ambitious pride,
　　　Fight for the rule of the rich fleecéd flocke,
　　　Their hornéd fronts so fierce on either side
　　　Do meete, that with the terrour of the shocke

7. Will was his guide; but will, of all the human faculties, is least fitted to be one's guide; it should itself be under the guidance of intelligence or truth.
8. Redcrosse's victory over the monster Errour did not give him the discrimination to pierce the deceptions of either Archimago or the false Una. His second trial will be against Sans foy—"without faith," atheism.

140 Astonied both, stand sencelesse as a blocke,
    Forgetfull of the hanging victory:
    So stood these twaine, unmovéd as a rocke,
    Both staring fierce, and holding idely
The broken reliques of their former cruelty.

                    17

145 The Sarazin sore daunted with the buffe
    Snatcheth his sword, and fiercely to him flies;
    Who well it wards, and quyteth° cuff with cuff: *requites*
    Each others equall puissaunce envies,
    And through their iron sides with cruell spies°   *looks*
150 Does seeke to perce: repining courage yields
    No foote to foe. The flashing fier flies
    As from a forge out of their burning shields,
And streames of purple bloud new dies the verdant fields.

                    18

    "Curse on that Crosse," quoth then the Sarazin,
155 "That keepes thy body from the bitter fit;°   *stroke*
    Dead long ygoe I wote thou haddest bin,
    Had not that charme from thee forwarnéd it:
    But yet I warne thee now assuréd sitt,
    And hide thy head." Therewith upon his crest
160 With rigour so outrageous he smitt,
    That a large share it hewd out of the rest,
And glauncing downe his shield, from blame him fairely blest.[9]

                    19

    Who thereat wondrous wroth, the sleeping spark
    Of native vertue gan eftsoones revive,
165 And at his haughtie helmet making mark,
    So hugely stroke, that it the steele did rive,
    And cleft his head. He tumbling downe alive,
    With bloudy mouth his mother earth did kis,
    Greeting his grave: his grudging ghost did strive
170 With the fraile flesh; at last it flitted is,
Whither the soules do fly of men, that live amis.

                    20

    The Lady when she saw her champion fall,
    Like the old ruines of a broken towre,
    Staid not to waile his woefull funerall,
175 But from him fled away with all her powre;
    Who after her as hastily gan scowre,°   *scurry*
    Bidding the Dwarfe with him to bring away
    The Sarazins shield, signe of the conqueroure.
    Her soone he overtooke, and bad to stay,
180 For present cause was none of dread her to dismay.

                    21

    She turning backe with ruefull countenaunce,
    Cride, "Mercy mercy Sir vouchsafe to show
    On silly° Dame, subject to hard mischaunce,   *innocent*

9. Preserved him from harm.

And to your mighty will." Her humblesse low
185 In so ritch weedes and seeming glorious show,
Did much emmove his stout heroicke heart,
And said, "Deare dame, your suddein overthrow
Much rueth° me; but now put feare apart,   grieves
And tell, both who ye be, and who that tooke your part."

22

190 Melting in teares, then gan she thus lament;
"The wretched woman, whom unhappy howre
Hath now made thrall to your commandément,
Before that angry heavens list to lowre,
And fortune false betraide me to your powre
195 Was (O what now availeth that I was!)
Borne the sole daughter of an Emperour,
He that the wide West under his rule has,
And high hath set his throne, where Tiberis doth pas.[1]

23

"He in the first flowre of my freshest age,
200 Betrothéd me unto the onely haire°   heir
Of a most mighty king, most rich and sage;
Was never Prince so faithfull and so faire,
Was never Prince so meeke and debonaire;°   gracious
But ere my hopéd day of spousall shone,
205 My dearest Lord fell from high honours staire,
Into the hands of his accursed fone,°   foes
And cruelly was slaine, that shall I ever mone.

24

"His blessed body spoild of lively breath,
Was afterward, I know not how, convaid
210 And fro me hid: of whose most innocent death
When tidings came to me unhappy maid,
O how great sorrow my sad soule assaid.°   afflicted
Then forth I went his woefull corse to find,
And many yeares throughout the world I straid,

---

1. The Tiber River runs through Rome. The lady's admission that she is the daughter of Rome (and hence the Roman Catholic Church) is an immediate clue to the fact that she is evil. Her appearance, as described in stanza 13, was, however, also full of clues. She resembles the Whore of Babylon (Revelation xvii.3–4): "and I saw a woman sit upon a scarlet coloured beast, full of names of blasphemy, having seven heads and ten horns. And the woman was arrayed in purple and scarlet colour, and decked with gold and precious stones and pearls, having a golden cup in her hand full of abominations and filthiness of her fornication." Her father, she says, is ruler of the West—but Una's father had the rule of both East *and* West (I.i.5): on the historical plane, the true church once embraced east and west whereas the false rules only the west; truth is universal and comprehends falsehood, which is partial. As the false church, she wears the pope's miter. The Roman church is an embodiment of villainy and evil in *The Faerie Queene* because this was a time of violent Protestant-Catholic controversy in both Europe and England, which had led to exchanges of Protestant and Catholic monarchs, bloodshed, and burnings; England had only recently emerged from its own religious strife. Popular fear of Catholicism was very real, and Spenser draws partly on the "bogey" images of this fear in erecting his figures of evil.

215   A virgin widow, whose deepe wounded mind
      With love, long time did languish as the striken hind.[2]

25

      "At last it chauncéd this proud Sarazin
         To meete me wandring, who perforce me led
         With him away, but yet could never win
220   The fort, that Ladies hold in soveraigne dread.
         There lies he now with foule dishonour dead,
         Who whiles he livde, was calléd proud Sans foy,
         The eldest of three brethren, all three bred
         Of one bad sire, whose youngest is Sans joy,
225   And twixt them both was borne the bloudy bold Sans loy.[3]

26

      "In this sad plight, friendlesse, unfortunate,
         Now miserable I Fidessa dwell,
         Craving of you in pitty of my state,
         To do none° ill, if please ye not do well."   no
230   He in great passion all this while did dwell,
         More busying his quicke eyes, her face to view,
         Then his dull eares, to heare what she did tell;
         And said, "Faire Lady hart of flint would rew
      The undeservéd woes and sorrowes, which ye shew.

27

235   "Henceforth in safe assuraunce may ye rest,
         Having both found a new friend you to aid,
         And lost an old foe, that did you molest:
         Better new friend than an old foe is[4] said."
         With chaunge of cheare the seeming simple maid
240   Let fall her eyen, as shamefast to the earth,
         And yeelding soft, in that she nought gain-said,
         So forth they rode, he feining seemely merth,
      And she coy lookes: so dainty they say maketh derth.[5]

28

      Long time they thus together traveiléd,
245   Till weary of their way, they came at last,
         Where grew two goodly trees, that faire did spred
         Their armes abroad, with gray mosse overcast,
         And their greene leaves trembling with every blast,°   breeze
         Made a calme shadow far in compasse round:

2. Her story is full of lies, inasmuch as she is not a "virgin widow," while Christ, the "Prince," is not "hid"; she is unaware that he has risen from the dead.
3. Literally, "without law." Sans foy means "without faith"; Sans joy, "without joy." *The Faerie Queene* is full of characters who come in sets—opposing principles or double and triple incarnations of the same principle. Una and this lady (falsely named Fidessa, or "faith"), for example, are in opposition; the three Saracens form a triad of degenerative qualities that Holiness must defeat. For Holiness, even untried, to defeat atheism ("without faith") was comparatively easy.
4. I.e., it is.
5. Proverbial: "what's dear is rare." Here, "coyness creates unsatisfied desire." Redcrosse is unaware of the falsehoods in the lady's story—as England was seduced again to the false church during the reign of Mary.

250   The fearefull Shepheard often there aghast
      Under them never sat, ne wont there sound
His mery oaten pipe, but shund th' unlucky ground.

29

But this good knight soone as he them can spie,
      For the coole shade him thither hastly got:
255   For golden Phoebus now ymounted hie,
      From fiery wheeles of his faire chariot
      Hurléd his beame so scorching cruell hot,
      That living creature mote it not abide;
      And his new Lady it enduréd not.
260   There they alight, in hope themselves to hide
From the fierce heat, and rest their weary limbs a tide.°   *time*

30

Faire seemely pleasaunce each to other makes,
      With goodly purposes there as they sit:
      And in his falséd fancy he her takes
265   To be the fairest wight that livéd yit;
      Which to expresse, he bends his gentle wit,
      And thinking of those braunches greene to frame
      A girlond for her dainty forehead fit,
      He pluckt a bough; out of whose rift there came
270   Small drops of gory bloud, that trickled downe the same.

31

Therewith a piteous yelling voyce was heard,
      Crying, "O spare with guilty hands to teare
      My tender sides in this rough rynd embard,°   *imprisoned*
      But fly, ah fly far hence away, for feare
275   Least to you hap, that happened to me heare,
      And to this wretched Lady, my deare love,
      O too deare love, love bought with death too deare."
      Astond he stood, and up his haire did hove°   *heave, raise*
And with that suddein horror could no member move.

32

280   At last whenas the dreadfull passion
      Was overpast, and manhood well awake,
      Yet musing at the straunge occasion,
      And doubting much his sence, he thus bespake;
      "What voyce of damnéd Ghost from Limbo[6] lake,
285   Or guilefull spright wandring in empty aire,
      Both which fraile men do oftentimes mistake,°   *mislead*
      Sends to my doubtfull eares these speaches rare,
And ruefull plaints, me bidding guiltlesse bloud to spare?"

33

Then groning deepe, "Nor damned Ghost," quoth he,
290   "Nor guilefull sprite to thee these wordes doth speake,
      But once a man Fradubio,° now a tree,   *Doubt*
      Wretched man, wretched tree; whose nature weake,

6. The abode of lost spirits.

A cruell witch her curséd will to wreake,
Hath thus transformed, and plast in open plaines,
Where Boreas° doth blow full bitter bleake,   the North Wind
And scorching Sunne does dry my secret vaines:
For though a tree I seeme, yet cold and heat me paines."

34
"Say on Fradubio then, or° man, or tree,"   whether
Quoth then the knight, "by whose mischievous arts
Art thou misshapéd thus, as now I see?
He oft finds med'cine, who his griefe imparts;
But double griefs afflict concealing harts,
As raging flames who striveth to suppresse."
"The author then," said he, "of all my smarts,
Is one Duessa[7] a false sorceresse,
That many errant° knights hath brought to wretchednesse.   wandering

35
"In prime of youthly yeares, when corage hot
The fire of love and joy of chevalree
First kindled in my brest, it was my lot
To love this gentle Lady, whom ye see,
Now not a Lady, but a seeming tree;
With whom as once I rode accompanyde,
Me chauncéd of a knight encountred bee,
That had a like faire Lady by his syde,
Like a faire Lady, but did fowle Duessa hyde.

36
"Whose forgéd beauty he did take in hand,[8]
All other Dames to have exceeded farre;
I in defence of mine did likewise stand,
Mine, that did then shine as the Morning starre:
So both to battell fierce arraungéd arre,
In which his harder fortune was to fall
Under my speare: such is the dye° of warre: hazard
His Lady left as a prise martiall,[9]
Did yield her comely person, to be at my call.

37
"So doubly loved of Ladies unlike faire,
Th' one seeming such, the other such indeede,
One day in doubt I cast for to compare,
Whether° in beauties glorie did exceede;   which one (of two)
A Rosy girlond was the victors meede:°   reward
Both seemde to win, and both seemde won to bee,
So hard the discord was to be agreede.
Fraelissa° was as faire, as faire mote bee,   Frailty
And ever false Duessa seemde as faire as shee.

38
"The wicked witch now seeing all this while
The doubtfull ballaunce equally to sway,

---

7. Duessa means "two," of double nature.

8. He maintained.
9. Spoil of battle.

What not by right, she cast to win by guile,
And by her hellish science raisd streight way
A foggy mist, that overcast the day,
And a dull blast, that breathing on her face,
340   Dimmed her former beauties shining ray,
And with foule ugly forme did her disgrace:
Then was she faire alone, when none was faire in place.[1]

39

"Then cride she out, 'Fye, fye, deforméd wight,
Whose borrowed beautie now appeareth plaine
345   To have before bewitchéd all mens sight;
O leave her soone, or let her soone be slaine.'
Her lothly visage viewing with disdaine,
Eftsoones I thought her such, as she me told,
And would have kild her; but with faignéd paine,
350   The false witch did my wrathfull hand withhold;
So left her, where she now is turnd to trëen mould.[2]

40

"Thens forth I tooke Duessa for my Dame,
And in the witch unweeting° joyd long time,   *unknowingly*
Ne ever wist, but that she was the same,
355   Till on a day (that day is every Prime,[3]
When Witches wont do penance for their crime)
I chaunst to see her in her proper hew,
Bathing her selfe in origane and thyme:[4]
A filthy foule old woman I did vew,
360 That ever to have toucht her, I did deadly rew.

41

"Her neather partes misshapen, monstruous,
Were hidd in water, that I could not see,
But they did seeme more foule and hideous,
Then womans shape man would beleeve to bee.
365   Thens forth from her most beastly companie
I gan refraine, in minde to slip away,
Soone as appeard safe opportunitie:
For danger great, if not assured decay°   *destruction*
I saw before mine eyes, if I were knowne to stray.

42

370 "The divelish hag by chaunges of my cheare°   *countenance*
Perceived my thought, and drownd in sleepie night,
With wicked herbes and ointments did besmeare
My bodie all, through charmes and magicke might,
That all my senses were bereavéd quight:
375   Then brought she me into this desert waste,
And by my wretched lovers side me pight,°   *pitched*
Where now enclosd in wooden wals full faste,
Banisht from living wights, our wearie dayes we waste."

1. Perhaps, "when nobody else was fair."
2. The form of a tree.
3. The first appearance of the new moon.
4. Two kinds of herbs; they were associated, in classical tradition, with witches like Scylla, Circe, and Medea.

43

"But how long time," said then the Elfin knight,
380   "Are you in this misforméd house to dwell?"
"We may not chaunge," quoth he, "this evil plight,
Till we be bathéd in a living well;
That is the terme prescribéd by the spell."
"O how," said he, "mote I that well out find,
385   That may restore you to your wonted well?"°   *well-being*
"Time and suffiséd fates to former kynd
Shall us restore, none else from hence may us unbynd."[5]

44

The false Duessa, now Fidessa hight,°   *called*
Heard how in vaine Fradubio did lament,
390   And knew well all was true. But the good knight
Full of sad feare and ghastly dreriment,°   *gloom*
When all this speech the living tree had spent,
The bleeding bough did thrust into the ground,
That from the bloud he might be innocent,
395   And with fresh clay did close the wooden wound:
Then turning to his Lady, dead with feare her found.

45

Her seeming dead he found with feignéd feare,
As all unweeting of that well she knew,[6]
And paynd himselfe with busie care to reare
400   Her out of carelesse° swowne. Her eylids blew   *unconscious*
And dimméd sight with pale and deadly hew
At last she up gan lift: with trembling cheare
Her up he tooke, too simple and too trew,
And oft her kist. At length all passéd feare,[7]
405   He set her on her steede, and forward forth did beare.

Canto III

Forsaken Truth long seekes her love,
    And makes the Lyon mylde,
Marres° blind Devotions mart,° and fals   *spoils / business*
    In hand of leachour vylde.

1

Nought is there under heav'ns wide hollownesse,
    That moves more deare compassion of mind,

5. The tale of a man imprisoned in a tree is paralleled by Virgil's *Aeneid* III. 27–42 and Ariosto's *Orlando Furioso* VI.26–53. His hesitation between Fraelissa and Duessa parallels Redcrosse's own spiritual state between Una and Duessa (the real name of "Fidessa," as line 388 casually informs us). The very name "Duessa" (two) reveals her falsity next to Una ("one"). Note that Fra-

dubio ("father doubt") cannot warn Redcrosse against Duessa, who is present at the whole recital: doubt is not, perhaps, a trustworthy help to Holiness. Doubt and frailty can only be helped by baptism (lines 381–82).
6. I.e., pretending ignorance of what she knew well.
7. I.e., having passed all fear.

Then beautie brought t'unworthy° wretchednesse   *undeserved*
Through envies snares or fortunes freakes unkind:
5   I, whether lately through her brightnesse blind,
Or through alleageance and fast fealtie,
Which I do owe unto all woman kind,
Feele my heart perst° with so great agonie,   *pierced*
When such I see, that all for pittie I could die.

2

10 And now it is empassionéd so deepe,
For fairest Unas sake, of whom I sing,
That my fraile eyes these lines with teares do steepe,
To thinke how she through guilefull handeling,
Though true as touch,° though daughter of a king,   *touchstone*
15 Though faire as ever living wight was faire,
Though nor in word nor deede ill meriting,
Is from her knight divorcéd in despaire
And her due loves derived° to that vile witches share.   *diverted*

3

Yet she most faithfull Ladie all this while
20 Forsaken, wofull, solitarie mayd
Farre from all peoples prease,° as in exile,   *press, crowd*
In wildernesse and wastfull deserts strayd,
To seeke her knight; who subtilly betrayd
Through that late vision, which th' Enchaunter wrought,
25 Had her abandond. She of nought affrayd,
Through woods and wastnesse wide him daily sought;
Yet wishéd tydings none of him unto her brought.

4

One day nigh wearie of the yrkesome way,
From her unhastie beast she did alight,
30 And on the grasse her daintie limbes did lay
In secret shadow,° farre from all mens sight: *shade*
From her faire head her fillet she undight,[8]
And laid her stole aside. Her angels face
As the great eye of heaven shynéd bright,
35 And made a sunshine in the shadie place;
Did never mortall eye behold such heavenly grace.

5

It fortunéd out of the thickest wood
A ramping Lyon rushéd suddainly,
Hunting full greedie after salvage blood:[9]
40 Soone as the royall virgin he did spy,
With gaping mouth at her ran greedily,
To have attonce devoured her tender corse:
But to the pray when as he drew more ny,
His bloudie rage asswagéd with remorse,
45 And with the sight amazd, forgat his furious forse.

---

8. She took off her headband   9. Wild game.

6

In stead thereof he kist her wearie feet,
    And lickt her lilly hands with fawning tong,
    As[1] he her wrongéd innocence did weet.°   *understand*
    O how can beautie maister the most strong,
50   And simple truth subdue avenging wrong?
    Whose yeelded pride and proud submission,
    Still dreading death, when she had markéd long,
    Her hart gan melt in great compassion,
And drizling teares did shed for pure affection.

7

55 "The Lyon Lord of everie beast in field,"
    Quoth she, "his princely puissance° doth abate   *power*
    And mightie proud to humble weake does yield,
    Forgetfull of the hungry rage, which late
    Him prickt, in pittie of my sad estate:°   *condition*
60   But he my Lyon, and my noble Lord,
    How does he find in cruell hart to hate
    Her that him loved, and ever most adord,
As the God of my life? why hath he me abhord?"

8

Redounding teares did choke th'end of her plaint,
65   Which softly ecchoed from the neighbour wood;
    And sad to see her sorrowfull constraint°   *affliction*
    The kingly beast upon her gazing stood;
    With pittie calmd, downe fell his angry mood.
    At last in close hart shutting up her paine,
70   Arose the virgin borne of heavenly brood,°   *parentage*
    And to her snowy Palfrey got againe,
To seeke her strayéd Champion, if she might attaine.°   *overtake*

9

The Lyon would not leave her desolate,
    But with her went along, as a strong gard
75   Of her chast person, and a faithfull mate
    Of her sad troubles and misfortunes hard:
    Still when she slept, he kept both watch and ward,
    And when she wakt, he waited diligent,
    With humble service to her will prepard:
80   From her faire eyes he tooke commaundement,
And ever by her lookes conceivéd her intent.[2]

10

Long she thus traveiléd through deserts wyde,
    By which she thought her wandring knight shold pas,
    Yet never shew of living wight espyde;
85   Till that at length she found the troden gras,

---

1. As though.
2. Whereas Redcrosse, the man, has confusedly abandoned truth, the lion, king of beasts, an animal under nature's law, follows truth instinctively. Lions revere the heroine in the romance *Sir Bevis of Hamptoun* and accompany the heroes of other medieval romances; they have long been associated with the British crown.

In which the tract° of peoples footing was,   *track*
    Under the steepe foot of a mountaine hore;°   *gray*
    The same she followes, till at last she has
    A damzell spyde slow footing her before,
90 That on her shoulders sad° a pot of water bore.   *heavy*

11

To whom approching she to her gan call,
    To weet, if dwelling place were nigh at hand;
    But the rude° wench her answered nought at all,   *ignorant*
    She could not heare, nor speake, nor understand;
95 Till seeing by her side the Lyon stand,
    With suddaine feare her pitcher downe she threw,
    And fled away: for never in that land
    Face of faire Ladie she before did vew,
And that dread Lyons looke her cast in deadly° hew.   *deathlike*

12

100 Full fast she fled, ne ever lookt behynd,
    As if her life upon the wager lay,
    And home she came, whereas her mother blynd
    Sate in eternall night: nought could she say,
    But suddaine catching hold, did her dismay
105 With quaking hands, and other signes of feare:
    Who full of ghastly fright and cold affray,
    Gan shut the dore. By this arrivéd there
Dame Una, wearie Dame, and entrance did requere.°   *request*

13

Which when none yeelded, her unruly Page
110 With his rude clawes the wicket° open rent,   *door*
    And let her in; where of his cruell rage
    Nigh dead with feare, and faint astonishment,
    She found them both in darkesome corner pent;°   *huddled*
    Where that old woman day and night did pray
115 Upon her beades devoutly penitent;
    Nine hundred *Pater nosters* every day,
And thrise nine hundred *Aves* she was wont to say.[3]

14

And to augment her painefull pennance more,
    Thrise every weeke in ashes she did sit,
120 And next her wrinkled skin rough sackcloth wore,
    And thrise three times did fast from any bit:°   *food*
    But now for feare her beads she did forget.
    Whose needlesse dread for to remove away,
    Faire Una faméd words and count'nance fit:
125 Which hardly doen, at length she gan them pray,
That in their cotage small, that night she rest her may.

---

3. "Them both" will be named in line 157. The old lady's name, Corceca, means "blind devotion." The (obviously Catholic) prayers that the two mouth are motivated by fear, not faith. Her daughter's name, "Abessa," suggests the monastic orders (i.e., "abbess") and (from *ab esse*, "non-being," "withdrawal") that she is superstition. Her timorous reaction to the Lyon was typically excessive, and her pitcher of water was perhaps emblematic of her fickle state.

15

The day is spent, and commeth drowsie night,
   When every creature shrowded is in sleepe;
   Sad Una downe her laies in wearie plight,
130   And at her feet the Lyon watch doth keepe:
   In stead of rest, she does lament, and weepe
For the late losse of her deare lovéd knight,
And sighes, and grones, and evermore does steepe
   Her tender brest in bitter teares all night,
135 All night she thinks too long, and often lookes for light.

16

Now when Aldeboran was mounted hie
Above the shynie Cassiopeias chaire,[4]
   And all in deadly sleepe did drownéd lie,
   One knockéd at the dore, and in would fare;
140   He knockéd fast,° and often curst, and sware,   *insistently*
   That readie entrance was not at his call:
For on his backe a heavy load he bare
Of nightly stelths and pillage severall,
Which he had got abroad by purchase° criminall.   *acquisition*

17

145 He was to weete[5] a stout and sturdie thiefe,
   Wont to robbe Churches of their ornaments,
   And poore mens boxes[6] of their due reliefe,
   Which given was to them for good intents;
   The holy Saints of their rich vestiments
150   He did disrobe, when all men carelesse slept,
   And spoild the Priests of their habiliments,°   *vestments*
Whiles none the holy things in safety kept;
Then he by cunning sleights in at the window crept.

18

And all that he by right or wrong could find,
155   Unto this house he brought, and did bestow
   Upon the daughter of this woman blind,
   Abessa daughter of Corceca slow,
   With whom he whoredome usd, that few did know,
   And fed her fat with feast of offerings,
160   And plentie, which in all the land did grow;
   Ne sparéd he to give her gold and rings:
And now he to her brought part of his stolen things.

19

Thus long the dore with rage and threats he bet,°   *beat*
   Yet of those fearefull women none durst rize,
165   The Lyon frayéd° them, him in to let: *terrify*
   He would no longer stay him to advize,
   But open breakes the dore in furious wize,

---

4. Aldebaran, in the constellation Taurus, mounts over the constellation Cassiopeia.
5. In fact.

6. A box for alms for the poor, especially one placed near the door of a church.

And entring is; when that disdainfull beast
　Encountring fierce, him suddaine doth surprize,
170　And seizing° cruell clawes on trembling brest,　　　　　*fastening*
Under his Lordly foot him proudly hath supprest.[7]

20

Him booteth not resist,[8] nor succour call,
　His bleeding hart is in the vengers hand,
　Who streight him rent in thousand peeces small,
175　And quite dismembred hath: the thirstie land
　Drunke up his life; his corse left on the strand.°　　　*ground*
　His fearefull friends weare out the wofull night,
　Ne dare to weepe, nor seeme to understand
　The heavie hap,° which on them is alight,　　　　　　*lot*
180　Affraid, least to themselves the like mishappen might.

21

Now when broad day the world discovered° has,　　　*revealed*
　Up Una rose, up rose the Lyon eke,
　And on their former journey forward pas,
　In wayes unknowne, her wandring knight to seeke,
185　With paines farre passing that long wandring Greeke,[9]
　That for his love refuséd deitie;
　Such were the labours of this Lady meeke,
　Still seeking him, that from her still did flie,
Then furthest from her hope, when most she weenéd nie.[1]

22

190　Soone as she parted thence, the fearetull twaine,
　That blind old woman and her daughter deare
　Came forth, and finding Kirkrapine there slaine,
　For anguish great they gan to rend their heare,
　And beat their brests, and naked flesh to teare.
195　And when they both had wept and wayld their fill,
　Then forth they ranne like two amazéd deare,
　Halfe mad through malice, and revenging will,[2]
To follow her, that was the causer of their ill.

23

Whom overtaking, they gan loudly bray,
200　With hollow howling, and lamenting cry,
　Shamefully at her rayling all the way,
　And her accusing of dishonesty,°　　　　　　　　*unchastity*
　That was the flowre of faith and chastity;
　And still amidst her rayling, she[3] did pray,
205　That plagues, and mischiefs, and long misery

---

7. The thief is named Kirkrapine (in line 192), which means "church robbery." That he brings illgotten gains to the house of superstition may represent the accumulation of the monastic estates and their sheltering under the privileges of the Roman church. By this interpretation, the lion becomes Henry VIII, who expropriated the monasteries.
8. It does no good to resist.
9. Odysseus, who renounced immortality and the love of the nymph Calypso for his wife Penelope.
1. Believed near.
2. Desire of revenge.
3. I.e., Corceca.

Might fall on her, and follow all the way,
And that in endlesse error° she might ever stray.   *wandering*

24

But when she saw her prayers nought prevaile,
    She backe returnéd with some labour lost;
    And in the way as she did weepe and waile,
210   A knight her met in mighty armes embost,°   *encased*
    Yet knight was not for all his bragging bost,
    But subtill Archimag, that Una sought
    By traynes° into new troubles to have tost: *tricks*
215   Of that old woman tydings he besought,
If that of such a Ladie she could tellen ought.

25

Therewith she gan her passion to renew,
    And cry, and curse, and raile, and rend her heare,
    Saying, that harlot she too lately knew,
220   That causd her shed so many a bitter teare,
    And so forth told the story of her feare:
    Much seeméd he to mone her haplesse chaunce,
    And after for that Ladie did inquere;
    Which being taught, he forward gan advaunce
225 His fair enchaunted steed, and eke his charméd launce.

26

Ere long he came, where Una traveild slow,
    And that wilde Champion wayting° her besyde: *attending*
    Whom seeing such, for dread he durst not show
    Himselfe too nigh at hand, but turnéd wyde
230   Unto an hill; from whence when she him spyde,
    By his like seeming shield, her knight by name
    She weend it was, and towards him gan ryde:
    Approching nigh, she wist° it was the same,   *believed*
And with faire fearefull humblesse towards him shee came.

27

235 And weeping said, "Ah my long lackéd Lord,
    Where have ye bene thus long out of my sight?
    Much fearéd I to have bene quite abhord,
    Or ought° have done, that ye displeasen might,   *aught*
    That should as death unto my deare hart light:[4]
240   For since mine eye your joyous sight did mis,
    My chearefull day is turnd to chearelesse night,
    And eke my night of death the shadow is;
But welcome now my light, and shining lampe of blis."

28

He thereto meeting[5] said, "My dearest Dame,
245   Farre be it from your thought, and fro my will,
    To thinke that knighthood I so much should shame,
    As you to leave, that have me lovéd still,
    And chose in Faery court of meere° goodwill,   *pure*
    Where noblest knights were to be found on earth:

---

4. I.e., be as a death-blow to my sad   5. Answering in like manner.
heart.

The earth shall sooner leave her kindly° skill   *natural*
To bring forth fruit, and make eternall derth,°   *desert*
Then I leave you, my liefe, yborne of heavenly berth.

29

"And sooth to say, why I left you so long,
  Was for to seeke adventure in strange place,
  Where Archimago said a felon strong
  To many knights did daily worke disgrace;
  But knight he now shall never more deface:
  Good cause of mine excuse; that mote° ye please   *may*
  Well to accept, and evermore embrace
  My faithfull service, that by land and seas
Have vowd you to defend, now then your plaint appease."

30

His lovely° words her seemd due recompence   *loving*
  Of all her passéd paines: one loving howre
  For many yeares of sorrow can dispence:°   *make amends*
  A dram of sweet is worth a pound of sowre:
  She has forgot, how many a wofull stowre°   *trouble*
  For him she late endured; she speakes no more
  Of past: true is, that true love hath no powre
  To looken backe; his eyes be fixt before.
Before her stands her knight, for whom she toyld so sore.

31

Much like, as when the beaten marinere,
  That long hath wandred in the Ocean wide,
  Oft soust° in swelling Tethys[6] saltish teare,   *soaked*
  And long time having tand his tawney hide
  With blustring breath of heaven, that none can bide,
  And scorching flames of fierce Orions hound,[7]
  Soone as the port from farre he has espide,
  His chearefull whistle merrily doth sound,
And Nereus crownes with cups;[8] his mates him
    pledg° around.   *toast*

32

Such joy made Una, when her knight she found;
  And eke th'enchaunter joyous seemd no lesse,
  Then the glad marchant, that does vew from ground.
  His ship farre come from watrie wildernesse,
  He hurles out vowes, and Neptune oft doth blesse:
  So forth they past, and all the way they spent
  Discoursing of her dreadfull late distresse,
  In which he askt her, what the Lyon ment:
Who told her all that fell° in journey as she went.   *befell*

33

They had not ridden farre, when they might see
  One pricking towards them with hastie heat,

6. The wife of Ocean; here, Ocean.
7. Sirius, the dog star, symbolizing hot weather (the "dog days").
8. Nereus is god of the Mediterranean, to whom the mariner in gratitude makes libations.

Full strongly armd, and on a courser free,
That through his fiercenesse fomed all with sweat,
And the sharpe yron° did for anger eat,   bit
When his hot ryder spurd his chauféd° side;   heated
295   His looke was sterne, and seeméd still to threat
Cruell revenge, which he in hart did hyde,
And on his shield Sans loy[9] in bloudie lines was dyde.

34

When nigh he drew unto this gentle payre
And saw the Red-crosse, which the knight did beare,
300   He burnt in fire, and gan eftsoones prepare
Himselfe to battell with his couchéd speare.
Loth was that other, and did faint through feare,
To taste th'untryed dint of deadly steele;
But yet his Lady did so well him cheare,
305   That hope of new good hap he gan to feele;
So bent° his speare, and spurnd his horse with yron heele.   lowered

35

But that proud Paynim° forward came so fierce,   pagan
And full of wrath, that with his sharp-head speare
Through vainely crosséd shield[1] he quite did pierce,
310   And had his staggering steede not shrunke for feare,
Through shield and bodie eke he should him beare:°   thrust
Yet so great was the puissance of his push,
That from his saddle quite he did him beare:
He tombling rudely downe to ground did rush,
315   And from his goréd wound a well of bloud did gush.[2]

36

Dismounting lightly from his loftie steed,
He to him lept, in mind to reave° his life,   take
And proudly said, "Lo there the worthie meed
Of him, that slew Sans foy with bloudie knife;
320   Henceforth his ghost freed from repining strife,
In peace may passen over Lethe[3] lake,
When mourning altars purgd° with enemies life,   cleansed
The blacke infernall Furies[4] doen aslake:°   appease
Life from Sans foy thou tookst, Sans loy shall from thee take."

37

325   Therewith in haste his helmet gan unlace,
Till Una cride, "O hold that heavie hand,
Deare Sir, what ever that thou be in place:[5]
Enough is, that thy foe doth vanquisht stand
Now at thy mercy: Mercie not withstand:

9. The name means "without law." Law
here is not, of course, merely state law,
but the law of the cosmos, of nature,
of civil government, and of man—the
law that holds all life, both above the
earth and on it, together. Hence "Sans
loy" stands for the loss of all order, or
chaos.
1. The cross on Archimago's shield was
false and did not give him the protection the Redcrosse knight received in his
fight with Sans foy; see I.ii.18.
2. This is true poetic justice: lawlessness defeats the devil.
3. A river in Hades whose water when
drunk caused forgetfulness.
4. Spirits of discord and revenge.
5. Whoever you are.

330 For he is one the truest knight alive,
    Though conquered now he lie on lowly land,
    And whilest him fortune favourd, faire did thrive
In bloudie field: therefore of life him not deprive."

38

Her piteous words might not abate his rage,
335   But rudely rending up his helmet, would
    Have slaine him straight: but when he sees his age,
    And hoarie head of Archimago old,
    His hastie hand he doth amazéd hold,
    And halfe ashaméd, wondred at the sight:
340   For the old man well knew he, though untold,
    In charmes and magicke to have wondrous might,
Ne ever wont in field, ne in round lists[6] to fight.

39

And said, "Why Archimago, lucklesse syre,
    What doe I see? what hard mishap is this,
345   That hath thee hither brought to taste mine yre?
    Or thine the fault, or mine the error is,
    In stead of foe to wound my friend amis?"
    He answered nought, but in a traunce still lay,
    And on those guilefull dazéd eyes of his
350   The cloud of death did sit. Which doen away,[7]
He left him lying so, ne would no lenger stay.

40

But to the virgin comes, who all this while
    Amaséd stands, her selfe so mockt° to see   *deceived*
    By him, who has the guerdon° of his guile,   *reward*
355   For so misfeigning her true knight to bee:
    Yet is she now in more perplexitie,
    Left in the hand of that same Paynim bold,
    From whom her booteth not at all to flie;
    Who by her cleanly garment catching hold,
360 Her from her Palfrey pluckt, her visage to behold.

41

But her fierce servant full of kingly awe
    And high disdaine, whenas his soveraine Dame
    So rudely handled by her foe he sawe,
    With gaping jawes full greedy at him came,
365   And ramping on his shield, did weene° the same   *intend*
    Have reft away with his sharpe rending clawes
    But he was stout, and lust did now inflame
    His corage more, that from his griping pawes
He hath his shield redeemed, and foorth his swerd he drawes.

42

370 O then too weake and feeble was the forse
    Of salvage beast, his puissance to withstand:
    For he was strong, and of so mightie corse,

---

6. **Enclosures for fighting tournaments.**   7. **When he recovered from the swoon.**

As ever wielded speare in warlike hand,
And feates of armes did wisely understand.
375 Eftsoones he perced through·his chaufed chest
With thrilling° point of deadly yron brand,°   *penetrating / sword*
And launcht° his Lordly hart: with death opprest   *pierced*
He roared aloud, whiles life forsooke his stubborne brest.[8]

43

Who now is left to keepe the forlorne maid
380 From raging spoile of lawlesse victors will?
Her faithfull gard removed, her hope dismaid,
Her selfe a yeelded pray to save or spill.°   *destroy*
He now Lord of the field, his pride to fill,
With foule reproches, and disdainfull spight·
385 Her vildly entertaines, and will or nill,·
Beares her away upon his courser light:
Her prayers nought prevaile; his rage is more of might.

44

And all the way, with great lamenting paine,
And piteous plaints she filleth his dull° eares,   *deaf*
390 That stony hart could riven have in twaine,
And all the way she wets with flowing teares:
But he enraged with rancor, nothing heares.
Her servile beast yet would not leave her so,
But followes her farre off, ne ought he feares,
395 To be partaker of her wandring woe,
More mild in beastly kind,° then that her beastly foe.   *nature*

Canto IV

To sinfull house of Pride, Duessa
guides the faithfull knight,
Where brothers death to wreak° Sansjoy   *avenge*
doth chalenge him to fight.

1

Young knight, what ever that dost armes professe,
And through long labours huntest after fame,
Beware of fraud, beware of ficklenesse,
In choice, and change of thy deare lovéd Dame,
5 Least thou of her beleeve too lightly blame,
And rash misweening doe thy hart remove:
For unto knight there is no greater shame,
Then lightnesse and inconstancie in love;
That doth this Redcrosse knights ensample° plainly prove.   *example*

2

10 Who after that he had faire Una lorne,°   *lost*
Through light misdeeming of her loialtie,   *misjudging*
And false Duessa in her sted had borne,

8. Nature's law is, perhaps, defenseless against human lawlessness. Sans loy's killing of the lion might also be taken as the momentary triumph of Catholicism under Mary Tudor.

Called Fidess', and so supposd to bee;
Long with her traveild, till at last they see
15   A goodly building, bravely garnishéd,°   *adorned*
The house of mightie Prince it seemd to bee:
And towards it a broad high way[9] that led,
All bare through peoples feet, which thither traveiléd.

3

Great troupes of people traveild thitherward
20   Both day and night, of each degree and place,°   *rank*
But few returnéd, having scapéd hard,
With balefull beggerie, or foule disgrace,
Which ever after in most wretched case,
Like loathsome lazars,° by the hedges lay.   *lepers*
25   Thither Duessa bad him bend his pace:
For she is wearie of the toilesome way,
And also nigh consuméd is the lingring day.

4

A stately Pallace built of squaréd bricke,
Which cunningly was without morter laid,
30   Whose wals were high, but nothing strong, nor thick,
And golden foile° all over them displaid,   *thin layer*
That purest skye with brightnesse they dismaid°:   *outdid*
High lifted up were many loftie towres,
And goodly galleries farre over laid,[1]
35   Full of faire windowes, and delightfull bowres;
And on the top a Diall told the timely howres.[2]

5

It was a goodly heape° for to behould,   *building*
And spake the praises of the workmans wit;
But full great pittie, that so faire a mould°   *structure*
40   Did on so weake foundation ever sit:
For on a sandie hill, that still did flit,°   *give way*
And fall away, it mounted was full hie,
That every breath of heaven shakéd it:
And all the hinder parts, that few could spie,
45 Were ruinous and old, but painted cunningly.

6

Arrivéd there they passéd in forth right;
For still to all the gates stood open wide,
Yet charge of them was to a Porter hight°   *committed*
Cald Malvenù,[3] who entrance none denide:
50   Thence to the hall, which was on every side
With rich array and costly arras dight:[4]
Infinite sorts of people did abide

---

9. "Broad is the way that leadeth to destruction" (Matthew vii.13).
1. Placed above.
2. The clock ("Diall") is illustrative of the power of time over the life of this world, as it is lived in the House of Pride. This proud elegant castle is reminiscent of Alcina's palace in *Orlando Furioso* VI.
3. The name means "unwelcome." In courtly-love allegories, the porter is often called "Bienvenu" or "Bel-accueil" ("welcome").
4. Decorated with costly wall hangings.

There waiting long, to win the wishéd sight
Of her, that was the Lady of that Pallace bright.

7

55 By them they passe, all gazing on them round,
     And to the Presence° mount; whose glorious vew   *reception hall*
     Their frayle amazéd senses did confound:
     In living Princes court none ever knew
     Such endlesse richesse, and so sumptuous shew;
60   Ne Persia selfe, the nourse of pompous pride
     Like ever saw. And there a noble crew
     Of Lordes and Ladies stood on every side,
Which with their presence faire, the place much beautifide.

8

High above all a cloth of State[5] was spred,
65   And a rich throne, as bright as sunny day,
     On which there sate most brave embellishéd[6]
     With royall robes and gorgeous array,
     A mayden Queene, that shone as Titans° ray,   *the sun's*
     In glistring gold, and peerelesse pretious stone:
70   Yet her bright blazing beautie did assay°   *attempt*
     To dim the brightnesse of her glorious throne,
As envying her selfe, that too exceeding shone.

9

Exceeding shone, like Phoebus fairest childe,
     That did presume his fathers firie wayne,°   *chariot*
75   And flaming mouthes of steedes unwonted wilde
     Through highest heaven with weaker° hand to rayne;   *too weak*
     Proud of such glory and advancement vaine,
     While flashing beames do daze his feeble eyen,
     He leaves the welkin° way most beaten plaine,   *skyey*
80   And rapt° with whirling wheeles, inflames the skyen,   *carried away*
With fire not made to burne, but fairely for to shyne.[7]

10

So proud she shynéd in her Princely state,°   *throne*
     Looking to heaven; for earth she did disdayne,
     And sitting high; for lowly° she did hate: *lowliness*
85   Lo underneath her scornefull feete, was layne
     A dreadfull Dragon with an hideous trayne,°   *tail*
     And in her hand she held a mirrhour bright,[8]
     Wherein her face she often vewéd fayne,
     And in her selfe-loved semblance tooke delight;
90 For she was wondrous faire, as any living wight.

---

5. Canopy.
6. Handsomely clad.
7. Phaëton tried to drive the chariot of Phoebus, his father, but set the skies on fire and fell, as Lucifer (Satan) fell from heaven. Lucifera (Pride) shines like Phaëton (line 82), which suggests

a similar fate. Although her House does not fall, it is seen first as glorious, then for what it really is.
8. Pride, and figures associated with her in Renaissance literature and art, often hold a mirror, emblematic of self-love.

11

Of griesly Pluto she the daughter was,
  And sad Proserpina the Queene of hell;
  Yet did she thinke her pearelesse worth to pas
  That parentage, with pride so did she swell,
95 And thundring Jove, that high in heaven doth dwell,
  And wield° the world, she clayméd for her syre,   *govern*
  Or if that any else did Jove excell:
  For to the highest she did still aspyre,
Or if ought higher were then that, did it desyre.

12

100 And proud Lucifera men did her call,
  That made her selfe a Queene, and crownd to be,
  Yet rightfull kingdome she had none at all,
  Ne heritage of native soveraintie,
  But did usurpe with wrong and tyrannie
105 Upon the scepter, which she now did hold:
  Ne ruld her Realmes with lawes, but pollicie,°   *conspiracy*
  And strong advizement of six wisards old,
That with their counsels bad her kingdome did uphold.

13

Soone as the Elfin knight in presence came,
110 And false Duessa seeming Lady faire,
  A gentle Husher,° Vanitie by name   *usher*
  Made rowme, and passage for them did prepaire:
  So goodly brought them to the lowest staire
  Of her high throne, where they on humble knee
115 Making obeyssance, did the cause declare,
  Why they were come, her royall state to see,
To prove° the wide report of her great Majestee.   *verify*

14

With loftie eyes, halfe loth to looke so low,
  She thankéd them in her disdainefull wise,
120 Ne other grace vouchsaféd them to show
  Of Princesse worthy, scarse them bad arise
  Her Lordes and Ladies all this while devise
  Themselves to setten forth to straungers sight:
  Some frounce° their curléd haire in courtly guise,   *frizzle*
125 Some prancke° their ruffes, and others trimly dight°   *display/adjust*
Their gay attire: each others greater pride does spight.

15

Goodly they all that knight do entertaine,
  Right glad with him to have increast their crew:
  But to Duess' each one himselfe did paine
130 All kindnesse and faire courtesie to shew;
  For in that court whylome° her well they knew: *formerly*
  Yet the stout Faerie mongst the middest° crowd   *thickest*
  Thought all their glorie vaine in knightly vew,
  And that great Princesse too exceeding prowd,
135 That to strange knight no better countenance allowd.

16

Suddein upriseth from her stately place
  The royall Dame, and for her coche doth call:

All hurtlen° forth, and she with Princely pace,   *rush*
As faire Aurora in her purple pall,°   *robe*
140   Out of the East the dawning day doth call:
So forth she comes: her brightnesse brode° doth blaze;   *abroad*
The heapes of people thronging in the hall,
Do ride° each other, upon her to gaze: *crowd*
Her glorious glitterand° light doth all mens eyes amaze.   *glittering*

17

145 So forth she comes, and to her coche does clyme,
Adornéd all with gold, and girlonds gay,
That seemd as fresh as Flora in her prime,
And strove to match, in royall rich array,
Great Junos golden chaire,° the which they say   *chariot*
150 The Gods stand gazing on, when she does ride
To Joves high house through heavens bras-pavéd way
Drawne of faire Pecocks, that excell in pride,
And full of Argus eyes their tailes dispredden wide.[9]

18

But this was drawne of six unequall beasts,
155 On which her six sage Counsellours did ryde,
Taught to obay their bestiall beheasts,
With like conditions to their kinds applyde:[1]
Of which the first, that all the rest did guyde,
Was sluggish Idlenesse the nourse of sin;
160 Upon a slouthfull Asse he chose to ryde,
Arayd in habit blacke, and amis° thin,   *hood, cape*
Like to an holy Monck, the service to begin.

19

And in his hand his Portesse° still he bare,   *breviary*
That much was worne, but therein little red,
165 For of devotion he had little care,
Still drownd in sleepe, and most of his dayes ded;
Scarse could he once uphold his heavie hed,
To looken, whether it were night or day:
May seeme the wayne° was very evill led,   *chariot*
170 When such an one had guiding of the way,
That knew not, whether right he went, or else astray.

20

From worldly cares himselfe he did esloyne,°   *withdraw*
And greatly shunnéd manly exercise,
From every worke he chalengéd essoyne,°   *excuse*
175 For contemplation sake: yet otherwise,
His life he led in lawlesse riotise;
By which he grew to grievous malady;
For in his lustlesse° limbs through evill guise°   *feeble/living*

9. The many-eyed monster Argus was set by Juno to watch Jupiter's love Io. When Mercury killed Argus, his eyes were put in the peacock's tail feathers.
1. The "sage Counsellours" do not guide their beasts, but are guided by them (i.e., by their bestial "kinds," or natures). This procession of the seven deadly sins—of which Pride is the queen, the chief sin—had a long tradition in medieval art and literature. And see Marlowe's *Dr. Faustus* (II.ii.111–64).

A shaking fever raignd continually:
180 Such one was Idlenesse, first of this company.

21

And by his side rode loathsome Gluttony,
  Deforméd creature, on a filthie swyne,
  His belly was up-blowne with luxury,
  And eke with fatnesse swollen were his eyne,
185 And like a Crane his necke was long and fyne,°   thin
  With which he swallowd up excessive feast,
  For want whereof poore people oft did pyne;°   starve
  And all the way, most like a brutish beast,
He spuéd up his gorge, that all did him deteast.

22

190 In greene vine leaves he was right fitly clad;
  For other clothes he could not weare for heat,
  And on his head an yvie girland had,
  From under which fast trickled downe the sweat:
  Still as he rode, he somewhat° still did eat,   something
195 And in his hand did beare a bouzing can,
  Of which he supt so oft, that on his seat
  His dronken corse he scarse upholden can,
In shape and life more like a monster, then a man.[2]

23

Unfit he was for any worldly thing,
200 And eke unhable once° to stirre or go,°   at all/walk
  Not meet to be of counsell to a king,
  Whose mind in meat and drinke was drownéd so,
  That from his friend he seldome knew his fo:
  Full of diseases was his carcas blew,°   livid
205 And a dry dropsie through his flesh did flow:
  Which by misdiet daily greater grew:
Such one was Gluttony, the second of that crew.

24

And next to him rode lustfull Lechery,
  Upon a bearded Goat, whose rugged haire,
210 And whally° eyes (the signe of gelosy,)   greenish
  Was like the person selfe, whom he did beare:
  Who rough, and blacke, and filthy did appeare,
  Unseemely man to please faire Ladies eye;
  Yet he of Ladies oft was lovéd deare,
215 When fairer faces were bid standenby:°   away
O who does know the bent of womens fantasy?

25

In a greene gowne he clothéd was full faire,
  Which underneath did hide his filthinesse,
  And in his hand a burning hart he bare,
220 Full of vaine follies, and new fanglenesse:°   fickleness
  For he was false, and fraught with ficklenesse,

2. The drunken old Silenus of Greek mythology (see Ovid's *Metamorphoses*) is echoed here.

And learnéd had to love with secret lookes,
And well could daunce, and sing with ruefulnesse,
And fortunes tell, and read in loving° bookes,   erotic
225 And thousand other wayes, to bait his fleshly hookes.

26

Inconstant man, that lovéd all he saw,
And lusted after all, that he did love,
Ne would his looser life be tide to law,
But joyd weake wemens hearts to tempt and prove°   try
230 If from their loyall loves he might then move;
Which lewdnesse fild him with reprochfull paine
Of that fowle evill,³ which all men reprove,
That rots the marrow, and consumes the braine:
Such one was Lecherie, the third of all this traine.

27

235 And greedy Avarice by him did ride,
Upon a Camell loaden all with gold;
Two iron coffers hong on either side,
With precious mettall full, as they might hold,
And in his lap an heape of coine he told;°   counted
240 For of his wicked pelfe his God he made,
And unto hell him selfe for money sold;
Accursed usurie was all his trade,
And right and wrong ylike in equall ballaunce waide.⁴

28

His life was nigh unto deaths doore yplast,
245 And thread-bare cote, and cobled shoes he ware,
Ne scarse good morsell all his life did tast,
But both from backe and belly still did spare,
To fill his bags, and richesse to compare;°   acquire
Yet chylde ne kinsman living had he none
250 To leave them to; but thorough daily care
To get, and nightly feare to lose his owne,
He led a wretched life unto him selfe unknowne.

29

Most wretched wight, whom nothing might suffise,
Whose greedy lust did lacke in greatest store,°   plenty
255 Whose need had end, but no end covetise,
Whose wealth was want, but whose plenty made him pore,
Who had enough, yet wishéd ever more;
A vile disease, and eke in foote and hand
A grievous gout tormented him full sore,
260 That well he could not touch, nor go, nor stand:
Such one was Avarice, the fourth of this faire band.

30

And next to him malicious Envie rode,
Upon a ravenous wolfe, and still did chaw

---

3. I.e., syphilis.   4. I.e., made no distinction between right and wrong.

Betweene his cankred teeth a venemous tode,
265 That all the poison ran about his chaw;°   *jaw*
But inwardly he chawéd his owne maw°   *entrails*
At neighbours wealth, that made him ever sad;
For death it was, when any good he saw,
And wept, that cause of weeping none he had,
270 But when he heard of harme, he wexéd wondrous glad.

31

All in a kirtle of discolourd say[5]
He clothéd was, ypainted full of eyes;
And in his bosome secretly there lay
An hatefull Snake, the which his taile uptyes
275 In many folds, and mortall sting implyes.°   *enfolds*
Still as he rode, he gnasht his teeth, to see
Those heapes of gold with griple° Covetyse,   *grasping*
And grudgéd at the great felicitie
Of proud Lucifera, and his owne companie.

32

280 He hated all good workes and vertuous deeds,
And him no lesse, that any like did use,
And who with gracious bread the hungry feeds,
His almes for want of faith he doth accuse;
So every good to bad he doth abuse:°   *twist*
285 And eke the verse of famous Poets witt
He does backebite, and spightfull poison spues
From leprous mouth on all, that ever writt:
Such one vile Envie was, that fifte in row did sitt.

33

And him beside rides fierce revenging Wrath,
290 Upon a Lion, loth for to be led;
And in his hand a burning brond° he hath,   *sword*
The which he brandisheth about his hed;
His eyes did hurle forth sparkles fiery red,
And staréd sterne on all, that him beheld,
295 As ashes pale of hew and seeming ded;
And on his dagger still his hand he held,
Trembling through hasty rage, when choler° in him sweld.   *anger*

34

His ruffin° raiment all was staind with blood,   *disarranged*
Which he had spilt, and all to rags yrent,°   *torn*
300 Through unadviséd rashnesse woxen wood,[6]
For of his hands he had no governement,°   *control*
Ne cared for bloud in his avengement:
But when the furious fit was overpast,
His cruell facts° he often would repent;   *actions*
305 Yet wilfull man he never would forecast,
How many mischieves should ensue his heedlesse hast.

5. Jacket of many-colored wool.   6. Grown insane.

35

Full many mischiefes follow cruell Wrath;
  Abhorréd bloudshed, and tumultuous strife,
  Unmanly° murder, and unthrifty scath,°   *inhuman/damage*
310 Bitter despight, with rancous rusty knife,
  And fretting griefe the enemy of life;
  All these, and many evils moe° haunt ire,   *more*
  The swelling Splene,° and Frenzy raging rife,   *malice*
  The shaking Palsey, and Saint Fraunces fire:[7]
315 Such one was Wrath, the last of this ungodly tire.°   *train*

36

And after all, upon the wagon beame
  Rode Sathan, with a smarting whip in hand,
  With which he forward lasht the laesie teme,
  So oft as Slowth still in the mire did stand.
320 Huge routs of people did about them band,
  Showting for joy, and still before their way
  A foggy mist had covered all the land;
  And underneath their feet, all scattered lay
Dead sculs and bones of men, whose life had gone astray.

37

325 So forth they marchen in this goodly sort,
  To take the solace° of the open aire,   *recreation*
  And in fresh flowring fields themselves to sport;
  Emongst the rest rode that false Lady faire,
  The fowle Duessa, next unto the chaire
330 Of proud Lucifera, as one of the traine:
  But that good knight would not so nigh repaire,°   *approach*
  Him selfe estraunging from their joyaunce vaine,
Whose fellowship seemd far unfit for warlike swaine.

38

So having solacéd themselves a space
335 With pleasaunce of the breathing° fields yfed,   *fragrant*
  They backe returnéd to the Princely Place;
  Whereas an errant knight in armes ycled,°   *clad*
  And heathnish shield, wherein with letters red
  Was writ Sans joy, they new arrivéd find:
340 Enflamed with fury and fiers hardy-hed,°   *audacity*
  He seemd in hart to harbour thoughts unkind,
And nourish bloudy vengeaunce in his bitter mind.[8]

39

Who when the shaméd shield[9] of slaine Sans foy
  He spied with that same Faery champions page,
345 Bewraying° him, that did of late destroy   *revealing*

---

7. St. Anthony's fire, erysipelas, or the flaming itch; appropriate to Wrath.
8. Sans joy ("without joy") stands, not simply for gloom or "no fun," but for *accidie*, loss of heart. Redcrosse's high-minded rejection of the seven deadly sins (lines 331–33) does not protect him from this darkness of the spirit.
9. With the arms reversed. See below, line 369.

His eldest brother, burning all with rage
He to him leapt, and that same envious gage[1]
Of victors glory from him snatcht away:
But th'Elfin knight, which ought° that warlike   *owned/trophy*
   wage,°
350   Disdaind to loose the meed he wonne in fray,
And him rencountring fierce, reskewd the noble pray.

40

Therewith they gan to hurtlen° greedily,   *skirmish*
   Redoubted battaile ready to darrayne,°   *contest*
   And clash their shields, and shake their swords on hy,
355   That with their sturre they troubled all the traine;
   Till that great Queene upon eternall paine
   Of high displeasure, that ensewen might,
   Commaunded them their fury to refraine,
   And if that either to that shield had right,
360   In equall lists they should the morrow next it fight.

41

"Ah dearest Dame," quoth then the Paynim bold,
   "Pardon the errour of enragéd wight,
   Whom great griefe made forget the raines to hold
   Of reasons rule, to see this recreant knight,
365   No knight, but treachour full of false despight
   And shamefull treason, who through guile hath slayn
   The prowest° knight, that ever field did fight,   *bravest*
   Even stout Sans foy (O who can then refrayn?)
Whose shield he beares renverst, the more to heape disdayn.

42

370 "And to augment the glorie of his guile,
   His dearest love[2] the faire Fidessa loe
   Is there possessed of° the traytour vile,   *by*
   Who reapes the harvest sowen by his foe,
   Sowen in bloudy field, and bought with woe:
375   That brothers hand shall dearely well requight
   So be, O Queene, you equall favour showe."
   Him litle answerd th'angry Elfin knight:
He never meant with words, but swords to plead his right.

43

But threw his gauntlet as a sacred pledge,
380   His cause in combat the next day to try:
   So been they parted both, with harts on edge,
   To be avenged each on his enimy.
   That night they pas in joy and jollity,
   Feasting and courting both in bowre and hall;
385   For Steward was excessive Gluttonie,
   That of his plenty pouréd forth to all;
Which doen,° the Chamberlain Slowth did to rest them call.   *done*

1. Envied prize.   2. I.e. Sans foy's.

44

Now whenas darkesome night had all displayd
   Her coleblacke curtein over brightest skye,
390 The warlike youthes on dayntie couches layd,
   Did chace away sweet sleepe from sluggish eye,
   To muse on meanes of hopéd victory.
   But whenas Morpheus[3] had with leaden mace
   Arrested all that courtly company,
395 Up-rose Duessa from her resting place,
And to the Paynims lodging comes with silent pace.

45

Whom broad awake she finds, in troublous fit,°   *mood*
   Forecasting, how his foe he might annoy,
   And him amoves with speaches seeming fit:
400 "Ah deare Sans joy, next dearest to Sans foy,
   Cause of my new griefe, cause of my new joy,
   Joyous, to see his ymage in mine eye,
   And greeved, to thinke how foe did him destroy,
   That was the flowre of grace and chevalrye;
405 Lo his Fidessa to thy secret faith I flye."

46

With gentle wordes he can° her fairely greet,   *did*
   And bad say on the secret of her hart.
   Then sighing soft, "I learne that litle sweet
   Oft tempred is," quoth she, "with muchell smart:
410 For since my brest was launcht° with lovely dart   *pierced*
   Of deare Sans foy, I never joyéd howre,
   But in eternall woes my weaker hart
   Have wasted, loving him with all my powre,
And for his sake have felt full many an heavie stowre.°   *grief*

47

415 "At last when perils all I weenéd past,
   And hoped to reape the crop of all my care,
   Into new woes unweeting° I was cast,   *unknowing*
   By this false faytor,° who unworthy ware   *deceiver*
   His worthy shield, whom he with guilefull snare
420 Entrappéd slew, and brought to shamefull grave.
   Me silly° maid away with him he bare,   *innocent*
   And ever since hath kept in darksome cave,
For that I would not yeeld, that° to Sans foy I gave.   *what*

48

"But since faire Sunne hath sperst° that lowring clowd, *dispersed*
425 And to my loathéd life now shewes some light,
   Under your beames I will me safely shroud,
   From dreaded storme of his disdainfull spight:
   To you th'inheritance belongs by right
   Of brothers prayse, to you eke longs° his love.   *belongs*
430 Let not his love, let not his restlesse spright°   *ghost*
   Be unrevenged, that calles to you above
From wandring Stygian[4] shores, where it doth endlesse move."

---

3. The god of sleep.   4. Of the river Styx, in the underworld.

49

Thereto said he, "Faire Dame be nought dismaid
 For sorrowes past; their griefe is with them gone:
435 Ne yet of present perill be affraid;
 For needlesse feare did never vantage° none,   *aid*
 And helplesse hap it booteth not to mone.
 Dead is Sans-foy, his vitall paines are past,
 Though greevéd ghost for vengeance deepe do grone:
440 He lives, that shall him pay his dewties° last,   *rites*
And guiltie Elfin bloud shall sacrifice in hast."

50

"O but I feare the fickle freakes,"[5] quoth shee,
 "Of fortune false, and oddes of armes in field."
 "Why dame," quoth he, "what oddes can ever bee,
445 Where both do fight alike, to win or yield?"
 "Yea but," quoth she, "he beares a charméd shield,
 And eke enchaunted armes, that none can perce,
 Ne none can wound the man, that does them wield."
 "Charmd or enchaunted," answerd he then ferce,° *fiercely*
450 "I no whit reck, ne you the like need to reherce.° *recount*

51

"But faire Fidessa, sithens° fortunes guile,   *since*
 Or enimies powre hath now captivéd you,
 Returne from whence ye came, and rest a while
 Till morrow next, that I the Elfe subdew,
455 And with Sans foyes dead dowry you endew."[6]
 "Ay me, that is a double death," she said,
 "With proud foes sight my sorrow to renew:
 Where ever yet I be, my secrete aid
Shall follow you." So passing forth she him obaid.

Canto V

The faithfull knight in equall field
subdewes his faithlesse foe,
Whom false Duessa saves, and for
his cure to hell does goe.

1

The noble hart, that harbours vertuous thought,
 And is with child of glorious great intent,
 Can never rest, untill it forth have brought
 Th'eternall brood of glorie excellent:[7]
5 Such restlesse passion did all night torment
 The flaming corage of that Faery knight,
 Devizing, how that doughtie turnament
 With greatest honour he atchieven might;
Still did he wake, and still did watch for dawning light.

---

5. Unpredictable tricks.
6. I.e., endow you with the dowry of the dead Sans foy.

7. That good is manifested only in action, not in mere intent, is an important commonplace of Renaissance thinking.

2

10 At last the golden Orientall gate
     Of greatest heaven gan to open faire,
     And Phoebus fresh, as bridegrome to his mate,
     Came dauncing forth, shaking his deawie haire:
     And hurld his glistring beames through gloomy aire.
15   Which when the wakeful Elfe perceived, streight way
     He started up, and did him selfe prepaire,
     In sun-bright armes, and battailous array:
  For with that Pagan proud he combat will that day.

3

  And forth he comes into the commune hall,
20   Where earely waite him many a gazing eye,
     To weet what end to straunger knights may fall.
     There many Minstrales maken melody,
     To drive away the dull melancholy,
     And many Bardes, that to the trembling chord
25   Can tune their timely° voyces cunningly,   *measured*
     And many Chroniclers, that can record
  Old loves, and warres for ladies doen by many a Lord.

4

  Soone after comes the cruell Sarazin,
     In woven maile all arméd warily,
30   And sternly lookes at him, who not a pin
     Does care for looke of living creatures eye.
     They bring them wines of Greece and Araby,
     And daintie spices fetcht from furthest Ynd,°   *India*
     To kindle heat of courage privily:°   *within*
35   And in the wine a solemne oth they bynd
  T'observe the sacred lawes of armes, that are assynd.

5

  At last forth comes that far renowméd Queene,
     With royall pomp and Princely majestie;
     She is ybrought unto a paléd° greene,   *fenced*
40   And placéd under stately canapee,°   *canopy*
     The warlike feates of both those knights to see.
     On th'other side in all mens open vew
     Duessa placéd is, and on a tree
     Sans-foy his shield is hangd with bloudy hew:
45 Both those the lawrell girlonds to the victor dew.

6

  A shrilling trompet sownded from on hye,
     And unto battaill bad them selves addresse:
     Their shining shieldes about their wrestes° they tye,   *wrists*
     And burning blades about their heads do blesse,°   *brandish*
50   The instruments of wrath and heavinesse:
     With greedy force each other doth assayle,
     And strike so fiercely, that they do impresse

Deepe dinted furrowes in the battred mayle;
The yron walles to ward their blowes are weake and fraile.

7

55 The Sarazin was stout, and wondrous strong,
     And heapéd blowes like yron hammers great:
     For after bloud and vengeance he did long.
     The knight was fiers, and full of youthly heat:
     And doubled strokes, like dreaded thunders threat:
60   For all for prayse and honour he did fight.
     Both stricken strike, and beaten both do beat,
     That from their shields forth flyeth firie light,
And helmets hewen deepe, shew marks of eithers might.

8

So th'one for wrong, the other strives for right:
65   As when a Gryfon[8] seizéd of his pray,
     A Dragon fiers encountreth in his flight,
     Through widest ayre making his ydle way,
     That would his rightfull ravine° rend away: *prey*
     With hideous horrour both together smight,
70   And souce° so sore, that they the heavens affray: *strike*
     The wise Southsayer° seeing so sad sight,   *soothsayer*
Th'amazéd vulgar tels of warres and mortall fight.

9

So th'one for wrong, the other strives for right,
     And each to deadly shame would drive his foe:
75   The cruell steele so greedily doth bight
     In tender flesh, that streames of bloud down flow,
     With which the armes, that earst so bright did show,
     Into a pure vermillion now are dyde:
     Great ruth in all the gazers harts did grow,
80   Seeing the goréd woundes to gape so wyde,
That victory they dare not wish to either side.

10

At last the Paynim chaunst to cast his eye,
     His suddein° eye, flaming with wrathfull fyre,   *darting*
     Upon his brothers shield, which hong thereby:
85   Therewith redoubled was his raging yre,
     And said, "Ah wretched sonne of wofull syre,
     Doest thou sit wayling by black Stygian lake,
     Whilest here thy shield is hangd for victors hyre,°   *reward*
     And sluggish german[9] doest thy forces slake,
90 To after-send his foe, that him may overtake?

11

"Goe caytive° Elfe, him quickly overtake,   *wretched*
     And soone redeeme from his long wandring woe;
     Goe guiltie ghost, to him my message make,
     That I his shield have quit° from dying foe."   *rescued*

8. A legendary monster, half eagle, half   9. I.e., his brother (Sans foy).
lion.

95   Therewith upon his crest he stroke him so,
       That twise he reeléd, readie twise to fall;
       End of the doubtfull battell deeméd tho°   *then*
       The lookers on, and lowd to him gan call
   The false Duessa, "Thine the shield, and I, and all."[1]

12

100   Soone as the Faerie heard his Ladie speake,
       Out of his swowning dreame he gan awake,
       And quickning° faith, that earst was woxen weake,   *vitalizing*
       The creeping deadly cold away did shake:
       Tho moved with wrath, and shame, and Ladies sake,
105   Of all attonce he cast° avengd to bee,   *determined*
       And with so'exceeding furie at him strake,
       That forcéd him to stoupe upon his knee;
   Had he not stoupéd so, he should have cloven bee,

13

   And to him said, "Goe now proud Miscreant,
110   Thy selfe thy message doe° to german deare,   *give*
       Alone he wandring thee too long doth want:
       Goe say, his foe thy shield with his doth beare."
       Therewith his heavie hand he high gan reare,
       Him to have slaine; when loe a darkesome clowd
115   Upon him fell: he no where doth appeare,
       But vanisht is. The Elfe him cals alowd,
   But answer none receives: the darknes him does shrowd.[2]

14

   In haste Duessa from her place arose,
       And to him running said, "O prowest° knight,   *bravest*
120   That ever Ladie to her love did chose,
       Let now abate the terror of your might,
       And quench the flame of furious despight,
       And bloudie vengeance; lo th'infernall powres
       Covering your foe with cloud of deadly night,
125   Have borne him hence to Plutoes balefull bowres.
   The conquest yours, I yours, the shield, and glory yours."

15

   Not all so satisfide, with greedie eye
       He sought all round about, his thirstie blade
       To bath in bloud of faithlesse enemy;
130   Who all that while lay hid in secret shade:
       He standes amazéd, how he thence should fade.
       At last the trumpets Triumph sound on hie,
       And running Heralds humble homage made,
       Greeting him goodly with new victorie,
135   And to him brought the shield, the cause of enmitie.

1. Duessa is, of course, calling to Sans joy, but Redcrosse (lines 100 ff.) hears her as "Fidessa."
2. This inconclusive ending to the fight is a traditional epic device. Cf., in *Iliad* III, the battle between Menelaus and Paris and *Paradise Lost* IV. In Tasso's *Gerusalemme Liberata* (VII.44–45) the enchantress Armida protects Rambaldo in like manner.

16

Wherewith he goeth to that soveraine Queene,
And falling her before on lowly knee,
To her makes present of his service seene:[3]
Which she accepts, with thankes, and goodly gree,°   *favor*
140 Greatly advauncing° his gay chevalree.   *extolling*
So marcheth home, and by her takes the knight,
Whom all the people follow with great glee,
Shouting, and clapping all their hands on hight,
That all the aire it fils, and flyes to heaven bright.

17

145 Home is he brought, and laid in sumptuous bed:
Where many skilfull leaches° him abide,°   *doctors/attend*
To salve his hurts, that yet still freshly bled.
In wine and oyle they wash his woundes wide,
And softly can embalme° on every side.   *anoint*
150 And all the while, most heavenly melody
About the bed sweet musicke did divide,[4]
Him to beguile of griefe and agony:
And all the while Duessa wept full bitterly.

18

As when a wearie traveller that strayes
155 By muddy shore of broad seven-mouthéd Nile,
Unweeting of the perillous wandring wayes,
Doth meet a cruell craftie Crocodile,
Which in false griefe hyding his harmefull guile,
Doth weepe full sore, and sheddeth tender teares:
160 The foolish man, that pitties all this while
His mournefull plight, is swallowed up unwares,
Forgetfull of his owne, that mindes anothers cares.

19

So wept Duessa untill eventide,
That° shyning lampes in Joves high house were light: *when*
165 Then forth she rose, ne lenger would abide,
But comes unto the place, where th'Hethen knight
In slombring swownd nigh voyd of vitall spright,
Lay covered with inchaunted cloud all day:
Whom when she found, as she him left in plight,
170 To wayle his woefull case she would not stay,
But to the easterne coast of heaven makes speedy way.

20

Where griesly Night, with visage deadly sad,
That Phoebus chearefull face durst never vew,
And in a foule blacke pitchie mantle clad,
175 She findes forth comming from her darkesome mew,°   *den*
Where she all day did hide her hated hew.
Before the dore her yron charet stood,

3. Proved. Redcrosse's act of idolatrous worship to Lucifera bodes ill for his spir- itual health.
4. Played variations.

Alreadie harnesséd for journey new;
And cole blacke steedes yborne of hellish brood,
180 That on their rustie bits did champ, as they were wood.[5]

21

Who when she saw Duessa sunny bright,
    Adornd with gold and jewels shining cleare,
    She greatly grew amazéd at the sight,
    And th'unacquainted light began to feare:
185   For never did such brightnesse there appeare,
    And would have backe retyred to her cave,
    Untill the witches speech she gan to heare,
    Saying, "Yet O thou dreaded Dame, I crave
Abide, till I have told the message, which I have."

22

190 She stayd, and foorth Duessa gan proceede,
    "O thou most auncient Grandmother of all,
    More old then Jove, whom thou at first didst breede,
    Or that great house of Gods caelestiall,
    Which wast begot in Daemogorgons hall,[6]
195   And sawst the secrets of the world unmade,[7]
    Why suffredst thou thy Nephewes° deare to fall   grandsons
    With Elfin sword, most shamefully betrade?
Lo where the stout Sans joy doth sleepe in deadly shade.

23

"And him before, I saw with bitter eyes
200   The bold Sans foy shrinke underneath his speare;
    And now the pray of fowles in field he lyes,
    Nor wayld of friends, nor laid on groning beare,°   bier
    That whylome was to me too dearely deare.
    O what of Gods then boots it to be borne,
205   If old Aveugles sonnes so evill heare?[8]
    Or who shall not great Nightes children scorne,
When two of three her Nephews are so fowle forlorne.

24

"Up then, up dreary Dame, of darknesse Queene,
    Go gather up the reliques of thy race,
210   Or else goe them avenge, and let be seene,
    That dreaded Night in brightest day hath place,
    And can the children of faire light deface."°   destroy
    Her feeling speeches some compassion moved
    In hart, and chaunge in that great mothers face:
215   Yet pittie in her hart was never proved
Till then: for evermore she hated, never loved.

25

And said, "Deare daughter rightly may I rew
    The fall of famous children borne of mee,

5. Mad. The description of night echoes not only descriptions in classical poetry but also the world of popular superstition in the English countryside.
6. I.e., in Chaos.
7. Before it was made.
8. I.e., are so badly thought of. "Aveugle" means "blind"; he is son of Night and father of Sans foy, Sans joy, and Sans loy.

And good successes, which their foes ensew:°   *attend*
220 But who can turne the streame of destinee,
Or breake the chayne of strong necessitee,
Which fast is tyde to Joves eternall seat?[9]
The sonnes of Day he favoureth, I see,
And by my ruines thinkes to make them great:
225 To make one great by others losse, is bad excheat.°   *profit*

26

"Yet shall they not escape so freely all;
For some shall pay the price of others guilt:
And he the man that made Sans foy to fall,
Shall with his owne bloud price that[1] he hath spilt.
230 But what art thou, that telst of Nephews kilt?"
"I that do seeme not I, Duessa am,"
Quoth she, "how ever now in garments gilt,
And gorgeous gold arayd I to thee came;
Duessa I, the daughter of Deceipt and Shame."

27

235 Then bowing downe her agéd backe, she kist
The wicked witch, saying; "In that faire face
The false resemblance of Deceipt, I wist°   *knew*
Did closely lurke; yet so true-seeming grace
It carried, that I scarse in darkesome place
240 Could it discerne, though I the mother bee
Of falshood, and root of Duessaes race.
O welcome child, whom I have longd to see,
And now have seene unwares. Lo now I go with thee."

28

Then to her yron wagon she betakes,
245 And with her beares the fowle welfavourd witch:
Through mirkesome aire her readie way she makes.
Her twyfold° Teme, of which two blacke as pitch,   *twofold*
And two were browne, yet each to each unlich,°   *unlike*
Did softly swim away, ne ever stampe,
250 Unlesse she chaunst their stubborne mouths to twitch;
Then foming tarre, their bridles they would champe,
And trampling the fine element,[2] would fiercely rampe.°   *rear*

29

So well they sped, that they be come at length
Unto the place, whereas the Paynim lay,
255 Devoid of outward sense, and native strength,
Coverd with charméd cloud from vew of day,
And sight of men, since his late luckelesse fray.
His cruell wounds with cruddy° bloud congealed,   *clotted*
They binden up so wisely, as they may,

---

9. The golden chain of concord or design that binds the entire universe; the image goes back as far as Homer (*Iliad* VIII.18–27) and was given classic statement by Boethius (*Consolation of Philosophy* II.8). Cf. ix.1.
1. I.e., pay for what.
2. The air.

₂₆₀ And handle softly, till they can be healed:
So lay him in her charet, close in night concealed.

30

And all the while she stood upon the ground,
    The wakefull dogs did never cease to bay,
    As giving warning of th'unwonted sound,
₂₆₅   With which her yron wheeles did them affray,
    And her darke griesly looke them much dismay;
    The messenger of death, the ghastly Owle
    With drearie shriekes did also her bewray;°   *reveal*
    And hungry Wolves continually did howle,
₂₇₀ At her abhorréd face, so filthy and so fowle.

31

Thence turning backe in silence soft they stole,
    And brought the heavie corse with easie pace
    To yawning gulfe of deepe Avernus hole.[3]
    By that same hole an entrance darke and bace
₂₇₅   With smoake and sulphure hiding all the place,
    Descends to hell: there creature never past,
    That backe returnéd without heavenly grace;
    But dreadfull Furies, which their chaines have brast,°   *burst*
    And damnéd sprights sent forth to make ill° men aghast.   *evil*

32

₂₈₀ By that same way the direfull dames doe drive
    Their mournefull charet, fild with rusty blood,
    And downe to Plutoes house are come bilive:°   *quickly*
    Which passing through, on every side them stood
    The trembling ghosts with sad amazéd mood,
₂₈₅   Chattring their yron teeth, and staring wide
    With stonie eyes; and all the hellish brood
    Of feends infernall flockt on every side,
    To gaze on earthly wight, that with the Night durst ride.

33

They pas the bitter waves of Acheron,
₂₉₀   Where many soules sit wailing woefully,
    And come to fiery flood of Phlegeton,
    Whereas the damnéd ghosts in torments fry,
    And with sharpe shrilling shriekes doe bootlesse cry,
    Cursing high Jove, the which them thither sent.
₂₉₅   The house of endlesse paine is built thereby,
    In which ten thousand sorts of punishment
    The curséd creatures doe eternally torment.

34

Before the threshold dreadfull Cerberus
    His three deforméd heads did lay along,°   *down*

---

3. In classical mythology, Avernus is Hell, where Pluto reigns (line 282). Acheron (line 289) and Phlegeton (line 291) are rivers in Hell. Cerberus (line 298), the three-headed dog, is guardian there. Stanzas 31–35 recall much of Aeneas's descent into Hell (Virgil, *Aeneid* VI.200, 239–40).

300　Curled with thousands adders venemous,
　　And lilléd° forth his bloudie flaming tong:　　　　　　　　*lolled*
　　At them he gan to reare his bristles strong,
　　And felly gnarre,[4] untill dayes enemy
　　Did him appease; then downe his taile he hong
305　And suffered them to passen quietly:
　　For she in hell and heaven had power equally.

35
　　There was Ixion turnéd on a wheele,
　　　For daring tempt the Queene of heaven to sin;
　　And Sisyphus an huge round stone did reele°　　　　　*roll*
310　Against an hill, ne might from labour lin;°　　　　　　*cease*
　　There thirstie Tantalus hong by the chin;
　　And Tityus fed a vulture on his maw;°　　　　　　　　*liver*
　　Typhoeus joynts were stretchéd on a gin,°　　　　　　*rack*
　　Theseus condemned to endlesse slouth° by law,　　　*sloth*
315　And fifty sisters water in leake° vessels draw.[5]　　　*leaky*

36
　　They all beholding worldly wights in place,
　　　Leave off their worke, unmindfull of their smart,
　　To gaze on them; who forth by them doe pace,
　　Till they be come unto the furthest part:
320　Where was a Cave ywrought by wondrous art,
　　Deepe, darke, uneasie, dolefull, comfortlesse,
　　In which sad Aesculapius farre a part
　　Emprisond was in chaines remedilesse,
　　For that Hippolytus rent corse he did redresse.[6]

37
325　Hippolytus a jolly° huntsman was,　　　　　　　　　　*fine*
　　　That wont in charet chace the foming Bore;
　　He all his Peeres in beautie did surpas,
　　But Ladies love as losse of time forbore:
　　His wanton stepdame[7] lovéd him the more,
330　But when she saw her offred sweets refused
　　Her love she turnd to hate, and him before
　　His father fierce of treason false accused,
　　And with her gealous termes his open eares abused.

38
　　Who all in rage his Sea-god syre[8] besought,
335　　Some curséd vengeance on his sonne to cast:

---

4. Savagely growl.
5. Ixion was being punished for attempting to seduce Juno; Sisyphus for refusing to pray to the gods; Tantalus for stealing the gods' nectar; Tityus for having tried to seduce Apollo's mother; the monster Typhoeus for creating unfavorable winds; Theseus for stealing Persephone from Hades; and the daughters of King Danaus for having killed their husbands on the wedding night.

Ovid, Virgil, and Homer are Spenser's sources here.
6. Aesculapius was god of medicine. Spenser draws most closely for the story of Hippolytus upon Boccaccio's *De Genealogica* (X.50), although Ovid and Virgil also tell the story.
7. Phaedra, the wife of his father, Theseus.
8. Poseidon (Neptune).

From surging gulf two monsters straight were brought,
With dread whereof his chasing steedes aghast,
Both charet swift and huntsman overcast.
His goodly corps on ragged cliffs yrent,
340 Was quite dismembred, and his members chast
Scattered on every mountaine, as he went,
That of Hippolytus was left no moniment.[9]

39

His cruell stepdame seeing what was donne,
Her wicked dayes with wretched knife did end,
345 In death avowing th'innocence of her sonne.
Which hearing his rash Syre, began to rend
His haire, and hastie tongue, that did offend:
Tho gathering up the relicks of his smart[1]
By Dianes meanes, who was Hippolyts frend,
350 Them brought to Aesculape, that by his art
Did heale them all againe, and joynéd every part.

40

Such wondrous science in mans wit to raine
When Jove avizd,° that could the dead revive,   *discovered*
And fates expiréd could renew againe,
355 Of endlesse life he might him not deprive,
But unto hell did thrust him downe alive,
With flashing thunderbolt ywounded sore:
Where long remaining, he did alwaies strive
Himselfe with salves to health for to restore,
360 And slake the heavenly fire, that raged evermore.

41

There auncient Night arriving, did alight
From her nigh wearie waine, and in her armes
To Aesculapius brought the wounded knight:
Whom having softly disarayd of armes,
365 Tho gan to him discover all his harmes,
Beseeching him with prayer, and with praise,
If either salves, or oyles, or herbes, or charmes
A fordonne° wight from dore of death mote raise,   *undone*
He would at her request prolong her nephews daies.

42

370 "Ah Dame," quoth he, "thou temptest me in vaine,
To dare the thing, which daily yet I rew,
And the old cause of my continued paine
With like attempt to like end to renew.
Is not enough, that thrust from heaven dew°   *fitting*
375 Here endlesse penance for one fault I pay,
But that redoubled crime with vengeance new
Thou biddest me to eeke?° Can Night defray°   *increase/appease*
The wrath of thundring Jove, that rules both night and day?"

9. I.e., no trace of identity.   1. I.e., his remains.

43

"Not so," quoth she; "but sith that heavens king
380 From hope of heaven hath thee excluded quight,
     Why fearest thou, that canst not hope for thing,
     And fearest not, that more thee hurten might,
     Now in the powre of everlasting Night?
     Goe to then, O thou farre renowméd sonne
385 Of great Apollo, shew thy famous might
     In medicine, that else° hath to thee wonne   *already*
Great paines, and greater praise, both never to be donne."° *ended*

44

Her words prevaild: And then the learnéd leach°   *doctor*
     His cunning hand gan to his wounds to lay,
390 And all things else, the which his art did teach:
     Which having seene, from thence arose away
     The mother of dread darknesse, and let stay
     Aveugles sonne there in the leaches cure,
     And backe returning tooke her wonted way,
395 To runne her timely race,² whilst Phoebus pure
In westerne waves his wearie wagon did recure.°   *refresh*

45

The false Duessa leaving noyous° Night,   *harmful*
     Returnd to stately pallace of dame Pride;
     Where when she came, she found the Faery knight
400 Departed thence, albe° his woundes wide   *although*
     Not throughly heald, unreadie were to ride.
     Good cause he had to hasten thence away;
     For on a day his wary Dwarfe had spide,
     Where in a dongeon deepe huge numbers lay
405 Of caytive° wretched thrals,° that wayléd night   *captive/slaves*
        and day.³

46

A ruefull sight, as could be seene with eie;
     Of whom he learnéd had in secret wise
     The hidden cause of their captivitie,
     How mortgaging their lives to Covetise,
410 Through wastfull Pride, and wanton Riotise,
     They were by law of that proud Tyrannesse⁴
     Provokt with Wrath, and Envies false surmise,
     Condemnéd to that Dongeon mercilesse,
Where they should live in woe, and die in wretchednesse.

47

415 There was that great proud king of Babylon,⁵
     That would compell all nations to adore,
     And him as onely God to call upon,
     Till him through celestiall doome° throwne out of dore, *judgment*
     Into an Oxe he was transformed of yore:
420 There also was king Croesus,⁶ that enhaunst°   *exalted*

2. Her measured (nightly) journey.
3. The Dwarfe here acts as a "wary"
conscience.
4. I.e., Lucifera, whose "law" is that of
destruction by sin. The noble sinners
named in stanzas 47–50 exemplify a
theme common to Renaissance morality,
the fall of princes.
5. Nebuchadnezzar (Daniel iii–iv).
6. King of Lydia, famous for his riches.

His heart too high through his great riches store;
And proud Antiochus,[7] the which advaunst
His curséd hand gainst God, and on his altars daunst.

48

And them long time before, great Nimrod[8] was,
425   That first the world with sword and fire warrayd;°   *ravaged*
And after him old Ninus farre did pas°   *surpass*
In princely pompe, of all the world obayd;
There also was that mightie Monarch layd
Low under all, yet above all in pride,
430   That name of native° syre did fowle upbrayd,   *natural*
And would as Ammons sonne[8a] be magnifide,
Till scornd of God and man a shamefull death he dide.

49

All these together in one heape were throwne,
Like carkases of beasts in butchers stall.
435   And in another corner wide were strowne
The antique ruines of the Romaines fall:[9]
Great Romulus the Grandsyre of them all,
Proud Tarquin, and too lordly Lentulus,
Stout Scipio, and stubborne Hanniball,
440   Ambitious Sylla, and sterne Marius,
High Caesar, great Pompey, and fierce Antonius.

50

Amongst these mighty men were wemen mixt,
Proud wemen, vaine, forgetfull of their yoke:
The bold Semiramis,[1] whose sides transfixt
445   With sonnes owne blade, her fowle reproches spoke;
Faire Sthenoboea,[2] that her selfe did choke
With wilfull cord, for wanting° of her will;   *lacking*
High minded Cleopatra, that with stroke
Of Aspes sting her selfe did stoutly kill:
450 And thousands moe the like, that did that dongeon fill.

51

Besides the endlesse routs of wretched thralles,
Which thither were assembled day by day,
From all the world after their wofull falles,
Through wicked pride, and wasted wealthes decay.
455   But most of all, which in that Dongeon lay
Fell from high Princes courts, or Ladies bowres,
Where they in idle pompe, or wanton play,
Consuméd had their goods, and thriftlesse howres,
And lastly throwne themselves into these heavy stowres.°   *disasters*

---

7. King of Syria, who tried to stamp out the Jewish religion (I Maccabees i.20–24).
8. A mighty hunter, associated with the Tower of Babel (Genesis x.9). Founder of Nineveh.
8a. Alexander the Great, occasionally worshiped as the son of Jupiter Ammon.
9. Romulus, founder of Rome; Tarquin, Roman tyrant; Lentulus, a conspirator with Catiline; Scipio, Roman general, conqueror of Carthage; Hannibal, Carthaginian general; Sulla, Roman civil war general; Marius, Sulla's rival; Julius Caesar; Pompey the Great; and Mark Anthony. All are memorialized in Plutarch's *Lives*.
1. Wife of Ninus.
2. Queen of King Proetus of Argos, who fell vainly in love with Bellerophon.

52

460 Whose case whenas the carefull Dwarfe had tould,
And made ensample of their mournefull sight
Unto his maister, he no lenger would
There dwell in perill of like painefull plight,
465 But early rose, and ere that dawning light
Discovered had the world to heaven wyde,
He by a privie Posterne° tooke his flight,   *gate*
That of no envious eyes he mote be spyde:[3]
For doubtlesse death ensewd, if any him descryde.

53

Scarse could he footing find in that fowle way,
470 For many corses, like a great Lay-stall°   *rubbish heap*
Of murdred men which therein strowéd lay,
Without remorse, or decent funerall:
Which all through that great Princesse pride did fall
And came to shamefull end. And them beside
475 Forth ryding underneath the castell wall,
A donghill of dead carkases he spide,
The dreadfull spectacle° of that sad house of Pride.   *example*

Canto VI

From lawlesse lust by wondrous grace
fayre Una is releast:
Whom salvage nation does adore,
and learnes her wise beheast.°   *bidding*

1

As when a ship, that flyes faire under saile,
An hidden rocke escapéd hath unwares,
That lay in waite her wrack for to bewaile,
The Marriner yet halfe amazéd stares
5 At perill past, and yet in doubt ne dares
To joy at his foole-happie oversight:
So doubly is distrest twixt joy and cares
The dreadlesse courage° of this Elfin knight,   *heart*
Having escapt so sad ensamples in his sight.

2

10 Yet sad he was that his too hastie speed
The faire Duess' had forst him leave behind;
And yet more sad, that Una his deare dreed°   *object of reverence*
Her truth had staind with treason so unkind;°   *unnatural*
Yet crime in her could never creature find,
15 But for his love, and for her owne selfe sake,
She wandred had° from one to other Ynd,   *would have*
Him for to seeke, ne ever would forsake,
Till her unwares the fierce Sansloy did overtake.

3. Redcrosse entered the House of Pride from above; he leaves it from below.

3

Who after Archimagoes fowle defeat,
20   Led her away into a forrest wilde,
     And turning wrathfull fire to lustfull heat,
     With beastly sin thought her to have defilde,
     And made the vassall of his pleasures vilde.°   *vile*
     Yet first he cast by treatie,° and by traynes,°   *persuasion/tricks*
25   Her to perswade, that stubborne fort to yilde:
     For greater conquest of hard love he gaynes,
That workes it to his will, then he that it constraines.°   *forces*

4

With fawning wordes he courted her a while,
     And looking lovely,° and oft sighing sore,   *lovingly*
30   Her constant hart did tempt with diverse guile:
     But wordes, and lookes, and sighes she did abhore,
     As rocke of Diamond stedfast evermore.[4]
     Yet for to feed his fyrie lustfull eye,
     He snatcht the vele, that hong her face before;
35   Then gan her beautie shine, as brightest skye,
And burnt his beastly hart t'efforce° her chastitye.   *violate*

5

So when he saw his flatt'ring arts to fayle,
     And subtile engines bet° from batteree,   *beaten*
     With greedy force he gan the fort assayle,
40   Whereof he weend possesséd soone to bee,
     And win rich spoile of ransackt chastetee.
     Ah heavens, that do this hideous act behold,
     And heavenly virgin thus outragéd see,
     How can ye vengeance just so long withhold,
45 And hurle not flashing flames upon that Paynim bold?

6

The pitteous maden carefull° comfortlesse,   *full of cares*
     Does throw out thrilling shriekes, and shrieking cryes,
     The last vaine helpe of womens great distresse,
     And with loud plaints importuneth the skyes,
50   That molten starres do drop like weeping eyes;
     And Phoebus flying so most shamefull sight,
     His blushing face in foggy cloud implyes,°   *buries*
     And hides for shame. What wit of mortall wight
Can now devise to quit a thrall[5] from such a plight?

7

55 Eternall providence exceeding thought,
     Where none appeares can make her selfe a way:
     A wondrous way it for this Lady wrought,
     From Lyons clawes to pluck the gripéd pray.
     Her shrill outcryes and shriekes so loud did bray,
60   That all the woodes and forestes did resownd;

4. The diamond was traditionally per-   made of diamond.
fect; Arthur's shield (I.vii.33) is also   5. Release a victim.

A troupe of Faunes and Satyres far away
  Within the wood were dauncing in a rownd,
Whiles old Sylvanus slept in shady arber sownd.[6]

8

Who when they heard that pitteous strainéd voice,
65 In hast forsooke their rurall meriment,
  And ran towards the far rebownded noyce,
  To weet, what wight so loudly did lament.
  Unto the place they come incontinent:°   *immediately*
  Whom when the raging Sarazin espide,
70 A rude, misshapen, monstrous rablement,
  Whose like he never saw, he durst not bide,
But got his ready steed, and fast away gan ride.[7]

9

The wyld woodgods arrivéd in the place,
  There find the virgin dolefull desolate,
75 With ruffled rayments, and faire blubbred face,
  As her outrageous foe had left her late,
  And trembling yet through feare of former hate;
  All stand amazéd at so uncouth° sight,   *strange*
  And gin to pittie her unhappie state,
80 All stand astonied at her beautie bright,
In their rude eyes unworthie° of so wofull plight. *undeserving*

10

She more amazed, in double dread doth dwell;
  And every tender part for feare does shake:
  As when a greedie Wolfe through hunger fell
85 A seely° Lambe farre from the flocke does take, *innocent*
  Of whom he meanes his bloudie feast to make,
  A Lyon spyes fast running towards him,
  The innocent pray in hast he does forsake,
  Which quit from death yet quakes in every lim
90 With chaunge of feare, to see the Lyon looke so grim.

11

Such fearefull fit assaid° her trembling hart,   *afflicted*
  Ne word to speake, ne joynt to move she had:
  The salvage nation feele her secret smart,
  And read her sorrow in her count'nance sad;
95 Their frowning forheads with rough hornes yclad,
  And rusticke horror[8] all a side doe lay,
  And gently grenning, shew a semblance glad
  To comfort her, and feare to put away,
Their backward bent knees teach[9] her humbly to obay.

---

6. Fauns and satyrs, creatures with men's bodies above the waist and goats' bodies below, noted in classical mythology for their sensuality, engage here in "rurall meriment"; Sylvanus, Roman god of the woods, is traditionally associated with fauns.

7. The "woodgods," like the Lyon of Canto iii, bear some natural goodness—unlike Sans loy, who is alien to nature. They perhaps represent religious belief and practice before Christianity.
8. Rough manner.
9. I.e., teach them.

12

100 The doubtfull Damzell dare not yet commit
      Her single° person to their barbarous truth,°   *solitary/honesty*
      But still twixt feare and hope amazd does sit,
      Late learnd what harme to hastie trust ensu'th,
      They in compassion of her tender youth,
105 And wonder of her beautie soveraine,
      Are wonne with pitty and unwonted ruth,
      And all prostrate upon the lowly plaine,
    Do kisse her feete, and fawne on her with count'nance faine.° *pleasant*

13

   Their harts she ghesseth by their humble guise,
110 And yieldes her to extremitie of time;[1]
      So from the ground she fearelesse doth arise,
      And walketh forth without suspect of crime:
      They all as glad, as birdes of joyous Prime,°   *springtime*
      Thence lead her forth, about her dauncing round,
115 Shouting, and singing all a shepheards ryme,
      And with greene braunches strowing all the ground,
    Do worship her, as Queene, with olive girlond cround.

14

   And all the way their merry pipes they sound,
      That all the woods with doubled Eccho ring,
120 And with their hornéd feet do weare the ground,
      Leaping like wanton kids in pleasant Spring.
      So towards old Sylvanus they her bring;
      Who with the noyse awakéd, commeth out,
      To weet the cause, his weake steps governing
125 An agéd limbs on Cypresse stadle° stout,   *staff*
    And with an yvie twyne his wast is girt about.

15

   Far off he wonders, what them makes so glad,
      Or° Bacchus merry fruit[2] they did invent,°   *whether/find*
      Or Cybeles franticke rites[3] have made them mad;
130 They drawing nigh, unto their God present
      That flowre of faith and beautie excellent.
      The God himselfe vewing that mirrhour rare,
      Stood long amazd, and burnt in his intent;[4]
      His owne faire Dryope now he thinkes not faire,
135 And Pholoe fowle, when her to this he doth compaire.[5]

16

   The woodborne people fall before her flat,
      And worship her as Goddesse of the wood;
      And old Sylvanus selfe bethinkes not, what
      To thinke of wight so faire, but gazing stood,

1. I.e., necessity of the time.
2. Wine grapes.
3. Orgiastic dances in worship of Cybele, goddess of the powers of Nature.
4. Glowed with intense concentration. Una is a "mirrhour rare" in that she reflects heavenly beauty.
5. Dryope and Pholoe were nymphs loved by Faunus and Pan; for Spenser, the names "Faunus," "Pan," and "Sylvanus" were apparently interchangeable.

140 In doubt to deeme her borne of earthly brood;
　　Sometimes Dame Venus selfe he seemes to see,
　　But Venus never had so sober mood;
　　Sometimes Diana he her takes to bee,
　　But misseth bow, and shaftes, and buskins° to her knee.　　*soft boots*

17

145 By vew of her he ginneth to revive
　　His ancient love, and dearest Cyparisse,[6]
　　And calles to mind his pourtraiture alive,[7]
　　How faire he was, and yet not faire to this,
　　And how he slew with glauncing dart amisse
150 A gentle Hynd, the which the lovely boy
　　Did love as life, above all worldly blisse;
　　For griefe whereof the lad n'ould° after joy,　　*would not*
　　But pynd away in anguish and selfe-wild annoy.°　　*suffering*

18

　　The wooddy Nymphes, faire Hamadryades[8]
155 Her to behold do thither runne apace,
　　And all the troupe of light-foot Naiades,[9]
　　Flocke all about to see her lovely face:
　　But when they vewéd have her heavenly grace,
　　They envie her in their malitious mind,
160 And fly away for feare of fowle disgrace:
　　But all the Satyres scorne their woody kind,
　　And henceforth nothing faire, but her on earth they find.

19

　　Glad of such lucke, the luckelesse lucky maid,
　　Did her content to please their feeble eyes,
165 And long time with that salvage people staid,
　　To gather breath in many miseries.
　　During which time her gentle wit she plyes,
　　To teach them truth, which worshipt her in vaine,
　　And made her th'Image of Idolatryes;
170 But when their bootlesse zeale she did restraine
　　From her own worship, they her Asse would worship fayn.[1]

20

　　It fortunéd a noble warlike knight
　　By just occasion to that forrest came,
　　To seeke his kindred, and the lignage right,°　　*true*
175 From whence he tooke his well deservéd name:
　　He had in armes abroad wonne muchell fame,
　　And fild far landes with glorie of his might,
　　Plaine, faithfull, true, and enimy of shame,
　　And ever loved to fight for Ladies right,
180 But in vaine glorious frayes he litle did delight.

---

6. A fair youth, beloved of Sylvanus, turned into a cypress tree.
7. I.e., his appearance when alive.
8. Nymphs whose lives depended upon the trees with which they were associated.
9. Water nymphs.
1. I.e., willingly. Natural goodness can give some recognition, albeit only externally, to Una. Though Una does her best to teach the satyrs true religion, they are idolaters even in the truth.

21

A Satyres sonne yborne in forrest wyld,
   By straunge adventure as it did betyde,
   And there begotten of a Lady myld,
   Faire Thyamis the daughter of Labryde,
185 That was in sacred bands of wedlocke tyde
   To Therion, a loose unruly swayne;[2]
   Who had more joy to raunge the forrest wyde,
   And chase the salvage beast with busie payne,[3]
Then serve his Ladies love, and wast in pleasures vayne.

22

190 The forlorne mayd did with loves longing burne,
   And could not lacke° her lovers company,   *be without*
   But to the wood she goes, to serve her turne,
   And seeke her spouse, that from her still does fly,
   And followes other game and venery:[4]
195 A Satyre chaunst her wandring for to find,
   And kindling coles of lust in brutish eye,
   The loyall links of wedlocke did unbind,
And made her person thrall unto his beastly kind.

23

So long in secret cabin there he held
200 Her captive to his sensuall desire,
   Till that with timely fruit her belly sweld,
   And bore a boy unto that salvage sire:
   Then home he suffred her for to retire,
   For ransome leaving him the late borne childe;
205 Whom till to ryper yeares he gan aspire,°   *grow up*
   He noursled up in life and manners wilde,
Emongst wild beasts and woods, from lawes of men exilde.

24

For all he taught the tender ymp,° was but   *child*
   To banish cowardize and bastard° feare;   *base*
210 His trembling hand he would him force to put
   Upon the Lyon and the rugged Beare,
   And from the she Beares teats her whelps to teare;
   And eke wyld roring Buls he would him make
   To tame, and ryde their backes not made to beare;
215 And the Robuckes in flight to overtake,
That every beast for feare of him did fly and quake.

25

Thereby so fearelesse, and so fell° he grew,   *fierce*
   That his owne sire and maister of his guise[5]

2. "Thyamis" means "passion," "Therion," "wild beast." Their child Satyrane
(he is named in line 249) ought to be
a savage creature, but instead his natural
goodness welcomes and reveres truth and
grace in Una with a higher understanding than the lion or the woodgods can
give.
3. Painstaking care.
4. The word means both "hunting" and
"sexual play."
5. Teacher of his manners.

Did often tremble at his horrid° vew,   *rough*
220   And oft for dread of hurt would him advise,
The angry beasts not rashly to despise,
Nor too much to provoke; for he would learne°   *teach*
The Lyon stoup to him in lowly wise,
(A lesson hard) and make the Libbard° sterne   *leopard*
225 Leave roaring, when in rage he for revenge did earne.°   *yearn*

26

And for to make his powre approvéd° more,   *extended*
Wyld beasts in yron yokes he would compell;
The spotted Panther, and the tuskéd Bore,
The Pardale° swift, and the Tigre cruell;   *panther*
230   The Antelope, and Wolfe both fierce and fell;
And them constraine in equall teme to draw.
Such joy he had, their stubborne harts to quell,
And sturdie courage tame with dreadfull aw,
That his beheast they feared, as a tyrans law.

27

235 His loving mother came upon a day
Unto the woods, to see her little sonne;
And chaunst unwares to meet him in the way,
After his sportes, and cruell pastime donne,
When after him a Lyonesse did runne,
240   That roaring all with rage, did lowd requere°   *demand*
Her children deare, whom he away had wonne:
The Lyon whelpes she saw how he did beare,
And lull in rugged armes, withouten childish feare.

28

The fearefull Dame all quakéd at the sight,
245   And turning backe, gan fast to fly away,
Untill with love revokt° from vaine affright,   *restrained*
She hardly yet perswaded was to stay,
And then to him these womanish words gan say;
"Ah Satyrane, my dearling, and my joy,
250   For love of me leave off this dreadfull play;
To dally thus with death, is no fit toy,
Go find some other play-fellowes, mine own sweet boy."

29

In these and like delights of bloudy game
He traynéd was, till ryper yeares he raught,°   *reached*
255   And there abode, whilst any beast of name
Walkt in that forest, whom he had not taught
To feare his force: and then his courage haught°   *high*
Desird of forreine foemen to be knowne,
And far abroad for straunge adventures sought:
260   In which his might was never overthrowne,
But through all Faery lond his famous worth was blown.

30

Yet evermore it was his manner faire,
   After long labours and adventures spent,
   Unto those native woods for to repaire,
265   To see his sire and ofspring° auncient.   *origin*
   And now he thither came for like intent;
   Where he unwares the fairest Una found,
   Straunge Lady, in so straunge habiliment,
   Teaching the Satyres, which her sat around,
270 Trew sacred lore, which from her sweet lips did redound.

31

He wondred at her wisedome heavenly rare,
   Whose like in womens wit he never knew;
   And when her curteous deeds he did compare,
   Gan her admire, and her sad sorrowes rew,
275   Blaming of Fortune, which such troubles threw,
   And joyd to make proofe of her crueltie
   On gentle Dame, so hurtlesse,° and so trew: *harmless*
   Thenceforth he kept her goodly company,
And learnd her discipline of faith and veritie.

32

280 But she all vowd unto the Redcrosse knight,
   His wandring perill closely° did lament,   *secretly*
   Ne in this new acquaintaunce could delight,
   But her deare heart with anguish did torment,
   And all her wit in secret counsels spent,
285   How to escape. At last in privie wise
   To Satyrane she shewéd her intent;
   Who glad to gain such favour, gan devise,
How with that pensive Maid he best might thence arise.°   *depart*

33

So on a day when Satyres all were gone,
290   To do their service to Sylvanus old,
   The gentle virgin left behind alone
   He led away with courage stout and bold.
   Too late it was, to Satyres to be told,
   Or ever hope recover her againe:
295   In vaine he seekes that having cannot hold.
   So fast he carried her with carefull paine,[6]
That they the woods are past, and come now to the plaine.

34

The better part now of the lingring day,
   They traveild had, when as they farre espide
300   A wearie wight forwandring° by the way,   *wandering along*
   And towards him they gan in hast to ride,
   To weet of newes, that did abroad betide,
   Or tydings of her knight of the Redcrosse.
   But he them spying, gan to turne aside,

6. Painstaking care.

305   For feare as seemd, or for some feignéd losse;
      More greedy they of newes, fast towards him do crosse.

35

    A silly° man, in simple weedes forworne,°   *simple/worn out*
      And solid with dust of the long dried way;
      His sandales were with toilesome travell torne,
310   And face all tand with scorching sunny ray,
      As he had traveild many a sommers day,
      Through boyling sands of Arabie and Ynde;
      And in his hand a Jacobs staffe,[7] to stay
      His wearie limbes upon: and eke behind,
315 His scrip° did hang, in which his needments he did bind.   *bag*

36

    The knight approching nigh, of him inquerd
      Tydings of warre, and of adventures new;
      But warres, nor new adventures none he herd.
      Then Una gan to aske, if ought he knew,
320   Or heard abroad of that her champion trew,
      That in his armour bare a croslet° red.   *small cross*
      "Aye me, Deare dame," quoth he, "well may I rew
      To tell the sad sight, which mine eies have red:°   *beheld*
    These eyes did see that knight both living and eke ded."

37

325 That cruell word her tender hart so thrild,° .   *pierced*
      That suddein cold did runne through every vaine,
      And stony horrour all her sences fild
      With dying fit, that downe she fell for paine.
      The knight her lightly rearéd up againe,
330   And comforted with curteous kind reliefe:
      Then wonne from death, she bad him tellen plaine
      The further processe° of her hidden griefe;   *account*
    The lesser pangs can beare, who hath endured the chiefe.

38

    Then gan the Pilgrim thus, "I chaunst this day,
335   This fatall day, that shall I ever rew,
      To see two knights in travell on my way
      (A sory sight) arraunged in battell new,
      Both breathing vengeaunce, both of wrathfull hew:
      My fearefull flesh did tremble at their strife,
340   To see their blades so greedily imbrew,°   *thrust*
      That drunke with bloud, yet thristed after life:
    What more? the Redcrosse knight was slaine with Paynim knife."

39

    "Ah dearest Lord," quoth she, "how might that bee,
      And he the stoutest knight, that ever wonne?"°   *fought*
345   "Ah dearest dame," quoth he, "how might I see
      The thing, that might not be, and yet was donne?"
      "Where is," said Satyrane, "that Paynims sonne,
      That him of life, and us of joy hath reft?"

7. I.e., pilgrim's staff.

"Not far away," quoth he, "he hence doth wonne°   stay
350 Foreby a fountaine, where I late him left
Washing his bloudy wounds, that through° the steele were cleft."   by

40

Therewith the knight thence marchéd forth in hast,
   Whiles Una with huge heavinesse opprest,
   Could not for sorrow follow him so fast;
355 And soone he came, as he the place had ghest,
   Whereas that Pagan proud him selfe did rest,
   In secret shadow by a fountaine side:
   Even he it was, that earst would have supprest°   violated
   Faire Una: whom when Satyrane espide,
360 With fowle reprochfull words he boldly him defide.

41

And said, "Arise thou cursed Miscreaunt,
   That hast with knightlesse guile and trecherous train°   deceit
   Faire knighthood fowly shamed, and doest vaunt
   That good knight of the Redcrosse to have slain:
365 Arise, and with like treason now maintain
   Thy guilty wrong, or else thee guilty yield."
   The Sarazin this hearing, rose amain,°   at once
   And catching up in hast his three square[8] shield,
   And shining helmet, soone him buckled to the field.

42

370 And drawing nigh him said, "Ah misborne° Elfe,   base-born
   In evill houre thy foes thee hither sent,
   Anothers wrongs to wreake upon thy selfe:
   Yet ill thou blamest me, for having blent°   stained
   My name with guile and traiterous intent;
375 That Redcrosse knight, perdie, I never slew,
   But had he beene, where earst his armes were lent,
   Th' enchaunter vaine his errour should not rew:
   But thou his errour shalt, I hope now proven trew."[9]

43

Therewith they gan, both furious and fell,
380 To thunder blowes, and fiersly to assaile
   Each other bent his enimy to quell,°   kill
   That with their force they perst both plate and maile,
   And made wide furrowes in their fleshes fraile,
   That it would pitty° any living eie.   bring pity to
385 Large floods of bloud adowne their sides did raile:°   flow
   But floods of bloud could not them satisfie:
   Both hungred after death: both chose to win, or die.

---

8. Triangular.
9. I.e., had Redcrosse been where his
arms were, the enchanter Archimago
would not have to regret his error in
fighting me. But you will now repeat his
error in fighting me and demonstrate
what an error it is.

44

So long they fight, and fell revenge pursue,
  That fainting each, themselves to breathen let,
390 And oft refreshéd, battell oft renue:
  As when two Bores with rancling malice met,
  Their gory sides fresh bleeding fiercely fret,°   *tear*
  Til breathlesse both them selves aside retire,
  Where foming wrath, their cruell tuskes they whet,
395 And trample th'earth, the whiles they may respire
Then backe to fight againe, new breathéd and entire.°   *refreshed*

45

So fiersly, when these knights had breathéd once,
  They gan to fight returne, increasing more
  Their puissant force, and cruell rage attonce,
400 With heapéd strokes more hugely, then before,
  That with their drerie° wounds and bloudy gore   *dreadful*
  They both deforméd, scarsely could be known.
  By this sad Una fraught with anguish sore,
  Led with their noise, which through the aire was thrown,
405 Arrived, where they in erth their fruitles bloud had sown.

46

Whom all so soone as that proud Sarazin
  Espide, he gan revive the memory
  Of his lewd lusts, and late attempted sin,
  And left the doubtfull battell hastily,
410 To catch her, newly offred to his eie:
  But Satyrane with strokes him turning, staid,
  And sternely bad him other businesse plie,
  Then hunt the steps of pure unspotted Maid:
Wherewith he all enraged, these bitter speaches said.

47

415 "O foolish faeries sonne, what furie mad
  Hath thee incenst, to hast thy dolefull fate?
  Were it not better, I that Lady had,
  Then that thou hadst repented it too late?
  Most sencelesse man he, that himselfe doth hate,
420 To love another. Lo then for thine ayd
  Here take thy lovers token on thy pate."
  So they to fight; the whiles the royall Mayd
Fled farre away, of that proud Paynim sore afrayd.

48

But that false Pilgrim, which that leasing° told,   *lying*
425 Being in deed old Archimage, did stay
  In secret shadow, all this to behold,
  And much rejoycéd in their bloudy fray:
  But when he saw the Damsell passe away
  He left his stond,° and her pursewd apace,   *place*

430 In hope to bring her to her last decay.°   *destruction*
     But for to tell her lamentable cace,
And eke this battels end, will need another place.

Canto VII

The Redcrosse knight is captive made
By Gyaunt proud opprest,
Prince Arthur meets with Una great-
ly with those newes distrest.

1

What man so wise, what earthly wit so ware,°   *wary*
   As to descry° the crafty cunning traine,   *perceive*
   By which deceipt doth maske in visour faire,
   And cast her colours dyéd deepe in graine,
5 To seeme like Truth, whose shape she well can faine,
   And fitting gestures to her purpose frame,
   The guiltlesse man with guile to entertaine?°   *receive*
   Great maistresse of her art was that false Dame,
The false Duessa, clokéd with Fidessaes name.

2

10 Who when returning from the drery Night,
   She fownd not in that perilous house of Pryde,
   Where she had left, the noble Redcrosse knight,
   Her hopéd pray, she would no lenger bide,
   But forth she went, to seeke him far and wide.
15 Ere long she fownd, whereas° he wearie sate,   *where*
   To rest him selfe, foreby° a fountaine side,   *beside*
   Disarméd all of yron-coted Plate,
And by his side his steed the grassy forage ate.

3

   He feedes upon the cooling shade, and bayes°   *bathes*
20   His sweatie forehead in the breathing wind,
   Which through the trembling leaves full gently playes
   Wherein the cherefull birds of sundry kind
   Do chaunt sweet musick, to delight his mind:
   The Witch approaching gan him fairely greet,
25   And with reproch of carelesnesse unkind
   Upbrayd, for leaving her in place unmeet,°   *unfitting*
With fowle words tempring faire, soure gall with hony sweet.

4

   Unkindnesse past, they gan of solace treat,
   And bathe in pleasaunce of the joyous shade,
30   Which shielded them against the boyling heat,
   And with greene boughes decking a gloomy glade,
   About the fountaine like a girlond made;
   Whose bubbling wave did ever freshly well,
   Ne ever would through fervent° sommer fade: *hot*
35   The sacred Nymph, which therein wont to dwell,
Was out of Dianes favour, as it then befell.

5

The cause was this: one day when Phoebe[1] fayre
   With all her band was following the chace,
   This Nymph, quite tyred with heat of scorching ayre
40 Sat downe to rest in middest of the race:
   The goddesse wroth gan fowly her disgrace,°   *scold*
   And bad the waters, which from her did flow,
   Be such as she her selfe was then in place.[2]
   Thenceforth her waters waxéd dull and slow,
45 And all that drunke thereof, did faint and feeble grow.

6

Hereof this gentle knight unweeting was,
   And lying downe upon the sandie graile,°   *gravel*
   Drunke of the streame, as cleare as cristall glas;
   Eftsoones his manly forces gan to faile,
50 And mightie strong was turnd to feeble fraile.
   His chaunged powres at first themselves not felt,
   Till crudled° cold his corage° gan assaile,   *curdled/vigor*
   And chearefull bloud in faintnesse chill did melt,
Which like a fever fit through all his body swelt.°   *raged*

7

55 Yet goodly court he made still to his Dame,
   Pour out in loosnesse on the grassy grownd,
   Both carelesse of his health, and of his fame:
   Till at the last he heard a dreadfull sownd,
   Which through the wood loud bellowing, did rebownd,
60 That all the earth for terrour seemed to shake,
   And trees did tremble. Th'Elfe therewith astownd,°   *amazed*
   Upstarted lightly from his looser make,°   *companion*
And his unready weapons gan in hand to take.[3]

8

But ere he could his armour on him dight,
65 Or get his shield, his monstrous enimy
   With sturdie steps came stalking in his sight,
   An hideous Geant horrible and hye,
   That with his talnesse seemd to threat the skye,
   The ground eke groned under him for dreed;
70 His living like saw never living eye,
   Ne durst behold: his stature did exceed
The hight of three the tallest sonnes of mortall seed.

9

The greatest Earth his uncouth mother was,
   And blustring Aeolus his boasted sire,[4]
75 Who with his breath, which through the world doth pas,
   Her hollow womb did secretly inspire,°   *breathe into*

1. I.e., Diana, goddess of the moon.
2. At that time.
3. Redcrosse is weakened by his encounter with the despair of Sans joy; he has been seduced by falsehood, Duessa; he has drunk of the waters of spiritual sloth: he is thus, now, an easy victim.

4. Aeolus was keeper of the winds. His son, the giant, is Orgoglio (named in line 122), which means "pride." That this sin, pride of the flesh, unchristian and unreasonable, should be the son of the gross earth and the "blustring" wind seems appropriate.

And fild her hidden caves with stormie yre,
That she conceived; and trebling the dew time,
In which the wombes of women do expire,°   *bring forth*
80   Brought forth this monstrous masse of earthly slime,
Puft up with emptie wind, and fild with sinfull crime.

10

So growen great through arrogant delight
Of th'high descent, whereof he was yborne,
And through presumption of his matchlesse might,
85   All other powres and knighthood he did scorne.
Such now he marcheth to this man forlorne,
And left to losse:° his stalking steps are stayde   *destruction*
Upon a snaggy Oke, which he had torne
Out of his mothers bowelles, and it made
90 His mortall mace, wherewith his foemen he dismayde.

11

That when the knight he spide, he gan advance
With huge force and insupportable mayne,[5]
And towardes him with dreadfull fury praunce;
Who haplesse, and eke hopelesse, all in vaine
95   Did to him pace, sad battaile to darrayne,°   *contest*
Disarmd, disgrast, and inwardly dismayde,[6]
And eke so faint in every joynt and vaine,
Through that fraile° fountaine, which him feeble made,   *enfeebling*
That scarsely could he weeld his bootlesse° single blade.   *futile*

12

100 The Geaunt strooke so maynly° mercilesse,   *mightily*
That could have overthrowne a stony towre,
And were not heavenly grace, that him did blesse,
He had beene pouldred° all, as thin as flowre: *powdered*
But he was wary of that deadly stowre,
105   And lightly lept from underneath the blow:
Yet so exceeding was the villeins powre,
That with the wind it did him overthrow,
And all his sences stound,° that still he lay full low.   *stunned*

13

As when that divelish yron Engin[7] wrought
110   In deepest Hell, and framd by Furies skill,   *explosive*
With windy Nitre and quick° Sulphur fraught,
And ramd with bullet round, ordaind to kill,
Conceiveth fire, the heavens it doth fill
With thundring noyse, and all the ayre doth choke,
115   That none can breath, nor see, nor heare at will,
Through smouldry cloud of duskish stincking smoke,
That th'onely breath[8] him daunts, who hath escapt the stroke.

---

5. Irresistable power.   7. I.e., cannon.
6. Dis-made, dissolved.   8. I.e., the blast alone.

14

So daunted when the Geaunt saw the knight,
His heavie hand he·heavéd up on hye,
₁₂₀ And him to dust thought to have battred quight,
Untill Duessa loud to him gan crye;
"O great Orgoglio, greatest under skye,
O hold thy mortall hand for Ladies sake,
Hold for my sake, and do him not to dye,
₁₂₅ But vanquisht thine eternall bondslave make,
And me thy worthy meed unto thy Leman take."⁹

15

He hearkned, and did stay from further harmes,
To gayne so goodly guerdon,° as she spake: *reward*
So willingly she came into his armes,
₁₃₀ Who her as willingly to grace° did take,   *favor*
And was posséssed of his new found make.°   *mate*
Then up he tooke the slombred sencelesse corse,
And ere he could out of his swowne awake,
Him to his castle brought with hastie forse,
₁₃₅ And in a Dongeon deepe him threw without remorse.

16

From that day forth Duessa was his deare,
And highly honourd in his haughtie eye,
He gave her gold and purple pall° to weare,   *robe*
And triple crowne set on her head full hye,¹
₁₄₀ And her endowd with royall majestye:
Then for to make her dreaded more of men,
And peoples harts with awfull terrour tye,
A monstrous beast ybred in filthy fen
He chose, which he had kept long time in darksome den.

17

₁₄₅ Such one it was, as that renowméd Snake
Which great Alcides in Stremona slew,
Long fostred in the filth of Lerna lake,
Whose many heads out budding ever new,
Did breed him endlesse labour to subdew:²
₁₅₀ But this same Monster much more ugly was;
For seven great heads out of his body grew,
An yron brest, and backe of scaly bras,
And all embrewd° in bloud, his eyes did shine as glas.   *stained*

9. I.e., take me, your worthy reward, as your mistress.
1. Duessa is attired like the Whore of Babylon in Revelation xvii.3–4; the triple crown is that of the papacy. See i.13, also i.22 and note.
2. The nine-headed Lernean hydra slain by Hercules (Alcides). The seven-headed monster is the red dragon of Revelation: "behold a great red dragon, having seven heads and ten horns, and seven crowns upon his heads * * * [whose] tail drew the third part of the stars of heaven, and did cast them to the earth * * * [he is] that old serpent, called the Devil, and Satan, which deceiveith the whole world" (xii.3–4,9). Pictures of the Beast of the Apocalypse illustrate medieval literature on the vices. On the historical plane, Spenser associates it with the Roman church.

18

His tayle was stretchéd out in wondrous length,
That to the house of heavenly gods it raught,°   reached
And with extorted powre, and borrowed strength,
The ever-burning lamps from thence it brought,
And prowdly threw to ground, as things of nought;
And underneath his filthy feet did tread
The sacred things, and holy heasts° foretaught.   commandments
Upon this dreadfull Beast with sevenfold head
He set the false Duessa, for more aw and dread.

19

The wofull Dwarfe, which saw his maisters fall,
Whiles he had keeping of his grasing steed,
And valiant knight become a caytive thrall,
When all was past, tooke up his forlorne weed,[3]
His mightie armour, missing most at need;
His silver shield, now idle maisterlesse;
His poynant° speare, that many made to bleed,   piercing
The ruefull moniments of heavinesse,
And with them all departes, to tell his great distresse.

20

He had not travaild long, when on the way
He wofull Ladie, wofull Una met,[4]
Fast flying from the Paynims greedy pray,°   clutch
Whilest Satyrane him from pursuit did let:°   prevent
Who when her eyes she on the Dwarfe had set,
And saw the signes, that deadly tydings spake,
She fell to ground for sorrowfull regret,
And lively breath her sad brest did forsake,
Yet might her pitteous hart be seene to pant and quake.

21

The messenger of so unhappie newes
Would faine have dyde: dead was his hart within,
Yet outwardly some little comfort shewes:
At last recovering hart, he does begin
To rub her temples, and to chaufe her chin,
And every tender part does tosse and turne:
So hardly he the flitted life does win,
Unto her native prison[5] to retourne:
Then gins her grievéd ghost° thus to lament and mourne.   spirit

22

"Ye dreary instruments of dolefull sight,
That doe this deadly spectacle behold,
Why do ye lenger feed on loathéd light,
Or liking find to gaze on earthly mould,°   form
Sith cruell fates the carefull° threeds unfould,   anguished
The which my life and love together tyde?

---

3. Abandoned garment.
4. Only in Faerie Land could the Dwarfe find Una so soon after Redcrosse's fortunes are at their lowest.
5. I.e., the body.

Now let the stony dart of senselesse cold
  Perce to my hart, and pas through every side,
And let eternall night so sad sight fro me hide.

23

"O lightsome day, the lampe of highest Jove,
  First made by him, mens wandring wayes to guyde,
  When darknesse he in deepest dongeon drove,
  Henceforth thy hated face for ever hyde,
  And shut up heavens windowes shyning wyde:
  For earthly sight can nought but sorrow breed,
  And late repentance, which shall long abyde.
  Mine eyes no more on vanitie shall feed,
But seeléd up with death, shall have their deadly meed."[6]

24

Then downe againe she fell unto the ground;
  But he her quickly rearéd up againe:
  Thrise did she sinke adowne in deadly swownd,
  And thrise he her revived with busie paine:
  At last when life recovered had the raine,°   *rein*
  And over-wrestled his strong enemie,
  With foltring tong, and trembling every vaine,
  "Tell on," quoth she, "the wofull Tragedie,
The which these reliques sad present unto mine eie.

25

"Tempestuous fortune hath spent all her spight,
  And thrilling sorrow throwne his utmost dart;
  Thy sad tongue cannot tell more heavy plight,
  Then that I feele, and habour in mine hart:
  Who hath endured the whole, can beare each part.
  If death it be, it is not the first wound,
  That launchéd° hath my brest with bleeding smart.   *pierced*
  Begin, and end the bitter balefull stound;°   *disaster*
If lesse, then that I feare, more favour I have found."

26

Then gan the Dwarfe the whole discourse declare,
  The subtill traines of Archimago old;
  The wanton loves of false Fidessa faire,
  Bought with the bloud of vanquisht Paynim bold:
  The wretched payre transformed to treen mould;[7]
  The house of Pride, and perils round about;
  The combat, which he with Sans joy did hould;
  The lucklesse conflict with the Gyant stout,
Wherein captived, of life or death he stood in doubt.

27

She heard with patience all unto the end,
  And strove to maister sorrowfull assay,[8]
  Which greater grew, the more she did contend,
  And almost rent her tender hart in tway;

6. Reward of death.   8. I.e., attack of sorrow.
7. Shape of a tree.

And love fresh coles unto her fire did lay:
240 For greater love, the greater is the losse.
Was never Ladie lovéd dearer° day,   *more dearly*
Then she did love the knight of the Redcrosse;
For whose deare sake so many troubles her did tosse.

28

At last when fervent sorrow slakéd was,
245 She up arose, resolving him to find
Alive or dead: and forward forth doth pas,
All as the Dwarfe the way to her assynd:°   *showed*
And evermore in constant carefull mind
She fed her wound with fresh renewéd bale;°   *anguish*
250 Long tost with stormes, and bet° with bitter wind,   *beat*
High over hils, and low adowne the dale,
She wandred many a wood, and measurd many a vale.

29

At last she chauncéd by good hap to meet
A goodly knight,[9] faire marching by the way
255 Together with his Squire, arayéd meet:
His glitterand° armour shinéd farre away,   *glittering*
Like glauncing light of Phoebus brightest ray;
From top to toe no place appearéd bare,
That deadly dint of steele endanger may:
260 Athwart his brest a bauldrick° brave he ware,   *sash*
That shynd, like twinkling stars, with stons most pretious rare.

30

And in the midst thereof one pretious stone
Of wondrous worth, and eke of wondrous mights,
Shapt like a Ladies head,[1] exceeding shone,
265 Like Hesperus° emongst the lesser lights,   *evening star*
And strove for to amaze the weaker sights;
Thereby his mortall blade full comely hong
In yvory sheath, ycarved with curious slights;°   *patterns*
Whose hilts were burnisht gold, and handle strong
270 Of mother pearle, and buckled with a golden tong.°   *pin*

31

His haughtie helmet, horrid° all with gold,   *bristling*
Both glorious brightnesse, and great terrour bred;
For all the crest a Dragon did enfold
With greedie pawes, and over all did spred

9. Prince Arthur, the supreme hero of the entire *Faerie Queene.* As Spenser explained to Ralegh, "So in the person of Prince Arthure I sette forth magnificence in particular, which vertue for that (according to Aristotle and the rest) it is the perfection of all the rest, and conteineth in it them all." Since, he says, "I mention [in each book] the deeds of Arthur appliable to that vertue which I write of in that book," and since the "virtue" in Book I is Holiness, Arthur will be not unlike Christ, or the power of Christian grace, in the ensuing episodes.
1. I.e., that of the Faerie Queene, Gloriana.

275 His golden wings: his dreadfull hideous hed
 Close couchéd on the bever,° seemed to throw   *visor*
 From flaming mouth bright sparkles fierie red,
 That suddeine horror to faint harts did show;
And scaly tayle was stretcht adowne his backe full low.

32

280 Upon the top of all his loftie crest,
 A bunch of haires discolourd° diversly,   *dyed*
 With sprincled pearle, and gold full richly drest,
 Did shake, and seemed to daunce for jollity,
 Like to an Almond tree ymounted hye
285 On top of greene Selinis all alone,
 With blossomes brave bedeckéd daintily;
 Whose tender locks do tremble every one
At every little breath, that under heaven is blowne.

33

His warlike shield all closely covered was,
290 Ne might of mortall eye be ever seene;
 Not made of steele, nor of enduring bras,
 Such earthly mettals soone consuméd bene:
 But all of Diamond perfect pure and cleene°   *clear*
 It framéd was, one massie entire mould,
295 Hewen out of Adamant rocke with engines keene,
 That point of speare it never percen could,
Ne dint of direfull sword divide the substance would.[2]

34

The same to wight he never wont disclose,
 But° when as monsters huge he would dismay,   *except*
300 Or daunt unequall armies of his foes,
 Or when the flying heavens he would affray;
 For so exceeding shone his glistring ray,
 That Phoebus golden face it did attaint,°   *dim*
 As when a cloud his beames doth over-lay;
305 And silver Cynthia° wexéd pale and faint,   *the moon*
As when her face is staynd with magicke arts constraint.°   *force*

35

No magicke arts hereof had any might,
 Nor bloudie wordes of bold Enchaunters call,
 But all that was not such, as seemd in sight,
310 Before that shield did fade, and suddeine fall:
 And when him list the raskall routes[3] appall,
 Men into stones therewith he could transmew,°   *change*
 And stones to dust, and dust to nought at all;
 And when him list the prouder lookes subdew,
315 He would them gazing blind, or turne to other hew.°   *form*

---

2. The diamond—unflawed, unpierce-
able, translucent—is emblematic of the
perfect faith which is Arthur's shield. Cf.
Ephesians vi.16: "Above all, taking the
shield of faith, wherewith ye shall be
able to quench all the fiery darts of the
wicked."
3. Unruly mobs.

36

Ne let it seeme, that credence this exceedes,
 For he that made the same, was knowne right well
 To have done much more admirable deedes.
 It Merlin was, which whylome° did excell   *formerly*
320 All living wightes in might of magicke spell:
 Both shield, and sword, and armour all he wrought
 For this young Prince, when first to armes he fell;
 But when he dyde, the Faerie Queene it brought
To Faerie lond, where yet it may be seene, if sought.[4]

37

325 A gentle youth, his dearely lovéd Squire
 His speare of heben° wood behind him bare,   *ebony*
 Whose harmefull head, thrice heated in the fire,
 Had riven many a brest with pikehead square;
 A goodly person, and could menage° faire   *control*
330 His stubborne steed with curbéd canon bit,[5]
 Who under him did trample as the aire,
 And chauft,° that any on his backe should sit;   *fretted*
The yron rowels into frothy fome he bit.

38

When as this knight nigh to the Ladie drew,
335 With lovely court he gan her entertaine;
 But when he heard her answers loth, he knew
 Some secret sorrow did her heart distraine:°   *oppress*
 Which to allay, and calme her storming paine,
 Faire feeling words he wisely gan display,
340 And for her humour fitting purpose faine,[6]
 To tempt the cause it selfe for to bewray;
Wherewith emmoved, these bleeding words she gan to say.

39

"What worlds delight, or joy of living speach
 Can heart, so plunged in sea of sorrowes deepe,
345 And heapéd with so huge misfortunes, reach?
 The carefull° cold beginneth for to creepe,   *afflicting*
 And in my heart his yron arrow steepe,
 Soone as I thinke upon my bitter bale:
 Such helplesse harmes yts better hidden keepe,
350 Then rip up griefe, where it may not availe,
My last left comfort is, my woes to weepe and waile."

40

"Ah Ladie deare," quoth then the gentle knight,
 "Well may I weene, your griefe is wondrous great;
 For wondrous great griefe groneth in my spright,°   *spirit*
355 Whiles thus I heare you of your sorrowes treat.
 But wofull Ladie let me you intrete,
 For to unfold the anguish of your hart:
 Mishaps are maistred by advice discrete,

---

4. I.e., Arthur's virtues may be seen   5. Cannon-bit; a smooth, round bit.
still in Queen Elizabeth's England.   6. I.e., suited his manner to her mood.

And counsell mittigates the greatest smart;
360 Found never helpe, who never would his hurts impart."

41

"O but," quoth she, "great griefe will not be tould,
  And can more easily be thought, then said."
"Right so"; quoth he, "but he, that never would,
  Could never: will to might gives greatest aid."
365 "But grief," quoth she, "does greater grow displaid,
  If then it find not helpe, and breedes despaire."
"Despaire breedes not," quoth he, "where faith is staid."°   *firm*
"No faith so fast," quoth she, "but flesh does paire."°   *impair*
"Flesh may empaire," quoth he, "but reason can repaire."

42

370 His goodly reason, and well guided speach
  So deepe did settle in her gratious thought,
  That her perswaded to disclose the breach,
  Which love and fortune in her heart had wrought,
  And said; "Faire Sir, I hope good hap hath brought
375 You to inquire the secrets of my griefe,
  Or that your wisedome will direct my thought,
  Or that your prowesse can me yield reliefe:
Then heare the storie sad, which I shall tell you briefe.

43

"The forlorne Maiden, whom your eyes have seene
380 The laughing stocke of fortunes mockeries,
  Am th'only daughter of a King and Queene,
  Whose parents deare, whilest equall destinies
  Did runne about,[7] and their felicities
  The favourable heavens did not envy,
385 Did spread their rule through all the territories,
  Which Phison and Euphrates floweth by,
And Gehons golden waves doe wash continually.[8]

44

"Till that their cruell curséd enemy,
  An huge great Dragon horrible in sight,
390 Bred in the loathly lakes of Tartary,°   *Tartarus (Hell)*
  With murdrous ravine,° and devouring might   *destruction*
  Their kingdome spoild, and countrey wasted quight:
  Themselves, for feare into his jawes to fall,
  He forst to castle strong to take their flight,
395 Where fast embard in mightie brasen wall,
He has them now foure yeres besiegd to make them thrall.

45

"Full many knights adventurous and stout
  Have enterprizd that Monster to subdew;
  From every coast that heaven walks about,
400 Have thither come the noble Martiall crew,
  That famous hard atchievements still pursew,

7. I.e., while impartial destinies surrounded them.

8. These three rivers flow in the Garden
of Eden (Genesis ii.11–14).

Yet never any could that girlond win,
But all still shronke,° and still he greater grew: quailed
All they for want of faith, or guilt of sin,
405 The pitteous pray of his fierce crueltie have bin.

46

"At last yledd° with farre reported praise,   led
Which flying fame throughout the world had spread,
Of doughtie knights, whom Faery land did raise,
That noble order hight° of Maidenhed,[9]   called
410 Forthwith to court of Gloriane I sped,
Of Gloriane great Queene of glory bright,
Whose kingdomes seat Cleopolis is red,[1]
There to obtaine some such redoubted knight,
That Parents deare from tyrants powre deliver might.

47

415 "It was my chance (my chance was faire and good)
There for to find a fresh unprovéd knight,
Whose manly hands imbrewed in guiltie blood
Had never bene, ne ever by his might
Had throwne to ground the unregarded right:
420 Yet of his prowesse proofe he since hath made
(I witnesse am) in many a cruell fight;
The groning ghosts of many one dismaide
Have felt the bitter dint of his avenging blade.

48

"And ye the forlorne reliques of his powre,
425 His byting sword, and his devouring speare,
Which have enduréd many a dreadfull stowre,°   conflict
Can speake his prowesse, that did earst you beare,
And well could rule: now he hath left you heare,
To be the record of his ruefull losse,
430 And of my dolefull disaventurous deare:[2]
O heavie record of the good Redcrosse,
Where have you left your Lord, that could so well you tosse?

49

"Well hopéd I, and faire beginnings had,
That he my captive langour should redeeme,[3]
435 Till all unweeting, an Enchaunter bad
His sence abusd, and made him to misdeeme
My loyalty, not such as it did seeme;
That° rather death desire, then such despight.   I, who
Be judge ye heavens, that all things right esteeme,
440 How I him loved, and love with all my might,
So thought I eke of him, and thinke I thought aright.

---

9. Historically, the Order of the Garter. Its emblem shows St. George killing the dragon.
1. Named. "Cleopolis" means "famous city." In the historical allegory, it is London, as Gloriana is Elizabeth. In other contexts, however, it may be Camelot or the earthly counterpart of the New Jerusalem.
2. Unfortunate lover.
3. I.e., relieve my state, captive to sadness.

50

"Thenceforth me desolate he quite forsooke,
   To wander, where wilde fortune would me lead,
   And other bywaies he himselfe betooke,
445 Where never foot of living wight did tread,
   That brought not backe the balefull body dead;[4]
   In which him chauncéd false Duessa meete,
   Mine onely foe, mine onely deadly dread,
   Who with her witchcraft and misseeming° sweete,   *deception*
450 Inveigled him to follow her desires unmeete.°   *improper*

51

"At last by subtill sleights she him betraid
   Unto his foe, a Gyant huge and tall,
   Who him disarméd, dissolute,° dismaid,   *enfeebled*
   Unwares surpriséd, and with mightie mall°   *club*
455 The monster mercilesse him made to fall,
   Whose fall did never foe before behold;
   And now in darkesome dungeon, wretched thrall,
   Remedilesse, for aie° he doth him hold;   *ever*
This is my cause of griefe, more great, then may be told."

52

460 Ere she had ended all, she gan to faint:
   But he her comforted and faire bespake,
   "Certes, Madame, ye have great cause of plaint,
   That stoutest heart, I weene, could cause to quake.
   But be of cheare, and comfort to you take:
465 For till I have acquit° your captive knight,   *freed*
   Assure your selfe, I will you not forsake."
   His chearefull words revived her chearelesse spright,
So forth they went, the Dwarfe them guiding ever right.

Canto VIII

Faire virgin to redeeme her deare
   brings Arthur to the fight:
Who slayes the Gyant, wounds the beast,
   and strips Duessa quight.

1

Ay me, how many perils doe enfold
   The righteous man, to make him daily fall?
   Were not, that heavenly grace doth him uphold,
   And stedfast truth acquite him out of all.
5 Her love is firme, her care continuall,
   So oft as he through his owne foolish pride,
   Or weakenesse is to sinfull bands° made thrall: *bonds*
   Else should this Redcrosse knight in bands have dyde,
For whose deliverance she this Prince doth thither guide.

4. I.e., who returned alive.

2

10 They sadly traveild thus, untill they came
   Nigh to a castle builded strong and hie:
   Then cryde the Dwarfe, "lo yonder is the same,
   In which my Lord my liege doth lucklesse lie,
   Thrall to that Gyants hatefull tyrannie:
15 Therefore, deare Sir, your mightie powres assay."
   The noble knight alighted by and by[5]
   From loftie steede, and bad the Ladie stay,
To see what end of fight should him befall that day.

3

So with the Squire, th'admirer of his might,
20 He marchéd forth towards that castle wall;
   Whose gates he found fast shut, ne living wight
   To ward° the same, nor answere commers call.   guard
   Then tooke that Squire an horne of bugle small,[6]
   Which hong adowne his side in twisted gold,
25 And tassels gay. Wyde wonders over all
   Of that same hornes great vertues weren told,
Which had approvéd° bene in uses manifold.   demonstrated

4

Was never wight, that heard that shrilling sound,
   But trembling feare did feele in every vaine;
30 Three miles it might be easie heard around,
   And Ecchoes three answered it selfe againe:
   No false enchauntment, nor deceiptfull traine
   Might once abide the terror of that blast,
   But presently was voide and wholly vaine:
35 No gate so strong, no locke so firme and fast,
But with that percing noise flew open quite, or brast.°   burst

5

The same before the Geants gate he blew,
   That all the castle quakéd from the ground,
   And every dore of freewill open flew.
40 The Gyant selfe dismaiéd with that sownd,
   Where he with his Duessa dalliance° fownd,   amorous play
   In hast came rushing forth from inner bowre,
   With staring countenance sterne, as one astownd,
   And staggering steps, to weet, what suddein stowre°   disturbance
45 Had wrought that horror strange, and dared his dreaded powre.

6

And after him the proud Duessa came,
   High mounted on her manyheaded beast,
   And every head with fyrie tongue did flame,
   And every head was crownéd on his creast,
50 And bloudie mouthéd with late cruell feast.[7]
   That when the knight beheld, his mightie shild

5. Immediately.
6. A "bugle" is a wild ox; the "wide
wonders" (marvelous tales) told of the
horn connect it with the horn of Roland
and the ram's horn of Joshua, with
which he razed the walls of Jericho
(Joshua vi.5).
7. Evidently the St. Bartholomew's Day
Massacre of 1572, in which the French
Huguenots (Protestants) were slaughtered.

Upon his manly arme he soone addrest,°   *adjusted*
  And at him fiercely flew, with courage fild,°   *filled*
And eger greedinesse° through every member thrild.   *desire*

7

55 Therewith the Gyant buckled him to fight,
      Inflamed with scornefull wrath and high disdaine,
      And lifting up his dreadfull club on hight,
      All armed with ragged snubbes° and knottie graine,   *snags*
      Him thought at first encounter to have slaine.
60   But wise and warie was that noble Pere,°   *peer*
      And lightly leaping from so monstrous maine,°   *force*
      Did faire avoide the violence him nere;
It booted nought, to thinke, such thunderbolts to beare.[8]

8

Ne shame he thought to shunne so hideous might:
65   The idle° stroke, enforcing furious way,   *inaccurate*
      Missing the marke of his misayméd sight
      Did fall to ground, and with his° heavie sway°   *its/force*
      So deepely dinted in the driven clay,
      That three yardes deepe a furrow up did throw:
70   The sad earth wounded with so sore assay,°   *assault*
      Did grone full grievous underneath the blow,
And trembling with strange feare, did like an earthquake show.

9

As when almightie Jove in wrathfull mood,
      To wreake° the guilt of mortall sins is bent,   *punish*
75   Hurles forth his thundring dart with deadly food,[9]
      Enrold in flames, and smouldring dreriment,
      Through riven cloudes and molten firmament;
      The fierce threeforkéd engin° making way,   *weapon*
      Both loftie towres and highest trees hath rent,
80   And all that might his angrie passage stay,
And shooting in the earth, casts up a mount of clay.

10

His boystrous° club, so buried in the ground,   *huge*
      He could not rearen up againe so light,
      But that the knight him at avantage found,
85   And whiles he strove his combred clubbe to quight°   *release*
      Out of the earth, with blade all burning bright
      He smote off his left arme, which like a blocke
      Did fall to ground, deprived of native might;
      Large streames of bloud out of the trunckéd stocke
90 Forth gushéd, like fresh water streame from riven rocke.[1]

11

Dismaiéd with so desperate deadly wound,
      And eke impatient of[2] unwonted paine,
      He loudly brayd with beastly yelling sound,
      That all the fields rebellowéd againe;

---

8. The ensuing battle may be taken as the struggle of the Protestant against the Roman church—or that of Christian grace against evil, the Antichrist.

9. Hatred (feud).
1. Cf. Exodus xvii.6, where Moses smites the rock and water flows forth.
2. Agonized by.

95 As great a noyse, as when in Cymbrian plaine
An heard of Bulles, whom kindly° rage doth sting,   *natural*
Do for the milkie mothers want complaine,[3]
And fill the fields with troublous bellowing,
The neighbour woods around with hollow murmur ring.

12

100 That when his deare Duessa heard, and saw
The evill stownd,° that daungerd her estate,   *blow*
Unto his aide she hastily did draw
Her dreadfull beast, who swolne with bloud of late
Came ramping forth with proud presumpteous gate,
105 And threatned all his heads like flaming brands.°   *torches*
But him the Squire made quickly to retrate,
Encountring fierce with single° sword in hand,   *only*
And twixt him and his Lord did like a bulwarke stand,

13

The proud Duessa full of wrathfull spight,
110 And fierce disdaine, to be affronted so,
Enforst her purple beast with all her might
That stop° out of the way to overthroe,   *obstacle*
Scorning the let° of so unequall foe: *obstruction*
But nathemore° would that courageous swayne   *never the more*
115 To her yeeld passage, gainst his Lord to goe,
But with outrageous strokes did him restraine,
And with his bodie bard the way atwixt them twaine.

14

Then tooke the angrie witch her golden cup,
Which still she bore, replete with magick artes; [4]
120 Death and despeyre did many thereof sup,
And secret poyson through their inner parts,
Th' eternall bale of heavie wounded harts;
Which after charmes and some enchauntments said,
She lightly sprinkled on his weaker° parts;   *too weak*
125 Therewith his sturdie courage soone was quayd,°   *quelled*
And all his senses were with suddeine dread dismayd.

15

So downe he fell before the cruell beast,
Who on his necke his bloudie clawes did seize,
That life nigh crusht out of his panting brest:
130 No powre he had to stirre, nor will to rize.
That when the carefull° knight gan well avise,   *watchful*
He lightly left the foe, with whom he fought,
And to the beast gan turne his enterprise;
For wondrous anguish in his hart it wrought,
135 To see his lovéd Squire into such thraldome brought.

16

And high advauncing his bloud-thirstie blade,

---

3. I.e., mourn the cows' absence.
4. Cf. the golden cup of the woman in Revelation, which is "full of abominations" (xvii.4), the chalice of the Roman church, and the cup of Circe (in *Odyssey* X).

Stroke one of those deforméd heads so sore,[5]
  That of his puissance proud ensample made;
  His monstrous scalpe° downe to his teeth it tore   *skull*
140   And that misforméd shape mis-shapéd more:
  A sea of bloud gusht from the gaping wound,
  That her gay garments staynd with filthy gore,
  And overflowéd all the field around;
That over shoes in bloud he waded on the ground.

                17

145 Thereat he roaréd for exceeding paine,
  That to have heard, great horror would have bred,
  And scourging th' emptie ayre with his long traine,
  Through great impatience° of his grievéd hed   *agony*
150   His gorgeous ryder from her loftie sted
  Would have cast downe, and trod in durtie myre,
  Had not the Gyant soone her succouréd;
Who all enraged with smart and franticke yre,
Came hurtling in full fierce, and forst the knight retyre.

                18

The force, which wont in two to be disperst,
155   In one alone left hand he now unites,
  Which is through rage more strong then both were erst;
  With which his hideous club aloft he dites,°   *raises*
  And at his foe with furious rigour smites,
  That strongest Oake might seeme to overthrow:
160   The stroke upon his shield so heavie lites,
  That to the ground it doubleth him full low:
What mortall wight could ever beare so monstrous blow?

                19

And in his fall his shield, that covered was,
  Did loose his vele° by chaunce, and open flew: *veil*
165   The light whereof, that heavens light did pas,°   *surpass*
  Such blazing brightnesse through the aier threw,
  That eye mote not the same endure to vew.
  Which when the Gyaunt spyde with staring° eye,   *awed*
  He downe let fall his arme, and soft withdrew
170   His weapon huge, that heavéd was on hye
For to have slaine the man, that on the ground did lye.

                20

And eke the fruitfull-headed° beast, amazed   *many-headed*
  At flashing beames of that sunshiny shield,
  Became starke blind, and all his senses dazed,
175   That downe he tumbled on the durtie field,
  And seemed himselfe as conqueréd to yield.
  Whom when his maistresse proud perceived to fall,
  Whiles yet his feeble feet for faintnesse reeld,
  Unto the Gyant loudly she gan call,
180 "O helpe Orgoglio, helpe, or else we perish all."

5. "I saw one of [the beast's] heads as it were wounded to death" (Revelation xiii.3).

21

At her so pitteous cry was much amooved
  Her champion stout, and for to ayde his frend,
  Againe his wonted angry weapon prooved:°   *tried*
  But all in vaine: for he has read his end
185 In that bright shield, and all their forces spend
  Themselves in vaine: for since that glauncing° sight,   *flashing*
  He hath no powre to hurt, nor to defend;
  As where th' Almighties lightning brond does light,
It dimmes the dazéd eyen, and daunts the senses quight.

22

190 Whom when the Prince, to battell new addrest,
  And threatning high his dreadfull stroke did see,
  His sparkling blade about his head he blest,°   *waved*
  And smote off quite his right leg by the knee,
  That downe he tombled; [6] as an aged tree,
195 High growing on the top of rocky clift,
  Whose hartstrings with keene steele nigh hewen be,
  The mightie trunck halfe rent, with ragged rift
Doth roll adowne the rocks, and fall with fearefull drift.°   *impact*

23

Or as a Castle rearéd high and round,
200 By subtile engins and malitious slight°   *magic*
  Is underminéd from the lowest ground,
  And her foundation forst,° and feebled quight,   *shattered*
  At last downe falles, and with her heapéd hight
  Her hastie ruine does more heavie make,
205 And yields it selfe unto the victours might;
  Such was this Gyaunts fall, that seemed to shake
The stedfast globe of earth, as it for feare did quake.

24

The knight then lightly leaping to the pray,
  With mortall steele him smot againe so sore,
210 That headlesse his unweldy bodie lay,
  All wallowd in his owne fowle bloudy gore,
  Which flowéd from his wounds in wondrous store.
  But soone as breath out of his breast did pas,
  That huge great body, which the Gyaunt bore,
215 Was vanisht quite, and of that monstrous mas
Was nothing left, but like an emptie bladder was.

25

Whose grievous fall, when false Duessa spide,
  Her golden cup she cast unto the ground,
  And crownéd mitre rudely threw aside;
220 Such percing griefe her stubborne hart did wound,
  That she could not endure that dolefull stound,°   *sorrow*
  But leaving all behind her, fled away:
  The light-foot Squire her quickly turned around,
  And by hard meanes enforcing her to stay,
225 So brought unto his Lord, as his deservéd pray.

6. Pride is not defeated all at once, but step by step; for the image of the tree,
cf. *Aeneid* II.626–31, among other sources.

26

The royall Virgin, which beheld from farre,
  In pensive plight, and sad perplexitie,
  The whole atchievement° of this doubtfull warre,   *course*
  Came running fast to greet his victorie,
230 With sober gladnesse, and myld modestie,
  And with sweet joyous cheare him thus bespake;
  "Faire braunch of noblesse, flowre of chevalrie,
  That with your worth the world amazéd make,
How shall I quite° the paines, ye suffer for my sake?   *requite*

27

235 "And you [7] fresh bud of vertue springing fast,
  Whom these sad eyes saw nigh unto deaths dore,
  What hath poore Virgin for such perill past,
  Wherewith you to reward? Accept therefore
  My simple selfe, and service evermore;
240 And he that high does sit, and all things see
  With equall° eyes, their merites to restore,°   *impartial/reward*
  Behold what ye this day have done for mee,
And what I cannot quite, requite with usuree.

28

"But sith the heavens, and your faire handeling°   *conduct*
245 Have made you maister of the field this day,
  Your fortune maister eke with governing,[8]
  And well begun end all so well, I pray,
  Ne let that wicked woman scape away;
  For she it is, that did my Lord bethrall,
250 My dearest Lord, and deepe in dongeon lay,
  Where he his better dayes hath wasted all.
O heare, how piteous he to you for ayd does call."

29

Forthwith he gave in charge unto his Squire,
  That scarlot whore to keepen carefully;
255 Whiles he himselfe with greedie ° great desire   *eager*
  Into the Castle entred forcibly,
  Where living creature none he did espye;
  Then gan he lowdly through the house to call:
  But no man cared to answere to his crye.
260 There raignd a solemne silence over all,
Nor voice was heard, nor wight was seene in bowre or hall.

30

At last with creeping crooked pace forth came
  An old old man, with beard as white as snow,
  That on a staffe his feeble steps did frame,
265 And guide his wearie gate both too and fro:
  For his eye sight him failéd long ygo,
  And on his arme a bounch of keyes he bore,
  The which unuséd rust did overgrow:
  Those were the keyes of every inner dore,
270 But he could not them use, but kept them still in store.

7. I.e., the Squire. Una's reward to the Squire who has done such faithful service in the war against Pride is itself an exemplary act of humility.
8. Secure your good fortune also by prudent management.

31

But very uncouth sight was to behold,
  How he did fashion his untoward° pace,   *awkward*
  For as he forward mooved his footing old,
  So backward still was turned his wrincled face,
275 Unlike to men, who ever as they trace,
  Both feet and face one way are wont to lead.
  This was the auncient keeper of that place,
  And foster father of the Gyant dead;
His name Ignaro did his nature right aread.[9]

32

280 His reverend haires and holy gravitie
  The knight much honord, as beseeméd well,[1]
  And gently askt, where all the people bee,
  Which in that stately building wont to dwell.
  Who answerd him full soft, he could not tell.
285 Againe he askt, where that same knight was layd,
  Whom great Orgoglio with his puissaunce fell
  Had made his caytive thrall; againe he sayde,
He could not tell: ne ever other answere made.

33

Then askéd he, which way he in might pas:
290 He could not tell, againe he answeréd.
  Thereat the curteous knight displeaséd was,
  And said, "Old sire, it seemes thou hast not red °   *recognized*
  How ill it sits with [2] that same silver hed
  In vaine to mocke, or mockt in vaine to bee:
295 But if thou be, as thou art pourtrahéd
  With natures pen, in ages grave degree,[3]
Aread in graver wise, what I demaund of thee."

34

His answere likewise was, he could not tell.
  Whose sencelesse speach, and doted ignorance
300 When as the noble Prince had markéd well,
  He ghest his nature by his countenance,
  And calmd his wrath with goodly temperance.
  Then to him stepping, from his arme did reach
  Those keyes, and made himselfe free enterance.
305 Each dore he openéd without any breach;°   *forcing*
There was no barre to stop, nor foe him to empeach.°   *hinder*

35

There all within full rich arayd he found,
  With royall arras and resplendent gold.
  And did with store of every thing abound,
310 That greatest Princes presence might behold.
  But all the floore (too filthy to be told)
  With bloud of guiltlesse babes, and innocents trew,

---

9. Make known. Doting ignorance ("Ignaro") is a fit servant for pride and the
false church; he has his counterparts in
Abessa and Corceca.

1. Seemed proper.
2. I.e., suits.
3. I.e., dignity.

Which there were slaine, as sheepe out of the fold,
Defiléd was, that dreadfull was to vew,
315 And sacred° ashes over it was strowéd new.   *accursed*

36

And there beside of marble stone was built
    An Altare, carved with cunning imagery,
    On which true Christians bloud was often spilt,
    And holy Martyrs often doen to dye,[4]
320   With cruell malice and strong tyranny:
    Whose blessed sprites from underneath the stone
    To God for vengeance cryde continually,[5]
    And with great griefe were often heard to grone,
That hardest heart would bleede, to heare their piteous mone.

37

325 Through every rowme he sought, and every bowr,
    But no where could he find that wofull thrall:
    At last he came unto an yron doore,
    That fast was lockt, but key found not at all
    Emongst that bounch, to open it withall;
330   But in the same a little grate was pight,°   *placed*
    Through which he sent his voyce, and lowd did call
    With all his powre, to weet, if living wight
Were houséd therewithin, whom he enlargen° might.   *release*

38

Therewith an hollow, dreary, murmuring voyce
335   These piteous plaints and dolours did resound;
    "O who is that, which brings me happy choyce°   *chance*
    Of death, that here lye dying every stound,°   *moment*
    Yet live perforce in balefull darkenesse bound?
    For now three Moones have changéd thrice their hew,°   *shape*
340   And have beene thrice hid underneath the ground,
    Since I the heavens chearefull face did vew,
O welcome thou, that doest of death bring tydings trew."

39

Which when that Champion heard, with percing point
    Of pitty deare° his hart was thrilléd sore,   *extreme*
345   And trembling horrour ran through every joynt,
    For ruth of gentle knight so fowle forlore:
    Which shaking off, he rent that yron dore,
    With furious force, and indignation fell;°   *fierce*
    Where entred in, his foot could find no flore,
350   But all a deepe descent, as darke as hell,
That breathéd ever forth a filthie banefull smell.

40

But neither darkenesse fowle, nor filthy bands,
    Nor noyous smell his purpose could withhold,
    (Entire affection hateth nicer° hands)   *too fastidious*

4. Put to death.
5. "And when he had opened the fifth seal, I saw under the altar the souls of them that were slain for the word of God, and for the testimony which they held: And they cried with a loud voice, saying, How long, O Lord, holy and true, dost thou not judge and avenge our blood on them that dwell on the earth?" (Revelation vi.9–10).

355 But that with constant zeale, and courage bold,
After long paines and labours manifold,
He found the meanes that Prisoner up to reare;
Whose feeble thighes, unhable to uphold
His pinéd° corse, him scarse to light could beare,   *wasted*
360 A ruefull spectacle of deathe and ghastly drere.°   *wretchedness*

41
His sad dull eyes deepe sunck in hollow pits,
Could not endure th' unwonted sunne to view;
His bare thin cheekes for want of better bits,°   *food*
And empty sides deceivéd° of their dew,   *cheated*
365 Could make a stony hart his hap to rew;
His rawbone armes, whose mighty brawnéd bowrs°   *muscles*
Were wont to rive steele plates, and helmets hew,
Were cleane consumed, and all his vitall powres
Decayd, and all his flesh shronk up like withered flowres.

42
370 Whom when his Lady saw, to him she ran
With hasty joy: to see him made her glad,
And sad to view his visage pale and wan,
Who earst in flowres of freshest youth was clad.
Tho° when her well of teares she wasted had,   *then*
375 She said, "Ah dearest Lord, what evill starre
On you hath frownd, and pourd his influence bad,
That of your selfe ye thus berobbéd arre,
And this misseeming hew⁶ your manly looks doth marre?

43
"But welcome now my Lord, in wele or woe,
380 Whose presence I have lackt to long a day;
And fie on Fortune mine avowéd foe,
Whose wrathfull wreakes° them selves do now alay.   *punishments*
And for these wrongs shall treble penaunce pay
Of treble good: good growes of evils priefe."⁷
385 The chearelesse man, whom sorrow did dismay,°   *unnerve*
Had no delight to treaten° of his griefe;   *speak*
His long enduréd famine needed more reliefe.

44
"Faire Lady," then said that victorious knight,⁸
"The things, that grievous were to do, or beare,
390 Them to renew, I wote, breeds no delight;
Best musicke breeds delight in loathing eare:
But th onely good, that growes of passéd feare,
Is to be wise, and ware° of like agein.   *wary*
This dayes ensample hath this lesson deare
395 Deepe written in my heart with yron pen,
That blisse may not abide in state of mortall men.

45
"Henceforth sir knight, take to you wonted strength,
And maister these mishaps with patient might;

6. Unseemly shape.   8. I.e., Arthur.
7. Endurance of evil.

Loe where your foe lyes stretcht in monstrous length,
400 And loe that wicked woman in your sight,[9]
The roote of all your care, and wretched plight,
Now in your powre, to let her live, or dye."
"To do her dye," quoth Una, "were despight,°   *spiteful*
And shame t'avenge so weake an enimy;
405 But spoile her of her scarlot robe, and let her fly."

46

So as she bad, that witch they disaraid,
And robd of royall robes, and purple pall,
And ornaments that richly were displaid;
Ne spared they to strip her naked all.
410 Then when they had despoild her tire° and call,°   *robe/headdress*
Such as she was, their eyes might her behold,
That her misshapéd parts did them appall,
A loathly, wrinckled hag, ill favoured, old,
Whose secret filth good manners biddeth not be told.

47

415 Her craftie head was altogether bald,
And as in hate of honorable eld,°   *age*
Was overgrowne with scurfe and filthy scald;°   *scabs*
Her teeth out of her rotten gummes were feld,°   *fallen*
And her sowre breath abhominably smeld;
420 Her dried dugs, like bladders lacking wind,
Hong downe, and filthy matter from them weld;
Her wrizled skin as rough, as maple rind,
So scabby was, that would have loathd all womankind.

48

Her neather parts, the shame of all her kind,[1]
425 My chaster Muse for shame doth blush to write;
But at her rompe she growing had behind
A foxes taile, with dong all fowly dight;°   *covered*
And eke her feete most monstrous were in sight;
For one of them was like an Eagles claw,
430 With griping talaunts armd to greedy fight,
The other like a Beares uneven° paw: *rough*
More ugly shape yet never living creature saw.[2]

49

Which when the knights beheld, amazd they were,
And wondred at so fowle deforméd wight.
435 "Such then," said Una, "as she seemeth here,
Such is the face of falshood, such the sight
Of fowle Duessa, when her borrowed light
Is laid away, and counterfesaunce° knowne."   *disguise*
Thus when they had the witch disrobéd quight,
440 And all her filthy feature° open showne,   *form*
They let her goe at will, and wander wayes unknowne.

9. Over there.
1. I.e., womankind.
2. Cf. Duessa with the House of Pride: fair above, foul below. Her filthiness is like that of Alcina in Ariosto's *Orlando Furioso*, VII.71–73. Cf. also Revelation xvii.16: "these shall hate the whore, and shall make her desolate and naked." Foxes (cf. line 427) were noted for cunning; eagles and bears (lines 429, 431) for rapacity, cruelty, and brutality.

50

She flying fast from heavens hated face,
  And from the world that her discovered wide,
  Fled to the wastfull wildernesse apace,
445 From living eyes her open shame to hide,
  And lurkt in rocks and caves long unespide.
  But that faire crew of knights, and Una faire
  Did in that castle afterwards abide,
  To rest them selves, and weary powres repaire,
450 Where store they found of all, that dainty was and rare.

Canto IX

His loves and lignage Arthur tells:
  The knights knit friendly bands:
  Sir Trevisan flies from Despayre,
  Whom Redcrosse knight withstands.

1

O goodly golden chaine,[3] wherewith yfere°   *together*
  The vertues linkéd are in lovely wize:
  And noble minds of yore allyéd were,
  In brave poursuit of chevalrous emprize,°   *adventure*
5 That none did others safety despize,
  Nor aid envy° to him, in need that stands,   *begrudge*
  But friendly each did others prayse devize
  How to advaunce with favourable hands,
As this good Prince redeemd the Redcrosse knight from bands.°*bonds*

2

10 Who when their powres, empaird through labour long,
  With dew repast they had recuréd° well,   *restored*
  And that weake captive wight now wexéd strong,
  Them list no lenger there at leasure dwell,
  But forward fare, as their adventures fell,
15 But ere they parted, Una faire besought
  That straunger knight his name and nation tell;
  Least so great good, as he for her had wrought,
Should die unknown, and buried be in thanklesse thought.

3

"Faire virgin," said the Prince, "ye me require
20 A thing without the compas[4] of my wit:
  For both the lignage and the certain Sire,
  From which I sprong, from me are hidden yit.
  For all so soone as life did me admit
  Into this world, and shewéd heavens light,
25 From mothers pap I taken was unfit:°   *unsuitably*
  And streight delivered to a Faery knight,
To be upbrought in gentle thewes° and martiall might.   *manners*

3. Stanza 1 opens with an invocation of
the golden chain of love or concord
which binds the world and the human
race together (cf. v.25 and note). It

will be reaffirmed in stanza 19 when the
two knights exchange symbolic gifts and
shake hands in token of fellowship.
4. I.e., beyond the reach of.

4

"Unto old Timon[5] he me brought bylive,°   *immediately*
   Old Timon, who in youthly yeares hath beene
30 In warlike feates th'expertest man alive,
   And is the wisest now on earth I weene;
   His dwelling is low in a valley greene,
   Under the foot of Rauran mossy hore,°   *gray*
   From whence the river Dee as silver cleene°   *pure*
35 His tombling billowes rolls with gentle rore:[6]
There all my dayes he traind me up in vertuous lore.

5

"Thither the great Magicien Merlin came,
   As was his use, ofttimes to visit me:
   For he had charge my discipline to frame,
40 And Tutours nouriture° to oversee.   *training*
   Him oft and oft I askt in privitie,
   Of what loines and what lignage I did spring:
   Whose aunswere bad me still assuréd bee,
   That I was sonne and heire unto a king,
45 As time in her just terme[7] the truth to light should bring."

6

"Well worthy impe,"° said then the Lady gent,°   *offspring/gentle*
   "And Pupill fit for such a Tutours hand.
   But what adventure, or what high intent
   Hath brought you hither into Faery land,
50 Aread° Prince Arthur, crowne of Martiall band?"   *declare*
   "Full hard it is," quoth he, "to read aright
   The course of heavenly cause, or understand
   The secret meaning of th'eternall might,
That rules mens wayes, and rules the thoughts of living wight.

7

55 "For whither he through fatall° deepe foresight   *prophetic*
   Me hither sent, for cause to me unghest,
   Or that fresh bleeding wound, which day and night
   Whilome° doth rancle in my riven brest,   *incessantly*
   With forcéd fury following his° behest,   *its*
60 Me hither brought by wayes yet never found,
   You to have helpt I hold my selfe yet blest."
   "Ah curteous knight," quoth she, "what secret wound
Could ever find,° to grieve the gentlest hart on ground?"   *succeed*

8

"Deare Dame," quoth he, "you sleeping sparkes awake,
65 Which trubled once, into huge flames will grow,
   Ne ever will their fervent fury slake
   Till living moysture into smoke do flow,
   And wasted° life do lye in ashes low.   *consumed*
   Yet sithens° silence lesseneth not my fire,   *since*

---

5. The name means "Honor."
6. The hill Rauran is in Wales; the river Dee also flows in, and forms part of the boundary of Wales. The Tudors (Queen Elizabeth's family) were originally Welsh, and the legends of Arthur had their beginnings in the Celtic mythology of early Wales.
7. Due course.

70 But told it flames, and hidden it does glow,
 I will revele, what ye so much desire:
Ah Love, lay downe thy bow, the whiles I may respire.°   *breathe*

9

"It was in freshest flowre of youthly yeares,
 When courage first does creepe in manly chest,
75 Then first the coale of kindly° heat appeares   *of nature*
 To kindle love in every living brest;
 But me had warnd old Timons wise behest,
 Those creeping flames by reason to subdew,
 Before their rage grew to so great unrest,
80 As miserable lovers use to rew,
Which still wex old in woe, whiles woe still wexeth new.

10

"That idle name of love, and lovers life,
 As losse of time, and vertues enimy
 I ever scornd, and joyd to stirre up strife,
85 In middest of their mournfull Tragedy,
 Ay wont to laugh, when them I heard to cry,
 And blow the fire, which them to ashes brent:°   *burned*
 Their God himselfe, grieved at my libertie,
 Shot many a dart at me with fiers intent,
90 But I them warded all with wary government.[8]

11

"But all in vaine: no fort can be so strong,
 Ne fleshly brest can arméd be so sound,
 But will at last be wonne with battrie° long,   *siege*
 Or unawares at disavantage found;
95 Nothing is sure, that growes on earthly ground:
 And who most trustes in arme of fleshly might,
 And boasts, in beauties chaine not to be bound,
 Doth soonest fall in disaventrous° fight.   *disastrous*
And yeeldes his caytive neck to victours most° despight.   *greatest*

12

100 "Ensample make of him your haplesse joy,
 And of my selfe now mated,° as ye see;   *overcome*
 Whose prouder° vaunt that proud avenging boy   *too proud*
 Did soone pluck downe, and curbd my libertie.
 For on a day prickt° forth with jollitie   *rode*
105 Of looser life, and heat of hardiment,°   *boldness*
 Raunging the forest wide on courser free,
 The fields, the floods, the heavens with one consent
Did seeme to laugh° on me, and favour mine intent.   *smile*

13

"For-wearied with my sports, I did alight
110 From loftie steed, and downe to sleepe me layd;
 The verdant gras my couch did goodly dight,°   *make*
 And pillow was my helmet faire displayd:

8. I.e., self-control. The descriptions here of Cupid's archery and of the siege of the castle of chastity (in the next stanza) have many echoes from the courtly-love traditions.

Whiles every sence the humour sweet embayd,°   *pervaded*
And slombring soft my hart did steale away,
115 Me seeméd, by my side a royall Mayd
Her daintie limbes full softly down did lay:
So faire a creature yet saw never sunny day.

14

"Most goodly glee° and lovely blandishment°   *pleasure/compliment*
She to me made, and bad me love here deare,
120 For dearely sure her love was to me bent,
As when just time expiréd[9] should appeare.
But whether dreames delude, or true it were,
Was never hart so ravisht with delight,
Ne living man like words did ever heare,
125 As she to me delivered all that night;
And at her parting said, She Queene of Faeries hight.[1]

15

"When I awoke, and found her place devoyd,°   *empty*
And nought but presséd gras, where she had lyen,
I sorrowed all so much, as earst I joyd,
130 And washéd all her place with watry eyen.
From that day forth I loved that face divine;
From that day forth I cast in carefull mind,
To seeke her out with labour, and long tyne,°   *hardship*
And never vow to rest, till her I find,
135 Nine monethes I seeke in vaine yet ni'll° that vow unbind."   *will not*

16

Thus as he spake, his visage wexéd pale,
And chaunge of hew great passion did bewray;
Yet still he strove to cloke his inward bale,°   *grief*
And hide the smoke, that did his fire display,
140 Till gentle Una thus to him gan say;
"Oh happy Queene of Faeries, that hast found
Mongst many, one that with his prowesse may
Defend thine honour, and thy foes confound:
True Loves are often sown, but seldom grow on ground."

17

145 "Thine, O then," said the gentle Redcrosse knight,
"Next to that Ladies love, shalbe the place,
O fairest virgin, full of heavenly light,
Whose wondrous faith, exceeding earthly race,
Was firmest fixt in mine extremest case.
150 And you, my Lord, the Patrone° of my life,   *protector*
Of that great Queene may well gaine worthy grace:
For onely worthy you through prowes priefe[2]
Yf living man mote worthy be, to be her liefe."°   *love*

9. The right occasion having arisen.
1. Was called. Gloriana is also, in the two principal allegories, Queen Elizabeth and Heavenly Grace. This is one of the passages where the "faery" nature of *The Faerie Queene* makes itself strongly felt. In the background are many folk- tales and ballads of a hero bewitched by the Queen of Faery. Note further the complex layering, by which Arthur, who is a character in Faery, has entered this world through a vision in a dream.
2. Demonstration of prowess.

18

So diversly discoursing of their loves,
The golden Sunne his glistring head gan shew,
And sad remembraunce now the Prince amoves,
With fresh desire his voyage to pursew:
Als° Una earnd° her traveill to renew. *so/yearned*
Then those two knights, fast friendship for to bynd,
And love establish each to other trew,
Gave goodly gifts, the signes of gratefull mynd,
And eke as pledges firme, right hands together joynd.

19

Prince Arthur gave a boxe of Diamond sure,° *flawless*
Embowd° with gold and gorgeous ornament, *bound*
Wherein were closd few drops of liquor pure,
Of wondrous worth, and vertue excellent,
That any wound could heale incontinent:° *immediately*
Which to requite, the Redcrosse knight him gave
A booke, wherein his Saveours testament
Was writ with golden letters rich and brave;
A worke of wondrous grace, and able soules to save.

20

Thus beene they parted, Arthur on his way
To seeke his love, and th'other for to fight
With Unas foe, that all her realme did pray.° *prey upon*
But she now weighing the decayéd plight,
And shrunken synewes of her chosen knight,
Would not a while her forward course pursew,
Ne bring him forth in face of dreadfull fight,
Till he recovered had his former hew:
For him to be yet weake and wearie well she knew.

21

So as they traveild, lo they gan espy
An arméd knight towards them gallop fast,
That seeméd from some fearéd foe to fly,
Or other griesly thing, that him agast.° *scared*
Still as he fled, his eye was backward cast,
As if his feare still followed him behind;
Als flew his steed, as he his bands had brast,
And with his wingéd heeles did tread the wind,
As he had beene a fole of Pegasus his kind.[3]

22

Nigh as he drew, they might perceive his head
To be unarmd, and curld uncombéd heares
Upstaring stiffe, dismayd with uncouth dread;
Nor drop of bloud in all his face appeares
Nor life in limbe: and to increase his feares,
In fowle reproch° of knighthoods faire degree,° *disgrace/position*
About his neck an hempen rope he weares,
That with his glistring armes does ill agree;[4]
But he of rope or armes has now no memoree.

3. I.e., like Pegasus (a flying horse).
4. The rope around his neck suggests attempts (past and future) at suicide—the reason for which becomes clear a few stanzas later.

23

The Redcrosse knight toward him crosséd fast,
 To weet, what mister° wight was so dismayd: *kind of*
 There him he finds all sencelesse and aghast,
 That of him selfe he seemd to be afrayd;
 Whom hardly he from flying forward stayd,
 Till he these wordes to him deliver might;
 "Sir knight, aread who hath ye thus arayd,
 And eke from whom make ye this hasty flight:
For never knight I saw in such misseeming° plight."   *unseemly*

24

He answerd nought at all, but adding new
 Feare to his first amazment, staring wide
 With stony eyes, and hartlesse hollow hew,
 Astonisht stood, as one that had aspide
 Infernall furies, with their chaines untide.
 Him yet againe, and yet againe bespake
 The gentle knight; who nought to him replide,
 But trembling every joynt did inly quake,
And foltring tongue at last these words seemd forth to shake.

25

"For Gods deare love, Sir knight, do me not stay;
 For loe he comes, he comes fast after mee."
 Eft° looking backe would faine have runne away;   *again*
 But he him forst to stay, and tellen free
 The secret cause of his perplexitie:
 Yet nathemore° by his bold hartie speach,   *not at all*
 Could his bloud-frosen hart emboldned bee,
 But through his boldnesse rather feare did reach,
Yet forst, at last he made through silence suddein breach.

26

"And am I now in safetie sure," quoth he,
 "From him, that would have forcéd me to dye?
 And is the point of death now turnd fro mee,
 That I may tell this haplesse history?"
 "Feare nought:" quoth he, "no daunger now is nye."
 "Then shall I you recount a ruefull cace,"
 Said he, "the which with this unlucky eye
 I late beheld, and had not greater grace
Me reft from it, had bene partaker of the place.[5]

27

"I lately chaunst (Would I had never chaunst)
 With a faire knight to keepen companee,
 Sir Terwin hight, that well himselfe advaunst
 In all affaires, and was both bold and free,
 But not so happie as mote happie bee:
 He loved, as was his lot, a Ladie gent,°   *noble*
 That him againe° loved in the least degree: *in return*
 For she was proud, and of too high intent,°   *ambition*
And joyd to see her lover languish and lament.

5. I.e., shared the same fate.

28

"From whom returning sad and comfortlesse,
245   As on the way together we did fare,
    We met that villen (God from him me blesse°)   *defend*
    That curséd wight, from whom I scapt why leare,°   *recently*
    A man of hell, that cals himselfe Despaire;[6]
    Who first us greets, and after faire areedes°   *tells*
250   Of tydings strange, and of adventures rare:
    So creeping close, as Snake in hidden weedes,
Inquireth of our states, and of our knightly deedes.

29

"Which when he knew, and felt our feeble harts
    Embost° with bale,° and bitter byting griefe,   *exhausted/sorrow*
255   Which love had launchéd with his deadly darts,
    With wounding words and termes of foule repriefe°   *insult*
    He pluckt from us all hope of due reliefe,
    That earst us held in love of lingring life;
    Then hopelesse hartlesse, gan the cunning thiefe
260   Perswade us die, to stint° all further strife: *end*
To me he lent this rope, to him a rustie knife.

30

"With which sad instrument of hastie death,
    That wofull lover, loathing lenger° light,   *longer*
    A wide way made to let forth living breath.
265   But I more fearefull, or more luckie wight,
    Dismayd with that deforméd dismall sight,
    Fled fast away, halfe dead with dying feare:[7]
    Ne yet assured of life by you, Sir knight,
    Whose like infirmitie like chaunce may beare:
270 But God you never let his charméd speeches heare."

31

"How may a man," said he, "with idle speach
    Be wonne, to spoyle the Castle of his health?"
    "I wote," quoth he, "whom triall° late did teach,   *experience*
    That like would not[8] for all this worldes wealth:
275   His subtill tongue, like dropping honny, mealt'th°   *melts*
    Into the hart, and searcheth every vaine,
    That ere one be aware, by secret stealth
    His powre is reft, and weakenesse doth remaine.
O never Sir desire to try° his guilefull traine."   *test*

32

280 "Certes," said he, "hence shall I never rest,
    Till I that treachours art have heard and tride;
    And you Sir knight, whose name mote° I request,   *might*
    Of grace do me unto his cabin guide."

6. Redcrosse has hitherto been the victim of pride and rashness; here, another spiritual vice, directly contrary, is met —the temptation to the ultimate Christian sin, the despair of God's grace. Such despair was a concern to Renaissance writers of religious and medical works. Robert Burton, in his *Anatomy of Melancholy* (1621), wrote that the despair "which concerns God * * * [is] opposite to hope, and a most pernicious sin * * * The part affected is the whole soul" ("Religious Melancholy," II.i.2).
7. Fear of death.
8. I.e., would not do the like again.

"I that hight Trevisan," quoth he, "will ride
285 Against my liking backe, to doe you grace:
  But nor for gold nor glee° will I abide   *glitter*
  By you, when ye arrive in that same place;
For lever° had I die, then see his deadly face."   *rather*

33

Ere long they come, where that same wicked wight
290 His dwelling has, low in an hollow cave,
  Farre underneath a craggie clift ypight,°   *placed*
  Darke, dolefull, drearie, like a greedie grave,
  That still for carrion carcases doth crave:
  On top whereof aye dwelt the ghastly Owle,
295 Shrieking his balefull note, which ever drave
  Farre from that haunt all other chearefull fowle;
And all about it wandring ghostes did waile and howle.

34

And all about old stockes and stubs of trees,
  Whereon nor fruit, nor leafe was ever seene,
300 Did hang upon the ragged rocky knees;°   *crags*
  On which had many wretches hangéd beene,
  Whose carcases were scattered on the greene,
  And throwne about the cliffs. Arrivéd there,
  That bare-head knight for dread and dolefull teene,°   *grief*
305 Would faine have fled, ne durst approachen neare,
But th'other forst him stay, and comforted in feare.

35

That darkesome cave they enter, where they find
  That curséd man, low sitting on the ground,
  Musing full sadly in his sullein mind;
310 His griesie° lockes, long growen, and unbound,   *gray*
  Disordred hong about his shoulders round,
  And hid his face; through which his hollow eyne
  Lookt deadly dull, and staréd as astound;
  His raw-bone cheekes through penurie and pine,°   *starvation*
315 Were shronke into his jawes, as° he did never dine.   *as if*

36

His garment nought but many ragged clouts,°   *cloths*
  With thornes together pind and patchéd was,
  The which his naked sides he wrapt abouts;
  And him beside there lay upon the gras
320 A drearie corse, whose life away did pas,
  All wallowd in his owne yet luke-warme blood,
  That from his wound yet welléd fresh alas;
  In which a rustie knife fast fixéd stood,
And made an open passage for the gushing flood.

37

325 Which piteous spectacle, approving trew
  The wofull tale that Trevisan had told,
  When as the gentle Redcrosse knight did vew,
  With firie zeale he burnt in courage bold,

Him to avenge, before his bloud were cold,
330   And to the villein said, "Thou damnéd wight,   *deed*
  The author of this fact,° we here behold,
  What justice can but judge against thee right,   *pay for*
With thine owne bloud to price° his bloud, here
      shed in sight?"

38

"What franticke fit," quoth he,[9] "hath thus distraught
335   Thee, foolish man, so rash a doome° to give?   *judgment*
  What justice ever other judgement taught,
  But he should die, who merites not to live?
  None else to death this man despayring drive,°   *drove*
  But his owne guiltie mind deserving death.
340   Is then unjust to each his due to give?
  Or let him die, that loatheth living breath?
Or let him die at ease, that liveth here uneath°?   *uneasily*

39

"Who travels by the wearie wandring way,
  To come unto his wishéd home in haste,
345   And meetes a flood, that doth his passage stay,
  Is not great grace to helpe him over past,
  Or free his feet, that in the myre sticke fast?
  Most envious man, that grieves at neighbours good,
  And fond,° that joyest in the woe thou hast,   *foolish*
350   Why wilt not let him passe, that long hath stood
Upon the banke, yet wilt thy selfe not passe the flood?

40

"He there does now enjoy eternall rest
  And happie ease, which thou doest want and crave,
  And further from it daily wanderest:
355   What if some litle paine the passage have,
  That makes fraile flesh to feare the bitter wave?
  Is not short paine well borne, that brings long ease,
  And layes the soule to sleepe in quiet grave?
  Sleepe after toyle, port after stormie seas,
360 Ease after warre, death after life does greatly please."[1]

41

The knight much wondred at his suddeine° wit,   *quick*
  And said, "The terme of life is limited,
  Ne may a man prolong, nor shorten it;
  The souldier may not move from watchfull sted,°   *position*
365   Nor leave his stand, untill his Captaine bed."°   *commands*
  "Who life did limit by almightie doome,"
  Quoth he,[2] "knowes best the termes establishéd;
  And he, that points the Centonell his roome,°   *station*
Doth license him depart at sound of morning droome."

---

9. I.e., Despaire.
1. Despaire's arguments on behalf of suicide as against a painful life are derived, like those of Hamlet in his third soliloquy (*Hamlet* III.i.56–88), principally from Seneca, Marcus Aurelius, and the ancient stoics, and from Old Testament utterings on divine justice.
2. I.e., Despaire.

42

370 "Is not his deed, what ever thing is donne,
 In heaven and earth? did not he all create
 To die againe? all ends that was begonne,
 Their times in his eternall booke of fate
 Are written sure, and have their certaine date.
375 Who then can strive with strong necessitie,
 That holds the world in his° still chaunging state,   *its*
 Or shunne the death ordaynd by destinie?
When houre of death is come, let none aske whence, nor why.

43

"The lenger life, I wote° the greater sin,   *know*
380 The greater sin, the greater punishment:
 All those great battels, which thou boasts to win,
 Through strife, and bloud-shed, and avengement,
 Now praysd, hereafter deare thou shalt repent:
 For life must life, and bloud must bloud repay.
385 Is not enough thy evill life forespent?
 For he, that once hath misséd the right way,
The further he doth goe, the further he doth stray.

44

"Then do no further goe, no further stray,
 But here lie downe, and to thy rest betake,
390 Th'ill to prevent, that life ensewen may.[3]
 For what hath life, that may it lovéd make,
 And gives not rather cause it to forsake?
 Feare, sicknesse, age, losse, labour, sorrow, strife,
 Paine, hunger, cold, that makes the hart to quake;
395 And ever fickle fortune rageth rife,
All which, and thousands mo° do make a loathsome life.   *more*

45

"Thou wretched man, of death hast greatest need,
 If in true ballance thou wilt weigh thy state:
 For never knight, that daréd warlike deede,
400 More lucklesse disaventures did amate:°   *appall*
 Witnesse the dongeon deepe, wherein of late
 Thy life shut up, for death so oft did call;
 And though good lucke prolongéd hath thy date,°   *span of life*
 Yet death then, would the like mishaps forestall,
405 Into the which hereafter thou maiest happen fall.

46

"Why then doest thou, O man of sin, desire
 To draw thy dayes forth to their last degree?
 Is not the measure of thy sinfull hire[4]
 High heapéd up with huge iniquitie,
410 Against the day of wrath,[5] to burden thee?
 Is not enough that to this Ladie milde
 Thou falséd hast thy faith with perjurie,
 And sold thy selfe to serve Duessa vilde,°   *vile*
With whom in all abuse thou hast thy selfe defilde?

3. I.e., to prevent the evil that will en-   4. Service to sin.
sue in the rest of your life.   5. Judgment Day.

47

415 "Is not he just, that all this doth behold
From highest heaven, and beares an equall° eye?   *impartial*
Shall he thy sins up in his knowledge fold,
And guiltie be of thine impietie?
Is not his law, Let every sinner die:
420 Die shall all flesh? what then must needs be donne,
Is it not better to doe willinglie,
Then linger, till the glasse be all out ronne?
Death is the end of woes: die soone, O faeries sonne."

48

The knight was much enmovéd with his speach,
425 That as a swords point through his hart did perse,
And in his conscience made a secret breach,
Well knowing true all, that he did reherse°   *recount*
And to his fresh remembrance did reverse°   *bring back*
The ugly vew of his deforméd crimes,
430 That all his manly powres it did disperse,
As he were charméd with inchaunted rimes,
That oftentimes he quakt, and fainted oftentimes.

49

In which amazement, when the Miscreant
Perceivéd him to waver weake and fraile,
435 Whiles trembling horror did his conscience dant,°   *daunt*
And hellish anguish did his soule assaile,
To drive him to despaire, and quite to quaile,°   *be dismayed*
He shewed him painted in a table° plaine,   *picture*
The damnéd ghosts, that doe in torments waile,
440 And thousand feends that doe them endlesse paine
With fire and brimstone, which for ever shall remaine.

50

The sight whereof so throughly him dismaid,
That nought but death before his eyes he saw,
And ever burning wrath before him laid,
445 By righteous sentence of th'Almighties law:
Then gan the villein him to overcraw,°   *exult over*
And brought unto him swords, ropes, poison, fire,
And all that might him to perdition draw;
And bad him choose, what death he would desire:
450 For death was due to him, that had provokt Gods ire.[6]

51

But when as none of them he saw him take,
He to him raught° a dagger sharpe and keene,   *reached*
And gave it him in hand: his hand did quake,
And tremble like a leafe of Aspin greene,
455 And troubled bloud through his pale face was seene
To come, and goe with tydings from the hart,
As it a running messenger had beene.
At last resolved to worke his finall smart,
He lifted up his hand, that backe againe did start.

---

6. Hamlet turned aside from suicide because of fear of the unknown; here, however, Redcrosse is tempted by the powerfully exciting allurement of death.

52

460 Which when as Una saw, through every vaine
  The crudled cold ran to her well of life,
  As in a swowne: but soone relived° againe,   *revived*
  Out of his hand she snatcht the curséd knife,
  And threw it to the ground, enragéd rife,°   *deeply*
465 And to him said, "Fie, fie, faint harted knight,
  What meanest thou by this reprochfull strife?
  Is this the battell, which thou vauntst to fight
With the fire-mouthéd Dragon, horrible and bright?

53

  "Come, come away, fraile, feeble, fleshly wight,
470 Ne let vaine words bewitch thy manly hart,
  Ne divelish thoughts dismay thy constant spright.
  In heavenly mercies hast thou not a part?
  Why shouldst thou then despeire, that chosen art?
  Where justice growes, there grows eke greater grace,
475 The which doth quench the brond of hellish smart,
  And that accurst hand-writing doth deface.°   *blot out*
Arise, Sir knight arise, and leave this curséd place."[7]

54

So up he rose, and thence amounted streight.
  Which when the carle° beheld, and saw his guest   *churl*
480 Would safe depart, for all his subtill sleight,
  He chose an halter from among the rest,
  And with it hung himselfe, unbid unblest.
  But death he could not worke himselfe thereby;
  For thousand times he so himselfe had drest,°   *made ready*
485 Yet nathelesse it could not doe him die,
Till he should die his last, that is eternally.[8]

Canto X

Her faithfull knight faire Una brings
to house of Holinesse,
Where he is taught repentance, and
the way to heavenly blesse.°   *bliss*

1

What man is he, that boasts of fleshly might,
  And vaine assurance of mortality,°   *immortality*
  Which all so soone, as it doth come to fight,
  Against spirituall foes, yeelds by and by,[1]
5 Or from the field most cowardly doth fly?
  Ne let the man ascribe it to his skill,
  That thorough grace hath gainéd victory.
  If any strength we have, it is to ill,

7. Una reminds Redcrosse of God's
mercy, the "greater grace" conspicuously missing from Despaire's eloquent
speeches.
8. Despaire cannot kill himself. Compare his fruitless suicide attempts with
Aesculapius's equally fruitless attempts
"himself with salves to health for to
restore" (I.v.40).
1. Immediately.

But all the good is Gods, both power and eke will.[2]

2

¹⁰ By that, which lately hapned, Una saw,
   That this her knight was feeble, and too faint;
   And all his sinews woxen weake and raw,°   *unready*
   Through long enprisonment, and hard constraint,
   Which he enduréd in his late restraint,
¹⁵   That yet he was unfit for bloudie fight:
   Therefore to cherish him with diets daint,°   *dainty*
   She cast to bring him, where he chearen° might,   *be cheered*
Till he recovered had his[3] late decayéd plight.

3

There was an auntient house not farre away,
²⁰   Renowmd throughout the world for sacred lore,
   And pure unspotted life: so well they say
   It governd was, and guided evermore,
   Through wisedome of a matrone grave and hore;°   *gray-haired*
   Whose onely joy was to relieve the needes
²⁵   Of wretched soules, and helpe the helpelesse pore:
   All night she spent in bidding of her bedes,[4]
And all the day in doing good and godly deedes.

4

Dame Caelia[5] men did her call, as thought
   From heaven to come, or thither to arise,
³⁰   The mother of three daughters, well upbrought
   In goodly thewes,° and godly exercise: *habits*
   The eldest two most sober, chast, and wise,
   Fidelia and Speranza virgins were,
   Though spousd,° yet wanting wedlocks solemnize; *bethrothed*
³⁵   But faire Charissa to a lovely fere°   *mate*
Was linckéd, and by him had many pledges dere.[6]

5

Arrivéd there, the dore they find fast lockt;
   For it was warely watchéd night and day,
   For feare of many foes: but when they knockt,
⁴⁰   The Porter opened unto them streight way:
   He was an agéd syre, all hory gray,
   With lookes full lowly cast, and gate full slow,
   Wont on a staffe his feeble steps to stay,
   Hight Humilta.° They passe in stouping low;   *humility*
⁴⁵ For streight and narrow was the way, which he did show.[7]

---

2. "For by grace are ye saved through faith; and that not of yourselves: it is the gift of God: Not of works, lest any men should boast" (Ephesians ii.8–9).
3. I.e., from his.
4. Saying prayers.
5. The name means "heavenly."
6. I.e., many children. The daughters' names mean "faith," "hope," and "charity." Cf. with them the three Saracens, Sans foy, Sans joy, and Sans loy: "faith" is the answer to atheism; "hope," the answer to empty despair; and "charity" (the highest law that embraces all other laws) the answer to chaos. "And now abideth faith, hope, charity, these three; but the greatest of these is charity" (I Corinthians xiii.13). Canto x, in which Spenser's didactic purpose is expressed with particular directness, is especially rich in scriptural references and echoes. Many aspects of the House of Holiness oppose their counterparts in the House of Pride (Canto iv).
7. "Strait is the gate, and narrow is the way, which leadeth unto life, and few there be that find it" (Matthew vii.14).

6

Each goodly thing is hardest to begin,
But entred in a spacious court they see,
Both plaine, and pleasant to be walkéd in,
Where them does meete a francklin° faire and free, *freeholder*
50 And entertaines with comely courteous glee,
His name was Zele, that him right well became,
For in his speeches and behaviour hee
Did labour lively to expresse the same,
And gladly did them guide, till to the Hall they came.

7

55 There fairely them receives a gentle Squire,
Of milde demeanure, and rare courtesie,
Right cleanly clad in comely sad° attire; *sober*
In word and deede that shewed great modestie,
And knew his good° to all of each degree, *proper respect*
60 Hight Reverence. He them with speeches meet
Does faire entreat; no courting nicetie,° *affectation*
But simple true, and eke unfainéd sweet,
As might become a Squire so great persons to greet.

8

And afterwards them to his Dame he leades,
65 That agéd Dame, the Ladie of the place:
Who all this while was busie at her beades:
Which doen, she up arose with seemely grace,
And toward them full matronely did pace.
Where when that fairest Una she beheld,
70 Whom well she knew to spring from heavenly race,
Her hart with joy unwonted inly sweld,
As feeling wondrous comfort in her weaker eld.° *older age*

9

And her embracing said, "O happie earth,
Whereon thy innocent feet doe ever tread,
75 Most vertuous virgin borne of heavenly berth,
That to redeeme thy woefull parents head,
From tyrans rage, and ever-dying dread,[8]
Hast wandred through the world now long a day;
Yet ceasest not thy wearie soles to lead,
80 What grace hath thee now hither brought this way?
Or doen thy feeble feet unweeting hither stray?

10

"Strange thing it is an errant° knight to see *wandering*
Here in this place, or any other wight,
That hither turnes his steps. So few there bee,
85 That chose the narrow path, or seeke the right:
All keepe the broad high way, and take delight
With many rather for to go astray,
And be partakers of their evill plight,
Then with a few to walke the rightest way;
90 O foolish men, why haste ye to your owne decay?"

8. Continuing fear of death.

11

"Thy selfe to see, and tyred limbs to rest,
    O matrone sage," quoth she, "I hither came,
    And this good knight his way with me addrest,
    Led with thy prayses and broad-blazéd fame,
95 That up to heaven is blowne." The auncient Dame
    Him goodly greeted in her modest guise,
    And entertaynd them both, as best became,
    With all the court'sies, that she could devise,
Ne wanted ought, to shew her bounteous or wise.

12

100 Thus as they gan of sundry things devise,°   *talk*
    Loe two most goodly virgins came in place,
    Ylinkéd arme in arme in lovely° wise,   *loving*
    With countenance demure, and modest grace,
    They numbred even steps and equall pace:
105 Of which the eldest, that Fidelia hight,
    Like sunny beames threw from her Christall face,
    That could have dazd the rash beholders sight,
And round about her head did shine like heavens light.[9]

13

She was araiéd all in lilly white,
110 And in her right hand bore a cup of gold,
    With wine and water fild up to the hight,
    In which a Serpent did himselfe enfold,
    That horrour made to all, that did behold;
    But she no whit did chaunge her constant mood:[1]
115 And in her other hand she fast did hold
    A booke, that was both signd and seald with blood,
Wherein darke things were writ, hard to be understood.[2]

14

Her younger sister, that Speranza hight,
    Was clad in blew, that her beseeméd well;
120 Not all so chearefull seeméd she of sight,[3]
    As was her sister; whether dread did dwell,
    Or anguish in her hart, is hard to tell:
    Upon her arme a silver anchor[4] lay,
    Whereon she leanéd ever, as befell:
125 And ever up to heaven, as she did pray,
Her stedfast eyes were bent, ne swarvéd other way.

15

They seeing Una, towards her gan wend,

9. Cf. the brightness of Arthur's shield, unveiled (viii.19).
1. Expression. The serpent in the cup is a symbol of St. John the Evangelist, whose faith was so great he could drink venom without harm. Contrast Duessa's cup (viii.14). The symbolic details in these portraits appear also in the allegorical figures in other works of Renaissance literature and art—particularly the emblem books.
2. The New Testament. See II Peter iii.16: "in which are some things hard to be understood, which they that are unlearned and unstable wrest, as they do also the other scriptures, unto their own destruction." Peter says this of St. Paul's writings, but it could also be said of many other parts of the New Testament—which is "signed and sealed with [the] blood" of Christ and the martyrs.
3. In appearance.
4. The iconographic symbol of hope.

Who them encounters with like courtesie;
  Many kind speeches they betwene them spend,
130 And greatly joy each other well to see:
  Then to the knight with shamefast° modestie   *humble*
  They turne themselves, at Unas meeke request,
  And him salute with well beseeming glee;
  Who faire them quites,° as him beseeméd best,   *returns the salute*
135 And goodly gan discourse of many a noble gest.°   *achievement*

16

Then Una thus; "But she your sister deare;
  The deare Charissa where is she become?
  Or wants she health, or busie is elsewhere?"
  "Ah no," said they, "but forth she may not come:
140 For she of late is lightned of her wombe,
  And hath encreast the world with one sonne more,[5]
  That her to see should be but troublesome."
  "Indeede," quoth she, "that should her trouble sore,
But thankt be God, that her encrease so° evermore."   *truly*

17

145 Then said the aged Caelia, "Deare dame,
  And you good Sir, I wote that of your toyle,
  And labours long, through which ye hither came,
  Ye both forwearied be: therefore a whyle
  I read° you rest, and to your bowres recoyle."[6]   *suggest*
150 Then calléd she a Groome, that forth him led
  Into a goodly lodge, and gan despoile°   *disrobe*
  Of puissant armes, and laid in easie bed;
His name was meeke Obedience rightfully aréd.°   *understood*

18

Now when their wearie limbes with kindly° rest,   *natural*
155 And bodies were refresht with due repast,
  Faire Una gan Fidelia faire request,
  To have her knight into her schoolehouse plaste,
  That of her heavenly learning he might taste,
  And heare the wisedome of her words divine.
160 She graunted, and that knight so much agraste,°   *favored*
  That she him taught celestiall discipline,
And opened his dull eyes, that light mote in them shine.

19

And that her sacred Booke, with bloud[7] ywrit,
  That none could read, except she did them teach,
165 She unto him discloséd every whit,
  And heavenly documents° thereout did preach,   *doctrines*
  That weaker whit of man could never reach,
  Of God, of grace, of justice, of free will,
  That wonder was to heare her goodly speach:
170 For she was able, with her words to kill,
And raise againe to life the hart, that she did thrill.°   *pierce*

5. Charity, the fruitful virtue, is often depicted pictorially as a mother with children.   6. Retire to your rooms.
7. I.e., the blood of Christ.

20

And when she list poure out her larger spright,[8]
 She would commaund the hastie Sunne to stay,
 Or backward turne his course from heavens hight;
175 Sometimes great hostes of men she could dismay,
 Dry-shod to passe, she parts the flouds in tway;
 And eke huge mountaines from their native seat
 She would commaund, themselves to beare away,
 And throw in raging sea with roaring threat.
180 Almightie God her gave such powre, and puissance great.[9]

21

The faithfull knight now grew in litle space,
 By hearing her, and by her sisters lore,
 To such perfection of all heavenly grace,
 That wretched world he gan for to abhore,
185 And mortall life gan loath, as thing forelore,
 Greeved with remembrance of his wicked wayes,
 And prickt with anguish of his sinnes so sore,
 That he desirde to end his wretched dayes:
So much the dart of sinfull guilt the soule dismayes.

22

190 But wise Speranza gave him comfort sweet,
 And taught him how to take assuréd hold
 Upon her silver anchor, as was meet;
 Else had his sinnes so great, and manifold
 Made him forget all that Fidelia told.
195 In this distresséd doubtfull agonie,
 When him his dearest Una did behold,
 Disdeining life, desiring leave to die,
She found her selfe assayld with great perplexitie.

23

And came to Caelia to declare her smart,
200 Who well acquainted with that commune plight,
 Which sinfull horror[1] workes in wounded hart,
 Her wisely comforted all that she might,
 With goodly counsell and advisement right;
 And streightway sent with carefull diligence,
205 To fetch a Leach,° the which had great insight   doctor
 In that disease of grievéd conscience,
And well could cure the same; His name was Patience.

24

Who comming to that soule-diseaséd knight,
 Could hardly him intreat, to tell his griefe:
210 Which knowne, and all that noyd° his heavie spright   troubled
 Well searcht, eftsoones he gan apply reliefe
 Of salves and med'cines, which had passing priefe,[2]

---

8. Full spiritual power.
9. Joshua made the sun stand still (Joshua x.12); Hezekiah made it turn backwards (II Kings xx.10); Gideon was victorious over the Midianites (Judges vii.7); Moses led the Israelites through the parted waters of the Red Sea (Exodus xiv.21–31); faith, said Christ, can move mountains (Matthew xxi.21). All these are miracles of faith.
1. Horror of sin.
2. Which had extraordinary power.

And thereto added words of wondrous might:[3]
  By which to ease he him recuréd briefe,°   *speedily*
215 And much asswaged the passion° of his plight,   *suffering*
  That he his paine endured, as seeming now more light.

25

But yet the cause and root of all his ill,
  Inward corruption, and infected sin,
  Not purged nor heald, behind remainéd still,
220 And festring sore did rankle yet within,
  Close° creeping twixt the marrow and the skin.   *secretly*
  Which to extirpe,° he laid him privily   *extirpate*
  Downe in a darkesome lowly place farre in,
  Whereas he meant his corrosives to apply,
225 And with streight° diet tame his stubborne malady.   *strict*

26

In ashes and sackcloth he did array
  His daintie corse, proud humors[4] to abate,
  And dieted with fasting every day,
  The swelling of his wounds to mitigate,
230 And made him pray both earely and eke late:
  And ever as superfluous flesh did rot
  Amendment readie still at hand did wayt,
  To pluck it out wth pincers firie whot,°   *hot*
  That soone in him was left no one corrupted jot.

27

235 And bitter Penance with an yron whip,
  Was wont him once to disple° every day: *discipline*
  And sharpe Remorse his hart did pricke and nip,
  That drops of bloud thence like a well did play;
  And sad Repentance uséd to embay°   *bathe*
240 His bodie in salt water smarting sore,
  The filthy blots of sinne to wash away.[5]
  So in short space they did to health restore
The man that would not live, but earst° lay at deathes dore.   *before*

28

In which his torment often was so great,
245 That like a Lyon he would cry and rore,
  And rend his flesh, and his owne synewes eat.
  His own deare Una hearing evermore
  His ruefull shriekes and gronings, often tore
  Her guiltlesse garments, and her golden heare,
250 For pitty of his paine and anguish sore;
  Yet all with patience wisely she did beare;
For well she wist, his crime could else be never cleare.

29

Whom thus recovered by wise Patience,
  And trew Repentance they to Una brought:
255 Who joyous of his curéd conscience,
  Him dearely kist, and fairely eke besought

3. I.e., absolution, or spiritual counseling generally.
4. Passions—i.e., pride.

5. "Wash me throughly from mine iniquity, and cleanse me from my sin" (Psalms li.2).

Himselfe to chearish,° and consuming thought   cheer
  To put away out of his carefull brest.
  By this Charissa, late in child-bed brought,
260 Was woxen strong, and left her fruitfull nest;
To her faire Una brought this unacquainted guest.

30

She was a woman in her freshest age,
  Of wondrous beauty, and of bountie° rare,   virtue
  With goodly grace and comely personage,
265 That was on earth not easie to compare;
  Full of great love, but Cupids wanton snare
  As hell she hated, chast in worke and will;
  Her necke and breasts were ever open bare,
  That ay thereof her babes might sucke their fill;
270 The rest was all in yellow robes arayéd still.[6]

31

A multitude of babes about her hong,
  Playing their sports, that joyd her to behold,
  Whom still she fed, whiles they were weake and young,
  But thrust them forth still, as they wexéd old:
275 And on her head she wore a tyre° of gold,   headdress
  Adornd with gemmes and owches° wondrous faire,   jewels
  Whose passing° price uneath° was to be told;   surpassing/scarcely
  And by her side there sate a gentle paire
Of turtle doves, she sitting in an yvorie chaire.

32

280 The knight and Una entring, faire her greet,
  And bid her joy of that her happie brood;
  Who them requites with court'sies seeming meet,°   appropriate
  And entertaines with friendly chearefull mood.
  Then Una her besought, to be so good,
285 As in her vertuous rules to schoole her knight,
  Now after all his torment well withstood,
  In that sad° house of Penaunce, where his spright   solemn
Had past the paines of hell, and long enduring night.

33

She was right joyous of her just request,
290 And taking by the hand that Faeries sonne,
  Gan him instruct in every good behest,
  Of love, and righteousness, and well to donne,[7]
  And wrath, and hatred warely to shonne,
  That drew on men Gods hatred, and his wrath,
295 And many soules in dolours° had fordonne:°   misery/destroyed
  In which when him she well instructed hath,
From thence to heaven she teacheth him the ready path.

34

Wherein his weaker° wandring steps to guide,   too weak
  An auncient matrone she to her does call,

6. Her yellow (saffron) robe is the emblem of fruitfulness. That she is "chast
in work and will" and hates "Cupids
wanton snare" does not contradict her
"multitude of babes"; Spenser is distinguishing between *eros* and *agape*,
sexual love and Christian love.
7. I.e., right action.

300   Whose sober lookes her wisedome well descride:°   *made known*
        Her name was Mercie, well knowne over all,
        To be both gratious, and eke liberall:
        To whom the carefull charge of him she gave,
        To lead aright, that he should never fall
305   In all his wayes through this wide worldés wave,°   *expanse*
    That Mercy in the end his righteous soule might save.

35

    The godly Matrone by the hand him beares
        Forth from her presence, by a narrow way,
        Scattred with bushy thornes, and ragged breares,°   *briers*
310   Which still before him she removed away,
        That nothing might his ready passage stay:
        And ever when his feet encombred were,
        Or gan to shrinke, or from the right to stray,
        She held him fast, and firmely did upbeare,
315 As carefull Nourse her child from falling oft does reare.

36

    Eftsoones unto an holy Hospitall,°   *retreat*
        That was fore°by the way, she did him bring,   *close*
        In which seven Bead-men[8] that had vowéd all
        Their life to service of high heavens king
320   Did spend their dayes in doing godly thing:
        Their gates to all were open evermore,
        That by the wearie way were traveiling,
        And one sate wayting ever them before,
    To call in commers-by, that needy were and pore.

37

325 The first of them that eldest was, and best,°   *chief*
        Of all the house had charge and governement,
        As Guardian and Steward of the rest:
        His office was to give entertainement
        And lodging, unto all that came, and went:
330   Not unto such, as could him feast againe,
        And double quite,° for that he on them spent,   *repay*
        But such, as want of harbour° did constraine: *shelter*
    Those for Gods sake his dewty was to entertaine.

38

    The second was as Almner° of the place,   *almoner*
335   His office was, the hungry for to feed,
        And thristy give to drinke, a worke of grace:
        He feard not once him selfe to be in need,
        Ne cared to hoord for those, whom he did breede:[9]
        The grace of God he layd up still in store,
340   Which as a stocke he left unto his seede;
        He had enough, what need him care for more?
    And had he lesse, yet some he would give to the pore.

39

    The third had of their wardrobe custodie,
        In which were not rich tyres,° nor garments gay,   *robes*

8. Men of prayer.   9. I.e., his children.

345 The plumes of pride, and wings of vanitie,
But clothes meet to keepe keene could° away,   *cold*
And naked nature seemely to aray;
With which bare wretched wights he dayly clad,
The images of God in earthly clay;
350 And if that no spare clothes to give he had,
His owne coate he would cut, and it distribute glad.

40

The fourth appointed by his office was,
Poore prisoners to relieve with gratious ayd,
And captives to redeeme with price of bras,°   *money*
355 From Turkes and Sarazins, which them had stayd;°   *held captive*
And though they faultie were, yet well he wayd,
That God to us forgiveth every howre
Much more then that, why° they in bands were layd,   *for which*
And he that harrow hell[1] with heavie stowre,
360 The faultie soules from thence brought to his heavenly bowre.

41

The fift had charge sicke persons to attend,
And comfort those, in point of death which lay;
For them most needeth comfort in the end,
When sin, and hell, and death do most dismay
365 The feeble soule departing hence away.
All is but lost, that living we bestow,°   *store up*
If not well ended at our dying day.
O man have mind of that last bitter throw;°   *throe*
For as the tree does fall, so lyes it ever low.

42

370 The sixt had charge of them now being dead,
In seemely sort their courses to engrave,°   *bury*
And deck with dainty flowres their bridall bed,
That to their heavenly spouse both sweet and brave
They might appeare, when he their soules shall save.
375 The wondrous workemanship of Gods owne mould,°   *image*
Whose face he made, all beasts to feare, and gave
All in his hand, even dead we honour should.
Ah dearest God me graunt, I dead be not defould.°   *abused*

43

The seventh now after death and buriall done,
380 Had charge the tender Orphans of the dead
And widowes ayd, least they should be undone:
In face of judgement[2] he their right would plead,
Ne ought the powre of mighty men did dread
In their defence, nor would for gold or fee
385 Be wonne their rightfull causes downe to tread:

---

1. I.e., Christ, who journeyed to hell to deliver those good people who lived before his time, according to a popular story in the Middle Ages. It originated in the apocryphal gospel of Nicodemus.
2. I.e., in court.
3. Always freely. The seven Bead-men here correspond to, and perform, the seven works of charity, or corporal mercy: lodging the homeless, feeding the hungry, clothing the naked, redeeming the captive, comforting the sick, honoring the dead, and succoring the orphan. Cf. the seven deadly sins in the House of Pride.

And when they stood in most necessitee,
He did supply their want, and gave them ever free.[3]

44

There when the Elfin knight arrivéd was,
  The first and chiefest of the seven, whose care
390 Was guests to welcome, towardes him did pas:
  Where seeing Mercie, that his steps up bare,°   *supported*
  And alwayes led, to her with reverence rare·
  He humbly louted° in meeke lowlinesse,   *bowed*
  And seemely welcome for her did prepare:
395 For of their order she was Patronesse,
  Albe° Charissa were their chiefest founderesse.   *although*

45

There she awhile him stayes, him selfe to rest,
  That to the rest more able he might bee:
  During which time, in every good behest
400 And godly worke of Almes and charitee
  She him instructed with great industree;
  Shortly therein so perfect he became,
  That from the first unto the last degree,
  His mortall life he learnéd had to frame
405 In holy righteousnesse, without rebuke or blame.

46

Thence forward by that painfull way they pas,
  Forth to an hill, that was both steepe and hy;
  On top whereof a sacred chappell was,
  And eke a litle Hermitage thereby,
410 Wherein an agéd holy man did lye,
  That day and night said his devotion,
  Ne other worldly busines did apply;
  His name was heavenly Contemplation;
Of God and goodnesse was his meditation.

47

415 Great grace that old man to him given had;
  For God he often saw from heavens hight,
  All° were his earthly eyen both blunt° and bad,   *although/dim*
  And through great age had lost their kindly° sight,   *natural*
  Yet wondrous quick and persant° was his spright,   *piercing*
420 As Eagles eye, that can behold the Sunne:
  That hill they scale with all their powre and might,
  That his frayle thighes nigh wearie and fordonne°   *exhausted*
Gan faile, but by her helpe the top at last he wonne.

48

There they do finde that godly agéd Sire,
425 With snowy lockes adowne his shoulders shed,
  As hoarie frost with spangles doth attire
  The mossy braunches of an Oke halfe ded.
  Each bone might through his body well be red,°   *observed*
  And every sinew seene through his long fast:
430 For nought he cared his carcas long unfed;
  His mind was full of spirituall repast,
And pynéd° his flesh, to keepe his body low and chast.   *starved*

49

Who when these two approching he aspide,
   At their first presence grew agrievéd sore,
435 That forst him lay his heavenly thoughts aside;
   And had he not that Dame respected more,°   *greatly*
   Whom highly he did reverence and adore,
   He would not once have movéd for the knight.
   They him saluted standing far afore;°   *away*
440 Who well them greeting, humbly did requight,
And asked, to what end they clomb° that tedious height. *had climbed*

50

"What end," quoth she, "should cause us take such paine,
   But that same end, which every living wight
   Should make his marke, high heaven to attaine?
445 Is not from hence the way, that leadeth right
   To that most glorious house, that glistreth bright
   With burning starres, and everliving fire,
   Whereof the keyes are to thy hand behight°   *entrusted*
   By wise Fidelia? she doth thee require,
450 To shew it to this knight, according his desire."

51

"Thrise happy man," said then the father grave,
   "Whose staggering steps thy steady hand doth lead,
   And shewes the way, his sinfull soule to save.
   Who better can the way to heaven aread.
455 Then thou thy selfe, that was both borne and bred
   In heavenly throne, where thousand Angels shine?
   Thou doest the prayers of the righteous sead°   *offspring*
   Present before the majestie divine,
And his avenging wrath to clemencie incline.

52

460 "Yet since thou bidst, thy pleasure shalbe donne.
   Then come thou man of earth, and see the way,
   That never yet was seene of Faeries sonne,
   That never leads the traveiler astray,
   But after labours long, and sad delay,
465 Brings them to joyous rest and endlesse blis.
   But first thou must a season fast and pray,
   Till from her bands the spright assoiléd° is,   *released*
And have her strength recured° from fraile infirmitis." *recovered*

53

That done, he leads him to the highest Mount;
470 Such one, as that same mighty man of God,
   The bloud-red billowes like a walléd front
   On either side disparted with his rod,
   Till that his army dry-foot through them yod,°   *went*
   Dwelt fortie dayes upon; where writ in stone
475 With bloudy letters by the hand of God,
   The bitter doome° of death and balefull mone   *judgment*
He did receive, whiles flashing fire about him shone.

54

Or like that sacred hill, whose head full hie,

Adornd with fruitfull Olives all arownd,
480 Is, as it were for endlesse memory
Of that deare Lord, who oft thereon was fownd,
For ever with a flowring girlond crownd:
Or like that pleasaunt Mount, that is for ay
Through famous Poets verse each where° renownd,   *everywhere*
485 On which the thrise three learned Ladies play
Their heavenly notes, and make full many a lovely lay.[4]

55

From thence, far off he unto him did shew
A litle path, that was both steepe and long,
Which to a goodly Citie led his vew;
490 Whose wals and towres were builded high and strong
Of perle and precious stone, that earthly tong
Cannot describe, nor wit of man can tell;
Too high a ditty° for my simple song;   *subject*
The Citie of the great king hight it well,
495 Wherein eternall peace and happinesse doth dwell.

56

As he thereon stood gazing, he might see
The blessed Angels to and fro descend
From highest heaven, in gladsome companee,
And with great joy into that Citie wend,
500 As commonly° as friend does with his frend.[5]   *generally*
Whereat he wondred much, and gan enquere,
What stately building durst so high extend
Her loftie towres unto the starry sphere,
And what unknowen nation there empeopled were.

57

505 "Faire knight," quoth he, "Hierusalem that is,
The new Hierusalem, that God has built
For those to dwell in, that are chosen his,
His chosen people purged from sinfull guilt,
With pretious bloud, which cruelly was spilt
510 On curséd tree, of that unspotted lam,
That for the sinnes of all the world was kilt:
Now are they Saints all in that Citie sam,°   *together*
More deare unto their God, then younglings to their dam."[6]

58

"Till now," said then the knight, "I weenéd well,
515 That great Cleopolis,[7] where I have beene,

---

4. The mountain is successively compared to Mount Sinai (lines 469–77), where Moses, after parting the "bloud-red billowes" of the Red Sea, received the tablets of the laws of Judaism; to the Mount of Olives (lines 478–82), associated with Christ; and to Mount Parnassus (lines 483–86), where dwelled the nine muses of art and poetry. This last has the effect of equating poetry with the profoundest religious experience —a tradition that Sidney's *Apology* also incorporates.

5. Cf. Jacob's ladder: "And he dreamed, and behold a ladder set up on the earth, and the top of it reached to heaven; and behold the angels of God ascending and descending on it" (Genesis xxviii.12).
6. The New Jerusalem is described in Revelation xxi-xxii; "the nations of them which are saved shall walk in the light of it" (xxi.24).
7. London, Camelot—and here, the earthly counterpart of the Heavenly Kingdom.

In which that fairest Faerie Queene doth dwell,
The fairest Citie was, that might be seene;
And that bright towre all.built of christall cleene,°   *clear*
Panthea,[8] seemd the brightest thing, that was:
520   But now by proofe all otherwise I weene;
For this great Citie that does far surpas,
And this bright Angels towre quite dims that towre of glas."

59

"Most trew," then said the holy aged man;
"Yet is Cleopolis for earthly frame,°   *structure*
525   The fairest peece, that eye beholden can:
And well beseemes all knights of noble name,
That covet in th'immortall booke of fame
To be eterniz'd, that same to haunt,°   *frequent*
And doen their service to that soveraigne Dame,
         reward
530   That glorie does to them for guerdon° graunt: *claim*
For she is heavenly borne, and heaven may justly vaunt.°

60

"And thou faire ymp, sprong out from English race,
         accounted
How ever now accompted° Elfins sonne,   *favor*
Well worthy doest thy service for her grace,°
535   To aide a virgin desolate foredonne.
But when thou famous victorie hast wonne,
And high emongst all knights has hong thy shield,
Thenceforth the suit° of earthly conquest shonne,   *pursuit*
And wash thy hands from guilt of bloudy field:
540   For bloud can nought but sin, and wars but sorrowes yield.

61

"Then seeke this path, that I to thee presage,°   *point out*
Which after all to heaven shall thee send;
Then peaceably thy painefull pilgrimage
To yonder same Hierusalem do bend,
545   Where is for thee ordaind a blessed end:
For thou emongst those Saints, whom thou doest see,
Shalt be a Saint, and thine owne nations frend
And Patrone: thou Saint George shalt calléd bee,
Saint George of mery England, the signe of victoree."[9]

62

550   "Unworthy wretch," quoth he, "of so great grace,
How dare I thinke such glory to attaine?"
"These that have it attaind, were in like cace,"
Quoth he, "as wretched, and lived in like paine."
"But deeds of armes must I at last be faine,
555   And Ladies love to leave so dearely bought?"
"What need of armes, where peace doth ay remaine,"
Said he, "and battailes none are to be fought?
As for loose loves are vaine, and vanish into nought."

---

8. Reminiscent of the temple of glass in Chaucer's *Hous of Fame;* perhaps intended to represent Richmond Palace or Westminster Abbey.
9. Spenser's conception of St. George, patron saint of England, draws on the *Legenda Aurea* (translated by Caxton in 1487); on pictures, tapestries, and pageants; and on folklore.

63

"O let me not," quoth he, "then turne againe
560 Backe to the world, whose joyes so fruitlesse are;
But let me here for aye in peace remaine,
Or streight way on that last long voyage fare,
That nothing may my present hope empare."°   *impair*
"That may not be," said he, "ne maist thou yit
565 Forgo that royall maides bequeathéd care,°   *charge*
Who did her cause into thy hand commit,
Till from her curséd foe thou have her freely quit."° *released*

64

"Then shall I soone," quoth he, "so God me grace,
Abet° that virgins cause disconsolate,   *support*
570 And shortly backe returne unto this place
To walke this way in Pilgrims poore estate.
But now aread, old father, why of late
Didst thou behight me borne of English blood,
Whom all a Faeries sonne doen nominate?"°   *name*
575 "That word shall I," said he, "avouchen° good,   *prove*
Sith to thee is unknowne the cradle of thy brood.

65

"For well I wote, thou springst from ancient race
Of Saxon kings, that have with mightie hand
And many bloudie battailes fought in place°   *there*
580 High reard their royall throne in Britane land,
And vanquisht them, unable to withstand:
From thence a Faerie thee unweeting reft,[1]
There as thou slepst in tender swadling band,
And her base Elfin brood there for thee left.
585 Such men do Chaungelings call, so chaungd by Faeries theft.

66

"Thence she thee brought into this Faerie lond,
And in an heapéd furrow did thee hyde,
Where thee a Ploughman all unweeting fond,
As he his toylesome teme that way did guyde,
590 And brought thee up in ploughmans state to byde,
Whereof Georgos he thee gave to name;[2]
Till prickt with courage, and thy forces pryde,
To Faery court thou cam'st to seeke for fame,
And prove thy puissaunt armes, as seemes thee best became."° *suited*

67

595 "O holy Sire," quoth he, "how shall I quight
The many favours I with thee have found,
That has my name and nation red aright,
And taught the way that does to heaven bound?"°   *go*
This said, adowne he lookéd to the ground,
600 To have returnd, but dazéd were his eyne,
Through passing° brightnesse, which did quite confound *surpassing*
His feeble sence, and too exceeding shyne.
So darke are earthly things compard to things divine.

1. Secretly stole.
2. *Georgos* is Greek for "farmer" (cf. Virgil's *Georgics*, on farming).

68

605

At last whenas himselfe he gan to find,
    To Una back he cast him to retire;
    Who him awaited still with pensive mind.
    Great thankes and goodly meed° to that good syre,   *gift*
    He thence departing gave for his paines hyre.°   *reward*
    So came to Una, who him joyd to see,
    And after litle rest, gan him desire,
    Of her adventure mindfull for to bee.
So leave they take of Caelia, and her daughters three.

(line 610 marked at "And after litle rest")

Canto XI

The knight with that old Dragon fights
two dayes incessantly:
The third him overthrowes, and gayns
most glorious victory.

1

High time now gan it wex° for Una faire,   *develop*
    To thinke of those her captive Parents deare,
    And their forwasted kingdome to repaire:[3]
    Whereto whenas they now approachéd neare,
    With hartie words her knight she gan to cheare,
    And in her modest manner thus bespake;
    "Deare knight, as deare, as ever knight was deare,
    That all these sorrowes suffer for my sake,
High heaven behold the tedious toyle, ye for me take.

(line 5 marked at "With hartie words")

2

"Now are we come unto my native soyle,
    And to the place, where all our perils dwell;
    Here haunts that feend, and does his dayly spoyle,
    Therefore henceforth be at your keeping well,[4]
    And ever ready for your foeman fell.
    The sparke of noble courage now awake,
    And strive your excellent selfe to excell;
    That shall ye evermore renowméd make,
Above all knights on earth, that batteill undertake."

(line 10 marked at "Now are we come"; line 15 marked at "The sparke of noble courage")

3

And pointing forth, "lo yonder is," said she,
    "The brasen towre in which my parents deare
    For dread of that huge feend emprisond be,
    Whom I from far see on the walles appeare,
    Whose sight my feeble° soule doth greatly cheare: *melancholy*
    And on the top of all I do espye
    The watchman wayting tydings glad to heare,
    That O my parents might I happily
Unto you bring, to ease you of your misery."

(line 20 marked at "The brasen towre"; line 25 marked at "The watchman wayting")

4

With that they heard a roaring hideous sound,

---

3. I.e., to restore their kingdom, laid   4. I.e., be alert to your responsibilities.
waste (by the dragon), to health.

That all the ayre with terrour filléd wide,
30   And seemd uneath° to shake the stedfast ground.   *almost*
  Eftsoones that dreadfull Dragon they espide,
  Where stretcht he lay upon the sunny side
  Of a great hill, himselfe like a great hill.
  But all so soone, as he from far descride
35   Those glistring armes, that heaven with light did fill,
He rousd himselfe full blith,° and hastned them   *eagerly/*
    untill.°   *toward*

5

Then bad the knight his Lady yede° aloofe,   *step*
  And to an hill her selfe withdraw aside,
  From whence she might behold that battailles proof°   *outcome*
40   And eke be safe from daunger far descryde:
  She him obayd, and turnd a little wyde.°   *aside*
  Now I thou sacred Muse,[5] most learned Dame,
  Faire ympe° of Phoebus, and his aged bride,[6]   *child*
  The Nourse of time, and everlasting fame,
45 That warlike hands ennoblest with immortall name;

6

O gently come into my feeble brest,
  Come gently, but not with that mighty rage,
  Wherewith the martiall troupes thou doest infest,°   *arouse*
  And harts of great Heroës doest enrage,
50   That nought their kindled courage may aswage,
  Soone as thy dreadfull trompe begins to sownd;
  The God of warre with his fiers equipage
  Thou doest awake, sleepe never he so sownd,
And scaréd nations doest with horrour sterne astown.°   *appall*

7

55 Faire Goddesse lay that furious fit° aside,   *mood*
  Till I of warres and bloudy Mars do sing[7]
  And Briton fields with Sarazin bloud bedyde,
  Twixt that great faery Queene and Paynim king,
  That with their horrour heaven and earth did ring,
60   A worke of labour long, and endlesse prayse:
  But now a while let downe that haughtie string,
  And to my tunes thy second tenor rayse,[8]
That I this man of God his godly armes may blaze.°   *describe*

8

By this the dreadfull Beast drew nigh to hand,
65   Halfe flying, and halfe footing in his hast,
  That with his largenesse measuréd much land,
  And made wide shadow under his huge wast;°   *girth*
  As mountaine doth the valley overcast.
  Approching nigh, he rearéd high afore
70   His body monstrous, horrible, and vast,
  Which to increase his wondrous greatnesse more,
Was swolne with wrath, and poyson, and with bloudy gore.

5. Calliope, muse of epic poetry, or Clio, muse of history.
6. I.e., Mnemosyne (memory).
7. Spenser refers to a projected book of *The Faerie Queene* which he never wrote.
8. The "haughtie" (high-pitched) mode would be appropriate to a large-scale epic war; the "second tenor" (lower in pitch) to this present battle.

9

And over, all with brasen scales was armd,
   Like plated coate of steele, so couchéd neare,[9]
75   That nought mote perce, ne might his corse be harmd
   With dint of sword, nor push of pointed speare;
   Which as an Eagle, seeing pray appeare,
   His aery Plumes doth rouze,° full rudely dight,   *shake*
   So shakéd he, that horrour was to heare,
80   For as the clashing of an Armour bright,
Such noyse his rouzéd scales did send unto the knight.

10

His flaggy° wings when forth he did display,   *drooping*
   Were like two sayles, in which the hollow wynd
   Is gathered full, and worketh speedy way:
85   And eke the pennes,° that did his pineons bynd,   *quills*
   Were like mayne-yards, with flying canvas lynd,
   With which whenas him list the ayre to beat,
   And there by force unwonted passage find,
90   The cloudes before him fled for terrour great,
And all the heavens stood still amazéd with his threat.

11

His huge long tayle wound up in hundred foldes,
   Does overspred his long bras-scaly backe,
   Whose wreathéd boughts° when ever he unfoldes,   *coils*
   And thicke entangled knots adown does slacke,
95   Bespotted as with shields of red and blacke,
   It sweepeth all the land behind him farre,
   And of three furlongs does but litle lacke;
   And at the point two stings in-fixéd arre,
Both deadly sharpe, that sharpest steele exceeden farre.

12

100   But stings and sharpest steele did far exceed[1]
   The sharpnesse of his cruell rending clawes;
   Dead was it sure, as sure as death in deed,
   What ever thing does touch his ravenous pawes,
   Or what within his reach he ever drawes.
105   But his most hideous head my toung to tell
   Does tremble: for his deepe devouring jawes
   Wide gapéd, like the griesly mouth of hell,
Through which into his darke abisse all ravin° fell.[2]   *prey, booty*

13

And that more wondrous was, in either jaw
110   Threeranckes of yron teeth enraungéd were,
   In which yet trickling bloud and gobbets raw
   Of late devouréd bodies did appeare,
   That sight thereof bred cold congealéd feare:
   Which to increase, and all at once to kill,
115   A cloud of smoothering smoke and sulphur seare°   *burning*

9. Closely overlaid.
1. I.e., were far exceeded by.
2. In emphasizing the deathly, hellish aspects of the dragon, this stanza reveals the stakes of the battle: holiness v. sin, the Protestant v. the Catholic churches, life v. death.

Out of his stinking gorge° forth steeméd still,   *maw*
That all the ayre about with smoke and·stench· did fill.

14

His blazing eyes, like two bright shining shields,
   Did burne with wrath, and sparkled living fyre;
120 As two broad Beacons, set in open fields,
   Send forth their flames farre off to every shyre,
   And warning give, that enemies conspyre,
   With fire and sword the region to invade;
125 So flamed his eyne with rage and rancorous yre:
   But farre within, as in a hollow glade,
Those glaring lampes were set, that made a dreadfull shade.[3]

15

So dreadfully he towards him did pas,
   Forelifting up aloft his speckled brest,
   And often bounding on the bruséd gras,
130 As for great joyance of his newcome guest.
   Eftsoones he gan advance his haughtie crest,
   As chafféd° Bore his bristles doth upreare,   *vexed*
   And shoke his scales to battell readie drest;
   That made the Redcrosse knight nigh quake for feare,
135 As bidding bold defiance to his foeman neare.

16

The knight gan fairely couch° his steadie speare,   *rest, aim*
   And fiercely ran at him with rigorous might:
   The pointed steele arriving rudely theare,
   His harder hide would neither perce, nor bight,
140 But glauncing by forth passéd forward right;
   Yet sore amovéd with so puissant push,
   The wrathfull beast about him turnéd light,°   *quickly*
   And him so rudely passing by, did brush
With his long tayle, that horse and man to ground did rush.

17

145 Both horse and man up lightly rose againe,
   And fresh encounter towards him addrest:
   But th' idle stroke yet backe recoyld in vaine,
   And found no place his° deadly point to rest.   *its*
   Exceeding rage enflamed the furious beast,
150 To be avengéd of so great despight;°   *outrage*
   For never felt his imperceable brest
   So wondrous force, from hand of living wight;
Yet had he proved° the powre of many a puissant knight. *tested*

18

Then with his waving wings displayéd wyde,
155 Himselfe up high he lifted from the ground,
   And with strong flight did forcibly divide
   The yielding aire, which nigh too feeble found
   Her flitting partes, and element unsound,

---

3. Cf. among other echoes, the great beast of Revelation (xiii.2): "And the beast which I saw was like unto a leopard, and his feet were as the feet of a bear, and his mouth as the mouth of a lion: and the dragon gave him his power, and his seat, and great authority."

To beare so great a weight: he cutting way
160 With his broad sayles, about him soaréd round:
At last low stouping with unweldie sway,[4]
Snatcht up both horse and man, to beare them quite away.

19

Long he them bore above the subject plaine,[5]
So farre as Ewghen[6] bow a shaft may send,
165 Till struggling strong did him at last constraine,
To let them downe before his flightés end:
As hagard° hauke presuming to contend   *untrained*
With hardie fowle, above his hable might,[7]
His wearie pounces° all in vaine doth spend,   *claws*
170 To trusse° the pray too heavie for his flight;   *seize*
Which comming downe to ground, does free it selfe by fight.

20

He so disseizéd of his gryping grosse,[8]
The knight his thrillant° speare againe assayd   *piercing*
In his bras-plated body to embosse,°   *plunge*
175 And three mens strength unto the stroke he layd;
Wherewith the stiffe beame quakéd, as affrayd,
And glauncing from his scaly necke, did glyde
Close under his left wing, then broad displayd.
The percing steele there wrought a wound full wyde,
180 That with the uncouth smart the Monster lowdly cryde.

21

He cryde, as raging seas are wont to rore,
When wintry storme his wrathfull wreck does threat,
The rolling billowes beat the ragged shore,
As they the earth would shoulder from her seat,
185 And greedie gulfe does gape, as he would eat
His neighbour element[9] in his revenge:
Then gin the blustring brethren[1] boldly threat,
To move the world from off his stedfast henge,°   *hinge*
And boystrous battell make, each other to avenge.

22

190 The steely head stucke fast still in his flesh,
Till with his cruell clawes he snatcht the wood,
And quite a sunder broke. Forth flowéd fresh
A gushing river of blacke goarie blood,
That drownéd all the land, whereon he stood;
195 The stream thereof would drive a water-mill.
Trebly augmented was his furious mood
With bitter sense of his deepe rooted ill,
That flames of fire he threw forth from his large noséthrill.

23

His hideous tayle then hurléd he about,
200 And therewith all enwrapt the nimble thyes

---

4. Ponderous force.
5. I.e., the ground below.
6. Yewen, of yew.
7. Able power.

8. Freed from his formidable grip.
9. I.e., earth.
1. I.e., the winds.

Of his froth-fomy steed, whose courage stout
Striving to loose the knot, that fast him tyes,
Himselfe in streighter bandes too rash implyes,
That to the ground he is perforce constraynd
05 To throw his rider: who can° quickly ryse   *began to*
From off the earth, with durty bloud distaynd,
For that reprochfull fall right fowly he disdaynd.

24
And fiercely tooke his trenchand° blade in hand,   *sharp*
With which he stroke so furious and so fell,
10 That nothing seemd the puissance could withstand:
Upon his crest the hardned yron fell,
But his more hardned crest was armd so well,
That deeper dint therein it would not make;
Yet so extremely did the buffe him quell,°   *dismay*
15 That from thenceforth he shund the like to take,
But when he saw them come, he did them still forsake.°   *avoid*

25
The knight was wrath to see his stroke beguyld,
And smote againe with more outrageous might;
But backe againe the sparckling steele recoyld,
20 And left not any marke, where it did light;
As if in Adamant rocke it had bene pight.°   *struck against*
The beast impatient of his smarting wound,
And of so fierce and forcible despight,
Thought with his wings to stye° above the ground;   *mount*
25 But his late wounded wing unserviceable found.

26
Then full of griefe and anguish vehement,
He lowdly brayd, that like was never heard,
And from his wide devouring oven sent
A flake° of fire, that flashing in his beard,   *flash*
30 Him all amazd, and almost made affeard;
The scorching flame sore swingéd° all his face,   *singed*
And through his armour all his bodie seard,
That he could not endure so cruell cace,
But thought his armes to leave, and helmet to unlace.

27
35 Not that great Champion of the antique world,
Whom famous Poetes verse so much doth vaunt,
And hath for twelve huge labours high extold,
So many furies and sharpe fits did haunt,
When him the poysoned garment did enchaunt
40 With Centaures bloud, and bloudie verses charmed,
As did this knight twelve thousand dolours daunt,
Whom fyrie steele now burnt, that earst him armed,
That erst him goodly armed, now most of all him harmed.[2]

---

2. Redcrosse's fire-baptism is compared
to the burning shirt of Nessus, which
killed Hercules, "that great Champion of
the antique world" (line 235); the metaphor of warfare and battle is here supplemented, as often in Spenser, by a
metaphor of healing and purgation.

28

Faint, wearie, sore, emboyléd, grievéd, brent°   *burned*
245   With heat, toyle, wounds, armes, smart, and inward fire
      That never man such mischiefes did torment;
      Death better were, death did he oft desire,
      But death will never come, when needes require.
      Whom so dismayd when that his foe beheld,
250   He cast to suffer him no more respire,°   *rest*
      But gan his sturdie sterne° about to weld,°   *tail/lash*
And him so strongly stroke, that to the ground him feld.

29

It fortunéd (as faire it then befell)
      Behind his backe unweeting, where he stood,
      Of auncient time there was a springing well,
255   From which fast trickled forth a silver flood,
      Full of great vertues, and for med'cine good.
      Whylome,° before that curséd Dragon got   *formerly*
      That happie land, and all with innocent blood
260   Defyld those sacred waves, it rightly hot°   *was called*
The Well of Life, ne yet his° vertues had forgot.   *its*

30

For unto life the dead it could restore,
      And guilt of sinfull crimes cleane wash away,
      Those that with sicknesse were infected sore,
265   It could recure, and aged long decay
      Renew, as one were borne that very day.
      Both Silo this, and Jordan did excell,
      And th' English Bath, and eke the german Spau,
      Ne can Cephise, nor Hebrus match this well:
270 Into the same the knight backe overthrowen, fell.[3]

31

Now gan the golden Phoebus for to steepe
      His fierie face in billowes of the west,
      And his faint steedes watred in Ocean deepe,
      Whiles from their journall° labours they did rest,   *daily*
275   When that infernall Monster, having kest°   *cast*
      His wearie foe into that living well,
      Can° high advaunce his broad discoloured brest,   *did*
      Above his wonted pitch,° with countenance fell,   *height*
And clapt his yron wings, as victor he did dwell.°   *remain*

32

280 Which when his pensive Ladie saw from farre,
      Great woe and sorrow did her soule assay,°   *attack*
      As weening that the sad end of the warre,
      And gan to highest God entirely° pray,   *earnestly*
      That fearéd chaunce° from her to turne away;   *fate*

3. In the old English metrical romance *Sir Bevis of Hampton*, the hero is saved in his fight with a dragon by a healing well; "a pure river of water of life" is also described in Revelation xxii.1–2. The Well of Life, with its baptismal powers of renewal, is successively compared to waters of the Bible, of England and Europe, and of classical antiquity. In Siloam (Silo) a blind man was cured by Christ (John ix.7); the crossing of the river Jordan saved the Jews (Deuteronomy xxvii.2–9), and Christ was baptized therein (Matthew iii.16); "Bath" and "Spau" (Spa) were famed for their medicinal waters; "Cephise" and "Hebrus" in Greece were noted for their clear streams.

285 With folded hands and knees full lowly bent
    All night she watcht, ne once adowne would lay
    Her daintie limbs in her sad dreriment,
But praying still did wake, and waking did lament.

33

    The morrow next gan early to appeare,
290   That Titan[4] rose to runne his daily race;
    But early ere the morrow next gan reare
    Out of the sea faire Titans deawy face,
    Up rose the gentle virgin from her place,
    And lookéd all about, if she might spy
295   Her loved knight to move his manly pace:
For she had great doubt of his safety,
Since late she saw him fall before his enemy.

34

    At last she saw, where he upstarted brave
    Out of the well, wherein he drenchéd lay;
300   As Eagle fresh out of the Ocean wave,
    Where he hath left his plumes all hoary gray,
    And deckt himselfe with feathers youthly gay,
    Like Eyas° hauke up mounts unto the skies,   *young*
    His newly budded pineons to assay,
305   And marveiles at himselfe, still as he flies:
So new this new-borne knight to battell new did rise.

35

    Whom when the damnéd feend so fresh did spy,
    No wonder if he wondred at the sight,
    And doubted, whether his late enemy
310   It were, or other new suppliéd knight.
    He, now to prove his late renewéd might,
    High brandishing his bright deaw-burning blade,
    Upon his crested scalpe so sore did smite,
    That to the scull a yawning wound it made:
315 The deadly dint his dulléd senses all dismaid.

36

    I wote not, whether the revenging steele
    Were hardnéd with that holy water dew,
    Wherein he fell, or sharper edge did feele,
    Or his baptizéd hands now greater° grew;   *stronger*
320   Or other secret vertue did ensew;
    Else never could the force of fleshly arme,
    Ne molten mettall in his bloud embrew:°   *plunge*
    For till that stownd° could never wight him harme,   *stunning blow*
By subtilty, nor slight,° nor might, nor mighty charme.   *trickery*

37

325 The cruell wound enragéd him so sore,
    That loud he yelléd for exceeding paine;
    As hundred ramping Lyons seemed to rore,
    Whom ravenous hunger did there to constraine:
    Then gan he tosse aloft his stretchéd traine,
330   And therewith scourge the buxome° aire so sore,   *yielding*

---

4. **When the sun.**

That to his force to yeelden it was faine;
Ne ought° his sturdie strokes might stand afore,   *anything*
That high trees overthrew, and rocks in peeces tore.

38

The same advauncing high above his head,
335 With sharpe intended° sting so rude him smot,   *shot out*
That to the earth him drove, as stricken dead,
Ne living wight would have him life behot:°   *granted*
The mortall sting his angry needle shot
Quite through his shield, and in his shoulder seasd,
340 Where fast it stucke, ne would there out be got:
The griefe thereof him wondrous sore diseasd,°   *afflicted*
Ne might his ranckling paine with patience be appeasd.[5]

39

But yet more mindfull of his honour deare,
Then of the grievous smart, which him did wring,°   *torment*
345 From loathéd soile he can° him lightly reare,   *began to*
And strove to loose the farre infixéd sting:
Which when in vaine he tryde with struggeling,
Inflamed with wrath, his raging blade he heft,
And strooke so strongly, that the knotty string
350 Of his huge taile he quite a sunder cleft,
Five joynts thereof he hewd, and but the stump him left.

40

Hart cannot thinke, what outrage, and what cryes,
With foule enfouldred[6] smoake and flashing fire,
The hell-bred beast threw forth unto the skyes,
355 That all was coveréd with darknesse dire:
Then fraught with rancour, and engorgéd° ire,   *choking*
He cast at once him to avenge for all,
And gathering up himselfe out of the mire,
With his uneven wings did fiercely fall
360 Upon his sunne-bright shield, and gript it fast withall.

41

Much was the man encombred with his hold,
In feare to lose his weapon in his paw,
Ne wist yet, how his talents° to unfold;   *talons*
Nor harder was from Cerberus greedie jaw
365 To plucke a bone, then from his cruell claw
To reave° by strength the gripéd gage° away: *seize/prize*
Thrise he assayd it from his foot to draw,
And thrise in vaine to draw it did assay,
It booted nought to thinke, to robbe him of his pray.

42

370 Tho when he saw no power might prevaile,
His trustie sword he cald to his last aid,
Wherewith he fiercely did his foe assaile,
And double blowes about him stoutly laid,
That glauncing fire out of the yron plaid;
375 As sparckles from the Andvile use to fly,

5. Redcrosse's wound suggests Christ's   6. Hurled out like thunder.
wounded side.

When heavie hammers on the wedge are swaid;°   *struck*
Therewith at last he forst him to unty°   *loosen*
One of his grasping feete, him to defend thereby.

43

The other foot, fast fixéd on his shield,
380 Whenas no strength, nor stroks mote him constraine
To loose, ne yet the warlike pledge to yield,
He smot thereat with all his might and maine,
That nought so wondrous puissance might sustaine;
Upon the joynt the lucky steele did light,
385 And made such way, that hewd it quite in twaine;
The paw yet misséd not his minisht° might,   *lessened*
But hong still on the shield, as it at first was pight.

44

For griefe thereof, and divelish despight,
From his infernall fournace forth he threw
390 Huge flames, that dimméd all the heavens light,
Enrold in duskish smoke and brimstone blew;
As burning Aetna from his boyling stew°   *cauldron*
Doth belch out flames, and rockes in peeces broke,
And ragged ribs of mountaines molten new
395 Enwrapt in coleblacke clouds and filthy smoke,
That all the land with stench, and heaven with horror choke.

45

The heate whereof, and harmefull pestilence
So sore him noyd,° that forst him to retire   *troubled*
A little backward for his best defence,
400 To save his bodie from the scorching fire,
Which he from hellish entrailes did expire.°   *breathe out*
It chaunst (eternall God that chaunce did guide)
As he recoyléd backward, in the mire
His nigh forwearied feeble feet did slide,
405 And downe he fell, with dread of shame sore terrifide.

46

There grew a goodly tree him faire beside,
Loaden with fruit and apples rosie red,
As they in pure vermilion had beene dide,
Whereof great vertues over all were red:°   *declared*
410 For happie life to all, which thereon fed,
And life eke everlasting did befall:
Great God it planted in that blessed sted°   *place*
With his almightie hand, and did it call
The Tree of Life, the crime of our first fathers fall.[7]

47

415 In all the world like was not to be found,
Save in that soile, where all good things did grow,
And freely sprong out of the fruitfull ground,
As incorrupted Nature did them sow,

7. In Genesis ii.9 appears the Tree of Life which God planted in the Garden of Eden. The "crime of our first fathers fall" is that Adam, in being banished from Eden, separated himself—and us—from the tree. The tree appears again in the New Jerusalem (Revelation xxii.2).

Till that dread Dragon all did overthrow.
420 Another like faire tree eke grew thereby,
Whereof who so did eat, eftsoones did know
Both good and ill: O mornefull memory:
That tree through one mans fault hath doen us all to dy.[8]

48

From that first tree forth flowd, as from a well,
425 A trickling streame of Balme, most soveraine
And daintie deare,[9] which on the ground still fell,
And overflowéd all the fertill plaine,
As it had deawéd bene with timely° raine: seasonable
Life and long health that gratious° ointment gave,   full of grace
430 And deadly woundes could heale, and reare againe
The senselesse corse appointed° for the grave.   made ready
Into that same he fell: which did from death him save.[1]

49

For nigh thereto the ever damnéd beast
Durst not approch, for he was deadly made,[2]
435 And all that life preservéd, did detest:
Yet he it oft adventured to invade.
By this the drouping day-light gan to fade,
And yeeld his roome to sad succeeding night,
Who with her sable mantle gan to shade
440 The face of earth, and wayes of living wight,
And high her burning torch set up in heaven bright.

50

When gentle Una saw the second fall
Of her deare knight, who wearie of long fight,
And faint through losse of bloud, moved not at all,
445 But lay as in a dreame of deepe delight,
Besmeard with pretious Balme, whose vertuous might
Did heale his wounds, and scorching heat alay,
Againe she stricken was with sore affright,
And for his safetie gan devoutly pray;
450 And watch the noyous° night, and wait for joyous day.   afflicting

51

The joyous day gan early to appeare,
And faire Aurora from the deawy bed
Of aged Tithone gan her selfe to reare,[3]
With rosie cheekes, for shame as blushing red;
455 Her golden lockes for haste were loosely shed
About her eares, when Una her did marke
Clymbe to her charet, all with flowers spred,
From heaven high to chase the chearelesse darke;
With merry note her loud salutes the mounting larke.

---

8. I.e., killed us. The tree described here is the Tree of Knowledge of Good and Evil in the Garden of Eden.
9. Precious.
1. A healing balm flowing from the tree of mercy is used by Seth to anoint Adam in the apocryphal Gospel of Nicodemus. This same balm is used later by Christ and is understood to be His blood. Christ's blood was shed to redeem mankind from eternal damnation.
2. I.e., a child of death.
3. Aurora is goddess of the dawn, Tithonus her husband ("aged" because he was granted everlasting life without everlasting youth).

52

460 Then freshly up arose the doughtie knight,
 All healéd of his hurts and woundés wide,
 And did himselfe to battell readie dight;
 Whose early foe awaiting him beside
 To have devourd, so soone as day he spyde,
465 When now he saw himselfe so freshly reare,
 As if late fight had nought him damnifyde,° injured
 He woxe dismayd, and gan his fate to feare;
Nathlesse° with wonted rage he him advauncéd neare. nevertheless

53

 And in his first encounter, gaping wide,
470 He thought attonce him to have swallowed quight,
 And rusht upon him with outragious pride;
 Who him r'encountring fierce, as hauke in flight,
 Perforce rebutted° backe. The weapon bright drove
 Taking advantage of his open jaw,
475 Ran through his mouth with so importune° might, violent
 That deepe emperst his darksome hollow maw,
And back retyrd, his life bloud forth with all did draw.

54

 So downe he fell, and forth his life did breath,
 That vanisht into smoke and cloudés swift;
480 So downe he fell, that th' earth him underneath
 Did grone, as feeble so great load to lift;
 So downe he fell, as an huge rockie clift,
 Whose false° foundation waves have washt away, insecure
 With dreadfull poyse° is from the mayneland rift, falling weight
485 And rolling downe, great Neptune doth dismay;
So downe he fell, and like an heapéd mountaine lay.

55

 The knight himselfe even trembled at his fall,
 So huge and horrible a masse it seemed;
 And his deare Ladie, that beheld it all,
490 Durst not approch for dread, which she misdeemed,° misjudged
 But yet at last, when as the direfull feend
 She saw not stirre, off-shaking vaine affright,
 She nigher drew, and saw that joyous end:
 Then God she praysd, and thankt her faithfull knight,
495 That had atchieved so great a conquest by his might.

Canto XII

Faire Una to the Redcrosse knight
betrouthéd is with joy:
Though false Duessa it to barre
her false sleights doe imploy.

1

Behold I see the haven nigh at hand,
 To which I meane my wearie course to bend;

Vere the maine shete, and beare up with the land,[4]
The which afore is fairely to be kend,°   recognized
5 And seemeth safe from stormes, that may offend;
There this faire virgin wearie of her way
Must landed be, now at her journeyes end:
There eke my feeble barke° a while may stay,   ship
Till merry wind and weather call her thence away.

2

10 Scarsely had Phoebus in the glooming East
Yet harnesséd his firie-footed teeme,
Ne reard above the earth his flaming creast,
When the last deadly smoke aloft did steeme,
That signe of last outbreathéd life did seeme
15 Unto the watchman on the castle wall;
Who thereby dead that balefull Beast did deeme,
And to his Lord and Ladie lowd gan call,
To tell, how he had seene the Dragons fatall fall.

3

Uprose with hastie joy, and feeble speed
20 That aged Sire, the Lord of all that land,
And lookéd forth, to weet, if true indeede
Those tydings were, as he did understand,
Which whenas true by tryall he out fond,
He bad to open wyde his brazen gate,
25 Which long time had bene shut, and out of hond[5]
Proclayméd joy and peace through all his state;
For dead now was their foe, which them forrayéd late.[6]

4

Then gan triumphant Trompets sound on hie,
That sent to heaven the ecchoéd report
30 Of their new joy, and happie victorie
Gainst him, that had them long opprest with tort,°   wrong
And fast imprisonéd in siegéd fort.
Then all the people, as in solemne feast,
To him assembled with one full consort,[7]
35 Rejoycing at the fall of that great beast,
From whose eternall bondage now they were releast.

5

Forth came that auncient Lord and aged Queene,
Arayd in antique robes downe to the ground,
And sad° habiliments right well beseene;°   dignified/proper
40 A noble crew about them waited round
Of sage and sober Peres, all gravely gownd;
Whom farre before did march a goodly band
Of tall young men, all hable armes to sownd,[8]
But now they laurell braunches bore in hand;
45 Glad signe of victorie and peace in all their land.

---

4. Release the mainsail line and sail toward the land. The metaphor in this
stanza echoes many classical authors and
Chaucer's *Troilus and Criseyde* (II.1–7).

5. Straightway.
6. Had recently ravaged.
7. All together.
8. Able to fight with weapons.

6

Unto that doughtie Conquerour they came,
   And him before themselves prostrating low,
   Their Lord and Patrone loud did him proclame,
   And at his feet their laurell boughes did throw.
50 Soone after them all dauncing on a row
   The comely virgins came, with girlands dight,
   As fresh as flowres in medow greene do grow,
   When morning deaw upon their leaves doth light:
And in their hands sweet Timbrels° all upheld   *tambourines*
   on hight.

7

55 And them before, the fry° of children young   *crowd*
   Their wanton° sports and childish mirth did play,   *playful*
   And to the Maydens sounding tymbrels sung
   In well attunéd notes, a joyous lay,
   And made delightfull musicke all the way,
60 Untill they came, where that faire virgin stood;
   As faire Diana in fresh sommers day
   Beholds her Nymphes, enraunged in shadie wood,
Some wrestle, some do run, some bathe in christall flood.

8

So she beheld those maydens meriment
65 With chearefull vew; who when to her they came,
   Themselves to ground with gratious humblesse bent,
   And her adored by honorable name,
   Lifting to heaven her everlasting fame:
   Then on her head they set a girland greene,
70 And crownéd her twixt earnest and twixt game; [9]
   Who in her selfe-resemblance well beseene,[1]
Did seeme such, as she was, a goodly maiden Queene.

9

And after all, the raskall many° ran,   *mob*
   Heapéd together in rude rablement,
75 To see the face of that victorious man:
   Whom all admired, as from heaven sent,
   And gazd upon with gaping wonderment.
   But when they came, where that dead Dragon lay,
   Stretcht on the ground in monstrous large extent,
80 The sight with idle° feare did them dismay,   *baseless*
Ne durst approch him nigh, to touch, or once assay.

10

Some feard, and fled; some feard and well it faynd;
   One that would wiser seeme, then all the rest,
   Warnd him not touch, for yet perhaps remaynd
85 Some lingring life within his hollow brest,
   Or in his wombe might lurke some hidden nest
   Of many Dragonets, his fruitfull seed;
   Another said, that in his eyes did rest
   Yet sparckling fire, and bad thereof take heed;
90 Another said, he saw him move his eyes indeed.

---

9. I.e., half in fun.   1. I.e., looking appropriately like herself.

11

One mother, when as her foolehardie chyld
  Did come too neare, and with his talants play,
  Halfe dead through feare, her litle babe revyld,°   *scolded*
  And to her gossips° gan in counsell say;   *women friends*
95   "How can I tell, but that his talants may
  Yet scratch my sonne, or rend his tender hand?"
  So diversly themselves in vaine they fray;°   *scare*
  Whiles some more bold, to measure him nigh stand,
To prove° how many acres he did spread of land.   *determine*

12

100 Thus flockéd all the folke him round about,
  The whiles that hoarie king, with all his traine,
  Being arrivéd, where that champion stout
  After his foes defeasance° did remaine,   *defeat*
  Him goodly greetes, and faire does entertaine,
105   With princely gifts of yvorie and gold,
  And thousand thankes him yeelds for all his paine.
  Then when his daughter deare he does behold,
Her dearely doth imbrace, and kisseth manifold.°   *many times*

13

And after to his Pallace he them brings,
110   With shaumes,[2] and trompets, and with Clarions sweet;
  And all the way the joyous people sings,
  And with their garments strowes the pavéd street:
  Whence mounting up, they find purveyance° meet   *provisions*
  Of all, that royall Princes court became,°   *suited*
115   And all the floore was underneath their feet
  Bespred with costly scarlot of great name,[3]
On which they lowly sit, and fitting purpose frame.

14

What needs me tell their feast and goodly guize,°   *mode of life*
  In which was nothing riotous nor vaine?
120   What needs of daintie dishes to devize,°   *talk*
  Of comely services, or courtly trayne?
  My narrow leaves cannot in them containe
  The large discourse[4] of royall Princes state.
  Yet was their manner then but bare and plaine:
125   For th' antique world excesse and pride did hate;[5]
Such proud luxurious pompe is swollen up but late.

15

Then when with meates and drinkes of every kinde
  Their fervent appetites they quenchéd had,
  That auncient Lord gan fit occasion finde,
130   Of straunge adventures, and of perils sad,
  Which in his travell him befallen had,
  For to demaund of his renowméd guest:
  Who then with utt'rance grave, and count'nance sad,
  From point to point, as is before exprest,
135 Discourst his voyage long, according his request.

---

2. Ancient wind instrument like an oboe.
3. I.e., famous scarlet cloth.
4. I.e., full description.
5. The question of "excesse" will be paramount in Book II, "The Legend of Sir Guyon, or of Temperance."

16

Great pleasure mixt with pittifull° regard,   *sympathetic*
   That godly King and Queene did passionate,[6]
   Whiles they his pittifull adventures heard,
   That oft they did lament his lucklesse state,
140 And often blame the too importune fate,
   That heapd on him so many wrathfull wreakes:°   *injuries*
   For never gentle knight, as he of late,
   So tosséd was in fortunes cruell freakes;
And all the while salt teares bedeawd the hearers cheaks.

17

145 Then said that royall Pere in sober wise:
   "Deare Sonne, great beene the evils, which ye bore
   From first to last in your late enterprise,
   That I note,° whether prayse, or pitty more: *know not*
   For never living man, I weene, so sore
150 In sea of deadly daungers was distrest;
   But since now safe ye seiséd° have the shore,   *reached*
   And well arrivéd are (high God be blest),
Let us devize of ease and everlasting rest."

18

"Ah dearest Lord," said then that doughty knight,
155 "Of ease or rest I may not yet devize;
   For by the faith, which I to armes have plight,
   I bounden am streight after this emprize,°   *enterprise*
   As that your daughter can ye well advize,
   Backe to returne to that great Faerie Queene,
160 And her to serve six yeares in warlike wize,
   Gainst that proud Paynim king, that workes her teene:°   *sorrow*
Therefore I ought crave pardon, till I there have beene."[7]

19

"Unhappie falles that hard necessitie,"
   Quoth he, "the troubler of my happie peace,
165 And vowéd foe of my felicitie;
   Ne I against the same can justly preace:°   *press*
   But since that band° ye cannot now release,   *obligation*
   Nor doen undo (for vowes may not be vaine),
   Soone as the terme of those six yeares shall cease,
170 Ye then shall hither backe returne againe,
The marriage to accomplish vowd betwixt you twain.

20

"Which for my part I covet to performe,
   In sort as through the world I did proclame,
   That who so kild that monster most deforme,
175 And him in hardy battaile overcame,
   Should have mine onely daughter to his Dame,°   *wife*

---

6. I.e., did feel and express.
7. That the marriage of Redcrosse and Una cannot be made final here and now signifies primarily that the final Christian triumph, the marriage of Christ and the true church will be achieved only at the end of time, the Day of Judgment. Meanwhile, the struggle against evil (and the Roman Church) continues.

And of my kingdome heire apparaunt bee:
Therefore since now to thee perteines the same,
By dew desert of noble chevalree,
180 Both daughter and eke kingdome, lo I yield to thee."

21

Then forth he calléd that his daughter faire,
The fairest Un' his onely daughter deare,
His onely daughter, and his onely heyre;
Who forth proceeding with sad° sober cheare,°   *grave/countenance*
185 As bright as doth the morning starre appeare
Out of the East, with flaming lockes bedight,°   *bedecked*
To tell that dawning day is drawing neare,
And to the world does bring long wishéd light;
So faire and fresh that Lady shewd her selfe in sight.

22

190 So faire and fresh, as freshest flowre in May;
For she had layd her mournefull stole aside,
And widow-like sad wimple° throwne away,   *veil*
Wherewith her heavenly beautie she did hide,
Whiles on her wearie journey she did ride;
195 And on her now a garment she did weare,
All lilly white, withoutten spot, or pride,°   *ornament*
That seemed like silke and silver woven neare,°   *tightly*
But neither silke nor silver therein did appeare.[8]

23

The blazing brightnesse of her beauties beame,
200 And glorious light of her sunshyny face[9]
To tell, were as to strive against the streame.
My ragged rimes are all too rude and bace,
Her heavenly lineaments for to enchace.°   *adorn*
Ne wonder; for her owne deare lovéd knight,
205 All° were she dayly with himselfe in place,   *although*
Did wonder much at her celestiall sight:
Oft had he seene her faire, but never so faire dight.

24

So fairely dight, when she in presence came,
She to her Sire made humble reverence,
210 And bowéd low, that her right well became,
And added grace unto her excellence:
Who with great wisdome, and grave eloquence
Thus gan to say. But eare° he thus had said,   *ere*
With flying speede, and seeming great pretence,°   *importance*
215 Came running in, much like a man dismaid,
A Messenger with letters, which his message said.

---

8. "The marriage of the Lamb is come, and his wife hath made herself ready. And to her was granted that she should be arrayed in fine linen, clean and white: for the fine linen is the righteousness of saints" (Revelation xix.7–8).
9. Revelation xxi.9, 11 describes the New Jerusalem as "the bride, the Lamb's wife * * * her light was like unto a store most precious." Contemplation showed Redcrosse the "real New Jerusalem" (xi.505–13); by these allusions, Spenser associates it with Una and her father's kingdom, Eden (now restored).

25

All in the open hall amazéd stood,
    At suddeinnesse of that unwarie° sight,   *unexpected*
    And wondred at his breathlesse hastie mood.
But he for nought would stay his passage right°   *direct*
    Till fast° before the king he did alight;   *close*
    Where falling flat, great humblesse he did make,
    And kist the ground, whereon his foot was pight;°   *placed*
    Then to his hands that writ° he did betake,   *document*
Which he disclosing, red thus, as the paper spake.

26

"To thee, most mighty king of Eden faire,
    Her greeting sends in these sad lines addrest,
    The wofull daughter, and forsaken heire
    Of that great Emperour of all the West;
    And bids thee be advizéd for the best,
    Ere thou thy daughter linck in holy band
    Of wedlocke to that new unknowen guest:
For he already plighted his right hand
Unto another love, and to another land.

27

"To me sad mayd, or rather widow sad,
    He was affiauncéd long time before,
    And sacred pledges he both gave, and had,
    False erraunt knight, infamous, and forswore:
    Witnesse the burning Altars, which° he swore,   *by which*
    And guiltie heavens of[1] his bold perjury,
    Which though he hath polluted oft of yore,
Yet I to them for judgement just do fly,
And them conjure t' avenge this shamefull injury.

28

"Therefore since mine he is, or° free or bond,   *whether*
    Or false or trew, or living or else dead,
    Withhold, O soveraine Prince, your hasty hond
    From knitting league with him, I you aread;°   *advise*
    Ne wene° my right with strength adowne to tread,   *think*
    Through weakenesse of my widowhed, or woe:
    For truth is strong, her rightfull cause to plead,
And shall find friends, if need requireth soe,
So bids thee well to fare, Thy neither friend, nor foe, Fidessa."

29

When he these bitter byting words had red,
    The tydings straunge did him abashéd make,
    That still he sate long time astonishéd
    As in great muse, ne word to creature spake.
    At last his solemne silence thus he brake,
    With doubtfull eyes fast fixéd on his guest:
    "Redoubted knight, that for mine onely sake
Thy life and honour late adventurest,
Let nought be hid from me, that ought to be exprest.

1. I.e., and heavens polluted by.

30

"What meane these bloudy vowes, and idle threats,
  Throwne out from womanish impatient mind?
  What heavens? what altars? what enragéd heates
265 Here heapéd up with termes of love unkind,°   *unnatural*
  My conscience cleare with guilty bands[2] would bind?
  High God be witnesse, that I guiltlesse ame.
  But if your selfe, Sir knight, ye faultie find,
  Or wrappéd be in loves of former Dame,
270 With crime do not it cover, but disclose the same."

31

To whom the Redcrosse knight this answere sent,
  "My Lord, my King, be nought hereat dismayd,
  Till well ye wote by grave intendiment,[3]
  What woman, and wherefore doth me upbrayd
275 With breach of love, and loyalty betrayd.
  It was in my mishaps, as hitherward
  I lately traveild, that unwares I strayd
  Out of my way, through perils straunge and hard;
That day should faile me, ere I had them all declard.

32

280 "There did I find, or rather I was found
  Of this false woman, that Fidessa hight,
  Fidessa hight the falsest Dame on ground,
  Most false Duessa, royall richly dight,
  That easie was t' invegle° weaker sight: *deceive*
285 Who by her wicked arts, and wylie skill,
  Too fasle and strong for earthly skill or might,
  Unwares me wrought unto her wicked will,
And to my foe betrayd, when least I fearéd ill."

33

Then steppéd forth the goodly royall Mayd,
290 And on the ground her selfe prostrating low,
  With sober countenaunce thus to him sayd:
  "O pardon me, my soveraigne Lord, to show
  The secret treasons, which of late I know
  To have bene wroght by that false sorceresse.
295 She onely she it is, that earst did throw
  This gentle knight into so great distresse,
That death him did awaite in dayly wretchednesse.

34

"And now it seemes, that she subornéd hath
  This craftie messenger with letters vaine,
300 To worke new woe and improvided scath,[4]
  By breaking of the band betwixt us twaine;
  Wherein she uséd hath the practicke paine[5]
  Of this false footman, clokt with simplenesse,
  Whom if ye please for to discover plaine,
305 Ye shall him Archimago find, I ghesse,
The falsest man alive; who tries shall find no lesse."

2. I.e., bonds of guilt.
3. I.e., serious investigation.
4. Unexpected harm.
5. Treacherous skill.

35

The king was greatly movéd at her speach,
  And all with suddein indignation fraight,°   *laden*
  Bad° on that Messenger rude hands to reach.   *bade*
310 Eftsoones the Gard, which on his state did wait,
  Attacht that faitor° false, and bound him strait: *impostor*
  Who seeming sorely chaufféd° at his band,   *angered*
  As chainéd Beare, whom cruell dogs do bait,
  With idle force did faine them to withstand,
315 And often semblaunce made to scape out of their hand.

36

But they him layd full low in dungeon deepe,
  And bound him hand and foote with yron chains.
  And with continuall watch did warely keepe;
  Who then would thinke, that by his subtile trains
320 He could escape fowle death or deadly paines?[6]
  Thus when that Princes wrath was pacifide,
  He gan renew the late forbidden banes,[7]
  And to the knight his daughter deare he tyde,
With sacred rites and vowes for ever to abyde.

37

325 His owne two hands the holy knots did knit,
  That none but death for ever can devide;
  His owne two hands, for such a turne most fit,
  The housling° fire did kindle and provide,   *sacramental*
  And holy water thereon sprinckled wide;[8]
330 At which the bushy Teade° a groome did light,   *marriage torch*
  And sacred lampe in secret chamber hide,
  Where it should not be quenchéd day nor night,
For feare of evill fates, but burnen ever bright.

38

Then gan they sprinckle all the posts with wine,
335 And made great feast to solemnize that day;
  They all perfumde with frankensense divine,
  And precious odours fetcht from far away,
  That all the house did sweat with great aray:
  And all the while sweete Musicke did apply
40 Her curious° skill, the warbling notes to play,   *intricate*
  To drive away the dull Melancholy;
The whiles one sung a song of love and jollity.

39

During the which there was an heavenly noise
  Heard sound through all the Pallace pleasantly,

---

6. "And he laid hold on the dragon, that old serpent, which is the Devil, and Satan, and bound him a thousand years, And cast him into the bottomless pit, and shut him up, and set a seal upon him, that he should deceive the nations no more, till the thousand years should be fulfilled: and after that he must be loosed a little season" (Revelation xx.2–3).
7. Banns, i.e., announcements of marriage.

8. So marriages in ancient times were solemnized with sacramental fire and water. Plutarch (*Roman Questions* 1) explains the practice on four counts, of which two may especially have interested Spenser: (a) fire is masculine and active, water feminine and relatively passive; (b) as fire and water are most usefully productive in combination, so the joining of male and female in marriage appropriately completes society.

345 Like as it had bene many an Angels voice,
    Singing before th' eternall majesty,
    In their trinall triplicities[9] on hye;
    Yet wist no creature, whence that heavenly sweet°   *delight*
    Proceeded, yet each one felt secretly°   *inwardly*
350 Himselfe thereby reft of his sences meet,°   *proper*
And ravishéd with rare impression in his sprite.[10]

40

Great joy was made that day of young and old,
    And solemne feast proclaimd throughout the land,
    That their exceeding merth may not be told:
355 Suffice it heare by signes to understand
    The usuall joyes at knitting of loves band.
    Thrise happy man the knight himselfe did hold,
    Posséssed of his Ladies hart and hand,
    And ever, when his eye did her behold,
360 His heart did seeme to melt in pleasures manifold.

41

Her joyous presence and sweet company
    In full content he there did long enjoy,
    Ne wicked envie, ne vile gealosy
    His deare delights were able to annoy:
365 Yet swimming in that sea of blisfull joy,
    He nought forgot, how he whilome had sworne,
    In case he could that monstrous beast destroy,
    Unto his Faerie Queene backe to returne:
The which he shortly did, and Una left to mourne.

42

370 Now strike your sailes ye jolly Mariners,
    For we be come unto a quiet rode,°   *harbor*
    Where we must land some of our passengers,
    And light this wearie vessell of her lode.
    Here she a while may make her safe abode,
375 Till she repairéd have her tackles spent,°   *worn out*
    And wants supplide. And then againe abroad
    On the long voyage whereto she is bent:
Well may she speede and fairely finish her intent.

9. The "trinall triplicities" are the nine angelic orders, divided, according to the pseudo-Areopagite, into three groups of three, the whole hierarchy corresponding to the nine spheres of the universe; what is heard in this stanza is, therefore, the music of the spheres.

10. Spirit. "Let us be glad and rejoice, and give honor to him: for the marriage of the Lamb is come" (Revelation xix.6). In Revelation, the marriage of Christ and the New Jerusalem signalizes the general redemption.

From The Second Booke of the Faerie Queene[1]

CONTAYNING

The Legend of Sir Guyon,

OR

OF TEMPERAUNCE

1

Right well I wote° most mighty Soveraine,   *know*
 That all this famous antique history,
 Of some th'aboundance of an idle braine
 Will judgéd be, and painted forgery,
5 Rather then matter of just° memory,   *well-founded*
 Sith none, that breatheth living aire, does know,
 Where is that happy land of Faéry,
 Which I so much do vaunt, yet no where show,
But vouch° antiquities, which no body can know. *assert*

2

10 But let that man with better sence advize,° *consider*
 That of the world least part to us is red:° *read, revealed*
 And dayly how through hardy enterprize,
 Many great Regions are discoveréd,
 Which to late age[2] were never mentionéd.
15 Who ever heard of th' Indian *Peru*?
 Or who in venturous vessell measuréd

1. Book II is the story of Guyon, who represents and becomes the virtue of Temperance (or moderation, self-control) as Redcross represented, and became, Holiness. Guyon's companion is a "palmer," a "sage and sober" pilgrim, who represents Reason, and accordingly is left behind on some adventures which lead Guyon on to sensuality. For example, though Guyon can overcome enemies which represent anger, fury, wrath, he is more vulnerable to the seductions of Acrasia's servant Phaedria, "modest Merth," who conducts him across her Idle Lake. He doesn't stay, but in this adventure he loses the help of the Palmer, Reason. There are not as many battles and jousts in Book II as in Book I, because Temperance is a virute which consists mainly of *not* doing things. The trials are appeals to the senses, so the eminent qualities of Book II are descriptive rather than narrative. Canto vii, the Cave of Mammon, corresponds roughly to the encounters with Orgoglio and Despair in Book I, but it is much more elaborately worked out and the atmosphere is especially notable. Guyon is not really tempted by Mammon's blandishments: there are some similarities here to the temptation of Christ by Satan. As Graham Hough says, (*A Preface to "The Faerie Queene,"* p. 157)

"Guyon never seems to be in danger from Mammon, and if he faints at the end it is not that his virtue has been shaken but that he is exhausted by long dwelling in a life-destroying atmosphere. The strength of the Mammon scenes partly depends on this; they depart from the conventional pattern of temptations presented and overcome to the subtler horror of a poisoned atmosphere, an air that suffocates while it repels." The Mammon episode gave Spenser the opportunity to present a trip to the underworld, conventional in the epic, and in typical Renaissance fashion he mixes classical and Christian motifs: among those seen in Hell are Tantalus and Pontius Pilate. Sir Guyon stays below three days, as Jonah had spent three days in the whale's belly and Jesus three days in the tomb. There is much of the old folklore element in the Cave of Mammon episode, also: Guyon must not eat anything while he is there, for fear an "ugly feend" who follows in his footsteps will tear him into a thousand pieces (stanzas 27 and 64). So Proserpina in the classical myth had to spend time in Hell because she ate something there, and in the ancient Eleusinian mystery rites initiates were followed by "furies" to make sure they followed the ritual exactly.
2. To recent times.

The Amazons huge river now found trew?
Or fruitfullest Virginia who did ever vew?[3]

3

Yet all these were, when no man did them know;
Yet have from wisest ages hidden beene:
And later times things more unknowne shall show.
Why then should witless man so much
    misweene°   *think wrongly*
That nothing is, but that which he hath seene?
What if within the Moones faire shining spheare?
What if in every other starre unseene
Of other worldes he happily° should heare?   *by chance*
He wonder would much more: yet such to some appeare.

4

Of Faerie lond yet if he more inquire,
By certaine signes here set in sundry place
He may it find; ne let him then admire,°   *wonder*
But yield his sence to be too blunt and bace,
That n'ote° without an hound fine footing trace.   *cannot*
And thou, O fairest Princesse under sky,
In this faire mirrhour maist behold thy face,
And thine owne realmes in lond of Faéry,
And in this antique Image[4] thy great auncestry.

5

The which O pardon me thus to enfold
In covert vele,[5] and wrap in shadowes light,
That feeble eyes your glory may behold,
Which else could not endure those beamés bright,
But would be dazled with exceeding light.
O pardon, and vouchsafe with patient eare
The brave adventures of this Faery knight
The good Sir Guyon gratiously to heare,
In whom great rule of Temp'raunce goodly doth appeare.

Canto VII [*The Cave of Mammon*]

Guyon findes Mammon in a delve,°   *pit, den*
   Sunning his threasure hore:°   *ancient*
  Is by him tempted, and led downe,
    To see his secret store.

1

As Pilot well expert in perilous wave,
That to a stedfast starre his course hath bent,
When foggy mistes, or cloudy tempests have

---

3. In 1584 Sir Walter Ralegh laid at the feet of the Virgin Queen his claim to newly discovered lands in North America; she named the country "Virginia." In the second edition of *The Faerie* *Queene* the dedication calls Elizabeth "Queene of England, Fraunce and Ireland, *and of Virginia*."
4. I.e., the poem.
5. Concealing veil.

The faithfull light of that faire lampe yblent,° *blinded*
5   And cover'd heaven with hideous dreriment,
Upon his card° and compas firmes his eye, *chart, map*
The maisters of his long experiment,° *experience*
And to them does the steddy helme apply,
Bidding his wingéd vessell fairely forward fly.

2

10 So Guyon having lost his trusty guide,[6]
Late left beyond that Ydle lake, proceedes
Yet on his way, of none accompanide;
And evermore himselfe with comfort feedes,
Of his owne vertues, and prayse-worthy deedes.
15   Long so he yode,° yet no adventure found, *went*
Which fame of her shrill trompet worthy reedes:° *considers*
For still he traveild through wide wastfull ground,
That nought but desert wildernesse shew'd all around.

3

At last he came unto a gloomy glade,
20   Cover'd with boughes and shrubs from heavens light,
Whereas he sitting found in secret shade
An uncouth, salvage,° and uncivile° wight, *savage / wild*
Of griesly hew, and fowle ill favour'd sight;
His face with smoke was tand, and eyes were bleard,
25   His head and beard with sout° were ill bedight,° *soot / covered*
His cole-blacke hands did seeme to have been seard
In smithes fire-spitting forge, and nayles like clawes appeard.

4

His yron coate all overgrowne with rust,
Was underneath envelopéd with gold,
30   Whose glistring glosse darkned with filthy dust,
Well it appearéd, to have beene of old
A worke of rich entayle,° and curious mould,[7] *carving*
Woven with antickes° and wild Imagery: *fantastic figures*
And in his lap a masse of coyne he told,° *counted*
35   And turned upsidowne, to feed his eye
And covetous desire with his huge threasury.

5

And round about him lay on every side
Great heapes of gold, that never could be spent:
Of which some were rude owre,° not purifide *ore*
40   Of Mulcibers devouring element;[8]
Some others were new driven,° and distent° *beaten / drawn out*
Into great Ingoes,° and to wedges square; *ingots*
Some in round plates withouten moniment;° *impression*
But most were stampt, and in their metall bare
45 The antique shapes of kings and kesars° straunge and rare. *caesars*

---

6. Guyon's guide, the Palmer, was left
behind when Phaedria ferried Guyon
over the Idle Lake in Canto vi.

7. Intricate design.
8. Mulciber, also known as Hephaestos
and Vulcan, was the classical god of fire.

6

Soone as he Guyon saw, in great affright
  And hast he rose, for to remove aside
  Those pretious hils from straungers envious sight,
  And downe them pouréd through an hole full wide,
50 Into the hollow earth, them there to hide.
  But *Guyon* lightly to him leaping, stayd
  His hand, that trembled, as one terrifyde;
  And though him selfe were at the sight dismayd,
Yet him perforce restrayed, and to him doubtfull sayd.

7

55 What art thou man, (if man at all thou art)
  That here in desert hast thin habitaunce,
  And these rich heapes of wealth doest hide apart
  From the worldes eye, and from her right usaunce?°   *usage*
  Thereat with staring eyes fixéd askaunce°   *as if*
60 In great disdaine, he answerd; Hardy Elfe,
  That darest vew my direfull countenaunce,
  I read° thee rash, and heedlesse of thy selfe,   *consider*
To trouble my still seate,° and heapes of pretious pelfe.°   *residence /*
                                                 plunder

8

God of the world and worldlings I me call,
65 Great Mammon, greatest god below the skye,
  That of my plenty poure out unto all,
  And unto none my graces do envye:°   *begrudge*
  Riches, renowme, and principality,
  Honour, estate, and all this worldés good,
70 For which men swinck° and sweat incessantly,   *labor*
  Fro me do flow into an ample flood,
And in the hollow earth have their eternall brood.°   *breeding place*

9

Wherefore if me thou deigne to serve and sew,°   *follow*
  At thy commaund lo all these mountaines bee;
75 Or if to thy great mind, or greedy vew
  All these may not suffise, there shall to thee
  Ten times so much be numbred francke and free.
  Mammon (said he) thy godheades vaunt° is vaine,   *boast*
  And idle offers of thy golden fee;°   *reward*
80 To them, that covet such eye-glutting gaine,
Proffer thy giftes, and fitter servaunts entertaine.

10

Me ill besits, that in der-doing° armes,   *courageous*
  And honours suit° my vowed dayes do spend,   *pursuit*
  Unto thy bounteous baytes, and pleasing charmes,
85 With which weake men thou witchest,° to attend: *bewitchest*
  Regard of worldly mucke doth fowly blend,°   *blind*
  And low abase the high heroicke spright,°   *spirit*

That joyes for crownes and kingdomes to contend;
Faire shields, gay steedes, bright armes be my delight:
90 Those be the riches fit for an advent'rous knight.

11

Vaine glorious Elfe (said he) doest not thou weet,° *know*
That money can thy wantes at will supply?
Sheilds, steeds, and armes, and all things for thee meet
It can purvay in twinckling of an eye;
95 And crownes and kingdomes to thee multiply.
Do not I kings create, and throw the crowne
Sometimes to him, that low in dust doth ly?
And him that raignd, into his rowme° thrust downe, *place*
And whom I lust,° do heape with glory and renowne? *please*

12

100 All otherwise (said he) I riches read,° *interpret*
And deeme them roote of all disquietnesse;
First got with guile, and then preserv'd with dread,
And after spent with pride and lavishnesse,
Leaving behind them griefe and heavinesse.
105 Infinite mischiefes of them do arize,
Strife, and debate, bloudshed, and bitternesse,
Outrageous wrong, and hellish covetize,° *covetousness*
That noble heart as great dishonour doth despize.

13

Ne thine be kingdomes, ne the scepters thine;
110 But realmes and rulers thou doest both confound,
And loyall truth to treason doest incline;
Witnesse the guiltlesse bloud pourd oft on ground,
The crownéd often slaine, the slayer cround,
The sacred Diademe in peeces rent,
115 And purple robe goréd with many a wound;
Castles surprizd, great cities sackt and brent:° *burned*
So mak'st thou kings, and gaynest wrongfull governement.

14

Long were to tell the troublous stormes, that tosse
The private state, and make the life unsweet:
120 Who° swelling sayles in Caspian sea doth crosse, *he who with*
And in frayle wood on Adrian° gulfe doth fleet,° *Adriatic / float*
Doth not, I weene, so many evils meet.
Then Mammon wexing wroth, And why then, said,
Are mortall men so fond° and undiscreet, *foolish*
125 So evill thing to seeke unto their ayd,
And having not complaine, and having it upbraid?

15

Indeede (quote he) through fowle intemperaunce,
Frayle men are oft capitiv'd to covetise:
But would they thinke, with how small allowaunce
130 Untroubled Nature doth her selfe suffise,

Such superfluities they would despise,
Which with sad cares empeach° our native joyes: *impair*
At the well head the purest streames arise:
But mucky filth his braunching armes annoyes,
135 And with uncomely weedes the gentle wave accloyes°.   *clogs*

16

The antique° world, in his first flowring youth,[9]   *ancient*
    Found no defect in his Creatours grace,
    But with glad thankes, and ureprovéd truth,
    The gifts of soveraigne bountie did embrace:
140 Like Angels life was then mens happy cace;
    But later ages pride, like corn-fed steed,
    Abusd her plenty, and fat swolne encreace
    To all licentious lust, and gan exceed
The measure of her meane,[1] and naturall first need.

17

145 Then gan a curséd hand the quiet wombe
    Of his great Grandmother with steele to wound,
    And the hid treasures in her sacred tombe,
    With Sacriledge to dig. Therein he found
    Fountaines of gold and silver to abound,
150 Of which the matter of his huge desire
    And pompous pride eftsoones° he did compound;   *presently*
    Then avarice gan through his veines inspire°   *breathe*
His greedy flames, and kindled life-devouring fire.

18

Sonne (said he then) let be thy bitter scorne,
155 And leave the rudenesse of that antique age
    To them, that liv'd therein in state forlorne;
    Thou that doest live in later times, must wage°   *barter*
    Thy workes for wealth, and life for gold engage.°   *hire out*
    If then thee list my offred grace to use,
160 Take what thou please of all this surplusage;
    If thee list not, leave have thou to refuse:
But thing refused, do not afterward accuse.

19

Me list not (said the Elfin knight) receave
    Thing offred, till I know it well be got,
165 Ne wote° I, but thou didst these goods bereave°   *know / remove*
    From rightfull owner by unrighteous lot,[2]
    Or that bloud guiltinesse or guile them blot.
    Perdy (quoth he) yet never eye did vew,
    Ne toung did tell,° ne hand these handled not,   *count*
170 But safe I have them kept in secret mew,°   *cave*
From heavens sight, and powre of all which them pursew.

---

9. Stanzas 16 and 17 present a traditional picture of the Golden Age, before
technology, pride, and avarice had
turned man into what he now is. The
next ages, Silver, Brazen, and Iron (the
present) showed gradual deterioration.
1. Limit of moderation.
2. Partition of plunder.

20

What secret place (quoth he) can safely hold
  So huge a masse, and hide from heavens eye?
  Or where hast thou thy wonne,° that so much gold   *home*
175 Thou canst preserve from wrong and robbery?
Come thou (quoth he) and see. So by and by
Through that thicke covert he him led, and found
A darkesome way, which no man could descry,°   *discover*
That deepe descended through the hollow ground,
180 And was with dread and horrour compasséd around.

21

At length they came into a larger space,
  That stretcht it selfe into an ample plaine,
  Through which a beaten broad high way did trace,
  That streight did lead to Plutoes griesly raine:[3]
185 By that wayes side, there sate infernall Payne,
  And fast beside him sat tumultuous Strife:
  The one in hand an yron whip did straine,°   *grip*
  The other brandishéd a bloudy knife,
And both did gnash their teeth, and both did threaten life.

22

190 On thother side in one consort° there sate,   *group*
  Cruell Revenge, and rancorous Despight,
  Disloyall Treason, and hart-burning Hate,
  But gnawing Gealosie out of their sight
  Sitting alone, his bitter lips did bight,
195 And trembling Feare still to and fro did fly,
  And found no place, where safe he shroud° him might,   *hide*
  Lamenting Sorrow did in darknesse lye,
And Shame his ugly face did hide from living eye.

23

And over them sad Horrour with grim hew,°   *aspect*
200 Did alwayes sore, beating his yron wings;
  And after him Owles and Night-ravens flew,
  The hatefull messengers of heavy° things,   *doleful*
  Of death and dolour telling sad tidings;
  Whiles sad Celeno,[4] sitting on a clift,
205 A song of bale° and bitter sorrow sings,   *misfortune*
  That hart of flint a sunder could have rift:°   *torn*
Which having ended, after him she flyeth swift.

24

All these before the gates of Pluto lay,
  By whom the passing, spake unto them nought.
210 But th' Elfin knight with wonder all the way

3. I.e., Pluto's horrible kingdom. Mammon was associated in Christian thought with wealth. According to the Sermon on the Mount, "where your treasure is, there will your heart be also. Ye cannot serve God and Mammon." The classical Plutus, god of wealth, and Pluto, god of the underworld, were often confused.
4. Celeno was a harpy in Virgil's *Aeneid* III.245–46. Harpies had the faces and breasts of women, but the wings and talons of birds. They were monsters of ill omen.

Did feed his eyes, and fild his inner thought.
At last him to a litle dore he brought,
That to the gate of Hell, which gaped wide,
Was next adjoyning, ne them parted ought:[5]
215 Betwixt them both was but a litle stride,
  That did the house of Richesse from hell-mouth divide.

25

Before the dore sat selfe-consuming Care,
  Day and night keeping wary watch and ward,
  For feare least Force or Fraud should unaware
220 Breake in, and spoile° the treasure there in gard: *steal*
  Ne would he suffer Sleepe once thither-ward
  Approch, albe° his drowsie den were next;   *although*
  For next to death is Sleepe to be compard:
  Therefore his house is unto his annext;
225 Here Sleep, there Richesse, and Hel-gate them both betwext.

26

So soone as Mammon there arriv'd, the dore
  To him did open, and affoorded way;
  Him followed eke Sir Guyon evermore,
  Ne darkenesse him, ne daunger might dismay.
230 Soone as he entred was, the dore streight way
  Did shut, and from behind it forth there lept
  An ugly feend, more fowle then dismall day,[6]
  The which with monstrous stalke behind him stept,
  And ever as he went, dew° watch upon him kept.   *due, proper*

27

235 Well hopéd he, ere long that hardy guest,
  If ever covetous hand, or lustfull eye,
  Or lips he layd on thing, that likt° him best,   *pleased*
  Or ever sleepe his eye-strings did untye,
  Should be his pray. And therefore still° on hye   *always*
240 He over him did hold his cruell clawes,
  Threatning with greedy gripe to do him dye
  And rend in peeces with his ravenous pawes,
  If ever he transgrest the fatall Stygian lawes.[7]

28

That houses forme within was rude and strong
245 Like an huge cave, hewne out of rocky clift,
  From whose rough vaut the ragged breaches° hong,   *stalactites*
  Embost with massy gold of glorious gift,°   *quality*
  And with rich metall loaded every rift,
  That heavy ruine they did seeme to threat;
250 And over them Arachne[8] high did lift
  Her cunning web, and spred her subtile net,
  Enwrappéd in fowle smoke and clouds more blacke then jet.

---

5. Nothing separated them.
6. Latin *dies mali*, "evil days." There were two in each month, the first and the seventh from last.
7. Laws of the underworld, so called from Styx, its boundary.
8. For her arrogance and excessive pride in her weaving, she was turned into a spider by Athena (Ovid, *Metamorphoses*).

29

Both roofe, and floore, and wals were all of gold,
  But overgrowne with dust and old decay,
255 And hid in darkenesse, that none could behold
  The hew thereof: for vew of chearefull day
  Did never in that house it selfe display,
  But a faint shadow of uncertain light;
  Such as a lamp, whose life does fade away:
260 Or as the Moone cloathed with clowdy night,
Does shew to him, that walkes in feare and sad affright.

30

In all that rowme was nothing to be seene,
  But huge great yron chests and coffers strong,
  All bard with double bends,° that none could   *bands/*
  weene°   *think*
265 Them to efforce° by violence or wrong;   *force open*
  On every side they placéd were along.
  But all the ground with sculs was scatteréd,
  And dead mens bones, which round about were flong,
  Whose lives, it seeméd, whilome° there were shed,   *in the past*
270 And their vile carcases now left unburiéd.

31

They forward passe, ne Guyon yet spoke word,
  Till that they came unto an yron dore,
  Which to them opened of his owne accord,
  And shewd of richesse such exceeding store,
275 As eye of man did never see before;
  Ne ever could within one place be found,
  Though all the wealth, which is, or was of yore,
  Could gathered be through all the world around,
And that above were added to that under ground.

32

280 The charge thereof unto a covetous Spright
  Commaunded was, who thereby did attend,
  And warily awaited day and night,
  From other covetous feends it to defend,
  Who it to rob and ransacke did intend.
285 Then Mammon turning to that warriour, said;
  Loe here the worldés blis, loe here the end,
  To which all men do ayme, rich to be made:
Such grace now to be happy, is before thee laid.

33

Certes (said he) I n'ill° thine offred grace,   *will not accept*
290 Ne to be made so° happy do intend: *thus*
  Another blis before mine eyes I place,
  Another happinesse, another end.
  To them, that list, these base regardes° I lend:° *aims / relinquish*
  But I in armes, and in atchievements brave,
295 Do rather choose my flitting houres to spend,
  And to be Lord of those that riches have,
Then them to have my selfe, and be their servile sclave.

34

Thereat the feend his gnashing teeth did grate,
  And griev'd, so long to lacke his greedy pray;[9]
300 For well he weenéd,° that so glorious bayte   *supposed*
  Would tempt his guest, to take thereof assay:°   *trial*
  Had he so doen, he had him snatcht away,
  More light then Culver° in the Faulcons fist.   *dove*
  Eternall God thee save from such decay.°   *ruin*
305 But whenas Mammon saw his purpose mist,
  Him to entrap unwares another way he wist.°   *thought of*

35

Thence forward he him led, and shortly brought
  Unto another rowme, whose dore forthright,
  To him did open, as it had beene taught:
310 Therein an hundred raunges weren pight,°   *placed*
  And hundred fornaces all burning bright;
  By every fornace many feends did bide,
  Deforméd creatures, horrible in sight,
  And every feend his busie paines applide,
315 To melt the golden metall, ready to be tride.°   *refined*

36

One with great bellowes gathered filling aire,
  And with forst wind the fewell did inflame;
  Another did the dying bronds° repaire   *burning logs*
  With yron toungs, and sprinckled oft the same
320 With liquid waves, fiers Vulcans rage to tame,
  Who maistring them, renewd his former heat;
  Some scumd the drosse, that from the metall came;
  Some stird the molten owre with ladles great;
  And every one did swincke,° and every one did sweat. *work*

37

325 But when as earthly wight they present saw,
  Glistring in armes and battailous° aray,   *warlike*
  From their whot worke they did themselves withdraw
  To wonder at the sight: for till that day,
  They never creature saw, that came that way.
330 Their staring eyes sparckling with fervent fire,
  And ugly shapes did nigh the man dismay,
  That were it not for shame, he would retire,
  Till that him thus bespake their soveraigne Lord and sire.

38

Behold, thou Faeries sonne, with mortall eye,
335 That° living eye before did never see: *what*
  The thing, that thou didst crave so earnestly,
  To weet, whence all the wealth late shewd by mee,
  Proceeded, lo now is reveald to thee.
  Here is the fountaine of the worldés good:

9. To be denied for so long the prey he desired.

340 Now therefore, if thou wilt enrichéd bee,
     Avise thee° well, and chaunge thy wilfull mood,   *consider*
   Least thou perhaps hereafter wish, and be withstood.

                          39
  Suffise it then, thou Money God (quoth hee)
     That all thine idle offers I refuse.
345 All that I need I have; what needeth mee
     To covet more, then I have cause to use?
       With such vaine shewes thy worldlings vile abuse:°   *delude*
       But give me leave to follow mine emprise.°   *enterprise*
       Mammon was much displeasd, yet no'te° he chuse,   *might not*
350 But beare the rigour of his bold mesprise,°   *contempt*
   And thence him forward led, him further to entise.

                         40
He brought him through a darksome narrow strait,
     To a broad gate, all built of beaten gold:
     The gate was open, but therein did wait
355 A sturdy villein, striding stiffe and bold,
     As if that highest God defie he would;
     In his right hand an yron club he held,
     But he himselfe was all of golden mould,
     Yet had both life and sence, and well could weld°   *wield*
360 That curséd weapon, when his cruell foes he queld.°   *killed*

                         41
Disdayne he calléd was, and did disdaine
     To be so cald, and who so did him call:
     Sterne was his looke, and full of stomacke° vaine,   *arrogance*
     His portaunce° terrible, and stature tall,   *bearing*
365 Far passing th' hight of men terrestriall;
     Like an huge Gyant of the Titans race,
     That made him scorne all creatures great and small,
     And with his pride all others powre deface:°   *destroy*
   More fit amongst blacke fiendes, then men do have his place.

                         42
370 Soone as those glitterand° armes he did espye,   *glittering*
     That with their brightnesse made that darknesse light,
     His harmefull club he gan to hurtle° hye,   *brandish*
     And threaten batteill to the Faery knight;
     Who likewise gan himselfe to batteill dight,°   *prepare*
375 Till Mammon did his hasty hand withhold,
     And counseld him abstaine from perilous fight:
     For nothing might abash the villein bold,
   Ne mortall steele emperce his miscreated mould.

                         43
So having him with reason pacifide,
380 And the fiers Carle° commaunding to forbeare,   *churl*
     He brought him in. The rowme was large and wide,
     As it some Gyeld° or solemne Temple weare: *guild, guild-hall*

Many great golden pillours did upbeare
The massy roofe, and riches huge sustayne,
385 And every pillour deckéd was full deare°   richly
With crownes and Diademes, and titles vaine,
Which mortall Princes wore, whiles they on earth did rayne.

44

A route° of people there assembled were,   crowd
Of every sort and nation under skye,
390 Which with great uprore preacéd° to draw nere   pressed
To th' upper part, where was advancéd hye
A stately siege° of soveraigne majestye;   seat
And thereon sat a woman gorgeous gay,
And richly clad in robes of royaltye,
395 That never earthly Prince in such aray
His glory did enhaunce, and pompous pride display.

45

Her face right wondrous faire did seeme to bee,
That her broad beauties beam great brightness threw
Through the dim shade, that all men might it see:
400 Yet was not that same her owne native hew,
But wrought by art and counterfetted shew,
Thereby more lovers unto her to call;
Nath'lesse most heavenly faire in deed and vew
She by creation was, till she did fall;
405 Thenceforth she sought for helps, to cloke her crime withall.

46

There, as in glistring glory she did sit,
She held a great gold chaine ylincked well,[1]
Whose upper end to highest heaven was knit,
And lower part did reach to lowest Hell;
410 And all that preace° did round about her swell,   crowd
To catchen hold of that long chaine, thereby
To clime aloft, and others to excell:
That was Ambition, rash desire to sty,°   rise
And every lincke thereof a step of dignity.

47

415 Some thought to raise themselves to high degree,
By riches and unrighteous reward,
Some by close shouldring,[2] some by flatteree;
Others through friends, others for base regard;°   bribes
And all by wrong wayes for themselves prepard.
420 Those that were up themselves, kept others low,
Those that were low themselves, held others hard,
Ne suffred them to rise or greater grow,
But every one did strive his fellow downe to throw.

48

Which whenas Guyon saw, he gan inquire,
425 What meant that preace about that Ladies throne,

1. The golden chain reaching to heaven appears in the *Iliad* VIII.19–22. Renaissance mythographers such as Natalis Comes took it to represent ambition.
2. Thrusting aside.

And what she was that did so high aspire.
Him Mammon answeréd; That goodly one,
Whom all that folke with such contention,
Do flocke about, my deare, my daughter is;
430 Honour and dignitie from her alone,
Derivéd are, and all this worldés blis
For which ye men do strive: few get, but many mis.

49
And faire Philotimé[3] she rightly hight,°   *is called*
The fairest wight that wonneth° under skye,   *lives*
435 But that this darksome neather world her light
Doth dim with horrour and deformitie,
Worthy of heaven and hye felicitie,
From whence the gods have her for envy thrust:
But sith thou hast found favour in mine eye,
440 Thy spouse I will her make, if that thou lust,°   *wish*
That she may thee advance for workes and merites just.

50
Gramercy° Mammon (said the gentle knight)   *Thanks*
For so great grace and offred high estate;
But I, that am fraile flesh and earthly wight,
445 Unworthy match for such immortall mate
My selfe well wote, and mine unequall fate;
And were I not, yet is my trouth yplight,
And love avowed to other Lady late,°   *recently*
That to remove the same I have no might:
450 To chaunge love causelesse is reproch to warlike knight.

51
Mammon emmovéd was with inward wrath;
Yet forcing it to faine,[4] him forth thence led
Through griesly shadowes by a beaten path,
Into a gardin goodly garnishéd
455 With hearbs and fruits, whose kinds mote not be red:°   *told*
Not such, as earth out of her fruitfull woomb
Throwes forth to men, sweet and well savouréd,
But direfull deadly blacke both leafe and bloom,
Fit to adorne the dead, and decke the drery toombe.

52
460 There mournful Cypresse grew in greatest store,
And trees of bitter Gall, and Heben sad,
Dead sleeping Poppy, and blacke Hellebore,
Cold Coloquintida, and Tetra mad,
Mortall Samnitis, and Cicuta bad,[5]
465 With which th' unjust Atheniens made to dy
Wise Socrates, who thereof quaffing glad
Pourd out his life, and last Philosophy
To the faire Critias his dearest Belamy.°   *good friend*

---

3. The name, in Greek, means love of distinction or ambition.
4. Hiding his anger.

5. Cicuta is hemlock. The other plants mentioned are poisonous or associated with death.

53

The Gardin of Proserpina this hight;°   *is called*
470 And in the midst thereof a silver seat,[6]
     With a thicke Arber goodly over dight,°   *spread*
     In which she often vsd from open heat
     Her selfe to shroud, and pleasures to entreat.°   *enjoy*
     Next thereunto did grow a goodly tree,
475 With braunches broad dispred° and body great,   *spread out*
     Clothed with leaves, that none the wood mote see
And loaden all with fruit as thicke as it might bee.

54

Their fruit were golden apples glistring bright,
     That goodly was their glory to behold,
480 On earth like never grew, ne living wight
     Like ever saw, but° they from hence were sold;° *unless / brought*
     For those, which Hercules with conquest bold
     Got from great Atlas daughters, hence began,
     And planted there, did bring forth fruit of gold:
     And those with which th' Eubaean young man wan°   *won*
Swift Atalanta, when through craft he her out ran.[7]

55

Here also sprong that goodly golden fruit,
     With which Acontius got his lover trew,
     Whom he had long time sought with fruitlesse suit:
490 Here eke that famous golden Apple grew,
     The which emongst the gods false Ate threw;
     For which th' Idaean Ladies disagreed,
     Till partiall° Paris dempt° it Venus dew,   *prejudiced / judged*
     And had of her, faire **Helen** for his meed,°   *reward*
495 That many noble Greekes and Trojans made to bleed.

56

The warlike elfe, much wondred at this tree,
     So faire and great, that shadowed all the ground,
     And his broad braunches, laden with rich fee,°   *bounty*
     Did stretch themselves without the utmost bound
500 Of this great gardin, compast° with a mound,   *surrounded*
     Which over-hanging, they themselves did steepe,
     In a blacke flood which flow'd about it round;
     That is the river of Cocytus deepe,[8]
In which full many soules do endlesse waile and weepe.

57

505 Which to behold, he clomb up to the banke,
     And looking downe, saw many damned wights,

6. The seat (mentioned again in Stanza 63) on which Theseus was condemned to sit in endless sloth. See Book I, Canto v, Stanza 35.
7. The famous golden apples from classical legend mentioned in these two stanzas are the apples of the Hesperides which Hercules had to steal as his eleventh labor; the apples tossed to the ground by Melanion of Euboea, causing the swift Atalanta to stop and pick them up, thereby losing the race to him; and finally, the apple which Ate, goddess of discord, tossed into a feast of the gods. It was marked "For the Fairest," and a contest arose among Venus, Juno, and Minerva, here called "*Idaean* Ladies" because the decision in favor of Venus was made on Mt. Ida by the prejudiced ("partiall") shepherd Paris.
8. A river of hell. The name means "lamentation" in Greek.

In those sad waves, which direfull deadly stanke,
Plongéd continually of° cruell Sprights,   *by*
That with their pitteous cryes, and yelling shrights,°   *shrieks*
510 They made the further shore resounden wide:
Emongst the rest of those same ruefull sights,
One cursed creature, he by chaunce espide,
That drenchéd lay full deepe, under the Garden side.

58

Deepe was he drenchéd to the upmost chin,
515 Yet gaped still, as coveting to drinke
Of the cold liquor, which he waded in,
And stretching forth his hand, did often thinke
To reach the fruit, which grew upon the brincke:
But both the fruit from hand, and floud from mouth
520 Did flie abacke, and made him vainely swinke:°   *labor*
The whiles he sterv'd° with hunger and with   *starved /*
   drouth°   *thirst*
He daily dyde, yet never throughly° dyen couth.° *thoroughly / could*

59

The knight him seeing labour so in vaine,
Askt who he was, and what he ment thereby:
525 Who groning deepe, thus answerd him againe;
Most curséd of all creatures under skye,
Lo Tantalus, I here tormented lye:
Of whom high Jove wont whylome feasted bee,[9]
Lo here I now for want of food doe dye:
530 But if that thou be such, as I thee see,
Of grace I pray thee, give to eat and drinke to mee.

60

Nay, nay, thou greedie Tantalus (quoth he)
Abide the fortune of thy present fate,
And unto all that live in high degree,°   *rank*
535 Ensample be of mind intemperate,
To teach them how to use their present state.
Then gan the cursed wretch aloud to cry,
Accusing highest Jove and gods ingrate,
And eke blaspheming heaven bitterly,
540 As authour of unjustice, there to let him dye.

61

He lookt a little further, and espyde
Another wretch, whose carkasse deepe was drent°   *submerged*
Within the river, which the same did hyde:
But both his hands most filthy feculent,°   *feces-laden*
545 Above the water were on high extent,°   *extended*
And faynd° to wash themselves incessantly;   *tried*
Yet nothing cleaner were for such intent,
But rather fowler seemed to the eye;
So lost his labour vaine and idle° industry.   *futile*

9. By whom Jove was formerly feasted. According to the Renaissance mythographer Natalis Comes, Tantalus was condemned to perpetual thirst because avaricious people can never get enough no matter how much wealth they have.

62

550 The knight him calling, askéd who he was,
  Who lifting up his head, him answered thus:
  I Pilate am the falsest Judge, alas,
  And most unjust, that by unrightéous
  And wicked doome,° to Jewes despiteous°   *verdict / cruel*
555 Delivered up the Lord of life to die,
  And did acquite a murdrer felonous;
  The whiles my hands I washt in puritie,
The whiles my soule was soyld with foule iniquitie.

63

Infinite moe,° tormented in like paine   *more*
560 He there beheld, too long here to be told:
  Ne Mammon would there let him long remaine,
  For terrour of the tortures manifold,
  In which the damnéd soules he did behold,
  But roughly him bespake. Thou fearefull foole,
565 Why takest not of that same fruit of gold,
  Ne sittest downe on that same silver stoole,
To rest thy wearie person, in the shadow coole.

64

All which he did, to doe him deadly fall
  In frayle intemperance through sinfull bayt;
570 To which if he inclinéd had at all,
  That dreadfull feend, which did behind him wayt,
  Would him have rent in thousand peeces strayt:° *straightaway*
  But he was warie wise in all his way,
  And well perceivéd his deceiptfull sleight,°   *trick*
575 Ne suffred lust° his safetie to betray;   *greed*
So goodly did beguile the Guyler° of the pray. *deceiver*

65

And now he has no long remainéd there,
  That vitall powres gan wexe both weake and wan,° *faint*
  For want of food, and sleepe, which two upbeare,
580 Like mightie pillours, this fraile life of man,
  That none without the same enduren can.
  For now three dayes of men were full outwrought,° *completed*
  Since he this hardie enterprize began:
  For thy° great Mammon fairely he besought, *therefore*
585 Into the world to guide him backe, as he him brought.

66

The God, though loth, yet was constraind t' obay,
  For lenger time, then that, no living wight
  Below the earth, might suffred° be to stay: *allowed*
  So backe againe, him brought to living light.
590 But all so soone as his enfeebled spright°   *spirit*
  Gan sucke this vitall aire into his brest,
  As overcome with too exceeding might,
  The life did flit away out of her nest,
And all his senses were with deadly fit opprest.

From *Canto XII*: [*The Bower of Bliss*]¹

42

370   Thence passing forth, they shortly do arrive,
      Whereas the Bowre of Blisse was situate;
      A place pickt out by choice of best alive,²
      That natures worke by art can imitate:
      In which what ever in this worldly state
375   Is sweet, and pleasing unto living sense,
      Or that may dayntiest fantasie aggrate,°   *please, satisfy*
      Was pouréd forth with plentifull dispence,°   *liberality*
  And made there to abound with lavish affluence.

43

  Goodly it was encloséd round about,
380   Aswell their entred guestes to keepe within,
      As those unruly beasts to hold without;
      Yet was the fence thereof but weake and thin;
      Nought feard their force, that fortilage° to win,   *fortalice, fort*
      But wisedomes powre, and temperaunces might,³
385   By which the mightiest things efforcéd bin:°   *were*
      And eke the gate was wrought of substaunce light,
  Rather for pleasure, then for battery or fight.

44

  Yt framéd was of precious yvory,
      That seemd a worke of admirable wit;
390   And therein all the famous history
      Of Jason and Medaea was ywrit;
      Her mighty charmes, her furious loving fit,

1. In the present selection from the last Canto, Sir Guyon and the Palmer visit and destroy the Bower of Bliss. The Bower functions, much as Lucifera's palace or Orgoglio's dungeon did in Book I, as an allegorical locale where a symbolic action takes place. Spenser had first shown his readers the Bower in Canto v; there Cymochles is found reclining "amidst a flock of Damzelles"; they are half-naked, wantonly flirtatious, while he, "like an Adder lurking in the weedes, / His wandring thought in deep desire does steepe." That was, however, only a preliminary glimpse.

The "Bower of Bliss," perhaps the most famous of Spenser's "set pieces," has been variously interpreted. In *The Allegory of Love*, C. S. Lewis argues convincingly that the Bower "is not a picture of lawless, that is, unwedded love as opposed to lawful love. It is a picture, one of the most powerful ever painted, of the whole sexual nature in disease. There is not a kiss or an embrace in the island: only male prurience and female provocation" (p. 332). This is especially true of Acrasia, the mistress of the Bower, whose name means both "excess" and "impotence"; she is seen (stanzas 77–79) statically posed, doing nothing, only *appearing* as the archetypal seductress. The Bower is certainly a place where sexuality is sterile, as the Garden of Adonis (in the following selection) is a place where it is fertile. Some readers may find, however, that imagery partly overflows moral intention. For example, the two girls bathing in a pool (stanzas 63–68) are assuredly pin-ups out of a man's magazine of the mid-20th century—and yet Spenser compares them to the morning star and to the Venus of Cyprus (lines 577–80).

2. I.e., the best living artists. The imitating of nature by art had been foreshadowed in Canto v, where "art, striving to compare / with nature, did an Arber greene dispred" (II.v.272–73). Nature is important to Sir Guyon, as it was not to Redcrosse, because temperance is attainable by unaided nature, whereas holiness requires the help of grace.

3. The fear is not of the physical force of Guyon and the Palmer but of the virtuous power of their temperance and wisdom.

His goodly conquest of the golden fleece,
His falséd faith, and love too lightly flit,
395 The wondred° Argo, which in venturous peece   admired
First through the Euxine seas bore all the flowr of Greece.

45

Ye might have seene the frothy billowes fry°   foam
Under the ship, as thorough them she went,
That seemd the waves were into yvory,
400 Or yvory into the waves were sent;
And other where the snowy substaunce sprent
With vermell,° like the boyes bloud therein shed,   vermilion
A piteous spectacle did represent,
And otherwhiles° with gold besprinkeléd;   elsewhere
405 Yt seemd th' enchaunted flame, which did Creüsa wed.[4]

46

All this, and more might in that goodly gate
Be red; that ever open stood to all,[5]
Which thither came: but in the Porch there sate
A comely personage of stature tall,
410 And semblaunce° pleasing, more than naturall,   appearance
That travellers to him seemd to entize;
His looser° garment to the ground did fall,   too loose
And flew about his heeles in wanton wize,
Not fit for speedy pace, or manly exercize.

47

415 They in that place him Genius° did call: guiding spirit
Not that celestiall powre, to whom the care
Of life, and generation of all
That lives, pertaines in charge particulare,
Who wondrous things concerning our welfare,
420 And straunge phantomes doth let us oft forsee,
And oft of secret ill bids us beware:
That is our Selfe, whom though we do not see,
Yet each doth in him selfe it well perceive to bee.

48

Therefore a God him sage Antiquity
425 Did wisely make, and good Agdistes call:
But this same was to that quite contrary,
The foe of life, that good envyes° to all,   grudges
That secretly doth us procure to fall,
Through guilefull semblaunts,° which he makes us see.   illusions

---

4. Jason, in his ship the *Argo*, sought the Golden Fleece of the king of Colchis; the witch Medea, the king's daughter, fell in love with him and used "her mighty charmes" to help him obtain it (lines 392–93). The "boyes bloud" (line 402) refers to Absyrtus, Medea's younger brother, whose body she cut into pieces and scattered, to delay her father's pursuit by making him stop to collect the fragments. Later, Jason deserted Medea for Creüsa; in revenge, Medea gave the girl a dress which burst into fire when she put it on; the flame consumed and thus "wed" her (line 405). This tale of unnatural "furious loving," with all its attendant violence, is appropriate to the Bower.

5. "Wide is the gate, and broad is the way, that leadeth to destruction, and many there be which go in thereat" (Matthew vii.13).

30   He of this Gardin had the governall,
And Pleasures porter was devizd° to bee,   *considered*
Holding a staffe in hand for more formalitee.

49

With diverse flowres he daintily was deckt,
And strowéd round about, and by his side
35   A mighty mazer° bowle of wine was set,   *drinking*
As if it had to him bene sacrifide;
Wherewith all new-come guests he gratifide:
So did he eke Sir Guyon passing by:
But he his idle curtesie defide,
440   And overthrew his bowle disdainfully;
And broke his staffe, with which he charméd semblants sly.[6]

50

Thus being entred, they behold around
A large and spacious plaine, on every side
Strowed with pleasauns,° whose faire grassy ground   *gardens*
445   Mantled with greene, and goodly beautifide
With all the ornaments of Floraes pride,
Wherewith her mother Art, as halfe in scorne
Of niggard Nature, like a pompous bride
Did decke her, and too lavishly adorne,
450   When forth from virgin bowre she comes in th' early morne.[7]

51

Thereto the Heavens alwayes Joviall,°   *propitious*
Lookt on them lovely,° still in stedfast state,   *lovingly*
Ne suffred storme nor frost on them to fall,
Their tender buds or leaves to violate,
455   Nor scorching heat, nor cold intemperate
T' afflict the creatures, which therein did dwell,
But the milde aire with season moderate
Gently attempred, and disposd so well,
That still it breathéd forth sweet spirit and holesome smell.

52

460   More sweet and holesome, then the pleasaunt hill
Of Rhodope, on which the Nimphe, that bore
A gyaunt babe, her selfe for griefe did kill;
Or the Thessalian Tempe, where of yore
Faire Daphne Phoebus hart with love did gore;
465   Or Ida, where the Gods loved to repaire,
When ever they their heavenly bowres forlore;[8]

6. I.e., raised deceitful apparitions. The rod and bowl are traditional emblems of enchantment (cf. for example, Duessa's cup, in I.viii.14).
7. Art no longer merely imitates nature but undertakes to supplant it, by excess.
8. Deserted. The nymph Rhodope, who had a "gyaunt babe," Athos, by Neptune (lines 460–62), was turned into a mountain; Daphne, another nymph, charmed Apollo so that he pursued her until she prayed for aid and was turned into a laurel tree; Mount Ida was the scene of the rape of Ganymede and the judgment of Paris, and the gods watched the Trojan War from its heights. These are all allusions to violent and unhappy passion—and yet the Bower is also compared to Mt. Parnassus, home of the Muses, and to the Garden of Eden.

Or sweet Parnasse, the haunt of Muses faire;
Or Eden selfe, if ought with Eden mote compaire.

53

Much wondred Guyon at the faire aspect
470   Of that sweet place, yet suffred no delight
    To sincke into his sence, nor mind affect,
    But passéd forth, and lookt still forward right,°   straight ahead
    Bridling his will, and maistering his might:
    Till that he came unto another gate;
475   No gate, but like one, being goodly dight
    With boughes and braunches, which did broad dilate°   spread out
Their clasping armes, in wanton wreathings intricate.

54

So fashionéd a Porch with rare device,
    Archt over head with an embracing vine,
480   Whose bounches hanging downe, seemed to entice
    All passers by, to tast their lushious wine
    And did themselves into their hands incline,
    As freely offering to be gatheréd:
    Some deepe empurpled as the Hyacint,
485   Some as the Rubine, laughing sweetly red,
Some like faire Emeraudes, not yet well ripenéd.

55

And them amongst, some were of burnisht gold,
    So made by art, to beautifie the rest,
    Which did themselves emongst the leaves enfold,
490   As lurking from the vew of covetous guest,
    That the weake bowes, with so rich load opprest,
    Did bowe adowne, as over-burdenéd.
    Under that Porch a comely dame did rest,
    Clad in faire weedes,° but fowle disorderéd,   garments
495 And garments loose, that seemd unmeet for womanhed.°   womanhood

56

In her left hand a Cup of gold she held,
    And with her right the riper° fruit did reach,   overripe
    Whose sappy liquor, that with fulnesse sweld,
    Into her cup she scruzd,° with daintie breach   crushed
500   Of her fine fingers, without fowle empeach,°   hindrance
    That so faire wine-presse made the wine more sweet:
    Thereof she usd to give to drinke to each,
    Whom passing by she happenéd to meet:
It was her guise,° all Straungers goodly so to greet.   custom

57

505 So she to Guyon offred it to tast;
    Who taking it out of her tender hond,
    The cup to ground did violently cast,
    That all in peeces it was broken fond,°   found
    And with the liquor stainéd all the lond.°   land
510   Whereat Excesse exceedingly was wroth,

Yet no'te° the same amend, ne yet withstond,   *knew not how to*
But suffered him to passe, all° were she loth;   *although*
Who nought regarding her displeasure forward goth.

58

₅₁₅

There the most daintie Paradise on ground,
    It selfe doth offer to his sober eye,
    In which all pleasures plenteously abound,
    And none does others happinesse envye:
    The painted flowres, the trees upshooting hye,
₅₂₀   The dales for shade, the hilles for breathing space,
    The trembling groves, the Christall running by;
    And that, which all faire workes doth most aggrace,°   *add grace to*
The art, which all that wrought, appearéd in no place.

59

₅₂₅

One would have thought (so cunningly, the rude,
    And scornéd parts were mingled with the fine)
    That nature had for wantonesse ensude°   *imitated*
    Art, and that Art at nature did repine;°   *complain*
    So striving each th' other to undermine,
    Each did the others worke more beautifie;
₅₃₀   So diff'ring both in willes, agreed in fine:[9]
    So all agreed through sweete diversitie,
This Gardin to adorne with all varietie.

60

And in the midst of all, a fountaine stood,
    Of richest substaunce, that on earth might bee,
    So pure and shiny, that the silver flood
₅₃₅   Through every channell running one might see;
    Most goodly it with curious imageree
    Was over-wrought, and shapes of naked boyes,
    Of which some seemd with lively jollitee,
    To fly about, playing their wanton toyes,°   *sports*
₅₄₀Whilest others did them selves embay° in liquid joyes.   *drench*

61

And over all, of purest gold was spred,
    A trayle of yvie in his native hew:
    For the rich metall was so colouréd,
    That wight, who did not well avised it vew,
₅₄₅   Would surely deeme it to be yvie trew:[1]
    Low his lascivious armes adown did creepe,
    That themselves dipping in the silver dew,
    Their fleecy flowres they tenderly did steepe,
Which° drops of Christall seemd for wantones°   *on which/wantonness*
    to weepe.

62

₅₅₀

Infinit streames continually did well
    Out of this fountaine, sweet and faire to see,

---

9. I.e., at the end. Art and nature harmonize with each other in effect, although antagonistic in intention.

1. The golden ivy has attracted much critical comment as an image of artifice with a touch of the repellent about it.

The which into an ample laver° fell,   *basin*
And shortly grew to so great quantitie,
That like a little lake it seemd to bee;
555 Whose depth exceeded not three cubits hight,
That through the waves one might the bottom see,
All pavéd beneath with Jasper shining bright,
That seemd the fountaine in that sea did sayle upright.

63

And all the margent round about was set,
560 With shady Laurell trees, thence to defend°   *ward off*
The sunny beames, which on the billowes bet,
And those which therein bathéd, mote offend.
As Guyon hapned by the same to wend,
Two naked Damzelles he therein espyde,
565 Which therein bathing, seeméd to contend,
And wrestle wantonly, ne cared to hyde,
Their dainty parts from vew of any, which them eyde.

64

Sometimes the one would lift the other quight
Above the waters, and then downe againe
570 Her plong, as over maisteréd by might,
Where both awhile would coveréd remaine,
And each the other from to rise restraine;
The whiles their snowy limbes, as through a vele,
So through the Christall waves appearéd plaine:
575 Then suddeinly both would themselves unhele,°   *uncover*
And th' amarous sweet spoiles to greedy eyes revele.

65

As that faire Starre, the messenger of morne,
His deawy face out of the sea doth reare:
Or as the Cyprian goddesse,[2] newly borne
580 Of th' Oceans fruitfull froth, did first appeare:
Such seeméd they, and so their yellow heare
Christalline humour[3] droppéd downe apace.
Whom such when Guyon saw, he drew him neare,
And somewhat gan relent his earnest pace,
585 His stubborne brest gan secret pleasaunce to embrace.

66

The wanton Maidens him espying, stood
Gazing a while at his unwonted guise;°   *manner*
Then th' one her selfe low duckéd in the flood,
Abasht, that her a straunger did avise:°   *see*
590 But th' other rather higher did arise,
And her two lilly paps aloft displayd,
And all, that might his melting hart entise
To her delights, she unto him bewrayed:°   *revealed*
The rest hid underneath, him more desirous made.

---

2. Venus (one of whose principal   3. Clear liquid.
shrines was on the island of Cyprus).

67

595 With that, the other likewise up arose,
    And her faire lockes, which formerly were bownd
    Up in one knot, she low adowne did lose: °   *loosen*
    Which flowing long and thick, her clothed arownd,
600   And th' yvorie in golden mantle gownd:
    So that faire spectacle from him was reft,
    Yet that, which reft it, no lesse faire was fownd:
    So hid in lockes and waves from lookers theft,
Nought but her lovely face she for his looking left.

68

Withall she laughéd, and she blusht withall,
605   That blushing to her laughter gave more grace,
    And laughter to her blushing, as did fall:
    Now when they spide the knight to slacke his pace,
    Them to behold, and in his sparkling face
    The secret signes of kindled lust appeare,
610   Their wanton meriments they did encreace,
    And to him beckned, to approach more neare,
And shewd him many sights, that courage cold could reare.[4]

69

On which when gazing him the Palmer saw,
    He much rebukt those wandring eyes of his,
615   And counseld well, him forward thence did draw.
    Now are they come nigh to the Bowre of blis
    Of her fond favorites so named amis:
    When thus the Palmer: "Now Sir, well avise;°   *take care*
    For here the end of all our travell is:
620   Here wonnes° Acrasia, whom we must surprise,   *dwells*
    Else she will slip away, and all our drift° despise."   *plan, effort*

70

Eftsoones they heard a most melodious sound,
    Of all that mote delight a daintie eare,
    Such as attonce might not on living ground,
625   Save in this Paradise, be heard elswhere:
    Right hard it was, for wight, which did it heare,
    To read, what manner musicke that mote bee:
    For all that pleasing is to living eare,
    Was there consorted in one harmonee,
630 Birdes, voyces, instruments, windes, waters, all agree.

71

The joyous birdes shrouded in chearefull shade,
    Their notes unto the voyce attempred° sweet;   *attuned*
    Th' Angelicall soft trembling voyces made
    To th' instruments divine respondence meet:°   *fitting*
635   The silver sounding instruments did meet°   *join*
    With the base murmure of the waters fall:
    The waters fall with difference discreet,°   *suitable*

---

4. That could arouse a cold spirit.

Now soft, now loud, unto the wind did call:
The gentle warbling wind low answered to all.[5]

72

640 There, whence that Musick seeméd heard to bee,
    Was the faire Witch her selfe now solacing,
    With a new Lover, whom through sorceree
    And witchcraft, she from farre did thither bring:
    There had him now layd a slombering,
645   In secret shade, after long wanton joyes:
    Whilst round about them pleasauntly did sing
    Many faire Ladies, and lascivious boyes,
That ever mixt their song with light licentious toyes.

73

And all that while, right over him she hong,
650   With her false eyes fast fixéd in his sight,
    As seeking medicine, whence she was stong,
    Or greedily depasturing° delight: *feeding on*
    And oft inclining downe with kisses light,
    For feare of waking him, his lips bedewd,
655   And through his humid eyes did sucke his spright,
    Quite molten into lust and pleasure lewd;
Wherewith she sighéd soft, as if his case she rewd.°   *pitied*

74

The whiles some one did chaunt this lovely lay:
    "Ah see, who so faire thing doest faine° to see   *delight*
660   In springing flowre the image of thy day;
    Ah see the Virgin Rose, how sweetly shee
    Doth first peepe forth with bashfull modestee
    That fairer seemes, the lesse ye see her may
    Lo see soone after, how more bold and free
665   Her baréd bosome she doth broad display;
Loe see soone after, how she fades, and falles away.

75

"So passeth, in the passing of a day,
    Of mortall life the leafe, the bud, the flowre,
    Ne more doth flourish after first decay,
670   That earst was sought to decke both bed and bowre,
    Of many a Ladie, and many a Paramowre: °   *lover*
    Gather therefore the Rose, whilest yet is prime
    For soone comes age, that will her pride deflowre:
    Gather the Rose of love, whilest yet is time,
675 Whilest loving thou mayst lovéd be with equal crime."

---

5. Taste, sight, smell, and sound are all titillated here; little is said, however, óf touching. Acrasia, whom we are about to see, bears many resemblances to Circe (not only the cool figure of *Odyssey* X, but the much more witchlike and seductive creature painted by Ovid) and to the enchantresses of Italian romance who derive from Circe, such as Acratia in Trissino's *L'Italia Liberata* and Armida in Tasso's *Gerusalemme Liberata*. In fact, much of the description in Canto xii is imitated from Armida's garden in that poem, and the rose song of stanzas 74 and 75 (a classic statement of the *carpe-diem* theme) is a direct translation.

76

He ceast, and then gan all the quire of birdes
  Their diverse notes t' attune unto his lay,
  As in approvance of his pleasing words.
  The constant paire heard all, that he did say,
680 Yet swarved not, but kept their forward way,
  Through many covert groves, and thickets close,
  In which they creeping did at last display°   *discover*
  That wanton Ladie, with her lover lose,°   *loose*
Whose sleepie head she in her lap did soft dispose.

77

685 Upon a bed of Roses she was layd,[6]
  As faint through heat, or dight to pleasant sin,
  And was arayd, or rather disarayd,
  All in a vele of silke and silver thin,
  That hid no whit her alablaster skin,
690 But rather shewd more white, if more might bee:
  More subtile web Arachne° cannot spin,   *the spider*
  Nor the fine nets, which oft we woven see
Of scorched deaw, do not in th' aire more lightly flee.°   *float*

78

Her snowy brest was bare to readie spoyle
695 Of hungry eies, which n'ote° therewith be fild,   *could not*
  And yet through languor of her late sweet toyle,
  Few drops, more cleare than Nectar, forth distild,
  That like pure Orient perles adowne it trild,°   *trickled*
  And her faire eyes sweet smyling in delight,
700 Moystened their fierie beames, with which she thrild
  Fraile harts, yet quenchéd not; like starry light
Which sparckling on the silent waves, does seeme more bright.

79

The young man sleeping by her, seemd to bee
  Some goodly swayne of honorable place,°   *rank*
705 That certés it great pittie was to see
  Him his nobilitie so foule deface;°   *disgrace*
  A sweet regard, and amiable grace,
  Mixed with manly sternnesse did appeare
  Yet sleeping, in his well proportioned face,
710 And on his tender lips the downy heare
Did now but freshly spring, and silken blossomes beare.

80

His warlike armes, the idle instruments
  Of sleeping praise, were hong upon a tree,
  And his brave shield, full of old moniments,
715 Was fowly ra'st,[7] that none the signes might see;
  Ne for them, ne for honour caréd hee,
  Ne ought, that did to his advauncement tend,

---

6. Prepared for.
7. Erased. The removal of the emblems   from his shield was the last disgrace of
                                    a knight.

But in lewd loves, and wastfull luxuree,
His dayes, his goods, his bodie he did spend:
720 O horrible enchantment, that him so did blend.°   *blind*

81

The noble Elfe,[8] and carefull Palmer drew
So nigh them, minding nought, but lustfull game,
That suddein forth they on them rusht, and threw
A subtile net, which onely for the same
725 The skilfull Palmer formally° did frame.   *scientifically*
So held them under fast, the whiles the rest
Fled all away for feare of fowler shame.
The faire Enchauntresse, so unwares opprest,
Tryde all her arts, and all her sleights, thence out to wrest.

82

730 And eke her lover strove: but all in vaine;
For that same net so cunningly was wound,
That neither guile, nor force might it distraine.°   *tear*
They tooke them both, and both them strongly bound
In captive bandes, which there they readie found:
735 But her in chaines of adamant he tyde;
For nothing else might keepe her safe and sound;
But Verdant[9] (so he hight) he soone untyde,
And counsell sage in steed thereof to him applyde.

83

But all those pleasant bowres and Pallace brave,
740 Guyon broke downe, with rigour pittilesse;
Ne ought their goodly workmanship might save
Them from the tempest of his wrathfulnesse,
But that their blisse he turned to balefulnesse:
Their groves he feld, their gardins did deface,.
745 Their arbers spoyle, their Cabinets° suppresse,   *summerhouses*
Their banket houses burne, their buildings race,°   *raze*
And of the fairest late, now made the fowlest place.

84

Then led they her away, and eke that knight
They with them led, both sorrowfull and sad:
750 The way they came, the same retourned they right,
Till they arrivéd, where they lately had
Charmed those wild-beasts, that raged with furie mad.
Which now awaking, fierce at them gan fly,
As in their mistresse reskew, whom they lad;°   *lead*
755 But them the Palmer soone did pacify.
Then Guyon askt, what meant those beastes, which there did ly.

85

Said he, "These seeming beasts are men indeed,
Whom this Enchauntresse hath transforméd thus,
Whylome her lovers, which her lusts did feed,
760 Now turned into figures hideous,

8. Knight of fairyland.
9. The name means "green" and may refer, therefore, to a young man in the springtime of his sensuality.

According to their mindes like monstruous."[10]
"Sad end," quoth he, "of life intemperate,
And mournefull meed of joyes delicious:
But Palmer, if it mote thee so aggrate,° *please*
765 Let them returnéd be unto their former state."

86

Streight way he with his vertuous staffe them strooke,
And streight of beasts they comely men became;
Yet being men they did unmanly looke,
And staréd ghastly, some for inward shame,
770 And some for wrath, to see their captive Dame:
But one above the rest in speciall,
That had an hog beene late, hight Grille by name,
Repinéd greatly, and did him miscall,° *abuse*
That had from hoggish forme him brought to naturall.

87

775 Said Guyon, "See the mind of beastly man,
That hath so soone forgot the excellence
Of his creation, when he life began,
That now he chooseth, with vile difference,° *change*
To be a beast, and lacke intelligence."
780 To whom the Palmer thus, "The donghill kind
Delights in filth and foule incontinence:
Let Grill be Grill, and have his hoggish mind,
But let us hence depart, whilest wether serves and wind."

From Book III, Canto VI[1]

[The Garden of Adonis]

30

In that same Gardin all the goodly flowres,
Wherewith dame Nature doth her beautifie,
And decks the girlonds of her paramoures,
265 Are fetcht: there is the first seminarie° *genetic source*
Of all things, that are borne to live and die,
According to their kindes. Long worke it were,

10. Circe had changed Odysseus' companions into swine, but Odysseus was empowered to release them. Cf. also the animals upon which the sins rode in I.v.
1. The "hero" of Book III is the lady Britomart, the representative of Chastity. By "chastity" is meant, however, not abstinence but a love that is devoted and active. The "Garden of Adonis" passage here reprinted is the "allegorical core" of the book, but unlike Orgoglio's castle or the Bower of Bliss, the knight does not enter upon any symbolic action therein; in fact, Britomart does not even appear.

The Garden of Adonis is part of a long literary tradition of earthly paradises, among them Homer's Garden of Alcinous (*Odyssey* VII) and Chaucer's Garden of Nature in the *Parliament of Fowls* (lines 120–308), and of gardens in courtly-love allegories. The broadly Neoplatonic ideas in stanzas 30–50 parallel classical and later sources such as the Myth of Er in Plato's *Republic*, the *Enneads* of Plotinus, and Arthur Golding's translation of Ovid's *Metamorphoses*. In Spenser's Garden all living things are formed and re-formed; as the center of generation and regeneration, it is the axis upon which the idea of love, as the life-producing power, turns. The Garden exhibits a picture of what love would be if man were not what he is.

Here to account the endlesse progenie
Of all the weedes,° that bud and blossome there;   *plants*
270 But so much as doth need, must needs be counted here.

31

It sited was in fruitfull soyle of old,
    And girt in with two walles on either side;
    The one of yron, the other of bright gold,
    That none might thorough breake, nor overstride:
275   And double gates it had, which opened wide,
    By which both in and out men moten° pas;   *could*
    Th' one faire and fresh, the other old and dride:
    Old Genius the porter of them was,
Old Genius, the which a double nature has.

32

280 He letteth in, he letteth out to wend,°   *go*
    All that to come into the world desire;
    A thousand thousand naked babes attend
    About him day and night, which doe require,
    That he with fleshly weedes would them attire:[2]
285   Such as him list, such as eternall fate
    Ordainéd hath, he clothes with sinfull mire,[3]
    And sendeth forth to live in mortall state,
Till they againe returne backe by the hinder gate.

33

After that they againe returnéd beene,
290   They in that Gardin planted be againe;
    And grow afresh, as they had never seene
    Fleshly corruption, nor mortall paine.
    Some thousand yeares so doen they there remaine;
    And then of him are clad with other hew,°   *form*
295   Or sent into the chaungefull world againe,
    Till thither they returne, where first they grew:
So like a wheele around they runne from old to new.

34

Ne needs there Gardiner to set, or sow,
    To plant or prune: for of their owne accord
300   All things, as they created were, doe grow,
    And yet remember well the mightie word,
    Which first was spoken by th' Almightie lord,
    That bad them to increase and multiply:
    Ne doe they need with water of the ford,°   *stream*
305   Or of the clouds to moysten their roots dry;
For in themselves eternall moisture they imply.°   *contain*

35

Infinite shapes of creatures there are bred,
    And uncouth° formes, which none yet ever knew,   *strange*
    And every sort is in a sundry° bed   *separate*

2. The "naked babes" may be taken as the "seeds" from which all life springs, or as souls in the pre-existent state. "Weedes" are clothes, so "fleshly weedes" are, here, the body.
3. I.e., the flesh.

310 Set by it selfe, andranckt in comely rew:°   *row, rank*
Some fit for reasonable soules t' indew,°   *put on*
Some made for beasts, some made for birds to weare,
And all the fruitfull spawne of fishes hew
In endlesse rancks along enraungéd were,
315 That seemed the Ocean could not containe them there.

36

Daily they grow, and daily forth are sent
Into the world, it to replenish more;
Yet is the stocke not lessenéd, nor spent,
But still remaines in everlasting store,
320 As it at first created was of yore.
For in the wide wombe of the world there lyes,
In hatefull darkenesse and in deepe horrore,
An huge eternall Chaos, which supplyes
The substances of natures fruitfull progenyes.

37

325 All things from thence doe their first being fetch,
And borrow matter, whereof they are made,
Which when as forme and feature it does ketch,[4]
Becomes a bodie, and doth then invade°   *enter*
The state of life, out of the griesly shade.
330 That substance is eterne, and bideth so,
Ne when the life decayes, and forme does fade,
Doth it consume, and into nothing go,
But chaungéd is, and often altred to and fro.

38

The substance is not chaunged, nor alteréd,
335 But th' only forme and outward fashion;°   *appearance*
For every substance is conditionéd
To change her hew, and sundry formes to don,
Meet for her temper and complexion:
For formes are variable and decay,
340 By course of kind,° and by occasion;   *nature*
And that faire flowre of beautie fades away,
As doth the lilly fresh before the sunny ray.[5]

39

Great enimy to it, and to all the rest,
That in the Gardin of Adonis springs,
345 Is wicked Time, who with his scyth addrest,°   *armed*
Does mow the flowring herbes and goodly things,
And all their glory to the ground downe flings,
Where they doe wither, and are fowly mard:
He flyes about, and with his flaggy° wings   *drooping*
350 Beates downe both leaves and buds without regard,
Ne ever pittie may relent his malice hard.

---

4. I.e., when it takes shape and outline.
5. While stanzas 30–35 emphasized the cyclical process of all life, stanzas 36–

38 describe the indestructible substance that persists through the cycles.

40

Yet pittie often did the gods relent,
    To see so faire things mard, and spoyléd quight:
    And their great mother Venus did lament
355   The losse of her deare brood, her deare delight:
    Her hart was pierst with pittie at the sight,
    When walking through the Gardin, them she spyde,
    Yet no'te[6] she find redresse for such despight.
    For all that lives, is subject to that law:
360 All things decay in time, and to their end do draw.

41

But were it not, that Time their troubler is,
    All that in this delightfull Gardin growes,
    Should happie be, and have immortall blis,
    For here all plentie, and all pleasure flowes,
365   For sweet love gentle fits° emongst them throwes,   *impulses*
    Without fell rancor, or fond gealosie;
    Franckly each paramour° his leman° knowes,   *lover / sweetheart*
    Each bird his mate, ne any does envie
    Their goodly meriment, and gay felicite.

42

370 There is continuall spring, and harvest there
    Continuall, both meeting at one time:[7]
    For both the boughes doe laughing blossomes beare,
    And with fresh colours decke the wanton Prime,°   *Spring*
    And eke attonce the heavy trees they clime,
375   Which seeme to labour under their fruits lode:
    The whiles the joyous birdes make their pastime
    Emongst the shadie leaves, their sweet abode,
    And their true loves without suspition tell abrode.

43

Right in the middest of that Paradise,
380   There stood a stately Mount, on whose round top
    A gloomy grove of mirtle trees did rise,
    Whose shadie boughes sharpe steele did never lop,
    Nor wicked beasts their tender buds did crop,
    But like a girlond compasséd the hight,
385   And from their fruitfull sides sweet gum did drop,
    That all the ground with precious deaw bedight,
    Threw forth most dainty odours, and most sweet delight.

44

And in the thickest covert of that shade,
    There was a pleasant arbour, not by art,
390   But of the trees owne inclination made,[8]
    Which knitting their rancke° braunches part to part,   *dense*
    With wanton yvie twyne entrayld athwart,
    And Eglantine, and Caprifole[9] emong,

---

6. Did not know how to.
7. The sexuality of the Garden is life-giving—unlike the sexuality of the Bower of Bliss, which was life-destroying. The Garden is untroubled by seasonal change, like other perfect gardens in Renaissance and medieval literature, which are types of an ideal world.
8. Unlike the Bower of Bliss, where art rivaled or supplanted nature, Venus's bower is entirely natural.
9. Honeysuckle or woodbine.

Fashiond above within their inmost part,
395   That nether Phoebus beams could through them throng,
Nor Aeolus sharp blast could worke them any wrong.

45

And all about grew every sort of flowre,
  To which sad lovers were transformed of yore;
  Fresh Hyacinthus, Phoebus paramoure,
400   And dearest love,
  Foolish Narcisse, that likes the watry shore,
  Sad Amaranthus, made a flowre but late,
  Sad Amaranthus, in whose purple gore
  Me seemes I see Amintas wretched fate,
405 To whom sweet Poets verse hath given endlesse date.[1]

46

There wont faire Venus often to enjoy
  Her deare Adonis joyous company,
  And reape sweet pleasure of the wanton boy;
410   There yet, some say, in secret he does ly,
  Lappéd in flowres and pretious spycery,
  By her hid from the world, and from the skill°   *knowledge*
  Of Stygian Gods, which doe her love envy;
  But she her selfe, when ever that she will,
Possesseth him, and of his sweetnesse takes her fill.

47

415 And sooth it seemes they say: for he may not
  For ever die, and ever buried bee
  In balefull night, where all things are forgot;
  All° be he subject to mortalitie,   *although*
  Yet is eterne in mutabilitie,
420   And by succession made perpetuall,
  Transforméd oft, and chaungéd diverslie:
  For him the Father of all formes they call;
Therefore needs mote he live, that living gives to all.[2]

48

There now he liveth in eternall blis,
425   Joying his goddesse, and of her enjoyd:
  Ne feareth he hence forth that foe of his,
  Which with his cruell tuske him deadly cloyd:°   *pierced*
  For that wilde Bore, the which him once annoyd,°   *injured*
  She firmely hath emprisonéd for ay,
430   That her sweet love his malice mote avoyd,

1. Hyacinthus was a youth loved by Apollo and Zephyrus; returning the love of the former, he was killed out of jealousy by the latter, and the flower known by his name sprang from his blood. Narcissus, enamored of his own reflection in a pool, died and was also transformed into a flower. "Amintas" is Spenser's name for Sir Philip Sidney, on whose death Spenser, like all the other poets of his day, produced a poem. All these young men, turned into flowers after being cut off in the flower of their lives, suggest the quality of Adonis's Garden; it is the place where unfulfilled potentialities are renewed, and spiritual vitality is restored to wounded ideals. "Amaranthus" completes this idea, for its name means, in Greek, the "undying, unfading flower"; it symbolizes spiritual immortality for Adonis and his group of handsome, unfulfilled young men.

2. Adonis might be taken to symbolize the changing forms of matter, which cannot be destroyed but remain "eterne in mutabilitie," line 419.

In a strong rocky Cave, which is they say,
Hewen underneath that Mount, that none him losen may.[3]

49

There now he lives in everlasting joy,
　With many of the Gods in company,
435　Which thither haunt, and with the wingéd boy[4]
　Sporting himselfe in safe felicity:
Who when he hath with spoiles and cruelty
Ransackt the world, and in the wofull harts
Of many wretches set his triumphes hye,
440　Thither resorts, and laying his sad darts
Aside, with faire Adonis playes his wanton parts.

50

And his true love faire Psyche with him playes,
　Faire Psyche to him lately reconcyld,
　After long troubles and unmeet upbrayes,°   *reproaches*
445　With which his mother Venus her revyld,°   *scolded*
　And eke himselfe her cruelly exyld:[5]
But now in stedfast love and happy state
She with him lives, and hath him borne a chyld,
　Pleasure, that doth both gods and men aggrate,°   *gratify*
450　Pleasure, the daughter of Cupid and Psyche late.

From Book VII: Two Cantos of Mutabilitie[1]

Canto VI

Proud Change (not pleasd, in mortall things,
　beneath the Moon, to raigne)
Pretends, as well of Gods, as Men,
　To be the Soveraine.

1

What man that sees the ever-whirling wheele
　Of Change, the which all mortall things doth sway,
　But that thereby doth find, and plainly feele,
　How MUTABILITY in them doth play

3. "Losen": set free. This stanza retells
the myth of Venus and Adonis. The boar
may stand for animal passion, violence,
and disorder.
4. I.e., Cupid—who, it should be noted,
never appeared in the Bower of Bliss.
5. Psyche, a beautiful princess, was
visited by her lover Cupid only at night.
Curious to see him, she lighted a lamp
while he was asleep accidentally dropped
some hot oil on him, and awakened him.
He was angry at her lack of trust and
left her; she wandered in search of him
and endured many hardships imposed by
Venus, who was jealous of her beauty.
She was finally reunited with Cupid and
made immortal. Her story has been
taken to represent the arduous purification, by trial and misfortune, of the
human soul.
1. Two cantos and two stanzas of another, called "the Mutability Cantos,"
were first published in 1609, ten years
after Spenser's death. According to the
title page, they "appear to be parcel of
some following book of *The Faerie
Queene*, under the legend of Constan-
cie." If so, they are a longer digression
from the story than any now in the
poem. These cantos give Spenser's reflections, influenced perhaps by Lucretius,
on change and permanence in the world
—a subject which fascinated the Elizabethan imagination.

5   Her cruell sports, to many mens decay?
     Which that to all may better yet appeare,
     I will rehearse that whylome I heard say,
     How she at first her selfe began to reare,
   Gainst all the Gods, and th' empire sought from them to beare.

2

10   But first, here falleth fittest to unfold
     Her antique race and linage ancient,
     As I have found it registred of old,
     In Faery Land mongst records permanent:
     She was, to weet, a daughter by descent
15   Of those old Titans,[2] that did whylome strive
     With Saturnes sonne for heavens regiment.°   *rule*
     Whom though high Jove of kingdome did deprive,
   Yet many of their stemme long after did survive.

3

     And many of them, afterwards obtained
20   Great power of Jove, and high authority;
     As Hecaté,[3] in whose almighty hand,
     He plac't all rule and principality,
     To be by her disposéd diversly,
     To Gods, and men, as she them list divide:
25   And drad Bellona,[4] that doth sound on hie
     Warres and allarums unto Nations wide,
   That makes both heaven and earth to tremble at her pride.

4

     So likewise did this Titanesse aspire,
     Rule and dominion to her selfe to gaine;
30   That as a Goddesse, men might her admire,
     And heavenly honours yield, as to them twaine.
     At first, on earth she sought it to obtaine;
     Where she such proofe and sad examples shewed
     Of her great power, to many ones great paine,
35   That not men onely (whom she soone subdewed)
   But eke all other creatures, her bad dooings rewed.

5

     For she the face of earthly things so changed,
     That all which Nature had establisht first
     In good estate, and in meet order ranged,
40   She did pervert, and all their statutes burst:
     And all the worlds faire frame (which none yet durst
     Of Gods or men to alter or misguide)
     She altered quite, and made them all accurst
     That God had blest; and did at first provide
45   In that still happy state for ever to abide.

---

2. The Titans were the sons and daughters of sky and earth; their king was Cronus (time). Jove, Cronus' son, dethroned him and established the rule of the gods. But some descendants of the original Titans, such as Prometheus, Hecate, and others, survived. Spenser invents another, a Titaness called Mutability.
3. Patroness of witchcraft.
4. Patroness of war and conflict.

6

Ne shee the lawes of Nature only brake,
  But eke of Justice, and of Policie;
And wrong of right, and bad of good did make,
  And death for life exchangéd foolishlie;
50 Since which, all living wights have learned to die,
  And all this world is woxen daily worse.
  O pittious worke of MUTABILITIE!
  By which, we all are subject to that curse,
And death in stead of life have suckéd from our Nurse.

7

55 And now, when all the earth she thus had brought
  To her behest, and thrallèd to her might,
  She gan to cast° in her ambitious thought,   resolve
  T' attempt the empire of the heavens hight,
  And Jove himself to shoulder from his right.
60 And first, she past the region of the ayre,
  And of the fire, whose substance thin and slight,
  Made no resistance, ne could her contraire,
But ready passage to her pleasure did prepaire.[5]

* * *

Canto VII

Pealing, from Jove, to Natur's Bar,
  bold Alteration pleades
Large Evidence: but Nature soone
  her righteous Doome areads.

1

Ah! whither doost thou now thou greater Muse[6]
  Me from these woods and pleasing forrests bring?
  And my fraile spirit (that dooth oft refuse
  This too high flight, unfit for her weake wing)
5 Lift up aloft, to tell of heavens King
  (Thy soveraine Sire) is fortunate successe,
  And victory, in bigger noates to sing,
  Which he obtained against that Titanesse,
That him of heavens Empire sought to dispossesse.

2

10 Yet sith I needs must follow thy behest,
  Doe thou my weaker wit with skill inspire,
  Fit for this turne; and in my feeble brest

---

5. In the rest of Canto vi Mutability journeys to the circle of the moon and tries to usurp the throne of Cynthia, but fails, and then proceeds to Jove's throne in heaven. He threatens to punish her for presumption, but she says Jove is a prejudiced judge and appeals to the goddess Nature. It is agreed that Nature's verdict will be accepted, and the grand session of this supreme court will be held on Arlo Hill in Ireland. In Canto vii Spenser proceeds to give some mythological history of Arlo, in his own neighborhood.
6. I.e., Clio, Muse of history.

Kindle fresh sparks of that immortall fire,
Which learned minds inflameth with desire
15   Of heavenly things: for, who but thou alone,
That art yborne of heaven and heavenly Sire,
Can tell things doen in heaven so long ygone;
So farre past memory of man that may be knowne.

3

Now, at the time that was before agreed,
20   The Gods assembled all on Arlo hill;[7]
As well those that are sprung of heavenly seed,
As those that all the other world doe fill,
And rule both sea and land unto their will:
Onely th' infernall Powers might not appeare;
25   Aswell for horror of their count'naunce ill,
As for th' unruly fiends which they did feare;
Yet Pluto and Proserpina were present there.

4

And thither also came all other creatures,
What-ever life or motion doe retaine,
30   According to their sundry kinds of features;
That Arlo scarsly could them all containe;
So full they filléd every hill and Plaine:
And had not Natures Sergeant (that is Order)
Them well disposéd by his busie paine,
35   And raungéd farre abroad in every border,
They would have causéd much confusion and disorder.

5

Then forth issewed (great goddesse) great dame Nature,
With goodly port and gracious Majesty:
Being far greater and more tall of stature
40   Then any of the gods or Powers on hie:
Yet certes by her face and physnomy,
Whether she man or woman inly were,
That could not any creature well descry:
For, with a veile that wimpled every where,
45   Her head and face was hid, that mote to none appeare.

6

That some doe say was so by skill devized,
To hide the terror of her uncouth hew,
From mortall eyes that should be sore agrized °   *horrified*
For that her face did like a Lion shew,
50   That eye of wight would not indure to view:
But others tell that it so beautious was,
And round about such beames of splendor threw,
That it the Sunne a thousand times did pass,
Ne could be seene, but like an image in a glass.

7

55   That well may seemen true: for, well I weene
That this same day, when she on Arlo sat,

7. Galteemore in southern Ireland, near Spenser's home, Kilcolman Castle.

Her garment was so bright and wondrous sheene,
That my fraile wit cannot devize to what
It to compare, nor finde like stuffe to that,
60 As those three sacred Saints, though else most wise,
Yet on mount Thabor quite their wits forgat,
When they their glorious Lord in strange disguise
Transfigured sawe; his garments so did daze their eyes.[8]

8

In a fayre Plaine upon an equall Hill,
65 She placéd was in a pavilion;
Not such as Crafts-men by their idle skill
Are wont for Princes states to fashion:
But th' earth her self of her owne motion,
Out of her fruitfull bosome made to growe
70 Most dainty trees; that, shooting up anon,
Did seeme to bow their bloosming heads full lowe,
For homage unto her, and like a throne did shew.

9

So hard it is for any living wight,
All her array and vestiments to tell,
That old Dan° Geffrey (in whose gentle spright°   Sir / spirit
75 The pure well head of Poesie did dwell)
In his *Foules parley* durst not with it mel,°   meddle
But it transferd to Alane, who he thought
Had in his *Plaint of kindes* described it well:[9]
80 Which who will read set forth so as it ought,
Go seek he out that Alane where he may be sought.

10

And all the earth far underneath her feete
Was dight with flowres, that voluntary grew
Out of the ground, and sent forth odours sweet;
85 Tenne thousand mores° of sundry sent and hew,   plants
That might delight the smell, or please the view:
The which, the Nymphes, from all the brooks thereby
Had gatheréd, which they at her foot-stoole threw;
That richer seemed then any tapestry,
90 That Princes bowres adorne with painted imagery.

11

And Mole[1] himselfe, to honour her the more,
Did deck himself in freshest faire attire,
And his high head, that seemeth alwaies hore
With hardned frosts of former winters ire,
95 He with an Oaken girlond now did tire,
As if the love of some new Nymph late seene,
Had in him kindled youthfull fresh desire,

8. Peter, James, and John saw Jesus transfigured on a mountain. See Matthew xvii.1–8.
9. Chaucer, in his *Parliament of Fowls*, lines 316–18, refers to Alanus de Insulis'
De Planctu Naturae as Aleyn's *Pleynt of Kind* ("Complaint of Nature").
1. The mountain range of which Arlo is the highest peak.

And made him change his gray attire to greene;
Ah gentle Mole! such joyance hath thee well beseene.

12

100 Was never so great joyance since the day,
 That all the gods whylome assembled were,
 On Haemus hill in their divine array,
 To celebrate the solemne bridall cheare,
 Twixt Peleus, and dame Thetis pointed there:[2]
105 Where Phoebus self, that god of Poets hight,
 They say did sing the spousall hymne full cleere,
 That all the gods were ravisht with delight
Of his celestiall song, and Musicks wondrous might.

13

 This great Grandmother of all creatures bred
110 Great Nature, ever young yet full of eld,°   *age*
 Still mooving, yet unmovéd from her sted;°   *place*
 Unseene of any, yet of all beheld;
 Thus sitting in her throne as I have teld,
 Before her came dame Mutabilitie,
115 And being lowe before her presence feld,°   *prostrated*
 With meek obaysance and humilitie,
Thus gan her plaintif Plea, with words to amplifie:

14

 "To thee O greatest goddesse, onely great,
 An humble suppliant loe, I lowely fly
120 Seeking for Right, which I of thee entreat;
 Who Right to all dost deal indifferently,
 Damning all Wrong and tortious° Injurie,   *wrongful*
 Which any of thy creatures doe to other
 (Oppressing them with power, unequally)
125 Sith of them all thou art the equall mother,
And knittest each to each, as brother unto brother.

15

 "To thee therefore of this same Jove I plaine,
 And of his fellow gods that faine to be,
 That challenge to themslves the whole worlds raign;
130 Of which, the greatest part is due to me,
 And heaven it selfe by heritage in Fee:[3]
 For, heaven and earth I both alike do deeme,
 Sith heaven and earth are both alike to thee;
 And, gods no more than men thou doest esteeme:
135 For, even the gods to thee, as men to gods do seeme.

16

 "Then weigh, O soveraigne goddesse, by what right
 These gods do claime the worlds whole soveraity;
 And that° is onely dew unto thy might   *that which*
 Arrogate to themselves ambitiously:

---

2. Mortal king and sea goddess, the parents of Achilles. "Pointed": appointed.   3. Legally.

140   As for the gods owne principality,
    Which Jove usurpes unjustly; that to be
    My heritage, Jove's self cannot deny,
    From my great Grandsire Titan, unto mee,
  Derived by dew descent; as is well knowen to thee.

17

145 "Yet mauger° Jove, and all his gods beside,   *despite*
    I doe possesse the worlds most regiment,°   *control*
    As, if ye please it into parts divide,
    And every parts inholders° to convent,°   *occupants / assemble*
    Shall to your eyes appeare incontinent.°   *immediately*
150   And first, the Earth (great mother of us all)
    That only seems unmoved and permanent,
    And unto Mutability not thrall;
  Yet is she changed in part, and eeke in generall.

18

  "For, all that from her springs, and is ybredde,
155 How-ever fayre it flourish for a time,
    Yet see we soone decay; and, being dead,
    To turne again unto their earthly slime:
    Yet, out of their decay and mortall crime,
    We daily see new creatures to arize;
160   And of their Winter spring another Prime,°   *springtime*
    Unlike in forme, and changed by strange disguise:
  So turne they still about, and change in restlesse wise.

19

  "As for her tenants; that is, man and beasts,
    The beasts we daily see massácred dy,
165 As thralls and vassalls unto mens beheasts:
    And men themselves doe change continually,
    From youth to eld, from wealth to poverty,
    From good to bad, from bad to worst of all.
    Ne doe their bodies only flit and fly:
170   But eeke their minds (which they immortall call)
  Still change and vary thoughts, as new occasions fall.

20

  "Ne is the water in more constant case;
    Whether those same on high, or these belowe.
    For, th' Ocean moveth stil, from place to place;
175 And every River still doth ebbe and flowe:
    Ne any Lake, that seems most still and slowe,
    Ne Poole so small, that can his smoothnesse holde,
    When any winde doth under heaven blowe;
    With which, the clouds are also tost and rolled;
180 Now like great Hills; and, streight, like sluces, them unfold.

21

  "So likewise are all watry living wights
    Still tost, and turnéd, with continuall change,
    Hever abyding in their stedfast plights.
    The fish, still floting, doe at randon range,

185 And never rest; but evermore exchange
 Their dwelling places, as the streames them carrie:
 Ne have the watry foules a certaine grange,°   *dwelling*
 Wherein to rest, ne in one stead do tarry;
But flitting still doe flie, and still their places vary.

     22
190 "Next is the Ayre: which who feeles not by sense
 (For, of all sense it is the middle meane[4])
 To flit still? and, with subtill influence
 Of his thin spirit, all creatures to maintaine,
 In state of life? O weake life! that does leane
195 On thing so tickle° as th' unsteady ayre;   *uncertain*
 Which every howre is changed, and altred cleane
 With every blast that bloweth fowle or faire:
The faire doth it prolong; the fowle doth it impaire.

     23
 "Therein the changes infinite beholde,
200 Which to her creatures every minute chaunce;
 Now, boyling hot: streight, friezing deadly cold:
 Now, faire sun-shine, that makes all skip and daunce:
 Streight, bitter storms and balefull countenance,
 That makes them all to shiver and to shake:
205 Rayne, hayle, and snowe do pay them sad penance,
 And dreadful thunder-claps (that make them quake)
With flames and flashing lights that thousand changes make.

     24
 "Last is the fire: which, though it live for ever,
 Ne can be quenchéd quite; yet, every day,
210 Wee see his parts, so soone as they do sever,
 To lose their heat, and shortly to decay;
 So, makes himself his owne consuming pray.
 Ne any living creatures doth he breed:
 But all, that are of others bredd, doth slay;
215 And, with their death, his cruell life dooth feed;
Nought leaving but their barren ashes, without seede.

     25
 "Thus, all these fower° (the which the ground-work bee   *four*
 Of all the world, and of all living wights)
 To thousand sorts of Change we subject see.
220 Yet are they changed (by other wondrous slights)
 Into themselves, and lose their native mights;
 The Fire to Aire, and th' Ayre to Water sheere,°   *clear*
 And Water into Earth: yet Water fights
 With Fire, and Aire with Earth approaching neere:
225 Yet all are in one body, and as one appeare.

     26
 "So, in them all raignes Mutabilitie;
 How-ever these, that Gods themselves do call,
 Of them doe claime the rule and soveraity:

4. The conductor or medium.

As, Vesta, of the fire aethereall;
230 Vulcan, of this, with us so usuall;[5]
Ops, of the earth; and Juno of the Ayre;
Neptune, of Seas; and Nymphes, of Rivers all.
For, all those Rivers to me subject are:
And all the rest, which they usurp, be all my share.

27

235 "Which to approven true, as I have told,
Vouchsafe, O goddesse, to thy presence call
The rest which doe the world in being hold:
As, times and seasons of the yeare that fall:
Of all the which, demand in generall,
240 Or judge thy selfe, by verdit of thine eye,
Whether to me they are not subject all."
Nature did yeeld thereto; and by-and-by,
Bade Order call them all, before her Majesty.

28

So, forth issewed the Seasons of the yeare;
245 First, lusty Spring, all dight in leaves of flowres
That freshly budded and new bloosmes did beare
(In which a thousand birds had built their bowres
That sweetly sung, to call forth Paramours):
And in his hand a javelin he did beare,
250 And on his head (as fit for warlike stoures°)   *combats*
A guilt engraven morion° he did weare;   *helmet*
That as some did him love, so others did him feare.

29

Then came the jolly Sommer, being dight
In a thin silken cassock coloured greene,
255 That was unlynéd all, to be more light:
And on his head a girlond well beseene
He wore, from which as he had chaufféd° been   *heated*
The sweat did drop; and in his hand he bore
A boawe and shaftes, as he in forrest greene
260 Had hunted late the Libbard° or the Bore,   *leopard*
And now would bathe his limbes, with labor heated sore.

30

Then came the Autumne all in yellow clad,
As though he joyéd in his plentious store,
Laden with fruits that made him laugh, full glad
265 That he had banisht hunger, which to-fore
Had by the belly oft him pinchéd sore.
Upon his head a wreath that was enrold
With eares of corne, of every sort he bore:
And in his hand a sickle he did holde,
270 To reape the ripened fruits the which the earth had yold.

5. Vesta, Roman goddess of the hearth, is assigned by Spenser to rule over the fire that is above the air, as Vulcan rules over earthly fire ("this, with us so usuall"). Ops, Roman goddess of plenty and fertility, rules the earth.

31

Lastly, came Winter cloathéd all in frize,[6]
  Chattering his teeth for cold that did him chill,
  Whil'st on his hoary beard his breath did freese;
  And the dull drops that from his purpled bill
275 As from a limbeck did adown distill.
  In his right hand a tippéd staffe he held,
  With which his feeble steps he stayéd still:
  For, he was faint with cold, and weak with eld;
That scarse his looséd limbes he hable was to weld.

32

280 These, marching softly, thus in order went,
  And after them, the Monthes all riding came;
  First, sturdy March[7] with brows full sternly bent,
  And arméd strongly, rode upon a Ram,
  The same which over Hellespontus swam:[8]
285 Yet in his hand a spade he also hent,
  And in a bag all sorts of seeds ysame,
  Which on the earth he strowéd as he went,
And fild her womb with fruitfull hope of nourishment.

33

Next came fresh Aprill full of lustyhed,
290 And wanton as a Kid whose horne new buds:
  Upon a Bull he rode, the same which led
  Europa floting through th' Argolick fluds:[9]
  His hornes were gilden all with golden studs
  And garnishéd with garlonds goodly dight
295 Of all the fairest flowres and freshest buds
  Which th' earth brings forth, and wet he seemed in sight
With waves, through which he waded for his loves delight.

34

Then came faire May, the fayrest mayd on ground,
  Deckt all with dainties of her seasons pryde,
300 And throwing flowres out of her lap around:
  Upon two brethrens shoulders she did ride,
  The twinnes of Leda;[1] which on eyther side
  Supported her like to their soveraine Queene.
  Lord! how all creatures laught, when her they spide,
305 And leapt and daunc't as they had ravisht beene!
And Cupid selfe about her fluttred all in greene.

35

And after her, came jolly June, arrayd
  All in greene leaves, as he a Player were;
  Yet in his time, he wrought as well as playd,

6. A coarse woolen cloth.
7. In the old calendar, the year began in March.
8. The ram with the golden fleece, on which Helle and her brother Phrixus flew through the air to escape an evil stepmother. Helle fell off into a body of water that was named after her: the Hellespont.
9. The bull was Jupiter in disguise. He swam with Europa to Crete. "Argolick": Greek.
1. Castor and Pollux (the zodiacal sign of Gemini). Each month brings its zodiacal sign to the conference.

³¹⁰ That by his plough-yrons mote right well appeare:
Upon a Crab he rode, that him did beare
With crooked crawling steps an uncouth pase,
And backward yode,° as Bargemen wont to fare   *went*
Bending their force contrary to their face,
³¹⁵ Like that ungracious crew which faines demurest grace.

36

Then came hot July boyling like to fire,
That all his garments he had cast away:
Upon a Lyon raging yet with ire
He boldly rode and made him to obay:
³²⁰ It was the beast that whylome did forray
The Nemaean forrest, till th' Amphytrionide²
Him slew, and with his hide did him array;
Behinde his back a sithe, and by his side
Under his belt he bore a sickle circling wide.

37

³²⁵ The sixt was August, being rich arrayd
In garment all of gold downe to the ground
Yet rode he not, but led a lovely Mayd
Forth by the lilly hand, the which was cround
With eares of corne, and full her hand was found;
³³⁰ That was the righteous Virgin,³ which of old
Lived here on earth, and plenty made abound;
But, after Wrong was loved and Justice solde,
She left th' unrighteous world and was to heaven extold.°   *raised*

38

Next him, September marchéd eeke on foote;
³³⁵ Yet was he heavy laden with the spoyle
Of harvests riches, which he made his boot,°   *booty*
And him enricht with bounty of the soyle:
In his one hand, as fit for harvests toyle,
He held a knife-hook; and in th' other hand
³⁴⁰ A paire of waights, with which he did assoyle°   *weigh*
Both more and lesse, where it in doubt did stand,
And equall gave to each as Justice duly scanned.

39

Then came October full of merry glee:
For, yet his noule was totty of the must,⁴
³⁴⁵ Which he was treading in the wine-fats see,
And of the joyous oyle, whose gentle gust°   *taste*
Made him so frollick and so full of lust:°   *pleasure*
Upon a dreadfull Scorpion he did ride,
The same which by Dianaes doom unjust
³⁵⁰ Slew great Orion:⁵ and eeke by his side
He had his ploughing share, and coulter⁶ ready tyde.

---

2. I.e., Hercules.
3. Astraea, who symbolized Justice.
4. I.e., his head was unsteady from the wine-mash. "Wine-fats see": wine vats' sea.
5. According to one legend, Orion boasted that he could kill anything that came from the earth. Indignant at his arrogance, Diana sent a scorpion which stung and killed him.
6. Cutting edge of a plow.

40

Next was November, he full grosse and fat,
    As fed with lard, and that right well might seeme;
    For, he had been a fatting hogs of late,
355   That yet his browes with sweat, did reek and steem,
    And yet the season was full sharp and breem;°   *bitter*
    In planting eeke he took no small delight:
    Whereon he rode, not easie was to deeme;
    For it a dreadfull Centaure was in sight,
360 The seed of Saturne and faire Naïs, Chiron hight.

41

And after him, came next the chill December:
    Yet he through merry feasting which he made,
    And great bonfires, did not the cold remember;
    His Saviours birth his mind so much did glad:
365   Upon a shaggy-bearded Goat he rode,
    The same wherewith Dan Jove in tender yeares,
    They say, was nourisht by th' Idaean mayd;[7]
    And in his hand a broad deepe boawle he beares;
    Of which, he freely drinks an health to all his peeres.

42

370 Then came old January, wrappéd well
    In many weeds to keep the cold away;
    Yet did he quake and quiver like to quell,°   *curdle*
    And blowe his nayles to warme them if he may:
    For, they were numbd with holding all the day
375   An hatchet keene, with which he felléd wood,
    And from the trees did lop the needlesse spray:
    Upon an huge great Earth-pot steane[8] he stood;
    From whose wide mouth, there flowéd forth the Romane floud.[9]

43

And lastly, came cold February, sitting
380   In an old wagon, for he could not ride;
    Drawne of two fishes for the season fitting,
    Which through the flood before did softly slyde
    And swim away: yet had he by his side
    His plough and harnesse fit to till the ground,
385   And tooles to prune the trees, before the pride
    Of hasting Prime did make them burgein round:
    So past the twelve Months forth, and their dew places found.

44

And after these, there came the Day, and Night,
    Riding together both with equall pase,
390   Th' one on a Palfrey blacke, the other white;
    But Night had covered her uncomely face
    With a black veile, and held in hand a mace,

---

7. Jove was saved by his mother Rhea from being eaten by Cronus, his father. He was brought up in Crete and suckled by a goat. The "Idaean mayd" is the nymph of a Mt. Ida in Crete.
8. Jar (here standing for the constellation Aquarius).
9. I.e., the Tiber River.

On top whereof the moon and stars were pight,°   *placed*
And sleep and darknesse round about did trace:
395   But Day did beare, upon his scepters hight,
The goodly Sun, encompast all with beamés bright.

45

Then came the Howres, faire daughters of high Jove,
And timely Night, the which were all endewed
With wondrous beauty fit to kindle love;
400   But they were Virgins all, and love eschewed,
That might forslack the charge to them foreshewed
By mighty Jove; who did them Porters make
Of heavens gate (whence all the gods issued)
Which they did dayly watch, and nightly wake
405 By even turnes, he ever did their charge forsake.

46

And after all came Life, and lastly Death;
Death with most grim and griesly visage seene,
Yet is he nought but parting of the breath;
Ne ought to see, but like a shade to weene,
410   Unbodiéd, unsouled, unheard, unseene.
But Life was like a faire young lusty boy,
Such as they faine Dan Cupid to have beene,
Full of delightfull health and lively joy,
Deckt all with flowres, and wings of gold fit to employ.

47

415 When these were past, thus gan the Titanesse:
"Lo, mighty mother, now be judge and say,
Whether in all thy creatures more or lesse
CHANGE doth not raign and beare the greatest sway:
For, who sees not, that Time on all doth pray?
420   But Times do change and move continually.
So nothing here long standeth in one stay:
Wherefore, this lower world who can deny
But to be subject still to Mutabilitie?"

48

Then thus gan Jove: "Right true it is, that these
425   And all things else that under heaven dwell
Are chaunged of Time, who doth them all disseise°   *deprive*
Of being: But, who is it (to me tell)
That Time himselfe doth move and still compell
To keepe his course? Is not that namely wee
430   Which poure that vertue from our heavenly cell,
That moves them all, and makes them changéd be?
So them we gods doe rule, and in them also thee."

49

To whom, thus Mutability: "The things
Which we see not how they are moved and swayd,
435 Ye may attribute to your selves as Kings,
And say they by your secret powre are made:
But what we see not, who shall us perswade?

But were they so, as ye them faine to be,
   Moved by your might, and ordred by your ayde;
440 Yet what if I can prove, that even yee
   Your selves are likewise changed, and subject unto mee?

50

"And first, concerning her that is the first,
   Even you faire Cynthia, whom so much ye make
   Joves dearest darling, she was bred and nurst
445 On Cynthus hill, whence she her name did take:
   Then is she mortall borne, how-so ye crake;°   *boast*
   Besides, her face and countenance every day
   We changéd see, and sundry forms partake,
450 So that *as changefull as the Moone* men use to say.

51

"Next, Mercury, who though he lesse appeare
   To change his hew, and alwayes seeme as one;
   Yet, he his course doth altar every yeare,
   And is of late far out of order gone:
455 So Venus eeke, that goodly Paragone,
   Though faire all night, yet is she darke all day;
   And Phoebus self, who lightsome is alone,
   Yet is he oft eclipséd by the way,
And fills the darkned world with terror and dismay.

52

460 "Now Mars that valiant man is changéd most:
   For, he some times so far runs out of square,
   That he his way doth seem quite to have lost,
   And cleane without his usuall sphere to fare;
   That even these Star-gazers stonisht are
465 At sight thereof, and damne their lying bookes:
   So likewise, grim Sir Saturne oft doth spare
   His sterne aspect, and calme his crabbéd lookes:
So many turning cranks these have, so many crookes.

53

"But you Dan Jove, that only constant are,
470 And King of all the rest, as ye do clame,
   Are you not subject eeke to this misfare?
   Then let me aske you this withouten blame,
   Where were ye borne? some say in Crete by name,
   Others in Thebes, and others other-where;
475 But wheresoever they commént the same,
   They all consent that ye begotten were,
And borne here in this world, ne other can appeare.

54

"Then are ye mortall borne, and thrall to me,
   Unlesse the kingdome of the sky yee make
480 Immortall, and unchangeable to bee;
   Besides, that power and vertue which ye spake,
   That ye here worke, doth many changes take,

And your owne natures change: for, each of you
That vertue have, or this, or that to make,
Is checkt and changéd from his nature trew,
485 By others opposition or obliquid view.[1]

55

"Besides, the sundry motions of your Spheares,
So sundry waies and fashions as clerkes° faine,   *learned men*
Some in short space, and some in longer yeares;
What is the same but alteration plaine?
490 Onely the starrie skie doth still remaine:
Yet do the Starres and Signes therein still move,
And even it self is moved, as wizards saine.[2]
But all that moveth, doth mutation love:
Therefore both you and them to me I subject prove.

56

495 "Then since within this wide great Universe
Nothing doth firme and permanent appeare,
But all things tost and turnéd by transverse:[3]
What then should let,° but I aloft should reare   *hinder*
My Trophee, and from all, the triumph beare?
500 Now judge then (O thou greatest goddesse trew!)
According as thy selfe doest see and heare,
And unto me addoom° that is my dew;   *decree, award*
That is the rule of all, all being ruled by you."

57

So having ended, silence long ensewed,
505 Ne Nature to or fro spake for a space,
But with firme eyes affixt, the ground still viewed.
Meane while, all creatures, looking in her face,
Expecting th' end of this so doubtfull case,
Did hang in long suspence what would ensew,
510 To whether side should fall the soveraigne place:
At length, she looking up with chearefull view,
The silence brake, and gave her doome in speeches few.

58

"I well consider all that ye have sayd,
And find that all things stedfastnes doe hate
515 And changéd be: yet being rightly wayd°   *weighed*
They are not changéd from their first estate;
But by their change their being doe dilate:
And turning to themselves at length againe,
Doe worke their owne perfection so by fate:
520 Then over them Change doth not rule and raigne;
But they raigne over change, and doe their states maintaine.

59

"Cease therefore daughter further to aspire,
And thee content thus to be ruled by me:
For thy decay thou seekst by thy desire;

---

1. A reference to the central idea of astrology—that each planet has a "virtue" that it sheds on earth; the effect is dependent upon its position and the position of other planets.
2. As scientists say.
3. I.e., crosswise.

525 But time shall come that all shall changéd bee,
And from thenceforth, none no more change shall see."
So was the Titaness put downe and whist,°   *silenced*
And Jove confirmed in his imperiall see.°   *position*
Then was that whole assembly quite dismist,
530 And Natur's selfe did vanish, whither no man wist.

The VIII Canto, Unperfite

1

When I bethinke me on that speech whyleare,
Of Mutability, and well it way:
Me seemes, that though she all unworthy were
Of the Heav'ns Rule; yet very sooth to say,
5 In all things else she beares the greatest sway.
Which makes me loath this state of life so tickle,°   *precarious*
And love of things so vaine to cast away;
Whose flowring pride, so fading and so fickle,
Short Time shall soon cut down with his consuming sickle.

2

10 Then gin I thinke on that which Nature sayd,
Of that same time when no more Change shall be,
But stedfast rest of all things firmely stayd
Upon the pillours of Eternity,
That is contrayr to Mutabilitie:
15 For, all that moveth, doth in Change delight:
But thence-forth all shall rest eternally
With Him that is the God of Sabbaoth hight:
O that great Sabbaoth God, graunt me that Sabaoths sight.

                           1590, 1596, 1609

From Amoretti[4]

Sonnet 1

Happy ye leaves when as those lilly hands,
Which hold my life in their dead doing[5] might,
Shall handle you and hold in loves soft bands,
Lyke captives trembling at the victors sight.
5 And happy lines, on which with starry light,
Those lamping eyes will deigne sometimes to look
And reade the sorrowes of my dying spright,°   *spirit*
Written with teares in harts close° bleeding book.   *secret*
And happy rymes bathed in the sacred brooke,

---

4. I.e., "little loves" or "little love poems." They are sonnets to a woman named Elizabeth—probably Elizabeth Boyle, who became Spenser's second wife. The sequence, or cycle, tells of a courtship (*Epithalamion*, with which they were published, is a song for a wedding). The *Amoretti* draws, like other sonnet cycles, upon characteristic and conventional themes and conceits; what is characteristically Spenserian about them is his understanding, and yoking, of the spirit and the flesh; see, for example, lines 9–12 of Sonnet 1. The rhyme scheme is *abab bcbc cdcd ee*, a difficult pattern requiring four words for two of the rhymes.

5. I.e., killing.

10 Of Helicon[6] whence she deriveéd is,
When ye behold that Angels blessed looke,
My soules long lackéd foode, my heavens blis.
Leaves, lines, and rymes, seeke her to please alone,
Whom if ye please, I care for other none.

Sonnet 34

Lyke as a ship that through the ocean wyde,
By conduct of some star doth make her way,
Whenas a storme hath dimd her trusty guyde,
Out of her course doth wander far astray.
5 So I whose star, that wont with her bright ray,
Me to direct, with cloudes is overcast,
Doe wander now in darknesse and dismay,
Through hidden perils round about me plast.°   *placed*
Yet hope I well, that when this storme is past
10 My Helice[7] the lodestar of my lyfe
Will shine again, and looke on me at last,
With lovely light to cleare my cloudy grief.
Till then I wander carefull° comfortlesse,   *full of cares*
In secret sorow and sad pensivenesse.

Sonnet 35

My hungry eyes through greedy covetize,
Still to behold the object of their paine,
With no contentment can themselves suffize:
But having pine° and having not complaine.   *starve*
5 For lacking it they cannot lyfe sustayne,
And having it they gaze on it the more:
In their amazement lyke Narcissus[8] vaine
Whose eyes him starved: so plenty makes me poore.
Yet are mine eyes so filled with the store°   *abundance*
10 Of that faire sight, that nothing else they brooke,
But lothe the things which they did like before,
And can no more endure on them to looke.
All this worlds glory seemeth vayne to me,
And all their showes but shadowes, saving she.

Sonnet 37

What guyle is this, that those her golden tresses,
She doth attyre under a net of gold:
And with sly° skill so cunningly them dresses,   *clever*
That which is gold or heare, may scarse be told?
5 Is it that mens frayle eyes, which gaze too bold,
She may entangle in that golden snare:
And being caught may craftily enfold,
Theyr weaker harts, which are not wel aware?
Take heed therefore, myne eyes, how ye doe stare
10 Henceforth too rashly on that guilefull net,

6. The "sacred brooke" is the Hippo-
crene, which flows from Mount Helicon,
the mountain sacred to the Muses. It
not only inspires the poet but here represents heaven, where his beloved originated.
7. The Big Dipper or North Star.
8. The beautiful youth in mythology
who fell in love with his own reflection.

In which if ever ye entrappéd are,
Out of her bands ye *by no means shall get.*
Fondnesse° it were for any being free,   *foolishness*
To covet fetters, though they golden bee.

Sonnet 54

Of this worlds theatre in which we stay,
My love like the spectator ydly sits
Beholding me that all the pageants play,
Disguysing diversly my troubled wits.
5   Sometimes I joy when glad occasion fits,
And mask in myrth lyke to a comedy:
Soone after when my joy to sorrow flits,
I waile and make my woes a tragedy.
Yet she, beholding me with constant eye,
10 Delights not in my merth nor rues my smart:
But when I laugh she mocks, and when I cry
She laughs and hardens evermore her heart.
What then can move her? if nor merth nor mone,°   *moan*
She is no woman, but a sencelesse stone.

Sonnet 59

Thrise happie she, that is so well assured
Unto her selfe and setled so in hart:
That nether will for better be allured,
Ne feard with worse to any chaunce to start:
5   But like a steddy ship doth strongly part
The raging waves and keepes her course aright:
Ne ought ° for tempest doth from it depart,   *at all*
Ne ought for fayrer weathers false delight.
Such selfe assurance need not feare the spight
10 Of grudging foes, ne favour seek of friends:
But in the stay of her owne stedfast might,
Nether to one her self nor other bends.
Most happy she that most assured doth rest,
But he most happy who such one loves best.

Sonnet 68

Most glorious Lord of lyfe, that on this day,[9]
Didst make thy triumph over death and sin:
And having harrowed hell,[1] didst bring away
Captivity thence captive us to win:
5   This joyous day, deare Lord, with joy begin,
And grant that we for whom thou diddest dye
Being with thy deare blood clene washt from sin,
May live for ever in felicity.
And that thy love we weighing worthily,
10 May likewise love thee for the same againe:

9. Easter Day.
1. In the apocryphal gospels, Christ descended into hell and led out those who had lived before his time that de- served to be saved. "Captivity thence captive" is a Biblical phrase, as in Judges v.12 and Ephesians iv.8.

And for thy sake that all lyke deare didst buy,
With love may one another entertayne.
So let us love, deare love, lyke as we ought,
Love is the lesson which the Lord us taught.[2]

Sonnet 70

Fresh spring the herald of loves mighty king,
In whose cote armour[3] richly are displayd
All sorts of flowers the which on earth do spring
In goodly colours gloriously arrayd.
5   Goe to my love, where she is carelesse layd,
Yet in her winters bowre not well awake:
Tell her the joyous time wil not be staid
Unlesse she doe him by the forelock take.
Bid her therefore her selfe soone ready make,
10   To wayt on love amongst his lovely crew:
Where every one that misseth then her make,°   mate, lover
Shall be by him amearest with penance dew.[4]
Make hast therefore sweet love, whilest it is prime,°*early morning*
For none can call againe the passéd time.

Sonnet 75[5]

One day I wrote her name upon the strand,
But came the waves and washéd it away:
Agayne I wrote it with a second hand,
But came the tyde, and made my paynes his pray.
5   "Vayne man," sayd she, "that doest in vaine assay,
A mortall thing so to immortalize,
For I my selve shall lyke to this decay,
And eek my name bee wypéd out lykewize."
"Not so," quod° I, "let baser things devize   quoth
10   To dy in dust, but you shall live by fame:
My verse your vertues rare shall eternize,
And in the heavens wryte your glorious name.
Where whenas death shall all the world subdew,
Our love shall live, and later life renew."

Sonnet 79

Men call you fayre, and you doe credit° it,   believe
For that your selfe ye dayly such doe see:
But the trew fayre, that is the gentle wit,
And vertuous mind, is much more praysd of me.
5   For all the rest, how ever fayre it be,
Shall turne to nought and loose that glorious hew:
But onely that is permanent and free
From frayle corruption, that doth flesh ensew.°   outlast
That is true beautie: that doth argue you

---

2. Cf. John xv.12: "This is my commandment, That ye love one another, as I have loved you."
3. Coat of arms.
4. I.e., have suitable penance imposed upon him.
5. The theme here expressed is an ancient and traditional one. Cf. Shakespeare's Sonnet 55, "Not marble, nor the gilded **monuments.**"

10   To be divine and borne of heavenly seed:
     Derived from that fayre Spirit, from whom al true
     And perfect beauty did at first proceed.
     He onely fayre, and what he fayre hath made:
     All other fayre, lyke flowres, untymely fade.

1595

Epithalamion[1]

     Ye learned sisters which have oftentimes
     Beene to me ayding, others to adorne:[2]
     Whom ye thought worthy of your gracefull rymes,
     That even the greatest did not greatly scorne
5   To heare theyr names sung in your simple layes,
     But joyéd in theyr prayse.
     And when ye list your owne mishaps to mourne,
     Which death, or love, or fortunes wreck did rayse,
     Your string could soone to sadder tenor° turne,   *mood*
10 And teach the woods and waters to lament
     Your dolefull dreriment.°   *sorrow*
     Now lay those sorrowfull complaints aside,
     And having all your heads with girland crownd,
     Helpe me mine owne loves prayses to resound,
15 Ne let the same of° any be envide: *by*
     So Orpheus did for his owne bride,[3]
     So I unto my selfe alone will sing,
     The woods shall to me answer and my Eccho ring.

     Early before the worlds light giving lampe,
20 His golden beame upon the hils doth spred,

1. An epithalamion is a wedding song or poem; its Greek name conveys that it was sung on the threshold of the bridal chamber. The genre was widely practiced by the Latin poets, particularly Catullus. Catullus wrote two kinds of epithalamion: one in an elevated ceremonial style, the other in a more private, lyric style; it is the latter style that Spenser follows. Common elements are the invocation to the Muses, the bringing home of the bride, the singing and dancing at the wedding party, and the preparations for the wedding night. The reader should be aware that the poem's merit is not in its "originality" but in its evocative, many-layered commingling of the conventions. Spenser blends with these conventional elements his own Irish setting and native folklore.

In addition, the *Epithalamion* is highly structured. First there is an introductory stanza, then two 10-stanza sections on each side of the two central stanzas about the church ceremony itself. Each of the 10-stanza sections is divided into units of 3-4-3. As A. Kent Hieatt has pointed out in his book, *Short Time's Endless Monument* (1960), the poem also has a surprising and complex numerical structure that reinforces the motif of the passage of time. For example, the poem has exactly 365 long lines (composed of five or more metrical feet) matching the number of days in the year. There are 24 stanzas, counting the envoy, matching the hours of one day and night. Of these stanzas, the first 16 describe the course of the day, in which the woods echo the various sounds; the last 8 describe the night, a time of silence in which the woods no longer echo. At the summer solstice (cf. line 266 and note) in the latitude of Ireland, night in fact falls after 16 hours of daylight.

To point to these elements of high artistry is not, of course, to explain why the *Epithalamion* is one of the great poems of the language. The subtle time structure serves to reinforce the idea implicit throughout the poem that this marriage has reference to all marriages; it emphasizes the endless cycle of time, measured by the passing of the hours and the years—as against which marriage, as a Christian sacrament, stands firm, "eterne in mutabilitie."

2. I.e., to write poems in praise of others (e.g., Queen Elizabeth in *The Faerie Queene*). The "learned sisters" are the Muses.

3. Orpheus, the most famous musician of classical antiquity, was equally famous for his love for his wife Eurydice.

Having disperst the nights unchearefull dampe,
Doe ye awake, and with fresh lustyhed°   *vigor*
Go to the bowre° of my belovéd love,   *bedchamber*
My truest turtle dove,
25   Bid her awake; for Hymen[4] is awake,
And long since ready forth his maske to move,
With his bright Tead[5] that flames with many a flake,°   *spark*
And many a bachelor to waite on him,
In theyr fresh garments trim.
30   Bid her awake therefore and soone her dight,°   *dress*
For lo the wishéd day is come at last,
That shall for al the paynes and sorrowes past,
Pay to her usury of long delight:
And whylest she doth her dight,
35   Doe ye to her of joy and solace sing,
That all the woods may answer and your eccho ring.

Bring with you all the Nymphes that you can heare[6]
Both of the rivers and the forrests greene:
And of the sea that neighbours to her neare,
40   Al with gay girlands goodly wel beseene.[7]
And let them also with them bring in hand,
Another gay girland
For my fayre love of lillyes and of roses,
Bound truelove wize[8] with a blew silke riband.
45   And let them make great store of bridale poses,°   *posies*
And let them eeke bring store of other flowers
To deck the bridale bowers.
And let the ground whereas her foot shall tread,
For feare the stones her tender foot should wrong
50   Be strewed with fragrant flowers all along,
And diapred lyke the discolored mead. [9]
Which done, doe at her chamber dore awayt,
For she will waken strayt, °   *straightway*
The whiles doe ye this song unto her sing,
55   The woods shall to you answer and your Eccho ring.

Ye Nymphes of Mulla[1] which with careful heed,
The silver scaly trouts doe tend full well,
And greedy pikes which use therein to feed,
(Those trouts and pikes all others doo excell)
60   And ye likewise, which keepe the rushy lake,
Where none doo fishes take,
Bynd up the locks the which hang scatterd light,
And in his waters which your mirror make,
Behold your faces as the christall bright,
65   That when you come whereas my love doth lie,
No blemish she may spie.

---

4. The god of marriage, who leads a "maske" or procession at weddings.
5. A ceremonial torch, associated with marriages since classical times.
6. I.e., that can hear you.
7. I.e., beautified.
8. I.e., in a love knot.
9. I.e., ornamented like the many-colored meadow.
1. The vale of Mulla, near Spenser's home in Ireland.

And eke ye lightfoot mayds which keepe the deere.[2]
That on the hoary mountayne use to towre,
And the wylde wolves which seeke them to devoure,
70 With your steele darts doo chace from comming neer
Be also present heere,
To helpe to decke her and to help to sing,
That all the woods may answer and your eccho ring.

Wake, now my love, awake; for it is time,
75 The Rosy Morne long since left Tithones bed,
All ready to her silver coche to clyme,
And Phoebus gins to shew his glorious hed.
Hark how the cheerefull birds do chaunt theyr laies
And carroll of loves praise.
80 The merry Larke hir mattins° sing aloft,   *morning prayers*
The thrust replyes, the Mavis descant[3] playes,
The Ouzell shrills, the Ruddock warbles soft,
So goodly all agree with sweet consent,
To this dayes merriment.
85 Ah my deere love why doe ye sleepe thus long,
When meeter were that ye should now awake,
T' away the comming of your joyous make,°   *mate*
And hearken to the birds lovelearnéd song,
The deawy leaves among.
90 For they of joy and pleasance to you sing,
That all the woods them answer and theyr eccho ring.

My love is now awake out of her dreame,
And her fayre eyes like stars that dimméd were
With darksome cloud, now shew theyr goodly beams
95 More bright then Hesperus° his head doth rere.   *evening star*
Come now ye damzels, daughters of delight,
Helpe quickly her to dight,
But first come ye fayre houres which were begot
In Joves sweet paradice, of Day and Night,
100 Which doe the seasons of the yeare allot,
And al that ever in this world is fayre
Doe make and still repayre.[4]
And ye three handmayds of the Cyprian Queene,[5]
The which doe still adorne her beauties pride,
105 Helpe to addorne my beautifullest bride:
And as ye her array, still throw betweene°   *now and then*
Some graces to be seene,
And as ye use to Venus, to her sing,
The whiles the woods shal answer and your eccho ring.

110 Now is my love all ready forth to come,
Let all the virgins therefore well awayt,

2. I.e., all wild animals, kept by the forest nymphs. To "towre" (a falconry term) is to occupy heights.
3. A melody or counterpoint written above a musical theme—a soprano obbligato. The "Mavis" is the thrush. The "Ouzell" is the blackbird (which sings in England); the "Ruddock," the European robin. The birds' concert is a convention of medieval love poetry.
4. In the passage of the hours, all things on earth change. "Still": continuously.
5. The Graces attending on Venus ("Cyprian Queene"), representing brightness, joy, and bloom.

And ye fresh boyes that tend upon her groome
Prepare your selves; for he is comming strayt.
Set all your things in seemely good aray°   *order*
115 Fit for so joyfull day,
The joyfulst day that ever sunne did see.
Faire Sun, shew forth thy favourable ray,
And let thy lifull° heat not fervent be   *lifegiving*
For feare of burning her sunshyny face,
120 Her beauty to disgrace.
O fayrest Phoebus, father of the Muse,
If ever I did honour thee aright,
Or sing the thing, that mote° they mind delight,   *might*
Doe not thy servants simple boone refuse,
125 But let this day let this one day be myne,
Let all the rest be thine.
Then I thy soverayne prayses loud wil sing,
That all the woods shal answer and theyr eccho ring.

Harke how the Minstrels gin to shrill aloud
130 Their merry Musick that resounds from far,
The pipe, the tabor, and the trembling Croud,[6]
That well agree withouten breach or jar.°   *discord*
But most of all the Damzels doe delite,
When they their tymbrels° smyte,   *tambourines*
135 And thereunto doe daunce and carrol sweet,
That all the sences they doe ravish quite,
The whyles the boyes run up and downe the street,
Crying aloud with strong confuséd noyce,
As if it were one voyce.
140 *Hymen iô Hymen, Hymen*[7] they do shout,
That even to the heavens theyr shouting shrill
Doth reach, and all the firmament doth fill,
To which the people standing all about,
As in approvance doe thereto applaud
145 And loud advaunce her laud,°   *praise*
And evermore they *Hymen Hymen* sing,
That al the woods them answer and theyr eccho ring.

Loe where she comes along with portly° pace   *stately*
Lyke Phoebe from her chamber of the East,
150 Arysing forth to run her mighty race,[8]
Clad all in white, that seemes° a virgin best.   *suits*
So well it her beseems that ye would weene
Some angell she had beene.
Her long loose yellow locks lyke golden wyre,
155 Sprinckled with perle, and perling° flowres a tweene, *winding*
Doe lyke a golden mantle her attyre,

---

6. Primitive fiddle; the "tabor" is a small drum. Spenser here designates Irish, not classical, instruments and music for the classical masque or ballet.
7. The name of the god of marriage, used as a conventional exclamation at weddings.
8. Phoebe is the moon, a virgin like the bride; the reference to her antici-pates the night.

And being crownéd with girland greene,
Seeme lyke some mayden Queene.
Her modest eyes abashéd to behold
160 So many gazers, as on her do stare,
Upon the lowly ground affixéd are.
Ne dare lift up her countenance too bold,
But blush to heare her prayses sung so loud,
So farre from being proud.
165 Nathlesse doe ye still loud her prayses sing.
That all the woods may answer and your eccho ring.

Tell me ye merchants daughters did ye see
So fayre a creature in your towne before,
So sweet, so lovely, and so mild as she,
170 Adornd with beautyes grace and vertues store,
Her goodly eyes lyke Saphyres shining bright,
Her forehead yvory white,
Her cheekes lyke apples which the sun hath rudded,°   made red
Her lips lyke cherryes charming men to byte,
175 Her brest like to a bowle of creame uncrudded,°   uncurdled
Her paps lyke lyllies budded,
Her snowie necke lyke to a marble towre,
And all her body like a pallace fayre,
Ascending uppe with many a stately stayre,
180 To honors seat and chastities sweet bowre.[9]
Why stand ye still ye virgins in amaze,
Upon her so to gaze,
Whiles ye forget your former lay to sing,
To which the woods did answer and your eccho ring.

185 But if ye saw that which no eyes can see,
The inward beauty of her lively spright,°   soul
Garnisht with heavenly guifts of high degree,
Much more then would ye wonder at that sight,
And stand astonisht lyke to those which red°   discern
190 Medusaes mazeful hed.[1]
There dwels sweet love and constant chastity,
Unspotted fayth and comely womanhood,
Regard of honour and mild modesty,
There vertue raynes as Queene in royal throne,
195 And giveth lawes alone.
The which the base° affections doe obay,   lower
And yeeld theyr services unto her will,
Ne thought of thing uncomely ever may
Thereto approch to tempt her mind to ill.
200 Had ye once seene these her celestial threasures,
And unrevealéd pleasures,
Then would ye wonder and her prayses sing,
That al the woods should answer and your echo ring.

---

9. The head, where the higher faculties are. The catalogue of qualities is a convention in love poetry. Cf. also The Song of Solomon iv–viii.

1. Medusa, one of the Gorgons, had serpents instead of hair (hence a "mazeful hed"): the effect on a beholder was to turn him to stone.

Open the temple gates unto my love,
205 Open them wide that she may enter in,
And all the postes adorne as doth behove,[2]
And all the pillours deck with girlands trim,
For to recyve this Saynt with honour dew,
That commeth in to you.
210 With trembling steps and humble reverence,
She commeth in, before th' almighties vew,
Of her ye virgins learne obedience,
When so ye come into those holy places,
To humble your proud faces:
215 Bring her up to th' high altar, that she may
The sacred ceremonies there partake,
The which do endless matrimony make,
And let the roring Organs loudly play
The praises of the Lord in lively notes,
220 The whiles with hollow throates
The Choristers the joyous Antheme sing,
That al the woods may answere and their eccho ring.

Behold whiles she before the altar stands
Hearing the holy priest that to her speakes
225 And blesseth her with his two happy hands,
How the red roses flush up in her cheekes,
And the pure snow with goodly vermill stayne,
Like crimsin dyde in grayne,°   *fast color*
That even th' Angels which continually,
230 About the sacred Altare doe remaine,
Forget their service and about her fly,
Ofte peeping in her face that seemes more fayre,
The more they on it stare.
But her sad° eyes still fastened on the ground,   *modest*
235 Are governéd with goodly modesty,
That suffers not one looke to glaunce awry,
Which may let in a little thought unsownd.
Why blush ye love to give to me your hand,
The pledge of all our band?°   *bond, tie*
240 Sing ye sweet Angels, Alleluya sing,
That all the woods may answere and your eccho ring.

Now al is done; bring home the bride againe,
Bring home the triumph of our victory,
Bring home with you the glory of her gaine,[3]
245 With joyance bring her and with jollity.
Never had man more joyfull day then this,
Whom heaven would heape with blis.
Make feast therefore now all this live long day,
This day for ever to me holy is,
250 Poure out the wine without restraint or stay,
Poure not by cups, but by the belly full,

2. As is proper. The doorposts were trimmed for weddings in classical times, and the custom was often referred to in classical and medieval love poetry.
3. I.e., the glory of gaining her.

Poure out to all that wull,°   *want it*
And sprinkle all the postes and wals with wine,
That they may sweat, and drunken be withall.
255 Crowne ye God Bacchus with a coronall,°   *flower garland*
And Hymen also crowne with wreathes of vine,
And let the Graces daunce unto the rest;
For they can doo it best:
The whiles the maydens doe theyr carroll sing,
260 To which the woods shal answer and theyr eccho ring.

Ring ye the bels, ye young men of the towne,
And leave your wonted labors for this day:
This day is holy; doe ye write it downe,
That ye for ever it remember may.
265 This day the sunne is in his chiefest hight,
With Barnaby the bright,[4]
From whence declining daily by degrees,
He somewhat loseth of his heat and light,
When once the Crab[5] behind his back he sees.
270 But for this time it ill ordainéd was,
To chose the longest day in all the yeare,
And shortest night, when longest fitter weare:
Yet never day so long, but late° would passe.   *at last*
Ring ye the bels, to make it weare away,
275 And bonefiers make all day,
And daunce about them, and about them sing:
That all the woods may answer, and your eccho ring.

Ah when will this long weary day have end,
And lende me leave to come unto my love?
280 How slowly do the houres theyr numbers spend?
How slowly does sad Time his feathers move?
Hast thee O fayrest Planet to thy home
Within the Westerne fome:
Thy tyred steedes long since have need of rest.
285 Long though it be, at last I see it gloome,
And the bright evening star with golden creast
Appeare out of the East.
Fayre childe of beauty, glorious lampe of love
That all the host of heaven in rankes doost lead,
290 And guydest lovers through the nightés dread,
How chearefully thou lookest from above,
And seemst to laugh atweene thy twinkling light
As joying in the sight
Of these glad many which for joy doe sing,
295 That all the woods them answer and their echo ring.

Now ceasse ye damsels your delights forepast;
Enough is it, that all the day was youres:
Now day is doen, and night is nighing fast:
Now bring the Bryde into the brydall boures.

4. St. Barnabas' Day, at the time of the summer solstice.
5. The constellation Cancer between Gemini and Leo. The sun, passing through the zodiac, leaves the Crab behind toward the end of July.

300 Now night is come, now soone her disaray,
And in her bed her lay;
Lay her in lillies and in violets,
And silken courteins over her display,°   *spread*
And odour sheetes, and Arras° coverlets.   *tapestry*
305 Behold how goodly my faire love does ly
In proud humility;
Like unto Maia,[6] when as Jove her tooke,
In Tempe, lying on the flowry gras,
Twixt sleepe and wake, after she weary was,
310 With bathing in the Acidalian brooke.
Now it is night, ye damsels may be gon,
And leave my love alone,
And leave likewise your former lay to sing:
The woods no more shal answere, nor your echo ring.

315 Now welcome night, thou night so long expected,
That long daies labour doest at last defray,°   *pay*
And all my cares, which cruell love collected,
Hast sumd in one, and cancelléd for aye:
Spread thy broad wing over my love and me,
320 That no man may us see,
And in thy sable mantle us enwrap,
From feare of perrill and foule horror free.
Let no false treason seeke us to entrap,
Nor any dread disquiet once annoy
325 The safety of our joy:
But let the night be calme and quietsome,
Without tempestuous storms or sad afray:
Lyke as when Jove with fayre Alcmena[7] lay,
When he begot the great Tirynthian groome:
330 Or lyke as when he with thy selfe[8] did lie,
And begot Majesty.
And let the mayds and yongmen cease to sing:
Ne let the woods them answer, nor theyr eccho ring.

Let no lamenting cryes, nor dolefull teares,
335 Be heard all night within nor yet without.
Ne let false whispers, breeding hidden feares,
Breake gentle sleepe with misconceivéd dout.
Let no deluding dreames, nor dreadful sights
Make sudden sad affrights;
340 Ne let housefyres, nor lightnings helpelesse harmes,
Ne let the Pouke,[9] nor other evill sprights,
Ne let mischivous witches with theyr charmes,
Ne let hob Goblins, names whose sence we see not,
Fray us with things that be not.
345 Let not the shriech Oule, nor the Storke be heard:

---

6. The eldest and most beautiful of the Pleiades.
7. The mother of Hercules ("the great Tirynthian groome").
8. I.e., night.
9. Puck, Robin Goodfellow—here more powerful and evil than Shakespeare made him.

Nor the night Raven that still deadly yels,[1]
Nor damnéd ghosts cald up with mighty spels,
Nor griesly vultures make us once affeard:
Ne let th'unpleasant Quyre of Frogs still croking
350   Make us to wish theyr choking.
Let none of these theyr drery accents sing;
Ne let the woods them answer, nor theyr eccho ring.

But let stil Silence trew night watches keepe,
That sacred peace may in assurance rayne,
355   And tymely sleep, when it is tyme to sleepe,
May poure his limbs forth on your[2] pleasant playne,
The whiles an hundred little wingéd loves,[3]
Like divers fethered doves,
Shall fly and flutter round about your bed,
360   And in the secret darke, that none reproves,
Their prety stealthes shal worke, and snares shal spread
To filch away sweet snatches of delight,
Conceald through covert night.
Ye sonnes of Venus, play your sports at will,
365   For greedy pleasure, carelesse of your toyes,°   *frivolities*
Thinks more upon her paradise of joyes,
Then what ye do, albe it good or ill.
All night therefore attend your merry play,
For it will soone be day:
370   Now none doth hinder you, that say or sing,
Ne will the woods now answer, nor your Eccho ring.

Who is the same, which at my window peepes?
Or whose is that faire face, that shines so bright,
Is it not Cinthia,[4] she that never sleepes,
375   But walkes about high heaven al the night?
O fayrest goddesse, do thou not envy
My love with me to spy:
For thou likewise didst love, though now unthought,° *unsuspected*
And for a fleece of woll,° which privily,   *wool*
380   The Latmian shephard[5] once unto thee brought,
His pleasures with thee wrought,
Therefore to us be favorable now;
And sith of wemens labours thou hast charge,[6]
And generation goodly dost enlarge,
385   Encline thy will t' effect our wishfull vow,
And the chast wombe informe with timely seed,
That may our comfort breed:
Till which we cease our hopefull hap to sing,
Ne let the woods us answere, nor our Eccho ring.

---

1. The owl and the night raven were
birds of ill omen; the stork, in Chaucer's
Parliament of Fowls, is called an avenger
of adultery. "Still": always.
2. I.e., Night's.
3. Cupids (or amoretti).
4. I.e., the moon.
5. Endymion, beloved by the moon.

The "fleece of woll," however, comes
from another story—that of Pan's enticement of the moon.
6. Diana (the moon, "Cinthia") is,
as Lucina, patroness of births; the "labours" are, of course, those of childbirth.

390 And thou great Juno, which with awful might
The lawes of wedlock still dost patronize,
And the religion of the faith first plight
With sacred rites hast taught to solemnize:
And eeke for comfort often calléd art
395 Of women in their smart,°   *labor*
Eternally bind thou this lovely band,
And all thy blessings unto us impart.
And thou glad Genius,[7] in whose gentle hand,
The bridale bowre and geniall bed remaine,
400 Without blemish or staine,
And the sweet pleasures of theyr loves delight
With secret ayde doest succour and supply,
Till they bring forth the fruitfull progeny,
Send us the timely fruit of this same night.
405 And thou fayre Hebe,[8] and thou Hymen free,
Grant that it may be so.
Til which we cease your further prayse to sing,
Ne any woods shal answer, nor your Eccho ring.

And ye high heavens, the temple of the gods,
410 In which a thousand torches flaming bright
Doe burne, that to us wretched earthly clods,
In dreadful darknesse lend desired light;
And all ye powers which in the same remayne,
More than we men can fayne,
415 Poure out your blessing on us plentiously,
And happy influence upon us raine,
That we may raise a large posterity,
Which from the earth, which they may long possesse,
With lasting happinesse,
420 Up to your haughty pallaces may mount,
And for the guerdon of theyr glorious merit
May heavenly tabernacles there inherit,
Of blessed Saints for to increase the count.
So let us rest, sweet love, in hope of this,
425 And cease till then our tymely joyes to sing,
The woods no more us answer, nor our eccho ring.

Song made in lieu of many ornaments,
With which my love should duly have bene dect,
Which cutting off through hasty accidents,
430 Ye would not stay your dew time to expect,
But promist both to recompens,
Be unto her a goodly ornament,
And for short time an endlesse moniment.[9]

1595

---

7. Patron of sex, pregnancy, reproduction. Cf. Genius in the Garden of Adonis (*The Faerie Queene* III.vi.31).
8. Patron of youth and freedom.
9. The envoy is traditionally apologetic in tone: the poem is offered as a substitute for wedding presents ("ornaments") that did not arrive in time for the wedding. But this elaborate poem is itself a "goodly ornament," for (in a final reference to the theme of time and eternity) it stands as a timeless monument of art to the passing day which it celebrates.

SIR WALTER RALEGH
(1552–1618)

The brilliant and versatile Ralegh was a soldier, courtier, poet, philosopher, explorer and colonizer, student of science, and historian. He is popularly known now as the founder of Virginia and the introducer of tobacco into Europe, but in his own time he was known for his skeptical mind, his great favor with the queen, his hatred of Spain, and, to Edmund Spenser and others, his poetry. The major part of his verse has not survived; it was a long poem to the queen called *Cynthia*; it was never printed and we have only a few stanzas in manuscript. Some of his shorter poems were very popular and were printed in anthologies or songbooks. His reply to Marlowe's *Passionate Shepherd* is only one of several such answers; both Donne and Herrick wrote them, but Ralegh's is the best. His poem *The Lie*, with its attacks upon social classes and institutions, in its turn provoked many answers. *Farewell, False Love* is an early poem of Ralegh's which was set to music by the composer William Byrd in 1588.

His prose is narrative, descriptive, and philosophical. He published in 1591, soon after the events it describes, his account of the heroic fight of his cousin, Sir Richard Grenville, with a greatly superior Spanish fleet. In 1595 he published a piece of propaganda for exploration with the title *The Discovery of the Large, Rich, and Beautiful Empire of Guiana, with a Relation of the Great and Golden City of Manoa, which the Spaniards call El Dorado, and the Provinces of Emeria, Arromaia, Amapaia and Other Countries, with their Rivers Adjoining.*

From 1603 to his execution in 1618 Ralegh was kept imprisoned in the Tower of London by King James, except for a period in 1617 when he made his ill-fated last voyage to Guiana. In prison he wrote his long, unfinished *History of the World*; it confines itself to the earliest times and does not deal with recent history because, as Ralegh remarked, he who follows truth too closely at the heels might get kicked in the teeth. The most famous passage in the *History* is at the end. An apostrophe to Death, it is a fine example of rotund 17th-century prose:

> O eloquent, just, and mighty Death! Whom none could advise, thou hast persuaded; what none hath dared, thou hast done; and whom the world hath flattered thou only hast cast out of the world and despised. Thou hast drawn together all the farfetched greatness, all the pride, cruelty, and ambition of man, and covered it all over with these two narrow words, *His jacet!* [Here lies]

Ralegh was a passionate man, like Hotspur and Hamlet, and of course he had enemies. Yet by 1618 popular sympathy was so much in his favor that, as Trevelyan said, "the ghost of Ralegh pursued the House of Stuart to the scaffold." Had he not earned a name as the founder of Virginia, the eloquent and grave historian, "a seafaring man, a soldier and a courtier," as he

described himself on the scaffold, he would still be the poet Spenser
praised, "the sommers nightingale" who

> tooke in hond
> My pipe, before that aeméuléd [imitated] of many,
> And plaid thereon; (for well that skil he cond) [knew]
> Himself as skilfull in that art as any.

The Nymph's Reply to the Shepherd

If all the world and love were young,
And truth in every shepherd's tongue,
These pretty pleasures might me move
To live with thee and be thy love.

Time drives the flocks from field to fold   5
When rivers rage and rocks grow cold,
And Philomel[1] becometh dumb;
The rest complains of cares to come.

The flowers do fade, and wanton fields
To wayward winter reckoning yields;   10
A honey tongue, a heart of gall,
Is fancy's spring, but sorrow's fall.

Thy gowns, thy shoes, thy beds of roses,
Thy cap, thy kirtle,[2] and thy posies
Soon break, soon wither, soon forgotten—   15
In folly ripe, in reason rotten.

Thy belt of straw and ivy buds,
Thy coral clasps and amber studs,
All these in me no means can move
To come to thee and be thy love.   20

But could youth last and love still breed,
Had joys no date[3] nor age no need,
Then these delights my mind might move
To live with thee and be thy love.

[On the Life of Man]

What is our life? a play of passion;
Our mirth the music of division;[4]
Our mothers' wombs the tiring-houses[5] be
Where we are dressed for this short comedy.
Heaven the judicious sharp spectator is,   5

---

1. The nightingale.
2. Skirt, outer petticoat.
3. Ending.
4. The more rapid accompaniment to,

or variation on, a musical theme.
5. Dressing rooms in an Elizabethan
theater.

That sits and marks still who doth act amiss;
Our graves that hide us from the searching sun
Are like drawn curtains when the play is done.
Thus march we, playing, to our latest rest,
Only we die in earnest—that's no jest.   10

                                              1612

[Sir Walter Ralegh to His Son]

Three things there be that prosper up apace
And flourish, whilst they grow asunder far,
But on a day, they meet all in one place,
And when they meet, they one another mar;
And they be these: the wood, the weed, the wag.   5
The wood is that which makes the gallow tree;
The weed is that which strings the hangman's bag;
The wag, my pretty knave, betokeneth thee.
Mark well, dear boy, whilst these assemble not,
Green springs the tree, hemp grows, the wag is wild, 10
But when they meet, it makes the timber rot;
It frets the halter, and it chokes the child.
Then bless thee, and beware, and let us pray
We part not with thee at this meeting day.

ca. 1600

Walsinghame[6]

"As you came from the holy land
   of Walsinghame,
Met you not with my true love
   by the way as you came?"

"How shall I know your true love,
   that have met many one   5
As I went to the holy land,
   that have come, that have gone?"

"She is neither white nor brown,
   but as the heavens fair:
There is none hath a form so divine   10
   in the earth or the air."

"Such an one did I meet, good sir,
   such an angelic face,
Who like a queen, like a nymph, did appear   15
   by her gait, by her grace."

6. A priory popular for pilgrimages before its destruction in 1538. There were several traditional ballads on the subject; Ralegh's imitation is a dialogue between an old man and a pilgrim. They speak alternately, until the last four stanzas, when the pilgrim speaks.

"She hath left me here all alone,
    all alone as unknown,
Who sometimes did lead me with herself,
    and me loved as her own."   20

"What's the cause that she leaves you alone
    and a new way doth take,
Who loved you once as her own
    and her joy did you make?"

"I have loved her all my youth,   25
    but now, old, as you see;
Love likes not the falling fruit
    from the withered tree."

"Know that love is a careless child
    and forgets promise past;   30
He is blind, he is deaf when he list
    and in faith never fast.

"His desire is a dureless[7] content
    and a trustless joy;
He is won with a world of despair   35
    and is lost with a toy.

"Of womenkind such indeed is the love,
    (or the word 'love' abused)
Under which many childish desires
    and conceits are excused.   40

"But Love is a durable fire
    in the mind ever burning—
Never sick, never old, never dead,
    from itself never turning."

The Lie

Go, soul, the body's guest,
Upon a thankless errand;
Fear not to touch the best;
The truth shall be thy warrant.
Go, since I needs must die,   5
And give the world the lie.

Say to the court, it glows
And shines like rotten wood;
Say to the church, it shows
What's good, and doth no good.   10
If church and court reply,
Then give them both the lie.

7. Transient.

Tell potentates, they live
Acting by others' action;
Not loved unless they give,
Not strong but by a faction. 15
If potentates reply,
Give potentates the lie.

Tell men of high condition,
That manage the estate, 20
Their purpose is ambition,
Their practice only hate.
And if they once reply,
Then give them all the lie.

Tell them that brave it[8] most, 25
They beg for more by spending,
Who, in their greatest cost,
Seek nothing but commending.
And if they make reply,
Then give them all the lie. 30

Tell zeal it wants devotion;
Tell love it is but lust;
Tell time it is but motion;
Tell flesh it is but dust.
And wish them not reply, 35
For thou must give the lie.

Tell age it daily wasteth;
Tell honor how it alters;
Tell beauty how she blasteth;
Tell favor how it falters. 40
And as they shall reply,
Give every one the lie.

Tell wit how much it wrangles
In tickle[9] points of niceness;
Tell wisdom she entangles 45
Herself in overwiseness.
And when they do reply,
Straight give them both the lie.

Tell physic of her boldness;
Tell skill it is pretension; 50
Tell charity of coldness;
Tell law it is contention.
And as they do reply,
So give them still the lie.

Tell fortune of her blindness; 55
Tell nature of decay;
Tell friendship of unkindness;
Tell justice of delay.

8. I.e., those who spend much on clothes.   9. Delicate.

And if they will reply,
Then give them all the lie.   60

Tell arts they have no soundness,
But vary by esteeming;
Tell schools they want profoundness,
And stand too much on seeming.
If arts and schools reply,   65
Give arts and schools the lie.

Tell faith it's fled the city;
Tell how the country erreth;
Tell manhood shakes off pity;
Tell virtue least preferreth.   70
And if they do reply,
Spare not to give the lie.

So when thou hast, as I
Commanded thee, done blabbing—
Although to give the lie   75
Deserves no less than stabbing—
Stab at thee he that will,
No stab the soul can kill.

ca. 1592

Farewell, False Love

Farewell, false love, the oracle of lies,
A mortal foe and enemy to rest;
An envious boy, from whom all cares arise,
A bastard vile, a beast with rage possessed;
A way of error, a temple full of treason,   5
In all effects contrary unto reason.

A poisoned serpent covered all with flowers,
Mother of sighs and murtherer of repose,
A sea of sorrows from whence are drawn such showers
As moisture lends to every grief that grows;   10
A school of guile, a net of deep deceit,
A gilded hook that holds a poisoned bait.

A fortress foiled[1] which reason did defend,
A siren song, a fever of the mind,
A maze wherein affection finds no end,   15
A raging cloud that runs before the wind,
A substance like the shadow of the sun,
A goal of grief for which the wisest run.

A quenchless fire, a nurse of trembling fear,
A path that leads to peril and mishap;   20
A true retreat of sorrow and despair,
An idle boy that sleeps in pleasure's lap,

1. Overthrown.

A deep distrust of that which certain seems,
A hope of that which reason doubtful deems.

Sith[2] then thy trains my younger years betrayed, 25
And for my faith ingratitude I find,
And sith repentance hath my wrongs bewrayed[3]
Whose course was ever contrary to kind—
False love, desire, and beauty frail, adieu!
Dead is the root whence all these fancies grew. 30

1588

The Author's Epitaph, Made By Himself[4]

Even such is time, which takes in trust
Our youth, our joys, and all we have,
And pays us but with age and dust,
Who in the dark and silent grave
When we have wandered all our ways
Shuts up the story of our days, 5
And from which earth, and grave, and dust
The Lord shall raise me up, I trust.

1628

A Report of the Truth of the Fight About the Isles of Azores This Last Summer[1] Betwixt the *Revenge*,[2] One of Her Majesty's Ships, and an Armada[3] of the King of Spain

Because the rumors are diversely spread, as well in England as in the Low Countries and elsewhere, of this late encounter between her Majesty's ships and the Armada of Spain; and that the Spaniards according to their usual manner fill the world with their vainglorious vaunts, making great appearance of victories, when on the contrary themselves are most commonly and shamefully beaten and dishonored; thereby hoping to possess the ignorant multitude by anticipating and forerunning false reports; it is agreeable with all good reason, for manifestation of the truth, to overcome falsehood and untruth, that the beginning, continuance, and success of this late honorable encounter of Sir Richard Grenville[4] and other her

2. Since; "trains": tricks, stratagems.
3. Revealed.
4. In the 17th century it was thought that Ralegh composed this poem the night before his execution and wrote it in his Bible. It is actually a version of the last stanza of a love poem, "Nature, That Washed Her Hands in Milk" (about 1592). Only the first three words and the final couplet are changed.
1. 1591.
2. A ship of 500 tons and 250 men. It

had been Drake's ship in the fight with the Armada, 1588.
3. A fleet of armed ships. Ralegh also uses the term for a single warship.
4. Ralegh's first cousin. Grenville, (ca. 1541–91) had commanded Ralegh's first expedition to colonize Roanoke Island in 1585. Ralegh's prose account is the chief source for Tennyson's famous ballad *The Revenge: A Ballad of the Fleet*, first published in 1878.

Majesty's captains, with the Armada of Spain, should be truly set down and published without partiality or false imaginations. And it is no marvel that the Spaniard should seek by false and slanderous pamphlets, advisoes, and letters, to cover their own loss and to derogate from others their due honors, especially in this fight being performed far off; seeing they were not ashamed in the year 1588, when they purposed the invasion of this land, to publish in sundry languages, in print, great victories in words, which they pleaded to have obtained against this realm; and spread the same in a most false sort over all parts of France, Italy, and elsewhere. When shortly after it was happily manifested in very deed to all nations how their navy, which they termed invincible, consisting of 140 sail[5] of ships, not only of their own kingdom but strengthened with the greatest argosies, Portugal carracks,[6] Florentines, and huge hulks of other countries, were by thirty of her Majesty's own ships of war, and a few of our own merchants, by the wise, valiant, and most advantageous conduction of the Lord Charles Howard, high admiral of England, beaten and shuffled together; even from the Lizard in Cornwall, first to Portland, where they shamefully left Don Pedro de Valdes with his mighty ship; from Portland to Calais, where they lost Hugo de Moncado, with the gallias[7] of which he was captain; and from Calais driven with squibs[8] from their anchors, were chased out of the sight of England, round about Scotland and Ireland. Where for the sympathy of their barbarous religion, hoping to find succor and assistance, a great part of them were crushed against the rocks, and those others that landed, being very many in number, were notwithstanding broken, slain, and taken, and so sent from village to village, coupled in halters, to be shipped into England. Where her Majesty of her princely and invincible disposition disdaining to put them to death, and scorning either to retain or entertain them, they were all sent back again to their countries, to witness and recount the worthy achievements of their invincible and dreadful navy. Of which the number of soldiers, the fearful burthen of their ships, the commanders' names of every squadron, with all other their magazines of provisions, were put in print, as an army and navy unresistible and disdaining prevention.[9] With all which so great and terrible an ostentation they did not in all their sailing round about England so much as sink or take one ship, bark, pinnace,[1] or cockboat[2] of ours, or ever burned so much as one sheepcote of this land. Whenas on the contrary Sir Francis Drake, with only eight hundred soldiers, not long before landed in their Indies and forced Santiago, Santo Domingo, Cartagena, and the forts of Florida. And after that Sir John Norris

---

5. Ralegh wrote "240"; the correction is Hakluyt's.
6. Large ships.
7. Galleys.

8. Exploding shot.
9. Scorning resistance.
1. A small two-masted ship.
2. Dory or lifeboat.

marched from Peniche in Portugal, with a handful of soldiers, to the gates of Lisbon, being above forty English miles. Where the earl of Essex himself and other valiant gentlemen braved the city of Lisbon, encamped at the very gates; from whence after many days' abode, finding neither promised party nor provision to batter,[3] they made retreat by land in despite of all their garrisons both of horse and foot.

In this sort I have a little digressed from my first purpose, only by the necessary comparison of theirs and our actions; the one covetous of honor without vaunt of ostentation; the other so greedy to purchase the opinion of their own affairs and by false rumors to resist the blasts of their own dishonors as they will not only not blush to spread all manner of untruths, but even for the least advantage, be it but for the taking of one poor adventurer of the English, will celebrate the victory with bonfires in every town, always spending more in faggots than the purchase was worth they obtained. Whenas we never yet thought it worth the consumption of two billets when we have taken eight or ten of their Indian ships at one time and twenty of the Brazil fleet. Such is the difference between true valor and ostentation, and between honorable actions and frivolous vainglorious vaunts. But now to return to my first purpose.

The Lord Thomas Howard, with six of her Majesty's ships, six victualers[4] of London, the bark *Ralegh*, and two or three pinnaces, riding at anchor near unto Flores, one of the westerly islands of the Azores, the last of August in the afternoon, had intelligence by one Captain Middleton of the approach of the Spanish Armada. Which Middleton being in a very good sailer had kept them company three days before, of good purpose, both to discover their forces the more, as also to give advice to my Lord Thomas of their approach. He had no sooner delivered the news but the fleet was in sight.

Many of our ships' companies were on shore in the island, some providing ballast for their ships, others filling of water and refreshing themselves from the land with such things as they could either for money or by force recover. By reason whereof our ships being all pestered and roomaging,[5] everything out of order, very light for want of ballast. And that which was most to our disadvantage, the one-half part of the men of every ship sick and utterly unserviceable. For in the *Revenge* there were ninety diseased; in the *Bonaventure* not so many in health as could handle her mainsail. For had not twenty men been taken out of a bark of Sir George Cary's, his being commanded to be sunk, and those appointed to her, she had hardly ever recovered England. The rest for the most part were in little better state. The names of her Majesty's ships were these as followeth: the *Defiance*, which was admiral, the *Revenge*, vice-ad-

3. **Seize** upon, strike.
4. Supply ships.

5. Busied with various occupations, and the cargo not arranged.

miral, the *Bonaventure* commanded by Captain Cross, the *Lion* by George Fenner, the *Foresight* by Mr. Thomas Vavasour, and the *Crane* by Duffield. The *Foresight* and the *Crane* being but small ships; only the other were of the middle size; the rest, besides the bark *Ralegh* commanded by Captain Thin, were victualers and of small force or none.

The Spanish fleet having shrouded their approach by reason of the island, were now so soon at hand as our ships had scarce time to weigh their anchors, but some of them were driven to let slip their cables and set sail. Sir Richard Grenville was the last weighed, to recover the men that were upon the island, which otherwise had been lost. The Lord Thomas with the rest very hardly recovered the wind, which Sir Richard Grenville not being able to do was persuaded by the master and others to cut his mainsail and cast about, and to trust to the sailing of his ship; for the squadron of Seville were on his weather bow. But Sir Richard utterly refused to turn from the enemy, alleging that he would rather choose to die than to dishonor himself, his country, and her Majesty's ship, persuading his company that he would pass through the two squadrons in despite of them, and enforce those of Seville to give him way. Which he performed upon divers of the foremost, who, as the mariners term it, sprang their luff,[6] and fell under the lee of the *Revenge*. But the other course had been the better, and might right well have been answered[7] in so great an impossibility of prevailing. Notwithstanding, out of the greatness of his mind he could not be persuaded.

In the meanwhile as he attended those which were nearest him, the great *San Philip* being in the wind of him and coming towards him becalmed his sails in such sort as the ship could neither make way nor feel the helm, so huge and high cargoed was the Spanish ship, being of a thousand and five hundred tons. Who after laid the *Revenge* aboard.[8] When he was thus bereft of his sails, the ships that were under his lee, luffing up, also laid him aboard; of which the next was the admiral of the Biscaines, a very mighty and puissant ship commanded by Brittandona. The said *Philip* carried three tier of ordnance on a side, and eleven pieces in every tier. She shot eight forthright out of her chase,[9] besides those of her stern ports.

After the *Revenge* was entangled with this *Philip*, four other boarded her; two on her larboard and two on her starboard. The fight thus beginning at three of the clock in the afternoon continued very terrible all that evening. But the great *San Philip* having received the lower tier of the *Revenge*, discharged with crossbarshot,[1] shifted herself with all diligence from her sides, utterly mis-

---

6. Headed into the wind too far.
7. Justified.
8. Came alongside.

9. Bow.
1. A ball with projecting bars.

liking her first entertainment. Some say that the ship foundered, but we cannot report it for truth unless we were assured.

The Spanish ships were filled with companies of soldiers, in some two hundred besides the mariners, in some five, in others eight hundred. In ours there were none at all, beside the mariners, but the servants of the commanders and some few voluntary gentlemen only. After many interchanged volleys of great ordnance and small shot, the Spaniards deliberated to enter the *Revenge*, and made divers attempts, hoping to force her by the multitudes of their armed soldiers and musketeers, but were still repulsed again and again, and at all times beaten back into their own ships or into the seas.

In the beginning of the fight the *George Noble* of London, having received some shot through her by the armadas, fell under the lee of the *Revenge* and asked Sir Richard what he would command him, being but one of the victualers and of small force. Sir Richard bid him save himself and leave him to his fortune.

After the fight had thus without intermission continued while the day lasted and some hours of the night, many of our men were slain and hurt, and one of the great galleons of the armada and the admiral of the hulks[2] both sunk, and in many other of the Spanish ships great slaughter was made. Some write that Sir Richard was very dangerously hurt almost in the beginning of the fight and lay speechless for a time ere he recovered. But two of the *Revenge's* own company, brought home in a ship of lime from the islands, examined by some of the lords and others, affirmed that he was never so wounded as that he forsook the upper deck, till an hour before midnight; and then being shot into the body with a musket, as he was a-dressing was again shot into the head, and withal his chirurgeon wounded to death. This agreeth also with an examination taken by Sir Francis Godolphin of four other mariners of the same ship being returned, which examination the said Sir Francis sent unto Master William Killigrew of her Majesty's privy chamber.

But to return to the fight, the Spanish ships which attempted to board the *Revenge*, as they were wounded and beaten off, so always others came in their places, she having never less than two mighty galleons by her sides and aboard her. So that ere the morning, from three of the clock the day before, there had fifteen several armadas assailed her; and all so ill approved their entertainment as they were by the break of day far more willing to hearken to a composition than hastily to make any more assaults or entries. But as the day increased, so our men decreased; and as the light grew more and more, by so much more grew our discomforts. For none appeared in sight but enemies, saving one small ship called the *Pilgrim*, commanded by Jacob Whiddon, who hovered all night to see the suc-

2. Chief of the supply ships.

cess, but in the morning bearing with the *Revenge*, was hunted like a hare amongst many ravenous hounds, but escaped.

All the powder of the *Revenge* to the last barrel was now spent, all her pikes broken, forty of her best men slain, and the most part of the rest hurt. In the beginning of the fight she had but one hundred free from sickness, and fourscore and ten sick, laid in hold upon the ballast. A small troop to man such a ship, and a weak garrison to resist so mighty an army. By those hundred all was sustained, the volleys, boardings, and enterings of fifteen ships of war, besides those which beat her at large. On the contrary, the Spanish were always supplied with soldiers brought from every squadron; all manner of arms and powder at will. Unto ours there remained no comfort at all, no hope, no supply either of ships, men, or weapons; the masts all beaten overboard, all her tackle cut asunder, her upper work altogether razed, and in effect evened she was with the water, but the very foundation or bottom of a ship, nothing being left overhead either for fight or defense.

Sir Richard, finding himself in this distress and unable any longer to make resistance, having endured in this fifteen hours' fight the assault of fifteen several armadas all by turns aboard him, and by estimation eight hundred shot of great artillery, besides many assaults and entries; and that himself and the ship must needs be possessed by the enemy, who were now all cast in a ring round him, the *Revenge* not able to move one way or other but as she was moved with the waves and billow of the sea; commanded the master gunner, whom he knew to be a most resolute man, to split and sink the ship; that thereby nothing might remain of glory or victory to the Spaniards, seeing in so many hours' fight and with so great a navy they were not able to take her, having had fifteen hours' time, above ten thousand[3] men, and fifty-and-three sail of men-of-war to perform it withal; and persuaded the company, or as many as he could induce, to yield themselves unto God and to the mercy of none else, but as they had like valiant resolute men repulsed so many enemies they should not now shorten the honor of their nation by prolonging their own lives for a few hours or a few days.

The master gunner readily condescended, and divers others; but the captain and the master were of another opinion, and besought Sir Richard to have care of them; alleging that the Spaniard would be as ready to entertain a composition as they were willing to offer the same; and that there being divers sufficient and valiant men yet living, and whose wounds were not mortal, they might do their country and prince acceptable service hereafter. And that whereas Sir Richard had alleged that the Spaniards should never glory to have taken one ship of her Majesty, seeing that they had so long

3. Hakluyt's correction of Ralegh's "15,000."

and so notably defended themselves, they answered that the ship had six foot water in hold, three shot under water which were so weakly stopped as with the first working of the sea she must needs sink, and was besides so crushed and bruised as she could never be removed out of the place.

And as the matter was thus in dispute, and Sir Richard refusing to hearken to any of those reasons, the master of the *Revenge* (while the captain won unto him the greater party) was convoyed aboard the general, Don Alfonso Baçan. Who finding none over-hasty to enter the *Revenge* again, doubting lest Sir Richard would have blown them up and himself, and perceiving by the report of the master of the *Revenge* his dangerous disposition, yielded that all their lives should be saved, the company sent for England, and the better sort to pay such reasonable ransom as their estate would bear, and in the mean season to be free from galley or imprisonment. To this he so much the rather condescended as well, as I have said, for fear of further loss and mischief to themselves, as also for the desire he had to recover Sir Richard Grenville; whom for his notable valor he seemed greatly to honor and admire.

When this answer was returned, and that safety of life was promised, the common sort being now at the end of their peril, the most drew back from Sir Richard and the master gunner, being no hard matter to dissuade men from death to life. The master gunner, finding himself and Sir Richard thus prevented and mastered by the greater number, would have slain himself with a sword, had he not been by force withheld and locked into his cabin. Then the general sent many boats aboard the *Revenge*, and divers of our men fearing Sir Richard's disposition stole away aboard the general and other ships. Sir Richard, thus overmatched, was sent unto by Alfonso Baçan to remove out of the *Revenge*, the ship being marvelous unsavory, filled with blood and bodies of dead and wounded men like a slaughterhouse. Sir Richard answered that he might do with his body what he list, for he esteemed it not, and as he was carried out of the ship he swounded, and reviving again desired the company to pray for him. The general used Sir Richard with all humanity, and left nothing unattempted that tended to his recovery, highly commending his valor and worthiness, and greatly bewailing the danger wherein he was, being unto them a rare spectacle and a resolution seldom approved, to see one ship turn toward so many enemies, to endure the charge and boarding of so many huge armadas, and to resist and repel the assaults and entries of so many soldiers. All which and more is confirmed by a Spanish captain of the same armada, and a present actor in the fight, who being severed from the rest in a storm was by the *Lion* of London, a small ship, taken, and is now prisoner in London.

* * *

To conclude, it hath ever to this day pleased God to prosper and defend her Majesty, to break the purposes of malicious enemies, of forsworn traitors, and of unjust practises and invasions. She hath ever been honored of the worthiest kings, served by faithful subjects, and shall by the favor of God resist, repel, and confound all whatsoever attempts against her sacred person or kingdom. In the meantime let the Spaniard and traitor vaunt of their success; and we her true and obedient vassals guided by the shining light of her virtues shall always love her, serve her, and obey her to the end of our lives.   1591

CHRISTOPHER MARLOWE
(1564–1593)

ca. 1587:   *Tamburlaine* produced, introducing blank verse,
                      "Marlowe's mighty line," to the stage.
ca. 1592–93: *Dr. Faustus*.

Christopher Marlowe was born two months before William Shakespeare. He was the son of a Canterbury shoemaker; in 1580 he went to Corpus Christi College, Cambridge, on a scholarship which was ordinarily awarded to students preparing for the ministry. He held the scholarship for the maximum time, six years, but did not take holy orders. Instead, he began to write plays. When he came to supplicate for his Master of Arts degree in 1587, the university was about to deny it to him on the grounds that he intended to go abroad to Reims, the center of Catholic intrigue and propaganda against Elizabeth, and remain there. But the Privy Council intervened and requested that, since Marlowe had done the queen good service, he be granted his degree at the next commencement "because it is not Her Majesty's pleasure that anyone employed as he had been in matters touching the benefit of his country should be defamed by those that are ignorant in the affairs he went about." Although much sensational information about Marlowe has been discovered in modern times, we are still "ignorant in the affairs he went about."

Before he left Cambridge, he had certainly written his tremendously successful play *Tamburlaine* and perhaps also, in collaboration with his younger Cambridge contemporary, Thomas Nashe, the tragedy of *Dido, Queen of Carthage*. *Tamburlaine*, which soon was followed by a sequel (*Tamburlaine*, Part II), dramatizes the exploits of a 14th-century Scythian shepherd who conquered much of the known world, as Alexander had before him. In some 16th-century narratives Tamburlaine is represented as the type of modern (i.e., Renaissance) man, and in others he is portrayed as God's Scourge. In Marlowe's play he is the vehicle for the expression of boundless energy and ambition, the impulse to strive constantly upward to absolute power. When one of his victims accuses him of bloody cruelty, Tamburlaine answers that ambition to rule is embedded in the laws of nature and in basic human psychology:

Nature, that framed us of four elements
Warring within our breasts for regiment,
Doth teach us all to have aspiring minds;
Our souls, whose faculties can comprehend
The wondrous architecture of the world
And measure every planet's wandering course,
Still climbing after knowledge infinite,
And always moving as the restless spheres,
Wills us to wear ourselves and never rest
Until we reach the ripest fruit of all,
That perfect bliss and sole felicity,
The sweet fruition of an earthly crown.

The English theater had heard nothing like this before. Here is a resonant, rhetorical blank verse, eminently suited to projection from the stage, and appropriate also, as it turned out, for the robust talents of the actor Edward Alleyn who happily appeared in time to portray Marlowe's heroes.

From the time of his first great success, when he was 23, Marlowe nad only six years to live. They were not calm years. In 1589 he was involved in a brawl with one William Bradley, in which the poet Thomas Watson intervened and killed Bradley. Both poets were jailed, but Watson got off on a plea of self-defense and Marlowe was released. In 1591 Marlowe was living in London with the playwright Thomas Kyd, who later gave information to the Privy Council accusing Marlowe of atheism and treason. On May 30, 1593, at the inn of the Widow Bull in Deptford, Marlowe was killed by a dagger thrust in an argument over the bill. In these six violent years, Marlowe composed five more plays: his sequel to *Tamburlaine*; *The Massacre at Paris*; two major tragedies, *The Jew of Malta* and *Dr. Faustus*; and a chronicle history play, *Edward II*. We do not know when he did his verse translations, of the *Amores* of Ovid and the first book of Lucan's *Pharsalia*, or the more original *Hero and Leander*. When he died, in 1593, he had created an immortal place for himself in English drama and poetry; if his contemporary, William Shakespeare, had died at the same age he would scarcely be known today.

Marlowe's major tragedies, *Tamburlaine*, *The Jew of Malta*, and *Dr. Faustus*, all portray a hero who passionately seeks power—the power of rule, the power of money, and the power of knowledge, respectively. Each of the heroes is an "overreacher," striving beyond the bounds of human capacity, or at least the limits imposed upon human achievement. The plots show these heroes finally defeated, but, as in all high tragedy, the values for which the hero stood emerge larger than the forces which defeat him.

From Hero and Leander[1]
From *The First Sestiad*

On Hellespont, guilty of true love's blood,
In view and opposite, two cities stood,

1. *Hero and Leander* is a poem of the mythological-erotic type which was highly popular in the 1590's, especially among readers of the aristocratic or courtier class. Shakespeare's *Venus and Adonis* is another example of the genre, for which the great classical model was Ovid. Marlowe, however, based his poem somewhat remotely upon a Greek original by Musaeus, an Alexandrian poet and grammarian of the 5th century A.D. Although the subject matter was

Sea-borderers, disjoined by Neptune's might;
The one Abydos, the other Sestos hight.[2]
At Sestos Hero dwelt; Hero the fair,   5
Whom young Apollo courted for her hair,
And offered as a dower his burning throne,
Where she should sit for men to gaze upon.
The outside of her garments were of lawn,[3]
The lining purple silk, with gilt stars drawn;   10
Her wide sleeves green, and bordered with a grove
Where Venus in her naked glory strove
To please the careless and disdainful eyes
Of proud Adonis, that before her lies;[4]
Her kirtle blue, whereon was many a stain,   15
Made with the blood of wretched lovers slain.[5]
Upon her head she ware a myrtle wreath,
From whence her veil reached to the ground beneath.
Her veil was artificial flowers and leaves,
Whose workmanship both man and beast deceives;   20
Many would praise the sweet smell as she passed,
When 'twas the odor which her breath forth cast;
And there for honey, bees have sought in vain,
And, beat from thence, have lighted there again.
About her neck hung chains of pebble-stone,   25
Which, lightened by her neck, like diamonds shone.
She ware no gloves, for neither sun nor wind
Would burn or parch her hands, but to her mind[6]
Or warm or cool them, for they took delight
To play upon those hands, they were so white.   30
Buskins[7] of shells all silvered, uséd she,
And branched with blushing coral to the knee,
Where sparrows perched, of hollow pearl and gold,
Such as the world would wonder to behold;
Those with sweet water oft her handmaid fills,   35
Which, as she went, would chirrup through the bills.
Some say, for her the fairest Cupid pined,
And looking in her face, was strooken blind.
But this is true: so like was one the other,
As he imagined Hero was his mother;[8]   40

drawn from classical authors, the qualities sought in these poems by Elizabethan poets and readers were their own: a richness of detail in the descriptions, exuberance of fancy and vividness in mythological invention, sensuous appeal in the erotic passages, and the conveying of a kind of remoteness which makes the action seem to take place in a recognizable but idealized world.

The poem is divided into "Sestiads" (i.e., cantos), a word coined from Hero's city, Sestos, which was opposite Abydos on the Hellespont (see lines 1–4). Marlowe completed only the First Sestiad (of which the initial 176 lines are here reprinted), and the Second. George Chapman later finished the poem.

2. Called.
3. A kind of fine linen or thin cambric.
4. Venus's love for the reluctant young hunter, Adonis, and his death in the boar hunt are told by Ovid and by Shakespeare in *Venus and Adonis*. "Kirtle": skirt.
5. The extravagant claim is made that many "wretched lovers" had committed suicide at her feet because Hero would not have them.
6. As she wished.
7. High shoes or boots.
8. I.e., Venus.

And oftentimes into her bosom flew,
About her naked neck his bare arms threw,
And laid his childish head upon her breast,
And with still panting rocked, there took his rest.
So lovely fair was Hero, Venus' nun,[9]   45
As Nature wept, thinking she was undone,
Because she took more from her than she left
And of such wondrous beauty her bereft;
Therefore, in sign her treasure suffered wrack,
Since Hero's time hath half the world been black.   50
Amorous Leander, beautiful and young,
(Whose tragedy divine Musaeus[1] sung)
Dwelt at Abydos; since him dwelt there none
For whom succeeding times make greater moan.
His dangling tresses that were never shorn,   55
Had they been cut and unto Colchos[2] borne,
Would have allured the vent'rous youth of Greece
To hazard more than for the Golden Fleece.
Fair Cynthia[3] wished his arms might be her sphere;
Grief makes her pale, because she moves not there.   60
His body was as straight as Circe's wand;[4]
Jove might have sipped out nectar from his hand.
Even as delicious meat is to the taste,
So was his neck in touching, and surpassed
The white of Pelops' shoulder.[5] I could tell ye   65
How smooth his breast was, and how white his belly,
And whose immortal fingers did imprint
That heavenly path, with many a curious[6] dint,
That runs along his back; but my rude pen
Can hardly blazon forth the loves of men,   70
Much less of powerful gods; let it suffice
That my slack[7] muse sings of Leander's eyes,
Those orient cheeks and lips, exceeding his
That leapt into the water for a kiss
Of his own shadow, and despising many,   75
Died ere he could enjoy the love of any.[8]
Had wild Hippolytus[9] Leander seen,
Enamored of his beauty had he been;
His presence made the rudest peasant melt,
That in the vast uplandish country dwelt;   80
The barbarous Thracian soldier, moved with naught,
Was moved with him, and for his favor sought.

9. The connotations of these two words are contradictory; Marlowe gets a similar effect elsewhere in the poem. Hero is a maiden in attendance at the temple of Venus, who is, of course, the goddess of love.
1. I.e., the author of the Greek poem upon which *Hero and Leander* is remotely based. He was sometimes confused with a legendary early Musaeus, supposed son of Orpheus—hence Marlowe calls him "divine."
2. A country in Asia where the Argo-
nauts ("the ven'trous youth of Greece") found the Golden Fleece.
3. The moon; "sphere": orbit.
4. The wand with which Circe, in the *Odyssey*, turned men into beasts.
5. Pelops, according to Ovid, had a shoulder of ivory.
6. Exquisite.
7. Dull. "Orient": shining.
8. An allusion to Narcissus.
9. Like Adonis, he preferred hunting to love.

Some swore he was a maid in man's attire,
For in his looks were all that men desire:
A pleasant smiling cheek, a speaking[1] eye,   85
A brow for love to banquet royally;
And such as knew he was a man, would say,
"Leander, thou art made for amorous play;
Why art thou not in love, and loved of all?
Though thou be fair, yet be not thine own thrall."   90
  The men of wealthy Sestos every year,
For his sake whom their goddess held so dear,
Rose-cheeked Adonis, kept a solemn feast.
Thither resorted many a wandering guest
To meet their loves; such as had none at all   95
Came lovers home from this great festival;
For every street, like to a firmament,
Glistered with breathing stars, who, where they went,
Frighted the melancholy earth, which deemed
Eternal heaven to burn, for so it seemed   100
As if another Phaëton[2] had got
The guidance of the sun's rich chariot.
But, far above the loveliest, Hero shined,
And stole away the enchanted gazer's mind;
For like sea nymphs' inveigling harmony,   105
So was her beauty to the standers by.
Nor that night-wandering pale and watery star[3]
(When yawning dragons draw her thirling[4] car
From Latmus' mount up to the gloomy sky,
Where, crowned with blazing light and majesty,   110
She proudly sits) more over-rules[5] the flood
Than she the hearts of those that near her stood.
Even as when gaudy nymphs pursue the chase,
Wretched Ixion's shaggy-footed race,[6]
Incensed with savage heat, gallop amain   115
From steep pine-bearing mountains to the plain,
So ran the people forth to gaze upon her,
And all that viewed her were enamored on her.
And as in fury of a dreadful fight,
Their fellows being slain or put to flight,   120
Poor soldiers stand with fear of death dead-strooken,
So at her presence all, surprised and tooken,
Await the sentence of her scornful eyes;
He whom she favors lives, the other dies.
There might you see one sigh, another rage,   125
And some, their violent passions to assuage,
Compile sharp satires; but alas, too late,
For faithful love will never turn to hate.

---

1. Expressive.
2. A son of the sun god, he drove his
father's chariot across the sky and almost burned up the world.
3. The moon.
4. Flying like a spear. Latmus was the
mountain where the moon visited her
lover, Endymion.
5. Rules over.
6. I.e., the centaurs, fathered by Ixion
upon a cloud. For his presumption in
loving Juno, Ixion was chained to a
wheel—hence "wretched."

And many, seeing great princes were denied,
Pined as they went, and thinking on her, died.   130
On this feast day, oh, curséd day and hour!
Went Hero thorough[7] Sestos, from her tower
To Venus' temple, where unhappily,
As after chanced, they did each other spy.
So fair a church as this had Venus none;   135
The walls were of discolored[8] jasper stone,
Wherein was Proteus carved, and o'erhead
A lively[9] vine of green sea-agate spread,
Where, by one hand, light-headed Bacchus hung,
And with the other, wine from grapes out-wrung.   140
Of crystal shining fair the pavement was;
The town of Sestos called it Venus' glass;
There might you see the gods in sundry shapes,
Committing heady[1] riots, incest, rapes;
For know that underneath this radiant floor   145
Was Danae's statue in a brazen tower;[2]
Jove slyly stealing from his sister's bed
To dally with Idalian Ganymed,[3]
And for his love Europa bellowing loud,
And tumbling with the rainbow in a cloud;   150
Blood-quaffing Mars heaving the iron net
Which limping Vulcan and his Cyclops set;[4]
Love kindling fire to burn such towns as Troy;
Silvanus weeping for the lovely boy[5]
That now is turned into a cypress tree,   155
Under whose shade the wood-gods love to be.
And in the midst a silver altar stood;
There Hero sacrificing turtles'[6] blood,
Veiled to the ground, veiling her eyelids close,
And modestly they opened as she rose;   160
Thence flew love's arrow with the golden head,[7]
And thus Leander was enamoréd.
Stone still he stood, and evermore he gazed,
Till with the fire that from his countenance blazed,
Relenting Hero's gentle heart was strook;   165
Such force and virtue hath an amorous look.
It lies not in our power to love or hate,
For will in us is overruled by fate.
When two are stripped, long ere the course begin
We wish that one should lose, the other win;   170

---

7. Through.
8. Of various colors.
9. Lifelike.
1. Passionate, violent. In the next lines, specific examples of the "riots, incest, rapes" are given.
2. Danaë, imprisoned in a tower, was visited by Jove in the form of a shower of gold. "His sister's": i.e., Juno's; she was also Jove's wife.
3. A beautiful youth whom Jove kidnaped from Mt. Ida (hence "Idalian").

In order to seduce Europa, Jove took the form of a "bellowing" bull.
4. Vulcan used a net to trap Venus, his wife, and Mars, "blood-quaffing" god of war, in the act of love.
5. I.e., Cyparissus, beloved of the wood god Sylvanus.
6. Turtledoves, symbolic of constancy in love.
7. The "golden head" of some of Cupid's arrows produced love; he had others, of lead, that produced dislike.

And one especially do we affect[8]
Of two gold ingots, like in each respect.
The reason no man knows, let it suffice,
What we behold is censured by our eyes.
Where both deliberate, the love is slight;   175
Who ever loved, that loved not at first sight?[9]

* * *

1598

The Passionate Shepherd to His Love[1]

Come live with me and be my love,
And we will all the pleasures prove[2]
That valleys, groves, hills, and fields,
Woods, or steepy mountain yields.

And we will sit upon the rocks,   5
Seeing the shepherds feed their flocks,
By shallow rivers to whose falls
Melodious birds sing madrigals.

And I will make thee beds of roses
And a thousand fragrant posies,   10
A cap of flowers, and a kirtle
Embroidered all with leaves of myrtle;

A gown made of the finest wool
Which from our pretty lambs we pull;
Fair lined slippers for the cold,   15
With buckles of the purest gold;

A belt of straw and ivy buds,
With coral clasps and amber studs:
And if these pleasures may thee move,
Come live with me, and be my love.   20

The shepherds' swains shall dance and sing
For thy delight each May morning:
If these delights thy mind may move,
Then live with me and be my love.

1599, 1600

8. Have affection for.
9. Shakespeare quotes this line in *As You Like It* (III.v.82).
1. This pastoral lyric of invitation is one of the most famous of Elizabethan songs, and a few lines from it are sung in Shakespeare's *Merry Wives of Windsor*. Many poets have written replies to it, the finest of which is by that other great Elizabethan romantic, Sir Walter Ralegh.
2. Test, experience.

Dr. Faustus   The date of Marlowe's *Dr. Faustus* is in dispute. Some authorities date it during the last year of the playwright's life, between the spring of 1592 and that of 1593, but others think it belongs in 1588–89, not long after the second part of *Tamburlaine*. The story was a striking one, often retold in ballad and pamphlet, and the play, which includes some of Marlowe's most magnificent poetry, was a theatrical success. In popular legend John Faustus, a Doctor of Divinity, sold his soul to the devil for further knowledge, of magic particularly, and was damned for it; Marlowe used as his source material a rather simple-minded German narrative called, in its English translation, *The History of the Damnable Life and Deserved Death of Doctor John Faustus*. He turned it into a powerful projection of the Renaissance lust for knowledge, set against the medieval insistence upon salvation as the individual's main and guiding concern upon earth. In the *Faustbook* which was his source, many farcical episodes showed the hero playing pranks with his newly-won power; whether Marlowe wrote the comic scenes in *Faustus* or turned them over to a collaborator like Samuel Rowley we cannot be sure. Recent critics have replied to the standard objection that the poetic and prose parts of the play conflict with each other by arguing that the discrepancy is intentionally ironic.

Some of the intellectual background of the play requires explanation for a 20th-century reader. He must understand that devils are real and are sometimes called "spirits"; that when Faustus asks for power to be a spirit and go invisible he is taking on some attributes of a devil, though of course he keeps his human soul; and that when he acquires Helen, who is a spirit, as his paramour, he has committed the sin of demoniality (intercourse with devils) and is beyond repentance. But although Marlowe's play should be read in the context of the thought and belief of the Middle Ages and Renaissance, it has also a timeless interest. The Faust legend has a relevant meaning in many periods; Goethe made it the subject of his masterpiece in the 19th century and Thomas Mann has treated it again in the 20th.

The text of *Dr. Faustus* has come down to us in two forms, both corrupt. It is one of the major triumphs of modern literary scholarship that Sir W. W. Greg, in his parallel-text edition of the two quartos and his conjectural reconstruction of what Marlowe and his collaborator originally wrote, has made *Dr. Faustus* a comprehensible play. The text here printed is based upon Greg's work.

The Tragical History
of the Life and Death of Doctor Faustus

Dramatis Personae

CHORUS
DR. JOHN FAUSTUS, *of the* University *of* Wittenberg
WAGNER, *his servant*
GOOD ANGEL *and* BAD ANGEL
VALDES *and* CORNELIUS, *magicians and friends of* FAUSTUS
THREE SCHOLARS, *students at the university*
LUCIFER, MEPHISTOPHILIS, *and* BELZEBUB, *devils*
ROBIN *and* DICK, *rustic clowns*
THE SEVEN DEADLY SINS

POPE ADRIAN
RAYMOND, *King of Hungary*
BRUNO, *a rival Pope, appointed by the* EMPEROR
CARDINALS OF FRANCE *and* PADUA
ARCHBISHOP OF RHEIMS
MARTINO, FREDERICK, *and* BENVOLIO, *gentlemen at the* EMPEROR'S
    court
CAROLUS (CHARLES) THE FIFTH, EMPEROR
DUKE OF SAXONY
DUKE *and* DUCHESS OF VANHOLT
HORSE-COURSER
CARTER
HOSTESS *of a tavern*
OLD MAN
SPIRITS *of* DARIUS, ALEXANDER *and his* PARAMOUR, *and* HELEN OF
    TROY
ATTENDANTS, MONKS *and* FRIARS, SOLDIERS, PIPER, *two* CUPIDS

Act I

[*Enter* CHORUS.[1]]

CHO. Not marching in the fields of Trasimene[2]
    Where Mars did mate the warlike Carthagens,
    Nor sporting in the dalliance of love
    In courts of kings where state[3] is overturned,
    Nor in the pomp of proud audacious deeds   5
    Intends our Muse to vaunt his heavenly verse:
    Only this, gentles, we must now perform,
    The form of Faustus' fortunes good or bad.
    And so to patient judgments we appeal
    And speak for Faustus in his infancy.   10
    Now is he born, his parents base of stock,
    In Germany within a town called Rhode;[4]
    At riper years to Wittenberg he went
    Whereas his kinsmen chiefly brought him up;
    So much he profits in divinity,   15
    The fruitful plot of scholarism graced,[5]
    That shortly he was graced with Doctor's name,
    Excelling all whose sweet delight disputes[6]
    In th' heavenly matters of theology,
    Till, swollen with cunning,[7] of a self-conceit,   20
    His waxen wings did mount above his reach
    And melting, heavens conspired his overthrow.[8]

1. A single actor who recited a prologue to an act or a whole play, and
occasionally delivered an epilogue.
2. The battle of Lake Trasimene (217
B.C.) was one of the Carthaginian leader
Hannibal's great victories. "Mate":
join with.
3. Political power.
4. Roda. Wittenberg, in the next line,
was the famous university where Martin Luther studied, as did Shakespeare's

Hamlet and Horatio; "whereas":
where.
5. Grazed. In line 17 "graced" refers
to the Cambridge word for permission
to proceed to a degree.
6. The usual academic exercises were
disputations, which took the place of
examinations.
7. Learning.
8. The reference is to the Greek myth
of Icarus, who flew too near the sun

For, falling to a devilish exercise
And glutted more with learning's golden gifts,
He surfeits upon curséd necromancy;[9]   25
Nothing so sweet as magic is to him,
Which he prefers before his chiefest bliss[1]—
And this the man that in his study sits.
    [*Draws the curtain*[2] *and exit.*]

SCENE 1

    [FAUSTUS *in his study.*]
FAUST. Settle thy studies, Faustus, and begin
    To sound the depth of that thou wilt profess.
    Having commenced, be a divine in show,
    Yet level[3] at the end of every art
    And live and die in Aristotle's works: 5
    Sweet Analytics,[4] 'tis thou hast ravished me!   [*Reads.*]
    Bene disserere est finis logicis—
    Is to dispute well logic's chiefest end?
    Affords this art no greater miracle?
    Then read no more; thou hast attained the end.   10
    A greater subject fitteth Faustus' wit:
    Bid ὂν χαὶ μὴ ὂν[5] farewell, Galen come,
    Seeing *ubi desinit philosophus, ibi incipit medicus;*[6]
    Be a physician, Faustus, heap up gold
    And be eternized for some wondrous cure.   [*Reads.*] 15
    Summum bonum medicinae sanitas[7]—
    The end of physic is our bodies' health:
    Why, Faustus, hast thou not attained that end?
    Is not thy common talk sound aphorisms?[8]
    Are not thy bills hung up as monuments   20
    Whereby whole cities have escaped the plague
    And thousand desperate maladies been cured?
    Yet art thou still but Faustus, and a man.
    Couldst thou make men to live eternally
    Or, being dead, raise them to life again,   25
    Then this profession were to be esteemed.
    Physic, farewell. Where is Justinian?[9]   [*Reads.*]
    Si una eademque res legatur duobus,
    Alter rem, alter valorem rei, etc.[1]—

on wings of feathers and wax made by
his father Daedalus. The wax melted
and he fell into the sea and was
drowned.
9. Black magic.
1. The salvation of his soul.
2. The curtain to the inner stage, behind the main stage, which serves here
as Faustus' study. "Draws" here means
"draws apart."
3. "Commenced": graduated, i.e., received the doctor's degree; "in show":
in external ·appearance; "level": aim.
4. The title of a treatise on logic by
Aristotle. The Latin means, "To carry
on a disputation well is the end or

purpose of logic."
5. "Being and not being," i.e., philosophy. Galen: the ancient authority on
medicine (2nd century A.D.).
6. "Where the philosopher leaves off
the physician begins."
7. "Good health is the object of medicine" (or "physic").
8. I.e., reliable medical pronounce-
ments. "Bills": prescriptions.
9. Roman emperor and authority on
law (483–565), author of the *Institutes.*
1. "If something is bequeathed to two
persons, one shall have the thing itself, the other something of equal
value." The next Latin phrase means:

A pretty case of paltry legacies!   30
Exhaereditare filium non potest pater nisi—
Such is the subject of the Institute
And universal body of the law.
This study fits a mercenary drudge
Who aims at nothing but external trash,   35
Too servile and illiberal for me.
When all is done, divinity is best.
Jerome's Bible,[2] Faustus, view it well: [*Reads.*]
Stipendium peccati mors est—Ha! *Stipendium, etc.*
The reward of sin is death? That's hard.   40
Si pecasse negamus, fallimur, et nulla est in nobis veritas[3]—
If we say that we have no sin
We deceive ourselves, and there's no truth in us.
Why then belike
We must sin and so consequently die,   45
Aye, we must die an everlasting death.
What doctrine call you this, *Che sera, sera:*[4]
What will be, shall be? Divinity, adieu!
These metaphysics[5] of magicians
And necromantic books are heavenly: 50
Lines, circles, signs, letters, and characters—
Aye, these are those that Faustus most desires.
O what a world of profit and delight,
Of power, of honor, of omnipotence,
Is promised to the studious artisan![6]   55
All things that move between the quiet[7] poles
Shall be at my command. Emperors and kings
Are but obeyed in their several provinces,
Nor can they raise the wind or rend the clouds;
But his dominion that exceeds in this   60
Stretcheth as far as doth the mind of man.
A sound magician is a demigod:
Here tire my brains to gain a deity!
Wagner!
        [*Enter* WAGNER.]
Commend me to my dearest friends,   65
The German Valdes and Cornelius;
Request them earnestly to visit me.
WAG. I will, sir.   [*Exit.*]
FAUST. Their conference will be a greater help to me
Than all my labors, plod I ne'er so fast.   70
        [*Enter the* GOOD ANGEL *and the* BAD ANGEL.]
G. ANG. O Faustus, lay that damnéd book aside
And gaze not on it, lest it tempt thy soul

"A father cannot disinherit his son unless."
2. The Latin translation, or "Vulgate,"
of St. Jerome (ca. 340–420). The Latin
(Romans vi.23) is translated in line
40.
3. I John i.8, translated in the next two

lines.
4. Translated in the first half of the
next line.
5. Basic principles.
6. I.e., a master of the occult arts,
such as necromancy.
7. Unmoving.

And heap God's heavy wrath upon thy head.
Read, read the Scriptures! That is blasphemy.
B. ANG. Go forward, Faustus, in that famous art   75
Wherein all nature's treasury is contained:
Be thou on earth, as Jove[8] is in the sky,
Lord and commander of these elements.
　　　[*Exeunt* ANGELS.]
FAUST. How am I glutted with conceit[9] of this!
Shall I make spirits fetch me what I please,   80
Resolve me of all ambiguities,
Perform what desperate enterprise I will?
I'll have them fly to India[1] for gold,
Ransack the ocean for orient pearl,
And search all corners of the new-found world[2]   85
For pleasant fruits and princely delicates;
I'll have them read me strange philosophy
And tell the secrets of all foreign kings;
I'll have them wall all Germany with brass
And make swift Rhine circle fair Wittenberg;   90
I'll have them fill the public schools[3] with silk
Wherewith the students shall be bravely clad;
I'll levy soldiers with the coin they bring,
And chase the Prince of Parma[4] from our land
And reign sole king of all our provinces;   95
Yea, stranger engines for the brunt of war
Than was the fiery keel[5] at Antwerp's bridge
I'll make my servile spirits to invent!
　　　[*Enter* VALDES *and* CORNELIUS.]
Come, German Valdes and Cornelius,
And make me blest with your sage conference.   100
Valdes, sweet Valdes and Cornelius,
Know that your words have won me at the last
To practice magic and concealéd arts;
Yet not your words only, but mine own fantasy
That will receive no object,[6] for my head   105
But ruminates on necromantic skill.
Philosophy is odious and obscure,
Both law and physic are for petty wits,
Divinity is basest of the three,
Unpleasant, harsh, contemptible, and vile;   110
'Tis magic, magic, that hath ravished me!
Then, gentle friends, aid me in this attempt,
And I, that have with concise syllogisms *form of reasoning in which two premises are made and a logical concl. drawn frm. thm*

8. God (a common substitution in
Elizabethan drama).
9. Filled with the idea.
1. "India" could mean the West Indies,
America, or Ophir (in the east).
2. The western hemisphere.
3. The university lecture rooms.
4. The Duke of Parma was the Spanish
governor general of the Low Countries
from 1579 to 1592.
5. A reference to the burning ship sent
by the Netherlanders in 1585 against
the barrier on the river Scheldt which
Parma had built as a part of the
blockade of Antwerp.
6. That will pay no attention to physical reality.

Graveled[7] the pastors of the German church,
And made the flowering pride of Wittenberg   115
Swarm to my problems[8] as the infernal spirits
On sweet Musaeus when he came to hell,
Will be as cunning as Agrippa[9] was
Whose shadows made all Europe honor him.

VALD. Faustus, these books, thy wit, and our experience   120
Shall make all nations to canonize us.
As Indian Moors[1] obey their Spanish lords
So shall the spirits of every element
Be always serviceable to us three:
Like lions shall they guard us when we please,   125
Like Almain rutters[2] with their horsemen's staves,
Or Lapland giants trotting by our sides;
Sometimes like women, or unwedded maids,
Shadowing more beauty in their airy brows
Than in the white breasts of the queen of love;   130
From Venice shall they drag huge argosies
And from America the golden fleece
That yearly stuffs old Philip's[3] treasury,
If learned Faustus will be resolute.

FAUST. Valdes, as resolute am I in this   135
As thou to live; therefore object it not.[4]

CORN. The miracles that magic will perform
Will make thee vow to study nothing else.
He that is grounded in astrology,
Enriched with tongues, well seen[5] in minerals,   140
Hath all the principles magic doth require.
Then doubt not, Faustus, but to be renowned
And more frequented for this mystery[6]
Than heretofore the Delphian oracle.
The spirits tell me they can dry the sea   145
And fetch the treasure of all foreign wrecks—
Aye, all the wealth that our forefathers hid
Within the massy[7] entrails of the earth.
Then tell me, Faustus, what shall we three want?

FAUST. Nothing, Cornelius. O this cheers my soul!   150
Come, show me some demonstrations magical
That I may conjure in some lusty[8] grove
And have these joys in full possession.

VALD. Then haste thee to some solitary grove
And bear wise Bacon's[9] and Albanus' works,   155

---

7. Confounded.
8. Lectures in logic and mathematics. Musaeus was a mythical singer, son of Orpheus; it was, however, the latter who charmed the denizens of hell with his music.
9. Cornelius Agrippa, German author of *The Vanity and Uncertainty of Arts and Sciences*, popularly supposed to have the power of calling up shades ("shadows") of the dead.

1. I.e., dark-skinned American Indians.
2. German horsemen.
3. Philip II, king of Spain.
4. I.e., don't make it a condition.
5. Expert.
6. Craft. The "Delphian oracle" was the oracle of Apollo at Delphi, much frequented in antiquity.
7. Massive.
8. Flourishing, beautiful.
9. Roger Bacon, the medieval friar and

The Hebrew Psalter and New Testament;
And whatsoever else is requisite
We will inform thee ere our conference cease.

CORN. Valdes, first let him know the words of art,
And then, all other ceremonies learned,   160
Faustus may try his cunning by himself.

VALD. First I'll instruct thee in the rudiments,
And then wilt thou be perfecter than I.

FAUST. Then come and dine with me, and after meat
We'll canvass every quiddity[1] thereof;   165
For ere I sleep I'll try what I can do:
This night I'll conjure[2] though I die therefore.   [*Exeunt.*]

SCENE 2

[*Enter two* SCHOLARS.]

1 SCH. I wonder what's become of Faustus, that was wont to
make our schools ring with *sic probo*.[3]

2 SCH. That shall we presently know; here comes his boy.[4]

[*Enter* WAGNER *carrying wine.*]

1 SCH. How now, sirrah; where's thy master?

WAG. God in heaven knows.   5

2 SCH. Why, dost not thou know then?

WAG. Yes, I know; but that follows not.

1 SCH. Go to, sirrah; leave your jesting and tell us where he is.

WAG. That follows not by force of argument, which you, being
licentiate,[5] should stand upon; therefore acknowledge your   10
error and be attentive.

2 SCH. Then you will not tell us?

WAG. You are deceived, for I will tell you. Yet if you were not
dunces you would never ask me such a question, for is he not
corpus naturale, and is not that *mobile*?[6] Then wherefore   15
should you ask me such a question? But that I am by nature
phlegmatic,[7] slow to wrath and prone to lechery (to love, I
would say), it were not for you to come within forty foot of
the place of execution,[8] although I do not doubt to see you
both hanged the next sessions. Thus having triumphed over   20
you, I will set my countenance like a precisian,[9] and begin
to speak thus: Truly, my dear brethren, my master is within
at dinner with Valdes and Cornelius, as this wine, if it could
speak, would inform your worships; and so the Lord bless you,
preserve you, and keep you, my dear brethren.   25

[*Exit.*]

scientist, popularly thought a magician.
"Albanus" is Pietro d'Albano, 13th-
century alchemist.
1. Essential feature.
2. Call up spirits.
3. "Thus I prove," a phrase in scholastic disputation.
4. Poor student earning his keep.
5. I.e., graduate students.
6. *Corpus naturale et mobile* (natural,
movable matter) was a scholastic definition of the subject matter of physics.
Wagner is here parodying the language
of learning he hears around the university.
7. Dominated by the phlegm, one of
the four humors of medieval medicine
and psychology.
8. I.e., the dining room.
9. A Puritan. The rest of his speech
is in the style of the Puritans.

1 SCH. O Faustus, then I fear that which I have long suspected,
That thou art fallen into that damnéd art
For which they two are infamous throughout the world.
2 SCH. Were he a stranger, not allied to me,
The danger of his soul would make me mourn.   30
But come, let us go and inform the Rector,[1]
It may be his grave counsel may reclaim him.
1 SCH. I fear me nothing will reclaim him now.
2 SCH. Yet let us see what we can do.

                                                    [*Exeunt.*]

SCENE 3

[*Enter* FAUSTUS *to conjure.*]
FAUST. Now that the gloomy shadow of the night,
Longing to view Orion's drizzling look,[2]
Leaps from the antarctic world unto the sky
And dims the welkin[3] with her pitchy breath,
Faustus, begin thine incantations   5
And try if devils will obey thy hest,
Seeing thou has prayed and sacrificed to them.
Within this circle is Jehovah's name
       [*He draws the circle[4] on the ground.*]
Forward and backward anagrammatized,
The breviated names of holy saints,
Figures of every adjunct[5] to the heavens   10
And characters of signs and erring stars,
By which the spirits are enforced to rise.
Then fear not, Faustus, but be resolute
And try the uttermost magic can perform.   [*Thunder.*]   15
Sint mihi dei Acherontis propitii! Valeat numen triplex
Iehovae! Ignei aerii aquatici terreni spiritus, salvete! Orientis
princeps Lucifer Belzebub, inferni ardentis monarcha, et De-
mogorgon, propitiamus vos, ut appareat et surgat Mephistophi-
lis![6]   20
       [FAUSTUS *pauses. Thunder still.*]
Quid tu moraris?[7] *Per Iehovam, Gehennam et consecratam*
aquam quam nunc spargo, signumque crucis quod nunc facio,
et per vota nostra, ipse nunc surgat nobis dicatus Mephistophi-
lis!

1. The head of a German university.
2. Orion appears at the beginning of winter. The phrase is a reminiscence of Virgil.
3. Sky.
4. I.e., the magic circle on the ground within which the spirits rise.
5. Heavenly body, thought to be joined to the solid firmament. "Characters of signs" are signs of the zodiac and the planets; "erring": wandering.
6. This first part of the incantation means: "May the gods of the lower regions favor me! Goodbye to the Trin-

ity! Hail, spirits of fire, air, water, and earth! Prince of the East, Belzebub, monarch of burning hell, and Demogorgon, we pray to you that Mephistophilis may appear and rise."
7. Nothing has happened, so Faustus. asks, "What are you waiting for?" and continues to conjure: "By Jehovah, Gehenna, and the holy water which I now sprinkle, and the sign of the cross which I now make, and by our vows, may Mephistophilis himself now rise to serve us."

[MEPHISTOPHILIS *in the shape of a dragon rises from the
earth outside the circle.*]
I charge thee to return and change thy shape;   25
Thou art too ugly to attend on me.
Go, and return an old Franciscan friar;
That holy shape becomes a devil best.   [*Exit* MEPH.]
I see there's virtue in my heavenly words:
Who would not be proficient in this art?   30
How pliant is this Mephistophilis,
Full of obedience and humility!
Such is the force of magic and my spells.
Now, Faustus, thou art conjurer laureate
That canst command great Mephistophilis: 35
Quin redis, Mephistophilis, fratris imagine![8]
    [*Re-enter* MEPHISTOPHILIS *like a Friar.*]
MEPH. Now, Faustus, what wouldst thou have me do?
FAUST. I charge thee wait upon me whilst I live
To do whatever Faustus shall command,
Be it be make the moon drop from her sphere   40
Or the ocean to overwhelm the world.
MEPH. I am a servant to great Lucifer
And may not follow thee without his leave:
No more than he commands must we perform.
FAUST. Did not he charge thee to appear to me?   45
MEPH. No, I came now hither of my own accord.
FAUST. Did not my conjuring speeches raise thee?
Speak!
MEPH. That was the cause, but yet *per accidens,*[9]
For when we hear one rack[1] the name of God,   50
Abjure the Scriptures and his Saviour Christ,
We fly in hope to get his glorious soul;
Nor will we come unless he use such means
Whereby he is in danger to be damned;
Therefore the shortest cut for conjuring.   55
Is stoutly to abjure the Trinity
And pray devoutly to the prince of hell.
FAUST. So I have done, and hold this principle,
There is no chief but only Belzebub
To whom Faustus doth dedicate himself.   60
This word "damnation" terrifies not me
For I confound hell in Elysium;
My ghost be with the old philosophers![2]
But leaving these vain trifles of men's souls—
Tell me, what is that Lucifer thy lord?   65
MEPH. Arch-regent and commander of all spirits.
FAUST. Was not that Lucifer an angel once?
MEPH. Yes, Faustus, and most dearly loved of God.

8. "Return, Mephistophilis, in the shape
of a friar."
9. By the immediate, not ultimate,
cause.
1. Torture (by anagrammatizing).

2. I.e., I regard heaven and hell indifferently; if the old (pre-Christian)
philosophers are damned, let me be
damned with them.

FAUST. How comes it, then, that he is prince of devils?   70

MEPH. O, by aspiring pride and insolence,
    For which God threw him from the face of heaven.

FAUST. And what are you that live with Lucifer?

MEPH. Unhappy spirits that fell with Lucifer,
    Conspired against our God with Lucifer,   75
    And are forever damned with Lucifer.

FAUST. Where are you damned?

MEPH. In hell.

FAUST. How comes it, then, that thou art out of hell?

MEPH. Why, this is hell, nor am I out of it: 80
    Thinkst thou that I who saw the face of God
    And tasted the eternal joys of heaven
    Am not tormented with ten thousand hells
    In being deprived of everlasting bliss?
    O Faustus, leave these frivolous demands   85
    Which strike a terror to my fainting soul!

FAUST. What, is great Mephistophilis so passionate
    For being deprived of the joys of heaven?
    Learn thou of Faustus manly fortitude
    And scorn those joys thou never shalt possess.   90
    Go, bear these tidings to great Lucifer:
    Seeing Faustus hath incurred eternal death
    By desperate thoughts against Jove's deity,
    Say he surrenders up to him his soul
    So he will spare him four and twenty years,   95
    Letting him live in all voluptuousness,
    Having thee ever to attend on me:
    To give me whatsoever I shall ask,
    To tell me whatsoever I demand,
    To slay mine enemies and aid my friends,   100
    And always be obedient to my will.
    Go, and return to mighty Lucifer,
    And meet me in my study at midnight
    And then resolve me of thy master's mind.[4]

MEPH. I will, Faustus.   [*Exit.*] 105

FAUST. Had I as many souls as there be stars
    I'd give them all for Mephistophilis!
    By him I'll be great emperor of the world,
    And make a bridge thorough the moving air
    To pass the ocean with a band of men;   110
    I'll join the hills that bind the Afric shore
    And make that country continent to Spain,
    And both contributory to my crown;
    The Emperor[5] shall not live but by my leave,
    Nor any potentate of Germany.   115
    Now that I have obtained what I desire
    I'll live in speculation[6] of this art
    Till Mephistophilis return again.   [*Exit.*]

3. Overcome by emotion.   5. The Holy Roman Emperor.
4. Give me his decision.   6. Contemplation.

SCENE 4

[*Enter* WAGNER *and the* CLOWN ⟨ROBIN.⟩[7]]

WAG. Come hither, sirrah boy.

CLOWN. Boy! O disgrace to my person! Zounds, boy in your face!
You have seen many boys with such pickadevaunts, I am sure.[8]

WAG. Sirrah, hast thou no comings in?[9]

CLOWN. Yes, and goings out too; you may see, sir.   5

WAG. Alas, poor slave. See how poverty jests in his nakedness: the
villain's out of service, and so hungry that I know he would
give his soul to the devil for a shoulder of mutton, though it
were blood-raw.

CLOWN. Not so, neither; I had need to have it well-roasted, and   10
good sauce to it, if I pay so dear, I can tell you.

WAG. Sirrah, wilt thou be my man and wait on me? And I will
make thee go like *Qui mihi discipulus.*[1]

CLOWN. What, in verse?

WAG. No, slave, in beaten silk and staves-acre.[2]   15

CLOWN. Staves-acre! that's good to kill vermin. Then, belike, if
I serve you I shall be lousy.

WAG. Why, so thou shalt be, whether thou dost it or no; for,
sirrah, if thou dost not presently bind thyself to me for seven
years, I'll turn all the lice about thee into familiars[3] and make 20
them tear thee in pieces.

CLOWN. Nay, sir, you may save yourself a labor, for they are as
familiar with me as if they paid for their meat and drink, I can
tell you.

WAG. Well, sirrah, leave your jesting and take these guilders.[4]   25

CLOWN. Yes, marry, sir, and I thank you, too.

WAG. So, now thou art to be at an hour's warning whenever and
wheresoever the devil shall fetch thee.

CLOWN. Here, take your guilders again, I'll none of 'em.

WAG. Not I, thou art pressed;[5] prepare thyself, for I will presently 30
raise up two devils to carry thee away. Banio! Belcher!

CLOWN. Belcher? And Belcher come here I'll belch him. I am not
afraid of a devil.

[*Enter two* DEVILS, *and the* CLOWN *runs up and down crying.*]

WAG. How now, sir! Will you serve me now?

CLOWN. Aye, good Wagner, take away the devil then.   35

WAG. Spirits, away!   [DEVILS *exeunt.*]

---

7. Not a court jester (as in some of
Shakespeare's plays), but the older-
fashioned stock character, a rustic
buffoon. The name "Robin" has been interpolated by later editors of the text;
all such interpolations, introduced for
clarity of understanding, are indicated
by the special brackets used here.
8. The point of the Clown's retort is
that he is a man and wears a beard
("pickadevaunt"). "Zounds": an oath
("God's wounds").

9. Income, but the Clown then puns on
the literal meaning.
1. "You who are my pupil" (the opening phrase of a poem on how students
should behave, from Lily's *Latin Grammar*). Wagner means, "like a proper
servant of a learned man."
2. A kind of delphinium used for killing vermin.
3. Familiar spirits, demons.
4. Money.
5. Impressed, i.e., hired.

Now, sirrah, follow me.

CLOWN. I will, sir. But hark you, master, will you teach me this
conjuring occupation?

WAG. Aye, sirrah, I'll teach thee to turn thyself to a dog, or a cat,
or a mouse, or a rat, or anything.   40

CLOWN. A dog, or a cat, or a mouse, or a rat! O brave[6] Wagner!

WAG. Villain, call me Master Wagner; and see that you walk attentively, and let your right eye be always diametrally[7] fixed
upon my left heel, that thou mayst *quasi vestigiis nostris in-
sistere*.[8]   45

CLOWN. Well, sir, I warrant you.   [*Exeunt*.]

Act II

SCENE 1

Is he undecided here?

[*Enter* FAUSTUS *in his study*.]

FAUST. Now, Faustus, must thou needs be damned,
Canst not be saved.
What boots[9] it, then, to think of God or heaven?
Away with such vain fancies, and despair—
Despair in God and trust in Belzebub.
Now go not backward, no, be resolute!   5
Why waverest? Something soundeth in mine ears:
"Abjure this magic, turn to God again!"
Aye, and Faustus will turn to God again.
To God? He loves thee not;   10
The God thou servest is thine own appetite,
Wherein is fixed the love of Belzebub.
To him I'll build an altar and a church
And offer lukewarm blood of newborn babes.
        [*Enter* GOOD ANGEL *and* BAD ANGEL.]
G. ANG. Sweet Faustus, leave that execrable art.   15
B. ANG. Go forward, Faustus, in that famous art.
FAUST. Contrition, prayer, repentance—what of them?
G. ANG. O they are means to bring thee unto heaven!
B. ANG. Rather illusions, fruits of lunacy,
That makes men foolish that do use them most.   20
G. ANG. Sweet Faustus, think of heaven and heavenly things.
B. ANG. No, Faustus, think of honor and of wealth.
        [⟨*Exeunt* ANGELS.⟩]
FAUST. Of wealth!
Why, the signiory of Emden[1] shall be mine.
When Mephistophilis shall stand by me   25
What power can hurt me? Faustus, thou art safe;
Cast no more doubts. Come, Mephistophilis,
And bring glad tidings from great Lucifer.
Is't not midnight? Come, Mephistophilis!

6. Marvelous, wonderful.
7. Diametrically.
8. A pedantic way of saying "follow
my footsteps."
9. Avails.
1. A wealthy German trade center.

Veni, veni, Mephistophile![2]   30
    [*Enter* MEPHISTOPHILIS.]
  Now tell me what saith Lucifer, thy lord?
MEPH. That I shall wait on Faustus whilst I live,
  So he will buy my service with his soul.
FAUST. Already Faustus hath hazarded that for thee.
MEPH. But, Faustus, thou must bequeath it solemnly   35
  And write a deed of gift with thine own blood,
  For that security craves Lucifer.
  If thou deny it, I must back to hell.
FAUST. Stay, Mephistophilis, and tell me what good
  Will my soul do thy lord?
MEPH.   Enlarge his kingdom.   40
FAUST. Is that the reason why he tempts us thus?
MEPH. *Solamen miseris socios habuisse doloris.*[3]
FAUST. Why, have you any pain that tortures others?
MEPH. As great as have the human souls of men.
  But tell me, Faustus, shall I have thy soul?   45
  And I will be thy slave, and wait on thee,
  And give thee more than thou hast wit to ask.
FAUST. Aye, Mephistophilis, I'll give it him.
MEPH. Then, Faustus, stab thine arm courageously,
  And bind thy soul that at some certain day   50
  Great Lucifer may claim it as his own,
  And then be thou as great as Lucifer.
FAUST. Lo, Mephistophilis, for love of thee
    [*Stabbing his arm.*]
  I cut mine arm, and with my proper[4] blood
  Assure my soul to be great Lucifer's.   55
  Chief lord and regent of perpetual night,
  View here the blood that trickles from mine arm
  And let it be propitious for my wish!
MEPH. But, Faustus,
  Write it in manner of a deed of gift.   60
FAUST. Aye, so I do. [*Writes.*] But, Mephistophilis,
  My blood congeals and I can write no more.
MEPH. I'll fetch thee fire to dissolve it straight.   [*Exit.*]
FAUST. What might the staying of my blood portend?
  Is it unwilling I should write this bill?[5]   65
  Why streams it not, that I may write afresh?
  "Faustus gives to thee his soul"—ah, there it stayed.
  Why shouldst thou not? Is not thy soul thine own?
  Then write again: "Faustus gives to thee his soul."
    [*Enter* MEPHISTOPHILIS *with a chafer*[6] *of fire.*]
MEPH. See, Faustus, here is fire; set it on.   70
FAUST. So: now the blood begins to clear again;
  Now will I make an end immediately.   [⟨*Writes.*⟩]

2. "Come, come, Mephistophilis!"   5. Contract.
3. "Misery loves company."   6. A portable grate.
4. Own.

MEPH. [*aside*] What will not I do to obtain his soul!

FAUST. *Consummatum est*[7]—this bill is ended;
And Faustus hath bequeathed his soul to Lucifer.   75
But what is this inscription on mine arm?
"*Homo, fuge!*"[8] Whither should I fly?
If unto God, he'll throw me down to hell.
My senses are deceived; here's nothing writ.
O yes, I see it plain: even here is writ   80
"*Homo, fuge!*" Yet shall not Faustus fly.

MEPH. I'll fetch him somewhat to delight his mind.   [*Exit.*]
          [*Re-enter* MEPHISTOPHILIS *with* DEVILS, *giving crowns and
          rich apparel to* FAUSTUS, *and dance, and then depart.*]

FAUST. What means this show?
Speak, Mephistophilis.

MEPH. Nothing, Faustus, but to delight thy mind   85
And let thee see what magic can perform.

FAUST. But may I raise such spirits when I please?

MEPH. Aye, Faustus, and do greater things than these.

FAUST. Then, Mephistophilis, receive this scroll,
A deed of gift of body and of soul;   90
But yet conditionally that thou perform
All covenant-articles between us both.

MEPH. Faustus, I swear by hell and Lucifer
To effect all promises between us made.

FAUST. Then hear me read it, Mephistophilis.   [⟨*Reads.*⟩]   95
"On these conditions following:
First, that Faustus may be a spirit in form and substance.
Secondly, that Mephistophilis shall be his servant and at his
command.
Thirdly, that Mephistophilis shall do for him, and bring him   100
whatsoever.
Fourthly, that he shall be in his chamber or house invisible.
Lastly, that he shall appear to the said John Faustus at all
times, in what form or shape soever he please.
I, John Faustus of Wittenberg, Doctor, by these presents do   105
give both body and soul to Lucifer, Prince of the East, and his
minister Mephistophilis, and furthermore grant unto them,
that four and twenty years being expired, the articles above
written inviolate, full power to fetch or carry the said John
Faustus, body and soul, flesh, blood, or goods, into their habi-   110
tation wheresoever.
                    By me John Faustus."

MEPH. Speak, Faustus, do you deliver this as your deed?

FAUST. Aye, take it, and the devil give thee good of it.

MEPH. Now, Faustus, ask what thou wilt.   115

FAUST. First will I question with thee about hell.
Tell me, where is the place that men call hell?

MEPH. Under the heavens.

---

7. "It is finished." A blasphemy, as these are the words of Christ on the Cross (see John xix.30).
8. "O man, flee!"

FAUST.   Aye, but whereabout?

MEPH. Within the bowels of these elements,
Where we are tortured and remain forever.   120
Hell hath no limits, nor is circumscribed
In one self place, for where we are is hell,
And where hell is there must we ever be;
And, to be short, when all the world dissolves
And every creature shall be purified,   125
All places shall be hell that is not heaven.

FAUST. I think hell's a fable.

MEPH. Aye, think so, till experience change thy mind.

FAUST. Why, thinkst thou that Faustus shall be damned?

MEPH. Aye, of necessity, for here's the scroll   130
In which thou hast given thy soul to Lucifer.

FAUST. Aye, and body too; but what of that?
Thinkst thou that Faustus is so fond[9] to imagine
That after this life there is any pain?
No, these are trifles and mere old wives' tales.   135

MEPH. But I am an instance to prove the contrary,
For I tell thee I am damned and now in hell.

FAUST. Nay, and this be hell I'll willingly be damned.
What, sleeping, eating, walking, and disputing?
But leaving off this, let me have a wife,   140
The fairest maid in Germany,
For I am wanton and lascivious
And cannot live without a wife.

MEPH. I prithee, Faustus, talk not of a wife.[1]

FAUST. Nay, sweet Mephistophilis, fetch me one. for I will have 145
one.

MEPH. Well, thou shalt have a wife. Sit there till I come. [⟨*Exit.*⟩]
[*Re-enter* MEPHISTOPHILIS *with a* DEVIL *dressed like a
woman, with fireworks.*]

FAUST. What sight is this?

MEPH. Now Faustus, how dost thou like thy wife?

FAUST. Here's a hot whore indeed! No, I'll no wife.   150

MEPH. Marriage is but a ceremonial toy,
And if thou lovest me, think no more of it.
I'll cull thee out the fairest courtesans
And bring them every morning to thy bed;
She whom thine eye shall like thy heart shall have,   155
Were she as chaste as was Penelope,[2]
As wise as Saba, or as beautiful
As was bright Lucifer before his fall.
Hold, take this book: peruse it thoroughly.
The iterating[3] of these lines brings gold,   160
The framing[4] of this circle on the ground

9. Foolish.
1. Mephistophilis cannot produce a wife for Faustus because marriage is a sacrament.
2. The wife of Ulysses, famed for chas-
tity and fidelity. "Saba": the Queen of Sheba.
3. Repeating.
4. Drawing.

Brings whirlwinds, tempests, thunder, and lightning;
Pronounce this thrice devoutly to thyself
And men in harness shall appear to thee,
Ready to execute what thou desirest.   165

FAUST. Thanks, Mephistophilis, yet fain would I have a book
wherein I might behold all spells and incantations, that I
might raise up spirits when I please.

MEPH. Here they are in this book.   [*There turn to them.*]

FAUST. Now would I have a book where I might see all characters 170
and planets of the heavens, that I might know their motions
and dispositions.

MEPH. Here they are too.   [*Turn to them.*]

FAUST. Nay, let me have one book more, and then I have done,
wherein I might see all plants, herbs, and trees that grow upon 175
the earth.

MEPH. Here they be.

FAUST. O thou art deceived!

MEPH. Tut, I warrant thee.   [*Turn to them.*]
     [⟨*Exeunt.*⟩][5]

SCENE 2

[*Enter* FAUSTUS *in his study and* MEPHISTOPHILIS.]

FAUST. When I behold the heavens then I repent
And curse thee, wicked Mephistophilis,
Because thou hast deprived me of those joys.

MEPH. 'Twas thine own seeking, Faustus, thank thyself.
But thinkest thou heaven is such a glorious thing?   5
I tell thee, Faustus, it is not half so fair
As thou or any man that breathes on earth.

FAUST. How provest thou that?

MEPH. 'Twas made for man; then he's more excellent.

FAUST. If heaven was made for man 'twas made for me.   10
I will renounce this magic and repent.
     [*Enter* GOOD ANGEL *and* BAD ANGEL.]

G. ANG. Faustus, repent; yet God will pity thee.

B. ANG. Thou art a spirit; God cannot pity thee.

FAUST. Who buzzeth in mine ears I am a spirit?[6]
Be I a devil, yet God may pity me.   15
Yea, God will pity me, if I repent.

B. ANG. Aye, but Faustus never shall repent.
     [*Exeunt* ANGELS.]

FAUST. My heart is hardened; I cannot repent.
Scarce can I name salvation, faith, or heaven,
But fearful echoes thunder in mine ears: 20
"Faustus, thou are damned!" Then guns and knives,
Swords, poison, halters, and envenomed steel

---

5. After this a comic scene has been lost from the text. In it, apparently the Clown, Robin, stole one of Faustus' conjuring books and left Wagner's serv-ice. He then became an hostler at an inn.
6. Evil spirit, devil.

Are laid before me to dispatch myself,
And long ere this I should have done the deed
Had not sweet pleasure conquered deep despair. 25
Have I not made blind Homer sing to me
Of Alexander's love and Oenon's death,[7]
And hath not he that built the walls of Thebes
With ravishing sound of his melodious harp[8]
Made music with my Mephistophilis? 30
Why should I die, then, or basely despair?
I am resolved Faustus shall not repent.
Come, Mephistophilis, let us dispute again
And reason of divine astrology.
Speak, are there many spheres above the moon? 35
Are all celestial bodies but one globe
As is the substance of this centric earth?[9]

MEPH. As are the elements, such are the heavens,
Even from the moon unto the empyreal orb,
Mutually folded in each other's spheres, 40
And jointly move upon one axletree
Whose termine[1] is termed the world's wide pole;
Nor are the names of Saturn, Mars, or Jupiter
Feigned, but are erring stars.

FAUST. But tell me, have they all one motion, both *situ et tem-* 45
pore?[2]

MEPH. All move from east to west in four and twenty hours upon
the poles of the world, but differ in their motions upon the
poles of the zodiac.[3]

FAUST. These slender questions Wagner can decide. 50
Hath Mephistophilis no greater skill?
Who knows not the double motion of the planets?
That the first is finished in a natural day;
The second thus, Saturn in thirty years, Jupiter in twelve, Mars
in four, the Sun, Venus, and Mercury in a year, the Moon in 55
twenty-eight days. These are freshmen's suppositions. But tell
me, hath every sphere a dominion or *intelligentia?*[4]

MEPH. Aye.

FAUST. How many heavens or spheres are there?

MEPH. Nine: the seven planets, the firmament, and the empyreal 60
heaven.

7. Alexander is another name for Paris, the lover of Oenone; later he deserted her and abducted Helen, causing the Trojan War. Oenone refused to heal the wounds Paris received in battle, and when he died of them she killed herself in remorse.
8. I.e., the legendary musician Amphion.
9. "Faustus asks whether all the apparently different heavenly bodies form really one globe, like the earth. Mephistophilis answers that like the elements, which are separate but combined, the heavenly bodies are separate, though their spheres are infolded, and they move on one axletree. Hence we are not in error in giving individual names to Saturn, Mars, or Jupiter; they are separate planets" (F. S. Boas). The "empyreal orb," or outermost sphere, was also called the empyrean.
1. End.
2. In position and time.
3. I.e., the common axletree on which all the spheres revolve.
4. I.e., an angel or intelligence (thought to be the source of motion in each sphere).

FAUST. But is there not *coelum igneum, et crystallinum?*[5]

MEPH. No, Faustus, they be but fables.

FAUST. Resolve me then in this one question: why are not conjunctions, oppositions, aspects, eclipses, all at one time, but in 65
   some years we have more, in some less?

MEPH. *Per inequalem motum respectu totius.*[6]

FAUST. Well, I am answered. Tell me, who made the world?

MEPH. I will not.

FAUST. Sweet Mephistophilis, tell me. 70

MEPH. Move me not, Faustus.

FAUST. Villain, have I not bound thee to tell me anything?

MEPH. Aye, that is not against our kingdom; this is.
   Thou art damned; think thou of hell.

FAUST. Think, Faustus, upon God that made the world! 75

MEPH. Remember this! [*Exit.*]

FAUST. Aye, go, accurséd spirit, to ugly hell;
   'Tis thou has damned distresséd Faustus' soul.
   Is 't too late?
          [*Enter* GOOD ANGEL *and* BAD ANGEL.]

B. ANG. Too late. 80

G. ANG. Never too late, if Faustus will repent.

B. ANG. If thou repent, devils will tear thee in pieces.

G. ANG. Repent, and they shall never raze[7] thy skin.
          [*Exeunt* ANGELS.]

FAUST. O Christ, my Saviour! my Saviour!
   Help to save distresséd Faustus' soul. 85
          [*Enter* LUCIFER, BELZEBUB, *and* MEPHISTOPHILIS.]

LUC. Christ cannot save thy soul, for he is just;
   There's none but I have interest in the same.

FAUST. O what art thou that lookst so terrible?

LUC. I am Lucifer,
   And this is my companion prince in hell. 90

FAUST. O Faustus, they are come to fetch thy soul!

BEL. We are come to tell thee thou dost injure us.

LUC. Thou call'st on Christ, contrary to thy promise.

BEL. Thou shouldst not think on God.

LUC. Think on the devil. 95

BEL. And his dam too.[8]

FAUST. Nor will I henceforth. Pardon me in this,
   And Faustus vows never to look to heaven,
   Never to name God or pray to him,
   To burn his Scriptures, slay his ministers, 100
   And make my spirits pull his churches down.

LUC. So shalt thou show thyself an obedient servant, and we will
   highly gratify thee for it.

BEL. Faustus, we are come from hell in person to show thee some

---

5. The "heaven of fire" and the "crystalline sphere," introduced by some of
the old authorities to explain the pre-
cession of the equinoxes.
6. "Because of their unequal velocities
within the system."
7. Scratch.
8. "The devil and his dam" was a common colloquial expression.

pastime. Sit down, and thou shalt behold the Seven Deadly 105
Sins appear to thee in their own proper shapes and likeness.

FAUST. That sight will be as pleasant to me as Paradise was to
Adam, the first day of his creation.

LUC. Talk not of Paradise or Creation, but mark the show. Go,
Mephistophilis, fetch them in. 110

[*Enter the* SEVEN DEADLY SINS,[9] *led by a piper*.]

Now, Faustus, question them of their names and dispositions.

FAUST. That shall I soon. What art thou, the first?

PRIDE. I am Pride. I disdain to have any parents. I am like to
Ovid's flea:[1] I can creep into every corner of a wench; sometimes like a periwig I sit upon her brow; next like a necklace 115
I hang about her neck; then like a fan of feathers I kiss her
lips; and then turning myself to a wrought smock[2] do what I
list. But fie, what a smell is here! I'll not speak another word
except the ground be perfumed and covered with cloth of
arras.[3] 120

FAUST. Thou art a proud knave indeed. What art thou, the
second?

COVET. I am Covetousness, begotten of an old churl in a leather
bag; and, might I now obtain my wish, this house, you and
all, should turn to gold, that I might lock you safe into my 125
chest. O my sweet gold!

FAUST. And what art thou, the third?

ENVY. I am Envy, begotten of a chimney-sweeper and an oyster-
wife. I cannot read, and therefore wish all books were burned.
I am lean with seeing others eat. O that there would come a 130
famine over all the world, that all might die, and I live alone;
then thou shouldst see how fat I'd be! But must thou sit and
I stand? Come down, with a vengeance!

FAUST. Out, envious wretch! But what art thou, the fourth?

WRATH. I am Wrath. I had neither father nor mother; I leapt 135
out of a lion's mouth when I was scarce an hour old, and ever
since have run up and down the world with these case of
rapiers, wounding myself when I could get none to fight withal.
I was born in hell; and look to it, for some of you shall be my
father. 140

FAUST. And what art thou, the fifth?

GLUT. I am Gluttony. My parents are all dead, and the devil a
penny they have left me but a small pension, and that buys
me thirty meals a day and ten bevers[4]—a small trifle to suffice
nature. I come of a royal pedigree: my father was a gammon[5] 145
of bacon, and my mother was a hogshead of claret wine. My

9. The Seven Deadly Sins are pride, avarice, gluttony, lust, sloth, envy, and anger. (They are deadly because other sins grow out of them.) They were frequently represented in medieval plays, sometimes in the rather grimly comic tone used here; in the old morality plays all the characters, not merely the sins, were abstractions.

1. A salacious medieval poem *Carmen de Pulice* ("The Flea") was attributed to Ovid.
2. A decorated or ornamented petticoat.
3. Arras in Flanders exported fine cloth used for tapestry hangings.
4. Snacks.
5. The lower side of pork, including the leg.

godfathers were these: Peter Pickle-herring and Martin Martle-
mas-beef. But my godmother, O, she was a jolly gentlewoman,
and well beloved in every good town and city: her name was
mistress Margery March-beer. Now, Faustus, thou hast heard 150
all my progeny;[6] wilt thou bid me to supper?

FAUST. Not I. Thou wilt eat up all my victuals.

GLUT. Then the devil choke thee!

FAUST. Choke thyself, glutton. What art thou, the sixth?

SLOTH. Heigh ho! I am Sloth. I was begotten on a sunny bank, 155
where I have lain ever since, and you have done me great injury
to bring me from thence; let me be carried thither again by
Gluttony and Lechery. Heigh ho! I'll not speak word more for
a king's ransom.

FAUST. And what are you, mistress minx, the seventh and last? 160

LECHERY. Who, I, sir? I am one that loves an inch of raw mutton[7] better than an ell of fried stockfish, and the first letter
of my name begins with Lechery.

LUC. Away, to hell, away! On, piper![8]
    [*Exeunt the* SINS.]

FAUST. O how this sight doth delight my soul! 165

LUC. Tut, Faustus, in hell is all manner of delight.

FAUST. O might I see hell and return again safe, how happy were
I then!

LUC. Faustus, thou shalt. At midnight I will send for thee. In
meantime peruse this book, and view it throughly, and thou 170
shalt turn thyself into what shape thou wilt.

FAUST. Thanks, mighty Lucifer; this will I keep as chary[9] as my
life.

LUC. Now Faustus, farewell.

FAUST. Farewell, great Lucifer. Come, Mephistophilis. 175
    [*Exeunt* OMNES.]

SCENE 3

[*Enter the* CLOWN (ROBIN).]

ROBIN. What, Dick, look to the horses there till I come again.
I have gotten one of Dr. Faustus' conjuring books, and now
we'll have such knavery as 't passes.
    [*Enter* DICK.]

DICK. What, Robin, you must come away and walk the horses.

ROBIN. I walk the horses! I scorn 't, faith: I have other matters 5
in hand; let the horses walk themselves and they will. "A *per
se*[1] a; t, h, e, the; o *per se* o; deny orgon, gorgon." Keep further
from me, O thou illiterate and unlearned hostler.

6. Ancestry, lineage.
7. Frequently a word of indecent meaning in Elizabethan English; here it
means the penis. "Ell": 45 inches;
"stockfish": dried cod.
8. The command to the piper who led
the procession of the Deadly Sins onto
the stage to strike up a tune for their
exit.
9. Carefully.
1. "A by itself," a method of reading
the letters of the alphabet taught to
children. Robin's semi-literacy is being
satirized. "Deny orgon, gorgon" is a
parody of Faustus' invocation of Demogorgon in I.iii.

DICK. 'Snails,[2] what has thou got there? a book? Why, thou canst
not tell ne'er a word on 't.   10

ROBIN. That thou shalt see presently. Keep out of the circle, I
say, lest I send you into the ostry[3] with a vengeance.

DICK. That's like, faith! You had best leave your foolery, for an
my master come, he'll conjure you, faith.

ROBIN. My master conjure me! I'll tell thee what; an my master   15
come here, I'll clap as fair a pair of horns on 's head as e'er
thou sawest in thy life.[4]

DICK. Thou needst not do that, for my mistress hath done it.

ROBIN. Aye, there be of us here have waded as deep into matters
as other men, if they were disposed to talk.   20

DICK. A plague take you! I thought you did not sneak up and
down after her for nothing. But I prithee tell me in good sadness, Robin, is that a conjuring book?

ROBIN. Do but speak what thou 't have me do, and I'll do 't. If
thou 't dance naked, put off thy clothes, and I'll conjure about 25
thee presently. Or if thou 't but to the tavern with me, I'll give
thee white wine, red wine, claret wine, sack, muscadine, mal-
mesey, and whippincrust,[5] hold-belly-hold, and we'll not pay
one penny for it.

DICK. O brave! Prithee let's to it presently, for I am as dry as a dog. 30

ROBIN. Come then, let's away.   [*Exeunt.*]

Act III

[*Enter* CHORUS.]

CHO. Learned Faustus,
　　To find the secrets of astronomy
　　Graven in the book of Jove's high firmament,
　　Did mount himself to scale Olympus' top.
　　Where sitting in a chariot burning bright   5
　　Drawn by the strength of yokéd dragons' necks,
　　He views the clouds, the planets, and the stars,
　　The tropics, zones, and quarters of the sky
　　From the bright circle of the hornéd moon
　　Even to the height of *Primum Mobile*;[6]   10
　　And whirling round with this circumference
　　Within the concave compass of the pole,
　　From east to west his dragons swiftly glide
　　And in eight days did bring him home again.
　　Not long he stayed within his quiet house   15
　　To rest his bones after his weary toil
　　But new exploits do hale him out again;
　　And mounted then upon a dragon's back
　　That with his wings did part the subtle air,
　　He now is gone to prove cosmography[7]   20

2. I.e., God's nails (on the Cross).
3. Stable.
4. A wife's infidelity was supposed in
legend, and in the standard Elizabethan
joke, to cause her husband to grow
horns.
5. Robin's pronunciation of "hippocras," a spiced wine.
6. The outermost sphere, the empyrean.
7. I.e., to test the accuracy of maps.

That measures coasts and kingdoms of the earth:
And, as I guess, will first arrive at Rome
To see the Pope and manner of his court
And take some part of holy Peter's feast,
The which this day is highly solemnized.   25
    [*Exit.*]

SCENE 1

    [*Enter* FAUSTUS *and* MEPHISTOPHILIS.]
FAUST. Having now, my good Mephistophilis,
  Passed with delight the stately town of Trier[8]
  Environed round with airy mountain tops,
  With walls of flint and deep-entrenchéd lakes,[9]
  Not to be won by any conquering prince;   5
  From Paris next coasting the realm of France,
  We saw the river Maine fall into Rhine,
  Whose banks are set with groves of fruitful vines;
  Then up to Naples, rich Campania,
  With buildings fair and gorgeous to the eye,   10
  Whose streets straight forth and paved with finest brick
  Quarter the town in four equivalents.
  There saw we learned Maro's[1] golden tomb,
  The way he cut, an English mile in length,
  Thorough a rock of stone in one night's space,   15
  From thence to Venice, Padua, and the rest,
  In midst of which a sumptuous temple[2] stands
  That threats the stars with her aspiring top,
  Whose frame is paved with sundry colored stones
  And roofed aloft with curious work in gold.   20
  Thus hitherto hath Faustus spent his time.
  But tell me now, what resting place is this?
  Hast thou, as erst I did command,
  Conducted me within the walls of Rome?
MEPH. I have, my Faustus, and for proof thereof   25
  This is the goodly palace of the Pope,
  And 'cause we are no common guests
  I choose his privy chamber for our use.
FAUST. I hope his Holiness will bid us welcome.
MEPH. All's one, for we'll be bold with his venison.   30
  But now, my Faustus, that thou mayst perceive
  What Rome contains for to delight thine eyes,
  Know that this city stands upon seven hills
  That underprop the groundwork of the same;
  Just through the midst runs flowing Tiber's stream,   35
  With winding banks that cut it in two parts
  Over the which four stately bridges lean

8. Treves (in Prussia).
9. Moats.
1. Virgil's. In medieval legend the Roman poet Virgil was considered a magician, and a tunnel ("way") on the promontory of Posilippo at Naples, near his tomb, was accredited to his magical powers.
2. I.e., St. Mark's in Venice.

That make safe passage to each part of Rome.
Upon the bridge called Ponte Angelo
Erected is a castle passing strong,   40
Where thou shalt see such store of ordnance
As that the double cannons forged of brass
Do match the number of the days contained
Within the compass of one complete year;
Besides the gates and high pyramides[3]   45
That Julius Caesar brought from Africa.

FAUST. Now by the kingdoms of infernal rule,
  Of Styx, Acheron, and the fiery lake
  Of ever-burning Phlegethon,[4] I swear
  That I do long to see the monuments   50
  And situation of bright-splendent Rome.
  Come, therefore, let's away.

MEPH. Nay, stay, my Faustus; I know you'd see the Pope
  And take some part of holy Peter's feast,
  The which in state and high solemnity   55
  This day is held through Rome and Italy
  In honor of the Pope's triumphant victory.

FAUST. Sweet Mephistophilis, thou pleasest me;
  Whilst I am here on earth let me be cloyed
  With all things that delight the heart of man.   60
  My four and twenty years of liberty
  I'll spend in pleasure and in dalliance,
  That Faustus' name, whilst this bright frame doth stand,
  May be admiréd through the furthest land.

MEPH. 'Tis well said, Faustus; come then, stand by me   65
  And thou shalt see them come immediately.

FAUST. Nay, stay, my gentle Mephistophilis,
  And grant me my request, and then I go.
  Thou knowst, within the compass of eight days
  We viewed the face of heaven, of earth, of hell;   70
  So high our dragons soared into the air
  That, looking down, the earth appeared to me
  No bigger than my hand in quantity.
  There did we view the kingdoms of the world,
  And what might please mine eye I there beheld.   75
  Then in this show let me an actor be,
  That this proud Pope may Faustus' cunning see.

MEPH. Let it be so, my Faustus, but first stay
  And view their triumphs[5] as they pass this way,
  And then devise what best contents thy mind,   80
  By cunning of thine art to cross the Pope
  Or dash the pride of this solemnity,
  To make his monks and abbots stand like apes
  And point like antics[6] at his triple crown,

3. *Py-rám-i-des,* a singular noun, meaning an obelisk.
4. Classical names for rivers of the underworld; symbolic of hell, they are appropriate as oaths for Faustus.
5. Parades.
6. Grotesque figures.

To beat the beads about the friars' pates 85
Or clap huge horns upon the cardinals' heads,
Or any villainy thou canst devise,
And I'll perform it, Faustus. Hark, they come!
This day shall make thee be admired in Rome.

> [*Enter the* CARDINALS *and* BISHOPS, *some bearing crosiers,*
> *some the pillars;* MONKS *and* FRIARS *singing their proces-*
> *sion; then the* POPE *and* RAYMOND, *King of Hungary,*
> *with* BRUNO *led in chains.*][7]

POPE. Cast down our footstool.
RAY.   Saxon Bruno, stoop, 90
Whilst on thy back his Holiness ascends
St. Peter's chair and state pontifical.
BRUNO. Proud Lucifer, that state belongs to me;
But thus I fall, to Peter, not to thee.
POPE. To me and Peter shalt thou groveling lie 95
And crouch before the papal dignity.
Sound trumpets, then, for thus St. Peter's heir
From Bruno's back ascends St. Peter's chair.

> [*A flourish while he ascends.*]

Thus as the gods creep on with feet of wool
Long ere with iron hands they punish men, 100
So shall our sleeping vengeance now arise
And smite with death thy hated enterprise.
Lord Cardinals of France and Padua,
Go forthwith to our holy consistory
And read among the statutes decretal 105
What, by the holy council held at Trent,[8]
The sacred synod hath decreed for him
That doth assume the papal government
Without election and a true consent.
Away and bring us word with speed. 110
1 CARD. We go, my lord.   [*Exeunt* CARDINALS.]
POPE. Lord Raymond—
FAUST. Go, haste thee, gentle Mephistophilis,
Follow the cardinals to the consistory,
And as they turn their superstitious books, 115
Strike them with sloth and drowsy idleness
And make them sleep so sound that in their shapes
Thyself and I may parley with this Pope,
This proud confronter of the Emperor,[9]
And in despite of all his holiness 120
Restore this Bruno to his liberty

---

7. "Crosiers": crosses borne before prelates; "the pillars" (of silver), however, are known to have been used by only two English cardinals, Wolsey and De la Pole. "Raymond, King of Hungary" is unknown to history. "Bruno" is likewise fictitious; he is the German pretender to the papal throne over whom the Pope has just triumphed (line 57).
8. The famous council of the Catholic Church which lasted from 1545 to 1563.
9. Holy Roman Emperor. Faustus refers to the conflict between the Pope and the Emperor; the former was victorious and captured the Emperor's choice for Pope, "Saxon Bruno."

And bear him to the states of Germany.

MEPH. Faustus, I go.

FAUST.   Dispatch it soon.
  The Pope shall curse that Faustus came to Rome.

    [*Exeunt* FAUSTUS *and* MEPHISTOPHILIS.]

BRUNO. Pope Adrian, let me have some right of law;   125
  I was elected by the Emperor.

POPE. We will depose the Emperor for that deed
  And curse the people that submit to him;
  Both he and thou shalt stand excommunicate
  And interdict from church's privilege   130
  And all society of holy men.
  He grows too proud in his authority,
  Lifting his lofty head above the clouds,
  And like a steeple overpeers the church,
  But we'll pull down his haughty insolence.   135
  And as Pope Alexander,[1] our progenitor,
  Trod on the neck of German Frederick,
  Adding this golden sentence to our praise,
  That Peter's heirs should tread on emperors
  And walk upon the dreadful adder's back,   140
  Treading the lion and the dragon down,
  And fearless spurn the killing basilisk;[2]
  So will we quell that haughty schismatic,
  And by authority apostolical
  Depose him from his regal government.   145

BRUNO. Pope Julius swore to princely Sigismond,
  For him and the succeeding popes of Rome,
  To hold the emperors their lawful lords.

POPE. Pope Julius did abuse the church's rights,
  And therefore none of his decrees can stand.   150
  Is not all power on earth bestowed on us?
  And therefore though we would we cannot err.
  Behold this silver belt, whereto is fixed
  Seven golden keys fast sealed with seven seals
  In token of our sevenfold power from heaven,   155
  To bind or loose, lock fast, condemn, or judge,
  Resign or seal, or whatso pleaseth us.
  Then he and thou and all the world shall stoop,
  Or be assuréd of our dreadful curse
  To light as heavy as the pains of hell.   160

    [*Enter* FAUSTUS *and* MEPHISTOPHILIS *like cardinals.*]

MEPH. Now tell me, Faustus, are we not fitted well?

FAUST. Yes, Mephistophilis, and two such cardinals
  Ne'er served a holy pope as we shall do.
  But whilst they sleep within the consistory
  Let us salute his reverend Fatherhood.   165

RAY. Behold, my lord, the cardinals are returned.

1. Pope Alexander III (1159–81) compelled the Emperor Frederick Barbarossa to submit to him.

2. A mythical monster capable of killing by a look.

POPE. Welcome, grave fathers, answer presently;[3]
    What have our holy council there decreed
    Concerning Bruno and the Emperor
    In quittance of their late conspiracy   170
    Against our state and papal dignity?
FAUST. Most sacred patron of the church of Rome,
    By full consent of all the synod
    Of priests and prelates it is thus decreed:
    That Bruno and the German Emperor   175
    Be held as lollards[4] and bold schismatics
    And proud disturbers of the church's peace.
    And if that Bruno by his own assent,
    Without enforcement of the German peers,
    Did seek to wear the triple diadem   180
    And by your death to climb St. Peter's chair,
    The statutes decretal have thus decreed:
    He shall be straight condemned of heresy
    And on a pile of fagots burned to death.
POPE. It is enough. Here, take him to your charge   185
    And bear him straight to Ponte Angelo,
    And in the strongest tower enclose him fast.
    Tomorrow, sitting in our consistory
    With all our college of grave cardinals,
    We will determine of his life or death.   190
    Here, take his triple crown along with you
    And leave it in the church's treasury.
    Make haste again, my good lord cardinals,
    And take our blessing apostolical.
MEPH. So, so. Was never devil thus blessed before!   195
FAUST. Away, sweet Mephistophilis, be gone;
    The cardinals will be plagued for this anon.
       [*Exeunt* FAUSTUS *and* MEPHISTOPHILIS *with* BRUNO.]
POPE. Go presently and bring a banquet forth,
    That we may solemnize St. Peter's feast
    And with Lord Raymond, King of Hungary,   200
    Drink to our late and happy victory.   [*Exeunt.*]

SCENE 2

    [*The banquet is brought in, and then enter* FAUSTUS *and*
    MEPHISTOPHILIS *in their own shapes.*]
MEPH. Now Faustus, come prepare thyself for mirth;
    The sleepy cardinals are hard at hand
    To censure Bruno, that is posted hence
    And on a proud-paced steed as swift as thought
    Flies o'er the Alps to fruitful Germany,   5
    There to salute the woeful Emperor.
FAUST. The Pope will curse them for their sloth today
    That slept both Bruno and his crown away.

3. Immediately.
4. Protestants, usually English followers of Wycliffe, the 14th-century religious reformer.

But now, that Faustus may delight his mind
And by their folly make some merriment,   10
Sweet Mephistophilis, so charm me here
That I may walk invisible to all
And do whate'er I please unseen of any.
MEPH. Faustus, thou shalt; then kneel down presently,
       Whilst on thy head I lay my hand   15
       And charm thee with this magic wand.
       First wear this girdle, then appear
       Invisible to all are here.
       The planets seven, the gloomy air,
       Hell, and the Furies' forkéd hair,   20
       Pluto's blue fire and Hecate's[5] tree
       With magic spells so compass thee
       That no eye may thy body see.
So, Faustus, now, for all their holiness,
    Do what thou wilt thou shalt not be discerned.   25
FAUST. Thanks, Mephistophilis. Now friars, take heed
Lest Faustus make your shaven crowns to bleed.
MEPH. Faustus, no more; see where the cardinals come.
    [*Enter* POPE *and all the lords, with* KING RAYMOND *and
    the* ARCHBISHOP OF RHEIMS. *Enter the two* CARDINALS
    with a book.*]
POPE. Welcome, lord cardinals; come, sit down.
    Lord Raymond, take your seat. Friars, attend,   30
    And see that all things be in readiness
    As best beseems this solemn festival.
1 CARD. First may it please your sacred holiness
    To view the sentence of the reverend synod
    Concerning Bruno and the Emperor.   35
POPE. What needs this question? Did I not tell you
    Tomorrow we would sit i' th' consistory
    And there determine of his punishment?
    You brought us word, even now, it was decreed
    That Bruno and the curséd Emperor   40
    Were by the holy council both condemned
    For loathéd lollards and base schismatics;
    Then wherefore would you have me view that book?
1 CARD. Your Grace mistakes; you gave us no such charge.
RAY. Deny it not; we all are witnesses   45
    That Bruno here was late delivered you,
    With his rich triple crown to be reserved
    And put into the church's treasury.
BOTH CARD. By holy Paul we saw them not.
POPE. By Peter, you shall die   50
    Unless you bring them forth immediately.

5. The goddess of magic and witch-craft, whose name the Elizabethans pronounced *Héc-at.* She is not known to have any special "tree"; the word may be a mistake for "three," since she was often represented as a triple goddess—of heaven, earth, and hell.

Hale them to prison! Lade their limbs with gyves![6]
False prelates, for this hateful treachery,
Cursed be your souls to hellish misery. [*Exeunt* CARDINALS.]
FAUST. So they are safe. Now, Faustus, to the feast;   55
  The Pope had never such a frolic guest.
POPE. Lord Archbishop of Rheims, sit down with us.
ARCH. I thank your Holiness.
FAUST. Fall to! The devil choke you an you spare!
POPE. Who's that spoke? Friars, look about.   60
  Lord Raymond, pray fall to. I am beholden
  To the Bishop of Milan for this so rare a present.
FAUST. I thank you, sir.
      [FAUSTUS *snatches the meat from the* POPE.]
POPE. How now! Who snatched the meat from me? Villains,
  why speak you not?   65
FRIAR. Here's nobody, if it like your Holiness.
POPE. My good Lord Archbishop, here's a most dainty dish
  Was sent me from a cardinal in France.
FAUST. I'll have that, too.
      [FAUSTUS *snatches the dish from the* POPE.]
POPE. What lollards do attend our Holiness   70
  That we receive such great indignity?
  Fetch me some wine.
FAUST. Aye, pray do, for Faustus is adry.
POPE. Lord Raymond, I drink unto your Grace.
FAUST. I pledge your Grace.   75
      [FAUSTUS *snatches the cup from the* POPE.]
POPE. My wine gone, too? Ye lubbers, look about
  And find the man that doth this villainy,
  Or by my sanctitude you all shall die.
  I pray, my lords, have patience at this troublesome banquet.
ARCH. Please your Holiness, I think it be some ghost crept out of 80
  purgatory and now is come unto your Holiness for his pardon.
POPE. It may be so;
  Go then, command our priests to sing a dirge
  To lay the fury of this same troublesome ghost.
  Once again, my lord, fall to.   85
      [*The* POPE *crosses himself.*]
FAUST. How now!
  Must every bit be spicéd with a cross?
  Well, use that trick no more, I would advise you.
      [*The* POPE *crosses himself.*]
  Well, there's the second time; aware the third;
  I give you fair warning.   90
      [*The* POPE *crosses himself again.*]
  Nay then, take that!
      [FAUSTUS *hits the* POPE *a box on the ear.*]
POPE. O, I am slain! Help me, my lords!
  O come and help to bear my body hence!

6. I.e., load their limbs with prisoners' shackles.

Damned be his soul forever for this deed.

[*Exeunt the* POPE *and his train.*]

MEPH. Now Faustus, what will you do now? For I can tell you 95
you'll be cursed with bell, book, and candle.[7]

FAUST. Bell, book, and candle; candle, book, and bell
Forward and backward, to curse Faustus to hell!

[*Enter all the* FRIARS *with bell, book, and candle to sing the dirge.*]

FRIAR. Come, brethren, let's about our business with good devotion. 100

[ALL *sing this:*]
Curséd be he that stole away his Holiness' meat from the
table—*maledicat dominus!*[8]
Curséd be he that struck his Holiness a blow on the face—
maledicat dominus!
Curséd be he that took Friar Sandelo a blow on the face— 105
maledicat dominus!
Curséd be he that disturbeth our holy dirge—*maledicat dominus!*
Curséd be he that took away his Holiness' wine—*maledicat
dominus! Et omnes sancti!*[9] Amen. 110

[FAUSTUS *and* MEPHISTOPHILIS *beat the* FRIARS, *and fling
fireworks among them, and so exeunt.*]

SCENE 3

[*Enter* CLOWN ⟨ROBIN⟩ *and* DICK *with a cup.*]

DICK. Sirrah Robin, we were best look that your devil can answer
the stealing of this same cup, for the vintner's boy follows us
at the hard heels.

ROBIN. 'Tis no matter, let him come! An he follow us I'll so conjure him as he was never conjured in his life, I warrant him. 5
Let me see the cup.

[*Enter* VINTNER.]

DICK. Here 'tis. Yonder he comes. Now, Robin, now or never
show thy cunning.

VINT. O, are you here? I am glad I have found you. You are a
couple of fine companions! Pray, where's the cup you stole 10
from the tavern?

ROBIN. How, how? We steal a cup? Take heed what you say! We
look not like cup-stealers, I can tell you.

VINT. Never deny it, for I know you have it, and I'll search you.

ROBIN. Search me? Aye, and spare not. Hold the cup, Dick! 15
Come, come; search me, search me.

VINT. Come on, sirrah, let me search you now.

DICK. Aye, aye, do; do. Hold the cup, Robin. I fear not your
searching. We scorn to steal your cups, I can tell you.

VINT. Never outface me for the matter, for sure the cup is be- 20
tween you two.

7. The traditional paraphernalia for
cursing and excommunication.

8. "May the Lord curse him!"
9. And all saints (also curse him).

ROBIN. Nay, there you lie. 'Tis beyond us both.

VINT. A plague take you! I thought 'twas your knavery to take it away. Come, give it me again.

ROBIN. Aye, much! When, can you tell?[1] Dick, make me a circle, 25
and stand close at my back and stir not for thy life. Vintner, you shall have your cup anon. Say nothing, Dick. O *per se* O; Demogorgon, Belcher and Mephistophilis!

[*Enter* MEPHISTOPHILIS.]

MEPH. Monarch of hell, under whose black survey
Great potentates do kneel with awful fear, 30
Upon whose altars thousand souls do lie,
How am I vexéd with these villains' charms!
From Constantinople am I hither brought
Only for pleasure of these damnéd slaves.   [*Exit* VINTNER.]

ROBIN. By Lady, sir, you have had a shrewd journey of it; will it 35
please you to take a shoulder of mutton to supper and a tester[2]
in your purse, and go back again?

DICK. Aye, I pray you heartily, sir; for we called you but in jest,
I promise you.

MEPH. To purge the rashness of this curséd deed, 40
First be thou turnéd to this ugly shape:
For apish deeds transforméd to an ape.

ROBIN. O brave! an ape! I pray, sir, let me have the carrying of
him about to show some tricks.

MEPH. And so thou shalt. Be thou transformed to a dog and 45
carry him upon thy back. Away! Be gone!

ROBIN. A dog! That's excellent! Let the maids look well to their
porridge pots, for I'll into the kitchen presently. Come, Dick,
come.

[*Exit* ROBIN *and* DICK.]

MEPH. Now with the flames of ever-burning fire 50
I'll wing myself and forthwith fly amain
Unto my Faustus, to the Great Turk's court.   [*Exit.*]

Act IV

[*Enter* CHORUS.]

CHO. When Faustus had with pleasure ta'en the view
Of rarest things and royal courts of kings,
He stayed his course and so returnéd home,
Where such as bear his absence but with grief,
I mean his friends and nearest companións, 5
Did gratulate his safety with kind words,
And in their conference of what befell
Touching his journey through the world and air,
They put forth questions of astrology
Which Faustus answered with such learned skill 10
As they admired and wondered at his wit.
Now is his fame spread forth in every land:

1. A common Elizabethan scornful re-   2. Sixpence.
tort.

Amongst the rest the Emperor is one,
Carolus the Fifth,[3] at whose palace now
Faustus is feasted 'mongst his noblemen.
What there he did in trial of his art   15
I leave untold, your eyes shall see performed.   [*Exit.*]

SCENE 1

[*Enter* MARTINO *and* FREDERICK *at several doors.*[4]]
MART. What ho! Officers, gentlemen!
  Hie to the presence to attend the Emperor.
  Good Frederick, see the rooms be voided straight;
  His Majesty is coming to the hall.
  Go back, and see the state in readiness.   5
FRED. But where is Bruno, our elected Pope,
  That on a fury's back came post from Rome?
  Will not his Grace consort[5] the Emperor?
MART. O yes, and with him comes the German conjurer,
  The learned Faustus, fame of Wittenberg,   10
  The wonder of the world for magic art;
  And he intends to show great Carolus
  The race of all his stout progenitors
  And bring in presence of his majesty
  The royal shapes and warlike semblances   15
  Of Alexander and his beauteous paramour.[6]
FRED. Where is Benvolio?
MART. Fast asleep, I warrant you;
  He took his rouse with stoups[7] of Rhenish wine
  So kindly yesternight to Bruno's health
  That all this day the sluggard keeps his bed.   20
FRED. See, see; his window's ope; we'll call to him.
MART. What ho, Benvolio!
    [*Enter* BENVOLIO *above at a window, in his nightcap,*
    buttoning.]
BENV. What a devil ail you two?
MART. Speak softly, sir, lest the devil hear you;   25
  For Faustus at the court is late arrived
  And at his heels a thousand furies wait
  To accomplish whatsoever the Doctor please.
BENV. What of this?
MART. Come, leave thy chamber first and thou shalt see   30
  This conjurer perform such rare exploits
  Before the Pope[8] and royal Emperor
  As never yet was seen in Germany.
BENV. Has not the Pope enough of conjuring yet?
  He was upon the devil's back late enough,
  And if he be so far in love with him   35
  I would he would post home to Rome with him again.

3. I.e., Emperor Charles V (1519–56).
4. I.e., at different entrances.
5. Accompany.
6. Alexander the Great and his mistress
  Thaïs.
7. Drank many full glasses.
8. Bruno.

FRED. Speak, wilt thou come and see this sport?

BENV. Not I.

MART. Wilt thou stand in thy window and see it, then? 40

BENV. Aye, and I fall not asleep i' th' meantime.

MART. The Emperor is at hand, who comes to see
What wonders by black spells may compassed be.

BENV. Well, go you to the Emperor. I am content for this once
to thrust my head out a window, for they say if a man be drunk 45
overnight the devil cannot hurt him in the morning. If that be
true, I have a charm in my head shall control him as well as the
conjurer, I warrant you.

    [*Exit* MARTINO *and* FREDERICK.]

SCENE 2

    [*A sennet.*[9] *Enter* CHARLES THE GERMAN EMPEROR, BRUNO,
the DUKE OF SAXONY, FAUSTUS, MEPHISTOPHILIS, FRED-
ERICK, MARTINO *and* ATTENDANTS. BENVOLIO *remains at
his window.*]

EMP. Wonder of men, renowned magician,
Thrice-learned Faustus, welcome to our court.
This deed of thine, in setting Bruno free
From his and our professéd enemy,
Shall add more excellence unto thine art 5
Than if by powerful necromantic spells
Thou couldst command the world's obedience.
Forever be beloved of Carolus;
And if this Bruno thou hast late redeemed
In peace possess the triple diadem 10
And sit in Peter's chair despite of chance,
Thou shalt be famous through all Italy
And honored of the German Emperor.

FAUST. These gracious words, most royal Carolus,
Shall make poor Faustus to his utmost power 15
Both love and serve the German Emperor
And lay his life at holy Bruno's feet.
For proof whereof, if so your Grace be pleased,
The Doctor stands prepared by power of art
To cast his magic charms that shall pierce through 20
The ebon gates of ever-burning hell
And hale the stubborn furies from their caves
To compass whatsoe'er your Grace commands.

BENV. [*aside*] Blood! He speaks terribly, but for all that I do not
greatly believe him. He looks as like a conjurer as the Pope to 25
a costermonger.[1]

EMP. Then Faustus, as thou late didst promise us,
We would behold that famous conqueror,
Great Alexander and his paramour,
In their true shapes and state majestical, 30
That we may wonder at their excellence.

9. A trumpet signal.   1. Fruitseller.

FAUST. Your Majesty shall see them presently.
Mephistophilis, away!
And with a solemn noise of trumpets' sound
Present before this royal Emperor   35
Great Alexander and his beauteous paramour.

MEPH. Faustus, I will.   [*Exit.*]

BENV. [*aside*] Well, master Doctor, an your devils come not away
quickly, you shall have me asleep presently. Zounds, I could eat
myself for anger to think I have been such an ass all this while 40
to stand gaping after the devil's governor, and can see nothing.

FAUST. [*aside*] I'll make you feel something anon if my art fail me
not.—
My lord, I must forewarn your Majesty
That when my spirits present the royal shapes   45
Of Alexander and his paramour,
Your Grace demand no questions of the King,
But in dumb silence let them come and go.

EMP. Be it as Faustus please; we are content.

BENV. [*aside*] Aye, Aye, and I am content, too. And thou bring   50
Alexander and his paramour before the Emperor, I'll be Actaeon[2] and turn myself into a stag.

FAUST. [*aside*] And I'll play Diana and send you the horns presently.

[*Sennet. Enter at one door the emperor* ALEXANDER, *at the
other* DARIUS. *They meet;* DARIUS *is thrown down;* ALEX-
ANDER *kills him, takes off his crown and, offering to go
out, his* PARAMOUR *meets him; he embraceth her and sets*
DARIUS' *crown upon her head and, coming back, both
salute the* EMPEROR, *who, leaving his state,[3] offers to embrace them, which* FAUSTUS *seeing, suddenly stays him.
Then trumpets cease and music sounds.*]

FAUST. My gracious lord, you do forget yourself;   55
These are but shadows, not substantial.

EMP. O pardon me; my thoughts are ravished so
With sight of this renownéd Emperor
That in mine arms I would have compassed him.
But Faustus, since I may not speak to them   60
To satisfy my longing thoughts at full,
Let me this tell thee: I have heard it said
That this fair lady, whilst she lived on earth,
Had on her neck a little wart or mole.
How may I prove that saying to be true?   65

FAUST. Your Majesty may boldly go and see.

EMP. Faustus, I see it plain;
And in this sight thou better pleasest me
Than if I gained another monarchy.

FAUST. Away, be gone!   [*Exit* SHOW.] 70
See, see, my gracious lord, what strange beast is yon, that

2. The hunter of classical legend who
happened to see the goddess Diana
bathing. In punishment he was changed
into a stag and pursued by his own
hounds.
3. Throne.

thrusts its head out at the window!

EMP. O wondrous sight! See, Duke of Saxony, two spreading
horns most strangely fastened upon the head of young Benvolio. 75

SAX. What, is he asleep, or dead?

FAUST. He sleeps, my lord, but dreams not of his horns.

EMP. This sport is excellent. We'll call and wake him. What ho!
Benvolio!

BENV. A plague upon you! Let me sleep a while. 80

EMP. I blame thee not to sleep, much, having such a head of thine
own.

SAX. Look up, Benvolio. 'Tis the Emperor calls.

BENV. The Emperor! Where? O zounds, my head!

EMP. Nay, and thy horns hold 'tis no matter for thy head, for 85
that's armed sufficiently.

FAUST. Why, how now, sir knight! What, hanged by the horns?
This is most horrible. Fie, fie! Pull in your head, for shame!
Let not all the world wonder at you.

BENV. Zounds, Doctor, is this your villainy? 90

FAUST. O, say not so, sir. The Doctor has no skill,
No art, no cunning to present these lords
Or bring before this royal Emperor
The mighty monarch, warlike Alexander?
If Faustus do it, you are straight resolved 95
In bold Actaeon's shape to turn a stag?
And therefore, my lord, so please your Majesty,
I'll raise a kennel of hounds shall hunt him so
As all his footmanship shall scarce prevail
To keep his carcass from their bloody fangs. 100
Ho, Belimote, Argiron, Asterote!

BENV. Hold, hold! Zounds, he'll raise up a kennel of devils, I
think, anon. Good my lord, entreat for me. 'Sblood, I am never
able to endure these torments.

EMP. Then good master Doctor, 105
Let me entreat you to remove his horns;
He has done penance now sufficiently.

FAUST. My gracious lord, not so much for injury done to me, as
to delight your Majesty with some mirth, hath Faustus justly
requited this injurious knight; which, being all I desire, I am 110
content to remove his horns.—Mephistophilis, transform him.
—And hereafter, sir, look you speak well of scholars.

BENV. [*aside*] Speak well of ye! 'Sblood, and scholars be such
cuckoldmakers to clap horns of honest men's heads o' this order, I'll ne'er trust smooth faces and small ruffs[4] more. But an 115
I be not revenged for this, would I might be turned to a gaping
oyster and drink nothing but salt water!

EMP. Come, Faustus. While the Emperor lives,
In recompense of this thy high desert,

4. I.e., scholars, who were often smooth-
shaven and did not wear the large
"ruffs" (collars) of courtiers. But

Faustus has a beard; see the next
scene.

Thou shalt command the state of Germany 120
And live beloved of mighty Carolus.   [*Exeunt* OMNES.]

SCENE 3

[*Enter* BENVOLIO, MARTINO, FREDERICK, *and* SOLDIERS.]

MART. Nay, sweet Benvolio, let us sway thy thoughts
    From this attempt against the conjurer.
BENV. Away! You love me not to urge me thus.
    Shall I let slip so great an injury
    When every servile groom jests at my wrongs   5
    And in their rustic gambols proudly say,
    "Benvolio's head was graced with horns today"?
    O, may these eyelids never close again
    Till with my sword I have that conjurer slain.
    If you will aid me in this enterprise,   10
    Then draw your weapons and be resolute;
    If not, depart. Here will Benvolio die,
    But Faustus' death shall quit[5] my infamy.
FRED. Nay, we will stay with thee, betide what may,
    And kill that Doctor if he come this way.   15
BENV. Then gentle Frederick, hie thee to the grove
    And place our servants and our followers
    Close in an ambush there behind the trees.
    By this I know the conjurer is near;
    I saw him kneel and kiss the Emperor's hand   20
    And take his leave laden with rich rewards.
    Then, soldiers, boldly fight. If Faustus die,
    Take you the wealth, leave us the victory.
FRED. Come, soldiers, follow me unto the grove;
    Who kills him shall have gold and endless love.   25
    [*Exit* FREDERICK *with the* SOLDIERS.]
BENV. My head is lighter than it was by th' horns,
    But yet my heart's more ponderous than my head
    And pants until I see that conjurer dead.
MART. Where shall we place ourselves, Benvolio?
BENV. Here will we stay to bide the first assault.   30
    O, were that damnéd hell-hound but in place
    Thou soon shouldst see me quit my foul disgrace.
    [*Enter* FREDERICK.]
FRED. Close, close! The hated conjurer is at hand
    And all alone comes walking in his gown;
    Be ready then and strike the peasant down.   35
BENV. Mine be that honor then. Now, sword, strike home!
    For horns he gave I'll have his head anon.
    [*Enter* FAUSTUS *wearing a false head.*]
MART. See, see, he comes.
BENV.   No words; this blow ends all;
    Hell take his soul, his body thus must fall.
FAUST. O!
                                                               40

5. Avenge.

FRED. Groan you, master Doctor?

BENV. Break may his heart with groans. Dear Frederick, see
Thus will I end his griefs immediately.
[*Cuts off the false head.*]

MART. Strike with a willing hand! His head is off.

BENV. The devil's dead; the furies now may laugh.   45

FRED. Was this that stern aspect, that awful frown,
Made the grim monarch of infernal spirits
Tremble and quake at his commanding charms?

MART. Was this that damnéd head whose art conspired
Benvolio's shame before the Emperor?   50

BENV. Aye, that's the head, and here the body lies
Justly rewarded for his villainies.

FRED. Come, let's devise how we may add more shame
To the black scandal of his hated name.

BENV. First, on his head, in quittance of my wrongs,   55
I'll nail huge forkéd horns and let them hang
Within the window where he yoked me first,
That all the world may see my just revenge.

MART. What use shall we put his beard to?

BENV. We'll sell it to a chimney-sweeper; it will wear out ten   60
birchen brooms, I warrant you.

FRED. What shall his eyes do?

BENV. We'll pull out his eyes, and they shall serve for buttons to
his lips to keep his tongue from catching cold.

MART. An excellent policy. And now, sirs, having divided him,   65
what shall the body do?
[*FAUSTUS rises.*]

BENV. Zounds, the devil's alive again!

FRED. Give him his head, for God's sake!

FAUST. Nay, keep it. Faustus will have heads and hands,
Aye, all your hearts, to recompense this deed.   70
Knew you not, traitors, I was limited
For four and twenty years to breathe on earth?
And had you cut my body with your swords
Or hewed this flesh and bones as small as sand,
Yet in a minute had my spirit returned   75
And I had breathed a man made free from harm.
But wherefore do I dally my revenge?
Asteroth, Belimoth, Mephistophilis!
[*Enter* MEPHISTOPHILIS *and other* DEVILS.]
Go, horse these traitors on your fiery backs
And mount aloft with them as high as heaven,   80
Then pitch them headlong to the lowest hell.
Yet stay, the world shall see their misery,
And hell shall after plague their treachery.
Go, Belimoth, and take this caitiff[6] hence
And hurl him in some lake of mud and dirt;   85
Take thou this other, drag him through the woods

6. Wretch.

Amongst the pricking thorns and sharpest briars,
Whilst with my gentle Mephistophilis
This traitor flies unto some steepy rock
That rolling down may break the villain's bones   90
As he intended to dismember me.
Fly hence, dispatch my charge immediately.
FRED. Pity us, gentle Faustus; save our lives!
FAUST. Away!
FRED. He must needs go that the devil drives.   95
                              [*Exeunt* SPIRITS *with the* KNIGHTS.]
           [*Enter the ambushed* SOLDIERS.]
1 SOLD. Come, sirs, prepare yourselves in readiness;
   Make haste to help these noble gentlemen;
   I heard them parley with the conjurer.
2 SOLD. See where he comes; dispatch, and kill the slave!
FAUST. What's here? An ambush to betray my life?   100
   Then, Faustus, try thy skill. Base peasants, stand!
   For lo, these trees remove at my command
   And stand as bulwarks 'twixt yourselves and me
   To shield me from your hated treachery;
   Yet to encounter this, your weak attempt,   105
   Behold an army comes incontinent.[7]
           [FAUSTUS *strikes the door, and enter a* DEVIL *playing on a
           drum; after him another bearing an ensign, and divers
           with weapons;* MEPHISTOPHILIS *with fireworks. They set
           upon the* SOLDIERS *and drive them out. Exeunt.*]

                    SCENE 4

           [*Enter at several doors* BENVOLIO, FREDERICK, *and* MAR-
           TINO, *their heads and faces bloody and besmeared with
           mud and dirt, all having horns on their heads.*]
MART. What ho, Benvolio!
BENV. Here! What, Frederick, ho!
FRED. O help me, gentle friend. Where is Martino?
MART. Dear Frederick, here—
   Half smothered in a lake of mud and dirt   5
   Through which the furies dragged me by the heels.
FRED. Martino, see! Benvolio's horns again.
MART. O misery! How now, Benvolio!
BENV. Defend me, heaven! Shall I be haunted still?
MART. Nay, fear not, man; we have no power to kill.   10
BENV. My friends transforméd thus! O hellish spite!
   Your heads are all set with horns.
FRED. You hit it right;
   It is your own you mean; feel on your head.
BENV. Zounds, horns again!   15
MART. Nay, chafe not, man; we are all sped.[8]
BENV. What devil attends this damned magician
   That spite of spite our wrongs are doubled?

----

7. Immediately.   8. Don't fret, man, we are all done for.

FRED. What may we do that we may hide our shames?
BENV. If we should follow him to work revenge,   20
    He'd join long asses' ears to those huge horns
    And make us laughingstocks to all the world.
MART. What shall we then do, dear Benvolio?
BENV. I have a castle joining near these woods,
    And thither we'll repair and live obscure   25
    Till time shall alter this our brutish shapes.
    Sith black disgrace hath thus eclipsed our fame,
    We'll rather die with grief than live with shame.

                                    [*Exeunt* OMNES.]

                        SCENE 5

        [*Enter* FAUSTUS *and the* HORSE-COURSER.[9]]

HOR. I beseech your Worship, accept of these forty dollars.[1]
FAUST. Friend, thou canst not buy so good a horse for so small a
    price. I have no great need to sell him, but if thou likest him
    for ten dollars more, take him, because I see thou hast a good
    mind to him.   5
HOR. I beseech you, sir, accept of this; I am a very poor man and
    have lost very much of late by horseflesh, and this bargain will
    set me up again.
FAUST. Well, I will not stand with thee; give me the money. Now,
    sirrah, I must tell you that you may ride him o'er hedge and   10
    ditch and spare him not; but—do you hear?—in any case ride
    him not into the water.
HOR. How, sir, not into the water? Why, will he not drink of all
    waters?
FAUST. Yes, he will drink of all waters, but ride him not into the 15
    water; o'er hedge and ditch or where thou wilt, but not into the
    water. Go bid the hostler deliver him unto you, and remember
    what I say.
HOR. I warrant you, sir. O joyful day! Now am I a made man for-
    ever.   20
        [*Exit.*]
FAUST. What art thou, Faustus, but a man condemned to die?
    Thy fatal time draws to a final end;
    Despair doth drive distrust into my thoughts.
    Confound these passions with a quiet sleep.
    Tush, Christ did call the thief upon the cross;[2]   25
    Then rest thee, Faustus, quiet in conceit.
                            [*He sits to sleep in his chair.*]
        [*Enter the* HORSE-COURSER *wet.*]
HOR. O, what a cozening Doctor was this! I riding my horse into
    the water, thinking some hidden mystery had been in the horse,
    I had nothing under me but a little straw, and had much ado
    to escape drowning. Well, I'll go rouse him and make him give 30

---

9. Horse-trader, traditionally a sharp
bargainer or cheat.
1. Common German coins; the word
originally comes from the German

Joachimsthaler.
2. In Luke xxiii.39–43 one of the two
thieves crucified with Jesus is promised
Paradise. "In conceit": in mind.

me my forty dollars again. Ho! sirrah Doctor, you cozening
scab! Master Doctor, awake and arise, and give me my money
again, for your horse is turned to a bottle³ of hay. Master Doc-
tor—
   [*He pulls off his leg.*]
Alas, I am undone! What shall I do? I have pulled off his leg. 35
FAUST. O help! Help! The villain hath murdered me!
HOR. Murder or not murder, now he has but one leg I'll outrun
   him and cast this leg into some ditch or other.
      [*Exit.*]
FAUST. Stop him, stop him, stop him! Ha ha ha! Faustus hath his
   leg again, and the horse-courser a bundle of hay for his forty 40
   dollars.
      [*Enter* WAGNER.]
FAUST. How now, Wagner! What news with thee?
WAG. If it please you, the Duke of Vanholt doth earnestly entreat
   your company and hath sent some of his men to attend you
   with provision fit for your journey.   45
FAUST. The Duke of Vanholt's an honorable gentleman, and one
   to whom I must be no niggard of my cunning. Come, away!

                         SCENE 6
      [*Enter* ROBIN, DICK, HORSE-COURSER, *and a* CARTER.]
CART. Come, my masters, I'll bring you to the best beer in Eu-
   rope— What ho, Hostess!—Where be these whores?⁴
      [*Enter* HOSTESS.]
HOST. How now! What lack you? What, my old guests, welcome.
ROBIN. Sirrah Dick, dost thou know why I stand so mute?
DICK. No, Robin, why is 't?
ROBIN. I am eighteen pence on the score,⁵ but say nothing; see if 5
   she have forgotten me.
HOST. Who's this that stands so solemnly by himself? What, my
   old guest!
ROBIN. O, hostess, how do you do? I hope my score stands still.   10
HOST. Aye, there's no doubt of that, for methinks you make no
   haste to wipe it out.
DICK. Why, hostess, I say, fetch us some beer.
HOST. You shall presently; look up into th' hall. There, ho!
      [*Exit.*]
DICK. Come, sirs; what shall we do now till mine hostess comes?   15
CART. Marry, sir, I'll tell you the bravest tale how a conjurer
   served me. You know Dr. Faustus?
HOR. Aye, a plague take him! Here's some on 's have cause to
   know him. Did he conjure thee too?
CART. I'll tell you how he served me. As I was going to Witten-   20
   berg t' other day, he met me and asked me what he should give
   me for as much hay as he could eat. Now, sir, I, thinking that
   a little would serve his turn, bade him take as much as he

3. Bundle.
4. I.e., the hostess and maids of the
inn.
5. Charged, not paid for.

would for three farthings. So he presently gave me my money and fell to eating; and, as I am a cursen man, he never left eating till he had eat up all my load of hay. 25

ALL. O monstrous; eat a whole load of hay!

ROBIN. Yes, yes; that may be, for I have heard of one that has eat a load of hay.[6]

HOR. Now, sirs, you shall hear now villainously he served me. I went to him yesterday to buy a horse of him, and he would by no means sell him under forty dollars. So, sir, because I knew him to be such a horse as would run over hedge and ditch and never tire, I gave him his money. So, when I had my horse, Dr. Faustus bade me ride him night and day and spare him no time; "But," quoth he, "in any case ride him not into the water." Now sir, I thinking the horse had had some quality that he would not have me know of, what did I but ride him into a great river, and when I came just in the midst my horse vanished away and I sat straddling upon a bottle of hay. 40

ALL. O brave Doctor! *seems to be satirical*

HOR. But you shall hear how bravely I served him for it. I went me home to his house, and there I found him asleep; I kept a hallowing and whooping in his ears, but all could not wake him. I seeing that, took him by the leg and never rested pulling till I had pulled me his leg quite off, and now 'tis at home in mine hostry.[7]

DICK. And has the Doctor but one leg then? That's excellent, for one of his devils turned me into the likeness of an ape's face.

CART. Some more drink, hostess! 50

ROBIN. Hark you, we'll into another room and drink awhile, and then we'll go seek out the Doctor.

[*Exeunt* OMNES.]

SCENE 7

[*Enter the* DUKE OF VANHOLT, *his* DUCHESS, FAUSTUS, *and* MEPHISTOPHILIS.]

DUKE. Thanks, master Doctor, for these pleasant sights; nor know I how sufficiently to recompense your great deserts in erecting that enchanted castle in the air, the sight whereof so delighted me as nothing in the world could please me more.

FAUST. I do think myself, my good lord, highly recompensed that 5 it pleaseth your Grace to think but well of that which Faustus hath performed. But gracious lady, it may be that you have taken no pleasure in those sights; therefore I pray you tell me what is the thing you most desire to have; be it in the world it shall be yours. I have heard that great-bellied women do long 10 for things that are rare and dainty.

DUCH. True, master Doctor, and since I find you so kind, I will make known unto you what my heart desires to have; and were it now summer, as it is January, a dead time of winter, I would

6. Comic expression for being drunk 7. Inn.
—to carry a jag (or load) of logs.

request no better meat than a dish of ripe grapes. ₁₅

FAUST. This is but a small matter.—Go, Mephistophilis, away!—
[*Exit* MEPHISTOPHILIS.]
Madam, I will do more than this for your content.
[*Enter* MEPHISTOPHILIS *again with the grapes.*]
Here, now taste ye these; they should be good, for they come
from a far country, I can tell you.

DUKE. This makes me wonder more than all the rest, that at this ₂₀
time of year, when every tree is barren of his fruit, from whence
you had these ripe grapes.

FAUST. Please it your Grace, the year is divided into two circles
over the whole world, so that when it is winter with us, in the
contrary circle it is likewise summer with them, as in India, ₂₅
Saba,[8] and such countries that lie far east, where they have
fruit twice a year. From whence, by means of a swift spirit that
I have, I had these grapes brought as you see.

DUCH. And trust me they are the sweetest grapes that e'er I tasted.
[*The* CLOWNS *bounce[9] at the gate within.*]

DUKE. What rude disturbers have we at the gate? ₃₀
Go pacify their fury, set it ope,
And then demand of them what they would have.
[*They knock again and call out to talk with* FAUSTUS.]

A SERVANT. Why, how now, masters, what a coil[1] is there!
What is the reason you disturb the Duke?

DICK. We have no reason for it, therefore a fig[2] for him! ₃₅

SERV. Why, saucy varlets! Dare you be so bold?

HOR. I hope, sir, we have wit enough to be more bold than welcome.

SERV. It appears so; Pray be bold elsewhere
And trouble not the Duke. ₄₀

DUKE. What would they have?

SERV. They all cry out to speak with Dr. Faustus.

CART. Aye, and we will speak with him.

DUKE. Will you, sir? Commit[3] the rascals!

DICK. Commit with us? He were as good commit with his father ₄₅
as commit with us.

FAUST. I do beseech your Grace, let them come in;
They are good subject for a merriment.

DUKE. Do as thou wilt, Faustus; I give thee leave.

FAUST. I thank your Grace.
[*Enter* ROBIN, DICK, CARTER, *and* HORSE-COURSER.]
Why, how now, my good friends? ₅₀
'Faith you are too outrageous; but come near,
I have procured your pardons. Welcome all!

ROBIN. Nay, sir, we will be welcome for our money, and we will
pay for what we take. What ho! Give 's half a dozen of beer
here, and be hanged. ₅₅

8. Sheba.
9. Bang.
1. Disturbance.
2. An obscene gesture, implying con-

tempt.
3. Put in jail. Dick puns on its other
meaning ("commit adultery"), from
the Ten Commandments.

FAUST. Nay, hark you, can you tell me where you are?

CART. Aye, marry, can I; we are under heaven.

SERV. Aye, but, sir saucebox, know you in what place?

HOR. Aye, aye, the house is good enough to drink in. Zounds, fill
us some beer, or we'll break all the barrels in the house and 60
dash out all your brains with your bottles.

FAUST. Be not so furious; come, you shall have beer.
My lord, beseech you give me leave awhile;
I'll gage my credit 'twill content your Grace.

DUKE. With all my heart, kind Doctor, please thyself; 65
Our servants and our court's at thy command.

FAUST. I humbly thank your Grace. Then fetch some beer.

HOR. Aye, marry, there spake a doctor indeed; and, faith, I'll
drink a health to thy wooden leg for that word.

FAUST. My wooden leg! What dost thou mean by that? 70

CART. Ha ha ha, dost hear him, Dick? He has forgot his leg.

HOR. Aye, he does not stand much upon that.

FAUST. No, faith, not much upon a wooden leg.

CART. Good lord, that flesh and blood should be so frail with
your worship! Do you not remember a horse-courser you sold 75
a horse to?

FAUST. Yes, I remember I sold one a horse.

CART. And do you remember you bid he should not ride him into
the water?

FAUST. Yes, I do very well remember that. 80

CART. And do you remember nothing of your leg?

FAUST. No, in good sooth.

CART. Then I pray remember your courtesy.

FAUST. I thank you, sir.

CART. 'Tis not so much worth. I pray you tell me one thing. 85

FAUST. What's that?

CART. Be both of your legs bedfellows every night together?

FAUST. Wouldst thou make a colossus[4] of me, that thou askest
me such questions?

CART. No, truly, sir, I would make nothing of you, but I would 90
fain know that.

   [*Enter* HOSTESS *with drink.*]

FAUST. Then I assure thee certainly they are.

CART. I thank you; I am fully satisfied.

FAUST. But wherefore dost thou ask?

CART. For nothing, sir; but methinks you should have a wooden 95
bedfellow to one of 'em.

HOR. Why, do you hear, sir, did not I pull off one of your legs
when you were asleep?

FAUST. But I have it again now I am awake; look you here, sir.

ALL. O horrible! Had the doctor three legs? 100

CART. Do you remember, sir, how you cozened me and eat up my
load of——

4. The huge statue which stood at the
entrance to the harbor at Rhodes; boats
sailed between its legs, and Dr. Faustus
is suggesting that the clowns are making his legs as important.

[FAUSTUS *charms him dumb*.]

DICK. Do you remember how you made me wear an ape's——

HOR. You whoreson conjuring scab, do you remember how you
cozened me of a ho—— 105

ROBIN. Ha' you forgotten me? You think to carry it away with
your hey-pass and your re-pass;[5] do you remember the dog's
fa——

[*Exeunt* CLOWNS.]

HOST. Who pays for the ale? Hear you, master Doctor, now you
have sent away my guests, I pray who shall pay me for my 110
a——

[*Exit* HOSTESS.]

DUCH. My lord,
We are much beholding to this learned man.

DUKE. So are we, madam, which we will recompense
With all the love and kindness that we may; 115
His artful sport drives all sad thoughts away.   [*Exeunt*.]

Act V

SCENE 1

[*Thunder and lightning. Enter* DEVILS *with covered dishes*;
MEPHISTOPHILIS *leads them into* FAUSTUS' *study. Then
enter* WAGNER.]

WAG. I think my master means to die shortly;
He has made his will and given me his wealth,
His house, his goods, and store of golden plate,
Besides two thousand ducats ready coined.
And yet I wonder, for if death were nigh 5
He would not banquet and carouse and swill
Amongst the students as even now he doth,
Who are at supper with such belly-cheer
As Wagner ne'er beheld in all his life.
See where they come; belike the feast is ended.   [*Exit*.] 10

[*Enter* FAUSTUS *and* MEPHISTOPHILIS *with two or three*
SCHOLARS.]

1 SCH. Master Doctor Faustus, since our conference about fair
ladies, which was the beautifullest in all the world, we have determined with ourselves that Helen of Greece was the ad-
mirablest lady that ever lived. Therefore, master Doctor, if
you will do us that favor as to let us see that peerless dame of 15
Greece whom all the world admires for majesty, we should
think ourselves much beholding unto you.

FAUST. Gentlemen,
For that I know your friendship is unfeigned,
And Faustus' custom is not to deny 20
The just requests of those that wish him well,
You shall behold that peerless dame of Greece,
No otherways for pomp and majesty

5. Traditional exclamations of a conjurer.

Than when Sir Paris crossed the seas with her
And brought the spoils to rich Dardania.[6]   25
Be silent, then, for danger is in words.
    [*Music sounds, and* HELEN *passeth over the stage.*]
2 SCH. Too simple is my wit to tell her praise
    Whom all the world admires for majesty.
3 SCH. No marvel though the angry Greeks pursued
    With ten years' war the rape of such a queen   30
    Whose heavenly beauty passeth all compare.
1 SCH. Since we have seen the pride of Nature's works
    And only paragon of excellence,
    Let us depart, and for this glorious deed
    Happy and blest be Faustus evermore.   35
FAUST. Gentlemen, farewell; the same I wish to you.
                                 [*Exeunt* SCHOLARS.]

    [*Enter an* OLD MAN.]
OLD MAN. O gentle Faustus, leave this damnéd art,
    This magic, that will charm thy soul to hell
    And quite bereave[7] thee of salvation.
    Though thou hast now offended like a man,   40
    Do not persevere in it like a devil.
    Yet, yet, thou hast an amiable soul
    If sin by custom grow not into nature;
    Then, Faustus, will repentance come too late;
    Then thou art banished from the sight of heaven.   45
    No mortal can express the pains of hell.
    It may be this my exhortation
    Seems harsh and all unpleasant; let it not;
    For, gentle son, I speak it not in wrath
    Or envy of thee, but in tender love   50
    And pity of thy future misery,
    And so have hope that this my kind rebuke,
    Checking thy body, may amend thy soul.
FAUST. Where art thou, Faustus? Wretch, what hast thou done?
    Damned art thou, Faustus, damned! Despair and die.   55
    [MEPHISTOPHILIS *gives him a dagger.*]
    Hell claims his right, and with a roaring voice
    Says, "Faustus, come; thine hour is almost come!"
    And Faustus now will come to do thee right.
OLD MAN. O stay, good Faustus, stay thy desperate steps!
    I see an angel hovers o'er thy head   60
    And with a vial full of precious grace
    Offers to pour the same into thy soul:
    Then call for mercy and avoid despair.
FAUST. Ah my sweet friend, I feel thy words
    To comfort my distresséd soul.   65
    Leave me awhile to ponder on my sins.
OLD MAN. Faustus, I leave thee, but with grief of heart,
    Fearing the ruin of thy hopeless soul.   [*Exit.*]

6. Troy.   7. Deprive.

FAUST. Accurséd Faustus, where is mercy now?
   I do repent and yet I do despair: 70
   Hell strives with grace for conquest in my breast.
   What shall I do to shun the snares of death?
MEPH. Thou traitor, Faustus, I arrest thy soul
   For disobedience to my sovereign lord.
   Revolt, or I'll in piecemeal tear thy flesh.   75
FAUST. I do repent I e'er offended him.
   Sweet Mephistophilis, entreat thy lord
   To pardon my unjust presumption,
   And with my blood again I will confirm
   The former vow I made to Lucifer.   80
MEPH. Do it then, Faustus, with unfeignéd heart
   Lest greater danger do attend thy drift.
FAUST. Torment, sweet friend, that base and aged man
   That durst dissuade me from thy Lucifer,
   With greatest torments that our hell affords.   85
MEPH. His faith is great; I cannot touch his soul;
   But what I may afflict his body with
   I will attempt, which is but little worth.
FAUST. One thing, good servant, let me crave of thee
   To glut the longing of my heart's desire: 90
   That I might have unto my paramour
   That heavenly Helen which I saw of late,
   Whose sweet embracings may extinguish clear
   These thoughts that do dissuade me from my vow,
   And keep mine oath I made to Lucifer.   95
MEPH. This, or what else my Faustus shall desire
   Shall be performed in twinkling of an eye.
      [*Enter* HELEN *again, passing over between two* CUPIDS.]
FAUST. Was this the face that launched a thousand ships
   And burnt the topless[8] towers of Ilium?
   Sweet Helen, make me immortal with a kiss.   100
   Her lips sucks forth my soul—see where it flies!
   Come, Helen, come, give me my soul again.
   Here will I dwell, for heaven is in these lips
   And all is dross that is not Helena.
      [*Enter* OLD MAN *and stands watching* FAUSTUS.]
   I will be Paris, and for love of thee   105
   Instead of Troy shall Wittenberg be sacked,
   And I will combat with weak Menelaus
   And wear thy colors on my pluméd crest;
   Yea, I will wound Achilles in the heel
   And then return to Helen for a kiss.   110
   O thou art fairer than the evening air
   Clad in the beauty of a thousand stars!
   Brighter art thou than flaming Jupiter
   When he appeared to hapless Semele,[9]

8. So high they seemed to have no tops.
9. A Theban girl, loved by Jupiter and destroyed by the fire of his lightning when he appeared to her in his full splendor.

More lovely than the monarch of the sky   115
In wanton Arethusa's azured arms,[1]
And none but thou shalt be my paramour!
    [*Exeunt* ALL *except the* OLD MAN.]
OLD MAN. Accursèd Faustus, miserable man,
    That from thy soul exclud'st the grace of heaven
    And fliest the throne of his tribunal seat.   120
    [*Enter the* DEVILS *to torment him.*]
    Satan begins to sift me with his pride.[2]
    As in this furnace God shall try my faith,
    My faith, vile hell, shall triumph over thee!
    Ambitious fiends, see how the heavens smiles
    At your repulse, and laughs your state to scorn.   125
    Hence, hell! for hence I fly unto my God.   [*Exeunt.*]

                          SCENE 2

    [*Thunder. Enter* LUCIFER, BELZEBUB, *and* MEPHISTOPHI-
    LIS.]
LUC. Thus from infernal Dis[3] do we ascend
    To view the subjects of our monarchy,
    Those souls which sin seals the black sons of hell.
    'Mong which as chief, Faustus, we come to thee,
    Bringing with us lasting damnation   5
    To wait upon thy soul; the time is come
    Which makes it forfeit.
MEPH.   And this gloomy night
    Here in this room will wretched Faustus be.
BEL. And here we'll stay
    To mark him how he doth demean himself.   10
MEPH. How should he but with desperate lunacy?
    Fond worldling, now his heart-blood dries with grief,
    His conscience kills it, and his laboring brain
    Begets a world of idle fantasies
    To overreach the devil, but all in vain.   15
    His store of pleasure must be sauced with pain.
    He and his servant Wagner are at hand;
    Both come from drawing Faustus' latest will.
    See where they come!
    [*Enter* FAUSTUS *and* WAGNER.]
FAUST. Say, Wagner, thou has perused my will;   20
    How dost thou like it?
WAG.   Sir, so wondrous well
    As in all humble duty I do yield
    My life and lasting service for your love.
    [*Enter the* SCHOLARS.]
FAUST. Gramercies, Wagner.—Welcome, gentlemen.
1 SCH. Now, worthy Faustus, methinks your looks are changed.   25

1. Arethusa was the nymph of a foun-   of the sky."
tain, as well as the fountain itself; no   2. I.e., to test me with his strength.
classical myth, however, records her   3. The underworld.
love affair with Jupiter, the "monarch

FAUST. Ah, gentlemen!

2 SCH. What ails Faustus?

FAUST. Ah, my sweet chamber-fellow, had I lived with thee, then had I lived still, but now must die eternally. Look, sirs! Comes he not? Comes he not? 30

1 SCH. O my dear Faustus, what imports this fear?

2 SCH. Is all our pleasure turned to melancholy?

3 SCH. He is not well with being over-solitary.

2 SCH. If it be so, we'll have physicians, and Faustus shall be cured. 35

3 SCH. 'Tis but a surfeit,[4] sir; fear nothing.

FAUST. A surfeit of deadly sin that hath damned both body and soul.

2 SCH. Yet, Faustus, look up to heaven: remember God's mercies are infinite. 40

FAUST. But Faustus' offense can ne'er be pardoned; the Serpent that tempted Eve may be saved, but not Faustus. Ah, gentlemen, hear me with patience, and tremble not at my speeches. Though my heart pants and quivers to remember that I have been a student here these thirty years, O would I had never seen 45 Wittenberg, never read book! And what wonders I have done all Germany can witness, yea all the world, for which Faustus hath lost both Germany and the world, yea heaven itself— heaven the seat of God, the throne of the blessed, the kingdom of joy, and must remain in hell forever, hell, ah hell, forever! 50 Sweet friends, what shall become of Faustus, being in hell forever?

3 SCH. Yet, Faustus, call on God.

FAUST. On God, whom Faustus hath abjured? on God, whom Faustus hath blasphemed? Ah, my God, I would weep, but the 55 devil draws in my tears! Gush forth, blood, instead of tears, yea life and soul! O he stays my tongue; I would lift up my hands but, see, they hold 'em, they hold 'em!

ALL. Who, Faustus?

FAUST. Why, Lucifer and Mephistophilis. 60
Ah, gentlemen, I gave them my soul for my cunning.

ALL. God forbid!

FAUST. God forbade it indeed, but Faustus hath done it: for vain pleasure of four and twenty years hath Faustus lost eternal joy and felicity. I writ them a bill with mine own blood; the date 65 is expired, this is the time, and he will fetch me.

1 SCH. Why did not Faustus tell us of this before, that divines might have prayed for thee?

FAUST. Oft have I thought to have done so, but the devil threatened to tear me in pieces if I named God, to fetch both body 70 and soul if I once gave ear to divinity; and now 'tis too late. Gentlemen, away, lest you perish with me!

2 SCH. O what may we do to save Faustus?

FAUST. Talk not of me, but save yourselves and depart.

4. Indigestion; the effects of overindulgence.

3 SCH. God will strengthen me: I will stay with Faustus.   75
1 SCH. Tempt not God, sweet friend, but let us into the next
  room, and there pray for him.
FAUST. Aye, pray for me, pray for me! And what noise soever ye
  hear, come not unto me, for nothing can rescue me.
2 SCH. Pray thou, and we will pray that God may have mercy   80
  upon thee.
FAUST. Gentlemen, farewell. If I live till morning I'll visit you;
  if not, Faustus is gone to hell.
ALL. Faustus, farewell.   [*Exeunt* SCHOLARS.]
MEPH. Aye, Faustus, now hast thou no hope of heaven;   85
  Therefore despair, think only upon hell,
  For that must be thy mansion, there to dwell.
FAUST. O thou bewitching fiend, 'twas thy temptation
  Hath robbed me of eternal happiness.
MEPH. I do confess it, Faustus, and rejoice.   90
  'Twas I, that when thou wert i' the way to heaven
  Damned up thy passage; when thou tookest the book
  To view the scriptures, then I turned the leaves
  And led thine eye.
  What, weepst thou? 'tis too late. Despair, farewell!   95
  Fools that will laugh on earth must weep in hell.   [*Exit.*]
      [*Enter the* GOOD ANGEL *and the* BAD ANGEL *at several
      doors.*]
G. ANG. Ah Faustus, if thou hadst given ear to me,
  Innumerable joys had followed thee,
  But thou didst love the world.
B. ANG.   Gave ear to me
  And now must taste hell's pains perpetually.   100
G. ANG. O what will all thy riches, pleasures, pomps
  Avail thee now?
B. ANG.   Nothing but vex thee more,
  To want in hell, that had on earth such store.
      [*Music while the throne descends.*[5]]
G. ANG. O, thou hast lost celestial happiness,
  Pleasures unspeakable, bliss without end.   105
  Hadst thou affected sweet divinity
  Hell or the devil had had no power on thee.
  Hadst thou kept on that way, Faustus, behold
  In what resplendent glory thou hadst sit
  In yonder throne, like those bright shining saints,   110
  And triumphed over hell; that hast thou lost.
  And now, poor soul, must thy good angel leave thee;
  The jaws of hell are open to receive thee.
      [*Exit. Hell is discovered.*]
B. ANG. Now Faustus, let thine eyes with horror stare
  Into that vast perpetual torture-house.   115
  There are the furies, tossing damnéd souls

5. A throne suspended by ropes descended to the stage near the end of many Elizabethan plays and was an expected theatrical display. Here the throne clearly symbolizes heaven, as the next speech shows.

On burning forks; their bodies boil in lead.
There are live quarters[6] broiling on the coals
That ne'er can die; this ever-burning chair
Is for o'ertortured souls to rest them in;   120
These that are fed with sops of flaming fire
Were gluttons and loved only delicates
And laughed to see the poor starve at their gates.
But yet all these are nothing; thou shalt see
Ten thousand tortures that more horrid be.   125
FAUST. O, I have seen enough to torture me.
B. ANG. Nay, thou must feel them, taste the smart of all;
He that loves pleasure must for pleasure fall.
And so I leave thee, Faustus, till anon;
Then wilt thou tumble in confusión.[7]   130
        [*Exit. The clock strikes eleven.*]
FAUST. Ah, Faustus,
Now hast thou but one bare hour to live
And then thou must be damned perpetually!
Stand still, you ever-moving spheres of heaven,
That time may cease and midnight never come;   135
Fair Nature's eye, rise, rise again, and make
Perpetual day; or let this hour be but
A year, a month, a week, a natural day,
That Faustus may repent and save his soul!
O *lente lente currite noctis equi.*[8]   140
The stars move still, time runs, the clock will strike,
The devil will come, and Faustus must be damned.
O, I'll leap up to my God! Who pulls me down?
See, see, where Christ's blood streams in the firmament!—
One drop would save my soul—half a drop! ah, my Christ!   145
Rend not my heart for naming of my Christ;
Yet will I call on him—O, spare me, Lucifer!
Where is it now? 'Tis gone; and see where God
Stretcheth out his arm and bends his ireful brows.
Mountains and hills, come, come and fall on me   150
And hide me from the heavy wrath of God,
No, no—
Then will I headlong run into the earth:
Earth, gape! O no, it will not harbor me.
You stars that reigned at my nativity,   155
Whose influence hath allotted death and hell,
Now draw up Faustus like a foggy mist
Into the entrails of yon laboring clouds
That when they vomit forth into the air,
My limbs may issue from their smoky mouths,   160
So that my soul may but ascend to heaven.
        [*The watch strikes.*]
Ah, half the hour is past; 'twill all be past anon.

6. Bodies.
7. Destruction, perdition.
8. "Slowly, slowly run, O horses of the night," adapted from a line in Ovid's *Amores.*

O God,
If thou wilt not have mercy on my soul,
Yet for Christ's sake whose blood hath ransomed me   165
Impose some end to my incessant pain:
Let Faustus live in hell a thousand years,
A hundred thousand, and at last be saved!
O, no end is limited to damnéd souls!
Why wert thou not a creature wanting soul?   170
Or why is this immortal that thou hast?
Ah, Pythagoras' *metempsychosis*[9]—were that true,
This soul should fly from me, and I be changed
Unto some brutish beast. All beasts are happy,
For when they die   175
Their souls are soon dissolved in elements,
But mine must live still[1] to be plagued in hell.
Cursed be the parents that engendered me!
No, Faustus, curse thyself, curse Lucifer
That hath deprived thee of the joys of heaven.   180
      [*The clock strikes twelve.*]
It strikes, it strikes! Now, body, turn to air
Or Lucifer will bear thee quick[2] to hell!
      [*Thunder and lightning.*]
O soul, be changed to little water drops
And fall into the ocean, ne'er be found.
My God, my God, look not so fierce on me!   185
      [*Enter* DEVILS.]
Adders and serpents, let me breathe awhile!
Ugly hell, gape not—come not, Lucifer—
I'll burn my books—ah, Mephistophilis!
      [*Exeunt* DEVILS *with* FAUSTUS.]

                         SCENE 3

      [*Enter the* SCHOLARS.]
1 SCH. Come, gentlemen, let us go visit Faustus,
      For such a dreadful night was never seen
      Since first the world's creation did begin,
      Such fearful shrieks and cries were never heard.
      Pray heaven the Doctor have escaped the danger.   5
2 SCH. O, help us heaven! See, here are Faustus' limbs
      All torn asunder by the hand of death.
3 SCH. The devils whom Faustus served have torn him thus;
      For 'twixt the hours of twelve and one, methought
      I heard him shriek and call aloud for help.   10
      At which self[3] time the house seemed all on fire
      With dreadful horror of these damnéd fiends.
      2 SCH. Well, gentlemen, though Faustus' end be such
      As every Christian heart laments to think on,
      Yet for he was a scholar once admired   15

9. Pythagoras' doctrine of the trans-   2. Alive.
migration of souls.   3. Same, exact.
1. Always.

For wondrous knowledge in our German schools,
We'll give his mangled limbs due burial;
And all the students, clothed in mourning black,
Shall wait upon his heavy[4] funeral.   [*Exeunt.*]
    [*Enter* CHORUS.]
CHO. Cut is the branch that might have grown full straight,   20
And burnéd is Apollo's laurel bough[5]
That sometime grew within this learnéd man.
Faustus is gone: regard his hellish fall,
Whose fiendful fortune may exhort the wise
Only to wonder at[6] unlawful things   25
Whose deepness doth entice such forward wits
To practice more than heavenly power permits.   [*Exit.*]
                                                      1604, 1616

4. Tragic, sorrowful.
5. Laurel is a symbol of wisdom and learning; Apollo was the god of divination, one of whose shrines was the oracle at Delphi. The image, though it sounds classical, is really Marlowe's.
6. I.e., to be content with observing with awe. "Fiendful fortune": devilish fate.

WILLIAM SHAKESPEARE
(1564–1616)

ca. 1588–92: In London as actor and playwright.
ca. 1592–98: Devotes himself mainly to chronicle histories and comedies.
ca. 1601–9: Period of the great tragedies and romantic comedies.
ca. 1610:   Retires to Stratford.

William Shakespeare was born in Stratford-on-Avon in April (probably April 23), 1564. His father was a citizen of some prominence who became an alderman and bailiff, but who later suffered financial reverses. Shakespeare presumably attended the Stratford grammar school, where he could have acquired a respectable knowledge of Latin, but he did not proceed to Oxford or Cambridge. There are legends about Shakespeare's youth but no documented facts. The first record we have of his life after his christening is that of his marriage in 1582 to Anne Hathaway. A daughter was born to the young Shakespeares in 1583 and twins, a boy and a girl, in 1585. We possess no information about his activities for the next seven years, but by 1592 he was in London as an actor and apparently well-known as a playwright, for Robert Greene refers to him resentfully in *A Groatsworth of Wit* as "an upstart crow, beautified with our feathers," who, "being an absolute *Johannes Factotum*, is in his own conceit the only Shake-scene in a country."

At this time, there were several companies of actors in London and in the provinces. What connection Shakespeare had with one or more of them before 1592 is conjectural, but we do know of his long and fruitful connection with the most successful troupe, the Lord Chamberlain's Men, who later, when James I came to the throne, became the King's Men. Shakespeare not only acted with this company, but eventually became a leading shareholder and the principal playwright. The company included some of the most famous actors of the day, such as Richard Burbage, who no doubt created the roles of Hamlet, Lear, and Othello, and Will Kempe and Robert Armin, who acted Shakespeare's clowns and fools. In 1599 the Chamberlain's Men built and occupied that best known of Elizabethan theaters, the Globe.

Shakespeare did not, in his early years, confine himself to the theater. In 1593 he published a mythological-erotic poem, *Venus and Adonis*, dedicated to the Earl of Southampton; in the next year he dedicated a "graver labor," *The Rape of Lucrece*, to the same noble patron. By 1597 Shakespeare had so prospered that he was able to purchase New Place, a handsome house in Stratford; he could now call himself a gentleman, as his father had been granted a coat of arms in the previous year.

Our first record of the playwright's actual work occurs in Francis Meres' *Palladis Tamia: Wit's Treasury* (1598), in which Meres compared English poets with the ancients; of Shakespeare he says, "As Plautus and Seneca are accounted the best for Comedy and Tragedy among the Latins, so Shakespeare among the English is the most excellent in both kinds for the stage." He goes on to list *Richard II, Richard III, Henry IV, King John, Titus Andronicus,* and *Romeo and Juliet* for tragedy and *Two Gentlemen of Verona, The Comedy of Errors, A Midsummer Night's Dream, The Merchant of Venice, Love's Labor's Lost,* and the unknown (or perhaps retitled) *Love's Labor's Won* as comedy. All of the plays Meres lists as tragedy (except for *Romeo and Juliet* and the very early *Titus Andronicus*) we would call chronicle history plays, a popular kind of drama based upon history books like Raphael Holinshed's *Chronicle* and presenting dramatically the events in the reigns of various English kings. About the turn of the century Shakespeare wrote his great romantic comedies, *As You Like It, Twelfth Night,* and *Much Ado About Nothing,* and his concluding history play in the Prince Hal series, *Henry V.* The next decade was the period of the great tragedies: *Hamlet, Macbeth, Othello, King Lear,* and *Antony and Cleopatra.*

About 1610 Shakespeare apparently retired to Stratford, though he continued to write, both by himself (*The Tempest*) and in collaboration (*Henry VIII*). This is the period of the "romances" or "tragicomedies," which include, besides *The Tempest, Cymbeline* and *The Winter's Tale.* Aside from his two early nondramatic poems, Shakespeare devoted his genius primarily to the stage. Meres mentioned in 1598, however, that he was known for "his sugared sonnets among his private friends"; the sonnets were published in 1609, apparently without his authorization. He contributed the strange and beautiful poem, *The Phoenix and the Turtle,* to an anthology in 1601.

The plays contain some of the finest songs ever written. They are of various types: the aubade, or morning song, the gay pastoral invitation, love songs of various kinds, the ballad sung by wandering minstrels, and the funeral dirge. They illustrate many sides of Shakespeare's genius—his incomparable lyric gift, his ready humor, and his marvelous sensitivity to the sights and sounds of English life, especially the life of the country.

The sonnets are Shakespeare's contribution to a popular vogue, but his cycle is quite unlike the other sonnet sequences of his day. Shakespeare's cycle suggests a story, though the details are vague, and there is doubt even whether the sonnets as published in 1609 are in the correct order. Certain motifs are clear: a series celebrating the beauty of a young man and urging him to marry; some sonnets to a lady; some sonnets (like 144) about a strange triangle of love involving two men and a woman; sonnets on the destructive power of time and the permanence of poetry; sonnets about a rival poet; and incidental sonnets of moral insight, like 129 and 146. The biographical background of the sonnets has aroused much speculation, but very little of it is convincing. The poems themselves are what is important. Though the vocabulary is often simple, the metaphorical style of the sonnets is rich. "Shall I compare thee to a summer's day" is a question which might lead to a very ordinary conceit; instead it introduces a profound meditation on time, change, and beauty.

The structure of the sonnet frequently reinforces the power of the metaphors; each quatrain in 73 develops an image of lateness, of approaching extinction—of a season, of a day, and of a fire, but they also apply to a life. The three quatrains may be equally and successively at work preparing for the conclusion in the couplet, or the first eight lines may contain a catalogue and the last six turn in quite a different direction, as in sonnet 29. The rhetorical strategy of the sonnets is also worth careful attention. Some begin with a purported reminiscence; some are imperative; others make an almost proverbial statement, then elaborate it. The imagery comes from a wide variety of sources: gardening, navigation, law, farming, business, pictorial art, astrology, domestic affairs. The moods are also not confined to what the Renaissance thought were those of the despairing Petrarchan lover; they include delight, pride, melancholy, shame, disgust, fear. It is evident that the poet of the sonnets is also the author of the great plays.

When Shakespeare died, in Stratford in 1616, no collected edition of his plays had been published. Some of them had been printed in separate editions ("quartos") without his editorial supervision, sometimes from his manuscripts, sometimes from playhouse prompt books, sometimes from pirated texts secured by shorthand reports of a performance or from reconstruction from memory by an actor or spectator.

In 1623, two members of Shakespeare's company, John Heminges and Henry Condell, published the great collection of all the plays they considered authentic; it is called the First Folio. They printed the best texts they had, according to their lights. The Folio contains an epistle "to the great variety of readers" which urges us to read Shakespeare again and again; if we do not like him, say Heminges and Condell, it is evident that we do not understand him. Another preliminary document in the First Folio is a poem by Shakespeare's great rival, critic, and opposite, Ben Jonson. In it he asserts the superiority of Shakespeare not only to other English playwrights but to the Greek and Latin masters. Jonson first states what has come to be a universal opinion:

> Triumph, my Britain, thou hast one to show
> To whom all scenes of Europe homage owe.
> He was not of an age, but for all time!

SONGS FROM THE PLAYS
When Daisies Pied[1]

SPRING

When daisies pied and violets blue
    And ladysmocks all silver-white
And cuckoobuds of yellow hue
    Do paint the meadows with delight,
The cuckoo then, on every tree,   5
Mocks married men;[2] for thus sings he,
              Cuckoo;
Cuckoo, cuckoo: Oh word of fear,
Unpleasing to a married ear!

When shepherds pipe on oaten straws,[3]   10
    And merry larks are plowmen's clocks,
When turtles tread,[4] and rooks, and daws,
    And maidens bleach their summer smocks,
The cuckoo then, on every tree,
Mocks married men; for thus sings he,   15
              Cuckoo;
Cuckoo, cuckoo: Oh word of fear,
Unpleasing to a married ear!

WINTER

When icicles hang by the wall
    And Dick the shepherd blows his nail[5]   20
And Tom bears logs into the hall,
    And milk comes frozen home in pail,
When blood is nipped and ways be foul,
Then nightly sings the staring owl,
              Tu-who;   25
Tu-whit, tu-who: a merry note,
While greasy Joan doth keel[6] the pot.

When all aloud the wind doth blow,
    And coughing drowns the parson's saw,[7]
And birds sit brooding in the snow,   30
    And Marian's nose looks red and raw,
When roasted crabs[8] hiss in the bowl,
Then nightly sings the staring owl,
              Tu-who;
Tu-whit, tu-who: a merry note   35
While greasy Joan doth keel the pot.

1. This song concludes *Love's Labour's Lost* (1594–95), one of Shakespeare's earliest comedies. Announced as a "Dialogue * * * in praise of the Owl and the Cuckoo," it provides a lyric commentary on the bittersweet mood that dominates the play's last scene. "Pied": variegated.
2. The cuckoo's song—"Cuckoo!"—is taken to mean "Cuckold!"
3. The reed pipes played by shepherds.
4. Turtledoves mate. The "larks" are "plowmen's clocks" because they sing at sunrise.
5. Warms his fingers by blowing on them.
6. Stir, to prevent boiling over.
7. Wise saying.
8. Crabapples.

Tell Me Where Is Fancy Bred[9]

Tell me where is fancy bred,
Or in the heart or in the head?
How begeot, how nourishéd?
    Reply, reply.
It is engendered in the eyes,   5
With gazing fed; and fancy dies
In the cradle where it lies.
    Let us all ring fancy's knell:
I'll begin it—Ding, dong, bell.
Ding, dong, bell.   10

Sigh No More, Ladies[1]

Sigh no more, ladies, sigh no more,
  Men were deceivers ever;
One foot in sea, and one on shore,
  To one thing constant never.
      Then sigh not so,   5
      But let them go,
And be you blithe and bonny,
Converting all your sounds of woe
  Into Hey nonny, nonny.

Sing no more ditties, sing no mo   10
  Of dumps [2] so dull and heavy;
The fraud of men was ever so,
  Since summer first was leavy.
      Then sigh not so,
      But let them go,   15
And be you blithe and bonny,
Converting all your sounds of woe
  Into Hey nonny, nonny.

Under the Greenwood Tree[3]

Under the greenwood tree
Who loves to lie with me,

---

9. *The Merchant of Venice* (1596–97) III.ii.63 ff.; sung while Bassanio is trying to choose between the caskets of gold, silver, and lead—one of which contains the token that will enable him to gain Portia as his wife. The song is perhaps intended to help Bassanio's choice: notice the number of words that rhyme with "lead." "Fancy" is a superficial love or liking for something attractive.
1. *Much Ado About Nothing* (1598–99) II.iii.64 ff.
2. Sad songs.
3. *As You Like It* (1599–1600) II.v.1 ff.; this song provides a comment on the happy existence of the banished Duke and his followers in the Forest of Arden, where life is "more sweet / Than that of painted pomp."

And turn his merry note
Unto the sweet bird's throat,[4]
Come hither, come hither, come hither: 5
　　Here shall he see
　　No enemy
But winter and rough weather.

　　Who doth ambition shun
　　And loves to live i' the sun,   10
　　Seeking the food he eats,
　　And pleased with what he gets,
Come hither, come hither, come hither:
　　Here shall he see
　　No enemy   15
But winter and rough weather.

Blow, Blow, Thou Winter Wind[5]

Blow, blow, thou winter wind,
Thou art not so unkind
　　As man's ingratitude;
Thy tooth is not so keen,
Because thou art not seen,   5
　　Although thy breath be rude.
Heigh-ho! sing, heigh-ho! unto the green holly:
Most friendship is feigning, most loving mere folly:
　　Then, heigh-ho, the holly!
　　This life is most jolly.   10

Freeze, freeze, thou bitter sky,
That dost not bite so nigh
　　As benefits forgot:
Though thou the waters warp,[6]
Thy sting is not so sharp   15
　　As friend remembered not.
Heigh-ho! sing, etc.

Oh Mistress Mine[7]

Oh mistress mine! where are you roaming?
Oh! stay and hear; your true love's coming,
　　That can sing both high and low.
Trip no further, pretty sweeting;
Journeys end in lovers meeting,   5
　　Every wise man's son doth know.

What is love? 'tis not hereafter;
Present mirth hath present laughter;
　　What's to come is still unsure:

---

4. I.e., improvise his song in harmony
with the bird's.
5. Also from *As You Like It* II.vii.
174 ff. The contrast here between nature and man's willful behavior is one
of the continuing themes of the play.
6. I.e., roughen by freezing.
7. *Twelfth Night* (1601-2) II.iii.40 ff.

In delay there lies no plenty;　　　　　　10
　Then come kiss me, sweet and twenty,
　　Youth's a stuff will not endure.

Take, Oh, Take Those Lips Away[8]

Take, Oh, take those lips away,
　That so sweetly were forsworn;
And those eyes, the break of day,
　Lights that do mislead the morn:
But my kisses bring again, bring again;　　　5
Seals of love, but sealed in vain, sealed in vain.

Fear No More the Heat o' the Sun[9]

Fear no more the heat o' the sun,
　Nor the furious winter's rages;
Thou thy worldly task hast done,
　Home art gone, and ta'en thy wages:
Golden lads and girls all must,　　　　　5
As [1] chimney-sweepers, come to dust.

Fear no more the frown o' the great;
　Thou art past the tyrant's stroke;
Care no more to clothe and eat;
　To thee the reed is as the oak:　　　　10
The scepter, learning, physic, must
All follow this, and come to dust.

Fear no more the lightning flash,
　Nor the all-dreaded thunder stone;[2]
Fear not slander, censure rash;　　　　　15
　Thou hast finished joy and moan:
All lovers young, all lovers must
Consign to thee, and come to dust.

No exorciser harm thee!
Nor no witchcraft charm thee!　　　　　20
Ghost unlaid forbear thee!
Nothing ill come near thee!
Quiet consummation have;
And renownéd be thy grave!

When Daffodils Begin to Peer[3]

When daffodils begin to peer,
　With heigh! the doxy[4] over the dale,

---

8. *Measure for Measure* (1604) IV.i. 1 ff.; Mariana's desolation at being jilted by her lover Angelo is poignantly conveyed in this song, which is sung at her first entrance.
9. A lament for the supposedly dead Imogen, sung in *Cymbeline* IV.ii.258 ff.
1. Like.
2. The sound of thunder was commonly thought to be caused by the falling of

stones or meteorites.
3. *The Winter's Tale* (1610–11) IV. iii.1 ff. Autolycus, ballad-singer, peddler, and rogue, makes his entrance singing this song, which not only effectively establishes his character but also helps to move the play from the wintry mood of the earlier scenes to the spring mood of the later scenes.
4. Girl or mistress (thieves' slang).

Why, then comes in the sweet o' the year;
    For the red blood reigns in the winter's pale.[5]

The white sheet bleaching on the hedge,[6]   5
    With heigh! the sweet birds, Oh, how they sing!
Doth set my pugging[7] tooth on edge;
    For a quart of ale is a dish for a king.

The lark, that tirra-lirra chants,
    With heigh! with heigh! the thrush and the jay,   10
Are summer songs for me and my aunts,[8]
    While we lie tumbling in the hay.

Full Fathom Five[9]

Full fathom five thy father lies;
    Of his bones are coral made;
Those are pearls that were his eyes:
    Nothing of him that doth fade,
But doth suffer a sea change   5
Into something rich and strange.
Sea nymphs hourly ring his knell:
    Ding-dong.
Hark! now I hear them—Ding-dong, bell.

Where the Bee Sucks, There Suck I[1]

Where the bee sucks, there suck I:
In a cowslip's bell I lie;
There I couch when owls do cry.
On the bat's back I do fly
After summer merrily.   5
Merrily, merrily shall I live now
Under the blossom that hangs on the bough.

Sonnets

3

Look in thy glass, and tell the face thou viewest
Now is the time that face should form another,
Whose fresh repair if now thou not renewest,

---

5. A pun on (1) a territory over which one has jurisdiction (2) lacking in color.
6. Laundry, dried or bleached on hedges, was sometimes stolen by passing vagabonds like Autolycus.
7. Thieving.
8. Girls or mistresses.
9. *The Tempest* (1611–12) I.ii.396 ff. Ariel, the airy spirit of the enchanted isle, sings this song to Ferdinand, prince of Naples. Ferdinand wonders at it: "The ditty does remember my drowned father. / This is no mortal business, nor no sound/ That the earth owes [owns]."
1. Also from *The Tempest* V.i.88 ff.: Ariel is happily anticipating the freedom of his future life.

Thou dost beguile the world, unbless some mother.
For where is she so fair whose uneared[2] womb   5
Disdains the tillage of thy husbandry?
Or who is he so fond[3] will be the tomb
Of his self-love, to stop posterity?
Thou art thy mother's glass,[4] and she in thee
Calls back the lovely April of her prime;   10
So thou through windows of thine age shalt see,
Despite of wrinkles, this thy golden time.
But if thou live rememb'red not to be,
Die single, and thine image dies with thee.

12

When I do count the clock that tells the time
And see the brave[5] day sunk in hideous night,
When I behold the violet past prime
And sable curls all silver'd o'er with white,
When lofty trees I see barren of leaves,   5
Which erst[6] from heat did canopy the herd,
And summer's green all girded up in sheaves
Borne on the bier with white and bristly beard—
Then of thy beauty do I question make
That thou among the wastes of time must go,   10
Since sweets and beauties do themselves forsake
And die as fast as they see others grow,
And nothing 'gainst Time's scythe can make defense
Save breed,[7] to brave him when he takes thee hence.

18

Shall I compare thee to a summer's day?
Thou art more lovely and more temperate:
Rough winds do shake the darling buds of May,
And summer's lease hath all too short a date:
Sometime too hot the eye of heaven shines   5
And often is his gold complexion dimmed;
And every fair from fair sometimes declines,
By chance or nature's changing course untrimmed;[8]
But thy eternal summer shall not fade,
Nor lose possession of that fair thou ow'st;[9]   10
Nor shall death brag thou wander'st in his shade,
When in eternal lines to time thou grow'st:
So long as men can breathe, or eyes can see,
So long lives this, and this gives life to thee.[1]

2. Unplowed.
3. Foolish.
4. Mirror.
5. Splendid.
6. Formerly.
7. Offspring; "to brave": to defy.
8. Stripped of gay apparel.

9. Ownest.
1. The boast of immortality for one's verse was a Renaissance convention and goes back to the classics. It implies, not egotism on the part of the poet, but a faith in the permanence of poetry.

29

When, in disgrace with fortune and men's eyes,
I all alone beweep my outcast state,
And trouble deaf heaven with my bootless² cries,
And look upon myself, and curse my fate,
Wishing me like to one more rich in hope,   5
Featured like him, like him with friends possessed,
Desiring this man's art and that man's scope,
With what I most enjoy contented least;
Yet in these thoughts myself almost despising,
Haply I think on thee—and then my state,³   10
Like to the lark at break of day arising
From sullen earth, sings hymns at heaven's gate;
For thy sweet love remembered such wealth brings
That then I scorn to change my state with kings.⁴

30

When to the sessions⁵ of sweet silent thought
I summon up remembrance of things past,
I sigh the lack of many a thing I sought,
And with old woes new wail⁶ my dear time's waste:
Then can I drown an eye, unused to flow,   5
For precious friends hid in death's dateless⁷ night,
And weep afresh love's long since canceled woe,
And moan the expense ⁸ of many a vanished sight:
Then can I grieve at grievances foregone,⁹
And heavily from woe to woe tell o'er   10
The sad account of fore-bemoanèd moan,
Which I new pay as if not paid before.
But if the while I think on thee, dear friend,
All losses are restored and sorrows end.

55

Not marble, nor the gilded monuments
Of princes, shall outlive this powerful rhyme;
But you shall shine more bright in these contents
Than unswept stone, besmeared with sluttish time.¹
When wasteful war shall statues overturn,   5
And broils root out the work of masonry,
Nor Mars his² sword nor war's quick fire shall burn
The living record of your memory.
'Gainst death and all-oblivious enmity³

---

2. Futile.
3. Condition, state of mind; but in line 14 there is a pun on "state" meaning chair of state, throne.
4. This sonnet and the next are companion pieces, one dealing with present troubles, the other with those past.
5. Sittings of court; "summon up" (line 2) continues the metaphor.
6. Bewail anew.

7. Endless.
8. Loss.
9. Old subjects for grief. "Tell": count.
1. I.e., than in a stone tomb or effigy which time wears away and covers with dust.
2. Mars's.
3. The enmity of oblivion, of being forgotten.

Shall you pace forth; your praise shall still find room   10
Even in the eyes of all posterity
That wear this world out to the ending doom.[4]
So, till the judgment that yourself arise,
You live in this, and dwell in lovers' eyes.

56

Sweet love, renew thy force; be it not said
Thy edge should blunter be than appetite,
Which but today by feeding is allayed,
Tomorrow sharpened in his former might.
So, love, be thou: although today thou fill   5
Thy hungry eyes even till they wink[5] with fullness,
Tomorrow see again, and do not kill
The spirit of love with a perpetual dullness.
Let this sad int'rim like the ocean be
Which parts the shore where two contracted new[6]   10
Come daily to the banks, that, when they see
Return of love, more blest may be the view;
Or call it winter, which, being full of care,
Makes summer's welcome thrice more wished, more rare.

60

Like as the waves make towards the pebbled shore,
So do our minutes hasten to their end;
Each changing place with that which goes before,
In sequent toil all forwards do contend.[7]
Nativity, once in the main[8] of light,   5
Crawls to maturity, wherewith being crowned,
Crooked eclipses 'gainst his glory fight,
And time that gave doth now his gift confound.
Time doth transfix the flourish [9] set on youth
And delves the parallels in beauty's brow,   10
Feeds on the rarities of nature's truth,
And nothing stands but for his scythe to mow.
And yet to times in hope [1] my verse shall stand,
Praising thy worth, despite his cruel hand.

71

No longer mourn for me when I am dead
Than you shall hear the surly sullen bell [2]
Give warning to the world that I am fled
From this vile world, with vilest worms to dwell:

4. Judgment Day. The next line is paraphrased, "Until you rise from the dead
on Judgment Day."
5. Close (not momentarily).
6. A newly engaged couple.
7. Toiling and following each other,
the waves struggle to press forward.
8. Broad expanse.

9. Remove the embellishment. "Delves
the parallels": digs the parallel furrows
(wrinkles). To "flourish" is also to
blossom.
1. Future times.
2. The bell was tolled to announce the
death of a member of the parish—
one stroke for each year of his life.

Nay, if you read this line, remember not   5
The hand that writ it; for I love you so,
That I in your sweet thoughts would be forgot,
If thinking on me then should make you woe.
Oh, if, I say, you look upon this verse
When I perhaps compounded am with clay,   10
Do not so much as my poor name rehearse,
But let your love even with my life decay;
Lest the wise world should look into your moan,
And mock you with me after I am gone.

73

That time of year thou mayst in me behold   *a*
When yellow leaves, or none, or few, do hang   *b*
Upon those boughs which shake against the cold, *a*
Bare ruined choirs, where late the sweet birds sang. *b*
In me thou see'st the twilight of such day   5
As after sunset fadeth in the west;
Which by and by black night doth take away,
Death's second self that seals up all in rest.
In me thou see'st the glowing of such fire,
That on the ashes of his youth doth lie,   10
As the deathbed whereon it must expire,
Consumed with that which it was nourished by.[3]
This thou perceiv'st, which makes thy love more strong,
To love that well which thou must leave ere long.

87

Farewell: thou art too dear[4] for my possessing,   *a*
And like enough thou know'st thy estimate.[5]   *b*
The charter[6] of thy worth gives thee releasing;   *a*
My bonds in thee are all determinate.[7]   *b*
For how do I hold thee but by thy granting,   *c*   5
And for that riches where is my deserving?   *d*
The cause of this fair gift in me is wanting,   *c*
And so my patent [8] back again is swerving.   *d*
Thyself thou gav'st, thy own worth then not knowing, *e*
Or me, to whom thou gav'st it, else mistaking;   *f*   10
So thy great gift, upon misprision[9] growing,   *e*
Comes home again, on better judgment making.   *f*
Thus have I had thee as a dream doth flatter,   *g*
In sleep a king, but waking no such matter.   *g*

94

They that have power to hurt and will do none,
That do not do the thing they most do show,[1]

---

3. Choked by the ashes of that which
once nourished its flame.
4. Expensive, beloved.
5. Value.
6. Deed, contract for property.

7. Expired.
8. Title.
9. Mistake, oversight.
1. Seem to do.

Who, moving others, are themselves as stone,
Unmovéd, cold, and to temptation slow;
They rightly do inherit heaven's graces   5
And husband nature's riches from expense; [2]
They are the lords and owners of their faces,
Others but stewards of their excellence.
The summer's flower is to the summer sweet,
Though to itself it only live and die,   10
But if that flower with base infection meet,
The basest weed outbraves his dignity:
For sweetest things turn sourest by their deeds;
Lilies that fester smell far worse than weeds.[3]

97

How like a winter hath my absence been
From thee, the pleasure of the fleeting year!
What freezings have I felt, what dark days seen!
What old December's bareness everywhere!
And yet this time removed was summer's time,   5
The teeming autumn big with rich increase,
Bearing the wanton burthen of the prime,[4]
Like widowed wombs after their lords' decease;
Yet this abundant issue seemed to me
But hope of orphans and unfathered fruit;   10
For summer and his pleasures wait on thee,
And, thou away, the very birds are mute;
Or, if they sing, 'tis with so dull a cheer
That leaves look pale, dreading the winter's near.

98

From you have I been absent in the spring,
When proud-pied[5] April, dressed in all his trim,
Hath put a spirit of youth in everything,
That heavy Saturn[6] laughed and leaped with him.
Yet nor the lays of birds, nor the sweet smell   5
Of different flowers in odor and in hue,
Could make me any summer's story tell,
Or from their proud lap pluck them where they grew;
Nor did I wonder at[7] the lily's white,
Nor praise the deep vermilion in the rose;   10
They were but sweet, but figures of delight,
Drawn after you, you pattern of all those.
Yet seemed it winter still, and, you away,
As with your shadow I with these did play.

2. I.e., they do not squander nature's gifts.
3. This line appears in *Edward III* (II. i.451), an apocryphal Shakespearean play licensed December 1, 1595.
4. Spring, which has engendered the lavish crop ("wanton burthen") that autumn is now left to bear.
5. Magnificent in many colors.
6. God of meloncholy.
7. Admire.

104

To me, fair friend, you never can be old,
For as you were when first your eye I eyed
Such seems your beauty still. Three winters cold
Have from the forests shook three summer's pride,
Three beauteous springs to yellow autumn turned   5
In process [8] of the seasons have I seen,
Three April perfumes in three hot Junes burned,
Since first I saw you fresh, which yet are green.
Ah, yet doth beauty, like a dial-hand, [9]
Steal from his figure, and no pace perceived;   10
So your sweet hue, which methinks still doth stand,
Hath motion, and mine eye may be deceived:
For fear of which, hear this, thou age unbred: [1]
Ere you were born was beauty's summer dead.

106

When in the chronicle of wasted [2] time
I see descriptions of the fairest wights,
And beauty making beautiful old rhyme
In praise of ladies dead and lovely knights,
Then, in the blazon [3] of sweet beauty's best,   5
Of hand, of foot, of lip, of eye, of brow,
I see their antique pen would have expressed
Even such a beauty as you master now.
So all their praises are but prophecies
Of this our time, all you prefiguring;   10
And, for they looked but with divining eyes,
They had not skill enough your worth to sing: [4]
For we, which now behold these present days,
Have eyes to wonder, but lack tongues to praise.

107

Not mine own fears, nor the prophetic soul
Of the wide world dreaming on things to come, [5]
Can yet the lease of my true love control,
Supposed as forfeit to a confinèd doom. [6]
The mortal moon hath her eclipse endured,   5
And the sad augurs mock their own presage; [7]
Incertainties now crown themselves assured,
And peace [8] proclaims olives of endless age.

8. Procession.
9. Hand of a watch.
1. Unborn generation.
2. Past.
3. Display.
4. Because ("for") they were able *only* ("but") to foresee prophetically.
5. This sonnet refers to contemporary events and the prophecies, common in Elizabethan almanacs, of disaster.
6. I.e., can yet put an end to my love, which I thought doomed to early forfeiture.

7. The "mortal moon" is Queen Elizabeth; her "eclipse" is probably her climacteric year, her 63rd (thought significant because the product of two "significant" numbers, 7 and 9), which ended in September, 1596. The sober astrologers ("sad augurs") now ridicule their own predictions ("presage") of catastrophe, since they turned out to be false.
8. Probably an agreement between Henry IV of France and Elizabeth.

Now with the drops of this most balmy time
My love looks fresh, and death to me subscribes,[9]   10
Since, spite of him, I'll live in this poor rhyme,
While he insults o'er dull and speechless tribes:
And thou in this shalt find thy monument,
When tyrants' crests and tombs of brass are spent.

110[1]

Alas, 'tis true I have gone here and there
And made myself a motley[2] to the view,
Gored[3] mine own thoughts, sold cheap what is most dear,
Made old offenses of affections new;[4]
Most true it is that I have looked on truth   5
Askance and strangely; but, by all above,
These blenches[5] gave my heart another youth,
And worse essays[6] proved thee my best of love.
Now all is done, have what shall have no end:
Mine appetite I never more will grind[7]   10
On newer proof, to try an older friend,
A god in love, to whom I am confined.
Then give me welcome, next my heaven the best,
Even to thy pure and most most loving breast.

116

Let me not to the marriage of true minds
Admit impediments.[8] Love is not love
Which alters when it alteration finds,
Or bends with the remover to remove:
Oh, no! it is an ever-fixéd mark,   5
That looks on tempests and is never shaken;
It is the star to every wandering bark,
Whose worth's unknown, although his height[9] be taken.
Love's not Time's fool, though rosy lips and cheeks
Within his[1] bending sickle's compass come;   10
Love alters not with his brief hours and weeks,
But bears it out even to the edge of doom.[2]
If this be error and upon me proved,
      I never writ, nor no man ever loved.

118

Like as, to make our appetites more keen,
With eager[3] compounds we our palate urge;

---

9. Submits.
1. This is the second in a group of sonnets that deal with the poet's absence from the friend and an unfaithfulness to him. The first three lines may refer to Shakespeare's career as an actor.
2. A clown (with a varicolored costume).
3. Wounded.
4. Offended by changing old friends for new.
5. Offenses.
6. Trials of what is worse.
7. Whet.
8. From the Marriage Service: "If any of you know cause or just impediment why these persons should not be joined together * * * "
9. The star's value is not known, though the star's "height" (altitude) may be known and used for practical navigation.
1. I.e., Time's (as also in line 11).
2. Brink of the Last Judgment.
3. Bitter.

As, to prevent our maladies unseen,
We sicken to shun sickness when we purge:[4]
Even so, being full of your ne'er-cloying sweetness,   5
To bitter sauces did I frame my feeding;
And, sick of welfare,[5] found a kind of meetness
To be diseased ere that there was true needing.
Thus policy in love, t' anticipate
The ills that were not, grew to faults assuréd,   10
And brought to medicine a healthful state,
Which, rank of goodness, would by ill be curéd.
But thence I learn, and find the lesson true,
Drugs poison him that so fell sick of you.

121

'Tis better to be vile than vile esteemed
When not to be receives reproach of being,[6]
And the just pleasure lost, which is so deemed
Not by our feeling but by others' seeing.
For why should others' false adulterate eyes   5
Give salutation to my sportive blood?[7]
Or on my frailties why are frailer spies,[8]
Which in their wills count bad what I think good?
No, I am that I am; and they that level[9]
At my abuses reckon up their own: 10
I may be straight though they themselves be bevel;[1]
By their rank thoughts my deeds must not be shown,
Unless this general evil they maintain:
All men are bad and in their badness reign.

129

Th' expense of spirit in a waste of shame
Is lust in action;[2] and till action, lust
Is perjured, murderous, bloody, full of blame,
Savage, extreme, rude, cruel, not to trust;
Enjoyed no sooner but despiséd straight: 5
Past reason hunted; and no sooner had,
Past reason hated, as a swallowed bait,
On purpose laid to make the taker mad:
Mad in pursuit, and in possession so;
Had, having, and in quest to have, extreme;   10
A bliss in proof[3] and proved, a very woe;

4. Take cathartics.
5. Replete with well-being; as in "rank of goodness" (line 12). "Sick of" does not have the modern meaning "tired of"; it rather means "sick with," here and in line 14.
6. I.e., it is better to be vicious than to be thought vicious when the innocent are thought vicious.
7. Others' falsified, lewdly corrupt eyes tempt me.

8. Men with more frailties.
9. Aim.
1. Crooked, slanting.
2. The word order here is inverted and slightly obscures the meaning. Lust, when put into action, expends "spirit" (life, vitality) in a "waste" (desert, with a possible pun on "waist," also) of shame.
3. A bliss during the experience.

Before, a joy proposed; behind, a dream.
All this the world well knows; yet none knows well
To shun the heaven that leads men to this hell.

130

My mistress' eyes are nothing like the sun;[4]
Coral is far more red than her lips' red;
If snow be white, why then her breasts are dun;
If hairs be wires, black wires grow on her head.
I have seen roses damasked,[5] red and white,   5
But no such roses see I in her cheeks;
And in some perfumes is there more delight
Than in the breath that from my mistress reeks.
I love to hear her speak, yet well I know
That music hath a far more pleasing sound;   10
I grant I never saw a goddess go;[6]
My mistress, when she walks, treads on the ground.
And yet, by heaven, I think my love as rare
As any she belied with false compare.

138

When my love swears that she is made of truth, *a*
I do believe her, though I know she lies, *b*
That she might think me some untutored youth, *a*
Unlearned in the world's false subtleties. *b*
Thus vainly thinking that she thinks me young, *c*   5
Although she knows my days are past the best,[7] *d*
Simply I credit her false-speaking tongue: *c*
On both sides thus is simple truth suppressed. *d*
But wherefore says she not she is unjust?[8] *e*
And wherefore say not I that I am old? *f*   10
Oh, love's best habit[9] is in seeming trust, *e*
And age in love loves not to have years told. *f*
Therefore I lie with her and she with me, *g*
And in our faults by lies we flattered be. *g*

144

Two loves I have of comfort and despair,
Which like two spirits do suggest me still:[1]
The better angel is a man right fair,
The worser spirit a woman, colored ill.[2]
To win me soon to hell, my female evil   5
Tempteth my better angel from my side,
And would corrupt my saint to be a devil,

4. An anti-Petrarchan sonnet. All of the details commonly attributed by other Elizabethan sonneteers to their ladies are here denied to the poet's mistress.
5. Variegated. The damask rose (supposedly from Damascus, originally) is pink.
6. **Walk.**

7. Shakespeare was 35 or younger when he wrote this sonnet (it first appeared in *The Passionate Pilgrim*, 1599). "Simply": like a simpleton.
8. Unfaithful.
9. Appearance, deportment.
1. Tempt me constantly.
2. Dark.

Wooing his purity with her foul pride.
And whether that my angel be turned fiend
Suspect I may, yet not directly tell;   10
But being both from[3] me, both to each friend,
I guess one angel in another's hell.
Yet this shall I ne'er know, but live in doubt,
Till my bad angel fire[4] my good one out.

146

Poor soul, the center of my sinful earth,
Lord of[5] these rebel powers that thee array,[6]
Why dost thou pine within and suffer dearth,
Painting thy outward walls so costly gay?
Why so large cost, having so short a lease,   5
Dost thou upon thy fading mansion spend?
Shall worms, inheritors of this excess,
Eat up thy charge? Is this thy body's end?
Then, soul, live thou upon thy servant's loss,
And let that pine to aggravate thy store;[7]   10
Buy terms[8] divine in selling hours of dross;
Within be fed, without be rich no more.
So shalt thou feed on death, that feeds on men,
And death once dead, there's no more dying then.

The Phoenix and the Turtle[1]

Let the bird of loudest lay,[2]
On the sole Arabian tree,
Herald sad and trumpet be,
To whose sound chaste wings obey.

3. Away from; "each": each other.
4. Drive out by fire.
5. An emendation. The Quarto repeats the last three words of line 1. Other suggestions are "Thrall to," "Starv'd by," "Press'd by," and leaving the repetition but dropping "that thee" in line 2
6. Dress out, often used in a military sense.
7. Let "that" (i.e., the body) deteriorate to increase ("aggravate") the soul's riches ("thy store").
8. Long periods; "dross": refuse, rubbish.
1. First published in Robert Chester's *Love's Martyr, or Rosalin's Complaint* (1601). It is part of an appendix containing "divers poetical essays" by other poets, all supposedly dealing with the same subject. This subject has something to do with a Welsh knight, Sir John Salusbury, and his lady. But Shakespeare's poem is not consistent with the other poems in the volume, for some of them celebrate the birth of offspring to the phoenix and the turtle, whereas Shakespeare says the birds died leaving no posterity. The phoenix is a legendary bird of Arabia: it perishes in flames and a new one arises from the ashes; only one is alive at a time. Queen Elizabeth, the Virgin Queen, was sometimes symbolized by the unique and virginal phoenix. The "turtle" (turtledove) is common in Elizabethan imagery as the most loving of birds. Bird poems were traditionally allegorical, from Chaucer's time on down, but the key to this allegory (if it is one) has been lost.
2. Cry or song. This stanza might be paraphrased, "Let the bird with the loudest voice proclaim from the perch of the phoenix ('Arabian tree'); all gentle birds ('chaste wings') will respond to the summons."

But thou shrieking harbinger,   5
Foul precurrer of the fiend,[3]
Augur of the fever's end,
To this troop come thou not near!

From this session interdict
Every fowl of tyrant wing,   10
Save the eagle, feathered king:
Keep the obsequy so strict.

Let the priest in surplice white,
That defunctive music can,[4]
Be the death-divining swan,   15
Lest the requiem lack his right.

And thou treble-dated[5] crow,
That thy sable gender mak'st
With the breath thou giv'st and tak'st,[6]
'Mongst our mourners shalt thou go.   20

Here the anthem doth commence:
Love and constancy is dead,
Phoenix and the turtle fled
In a mutual flame from hence.

So they loved as love in twain   25
Had the essence but in one;[7]
Two distincts, division none:
Number there in love was slain.

Hearts remote, yet not asunder;
Distance, and no space was seen   30
'Twixt this turtle and his queen;
But in them[8] it were a wonder.

So between them love did shine
That the turtle saw his right[9]
Flaming in the phoenix' sight: 35
Either was the other's mine.[1]

Property[2] was thus appalled,
That the self was not the same;
Single nature's double name
Neither two nor one was called.   40

3. Forerunner of the devil. "Harbinger": precursor. The screech owl is probably meant.
4. I.e., skilled in funeral ("defunctive") music. The swan was supposed to sing only once, just before its death.
5. Living three lifetimes.
6. "Sable gender": black offspring. The crow was supposed to conceive and lay its eggs through the bill.
7. They were originally two, but by love were united into one. Since one is singular, and not a number, "Number there in love was slain."
8. In any other case than theirs.
9. What was due him, love returned.
1. Rich source of wealth or treasure.
2. Peculiar or essential quality. "Property" is "appalled" to find that personality ("self") is obliterated in the union of the two. Accordingly it is impossible to say whether they were two or one.

Reason, in itself confounded,
Saw division grow together,[3]
To themselves yet either neither,
Simple were so well compounded;

That it cried, "How true a twain   45
Seemeth this concordant one!
Love hath reason, reason none,
If what parts can so remain."[4]

Whereupon it made this threne[5]
To the phoenix and the dove,   50
Co-supremes and stars of love,
As chorus to their tragic scene.

Threnos

Beauty, truth, and rarity,
Grace in all simplicity,
Here enclosed in cinders lie.   55

Death is now the phoenix' nest;
And the turtle's loyal breast
To eternity doth rest,

Leaving no posterity:
'Twas not their infirmity,   60
It was married chastity.

Truth may seem, but cannot be;
Beauty brag, but 'tis not she:[6]
Truth and Beauty buried be.

To this urn let those repair   65
That are either true or fair;
For these dead birds sigh a prayer.

1601

1 Henry IV   The title page of the first quarto edition of Shakespeare's 1 *Henry IV*, published in 1598, reads: "THE HISTORY OF HENRIE THE FOURTH; With the the battell at Shrewsburie, *betweene the King and Lord* Henry Percy, surnamed Henrie Hotspur of the North. *With the humorous conceits of Sir* John Falstalffe." It had been performed on the stage and at court before publication, and from that time to this it has remained one of Shakespeare's most popular plays.

Shakespeare had already inaugurated a new dramatic type by writing

3. Reason, which discriminates parts of a thing, is here confounded because the two parts are merged. Each element lost its identity in being fused with the other.
4. Love is more reasonable than reason, because it has proved that the separateness of entities (one of reason's laws) does not always hold true.
5. Threnody, funeral song.
6. Whatever may appear hereafter as truth or beauty will be only illusion. Real truth and beauty lie buried here.

four plays dealing with fairly recent English history, and had then gone
back to a period two centuries earlier to portray, in *Richard II*, the downfall of the weak, effeminate and poetic young King Richard ("that sweet
lovely rose," as he is called in this play) at the hands of the hard, efficient
Bolingbroke, who came to the throne as Henry IV. Before this seizure of
the crown there had been a prophecy, put by Shakespeare into the mouth
of the Bishop of Carlisle in *Richard II* (IV.i.136–44), of the dire consequences to follow:

> And if you crown him, let me prophesy,
> The blood of English shall manure the ground
> And future ages groan for this foul act;
> Peace shall go sleep with Turks and infidels,
> And in this seat of peace tumultuous wars
> Shall kin with kin and kind with kind confound;
> Disorder, horror, fear, and mutiny
> Shall here inhabit, and this land be called
> The field of Golgotha and dead men's skulls.

Shakespeare drew his historical material from the prose chronicle histories, specifically Raphael Holinshed's *Chronicles of England, Scotland,
and Ireland*, Samuel Daniel's historical poem *Civil Wars*, and an earlier
play, either the popular farcical piece called *The Famous Victories of
Henry V* or a lost play which was its source. His sources gave him the
portrait of a gay and reckless Prince of Wales and his roistering companions. Chief of these was a fat knight, Sir John Oldcastle; Shakespeare
at first used this name, but later, because of protests from the descendants
of that Protestant martyr, changed the name to Sir John Falstaff. This
character, whose "humorous conceits" are advertised on the title page, is
one of the greatest comic creations in all literature. Shakespeare continued
to exploit his inexhaustible exuberance through a sequel, *The Second Part
of Henry IV*, and a comedy of middle-class life, supposed to have been
written at Queen Elizabeth's command, *The Merry Wives of Windsor*.

The ominous wars of Carlisle's prophecy could thus be mixed with
hilarious fooling, but 1 *Henry IV* succeeds, not only as a comedy, but as
a serious play about character and history. The real hero is not King Henry
IV, nor the fat Falstaff, but Prince Hal, the handsome playboy who in
time of crisis reforms and saves his father's throne. He is the prince who
later became Henry V, the English national hero who reconquered France.

Shakespeare's theme in all his history plays is the importance of order
and degree, of the disruptive effects of civil strife and rebellion. But as he
matured as a dramatist (and 1 *Henry IV* stands at the beginning of his
great period of maturity), he found character to be more interesting than
the philosophy or events of history. How to demonstrate the kind of character that would make the English national hero was his problem, and
he solved it by a method of comparison and contrast, utilizing four men
of different types. At one extreme is Falstaff, who loves to eat, drink, joke,
and dramatize himself, and to whom anything as intangible as honor is
a mere word, a breath of air. Opposite in every way is Hotspur, fiery and
impatient, completely ambitious for honor and fame, scornful of the soft,
civilized arts of poetry and music, a hardheaded fanatic. A third type is
the wild Welshman Glendower, a believer in magic and a practitioner of

it, an accomplished poet yet a valiant, if superstitious, warrior, and an egotist like his ally Hotspur. Finally there is Prince Hal, whose sense of humor rivals Falstaff's, but who turns out to be the match for Hotspur in valor and his superior in knightly courtesy. It is worth noting that Shakespeare changed history in order to make this dramatic contrast: in Holinshed's *Chronicle* Hotspur is older than Prince Hal's father, but Shakespeare makes them contemporaries. It is in the excesses of the other three that we see the merits of the Prince's character illuminated. The four characters represent not only men but ways of life. And these ways of life are all relevant to fundamental questions about social and political responsibility, honor, and loyalty to a cause.

Some background in 15th-century English history, as Shakespeare understood it, is needed if we are to respond readily to the play. Henry Hereford, called Bolingbroke, was in exile in France when his father, John of Gaunt, died. He returned to England to claim his inheritance, and profited from the aid of the Percy family, powerful nobles in the north. The two brothers, Henry Percy, Earl of Northumberland, and Thomas Percy, Earl of Worcester, together with Northumberland's son Henry (called Hotspur) received Bolingbroke's oath at Doncaster (see V.i.32–58) to seize only his inheritance. But King Richard II was in Ireland fighting, having named Edmund Mortimer, Earl of March, his successor if he did not return. In the confused situation in England, Bolingbroke was able to collect enough power so that on Richard's return he could force him to abdicate and then have him killed in prison. Various troubles on the borders made the throne of the new king (Henry IV) insecure. Hotspur managed to defeat the Scots under Douglas at Holmedon (see I.i.62–75) and took many important prisoners. But Mortimer, in fighting against Glendower in Wales, was taken captive and married Glendower's daughter. Henry IV refused to ransom Mortimer, and the indignation of Mortimer's brother-in-law, Hotspur, led him to refuse to turn over his prisoners to the king. So came the conspiracy into being—and such a formidable opposition as that of the Percies, Douglas, Glendower, and certain disaffected churchmen like the Archbishop of York meant a critical danger to Henry's throne. The Battle of Shrewsbury, the climax of this play, decides the conflict.

Much critical comment has been devoted to the character of Falstaff. He has certain resemblances to the traditional *miles gloriosus* (braggart soldier) of Latin comedy, but he far transcends the type; he sometimes resembles the Vice, a comic character in the old morality plays, who is usually an allegorical personification of extreme self-indulgence or of a particular sin; and he often uses, or parodies, the language of the Puritans. Critics differ on whether Falstaff is really a coward or not, and on the question of how much he expects his lies to be believed. But everyone agrees about his inexhaustible vitality and resiliency. It is not surprising that he, like other immortal characters in literature, remains something of a mystery.

The First Part of
King Henry the Fourth

Dramatis Personae

KING HENRY THE FOURTH

HENRY, *Prince of Wales*

PRINCE JOHN OF LANCASTER } *Sons to the* KING

EARL OF WESTMORELAND

SIR WALTER BLUNT

THOMAS PERCY, *Earl of Worcester*

HENRY PERCY, *Earl of Northumberland*

HENRY PERCY, *surnamed* HOTSPUR, *his son*

EDMUND MORTIMER, *Earl of March*

RICHARD SCROOP, *Archbishop of York*

ARCHIBALD, *Earl of Douglas*

OWEN GLENDOWER

SIR RICHARD VERNON

SIR MICHAEL, *a friend to the* ARCHBISHOP OF YORK

SIR JOHN FALSTAFF

POINS

GADSHILL

PETO

BARDOLPH

LADY PERCY, *wife to* HOTSPUR, *and sister to* MORTIMER

LADY MORTIMER, *daughter to* GLENDOWER, *and wife to* MORTIMER

MISTRESS QUICKLY, *hostess of a tavern in Eastcheap*

LORDS, OFFICERS, SHERIFF, VINTNER, CHAMBERLAIN, DRAWERS, *two* CARRIERS, TRAVELERS, *and* ATTENDANTS

Act I

SCENE 1

[*Enter the* KING, PRINCE JOHN OF LANCASTER, THE EARL OF WESTMORELAND, SIR WALTER BLUNT, *with others.*]

KING. So shaken as we are, so wan with care,
  Find we a time for frighted peace to pant,[1]
  And breathe short-winded accents of new broils[2]
  To be commenced in stronds afar remote.
  No more the thirsty entrance[3] of this soil   5
  Shall daub her lips with her own children's blood;
  No more shall trenching war channel her fields,
  Nor bruise her flowerets with the arméd hoofs
  Of hostile paces:[4] those opposéd eyes,
  Which, like the meteors of a troubled heaven,   10
  All of one nature, of one substance bred,
  Did lately meet in the intestine shock[5]
  And furious close of civil butchery,
  Shall now, in mutual well-beseeming ranks,

1. I.e., let us allow peace to catch her breath.
2. I.e., news of new wars; "stronds": strands, regions.
3. Surface.
4. The tread of war horses.
5. Internal violence; "close": encounter.

March all one way and be no more opposed   15
Against acquaintance, kindred, and allies.
The edge of war, like an ill-sheathéd knife,
No more shall cut his master: therefore, friends,
As far as to the sepulcher of Christ,
Whose soldier now, under whose blessed cross   20
We are impresséd and engaged to fight,
Forthwith a power[6] of English shall we levy,
Whose arms were molded in their mother's womb
To chase these pagans in those holy fields
Over whose acres walked those blessed feet   25
Which fourteen hundred years ago were nailed
For our advantage on the bitter cross.
But this our purpose now is twelve month old,
And bootless[7] 'tis to tell you we will go.
Therefore we meet not now:[8] then let me hear   30
Of you, my gentle cousin Westmoreland,
What yesternight our council did decree
In forwarding this dear expedience.[9]

WEST. My liege, this haste was hot in question,[1]
And many limits of the charge set down   35
But yesternight, when all athwart[2] there came
A post from Wales loaden with heavy news,
Whose worst was that the noble Mortimer,
Leading the men of Herefordshire to fight
Against the irregular[3] and wild Glendower,   40
Was by the rude hands of that Welshman taken,
A thousand of his people butcheréd,
Upon whose dead corpse[4] there was such misuse,
Such beastly shameless transformatión,
By those Welshwomen done as may not be   45
Without much shame retold or spoken of.

KING. It seems then that the tidings of this broil
Brake off our business for the Holy Land.

WEST. This matched with other did, my gracious lord,
For more uneven and unwelcome news   50
Came from the north, and thus it did import:
On Holyrood Day[5] the gallant Hotspur there,
Young Harry Percy, and brave Archibald,
That ever-valiant and approvéd Scot,
At Holmedon met,   55
Where they did spend a sad and bloody hour;
As by discharge of their artillery,
And shape of likelihood,[6] the news was told;
For he that brought them[7] in the very heat

6. Army. He is planning a crusade, in
expiation of his guilt for the death of
Richard II.
7. Useless.
8. I.e., that is not the reason for our
present meeting. "Cousin": kinsman.
9. Important, urgent matter.
1. Actively discussed. "Limits of the
charge": assignment of commands.

2. Interrupting, crossing our purpose.
"Post": messenger.
3. Guerilla.
4. Bodies.
5. Holy Cross Day (Sept. 14).
6. Probable inference. "As": since.
7. I.e., the news (usually a plural in
Shakespeare). "Pride": height; literally, the top of a falcon's flight.

And pride of their contention did take horse, 60
Uncertain of the issue any way.
KING. Here is a dear, a true industrious friend,
Sir Walter Blunt, new lighted from his horse,
Stained with the variation of each soil
Betwixt that Holmedon and this seat of ours; 65
And he hath brought us smooth and welcome news.
The Earl of Douglas is discomfited;
Ten thousand bold Scots, two and twenty knights
Balked[8] in their own blood did Sir Walter see
On Holmedon's plains. Of prisoners Hotspur took 70
Mordake Earl of Fife, and eldest son
To beaten Douglas, and the Earl of Athol,
Of Murray, Angus, and Menteith;
And is not this an honorable spoil,
A gallant prize? ha, cousin, is it not? 75
WEST. In faith,
It is a conquest for a prince to boast of.
KING. Yea, there thou mak'st me sad and mak'st me sin
In envy that my Lord Northumberland
Should be the father to so blest a son, 80
A son who is the theme of honor's tongue,
Amongst a grove the very straightest plant,
Who is sweet Fortune's minion[9] and her pride;
Whilst I, by looking on the praise of him,
See riot and dishonor stain the brow 85
Of my young Harry. O that it could be proved
That some night-tripping fairy had exchanged
In cradle-clothes our children where they lay,
And called mine Percy, his Plantagenet!
Then would I have his Harry, and he mine. 90
But let him from my thoughts. What think you, coz,
Of this young Percy's pride? The prisoners
Which he in this adventure hath surprised
To his own use he keeps, and sends me word
I shall have none but Mordake Earl of Fife. 95
WEST. This is his uncle's teaching, this is Worcester,
Malevolent to you in all aspects,[1]
Which makes him prune himself,[2] and bristle up
The crest of youth against your dignity.
KING. But I have sent for him to answer this; 100
And for this cause awhile we must neglect
Our holy purpose to Jerusalem.
Cousin, on Wednesday next our council we
Will hold at Windsor, so inform the lords;
But come yourself with speed to us again, 105
For more is to be said and to be done
Than out of anger can be utteréd.
WEST. I will, my liege. [*Exeunt.*]

8. Heaped.
9. Favorite.
1. Hostile in every way. The figure is from astrology.
2. Plume himself. "Bristle up" and "crest" continue the image, which is that of a fighting cock.

SCENE 2

[*Enter* HENRY, PRINCE OF WALES, *and* SIR JOHN FALSTAFF.]

FAL. Now Hal, what time of day is it, lad?

PRINCE. Thou art so fat-witted with drinking of old sack,[3] and un-
buttoning thee after supper, and sleeping upon benches after
noon, that thou hast forgotten to demand that truly which
thou wouldst truly know. What a devil hast thou to do with   5
the time of the day? Unless hours were cups of sack, and minutes capons, and clocks the tongues of bawds, and dials the
signs of leaping-houses,[4] and the blessed sun himself a fair hot
wench in flame-colored taffeta, I see no reason why thou
shouldst be so superfluous to demand the time of the day.   10

FAL. Indeed you come near me now, Hal, for we that take purses
go by the moon and the seven stars, and not by Phoebus,[5] he,
"that wandering knight so fair." And I prithee, sweet wag,
when thou art king, as, God save thy grace—majesty I should
say, for grace[6] thou wilt have none—   15

PRINCE. What, none?

FAL. No, by my troth, not so much as will serve to be prologue
to an egg and butter.

PRINCE. Well, how then? come, roundly, roundly.[7]

FAL. Marry then, sweet wag, when thou art king, let not us that   20
are squires of the night's body[8] be called thieves of the day's
beauty; let us be Diana's foresters, gentlemen of the shade,
minions of the moon; and let men say we be men of good
government, being governed as the sea is, by our noble and
chaste mistress the moon, under whose countenance we steal.   25

PRINCE. Thou sayest well, and it holds well too, for the fortune
of us that are the moon's men doth ebb and flow like the sea,
being governed as the sea is by the moon. As for proof now:
a purse of gold most resolutely snatched on Monday night and
most dissolutely spent on Tuesday morning, got with swearing   30
"Lay by" and spent with crying "Bring in," now in as low an
ebb as the foot of the ladder and by and by in as high a flow
as the ridge of the gallows.[9]

FAL. By the Lord thou sayest true, lad. And is not my hostess of
the tavern a most sweet wench?   35

PRINCE. As the honey of Hybla,[1] my old lad of the castle. And is
not a buff jerkin a most sweet robe of durance?[2]

3. Sherry.
4. Whorehouses.
5. The sun. Falstaff then quotes from
a popular ballad.
6. A triple pun: (1) "your Grace,"
the correct manner of addressing a
prince or duke; (2) the divine influence
which produces sanctity; and (3) a
short prayer before a meal—hence
Falstaff's allusion to "egg and butter,"
a common hasty breakfast.
7. Plainly.
8. Two puns are involved: a "squire
of the body" was an attendant on a
knight, and "body" would be pronounced *bawdy.* "Beauty" also puns
with "booty" (which thieves take);

Diana is, of course, the moon goddess.
9. "Lay by": i.e., hand over (a robber's command to his victim); "bring
in": a customer's command for more
drink at a tavern. The "foot of the
ladder" is at the bottom of the gallows
(robbery was a hanging offense);
the "ridge" is the crosspiece at the
top.
1. A town in Sicily, famous for honey;
"old lad of the castle" is a reference
to Falstaff's original name, Oldcastle.
2. A "buff jerkin" was the leather
jacket worn by a sheriff's sergeant;
"durance" is a pun: (1) lasting quality
and (2) imprisonment.

FAL. How now, how now, mad wag! what, in thy quips and thy
quiddities?[3] what a plague have I to do with a buff jerkin?

PRINCE. Why, what a pox have I to do with my hostess of the 40
tavern?

FAL. Well, thou hast called her to a reckoning many a time and
oft.

PRINCE. Did I ever call for thee to pay thy part?

FAL. No, I'll give thee thy due, thou hast paid all there. 45

PRINCE. Yea, and elsewhere, so far as my coin would stretch,
and where it would not I have used my credit.

FAL. Yea, and so used it that were it not here apparent that thou
art heir apparent[4]—but I prithee, sweet wag, shall there be
gallows standing in England when thou art king? and resolu- 50
tion thus fobbed as it is with the rusty curb of old father antic
the law?[5] Do not thou, when thou art king, hang a thief.

PRINCE. No, thou shalt.

FAL. Shall I? O rare! By the Lord, I'll be a brave judge.

PRINCE. Thou judgest false already; I mean thou shalt have the 55
hanging of the thieves and so become a rare hangman.

FAL. Well, Hal, well; and in some sort it jumps with my humor[6]
as well as waiting in the court, I can tell you.

PRINCE. For obtaining of suits?[7]

FAL. Yea, for obtaining of suits, whereof the hangman hath no 60
lean wardrobe. 'Sblood,[8] I am as melancholy as a gib cat or a
lugged bear.

PRINCE. Or an old lion, or a lover's lute.

FAL. Yea, or the drone of a Lincolnshire bagpipe.

PRINCE. What sayest thou to a hare, or the melancholy of Moor- 65
ditch?[9]

FAL. Thou hast the most unsavory similes and art indeed the
most comparative,[1] rascalliest, sweet young prince. But Hal,
I prithee, trouble me no more with vanity. I would to God
thou and I knew where a commodity of good names were to be 70
bought. An old lord of the council rated[2] me the other day in
the street about you, sir, but I marked him not; and yet he
talked very wisely, but I regarded him not; and yet he talked
wisely, and in the street too.

PRINCE. Thou didst well, for wisdom cries out in the streets and 75
no man regards it.[3]

FAL. O, thou hast damnable iteration[4] and art indeed able to
corrupt a saint. Thou hast done much harm upon me, Hal,
God forgive thee for it! Before I knew thee, Hal, I knew noth-

3. Quibbles.
4. "Here" and "heir" would pun in
Elizabethan pronunciation.
5. "Resolution": bravery; "fobbed":
cheated; "antic": a clown.
6. I.e., agrees with my disposition.
7. Special favors, but "clothing" in
the next line. The hangman was given
the clothes of his victims.
8. God's blood, a common oath. "Gib
cat": tomcat; "lugged": baited (in the
bear-baiting pits a bear was attacked by

dogs as a public amusement).
9. The "hare" was traditionally associated with melancholy; Moorditch was
a foul-smelling ditch on the outskirts
of London.
1. Affecting wit, dealing in comparisons.
2. Scolded, berated.
3. Prince Hal is quoting Proverbs i.
20 and 24.
4. Repetition, especially of sacred
texts.

ing, and now am I, if a man should speak truly, little better 80
than one of the wicked. I must give over this life, and I will
give it over; by the Lord, an[5] I do not, I am a villain; I'll be
damned for never a king's son in Christendom.

PRINCE. Where shall we take a purse tomorrow, Jack?

FAL. Zounds, where thou wilt, lad; I'll make one; an I do not, 85
call me villain and baffle[6] me.

PRINCE. I see a good amendment of life in thee—from praying
to purse-taking.

FAL. Why, Hal, 'tis my vocation,[7] Hal; 'tis no sin for a man to
labor in his vocation. 90

[*Enter* POINS.]

Poins! Now shall we know if Gadshill[8] have set a match. O, if
men were to be saved by merit, what hole in hell were hot
enough for him? This is the most omnipotent villain that ever
cried "stand" to a true man.

PRINCE. Good morrow, Ned. 95

POINS. Good morrow, sweet Hal. What says Monsieur Remorse?
what says Sir John Sack and Sugar? Jack! how agrees the devil
and thee about thy soul, that thou soldest him on Good Friday last for a cup of Madeira and a cold capon's leg?

PRINCE. Sir John stands to his word; the devil shall have his bar- 100
gain, for he was never yet a breaker of proverbs; he will give
the devil his due.

POINS. Then art thou damned for keeping thy word with the
devil.

PRINCE. Else he had been damned for cozening[9] the devil. 105

POINS. But my lads, my lads, tomorrow morning by four o'clock,
early at Gadshill, there are pilgrims going to Canterbury with
rich offerings, and traders riding to London with fat purses.
I have vizards[1] for you all, you have horses for yourselves; Gadshill lies tonight in Rochester; I have bespoke supper tomorrow 110
night in Eastcheap; we may do it as secure as sleep. If you will
go, I will stuff your purses full of crowns; if you will not, tarry
at home and be hanged.

FAL. Hear ye, Yedward, if I tarry at home and go not, I'll hang
you for going. 115

POINS. You will, chops?[2]

FAL. Hal, wilt thou make one?

PRINCE. Who, I rob? I a thief? not I, by my faith.

FAL. There's neither honesty, manhood, nor good fellowship in
thee, nor thou camest not of the blood royal,[3] if thou darest 120

5. If.
6. A knight in the days of chivalry was "baffled" or disgraced by having his shield hung upside down. Falstaff may mean "hang me up by the heels." "Zounds": a common oath, a contraction of "by God's wounds" (i.e., Jesus' wounds on the Cross).
7. Falstaff is here making fun of the Puritan doctrine of "calling" or vocation, based on the parable of the talents (see Matthew xxv.25 ff.).
8. Gadshill is both a man and a

place: the place is a hill 27 miles from London on the road to Rochester; it was notorious for robberies. The man, so called from the place, is the thieves' "setter," who arranges when and where the robbery will occur.
9. Cheating.
1. Masks.
2. Fat face.
3. A pun: the coin called a "royal" was worth ten shillings. "Stand for" also puns: it means both "represent" and "fight for."

not stand for ten shillings.

PRINCE. Well then, once in my days I'll be a madcap.

FAL. Why, that's well said.

PRINCE. Well, come what will, I'll tarry at home.

FAL. By the Lord, I'll be a traitor then, when thou art king.   125

PRINCE. I care not.

POINS. Sir John, I prithee leave the prince and me alone; I will
lay him down such reasons for this adventure that he shall go.

FAL. Well, God give thee the spirit of persuasion and him the
ears of profiting, that what thou speakest may move and what   130
he hears may be believed, that the true prince may, for recreation sake, prove a false thief; for the poor abuses of the time
want countenance.⁴ Farewell; you shall find me in Eastcheap.

PRINCE. Farewell, thou latter spring, farewell, Allhallown summer!⁵

     [⟨*Exit* FALSTAFF.⟩]⁶

POINS. Now, my good sweet honey lord, ride with us tomorrow;   135
I have a jest to execute that I cannot manage alone. Falstaff,
Bardolph, Peto, and Gadshill shall rob those men that we have
already waylaid; yourself and I will not be there, and when
they have the booty, if you and I do not rob them, cut this
head off from my shoulders.   140

PRINCE. How shall we part with them in setting forth?

POINS. Why, we will set forth before or after them, and appoint
them a place of meeting, wherein it is at our pleasure to fail,
and then will they adventure upon the exploit themselves,
which they shall have no sooner achieved but we'll set upon   145
them.

PRINCE. Yea, but 'tis like that they will know us by our horses, by
our habits,⁷ and by every other appointment to be ourselves.

POINS. Tut, our horses they shall not see—I'll tie them in the
wood; our vizards we will change after we leave them: and,   150
sirrah, I have cases of buckram for the nonce,⁸ to immask our
noted outward garments.

PRINCE. Yea, but I doubt they will be too hard for us.

POINS. Well, for two of them, I know them to be as true-bred
cowards as ever turned back; and for the third, if he fight   155
longer than he sees reason, I'll forswear arms. The virtue of this
jest will be the incomprehensible lies that this same fat rogue
will tell us when we meet at supper: how thirty at least he
fought with; what wards,⁹ what blows, what extremities he endured; and in the reproof of this lies the jest.   160

PRINCE. Well, I'll go with thee. Provide us all things necessary

---

4. A satirical reference to the common
complaint that the nobility did not
properly give "countenance" to (i.e.,
encourage) good causes, and to the
Puritan habit of attacking the "abuses
of the time." This entire speech parodies the language of the Puritans.
5. I.e., Indian summer. The two epithets are intended to suggest how unseasonable it is for Falstaff, an old
man, to be engaged in youthful, hood-

lum exploits.
6. This stage direction, like some others
in the play, does not appear in the
earliest editions; it was added by a
later editor. All such interpolated directions are indicated in our text by
the special brackets used here.
7. Clothes.
8. I.e., outer clothes (of a coarse, stiff
cloth) for the occasion.
9. Guards in fencing.

and meet me tomorrow night[1] in Eastcheap; there I'll sup.
Farewell.

POINS. Farewell, my lord. [*Exit* POINS.]

PRINCE. I know you all, and will awhile uphold   165
The unyoked humor[2] of your idleness;
Yet herein will I imitate the sun,
Who doth permit the base contagious clouds
To smother up his beauty from the world,
That, when he please again to be himself,   170
Being wanted, he may be more wondered at
By breaking through the foul and ugly mists
Of vapors that did seem to strangle him.
If all the year were playing holidays,
To sport would be as tedious as to work;   175
But when they seldom come, they wished for come,
And nothing pleaseth but rare accidents.
So, when this loose behavior I throw off
And pay the debt I never promiséd,
By how much better than my word I am,   180
By so much shall I falsify men's hopes,
And like bright metal on a sullen ground,[3]
My reformation, glittering o'er my fault,
Shall show more goodly and attract more eyes
Than that which hath no foil[4] to set it off.   185
I'll so offend to make offense a skill,[5]
Redeeming time when men think least I will. [*Exit.*]

SCENE 3

[*Enter the* KING, NORTHUMBERLAND, WORCESTER, HOT-
SPUR, SIR WALTER BLUNT, *with others.*]

KING. My blood hath been too cold and temperate,
Unapt to stir at these indignities,
And you have found me,[6] for accordingly
You tread upon my patience; but be sure
I will from henceforth rather be myself,   5
Mighty and to be feared, than my condition,[7]
Which hath been smooth as oil, soft as young down,
And therefore lost that title of respect
Which the proud soul ne'er pays but to the proud.

WOR. Our house, my sovereign liege, little deserves   10
The scourge of greatness to be used on it,

---

1. Either the text should read "to-night" (before the robbery) or else Shakespeare intends to show Prince Hal's mind intent, not on the robbery, but on its aftermath. The soliloquy of the Prince that follows has provoked much critical discussion. Read psychologically, it makes Hal seem like a prig and a self-conscious schemer, but this surely was not Shakespeare's intention. Rather, the speech belongs to the old dramatic convention in which the speaker steps out of character for a moment to deliver a message from the playwright to the audience.
2. Undisciplined whim.
3. Dull background.
4. I.e., contrast.
5. Piece of good policy. "Redeeming time": making good use of time, following the advice given to Christians in a non-Christian world. See Ephesians v.16.
6. Discovered this to be true.
7. Disposition.

And that same greatness too which our own hands
Have holp[8] to make so portly.
NORTH. My lord—
KING. Worcester, get thee gone, for I do see   15
  Danger and disobedience in thine eye;
  O, sir, your presence is too bold and peremptory,
  And majesty might never yet endure
  The moody frontier of a servant brow.[9]
  You have good leave to leave us; when we need   20
  Your use and counsel we shall send for you.   [*Exit* WOR.]
  You were about to speak.   [⟨*to* NORTH.⟩]
NORTH.   Yea, my good lord.
  Those prisoners in your highness' name demanded,
  Which Harry Percy here at Holmedon took,
  Were, as he says, not with such strength denied   25
  As is delivered to your majesty.
  Either envy therefore or misprisión[1]
  Is guilty of this fault, and not my son.
HOT. My liege, I did deny no prisoners.
  But I remember, when the fight was done,   30
  When I was dry with rage and extreme toil,
  Breathless and faint, leaning upon my sword,
  Came there a certain lord, neat and trimly dressed,
  Fresh as a bridegroom, and his chin new reaped
  Showed like a stubble-land at harvest-home;   35
  He was perfuméd like a milliner,[2]
  And 'twixt his finger and his thumb he held
  A pouncet box,[3] which ever and anon
  He gave his nose and took 't away again;
  Who therewith angry, when it next came there,   40
  Took it in snuff;[4] and still he smiled and talked,
  And as the soldiers bore dead bodies by,
  He called them untaught knaves, unmannerly,
  To bring a slovenly[5] unhandsome corse
  Betwixt the wind and his nobility.   45
  With many holiday and lady terms[6]
  He questioned me; amongst the rest, demanded
  My prisoners in your majesty's behalf.
  I then, all smarting with my wounds being cold,
  To be so pestered with a popinjay,[7]   50
  Out of my grief and my impatience
  Answered neglectingly I know not what,
  He should, or he should not; for he made me mad
  To see him shine so brisk and smell so sweet

8. Helped; "portly": stately.
9. I.e., a servant's brow showing defiance, like a fortification ("frontier").
1. "Envy": malice; "misprision": mistake.
2. Not a maker of hats, but a dealer in perfumes, women's gloves, etc.
3. Perfume box.
4. I.e., was annoyed at it, with a pun on "snuffing it up."
5. Nasty, disgusting; "corse": corpse, body.
6. Affected and effeminate language (not "everyday" English).
7. Parrot.

And talk so like a waiting-gentlewoman   55
Of guns and drums and wounds—God save the mark!—
And telling me the sovereign'st thing on earth
Was parmaceti[8] for an inward bruise,
And that it was great pity, so it was,
This villanous saltpeter[9] should be digged   60
Out of the bowels of the harmless earth,
Which many a good tall[1] fellow had destroyed
So cowardly, and but for these vile guns
He would himself have been a soldier.
This bald[2] unjointed chat of his, my lord,   65
I answered indirectly as I said,
And I beseech you, let not his report
Come current[3] for an accusation
Betwixt my love and your high majesty.

BLUNT. The circumstance considered, good my lord,   70
  Whate'er Lord Harry Percy then had said
  To such a person and in such a place,
  At such a time, with all the rest retold,
  May reasonably die and never rise
  To do him wrong or any way impeach   75
  What then he said, so he unsay it now.

KING. Why, yet[4] he doth deny his prisoners,
  But with proviso and exception,
  That we at our own charge shall ransom straight
  His brother-in-law, the foolish Mortimer,   80
  Who, on my soul, hath willfully betrayed
  The lives of those that he did lead to fight
  Against that great magician, damned Glendower,
  Whose daughter, as we hear, the Earl of March
  Hath lately married. Shall our coffers then   85
  Be emptied to redeem a traitor home?
  Shall we buy treason? and indent with fears,[5]
  When they have lost and forfeited themselves?
  No, on the barren mountains let him starve;
  For I shall never hold that man my friend   90
  Whose tongue shall ask me for one penny cost
  To ransom home revolted Mortimer.

HOT. Revolted Mortimer!
  He never did fall off, my sovereign liege,
  But by the chance of war. To prove that true   95
  Needs no more but one tongue for all those wounds,
  Those mouthéd wounds[6] which valiantly he took
  When on the gentle Severn's sedgy bank
  In single opposition, hand to hand,

---

8. Spermaceti, whale oil used as an ointment.
9. Used in gunpowder.
1. Brave.
2. Trivial. "Indirectly": negligently.
3. Be considered valid.
4. I.e., even after all this (the strong use of "yet"). "But": except.

5. Enter into a contract with cowards.
6. Wounds are often likened to mouths in Shakespeare. The image may derive from their appearance and from the idea that they could speak as witnesses to what caused them. Cf. *Julius Caesar* III.ii.229–31 and *Richard III* I.ii. 55–56.

He did confound the best part of an hour 100
In changing hardiment[7] with great Glendower;
Three times they breathed[8] and three times did they drink
Upon agreement of swift Severn's flood,
Who then, affrighted with their bloody looks,
Ran fearfully among the trembling reeds, 105
And hid his crisp[9] head in the hollow bank
Bloodstainéd with these valiant combatants.
Never did bare and rotten policy[1]
Color her working with such deadly wounds,
Nor never could the noble Mortimer 110
Receive so many, and all willingly;
Then let not him be slandered with revolt.

KING. Thou dost belie him, Percy, thou dost belie him;
He never did encounter with Glendower.
I tell thee, 115
He durst as well have met the devil alone
As Owen Glendower for an enemy.
Art thou not ashamed? But, sirrah,[2] henceforth
Let me not hear you speak of Mortimer;
Send me your prisoners with the speediest means, 120
Or you shall hear in such a kind from me
As will displease you. My Lord Northumberland,
We license your departure with your son.
Send us your prisoners, or you will hear of it.
    [*Exeunt* KING, ⟨BLUNT, *and train.*⟩]

HOT. An if the devil come and roar for them 125
I will not send them; I will after straight
And tell him so, for I will ease my heart
Albeit I make a hazard of my head.

NORTH. What, drunk with choler?[3] stay and pause awhile.
Here comes your uncle.
    [*Enter* WORCESTER.]

HOT.   Speak of Mortimer! 130
Zounds, I will speak of him, and let my soul
Want mercy if I do not join with him;
Yea, on his part[4] I'll empty all these veins,
And shed my dear blood drop by drop in the dust,
But I will lift the downtrod Mortimer 135
As high in the air as this unthankful king,
As this ingrate and cankered[5] Bolingbroke.

NORTH. Brother, the king hath made your nephew mad.

WOR. Who struck this heat up after I was gone?

HOT. He will, forsooth, have all my prisoners; 140
And when I urged the ransom once again
Of my wife's brother, then his check looked pale,
And on my face he turned an eye of death,

7. Testing prowess and exchanging blows. "Confound": spend.
8. Paused for breath.
9. I.e., curly (because of the waves).
1. Craftiness or conspiracy; "color": disguise.
2. A form of "Sir," but used familiarly, and sometimes, as here, with a tone of contempt. "Speak of": i.e., even mention (an emphatic sense of "speak").
3. Anger.
4. Behalf.
5. Ungrateful and malignant.

Trembling even at the name of Mortimer.

wor. I cannot blame him; was not he proclaimed   145
  By Richard, that dead is, the next of blood?

north. He was—I heard the proclamation;
  And then it was when the unhappy king
  (Whose wrongs in us God pardon![6]) did set forth
  Upon his Irish expeditión;   150
  From whence he intercepted did return
  To be deposed and shortly murderéd.

wor. And for whose death we in the world's wide mouth
  Live scandalized and foully spoken of.

hot. But soft, I pray you; did King Richard then   155
  Proclaim my brother[7] Edmund Mortimer
  Heir to the crown?

north.   He did; myself did hear it.

hot. Nay, then I cannot blame his cousin king
  That wished him on the barren mountains starve.
  But shall it be that you, that set the crown   160
  Upon the head of this forgetful man
  And for his sake wear the detested blot
  Of murderous subornation[8]—shall it be
  That you a world of curses undergo,
  Being the agents, or base second means,[9]   165
  The cords, the ladder, or the hangman rather?
  O pardon me that I descend so low
  To show the line and the predicament
  Wherein you range[1] under this subtle king!
  Shall it for shame be spoken in these days,   170
  Or fill up chronicles in time to come,
  That men of your nobility and power
  Did gage[2] them both in an unjust behalf,
  As both of you—God pardon it!—have done,
  To put down Richard, that sweet lovely rose,   175
  And plant this thorn, this canker,[3] Bolingbroke?
  And shall it in more shame be further spoken,
  That you are fooled, discarded, and shook off
  By him for whom these shames ye underwent?
  No; yet time serves wherein you may redeem   180
  Your banished honors and restore yourselves
  Into the good thoughts of the world again,
  Revenge the jeering and disdained[4] contempt
  Of this proud king, who studies day and night
  To answer all the debt he owes to you   185
  Even with the bloody payment of your deaths:
  Therefore, I say—

wor.   Peace, cousin, say no more;
  And now I will unclasp a secret book,

6. I.e., God pardon in us the wrongs we did to him.
7. Brother-in-law.
8. I.e., the stain of aiding and abetting murder.
9. Tools, helpers.
1. I.e., to show the position and the category (or class) in which you are placed.
2. Pledge; "behalf": cause.
3. "Canker" meant not only a wild rose but also a diseased spot (a cancer).
4. Disdainful.

And to your quick-conceiving discontents
I'll read you matter deep and dangerous,   190
As full of peril and adventurous spirit
As to o'er-walk a current roaring loud
On the unsteadfast footing of a spear.[5]

HOT. If he fall in, good night, or sink or swim;
Send danger from the east unto the west,   195
So honor cross it from the north to south,
And let them grapple; O, the blood more stirs
To rouse a lion than to start[6] a hare!

NORTH. Imagination of some great exploit
Drives him beyond the bounds of patience.   200

HOT. By heaven, methinks it were an easy leap
To pluck bright honor from the pale-faced moon,
Or dive into the bottom of the deep,
Where fathom line could never touch the ground,
And pluck up drownèd honor by the locks,   205
So he that doth redeem her thence might wear
Without corrival[7] all her dignities;
But out upon this half-faced fellowship![8]

WOR. He apprehends a world of figures[9] here,
But not the form of what he should attend.   210
Good cousin, give me audience for a while.

HOT. I cry you mercy.

WOR.   Those same noble Scots
That I have prisoners—

HOT.   I'll keep them all;
By God, he shall not have a Scot of them;
No, if a Scot would save his soul he shall not.   215
I'll keep them, by this hand.

WOR.   You start away
And lend no ear unto my purposes.
Those prisoners you shall keep.

HOT.   Nay, I will; that's flat.
He said he would not ransom Mortimer,
Forbade my tongue to speak of Mortimer,   220
But I will find him when he lies asleep,
And in his ear I'll holla "Mortimer!"
Nay,
I'll have a starling shall be taught to speak[1]
Nothing but "Mortimer," and give it him   225
To keep his anger still in motion.

WOR. Hear you, cousin, a word.

HOT. All studies here I solemnly defy,
Save how to gall[2] and pinch this Bolingbroke;
And that same sword-and-buckler[3] Prince of Wales,   230
But that I think his father loves him not

---

5. A spear laid down as a foot-bridge.
6. Arouse, in hunting.
7. Rival.
8. Miserable sharing (of honor) with someone else.
9. Rhetorical figures of speech.

1. Starlings used to be taught to speak, as parrots are now.
2. Irritate.
3. Weapons used not by gentlemen but by servants or rustic clowns.

And would be glad he met with some mischance,
I would have him poisoned with a pot of ale.[4]
WOR. Farewell, kinsman; I'll talk to you
When you are better tempered to attend.   235
NORTH. Why, what a wasp-stung and impatient fool
Art thou to break into this woman's mood,
Tying thine ear to no tongue but thine own!
HOT. Why, look you, I am whipped and scourged with rods,
Nettled and stung with pismires,[5] when I hear   240
Of this vile politician Bolingbroke.
In Richard's time—what do you call the place?—
A plague upon it, it is in Gloucestershire—
'Twas where the madcap duke his uncle kept,[6]
His uncle York, where I first bowed my knee   245
Unto this king of smiles, this Bolingbroke—
'Sblood!—
When you and he came back from Ravenspurgh.
NORTH. At Berkeley castle.
HOT. You say true.   250
Why, what a candy deal of courtesy
This fawning greyhound[7] then did proffer me!
"Look when his infant fortune came to age,"
And "gentle Harry Percy," and "kind cousin";
O, the devil take such cozeners![8] God forgive me!   255
Good uncle, tell your tale; I have done.
WOR. Nay, if you have not, to it again;
We will stay your leisure.
HOT.   I have done, i' faith.
WOR. Then once more to your Scottish prisoners.
Deliver them up without their ransom straight,   260
And make the Douglas' son your only mean
For powers in Scotland, which, for divers reasons
Which I shall send you written, be assured
Will easily be granted. You, my lord, [⟨*to* NORTHUMBERLAND⟩]
Your son in Scotland being thus employed,   265
Shall secretly into the bosom creep
Of that same noble prelate well beloved,
The archbishop.
HOT. Of York, is it not?
WOR. True; who bears hard   270
His brother's death at Bristol, the Lord Scroop.
I speak not this in estimation,[9]
As what I think might be, but what I know
Is ruminated, plotted, and set down,
And only stays but to behold the face   275
Of that occasion that shall bring it on.

4. The drink of the lower classes.
5. Ants.
6. Lived.
7. A complex image which occurs· in Shakespeare several times (cf. *Hamlet* III.ii.65–67 and *Antony and Cleopatra* IV.xii.20–23). The idea of fawning or flattery called up to Shakespeare's mind the image of a dog begging for sweet-meats ("candy").
8. Cheaters, with of course a pun on the word "cousin."
9. I.e., guessing.

HOT. I smell it; upon my life, it will do well.

NORTH. Before the game is afoot, thou still let'st slip.[1]

HOT. Why, it cannot choose but be a noble plot;
    And then the power of Scotland and of York   280
    To join with Mortimer, ha?

WOR.   And so they shall.

HOT. In faith, it is exceedingly well aimed.

WOR. And 'tis no little reason bids us speed,
    To save our heads by raising of a head;[2]
    For, bear ourselves as even as we can,   285
    The king will always think him in our debt,
    And think we think ourselves unsatisfied,
    Till he hath found a time to pay us home;
    And see already how he doth begin
    To make us strangers to his looks of love.   290

HOT. He does, he does; we'll be revenged on him.

WOR. Cousin, farewell. No further go in this
    Than I by letters shall direct your course.
    When time is ripe, which will be suddenly,
    I'll steal to Glendower and Lord Mortimer,   295
    Where you and Douglas and our powers at once,
    As I will fashion it, shall happily meet,
    To bear our fortunes in our own strong arms,
    Which now we hold at much uncertainty.

NORTH. Farewell, good brother; we shall thrive, I trust.   300

HOT. Uncle, adieu; O, let the hours be short
    Till fields and blows and groans applaud our sport!   [*Exeunt.*]

Act II

SCENE 1

[*Enter a* CARRIER *with a lantern in his hand.*]

FIRST CAR. Heigh-ho! an it be not four by the day, I'll be hanged;
Charles' wain[3] is over the new chimney, and yet our horse not
packed. What, ostler!

OST. [*within*] Anon, anon.

FIRST CAR. I prithee, Tom, beat Cut's saddle,[4] put a few flocks 5
in the point; poor jade, is wrung in the withers out of all cess.[5]
    [*Enter another* CARRIER.]

SEC. CAR. Peas and beans are as dank here as a dog, and that is the
next way to give poor jades the bots;[6] this house is turned upside down since Robin Ostler died.

FIRST CAR. Poor fellow, never joyed since the price of oats rose; 10
it was the death of him.

SEC. CAR. I think this be the most villainous house in all London

1. An image from hunting. The meaning is: "You always ('still') release the
dogs before we are ready to pursue the
game."
2. Raising an army.
3. The constellation of the Great Bear
or Big Dipper.
4. The saddle was beaten to make it
soft; "Cut" is a name for a horse with
a docked tail. "Flocks in the point":
pieces of wool under the point of the
saddle.
5. I.e., is sore in the shoulders excessively.
6. I.e., that is the easiest way to give
poor nags worms in the stomach.

road for fleas; I am stung like a tench.[7]

FIRST CAR. Like a tench! by the mass, there is ne'er a king christen[8] could be better bit than I have been since the first cock. 15

SEC. CAR. Why, they will allow us ne'er a jordan, and then we leak in your chimney, and your chamber-lye breeds fleas like a loach.[9]

FIRST CAR. What, ostler! come away and be hanged, come away! 20

SEC. CAR. I have a gammon[1] of bacon and two razes of ginger, to be delivered as far as Charing Cross.

FIRST CAR. God's body! the turkeys in my pannier[2] are quite starved. What, ostler! A plague on thee, hast thou never an eye in thy head? canst not hear? An 'twere not as good deed as 25 drink to break the pate on thee, I am a very villain. Come and be hanged! hast no faith in thee?

　　　[*Enter* GADSHILL.]

GADS. Good morrow, carriers. What's o'clock?

FIRST CAR. I think it be two o'clock.

GADS. I prithee lend me thy lantern to see my gelding in the 30 stable.

FIRST CAR. Nay, by God, soft; I know a trick worth two of that, i' faith.

GADS. I pray thee lend me thine.

SEC. CAR. Aye, when? canst tell?[3] Lend me thy lantern, quoth 35 he? marry, I'll see thee hanged first.

GADS. Sirrah carrier, what time do you mean to come to London?

SEC. CAR. Time enough to go to bed with a candle, I warrant thee. Come, neighbor Mugs, we'll call up the gentlemen; they will along with company, for they have great charge.[4] 40

　　　[*Exeunt* ⟨CARRIERS.⟩]

GADS. What ho! chamberlain!

CHAM. [*within*] At hand, quoth pickpurse.

GADS. That's even as fair as At hand, quoth the chamberlain, for thou variest no more from picking of purses than giving direction[5] doth from laboring; thou layest the plot how. 45

　　　[*Enter* CHAMBERLAIN.]

CHAM. Good morrow, Master Gadshill. It holds current[6] that I told you yesternight; there's a franklin[7] in the weald of Kent hath brought three hundred marks with him in gold—I heard him tell it to one of his company last night at supper—a kind of auditor,[8] one that hath abundance of charge too, God 50 knows what. They are up already and call for eggs and butter;

---

7. A fish covered with red spots, like fleabites.
8. Christian king.
9. "Jordan": chamber pot; "chamber-lye": urine. The "loach" is a fish which breeds prolifically.
1. Haunch; "razes": roots.
2. Basket.
3. A colloquial expression of contemptuous refusal.
4. Valuable cargo.
5. A pun: "giving direction" means

supervising, as contrasted with "laboring," but it was also the name for informing thieves about the journeys of prospective victims (laying "the plot how").
6. Remains true.
7. A freeholder, just below a gentleman in rank. "Weald of Kent": a section of that county, formerly wooded.
8. Revenue officer; "abundance of charge": considerable property.

they will away presently.[9]

GADS. Sirrah, if they meet not with Saint Nicholas' clerks,[1] I'll give thee this neck.

CHAM. No, I'll none of it; I pray thee, keep that for the hang- 55
man, for I know thou worshipest Saint Nicholas as truly as a man of falsehood may.

GADS. What talkest thou to me of the hangman? if I hang, I'll make a fat pair of gallows; for if I hang, old Sir John hangs with me, and thou knowest he is no starveling. Tut! there are 60 other Trojans[2] that thou dreamest not of, the which for sport sake are content to do the profession some grace, that would, if matters should be looked into, for their own credit sake make all whole. I am joined with no foot land-rakers,[3] no long-staff sixpenny strikers, none of these mad mustachio purple- 65 hued maltworms,[4] but with nobility and tranquility, burgo-masters and great oneyers, such as can hold in, such as will strike sooner than speak, and speak sooner than drink, and drink sooner than pray; and yet, zounds, I lie, for they pray continually to their saint, the commonwealth, or rather, not 70 pray to her but prey on her, for they ride up and down on her and make her their boots.[5]

CHAM. What, the commonwealth their boots? will she hold out water in foul way?

GADS. She will, she will; justice hath liquored her. We steal as in 75 a castle, cocksure; we have the receipt of fern seed,[6] we walk invisible.

CHAM. Nay, by my faith, I think you are more beholding to the night than to fern seed for your walking invisible.

GADS. Give me thy hand; thou shalt have a share in our purchase,[7] 80 as I am a true man.

CHAM. Nay, rather let me have it, as you are a false thief.

GADS. Go to; *homo* is a common name to all men. Bid the ostler bring my gelding out of the stable. Farewell, you muddy[8] knave.

[*Exeunt.*]

SCENE 2

[*Enter* PRINCE *and* POINS.]

POINS. Come shelter, shelter; I have removed Falstaff's horse, and he frets like a gummed velvet.[9]

PRINCE. Stand close.

[*Enter* FALSTAFF.]

FAL. Poins! Poins, and be hanged! Poins!

PRINCE. Peace, ye fat-kidneyed rascal! what a brawling dost thou 5
keep!

FAL. Where's Poins, Hal?

9. At once.
1. Highwaymen.
2. Roisterers, good fellows.
3. Footpads; "sixpenny strikers": small-time thieves.
4. Flushed, swaggering barflies. "Oney-ers": dignitaries; "hold in": keep se-cret.
5. Booty.

6. I.e., we have the recipe for fern seed (supposed to make one invisible). "Liquored": greased.
7. Takings.
8. Muddle-headed.
9. Cheap velvet was treated with gum to make the pile stiff; as a result it soon fretted or wore away. "Stand close": hide.

PRINCE. He is walked up to the top of the hill; I'll go seek him.
> [⟨*He pretends to go, but hides onstage with* POINS.⟩]

FAL. I am accursed to rob in that thief's company; the rascal
hath removed my horse, and tied him I know not where. If 10
I travel but four foot by the squier[1] further afoot, I shall break
my wind. Well, I doubt not but to die a fair death for all this,
if I 'scape hanging for killing that rogue. I have forsworn his
company hourly any time this two and twenty years, and yet
I am bewitched with the rogue's company. If the rascal have 15
not given me medicines to make me love him, I'll be hanged;
it could not be else; I have drunk medicines. Poins! Hal! a
plague upon you both! Bardolph! Peto! I'll starve ere I'll rob
a foot further. An 'twere not as good a deed as drink to turn
true man and to leave these rogues, I am the veriest varlet 20
that ever chewed with a tooth. Eight yards of uneven ground
is threescore and ten miles afoot with me, and the stony-hearted
villains know it well enough; a plague upon it when thieves
cannot be true one to another! [*They whistle.*] Whew! A
plague upon you all! Give me my horse, you rogues; give me 25
my horse, and be hanged!

PRINCE. Peace, ye fat-guts! lie down; lay thine ear close to the
ground and list if thou canst hear the tread of travelers.

FAL. Have you any levers to lift me up again, being down?
'Sblood, I'll not bear my own flesh so far afoot again for all 30
the coin in thy father's exchequer. What a plague mean ye to
colt[2] me thus?

PRINCE. Thou liest; thou art not colted, thou art uncolted.

FAL. I prithee, good Prince, Hal, help me to my horse, good king's
son. 35

PRINCE. Out, ye rogue! shall I be your ostler?

FAL. Go hang thyself in thine own heir-apparent garters! If I be
ta'en, I'll peach for this. An I have not ballads made on you
all and sung to filthy tunes, let a cup of sack be my poison;
when a jest is so forward, and afoot too! I hate it. 40

> [*Enter* GADSHILL, ⟨BARDOLPH *and* PETO *with him.*⟩]

GADS. Stand.

FAL. So I do, against my will.

POINS. O, 'tis our setter; I know his voice. Bardolph, what news?

BARD. Case[3] ye, case ye, on with your vizards; there's money of
the king's coming down the hill; 'tis going to the king's ex- 45
chequer.

FAL. You lie, you rogue; 'tis going to the king's tavern.

GADS. There's enough to make us all.

FAL. To be hanged.

PRINCE. Sirs, you four shall front them in the narrow lane; Ned 50
Poins and I will walk lower; if they 'scape from your encounter,
then they light on us.

PETO. How many be there of them?

GADS. Some eight or ten.

FAL. Zounds, will they not rob us? 55

1. Ruler, yardstick.
2. Trick.
3. Mask.

PRINCE. What, a coward, Sir John Paunch?

FAL. Indeed, I am not John of Gaunt your grandfather, but yet no coward, Hal.

PRINCE. Well, we leave that to the proof.

POINS. Sirrah Jack, thy horse stands behind the hedge; when thou needest him, there thou shalt find him. Farewell, and stand fast. 60

FAL. Now cannot I strike him, if I should be hanged.

PRINCE. [⟨aside to POINS⟩] Ned, where are our disguises?

POINS. [⟨aside⟩] Here, hard by; stand close. 65

[⟨Exeunt PRINCE and POINS.⟩]

FAL. Now, my masters, happy man be his dole,[4] say I; every man to his business.

[Enter the TRAVELERS.]

FIRST TRAV. Come, neighbor, the boy shall lead our horses down the hill; we'll walk afoot awhile, and ease our legs.

THIEVES. Stand! 70

TRAVELERS. Jesus bless us!

FAL. Strike; down with them; cut the villains' throats. Ah, whoreson caterpillars,[5] bacon-fed knaves, they hate us youth! Down with them, fleece them.

TRAVELERS. O, we are undone, both we and ours forever! 75

FAL. Hang ye, gorbellied[6] knaves, are ye undone? No, ye fat chuffs, I would your store were here! On, bacons, on! What, ye knaves, young men must live! You are grand jurors, are ye? we'll jure ye, faith.

[Here they rob them and bind them. Exeunt.]
[Enter the PRINCE and POINS.]

PRINCE. The thieves have bound the true men. Now could thou and I rob the thieves and go merrily to London; it would be argument[7] for a week, laughter for a month, and a good jest forever. 80

POINS. Stand close; I hear them coming.

[Enter the THIEVES again.]

FAL. Come, my masters, let us share, and then to horse before day. An the Prince and Poins be not two arrant cowards, there's no equity stirring;[8] there's no more valor in that Poins than in a wild duck. 85

PRINCE. Your money!

POINS. Villains!

[As they are sharing, the PRINCE and POINS set upon them; they all run away; and FALSTAFF, after a blow or two, runs away too, leaving the booty behind them.] 90

PRINCE. Got with much ease. Now merrily to horse;
The thieves are all scattered and possessed with fear
So strongly that they dare not meet each other;
Each takes his fellow for an officer.
Away, good Ned. Falstaff sweats to death, 95

4. I.e., good luck!
5. "Caterpillars of the commonwealth" was a common phrase, referring to rogues. Falstaff here applies ridiculously inappropriate terms to the travelers
and to himself (e.g., "youth").
6. Fat; "chuffs": misers.
7. Subject of stories.
8. There's no justice.

And lards the lean earth as he walks along;
Were 't not for laughing, I should pity him.

POINS. How the rogue roared!   [*Exeunt.*]

SCENE 3

[*Enter* HOTSPUR, *alone, reading a letter.*]

HOT. "But for mine own part, my lord, I could be well contented
to be there, in respect of the love I bear your house." "He
could be contented"; why is he not, then? "In respect of the
love he bears our house," he shows in this, he loves his own
barn better than he loves our house. Let me see some more. 5
"The purpose you undertake is dangerous." Why, that's certain. 'Tis dangerous to take a cold, to sleep, to drink; but I tell
you, my lord fool, out of this nettle, danger, we pluck this
flower, safety. "The purpose you undertake is dangerous, the
friends you have named uncertain, the time itself unsorted,⁹ 10
and your whole plot too light for the counterpoise of so great
an opposition." Say you so, say you so? I say unto you again,
you are a shallow cowardly hind,¹ and you lie. What a lack-
brain is this! By the Lord, our plot is a good plot as ever was
laid, our friends true and constant; a good plot, good friends, 15
and full of expectation; an excellent plot, very good friends.
What a frosty-spirited rogue is this! Why, my lord of York²
commends the plot and the general course of the action.
Zounds, an I were now by this rascal I could brain him with
his lady's fan. Is there not my father, my uncle, and myself? 20
Lord Edmund Mortimer, my lord of York, and Owen Glendower? is there not besides the Douglas? have I not all their
letters to meet me in arms by the ninth of the next month, and
are they not some of them set forward already? What a pagan
rascal is this, an infidel! Ha! you shall see now in very sincerity 25
of fear and cold heart, will he to the king and lay open all our
proceedings. O, I could divide myself and go to buffets,³ for
moving such a dish of skim milk with so honorable an action!
Hang him! let him tell the king. We are prepared; I will set
forward tonight. 30

[*Enter his* LADY.]

How now, Kate! I must leave you within these two hours.

LADY. O, my good lord, why are you thus alone?
For what offense have I this fortnight been
A banished woman from my Harry's bed?
Tell me, sweet lord, what is 't that takes from thee 35
Thy stomach,⁴ pleasure, and thy golden sleep?
Why dost thou bend thine eyes upon the earth,
And start so often when thou sit'st alone?
Why hast thou lost the fresh blood in thy cheeks,
And given my treasures and my rights of thee 40
To thick-eyed musing and cursed melancholy?
In thy faint slumbers I by thee have watched
And heard thee murmur tales of iron wars,

9. Unsuitable.
1. Peasant.
2. The Archbishop of York.

3. Split myself in two and let the parts
fight each other; "moving": urging.
4. Appetite.

Speak terms of manage[5] to thy bounding steed,
Cry "Courage! to the field!" And thou hast talked   45
Of sallies and retires, of trenches, tents,
Of palisadoes, frontiers, parapets,
Of basilisks, of cannon, culverin,[6]
Of prisoners' ransom and of soldiers slain,
And all the currents of a heady fight.   50
Thy spirit within thee hath been so at war
And thus hath so bestirred thee in thy sleep
That beads of sweat have stood upon thy brow
Like bubbles in a late-disturbéd stream,
And in thy face strange motions have appeared   55
Such as we see when men restrain their breath
On some great sudden hest.[7] O, what portents are these?
Some heavy business hath my lord in hand
And I must know it, else he loves me not.

HOT. What, ho!
         [⟨*Enter* SERVANT.⟩]
                  Is Gilliams with the packet gone?   60
SERV. He is, my lord, an hour ago.
HOT. Hath Butler brought those horses from the sheriff?
SERV. One horse, my lord, he brought even now.
HOT. What horse? a roan, a crop-ear, is it not?
SERV. It is, my lord.
HOT.   That roan shall be my throne.   65
  Well, I will back[7a] him straight; O Esperance![8]
  Bid Butler lead him forth into the park.   [⟨*Exit* SERVANT.⟩]
LADY. But hear you, my lord.
HOT. What say'st thou, my lady?
LADY. What is it carries you away?
HOT. Why, my horse, my love, my horse.   70
LADY. Out, you mad-headed ape!
  A weasel hath not such a deal of spleen[9]
  As you are tossed with. In faith
  I'll know your business, Harry, that I will.
  I fear my brother Mortimer doth stir   75
  About his title, and hath sent for you
  To line[1] his enterprise; but if you go—
HOT. So far afoot, I shall be weary, love.
LADY. Come, come, you paraquito, answer me   80
  Directly unto this question that I ask;
  In faith, I'll break thy little finger, Harry,
  An if thou wilt not tell me all things true.
HOT. Away,
  Away, you trifler! Love! I love thee not,   85

5. Horsemanship.
6. Three kinds of artillery (named here in decreasing order of weight).
7. Command.
7a. Mount.
8. The battle cry of the Percies: "Hope!"
9. The spleen was supposed to be the source of sudden and violent emotions; the weasel was considered a very impetuous animal.
1. Support.

I care not for thee, Kate; this is no world
To play with mammets and to tilt with lips;
We must have bloody noses and cracked crowns,[2]
And pass them current too. God's me, my horse!
What say'st thou, Kate? what wouldst thou have with me?   90
LADY. Do you not love me? do you not, indeed?
  Well, do not then, for since you love me not
  I will not love myself. Do you not love me?
  Nay, tell me if you speak in jest or no.
HOT. Come, wilt thou see me ride?   95
  And when I am o' horseback, I will swear
  I love thee infinitely. But hark you, Kate,
  I must not have you henceforth question me
  Whither I go, nor reason whereabout;
  Whither I must, I must; and, to conclude,   100
  This evening must I leave you, gentle Kate.
  I know you wise, but yet no farther wise
  Than Harry Percy's wife; constant you are,
  But yet a woman, and for secrecy
  No lady closer; for I well believe   105
  Thou wilt not utter what thou dost not know,
  And so far will I trust thee, gentle Kate.
LADY. How! so far?
HOT. Not an inch further. But hark you, Kate,
  Whither I go, thither shall you go too;   110
  Today will I set forth, tomorrow you.
  Will this content you, Kate?
LADY.   It must of force.   [*Exeunt.*]

SCENE 4

[*Enter the* PRINCE *and* POINS.]

PRINCE. Ned, prithee come out of that fat[3] room, and lend me
  thy hand to laugh a little.
POINS. Where hast been, Hal?
PRINCE. With three or four loggerheads[4] amongst three or fourscore hogsheads. I have sounded the very bass string of humil-   5
  ity. Sirrah, I am sworn brother to a leash of drawers,[5] and can
  call them all by their christen names, as Tom, Dick, and Francis. They take it already upon their salvation, that though I be
  but Prince of Wales, yet I am the king of courtesy, and tell me
  flatly I am no proud Jack, like Falstaff, but a Corinthian,[6] a lad   10
  of mettle, a good boy—by the Lord, so they call me—and when
  I am king of England I shall command all the good lads in
  Eastcheap. They call drinking deep, dyeing scarlet, and when
  you breathe in your watering[7] they cry "hem!" and bid you
  play it off. To conclude, I am so good a proficient in one quar-   15
  ter of an hour that I can drink with any tinker in his own lan-

2. Broken heads, with a pun on
"crowns" as coins. "Mammets": breasts.
3. Vat. This establishes that the scene is
a tavern.

4. Blockheads.
5. Group of tapsters, waiters.
6. Good fellow.
7. Drinking.

guage during my life. I tell thee, Ned, thou hast lost much
honor, that thou wert not with me in this action. But, sweet
Ned—to sweeten which name of Ned, I give thee this pennyworth of sugar, clapped even now into my hand by an under-
skinker,[8] one that never spake other English in his life than
"Eight shillings and sixpence," and "You are welcome," with
this shrill addition, "Anon, anon, sir! Score a pint of bastard
in the Half-Moon,"[9] or so. But, Ned, to drive away the time
till Falstaff come, I prithee do thou stand in some by-room,
while I question my puny drawer to what end he gave me the
sugar, and do thou never leave calling "Francis," that his tale
to me may be nothing but "Anon." Step aside, and I'll show
thee a precedent.

POINS. Francis!

PRINCE. Thou art perfect.

POINS. Francis! [⟨*Exit* POINS.⟩]

[*Enter* DRAWER.]

FRAN. Anon, anon, sir. Look down into the Pomgarnet,[1] Ralph.

PRINCE. Come hither, Francis.

FRAN. My lord?

PRINCE. How long hast thou to serve,[2] Francis?

FRAN. Forsooth, five years, and as much as to—

POINS. [*within*] Francis!

FRAN. Anon, anon, sir.

PRINCE. Five year! by'r Lady, a long lease for the clinking of
pewter. But, Francis, darest thou be so valiant as to play the
coward with thy indenture and show it a fair pair of heels and
run from it?

FRAN. O Lord, sir, I'll be sworn upon all the books in England, I
could find in my heart—

POINS. [*within*] Francis!

FRAN. Anon, sir.

PRINCE. How old art thou, Francis?

FRAN. Let me see—about Michaelmas next I shall be—

POINS. [*within*] Francis!

FRAN. Anon, sir. Pray stay a little, my lord.

PRINCE. Nay, but hark you, Francis: for the sugar thou gavest
me, 'twas a pennyworth, was't not?

FRAN. O Lord, I would it had been two!

PRINCE. I will give thee for it a thousand pound; ask me when
thou wilt, and thou shalt have it.

POINS. [*within*] Francis!

FRAN. Anon, anon.

PRINCE. Anon, Francis? No, Francis, but tomorrow, Francis; or
Francis, o' Thursday, or indeed, Francis, when thou wilt. But,

Francis!

FRAN. My lord?

PRINCE. Wilt thou rob this leathern-jerkin,[3] crystal-button, not-pated, agate-ring, puke-stocking, caddis-garter, smooth-tongue, Spanish-pouch—   65

FRAN. O Lord, sir, who do you mean?

PRINCE. Why, then, your brown bastard is your only drink, for look you, Francis, your white canvas doublet will sully. In Barbary, sir, it cannot come to so much.[4]

FRAN. What, sir?   70

POINS. [*within*] Francis!

PRINCE. Away, you rogue, dost thou not hear them call?
      [*Here they both call him; the drawer stands amazed, not knowing which way to go.*]
      [*Enter* VINTNER.]

VINT. What, stand'st thou still, and hear'st such a calling? Look to the guests within. [*Exit* FRANCIS.] My lord, old Sir John with half-a-dozen more are at the door; shall I let them in?   75

PRINCE. Let them alone awhile, and then open the door. [*Exit* VINTNER.] Poins!
      [*Enter* POINS.]

POINS. Anon, anon, sir.

PRINCE. Sirrah, Falstaff and the rest of the thieves are at the door; shall we be merry?   80

POINS. As merry as crickets, my lad. But hark ye, what cunning match have you made with this jest of the drawer? come, what's the issue?

PRINCE. I am now of all humors[5] that have showed themselves humors since the old days of goodman Adam to the pupil[6] age   85
of this present twelve o'clock at midnight.
      [⟨*Enter* FRANCIS.⟩]
      What's o'clock, Francis?

FRAN. Anon, anon, sir.   [⟨*Exit.*⟩]

PRINCE. That ever this fellow should have fewer words than a parrot, and yet the son of a woman! His industry is upstairs   90
and downstairs, his eloquence the parcel[7] of a reckoning. I am not yet of Percy's mind, the Hotspur of the north, he that kills me some six or seven dozen of Scots at a breakfast, washes his hands, and says to his wife "Fie upon this quiet life! I want work." "O my sweet Harry," says she, "how many hast thou   95
killed today?" "Give my roan horse a drench," says he, and answers "Some fourteen," an hour after, "a trifle, a trifle." I prithee, call in Falstaff; I'll play Percy, and that damned brawn shall play Dame Mortimer his wife. "Rivo!"[8] says the drunkard. Call in ribs, call in tallow.   100
      [*Enter* FALSTAFF, ⟨GADSHILL, BARDOLPH, *and* PETO, FRAN-

---

3. Leather-jacketed; "not-pated": with short hair; "puke": dark gray; "caddis": worsted tape.
4. Deliberate nonsense to confuse Francis, and one of the first instances of doubletalk in English literature.

5. Temperaments, dispositions.
6. Youthful.
7. Item.
8. Drink up!

cis *following with wine.*)]

POINS. Welcome, Jack; where hast thou been?

FAL. A plague of all cowards, I say, and a vengeance too, marry
and amen! Give me a cup of sack, boy. Ere I lead this life long,
I'll sew nether stocks[9] and mend them and foot them too. A
plague of all cowards! Give me a cup of sack, rogue. Is there no 105
virtue extant? [*He drinks.*]

PRINCE. Didst thou ever see Titan[1] kiss a dish of butter, pitiful-
hearted butter that melted at the sweet tale of the sun's? If
thou didst, then behold that compound.

FAL. You rogue, here's lime in this sack too;[2] there is nothing but 110
roguery to be found in villainous man, yet a coward is worse
than a cup of sack with lime in it. A villainous coward! Go thy
ways, old Jack, die when thou wilt; if manhood, good manhood,
be not forgot upon the face of the earth, then am I a shotten
herring.[3] There lives not three good men unhanged in Eng- 115
land, and one of them is fat and grows old. God help the while;
a bad world, I say. I would I were a weaver; I could sing psalms[4]
or anything. A plague of all cowards, I say still.

PRINCE. How now, woolsack, what mutter you?

FAL. A king's son! If I do not beat thee out of thy kingdom with 120
a dagger of lath, and drive all thy subjects afore thee like a flock
of wild geese, I'll never wear hair on my face more. You Prince
of Wales!

PRINCE. Why, you whoreson round man, what's the matter?

FAL. Are not you a coward? answer me to that; and Poins there? 125

POINS. Zounds, ye fat paunch, an ye call me coward, by the Lord
I'll stab thee.

FAL. I call thee coward! I'll see thee damned ere I call thee coward; but I would give a thousand pound I could run as fast as
thou canst. You are straight enough in the shoulders, you 130
care not who sees your back; call you that backing of your
friends? A plague upon such backing! give me them that will
face me. Give me a cup of sack; I am a rogue if I drunk today.

PRINCE. O villain! thy lips are scarce wiped since thou drunkest
last. 135

FAL. All's one for that. [*He drinks.*] A plague of all cowards, still
say I.

PRINCE. What's the matter?

FAL. What's the matter! there be four of us here have ta'en a
thousand pound this day morning. 140

PRINCE. Where is it, Jack? where is it?

FAL. Where is it? taken from us it is—a hundred upon poor four
of us.

PRINCE. What, a hundred, man?

FAL. I am a rogue if I were not at half-sword[5] with a dozen of 145
them two hours together. I have 'scaped by miracle. I am

9. Stockings.
1. The sun.
2. Lime was used to make wine sparkle.
3. A herring that has cast its spawn
and is lean.
4. Protestant weavers from Flanders
were notorious for singing psalms.
5. At half a sword's length.

eight times thrust through the doublet, four through the hose, my buckler cut through and through, my sword hacked like a handsaw—*ecce signum!*[6] I never dealt better since I was a man; all would not do. A plague of all cowards! Let them speak; if they speak more or less than truth, they are villains and the sons of darkness.

PRINCE. Speak, sirs; how was it?

GADS. We four set upon some dozen—

FAL. Sixteen at least, my lord.

GADS. And bound them.

PETO. No, no, they were not bound.

FAL. You rogue, they were bound, every man of them, or I am a Jew else, an Ebrew Jew.

GADS. As we were sharing, some six or seven fresh men set upon us—

FAL. And unbound the rest, and then come in the other.

PRINCE. What, fought you with them all?

FAL. All! I know not what you call all, but if I fought not with fifty of them, I am a bunch of radish; if there were not two or three and fifty upon poor old Jack, then am I no two-legged creature.

PRINCE. Pray God you have not murdered some of them.

FAL. Nay, that's past praying for; I have peppered two of them. Two I am sure I have paid, two rogues in buckram suits. I tell thee what, Hal, if I tell thee a lie, spit in my face, call me horse. Thou knowest my old ward;[7] here I lay, and thus I bore my point. Four rogues in buckram let drive at me—

PRINCE. What, four? thou saidst but two even now.

FAL. Four, Hal; I told thee four.

POINS. Aye, aye, he said four.

FAL. These four came all a-front, and mainly[8] thrust at me. I made me no more ado but took all their seven points in my target,[9] thus.

PRINCE. Seven? why, there were but four even now.

FAL. In buckram.

POINS. Aye, four, in buckram suits.

FAL. Seven, by these hilts, or I am a villain else.

PRINCE. Prithee, let him alone; we shall have more anon.

FAL. Dost thou hear me, Hal?

PRINCE. Aye, and mark thee too, Jack.

FAL. Do so, for it is worth the listening to. These nine in buckram that I told thee of—

PRINCE. So, two more already.

FAL. Their points being broken—

POINS. Down fell their hose.[1]

FAL. Began to give me ground; but I followed me close, came in foot and hand, and with a thought seven of the eleven I paid.

6. Here's the proof!
7. Defense; "here I lay": this was my stance.
8. Strongly.
9. Shield.
1. Poins puns on the other meaning of "points": the laces used to tie up trousers ("hose").

PRINCE. O monstrous! eleven buckram men grown out of two!

FAL. But, as the devil would have it, three misbegotten knaves 195 in Kendal green came at my back and let drive at me, for it was so dark, Hal, that thou couldst not see thy hand.

PRINCE. These lies are like their father that begets them—gross as a mountain, open, palpable. Why, thou clay-brained guts, thou knotty-pated fool, thou whoreson, obscene, greasy tallow- 200 catch²—

FAL. What, art thou mad? art thou mad? is not the truth the truth?

PRINCE. Why, how couldst thou know these men in Kendal green, when it was so dark thou couldst not see thy hand? come, tell 205 us your reason. What sayest thou to this?

POINS. Come, your reason, Jack, your reason.

FAL. What, upon compulsion? Zounds, an I were at the strappado,³ or all the racks in the world, I would not tell you on compulsion. Give you a reason on compulsion! if reasons⁴ 210 were as plentiful as blackberries, I would give no man a reason upon compulsion, I.

PRINCE. I'll be no longer guilty of this sin; this sanguine coward, this bed-presser, this horseback-breaker, this huge hill of flesh— 215

FAL. 'Sblood, you starveling, you eelskin, you dried neat's tongue, you bull's pizzle, you stockfish!⁵ O for breath to utter what is like thee! you tailor's yard, you sheath, you bow case, you vile standing-tuck⁶—

PRINCE. Well, breathe awhile, and then to it again; and when 220 thou hast tired thyself in base comparisons, hear me speak but this.

POINS. Mark, Jack.

PRINCE. We two saw you four set on four and bound them, and were masters of their wealth. Mark now, how a plain tale shall 225 put you down. Then did we two set on you four; and, with a word, outfaced you from your prize, and have it, yea, and can show it you here in the house; and, Falstaff, you carried your guts away as nimbly, with as quick dexterity, and roared for mercy and still run and roared, as ever I heard bullcalf. What a 230 slave art thou, to hack thy sword as thou hast done, and then say it was in fight! What trick, what device, what starting-hole,⁷ canst thou now find out to hide thee from this open and apparent shame?

POINS. Come, let's hear, Jack; what trick hast thou now? 235

FAL. By the Lord, I knew ye as well as he that made ye. Why, hear you, my masters: was it for me to kill the heir apparent? should I turn upon the true prince? why, thou knowest I am

---

2. Piece of tallow from which chandlers made candles.
3. A method of torture; "racks": another method.
4. A pun on the word "raisin," which was spelled and pronounced like "rea-son" in Elizabethan England.
5. I.e., you ox tongue, you bull's penis, you dried cod!
6. Stiff rapier.
7. Evasion.

as valiant as Hercules; but beware instinct; the lion will not touch the true prince.[8] Instinct is a great matter; I was now a coward on instinct. I shall think the better of myself and thee during my life; I for a valiant lion, and thou for a true prince. But, by the Lord, lads, I am glad you have the money. Hostess, clap to the doors; watch tonight, pray tomorrow. Gallants, lads, boys, hearts of gold, all the titles of good fellowship come to you! What, shall we be merry? shall we have a play extempore?

PRINCE. Content; and the argument[9] shall be thy running away.

FAL. Ah, no more of that, Hal, an thou lovest me!

[*Enter* HOSTESS.]

HOST. O Jesu, my lord the prince!

PRINCE. How now, my lady the hostess! what sayest thou to me?

HOST. Marry, my lord, there is a nobleman of the court at door would speak with you; he says he comes from your father.

PRINCE. Give him as much as will make him a royal[1] man, and send him back again to my mother.

FAL. What manner of man is he?

HOST. An old man.

FAL. What doth gravity out of his bed at midnight? Shall I give him his answer?

PRINCE. Prithee, do, Jack.

FAL. Faith, and I'll send him packing. [*Exit.*]

PRINCE. Now, sirs. By 'r Lady, you fought fair; so did you, Peto; so did you, Bardolph; you are lions too, you ran away upon instinct, you will not touch the true prince; no, fie!

BARD. Faith, I ran when I saw others run.

PRINCE. Faith, tell me now in earnest, how came Falstaff's sword so hacked?

PETO. Why, he hacked it with his dagger, and said he would swear truth out of England but he would make you believe it was done in fight, and persuaded us to do the like.

BARD. Yea, and to tickle our noses with speargrass to make them bleed, and then to beslubber our garments with it and swear it was the blood of true men. I did that I did not this seven year before, I blushed to hear his monstrous devices.

PRINCE. O villain, thou stolest a cup of sack eighteen years ago, and wert taken with the manner,[2] and ever since thou hast blushed extempore. Thou hadst fire[3] and sword on thy side, and yet thou rannest away; what instinct hadst thou for it?

BARD. My lord, do you see these meteors? do you behold these exhalations?

PRINCE. I do.

BARD. What think you they portend?

PRINCE. Hot livers and cold purses.[4]

8. In many medieval romances the lion, as king of beasts, shows respect for royalty.
9. Plot or story.
1. A "royal" was half of a pound sterling, a "noble" was a third.
2. In the act.
3. "Fire" and the allusions to "meteors" and "exhalations" (shooting stars) refer to Bardolph's red nose.
4. I.e., drunkenness and poverty.

BARD. Choler, my lord, if rightly taken.

PRINCE. No, if rightly taken, halter.   285

[*Enter* FALSTAFF.]

Here comes lean Jack, here comes bare-bone. How now, my
sweet creature of bombast,[5] how long is 't ago, Jack, since thou
sawest thine own knee?

FAL. My own knee! when I was about thy years, Hal, I was not
an eagle's talon in the waist; I could have crept into any alder- 290
man's thumb ring. A plague of sighing and grief—it blows a
man up like a bladder. There's villainous news abroad; here
was Sir John Bracy from your father; you must to the court
in the morning. That same mad fellow of the north, Percy, and
he of Wales, that gave Amamon[6] the bastinado and made 295
Lucifer cuckold and swore the devil his true liegeman upon the
cross of a Welsh hook[7]—what a plague call you him?

POINS. O, Glendower.

FAL. Owen, Owen, the same; and his son-in-law Mortimer, and
old Northumberland, and that sprightly Scot of Scots, Doug- 300
las, that runs o' horseback up a hill perpendicular—

PRINCE. He that rides at high speed and with his pistol kills a
sparrow flying.

FAL. You have hit it.

PRINCE. So did he never the sparrow.   305

FAL. Well, that rascal hath good mettle in him; he will not run.

PRINCE. Why, what a rascal art thou then, to praise him so for
running!

FAL. O' horseback, ye cuckoo; but afoot he will not budge a foot.

PRINCE. Yes, Jack, upon instinct.   310

FAL. I grant ye, upon instinct. Well, he is there too, and one
Mordake, and a thousand blue-caps[8] more. Worcester is stolen
away tonight; thy father's beard is turned white with the news;
you may buy land now as cheap as stinking mackerel.

PRINCE. Why then, it is like, if there come a hot June, and this 315
civil buffeting hold, we shall buy maidenheads as they buy
hobnails, by the hundreds.

FAL. By the mass, lad, thou sayest true; it is like we shall have
good trading that way. But tell me, Hal, art not thou horrible
afeard? thou being heir apparent, could the world pick thee 320
out three such enemies again as that fiend Douglas, that spirit
Percy, and that devil Glendower? Art thou not horribly afraid?
doth not thy blood thrill at it?

PRINCE. Not a whit, i' faith; I lack some of thy instinct.

FAL. Well, thou wilt be horribly chid tomorrow when thou com- 325
est to thy father; if thou love me, practice an answer.

PRINCE. Do thou stand for[9] my father and examine me upon the
particulars of my life.

FAL. Shall I? Content. This chair shall be my state,[1] this dagger

---

5. Padding, stuffing.
6. A devil. "Bastinado": a beating,
cudgelling.
7. A long spear with a hook on it.

8. Scots.
9. Represent.
1. Throne.

my scepter, and this cushion my crown. 330

PRINCE. Thy state is taken for a joint-stool,[2] thy golden scepter for a leaden dagger, and thy precious rich crown for a pitiful bald crown!

FAL. Well, an the fire of grace be not quite out of thee, now shalt thou be moved. Give me a cup of sack to make my eyes 335 look red, that it may be thought I have wept, for I must speak in passion, and I will do it in King Cambyses'[3] vein.

PRINCE. Well, here is my leg.[4]

FAL. And here is my speech. Stand aside, nobility.

HOST. O Jesu, this is excellent sport, i' faith! 340

FAL. Weep not, sweet queen, for trickling tears are vain.

HOST. O, the father, how he holds his countenance!

FAL. For God's sake, lords, convey my tristful queen,
For tears do stop the floodgates of her eyes.

HOST. O Jesu, he doth it as like one of these harlotry players as 345 ever I see!

FAL. Peace, good pint pot, peace, good ticklebrain. Harry, I do not only marvel where thou spendest thy time, but also how thou art accompanied, for though the camomile,[5] the more it is trodden on the faster it grows, so youth, the more it is 350 wasted the sooner it wears. That thou art my son, I have partly thy mother's word, partly my own opinion, but chiefly a villainous trick of thine eye and a foolish hanging of thy nether lip that doth warrant[6] me. If then thou be son to me, here lies the point; why, being son to me, art thou so pointed at? Shall 355 the blessed sun of heaven prove a micher[7] and eat blackberries? a question not to be asked. Shall the son of England prove a thief and take purses? a question to be asked. There is a thing, Harry, which thou hast often heard of and it is known to many in our land by the name of pitch. This pitch, as an- 360 cient writers do report, doth defile; so doth the company thou keepest: for, Harry, now I do not speak to thee in drink but in tears, not in pleasure but in passion, not in words only, but in woes also: and yet there is a virtuous man whom I have often noted in thy company, but I know not his name. 365

PRINCE. What manner of man, an it like your majesty?

FAL. A goodly portly man, i' faith, and a corpulent; of a cheerful look, a pleasing eye and a most noble carriage, and, as I think, his age some fifty, or, by 'r Lady, inclining to threescore; and now I remember me, his name is Falstaff. If that man should 370 be lewdly given, he deceiveth me, for, Harry, I see virtue in his looks. If then the tree may be known by the fruit, as the fruit by the tree, then, peremptorily I speak it, there is virtue in that Falstaff; him keep with, the rest banish. And tell me

2. An ordinary stool, made by a joiner (carpenter).
3. Like the bombastic hero of the old play *Cambyses*.
4. I.e., he bows, makes an obeisance.
5. An aromatic herb. The style in this speech is a parody of Euphuism, the ornate, elaborate, balanced style popular by Lyly's *Euphues*.
6. Assure.
7. Truant.

now, thou naughty varlet, tell me, where hast thou been this 375 month?

PRINCE. Dost thou speak like a king? Do thou stand for me, and I'll play my father.

FAL. Depose me? if thou dost it half so gravely, so majestically, both in word and matter, hang me up by the heels for a 380 rabbit-sucker[8] or a poulter's hare.

PRINCE. Well, here I am set.[9]

FAL. And here I stand; judge, my masters.

PRINCE. Now, Harry, whence come you?

FAL. My noble lord, from Eastcheap. 385

PRINCE. The complaints I hear of thee are grievous.

FAL. 'Sblood, my lord, they are false: nay, I'll tickle ye for a young prince, i' faith.

PRINCE. Swearest thou, ungracious boy? thenceforth ne'er look on me. Thou art violently carried away from grace; there is a 390 devil haunts thee in the likeness of an old fat man; a tun[1] of man is thy companion. Why dost thou converse with that trunk of humors, that bolting-hutch[2] of beastliness, that swollen parcel of dropsies, that huge bombard of sack, that stuffed cloak-bag of guts, that roasted Manningtree[3] ox with the pud- 395 ding in his belly, that reverend vice, that gray iniquity, that father ruffian, that vanity in years? Wherein is he good, but to taste sack and drink it? wherein neat and cleanly, but to carve a capon and eat it? wherein cunning, but in craft? wherein crafty, but in villainy? wherein villainous, but in all things? 400 wherein worthy, but in nothing?

FAL. I would your grace would take me with you; whom means your grace?

PRINCE. That villainous abominable misleader of youth, Falstaff, that old white-bearded Satan. 405

FAL. My lord, the man I know.

PRINCE. I know thou dost.

FAL. But to say I know more harm in him than in myself were to say more than I know. That he is old the more the pity, his white hairs do witness it; but that he is, saving your reverence, 410 a whoremaster, that I utterly deny. If sack and sugar be a fault, God help the wicked! if to be old and merry be a sin, then many an old host that I know is damned; if to be fat be to be hated, then Pharaoh's lean kine[4] are to be loved. No, my good lord, banish Peto, banish Bardolph, banish Poins, 4 5 but for sweet Jack Falstaff, kind Jack Falstaff, true Jack Falstaff, valiant Jack Falstaff, and therefore more valiant, being as he is old Jack Falstaff, banish not him thy Harry's company, banish not him thy Harry's company; banish plump Jack, and ban-

---

8. Suckling rabbit.
9. Seated.
1. Large barrel.
2. Trough; "bombard": leather wine vessel.
3. Town in Essex, noted for barbecues;

"pudding": sausage. The "vice" was a comic character in the old morality plays. Falstaff is in some respects a descendant of this type-character.
4. In the dream Joseph interpreted. See Genesis xli.19–21.

ish all the world.

PRINCE. I do, I will.   [⟨*A knocking heard.*⟩] ⁴²⁰
                                   [⟨*Exeunt* HOSTESS *and* BARDOLPH.⟩]
      [*Enter* BARDOLPH, *running.*]

BARD. O, my lord, my lord, the sheriff with a most monstrous
      watch is at the door.

FAL. Out, ye rogue! Play out the play; I have much to say in the
      behalf of that Falstaff.   ⁴²⁵
      [*Enter the* HOSTESS.]

HOST. O Jesu, my lord, my lord!

FAL. Heigh, heigh! the devil rides upon a fiddlestick;⁵ what's the
      matter?

HOST. The sheriff and all the watch are at the door; they are come
      to search the house. Shall I let them in?   ⁴³⁰

FAL. Dost thou hear, Hal? never call a true piece of gold a coun-
      terfeit; thou art essentially mad, without seeming so.⁶

PRINCE. And thou a natural coward, without instinct.

FAL. I deny your major;⁷ if you will deny the sheriff, so; if not,
      let him enter. If I become not a cart as well as another man, ⁴³⁵
      a plague on my bringing up! I hope I shall as soon be strangled
      with a halter as another.⁸

PRINCE. Go hide thee behind the arras;⁹ the rest walk up above.
      Now, my masters, for a true face and good conscience.

FAL. Both which I have had; but their date is out,¹ and therefore ⁴⁴⁰
      I'll hide me.

PRINCE. Call in the sheriff.

                              [*Exeunt* ⟨*all except the* PRINCE *and* POINS.⟩]
            [*Enter* SHERIFF *and the* CARRIER.]

      Now, master sheriff, what is your will with me?

SHER. First pardon me, my lord. A hue and cry
      Hath followed certain men unto this house.   ⁴⁴⁵

PRINCE. What men?

SHER. One of them is well known, my gracious lord,
      A gross fat man.

CAR.   As fat as butter.

PRINCE. The man, I do assure you, is not here,
      For I myself at this time have employed him,   ⁴⁵⁰
      And, sheriff, I will engage my word to thee
      That I will by tomorrow dinnertime
      Send him to answer thee or any man
      For anything he shall be charged withal;
      And so let me entreat you leave the house.   ⁴⁵⁵

SHER. I will, my lord. There are two gentlemen

5. I.e., there's a commotion.
6. I.e., don't give a true man (me, Falstaff) away as a thief. He goes on to accuse the prince, in his reversal of values in the play scene, of being out of his mind, though he appears rational.
7. Your major premise (that I, Falstaff, am a coward).
8. I.e., I hope my fat neck will not make the process of strangling on the gallows longer for me than for the rest of you. The "cart" is the wagon on which criminals were taken to be hanged.
9. The hangings or draperies. On the Elizabethan stage these would conceal the inner stage. "Up above": on the balcony.
1. Lease has expired.

Have in this robbery lost three hundred marks.

PRINCE. It may be so; if he have robbed these men
  He shall be answerable; and so farewell.

SHER. Good night, my noble lord.   460

PRINCE. I think it is good morrow, is it not?

SHER. Indeed, my lord, I think it be two o'clock.

  [*Exeunt* (SHERIFF *and* CARRIER.)]

PRINCE. This oily rascal is known as well as Paul's.[2] Go call him
  forth.

POINS. Falstaff!—Fast asleep behind the arras, and snorting like 465
  a horse.

PRINCE. Hark, how hard he fetches breath. Search his pockets.
  [*He searcheth his pockets, and findeth certain papers.*] What
  hast thou found?

POINS. Nothing but papers, my lord.   470

PRINCE. Let's see what they be: read them.

POINS. [*reads*] "Item, a capon. . . . . .   2s. 2d.
        Item, sauce. . . . . .   4d.
        Item, sack, two gallons. . 5s. 8d.
        Item, anchovies and sack   475
            after supper. . . . . 2s. 6d.
        Item, bread. . . . . .   ob."[3]

PRINCE. O monstrous! but one halfpennyworth of bread to this
  intolerable deal of sack! What there is else, keep close; we'll
  read it at more advantage; there let him sleep till day. I'll to 480
  the court in the morning. We must all to the wars, and thy
  place shall be honorable. I'll procure this fat rogue a charge
  of foot,[4] and I know his death will be a march of twelvescore.
  The money shall be paid back again with advantage. Be with
  me betimes[5] in the morning, and so good morrow, Poins.   485

POINS. Good morrow, good my lord.   [*Exeunt.*]

Act III

SCENE 1

[*Enter* HOTSPUR, WORCESTER, LORD MORTIMER, *and* OWEN
  GLENDOWER.]

MORT. These promises are fair, the parties sure,
  And our induction[6] full of prosperous hope.

HOT. Lord Mortimer, and cousin Glendower,
  Will you sit down?
  And uncle Worcester; a plague upon it,   5
  I have forgot the map.

GLEND.   No, here it is.
  Sit, cousin Percy, sit, good cousin Hotspur,
  For by that name as oft as Lancaster
  Doth speak of you, his cheek looks pale and with

2. St. Paul's Cathedral.
3. Oble, a halfpenny.
4. Company of infantry. "Twelve-

score": i.e., 240 yards.
5. Early.
6. Initial step.

A rising sigh he wisheth you in heaven.   10
HOT. And you in hell as often as he hears Owen Glendower spoke
    of.
GLEND. I cannot blame him; at my nativity
    The front[7] of heaven was full of fiery shapes,
    Of burning cressets, and at my birth   15
    The frame and huge foundation of the earth
    Shaked like a coward.
HOT. Why, so it would have done at the same season if your
    mother's cat had but kittened, though yourself had never been
    born.   20
GLEND. I say the earth did shake when I was born.
HOT. And I say the earth was not of my mind,
    If you suppose as fearing you it shook.
GLEND. The heavens were all on fire, the earth did tremble.
HOT. O then the earth shook to see the heavens on fire,   25
    And not in fear of your nativity.
    Diseaséd nature oftentimes breaks forth
    In strange eruptions; oft the teeming earth
    Is with a kind of colic pinched and vexed
    By the imprisoning of unruly wind   30
    Within her womb, which for enlargement striving
    Shakes the old beldam[8] earth and topples down
    Steeples and moss-grown towers. At your birth
    Our grandam earth, having this distemperature,[9]
    In passion shook.
GLEND.   Cousin, of many men   35
    I do not bear these crossings. Give me leave
    To tell you once again that at my birth
    The front of heaven was full of fiery shapes,
    The goats ran from the mountains, and the herds
    Were strangely clamorous to the frighted fields.   40
    These signs have marked me extraordinary,
    And all the courses of my life do show
    I am not in the roll of common men.
    Where is he living, clipped in with[1] the sea
    That chides the banks of England, Scotland, Wales,   45
    Which calls me pupil or hath read to me?
    And bring him out that is but woman's son
    Can trace me in the tedious ways of art[2]
    And hold me pace in deep experiments.
HOT. I think there's no man speaks better Welsh. I'll to dinner.   50
MORT. Peace, cousin Percy; you will make him mad.
GLEND. I can call spirits from the vasty deep.
HOT. Why, so can I, or so can any man;
    But will they come when you do call for them?
GLEND. Why, I can teach you, cousin, to command   55
    The devil.

7. The forehead. "Cressets": lamps.   1. Within the limits of.
8. Old woman.   2. Follow me in practicing difficult
9. Ailment.   magic.

HOT. And I can teach thee, coz, to shame the devil
    By telling truth; tell truth and shame the devil.[3]
    If thou have power to raise him, bring him hither,
    And I'll be sworn I have power to shame him hence.   60
    O, while you live, tell truth and shame the devil!
MORT. Come, come, no more of this unprofitable chat.
GLEND. Three times hath Henry Bolingbroke made head
    Against my power, thrice from the banks of Wye
    And sandy-bottomed Severn have I sent him   65
    Bootless[4] home and weather-beaten back.
HOT. Home without boots, and in foul weather too!
    How 'scapes he agues,[5] in the devil's name?
GLEND. Come, here is the map; shall we divide our right
    According to our threefold order ta'en?[6]   70
MORT. The archdeacon hath divided it
    Into three limits very equally:
    England, from Trent and Severn hitherto,
    By south and east is to my part assigned;
    All westward, Wales beyond the Severn shore,   75
    And all the fertile land within that bound,
    To Owen Glendower; and, dear coz, to you
    The remnant northward lying off from Trent;
    And our indentures tripartite are drawn,
    Which being sealéd interchangeably,   80
    A business that this night may execute,
    Tomorrow, cousin Percy, you and I
    And my good Lord of Worcester will set forth
    To meet your father[7] and the Scottish power,
    As is appointed us, at Shrewsbury.   85
    My father Glendower is not ready yet,
    Nor shall we need his help these fourteen days.
    Within that space you may have drawn together
    Your tenants, friends, and neighboring gentlemen.
GLEND. A shorter time shall send me to you, lords,   90
    And in my conduct shall your ladies come,
    From whom you now must steal and take no leave,
    For there will be a world of water shed
    Upon the parting of your wives and you.
HOT. Methinks my moiety,[8] north from Burton here,   95
    In quantity equals not one of yours;
    See how this river comes me cranking[9] in,
    And cuts me from the best of all my land
    A huge half-moon, a monstrous cantle[1] out.
    I'll have the current in this place dammed up;   100
    And here the smug[1a] and silver Trent shall run

3. A proverb.
4. Unsuccessful; but Hotspur takes it in the other sense.
5. Fevers and chills.
6. Divide our property according to the arrangement for division into three parts.
7. Father-in-law.
8. Part, share.
9. Curving.
1. Corner.
1a. Smooth.

In a new channel, fair and evenly;
It shall not wind with such a deep indent
To rob me of so rich a bottom[2] here.
GLEND. Not wind? it shall, it must; you see it doth.   105
MORT. Yea, but
Mark how he bears his course, and runs me up
With like advantage on the other side;
Gelding the opposéd continent[3] as much
As on the other side it takes from you.   110
WOR. Yea, but a little charge will trench him here
And on this north side win this cape of land,
And then he runs straight and even.
HOT. I'll have it so; a little charge will do it.
GLEND. I'll not have it altered.
HOT.   Will not you?   115
GLEND. No, nor you shall not.
HOT.   Who shall say me nay?
GLEND. Why, that will I.
HOT. Let me not understand you then; speak it in Welsh.
GLEND. I can speak English, lord, as well as you,
For I was trained up in the English court,   120
Where, being but young, I framéd to the harp
Many an English ditty lovely well
And gave the tongue a helpful ornament,
A virtue that was never seen in you.
HOT. Marry,   125
And I am glad of it with all my heart;
I had rather be a kitten and cry mew
Than one of these same meter ballad-mongers;
I had rather hear a brazen canstick turned,[4]
Or a dry wheel grate on the axletree,   130
And that would set my teeth nothing on edge,
Nothing so much as mincing[5] poetry;
'Tis like the forced gait of a shuffling nag.
GLEND. Come, you shall have Trent turned.
HOT. I do not care; I'll give thrice so much land   135
To any well-deserving friend;
But in the way of bargain, mark ye me,
I'll cavil[6] on the ninth part of a hair.
Are the indentures drawn? shall we be gone?
GLEND. The moon shines fair; you may be away by night.   140
I'll haste the writer, and withal
Break with[7] your wives of your departure hence.
I am afraid my daughter will run mad,
So much she doteth on her Mortimer.   [*Exit.*]
MORT. Fie, cousin Percy, how you cross my father!   145
HOT. I cannot choose; sometime he angers me

2. Valley.
3. I.e., cutting off from the opposite side.
4. A brass candlestick turned on a lathe.
5. Affected.
6. Quibble.
7. Inform.

With telling me of the moldwarp[8] and the ant,
Of the dreamer Merlin and his prophecies,
And of a dragon and a finless fish,
A clip-winged griffin and a molten raven,   150
A couching lion and a ramping[9] cat,
And such a deal of skimble-skamble stuff
As puts me from my faith. I tell you what;
He held me last night at least nine hours
In reckoning up the several devils' names   155
That were his lackeys. I cried "hum" and "well, go to,"
But marked him not a word. O, he is as tedious
As a tired horse, a railing[1] wife,
Worse than a smoky house. I had rather live
With cheese and garlic in a windmill,[2] far,   160
Than feed on cates and have him talk to me
In any summer house in Christendom.

MORT. In faith, he is a worthy gentleman,
    Exceedingly well read, and profited
    In strange concealments,[3] valiant as a lion   165
    And wondrous affable and as bountiful
    As mines of India. Shall I tell you, cousin?
    He holds your temper[4] in a high respect
    And curbs himself even of his natural scope
    When you come 'cross his humor; faith, he does.   170
    I warrant you that man is not alive
    Might so have tempted him as you have done
    Without the taste of danger and reproof;
    But do not use it oft, let me entreat you.

WOR. In faith, my lord, you are too willful-blame,   175
    And since your coming hither have done enough
    To put him quite beside his patience.
    You must needs learn, lord, to amend this fault.
    Though sometimes it show greatness, courage, blood[5]—
    And that's the dearest grace it renders you—   180
    Yet oftentimes it doth present harsh rage,
    Defect of manners, want of government,[6]
    Pride, haughtiness, opinion, and disdain;
    The least of which haunting a nobleman
    Loseth men's hearts and leaves behind a stain   185
    Upon the beauty of all parts besides,
    Beguiling them of commendation.

HOT. Well, I am schooled; good manners be your speed!
    Here come our wives, and let us take our leave.

8. Mole. According to the chronicler Holinshed there were prophecies in which Henry IV was referred to as "a moldwarp, cursed of God." Merlin was the famous prophet of King Arthur's court; many later prophecies were attributed to him.
9. "Couching" and "ramping" are Hotspur's versions of the heraldic terms "couchant" (lying down) and "ramp-ant" (erect, on hind feet).
1. Nagging.
2. Cheese and garlic would be smelly, and the living quarters in a mill would be noisy. "Cates": delicacies.
3. Experienced in secret mysteries.
4. Character.
5. Breeding, blood-lines.
6. Self-control. "Opinion": arrogance.

[*Enter* GLENDOWER *with the ladies.*]

MORT. This is the deadly spite that angers me;   190
  My wife can speak no English, I no Welsh.
GLEND. My daughter weeps; she will not part with you,
  She'll be a soldier too, she'll to the wars.
MORT. Good father, tell her that she and my aunt Percy
  Shall follow in your conduct speedily.   195
    [GLENDOWER SPEAKS *to her in Welsh, and she answers*
    him in the same.]
GLEND. She is desperate here; a peevish self-willed harlotry,[7] one
  that no persuasion can do good upon.
    [*The lady speaks in Welsh.*]
MORT. I understand thy looks; that pretty Welsh
  Which thou pour'st down from these swelling heavens[8]
  I am too perfect in; and, but for shame,   200
  In such a parley should I answer thee.
    [*The lady speaks again in Welsh.*]
  I understand thy kisses and thou mine,
  And that's a feeling disputation,
  But I will never be a truant, love,
  Till I have learned thy language, for thy tongue   205
  Makes Welsh as sweet as ditties highly penned,
  Sung by a fair queen in a summer's bower,
  With ravishing division,[9] to her lute.
GLEND. Nay, if you melt, then will she run mad.
    [*The lady speaks again in Welsh.*]
MORT. O, I am ignorance itself in this!   210
GLEND. She bids you on the wanton rushes[1] lay you down
  And rest your gentle head upon her lap,
  And she will sing the song that pleaseth you
  And on your eyelids crown the god of sleep,
  Charming your blood with pleasing heaviness,   215
  Making such difference 'twixt wake and sleep
  As is the difference betwixt day and night
  The hour before the heavenly-harnessed team[2]
  Begins his golden progress in the east.
MORT. With all my heart I'll sit and hear her sing;   220
  By that time will our book,[3] I think, be drawn.
GLEND. Do so;
  And those musicians that shall play to you
  Hang in the air a thousand leagues from hence,
  And straight they shall be here; sit, and attend.   225
HOT. Come, Kate, thou art perfect in lying down; come, quick,
  quick, that I may lay my head in thy lap.
LADY P. Go, ye giddy goose.

---

7. Wench; used affectionately, not seriously (Juliet's father applies the same phrase to her in *Romeo and Juliet*).
8. I.e., tears from her eyes. "Answer thee": cry likewise.
9. Musical variation.
1. The dry reeds used as a floor covering in Elizabethan England.
2. The horses of the sun.
3. The indenture.

[*The music plays.*]

HOT. Now I perceive the devil understands Welsh,
And 'tis no marvel, he is so humorous.[4]   230
By 'r Lady, he is a good musician.

LADY P. Then should you be nothing but musical, for you are altogether governed by humors. Lie still, ye thief, and hear the
lady sing in Welsh.

HOT. I had rather hear Lady, my brach,[5] howl in Irish.   235

LADY P. Wouldst thou have thy head broken?

HOT. No.

LADY P. Then be still.

HOT. Neither; 'tis a woman's fault.[6]

LADY P. Now God help thee.   240

HOT. To the Welsh lady's bed.

LADY P. What's that?

HOT. Peace! she sings.

[*Here the lady sings a Welsh song.*]

HOT. Come, Kate, I'll have your song too.

LADY P. Not mine, in good sooth.   245

HOT. Not yours, in good sooth! Heart! you swear like a comfit-
maker's[7] wife. "Not you, in good sooth," and "as true as I
live," and "as God shall mend me," and "as sure as day,"
And givest such sarcenet[8] surety for thy oaths
As if thou never walk'st further than Finsbury.   250
Swear me, Kate, like a lady as thou art,
A good mouth-filling oath, and leave "in sooth,"
And such protest of pepper-gingerbread,[9]
To velvet-guards and Sunday citizens.
Come, sing.   255

LADY P. I will not sing.

HOT. 'Tis the next way to turn tailor, or be redbreast teacher.[1]
An the indentures be drawn, I'll away within these two hours;
and so, come in when ye will.   [*Exit.*]

GLEND. Come, come, Lord Mortimer, you are as slow   260
As hot Lord Percy is on fire to go.
By this our book is drawn; we will but seal,
And then to horse immediately.

MORT.   With all my heart. [*Exeunt.*]

SCENE 2

[*Enter the* KING, PRINCE OF WALES, *and others.*]

KING. Lords, give us leave; the Prince of Wales and I

4. Capricious, governed by humors.
5. My bitch hound, Lady.
6. Hotspur sarcastically reverses the usual saying about women and talkativeness.
7. Confectioner's.
8. Thin silk. Finsbury: a recreation ground outside London, frequented by citizens and their wives on Sundays, but not by ladies of Lady Percy's class.
9. I.e., such tame oaths, as crumbly and unsubstantial as gingerbread. "Velvet-guards": respectable people of the middle class, who wore velvet stripes on their clothes; "Sunday citizens": city folk out for a stroll on Sunday.
1. I.e., it is the easiest way to become a tailor (supposedly tailors sang at their work) or a person who teaches birds to sing. Hotspur is equally scornful of music and of people who work for a living.

Must have some private conference; but be near at hand,
For we shall presently have need of you.   [*Exeunt* LORDS.]
I know not whether God will have it so
For some displeasing service I have done,   5
That, in his secret doom, out of my blood[2]
He'll breed revengement and a scourge for me;
But thou dost in thy passages[3] of life
Make me believe that thou art only marked
For the hot vengeance and the rod of heaven   10
To punish my mistreadings.[4] Tell me else,
Could such inordinate and low desires,
Such poor, such bare, such lewd,[5] such mean attempts,
Such barren pleasures, rude society
As thou art matched withal and grafted to   15
Accompany the greatness of thy blood
And hold their level with thy princely heart?
PRINCE. So please your majesty, I would I could
   Quit[6] all offenses with as clear excuse
   As well as I am doubtless I can purge   20
   Myself of many I am charged withal;
   Yet such extenuation let me beg,
   As, in reproof of many tales devised
   (Which oft the ear of greatness needs must hear)
   By smiling pickthanks[7] and base newsmongers,   25
   I may, for some things true, wherein my youth
   Hath faulty wandered and irregular,
   Find pardon on my true submissión.
KING. God pardon thee; yet let me wonder, Harry,
   At thy affections, which doth hold a wing   30
   Quite from the flight of all thy ancestors.
   Thy place in council thou hast rudely lost,
   Which by thy younger brother is supplied,
   And art almost an alien to the hearts
   Of all the court and princes of my blood.   35
   The hope and expectation of thy time[8]
   Is ruined, and the soul of every man
   Prophetically do forethink thy fall.
   Had I so lavish of my presence been,
   So common-hackneyed in the eyes of men,   40
   So stale and cheap to vulgar company,
   Opinion,[9] that did help me to the crown,
   Had still kept loyal to possessión
   And left me in reputeless banishment,
   A fellow of no mark nor likelihood.   45
   By being seldom seen, I could not stir

2. Through my son.
3. Actions.
4. False steps, misdeeds.
5. Low.
6. Acquit myself of. "Doubtless": sure.
7. Flatterers; "newsmongers": tattle-tales.
8. Lifetime.
9. Popularity, public opinion. "Possession": i.e., the possessor, Richard II.

But like a comet I was wondered at,
That men would tell their children "This is he";
Others would say "Where, which is Bolingbroke?"
And then I stole all courtesy from heaven, 50
And dressed myself in such humility
That I did pluck allegiance from men's hearts,
Loud shouts and salutations from their mouths,
Even in the presence of the crownéd king.
Thus did I keep my person fresh and new, 55
My presence like a robe pontifical,
Ne'er seen but wondered at; and so my state,[1]
Seldom but sumptuous, showed like a feast
And wan[2] by rareness such solemnity.
The skipping king, he ambled up and down 60
With shallow jesters and rash bavin wits,[3]
Soon kindled and soon burnt, carded his state,
Mingled his royalty with capering fools,
Had his great name profanéd with their scorns
And gave his countenance[4] against his name 65
To laugh at gibing boys and stand the push
Of every beardless vain comparative,[5]
Grew a companion to the common streets,
Enfeoffed himself to popularity,[6]
That, being daily swallowed by men's eyes, 70
They surfeited with honey and began
To loathe the taste of sweetness, whereof a little
More than a little is by much too much.
So when he had occasion to be seen
He was but as the cuckoo is in June,[7] 75
Heard, not regarded, seen, but with such eyes
As, sick and blunted with community,[8]
Afford no extraordinary gaze
Such as is bent on sunlike majesty
When it shines seldom in admiring eyes, 80
But rather drowsed and hung their eyelids down,
Slept in his face[9] and rendered such aspéct
As cloudy men use to their adversaries,
Being with his presence glutted, gorged, and full.
And in that very line, Harry, standest thou, 85
For thou hast lost thy princely privilege
With vile participation.[1] Not an eye
But is a-weary of thy common sight,

1. Public ceremonial appearances.
2. Won. "Such solemnity": i.e., the greatest possible majestic effect (an intensive use of "such"). King Henry's theory of public relations is of course not based upon the assumption of a democratic society.
3. "Rash": quick; "bavin": brushwood; the image is explained in the next line. "Carded his state": degraded his royal dignity; "card" also means "to adulterate wine."
4. Authority; "name": reputation.
5. Shallow satirical pretender to wit.
6. Made himself the common property of the public.
7. The cuckoo is noticed in April, when its song is first heard; by June it is commonplace.
8. Commonness.
9. I.e., yawned in his face. "Aspect": looks; "cloudy": sullen.
1. Association with vile companions.

Save mine, which hath desired to see thee more,
Which now doth that I would not have it do, 90
Make blind itself with foolish tenderness.

PRINCE. I shall hereafter, my thrice gracious lord,
Be more myself.

KING.   For all the world
As thou art to this hour was Richard then
When I from France set foot at Ravenspurgh, 95
And even as I was then is Percy now.
Now, by my scepter and my soul to boot,
He hath more worthy interest to the state
Than thou the shadow of succession;[2]
For of no right, nor color like to right, 100
He doth fill fields with harness in the realm,
Turns head against the lion's arméd jaws,[3]
And, being no more in debt to years than thou,
Leads ancient lords and reverend bishops on
To bloody battles and to bruising arms. 105
What never-dying honor hath he got
Against renownéd Douglas! whose high deeds,
Whose hot incursions and great name in arms
Holds from all soldiers chief majority
And military title capital[4] 110
Through all the kingdoms that acknowledge Christ.
Thrice hath this Hotspur, Mars in swaddling clothes,
This infant warrior, in his enterprises
Discomfited great Douglas, ta'en him once,
Enlargéd[5] him and made a friend of him, 115
To fill the mouth of deep defiance up[6]
And shake the peace and safety of our throne.
And what say you to this? Percy, Northumberland,
The Archbishop's grace of York, Douglas, Mortimer,
Capitulate[7] against us and are up. 120
But wherefore do I tell these news to thee?
Why, Harry, do I tell thee of my foes,
Which art my nearest and dearest enemy?
Thou that art like enough through vassal fear,
Base inclination and the start of spleen,[8] 125
To fight against me under Percy's pay,
To dog his heels and curtsy at his frowns,
To show how much thou art degenerate.

PRINCE. Do not think so; you shall not find it so;
And God forgive them that so much have swayed 130
Your majesty's good thoughts away from me.

---

2. I.e., Hotspur's claim to the throne
is more solid, because of his achievements, than is Hal's, which rests only
on shadowy rights of succession by
birth. "Color": false pretense.
3. I.e., takes military action against
the king's army. "Harness": armor.
4. Has the greatest reputation among

soldiers. "Incursions": raids; "majority": superiority.
5. Freed.
6. I.e., to make the voice of defiance
full in volume.
7. Make agreements; "up": in arms.
8. Unreasoning impulse.

I will redeem all this on Percy's head
And in the closing of some glorious day
Be bold to tell you that I am your son,
When I will wear a garment all of blood   135
And stain my favors⁹ in a bloody mask,
Which, washed away, shall scour my shame with it;
And that shall be the day, whene'er it lights,
That this same child of honor and renown,
This gallant Hotspur, this all-praiséd knight,   140
And your unthought-of Harry chance to meet.
For every honor sitting on his helm—
Would they were multitudes, and on my head
My shames redoubled!—for the time will come
That I shall make this northern youth exchange   145
His glorious deeds for my indignities.
Percy is but my factor,¹ good my lord,
To engross up glorious deeds on my behalf,
And I will call him to so strict account,
That he shall render every glory up,   150
Yea, even the slightest worship² of his time,
Or I will tear the reckoning from his heart.
This in the name of God I promise here,
The which if He be pleased I shall perform,
I do beseech your majesty, may salve   155
The long-grown wounds of my intemperance;
If not, the end of life cancels all bands,³
And I will die a hundred thousand deaths
Ere break the smallest parcel of this vow.

KING. A hundred thousand rebels die in this;   160
Thou shalt have charge and sovereign trust herein.
    [*Enter* BLUNT.]
How now, good Blunt? thy looks are full of speed.

BLUNT. So hath the business that I come to speak of.
Lord Mortimer of Scotland hath sent word
That Douglas and the English rebels met   165
The eleventh of this month at Shrewsbury;
A mighty and a fearful head⁴ they are,
If promises be kept on every hand,
As ever offered foul play in a state.

KING. The Earl of Westmoreland set forth today,   170
With him my son, Lord John of Lancaster,
For this advertisement⁵ is five days old.
On Wednesday next, Harry, you shall set forward;
On Thursday we ourselves will march. Our meeting
Is Bridgenorth and, Harry, you shall march   175
Through Gloucestershire, by which account,⁶

9. Features.
1. Agent; "engross up": collect, acquire.
2. Honor.
3. Bonds, debts.
4. Power.
5. News.
6. Method. "Our business valued"; according to estimates.

Our business valued, some twelve days hence
Our general forces at Bridgenorth shall meet.
Our hands are full of business: let's away;
Advantage feeds him fat while men delay.[7]   [*Exeunt.*] 180

SCENE 3

[*Enter* FALSTAFF *and* BARDOLPH.]

FAL. Bardolph, am I not fallen away vilely since this last action?[8]
do I not bate? do I not dwindle? Why, my skin hangs about
me like an old lady's loose gown; I am withered like an old
applejohn.[9] Well, I'll repent, and that suddenly, while I am
in some liking; I shall be out of heart shortly, and then I shall 5
have no strength to repent. An I have not forgotten what the
inside of a church is made of, I am a peppercorn, a brewer's
horse. The inside of a church! Company, villainous company,
hath been the spoil of me.

BARD. Sir John, you are so fretful you cannot live long.   10

FAL. Why, there is it; come sing me a bawdy song, make me
merry. I was as virtuously given as a gentleman need to be:
virtuous enough; swore little; diced not above seven times a
week; went to a bawdyhouse not above once in a quarter—of an
hour; paid money that I borrowed three or four times; lived 15
well and in good compass; and now I live out of all order, out
of all compass.

BARD. Why, you are so fat, Sir John, that you must needs be out
of all compass, out of all reasonable compass, Sir John.

FAL. Do thou amend thy face, and I'll amend my life; thou art 20
our admiral,[1] thou bearest the lantern in the poop, but 'tis in
the nose of thee; thou art the Knight of the Burning Lamp.

BARD. Why, Sir John, my face does you no harm.

FAL. No, I'll be sworn; I make as good use of it as many a man
doth of a death's-head or a *memento mori.*[2] I never see thy 25
face but I think upon hell-fire and Dives[3] that lived in purple,
for there he is in his robes, burning, burning. If thou wert any
way given to virtue, I would swear by thy face; my oath should
be "By this fire, that's God's angel"; but thou art altogether
given over, and wert indeed, but for the light in thy face, the 30
son of utter darkness. When thou rannest up Gadshill in the
night to catch my horse, if I did not think thou hadst been an
ignis fatuus[4] or a ball of wildfire, there's no purchase in money.
O, thou art a perpetual triumph,[5] an everlasting bonfire light!
Thou hast saved me a thousand marks in links[6] and torches, 35
walking with thee in the night betwixt tavern and tavern, but

---

7. I.e., the rebels' "advantage" (opportunity) grows as the king's men delay.
8. I.e., the Gadshill robbery; "bate":
lose weight.
9. A keeping apple with a wrinkled
skin. "In some liking": in good condition.
1. Flagship.

2. I.e., a skull or some other reminder
of death.
3. The rich man who would not give
food to Lazarus and was punished in
hell for it. See Luke xvi.19–31.
4. Will-o'-the-wisp; "wildfire": a firework used for military purposes.
5. Illumination at a public festival.
6. Small torches carried at night.

the sack that thou hast drunk me would have bought me lights
as good cheap at the dearest chandler's[7] in Europe. I have maintained that salamander of yours with fire any time this two and
thirty years, God reward me for it.   40

BARD. 'Sblood, I would my face were in your belly!

FAL. God-a-mercy! so should I be sure to be heartburned.

    [*Enter* HOSTESS.]

How now, Dame Partlet[8] the hen! have you inquired yet who
picked my pocket?

HOST. Why, Sir John, what do you think, Sir John? do you think   45
I keep thieves in my house? I have searched, I have inquired,
so has my husband, man by man, boy by boy, servant by servant; the tithe[9] of a hair was never lost in my house before.

FAL. Ye lie, hostess; Bardolph was shaved and lost many a hair,
and I'll be sworn my pocket was picked. Go to, you are a   50
woman, go.

HOST. Who, I? no, I defy thee; God's light, I was never called
so in mine own house before.

FAL. Go to, I know you well enough.

HOST. No, Sir John; you do not know me, Sir John. I know   55
you, Sir John; you owe me money, Sir John, and now you
pick a quarrel to beguile me of it; I bought you a dozen of
shirts to your back.

FAL. Dowlas,[1] filthy dowlas; I have given them away to bakers'
wives, and they have made bolters of them.   60

HOST. Now, as I am a true woman, holland[2] of eight shillings an
ell. You owe money here besides, Sir John, for your diet and
by-drinkings,[3] and money lent you, four and twenty pound.

FAL. He had his part of it; let him pay.

HOST. He? alas, he is poor; he hath nothing.   65

FAL. How! poor? look upon his face; what call you rich? let them
coin his nose, let them coin his cheeks; I'll not pay a denier.[4]
What, will you make a younker of me? shall I not take mine
ease in mine-inn but I shall have my pocket picked? I have lost
a seal ring of my grandfather's worth forty mark.[5]   70

HOST. O Jesu, I have heard the prince tell him I know not how
oft that that ring was copper.

FAL. How! the prince is a Jack,[6] a sneak-up; 'sblood, an he were
here, I would cudgel him like a dog if he would say so.

    [*Enter the* PRINCE ⟨*and* POINS⟩, *marching, and* FALSTAFF
    meets them playing upon his truncheon like a fife.]

How now, lad, is the wind in that door, i' faith? must we all   75
march?

---

7. Candlemaker's. "Salamanders" were
lizards that supposedly lived in fire
and ate it.
8. A nickname from the hen in Chaucer's Nun's Priest's Tale; in Shakespeare's time a conventional name for
a scolding woman.
9. Tenth part.
1. A coarse cloth. "Bolters": sieves for

flour.
2. Fine linen; "ell": 45 inches.
3. Drinks between meals.
4. French penny, worth a tenth of an
English penny. "Younker": youngster,
novice.
5. A mark was worth two-thirds of a
pound.
6. Rascal; "sneak-up": a sneak.

BARD. Yea, two and two, Newgate fashion.[7]

HOST. My lord, I pray you hear me.

PRINGE. What sayest thou, Mistress Quickly? How doth thy husband? I love him well; he is an honest man.   80

HOST. Good my lord, hear me.

FAL. Prithee let her alone, and list to me.

PRINCE. What sayest thou, Jack?

FAL. The other night I fell asleep here behind the arras and had my pocket picked; this house is turned bawdyhouse, they pick 85 pockets.

PRINCE. What didst thou lose, Jack?

FAL. Wilt thou believe me, Hal? three or four bonds of forty pound apiece, and a seal ring of my grandfather's.

PRINCE. A trifle, some eightpenny matter.   90

HOST. So I told him, my lord, and I said I heard your grace say so; and, my lord, he speaks most vilely of you, like a foulmouthed man as he is, and said he would cudgel you.

PRINCE. What, he did not?

HOST. There's neither faith, truth, nor womanhood in me else. 95

FAL. There's no more faith in thee than in a stewed prune,[8] nor no more truth in thee than in a drawn fox, and for womanhood Maid Marian may be the deputy's wife of the ward to thee.[9] Go, you thing, go.

HOST. Say, what thing, what thing?   100

FAL. What thing! why, a thing to thank God on.

HOST. I am no thing to thank God on, I would thou shouldst know it; I am an honest man's wife, and, setting thy knighthood aside,[1] thou art a knave to call me so.

FAL. Setting thy womanhood aside, thou art a beast to say other- 105 wise.

HOST. Say, what beast, thou knave, thou?

FAL. What beast? why, an otter.

PRINCE. An otter, Sir John, why an otter?

FAL. Why, she's neither fish nor flesh, a man knows not where 110 to have her.[2]

HOST. Thou art an unjust man in saying so; thou or any man knows where to have me, thou knave, thou!

PRINCE. Thou sayest true, hostess, and he slanders thee most grossly.   115

HOST. So he doth you, my lord, and said this other day you ought[3] him a thousand pound.

PRINCE. Sirrah, do I owe you a thousand pound?

FAL. A thousand pound, Hal! A million. Thy love is worth a mil-

7. Chained together, like prisoners at Newgate.
8. Stewed prunes were commonly served in bawdyhouses, as a supposed protection against venereal disease. "Drawn": hunted.
9. "Maid Marian" was a female character of low morals in the popular Robin Hood plays; a "deputy's wife of the ward" would be a respectable woman.
1. I.e., ignoring, or intending no disrespect to, the rank of knighthood. Falstaff intentionally misunderstands the phrase.
2. I.e., how to understand her. But the Hostess' retort is, unconsciously, equivalent to saying that she is completely promiscuous.
3. Owed.

lion; thou owest me thy love.   120

HOST. Nay, my lord, he called you Jack, and said he would cudgel
  you.

FAL. Did I, Bardolph?

BARD. Indeed, Sir John, you said so.

FAL. Yea, if he said my ring was copper.   125

PRINCE. I say 'tis copper; darest thou be as good as thy word now?

FAL. Why, Hal, thou knowest, as thou art but man, I dare; but
  as thou art prince, I fear thee as I fear the roaring of the lion's
  whelp.

PRINCE. And why not as the lion?   130

FAL. The king himself is to be feared as the lion; dost thou think
  I'll fear thee as I fear thy father? Nay, an I do, I pray God my
  girdle⁴ break.

PRINCE. O, if it should, how would thy guts fall about thy knees!
  But, sirrah, there's no room for faith, truth, nor honesty in this 135
  bosom of thine; it is all filled up with guts and midriff. Charge
  an honest woman with picking thy pocket! Why, thou whoreson, impudent, embossed rascal,⁵ if there were anything in thy
  pocket but tavern-reckonings, memorandums of bawdyhouses,
  and one poor pennyworth of sugar candy to make thee long- 140
  winded, if thy pocket were enriched with any other injuries but
  these, I am a villain. And yet you will stand to it, you will not
  pocket up wrong; art thou not ashamed?

FAL. Dost thou hear, Hal? thou knowest in the state of innocency
  Adam fell, and what should poor Jack Falstaff do in the days 145
  of villainy? Thou seest I have more flesh than another man,
  and therefore more frailty. You confess then, you picked my
  pocket?

PRINCE. It appears so by the story.

FAL. Hostess, I forgive thee; go make ready breakfast, love thy 150
  husband, look to thy servants, cherish thy guests; thou shalt
  find me tractable to any honest reason; thou seest I am pacified
  still. Nay, prithee begone. [*Exit* HOSTESS.] Now, Hal, to the
  news at court; for the robbery, lad, how is that answered?

PRINCE. O, my sweet beef, I must still be good angel to thee; the 155
  money is paid back again.

FAL. O, I do not like that paying back; 'tis a double labor.

PRINCE. I am good friends with my father and may do anything.

FAL. Rob me the exchequer the first thing thou doest, and do it
  with unwashed hands too.   160

BARD. Do, my lord.

PRINCE. I have procured thee, Jack, a charge of foot.⁶

FAL. I would it had been of horse. Where shall I find one that
  can steal well? O for a fine thief, of the age of two and twenty
  or thereabouts! I am heinously unprovided. Well, God be 165
  thanked for these rebels, they offend none but the virtuous; I

---

4. Belt.
5. Swollen rascal; "embossed" was also
a technical term in hunting, applied to
a deer which was exhausted and foaming at the mouth.
6. Command of a company of foot-
soldiers. "Horse": cavalry.

laud them, I praise them.

PRINCE. Bardolph!

BARD. My lord?

PRINCE. Go bear this letter to Lord John of Lancaster, to my 170
brother John; this to my Lord of Westmoreland. [*Exit* BAR-
DOLPH.] Go, Poins, to horse, to horse; for thou and I have
thirty miles to ride yet ere dinnertime. [*Exit* POINS.] Jack, meet
me tomorrow in the Temple Hall at two o'clock in the after-
noon. 175
There shalt thou know thy charge, and there receive
Money and order for their furniture.[7]
The land is burning, Percy stands on high,
And either we or they must lower lie. [⟨*Exit.*⟩]

FAL. Rare words, brave world! Hostess, my breakfast, come. 180
O, I could wish this tavern were my drum![7a] [*Exit.*]

Act IV

SCENE 1

[*Enter* HOTSPUR, WORCESTER, *and* DOUGLAS.]

HOT. Well said, my noble Scot. If speaking truth
In this fine age were not thought flattery,
Such attribution should the Douglas have
As not a soldier of this season's stamp
Should go so general current[8] through the world. 5
By God, I cannot flatter; I do defy
The tongues of soothers,[9] but a braver place
In my heart's love hath no man than yourself;
Nay, task me to my word,[1] approve me, lord.

DOUG. Thou art the king of honor; 10
No man so potent breathes upon the ground
But I will beard him.[2]

HOT. Do so, and 'tis well.

[*Enter a* MESSENGER *with letters.*]
What letters hast thou there?—I can but thank you.

MESS. These letters come from your father.

HOT. Letters from him! why comes he not himself? 15

MESS. He cannot come, my lord; he is grievous sick.

HOT. Zounds! how has he the leisure to be sick
In such a justling[3] time? Who leads his power?
Under whose government come they along?

MESS. His letters bears his mind, not I, my lord. 20

WOR. I prithee tell me, doth he keep his bed?

MESS. He did, my lord, four days ere I set forth,
And at the time of my departure thence

---

7. Furnishings, equipment.
7a. Headquarters.
8. I.e., that not a soldier of this year's coinage should achieve such currency. "Attribution": praise.
9. Flatterers; "braver": more distin-

guished.
1. Compare my actions with my speech. "Approve": prove, test.
2. I.e., I will take on anybody, however powerful.
3. Turbulent.

He was much feared by[4] his physiciáns.

WOR. I would the state of time had first been whole   25
    Ere he by sickness had been visited;
    His health was never better worth than now.

HOT. Sick now! droop now! this sickness doth infect
    The very lifeblood of our enterprise;
      'Tis catching hither, even to our camp.   30
    He writes me here that inward sickness—
    And that his friends by deputation could not
    So soon be drawn,[5] nor did he think it meet
    To lay so dangerous and dear a trust
    On any soul removed but on his own.   35
    Yet doth he give us bold advertisement
    That with our small conjunction[6] we should on
    To see how fortune is disposed to us;
    For, as he writes, there is no quailing now,
    Because the king is certainly possessed[7]   40
    Of all our purposes. What say you to it?

WOR. Your father's sickness is a maim to us.

HOT. A perilous gash, a very limb lopped off;
    And yet in faith it is not; his present want[8]
    Seems more than we shall find it. Were it good   45
    To set the exact wealth of all our states
    All at one cast, to set so rich a main[9]
    On the nice hazard of one doubtful hour?
    It were not good, for therein should we read
    The very bottom and the soul of hope,[1]   50
    The very list, the very utmost bound
    Of all our fortunes.

DOUG.   Faith, and so we should,
    Where now remains a sweet reversión.[2]
    We may boldly spend upon the hope of what
    Is to come in;   55
    A comfort of retirement[3] lives in this.

HOT. A rendezvous, a home to fly unto,
    If that the devil and mischance look big
    Upon the maidenhead of our affairs.[4]

WOR. But yet I would your father had been here.   60
    The quality and hair[5] of our attempt
    Brooks no division; it will be thought
    By some that know not why he is away
    That wisdom, loyalty, and mere dislike
    Of our proceedings kept the earl from hence.   65

4. Feared for by. "State of time": public affairs.
5. Could not quickly be organized under a deputy. "Soul removed": other person.
6. Unified forces.
7. Informed.
8. Our present awareness of his absence.
9. Stake, in betting; "nice hazard": risky chance.
1. Foundation and essence of our expectations. "List": limit.
2. A fund to be inherited in the future.
3. Sustaining place to fall back on.
4. I.e., threaten the beginning of our affairs.
5. Character; "brooks": allows.

And think how such an apprehensión
May turn the tide of fearful factión[6]
And breed a kind of question in our cause,
For well you know we of the offering[7] side
Must keep aloof from strict arbitrement,   70
And stop all sight-holes, every loop[8] from whence
The eye of reason may pry in upon us.
This absence of your father's draws a curtain,
That shows the ignorant a kind of fear
Before not dreamt of.

HOT.   You strain too far.   75
I rather of his absence make this use:
It lends a luster and more great opinion,
A larger dare to our great enterprise,
Than if the earl were here, for men must think,
If we without his help can make a head   80
To push against a kingdom, with his help
We shall o'erturn it topsy-turvy down.
Yet all goes well, yet all our joints are whole.

DOUG. As heart can think; there is not such a word
Spoke of in Scotland as this term of fear.   85

    [*Enter* SIR RICHARD VERNON.]

HOT. My cousin Vernon, welcome, by my soul!

VER. Pray God my news be worth a welcome, lord.
The Earl of Westmoreland, seven thousand strong,
Is marching hitherwards; with him Prince John.

HOT. No harm; what more?

VER.   And further I have learned   90
The king himself in person is set forth,
Or hitherwards intended speedily,
With strong and mighty preparatión.

HOT. He shall be welcome too. Where is his son,
The nimble-footed madcap Prince of Wales,   95
And his comrades that daft[9] the world aside
And bid it pass?

VER.   All furnished, all in arms,
All plumed like estridges[1] that with the wind
Bated, like eagles having lately bathed,
Glittering in golden coats like images,   100
As full of spirit as the month of May,
And gorgeous as the sun at midsummer,
Wanton as youthful goats, wild as young bulls.
I saw young Harry, with his beaver[2] on,
His cushes on his thighs, gallantly armed,   105
Rise from the ground like feathered Mercury,
And vaulted with such ease into his seat,

---

6. Conspiracy.
7. Challenging. "Arbitrement": investigation.
8. Loophole.
9. Push.

1. Ostriches; "bated": fluttering their wings.
2. Helmet. "Cushes": cuisses, armor for the thighs.

As if an angel dropped down from the clouds,
To turn and wind³ a fiery Pegasus
And witch the world with noble horsemanship.   110
HOT. No more, no more. Worse than the sun in March
This praise doth nourish agues.⁴ Let them come;
They come like sacrifices in their trim,
And to the fire-eyed maid of smoky war⁴ᵃ
All hot and bleeding will we offer them;   115
The mailéd Mars shall on his altar sit
Up to the ears in blood. I am on fire
To hear this rich reprisal⁵ is so nigh
And yet not ours. Come, let me taste my horse,
Who is to bear me like a thunderbolt   120
Against the bosom of the Prince of Wales;
Harry to Harry shall, hot horse to horse,
Meet and ne'er part till one drop down a corse.
O that Glendower were come!
VER.   There is more news;
I learned in Worcester, as I rode along,   125
He cannot draw his power this fourteen days.
DOUG. That's the worst tidings that I hear of yet.
WOR. Aye, by my faith, that bears a frosty sound.
HOT. What may the king's whole battle⁶ reach unto?
VER. To thirty thousand.
HOT.   Forty let it be;   130
My father and Glendower being both away,
The powers of us may serve so great a day.
Come, let us take a muster speedily;
Doomsday is near; die all, die merrily.
DOUG. Talk not of dying; I am out out of fear   135
Of death or death's hand for this one-half year.   [*Exeunt.*]

SCENE 2

[*Enter* FALSTAFF *and* BARDOLPH.]
FAL. Bardolph, get thee before to Coventry; fill me a bottle of
sack, our soldiers shall march through. We'll to Sutton Co'fil'⁶ᵃ
tonight.
BARD. Will you give me money, captain?
FAL. Lay out, lay out.   5
BARD. This bottle makes an angel.⁷
FAL. An if it do, take it for thy labor; and if it make twenty, take
them all; I'll answer the coinage. Bid my lieutenant Peto
meet me at town's end.
BARD. I will, captain; farewell.   [*Exit.*]   10
FAL. If I be not ashamed of my soldiers, I am a soused gurnet.⁸
I have misused the king's press damnably. I have got in ex-

---

3. Direct. "Pegasus": winged horse.
4. Fevers. Malaria was thought to be caused by vapors from the marshes, drawn up by the sun in spring.
4a. Bellona, goddess of war.
5. Prize.

6. Army.
6a. Sutton Coldfield, about 25 miles from Coventry.
7. Ten shillings' worth.
8. Pickled anchovy. "Press": the draft or impressment of soldiers into service.

change of a hundred and fifty soldiers three hundred and odd pounds. I press me none but good householders, yeomen's sons, inquire me out contracted bachelors, such as had been asked twice on the banns,[9] such a commodity[1] of warm slaves as had as lieve hear the devil as a drum, such as fear the report of a caliver worse than a struck fowl or a hurt wild duck. I pressed me none but such toasts-and-butter[2] with hearts in their bellies no bigger than pins' heads, and they have bought out their services, and now my whole charge consists of ancients,[3] corporals, lieutenants, gentlemen of companies, slaves as ragged as Lazarus in the painted cloth where the glutton's dogs licked his sores, and such as indeed were never soldiers, but discarded unjust serving-men, younger sons to younger brothers, revolted tapsters and ostlers trade-fallen,[4] the cankers of a calm world and a long peace, ten times more dishonorable ragged than an old-fac'd ancient,[5] and such have I to fill up the rooms of them that have bought out their services, that you would think that I had a hundred and fifty tattered prodigals lately come from swine-keeping, from eating draff[6] and husks. A mad fellow met me on the way and told me I had unloaded all the gibbets and pressed the dead bodies. No eye hath seen such scarecrows. I'll not march through Coventry with them, that's flat; nay, and the villains march wide betwixt the legs, as if they had gyves[7] on, for indeed I had the most of them out of prison. There's but a shirt and a half in all my company, and the half shirt is two napkins tacked together and thrown over the shoulders like a herald's coat without sleeves, and the shirt, to say the truth, stolen from my host at Saint Alban's, or the red-nose innkeeper of Daventry. But that's all one; they'll find linen enough on every hedge.[8]

[*Enter the* PRINCE *and the Lord of* WESTMORELAND.]

PRINCE. How now, blown Jack! how now, quilt!

FAL. What, Hal, how now, mad wag! what a devil dost thou in Warwickshire? My good Lord of Westmoreland, I cry you mercy; I thought your honor had already been at Shrewsbury.

WEST. Faith, Sir John, 'tis more than time that I were there, and you too; but my powers are there already. The king, I can tell you, looks for us all; we must away all night.

FAL. Tut, never fear me; I am as vigilant as a cat to steal cream.

PRINCE. I think, to steal cream indeed, for thy theft hath already made thee butter. But tell me, Jack, whose fellows are these that come after?

FAL. Mine, Hal, mine.

PRINCE. I did never see such pitiful rascals.

---

9. Notice of approaching marriage, announced three times publicly in church before the marriage could take place.
1. "Commodity": collection; "warm": well-to-do; "caliver": musket.
2. Sissies.
3. Ensigns.
4. Hostlers out of work; "cankers":

canker worms.
5. Frayed flag.
6. Garbage. The prodigal son, in the Bible, fed on husks before returning to the paternal board.
7. Leg-irons.
8. Laundry was customarily hung on hedges to dry.

FAL. Tut, tut, good enough to toss,[9] food for powder, food for powder; they'll fill a pit as well as better; tush, man, mortal men, mortal men.

WEST. Aye, but, Sir John, methinks they are exceeding poor and bare, too beggarly. 60

FAL. Faith, for their poverty I know not where they had that, and for their bareness I am sure they never learned that of me.

PRINCE. No, I'll be sworn, unless you call three fingers on the ribs bare. But, sirrah, make haste; Percy is already in the field.

FAL. What, is the king encamped? 65

WEST. He is, Sir John; I fear we shall stay too long.

FAL. Well,
　To the latter end of a fray and the beginning of a feast
　Fits a dull fighter and a keen guest. [*Exeunt.*]

SCENE 3

[*Enter* HOTSPUR, WORCESTER, DOUGLAS, *and* VERNON.]

HOT. We'll fight with him tonight.

WOR. 　　　　　　　　It may not be.

DOUG. You give him then advantage.

VER. 　　　　　　　　Not a whit.

HOT. Why say you so? looks he not for supply?

VER. So do we.

HOT. 　　　　His is certain, ours is doubtful.

WOR. Good cousin, be advised; stir not tonight. 5

VER. Do not, my lord.

DOUG. 　　　　　　You do not counsel well;
　You speak it out of fear and cold heart.

VER. Do me no slander, Douglas; by my life,
　And I dare well maintain it with my life,
　If well-respected honor bid me on, 10
　I hold as little counsel with weak fear
　As you, my lord, or any Scot that this day lives.
　Let it be seen tomorrow in the battle
　Which of us fears.

DOUG. 　　　　Yea, or tonight.

VER. 　　　　　　　　Content.

HOT. Tonight, say I. 15

VER. Come, come, it may not be. I wonder much,
　Being men of such great leading as you are,
　That you foresee not what impediments
　Drag back our expedition;[1] certain horse
　Of my cousin Vernon's are not yet come up, 20
　Your uncle Worcester's horse came but today,
　And now their pride and mettle is asleep,
　Their courage with hard labor tame and dull,
　That not a horse is half the half of himself.

HOT. So are the horses of the enemy 25

9. I.e., on a pike, or long spear. 　　1. Retard our speed.

In general, journey-bated² and brought low;
The better part of ours are full of rest.

WOR. The number of the king exceedeth ours;
For God's sake, cousin, stay till all come in.

[*The trumpet sounds a parley. Enter* SIR WALTER BLUNT.]

BLUNT. I come with gracious offers from the king,   30
If you vouchsafe me hearing and respect.

HOT. Welcome, Sir Walter Blunt; and would to God
You were of our determinatión!
Some of us love you well, and even those some
Envy your great deservings and good name   35
Because you are not of our quality,³
But stand against us like an enemy.

BLUNT. And God defend⁴ but still I should stand so,
So long as out of limit and true rule
You stand against anointed majesty.   40
But to my charge. The king hath sent to know
The nature of your griefs, and whereupon
You conjure from the breast of civil peace
Such bold hostility, teaching his duteous land
Audacious cruelty. If that the king   45
Have any way your good deserts forgot,
Which he confesseth to be manifold,
He bids you name your griefs, and with all speed
You shall have your desires with interest
And pardon absolute for yourself and these   50
Herein misled by your suggestión.

HOT. The king is kind, and well we know the king
Knows at what time to promise, when to pay.
My father and my uncle and myself
Did give him that same royalty he wears;   55
And when he was not six and twenty strong,
Sick in the world's regard, wretched and low,
A poor unminded outlaw sneaking home,
My father gave him welcome to the shore;
And when he heard him swear and vow to God   60
He came but to be Duke of Lancaster,
To sue his livery⁵ and beg his peace,
With tears of innocency and terms of zeal,
My father, in kind heart and pity moved,
Swore him assistance and performed it too.   65
Now when the lords and barons of the realm
Perceived Northumberland did lean to him,
The more and less came in with cap and knee,
Met him in boroughs, cities, villages,
Attended him on bridges, stood in lanes,   70
Laid gifts before him, proffered him their oaths,

---

2. Tired from travel.
3. Fellowship, party.
4. Forbid; "still": always.

5. I.e., claim title to his late father's lands (held by King Richard II).

Gave him their heirs as pages, followed him
Even at the heels in golden multitudes.
He presently, as greatness knows itself,
Steps me a little higher than his vow, 75
Made to my father while his blood was poor
Upon the naked shore at Ravenspurgh,
And now, forsooth, takes on him to reform
Some certain edicts and some strait[6] decrees
That lie too heavy on the commonwealth, 80
Cries out upon abuses, seems to weep
Over his country's wrongs, and by this face,
This seeming brow of justice, did he win
The hearts of all that he did angle for;
Proceeded further, cut me off the heads 85
Of all the favorites that the absent king
In deputation left behind him here,
When he was personal[7] in the Irish war.

BLUNT. Tut, I came not to hear this.

HOT.   Then to the point.
In short time after he deposed the king, 90
Soon after that deprived him of his life,
And in the neck of that tasked[8] the whole state;
To make that worse, suffered his kinsman March
(Who is, if every owner were well placed,
Indeed his king) to be engaged[9] in Wales, 95
There without ransom to lie forfeited;
Disgraced[1] me in my happy victories,
Sought to entrap me by intelligence,[2]
Rated mine uncle from the council board,
In rage dismissed my father from the court, 100
Broke oath on oath, committed wrong on wrong,
And in conclusion drove us to seek out
This head of safety,[3] and withal to pry
Into his title, the which we find
Too indirect for long continuance. 105

BLUNT. Shall I return this answer to the king?

HOT. Not so, Sir Walter; we'll withdraw awhile.
Go to the king, and let there be impawned[4]
Some surety for a safe return again,
And in the morning early shall mine uncle 110
Bring him our purposes; and so farewell.

BLUNT. I would you would accept of grace and love.

HOT. And may be so we shall.

BLUNT.   Pray God you do.   [*Exeunt.*]

6. Strict.
7. Actively participating in person.
8. I.e., immediately after that, (he) taxed.
9. Pawned as a hostage.

1. I.e., did not favor.
2. Spying; "rated": angrily dismissed.
3. Army for our safety.
4. Pledged; "surety": guarantee.

SCENE 4

[*Enter the* ARCHBISHOP OF YORK *and* SIR MICHAEL.]

ARCH. Hie, good Sir Michael; bear this sealéd brief[5]
  With wingéd haste to the lord marshal,
  This to my cousin Scroop, and all the rest
  To whom they are directed. If you knew
  How much they do import you would make haste.   5
SIR M. My good lord,
  I guess their tenor.
ARCH.   Like enough you do.
  Tomorrow, good Sir Michael, is a day
  Wherein the fortune of ten thousand men
  Must bide the touch;[6] for, sir, at Shrewsbury,   10
  As I am truly given to understand,
  The king with mighty and quick-raiséd power
  Meets with Lord Harry; and I fear, Sir Michael,
  What with the sickness of Northumberland,
  Whose power was in the first proportión,[7]   15
  And what with Owen Glendower's absence thence,
  Who with them was a rated[8] sinew too
  And comes not in, o'er-ruled by prophecies—
  I fear the power of Percy is too weak
  To wage an instant trial with the king.   20
SIR M. Why, my good lord, you need not fear;
  There is Douglas and Lord Mortimer.
ARCH. No, Mortimer is not there.
SIR M. But there is Mordake, Vernon, Lord Harry Percy,
  And there is my Lord of Worcester and a head   25
  Of gallant warriors, noble gentlemen.
ARCH. And so there is; but yet the king hath drawn
  The special head[9] of all the land together:
  The Prince of Wales, Lord John of Lancaster,
  The noble Westmoreland, and warlike Blunt,   30
  And many more corrivals[1] and dear men
  Of estimation and command in arms.
SIR M. Doubt not, my lord, they shall be well opposed.
ARCH. I hope no less, yet needful 'tis to fear,
  And to prevent the worst, Sir Michael, speed;   35
  For if Lord Percy thrive not, ere the king
  Dismiss his power, he means to visit[2] us,
  For he hath heard of our confederacy,
  And 'tis but wisdom to make strong against him;
  Therefore make haste. I must go write again   40
  To other friends; and so farewell, Sir Michael.   [*Exeunt.*]

5. Letter.
6. Stand the test.
7. The largest part.
8. Highly regarded.

9. Principal army.
1. Associates; "dear": noble.
2. Attack.

Act V

[*Enter the* KING, PRINCE OF WALES, PRINCE JOHN OF
LANCASTER, SIR WALTER BLUNT, *and* FALSTAFF.]

KING. How bloodily the sun begins to peer
  Above yon busky[3] hill! The day looks pale
  At his distemperature.[4]
PRINCE.   The southern wind
  Doth play the trumpet to his purposes,[5]
  And by his hollow whistling in the leaves   5
  Foretells a tempest and a blustering day.
KING. Then with the losers let it sympathize,
  For nothing can seem foul to those that win.
    [*The trumpet sounds. Enter* WORCESTER ⟨*and* VERNON.⟩]
  How now, my lord of Worcester! 'Tis not well
  That you and I should meet upon such terms   10
  As now we meet. You have deceived our trust
  And made us doff our easy robes of peace,
  To crush[6] our old limbs in ungentle steel;
  This is not well, my lord, this is not well.
  What say you to it? will you again unknit   15
  This churlish knot of all-abhorréd war
  And move in that obedient orb[7] again
  Where you did give a fair and natural light,
  And be no more an exhaled meteor,[8]
  A prodigy of fear and a portent   20
  Of broachéd mischief to the unborn times?[9]
WOR. Hear me, my liege:
  For mine own part I could be well content
  To entertain the lag end of my life
  With quiet hours, for I do protest   25
  I have not sought the day of this dislike.
KING. You have not sought it! how comes it then?
FAL. Rebellion lay in his way, and he found it.
PRINCE. Peace, chewet,[1] peace!
WOR. It pleased your majesty to turn your looks   30
  Of favor from myself and all our house,
  And yet I must remember[2] you, my lord,
  We were the first and dearest of your friends.
  For you my staff of office did I break
  In Richard's time, and posted day and night   35
  To meet you on the way and kiss your hand

---

3. Wooded.
4. I.e., the sun's illness or malevolence.
5. I.e., the sun's intentions; the southern wind supports them.
6. Enfold, cramp.
7. Regular orbit, as of a planet.
8. Meteors were thought to be made of gas exhaled by a planet and were com-

monly associated with civil commotion.
9. I.e., of harm or disaster opened up ("broached") to plague the future. Note that "mischief" conveyed a stronger meaning to Shakespeare than it does to us.
1. Chattering bird.
2. Remind.

When yet you were in place and in account
Nothing so strong and fortunate as I.
It was myself, my brother, and his son
That brought you home and boldly did outdare   40
The dangers of the time. You swore to us,
And you did swear that oath at Doncaster,
That you did nothing purpose 'gainst the state
Nor claim no further than your new-fall'n right,
The seat of Gaunt, dukedom of Lancaster.   45
To this we swore our aid. But in short space
It rained down fortune showering on your head
And such a flood of greatness fell on you,
What with our help, what with the absent king,
What with the injuries of a wanton time,   50
The seeming sufferances[3] that you had borne,
And the contrarious winds that held the king
So long in his unlucky Irish wars
That all in England did repute him dead;
And from this swarm of fair advantages   55
You took occasion to be quickly wooed
To gripe the general sway[4] into your hand,
Forgot your oath to us at Doncaster,
And being fed by us you used us so
As that ungentle gull[5] the cuckoo's bird   60
Useth the sparrow, did oppress our nest,
Grew by our feeding to so great a bulk
That even our love durst not come near your sight
For fear of swallowing;[6] but with nimble wing
We were enforced for safety sake to fly   65
Out of your sight and raise this present head,
Whereby we stand opposéd by such means
As you yourself have forged against yourself
By unkind usage, dangerous countenance,[7]
And violation of all faith and troth   70
Sworn to us in your younger enterprise.
KING. These things indeed you have articulate,[8]
Proclaimed at market crosses, read in churches,
To face the garment of rebellión
With some fine color that may please the eye   75
Of fickle changelings and poor discontents,
Which gape and rub the elbow at the news
Of hurlyburly innovatión;
And never yet did insurrection want
Such water colors to impaint his cause,   80
Nor moody beggars starving for a time
Of pellmell havoc and confusión.
PRINCE. In both our armies there is many a soul

---

3. Sufferings.
4. Seize power over the whole state.
5. Rude nestling; the cuckoo hatches
its young in other birds' nests.
6. Being swallowed.
7. Threatening looks.
8. Drawn up in detail.

Shall pay full dearly for this encounter;
If once they join in trial. Tell your nephew   85
The Prince of Wales doth join with all the world
In praise of Henry Percy; by my hopes,
This present enterprise set off his head,[9]
I do not think a braver gentleman,
More active-valiant or more valiant-young,   90
More daring or more bold, is now alive
To grace this latter age with noble deeds.
For my part, I may speak it to my shame,
I have a truant been to chivalry—
And so I hear he doth account me too—   95
Yet this before my father's majesty:
I am content that he shall take the odds
Of his great name and estimation,
And will, to save the blood on either side,
Try fortune with him in a single fight.   100
KING. And, Prince of Wales, so dare we venture thee,
Albeit considerations infinite
Do make[1] against it. No, good Worcester, no,
We love our people well; even those we love
That are misled upon your cousin's part;   105
And, will they take the offer of our grace,
Both he and they and you, yea, every man
Shall be my friend again and I'll be his.
So tell your cousin, and bring me word
What he will do; but if he will not yield,   110
Rebuke and dread correction wait on[2] us
And they shall do their office. So, be gone;
We will not now be troubled with reply.
We offer fair; take it advisedly.
    [*Exit* WORCESTER ⟨*and* VERNON.⟩]
PRINCE. It will not be accepted, on my life;   115
The Douglas and the Hotspur both together
Are confident against the world in arms.
KING. Hence, therefore, every leader to his charge,
For on their answer will we set on them,
And God befriend us, as our cause is just!   120
    [*Exeunt all but the* PRINCE *and* FALSTAFF.]
FAL. Hal, if thou see me down in the battle and bestride me, so;
    'tis a point of friendship.
PRINCE. Nothing but a colossus can do thee that friendship. Say
    thy prayers, and farewell.
FAL. I would 'twere bedtime, Hal, and all well.   125
PRINCE. Why, thou owest God a death.   [⟨*Exit.*⟩]
FAL. 'Tis not due yet; I would be loath to pay him before his day.
    What need I be so forward with him that calls not on me?
    Well, 'tis no matter; honor pricks me on. Yea, but how if honor

9. Deducted from his account.   2. Accompany.
1. Weigh.

prick me off when I come on? How then? can honor set to a ₁₃₀
leg? No. Or an arm? No. Or take away the grief of a wound?
No. Honor hath no skill in surgery, then? No. What is honor?
A word. What is in that word honor? what is that honor? Air.
A trim reckoning![13] Who hath it? He that died o' Wednesday.
Doth he feel it? No. Doth he hear it? No. 'Tis insensible,[4] ₁₃₅
then? Yea, to the dead. But will it not live with the living? No.
Why? Detraction will not suffer it. Therefore I'll none of it;
Honor is a mere scutcheon.[5] And so ends my catechism. [*Exit.*]

SCENE 2

[*Enter* WORCESTER *and* SIR RICHARD VERNON.]

WOR. O no, my nephew must not know, Sir Richard,
    The liberal and kind offer of the king.
VER. 'Twere best he did.
WOR.   Then are we all undone.
    It is not possible, it cannot be,
    The king should keep his word in loving us;   5
    He will suspect us still and find a time
    To punish this offense in other faults.
    Suspicion all our lives shall be stuck full of eyes,
    For treason is but trusted like the fox
    Who, ne'er so tame, so cherished and locked up,   10
    Will have a wild trick of his ancestors;
    Look how we can, or sad or merrily,
    Interpretation will misquote our looks,
    And we shall feed like oxen at a stall,
    The better cherished, still the nearer death.   15
    My nephew's trespass may be well forgot;
    It hath the excuse of youth and heat of blood
    And an adopted name of privilege,[6]
    A harebrained Hotspur, governed by a spleen.
    All his offenses live upon my head   20
    And on his father's; we did train him on,
    And, his corruption being ta'en from us,[7]
    We, as the spring of all, shall pay for all.
    Therefore, good cousin, let not Harry know
    In any case the offer of the king.   25
VER. Deliver what you will; I'll say 'tis so.
    Here comes your cousin.

[*Enter* HOTSPUR ⟨*and* DOUGLAS.⟩]

HOT. My uncle is returned;
    Deliver up my Lord of Westmoreland.
    Uncle, what news?   30
WOR. The king will bid you battle presently.[8]
DOUG. Defy him by the Lord of Westmoreland.

---

3. A fine totaling of the bill.
4. Not capable of being felt.
5. A coat of arms, as often put on a tombstone.
6. A nickname which gives him privileges. "Spleen": impetuous temperament.
7. Being attributed to. "Train": entice.
8. Immediately.

HOT. Lord Douglas, go you and tell him so.
DOUG. Marry, and shall, and very willingly.   [*Exit.*]
WOR. There is no seeming mercy in the king.   35
HOT. Did you beg any? God forbid!
WOR. I told him gently of our grievances,
    Of his oath-breaking, which he mended thus,
    By now forswearing[9] that he is forsworn;
    He calls us rebels, traitors, and will scourge   40
    With haughty arms this hateful name in us.
        [*Enter* DOUGLAS.]
DOUG. Arm, gentlemen, to arms! for I have thrown
    A brave defiance in King Henry's teeth,
    And Westmoreland, that was engaged,[1] did hear it,
    Which cannot choose but bring him quickly on.   45
WOR. The Prince of Wales stepped forth before the king,
    And, nephew, challenged you to single fight.
HOT. O, would the quarrel lay upon our heads,
    And that no man might draw short breath today
    But I and Harry Monmouth! Tell me, tell me,   50
    How showed his tasking?[2] seemed it in contempt?
VER. No, by my soul; I never in my life
    Did hear a challenge urged more modestly,
    Unless a brother should a brother dare
    To gentle exercise and proof of arms.   55
    He gave you all the duties of a man,
    Trimmed up your praises with a princely tongue,
    Spoke your deservings like a chronicle,
    Making you ever better than his praise
    By still dispraising praise valued with you;   60
    And, which became him like a prince indeed,
    He made a blushing cital[3] of himself,
    And chid his truant youth with such a grace
    As if he mastered there a double spirit
    Of teaching and of learning instantly.   65
    There did he pause; but let me tell the world,
    If he outlive the envy of this day,
    England did never owe[4] so sweet a hope,
    So much misconstrued in his wantonness.
HOT. Cousin, I think thou art enamoured   70
    On his follies; never did I hear
    Of any prince so wild a libertine.
    But be he as he will, yet once ere night
    I will embrace him with a soldier's arm,
    That he shall shrink under my courtesy.   75
    Arm, arm with speed; and, fellows, soldiers, friends,
    Better consider what you have to do
    Than I, that have not well the gift of tongue,

9. Swearing falsely.
1. Held as a hostage.
2. Challenge.

3. Mention, recital.
4. Own. "Wantonness": frivolity.

Can lift your blood up with persuasión.

    [*Enter a* MESSENGER.]

MESS. My lord, here are letters for you.   80

HOT. I cannot read them now.

  O gentlemen, the time of life is short!

  To spend that shortness basely were too long,

  If life did ride upon a dial's point,[5]

  Still ending at the arrival of an hour;   85

  And if we live, we live to tread on kings,

  If die, brave death when princes die with us!

  Now, for our consciences, the arms are fair,

  When the intent of bearing them is just.

      [*Enter another* MESSENGER.]

MESS. My lord, prepare; the king comes on apace.   90

HOT. I thank him that he cuts me from my tale,

  For I profess not talking; only this—

  Let each man do his best; and here draw I

  A sword whose temper I intend to stain

  With the best blood that I can meet withal   95

  In the adventure of this perilous day.

  Now, Esperance! Percy![6] and set on.

  Sound all the lofty instruments of war,

  And by that music let us all embrace;

  For, heaven to earth,[7] some of us never shall   100

  A second time do such a courtesy.

      [*The trumpets sound. They embrace and exeunt.*]

SCENE 3

    [*The* KING *enters with his power. Alarum*[8] *to the battle.
    Then enter* DOUGLAS *and* SIR WALTER BLUNT.]

BLUNT. What is thy name, that in the battle thus

  Thou crossest me? what honor dost thou seek

  Upon my head?

DOUG.   Know then, my name is Douglas,

  And I do haunt thee in the battle thus

  Because some tell me that thou art a king.[9]   5

BLUNT. They tell thee true.

DOUG. The Lord of Stafford dear[1] today hath bought

  Thy likeness, for instead of thee, King Harry,

  This sword hath ended him; so shall it thee,

  Unless thou yield thee as my prisoner.   10

BLUNT. I was not born a yielder, thou proud Scot,

  And thou shalt find a king that will revenge

  Lord Stafford's death.   [*They fight.* DOUGLAS *kills* BLUNT.]

      [*Enter* HOTSPUR.]

---

5. Hand of a clock; "still": always. Hotspur's meaning (in lines 83–85) is that a base life would be too long even if it lasted only an hour.
6. Hope, Percy! (the family motto).
7. I.e., the odds are heaven to earth that.
8. Trumpet signal.
9. Blunt and others are dressed to look like the king.
1. Expensively.

HOT. O Douglas, hadst thou fought at Holmedon thus,
  I never had triumphed upon a Scot.   15
DOUG. All's done, all's won; here breathless lies the king.
HOT. Where?
DOUG. Here.
HOT. This, Douglas? No, I know this face full well;
  A gallant knight he was, his name was Blunt;   20
  Semblably furnished like the king himself.
DOUG. Ah fool, go with thy soul whither it goes!
  A borrowed title hast thou bought too dear;
  Why didst thou tell me that thou wert a king?
HOT. The king hath many marching in his coats.   25
DOUG. Now, by my sword, I will kill all his coats;
  I'll murder all his wardrobe, piece by piece,
  Until I meet the king.
HOT.   Up and away!
  Our soldiers stand full fairly for the day.   [*Exeunt.*]
       [*Alarum. Enter* FALSTAFF *alone.*]
FAL. Though I could 'scape shot-free[2] at London, I fear the shot   30
  here; here's no scoring but upon the pate. Soft, who are you?
  Sir Walter Blunt; there's honor for you, here's no vanity! I
  am as hot as molten lead, and as heavy too; God keep lead out
  of me! I need no more weight than mine own bowels. I have
  led my ragamuffins where they are peppered; there's not three   35
  of my hundred and fifty left alive, and they are for the town's
  end, to beg during life. But who comes here?
       [*Enter the* PRINCE.]
PRINCE. What, stand'st thou idle here? lend me thy sword;
  Many a nobleman lies stark and stiff
  Under the hoofs of vaunting enemies,   40
  Whose deaths are yet unrevenged; I prithee, lend me thy sword.
FAL. O Hal, I prithee give me leave to breathe awhile. Turk Greg-
  ory[3] never did such deeds in arms as I have done this day. I
  have paid Percy, I have made him sure.
PRINCE. He is indeed, and living to kill thee. I prithee, lend me   45
  thy sword.
FAL. Nay, before God, Hal, if Percy be alive, thou get'st not
  my sword; but take my pistol if thou wilt.
PRINCE. Give it me; what, is it in the case?
FAL. Aye, Hal; 'tis hot, 'tis hot; there's that will sack a city.   50
       [*The* PRINCE *draws it out, and finds it to be a bottle of
       sack.*]
PRINCE. What, is it a time to jest and dally now?
       [*He throws the bottle at him. Exit.*]
FAL. Well, if Percy be alive, I'll pierce him. If he do come in my
  way, so; if he do not, if I come in his willingly, let him make a

2. Scot-free, without paying the bill at a tavern; "scoring" continues the pun; it means (1) marking up a charge; (2) cutting with a sword.

3. Falstaff combines Pope Gregory VII, of whom fantastic stories were told, with "Turk" (the Turks were noted for ferocity).

carbonado⁴ of me. I like not such grinning honor as Sir Walter
hath; give me life, which if I can save, so; if not, honor comes 55
unlooked for, and there's an end.   [*Exit.*]

SCENE 4

[*Alarum. Excursions.⁵ Enter the* KING, *the* PRINCE, PRINCE
JOHN OF LANCASTER, *and* EARL OF WESTMORELAND.]

KING. I prithee,
    Harry, withdraw thyself; thou bleed'st too much.
    Lord John of Lancaster, go you with him.
LAN. Not I, my lord, unless I did bleed too.
PRINCE. I beseech your majesty, make up,⁶   5
    Lest your retirement do amaze your friends.
KING. I will do so.
    My Lord of Westmoreland, lead him to his tent.
WEST. Come, my lord, I'll lead you to your tent.
PRINCE. Lead me, my lord? I do not need your help,   10
    And God forbid a shallow scratch should drive
    The Prince of Wales from such a field as this,
    Where stained nobility lies trodden on,
    And rebels' arms triumph in massacres!
LAN. We breathe too long; come, cousin Westmoreland,   15
    Our duty this way lies; for God's sake, come.
      [⟨*Exeunt* PRINCE JOHN *and* WESTMORELAND.⟩]
PRINCE. By God, thou hast deceived me, Lancaster;
    I did not think thee lord of such a spirit.
    Before, I loved thee as a brother, John,
    But now I do respect thee as my soul.   20
KING. I saw him hold Lord Percy at the point
    With lustier maintenance than I did look for
    Of such an ungrown warrior.
PRINCE.   O, this boy
    Lends mettle to us all!   [*Exit.*]
      [*Enter* DOUGLAS.]
DOUG. Another king! they grow like Hydra's heads.⁷   25
    I am the Douglas, fatal to all those
    That wear those colors on them; what art thou,
    That counterfeit'st the person of a king?
KING. The king himself, who, Douglas, grieves at heart
    So many of his shadows thou hast met   30
    And not the very king. I have two boys
    Seek Percy and thyself about the field,
    But seeing thou fall'st on me so luckily
    I will assay thee; so defend thyself.
DOUG. I fear thou art another counterfeit,   35
    And yet, in faith, thou bearest thee like a king;
    But mine I am sure thou art, whoe'er thou be,

4. A cubed steak.
5. Brief appearances and exits of soldiers fighting.
6. Advance; "amaze": dismay.

7. The heads of this fabulous monster
grew back faster than they could be
cut off.

And thus I win thee.

[*They fight; the* KING *being in danger, enter* PRINCE OF WALES.]

PRINCE. Hold up thy head, vile Scot, or thou art like
Never to hold it up again! the spirits   40
Of valiant Shirley, Stafford, Blunt, are in my arms;
It is the Prince of Wales that threatens thee,
Who never promiseth but he means to pay.

[*They fight;* DOUGLAS *flieth.*]

Cheerly, my lord; how fares your grace?
Sir Nicholas Gawsey hath for succor sent,   45
And so hath Clifton; I'll to Clifton straight.

KING. Stay, and breathe awhile.
Thou hast redeemed thy lost opinión,
And showed thou makest some tender of[8] my life
In this fair rescue thou hast brought to me.   50

PRINCE. O God, they did me too much injury
That ever said I hearkened for your death.
If it were so, I might have let alone
The insulting hand of Douglas over you,
Which would have been as speedy in your end   55
As all the poisonous potions in the world
And saved the treacherous labor of your son.

KING. Make up to Clifton; I'll to Sir Nicholas Gawsey.   [*Exit.*]

[*Enter* HOTSPUR.]

HOT. If I mistake not, thou art Harry Monmouth.

PRINCE. Thou speak'st as if I would deny my name.   60

HOT. My name is Harry Percy.

PRINCE.   Why then I see
A very valiant rebel of the name.
I am the Prince of Wales, and think not, Percy,
To share with me in glory any more:
Two stars keep not their motion in one sphere,[9]   65
Nor can one England brook a double reign
Of Harry Percy and the Prince of Wales.

HOT. Nor shall it, Harry, for the hour is come
To end the one of us; and would to God
Thy name in arms were now as great as mine!   70

PRINCE. I'll make it greater ere I part from thee,
And all the budding honors on thy crest
I'll crop to make a garland for my head.

HOT. I can no longer brook thy vanities.   [*They fight.*]

[*Enter* FALSTAFF.]

FAL. Well said, Hal, to it, Hal! Nay, you shall find no boy's play   75
here, I can tell you.

[*Enter* DOUGLAS; *he fighteth with* FALSTAFF, *who falls
down as if he were dead.* ⟨*Exit* DOUGLAS.⟩ *The* PRINCE
killeth PERCY.]

8. I.e., you have some concern for.   9. Orbit. "Brook": endure.
"Opinion": reputation.

HOT. O Harry, thou hast robbed me of my youth!
    I better brook the loss of brittle life
    Than those proud titles thou hast won of me;
    They wound my thoughts worse than thy sword my flesh;   80
    But thought's the slave of life, and life time's fool,
    And time, that takes survey of all the world,
    Must have a stop. O, I could prophesy,
    But that the earthy and cold hand of death
    Lies on my tongue; no, Percy, thou art dust,   85
    And food for—   [⟨*Dies.*⟩]
PRINCE. For worms, brave Percy; fare thee well, great heart!
    Ill-weaved ambition, how much art thou shrunk!
    When that this body did contain a spirit
    A kingdom for it was too small a bound,   90
    But now two paces of the vilest earth
    Is room enough; this earth that bears thee dead
    Bears not alive so stout[1] a gentleman.
    If thou wert sensible of courtesy,
    I should not make so dear[2] a show of zeal;   95
    But let my favors hide thy mangled face[3]
    And, even in thy behalf, I'll thank myself
    For doing these fair rites of tenderness.
    Adieu, and take thy praise with thee to heaven;
    Thy ignominy sleep with thee in the grave,   100
    But not remembered in thy epitaph!
      [*He spieth* FALSTAFF *on the ground.*]
    What, old acquaintance, could not all this flesh
    Keep in a little life? Poor Jack, farewell;
    I could have better spared a better man.
    O, I should have a heavy miss of thee,   105
    If I were much in love with vanity!
    Death hath not struck so fat a deer today,
    Though many dearer,[4] in this bloody fray.
    Emboweled will I see thee by and by;
    Till then in blood by noble Percy lie.   [*Exit.*]   110
FAL. [*rising up*] Emboweled! if thou embowel me today, I'll give
    you leave to powder[5] me and eat me tomorrow. 'Sblood, 'twas
    time to counterfeit, or that hot termagant[6] Scot had paid me
    scot and lot too. Counterfeit? I lie, I am no counterfeit; to die
    is to be a counterfeit, for he is but the counterfeit of a man   115
    who hath not the life of a man; but to counterfeit dying when
    a man thereby liveth is to be no counterfeit, but the true and
    perfect image of life indeed. The better part[7] of valor is discre-
    tion, in the which better part I have saved my life. Zounds, I
    am afraid of this gunpowder Percy, though he be dead; how if   120
    he should counterfeit too and rise? By my faith, I am afraid he
    would prove the better counterfeit. Therefore I'll make him

---

1. Valiant.
2. Open.
3. Prince Hal here covers Hotspur's face with a scarf.
4. Nobler. "Emboweled": embalmed.
5. Pickle.
6. Violent; "scot and lot": completely.
7. Quality, not "portion."

sure; yea, and I'll swear I killed him. Why may not he rise as
well as I? Nothing confutes me but eyes, and nobody sees me.
Therefore, sirrah [*stabbing him*], with a new wound in your 125
thigh, come you along with me.

      [*He takes up* HOTSPUR *on his back.*]
  [*Enter the* PRINCE *and* JOHN OF LANCASTER.]

PRINCE. Come, brother John, full bravely hast thou fleshed[8]
 Thy maiden sword.

LAN.   But soft, whom have we here?
 Did you not tell me this fat man was dead?

PRINCE. I did; I saw him dead,   130
 Breathless and bleeding on the ground. Art thou alive?
 Or is it fantasy[9] that plays upon our eyesight?
 I prithee speak; we will not trust our eyes
 Without our ears; thou art not what thou seem'st.

FAL. No, that's certain, I am not a double man; but if I be not 135
Jack Falstaff, then am I a Jack.[1] There is Percy [*throwing the
body down*]; if your father will do me any honor, so; if not, let
him kill the next Percy himself. I look to be either earl or duke,
I can assure you.

PRINCE. Why, Percy I killed myself and saw thee dead. 140

FAL. Didst thou? Lord, Lord, how this world is given to lying! I
grant you I was down and out of breath, and so was he; but we
rose both at an instant and fought a long hour by Shrewsbury
clock. If I may be believed, so; if not, let them that should reward valor bear the sin upon their own heads. I'll take it upon 145
my death, I gave him this wound in the thigh; if the man were
alive and would deny it, zounds, I would make him eat a piece
of my sword.

LAN. This is the strangest tale that ever I heard.

PRINCE. This is the strangest fellow, brother John.   150
 Come, bring your luggage nobly on your back;
 For my part, if a lie may do thee grace,
 I'll gild it with the happiest terms I have.

  [*A retreat is sounded.*]

 The trumpet sounds retreat;[2] the day is ours.
 Come, brother, let us to the highest[3] of the field, 155
 To see what friends are living, who are dead.

  [*Exeunt* ⟨PRINCE OF WALES *and* LANCASTER.⟩]

FAL. I'll follow, as they say, for reward. He that rewards me, God
reward him! If I do grow great,[4] I'll grow less, for I'll purge and
leave sack, and live cleanly as a nobleman should do. [*Exit.*]

SCENE 5

 [*The trumpets sound. Enter the* KING, PRINCE OF WALES,
 PRINCE JOHN OF LANCASTER, EARL OF WESTMORELAND,
 with WORCESTER *and* VERNON *prisoners.*]

8. Initiated.
9. Illusion.
1. I.e., a worthless fellow.
2. The signal to stop pursuit of the

defeated enemy.
3. Highest part.
4. I.e., become "either earl or duke."
"Purge": take cleansing medicines.

KING. Thus ever did rebellion find rebuke.
Ill-spirited Worcester, did not we send grace,
Pardon, and terms of love to all of you?
And wouldst thou turn our offers contrary,
Misuse the tenor of thy kinsman's trust?   5
Three knights upon our party slain today,
A noble earl and many a creature else
Had been alive this hour,
If like a Christian thou hadst truly borne
Betwixt our armies true intelligence.   10
WOR. What I have done my safety urged me to,
And I embrace this fortune patiently,
Since not to be avoided it falls on me.
KING. Bear Worcester to the death and Vernon too;
Other offenders we will pause upon.   15
    [*Exeunt* WORCESTER *and* VERNON ⟨*guarded.*⟩]
How goes the field?
PRINCE. The noble Scot, Lord Douglas, when he saw
The fortune of the day quite turned from him,
The noble Percy slain, and all his men
Upon the foot of fear,[5] fled with the rest,   20
And falling from a hill he was so bruised
That the pursuers took him. At my tent
The Douglas is, and I beseech your grace
I may dispose of him.
KING.   With all my heart.
PRINCE. Then, brother John of Lancaster, to you   25
This honorable bounty shall belong;
Go to the Douglas and deliver him
Up to his pleasure, ransomless and free;
His valor shown upon our crests today
Hath taught us how to cherish such high deeds   30
Even in the bosom of our adversaries.
LAN. I thank your grace for this high courtesy,
Which I shall give away immediately.
KING. Then this remains, that we divide our power.
You, son John and my cousin Westmoreland,   35
Towards York shall bend you with your dearest[6] speed
To meet Northumberland and the prelate Scroop,
Who, as we hear, are busily in arms;
Myself and you, son Harry, will towards Wales
To fight with Glendower and the Earl of March.   40
Rebellion in this land shall lose his sway,
Meeting the check of such another day;
And since this business so fair is done,
Let us not leave till all our own be won.   [*Exeunt.*]
                                                 1598

5. Fleeing in panic.   6. Greatest.

King Lear *King Lear* is one of Shakespeare's major tragedies, in the
company of *Hamlet, Macbeth, Othello,* and *Antony and Cleopatra.* It is
even on a grander scale than any of them, for it involves not only the world
in which human events take place, but the elements themselves—the realm
of Nature. Whether the cosmos is friendly to man, or indifferent to him, or
hostile to his aims and aspirations is a subject which the writer of tragedy
explores. From the Book of Job through the great Greek tragedies and on
to Shakespeare the tragic dramatist shows man suffering and trying to find
the meaning of his suffering. As Richard Sewall has put it (*Tragedy:
Modern Essays in Criticism,* ed. Laurence Michel and Richard B. Sewall, p.
124), "the essence of his nature is brought out by suffering: 'I suffer, I will
to suffer, I learn by suffering; therefore I am.'"

The anguish of the tragic hero arises from his uncertain knowledge of
himself and of people around him; from his awareness that good and evil
are distributed in no obvious or logical way, and that what seems at first to
be good is in fact evil; and from his desperate question whether there are
"justicers" above, and if so, how they can possibly allow the world to go on
as it does.

King Lear was written sometime between 1603 and 1606, probably in
1604 or 1605. It, together with the other great tragedies, comes in a period
after the sunny comedies *Much Ado About Nothing, As You Like It,* and
Twelfth Night, and before the dramatic romances of Shakespeare's final
period, *Cymbeline, The Winter's Tale,* and *The Tempest.* Although there
is a certain concentration on a particular type of play in each of these three
periods of Shakespeare's life, it would be rash to draw any conclusions
about the dramatist's biography from this. Mozart wrote some of his gayest
music when his personal life was miserable.

Structurally, *King Lear* has two plots, and more than in any other play of
Shakespeare, the two plots reinforce each other. They both have to do with
the relationship between parents and children. One plot involves three
daughters and a father; the other displays a father and two sons, one legitimate and the other illegitimate. The plots are woven together intimately;
they do not touch each other merely by coincidence. Shakespeare drew
them from widely different sources: the main plot of King Lear and his
three daughters came from an old chronicle play (not a tragedy) called *The
True Chronicle History of King Leir and his Three Daughters,* supplemented by treatments of the story in Holinshed's *Chronicle,* Spenser's
Faerie Queene, and perhaps others. The plot of Gloucester and his two sons
comes from Sir Philip Sidney's popular romance, *The Countess of Pembroke's Arcadia.*

The play has many themes, persistently touched upon and handled in
various ways. A major one is Nature, and the word has many meanings in
the play. Nature was thought of in the Middle Ages as a goddess; she was
also called (in Chaucer, for example) "Kind." The word "kind" and its
derivatives have both senses in Shakespeare, and the words "nature" and
"natural" have many connotations. "Natural" sometimes means "virtuous,"
as showing "natural" feelings for a parent or child. But "natural" may also
mean the opposite of law and custom. "Nature" is not only the physical

world, but also that part of nature that we call "human nature." What is truly "natural" in that sphere is a mystery. "Is there any cause in nature that makes these hard hearts?" asks Lear in his misery.

As he had done in some earlier plays, for example *Romeo and Juliet* and *Julius Caesar*, Shakespeare makes belief in astrology, the influence of the stars on human affairs, an important theme in *King Lear*. The characters take different points of view on this question, and we must not suppose that any one of them is necessarily giving the author's opinion. Belief in the stars is only one form of a great tragic dilemma: is what happens to us the result of fate or destiny, or do we bring our disasters upon ourselves?

Another great theme is the learning of wisdom. How is it done? By observation, using the eyes? By abandoning what we had supposed was wisdom and assuming that we are fools? By turning off the rational brain and trusting to the emotions? It has been suggested above that in tragedy man learns by suffering. In *King Lear* this suffering takes every form, physical and mental, and sometimes both. "How sharper than a serpent's tooth it is to have a thankless child!" says the old king. One of the ways the proud and arrogant must learn wisdom is by being stripped—stripped of their luxuries, their status, their power, and reduced to the level of beasts. It is noteworthy that this stripping process is one which can be done by one's enemies or by the elements, or by both.

The theme of "service" is a common one in Shakespeare. Service meant something different in the class society of the seventeenth century from what it means in our more democratic time. We are used to service stations and service industries, but in Shakespeare's time service was associated closely with rank, and it implied, or could imply, a degree of personal dedication which we would find strange. An earl, banished, disguises himself and applies to be a servant—a sensational situation in the eyes of Shakespeare's audience. Or servants resisting the evil actions of their masters—almost incredible. The roles of the Fool, Oswald, and Kent will not be clear unless we recall the earlier conception of service.

Though irony is very common in tragedy (that Gloucester doesn't "see" until he has lost his eyes is an example of irony) the comic element is not —except in Shakespeare. The porter in *Macbeth* is a famous instance. In *Lear* the Fool is partly comic, not in the free-hearted way of the fool Feste in *Twelfth Night*, but in the critical, satirical mode of Touchstone in *As You Like It*, only more so. The court jester, called "Fool" not because he was foolish, had a certain freedom which courtiers did not have. He could be threatened with whipping, as a child could, but he was treated affectionately by his master as long as he amused him. The Fool in *Lear* may be "a pestilent gall" to his master when he reminds him of his folly, but the King clearly loves him.

Love is a great force in the play, when it is finally discovered. It cannot be measured by numbers, as Lear first tries to do. Justice and pity may be relative, and they are vitally important in society, but in the great catastrophe at the end it is the love of Lear and Cordelia that surmounts even their destruction.

The Tragedy of King Lear

Dramatis Personae

KING LEAR
KING OF FRANCE
DUKE OF BURGUNDY
DUKE OF CORNWALL
DUKE OF ALBANY
EARL OF KENT
EARL OF GLOUCESTER
EDGAR, *son to* GLOUCESTER
EDMUND, *bastard son to* GLOUCESTER
CURAN, *a courtier*
OLD MAN, *tenant to* GLOUCESTER
DOCTOR
FOOL
OSWALD, *steward to* GONERIL
A CAPTAIN *employed by* EDMUND
GENTLEMAN *attendant on* CORDELIA
A HERALD
SERVANTS *to* CORNWALL
GONERIL ⎫
REGAN   ⎬ *daughters to* LEAR
CORDELIA ⎭
KNIGHTS *attending on* LEAR, OFFICERS, MESSENGERS, SOLDIERS,
ATTENDANTS

Act I

SCENE 1

[*Enter* KENT, GLOUCESTER, *and* EDMUND.]

KENT. I thought the king had more affected[1] the Duke of
Albany than Cornwall.

GLOU. It did always seem so to us: but now, in the division of
the kingdom, it appears not which of the dukes he values
most; for equalities are so weighed, that curiosity in neither   5
can make choice of either's moiety.[2]

KENT. Is not this your son, my lord?

GLOU. His breeding, sir, hath been at my charge: I have so often
blushed to acknowledge him, that now I am brazed[3] to it.

KENT. I cannot conceive[4] you.   10

GLOU. Sir, this young fellow's mother could: whereupon she grew

1. Regard for; "Albany" is Scotland.
2. I.e., shares are so evenly balanced that careful consideration cannot decide whose part is greater.
3. Hardened.
4. Understand, with a pun on "become pregnant."

round-wombed, and had, indeed, sir, a son for her cradle ere she had a husband for her bed. Do you smell a fault?

KENT. I cannot wish the fault undone, the issue of it being so proper.[5]   15

GLOU. But I have, sir, a son by order of law, some year elder than this, who yet is no dearer in my account: though this knave came something saucily into the world before he was sent for, yet was his mother fair; there was good sport at his making, and the whoreson must be acknowledged. Do you   20 know this noble gentleman, Edmund?

EDM. No, my lord.

GLOU. My lord of Kent. Remember him hereafter as my honorable friend.

EDM. My services to your lordship.   25

KENT. I must love you, and sue to know you better.

EDM. Sir, I shall study deserving.

GLOU. He hath been out[6] nine years, and away he shall again. [*Sound a sennet.*[7]] The king is coming.

   [*Enter one bearing a coronet, then* KING LEAR, CORNWALL,
   ALBANY, GONERIL, REGAN, CORDELIA, *and* ATTENDANTS.]

LEAR. Attend the lords of France and Burgundy, Gloucester.   30

GLOU. I shall, my liege.   [*Exeunt* GLOUCESTER *and* EDMUND.]

LEAR. Meantime we shall express our darker[8] purpose.
   Give me the map there. Know that we have divided
   In three our kingdom; and 'tis our fast intent
   To shake all cares and business from our age;   35
   Conferring them on younger strengths, while we
   Unburthened crawl toward death. Our son of Cornwall,
   And you, our no less loving son of Albany,
   We have this hour a constant will to publish
   Our daughters' several dowers, that future strife   40
   May be prevented now. The princes, France and Burgundy,
   Great rivals in our youngest daughter's love,
   Long in our court have made their amorous sojourn,
   And here are to be answered. Tell me, my daughters,—
   Since now we will divest us, both of rule,   45
   Interest[9] of territory, cares of state,—
   Which of you shall we say doth love us most?
   That we our largest bounty may extend
   Where nature doth with merit challenge.[1] Goneril,
   Our eldest-born, speak first.   50

GON. Sir, I love you more than words can wield the matter;[2]
   Dearer than eye-sight, space, and liberty;
   Beyond what can be valued, rich or rare;
   No less than life, with grace, health, beauty, honor;
   As much as child e'er loved, or father found;   55

5. Handsome.
6. Abroad.
7. A distinctive set of notes on a trumpet, announcing the arrival of that particular person to whom the notes belong.
8. More secret.
9. Possession.
1. I.e., where nature plus merit can make the greatest claim for reward.
2. Handle the theme.

A love that makes breath poor, and speech unable;
Beyond all manner of so much I love you.
COR. [*aside*] What shall Cordelia do? Love, and be silent.
LEAR. Of all these bounds, even from this line to this,
  With shadowy forests and with champains[3] riched,   60
  With plenteous rivers and wide-skirted meads,[4]
  We make thee lady: to thine and Albany's issue
  Be this perpetual. What says our second daughter,
  Our dearest Regan, wife to Cornwall? Speak.
REG. Sir, I am made   65
  Of the self-same metal[5] that my sister is,
  And prize me at her worth. In my true heart
  I find she names my very deed of love;
  Only she comes too short, that I profess
  Myself an enemy to all other joys,   70
  Which the most precious square of sense[6] possesses,
  And find I am alone felicitate[7]
  In your dear highness' love.
COR.   [*aside*] Then poor Cordelia!
  And yet not so; since, I am sure, my love's
  More richer than my tongue.   75
LEAR. To thee and thine hereditary ever
  Remain this ample third of our fair kingdom;
  No less in space, validity,[8] and pleasure,
  Than that conferred on Goneril. Now, our joy,
  Although the last, not least; to whose young love   80
  The vines of France and milk of Burgundy
  Strive to be interessed,[9] what can you say to draw
  A third more opulent than your sisters? Speak.
COR. Nothing, my lord.
LEAR. Nothing?   85
COR. Nothing.
LEAR. Nothing can come of nothing. Speak again.
COR. Unhappy that I am, I cannot heave
  My heart into my mouth. I love your majesty
  According to my bond;[1] nor more nor less.   90
LEAR. How, how, Cordelia! mend your speech a little,
  Lest it may mar your fortunes.
COR.   Good my lord,
  You have begot me, bred me, loved me; I
  Return those duties back as are right fit,
  Obey you, love you, and most honor you.   95
  Why have my sisters husbands, if they say
  They love you all? Haply, when I shall wed,
  That lord whose hand must take my plight[2] shall carry

---

3. Unwooded plains.
4. Meadows.
5. The stuff (mettle) of which a person,
or his character, is made.
6. Sensitive feeling.
7. I.e., can only be happy.
8. Value.

9. Closely united.
1. The word is ambiguous. It can mean
filial obligation, one's "bounden duty,"
or it can mean the strict terms of a contract, as in *The Merchant of Venice*.
2. The pledge in the marriage service:
"And thereto I plight thee my troth."

Half my love with him, half my care and duty.
Sure, I shall never marry like my sisters,   100
To love my father all.

LEAR. But goes thy heart with this?

COR. Ay, good my lord.

LEAR. So young, and so untender?

COR. So young, my lord, and true.   105

LEAR. Let it be so! Thy truth, then, be thy dower!
For, by the sacred radiance of the sun,
The mysteries of Hecate,[3] and the night;
By all the operation of the orbs[4]
From whom we do exist and cease to be;   110
Here I disclaim all my paternal care,
Propinquity and property of blood,[5]
And as a stranger to my heart and me
Hold thee, from this, for ever. The barbarous Scythian,[6]
Or he that makes his generation messes   115
To gorge his appetite,[7] shall to my bosom
Be as well neighbored, pitied, and relieved,
As thou my sometime daughter.

KENT.   Good my liege,—

LEAR. Peace, Kent!
Come not between the dragon and his wrath.[8]   120
I loved her most, and thought to set my rest[9]
On her kind nursery. Hence, and avoid my sight!
So be my grave my peace, as here I give
Her father's heart from her! Call France; who stirs?
Call Burgundy. Cornwall and Albany,   125
With my two daughters' dowers digest[1] this third:
Let pride, which she calls plainness, marry her.
I do invest you jointly with my power,
Pre-eminence, and all the large effects
That troop with majesty. Ourself, by monthly course,   130
With reservation of an hundred knights,
By you to be sustained, shall our abode
Make with you by due turns. Only we still retain
The name, and all the additions to a king;[2]
The sway, revenue, execution of the rest,   135
Beloved sons, be yours; which to confirm,
This coronet part betwixt you.

KENT.   Royal Lear,
Whom I have ever honored as my king,
Loved as my father, as my master followed,

---

3. The secret rites of the goddess of the lower world.
4. Planets.
5. Near relationship and identity of blood.
6. The nomadic Scythians were supposed to be the most barbarous people of antiquity.
7. A cannibal who eats his own children.
8. A dragon was on the crest of ancient British kings, and in Shakespeare the dragon is often a symbol of wrath.
9. Not only "to seek my repose" but also "to bet everything I have," an expression from the card game primero.
1. Absorb.
2. Royal titles, honors, ceremony. He intends to give up only his wealth and power.

As my great patron thought on in my prayers— 140
LEAR. The bow is bent and drawn, make from the shaft.[3]
KENT. Let it fall rather, though the fork[4] invade
    The region of my heart: be Kent unmannerly,
    When Lear is mad. What wilt thou do, old man?
    Think'st thou that duty shall have dread to speak, 145
    When power to flattery bows? To plainness honor's bound,
    When majesty stoops to folly.[5] Reverse thy doom,[6]
    And, in thy best consideration, check
    This hideous rashness. Answer my life my judgment,
    Thy youngest daughter does not love thee least; 150
    Nor are those empty-hearted whose low sound
    Reverbs no hollowness.[7]
LEAR.   Kent, on thy life, no more.
KENT. My life I never held but as a pawn
    To wage against thy enemies; nor fear to lose it,
    Thy safety being the motive.
LEAR.   Out of my sight! 155
KENT. See better, Lear; and let me still remain
    The true blank of thine eye.[8]
LEAR. Now, by Apollo,—
KENT.   Now, by Apollo, king,
    Thou swear'st thy gods in vain.[9]
LEAR.   O, vassal! miscreant!
                  [*Laying his hand on his sword.*]
ALB. }
CORN. }   Dear sir, forbear. 160
KENT. Do;
    Kill thy physician, and the fee bestow
    Upon thy foul disease. Revoke thy doom;
    Or, whilst I can vent clamor from my throat,
    I'll tell thee thou dost evil.
LEAR.   Hear me, recreant![1] 165
    On thine allegiance, hear me!
    Since thou hast sought to make us break our vow,
    Which we durst never yet, and with strained[2] pride
    To come between our sentence and our power,
    Which nor our nature nor our place can bear, 170
    Our potency made good, take thy reward.
    Five days we do allot thee, for provision
    To shield thee from diseases[3] of the world;
    And on the sixth to turn thy hated back
    Upon our kingdom: if, on the tenth day following, 175

3. I have drawn the bow; you had better avoid the arrow I am about to shoot at you.
4. An arrowhead with two prongs.
5. A common rhetorical device in Shakespeare, the substitution of the abstract for the concrete.
6. Judgment, sentence.
7. That Cordelia says little and speaks softly does not mean that she is hollow (insincere).

8. The bull's-eye of a target.
9. Classical gods are invoked throughout to heighten the pagan atmosphere. But there is frequent questioning as to whether those, or any, gods exist and if they do, whether they can be invoked. The word *miscreant*, which Lear calls Kent, used to mean "misbeliever."
1. Traitor.
2. Forced, unnatural.
3. Difficulties.

Thy banished trunk be found in our dominions,
The moment is thy death. Away! by Jupiter,
This shall not be revoked.
KENT. Fare thee well, king. Sith thus thou wilt appear,
    Freedom lives hence, and banishment is here.[4]   180
    [*To* CORDELIA.] The gods to their dear shelter take thee,
        maid,
    That justly think'st, and hast most rightly said!
    [*To* REGAN *and* GONERIL.] And your large speeches may your
        deeds approve,
    That good effects may spring from words of love.[5]
    Thus Kent, O princes, bids you all adieu;   185
    He'll shape his old course in a country new.   [*Exit.*]
    [*Flourish. Re-enter* GLOUCESTER, *with* FRANCE, BURGUNDY,
      and ATTENDANTS.]
GLOU. Here's France and Burgundy, my noble lord.
LEAR. My lord of Burgundy,
    We first address towards you, who with this king
    Hath rivaled for our daughter. What, in the least,   190
    Will you require in present dower with her,
    Or cease your quest of love?
BUR.   Most royal majesty,
    I crave no more than what your highness offered,
    Nor will you tender less.
LEAR.   Right noble Burgundy,
    When she was dear to us, we did hold her so;[6]   195
    But now her price is fallen. Sir, there she stands;
    If aught within that little seeming substance,[7]
    Or all of it, with our displeasure pieced,[8]
    And nothing more, may fitly like your grace,
    She's there, and she is yours.
BUR.   I know no answer.   200
LEAR. Will you, with those infirmities she owes,[9]
    Unfriended, new-adopted to our hate,
    Dowered with our curse, and strangered with our oath,
    Take her, or leave her?
BUR.   Pardon me, royal sir;
    Election makes not up[1] on such conditions.   205
LEAR. Then leave her, sir; for, by the power that made me,
    I tell you all her wealth. [*to* FRANCE] For you, great king,
    I would not from your love make such a stray[2]
    To match you where I hate; therefore beseech you
    To avert your liking a more worthier way   210

4. I.e., to stay here would be a punishment like being banished, and going
away is not a punishment, but an escape
to freedom.
5. May your actions correspond to your
speeches, so words promising love may
have good results. Kent's rhyming lines
are ironical, moralistic, and constitute a
kind of formal farewell.
6. Punning on the word "dear"—"beloved" and "expensive."
7. That small appearance of reality.
8. Attached to it.
9. Owns.
1. Choice is not made.
2. Stray so far.

Than on a wretch whom nature is ashamed
Almost to acknowledge hers.
FRANCE.   This is most strange,
That she, that even but now was your best object,
The argument[3] of your praise, balm of your age,
Most best, most dearest, should in this trice of time   215
Commit a thing so monstrous, to dismantle
So many folds of favor. Sure, her offense
Must be of such unnatural degree,
That monsters it, or your fore-vouched affection
Fall'n into taint;[4] which to believe of her,   220
Must be a faith that reason without miracle
Could never plant in me.
COR.   I yet beseech your majesty,—
If for I want that glib and oily art,
To speak and purpose not,—since what I well intend,
I'll do't before I speak,—that you make known   225
It is no vicious blot, murder, or foulness,
No unchaste action, or dishonored step,
That hath deprived me of your grace and favor;
But even for want of that for which I am richer,
A still-soliciting[5] eye, and such a tongue   230
As I am glad I have not, though not to have it
Hath lost me in your liking.
LEAR.   Better thou
Hadst not been born than not to have pleased me better.
FRANCE. Is it but this,—a tardiness in nature[6]
Which often leaves the history unspoke   235
That it intends to do? My lord of Burgundy,
What say you to the lady? Love's not love
When it is mingled with regards that stands
Aloof from th' entire point. Will you have her?
She is herself a dowry.
BUR.   Royal Lear,   240
Give but that portion which yourself proposed,
And here I take Cordelia by the hand,
Duchess of Burgundy.
LEAR. Nothing! I have sworn; I am firm.
BUR. I am sorry, then, you have so lost a father   245
That you must lose a husband.
COR.   Peace be with Burgundy!
Since that respects of fortune[7] are his love,
I shall not be his wife.
FRANCE. Fairest Cordelia, that art most rich, being poor;
Most choice, forsaken; and most loved, despised!   250

3. Main object of love and favor; "argument": subject.
4. Her offense must be unnatural and monstrous, or else your previously expressed affection for her must have been error.
5. Always pleading.
6. Natural shyness.
7. Considerations of money.

Thee and thy virtues here I seize upon:
Be it lawful I take up what's cast away.
Gods, gods! 't is strange that from their cold'st neglect
My love should kindle to inflamed respect.[8]
Thy dowerless daughter, king, thrown to my chance,   255
Is queen of us, of ours, and our fair France.
Not all the dukes of waterish Burgundy
Can buy this unprized precious maid of me.
Bid them farewell, Cordelia, though unkind;[9]
Thou losest here, a better where to find.   260
LEAR. Thou hast her, France; let her be thine; for we
Have no such daughter, nor shall ever see
That face of hers again. Therefore be gone
Without our grace, our love, our benison.
Come, noble Burgundy.   265

[*Flourish. Exeunt all but* FRANCE, GONERIL, REGAN, *and*
CORDELIA.]

FRANCE. Bid farewell to your sisters.
COR. The jewels of our father, with washed eyes[1]
Cordelia leaves you. I know you what you are,
And like a sister am most loath to call
Your faults as they are named. Use well our father.   270
To your professed bosoms[2] I commit him;
But yet, alas, stood I within his grace,
I would prefer him to a better place.
So, farewell to you both.
REG. Prescribe not us our duties.
GON.   Let your study   275
Be to content your lord, who hath received you
At fortune's alms.[3] You have obedience scanted,
And well are worth the want that you have wanted.[4]
COR. Time shall unfold what pleated cunning hides:
Who cover faults, at last shame them derides.   280
Well may you prosper!
FRANCE.   Come, my fair Cordelia.

[*Exeunt* FRANCE *and* CORDELIA.]

GON. Sister, it is not a little I have to say of what most nearly
appertains to us both. I think our father will hence to-night.
REG. That's most certain, and with you; next month with us.
GON. You see how full of changes his age is; the observation we   285
have made of it hath not been little: he always loved our sister
most; and with what poor judgment he hath now cast her off
appears too grossly.[5]

8. Passionate regard.
9. Unnatural and cruel. The rhyming lines here, as in Kent's farewell, are ceremonial and sententious.
1. Tears.
2. Referring to the love they claimed they felt.
3. As a petty charity, not a bounteous gift.
4. You have come short of obedience, and this lack is just about what you are worth.
5. Such chorus-like comments, a convention in Shakespeare, guide the audience's response; they are not intended to characterize the speakers.

REG. 'Tis the infirmity of his age; yet he hath ever but slenderly
  known himself.   290
GON. The best and soundest of his time hath been but rash; then
  must we look to receive from his age, not alone the imperfections of long-engraffed condition, but therewithal the unruly
  waywardness that infirm and choleric years bring with them.
REG. Such unconstant starts[6] are we like to have from him as   295
  this of Kent's banishment.
GON. There is further compliment of leave-taking between
  France and him. Pray you, let's hit[7] together: if our father
  carry authority with such dispositions as he bears, this last[8]
  surrender of his will but offend us.   300
REG. We shall further think on 't.
GON. We must do something, and i' the heat.[9]   [*Exeunt.*]

SCENE 2

[*Enter* EDMUND, *with a letter.*]
EDM. Thou, nature, art my goddess; to thy law
  My services are bound. Wherefore should I
  Stand in the plague of custom,[1] and permit
  The curiosity[2] of nations to deprive me,
  For that I am some twelve or fourteen moonshines   5
  Lag of a brother? Why bastard? wherefore base?
  When my dimensions are as well compact,[3]
  My mind as generous[4] and my shape as true,
  As honest[5] madam's issue? Why brand they us
  With base? with baseness? bastardy? base, base?   10
  Who, in the lusty stealth of nature, take
  More composition and fierce quality[6]
  Than doth, within a dull, stale, tired bed,
  Go to creating a whole tribe of fops,
  Got 'tween asleep and wake? Well, then,   15
  Legitimate Edgar, I must have your land.
  Our father's love is to the bastard Edmund
  As to the legitimate. Fine word,—'legitimate'!
  Well, my legitimate, if this letter speed,[7]
  And my invention thrive, Edmund the base   20
  Shall top the legitimate. I grow; I prosper.
  Now, gods, stand up for bastards!
    [*Enter* GLOUCESTER.]
GLOU. Kent banished thus? and France in choler parted?
  And the king gone tonight? subscribed[8] his power?

6. Sudden jerks (as from a skittish
horse).
7. Agree.
8. Recent.
9. While the iron's hot (proverbial).
1. Be dependent on diseased custom.
2. Scrupulousness.

3. My proportions are as well made.
4. Noble, aristocratic.
5. Chaste.
6. A fuller mixture and more energy
7. Prosper; "invention": plot.
8. Surrendered.

Confined to exhibition?[9] All this done   25
Upon the gad?[1] Edmund, how now! what news?

EDM. So please your lordship, none.   [*Putting up the letter.*]

GLOU. Why so earnestly seek you to put up that letter?

EDM. I know no news, my lord.

GLOU. What paper were you reading?   30

EDM. Nothing, my lord.

GLOU. No? What needed, then, that terrible dispatch of it into
your pocket? the quality[2] of nothing hath not such need to
hide itself. Let's see. Come, if it be nothing, I shall not need
spectacles.   35

EDM. I beseech you, sir, pardon me. It is a letter from my
brother, that I have not all o'er-read; and for so much as I
have perused, I find it not fit for your o'er-looking.

GLOU. Give me the letter, sir.

EDM. I shall offend, either to detain or give it. The contents, as 40
in part I understand them, are to blame.

GLOU. Let's see, let's see.

EDM. I hope, for my brother's justification, he wrote this but as
an essay or taste[3] of my virtue.

GLOU. [*reads*] "This policy and reverence[4] of age makes the 45
world bitter to the best of our times; keeps our fortunes from
us till our oldness cannot relish them. I begin to find an idle
and fond[5] bondage in the oppression of aged tyranny; who
sways, not as it hath power, but as it suffered.[6] Come to
me, that of this I may speak more. If our father would sleep 50
till I waked him, you should enjoy half his revenue for ever,
and live the beloved of your brother, EDGAR."
Hum—conspiracy!—"Sleep till I waked him,—you should enjoy half his revenue,"—My son Edgar! Had he a hand to write
this? a heart and brain to breed it in?—When came this to 55
you? who brought it?

EDM. It was not brought me, my lord; there's the cunning of it;
I found it thrown in at the casement of my closet.[7]

GLOU. You know the character[8] to be your brother's?

EDM. If the matter were good, my lord, I durst swear it were his; 60
but, in respect of that, I would fain think it were not.

GLOU. It is his.

EDM. It is his hand, my lord; but I hope his heart is not in the
contents.

GLOU. Hath he never heretofore sounded[9] you in this business? 65

EDM. Never, my lord. But I have heard him oft maintain it to be
fit, that, sons at perfect age, and fathers declining, the father
should be as ward to the son, and the son manage his revenue.

GLOU. O villain, villain! His very opinion in the letter! Abhorred

---

9. A small allowance.
1. Suddenly.
2. Nature.
3. Test or trial.
4. Custom of reverencing.
5. Foolish.

6. Who rules not through power, but by
our permission.
7. Private room.
8. Handwriting.
9. Tested the depth (a nautical metaphor).

villain! Unnatural, detested, brutish villain! worse than bru- 70
tish! Go, sirrah, seek him. I'll apprehend him. Abominable villain! Where is he?

EDM. I do not well know, my lord. If it shall please you to suspend your indignation against my brother till you can derive
from him better testimony of his intent, you shall run a cer- 75
tain course; where, if you violently proceed against him, mistaking his purpose, it would make a great gap in your own
honor and shake in pieces the heart of his obedience. I dare
pawn down my life for him that he hath wrote this to feel my
affection to your honor, and to no further pretense of danger.[1] 80

GLOU. Think you so?

EDM. If your honor judge it meet, I will place you where you
shall hear us confer of this, and by an auricular assurance[2]
have your satisfaction; and that without any further delay than
this very evening. 85

GLOU. He cannot be such a monster—

EDM. Nor is not, sure.

GLOU. To his father, that so tenderly and entirely loves him.
Heaven and earth! Edmund, seek him out; wind me into[3]
him, I pray you; frame the business after your own wisdom. I 90
would unstate myself, to be in a due resolution.[4]

EDM. I will seek him, sir, presently[5]; convey the business as I
shall find means, and acquaint you withal.

GLOU. These late[6] eclipses in the sun and moon portend no good
to us. Though the wisdom of nature can reason it thus and 95
thus,[7] yet nature finds itself scourged by the sequent effects.
Love cools, friendship falls off, brothers divide; in cities,
mutinies;[8] in countries, discord; in palaces, treason; and the
bond cracked 'twixt son and father. This villain of mine comes
under the prediction; there's son against father. The king falls 100
from bias of nature;[9] there's father against child. We have
seen the best of our time. Machinations, hollowness, treachery, and all ruinous disorders, follow us disquietly to our
graves. Find out this villain, Edmund; it shall lose thee nothing; do it carefully. And the noble and true-hearted Kent ban- 105
ished! his offence, honesty! 'Tis strange.   [*Exit.*]

EDM. This is the excellent foppery[1] of the world, that, when we
are sick in fortune, often the surfeit of our own behavior, we
make guilty of[2] our disasters the sun, the moon, and the stars;
as if we were villains by necessity; fools by heavenly compul- 110
sion;   knaves,   thieves,   and   treachers,   by   spherical
predominance;[3] drunkards, liars, and adulterers, by an

enforced obedience of planetary influence; and all that we are
evil in, by a divine thrusting on.[4] An admirable evasion of
whore-master man, to lay his goatish[5] disposition to the
charge of a star! My father compounded with my mother
under the dragon's tail, and my nativity was under Ursa
Major, so that it follows, I am rough and lecherous. Fut![6] I
should have been that I am, had the maidenliest star in the
firmament twinkled on my bastardizing. Edgar—

[*Enter* EDGAR.]

and pat he comes like the catastrophe of the old comedy.[7] My
cue is villanous melancholy, with a sigh like Tom o' Bedlam.[8]
O, these eclipses do portend these divisions![9] Fa, sol, la, mi.

EDG. How now, brother Edmund? What serious contemplation
are you in?

EDM. I am thinking, brother, of a prediction I read this other
day, what should follow these eclipses.

EDG. Do you busy yourself about that?

EDM. I promise you, the effects he writes of succeed[1] unhappily;
as of unnaturalness between the child and the parent; death,
dearth,[2] dissolutions of ancient amities; divisions in state,
menaces and maledictions against king and nobles; needless
diffidences,[3] banishment of friends, dissipation of cohorts,[4]
nuptial breaches, and I know not what.

EDG. How long have you been a sectary astronomical?[5]

EDM. Come, come! When saw you my father last?

EDG. Why, the night gone by.

EDM. Spake you with him?

EDG. Ay, two hours together.

EDM. Parted you in good terms? Found you no displeasure in
him by word or countenance?

EDG. None at all.

EDM. Bethink yourself wherein you may have offended him; and
at my entreaty forbear his presence till some little time hath
qualified[6] the heat of his displeasure; which at this instant so
rageth in him, that with the mischief of your person it would
scarcely allay.

EDG. Some villain hath done me wrong.

EDM. That's my fear. I pray you, have a continent[7] forbearance
till the speed of his rage goes slower; and, as I say, retire with
me to my lodging, from whence I will fitly[8] bring you to hear
my lord speak. Pray ye, go! There's my key. If you do stir

---

4. Supernatural instigation.
5. Lecherous.
6. Christ's foot: an oath.
7. Like the conclusion in an old comedy, often hurriedly patched up to bring the play to an end.
8. A mad beggar. "Bedlam" comes from Bethlehem Hospital, an asylum for the insane in London.
9. Disunions. But "divisions" was also a

musical term, meaning "runs."
1. Turn out.
2. Famine.
3. Distrusts.
4. Breaking up of army units.
5. Believer in astrology.
6. Lessened.
7. Restrained.
8. Suitably.

abroad, go armed.

EDG. Armed, brother?

EDM. Brother, I advise you to the best. Go armed. I am no 155
honest man if there be any good meaning[9] towards you. I have
told you what I have seen and heard; but faintly, nothing like
the image and horror[1] of it. Pray you, away!

EDG. Shall I hear from you anon?

EDM. I do serve you in this business. [*Exit* EDGAR.] 160
    A credulous father, and a brother noble,
    Whose nature is so far from doing harms,
    That he suspects none; on whose foolish honesty
    My practices ride easy! I see the business.
    Let me, if not by birth, have lands by wit: 165
    All with me's meet that I can fashion fit. [*Exit.*]

SCENE 3

[*Enter* GONERIL, *and* OSWALD, *her steward.*]

GON. Did my father strike my gentleman for chiding of his fool?

OSW. Yes, madam.

GON. By day and night[2] he wrongs me; every hour
    He flashes into one gross crime[3] or other,
    That sets us all at odds. I'll not endure it. 5
    His knights grow riotous, and himself upbraids us
    On every trifle. When he returns from hunting,
    I will not speak with him. Say I am sick.
    If you come slack of[4] former services,
    You shall do well; the fault of it I'll answer.[5] 10

OSW. He's coming, madam; I hear him. [*Horns within.*]

GON. Put on what weary negligence you please,
    You and your fellows. I'd have it come to question.[6]
    If he dislike it, let him to our sister,
    Whose mind and mine, I know, in that are one, 15
    Not to be overruled. Idle old man,
    That still would manage those authorities
    That he hath given away! Now, by my life,
    Old fools are babes again, and must be used
    With checks as flatteries,—when they are seen abused.[7] 20
    Remember what I tell you.

OSW.   Well, madam.

GON. And let his knights have colder looks among you.
    What grows of it, no matter; advise your fellows so.
    I would breed from hence occasions,[8] and I shall,
    That I may speak. I'll write straight[9] to my sister, 25
    To hold my very course. Prepare for dinner. [*Exeunt.*]

---

9. Intention.
1. Horrible reality.
2. An oath. See I.i.111–112.
3. Offense, not necessarily a violation of law.
4. Fall short of.
5. Be answerable for.

6. Made an issue of.
7. Must be corrected by rebukes rather than flatteries when they are seen to be deluded.
8. Chances.
9. Immediately.

SCENE 4

[*Enter* KENT, *disguised.*]

KENT. If but as well I other accents borrow,
　That can my speech defuse,[1] my good intent
　May carry through itself to that full issue
　For which I razed my likeness.[2] Now, banished Kent,
　If thou canst serve where thou dost stand condemned,　　　5
　So may it come, thy master, whom thou lovest,
　Shall find thee full of labors.

　　　[*Horns within. Enter* LEAR, KNIGHTS, *and* ATTENDANTS.]

LEAR. Let me not stay a jot[3] for dinner; go get it ready. [*Exit
　an* ATTENDANT.] How now! What art thou?

KENT. A man, sir.　　　　　　　　　　　　　　　　　　　　　10

LEAR. What dost thou profess?[4] What wouldst thou with us?

KENT. I do profess to be no less than I seem; to serve him truly
　that will put me in trust; to love him that is honest; to con-
　verse with him that is wise and says little; to fear judgment; to
　fight when I cannot choose; and to eat no fish.[5]　　　　　15

LEAR. What art thou?

KENT. A very honest-hearted fellow, and as poor as the king.

LEAR. If thou be as poor for a subject as he is for a king, thou art
　poor enough. What wouldst thou?

KENT. Service.　　　　　　　　　　　　　　　　　　　　　20

LEAR. Who wouldst thou serve?

KENT. You.

LEAR. Dost thou know me, fellow?

KENT. No, sir; but you have that in your countenance[6] which I
　would fain call master.　　　　　　　　　　　　　　　　25

LEAR. What's that?

KENT. Authority.

LEAR. What services canst thou do?

KENT. I can keep honest counsel, ride, run, mar a curious[7] tale
　in telling it, and deliver a plain message bluntly. That which　30
　ordinary men are fit for, I am qualified in; and the best of me
　is diligence.

LEAR. How old art thou?

KENT. Not so young, sir, to love a woman for singing, nor so
　old to dote on her for anything. I have years on my back forty-　35
　eight.

LEAR. Follow me; thou shalt serve me. If I like thee no worse
　after dinner, I will not part from thee yet. Dinner, ho dinner!
　Where's my knave?[8] my fool? Go you, and call my fool hither.

　　　　　　　　　　　　　　　　　　　　　[*Exit an* ATTENDANT.]

　[*Enter* OSWALD.]

1. If I can speak like someone else, so
that my voice is disguised.
2. Changed my appearance (put on this
disguise).
3. Wait a moment.
4. What is your trade or calling? But
Kent takes the word "profess" in another sense—to assert, believe.

5. To know that I must face judgment
and act accordingly; to fight when I cannot avoid it; and to be a loyal Protestant, not a Catholic who eats fish on
Friday.
6. Bearing.
7. Intricate, complicated.
8. Boy.

LEAR. You, you, sirrah,[9] where's my daughter? 40

OSW. So please you,— [*Exit.*]

LEAR. What says the fellow there? Call the clotpoll[1] back. [*Exit a* KNIGHT.] Where's my fool, ho? I think the world's asleep.
    [*Re-enter* KNIGHT.]
    How now! where's that mongrel?

KNIGHT. He says, my lord, your daughter is not well. 45

LEAR. Why came not the slave back to me when I called him?

KNIGHT. Sir, he answered me in the roundest[2] manner, he would not.

LEAR. He would not!

KNIGHT. My lord, I know not what the matter is; but, to my 50 judgment, your highness is not entertained[3] with that ceremonious affection as you were wont,[4] there's a great abatement of kindness appears as well in the general dependants as in the duke himself also and your daughter.

LEAR. Ha! sayest thou so? 55

KNIGHT. I beseech you pardon me, my lord, if I be mistaken; for my duty cannot be silent when I think your highness wronged.

LEAR. Thou but rememberest me of mine own conception. I have perceived a most faint neglect of late; which I have rather blamed as mine own jealous curiosity[5] than as a very 60 pretence and purpose of unkindness. I will look further into 't. But where's my fool? I have not seen him this two days.

KNIGHT. Since my young lady's going into France, sir, the fool hath much pined away.

LEAR. No more of that; I have noted it well. Go you and tell my 65 daughter I would speak with her. [*Exit* KNIGHT.] Go you, call hither my fool. [*Exit an* ATTENDANT.]
    [*Re-enter* OSWALD.]
    O, you sir, you! Come you hither, sir. Who am I, sir?

OSW. My lady's father.

LEAR. "My lady's father"! My lord's knave! You whoreson dog! 70 you slave! you cur!

OSW. I am none of these, my lord; I beseech your pardon.

LEAR. Do you bandy[6] looks with me, you rascal?
    [*Striking him.*]

OSW. I'll not be struck, my lord.

KENT. Nor tripped neither, you base foot-ball player.[7] 75
    [*Tripping up his heels.*]

LEAR. I thank thee, fellow; thou servest me, and I'll love thee.

KENT. Come, sir, arise, away! I'll teach you differences.[8] Away, away! If you will measure your lubber's length[9] again, tarry; but away! Go to! Have you wisdom? so.

---

9. An address to a social inferior or stranger.
1. Clod-pate, blockhead.
2. Plainest, rudest.
3. Treated.
4. Accustomed.
5. Suspicious watchfulness.
6. Hit back and forth, as in tennis.

7. Elizabethan football, not the modern sport, was played only by lower-class ruffians, and, according to a contemporary, was marked by "fighting, brawling, contention, quarrel-picking, murder, homicide, and great effusion of blood."
8. Social rank and position.
9. Be knocked down.

[*Pushes* OSWALD *out.*]

LEAR. Now, my friendly knave, I thank thee: there's earnest[1] 80
of thy service.   [*Giving* KENT *money.*]
   [*Enter* FOOL.]

FOOL. Let me hire him too. Here's my coxcomb.
                [*Offering* KENT *his cap.*]

LEAR. How now, my pretty knave! How dost thou?

FOOL. Sirrah, you were best take my coxcomb.

KENT. Why, fool?   85

FOOL. Why, for taking one's part that's out of favor. Nay, an
   thou canst not smile as the wind sits, thou'lt catch cold
   shortly.[2] There, take my coxcomb! Why, this fellow has banished two on's daughters, and did the third a blessing against
   his will. If thou follow him, thou must needs wear my cox-   90
   comb. How now, nuncle![3] Would I had two coxcombs and
   two daughters!

LEAR. Why, my boy?

FOOL. If I gave them all my living, I'd keep my coxcombs myself.
   There's mine; beg another of thy daughters.   95

LEAR. Take heed, sirrah; the whip.

FOOL. Truth's a dog must to kennel; he must be whipped out,
   when Lady the brach[4] may stand by the fire and stink.

LEAR. A pestilent gall to me!

FOOL. Sirrah, I'll teach thee a speech.   100

LEAR. Do.

FOOL. Mark it, nuncle:
          Have more than thou showest,
          Speak less than thou knowest,
          Lend less than thou owest,[5]   105
          Ride more than thou goest,
          Learn more than thou trowest,
          Set less than thou throwest;[6]
          Leave thy drink and thy whore,
          And keep in-a-door,   110
          And thou shalt have more
          Than two tens to a score.[7]

KENT. This is nothing, fool.

FOOL. Then 'tis like the breath of an unfeed lawyer; you gave
   me nothing for 't. Can you make no use of nothing, nuncle? 115

LEAR. Why, no, boy; nothing can be made out of nothing.

FOOL. [*to* KENT] Prithee, tell him, so much the rent of his land
   comes to. He will not believe a fool.

LEAR. A bitter fool!

FOOL. Dost thou know the difference, my boy, between a bitter 120

---

1. A small sum paid in advance.
2. If you can't please the party in power, you will be thrown out.
3. Contraction of "mine uncle"—a form of address used by fools to their male superiors.
4. Bitch. "Lady" was a common name for a female dog (see *1 Henry IV*,

III.i.235).
5. Ownest; "goest": walk.
6. Don't put all your winnings on one cast of the dice.
7. You will have more than twenty shillings to the pound; i.e., you will save money.

fool and a sweet fool?

LEAR. No, lad; teach me.

FOOL.   That lord that counseled thee
                          To give away thy land,
                     Come place him here by me,   125
                          Do thou for him stand:
                     The sweet and bitter fool
                          Will presently appear;
                     The one in motley here,
                          The other found out there.   130

LEAR. Dost thou call me fool, boy?

FOOL. All thy other titles thou hast given away; that thou wast born with.

KENT. This is not altogether fool, my lord.

FOOL. No, faith, lords and great men will not let me; if I had a 135 monopoly[8] out, they would have part on 't: and ladies too, they will not let me have all fool to myself; they 'll be snatching. Give me an egg, uncle, and I'll give thee two crowns.

LEAR. What two crowns shall they be?

FOOL. Why, after I have cut the egg i' the middle, and eat up 140 the meat, the two crowns of the egg. When thou clovest thy crown i' the middle, and gavest away both parts, thou borest thy ass on thy back o'er the dirt.[9] Thou hadst little wit in thy bald crown, when thou gavest thy golden one away. If I speak like myself in this, let him be whipped that first finds it so.   145
     [*singing*]
               Fools had ne'er less wit in a year;
                    For wise men are grown foppish,
               They know not how their wits to wear,
                    Their manners are so apish.

LEAR. When were you wont to be so full of songs, sirrah?   150

FOOL. I have used it, nuncle, ever since thou madest thy daughters thy mother; for when thou gavest them the rod, and put'st down thine own breeches,
     [*singing*]
               Then they for sudden joy did weep,
                    And I for sorrow sung,   155
               That such a king should play bo-peep,[1]
                    And go the fools among.
Prithee, nuncle, keep a schoolmaster that can teach thy fool to lie. I would fain learn to lie.

LEAR. An you lie, sirrah, we'll have you whipped.   160

FOOL. I marvel what kin thou and thy daughters are. They'll have me whipped for speaking true, thou'lt have me whipped for lying; and sometimes I am whipped for holding my peace. I had rather be any kind o' thing than a fool; and yet I would not be thee, nuncle; thou hast pared thy wit o' both sides, and 165

---

8. That monopolies on certain imports and raw materials were granted to courtiers was a source of common complaint.

9. Mud. In an Aesop fable, a man carries his ass instead of riding it.

1. Hide-and-go-seek.

left nothing i' the middle. Here comes one o' the parings.
    [*Enter* GONERIL.]
LEAR. How now, daughter! What makes that frontlet[2] on? Me-
    thinks you are too much of late i' the frown.
FOOL. Thou wast a pretty fellow when thou hadst no need to
    care for her frowning; now thou art an O without a figure.[3] I 170
    am better than thou art now; I am a fool, thou art nothing.
    [*To* GON.] Yes, forsooth, I will hold my tongue; so your face
    bids me, though you say nothing.   Mum, mum,
               He that keeps nor crust nor crum,
               Weary of all, shall want some. 175
    [*Pointing to* LEAR.] That's a shelled peascod.[4]
GON. Not only, sir, this your all-licensed fool,
    But other of your insolent retinue
    Do hourly carp and quarrel, breaking forth
    In rank[6] and not-to-be-endured riots. 180
    I had thought, by making this well known unto you,
    To have found a safe[7] redress; but now grow fearful,
    By what yourself too late have spoke and done,
    That you protect this course, and put it on[8]
    By your allowance; which if you should, the fault 185
    Would not 'scape censure, nor the redresses sleep,
    Which, in the tender of a wholesome weal,[9]
    Might in their working do you that offense,
    Which else were shame, that then necessity
    Will call discreet proceeding. 190
FOOL. For, you know, nuncle,
        The hedge-sparrow fed the cuckoo so long,
        That it had it[1] head bit off by it young.
    So, out went the candle, and we were left darkling.[2]
LEAR. Are you our daughter? 195
GON. Come, sir.
    I would you would make use of that good wisdom,
    Whereof I know you are fraught,[3] and put away
    These dispositions, that of late transform you
    From what you rightly are. 200
FOOL. May not an ass know when the cart draws the horse?
    Whoop, Jug! I love thee.[4]
LEAR. Doth any here know me? This is not Lear.
    Doth Lear walk thus? speak thus? Where are his eyes?
    Either his notion[5] weakens, his discernings 205
    Are lethargied—Ha! waking? 'Tis not so.

---

2. I.e., frown (literally, a band worn on the forehead).
3. A zero without a number before it.
4. A shelled or empty peapod.
5. Permitted to say or do anything.
6. Gross.
7. Sure.
8. Instigate it.
9. Out of our concern for a healthy so-ciety "redresses."
1. Its. The couplet sounds like a prov-erb.
2. In the dark.
3. Well furnished.
4. A bit of nonsense, probably accompan-ied by a caper. "Jug" is a nickname for "Joan."
5. Intellectual power.

Who is it that can tell me who I am?

FOOL. Lear's shadow.

LEAR. I would learn that;[6] for, by the marks of sovereignty,
knowledge, and reason, I should be false—persuaded I had 210
daughters.

FOOL. Which they will make an obedient father.

LEAR. Your name, fair gentlewoman?

GON. This admiration,[7] sir, is much o' the savor
Of other your new pranks. I do beseech you   215
To understand my purposes aright.
As you are old and reverend, you should be wise.
Here do you keep a hundred knights and squires;
Men so disordered, so deboshed[8] and bold,
That this our court, infected with their manners,   220
Shows[9] like a riotous inn. Epicurism and lust
Make it more like a tavern or a brothel
Than a graced[1] palace. The shame itself doth speak
For instant remedy, be then desired
By her, that else will take the thing she begs,   225
A little to disquantity[2] your train;
And the remainder that shall still depend,[3]
To be such men as may besort your age,
And know themselves and you.

LEAR.   Darkness and devils!
Saddle my horses! call my train together!   230
Degenerate bastard! I'll not trouble thee.
Yet have I left a daughter.

GON. You strike my people, and your disordered rabble
Make servants of their betters.

            [Enter ALBANY.]

LEAR. Woe that too late repents![4]—[to ALB.]   235
O, sir, are you come?
Is it your will? Speak, sir. Prepare my horses!
Ingratitude, thou marble-hearted fiend,
More hideous when thou show'st thee in a child
Than the sea-monster!

ALB.   Pray, sir, be patient.   240

LEAR. [to GON.] Detested kite![5] thou liest:
My train are men of choice and rarest parts,
That all particulars of duty know,
And in the most exact regard support
The worships of their name. O most small fault,   245
How ugly didst thou in Cordelia show!
That, like an engine, wrench'd my frame of nature

6. The answer to his question. He ignores the Fool's answer.
7. Pretended astonishment, wondering
who I am.
8. Debauched.
9. Appears.
1. Honorable.

2. Decrease in size.
3. Wait on you as dependents.
4. Woe to him who repents too late (a
proverbial expression).
5. The carrion crow. In Shakespeare, a
despicable creature symbolic of cowardice, meanness, cruelty, and death.

From the fixed place;[6] drew from my heart all love,
And added to the gall.[7] O Lear, Lear, Lear!
Beat at this gate, that let thy folly in,   [*striking his head*]   250
And thy dear judgment out! Go, go, my people.

ALB. My lord, I am guiltless, as I am ignorant
  Of what hath moved you.

LEAR.   It may be so, my lord.
  Hear, Nature, hear! dear goddess, hear!
  Suspend thy purpose, if thou didst intend   255
  To make this creature fruitful!
  Into her womb convey sterility!
  Dry up in her the organs of increase;
  And from her derogate[8] body never spring
  A babe to honor her! If she must teem,[9]   260
  Create her child of spleen, that it may live
  And be a thwart, disnatured [1]torment to her!
  Let it stamp wrinkles in her brow of youth;
  With cadent[2] tears fret channels in her cheeks;
  Turn all her mother's pains and benefits[3]   265
  To laughter and contempt, that she may feel
  How sharper than a serpent's tooth it is
  To have a thankless child! Away, away!   [*Exit.*]

ALB. Now, gods that we adore, whereof comes this?

GON. Never afflict yourself to know the cause;   270
  But let his disposition have that scope
  That dotage gives it.
      [*Re-enter* LEAR.]

LEAR. What, fifty of my followers at a clap?
  Within a fortnight?

ALB.   What's the matter, sir?

LEAR. I'll tell thee. [*to* GON.] Life and death! I am ashamed   275
  That thou hast power to shake my manhood thus;
  That these hot tears, which break from me perforce,
  Should make thee worth them. Blasts and fogs upon thee!
  The untented woundings[4] of a father's curse
  Pierce every sense about thee! Old fond[5] eyes,   280
  Beweep this cause again, I'll pluck ye out,
  And cast you, with the waters that you lose,
  To temper[6] clay. Yea, is it come to this?
  Let it be so. Yet have I left a daughter,
  Who, I am sure, is kind and comfortable.[7]   285
  When she shall hear this of thee, with her nails
  She'll flay thy wolvish visage. Thou shalt find
  That I'll resume the shape which thou dost think

---

6. I.e., which, like a pulley or lever, moved a larger thing (my natural frame or disposition) from its regular place.
7. And put the bitter fluid, gall, there in place of love.
8. Debased.
9. Have children.
1. Perverse, unnatural.

2. Falling.
3. Maternal cares.
4. Wounds too deep to be cleaned with a "tent"—a roll of lint.
5. Foolish.
6. Moisten.
7. Willing to give comfort.

I have cast off for ever; thou shalt
                    [Exeunt LE
GON. Do you mark that, my lord?
ALB. I cannot be so partial, Goneril,
    To the great love I bear you,—
GON. Pray you, content.[8] What, Oswald, ho!
    You sir, more knave than fool, after your master!
FOOL. Nuncle Lear, nuncle Lear, tarry and take the
    thee.

             A fox, when one has caught her,
             And such a daughter,
             Should sure to the slaughter,
             If my cap would buy a halter: 300
             So the fool follows after.[9]   [Exit.]
GON. This man hath had good counsel!—a hundred knights?
    'T is politic[1] and safe to let him keep
    At point[2] a hundred knights? Yes, that on every dream,
    Each buzz,[3] each fancy, each complaint, dislike,   305
    He may enguard his dotage with their powers,
    And hold our lives in mercy.[4] Oswald, I say!
ALB. Well, you may fear too far.
GON.   Safer than trust too far:
    Let me still[5] take away the harms I fear,
    Not fear still to be taken. I know his heart.   310
    What he hath uttered I have writ my sister.
    If she sustain him and his hundred knights,
    When I have showed the unfitness,—
        [Re-enter OSWALD.]
                        How now, Oswald!
    What, have you writ that letter to my sister?
OSW. Yes, madam.   315
GON. Take you some company, and away to horse!
    Inform her full of my particular fear,
    And thereto add such reasons of your own
    As may compact[6] it more. Get you gone,
    And hasten your return. [Exit OSWALD.] No, no, my lord,320
    This milky gentleness and course[7] of yours
    Though I condemn not, yet, under pardon,
    You are much more attaxed[8] for want of wisdom
    Than praised for harmful mildness.[9]
ALB. How far your eyes may pierce I cannot tell: 325
    Striving to better, oft we mar what's well.
GON. Nay, then—
ALB. Well, well; the event.[1]   [Exeunt.]

8. Be quiet.   5. Always.
9. The rhyming words were pronounced 6. Confirm.
"hauter" and "auter."   7. This mild and gentle course of action.
1. Prudent.   8. Criticized.
2. In armed readiness.   9. Dangerous lenity.
3. Rumor.   1. The outcome.
4. In jeopardy.

d FOOL.]

oucester with these letters.[2] Acquaint
                  er with any thing you know than comes
                  out of[3] the letter. If your diligence be not
                  be there afore you.
                  not sleep, my lord, till I have delivered your letter. 5
[*Exit.*]

OOL. If a man's brains were in 's heels, were't not in danger
of kibes?[4]

LEAR. Ay, boy.

FOOL. Then, I prithee, be merry; thy wit shall ne'er go slipshod.[5]   10

LEAR. Ha, ha, ha!

FOOL. Shalt see thy other daughter will use thee kindly;[6] for
though she's as like this as a crab's[7] like an apple, yet I can
tell what I can tell.

LEAR. Why, what canst thou tell, my boy?   15

FOOL. She will taste as like this as a crab does to a crab. Thou
canst tell why one's nose stands i' the middle on's[8] face?

LEAR. No.

FOOL. Why, to keep one's eyes of either side's nose, that what a
man cannot smell out, 'a may spy into.   20

LEAR. I did her wrong—

FOOL. Canst tell how an oyster makes his shell?

LEAR. No.

FOOL. Nor I neither; but I can tell why a snail has a house.

LEAR. Why?   25

FOOL. Why, to put his head in; not to give it away to his daughters, and leave his horns without a case.[9]

LEAR. I will forget my nature. So kind a father! Be my horses
ready?

FOOL. Thy asses are gone about 'em. The reason why the seven   30
stars are no moe[1] than seven is a pretty reason.

LEAR. Because they are not eight?

FOOL. Yes, indeed. Thou wouldst make a good fool.

LEAR. To take 't again perforce! Monster ingratitude!

FOOL. If thou wert my fool, nuncle, I'd have thee beaten for   35
being old before thy time.

LEAR. How's that?

FOOL. Thou shouldst not have been old till thou hadst been
wise.

LEAR. O, let me not be mad, not mad, sweet heaven!   40
Keep me in temper; I would not be mad!

---

2. This letter.
3. Question arising from.
4. Chilblains.
5. Wearing slippers, as would someone
who was suffering from chilblains.
6. (1) Affectionately; (2) according to
nature.

7. Crab apple, usually sour.
8. Of his.
9. The fool makes the cynical but common Elizabethan assumption that every
married man is a cuckold.
1. More; "pretty": apt, cogent.

[*Enter* GENTLEMAN.]
How now! Are the horses ready?
GENT. Ready, my lord.
LEAR. Come, boy.
FOOL. She that's a maid now, and laughs at my departure,   45
    Shall not be a maid long, unless things be cut shorter.[2]

[*Exeunt.*]

Act II

SCENE 1

[*Enter* EDMUND *and* CURAN *meeting.*]
EDM. Save thee, Curan.
CUR. And you, sir. I have been with your father, and given him
    notice that the Duke of Cornwall and Regan his duchess will
    be here with him this night.
EDM. How comes that?   5
CUR. Nay, I know not. You have heard of the news abroad—I
    mean the whispered ones, for they are yet but ear-bussing
    arguments?[3]
EDM. Not I. Pray you, what are they?
CUR. Have you heard of no likely wars toward,[4] 'twixt the Dukes   10
    of Cornwall and Albany?
EDM. Not a word.
CUR. You may do, then, in time. Fare you well, sir.   [*Exit.*]
EDM. The duke be here tonight? The better! best!
    This weaves itself perforce into my business.   15
    My father hath set guard to take my brother;
    And I have one thing, of a queasy[5] question,
    Which I must act. Briefness and fortune, work!
    Brother, a word! Descend! Brother, I say!
        [*Enter* EDGAR.]
    My father watches. O sir, fly this place!   20
    Intelligence is given where you are hid.
    You have now the good advantage of the night.
    Have you not spoken 'gainst the Duke of Cornwall?
    He's coming hither; now, i' the night, i' the haste,
    And Regan with him: have you nothing said   25
    Upon his party[6] 'gainst the Duke of Albany?
    Advise yourself.
EDG.   I am sure on't, not a word.
EDM. I hear my father coming. Pardon me!
    In cunning[7] I must draw my sword upon you:

---

2. Addressed to the audience. An Elizabethan dirty joke: the maiden who
laughs at me will lose her virginity soon
unless all young men are castrated.
3. Whispered rumors.
4. Impending.

5. Requiring delicate management, but
also rather nauseating.
6. On his side.
7. As a trick (to avoid suspicion of col-
lusion).

Draw; seem to defend yourself; now quit you well.[8]   30
Yield! Come before my father. Light, ho, here!
Fly, brother. Torches, torches! So, farewell.   [*Exit* EDGAR.]
Some blood drawn on me would beget opinion[9]
                                    [*Wounds his arm.*]
Of my more fierce endeavor. I have seen drunkards
Do more than this in sport. Father, father!   35
Stop, stop! No help?
        [*Enter* GLOUCESTER, *and* SERVANTS *with torches.*]
GLOU. Now, Edmund, where's the villain?
EDM. Here stood he in the dark, his sharp sword out,
    Mumbling of wicked charms, conjuring the moon
    To stand auspicious mistress,—
GLOU.   But where is he?   40
EDM. Look, sir, I bleed.
GLOU.   Where is the villain, Edmund?
EDM. Fled this way, sir. When by no means he could—
GLOU. Pursue him, ho! Go after. [*Exeunt some* SERVANTS.] By
    no means what?
EDM. Persuade me to the murder of your lordship;   45
    But that[1] I told him, the revenging gods
    'Gainst parricides did all their thunders bend;
    Spoke, with how manifold and strong a bond
    The child was bound to the father; sir, in fine,
    Seeing how loathly opposite[2] I stood   50
    To his unnatural purpose, in fell motion,[3]
    With his prepared sword, he charges home
    My unprovided body, lanched[4] mine arm:
    But when he saw my best alarumed spirits,
    Bold in the quarrel's right, roused to the encounter,   55
    Or whether gasted[5] by the noise I made,
    Full suddenly he fled.
GLOU.   Let him fly far.
    Not in this land shall he remain uncaught;
    And found—dispatch.[6] The noble duke my master,
    My worthy arch and patron,[7] comes to-night: 60
    By his authority I will proclaim it,
    That he which finds him shall deserve our thanks,
    Bringing the murderous caitiff[8] to the stake;
    He that conceals him, death.
EDM. When I dissuaded him from his intent,   65
    And found him pight[9] to do it, with curst speech
    I threatened to discover him. He replied,
    "Thou unpossessing bastard! dost thou think
    If I would stand against thee, would the reposal
    Of any trust, virtue, or worth in thee   70

8. Fight vigorously.
9. Persuade people.
1. When.
2. Bitterly opposed.
3. Deadly thrust.
4. Wounded.

5. Frightened.
6. I.e., when he is captured, let him be killed.
7. Chief patron.
8. Wretch.
9. Determined; "curst": angry.

Make thy words faithed?[1] No. What I should deny,—
As this I would; ay, though thou didst produce
My very character,[2]—I'd turn it all
To thy suggestion, plot, and damned practice:
And thou must make a dullard of the world,   75
If they not thought the profits of my death
Were very pregnant and potential spurs
To make thee seek it."
GLOU.   Strong and fastened[3] villain!
Would he deny his letter? I never got[4] him. [*Tucket within.*]
Hark, the Duke's trumpets! I know not why he comes.   80
All ports[5] I'll bar; the villain shall not 'scape;
The duke must grant me that. Besides, his picture
I will send far and near, that all the kingdom
May have due note of him; and of my land,
Loyal and natural[6] boy, I'll work the means   85
To make thee capable.[7]
          [*Enter* CORNWALL, REGAN, *and* ATTENDANTS.]
CORN. How now, my noble friend! Since I came hither,
     (Which I can call but now) I have heard strange news.
REG. If it be true, all vengeance comes too short
     Which can pursue the offender. How dost, my lord?   90
GLOU. O, madam, my old heart is cracked, is cracked!
REG. What, did my father's godson seek your life?
     He whom my friend named? Your Edgar?
GLOU. O, lady, lady, shame would have it hid!
REG. Was he not companion with the riotous knights   95
     That tend upon my father?
GLOU. I know not, madam. 'Tis too bad, too bad!
EDM. Yes, madam, he was of that consórt.[8]
REG. No marvel, then, though he were ill affected.[9]
     'Tis they have put him on[1] the old man's death,   100
     To have th' expense and waste of his revénues.
     I have this present evening from my sister
     Been well informed of them; and with such cautions
     That if they come to sojourn at my house,
     I'll not be there.
CORN.   Nor I, assure thee, Regan.   105
     Edmund, I hear that you have shown your father
     A child-like[2] office.
EDM.   'Twas my duty, sir.
GLOU. He did bewray[3] his practice, and received
     This hurt you see, striving to apprehend him.
CORN. Is he pursued?
GLOU.   Ay, my good lord.   110

CORN. If he be taken, he shall never more
    Be feared of doing harm.[4] Make your own purpose,
    How in my strength you please. For you, Edmund,
    Whose virtue and obedience doth this instant
    So much commend itself, you shall be ours.   115
    Natures of such deep trust we shall much need;
    You we first seize on.
EDM.   I shall serve you, sir,
    Truly, however else.
GLOU.   For him I thank your grace.
CORN. You know not why we came to visit you,—
REG. Thus out of season, threading[5] dark-eyed night.   120
    Occasions, noble Gloucester, of some poise,[6]
    Wherein we must have use of your advice:
    Our father he hath writ, so hath our sister,
    Of differences, which I least thought of fit
    To answer from our home. The several messengers   125
    From hence attend dispatch.[7] Our good old friend,
    Lay comforts to your bosom, and bestow
    Your needful counsel to our business,
    Which craves the instant use.[8]
GLOU.   I serve you, madam.
    Your graces are right welcome.   *[Exeunt.]* 130

SCENE 2

[*Enter* KENT *and* OSWALD, *severally.*]
OSW. Good dawning to thee, friend. Art of this house?
KENT. Ay.
OSW. Where may we set our horses?
KENT. I' the mire.
OSW. Prithee, if thou lovest me, tell me.   5
KENT. I love thee not.
OSW. Why, then, I care not for thee.
KENT. If I had thee in Lipsbury pinfold,[9] I would make thee care
    for me.
OSW. Why dost thou use me thus? I know thee not.   10
KENT. Fellow, I know thee.
OSW. What dost thou know me for?
KENT. A knave; a rascal; an eater of broken meats[1]; a base,
    proud, shallow, beggarly, three-suited, hundred-pound, filthy,
    worsted-stocking knave;[2] a lily-livered, action-taking[3] knave; a 15
    whoreson, glass-gazing, superserviceable, finical rogue; one-

---

4. Be a public danger.
5. Making our way through.
6. Weight, importance.
7. Are waiting to be sent off.
8. Must be done immediately.
9. An obscure expression, possibly meaning "between my teeth."
1. One who lives on scraps.

2. Servants were provided with three suits a year; Oswald's total resources would not be over a hundred pounds; he wears only worsted stockings (gentlemen wore silk).
3. One who goes to law instead of fighting; a coward.

trunk-inheriting[4] slave; one that wouldst be a bawd in way of
good service, and art nothing but the composition of a knave,
beggar, coward, pandar, and the son and heir of a mongrel
bitch; one whom I will beat into clamorous whining, if thou   20
deniest the least syllable of thy addition.[5]

osw. Why, what a monstrous fellow art thou, thus to rail on one
that is neither known of thee nor knows thee!

kent. What a brazen-faced varlet art thou, to deny thou knowest
me! Is it two days ago since I tripped up thy heels, and beat   25
thee before the king? Draw, you rogue! For, though it be
night, yet the moon shines. I'll make a sop of the moonshine[6]
of you. Draw, you whoreson cullionly barber-monger, draw![7]

                                              [*Drawing his sword.*]

osw. Away! I have nothing to do with thee.

kent. Draw, you rascal! You come with letters against the king,   30
and take Vanity the puppet's[8] part against the royalty of her
father. Draw, you rogue, or I'll so carbonado[9] your shanks!
Draw, you rascal! Come your ways!

osw. Help, ho! murther! help!

kent. Strike, you slave! Stand, rogue! Stand, you neat slave!   35
Strike!   [*Beating him.*]

osw. Help, ho! murther! murther!

     [*Enter* edmund *with his rapier drawn,* cornwall,
     regan, gloucester, *and* servants.]

edm. How now! What's the matter?   [*Parts them.*]

kent. With you, goodman boy, an you please! Come, I'll
flesh[1] ye! Come on, young master!   40

glou. Weapons! arms! What's the matter here?

corn. Keep peace, upon your lives!
     He dies that strikes again. What is the matter?

reg. The messengers from our sister and the king.

corn. What is your difference? Speak.   45

osw. I am scarce in breath, my lord.

kent. No marvel, you have so bestirred your valor. You cowardly
rascal, nature disclaims in thee; a tailor made thee.[2]

corn. Thou art a strange fellow. A tailor make a man?

kent. Ay, a tailor, sir. A stone-cutter or a painter could not have   50
made him so ill, though he had been but two hours at the
trade.

corn. Speak yet, how grew your quarrel?

osw. This ancient ruffian, sir, whose life I have spared at suit of[3]
his gray beard,—   55

---

4. One whose entire possessions would
fit in one trunk.
5. Titles.
6. Full of holes, so the moon will shine
through.
7. A base fellow who hangs around barber shops.
8. I.e., Goneril. Vanity was a character
in the morality plays, which were often
performed by puppets.
9. Score, cut cross-wise.
1. Initiate.
2. You are so cowardly that nature denies making you; a tailor made you (alluding to the proverb that it takes nine
tailors to make a man).
3. Because of a plea by.

KENT. Thou whoreson zed! thou unnecessary letter![4] My lord, if
you will give me leave, I will tread this unbolted[5] villain into
mortar, and daub the walls of a jakes[6] with him. Spare my
gray beard, you wagtail?[7]

CORN. Peace, sirrah!   60
You beastly knave, know you no reverence?

KENT. Yes, sir, but anger hath a privilege.

CORN. Why art thou angry?

KENT. That such a slave as this should wear a sword,[8]
Who wears no honesty. Such smiling rogues as these,   65
Like rats, oft bite the holy cords a-twain
Which are too intrinse t' unloose;[9] smooth every passion
That in the natures of their lords rebel;
Bring oil to fire, snow to their colder moods;
Renege, affirm, and turn their halcyon beaks[1]   70
With every gale and vary[2] of their masters,
Knowing nought, like dogs, but following.
A plague upon your epileptic visage!
Smile you my speeches, as I were a fool?
Goose, if I had you upon Sarum plain   75
I'ld drive ye cackling home to Camelot.[3]

CORN. What, art thou mad, old fellow?

GLOU. How fell you out? say that.

KENT. No contraries hold more antipathy
Than I and such a knave.   80

CORN. Why dost thou call him knave? What's his offense?

KENT. His countenance likes[4] me not.

CORN. No more, perchance, does mine, nor his, nor hers.

KENT. Sir, 'tis my occupation to be plain.
I have seen better faces in my time   85
Than stands on any shoulder that I see
Before me at this instant.

CORN.   This is some fellow,
Who, having been praised for bluntness, doth affect
A saucy roughness, and constrains the garb
Quite from his nature.[5] He cannot flatter, he,   90
An honest mind and plain, he must speak truth!
An they will take it, so; if not, he's plain.
These kind of knaves I know, which in this plainness
Harbor more craft[6] and more corrupter ends

---

4. Zed, still the English name for the
letter *z*, is unnecessary because its sound
can be expressed by *s*.
5. Coarse, unsifted.
6. Privy.
7. A bird that bobs its head up and
down constantly.
8. Swords were supposed to be worn
only by gentlemen, and Oswald is a
mere parasitic servant.
9. Bite in two the holy cords of affection
(between daughter and father, for instance), which are too intricately tied to

be undone in any natural way.
"Smooth": flatter.
1. Deny, affirm, and turn with the wind,
as a halcyon or kingfisher was supposed
to when hung up by the neck.
2. Varying gale.
3. Salisbury (Sarum) Plain had flocks of
geese on it. Camelot was the legendary
castle of King Arthur, sometimes located
at Winchester.
4. Pleases.
5. Distorts the nature of plain speech.
6. Deceit.

Than twenty silly ducking observants 95
 That stretch their duties nicely.[7]
KENT. Sir, in good sooth, in sincere verity,
 Under the allowance of your great aspect,
 Whose influence, like the wreath of radiant fire
 On flickering Phoebus' front,[8]
CORN.   What mean'st by this? 100
KENT. To go out of my dialect, which you discommend so much.
 I know, sir, I am no flatterer. He that beguiled you in a plain
 accent was a plain knave; which for my part I will not be,
 though I should win your displeasure to entreat me to 't.
CORN. What was the offense you gave him? 105
OSW. I never gave him any:
 It pleased the king his master very late
 To strike at me, upon his misconstruction,[9]
 When he, conjunct,[1] and flattering his displeasure,
 Tripped me behind; being down, insulted, railed, 110
 And put upon him such a deal of man,
 That worthied him, got praises of the king
 For him attempting who was self-subdued;[2]
 And, in the fleshment[3] of this dread exploit,
 Drew on me here again.
KENT.   None of these rogues and cowards 115
 But Ajax is their fool.[4]
CORN. Fetch forth the stocks!
 You stubborn miscreant knave, you reverent braggart,
 We'll teach you—
KENT.   Sir, I am too old to learn.
 Call not your stocks for me. I serve the king; 120
 On whose employment I was sent to you:
 You shall do small respect, show too bold malice
 Against the grace and person of my master,
 Stocking his messenger.
CORN. Fetch forth the stocks! As I have life and honor, 125
 There shall he sit till noon.
REG. Till noon? Till night, my lord, and all night too!
KENT. Why, madam, if I were your father's dog,
 You should not use me so.
REG.   Sir, being his knave, I will.
CORN. This is a fellow of the self-same color 130
 Our sister speaks of. Come, bring away the stocks!
                        [*Stocks brought out.*]
GLOU. Let me beseech your grace not to do so.
 His fault is much, and the good king his master

7. Than twenty obsequious servants who precisely adopt the manners prescribed for them.
8. Kent, mimicking the flattery of servants like Oswald, addresses Cornwall as if he were a planet, comparable to the sun.
9. Misunderstanding.

1. Taking the king's side.
2. Made himself out to be a hero, won honor for himself . . . for attacking someone who wouldn't fight.
3. Furious excitement.
4. In Shakespeare's *Troilus and Cressida* the cowardly, malicious Thersites treats the plain-spoken warrior Ajax as a fool.

Will check[5] him for't. Your purposed low correction
Is such as basest and contemned'st wretches   135
For pilferings and most common trespasses
Are punished with: the king must take it ill,
That he, so slightly valued in his messenger,
Should have him thus restrained.
CORN.   I'll answer[6] that.
REG. My sister may receive it much more worse,   140
    To have her gentleman abused, assaulted,
    For following her affairs. Put in his legs.
                            [KENT *is put in the stocks.*]
    Come, my good lord, away.
                    [*Exeunt all but* GLOUCESTER *and* KENT.]
GLOU. I am sorry for thee, friend: 'tis the duke's pleasure,
    Whose disposition, all the world well knows,   145
    Will not be rubbed nor stopped: I'll entreat for thee.
KENT. Pray, do not, sir. I have watched[7] and traveled hard;
    Some time I shall sleep out, the rest I'll whistle.
    A good man's fortune may grow out at heels:
    Give you good morrow!   150
GLOU. The duke's to blame in this; 't will be ill-taken.   [*Exit.*]
KENT. Good king, that must approve the common saw,[8]
    Thou out of heaven's benediction comest
    To the warm sun!
    Approach, thou beacon to this under globe,[9]   155
    That by thy comfortable beams I may
    Peruse this letter! Nothing almost sees miracles
    But misery.[1] I know 'tis from Cordelia,
    Who hath most fortunately been informed
    Of my obscuréd course; [*reads*] "and shall find time   160
    From this enormous state, seeking to give
    Losses their remedies." All weary and o'er-watched,
    Take vantage, heavy eyes, not to behold
    This shameful lodging.
    Fortune, good night; smile once more; turn thy wheel![2] 165
                                            [*Sleeps.*]

                        SCENE 3

        [*Enter* EDGAR.]
EDG. I heard myself proclaimed;
    And by the happy hollow of a tree
    Escaped the hunt. No port is free; no place,
    That guard, and most unusual vigilance,
    Does not attend my taking. Whiles I may 'scape,   5

5. Rebuke.
6. Be answerable for.
7. Gone without sleep.
8. Confirm the common saying.
9. I.e., the sun.

1. For those in misery, any relief seems almost miraculous.
2. Bring good fortune in place of the present bad. The goddess Fortuna was often portrayed turning a wheel.

I will preserve myself; and am bethought
To take the basest and most poorest shape
That ever penury, in contempt of man,
Brought near the beast.[3] My face I'll grime with filth,
Blanket my loins, elf[4] all my hair in knots,   10
And with presented nakedness out-face
The winds and persecutions of the sky.
The country gives me proof[5] and precedent
Of Bedlam beggars,[6] who, with roaring voices,
Strike in their numbed and mortified bare arms   15
Pins, wooden pricks, nails, sprigs of rosemary;
And with this horrible object,[7] from low farms,
Poor pelting[8] villages, sheep-cotes, and mills,
Sometime with lunatic bans,[9] sometime with prayers,
Enforce their charity. Poor Turlygod! poor Tom![1]   20
That's something yet! Edgar I nothing am.   [*Exit.*]

SCENE 4

[*Enter* LEAR, FOOL, *and* GENTLEMAN.]
LEAR. 'Tis strange that they should so depart from home,
And not send back my messenger.
GENT.   As I learned,
The night before there was no purpose in them
Of this remove.[2]
KENT.   Hail to thee, noble master!
LEAR. Ha!   5
Makest thou this shame thy pastime?[3]
KENT.   No, my lord.
FOOL. Ha, ha! he wears cruel garters.[4] Horses are tied by the
heads, dogs and bears by the neck, monkeys by the loins, and
men by the legs. When a man's over-lusty at legs, then he
wears wooden nether-stocks.[5]   10
LEAR. What's he that hath so much thy place mistook
To set thee here?
KENT.   It is both he and she;
Your son and daughter.
LEAR. No.
KENT. Yes.   15
LEAR. No, I say.
KENT. I say, yea.
LEAR. No, no, they would not!

3. I have got the idea of taking the basest and poorest shape that poverty ever
brought a man to, making him like a
beast.
4. Tangle.
5. Example.
6. See note 8, p. 922, above.
7. Spectacle.
8. Paltry.

9. Curses.
1. See note 8, p. 922, above.
2. Change of residence.
3. Are you in this disgraceful situation
as a joke?
4. A pun on "crewel," thin worsted
yarn, which was used for garters.
5. Stockings.

KENT. Yes, yes, they have!

LEAR. By Jupiter, I swear, no! 20

KENT. By Juno, I swear, aye!

LEAR.   They durst not do 't;
They would not, could not do 't. 'Tis worse than murder,
To do upon respect[6] such violent outrage.
Resolve me, with all modest haste, which way
Thou mightst deserve, or they impose, this usage, 25
Coming from us.

KENT.   My lord, when at their home
I did commend your highness' letters to them,
Ere I was risen from the place that showed
My duty kneeling, came there a reeking post,
Stewed in his haste, half breathless, panting forth 30
From Goneril his mistress, salutations;
Delivered letters, spite of intermission,
Which presently they read; on whose contents,[7]
They summoned up their meiny,[8] straight took horse;
Commanded me to follow, and attend 35
The leisure of their answer, gave me cold looks,
And meeting here the other messenger,
Whose welcome, I perceived, had poisoned mine,—
Being the very fellow that of late
Displayed so saucily against your highness,— 40
Having more man than wit about me, drew.
He raised the house with loud and coward cries.
Your son and daughter found this trespass worth
The shame which here it suffers.

FOOL. Winter's not gone yet, if the wild-geese fly that way.[9] 45
                Fathers that wear rags
                   Do make their children blind;
                But fathers that bear bags[1]
                   Shall see their children kind.
                Fortune, that arrant whore, 50
                   Ne'er turns the key[2] to the poor.
But, for all this, thou shalt have as many dolors for thy daughters as thou canst tell in a year.[3]

LEAR. O, how this mother swells up toward my heart!
Hysterica passio, down, thou climbing sorrow, 55
Thy element's below![4] Where is this daughter?

KENT. With the earl, sir, here within.

LEAR.   Follow me not; stay here.
                                   [*Exit.*]

GENT. Made you no more offenses but what you speak of?

KENT. None. How chance the king comes with so small a train?

---

6. (1) Upon the respect due a King's messenger; (2) deliberately.
7. Getting the message.
8. Household.
9. A pseudo-proverb meaning things are still in a bad way.
1. Hang on to the moneybags.
2. Opens the door.

3. Punning on dolors (sorrows) and dollars (coins) and on tell (narrate) and tell (count).
4. The mother, or *hysterica passio*, was a hysteria supposedly marked by a rising of wind from the belly to the heart and finally to the throat.

FOOL. An thou hadst been set i' the stocks for that question, 60
thou hadst well deserved it.

KENT. Why, fool?

FOOL. We'll set thee to school to an ant, to teach thee there's no
laboring i' the winter. All that follow their noses are led by
their eyes but blind men, and there's not a nose among twenty 65
but can smell him that's stinking. Let go thy hold when a
great wheel runs down a hill, lest it break thy neck with following it; but the great one that goes up the hill, let him draw
thee after. When a wise man gives thee better counsel, give
me mine again. I would have none but knaves follow it, since 70
a fool gives it.

> That sir which serves and seeks for gain,
> And follows but for form,
> Will pack[5] when it begins to rain,
> And leave thee in the storm.
> But I will tarry; the fool will stay, 75
> And let the wise man fly.
> The knave turns fool that runs away;
> The fool no knave, perdy.[6]

KENT. Where learned you this, fool? 80

FOOL. Not i' the stocks, fool.

[*Re-enter* LEAR, *with* GLOUCESTER.]

LEAR. Deny to speak with me? They are sick? they are weary?
They have traveled all the night? Mere fetches;[7]
The images of revolt and flying off.
Fetch me a better answer.

GLOU.   My dear lord, 85
You know the fiery quality of the duke;
How unremoveable and fixed he is
In his own course.

LEAR. Vengeance! plague! death! confusion!
Fiery? what quality? Why, Gloucester, Gloucester, 90
I'd speak with the Duke of Cornwall and his wife.

GLOU. Well, my good lord, I have informed them so.

LEAR. Informed them! Dost thou understand me, man?

GLOU. Ay, my good lord.

LEAR. The king would speak with Cornwall; the dear father 95
Would with his daughter speak, commands her service.
Are they informed of this? My breath and blood!
Fiery? the fiery duke? Tell the hot duke that—
No, but not yet. May be he is not well.
Infirmity doth still neglect all office[8] 100
Whereto our health is bound; we are not ourselves
When nature, being oppressed, commands the mind
To suffer with the body. I'll forbear;
And am fallen out with my more headier will,[9]
To take[1] the indisposed and sickly fit 105

---

5. Be off.
6. Assuredly (*per Dieu*).
7. Tricks, ruses.

8. Duty.
9. Am at odds with my impetuous will.
1. For taking.

For the sound man. Death on my state![2] Wherefore
[*looking on* KENT]
Should he sit here? This act persuades me
That this remotion of the duke and her
Is practice only.[3] Give me my servant forth.
Go tell the duke and 's wife I'd speak with them,   110
Now, presently![4] Bid them come forth and hear me,
Or at their chamber-door I'll beat the drum
Till it cry sleep to death.[5]

GLOU. I would have all well betwixt you.   [*Exit.*]

LEAR. O me, my heart, my rising heart! but, down!   115

FOOL. Cry to it, nuncle, as the cockney did to the eels when she
put 'em i' the paste[6] alive; she knapped 'em o' the coxcombs
with a stick, and cried "Down, wantons, down!" 'Twas her
brother that, in pure kindness to his horse, buttered his hay.

[*Enter* CORNWALL, REGAN, GLOUCESTER, *and* SERVANTS.]

LEAR. Good morrow to you both.

CORN.   Hail to your grace!   120
[KENT *is set at liberty.*]

REG. I am glad to see your highness.

LEAR. Regan, I think you are; I know what reason
I have to think so. If thou shouldst not be glad,
I would divorce me from thy mother's tomb,
Sepulchring an adultress. [*To* KENT.] O, are you free?   125
Some other time for that. Belovéd Regan,
Thy sisters' naught. O Regan, she hath tied
Sharp-toothed unkindness, like a vulture, here![7]
[*Points to his heart.*]
I can scarce speak to thee; thou'lt not believe
With how depraved a quality—O Regan!   130

REG. I pray you, sir, take patience. I have hope
You less know how to value her desert
Than she to scant[8] her duty.

LEAR.   Say, how is that?

REG. I cannot think my sister in the least
Would fail her obligation. If, sir, perchance   135
She have restrained the riots of your followers,
'Tis on such ground, and to such wholesome end,
As clears her from all blame.

LEAR. My curses on her!

REG.   O, sir, you are old;   140
Nature in you stands on the very verge
Of her confine. You should be ruled and led
By some discretion,[9] that discerns your state
Better than you yourself. Therefore, I pray you,
That to our sister you do make return;

2. Royal power.
3. This removal of the Duke and Regan
is a mere trick.
4. Immediately.
5. Until its sound kills sleep.
6. Meat pie.

7. Lear calls himself a kind of Prometheus, who suffered the punishment of having an eagle feed on his liver.
8. Be neglectful of.
9. I.e., some discreet person.

Say you have wronged her, sir.

LEAR.   Ask her forgiveness?   145
  Do you but mark how this becomes the house:[1]
  "Dear daughter, I confess that I am old; [*kneeling*]
  Age is unnecessary. On my knees I beg
  That you'll vouchsafe me raiment, bed, and food."

REG. Good sir, no more! These are unsightly tricks.   150
  Return you to my sister.

LEAR.   [*Rising.*] Never, Regan!
  She hath abated[2] me of half my train;
  Looked black upon me; struck me with her tongue
  Most serpent-like, upon the very heart.
  All the stored vengeances of heaven fall   155
  On her ingrateful top! Strike her young bones,[3]
  You taking[4] airs, with lameness!

CORN.   Fie, sir, fie!

LEAR. You nimble lightnings, dart your blinding flames
  Into her scornful eyes! Infect her beauty,
  You fen-sucked fogs, drawn by the powerful sun,   160
  To fall and blast her pride!

REG. O the blest gods! so will you wish on me,
  When the rash mood is on.

LEAR. No, Regan, thou shalt never have my curse.
  Thy tender-hefted[5] nature shall not give   165
  Thee o'er to harshness. Her eyes are fierce; but thine
  Do comfort and not burn. 'Tis not in thee
  To grudge my pleasures, to cut off my train,
  To bandy hasty words, to scant my sizes,[6]
  And in conclusion to oppose the bolt   170
  Against my coming in. Thou better know'st
  The offices[7] of nature, bond of childhood,
  Effects of courtesy, dues of gratitude;
  Thy half o' the kingdom hast thou not forgot,
  Wherein I thee endowed.

REG.   Good sir, to the purpose.   175

LEAR. Who put my man i' the stocks?   [*Tucket within.*]

CORN.   What trumpet's that?

REG. I know't, my sister's. This approves[8] her letter,
  That she would soon be here.
    [*Enter* OSWALD.]
             Is your lady come?

LEAR. This is a slave, whose easy-borrowed pride
  Dwells in the fickle grace of her he follows.   180
  Out, varlet, from my sight!

CORN.   What means your grace?

1. Our family, the royal family of Britain.
2. Deprived.
3. Unborn child (an expression from the old *King Leir*).
4. Infecting.
5. Gentle.
6. Allowances.
7. Duties.
8. Confirms.

LEAR. Who stocked my servant? Regan, I have good hope
 Thou didst not know on 't. [*Enter* GONERIL.] Who comes
  here? O heavens,
 If you do love old men, if your sweet sway
 Allow obedience, if yourselves are old,   185
 Make it your cause! Send down, and take my part!
 [*To* GON.] Art not ashamed to look upon this beard?
 O Regan, wilt thou take her by the hand?
GON. Why not by the hand, sir? How have I offended?
 All's not offense that indiscretion finds   190
 And dotage terms so.[9]
LEAR.   O sides, you are too tough!
 Will you yet hold? How came my man i' the stocks?
CORN. I set him there, sir; but his own disorders
 Deserved much less advancement[1]
LEAR.   You! did you?
REG. I pray you, father, being weak, seem so.   195
 If, till the expiration of your month,
 You will return and sojourn with my sister,
 Dismissing half your train, come then to me.
 I am now from home, and out of that provision
 Which shall be needful for your entertainment.   200
LEAR. Return to her, and fifty men dismissed?
 No, rather I abjure all roofs, and choose
 To wage against the enmity o' the air;
 To be a comrade with the wolf and owl,—
 Necessity's sharp pinch! Return with her?   205
 Why, the hot-blooded[2] France, that dowerless took
 Our youngest born, I could as well be brought
 To knee his throne, and, squire-like, pension beg
 To keep base life afoot. Return with her?
 Persuade me rather to be slave and sumpter[3]   210
 To this detested groom.   [*Pointing at* OSWALD.]
GON.   At your choice, sir.
LEAR. I prithee, daughter, do not make me mad.
 I will not trouble thee, my child; farewell.
 We'll no more meet, no more see one another.
 But yet thou art my flesh, my blood, my daughter;   215
 Or rather a disease that's in my flesh,
 Which I must needs call mine. Thou art a boil,
 A plague-sore, an embossed carbuncle,[4]
 In my corrupted blood. But I'll not chide thee;
 Let shame come when it will, I do not call it.   220
 I do not bid the Thunder-bearer[5] shoot,
 Nor tell tales of thee to high-judging Jove.
 Mend when thou canst; be better at thy leisure.

---

9. Not everything is an offense that poor
judgment finds so and senility calls so.
1. His own misconduct deserved less
promotion.

2. Passionate.
3. Packhorse.
4. Swollen tumor.
5. I.e., Jove.

I can be patient, I can stay with Regan,
I and my hundred knights.
REG.   Not altogether so.   225
  I looked not for you yet, nor am provided
  For your fit welcome. Give ear, sir, to my sister;
  For those that mingle reason with your passion
  Must be content to think you old, and so—
  But she knows what she does.
LEAR.   Is this well spoken?   230
REG. I dare avouch it, sir. What, fifty followers?
  Is it not well? What should you need of more?
  Yea, or so many, sith that[6] both charge and danger
  Speak 'gainst so great a number? How, in one house,
  Should many people, under two commands,   235
  Hold amity? 'T is hard; almost impossible.
GON. Why might not you, my lord, receive attendance
  From those that she calls servants, or from mine?
REG. Why not, my lord? If then they chanced to slack you,
  We could control them. If you will come to me,—   240
  For now I spy a danger,—I entreat you
  To bring but five-and-twenty. To no more
  Will I give place or notice.
LEAR. I gave you all—
REG.   And in good time you gave it.
LEAR. Made you my guardians, my depositaries;   245
  But kept a reservation[7] to be followed
  With such a number. What, must I come to you
  With five-and-twenty, Regan? Said you so?
REG. And speak't again, my lord; no more with me.
LEAR. Those wicked creatures yet do look well-favored,   250
  When others are more wicked; not being the worst
  Stands in some rank of praise. [*To* GON.] I'll go with thee:
  Thy fifty yet doth double five-and-twenty,
  And thou art twice her love.
GON.   Hear me, my lord.
  What need you five-and-twenty, ten, or five,   255
  To follow in a house where twice so many
  Have a command to tend you?
REG.   What need one?
LEAR. O, reason not the need! Our basest beggars
  Are in the poorest thing superfluous.[8]
  Allow not nature more than nature needs,   260
  Man's life's as cheap as beast's. Thou art a lady;
  If only to go warm were gorgeous,
  Why, nature needs not what thou gorgeous wear'st,
  Which scarcely keeps thee warm.[9] But, for true need,—

6. Since.
7. Made you my stewardesses and trustees, but kept a reserve clause.
8. Our poorest beggars, if they own anything at all, have more than they need.

9. I.e., if dressing warmly is to be gorgeous, you are both more and less than that; for the gorgeous lady's clothes you wear are too scanty to keep you warm.

You heavens, give me that patience, patience I need!   265
You see me here, you gods, a poor old man,
As full of grief as age; wretched in both!
If it be you that stirs these daughters' hearts
Against their father, fool me not so much[1]
To bear it tamely; touch me with noble anger,   270
And let not women's weapons, water-drops,
Stain my man's cheeks! No, you unnatural hags,
I will have such revenges on you both,
That all the world shall—I will do such things,—
What they are, yet I know not; but they shall be   275
The terrors of the earth! You think I'll weep;
No, I'll not weep.
I have full cause of weeping, but this heart
Shall break into a hundred thousand flaws[2]
Or ere I'll weep. O fool, I shall go mad!   280

> [*Exeunt* LEAR, GLOUCESTER, KENT, *and* FOOL.
> *Storm and tempest.*]

CORN. Let us withdraw; 't will be a storm.
REG. This house is little; the old man and his people
  Cannot be well bestowed.
GON. 'Tis his own blame; hath put himself from rest,[3]
  And must needs taste his folly.   285
REG. For his particular,[4] I'll receive him gladly,
  But not one follower.
GON.   So am I purposed.
  Where is my lord of Gloucester?
CORN. Followed the old man forth. He is returned.

> [*Re-enter* GLOUCESTER.]

GLOU. The king is in high rage.
CORN.   Whither is he going?   290
GLOU. He calls to horse, but will I know not whither.
CORN. 'Tis best to give him way; he leads himself.
GON. My lord, entreat him by no means to stay.
GLOU. Alack, the night comes on, and the bleak winds
  Do sorely ruffle.[5] For many miles about   295
  There's scarce a bush.[6]
REG.   O, sir, to willful men,
  The injuries that they themselves procure
  Must be their schoolmasters. Shut up your doors.
  He is attended with a desperate train;[7]
  And what they may incense him to, being apt   300
  To have his ear abused, wisdom bids fear.
CORN. Shut up your doors, my lord; 'tis a wild night.
  My Regan counsels well. Come out o' the storm.   [*Exeunt.*]

---

1. Don't make me such a fool as.
2. Fragments.
3. He has separated himself from peace of mind.
4. As for himself alone.
5. Violently rage.
6. The Quarto reads "not a bush." The contradiction between either of these statements and Edgar's hollow tree in II.iii.2, has often been noticed.
7. There is no other indication that in these scenes Lear is accompanied by "a desperate train" (his knights).

Act III

SCENE 1

[*Storm still. Enter* KENT *and a* GENTLEMAN, *at several doors.*]

KENT. Who's there, besides foul weather?

GENT. One minded like the weather, most unquietly.

KENT. I know you. Where's the king?

GENT. Contending with the fretful elements;
Bids the wind blow the earth into the sea,   5
Or swell the curlèd waters 'bove the main,[8]
That things might change or cease; tears his white hair,
Which the impetuous blasts, with eyeless rage,
Catch in their fury, and make nothing of;[9]
Strives in his little world of man[1] to out-scorn   10
The to-and-fro-conflicting wind and rain.
This night, wherein the cub-drawn bear would couch,[2]
The lion and the belly-pinchèd wolf
Keep their fur dry, unbonneted he runs,
And bids what will take all.[3]

KENT.   But who is with him?   15

GENT. None but the fool, who labors to out-jest
His heart-struck injuries.[4]

KENT.   Sir, I do know you;
And dare, upon the warrant of my note,
Commend a dear thing to you.[5] There is division,
Although as yet the face of it be covered   20
With mutual cunning, 'twixt Albany and Cornwall;
Who have—as who have not, that their great stars
Throned and set high?—servants, who seem no less,
Which are to France the spies and speculations
Intelligent of our state.[6] What hath been seen,   25
Either in snuffs and packings[7] of the dukes,
Or the hard rein which both of them have borne
Against the old kind king; or something deeper,
Whereof perchance these are but furnishings;[8]
But, true it is, from France there comes a power   30
Into this scattered kingdom; who already,
Wise in our negligence, have secret feet
In some of our best ports, and are at point[9]
To show their open banner. Now to you:

---

8. Land; "things": everything.
9. Show no respect for (opposite of "make much of").
1. I.e., microcosm.
2. The bear, sucked dry by its cubs and ravenously hungry, would nevertheless lie in its lair instead of seeking food.
3. A gambler's cry on the last throw of the dice—a cry of desperation.
4. To counter with his jests the injuries which have struck Lear to the heart.

5. Dare, on the basis of my knowledge of you, to entrust an important matter to you.
6. Who are France's spies and intelligence agents in our country.
7. Quarrels and plots against each other.
8. Trimmings.
9. Who already, taking advantage of our negligence, have gained a secret foothold and are ready.

If on my credit you dare build so far   35
To make your speed to Dover, you shall find
Some that will thank you, making just report
Of how unnatural and bemadding sorrow
The king hath cause to plain.[1]
I am a gentleman of blood and breeding;   40
And, from some knowledge and assurance,[2] offer
This office to you.
GENT. I will talk further with you.
KENT.   No, do not.
For confirmation that I am much more
Than my out-wall, open this purse, and take   45
What it contains. If you shall see Cordelia,—
As fear not but you shall,—show her this ring,
And she will tell you who your fellow is
That yet you do not know. Fie on this storm!
I will go seek the king.   50
GENT. Give me your hand. Have you no more to say?
KENT. Few words, but, to effect,[3] more than all yet;
That, when we have found the king,—in which your pain
That way, I'll this,[4]—he that first lights on him
Holla the other.   [*Exeunt severally.*] 55

SCENE 2

[*Enter* LEAR *and* FOOL. *Storm still.*]
LEAR. Blow, winds, and crack your cheeks![5] rage! blow!
You cataracts and hurricanoes,[6] spout
Till you have drenched our steeples, drowned the cocks![7]
You sulphurous and thought-executing fires,[8]
Vaunt-couriers to oak-cleaving thunderbolts,   5
Singe my white head! And thou, all-shaking thunder,
Smite flat the thick rotundity o' the world!
Crack Nature's molds, all germens spill at once,[9]
That make ingrateful man!
FOOL. O nuncle, court holy-water[1] in a dry house is better than 10
this rain-water out o' door. Good nuncle, in, and ask thy daugh-
ters' blessing! Here's a night pities neither wise man nor fool.
LEAR. Rumble thy bellyful! Spit, fire! spout, rain!
Nor rain, wind, thunder, fire, are my daughters:
I tax not you, you elements, with unkindness;[2]   15

---

1. For making accurate report of the unnatural and maddening sorrow that the
king can justifiably complain of.
2. Trustworthy information.
3. In importance.
4. In which troublesome task, you go
that way, I'll go this.
5. In contemporary maps, winds were
represented by faces with their cheeks
puffed out, blowing.

6. Both words mean "waterspouts."
7. Weathercocks.
8. Lightning flashes which work ("execute") faster than thought.
9. Crack the molds Nature uses and destroy the seeds that make the ungrateful
creature, man.
1. I.e., flattery.
2. I do not charge you elements with unnaturalness.

I never gave you kingdom, called you children,
You owe me no subscription.[3] Then let fall
Your horrible pleasure. Here I stand, your slave,
A poor, infirm, weak, and despised old man.
But yet I call you servile ministers,[4]   20
That have with two pernicious daughters joined
Your high engendered battles[5] 'gainst a head
So old and white as this. O! O! 't is foul!
FOOL. He that has a house to put 's head in has a good head-
piece,[6]   25

            The cod-piece that will house
               Before the head has any,
            The head and he shall louse;
               So beggars marry many.[7]
            The man that makes his toe   30
               What he his heart should make
            Shall of a corn cry woe,
               And turn his sleep to wake.[8]
For there was never yet fair woman but she made mouths in a
glass.[9]   35
LEAR. No, I will be the pattern of all patience; I will say nothing.
      [*Enter* KENT.]
KENT. Who's there?
FOOL. Marry, here 's grace and a cod-piece;[1] that's a wise man and
a fool.
KENT. Alas, sir, are you here? things that love night   40
Love not such nights as these; the wrathful skies
Gallow the very wanderers of the dark,[2]
And make them keep their caves. Since I was man,
Such sheets of fire, such bursts of horrid thunder,
Such groans of roaring wind and rain, I never   45
Remember to have heard. Man's nature cannot carry
The affliction nor the fear.
LEAR.   Let the great gods,
That keep this dreadful pother o'er our heads,
Find out their enemies now.[3] Tremble, thou wretch,
That hast within thee undivulgéd crimes,   50
Unwhipped of justice. Hide thee, thou bloody hand;
Thou perjured, and thou simular of virtue
That are incestuous.[4] Caitiff, to pieces shake,
That under covert and convenient seeming

3. Submission, obedience.
4. Slavish agents.
5. Your heaven-born battalions.
6. (1) Helmet; (2) skull.
7. Codpiece: penis (from the piece of clothing covering it). "The man that be-gets children before he has a house will surely become a lousy vagabond. Thus it is that many beggars get married" (Kittredge's note).
8. The man who exchanges the place of his toe and his heart will get a corn on his heart that will hurt so he can't sleep at night.
9. A quasi-proverbial saying about the vanity of women. "Made mouths": made faces.
1. Grace refers to a noble person; the codpiece was prominent in a clown's costume.
2. Terrify the wild beasts.
3. By the terror inspired in guilty people.
4. You perjurer, and you incestuous man who pretends to be virtuous.

Hast practiced on man's life.[5] Close pent-up guilts   55
Rive your concealing continents, and cry
These dreadful summoners grace.[6] I am a man
More sinned against than sinning.
KENT.   Alack, bare-headed
Gracious my lord, hard by here is a hovel;
Some friendship will it lend you 'gainst the tempest.   60
Repose you there, while I to this hard house—
More harder than the stones whereof 'tis raised,
Which even but now, demanding after you,
Denied me to come in—return, and force
Their scanted courtesy.
LEAR.   My wits begin to turn.   65
Come on, my boy. How dost, my boy? Art cold?
I am cold myself. Where is this straw, my fellow?
The art of our necessities is strange,
That can make vile things precious.[7] Come, your hovel.
Poor fool and knave, I have one part in my heart   70
That's sorry yet for thee.
FOOL. [*singing*]
        He that has and a little tiny wit,—
            With hey, ho, the wind and the rain,—
        Must make content with his fortunes fit,
            For the rain it raineth every day.[8]   75
LEAR. True, my good boy. Come, bring us to this hovel.
                              [*Exeunt* LEAR *and* KENT.]
FOOL. This is a brave night to cool a courtesan.[9]
    I'll speak a prophecy ere I go:
        When priests are more in word than matter;
        When brewers mar their malt with water;   80
        When nobles are their tailors' tutors;
        No heretics burned, but wenches' suitors;
        When every case in law is right;
        No squire in debt, nor no poor knight;
        When slanders do not live in tongues,   85
        Nor cutpurses come not to throngs;
        When usurers tell their gold i' the field,
        And bawds and whores do churches build;
        Then shall the realm of Albion
        Come to great confusion.   90
        Then comes the time, who lives to see 't,

---

5. Wretch, who in clever and plausible deception has plotted a murder.
6. Carefully hidden crimes, burst out of the covering that hides you and beg mercy from these dreadful ministers of justice.
7. Necessity has a kind of strange magic which can make worthless things precious.

8. An adaptation of one verse of a song sung by Feste, the fool, at the end of Shakespeare's *Twelfth Night*. Lear's Fool alters it to emphasize the lack of wit of himself and his master.
9. A fine night to cool the lust of a courtesan.

That going shall be used with feet.
This prophecy Merlin shall make; for I live before his time.[1]
[Exit.]

SCENE 3

[Enter GLOUCESTER *and* EDMUND.]
GLOU. Alack, alack, Edmund, I like not this unnatural dealing.[2]
When I desired their leave that I might pity him, they took from
me the use of mine own house; charged me, on pain of their perpetual displeasure, neither to speak of him, entreat for him, nor
any way sustain him.   5
EDM. Most savage and unnatural!
GLOU. Go to;[3] say you nothing. There's a division betwixt the
dukes, and a worse matter than that. I have received a letter
this night; 'tis dangerous to be spoken; I have locked the letter
in my closet.[4] These injuries the king now bears will be re-   10
venged home; there's part of a power already footed; we must
incline to the king.[5] I will seek him, and privily relieve him.
Go you and maintain talk with the duke, that my charity be
not of him perceived if he ask for me, I am ill, and gone to
bed. Though I die for it, as no less is threatened me, the king   15
my old master must be relieved. There is some strange thing
toward, Edmund; pray you, be careful.   *[Exit.]*
EDM. This courtesy, forbid thee,[6] shall the duke
Instantly know, and of that letter too.
This seems a fair deserving, and must draw me[7]   20
That which my father loses—no less than all.
The younger rises when the old doth fall.   *[Exit.]*

SCENE 4

[Enter LEAR, KENT, *and* FOOL.]
KENT. Here is the place, my lord; good my lord, enter:
The tyranny of the open night's[8] too rough
For nature to endure.   *[Storm still.]*
LEAR. Let me alone.

---

1. The "when . . . then" formula was a
traditional medieval satiric mode in
which the poet ticked off one abuse after
another: when all are remedied, all will
be well. One of the old "whens," erroneously thought to be by Chaucer, was
called Merlin's Prophecy; the Fool, in
identifying it, emphasizes the antiquity of
the *Lear* setting.
2. I.e., unnatural behavior of Regan and
Cornwall.

3. Enough.
4. Private room.
5. These injuries the king suffers will be
revenged to the full; part of an army is
already landed; we must be on the side
of the king.
6. Forbidden to you.
7. This deserves reward and must get for
me.
8. Night in the open.

KENT. Good my lord, enter here.

LEAR.   Wilt break my heart?   5

KENT. I had rather break mine own. Good my lord, enter.

LEAR. Thou think'st 'tis much that this contentious storm
  Invades us to the skin. So 'tis to thee;
  But where the greater malady is fixed,[9]
  The lesser is scarce felt. Thou'dst shun a bear;   10
  But if thy flight lay toward the raging sea,
  Thou'dst meet the bear i' the mouth. When the mind's free,
  The body's delicate.[1] The tempest in my mind
  Doth from my senses take all feeling else
  Save what beats there. Filial ingratitude!   15
  Is it not as this mouth should tear this hand
  For lifting food to 't? But I will punish home.[2]
  No, I will weep no more. In such a night
  To shut me out! Pour on; I will endure.
  In such a night as this! O Regan, Goneril!   20
  Your old kind father, whose frank heart gave all,—
  O, that way madness lies; let me shun that;
  No more of that.

KENT.   Good my lord, enter here.

LEAR. Prithee, go in thyself; seek thine own ease:
  This tempest will not give me leave to ponder   25
  On things would hurt me more. But I'll go in.
  [*To the* FOOL.] In, boy; go first. You houseless poverty,[3]—
  Nay, get thee in. I'll pray, and then I'll sleep.

                              [FOOL *goes in.*]

  Poor naked wretches, whereso'er you are,
  That bide[4] the pelting of this pitiless storm,   30
  How shall your houseless heads and unfed sides,
  Your looped and windowed raggedness,[5] defend you
  From seasons such as these? O, I have ta'en
  Too little care of this! Take physic, pomp;
  Expose thyself to feel what wretches feel,   35
  That thou mayst shake the superflux to them,
  And show the heavens more just.[6]

EDG. [*within*] Fathom and half, fathom and half![7]
  Poor Tom!   [*The* FOOL *runs out from the hovel.*]

FOOL. Come not in here, nuncle, here's a spirit.   40
  Help me, help me!

KENT. Give me thy hand. Who's there?

FOOL. A spirit, a spirit! He says his name's poor Tom.

KENT. What are thou that dost grumble there i' the straw? Come
  forth.   45

9. Chronic, incurable.
1. When the mind is at ease, the body is sensitive to physical pain.
2. Thoroughly.
3. The Fool is addressed.
4. Endure.
5. How shall your uncovered heads and unfed bodies, your tattered rags full of holes, like windows in a house.
6. Shake off the surplus you enjoy to the poor and show that the heavens distribute some kind of justice.
7. The rains are so heavy that Poor Tom pretends they are at sea and he is taking soundings.

[*Enter* EDGAR *disguised as a madman.*]

EDG. Away! the foul fiend follows me!

Through the sharp hawthorn blows the cold wind.

Humh! go to thy cold bed, and warm thee.[8]

LEAR. Hast thou given all to thy two daughters? And art thou
come to this?　　　　　　　　　　　　　　　　　　　　　50

EDG. Who gives any thing to poor Tom? whom the foul fiend
hath led through fire and through flame, through ford and
whirlpool, o'er bog and quagmire; that hath laid knives under
his pillow and halters in his pew; set ratsbane by his porridge;[9]
made him proud of heart, to ride on a bay trotting-horse over　55
four-inched bridges, to course[1] his own shadow for a traitor.
Bless thy five wits! Tom's a-cold,—O, do, de, do de, do de.
Bless thee from whirlwinds, star-blasting, and taking![2] Do poor
Tom some charity, whom the foul fiend vexes: there could I
have him now,—and there,—and there again, and there.　60
　　　　　　　　　　　　　　　　　　　　[*Storm still.*]

LEAR. What, has his daughters brought him to this pass?
Couldst thou save nothing? Didst thou give them all?

FOOL. Nay, he reserved a blanket, else we had been all shamed.

LEAR. Now, all the plagues that in the pendulous air
Hang fated o'er men's faults light on thy daughters!　　　65

KENT. He hath no daughters, sir.

LEAR. Death, traitor! nothing could have subdued nature
To such a lowness but his unkind[3] daughters.
Is it the fashion that discarded fathers
Should have thus little mercy on their flesh?[4]　　　　　70
Judicious punishment! 't was this flesh begot
Those pelican daughters.[5]

EDG. Pillicock sat on Pillicock-hill.
Halloo, halloo, loo, loo!

FOOL. This cold night will turn us all to fools and madmen.　75

EDG. Take heed o' the foul fiend; obey thy parents; keep thy
word justly; swear not; commit not with man's sworn spouse;
set not thy sweet heart on proud array. Tom's a-cold.

LEAR. What hast thou been?

EDG. A serving-man, proud in heart and mind; that curled my　80
hair; wore gloves in my cap;[6] served the lust of my mistress'
heart, and did the act of darkness with her; swore as many
oaths as I spake words, and broke them in the sweet face of
heaven: one that slept in the contriving of lust, and waked to
do it. Wine loved I deeply, dice dearly; and in woman out-　85

8. Poor Tom, pursued as he thinks by
the devil, quotes snatches of old songs
and plays. "Humh" signifies his shivering, as does "do de" in line 57.
9. The devil tried to capture souls of
madmen by tempting them to the sin of
suicide.
1. Chase.
2. Malign influences of planets and spirits. Lear picks up the theme in lines 64–
65.
3. Unnatural.
4. Lear notices the pins and splinters
Edgar has stuck into his arm.
5. In legend the pelican was supposed to
feed its offspring with its own blood.
The word reminds Edgar of a children's
rhyme.
6. As a favor from his mistress.

paramoured the Turk. False of heart, light of ear, bloody of
hand; hog in sloth, fox in stealth, wolf in greediness, dog in
madness, lion in prey. Let not the creaking of shoes nor the
rustling of silks betray thy poor heart to woman. Keep thy foot
out of brothels, thy hand out of plackets,[7] thy pen from lend- 90
ers' books, and defy the foul fiend. Still through the hawthorn
blows the cold wind: Says suum, mun, ha, no, nonny. Dolphin
my boy, my boy, sessa! let him trot by.[8]   [*Storm still.*]

LEAR. Why, thou wert better in thy grave than to answer with
thy uncovered body this extremity of the skies. Is man no 95
more than this? Consider him well. Thou owest the worm no
silk, the beast no hide, the sheep no wool, the cat[9] no perfume. Ha! here's three on's are sophisticated![1] Thou art the
thing itself; unaccommodated[2] man is no more but such a
poor, bare, forked animal as thou art. Off, off, you lendings! 100
come, unbutton here.   [*Tearing off his clothes.*]

FOOL. Prithee, nuncle, be contented; 'tis a naughty[3] night to
swim in. Now a little fire in a wild field were like an old lecher's heart; a small spark, all the rest on's body cold. Look, here
comes a walking fire.   105

          [*Enter* GLOUCESTER, *with a torch.*]

EDG. This is the foul fiend Flibbertigibbet. He begins at curfew,
and walks till the first cock.[4] He gives the web and the pin,[5]
squinies[5] the eye, and makes the hare-lip; mildews the white[6]
wheat, and hurts the poor creature of earth.

          St. Withold footed thrice the old;   110
          He met the night-mare and her nine-fold;
          Bid her alight,
          And her troth plight,
          And, aroint thee, witch, aroint thee![7]

KENT. How fares your grace?   115
LEAR. What's he?
KENT. Who's there? What is't you seek?
GLOU. What are you there? Your names?
EDG. Poor Tom, that eats the swimming frog, the toad, the tad-
pole, the wall-newt and the water;[8] that in the fury of his 120
heart, when the foul fiend rages, eats cow-dung for sallets;[9]
swallows the old rat and the ditch-dog; drinks the green
mantle of the standing-pool; who is whipped from tithing to
tithing,[1] and stock-punished, and imprisoned; who hath had
three suits to his back, six shirts to his body, horse to ride, and 125
weapon to wear;

But mice and rats, and such small deer,[2]
Have been Tom's food for seven long year.
    Beware my follower. Peace, Smulkin; peace, thou fiend!
GLOU. What, hath your grace no better company?   130
EDG. The prince of darkness is a gentleman. Modo he's call'd,
    and Mahu.
GLOU. Our flesh and blood is grown so vile, my lord,
    That it doth hate what gets it.
EDG. Poor Tom's a-cold.   135
GLOU. Go in with me. My duty cannot suffer[3]
    To obey in all your daughters' hard commands:
    Though their injunction be to bar my doors,
    And let this tyrannous night take hold upon you
    Yet have I ventured to come seek you out.   140
    And bring you where both fire and food is ready.
LEAR. First let me talk with this philosopher.[4]
    What is the cause of thunder?
KENT. Good my lord, take his offer; go into the house.
LEAR. I'll take a word with this same learned Theban.[5]   145
    What is your study?
EDG. How to prevent[6] the fiend, and to kill vermin.
LEAR. Let me ask you one word in private.
KENT. Importune him once more to go, my lord;
    His wits begin to unsettle.
GLOU.   Canst thou blame him? [Storm still.] 150
    His daughters seek his death; ah, that good Kent!
    He said it would be thus, poor banished man!
    Thou say'st the king grows mad; I'll tell thee, friend,
    I am almost mad myself. I had a son,
    Now outlawed from my blood. He sought my life,   155
    But lately, very late. I loved him, friend;
    No father his son dearer. True to tell thee,
    The grief hath crazed my wits. What a night's this!
    I do beseech your grace,—
LEAR.   O, cry you mercy,[7] sir.
    Noble philosopher, your company.   160
EDG. Tom's a-cold.
GLOU. In, fellow, there, into the hovel; keep thee warm.
LEAR. Come, let's in all.
KENT.   This way, my lord.
LEAR.   With him!
    I will keep still[8] with my philosopher.
KENT. Good my lord, soothe[9] him; let him take the fellow.   165
GLOU. Take him you on.
KENT. Sirrah, come on; go along with us.
LEAR. Come, good Athenian.

2. Animals.
3. Allow me.
4. Natural philosopher, scientist.
5. Lear in his madness takes Poor Tom
for a learned man from abroad: Thebes,
Athens, or Persia (III.vi.74).
6. Avoid.
7. I beg your pardon.
8. Remain always.
9. Humor.

GLOU. No words, no words: hush.

EDG. Child Rowland to the dark tower came,[1]   170
  His word was still,—Fie, foh, and fum,
  I smell the blood of a British man.   [*Exeunt.*]

SCENE 5

[*Enter* CORNWALL *and* EDMUND.]

CORN. I will have my revenge ere I depart his house.

EDM. How, my lord, I may be censured, that nature thus gives
  way to loyalty, something fears me to think of.[2]

CORN. I now perceive, it was not altogether your brother's evil
  disposition made him seek his death; but a provoking merit,[3]   5
  set a-work by a reproveable badness in himself.

EDM. How malicious is my fortune, that I must repent to be just!
  This is the letter he spoke of, which approves him an intelligent party[4] to the advantages of France. O heavens! that this
  treason were not, or not I the detector!   10

CORN. Go with me to the duchess.

EDM. If the matter of this paper be certain, you have mighty
  business in hand.

CORN. True or false, it hath made thee Earl of Gloucester. Seek
  out where thy father is, that he may be ready for our   15
  apprehension.[5]

EDM. [*aside*] If I find him comforting the king, it will stuff his
  suspicion more fully.—I will persever in my course of loyalty, though the conflict be sore between that and my blood.[6]

CORN. I will lay trust upon thee, and thou shalt find a dearer   20
  father in my love.   [*Exeunt.*]

SCENE 6

[*Enter* GLOUCESTER, LEAR, KENT, FOOL , *and* EDGAR.]

GLOU. Here is better than the open air; take it thankfully. I will
  piece out the comfort with what addition I can; I will not be
  long from you.

KENT. All the power of his wits have given sway to his impatience: the gods reward your kindness!   [*Exit* GLOUCESTER.]   5

EDG. Fraretetto calls me; and tells me Nero is an angler in the
  lake of darkness.[7] Pray, innocent, and beware the foul fiend.

FOOL. Prithee, nuncle, tell me whether a madman be a gentleman or a yeoman?

LEAR. A king, a king!   10

---

1. "Child": a candidate for knighthood.
The line may be from a lost ballad;
Browning built a notable poem on it.
"Word": motto, which absurdly comes
from *Jack the Giant Killer*.
2. "What people will think of me, since
my natural feelings as a son thus give
way to loyalty, rather frightens me"
(Muir's note).
3. A quality in him deserved death.
4. Which proves him a spy.
5. Arrest.
6. Filial feelings.
7. Fraretetto is the name of one of his
demons. The Emperor Nero is a fisherman in Chaucer's *Monk's Tale*.

FOOL. No, he's a yeoman that has a gentleman to his son; for
   he's a mad yeoman that sees his son a gentleman before him.
LEAR. To have a thousand with red burning spits
   Come hissing in upon 'em,—
EDG. The foul fiend bites my back.   15
FOOL. He's mad that trusts in the tameness of a wolf, a horse's
   health,[8] a boy's love, or a whore's oath.
LEAR. It shall be done; I will arraign them straight.[9]
   [*To* EDGAR.] Come, sit thou here, most learned justicer;
   [*to the* FOOL] Thou, sapient sir, sit here. Now, you she
   foxes!   20
EDG. Look, where he stands and glares! Wantest thou eyes at
   trial, madam?[1]
             Come o'er the bourn, Bessy, to me,—
FOOL.   Her boat hath a leak,
             And she must not speak   25
         Why she dares not come over to thee.
EDG. The foul fiend haunts poor Tom in the voice of a nightin-
   gale. Hopdance cries in Tom's belly for two white herring.
   Croak not, black angel; I have no food for thee.[2]
KENT. How do you, sir? Stand you not so amazed: 30
   Will you lie down and rest upon the cushions?
LEAR. I'll see their trial first. Bring in the evidence.
   [*To* EDGAR.] Thou robed man of justice, take thy place;
   [*to the* FOOL] And thou, his yoke-fellow of equity,[3]
   Bench by his side: [*to* KENT] you are o' the commission,   35
   Sit you too,
EDG. Let us deal justly.
             Sleepest or wakest thou, jolly shepherd?
             Thy sheep be in the corn;
         And for one blast of thy minikin mouth,   40
             Thy sheep shall take no harm.[4]
   Pur! the cat is gray.
LEAR. Arraign her first; 'tis Goneril. I here take my oath before
   this honorable assembly, she kicked the poor king her father.
FOOL. Come hither, mistress. Is your name Goneril?   45
LEAR. She cannot deny it.
FOOL. Cry you mercy, I took you for a joint-stool.[5]
LEAR. And here's another, whose warped looks proclaim
   What store[6] her heart is made on. Stop her there!
   Arms, arms, sword, fire! Corruption in the place!   50

---

8. Horses were supposed to be more
subject to ailments than other animals.
9. I will legally try them (Goneril and
Regan) right now.
1. Poor Tom points to Frateretto and
asks the imaginary Goneril if she minds
having onlookers at her trial. He then
quotes (or sings) in a line from a ballad
which a lover addresses his sweetheart.
"Bourn": brook.
2. The growling of his stomach from
hunger Tom takes to be the croaking of

the foul fiend.
3. I.e., judicial colleague.
4. Another ballad stanza. "Minikin":
delicate, dainty.
5. The comment is a common one meaning "Pardon me; I didn't notice you,"
but the comedy is richer, and more like
the Fool, if an actual stool is addressed.
"Joint stool": a low stool made by
joiner (carpenter).
6. Material.

False justicer, why hast thou let her 'scape?

EDG. Bless thy five wits!

KENT. O pity! Sir, where is the patience now,
That you so oft have boasted to retain?

EDG. [*aside*] My tears begin to take his part so much,   55
They'll mar my counterfeiting.[7]

LEAR. The little dogs and all,
Tray, Blanch, and Sweet-heart, see, they bark at me.[8]

EDG. Tom will throw his head at them. Avaunt, you curs!

> Be thy mouth or black or white,   60
> Tooth that poisons if it bite;
> Mastiff, greyhound, mongrel grim,
> Hound or spaniel, brach or lym,
> Or bobtail tike or trundle-tail.
> Tom will make them weep and wail: 65
> For, with throwing thus my head,
> Dogs leap the hatch, and all are fled.[9]

Do de, de, de. Sessa! Come, march to wakes and fairs and
market-towns. Poor Tom, thy horn is dry.[1]

LEAR. Then let them anatomize[2] Regan; see what breeds about   70
her heart. Is there any cause in nature that makes these hard
hearts? [*To* EDGAR.] You, sir, I entertain for one of my hundred; I do not like the fashion of your garments. You will say
they are Persian attire; but let them be changed.

KENT. Now, good my lord, lie there and rest awhile.   75

LEAR. Make no noise, make no noise; draw the curtains. So, so,
so. We'll go to supper i' the morning. So, so so.[3]

FOOL. And I'll go to bed at noon.

[*Re-enter* GLOUCESTER.]

GLOU. Come hither, friend. Where is the king my master?

KENT. Here, sir; but trouble him not; his wits are gone.   80

GLOU. Good friend, I prithee, take him in thy arms;
I have o'erheard a plot of death upon him:
There is a litter ready; lay him in 't
And drive towards Dover, friend, where thou shalt meet
Both welcome and protection. Take up thy master.   85
If thou shouldst dally half an hour, his life,
With thine, and all that offer to defend him,
Stand in assured loss. Take up, take up!
And follow me, that will to some provision
Give thee quick conduct.

KENT.   Oppresséd nature sleeps: 90
This rest might yet have balmed thy broken sinews,
Which, if convenience will not allow,

---

7. Spoil my pretense.
8. Lear in his delirium thinks that his own dogs have sided with his daughters and now bark at him.
9. Another improvised charm. "Brach or lym": bitch or bloodhound; "hatch": the lower half of a divided door.

1. Beggars carried a horn to hold the drinks they begged.
2. Dissect.
3. The curtains are the curtains of his bed at home. He is aware that he should have supped before going to bed.

Stand in hard cure.[4] [*To the* FOOL.] Come, help to bear thy
  master:
Thou must not stay behind.

GLOU.   Come come, away.
                          [*Exeunt all but* EDGAR.]

EDG. When we our betters see bearing our woes,   95
  We scarcely think our miseries our foes.
  Who alone suffers suffers most i' the mind,
  Leaving free[5] things and happy shows behind:
  But then the mind much sufferance doth o'erskip
  When grief hath mates, and bearing[6] fellowship.   100
  How light and portable my pain seems now,
  When that which makes me bend makes the king bow;
  He childed as I fathered! Tom, away!
  Mark the high noises, and thyself bewray[7]
  When false opinion, whose wrong thought defiles thee,   105
  In thy just proof repeals and reconciles thee.[8]
  What will hap more tonight, safe 'scape the king!
  Lurk, lurk.[9]   [*Exit.*]

                    SCENE 7

    [*Enter* CORNWALL, REGAN, GONERIL, EDMUND, *and* SER-
    VANTS.]

CORN. Post speedily to my lord your husband; show him this
  letter. The army of France is landed. Seek out the villain
  Gloucester.   [*Exeunt some of the* SERVANTS.]

REG. Hang him instantly.

GON. Pluck out his eyes.   5

CORN. Leave him to my displeasure. Edmund, keep you our sister company. The revenges we are bound to[1] take upon your
  traitorous father are not fit for your beholding. Advise the
  duke, where you are going, to a most festinate[2] preparation.
  We are bound to the like. Our posts shall be swift and in-   10
  telligent betwixt us. Farewell, dear sister: farewell, my lord
  of Gloucester.

    [*Enter* OSWALD.]

  How now! Where's the king?

OSW. My lord of Gloucester hath conveyed him hence.
  Some five or six and thirty of his knights,   15
  Hot questrists[3] after him, met him at gate;
  Who, with some other of the lords dependants,
  Are gone with him towards Dover; where they boast
  To have well-armed friends.

---

4. This rest might have restored your racked nerves, which can hardly be cured without it.
5. Carefree.
6. Endurance, suffering.
7. Notice signs of discord among the powerful, and reveal yourself.
8. When the false charges which hurt you so much are proved unfounded and you are called back from exile and reconciled with your father.
9. Remain in hiding.
1. Ready to.
2. Rapid.
3. Seekers.

CORN.   Get horses for your mistress.

GON. Farewell, sweet lord, and sister.   20

CORN. Edmund, farewell.

                [Exeunt GONERIL, EDMUND, *and* OSWALD.]

  Go seek the traitor Gloucester,

  Pinion him like a thief, bring him before us.

                  [Exeunt other SERVANTS.]

  Though well we may not pass upon his life

  Without the form of justice, yet our power   25

  Shall do a courtesy to[4] our wrath, which men

  May blame, but not control. Who's there? the traitor?

        [Enter GLOUCESTER, *brought in by two or three.]*

REG. Ingrateful fox! 'tis he.

CORN. Bind fast his corky[5] arms.

GLOU. What mean your graces? Good my friends, consider   30

  You are my guests. Do me no foul play, friends.

CORN. Bind him, I say.   *[*SERVANTS *bind him.]*

REG.   Hard, hard. O filthy[6] traitor!

GLOU. Unmerciful lady as you are, I'm none.

CORN. To this chair bind him. Villain, thou shalt find—

                *[*REGAN *plucks his beard.]*

GLOU. By the kind gods, 'tis most ignobly done   35

  To pluck me by the beard.

REG. So white, and such a traitor!

GLOU.   Naughty[7] lady,

  These hairs, which thou dost ravish from my chin,

  Will quicken,[8] and accuse thee. I am your host.

  With robbers' hands my hospitable favors   40

  You should not ruffle[9] thus. What will you do?

CORN. Come, sir, what letters had you late from France?

REG. Be simple answerer,[1] for we know the truth.

CORN. And what confederacy have you with the traitors

  Late footed[2] in the kingdom?   45

REG. To whose hands have you sent the lunatic king?

  Speak.

GLOU. I have a letter guessingly set down,

  Which came from one that's of a neutral heart,

  And not from one opposed.

CORN.   Cunning.

REG.   And false.   50

CORN. Where hast thou sent the king?

GLOU. To Dover.

REG. Wherefore to Dover? Wast thou not charged at peril—

CORN. Wherefore to Dover? Let him first answer that.

GLOU. I am tied to the stake, and I must stand the course.[3]   55

---

4. Yield to.
5. Dry and withered.
6. Odious.
7. Wicked.
8. Come to life.

9. Do violence to.
1. I.e., frank.
2. Recently landed.
3. The image is of a bear tied to a stake and baited by dogs.

REG. Wherefore to Dover, sir?

GLOU. Because I would not see thy cruel nails
    Pluck out his poor old eyes; nor thy fierce sister
    In his anointed[4] flesh stick boarish fangs.
    The sea, with such a storm as his bare head   60
    In hell-black night endured, would have buoyed up,
    And quenched the stelléd fires.[5]
    Yet, poor old heart, he holp the heavens to rage.
    If wolves had at thy gate howled that dern[6] time,
    Thou shouldst have said "Good porter, turn the key."   65
    All cruels else subscribed.[7] But I shall see
    The wingéd vengeance overtake such children.

CORN. See 't shalt thou never. Fellows, hold the chair.
    Upon these eyes of thine I'll set my foot.

GLOU. He that will think to live till he be old,   70
    Give me some help! O cruel! O ye gods!

REG. One side will mock another. The other too!

CORN. If you see vengeance,—

FIRST SERV.   Hold your hand, my lord:
    I have served you ever since I was a child;
    But better service have I never done you   75
    Than now to bid you hold.

REG. How now, you dog!

FIRST SERV. If you did wear a beard upon your chin,
    I'd shake it on this quarrel.

REG. What do you mean?   80

CORN. My villain!   [*They draw and fight.*]

FIRST SERV. Why, then, come on, and take the chance of anger.

REG. Give me thy sword. A peasant stand up thus!
                [*Takes a sword, and runs at him behind.*]

FIRST SERV. O, I am slain! My lord, you have one eye left
    To see some mischief on him. O!   [*Dies.*] 85

CORN. Lest it see more, prevent it. Out, vile jelly!
    Where is thy luster now?

GLOU. All dark and comfortless. Where's my son Edmund?
    Edmund, enkindle all the sparks of nature,
    To quit this horrid act.[8]

REG.   Out,[9] treacherous villain!   90
    Thou call'st on him that hates thee. It was he
    That made the overture[1] of thy treasons to us;
    Who is too good to pity thee.

GLOU. O my follies! Then Edgar was abused.
    King gods, forgive me that, and prosper him!   95

REG. Go thrust him out at gates, and let him smell
    His way to Dover.   [*Exit one with* GLOUCESTER.]

---

4. As a king.
5. Would have risen up and quenched the fires of the stars.
6. Dire, dread.
7. I.e., all other cruel creatures submitted to the fury of the storm, but you did not.
8. Arouse all your filial feelings to revenge this horrid act.
9. Out upon you! (a curse).
1. Disclosure.

How is't, my lord? how look you?[2]

CORN. I have received a hurt. Follow me, lady;
Turn out that eyeless villain. Throw this slave   100
Upon the dunghill. Regan, I bleed apace.
Untimely comes this hurt. Give me your arm.
    [*Exit* CORNWALL *led by* REGAN.]

SEC. SERV. I'll never care what wickedness I do,
If this man come to good.

THIRD SERV.   If she live long,
And in the end meet the old[3] course of death,   105
Women will all turn monsters.

SEC. SERV. Let's follow the old earl, and get the Bedlam
To lead him where he would. His roguish madness
Allows itself to any thing.[4]

THIRD SERV. Go thou; I'll fetch some flax and whites of eggs[5]   110
To apply to his bleeding face. Now, heaven help him!
    [*Exeunt severally.*]

Act IV

SCENE 1

[*Enter* EDGAR.]

EDG. Yet better thus, and known to be contemned
Than still contemned and flattered.[6] To be worst,
The lowest and most dejected thing of fortune,
Stands still in esperance, lives not in fear.[7]
The lamentable change is from the best;   5
The worst returns to laughter. Welcome, then,
Thou unsubstantial air that I embrace!
The wretch that thou hast blown unto the worst
Owes nothing to thy blasts. But who comes here?
    [*Enter* GLOUCESTER, *led by an* OLD MAN.]
My father, poorly led? World, world, O world!   10
But that thy strange mutations make us hate thee,
Life would not yield to age.[8]

OLD MAN. O, my good lord, I have been your tenant, and your
father's tenant, these fourscore years.

GLOU. Away, get thee away! Good friend, be gone.   15
Thy comforts can do me no good at all;
Thee they may hurt.

OLD MAN. Alack, sir, you cannot see your way.

GLOU. I have no way, and therefore want no eyes;

2. How do you seem to be?
3. Natural.
4. Since he is a mad vagabond (rogue) he will not be called to account.
5. The usual application for wounds in the eyes.
6. I.e., it is better to be a beggar, publicly known to be condemned, than always ("still") to be condemned by flattery, as a prince is.
7. The one cast to the bottom by fortune can hope to move up; he doesn't fear falling lower.
8. "The only thing that makes us grow old and die is our hatred of life in this world, and that hatred is caused by the strange vicissitudes of fortune" (Kittredge's note).

I stumbled when I saw. Full oft 'tis seen,   20
Our means secure us, and our mere defects
Prove our commodities.[9] O dear son Edgar,
The food of thy abuséd father's wrath![1]
Might I but live to see thee in my touch,
I'd say I had eyes again!

OLD MAN.   How now! Who's there?   25

EDG. [*aside*] O gods! Who is't can say "I am at the worst"?
  I am worse than e'er I was.

OLD MAN.   'Tis poor mad Tom.

EDG. [*aside*] And worse I may be yet: the worst is not
  So long as we can say "This is the worst."

OLD MAN. Fellow, where goest?

GLOU.   Is it a beggar-man?   30

OLD MAN. Madman and beggar too.

GLOU. He has some reason, else he could not beg.
  I' the last night's storm I such a fellow saw;
  Which made me think a man a worm.[2] My son
  Came then into my mind, and yet my mind   35
  Was then scarce friends with him. I have heard more since.
  As flies to wanton[3] boys are we to the gods;
  They kill us for their sport.

EDG.   [*aside*] How should this be?
  Bad is the trade that must play fool to sorrow,
  Angering itself and others.—Bless thee, master!   40

GLOU. Is that the naked fellow?

OLD MAN.   Ay, my lord.

GLOU. Then, prithee, get thee gone. If, for my sake,
  Thou wilt o'ertake us, hence a mile or twain,
  I' the way toward Dover, do it for ancient[4] love;
  And bring some covering for this naked soul,   45
  Who I'll entreat to lead me.

OLD MAN.   Alack, sir, he is mad.

GLOU. 'Tis the times' plague, when madmen lead the blind.
  Do as I bid thee, or rather do thy pleasure;
  Above the rest,[5] be gone.

OLD MAN. I'll bring him the best 'parel that I have,   50
  Come on 't what will.   [*Exit.*]

GLOU. Sirrah, naked fellow,—

EDG. Poor Tom's a-cold. [*aside*] I cannot daub it further.[6]

GLOU. Come hither, fellow.

EDG. [*aside*] And yet I must.—Bless thy sweet eyes, they bleed. 55

GLOU. Know'st thou the way to Dover?

EDG. Both stile and gate, horse-way and foot-path. Poor Tom
  hath been scared out of his good wits. Bless thee, good man's

---

9. I.e., a truth often observed is that prosperity makes us careless but adversity proves to be our best possession.
1. The one on whom his father fed his anger.
2. "How much less man, that is a worm" (Job xxv.6).
3. Sportive, playful.
4. Former, bygone.
5. All.
6. Pretend anymore.

son, from the foul fiend! Five fiends have been in Poor Tom
at once; of lust, as Obidicut; Hobbididance, prince of dumb- 60
ness; Mahu, of stealing; Modo, of murder; Flibbertigibbet, of
mopping and mowing,[7] who since possesses chambermaids
and waiting-women. So, bless thee, master!
GLOU. Here, take this purse, thou whom the heavens' plagues
Have humbled to all strokes.[8] That I am wretched 65
Makes thee the happier. Heavens, deal so still!
Let the superfluous and lust-dieted[9] man,
That slaves your ordinance,[1] that will not see
Because he doth not feel, feel your power quickly;
So distribution should undo excess, 70
And each man have enough. Dost thou know Dover?
EDG. Ay, master.
GLOU. There is a cliff, whose high and bending[2] head
Looks fearfully in the confinèd deep.[3]
Bring me but to the very brim of it, 75
And I'll repair the misery thou dost bear
With something rich about me. From that place
I shall no leading need.
EDG.   Give me thy arm.
Poor Tom shall lead thee.   [*Exeunt.*]

SCENE 2

[*Enter* GONERIL *and* EDMUND.]
GON. Welcome, my lord. I marvel our mild husband
Not met us on the way.[4]
        [*Enter* OSWALD.]
                              Now where's your master?
OSW. Madam, within, but never man so changed.
I told him of the army that was landed;
He smiled at it. I told him you were coming; 5
His answer was "The worse." Of Gloucester's treachery,
And of the loyal service of his son,
When I informed him, then he called me sot,[5]
And told me I had turned the wrong side out.
What most he should dislike seems pleasant to him; 10
What like, offensive.
GON. [*to* EDM.] Then shall you go no further.
It is the cowish[6] terror of his spirit,
That dares not undertake. He'll not feel wrongs
Which tie him to an answer.[7] Our wishes on the way 15

---

7. Making faces.
8. Have brought so low as to accept
humbly the bitterest strokes of Fortune.
9. Overly self-indulgent.
1. Makes your law subject to him.
2. Beetling.
3. Look into the sea, hemmed in by
cliffs.

4. I.e., from Gloucester's castle; they
have arrived at Goneril and Albany's
castle.
5. Fool.
6. Cowardly.
7. He will overlook offenses which
would require him to punish.

May prove effects.[8] Back, Edmund, to my brother;
Hasten his musters and conduct his powers.
I must change arms at home, and give the distaff
Into my husband's hands. This trusty servant
Shall pass between us. Ere long you are like to hear,   20
If you dare venture in your own behalf,
A mistress's command. Wear this; spare a speech;

                                        [*Giving a favor.*]

Decline your head. This kiss, if it durst speak,
Would stretch thy spirits up into the air.
Conceive, and fare thee well.   25
EDM. Yours in the ranks of death.[9]
GON.   My most dear Gloucester!

                                        [*Exit* EDMUND.]

O, the difference of man and man!
To thee a woman's services are due:
My foot usurps my body.[1]
OSW.   Madam, here comes my lord.
OSW. Madam, here comes my lord.   [*Exit.*]   30
        [*Enter* ALBANY.]
GON. I have been worth the whistle.[2]
ALB.   O Goneril!
You are not worth the dust which the rude wind
Blows in your face. I fear your disposition.
That nature, which contemns it origin,
Cannot be bordered certain in itself.[3]   35
She that herself will sliver and disbranch
From her material sap, perforce must wither
And come to deadly use.[4]
GON. No more; the text is foolish.[5]
ALB. Wisdom and goodness to the vile seem vile;   40
Filths savor but themselves. What have you done?
Tigers, not daughters, what have you performed?
A father, and a gracious aged man,
Whose reverence even the head-lugged[6] bear would lick,
Most barbarous, most degenerate, have you madded.   45
Could my good brother suffer you to do it?
A man, a prince, by him so benefited!
If that the heavens do not their visible spirits[7]
Send quickly down to tame these vild[8] offenses,

8. Our desires expressed on the way here (that you might take Albany's place as my husband) may be fulfilled. "Brother": brother-in-law, Cornwall.
9. Some critics see sexual innuendoes in "spirits," "conceive," and "death."
1. I.e., "a woman might justly adore Edmund, but Albany in the role of husband is as if the foot presumed to control the whole body" (Brooke's note).
2. Goneril, commenting bitterly on Albany's failure to meet her on the way refers to a proverb, "It is a poor dog that is not worth the whistling."
3. I have fears concerning your disposition. The nature that renounces its source cannot be trusted to keep within natural or moral limits.
4. I.e., she who cuts herself off from the tree that gave her life must be a withered branch, ready for burning ("deadly use").
5. She suggests that Albany is starting to preach a sermon, and she will hear no more of it.
6. Tugged along by a chain around its head.
7. Lightning and thunderbolt, as distinguished from invisible spirits.
8. Vile.

It will come,   50
Humanity must perforce prey on itself,
Like monsters of the deep.
GON.   Milk-livered man!
That bear'st a cheek for blows,[9] a head for wrongs:
Who hast not in thy brows an eye discerning
Thine honor from thy suffering; that not know'st   55
Fools do those villains pity who are punished
Ere they have done their mischief. Where's thy drum?
France spreads his banners in our noiseless[1] land,
With pluméd helm thy state[2] begins to threat;
Whiles thou, a moral[3] fool, sit'st still, and criest   60
"Alack, why does he so?"
ALB.   See thyself, devil!
Proper deformity shows not in the fiend
So horrid as in woman.[4]
GON.   O vain fool!
ALB. Thou changéd and self-covered thing, for shame,
Be-monster not thy feature.[5] Were't my fitness   65
To let these hands obey my blood,[6]
They are apt enough to dislocate and tear
Thy flesh and bones. Howe'er thou art a fiend,
A woman's shape doth shield thee.
GON. Marry, your manhood! mew!   70
[Enter a MESSENGER.]
ALB. What news?
MESS. O, my good lord, the Duke of Cornwall's dead;
Slain by his servant, going to put out
The other eye of Gloucester.
ALB.   Gloucester's eyes?
MESS. A servant that he bred, thrilled with remorse,[7]   75
Opposed against the act, bending his sword
To his great master; who, thereat enraged,
Flew on him, and amongst them felled him dead;
But not without that harmful stroke, which since
Hath plucked him after.
ALB.   This shows you are above,   80
You justicers, that these our nether crimes[8]
So speedily can venge! But, O poor Gloucester!
Lost he his other eye?
MESS.   Both, both, my lord.
This letter, madam, craves a speedy answer;

---

9. To be understood in the light of Matthew v.39, "whosoever shall smite thee on thy right cheek, turn to him the other also," though King Lear has a pre-Christian setting.
1. Because the drum of Albany's army has not yet sounded.
2. Throne, power.
3. Moralizing.
4. The ugliness which is natural ("proper") in a demon is not so horrid as in a woman.
5. I.e., you hypocrite, do not allow your whole shape ("feature") to become that of a monster.
6. Passion.
7. A servant he had brought up, pierced by compassion.
8. I.e., you judges, that these crimes here below, on earth.

'T is from your sister.   85
GON. [*aside*] One way I like this well;
   But being a widow, and my Gloucester with her,
   May all the building in my fancy pluck
   Upon my hateful life.⁹ Another way,
   The news is not so tart.—I'll read, and answer.   [*Exit.*] 90
ALB. Where was his son when they did take his eyes?
MESS. Come with my lady hither.
ALB.   He is not here.
MESS. No, my good lord; I met him back again.¹
ALB. Knows he the wickedness?
MESS. Ay, my good lord; 'twas he informed against him;   95
   And quit the house on purpose, that their punishment
   Might have the freer course.
ALB.   Gloucester, I live
   To thank thee for the love thou show'dst the king,
   And to revenge thine eyes. Come hither, friend.
   Tell me what more thou know'st.   [*Exeunt.*] 100

SCENE 3

[*Enter* KENT *and a* GENTLEMAN.]
KENT. Why the King of France is so suddenly gone back know
   you the reason?
GENT. Something he left imperfect in the state, which since his
   coming forth is thought of; which imports to the kingdom so
   much fear and danger, that his personal return was most   5
   required and necessary.
KENT. Who hath he left behind him general?
GENT. The Marshall of France, Monsieur LaFar.
KENT. Did your letters pierce² the queen to any demonstration
   of grief?   10
GENT. Ay, sir. She took them, read them in my presence;
   And now and then an ample tear trilled³ down
   Her delicate cheek. It seemed she was a queen
   Over her passion, who, most rebel-like,
   Sought to be king o'er her.
KENT.   O, then it moved her.   15
GENT. Not to a rage. Patience and sorrow strove
   Who should express her goodliest. You have seen
   Sunshine and rain at once: her smiles and tears
   Were like, a better way.⁴ Those happy smilets,
   That played on her ripe lip, seemed not to know   20
   What guests were in her eyes, which parted thence,
   As pearls from diamonds dropped. In brief,
   Sorrow would be a rarity most beloved,
   If all could so become it.

9. May destroy all my castles in the air   2. Move.
and make my life hateful to me.   3. Trickled.
1. On the way back.   4. But in a better fashion.

KENT.   Made she no verbal question?
GENT. 'Faith, once or twice she heaved the name of "father"   25
  Pantingly forth, as if it pressed her heart;
  Cried "Sisters! sisters! Shame of ladies! sisters!
  Kent! father! sisters! What, i' the storm? i' the night?
  Let pity not be believed!" There she shook
  The holy water from her heavenly eyes,   30
  And clamor moistened.[5] Then away she started
  To deal with grief alone.
KENT.   It is the stars,
  The stars above us, govern our conditions;[6]
  Else one self mate and make[7] could not beget
  Such different issues. You spoke not with her since?   35
GENT. No.
KENT. Was this before the king returned?
GENT.   No, since.
KENT. Well, sir, the poor distressed Lear's i' the town;
  Who sometime, in his better tune,[8] remembers
  What we are come about, and by no means   40
  Will yield to see his daughter.
GENT.   Why, good sir?
KENT. A sovereign shame so elbows him; his own unkindness,
  That stripped her from his benediction, turned her
  To foreign casualties,[9] gave her dear rights
  To his dog-hearted daughters, these things sting   45
  His mind so venomously, that burning shame
  Detains him from Cordelia.
GENT.   Alack, poor gentleman!
KENT. Of Albany's and Cornwall's powers you heard not?
GENT. 'Tis so, they are afoot.
KENT. Well, sir, I'll bring you to our master Lear,   50
  And leave you to attend him. Some dear cause[1]
  Will in concealment wrap me up awhile;
  When I am known aright, you shall not grieve
  Lending me this acquaintance. I pray you, go
  Along with me.   [*Exeunt.*] 55

SCENE 4

  [*Enter, with drum and colors,* CORDELIA, DOCTOR, *and*
    SOLDIERS.]
COR. Alack, 'tis he! Why, he was met even now
  As mad as the vexed[2] sea; singing aloud;
  Crowned with rank fumiter and furrow-weeds,
  With hor-docks, hemlock, nettles, cuckoo-flowers,
  Darnel,[3] and all the idle weeds that grow   5

---

5. "Followed her cries of sorrow with
tears" (Kittredge's note).
6. Characters.
7. Mate.
8. In his lucid intervals.

9. Chances.
1. Important reason.
2. Turbulent.
3. All common weeds.

In our sustaining corn. A century[4] send forth;
Search every acre in the high-grown field,
And bring him to our eye. [*Exit an* OFFICER.] What can
  man's wisdom
In the restoring his bereaved sense?[5]
He that helps him take all my outward worth.   10
DOCT. There is means, madam.
  Our foster-nurse of nature is repose,
  The which he lacks. That to provoke in him,
  Are many simples operative, whose power
  Will close the eye of anguish.[6]
COR.   All blest secrets,   15
  All you unpublished virtues of the earth,
  Spring with my tears![7] be aidant and remediate[8]
  In the good man's distress! Seek, seek for him;
  Lest his ungoverned rage dissolve the life
  That wants the means to lead it.[9]
      [*Enter a* MESSENGER.]
MESS.   News, madam;   20
  The British powers are marching hitherward.
COR. 'Tis known before; our preparation stands
  In expectation of them. O dear father,
  It is thy business that I go about;
  Therefore great France   25
  My mourning and important[1] tears hath pitied.
  No blown[2] ambition doth our arms incite,
  But love, dear love, and our aged father's right.
  Soon may I hear and see him!   [*Exeunt.*]

SCENE 5

    [*Enter* REGAN *and* OSWALD.]
REG. But are my brother's powers set forth?
OSW.   Ay, madam.
REG. Himself in person there?
OSW. Madam, with much ado.[3]
  Your sister is the better soldier.
REG. Lord Edmund spake not with your lord at home?   5
OSW. No, madam.
REG. What might import my sister's letter to him?
OSW. I know not, lady.
REG. Faith, he is posted hence on serious matter.
  It was great ignorance,[4] Gloucester's eyes being out,   10

4. A hundred soldiers.
5. I.e., what can medical science do to restore his lost sanity?
6. I.e., sleep, which he lacks, is nature's fostering nurse, and we have many powerful herbs ("simples") which will deaden his pain and put him to sleep.
7. May all unknown herb remedies spring up, watered by my tears.
8. Helpfully remedial.
9. Lest his mad frenzy take his life, since he is without the "means" (i.e., reason) to lead it.
1. Importuning.
2. Puffed up, inflated.
3. After much persuasion.
4. Folly.

To let him live. Where he arrives he moves
All hearts against us. Edmund, I think, is gone,
In pity of his misery, to dispatch
His nighted[5] life; moreover, to descry
The strength o' the enemy.   15

OSW. I must needs after him, madam, with my letter.

REG. Our troops set forth tomorrow. Stay with us;
The ways are dangerous.

OSW.   I may not, madam:
My lady charged my duty in this business.

REG. Why should she write to Edmund? Might not you   20
Transport her purposes by word? Belike,
Something—I know not what. I'll love thee much,
Let me unseal the letter.

OSW.   Madam, I had rather—

REG. I know your lady does not love her husband;
I am sure of that; and at her late being here   25
She gave strange oeillades[6] and most speaking looks
To noble Edmund. I know you are of her bosom.[7]

OSW. I, madam?

REG. I speak in understanding; y'are, I know't.
Therefore I do advise you, take this note:[8]   30
My lord is dead; Edmund and I have talked;
And more convenient is he for my hand
Than for your lady's. You may gather more.
If you do find him, pray you, give him this;[9]
And when your mistress hears thus much[1] from you,   35
I pray, desire her call her wisdom to her.
So, fare you well.
If you do chance to hear of that blind traitor,
Preferment falls on him that cuts him off.

OSW. Would I could meet him, madam! I should show   40
What party I do follow.

REG. Fare thee well.   [Exeunt.]

SCENE 6

[Enter GLOUCESTER, and EDGAR dressed like a peasant.]

GLOU. When shall we come to the top of that same hill?

EDG. You do climb up it now. Look how we labor.

GLOU. Methinks the ground is even.

EDG.   Horrible steep.
Hark, do you hear the sea?

GLOU.   No, truly.

EDG. Why, then, your other senses grow imperfect   5
By your eyes' anguish.

GLOU.   So may it be, indeed.
Methinks thy voice is altered, and thou speakest

5. Darkened through blindness.   8. Take note of what I say.
6. Amorous glances.   9. A love-token.
7. In her confidence.   1. What I have told her.

In better phrase and matter than thou didst.
EDG. Y'are much deceived. In nothing am I changed
But in my garments.
GLOU.   Methinks y'are better spoken.   10
EDG. Come on, sir; here's the place. Stand still. How fearful
And dizzy 'tis, to cast one's eyes so low!
The crows and choughs[2] that wing the midway air
Show scarce so gross[3] as beetles. Halfway down
Hangs one that gathers sampire,[4] dreadful trade!   15
Methinks he seems no bigger than his head.
The fishermen, that walk upon the beach,
Appear like mice; and yond tall anchoring bark,
Diminished to her cock;[5] her cock, a buoy
Almost too small for sight. The murmuring surge,   20
That on the unnumbered idle pebble[6] chafes,
Cannot be heard so high. I'll look no more,
Lest my brain turn, and the deficient sight[7]
Topple down headlong.
GLOU.   Set me where you stand.
EDG. Give me your hand. You are now within a foot   25
Of th' extreme verge. For all beneath the moon
Would I not leap upright.
GLOU.   Let go my hand.
Here, friend, 's another purse; in it a jewel
Well worth a poor man's taking. Fairies and gods
Prosper it with thee! Go thou farther off;   30
Bid me farewell, and let me hear thee going.
EDG. Now fare you well, good sir.
GLOU.   With all my heart.
EDG. [aside] Why I do trifle thus with his despair
Is done to cure it.
GLOU. [kneeling] O you mighty gods!   35
This world I do renounce, and, in your sights,
Shake patiently my great affliction off.
If I could bear it longer, and not fall
To quarrel with your great opposeless[8] wills,
My snuff and loathéd part of nature[9] should   40
Burn itself out. If Edgar live, O, bless him!
Now, fellow, fare thee well.   [He falls forward and swoons.]
EDG.   Gone, sir; farewell.—
And yet I know not how conceit[1] may rob
The treasury of life, when life itself
Yields[2] to the theft. Had he been where he thought,   45
By this had thought been past. Alive or dead?

2. Jackdaws.
3. Large.
4. An aromatic plant used in pickling.
5. Cockboat.
6. Innumerable barren pebbles.
7. My vision being distorted.
8. Succumb to rebellion against. "Op-

poseless": irresistible.
9. Snuff: burnt part of a wick. The remainder of his life, loathsome to him, would be a snuff.
1. Imagination, delusion.
2. Consents.

Ho, you sir! friend! Hear you, sir? speak!
Thus might he pass indeed. Yet he revives.
What are you, sir?

GLOU.   Away, and let me die.

EDG. Hadst thou been aught but gossamer, feathers, air,   50
So many fathom down precipitating,[3]
Thou'dst shivered like an egg; but thou dost breathe;
Hast heavy substance;[4] bleed'st not; speak'st; art sound.
Ten masts at each[5] make not the altitude
Which thou hast perpendicularly fell.   55
Thy life's a miracle. Speak yet again.

GLOU. But have I fallen, or no?

EDG. From the dread summit of this chalky bourn.[6]
Look up a-height; the shrill-gorged[7] lark so far
Cannot be seen or heard. Do but look up.   60

GLOU. Alack, I have no eyes.
Is wretchedness deprived that benefit,
To end itself by death? 'Twas yet some comfort,
When misery could beguile[8] the tyrant's rage,
And frustrate his proud will.

EDG.   Give me your arm.   65
Up—so. How is 't? Feel you your legs? You stand.

GLOU. Too well, too well.

EDG.   This is above all strangeness.
Upon the crown o' the cliff, what thing was that
Which parted from you?

GLOU.   A poor unfortunate beggar.

EDG. As I stood here below, methought his eyes   70
Were two full moons; he had a thousand noses,
Horns whelked and waved like the enridgéd sea:
It was some fiend. Therefore, thou happy father,[9]
Think that the clearest[1] gods, who make them honors
Of men's impossibilities, have preserved thee.   75

GLOU. I do remember now. Henceforth I'll bear
Affliction till it do cry out itself
"Enough, enough," and die. That thing you speak of,
I took it for a man; often 't would say
"The fiend, the fiend"—he led me to that place.   80

EDG. Bear free[2] and patient thoughts. But who comes here?
    [*Enter* LEAR, *fantastically dressed with wild flowers.*]
The safer sense will ne'er accommodate
His master thus.[3]

LEAR. No, they cannot touch me for coining; I am the king

---

3. Falling headlong.
4. Substantial weight.
5. End to end.
6. Boundary (i.e., the cliff).
7. Shrill-throated.
8. Cheat.

9. Old man (Edgar does not reveal his identity).
1. Glorious.
2. Happy.
3. A man in his right senses would never dress this way.

himself.[4]   85

EDG. O thou side-piercing sight!

LEAR. Nature's above art in that respect. There's your press-
money.[5] That fellow handles his bow like a crow-keeper.[6]
Draw me a clothier's yard.[7] Look, look, a mouse! Peace, peace;
this piece of toasted cheese will do 't. There's my gauntlet;[8] 90
I'll prove it on a giant. Bring up the brown bills.[9] O, well
flown, bird! i' the clout, i' the clout.[1] Hewgh! Give the word.[2]

EDG. Sweet marjoram.

LEAR. Pass.

GLOU. I know that voice.   95

LEAR. Ha! Goneril, with a white beard! They flattered me like a
dog; and told me I had white hairs in my beard ere the black
ones were there. To say "aye" and "no" to everything that I
said![3]—"Aye" and "no" too was no good divinity. When the
rain came to wet me once, and the wind to make me chatter; 100
when the thunder would not peace at my bidding; there I
found 'em, there I smelt 'em out. Go to, they are not men o'
their words! They told me I was everything. 'Tis a lie, I am
not ague-proof.

GLOU. The trick[4] of that voice I do well remember.   105
Is 't not the king?

LEAR.   Aye, every inch a king!
When I do stare, see how the subject quakes.
I pardon that man's life. What was thy cause?[5]
Adultery? Thou shalt not die. Die for adultery? No. The wren
goes to 't, and the small gilded fly does lecher in my sight. 110
Let copulation thrive; for Gloucester's bastard son was kinder
to his father than my daughters got 'tween the lawful sheets.
To 't, luxury, pell-mell![6] for I lack soldiers. Behold yond
simpering dame, whose face between her forks presages
snow;[7] that minces virtue, and does shake the head to hear 115
of pleasure's name, the fitchew, nor the soiléd horse, goes
to 't with a more riotous appetite.[8] Down from the waist they
are Centaurs,[9] though women all above. But to the girdle do

---

4. The king had the exclusive privilege
of coining.
5. Money paid to recruits.
6. Scarecrow.
7. The standard English arrow was a
cloth-yard long.
8. A glove thrown down as a challenge
to a duel.
9. Halberds or pikes, painted brown to
resist rust.
1. The bull's-eye.
2. Password. Edgar chooses the name of
a herb supposed to be good for diseases of the brain.
3. I.e., to agree with me always, as flat-

terers do. "No good divinity": i.e., bad
theology. Several Biblical texts say that
your *aye* should mean aye, and your *no*,
no.
4. Peculiarity.
5. Legal charge, offense.
6. Promiscuously: "luxury": lust.
7. I.e., whose face presages snow between her forks (legs).
8. I.e., neither the polecat nor the well-
fed horse pursues sex more violently.
9. Creatures in Greek mythology, half
human, half horse, supposed to be extremely lustful.

the gods inherit,[1] beneath is all the fiends'; there's hell, there's darkness, there's the sulphurous pit, burning, scalding, stench, consumption! Fie, fie, fie! pah! pah! Give me an ounce of civet,[2] good apothecary, to sweeten my imagination. There's money for thee. 120

GLOU. O, let me kiss that hand!

LEAR. Let me wipe it first; it smells of mortality. 125

GLOU. O ruined piece[3] of nature! This great world[4] Shall so wear out to nought. Dost thou know me?

LEAR. I remember thine eyes well enough. Dost thou squiny[5] at me? No, do thy worst, blind Cupid; I'll not love. Read thou this challenge; mark but the penning of it. 130

GLOU. Were all the letters suns, I could not see one.

EDG. [*aside*] I would not take this from report. It is, And my heart breaks at it.

LEAR. Read.

GLOU. What, with the case of eyes?[6] 135

LEAR. O, ho, are you there with me? No eyes in your head, nor no money in your purse? Your eyes are in a heavy case, your purse in a light.[7] Yet you see how this world goes.

GLOU. I see it feelingly.

LEAR. What, art mad? A man may see how this world goes with no eyes. Look with thine ears. See how yond justice rails upon yond simple[8] thief. Hark, in thine ear. Change places and, handy-dandy,[9] which is the justice, which is the thief? Thou hast seen a farmer's dog bark at a beggar? 140

GLOU. Aye, sir. 145

LEAR. And the creature[1] run from the cur? There thou mightst behold the great image of authority: a dog's obeyed in office.
Thou rascal beadle,[2] hold thy bloody hand!
Why dost thou lash that whore? Strip thine own back;
Thou hotly lusts to use her in that kind 150
For which thou whipp'st her. The usurer hangs the cozener.[3]
Through tattered clothes small vices do appear;
Robes and furred gowns hide all. Plate sin with gold,
And the strong lance of justice hurtless breaks;
Arm it in rags, a pigmy's straw does pierce it. 155

---

1. I.e., the gods rule only down to the belt.
2. Perfume.
3. Masterpiece. It was commonplace to consider man the masterpiece of Nature's creation.
4. The universe.
5. Squint.
6. Eye sockets.
7. I.e., your eyes are in a sad plight (with a pun on "case" as socket) and your purse in a pleasant one (with a pun on "light" as "of little weight" and perhaps also "visible").
8. Low-class, ordinary.
9. A child's game in which one is asked to tell which closed fist contains an object.
1. Human being.
2. Minor constable.
3. The judge practices usury but hangs a small cheater.

None does offend, none, I say, none; I'll able 'em;[4]
Take that of me,[5] my friend, who have the power
To seal the accuser's lips. Get thee glass eyes;
And, like a scurvy politician,[6] seem
To see the things thou dost not. Now, now, now, now!   160
Pull off my boots. Harder, harder! So.[7]

EDG. O, matter and impertinency[8] mixed!
Reason in madness!

LEAR. If thou wilt weep[9] my fortunes, take my eyes.
I know thee well enough; thy name is Gloucester: 165
Thou must be patient. We came crying hither;
Thou knows't, the first time that we smell the air,
We wail and cry. I will preach to thee. Mark.

GLOU. Alack, alack the day!

LEAR. When we are born, we cry that we are come   170
To this great stage of fools. This' a good block;[1]
It were a delicate stratagem, to shoe
A troop of horse with felt. I'll put 't in proof;[2]
And when I have stol'n upon these sons-in-law,
Then, kill, kill, kill, kill, kill, kill!   175

[*Enter a* GENTLEMEN, *with* ATTENDANTS.]

GENT. O, here he is; lay hand upon him. Sir,
Your most dear daughter—

LEAR. No rescue? What, a prisoner? I am even
The natural food of fortune. Use me well;
You shall have ransom. Let me have surgeons;   180
I am cut to the brains.

GENT.   You shall have any thing.

LEAR. No seconds?[3] all myself?
Why, this would make a man a man of salt,[4]
To use his eyes for garden water-pots,
Aye, and laying autumn's dust.

GENT.   Good sir—   185

LEAR. I will die bravely, like a smug bridegroom.[5] What!
I will be jovial. Come, come; I am a king,
My masters, know you that?

GENT. You are a royal one, and we obey you.

LEAR. Then there's life in't. Nay, if you get it, you shall get it   190
with running. Sa, sa, sa, sa.[6]

[*Exit running;* ATTENDANTS *follow.*]

4. Authorize.
5. He hands him an imaginary pardon.
6. A vile trickster, a Machiavellian.
7. Lear imagines that he has just come in from hunting, as in I.iv.
8. Sense and nonsense.
9. Cry over.
1. "All the world's a stage" is a commonplace. Lear then thinks of the "stage" as a platform to preach from, but the word "block" suggests a mount-ing-block for getting on horseback, and, in another sense, hats, whence "felt."
2. Try the experiment.
3. Helpers.
4. Because of his tears.
5. "Bravely": (1) courageously; (2) in fine clothes. "Smug": neat.
6. I.e., the case is not yet desperate; but if you want me, you will have to catch me. "Sa, sa": a hunting cry, urging the hounds to greater speed.

GENT. A sight most pitiful in the meanest wretch,
    Past speaking of in a king! Thou hast one daughter,
    Who redeems nature from the general curse
    Which twain have brought her to.   195
EDG. Hail, gentle⁷ sir.
GENT.   Sir, speed you. What's your will?
EDG. Do you hear aught, sir, of a battle toward?⁸
GENT. Most sure and vulgar.⁹ Everyone hears that,
    Which can distinguish sound.
EDG.   But, by your favor,
    How near's the other army?   200
GENT. Near and on speedy foot. The main descry
    Stands on the hourly thought.¹
EDG. I thank you, sir. That's all.
GENT. Though that the queen on special cause is here,
    Her army is moved on.
EDG.   I thank you, sir.   [*Exit* GENT.] 205
GLOU. You ever-gentle gods, take my breath from me;
    Let not my worser spirit² tempt me again
    To die before you please!
EDG.   Well pray you, father.
GLOU. Now, good sir, what are you?
EDG. A most poor man, made tame to fortune's blows;   210
    Who, by the art of known and feeling sorrows,
    Am pregnant to³ good pity. Give me your hand,
    I'll lead you to some biding.⁴
GLOU.   Hearty thanks.
    The bounty and the benison of heaven
    To boot, and boot!   215
        [*Enter* OSWALD.]
OSW. A proclaimed prize! Most happy!
    That eyeless head of thine was first framed flesh
    To raise my fortunes. Thou old unhappy traitor,
    Briefly thyself remember.⁵ The sword is out
    That must destroy thee.
GLOU.   Now let thy friendly hand   220
    Put strength enough to 't.   [EDGAR *interposes.*]
OSW.   Wherefore, bold peasant.
    Darest thou support a published⁶ traitor? Hence,
    Lest that the infection of his fortune take
    Like hold on thee. Let go his arm.
EDG. Chill not let go, zir, without vurther 'casion.⁷   225
OSW. Let go, slave, or thou diest!
EDG. Good gentleman, go your gait, and let poor volk pass. An
    chud⁸ ha' bin zwaggered out of my life, 't would not ha' bin

7. Noble.   4. Abode.
8. In preparation.   5. Remember your sins and repent.
9. Common knowledge.   6. Proclaimed.
1. We expect to descry the main force   7. Conventional rustic dialect, similar to
within the hour.   that of Somersetshire. "Chill": I will.
2. My evil genius.   8. If I should.
3. Susceptible to.

zo long as 'tis by a vortnight. Nay, come not near th' old
man; keep out, che vor ye, or ise try whether your costard or₂₃₀
my ballow be the harder.⁹ Chill be plain with you.

osw. Out, dunghill!

edg. Chill pick your teeth, zir. Come! No matter vor your foins.¹

> [*They fight, and* edgar *knocks him down.*]

osw. Slave, thou hast slain me. Villain, take my purse.
 If ever thou wilt thrive, bury my body;
 And give the letters² which thou find'st about me   235
 To Edmund earl of Gloucester. Seek him out
 Upon the British party. O, untimely death!
 Death!   [*He dies.*]

edg. I know thee well: a serviceable villain;   240
 As duteous to the vices of thy mistress
 As badness would desire.

glou.   What, is he dead?

edg. Sit you down, father; rest you.
 Let's see his pockets; the letters that he speaks of
 May be my friends. He's dead; I am only sorry   245
 He had no other death'sman. Let us see.
 Leave, gentle wax;³ and, manners blame us not.
 To know our enemies' minds, we'd rip their hearts;
 Their papers, is more lawful.
 [*Reads.*] "Let our reciprocal vows be remembered. You have₂₅₀
many opportunities to cut him off.⁴ If your will want not,
time and place will be fruitfully offered. There is nothing
done, if he return the conqueror. Then am I the prisoner, and
his bed my jail; from the loathed warmth wherof deliver me,
and supply the place for your labor.   255
        "Your—wife, so I would say—
         "Affectionate servant,⁵
           "goneril."

O undistinguished space of woman's will!⁶
A plot upon her virtuous husband's life;   260
And the exchange my brother! Here, in the sands,
Thee I'll rake up, the post unsanctified⁷
Of murderous lechers; and in the mature time⁸
With this ungracious paper strike the sight
Of the death-practiced⁹ duke. For him 'tis well   265
That of thy death and business I can tell.

glou. The king is mad. How stiff¹ is my vile sense,
 That I stand up, and have ingenious feeling
 Of my huge sorrows! Better I were distract;
 So should my thoughts be fenced from my griefs,   270

---

9. Keep out, I warrant you, or I'll see
whether your head or my cudgel is harder.
1. Thrusts.
2. I.e., letter.
3. By your leave, gentle wax (as he un-
seals the letter).

4. I.e., kill Albany.
5. I.e., lover.
6. O limitless extent of woman's lust.
7. Unholy letter-carrier.
8. When time is ripe.
9. Whose death was plotted.
1. Unbending.

And woes by wrong imaginations lose
The knowledge of themselves.[2]

EDG.   Give me your hand.

                                        [*Drum afar off.*]

Far off, methinks, I hear the beaten drum.
Come, father, I'll bestow you with a friend.   [*Exeunt.*]

SCENE 7

[*Enter* CORDELIA, KENT, DOCTOR, *and a* GENTLEMAN.]

COR. O thou good Kent, how shall I live and work,
To match thy goodness? My life will be too short,
And every measure fail me.[3]

KENT. To be acknowledged, madam, is o'erpaid.
All my reports go with the modest truth;   5
Nor more nor clipped, but so.[4]

COR.   Be better suited.
These weeds are memories of those worser hours.[5]
I prithee, put them off.

KENT.   Pardon me, dear madam;
Yet to be known shortens my made intent.[6]
My boon I make it, that you know me not   10
Till time and I think meet.

COR. Then be 't so, my good lord. [*To the* DOCTOR.] How does
    the king?

DOCT. Madam, sleeps still.

COR. O you kind gods,
Cure this great breach in his abuséd nature!   15
The untuned and jarring senses, O, wind up
Of this child-changéd father![7]

DOCT.   So please your majesty
That we may wake the king? He hath slept long.

COR. Be governed by your knowledge, and proceed
I' the sway of your own will. Is he arrayed?[8]   20

    [*Enter* LEAR *in a chair carried by* SERVANTS.]

GENT. Aye, madam. In the heaviness of his sleep
We put fresh garments on him.

DOCT. Be by, good madam, when we do awake him;
I doubt not of his temperance.[9]

COR.   Very well.   [*Music.*]

DOCT. Please you, draw near. Louder the music there!   25

COR. O my dear father! Restoration hang
Thy medicine on my lips; and let this kiss
Repair those violent harms that my two sisters

---

2. I.e., I would be better off mad; then
my troubles would be separated from my
thoughts and accordingly would have no
knowledge of themselves.
3. Since Kent's goodness is immeasurable.
4. Neither amplified nor abbreviated, but
accurate.

5. Be better dressed. These clothes recall
your hours of trouble.
6. I am not ready to be known yet.
7. Tune up the out-of-tune senses of this
father who is changed into a child.
8. Dressed.
9. Normality.

Have in thy reverence made!¹

KENT.   Kind and dear princess!

COR. Had you not been their father, these white flakes   30
    Had challenged pity of them.² Was this a face
    To be opposed against the warring winds?
    To stand against the deep dread-bolted thunder?
    In the most terrible and nimble stroke
    Of quick, cross lightning? to watch—poor perdu!—   35
    With this thin helm?³ Mine enemy's dog,
    Though he had bit me, should have stood that night
    Against my fire; and wast thou fain, poor father,
    To hovel thee with swine, and rogues forlorn,
    In short and musty straw? Alack, alack!   40
    'Tis wonder that thy life and wits at once
    Had not concluded all. He wakes; speak to him.

DOCT. Madam, do you; 'tis fittest.

COR. How does my royal lord? How fares your majesty?

LEAR. You do me wrong to take me out o' the grave.   45
    Thou art a soul in bliss; but I am bound
    Upon a wheel of fire, that mine own tears
    Do scald like molten lead.⁴

COR.   Sir, do you know me?

LEAR. You are a spirit, I know. When did you die?

COR. Still, still, far wide!⁵   50

DOCT. He's scarce awake. Let him alone awhile.

LEAR. Where have I been? Where am I? Fair daylight?
    I am mightily abused.⁶ I should e'en die with pity,
    To see another thus. I know not what to say.
    I will not swear these are my hands. Let's see.   55
    I feel this pin prick. Would I were assured
    Of my condition!

COR.   O, look upon me, sir,
    And hold your hands in benediction o'er me:
    No, sir, you must not kneel.

LEAR. Pray, do not mock me.   60
    I am a very foolish fond⁷ old man,
    Fourscore and upward, not an hour more nor less;
    And, to deal plainly,
    I fear I am not in my perfect mind.
    Methinks I should know you, and know this man;   65
    Yet I am doubtful; for I am mainly⁸ ignorant
    What place this is; and all the skill I have
    Remembers not these garments; nor I know not
    Where I did lodge last night. Do not laugh at me;

---

1. Have done to you, who should be treated with reverence.
2. These white hairs would have claimed pity from them.
3. Poor solitary sentinel, with this thin head protection (his hair).
4. In the New Testament Apocrypha the damned in hell are tormented on wheels of fire.
5. Wandering in the mind.
6. Deluded.
7. In his dotage.
8. Completely.

For, as I am a man, I think this lady   70
  To be my child Cordelia.
COR.   And so I am, I am.
LEAR. Be your tears wet? Yes, faith. I pray, weep not.
  If you have poison for me, I will drink it.
  I know you do not love me; for your sisters
  Have, as I do remember, done me wrong.   75
  You have some cause, they have not.
COR.   No cause, no cause.
LEAR. Am I in France?
KENT.   In your own kingdom, sir.
LEAR. Do not abuse[9] me.
DOCT. Be comforted, good madam. The great rage,[1]
  You see, is killed in him; and yet it is danger   80
  To make him even o'er the time he has lost.[2]
  Desire him to go in. Trouble him no more
  Till further settling.[3]
COR. Will't please your highness walk?
LEAR.   You must bear with me:
  Pray you now, forget and forgive. I am old and foolish.   85
                    [*Exeunt all but* KENT *and* GENTLEMAN.]
GENT. Holds it true, sir, that the Duke of Cornwall was so slain?
KENT. Most certain, sir.
GENT. Who is conductor[4] of his people?
KENT. As 'tis said, the bastard son of Gloucester.
GENT. They say Edgar, his banished son, is with the Earl of Kent 90
  in Germany.
KENT. Report is changeable.'Tis time to look about. The powers
  of the kingdom approach apace.[5]
GENT. The arbitrement[6] is like to be bloody. Fare you well, sir.
                                                      [*Exit.*]

KENT. My point and period will be throughly wrought,[7]   95
  Or well or ill, as this day's battle's fought.   [*Exit.*]

Act V

SCENE 1

[*Enter, with drum and colors,* EDMUND, REGAN, GENTLE-
  MEN, *and* SOLDIERS.]
EDM. Know of the duke if his last purpose hold,
  Or whether since he is advised by aught
  To change the course.[8] He's full of alteration
  And self-reproving. Bring his constant pleasure.[9]
                    [*To a* GENTLEMAN, *who goes out.*]

9. Delude.
1. Violent delirium.
2. I.e., it is dangerous to make him go over his recent experiences.
3. Till he has calmed down.
4. Leader.
5. The British forces are approaching rapidly.
6. Decisive battle.
7. The end and purpose of my life will be completely worked out.
8. Find out from Albany if he still intends to fight or has changed his mind.
9. Fixed decision.

REG. Our sister's man is certainly miscarried.[1]   5
EDM. 'Tis to be doubted,[2] madam.
REG.   Now, sweet lord,
  You know the goodness I intend upon you.
  Tell me—but truly—but then speak the truth,
  Do you not love my sister?
EDM.   In honored love.
REG. But have you never found my brother's way   10
  To the forfended[3] place?
EDM.   That thought abuses you.
REG. I am doubtful that you have been conjunct
  And bosomed with her, as far as we call hers.[4]
EDM. No, by mine honor, madam.
REG. I never shall endure her. Dear my lord,   15
  Be not familiar with her.
EDM.   Fear me not.
  She and the duke her husband!
    [*Enter, with drum and colors,* ALBANY, GONERIL, *and*
      SOLDIERS.]
GON. [*aside*] I had rather lose the battle than that sister
  Should loosen[5] him and me.
ALB. Our very loving sister, well be-met.   20
  Sir, this I hear: the king is come to his daughter,
  With others whom the rigor of our state[6]
  Forced to cry out. Where I could not be honest,
  I never yet was valiant. For this business,
  It toucheth us, as France invades our land,   25
  Not bolds the king, with others, whom, I fear,
  Most just and heavy causes make oppose.[7]
EDM. Sir, you speak nobly.
REG.   Why is this reasoned?[8]
GON. Combine together 'gainst the enemy;
  For these domestic and particular broils   30
  Are not the question here.
ALB.   Let's then determine
  With the ancient of war on our proceeding.[9]
EDM. I shall attend you presently at your tent.
REG. Sister, you'll go with us?
GON. No.   35
REG. 'Tis most convenient; pray you, go with us.
GON. [*aside*] O, ho, I know the riddle.—I will go.
    [*As they are going out, enter* EDGAR *disguised.*]
EDG. If e'er your grace had speech with man so poor,
  Hear me one word.

1. I.e., Oswald has certainly come to
harm.
2. Feared.
3. Forbidden.
4. I am afraid you have been intimate
with her, in every sense of the word.
5. Separate.
6. Harshness of our rule.

7. It concerns us because France invades
our land, but not because it supports the
king and others who have great and justified grievances and for that reason oppose us.
8. Why discuss it?
9. Consult with veterans on our strategy.

ALB.   I'll overtake you. Speak.
                              [*Exeunt all but* ALBANY *and* EDGAR.]
EDG. Before you fight the battle, ope this letter.   40
  If you have victory, let the trumpet sound
  For him that brought it. Wretched though I seem,
  I can produce a champion that will prove
  What is avouched[1] there. If you miscarry,
  Your business of the world hath so an end,   45
  And machination[2] ceases. Fortune love you!
ALB. Stay till I have read the letter.
EDG.   I was forbid it.
  When time shall serve, let but the herald cry,
  And I'll appear again.
ALB. Why, fare thee well. I will o'erlook[3] thy paper.   50
                              [*Exit* EDGAR.]

      [*Re-enter* EDMUND.]
EDM. The enemy's in view; draw up your powers.
  Here is the guess of their true strength and forces
  By diligent discovery; but your haste
  Is now urged on you.
ALB.   We will greet the time.[4] [*Exit.*]
EDM. To both these sisters have I sworn my love;   55
  Each jealous of the other, as the stung
  Are of the adder. Which of them shall I take?
  Both? one? or neither? Neither can be enjoyed,
  If both remain alive. To take the widow
  Exasperates, makes mad her sister Goneril;   60
  And hardly shall I carry out my side,
  Her husband being alive. Now then we'll use
  His countenance[5] for the battle; which being done,
  Let her who would be rid of him devise
  His speedy taking off.[6] As for the mercy   65
  Which he intends to Lear and to Cordelia,
  The battle done, and they within our power,
  Shall never see his pardon; for my state
  Stands on me to defend, not to debate.[7]   [*Exit.*]

                        SCENE 2

      [*Alarum within. Enter, with drum and colors,* LEAR,
      CORDELIA, *and* SOLDIERS, *over the stage; and exeunt.*]
      [*Enter* EDGAR *and* GLOUCESTER.]
EDG. Here, father,[8] take the shadow of this tree
  For your good host; pray that the right may thrive:

---

1. Asserted; "miscarry": are defeated.
2. Plotting.
3. Read.
4. Meet the emergency.
5. Authority.
6. Killing.
7. My interests require me to act, not discuss moral considerations.
8. Old man (Edgar has not revealed his identity).

If ever I return to you again,
I'll bring you comfort.

GLOU.   Grace go with you, sir!   [*Exit* EDGAR.]

[*Alarum and retreat within. Re-enter* EDGAR.]

EDG. Away, old man! give me thy hand! away!   5
King Lear hath lost, he and his daughter ta'en.
Give me thy hand! come on!

GLOU. No farther, sir; a man may rot even here.

EDG. What, in ill thoughts again? Men must endure
Their going hence, even as their coming hither;   10
Ripeness is all. Come on!   [*Exeunt.*]

SCENE 3

[*Enter, in conquest, with drum and colors,* EDMUND;
LEAR *and* CORDELIA, *prisoners;* CAPTAIN, SOLDIERS, &c.]

EDM. Some officers take them away. Good guard,
Until their greater pleasures first be known
That are to censure them.[9]

COR.   We are not the first
Who, with best meaning, have incurred the worst.
For thee, oppresséd king, am I cast down;   5
Myself could else out-frown false Fortune's frown.
Shall we not see these daughters and these sisters?

LEAR. No, no, no, no! Come, let's away to prison.
We two alone will sing like birds i' the cage.
When thou dost ask me blessing, I'll kneel down,[1]   10
And ask of thee forgiveness. So we'll live,
And pray, and sing, and tell old tales, and laugh
At gilded butterflies,[2] and hear poor rogues
Talk of court news; and we'll talk with them too,
Who loses and who wins; who 's in, and who 's out;   15
And take upon 's the mystery of things,[3]
As if we were Gods' spies; and we'll wear out,
In a walled prison, packs and sects of great ones,[4]
That ebb and flow by the moon.

EDM.   Take them away.

LEAR. Upon such sacrifices,[5] my Cordelia,   20
The gods themselves throw incense. Have I caught thee?
He that parts us shall bring a brand from heavens,
And fire us hence like foxes.[6] Wipe thine eyes;
The good-years shall devour them, flesh and fell,[7]
Ere they shall make us weep! We'll see 'em starved first.   25

9. Until we know the wishes of the higher authorities who are to judge them.
1. It was considered shocking for a parent to kneel to his child.
2. Foppish courtiers.
3. Profess to understand the mysterious course of events.
4. We will outlast, in prison, cliques and parties.
5. As their renunciation of the world.
6. I.e., smoke us out as hunters smoke foxes from their holes.
7. Time shall devour them, flesh and skin.

Come.   [*Exeunt* LEAR *and* CORDELIA, *guarded.*]

EDM. Come hither, captain; hark.
Take thou this note [*giving a paper*]. Go follow them to
    prison:
One step I have advanced thee. If thou dost
As this instructs thee, thou dost make thy way   30
To noble fortunes. Know thou this, that men
Are as the time is. To be tender-minded
Does not become a sword. Thy great employment
Will not bear question.[8] Either say thou'lt do 't,
Or thrive by other means.

CAPT.   I'll do 't, my lord.   35

EDM. About it; and write happy[9] when thou hast done.
Mark, I say, instantly; and carry it so
As I have set it down.[1]

CAPT. I cannot draw a cart, nor eat dried oats;
If it be a man's work, I'll do 't.   [*Exit.*] 40
    [*Flourish. Enter* ALBANY, GONERIL, REGAN, *another*
    CAPTAIN, *and* SOLDIERS.]

ALB. Sir, you have showed today your valiant strain,
And fortune led you well. You have the captives
That were the opposites of this day's strife.
We do require them of you, so to use them
As we shall find their merits and our safety   45
May equally determine.

EDM.   Sir, I thought it fit
To send the old and miserable king
To some retention and appointed guard;
Whose age has charms in it, whose title more,
To pluck the common bosom on his side,   50
And turn our impressed lances in our eyes[2]
Which do command them. With him I sent the queen;
My reason all the same; and they are ready
Tomorrow, or at further space, t' appear
Where you shall hold your session. At this time   55
We sweat and bleed; the friend hath lost his friend;
And the best quarrels, in the heat, are cursed
By those that feel their sharpness.[3]
The question of Cordelia and her father
Requires a fitter place.

ALB.   Sir, by your patience,   60
I hold you but a subject of this war,
Not as a brother.

REG.   That's as we list to grace him.[4]

8. Cannot be discussed.
9. Consider yourself fortunate.
1. Do it immediately and do it just as I
have written it down.
2. I.e., to win popular support and turn

conscripted soldiers against us.
3. I.e., the best causes are injured by
high feelings.
4. That depends on how much I please
to honor him.

Methinks our pleasure might have been demanded,
Ere you had spoken so far. He led our powers;
Bore the commission of my place and person;   65
The which immediacy[5] may well stand up,
And call itself your brother.
GON.   Not so hot!
In his own grace he doth exalt himself,
More than in your addition.[6]
REG.   In my rights,
By me invested, he compeers the best.[7]   70
GON. That were the most, if he should husband you.
REG. Jesters do oft prove prophets.
GON.   Holla, holla!
That eye that told you so looked but a-squint.
REG. Lady, I am not well; else I should answer
From a full-flowing stomach.[8] General,   75
Take thou my soldiers, prisoners, patrimony:
Dispose of them, of me; the walls[9] are thine.
Witness the world, that I create thee here
My lord and master.
GON.   Mean you to enjoy him?
ALB. The let-alone lies not in your good will.   80
EDM. Nor in thine, lord.
ALB.   Half-blooded fellow, yes.
REG. [*to* EDMUND] Let the drum strike, and prove my title
thine.
ALB. Stay yet; hear reason. Edmund, I arrest thee
On[1] capital treason; and, in thine attaint,
This gilded serpent [*pointing to* GONERIL]. For your claim, fair
sister,   85
I bar it in the interest of my wife;
'Tis she is sub-contracted to this lord,
And I, her husband, contradict your banes.[2]
If you will marry, make your loves to me,
My lady is bespoke.
GON.   An interlude![3]   90
ALB. Thou art armed, Gloucester. Let the trumpet sound.
If none appear to prove upon thy head
Thy heinous, manifest, and many treasons,
There is my pledge [*throwing down a glove*]; I'll prove it on
thy heart,
Ere I taste bread, thou art in nothing less   95
Than I have proclaimed thee.

---

5. I.e., being my immediate representative.
6. He ranks higher by his own qualities than by the titles you confer on him.
7. By virtue of the rights I have vested in him, he equals the highest rank.
8. From a tide of high resentment.

9. I.e., Regan's person, referring to the common conceit that the lady is a castle, besieged by her lover.
1. For.
2. Banns (announcements in church of an impending marriage).
3. I.e., what a drama this is!

REG. Sick, O, sick!

GON. [*aside*] If not, I'll ne'er trust medicine.[4]

EDM. There 's my exchange [*throwing down a glove*]. What in
the world he is
That names me traitor, villain-like he lies.
Call by thy trumpet. He that dares approach, 100
On him, on you, who not? I will maintain[5]
My truth and honor firmly.

ALB. A herald, ho!

EDM. A herald, ho, a herald!

ALB. Trust to thy single virtue[6]; for thy soldiers,
All levied in my name, have in my name 105
Took their discharge.

REG. My sickness grows upon me.

ALB. She is not well; convey her to my tent. [*Exit* REGAN, *led.*]
[*Enter a* HERALD.]
Come hither, herald,—Let the trumpet sound,—
And read out this.

CAPT. Sound, trumpet! [*A trumpet sounds.*]

HER. [*reads*] "If any man of quality or degree within the lists 110
of the army will maintain upon Edmund, supposed Earl of
Gloucester, that he is a manifold traitor, let him appear by the
third sound of the trumpet. He is bold in his defense."

EDM. Sound! [*First trumpet.*]

HER. Again! [*Second trumpet.*] 115

HER. Again! [*Third trumpet.*]
[*Trumpet answers within.*]
[*Enter* EDGAR, *at the third sound, armed, with a trumpet
before him.*]

ALB. Ask him his purposes, why he appears
Upon this call o' the trumpet.

HER. What are you?
Your name, your quality? and why you answer
This present summons?

EDG. Know, my name is lost; 120
By treason's tooth bare-gnawn and canker-bit.[7]
Yet am I noble as the adversary
I come to cope.

ALB. Which is that adversary?

EDG. What's he that speaks for Edmund Earl of Gloucester?

EDM. Himself. What say'st thou to him?

EDG. Draw thy sword, 125
That, if my speech offend a noble heart,
Thy arm may do thee justice. Here is mine.
Behold, it is the privilege of mine honors,
My oath, and my profession. I protest,

---

4. Poison.
5. Prove in combat.
6. Your own personal strength.

7. I.e., gnawn and eaten by the tooth of
the caterpillar treason.

Maugre[8] thy strength, youth, place, and eminence,   130
Despite thy victor sword and fire-new[9] fortune,
Thy valor and thy heart, thou art a traitor;
False to thy gods, thy brother, and thy father;
Conspirant 'gainst this high-illustrious prince;
And, from the extremest upward of thy head   135
To the descent and dust below thy foot,
A most toad-spotted traitor. Say thou "No,"
This sword, this arm, and my best spirits, are bent
To prove upon thy heart, whereto I speak,
Thou liest.

EDM.   In wisdom I should ask thy name;   140
But, since thy outside looks so fair and warlike
And that thy tongue some say[1] of breeding breathes,
What safe and nicely I might well delay
By rule of knighthood, I disdain and spurn.
Back do I toss these treasons to thy head;   145
With the hell-hated lie o'erwhelm thy heart;
Which, for they yet glance by and scarcely bruise,
This sword of mine shall give them instant way,
Where they shall rest for ever. Trumpets, speak!
                    [*Alarums. They fight.* EDMUND *falls.*]

ALB. Save him, save him![2]

GON.   This is practice,[3] Gloucester: 150
By the law of arms thou wast not bound to answer
An unknown opposite. Thou art not vanquished,
But cozened and beguiled.

ALB.   Shut your mouth, dame,
Or with this paper shall I stople it.[4]
Thou worse than any name, read thine own evil.   155
No tearing, lady! I perceive you know it.
                    [*Gives the letter to* EDMUND.]

GON. Say, if I do, the laws are mine, not thine.
Who can arraign me for 't?

ALB.   Most monstrous! oh!
Know'st thou this paper?

GON.   Ask me not what I know.   [*Exit.*]

ALB. Go after her: she's desperate; govern her.   160

EDM. What you have charged me with, that have I done;
And more, much more; the time will bring it out.
'Tis past, and so am I. But what art thou
That hast this fortune[5] on me? If thou 'rt noble,
I do forgive thee.

EDG.   Let's exchange charity.   165

8. Despite.
9. Brand new.
1. Smack.
2. A puzzle, variously explained. Dr. Johnson thought Albany wanted Edmund's life saved temporarily so he
could be proved guilty; other editors give the line to Goneril.
3. Trickery.
4. Plug it up.
5. This downfall, turn of the wheel of Fortune. Cf. line 204, below.

I am no less in blood than thou art, Edmund;
If more, the more thou hast wronged me.
My name is Edgar, and thy father's son.
The gods are just, and of our pleasant vices
Make instruments to plague us.   170
The dark and vicious place where thee he got[6]
Cost him his eyes.

EDM.   Thou hast spoken right, 'tis true;
The wheel is come full circle! I am here.

ALB. Methought thy very gait did prophesy
A royal nobleness. I must embrace thee.   175
Let sorrow split my heart, if ever I
Did hate thee or thy father!

EDG.   Worthy prince. I know 't.

ALB. Where have you hid yourself?
How have you known the miseries of your father?

EDG. By nursing them, my lord. List a brief tale;   180
And when 'tis told, O, that my heart would burst!
The bloody proclamation to escape,
That followed me so near,—O, our lives' sweetness!
That we the pain of death would hourly die
Rather than die at once![7]—taught me to shift   185
Into a madman's rags; to assume a semblance
That very dogs disdained; and in this habit
Met I my father with his bleeding rings,
Their precious stones new lost; became his guide,
Led him, begged for him, saved him from despair;   190
Never,—O fault!—revealed myself unto him,
Until some half-hour past, when I was armed:
Not sure, though hoping, of this good success,
I asked his blessing, and from first to last
Told him my pilgrimage. But his flawed heart,—   195
Alack, too weak the conflict to support!—
'Twixt two extremes of passion, joy and grief,
Burst smilingly.

EDM.   This speech of yours hath moved me,
And shall perchance do good; but speak you on;
You look as you had something more to say.   200

ALB. If there be more, more woeful, hold it in;
For I am almost ready to dissolve,[8]
Hearing of this.

EDG.   This would have seemed a period
To such as love not sorrow; but another,
To amplify too much would make much more,   205
And top extremity.[9]

---

6. Begot.
7. I.e., how sweet life must be to persuade us to go on dying every hour rather than dying once for all.
8. Melt in tears.

9. This would have seemed the end to those who don't love sorrow; only another sorrow, if I were to tell all about it, would go beyond that extreme limit.

Whilst I was big[1] in clamor came there in a man,
Who, having seen me in my worst estate,
Shunned my abhorred society; but then, finding
Who 'twas that so endured, with his strong arms   210
He fastened on my neck, and bellowed out
As he'd burst heaven; threw him on[2] my father;
Told the most piteous tale of Lear and him
That ever ear received; which in recounting
His grief grew puissant, and the strings of life   215
Began to crack. Twice then the trumpets sounded,
And there I left him tranced.[3]

ALB.   But who was this?
EDG. Kent, sir, the banished Kent; who in disguise
     Followed his enemy king, and did him service
     Improper for a slave.[4]   220

          [*Enter a* GENTLEMAN, *with a bloody knife.*]

GENT. Help, help, O, help!
EDG.   What kind of help?
ALB.   Speak, man.
EDG. What means that bloody knife?
GENT.   'Tis hot, it smokes,
     It came even from the heart of—O, she's dead!
ALB. Who dead? speak, man.
GENT. Your lady, sir, your lady! and her sister   225
     By her is poisoned; she hath confessed it.
EDM. I was contracted to them both. All three
     Now marry in an instant.

          [*Enter* KENT.]

EDG.   Here comes Kent.
ALB. Produce their bodies, be they alive or dead:
     This judgment of the heavens, that makes us tremble,   230
     Touches us not with pity.   [*Exit* GENTLEMAN.]
                    O, is this he?
     The time will not allow the compliment[5]
     Which very manners urges.
KENT.   I am come
     To bid my king and master aye good night.
     Is he not here?
ALB.   Great thing of us forgot!   235
     Speak, Edmund, where's the king? and where's Cordelia?
     See'st thou this object, Kent?

          [*The bodies of* GONERIL *and* REGAN *are brought in.*]

KENT. Alack, why thus?
EDM.   Yet Edmund was beloved.
     The one the other poisoned for my sake,

---

1. Loud.
2. Embraced.
3. Senseless.
4. I.e., followed the king who was hostile to him and did service for him you
wouldn't ask a slave to do.
5. Ceremony.

And after slew herself. 240

ALB. Even so. Cover their faces.

EDM. I pant for life. Some good I mean to do,
Despite of mine own nature. Quickly send,
Be brief in it, to the castle; for my writ
Is on the life of Lear and on Cordelia: 245
Nay, send in time.

ALB.   Run, run, O, run!

EDG. To who, my lord? Who hath the office? send
Thy token of reprieve.

EDM.   Well thought on. Take my sword,
Give it the captain.

ALB.   Haste thee for thy life.   [*Exit* EDGAR.] 250

EDM. He hath commission from thy wife and me
To hang Cordelia in the prison, and
To lay the blame upon her own despair,
That she fordid[6] herself.

ALB. The gods defend her! Bear him hence awhile. 255
               [EDMUND *is borne off.*]
     [*Re-enter* LEAR, *with* CORDELIA *dead in his arms;* EDGAR,
       CAPTAIN, *and others following.*]

LEAR. How, howl, howl, howl! O, you are men of stones:
Had I your tongues and eyes, I'd use them so
That heaven's vault should crack. She's gone forever!
I know when one is dead, and when one lives;
She's dead as earth. Lend me a looking-glass; 260
If that her breath will mist or strain the stone,[7]
Why, then she lives.

KENT.   Is this the promised end?[8]

EDG. Or image of that horror?

ALB.   Fall, and cease![9]

LEAR. This feather stirs; she lives! If it be so,
It is a chance which does redeem all sorrows 265
That ever I have felt.

KENT. [*kneeling*] O my good master!

LEAR. Prithee, away.

EDG.   'Tis noble Kent, your friend.

LEAR. A plague upon you, murderers, traitors all!
I might have saved her; now she's gone for ever! 270
Cordelia, Cordelia! stay a little. Ha!
What is 't thou say'st? Her voice was ever soft,
Gentle, and low, an excellent thing in woman.
I killed the slave that was a-hanging thee.

CAPT. 'Tis true, my lords, he did.

LEAR.   Did I not, fellow? 275
I have seen the day, with my good biting falchion[1]

---

6. Destroyed.
7. Mirror (of polished crystal).
8. Doomsday, the Last Judgment.

9. Let the heavens fall, and everything
come to an end.
1. Light sword.

I would have made them skip: I am old now,
And these same crosses[2] spoil me. Who are you?
Mine eyes are not o' the best. I'll tell you straight.[3]

KENT. If fortune brag of two she loved and hated,   280
    One of them we behold.

LEAR. This is a dull sight. Are you not Kent?

KENT.   The same,
    Your servant Kent. Where is your servant Caius?

LEAR. He's a good fellow, I can tell you that;
    He'll strike, and quickly too. He's dead and rotten.   285

KENT. No, my good lord; I am the very man,—

LEAR. I'll see that straight.

KENT. That, from your first of difference and decay,[4]
    Have followed your sad steps.

LEAR.   You are welcome hither.

KENT. Nor no man else. All's cheerless, dark, and deadly.   290
    Your eldest daughters have fordone themselves,
    And desperately[5] are dead.

LEAR.   Aye, so I think.

ALB. He knows not what he says; and vain it is
    That we present us to him.

EDG.   Very bootless.[6]
    [*Enter a* CAPTAIN.]

CAPT. Edmund is dead, my lord.

ALB.   That's but a trifle here.   295
    You lords and noble friends, know our intent.
    What comfort to this great decay[7] may come
    Shall be applied. For us, we will resign,
    During the life of this old majesty,
    To him our absolute power; [*to* EDGAR *and* KENT] you, to your
        rights;   300
    With boot, and such addition[8] as your honors
    Have more than merited. All friends shall taste
    The wages of their virtue, and all foes
    The cup of their deserving. O, see, see!

LEAR. And my poor fool[9] is hanged! No, no, no life!   305
    Why should a dog, a horse, a rat, have life,
    And thou no breath at all? Thou'lt come no more,
    Never, never, never, never, never!
    Pray you, undo this button. Thank you, sir.
    Do you see this? Look on her, look, her lips,   310
    Look there, look there!   [*Dies.*]

EDG.   He faints! My lord, my lord!

KENT. Break, heart; I prithee, break!

2. Troubles, frustrations.
3. Straightway.
4. Beginning of change and decline in fortunes.
5. From despair.

6. Futile.
7. This great man ruined.
8. More besides, and such titles.
9. An affectionate term, referring to Cordelia.

EDG.   Look up, my lord.

KENT. Vex not his ghost.[1] O, let him pass! He hates him much

    That would upon the rack of this tough world

    Stretch him out longer.[2]

EDG.   He is gone, indeed.   315

KENT. The wonder is, he hath endured so long.

    He but usurped his life.

ALB. Bear them from hence. Our present business

    Is general woe. [*to* KENT *and* EDGAR] Friends of my soul,

        you twain

    Rule in this realm, and the gored[3] state sustain.   320

KENT. I have a journey, sir, shortly to go;

    My master calls me, I must not say no.

EDG. The weight of this sad time we must obey;

    Speak what we feel, not what we ought to say.

    The oldest hath borne most; we that are young   325

    Shall never see so much, nor live so long.[4]

                         [*Exeunt, with dead march.*]

1604–5   1608

1. Departing spirit.
2. The rack was an instrument of torture in which the victim's arms and legs were pulled, even to dislocation.
3. Wounded.
4. These lines are given to Albany in the Quarto, to Edgar in the Folio. Editors who follow the Quarto argue that Shakespeare always gives the concluding speech in a tragedy to the highest-ranking person who survives. Those who follow the Folio say that Edgar must reply to Albany's "Friends of my soul" and that "we that are young" suits Edgar better than Albany. In effect, Edgar tacitly accepts the commission to rule which Kent has had to decline, so he is the highest-ranking survivor.

Sixteenth-Century Lyrics

The 16th century was one of the great ages for lyric poetry in English. As J. J. Jusserand puts it, in his *Literary History of the English People*, "Indefatigable, the poets now sing verses worthy of remembrance, on every subject, amorous, religious, epic, satirical, pastoral, didactic, moving from the world of insects to the world of heroes. Songs rise naturally to their lips, no one knows why, they do not know why."

The lyrics written by courtiers, in the first half of the century as well as later, were poems intended to be set to music and sung. In the courts of all the Tudor sovereigns music flourished; skill in composition was an excellent qualification for a servant, and noblemen, even crowned heads themselves, pursued the art. Sometimes a courtly poet would compose new words to a popular tune. The songs of Wyatt and other courtiers collected in *Tottel's Miscellany* are only a remnant of the large amount of lyrical verse written in the courts of Henry VIII and Edward VI. The courtly "makers," as they have been called, were of course able to imitate and borrow foreign stanza forms and popular themes from the poetry of Italy and France. But at their best they wrote lyrics in the native English tradition also, and the fusing of native and foreign strains may well be the best reason for the flourishing of lyric poetry in the last decades of the century.

In Shakespeare's *Twelfth Night*, the Duke calls upon a court jester to repeat a song he has heard him sing:

> O fellow, come, the song we had last night.
> Mark it, Cesario; it is old and plain.
> The spinsters and the knitters in the sun,
> And the free maids that weave their thread with bones,
> Do use to chant it. It is silly sooth,
> And dallies with the innocence of love
> Like the old age.

Singing at court is pictured here; moreover, it is part of a play, thereby illustrating another source of lyric poetry in Elizabethan England: the drama. Acting companies used boys to play their female parts, and often these boys had been trained as singers; the playwright would provide them opportunities to display their talents. In Thomas Dekker's play of craftsmen's life, *The Shoemakers' Holiday*, the workers sing while they cobble shoes, and Shakespeare's gravedigger, in *Hamlet*, sings while he works.

The popular ballad, with its simple four-line stanza form, of anonymous or perhaps composite authorship, can be traced back to the 15th century, and, with the invention of printing, a more commercial form, the broad-

995

side ballad, became popular. Copies of broadside ballads were sold by traveling peddlers like Autolycus in Shakespeare's *Winter's Tale*; they were often crude affairs, and exploited the latest murder or scandal like the sensational newspaper of modern times.

At the other extreme were the two kinds of art song, the madrigal and the air. A madrigal is a song for two or more voices in counterpoint, usually a setting of a poem expressing the woes of the Petrarchan lover, although any subject is possible. The music is highly imitative of the meaning of the words, but since the separate voices are usually not on the same word at the same time, it is often difficult to understand a madrigal being sung. There is evidence that many Elizabethans could sing a part in a madrigal at sight—a feat which now requires a high degree of musical training. The words must be contained within one rather short stanza, since the music is so closely adapted to the meaning and since phrases are repeated many times in the different voices.

The air, a much less complicated musical form, used words arranged in stanzas; it was a single, recurring melody for the voice with a three-part accompaniment on the lute. Words written for the lute-song or air were much more frequently excellent lyric poems than the words written for madrigals, which tended to be not much more than epigrams. The finest poet of airs was Thomas Campion, who was also a composer. He had a remarkably sensitive ear and a thorough understanding of the problems of versification and musical setting. The genius of Campion and of Ben Jonson solved the vexed problem of whether English quantitative verse (verse which relies upon length and duration of syllables, rather than accent) could be successful.

The 16th century produced more anonymous lyrics than it did lyrics the authors of which can be identified. There are several reasons for this. The Elizabethan period shared the medieval idea that pride of individual authorship was unimportant. Moreover many poems circulated in manuscript and were copied into manuscript books one after the other, without particular care for identifying authorship. Sometimes publishers obtained such collections and printed them, either not knowing or not caring about the authorship of individual poems. The first great 16th-century anthology, *Tottel's Miscellany* (1557), has a large number of poems attributed to "Uncertain Authors," only a few of whom have been identified up to the present time; a very popular anthology at the end of the century, *The Phoenix Nest*, gives no name at all for some poems and attributes others to "Ignoto."

Another reason for the survival of anonymous poems was that they were often the lyrics for songs. The composer published his musical settings with the words, so that they could be sung, but few publishers gave credit to the author of the words. An exception was Thomas Campion. There was a casualness about authorship that seems strange to us. Aristocrats and courtiers, though they wrote poetry, often did not wish to be known as writers—it would seem beneath them. On the other hand, the art was less specialized in those days: lawyers, statesmen, explorers, parsons, soldiers, merchants—it was a rare Elizabethan who would not try his hand at a verse.

JOHN SKELTON
(ca. 1460–1529)

According to one of the jest-book tales, John Skelton suddenly interrupted one of his sermons to ask the members of his congregation why they had complained that he kept a fair wench in the rectory. To be sure, he said, he did keep a fair wench; she was fairer than his parishioners' wives and had given him a son. Holding the child up naked before the congregation, he exclaimed, "How say you, neighbors all? Is not this child as fair as is the best of all yours? It hath nose, eyes, hands, and feet, as well as any of yours. It is not like a pig, nor a calf, nor like no foul nor no monstrous beast. If I had brought forth this child without arms or legs, or that it were deformed being a monstrous thing, I would never have blamed you to have complained to the Bishop of me, but to complain without a cause! I say as I said before, in my antetheme, *vos estis*, you be, and have been, and will and shall be knaves to complain of me without a cause reasonable."

Many and colorful were the stories circulated about the mad wag Skelton —who was also the major poet of the first quarter of the century, with the title of Poet Laureate from both Oxford and Cambridge. He was famous as a rhetorician and a translator, and he was also, for a time, tutor to the young Henry VIII. He took orders and, after writing *The Bowge of Court*, a satire on courtiers and court life, retired about 1504, became rector of the parish church at Diss, in Norfolk. By 1512 he had returned to the court, appointed King's Orator. He moved to a house in the sanctuary of Westminster in 1518, and shortly thereafter began his vituperous attacks upon Cardinal Wolsey, the great prelate-statesman, beginning with *Colin Clout* (1519) and continuing with *Speak, Parrot* (1521) and *Why Come Ye Not to Court?* (1522–23). Wolsey had him imprisoned for a time but later released him.

While in retirement at Diss, he began to write poetry in a "plain style" that rejected ornate rhetorical devices and aureate language. His satires gain some of their most startling effects by mixing high and low styles. These "open satires," as they are called, are written in short rhymed lines that to the modern ear resemble doggerel, although something like this form was probably familiar enough to readers of medieval satire. A Skeltonic line may have from two to five beats, and the lines can keep on rhyming until the resources of the language give out. To many of his poems, particularly the satires, this strange meter is singularly appropriate. *The Tunning of Elinour Rumming* is, for example, a wonderfully disordered, clattering portrait of an alewife that reminds one of Brueghel's paintings in its realism, and the Skeltonics do much to contribute to the effect of disorder. The lines give the voice of the narrator of the satires a breathless urgency much admired by Robert Graves and W. H. Auden, among other modern poets. Skelton's satires draw upon a long tradition of medieval anti-clerical satire, but he brings a fresh voice to the genre.

Skelton's lyrics also partake of traditional medieval modes which the poet

makes his own. To the three-part song *Mannerly Margery*, a traditional
ballad of the clerk and the serving-maid, he gives an ironic ending. His
rather salacious *Lullay, Lullay* is a parody on traditional lullabies in which
the Virgin Mary rocks the Christ child in her lap. In such poems we hear
a genuine music and find, as always, the impress of the distinctive character
of their author.

From Colin Clout[1]

And if ye stand in doubt
Who brought this rhyme about,
My name is Colin Clout.
I purpose to shake out
5   All my conning° bag,   *learning*
Like a clerkly hag.[2]
For though my rhyme be ragged,
Tattered and jagged,
Rudely rain-beaten,
10   Rusty and moth-eaten,
If ye take well therewith,
It hath in it some pith.
For, as far as I can see,
It is wrong with each degree.
15   For the temporality°   *laymen*
Accuseth the spirituality;
The spiritual again
Doth grudge and complain
Upon the temporal men;
20   Thus, each of other blother°   *babble*
The one against the other.
Alas, they make me shudder!
For in hugger-mugger°   *haste*
The Church is put in fault;
25   The prelates been so haut,°   *haughty*
They say, and look so high
As though they woulde fly
Above the starry sky.

                                                     1519

Upon a Dead Man's Head

*That was sent to him from an honorable gentlewoman for a token,
Skelton, Laureate, devised this ghostly*[3] *meditation in English
covenable,*[4] *in sentence, commendable, lamentable, lacrimable,
profitable for the soul.*

1. These are lines 47–74, comprising
part of the introductory matter. Colin
Clout, the narrator, here introduces the
theme of the whole long poem, in the
characteristically jagged Skeltonic line.
2. Old scholar.
3. Spiritual.
4. Suitable; "in sentence": in meaning.

Your ugly token
My mind hath broken
From worldly lust;
For I have discussed,
5   We are but dust
And die we must.

It is general
To be mortal;
I have well espied
10   No man may him hide
From Death hollow-eyed
With sinews wyderéd°   *withered*
With bones shyderéd,°   *shattered*
With his worm-eaten maw
15   And his ghastly jaw
Gaping aside,
Naked of hide,
Neither flesh nor fell.°   *skin*

Then, by my counsel
20   Look that ye spell°   *study*
Well this gospel,
For whereso we dwell
Death will us quell
And with us mell.°   *mix*

25   For all our pampered paunches
There may no fraunchis°   *franchise*
Nor worldly bliss
Redeem us from this:
Our days be dated
30   To be checkmated
With draughtes of death
Stopping our breath;
Our eyen sinking,
Our bodies stinking,
35   Our gummes grinning,
Our soules brinning.°   *burning*

To whom, then, shall we sue
For to have rescue
But to sweet Jesu
40   On us then for to rue?
O goodly child
Of Mary mild
Then be our shield,
That we be not exiled
45   To the dyne° dale   *dark*

Of bootless bale[5]
Nor to the lake
Of fiendes° black.   *devils*

50   But grant us grace
To see thy face
And to purchase
Thine heavenly place
And thy palace
Full of solace
55   Above the sky
That is so high,
Eternally
To behold and see
The Trinity.

Amen.

Myrres vous y.[6]

ca.1498

Mannerly Margery Milk and Ale[7]

Aye, beshrew you, by my fay,[8]
These wanton clerks be nice° alway,   *foolish*
Avaunt, avaunt, my popinjay!
"What, will you do nothing but play?"
5   Tilly vally straw, let be I say!
Gup,[9] Christian Clout, gup, Jack of the Vale!
With Mannerly Margery milk and ale.

"By God, ye be a pretty pode,°   *toad*
And I love you an whole cartload."
10   Straw, James Foder, ye play the fode,°   *deceiver, seducer*
I am no hackney for your rod:°   *riding*
Go watch a bull, your back is broad!
Gup, Christian Clout, gup, Jack of the Vale!
With Mannerly Margery milk and ale.

15   Ywis° ye deal uncourteously;   *certainly*
What, would ye frumple° me? now fie!   *rumple, tumble*
"What, and ye shall not be my pigsny?"°   *darling*
By Christ, ye shall not, no hardily:
I will not be japped° bodily!   *tricked, deceived*
20   Gup, Christian Clout, gup, Jack of the Vale!
With Mannerly Margery milk and ale.

"Walk forth your way, ye cost me naught;
Now have I found that I have sought:

5. Irremediable sorrow.
6. See yourself in it.
7. The clerk's lines are in quotation marks; Margery sings the rest, except the chorus lines, which are sung by a bass.
8. "Beshrew": curse (not used seriously); "fay": faith.
9. Contracted from "go up."

The best cheap flesh that ever I bought."
25   Yet, for his love that hath all wrought,
Wed me, or else I die for thought.
Gup, Christian Clout, your breath is stale!
Go, Mannerly Margery milk and ale!
Gup, Christian Clout, gup, Jack of the Vale!
30   With Mannerly Margery milk and ale.

ca. 1510   1523

Lullay, Lullay, Like a Child

With lullay, lullay, like a child,
Thou sleepest too long, thou art beguiled.°   *deceived*

"My darling dear, my daisy flower,
Let me," quod° he, "lie in your lap."   *quoth*
5   "Lie still," quod she, "my paramour,
Lie still, hardily,° and take a nap."   *confidently*
His head was heavy, such was his hap,
All drowsy dreaming, drowned in sleep,
That of his love he took no keep.
10   With hey, lullay, lullay, like a child,
Thou sleepest too long, thou art beguiled.

With ba, ba, ba![1] and bas, bas, bas!
She cherished him, both cheek and chin,
That he wist never where he was,
15   He had forgotten all deadly sin.
He wanted wit her love to win,
He trusted her payment and lost all his pay;
She left him sleeping and stale° away,   *stole*
With hey, lullay, lullay, like a child,
20   Thou sleepest too long, thou art beguiled.

The rivers rough, the waters wan,
She spared not to wet her feet;
She waded over, she found a man
That halséd° her heartily and kissed her sweet—   *embraced*
25   Thus after her cold she caught a heat.
"My lief," she said, "routeth[2] in his bed;
Ywis° he hath an heavy head."   *certainly*
With hey, lullay, lullay, like a child,

Thou sleepest too long, thou are beguiled.
30   What dreamest thou, drunkard, drowsy pate?
Thy lust and liking is from thee gone.
Thou blinkard blowboll,[3] thou wakest too late.

---

1. The "by" of *lullaby;* "bas, bas, bas":   2. My lover snores.
kiss, kiss, kiss.   3. Blink-eyed drunkard.

> Behold thou liest, luggard,° alone!   sluggard
> Well may thou sigh, well may thou groan,
> To deal with her so cowardly.
35   Ywis, pole-hatchet,° she bleared thine eye.   barfly

1490–1503

SIR EDWARD DYER

(1543–1607)

Dyer was a courtier, a friend of Sir Philip Sidney, and a patron of poets. Since he published nothing himself, not much poetry has survived that can be confidently assigned to him. But his contemporaries, such as Nashe, thought that he was the first "that repurified poetry from arts pedantism [presumably the learned language of the university] and that instructed it to speak courtly." His best-known lyric, *My Mind to Me a Kingdom Is*, is one of the great expressions in English of the ideal of *otium* or the contented mind. It is of course related to the idyllic simplicity of pastoral, and to the glorification of the mean estate (moderate living) in Surrey's poem *My Friend, the Things That Do Attain*.

My Mind to Me a Kingdom Is

> My mind to me a kingdom is;
>   Such present joys therein I find
> That it excels all other bliss
>   That earth affords or grows by kind.[1]
> Though much I want[2] which most would have,   5
> Yet still my mind forbids to crave.
>
> No princely pomp, no wealthy store,
>   No force to win the victory,
> No wily wit to salve a sore,
>   No shape to feed a loving eye;   10
> To none of these I yield as thrall.
> For why[3] my mind doth serve for all.
>
> I see how plenty suffers oft,
>   And hasty climbers soon do fall;
> I see that those which are aloft   15
>   Mishap doth threaten most of all;
> They get with toil, they keep with fear.
> Such cares my mind could never bear.
>
> Content I live, this is my stay;
>   I seek no more than may suffice;   20
> I press to bear no haughty sway;
>   Look, what I lack my mind supplies;

1. Nature.
2. Lack.
3. Because.

Lo, thus I triumph like a king,
Content with that my mind doth bring.

Some have too much, yet still do crave;   25
   I little have, and seek no more.
They are but poor, though much they have,
   And I am rich with little store.
They poor, I rich; they beg, I give;
They lack, I leave; they pine, I live.   30

I laugh not at another's loss;
   I grudge not at another's gain;
No worldly waves my mind can toss;
   My state at one doth still remain.
I fear no foe, I fawn no friend;   35
I loathe not life, nor dread my end.

Some weigh their pleasure by their lust,
   Their wisdom by their rage of will;
Their treasure is their only trust;
   A cloakéd craft their store of skill.   40
But all the pleasure that I find
Is to maintain a quiet mind.

My wealth is health and perfect ease;
   My conscience clear my choice defense;
I neither seek by bribes to please,   45
   Nor by deceit to breed offense.
Thus do I live; thus will I die.
Would all did so as well as I!

1588

FULKE GREVILLE, LORD BROOKE

(1554–1628)

Greville was a successful courtier, philosopher, poet, and patron of poets.
He led a long and prosperous life, which he summed up in the epitaph he
composed for himself: "Servant to Queen Elizabeth, Councillor to King
James, and Friend to Sir Philip Sidney." He wrote a biography of Sidney
which was not published until 1652. His poetry consists of *Caelica*, a
collection of short poems, written probably during Elizabeth's reign but not
published, for the most part, until after Greville's death, two closet dramas,
and several long poems or treatises on Learning, Fame and Honor, Wars,
Monarchy, and Religion. He kept revising his poems, and the dates of their
composition are very uncertain. His philosophical bent and his untraditional
handling of conceits have caused critics to say that he was a metaphysical
poet ahead of his time.

   Greville never married during his long life, but a chronicler of his times wrote of him that he lived and died a constant courtier of the ladies. Whether his Myra, Caelica, or Cynthia represent real or imaginary loves remains a mystery. His reputation as a poet has been gradually increasing in the last thirty years, and significant critical and biographical work on him has been published.

From Caelica

All my senses, like beacons' flame,
Gave alarum to desire
To take arms in Cynthia's name,
And set all my thoughts on fire.
Fury's wit persuaded me,   5
Happy love was hazard's heir,
Cupid did best shoot and see
In the night where smooth is fair;
Up I start believing well
To see if Cynthia were awake.   10
Wonders, I saw, who can tell?
And thus unto myself I spake:
"Sweet god Cupid where am I,
That, by pale Diana's light
Such rich beauties do espy   15
As harm our senses with delight?
Am I borne up to the skies?
See where Jove and Venus shine,
Showing in her heavenly eyes
That desire is divine.   20
Look where lies the Milken Way,
Way unto that dainty throne,
Where while all the gods would play,
Vulcan thinks to dwell alone."[1]
I gave reins to this conceit,   25
Hope went on the wheel of[2] lust;
Fancy's scales are false of weight,
Thoughts take thought[3] that go of trust.
I stepped forth to touch the sky;
I a god by Cupid dreams,[4]   30
Cynthia who did naked lie,
Runs away like silver streams,
Leaving hollow banks behind,
Who can neither forward move,
Nor, if rivers be unkind,   35
Turn away or leave to love.

1. Vulcan was the husband of Venus, who cuckolded him with Mars.
2. Was carried along by.
3. Are anxious.
4. He imagines himself Cupid, among the gods.

There stand I, like Arctic Pole,
Where Sol passeth o'er the line,[5]
Mourning my benighted soul,
Which so loseth light divine.   40
There stand I like men that preach
From the execution place,
At their death content to teach
All the world with their disgrace.
He that lets his Cynthia lie   45
Naked on a bed of play,
To say prayers ere she die,
Teacheth Time to run away.
Let no love-desiring heart
In the stars go seek his fate;   50
Love is only Nature's art;
Wonder hinders love and hate.
None can well behold with eyes
But what underneath him lies.

1633

From Mustapha

Chorus Sacerdotum[1]

Oh wearisome condition of humanity!
Born under one law, to another bound;
Vainly begot, and yet forbidden vanity;
Created sick, commanded to be sound.
What meaneth Nature by these diverse laws?   5
Passion and reason, self-division cause.
Is it the mark[2] or majesty of power
To make offenses that it may forgive?
Nature herself doth her own self deflower
To hate those errors she herself doth give.   10
For how should man think that he may not do[3]
If Nature did not fail, and punish too?
Tyrant to others, to herself unjust,
Only commands things difficult and hard;
Forbids us all things which it knows is lust,[4]   15
Makes easy pains, unpossible reward.
If Nature did not take delight in blood,
She would have made more easy ways to good.
We that are bound by vows, and by promotion,[5]
With pomp of holy sacrifice and rites,   20

5. The equator.
1. "Chorus of Priests" from the closet tragedy *Mustapha*.
2. Target or aim.
3. Why should any action be forbidden?
4. Which we naturally desire.
5. Appointment as priests.

To teach belief in good and still devotion,
To preach of Heaven's wonders and delights;
Yet when each of us in his own heart looks,
He finds the God there far unlike his books.

                                                    1609

ROBERT SOUTHWELL
(1561–1595)

Father Robert Southwell, S.J., was the younger son of a prominent English family who went to the English seminary for Catholics at Douai as a youth, then to Rome, where he entered the Society of Jesus. In 1586 he returned to England. His mission was a dangerous one, and he probably foresaw the martyrdom he was to suffer in 1595. He wrote a good deal of religious prose and verse; the most famous of his lyrics is *The Burning Babe*. Ben Jonson remarked to William Drummond of Hawthornden that if he had written *The Burning Babe* he would have been willing to destroy many of his own poems.

The Burning Babe

As I in hoary winter's night stood shivering in the snow,
Surprised I was with sudden heat which made my heart to glow;
And lifting up a fearful eye to view what fire was near,
A pretty babe all burning bright did in the air appear;
Who, scorchéd with excessive heat, such floods of tears did shed   5
As though his floods should quench his flames which with his tears
       were fed.
"Alas," quoth he, "but newly born in fiery heats I fry,[1]
Yet none approach to warm their hearts or feel my fire but I!
My faultless breast the furnace is, the fuel wounding thorns,
Love is the fire, and sighs the smoke, the ashes shame and scorns;   10
The fuel justice layeth on, and mercy blows the coals,
The metal in this furnace wrought are men's defiléd souls,
For which, as now on fire I am to work them to their good,
So will I melt into a bath to wash them in my blood."
With this he vanished out of sight and swiftly shrunk away,   15
And straight I calléd unto mind that it was Christmas day.

                                                    1602

1. Burn.

SAMUEL DANIEL
(1562–1619)

Samuel Daniel, translator, historian, and poet, was a follower of the Countess of Pembroke, Sidney's sister. He wrote classical tragedies, a verse history
of the *Civil Wars Between the Two Houses of Lancaster and York* (1594–
1609), a late defense of learning in *Musophilus*, and one of the better
Elizabethan sonnet cycles, *Delia* (1592). His *Defense of Rhyme* (1603),
written in answer to Thomas Campion's criticisms of the use of rhyme, is
an important contribution to the critical debates of the time. As a lyric
poet, Daniel is restrained, quiet, and eloquent.

From Delia

33

When men shall find thy flower, thy glory pass,
And thou, with careful brow sitting alone,
Receivéd hast this message from thy glass,
That tells thee truth, and says that all is gone,
Fresh shalt thou see in me the wounds thou madest,   5
Though spent thy flame, in me the heat remaining,
I that have loved thee thus before thou fadest,
My faith shall wax, when thou art in thy waning.
The world shall find this miracle in me,
That fire can burn when all the matter's spent;   10
Then what my faith hath been thyself shall see,
And that thou wast unkind thou mayst repent.
Thou mayst repent that thou hast scorned my tears,
When winter snows upon thy golden hairs.

45

Care-charmer Sleep, son of the sable Night,
Brother to Death, in silent darkness born,
Relieve my languish and restore the light;
With dark forgetting of my cares, return.
And let the day be time enough to mourn   5
The shipwreck of my ill-adventured youth;
Let waking eyes suffice to wail their scorn
Without the torment of the night's untruth.
Cease, dreams, th' imagery of our day desires,
To model forth the passions of the morrow;   10
Never let rising sun approve you liars,

To add more grief to aggravate my sorrow.
Still let me sleep, embracing clouds in vain,
And never wake to feel the day's disdain.

46

Let others sing of knights and paladins
In aged accents and untimely[1] words,
Paint shadows in imaginary lines
Which well the reach of their high wits records;
But I must sing of thee and those fair eyes.   5
Authentic shall my verse in time to come,
When yet th' unborn shall say, "Lo where she lies,
Whose beauty made him speak that else was dumb."
These are the arks, the trophies I erect,
That fortify thy name against old age;   10
And these thy sacred virtues must protect
Against the dark and time's consuming rage.
Though th' error of my youth they shall discover,
Suffice, they show I lived and was thy lover.

1592

1. Obsolete.

MICHAEL DRAYTON
(1563–1631)

Drayton's long career as a poet extended from the early 1590's until well
on in the 17th century. He was born about a year earlier than Shakespeare
and in the same county, Warwickshire. He collaborated in plays, wrote
sonnets, pastorals, odes, poetic epistles, and a versified history called *The
Barons' Wars*, but he intended as his masterpiece a 30,000-line historical-
geographical poem about the English countryside called *Poly-Olbion*. His
lifelong devotion to Anne Goodere, Lady Rainsford, is memorialized in
his sonnets to a lady called Idea. He revised his sonnets and added to them
as they were republished, so one can trace his development from an Elizabethan to a 17th-century poet. He wrote of himself:

"My muse is rightly of the English strain
That cannot long one fashion entertain."

From Idea

6

How many paltry, foolish, painted things,
That now in coaches trouble every street,
Shall be forgotten, whom no poet sings,

Ere they be well wrapped in their winding sheet?
Where[1] I to thee eternity shall give
When nothing else remaineth of these days,
And queens hereafter shall be glad to live
Upon the alms of thy superfluous praise.
Virgins and matrons, reading these my rhymes,
Shall be so much delighted with thy story
That they shall grieve they lived not in these times
To have seen thee, their sex's only glory;
So shalt thou fly above the vulgar throng,
Still to survive in my immortal song.

1619

37

Dear, why should you command me to my rest
When now the night doth summon all to sleep?
Methinks this time becometh lovers best;
Night was ordained together friends to keep.
How happy are all other living things
Which, though the day disjoin by several flight,
The quiet evening yet together brings,
And each returns unto his love at night.
O thou, that art so courteous else to all,
Why shouldst thou, Night, abuse me only thus,
That every creature to his kind doth call
And yet 'tis thou dost only sever us.
Well could I wish it would be ever day
If when night comes you bid me go away.

1602

50

As in some countries far removed from hence
The wretched creature destinéd to die,
Having the judgment due to his offense,
By surgeons begged, their art on him to try;
Which on the living work without remorse,
First make incision on each mastering[2] vein,
Then staunch the bleeding, then trans-pierce the corse,
And with their balms recure the wounds again;
Then poison, and with physic him restore;
Not that they fear the hopeless man to kill,
But their experience to increase the more;
Even so my mistress works upon my ill
By curing me and killing me each hour
Only to show her beauty's sovereign power.

1605

1. Whereas.   2. Master, principal.

61

Since there's no help, come let us kiss and part;
Nay, I have done, you get no more of me,
And I am glad, yea glad with all my heart
That thus so cleanly I myself can free;
Shake hands forever, cancel all our vows,   5
And when we meet at any time again,
Be it not seen in either of our brows
That we one jot of former love retain.
Now at the last gasp of love's latest breath,
When, his pulse failing, passion speechless lies,   10
When faith is kneeling by his bed of death,
And innocence is closing up his eyes;
Now if thou wouldst, when all have given him over,
From death to life thou mightst him yet recover.

1619

THOMAS NASHE
(1567–1601)

Nashe was a graduate of Cambridge. He wrote one of the best Elizabethan
novels, *The Unfortunate Traveler*, and a number of plays, usually in
collaboration. He was chiefly known in his time, however, for his breezy,
vigorous pamphlets in a running battle with Gabriel Harvey. This quarrel
became so violent that in 1599 the authorities ordered that "all Nashe's
books and Doctor Harvey's books be taken wheresoever they may be found
and that none of their books ever be printed hereafter." The two lyrics
of very different moods, *Spring, the Sweet Spring* and *A Litany*, are songs
from *A Pleasant Comedy Called Summer's Last Will and Testament*,
acted before the Archbishop of Canterbury in his palace at Croydon in
1592 and published in 1600.

Spring, the Sweet Spring

Spring, the sweet spring, is the year's pleasant king,
Then blooms each thing, then maids dance in a ring,
Cold doth not sting, the pretty birds do sing:
    Cuckoo, jug-jug, pu-we, to-witta-woo![1]

The palm and may make country houses gay,   5
Lambs frisk and play, the shepherds pipe all day,
And we hear aye birds tune this merry lay:
    Cuckoo, jug-jug, pu-we, to-witta-woo!

---

1. The calls of the cuckoo, the nightingale, the lapwing, and the owl respectively.

The fields breathe sweet, the daisies kiss our feet,
Young lovers meet, old wives a-sunning sit,   10
In every street these tunes our ears do greet:
   Cuckoo, jug-jug, pu-we, to-witta-woo!
     Spring, the sweet spring!

A Litany in Time of Plague

Adieu, farewell, earth's bliss;
This world uncertain is;
Fond[2] are life's lustful joys;
Death proves them all but toys;[3]
None from his darts can fly;   5
I am sick, I must die.
   Lord, have mercy on us!

Rich men, trust not in wealth,
Gold cannot buy you health;
Physic himself must fade.   10
All things to end are made,
The plague full swift goes by;
I am sick, I must die.
   Lord, have mercy on us!

Beauty is but a flower   15
Which wrinkles will devour;
Brightness falls from the air;
Queens have died young and fair;
Dust hath closed Helen's eye.
I am sick, I must die.   20
   Lord, have mercy on us!

Strength stoops unto the grave,
Worms feed on Hector brave;
Swords may not fight with fate,
Earth still holds ope her gate.   25
"Come, come!" the bells do cry.
I am sick, I must die.
   Lord, have mercy on us.

Wit with his wantonness
Tasteth death's bitterness;   30
Hell's executioner
Hath no ears for to hear
What vain art can reply.

2. Foolish.   3. Trifles.

I am sick, I must die.
    Lord, have mercy on us. 35

Haste, therefore, each degree,
To welcome destiny;
Heaven is our heritage,
Earth but a player's stage;
Mount we unto the sky. 40
I am sick, I must die.
    Lord, have mercy on us.

1592   1600

THOMAS CAMPION
(1567–1620)

Thomas Campion was a law student, a physician, a composer, and a poet. His first poetic attempts were in Latin. His love of classical, quantitative versification carried over into his English poems and songs, as well as into his critical theory, which he expounded in his *Observations in the Art of English Poesy*. (In quantitative verse the syllables are arranged in pattern according to their length and duration, rather than according to accent or stress; cf. Campion's *Rose-Cheeked Laura*.) But his greatest achievement as a lyric poet—and he is one of the very best in the language—comes from the fact that he was both poet and composer. He says in the preface to one of his books, "I have chiefly aimed to couple my words and notes lovingly together, which will be much for him to do that hath not power over both."

My Sweetest Lesbia[1]

My sweetest Lesbia, let us live and love,
And though the sager sort our deeds reprove,
Let us not weigh them. Heaven's great lamps do dive
Into their west, and straight again revive,
But soon as once set is our little light, 5
Then must we sleep one ever-during night.

If all would lead their lives in love like me,
Then bloody swords and armor should not be;
No drum nor trumpet peaceful sleeps should move,
Unless alarm came from the camp of love. 10
But fools do live, and waste their little light,
And seek with pain their ever-during night.

1. Imitated and partly translated from a poem by Catullus (87–ca. 54 B.C.), the Latin lyric poet who often celebrated the charms of Lesbia in his verses. This and the two lyrics which follow appeared in *A Book of Airs*, which contains Campion's first work as a composer.

When timely death my life and fortune ends,
Let not my hearse be vexed with mourning friends,
But let all lovers, rich in triumph, come   15
And with sweet pastimes grace my happy tomb;
And Lesbia, close up thou my little light,
And crown with love my ever-during night.

1601

When to Her Lute Corinna Sings

When to her lute Corinna sings,
Her voice revives the leaden strings,
And doth in highest notes appear
As any challenged echo clear;
But when she doth of mourning speak,   5
Ev'n with her sighs the strings do break.

And as her lute doth live or die,
Led by her passion, so must I:
For when of pleasure she doth sing,
My thoughts enjoy a sudden spring,   10
But if she doth of sorrow speak,
Ev'n from my heart the strings do break.

1601

When Thou Must Home to Shades of Underground

When thou must home to shades of underground,
And there arrived, a new admiréd guest,
The beauteous spirits do engirt thee round,
White Iope,[2] blithe Helen, and the rest,
To hear the stories of thy finished love   5
From that smooth tongue whose music hell can move,

Then wilt thou speak of banqueting delights,
Of masques and revels which sweet youth did make,
Of tourneys and great challenges of knights,
And all these triumphs for thy beauty's sake;   10
When thou hast told these honors done to thee,
Then tell, Oh tell, how thou didst murther me.

1601

Rose-cheeked Laura[3]

Rose-cheeked Laura, come,
Sing thou smoothly with thy beauty's

2. Daughter of Aeolus, also known as Cassiopeia.
3. Written by Campion to illustrate his theories of versification in *Observa-* *tions in the Art of English Poesy*, this song is a brilliant example of the way in which quantitative verse can be made musically effective in English.

Silent music, either other
    Sweetly gracing.

Lovely forms do flow   5
From concent⁴ divinely framed;
Heav'n is music, and thy beauty's
    Birth is heavenly.

These dull notes we sing
Discords need for helps to grace them;   10
Only beauty purely loving
    Knows no discord,

But still moves delight,
Like clear springs renewed by flowing,
Ever perfect, ever in them-   15
    Selves eternal.
                       1602

What If a Day

What if a day, or a month, or a year
Crown thy delights with a thousand sweet contentings?
Cannot a chance of a night or an hour
Cross thy desires with as many sad tormentings?
    Fortune, honor, beauty, youth   5
    Are but blossoms dying;
    Wanton pleasure, doting love
    Are but shadows flying.
    All our joys are but toys,
    Idle thoughts deceiving;   10
    None have power of an hour
    In their lives' bereaving.

Earth's but a point to the world, and a man
Is but a point to the world's compared centure;⁵
Shall then the point of a point be so vain   15
As to triumph in a sely⁶ point's adventure?
    As is hazard that we have,
    There is nothing biding;
    Days of pleasure are like streams
    Through fair meadows gliding.   20
    Weal and woe, time doth go,
    Time is never turning;
    Secret fates guide our states,
    Both in mirth and mourning.
                       1606

4. Playing or singing together in harmony.
5. Circumference (literally, a belt or girdle).
6. Innocent, insignificant.

Never Love Unless You Can

Never love unless you can
Bear with all the faults of man;
Men sometimes will jealous be,
Though but little cause they see,
And hang the head, as discontent,   5
And speak what straight they will repent.

Men that but one saint adore
Make a show of love to more;
Beauty must be scorned in none,
Though but truly served in one;   10
For what is courtship but disguise?
True hearts may have dissembling eyes.

Men when their affairs require
Must a while themselves retire,
Sometimes hunt, and sometimes hawk,   15
And not ever sit and talk.
If these and such like you can bear,
Then like, and love, and never fear.

1617

There Is a Garden in Her Face

There is a garden in her face,
Where roses and white lilies grow,
A heavenly paradise is that place,
Wherein all pleasant fruits do flow.
There cherries grow, which none may buy   5
Till "Cherry ripe!"[7] themselves do cry.

Those cherries fairly do enclose
Of orient pearl a double row;
Which when her lovely laughter shows,
They look like rosebuds filled with snow.   10
Yet them nor peer nor prince can buy,
Till "Cherry ripe!" themselves do cry.

Her eyes like angels watch them still;
Her brows like bended bows do stand,
Threatening with piercing frowns to kill   15
All that attempt with eye or hand
Those sacred cherries to come nigh,
Till "Cherry ripe!" themselves do cry.

1617

7. A familiar cry of London street vendors.

Think'st Thou to Seduce Me Then[1]

Think'st thou to seduce me then with words that have no meaning?
Parrots so can learn to prate, our speech by pieces gleaning;
Nurses teach their children so about the time of weaning.

Learn to speak first, then to woo; to wooing much pertaineth;
He that courts us, wanting art, soon falters when he feigneth,   5
Looks asquint on his discourse,[2] and smiles when he complaineth.

Skillful anglers hide their hooks, fit baits for every season;
But with crooked pins fish thou, as babes do that want reason:
Gudgeons[3] only can be caught with such poor tricks of treason.

Ruth[4] forgive me, if I erred from human heart's compassion,   10
When I laughed sometimes too much to see thy foolish fashion;
But, alas, who less could do that found so good occasion?

                              1617

Fain Would I Wed

Fain would I wed a fair young man that night and day could please
    me,
When my mind or body grieved that had the power to ease me.
Maids are full of longing thoughts that breed a bloodless sickness,
And that, oft I hear men say, is only cured by quickness.
Oft I have been wooed and praised, but never could be movéd;   5
Many for a day or so I have most dearly lovéd,
But this foolish mind of mine straight loathes the thing resolvéd;
If to love be sin in me, that sin is soon absolvéd.
Sure I think I shall at last fly to some holy order;
When I once am settled there, then can I fly no farther.   10
Yet I would not die a maid, because I had a mother,
As I was by one brought forth, I would bring forth another.

                              1617

---

1. In this poem and the one following, Campion assumes the voice of a female speaker; the procedure is rare enough among early poets to call for comment. Both poems are written in the old-fashioned metrical form known as "fourteeners"—verses of fourteen or fifteen sylla-bles, with seven accented beats.
2. Looks away from the lady to check on his script.
3. Small fish.
4. Pity, which misled the girl into seeming too complaisant.

ANONYMOUS LYRICS[1]

Back and Side Go Bare, Go Bare[2]

Back and side go bare, go bare,
  Both foot and hand go cold;
But, belly, God send thee good ale enough,
  Whether it be new or old.

I cannot eat but little meat,   5
  My stomach is not good;
But sure I think that I can drink
  With him that wears a hood.[3]
Though I go bare, take ye no care,
  I am nothing a-cold;   10
I stuff my skin so full within
  Of jolly good ale and old.
Back and side go bare, go bare, etc.

I love no roast but a nut-brown toast,[4]
  And a crab laid in the fire;   15
A little bread shall do me stead,
  Much bread I not desire.
No frost nor snow, no wind, I trow,[5]
  Can hurt me if I would,
I am so wrapped, and throughly lapped   20
  Of jolly good ale and old.
Back and side go bare, etc.

And Tib my wife, that as her life
  Loveth well good ale to seek,
Full oft drinks she, till ye may see   25
  The tears run down her cheeks.
Then doth she troll[6] to me the bowl,
  Even as a maltworm should,
And saith, "Sweetheart, I took my part
  Of this jolly good ale and old."   30
Back and side go bare, etc.

---

1. For discussion, see the introduction to the Lyrics section.
2. One of the best of English drinking songs, this is sung in *Gammer Gurton's Needle,* a pioneer play in the development of native English comedy. The play is often ascribed to a "Mr. S., Master of Art," who probably wrote it for performance at Cambridge University.
3. Specifically, with a monk; generally, with anybody.
4. Toast was often dipped in beverages; "crab": crab apple.
5. Think, suppose.
6. Pass.

Now let them drink, till they nod and wink,
    Even as good fellows should do;
They shall not miss to have the bliss
    Good ale doth bring men to;   35
And all poor souls that have scoured bowls
    Or have them lustily trolled,
God save the lives of them and their wives,
    Whether they be young or old.

Back and side go bare, go bare,   40
    Both foot and hand go cold;
But, belly, God send thee good ale enough,
    Whether it be new or old.

                       1575

Though Amaryllis Dance in Green[7]

Though Amaryllis dance in green
    Like fairy queen;
    And sing full clear
Corinna can, with smiling, cheer.
Yet since their eyes make heart so sore,
Heigh ho, heigh ho, 'chill[8] love no more.   5

My sheep are lost for want of food,
    And I so wood,[9]
    That all the day
I sit and watch a herdmaid gay,   10
Who laughs to see me sigh so sore,
Heigh ho, heigh ho, 'chill love no more.

Her loving looks, her beauty bright
    Is such delight,
    That all in vain   15
I love to like and lose my gain,
For her that thanks me not therefor,
Heigh ho, heigh ho, 'chill love no more.

Ah wanton eyes, my friendly foes,
    And cause of woes,   20
    Your sweet desire
Breeds flames of ice and freeze in fire.
Ye scorn to see me weep so sore,
Heigh ho, heigh ho, 'chill love no more.

---

7. William Byrd set this anonymous lyric to music in his song book entitled *Psalms, Sonnets, and Songs of Sadness and Piety*. It is a "ballet"— a dance-song of short stanzas with refrain—an appropriate form for this quaint rustic song of the renunciation of love.
8. The rustic dialect form for "I will": (i)ch (w)ill.
9. Frantic.

Love ye who list, I force him not,   25
    Sith, God it wot,
    The more I wail,
The less my sighs and tears prevail.
What shall I do but say therefore,
Heigh ho, heigh ho, 'chill love no more.
                               30
                              1588

Come Away, Come, Sweet Love![1]

Come away, come, sweet love! The golden morning breaks;
All the earth, all the air of love and pleasure speaks.
    Teach thine arms then to embrace,
    And sweet rosy lips to kiss,
    And mix our souls in mutual bliss;   5
    Eyes were made for beauty's grace,
    Viewing, rueing love-long pain,
    Procured by beauty's rude disdain.

Come away, come, sweet love! The golden morning wastes,
While the sun from his sphere his fiery arrows casts   10
    Making all the shadows fly,
    Playing, staying in the grove
    To entertain the stealth of love.
    Thither, sweet love, let us hie,
    Flying, dying in desire,   15
    Winged with sweet hopes and heavenly fire.

Come away, come, sweet love! Do not in vain adorn
Beauty's grace, that should rise like to the naked morn.
    Lilies on the riverside
    And fair Cyprian[2] flowers new-blown   20
    Desire no beauties but their own,
    Ornament is nurse of pride;
    Pleasure measure love's delight.
    Haste then, sweet love, our wishéd flight!

                               1597

Thule, the Period of Cosmography[3]

Thule, the period of cosmography,
    Doth vaunt of Hecla,[4] whose sulphurious fire

1. An aubade (or morning song to one's lady), set to music by John Dowland in his *First Book of Songs or Airs.* Dowland (1563–1626) was a famous composer and lutenist.
2. Pertaining to Venus, the Cyprian goddess; hence, spring flowers.
3. "Thule" or "Ultima Thule" was a general name for the Arctic; "period of cosmography" suggests the end point of navigation, a full stop. This remarkable poem, which draws upon Elizabethan interest in exploration and discovery to illustrate the conventional pangs of a lover, first appeared in a book of madrigals by Thomas Weelkes.
4. A volcano in Iceland.

Doth melt the frozen clime and thaw the sky;
    Trinacrian Aetna's[5] flames ascend not higher.
These things seem wondrous, yet more wondrous I,   5
Whose heart with fear doth freeze, with love doth fry.

The Andalusian[6] merchant, that returns
    Laden with cochineal and China dishes,
Reports in Spain how strangely Fogo[7] burns
    Amidst an ocean full of flying fishes.   10
These things seem wondrous, yet more wondrous I,
Whose heart with fear doth freeze, with love doth fry.

                                                                  1600

Madrigal[8]

My love in her attire doth show her wit,
    It doth so well become her;
For every season she hath dressings fit,
    For winter, spring, and summer.
No beauty she doth miss   5
When all her robes are on;
But beauty's self she is
When all her robes are gone.

                                                                  1602

Weep You No More, Sad Fountains[9]

Weep you no more, sad fountains;
    What need you flow so fast?
Look how the snowy mountains
    Heaven's sun doth gently waste.
But my sun's heavenly eyes   5
    View not your weeping,
    That now lie sleeping
Softly, now softly lies
    Sleeping.

Sleep is a reconciling,   10
    A rest that peace begets.
Doth not the sun rise smiling
    When fair at even he sets?

5. Mt. Etna, a volcano in Sicily ("Trinacria").
6. From southern Spain. "Cochineal":
a red dye.
7. Fuego, a volcano in Guatemala.
8. This sophisticated courtly lyric was
printed in an anthology entitled *A
Poetical Rhapsody* (1602).

9. This anonymous lyric comes from
another song book of John Dowland's
(his *Third and Last Book of Songs or
Airs*). Like a number of other song-
book lyrics which were apparently
written only with the object of being
set to music, its versification is quantitative.

Rest you then, rest, sad eyes,
   Melt not in weeping   15
   While she lies sleeping
Softly, now softly lies
    Sleeping.

1603

The Silver Swan[1]

The silver swan, who living had no note.
When death approached, unlocked her silent throat;
Leaning her breast against the reedy shore,
Thus sung her first and last, and sung no more:
  "Farewell, all joys; Oh death, come close mine eyes;   5
More geese than swans now live, more fools than wise."

1612

1. From Orlando Gibbons' *First Set of Madrigals and Motets*. In this short lyric, Gibbons, who was one of the last of the madrigalists, may be mourning the demise of his art.

Prose of the Sixteenth Century

Three mind-shattering experiences struck England in quick succession during the first quarter of the 16th century. They were the humanism of the Italian Renaissance, which for a hundred years had been moving north across Europe, the Reformation of the Roman church set in motion by Martin Luther, and the discovery of the New World by Christopher Columbus. The broad impact of the Renaissance on English culture is richly represented in the poetry and drama of the Elizabethan age from Sidney, Spenser, and Marlowe to Shakespeare and Donne. But English prose, as it existed during most of the 15th and 16th centuries, was not an instrument in which anyone felt very much confidence; it was not, therefore, much exercised in works of "high" literature. Malory is the sole exception, but Malory writes a variety of English prose akin to early epic poetry—incantatory, evocative, indefinite. A modern English prose style was forged only gradually, in the exploration and exposition of urgent practical problems—among the chief of which were the issues posed by the Reformation of the church, and the speculations aroused by the discovery of new continents and unknown civilizations.

THE ENGLISH REFORMATION

When Martin Luther nailed his 95 theses to the cathedral door at Wittenberg on the first of November, 1517, neither he nor anyone else knew what he was doing. Luther thought he was simply opening up some topics for academic discussion. But his ideas were hailed as, and immediately became, the slogans of a mass revolution, which swept Luther and the entire Christian world into deep waters of thought and feeling which had never before been sounded.

For medieval man, the Roman Catholic apostolic church was a universal, infallible, omnicompetent guide to the conduct of life from cradle to grave. He walked hand in hand with it, consulting its spokesmen at regular intervals, corrected by its discipline, comforted by its sacraments, sustained by its promises. The Bible, being in a special language which only clergymen could read, served to guide them, and they guided the laity. The ordinary man did not need to have a highly developed religious conscience (which is rather like a magnetic compass to navigate by) because he had something better—an infallible, divinely inspired, constant companion. Thus arose the vast system of confession, penanace, and absolution, of indulgences and pardons and remission of sins, which gave the Catholic hierarchy so much power over their flock. Under the circumstances, it mattered hardly at all that the Bible, the order of the Mass, and most of the theological discussions were in Latin, which the layman could not understand. Understanding was not really part of his function.

But when Luther revolted against the ancient church, was cast out by it, and founded his own church, he did so in the name of a conscience—his own—enlightened by a personal reading of the Scriptures. Two conse-quences immediately followed. To decide rationally whether Luther, or the Pope, or some third party was right, everyone had to read the Bible for himself. That is no light undertaking at best, for it is a long, hard book, confusing and apparently contradictory in many passages. Before most of us can even start to read this gigantic compendium of history, prophecy, and moral instruction, it has to be translated from the original Hebrew and Greek into the different vernaculars. That is a job of inconceivable complex-ity, at which scholars have been laboring from Luther's day to our own. And since membership in any particular church was now essentially volun-tary, the whole focus of the religious service shifted, from adoration and lustration (as by the Mass) to persuasion and edification (as by the sermon). Finally, books of controversial and polemical divinity began to be written in the national languages, not only between Catholic and Protestant champions, but by different Protestant groups against one another. By study-ing these controversies, hearing these sermons, reading the Bible con-stantly, and purifying his conscience as much as possible, each man (it was supposed) could decide for himself what was the safest way to salvation.

Though the English Reformation under Henry VIII was more gradual, more moderate, and far less violent than it was on the Continent, the same basic changes took place nonetheless. The first reformers in England were among the first translators of the Bible; William Tyndale, boldest and most influential of the group, paid for his pioneer's assurance by being burned at the stake. Yet within three years of his death in 1536, an English Bible was on public sale everywhere in the land; and there can be no doubt that the impulse to read the Bible, and learn about one's eternal destination, was responsible for a tremendous forward leap in the basic literacy of the nation.

Tyndale, a man of unusual energy and scholarship, translated direct from the Greek and Hebrew texts of his day, such as they were; but many other versions appeared in which the translators made use of Luther's German, the old Latin version prepared by Saint Jerome in the 4th century and known as the "Vulgate," and some of the French versions used by Calvin's church in Geneva. Bibles started to accumulate marginal notes, often betraying particular sectarian purposes; at the same time, the English tongue itself, into which the Bible was being translated, was in a state of rapid change. Thus, interpreting the translations themselves sometimes became a problem; and when serious doctrinal questions could be answered in different ways on the basis of different Bibles, it became clear that some-thing definitive was called for. When the English Puritan party met with King James, shortly after his accession, one of their requests was for a new translation of the Bible; that was just about the only one of their requests that he granted, and the result was the Bible that we know today as the "King James version." It was executed by a committee of scholars, who consulted not only the original versions in the original tongues but all the versions done since. This sounds like a sure recipe for translational disaster, but in fact the King James version is one of the great triumphs in the his-tory of this exasperating art. The translators were men of unusual learning and literary skill; they also had the good sense to lean heavily on the work of William Tyndale who, working alone, in exile, and under constant threat of persecution, cast the English Bible singlehandedly into a form it has never relinquished.

More important even than the fact of translation into the vernacular was the special importance conferred on the Bible by the special English habit of Bible-reading. Until comparatively recent years, in both England and America, the Bible was pretty sure to be found in every household—often enough, the only book there. It was read and reread, privately and around the fireplace, for entertainment and consolation and instruction. It was memorized. It became the traditional place in which to record the details of family history. It was consulted on every occasion in life. As a result, its powerful, poetic images were absorbed into normal English speech, its rhythms and formulas were taken up into the language, like those of no other book in history. The good Samaritan, the golden rule, the promised land, the parable of the talents, scribes and pharisees, shibboleths and sermons on the mount, Philistines, the land of milk and honey, and manna from heaven—there is no end to the phrases and metaphors and concepts that came flooding into our language through the medium of Bible-translations and Bible-study.

As if this were not enough, the Bible had a special day set aside for it, when everybody without exception went to church, often twice a day, to hear the Word of God expounded, interpreted, and applied. In those days long before newspapers, postal service, or other public communications, sermons served many public social functions. They were vehicles of scandal and edification, of government or social propaganda, they were social entertainment, intellectual exercise, and the seed, sometimes, for a whole week's conversation in the life of a sleepy village. Preachers naturally adapted their prose styles to appeal to the special circumstances of their congregations and to the special message they wanted to deliver. We see a striking instance of this in the homely, yet tough-minded, sermons of Bishop Latimer. Latimer's harshest words are directed against the church hierarchy and those who allow that hierarchy to manage their religious life. His praise of the plower is praise of the hard-working pastor, who works closely with his hard-working flock, so that their common individual efforts may conduct them to an immortal harvest.

That was the happy, the ideal aspect of the Protestant enterprise. But from the beginning, men found it hard to agree on that rule of Christian conduct which, everyone supposed, was to become evident through diligent study of the scriptures. The strict rules laid down by John Calvin for the church at Geneva, Switzerland, and imitated by John Knox in the reformed Kirk of Scotland, represented one popular pattern. From their fondness for talking about the "purification" of the church, these people became known as "puritans." The actual church discipline they proposed was called "presbyterian" because it gave primary authority to the presbyters, or priests, gathered together in special disciplinary assemblies. By contrast, the bishop gave his name (the Latin title is "episcopus") to episcopalianism. But Elizabeth set her face steadily against these changes in doctrine and discipline that the Puritans proposed; she ordered her bishops to take increasingly severe measures against presbyterian puritanism. Denied freedom to legislate change, the reformers accordingly undertook a campaign of propaganda. At first their books, like those of their opponents, were solemn and weighty, full of Biblical citations and academic syllogisms. But as the Puritans despaired of making headway on this front, and saw the Elizabethan censorship growing stricter, some of them turned to the underground press, publishing (1588–90) under the pseudonym of "Martin Marprelate" a series of satirical tracts which argued against the bishops, not formally and directly, but with quips and japes and invective. The Marprelate tracts are the finest prose satires of the Elizabethan age, and they emphasize the tendency of controversy to seek out and use popular forms. But their practical effects were nil. The Elizabethan police sought out the secret press (it was being carried around the country in the back of a haywagon), and the men responsible disappeared into prison, where, conveniently, while waiting for trial, several of them died.

It came thus as the climax of an increasingly bitter controversy within the English church between puritan Presbyterians and conservative Episcopalians—a controversy which had already lasted almost fifty years—when Richard Hooker brought forth in 1594 the first part of his monumental treatise, *Of the Laws of Ecclesiastical Polity*. It is a forbidding title and a rigorous book; but it can still be read for pleasure, and it fully deserves its reputation as the first finished monument of modern English prose. *Suaviter in modo, fortiter in re* is the appropriate Latin tag: "softly as far as words go, but no compromise on principles." Gently, slowly, irresistibly, with manifold expressions of Christian charity, and with remorseless logic, Hooker crushes his antagonists like a boa constrictor enveloping a rabbit. His premises are laid so widely and deeply that one can hardly disagree with them and retain any pretense to rationality; then gradually he begins to tighten his conclusions. If the Puritan revolution, based on conscience, could have been stopped by careful logic or judicious common sense, Hooker's book would doubtless have stopped it. But conscience is a prickly, uncontrollable force, and the Puritans would not be argued out of their conscientious objections to the discipline of the English church. With or without logic, they continued to fulminate and agitate, with consequences which can be learned in the section of this anthology devoted to the 17th century.

THE NEW WORLD

The discovery of America was accomplished by an Italian in the service of the Spanish crown; Spaniards explored and conquered the great kingdoms of Mexico and Peru, while Portuguese navigators first turned the Cape of Good Hope on their way to India, and the tip of South America on their way around the world. The English were thus relative latecomers to the work of exploring and exploiting the New World. Sir Walter Ralegh attempted the first wretched and unsuccessful colony in Virginia fully a hundred years after Pope Alexander VI had categorically divided the New World between Spain and Portugal. By that time there were well-established Portuguese colonies up and down the coast of South America and India; and the Spanish were entrenched not only in Mexico and the American southwest, but in Florida and California. But though the English were slow in starting to compete with their Latin rivals, the voyages of discovery struck at English imaginations almost as soon as they were known. Gold and silver were the loot that stirred practical men to action: but the idea of a separate, remote civilization based on a new and different dispensation from God was also deeply appealing. One classic expression of it is found in More's *Utopia* (1516). No doubt the basic moral principles of that rather severe never-never land rise from More's deeply religious hostility to avarice, luxury, and lust, traditional vices long denounced by the church. But the form of the book, as a half-serious traveler's tale, was surely suggested by the explorer's tales circulating through all the ports and trading centers of Europe. Most of the preoccupations of Renaissance Europe thus got knotted up in this crucial little book. Could a humane and wise counselor—a humanist—hope to have any influence on a greedy and irrational ruler? What sort of good life could men achieve without the advantage of Christian faith, by the mere light of reason? Might there not be peoples somewhere in the world whose simplicity of manners and natural honesty put to shame the cruelty and corruption of modern Europe? Despite his jocose manner, More was terribly in earnest about these questions; and it is therefore significant that he avoided using English altogether, and wrote his book in Latin. Doubtless he wanted to reach an international audience of humanists on the Continent; conceivably, he thought some of his speculations too radical to be trusted directly to a popular audience. But in addition, the English prose available to him was too cumbersome, too heavy and awkward in its syntax, too poor in its vocabulary, to express the ironic nuances of More's thought. One need only consult the first translation into English of More's little book—that done by Raphe Robynson in 1551—to sense the many problems that English prose of the early 16th century interposed between a writer and his thought.

More, as a learned humanist, a constitutional lawyer, and an international diplomat, had such deep bonds with the Latin tongue that it must surely have been easier for him to cast the *Utopia* in Latin than in English. But the roughnecks, freebooters, and adventurers who represented England on the high seas during the latter part of the 16th century were another breed entirely. They used English because they had to, and under their hands and those of their sympathizers, it gradually grew toward a more forceful and evocative instrument of expression. Men like Drake, Hawkins, Ralegh, Cabot, Grenville, Gilbert, and Frobisher often stood on a very ambiguous legal footing when they put to sea. They did not generally intend to establish colonies and they were not equipped to do any serious mining. Since England was generally on terms of uneasy peace with Spain, they were not officially entitled to attack Spanish settlements or hijack Spanish galleons; yet the backers and investors who raised money to fit them out expected a rich return on their investment. So that, half-pirates and half-patriots, operating half a world away from any effective police power, the English seadogs made it their business to pick up whatever they could find wherever they happened to come across it. Occasionally one of them, or one of their crew, would write up an account of a voyage, partly as a recruiting pamphlet, partly by way of inducing potential capitalists to put up more money. These accounts made stirring stories; they bolstered English patriotic feeling against the traditional enemies, Spain and the Papacy; and they brought literature out of the sometimes precious atmosphere of the court and into the world of adventurous action. The man chiefly responsible for collecting, editing, and sometimes retelling these stories was Richard Hakluyt, a romantically minded clergyman who published, first in 1589 and then in a much enlarged version of 1598–1600, the *Principal Navigations, Voyages, and Discoveries of the English Nation.* By the time these books appeared, everyone in England was aware that the great victory over the Spanish Armada in 1588 had been the work of divine providence working hand in glove with these hard-bitten adventurers. Quite apart from this glorious myth, there were of course practical technical reasons for the English victory. Their little ships could sail circles around the heavy Spanish vessels, many of which were built for the less violent seas of the Mediterranean; and the English guns, being forged to finer tolerances, far outranged the Spanish cannon and so could hammer the Spanish ships with impunity. Finally, the English were just plain lucky in the terrible weather which blew up the Channel in the late summer of 1588. But in the moment of victory, God shared the glory with His Englishmen; it was a protestant as well as a national triumph, and Hakluyt's anthology became a permanent part of the national legend.

Plain, practical prose, often on technical or scientific topics, and cast in the common, vernacular speech, flourished in England during the latter years of Elizabeth; it was a development largely unlike anything on the Continent. On the whole, the universities, which tended to be conservative, had little part on this activity. But the lectures established by Sir Thomas Gresham in the City of London were free for all to attend, and they were mostly in English. They provided the foundations for a practical vernacular technology, a pragmatic mingling of learned theory with homely practice, which could not fail to be profoundly influential, both on the material culture of England and on the language Englishmen spoke. In 1600 Sir William Gilbert published in Latin his great treatise on magnetism, as Sir William Harvey in 1628 announced the circulation of the blood in the learned language. But Harvey's theory had been set forth in English lectures twelve years before he published to the learned world at large; and Gilbert worked closely with the navigators and mariners of English vessels in developing both his learned theories and some practical applications of them.

Meanwhile, scholars, clergymen, and courtiers were experimenting with literary ways to make English more sonorous and rhetorically more complex; and not all these experiments were without influence. During the last half of the century, English vocabulary was enormously enriched by a mass of words adapted from Greek and Latin originals; some evidently seemed artificial or pretentious, and were dropped, but many others were permanently adopted into the language. Whether Cicero or Seneca or some other classical author was the best model for an English prose stylist was much debated; the point was never conclusively settled, but the parties sometimes emerged from their dispute with a widened range of stylistic possibilities before them. Writers of pastoral prose, like Sidney in his *Arcadia,* emphasized the artificiality of their genre by deliberately using formal rhetorical devices culled from the Greek sophists and rhetoricians. The short-lived fad of "Euphuism"—an experiment in exaggerated, aphoristic, sententious prose begun by John Lyly in 1579 and concluded by the same author in 1580, seems nowadays almost parodic in its artificiality; but it attests to the taste of the age for gorgeous inventions and dainty devices. On a more serious level, churchmen like Lancelot Andrewes and John Donne, who preached often before learned and intellectually restless auditories, were under strong temptation to dazzle with flights of rhetoric, showers of metaphor, intricate paradoxes, and multilingual puns.

During the last years of Elizabeth, after the great triumph of Armada, a curious hardening of lines and sharpening of attitudes is felt to take place. The party which calls itself the "court" grows increasingly remote from and hostile to that known as the "country." At the same time, the church hierarchy, directly and intimately connected with the court, moves ever further away from the homely and painful preachers of the Word who called themselves Puritans. Like the nation itself, English prose style seems to be dividing between the plain and the intricate, the unadorned and the complexly decorated. With the useful help of historical hindsight, we can see the savage storms of the 17th century building up behind a symptom as slight as the two prose styles of the later 16th century. Their working out is reserved for the next hundred years.

The English Reformation

TRANSLATING THE BIBLE (Isaiah liii.3–6)

The English Reformation made it imperative to read the Bible for oneself; hence fewer tasks were more important than rendering the Bible from its Greek and Hebrew originals into the vernacular. In England William Tyndale began his translation in 1523; he had to do it surreptitiously and outside the country; he finally suffered martyrdom for his efforts. In 1530 a royal proclamation condemned Tyndale's translation and all other versions in the vulgar tongue. Then in 1535 Miles Coverdale published, in Zürich, the first complete Bible in English. By this time the official attitude was changing, and in 1540 the so-called Great Bible was published, the first English Bible issued with official sanction—evidence of the extent of the breach between the English church and the Church of Rome.

The Geneva Bible (1560) was the work of Protestant refugees who fled to the Continent in the reign of the Catholic Queen Mary. It was the first Bible to divide the chapters into verses in the modern manner, and the first English Bible to be printed in Roman type rather than the old black letter or Gothic type. It was handy in size, and in many instances more accurate than its predecessors, but the marginal commentary was strongly biased in the Protestant direction. The Bishops' Bible (1568) was an attempt on the part of the Elizabethan church to counter the extreme Protestantism of the Geneva Bible. The bishops who sponsored it could indeed insist that their Bible be the official one used in churches, but the people continued to read the Geneva Bible at home, and its influence remained very great throughout the century. A Catholic translation into English, based upon the Latin Vulgate, was a belated concession to the demand for the scriptures in the vernacular. It was published by English refugees abroad, the New Testament at Rheims in 1582 and the Old Testament at Douai in 1609–10. Though it was outside the main English tradition, it was not without its influence upon the King James Version which was to follow.

King James did not like the popular Geneva Bible (some of its commentary was not highly favorable to kings). As a part of the religious settlement which took place early in his reign, he authorized a group of translators to make a new version of the Bible in English. The resulting work has been called "the noblest monument of English prose"; it owes more to Tyndale than to any other predecessor, but it has extraordinary beauties of its own. We have chosen to reprint versions of a passage from Isaiah that shows the King James Version at its most felicitous. Our last example comes from the New English Bible of 1970.

Translating the Bible (Isaiah liii.3–6)

From *The Great Bible*

He is despised and abhorred of men. He is such a man as is afull of sorrow and as hath good experience of infirmities. We have reckoned him so vile that we hid our faces from him. Yea, he was despised and therefore we regarded him not.

Howbeit he only hath taken on him our infirmities and borne our pains. Yet we did judge him, as though he were plagued and cast down of God and punished.

Whereas he (notwithstanding) was wounded for our offenses and smitten for our wickedness. For the chastisement of our peace was laid upon him and with his stripes we are healed.

As for us, we have gone all astray, like sheep; every one hath turned his own way. But the Lord hath heaped together upon him the iniquity of us all.

1539–40

From *The Coverdale Bible*

He shall be the most simple and despised of all which yet hath good experience of sorrows and infirmities. We shall reckon him so simple and so vile that we shall hide our faces from him.

Howbeit of a truth he only taketh away our infirmity and beareth our pain, yet we shall judge him as though he were plagued and cast down of God.

Whereas he, notwithstanding, shall be wounded for our offenses and smitten for our wickedness. For the pain of our punishment shall be laid upon him and with his stripes shall we be healed.

As for us we go all astray, like sheep. Every one turneth his own way. But through him the Lord pardoneth all our sins.

1550

From *The Geneva Bible*

He is despised and rejected of men. He is a man full of sorrows and hath experience of infirmities. We hid as it were our faces from him. He was despised and we esteemed him not.

Surely he hath borne our infirmities and carried our sorrows; yet we did judge him as plagued, and smitten of God, and humbled.

But he was wounded for our transgressions; he was broken for our iniquities; the chastisement of our peace was upon him, and with his stripes we are healed.

All we like sheep have gone astray. We have turned every one to his own way, and the Lord hath laid upon him the iniquity of us all.

1560

From *The King James Bible*

He is despised and rejected of men; a man of sorrows, and acquainted with grief. And we hid as it were our faces from him. He was despised, and we esteemed him not.

Surely he hath borne our griefs and carried our sorrows; yet we did esteem him stricken, smitten of God, and afflicted.

But he was wounded for our transgressions; he was bruised for our iniquities. The chastisement of our peace was upon him, and with his stripes we are healed.

All we like sheep have gone astray; we have turned every one to his own way; and the Lord hath laid on him the iniquity of us all.

1611

From *The New English Bible*

He was despised, he shrank from the sight of men,
    tormented and humbled by suffering;
    we despised him, we held him of no account,
    a thing from which men turn away their eyes.

Yet on himself he bore our sufferings,
    our torments he endured,
    while we counted him smitten by God,
    struck down by disease and misery;

but he was pierced for our transgressions,
    tortured for our iniquities;
    the chastisement he bore is health for us
    and by his scourging we are healed.

We had all strayed like sheep,
    each of us had gone his own way;
    but the Lord laid upon him
    the guilt of us all.

1970

HUGH LATIMER

(ca. 1492–1555)

The foremost preacher of that part of the English Reformation which ended with the accession of Henry VIII's Catholic daughter Mary in 1553, Latimer was hailed by his Protestant admirers as the apostle to the English. During this period the English church was separated from Rome, the monasteries were destroyed and the consequent economic redistribution strengthened the power of the crown, and the Bible was made available to the people in their own tongue. In all of this process Latimer was extremely influential. The ambassador of the emperor Charles V wrote in 1535 that Latimer had made more heretics than Luther.

Latimer was for a time Bishop of Worcester in the reign of Henry VIII, but he resigned his see and reached his greatest fame as a preacher in the short reign of Edward VI (1547–53). During Lent of 1549 he preached seven Friday sermons at court which were taken down in some kind of shorthand by a devoted follower, one Thomas Some, and published. In the previous year he had preached a series of sermons at Paul's Cross, in behalf of the government, but unfortunately only one of them has survived. It is the famous sermon on the plowers. Latimer sustains his homely metaphor of preachers as plowmen through a long discourse, but his style is chiefly remarkable for its vivid concreteness, his familiar illustrations, and his satirical descriptions of nonpreaching prelates and superstitious Catholics.

When Mary came to the throne in 1553, that phase of the English Reformation was over. The most prominent leaders of it—Thomas Cranmer, Archbishop of Canterbury; Nicholas Ridley, Bishop of London; and Hugh Latimer—were condemned as heretics. In 1554 they were compelled to engage in a disputation at Oxford on the doctrine of the Mass. Following that, parliament reenacted an old statute for the punishment of heretics (it had been repealed in Edward's reign) and passed the Great Act of Reconciliation with Rome. As a consequence, the Oxford Martyrs, as they are now called, were burned at the stake, Ridley and Latimer together and Cranmer separately. The account of Latimer's death in Foxe's *Acts and Monuments* is the most famous narrative in that famous book.

From Sermon of the Plowers

ROMANS XV.4

Quæcunque scripta sunt ad nostram doctrinam scripta sunt.

"All things which are written, are written for our erudition and knowledge. All things that are written in God's book, in the Bible book, in the book of the holy scripture, are written to be our doctrine."

I told you in my first sermon, honorable audience, that I purposed to declare unto you two things. The one, what seed should be sown in God's field, in God's plow land; and the other, who should be the sowers: that is to say, what doctrine is to be taught in Christ's church and congregation, and what men should be the teachers and preachers of it. The first part I have told you in the three sermons past, in which I have assayed[1] to set forth my plow, to prove what I could do. And now I shall tell you who be the plowers: for God's word is a seed to be sown in God's field, that is, the faithful congregation, and the preacher is the sower. And it is in the gospel: *Exivit qui seminat seminare semen suum.* "He that soweth," the husbandman, the plowman, "went forth to sow his seed,"[2] so that a preacher is resembled to a plowman, as it is in another place: *Nemo admota aratro manu, et a tergo respiciens, aptus est regno Dei.* "No man that putteth his hand to the plow and looketh back, is apt for the kingdom of God."[3] That is to say, let no preacher be negligent in doing his office. Albeit this is one of the places that hath been racked,[4] as I told you of racking scriptures. And I have been one of them myself that hath racked it, I cry God mercy for it, and have been one of them that have believed and have expounded it against religious persons that would forsake their order which they had professed, and would go out of their cloister: whereas indeed it toucheth not monkery, nor maketh any thing at all for any such matter; but it is directly spoken of diligent preaching of the word of God.

For preaching of the gospel is one of God's plow-works, and the preacher is one of God's plowmen. Ye may not be offended with my similitude, in that I compare preaching to the labor and work of plowing, and the preacher to a plowman. Ye may not be offended with this my similitude; for I have been slandered of some persons for such things. It hath been said of me: "Oh, Latimer! nay, as for him, I will never believe him while I live, nor never trust him; for he likened our blessed Lady to a saffron-bag," where indeed I never used that similitude. But it was as I have said unto you before now, according to that which Peter saw before in the spirit of prophecy, and said, that there should come afterward men *per quos via veritatis maledictis afficeretur,* there should come fellows "by whom the way of truth should be ill spoken of"[5] and slandered. But in case I had used this similitude, it had not been to be reproved, but might have been without reproach. For I might have said thus: as the saffron-bag that hath been full of saffron, or hath had saffron in it, doth ever after savor and smell of the sweet saffron that it contain-

1. Tried. The "three sermons past" were never printed.
2. Matthew xiii.3.
3. Luke ix.62.
4. Given a forced or strained interpretation.
5. II Peter ii.2.

eth; so our blessed Lady, which conceived and bare Christ in her womb, did ever after resemble the manners and virtues of that precious babe which she bare. And what had our blessed Lady been the worse for this? or what dishonor was this to our blessed Lady? But as preachers must be ware and circumspect that they give not any just occasion to be slandered and ill spoken of by the hearers, so must not the auditors be offended without cause. For heaven is in the gospel likened to a mustard-seed. It is compared also to a piece of leaven; as Christ saith, that at the last day he will come like a thief: and what dishonor is this to God? or what derogation is this to heaven? Ye may not then, I say, be offended with my similitude, for because I liken preaching to a plowman's labor, and a prelate to a plowman. But now you will ask me whom I call a prelate. A prelate is that man, whatsoever he be, that hath a flock to be taught of him; whosoever hath any spiritual charge in the faithful congregation, and whosoever he be that hath cure of soul.[6] And well may the preacher and the plowman be likened together. First for their labor of all seasons of the year. For there is no time of the year in which the plowman hath not some special work to do: as in my country in Leicestershire, the plowman hath a time to set forth, and to assay his plow, and other times for other necessary works to be done. And then they also may be likened together for the diversity of works and variety of offices that they have to do. For as the plowman first setteth forth his plow, and then tilleth his land, and breaketh it in furrows, and sometime ridgeth it up again; and at another time harroweth it, and clotteth[7] it, and sometime dungeth it, and hedgeth it, diggeth it, and weedeth it, purgeth and maketh it clean: so the prelate, the preacher, hath many divers offices to do. He hath first a busy work to bring his parishioners to a right faith, as Paul calleth it. And not a swerving faith, but to a faith that embraceth Christ, and trusteth to his merits; a lively faith, a justifying faith, a faith that maketh a man righteous, without respect of works: as ye have it very well declared and set forth in the Homily.[8] He hath then a busy work, I say, to bring his flock to a right faith, and then to confirm them in the same faith: now casting them down with the law, and with threatenings of God for sin; now ridging them up again with the gospel, and with the promises of God's favor; now weeding them, by telling them their faults, and making them forsake sin; now clotting them, by breaking their stony hearts, and by making them supple-hearted, and making them to have hearts of flesh, that is, soft hearts, and apt for doctrine to enter in; now teaching to know God rightly, and to know their duty to God and to their neighbors; now exhorting them, when they know their duty,

---

6. Care of souls, pastoral duties.
7. Breaks up clods.
8. One of the homilies or sermons printed and ordered by royal authority to be read in church.

that they do it, and be diligent in it; so that they have a continual work to do. Great is their business, and therefore great should be their hire. They have great labors, and therefore they ought to have good livings, that they may commodiously feed their flock; for the preaching of the word of God unto the people is called meat. Scripture calleth it meat; not strawberries, that come but once a year, and tarry not long, but are soon gone: but it is meat, it is no dainties. The people must have meat that must be familiar and continual, and daily given unto them to feed upon. Many make a strawberry of it, ministering it but once a year; but such do not the office of good prelates. For Christ saith: *Quis putas esse servus prudens et fidelis? qui dat cibum in tempore.* "Who think you is a wise and a faithful servant? he that giveth meat in due time."[9] So that he must at all times convenient preach diligently. Therefore saith he: "Who trow[1] ye is a faithful servant?" He speaketh it as though it were a rare thing to find such a one, and as though he should say, there be but a few of them to find in the world. And how few of them there be throughout this realm that give meat to their flock as they should do, the Visitors[2] can best tell. Too few, too few, the more is the pity, and never so few as now.

By this then it appeareth that a prelate, or any that hath cure of soul, must diligently and substantially work and labor. Therefore saith Paul to Timothy: *Qui episcopatum desiderat, hic bonum opus desiderat*: "He that desireth to have the office of a bishop," or a prelate, "that man desireth a good work."[3] Then if it be good work, it is work. Ye can make but a work of it. It is God's work, God's plow, and that plow God would have still[4] going. Such then as loiter and live idly, are not good prelates or ministers. And of such as do not preach and teach, nor do not their duties, God saith by his prophet Jeremy: *Maledictus qui facit opus Dei fradulenter;* "guilefully" or "deceitfully": some books have *negligenter*, "negligently" or "slackly."[5] How many such prelates, how many such bishops, Lord, for thy mercy, are there now in England? And what shall we in this case do? shall we company with them? O Lord, for thy mercy! shall we not company with them? O Lord, whither shall we flee from them? But "cursed be he that doth the work of God negligently or guilefully." A sore word for them that are negligent in discharging their office, or have done it fraudulently; for that is the thing that maketh the people ill.

* * *

But now methinketh I hear one say unto me: Wot ye what you say? Is it a work? Is it a labor? How then hath it happened that we have had so many hundred years so many unpreaching prelates, lording loiterers, and idle ministers? Ye would have me here to

---

9. Matthew xxiv.45.
1. Think.
2. Ecclesiastical inspectors.

3. I Timothy iii.1.
4. Always.
5. Jeremiah xlviii.10.

make answer, and to show the cause thereof. Nay, this land is not for me to plow; it is too stony, too thorny, too hard for me to plow. They have so many things that make for them, so many things to lay for themselves, that it is not for my weak team to plow them. They have to lay for themselves long customs, ceremonies, and authority, placing in Parliament, and many things more. And I fear me this land is not yet ripe to be plowed; for, as the saying is, it lacketh weathering: this gear[6] lacketh weathering; at least way it is not for me to plow. For what shall I look for among thorns, but pricking and scratching? What among stones, but stumbling? What (I had almost said) among serpents, but stinging? But this much I dare say, that since lording and loitering hath come up, preaching hath come down, contrary to the Apostles' times. For they preached and lorded not, and now they lord and preach not. For they that be lords will ill go to plow. It is no meet office for them. It is not seeming for their estate. Thus came up lording loiterers. Thus crept in unpreaching prelates; and so have they long continued. For how many unlearned prelates have we now at this day? And no marvel: for if the plowmen that now be were made lords, they would clean give over plowing, they would leave off their labor, and fall to lording outright, and let the plow stand. And then both plows not walking, nothing should be in the commonweal but hunger. For ever since the prelates were made lords and nobles, the plow standeth, there is no work done, the people starve. They hawk, they hunt, they card, they dice, they pastime in their prelacies with gallant gentlemen, with their dancing minions, and with their fresh companions, so that plowing is set aside. And by the lording and loitering, preaching and plowing is clean gone. And thus if the plowmen of the country were as negligent in their office as prelates be, we should not long live, for lack of sustenance. * * *

But now for the fault of unpreaching prelates, methink I could guess what might be said for excusing of them. They are so troubled with lordly living, they be so placed in palaces, couched in courts, ruffling in their rents,[7] dancing in their dominions, burdened with ambassages, pampering of their paunches, like a monk that maketh his jubilee; munching in their mangers, and moiling[8] in their gay manors and mansions, and so troubled with loitering in their lordships, that they cannot attend it. They are otherwise occupied, some in the king's matters, some are ambassadors, some of the privy council, some to furnish the court, some are Lords of the Parliament, some are Presidents,[9] and some Comptrollers of mints.

Well, well. Is this their duty? Is this their office? Is this their calling? Should we have ministers of the church to be comptrollers of the mints? Is this a meet office for a priest that hath cure of souls?

6. State of affairs.
7. Swaggering in their riches.
8. Working hard.

9. I.e., Lord President of the Privy Council, advisors to the sovereign.

Is this his charge? I would here ask one question: I would fain know who controlleth the devil at home at his parish, while he controlleth the mint? If the Apostles might not leave the office of preaching to be deacons, shall one leave it for minting? I cannot tell you; but the saying is, that since priests have been minters, money hath been worse than it was before. And they say that the evilness of money hath made all things dearer. * * *

And now I would ask a strange question: who is the most diligentest bishop and prelate in all England, that passeth all the rest in doing his office? I can tell, for I know him who it is, I know him well. But now I think I see you listening and hearkening, that I should name him. There is one that passeth all the other, and is the most diligent prelate and preacher in all England. And will ye know who it is? I will tell you. It is the Devil. He is the most diligent preacher of all other; he is never out of his diocese; he is never from his cure; ye shall never find him unoccupied; he is ever in his parish; he keepeth residence at all times; ye shall never find him out of the way: call for him when you will, he is ever at home; the diligentest preacher in all the realm; he is ever at his plow: no lording nor loitering can hinder him; he is ever applying his business, ye shall never find him idle, I warrant you. And his office is to hinder religion, to maintain superstition, to set up idolatry, to teach all kind of popery. He is ready as can be wished, for to set forth his plow; to devise as many ways as can be to deface and obscure God's glory. Where the Devil is resident, and hath his plow going, there away with books, and up with candles; away with Bibles, and up with beads; away with the light of the gospel, and up with the light of candles, yea, at noondays. Where the Devil is resident, that he may prevail, up with all superstition and idolatry; censing, painting of images, candles, palms, ashes, holy water, and new service of men's inventing;[1] as though man could invent a better way to honor God with, than God himself hath appointed. Down with Christ's cross, up with purgatory pickpurse, up with him, the popish purgatory, I mean. Away with clothing the naked, the poor and impotent; up with decking of images and gay garnishing of stocks and stones. Up with man's traditions and his laws, down with God's traditions and his most holy word. Down with the old honor due to God, and up with the new god's honor: let all things be done in Latin. There must be nothing but Latin, not as much as *Memento homo quod cinis es, et in cinerem reverteris*: "Remember, man, that thou art ashes, and into ashes thou shalt return":[2] which be the words that the minister speaketh to the ignorant people, when he giveth them ashes upon Ash Wednesday; but it must be spoken in Latin: God's word may in no wise be translated into English.

---

1. All, in Latimer's view, papist "superstition and idolatry."

2. Genesis iii.19.

O that our prelates would be as diligent to sow the corn of good doctrine, as Satan is to sow cockle and darnel! [3]* * *

* * * And this is the prick,[4] this is the mark at the which the Devil shooteth, to evacuate the cross of Christ, and to mingle the institution of the Lord's Supper; the which although he cannot bring to pass, yet he goeth about by his sleights and subtle means to frustrate the same; and these fifteen hundred years he hath been a doer, only purposing to evacuate Christ's death, and to make it of small efficacy and virtue. For whereas Christ, according as the serpent was lift up in wilderness, so would he himself to be exalted, that thereby as many as trusted in him should have salvation. But the Devil would none of that. They would have us saved by a daily oblation propitiatory,[5] by a sacrifice expiatory, or remissory.

Now if I should preach in the country, among the unlearned, I would tell what propitiatory, expiatory, and remissory is; but here is a learned auditory, yet for them that be unlearned I will expound it. Propitiatory, expiatory, remissory, or satisfactory, for they signify all one thing in effect, and is nothing else but a thing whereby to obtain remission of sins, and to have salvation. And this way the Devil used to evacuate the death of Christ, that we might have affiance[6] in other things, as in the daily sacrifice of the priest; whereas Christ would have us to trust in his only sacrifice. So he was: *Agnus occisus ab origine mundi*, "The Lamb that hath been slain from the beginning of the world";[7] and therefore he is called *juge sacrificium*, "a continual sacrifice,"[8] and not for the continuance of the Mass, as the blanchers[9] have blanched it, and wrested it; and as I myself did once mistake it. But Paul saith, *per semetipsum purgatio facta*, "by himself," and by none other, Christ "made purgation" and satisfaction for the whole world.[1]

* * *

Then let us trust upon his only death, and look for none other sacrifice propitiatory, than the same bloody sacrifice, the lively sacrifice; and not the dry sacrifice, but a bloody sacrifice. For Christ himself said, *consummatum est*: "It is perfectly finished":[2] I have taken at my Father's hand the dispensation of redeeming mankind. I have wrought man's redemption, and have dispatched the matter. Why then mingle ye him? Why do ye divide him? Why make you of him more sacrifices than one? Paul saith, *Pascha nostrum immolatus est Christus*: "Christ our passover is offered up";[3] so that the thing is done, and Christ hath done it, and he hath done it *semel*, "once for all." And it was a bloody sacrifice, not a dry sacrifice.

3. Weeds.
4. Bull's-eye.
5. In the Catholic service, the offering of bread and wine in the eucharist.
6. Faith.
7. Revelation xiii.8.
8. Daniel viii.11.
9. Distorters, perverters of the true meaning.
1. Hebrews i.3.
2. John xix.30; Christ's last words on the Cross.
3. I Corinthians v.7.

Why then, it is not the Mass that availeth or profiteth for the quick and the death. Woe worth[4] thee, O Devil, woe worth thee, that hast prevailed so far and so long, that hast made England to worship false gods, forsaking Christ their Lord! Woe worth thee, Devil, woe worth thee, Devil and all thy angels! If Christ by his death draweth all things to himself, and draweth all men to salvation, and to heavenly bliss, that trust in him; then the priests at the Mass, at the popish Mass, I say, what can they draw, when Christ draweth all, but lands and goods from the right heirs? The priests draw goods and riches, benefices and promotions to themselves; and such as believed in their sacrifice they draw to the Devil. But Christ it is that draweth souls unto him by his bloody sacrifice. What have we to do then but *epulari in Domino*, "to eat in the Lord" at his Supper?[5]

What other service have we to do to him? and what other sacrifice have we to offer, but the mortification of our flesh? What other oblation have we to make, but of obedience, of good living, of good works, and of helping our neighbors? But as for our redemption, it is done already, it cannot be better. Christ hath done that thing so well, that it cannot be amended. It cannot be devised how to make that any better than he hath done it. * * *

* * * And good hope there is, that it shall be likewise here in England; for the King's Majesty is so brought up in knowledge, virtue, and godliness, that it is not to be mistrusted but that we shall have all things well, and that the glory of God shall be spread abroad throughout all parts of the realm, if the prelates will diligenty apply their plow, and be preachers rather than lords. But our blanchers, which will be lords, and no laborers, when they are commanded to go and be resident upon their cures, and preach in their benefices, they would say, "What? I have set a deputy there; I have a deputy that looketh well to my flock, and the which shall discharge my duty." "A deputy," quoth he! I looked for that word all this while. And what a deputy must he be, trow ye? Even one like himself: he must be a canonist; that is to say, one that is brought up in the study of the Pope's laws and decrees; one that will set forth papistry as well as himself will do; and one that will maintain all superstition and idolatry; and one that will nothing at all, or else very weakly, resist the Devil's plow: yea, happy it is if he take not part with the Devil; and where he should be an enemy to him, it is well if he take not the Devil's part against Christ. But in the mean time the prelates take their pleasures. They are lords, and no laborers, but the Devil is diligent at his plow. He is no unpreaching prelate. He is no lordly loiterer from his cure, but a busy plowman; so that among all the prelates, and among all the pack of them that

---

4. Betide.   5. I Corinthians xi.20.

have cure, the Devil shall go for my money, for he still applieth his business. Therefore, ye unpreaching prelates, learn of the Devil to be diligent in doing of your office. Learn of the Devil. And if you will not learn of God nor good men, for shame learn of the Devil, *ad erubescentiam vestram dico,* "I speak it for your shame."[6] If you will not learn of God, nor good men, to be diligent in your office, learn of the Devil. Howbeit there is now very good hope that the King's Majesty, being by the help of good governance of his most honorable counselors, he is trained and brought up in learning and knowledge of God's word, will shortly provide a remedy, and set an order herein, which thing that it may so be, let us pray for him. Pray for him, good people, pray for him. Ye have great cause and need to pray for him.

1548

6. I Corinthians vi.5.

JOHN FOXE

(1516–1587)

John Foxe's career at Oxford University, where he had become a fellow of Magdalen College, was interrupted when his Puritan convictions led him to protest too energetically against some of the college rules and practices. For some years he then served as a tutor to the children of various great houses; but when Mary became queen in 1553, and the persecutions of Protestants began, he fled to the Continent. His great book was already under way, though it was in Latin and had not yet really focused on its main subject. In its first version (Strasbourg, 1554) it was a history of the persecutions suffered by the early Protestants, particularly Wycliffe and John Hus. But the book grew and grew under his hands, as he received from England accounts of the hideous tortures and persecutions being inflicted on the Protestants there. When Elizabeth came to the throne in 1558, Foxe returned at once to England, and there he translated his previous Latin volume, adding to it hundreds of stories (many true, some doubtful, some ridiculous) all tending to show the horrible malice of Catholic persecutors and the saintly sufferings of Protestant martyrs. The English edition was published in 1563; its title was *Acts and Monuments of these latter and perilous days, touching matters of the church, wherein are comprehended and described the great persecution and horrible troubles that have been wrought and practices by the Romish prelates from the year of Our Lord a thousand to the time now present.* It was immediately and enormously popular. Foxe saw life melodramatically, in terms of black and white; and he tended to believe without questioning it too closely any good story that confirmed his prejudices. As a result his book soon grew to enormous dimensions—in its final version, to over 6,000 folio pages, containing 4 mil-

lion words. Apart from fanning the flames of anti-Catholic feeling, Foxe
had an immense influence upon English nationalism; his stories tended to
show that England was the land of the chosen people, and that, in passing
through the fiery trials of Marian persecution, the Protestant martyrs were
simply preparing the way for a glorious destiny in which England would
lead the way toward the kingdom of God on earth. Foxe's second edition, in
1570, was so impressive that a copy of it was required to be placed, with
the Bible, in every English church.

From Acts and Monuments

OF THESE LATTER AND PERILOUS DAYS, TOUCHING MATTERS OF
THE CHURCH, WHEREIN ARE COMPREHENDED AND DESCRIBED THE
GREAT PERSECUTION AND HORRIBLE TROUBLES THAT HAVE BEEN
WROUGHT AND PRACTICES BY THE ROMISH PRELATES FROM THE
YEAR OF OUR LORD A THOUSAND TO THE TIME NOW PRESENT

The Behavior of Dr. Ridley and Master Latimer, at the Time of Their Death, which was the Sixteenth of October, an. 1555

Upon the north side of the town, in the ditch over against Balliol
College, the place of execution was appointed; and for fear of any
tumult that might arise, to let the burning of them, the Lord Williams was commanded by the queen's letters (and the householders
of the city) to be there assistant, sufficiently appointed. And when
everything was in a readiness, the prisoners were brought forth by
the mayor and the bailiffs.

Master Ridley had a fair black gown furred, and faced with
foins,[1] such as he was wont to wear being bishop, and a tippet of
velvet furred likewise about his neck, a velvet nightcap upon his
head, and a corner cap upon the same, going in a pair of slippers to
the stake, and going between the mayor and an alderman, etc. After
him came Master Latimer in a poor Bristol frieze frock all worn,
with his buttoned cap, and a kerchief on his head all ready to the
fire, a new long shroud hanging over his hose down to the feet;
which at the first sight stirred men's hearts to rue upon them,
beholding on the one side the honor they sometime had, and on
the other, the calamity whereunto they were fallen.

Master Doctor Ridley, as he passed towards Bocardo,[2] looking up
where Master Cranmer did lie, hoping belike to have seen him at
the glass window and to have spoken unto him. But then Master
Cranmer was busy with Friar Soto and his fellows, disputing

1. Fur trimmings.   2. The prison in Oxford.

together, so that he could not see him through that occasion. Then Master Ridley, looking back, espied Master Latimer coming after, unto whom he said, "Oh, be ye there?" "Yea," said Master Latimer, "have after as fast as I can follow." So he following a pretty way off, at length they came both to the stake, one after the other, where first Dr. Ridley entering the place, marvelous earnestly holding up both his hands, looked towards heaven. Then shortly after espying Master Latimer, with a wondrous cheerful look, ran to him, embraced, and kissed him; and, as they that stood near reported, comforted him saying, "Be of good heart, brother, for God will either assuage the fury of the flame, or else strengthen us to abide it." With that went he to the stake, kneeled down by it, kissed it, and most effectuously prayed, and behind him Master Latimer kneeled, as earnestly calling upon God as he. After they arose, the one talked with the other a little while, till they which were appointed to see the execution removed themselves out of the sun. What they said I can learn of no man.

Then Dr. Smith,[3] of whose recantation in King Edward's time ye heard before, began his sermon to them upon this text of St. Paul in the 13 chap. of the first epistle to the Corinthians: *"Si corpus meum tradam igni, charitatem autem non habeam, nihil inde utilitatis capio,"* that is, "If I yield my body to the fire to be burned and have not charity, I shall gain nothing thereby." Wherein he alleged that the goodness of the cause, and not the order of death, maketh the holiness of the person; which he confirmed by the examples of Judas, and of a woman in Oxford that of late hanged herself, for that they, and such like as he recited, might then be adjudged righteous, which desperately sundered their lives from their bodies, as he feared that those men that stood before him would do. But he cried still to the people to beware of them, for they were heretics, and died out of the church. And on the other side, he declared their diversities in opinions, as Lutherans, Oecolampadians, Zwinglians,[4] of which sect they were, he said, and that was the worst; but the old church of Christ and the Catholic faith believed far otherwise. At which place they lifted up both their hands and eyes to heaven, as it were calling God to witness of the truth; the which countenance they made in many other places of his sermon, whereas they thought he spake amiss. He ended with a very short exhortation to them to recant, and come home again to the church, and save their lives and souls, which else were condemned. His sermon was scant in all a quarter of an hour.

Dr. Ridley said to Master Latimer, "Will you begin to answer

---

3. Richard Smith, D.D. (1500–63); he had recanted in 1547 but later repudiated his recantation.
4. Followers, respectively, of Martin Luther (1483–1546), founder of the reformation in Germany; Johann Oecolampadius (1482–1531), organizer of Protestantism at Basle; Ulrich Zwingli (1484–1531), organizer of Protestantism in Zürich.

the sermon, or shall I?" Master Latimer said: "Begin you first, I pray you." "I will," said Master Ridley.

Then the wicked sermon being ended, Dr. Ridley and Master Latimer kneeled down upon their knees towards my Lord Williams of Tame, the vice-chancellor of Oxford, and divers other commissioners appointed for that purpose, which sat upon a form thereby. Unto whom Master Ridley said: "I beseech you, my lord, even for Christ's sake, that I may speak but two or three words." And whilst my lord bent his head to the mayor and vice-chancellor, to know (as it appeared) whether he might give him leave to speak, the bailiffs and Dr. Marshall, vice-chancellor, ran hastily unto him, and with their hands stopped his mouth, and said: "Master Ridley, if you will revoke your erroneous opinions, and recant the same, you shall not only have liberty so to do, but also the benefit of a subject; that is, have your life." "Not otherwise?" said Master Ridley. "No," quoth Dr. Marshall. "Therefore if you will not so do, then there is no remedy but you must suffer for your deserts." "Well," quoth Master Ridley, "so long as the breath is in my body, I will never deny my Lord Christ, and his known truth; God's will be done in me!" And with that he rose up and said with a loud voice: "Well then, I commit our cause to almighty God, which shall indifferently judge all." To whose saying, Master Latimer added his old posy,[5] "Well! There is nothing hid but it shall be opened." And he said he could answer Smith well enough, if he might be suffered.

Incontinently they were commanded to make them ready, which they with all meekness obeyed. Master Ridley took his gown and his tippet,[6] and gave it to his brother-in-law Master Shipside, who all his time of imprisonment, although he might not be suffered to come to him, lay there at his own charges to provide him necessaries, which from time to time he sent him by the sergeant that kept him. Some other of his apparel that was little worth, he gave away; other the bailiffs took. He gave away besides divers other small things to gentlemen standing by, and divers of them pitifully weeping, as to Sir Henry Lea he gave a new groat; and to divers of my Lord Williams' gentlemen some napkins, some nutmegs, and races of ginger; his dial, and such other things as he had about him, to everyone that stood next him. Some plucked the points of his hose. Happy was he that might get any rag of him. Master Latimer gave nothing, but very quickly suffered his keeper to pull off his hose and his other array, which to look unto was very simple; and being stripped into his shroud, he seemed as comely a person to them that were present as one should lightly see; and whereas in his clothes he

---

5. Motto.
6. "This was no Popish tippet, but made only to keep his neck warm" [Foxe's note].

appeared a withered and crooked silly old man, he now stood bolt upright, as comely a father as one might lightly behold.

Then Master Ridley, standing as yet in his truss,[7] said to his brother: "It were best for me to go in my truss still." "No," quoth his brother, "it will put you to more pain; and the truss will do a poor man good." Whereunto Master Ridley said: "Be it, in the name of God"; and so unlaced himself. Then being in his shirt, he stood upon the foresaid stone, and held up his hand and said: "Oh heavenly Father, I give unto thee most hearty thanks, for that thou hast called me to be a professor of thee, even unto death. I beseech thee, Lord God, take mercy upon this realm of England, and deliver the same from all her enemies."

Then the smith took a chain of iron, and brought the same about both Dr. Ridley's and Master Latimer's middles; and as he was knocking in a staple, Dr. Ridley took the chain in his hand, and shaked the same, for it did gird in his belly, and looking aside to the smith, said: "Good fellow, knock it in hard, for the flesh will have his course." Then his brother did bring him gunpowder in a bag, and would have tied the same about his neck. Master Ridley asked what it was. His brother said, "Gunpowder." "Then," said he, "I take it to be sent of God; therefore I will receive it as sent of him. And have you any," said he, "for my brother?" meaning Master Latimer. "Yea, sir, that I have," quoth his brother. "Then give it unto him," said he, "betime; lest ye come too late." So his brother went, and carried of the same gunpowder unto Master Latimer.

In the meantime Dr. Ridley spake unto my Lord Williams, and said: "My lord, I must be a suitor unto your lordship in the behalf of divers poor men, and specially in the cause of my poor sister; I have made a supplication to the Queen's Majesty in their behalfs. I beseech your lordship for Christ's sake, to be a mean to her Grace for them. My brother here hath the supplication, and will resort to your lordship to certify you hereof. There is nothing in all the world that troubleth my conscience, I praise God, this only excepted. Whiles I was in the see of London divers poor men took leases of me, and agreed with me for the same. Now I hear say the bishop[8] that now occupieth the same room will not allow my grants unto them made, but contrary unto all law and conscience hath taken from them their livings, and will not suffer them to enjoy the same. I beseech you, my lord, be a mean for them; you shall do a good deed, and God will reward you."

Then they brought a faggot, kindled with fire, and laid the same

---

7. A close-fitting body-garment or jacket.
8. Edmund Bonner (ca. 1500–69); he had preceded Ridley as Bishop of London during the reign of Edward VI, and became Bishop again on Mary's accession.

down at Dr. Ridley's feet. To whom Master Latimer spake in this manner: "Be of good comfort, Master Ridley, and play the man. We shall this day light such a candle, by God's grace, in England, as I trust shall never be put out."

And so the fire being given unto them, when Dr. Ridley saw the fire flaming up toward him, he cried with a wonderful loud voice: "*In manus tuas, Domine, commendo spiritum meum; Domine, recipe spiritum meum.*" And after, repeated this latter part often in English, "Lord, Lord, receive my spirit"; Master Latimer crying as vehemently on the other side, "Oh Father of heaven, receive my soul!" who received the flame as it were embracing of it. After, as he had stroked his face with his hands, and as it were bathed them a little in the fire, he soon died (as it appeared) with very little pain or none. And thus much concerning the end of this old and blessed servant of God, Master Latimer, for whose laborious travails, fruitful life, and constant death the whole realm hath cause to give great thanks to almighty God.

But Master Ridley, by reason of the evil making of the fire unto him, because the wooden faggots were laid about the gosse[9] and over-high built, the fire burned first beneath, being kept down by the wood; which when he felt, he desired them for Christ's sake to let the fire come unto him. Which when his brother-in-law heard, but not well understood, intending to rid him out of his pain (for the which cause he gave attendance), as one in such sorrow not well advised what he did, heaped faggots upon him, so that he clean covered him, which made the fire more vehement beneath, that it burned clean all his nether parts, before it once touched the upper; that that made him leap up and down under the faggots, and often desire them to let the fire come unto him, saying, "I cannot burn." Which indeed appeared well; for, after his legs were consumed by reason of his struggling through the pain (whereof he had no release, but only his contentation[1] in God), he showed that side toward us clean, shirt and all untouched with flame. Yet in all this torment he forgat not to call upon God still, having in his mouth, "Lord have mercy upon me," intermingling this cry, "Let the fire come unto me, I cannot burn." In which pains he labored till one of the standers-by with his bill[2] pulled off the faggots above, and where he saw the fire flame up, he wrested himself unto that side. And when the flame touched the gunpowder, he was seen stir no more, but burned on the other side, falling down at Master Latimer's feet. Which some said happened by reason that the chain loosed; other said that he fell over the chain by reason of the poise of his body and the weakness of the nether limbs.

Some said that before he was like to fall from the stake, he

---

9. Gorse, used as kindling.
1. Satisfaction.

2. A long staff terminating in a hook-shaped blade.

desired them to hold him to it with their bills. Howsoever it was, surely it moved hundreds to tears, in beholding the horrible sight; for I think there was none that had not clean exiled all humanity and mercy which would not have lamented to behold the fury of the fire so to rage upon their bodies. Signs there were of sorrow on every side. Some took it grievously to see their deaths, whose lives they held full dear; some pitied their persons, that thought their souls had no need thereof. His brother moved many men, seeing his miserable case, seeing (I say) him compelled to such infelicity, that he thought then to do him best service when he hastened his end. Some cried out of the luck, to see his endeavor (who most dearly loved him, and sought his release) turn to his greater vexation and increase of pain. But whoso considered their preferments in time past, the places of honor that they sometime occupied in this commonwealth, the favor they were in with their princes, and the opinion of learning they had, could not choose but sorrow with tears to see so great dignity, honor, and estimation, so necessary members sometime accounted, so many godly virtues, the study of so many years, such excellent learning, to be put into the fire and consumed in one moment. Well! dead they are, and the reward of this world they have already. What reward remaineth for them in heaven, the day of the Lord's glory, when he cometh with his saints, shall shortly, I trust, declare.

1563

"MARTIN MARPRELATE"

"Martin Marprelate" was the pseudonym of several Puritan pamphleteers, among them Job Throckmorton and John Penry, who attacked the established clergy of the Church of England, and especially the lordly bishops and archbishops, between 1588 and 1593. An answer to an early Marprelate tract was prepared by Thomas Cooper, Bishop of Winchester, who of course defended episcopacy as divinely ordained and historically respectable. This answer was called *An Admonition to the People of England* and was written in a dignified style, suitable for a bishop. But Martin was appealing to a popular audience, so he used a colloquial, informal, sometimes scurrilous style. The *Admonition* was signed only by the author's initials, T. C., perhaps to mislead readers into thinking the author was the prominent Puritan, Thomas Cartwright. But Martin was not deceived, and he played on the Bishop's name in the title of his reply. "Hay any work for a cooper?" was a common London street cry meaning "Have you any work for a cooper (barrel-maker) to do?" The vituperative character of the language may seem strange to modern readers, especially when the content has to do with religion, but this remained the prevailing style in controversy through the next century and can be observed in some of the prose of John Milton.

From Hay Any Work for Cooper

[Church Government]

Your reasons for the defense of your hierarchy and the keeping out of Christ's government, used by this profane T. C., are already answered. They show what profane beasts you are. I will here repeat them. But here, first, the reader is to know what answer this T. C. maketh unto the syllogisms, whereby I prove all lord bishops to be petty popes and petty antichrists. I assure you no other than this: he flatly denieth the conclusion, whereas he might (if he had any learning in him, or had read anything) know that every dunstical[1] logician giveth this for an inviolable precept, that the conclusion is not to be denied. For that must needs be true, if the major and minor[2] be true; he in omitting the major and minor, because he was not able to answer, thereby granteth the conclusion to be true. His answer unto the conclusion is, that all lord bishops were not petty popes, because Cranmer, Ridley, Hooper,[3] were not petty popes. They were not petty popes because they were not reprobates. As though—you block, you!—every petty pope and every petty antichrist were a reprobate. Why, no man can deny Gregory the Great[4] to be a petty pope and a petty antichrist. For he was the next immediate pope before Boniface I, that known antichrist; and yet this Gregory left behind him undoubted testimonies of a chosen child of God. So might they; and yet be petty popes, in respect of their office. Profane T. C.'s first and second reason for the lawfulness of our church government! And what though good men gave their consent unto our church government, or writing unto bishops gave them their lordly titles? Are their offices therefore lawful? Then, so is the Pope's office. For Erasmus was a good man, you cannot deny; and yet he both allowed of the Pope's offices since his calling,[5] and writing unto him gave him his titles. So did Luther since his calling also, for he dedicated his book of Christian Liberty unto Pope Leo X. The book and his Epistle unto the Pope are both in English. Here I would wish the magistrate to mark what good reasons you are able to afford for your hierarchy.

Thirdly, saith profane T. C., page 75, all churches have not the government of pastors and doctors; but Saxony and Denmark have lord bishops.[6] You are a great statesman, undoubtedly, T. C., that understand the state of other churches so well. But herein the

---

1. Hairsplitting, after Duns Scotus, medieval philosopher.
2. I.e., premises.
3. Thomas Cranmer, Nicholas Ridley, and John Hooper were all bishops and martyrs during the reign of Mary.
4. Saint Gregory I, Pope 590–604. The following statement about Boniface I is

a factual error. He was Pope 418–422.
5. "Calling of grace," i.e., becoming a Protestant.
6. Cooper maintained that the "superintendents" in the Protestant churches of Saxony and Denmark were equivalent to bishops and archbishops.

impudency of a proud fool appeareth egregiously. As though the testimony of a silly schoolmaster,[7] being also as unlearned as a man of that trade and profession can be with any honesty, would be believed against known experience. Yes, but Saxony and Denmark have superintendents; what then? Ergo, lord archbishops and bishops? I deny it. Though other churches had lord archbishops and bishops, this proveth nothing but that other churches are maimed and have their imperfections. Your reason is this: other good churches are deformed, therefore ours must be so too. The king's son is lame, therefore the children of no subjects must go upright. And these be all the good reasons which you can bring for the government of archbishops and bishops against the government of Christ. You reason thus: it[8] must not be admitted into this kingdom, for then civilians shall not be able to live in that estimation and wealth wherein they now do. Carnal and senseless beasts, who are not ashamed to prefer the outward state of men before the glory of Christ's kingdom. Here again, let the magistrate and other readers consider, whether it be not time that such brutish men shall be looked into. Which reason thus: The body of Christ, which is the church, must needs be maimed and deformed in this commonwealth, because other civilians should not be able to live. Why, you enemies to the State, you traitors to God and his Word, you Mar-Prince, Mar-Law, Mar-Magistrate, Mar-Church, and Mar-Commonwealth,[9] do you not know that the world should rather go a-begging than that the glory of God, by maiming His church, should be defaced? Who can abide this indignity?

1589

7. Cooper had formerly been headmaster of the Magdalen School, Oxford.
8. I.e., the "government of Christ" or the Puritan system of church government.

"Civilians": laymen made rich by the plundering of the monasteries.
9. Names given to Martin Marprelate in Cooper's pamphlet.

RICHARD HOOKER
(1554–1600)

Out of the long and bitter controversy over the government of the church in 16th-century England emerged one literary masterpiece. It is a long work in eight books called *Of the Laws of Ecclesiastical Polity* (that is, the governmental system of the church). The author was Richard Hooker, a scholar and minister who accomplished the extraordinary feat of engaging in the bitterest dispute of his time and maintaining a calm, reasonable manner. In 1585 Hooker was Master of the Temple (in modern terms, a dean of a law school); one of his subordinates was a Puritan lecturer named Walter Travers. Between them a running debate developed on the burning question of how the church should be governed. The Puritan view was that no organization or authority in the church was valid unless it was based clearly and specifically upon the Bible; the whole hierarchical system of the English church, with its deacons, priests, bishops, and archbishops, was accordingly wrong. The position Hooker undertook to defend was that the Scriptures, or divine revelation, are not the only guide given to men for organizing and administering the Christian church. A more important guide is the law of nature, which is also divinely given; this law can be discovered by the use of human reason.

In his great book, which grew out of his controversy with Travers, Hooker therefore had to explain how the law of nature justified the existing organization of the English church. Book I of *Ecclesiastical Polity* deals with laws in general and their various kinds, picturing a universe operating under natural and divine law and founded upon reason. Book II deals with the nature, authority, and adequacy of Scripture. Book III concerns the scriptural bases for worship and government. Book IV defends the rites and ceremonies of the English church, and Book V, longer than the first four together, is a commentary on *The Book of Common Prayer*. Books VI, VII, and VIII deal with various embodiments of authority—elders, bishops, kings, and popes.

Hooker was a close and effective reasoner; he relied not upon the fiery invective or impassioned rhetoric which characterized most disputants of his time, but rather upon a calm, reasonable, tolerant approach. His defense of existing ecclesiastical practices went back to fundamental principles, to a philosophy of nature and of man's place in it, of his relation to God and to his fellow men. It is this world view which makes Hooker's book of interest when the controversy over church organization has long since died down. And the prose in which Hooker sets forth his world view is the finest prose of the Elizabethan age. King James I is quoted by Izaak Walton, Hooker's 17th-century biographer, as saying, "I observe there is in Mr. Hooker no affected language; but a grave, comprehensive, clear manifestation of reason, and that backed with the authority of the Scriptures, the fathers and schoolmen, and with all law both sacred and civil. And, though others may write well, yet in the next age they will be forgotten; but doubtless there is in every page of Mr. Hooker's book the picture of a divine soul, such pictures of truth and reason, and drawn in so sacred colors, that they shall never fade but give an immortal memory to the author."

From Of the Laws of Ecclesiastical Polity
From *The Preface*

[ON MODERATION IN CONTROVERSY]

* * * Amongst ourselves, there was in King Edward's days some question moved by reason of a few men's scrupulosity touching certain things.[1] And beyond seas, of them which fled in the days of

1. During the short reign of the boy king, Edward VI (1547–53), the reformation begun under Henry VIII was carried further. Services were held in English, images were banished from the church, and the use of holy water was forbidden. During the following reign of Mary, a Catholic, many Protestant reformers fled abroad and there were influenced by the Calvinist doctrines and practices of the "Church of Geneva."

Queen Mary, some contenting themselves abroad with the use of their own service book at home authorized before their departure out of the realm, others liking better the common prayer book of the Church of Geneva translated, those smaller contentions before begun were by this mean somewhat increased. Under the happy reign of Her Majesty which now is, the greatest matter a while contended for was the wearing of the cap and surplice,[2] till there came *Admonitions Directed unto the High Court of Parliament,* by men who, concealing their names, thought it glory enough to discover their minds and affections, which were now universally bent even against all the orders and laws wherein this Church is found unconformable to the platform of Geneva. Concerning the defender of which admonitions, all that I mean to say is this: "There will come a time when three words uttered with charity and meekness shall receive a far more blessed reward than three thousand volumes written with disdainful sharpness of wit." But the manner of men's writing must not alienate our hearts from the truth if it appear they have the truth, as the followers of the same defender do think he hath, and in that persuasion they follow him no otherwise than himself doth Calvin, Beza[3] and others, with the like persuasion that they in this cause had the truth. We being as fully persuaded otherwise, it resteth that some kind of trial be used to find out which part is in error.

The first mean whereby Nature teacheth men to judge good from evil, as well in laws as in other things, is the force of their own discretion. Hereunto therefore Saint Paul referreth oftentimes his own speech to be considered by them that heard him, "I speak as to them which have understanding; judge ye what I say."[4] Again, afterward, "Judge in yourselves, is it comely that a woman pray uncovered?" The exercise of this kind of judgment our Saviour requireth in the Jews.[5] In them of Berea the Scripture commendeth it. Finally, whatsoever we do, if our own secret judgment consent not unto it as fit and good to be done, the doing of it, to us, is sin, although the thing itself be allowable. Saint Paul's rule therefore generally is, "Let every man in his own mind be fully persuaded of that thing which he either alloweth or doth."[6] Some things are so familiar and plain that truth from falsehood and good from evil is most easily discerned in them, even by men of no deep capacity.

2. The extreme Protestants or "Puritans" were opposed to the daily wearing of cap and gown by the clergy and the wearing of the surplice in church. This "Vestiarian controversy" was at its height in the 1560's. The *"Admonitions Directed unto the High Court of Parliament,"* by John Field and Thomas Wilcox (1572), attacked not only conventional clerical dress but the Prayer Book, episcopacy, and the whole structure of the Church of England.

3. John Calvin (1509–64) and Theodore Beza (1519–1605), two leading Protestant reformers on the Continent.
4. I Corinthians x.15. The next quotation is from I Corinthians xi.13.
5. See Luke xii.57. "Them of Berea": the inhabitants of the Macedonian city of Berea who "received the word with all readiness of mind" when Paul preached to them, according to Acts xiv.10–11.
6. See Romans xiv.5.

And of that nature, for the most part are things absolutely unto all men's salvation necessary, either to be held or denied, either to be done or avoided. For which cause Saint Augustine acknowledgeth that they are not only set down, but also plainly set down in scripture, so that he which heareth or readeth may, without any great difficulty, understand. Other things also there are belonging, though in a lower degree of importance, unto the offices of Christian men, which, because they are more obscure, more intricate and hard to be judged of, therefore God hath appointed some to spend their whole time principally in the study of things divine, to the end that in these more doubtful cases their understanding might be a light to direct others. "If the understanding power or faculty of the soul be," saith the Grand Physician,[7] "like unto the bodily sight, not of equal sharpness in all, what can be more convenient than that, even as the dark-sighted man is directed by the clear about things visible, so likewise in matters of deeper discourse the wise in heart do show the simple where his way lieth?" In the doubtful cases of law, what man is there who seeth not how requisite it is that professors of skill in that faculty be our directors? So is it in all other kinds of knowledge. And even in this kind likewise the Lord hath himself appointed that "the Priest's lips should preserve knowledge, and that other men should seek the truth at his mouth, because he is the messenger of the Lord of Hosts."[8] Gregory Nazianzen, offended at the people's too great presumption in controlling the judgment of them to whom in such cases they should rather have submitted their own, seeketh by earnest entreaty to stay them within their bounds: "Presume not, ye that are sheep, to make yourselves guides of them that should guide you; neither seek ye to overskip the fold which they about you have pitched. It sufficeth for your part, if ye can well frame yourselves to be ordered. Take not upon you to judge your judges, nor to make them subject to your laws who should be a law to you. For God is not a God of sedition and confusion but of order and of peace." But ye will say that if the guides of the people be blind, the common sort of men must not close up their own eyes and be led by the conduct of such; if the priest be partial in the law, the flock must not therefore depart from the ways of sincere truth, and in simplicity yield to be followers of him for his place' sake and office over them. Which thing, though in itself most true, is in your defense notwithstanding weak; because the matter wherein ye think that ye see and imagine that your ways are sincere is of far deeper consideration than any one amongst five hundred of you conceiveth. Let the vulgar sort amongst

---

7. I.e., Galen, Greek physician of the 2d century A.D., whose works were long accepted as the highest medical authority.

8. See Malachi ii.7. "Gregory Nazianzen" is St. Gregory of Nazianzus, a 4th-century bishop.

you know that there is not the least branch of the cause wherein they are so resolute but to the trial of it a great deal more appertaineth than their concept doth reach unto. I write not this in disgrace of the simplest that way given,[9] but I would gladly they knew the nature of that cause wherein they think themselves thoroughly instructed and are not; by means whereof they daily run themselves, without feeling their own hazard, upon the dint of the Apostle's sentence against evil speakers as touching things wherein they are ignorant.[1] If it be granted a thing unlawful for private men, not called into public consultation, to dispute which is the best state of civil polity, with a desire of bringing in some other kind than that under which they already live, for of such disputes I take it his meaning was—if it be a thing confessed that of such questions they cannot determine without rashness, inasmuch as a great part of them consisteth in special circumstances, and for one kind as many reasons may be brought as for another—is there any reason in the world why they should better judge what kind of regiment[2] ecclesiastical is the fittest? For in the civil state more insight and, in those affairs, more experience a great deal needs be granted them, than in this they can possibly have. When they which write in defense of your discipline and commend it unto the highest[3] not in the least cunning manner, are forced notwithstanding to acknowledge that with whom the truth is they know not, they are not certain—what certainty or knowledge can the multitude have thereof? Weigh what doth move the common sort so much to favor this innovation and it shall soon appear unto you that the force of particular reasons which for your several opinions are alleged is a thing whereof the multitude never did nor could consider as to be therewith wholly carried; but certain general inducements are used to make salable your cause in gross; and when once men have cast a fancy towards it, any slight declaration of specialties will serve to lead forward men's inclinable and prepared minds. The method of winning the people's affection unto a general liking of "the Cause," for so ye term it, hath been this: First, in the hearing of the multitude, the faults, especially of higher callings, are ripped up with marvelous exceeding severity and sharpness of reproof, which being oftentimes done, begetteth a great good opinion of integrity, zeal, and holiness to such constant reprovers of sin as by likelihood would never be so much offended at that which is evil, unless themselves were singularly

9. I.e., I am not disparaging ordinary, uneducated people.
1. Ignorant people run the risk of the condemnation of the apostle Peter: "But these, as natural brute beasts, made to be taken and destroyed, speak evil of the things that they understand not; and shall utterly perish in their own corruption" (II Peter ii.12).
2. Government.
3. I.e., Queen Elizabeth. The *Humble Petition of the Commonalty* (1588) said, "we are very babes and children, not knowing our right hand from our left in matters that concern the Kingdom of Heaven." "Cunning": learned.

good. The next thing hereunto is to impute all faults and corruptions wherewith the world aboundeth unto the kind of ecclesiastical government established. Wherein, as by reproving faults, they purchased unto themselves with the multitude a name to be virtuous; so by finding out this kind of cause they obtain to be judged wise above others, whereas in truth unto the form even of Jewish government, which the Lord himself, they all confess, did establish, with like show of reason they might impute those faults which the prophets condemn in the governors of that commonwealth as to the English kind of regiment ecclesiastical (whereof also God himself though in other sort is author), the stains and blemishes found in our state, which springing from the root of human frailty and corruption, not only are, but have always been more or less—yea, and for anything we know to the contrary will be till the world's end—complained of, what form of government soever take place. Having gotten thus much sway in the hearts of men, a third step is to propose their own form of church government as the only sovereign remedy of all evils, and to adorn it with all the glorious titles that may be. And the nature, as of men that have sick bodies, so likewise of the people in the crazedness of their minds possessed with dislike and discontentment at things present, is to imagine that anything the virtue whereof they hear commended would help them, but that most which they least have tried. The fourth degree of inducement is by fashioning the very notions and conceits[4] of men's minds in such sort that when they read the Scriptures they may think that everything soundeth towards the advancement of that discipline and to the utter disgrace of the contrary. Pythagoras, by bringing up his scholars in the speculative knowledge of numbers, made their conceits therein so strong that when they came to the contemplation of things natural they imagined that in every particular thing they even beheld, as it were with their eyes, how the elements of number gave essence and being to the works of nature. A thing in reason impossible, which notwithstanding through their misfashioned preconceit appeared unto them no less certain than if nature had written it in the very foreheads of all the creatures of God. * * *

From *Book I, Chapter 3*
[THE LAW OF NATURE]

* * * Now if Nature should intermit her course and leave altogether, though it were but for a while, the observation of her own laws; if those principal and mother elements of the world, whereof all things in this lower world are made, should lose the qualities which they now have; if the frame of that heavenly arch erected

---

4. Concepts.

over our heads should loosen and dissolve itself; if celestial spheres should forget their wonted motions and by irregular volubility turn themselves any way as it might happen; if the prince of the lights of heaven which now as a giant doth run his unwearied course, should as it were through a languishing faintness begin to stand and to rest himself; if the moon should wander from her beaten way, the times and seasons of the year blend themselves by disordered and confused mixture, the winds breathe out their last gasp, the clouds yield no rain, the earth be defeated of heavenly influence, the fruits of the earth pine away as children at the withered breasts of their mother no longer able to yield them relief, what would become of man himself, whom these things now do all serve? See we not plainly that obedience of creatures unto the law of Nature is the stay of the whole world? Notwithstanding with Nature it cometh sometimes to pass as with art. Let Phidias[5] have rude and obstinate stuff to carve, though his art do that it should, his work will lack that beauty which otherwise in fitter matter it might have had. He that striketh an instrument with skill may cause notwithstanding a very unpleasant sound if the string whereon he striketh chance to be uncapable of harmony. In the matter whereof natural things consist, that of Theophrastus[6] taketh place, "much of it is oftentimes such as will by no means yield to receive that impression which were best and most perfect." Which defect in the matter of things natural, they who gave themselves unto the contemplation of Nature among the heathen observed often; but the true original cause thereof divine malediction,[7] laid for the sin of man upon those creatures which God had made for the use of man. This, being an article of that saving truth which God hath revealed unto his church, was above the reach of their merely natural capacity and understanding. But howsoever these swervings are now and then incident into the course of Nature, nevertheless so constantly the laws of Nature are by natural agents observed, that no man denieth but those things which Nature worketh are wrought either always or for the most part after one and the same manner. * * *

From *Book I, Chapter 8*

[ON COMMON SENSE]

* * * The general and perpetual voice of men is as the sentence[8] of God himself. For that which all men have at all times learned, Nature herself must needs have taught, and God being the author of Nature, her voice is but his instrument. By her from Him we re-

5. The greatest of ancient Greek sculptors (5th century B.C.).
6. Greek writer of the 3rd century B.C., a follower of Aristotle and inventor of the type of essay called the "character," which in concise form

delineated a type of person.
7. God's curse in Eden, which fell not only upon sinful man but upon the earth as well.
8. Wisdom.

ceive whatsoever in such sort we learn. Infinite duties there are, the goodness whereof is by this rule sufficiently manifested, although we had no warrant besides to approve them. The apostle St. Paul having speech concerning the heathen saith of them "They are a law unto themselves."[9] His meaning is, that by force of the light of reason wherewith God illuminateth everyone which cometh into the world, men being enabled to know truth from falsehood, and good from evil, do thereby learn in many things what the will of God is; which will himself not revealing by any extraordinary means unto them, but they by natural discourse attaining the knowledge thereof, seem the makers of those laws which indeed are his, and they but only the finders of them out. A law therefore generally taken is a directive rule unto goodness of operation. The rule of divine operations outward is the definite appointment of God's own wisdom set down within himself. The rule of natural agents that work by simple necessity is the determination of the wisdom of God, known to God himself, the principal director of them, but not unto them that are directed to execute the same. The rule of natural agents which work after a sort of their own accord, as the beasts do, is the judgment of common sense or fancy concerning the sensible[1] goodness of those objects wherewith they are moved. The rule of ghostly or immaterial natures, as spirits and angels, is their intuitive intellectual judgment concerning the amiable beauty and high goodness of that object, which with unspeakable joy and delight doth set them on work. The rule of voluntary agents on earth is the sentence that reason giveth concerning the goodness of those things which they are to do. And the sentences which reason giveth are some more, some less general, before it come to define in particular actions what is good. The main principles of reason are in themselves apparent. For to make nothing evident of itself unto man's understanding were to take away all possibility of knowing anything. And herein that of Theophrastus is true, "They that seek a reason of all things do utterly overthrow reason." * * *

From *Book I, Chapter 9*
[NATURE, RIGHTEOUSNESS, AND SIN]

Now the due observation of this law which reason teacheth us cannot but be effectual unto their great good that observe the same. For we see the whole world and each part thereof so compacted[2] that as long as each thing performeth only that work which is natural unto it, it thereby preserveth both other things and also itself. Contrariwise, let any principal thing, as the sun or moon, or any one of

9. Romans ii.14.
1. Perceptible by the senses.

2. Agreed.

the heavens or elements, but once cease or fail, or swerve, and who does not easily conceive that the sequel thereof would be ruin both to itself and whatsoever dependeth upon it? And is it possible that man, being not only the noblest creature in the world, but even a very world in himself, his transgressing the law of his nature should draw no manner of harm after it? Yes, tribulation and anguish unto every soul that doth evil. Good doth follow unto all things by observing the course of their nature, and on the contrary side, evil by not observing it, but not unto natural agents that good which we call reward, not that evil which we properly term punishment. The reason whereof is because amongst creatures in this world, only man's observation of the law of his nature is Righteousness, only man's transgression Sin. And the reason of this is his manner of observing or transgressing the law of his nature. He doth not otherwise than voluntarily the one or the other. What we do against our wills, or constrainedly, we are not properly said to do it, because the motive cause of doing it is not in ourselves, but carrieth us, as if the wind should drive a feather in the air, we no whit furthering that whereby we are driven. In such cases therefore the evil which is done moveth compassion; men are pitied for it, as being rather miserable in such respect than culpable. * * *

From *Book I, Chapter* 10
[THE FOUNDATIONS OF SOCIETY]

That which hitherto we have set down is, I hope, sufficient to show their brutishness which imagine that religion and virtue are only as men will accompt of[3] them, that we might make as much accompt, if we would, of the contrary, without any harm unto ourselves, and that in Nature they are as indifferent one as the other. We see then how Nature itself teacheth laws and statutes to live by. The laws which have been hitherto mentioned do bind men absolutely, even as they are men, although they have never any settled fellowship, never any solemn agreement amongst themselves what to do or not to do. But forasmuch as we are not by ourselves sufficient to furnish ourselves with competent store of things needful for such a life as our nature doth desire, a life fit for the dignity of man, therefore to supply those defects and imperfections which are in us living single and solely, by ourselves, we are naturally induced to seek communion and fellowship with others. This was the cause of men's uniting themselves at the first in politic societies, which societies could not be without government, nor government without a distinct kind of law from that which hath been already declared. Two foundations there are which bear up public societies,

3. Value.

the one a natural inclination whereby all men desire a sociable life and fellowship, the other an order expressly or secretly agreed upon, touching the manner of their union in living together. The latter is that which we call the law of a commonweal,[4] the very soul of a politic body, the parts whereof are by law animated, held together and set on work in such actions as the common good requireth. Laws politic, ordained for external order and regiment amongst men, are never framed as they should be, unless presuming the will of man to be inwardly obstinate, rebellious, and averse from all obedience unto the sacred laws of his nature—in a word, unless presuming man to be in regard of his depraved mind little better than a wild beast—they do accordingly provide notwithstanding so to frame his outward actions that they be no hindrance unto the common good for which societies are instituted; unless they do this, they are not perfect. It resteth therefore that we consider how Nature findeth out such laws of government as serve to direct even nature depraved to a right end. All men desired to lead in this world an happy life. That life is led most happily, wherein all virtue is exercised without impediment or let. The Apostle[5] in exhorting men to contentment, although they have in this world no more than very bare food and raiment, giveth us thereby to understand that those are even the lowest of things necessary; that if we should be stripped of all those things without which we might possibly be, yet these must be left, that destitution in these is such an impediment, as till it be removed, suffereth not the mind of man to admit any other care. For this cause first God assigned Adam maintenance of life and then appointed him a law to observe. For this cause after men began to grow to a number, the first thing we read they gave themselves unto was the tilling of the earth and the feeding of cattle. Having by this mean whereon to live, the principal actions of their life afterward are noted by the exercise of their religion. True it is that the Kingdom of God must be the first thing in our purposes and desires. But inasmuch as righteous life presupposeth life, inasmuch as to live virtuously it is impossible except we live, therefore the first impediment which naturally we endeavor to remove is penury and want of things without which we cannot live. Unto life many implements are necessary; moe,[6] if we seek, as all men naturally do, such a life as hath in it joy, comfort, delight and pleasure. To this end we see how quickly sundry arts mechanical were found out in the very prime of the world. As things of greatest necessity are always first provided for, so things of greatest dignity are most accompted of by all such as judge rightly. Although therefore riches be a thing which every man wisheth, yet no man of judgment can esteem it better to be rich than wise, virtuous, and religious. If we be both or

---

4. Commonwealth. Originally the "common good."

5. Paul, in I Timothy vi.8.

6. More.

either of these, it is not because we are so born. For into the world
we come as empty of the one as of the other, as naked in mind as
we are in body. Both which necessities of man had at the first no
other helps and supplies than only domestical, such as that which
the prophet[7] implieth, saying, "Can a mother forget her child?",
such as that which the Apostle[8] mentioneth, saying, "He that careth
not for his own is worse than an infidel"; such as that concerning
Abraham, "Abraham will command his sons and his household after
him that they keep the way of the Lord."[9] But neither that which
we learn of ourselves, nor that which others teach us, can prevail
where wickedness and malice have taken deep root. If therefore
when there was but as yet one only family in the world, no means
of instruction human or divine could prevent effusion of blood, how
could it be chosen but that when families were multiplied and
increased upon earth, after separation each providing for itself, envy,
strife, contention, and violence must grow amongst them? For hath
not Nature furnished man with wit and valor, as it were with armor,
which may be used as well unto extreme evil as good? Yea, were
they not used by the rest of the world unto evil, unto the contrary
only by Seth, Enoch, and those few the rest in that line?[1] We all
make complaint of the iniquity of our times; not unjustly, for the
days are evil. But compare them with those times wherein there were
no civil societies, with those times wherein there was as yet no manner of public regiment established, with those times wherein there
were not above eight persons righteous living upon the face of the
earth, and we have surely good cause to think that God hath blessed
us exceedingly and hath made us behold most happy days. To take
away all such mutual grievances, injuries, and wrongs, there was no
way but only by growing into composition and agreement amongst
themselves by ordaining some kind of government public and by
yielding themselves subject thereunto, that unto whom they granted
authority to rule and govern, by them the peace, tranquility, and
happy estate of the rest might be procured. * * *

From *Book I, Chapter* 12

[THE NEED FOR LAW]

* * * The first principles of the law of nature are easy: hard
it were to find men ignorant of them; but concerning the duty which
Nature's law doth require at the hands of men in a number of
things particular, so far hath the natural understanding even of
sundry whole nations been darkened, that they have not discerned—
no, not gross iniquity—to be sin. Again, being so prone as we are

---

7. Isaiah (xlix.17).
8. Paul, in I Timothy v.8.
9. Genesis xviii.19.
1. The virtuous line of Seth is described in Genesis iv.25–26. It was in
the time of Seth and his son Enos that
"men began to call upon the name of
the Lord."

to fawn upon ourselves, and to be ignorant as much as may be of our own deformities, without the feeling sense whereof we are most wretched, even so much the more because not knowing them we cannot as much as desire to have them taken away, how should our festered sores be cured but that God hath delivered a law as sharp as the two-edged sword, piercing the very closest and most unsearchable corners of the heart which the law of nature can hardly, human laws by no means possible, reach unto? Hereby we know even secret concupiscence to be sin, and are made fearful to offend, though it be but in a wandering cogitation. * * *

1593

The New World

SIR THOMAS MORE
(1478–1535)

1514–16: Writing *Utopia*.
1532:   Resigns as Lord Chancellor after refusing to take oath to support Act of Succession and Supremacy.

More's famous philosophical romance *Utopia* (the name means "nowhere") is the father of a whole class of writings, from Bacon's *New Atlantis* (1626), through Swift's *Gulliver's Travels* (1726), Butler's *Erewhon* (1872), and Bellamy's *Looking Backward* (1888), to the "science fiction" stories of the present. But More's book has its own ancestry. It derives in part from Plato's *Republic* (and hence is philosophical) and in part from the accounts of travelers like Amerigo Vespucci (1507) and hence is romantic. It is a major monument of the great Christian humanist awakening of which Pico della Mirandola (1463–94), Desiderius Erasmus (ca. 1466–1536), and More himself were the most brilliant figures. Since the first of these was Italian, the second Dutch, and the third English, the movement was obviously international; *Utopia* was written in Latin, the international language.

Utopia represents itself as a traveler's tale, told by a veteran mariner (who is also a philosopher) to a group of somewhat skeptical companions as they sit in a garden one afternoon in Antwerp, in Holland. It is divided into two books. In the first, written in dialogue form, the corruption of European civil life is criticized. In the second, the traveler Raphael Hythloday describes the institutions of Utopia, with many ironic references to the real world with which the listeners are familiar.

Utopia is thus not presented as a mere dream or impractical fancy, as the modern use of the word "utopian" sometimes suggests. It is the fruit of More's serious thought—though he was never wholly serious—on the great social problems of his time. More felt, very strongly, the value of the ideals embodied in the rules of the monastic orders. Yet he was himself a man of the world, a lawyer and negotiator; he saw how far from realization in practice were the social ideals he admired. Central to his thought is the idea of community of property, for which he had a precedent in Plato as well as in the rules of the monastic orders; no fundamental reform in society is possible until private property is abolished. Yet it is typical of More's carefully balanced method that a standard defense of private property is put into the mouth of More as a character in the dialogue, against the position of the main speaker, Hythloday.

More's life was even more remarkable than his writings. He was born in London, the son of a prominent lawyer; as a boy he served in Archbishop Morton's household, then proceeded to Oxford and the Inns of Court. He became a friend of Erasmus, the great humanist, scholar, and editor of the New Testament; it was to More that Erasmus dedicated his satire *The Praise of Folly*. Soon after he wrote *Utopia* More rose to positions of great responsibility under King Henry VIII: Master of Requests, Privy Councillor, Speaker of the House of Commons, and finally Lord Chancellor. In 1532, after the king's marriage to Anne Boleyn, More refused to take the oath for the Act of Succession and Supremacy. Although he had compromised before, as any successful administrator must, his conscience would not permit him to assert that any temporal lord, even Henry, could or ought to be head of that spiritual body, the church. From the point of view of the government, his refusal was treason, and he was condemned to death; efforts, including those of his wife, to reconcile him with Henry failed, and in 1535 he was executed. No death in English history is more famous: as he mounted the shaky steps to the scaffold, he said to the sheriff's officer, "I pray you, Master Lieutenant, see me safe up, and for my coming down let me shift for myself"; as he put his head on the block he moved his beard aside, remarking that his beard had done the king no offense. He was of course certain that he was not dying for treason, but in and for the faith of the Catholic Church. Four hundred years later he was canonized by the church as St. Thomas More.

From Utopia[1]

From *Book I*

The most victorious and triumphant King of England, Henry the Eighth of that name, in all royal virtues a prince most peerless, had recently some differences with Charles,[2] the most serene Prince of Castile, and sent me into Flanders to negotiate and compose matters between them. I was colleague and companion to that incomparable man, Cuthbert Tunstall,[3] whom the king lately made Master of the Rolls to the great satisfaction of all. I will say nothing of this man, not because I fear the testimony of a friend will be questioned, but because his learning and virtues are greater than I can describe. And also they are so well-known that they do not need my commenda-

---

1. The translation from which these selections are taken is by H. S. V. Ogden (1949).
2. The future Emperor Charles V; the differences had to do with the wool trade. The negotiations took place in 1515 and 1516.
3. Cuthbert Tunstall, later Bishop of London and of Durham, was one of More's closest friends.

tion, unless I would, according to the proverb, "Show the sun with a lantern."

The men appointed by the prince to treat with us, all excellent men, met us at Bruges according to agreement. The chief man among them and their leader was the Margrave of Bruges, a distinguished man. But the wisest and best spoken was George Temse, the Provost of Cassel, a man eloquent both by nature and training, very learned in the law, and most skillful in affairs through his capacity and long practice. After we had met several times and could not come to an agreement, they went to Brussels for some days to learn their prince's pleasure.

Meanwhile I went to Antwerp, since our business permitted it. Of those who visited me while I was there, Peter Giles[4] was more congenial to me than any of the others. He was a native of Antwerp, a man much respected there and worthy of the highest regard. I do not know of a more cultivated or a better bred young man anywhere. He is, indeed, the best and most learned of men, and besides, very courteous to all. To his intimates he is so loving, so trustworthy, and so deeply affectionate that it would be very hard to find another friend like him anywhere. No man is more modest or more candid. No man unites more simplicity with prudence. His conversation is so pleasant, and so witty without vulgarity, that the fervent desire I felt to see my native country and my wife and children (from whom I had been away more than four months) was much eased by his company.

One day after I had heard mass at Notre Dame, the most beautiful and most frequented church in Antwerp, I was about to return to my lodgings when I happened to see him talking with a stranger, a man well advanced in years. The stranger had a sunburned face, a long beard, and a cloak hanging carelessly from his shoulders. From his appearance and clothing I took him to be a seaman. When Peter saw me, he approached and greeted me. As I was returning his salutation, he took me aside, and pointing to the stranger, said, "Do you see that man? I was just thinking of bringing him to you."

"He would have been very welcome on your account," I answered.

"And on his own, too," he said, "if you knew him, for there is no man alive who can tell you so much about unknown peoples and countries. And I know that you are most eager for such information."

"Then," said I, "I did not guess badly, for at first sight I took him for a seaman."

4. Peter Giles, or Petrus Aegidius, was town clerk of Antwerp, a humanist and friend of Erasmus. He arranged for the first printing of *Utopia*.

"No," he replied, "you are mistaken, for he has sailed not as the sailor Palinurus, but as Ulysses, or rather as Plato.[5] This Raphael, surnamed Hythloday (for so he is called), though not ignorant of the Latin tongue, is eminently learned in the Greek. He has applied himself more particularly to Greek because he has given himself wholly to philosophy, in which he knew that the Romans have left us nothing that is valuable except what is to be found in Seneca and Cicero. He was so desirous of seeing the world that he divided his patrimony among his brothers (he is Portuguese by birth), and threw in his lot with Americus Vespucius. He took part in the last three of Vespucius's four voyages, accounts of which are now published. But he did not return home with him on the last voyage. After much effort, he won permission from Americus to be one of the twenty-four who were left in a fort at the farthest place at which they touched in their last voyage. Being left thus was highly gratifying to a man who gave more thought to his travels than to his burial place, and who often used to say that one who has no grave is covered by the sky and that the road to heaven is equally short from all places.

"Yet this disposition of mind would have cost him dear if God had not been very gracious to him. After the departure of Vespucius he traveled over many countries with five companions from the fort. At last by singular good fortune he got to Ceylon and from thence to Calcutta, where he very happily found some Portuguese ships. And so, beyond anyone's expectation, he came back to his own country."

When Peter had told me this, I thanked him for his kindness in wishing to make me acquainted with a man whose conversation he knew would be so acceptable to me, and I turned toward Raphael. Upon that Raphael and I greeted one another. And after the ordinary civilities of strangers upon their first meeting, we all went to my house. There in the garden we sat down on a grassy bank and conversed.

He told us that when Vespucius had sailed away, he and his companions that had stayed behind in the fort often met the people of the country, and by fair and gentle speech gradually won their favor. Before long they came to dwell with them quite safely and even familiarly. He also told us that they were esteemed by the prince (I have forgotten his name and his country), who furnished them plentifully with all things necessary, and who also gave them the means of traveling, both boats when they went by

---

5. Palinurus, Aeneas' pilot, fell overboard when asleep and drowned. He is here contrasted with Ulysses, who was regarded as the type of the thoughtful, observant traveler. Plato is cited as the profound philosopher; his *Republic* strongly influenced *Utopia*. Raphael Hythloday is an invented character; his last name is coined from Greek words meaning "a skilled conveyer of trifles or nonsense."

water and wagons when they traveled overland. He sent with them a faithful guide who was to introduce and recommend them to such other princes as they had a mind to see. After many days' journey, they came to towns and cities, and to commonwealths that were both well peopled and happily governed.

Under the equator and as far on both sides of it as the sun moves, there lie vast deserts parched with the perpetual heat of the sun. The whole region is desolate and gloomy, savage and uncultivated, inhabited by wild beasts and serpents, and by a few men as wild and dangerous as the beasts themselves. As they went on, conditions gradually grew milder. The heat was less burning, the earth greener, and even the beasts less fierce. At last they found nations, cities, and towns that had mutual commerce among themselves and with their neighbors, and that traded by sea and land with remote countries. From then on, he said, they were able to visit many lands on all sides, for they were welcome on board any ship about to make a voyage.

The first vessels that they saw were flat-bottomed, with sails made of close-woven reeds and wicker, or in some places of leather. Farther on they found ships made with round keels and canvas sails, in all ways like our ships. The seamen were skillful both in sailing and in navigation. They were most grateful to him, Raphael said, for showing them the use of the compass, of which they had been ignorant. For that reason they had sailed with great caution and only in summer. Now they have such confidence in the compass that they no longer fear winter, and are carefree rather than safe. This discovery, which they thought so much to their advantage, may become the cause of much mischief to them through their imprudence.

It would take too long to set forth all that Raphael told us he had observed, and it would be a digression from our present purpose. Perhaps in another place we shall tell more about the things that are worth knowing, especially about the wise and prudent institutions that he observed among the civilized nations. We asked him many questions about such things and he answered us very willingly. We made no inquiries, however, about monsters, which are common enough. Scyllas, ravenous harpies,[6] and cannibals are easy to find anywhere, but it is not so easy to find states that are well and wisely governed.

While he told us of many things which are amiss among those new-found nations, he also reckoned up not a few things from which patterns might be taken for correcting the errors of our

---

6. "Scyllas" were horrible monsters, like that which dwelt in a cave in the rock Scylla in the *Odyssey;* she had twelve feet and six heads, with three rows of teeth in each head. "Harpies" were large birds with faces of women pale with hunger and long, sharp claws.

own cities and kingdoms. These I shall treat in another place,[7] as I have said. Now I intend to relate only what he told us about the manners and laws of the Utopians, first setting forth the occasion that led us to speak of that commonwealth. Raphael had been talking very wisely about the numerous errors and also the wise institutions found both among those nations and us, speaking as intimately about the customs and government of each place he had visited as though he had lived there all his life. Peter was struck with admiration.

"I wonder, Master Raphael," he said, "why you do not enter some king's service, for I know of no prince who would not be eager to have you. Your learning and your knowledge of places and men would entertain him pleasantly, while your advice and your examples would be invaluable. Thus you would serve your own interest and be useful to all your friends."

"I am not greatly concerned about my friends," he said, "for I have already done my duty toward them. While I was still young and healthy, I distributed among my relations and friends the possessions which other men do not part with till they are old and sick (and then only grudgingly and because they can no longer keep them). I think my friends should rest content with this and not expect that for their sake I should enslave myself to any king whatsoever."

"Well said," Peter replied, "but I do not mean that you should be a slave to any king, only that you should be of service to him."

"The difference is a mere matter of words," Raphael replied.

"As you will," said Peter, "but I do not see any other way in which you can be so useful either to your friends or to the public, to say nothing of making yourself happier."

"Happier?" exclaimed Raphael. "Would a way of life so abhorrent to my nature make my life happier? Now I live as I will, and I believe very few courtiers can say that. As a matter of fact, there are so many men courting the favor of the great that it will be no great loss if they have to do without me or others like me."

Then I said, "It is clear, Master Raphael, that you desire neither wealth nor power, and indeed I value and admire such a man much more than I do any of the great men in the world. Yet I think, if you would give your time and effort to public affairs, you would do a thing worthy of a generous and philosophical nature like yours, even though you might not enjoy it. You could best perform such a service by belonging to the council of some great prince, whom you would urge on to whatever is noble and just. I know you would do this, if you were in such a post. And your efforts would be effective, because a people's welfare or misery

7. See Book II below.

flows wholly from their prince, as from a never-failing spring. Your
learning is so full, even when not combined with experience, and
your experience so great, even without learning, that you would
be an exceptional councilor to any king whatsoever."

"You are doubly mistaken, my dear More," said he, "both in
your opinion of me and in your estimate of the situation itself. I
do not have that capacity which you fancy to be in me, and if I
had it, the public would not be any better off through the sacrifice
of my leisure; for most princes apply themselves to warlike pursuits (in which I have no skill or interest) rather than to the useful
arts of peace. They are generally more set on acquiring new kingdoms rightly or wrongly, than on governing well those that they
already have. Moreover the councilors of kings are so wise that
they need no advice from others (or at least so it seems to themselves). At the same time they accept and even applaud the most
absurd statements of men whose favor they seek for the sake of
standing well with the prince. It is natural that each man should
flatter himself by thinking his own opinions best. The old crow
loves his young and the ape his cubs. Now in a court made up of
those who envy all others and admire only themselves, if a man
should propose something that he had read in history or observed
in his travels, the other councilors would fear that their whole reputation for wisdom was in danger, and that they would be regarded
as plain fools unless they could show his suggestion was weak and
defective. If all else failed, they would take refuge in the retort
that such and such things pleased our ancestors and would that
we could match their wisdom! With this they would settle down
as though they had said the last word on the subject and as though
there were a terrible danger in finding a man wiser than our ancestors in anything. We readily follow whatever they did, as though
it were necessarily best. But if something better is proposed, we
seize the excuse of reverence for past times and cling to it doggedly.
I have met with these proud, absurd, and morose judgments in
many places, and once even in England. * * * "

From *Book II*

1. THEIR COUNTRY AND AGRICULTURE

The island of Utopia is two hundred miles in breadth in the
middle part where it is widest, and it is nowhere much narrower than
this except toward the two ends. These ends, drawn around in a
five-hundred-mile curve, make the island crescent-shaped. Between
the horns of the crescent, which are some eleven miles apart, the
sea comes in and spreads into a great bay. Being well secured from
the wind, the bay does not rage with great waves, but is quite like

a lake. This makes nearly the whole inner coast a harbor, greatly facilitating mutual trade. But the entrance into the bay, what with shallows on one side and rocks on the other, is very dangerous. Near the middle there is one rock that rises above the water, and so is not dangerous. On the top of it a tower has been built, in which a garrison is kept. The other rocks lie under water and are very treacherous. The channels are known only to the Utopians, so if any stranger should chance to enter the bay without one of their pilots, he would run a great danger of shipwreck. Even they themselves could not enter safely if some marks on the coast did not direct their way. If these were shifted even a little, any fleet coming against them, no matter how great it was, would certainly be lost.

On the other side of the island there are likewise many harbors, and the coast is so fortified by nature and art that a small number of men could hold off the attack of a great force. They say (and the appearance of the place bears this out) that their land was once not an island. But Utopus, who conquered the country and gave it his name (it was previously called Abraxa),[1] brought its rude and uncivilized inhabitants to such a high level of culture and humanity that now they excel all other people in that part of the world. When he had subdued them, he cut a channel fifteen miles long where their land joined the continent and thus brought the sea entirely around their land. He not only forced the natives to work at it, but his soldiers too, so that the natives would not think they were treated like slaves. By putting so many men to work, he finished the project quickly, and the neighbors, who at first had laughed at his folly, were struck with admiration and terror at his success.

There are fifty-four cities on the island, all large and well built, and with the same language, customs, institutions, and laws. All of them are built on the same plan, as far as the location permits. The nearest are at least twenty-four miles apart, and those that are farthest are not so far but that a man can go on foot from one city to the next in a day.

Once a year each city sends three of its wisest elders to Amaurot[2] to consult about their common concerns. Amaurot is the chief city of the island and lies near its center, so that it is the most convenient place for the elders to meet. Every city has enough ground assigned to it so that it has at least ten miles of farm land in every direction. Where the cities are farther apart, they have more ground. No city desires to enlarge its bounds, for the inhabitants consider themselves husbandmen rather than landlords. They have built houses all over the countryside, well designed and fur-

1. From Greek, "not small."
2. The name is coined from a Greek adjective meaning "dim, obscure"—a suitable name for the capital of "Nowhere."

nished with farm equipment. These houses are inhabited by citizens who come to the country by turns to dwell in them. No country household has fewer than forty men and women in it, besides two bondmen.[3] A master and mistress, serious and mature persons, are in charge of each household. A magistrate is placed over every thirty households. Every year twenty from each household move back to the city, after completing a two-year turn in the country. In their place twenty others are sent out from town, to learn farm work from those that have already been in the country for a year and are somewhat skilled in it. In turn they must teach those who come the following year. If they were all equally ignorant of farm work and new to it, they might damage the crops through ignorance. This custom of shifting the farm workers is established in order that no one will have to do this hard work against his will for more than two years, but many of them ask to stay longer because they take a natural delight in farm life.

The farm workers till the soil, care for the cattle, hew wood, and take it to the city by land or water, as is most convenient. They breed an enormous number of chickens by a marvelous method. Men hatch the eggs, not hens, by keeping them in a warm place at an even temperature. The chicks, as soon as they come out of the shell, recognize and follow men instead of their mothers.

They raise very few horses, but these are full of mettle and are kept only for exercising the youth in the art of horsemanship. For the work of plowing and hauling they employ only oxen. They think horses are stronger than oxen, but they find that oxen can hold out longer and are less subject to disease, and so can be kept with less cost and effort. Moreover, when they are too old for work, they can be used for meat.

They raise grain only for bread. They drink wine, apple or pear cider, or water, sometimes clear, but often mixed with honey or licorice, of which they have an abundance. Although they know just how much grain each city and its district will consume, they sow more grain and breed more cattle than they need for their own use, and share the surplus with their neighbors. When they need goods on the farms which they do not make there, they get them from the town magistrates without giving anything in exchange. This is not inconvenient, since most of them go to town once a month, especially on holidays. When harvest time comes, the country magistrates notify the towns how many hands will be needed. The harvesters come at the right time, and commonly get in the whole harvest in one fair day.

---

3. More provides for a few bondmen or slaves in Utopia, to perform tasks unfit for citizens, such as slaughtering. Bondage is usually a punishment for serious crimes.

7. THEIR GOLD AND SILVER, AND HOW THEY KEEP IT

Therefore[4] they have accumulated an inestimable amount of gold and silver, but they do not keep it in the form of treasure. I am reluctant to tell you how they keep it, for fear you will not believe me. I would not have believed it myself if anyone had told me about it—not unless I had seen it with my own eyes. It is almost always true that the more different anything is from what people are used to, the harder it is to believe. In view of the fact that the Utopians' customs are so different from ours, a shrewd judge will not be surprised to find that they do not use gold and silver at all as we do. Since they keep gold and silver only for grave contingencies, they take care that in the meantime no one shall value these metals more than they deserve. Iron is obviously greatly superior to either. Men can no more do without iron than without fire and water. But gold and silver have no indispensable qualities. Human folly has made them precious only because of their scarcity. Nature, like a wise and generous parent, has placed the best things everywhere and in the open, such as air and water and the earth itself, but she has hidden vain and useless things in remote and faraway places.

If they kept their gold and silver guarded in a tower, foolish people might suspect the prince and senate[5] of deceiving the citizens and aiming at some advantage for themselves. If they made plate and wrought-metal work out of them, they would not want to give up such articles and melt them down to pay mercenaries. To solve the problem, they have thought out a plan as much in accord with their institutions as it is contrary to ours. The plan seems incredible to us (except to those of us who are very wise), because we regard gold as of great value and hoard it carefully. While their eating and drinking utensils are made of china and glass, beautiful but inexpensive, their chamber pots and stools both in their public halls and their homes are made of gold and silver. They also use these metals for the chains and fetters of their bondmen. They hang gold rings from the ears of criminals, place gold rings on their fingers, gold collars around their necks, and gold crowns on their heads. Thus they hold gold and silver up to scorn in every way.

The result is that when there is need to part with these metals, which others give up as painfully as if their vitals were being torn out, none of the Utopians regard it as any more than the loss of a penny, so to speak. They find pearls on their shores and

4. More has explained (in a section here omitted) that the Utopians hire mercenary soldiers in time of war and pay them very highly; enemy soldiers often desert to them.

5. The prince, as More has earlier explained, is chosen for life by the senate, whose members are selected by an assembly, whose members in turn are elected from households.

diamonds and carbuncles[6] on certain rocks, but they do not search for them. If they find them by chance, they polish them and adorn their younger children with them. As children they take pride and pleasure in such ornaments, and consequently put them aside when they are older and observe that only children use such baubles. This results from their own sense of propriety and not from their parents' commands, just as our children throw away their nuts,[7] amulets, and dolls, when they grow up.

Different customs and institutions produce quite different ideas and attitudes, a truth I never saw better illustrated than in the behavior of the Anemolian[8] ambassadors, who came to Amaurot while I was there. Because they came to discuss important business, three citizens from each city had come to Amaurot ahead of time. The ambassadors from neighboring states, at least those who had been there before, knew that fine clothing was not esteemed among the Utopians, that silk was scorned, and that gold was considered a shameful thing. They came as plainly clothed as possible. But when the Anemolians, who lived far away and had little intercourse with the Utopians, saw that all the people wore the same coarse clothing, they took it for granted that they did not have anything else. They themselves, being a proud rather than a wise people, decided to dress themselves gloriously like gods and dazzle the eyes of the poor Utopians by the splendor of their garb. The three ambassadors made their entry accompanied by a hundred attendants, all dressed in varicolored clothing, many in silk. Since they were nobles at home, the ambassadors wore cloaks of cloth of gold, necklaces and earrings of gold, gold rings on their fingers, caps hung with gold chains studded with pearls and other jewels, in short decked out with all those things which among the Utopians were considered badges of slavery, signs of punishment, or toys for children. It was a sight to see how high they held their heads when they compared their clothing with that of the Utopians, for the people had swarmed out into the streets. It was no less amusing to think how far they were from creating the impression which they had expected to make, for in the eyes of all the Utopians, except for those few who had visited other states, all this pomp and splendor seemed shameful. The Utopians saluted all the lowest people as lords and paid no respect at all to the ambassadors themselves, because they seemed to be dressed as slaves with their gold chains. And you might have seen children, who had already thrown away their pearls and gems, nudge their mothers upon seeing the jewels in the ambassadors' caps, and say, "Look, mother! See that big fool who wears pearls and gems, as if he were a little boy!"

6. Rubies.
7. Marbles.

8. Coined from the Greek for "windy."

Then she would say seriously, "Hush, my boy. I think he is one of the ambassadors' fools." Others found fault with the golden chains for being useless and so light that any slave might break them, and so loose that a person when he wished could shake them off, and run away. But after the ambassadors had spent one day and then another there, and had seen the great quantity of cheap gold and silver which was scorned as much by the Utopians as it was held in respect by the Anemolians, and when they had learned also that there was more gold and silver in the chains and fetters of a single slave than in the apparel of all three ambassadors, then their feathers fell. Somewhat shamefacedly they laid aside all the finery in which they had strutted, but they did so willingly, as they had conversed with the Utopians and learned their customs and ideas.

12. THEIR MARRIAGE CUSTOMS

A woman is not married before eighteen, nor a man before twenty-two. If a man (or woman) is convicted of an illict affair before marriage, he is severely punished and marriage is denied him for his whole life, unless a prince's pardon remits the punishment. The master and mistress of the household in which the offense has occured are in disgrace for having been remiss in their duty. The reason for punishing this offense so severely is the fear that few would unite in married love, to spend their whole lives with one person and put up with all the annoyances of marriage, unless they were rigorously restrained from promiscuity.

In the choice of wives they carefully follow a custom which seemed to us foolish and absurd. Before marriage some responsible and honorable woman, either a virgin or a widow, presents the woman naked to her suitor and after that some upright man presents the suitor naked to the woman. We laughed at this and condemned it as foolish. On the contrary they wonder at the stupidity of other people, who are exceedingly cautious in matters involving only a little money. For example, men will refuse to buy a colt, unless they take off its saddle and harness, which might conceal a sore. But in the choice of a mate, on which one's happiness depends for the rest of one's life, they act carelessly. They leave all but a hand's-breadth of the woman's face covered with clothing and judge her by it, so that in marrying a couple runs a great risk of mutual dislike if later anything in either's body should offend the other. Not all men are so wise that they consider only a woman's behavior. And even wise men think that physical beauty in wives adds not a little to the virtues of the mind. Certainly some deformity may lurk underneath clothing which will alienate a man from his wife when it is too late to be separated from her. If such a deformity is discovered after marriage, a man must bear his lot, so the Utopians think care ought to be taken by law that no one be deceived.

There is all the more reason for their taking this precaution, because in that part of the world they alone are monogamists. Their marriages are broken only by death. They do not allow divorce except for adultery or insufferable waywardness on the part of either spouse. The injured person is given permission to change spouses by the senate, but the guilty party is considered disreputable and for the rest of his life is forbidden to remarry. They do not allow a husband to put away his wife against her will because of some bodily misfortune. They consider it a matter of cruelty and disloyalty to desert one's spouse when most in need of comfort, especially in old age (which is itself really a sickness, since it brings sickness in its train). It happens occasionally that when a married couple cannot agree well together and when they have found other persons with whom they hope to live more happily, they separate by mutual consent and contract new marriages, but only with the consent of the senate. Such divorces are not allowed unless the senators and their wives have made careful inquiry into the grounds for it. They allow them unwillingly, for they know that it weakens the love of married couples to leave the door open to easy new marriages.

They punish adulterers with the severest bondage. If both parties are married, they are divorced, and the injured persons may be married to one another or to someone else. But if either of the injured parties continues to love the undeserving spouse, then the couple may live together in marriage, provided the innocent person is willing to share in the labor to which bondmen are condemned. Sometimes it happens that the repentance of the guilty person so moves the prince to pity that he grants both of them freedom once more. If anyone commits adultery a second time, his punishment is death.

16. THE RELIGION OF THE UTOPIANS

There are different kinds of religion throughout the island, as well as in each city. Some worship the sun as a god, others the moon, and still others some one of the planets. Others worship some man pre-eminent in virtue or glory, not only as a god, but as the supreme god. But by far the greatest number of the Utopians, and among these the wisest, worship none of these. They think there is one unknown, eternal, infinite, and unknowable deity, transcending human comprehension and pervading the whole universe not physically but in virtue and power. Him they call Father of all. They acknowledge that from Him alone comes the beginning, increase, progress, change, and end of all things. They do not offer divine honors to any other god.

Though they hold different beliefs on other matters of religion, all the Utopians agree with their wiser sort in this, that there is only one supreme power, the Maker and Ruler of the universe, whom they all call in their native language Mithra. But they differ as to who he is; some think he is one god, others another. But whatever god each person regards as the chief god, they all agree in thinking that God is the very Being to whose power and majesty the supremacy over all things is attributed by universal consent.

By degrees all the Utopians are coming to forsake their various superstitions and to agree upon this one religion that seems to excel the others in reason. No doubt the other religions would have vanished long ago, had it not happened that whenever one of the Utopians who was planning to change his religion met with misfortune, the rest regarded it not as an accident but as something sent by a divinity as a punishment for the desertion of his worship.

We told them of the name, doctrine, manner of life, and miracles of Christ, and of the wonderful constancy of the many martyrs, who willingly sacrificed their blood to bring so many nations far and wide to Christianity. You will hardly believe with what favorably disposed minds they received this account, either because God secretly incited them or because this religion is most like the belief already very strong among them. I thought that they were also somewhat influenced by learning that Christ instituted community of goods and that this custom was still in practice among the most sincere of the Christians. Whatever the reason, many came over to our religion and were baptized. Two of our number had died and none of us four survivors, I regret to say, were priests, so though they received instruction in other matters they did not receive those sacraments which in our religion only priests can administer. But they understand them and long for them ardently. In fact, they argue vigorously with one another as to whether a man chosen from among them without the Pope's authorization would have the true character of a priest. Though they seemed determined to choose such a one, they had not chosen him at the time of my leaving.

Those among them that have not yet accepted the Christian religion do not restrain others from it nor abuse the converts to it. While I was there, only one man among the Christians was punished. This newly baptized convert, in spite of all our advice, was preaching in public on the Christian worship more zealously than wisely. He grew so heated that he not only put our worship before all others, but also condemned all other rites as profane and loudly denounced their celebrants as wicked and impious men fit for hellfire. After he had been preaching these things for a long time, they seized him. They convicted him not on a charge of disparaging their religion, but of arousing public disorder among the people, and sentenced him to exile. For they count it among their oldest institutions that no man shall be made to suffer for his religion.

In the early days King Utopus learned that before his coming the inhabitants had quarreled violently over religion. He found that it was easy to conquer them all, because the different sects in fighting for their country fought by themselves instead of together. Therefore after his victory he decreed that each man might follow whatever religion he wished and might try to persuade others to join it amicably and temperately and without bitterness toward others. If persuasion failed, a person was forbidden to use force or to indulge in wrangling. If anyone argued for his religion contentiously, he was to be punished by exile or bondage.

Utopus made this law partly for the sake of peace, which he saw was in danger of being completely destroyed by constant strife and implacable hatred, and partly for the sake of religion. He did not venture to make dogmatic decisions in regard to religion, perhaps from some idea that God likes and inspires a variety and multiplicity of worship. He deemed it foolish and insolent for anyone to try to make all men accept his own beliefs by force and by threats. If one religion is true and the others false, and if men use reason and moderation, he clearly foresaw that the truth would prevail by its own strength. But if men fight and riot, as evil and headstrong men will do, then the best and holiest religion in the world will be crowded out by the emptiest superstitions, like wheat choked by thorns and briars. So he imposed no one religion on his people, and left each man free to believe what he would, with one exception. He made a solemn and severe law against any who sink so far below the dignity of human nature as to think that the soul dies with the body, or that the universe is carried along by chance without an over-ruling providence.

The Utopians believe that after this life there are punishments for wickedness and rewards for virtue. They consider one who thinks otherwise as hardly a man, since he has degraded the human soul to the low level of a beast's body. Such a man they do not count fit for human society, for if he dares, he will scorn all its laws and customs. Who can doubt that a man who fears nothing but the law and apprehends nothing after death would secretly flout his country's laws or break them by force to satisfy his greed? Therefore no preferment is awarded to one with such views, and no magistracy or any public responsibility is entrusted to him. Instead, he is generally looked down upon as a man of worthless and sordid nature. Yet they do not punish such a man further, for they are persuaded that no one can make himself believe anything at will. Nor do they force him by threats to conceal his thoughts, and so open the door to deceit and lying, which they detest as the next thing to fraud. But they take care that he does not argue for his opinions, especially before the common people. They permit and even encourage him to discuss these matters with their priests and other serious men, in full confidence that finally his mad opinions will yield to reason.

There are others, in fact a considerable number, who go to the opposite extreme, and believe that the souls of animals are immortal, though not comparable with the human soul in excellence nor capable of as great happiness. These men are not thought to be bad or altogether lacking in reason, and their opinion is not discouraged.

Almost all the Utopians believe so firmly that man's happiness after death is endless, that they lament sickness but not death. They only mourn a man's death if they see that he parts with life reluctantly. This they take as a very bad sign, as if his soul dreaded death because of hopelessness or from some secret and guilty foreboding of impending punishment. The coming of a man who does not run gladly at the call, but is dragged off like a shirker, cannot be pleasing to God. They feel horror at such a death, and after carrying out the body in sorrow and with silent prayers to God mercifully to pardon the man's weakness, they bury the body in the earth. When a man dies cheerfully and full of good hope, they do not grieve, but follow the body singing, earnestly commending the man's soul to God. Then they cremate him reverently rather than sadly, and in the place where the funeral pyre was made, they set up a tombstone with the dead man's honors engraved upon it. When they return from the funeral, they relate his life and good deeds, and no part of his life is more frequently nor more gladly rehearsed than his cheerful death.

They think that remembering his good qualities is a powerful incitement to virtue among the living and the most pleasing honor to the dead. For they believe that the dead are present among us and hear the talk about themselves, though they are invisible through the dullness of human sight. They think that the dead, in keeping with their happy condition, can go where they want, and in affectionate loyalty visit those they loved and esteemed during their lives. They also believe that in good men these affections, like other good things, are increased rather than decreased after death, and that the dead come among the living observing their words and deeds. Consequently they enter into their undertakings all the more confidently because of their trust in such protectors. And they are deterred from secret wrongdoing by the belief that their forefathers are present.

They laugh at auguries and other superstitious forms of divination that are common among other nations. But they revere miracles which cannot flow from the powers of nature, looking on them as the works and witnesses of God. They say that such miracles have frequently occurred among them. Sometimes they have won safety and success amid great dangers and uncertainties through public prayers offered with assured confidence.

They hold that the careful observation of nature and the reflection on it and the reverence that arises from this is a kind of worship very pleasing to God. * * *

Now I have described to you as truthfully as I could the structure of this commonwealth, which I think the best, and indeed the only one which can rightfully be called by that name. In other places where they speak of the common good, every man is looking out for his own good. But in Utopia where there is no private property and where they zealously pursue the public business, there the name commonwealth is doubly deserved. Elsewhere, even though the state is prosperous, most men know that they may die of hunger if they do not look out for themselves, and so they are forced to take care of themselves rather than other people. In Utopia where everything belongs to everybody, they know that if the public warehouses and granaries are full, no one will lack anything for his personal use.

Among them there is no maldistribution of goods, nor is anyone poor and indigent. When no one owns anything, all are rich. What greater riches can there be than to live cheerfully and serenely, free from all anxieties, without worries about making a living and unvexed by the complaints of one's wife about money? No one has to worry about his son's being poor, or about his daughter's dowry. Each man's livelihood and happiness are secure, and the same is true of all his relations, his wife, sons, grandsons, great-grandsons, and the whole line of descendants that highborn men assume will follow them. Why should he look forward to less, since those who can no longer work are cared for as well as those who do?

How could anyone dare to compare the justice of the Utopians with that of other nations? If there is any trace of justice or equity among other nations, may I perish among them! What justice is there in this, that a nobleman, a goldsmith,[9] a moneylender, or some other man who does nothing at all for a living or does something that is of no use to the public, lives a sumptuous and elegant life? In the meantime a servant, a driver, a blacksmith, or a farmer works as hard as a beast at labor so necessary that the commonwealth could not last a year without it. Yet they earn so poor a living and lead such miserable lives that their condition seems worse than that of draft animals. Beasts do not work so incessantly and do not live

9. I.e., a banker.

much worse—in fact they live better—and they have no worries about the future. But workingmen are burdened with barren and fruitless toil, and live in fear of want in their old age. Their daily wage is insufficient to support them for the present, so they can have no surplus to lay up for the future.

Is not a government unjust and ungrateful that squanders rich rewards on noblemen (as they are called), goldsmiths, and others that do not work but live only by flattery or by catering to useless pleasures? And is it just for a government to ignore the welfare of farmers, charcoal burners, servants, drivers, and blacksmiths, without whom the commonwealth could not exist at all? After their best years have been consumed by labor and they are worn out by age and sickness, they are still penniless, and the thankless state, unmindful of their many great services, rewards them with nothing but a miserable death. Furthermore the rich constantly try to whittle away something from the pitiful wages of the poor by private fraud and even by public laws. To pay so little to men who deserve the best from the state is in itself unjust, yet it is made "just" legally by passing a law.

So when I weigh in my mind all the other states which flourish today, so help me God, I can discover nothing but a conspiracy of the rich, who pursue their own aggrandizement under the name and title of the Commonwealth. They devise ways and means to keep safely what they have unjustly acquired, and to buy up the toil and labor of the poor as cheaply as possible and oppress them. When these schemes of the rich become established by the government, which is meant to protect the poor as well as the rich, then they are law. With insatiable greed these wicked men divide among themselves the goods which would have been enough for all.

And yet they are far short of the happiness of the Utopians, who have abolished the use of money, and with it greed. What evils they avoid! What a multitude of crimes they prevent! Everyone knows that frauds, thefts, quarrels, contentions, uprisings, murders, betrayals, and poisonings (evils which are commonly punished rather than checked by the severities of the law) would wither away if money were eradicated! Fear, anxiety, worry, care, toil, and sleepless nights would disappear at the same time as money! Even poverty, which seems to need money more than anything else for its relief, would vanish if money were gone.

To see this more clearly, consider this one example. Take some poor and unfruitful year in which hunger has carried off many thousands of men. If the barns of the rich were searched at the end of the year, I maintain that enough grain would be found to feed everyone, and to save those who died from the famine and from the plague caused by the famine. How easily the bare needs of life might be provided, if money, which is meant to procure us the necessities of life, did not itself deter us! Certainly rich men know this. They also know that it would be more practicable to provide the necessities of life for everyone than to supply superfluities for a few, and much better to eradicate our innumerable evils than to be burdened with great concentrations of wealth.

If that one monster pride, the first and foremost of all evils, did not forbid it, the whole world would doubtless have adopted the laws of the Utopians long before this, drawn on by a rational perception of what each man's true interest is or else by the authority of Christ our Saviour, who in His great wisdom knows what is best and in His loving kindness bids us do it. Pride measures her prosperity not by her own goods but by others' wants. Pride would not deign to be a goddess, if there were no inferiors she could rule and triumph over. Her happiness shines brightly only in comparison to others' misery, and their poverty binds them and hurts them the more as her wealth is displayed. Pride is the infernal serpent that steals into the hearts of men, thwarting and holding them back from choosing the better way of life.

Pride is far too deeply rooted in men's hearts to be easily torn out. I am glad, therefore, that the Utopians have achieved their social organization, which I wish all mankind would imitate. Their institutions give their commonwealth a moral and social foundation for living happy lives, and as far as man can predict, these institutions will last forever. Because they have rooted out ambition and strife along with other vices, they are in no danger of civil wars, which have ruined many states that seemed secure. And as long as they maintain sound institutions and domestic harmony, they can never be overcome by the envious rulers near by, who have often attempted their ruin in vain.

Thus Raphael finished speaking. I admit that not a few things in the manners and laws of the Utopians seemed very absurd to me: their way of waging war, their religious customs, as well as other matters, but especially the keystone of their entire system, namely, their communal living without the use of money. This one thing takes away all the nobility, magnificence, splendor, and majesty which public opinion commonly regards as the true ornaments of a nation. But I saw that Raphael was tired with talking, and I was not sure that he could bear contradiction in these matters. I remembered that he had spoken ill of certain men who feared they would not be thought wise unless they could find something to criticize in other men's opinions.

So with praise for the Utopian institutions and for his account of them, I took him by the hand and led him in to supper, adding that we would find some other time for considering these things more thoroughly and for talking with him in greater detail about them. I hope that such an opportunity may come sometime. Meanwhile I cannot agree with everything that he said, though he was singularly well informed and also highly experienced in worldly affairs. Yet I must confess that there are many things in the Utopian Commonwealth that I wish rather than expect to see followed among our citizens.

1514–16   1516

HAKLUYT'S VOYAGES

For its knowledge of the sea dogs and the rise of English sea power the world is indebted to a self-effacing, industrious clergyman, "Richard Hakluyt, Preacher" (1553–1616). He was born, probably in London, in 1553, educated at Westminster School and Christ Church, Oxford, where he received his B.A. in 1574 and his M.A. three years later.

As a boy he visited his older cousin Richard, in the Middle Temple, and became so interested in the maps and globes he saw there that he dedicated the rest of his life to the study of English exploration. At Oxford he read all the extant travels in Greek, Latin, Italian, English, Spanish, and Portuguese. In 1582 he published his first book, *Divers Voyages touching The Discovery of America*, dedicated to Sir Philip Sidney. A year later he considered taking part in Gilbert's second voyage, but instead for five years took the post of chaplain to Sir Edward Stafford, ambassador to Paris. During this time he worked tirelessly bringing together all the accounts of the English voyages he could in any way secure. In 1589 he published the first folio editions of *The Principal Navigations, Traffics, Voyages, and Discoveries of the English Nation*, and enlarged it to a three-volume folio edition in 1598–1600.

Hakluyt was a conscientious editor of enormous industry. He was faithful to his sources and was judicious in cutting and revising ornately written accounts of voyages which came into his hands. To seek out the only living survivor of a Labrador expedition of 1536, he once traveled two hundred miles. He searched English and Continental libraries and talked with English and foreign sailors on their returns from voyages. He knew every mapmaker, traveler, merchant-adventurer, explorer, imperialist of his time; and even the great men of the court—Sidney, Walsingham, Howard—passed on what they knew to him. He never sailed himself, but he knew more than any sailor.

He was a quiet, pious man, but above all (as Professor Raleigh says) he was a "zealot for the map and flag." He received ecclesiastical preferment, finally becoming archdeacon of Westminster in 1603. At his death in 1616 his manuscripts passed to the Reverend Samuel Purchas, who published further accounts of the voyages based on Hakluyt's collections.

Throughout the *Principal Navigations* one can see constant strains of British character and the qualities which make the great collection so representative of the Elizabethan spirit. The desire to see new worlds is interwoven with the lust for gold and with the hope of conquest. Along with the expressed missionary idea of adding new nations to Protestantism is the mounting hatred of Spain. The dogged energy and zeal of English navigators and seamen, which few praise even from their enemies, is graphically depicted. Fighters like Drake, Hawkins, and Grenville, dreamers such as Ralegh, empire visionaries like Gilbert, and gentlemen-adventurers like Essex crowd Hakluyt's pages.

From The Principal Navigations, Traffics, Voyages, and Discoveries of the English Nation

From *A brief and true report of the new-found land of Virginia: of the commodities there found, and to be raised, as well merchantable as others. Written by Thomas Hariot, servant to Sir Walter Ralegh, a member of the colony and there employed in discovering a full twelve-month.*[1]

OF THE NATURE AND MANNERS OF THE PEOPLE

It resteth I speak a word or two of the natural inhabitants, their natures and manners, leaving large discourse thereof until time more convenient hereafter. Now only so far forth, as that you may know how they in respect of troubling our inhabiting and planting, are not to be feared, but that they shall have cause both to fear and love us, that shall inhabit with them.

They are a people clothed with loose mantles made of deerskins, and aprons of the same round about their middles, all else naked, of such a difference of stature only as we in England, having no edge tools or weapons of iron or steel to offend us withal, neither know they how to make any. Those weapons that they have, are only bows made of witch hazel and arrows of reeds, flat-edged truncheons also of wood about a yard long, neither have they anything to defend themselves but targets[2] made of barks, and some armors made of sticks wickered together with thread.

Their towns are but small, and near the seacoast but few, some containing but ten or twelve houses, some twenty; the greatest that we have seen has been but of thirty houses. If they be walled, it is only done with barks of trees made fast to stakes, or else with poles only fixed upright and close one by another.

1. This was "The third voyage made by a ship sent in the year 1586, to the relief of the Colony planted in Virginia, at the sole charges of Sir Walter Ralegh" (*The Principal Navigations*, Hakluyt Society ed., VIII, 346). The expedition was under the leadership of Sir Richard Greville. Thomas Hariot (1560– 1621) was a mathematician and astronomer, mathematical tutor to Ralegh, and surveyor on the 1586 voyage. His *Brief and True Report* was first issued in 1588; Hakluyt included it in *The Principal Navigations* in 1600.
2. Shields.

Their houses are made of small poles, made fast at the tops in round form after the manner as is used in many arbories in our gardens of England, in most towns covered with barks, and in some with artificial mats made of long rushes, from the tops of the houses down to the ground. The length of them is commonly double to the breadth; in some places they are but twelve and sixteen yards long, and in some other we have seen of four-and-twenty.

In some places of the country, one only town belongs to the government of a *Wiroans* or Chief Lord, in other some two or three, in some six, eight, and more. The greatest Wiroans that yet we had dealing with had but eighteen towns in his government and able to make not above seven or eight hundred fighting men at the most. The language of every government is different from any other, and the further they are distant, the greater is the difference.

Their manner of wars amongst themselves is either by sudden surprising one another most commonly about the dawning of the day, or moonlight, or else by ambushes, or some subtle devices. Set battles are very rare, except it fall out where there are many trees, where either party may have some hope of defense, after the delivery of every arrow, in leaping behind some or other.

If there fall out any wars between us and them, what their fight is likely to be, we having advantages against them so many manner of ways, as by our discipline, our strange weapons and devices else, especially ordnance great and small, it may easily be imagined, by the experience we have had in some places, the turning up of their heels against us in running away was their best defense.

In respect of us they are a people poor, and for want of skill and judgment in the knowledge and use of our things, do esteem our trifles before things of greater value. Notwithstanding, in their proper manner (considering the want of such means as we have), they seem very ingenious. For although they have no such tools, nor any such crafts, sciences, and arts as we, yet in those things they do, they show excellency of wit.[3] And by how much they upon due consideration shall find our manner of knowledges and crafts to exceed theirs in perfection, and speed for doing or execution, by so much the more is it probable that they should desire our friendship and love, and have the greater respect for pleasing and obeying us. Whereby may be hoped, if means of good government be used, that they may in short time be brought to civility and the embracing of true religion.

Some religion they have already, which although it be far from the truth, yet being as it is, there is hope it may be the easier and sooner reformed.

They believe that there are many gods, which they call *Mantoac*,

3. I.e., intelligence.

but of different sorts and degrees, one only chief and great god, which hath been from all eternity. Who, as they affirm, when he purposed to make the world, made first other gods of a principal order to be as means and instruments to be used in the creation and government to follow, and after the sun, moon, and stars as petty gods, and the instruments of the other order more principal. First, they say, were made waters, out of which by the gods was made all diversity of creatures that are visible or invisible.

For mankind, they say a woman was made first which, by the working of one of the gods, conceived and brought forth children. And in such sort, they say, they had their beginning. But how many years or ages have passed since, they say they can make no relation, having no letters nor other such means as we to keep records of the particularities of times past, but only tradition from father to son.

They think that all the gods are of human shape, and therefore, they represent them by images in the forms of men, which they call *Kewasowok*, one alone is called *Kewas*. These they place in houses appropriate or temples, which they call *Machicomuck*, where they worship, pray, sing, and make many times offering unto them. In some Machicomuck, we have seen but one Kewas, in some two, and in other some three. The common sort think them to be also gods.

They believe also the immortality of the soul that, after this life as soon as the soul is departed from the body, according to the works it hath done, it is either carried to heaven, the habitat of gods, there to enjoy perpetual bliss and happiness, or else to a great pit or hole, which they think to be in the furthest parts of their part of the world toward the sunset, there to burn continually. The place they call *Popogusso*.

For the confirmation of this opinion, they told me two stories of two men that had been lately dead and revived again. The one happened, but a few years before our coming into the country, of a wicked man, which having been dead and buried, the next day the earth of the grave being seen to move, was taken up again, who made declaration where his soul had been. That is to say, very near entering into Popogusso, had not one of the gods saved him, and gave him leave to return again and teach his friends what they should do to avoid that terrible place of torment. The other happened in the same year we were there, but in a town that was sixty miles from us, and it was told me for strange news, that one being dead, buried, and taken up again as the first, showed that although his body had lain dead in the grave, yet his soul was alive and had traveled far in a long broad way, on both sides whereof grew most delicate and pleasant trees, bearing more rare and excellent fruits, than ever he had seen before or was able to express, and at length came to most brave and fair houses, near which he met his father that had been dead before, who gave him great charge to go back again and show his friends what good they were to do to enjoy the pleasures of that place, which when he had done he should after come again.

What subtlety soever be in the Wiroances and priests, this opinion worked so much in many of the common and simple sort of people, that it maketh them have great respect to their governors, and also great care what they do, to avoid torment after death, and to enjoy bliss, although notwithstanding there is punishment ordained for malefactors, as stealers, whoremongers, and other sort of wicked-doers, some punished with death, some with forfeitures,[4] some with beating, according to the greatness of the facts.

And this is the sum of their religion, which I learned by having special familiarity with some of their priests. Wherein they were not so sure grounded, nor gave such credit to their traditions and stories, but through conversing with us they were brought into great doubts of their own, and no small admiration of ours, with earnest desire in many, to learn more than we had means for want of perfect utterance in their language to express.

Most things they saw with us, as mathematical instruments, sea compasses, the virtue of the lodestone in drawing iron, a perspective glass whereby was showed many strange sights,[5] burning glasses, wild fireworks, guns, hooks, writing and reading, spring-clocks that seem to go of themselves, and many other things that we had were so strange unto them, and so far exceeded their capacities to comprehend the reason and means how they should be made and done, that they thought they were rather the works of gods than of men, or at the leastwise, they had been given and taught us by the gods. Which made many of them have such opinion of us, as that if they knew not the truth of God and religion already, it was rather to be had from us whom God so specially loved, than from a people that were so simple as they found themselves to be in comparison of us. Whereupon greater credit was given unto that we spoke of, concerning such matters.

Many times and in every town where I came, according as I was able, I made declaration of the contents of the Bible, that therein was set forth the true and only God, and his mighty works, that therein was contained the true doctrine of salvation through Christ, with many particulars of miracles and chief points of religion, as I was able then to utter, and thought fit for the time. And although I told them the book materially and of itself was not of any such virtue, as I thought they did conceive, but only the doctrine therein contained, yet would many be glad to touch it, to embrace it, to kiss it, to hold it to their breasts and heads, and stroke over all their

4. Fines.
5. The "perspective glass" was a tele- scope; the "burning glass" a mirror used to concentrate the sun's rays.

body with it, to show their hungry desire of that knowledge which was spoken of.

The Wiroans with whom we dwelt, called Wingina, and many of his people would be glad many times to be with us at our prayers, and many times call upon us both in his own town, as also in others whither he sometimes accompanied us, to pray and sing psalms, hoping thereby to be partaker of the same effects which we by that means also expected.

Twice this Wiroans was so grievously sick that he was like to die, and as he lay languishing, doubting of any help by his own priests, and thinking he was in such danger for offending us and thereby our God, sent for some of us to pray and be a means to our God that it would please him either that he might live, or after death dwell with him in bliss, so likewise were the requests of many others in the like case.

On a time also when their corn began to wither by reason of a drought which happened extraordinarily, fearing that it had come to pass by reason that in something they had displeased us, many would come to us and desire us to pray to our God of England, that he would preserve their corn, promising that when it was ripe we also should be partakers of the fruit.

* * * Some people could not tell whether to think us gods or men, and the rather because that all the space of their sickness, there was no man of ours known to die, or that was specially sick. They noted also that we had no women amongst us, neither that we did care for any of theirs.

Some, therefore, were of opinion that we were not born of women, and therefore not mortal, but that we were men of an old generation many years past, then risen again to immortality.

Some would likewise seem to prophesy that there were more of our generation yet to come to kill theirs and take their places as some thought the purpose was, by that which was already done. Those that were immediately to come after us they imagined to be in the air, yet invisible and without bodies, and that they by our entreaty and for the love of us did make the people to die in that sort as they did, by shooting invisible bullets into them.

To confirm this opinion, their physicians (to excuse their ignorance in curing the disease) would not be ashamed to say, but earnestly make the simple people believe that the strings of blood that they sucked out of the sick bodies, were the strings wherewithal the invisible bullets were tied and cast. Some also thought that we shot them ourselves out of our pieces, from the place where we dwelt, and killed the people in any town that had offended us, as we listed, how far distant from us soever it were. And other some said that it was the special work of God for our sakes, as we ourselves have cause in some sort to think no less, whatsoever some do, or may imagine to the contrary, specially some astrologers, knowing of the eclipse of the sun which we saw the same year before in our voyage thitherward, which unto them appeared very terrible. And also of a comet which began to appear but a few days before the beginning of the said sickness. But to exclude them from being the special causes of so special an accident, there are further reasons than I think fit at this present to be alleged. These their opinions I have set down the more at large, that it may appear unto you that there is good hope they may be brought through discreet dealing and government to the embracing of the truth, and consequently to honor, obey, fear, and love us.

And although some of our company towards the end of the year showed themselves too fierce in slaying some of the people in some towns, upon causes that on our part might easily enough have been borne withal, yet notwithstanding, because it was on their part justly deserved, the alteration of their opinions generally and for the most part concerning us is the less to be doubted. And whatsoever else they may be, by carefulness of ourselves need nothing at all to be feared.

The course which Sir Francis Drake held from the haven of Guatulco in the South Sea on the back side of Nueva Espanna to the northwest of California as far as forty-three degrees, and his return back along the said coast to thirty-eight degrees, where finding a fair and goodly haven,[6] he landed; and staying there many weeks, and discovering many excellent things in the country and great show of rich mineral matter and being offered the dominion of the country by the lord of the same, he took possession thereof in the behalf of her Majesty, and named it Nova Albion.

We kept our course from the Isle of Cano, which lieth in eight degrees of northerly latitude, and within two leagues of the main of Nicaragua, where we calked and trimmed our ship, along the coast of Nueva Espanna, until we came to the haven and town of Guatulco, which, as we were informed, had but seventeen Spaniards dwelling in it, and we found it to stand in fifteen degrees and fifty minutes.

As soon as we were entered this haven we landed, and went presently to the town and to the town house, where we found a judge sitting in judgment, he being associate with three other officers, upon three Negroes that had conspired the burning of the town, both which judges and prisoners we took, and brought them a-shipboard and caused the chief judge to write his letter to the town, to command all the townsmen to avoid, that we might safely water there. Which being done, and they departed, we ransacked the

6. I.e., San Francisco Bay. "Guatulco": Acapulco.

town and in one house we found a pot of the quantity of a bushel full of royals[7] of plate, which we brought to our ship.

And here one Thomas Moone, one of our company, took a Spanish gentleman as he was flying out of the town, and searching him, he found a chain of gold about him and other jewels, which we took and so let him go.

At this place our general among other Spaniards, set ashore his Portugal pilot, which he took at the Island of Cape Verde, out of a ship of Saint Marie port of Portugal, and having set them ashore, we departed thence.

Our general at this place and time thinking himself both in respect of his private injuries received from the Spaniards, as also of their contempts and indignities offered to our country and prince in general, sufficiently satisfied, and revenged, and supposing that her Majesty at his return would rest contented with this service, purposed to continue no longer upon the Spanish coasts, but began to consider and to consult of the best way for his country.

He thought it not good to return by the straits, for two special causes: the one, lest the Spaniards should there wait and attend for him in great number and strength, whose hands he, being left but one ship, could not possibly escape. The other cause was the dangerous situation of the mouth of the straits of the south side, with continual storms raining and blustering, as he found by experience, besides the shoals and sands upon the coast. Wherefore he thought it not a good course to adventure that way. He resolved therefore to avoid these hazards, to go forward to the islands of the Malucas, and there hence to sail the course of the Portugals by the Cape of Bona Sperança.

Upon this resolution, he began to think of his best way for the Malucas, and finding himself, where he now was, becalmed, he saw that of necessity he must be enforced to take a Spanish course, namely to sail somewhat northerly to get a wind. We therefore set sail and sailed 800 leagues at the least for a good wind, and thus much we sailed from the 16th of April (after our old style) till the third of June.

The fifth day of June, being in forty-three degrees towards the Arctic pole, being speedily come out of the extreme heat, we found the air so cold, that our men being pinched with the same, complained of the extremity thereof, and the further we went, the more the cold increased upon us, whereupon we thought it best for that time to seek land, and did so, finding it not mountainous, but low plainland, and we drew back again without landing, till we came within thirty-eight degrees towards the line. In which height it pleased God to send us into a fair and good bay, with a good wind to enter the same.

7. Gold coins.

In this bay we anchored the seventeenth of June, and the people of the country, having their houses close by the water's side, showed themselves unto us, and sent a present to our general.

When they came unto us, they greatly wondered at the things which we brought, but our general, according to his natural and accustomed humanity, courteously entreated them, and liberally bestowed on them necessary things to cover their nakedness, whereupon they supposed us to be gods, and would not be persuaded to the contrary. The presents which they sent unto our general were feathers and cawls[8] of net work.

Their houses are digged round about with earth, and have from the uttermost brims of the circle clefts of wood set upon them, joining close together at the top like a spire steeple, which by reason of that closeness are very warm.

Their bed is the ground with rushes strawed on it, and lying about the house, they have the fire in the midst. The men go naked, the women take bulrushes and kemb[9] them after the manner of hemp, and thereof make their loose garments, which being knit about their middles, hang down about their hips, having also about their shoulders a skin of deer, with the hair upon it. These women are very obedient and serviceable to their husbands.

After they were departed from us, they came and visited us the second time, and brought with them feathers and bags of tobacco for presents. And when they came to the top of the hill, at the bottom whereof we had pitched our tents, they stayed themselves, where one appointed for speaker wearied himself with making a long oration, which done, they left their bows upon the hill and came down with their presents.

In the meantime the women remaining on the hill, tormented themselves lamentably, tearing their flesh from their cheeks, whereby we perceived that they were about a sacrifice. In the meantime our general, with his company, went to prayer, and to reading of the Scriptures, at which exercise they were attentive and seemed greatly to be affected with it. But when they were come unto us they restored again unto us those things which before we had bestowed upon them.

The news of our being there being spread through the country, the people that inhabited round about came down, and amongst them the king himself, a man of a goodly stature, and comely personage,[1] with many other tall and warlike men, before whose coming were sent two ambassadors to our general, to signify that their king was coming, in doing of which message, their speech was continued about half an hour. This ended, they by signs requested

---

8. Hakluyt prints "cals," which may be netted baskets, or "cauls," netted caps or headdresses.
9. Comb.
1. Appearance.

our general to send something by their hand to their king, as a token that his coming might be in peace. Wherein our general having satisfied them, they returned with glad tidings to their king, who marched to us with a princely majesty, the people crying continually after their manner, and as they drew near unto us, so did they strive to behave themselves in their actions with comeliness.

In the forefront was a man of goodly personage, who bare the scepter or mace before the king, whereupon hanged two crowns, a less and a bigger, with three chains of a marvelous length. The crowns were made of knit-work wrought artificially with feathers of divers colors. The chains were made of a bony substance, and few be the persons among them that are admitted to wear them, and of that number also the persons are stinted, as some ten, some twelve, etc. Next unto him which bare the scepter, was the king himself, with his guard about his person, clad with cony[2] skins and other skins. After them followed the naked common sort of people, every one having his face painted, some with white, some with black, and other colors, and having in their hands one thing or other for a present, not so much as their children, but they also brought their presents.

In the meantime, our general gathered his men together, and marched within his fenced place, making against their approaching a very warlike show. They being trooped together in their order, and a general salutation being made, there was presently a general silence. Then he that bare the scepter before the king, being informed by another, whom they assigned to that office, with a manly and lofty voice, proclaimed that which the other spake to him in secret, continuing half an hour, which ended, and a general amen, as it were, given, the king, with the whole number of men and women (the children excepted) came down without any weapon, who descending to the foot of the hill, set themselves in order.

In coming towards our bulwarks and tents, the scepter-bearer began a song, observing his measures in a dance, and that with a stately countenance, whom the king with his guard, and every degree of persons following, did in like manner sing and dance, saving only the women, which danced and kept silence. The general permitted them to enter withour our bulwark, where they continued their song and dance a reasonable time. When they had satisfied themselves, they made signs to our general to sit down, to whom the king, and divers others made several orations, or rather supplication, that he would take their province and kingdom into his hand, and become their king, making signs that they would resign unto

2. Rabbit.

him their right and title of the whole land, and become his subjects. In which to persuade us the better, the king and the rest with
one consent and with great reverence, joyfully singing a song, did
set the crown upon his head, enriched his neck with all their chains
and offered unto him many other things, honoring him by the
name of *Hioh*, adding thereunto, as it seemed, a sign of triumph,
which thing our general thought not meet to reject, because he
knew not what honor and profit it might be to our country. Wherefore in the name, and to the use of her Majesty, he took the scepter, crown, and dignity of the said country in his hands, wishing
that the riches and treasure thereof might so conveniently be transported to the enriching of her kingdom at home, as it aboundeth in
the same.

The common sort of the people leaving the king and his guard
with our general, scattered themselves together with their sacrifices
among our people, taking a diligent view of every person; and such
as pleased their fancy (which were the youngest) they, enclosing
them about, offered their sacrifices unto them with lamentable
weeping, scratching, and tearing the flesh from their faces with
their nails, whereof issued abundance of blood. But we used signs to
them of disliking this, and stayed their hands from force, and
directed them upwards to the living God, whom only they ought to
worship. They showed unto us their wounds, and craved help of
them at our hands, whereupon we gave them lotions, plasters, and
ointments agreeing to the state of their griefs, beseeching God to
cure their diseases. Every third day they brought their sacrifices
unto us, until they understood our meaning, that we had no pleasure in them. Yet they could not be long absent from us, but daily
frequented our company to the hour of our departure, which departure seemed so grievous unto them, that their joy was turned into
sorrow. They entreated us, that being absent we would remember
them, and by stealth provided a sacrifice, which we disliked.

Our necessary business being ended, our general with his company traveled up into the country into their villages, where we
found herds of deer by a thousand in a company, being most large
and fat of body.

We found the whole country to be a warren of a strange kind of
conies, their bodies in bigness as be the Barbary conies, their heads
as the heads of ours, the feet of a want,[3] and the tail of a rat, being
of great length; under her chin on either side a bag into the which
she gathered her meat when she hath filled her belly abroad. The
people eat their bodies and make great account of their skins, for
their king's coat was made of them.

---

3. Mole.

Our general called this country, Nova Albion, and that for two causes: the one in respect of the white banks and cliffs, which lie towards the sea, and the other, because it might have some affinity with our country in name, which sometime was so called.

There is no part of earth here to be taken up, wherein there is not some special likelihood of gold or silver.

At our departure hence our general set up a monument of our being there, as also of her Majesty's right and title to the same, namely, a plate nailed upon a fair great post, whereupon was engraven her Majesty's name, the day and year of our arrival there, with the free giving up of the province and people into her Majesty's hands, together with her Highness' picture and arms,[4] in a piece of sixpence of current English money under the plate, whereunder was also written the name of our general.

It seemeth that the Spaniards hitherto had never been in this part of the country, neither did ever discover the land by many degrees to the southwards of this place.

1600

4. This brass plate is presently in the Library of the University of California.

The Seventeenth Century

(1603-1660)

(1588: The Spanish Armada.)
1603: Death of Elizabeth Tudor, accession of James Stuart.
1605: The Gunpowder Plot; last effort of English Catholic extremists.
1620: First emigration of Pilgrims to the New World.
1625: Death of James I, accession of Charles I.
1641: Outbreak of Civil War: closing of the theaters.
1649: Execution of Charles I, beginning of Commonwealth and Protectorate, known inclusively as the Interregnum (1649–60).
1660: End of the Protectorate, Restoration of Charles II.
(1688: Abdication of James II, last Stuart king of England.)

In its narrowest definition, the "17th century" reaches from the accession of the first Stuart king (James I) in 1603 to the restoration of the third (Charles II) in 1660. But the events of those years are meaningful only if seen in a pattern extending from 1588 to 1688. Between these two outer dates occurred those massive social events which, in their cumulative effect, bridge the gap between the Tudor autocracy of the 16th century and the ill-defined but functioning constitutional monarchy of the 18th century. At the center of the period lies the Puritan Revolution of 1640–60. The quarrels and controversies which culminated in this upheaval began to make themselves felt shortly after 1588; its tremors and aftershocks largely subsided after 1688. In more senses than one, the Revolution was the central event of the century.

Armada year marked a decisive turning point in the reign of Elizabeth. Like most of her subjects, she had expected the nation's supreme triumph over a long-awaited, much-hated invader to release a tide of patriotic good feeling. Nothing of the sort happened; on the contrary. Social problems which had long lain suppressed in the interests of national unity suddenly surfaced when the nation was secure. They gave rise to bitter and divisive quarrels, fought out for the most part between the aging queen and her successive parliaments. There were disputes over the government of the church, disputes over foreign policy, disputes over monopolies and special forms of economic privilege, disputes over parliamentary rights and immunities.

These were conflicts too deep to be solved by the queen's traditional measures of cajolery and grandiose rhetoric; and they were not solved, nor even alleviated. Neither did the peaceful accession of James, the first English monarch of the Stuart family, serve to mollify these quarrels; they festered throughout his reign, and grew inflamed under the autocratic rule of his son, Charles I. By 1640 they were ready to flare into full-scale revolution, and flare they did. In the wars that followed, the forces of insurrection were successful in one of their aims (they rendered Charles powerless), but not in another (they failed to set up a stable government, free from the faults of the one they had destroyed). The military dictatorship (1649–60) established first by Oliver Cromwell under the name of Commonwealth and then maintained even after his death as a Protectorate was no more than a makeshift effort to contain a political instability that had got out of hand. When Charles II was recalled from exile (1660) and put back on his father's throne but without his father's powers, it became clear that England was bound to have, in religion and politics, some sort of organization looser than anyone had anticipated, looser than anyone really wanted. But its exact form was subject to constant pulling and hauling among the parties, and no solid settlement was reached till 1688, when Charles's brother and successor, James II, was ejected from the throne and sent into exile. After 1688, its social problems compromised if not solved, the country settled down to a long constitutional nap under a series of monarchs who made little trouble for their parliaments and therefore had little trouble with their thrones. The crisis was over.

Though infinitely complex in details, the main social problems which exercised the 17th century can be broadly stated, with their solutions, in two sentences. In the religious sphere, the basic issue was: How far should the reformation of the Protestant church be carried? and the solution accomplished in 1688 was, "As far as each individual self-defined religious group wants." In the sphere of constitutional politics, the basic issue was: How much authority should the monarch have independent of the parliament? and the solution accomplished in 1688 was, "Almost none."

BEFORE AND AFTER THE PURITAN REVOLT

To visualize the immense changes wrought by the crisis years of the Puritan Revolt, and their relation to the quality of English literature, it may be useful to anatomize very roughly the value-structure of English society before and after the event. Oversimplifications are inevitable, but necessary to point up a set of broad changes which actually took place; and definitions are possible because the Revolution was preceded and followed by periods of relative order and tranquillity. Under Elizabeth Tudor the court was the undisputed center of national authority, influence, power, reward, and intellectual inspiration. Careers were made and fortunes established through court connections. London was the center of the kingdom, and the court was the unchallenged center of London. Particularly was this true in matters of the intellect, of literature and the arts. The characteristic forms of literature under Elizabeth were courtly. Courtiers patronized the theater by attending plays (of which the middle class generally disapproved) and by lending the prestige of their names to different acting companies. The sonnet sequence, the pastoral romance (Sidney's *Arcadia*), the chivalric allegory (Spenser's *Faerie Queene*), the learned sermon, the erotic idyll (*Hero and Leander* or *Venus and Adonis*), the masque, the epic—all these were courtly forms, implying courtly readers. Patronage flowed, when it flowed at all, from courtly donors; and, apart from the precarious rewards of the theater, patronage was almost the only way for a man to live by his writing. The same pattern continued under the first two Stuarts, James I and Charles I. Whether in his sermons or in his poems, a man like Donne wrote primarily for courtiers. Versatile and various as he was, Ben Jonson channeled almost all his energies into writing for court and courtiers. Carew, Suckling, Lovelace, and a host of lesser writers were themselves courtiers, simply in the sense that they spent much of their time at court. A man like George Herbert was much remarked because he could have been a courtier and chose not to be. There were exceptions, of course; country doctors and rural parsons sometimes exercised themselves in literature. But the court influence was predominant, and so far as a literary society existed, it took its tone from the court. Because court circles were narrow, a poet did not have to wait for publication in order to be widely known among his fellow poets. Manuscript collections of poems by one author, or by several, circulated through the court; a poem could become popular, be set to music several times over, and yet never appear in print. The books that were printed generally appeared in small editions, and being destined for a particular audience, could take a good deal for granted in the way of special background and training. A court preacher like Lancelot Andrewes assumed in his hearers acquaintance with at least the rudiments of three ancient languages; Sir Philip Sidney in the *Arcadia* assumed familiarity with the traditions and conventions of courtly behavior. For court society had many characteristic and distinctive values. It implied a belief in hierarchical order within a strict framework of uniformity, involving obedience to the national church, loyalty to the national monarch. Within that framework, it tended to produce intricate, allusive, and highly decorative writing. Courtiers generally valued the heroic passions—love (but not necessarily marriage), warfare (largely free of a political context), and devotional piety (quite apart from practical morality). The controlling principle behind all these distinctions was an emphasis upon honor as the supreme principle in life, not to be estimated in any way by criteria of mere prudence. Literature written within this framework and primarily for readers who accepted it tended generally to reflect its arrangement of values.

After 1660, and even more strikingly after 1688, the pattern of values was quite different. For one thing, the court was no longer an unchallenged center of intellectual and literary influence. It did not have the power, social and financial, to be anything of the sort. For now money and influence no longer flowed exclusively from the court. London City (a network of banks and merchants, jobbers, financiers, brokers, tradesmen, and credit-managers) was one rival source of power and influence; Parliament itself, which in 1688 would assert decisive power over the throne by expelling James II and appointing a Dutchman to be his successor as William III, was another. Instead of standing above interest as the sole fountain of honor, the court thus became in effect one of several competing interests. The relatively conservative "landed interest" tended toward the court, as the more innovative "money interest" found its chief support in the City; and Parliament men, ranking themselves under the deliberately meaningless nicknames of "Tory" and "Whig," sided with either interest as they chose or with both as they found the occasion proper. One's connection with an interest was not through the inflexible principle of honor, but through the flexible one of . . . interest.

In precisely the same way, the established church, which had once claimed to be the sole guardian of men's spiritual welfare and therefore of their worldly behavior—the authoritative voice disciplining every Englishman's private interests—became after 1660 simply one of many possible religious communities. The Puritan sects, originally factions within the English church, had been freed to multiply and develop their independence during the Interregnum; after the Restoration, they could not be got back into the English (Anglican) church by force or persuasion. When several sects exist side by side in open competition, they are all voluntary. Each interprets Scripture after its own fashion, each follows its own moral code, each tries to attract proselytes, all agree in not trying to persecute one another. But that creates problems of discipline; if a member does not like the social code of his sect, he transfers to a more understanding sect, or out of them all. When neither monarch nor church could control social and economic behavior, most of it passed out of control altogether. For morality in a social or business sense applies mainly to people, considered as responsible economic agents; and the new forms of economic organization involved either artificial personalities or legal fictions to which moral laws do not apply. Corporations and joint-stock companies, cartels and syndicates, mutual-aid societies and credit unions, banks and bankers' combines (a whole gamut of anonymous voluntary associations) began to develop England piecemeal, amorphously, after the fashion of a modern capitalist nation. New money brought to the fore new men, enterprising and respectable, but with few pretensions to courtly manners or intellectual sophistication. The literature which appealed to them was less dogmatic and moralistic than the old hell-and-damnation puritanism; it was more serious than the frankly bawdy wit of the Restoration stage. Observing these and other divergencies of taste, enterprising publishers began to aim their products at a particular market, in which they specialized. Before long, they were hiring writers to turn out titles on order. The "booksellers," as they were called, thus replaced the older courtly patrons as makers of public taste. Authors who wrote to order at the bidding of publishers became known collectively, from the cheap lodgings where they congregated, as Grub Street authors. For them, at least, the change from a society organized around honor to one organized around interest was very palpable indeed.

Around the broad social changes sketched above there took place a set of intellectual and spiritual changes, no less striking and significant. The Elizabethan monarchy and church had been hierarchical in organization because that was thought to be the inevitable structure of things, the natural pattern of the world. Every creature had his place in the great order of divine appointments; and the different families of being were bound together by a chain of universal analogy. The king was to his subjects as Michael was to the other archangels, as the bishop was to his pastors, as the lion was to other beasts, as the eagle was to other birds, as the diamond was to other stones, as gold was to other metals. The head ruled the other parts of the body because, as the seat of reason, it was nobler. Reason, which ruled in man, made him natural head of the family because passion was thought to rule in woman. The king was head of the body politic; in him, reason ruled as it ought, over the passionate and tumultuous multitude. And all this ruling was necessary because of Adam's fall, as a result of which not only human psychology but the whole structure of the universe had been disordered. Though they differed over the form of the rule and the name of the ruler, almost all the contestants in the civil wars agreed that the people needed strict discipline of some sort, because in themselves they were radically imperfect. While the various leaders were disputing over details, the people, simply as a result of slow experience (by living under an "illegitimate" authority, without any sort of religious conformity), demonstrated that they were less imperfect, and needed less rigid discipline, than had been supposed.

One universal truth emerged from the Revolution and Civil Wars—that no one universal truth was to be had, whether by sword, by prayer, or by study. Nor was it really needed. Individuals, it seemed, could hold differing views about foreign policy, the nature of Christ's presence in the sacrament, or the lawfulness of infant baptism, without necessarily precipitating social chaos. A single true belief in these matters, and in many, many others, was evidently unnecessary. And thus the whole notion of human beings as radically fallen creatures, who needed a special saving truth and a dose of stiff discipline to redeem their faults began fading toward obsolescence. A reasonable person (one who behaved sensibly and didn't bother his or her neighbor) seemed to be almost as good as need be. In a long list of controversies, over which people had once been willing to slit throats, it turned out that nobody was right and nobody was wrong. And thus the English community changed from one founded on the concepts of hierarchy, uniformity, and personal relatedness, to one founded on the concepts of multiplicity, disparity, and toleration. In less than a hundred years, the nation had passed from enlightened, inept autocracy to a vigorous, materialistic pluralism.

LITERARY CROSS-CURRENTS

With the obvious and immensely important exception of Milton, hardly any of the high literature (*belles lettres*) of the 17th century was the work of Puritans or men sympathetic to the Puritan cause. This is hardly surprising. Many early Puritans looked with misgivings on the secular imagination. They mistrusted literature on the same principle that they mistrusted statues (graven idols), church music, and elaborate religious rituals. These were all allurements and enticings of the sensual world; they threatened to contaminate and diffuse the pure spiritual energy of divinely infused faith. Yet a sense of deep disquiet, of ancient traditions under challenge, is everywhere felt in the early 17th century; and it can hardly be accounted for except as a response to the growing challenge—social, political, and religious—which ultimately took form in the Revolt.

One may well think of the metaphysical poets who followed Donne (Herbert, Crashaw, Vaughan, Cowley, Cleveland) as trying to draw out the traditional lyric of love and devotion by stretching it, under deliberate mental pressure, to encompass new unities from which a sense of strain and violent effort was rarely absent. In the opposite direction, Jonson and his "sons" the Cavalier poets (Carew, Herrick, Suckling, Waller, Davenant) generally tried to compress and limit their poems, giving them a high finish and a strong sense of easy domination at the expense of their explicit intellectual content. Though these alternate "schools" do not by any means represent watertight compartments (Donne himself wrote some Jonsonian-style poems, Jonson some which sound quite like Donne), the broad contrast of "Cavalier" with "metaphysical" does describe two major poetic alternatives of the early century. Yet both styles were wholly inadequate containers for the sort of gigantic energy which Milton, for example, was seeking to express.

For Milton, with his deep sense of moral imperative, his heroic ambitions for poetry, his proud Englishness, all the fashionable verses of his contemporaries must have seemed unbearably constricting. Like any great poet, Milton was capable of profiting from the study of craftsmen whom he had no intention of imitating; and he did profit by a study of Donne and Jonson, we may be sure. But for his central inspiration he reached back beyond both metaphysicals and cavaliers, to the figure of Spenser. In his youth particularly his mind ran to Spenserian projects—chivalric romances based on Arthurian themes or sometimes on scriptural stories. Milton's style was thus fully formed by the period of the late 1630's—he found his voice, it is usual to say, in *Lycidas* (1637)—but what he defined as his "duty" kept him through the next twenty years at the uncongenial labor of producing topical prose pamphlets on public affairs. When he finally brought it forth in 1667, *Paradise Lost* appeared to be a poem written by a man formed in one civilization for an audience reared in another.

In fact, Milton's poem had some trouble finding even that "fit audience though few" which the poet hoped for it; the poem actually had to make its own audience, as it started to do toward the end of the century. (One of its strongest sponsors was Lord Somers, chief legal craftsman of the 1688 settlement.) Milton's gains were made partly at the expense, and partly with the help, of the Restoration's most representative poet, John Dryden. The heroic couplets which were Dryden's favored poetic vehicle had developed only gradually, in the hands of the Cavalier poets, from a rather jolting and irregular meter toward the poised and sinewy units out of which Dryden built his verse-paragraphs. These couplets were less choked with learning than Milton's blank verse; their sentence-units were shorter, and logical or pseudo-logical argumentation played a greater part in the structure. Dryden is more a poet of statement, Milton more a poet of suggestion. But both are architects in verse, though Milton builds a cathedral, Dryden an elegant townhouse. And it is pleasant to record that the lesser poet, who had received so much public acclaim, was generous in his appreciation of the greater poet, who knew so little of it.

During the twenty years of Puritan rule at mid-century, most of the theaters were closed and hardly anything was written for the stage; during this period, most of the old actors and playwrights died, and the revival of the English stage after 1660 depended very largely on the work of one man, Sir William Davenant, and on the example of the French stage, then at its height. Shakespeare's emulators and successors under the first two Stuarts were much influenced by the melancholy then so largely prevalent; the dark, oppressive mood is almost unbroken in the work of tragic writers such as Webster, Ford, Tourneur, and Middleton. But alongside this somber and sometimes morbid tragedy, almost serving as relief from it, flourished a great variety of tragicomic spectacles, romantic comedies, and pastoral fantasies. Very often these plays were influenced by the masques so popular at court

—that is, they included a great deal in the way of spectacle, display, pageant, music, and sometimes fantasy. Though Shakespeare was long dead, though Jonson was in his dotage, and though none of the successors to these two men met their measure, the stage continued vigorously active right up to the Civil War. But then the theaters were shut, abruptly and apparently forever. When they reopened in 1660, they were forced at first to rely on a backlog of twenty-year-old plays. But gradually they built up a repertoire of comedies (generally bawdy) and tragedies in the rhetorical, declamatory manner which gave them, quite as much as the heroic couplets in which they were cast, the name of "heroic tragedies." Both these fashions, like so much else in the Reformation, were extreme and temporary. Dryden, who practiced both modes, lived to see them both at an end—the heroic tragedies under the weight of their own pomposity, the bawdy comedies under the attack of an infuriated clergyman, Jeremy Collier.

Beyond, perhaps outside, literature as such lies a change in the intellectual tone of the century which cannot be ignored, hard as it is to describe. The great minds of the early century were lawyers and theologians. Coke, Bacon, Selden, and Spelman among the lawyers, Laud, Andrewes, Cudworth, Ussher, and Chillingworth among the theologians were men famous in their generation. Among the lawyers, some are still consulted as authorities to this day—Coke is a name to conjure with in English law, and Selden's treatise on *Titles of Honor* is obsolete only because the subject itself is. As for the theologians, their work too has ceased to be "relevant"; but a brief browsing expedition through the "Library of Anglo-Catholic Theology" cannot fail to convince the student that they were men who worked—in their chosen trade—to very high standards of precise and authoritative scholarship. And yet, as the century's intellectual weather changed, these disciplines ceased to be at the center of things. There were great lawyers after 1660, but they were not the makers and shakers of society; there were famous clergymen, but they were not the builders of society's central codes of belief. Starting about mid-century, the great names belong to other disciplines—they are scientists like the astronomers Hooke and Halley, the physicist Robert Boyle, Locke the physician-philosopher, John Wallis and Sir Isaac Newton the mathematicians, William Harvey the anatomist. Few of them set out consciously to reconstruct an entire view of the cosmos, and Sir Isaac, who did so most successfully, retained to the end streaks and patches of the old beliefs. (He wrote a commentary on the Book of Revelation which has rather baffled those who admire his scientific work.) But the coming of a secular, materialist world view was in the air; even before the Puritans were forced to give up their dream of a community of saints, the tide had set and was ebbing rapidly another way.

BIRTH AND DEATH OF LITERARY FORMS

The stress and strain of a revolutionary age can thus be read at large in the century's literature, from the somber, sluggish melancholy of the early decades, through the hoarse, incoherent warfare of the middle years, to the slow firming up of new standards of decorum and correctness after 1660. Still another mark of violent change is provided by the number of literary forms which perished in the course of the century, even as others were being born.

Sonnets, for example, were all the rage in the last years of Elizabeth, the first years of James. Almost always they dealt with erotic themes, often they were linked together in sequences to suggest, if not to tell, a story. Donne turned the sonnet primarily to religious themes (of his *Songs and Sonnets*, only one, and it irregular, is actually a sonnet); Milton's sonnets are few and mostly political. And thereafter sonnets largely faded from the poetic repertory. Like epic poetry in our own day, sonnets just disappeared. Allegory suffered an even more curious fate. It was of course the essential method of Spenser's great poem, and a major ingredient in Milton's; the "highest" and most demanding poetry of the earlier age made use of it. But then again, in the last half of the century, it largely faded from view. Dryden did not accommodate his mind easily to allegory; when he did use it (as in *The Hind and the Panther*), there was a kind of grotesque comedy about it, as if the form were fundamentally a joke. Serious and explicit allegory had slid far down the social scale; it was now the natural mode for an inspired primitive like Bunyan.

Before the killing frosts of Puritanism, the masque and madrigal both perished. The one was a courtly, the other a popular, form; but both were suspect as vain, sensual, and worldly. Madrigals, as a blend of folk- and art-songs deeply rooted in the indigenous culture, were particularly to be regretted. For many years they had been sung in the yeoman's home or merchant's parlor, to the accompaniment of a chest of viols, that is, a consort of stringed instruments. Many involved complex polyphonic harmonies; many had been composed by distinguished musicians. But because it was an art that tended to make men happy with their present state, instead of wretched and guilty as they should have been, the Puritans disapproved: they wanted, instead of a "nest of singing birds," a nation of psalm-singers. So all the folk-arts and folk-customs faded—rounds and carols and madrigals, square-dancing, Maypoles, and rural games—to make way for the dreary, vacant English sabbath.

Despite the immense examples of Shakespeare and Milton, blank verse lost ground during the century to the rhymed couplet. Couplets had been written, in one form or another, since Chaucer's day, but only after midcentury did they take on the smooth, antithetical energy best exemplified in the opening lines of *Absalom and Achitophel*. They are a superb meter for argumentation—which was what Dryden did best. Alongside this regularizing of poetic surfaces went a vogue for extravagant and irregular odes after the manner of the Greek lyric poet Pindar. Jonson had known Pindar's work, and the *Ode on Cary and Morison* illustrates the rather severe conception he had of Pindaric form. Abraham Cowley in his *Pindarique Odes* (1656) set the example for greater irregularity in an effort to simulate greater violence of feeling, and his example was followed by Dryden, and later by Gray, not to speak of Wordsworth. Dryden's odes were sometimes set to music after a fashion imported from Italy and known by the Italian name of *oratorio*. He also wrote texts for operas, including one based on Milton's epic; opera too was an exotic form imported from Italy via France. After the indigenous madrigal and masque perished, their place was filled by imported oratorios and operas.

Satire, which had been a self-conscious novelty at the beginning of the century, was a well-established, almost a normal mode of poetry by the end;

more explanation was called for when one didn't write satire than when one did. In the process, satire grew subtler and more various; the satirist recognized his responsibility to divert the reader as well as to insult his antagonist. Indeed, a whole new tone of gentlemanly discourse grew up after the Restoration; it went by the name of "raillery," or sometimes "banter"—and while silly things could be said in it, so too could serious and important truths, about which nonetheless a gentleman might not want to show himself too earnest. Below satire, burlesque was still another literary device to which the 17th century gave birth, with the aid of France. After the unrelieved earnestness of the Puritans, derision and buffoonery became the order of the day; and with the advent of burlesque, we find ourselves on the very threshold of the modern novel, which Henry Fielding was to define in memorable words as "a comic epic in prose." One reason why he felt that way was undoubtedly that he began his literary career as a writer of stage-burlesques.

In all these manifold ways, the 17th century changed not only the tone of literature, but the very definition of what literature could be. Like all great cultural shifts, this one was too complex to be captured in a single phrase or attributed to a single cause. It had neither a fixed beginning nor a precise end. Yet in the seamless web of history we can hardly fail to notice new colors and textures which, over the course of the 17th century, enter into the warp and woof of the nation's literary as of its social life, to make it look and feel like a whole new piece of cloth.

JOHN WEBSTER

(1580?–1625)

Though Shakespeare seems, in our eyes, to tower above all his contemporaries, and was by no means without honor in his own day, it is only by comparison with him that the Stuart playwrights look small. In any other age of English literature a group of writers which included not only Ben Jonson but John Ford, John Webster, Cyril Tourneur, Francis Beaumont, John Marston, John Fletcher, and Thomas Middleton would have been the climactic glory of the English stage. Such a galaxy of talent, working at a level just short of supreme, we shall not see again. To select only one of these various and gifted men for representation is to do injustice to the rest; but if one it must be, Webster should be the man. As a poet, he is scarcely less powerful than Shakespeare himself, though his range is more restricted. He is a poet of moods, and of certain specific moods, which his age tended to group under the heading of "melancholy." Melancholy is a state of psychic arrest, of morbid inwardness, of fixation and paralysis; and to the exploration of this mood Webster sacrificed some of the movement and even the logic of his plots. Like Hamlet, the central consciousness responds eloquently and imaginatively to his dark circumstances, but is incapable of decisive action to change them. In *The Duchess of Malfi*, Daniel de Bosola is such a man. His inclinations are basically virtuous, but he has been soured and embittered by failure; a soldier and a scholar by profession, he has been reduced to playing what he knows is the mean role of a household spy. Out of his diseased imagination he thus becomes a sardonic wit and a grotesque, violent poet. This poetry of his mirrors the world in which he has fallen, a foul, stagnant, sumptuous sink of corruption, such as 17th-century Englishmen, with their strong Protestant feelings, imagined 16th-century, pre-Reformation Italy to have been.

Webster was obviously fascinated by the diseased and sophisticated corruption which he attributed to the Italy of the Borgias; and he used it as a background against which to pose the figure of his Duchess, one of the freest and most positive women in all English drama. In boldly asserting her right to choose a husband without regard to her family or her social class, the Duchess far transcends the standards of her age. Webster clearly expects us to admire both the assured sensitivity of her impulses and the perfect self-command with which she meets her final fate.

Though his plots are less artfully put together than Shakespeare's, Webster is capable of tremendous poetic flashes. His scenes of brooding terror are lit by fitful lightnings of the imagination, as when Ferdinand, faced with his sister's corpse, at last sees what his insane furies have meant. As for the man who created these lurid nightmares, we know little or nothing about his personal life. He was the son of a tailor, and may himself have plied the needle for a time. He collaborated with other playwrights, but came into his own style when he emancipated himself from that dependence. He professed to be a slow writer, and he drew heavily on his reading in the course of composition. Modern scholarship has found a literary source for nearly every phrase and concept in his plays. But, trite though it is to say so, what he made of his reading is distinctively his own. His art is one of brilliant highlights and black shadows of furtive and dangerous intrigue carried out in the flickering light of hell-fire; it serves to illumine one unflawed character who accepts without faltering or cringing the ultimate test.

The Duchess of Malfi

Dramatis Personae

FERDINAND, *Duke of Calabria*
THE CARDINAL, *his brother*
ANTONIO BOLOGNA, *steward of the household to the* DUCHESS
DELIO, *his friend*
DANIEL DE BOSOLA, *gentleman of the horse to the* DUCHESS
CASTRUCCIO
MARQUIS OF PESCARA
COUNT MALATESTE
SILVIO, *a Lord, of Milan*⎫
RODERIGO   ⎬ *gentlemen attending on the* DUCHESS
GRISOLAN   ⎭
DOCTOR
Several MADMEN, PILGRIMS, EXECUTIONERS, OFFICERS, ATTEND-
    ANTS, *&c.*
THE DUCHESS OF MALFI, *sister of* FERDINAND *and the* CARDINAL
CARIOLA, *her woman*
JULIA, CASTRUCCIO's *wife, and the* CARDINAL's *mistress*
OLD LADY, LADIES, *and* CHILDREN

SCENE. *Amalfi, Rome, and Milan*

Act I

SCENE 1. *Amalfi; a hall in the* DUCHESS's *palace.*

[*Enter* ANTONIO *and* DELIO.]
DELIO. You are welcome to your country, dear Antonio;
    You have been long in France, and you return
    A very formal Frenchman in your habit.[1]
    How do you like the French court?
ANTONIO.   I admire it:
    In seeking to reduce both state and people   5
    To a fixed order, their judicious king
    Begins at home; quits[2] first his royal palace
    Of flattering sycophants, of dissolute
    And infamous persons, which he sweetly terms
    His master's masterpiece, the work of Heaven;   10

1. An absolute Frenchman in your man-   2. Liberates, frees.
ners.

Considering duly that a prince's court
Is like a common fountain, whence should flow
Pure silver drops in general, but if 't chance
Some cursed example poison't near the head,
Death and diseases through the whole land spread.   15
And what is 't makes this blessed government
But a most provident council; who dare freely
Inform him the corruption of the times?
Though some o' th' court hold it presumption
To instruct princes what they ought to do,   20
It is a noble duty to inform them
What they ought to foresee. Here comes Bosola.
The only court-gall;[3] yet I observe his railing
Is not for simple love of piety.
Indeed, he rails at those things which he wants;   25
Would be as lecherous, covetous, or proud,
Bloody, or envious, as any man,
If he had means to be so. Here's the Cardinal.
    [*Enter the* CARDINAL *and* BOSOLA.]
BOSOLA. I do haunt you still.
CARDINAL. So.   30
BOSOLA. I have done you better service than to be slighted thus.
    Miserable age, where the only reward of doing well is the
    doing of it!
CARDINAL. You enforce your merit too much.
BOSOLA. I fell into the galleys[4] in your service; where, for two 35
    years together, I wore two towels instead of a shirt, with a
    knot on the shoulder, after the fashion of a Roman mantle.
    Slighted thus? I will thrive some way. Blackbirds fatten best in
    hard weather; why not I in these dog-days?[5]
CARDINAL. Would you could become honest!   40
BOSOLA. With all your divinity do but direct me the way to it. I
    have known many travel far for it, and yet return as arrant
    knaves as they went forth, because they carried themselves
    always along with them. [*Exit* CARDINAL.] Are you gone?
    Some fellows, they say, are possessed with the devil, but this 45
    great fellow were able to possess the greatest devil, and make
    him worse.
ANTONIO. He hath denied thee some suit?
BOSOLA. He and his brother are like plum-trees that grow crooked
    over standing-pools; they are rich and o'er-laden with fruit, but 50
    none but crows, pies, and caterpillars feed on them.[6] Could I
    be one of their flattering panders, I would hang on their ears

3. Court-satirist, but with the overtone of a disease, a blight.
4. Service at the oar of a Mediterranean galley was the last penalty this side of torture and execution, a 50-percent death sentence.
5. The hot, sultry season of midsummer. Being naturally an ill-omened creature, like a blackbird, Bosola thinks he may thrive under oppression.
6. "Standing-pools": stagnant, therefore poisonous, waters; "pies": magpies, birds of evil omen like blackbirds. By "panders," Bosola does not mean actual pimps, but slavish hangers-on, ready to perform any low office. The violence of these metaphors evidences the sickness of the speaker's mind.

like a horseleech till I were full and then drop off. I pray, leave
me. Who would rely upon these miserable dependencies, in
expectation to be advanced tomorrow? What creature ever fed 55
worse than hoping Tantalus?[7] Nor ever died any man more
fearfully than he that hoped for a pardon. There are rewards
for hawks and dogs when they have done us service; but for a
soldier that hazards his limbs in a battle, nothing but a kind
of geometry is his last supportation. 60

DELIO. Geometry?

BOSOLA. Aye, to hang in a fair pair of slings, take his latter swing
in the world upon an honorable pair of crutches, from hospital
to hospital. Fare ye well, sir: and yet do not you scorn us; for
places in the court are but like beds in the hospital, where this 65
man's head lies at that man's foot, and so lower and lower.
[*Exit.*]

DELIO. I knew this fellow seven years[8] in the galleys
For a notorious murder; and 'twas thought
The Cardinal suborned it. He was released 70
By the French general, Gaston de Foix,
When he recovered Naples.[9]

ANTONIO.   'Tis great pity
He should be thus neglected; I have heard
He's very valiant. This foul melancholy
Will poison all his goodness; for, I'll tell you,
If too immoderate sleep be truly said 75
To be an inward rust unto the soul,
It then doth follow want of action
Breeds all black malcontents; and their close rearing,
Like moths in cloth, do hurt for want of wearing.[1]

DELIO. The presence 'gins to fill: you promised me 80
To make me the partaker of the natures
Of some of your great courtiers.

ANTONIO.   The Lord Cardinal's,
And other strangers that are now in court?
I shall. Here comes the great Calabrian duke.

[*Enter* FERDINAND, CASTRUCCIO, SILVIO, RODERIGO,
GRISOLAN, *and* ATTENDANTS.]

FERDINAND. Who took the ring oftenest?[2] 85

SILVIO. Antonio Bologna, my lord.

FERDINAND. Our sister duchess' great-master of her household?

---

7. Tantalus, in classical mythology, was
tantalized by the constant presence
under his nose of delicious food and
drink which, though he was starving, he
could never reach.
8. In speaking to the Cardinal himself
(above, line 35), Bosola mentions only
two years.
9. Since Gaston de Foix was active in
Italy during the early 1500's, this circumstance establishes the time of the tragedy
as about 100 years before the time
Webster wrote. Ferdinand and the Cardinal are Spaniards established in Italy,

like the notorious house of Borgia (incestuous, simoniacal Pope Alexander VI
and his two illegitimate children Cesare
and Lucrezia), also active at the beginning of the 16th century.
1. Because they don't have anything to
do, malcontents suffer from moths as do
clothes which have not been worn for a
long time. "The presence": the assemblage of the court.
2. A common game around court, used
in training for tourneys, involved catching a hanging ring on the tip of a lance.

Give him the jewel. When shall we leave this sportive action,
and fall to action indeed?

CASTRUCCIO. Methinks, my lord, you should not desire to go to 90
war in person.

FERDINAND. Now for some gravity. Why, my lord?

CASTRUCCIO. It is fitting a soldier arise to be a prince, but not
necessary a prince descend to be a captain.

FERDINAND. No? 95

CASTRUCCIO. No, my lord, he were far better do it by a deputy.

FERDINAND. Why should he not as well sleep or eat by a deputy?
This might take idle, offensive, and base office from him,
whereas the other deprives him of honor.

CASTRUCCIO. Believe my experience, that realm is never long in 100
quiet where the ruler is a soldier.

FERDINAND. Thou told'st me thy wife could not endure fighting.

CASTRUCCIO. True, my lord.

FERDINAND. And of a jest she broke of a captain she met full of
wounds. I have forgot it. 105

CASTRUCCIO. She told him, my lord, he was a pitiful fellow, to
lie, like the children of Israel, all in tents.[3]

FERDINAND. Why, there's a wit were able to undo all the
chirurgeons[4] o' the city; for although gallants should quarrel
and had drawn their weapons and were ready to go to it, yet 110
her persuasions would make them put up.

CASTRUCCIO. That she would, my lord.

FERDINAND. How do you like my Spanish gennet?[5]

RODERIGO. He is all fire.

FERDINAND. I am of Pliny's opinion, I think he was begot by the 115
wind; he runs as if he were ballassed[6] with quicksilver.

SILVIO. True, my lord, he reels from the tilt often.[7]

RODERIGO *and* GRISOLAN. Ha, ha, ha!

FERDINAND. Why do you laugh? Methinks, you that are courtiers
should be my touchwood, take fire when I give fire; that is, 120
laugh but when I laugh, were the subject never so witty.

CASTRUCCIO. True, my lord, I myself have heard a very good jest,
and have scorned to seem to have so silly a wit as to understand it.

FERDINAND. But I can laugh at your fool, my lord. 125

CASTRUCCIO. He cannot speak, you know, but he makes faces:
my lady cannot abide him.

FERDINAND. No?

CASTRUCCIO. Nor endure to be in merry company, for she says
too much laughing and too much company fills her too full of 130
the wrinkle.

FERDINAND. I would, then, have a mathematical instrument

---

3. The lady's pun plays on the name for
lint bandages, "tents."
4. Surgeons.
5. Sometimes "jennet": a small Spanish
horse of Arabian stock.
6. Ballasted. Pliny in his natural history

tells about some Spanish horses generated by a swift wind (VIII.lxvii).
7. "Reeling from the tilt" involves a
double meaning: recoiling from the shock
of a charge, and rolling about like quicksilver on a tilted table.

made for her face, that she might not laugh out of compass.[8]
I shall shortly visit you at Milan, Lord Silvio.

SILVIO. Your grace shall arrive most welcome.   135

FERDINAND. You are a good horseman, Antonio. You have excellent riders in France. What do you think of good horsemanship?

ANTONIO. Nobly, my lord: as out of the Grecian horse issued
many famous princes, so out of brave horsemanship arise the   140
first sparks of growing resolution that raise the mind to noble
action.

FERDINAND. You have bespoke it worthily.

SILVIO. Your brother, the Lord Cardinal, and sister duchess.

          [*Re-enter* CARDINAL, *with* DUCHESS, CARIOLA, *and* JULIA.]

CARDINAL. Are the galleys come about?

GRISOLAN.   They are, my lord.   145

FERDINAND. Here's the Lord Silvio is come to take his leave.

DELIO. Now, sir, your promise. What's that Cardinal?
I mean his temper? They say he's a brave fellow,
Will play[9] his five thousand crowns at tennis, dance,
Court ladies, and one that hath fought single combats.   150

ANTONIO. Some such flashes superficially hang on him for form;
but observe his inward character: he is a melancholy churchman; the spring in his face is nothing but the engendering of
toads; where he is jealous of any man, he lays worse plots for
them than ever was imposed on Hercules, for he strews in his   155
way flatterers, panders, intelligencers, atheists, and a thousand
such political monsters.[1] He should have been Pope; but instead of coming to it by the primitive decency of the Church,
he did bestow bribes so largely and so impudently as if he
would have carried it away without Heaven's knowledge. 160
Some good he hath done——

DELIO. You have given too much of him. What's his brother?

ANTONIO. The duke there? A most perverse and turbulent nature.
What appears in him mirth is merely outside;
If he laugh heartily, it is to laugh   165
All honesty out of fashion.

DELIO.   Twins?

ANTONIO.   In quality.
He speaks with others' tongues, and hears men's suits
With others' ears; will seem to sleep o' th' bench
Only to entrap offenders in their answers;
Dooms men to death by information;[2]   170
Rewards by hearsay.

DELIO.   Then the law to him
Is like a foul black cobweb to a spider:
He makes of it his dwelling and a prison
To entangle those shall feed him.

8. Excessively; with a pun on the drafts-
man's compass.
9. Wager.
1. "Intelligencers": spies. The Cardinal
sets traps and dangers before his enemies as many and as formidable as the
labors of Hercules.
2. On the basis of secret reports.

ANTONIO. Most true:
  He never pays debts unless they be shrewd turns,[3]   175
  And those he will confess that he doth owe.
  Last, for his brother there, the Cardinal,
  They that do flatter him most say oracles
  Hang at his lips; and verily I believe them,
  For the devil speaks in them.   180
  But for their sister, the right noble duchess,
  You never fixed your eye on three fair medals
  Cast in one figure, of so different temper.
  For her discourse, it is so full of rapture,
  You only will begin then to be sorry   185
  When she doth end her speech, and wish, in wonder,
  She held it less vainglory to talk much,
  Than your penance to hear her: whilst she speaks,
  She throws upon a man so sweet a look,
  That it were able to raise one to a galliard[4]   190
  That lay in a dead palsy, and to dote
  On that sweet countenance; but in that look
  There speaketh so divine a continence
  As cuts off all lascivious and vain hope.
  Her days are practiced in such noble virtue   195
  That sure her nights, nay, more, her very sleeps,
  Are more in heaven than other ladies' shrifts.[5]
  Let all sweet ladies break their flattering glasses,
  And dress themselves in her.
DELIO. Fie, Antonio,
  You play the wire-drawer[6] with her commendations.   200
ANTONIO. I'll case the picture up: only thus much;
  All her particular worth grows to this sum,
  She stains[7] the time past, lights the time to come.
CARDINAL. You must attend my lady in the gallery,
  Some half an hour hence.
ANTONIO. I shall.   205
        [*Exteunt* ANTONIO *and* DELIO.]
FERDINAND. Sister, I have a suit to you.
DUCHESS. To me, sir?
FERDINAND. A gentleman here, Daniel de Bosola,
  One that was in the galleys—
DUCHESS. Yes, I know him.
FERDINAND. A worthy fellow he is. Pray, let me entreat for
  The provisorship of your horse.
DUCHESS. Your knowledge of him.   210
  Commends him and prefers him.
FERDINAND. Call him hither.
        [*Exit* ATTENDANT.]
  We are now upon parting. Good Lord Silvio,
  Do us commend to all our noble friends

3. Tricks to serve his own advantage.
4. A gay and lively dance.
5. Confessions.
6. Draw out her praises excessively;

"case the picture": frame it.
7. Darkens (by comparison with her brilliance).

At the leaguer.[8]

SILVIO.   Sir, I shall.

DUCHESS.   You are for Milan?   215

SILVIO. I am.

DUCHESS. Bring the caroches. We'll bring you down
To the haven.[9] [*Exeunt all but* FERDINAND *and the* CARDINAL.]

CARDINAL. Be sure you entertain that Bosola
For your intelligence:[1] I would not be seen in 't;
And therefore many times I have slighted him   220
When he did court our furtherance, as this morning.

FERDINAND. Antonio, the great-master of her household,
Had been far fitter.

CARDINAL.   You are deceived in him:
His nature is too honest for such business.
He comes: I'll leave you.   [*Exit.*]
        [*Re-enter* BOSOLA.]

BOSOLA.   I was lured to you.   225

FERDINAND. My brother, here, the Cardinal could never
Abide you.

BOSOLA. Never since he was in my debt.

FERDINAND. Maybe some oblique character in your face
Made him suspect you

BOSOLA.   Doth he study physiognomy?   230
There's no more credit to be given to th' face
Than to a sick man's urine, which some call
The physician's whore because she cozens[2] him.
He did suspect me wrongfully.

FERDINAND.   For that   235
You must give great men leave to take their times.
Distrust doth cause us seldom be deceived:
You see, the oft shaking of the cedar-tree
Fastens it more at root.

BOSOLA.   Yet, take heed;
For to suspect a friend unworthily   240
Instructs him the next way to suspect you,
And prompts him to deceive you.

FERDINAND. [*giving him money*] There's gold.

BOSOLA.   So:
What follows? Never rained such showers as these
Without thunderbolts i' th' tail of them. Whose throat must
    I cut?

FERDINAND. Your inclination to shed blood rides post
Before my occasion to use you. I give you that   245
To live i' th' court here, and observe the duchess;
To note all the particulars of her havior,
What suitors do solicit her for marriage,

8. A gathering of the armies, as at a
siege.
9. Harbor; "caroches": carriages.

1. I.e., be sure to hire Bosola as your
spy.
2. Tricks.

And whom she best affects. She's a young widow:
I would not have her marry again.

BOSOLA.   No, sir?   250

FERDINAND. Do not you ask the reason, but be satisfied
I say I would not.

BOSOLA.   It seems you would create me
One of your familiars.[3]

FERDINAND.   Familiar? What's that?

BOSOLA. Why, a very quaint invisible devil in flesh,   255
An intelligencer.

FERDINAND. Such a kind of thriving thing
I would wish thee, and ere long thou may'st arrive
At a higher place by 't.

BOSOLA.   Take your devils,
Which hell calls angels;[4] these cursed gifts would make   260
You a corrupter, me an impudent traitor;
And should I take these, they'd take me to hell.

FERDINAND. Sir, I'll take nothing from you that I have given:
There is a place that I procured for you
This morning, the provisorship o' th' horse;
Have you heard on 't?   265

BOSOLA.   No.

FERDINAND. 'Tis yours. Is't not worth thanks?

BOSOLA. I would have you curse yourself now, that your bounty,
Which makes men truly noble, e'er should make me
A villain. Oh, that to avoid ingratitude
For the good deed you have done me, I must do   270
All the ill man can invent! Thus the devil
Candies all sins o'er; and what heaven terms vile,
That names he complimental.

FERDINAND.   Be yourself;
Keep your old garb of melancholy; 'twill express
You envy those that stand above your reach,   275
Yet strive not to come near 'em: this will gain
Access to private lodgings, where yourself
May, like a politic dormouse—

BOSOLA.   As I have seen some
Feed in a lord's dish, half asleep, not seeming
To listen to any talk; and yet these rogues   280
Have cut his throat in a dream. What's my place?
The provisorship o' th' horse? Say, then, my corruption
Grew out of horse-dung. I am your creature.

FERDINAND.   Away! [*Exit.*]

BOSOLA. Let good men, for good deeds, covet good fame,
Since place and riches oft are bribes of shame: 285
Sometimes the devil doth preach.   [*Exit.*]

---

3. Evil spirits, agents of the devil.
4. Gold coins were known, from the image on them, as angels.

SCENE 2

[*Enter* FERDINAND, DUCHESS, CARDINAL, *and* CARIOLA.]

CARDINAL. We are to part from you, and your own discretion.
  Must now be your director.
FERDINAND.   You are a widow:
  You know already what man is; and therefore
  Let not youth, high promotion, eloquence—
CARDINAL.   No,
  Nor any thing without the addition, honor,   5
  Sway your high blood.
FERDINAND. Marry! They are most luxurious
  Will wed twice.
CARDINAL.   Oh, fie!
FERDINAND.   Their lives are more spotted
  Than Laban's sheep.[5]
DUCHESS.   Diamonds are of most value,
  They say, that have passed through most jewelers' hands.   10
FERDINAND. Whores by that rule are precious.
DUCHESS.   Will you hear me?
  I'll never marry.
CARDINAL. So most widows say;
  But commonly that motion[6] lasts no longer
  Than the turning of an hour-glass; the funeral sermon
  And it end both together.
FERDINAND.   Now hear me: 15
  You live in a rank pasture, here, i' th' court;
  There is a kind of honey-dew[7] that's deadly;
  'Twill poison your fame; look to't: be not cunning;
  For they whose faces do belie their hearts
  Are witches ere they arrive at twenty years,   20
  Aye, and give the devil suck.
DUCHESS.   This is terrible good counsel.
FERDINAND. Hypocrisy is woven of a fine small thread,
  Subtler than Vulcan's engine:[8] yet, believe't,
  Your darkest actions, nay, your privatest thoughts,
  Will come to light.
CARDINAL.   You may flatter yourself,   25
  And take your own choice; privately be married
  Under the eaves of night—
FERDINAND.   Think't the best voyage
  That e'er you made; like the irregular crab,
  Which, though't goes backward, thinks that it goes right
  Because it goes its own way; but observe,   30
  Such weddings may more properly be said
  To be executed than celebrated.

---

5. Dividing his flock with Jacob, Laban took the speckled sheep (Genesis xxx.31–33); the liver as seat of the passions was thought to be diseased when discolored.

6. Impulse, notion.
7. A sweet, sticky substance left on plants by aphids.
8. The net in which Vulcan, Venus' husband, caught her misbehaving with Mars.

CARDINAL.   The marriage night
  Is the entrance into some prison.
FERDINAND.   And those joys,
  Those lustful pleasures, are like heavy sleeps
  Which do forerun man's mischief.
CARDINAL.   Fare you well.   35
  Wisdom begins at the end: remember it.   [*Exit.*]
DUCHESS. I think this speech between you both was studied,
  It came so roundly off.
FERDINAND.   You are my sister;
  This was my father's poniard,[9] do you see?
  I'd be loth to see 't look rusty, 'cause 'twas his.   40
  I would have you to give o'er these chargeable[1] revels:
  A visor and a mask are whispering-rooms
  That were never built for goodness—fare ye well—
  And women like that part which, like the lamprey,[2]
  Hath never a bone in 't.
DUCHESS.   Fie, sir!
FERDINAND.   Nay,   45
  I mean the tongue; variety of courtship.
  What cannot a neat knave with a smooth tale
  Make a woman believe? Farewell, lusty widow.   [*Exit.*]
DUCHESS. Shall this move me? If all my royal kindred
  Lay in my way unto this marriage,   50
  I'd make them my low footsteps; and even now,
  Even in this hate, as men in some great battles,
  By apprehending danger, have achieved
  Almost impossible actions (I have heard soldiers say so),
  So I through frights and threatenings will assay   55
  This dangerous venture. Let old wives report
  I winked and chose a husband. Cariola,
  To thy known secrecy I have given up
  More than my life—my fame.
CARIOLA.   Both shall be safe,
  For I'll conceal this secret from the world   60
  As warily as those that trade in poison
  Keep poison from their children.
DUCHESS.   Thy protestation
  Is ingenious and hearty:[3] I believe it.
  Is Antonio come?
CARIOLA.   He attends you.
DUCHESS.   Good dear soul,
  Leave me, but place thyself behind the arras,[4]   65
  Where thou mayst overhear us. Wish me good speed,
  For I am going into a wilderness

9. Dagger.
1. Expensive; "visor": a half-mask, worn
by ladies at carnivals, theaters, and other
dubious resorts.
2. "Lamprey": eel. They do, of course,
have bones, but for the purposes of the

Duke's insinuation they are better without.
3. Sincere and from the heart.
4. Tapestries were often hung in Renaissance palaces to moderate the chill of
the bare walls.

Where I shall find nor path nor friendly clue
To be my guide.   [CARIOLA *goes behind the arras.*]
     [*Enter* ANTONIO.]
                         I sent for you: sit down;
Take pen and ink, and write. Are you ready?
ANTONIO.   Yes.   70
DUCHESS. What did I say?
ANTONIO. That I should write somewhat.
DUCHESS.   Oh, I remember.
After these triumphs and this large expense,
It's fit, like thrifty husbands,[5] we inquire
What's laid up for tomorrow.   75
ANTONIO. So please your beauteous excellence.
DUCHESS.   Beauteous?
Indeed, I thank you: I look young for your sake;
You have ta'en my cares upon you.
ANTONIO.   I'll fetch your grace
The particulars of your revenue and expense.
DUCHESS. Oh, you are an upright treasurer: but you mistook;   80
For when I said I meant to make inquiry
What's laid up for tomorrow, I did mean
What's laid up yonder for me.
ANTONIO.   Where?
DUCHESS.   In heaven.
I am making my will (as 'tis fit princes should,
In perfect memory), and I pray sir, tell me,   85
Were not one better make it smiling thus
Than in deep groans and terrible ghastly looks,
As if the gifts we parted with procured[6]
That violent distraction?
ANTONIO.   O, much better.
DUCHESS. If I had a husband now, this care were quit: 90
But I intend to make you overseer.
What good deed shall we first remember? Say.
ANTONIO. Begin with that first good deed begun i' th' world
After man's creation, the sacrament of marriage:
I'd have you first provide for a good husband;   95
Give him all.
DUCHESS. All?
ANTONIO.   Yes, your excellent self.
DUCHESS. In a winding-sheet?
ANTONIO.   In a couple.
DUCHESS. Saint Winfred, that were a strange will![7]
ANTONIO. 'Twere stranger if there were no will in you
To marry again.   100
DUCHESS.   What do you think of marriage?

5. Though used here in its original sense
of one who preserves and safeguards
property, the word shows where the
Duchess' thoughts are tending.
6. Brought on.
7. Saint Winfred, Welsh virgin and martyr, is an odd saint for the Duchess of
Malfi to swear on.

ANTONIO. I take't, as those that deny purgatory;
   It locally contains or heaven or hell;
   There's no third place in 't.
DUCHESS.   How do you affect it?[8]
ANTONIO. My banishment, feeding my melancholy,
   Would often reason thus—
DUCHESS.   Pray, let's hear it.   105
ANTONIO. Say a man never marry, nor have children,
   What takes that from him? Only the bare name
   Of being a father, or the weak delight
   To see the little wanton ride a-cock-horse
   Upon a painted stick, or hear him chatter   110
   Like a taught starling.
DUCHESS.   Fie, fie, what's all this?
   One of your eyes is bloodshot; use my ring to 't,
   They say 'tis very sovereign.[9] 'Twas my wedding-ring,
   And I did vow never to part with it
   But to my second husband.
ANTONIO.   You have parted with it now.   115
DUCHESS. Yes, to help your eyesight.
ANTONIO.   You have made me stark blind.
DUCHESS.   How?
ANTONIO. There is a saucy and ambitious devil
   Is dancing in this circle.[1]
DUCHESS.   Remove him.
ANTONIO.   How?
DUCHESS. There needs small conjuration, when your finger
   May do it: thus; is it fit?
         [*She puts the ring upon his finger; he kneels.*]
ANTONIO.   What said you?
DUCHESS.   Sir,   120
   This goodly roof of yours[2] is too low built;
   I cannot stand upright in 't nor discourse,
   Without I raise it higher: raise yourself;
   Or, if you please, my hand to help you: so.   [*Raises him.*]
ANTONIO. Ambition, madam, is a great man's madness,   125
   That is not kept in chains and close-pent rooms,
   But in fair lightsome lodgings, and is girt
   With the wild noise of prattling visitants,
   Which makes it lunatic beyond all cure.
   Conceive not I am so stupid but I aim   130
   Whereto your favors tend; but he's a fool
   That, being a-cold, would thrust his hands i' th' fire
   To warm them.
DUCHESS.   So, now the ground's broke,
   You may discover what a wealthy mine

---

8. Feel about it.
9. Healing, but with an additional overtone implying royal power.
1. To conjure up a devil, the necromancer first draws a charmed circle on the ground—like the duchess' ring.
2. His head as he kneels before her.

I make you lord of.

ANTONIO.   O my unworthiness!   135

DUCHESS. You were ill to sell yourself:
This darkening of your worth is not like that
Which tradesmen use i' th' city, their false lights
Are to rid bad wares off[3] and I must tell you,
If you will know where breathes a complete man   140
(I speak it without flattery), turn your eyes,
And progress through yourself.

ANTONIO.   Were there nor heaven
Nor hell, I should be honest: I have long served virtue,
And ne'er ta'en wages of her.

DUCHESS.   Now she pays it.   145
The misery of us that are born great!
We are forced to woo, because none dare woo us;
And as a tyrant doubles with his words
And fearfully equivocates, so we
Are forced to express our violent passions   150
In riddles and in dreams, and leave the path
Of simple virtue, which was never made
To seem the thing it is not. Go, go brag
You have left me heartless; mine is in your bosom:
I hope 'twill multiply love there. You do tremble:
Make not your heart so dead a piece of flesh,   155
To fear more than to love me. Sir, be confident:
What is 't distracts you? This is flesh and blood, sir;
'Tis not the figure cut in alabaster
Kneels at my husband's tomb. Awake, awake, man!
I do here put off all vain ceremony,   160
And only do appear to you a young widow
That claims you for her husband, and, like a widow,
I use but half a blush in 't.

ANTONIO.   Truth speak for me;
I will remain the constant sanctuary
Of your good name.

DUCHESS.   I thank you, gentle love: 165
And 'cause you shall not come to me in debt,
Being now my steward, here upon your lips
I sign your *Quietus est.*[4] This you should have begged now;
I have seen children oft eat sweetmeats thus,
As fearful to devour them too soon.   170

ANTONIO. But for your brothers?

DUCHESS.   Do not think of them.
All discord without this circumference[5]
Is only to be pitied, and not feared;
Yet, should they know it, time will easily
Scatter the tempest.

3. Tradesmen in the city display their
goods in a poor light, so the defects
won't be seen.

4. The legal formula for marking a bill
"Paid" or "Acquitted."
5. Their arms around one another.

ANTONIO.   These words should be mine,   175
 And all the parts you have spoke, if some part of it
 Would not have savored flattery.
DUCHESS.   Kneel.
         [CARIOLA *comes from behind the arras.*]
ANTONIO.   Ha!
DUCHESS. Be not amazed; this woman's of my counsel:
 I have heard lawyers say, a contract in a chamber
 Per verba de presenti[6] is absolute marriage.   180
        [*She and* ANTONIO *kneel.*]
 Bless, heaven, this sacred gordian,[7] which let violence
 Never untwine!
ANTONIO. And may our sweet affections, like the spheres,
 Be still in motion!
DUCHESS.   Quickening, and make
 The like soft music!   185
ANTONIO. That we may imitate the loving palms,
 Best emblem of a peaceful marriage, that ne'er
 Bore fruit, divided!
DUCHESS.   What can the Church force more?
ANTONIO. That fortune may not know an accident,
 Either of joy or sorrow, to divide   190
 Our fixéd wishes!
DUCHESS.   How can the Church build faster?[8]
 We now are man and wife, and 'tis the Church
 That must but echo this. Maid, stand apart:
 I now am blind.[9]
ANTONIO.   What's your conceit in this?
DUCHESS. I would have you lead your fortune by the hand 195
 Unto your marriage bed
 (You speak in me this, for we now are one);
 We'll only lie, and talk together, and plot
 To appease my humorous kindred; and if you please,
 Like the old tale in "Alexander and Lodowick,"   200
 Lay a naked sword between us, keep us chaste.[1]
 Oh, let me shroud my blushes in your bosom,
 Since 'tis the treasury of all my secrets!
       [*Exeunt* DUCHESS *and* ANTONIO.]
CARIOLA. Whether the spirit of greatness or of woman
 Reign most in her, I know not; but it shows   205
 A fearful madness: I owe her much of pity.   [*Exit.*]

---

6. "Through words in the present tense" —not, as commonly supposed, and perhaps by Webster himself, "On the words of a witness." In canon law, the duchess is right; her agreement with Antonio to consider themselves married is a valid contract with or without priest, ceremony, or even the presence of a witness.
7. Knot.
8. More securely, with a pun on "swifter."

9. The phrase "Maid, stand apart" is addressed to Cariola. In shutting her eyes and rejecting all support, the Duchess dramatizes the quality of her choice.
1. Alexander and Lodowick were look-a-like friends in an old ballad. For purely virtuous reasons, one slept with the wife of the other, but with the precaution indicated.

Act II

SCENE 1

[*Enter* BOSOLA *and* CASTRUCCIO.]

BOSOLA. You say you would fain be taken for an eminent courtier?

CASTRUCCIO. 'Tis the very main of my ambition.

BOSOLA. Let me see: you have a reasonable good face for 't already, and your nightcap expresses your ears sufficient largely. I would have you learn to twirl the strings of your band[2] with a good grace, and in a set speech, at th' end of every sentence, to hum three or four times, or blow your nose till it smart again, to recover your memory. When you come to be a president in criminal causes, if you smile upon a prisoner, hang him, but if you frown upon him and threaten him, let him be sure to 'scape the gallows.

CASTRUCCIO. I would be a very merry president.

BOSOLA. Do not sup o' night's; 'twill beget you an admirable wit.

CASTRUCCIO. Rather it would make me have a good stomach to quarrel; for they say, your roaring boys[3] eat meat seldom, and that makes them so valiant. But how shall I know whether the people take me for an eminent fellow?

BOSOLA. I will teach a trick to know it: give out you lie a-dying, and if you hear the common people curse you, be sure you are taken for one of the prime nightcaps.[4]

[*Enter an* OLD LADY.]

You come from painting now.

OLD LADY. From what?

BOSOLA. Why, from your scurvy face-physic. To behold thee not painted inclines somewhat near a miracle; these in thy face here were deep ruts and foul sloughs the last progress.[5] There was a lady in France that, having had the smallpox, flayed the skin off her face to make it more level; and whereas before she looked like a nutmeg-grater, after she resembled an abortive hedgehog.

OLD LADY. Do you call this painting?

BOSOLA. No, no, but you call it careening of an old morphewed lady, to make her disembogue again:[6] there's rough-cast phrase to your plastic.

OLD LADY. It seems you are well acquainted with my closet.

BOSOLA. One would suspect it for a shop of witchcraft, to find in it the fat of serpents, spawn of snakes, Jews' spittle, and their young children's ordure; and all these for the face. I would sooner eat a dead pigeon taken from the soles of the feet of

---

2. The elaborate ruff of the day had strings attached to it.
3. London town-bullies. (Webster's Amalfi has about it an occasional touch of Cheapside.)
4. Roughs who roamed the streets at night.

5. A progress was a formal royal journey of state.
6. Scraping ("careening") of an old, scaly ("morphewed") ship ("lady") to fit her for the ocean ("making her disembogue") again.

one sick of the plague than kiss one of you fasting.[7] Here are 40
two of you, whose sin of your youth is the very patrimony of
the physician; makes him renew his foot-cloth with the
spring,[8] and change his high-priced courtesan with the fall of
the leaf. I do wonder you do not loathe yourselves. Observe
my meditation now. 45
What thing is in this outward form of man
To be beloved? We account it ominous,
If nature do produce a colt, or lamb,
A fawn, or goat, in any limb resembling
A man, and fly from 't as a prodigy: 50
Man stands amazed to see his deformity
In any other creature but himself.
But in our own flesh, though we bear diseases
Which have their true names only ta'en from beasts—
As the most ulcerous wolf and swinish measle[9]— 55
Though we are eaten up of lice and worms,
And though continually we bear about us
A rotten and dead body, we delight
To hide it in rich tissue: all our fear,
Nay, all our terror, is lest our physician 60
Should put us in the ground to be made sweet—
Your wife's gone to Rome: you two couple, and get you
To the wells at Lucca to recover your aches.[1]
I have other work on foot. [*Exeunt* CASTRUCCIO *and* OLD LADY.]
I observe our duchess 65
Is sick a-days: she pukes, her stomach seethes,
The fins of her eye-lids look most teeming blue,
She wanes i' th' cheek, and waxes fat i' th' flank,
And contrary to our Italian fashion,
Wears a loose-bodied gown: there's somewhat in 't. 70
I have a trick may chance discover it,
A pretty one; I have bought some apricocks,[2]
The first our spring yields.
     [*Enter* ANTONIO *and* DELIO.]
DELIO.   And so long since married?
  You amaze me.
ANTONIO.   Let me seal your lips for ever:
  For, did I think that anything but th' air 75
  Could carry these words from you, I should wish
  You had no breath at all. [*turning to* BOSOLA] Now, sir, in
    your contemplation?

7. Centuries of traditional invective
about women's cosmetic practices, and
some contemporary practices and superstitions, lie behind this speech. Freshly
killed pigeons were indeed applied to the
feet of plague-victims, and fasting was
supposed to cause bad breath.
8. The physician grows rich on those
who have outworn their youth; every
spring he buys a new harness for his
horse and every fall a new mistress for
himself.
9. "Wolf" and "measle": an ulcerous
skin disease (lupus) and an infection of
swine.
1. The wells at Lucca are the mineral
springs at nearby Montecatini, then as
now renowned as a place to "take the
cure."
2. The old spelling "apricots," emphasizing the derivation of the name
from Latin *praecox*, "early ripener."

You are studying to become a great wise fellow?

BOSOLA. Oh, sir, the opinion of wisdom is a foul tetter[3] that 80
runs all over a man's body. If simplicity direct us to have no
evil, it directs us to a happy being, for the subtlest folly proceeds from the subtlest wisdom. Let me be simply honest.

ANTONIO. I do understand your inside.

BOSOLA.   Do you so?

ANTONIO. Because you would not seem to appear to th' world 85
Puffed up with your preferment, you continue
This out-of-fashion melancholy. Leave it, leave it.

BOSOLA. Give me leave to be honest in any phrase, in any compliment whatsoever. Shall I confess myself to you? I look no
higher than I can reach: they are the gods that must ride on 90
winged horses. A lawyer's mule of a slow pace will both suit
my disposition and business; for, mark me, when a man's
mind rides faster than his horse can gallop, they quickly both
tire.

ANTONIO. You would look up to heaven, but I think 95
The devil, that rules i' th' air, stands in your light.

BOSOLA. Oh, sir, you are lord of the ascendant,[4] chief man with
the duchess; a duke was your cousin-german removed. Say you
were lineally descended from King Pepin,[5] or he himself, what
of this? Search the heads of the greatest rivers in the world, 100
you shall find them but bubbles of water. Some would think
the souls of princes were brought forth by some more weighty
cause than those of meaner persons: they are deceived, there's
the same hand to them; the like passions sway them; the same
reason that makes a vicar go to law for a tithe-pig,[6] and undo 105
his neighbors, makes them spoil a whole province, and batter
down goodly cities with the cannon.

      [*Enter* DUCHESS *and* LADIES.]

DUCHESS. Your arm, Antonio; do I not grow fat?
I am exceeding short-winded. Bosola,
I would have you, sir, provide for me a litter, 110
Such a one as the Duchess of Florence rode in.

BOSOLA. The duchess used one when she was great with child.

DUCHESS. I think she did. Come hither, mend my ruff;
Here, when?
Thou art such a tedious lady, and thy breath smells 115
Of lemon-peels.[7] Would thou hadst done! Shall I swoon
Under thy fingers! I am so troubled
With the mother![8]

BOSOLA. [*aside*] I fear too much.

DUCHESS.   I have heard you say

---

3. Scab.
4. In astrology, favored by the stars just
coming into predominant influence.
5. Father of Charlemagne, and thus
source of a great dynasty.
6. A parson was entitled to a tenth
(tithe) of his parishioners' increase, but
would be considered mean if he sued for

the tenth part of his neighbor's newborn
piglet.
7. Lemon-peels were sometimes chewed
to sweeten the breath. "Tedious":
clumsy.
8. "The mother" is intestinal gas, sour
stomach, but with a second meaning not
lost on Bosola.

That the French courtiers wear their hats on 'fore 120
  The king.
ANTONIO. I have seen it.
DUCHESS.   In the presence?
ANTONIO.   Yes.
DUCHESS. Why should not we bring up that fashion? 'Tis
  Ceremony more than duty that consists
  In the removing of a piece of felt. 125
  Be you the example to the rest o' th' court;
  Put on your hat first.
ANTONIO.   You must pardon me.
  I have seen, in colder countries than in France,
  Nobles stand bare to th' prince, and the distinction
  Methought showed reverently. 130
BOSOLA. I have a present for your grace.
DUCHESS.   For me, sir?
BOSOLA. Apricocks, madam.
DUCHESS.   O, sir, where are they?
  I have heard of none to-year.
BOSOLA. [*aside*]   Good; her color rises.
DUCHESS. Indeed, I thank you: they are wondrous fair ones.
  What an unskillful fellow is our gardener! 135
  We shall have none this month.
BOSOLA.   Will not your grace pare them?
DUCHESS. No. They taste of musk, methinks; indeed they do.
BOSOLA. I know not: yet I wish your grace had pared 'em.
DUCHESS. Why?
BOSOLA. I forgot to tell you, the knave gardener, 140
  Only to raise his profit by them the sooner,
  Did ripen them in horse-dung.[9]
DUCHESS.   O, you jest.
  You shall judge: pray taste one.
ANTONIO.   Indeed, madam,
  I do not love the fruit.
DUCHESS.   Sir, you are loath
  To rob us of our dainties: 'tis a delicate fruit; 145
  They say they are restorative.
BOSOLA.   'Tis a pretty art,
  This grafting.
DUCHESS. 'Tis so; a bettering of nature.
BOSOLA. To make a pippin grow upon a crab,
  A damson on a blackthorn. [*aside*] How greedily she eats
    them! 150
  A whirlwind strike off these bawd farthingales![1]
  For, but for that and the loose-bodied gown,
  I should have discovered apparently[2]
  The young springal[3] cutting a caper in her belly.

9. The heat of decomposing manure was widely supposed to have special virtues; but Bosola is thinking also of his post as provisor of the horse.

1. Early hoop-skirts, capable of concealing the figure.
2. Easily, certainly.
3. Colt, youngster.

DUCHESS. I thank you, Bosola. They were right good ones, 155
    If they do not make me sick.
ANTONIO.   How now, madam?
DUCHESS. This green fruit and my stomach are not friends;
    How they swell me!
BOSOLA. [*aside*] Nay, you are too much swelled already.
DUCHESS. Oh, I am in an extreme cold sweat!
BOSOLA.   I am very sorry. 160
DUCHESS. Lights to my chamber! O good Antonio,
    I fear I am undone!
DELIO.   Lights there, lights!
    [*Exeunt* DUCHESS *and* LADIES. *Exit, on the other side,* BOSOLA.]
ANTONIO. O my most trusty Delio, we are lost!
    I fear she's fall'n in labor; and there's left
    No time for her remove.
DELIO.   Have you prepared 165
    Those ladies to attend her? and procured
    That politic safe conveyance for the midwife
    Your duchess plotted?
ANTONIO. I have.
DELIO.   Make use, then, of this forced occasion:
    Give out that Bosola hath poisoned her 170
    With these apricocks; that will give some color
    For her keeping close.
ANTONIO.   Fie, fie, the physicians
    Will then flock to her.
DELIO.   For that you may pretend
    She'll use some prepared antidote of her own,
    Lest the physicians should re-poison her, 175
ANTONIO. I am lost in amazement: I know not what to think
    on 't.   [*Exeunt.*]

SCENE 2

    [*Enter* BOSOLA.]
BOSOLA. So, so, there's no question but her tetchiness[4] and most
    vulturous eating of the apricocks are apparent signs of breed-
    ing.
    [*Enter an* OLD LADY.]
    Now?
OLD LADY. I am in haste, sir. 5
BOSOLA. There was a young waiting-woman had a monstrous
    desire to see the glass-house[5]——
OLD LADY. Nay, pray let me go.
BOSOLA. And it was only to know what strange instrument it
    was should swell up a glass to the fashion of a woman's belly. 10
OLD LADY. I will hear no more of the glass-house. You are still

4. Irritability.
5. Where bottles were blown, near the theater in Blackfriars.

abusing women?

BOSOLA. Who, I? No; only, by the way now and then, mention
your frailties. The orange-tree bears ripe and green fruit and
blossoms all together; and some of you give entertainment for 15
pure love, but more for more precious reward. The lusty spring
smells well, but drooping autumn tastes well. If we have the
same golden showers that rained in the time of Jupiter the
thunderer, you have the same Danaës still,[6] to hold up their
laps to receive them. Didst thou never study the mathematics? 20

OLD LADY. What's that sir?

BOSOLA. Why, to know the trick how to make a many lines meet
in one center. Go, go, give your foster-daughters good counsel:
tell them, that the devil takes delight to hang at a woman's
girdle, like a false rusty watch, that she cannot discern how 25
the time passes.   [*Exit* OLD LADY.]

    [*Enter* ANTONIO, DELIO, RODERIGO, *and* GRISOLAN.]

ANTONIO. Shut up the court-gates.

RODERIGO.   Why, sir? what's the danger?

ANTONIO. Shut up the posterns[7] presently, and call
All the officers o' th' court.

GRISOLAN.   I shall instantly.   [*Exit.*]

ANTONIO. Who keeps the key o' th' park gate?

RODERIGO.   Forobosco.   30

ANTONIO. Let him bring 't presently.

    [*Re-enter* GRISOLAN *with* SERVANTS.]

1 SERVANT. O, gentlemen o' the court, the foulest treason!

BOSOLA. [*aside.*] If that these apricocks should be poisoned now.
Without my knowledge!

1 SERVANT.   There was taken even now
A Switzer[8] in the duchess' bedchamber—

2 SERVANT.   A Switzer?   35

1 SERVANT. With a pistol in his great cod-piece.[9]

BOSOLA.   Ha, ha, ha!

1 SERVANT. The cod-piece was the case for 't.

2 SERVANT.   There was
A cunning traitor: who would have searched his cod-piece?

1 SERVANT. True, if he had kept out of the ladies' chambers.
And all the molds of his buttons were leaden bullets.   40

2 SERVANT. O wicked cannibal!
A fire-lock in 's cod-piece!

1 SERVANT.   'Twas a French plot,
Upon my life.

2 SERVANT. To see what the devil can do!

ANTONIO. Are all the officers here?

SERVANTS.   We are.

ANTONIO.   Gentlemen,   45

---

6. Jupiter's success in wooing Danaë in
a shower of gold traditionally illustrates
female venality.
7. Outer gates of a castle or palace.

8. Swiss guard.
9. An outsize flap worn on the front of
men's trunk hose.

We have lost much plate[1] you know, and but this evening
Jewels, to the value of four thousand ducats,
Are missing in the duchess' cabinet.
Are the gates shut?
SERVANT.   Yes.
ANTONIO.   'Tis the duchess' pleasure
    Each officer be locked into his chamber   50
    Till the sun-rising; and to send the keys
    Of all their chests and of their outward doors
    Into her bed-chamber. She is very sick.
RODERIGO. At her pleasure.
ANTONIO.   She entreats you take 't not ill:
    The innocent shall be the more approved by it.   55
BOSOLA. Gentlemen o' th' wood-yard, where's your Switzer now?
1 SERVANT. By this hand, 'twas credibly reported by one o' th'
    black guard.[2]   [*Exeunt all except* ANTONIO *and* DELIO.]
DELIO. How fares it with the duchess?
ANTONIO.   She's exposed
    Unto the worst of torture, pain, and fear.
DELIO. Speak to her all happy comfort.   60
ANTONIO. How I do play the fool with mine own danger!
    You are this night, dear friend, to post to Rome;
    My life lies in your service.
DELIO.   Do not doubt me.
ANTONIO. Oh, 'tis far from me, and yet fear presents me
    Somewhat that looks like danger.
DELIO.   Believe it,   65
    'Tis but the shadow of your fear, no more;
    How superstitiously we mind our evils!
    The throwing down salt, or crossing of a hare,
    Bleeding at nose, the stumbling of a horse,
    Or singing of a cricket, are of power   70
    To daunt whole man in us. Sir, fare you well:
    I wish you all the joys of a blessed father:
    And, for my faith, lay this unto your breast,
    Old friends, like old swords, still are trusted best.   [*Exit.*]
            [*Enter* CARIOLA.]
CARIOLA. Sir, you are the happy father of a son: 75
    Your wife commends him to you.
ANTONIO.   Blessed comfort!
    For Heaven's sake tend her well: I'll presently
    Go set a figure for 's nativity.[3]   [*Exeunt.*]

SCENE 3

            [*Enter* BOSOLA, *with a dark lantern.*]
BOSOLA. Sure I did hear a woman shriek: list, ha!

1. Massive gold and silver dishes, a frequent form of wealth in the days before
banks.
2. Kitchen-scullions; the "wood-yard" is

a source of firewood for kitchen and fire-
places.
3. Cast his horoscope.

And the sound came, if I received it right,
From the duchess' lodgings. There's some stratagem
In the confining all our courtiers
To their several wards: I must have part of it;   5
My intelligence will freeze else.⁴ List, again!
It may be 'twas the melancholy bird,
Best friend of silence and of solitariness,
The owl, that screamed so. Ha! Antonio?

   [*Enter* ANTONIO *with a candle, his sword drawn.*]

ANTONIO. I heard some noise. Who's there? What art thou?
  Speak.   10
BOSOLA. Antonio? Put not your face nor body
  To such a forced expression of fear.
  I am Bosola, your friend.
ANTONIO.   Bosola!
  [*aside*] This mole does undermine me. Heard you not
  A noise even now?
BOSOLA.   From whence?
ANTONIO.   From the duchess' lodging.   15
BOSOLA. Not I. Did you?
ANTONIO.   I did, or else I dreamed.
BOSOLA. Let's walk towards it.
ANTONIO.   No, it may be 'twas
  But the rising of the wind.
BOSOLA.   Very likely.
  Methinks 'tis very cold, and yet you sweat:
  You look wildly.
ANTONIO.   I have been setting a figure⁵
  For the duchess' jewels.   20
BOSOLA.   Ah, and how falls your question?
  Do you find it radical?⁶
ANTONIO.   What's that to you?
  'Tis rather to be questioned what design,
  When all men were commanded to their lodgings,
  Makes you a night-walker.
BOSOLA.   In sooth, I'll tell you: 25
  Now all the court's asleep, I thought the devil
  Had least to do here; I came to say my prayers;
  And if it do offend you I do so,
  You are a fine courtier.
ANTONIO. [*aside*] This fellow will undo me.   30
  You gave the duchess apricocks today:
  Pray Heaven they were not poisoned!
BOSOLA.   Poisoned? A Spanish fig⁷
  For the imputation!
ANTONIO.   Traitors are ever confident
  Till they are discovered. There were jewels stolen, too;

---

4. All my news will be cold.
5. Establishing the loss involved. But Bosola takes the expression astrologically, as if Antonio were casting a horo-scope.
6. Indicative, significant.
7. An obscene gesture, which Bosola doubtless makes onstage.

In my conceit, none are to be suspected   35
More than yourself.
BOSOLA.   You are a false steward.
ANTONIO. Saucy slave, I'll pull thee up by the roots.
BOSOLA. Maybe the ruin will crush you to pieces.
ANTONIO. You are an impudent snake indeed, sir:
    Are you scarce warm, and do you show your sting?   40
    You libel well, sir.
BOSOLA.   No, sir: copy it out,
    And I will set my hand to 't.[8]
ANTONIO. [*aside*]   My nose bleeds.
    One that were superstitious would count
    This ominous, when it merely comes by chance:
    Two letters, that are wrought here for my name,   45
    Are drowned in blood!
    Mere accident. For you, sir, I'll take order
    I' th' morn you shall be safe: [*aside*] 'tis that must color
    Her lying-in: sir, this door you pass not:
    I do not hold it fit that you come near   50
    The duchess' lodgings, till you have quit yourself.
    [*aside*] The great are like the base, nay, they are the same,
    When they seek shameful ways to avoid shame.   [*Exit.*]
BOSOLA. Antonio hereabout did drop a paper:
    Some of your help, false friend: [*Opening his lantern.*] Oh,
        here it is.   55
    What's here? A child's nativity calculated?   [*Reads.*]
    'The duchess was delivered of a son, 'tween the hours twelve
    and one in the night, *Anno Dom.* 1504,' that's this year—'*de-
    cimo nono Decembris.*'[9]—that's this night,—'taken according
    to the meridian of Malfi,'—that's our duchess: happy discov-   60
    ery! 'The lord of the first house being combust[1] in the ascend-
    ant, signifies short life; and Mars being in a human sign,
    joined to the tail of the Dragon, in the eighth house, doth
    threaten a violent death. *Caetera non scrutantur.*'[2]
    Why, now 'tis most apparent: this precise[3] fellow   65
    Is the duchess' bawd: I have it to my wish!
    This is a parcel of intelligency
    Our courtiers were cased up for: it needs must follow
    That I must be committed on pretense
    Of poisoning her; which I'll endure, and laugh at.   70
    If one could find the father now! But that
    Time will discover. Old Castruccio
    I' th' morning posts to Rome: by him I'll send
    A letter that shall make her brothers' galls
    O'erflow their livers. This was a thrifty way.   75

---

8. Bosola denies the charge of under-handed malignancy, not by denying malignancy, but by offering to make it public.
9. The 19th of December.
1. Afire.

2. The rest is not to be seen. Mars and the Dragon are sinister signs, even separately; fatal together.
3. This very fellow, but also implying that Antonio acts like a Puritan, a "precisian." "Bawd": procurer.

Though lust do mask in ne'er so strange disguise,
She's oft found witty, but is never wise.   [*Exit.*]

SCENE 4. *The palace of the* CARDINAL *at Rome.*

[*Enter* CARDINAL *and* JULIA.]

CARDINAL. Sit. Thou art my best of wishes. Prithee, tell me
What trick didst thou invent to come to Rome
Without thy husband.

JULIA.   Why, my lord, I told him
I came to visit an old anchorite[4]
Here for devotion.

CARDINAL.   Thou are a witty false one,   5
I mean, to him.

JULIA.   You have prevailed with me
Beyond my strongest thoughts! I would not now
Find you inconstant.

CARDINAL.   Do not put thyself
To such a voluntary torture, which proceeds
Out of your own guilt.

JULIA.   How, my lord?

CARDINAL.   You fear   10
My constancy, because you have approved[5]
Those giddy and wild turnings in yourself.

JULIA. Did you e'er find them?

CARDINAL.   Sooth, generally for women;
A man might strive to make glass malleable,
Ere he should make them fixed.

JULIA.   So, my lord.   15

CARDINAL. We had need go borrow that fantastic glass
Invented by Galileo the Florentine[6]
To view another spacious world i' th' moon,
And look to find a constant woman there.

JULIA. This is very well, my lord.

CARDINAL.   Why do you weep?   20
Are tears your justification? The self-same tears
Will fall into your husband's bosom, lady,
With a loud protestation that you love him
Above the world. Come, I'll love you wisely,
That's jealously, since I am very certain   25
You cannot make me cuckold.

JULIA.   I'll go home
To my husband.

CARDINAL.   You may thank me, lady,
I have taken you off your melancholy perch,
Bore you upon my fist, and showed you game,

---

4. Hermit.
5. Experienced.
6. In 1504, Galileo's telescope was more than 100 years in the future, but the reference was topical for Webster's audience.

And let you fly at it.[7] I pray thee, kiss me.   30
When thou wast with thy husband, thou wast watched
Like a tame elephant: still you are to thank me:
Thou hadst only kisses from him and high feeding;
But what delight was that? 'Twas just like one
That hath a little fingering on the lute,   35
Yet cannot tune it: still you are to thank me.

JULIA. You told me of a piteous wound i' th' heart
And a sick liver, when you wooed me first,
And spake like one in physic.[8]   [A *knock is heard.*]

CARDINAL.   Who's that?
          [*Enter* SERVANT.]
Rest firm, for my affection to thee,   40
Lightning moves slow to 't.[9]

SERVANT.   Madam, a gentleman,
That's come post from Malfi, desires to see you.

CARDINAL. Let him enter. I'll withdraw.   [*Exit.*]

SERVANT.   He says
Your husband, old Castruccio, is come to Rome,
Most pitifully tired with riding post.[1]   [*Exit.*] 45
          [*Enter* DELIO.]

JULIA. Signior Delio! [*aside*] 'tis one of my old suitors.

DELIO. I was bold to come and see you.

JULIA.   Sir, you are welcome.

DELIO. Do you lie here?

JULIA.   Sure, your own experience
Will satisfy you no: our Roman prelates
Do not keep lodging for ladies.

DELIO.   Very well.   50
I have brought you no commendations from your husband,
For I know none by him.

JULIA.   I hear he's come to Rome.

DELIO. I never knew man and beast, of a horse and a knight,
So weary of each other: if he had had a good back,
He would have undertook to have borne his horse,   55
His breech was so pitifully sore.

JULIA.   Your laughter
Is my pity.

DELIO. Lady, I know not whether
You want money, but I have brought you some.

JULIA. From my husband?

DELIO.   No, from mine own allowance.

JULIA.   I must hear the condition, ere I be bound to take it. 60

DELIO. Look on't, 'tis gold: hath it not a fine color?

JULIA. I have a bird more beautiful.

DELIO. Try the sound on 't.

7. The Cardinal speaks of himself as a falconer training a bird (Julia).
8. Like a man under a doctor's care.
9. By comparison.

1. When riding post, one changed horses at regular intervals without stopping to rest oneself.

JULIA. A lute-string far exceeds it:
It hath no smell, like cassia or civet;
Nor is it physical,[2] though some fond doctors 65
Persuade us seethe 't in cullises.[3] I'll tell you,
This is a creature bred by——
    [*Re-enter* SERVANT.]
SERVANT. Your husband's come,
Hath delivered a letter to the Duke of Calabria
That, to my thinking, hath put him out of his wits. [*Exit.*]
JULIA. Sir, you hear: 70
Pray, let me know your business and your suit
As briefly as can be.
DELIO. With good speed: I would wish you,
At such time as you are non-resident
With your husband, my mistress. 75
JULIA. Sir, I'll go ask my husband if I shall,
And straight return your answer. [*Exit.*]
DELIO. Very fine!
Is this her wit, or honesty, that speaks thus?
I heard one say the duke was highly moved
With a letter sent from Malfi. I do fear 80
Antonio is betrayed: how fearfully
Shows his ambition now! Unfortunate fortune!
They pass through whirlpools, and deep woes do shun,
Who the event weigh ere the action's done.[4] [*Exit.*]

SCENE 5

[*Enter* CARDINAL, *and* FERDINAND *with a letter.*]
FERDINAND. I have this night digged up a mandrake.[5]
CARDINAL. Say you?
FERDINAND. And I am grown mad with 't.
CARDINAL. What's the prodigy?
FERDINAND. Read there—a sister damned: she's loose i' th' hilts;[6]
Grown a notorious strumpet.
CARDINAL. Speak lower.
FERDINAND. Lower?
Rogues do not whisper 't now, but seek to publish 't 5
(As servants do the bounty of their lords)
Aloud; and with a covetous searching eye,
To mark who note them. O, confusion seize her!
She hath had most cunning bawds to serve her turn,
And more secure conveyances for lust 10
Than towns of garrison for service.
CARDINAL. Is 't possible?

2. Medicinally valuable.
3. Boil it up in a broth.
4. I.e., who look ahead at the consequences of their actions.
5. A fabulous root, violently aphrodisiac
but also deadly poison. Both aspects
apply to Ferdinand.
6. I.e., promiscuous; literally, a sword
which is too limber.

Can this be certain?

FERDINAND.   Rhubarb, oh, for rhubarb[7]
To purge this choler! Here's the cursèd day
To prompt my memory, and here 't shall stick
Till of her bleeding heart I make a sponge   15
To wipe it out.

CARDINAL.   Why do you make yourself
So wild a tempest?

FERDINAND.   Would I could be one,
That I might toss her palace 'bout her ears,
Root up her goodly forests, blast her meads.[8]
And lay her general territory as waste   20
As she hath done her honors.

CARDINAL.   Shall our blood,
The royal blood of Aragon and Castile,
Be thus attainted?

FERDINAND.   Apply desperate physic:
We must not now use balsamum,[9] but fire,
The smarting cupping-glass, for that 's the mean   25
To purge infected blood, such blood as hers.
There is a kind of pity in mine eye,
I'll give it to my handkercher; and now 'tis here,
I'll bequeath this to her bastard.

CARDINAL.   What to do?

FERDINAND. Why, to make soft lint for his mother's wounds,   30
When I have hewed her to pieces.

CARDINAL.   Cursèd creature!
Unequal nature, to place women's hearts
So far upon the left side![1]

FERDINAND.   Foolish men,
That e'er will trust their honor in a bark
Made of so slight weak bulrush as is woman,   35
Apt every minute to sink it!

CARDINAL. Thus ignorance, when it hath purchased honor,
It cannot wield it.

FERDINAND.   Methinks I see her laughing—
Excellent hyena! Talk to me somewhat, quickly,
Or my imagination will carry me   40
To see her in the shameful act of sin.

CARDINAL. With whom?

FERDINAND. Happily[2] with some strong-thighed bargeman,
Or one o' the woodyard that can quoit the sledge[3]
Or toss the bar, or else some lovely squire   45
That carries coals up to her privy lodgings.

---

7. Rhubarb, as a laxative, was supposed
to be good for the high pressures of
choler, hot-burning rage.
8. Open fields.
9. Balm, a gentle remedy, gives way to
cautery ("fire") and the "cupping-glass,"
by which people were bled.
1. The left is the sinister, or unlucky,
side.
2. Probably, haply.
3. Wield the sledgehammer, used in
splitting logs for firewood.

CARDINAL. You fly beyond your reason.

FERDINAND.   Go to, mistress!
'Tis not your whore's milk that shall quench my wild fire,
But your whore's blood.

CARDINAL. How idly shows this rage, which carries you,   50
As men conveyed by witches through the air,
On violent whirlwinds! This intemperate noise
Fitly resembles deaf men's shrill discourse,
Who talk aloud, thinking all other men
To have their imperfection.

FERDINAND.   Have not you   55
My palsy?

CARDINAL. Yes, I can be angry, but
Without this rupture: there is not in nature
A thing that makes man so deformed, so beastly,
As doth intemperate anger. Chide yourself.
You have divers men who never yet expressed   60
Their strong desire of rest but by unrest,
By vexing of themselves. Come, put yourself
In tune.

FERDINAND. So; I will only study to seem
The thing I am not. I could kill her now,
In you, or in myself; for I do think   65
It is some sin in us heaven doth revenge
By her.

CARDINAL. Are you stark mad?

FERDINAND.   I would have their bodies
Burnt in a coal-pit with the ventage stopped,
That their cursed smoke might not ascend to heaven;
Or dip the sheets they lie in in pitch or sulphur,   70
Wrap them in 't, and then light them like a match;
Or else to-boil their bastard to a cullis,
And give 't his lecherous father to renew
The sin of his back.[4]

CARDINAL.   I'll leave you.

FERDINAND.   Nay, I have done.
I am confident, had I been damned in hell,   75
And should have heard of this, it would have put me
Into a cold sweat. In, in; I'll go sleep.
Till I know who leaps my sister, I'll not stir:
That known, I'll find scorpions to string my whips,[5]
And fix her in a general eclipse.   [*Exeunt.*]   80

---

4. Only boiling down the bastard to a broth ("cullis") and feeding him to his father, as Atreus did to Thyestes in Greek legend, will satisfy Ferdinand. Thus the father will be made to "renew" (repair, atone for) the sin of his back in begetting the child.

5. Tipping the thongs of a whip with "scorpions" (tips of jagged steel or lead that sting and bite the flesh) is an old metaphor for aggravated punishment.

Act III

SCENE 1. *Amalfi.*

[*Enter* ANTONIO *and* DELIO.]

ANTONIO. Our noble friend, my most beloved Delio!
  Oh, you have been a stranger long at court;
  Came you along with the Lord Ferdinand?
DELIO. I did, sir. And how fares your noble duchess?
ANTONIO. Right fortunately well: she's an excellent   5
  Feeder of pedigrees; since you last saw her,
  She hath had two children more, a son and daughter.
DELIO. Methinks 'twas yesterday: let me but wink,
  And not behold your face, which to mine eye
  Is somewhat leaner, verily I should dream   10
  It were within this half-hour.
ANTONIO. You have not been in law, friend Delio,
  Nor in prison, nor a suitor at the court,
  Nor begged the reversion of some great man's place,
  Nor troubled with an old wife, which doth make   15
  Your time so insensibly hasten.[6]
DELIO.   Pray, sir, tell me.
  Hath not this news arrived yet to the ear
  Of the lord cardinal?
ANTONIO.   I fear it hath:
  The Lord Ferdinand, that's newly come to court,
  Doth bear himself right dangerously.
DELIO.   Pray, why?   20
ANTONIO. He is so quiet that he seems to sleep
  The tempest out, as dormice do in winter.
  Those houses that are haunted are most still
  Till the devil be up.
DELIO.   What say the common people?
ANTONIO. The common rabble do directly say   25
  She is a strumpet.
DELIO.   And your graver heads
  Which would be politic, what censure they?
ANTONIO. They do observe I grow to infinite purchase,
  The left hand way,[7] and all suppose the duchess
  Would amend it, if she could; for, say they,   30
  Great princes, though they grudge their officers
  Should have such large and unconfinéd means
  To get wealth under them, will not complain,
  Lest thereby they should make them odious
  Unto the people; for other obligation   35
  Of love or marriage between her and me
  They never dream of.
DELIO.   The Lord Ferdinand
  Is going to bed.

---

6. I.e., This is what makes your time
pass imperceptibly ("insensibly") by.

7. I.e., they think I am getting rich dis-
honestly.

[*Enter* DUCHESS, FERDINAND, *and* BOSOLA.]
FERDINAND. I'll instantly to bed,
  For I am weary.—I am to bespeak
  A husband for you.
DUCHESS.   For me, sir? Pray, who is 't?   40
FERDINAND. The great Count Malateste.
DUCHESS.   Fie upon him!
  A count? He's a mere stick of sugar-candy;
  You may look quite through him. When I choose
  A husband, I will marry for your honor.
FERDINAND. You shall do well in 't. How is 't, worthy Antonio? 45
DUCHESS. But, sir, I am to have private conference with you
  About a scandalous report is spread
  Touching mine honor.
FERDINAND.   Let me be ever deaf to 't:
  One of Pasquil's paper bullets,[8] court-calumny,
  A pestilent air, which princes' palaces   50
  Are seldom purged of. Yet, say that it were true,
  I pour it in your bosom, my fixed love
  Would strongly excuse, extenuate, nay, deny
  Faults, were they apparent in you. Go, be safe
  In your own innocency.
DUCHESS. [aside]   O blessèd comfort!   55
  This deadly air is purged.
              [*Exeunt* DUCHESS, ANTONIO, *and* DELIO.]
FERDINAND.   Her guilt treads on
  Hot-burning coulters.[9] Now, Bosola,
  How thrives our intelligence?
BOSOLA.   Sir, uncertainly
  'Tis rumored she hath had three bastards, but
  By whom we may go read i' th' stars.
FERDINAND.   Why, some   60
  Hold opinion all things are written there.
BOSOLA. Yes, if we could find spectacles to read them.
  I do suspect there hath been some sorcery
  Used on the duchess.
FERDINAND.   Sorcery? To what purpose?
BOSOLA. To make her dote on some desertless fellow   65
  She shames to acknowledge.
FERDINAND.   Can your faith give way
  To think there's power in potions or in charms,
  To make us love whether we will or no?
BOSOLA. Most certainly.
FERDINAND. Away! These are mere gulleries,[1] horrid things,   70
  Invented by some cheating mountebanks
  To abuse us. Do you think that herbs or charms

---

8. Anonymous satires were traditionally pasted on the statue of Pasquillo, or Pasquino, near Piazza Navona in Rome, and attributed to his authorship.
9. Medieval virginity-inquests customarily required the questioned lady to walk barefoot over red-hot plowshares ("coulters").
1. Deceits.

Can force the will? Some trials have been made
In this foolish practice, but the ingredients
Were lenitive poisons,[2] such as are of force   75
To make the patient mad; and straight the witch
Swears by equivocation they are in love.
The witchcraft lies in her rank blood. This night
I will force confession from her. You told me
You had got, within these two days, a false key   80
Into her bedchamber.
BOSOLA.   I have.
FERDINAND.   As I would wish.
BOSOLA. What do you intend to do?
FERDINAND.   Can you guess?
BOSOLA.   No.
FERDINAND. Do not ask, then:
He that can compass me, and know my drifts,
May say he hath put a girdle 'bout the world,   85
And sounded all her quicksands.
BOSOLA.   I do not
Think so.
FERDINAND. What do you think, then, pray?
BOSOLA.   That you
Are your own chronicle too much, and grossly
Flatter yourself.
FERDINAND.   Give me thy hand; I thank thee:
I never gave pension but to flatterers,   90
Till I entertained thee. Farewell.
That friend a great man's ruin strongly checks,
Who rails into his belief all his defects.   [*Exeunt.*]

SCENE 2. *The Bedchamber of the* DUCHESS.

[*Enter* DUCHESS, ANTONIO, *and* CARIOLA.]
DUCHESS. Bring me the casket hither, and the glass.
You get no lodging here tonight, my lord.
ANTONIO. Indeed, I must persuade one.
DUCHESS.   Very good:
I hope in time 'twill grow into a custom,
That noblemen shall come with cap and knee   5
To purchase a night's lodging of their wives.
ANTONIO. I must lie here.
DUCHESS.   Must! You are a lord of misrule.[3]
ANTONIO. Indeed, my rule is only in the night.
DUCHESS. To what use will you put me?
ANTONIO.   We'll sleep together.
DUCHESS. Alas, what pleasure can two lovers find in sleep!   10

2. Secret, slow-working poisons.
3. The mock-monarch of a carnival festival.

CARIOLA. My lord, I lie with her often, and I know
　She'll much disquiet you.
ANTONIO. 　　　　　　　See, you are complained of.
CARIOLA. For she's the sprawling'st bedfellow.
ANTONIO. 　　　　　　　　　　　　I shall like her
　The better for that.
CARIOLA. 　　　　　　Sir, shall I ask you a question?
ANTONIO. Oh, I pray thee, Cariola.
CARIOLA. 　　　　　　　　Wherefore still, when you lie 　15
　With my lady, do you rise so early?
ANTONIO. 　　　　　　　　Laboring men
　Count the clock oftenest, Cariola, are glad
　When their task's ended.
DUCHESS. 　　　　　　I'll stop your mouth. 　　[*Kisses him.*]
ANTONIO. Nay, that's but one; Venus had two soft doves
　To draw her chariot; I must have another— 　　　　　20
　　　　　　　　　　　　　[*She kisses him again.*]
　When wilt thou marry, Cariola?
CARIOLA. 　　　　　　　　Never, my lord.
ANTONIO. Oh, fie upon this single life! Forgo it.
　We read how Daphne, for her peevish flight,
　Became a fruitless bay-tree; Syrinx turned
　To the pale empty reed; Anaxarete 　　　　　　　25
　Was frozen into marble: whereas those
　Which married, or proved kind unto their friends,
　Were by a gracious influence transhaped
　Into the olive, pomegranate, mulberry.
　Became flowers, precious stones, or eminent stars.[4] 　　30
CARIOLA. This is a vain poetry, but I pray you tell me,
　If there were proposed me, wisdom, riches, and beauty,
　In three several young men, which should I choose?
ANTONIO. 'Tis a hard question: this was Paris' case,
　And he was blind in 't, and there was great cause; 　　35
　For how was 't possible he could judge right,
　Having three amorous goddesses in view,
　And they stark naked? 'Twas a motion[5]
　Were able to benight the apprehension
　Of the severest counsellor of Europe. 　　　　　　40
　Now I look on both your faces so well formed,
　It puts me in mind of a question I would ask.
CARIOLA. What is 't?
ANTONIO. 　　　　I do wonder why hard-favored ladies,

---

4. The olive was created by Athene; the mulberry gained its color from the blood of Pyramus and Thisbe; the pomegranate seems to have no particular mythological origin. Most of the other stories of ladies being transformed for complying, or not complying, with the solicitations of a god are from Ovid, *Metamorphoses.*
5. Spectacle. Paris had to choose between Hera, Athena, and Aphrodite, goddesses of marriage, wisdom, and love; his selecting the latter led to the Trojan war.

For the most part, keep worse-favored waiting-women
To attend them, and cannot endure fair ones.   45
DUCHESS. Oh, that's soon answered.
  Did you ever in your life know an ill painter
  Desire to have his dwelling next door to the shop
  Of an excellent picture-maker? 'Twould disgrace
  His face-making, and undo him. I prithee,   50
  When were we so merry?—My hair tangles.
ANTONIO. Pray thee, Cariola, let's steal forth the room,
  And let her talk to herself: I have divers times
  Served her the like, when she hath chafed extremely.
  I love to see her angry. Softly, Cariola.   55
                         [*Exeunt* ANTONIO *and* CARIOLA.]
DUCHESS. Doth not the color of my hair 'gin to change?
  When I wax gray, I shall have all the court
  Powder their hair with arras,[6] to be like me.
  You have cause to love me; I entered you into my heart
  Before you would vouchsafe to call for the keys.   60
        [*Enter* FERDINAND *behind.*]
  We shall one day have my brothers take you napping;
  Methinks his presence, being now in court,
  Should make you keep your own bed; but you'll say
  Love mixed with fear is sweetest. I'll assure you,
  You shall get no more children till my brothers   65
  Consent to be your gossips.[7] Have you lost your tongue?
                        [*She turns and sees* FERDINAND.]
  'Tis welcome:
  For know, whether I am doomed to live or die,
  I can do both like a prince.
FERDINAND.   Die, then, quickly! [*Giving her a poniard.*]
  Virtue, where art thou hid? What hideous thing   70
  Is it that doth eclipse thee?
DUCHESS.   Pray, sir, hear me.
FERDINAND. Or is it true thou art but a bare name,
  And no essential thing?
DUCHESS.   Sir—
FERDINAND.   Do not speak.
DUCHESS. No, sir: I will plant my soul in mine ears, to hear you.
FERDINAND. O most imperfect light of human reason,   75
  That mak'st us so unhappy to foresee
  What we can least prevent! Pursue thy wishes,
  And glory in them: there's in shame no comfort
  But to be past all bounds and sense of shame.
DUCHESS. I pray, sir, hear me. I am married.
FERDINAND.   So!   80
DUCHESS. Haply,[8] not to your liking: but for that,
  Alas, your shears do come untimely now

---

6. Orris-root, used in powdered form to   baptism.
make hair artificially gray.   8. Perhaps.
7. Intimate friends, but also sponsors in

To clip the bird's wings that's already flown!
Will you see my husband?
FERDINAND.   Yes, if I could change
  Eyes with a basilisk.[9]
DUCHESS.   Sure, you came hither   85
  By his confederacy.
FERDINAND.   The howling of a wolf
  Is music to thee, screech-owl: prithee, peace.
  Whate'er thou art that hast enjoyed my sister,
  For I am sure thou hear'st me, for thine own sake
  Let me not know thee. I came hither prepared   90
  To work thy discovery; yet am now persuaded
  It would beget such violent effects
  As would damn us both. I would not for ten millions
  I had beheld thee: therefore use all means
  I never may have knowledge of thy name;   95
  Enjoy thy lust still, and a wretched life,
  On that condition. And for thee, vile woman,
  If thou do wish thy lecher may grow old
  In thy embracements, I would have thee build
  Such a room for him as our anchorites   100
  To holier use inhabit. Let not the sun
  Shine on him till he's dead; let dogs and monkeys
  Only converse with him, and such dumb things
  To whom nature denies use to sound his name;
  Do not keep a paraquito,[1] lest she learn it;   105
  If thou do love him, cut out thine own tongue,
  Lest it bewray him.
DUCHESS.   Why might not I marry?
  I have not gone about in this to create
  Any new world or custom.
FERDINAND.   Thou art undone;
  And thou hast ta'en that massy sheet of lead   110
  That hid thy husband's bones, and folded it
  About my heart.
DUCHESS.   Mine bleeds for 't.
FERDINAND.   Thine? Thy heart?
  What should I name't unless a hollow bullet
  Filled with unquenchable wild-fire?
DUCHESS.   You are in this,
  Too strict, and were you not my princely brother,   115
  I would say, too willful. My reputation
  Is safe.
FERDINAND. Dost thou know what reputation is?
  I'll tell thee—to small purpose, since the instruction
  Comes now too late.   120
  Upon a time Reputation, Love, and Death,

---

9. The mythical basilisk was fabled to   1. Parrot.
kill with a glance.

Would travel o'er the world; and it was concluded
That they should part, and take three several ways.
Death told them, they should find him in great battles,
Or cities plagued with plagues. Love gives them counsel   125
To inquire for him 'mongst unambitious shepherds,
Where dowries were not talked of, and sometimes
'Mongst quiet kindred that had nothing left
By their dead parents. "Stay," quoth Reputation,
"Do not forsake me; for it is my nature,   130
If once I part from any man I meet,
I am never found again." And so for you:
You have shook hands with Reputation,
And made him invisible. So, fare you well.
I will never see you more.

DUCHESS.   Why should only I,   135
Of all the other princes of the world,
Be cased up, like a holy relic? I have youth
And a little beauty.

FERDINAND.   So you have some virgins
That are witches. I will never see thee more.   [*Exit.*]

[*Enter* ANTONIO *with a pistol, and* CARIOLA.]

DUCHESS. You saw this apparition?

ANTONIO.   Yes. We are   140
Betrayed. How came he hither? I should turn
This to thee, for that.   [*Pointing the pistol at* CARIOLA.]

CARIOLA.   Pray, sir, do; and when
That you have cleft my heart, you shall read there
Mine innocence.

DUCHESS.   That gallery gave him entrance.

ANTONIO. I would this terrible thing would come again,   145
That, standing on my guard, I might relate
My warrantable[2] love.   [*She shows the poniard.*]
                    Ha! What means this?

DUCHESS. He left this with me.

ANTONIO.   And it seems did wish
You would use it on yourself.

DUCHESS.   His action seemed
To intend so much.

ANTONIO.   This hath a handle to 't   150
As well as a point: turn it towards him, and
So fasten the keen edge in his rank gall.   [*Knocking within.*]
How now! Who knocks? More earthquakes?

DUCHESS.   I stand
As if a mine beneath my feet were ready
To be blown up.

CARIOLA.   'Tis Bosola.

DUCHESS.   Away!   155
O misery! Methinks unjust actions

2. Legitimate, defensible.

Should wear these masks and curtains, and not we.
You must instantly part hence: I have fashioned it
Already.   [*Exit* ANTONIO.]
            [*Enter* BOSOLA.]
BOSOLA. The duke your brother is ta'en up in a whirlwind, 160
Hath took horse, and 's rid post to Rome.
DUCHESS. So late?
BOSOLA. He told me, as he mounted into th' saddle,
You were undone.
DUCHESS.   Indeed, I am very near it.
BOSOLA. What's the matter?
DUCHESS. Antonio, the master of our household, 165
Hath dealt so falsely with me in 's accounts:
My brother stood engaged with me for money
Ta'en up of certain Neapolitan Jews,
And Antonio lets the bonds be forfeit.[3]
BOSOLA. Strange!—[*aside*] This is cunning.
DUCHESS.   And hereupon 170
My brother's bills at Naples are protested
Against.[4]—Call up our officers.
BOSOLA.   I shall.   [*Exit.*]
            [*Re-enter* ANTONIO.]
DUCHESS. The place that you must fly to is Ancona:[5]
Hire a house there; I'll send after you
My treasure and my jewels. Our weak safety 175
Runs upon enginous wheels:[6] short syllables
Must stand for periods. I must now accuse you
Of such a feignèd crime as Tasso calls
Magnanima menzogna, a noble lie,
'Cause it must shield our honors. Hark! They are coming. 180
        [*Re-enter* BOSOLA *and* OFFICERS.]
ANTONIO. Will your grace hear me?
DUCHESS. I have got well by you; you have yielded me
A million of loss: I am like to inherit
The people's curses for your stewardship.
You had the trick in audit-time to be sick, 185
Till I had signed your *quietus*;[7] and that cured you
Without help of a doctor. Gentlemen,
I would have this man be an example to you all;
So shall you hold my favor; I pray, let him;[8]
For h'as done that, alas, you would not think of, 190
And, because I intend to be rid of him,
I mean not to publish. [*to* ANTONIO] Use your fortune else-
where.

3. I.e., my brother advanced me some money in the form of notes, which I sent to Neapolitan money-lenders; now Antonio has let them call on the Duke for payment.
4. I.e., the Duke of Calabria's checks have bounced.
5. Ancona lies on the Adriatic coast of Italy, across the peninsula from Amalfi and well to the north.
6. Automatic wheels.
7. Receipt.
8. Release him.

ANTONIO. I am strongly armed to brook my overthrow;
As commonly men bear with a hard year,
I will not blame the cause on 't; but do think   195
The necessity of my malevolent star
Procures this, not her humor. Oh, the inconstant
And rotten ground of service! You may see,
'Tis even like him, that in a winter night,
Takes a long slumber o'er a dying fire,   200
A-loth to part from 't; yet parts thence as cold
As when he first sat down.
DUCHESS.   We do confiscate,
Towards the satisfying of your accounts,
All that you have.
ANTONIO.   I am yours, and 'tis very fit
All mine should be so.
DUCHESS.   So, sir, you have your pass.[9]   205
ANTONIO. You may see, gentlemen, what 'tis to serve
A prince with body and soul.   [*Exit.*]
BOSOLA. Here's an example for extortion: what moisture is drawn
out of the sea, when foul weather comes, pours down, and
runs into the sea again.   210
DUCHESS. I would know what are your opinions of this Antonio.
SECOND OFFICER. He could not abide to see a pig's head gaping:
I thought your grace would find him a Jew.[1]
THIRD OFFICER. I would you had been his officer, for your own
sake.   215
FOURTH OFFICER. You would have had more money.
FIRST OFFICER. He stopped his ears with black wool, and to
those came to him for money said he was thick of hearing.
SECOND OFFICER. Some said he was an hermaphrodite, for he
could not abide a woman.   220
FOURTH OFFICER. How scurvy proud he would look when the
treasury was full! Well, let him go!
FIRST OFFICER. Yes, and the chippings of the buttery fly after
him, to scour his gold chain![2]
DUCHESS. Leave us. [*Exeunt* OFFICERS.] What do you think of 225
these?
BOSOLA. That these are rogues that in 's prosperity, but to have
waited on his fortune, could have wished his dirty stirrup riveted through their noses, and followed after 's mule, like a
bear in a ring; would have prostituted their daughters to his 230
lust; made their first-born intelligencers; thought none happy
but such as were born under his blessed planet, and wore his
livery: and do these lice drop off now? Well, never look to
have the like again:[3] he hath left a sort of flattering rogues

9. Passport, leave to depart.
1. Jews were identified by their antipathy
to pork; but the assumptions here are
deliberately ridiculous.
2. A gold chain was the steward's tradi-

tional badge of office. Bread crumbs (the
"chippings of the buttery") were used
to polish gold and silver plate.
3. I.e., a servant as good as he was.

behind him; their doom must follow. Princes pay flatterers in 235
their own money: flatterers dissemble their vices, and they dissemble their lies; that's justice. Alas, poor gentleman!

DUCHESS. Poor? He hath amply filled his coffers.

BOSOLA. Sure, he was too honest. Pluto, the god of riches, when
he 's sent by Jupiter to any man, he goes limping, to signify 240
that wealth that comes on God's name comes slowly; but
when he 's sent on the devil's errand, he rides post and comes
in by scuttles.[4] Let me show you what a most unvalued jewel
you have in a wanton humor thrown away, to bless the man
shall find him. He was an excellent courtier and most faithful; 245
a soldier that thought it as beastly to know his own value too
little as devilish to acknowledge it too much. Both his virtue
and form deserved a far better fortune: his discourse rather
delighted to judge itself than show itself; his breast was filled
with all perfection, and yet it seemed a private whispering- 250
room,[5] it made so little noise of 't.

DUCHESS. But he was basely descended.

BOSOLA. Will you make yourself a mercenary herald, rather to
examine men's pedigrees than virtues? You shall want[6] him:
for know, an honest statesman to a prince is like a cedar 255
planted by a spring; the spring bathes the tree's root, the
grateful tree rewards it with his shadow: you have not done so.
I would sooner swim to the Bermoothes[7] on two politicians'
rotten bladders, tied together with an intelligencer's heart-
string, than depend on so changeable a prince's favor. Fare 260
thee well, Antonio! Since the malice of the world would needs
down with thee, it cannot be said yet that any ill happened
unto thee, considering thy fall was accompanied with virtue.

DUCHESS. Oh, you render me excellent music!

BOSOLA.   Say you?

DUCHESS. This good one that you speak of is my husband.   265

BOSOLA. Do I not dream? Can this ambitious age
    Have so much goodness in 't as to prefer
    A man merely for worth, without these shadows
    Of wealth and painted honors? Possible?

DUCHESS. I have had three children by him.

BOSOLA.   Fortunate lady!   270
    For you have made your private nuptial bed
    The humble and fair seminary of peace.
    No question but many an unbeneficed scholar[8]
    Shall pray for you for this deed, and rejoice
    That some preferment in the world can yet   275
    Arise from merit. The virgins of your land
    That have no dowries shall hope your example

---

4. In haste. Unvalued: invaluable.
5. Confessional-booth.
6. Miss.
7. The Bermudas, unknown in 1504, but

very topical a hundred years later, when
the play was written.
8. A scholar without an official appointment.

Will raise them to rich husbands. Should you want
Soldiers, 'twould make the very Turks and Moors
Turn Christians, and serve you for this act.   280
Last, the neglected poets of your time,
In honor of this trophy of a man,
Raised by that curious engine, your white hand,
Shall thank you, in your grave, for 't; and make that
More reverend than all the cabinets[9]   285
Of living princes. For Antonio,
His fame shall likewise flow from many a pen,
When heralds shall want coats to sell to men.

DUCHESS. As I taste comfort in this friendly speech,
So would I find concealment.   290

BOSOLA.   Oh, the secret of my prince,
Which I will wear on th' inside of my heart!

DUCHESS. You shall take charge of all my coin and jewels,
And follow him; for he retires himself
To Ancona.

BOSOLA.   So.

DUCHESS.   Whither, within few days,   295
I mean to follow thee.

BOSOLA.   Let me think:
I would wish your grace to feign a pilgrimage
To our Lady of Loreto[1], scarce seven leagues
From fair Ancona; so may you depart
Your country with more honor, and your flight   300
Will seem a princely progress, retaining
Your usual train about you.

DUCHESS.   Sir, your direction
Shall lead me by the hand.

CARIOLA.   In my opinion,
She were better progress to the baths at Lucca,
Or go visit the Spa in Germany;   305
For, if you will believe me, I do not like
This jesting with religion, this feigned
Pilgrimage.

DUCHESS. Thou art a superstitious fool.
Prepare us instantly for our departure.   310
Past sorrows, let us moderately lament them;
For those to come, seek wisely to prevent them.

                        [*Exit* DUCHESS, *with* CARIOLA.]

BOSOLA. A politician is the devil's quilted anvil;
He fashions all sins on him, and the blows
Are never heard: he may work in a lady's chamber,   315
As here for proof. What rests but I reveal
All to my lord? Oh, this base quality
Of intelligencer! Why, every quality i' th' world
Prefers but gain or commendation:

9. Reception-rooms. She will be more
honored in her grave than living princes
in their courts.

1. The shrine of the Virgin at Loreto was
famous throughout Europe.

Now for this act I am certain to be raised,   320
And men that paint weeds to the life are praised.

SCENE 3. *Rome.*

[*Enter* CARDINAL, FERDINAND, MALATESTE, PESCARA,
SILVIO, DELIO.]

CARDINAL. Must we turn soldier, then?

MALATESTE.   The emperor,[2]
Hearing your worth that way, ere you attained
This reverend garment, joins you in commission
With the right fortunate soldier the Marquis of Pescara.
And the famous Lannoy.

CARDINAL.   He that had the honor   5
Of taking the French king prisoner?[3]

MALATESTE.   The same.
Here's a plot drawn for a new fortification
At Naples.   [*They talk apart.*]

FERDINAND. This great Count Malateste, I perceive,
Hath got employment?

DELIO.   No employment, my lord;   10
A marginal note in the muster-book, that he is
A voluntary lord.

FERDINAND.   He 's no soldier?

DELIO. He has worn gunpowder in 's hollow tooth for the
toothache.[4]

SILVIO. He comes to the leaguer[5] with a full intent   15
To eat fresh beef and garlic, means to stay
Till the scent be gone, and straight return to court.

DELIO. He hath read all the late service as the city chronicle
relates it, and keeps two pewterers going, only to express battles in model.[6]   20

SILVIO. Then he'll fight by the book.

DELIO. By the almanac, I think, to choose good days and shun
the critical. That's his mistress' scarf.

SILVIO. Yes, he protests he would do much for that taffeta.

DELIO. I think he would run away from a battle, to save it from   25
taking prisoner.

SILVIO. He is horribly afraid gunpowder will spoil the perfume on
't.

DELIO. I saw a Dutchman break his pate once for calling him
pot-gun;[7] he made his head have a bore in 't like a musket.   30

---

2. The Spanish Emperor, Charles V. The
transformation of the Cardinal to a soldier (which has no consequence for the
action of the play) again recalls Cesare
Borgia, who was created a cardinal by his
father, Alexander VI, before he resigned
the office and became famous, or infamous, as a soldier.
3. Charles de Lannoy, Belgian by origin,
did indeed capture Francis I at Pavia,
but only in 1525, 21 years after the date
of the play's supposed action.
4. Saltpeter was sometimes used against
the toothache.
5. Assembly, muster of the troops.
6. He has studied all the recent military
history as it's represented on pewter
dishes, and employs two craftsmen of his
own to keep him up to date.
7. Loudmouth.

SILVIO. I would he had made a touchhole to 't. He is indeed a
guarded sumpter-cloth,[8] only for the remove of the court.

[*Enter* BOSOLA *and speaks to* FERDINAND *and the*
CARDINAL.]

PESCARA. Bosola arrived? What should be the business?
Some falling-out amongst the cardinals.
These factions amongst great men, they are like   35
Foxes; when their heads are divided,
They carry fire in their tails, and all the country
About them goes to wrack for 't.[9]

SILVIO.   What's that Bosola?

DELIO. I knew him in Padua—a fantastical scholar, like such who
study to know how many knots were in Hercules' club, of   40
what color Achilles' beard was, or whether Hector were not
troubled with the toothache. He hath studied himself half
blear-eyed to know the true symmetry of Caesar's nose by a
shoeing-horn; and this he did to gain the name of a speculative man.[1]   45

PESCARA. Mark Prince Ferdinand:
A very salamander lives in 's eye,
To mock the eager violence of fire.[2]

SILVIO. That Cardinal hath made more bad faces with his oppression than ever Michael Angelo[3] made good ones: he lifts up   50
's nose, like a foul porpoise before a storm.

PESCARA. The Lord Ferdinand laughs.

DELIO. Like a deadly cannon that lightens ere it smokes.

PESCARA. These are your true pangs of death,
The pangs of life, that struggle with great statesmen.   55

DELIO. In such a deformed silence witches whisper
Their charms.

CARDINAL. Doth she make religion her riding-hood
To keep her from the sun and tempest?

FERDINAND.   That,
That damns her. Methinks her fault and beauty,   60
Blended together, show like leprosy,
The whiter, the fouler. I make it a question
Whether her beggarly brats were ever christened.

CARDINAL. I will instantly solicit the state of Ancona.
To have them banished.

FERDINAND.   You are for Loreto?   65
I shall not be at your ceremony; fare you well.
Write to the Duke of Malfi, my young nephew

8. He is an empty ceremony, a mere formality. "Touchhole": where the match
was applied to set off a cannon.
9. Samson once tied some foxes together
by the tail and set them afire to burn
down the cornfields of the Philistines
(Judges XV).
1. Scholarship was the traditional cause
of melancholy, especially when exercised
on impossible, useless questions like
these.
2. The salamander, or water-lizard, was
supposed to be so cold and wet of constitution that it could live in fire; Ferdinand is cold in his rage.
3. Michelangelo Buonarroti, the great
Florentine painter and sculptor.

She had by her first husband, and acquaint him
With 's mother's honesty.
BOSOLA.   I will.
FERDINAND.   Antonio!
A slave that only smelled of ink and counters,   70
And never in 's life looked like a gentleman,
But in the audit-time. Go, go presently,[4]
Draw me out an hundred and fifty of our horse,
And meet me at the fort-bridge.   [*Exeunt.*]

SCENE 4. *The Shrine of Our Lady of Loreto.*

[*Enter* TWO PILGRIMS.]
FIRST PILGRIM. I have not seen a goodlier shrine than this;
Yet I have visited many.
SECOND PILGRIM.   The Cardinal of Aragon
Is this day to resign his cardinal's hat:
His sister duchess likewise is arrived
To pay her vow of pilgrimage. I expect   5
A noble ceremony.
FIRST PILGRIM. No question. They come.
[*Here the ceremony of the* CARDINAL's *installment, in
the habit of a soldier, is performed in delivering up his
cross, hat, robes, and ring, at the shrine, and investing
him with sword, helmet, shield, and spurs; then* ANTONIO,
the DUCHESS, *and their children, having presented them-
selves at the shrine, are, by a form of banishment in
dumb-show expressed towards them by the* CARDINAL *and
the state of Ancona, banished: during all which ceremony, this ditty is sung, to very solumn music, by divers
churchmen.*]
Arms and honors deck thy story,
To thy fame's eternal glory!
Adverse fortune ever fly thee;   10
No disastrous fate come nigh thee!

I alone will sing thy praises,
Whom to honor virtue raises;
And thy study, that divine is,
Bent to martial discipline is.   15
Lay aside all those robes lie by thee;
Crown thy arts with arms, they'll beautify thee.

O worthy of worthiest name, adorned in this manner,
Lead bravely thy forces on under war's warlike banner!
Oh, mayst thou prove fortunate in all martial courses!   20
Guide thou still by skill in arts and forces!

4. At once.

Victory attend thee nigh, whilst fame sings loud thy powers;
Triumphant conquest crown thy head, and blessings pour
  down showers!⁵   [*Exeunt all except the* TWO PILGRIMS.]

FIRST PILGRIM. Here's a strange turn of state! Who would have
  thought
So great a lady would have matched herself   25
Unto so mean a person? Yet the Cardinal
Bears himself much too cruel.

SECOND PILGRIM.   They are banished.

FIRST PILGRIM. But I would ask what power hath this state
Of Ancona to determine of a free prince?

SECOND PILGRIM. They are a free state, sir, and her brother
  showed.   30
How that the Pope, fore-hearing of her looseness,
Hath seized into th' protection of the Church
The dukedom which she held as dowager.⁶

FIRST PILGRIM. But by what justice?

SECOND PILGRIM.   Sure, I think by none,
Only her brother's instigation.   35

FIRST PILGRIM. What was it with such violence he took
Off from her finger?

SECOND PILGRIM.   'Twas her wedding-ring,
Which he vowed shortly he would sacrifice
To his revenge.

FIRST PILGRIM.   Alas, Antonio!
If that a man be thrust into a well,   40
No matter who sets hands to 't, his own weight
Will bring him sooner to th' bottom. Come, let's hence.
Fortune makes this conclusion general,
All things do help th' unhappy man to fall.   [*Exeunt.*]

SCENE 5. *Near Loreto.*

[*Enter* DUCHESS, ANTONIO, CHILDREN, CARIOLA, *and*
SERVANTS.]

DUCHESS. Banished Ancona!

ANTONIO.   Yes, you see what power
Lightens in great men's breath.

DUCHESS.   Is all our train
Shrunk to this poor remainder?

ANTONIO.   These poor men,
Which have got little in your service, vow
To take your fortune, but your wiser buntings,⁷   5
Now they are fledged, are gone.

DUCHESS.   They have done wisely.

5. This song is not very suitable to the scene, and Webster, in the edition of 1623, denied writing it.
6. The Duchess held Malfi only as guardian for her son, the still youthful Duke.
7. Migratory birds; "take": accept.

This puts me in mind of death: physicians thus,
With their hands full of money, use to give o'er
Their patients.
ANTONIO.   Right[8] the fashion of the world:
From decayed fortunes every flatterer shrinks;   10
Men cease to build where the foundation sinks.
DUCHESS. I had a very strange dream tonight.
ANTONIO.   What was 't?
DUCHESS. Methought I wore my coronet of state,
And on a sudden all the diamonds
Were changed to pearls.
ANTONIO.   My interpretation   15
Is, you'll weep shortly, for to me the pearls
Do signify your tears.
DUCHESS.   The birds that live
I' th' field on the wild benefit of nature
Live happier than we; for they may choose their mates,
And carol their sweet pleasures to the spring.   20
    [*Enter* BOSOLA *with a letter.*]
BOSOLA. You are happily o'erta'en.
DUCHESS.   From my brother?
BOSOLA. Yes, from the Lord Ferdinand your brother
All love and safety.
DUCHESS.   Thou dost blanch[9] mischief,
Wouldst make it white. See, see, like to calm weather
At sea before a tempest, false hearts speak fair   25
To those they intend most mischief.
    "Send Antonio to me; I want his head in a business."
A politic equivocation!
He doth not want your counsel, but your head;
That is, he cannot sleep till you be dead.   30
And here's another pitfall that's strewed o'er
With roses: mark it, 'tis a cunning one:
    "I stand engaged for your husband for several debts at
Naples: let not that trouble him; I had rather have his
heart than his money."   35
And I believe so too.
BOSOLA.   What do you believe?
DUCHESS. That he so much distrusts my husband's love,
He will by no means believe his heart is with him
Until he see it: the devil is not cunning
Enough to circumvent us in riddles.   40
BOSOLA. Will you reject that noble and free league
Of amity and love which I present you?
DUCHESS. Their league is like that of some politic kings,
Only to make themselves of strength and power
To be our after-ruin: tell them so.   45
BOSOLA. And what from you?
ANTONIO.   Thus tell him: I will not come.

8. Exactly.   9. Whitewash, cover up.

BOSOLA. And what of this?   [*Pointing to the letter.*]
ANTONIO.   My brothers have dispersed
  Blood-hounds abroad; which till I hear are muzzled,
  No truce, though hatched with ne'er such politic skill,
  Is safe, that hangs upon our enemies' will.   50
  I'll not come at them.
BOSOLA.   This proclaims your breeding:
  Every small thing draws a base mind to fear,
  As the adamant draws iron.[1] Fare you well, sir;
  You shall shortly hear from 's.   [*Exit.*]
DUCHESS.   I suspect some ambush;
  Therefore, by all my love I do conjure you   55
  To take your eldest son, and fly towards Milan.
  Let us not venture all this poor remainder
  In one unlucky bottom.[2]
ANTONIO.   You counsel safely.
  Best of my life, farewell. Since we must part,
  Heaven hath a hand in 't, but no otherwise   60
  Than as some curious artist[3] takes in sunder
  A clock or watch, when it is out of frame,
  To bring 't in better order.
DUCHESS.   I know not
  Which is best, to see you dead, or part with you.
  Farewell, boy.   65
  Thou art happy that thou hast not understanding
  To know thy misery; for all our wit
  And reading brings us to a truer sense
  Of sorrow. In the eternal church, sir,
  I do hope we shall not part thus.
ANTONIO.   Oh, be of comfort!   70
  Make patience a noble fortitude,
  And think not how unkindly we are used:
  Man, like to cassia, is proved best being bruised.[4]
DUCHESS. Must I, like to a slave-born Russian,
  Account it praise to suffer tyranny?   75
  And yet, O heaven, thy heavy hand is in 't!
  I have seen my little boy oft scourge his top,[5]
  And compared myself to 't: naught made me e'er
  Go right but heaven's scourge-stick.
ANTONIO.   Do not weep:
  Heaven fashioned us of nothing, and we strive   80
  To bring ourselves to nothing. Farewell, Cariola,
  And thy sweet armful. If I do never see thee more,
  Be a good mother to your little ones,
  And save them from the tiger. Fare you well.

---

1. As the loadstone draws iron.
2. The metaphor is mercantile; let's not load all our cargo in one ship ("bottom").
3. Clever craftsman; "out of frame": not working.
4. Man, like cinnamon-bark, is most aromatic (virtuous) when pressed (oppressed).
5. Boys used to make tops spin by whipping them.

DUCHESS. Let me look upon you once more, for that speech   85
    Came from a dying father. Your kiss is colder
    Than that I have seen an holy anchorite
    Give to a dead man's skull.
ANTONIO. My heart is turned to a heavy lump of lead,
    With which I sound my danger. Fare you well.   90
                   [*Exeunt* ANTONIO *and his son.*]
DUCHESS. My laurel is all withered.
CARIOLA. Look, madam, what a troop of arméd men
    Make toward us.
DUCHESS.   Oh, they are very welcome:
    When Fortune's wheel[6] is over-charged with princes,
    The weight makes it move swift: I would have my ruin   95
    Be sudden.
        [*Enter* BOSOLA *vizarded,*[7] *with a guard.*]
        I am your adventure,[8] am I not?
BOSOLA. You are. You must see your husband no more.
DUCHESS. What devil art thou that counterfeits heaven's thunder?
BOSOLA. Is that terrible? I would have you tell me whether
    Is that note worse that frights the silly birds   100
    Out of the corn, or that which doth allure them
    To the nets? You have hearkened to the last too much.
DUCHESS. Oh, misery! Like to a rusty o'ercharged cannon,
    Shall I never fly in pieces?—Come, to what prison?
BOSOLA. To none.
DUCHESS.   Whither, then?
BOSOLA.   To your palace.
DUCHESS.   I have heard   105
    That Charon's boat serves to convey all o'er[9]
    The dismal lake, but brings none back again.
BOSOLA. Your brothers mean you safety and pity.
DUCHESS.   Pity!
    With such a pity men preserve alive
    Pheasants and quails, when they are not fat enough   110
    To be eaten.
BOSOLA. These are your children?
DUCHESS.   Yes.
BOSOLA.   Can they prattle?
DUCHESS. No.
    But I intend, since they were born accursed,
    Curses shall be their first language.
BOSOLA.   Fie, madam!
    Forget this base, low fellow—
DUCHESS.   Were I a man,   115

---

6. The wheel of fortune is an ancient emblem of mutability; men have their fixed positions on it, and rise or fall as it turns.
7. Bosola wears a mask.
8. I.e., I am what you're looking for, am I not?
9. In classical mythology, Charon transports the souls of the dead across the river Styx to Hades.

I'd beat that counterfeit face into thy other.[1]
BOSOLA. One of no birth.[2]
DUCHESS. Say that he was born mean,
   Man is most happy when 's own actions
   Be arguments and examples of his virtue.
BOSOLA. A barren, beggarly virtue! 120
DUCHESS. I prithee, who is greatest? Can you tell?
   Sad tales befit my woe: I'll tell you one.
   A salmon, as she swam unto the sea,
   Met with a dog-fish, who encounters her
   With this rough language: "Why art thou so bold 125
   To mix thyself with our high state of floods,
   Being no eminent courtier, but one
   That for the calmest and fresh time o' the year
   Dost live in shallow rivers, rank'st thyself
   With silly smelts and shrimps? And darest thou 130
   Pass by our dog-ship without reverence?"
   "Oh!" quoth the salmon, "sister, be at peace:
   Thank Jupiter we both have passed the net!
   Our value never can be truly known,
   Till in the fisher's basket we be shown: 135
   I' th' market then my price may be the higher,
   Even when I am nearest to the cook and fire."
   So to great men the moral may be stretchéd;
   Men oft are valued high, when they're most wretched.
   But come, whither you please. I am armed 'gainst misery; 140
   Bent to all sways of the oppressor's will:
   There's no deep valley but near some great hill. [*Exeunt.*]

Act IV

SCENE 1. *Amalfi.*

[*Enter* FERDINAND *and* BOSOLA.]
FERDINAND. How doth our sister duchess bear herself
   In her imprisonment?
BOSOLA. Nobly. I'll describe her.
   She's sad as one long used to 't, and she seems
   Rather to welcome the end of misery
   Than shun it; a behavior so noble 5
   As gives a majesty to adversity:
   You may discern the shape of loveliness
   More perfect in her tears than in her smiles;
   She will muse for hours together; and her silence,
   Methinks, expresseth more than if she spake. 10
FERDINAND. Her melancholy seems to be fortified
   With a strange disdain.

---

1. I.e., I'd push your mask down your   2. Of low rank by birth.
throat.

BOSOLA.   'Tis so; and this restraint,
  Like English mastiffs that grow fierce with tying,
  Makes her too passionately apprehend
  Those pleasures she's kept from.
FERDINAND.   Curse upon her!
  I will no longer study in the book
  Of another's heart. Inform her what I told you.   [*Exit.*]
    [*Enter* DUCHESS.]
BOSOLA. All comfort to your grace!
DUCHESS.   I will have none.
  Pray thee, why dost thou wrap thy poisoned pills
  In gold and sugar?   20
BOSOLA. Your elder brother, the Lord Ferdinand,
  Is come to visit you, and sends you word,
  'Cause once he rashly made a solemn vow
  Never to see you more, he comes i' th' night,
  And prays you gently neither torch nor taper   25
  Shine in your chamber. He will kiss your hand
  And reconcile himself, but for his vow
  He dares not see you.
DUCHESS.   At his pleasure. Take hence the lights.
  He's come.
    [*Enter* FERDINAND.]
FERDINAND. Where are you?
DUCHESS.   Here, sir.
FERDINAND.   This darkness suits you well. 30
DUCHESS. I would ask you pardon.
FERDINAND.   You have it; for I account it
  The honorabl'st revenge, where I may kill,
  To pardon. Where are your cubs?
DUCHESS.   Whom?
FERDINAND.   Call them your children;
  For though our national law distinguish bastards
  From true legitimate issue, compassionate nature   35
  Makes them all equal.
DUCHESS.   Do you visit me for this?
  You violate a sacrament o' th' Church
  Shall make you howl in hell for 't.
FERDINAND.   It had been well
  Could you have lived thus always; for, indeed,
  You were too much i' th' light—but no more—   40
  I come to seal my peace with you. Here's a hand
        [*Gives her a dead man's hand.*]
  To which you have vowed much love; the ring upon 't
  You gave.
DUCHESS. I affectionately kiss it.
FERDINAND. Pray, do, and bury the print of it in your heart.
  I will leave this ring with you for a love-token,   45
  And the hand as sure as the ring; and do not doubt
  But you shall have the heart, too. When you need a friend,

Send it to him that owed[3] it; you shall see
Whether he can aid you.
DUCHESS.   You are very cold;
I fear you are not well after your travel.   50
Ha! Lights! Oh, horrible!
FERDINAND.   Let her have lights enough. [*Exit.*]
DUCHESS. What witchcraft doth he practice, that he hath left
A dead man's hand here?
    [*Here is discovered, behind a traverse,[4] the artificial fig-
    ures of Antonio and his children, appearing as if they
    were dead.*]
BOSOLA. Look you, here's the piece from which 'twas ta'en.
He doth present you this sad spectacle,   55
That, now you know directly they are dead,
Hereafter you may wisely cease to grieve
For that which cannot be recovered.
DUCHESS. There is not between heaven and earth one wish
I stay for after this: it wastes[5] me more   60
Than were't my picture, fashioned out of wax,
Stuck with a magical needle, and then buried
In some foul dunghill; and yond's an excellent property[6]
For a tyrant, which I would account mercy.
BOSOLA.   What's that?
DUCHESS. If they would bind me to that lifeless trunk   65
And let me freeze to death.
BOSOLA.   Come, you must live.
DUCHESS. That's the greatest torture souls feel in hell,
In hell, that they must live, and cannot die.
Portia,[7] I'll new-kindle thy coals again,
And revive the rare and almost dead example   70
Of a loving wife.
BOSOLA.   Oh, fie! Despair? Remember
You are a Christian.
DUCHESS.   The Church enjoins fasting:
I'll starve myself to death.
BOSOLA.   Leave this vain sorrow.
Things being at the worst begin to mend: the bee
When he hath shot his sting into your hand, may then   75
Play with your eyelid.
DUCHESS.   Good comfortable fellow,
Persuade a wretch that's broke upon the wheel
To have all his bones new set; entreat him live
To be executed again. Who must dispatch me?
I account this world a tedious theater,   80

---

3. Owned.
4. A translucent screen or curtain.
5. Consumes, as by secret disease; witches were supposed to be able to "waste" their enemies by making wax images and tormenting them as indicated below.
6. There's an excellent scheme.
7. Portia, the wife of Brutus, committed suicide by swallowing hot coals.

For I do play a part in 't 'gainst my will.
BOSOLA. Come, be of comfort; I will save your life,
DUCHESS.   Indeed,
   I have not leisure to tend so small a business.
BOSOLA. Now, by my life, I pity you.
DUCHESS.   Thou art a fool, then,
   To waste thy pity on a thing so wretched   85
   As cannot pity itself. I am full of daggers.
   Puff, let me blow these vipers from me.
      [*Enter* SERVANT.]
   What are you?
SERVANT.   One that wishes you long life.
DUCHESS. I would thou wert hanged for the horrible curse
   Thou hast given me. I shall shortly grow one   90
   Of the miracles of pity. I'll go pray—
   No, I'll go curse.
BOSOLA.   Oh, fie!
DUCHESS.   I could curse the stars—
BOSOLA. Oh, fearful!
DUCHESS. And those three smiling seasons of the year
   Into a Russian winter, nay, the world   95
   To its first chaos.[8]
BOSOLA.   Look you, the stars shine still.
DUCHESS. Oh, but you must
   Remember, my curse hath a great way to go.
   Plagues, that make lanes through largest families,
   Consume them!   100
BOSOLA. Fie, lady!
DUCHESS.   Let them, like tyrants,
   Never be remembered but for the ill they have done;
   Let all the zealous prayers of mortified
   Churchmen forget them!
BOSOLA.   Oh, uncharitable!
DUCHESS. Let Heaven a little while cease crowning martyrs   105
   To punish them!
   Go, howl them this, and say, I long to bleed:
   It is some mercy when men kill with speed.
                          [*Exeunt* DUCHESS *and* SERVANT.]
      [*Re-enter* FERDINAND.]
FERDINAND. Excellent, as I would wish; she's plagued in art:
   These presentations are but framed in wax   110
   By the curious master in that quality,
   Vincentio Lauriola,[9] and she takes them
   For true substantial bodies.
BOSOLA.   Why do you do this?
FERDINAND. To bring her to despair.

---

8. A Russian winter would last all year
long.
9. The art of wax modeling was common

enough, but the name of the artist seems
to be imaginary.

BOSOLA.   'Faith, end here,
  And go no farther in your cruelty.   115
  Send her a penitential garment to put on
  Next to her delicate skin, and furnish her
  With beads and prayer-books.
FERDINAND.   Damn her! That body of hers,
  While that my blood ran pure in 't, was more worth
  Than that which thou wouldst comfort, called a soul.   120
  I will send her masks of common courtesans,
  Have her meat served up by bawds and ruffians,
  And, 'cause she'll needs be mad, I am resolved
  To remove forth the common hospital
  All the mad-folk, and place them near her lodging;   125
  There let them practice together, sing and dance,
  And act their gambols to the full o' th' moon:
  If she can sleep the better for it, let her.
  Your work is almost ended.
BOSOLA.   Must I see her again?
FERDINAND. Yes.
BOSOLA.   Never.
FERDINAND.   You must.   130
BOSOLA.   Never in mine own shape;
  That's forfeited by my intelligence[1]
  And this last cruel lie. When you send me next,
  The business shall be comfort.
FERDINAND.   Very likely.
  Thy pity is nothing of kin to thee.[2] Antonio   135
  Lurks about Milan: thou shalt shortly thither
  To feed a fire as great as my revenge,
  Which ne'er will slack till it have spent his fuel.
  Intemperate agues make physicians cruel.   [*Exeunt.*]

SCENE 2

[*Enter* DUCHESS *and* CARIOLA.]
DUCHESS. What hideous noise was that?
CARIOLA.   'Tis the wild consort
  Of madmen, lady, which your tyrant brother
  Hath placed about your lodging. This tyranny,
  I think, was never practiced till this hour.
DUCHESS. Indeed, I thank him. Nothing but noise and folly   5
  Can keep me in my right wits, whereas reason
  And silence make me stark mad. Sit down;
  Discourse to me some dismal tragedy.
CARIOLA. Oh, 'twill increase your melancholy.
DUCHESS.   Thou are deceived:
  To hear of greater grief would lessen mine.   10

---

1. I.e., I can't do that because she   2. I.e., pity doesn't suit you very well.
knows now I've played the spy on her.

This is a prison?

CARIOLA.   Yes, but you shall live
To shake this durance off.

DUCHESS.   Thou art a fool:
The robin-redbreast and the nightingale
Never live long in cages.

CARIOLA.   Pray, dry your eyes.
What think you of, madam?

DUCHESS.   Of nothing; when I muse thus, 15
I sleep.

CARIOLA.   Like a madman, with your eyes open?

DUCHESS. Dost thou think we shall know one another in th'
other world?

CARIOLA. Yes, out of question.

DUCHESS.   Oh, that it were possible
We might but hold some two days' conference
With the dead! From them I should learn somewhat, I am
sure,   20
I never shall know here. I'll tell thee a miracle;
I am not mad yet, to my cause of sorrow:
Th' heaven o'er my head seems made of molten brass,
The earth of flaming sulphur, yet I am not mad.
I am acquainted with sad misery   25
As the tanned galley-slave is with his oar;
Necessity makes me suffer constantly,
And custom makes it easy. Who do I look like now?

CARIOLA. Like to your picture in the gallery,
A deal of life in show, but none in practice,   30
Or rather like some reverend monument
Whose ruins are even pitied.

DUCHESS.   Very proper.
And Fortune seems only to have her eyesight
To behold my tragedy.
How now! What noise is that?
        [*Enter* SERVANT.]

SERVANT.   I am come to tell you   35
Your brother hath intended you some sport.
A great physician, when the Pope was sick
Of a deep melancholy, presented him
With several sorts of madmen, which wild object
Being full of change and sport, forced him to laugh,   40
And so the imposthume[3] broke. The self-same cure
The duke intends on you.

DUCHESS.   Let them come in.

SERVANT. There's a mad lawyer; and a secular priest;
A doctor that hath forfeited his wits
By jealousy; an astrologian   45
That in his works said such a day o' the' month
Should be the day of doom, and, failing of 't,
Ran mad; an English tailor crazed i' th' brain

3. Boil.

With the study of new fashions; a gentleman-usher[4]
Quite beside himself with care to keep in mind   50
The number of his lady's salutations
Or 'How do you's' she employed him in each morning;
A farmer, too, an excellent knave in grain,
Mad 'cause he was hindered transportation:
And let one broker that's mad loose to these,   55
You'd think the devil were among them.[5]

DUCHESS. Sit, Cariola. Let them loose when you please,
For I am chained to endure all your tyranny.

[*Enter* MADMEN.]
[*Here by a* MADMAN *this Song is sung to a dismal kind
of music.*]

Oh, let us howl some heavy note,
    Some deadly dogged howl,   60
Sounding as from the threatening throat
    Of beasts and fatal fowl!
As ravens, screech-owls, bulls, and bears,
    We'll bell, and bawl our parts,
Till irksome noise have cloyed your ears   65
    And corrosived your hearts.
At last, whenas our choir wants breath,
    Our bodies being blest,
We'll sing, like swans, to welcome death,
    And die in love and rest.   70

FIRST MADMAN. Doom's-day not come yet? I'll draw it nearer by
a perspective,[6] or make a glass that shall set all the world on
fire upon an instant. I cannot sleep; my pillow is stuffed with
a litter of porcupines.

SECOND MADMAN. Hell is a mere glass-house, where the devils are   75
continually blowing up women's souls on hollow irons, and
the fire never goes out.

THIRD MADMAN. I will lie with every woman in my parish the
tenth night; I will tithe them over like haycocks.

FOURTH MADMAN. Shall my pothecary out-go me because I am a   80
cuckold? I have found out his roguery; he makes alum of his
wife's urine, and sells it to Puritans that have sore throats with
overstraining.

FIRST MADMAN. I have skill in heraldry.

SECOND MADMAN. Hast?   85

FIRST MADMAN. You do give for your crest a woodcock's head
with the brains picked out on 't; you are a very ancient gentleman.

THIRD MADMAN. Greek is turned Turk: we are only to be saved
by the Helvetian translation.[7]   90

---

4. Doorkeeper.
5. All the madmen have lost their wits
in the pursuit of their trades; lead them
to a broker, who might get them back to
work again, and they'll be madder than
ever.
6. Telescope.
7. The Geneva Bible; but how it would
help with the Greeks and Turks is clear
only to the lunatic.

FIRST MADMAN. Come on, sir, I will lay the law to you.

SECOND MADMAN. Oh, rather lay a corrosive: the law will eat to the bone.

THIRD MADMAN. He that drinks but to satisfy nature is damned.

FOURTH MADMAN. If I had my glass[8] here, I would show a sight 95 should make all the women here call me mad doctor.

FIRST MADMAN. What's he? A rope-maker?

SECOND MADMAN. No, no, no, a snuffling knave that, while he shows the tombs, will have his hand in a wench's placket.

THIRD MADMAN. Woe to the caroche[9] that brought home my 100 wife from the masque at three o'clock in the morning! It had a large feather-bed in it.

FOURTH MADMAN. I have pared the devil's nails forty times, roasted them in raven's eggs, and cured agues with them.

THIRD MADMAN. Get me three hundred milchbats, to make pos- 105 sets to procure sleep.[1]

FOURTH MADMAN. All the college may throw their caps at me: I have made a soap boiler costive; it was my masterpiece.

> [*Here the dance, consisting of eight* MADMEN, *with music answerable thereunto; after which* BOSOLA, *like an old man, enters.*]

DUCHESS. Is he mad too?

SERVANT.   Pray, question him. I'll leave you.

> [*Exeunt* SERVANT *and* MADMEN.]

BOSOLA. I am come to make thy tomb.

DUCHESS.   Ha! My tomb?   110
Thou speak'st as if I lay upon my deathbed,
Gasping for breath. Dost thou perceive me sick?

BOSOLA. Yes, and the more dangerously, since thy sickness
Is insensible.[2]

DUCHESS. Thou art not mad, sure. Dost know me?   115

BOSOLA. Yes.

DUCHESS.   Who am I?

BOSOLA. Thou art a box of worm-seed, at best but a salvatory of green mummy.[3] What's this flesh? A little crudded[4] milk, fantastical puff-paste. Our bodies are weaker than those paper-prisons boys use to keep flies in, more contemptible, since ours 120 is to preserve earthworms. Didst thou ever see a lark in a cage? Such is the soul in the body: this world is like her little turf of grass, and the heaven o'er our heads, like her looking-glass, only gives us a miserable knowledge of the small compass of our prison.   125

DUCHESS. Am not I thy duchess?

BOSOLA. Thou art some great woman, sure, for riot[5] begins to sit

8. Looking-glass.
9. Carriage.
1. It is a mad idea indeed that toddies ("possets") made of bat's milk would put people to sleep.
2. Imperceptible.
3. "Worm-seed" is a matter whose ultimate end is the generation of worms. "A salvatory of green mummy": the substance of mummified bodies was considered medicinal. The living body is a box ("salvatory") of such medicine, only not yet ready for use.
4. Curdled.
5. Debauchery.

on thy forehead, clad in gray hairs, twenty years sooner than on a merry milkmaid's. Thou sleep'st worse than if a mouse should be forced to take up her lodging in a cat's ear: a little infant that breeds its teeth,[6] should it lie with thee, would cry out, as if thou wert the more unquiet bedfellow. 130

DUCHESS. I am Duchess of Malfi still.

BOSOLA. That makes thy sleep so broken:
Glories, like glow-worms, afar off shine bright, 135
But, looked to near, have neither heat nor light.

DUCHESS. Thou art very plain.

BOSOLA. My trade is to flatter the dead, not the living; I am a tomb-maker.

DUCHESS. And thou com'st to make my tomb? 140

BOSOLA. Yes.

DUCHESS. Let me be a little merry. Of what stuff wilt thou make it?

BOSOLA. Nay, resolve me first, of what fashion?

DUCHESS. Why, do we grow fantastical in our deathbed? Do we 145
affect fashion in the grave?

BOSOLA. Most ambitiously. Princes' images on their tombs do not lie, as they were wont, seeming to pray up to heaven, but with their hands under their cheeks, as if they died of the tooth-ache. They are not carved with their eyes fixed upon the stars, 150
but as their minds were wholly bent upon the world, the self-same way they seem to turn their faces.

DUCHESS. Let me know fully therefore the effect
Of this thy dismal preparation,
This talk fit for a charnel.

BOSOLA.   Now I shall. 155
[*Enter* EXECUTIONERS, *with a coffin, cords, and a bell.*]
Here is a present from your princely brothers;
And may it arrive welcome, for it brings
Last benefit, last sorrow.

DUCHESS.   Let me see it:
I have so much obedience in my blood,
I wish it in their veins to do them good. 160

BOSOLA. This is your last presence-chamber.[7]

CARIOLA.   O my sweet lady!

DUCHESS. Peace; it affrights not me.

BOSOLA.   I am the common bellman,
That usually is sent to condemned persons
The night before they suffer.

DUCHESS.   Even now
Thou said'st thou wast a tomb-maker.

BOSOLA.   'Twas to bring you 165
By degrees to mortification.[8] Listen.

6. A teething infant.
7. The room in which a person of quality (duchess or prince) received courtiers and diplomats.
8. Repentance, but also death and de-
composition.

Hark, now every thing is still
The screech-owl and the whistler[9] shrill
Call upon our dame aloud,
And bid her quickly don her shroud!   170
Much you had of land and rent:
Your length in clay's now competent:[1]
A long war disturbed your mind;
Here your perfect peace is signed.
Of what is 't fools make such vain keeping?   175
Sin their conception, their birth weeping,
Their life a general mist of error,
Their death a hideous storm of terror.
Strew your hair with powders sweet,
Don clean linen, bathe your feet,   180
And (the foul fiend more to check)
A crucifix let bless your neck:
'Tis now full tide 'tween night and day;
End your groan, and come away.

CARIOLA. Hence, villains, tyrants, murderers! Alas!   185
What will you do with my lady? Call for help.

DUCHESS. To whom? To our next neighbors? They are madfolks.

BOSOLA. Remove that noise.

DUCHESS.   Farewell, Cariola.
In my last will I have not much to give:
A many hungry guests have fed upon me;   190
Thine will be a poor reversion.

CARIOLA.   I will die with her.

DUCHESS. I pray thee, look thou giv'st my little boy
Some syrup for his cold, and let the girl
Say her prayers ere she sleep.

    [CARIOLA is forced out by the EXECUTIONERS.]
    Now what you please.
What death?

BOSOLA.   Strangling;   195
Here are your executioners.

DUCHESS.   I forgive them:
The apoplexy, catarrh, or cough o' th' lungs,
Would do as much as they do.

BOSOLA. Doth not death fright you?

DUCHESS.   Who would be afraid on 't,
Knowing to meet such excellent company   200
In th' other world?

BOSOLA.   Yet, methinks,
The manner of your death should much afflict you:
This cord should terrify you.

DUCHESS.   Not a whit.
What would it pleasure me to have my throat cut

---

9. A bird premonitory of death.   1. Sufficient.

With diamonds? Or to be smothered   205
With cassia?[2] Or to be shot to death with pearls?
I know death hath ten thousand several doors
For men to take their exits, and 'tis found
They go on such strange geometrical hinges,
You may open them both ways.—Any way, for heaven sake,   210
So I were out of your whispering. Tell my brothers
That I perceive death, now I am well awake,
Best gift is they can give or I can take.
I would fain put off my last woman's fault,
I'd not be tedious to you.
EXECUTIONER.   We are ready.   215
DUCHESS. Dispose my breath how please you, but my body
Bestow upon my women, will you?
EXECUTIONER.   Yes.
DUCHESS. Pull, and pull strongly, for your able strength
Must pull down heaven upon me—
Yet stay; heaven-gates are not so highly arched   220
As princes' palaces; they that enter there
Must go upon their knees [*Kneels*]. Come, violent death.
Serve for mandragora[3] to make me sleep!
Go tell my brothers, when I am laid out,
They then may feed in quiet.   [*They strangle her.*] 225
BOSOLA. Where's the waiting woman? Fetch her: some other
Strangle the children.
            [*Exeunt* EXECUTIONERS, *some of whom return with*
            CARIOLA.]
Look you, there sleeps your mistress.
CARIOLA.   Oh, you are damned
Perpetually for this! My turn is next.
Is 't not so ordered?
BOSOLA.   Yes, and I am glad   230
You are so well prepared for 't.
CARIOLA.   You are deceived, Sir,
I am not prepared for 't, I will not die;
I will first come to my answer, and know
How I have offended.
BOSOLA.   Come, dispatch her.
You kept her counsel; now you shall keep ours.   235
CARIOLA. I will not die, I must not; I am contracted
To a young gentleman.
EXECUTIONER.   Here's your wedding-ring.
CARIOLA. Let me but speak with the duke; I'll discover
Treason to his person.
BOSOLA.   Delays! Throttle her.
EXECUTIONER. She bites and scratches.
CARIOLA.   If you kill me now,   240
I am damned; I have not been at confession

2. Cinnamon.
3. The word is used loosely for a stupefying drug.

This two years.

BOSOLA. [*to* EXECUTIONERS] When!

CARIOLA.   I am quick with child.

BOSOLA.   Why, then,
  Your credit's saved.[4]   [*They strangle* CARIOLA.]
             Bear her into th' next room;
  Let this lie still.
       [*Exeunt the* EXECUTIONERS *with the body of* CARIOLA.]
       [*Enter* FERDINAND.]

FERDINAND. Is she dead?

BOSOLA.   She is what   245
  You'd have her. But here begin your pity.
                [*Shows the children strangled.*]
  Alas, how have these offended?

FERDINAND.   The death
  Of young wolves is never to be pitied.

BOSOLA.   Fix
  Your eye here.

FERDINAND. Constantly.

BOSOLA.   Do you not weep?
  Other sins only speak; murder shrieks out: 250
  The element of water moistens the earth,
  But blood flies upwards and bedews the heavens.

FERDINAND. Cover her face; mine eyes dazzle: she died young.

BOSOLA. I think not so; her infelicity
  Seemed to have years too many.

FERDINAND.   She and I were twins;   255
  And should I die this instant, I had lived
  Her time to a minute.

BOSOLA.   It seems she was born first:
  You have bloodily approved[5] the ancient truth,
  That kindred commonly do worse agree
  Than remote strangers.

FERDINAND.   Let me see her face   260
  Again. Why didst not thou pity her? What
  An excellent honest man mightst thou have been,
  If thou hadst borne her to some sanctuary!
  Or, bold in a good cause, opposed thyself,
  With thy advancéd sword above thy head,   265
  Between her innocence and my revenge!
  I bade thee, when I was distracted of my wits,
  Go kill my dearest friend, and thou hast done 't.
  For let me but examine well the cause:
  What was the meanness of her match to me?   270
  Only I must confess I had a hope,
  Had she continued widow, to have gained
  An infinite mass of treasure by her death:
  And that was the main cause, her marriage,

---

4. Your reputation will now be safe.   5. Given proof of.

That drew a stream of gall quite through my heart.   275
For thee, as we observe in tragedies
That a good actor many times is cursed
For playing a villain's part, I hate thee for 't,
And, for my sake, say thou hast done much ill well.

BOSOLA. Let me quicken your memory, for I perceive   280
    You are falling into ingratitude: I challenge
    The reward due to my service.

FERDINAND.   I'll tell thee
    What I'll give thee.

BOSOLA.   Do.

FERDINAND.   I'll give thee a pardon
    For this murder.

BOSOLA.   Ha!

FERDINAND.   Yes, and 'tis
    The largest bounty I can study to do thee.   285
    By what authority didst thou execute
    This bloody sentence?

BOSOLA.   By yours.

FERDINAND.   Mine! Was I her judge?
    Did any ceremonial form of law
    Doom her to not-being? Did a complete jury
    Deliver her conviction up i' th' court?   290
    Where shalt thou find this judgment registered,
    Unless in hell? See, like a bloody fool,
    Thou'st forfeited thy life, and thou shalt die for 't.

BOSOLA. The office of justice is perverted quite
    When one thief hangs another. Who shall dare   295
    To reveal this?

FERDINAND. Oh, I'll tell thee;
    The wolf shall find her grave, and scrape it up,
    Not to devour the corpse, but to discover
    The horrid murder.

BOSOLA.   You, not I, shall quake for 't.

FERDINAND. Leave me.

BOSOLA.   I will first receive my pension.   300

FERDINAND. You are a villain.

BOSOLA.   When your ingratitude
    Is judge, I am so.

FERDINAND. Oh, horror, that not the fear
    Of Him which binds the devils can prescribe man
    obedience! Never look upon me more.

BOSOLA. Why, fare thee well.   305
    Your brother and yourself are worthy men:
    You have a pair of hearts are hollow graves,
    Rotten, and rotting others; and your vengeance,
    Like two chained bullets, still goes arm in arm.
    You may be brothers, for treason, like the plague,
    Doth take much in a blood.[6] I stand like one   310

6. Treason and plague run in certain families.

That long hath ta'en a sweet and golden dream.
I am angry with myself, now that I wake.
FERDINAND. Get thee into some unknown part o' th' world,
    That I may never see thee.
BOSOLA.   Let me know   315
    Wherefore I should be thus neglected. Sir,
    I served your tyranny, and rather strove
    To satisfy yourself than all the world,
    And though I loathed the evil, yet I loved
    You that did counsel it; and rather sought   320
    To appear a true servant than an honest man.
FERDINAND. I'll go hunt the badger by owl-light:
    'Tis a deed of darkness.   *[Exit.]*
BOSOLA. He's much distracted. Off, my painted honor!
    While with vain hopes our faculties we tire,   325
    We seem to sweat in ice and freeze in fire.
    What would I do, were this to do again?
    I would not change my peace of conscience
    For all the wealth of Europe.—She stirs; here's life.
    Return, fair soul, from darkness, and lead mine   330
    Out of this sensible[7] hell. She's warm, she breathes.
    Upon thy pale lips I will melt my heart,
    To store them with fresh color.—Who's there!
    Some cordial[8] drink!—Alas! I dare not call:
    So pity would destroy pity.—Her eye opes,   335
    And heaven in it seems to ope, that late was shut,
    To take me up to mercy.
DUCHESS. Antonio!
BOSOLA.   Yes, madam, he is living;
    The dead bodies you saw were but feigned statues:
    He's reconciled to your brothers: the Pope hath wrought   340
    The atonement.
DUCHESS.   Mercy!   *[She dies.]*
BOSOLA. Oh, she's gone again! There the cords of life broke.
    Oh, sacred innocence, that sweetly sleeps
    On turtles'[9] feathers, whilst a guilty conscience
    Is a black register wherein is writ   345
    All our good deeds and bad, a perspective[1]
    That shows us hell! That we cannot be suffered
    To do good when we have a mind to it!
    This is manly sorrow; these tears, I am very certain,
    Never grew in my mother's milk. My estate   350
    Is sunk below the degree of fear. Where were
    These penitent fountains while she was living?
    Oh, they were frozen up! Here is a sight
    As direful to my soul as is the sword
    Unto a wretch hath slain his father. Come, I'll bear thee   355
    Hence, and execute thy last will; that's deliver

7. Material, tangible.
8. Restorative.
9. Turtle doves, emblems of a loving
couple.
1. Picture.

Thy body to the reverend dispose[2]
Of some good women: that the cruel tyrant
Shall not deny me. Then I'll post to Milan,
Where somewhat I will speedily enact   360
Worth my dejection.   [*Exit with the body.*]

Act V

SCENE 1. *A Public Place in Milan.*

[*Enter* ANTONIO *and* DELIO.]

ANTONIO. What think you of my hope of reconcilement
　To the Aragonian brethren?
DELIO.　　　　　　　　　I misdoubt it;
　For though they have sent their letters of safe-conduct
　For your repair to Milan, they appear
　But nets to entrap you. The Marquis of Pescara,   5
　Under whom you hold certain land in cheat,[3]
　Much 'gainst his noble nature hath been moved
　To seize those lands, and some of his dependents
　Are at this instant making it their suit
　To be invested in your revenues.[4]   10
　I cannot think they mean well to your life
　That do deprive you of your means of life,
　Your living.
ANTONIO.　　　You are still an heretic
　To any safety I can shape myself.[5]
DELIO. Here comes the marquis. I will make myself   15
　Petitioner for some part of your land,
　To know whither it is flying.
ANTONIO.　　　　　　　　I pray do.   [*Withdraws.*]
　　　　[*Enter* PESCARA.]
DELIO. Sir, I have a suit to you.
PESCARA.　　　　　　　　To me?
DELIO. An easy one.
　There is the citadel of Saint Bennet,[6]   20
　With some demesnes, of late in the possession
　Of Antonio Bologna; please you bestow them on me.
PESCARA. You are my friend, but this is such a suit,
　Nor fit for me to give, nor you to take.
DELIO. No, sir?
PESCARA.　　　I will give you ample reason for 't   25
　Soon in private. Here's the Cardinal's mistress.
　　　　[*Enter* JULIA.]
JULIA. My lord, I am grown your poor petitioner,
　And should be an ill beggar, had I not

---

2. Disposition.
3. Escheat, in default of legal heirs.
4. I.e., to be given your rents.
5. I.e., you still don't give me any hope

of safety that I can believe in. "Heretic": unbeliever.
6. Saint Benedict; "demesnes": associated estates.

A great man's letter here, the Cardinal's,
To court you in my favor. [*Gives a letter.*]
PESCARA. He entreats for you 30
The citadel of Saint Bennet, that belonged
To the banished Bologna.
JULIA. Yes.
PESCARA. I could not
Have thought of a friend I could rather pleasure with it;
'Tis yours.
JULIA. Sir, I thank you; and he shall know
How doubly I am engaged both in your gift, 35
And speediness of giving, which makes your grant
The greater. [*Exit.*]
ANTONIO. [*aside*] How they fortify themselves
With my ruin!
DELIO. Sir, I am little bound to you.
PESCARA. Why?
DELIO. Because you denied this suit to me, and gave 't
To such a creature.
PESCARA. Do you know what it was? 40
It was Antonio's land, not forfeited
By course of law, but ravished from his throat
By the Cardinal's entreaty. It were not fit
I should bestow so main a piece of wrong
Upon my friend; 'tis a gratification 45
Only due to a strumpet, for it is injustice.
Shall I sprinkle the pure blood of innocents
To make those followers I call my friends
Look ruddier upon me? I am glad
This land, ta'en from the owner by such wrong, 50
Returns again unto so foul an use
As salary for his lust. Learn, good Delio,
To ask noble things of me, and you shall find
I'll be a noble giver.
DELIO. You instruct me well.
ANTONIO. [*aside*] Why, here's a man now would fright impu-
dence. 55
From sauciest beggars.
PESCARA. Prince Ferdinand's come to Milan,
Sick, as they give out, of an apoplexy,
But some say 'tis a frenzy. I am going
To visit him. [*Exit.*]
ANTONIO. 'Tis a noble old fellow.
DELIO. What course do you mean to take, Antonio? 60
ANTONIO. This night I mean to venture all my fortune,
Which is no more than a poor lingering life,
To the Cardinal's worst of malice. I have got
Private access to his chamber, and intend
To visit him about the mid of night, 65
As once his brother did our noble duchess.
It may be that the sudden apprehension

Of danger—for I'll go in mine own shape—
When he shall see it fraught with love and duty,
May draw the poison out of him, and work   70
A friendly reconcilement. If it fail,
Yet it shall rid me of this infamous calling,
For better fall once than be ever falling.
DELIO. I'll second you in all danger, and, howe'er,
My life keeps rank with yours.
ANTONIO.   You are still my loved   75
And best friend.   [*Exeunt.*]

SCENE 2

[*Enter* PESCARA *and* DOCTOR.]
PESCARA. Now, doctor, may I visit your patient?
DOCTOR. If 't please your lordship: but he's instantly[7]
To take the air here in the gallery
By my direction.
PESCARA.   Pray thee, what's his disease?
DOCTOR. A very pestilent disease, my lord,   5
They call lycanthropia.[8]
PESCARA.   What's that?
I need a dictionary to 't.
DOCTOR.   I'll tell you.
In those that are possessed with 't there o'erflows
Such melancholy humor, they imagine
Themselves to be transformed into wolves;   10
Steal forth to churchyards in the dead of night,
And dig dead bodies up: as two nights since
One met the duke 'bout midnight in a lane
Behind Saint Mark's Church, with the leg of a man
Upon his shoulder; and he howled fearfully;   15
Said he was a wolf, only the difference
Was, a wolf's skin was hairy on the outside,
His on the inside; bade them take their swords,
Rip up his flesh, and try. Straight I was sent for,
And, having ministered to him, found his grace   20
Very well recovered.
PESCARA. I'm glad on 't.
DOCTOR. Yet not without some fear
Of a relapse. If he grow to his fit again,
I'll go a nearer way to work with him
Than ever Paracelsus[9] dreamed of: if   25
They'll give me leave, I'll buffet his madness
Out of him. Stand aside; he comes.
      [*Enter* FERDINAND, MALATESTE, CARDINAL, *and* BOSOLA.]

7. Very shortly.
8. The mental aberration that produces
werewolves—as the Doctor will shortly
explain.
9. Paracelsus, the great Swiss alchemist,

famous for his cures by sympathetic
magic. Though anachronistic in this play,
he would be well known to Webster's
audience.

FERDINAND. Leave me.

MALATESTE. Why doth your lordship love this solitariness?

FERDINAND. Eagles commonly fly alone: they are crows, daws, 30
and starlings that flock together. Look, what's that follows
me?

MALATESTE. Nothing, my lord.

FERDINAND. Yes.

MALATESTE. 'Tis your shadow. 35

FERDINAND. Stay it; let it not haunt me.

MALATESTE. Impossible, if you move, and the sun shine.

FERDINAND. I will throttle it. [*Throws himself on the ground.*]

MALATESTE. O, my lord, you are angry with nothing.

FERDINAND. You are a fool: how is 't possible I should catch my 40
shadow, unless I fall upon 't? When I go to hell, I mean to
carry a bribe; for, look you, good gifts evermore make way for
the worst persons.

PESCARA. Rise, good my lord.

FERDINAND. I am studying the art of patience. 45

PESCARA. 'Tis a noble virtue.

FERDINAND. To drive six snails before me from this town to
Moscow; neither use goad nor whip to them, but let them
take their own time—the patient'st man i' th' world match
me for an experiment—and I'll crawl after like a sheep-biter.[1] 50

CARDINAL. Force him up. [*They raise him.*]

FERDINAND. Use me well, you were best. What I have done, I
have done: I'll confess nothing.

DOCTOR. Now let me come to him. Are you mad, my lord? Are
you out of your princely wits? 55

FERDINAND. What's he?

PESCARA. Your doctor.

FERDINAND. Let me have his beard sawed off, and his eyebrows
filed more civil.

DOCTOR. I must do mad tricks with him, for that's the only way 60
on 't. I have brought your grace a salamander's skin to keep
you from sunburning.[2]

FERDINAND. I have cruel sore eyes.

DOCTOR. The white of a cockatrix's[3] egg is present remedy.

FERDINAND. Let it be a new laid one, you were best. Hide me 65
from him: physicians are like kings—they brook no contradiction.

DOCTOR. Now he begins to fear me: now let me alone with him.

CARDINAL. How now? Put off your gown?

DOCTOR. Let me have some forty urinals filled with rosewater: he 70
and I'll go pelt one another with them. Now he begins to fear
me. Can you fetch a frisk, sir?[4] Let him go, let him go, upon
my peril: I find by his eye he stands in awe of me; I'll make

1. A sheepdog, nipping at the heels of
his flock.
2. The ideas are deliberately crazy: the
Doctor is trying to enter into Ferdinand's frenzy in order gradually to draw

him out.
3. A fabulous, and deadly poisonous,
serpent, supposed to be hatched of a
cock's egg.
4. Cut a caper, dance a jig.

him as tame as a dormouse.   75

FERDINAND. Can you fetch your frisks, sir? I will stamp him into
   a cullis, flay off his skin, to cover one of the anatomies[5] this
   rogue hath set i' th' cold yonder in Barber-Chirurgeons'-Hall.
   Hence, hence! You are all of you like beasts for sacrifice:
   there's nothing left of you but tongue and belly, flattery and
   lechery.   [*Exit.*] 80

PESCARA. Doctor, he did not fear you throughly.

DOCTOR.   True;
   I was somewhat too forward.

BOSOLA.   Mercy upon me,
   What a fatal judgment hath fall'n upon this Ferdinand!

PESCARA. Knows your grace what accident hath brought
   Unto the prince this strange distraction?   85

CARDINAL. [*aside*] I must feign somewhat. Thus they say it grew.
   You have heard it rumored, for these many years
   None of our family dies but there is seen
   The shape of an old woman, which is given
   By tradition to us to have been murdered   90
   By her nephews for her riches. Such a figure
   One night, as the prince sat up late at 's book,
   Appeared to him; when, crying out for help,
   The gentlemen of's chamber found his grace
   All on a cold sweat, altered much in face   95
   And language; since which apparition,
   He hath grown worse and worse, and I much fear
   He cannot live.

BOSOLA.   Sir, I would speak with you.

PESCARA. We'll leave your grace,
   Wishing to the sick prince, our noble lord,   100
   All health of mind and body.

CARDINAL.   You are most welcome.

         [*Exeunt* PESCARA, MALATESTE, *and* DOCTOR.]
   Are you come? So. [*aside*] This fellow must not know
   By any means I had intelligence[6]
   In our duchess' death; for, though I counseled it,
   The full of all th' engagement seemed to grow   105
   From Ferdinand.—Now, sir, how fares our sister?
   I do not think but sorrow makes her look
   Like to an oft-dyed garment: she shall now
   Taste comfort from me. Why do you look so wildly?
   Oh, the fortune of your master here the prince   110
   Dejects you, but be you of happy comfort:
   If you'll do one thing for me I'll entreat,
   Though he had a cold tombstone o'er his bones,
   I'll make you what you would be.

BOSOLA.   Anything;

---

5. Anatomical skeletons hung up in the
surgeon's college, which Ferdinand proposes to cover with the Doctor's flayed
skin.
6. Had a hand in.

Give it me in a breath, and let me fly to 't: 115
They that think long small expedition win,
For musing much o' th' end cannot begin.
　　[*Enter* JULIA.]
JULIA. Sir, will you come in to supper?
CARDINAL. 　　　　　　　　I am busy;
　Leave me.
JULIA. [*aside*] What an excellent shape hath that fellow! [Exit.]120
CARDINAL. 'Tis thus. Antonio lurks here in Milan:
　Inquire him out, and kill him. While he lives,
　Our sister cannot marry, and I have thought
　Of an excellent match for her. Do this, and style me
　Thy advancement.[7] 125
BOSOLA. But by what means shall I find him out?
CARDINAL. There is a gentleman called Delio
　Here in the camp, that hath been long approved
　His loyal friend. Set eye upon that fellow;
　Follow him to mass; maybe Antonio, 130
　Although he do account religion
　But a school-name,[8] for fashion of the world
　May accompany him; or else go inquire out
　Delio's confessor, and see if you can bribe
　Him to reveal it. There are a thousand ways 135
　A man might find to trace him; as to know
　What fellows haunt the Jews for taking up
　Great sums of money, for sure he's in want;
　Or else to go to th' picture-makers, and learn
　Who bought her picture lately. Some of these 140
　Haply may take.
BOSOLA. 　　　　Well, I'll not freeze i' th' business:
　I would see that wretched thing, Antonio,
　Above all sights i' th' world.
CARDINAL. 　　　　　　　Do, and be happy. [*Exit.*]
BOSOLA. This fellow doth breed basilisks in 's eyes,
　He's nothing else but murder; yet he seems 145
　Not to have notice of the duchess' death.
　'Tis his cunning: I must follow his example;
　There cannot be a surer way to trace
　Than that of an old fox.
　　[*Re-enter* JULIA, *with a pistol.*] 150
JULIA. So, sir, you are well met.
BOSOLA. How now?
JULIA. 　　　　Nay, the doors are fast enough.
　Now, sir,
　I will make you confess your treachery.
BOSOLA. Treachery?
JULIA. Yes,
　Confess to me which of my women 'twas 155

7. Look to me for your promotion. 　　　8. Just an idle phrase.

You hired to put love-powder into my drink?

BOSOLA. Love-powder?

JULIA.   Yes, when I was at Malfi.
Why should I fall in love with such a face else?
I have already suffered for thee so much pain,
The only remedy to do me good   160
Is to kill my longing.

BOSOLA.   Sure, your pistol holds
Nothing but perfumes or kissing-comfits.[9]
Excellent lady! You have a pretty way on 't
To discover your longing. Come, come, I'll disarm you,
And arm you thus:[1] yet this is wondrous strange.   165

JULIA. Compare thy form and my eyes together, you'll find
My love no such great miracle. Now you'll say
I am wanton: this nice modesty in ladies
Is but a troublesome familiar[2] that haunts them.

BOSOLA. Know you me, I am a blunt soldier.

JULIA.   The better: 170
Sure, there wants[3] fire where there are no lively sparks
Of roughness.

BOSOLA.   And I want compliment.[4]

JULIA.   Why, ignorance
In courtship cannot make you do amiss,
If you have a heart to do well.

BOSOLA.   You are very fair.   175

JULIA. Nay, if you lay beauty to my charge,
I must plead unguilty.

BOSOLA.   Your bright eyes carry
A quiver of darts in them sharper than sunbeams.

JULIA. You will mar me with commendation,
Put yourself to the charge of courting me,   180
Whereas now I woo you.

BOSOLA. [*aside*] I have it, I will work upon this creature.—
Let us grow most amorously familiar.
If the great Cardinal now should see me thus,
Would he not count me a villain?

JULIA.   No; he might   185
Count me a wanton, not lay a scruple
Of offence on you; for if I see and steal
A diamond, the fault is not i' th' stone,
But in me the thief that purloins it. I am sudden
With you: we that are great women of pleasure   190
Use to cut off these uncertain wishes
And unquiet longings, and in an instant join
The sweet delight and the pretty excuse together.
Had you been i' th' street, under my chamber-window,

9. Candies to sweeten the breath.
1. Disarm (by taking away her pistol and kissing her); arm (by embracing her).
2. An irksome ghost.
3. Lacks, is missing.
4. I don't have the gift of flattery.

Even there I should have courted you.

BOSOLA.   Oh, you are   195
An excellent lady!

JULIA.   Bid me do somewhat for you
Presently⁵ to express I love you.

BOSOLA.   I will;
And if you love me, fail not to effect it.
The Cardinal is grown wondrous melancholy;
Demand the cause, let him not put you off   200
With feigned excuse; discover the main ground on 't.

JULIA. Why would you know this?

BOSOLA.   I have depended on him,
And I hear that he is fallen in some disgrace
With the emperor: if he be, like the mice
That forsake falling houses, I would shift   205
To other dependence.

JULIA.   You shall not need
Follow the wars: I'll be your maintenance.

BOSOLA. And I your loyal servant: but I cannot
Leave my calling.

JULIA.   Not leave an ungrateful
General for the love of a sweet lady?   210
You are like some cannot sleep in feather-beds,
But must have blocks for their pillows.

BOSOLA.   Will you do this?

JULIA. Cunningly.

BOSOLA. Tomorrow I'll expect th' intelligence.

JULIA. Tomorrow? Get you into my cabinet;   215
You shall have it with you. Do not delay me,
No more than I do you: I am like one
That is condemned; I have my pardon promised,
But I would see it sealed. Go, get you in:
You shall see me wind my tongue about his heart   220
Like a skein of silk.   [*Exit* BOSOLA.]
      [*Re-enter* CARDINAL.]

CARDINAL.   Where are you?
      [*Enter* SERVANTS.]

SERVANTS.   Here.

CARDINAL. Let none, upon your lives, have conference
With the Prince Ferdinand, unless I know it.
[*aside*] In this distraction he may reveal
The murder.—   [*Exeunt* SERVANTS.]
                  Yond's my lingering consumption: 225
I am weary of her, and by any means
Would be quit of.

JULIA.   How now, my lord? What ails you?

CARDINAL. Nothing.

JULIA. Oh, you are much altered: come, I must be

---

5. Immediately.

Your secretary, and remove this lead 230
From off your bosom.[6] What's the matter?

CARDINAL. I may not
Tell you.

JULIA. Are you so far in love with sorrow
You cannot part with part of it? Or think you
I cannot love your grace when you are sad
As well as merry? Or do you suspect 235
I, that have been a secret to your heart
These many winters, cannot be the same
Unto your tongue?

CARDINAL. Satisfy thy longing—
The only way to make thee keep my counsel
Is not to tell thee.

JULIA. Tell your echo this, 240
Or flatterers, that like echoes still report
What they hear though most imperfect, and not me;
For if that you be true unto yourself,
I'll know.

CARDINAL. Will you rack[7] me?

JULIA. No, judgment shall
Draw it from you: it is an equal fault, 245
To tell one's secrets unto all or none.

CARDINAL. The first argues folly.

JULIA. But the last, tyranny.

CARDINAL. Very well. Why, imagine I have committed
Some secret deed which I desire the world
May never hear of.

JULIA. Therefore may not I know it? 250
You have concealed for me as great a sin
As adultery. Sir, never was occasion
For perfect trial of my constancy
Till now: sir, I beseech you——

CARDINAL. You'll repent it.

JULIA. Never. 255

CARDINAL. It hurries thee to ruin: I'll not tell thee.
Be well advised, and think what danger 'tis
To receive a prince's secrets: they that do,
Had need have their breasts hooped with adamant
To contain them. I pray thee, yet be satisfied; 260
Examine thine own frailty; 'tis more easy
To tie knots than unloose them: 'tis a secret
That, like a lingering poison, may chance lie
Spread in thy veins, and kill thee seven year hence.

JULIA. Now you dally with me.

CARDINAL. No more; thou shalt know it. 265
By my appointment the great Duchess of Malfi
And two of her young children, four nights since,

6. Secretaries opened letters addressed to
their masters by removing the heavy lead
seals.
7. Will you put me to the torture?

Were strangled.

JULIA.   O. Heaven! Sir, what have you done!

CARDINAL. How now? How settles this? Think you your bosom
  Will be a grave dark and obscure enough   270
  For such a secret?

JULIA.   You have undone yourself, sir.

CARDINAL. Why?

JULIA.   It lies not in me to conceal it.

CARDINAL.   No?
  Come, I will swear you to 't upon this book.

JULIA. Most religiously.

CARDINAL.   Kiss it.   [*She kisses the book.*]
                    Now you shall
  Never utter it; thy curiosity   275
  Hath undone thee: thou'rt poisoned with that book.
  Because I knew thou couldst not keep my counsel,
  I have bound thee to 't by death.
      [*Re-enter* BOSOLA.]

BOSOLA.   For pity sake,
  Hold!

CARDINAL. Ha! Bosola?

JULIA.   I forgive you
  This equal piece of justice you have done;   280
  For I betrayed your counsel to that fellow:
  He overheard it; that was the cause I said
  It lay not in me to conceal it.

BOSOLA.   O foolish woman,
  Couldst not thou have poisoned him?

JULIA.   'Tis weakness,
  Too much to think what should have been done. I go   285
  I know not whither.   [*Dies.*]

CARDINAL.   Wherefore com'st thou hither?

BOSOLA. That I might find a great man like yourself,
  Not out of his wits as the Lord Ferdinand,
  To remember my service.

CARDINAL.   I'll have thee hewed in pieces.

BOSOLA. Make not yourself such a promise of that life   290
  Which is not yours to dispose of.

CARDINAL.   Who placed thee here?

BOSOLA. Her lust, as she intended.

CARDINAL.   Very well.
  Now you know me for your fellow-murderer.

BOSOLA. And wherefore should you lay fair marble colors[8]
  Upon your rotten purposes to me?   295
  Unless you imitate some that do plot great treasons,
  And when they have done, go hide themselves i' th' graves
  Of those were actors in 't?

CARDINAL.   No more; there is

---

8. Plaster was often painted to look like marble.

A fortune attends thee.

BOSOLA. Shall I go sue
To Fortune any longer? 'Tis the fool's 300
Pilgrimage.

CARDINAL. I have honors in store for thee.

BOSOLA. There are a many ways that conduct to seeming
Honor, and some of them very dirty ones.

CARDINAL. Throw
To the devil thy melancholy. The fire burns well;
What need we keep a stirring of 't, and make 305
A greater smother? Thou wilt kill Antonio?

BOSOLA. Yes.

CARDINAL. Take up that body.

BOSOLA. I think I shall
Shortly grow the common bearer for churchyards.

CARDINAL. I will allow thee some dozen of attendants
To aid thee in the murder. 310

BOSOLA. Oh, by no means. Physicians that apply horse-leeches to
any rank swelling use to cut off their tails, that the blood may
run through them the faster: let me have no train[9] when I go
to shed blood, lest it make me have a greater when I ride to
the gallows. 315

CARDINAL. Come to me after midnight, to help to remove
That body to her own lodging: I'll give out
She died o' th' plague; 'twill breed the less inquiry
After her death.

BOSOLA. Where's Castruccio her husband?

CARDINAL. He's rode to Naples, to take possession 320
Of Antonio's citadel.

BOSOLA. Believe me, you have done
A very happy turn.

CARDINAL. Fail not to come.
There is the master-key of our lodgings, and by that
You may conceive what trust I plant in you.

BOSOLA. You shall find me ready. [*Exit* CARDINAL.]
O poor Antonio, 325
Though nothing be so needful to thy estate
As pity, yet I find nothing so dangerous;
I must look to my footing:
In such slippery ice-pavements men had need
To be frost-nailed well; they may break their necks else; 330
The precedent's here afore me. How this man
Bears up in blood! Seems fearless! Why, 'tis well:
Security some men call the suburbs of hell,
Only a dead wall between.[1] Well, good Antonio,
I'll seek thee out, and all my care shall be 335

---

9. Followers. Criminals, dragged through
the streets to be hanged at Tyburn, were
followed by crowds of the idle, the sadistic, and their own fellow criminals.

1. When men are close to hell, with only
a dead wall between—but the wall isn't
altogether dead, as we soon see—they
can live securely there.

To put thee into safety from the reach
Of these most cruel biters that have got
Some of thy blood already. It may be,
I'll join with thee in a most just revenge:
The weakest arm is strong enough that strikes   340
With the sword of justice. Still methinks the duchess
Haunts me. There, there, 'tis nothing but my melancholy.
O Penitence, let me truly taste thy cup,
That throws men down only to raise them up!   [*Exit.*]

SCENE 3. A *Fortification at Milan.*

[*Enter* ANTONIO *and* DELIO. *Echo from the* DUCHESS'
grave.]

DELIO. Yond's the Cardinal's window. This fortification
Grew from the ruins of an ancient abbey;
And to yond side o' th' river lies a wall,
Piece of a cloister, which in my opinion
Gives the best echo that you ever heard,   5
So hollow and so dismal, and withal
So plain in the distinction of our words,
That many have supposed it is a spirit
That answers.

ANTONIO.   I do love these ancient ruins.
We never tread upon them but we set   10
Our foot upon some reverend history:
And, questionless, here in this open court,
Which now lies naked to the injuries
Of stormy weather, some men lie interred
Loved the church so well, and gave so largely to 't,   15
They thought it should have canopied their bones
Till doomsday; but all things have their end:
Churches and cities, which have diseases
Like to men, must have like death that we have.

ECHO. "Like death that we have."   20

DELIO. Now the echo hath caught you.

ANTONIO.   It groaned, methought, and gave
A very deadly accent.

ECHO.   "Deadly accent."

DELIO. I told you 'twas a pretty one: you may make it
A huntsman, or a falconer, a musician   25
Or a thing of sorrow.

ECHO.   "A thing of sorrow."

ANTONIO. Aye, sure, that suits it best.

ECHO.   "That suits it best."

ANTONIO. 'Tis very like my wife's voice.

ECHO.   "Aye, wife's voice."

DELIO. Come, let's walk further from 't. I would not have you
Go to th' Cardinal's tonight: do not.

ECHO.   "Do not."   30

DELIO. Wisdom doth not more moderate wasting sorrow
    Than time: take time for 't; be mindful of thy safety.
ECHO. ."Be mindful of thy safety."
ANTONIO.   Necessity compels me:
    Make scrutiny throughout the passes of
    Your own life, you'll find it impossible   35
    To fly your fate.
ECHO.   "Oh, fly your fate."
DELIO.   Hark!
    The dead stones seem to have pity on you, and give you
    Good counsel.
ANTONIO.   Echo, I will not talk with thee,
    For thou art a dead thing.
ECHO.   "Thou art a dead thing."
ANTONIO. My duchess is asleep now,   40
    And her little ones, I hope sweetly: O Heaven,
    Shall I never see her more?
ECHO.   "Never see her more."
ANTONIO. I marked not one repetition of the echo
    But that, and on the sudden a clear light
    Presented me a face folded in sorrow.   45
DELIO. Your fancy merely.
ANTONIO.   Come, I'll be out of this ague,
    For to live thus is not indeed to live;
    It is a mockery and abuse of life.
    I will not henceforth save myself by halves;
    Lose all, or nothing.
DELIO.   Your own virtue save you!   50
    I'll fetch your eldest son, and second[2] you:
    It may be that the sight of his own blood
    Spread in so sweet a figure[3] may beget
    The more compassion. However, fare you well.
    Though in our miseries Fortune have a part,   55
    Yet in our noble sufferings she hath none:
    Contempt of pain, that we may call our own.   *[Exeunt.]*

SCENE 4. A *Room in the* CARDINAL's *Palace.*

[*Enter* CARDINAL, PESCARA, MALATESTE, RODERICO, *and*
    GRISOLAN.]
CARDINAL. You shall not watch tonight by the sick prince;
    His grace is very well recovered.
MALATESTE. Good my lord, suffer[4] us.
CARDINAL.   Oh, by no means;
    The noise and change of object in his eye
    Doth more distract him. I pray, all to bed;   5

2. Back you up.   4. Allow.
3. Face.

And though you hear him in his violent fit,
Do not rise, I entreat you.
PESCARA.   So, sir; we shall not.
CARDINAL. Nay, I must have you promise upon your honors,
   For I was enjoined to 't by himself; and he seemed
   To urge it sensibly.[5]
PESCARA.   Let our honors bind   **10**
   This trifle.
CARDINAL. Nor any of your followers.
MALATESTE.   Neither.
CARDINAL. It may be, to make trial of your promise,
   When he's asleep, myself will rise and feign
   Some of his mad tricks, and cry out for help,
   And feign myself in danger.
MALATESTE.   If your throat were cutting,   **15**
   I'd not come at you, now I have protested against it.
CARDINAL. Why, I thank you.
GRISOLAN.   'Twas a foul storm tonight.
RODERIGO. The Lord Ferdinand's chamber shook like an osier.[6]
MALATESTE. 'Twas nothing but pure kindness in the devil,
   To rock his own child.   [*Exeunt all except the* CARDINAL.] **20**
CARDINAL. The reason why I would not suffer these
   About my brother, is, because at midnight
   I may with better privacy convey
   Julia's body to her own lodging. Oh, my conscience!
   I would pray now, but the devil takes away my heart   **25**
   For having any confidence in prayer.
   About this hour I appointed Bosola
   To fetch the body: when he hath served my turn,
   He dies.   [*Exit.*]
     [*Enter* BOSOLA.]
BOSOLA. Ha! 'Twas the Cardinal's voice; I heard him name   **30**
   Bosola and my death. Listen! I hear
   One's footing.
     [*Enter* FERDINAND.]
FERDINAND.   Strangling is a very quiet death.
BOSOLA. [*aside*] Nay, then, I see I must stand upon my guard.
FERDINAND. What say to that? Whisper softly; do you agree to
   't? So; it must be done i' th' dark: the Cardinal would not for **35**
   a thousand pounds the doctor should see it.   [*Exit.*]
BOSOLA. My death is plotted; here's the consequence of murder.
   We value not desert nor Christian breath,
   When we know black deeds must be cured with death.
     [*Enter* ANTONIO *and* SERVANT.]
SERVANT. Here stay, sir and be confident, I pray:
   I'll fetch you a dark lantern.   [*Exit.*]
ANTONIO.   Could I take him
   At his prayers, there were hope of pardon.

---

5. With real feeling.   6. Reed.

BOSOLA.   Fall right, my sword! [*Stabs him.*]
  I'll not give thee so much leisure as to pray.
ANTONIO. Oh, I am gone! Thou hast ended a long suit[7]
  In a minute.
BOSOLA.   What art thou?
ANTONIO.   A most wretched thing,   45
  That only have thy benefit in death,
  To appear myself.
    [*Re-enter* SERVANT *with a lantern.*]
SERVANT.   Where are you, sir?
ANTONIO. Very near my home. Bosola?
SERVANT.   Oh, misfortune!
BOSOLA. Smother thy pity; thou art dead else. Antonio?
  The man I would have saved 'bove mine own life!   50
  We are merely the stars' tennis-balls, struck and bandied
  Which way please them.[8] O good Antonio,
  I'll whisper one thing in thy dying ear
  Shall make thy heart break quickly! Thy fair duchess
  And two sweet children——
ANTONIO.   Their very names   55
  Kindle a little life in me.
BOSOLA.   Are murdered.
ANTONIO. Some men have wished to die
  At the hearing of sad tidings; I am glad
  That I shall do 't in sadness: I would not now
  Wish my wounds balmed nor healed, for I have no use   60
  To put my life to. In all our quest of greatness,
  Like wanton boys, whose pastime is their care,
  We follow after bubbles blown in th' air.
  Pleasure of life, what is 't? Only the good
  Hours of an ague; merely a preparative   65
  To rest, to endure vexation. I do not ask
  The process of my death; only commend me
  To Delio.
BOSOLA.   Break, heart!
ANTONIO.   And let my son
  Fly the courts of princes.   [*Dies.*]
BOSOLA.   Thou seem'st
  To have loved Antonio?
SERVANT.   I brought him hither,   70
  To have reconciled him to the Cardinal.
BOSOLA. I do not ask thee that.
  Take him up, if thou tender thine own life,
  And bear him where the lady Julia
  Was wont to lodge. Oh, my fate moves swift;   75

7. Antonio thinks it is the Cardinal, to whom he was addressing his "suit" (plea for reconciliation), who has murdered him.

8. The power of the stars over men's lives was a Renaissance commonplace.

I have this Cardinal in the forge already;
Now I'll bring him to th' hammer. Oh direful misprision![9]
I will not imitate things glorious,
No more than base; I'll be mine own example.
On, on, and look thou represent, for silence,   80
The thing thou bear'st.[1]   [*Exeunt.*]

SCENE 5

[*Enter* CARDINAL, *with a book.*]
CARDINAL. I am puzzled in a question about hell:
He says, in hell there's one material fire,
And yet it shall not burn all men alike.
Lay him by. How tedious is a guilty conscience!
When I look into the fish-ponds in my garden,   5
Methinks I see a thing armed with a rake,
That seems to strike at me.
     [*Enter* BOSOLA, *and* SERVANT *bearing* ANTONIO'S *body.*]
                 Now, art thou come?
Thou look'st ghastly:
There sits in thy face some great determination
Mixed with some fear.
BOSOLA.   Thus it lightens into action: 10
I am come to kill thee.
CARDINAL.   Ha! Help! Our guard!
BOSOLA. Thou art deceived; they are out of thy howling.
CARDINAL. Hold; and I will faithfully divide
Revenues with thee.
BOSOLA.   Thy prayers and proffers
Are both unseasonable.
CARDINAL.   Raise the watch!   15
We are betrayed!
BOSOLA.   I have confined your flight:[2]
I'll suffer your retreat to Julia's chamber,
But no further.
CARDINAL.   Help! We are betrayed!
     [*Enter, above,* PESCARA, MALATESTE, RODERIGO, *and* GRI-
     SOLAN.]
MALATESTE. Listen.
CARDINAL.   My dukedom for rescue!
RODERIGO.   Fie upon   20
His counterfeiting!
MALATESTE.   Why, 'tis not the Cardinal.
RODERIGO. Yes, yes, 'tis he, but I'll see him hanged
Ere I'll go down to him.

---

9. Error.   carrying.
1. I.e., be as still as the corpse you're   2. Cut off your escape.

CARDINAL.   Here's a plot upon me;
I am assaulted! I am lost, unless some rescue.

GRISOLAN. He doth this pretty well, but it will not serve   25
To laugh me out of mine honor.

CARDINAL.   The sword's at my throat!

RODERIGO. You would not bawl so loud then.

MALATESTE.   Come, come,
Let's go to bed. He told us thus much aforehand.

PESCARA. He wished you should not come at him; but, believe't,
The accent of the voice sounds not in jest: 30
I'll down to him, howsoever, and with engines[3]
Force ope the doors.   [*Exit above.*]

RODERIGO.   Let's follow him aloof,[4]
And note how the Cardinal will laugh at him.
          [*Exeunt, above,* MALATESTE, RODERIGO, *and* GRISOLAN.]

BOSOLA. There's for you first,   [*He kills the* SERVANT.]
'Cause you shall not unbarricade the door   35
To let in rescue.

CARDINAL.   What cause hast thou to pursue my life?

BOSOLA.   Look there.

CARDINAL. Antonio?

BOSOLA.   Slain by my hand unwittingly.
Pray, and be sudden: when thou killed'st thy sister,
Thou took'st from Justice her most equal balance,   40
And left her naught but her sword.

CARDINAL.   Oh, mercy!

BOSOLA. Now, it seems thy greatness was only outward;
For thou fall'st faster of thyself than calamity
Can drive thee. I'll not waste longer time; there! [*Stabs him.*]

CARDINAL. Thou hast hurt me.

BOSOLA.   Again!   [*Stabs him again.*]

CARDINAL.   Shall I die like a leveret,[5]   45
Without any resistance? Help, help, help!
I am slain!
          [*Enter* FERDINAND.]

FERDINAND. Th' alarum? Give me a fresh horse;
Rally the vaunt-guard, or the day is lost.
Yield, yield! I give you the honor of arms,
Shake my sword over you; will you yield?[6]   50

CARDINAL. Help me; I am your brother!

FERDINAND.   The devil!
My brother fight upon the adverse party?
          [*He wounds the* CARDINAL, *and, in the scuffle, gives* BO-
          SOLA *his death-wound.*]

3. Bars and beams.
4. At a distance.
5. A baby hare, a defenseless creature.
6. It won't do to look for too much sense in Ferdinand's wild cries; he thinks he's on the field of battle and offering the "honor of arms" (liberal surrender terms) to his foes.

There flies your ransom.

CARDINAL. O justice!

I suffer now for what hath former been: 55
Sorrow is held the eldest child of sin.

FERDINAND. Now you're brave fellows. Caesar's fortune was
harder than Pompey's; Caesar died in the arms of prosperity,
Pompey at the feet of disgrace. You both died in the field.
The pain's nothing: pain many times is taken away with the 60
apprehension of greater, as the toothache with the sight of a
barber that comes to pull it out: there's philosophy for you.

BOSOLA. Now my revenge is perfect. Sink, thou main cause
                           [*He kills* FERDINAND.]
Of my undoing! The last part of my life
Hath done me best service.   65

FERDINAND. Give me some wet hay; I am broken-winded. I do
account this world but a dog-kennel: I will vault credit and
affect high pleasures beyond death.[7]

BOSOLA. He seems to come to himself, now he's so near
The bottom.

FERDINAND. My sister, O my sister! There's the cause on 't.   70
Whether we fall by ambition, blood, or lust,
Like diamonds we are cut with our own dust.   [*Dies.*]

CARDINAL. Thou hast thy payment, too.

BOSOLA. Yes, I hold my weary soul in my teeth.
'Tis ready to part from me. I do glory   75
That thou, which stood'st like a huge pyramid
Begun upon a large and ample base,
Shalt end in a little point, a kind of nothing.
    [*Enter, below,* PESCARA, MALATESTE, RODERIGO, *and*
    GRISOLAN.]

PESCARA. How now, my lord?

MALATESTE.   O sad disaster!

RODERIGO.   How
Comes this?   80

BOSOLA. Revenge for the Duchess of Malfi murdered
By th' Aragonian brethren; for Antonio
Slain by this hand; for lustful Julia
Poisoned by this man; and lastly for myself,
That was an actor in the main of all,   85
Much 'gainst mine own good nature, yet i' th' end
Neglected.

PESCARA. How now, my lord?

CARDINAL. Look to my brother: he gave us these large wounds
As we were struggling here i' the rushes.[8] And now,   90
I pray, let me be laid by and never thought of.   [*Dies.*]

---

7. Worn-out horses are said to be broken-winded. The last sentence implies that
he expects no more of this life and looks
forward only to the next one.

8. Reed mats laid down over Elizabethan
floors in lieu of carpets.

PESCARA. How fatally, it seems, he did withstand
His own rescue!
MALATESTE.   Thou wretched thing of blood,
How came Antonio by his death?
BOSOLA.   In a mist;
I know not how: such a mistake as I   95
Have often seen in a play. Oh, I am gone!
We are only like dead walls or vaulted graves,
That, ruined, yield no echo. Fare you well.
It may be pain, but no harm, to me to die
In so good a quarrel. Oh, this gloomy world!   100
In what a shadow, or deep pit of darkness,
Doth, womanish and fearful, mankind live!
Let worthy minds ne'er stagger in distrust
To suffer death or shame for what is just:
Mine is another voyage.   [*Dies.*] 105
PESCARA. The noble Delio, as I came to the palace,
Told me of Antonio's being here, and showed me
A pretty gentleman, his son and heir.
        [*Enter* DELIO *and* ANTONIO'S SON.]
MALATESTE. O sir,
You come too late!
DELIO.   I heard so, and was armed[9] for 't   110
Ere I came. Let us make noble use
Of this great ruin; and join all our force
To establish this young hopeful gentleman
In 's mother's right. These wretched eminent things
Leave no more fame behind 'em, than should one   115
Fall in a frost, and leave his print in snow;
As soon as the sun shines, it ever melts,
Both form and matter. I have ever thought
Nature doth nothing so great for great men
As when she's pleased to make them lords of truth: 120
Integrity of life is fame's best friend,
Which nobly, beyond death, shall crown the end. [*Exeunt.*]

performed, 1614   *published*, 1623

9. Inwardly prepared.

JOHN DONNE
(1572–1631)

1601: Secret marriage to Ann More.
1615: Sacred orders.
1633: First publication of *Songs and Sonnets*.

There are two distinct but related authors known as John Donne. First is the scandalous young spark, who wrote bawdy and cynical verses—Jack Donne, the rake. Then there is the gravely witty, passionately religious divine, who wrote verses to his God as ardent as those he had once addressed to his mistresses. This is Dr. John Donne, the Dean of St. Paul's. Yet the key to both men is the same; it is a kind of restless, searching energy, which scorns the easy platitude and the smooth, empty phrase; which is vivid, immediate, troubling; and which makes the reading of Donne's poetry an imaginative and intellectual struggle and an all-absorbing experience.

Donne was born into an old Roman Catholic family, at a time when anti-Catholic feeling in England was near its height. His faith barred him from many of the usual avenues of success, and his point of view was always that of an insecure outsider. Though he attended both Oxford and Cambridge Universities, as well as Lincoln's Inn (where barristers got their training), he never took any academic degrees and never practiced law. After quietly abandoning Catholicism some time during the 1590's, he had scruples about becoming an Anglican. He had no gift for commerce, and though he inherited money from his father (who died when Donne was only 4), it was far from enough to render him independent. Hence he had to make his way in the world indirectly—by wit, charm, learning, valor, and above all, favor. Partly from sheer intellectual curiosity, he read enormously in divinity, medicine, law, and the classics; he wrote to display his learning and wit. He traveled on the Continent, especially, it would seem, to Spain; even in later years, he was an inveterate voyager. With Ralegh and Essex he took part in two hit-and-run expeditions against Cadiz and the Azores. He put himself in the way of court employment, danced attendance on great court ladies, and generally lived the life of a brilliant young man hopeful of preferment.

When in 1598 Donne was appointed private secretary to Sir Thomas Egerton, the Lord Keeper, his prospects for worldly advancement seemed good. He sat in Elizabeth's last parliament and moved in court circles. But in 1601 he secretly married Lady Egerton's niece, 16-year-old Ann More, and thereby ruined his own worldly hopes. The marriage turned out happily, but Donne's imprudence was never forgiven. Sir George More had Donne imprisoned and dismissed from his post; and for the next dozen years, the poet had to struggle at a series of makeshift employments to support his growing family. As a man of 35, Donne was far from the brilliant young gallant of the 1590's; sick, poor, and unhappy, he was composing, but not publishing, a treatise on the lawfulness of suicide (*Biathanatos*). As he approached 40, he was engaged with Thomas Morton, Dean of Gloucester, in composing anti-Catholic polemics (*Pseudo-Martyr*, 1610; *Ignatius his Conclave*, 1611). In return for patronage from Sir Robert Drury, he wrote in 1611 and 1612 a pair of long poems, *The Anniversaries*, on the death of Sir Robert's daughter Elizabeth. None of these activities represent a full employment of Donne's volcanic intellectual energy. To be sure, Donne's social position need not be painted too blackly. He had friends among the courtiers, politicians, poets, and clergy—Mrs. Magdalen Herbert and her sons George and Edward, Ben Jonson, Sir Henry Goodyere, and Sir Henry Wotton among them. He was never quite without resources. Yet, broadly speaking, the middle years of Donne's life were a period of searching, uncertainty, and unhappiness.

Though Donne had flatly refused in 1607 to take Anglican orders, King James was certain that he would some day make a great Anglican preacher. Hence he declared that Donne could have no preferment or employment from him, except in the church. Finally, in 1615, Donne overcame his scruples, not the least of which was the fear of seeming ambitious, and entered the ministry. He was promptly appointed Reader in Divinity at Lincoln's Inn. In the 17th century, among court circles and at the Inns of Court where lawyers congregated, preaching was at once a form of spiritual devotion, an intellectual exercise, and a dramatic entertainment. Donne's metaphorical style, bold erudition, and dramatic wit at once established him as a great preacher in an age of great preachers. Fully 160 of his sermons survive. In 1621 he was made Dean of St. Paul's, where he preached to great congregations of "City" lawyers, courtiers, merchants, and tradesmen. In addition, his private devotions were published in 1624, and he continued to write sacred poetry till the very end of his life. Obsessed with the idea of death, Donne preached what was called his own funeral sermon just a few weeks before he died, and is supposed to have written the last, and one of the greatest, of his poems on his deathbed. He even had his portrait painted in his shroud.

The poetry of Donne represents a sharp break with most of that written by his predecessors and contemporaries. Much Elizabethan verse is decorative and flowery in its quality. Its images adorn, its meter is mellifluous. Image harmonizes with image, and line swells almost predictably into line. Donne's poetry, on the other hand, is written very largely in *conceits*—concentrated images which involve an element of dramatic contrast, of strain, or of intellectual difficulty. Most of the traditional "flowers of rhetoric" disappear completely. For instance, in his love poetry one never encounters bleeding hearts, cheeks like roses, lips like cherries, teeth like pearls, or Cupid shooting the arrows of love. The tears which flow in *A Valediction: of Weeping* are different from, and more complex than, the ordinary saline fluid of unhappy lovers; they are ciphers, naughts, symbols of the world's emptiness without the beloved; or else, suddenly reflecting her image, they are globes, worlds, they contain the sum of things. The poet who plays with conceits not only displays his own ingenuity; he may see into the nature of the world as deeply as the philosopher. Donne's conceits in particular leap continually in a restless orbit from the personal to the cosmic and back again.

Donne's rhythms are colloquial and various. He likes to twist and distort not only ideas, but metrical patterns and grammar itself. In the satires, which Renaissance writers understood to be "harsh" and "crabbed" as a genre, Donne's distortions often threaten to choke off the stream of expression entirely. But in the lyrics (both those which are worldly and those which are religious in theme), as in the elegies and sonnets, the verse never fails of a complex and memorable melody. Donne had an unusual gift, rather like that of a modern poet, T. S. Eliot, for striking off phrases which ring in the mind like a silver coin. They are two masters of the colloquial style, removed alike from the dignified, weighty manner of Milton and the sugared sweetness of the Elizabethans.

Donne and his followers are known to literary history as the "metaphysical school" of poets. Strictly speaking, this is a misnomer; there was no organized group of poets who imitated Donne, and if there had been, they would not have called themselves "metaphysical" poets. That term was invented by Dryden and Dr. Johnson. But the influence of Donne's poetic style was widely felt, especially by men whose taste was formed before 1660. George Herbert, Richard Crashaw, Henry Vaughan, Andrew Marvell, and Abraham Cowley are only the best known of those on whom Donne's influence is recognizable. The great change of taste which took place in 1660 threw Donne and the "conceited" style out of fashion; during the 18th and 19th centuries both he and his followers were rarely read and still more rarely appreciated. Finally, in the late 19th and early 20th centuries, three new editions of Donne appeared, of which Sir H. J. C. Grierson's, published in 1912, was quickly accepted as standard. By clarifying and purifying the often-garbled text, Grierson did a great deal to make Donne's poetry more available to the modern reader. Almost at once it started to exert an influence on modern poetic practice, the modern poets being hungry for a "tough" style which would free them from the worn-out rhetoric of late 19th-century romanticism. And Donne's status among the English poets quickly climbed from that of a curiosity to that of an acknowledged master.

No more than a couple of the poems on which Donne's modern reputation is built were published during his lifetime, though most of them were widely circulated through court and literary circles in handwritten copies. There were practical reasons for this halfway state of affairs. Many of the poems would have constituted black marks on Donne's reputation as an earnest and godly divine; and because they were difficult and allusive, only a few people wanted to read them. Thus Donne was known, outside the relatively limited circles which had access to manuscipt-collections, primarily as a preacher and devotional writer. But in these capacities he was tremendously productive and influential.

It has been said that there are two sorts of preachers—those who stand before us as representatives of God and explain His Word to us, and those who stand before God and explain our problems to Him. Certainly, John Donne belonged with the second group. He was a passionately human preacher, little interested in expounding dogma or laying down the rules of practical morality. What he presented to his hearers, in long, nervous periods, rich in poetic imagery and graphic detail, was a film in close-up of the

Christian drama—sin, guilt, contrition, repentance, faith, death, and transfiguration—with John Donne cast in the leading role. No other preacher in English could speak like Donne of the personal experience of entering heaven, and convey the sense that he had actually experienced in his own person every last detail of what he described.

Donne's acting impulses were not satisfied in the pulpit, though he preached an enormous number of immensely popular sermons; his whole life became a performance, upon which he commented, for public edification. Thus, his private prayers and devotions, written on the occasion of a serious sickness in 1623, promptly became a book (*Devotions upon Emergent Occasions*) in 1624. Readers of all sorts hastened to enjoy the pleasing anxieties and spiritual adventures of a devout and witty Christian wavering on the brink of eternity. To call the book a kind of existential soap-opera is doubtless too harsh, but it suggests some of the flamboyance with which Donne exploited his personal situation for purposes of pathetic and passionate instruction.

The basic text which follows is that of Sir Herbert Grierson (1912), but it has been modified, wherever sensible improvement seemed possible, and sometimes supplemented, by that of Dame Helen Gardner (*Divine Poems*, 1952, and *The Elegies and the Songs and Sonnets*, 1964).

The Good-Morrow

I wonder, by my troth, what thou and I
Did, till we loved? Were we not weaned till then,
But sucked on country pleasures, childishly?
Or snorted we in the seven sleepers' den?[1]
'Twas so; But this, all pleasures fancies be.   5
If ever any beauty I did see,
Which I desired, and got, 'twas but a dream of thee.

And now good morrow to our waking souls,
Which watch not one another out of fear;
For love all love of other sights controls,   10
And makes one little room an everywhere.
Let sea-discoverers to new worlds have gone,
Let maps to other,[2] worlds on worlds have shown,
Let us possess one world; each hath one, and is one.

My face in thine eye, thine in mine appears,[3]   15
And true plain hearts do in the faces rest;
Where can we find two better hemispheres
Without sharp North, without declining West?

1. Both Christian and Mohammedan authors recite the legend of seven youths of Ephesus, who hid in a cave from the persecutions of Decius, and slept there for 187 years. "Sucked" and "snorted" are words carefully chosen for their impact on the love poem.
2. I.e., let us concede that maps to other investigators have shown, etc. ("other" is an archaic plural form). In line 14 an alternative reading is "Let us possess *our* world" (from Dame Gardner).
3. Reflected in the pupils of one another's eyes, the lovers are, and possess, worlds of their own.

Whatever dies was not mixed equally;[4]
If our two loves be one, or thou and I
Love so alike that none do slacken, none can die.   20

                                                        1633

Song

    Go and catch a falling star,
      Get with child a mandrake root,[1]
    Tell me where all past years are,
      Or who cleft the Devil's foot,
    Teach me to hear mermaids[2] singing,   5
    Or to keep off envy's stinging,
         And find
         What wind
    Serves to advance an honest mind.

    If thou beest born to strange sights,   10
      Things invisible to see,
    Ride ten thousand days and nights,
      Till age snow white hairs on thee,
    Thou, when thou return'st, wilt tell me
    All strange wonders that befell thee,   15
         And swear
         No where
    Lives a woman true, and fair.

    If thou find'st one, let me know,
      Such a pilgrimage were sweet;   20
    Yet do not, I would not go,
      Though at next door we might meet;
    Though she were true when you met her,
    And last till you write your letter,
         Yet she
         Will be   25
    False, ere I come, to two, or three.

                                                        1633

The Undertaking

    I have done one braver thing
      Than all the Worthies[1] did,

4. Scholastic philosophy taught that when the elements were imperfectly ("not equally") mixed, matter was mortal and mutable; but when they were perfectly mixed, it was undying and unchanging. The dividing line between these two natures was the sphere of the moon.

1. The mandrake root, or mandragora, forked like the lower part of the human body, was highly reputed as an aphrodis-iac; to get one with child is a supreme impossibility.

2. Identified with the sirens, whose song only the wily Odysseus survived.

1. According to medieval legend, the Nine Worthies, or supreme heroes of history, included three Jews (Joshua, David, Judas Maccabeus), three pagans (Hector, Alexander, Julius Caesar), and three Christians (Arthur, Charlemagne, Godfrey of Bouillon).

And yet a braver thence doth spring,
　　Which is, to keep that hid.

It were but madness now t' impart　　　　　　5
　　The skill of specular stone,[2]
When he which can have learned the art
　　To cut it, can find none.

So, if I now should utter this,
　　Others (because no more　　　　　　　　10
Such stuff to work upon, there is)
　　Would love but as before.

But he who loveliness within
　　Hath found, all outward loathes,
For he who color loves, and skin,　　　　　15
　　Loves but their oldest clothes.

If, as I have, you also do
　　Virtue attired in woman see,
And dare love that, and say so too,
　　And forget the He and She;　　　　　　20

And if this love, though placéd so,
　　From profane men you hide,
Which will no faith on this bestow,
　　Or, if they do, deride;

Then you have done a braver thing　　　　25
　　Than all the Worthies did;
And a braver thence will spring,
　　Which is, to keep that hid.

　　　　　　　　　　　　　　　　　　1633

The Indifferent

I can love both fair and brown,[1]
Her whom abundance melts, and her whom want betrays,
Her who loves loneness best, and her who masks and plays,
Her whom the country formed, and whom the town,
Her who believes, and her who tries,[2]　　　　　5
Her who still weeps with spongy eyes,
And her who is dry cork, and never cries;
I can love her, and her, and you, and you,
I can love any, so she be not true.

2. A transparent or translucent material, reputed to have been used in antiquity for mirrors (in Latin, *speculae*), but no longer known.

1. Both blonde and brunette.
2. "Attempts to believe" and "tries things out."

Will no other vice content you?
Will it not serve your turn to do as did your mothers? [10]
Or have you all old vices spent, and now would find out others?
Or doth a fear that men are true torment you?
O we are not, be not you so;
Let me, and do you, twenty know.
Rob me, but bind me not, and let me go. [15]
Must I, who came to travail[3] thorough you
Grow your fixed subject, because you are true?

Venus heard me sigh this song,
And by love's sweetest part, variety, she swore,
She heard not this till now; and that it should be so no more. [20]
She went, examined, and returned ere long,
And said, Alas, some two or three
Poor heretics in love there be,
Which think to 'stablish dangerous constancy.
But I have told them, Since you will be true, [25]
You shall be true to them who are false to you.

1633

The question of persona

The Canonization

irritated or fed up

For God's sake hold your tongue, and let me love,
    Or chide my palsy, or my gout,
My five gray hairs, or ruined fortune, flout, *shows experience*
    With wealth your state, your mind with arts improve,
        Take you a course, get you a place,[1] *advice* [5]
        Observe His Honor, or His Grace,
Or the King's real, or his stamped face[2] *Find out what it's all about*
        Contemplate; what you will, approve,[3]
        So you will let me love.

Alas, alas, who's injured by my love? *questioning* [10]
    What merchant's ships have my sighs drowned?
Who says my tears have overflowed his ground?
    When did my colds a forward spring remove?[4]
        When did the heats which my veins fill
        Add one man to the plaguy bill?[5] *philosophical* [15]
Soldiers find wars, and lawyers find out still

---

3. "Grief, sorrow," but also "journey, travel."
1. "Take you a course": not necessarily of physic or instruction, but in the general sense of "settling yourself in life." A "place" is an appointment, at court or elsewhere.

2. On coins.
3. Put to proof, find by experience.
4. By freezing a fountain or blighting a season.
5. Deaths from the hot-weather plague were recorded, by parish, in weekly lists.

Litigious men, which quarrels move,
Though she and I do love.

Call us what you will, we are made such by love;
    Call her one, me another fly,
We're tapers too, and at our own cost die,[6]
    And we in us find the eagle and the dove.[7]
        The phoenix riddle hath more wit
        By us: we two being one, are it.
So, to one neutral thing both sexes fit.
    We die and rise the same, and prove
    Mysterious by this love.

We can die by it, if not live by love,
    And if unfit for tombs and hearse
Our legend be, it will be fit for verse;
    And if no piece of chronicle we prove,
        We'll build in sonnets pretty rooms;
        As well a well-wrought urn becomes
The greatest ashes, as half-acre tombs,
    And by these hymns,[8] all shall approve
    Us canonized for love:

And thus invoke us: You whom reverend love
    Made one another's hermitage;
You, to whom love was peace, that now is rage;
    Who did the whole world's soul contract,[9] and drove
        Into the glasses of your eyes
        (So made such mirrors, and such spies,
That they did all to you epitomize)
    Countries, towns, courts: Beg from above
    A pattern of your love![1]

20

25

30

35

40

45

1633

---

6. Like the "fly," a symbol of transitory life, we are burned up in "tapers,"
which consume themselves. There is a
hint here of the old superstition that
every act of intercourse subtracts a
day from one's life. (To "die," in the
punning terminology of the 17th century, was to consummate the act of
sex.)
7. The eagle and the dove are symbols
of earthly wisdom (strength) and heavenly meekness (purity), the latter paradoxically more powerful than the
former. The phoenix, in general mythology, was a fabulous Arabian bird, only
one of which existed at any one time.
After living a thousand years, it lit its
own funeral pyre, jumped in, and sang
its funeral song as it was consumed—
then rose triumphantly from its ashes,
a new bird. Thus it was a symbol of

immortality, as well as of desire rising
from its own exhaustion. "Eagle" and
"dove" are also alchemical terms for
processes leading to the rise of "phoenix," a stage in the transmutation of
metals.
8. Donne's own poems, transformed into
hymns in a new love-religion; "all":
posterity.
9. In line 40 Dame Helen Gardner reads
"extract" for "contract."
1. The poet and his mistress, turned to
saints, are implored by the rest of the
population to get from heaven
("above") a pattern of their love for
general distribution. "Countries, towns,
courts" are objects of the verb "drove";
the notion that eyes both see and reflect
the outside world, and so "contain" it
doubly, was very delightful to Donne.

The Apparition

When by thy scorn, O murderess, I am dead,
And that thou thinkst thee free
From all solicitation from me,
Then shall my ghost come to thy bed,
And thee, feigned vestal,[1] in worse arms shall see;   5
Then thy sick taper will begin to wink,
And he whose thou art then, being tired before,
Will, if thou stir, or pinch to wake him, think
     Thou call'st for more,
And in false sleep will from thee shrink,   10
And then, poor aspen wretch,[2] neglected thou
Bathed in a cold quicksilver sweat[3] wilt lie
     A verier ghost than I;
What I will say, I will not tell thee now,
Lest that preserve thee; and since my love is spent,   15
I had rather thou shouldst painfully repent,
Than by my threatenings rest still innocent.

                     1633

Love's Alchemy

Some that have deeper digged love's mine than I,
Say where his centric happiness doth lie;
     I have loved, and got, and told,
But should I love, get, tell, till I were old,
I should not find that hidden mystery;   5
     O, 'tis imposture all:
And as no chemic yet the elixir got,[1]
     But glorifies his pregnant pot,[2]
     If by the way to him befall
Some odoriferous thing, or medicinal;   10
     So lovers dream a rich and long delight,
     But get a winter-seeming summer's night.[3]

Our ease, our thrift, our honor, and our day,
Shall we for this vain bubble's shadow pay?
     Ends love in this, that my man   15

1. In Roman history the "vestals" were sacred virgins.
2. Aspen leaves flutter in the slightest breeze.
3. Sweating in terror; with an added innuendo from the circumstance that quicksilver (mercury) was a stock prescription for veneral disease.

1. "Chemic": alchemist; "the elixir": a magic medicine sought by alchemists and reputed to heal all ills.
2. Praises his fertile (and wombshaped) retort.
3. A night cold as in winter and short as in summer.

Can be as happy as I can if he can
Endure the short scorn of a bridegroom's play?
    That loving wretch that swears,
'Tis not the bodies marry, but the minds,
        Which he in her angelic finds,   20
        Would swear as justly that he hears,
In that day's rude hoarse minstrelsy, the spheres.[4]
    Hope not for mind in women; at their best
    Sweetness and wit they are, but mummy, possessed.[5]

                                                    1633

The Flea

Mark but this flea, and mark in this,
How little that which thou deniest me is;
Me it sucked first, and now sucks thee,
And in this flea our two bloods mingled be;
Thou know'st that this cannot be said   5
A sin, or shame, or loss of maidenhead,
    Yet this enjoys before it woo,
    And pampered swells with one blood made of two,
    And this, alas, is more than we would do.[1]

Oh stay, three lives in one flea spare,   10
Where we almost, nay more than married, are.
This flea is you and I, and this
Our marriage bed and marriage temple is;
Though parents grudge, and you, we are met,
And cloistered in these living walls of jet,   15
    Though use[2] make you apt to kill me
    Let not to that, self-murder added be,
    And sacrilege, three sins in killing three.

Cruel and sudden, hast thou since
Purpled thy nail, in blood of innocence?[3]   20
Wherein could this flea guilty be,
Except in that drop which it sucked from thee?
Yet thou triumph'st, and say'st that thou
Find'st not thy self nor me the weaker now;
    'Tis true, then learn how false tears be;   25

4. The perfect harmony of the planets, moving in concentric crystalline spheres, is contrasted with the charivari, a boisterous serenade for pots, pans, and trumpets, performed on the wedding night.
5. Almost all punctuation for the last two lines represents conjectures by modern editors. There might equally well be commas after "best" and "wit." The last word, "possessed," may modify "mummy," meaning "mummy with a

demon in it," or else "they," meaning "women who, when you have possessed them, are nothing but dried mummy."
1. I e., we, alas, don't dare hope for this consummation of our love, which the flea freely accepts. The idea of swelling suggests that of pregnancy.
2. Custom.
3. Like Herod, Donne's mistress has slaughtered the innocents, and is now clothed in imperial purple.

Just so much honor, when thou yield'st to me,
Will waste, as this flea's death took life from thee.

1633

The Curse

Who ever guesses, thinks, or dreams he knows
Who is my mistress, wither by this curse;
    His only, and only his purse
    May some dull heart to love dispose,[1]
And she yield then to all that are his foes;   5
    May he be scorned by one whom all else scorn,
    Forswear to others what to her h' hath sworn,
    With fear of missing, shame of getting, torn:

Madness his sorrow, gout his cramp, may he
Make, by but thinking, who hath made him such: 10
    And may he feel no touch
    Of conscience, but of fame, and be
Anguished, not that 'twas sin, but that 'twas she:
    In early and long scarceness may he rot,
    For land which had been his, if he had not   15
    Himself incestuously an heir begot:

May he dream treason, and believe that he
Meant to perform it, and confess, and die,
    And no record tell why:
    His sons, which none of his may be,   20
Inherit nothing but his infamy:
    Or may he so long parasites have fed,
    That he would fain be theirs whom he hath bred,[2]
    And at the last be circumcised for bread:

The venom of all stepdames, gamesters' gall,[3]   25
What tyrants and their subjects interwish,
    What plants, mines, beasts, fowl, fish,
    Can contribute, all ill which all
Prophets or poets spake; and all which shall
    Be annexed in schedules[4] unto this by me,   30
    Fall on that man; for if it be a she,
    Nature beforehand hath out-cursed me.

1633

---

1. I.e., may some dull heart fall in love with him for his only purse, and only for that.
2. I.e., may he have so many parasites that he'll have to be parasitic on them —and finally convert to Judaism.
3. Stepmothers and gamblers are represented as particularly malicious; tyrants are understood to wish the death of their subjects, and vice versa.
4. Codicils.

The Bait[1]

Come live with me and be my love,
And we will some new pleasures prove,
Of golden sands and crystal brooks,
With silken lines and silver hooks.

There will the river whispering run,   5
Warmed by thine eyes more than the sun.
And there th' enamored fish will stay,
Begging themselves they may betray.

When thou wilt swim in that live bath,
Each fish, which every channel hath,   10
Will amorously to thee swim,
Gladder to catch thee, than thou him.

If thou, to be so seen, beest loath,
By sun or moon, thou darkenest both;
And if myself have leave to see,   15
I need not their light, having thee.

Let others freeze with angling reeds,
And cut their legs with shells and weeds,
Or treacherously poor fish beset
With strangling snare, or windowy net.   20

Let coarse bold hands from slimy nest
The bedded fish in banks out-wrest,
Or curious traitors, sleave-silk flies,[2]
Bewitch poor fishes' wandering eyes.

For thee, thou needest no such deceit,   25
For thou thyself art thine own bait;
That fish that is not catched thereby,
Alas, is wiser far than I.

1633

A Valediction: Forbidding Mourning[1]

As virtuous men pass mildly away,
And whisper to their souls to go,

1. This poem is Donne's response to Marlowe's *Passionate Shepherd to His Love.* Another of the many replies was Ralegh's *Nymph's Reply to the Shepherd.*
2. Flies of unraveled silk, floss-silk.
1. The particularly serious and steady tone of this poem may be due to the circumstances of its composition. Izaak

Walton tells us it was addressed to Donne's wife on the occasion of his trip to the Continent in 1612. Donne had many forebodings of misfortune, which were verified when his wife gave birth to a stillborn child during his absence.

Whilst some of their sad friends do say
    The breath goes now, and some say, No;

So let us melt, and make no noise,   5
    No tear-floods, nor sigh-tempests move,
'Twere profanation of our joys
    To tell the laity our love.

Moving of th' earth brings harms and fears,
    Men reckon what it did and meant;   10
But trepidation of the spheres,
    Though greater far, is innocent.[2]

Dull sublunary[3] lovers' love
    (Whose soul[4] is sense) cannot admit
Absence, because it doth remove   15
    Those things which elemented[5] it.

But we by a love so much refined
    That our selves know not what it is,
Inter-assuréd of the mind,
    Care less, eyes, lips, and hands to miss.   20

Our two souls therefore, which are one,
    Though I must go, endure not yet
A breach, but an expansion,
    Like gold to airy thinness beat.

If they be two, they are two so   25
    As stiff twin compasses are two;
Thy soul, the fixed foot, makes no show
    To move, but doth, if th' other do.

And though it in the center sit,
    Yet when the other far doth roam,   30
It leans and hearkens after it,
    And grows erect, as that comes home.

Such wilt thou be to me, who must
    Like th' other foot, obliquely run;
Thy firmness makes my circle just,   35
    And makes me end where I begun.[6]

1633

2. I.e., earthquakes are thought to threaten evil consequences, but the variations of the spheres from true circularity, though they involve greater motions, are not considered sinister. "Trepidation of the spheres" (literally, "shuddering") was an additional arbitrary motion of the eighth sphere, introduced into the Ptolemaic system about the year 950 to account for certain celestial phenomena which were really due to the wobbling of the earth on its axis.
3. Beneath the moon, therefore mundane and subject to change.
4. Essence.
5. Composed.
6. The circle is an emblem of perfection; cf. also the motto of Mary, Queen of Scots, "In my end is my beginning." An excitingly complex, if perhaps overly medieval, reading of the poem is offered by John Freccero in *ELH*, **XXX** (December, 1963), 335–376.

The Ecstasy

Where, like a pillow on a bed,
    A pregnant bank swelled up to rest
The violet's reclining head,
    Sat we two, one another's best.
Our hands were firmly cemented   5
    With a fast balm, which thence did spring.
Our eye-beams twisted, and did thread
    Our eyes upon one double string;[1]
So to intergraft our hands, as yet
    Was all our means to make us one;   10
And pictures in our eyes to get
    Was all our propagation.
As 'twixt two equal armies, Fate
    Suspends uncertain victory,
Our souls (which to advance their state,   15
    Were gone out) hung 'twixt her and me.
And whilst our souls negotiate there,
    We like sepulchral statues lay;
All day the same our postures were,
    And we said nothing all the day.   20
If any, so by love refined
    That he soul's language understood,
And by good love were grown all mind,
    Within convenient distance stood,
He (though he know not which soul spake,   25
    Because both meant, both spake the same)
Might thence a new concoction[2] take,
    And part far purer than he came.
This ecstasy doth unperplex,[3]
    We said, and tell us what we love;   30
We see by this it was not sex;
    We see we saw not what did move;[4]
But as all several souls contain
    Mixture of things, they know not what,
Love these mixed souls doth mix again,   35
    And makes both one, each this and that.
A single violet transplant,
    The strength, the color, and the size
(All which before was poor, and scant)
    Redoubles still, and multiplies.   40

1. Joining hands and eyes is the only intercourse of the two lovers: "eye-beams" are invisible shafts of light, thought of as going out of the eyes and so enabling one to see things.

2. Purified mixture.
3. I.e., separate and clarify.
4. I.e., we see that we did not understand before what motivated ("did move") us.

When love, with one another so
  Interinanimates two souls,
That abler soul, which thence doth flow,
  Defects of loneliness controls.[5]
We then, who are this new soul, know,   45
  Of what we are composed, and made,
For, th' atomies[6] of which we grow,
  Are souls, whom no change can invade.
But O alas, so long, so far
  Our bodies why do we forbear?   50
They are ours, though they are not we; we are
  The intelligences, they the sphere.[7]
We owe them thanks because they thus,
  Did us to us at first convey,
Yielded their forces, sense, to us,   55
  Nor are dross to us, but allay.[8]
On man heaven's influence works not so
  But that it first imprints the air,[9]
So soul into the soul may flow,
  Though it to body first repair.   60
As our blood labors to beget
  Spirits as like souls as it can,[1]
Because such fingers need to knit
  That subtle knot which makes us man:
So must pure lovers' souls descend   65
  T' affections, and to faculties
Which sense may reach and apprehend;
  Else a great Prince in prison lies.
To our bodies turn we then, that so
  Weak men on love revealed may look;   70
Love's mysteries in souls do grow,
  But yet the body is his book.[2]
And if some lover, such as we,
  Have heard this dialogue of one,[3]
Let him still mark us; he shall see   75
  Small change when we are to bodies gone.

1633

5. The "abler soul" which derives from the union of two lesser ones can eliminate the loneliness with which each in itself is afflicted.

6. Atoms.

7. Medieval astronomers believed that the planets, set in crystalline spheres, were inhabited by "intelligences" which guided and controlled them. Similarly, Donne says, our bodies are guided and controlled by our selves.

8. "Dross" is an impurity which weakens metal, "allay" (alloy) an impurity which strengthens it. Our bodies contribute sensation ("sense") to the soul, and so reinforce it.

9. Astrological influences were thought to work on man through the surrounding air.

1. "Animal spirits" were thought to be begotten by the blood, to serve as intermediaries between body and soul.

2. I.e., love, a god within man, puts forth in the body a book where his mysteries may be read (as God the Creator put forth the book of Nature and the book of Scripture).

3. The characteristic Donne poem might be described as a "dialogue of one."

Lovers' Infiniteness

If yet I have not all[1] thy love,
Dear, I shall never have it all;
I cannot breathe one other sigh to move,
Nor can entreat one other tear to fall;
All my treasure, which should purchase thee,   5
Sighs, tears, and oaths, and letters, I have spent.
Yet no more can be due to me
Than at the bargain made was meant;
If then thy gift of love were partial,
That some to me, some should to others fall,   10
    Dear, I shall never have thee all.

Or if then thou gavest me all,
All was but all which thou hadst then;
But if in thy heart since there be or shall
New love created be by other men,   15
Which have their stocks entire, and can in tears,
In sighs, in oaths, and letters outbid me,
This new love may beget new fears,
For this love was not vowed by thee.
And yet it was, thy gift being general;   20
The ground, thy heart, is mine; whatever shall
    Grow there, dear, I should have it all.

Yet I would not have all yet.
He that hath all can have no more;
And since my love doth every day admit   25
New growth, thou shouldst have new rewards in store.
Thou canst not every day give me thy heart;
If thou canst give it, then thou never gavest it.
Love's riddles are, that though thy heart depart,
It stays at home, and thou with losing savest it.   30
But we will have a way more liberal
Than changing hearts, to join them;[2] so we shall
    Be one, and one another's all.

                                  1633

The Sun Rising

    Busy old fool, unruly sun,
      Why dost thou thus,
Through windows and through curtains call on us?

1. The influence of Donne's legal training is very clear here; the poem is a series of technical verbal quibbles on the word "all."

2. To join hearts is more liberal than to "change" (exchange) them; "liberal" implies amorous generosity, also relief from legal hairsplitting.

Must to thy motions lovers' seasons run?
    Saucy pedantic wretch, go chide   5
    Late school boys and sour prentices,
  Go tell court huntsmen that the King will ride,
  Call country ants to harvest offices;[1]
Love, all alike, no season knows nor clime,
Nor hours, days, months, which are the rags of time.   10

    Thy beams, so reverend and strong
    Why shouldst thou think?
I could eclipse and cloud them with a wink,
But that I would not lose her sight so long;
    If her eyes have not blinded thine,   15
    Look, and tomorrow late, tell me,
  Whether both th' Indias of spice and mine[2]
  Be where thou leftst them, or lie here with me.
Ask for those kings whom thou saw'st yesterday,
And thou shalt hear, All here in one bed lay.   20

    She is all states, and all princes, I,
    Nothing else is.
Princes do but play us; compared to this,
All honor's mimic, all wealth alchemy.[3]
    Thou, sun, art half as happy as we,   25
    In that the world's contracted thus;
  Thine age asks ease, and since thy duties be
  To warm the world, that's done in warming us.
Shine here to us, and thou art everywhere;
This bed thy center is,[4] these walls, thy sphere.
                               30

                                1633

Air and Angels

Twice or thrice had I loved thee,
Before I knew thy face or name;
So in a voice, so in a shapeless flame,
Angels affect us oft, and worshipped be;
    Still when, to where thou wert, I came,   5
Some lovely glorious nothing I did see.
    But since my soul, whose child love is,
Takes limbs of flesh, and else could nothing do,[1]
    More subtle than the parent is
Love must not be, but take a body too;   10
    And therefore what thou wert, and who,
    I bid love ask, and now
That it assume thy body I allow,
And fix itself in thy lip, eye, and brow.

---

1. Harvest chores, duties.
2. The India of "spice" is East India, that of "mine" (gold), the West Indies.
3. I.e., fraudulent.

4. The "center" of the sun's orbit.
1. As my soul could not function unless it were in a body, so love, which is the soul's child, must also be corporeal.

Whilst thus to ballast love I thought,   15
And so more steadily to have gone,
With wares which would sink admiration,
I saw I had love's pinnace overfraught;[2]
  Every thy hair for love to work upon
Is much too much, some fitter must be sought;   20
  For, nor in nothing, nor in things
Extreme and scatt'ring[3] bright, can love inhere.
   Then as an angel, face and wings
Of air, not pure as it, yet pure doth wear,
  So thy love may be my love's sphere.[4]   25
   Just such disparity
As is 'twixt air and angels' purity,
'Twixt women's love and men's will ever be.

          1633

Break of Day[1]

'Tis true, 'tis day; what though it be?
O wilt thou therefore rise from me?
Why should we rise, because 'tis light?
Did we lie down, because 'twas night?
Love, which in spite of darkness brought us hither,   5
Should in despite of light keep us together.

Light hath no tongue, but is all eye;
If it could speak as well as spy,
This were the worst that it could say,
That being well, I fain would stay,   10
And that I loved my heart and honor so,
That I would not from him, that had them, go.

Must business thee from hence remove?
O, that's the worst disease of love.
The poor, the foul, the false, love can   15
Admit, but not the busied man.
He which hath business, and makes love, doth do
Such wrong, as when a married man doth woo.

          1633

---

2. **Her physical beauty** (his "wares") would sink admiration—i.e., overwhelm wonder itself. This is too much ballast for love's "pinnace" (a small boat).
3. Diffused, dazzling.
4. Some Scholastic philosophers held that angels, when they appeared to men, assumed a body of air. Such a body, though pure, was less so than the angel's spiritual being. Similarly, women's love, which Donne thinks *less* pure than that of men, may still serve as the receptacle ("sphere") for the love of men.

1. Modeled on the Provençal aubade, or song of the lovers' parting at dawn, this poem is a departure for Donne in that it assumes a feminine point of view. As a rule, he is among the most consistently masculine of poets.

A Valediction: Of Weeping

Let me pour forth
My tears before thy face whilst I stay here,
For thy face coins them, and thy stamp they bear,
And by this mintage they are something worth,
    For thus they be   5
    Pregnant of thee;
Fruits of much grief they are, emblems of more—
When a tear falls, that Thou falls which it bore,
So thou and I are nothing then, when on a diverse shore.[1]

    On a round ball   10
A workman that hath copies by, can lay
An Europe, Afric, and an Asia,
And quickly make that, which was nothing, all;[2]
    So doth each tear
    Which thee doth wear,   15
A globe, yea world, by that impression grow,
Till thy tears mixed with mine do overflow
This world; by waters sent from thee, my heaven dissolvèd so.[3]

    O more than moon,
Draw not up seas to drown me in thy sphere;
Weep me not dead, in thine arms, but forbear   20
To teach the sea what it may do too soon.
    Let not the wind
    Example find
To do me more harm than it purposeth;   25
Since thou and I sigh one another's breath,
Whoe'er sighs most is cruelest, and hastes the other's death.[4]

                         1633

The Funeral

Whoever comes to shroud me, do not harm
    Nor question much
That subtle wreath of hair which crowns my arm;
The mystery, the sign you must not touch,
    For 'tis my outward soul,   5
Viceroy to that, which then to heaven being gone,

---

1. The loss of the lovers in their separation is figured in the fall of a tear which contains the image of the mistress.
2. I.e., on a blank globe an artist can draw the world, and so convert a cipher, the image of nothingness, to the whole world.
3. In describing Creation, Genesis i.6–7 makes mention of certain heavenly waters, some above and some below the firmament. Their existence and function has been much debated by Bible scholars.
4. The breath of life has been interchanged between the lovers.

Will leave this to control,
And keep these limbs, her[1] provinces, from dissolution.

For if the sinewy thread[2] my brain lets fall
    Through every part   10
Can tie those parts and make me one of all;
These hairs, which upward grew, and strength and art
    Have from a better brain,
Can better do it; except she meant that I
    By this should know my pain,   15
As prisoners then are manacled, when they're condemned to die.

Whate'er she meant by it, bury it with me,
    For since I am
Love's martyr, it might breed idolatry,
If into others' hands these relics came;
    As 'twas humility[3]   20
To afford to it all that a soul can do,
    So 'tis some bravery,
That since you would save none of me, I bury some of you.

                            1633

The Relic

When my grave is broke up again
Some second guest to entertain
(For graves have learned that woman-head[1]
To be to more than one a bed),
    And he that digs it, spies   5
A bracelet of bright hair about the bone,
    Will he not let us alone,
And think that there a loving couple lies,
Who thought that this device might be some way
To make their souls, at the last busy day,   10
Meet at this grave, and make a little stay?

If this fall in a time, or land,
Where mis-devotion[2] doth command,
Then he that digs us up, will bring
Us to the Bishop and the King,   15
    To make us relics; then
Thou shalt be a Mary Magdalen, and I
    A something else thereby;[3]

---

1. The soul's, but also the mistress's; compare "she," below, line 14.
2. The spinal cord and nervous system.
3. It was humility to grant, in the first thirteen and a half lines of the poem, that her hair could act as a soul; it is also "bravery" (defiance) to bury a part of the mistress in revenge for her cruelty.

1. I.e., characteristic of women. On the re-use of graves, see Sir Thomas Browne's *Urn-Burial* and *Hamlet* V.i.
2. False devotion, superstition. Donne seems to have in mind Roman Catholicism.
3. The rhythm of "something else" suggests the complete but blasphemous parallel, "Jesus Christ."

All women shall adore us, and some men;
And since at such time, miracles are sought,   20
I would have that age by this paper taught
What miracles we harmless lovers wrought.

    First, we loved well and faithfully,
    Yet knew not what we loved, nor why,
    Difference of sex no more we knew,   25
    Than our guardian angels do;
        Coming and going, we
Perchance might kiss, but not between those meals;[4]
        Our hands ne'er touched the seals,
Which nature, injured by late law, sets free:
These miracles we did; but now, alas,   30
All measure and all language I should pass,
Should I tell what a miracle she was.

                            1633

Elegy I. Jealousy[1]

Fond[2] woman, which wouldst have thy husband die,
And yet complainst of his great jealousy:
If, swoll'n with poison, he lay in's last bed,
His body with a cere-bark[3] covered,
Drawing his breath as thick and short as can   5
The nimblest crocheting musician,[4]
Ready with loathsome vomiting to spew
His soul out of one hell into a new,
Made deaf with his poor kindred's howling cries,
Begging with few feign'd tears great legacies,   10
Thou would'st not weep, but jolly and frolic be,
As a slave which tomorrow should be free;
Yet weep'st thou when thou seest him hungrily
Swallow his own death, heart's-bane jealousy.
Oh give him many thanks, he is courteous,   15
That in suspecting kindly warneth us.
We must not, as we used, flout openly
In scoffing riddles his deformity;
Nor at his board together being sat
With words nor touch, scarce looks, adulterate.[5]   20

4. The kiss of salutation and parting was, in the 17th century, a peculiarly English custom; the passage that follows seems to suggest some greater intimacy, permitted by nature, but unjustly abridged by "late law." It is hard to imagine what Donne had in mind here; he was not opposed to the sacrament of matrimony, and the laws of marriage could not be called "late," i.e., recent.

1. The situation is that of Ovid's more cynical poems (there are clear parallels with *Amores* I.iv): wife and lover are brutally unscrupulous in taking advantage of the hateful husband.
2. Foolish.
3. Cere-cloth is the waxed cloth in which a corpse is wrapped for the grave; the husband's corrupting skin ("bark") is already forming a grave-cloth for him.
4. Crochets (pronounced to rhyme with "pockets") are quarter-notes, to be played very fast.
5. Commit adultery.

Nor when he swoll'n and pampered with great fare
Sits down and snorts, caged in his basket chair,
Must we usurp his own bed any more,
Nor kiss and play in his house, as before.
Now I see many dangers; for that is   25
His realm, his castle, and his diocese.
But if, as envious men, which would revile
Their prince, or coin his gold, themselves exile
Into another country, and do it there,
We play in another house, what should we fear?   30
There we will scorn his household policies,
His silly plots and pensionary spies,
As the inhabitants of Thames' right side
Do London's mayor,[6] or Germans the Pope's pride.

                                             1633

Elegy XIX. Going to Bed

Come, Madam, come, all rest my powers defy,
Until I labor, I in labor lie.[1]
The foe oft-times, having the foe in sight,
Is tired with standing though he never fight.
Off with that girdle, like heaven's zone glittering,   5
But a far fairer world encompassing.
Unpin that spangled breastplate which you wear
That th' eyes of busy fools may be stopped there.
Unlace yourself, for that harmonious chime
Tells me from you that now it is bed-time.   10
Off with that happy busk,[2] which I envy,
That still can be and still can stand so nigh.
Your gown going off, such beauteous state reveals
As when from flowery meads th' hill's shadow steals.
Off with that wiry coronet and show   15
The hairy diadem which on you doth grow:
Now off with those shoes, and then safely tread
In this love's hallowed temple, this soft bed.
In such white robes, heaven's angels used to be
Received by men; thou, angel, bring'st with thee   20
A heaven like Mahomet's paradise;[3] and though
Ill spirits walk in white, we easily know
By this these angels from an evil sprite,
Those set our hairs, but these our flesh upright.
    License my roving hands, and let them go   25
Before, behind, between, above, below.
O my America! my new-found-land,

---

6. Suburban inhabitants of the "liberties" on the south bank of the Thames were beyond the jurisdiction of the municipal authorities. Houses of prostitution were therefore frequent there. Donne is not trying to compliment the lady.

1. "Labor" in the sense of "get to work" and in the sense of "distress."
2. Corset.
3. Populated by seductive houris, for the delectation of the faithful.

My kingdom, safeliest when with one man manned,
My mine of precious stones, my empery,
How blest am I in this discovering thee!   30
To enter in these bonds is to be free;
There where my hand is set, my seal shall be.[4]
     Full nakedness! All joys are due to thee,
As souls unbodied, bodies unclothed must be,
To taste whole joys. Gems which you women use   35
Are like Atalanta's balls,[5] cast in men's views,
That when a fool's eye lighteth on a gem,
His earthly soul may covet theirs, not them.
Like pictures, or like books' gay coverings, made
For laymen, are all women thus arrayed;   40
Themselves are mystic books, which only we
(Whom their imputed grace will dignify)
Must see revealed.[6] Then since that I may know,
As liberally as to a midwife, show
Thyself: cast all, yea, this white linen hence,   45
There is no penance due to innocence.
     To teach thee, I am naked first; why then
What need'st thou have more covering than a man?

                         1669

4. The jokes mingle law with sex; having signed the document with his hand, he will now seal it, and in the bond of their relationship he will find freedom.
5. Atalanta, running a race against her suitor Hippomenes, was beaten when he dropped golden balls (apples) for her to pick up. Donne, for reasons of his own, reverses the story.
6. By granting favors to their lovers, women impute to them grace which they don't deserve, as God imputes grace to undeserving sinners. Laymen can only look at the covers of mystic books (women); but "we" who have saving grace can read them.

Satire III, Religion

For the first time in English literary history, the mode of satire flourished in the last decade of Elizabeth's reign and under the first two Stuarts. Many social circumstances contributed to its popularity: a surplus of clever young men without jobs, bitter antipathies between social classes and groups, and a general spirit of disillusion and doubt which has been characterized as "Jacobean melancholy."

Out of this mood of prolonged doubt, search, and obstinate questioning came the five satires of John Donne. *Satire III, Religion* is not a satire in the customary sense of a mocking attack on some person or custom. It is a strenuous, inconclusive discussion of an acute theological problem: How may a man recognize the true church, to which all Christians claim to belong? The person to whom it is addressed is evidently a man without specific religious commitment, but with a great and anxious interest in religion, and a specially nervous feeling that the claims of Roman Catholicism may be justified. He has been a sailor, a soldier, a bit of a rake, a bit of a theologian; he has more than a smattering of law. In many small ways, he reminds us of young Jack Donne himself. But the most characteristic thing about this poem on the search for certainty is the toughness of mind which it evinces throughout. Donne's images have a raw, contemptuous

force, his phrasing is clipped, his grammar and his meter are twisted by
the energy of his argument. He has no easy answer for the question raised,
and makes no effort to charm or lull the reader. His poem is sheer display
of intellectual force, a pointed, inconclusive game of mind.

Satire III, Religion

Kind pity chokes my spleen; brave scorn forbids
Those tears to issue which swell my eyelids;
I must not laugh, nor weep sins, and be wise,
Can railing then cure these worn maladies?
Is not our mistress, fair Religion,   5
As worthy of all our souls' devotion,
As virtue was to the first blinded age?[1]
Are not heaven's joys as valiant to assuage
Lusts, as earth's honor was to them?[2] Alas,
As we do them in means, shall they surpass   10
Us in the end, and shall thy father's spirit
Meet blind philosophers in heaven, whose merit
Of strict life may be imputed faith,[3] and hear
Thee, whom he taught so easy ways and near
To follow, damned? O, if thou dar'st, fear this;   15
This fear great courage and high valor is.
Dar'st thou aid mutinous Dutch,[4] and dar'st thou lay
Thee in ships, wooden sepulchers, a prey
To leaders' rage, to storms, to shot, to dearth?
Dar'st thou dive seas and dungeons of the earth?   20
Hast thou courageous fire to thaw the ice
Of frozen North discoveries? and thrice
Colder than salamanders,[5] like divine
Children in the oven,[6] fires of Spain, and the line,
Whose countries limbecks to our bodies be,   25
Canst thou for gain bear?[7] And must every he
Which cries not, "Goddess!" to thy mistress, draw,[8]
Or eat thy poisonous words? Courage of straw!
O desperate coward, wilt thou seem bold, and
To thy foes and his[9] (who made thee to stand   30

1. The age of paganism, blind to the light of Christianity, but capable of following natural morality ("virtue").
2. I.e., hope of heaven should be as powerful ("valiant") an antidote to sin in us as earthly honor was to "them"—the pagans.
3. Even without Christian faith, pagan philosophers may achieve heaven (see *The Divine Comedy, Paradiso* XX) by an extraordinary display of virtue which causes faith to be imputed to them.
4. The Dutch continually enlisted English volunteers in their rebellious wars against the Spaniards. Donne had never fought in Flanders, though he had sailed twice against the Spaniards, to Cadiz and the Azores.
5. The salamander was traditionally so cold-blooded that it could live even in a fire.
6. The "divine children in the oven" are Shadrach, Meshach, and Abednego, rescued from the fiery furnace in Daniel iii.
7. The object of "bear" is "fires of Spain, and the line"—Inquisitorial and equatorial heats, which roast men as chemists heat materials in "limbecks" (alembics, or retorts for distilling).
8. I.e., fight a duel.
9. God's.

Sentinel in his world's garrison) thus yield,
And for forbidden wars, leave th' appointed field?
Know thy foes: The foul Devil (whom thou
Strivest to please) for hate, not love, would allow
Thee fain his whole realm to be quit;[1] and as   35
The world's all parts[2] wither away and pass,
So the world's self, thy other loved foe, is
In her decrepit wane, and thou, loving this,
Dost love a withered and worn strumpet; last,
Flesh (itself's death) and joys which flesh can taste,   40
Thou lovest; and thy fair goodly soul, which doth
Give this flesh power to taste joy, thou dost loathe.
Seek true religion. O, where? Mirreus,[3]
Thinking her unhoused here, and fled from us,
Seeks her at Rome; there, because he doth know   45
That she was there a thousand years ago.
He loves her rags so, as we here obey
The statecloth[4] where the Prince sat yesterday.
Crantz to such brave loves will not be enthralled,
But loves her only, who at Geneva is called   50
Religion—plain, simple, sullen, young,
Contemptuous, yet unhandsome; as among
Lecherous humors,[5] there is one that judges
No wenches wholesome but coarse country drudges.
Graius stays still at home here, and because   55
Some preachers, vile ambitious bawds, and laws
Still new, like fashions, bid him think that she
Which dwells with us, is only perfect, he
Embraceth her whom his Godfathers will
Tender to him, being tender, as wards still   60
Take such wives as their guardians offer, or
Pay values.[6] Careless Phrygius doth abhor
All, because all cannot be good, as one
Knowing some women whores, dares marry none.
Graccus loves all as one, and thinks that so   65
As women do in divers countries go
In divers habits, yet are still one kind,
So doth, so is religion; and this blind-
ness too much light breeds; but unmoved thou
Of force must one, and forced but one allow;   70
And the right;[7] ask thy father which is she,

1. I.e., the Devil would gladly give you
a free hand with his whole kingdom.
2. All parts of the world. It was a common belief in the 17th century that the
world was getting old and decrepit.
3. The imaginary characters in this
passage represent different creeds. "Mirreus" is a Roman Catholic, "Crantz" a
Geneva Presbyterian, "Graius" an
Erastian (i.e., believing in any religion
sponsored by the state), "Phrygius" a
skeptic, and "Graccus" a Universalist.
4. The royal canopy, a symbol of kingly

power.
5. Tempers, temperaments.
6. Young men (of "tender" years) might
reject the wives offered ("tendered")
them by their guardians; but, if they
did so, had to pay "values," i.e. fines.
7. I.e., being blind to the differences
between religions, Graccus has too
much light to see anything (lines 68–
69). But the poet insists that without
being swayed by human pressures, we
must find just one true religion, "the
right" true religion.

Let him ask his; though truth and falsehood be
Near twins, yet truth a little elder is;
Be busy to seek her, believe me this,
He's not of none, nor worst, that seeks the best.[8]   75
To adore, or scorn an image, or protest,
May all be bad; doubt wisely; in strange way
To stand inquiring right, is not to stray;
To sleep, or run wrong, is. On a huge hill,
Cragged and steep, Truth stands, and he that will   80
Reach her, about must, and about must go,
And what the hill's suddenness resists, win so;
Yet strive so, that before age, death's twilight,
Thy soul rest, for none can work in that night.
To will[9] implies delay, therefore now do.   85
Hard deeds, the body's pains; hard knowledge too
The mind's endeavors reach,[1] and mysteries
Are like the sun, dazzling, yet plain to all eyes.
Keep the truth which thou hast found; men do not stand
In so ill case here, that God hath with his hand   90
Signed kings' blank charters to kill whom they hate,
Nor are they vicars, but hangmen to fate.[2]
Fool and wretch, wilt thou let thy soul be tied
To man's laws, by which she shall not be tried
At the last day? O, will it then boot thee   95
To say a Philip, or a Gregory,
A Harry, or a Martin taught thee this?[3]
Is not this excuse for mere contraries
Equally strong? Cannot both sides say so?
That thou mayest rightly obey power, her bounds know;   100
Those passed, her nature and name is changed; to be
Then humble to her is idolatry.[4]
As streams are, power is; those blest flowers that dwell
At the rough stream's calm head, thrive and do well,
But having left their roots, and themselves given   105
To the stream's tyrannous rage, alas, are driven
Through mills, and rocks, and woods, and at last, almost
Consumed in going, in the sea are lost.
So perish souls, which more choose men's unjust
Power from God claimed, than God himself to trust.   110

1633

8. The man who seeks the best church is neither an unbeliever nor the worst sort of believer.
9. To intend a future action.
1. I.e., the body's pains achieve ("reach") hard deeds; the mind's endeavors will reach hard knowledge.
2. Human authority does not represent divine justice on earth; men are not God's vicars on earth (the hit here is at both the Pope and the secular monarch), but his hangmen at best—agents through whom his justice is fulfilled without carte blanche ("blank charters") to use their own judgments.
3. "Philip" is Philip II of Spain, and "Gregory" any one of several Pope Gregories (VII, XIII, XIV); "Harry" is England's Henry VIII, and "Martin" is Martin Luther. Laymen and clergy, Protestants and Catholics, all are covered. "Boot": profit.
4. I.e., when the true limits of ecclesiastical power have been passed, obedience becomes idolatry.

Good Friday, 1613. Riding Westward

Let man's soul be a sphere, and then, in this,
The intelligence that moves, devotion is,[1]
And as the other spheres, by being grown
Subject to foreign motions, lose their own,
And being by others hurried every day,   5
Scarce in a year their natural form obey;
Pleasure or business, so, our souls admit
For their first mover, and are whirled by it.[2]
Hence is 't, that I am carried towards the West
This day, when my soul's form bends towards the East.   10
There I should see a Sun,[3] by rising, set,
And by that setting endless day beget:
But that Christ on this cross did rise and fall,
Sin had eternally benighted all.
Yet dare I almost be glad I do not see   15
That spectacle, of too much weight for me.
Who sees God's face, that is self-life, must die;
What a death were it then to see God die?
It made his own lieutenant, Nature, shrink;
It made his footstool crack, and the sun wink.[4]   20
Could I behold those hands which span the poles,
And tune all spheres at once, pierced with those holes?
Could I behold that endless height which is
Zenith to us, and our antipodes,[5]
Humbled below us? Or that blood which is   25
The seat of all our souls, if not of His,
Make dirt of dust, or that flesh which was worn
By God, for his apparel, ragg'd and torn?
If on these things I durst not look, durst I
Upon his miserable mother cast mine eye,   30
Who was God's partner here, and furnished thus
Half of that sacrifice which ransomed us?
Though these things, as I ride, be from mine eye,
They are present yet unto my memory,
For that looks towards them; and Thou look'st towards me, 35
O Saviour, as Thou hang'st upon the tree.
I turn my back to Thee but to receive
Corrections, till Thy mercies bid Thee leave.
O think me worth Thine anger; punish me;
Burn off my rusts and my deformity;   40

1. As intelligences guide the visible planets, devotion is or should be the guiding principle of man's life.
2. I.e., spheres are deflected from their true orbits by outside influences; so our souls are deflected by business or pleasure.
3. The sun-Son pun was an ancient one.
Christ, the Son of God, set when he rose on the Cross, and his setting (death) gave rise to the Christian era.
4. An earthquake and eclipse supposedly accompanied the Crucifixion.
5. "Zenith" and "antipodes" are the highest and farthest reach of heaven.

Restore Thine image so much, by Thy grace,
That Thou may'st know me, and I'll turn my face.

1633

From Holy Sonnets[1]

1

Thou hast made me, and shall Thy work decay?
Repair me now, for now mine end doth haste;
I run to death, and death meets me as fast,
And all my pleasures are like yesterday.
I dare not move my dim eyes any way,　　　　　5
Despair behind, and death before doth cast
Such terror, and my feeble flesh doth waste
By sin in it, which it towards hell doth weigh.
Only Thou art above, and when towards Thee
By Thy leave I can look, I rise again;　　　　　10
But our old subtle foe so tempteth me
That not one hour myself I can sustain.
Thy grace may wing me to prevent his art,
And Thou like adamant draw mine iron heart.[2]

1633

5

I am a little world made cunningly
Of elements, and an angelic sprite;[3]
But black sin hath betrayed to endless night
My world's both parts, and O, both parts must die.
You which beyond that heaven which was most high　　5
Have found new spheres, and of new lands can write,[4]
Pour new seas in mine eyes, that so I might
Drown my world with my weeping earnestly,
Or wash it if it must be drowned no more.[5]

1. Several of the *Holy Sonnets* contain specific indications of date; number 17 makes reference to the recent death of Donne's wife (August 15, 1617) and number 18 may have been inspired by the Elector Palatine's defeat (October 29, 1620). But most are considerably earlier (1609–10). They are nineteen in number, conventional in their rhyme scheme and broad metrical pattern, but rhythmically bold, powerful in their imagery, and marked by deep emotional coloring. Donne's religion was never a secure or comfortable experience; his *Holy Sonnets* are documents which mingle anguished despair with no less anguished hope. And in a sonnet like *Holy Sonnet 14*, his faith rises to a series of knotted paradoxes involving coercion and submission, which would be revolting were it not for the full and evident sincerity of the mind to which they were inevitable.

2. "Wing": strengthen; "prevent": counteract; "adamant": loadstone. Note throughout the sonnets a combination of strong imperatives and protestations of abject helplessness which determines the tone of Donne's religious feeling.

3. Both body and soul—the former made of "elements," the latter "angelic sprite" (spirit).

4. Donne asks the astronomers and explorers to find new oceans for tears to weep or waters to wash away his sins.

5. God promised (Genesis ix.11) after Noah's experience that the earth would never again be flooded.

But O, it must be burnt! Alas, the fire   10
Of lust and envy have burnt it heretofore,
And made it fouler; let their flames retire,
And burn me, O Lord, with a fiery zeal
Of Thee and Thy house, which doth in eating heal.[6]

1635

7

At the round earth's imagined corners,[7] blow
Your trumpets, angels; and arise, arise
From death, you numberless infinities
Of souls, and to your scattered bodies go;
All whom the flood did, and fire shall, o'erthrow,   5
All whom war, dearth, age, agues, tyrannies,
Despair, law, chance hath slain, and you whose eyes
Shall behold God, and never taste death's woe.[8]
But let them sleep, Lord, and me mourn a space;
For, if above all these, my sins abound,   10
'Tis late to ask abundance of Thy grace
When we are there. Here on this lowly ground,
Teach me how to repent; for that's as good
As if Thou hadst sealed my pardon with Thy blood.

1633

10

Death, be not proud, though some have callèd thee
Mighty and dreadful, for thou art not so;
For those whom thou think'st thou dost overthrow
Die not, poor Death, nor yet canst thou kill me.
From rest and sleep, which but thy pictures be,   5
Much pleasure; then from thee much more must flow,
And soonest our best men with thee do go,
Rest of their bones, and soul's delivery.[9]
Thou art slave to fate, chance, kings, and desperate men,
And dost with poison, war, and sickness dwell,   10
And poppy[1] or charms can make us sleep as well
And better than thy stroke; why swell'st thou then?
One short sleep past, we wake eternally
And death shall be no more; Death, thou shalt die.

1633

6. See Psalm lxix.9: "For the zeal of
thine house hath eaten me up." The
passage involves three sorts of flame—
those of the Last Judgment; those of
lust and envy; and those of zeal, which
alone heal.
7. Donne may have been thinking of
the angels on old maps, who blow their
trumpets to the four points of the compass. See also Revelation vii.1.

8. See Matthew xvi.28, Mark ix.1, and
Luke ix.27, where the worthies are described who ascended directly to heaven
from this life.
9. I.e., our best men go with you to
find rest for their bones and freedom
("delivery") for their souls.
1. Opium. "Why swell'st thou then?":
why do you puff with pride?

14

Batter my heart, three-personed God; for You
As yet but knock, breathe, shine, and seek to mend;
That I may rise and stand, o'erthrow me, and bend
Your force to break, blow, burn, and make me new.
I, like an usurped town, to another due,   5
Labor to admit You, but O, to no end;
Reason, Your viceroy in me, me should defend,
But is captived, and proves weak or untrue.
Yet dearly I love You, and would be loved fain,
But am bethrothed unto Your enemy.   10
Divorce me, untie or break that knot again;
Take me to You, imprison me, for I,
Except You enthrall me, never shall be free,
Nor ever chaste, except You ravish me.

1633

18

Show me, dear Christ, Thy spouse so bright and clear.[2]
What! is it she which on the other shore
Goes richly painted? or which, robbed and tore,
Laments and mourns in Germany and here?[3]
Sleeps she a thousand, then peeps up one year? 5
Is she self-truth, and errs? now new, now outwore?
Doth she, and did she, and shall she evermore
On one, on seven, or on no hill appear?[4]
Dwells she with us, or like adventuring knights
First travel[5] we to seek, and then make love? 10
Betray, kind husband, Thy spouse to our sights,
And let mine amorous soul court Thy mild dove,
Who is most true and pleasing to Thee then
When she is embraced and open to most men.

1899

A Hymn to Christ, at the Author's Last Going into Germany[6]

In what torn ship soever I embark,
That ship shall be my emblem of Thy ark;

2. "What are the marks of a true church?" was a deeply fought field of interdenominational debate in the 17th century. Few Anglican clergymen would have expressed an indecision as universal as Donne's in this sonnet. Its skepticism, and a sense that versifying did not beseem a clergyman, kept the sonnet out of all 17th-century editions.
3. The Church of Rome is "she which goes richly painted on the other shore";

she is contrasted with the reformed churches "in Germany and here."
4. The Mount of Olives, the seven hills of Rome, and (perhaps) by Lake Geneva or in the town of Canterbury.
5. The 17th-century spelling, *travaile*, includes the idea of labor.
6. Donne went to Germany as chaplain to the Earl of Doncaster in 1619; the mission was a diplomatic one, to the King and Queen of Bohemia.

What sea soever swallow me, that flood
Shall be to me an emblem of Thy blood;
Though Thou with clouds of anger do disguise   5
Thy face, yet through that mask I know those eyes,
    Which, though they turn away sometimes,
        They never will despise.

I sacrifice this island unto Thee,
And all whom I loved there, and who loved me;   10
When I have put our seas twixt them and me,
Put Thou Thy seas betwixt my sins and Thee.
As the tree's sap doth seek the root below
In winter, in my winter now I go
    Where none but Thee, th' eternal root   15
        Of true love, I may know.

Nor Thou nor Thy religion dost control
The amorousness of an harmonious soul,
But Thou would'st have that love Thyself; as Thou
Art jealous, Lord, so I am jealous now;   20
Thou lov'st not, till from loving more,[7] Thou free
My soul; whoever gives, takes liberty;
    Oh, if Thou car'st not whom I love,
        Alas, Thou lov'st not me.

Seal then this bill of my divorce to all   25
On whom those fainter beams of love did fall;
Marry those loves, which in youth scattered be
On fame, wit, hopes (false mistresses), to Thee.
Churches are best for prayer that have least light:
To see God only, I go out of sight;   30
    And to 'scape stormy days, I choose
        An everlasting night.

                       1633

Hymn to God My God, in My Sickness[1]

Since I am coming to that holy room
    Where, with Thy choir of saints for evermore,
I shall be made Thy music; as I come
    I tune the instrument here at the door,
    And what I must do then, think here before.   5

Whilst my physicians by their love are grown
    Cosmographers, and I their map, who lie
Flat on this bed, that by them may be shown

---

7. From loving elsewhere. Donne is playing with the idea, "To give me true love you must take away my freedom to love elsewhere."

1. Izaak Walton, Donne's first biographer, says this poem was written March 23, 1631, eight days before Donne's death.

That this is my southwest discovery[2]
Per fretum febris,[3] by these straits to die,   10

I joy, that in these straits, I see my West;[4]
    For, though their currents yield return to none,
What shall my West hurt me? As West and East
    In all flat maps (and I am one) are one,
        So death doth touch the resurrection.   15

Is the Pacific Sea my home? Or are
    The Eastern riches? Is Jerusalem?
Anyan,[5] and Magellan, and Gibraltar,
    All straits, and none but straits, are ways to them,
        Whether where Japhet dwelt, or Cham, or Shem.[6]   20

We think that Paradise and Calvary,
    Christ's cross, and Adam's tree, stood in one place;
Look, Lord, and find both Adams met in me;
    As the first Adam's sweat surrounds my face,
        May the last Adam's blood my soul embrace.   25

So, in his purple wrapped,[7] receive me, Lord;
    By these his thorns give me his other crown;
And, as to others' souls I preached Thy word,
    Be this my text, my sermon to mine own;
        Therefore that he may raise the Lord throws down.   30

1635

A Hymn to God the Father[1]

Wilt Thou forgive that sin where I begun,
    Which is my sin, though it were done before?
Wilt Thou forgive that sin through which I run,
    And do run still, though still I do deplore?
        When Thou hast done, Thou hast not done,   5
        For I have more.

Wilt Thou forgive that sin which I have won
    Others to sin? and made my sin their door?
Wilt Thou forgive that sin which I did shun
    A year or two, but wallowed in a score?   10
        When Thou hast done, Thou hast not done,
        For I have more.

---

2. The Straits of Magellan, or something spiritual which is analogous to them.
3. I.e., through the straits of fever.
4. Where the sun sets, hence where life ends.
5. The Bering Straits.
6. Japhet, Cham (Ham), and Shem were the three sons of Noah by whom the world was repopulated after the Flood (Genesis x). The descendants of Japhet were thought to inhabit Europe, those of Ham Africa, and those of Shem Asia.
7. The purple of Christ is his blood; also a royal garment.
1. Even in poetry of unquestioned seriousness, Donne's mind expressed itself naturally in puns; there are several in this short hymn, which Walton tells us was written during Donne's illness of 1623.

I have a sin of fear, that when I have spun
My last thread, I shall perish on the shore;
Swear by Thy self, that at my death Thy Son   15
Shall shine as he shines now and heretofore;
And, having done that, Thou hast done,
I fear no more.

1633

From Devotions upon Emergent Occasions[1]

Meditation IV

Medicusque vocatur.
The physician is sent for.

It is too little to call man a little world; except God, man is a
diminutive to nothing.[2] Man consists of more pieces, more parts,
than the world; than the world doth, nay, than the world is. And if
these pieces were extended and stretched out in man as they are in
the world, man would be the giant and the world the dwarf; the
world but the map, and the man the world. If all the veins in our
bodies were extended to rivers, and all the sinews to veins of mines,
and all the muscles that lie upon one another to hills, and all the
bones to quarries of stones, and all the other pieces to the proportion of those which correspond to them in the world, the air would
be too little for this orb of man to move in, the firmament would be
but enough for this star. For as the whole world hath nothing to
which something in man doth not answer, so hath man many pieces
of which the whole world hath no representation. Enlarge this meditation upon this great world, man, so far as to consider the
immensity of the creatures this world produces. Our creatures are
our thoughts, creatures that are born giants, that reach from east to
west, from earth to heaven, that do not only bestride all the sea and

1. Donne's private devotions were written
during an attack of illness in the winter
of 1623. They describe in detail the
stages of Donne's disease and recovery;
each stage comprises a meditation on
the human condition, an expostulation
and debate with God, and a prayer to
Him. The book was published almost
immediately it was written, and to
great effect—the blend of private feeling and public moralizing rendering it
particularly accessible to 17th-century
readers. And its eloquent periods have
provided a title for at least one major
modern novel (see Meditation XVII).

"Emergent" occasions are those which
arise casually or unexpectedly.
Donne's Latin epigraphs are followed
by his English translations, some of
them very free ones indeed.
2. Donne's meditation is built on the
Renaissance notion that man is a microcosm, a little world, analogous in every
respect to the macrocosm, or big
world, outside. But in playing with this
notion, Donne paradoxically reverses it,
arguing for a moment that man is a
giant and the world his diminished representation.

land, but span the sun and firmament at once: my thoughts reach all, comprehend all.

Inexplicable mystery! I their creator am in a close prison, in a sick bed, anywhere, and any one of my creatures, my thoughts, is with the sun, and beyond the sun, overtakes the sun, and overgoes the sun in one pace, one step, everywhere. And then as the other world produces serpents and vipers, malignant and venomous creatures, and worms and caterpillars, that endeavor to devour that world which produces them, and monsters compiled and complicated of divers parents and kinds, so this world, our selves, produces all these in us, producing diseases and sicknesses of all those sorts; venomous and infectious diseases, feeding and consuming diseases, and manifold and entangled diseases made up of many several ones. And can the other world name so many venomous, so many consuming, so many monstrous creatures, as we can diseases, of all these kinds? O miserable abundance, O beggarly riches! How much do we lack of having remedies for every disease when as yet we have not names for them?

But we have a Hercules against these giants, these monsters: that is the physician. He musters up all the resources of the other world to succor this, all nature to relieve man. We have the physician but we are not the physician. Here we shrink in our proportion, sink in our dignity in respect of very mean creatures who are physicians to themselves. The hart that is pursued and wounded, they say, knows an herb which, being eaten, throws off the arrow: a strange kind of vomit.[3] The dog that pursues it, though he be subject to sickness, even proverbially knows his grass that recovers him. And it may be true that the drugger is as near to man as to other creatures; it may be that obvious and present simples, easy to be had, would cure him; but the apothecary is not so near him, nor the physician so near him, as they two are to other creatures. Man hath not that innate instinct to apply these natural medicines to his present danger, as those inferior creatures have. He is not his own apothecary, his own physician, as they are. Call back therefore thy meditation again, and bring it down. What's become of man's great extent and proportion, when himself shrinks himself and consumes himself to a handful of dust? What's become of his soaring thoughts, his compassing thoughts, when himself brings himself to the ignorance, to the thoughtlessness of the grave? His diseases are his own, but the physician is not; he hath them at home, but he must send for the physician.

3. The deer who knows by instinct how to cure his poisoned wound by eating of an herb which is naturally antithetical to poison recurs frequently in Renaissance literature; a major source was Pliny's *Natural History* VIII.41. "Simples": herbs; "drugger": druggist.

Meditation XIV

Idque notant criticis medici evenisse diebus.

The physicians observe these accidents to have fallen upon the critical days.

I would not make man worse than he is, nor his condition more miserable than it is. But could I though I would? As a man cannot flatter God nor overpraise him, so a man cannot injure man nor undervalue him. Thus much must necessarily be presented to his remembrance, that those false happinesses which he hath in this world have their times and their seasons and their critical days; and they are judged and denominated according to the times when they befall us. What poor elements are our happinesses made of if time, time which we can scarce consider to be anything, be an essential part of our happiness! All things are done in some place; but if we consider place to be no more but the next hollow superficies of the air, alas! how thin and fluid a thing is air, and how thin a film is a superficies, and a superficies of air! All things are done in time too; but if we consider time to be but the measure of motion, and howsoever it may seem to have three stations, past, present, and future, yet the first and last of these are not (one is not now, and the other is not yet) and that which you call *present* is not now the same that it was when you began to call it so in this line (before you sound that word *present* or that monosyllable *now*, the present and the now is past). If this imaginary half-nothing, time, be of the essence of our happinesses, how can they be thought durable? Time is not so; how can they be thought to be? Time is not so; not so considered in any of the parts thereof. If we consider eternity, into that time never entered; eternity is not an everlasting flux of time, but time is a short parenthesis in a long period; and eternity had been the same as it is, though time had never been. If we consider, not eternity, but perpetuity; not that which had no time to begin in, but which shall outlive time and be, when time shall be no more, what a minute is the life of the durablest creature compared to that! and what a minute is man's life in respect of the sun's or of a tree! and yet how little of our life is occasion, opportunity to receive good in; and how little of that occasion do we apprehend and lay hold of! How busy and perplexed a cobweb is the happiness of man here, that must be made up with a watchfulness to lay hold upon occasion, which is but a little piece of that which is nothing, time! And yet the best things are nothing without that. Honors, pleasures, possessions presented to us out of time, in our decrepit and distasted[4] and unapprehensive age, lose their office and lose their name; they are not honors to us

4. Having lost the sense of taste.

that shall never appear nor come abroad into the eyes of the people to receive honor from them who give it; nor pleasures to us who have lost our sense to taste them; nor possessions to us who are departing from the possession of them. Youth is their critical day; that judges them, that denominates them, that inanimates and informs them, and makes them honors and pleasures and possessions; and when they come in an unapprehensive age, they come as a cordial when the bell rings out,[5] as a pardon when the head is off. We rejoice in the comfort of fire, but does any man cleave to it at mid-summer? We are glad of the freshness and coolness of a vault, but does any man keep his Christmas there? or are the pleasures of the spring acceptable in autumn? If happiness be in the season or in the climate, how much happier then are birds than men, who can change the climate and accompany and enjoy the same season ever.

Meditation XVII

Nunc lento sonitu dicunt, morieris.

Now this bell tolling softly for another, says to me, Thou must die.

Perchance he for whom this bell tolls may be so ill as that he knows not it tolls for him; and perchance I may think myself so much better than I am, as that they who are about me and see my state may have caused it to toll for me, and I know not that. The church is catholic, universal, so are all her actions; all that she does belongs to all. When she baptizes a child, that action concerns me; for that child is thereby connected to that body which is my head too,[6] and ingrafted into that body whereof I am a member. And when she buries a man, that action concerns me: all mankind is of one author and is one volume; when one man dies, one chapter is not torn out of the book, but translated[7] into a better language; and every chapter must be so translated. God employs several translators; some pieces are translated by age, some by sickness, some by war, some by justice; but God's hand is in every translation, and his hand shall bind up all our scattered leaves again for that library where every book shall lie open to one another. As therefore the bell that rings to a sermon calls not upon the preacher only, but upon the congregation to come, so this bell calls us all; but how much more me, who am brought so near the door by this sickness. There was a contention as far as a suit[8] (in which piety and dignity, religion and estimation,[9] were mingled) which of the religious orders should ring to prayers first in the morning; and it was determined that they should ring first that rose earliest. If we understand aright

---

5. A "cordial" (medicine) which arrives when the parish bell is already tolling is a bit too late.
6. I.e., the Christian church is the head of all men, as well as a body composed of its members.

7. Literally, "carried across"; hence, on the spiritual level, exalted from one sphere to another.
8. Controversy which went as far as a lawsuit.
9. Self-esteem.

the dignity of this bell that tolls for our evening prayer, we would be glad to make it ours by rising early, in that application, that it might be ours as well as his whose indeed it is. The bell doth toll for him that thinks it doth; and though it intermit again, yet from that minute that that occasion wrought upon him, he is united to God. Who casts not up his eye to the sun when it rises? but who takes off his eye from a comet when that breaks out? Who bends not his ear to any bell which upon any occasion rings? but who can remove it from that bell which is passing a piece of himself out of this world? No man is an island, entire of itself; every man is a piece of the continent, a part of the main.[1] If a clod be washed away by the sea, Europe is the less, as well as if a promontory were, as well as if a manor of thy friend's or of thine own were. Any man's death diminishes me because I am involved in mankind, and therefore never send to know for whom the bell tolls; it tolls for thee. Neither can we call this a begging of misery or a borrowing of misery, as though we were not miserable enough of ourselves but must fetch in more from the next house, in taking upon us the misery of our neighbors. Truly it were an excusable covetousness if we did; for affliction is a treasure, and scarce any man hath enough of it. No man hath affliction enough that is not matured and ripened by it and made fit for God by that affliction. If a man carry treasure in bullion, or in a wedge of gold, and have none coined into current money, his treasure will not defray him as he travels. Tribulation is treasure in the nature of it, but it is not current money in the use of it, except we get nearer and nearer our home, heaven, by it. Another man may be sick too, and sick to death, and this affliction may lie in his bowels as gold in a mine and be of no use to him; but this bell that tells me of his affliction digs out and applies that gold to me, if by this consideration of another's danger I take mine own into contemplation and so secure myself by making my recourse to my God, who is our only security.

1623   1624

From Sermon LXVI

[*On the Weight of Eternal Glory*]

All our life is a continual burden, yet we must not groan; a continual squeezing, yet we must not pant; and as in the tenderness of our childhood, we suffer and yet are whipped if we cry, so we are complained of if we complain, and made delinquents if we call the times ill. And that which adds weight to weight and multiplies the sadness of this consideration is this: that still the best men have

---

1. Mainland.

had most laid upon them. As soon as I hear God say that he hath found "an upright man, that fears God and eschews evil," in the next lines I find a commission to Satan to bring in Sabeans and Chaldeans upon his cattle and servants, and fire and tempest upon his children, and loathsome diseases upon himself.[1] As soon as I hear God say that he hath found "a man according to his own heart," I see his sons ravish his daughters and then murder one another, and then rebel against the father and put him into straits for his life.[2] As soon as I hear God testify of Christ at his baptism, "This is my beloved Son in whom I am well pleased" I find that Son of his "led up by the Spirit, to be tempted of the devil."[3] And after I hear God ratify the same testimony again, at his transfiguration ("This is my beloved Son in whom I am well pleased,"), I find that beloved Son of his deserted, abandoned, and given over to scribes, and Pharisees, and publicans, and Herodians,[4] and priests, and soldiers, and people, and judges, and witnesses, and executioners; and he that was called the beloved Son of God and made partaker of the glory of heaven, in this world, in his transfiguration, is made now the sewer of all the corruption, of all the sins of this world, as no Son of God but a mere man, as no man but a contemptible worm. As though the greatest weakness in this world were man, and the greatest fault in man were to be good, man is more miserable than other creatures, and good men more miserable than any other men.

But then there is *Pondus Gloriae*, an exceeding weight of eternal glory, that turns the scale; for as it makes all worldly prosperity as dung, so it makes all worldly adversity as feathers. And so it had need, for in the scale against it there are not only put temporal afflictions, but spiritual too; and to these two kinds we may accommodate those words, "He that falls upon this stone" (upon temporal afflictions) may be bruised, broken, "but he upon whom that stone falls" (spiritual afflictions) "is in danger to be ground to powder."[5] And then the great and yet ordinary danger is that these spiritual afflictions grow out of temporal: murmuring and diffidence in God and obduration, out of worldly calamities; and so against nature, the fruit is greater and heavier than the tree, spiritual heavier than temporal afflictions.

* * *

Let me wither and wear out mine age in a discomfortable, in an unwholesome, in a penurious prison, and so pay my debts with my bones and recompense the wastefulness of my youth with the beggary of mine age; let me wither in a spittle[6] under sharp and foul

---

1. This is the story of the Book of Job.
2. The story of David.
3. The temptation on the mount, Matthew iv.1–11.
4. Followers of Herod, listed among the enemies of Christ.
5. Matthew xxi.44. "Diffidence": mistrust, loss of faith.
6. Hospital.

and infamous diseases, and so recompense the wantonness of my youth with that loathsomeness in mine age; yet if God withdraw not his spiritual blessings, his grace, his patience, if I can call my suffering his doing, my passion his action, all this that is temporal is but a caterpillar got into one corner of my garden, but a mildew fallen upon one acre of my corn; the body of all, the substance of all is safe as long as the soul is safe. But when I shall trust to that which we call a good spirit, and God shall deject and impoverish and evacuate that spirit, when I shall rely upon a moral constancy, and God shall shake, and enfeeble, and enervate, destroy and demolish that constancy, when I shall think to refresh myself in the serenity and sweet air of a good conscience, and God shall call up the damps and vapors of hell itself and spread a cloud of diffidence and an impenetrable crust of desperation upon my conscience; when health shall fly from me and I shall lay hold upon riches to succor me and comfort me in my sickness, and riches shall fly from me, and I shall snatch after favor and good opinion to comfort me in my poverty; when even this good opinion shall leave me and calumnies and misinformations shall prevail against me; when I shall need peace because there is none but thou, O Lord, that should stand for me, and then shall find that all the wounds that I have, come from thy hand, all the arrows that stick in me, from thy quiver; when I shall see that because I have given myself to my corrupt nature, thou hast changed thine; and because I am all evil towards thee, therefore thou hast given over being good towards me: when it comes to this height, that the fever is not in the humors but in the spirits,[7] that mine enemy is not an imaginary enemy, fortune, nor a transitory enemy, malice in great persons, but a real and an irresistible and an inexorable and an everlasting enemy, The Lord of Hosts himself, The Almighty God himself, the Almighty God himself only knows the weight of this affliction, and except he put in that *Pondus Gloriae*, that exceeding weight of an eternal glory, with his own hand, into the other scale, we are weighed down, we are swallowed up, irreparably, irrevocably, irrecoverably, irremediably.

* * *

If you look upon this world in a map, you find two hemispheres, two half worlds. If you crush heaven into a map, you may find two hemispheres too, two half heavens; half will be joy, and half will be glory, for in these two (the joy of heaven and the glory of heaven) is all heaven often represented unto us. And as of those two hemispheres of the world, the first hath been known long before, but the other (that of America, which is the richer in treasure), God reserved for later discoveries; so though he reserve that hemisphere

---

7. I.e., not superficial but in the root and marrow of my existence.

of heaven which is the glory thereof, to the resurrection, yet the other hemisphere, the joy of heaven, God opens to our discovery and delivers for our habitation even whilst we dwell in this world. * * * First think, that as a man must have some land or else he cannot be in wardship, so a man must have some of the love of God or else he could not fall under God's correction; God would not give him his physic, God would not study his cure, if he cared not for him. And then think also, that if God afford thee the shadow of his wings, that is, consolation, respiration, refreshing, though not a present and plenary deliverance in thy afflictions, not to thank God is a murmuring, and not to rejoice in God's ways is an unthankfulness. Howling is the noise of hell, singing the voice of heaven; sadness the damp of hell, rejoicing the serenity of heaven. And he that hath not this joy here, lacks one of the best pieces of his evidence for the joys of heaven, and hath neglected or refused that earnest by which God uses to bind his bargain, that true joy in this world shall flow into the joy of heaven as a river flows into the sea; this joy shall not be put out in death and a new joy kindled in me in heaven; but as my soul, as soon as it is out of my body, is in heaven and does not stay for the possession of heaven nor for the fruition of the sight of God till it be ascended through air, and fire, and moon, and sun, and planets, and firmament, to that place which we conceive to be heaven, but without the thousandth part of a minute's stop, as soon as it issues, is in a glorious light, which is heaven (for all the way to heaven is heaven; and as those angels which came from heaven hither, bring heaven with them and are in heaven here, so that soul that goes to heaven meets heaven here; and as those angels do not divest heaven by coming, so these souls invest heaven, in their going). As my soul shall not go towards heaven but go by heaven to heaven, to the heaven of heavens, so the true joy of a good soul in this world is the very joy of heaven. * * *

1625   1640

BEN JONSON

(1572–1637)

1598: *Every Man in his Humor,* Jonson's first play.
1610: *The Alchemist.*
1616: Jonson appointed poet laureate; publishes his *Works.*
1618: *Pleasure Reconciled to Virtue.*
1630: Quarrel with Inigo Jones.

Ben Jonson did so many different things in the literary world of the early 17th century, and made use of so many different styles to do them, that he is very hard to see as a whole person. Actor, playwright, poet and poet laureate, scholar, critic, translator, man of letters, and head, for the first time in English, of a literary "school," the so-called "sons of Ben," he was a giant of a man. Yet we cannot easily take a perspective of him.

Jonson's life was tough and turbulent. After his father's early death, Ben was adopted in infancy by a bricklayer and educated by the great classical scholar and antiquarian William Camden, before necessity drove him to enter the army. In Flanders, where the Dutch with English help were warring against the Spaniards, he fought singlehanded with one of the enemy before the massed armies, and killed his man. Returning to England about 1595, he began to work as an actor and playwright but was drawn from one storm center to another. He killed a fellow-actor in a duel, and escaped the gallows only by pleading "benefit of clergy" (i.e., by proving he could read and write, which entitled him to plead before a more lenient court). He was jailed for insulting the Scottish nation at a time when King James was newly arrived from Scotland. He took furious part in an intricate set of literary wars with his fellow-playwrights. Having converted to Catholicism, he was the object of deep suspicion after the Gunpowder Plot of Guy Fawkes (1605), when the phobia against his religion reached its height. Yet he rode out all these troubles, growing mellower as he grew older, and in his latter years became the unofficial literary dictator of London, the king's pensioned poet, a favorite around the court, and the good friend of men like Shakespeare, Donne, Francis Beaumont, John Selden, Francis Bacon, dukes, diplomats, and distinguished folk generally. In addition, he engaged the affection of younger men (poets like Robert Herrick, Thomas Carew, and Sir John Suckling, speculative thinkers like Lord Falkland and Sir Kenelm Digby), who delighted to christen themselves "sons of Ben." Sons of Ben provided the nucleus of the entire "Cavalier school" of English poets.

The first of Jonson's great plays was *Every Man in His Humor*, in which Shakespeare acted a leading role. It was also the first of the so-called "comedies of humors," in which the prevailing eccentricities and ruling passions of men (i.e., their "humors") were exposed to satiric deflation. Though Jonson's classical tragedy *Sejanus* (1603) has not been much liked (it is gloomy in mood, static in action, and weighty with antiquarian lore), *Volpone* (1606) and *The Alchemist* (1610) are two supreme satiric comedies of the English stage. Both have been repeatedly "adapted" and "modernized," but even now the original texts are likely to seem more lively and vital than the versions. Meanwhile, starting in 1605, Jonson began writing for the court a series of masques—elaborate semi-theatrical displays involving spectacle, allegory, and compliment to the king or queen. Thus he became closely involved with the life of the court, a connection which was formalized in 1616, when he was appointed poet laureate with a substantial pension. In the same year, he published in a splendid volume his collected *Works*, a body of poetry to which he kept adding in the years before his death. Though his later plays were not very successful, he turned out many occasional poems, verse letters, translations, complimentary verses before other men's volumes—finding in all these different forms a grave, incisive pattern of formal speech through which the reverberations of his immense classical learning make themselves heard.

The bulk of Jonson's poetry falls, without undue strain, into five groups, based mostly on stylistic qualities. He wrote a number of poems of festive ceremony, poems which celebrate those qualities of ordered richness and dignified delight which represent his image of the good life. A poem like *To Penshurst* turns a physical building and its surrounding countryside into an emblem of modest yet noble opulence; the poem *On Inviting a Friend to Supper* is an imitation of Horace, yet its tonality is thoroughly English, and the "modest little supper" to which he invites his friend would scandalize a modern weight-watcher. Quite a different side of Jonson's talent is represented by his elegies and epitaphs; they are brief, full, simple poems, such as one could imagine being carved on a marble slab—direct, impersonal, inevitable. Allied to these are his compliments and tributes; often prefixed to his friends' books, but sometimes simple tributes of friendship and admiration, they summarize warmly yet judiciously a man's character and achievement. Jonson the pure poet finds expression in his songs, sometimes from the plays and masques but sometimes standing alone, often intended for musical accompaniment, but generally beautifully melodic, even without it. Finally, Jonson wrote (in imitation of the Roman poet Martial) a great number of epigrams, sometimes lewd, sometimes nasty, occasionally funny. We have lost the taste for this sort of thing today, but epigrams were a vital Renaissance genre, and Jonsons' profane epigrams can usefully be compared to Crashaw's sacred ones.

Jonson took his calling as a poet with the greatest seriousness, asserting the dignity of the profession with (sometimes) a kind of pedantry and emphasis that contrasts with Shakespeare's extraordinary anonymity. When Jonson published his collected works—*The Works of Benjamin Jonson*—in 1616, it was the first time an English author had been so presumptuous. Yet he succeeded in making the fact of professional authorship somehow respectable; an author like Dryden, who owed so much to Jonson on stylistic grounds, owed him a social debt as well. His career stood on foundations which Ben, with his pedantry and his pugnacity, was the first to lay down.

To Penshurst[1]

Thou art not, Penshurst, built to envious show,
Of touch[2] or marble; nor canst boast a row
Of polished pillars, or a roof of gold;
Thou hast no lantern, whereof tales are told,
Or stair, or courts; but stand'st an ancient pile,   5
And, these[3] grudged at, art reverenced the while.
Thou joy'st in better marks, of soil, of air,
Of wood, of water; therein thou art fair.
Thou hast thy walks for health, as well as sport;
Thy mount, to which the dryads[4] do resort,   10
Where Pan and Bacchus their high feasts have made,

1. The country seat of the Sidney family (famous for Sir Philip) in Kent; Jonson's is one of the first English poems celebrating a specific place (later examples are *Cooper's Hill* by John Denham and *Windsor Forest* by Alexander Pope).

2. Touchstone, i.e., basanite, a pure black, finely grained, and therefore expensive variety of basalt. "Lantern": cupola.
3. More pretentious houses.
4. Wood nymphs.

Beneath the broad beech and the chestnut shade;
That taller tree, which of a nut was set
At his great birth where all the Muses met.[5]
There in the writhéd bark are cut the names   15
Of many a sylvan, taken with his flames;[6]
And thence the ruddy satyrs oft provoke
The lighter fauns to reach thy Lady's Oak.[7]
Thy copse too, named of Gamage,[8] thou hast there,
That never fails to serve thee seasoned deer   20
When thou wouldst feast or exercise thy friends.
The lower land, that to the river bends,
Thy sheep, thy bullocks, kine, and calves do feed;
The middle grounds thy mares and horses breed.
Each bank doth yield thee conies;[9] and the tops,   25
Fertile of wood, Ashore and Sidney's copse,[1]
To crown thy open table, doth provide
The purpled pheasant with the speckled side;
The painted partridge lies in every field,
And for thy mess is willing to be killed.   30
And if the high-swollen Medway[2] fail thy dish,
Thou hast thy ponds, that pay thee tribute fish,
Fat aged carps that run into thy net,
And pikes, now weary their own kind to eat,
As loath the second draught or cast to stay,   35
Officiously at first themselves betray;
Bright eels that emulate them, and leap on land
Before the fisher, or into his hand.
Then hath thy orchard fruit, thy garden flowers,
Fresh as the air, and new as are the hours.   40
The early cherry, with the later plum,
Fig, grape, and quince, each in his time doth come;
The blushing apricot and woolly peach
Hang on thy walls, that every child may reach.
And though thy walls be of the country stone,   45
They are reared with no man's ruin, no man's groan;
There's none that dwell about them wish them down;
But all come in, the farmer and the clown,[3]
And no one empty-handed, to salute
Thy lord and lady, though they have no suit.   50
Some bring a capon, some a rural cake,
Some nuts, some apples; some that think they make
The better cheeses bring them, or else send
By their ripe daughters, whom they would commend

---

5. Sir Philip Sidney was born at Penshurst; an oak tree, planted the day of his birth, is still shown as "Sidney's oak."
6. Woodsman, in love because of reading Sidney's sonnets.
7. Lady Leicester's oak, named after a lady of the house who once entered into labor under its branches. "Provoke": challenge to a race.

8. Lady Barbara Gamage gave her name to a grove near the entrance of the park.
9. Rabbits.
1. "Ashore and Sidney's copse" are little woods and spinneys, lovingly enumerated by Jonson. They still survive, under their ancient names.
2. The local river.
3. Yokel.

This way to husbands, and whose baskets bear   55
An emblem of themselves in plum or pear.
But what can this (more than express their love)
Add to thy free provisions, far above
The need of such? whose liberal board doth flow
With all that hospitality doth know;   60
Where comes no guest but is allowed to eat,
Without his fear, and of thy lord's own meat;
Where the same beer and bread, and selfsame wine,
That is his lordship's shall be also mine,
And I not fain to sit (as some this day   65
At great men's tables), and yet dine away.[4]
Here no man tells[5] my cups; nor, standing by,
A waiter doth my gluttony envy,
But gives me what I call, and lets me eat;
He knows below he shall find plenty of meat.   70
Thy tables hoard not up for the next day;
Nor, when I take my lodging, need I pray
For fire, or lights, or livery;[6] all is there,
As if thou then wert mine, or I reigned here:
There's nothing I can wish, for which I stay.[7]   75
That found King James when, hunting late this way
With his brave son, the prince, they saw thy fires
Shine bright on every hearth, as the desires
Of thy Penates[8] had been set on flame
To entertain them; or the country came   80
With all their zeal to warm their welcome here.
What (great I will not say, but) sudden cheer
Didst thou then make 'em! and what praise was heaped
On thy good lady then, who therein reaped
The just reward of her high housewifery;   85
To have her linen, plate, and all things nigh,
When she was far; and not a room but dressed
As if it had expected such a guest!
These, Penshurst, are thy praise, and yet not all.
Thy lady's noble, fruitful, chaste withal.   90
His children thy great lord may call his own,
A fortune in this age but rarely known.
They are, and have been, taught religion; thence
Their gentler spirits have sucked innocence.
Each morn and even they are taught to pray,   95
With the whole household, and may, every day,
Read in their virtuous parents' noble parts
The mysteries of manners, arms, and arts.
Now, Penshurst, they that will proportion[9] thee

---

4. Because the tables were so large, different courses might be served at different ends—hence the possibility of sitting at a man's table, yet dining away.
5. Counts.
6. Rations, food.
7. Wait.
8. Roman household gods. A room in the house is still known as "King James's room."
9. Compare.

With other edifices, when they see   100
   Those proud, ambitious heaps, and nothing else,
May say their lords have built, but thy lord dwells.

1616

Inviting a Friend to Supper

Tonight, grave sir, both my poor house and I
   Do equally desire your company:
Not that we think us worthy such a guest,
   But that your worth will dignify our feast
With those that come; whose grace may make that seem   5
   Something, which else could hope for no esteem.
It is the fair acceptance, Sir, creates
   The entertainment perfect: not the cates.[1]
Yet shall you have, to rectify your palate,
   An olive, capers, or some better salad   10
Ushering the mutton; with a short-legged hen,
   If we can get her, full of eggs, and then
Lemons and wine for sauce; to these, a coney
   Is not to be despaired of for our money;
And though fowl now be scarce, yet there are clerks,[2]   15
   The sky not falling, think we may have larks.
I'll tell you of more, and lie, so you will come:
   Of partridge, pheasant, wood-cock, of which some
May yet be there; and godwit if we can,
   Knot, rail, and ruff, too.[3] Howsoe'er, my man   20
Shall read a piece of Virgil, Tacitus,
   Livy, or of some better book to us,
Of which we'll speak our minds amidst our meat;
   And I'll profess[4] no verses to repeat.
To this, if aught appear which I not know of,   25
   That will the pastry, not my paper, show off.[5]
Digestive cheese and fruit there sure will be;
   But that which most doth take my muse and me
Is a pure cup of rich Canary wine,
   Which is the Mermaid's[6] now, but shall be mine;   30
Of which, had Horace or Anacreon tasted,
   Their lives, as do their lines, till now had lasted.
Tobacco, Nectar, or the Thespian spring
   Are all but Luther's beer to this I sing.[7]

1. Dishes.
2. Scholars; pronounced "clarks." A "coney" is a rabbit.
3. The treat of the feast will be these various game-birds respectively curlew, snipe, sandpiper, and corn crake.
4. Undertake, promise.
5. Jonson's promise not to recite his poetry is ironically qualified; poems may appear, but they will be on sheets of paper under pies, not for declamation.

6. The Mermaid tavern, famous haunt of the poets; sweet wine from the Canary Islands was very popular in England. Horace and Anacreon (the one in Latin, the other in Greek) wrote many poems in praise of good wine.
7. The Thespian spring is Castalia, haunt of the muses; compared to Canary, all these other intoxicants are no better than Luther's beer, i.e., weak stuff.

Of this we will sup free but moderately,   35
   And we will have no Pooly or Parrot[8] by,
Nor shall our cups make any guilty men,
   But at our parting we shall be as when
We innocently met. No simple word
   That shall be uttered at our mirthful board   40
Shall make us sad next morning; or affright
   The liberty that we'll enjoy tonight.

1616

Slow, Slow, Fresh Fount[1]

Slow, slow, fresh fount, keep time with my salt tears;
Yet slower, yet, O faintly, gentle springs!
List to the heavy part the music bears,
Woe weeps out her division,[2] when she sings.
    Droop herbs and flowers;   5
    Fall grief in showers;
Our beauties are not ours. O, I could still,
Like melting snow upon some craggy hill,
    Drop, drop, drop, drop,[3]   10
Since nature's pride is now a withered daffodil.

1600

Queen and Huntress[1]

Queen and huntress, chaste and fair,
Now the sun is laid to sleep,
Seated in thy silver chair,
State in wonted manner keep;
Hesperus entreats thy light,   5
Goddess excellently bright.

Earth, let not thy envious shade
Dare itself to interpose;
Cynthia's shining orb was made
Heaven to clear, when day did close.   10
Bless us then with wishéd sight,
Goddess excellently bright.

---

8. Pooly and Parrot were government spies though their conjunction also suggests a talkative bird, Poll Parrot. Jonson, as a Roman Catholic, had reason to be wary of undercover agents.
1. From the satiric comedy *Cynthia's Revels* (1600). It deals with the sin of self-love, and this famous lyric is a lament sung by Echo for Narcissus, who was entranced by his own image and ultimately transformed into a flower.

2. Grief, but also a rapid, melodic passage of music.
3. This line shows how far Jonson could go in adapting his verse to the needs of a composer.
1. Also from *Cynthia's Revels*, this song is sung by Hesperus, the evening star, to Cynthia, or Diana, goddess of chastity and the moon—with whom Queen Elizabeth was, almost automatically, equated.

Lay thy bow of pearl apart,
And thy crystal-shining quiver;
Give unto the flying hart   15
Space to breathe, how short soever.
Thou that mak'st a day of night,
Goddess excellently bright.

1600

Songs *from* The Vision of Delight

CHOIR:

In curious knots and mazes[1] so
The spring at first was taught to go;
And Zephyr[2] when he came to woo
His Flora had their motions too,
  And thence did Venus learn to lead   5
  Th' Idalian brawls,[3] and so to tread
As if the wind, not she, did walk,
Nor pressed a flower, nor bowed a stalk.

AURORA:[4]

I was not wearier where I lay
By frozen Tithon's side tonight   10
Than I am willing now to stay
And be a part of your delight.
  But I am urgéd by the day,
Against my will, to bid you come away.

CHOIR:

They yield to Time, and so must all.   15
As Night to sport, Day doth to action call,
  Which they the rather do obey,
Because the Morn with roses strews the way.

1617   1631

Song: To Celia[1]

Drink to me only with thine eyes,
And I will pledge with mine;
Or leave a kiss but in the cup,
And I'll not look for wine.

1. The interwoven motions of the dancers compared to the approach of spring.
2. Zephyr, the mild west wind, was described as the intimate of various nature deities, including Flora, goddess of flowers.
3. The dances of Venus on Mt. Ida were legendary. "Brawls": dances.
4. Aurora (dawn) was the unwilling bride of chilly old Tithonus (who was granted eternal life, but without eternal youth); hence she was eager to come to the night's entertainment and is reluctant to break it up.

1. These famous lines are a patchwork of five separate passages in the *Epistles* of Philostratus, a Greek sophist of the 3rd century A.D. Jonson very carefully reworded the phrases (there are several early MS. versions of the poem) into this classic lyric.

The thirst that from the soul doth rise,   5
Doth ask a drink divine:
But might I of Jove's nectar sup,
I would not change for thine.

I sent thee late a rosy wreath,
Not so much honoring thee,   10
As giving it a hope, that there
It could not withered be.
But thou thereon did'st only breathe,
And sent'st it back to me;
Since when it grows and smells, I swear,   15
Not of itself, but thee.

                                        1616

Come, My Celia[1]

Come, my Celia, let us prove,[2]
While we can, the sports of love;
Time will not be ours forever;
He at length our good will sever.
Spend not then his gifts in vain.   5
Suns that set may rise again;
But if once we lose this light,
'Tis with us perpetual night.
Why should we defer our joys?
Fame and rumor are but toys.   10
Cannot we delude the eyes
Of a few poor household spies,
Or his easier ears beguile,
So removéd by our wile?
'Tis no sin love's fruit to steal;   15
But the sweet thefts to reveal,
To be taken, to be seen,
These have crimes accounted been.

                                        1606

In the Person of Woman-kind

A SONG APOLOGETIC

Men, if you love us, play no more
    The fools or tyrants with your friends,
To make us still sing o'er and o'er
    Our own false praises for your ends:
        We have both wits and fancies too,   5
        And if we must, let's sing of you.

---

1. This song is sung by Volpone, in the comedy of the same name. It paraphrases a poem by Catullus.
2. Experience.

Nor do we doubt but that we can,
 If we would search with care and pain,
Find some one good in some one man;
  So going thorough[1] all your strain,   10
   We shall at last of parcels make
   One good enough for a song's sake.

And as a cunning painter takes
 In any curious piece you see
More pleasure while the thing he makes   15
 Than when 'tis made, why so will we.
   And having pleased our art, we'll try
   To make a new, and hang that by.

On My First Daughter

Here lies, to each her parents' ruth,[2]
Mary, the daughter of their youth;
Yet all heaven's gifts being heaven's due,
It makes the father less to rue.
At six months' end she parted hence   5
With safety of her innocence;
Whose soul heaven's queen, whose name she bears,
In comfort of her mother's tears,
Hath placed amongst her virgin-train:
Where, while that severed doth remain,   10
This grave partakes the fleshly birth;
Which cover lightly, gentle earth!

                1616

On My First Son

Farewell, thou child of my right hand,[3] and joy;
My sin was too much hope of thee, loved boy:
Seven years thou wert lent to me, and I thee pay,
Exacted by thy fate, on the just day.
O could I lose all father[4] now! for why   5
Will man lament the state he should envy,
To have so soon 'scaped world's and flesh's rage,
And, if no other misery, yet age?
Rest in soft peace, and asked, say, "Here doth lie
Ben Jonson his best piece of poetry."   10

1. "Thorough" could be used for "through" in the 17th century when the meter required it.
2. Grief. There is no sure identification of Jonson's daughter, nor a positive date of composition for the poem.
3. "Child of the right hand" is a literal translation of the Hebrew name "Benjamin," which implies the meanings "dexterous" or "fortunate." The boy was born in 1596, and died on his birthday in 1603.
4. Relinquish all thoughts of being a father.

For whose sake henceforth all his vows be such
As what he loves may never like too much.[5]

1616

Epitaph on Elizabeth, L. H.[6]

Wouldst thou hear what man can say
In a little? Reader, stay.
Underneath this stone doth lie
As much beauty as could die;
Which in life did harbor give   5
To more virtue than doth live.
If at all she had a fault,
Leave it buried in this vault.
One name was Elizabeth;
Th' other, let it sleep with death: 10
Fitter, where it died, to tell,
Than that it lived at all. Farewell!

1616

To the Memory of My Beloved Master
William Shakespeare

AND WHAT HE HATH LEFT US[1]

To draw no envy, Shakespeare, on thy name,
Am I thus ample to thy book and fame,
While I confess thy writings to be such
As neither man nor Muse can praise too much.
'Tis true, and all men's suffrage.[2] But these ways   5
Were not the paths I meant unto thy praise:
For silliest ignorance on these may light,
Which, when it sounds at best, but echoes right;
Or blind affection,[3] which doth ne'er advance
The truth, but gropes, and urgeth all by chance;   10
Or crafty malice might pretend this praise,
And think to ruin where it seemed to raise.
These are as some infamous bawd or whore
Should praise a matron. What could hurt her more?
But thou art proof against them, and, indeed,   15
Above th' ill fortune of them, or the need.

5. The obscure grammar of the last lines seems to refer back to the feeling in line 2, that too much affection is fatal to the loved one.
6. The subject of this epitaph may have been Elizabeth, Lady Hatton; but, in fact, her name has slept with death.
1. This poem was prefixed to the first folio of Shakespeare's plays, published in 1623.
2. Agreement, consent.
3. Prejudice.

I therefore will begin. Soul of the age!
The applause! delight! the wonder of our stage!
My Shakespeare, rise; I will not lodge thee by
Chaucer or Spenser, or bid Beaumont lie   20
A little further to make thee a room:[4]
Thou art a monument without a tomb,
And art alive still while thy book doth live,
And we have wits to read and praise to give.
That I not mix thee so, my brain excuses,   25
I mean with great, but disproportioned[5] Muses;
For, if I thought my judgment were of years,
I should commit thee surely with thy peers,
And tell how far thou didst our Lyly outshine,
Or sporting Kyd, or Marlowe's mighty line.[6]   30
And though thou hadst small Latin and less Greek,[7]
From thence to honor thee I would not seek
For names, but call forth thund'ring Aeschylus,
Euripides, and Sophocles to us,
Pacuvius, Accius, him of Cordova dead,[8]   35
To life again, to hear thy buskin[9] tread
And shake a stage; or, when thy socks were on,
Leave thee alone for the comparison
Of all that insolent Greece or haughty Rome
Sent forth, or since did from their ashes come.   40
Triumph, my Britain; thou hast one to show
To whom all scenes[1] of Europe homage owe.
He was not of an age, but for all time!
And all the Muses still were in their prime
When like Apollo he came forth to warm   45
Our ears, or like a Mercury to charm
Nature herself was proud of his designs,
And joyed to wear the dressing of his lines,
Which were so richly spun, and woven so fit,
As, since, she will vouchsafe no other wit: 50
The merry Greek, tart Aristophanes,
Neat Terence, witty Plautus[2] now not please,
But antiquated and deserted lie,

---

4. Chaucer, Spenser, and Francis Beaumont were buried in Westminster Abbey; Shakespeare, of course, in Stratford. Jonson endorses the separation; Shakespeare should not be crowded.
5. Not comparable.
6. John Lyly, Thomas Kyd, and Christopher Marlowe, Elizabethan dramatists put in the shade by Shakespeare.
7. Shakespeare had, by modern standards, a very adequate command of Latin; Jonson is speaking from the lofty height of his own remarkable scholarship. Shakespeare's French and Italian (he was competent in both tongues) Jonson does not think worthy of mention.

8. Marcus Pacuvius and Lucius Accius (2nd century B.C.) and "him of Cordova," Seneca the Younger (1st century A.D.), the greatest of the Latin tragedians. Only fragments survive of the plays of Pacuvius and Accius; Jonson's comparisons are more pedantic, in these instances, than relevant.
9. The symbol of tragedy, as contrasted with "socks" (in the next line), symbols of comedy.
1. Stages.
2. Aristophanes, the great Greek satirist and comic writer; Terence and Plautus (3rd and 2nd centuries B.C.), Roman writers of comedy.

As they were not of Nature's family.
Yet must I not give Nature all; thy Art,   55
My gentle Shakespeare, must enjoy a part.
For though the poet's matter Nature be,
His Art doth give the fashion; and that he
Who casts to write a living line must sweat
(Such as thine are) and strike the second heat   60
Upon the muses' anvil; turn the same,
And himself with it, that he thinks to frame,
Or for the laurel he may gain a scorn;
For a good poet's made as well as born.
And such wert thou! Look how the father's face   65
Lives in his issue; even so the race
Of Shakespeare's mind and manners brightly shines
In his well-turned and true-filed lines,
In each of which he seems to shake a lance,[3]
As brandished at the eyes of ignorance.   70
Sweet swan of Avon, what a sight it were
To see thee in our waters yet appear,
And make those flights upon the banks of Thames
That so did take Eliza and our James![4]
But stay; I see thee in the hemisphere   75
Advanced and made a constellation there![5]
Shine forth, thou star of poets, and with rage
Or influence[6] chide or cheer the drooping stage,
Which, since thy flight from hence, hath mourned like night,
And despairs day, but for thy volume's light.   80

1623

To John Donne

Donne, the delight of Phoebus and each Muse,
Who, to thy one, all other brains refuse;[1]
Whose every work, of thy most early wit,
Came forth example and remains so yet;
Longer a-knowing than most wits do live,   5
And which no affection praise enough can give.
To it[2] thy language, letters, arts, best life,
Which might with half mankind maintain a strife.
All which I meant to praise, and yet I would,
But leave, because I cannot as I should.   10

1616

---

3. Pun on Shake-speare.
4. Queen Elizabeth and King James.
5. Heroes and demigods were typically exalted after death to a place among the stars.
6. "Rage" and "influence" describe the supposed effects of the planets on earthly affairs. "Rage" also implies poetic inspiration.

1. The word "refuse" could imply a reproach against Donne's obscurity, a notion of egotism ("refusal" involving preference of one over others), or the idea of welding (re-fusing) lesser minds to a greater.
2. The verb "add" is understood.

To the Immortal Memory and Friendship of That Noble Pair, Sir Lucius Cary and Sir H. Morison[1]

The Turn

Brave infant of Saguntum, clear[2]
Thy coming forth in that great year
When the prodigious Hannibal did crown
His rage, with razing your immortal town.
Thou, looking then about   5
E'er thou wert half got out,
Wise child, didst hastily return
And mad'st thy mother's womb thine urn.
How summed a circle[3] didst thou leave mankind
Of deepest lore, could we the center find!   10

The Counter-Turn

Did wiser nature draw thee back
From out the horror of that sack,
Where shame, faith, honor, and regard of right
Lay trampled on?—the deeds of death and night
Urged, hurried forth, and hurled   15
Upon th' affrighted world?
Sword, fire, and famine, with fell fury met,
And all on utmost ruin set:
As, could they but life's miseries foresee,
No doubt all infants would return like thee.   20

The Stand

For what is life if measured by the space,
Not by the act?
Or maskéd man, if valued by his face,
Above his fact?
Here's one outlived his peers   25
and told forth fourscore years:
He vexéd time, and busied the whole state,
Troubled both foes and friends,
But ever to no ends:
What did this stirrer but die late?   30
How well at twenty had he fall'n or stood!
For three of his four-score, he did no good.

---

1. Henry Morison died in 1629 at the age of only twenty; his good friend Lucius Cary was a year or two younger. Jonson's ode is modeled on those of Pindar, with their triple pattern of strophe, antistrophe, and epode, translated literally by Jonson as turn, counterturn, and stand. These divisions served, when the Greek odes were recited in a theater, to distinguish which part of the chorus chanted them; in English odes, they serve simply to formalize the structure.
2. Explain, describe. Pliny tells the story of the infant born while Sagunto, in Spain, was being assaulted by Hannibal; he dived back into his mother's womb (setting a record for brevity), and was buried there.
3. How complete a lesson.

The Turn

He[4] entered well, by virtuous parts,
Got up and thrived with honest arts:
He purchased friends and fame and honors then,   35
And had his noble name advanced with men;
But, weary of that flight,
He stooped in all men's sight
To sordid flatteries, acts of strife,
And sunk in that dead sea of life   40
So deep, as he did then death's waters sup;
But that the cork of title buoyed him up.

The Counter-Turn

Alas, but Morison fell young;—
He never fell, thou fall'st,[5] my tongue.
He stood, a soldier, to the last right end,   45
A perfect patriot and a noble friend,
But most a virtuous son.
All offices[6] were done
By him, so ample, full, and round
In weight, in measure, number, sound,   50
As, though his age imperfect might appear,
His life was of humanity the sphere.

The Stand

Go now, and tell out[7] days summed up with fears,
And make them years;
Produce thy mass of miseries on the stage   55
To swell thine age;
Repeat of things a throng,
To show thou hast been long,
Not lived; for life doth her great actions spell,
By what was done and wrought   60
In season, and so brought
To light: her measures are, how well
Each syllab'e answered, and was formed how fair;
These make the lines of life, and that's her air.[8]

The Turn

It is not growing like a tree   65
In bulk, doth make man better be,
Or standing long an oak, three hundred year,
To fall a log at last, dry, bald, and sere:
A lily of a day
Is fairer far in May   70

---

4. I.e., another man, a separate example.
5. Slip, with a latent pun on Latin *fallor*, "to make a slip of the tongue."
6. Duties of life.
7. Count, number.

8. Life is a poem set to music, the music of its meaning. Life's "measures" are its metrical patterns, as well as the standards by which it is judged.

Although it fall and die that night;
It was the plant and flower of light.
In small proportions we just beauties see,
And in short measures life may perfect be.

The Counter-Turn

Call, noble Lucius, then for wine,   75
And let thy looks with gladness shine:
Accept this garland, plant it on thy head,
And think, nay, know, thy Morison's not dead.
He leaped the present age,
Possessed with holy rage,   80
To see that bright, eternal day,
Of which we priests and poets say
Such truths as we expect for happy men,
And there he lives with memory: and Ben

The Stand

Jonson, who sung this of him ere he went   85
Himself to rest,
Or taste a part of that full joy he meant
To have expressed
In this bright Asterism:[9]
Where it were friendship's schism   90
(Were not his Lucius long with us to tarry)
To separate these twi-
Lights, the Dioscuri;[1]
And keep the one half from his Harry.
But fate doth so alternate the design,   95
Whilst that in heaven, this light on earth must shine.

The Turn

And shine as you exalted are,
Two names of friendship, but one star,
Of hearts the union. And those not by chance
Made, or indentured, or leased out t' advance   100
The profits for a time.
No pleasures vain did chime
Of rhymes or riots at your feasts,
Orgies of drink, or feigned protests;
But simple love of greatness and of good   105
That knits brave minds and manners, more than blood.

The Counter-Turn

This made you first to know the Why
You liked, then after to apply
That liking; and approach so one the tother,

9. Constellation.
1. Castor and Pollux, the Dioscuri, are stars comprising the constellation of Gemini, or the twins.

Till either grew a portion of the other;   110
    Each styled by his end,
    The copy of his friend.
You lived to be the great surnames
And titles by which all made claims
Unto the Virtue. Nothing perfect done,   115
But as a Cary or a Morison.

The Stand

And such a force the fair example had,
    As they that saw
The good and durst not practice it, were glad
    That such a law   120
    Was left yet to mankind,
    Where they might read and find
Friendship in deed was written, not in words,
    And with the heart, not pen,
    Of two so early men,   125
    Whose lives her rolls were, and records,
Who, ere the first down blooméd on the chin
Had sowed these fruits, and got the harvest in.

1629   1640

Ode to Himself[1]

Come leave the loathéd stage,
    And the more loathsome age,
Where pride and impudence, in faction knit,
    Usurp the chair of wit!
Indicting and arraigning every day   5
    Something they call a play.
    Let their fastidious, vain
    Commission of the brain
Run on and rage, sweat, censure, and condemn;
They were not made for thee, less thou for them.   10

    Say that thou pour'st them wheat,
    And they will acorns eat;
'Twere simple fury still thyself to waste
    On such as have no taste!
To offer them a surfeit of pure bread,   15
    Whose appetites are dead!
    No, give them grains their fill,
    Husks, draff to drink and swill:[2]
If they love lees, and leave the lusty wine,
Envy them not; their palate's with the swine.   20

---

1. The failure of Jonson's *The New Inn* (1629) inspired this heroic assault on criticism and the public taste.

2. Jonson gets into one line three words which suggest pig-food.

No doubt some moldy tale,
  Like *Pericles*,[3] and stale
As the shrieve's crusts, and nasty as his fish—
    Scraps, out every dish
Thrown forth and raked into the common tub,   25
    May keep up the Play-club:
  There, sweepings do as well
  As the best-ordered meal;
For who the relish of these guests will fit
Needs set them but the alms basket of wit.   30

And much good do 't you then:
  Brave plush and velvet men
Can feed on orts;[4] and, safe in your stage clothes,
    Dare quit, upon your oaths,
The stagers and the stage-wrights too, your peers,[5]   35
    Of larding your large ears
  With their foul comic socks,
  Wrought upon twenty blocks;
Which, if they are torn, and turned, and patched enough,
The gamesters share your guilt, and you their stuff.   40

Leave things so prostitute
  And take th' Alcaic lute;[6]
Or thine own Horace, or Anacreon's lyre;
    Warm thee by Pindar's fire:
And though thy nerves be shrunk, and blood be cold,   45
    Ere years have made thee old,
  Strike that disdainful heat
  Throughout, to their defeat,
As curious fools, and envious of thy strain,
May, blushing, swear no palsy's in thy brain.   50

But when they hear thee sing
  The glories of thy king,
His zeal to God and his just awe o'er men,
    They may, blood-shaken then,
Feel such a flesh-quake to possess their powers   55
    As they shall cry, "Like ours,
  In sound of peace or wars,
  No harp e'er hit the stars
In tuning forth the acts of his sweet reign,
And raising Charles his chariot 'bove his Wain."[7]   60

1629   1640

3. Shakespeare's play, at least in part (printed 1609), which Jonson compares to poorhouse fare.
4. Scraps.
5. This fourth stanza turns toward an attack on the players and playwrights themselves, whom Jonson holds responsible for the low state of public taste. His anger here comes close to incoherence, and the plain sense of the stanza is most unclear.
6. That of Alcaeus, who lived ca. 600 B.C., and became famous, along with Horace, Anacreon, and Pindar, among the greatest lyric poets.
7. Jonson's poetry will elevate the chariot of Charles I (symbol of his royal power) above Charles's Wain (the seven bright stars of Ursa Major) among the constellations.

Pleasure Reconciled to Virtue

In the opening pages of his famous study, *The Civilization of the Renaissance in Italy*, Jacob Burckhardt eloquently describes the many pageants, tourneys, triumphs, and festal displays that were a striking feature of courtly and urban life in those days. England too, and as late as the first third of the 17th century, fostered these semi-dramatic ceremonials, under the title of masques. In its whole social and literary structure the masque stood quite apart from the stage play. It was performed by noble amateurs, not professional players, and performed, as a rule, only once, perhaps as the climax of "revels" which were tied strictly to a calendar date. The aim of the masque was not to make money, but to lose it, in great quantities and with maximum splendor. The masque did not try to create or maintain an intact illusion by separating the audience sharply from the action; rather, it mingled the audience off-stage with the actors on-stage, either inviting the audience to join the dance (as in *Pleasure Reconciled to Virtue*) or leading the players off the stage in an act of homage or deference to the chief person in the audience (as in Milton's *Comus*). The masque had many elements of an audience-participation game. Especially when produced at court, it made use of elaborate and expensive "machinery"—sets far more intricate than any the playhouses could afford. It involved many musicians, special dancers, and extravagant costumes; it jumbled the heraldic and mythical figures together in strange profusion; it was both comic and serious, and anything but realistic. The three constant elements of the masque were a rich spectacle (with both song and dance), a moral allegory, and a courtly compliment. In weaving these traditional ingredients together, Jonson, with his special gifts of learning, fantasy, and lucid eloquence, showed particular mastery. He wrote nearly thirty masques in all, of which *Pleasure Reconciled to Virtue* may be taken as typical.

The reader should not look for too much narrative logic in Jonson's masque, which shifts scenes and characters, not according to the sequences of a story, but to provide good "production numbers." Comus appears at the beginning of the masque, but only to sing a song and do a wild dance with his "crew." Hercules is present, because he once had to make a hard choice between pleasure and virtue; but as this choice is no longer necessary, he soon fades into the role of a spectator. There is another grotesque dance (an "antimasque" or "antic masque") of pygmies. This comic dance serves to prepare for, and contrast with, the elegant and polished dances performed by the gentry at the end of the masque; its specific form in Jonson's masque was probably determined by the presence of some dwarfs among the court jesters who wanted a part in the action. Finally, the true masquers take possession of the stage; they are a group of court lords, led by Prince Charles, richly dressed and wearing masks, but obviously recognizable in their own persons. They perform a series of intricate figures, descend into the audience to invite forth their ladies, and perform one other formal dance before the festivities become general.

These last dances of the masque are all under the guidance of Daedalus, the master-craftsman of ancient Greece, who is shown to be capable of reconciling pleasure with virtue, life with artifice, and the court with its own fantastic mirror-image in the masque. If Hercules in the masque reminds us of Jonson himself (teased by spiteful but impotent pygmies), the figure of Daedalus can scarcely fail to suggest Jonson's partner in masque-making, Inigo Jones. Jones was a student of continental art and architecture, a practicing architect under the special influence of Palladio, the Italian master, and an adviser to many aristocratic art-collectors; in his own line, he was quite as remarkable and influential a man as Jonson himself. The two men quarrelled violently and permanently in later years; but Jones was far and away the most sophisticated stage-designer and deviser of stage-effects in his time; we know he was responsible for the production of *Pleasure Reconciled to Virtue*; and Jonson would have enjoyed paying this elegant tribute to him as Daedalus, the fabulous artificer.

Pleasure Reconciled to Virtue

A MASQUE. AS IT WAS PRESENTED AT COURT BEFORE KING JAMES. 1618.

The scene was the mountain Atlas, who had his top ending in the figure of an old man, his head and beard all hoary and frost as if his shoulders were covered with snow; the rest wood and rock. A grove of ivy at his feet, out of which, to a wild music of cymbals, flutes and tabors, is brought forth Comus,[1] *the god of cheer, or the belly, riding in triumph, his head crowned with roses and other flowers, his hair curled; they that wait upon him crowned with ivy, their javelins done about with it; one of them going with Hercules his bowl bare before him, while the rest presented him with this*

HYMN

Room, room! make room for the bouncing belly.
First father of sauce, and deviser of jelly;
Prime master of arts, and the giver of wit,
That found out the excellent engine, the spit,
The plow and the flail, the mill and the hopper,   5
The hutch and the bolter, the furnace and copper,
The oven, the bavin, the mawkin, the peel,
The hearth and the range, the dog and the wheel.[2]
He, he first invented the hogshead and tun,
The gimlet and vice too, and taught them to run.   10
And since, with the funnel, an Hippocras bag
He's made of himself, that now he cries swag.[3]

1. Comus is the traditional classical and Renaissance figure of sensual indulgence; many of his properties here (ivy, wild music, and the flowing bowl) suggest his kinship with Dionysus. The bowl of Hercules, given him by the Sun-god, was so big that the hero sailed across the ocean in it. At the root of the masque is the ancient story that early in his life Hercules had to choose between a life of easy pleasure and one of strenuous virtue. But now, under King James, the two principles are at last going to be reconciled. Jonson's stage directions, being partly descriptive (for the reader), partly instructive (for the performer), are rather casual about observing consistency of tense.

2. "Hutch" (bin), "mill," and "hopper" were used in grinding grain; bavin, mawkin, and peel are different sorts of apparatus used in a bake-shop. A dog harnessed to a wheel served to keep a roasting-spit turning.

3. "Gimlet" and "vice" are tools for tapping a keg. A "Hippocras bag" is a cloth filter for clearing wine; and to "cry swag" is to reveal a drooping, pendulous belly.

Which shows, though the pleasure be but of four inches,
Yet he is a weasel, the gullet that pinches,
Of any delight, and not spares from the back   15
Whatever to make of the belly a sack.[4]
Hail, hail, plump paunch! O the founder of taste
For fresh meats, or powdered, or pickle, or paste;
Devourer of broiled, baked, roasted or sod,[5]
And emptier of cups, be they even or odd;   20
All which have now made thee so wide i' the waist
As scarce with no pudding thou art to be laced;
But eating and drinking until thou dost nod,
Thou break'st all thy girdles, and break'st forth a god.

To this, the Bowl-bearer.

Do you hear, my friends? to whom did you sing all this now? 25
Pardon me only that I ask you, for I do not look for an answer;
I'll answer myself. I know it is now such a time as the Saturnals[6]
for all the world, that every man stands under the eaves of his
own hat and sings what pleases him; that's the right and the liberty of it. Now you sing of god Comus here, the Belly-god. I say 30
it is well, and I say it is not well. It is well as it is a ballad, and
the belly worthy of it, I must needs say, an 'twere forty yards of
ballad more—as much ballad as tripe. But when the belly is not
edified by it, it is not well; for where did you ever read or hear
that the belly had any ears? Come, never pump for an answer, for 35
you are defeated. Our fellow Hunger there, that was as ancient a
retainer to the belly as any of us, was turned away for being
unseasonable—not unreasonable, but unseasonable—and now is
he (poor thin-gut) fain to get his living with teaching of starlings, magpies, parrots and jackdaws, those things he would have 40
taught the belly. Beware of dealing with the belly; the belly will
not be talked to, especially when he is full. Then there is no venturing upon Venter;[7] he will blow you all up; he will thunder
indeed, la: some in derision call him the father of farts. But I say
he was the first inventor of great ordnance, and taught us to dis- 45
charge them on festival days. Would we had a fit feast for him, i'
faith, to show his activity: I would have something now fetched
in to please his five senses, the throat; or the two senses, the eyes.
Pardon me for my two senses; for I that carry Hercules' bowl[8] in
the service may see double by my place, for I have drunk like a
frog today. I would have a tun now brought in to dance, and so
many bottles about him. Ha! You look as if you would make a 50
problem of this. Do you see? Do you see? a problem: why bot-

4. The gullet, though only four inches
long, is a harsh master; it imposes the
belly's great weight on the back.
5. Boiled.
6. The Roman Saturnalia, which came
about the end of the year, were a time
of license; Jonson compares them to the

twelfth-night festivities in the English
court, at which this masque was produced.
7. Belly, in Latin.
8. To carry Hercules' bowl would clearly
imply drinking a lot. "Tun": barrel.

tles? and why a tun? and why a tun? and why bottles to dance? I
say that men that drink hard and serve the belly in any place of 55
quality (as *The Jovial Tinkers,* or *The Lusty Kindred*[9]) are living
measures of drink, and can transform themselves, and do every
day, to bottles or tuns when they please; and when they have
done all they can, they are, as I say again (for I think I said
somewhat like it afore) but moving measures of drink; and there 60
is a piece in the cellar can hold more than all they. This will I
make good if it please our new god but to give a nod; for the
belly does all by signs, and I am all for the belly, the truest clock
in the world to go by.

Here the first antimasque[1] *danced by men in the shape of bottles,*
tuns, etc., after which,

HERCULES. What rites are these? Breeds earth more monsters yet?65
  Antaeus[2] scarce is cold: what can beget
  This store?—and stay! such contraries upon her?
  Is earth so fruitful of her own dishonor?
  Or 'cause his vice was inhumanity,
  Hopes she by vicious hospitality   70
  To work an expiation first?[3] and then
  (Help, Virtue!) these are sponges and not men.
  Bottles? mere vessels? half a tun of paunch?
  How? and the other half thrust forth in haunch?
  Whose feast? the belly's! Comus'! and my cup   75
  Brought in to fill the drunken orgies up
  And here abused! that was the crowned reward
  Of thirsty heroes after labor hard!
  Burdens and shames of nature, perish, die;
  For yet you never lived, but in the sty   80
  Of vice have wallowed, and in that swine's strife
  Been buried under the offense of life.
  Go, reel and fall under the load you make,
  Till your swoll'n bowels burst with what you take.
  Can this be pleasure, to extinguish man?   85
  Or so quite change him in his figure? Can
  The belly love his pain, and be content
  With no delight but what's a punishment?
  These monsters plague themselves, and fitly, too,
  For they do suffer what and all they do.   90
  But here must be no shelter, nor no shroud
  For such: sink grove, or vanish into cloud!

9. These seem to be names of taverns.
1. The antimasque, or antic masque, was
a group of dancers, grotesquely or comically dressed, who served to contrast
with the main group of masquers.
2. Antaeus, an earth-born giant, whom
Hercules destroyed in the course of his
labors. As his favored sport was wrestling, and he grew stronger every time he
touched the ground, Hercules had to kill
him by holding him in the air till he
died.
3. Hercules thinks that Comus is another
child of earth. Earth, he supposes, is
trying to expiate her guilt by producing
one monster after another.

After this the whole grove vanished, and the whole music was discovered, sitting at the foot of the mountain, with Pleasure and Virtue seated above them. The choir invited Hercules to rest with this

SONG

Great friend and servant of the good,
Let cool awhile thy heated blood,
And from thy mighty labor cease.   95
Lie down, lie down,
And give thy troubled spirits peace,
Whilst Virtue, for whose sake
Thou dost this godlike travail take,
May of the choicest herbage[4] make,   100
Here on this mountain bred,
A crown, a crown
For thy immortal head.

Here Hercules lay down at their feet, and the second antimasque, which was of pygmies, appeared.

1ST PYGMY. Antaeus dead and Hercules yet live!
Where is this Hercules? What would I give   105
To meet him now? Meet him? nay three such other,
If they had hand in murder of our brother![5]
With three? with four, with ten, nay, with as many
As the name yields! Pray anger there be any
Whereon to feed my just revenge, and soon!   110
How shall I kill him? Hurl him 'gainst the moon,
And break him in small portions! Give to Greece
His brain, and every tract of earth a piece!
2ND PYGMY. He is yonder.
1ST PYGMY. Where?   115
3RD PYGMY. At the hill foot, asleep.
1ST PYGMY. Let one go steal his club.
2ND PYGMY. My charge; I'll creep.
4TH PYGMY. He's ours.
1ST PYGMY. Yes, peace.
3RD PYGMY. Triumph, we have him, boy.   120
4TH PYGMY. Sure, sure, he's sure.
1ST PYGMY. Come, let us dance for joy.

At the end of their dance they thought to surprise him, when sud-

4. Plants and branches; "travail": labor, trouble.
5. Pygmies and giants, minimals and maximals, are disproportioned offspring of mere earth, therefore brothers to one another. The pygmies don't know how many Hercules-figures there are, because so many tales were told about the hero that even Renaissance mythographers were forced to think there must have been several persons of that name.

*denly, being awaked by the music, he roused himself, and they all
ran into holes.*

SONG

CHOIR. Wake, Hercules, awake: but heave up thy black eye,
　　'Tis only asked from thee to look and these will die,　　125
　　　　　Or fly.
　　　　Already they are fled,
　　　Whom scorn had else left dead.

*At which Mercury descended from the hill with a garland of poplar
to crown him.*

MERCURY. Rest still, thou active friend of Virtue: these
　　Should not disturb the peace of Hercules.　　130
　　Earth's worms and honor's dwarfs, at too great odds,
　　Prove or provoke the issue of the gods.
　　See here a crown the agèd hill hath sent thee,
　　My grandsire Atlas, he that did present thee
　　With the best sheep that in his fold were found,　　135
　　Or golden fruit in the Hesperian ground,
　　For rescuing his fair daughters, then the prey
　　Of a rude pirate, as thou cam'st this way;
　　And taught thee all the learning of the sphere,
　　And how, like him, thou might'st the heavens up-bear,　　140
　　As that thy labor's virtuous recompense.[6]
　　He, though, a mountain now, hath yet the sense
　　Of thanking thee for more, thou being still
　　Constant to goodness, guardian of the hill;
　　Antaeus, by thee suffocated here,　　145
　　And the voluptuous Comus, god of cheer,
　　Beat from his grove, and that defaced. But now
　　The time's arrived that Atlas told thee of: how
　　By unaltered law, and working of the stars,
　　There should be a cessation of all jars[7]　　150
　　'Twixt Virtue and her noted opposite,
　　Pleasure; that both should meet here in the sight
　　Of Hesperus, the glory of the west,[8]
　　The brightest star, that from his burning crest
　　Lights all on this side the Atlantic seas　　155
　　As far as to thy pillars, Hercules.[9]
　　See where he shines, Justice and Wisdom placed
　　About his throne, and those with Honor graced,

---

6. When Hercules was seeking the golden apples of the Hesperides, he took for a while Atlas' job of holding up the heavens, so the giant could wade out in the ocean and get the apples. Atlas himself was originally an astronomer, and thus knew "all the learning of the sphere."

7. Quarrels.

8. Jonson followed the mythographers in making Hesperus a brother of Atlas; as the evening star and guardian of the western isles, he identifies easily with King James.

9. The "pillars of Hercules" are the straits of Gibraltar.

Beauty and Love! It is not with his brother
Bearing the world, but ruling such another   160
Is his renown.[1] Pleasure, for his delight
Is reconciled to Virtue, and this night
Virtue brings forth twelve princes have been bred
In this rough mountain and near Atlas' head,
The hill of knowledge; one and chief of whom   165
Of the bright race of Hesperus is come,
Who shall in time the same that he is be,
And now is only a less light than he.[2]
These now she trusts with Pleasure, and to these
She gives an entrance to the Hesperides,   170
Fair Beauty's garden; neither can she fear
They should grow soft or wax effeminate here,
Since in her sight and by her charge all's done,
Pleasure the servant, Virtue looking on.[3]

*Here the whole choir of music called the twelve masquers forth
from the lap of the mountain, which then opened with this*

SONG

Ope, agèd Atlas, open then thy lap,   175
And from thy beamy bosom strike a light,
That men may read in thy mysterious map
          All lines
          And signs
Of royal education and the right,   180
      See how they come and show,
      That are but born to know,
          Descend,
          Descend,
    Though pleasure lead,   185
      Fear not to follow:
They who are bred
          Within the hill
          Of skill
May safely tread   190
      What path they will,
No ground of good is hollow.

In their descent from the hill Daedalus[4] came down before them.

1. As Hesperus, King James does not
hold up the sky, like his brother Atlas,
but rules over a special world of his
own, England.
2. Tradition has it that Prince Charles
was one of the masquers; he was just 18
at the time, and it was his first masque.
3. Having grown up inside Atlas itself,
so that virtue comes naturally to them,
the masquers can now be allowed to
mingle freely with the daughters of Hesperus, in pursuit of pleasure.
4. Daedalus, the mythical Greek maker
of mazes, acts here as master of the intricate steps of the dance which interweaves pleasure wtih virtue under the
guidance of art.

HERCULES. But Hermes, stay a little, let me pause:
  Who's this that leads?
MERCURY.   A guide that gives them laws
  To all their motions: Daedalus the wise.   195
HERCULES. And doth in sacred harmony comprise
  His precepts?
MERCURY.   Yes.
HERCULES.   They may securely prove[5]
  Then, any labyrinth, though it be of love.

Here, while they put themselves in form, Daedalus has his first

SONG

  Come on, come on! and where you go,
    So interweave the curious knot,   200
  As ev'n th' observer scarce may know
    Which lines are Pleasure's and which not.

  First, figure out the doubtful way
    At which awhile all youth should stay,[6]
  Where she and Virtue did contend   205
    Which should have Hercules to friend.

  Then, as all actions of mankind.
    Are but a labyrinth or maze,
  So let your dances be entwined,
    Yet not perplex men unto gaze;   210

  But measured, and so numerous too,
    As men may read each act you do,
  And when they see the graces meet,
    Admire the wisdom of your feet.

  For dancing is an exercise   215
    Not only shows the mover's wit,
  But maketh the beholder wise,
    As he hath power to rise to it.

The first dance.

After which Daedalus again.

SONG 2

  O more, and more! this was so well
    As praise wants half his voice to tell;   220

5. Experience.
6. The dancers are to "figure out" the doubtful moment of Hercules' choice in the sense of illustrating it; they are beyond the occasion of making it themselves, having already reconciled pleasure with virtue.

Again yourselves compose;
And now put all the aptness on
    Of figure, that proportion
        Or color can disclose.

That if those silent arts were lost,   225
Design and picture, they might boast
        From you a newer ground;[7]
Instructed to the height'ning sense
    Of dignity and reverence
        In your true motions found: 230

Begin, begin; for look, the fair
Do longing listen to what air
    You form your second touch;[8]
That they may vent their murmuring hymns
Just to the tune you move your limbs,   235
    And wish their own were such.

Make haste, make haste, for this
    The labyrinth of beauty is.

The second dance:

That ended, Daedalus.

SONG 3

It follows now you are to prove
The subtlest maze of all, that's love,   240
    And if you stay too long,
    The fair will think you do 'em wrong,

Go choose among—but with a mind
    As gentle as the stroking wind
        Runs o'er the gentler flowers.   245
And so let all your actions smile
    As if they meant not to beguile
        The ladies, but the hours.

Grace, laughter and discourse may meet,
    And yet the beauty not go less: 250
For what is noble should be sweet,
    But not dissolved in wantonness.

Will you that I give the law
    To all your sport, and sum it?

7. Put on the "aptness of figure," i.e., significance of expression, of which art (proportion or color) is capable; thus, if design and picture, the silent arts, were lost, they could be rebuilt out of the dance alone.
8. Endeavor.

It should be such should envy draw,   255
But ever overcome it.

Here they danced with the ladies, and the whole revels followed;[9]
which ended, Mercury called to Daedalus in this following speech,
which was after repeated in song by two trebles, two tenors, a bass,
and the whole chorus.

SONG 4

An eye of looking back were well,
  Or any murmur that would tell
    Your thoughts, how you were sent
      And went,   260
To walk with Pleasure, not to dwell.

These, these are hours by Virtue spared
  Herself, she being her own reward,
    But she will have you know
      That though   265
Her sports be soft, her life is hard.

You must return unto the hill,
  And there advance
With labor, and inhabit still
  That height and crown   270
From whence you ever may look down
  Upon triúmphed Chance.

She, she it is, in darkness shines.
  'Tis she that still herself refines
    By her own light, to every eye   275
More seen, more known when Vice stands by.
  And though a stranger here on earth,
    In heaven she hath her right of birth.
      There, there is Virtue's seat,
Strive to keep her your own;   280
  'Tis only she can make you great,
Though place here make you known.

After which, they danced their last dance, and returned into the
scene, which closed and was a mountain again as before.

And so it ended.

This pleased the king so well, as he would see it again; when it was
presented with these additions.[1]

1618   1640

9. Group of onlookers and courtiers.   masque, *For the Honor of Wales.*
1. The "additions" were another short

ROBERT HERRICK

(1591–1674)

What little personal history Robert Herrick had was always too much for him; the decisions he had to take were mostly forced on him, and he accepted them as misfortunes. Yet he is the happiest of English poets. The son of a prosperous London goldsmith, he was slow in taking his degrees, slower still in finding himself a career. Clearly he would have liked nothing better than a life of leisured study in London, talking literature and drinking sack with his hero Ben Jonson, while polishing his verses. But social pressures were insistent; he took orders in the church and moved reluctantly to a parish at Dean Prior, in Devonshire.

As a Londoner, he did not much like the rough West Country or its people, but he gradually adapted to both, settling placidly into his bachelor quarters and secreting poems as a hen lays eggs. For the purposes of these poems, he invented for himself dozens of imaginary mistresses—hectic, bewitching creatures with exotic names; but the maid who kept house for him was prophetically named Prudence. At the top of his poetic bent, in *Corinna's Going A-Maying*, Herrick produced a truly major lyric on the central theme of his life, the happy reconciliation of nature and nature's god. But most of his poetic work was casual, even trivial. He dwelt easily in the here and now, making playful verses out of his pets, his pleasures, his momentary peeves. He wrote against Devonshire, and then for it; about his cat, and his spaniel Tracy, and his maid Prudence; a farewell to sack (heart-rending) and a return to it (joyous). A recurrent theme in his verse is a playful, personal paganism—private sacrifices to household gods, tiny rituals and allusions to ancient creeds only half-seriously taken. The Puritans would have been scandalized had they realized that this minister of the holy gospel was at least half a pagan, and didn't even have the grace to be ashamed of the fact.

Herrick himself did not advertise his beliefs; but when the storm of civil war broke, and the Puritans came to power, they dispossessed him anyhow, and Herrick came down to London with the fruits of his exile. They were published early in 1648 in a fat little octavo volume with two titles, *Hesperides* for the secular poems, and *Noble Numbers* for those with sacred subjects. Altogether, there were over 1,200 poems in this one volume, the only publication of Herrick's life. But the time was not right for tiny, playful lyrics; nobody noticed *Hesperides*, either to applaud or deplore; and Herrick disappeared in silence and oblivion, not to be restored to English literature till the 19th century. He did manage to survive the harsh weather of Puritanism till King Charles was restored in 1660; and that restoration brought him back to Dean Prior, where he lived out his last years quietly, dying at the ripe age of 83.

Jonson taught Herrick the art of the polished trifle, the light touch, and the quiet mood. For both of them life was a sacrament—and Herrick brought to that sometimes portentous view of things a modesty and sense of proportion that are uniquely his own.

The Argument[1] of His Book

I sing of brooks, of blossoms, birds, and bowers,
Of April, May, of June, and July flowers.
I sing of Maypoles, hock carts, wassails, wakes,[2]
Of bridegrooms, brides, and of their bridal cakes.
I write of youth, of love, and have access   5
By these to sing of cleanly wantonness.[3]
I sing of dews, of rains, and, piece by piece,
Of balm, of oil, of spice, and ambergris.[4]
I sing of times trans-shifting, and I write
How roses first came red and lilies white.   10
I write of groves, of twilights, and I sing
The court of Mab and of the fairy king.[5]
I write of hell; I sing (and ever shall)
Of heaven, and hope to have it after all.

                                        1648

His Prayer to Ben Jonson

When I a verse shall make,
Know I have prayed thee,
For old religion's sake,[1]
Saint Ben to aid me.

Make the way smooth for me   5
When I, thy Herrick,
Honoring thee, on my knee,
Offer my lyric.

Candles I'll give to thee
And a new altar;   10
And thou Saint Ben shalt be
Writ in my psalter.

                                        1648

To the Water Nymphs Drinking at the Fountain

Reach with your whiter hands to me
Some crystal of the spring;

1. Subject matter.
2. "Hock carts" carried home the last load of the harvest; therefore adorned and celebrated. "Wakes": festive, not funerary occasions, to commemorate the dedication of a parish church.
3. Good fun, but already tinged with the lascivious overtone the word carries today.
4. Ambergris is used in making perfumes; hence it carries the overtone of something rare and delectable.
5. Mab was by long-standing tradition queen of the fairies and wife of King Oberon. See Shakespeare, *A Midsummer Night's Dream.*
1. The Puritans were hostile to the invocation of saints, above all such "saints" as Ben Jonson. Herrick plays on the fact that Jonson was a Catholic (of the "old religion"), as well as a saint in the mock-religion of poetry.

And I about the cup shall see
   Fresh lilies flourishing.

Or else, sweet nymphs, do you but this—   5
   To the glass your lips incline;
And I shall see by that one kiss
   The water turned to wine.

                       1648

To the Virgins, to Make Much of Time

Gather ye rosebuds while ye may,
   Old time is still a-flying;
And this same flower that smiles today
   Tomorrow will be dying.

The glorious lamp of heaven, the sun,   5
   The higher he's a-getting,
The sooner will his race be run,
   And nearer he's to setting.

That age is best which is the first,
   When youth and blood are warmer;   10
But being spent, the worse, and worst
   Times still succeed the former.

Then be not coy, but use your time,
   And, while ye may, go marry;
For, having lost but once your prime,   15
   You may forever tarry.

                       1648

Corinna's Going A-Maying

Get up! get up for shame! the blooming morn
Upon her wings presents the god unshorn.[1]
   See how Aurora throws her fair
   Fresh-quilted colors through the air:[2]
   Get up, sweet slug-a-bed, and see   5
   The dew bespangling herb and tree.
Each flower has wept and bowed toward the east
Above an hour since, yet you not dressed;
   Nay, not so much as out of bed?
   When all the birds have matins said,   10
   And sung their thankful hymns, 'tis sin,

1. Apollo, the sun god, whose hair (the rays of the sun) is never cut. For a discussion of the poem, and Apollo's rôle in it, see Cleanth Brooks, *The Well-Wrought Urn* (New York, 1947), Ch. 4.

2. Aurora, goddess of the dawn, is both tossing her blankets aside, like one anxious to be up, and spreading over the earth a freshly composed coverlet of light.

Nay, profanation to keep in,
Whenas a thousand virgins on this day
Spring, sooner than the lark, to fetch in May.[3]

Rise, and put on your foliage, and be seen   15
To come forth, like the springtime, fresh and green,
    And sweet as Flora.[4] Take no care
    For jewels for your gown or hair;
    Fear not; the leaves will strew
    Gems in abundance upon you;   20
Besides, the childhood of the day has kept,
Against you come, some orient[5] pearls unwept;
    Come and receive them while the light
    Hangs on the dew-locks of the night,
    And Titan[6] on the eastern hill   25
    Retires himself, or else stands still
Till you come forth. Wash, dress, be brief in praying:
Few beads[7] are best when once we go a-Maying.

Come, my Corinna, come; and, coming, mark
How each field turns a street,[8] each street a park   30
    Made green and trimmed with trees: see how
    Devotion gives each house a bough
    Or branch: each porch, each door ere this,
    An ark, a tabernacle is,[9]
Made up of whitethorn neatly interwove,   35
As if here were those cooler shades of love.
    Can such delights be in the street
    And open fields, and we not see 't?
    Come, we'll abroad; and let's obey
    The proclamation made for May,   40
And sin no more, as we have done, by staying;
But, my Corinna, come, let's go a-Maying.

There's not a budding boy or girl this day
But is got up and gone to bring in May;
    A deal of youth, ere this, is come   45
    Back, and with whitethorn laden home.
    Some have dispatched their cakes and cream
    Before that we have left to dream;
And some have wept, and wooed, and plighted troth,

3. On May Day morning, it was the custom to gather whitethorn blossoms and trim the house with them (see below, lines 30–35).
4. Flora, the Roman goddess of flowers and vegetation, had her festival in the spring.
5. Eastern, as pearls come from the Orient, but also rosy and glowing like the rising sun. "Against": until.
6. The sun.

7. A casual term for prayers, but with overtones of the old (Catholic) religion, which in the next stanza is playfully converted into, and identified with, the worship of nature.
8. Turns into a street.
9. The doorways, ornamented with whitethorn, are like the Hebrew Ark of the Covenant; May sprigs are the central mystery of the religion of nature.

And chose their priest, ere we can cast off sloth.   50
 Many a green-gown[1] has been given,
 Many a kiss, both odd and even;[2]
 Many a glance, too, has been sent
 From out the eye, love's firmament;
Many a jest told of the keys betraying   55
This night, and locks picked; yet we're not a-Maying.

Come, let us go while we are in our prime,
And take the harmless folly of the time.
 We shall grow old apace, and die
 Before we know our liberty.   60
 Our life is short, and our days run
 As fast away as does the sun;
And, as a vapor or a drop of rain
Once lost, can ne'er be found again;
 So when or you or I are made   65
 A fable, song, or fleeting shade,
 All love, all liking, all delight
 Lies drowned with us in endless night.
Then while time serves, and we are but decaying,
Come, my Corinna, come, let's go a-Maying.   70

           1648

Delight in Disorder

 A sweet disorder in the dress
 Kindles in clothes a wantonness.[3]
 A lawn[4] about the shoulders thrown
 Into a fine distractión;
 An erring[5] lace, which here and there   5
 Enthralls the crimson stomacher;[6]
 A cuff neglectful, and thereby
 Ribbons to flow confusedly;
 A winning wave, deserving note,
 In the tempestuous petticoat;   10
 A careless shoestring, in whose tie
 I see a wild civility;
 Do more bewitch me than when art
 Is too precise[7] in every part.

           1648

---

1. Got by rolling in the grass.
2. Kisses are odd and even in kissing games.
3. Most of the terms used to describe the ladies' clothing have an ethical or social overtone.
4. A scarf of fine linen.

5. Wandering, floating.
6. The lower part of the bodice.
7. "Precise" and "precision" were terms used freely of Puritans; Herrick, in praising feminine disarray, is defining the "sprezzatura," or careless grace, of his own cavalier art.

Upon Julia's Clothes

Whenas in silks my Julia goes,
Then, then, methinks, how sweetly flows
That liquefaction of her clothes.

Next, when I cast mine eyes, and see
That brave[1] vibration, each way free, 5
O, how that glittering taketh me!

1648

His Grange, or Private Wealth

Though clock
To tell how night draws hence I've none,
A cock
I have to sing how day draws on.
I have 5
A maid (my Prue) by good luck sent
To save
That little fates me gave or lent.
A hen
I keep, which creaking day by day, 10
Tells when
She goes her long white egg to lay.
A goose
I have, which with a jealous care,
Lets loose 15
Her tongue, to tell what danger's near.
A lamb
I keep (tame), with my morsels fed,
Whose dam
An orphan left him (lately dead). 20
A cat
I keep, that plays about my house,
Grown fat
With eating many a miching[2] mouse.
To these 25
A *Tracy* I do keep, whereby
I please
The more my rural privacy;
Which are
But toys, to give my heart some ease. 30
Where care
None is, slight things do lightly please.

1648

1. Glorious, splendid.
2. Thieving. Tracy was the name of Herrick's spaniel.

Upon Prue, His Maid

In this little urn is laid
Prudence Baldwin, once my maid,
From whose happy spark here let
Spring the purple violet.

1648

Upon His Spaniel Tracy

Now thou art dead, no eye shall ever see,
For shape and service, spaniel like to thee.
This shall my love do, give thy sad death one
Tear, that deserves of me a millión.

1648

Dreams

Here we are all, by day; by night, we're hurled
By dreams, each one into a several[1] world.

1648

To Lar[2]

No more shall I, since I am driven hence,
Devote to thee my grains of frankincense.
No more shall I from mantle-trees[3] hang down,
To honor thee, my little parsley crown:
No more shall I (I fear me) to thee bring   5
My chives of garlic for an offering.
No more shall I, from henceforth, hear a choir
Of merry crickets by my country fire.
Go where I will, thou lucky Lar stay here,
Warm by a glittering chimney all the year.   10

1648

---

1. Different.
2. The Roman Lar was a household god associated with the hearth and the family-center; he would normally be paid just such familiar, homely honors as Herrick describes—a bit of incense, an occasional bit of herb or savory seasoning. The poem was evidently written when Herrick was ejected from his living by the Puritans.
3. Mantlepiece.

His Return to London

From the dull confines of the drooping West,
To see the day spring from the pregnant East,
Ravished in spirit, I come, nay more, I fly
To thee, blest place of my nativity!
Thus, thus with hallowed foot I touch the ground   5
With thousand blessings by thy fortune crowned.
O fruitful genius! that bestowest here
An everlasting plenty, year by year;
O place! O people! Manners framed to please
All nations, customs, kindreds, languages!   10
I am a free-born Roman;[1] suffer then
That I amongst you live a citizen.
London my home is: though by hard fate sent
Into a long and irksome banishment;
Yet since called back; henceforward let me be,   15
O native country, repossessed by thee!
For, rather than I'll to the West return,
I'll beg of thee first here to have mine urn.
Weak I am grown, and must in short time fall;
Give thou my sacred relics burial.[2]   20

1648

1. A Roman born in the city was said to be "free of it," i.e., entitled to its liberties.

2. As a priest and a poet, Herrick might without immodesty claim that his "relics" were sacred.

GEORGE HERBERT
(1593–1633)

George Herbert was the fifth son of an ancient and distinguished Welsh family. His father died when he was young, and he was brought up by his mother, Magdalen Herbert, a friend of Donne's, and a lady eminent both for her piety and her love of letters. After taking his degrees with distinction at the University of Cambridge, George Herbert was elected Public Orator of the university. It was a post carrying dignity and even some authority: its incumbent was called on to express, in the florid Latin of the day, the sentiments of the university on public occasions. Other men had used the post as a steppingstone to high political office; and Herbert seems to have had this idea, at least briefly, in mind. But the death of his patrons, and the bent of his own temper, soon drew him in another direction. In 1626 he took a minor office in the church; in 1629 he married Jane Danvers; and in 1630 he accepted the living of Bemerton, in Salisbury, and took orders.

Many younger sons of highly connected houses entered the church in those days—picking up a sinecure here and a nonresident ministry there; accepting the pay, and letting the work be done by underpaid curates; filling the offices of the church, perhaps without scandal, but also without the least breath of spiritual fervor. At Bemerton, on the contrary, George Herbert became at once what the age delighted to recognize as "a learned, godly, and painful divine." He preached and prayed; he rebuilt the church out of his own pocket; he visited the poor, consoled the sick, and sat by the bed of the dying—administering true pastoral care to the plowman and the peer alike. "Holy Mr. Herbert" became the talk of the countryside in the three short years of his ministry, before he died of consumption. And during these years, he completed the volume of poems known as *The Temple*, which was published shortly after his death, in 1633, by the friend to whom it had been left. His fame rests on this volume, and all our selections are taken from it.

As a poet, Herbert is quiet, inward, subtle, graceful, and neat. Working within the great tradition of Christian types and imagery, he delights in using quaint devices and homely images. But his spiritual feeling is to an extraordinary degree pure and fresh and free. Donne may be described as the poet of religious doubt, of strain, of anxiety; Herbert is the poet of religious faith, of submission, of acceptance. Both are classified as "metaphysical" poets; both use "conceited" and ingenious images; but Herbert, in a poem like *Love*, for example, allows his meaning to unfold from the situation gently like a flower, where Donne would be tugging at it or arguing with a mock opponent. Herbert is never flashy, nor even strongly dramatic; like the church he served, he is devoted to the quiet middle way. Yet his quiet is never the quiet of emotional poverty or torpor. Herbert's moods are as changeable as the English weather; but underneath them one hears the uninterrupted murmur of prayer, the serene wisdom of a thousand years of faith. The ancient forms were ever George Herbert's chief delight; his poetry, from which the concept of "freshness" is rarely absent, is like the parish church—an intricate, ancient structure, rich in traditional designs, which is open for the humblest and simplest person to enter.

Virtue

Sweet day, so cool, so calm, so bright,
   The bridal of the earth and sky:
The dew shall weep thy fall tonight;
    For thou must die.

Sweet rose, whose hue, angry and brave,[1]   5
   Bids the rash gazer wipe his eye:
Thy root is ever in its grave,
    And thou must die.

Sweet spring, full of sweet days and roses,
   A box where sweets[2] compacted lie;   10
My music shows ye have your closes,[3]
    And all must die.

Only a sweet and virtuous soul,
   Like seasoned timber, never gives;
But though the whole world turn to coal,[4]   15
    Then chiefly lives.

                      1633

Man

My God, I heard this day
That none doth build a stately habitation,
   But he that means to dwell therein.
   What house more stately hath there been,
Or can be, than is man? to whose creation   5
   All things are in decay.[1]

   For man is every thing
And more; he is a tree, yet bears more fruit;
   A beast, yet is or should be more;
Reason and speech we only bring.   10

1. "Angry": having the hue of anger, red. "Brave": splendid. Both adjectives indicate the arrogant yet pathetic defiance of beauty in the face of time.
2. Perfumes.
3. Concluding cadences. The expression shows that Herbert intended his poem to be sung—as it has, in fact, often been.
4. Be reduced to a cinder at the Last Judgment. See II Peter iii.10.
1. By comparison with created man, all things are in decay.

Parrots may thank us, if they are not mute:
    They go upon the score.[2]

    Man is all symmetry,
Full of proportions, one limb to another,
    And all to all the world besides;   15
    Each part may call the farthest, brother;
For head with foot hath private amity,
    And both with moons and tides.

    Nothing hath got so far
But man hath caught and kept it as his prey   20
    His eyes dismount the highest star:
    He is in little all the sphere.
Herbs gladly cure our flesh; because that they
    Find their acquaintance there.

    For as the winds do blow,   25
The earth doth rest, heav'n move, and fountains flow;
    Nothing we see but means our good,
    As our delight, or as our treasure.
The whole is either our cupboard of food,
    Or cabinet of pleasure.   30

    The stars have us to bed;
Night draws the curtain which the sun withdraws,
    Music and light attend our head.
    All things unto our flesh are kind
In their descent and being; to our mind   35
    In their ascent and cause.

    Each thing is full of duty.
Waters united are our navigation,
    Distinguishèd, our habitation;
    Below, our drink; above, our meat;   40
Both are our cleanliness. Hath one such beauty?[3]
    Then how are all things neat!

    More servants wait on man
Than he'll take notice of; in every path,
    He treads down that which doth befriend him,   45

2. Man has a vegetable, an animal, and a spiritual nature; he's the only creature which speaks and reasons. Parrots may seem to be an exception to the first of these rules, but they talk on credit (because we taught them how).
3. All the elements serve us multiply, for instance water. Oceans are valuable for navigation; the earth was created by dividing waters from waters (Genesis i.6–7); on earth water is drink, from above (as dew or manna), food. If one element can serve so richly. how beautiful is the sum of things.

When sickness makes him pale and wan.[4]
O mighty love! Man is one world, and hath
    Another to attend him.

    Since then, my God, thou hast
So brave a palace built: O, dwell in it,   50
    That it may dwell with thee at last!
    Till then, afford us so much wit,
That, as the world serves us, we may serve thee,
    And both, thy servants be.

              1633

The Pilgrimage

I traveled on, seeing the hill where lay
    My expectation.
    A long it was and weary way.
    The gloomy cave of desperation
I left on th'one, and on the other side   5
    The rock of pride.[1]

And so I came to fancy's meadow, strowed
    With many a flower;
    Fain would I here have made abode,
    But I was quickened by my hour.   10
So to care's copse I came, and there got through
    With much ado.

That led me to the wild of passion, which
    Some call the wold[2]—
    A wasted place but sometimes rich.   15
    Here I was robbed of all my gold
Save one good angel,[3] which a friend had tied
    Close to my side.

At length I got unto the gladsome hill
    Where lay my hope,   20
    Where lay my heart; and, climbing still,
    When I had gained the brow and top,
A lake of brackish waters on the ground
    Was all I found.

4. Man thoughtlessly treads down the herb that will cure him when he's sick.
1. The spiritual pilgrimage or search through allegorical perils was a frequent literary motif long before Bunyan's *Pilgrim's Progress*; compare Henry Vaughan's *Regeneration*, below.
2. Upland moor country.
3. A golden coin as well as (punningly) a guardian angel.

With that abashed, and struck with many a sting   25
      Of swarming fears,
    I fell, and cried, "Alas, my king!
      Can both the way and end be tears?"
Yet taking heart I rose, and then perceived
      I was deceived: 30

My hill was further; so I flung away,
      Yet heard a cry,
    Just as I went: *None goes that way*
    And lives: "If that be all," said I,
"After so foul a journey, death is fair,   35
      And but a chair."[4]

                    1633

Easter Wings[1]

Lord, who createdst man in wealth and store,[2]
  Though foolishly he lost the same,
    Decaying more and more
      Till he became
        Most poor: 5
        With thee
        O let me rise
    As larks, harmoniously,
  And sing this day thy victories:
Then shall the fall further the flight in me.   10

My tender age in sorrow did begin:
  And still with sickness and shame
    Thou didst so punish sin,
      That I became
        Most thin.   15
        With thee
        Let me combine,
    And feel this day thy victory;
  For, if I imp[3] my wing on thine,
Affliction shall advance the flight in me.   20

                    1633

4. "Chair" implies rest and immobility, but also, in the sense of "sedan chair," a conveyance.

1. This poem and *The Altar* (below) are "shaped verses," which represent, by the typographical shape of the poem on the page, some part of the subject. Though sometimes condemned as "false wit," this sort of poem has appealed to an occasional author from Hellenistic times to the present. Among recent examples are *Vision and Prayer* by Dylan Thomas and *Un Coup de Dés* by Stéphane Mallarmé. The most amazing poet in this mode was a Byzantine pedant, Publius Optatian Porphyry, who printed his poems in two colors of ink, and got them to represent triremes and other complicated objects. Early editions of Herbert print *Easter Wings* with the lines running vertically.

2. Abundance.

3. Graft (a technical term from falconry).

The Altar

A broken ALTAR, Lord, thy servant rears,
Made of a heart, and cemented with tears:
  Whose parts are as thy hand did frame;
  No workman's tool hath touched the same.[1]
        A HEART alone   5
        Is such a stone,
        As nothing but
        Thy power doth cut.
        Wherefore each part
        Of my hard heart   10
        Meets in this frame,
        To praise thy Name:
  That, if I chance to hold my peace,
  These stones to praise thee may not cease.[2]
Oh let thy blessed SACRIFICE be mine,   15
And sanctify this ALTAR to be thine.

                         1633

The Flower

    How fresh, oh Lord, how sweet and clean
Are thy returns! even as the flowers in spring;
    To which, besides their own demesne,[1]
The late-past frosts tributes of pleasure bring.
        Grief melts away   5
        Like snow in May,
    As if there were no such cold thing.

    Who would have thought my shriveled heart
Could have recovered greenness? It was gone
    Quite underground; as flowers depart   10
To see their mother-root, when they have blown,[2]
        Where they together
        All the hard weather,
    Dead to the world, keep house unknown.

---

1. A reference to Exodus xx.25, in which the Lord enjoins Moses to build an altar without using cut stone or any tools. Herbert's book was titled *The Temple*, and many individual poems are about particular parts of a church—tne porch, the windows, the floor, the lock and key, or the altar.

2. Herbert wants his poem to praise God whether or not it is being read or spoken. There is also a reference to Luke xix.40: "I tell you that, if these should hold their peace, the stones would immediately cry out." Herbert's poetry, like Milton's, is rich to overflowing in Scriptural echoes.

1. Estate of one's own (here, beauty or pleasure). The word, spelled *demean* in the original text, may also be a short form of "demeanor," i.e., bearing.

2. Bloomed.

These are thy wonders, Lord of power,   15
Killing and quickening, bringing down to hell
     And up to heaven in an hour;
Making a chiming of a passing-bell.[3]
          We say amiss
          This or that is:[4]   20
     Thy word is all, if we could spell.

     Oh that I once past changing were,
Fast in thy Paradise, where no flower can wither!
     Many a spring I shoot up fair,
Offering[5] at heaven, growing and groaning thither;   25
          Nor doth my flower
          Want a spring shower,[6]
     My sins and I joining together.

     But while I grow in a straight line,
Still upwards bent, as if heaven were mine own,   30
     Thy anger comes, and I decline:
What frost to that? what pole is not the zone
          Where all things burn,
          When thou dost turn,
     And the least frown of thine is shown?[7]   35

     And now in age I bud again,
After so many deaths I live and write;
     I once more smell the dew and rain,
And relish versing. Oh, my only light,
          It cannot be   40
          That I am he
     On whom thy tempests fell all night.

     These are thy wonders, Lord of love,
To make us see we are but flowers that glide;[8]
          Which when we once can find and prove,[9]   45
     Thou hast a garden for us where to bide;
          Who would be more,
          Swelling through store,
     Forfeit their Paradise by their pride.

1633

---

3. The passing-bell, intended to mark the death of a parishioner, is tolled in a monotone; a chiming offers pleasant variety.
4. I.e., that a thing exists in its own nature.
5. Aiming.
6. The tears of contrition produced by the "joining together" of the poet's conscience and his sins.
7. Lines 32–35 may be paraphrased: "What cold compares to God's anger? Compared to God's wrath, what polar chill would not seem like the heat of the equator?"
8. Pass silently away.
9. Experience.

The Collar

I struck the board[1] and cried, "No more;
      I will abroad!
What? shall I ever sigh and pine?
My lines and life are free, free as the road,
    Loose as the wind, as large as store.   5
        Shall I be still in suit?[2]
Have I no harvest but a thorn
To let me blood, and not restore
What I have lost with cordial[3] fruit?
        Sure there was wine   10
Before my sighs did dry it; there was corn
    Before my tears did drown it.
Is the year only lost to me?
    Have I no bays[4] to crown it,
No flowers, no garlands gay? all blasted?   15
        All wasted?
Not so, my heart; but there is fruit,
      And thou hast hands.
Recover all thy sigh-blown age
On double pleasures: leave thy cold dispute   20
Of what is fit and not. Forsake thy cage,
      Thy rope of sands,[5]
Which petty thoughts have made, and made to thee
    Good cable, to enforce and draw,
        And be thy law,   25
While thou didst wink[6] and wouldst not see.
      Away! take heed;
      I will abroad.
Call in thy death's-head[7] there; tie up thy fears.
      He that forbears   30
    To suit and serve his need,
      Deserves his load."
But as I raved and grew more fierce and wild
      At every word,
Methought I heard one calling, *Child!*
      And I replied, *My Lord.*   35

1633

1. Table.
2. In attendance, waiting on someone for a favor.
3. Giving heart's ease, restorative.
4. The poet's wreath, here used as a general symbol of festivity.
5. Christian restrictions on behavior, which the "petty thoughts" of the docile believer have made "good cable," i.e., strong.
6. Shut your eyes (to the real weakness of the church's injunctions).
7. The skull which reminds the penitent of approaching death.

The Pulley

When God at first made man,
Having a glass of blessings standing by,
  "Let us," said he, "pour on him all we can.
Let the world's riches, which dispersèd lie,
    Contract into a span."   5

  So strength first made a way;
Then beauty flowed, then wisdom, honor, pleasure.
  When almost all was out, God made a stay,
Perceiving that, alone of all his treasure,
    Rest in the bottom lay.[1]   10

  "For if I should," said he,
"Bestow this jewel also on my creature,
  He would adore my gifts instead of me,
And rest in Nature, not the God of Nature;
    So both should losers be.   15

  "Yet let him keep the rest,
But keep them with repining restlessness.
  Let him be rich and weary, that at least,
If goodness lead him not, yet weariness
    May toss him to my breast."   20

Discipline

Throw away thy rod,
Throw away thy wrath:
        O my God,
Take the gentle path.

  For my heart's desire   5
Unto thine is bent:
        I aspire
To a full consent.

  Not a word or look
I affect to own,
        But by book,   10
And thy book alone.[2]

  Though I fail, I weep:
Though I halt in pace,

---

1. "Rest" in the poem has two senses ("remainder" and "repose"); Herbert works them against one another. This seesaw suggests the pulley, which can draw us to God one way or the other.
2. Disclaiming all independence, Herbert describes himself as an actor, who will speak only "by the book."

> Yet I creep   15
> To the throne of grace.
>
> Then let wrath remove;
> Love will do the deed:
> For with love
> Stony hearts will bleed.   20
>
> Love is swift of foot;
> Love's a man of war,[3]
> And can shoot,
> And can hit from far.
>
> Who can 'scape his bow?   25
> That which wrought on thee,
> Brought thee low,
> Needs must work on me.
>
> Throw away thy rod;
> Though man frailties hath,   30
> Thou art God:
> Throw away thy wrath.

1633

Jordan (I) [1]

> Who says that fictions only and false hair
> Become a verse? Is there in truth no beauty?
> Is all good structure in a winding stair?
> May no lines pass, except they do their duty
> Not to a true, but painted chair?[2]   5
>
> Is it no verse, except enchanted groves
> And sudden arbors shadow coarse-spun lines?[3]
> Must purling streams refresh a lover's loves?
> Must all be veiled while he that reads, divines,
> Catching the sense at two removes?   10

3. The jubilant song sung by Moses in Exodus xv calls the Lord "a man of war"; but Herbert is thinking also, and without any apparent sense of contradiction, about Cupid, another divine bowman.

1. Both poems titled *Jordan* are about complexity and simplicity; "crossing Jordan" is of course a symbol for entering into the Promised Land, and it seems likely that Herbert means to indicate by his title that for one who has crossed the river (i.e., come into God's country), many worldly complexities cease to be necessary or desirable.

2. May no poems ("lines") pass as good unless they make a reverence ("do their duty") to a false throne? It has often been the custom for men to bow before a throne, whether it was occupied or not (see Donne, *Satire III*, lines 47–48); but to require bowing to a throne in a painting (i.e., an artificial throne), would be excessive. Herbert implies that earthly love is a mere painted imitation of divine love.

3. "Sudden": i.e., that appear unexpectedly (an artificial effect much sought after in landscape gardening). "Shadow": overshadow, cause to be overlooked. Herbert is suggesting that flashy dramatic effects obscure poor craftsmanship. So far as it applies to anyone in particular, "coarse-spun lines" may be taken as referring to Donne.

Shepherds are honest people; let them sing:
    Riddle who list, for me, and pull for prime:[4]
I envy no man's nightingale or spring;
    Nor let them punish me with loss of rhyme,
        Who plainly say, *My God, My King.*   15

                                1633

Jordan (II)

When first my lines of heavenly joys made mention,
    Such was their luster, they did so excel,
That I sought out quaint words, and trim invention;
    My thoughts began to burnish,[1] sprout, and swell,
Curling with metaphors a plain intention,   5
    Decking the sense, as if it were to sell.[2]

Thousands of notions in my brain did run,
    Offering their service, if I were not sped:[3]
I often blotted what I had begun;
    This was not quick[4] enough, and that was dead.   10
Nothing could seem too rich to clothe the sun,
    Much less those joys which trample on his head.[5]

As flames do work and wind when they ascend,
    So did I weave myself into the sense;
But while I bustled, I might hear a friend   15
    Whisper, "How wide[6] is all this long pretense!
There is in love a sweetness ready penned:
    Copy out only that, and save expense."

                                  1633

Hope

I gave to Hope a watch of mine: but he
    An anchor gave to me.[1]
Then an old prayer-book I did present,

---

4. To draw a lucky card in the card game of "primero." Herbert implies that anyone who understands one of the complex poems he is describing (and parodying) has made a wild and lucky guess.
1. Expand, burgeon.
2. For sale.
3. Suited, supplied.
4. Lively, alive.
5. The "joys which trample on" the sun's head are those of the Son.
6. Irrelevant, "wide of the mark."
1. The game is a parlor-game in which wordless emblems are exchanged; each of them can be translated into a religious statement. The poet's gifts all suggest impatience after long service; the counter-gifts all imply, "Not yet." An anchor is the emblem of faith, and an "optic" is a telescope.

And he an optic sent.
With that I gave a vial full of tears,   5
But he a few green ears.
Ah, loiterer! I'll no more, no more I'll bring;
I did expect a ring.

1633

Denial

When my devotions could not pierce
Thy silent ears;
Then was my heart broken, as was my verse:
My breast was full of fears
And disorder: 5

My bent thoughts, like a brittle bow,
Did fly asunder:
Each took his way; some would to pleasure go,
Some to the wars and thunder
Of alarms.   10

As good go anywhere, they say,
As to benumb
Both knees and heart in crying night and day,
Come, come, my God, O come!
But no hearing.   15

O that thou shouldst give dust a tongue
To cry to thee,
And then not hear it crying! All day long
My heart was in my knee,[1]
But no hearing.   20

Therefore my soul lay out of sight,
Untuned, unstrung:
My feeble spirit, unable to look right,
Like a nipped blossom, hung
Discontented.   25

O cheer and tune my heartless breast;
Defer no time,
That so thy favors granting my request,
They and my mind may chime,[2]
And mend my rhyme.   30

1633

1. I.e., my heart was bowed and bent, like my knee, in reverence.
2. Agree. The rhyming of the last two lines, coming to restore the harmony of this stanza, illustrates Herbert's hope of harmony with God.

Sin's Round

Sorry I am, my God, sorry I am
That my offenses course it in a ring.
My thoughts are working like a busy flame,
Until their cockatrice[1] they hatch and bring:
And when they once have perfected their draughts,[2]   5
My words take fire from my inflaméd thoughts.

My words take fire from my inflaméd thoughts,
Which spit it forth like the Sicilian hill.[3]
They vent[4] the wares, and pass them with their faults,
And by their breathing ventilate[5] the ill.   10
But words suffice not, where are lewd intentions:
My hands do join to finish the inventions.

My hands do join to finish the inventions:
And so my sins ascend three stories high,[6]
As Babel grew, before there were dissensions.   15
Yet ill deeds loiter not: for they supply
New thoughts of sinning: wherefore, to my shame,
Sorry I am, my God, sorry I am.

    1633

Aaron

Holiness on the head,
Light and perfections on the breast,
Harmonious bells below, raising the dead
To lead them unto life and rest:
Thus are true Aarons dressed.[1]   5

Profaneness in my head,
Defects and darkness in my breast,
A noise of passions ringing me for dead
Unto a place where is no rest:
Poor priest, thus am I dressed.   10

1. A fabulous creature, sometimes identified with the basilisk, hatched by a viper out of a cock's egg and partaking of both natures, but infinitely more deadly than either. Here it is an image for sin.
2. This word, always pronounced and sometimes spelled *drafts* nowadays, was pronounced in the 17th century to rhyme with "naughts."
3. Mt. Etna, a volcano.
4. Vend; also "let forth" or "give vent to."

5. Increase, augment; also "give breath to." The word is a reminder that the cockatrice could kill creatures simply by breathing on them.
6. I.e., thoughts, words, hands—like the Tower of Babel.
1. Exodus xxviii describes in great detail the garments to be worn by Aaron as high priest. Note that there are five letters in the name "Aaron," five stanzas in the poem, and five lines in each stanza.

Only another head
I have, another heart and breast,
Another music, making live, not dead,
Without whom I could have no rest:
In him I am well dressed.

15

Christ is my only head,
My alone only heart and breast,
My only music, striking me even dead,
That to the old man I may rest,
And be in him new dressed.[2]

20

So, holy in my head,
Perfect and light in my dear breast,
My doctrine tuned by Christ, who is not dead,
But lives in me while I do rest,
Come, people; Aaron's dressed.

25

1633

Love (III)

Love bade me welcome: yet my soul drew back,
    Guilty of dust and sin.
But quick-eyed Love, observing me grow slack[1]
    From my first entrance in,
Drew nearer to me, sweetly questioning
    If I lacked anything.[2]

5

"A guest," I answered, "worthy to be here":
    Love said, "You shall be he."
"I, the unkind, ungrateful? Ah, my dear,
    I cannot look on thee."
Love took my hand, and smiling did reply,
    "Who made the eyes but I?"

10

"Truth, Lord; but I have marred them; let my shame
    Go where it doth deserve."
"And know you not," says Love, "who bore the blame?"
    "My dear, then I will serve."
"You must sit down," says Love, "and taste my meat."
    So I did sit and eat.

15

1633

2. As the clapper strikes the bell and makes music of it, Christ strikes the priest, killing the Old Adam (the "old man," i.e., human frailty) in him, and raising the regenerate soul.

1. Backward.
2. The first question of shopkeepers and tavern waiters to an entering customer would be "What d'ye lack?" (i.e., want).

RICHARD CRASHAW

(ca. 1613–1649)

Richard Crashaw is a phenomenon unique in Anglo-Saxon taste; there is really no other English poet who is much like him. His roots seem to be sunk less in English literature than in Italian and neo-Latin writings. His personal background was thoroughly English (his father was a noted Puritan clergyman, and his academic training was at Cambridge), but from the first he was devoted to ritual, ceremony, and ecclesiastical exercise. This habit of mind ultimately led him out of the English church altogether, and into Roman Catholicism—the church, as many Englishmen considered it, of the scarlet woman and of Antichrist himself. But, for one of Crashaw's ardent devotional temperament, it was a natural home. In terms of chronological time, Crashaw spent only the last five or six years of his life on the Continent and in the church of Rome; but in terms of his spiritual development, he never belonged anywhere else.

Poetically, Crashaw was a follower of George Herbert, as the title of his second volume (*Steps to the Temple*) suggests. But the feeling one gets from the two poets is altogether different. There is a little streak of quaint and homely imagery in Herbert; Crashaw exaggerates it toward the grotesque. In this practice he was following the writers of emblem-books—volumes in which a picture with allegorical meanings stood at the head of a poem explaining those meanings. He was also influenced by a widespread school of Jesuit writers of sacred Latin epigrams, and by the great Italian writer of conceits (*concetti*) Giambattista Marino, the first book of whose poem *The Massacre of the Innocents* Crashaw translated. All these influences—plus, of course, his own ardent temperament—pushed Crashaw toward the exploitation of far-fetched, almost perverse parallels, in which familiar physical objects not only stood for, but were sometimes distorted by, extravagant spiritual pressures. The method hardly allowed for any interest in "decorum," in the traditional sense of tonal harmony—and that, of course, is an assumption about the proper character of poetry that has prevailed very generally, until recent times. Thus Crashaw was bitterly ridiculed during the 19th and early 20th centuries for lines like those in *The Weeper*, his poem on the tears of Saint Mary Magdalen:

> And now where'er he strays
> Among the Galilean mountains
> Or more unwelcome ways,
> He's followed by two faithful fountains,
> Two walking baths; two weeping motions;
> Portable and compendious oceans.

The ludicrous effect produced by these lines isn't open to much question, any more than is the macabre effect produced by that little epigram on

Luke 11 (below, p. 188). But in seeking these effects, it is evident that
Crashaw was a conscious and deliberate craftsman working in an established
tradition which on the Continent often goes by the name of "baroque."
Whether this term is worth importing into English literary history in order
to take care of a largely isolated figure like Crashaw may be argued. Undeniably, it opens the way to many suggestive parallels, with Continental poetry
and with developments in the sister arts. In any event, we of the modern
world, with the violent and unresolved images of modern literature and the
surrealist phantasmagoria behind us, seem better equipped to appreciate the
poetry of Crashaw than readers have been for several hundred years past.

Since the image is so violent in Crashaw, the structure of his poems is
often less strict than an English reader is used to; they wander from image
to image, without seeming to "get anywhere." He wrote many of his poems
several times over, in differing versions; the same images and stanzas will
recur, but in an entirely different order, without any sign that the poem "as
a whole" (if it is a whole) has suffered in any way. For the effect at which
he aims is a phantasmagoria, a blurring together of erotic and spiritual, tortured and ecstatic, infantile and sadistic themes. This doesn't preclude wit,
even cheerful wit, but it's wit under the impulsion of a more consuming
religious passion than English devotional writers before Gerard Manley
Hopkins generally display. Like Saint Teresa of Avila, the Spanish mystic
whom Crashaw admired so much, he yearned to be eaten up by the zeal of
God's house—a spiritual act of faith to whose ecstatic paradoxes his best
poetry does spectacular justice.

Crashaw's publications were not many. In 1634 he published a book of
Sacred Epigrams in Greek and Latin; a volume titled *Steps to the Temple
(with Other Delights of the Muses)* appeared in 1646; and in 1652, a
volume published in Paris under the title of *Carmen Deo Nostro* collected
his final writings. Some new material has since been added from manuscript
collections; and Crashaw has enjoyed, of late years, a genuine revival of
popular favor, after long years of hostility, neglect, and, at best, condescension.

A special feature of Crashaw's poetry, in the manuscripts as well as the
printed volumes, is the styling of his poem's titles. They are elaborately
constructed in different sorts of lettering, the lines piled on top of one
another to create outsize typographical façades, like the weighty fronts of
baroque churches. The titles to *The Flaming Heart* and the poem *To the
Countess of Denbigh* are reproduced here from the 1652 edition.

The Flaming Heart   Saint Teresa of Avila, a 16th-century Spanish

mystic, was one of the great figures of the Catholic counter-reformation.
Her autobiography, describing not only her practical problems in establishing her ascetic order of barefoot Carmelites, but a series of ecstatic trances
and visions which brought her close to the Heavenly Vision itself, was immediately popular throughout all Europe. Gian Lorenzo Bernini, the great
Italian sculptor and architect, created the ultimate baroque statue of Saint
Teresa, which stands to this day in the church of Santa Maria della Vitto-
ria, in Rome. It shows the saint in an attitude of ecstatic, swooning abandonment, while a somewhat juvenile seraph stands over her, in the act of

plunging a golden arrow into her heart. The statue is based on a famous passage of the autobiography.

Bernini's statue was not actually unveiled till after Crashaw's death, and though the poet was in Rome and could easily have learned about the statue, or seen it by visiting Bernini's studio, there is no definite proof that he actually did so. In any case, what he says in the poem about a "picture" applies perfectly to Bernini's statue: the seraph *is* a weak and childish figure, the saint an embodiment of sensual and religious passion. The reversal of roles with which the poet plays in the first part of his poem makes an effective literary game; but it isn't clear what sort of picture or statue would express his preferred conception of the saint. What excites him—and Bernini too, for that matter—is the moment of total absorption in the divine, the ecstatic union. For Puritans this is too fleshly an experience to be sacred, but for those who respond to imaginative challenge, holding these two elements in balance is a special and perilous delight.

The Flaming Heart
Vpon the Book and
picture of the seraphicall saint

TERESA,
(AS SHE IS VSVALLY EX-
pressed with a SERAPHIM
biside her.)[1]

Well-meaning readers! you that come as friends,
And catch the precious name this piece pretends;[2]
Make not too much haste to admire
That fair-cheeked fallacy of fire.
That is a Seraphim, they say,   5
And this the great Teresia.
Readers, be ruled by me, and make
Here a well-placed and wise mistake:
You must transpose the picture quite
And spell it wrong to read it right;   10
Read *him* for *her* and *her* for *him*,
And call the Saint the Seraphim.
    Painter, what didst thou understand,
To put her dart into his hand!
See, even the years and size of him   15
Shows this the Mother Seraphim.
This is the mistress-flame; and duteous he,
Her happy fire-works here comes down to see.
O most poor-spirited of men!
Had thy cold pencil kissed her pen[3]   20

---

1. Crashaw does not know (or perhaps care) that "seraphim" is the plural form of the singular "seraph"; ('seraphs" are distinguished among angels by dwelling continually in the fire of divine love.
2. Puts forward.
3. I.e., if you'd only been properly inspired by her book.

Thou couldst not so unkindly err
To show us this faint shade for her.
Why, man, this speaks pure mortal frame,
And mocks with female frost love's manly frame.
One would suspect thou mean'st to paint   25
Some weak, inferior, woman saint.
But had thy pale-faced purple took
Fire from the burning cheeks of that bright book,
Thou wouldst on her have heaped up all
That could be found seraphical: 30
Whate'er this youth of fire wears fair,
Rosy fingers, radiant hair,
Glowing cheek and glistering wings,
All those fair and flagrant[4] things,
But before all, that fiery dart   35
Had filled the hand of this great heart.
   Do then as equal right requires,
Since his the blushes be, and hers the fires,
Resume and rectify thy rude design,
Undress thy seraphim into mine.   40
Redeem this injury of thy art,
Give him the veil, give her the dart.
   Give him the veil, that he may cover
The red cheeks of a rivaled lover,
Ashamed that our world now can show   45
Nests of new Seraphims here below.[5]
   Give her the dart, for it is she
(Fair youth) shoots both thy shaft and thee.
Say, all ye wise and well-pierced hearts
That live and die amidst her darts,   50
What is it your tasteful spirits do prove
In that rare life of her and love?
Say and bear witness. Sends she not
A Seraphim at every shot?
What magazines of immortal arms there shine!   55
Heaven's great artillery in each love-spun line.
Give then the dart to her who gives the flame,
Give him the veil who kindly takes the shame.
   But if it be the frequent fate
Of worst faults to be fortunate;   60
If all's prescription, and proud wrong
Hearkens not to an humble song,
For all the gallantry of him,
Give me the suffering Seraphim.[6]
His be the bravery of all those bright things, 65
The glowing cheeks, the glistering wings,
The rosy hand, the radiant dart;

---

4. Burning (from Latin *flagrare*).
5. Teresa burns on earth in the element of fire, as seraphim do in heaven.
6. If Teresa can't be transformed into the angel, as he would like, Crashaw still prefers her as the "suffering Seraphim."

Leave her alone the Flaming Heart.
　　Leave her that, and thou shalt leave her
Not one loose shaft, but love's whole quiver.　　　　70
For in love's field was never found
A nobler weapon than a wound.
Love's passives are his activ'st part,
The wounded is the wounding heart.
O heart! the equal poise of love's both parts,　　　75
Big alike with wounds and darts,
Live in these conquering leaves,[7] live all the same;
And walk through all tongues one triumphant flame.
Live here, great heart; and love and die and kill,
And bleed and wound; and yield and conquer still.　　80
Let this immortal life, where'er it comes,
Walk in a crowd of loves and martyrdoms.
Let mystic deaths wait on 't, and wise souls be
The love-slain witnesses of this life of thee:
O sweet incendiary! show here thy art,　　　　85
Upon this carcass of a hard, cold heart;[8]
Let all thy scattered shafts of light, that play
Among the leaves of thy large books of day,[9]
Combined against this breast, at once break in
And take away from me myself and sin!
This gracious robbery shall thy bounty be,　　　90
And my best fortunes such fair spoils of me.[1]
O thou undaunted daughter of desires!
By all thy dower of lights and fires;
By all the eagle in thee, all the dove;[2]
By all thy lives and deaths of love;　　　　95
By thy large draughts of intellectual day,
And by thy thirsts of love more large than they;
By all thy brim-filled bowls of fierce desire,
By thy last morning's draught of liquid fire;　　　100
By the full kingdom of that final kiss
That seized thy parting soul, and sealed thee His;
By all the heavens thou hast in Him,
Fair sister of the seraphim,
By all of Him we have in thee,　　　　105
Leave nothing of myself in me!
Let me so read thy life that I
Unto all life of mine may die!

　　　　　　　　　　　　　　　　　　　　　　1652

---

7. I.e., the leaves of St. Teresa's book.
8. After being Saint Teresa's, the heart is now Crashaw's.
9. Books filled with intellectual and spiritual light.
1. I.e., my best fortune will be to be despoiled in this way.

2. The eagle symbolizes wisdom, for its lofty flight and ability to look into the sun's eye; the dove symbolizes mercy. Cf. Donne's *Canonization*, line 22.

Non Vi.[1]

'Tis not the work of force but skill
To find the way into man's will.
'Tis loue alone can hearts unlock.
Who knowes the WORD, *he needs not knock.*

To the Noblest & best of Ladyes, the Countesse of Denbigh.

Perswading her to Resolution in Religion, & to render her selfe without further delay into the Communion of the Catholick Church.[2]

What heaven-entreated heart is this,
Stands trembling at the gate of bliss,
Holds fast the door, yet dares not venture
Fairly to open it, and enter?
Whose definition is a doubt   5
'Twixt life and death, 'twixt in and out.
Say, lingering fair! why comes the birth

1. Not by force. The emblem, which expresses a moral question and answer through a picture and appended poem, was popular throughout Europe in the late Renaissance. The heart here has a hinge on the right to show that it can be opened, but it is sealed on the left with a scroll or phylactery inscribed with certain Biblical phrases, standing for the Word or the Law. Only knowledge of the Word enables one to open the heart.
2. Lords and ladies with religious doubts and scruples were the object of tremendous attention during the 17th century. Anxious conferences were held, with priests of all faiths eager to put their views before a possible influential convert; accounts of these conferences were published, disputed, analyzed, and presented to the perplexed for their guidance. Susan, Countess of Denbigh, had been widowed in 1643, when her husband was killed fighting for the king; she had gone with the queen to Paris in 1644. and there, in a thoroughly Catholic environment, had begun contemplating conversion. The queen was a lifelong Catholic, Crashaw, though simply another member of the court in exile, was a new convert; pressure on the lady was therefore very strong to abjure her Anglicanism. As is his wont, Crashaw uses all the imagery of erotic persuasion in urging the Countess to "yield the fort and let life in."

Of your brave soul so slowly forth?
Plead your pretenses (O you strong
In weakness!) why you choose so long   10
In labor of your self to lie,
Not daring quite to live nor die.
Ah, linger not, loved soul! a slow
And late consent was a long no;
Who grants at last, long time tried,   15
And did his best to have denied.
What magic bolts, what mystic bars,
Maintain the will in these strange wars!
What fatal yet fantastic bands
Keep the free heart from its own hands!   20
So when the year takes cold, we see
Poor waters their own prisoners be.
Fettered and locked up fast they lie
In a sad self-captivity.
Th' astonished nymphs their flood's strange fate deplore,   25
To see themselves their own severer shore.
    Thou that alone canst thaw this cold,
And fetch the heart from its stronghold,
Almighty Love! end this long war,
And of a meteor make a star.   30
O fix this fair Indefinite;
And 'mongst thy shafts of sovereign light
Choose out that sure decisive dart
Which has the key of this close heart,
Knows all the corners of 't, and can control   35
The self-shut cabinet of an unsearched soul.
O let it be at last love's hour!
Raise this tall trophy of thy power;
Come once the conquering way, not to confute,
But kill this rebel-word, *irresolute*,   40
That so, in spite of all this peevish strength
Of weakness, she may write, *resolved at length*.
    Unfold at length, unfold, fair flower,
And use the season of love's shower.
Meet his well-meaning wounds, wise heart,   45
And haste to drink the wholesome dart,
That healing shaft which heaven till now
Hath in love's quiver hid for you.
O dart of love! arrow of light!
O happy you, if it hit right;   50
It must not fall in vain, it must
Not mark the dry, regardless dust.
Fair one, it is your fate, and brings
Eternal worlds upon its wings.
Meet it with wide-spread arms, and see   55
Its seat your soul's just center be.
Disband dull fears; give faith the day.
To save your life, kill your delay.

It is love's siege, and sure to be
Your triumph, though his victory.   60
'Tis cowardice that keeps this field,
And want of courage not to yield.
Yield, then, O yield, that love may win
The fort at last, and let life in.
Yield quickly, lest perhaps you prove   65
Death's prey before the prize of love.
This fort of your fair self, if 't be not won,
He is repulsed indeed; but you are undone.

                                                           1652

On Our Crucified Lord, Naked and Bloody

Th' have left Thee naked, Lord, O that they had;
This garment too I would they had denied.
Thee with Thyself they have too richly clad,
Opening the purple wardrobe of Thy side.
    O never could be found garments too good   5
    For Thee to wear, but these, of Thine own blood.

                                                           1646

To the Infant Martyrs[1]

Go, smiling souls, your new-built cages[2] break,
In heaven you'll learn to sing, ere here to speak,
Nor let the milky fonts that bathe your thirst
                    Be your delay;
    The place that calls you hence is, at the worst,   5
                    Milk all the way.[3]

                                                           1646

I Am the Door

And now Th' art set wide ope, the spear's sad art,
Lo! hath unlocked Thee at the very heart;
    He to himself (I fear the worst)
        And his own hope
    Hath shut these doors of heaven, that durst   5
        Thus set them ope.

                                                           1646

1. This poem, and the five which follow, were originally published in Latin, as sacred epigrams; but also appeared in *Steps to the Temple*, translated into English.
2. I.e., the bodies which confine them to an earthly existence.
3. The Milky Way will replace their mothers' milk, at the worst; at best, they may rise even higher in the heavens.

Luke 11

Blessed be the paps which Thou hast sucked.

Suppose He had been tabled at thy teats,
    Thy hunger feels not what He eats;
He'll have his teat ere long (a bloody one),
    The Mother then must suck the Son.

                                      1646

Upon the Infant Martyrs

To see both blended in one flood,
The mothers' milk, the children's blood,
Make me doubt if heaven will gather
Roses hence, or lilies rather.

                                      1646

Luke 7

She began to wash His feet with tears and wipe them with the hairs of her head.

Her eyes' flood licks His feet's fair stain,
Her hairs' flame licks that up again.
This flame thus quenched hath brighter beams;
This flood thus stained fairer streams.

                                      1646

On the Wounds of Our Crucified Lord

O these wakeful wounds of Thine!
    Are they mouths? or are they eyes?
Be they mouths, or be they eyne,[1]
    Each bleeding part some one supplies.[2]

Lo! a mouth, whose full-bloomed lips   5
    At too dear a rate are roses.
Lo! a bloodshot eye! that weeps
    And many a cruel tear discloses.

O thou that on this foot hast laid
    Many a kiss and many a tear,   10

1. An old plural form of "eyes."   2. I.e., each wound of Christ's supplies either an eye or a mouth.

Now thou shalt have all repaid,
  Whatsoe'er thy charges were.

This foot hath got a mouth and lips
  To pay the sweet sum of thy kisses;
To pay thy tears, an eye that weeps   15
  Instead of tears such gems as this is.

The difference only this appears
  (Nor can the change offend),
The debt is paid in ruby-tears
  Which thou in pearls didst lend.   20

                           1646

HENRY VAUGHAN

(1621–1695)

The doctrines of mystic correspondence (that is, of analogical relations between the world of creatures and the world of spirits), which had been publicly accepted philosophy during the Middle Ages, and which the genius of Donne had daringly revitalized in the late 16th century, faded during the 17th century before the rising rationalism and materialism which culminated in Hobbes, Locke, and Newton. One of the last figures to give full-voiced expression to it was a Welsh country doctor with special interest in the occult, Henry Vaughan.

Like Herrick, Vaughan enjoyed only a brief interlude of poetry in his long life. His career as a student at Oxford was interrupted by the civil wars, in which he took a brief part on the king's side. But after the royal defeat, he retired to his native Wales and began to practice medicine—as men could do in those days, without many preliminaries. (A treatise of *Hermetical Physic,* which he published in 1655, is reproduced in L. C. Martin's edition of Vaughan's *Works,* Vol. II; it gives some curious notions of his medical practice. But fortunately the Welsh are by nature a sturdy race.) In 1650 he published a thin volume of verse titled *Silex Scintillans,* The Fiery Flint; this was followed immediately by a second book called *Olor Iscanus,* or The Swan of Usk (1651). Both titles make rather erudite reference to Vaughan's Welsh ancestry and habitat: Wales is rough, rocky country, the home of hard men as well as of flinty hearts; and Usk is a little brook that flows near Vaughan's native town of Scethrog hard by Llansantffraed. *Silex Scintillans* was reprinted in 1655, with the addition of a second part—and that was, effectually, Vaughan's poetic career.

The major influences on Vaughan were evidently two. George Herbert's poetry made a great impression on the poet, and his verses are full of echoes from *The Temple.* More remarkably, Vaughan's twin brother Thomas was an esoteric, hermetic philosopher, an alchemist and a student of the occult correspondences of things. Vaughan's poems often imply some knowledge of these "secret doctrines" of the alchemical philosophers—doctrines in which folklore, sympathetic magic, religion, and the rudiments of scientific method rub elbows under the aegis of the mythical Egyptian teacher Hermes Trismegistus.

But though they are "occult" in their undertones and overtones, Vaughan's best poems are direct and untangled in their expression. They tend to start with a brilliant phrase or set of phrases and trail off into relatively prosaic meditations. Sparkles of poetic brightness attend most of his writings; but they glow irregularly and fade under the unsteady breath of the poet's personal inspiration. When that inspiration is up, he sees, or tries to see, through the veil of things, to the spiritual quick of life lying just under its commonplace, material surface. There is a kind of silver-gray purity in Vaughan's finest work, which, though comparable to Herbert's and tangibly influenced by it, is more nervous and restive, more apt to dissolve the physical book under our hands (as his last poem does), turning it into the living mind and immediate soul of a man.

The Retreat

Happy those early days! when I
Shined in my angel infancy.
Before I understood this place
Appointed for my second race,[1]
Or taught my soul to fancy aught   5
But a white, celestial thought;
When yet I had not walked above
A mile or two from my first love,
And looking back, at that short space,
Could see a glimpse of His bright face;   10
When on some gilded cloud or flower
My gazing soul would dwell an hour,
And in those weaker glories spy
Some shadows of eternity;
Before I taught my tongue to wound   15
My conscience with a sinful sound,
Or had the black art to dispense
A several[2] sin to every sense,
But felt through all this fleshly dress
Bright shoots of everlastingness.   20
    O, how I long to travel back,
And tread again that ancient track!
That I might once more reach that plain
Where first I left my glorious train,
From whence th' enlightened spirit sees   25

1. The "second race" suggests, dimly, a doctrine of pre-existence. Comparisons are often made with Wordsworth's *Ode:*   *Intimations of Immortality.*
2. Different.

That shady city of palm trees.[3]
But, ah! my soul with too much stay[4]
Is drunk, and staggers in the way.
Some men a forward motion love;
But I by backward steps would move,   30
And when this dust falls to the urn,
In that state I came, return.

1650

Regeneration

A ward, and still in bonds, one day
    I stole abroad;
It was high spring, and all the way
   Primrosed and hung with shade;
    Yet was it frost within,
      And surly winds   5
Blasted my infant buds, and sin
   Like clouds eclipsed my mind.

Stormed thus, I straight perceived my spring
    Mere stage and show,   10
My walk a monstrous, mountained thing,
   Roughcast with rocks and snow;
    And as a pilgrim's eye,
      Far from relief,
Measures the melancholy sky,   15
   Then drops and rains for grief,

So sighed I upwards still; at last
    'Twixt steps and falls
I reached the pinnacle, where placed
    I found a pair of scales;   20
    I took them up and laid
      In th' one, late pains;
The other smoke and pleasures weighed,
   But proved the heavier grains.[1]

With that some cried, "Away!" Straight I   25
    Obeyed, and led
Full east, a fair, fresh field could spy;
    Some called it Jacob's bed,[2]
    A virgin soil which no
      Rude feet ere trod,   30

---

3. The New Jerusalem, the Heavenly City (see Deuteronomy xxxiv.3).
4. Delay.
1. Vaughan's spiritual adventure can only be described darkly. After his purgatorial ascent, smoke and pleasures prove heavier than "late pains"; i.e., the vanity of his mind outweighs its recent turning to repentance.
2. Jacob, who wrestled with an angel and ascended directly to heaven on a ladder, is here a type of the mystical visionary.

Where, since he stepped there, only go
    Prophets and friends of God.

Here I reposed; but scarce well set,
    A grove descried
Of stately height, whose branches met   35
    And mixed on every side;
    I entered, and once in,
      Amazed to see 't,
Found all was changed, and a new spring
    Did all my senses greet.   40

The unthrift sun shot vital gold,
    A thousand pieces,
And heaven its azure did unfold,
    Checkered with snowy fleeces;
    The air was all in spice,   45
    And every bush
A garland wore; thus fed my eyes,
    But all the ear lay hush.[3]

Only a little fountain lent
    Some use for ears,   50
And on the dumb shades language spent,
    The music of her tears;
    I drew her near, and found
      The cistern full
Of divers stones, some bright and round,   55
    Others ill-shaped and dull.[4]

The first, pray mark, as quick as light
    Danced through the flood,

But the last, more heavy than the night,
    Nailed to the center stood;   60
    I wondered much, but tired
      At last with thought,
My restless eye that still desired
    As strange an object brought.

It was a bank of flowers, where I descried,   65
    Though 'twas midday,
Some fast asleep, others broad-eyed
    And taking in the ray;
    Here, musing long, I heard
      A rushing wind   70
Which still increased, but whence it stirred
    No where I could not find.

I turned me round, and to each shade
    Dispatched an eye

3. Quiet.
4. The stones may be thoughts, images, and concepts in the "little fountain" of inspiration; the imagery is no doubt tinged with alchemical symbolism, as well.

To see if any leaf had made 75
    Least motion or reply,
  But while I listening sought
    My mind to ease
By knowing where 'twas, or where not,
  It whispered, "Where I please."[5] 80

"Lord," then said I, "on me one breath,
And let me die before my death!"

                        1650

Corruption

Sure it was so. Man in those early days
  Was not all stone and earth;
He shined a little, and by those weak rays
  Had some glimpse of his birth.
He saw heaven o'er his head, and knew from whence 5
  He came, condemnéd, hither;
And, as first love draws strongest, so from hence
  His mind sure progressed thither.
Things here were strange unto him: sweat and till,
  All was a thorn or weed: 10
Nor did those last, but (like himself) died still
  As soon as they did seed.
They seemed to quarrel with him, for that act
  That felled him foiled them all:
He drew the curse upon the world, and cracked 15
  The whole frame with his fall.[1]
This made him long for home, as loath to stay
  With murmurers and foes;
He sighed for Eden, and would often say,
  "Ah! what bright days were those!" 20
Nor was heaven cold unto him; for each day
  The valley or the mountain
Afforded visits, and still paradise lay
  In some green shade or fountain.
Angels lay leiger[2] here; each bush and cell, 25
  Each oak and highway knew them;
Walk but the fields, or sit down at some well,
  And he was sure to view them.
Almighty Love! where art Thou now? Mad man
  Sits down and freezeth on; 30
He raves, and swears to stir nor fire, nor fan,

---

5. John iii.8: "The wind bloweth where it listeth, and thou hearest the sound thereof, but canst not tell whence it cometh, and whither it goeth: so is every one that is born of the Spirit." Cf. also the inspiring breath by which God breathed life into man (Genesis ii.7).
1. Compare *Paradise Lost* X.650 ff.
2. As resident ambassadors (from heaven).

But bids the thread be spun.[3]
I see, Thy curtains are close-drawn; Thy bow
   Looks dim, too, in the cloud;
Sin triumphs still, and man is sunk below   35
   The center, and his shroud.
All's in deep sleep and night: thick darkness lies
   And hatcheth o'er Thy people—
But hark! what trumpet's that? what angel cries,
   "Arise! thrust in Thy sickle"?[4]   40

1650

The World

I saw eternity the other night
Like a great ring of pure and endless light,
   All calm as it was bright;
And round beneath it, Time, in hours, days, years,
   Driven by the spheres,[1]   5
Like a vast shadow moved, in which the world
   And all her train were hurled.
The doting lover in his quaintest[2] strain
   Did there complain;
Near him, his lute, his fancy, and his flights,[3]   10
   Wit's sour delights,
With gloves and knots,[4] the silly snares of pleasure,
   Yet his dear treasure,
All scattered lay, while he his eyes did pour
   Upon a flower.   15

The darksome statesman, hung with weights and woe,
Like a thick midnight fog, moved there so slow
   He did nor stay nor go;
Condemning thoughts, like sad eclipses, scowl
   Upon his soul,   20
And clouds of crying witnesses without
   Pursued him with one shout.
Yet digged the mole, and, lest his ways be found,
   Worked underground,
Where he did clutch his prey. But One did see   25
   That policy:[5]
Churches and altars fed him; perjuries
   Were gnats and flies;

---

3. Man is willing to do none of the work of salvation, but expects all the rewards.
4. Revelation xiv.15: "And another angel came out of the temple, crying with a loud voice to him that sat on the cloud, 'Thrust in thy sickle and reap * * * '" The time to harvest is now.
1. The concentric spheres of Ptolemaic astronomy.
2. Most elaborate.
3. Light arrows, as used by Cupid.
4. Love knots.
5. Strategy. The "mole" (i.e., the "darksome statesman," line 16) worked underground to avoid detection; but He who marks the fall of a sparrow was not deceived.

It rained about him blood and tears; but he
    Drank them as free.[6]   30

The fearful miser on a heap of rust
Sat pining all his life there, did scarce trust
    His own hands with the dust;
Yet would not place[7] one piece above, but lives
    In fear of thieves.   35
Thousands there were as frantic as himself,
    And hugged each one his pelf:
The downright epicure placed heaven in sense,[8]
    And scorned pretense;
While others, slipped into a wide excess,   40
    Said little less;
The weaker sort, slight, trivial wares enslave,
    Who think them brave;[9]
And poor, despiséd Truth sat counting by[1]
    Their victory.   45
Yet some, who all this while did weep and sing,
And sing and weep, soared up into the ring;
    But most would use no wing.
"O fools!" said I, "thus to prefer dark night
    Before true light!   50
To live in grots and caves, and hate the day
    Because it shows the way,
The way which from this dead and dark abode
    Leads up to God,
A way where you might tread the sun and be   55
    More bright than he!"
But, as I did their madness so discuss,
    One whispered thus:
"This ring the bridegroom did for none provide,
    But for His bride."[2]   60

        1650

They Are All Gone into the World of Light!

They are all gone into the world of light!
    And I alone sit lingering here;
Their very memory is fair and bright,
    And my sad thoughts doth clear.[1]

It glows and glitters in my cloudy breast   5
    Like stars upon some gloomy grove,
Or those faint beams in which this hill is dressed
    After the sun's remove.

6. I.e., as freely as they rained.
7. Invest.
8. Found his heaven in the senses.
9. Fine, flashy.
1. Watching.

2. See Revelation xix.7–9 and xxi for the marriage of the Lamb and the bride (Christ and His church).
1. Brighten.

I see them walking in an air of glory,
    Whose light doth trample on my days;   10
My days, which are at best but dull and hoary,
    Mere glimmering and decays.

O holy hope, and high humility,
    High as the heavens above!
These are your walks, and you have showed them me   15
    To kindle my cold love.

Dear, beauteous death! the jewel of the just,
    Shining nowhere but in the dark;
What mysteries do lie beyond thy dust,
    Could man outlook that mark![2]   20

He that hath found some fledged bird's nest may know
    At first sight if the bird be flown;
But what fair well[3] or grove he sings in now,
    That is to him unknown.

And yet, as angels in some brighter dreams   25
    Call to the soul when man doth sleep,
So some strange thoughts transcend our wonted themes,
    And into glory peep.

If a star were confined into a tomb,
    Her captive flames must needs burn there;   30
But when the hand that locked her up gives room,
    She'll shine through all the sphere.

O Father of eternal life, and all
    Created glories under Thee!
Resume Thy spirit from this world of thrall[4]   35
    Into true liberty!

Either disperse these mists, which blot and fill
    My perspective[5] still as they pass;
Or else remove me hence unto that hill[6]
    Where I shall need no glass.
            40

              1655

Man

    Weighing the steadfastness and state
Of some mean things which here below reside,
    Where birds, like watchful clocks, the noiseless date
        And intercourse of times divide,
    Where bees at night get home and hive, and flowers,   5

---

2. Limit.
3. Spring.
4. I.e., take back the spirit which you have made from this world of slavery.

5. Literally, "telescope," but more freely, "distant vision."
6. Sion hill (figuratively, Abraham's bosom).

Early as well as late,
Rise with the sun and set in the same bowers;

I would (said I) my God would give
The staidness of these things to man! for these
To His divine appointments ever cleave,   10
    And no new business breaks their peace;
The birds nor sow nor reap, yet sup and dine;
        The flowers without clothes live,
Yet Solomon was never dressed so fine.[1]

Man hath still either toys or care;[2]   15
He hath no root, nor to one place is tied,
But ever restless and irregular
    About this earth doth run and ride.
He knows he hath a home, but scarce knows where;
        He says it is so far   20
That he hath quite forgot how to go there.

He knocks at all doors, strays and roams,
Nay, hath not so much wit as some stones[3] have,
Which in the darkest nights point to their homes,
    By some hid sense their Maker gave;   25
Man is the shuttle, to whose winding quest
        And passage through these looms
God ordered motion, but ordained no rest.

                                        1650

Silence and Stealth of Days!

Silence and stealth of days! 'tis now
        Since thou art gone[1]
Twelve hundred hours, and not a brow
        But clouds hang on.
As he that in some cave's thick damp,   5
        Locked from the light,
Fixeth a solitary lamp
        To brave the night,
And walking from his sun, when past
        That glimmering ray,   10
Cuts through the heavy mists in haste
        Back to his day,[2]

---

1. Cf. Matthew vi.26–29.
2. Diversions or grief.
3. Loadstones.
1. As indicated below, lines 27–28, the poem is on the loss of Vaughan's brother—not his twin brother Thomas, the hermetic philosopher, who did not die till 1666, but his younger brother William, who died in July, 1648.
2. The miner fixes his lamp halfway down the dark shaft, ventures a little beyond it, but then beats a hasty retreat.

So o'er fled minutes I retreat
    Unto that hour
Which showed thee last, but did defeat   15
    Thy light and power;
I search and rack my soul to see
    Those beams again,
But nothing but the snuff[3] to me
    Appeareth plain,   20
That dark and dead sleeps in its known
    And common urn;
But those[4] fled to their maker's throne,
    There shine and burn.
O could I track them! but souls must   25
    Track one the other,
And now the spirit, not the dust,
    Must be thy brother.
Yet I have one Pearl,[5] by whose light
    All things I see,   30
And in the heart of earth and night,
    Find heaven and thee.

                  1655

Unprofitableness

How rich, O Lord! how fresh thy visits are!
   'Twas but just now my bleak leaves hopeless hung,
    Sullied with dust and mud;
Each snarling blast shot through me, and did share[1]
Their youth and beauty; cold showers nipped and wrung   5
    Their spiciness and blood.
But since thou didst in one sweet glance survey
   Their sad decays, I flourish, and once more
    Breathe all perfumes and spice;
I smell a dew like myrrh, and all the day   10
Wear in my bosom a full sun; such store
    Hath one beam from thy eyes.
But, ah, my God! what fruit hast thou of this?
   What one poor leaf did ever I let[2] fall
    To wait upon thy wreath?   15
Thus thou all day a thankless weed dost dress,
And when th' hast done, a stench or fog is all
    The odor I bequeath.

                  1650

---

3. The wick of the lamp; also, metaphorically, the bodily form of the brother.
4. The reference is back to "light and power."
5. The Bible.

1. Cut away; the word "share" derives from, and is here used for, "shear."
2. The original printed text reads "yet"; corrected to avoid a strained construction.

ANDREW MARVELL
(1621–1678)

Andrew Marvell was one of those quiet men of wit and spirit whose voices generally go unheard during the storm and turmoil of revolution. He attended Cambridge; but after graduating B.A. in 1638 and traveling abroad for some years, he disappears from the biographer's view, turning up around 1650 as tutor to the daughter of Sir Thomas Fairfax, Lord-General of the Parliamentary forces. Here, at the family seat in Yorkshire, Nun Appleton House, Marvell seems to have written many if not most of his English poems. They are playful miniatures, for the most part, which display a genius for catching in a phrase some glancing overtone of serious, almost profound, reflection. Yet their learning, like their serious intent, is hidden beneath a graceful, humorous surface, and they suggest that Marvell must have been a delightful tutor to the little girl who was growing up to be the daughter of a great house.

In 1657 Marvell was appointed assistant to the blind Latin Secretary for the Commonwealth, John Milton; and in his quiet way, he seems to have been responsible after the Restoration for saving Milton from imprisonment and possible execution. Starting in 1659, Marvell was returned M.P. for his home town of Hull, and he continued to represent it in a businesslike way until his death. He was a good committee man, though not a public speaker, and devoted to the interests of Hull. His letters to his constituents are valuable historical documents; but one would never guess from reading them that their author was an accomplished poet.

And in fact, when Marvell died, he was known to the world simply as the author of a few rough-and-ready satires in prose and verse which had been printed during the Restoration. His "serious" verse was only published three years after his death, by a woman who gave herself out as his widow but had really been his housekeeper. The reputation of these poems has made its way slowly, but steadily; and it has never stood higher than in our own time. For it is now clear that Marvell's is the most major minor verse in English. Playful, casual, and witty in tone, always light on its metrical feet and exact in its diction, it displays depth and intellectual hardness in unexpected places; its texture is extraordinarily rich. One need only glance at the famous *To His Coy Mistress* to see these qualities exemplified. At first it looks like a dozen other poems on the *carpe diem* theme: slight, singsong, and semi-serious, it urges on the lady enjoyment of the present hour. But soon the four-beat couplet is made to sound deep and hollow, is made to reverberate like a bell as well as pattering like a nursery rhyme; and a vision of the grinning grave and the deserts of eternity rises out of Marvell's gallant compliments to a pretty girl. It is a slight thing—yet its three paragraphs are nailed to the stiff logic of the syllogism, and its delicately balanced feelings reach out to embrace more than, for so slight a structure, seems possible.

To His Coy Mistress

Had we but world enough, and time,
This coyness, lady, were no crime.
We would sit down, and think which way
To walk, and pass our long love's day.
Thou by the Indian Ganges' side   5
Shouldst rubies find; I by the tide
Of Humber would complain.[1] I would
Love you ten years before the flood,
And you should, if you please, refuse
Till the conversion of the Jews.[2]   10
My vegetable love should grow
Vaster than empires and more slow;
An hundred years should go to praise
Thine eyes, and on thy forehead gaze;
Two hundred to adore each breast,   15
But thirty thousand to the rest;
An age at least to every part,
And the last age should show your heart.
For, lady, you deserve this state,[3]
Nor would I love at lower rate.   20
    But at my back I always hear
Time's wingéd chariot hurrying near;
And yonder all before us lie
Deserts of vast eternity.
Thy beauty shall no more be found,   25
Nor, in thy marble vault, shall sound
My echoing song; then worms shall try
That long-preserved virginity,
And your quaint honor turn to dust,
And into ashes all my lust: 30
The grave's a fine and private place,
But none, I think, do there embrace.
    Now therefore, while the youthful hue
Sits on thy skin like morning dew,[4]
And while thy willing soul transpires[5]   35
At every pore with instant fires,
Now let us sport us while we may,
And now, like amorous birds of prey,

1. Compared to the gorgeous Oriental Ganges, the Humber (which flows through Marvell's home town of Hull) is a dull and unassuming little stream. "Complain" implies songs of plaintive love.
2. According to popular chronology, the Jews were to be converted just before the Last Judgment.
3. Dignity.
4. The text reads "glew"—an odious reading. "Lew" (meaning "warmth") has also been suggested, but it was obsolete long before Marvell wrote.
5. Breathes forth. "Instant fires": immediate, present enthusiasm.

Rather at once our time devour
Than languish in his slow-chapped[6] power.   40
Let us roll all our strength and all
Our sweetness up into one ball,
And tear our pleasures with rough strife
Thorough the iron gates of life:
Thus, though we cannot make our sun   45
Stand still, yet we will make him run.[7]

1681

Mourning

You, that decipher out the fate
    Of human offsprings from the skies,
What mean these infants which, of late,
    Spring from the stars of Chlora's eyes?

Her eyes confused, and doubled o'er   5
    With tears suspended ere they flow,
Seem bending upwards to restore
    To Heaven, whence it came, their woe.

When, molding of the watery spheres,[1]
    Slow drops untie themselves away,   10
As if she with those precious tears
    Would strew the ground where Strephon lay.

Yet some affirm, pretending art,
    Her eyes have so her bosom drowned,
Only to soften, near her heart,   15
    A place to fix another wound.

And while vain pomp does her restrain
    Within her solitary bower,
She courts herself in amorous rain,
    Herself both Danaë and the shower.[2]   20

Nay others, bolder, hence esteem
    Joy now so much her master grown,
That whatsoever does but seem
    Like grief is from her windows thrown.

Nor that she pays, while she survives,   25
    To her dead love this tribute due,

6. Slow-jawed. Time is envisaged as slowly chewing up the world and the people in it.
7. In the final lines, lover and mistress triumphantly reverse their relation to time, eating it avidly like birds of prey instead of being eaten by it, forcing the sun to race after them instead of fruitlessly imploring it to stand still.
1. Taking the shape of watery spheres.
2. Zeus wooed Danaë in a shower of gold.

But casts abroad these donatives[3]
    At the installing of a new.

How wide they dream! the Indian slaves,
    That sink for pearl through seas profound,   30
Would find her tears yet deeper waves
    And not of one the bottom sound.

I yet my silent judgment keep,
    Disputing not what they believe;
But sure as oft as women weep   35
    It is to be supposed they grieve.

                  1681

The Garden

How vainly men themselves amaze
To win the palm, the oak, or bays,[1]
And their incessant labors see
Crowned from some single herb, or tree,
Whose short and narrow-vergéd shade   5
Does prudently their toils upbraid;
While all flowers and all trees do close[2]
To weave the garlands of repose!

    Fair Quiet, have I found thee here,
And Innocence, thy sister dear?   10
Mistaken long, I sought you then
In busy companies of men.
Your sacred plants, if here below,
Only among the plants will grow;
Society is all but rude   15
To this delicious solitude.

    No white nor red was ever seen
So amorous as this lovely green.
Fond lovers, cruel as their flame,
Cut in these trees their mistress' name: 20
Little, alas, they know or heed
How far these beauties hers exceed!
Fair trees, wheresoe'er your barks I wound,
No name shall but your own be found.[3]

    When we have run our passion's heat,   25
Love hither makes his best retreat.
The gods, that mortal beauty chase,

3. Largesse, gifts of public charity.
1. Crowns, respectively, for athletics, civic merit, and poetry. "Amaze": bewilder.

2. Unite.
3. Marvell proposes to carve on the bark of trees, not "Sylvia" or "Laura," but "Beech" and "Oak."

Still in a tree did end their race:
Apollo hunted Daphne so,
Only that she might laurel grow;[4]
And Pan did after Syrinx speed,
Not as a nymph, but for a reed.   30

    What wondrous life is this I lead!
Ripe apples drop about my head;
The luscious clusters of the vine   35
Upon my mouth do crush their wine;
The nectarine and curious[5] peach
Into my hands themselves do reach;
Stumbling on melons, as I pass,
Insnared with flowers, I fall on grass.   40

    Meanwhile the mind, from pleasure less,[6]
Withdraws into its happiness;
The mind, that ocean where each kind
Does straight its own resemblance find;[7]
Yet it creates, transcending these,   45
Far other worlds and other seas,
Annihilating all that's made
To a green thought in a green shade.[8]

    Here at the fountain's sliding foot,
Or at some fruit tree's mossy root,   50
Casting the body's vest[9] aside,
My soul into the boughs does glide:
There, like a bird, it sits and sings,
Then whets[1] and combs its silver wings,
And, till prepared for longer flight,   55
Waves in its plumes the various light.[2]

    Such was that happy garden-state,
While man there walked without a mate:
After a place so pure and sweet,
What other help could yet be meet![3]   60
But 'twas beyond a mortal's share
To wander solitary there:
Two paradises 'twere in one
To live in paradise alone.

4. Ovid tells (in *Metamorphoses*) how Apollo hunted Daphne until she turned into a laurel, and how Pan pursued Syrinx until she became a reed, out of which he made Panpipes.
5. Exquisite.
6. Diminished and drawn in on itself to savor the pleasure.
7. Every creature on earth was popularly supposed to have its counterpart in the ocean; thus the mind is an ocean because it contains a counterpart to everything on earth.
3. Genesis ii.18 records the Lord's decision to make "an help meet" for Adam— *i.e.,* Eve.
8. The garden is a symbol of the contemplative life as contrasted with the active life; and green, distinguished from the white of innocence and the red of passion (line 17), connotes a way of life which is cool and detached from human concerns.
9. Vestment, garment.
1. Preens.
2. The many-colored light of this world, contrasted with the white radiance of eternity.

> How well the skillful gardener drew   65
> Of flowers and herbs this dial[4] new,
> Where, from above, the milder sun
> Does through a fragrant zodiac run;
> And as it works, th' industrious bee
> Computes its time as well as we!   70
> How could such sweet and wholesome hours
> Be reckoned but with herbs and flowers?

1681

The Mower, Against Gardens

Luxurious man,[1] to bring his vice in use,
    Did after him the world seduce,
And from the fields the flowers and plants allure,
    Where Nature was most plain and pure.
He first enclosed within the gardens square   5
    A dead and standing pool of air,
And a more luscious earth for them did knead,
    Which stupefied them while it fed.
The pink grew then as double as his mind;[2]
    The nutriment did change the kind.   10
With strange perfumes he did the roses taint;
    And flowers themselves were taught to paint.
The tulip white did for complexion seek,
    And learned to interline its cheek;
Its onion root they then so high did hold,   15
    That one was for a meadow sold:[3]
Another world was searched through oceans new,
    To find the marvel of Peru;[4]
And yet these rarities might be allowed
    To man, that sovereign thing and proud,   20
Had he not dealt between the bark and tree,[5]
    Forbidden mixtures there to see.
No plant now knew the stock from which it came;
    He grafts upon the wild the tame,
That the uncertain and adulterate fruit   25
    Might put the palate in dispute.
His green seraglio has its eunuchs too,
    Lest any tyrant him outdo;
And in the cherry he does Nature vex,
    To procreate without a sex.   30

4. Clock. While the growth and decline of the garden measure the passage of time, the sun, a milder clock, runs through the zodiac, or constellation of the seasons.
1. Luxury-loving, voluptuous man, who wants to popularize ("bring in use") his own vices.
2. The double pink or carnation is a product of sophisticated, therefore hypo-critical ("double"), minds.
3. A great boom in tulip bulbs took place in Holland during the 17th century; Marvell's line was therefore, on occasion, strictly accurate.
4. *Mirabilis Jalapa*, the four o'clock, a flower found originally in South America.
5. By grafting.

'Tis all enforced, the fountain and the grot,
   While the sweet fields do lie forgot,
Where willing Nature does to all dispense
   A wild and fragrant innocence;
And fauns and fairies do the meadows till   35
   More by their presence than their skill.
Their statues polished by some ancient hand,
   May to adorn the gardens stand;
But, howsoe'er the figures do excel,
   The gods themselves with us do dwell.   40

                                      1681

A Dialogue Between the Soul and Body

SOUL.   O, who shall from this dungeon raise
          A soul enslaved so many ways? [1]
          With bolts of bones, that fettered stands
          In feet; and manacled in hands.
          Here blinded with an eye; and there   5
          Deaf with the drumming of an ear;
          A soul hung up, as 'twere, in chains
          Of nerves, and arteries, and veins;
          Tortured, besides each other part,
          In a vain head and double heart?   10

BODY.   O, who shall me deliver whole
          From bonds of this tyrannic soul?
          Which, stretched upright, impales me so
          That mine own precipice[2] I go;
          And warms and moves this needless frame[3]   15
          (A fever could but do the same),
          And, wanting where[4] its spite to try,
          Has made me live to let me die.
          A body that could never rest
          Since this ill spirit it possessed.   20

SOUL.   What magic could me thus confine
          Within another's grief to pine?
          Where, whatsoever it complain,
          I feel, that cannot feel,[5] the pain;
          And all my care itself employs,   25
          That to preserve which me destroys;
          Constrained not only to endure

1. The soul speaks almost in the words of St. Paul's epistle to the Romans vii.24: "O wretched man that I am! who shall deliver me from the body of this death?" The body's speech mirrors or parodies that of the soul.
2. Possession of a soul is the reason why man walks erect, facing the heavens, instead of prowling the earth like a brute; but it is also the reason why he can fall and be damned, as brutes cannot; so the soul is an interior precipice.
3. This frame, which does not need it.
4. Lacking an object.
5. The soul can "feel" (sympathize) even though it "cannot feel" (has no power of physical sensation).

Diseases, but, what's worse, the cure;
And, ready oft the port to gain,
Am shipwrecked into health again.   30

BODY.   But Physic[6] yet could never reach
The maladies thou me dost teach;
Whom first the cramp of hope does tear,
And then the palsy shakes of fear;
The pestilence of love does heat,   35
Or hatred's hidden ulcer eat;
Joy's cheerful madness does perplex,
Or sorrow's other madness vex;
Which knowledge forces me to know,
And memory will not forego;   40
What but a soul could have the wit
To build me up for sin so fit?
So architects do square and hew
Green trees that in the forest grew.[7]

1681

The Definition of Love

My Love is of a birth as rare
As 'tis, for object, strange and high;
It was begotten by Despair
Upon Impossibility.

Magnanimous Despair alone   5
Could show me so divine a thing,
Where feeble Hope could ne'er have flown
But vainly flapped its tinsel wing.

And yet I quickly might arrive
Where my extended soul is fixed;[1]   10
But Fate does iron wedges drive,
And always crowds itself betwixt.

For Fate with jealous eye does see
Two perfect loves, nor lets them close;[2]
Their union would her ruin be,   15
And her tyrannic power depose.[3]

And therefore her decrees of steel
Us as the distant poles have placed
(Though Love's whole world on us doth wheel),
Not by themselves to be embraced,   20

6. Medicine.
7. The body asserts that it has been
trimmed and squared to an alien purpose, instead of being allowed to grow
freely and naturally, as in the forest.
1. Marvell thinks of his soul as having
gone out of his body ("extended") and

attached ("fixed") itself to his mistress.
2. Unite.
3. Fate, and its agents Time and
Change, would none of them have any
power against a perfect mixture of the
elements.

Unless the giddy heaven fall,
And earth some new convulsion tear,
And, us to join, the world should all
Be cramped into a planisphere.[4]

As lines, so loves oblique may well   25
Themselves in every angle greet;[5]
But ours, so truly parallel,
Though infinite, can never meet.

Therefore the love which us doth bind,
But Fate so enviously debars,   30
Is the conjunction of the mind,
And opposition of the stars.[6]

                                                       1681

Bermudas

Where the remote Bermudas ride,
In th' ocean's bosom unespied,
From a small boat that rowed along,
The listening winds received this song:

"What should we do but sing His praise,   5
That led us through the watery maze
Unto an isle so long unknown,
And yet far kinder than our own?
Where He the huge sea monsters wracks,
That lift the deep upon their backs;[1]   10
He lands us on a grassy stage,
Safe from the storms, and prelate's rage.[2]
He gave us this eternal spring
Which here enamels everything,
And sends the fowls to us in care,   15
On daily visits through the air;
He hangs in shades the orange bright,
Like golden lamps in a green night,
And does in the pomegranates close
Jewels more rich than Ormus[3] shows;   20
He makes the figs our mouths to meet,
And throws the melons at our feet;
But apples[4] plants of such a price,

---

4. A flat sphere, literally absurd, but describing a kind of astrological projection in which the world was represented in two dimensions and the poles were united.
5. "Oblique" includes the meaning of "deviating from right conduct or thought"; oblique loves, like oblique lines, touch in angles (corners), but Marvell's love and the lady's, being parallel and perfect, can never touch.

6. "Conjunction" and "opposition" are technical terms from astronomy, here yoked to Marvell's "definition."
1. See Milton's use of the same sea fable in *Paradise Lost* I.203 ff. "Wracks": shipwrecks, destroys.
2. Storms at sea are quietly equated with bishops as sources of peril.
3. Pearl- and jewel-trading center in the Persian Gulf.
4. Pineapples.

No tree could ever bear them twice;
With cedars, chosen by His hand,   25
From Lebanon, He stores the land;
And makes the hollow seas, that roar,
Proclaim the ambergris[5] on shore;
He cast (of which we rather boast)
The Gospel's pearl upon our coast,   30
And in these rocks for us did frame
A temple, where to sound His name.
O! let our voice His praise exalt,
Till it arrive at heaven's vault,
Which, thence (perhaps) rebounding, may   35
Echo beyond the Mexique Bay."[6]

Thus sung they in the English boat,
An holy and a cheerful note;
And all the way, to guide their chime,
With falling oars they kept the time.   40

1681

On *Paradise Lost*[1]

When I beheld the poet, blind yet bold,
In slender book his vast design unfold,
Messiah crowned, God's reconciled decree,
Rebelling angels, the forbidden tree,
Heaven, Hell, Earth, Chaos, all—the argument   5
Held me a while, misdoubting his intent,
That he would ruin (for I saw him strong)
The sacred truths to fable and old song
(So Samson groped the temple's posts in spite)[2]
The world o'erwhelming to revenge his sight.   10
Yet as I read, soon growing less severe,
I liked his project, the success did fear;
Through that wide field how he his way should find
O'er which lame faith leads understanding blind;
Lest he perplexed the things he would explain,   15
And what was easy he should render vain.
Or if a work so infinite he spanned,
Jealous I was that some less skillful hand

---

5. "Proclaim," a kind of learned joke, suggests the seas roaring to announce their bounty. Ambergris is an expensive, mysterious, soapy substance found in sperm whales and used in the manufacture of perfumes (see *Moby Dick*, Chapter XCII).
6. The Gulf of Mexico.
1. This poem was prefixed to the second (1674) edition of *Paradise Lost*; Marvell

wrote as an old friend and former colleague of Milton's, but with a note of respect that cannot be overlooked.
2. Blind Samson, brought into the temple of the Philistines to make them sport, pulled down the roof on himself and his enemies. Marvell had doubtless read Milton's tragedy, *Samson Agonistes*, published in 1671, three years before the present poem.

(Such as disquiet always what is well,
And by ill imitating would excel)   20
Might hence presume the whole creation's day
To change in scenes, and show it in a play.[3]
   Pardon me, mighty poet, nor despise
My causeless, yet not impious, surmise.
But I am now convinced, and none will dare   25
Within thy labors to pretend a share.
Thou hast not missed one thought that could be fit,
And all that was improper dost omit,
So that no room for writers is here left
But to detect their ignorance or theft.   30
   That majesty which through thy work doth reign
Draws the devout, deterring the profane.
And things divine thou treat'st of in such state
As them preserves, and thee, inviolate.
At once delight and horror on us seize,   35
Thou sing'st with so much gravity and ease;
And above human flight dost soar aloft
With plume so strong, so equal, and so soft.
The bird named from that paradise you sing
So never flags, but always keeps on wing.[4]   40
   Where could'st thou words of such a compass find?
Whence furnish such a vast expense of mind?
Just heaven thee like Tiresias to requite
Rewards with prophecy thy loss of sight.[5]
   Well might'st thou scorn thy readers to allure   45
With tinkling rhyme, of thy own sense secure;
While the Town-Bays[6] writes all the while and spells,
And like a pack-horse tires without his bells.
Their fancies like our bushy-points appear,
The poets tag them, we for fashion wear.[7]   50
I too, transported by the mode, offend,
And while I meant to praise thee, must commend.[8]
Thy verse, created like thy theme sublime
In number, weight, and measure, needs not rhyme.

1674

3. Here, as elsewhere (see note 6, below), Marvell shows himself jealously aware of Dryden, who had asked for and received (though grudgingly) Milton's permission to cast *Paradise Lost* in the form of an opera.
4. The bird of paradise was thought to have no feet, and thus to remain perpetually in flight.
5. Tiresias is one of the blind prophet-poets whom Milton himself invokes in Book III of *Paradise Lost* (line 36) as one of his prototypes.
6. Dryden had been parodied in a farce called *The Rehearsal* (1671) under the name "Mr. Bays." (The poet laureate was supposed to wear a crown of bay-leaves.) Marvell is glancing at Dryden's fondness for rhymed couplets.
7. The comparison of rhyme to points and tags (little silver decorations on the laces used to fasten hose to doublet) was a commonplace; Milton is said to have told Dryden, rather stiffly, "You may tag my verses."
8. "Commend" implies explanation, almost apology; praise would be straightforward eulogy. Marvell can only mean that Milton stands outside the fashions of his own day, and above them.

An Horatian Ode

UPON CROMWELL'S RETURN FROM IRELAND [1]

The forward youth that would appear,
Must now forsake his Muses dear,
    Nor in the shadows sing
    His numbers languishing:

'Tis time to leave the books in dust,   5
And oil the unuséd armor's rust;
    Removing from the wall
    The corselet of the hall.[2]

So restless Cromwell could not cease
In the inglorious arts of peace,   10
    But through adventurous war
    Urgéd his active star;

And, like the three-forked lightning, first
Breaking the clouds where it was nursed,
    Did thorough his own side   15
    His fiery way divide:[3]

For 'tis all one to courage high,
The emulous, or enemy;
    And with such, to enclose,
    Is more than to oppose;   20

Then burning through the air he went,
And palaces and temples rent;
    And Caesar's head at last
    Did through his laurels blast.[4]

---

1. Cromwell returned from conquering Ireland in May, 1650, about 18 months after the execution of Charles I. The two events were vaguely but persistently connected: Cromwell's victory over the Irish was somehow a "vindication" of his career to this point, a sign that God did not disapprove of his laying violent hands on the sacred person of the monarch. The title phrase, "An Horatian Ode," promises a poem of cool and balanced judgment, not "enthusiastic" or heroic like the odes of Pindar. For the political background of Marvell's poem, see John M. Wallace, "Marvell's Horatian Ode," *PMLA* 77 (1962), 33–45.
2. The "forward youth" who removes armor from the wall owes something to a similar figure in the first book of Lucan's *Pharsalia*, which is also a poem about force, justice, and civil war. Andrew Marvell was not by any means

dropping books and picking up armor in 1650.
3. Cromwell had begun as a relatively inconspicuous Presbyterian, but soon became the leader of the more radical group variously known as the "Rump" or the "Independents." The "three-forked lightning" he wields identifies him with Zeus; and his giving birth (to himself, presumably) through his own side (party, of course, but a part of the body, too) might remind a reader of Athena's birth through Zeus's ear.
4. Laurels were used for royal crowns precisely because they were supposed to protect from lightning. "Caesar," of course, is Charles I. Cromwell's acts with his thunderbolt (smashing palaces, temples, and at last Caesar's head through its laurels) suggest a tyrannical God. Yet Caesar was a tyrant too.

'Tis madness to resist or blame   25
The face of angry Heaven's flame;
    And if we would speak true,
    Much to the man is due,

Who from his private gardens, where
He lived reservéd and austere,   30
    As if his highest plot
    To plant the bergamot;[5]

Could by industrous valor climb
To ruin the great work of Time,
    And cast the kingdom old,   35
    Into another mold;

Though Justice against Fate complain,
And plead the ancient rights in vain;
    But those do hold or break,
    As men are strong or weak.   40

Nature that hateth emptiness,
Allows of penetration less,
    And therefore must make room
    Where greater spirits come.

What field of all the civil wars   45
Where his were not the deepest scars?
    And Hampton shows what part
    He had of wiser art;[6]

Where, twining subtle fears with hope,
He wove a net of such a scope   50
    That Charles himself might chase
    To Caresbrooke's narrow case,

That thence the royal actor borne,
The tragic scaffold might adorn;
    While round the arméd bands   55
    Did clap their bloody hands.

He nothing common did or mean
Upon that memorable scene,
    But with his keener eye
    The ax's edge did try;[7]   60

5. Bergamot is a variety of pear; but its etymology (from the Turkish, "prince's pear") may conceal the insinuation that Cromwell had been plotting for power even in his early days of "private" life. The whole poem is full of puns (cf. "enclose," line 19, "mold," line 36) for the reader to seek out.
6. Hampton Court, where Charles I was confined shortly before his execution. It was popularly said that Cromwell connived at his momentary escape to Carisbrooke Castle on the Isle of Wight in order to convince the doubtful Parliament that the king could not be trusted and must be executed.
7. Latin uses one word, *acies*, for the front of a battle line, the edge of a sword- or ax-blade, and the beam of an eye.

Nor called the gods with vulgar spite
To vindicate his helpless right;
    But bowed his comely head
    Down, as upon a bed.

This was that memorable hour,   65
Which first assured the forcéd power;
    So when they did design
    The capitol's first line,

A bleeding head where they begun,
Did fright the architects to run;   70
    And yet in that the state
    Foresaw its happy fate.[8]

And now the Irish are ashamed
To see themselves in one year tamed;
    So much one man can do,   75
    That does both act and know.

They can affirm his praises best,
And have, though overcome, confessed
    How good he is, how just,
    And fit for highest trust.   80

Nor yet grown stiffer with command,
But still in the republic's hand—
    How fit he is to sway,
    That can so well obey.

He to the Commons' feet presents   85
A kingdom for his first year's rents;
    And, what he may, forbears
    His fame to make it theirs;

And has his sword and spoils ungirt,
To lay them at the public's skirt: 90
    So, when the falcon high
    Falls heavy from the sky,

She, having killed, no more does search,
But on the next green bough to perch;
    Where, when he first does lure,   95
    The falconer has her sure.

What may not then our isle presume,
While victory his crest does plume!
    What may not others fear,
    If thus he crown each year!   100

8. When foundations were being dug for the temple of Jupiter at Rome, Pliny tells us, the workmen uncovered a bloody head. They at first thought it an ill omen but then were persuaded to consider it a token that Rome would be the head (*caput*) of an empire; hence the name of the temple, Jupiter Capitolinus, and of the hill on which it stood, the Capitoline. The tale may well imply a generic relation between civilization and violence.

A Caesar he ere long to Gaul,
To Italy an Hannibal,
    And to all states not free,
    Shall climactéric be.[9]

The Pict no shelter now shall find   105
Within his party-colored mind,
    But from this valor sad,
    Shrink underneath the plaid;[1]

Happy if in the tufted brake
The English hunter him mistake,   110
    Nor lay his hounds in near
    The Caledonian[2] deer.

But thou, the war's and fortune's son,
March indefatigably on;
    And for the last effect,   115
    Still keep thy sword erect;[3]

Besides the force it has to fright
The spirits of the shady night,
    The same arts that did gain
    A power must it maintain.[4]   120

                                  1681

---

9. Neither Caesar nor Hannibal brought, or pretended to bring, freedom to the lands they attacked. "Climactéric": a period of crucial change in human life (for better or worse), popularly supposed to occur when 9 joined with 7 in man's age, i.e., in his 63rd year.

1. Early inhabitants of Scotland were called Picts because their warriors painted themselves many colors (Latin, *pictus*: painted); Marvell is playing with an image of the Scotch as divided by factions (parties) into as many colors as Scotch plaids.

2. Scotch.

3. The sword is being carried "erect,"

i.e., with the bare blade up, not the cross of the handle. Naked power, not religion, is to be the ensign of Cromwell's rule.

4. The last lines of the poem seem to paraphrase a saying of Christ's to the effect that they who take the sword shall perish with the sword (Matthew xxvi.52); from Cromwell's point of view, it is not a very reassuring ending to the poem. Yet when the poem was printed, in 1681, the censor of Charles II thought it politically subversive, and had it physically cut out of all the copies of Marvell's poems except (fortunately) one.

JOHN MILTON
(1608–1674)

    1637:   *Lycidas.*
    1640–60: The pamphlet wars.
    1651:   Blindness.
    1667:   *Paradise Lost.*

The life of John Milton falls conveniently into three divisions. There is a period of youthful education and apprenticeship, which culminates in the writing of *Lycidas* (1637) and Milton's foreign travels (1638–39).

There is a period of prose and controversy (1640–60), when almost all his verse was occasional, and when his major preoccupations were political and social; and finally, there are the last fourteen years of his life, when he returned to literature, a mature and somewhat embittered figure, to publish his three great poems, *Paradise Lost* (1667), *Paradise Regained* (1671), and *Samson Agonistes* (1671).

Milton was born at Bread Street in Cheapside, the elder son of what we would nowadays probably call a real-estate man. From the beginning, Milton showed prodigious gifts as a student of languages. At St. Paul's School he mastered Latin and Greek, and before long he was adept in most modern European tongues, as well as Hebrew. Sent to Christ's College, Cambridge, he proceeded B.A. in 1629 and M.A. in 1632, meanwhile continuing to read voraciously and writing (too infrequently for his own satisfaction) an occasional poem. In the normal course of events, a career like this would have culminated in ordination to the ministry and a position in the church. Both Milton and his parents seem to have anticipated this. But after taking his M.A., Milton, who disliked the trend of civil and religious affairs in England, did not take orders; instead, he retired to his father's country house at Horton in Buckinghamshire, and for five more years, under his own direction, read day and night. It seems likely that Milton, in his time, read just about everything that was ever written in English, Latin, Greek, and Italian. (Of course, he had the Bible by heart.) In 1634 he wrote, at the invitation of a nearby noble family, the masque known as *Comus*; and in 1637 he contributed to a volume memorializing a college classmate the elegy of *Lycidas*. Finally, in 1638, his most indulgent father sent this most voracious of students abroad, to put the finishing touches on an already splendid education. For two years, Milton traveled on the Continent, visiting famous literary figures and scenes; then, hearing rumors of impending troubles in England, he returned home in 1639.

Of Milton's complex and troubled career in controversy we need not say much. It too is divided in three phases. He began by publishing antiprelatical tracts, against the government of the church by bishops. These are rough, knockabout, name-calling tracts in the style of the times, which take a popular position on a relatively popular issue. But Milton's next venture procured him a reputation as a radical. In June, 1642, he married Mary Powell. Within six weeks, she left him, to return to her parents' house; and from 1643 to 1645, Milton published a series of pamphlets advocating that divorce be granted on the grounds of incompatibility. Clearly his personal situation had influenced his social judgment; just as clearly, respectable Englishmen, who were disturbed by the troubles of the time, were bound to feel that "divorce at pleasure" represented the end of all social order, the coming of complete anarchy. Milton not only effected no change in the divorce laws, he largely discredited himself by his divorce pamphlets. His last undertaking was more worthy of his gifts. After the execution of Charles I, in 1649, he published a series of Latin disputations against Continental critics of the regime, defending the actions of Parliament in executing Charles. In the middle of this work, he went blind, as the result of eyestrain continued over many years. By the use of secretaries and amanuenses, however, he was able to fulfill his duties as

Latin Secretary to Cromwell's Council of State, and to contribute very substantially to the diplomatic dignity of the new government.

Meanwhile, his first wife returned to him, and having born him three daughters, died in 1652. In 1656 Milton married Katharine Woodcock, who died in childbirth, in 1658. Finally, in 1660, the whole political movement for which Milton had sacrificed so much, went to smash. Though Milton boldly published pamphlets in its support to the very last minute, the Good Old Cause was defeated, and Charles II recalled from his travels. For a time under the Restoration, Milton was imprisoned and in danger of his life; but friends intervened, and he escaped with a fine and the loss of most of his property.

In 1663 Milton married his third wife, Elizabeth Minshull; and in blindness, poverty, defeat, and relative isolation, he set about completing a poem "justifying the ways of God to men," which he had first envisaged many years before. It was published in 1667, as *Paradise Lost*; and despite the many difficulties which it presented, despite its unfamiliar meter (blank verse was rare outside drama), despite the unpopularity of its attitudes and Milton's reputation as a dangerous man, it was recognized at once as a supreme epic achievement. In 1671 Milton published *Paradise Regained*, an epic poem in four books describing Christ's temptation in the wilderness, and *Samson Agonistes*, a "closet" tragedy (i.e., not intended for the stage). He died, of complications arising from gout, in 1674.

In the writings of Milton, the work of two tremendous intellectual and social movements comes to a head. The Renaissance is responsible for the rich and complex texture of Milton's style, the multiplicity of its classical references, its wealth of ornament and decoration. *Paradise Lost*, being an epic, not only challenges comparison with Homer and Virgil, it undertakes to encompass the whole life of mankind—war, love, religion, Hell, Heaven, the cosmos. It is a poem vastly capacious of worldly experience. On the other hand, the Reformation speaks with equal, if not greater, authority in Milton's earnest and individually-minded Christianity. The great epic, which resounds with the grandeur and multiplicity of the world, is also a poem the central actions of which take place inwardly, at the core of man's conscience. Adam's fate culminates in an act of passive suffering, not of active heroism. He does not kill Hector or Turnus, much less Satan, he picks up the burden of worldly existence, and triumphs over his guilt by admitting it and repenting of it.

These two contrasting aspects of Milton's life and thought place him among the Christian humanists. His literary art places him in the small circle of great epic writers.

On Shakespeare[1]

What needs my Shakespeare for his honored bones
The labor of an age in piléd stones,
Or that his hallowed relics should be hid

---

1. Milton's tribute to Shakespeare appeared in the Second Folio of the plays.

Under a star-ypointing pyramid?[2]
Dear son of memory, great heir of fame,   5
What need'st thou such weak witness of thy name?
Thou in our wonder and astonishment
Hast built thyself a livelong monument.
For whilst to th' shame of slow-endeavoring art,
Thy easy numbers flow, and that each heart   10
Hath from the leaves of thy unvalued book[3]
Those delphic lines with deep impression took,
Then thou, our fancy of itself bereaving,
Dost make us marble with too much conceiving;[4]
And so sepulchered in such pomp dost lie,   15
That kings for such a tomb would wish to die.

1632

L'Allegro[1]

Hence loathéd Melancholy
   Of Cerberus[2] and blackest midnight born,
In Stygian[3] cave forlorn
   'Mongst horrid shapes, and shrieks, and sights unholy,

2. "Star-ypointing" uses one of Spenser's archaic "y-" prefixes to eke out the meter. (Note also the interpolated "that" in line 10, serving the same purpose.) Milton's poem begins by answering the common complaint of the day, that Shakespeare should have been buried in some place more splendid than Stratford. Shakespeare is described as the "son of memory" because that makes him a brother of the muses, daughters of Mnemosyne ("memory") by Zeus.
3. Beyond all value, invaluable book.
4. The monuments of Shakespeare's tomb are all the enchanted and motionless readers of his book.
1. *L'Allegro* and *Il Penseroso* are a pair of companion-poems, probably written around 1630 or 1631, in those dancing tetrameter couplets which are so hard to keep from degenerating into singsong, and so delightful when controlled. Milton's handling of this difficult meter may be compared with virtuoso performances like those of Marvell (*To · His Coy Mistress*), Keats (*Lines on the Mermaid Tavern*) and A. E. Housman (*Terence, This Is Stupid Stuff*).
   The titles are almost untranslatable, which is why Milton did not translate them. But within the framework of two contrasted days, we see the cheerful, sociable man, and the melancholy, contemplative man in their typical spiritual attitudes. Milton's interest in the typical accounts for the striking generality of the pictures: "And every shepherd tells his tale / Under the hawthorn in the dale"—there is no effort to create an individual shepherd in a particular setting. All the shepherds in all the dales for miles around are telling one story or another, each under his own hawthorn bush. But Milton's focus is on the mind that sees, and on the tone which it casts over a landscape. The cheerful man infuses his world with contagious cheerfulness; the melancholy man casts over the events of his day (which, as events, are not very different) a pervasive veil of melancholy. The backgrounds of this complex contemplative mood may be explored in Burton's famous *Anatomy of Melancholy;* in a more recent book, Erwin Panofsky's study, *Albrecht Dürer,* where it occurs in connection with Dürer's magnificent engraving of Melancholia; or in Saxl, Panofsky, and Klibansky's immense study, *Saturn and Melancholy* (1964). There is a history of literary cheerfulness, too—*The Happy Man,* by Maren Sofie Røstvig (1954).
   Milton's poems stand in contrast to one another, but the contrasts are shaded, not glaring; there is no effort to "decide" the conflict, or to make melancholy black and cheerfulness convivial. Both poems exist in a reflective half-light, as little idyls of description which for sheer elegance and charm have rarely been equaled.
2. The three-headed hell-hound of classical mythology.
3. I.e., near the river Styx, the river of the underworld.

Find out some uncouth cell, 5
    Where brooding Darkness spreads his jealous wings,
And the night-raven sings;
    There under ebon shades, and low-browed rocks,
As ragged as thy locks,
    In dark Cimmerian[4] desert ever dwell. 10
But come thou goddess fair and free,
In Heaven yclept Euphrosyne,[5]
And by men, heart-easing Mirth,
Whom lovely Venus at a birth
With two sister Graces more 15
To ivy-crownéd Bacchus bore;[6]
Or whether (as some sager sing)[7]
The frolic wind that breathes the spring,
Zephyr with Aurora playing,
As he met her once a-Maying, 20
There on beds of violets blue,
And fresh-blown[8] roses washed in dew,
Filled her with thee a daughter fair,
So buxom,[9] blithe, and debonair.
Haste thee nymph, and bring with thee 25
Jest and youthful Jollity,
Quips and Cranks,[1] and wanton Wiles,
Nods, and Becks, and wreathéd Smiles,
Such as hang on Hebe's[2] cheek,
And love to live in dimple sleek; 30
Sport that wrinkled Care derides,
And Laughter, holding both his sides.
Come, and trip it as ye go
On the light fantastic toe,
And in thy right hand lead with thee, 35
The mountain nymph, sweet Liberty;
And if I give thee honor due,
Mirth, admit me of thy crew
To live with her and live with thee,
In unreprovéd pleasures free; 40
To hear the lark begin his flight,
And, singing, startle the dull night,
From his watch-tower in the skies,
Till the dappled dawn doth rise;
Then to come[3] in spite of sorrow, 45
And at my window bid good morrow,
Through the sweetbriar, or the vine,

4. The Cimmerians, who gave their name to Crimea, were supposed to live on the outer edge of the world, in perpetual twilight.
5. Euphrosyne, Aglaia, and Thalia were the Graces, daughters (according to one story) of Zeus himself, and goddesses of beauty and delight. "Yclept": called.
6. Bacchus is god of wine.
7. The "sager" (poets) who describe the Graces as born of Zephyr and Aurora are in fact John Milton himself; he invented this version of the myth.
8. Newly opened.
9. Lively.
1. Jokes. "Becks": curtseys.
2. Goddess of youth and cupbearer to the other gods. Pronounced *Hee-bee*.
3. I.e., then admit me to come.

Or the twisted eglantine.
While the cock with lively din,
Scatters the rear of darkness thin,   50
And to the stack, or the barn door,
Stoutly struts his dames before;
Oft listening how the hounds and horn
Cheerly rouse the slumbering morn,
From the side of some hoar hill,   55
Through the high wood echoing shrill.
Sometime walking not unseen
By hedgerow elms, on hillocks green,
Right against the eastern gate,
Where the great sun begins his state,[4]   60
Robed in flames, and amber light,
The clouds in thousand liveries dight;[5]
While the plowman near at hand,
Whistles o'er the furrowed land,
And the milkmaid singeth blithe,   65
And the mower whets his scythe,
And every shepherd tells his tale,
Under the hawthorn in the dale.
Straight mine eye hath caught new pleasures
Whilst the landscape round it measures,   70
Russet lawns and fallows gray,
Where the nibbling flocks do stray,
Mountains on whose barren breast
The laboring clouds do often rest;
Meadows trim with daisies pied,[6]   75
Shallow brooks, and rivers wide.
Towers and battlements it sees
Bosomed high in tufted trees,
Where perhaps some beauty lies,
The cynosure[7] of neighboring eyes.   80
Hard by, a cottage chimney smokes,
From betwixt two aged oaks,
Where Corydon and Thyrsis[8] met,
Are at their savory dinner set
Of herbs, and other country messes,   85
Which the neat-handed Phyllis dresses;
And then in haste her bower she leaves,
With Thestylis to bind the sheaves;
Or if the earlier season lead
To the tanned haycock in the mead.   90
Sometimes with secure delight
The upland hamlets will invite,
When the merry bells ring round

4. Procession.
5. Dressed.
6. Dappled.
7. Literally, the bright polestar, by which mariners steer; here, a splendid, eminent object, much gazed at.
8. Since the days of Theocritus, the names "Corydon," "Thyrsis," "Phyllis," and "Thestylis" have been traditional shepherds' names.

And the jocund rebecks⁹ sound
To many a youth and many a maid,   95
Dancing in the checkered shade;
And young and old come forth to play
On a sunshine holiday,
Till the livelong daylight fail;
Then to the spicy nut-brown ale,   100
With stories told of many a feat,
How fairy Mab¹ the junkets eat;
She was pinched and pulled, she said,
And he, by Friar's lantern led,
Tells how the drudging goblin² sweat   105
To earn his cream-bowl, duly set,
When in one night, ere glimpse of morn,
His shadowy flail hath threshed the corn
That ten day-laborers could not end;
Then lies him down the lubber fiend,³   110
And, stretched out all the chimney's length,
Basks at the fire his hairy strength;
And crop-full out of doors he flings
Ere the first cock his matin rings.
Thus done the tales, to bed they creep,   115
By whispering winds soon lulled asleep.
Towered cities please us then,
And the busy hum of men,
Where throngs of knights and barons bold,
In weeds⁴ of peace high triumphs hold,   120
With store of ladies, whose bright eyes
Rain influence,⁵ and judge the prize
Of wit, or arms, while both contend
To win her grace, whom all commend.
There let Hymen⁶ oft appear   125
In saffron robe, with taper clear,
And pomp, and feast, and revelry,
With masque, and antique pageantry;
Such sights as youthful poets dream
On summer eves by haunted stream.   130
Then to the well-trod stage anon,
If Jonson's learned sock⁷ be on,
Or sweetest Shakespeare, fancy's child,
Warble his native wood-notes wild.

9. A rebeck is a small three-stringed fiddle; "jocund" implies a festive occasion.
1. Queen Mab, wife of Oberon, the fairy king. "She" and "he" in the next two lines are country folk, telling of their experiences with the fairies.
2. Robin Goodfellow, alias Puck, Pook, or Hobgoblin. "Friar's lantern": will-o'-the-wisp.
3. Oafish spirit.
4. Garments. "Triumphs": festive ceremonies.

5. The ladies' eyes are stars, and so have astrological influence over the men.
6. Roman god of marriage, wearing a yellow ("saffron") robe.
7. A low-heeled slipper, worn by actors in classical comedy, and often contrasted with the buskin (high-heeled boot) appropriate to tragedy. The contrast of Jonson as a "learned" poet with Shakespeare as a "natural" one was conventional.

And ever against eating cares[8]   135
Lap me in soft Lydian airs,[9]
Married to immortal verse
Such as the meeting soul may pierce
In notes, with many a winding bout[1]
Of linkéd sweetness long drawn out,   140
With wanton heed, and giddy cunning,
The melting voice through mazes running;
Untwisting all the chains that tie
The hidden soul of harmony;
That Orpheus' self[2] may heave his head   145
From golden slumber on a bed
Of heaped Elysian flowers, and hear
Such strains as would have won the ear
Of Pluto, to have quite set free
His half-regained Eurydice.   150
These delights if thou canst give,
Mirth, with thee I mean to live.

ca. 1631   1645

Il Penseroso

Hence vain deluding Joys,
   The brood of Folly without father bred.
How little you bestead,[3]
   Or fill the fixéd mind with all your toys;[4]
Dwell in some idle brain,   5
   And fancies fond[5] with gaudy shapes possess,
As thick and numberless
   As the gay motes that people the sunbeams,
Or likest hovering dreams,
   The fickle pensioners[6] of Morpheus' train.   10
But hail thou Goddess, sage and holy,
Hail, divinest Melancholy,
Whose saintly visage is too bright
To hit[7] the sense of human sight;
And therefore to our weaker view,   15
O'erlaid with black, staid Wisdom's hue.
Black, but such as in esteem,

8. "Eating cares" is but one of many classical phrases in the poem; it is from Horace, *Odes* II.xi.18 (*curas edaces*).
9. "Lydian" airs in music would be soft, languishing, sensual—unlike the chaste Dorian and brisk Ionian.
1. A musical "run" passage.
2. Orpheus went to the underworld to regain his wife Eurydice, and by his music dissolved the guardians of Hades in tears. But as they left, he violated the condition of her release by looking back at her, and so lost her again. Milton uses the Orpheus story again in *Il Penseroso, Lycidas,* and *Paradise Lost* VII.32 ff.
3. Avail, help.
4. Trifles.
5. Foolish.
6. Followers. Morpheus is the god of sleep; the melancholy man feels the cheerful man lives in a dream.
7. Suit, agree with.

Prince Memnon's sister[8] might beseem,
Or that starred Ethiope queen[9] that strove
To set her beauty's praise above   20
The sea nymphs, and their powers offended.
Yet thou art higher far descended;
Thee bright-haired Vesta long of yore
To solitary Saturn bore;[1]
His daughter she (in Saturn's reign   25
Such mixture was not held a stain).
Oft in glimmering bowers and glades
He met her, and in secret shades
Of woody Ida's inmost grove,
While yet there was no fear of Jove.   30
Come pensive nun, devout and pure,
Sober, steadfast, and demure,
All in a robe of darkest grain,[2]
Flowing with majestic train,
And sable stole of cypress lawn[3]   35
Over thy decent shoulders drawn.
Come, but keep thy wonted state,
With even step and musing gait,
And looks commercing with the skies,
Thy rapt soul sitting in thine eyes: 40
There held in holy passion still,
Forget thyself to marble, till
With a sad leaden downward cast,
Thou fix them on the earth as fast.
And join with thee calm Peace and Quiet,   45
Spare Fast, that oft with gods doth diet,
And hears the Muses in a ring
Aye round about Jove's altar sing.
And add to these retired Leisure,
That in trim gardens takes his pleasure;   50
But first, and chiefest, with thee bring,
Him that yon soars on golden wing,
Guiding the fiery-wheeléd throne,
The cherub Contemplation;[4]
And the mute Silence hist along   55

8. Memnon in *Odyssey* XI was a handsome Ethiopian prince who fought for Troy; his sister, mentioned not by Homer but by later commentators, was Hemera.
9. Cassiopeia, who was "starred" (i.e., turned into a constellation) for bragging that her daughter Andromeda or she herself (Milton follows this second version) was more beautiful than the sea nymphs.
1. Vesta was a goddess of purity; Milton invented the story of her connection with Saturn on Mt. Ida in Crete, and of her giving birth to Melancholy.

But Saturn helps out the poem because he was a primitive deity (hence melancholy is "natural") and because a saturnine complexion is said to show a dark and melancholy disposition.
2. Color.
3. "Cypress": a dark, delicate cloth (originally Cyprus, from the island; but the cypress is also the tree of death). "Lawn": a transparent, gauzy material, much like crape. "Decent": comely, proper.
4. The cherub Contemplation is suggested by the Biblical vision of Ezekiel.

'Less Philomel[5] will deign a song,
In her sweetest, saddest plight,
Smoothing the rugged brow of night,
While Cynthia[6] checks her dragon yoke
Gently o'er th' accustomed oak; 60
Sweet bird that shunn'st the noise of folly,
Most musical, most melancholy!
Thee chantress oft the woods among,
I woo to hear thy evensong;
And missing thee, I walk unseen 65
On the dry smooth-shaven green,
To behold the wandering moon,
Riding near her highest noon,
Like one that had been led astray
Through the Heaven's wide pathless way; 70
And oft as if her head she bowed,
Stooping through a fleecy cloud.
Oft on a plat[7] of rising ground,
I hear the far-off curfew sound,
Over some wide-watered shore, 75
Swinging slow with sullen roar;
Or if the air will not permit,
Some still removéd place will fit,
Where glowing embers through the room
Teach light to counterfeit a gloom 80
Far from all resort of mirth,
Save the cricket on the hearth,
Or the bellman's[8] drowsy charm,
To bless the doors from nightly harm;
Or let my lamp at midnight hour 85
Be seen in some high lonely tower,
Where I may oft outwatch the Bear,[9]
With thrice great Hermes,[1] or unsphere
The spirit of Plato to unfold
What worlds, or what vast regions hold 90
The immortal mind that hath forsook
Her mansion in this fleshly nook;
And of those demons[2] that are found
In fire, air, flood, or underground,
Whose power hath a true consent[3] 95
With planet, or with element.

5. The nightingale, whose song is traditionally one of grief. "Hist": summon.
6. Goddess of the moon, and of the underworld as well, she drives a pair of sleepless dragons.
7. Plot, flat open space.
8. The night watchman in little villages rang a bell to call the hours.
9. Since the Great Bear never sets, outwatching it is a major enterprise.
1. The Egyptian god Thoth or Hermes, to whom were attributed various esoteric books of the 3rd and 4th centuries A.D.; under the name of Hermes Trismegistus he later became a patron of magicians and alchemists. To "unsphere" Plato is to call Plato back to earth from the sphere he now inhabits.
2. Not devils, but classical beings akin to heroes, halfway between gods and men. There were four sorts of demons, corresponding to the four elements, each with a corresponding planet.
3. Mysterious agreement.

Some time let gorgeous Tragedy
In sceptered pall[4] come sweeping by,
Presenting Thebes', or Pelops' line,
Or the tale of Troy divine.[5]   100
Or what (though rare) of later age
Ennobled hath the buskined[6] stage.
But, O sad virgin, that thy power
Might raise Musaeus[7] from his bower,
Or bid the soul of Orpheus[8] sing   105
Such notes as, warbled to the string,
Drew iron tears down Pluto's cheek,
And made Hell grant what Love did seek.
Or call up him[9] that left half told
The story of Cambuscan bold,   110
Of Camball, and of Algarsife,
And who had Canacee to wife,
That owned the virtuous[1] ring and glass,
And of the wondrous horse of brass,
On which the Tartar king did ride;   115
And if aught else great bards beside
In sage and solemn tunes have sung,
Of tourneys and of trophies hung,
Of forests and enchantments drear,
Where more is meant than meets the ear.[2]   120
Thus, Night, oft see me in thy pale career,
Till civil-suited morn appear,[3]
Not tricked and frounced as she was wont,
With the Attic boy to hunt,
But kerchiefed in a comely cloud,   125
While rocking winds are piping loud,
Or ushered with a shower still,
When the gust hath blown his fill,
Ending on the rustling leaves,
With minute-drops from off the eaves.   130
And when the sun begins to fling
His flaring beams, me, Goddess, bring
To archéd walks of twilight groves,
And shadows brown that Sylvan[4] loves
Of pine or monumental oak,   135
Where the rude ax with heavéd stroke,
Was never heard the nymphs to daunt,

4. Royal robe (from Latin *palla*, the robe of tragic actors).
5. Tragedies about the royal line of Thebes would include Sophocles' Oedipus cycle; those about the line of Pelops, Aeschylus' *Oresteia;* and those about Troy, Euripides' *Trojan Women.*
6. The buskin of tragedy, contrasted with the sock of comedy.
7. A mythical poet-priest of the pre-Homeric age, supposedly son or pupil of the equally mythical Orpheus.
8. For the story of Orpheus, see *L'Allegro*, line 145, and note.
9. I.e., Chaucer, who in the Squire's Tale left the tale of Cambuscan half told.
1. Having special power.
2. A capsule description of allegory.
3. The goddess Aurora, who once fell in love with Cephalus ("the Attic boy," line 124), and used to go hunting with him. "Tricked and frounced": adorned and frizzled.
4. Roman god of the woodlands.

Or fright them from their hallowed haunt.
There in close covert by some brook,
Where no profaner eye may look,   140
Hide me from day's garish eye,
While the bee with honeyed thigh,
That at her flowery work doth sing,
And the waters murmuring
With such consort⁵ as they keep,   145
Entice the dewy-feathered sleep;
And let some strange mysterious dream,
Wave at his wings in airy stream,
Of lively portraiture displayed,
Softly on my eyelids laid.⁶   150
And as I wake, sweet music breathe
Above, about, or underneath,
Sent by some spirit to mortals good,
Or th' unseen genius⁷ of the wood.
But let my due feet never fail   155
To walk the studious cloister's pale,⁸
And love the high embowéd roof,
With antic⁹ pillars massy proof,
And storied windows¹ richly dight,
Casting a dim religious light.   160
There let the pealing organ blow,
To the full-voiced choir below,
In service high, and anthems clear,
As may with sweetness, through mine ear,
Dissolve me into ecstasies,   165
And bring all heaven before mine eyes.
And may at last my weary age
Find out the peaceful hermitage,
The hairy gown and mossy cell,
Where I may sit and rightly spell²   170
Of every star that Heaven doth show,
And every herb that sips the dew
Till old experience do attain
To something like prophetic strain.
These pleasures, Melancholy, give,   175
And I with thee will choose to live.

ca. 1631   1645

5. Accompaniment.
6. Milton's syntax gets loose and dreamy too, here. He means, "Let some strange dream wave at the wings of sleep, while a stream of vivid pictures passes softly over my eyelids."
7. Guardian angel.
8. Enclosure.
9. I.e., covered with quaint, grotesque, or antic carvings; but "antique," which derives from the same Latin root, was not excluded from the sense. "Massy proof": massive and strong.
1. I.e., with stories told by stained-glass images. "Dight": dressed.
2. Study. The melancholy man wants to think his way into the cosmos until he becomes a prophet.

Comus   After finishing his formal academic work at Cambridge, Milton
was living at his father's country house in Horton, Buckinghamshire, and
pursuing a course of independent postgraduate reading, when chance
brought him into contact with the Edgerton family, who owned property in
the neighborhood. They were a widespread family, with estates, positions,
and connections—distinguished upper-echelon civil servants, distantly related to the Sidneys. Having occasions to celebrate, they asked young Mr.
Milton to compose for them some ceremonial verses. The first of these semi-
dramatic pieces was a short spectacle named "Arcades" written perhaps for
the birthday, and certainly in honor, of the Countess Dowager of Derby. The
second was the masque now known to us as *Comus*, written in 1634 to
celebrate the appointment of her stepson, the Earl of Bridgewater, as Lord
President of Wales.

Socially speaking, Milton's two masques were altogether different from
those of Ben Jonson. It was a family entertainment that Milton was asked
to create; *Comus* was performed mainly by children, not sophisticated courtiers; it required little scenery, costuming, or machinery, and that little
quite simple. Compared with the court-masques, its budget was tiny. Perhaps for these reasons, Milton evidently felt free to make of *Comus* a personal statement rich in complex implication. The basic story of a temptation triumphantly resisted he found in the conventional Renaissance moral
reading of *Odyssey* X, describing the adventures of Odysseus on Circe's isle;
it needed only a little modification to take account of the very limited
troupe of actors at Milton's disposal, among whom the three young children of the Earl had to be given prominent parts. More importantly, the
fable answered to a lifelong preoccupation of the poet's mind. One could
define this central theme as the quarrel between a strongly sensual temperament and a powerful nay-saying sense of personal morality. On these terms
the verbal "debate" between the Lady and Comus articulates a quarrel
between two aspects of the poet himself. Certainly the dispute between easy
sensual indulgence and moral self-control based on a vigilant conscience
runs like a red thread through most of Milton's major works. But in *Comus*
one sees it rising toward a particularly idealistic, spiritualized solution. In
the formal argument, between Comus speaking for sense and the Lady
speaking for virginity, both parties overstate and rigidify the claims involved
in their opposed positions. Comus, pretending devotion to Nature, would
reduce the Lady to a promiscuous party-girl; her answers, protesting eternal
virginity, suggest that she belongs in a nunnery. But in the Attendant Spirit's epilogue we get a final, carefully balanced glimpse of Venus and Adonis,
Psyche and Cupid—images of erotic fulfillment from which the gross and
sensual elements have been purged, existing forever in a heaven of transcendent desire. Such love as this, Milton seems to suggest, would be no
derogation from the lady's much-tried chastity; yet it is in no way narrow,
negative, or—as we would say—puritanical.

Comus is written in a mixture of several different styles, lyric, dramatic,
and declamatory; it is often erudite and allusive, just as often charmingly
naïve and earnest. From time to time it rhymes, and then breaks off; it
pauses to imitate an archaic style of Greek dialogue. The action is set in a

vaguely defined place and time compounded of Shropshire and Arcadia,
1634 and mythological antiquity. Without ever being explicitly mentioned,
Christian moral values are everywhere present in the masque. Perhaps it is
their unusual hidden movement, behind the action, from opposition to
nature toward reconciliation with nature that has made this youthful allegory so puzzling to modern commentators.

A Mask Presented at Ludlow Castle, 1634 (*Comus*) [1]

The Persons:

The ATTENDANT SPIRIT, *afterwards in the habit of* THYRSIS[2]
COMUS *with his Crew*
The LADY
FIRST BROTHER
SECOND BROTHER
SABRINA, *the Nymph*

The chief persons which presented, were:

The LORD BRACKLEY.[3]
Mr. THOMAS EGERTON, *his Brother.*
The LADY ALICE EGERTON.

The first scene discovers a wild wood.

The ATTENDANT SPIRIT descends or enters.

Before the starry threshold of Jove's court[4]
My mansion is, where those immortal shapes
Of bright aërial spirits live ensphered
In regions mild of calm and serene air,
Above the smoke and stir of this dim spot,   5
Which men call earth, and with low-thoughted care
Confined and pestered in this pinfold here,[5]
Strive to keep up a frail and feverish being,
Unmindful of the crown that virtue gives
After this mortal change, to her true servants   10
Amongst the enthroned gods on sainted seats.
Yet some there be that by due steps aspire
To lay their just hands on that golden key
That opes the palace of eternity:

1. Milton's masque had at first no other
title than "A Mask Presented at Ludlow
Castle"; it came to be generally known
as *Comus* only after Milton's death.
"Ludlow Castle" is in Shropshire, near
the Welsh border, in the west of England.
2. Henry Lawes, who composed the
music for *Comus*, probably played the
part of Thyrsis. "Attendant Spirit": a
guardian, a good daemon, a virtuous

spirit, but not quite an angel.
3. Lord Brackley was the Earl of Bridgewater's elder son; he was 11 years old
when the masque was presented, his
brother Thomas was just 9, and their sister, the Lady Alice, was 15.
4. The Attendant Spirit comes from outside the court of Jove, a bright aërial
spirit from the middle regions between
heaven and earth.
5. Cattle-pen.

To such my errand is, and but for such,   15
I would not soil these pure ambrosial weeds
With the rank vapors of this sin-worn mold.
  But to my task. Neptune, besides the sway
Of every salt flood and each ebbing stream,
Took in by lot 'twixt high and nether Jove[6]   20
Imperial rule of all the sea-girt isles
That like to rich and various gems inlay
The unadornéd bosom of the deep;
Which he to grace his tributary gods
By course commits to several government,   25
And gives them leave to wear their sapphire crowns,
And wield their little tridents; but this isle,
The greatest and the best of all the main,
He quarters to his blue-haired deities;[7]
And all this tract that fronts the falling sun   30
A noble peer of mickle trust and power
Has in his charge, with temper'd awe to guide
An old and haughty nation proud in arms;
Where his fair offspring nursed in princely lore,
Are coming to attend their father's state   35
And new-entrusted scepter.[8] But their way
Lies through the perplexed paths of this drear wood,[9]
The nodding horror of whose shady brows
Threats the forlorn and wandering passenger;
And here their tender age might suffer peril,   40
But that by quick command from sovereign Jove
I was dispatched for their defense and guard;
And listen why, for I will tell ye now
What never yet was heard in tale or song
From old or modern bard, in hall or bower.[1]   45
  Bacchus that first from out the purple grape
Crushed the sweet poison of misuséd wine,
After the Tuscan mariners transformed,
Coasting the Tyrrhene shore, as the winds listed,
On Circe's island fell. (Who knows not Circe,   50
The daughter of the sun? Whose charmed cup
Whoever tasted, lost his upright shape,
And downward fell into a groveling swine.)[2]

6. "High" Jove was Jupiter, king of the gods, resident on Olympus; "nether" Jove was Dis or Pluto, resident in hell; Neptune, between them, took in not only the oceans but all the islands in them, including Britain.
7. England, Ireland, Scotland, and Wales are the quarters of Britain; the part that "fronts the falling sun" is the western part, i.e., Wales.
8. The Earl of Bridgewater, in whose honor the masque was given, had just been appointed Lord President of Wales —hence the compliments to "an old and haughty nation proud in arms."
9. The wood is not only the park around Ludlow Castle but, allegorically, the tangled forest of life, as in Dante.
1. The story told by the Attendant Spirit is indeed unknown to classical antiquity, though grafted onto classical mythology.
2. Ovid tells in the *Metamorphoses* (III) how Bacchus turned into dolphins some Italian pirates who tried to kidnap him. Circe's island was supposed to lie in the Tyrrhenian Sea, off the west coast of Italy. Circe the enchantress was a daughter of Helios the sun-god; the major classical fable involving her is *Odyssey* X, which describes how she enchanted and transformed Odysseus' men, but not wily Odysseus himself.

This nymph that gazed upon his clustering locks,
With ivy berries wreathed, and his blithe youth, 55
Had by him, ere he parted thence, a son
Much like his father, but his mother more,
Whom therefore she brought up, and Comus named:[3]
Who, ripe and frolic of his full grown age,
Roving the Celtic and Iberian fields, 60
At last betakes him to this ominous wood,
And in thick shelter of black shades embowered,
Excels his mother at her mighty art,
Offering to every weary traveler
His orient liquor in a crystal glass, 65
To quench the drought of Phœbus,[4] which as they taste,
(For most do taste through fond intemperate thirst)
Soon as the potion works, their human countenance,
Th' express resemblance of the gods, is changed
Into some brutish form of wolf, or bear, 70
Or ounce,[5] or tiger, hog, or bearded goat,
All other parts remaining as they were.
And they, so perfect is their misery,
Not once perceive their foul disfigurement,
But boast themselves more comely than before, 75
And all their friends and native home forget,
To roll with pleasure in a sensual sty.
Therefore when any favored of high Jove
Chances to pass through this adventurous glade,
Swift as the sparkle of a glancing star 80
I shoot from heaven to give him safe convoy,
As now I do. But first I must put off
These my sky robes spun out of Iris' woof,[6]
And take the weeds and likeness of a swain
That to the service of this house belongs, 85
Who with his soft pipe and smooth-dittied song
Well knows to still the wild winds when they roar,
And hush the waving woods, nor of less faith,
And in this office of his mountain watch
Likeliest, and nearest to the present aid 90
Of this occasion. But I hear the tread
Of hateful steps, I must be viewless[7] now.

COMUS *enters with a charming rod in one hand, his glass in the other; with him a rout of monsters, headed like sundry sorts of wild beasts, but otherwise like men and women, their apparel glistering. They come in making a riotous and unruly noise, with torches in their hands.*

3. Comus, in Jonson's earlier masque *Pleasure Reconciled to Virtue* (above), was a gross belly-god; Milton makes him younger, gayer, more attractive. The "Celtic" (French) and "Iberian" (Spanish) "fields" define the path by which he got from Italy to wild Wales.
4. Thirst caused by the sun. Orient liq-
uor glitters like the rising (orient) sun, perhaps because it has an oriental pearl in it.
5. Lynx.
6. Robes woven from the colors of the rainbow ("Iris"); "weeds": clothing.
7. Invisible.

COMUS. The star that bids the shepherd fold[8]
  Now the top of heaven doth hold,
  And the gilded car of day   95
  His glowing axle doth allay
  In the steep Atlantic stream,
  And the slope sun his upward beam
  Shoots against the dusky pole,
  Pacing toward the other goal   100
  Of his chamber in the east.
  Meanwhile welcome joy and feast,
  Midnight shout and revelry,
  Tipsy dance and jollity.
  Braid your locks with rosy twine   105
  Dropping odors, dropping wine.
  Rigor now is gone to bed,
  And advice with scrupulous head,
  Strict age, and sour severity,
  With their grave saws[9] in slumber lie.   110
  We that are of purer fire
  Imitate the starry choir,
  Who in their nightly watchful spheres,
  Lead in swift round the months and years.
  The sounds and seas with all their finny drove   115
  Now to the moon in wavering morris[1] move,
  And on the tawny sands and shelves
  Trip the pert fairies and the dapper elves;
  By dimpled brook and fountain brim,
  The wood-nymphs decked with daisies trim,   120
  Their merry wakes and pastimes keep:
  What hath night to do with sleep?
  Night hath better sweets to prove,
  Venus now wakes, and wakens love.
  Come let us our rites begin,   125
  'Tis only daylight that makes sin,
  Which these dun shades will ne'er report.
  Hail goddess of nocturnal sport,
  Dark veiled Cotytto,[2] to whom the secret flame
  Of midnight torches burns; mysterious dame,   130
  That ne'er art called but when the dragon womb
  Of Stygian darkness spits her thickest gloom,
  And makes one blot of all the air,
  Stay thy cloudy ebon chair
  Wherein thou rid'st with Hecat',[3] and befriend   135
  Us thy vowed priests, till utmost end
  Of all thy dues be done, and none left out,
  Ere the blabbing eastern scout,

---

8. Hesperus the evening star bids the shepherd return his flocks to their fold for the night.
9. Maxims.
1. The wavering morris-dance of the waters is the recurrent tides.

2. The Thracian goddess Cotytto was linked with Hecate (pronounced with three syllables) as patroness of witchcraft and nocturnal license.
3. Hecate, the chief classical goddess of witchcraft and sorcery.

The nice morn on th' Indian steep,[4]
From her cabined loophole peep,   140
And to the telltale sun descry
Our concealed solemnity.
Come, knit hands, and beat the ground,
In a light fantastic round.

The Measure

Break off, break off, I feel the different pace   145
Of some chaste footing near about this ground.
Run to your shrouds within these brakes and trees;
Our number may affright: some virgin sure
(For so I can distinguish by mine art)
Benighted in these woods. Now to my charms,   150
And to my wily trains; I shall ere long
Be well stocked with as fair a herd as grazed
About my mother Circe. Thus I hurl
My dazzling spells into the spongy air,
Of power to cheat the eye with blear illusion,   155
And give it false presentments,[5] lest the place
And my quaint habits breed astonishment,
And put the damsel to suspicious flight,
Which must not be, for that's against my course.
I under fair pretense of friendly ends   160
And well placed words of glozing[6] courtesy,
Baited with reasons not unplausible,
Wind me into the easy-hearted man,
And hug him into snares. When once her eye
Hath met the virtue of this magic dust,   165
I shall appear some harmless villager
Whom thrift keeps up about his country gear;
But here she comes, I fairly step aside,
And hearken if I may her business hear.

THE LADY *enters.*

LADY. This way the noise was, if mine ear be true,   170
    My best guide now; methought it was the sound
    Of riot and ill-managed merriment,
    Such as the jocund flute or gamesome pipe
    Stirs up among the loose unlettered hinds,[7]
    When for their teeming flocks and granges full   175
    In wanton dance they praise the bounteous Pan,[8]
    And thank the gods amiss. I should be loath
    To meet the rudeness and swilled insolence
    Of such late wassailers;[9] yet O where else

4. Milton imagines a European lookout stationed in the Himalayas to watch for the approach of morning from the East.
5. Comus probably flung some confetti in the air to represent magic dust.
6. Deceitful, flattering.
7. Countrymen.
8. God in general, but also the special god of shepherds and farmers.
9. Drinkers.

Shall I inform my unacquainted feet 180
In the blind mazes of this tangled wood?
My brothers, when they saw me wearied out
With this long way, resolving here to lodge
Under the spreading favor of these pines,
Stepped as they said to the next thicket side 185
To bring me berries, or such cooling fruit
As the kind hospitable woods provide.
They left me then, when the gray-hooded ev'n
Like a sad votarist in palmer's weed
Rose from the hindmost wheels of Phœbus' wain.[1] 190
But where they are, and why they came not back,
Is now the labor of my thoughts; 'tis likeliest
They had engaged their wandering steps too far,
And envious darkness, ere they could return,
Had stole them from me; else O thievish night 195
Why shouldst thou, but for some felonious end,
In thy dark lantern thus close up the stars,
That nature hung in heaven, and filled their lamps
With everlasting oil, to give due light
To the misled and lonely traveler? 200
This is the place, as well as I may guess,
Whence even now the tumult of loud mirth
Was rife and perfect in my listening ear,
Yet nought but single darkness do I find.
What might this be? A thousand fantasies 205
Begin to throng into my memory,
Of calling shapes and beckoning shadows dire,
And airy tongues that syllable men's names
On sands and shores and desert wildernesses.
These thoughts may startle well, but not astound 210
The virtuous mind, that ever walks attended
By a strong siding champion, conscience.——
O welcome pure-eyed faith, white-handed hope,
Thou hovering angel girt with golden wings,
And thou unblemished form of chastity,[2] 215
I see ye visibly, and now believe
That he, the supreme good, t' whom all things ill
Are but as slavish officers of vengeance.
Would send a glistering guardian, if need were,
To keep my life and honor unassailed. 220
Was I deceived, or did a sable cloud
Turn forth her silver lining on the night?
I did not err, there does a sable cloud
Turn forth her silver lining on the night,

1. As the chariot of the sun (Phoebus' wagon) disappeared over the horizon, evening rose behind it, like a gray, hooded pilgrim.
2. Milton must have expected his new triad of Faith, Hope, and Chastity to strike sharply on ears accustomed to the old formula of Faith, Hope and Charity. The difference is worth some meditation.

And casts a gleam over this tufted grove.   225
I cannot hallo to my brothers, but
Such noise as I can make to be heard farthest
I'll venture, for my new enlivened spirits
Prompt me; and they perhaps are not far off.

SONG

Sweet Echo, sweetest nymph that livest unseen   230
        Within thy airy shell
  By slow Meander's³ margent green,
And in the violet-embroidered vale
    Where the love-lorn nightingale
Nightly to thee her sad song mourneth well.   235

Canst thou not tell me of a gentle pair
    That likest thy Narcissus⁴ are?
      O if thou have
    Hid them in some flowery cave,
      Tell me but where,   240
Sweet queen of parley, daughter of the sphere,
  So mayst thou be translated to the skies,
And give resounding grace to all heav'n's harmonies.⁵

COMUS. Can any mortal mixture of earth's mold
  Breathe such divine enchanting ravishment?   245
  Sure something holy lodges in that breast,
  And with these raptures moves the vocal air
  To testify his hidden residence;
  How sweetly did they float upon the wings
  Of silence, through the empty-valuted night,   250
  At every fall smoothing the raven down
  Of darkness till it smiled: I have oft heard
  My mother Circe with the sirens three,
  Amidst the flowery kirtled Naiades,⁶
  Culling their potent herbs and baleful drugs,   255
  Who as they sung, would take the prisoned soul,
  And lap it in Elysium; Scylla wept,
  And chid her barking waves into attention,
  And fell Charybdis murmured soft applause:⁷
  Yet they in pleasing slumber lulled the sense,   260
  And in sweet madness robbed it of itself,

---

3. Meander is a slow-moving, winding river in Asia Minor, famous for its twisting and turning.
4. The beautiful young man of Greek mythology who fell in love with his own reflection, pined away, and became the flower which now bears his name.
5. Echo is "queen of parley" because she talks so much, and "daughter of the sphere" because her voice bounces off the vault of heaven.
6. Milton imagines Circe keeping company with the sirens and Naiades (sea-nymphs) because they were all seductive-destructive goddesses dwelling by the seaside.
7. Scylla and Charybdis were another pair of deadly females dwelling by the sea, the first a many-headed monster, the second a whirlpool.

But such a sacred and home-felt delight,
Such sober certainty of waking bliss,
I never heard till now. I'll speak to her
And she shall be my queen. Hail foreign wonder,   265
Whom certain these rough shades did never breed,
Unless the goddess that in rural shrine
Dwell'st here with Pan or Silvan,[8] by blest song
Forbidding every bleak unkindly fog
To touch the prosperous growth of this tall wood.   270
LADY. Nay gentle shepherd, ill is lost that praise
That is addressed to unattending ears;
Not any boast of skill, but éxtreme shift
How to regain my severed company,
Compelled me to awake the courteous echo   275
To give me answer from her mossy couch.
COMUS. What chance, good lady, hath bereft you thus?[9]
LADY. Dim darkness and this leafy labyrinth.
COMUS. Could that divide you from near-ushering guides?
LADY. They left me weary on a grassy turf.   280
COMUS. By falsehood, or discourtesy, or why?
LADY. To seek i' th' valley some cool friendly spring.
COMUS. And left your fair side all unguarded, Lady?
LADY. They were but twain, and purposed quick return.
COMUS. Perhaps forestalling night prevented them.   285
LADY. How easy my misfortune is to hit!
COMUS. Imports their loss, beside the present need?
LADY. No less than if I should my brothers lose.
COMUS. Were they of manly prime, or youthful bloom?
LADY. As smooth as Hebe's[1] their unrazored lips.   290
COMUS. Two such I saw, what time the labored ox
In his loose traces from the furrow came,
And the swinked[2] hedger at his supper sat;
I saw them under a green mantling vine
That crawls along the side of yon small hill,   295
Plucking ripe clusters from the tender shoots;
Their port was more than human, as they stood;
I took it for a fairy vision
Of some gay creatures of the element
That in the colors of the rainbow live   300
And play i' th' plighted[3] clouds. I was awe-struck,
And as I passed, I worshipped; if those you seek,
It were a journey like the path to heaven
To help you find them.
LADY.   Gentle villager,
What readiest way would bring me to that place?   305

---

8. Pan and Silvanus were classical na-
ture-deities. The words "you are" are understood, after "unless."
9. The exchange of conversation by alternating lines of verse was popular in
Greek drama, under the name of sti-
chomythia; Milton imitates it here as
part of his complex of styles.
1. Hebe (pronounced Hee-bee) was goddess of youth and spring, as well as
cup-bearer to all the other gods.
2. Exhausted.
3. Plaited, interwoven.

COMUS. Due west it rises from this shrubby point.
LADY. To find out that, good shepherd, I suppose,
    In such a scant allowance of star-light,
    Would overtask the best land-pilot's art,
    Without the sure guess of well-practiced feet.   310
COMUS. I know each lane and every alley green,
    Dingle or bushy dell of this wild wood,
    And every bosky bourn[4] from side to side,
    My daily walks and ancient neighborhood,
    And if your stray attendance be yet lodged,   315
    Or shroud within these limits, I shall know
    Ere morrow wake or the low-roosted lark
    From her thatched pallet rouse; if otherwise,
    I can conduct you, lady, to a low
    But loyal cottage, where you may be safe   320
    Till further quest.
LADY.   Shepherd, I take thy word,
    And trust thy honest offered courtesy,
    Which oft is sooner found in lowly sheds
    With smoky rafters, than in tap'stry halls
    And courts of princes, where it first was named,[5]   325
    And yet is most pretended: In a place
    Less warranted than this or less secure
    I cannot be, that I should fear to change it.
    Eye me blessed providence, and square my trial
    To my proportioned strength. Shepherd lead on.—   330

The Two BROTHERS.

ELDER BROTHER. Unmuffle ye faint stars, and thou fair moon
    That wont'st to love the traveler's benison,
    Stoop thy pale visage through an amber cloud,
    And disinherit Chaos, that reigns here
    In double night of darkness and of shades;   335
    Or if your influence be quite dammed up
    With black usurping mists, some gentle taper,
    Though a rush candle from the wicker hole
    Of some clay habitation, visit us
    With thy long leveled rule of streaming light,   340
    And thou shalt be our star of Arcady
    Or Tyrian cynosure.[6]
SECOND BROTHER.   Or if our eyes
    Be barred that happiness, might we but hear
    The folded flocks penned in their wattled cotes,[7]
    Or sound of pastoral reed with oaten stops,   345

4. Wooded brook; "dingle": vale.
5. The lady's moralizing on the frequency of courtesy outside of courts expresses an easy commonplace, perhaps copied from Ariosto; Milton was not yet an ardent republican.
6. Ovid tells how Arca, Jove's son by the Arcadian princess Callisto, became the constellation Ursa Minor, one of whose elements is the Pole Star, called also the Tyrian Cynosure because Phoenician seamen from Tyre used it to navigate by. ("Cynosure": dog-tail, i.e., pointer.)
7. Pens made of reeds (wattles).

Or whistle from the lodge, or village cock
Count the night watches to his feathery dames,
'Twould be some solace yet, some little cheering
In this close dungeon of innumerous boughs.
But O that hapless virgin our lost sister,   350
Where may she wander now, whither betake her
From the chill dew, amongst rude burs and thistles?
Perhaps some cold bank is her bolster now,
Or 'gainst the rugged bark of some broad elm
Leans her unpillowed head fraught with sad fears.   355
What if in wild amazement and affright,
Or while we speak, within the direful grasp
Of savage hunger or of savage heat?
ELDER BROTHER. Peace, brother, be not over-exquisite
To cast the fashion of uncertain evils;   360
For grant they be so, while they rest unknown,
What need a man forestall his date of grief,
And run to meet what he would most avoid?
Or if they be but false alarms of fear,
How bitter is such self-delusion?   365
I do not think my sister so to seek,
Or so unprincipled in virtue's book
And the sweet peace that goodness bosoms ever,
As that the single want of light and noise
(Not being in danger, as I trust she is not)   370
Could stir the constant mood of her calm thoughts,
And put them into misbecoming plight.
Virtue could see to do what virtue would
By her own radiant light, though sun and moon
Were in the flat sea sunk. And wisdom's self   375
Oft seeks to sweet retired solitude,
Where with her best nurse contemplatión
She plumes her feathers, and lets grow her wings
That in the various bustle of resort
Were all to-ruffled, and sometimes impaired.   380
He that has light within his own clear breast
May sit i' th' center,[8] and enjoy bright day,
But he that hides a dark soul and foul thoughts
Benighted walks under the midday sun;
Himself is his own dungeon.
SECOND BROTHER.   'Tis most true   385
That musing meditation most affects
The pensive secrecy of desert cell,
Far from the cheerful haunt of men and herds,
And sits as safe as in a senate-house;
For who would rob a hermit of his weeds,   390
His few books, or his beads, or maple dish,
Or do his gray hairs any violence?

---

8. I.e., at the center of the universe, which is the center of the earth.

But beauty, like the fair Hesperian tree[9]
Laden with blooming gold, had need the guard
Of dragon watch with unenchanted eye,   395
To save her blossoms and defend her fruit
From the rash hand of bold incontinence.
You may as well spread out the unsunned heaps
Of miser's treasure by an outlaw's den,
And tell me it is safe, as bid me hope   400
Danger will wink on opportunity,
And let a single helpless maiden pass
Uninjured in this wild surrounding waste.
Of night or loneliness it recks me not,[1]
I fear the dread events that dog them both,   405
Lest some ill-greeting touch attempt the person
Of our unowned sister.
ELDER BROTHER.   I do not, brother,
Infer as if I thought my sister's state
Secure without all doubt or controversy:
Yet where an equal poise of hope and fear   410
Does arbitrate th' event, my nature is
That I incline to hope rather than fear,
And gladly banish squint suspicion.
My sister is not so defenseless left
As you imagine; she has a hidden strength   415
Which you remember not.
SECOND BROTHER.   What hidden strength,
Unless the strength of heaven, if you mean that?
ELDER BROTHER. I mean that too, but yet a hidden strength
Which if heaven gave it, may be termed her own;
'Tis chastity, my brother, chastity: 420
She that has that, is clad in complete steel,
And like a quivered nymph with arrows keen[2]
May trace huge forests and unharbored heaths,
Infamous hills and sandy perilous wilds,
Where through the sacred rays of chastity,   425
No savage fierce, bandit or mountaineer
Will dare to soil her virgin purity:
Yea there, where very desolation dwells,
By grots and caverns shagged with horrid shades,
She may pass on with unblenched majesty,   430
Be it not done in pride or in presumption.
Some say no evil thing that walks by night
In fog or fire, by lake or moorish fen,[3]
Blue meager hag or stubborn unlaid ghost

---

9. As one of his many labors, Hercules had to gather golden apples from the garden of the Hesperides, or Western Islands; they were said to be guarded by a ferocious, wakeful dragon.
1. It doesn't disturb me.
2. Diana, goddess of chastity, was followed to the hunt by nymphs armed with bow and arrow.
3. Will-o'-the-wisps and suchlike ghostly apparitions were thought to delight in luring simple travelers into deadly swamps ("moorish fens").

That breaks his magic chains at curfew time, 435
No goblin or swart fairy of the mine,
Hath hurtful power o'er true virginity.
Do ye believe me yet, or shall I call
Antiquity from the old schools of Greece
To testify the arms of chastity? 440
Hence had the huntress Dian her dread bow,
Fair silver-shafted queen forever chaste,
Wherewith she tamed the brinded lioness
And spotted mountain pard, but set at nought
The frivolous bolt of Cupid; gods and men 445
Feared her stern frown, and she was queen o' th' woods.
What was that snaky-headed Gorgon shield
That wise Minerva wore, unconquered virgin,[4]
Wherewith she freezed her foes to congealed stone,
But rigid looks of chaste austerity 450
And noble grace that dashed brute violence
With sudden adoration and blank awe?
So dear to heaven is saintly chastity,
That when a soul is found sincerely so,
A thousand liveried angels lackey her, 455
Driving far off each thing of sin and guilt,
And in clear dream and solemn vision
Tell her of things that no gross ear can hear,
Till oft converse with heavenly habitants
Begin to cast a beam on th' outward shape, 460
The unpolluted temple of the mind,
And turns it by degrees to the soul's essence,
Till all be made immortal: but when lust
By unchaste looks, loose gestures, and foul talk,
But most by lewd and lavish act of sin, 465
Lets in defilement to the inward parts,
The soul grows clotted by contagión,
Imbodies and imbrutes, till she quite lose
The divine property of her first being.
Such are those thick and gloomy shadows damp 470
Oft seen in charnel vaults and sepulchers,
Lingering and sitting by a new-made grave,
As loath to leave the body that it loved,
And linked itself by carnal sensuality
To a degenerate and degraded state. 475

SECOND BROTHER. How charming is divine philosophy!
  Not harsh and crabbéd as dull fools suppose,
  But musical as is Apollo's lute,
  And a perpetual feast of nectared sweets,
  Where no crude surfeit reigns.

ELDER BROTHER.   List, list, I hear 480
  Some far-off hallo break the silent air.

4. In *Iliad* V, Homer describes Minerva   Gorgon face on it; the Gorgon turned to
or Athena as carrying a shield with a   stone whoever looked on it.

SECOND BROTHER. Methought so too; what should it be?

ELDER BROTHER.   For certain
    Either some one like us night-foundered here,
    Or else some neighbor woodman, or at worst,
    Some roving robber calling to his fellows.   485

SECOND BROTHER. Heaven keep my sister! Again, again, and near!
    Best draw, and stand upon our guard.

ELDER BROTHER.   I'll hallo;
    If he be friendly he comes well, if not,
    Defense is a good cause, and heaven be for us.

        The ATTENDANT SPIRIT *habited like a shepherd.*

    That hallo I should know; what are you? speak;   490
    Come not too near, you fall on iron stakes[5] else.

SPIRIT. What voice is that? my young lord? speak again.

SECOND BROTHER. O brother, 'tis my father's shepherd sure.

ELDER BROTHER. Thyrsis? Whose artful strains have oft delayed
    The huddling brook to hear his madrigal,   495
    And sweetened every musk rose of the dale.
    How cam'st thou here, good swain? hath any ram
    Slipped from the fold, or young kid lost his dam,
    Or straggling wether the pent flock forsook?
    How couldst thou find this dark sequestered nook?   500

SPIRIT. O my loved master's heir and his next joy,
    I came not here on such a trivial toy
    As a strayed ewe, or to pursue the stealth
    Of pilfering wolf; not all the fleecy wealth
    That doth enrich these downs, is worth a thought   505
    To this my errand, and the care it brought.
    But O my virgin lady, where is she?
    How chance she is not in your company?

ELDER BROTHER. To tell thee sadly, shepherd, without blame,
    Or our neglect, we lost her as we came.   510

SPIRIT. Ay me unhappy! then my fears are true.

ELDER BROTHER. What fears good Thyrsis? Prithee briefly show.

SPIRIT. I'll tell ye; 'tis not vain or fabulous,
    (Though so esteemed by shallow ignorance)
    What the sage poets taught by th' heavenly muse   515
    Storied of old in high immortal verse
    Of dire Chimeras and enchanted isles,
    And rifted rocks whose entrance leads to hell,[6]
    For such there be, but unbelief is blind.
        Within the navel of this hideous wood,   520
    Immured in cypress shades, a sorcerer dwells,
    Of Bacchus and of Circe born, great Comus,
    Deep skilled in all his mother's witcheries,

---

5. Drawn swords.
6. The Attendant Spirit is fond of lecturing on mythology, which he presents as
a pathway to religious truth. Here the
chimeras (fabulous monsters), enchanted
islands, and portals to hell are mentioned to render more credible the existence, in 1634 Wales, of Comus, a classical deity.

And here to every thirsty wanderer,
By sly enticement gives his baneful cup,   525
With many murmurs mixed, whose pleasing poison
The visage quite transforms of him that drinks,
And the inglorious likeness of a beast
Fixes instead, unmolding reason's mintage
Charactered in the face; this have I learnt   530
Tending my flocks hard by i' th' hilly crofts[7]
That brow this bottom glade, whence night by night
He and his monstrous rout are heard to howl
Like stabled wolves, or tigers at their prey,
Doing abhorréd rites to Hecate   535
In their obscuréd haunts of inmost bowers.
Yet have they many baits and guileful spells
To inveigle and invite th' unwary sense
Of them that pass unweeting by the way.
This evening late, by then the chewing flocks   540
Had ta'en their supper on the savory herb
Of knotgrass dew-besprent, and were in fold,
I sat me down to watch upon a bank
With ivy canopied, and interwove
With flaunting honeysuckle, and began,   545
Wrapped in a pleasing fit of melancholy,
To meditate my rural minstrelsy,[8]
Till fancy had her fill; but ere a close
The wonted roar was up amidst the woods,
And filled the air with barbarous dissonance,   550
At which I ceased, and listened them a while,
Till an unusual stop of sudden silence
Gave respite to the drowsy-flighted steeds
That draw the litter of close-curtained sleep;[9]
At last a soft and solemn-breathing sound   555
Rose like a steam of rich distilled perfumes,
And stole upon the air, that even silence
Was took ere she was ware, and wished she might
Deny her nature, and be never more,
Still to be so displaced. I was all ear,   560
And took in strains that might create a soul
Under the ribs of death; but O ere long
Too well I did perceive it was the voice
Of my most honored lady, your dear sister.
Amazed I stood, harrowed with grief and fear,   565
And "O poor hapless nightingale," thought I,
"How sweet thou sing'st, how near the deadly snare!"
Then down the lawns I ran with headlong haste
Through paths and turnings often trod by day,
Till guided by mine ear I found the place   570

---

7. Hillside cottages; "brow": overlook.   9. Sleep, being sleepy, rides in a closed
8. Play my country pipe.   carriage drawn by drowsy horses.

Where that damned wizard hid in sly disguise
(For so by certain signs I knew) had met
Already, ere my best speed could prevent,
The aidless innocent lady his wished prey,
Who gently asked if he had seen such two,   575
Supposing him some neighbor villager;
Longer I durst not stay, but soon I guessed
Ye were the two she meant; with that I sprung
Into swift flight, till I had found you here,
But further know I not.

SECOND BROTHER.   O night and shades,   580
How are ye joined with hell in triple knot
Against th' unarmed weakness of one virgin
Alone and helpless! Is this the confidence
You gave me, brother?

ELDER BROTHER.   Yes, and keep it still,
Lean on it safely, not a period   585
Shall be unsaid for me: against the threats
Of malice or of sorcery, or that power
Which erring men call chance, this I hold firm;
Virtue may be assailed but never hurt,
Surprised by unjust force but not enthralled,   590
Yea, even that which mischief meant most harm
Shall in the happy trial prove most glory.
But evil on itself shall back recoil,
And mix no more with goodness, when at last
Gathered like scum, and settled to itself,   595
It shall be in eternal restless change
Self-fed and self-consumed;[1] if this fail,
The pillared firmament is rottenness,
And earth's base built on stubble. But come, let's on.
Against th' opposing will and arm of heaven   600
May never this just sword be lifted up,
But for that damn'd magician, let him be girt
With all the grisly legions that troop
Under the sooty flag of Acheron,
Harpies and Hydras, or all the monstrous forms   605
'Twixt Africa and Ind,[2] I'll find him out,
And force him to restore his purchase[3] back,
Or drag him by the curls to a foul death,
Curs'd as his life.

SPIRIT. Alas, good venturous youth,
I love thy courage yet and bold emprise,   610
But here thy sword can do thee little stead;
Far other arms and other weapons must
Be those that quell the might of hellish charms.

---

1. After the Last Judgment, evil will be cut off from the rest of the world and allowed to burn itself up.
2. "Acheron": one of the rivers of hell, here standing for hell itself. "Harpies" are filthy, voracious birds, "Hydras" many-headed monsters. Africa and India were thought to be the abode of many strange, terrifying creatures.
3. Prey.

He with his bare wand can unthread thy joints,
And crumble all thy sinews.

ELDER BROTHER.   Why, prithee shepherd,   615
How durst thou then thyself approach so near
As to make this relation?

SPIRIT.   Care and utmost shifts
How to secure the lady from surprisal,
Brought to my mind a certain shepherd lad[4]
Of small regard to see to, yet well skilled   620
In every virtuous plant and healing herb
That spreads her verdant leaf to th' morning ray.
He loved me well, and oft would beg me sing,
Which when I did, he on the tender grass
Would sit, and hearken even to ecstasy,   625
And in requital ope his leathern scrip,
And show me simple[5] of a thousand names,
Telling their strange and vigorous faculties;
Amongst the rest a small unsightly root,
But of divine effect, he culled me out;   630
The leaf was darkish, and had prickles on it,
But in another country, as he said,
Bore a bright golden flower, but not in this soil:
Unknown, and like esteemed, and the dull swain
Treads on it daily with his clouted shoon,   635
And yet more med'cinal is it than that moly
That Hermes once to wise Ulysses gave;[6]
He called it haemony,[7] and gave it me,
And bade me keep it as of sovereign use
'Gainst all enchantments, mildew blast, or damp,   640
Or ghastly furies' apparition;
I pursed it up, but little reckoning made,
Till now that this extremity compelled,
But now I find it true; for by this means
I knew the foul enchanter though disguised,   645
Entered the very lime-twigs of his spells,
And yet came off: if you have this about you
(As I will give you when we go) you may
Boldly assault the necromancer's hall;
Where if he be, with dauntless hardihood   650

4. Avid allegorizers say that the "simple shepherd lad" is Milton himself. How this improves the passage—if it does—each reader must decide on his own.
5. Herbs, so called because they were used straight, as nature made them, without any artificial preparation.
6. The moly used by Ulysses for protection against Circe (*Odyssey* X) was an imaginary magic vegetable, much discussed by Renaissance commentators, mythographers, and over-credulous botanists. Pictures of it abound in botanical textbooks, and theories about the source of its magic power were equally numerous. Generally, though not universally, it bore the allegorical significance of temperance, and Milton himself used it that way in his first Latin elegy.
7. Like moly, haemony can represent many qualities and concepts. Haemonia is Thessaly, a land of magic and witchcraft; the Greek word for "blood" (*haemo*, as in *haemoglobin*), is close to hand; and moly was often compared with a plant called "Christ's thorn," which Milton might have wanted to suggest. Some of these associations may imply religious, others moral significance.

And brandished blade rush on him, break his glass,
And shed the luscious liquor on the ground,
But seize his wand; though he and his cursed crew
Fierce sign of battle make, and menace high,
Or like the sons of Vulcan[8] vomit smoke,   655
Yet will they soon retire, if he but shrink.
ELDER BROTHER.   Thyrsis lead on apace, I'll follow thee,
And some good angel bear a shield before us.

*The scene changes to a stately palace set out with all manner of
deliciousness; soft music, tables spread with all dainties.* COMUS
appears with his rabble, and the LADY *set in an enchanted chair,
to whom he offers his glass, which she puts by, and goes about to
rise.*

COMUS. Nay lady, sit; if I but wave this wand,
Your nerves are all chained up in alabaster,   660
And you a statue; or as Daphne was,
Root-bound, that fled Apollo.[9]
LADY.   Fool, do not boast,
Thou canst not touch the freedom of my mind
With all thy charms, although this corporal rind
Thou hast immanacled, while heaven sees good.   665
COMUS. Why are you vexed, lady? why do you frown?
Here dwell no frowns, nor anger, from these gates
Sorrow flies far: See, here be all the pleasures
That fancy can beget on youthful thoughts,
When the fresh blood grows lively, and returns   670
Brisk as the April buds in primrose-season.
And first behold this cordial julep here,
That flames and dances in his crystal bounds
With spirits of balm and fragrant syrups mixed.
Not that Nepenthes which the wife of Thone   675
In Egypt gave to Jove-born Helena[1]
Is of such power to stir up joy as this,
To life so friendly, or so cool to thirst.
Why should you be so cruel to yourself,
And to those dainty limbs which nature lent   680
For gentle usage and soft delicacy?
But you invert the covenants of her trust,
And harshly deal like an ill borrower
With that which you received on other terms,
Scorning the unexempt condition   685
By which all mortal frailty must subsist,
Refreshment after toil, ease after pain,
That have been tired all day without repast,
And timely rest have wanted; but, fair virgin,

---

8. The "sons of Vulcan" (fire, soot, ashes) live in volcanoes and other erupting caverns, to which they retreat after a first fierce onslaught.
9. Daphne, pursued by amorous Apollo, turned into a laurel tree to escape him

(Ovid, *Metamorphoses* I).
1. In *Odyssey* IV, Menelaus describes how he and Helen, returning from Troy, were entertained with a drink of nepenthe by the Egyptian Thone and his Greek wife.

This will restore all soon.
LADY.   'Twill not, false traitor,   690
'Twill not restore the truth and honesty
That thou hast banished from thy tongue with lies.
Was this the cottage and the safe abode
Thou told'st me of? What grim aspécts are these,
These ugly-headed monsters? Mercy guard me!   695
Hence with thy brewed enchantments, foul deceiver;
Hast thou betrayed my credulous innocence
With vizored falsehood and base forgery,
And wouldst thou seek again to trap me here
With lickerish[2] baits fit to ensnare a brute?   700
Were it a draught for Juno when she banquets,
I would not taste thy treasonous offer; none
But such as are good men can give good things,
And that which is not good, is not delicious
To a well-governed and wise appetite.   705
COMUS. O foolishness of men! that lend their ears
To those budge[3] doctors of the Stoic fur,
And fetch their precepts from the Cynic tub,
Praising the lean and sallow abstinence.
Wherefore did nature pour her bounties forth   710
With such a full and unwithdrawing hand,
Covering the earth with odors, fruits, and flocks,
Thronging the seas with spawn innumerable,
But all to please and sate the curious taste?
And set to work millions of spinning worms   715
That in their green shops weave the smooth-haired silk
To deck her sons; and that no corner might
Be vacant of her plenty, in her own loins
She hutched th' all-worshipped ore and precious gems
To store her children with. If all the world   720
Should in a pet of temperance feed on pulse,[4]
Drink the clear stream, and nothing wear but frieze,
Th'all-giver would be unthanked, would be unpraised,
Not half his riches known, and yet despised,
And we should serve him as a grudging master,   725
As a penurious niggard of his wealth,
And live like nature's bastards, not her sons,
Who would be quite surcharged with her own weight,
And strangled with her waste fertility;
Th' earth cumbered, and the winged air darked with plumes,   730
The herds would over-multitude their lords,
The sea o'erfraught would swell, and th' unsought diamonds
Would so emblaze the forehead of the deep,
And so bestud with stars, that they below

2. Delicious, but with the added implication of "lustful."
4. Lamb's wool, used to line academic gowns. Comus imagines the different schools of philosophy distinguished by different trims on their gowns—naturally, the cynics would have the coarsest. They get their lessons from Diogenes, who showed his contempt for material possessions by living in a tub.
4. Beans; "frieze": coarse woolen cloth.

Would grow inured to light, and come at last 735
To gaze upon the sun with shameless brows.[5]
List lady, be not coy, and be not cozened
With that same vaunted name virginity;
Beauty is nature's coin, must not be hoarded,
But must be current, and the good thereof 740
Consists in mutual and partaken bliss,
Unsavory in th' enjoyment of itself.
If you let slip time, like a neglected rose
It withers on the stalk with languished head.
Beauty is nature's brag, and must be shown 745
In courts, at feasts, and high solemnities
Where most may wonder at the workmanship;
It is for homely features to keep home,
They had their name thence; coarse complexións
And cheeks of sorry grain[6] will serve to ply 750
The sampler, and to tease the housewife's wool.
What need a vermeil-tinctured lip for that,
Love-darting eyes, or tresses like the morn?
There was another meaning in these gifts,
Think what, and be advised; you are but young yet. 755
LADY. I had not thought to have unlocked my lips
In this unhallowed air, but that this juggler
Would think to charm my judgment, as mine eyes,
Obtruding false rules pranked in reason's garb.
I hate when vice can bolt[6a] her arguments, 760
And virtue has no tongue to check her pride:
Impostor, do not charge most innocent nature,
As if she would her children should be riotous
With her abundance; she, good cateress,
Means her provision only to the good 765
That live according to her sober laws
And holy dictate of spare temperance.
If every just man that now pines with want
Had but a moderate and beseeming share
Of that which lewdly-pampered luxury 770
Now heaps upon some few with vast excess,
Nature's full blessings would be well dispensed
In unsuperfluous even proportion,
And she no whit encumbered with her store;
And then the giver would be better thanked, 775
His praise due paid, for swinish gluttony
Ne'er looks to heaven amidst his gorgeous feast,
But with besotted base ingratitude

5. Gold and diamonds were thought to "grow" underground by the secret influence of the sun; if they grew too much, Comus argues, "they below" (he carefully doesn't say who) would get used to the bright lights and come out.
6. Comus' entire argument, especially the comparison with a rose, recapitulates the familiar Renaissance theme of *carpe diem*, "seize the day." "Sorry grain": drab colors; "vermeil-tinctured": scarlet-colored. The argument that ugly girls are good enough for wives but pretty girls can go partying has something deliberately sophistical about it.
6a. Blurt out.

Crams, and blasphemes his feeder. Shall I go on?
Or have I said enough? To him that dares   780
Arm his profane tongue with contemptuous words
Against the sun-clad power of chastity
Fain would I something say, yet to what end?
Thou hast nor ear nor soul to apprehend
The sublime notion and high mystery   785
That must be uttered to unfold the sage
And serious doctrine of virginity,
And thou art worthy that thou shouldst not know
More happiness than this thy present lot.
Enjoy your dear wit and gay rhetoric   790
That hath so well been taught her dazzling fence,[7]
Thou art not fit to hear thyself convinced;
Yet should I try, the uncontrolléd worth
Of this pure cause would kindle my rapt spirits
To such a flame of sacred vehemence,   795
That dumb things would be moved to sympathize,
And the brute earth would lend her nerves, and shake,
Till all thy magic structures reared so high,
Were shattered into heaps o'er thy false head.
COMUS. She fables not, I feel that I do fear   800
Her words set off by some superior power:
And though not mortal, yet a cold shuddering dew
Dips me all o'er, as when the wrath of Jove
Speaks thunder and the chains of Erebus[8]
To some of Saturn's crew. I must dissemble,   805
And try her yet more strongly. Come, no more,
This is mere moral babble, and direct
Against the canon laws of our foundation;[9]
I must not suffer this, yet 'tis but the lees
And settlings of a melancholy blood;   810
But this will cure all straight, one sip of this
Will bathe the drooping spirits in delight
Beyond the bliss of dreams. Be wise, and taste.—

The BROTHERS *rush in with swords drawn, wrest his glass out of his hand, and break it against the ground; his rout[1] make sign of resistance, but are all driven in; the* ATTENDANT SPIRIT *comes in.*

SPIRIT. What, have you let the false enchanter scape?
O ye mistook, ye should have snatched his wand   815
And bound him fast; without his rod reversed,
And backward mutters of dissevering power,
We cannot free the lady that sits here
In stony fetters fixed and motionless;
Yet stay, be not disturbed, now I bethink me,   820
Some other means I have which may be used,

7. The art of fence, wordplay by analogy with sword play.
8. Jove killed his father Saturn and threw into hell ("Erebus") the whole generation of Titans and Giants who had supported the old ruler.
9. Comus pretends that his religion of lust and greed is a "foundation" like a monastery and is ruled by its own canon laws. "Lees": dregs.
1. Crowd of followers.

Which once of Meliboeus[2] old I learnt,
The soothest shepherd that ere piped on plains.
   There is a gentle nymph not far from hence,
That with moist curb sways the smooth Severn stream,   825
Sabrina is her name, a virgin pure;
Whilom she was the daughter of Locrine,
That had the scepter from his father Brute.[3]
She, guiltless damsel, flying the mad pursuit
Of her enragéd stepdam Gwendolen,   830
Commended her fair innocence to the flood
That stayed her flight with his cross-flowing course.
The water nymphs that in the bottom played,
Held up their pearléd wrists and took her in,
Bearing her straight to aged Nereus' hall,[4]   835
Who piteous of her woes, reared her lank head,
And gave her to his daughters to imbathe
In nectared lavers strewed with asphodel,
And through the porch and inlet of each sense
Drop in ambrosial oils till she revived   840
And underwent a quick immortal change,
Made goddess of the river; still she retains
Her maiden gentleness, and oft at eve
Visits the herds along the twilight meadows,
Helping all urchin blasts,[5] and ill-luck signs   845
That the shrewd meddling elf delights to make,
Which she with precious vialed liquors heals.
For which the shepherds at their festivals
Carol her goodness loud in rustic lays,
And throw sweet garland wreaths into her stream   850
Of pansies, pinks, and gaudy daffodils.
And, as the old swain said, she can unlock
The clasping charm and thaw the numbing spell,
If she be right invoked in warbled song,
For maidenhood she loves, and will be swift   855
To aid a virgin, such as was herself,
In hard-besetting need. This will I try
And add the power of some adjuring verse.

SONG

    Sabrina fair
        Listen where thou art sitting   860
    Under the glassy, cool, translucent wave,

---

2. "Meliboeus" is a traditional shepherd's name; it's doubtful if Milton had a particular person in mind, but it may have been Spenser.
3. The story of Sabrina was retold by Spenser (*Faerie Queene* II) from an original medieval version by Geoffrey of Monmouth. She was a girl descended through Locrinus from Brute (Brutus), the Trojan founder of Britain; her wicked stepmother Gwendolen so persecuted her that she drowned in the Severn, thus giving the river her name.
4. Nereus, an ancient sea-god, took care of her corpse: his daughters supervised her change into the patron saint of the river.
5. Plant diseases supposed to be spread by hedgehogs ("urchins"). The "meddling elf": Robin Goodfellow, or Puck.

In twisted braids of lilies knitting
The loose train of thy amber-dropping hair;
   Listen for dear honor's sake,
   Goddess of the silver lake,   865
      Listen and save.
Listen and appear to us
In name of great Oceanus,
By the earth-shaking Neptune's mace
And Tethys' grave majestic pace,   870
By hoary Nereus' wrinkled look,
And the Carpathian wizard's hook,
By scaly Triton's winding shell,
And old soothsaying Glaucus' spell,
By Leucothea's lovely hands   875
And her son that rules the strands,
By Thetis' tinsel-slipper'd feet,
And the songs of Sirens sweet,
By dead Parthenope's dear tomb,
And fair Ligea's golden comb,   880
Wherewith she sits on diamond rocks
Sleeking her soft alluring locks,
By all the Nymphs that nightly dance
Upon thy streams with wily glance,
Rise, rise, and heave thy rosy head   885
From thy coral-paven bed,
And bridle in thy headlong wave,[6]
Till thou our summons answered have.
      Listen and save.

SABRINA *rises, attended by water-nymphs, and sings:*

   By the rushy-fringéd bank,   890
Where grows the willow and the osier dank,
   My sliding chariot stays,
Thick set with agate and the azurn sheen
Of turquoise blue and emerald green
   That in the channel strays,   895
Whilst from off the waters fleet
Thus I set my printless feet
O'er the cowslip's velvet head,
   That bends not as I tread;
Gentle swain at thy request   900
   I am here.

SPIRIT. Goddess dear
   We implore thy powerful hand

---

6. The incantation invokes numerous wa-
ter-deities: Oceanus and his wife Tethys,
Neptune the sea-god and Triton his herald, Proteus the "Carpathian wizard"
(Virgil says in *Georgic* IV that he lived
in the Carpathian sea between Rhodes
and Crete), and Glaucus, whom Spenser
mentions as a soothsayer (*Faerie Queene*
IV.11). Leucothea was a sea-nymph who
rescued Odysseus from drowning (*Odyssey* V); Thetis was the sea-nymph
mother of Achilles; Parthenope and
Ligea were sirens who lived near Naples.

To undo the charmèd band
Of true virgin here distressed   905
Through the force and through the wile
Of unblest enchanter vile.
SABRINA. Shepherd 'tis my office best
To help ensnarèd chastity;
Brightest lady look on me,   910
Thus I sprinkle on thy breast
Drops that from my fountain pure
I have kept of precious cure,
Thrice upon thy finger's tip,
Thrice upon thy rubied lip;   915
Next this marble venomed seat
Smeared with gums of glutinous heat
I touch with chaste palms moist and cold.
Now the spell hath lost his hold;
And I must haste ere morning hour   920
To wait in Amphitrite's bower.[7]

    SABRINA *descends, and the* LADY *rises out of her seat.*

SPIRIT. Virgin, daughter of Locrine
Sprung of old Anchises' line,[8]
May thy brimmèd waves for this
Their full tribute never miss   925
From a thousand petty rills,
That tumble down the snowy hills:
Summer drouth or singed air
Never scorch thy tresses fair,
Nor wet October's torrent flood   930
Thy molten crystal fill with mud;
May thy billows roll ashore
The beryl and the golden ore,
May thy lofty head be crowned
With many a tower and terrace round,   935
And here and there thy banks upon
With groves of myrrh and cinnamon.
    Come lady, while heaven lends us grace,
Let us fly this cursèd place,
Lest the sorcerer us entice   940
With some other new device.
Not a waste or needless sound
Till we come to holier ground.
I shall be your faithful guide.
Through this gloomy covert wide,   945
And not many furlongs thence
Is your father's residence,

---

7. Amphitrite was the wife of Neptune.
8. Anchises, the father of Aeneas, was also—by the kind of fantastic genealogy easily accessible to Renaissance writers —an ancestor of Brutus and hence of Sabrina.

Where this night are met in state
Many a friend to gratulate
His wishéd presence, and beside   950
All the swains that there abide,
With jigs and rural dance resort.
We shall catch them at their sport,
And our sudden coming there
Will double all their mirth and cheer;   955
Come let us haste, the stars grow high,
But night sits monarch yet in the mid sky.

The scene changes, presenting Ludlow town and the President's[9]
castle, then come in country-dancers, after them the ATTENDANT
SPIRIT, *with the two* BROTHERS *and the* LADY.

SONG

SPIRIT. Back shepherds, back, enough your play,
          Till next sun-shine holiday;
          Here be without duck or nod[1]   960
          Other trippings to be trod
          Of lighter toes, and such court guise
          As Mercury did first devise
          With the mincing Dryades[2]
          On the lawns and on the leas.   965

This second song presents them to their father and mother.

          Noble lord, and lady bright,
          I have brought ye new delight,
          Here behold so goodly grown
          Three fair branches of your own.
          Heaven hath timely tried their youth,   970
          Their faith, their patience, and their truth,
          And sent them here through hard assays
          With a crown of deathless praise,
              To triumph in victorious dance
          O'er sensual folly and intemperance.   975

          The dances ended, the Spirit epiloguizes.

SPIRIT. To the ocean now I fly,
          And those happy climes that lie
          Where day never shuts his eye,
          Up in the broad fields of the sky:
          There I suck the liquid air   980
          All amidst the gardens fair
          Of Hesperus, and his daughters three
          That sing about the golden tree:[3]

9. The Earl of Bridgewater was newly appointed Lord President of Wales.
1. Characteristic motions of peasant dances, as opposed to the smoother figures of court dances. After the folk, the gentry display their skill.
2. Mercury, footing it with the "Dryades" (wood-nymphs), invented court-dancing.
3. The tree in the garden of the Hesperides, containing the golden apples.

Along the crispéd shades and bowers
Revels the spruce and jocund spring, 985
The graces and the rosy-bosomed hours,
Thither all their bounties bring,
That there eternal summer dwells,
And west winds with musky wing
About the cedarn alleys fling 990
Nard and cassia's balmy smells.[4]
Iris there with humid bow,
Waters the odorous banks that blow
Flowers of more mingled hue
Than her purfled scarf can shew, 995
And drenches with Elysian dew
(List mortals, if your ears be true)
Beds of hyacinth and roses
Where young Adonis oft reposes,[5]
Waxing well of his deep wound 1000
In slumber soft, and on the ground
Sadly sits th' Assyrian queen;
But far above in spangled sheen
Celestial Cupid her fam'd son advanced,
Holds his dear Psyche sweet entranced 1005
After her wandering labors long,
Till free consent the gods among
Make her his eternal bride,
And from her fair unspotted side
Two blissful twins are to be born, 1010
Youth and Joy; so Jove hath sworn.

But now my task is smoothly done,
I can fly, or I can run
Quickly to the green earth's end
Where the bowed welkin[6] slow doth bend, 1015
And from thence can soar as soon
To the corners of the moon.

Mortals that would follow me,
Love virtue, she alone is free,
She can teach ye how to climb 1020
Higher than the sphery chime;
Or if virtue feeble were,
Heaven itself would stoop to her.[7]

1634   1637

4. Aromatic roots and barks. Iris, goddess of the rainbow, wears a "purfled," i.e., embroidered, scarf.
5. Spenser describes (in *Faerie Queene* III.6) the Garden of Adonis, a kind of half-Heaven where Venus preserves, after his death, her unfortunate lover Adonis. Because this happened in the Middle East, she is "the Assyrian queen." Cupid and Psyche are another pair of mythical lovers, unfortunate on this earth, translated to another sphere, and there spiritualized to illustrate the reconciliation of love and virtue.
6. Heaven.
7. Here again critical debate has flourished. Has heaven in fact "stooped" (like a falcon dropping to its prey or a tall man bending down) to help the young people—or have they made it on their own? If grace has combined with virtue in bringing the lady safely to her father's house, in what proportion are these two energies to be seen as operating?

Lycidas   This poem is a pastoral elegy; that is, it uses the sometimes artificial imagery supplied by an idyllic shepherd's existence to bewail the loss of a friend. Among its many predecessors in the Renaissance and in classical antiquity are poems by Spenser, Ronsard, Castiglione, Mantuan, Petrarch, Virgil, Theocritus, Moschus, and Bion; its successors include poems like *Adonais* by Shelley and *Thyrsis* by Matthew Arnold. T. P. Harrison and H. J. Leon have collected in *The Pastoral Elegy* (1939) a selection of poems from the tradition.

All pastoral poems enjoy the privilege of saying something about the world as a whole while seeming to talk simply of an artificial play-society; they are irresistibly allegorical. They have certain conventions—the swain (i.e., the shepherd) is ignorant but unspoiled, naturally virtuous, inherently poetic; life is pleasant and easy, yet just for this reason the basic human preoccupations stand out. The pastoral elegy has a further list of conventions—a history of past friendship, a questioning of destiny, a procession of mourners, a laying-on of flowers, a consolation, and usually a refrain. Milton adapted all but the last of these to *Lycidas*.

Edward King, who was the occasion of the poem if not its subject, was a fellow student of Milton's at Cambridge. Milton says he was a poet, and he was in the church. While proceeding to his new parish in Ireland, he was drowned, in 1637; and Milton joined with his schoolfellows, the following year, to produce a little memorial volume. *Justa Edouardo King* includes 35 poems, mostly in Latin; only *Lycidas* is of literary consequence.

It is written in a flowing, extended manner, with many run-on lines and great impetus, predominantly in pentameter, but with many variations of line length, and an irregular rhyme scheme including ten unrhymed lines and two perfectly formed stanzas of ottava rima. Many of these technical qualities are reminiscent of the Italian *canzone* or song, but most of them had been exemplified previously in Spenser's *Epithalamion*.

There are usually taken to be three explicit climaxes in *Lycidas*, each having to do with an aspect of the shepherd's life and with a problem which Milton wished to pose regarding the meaning of existence. Apollo answers his first question about the reward of poetry; St. Peter answers a second question, about the spiritual shepherd who betrays his flock; and finally Lycidas is translated into the Christian Paradise, to be at one with the Lamb of God, the Good Shepherd, the supreme giver of poetic fame, and the proper subject of all song. Subordinate patterns of imagery include vegetation and nature deities, water and water gods, who serve an immense variety of purposes.

Lycidas

IN THIS MONODY[1] THE AUTHOR BEWAILS A LEARNED FRIEND,
UNFORTUNATELY DROWNED IN HIS PASSAGE FROM CHESTER
ON THE IRISH SEAS, 1637. AND BY OCCASION FORETELLS
THE RUIN OF OUR CORRUPTED CLERGY,
THEN IN THEIR HEIGHT.

Yet once more, O ye laurels, and once more
Ye myrtles brown, with ivy never sere,[2]
I come to pluck your berries harsh and crude,[3]
And with forced fingers rude,
Shatter your leaves before the mellowing year.   5
Bitter constraint, and sad occasion dear,[4]
Compels me to disturb your season due;
For Lycidas is dead, dead ere his prime,
Young Lycidas, and hath not left his peer.
Who would not sing for Lycidas? He knew   10
Himself to sing, and build the lofty rhyme.
He must not float upon his watery bier
Unwept, and welter to the parching wind,
Without the meed[5] of some melodious tear.
  Begin then, sisters of the sacred well[6]   15
That from beneath the seat of Jove doth spring,
Begin, and somewhat loudly sweep the string.
Hence with denial vain, and coy excuse;
So may some gentle Muse
With lucky words favor my destined urn,[7]   20
And as he passes turn,
And bid fair peace be to my sable shroud.
For we were nursed upon the selfsame hill,
Fed the same flock, by fountain, shade, and rill.
  Together both, ere the high lawns[8] appeared   25
Under the opening eyelids of the morn,
We drove afield, and both together heard
What time the grayfly winds her sultry horn,[9]
Battening our flocks with the fresh dews of night,
Oft till the star that rose at evening bright   30

1. A song sung in Greek drama by a single voice. This Miltonic headnote was added in the edition of 1645.
2. "Laurels" for the crown of poetry given by Apollo; "myrtles" for the undying love granted by Venus; "ivy," the plant of Bacchus. All three plants are evergreens associated with poetic inspiration.
3. Unripe.
4. Heartfelt, profoundly moving; but also, in the 17th century, with overtones of "dire."
5. Reward.
6. The nine sister Muses were reported to dwell by various springs or "wells"; most likely Milton had in mind that of Aganippe near Mt. Helicon.
7. The speaker suggests that if he sings for Lycidas, "some gentle Muse" (i.e., poet) may some day sing for him.
8. Upland pastures.
9. I.e., heard the grayfly when she buzzes ("winds her sultry horn"). "Battening": feeding.

Toward Heaven's descent had sloped his westering wheel.
Meanwhile the rural ditties were not mute,
Tempered to th' oaten flute,[1]
Rough satyrs danced, and fauns with cloven heel
From the glad sound would not be absent long,   35
And old Damoetas[2] loved to hear our song.
    But O the heavy change, now thou art gone,
Now thou art gone, and never must return!
Thee, shepherd, thee the woods and desert caves,
With wild thyme and the gadding[3] vine o'ergrown,   40
And all their echoes mourn.
The willows and the hazel copses green
Shall now no more be seen,
Fanning their joyous leaves to thy soft lays.
As killing as the canker[4] to the rose,   45
Or taint-worm to the weanling herds that graze,
Or frost to flowers that their gay wardrobe wear,
When first the white thorn blows;[5]
Such, Lycidas, thy loss to shepherd's ear.
    Where were ye, nymphs,[6] when the remorseless deep   50
Closed o'er the head of your loved Lycidas?
For neither were ye playing on the steep,
Where your old Bards, the famous Druids[7] lie,
Nor on the shaggy top of Mona high,[8]
Nor yet where Deva spreads her wizard stream: 55
Ay me! I fondly dream—
Had ye been there—for what could that have done?
What could the Muse[9] herself that Orpheus bore,
The Muse herself, for her inchanting[1] son
Whom universal Nature did lament,   60
When by the rout[2] that made the hideous roar,
His gory visage down the stream was sent,
Down the swift Hebrus to the Lesbian shore?
    Alas! What boots[3] it with incessant care
To tend the homely slighted shepherd's trade,   65
And strictly meditate the thankless Muse?[4]

1. Traditional Panpipes, played by shepherds.
2. A type name from pastoral poetry, possibly referring to some specific tutor at Cambridge.
3. Straggling.
4. Cankerworm.
5. Blossoms (as in the surviving expression, "full-blown").
6. Nature deities.
7. The Druids, priestly poet-kings of Celtic Britain, worshiped the forces of nature. They lie dead in their burying ground on the mountain ("steep") Kerig-y-Druidion in Wales.
8. "Mona" is the island of Anglesey. "Deva" is the river Dee in Cheshire. The Dee was magic ("wizard") because the size and position of its shifting stream foretold prosperity or dearth for the land. All the places mentioned in lines 52–55 are in the West Country, near where King drowned.
9. Calliope, Muse of epic poetry, was the mother of Orpheus.
1. "Inchanting" implies both song and magic; the root word survives as "incantation."
2. Orpheus was torn to pieces by a mob ("rout") of screaming Thracian women, who threw his gory head into the river Hebrus, down which it floated, still singing, and out to Lesbos in the Aegean. The fate of Orpheus and the Druids suggests that nature everywhere is indifferent to the destruction of the poet.
3. Profits.
4. Study to write poetry (the phrase is Virgil's).

Were it not better done as others use,
To sport with Amaryllis in the shade,
Or with the tangles of Neaera's hair?[5]
Fame is the spur that the clear spirit doth raise   70
(That last infirmity of noble mind)
To scorn delights, and live laborious days;
But the fair guerdon[6] when we hope to find,
And think to burst out into sudden blaze,
Comes the blind Fury[7] with th' abhorréd shears,   75
And slits the thin spun life. "But not the praise,"
Phoebus[8] replied, and touched my trembling ears;
"Fame is no plant that grows on mortal soil,
Not in the glistering foil[9]
Set off to th' world, nor in broad rumor lies,   80
But lives and spreads aloft by those pure eyes,
And perfect witness of all-judging Jove;
As he pronounces lastly on each deed,
Of so much fame in Heaven expect thy meed."

    O fountain Arethuse,[1] and thou honored flood,   85
Smooth-sliding Mincius, crowned with vocal reeds,
That strain I heard was of a higher mood.
But now my oat[2] proceeds,
And listens to the herald of the sea[3]
That came in Neptune's plea.   90
He asked the waves, and asked the felon winds,
"What hard mishap hath doomed this gentle swain?"
And questioned every gust of rugged wings
That blows from off each beakéd promontory;
They knew not of his story,   95
And sage Hippotades[4] their answer brings,
That not a blast was from his dungeon strayed,
The air was calm, and on the level brine,
Sleek Panope[5] with all her sisters played.
It was that fatal and perfidious bark   100
Built in th' eclipse,[6] and rigged with curses dark,

---

5. "Amaryllis" and "Neaera," conventional names for pretty nymphs, a passing hour's diversion for idle shepherds.
6. Reward.
7. Atropos, one of the three Fates, bearing scissors with which she cuts the thread of human life. Milton, to suggest the bitterness of death, makes her an avenging Fury.
8. Phoebus Apollo, god of poetic inspiration. Touching the ears of one's hearers was a traditional Roman way of asking them to remember something that had been said (Virgil, *Eclogues* VI; Horace, *Satires* I.ix.77).
9. Cheap, flashy metal, used to add glitter to glass gems.
1. Arethusa was a fountain in Sicily, Mincius a river in Lombardy, the former associated with the pastorals of Theocritus, the latter with those of Virgil. Arethusa was originally a nymph who went bathing in the river Alpheus, in Arcadian Greece. The river god grew enamored, and gave chase; she dove into the ocean and fled undersea to Sicily, where she came up as a fountain. Milton plays here with the idea of his pastoral going underground while the "strain of a higher mood" (line 87) is heard.
2. Pipe, hence song.
3. Neptune's "herald" is Triton, pleading his master's innocence in the death of Lycidas.
4. Aeolus, god of winds, and son of Hippotas.
5. The chief Nereid or sea nymph.
6. I.e., time of the worst possible luck.

That sunk so low that sacred head of thine.

    Next Camus,[7] reverend sire, went footing slow,
His mantle hairy, and his bonnet sedge,
Inwrought with figures dim, and on the edge   105
Like to that sanguine flower inscribed with woe.[8]
"Ah! who hath reft," quoth he, "my dearest pledge?"
    Last came and last did go
The pilot of the Galilean lake,[9]
Two massy keys he bore of metals twain   110
(The golden opes, the iron shuts amain[1]).
He shook his mitered locks,[2] and stern bespake:
"How well could I have spared for thee, young swain,
Enow[3] of such as for their bellies' sake,
Creep and intrude, and climb into the fold!   115
Of other care they little reckoning make,
Than how to scramble at the shearers' feast,
And shove away the worthy bidden guest.
Blind mouths![4] That scarce themselves know how to hold
A sheep-hook,[5] or have learned aught else the least   120
That to the faithful herdsman's art belongs!
What recks it them?[6] What need they? They are sped;
And when they list,[7] their lean and flashy songs
Grate on their scrannel[8] pipes of wretched straw.
The hungry sheep look up, and are not fed,   125
But swoln with wind, and the rank mist they draw,
Rot inwardly, and foul contagion spread,
Besides what the grim wolf with privy paw[9]
Daily devours apace, and nothing said.
But that two-handed engine at the door[1]   130
Stands ready to smite once, and smite no more."
    Return, Alpheus,[2] the dread voice is past,
That shrunk thy streams; return, Sicilian muse,

---

7. God of the river Cam (properly, Granta), representing the ancient University of Cambridge, but slow and shaggy like the stream.

8. The bonnet and mantle of Camus have marks of woe on the edge like the *AI AI* supposedly found on the hyacinth, a "sanguine flower" sprung from the blood of a youth killed accidentally by Apollo.

9. St. Peter, originally a fisherman on Lake Tiberias in Galilee, was first founder and bishop of the Christian church; his keys open and shut the gates to heaven.

1. Literally "in full force," "exceedingly"; in this context, "for good," "once and for all."

2. He wears the bishop's miter.

3. An old plural form of "enough," used here with contemptuous intensification, as if to say, "enough and more than enough."

4. This audacious metaphor, as of tapeworms, takes on new depth when one notes that the word *episcopus* (bishop)

originally meant "over-seer" and a "pastor" is properly one who feeds his flock.

5. The bishop's staff, or crozier, is made in the form of a shepherd's crook.

6. What do they care? "They are sped": i.e., they have prospered in a worldly sense; but also, "their doom is sealed."

7. Choose (that is, choose to play on their pipes, as shepherds should); but with the secondary meaning of "listen."

8. Harsh, meager. Milton's is the first recorded literary use of the word in English; it existed previously only in a North-Country dialect.

9. I.e., Roman Catholicism, whose agents operated in secret.

1. Many guesses as to the specific meaning of the "two-handed engine" are on record; it may be St. Peter's keys, the two houses of Parliament, or a big sword, but there is no harm in letting it remain an indistinct, apocalyptic instrument of revenge.

2. With the return of Alpheus, the pastoral mode of the poem revives (see

And call the vales, and bid them hither cast
Their bells and flowerets of a thousand hues.   135
Ye valleys low where the mild whispers use,[3]
Of shades and wanton winds, and gushing brooks,
On whose fresh lap the swart star[4] sparely looks,
Throw hither all your quaint enameled eyes,
That on the green turf suck the honeyed showers,   140
And purple all the ground with vernal flowers.
Bring the rathe[5] primrose that forsaken dies.
The tufted crow-toe, and pale jessamine,
The white pink, and the pansy freaked[6] with jet,
The glowing violet,   145
The musk-rose, and the well attired woodbine.
With cowslips wan that hang the pensive head,
And every flower that sad embroidery wears:
Bid amaranthus[7] all his beauty shed,
And daffadillies fill their cups with tears,   150
To strew the laureate hearse[8] where Lycid lies.
For so to interpose a little ease,
Let our frail thoughts dally with false surmise.[9]
Ay me! Whilst thee the shores and sounding seas
Wash far away, where'er thy bones are hurled,   155
Whether beyond the stormy Hebrides,[1]
Where thou perhaps under the whelming tide
Visit'st the bottom of the monstrous world;
Or whether thou, to our moist vows denied,
Sleep'st by the fable of Bellerus old,[2]   160
Where the great vision of the guarded mount
Looks toward Namancos and Bayona's hold;[3]
Look homeward angel now, and melt with ruth:[4]
And, O ye dolphins,[5] waft the hapless youth.
    Weep no more, woeful shepherds, weep no more,   165
For Lycidas your sorrow is not dead,

above, lines 85–87), and a catalogue of flowers serves, as in Castiglione's *Alcon*, to "interpose a little ease."

3. I.e., are used or accustomed to be heard.

4. The Dog Star, Sirius, which during the heats of late summer "looks sparely" (witheringly) on the vegetation.

5. Early.

6. Flecked (the early verb survives in our word "freckle").

7. The amaranth is an imaginary flower that never fades; but for Lycidas it will.

8. Bier decked with laurels (see line 1).

9. The "false surmise" is that the body of Lycidas has been recovered and can receive Christian burial.

1. Islands off the coast of Scotland, representing the northern terminus of the Irish Sea.

2. The fabulous giant Bellerus is supposed to lie buried on Land's End in Cornwall.

3. St. Michael's Mount, in Cornwall, from which the archangel is envisioned as looking south, over miles of open Atlantic, across the Bay of Biscay, to Bayona and the stronghold of Namancos in northern Spain, where the historical Catholic enemy of Protestant England lay entrenched.

4. Michael is implored to look homeward, relaxing his stern guard for a moment of grief and pity ("ruth").

5. Dolphins, admirable sea beasts, brought the Greek poet Arion safely ashore for love of his verses, and also wafted the dead body of Melicertes to land, where he was promptly transformed to a sea god, Palaemon.

Sunk though he be beneath the watery floor,
So sinks the day-star[6] in the ocean bed,
And yet anon repairs his drooping head,
And tricks[7] his beams, and with new-spangled ore,   170
Flames in the forehead of the morning sky:
So Lycidas sunk low, but mounted high,
Through the dear might of him that walked the waves,
Where other groves, and other streams along,
With nectar pure his oozy locks he laves,   175
And hears the unexpressive nuptial song,[8]
In the blest kingdoms meek of joy and love.
There entertain him all the saints above,
In solemn troops and sweet societies
That sing, and singing in their glory move,   180
And wipe the tears forever from his eyes.
Now, Lycidas, the shepherds weep no more;
Henceforth thou art the genius[9] of the shore,
In thy large recompense, and shalt be good
To all that wander in that perilous flood.   185
 Thus sang the uncouth swain[1] to th' oaks and rills,
While the still morn went out with sandals gray;
He touched the tender stops of various quills,[2]
With eager thought warbling his Doric[3] lay:
And now the sun had stretched out all the hills,   190
And now was dropped into the western bay;
At last he rose, and twitched his mantle blue:
Tomorrow to fresh woods, and pastures new.

1637

How Soon Hath Time

How soon hath Time, the subtle thief of youth,
 Stoln on his wing my three and twentieth year!
My hasting days fly on with full career,
 But my late spring no bud or blossom show'th.
Perhaps my semblance might deceive the truth,   5
 That I to manhood am arrived so near,
 And inward ripeness doth much less appear,
That some more timely-happy spirits endu'th.[1]

---

6. The sun.
7. Dresses.
8. Inexpressible hymn of joy, sung at "the marriage supper of the Lamb" (Revelation xix).
9. One who by divine appointment haunts a locality (in this case, "the shore") where he suffered and died,

protecting others who might undergo a fate like his own.
1. Unlettered shepherd (a stock convention of this supremely literary form).
2. The oaten stalks of Panpipes.
3. Rustic, simple.
1. Endoweth.

Yet be it less or more, or soon or slow,
    It shall be still in strictest measure even[2]   10
    To that same lot, however mean or high,
Toward which Time leads me, and the will of Heaven;
    All is, if I have grace to use it so,
    As ever in my great Taskmaster's eye.[3]

1631   1645

On the New Forcers of Conscience Under the Long Parliament[1]

Because you have thrown off your prelate lord,[2]
    And with stiff vows renounced his liturgy,
    To seize the widowed whore Plurality[3]
From them whose sin ye envied, not abhorred,
Dare ye for this adjure the civil sword   5
    To force our consciences that Christ set free,
    And ride us with a classic hierarchy[4]
Taught ye by mere A. S. and Rutherford?[5]
Men whose life, learning, faith, and pure intent
    Would have been held in high esteem with Paul   10
    Must now be named and printed heretics
By shallow Edwards and Scotch what d'ye call:[6]
    But we do hope to find out all your tricks,
    Your plots and packing worse than those of Trent,[7]
              That so the Parliament   15
May with their wholesome and preventive shears
Clip your phylacteries,[8] though balk your ears,

2. Equal, adequate. Whenever it appears and however much it amounts to, Milton's inner growth will be adequate to the destiny which time and heaven are preparing.

3. The last two lines are enigmatic; their sense depends on whether one reads the "all" of line 13 as referring to time or talent.

1. "The new forcers of conscience" are Presbyterians, whom Milton at first supported against the Episcopalians (Church-of-England men). Now, under the Puritan-dominated Long Parliament, he finds them as bad as their predecessors ("whose sin ye envied, not abhorred"). The sonnet proper has 14 lines followed by two "tails" of three lines each; in Italy, where it was common, this was called a *sonnetto caudato,* or "tailed sonnet."

2. Bishop.

3. I.e., the comfortable, and sometimes necessary, practice of one priest's holding several livings at once.

4. A church discipline made up on the Presbyterian model of synods or classes,

ecclesiastical governing boards with strong powers over the laity.

5. Adam Stuart and Samuel Rutherford, Presbyterian pamphleteers, whose full names Milton does not deign to give.

6. Thomas Edwards, alarmed by the spread of heresies, began to describe them in a book picturesquely titled *Gangraena* (1645–46). Before giving up in despair, he wrote three fat volumes, including a denunciation of Milton, whom he described unjustly as an advocate of "divorce at pleasure." "Scotch what d'ye call" is Milton's humanistic sneer at the unpronounceability of Scottish names.

7. I.e., of the Council of Trent, held by the Papacy in consequence of the Reformation; it was widely reported to have been the scene of political jockeying.

8. Little scrolls, containing texts from the Pentateuch, worn by orthodox Jews to remind them of the Law. Milton uses them here as symbols of superstition. **Mutilation by having one's ears cut**

And succor our just fears
When they shall read this clearly in your charge:
New presbyter is but *old priest* writ large.   20

ca. 1646   1673

On the Late Massacre in Piedmont[1]

Avenge, O Lord, thy slaughtered saints, whose bones
  Lie scattered on the Alpine mountains cold,
  Even them who kept thy truth so pure of old
  When all our fathers worshiped stocks and stones,
Forget not: in thy book record their groans   5
  Who were thy sheep and in their ancient fold
  Slain by the bloody Piemontese that rolled
  Mother with infant down the rocks. Their moans
The vales redoubled to the hills, and they
  To Heaven. Their martyred blood and ashes sow   10
  O'er all th' Italian fields where still doth sway
The triple tyrant:[2] that from these may grow
  A hundredfold, who having learnt thy way
  Early may fly the Babylonian woe.[3]

1655   1673

When I Consider How My Light Is Spent[1]

When I consider how my light is spent
  Ere half my days, in this dark world and wide,
  And that one talent which is death to hide,
  Lodged with me useless, though my soul more bent
To serve therewith my Maker, and present   5
  My true account, lest he returning chide;
  "Doth God exact day-labor, light denied?"
  I fondly[2] ask; but Patience to prevent

off was a common punishment for sedition, and several Presbyterian leaders had suffered it. Milton's MS. read, "Clip ye as close as marginal P——'s ears," but the jeer was too brutal. William Prynne, whose books had many footnotes in the margins, and whose ears had twice been cropped, had suffered for a cause in which Milton at the time believed; and his final version of the line is gentler.
1. The Waldenses were a heretical sect, probably of Eastern origin by way of Venice: they lived in the valleys of northern Italy ("the Piedmont") and southern France, professing a creed which was particularly akin to Protestantism in its avoidance of graven images ("stocks and stones"). The under-

standing which had allowed them freedom of worship was terminated in 1655, and the massacre which ensued was widely protested by the Protestant powers of Europe. Milton, as Latin secretary to Cromwell, wrote several indignant letters.
2. I.e., the Pope, wearing his tiara with three crowns.
3. Protestants in Milton's day frequently identified the Roman Church with the "whore of Babylon" (Revelation xvii, xviii).
1. Milton's sonnet on his blindness is very close, in theme, to that on his 23rd birthday. But the absolute repose of the latter sonnet's final line is beyond anything in the earlier one.
2. Foolishly. "Prevent": forestall.

That murmur, soon replies, "God doth not need
    Either man's work or his own gifts; who best   10
    Bear his mild yoke, they serve him best. His state
Is kingly. Thousands at his bidding speed
    And post o'er land and ocean without rest:
    They also serve who only stand and wait."

1655   1673

Methought I Saw My Late Espoused Saint

Methought I saw my late espouséd saint
    Brought to me like Alcestis[1] from the grave,
    Whom Jove's great son to her glad husband gave,
    Rescued from death by force though pale and faint.
Mine, as whom washed from spot of childbed taint,   5
    Purification in the old law did save,[2]
    And such, as yet once more I trust to have
    Full sight of her in Heaven without restraint,
Came vested all in white, pure as her mind.
    Her face was veiled, yet to my fancied sight,   10
    Love, sweetness, goodness, in her person shined
So clear, as in no face with more delight.
    But O, as to embrace me she inclined,
    I waked, she fled, and day brought back my night.

1658   1673

To My Friend, Mr. Henry Lawes, on His Airs[1]

Harry, whose tuneful and well measur'd song
    First taught our English music how to span
    Words with just note and accent, not to scan
    With Midas' ears,[2] committing short and long,
Thy worth and skill exempts thee from the throng,   5
    With praise enough for envy to look wan;
    To after age thou shalt be writ the man
    That with smooth air couldst humor best our tongue.
Thou honor'st verse, and verse must lend her wing
    To honor thee, the priest of Phoebus' choir[3]   10

1. Alcestis, wife of Admetus, was rescued from the underworld by Hercules ("Jove's great son").
2. The old law, prescribing periods for the purification of women after childbirth, is found in Leviticus xii. The compression of line 5 is perhaps extreme; expanded, it would read, "My wife, like the woman whom when washed from spot of childbed taint," etc.
1. Henry Lawes, who composed the original music for Milton's *Comus*, was a real innovator in the art of setting poems to music; he brought the two elements into closer harmony than anyone had achieved before.
2. Ovid tells, in *Metamorphoses* XI, how Midas was given ass's ears because he preferred Pan's pipes to the music of Apollo. "Committing": confusing, setting into conflict with one another.
3. The choir of Phoebus consists of the muses.

That tun'st their happiest lines in hymn, or story.
Dante shall give fame leave to set thee higher
Than his Casella,[4] whom he woo'd to sing,
Met in the milder shades of Purgatory.

1648

From Areopagitica[1]

* * * In Athens, where books and wits were ever busier than
in any other part of Greece, I find but only two sorts of writings
which the magistrate cared to take notice of: those either blasphemous and atheistical, or libelous. Thus the books of Protagoras were
by the judges of Areopagus commanded to be burnt, and himself
banished the territory for a discourse begun with his confessing not
to know *whether there were gods, or whether not.*[2] And against
defaming, it was decreed that none should be traduced by name, as
was the manner of Vetus Comoedia,[3] whereby we may guess how
they censured libeling: and this course was quick enough, as Cicero
writes, to quell both the desperate wits of other atheists, and the
open way of defaming, as the event showed. Of other sects and

4. Dante met Casella (*Purgatory* II) on
the lower slopes of the mountain, and
persuaded him to sing.
1. *Areopagitica* appeared on November
24, 1644. The title means "things to
be said before the Areopagus." The
Areopagus was an ancient, powerful,
and much-respected tribunal in Athens,
before which Isocrates, in 355 B.C., delivered a famous speech. Milton's title
implies a comparison between the Areopagus and the English Parliament, and
this comparison may be thought to
validate, in some degree, the florid,
oratorical tone of the tract.
  Areopagitica is a plea for the liberty
of unlicensed printing; its occasion was
a severe ordinance for the control of
printing which had been passed by Parliament on June 14, 1643. This ordinance, however disagreeable at the moment, was no striking novelty in English history. On the contrary, control of
the press had been actively exercised
by all the Tudors and both the early
Stuarts. The aim of this government
regulation was traditionally defined as
the preservation of order and uniformity in church and state; but it also
had an economic motive. Unlicensed
printers threatened a monopoly enjoyed by the twenty licensed printers
of London. Thus the censorship laws
familiar to Englishmen had generally
been strictly defined and had bristled

with penalties. But to enforce them
was another matter entirely. Tudor and
Stuart police forces being what they
were, few printers or authors had to
worry about the consequences of going
to print without a license. As a matter
of fact, *Areopagitica* was itself unlicensed, Milton's third unlicensed
pamphlet since the passage of the
Ordinance for Printing only seventeen
months before.
  Thus the practical effects of the
Ordinance for Printing were less important (particularly, we may be sure,
in Milton's eyes) than the principle
involved. Having taken the lead in destroying the licensing system of the
Stuarts, Parliament was now setting
up a censorship of its own. After a
long prologue, Milton's first approach
to his subject was to undertake a condensed history of censorship intended
to discredit the institution by showing
that only degenerate cultures ever made
use of it.
2. It was in the 5th century B.C. that
the sophist Protagoras of Abdera was
censured in the manner described;
Cicero wrote approvingly of this action in his treatise *On the Nature of
the Gods* I.xxiii.
3. The "Old Comedy" of Aristophanes
dealt with individuals, unlike the "New
Comedy" of Menander, which dealt
with types.

opinions, though tending to voluptuousness and the denying of Divine Providence, they took no heed. Therefore we do not read that either Epicurus, or that libertine school of Cyrene, or what the Cynic impudence uttered, was ever questioned by the laws.[4] Neither is it recorded that the writings of those old comedians were suppressed, though the acting of them were forbid; and that Plato commended the reading of Aristophanes, the loosest of them all, to his royal scholar Dionysius,[5] is commonly known, and may be excused, if holy Chrysostom, as is reported, nightly studied so much the same author and had the art to cleanse a scurrilous vehemence into the style of a rousing sermon.[6] * * *

And that the primitive councils and bishops were wont only to declare what books were not commendable, passing no further, but leaving it to each one's conscience to read or to lay by, till after the year 800, is observed already by Padre Paolo, the great unmasker of the Trentine Council.[7] After which time the Popes of Rome, engrossing what they pleased of political rule into their own hands, extended their dominion over men's eyes, as they had before over their judgments, burning and prohibiting to be read what they fancied not; yet sparing in their censures, and the books not many which they so dealt with: till Martin the Fifth, by his bull, not only prohibited, but was the first that excommunicated the reading of heretical books; for about that time Wycliffe and Huss[8] growing terrible, were they who first drove the papal court to a stricter policy of prohibiting. Which course Leo the Tenth and his successors followed, until the Council of Trent and the Spanish Inquisition engendering together brought forth, or perfected, those catalogues and expurging indexes,[9] that rake through the entrails of many an old good author with a violation worse than any could

4. Epicurus (4th and 3rd centuries B.C.) thought the gods had no influence on human affairs, but he did not deny their existence; therefore he was free of censorship. Aristippus of Cyrene, the pupil of Socrates, was like Epicurus in making pleasure the end of life. His school was known, from the Greek word for "pleasure," as the school of Hedonism; but, like Epicurus, he is misunderstood as a sensualist. Diogenes was the most famous of the Cynics, who often affected a rude and truculent disposition ("Cynic impudence"). All these philosophers flourished in and about the 4th century B.C.
5. That Plato told Dionysius, tyrant of Syracuse, to read Aristophanes is an ancient tradition. St. John Chrysostom, archbishop of Constantinople in the 4th century, is said to have hated the stage plays of his own day but profited from a constant perusal of Aristophanes.
6. After working his way through the various cities of Greece and the meager

records of Roman censorship, Milton takes his readers to the ages of primitive Christianity, where he finds no positive censorship, merely an occasional recommendation of certain books to be read or not to be read.
7. Father Paolo Sarpi (d. 1623) was a Venetian historian who opposed papal claims to secular authority. His *History of the Council of Trent* was favorite reading matter for Protestants, since it described in graphic detail the "plots and packing" which went on behind the scenes of the Counter-Reformation. See Milton's sonnet *On the New Forcers of Conscience*, line 14.
8. John Wycliffe (d. 1384) was an English church reformer and translator of the Bible; John Huss (burned at the stake in 1415) was a Bohemian reformer of similar tendencies.
9. Literally from the Latin, *indices expurgatorii*, lists of books forbidden to Catholics.

be offered to his tomb.

Nor did they stay in matters heretical, but any subject that was not to their palate, they either condemned in a Prohibition, or had it straight into the new purgatory of an Index. To fill up the measure of encroachment, their last invention was to ordain that no book, pamphlet, or paper should be printed (as if St. Peter had bequeathed them the keys of the press also out of paradise) unless it were approved and licensed under the hands of two or three glutton friars. For example:[1]

Let the Chancellor Cini be pleased to see if in this present work be contained aught that may withstand the printing.
                    Vincent Rabatta, Vicar of Florence.

I have seen this present work, and find nothing athwart the Catholic faith and good manners: in witness whereof I have given, etc.
                    Nicolò Cini, Chancellor of Florence.

Attending the precedent relation, it is allowed that this present work of Davanzati may be printed.
                    Vincent Rabatta, etc.

It may be printed, July 15.
                    Friar Simon Mompei d'Amelia, Chancellor
                    of the holy office in Florence.

Sure they have a conceit,[2] if he of the bottomless pit had not long since broke prison, that this quadruple exorcism would bar him down. I fear their next design will be to get into their custody the licensing of that which they say Claudius intended,[3] but went not through with. Vouchsafe to see another of their forms, the Roman stamp:

Imprimatur, If it seem good to the reverend master of the holy palace.
                    Belcastro, Vicegerent.

Imprimatur, Friar Nicolò Rodolphi, Master of the holy palace.

Sometimes five Imprimaturs are seen together dialogue-wise in the piazza of one title page, complimenting and ducking each to other with their shaven reverences, whether the author, who stands by in perplexity at the foot of his epistle, shall to the press or to the sponge.[4] These are the pretty responsories, these are the dear antiphonies, that so bewitched of late our prelates and their chaplains

---

1. Milton's examples come from a book on *The English Schism*, translated by Bernardo Davanzati from the original of an English Jesuit.
2. Notion.
3. The Roman historian Suetonius says that Claudius once planned to tax the act of breaking wind. Milton's note refers to this impractical scheme in the decent obscurity of a learned language.
4. I.e., the eraser. In the next sentence, "responsories" and "antiphonies" are ecclesiastical services after the pattern of a dialogue.

with the goodly echo they made; and besotted us to the gay imitation of a lordly Imprimatur, one from Lambeth House, another
from the west end of Paul's;[5] so apishly Romanizing, that the
word of command still was set down in Latin; as if the learned
grammatical pen that wrote it would cast no ink without Latin; or
perhaps, as they thought, because no vulgar tongue was worthy to
express the pure conceit of an Imprimatur; but rather, as I hope,
for that our English, the language of men ever famous and foremost in the achievements of liberty, will not easily find servile
letters enow to spell such a dictatory presumption English.[6] * * *

   Good and evil we know in the field of this world grow up together
almost inseparably; and the knowledge of good is so involved and
interwoven with the knowledge of evil, and in so many cunning
resemblances hardly to be discerned, that those confused seeds
which were imposed on Psyche as an incessant labor to cull out and
sort asunder,[7] were not more intermixed. It was from out the rind
of one apple tasted, that the knowledge of good and evil, as two
twins cleaving together, leaped forth into the world. And perhaps
this is that doom which Adam fell into of knowing good and evil,
that is to say of knowing good by evil.

   As therefore the state of man now is, what wisdom can there
be to choose, what continence to forbear without the knowledge of
evil? He that can apprehend and consider vice with all her baits and
seeming pleasures, and yet abstain, and yet distinguish, and yet
prefer that which is truly better, he is the true wayfaring[8] Christian.
I cannot praise a fugitive and cloistered virtue, unexercised and un-
breathed, that never sallies out and sees her adversary, but slinks out
of the race where that immortal garland[9] is to be run for, not
without dust and heat. Assuredly we bring not innocence into the
world, we bring impurity much rather; that which purifies us is trial,
and trial is by what is contrary. That virtue therefore which is but
a youngling in the contemplation of evil, and knows not the utmost
that vice promises to her followers, and rejects it, is but a blank
virtue, not a pure; her whiteness is but an excremental[1] whiteness;
which was the reason why our sage and serious poet Spenser (whom
I dare be known to think a better teacher than Scotus or Aquinas),[2]

5. Lambeth House is the Archbishop
of Canterbury's London home. "Paul's"
is St. Paul's Cathedral, headquarters
of the Bishop of London. Under the
prerogative government of Charles,
these were the two chief censors.
6. Having finished with the history of
censorship, Milton proceeds to argue
more generally that the institution
itself is evil and unchristian. As God
left man free to choose among the
many physical foods of this world,
urging only temperance, so he left him
free to pick and choose among ideas.
7. Angry at her son Cupid's love for

Psyche, Venus set Psyche to sorting
out a vast mound of mixed seeds; but
the ants took pity on her, and did the
work. See Apuleius, *The Golden Ass.*
8. There has been debate whether this
word should be read "wayfaring" or
"warfaring," but in the image of
Christian life as a pilgrimage, a crusade, the two ideas are united.
9. The crown of righteousness, the garland of virtue.
1. Exterior (like a whited sepulcher,
covering corruption within).
2. Duns Scotus and Thomas Aquinas,
taken as types of the Scholastic theo-

describing true temperance under the person of Guyon, brings him in with his palmer through the cave of Mammon and the bower of earthly bliss, that he might see and know, and yet abstain.

Since therefore the knowledge and survey of vice is in this world so necessary to the constituting of human virtue, and the scanning of error to the confirmation of truth, how can we more safely, and with less danger, scout into the regions of sin and falsity than by reading all manner of tractates and hearing all manner of reason? And this is the benefit which may be had of books promiscuously read.

But of the harm that may result hence, three kinds are usually reckoned. First, is feared the infection that may spread; but then all human learning and controversy in religious points must remove out of the world, yea, the Bible itself; for that ofttimes relates blasphemy not nicely,[3] it describes the carnal sense of wicked men not unelegantly, it brings in holiest men passionately murmuring against Providence through all the arguments of Epicurus:[4] in other great disputes it answers dubiously and darkly to the common reader: and ask a Talmudist what ails the modesty of his marginal Keri, that Moses and all the prophets cannot persuade him to pronounce the textual Chetiv.[5] For these causes we all know the Bible itself put by the papist into the first rank of prohibited books. The ancientest Fathers must be next removed, as Clement of Alexandria, and that Eusebian book of evangelic preparation, transmitting our ears through a hoard of heathenish obscenities to receive the Gospel.[6] Who finds not that Irenaeus, Epiphanius, Jerome, and others discover[7] more heresies than they well confute, and that oft for heresy which is the truer opinion?[8] * * *

Impunity and remissness, for certain, are the bane of a commonwealth; but here the great art lies, to discern in what the law is to bid restraint and punishment, and in what things persuasion only is to work. If every action which is good or evil in man at ripe years were to be under pittance[9] and prescription and compulsion, what were virtue but a name, what praise could be then due to

---

logian. The passage of Spenser referred to is *Faerie Queene* II.vii.

3. Daintily.

4. See the Book of Ecclesiastes.

5. "Keri" are the marginal comments of rabbinical scholars on the "Chetiv" of the Bible, the text itself. When the text was too free-spoken for later commentators, Keri was sometimes read in place of Chetiv.

6. Eusebius' *Preparatio Evangelica*, like many early Christian books of polemic, describes heathen wickedness in fascinating detail, as an encouragement to Christan faith. St. Irenaeus, St. Epiphanius, St. Jerome, and even that ancient and edifying convert, Clement of Alexandria, are all subject to this charge.

7. Describe (and so preserve, report).

8. Milton now argues that books cannot pervert men unless they are given force and vitality by a teacher, who, if he is a good teacher, needs no books. A fool, he urges, can find material for his folly in the best books, and a wise man material for his wisdom in the worst. Plato, indeed, recommended censorship in his *Republic;* but in real life one cannot censor books without censoring ballads, fiddlers, clothing, conversation, and social life as a whole.

9. Rationing.

well-doing, what gramercy[1] to be sober, just, or continent?

Many there be that complain of Divine Providence for suffering Adam to transgress; foolish tongues! when God gave him reason, he gave him freedom to choose, for reason is but choosing; he had been else a mere artificial Adam, such an Adam as he is in the motions.[2] We ourselves esteem not of that obedience, or love, or gift, which is of force: God therefore left him free, set before him a provoking object, ever almost in his eyes; herein consisted his merit, herein the right of his reward, the praise of his abstinence. Wherefore did he create passions within us, pleasures round about us, but that these rightly tempered are the very ingredients of virtue? They are not skillful considerers of human things, who imagine to remove sin by removing the matter of sin; for, besides that it is a huge heap increasing under the very act of diminishing, though some part of it may for a time be withdrawn from some persons, it cannot from all, in such a universal thing as books are; and when this is done, yet the sin remains entire. Though ye take from a covetous man all his treasure, he has yet one jewel left, ye cannot bereave him of his covetousness. Banish all objects of lust, shut up all youth into the severest discipline that can be exercised in any hermitage, ye cannot make them chaste that came not thither so: such great care and wisdom is required to the right managing of this point.

Suppose we could expel sin by this means; look how much we thus expel of sin, so much we expel of virtue: for the matter of them both is the same; remove that, and ye remove them both alike. This justifies the high providence of God, who, though he commands us temperance, justice, continence, yet pours out before us, even to a profuseness, all desirable things, and gives us minds that can wander beyond all limit and satiety. Why should we then affect a rigor contrary to the manner of God and of nature, by abridging or scanting those means, which books freely permitted are, both to the trial of virtue and the exercise of truth?[3] * * *

Well knows he who uses to consider, that our faith and knowledge thrives by exercise, as well as our limbs and complexion.[4] Truth is compared in Scripture to a streaming fountain; if her waters flow not in a perpetual progression, they sicken into a muddy pool of conformity and tradition. A man may be a heretic in the truth; and if he believe things only because his pastor says so, or the Assembly so determines, without knowing other reason, though his

---

1. Reward, thanks.
2. Puppet shows.
3. Censorship, Milton urges, is a vulgar, mechanical job; no man of intelligence will undertake it, and a dunderhead will make serious blunders. Finally, to put stupid men in authority over intelligent ones will discourage the pursuit of learning on every hand, except so far as censorship, by giving authority to banned books, will encourage men to seek out and cling to perverse opinions.
4. Constitution, regarded as the proper mingling of certain qualities in one's body.

belief be true, yet the very truth he holds becomes his heresy. There is not any burden that some would gladlier post off to another than the charge and care of their religion. There be, who knows not that there be, of Protestants and professors[5] who live and die in as arrant an implicit faith as any lay papist of Loretto.[6] A wealthy man, addicted to his pleasure and to his profits, finds religion to be a traffic so entangled, and of so many piddling accounts, that of all mysteries he cannot skill[7] to keep a stock going upon that trade. What should he do? Fain he would have the name to be religious, fain he would bear up with his neighbors in that. What does he therefore, but resolves to give over toiling, and to find himself out some factor,[8] to whose care and credit he may commit the whole managing of his religious affairs; some divine of note and estimation that must be. To him he adheres, resigns the whole warehouse of his religion, with all the locks and keys, into his custody; and indeed makes the very person of that man his religion; esteems his associating with him a sufficient evidence and commendatory of his own piety. So that a man may say his religion is now no more within himself, but is become a dividual[9] movable, and goes and comes near him, according as that good man frequents the house. He entertains him, gives him gifts, feasts him, lodges him; his religion comes home at night, prays, is liberally supped, and sumptuously laid to sleep, rises, is saluted, and after the malmsey, or some well-spiced brewage, and better breakfasted than He whose morning appetite would have gladly fed on green figs between Bethany and Jerusalem,[1] his religion walks abroad at eight, and leaves his kind entertainer in the shop trading all day without his religion.

Another sort there be who, when they hear that all things shall be ordered, all things regulated and settled, nothing written but what passes through the custom-house of certain publicans that have the tonnaging and poundaging[2] of all free-spoken truth, will straight give themselves up into your hands, make 'em and cut 'em out what religion ye please: there be delights, there be recreations and jolly pastimes that will fetch the day about from sun to sun, and rock the tedious year as in a delightful dream. What need they torture their heads with that which others have taken so strictly and so unalterably into their own purveying? These are the fruits which a dull ease and cessation of our knowledge will bring forth among the people. How goodly and how to be wished were

---

5. "Professors" in this context are people professing the Protestant faith.
6. A famous Catholic shrine.
7. Trades he cannot manage.
8. Agent.
9. I.e., separate or separable. Milton is describing the common institution of the household chaplain.

1. Mark xi.12–13. Jesus, hungry, found nothing but leaves on the fig tree, for the time of the figs was not yet.
2. "Publicans": tax collectors. Tonnage and poundage were excise taxes levied illegally by the king before 1641, and therefore specially odious to Milton's readers.

such an obedient unanimity as this, what a fine conformity would it starch us all into! Doubtless a staunch and solid piece of framework, as any January could freeze together.[3] * * *

Truth indeed came once into the world with her Divine Master, and was a perfect shape most glorious to look on: but when he ascended, and his apostles after him were laid asleep, then straight arose a wicked race of deceivers, who, as that story goes of the Egyptian Typhon with his conspirators, how they dealt with the good Osiris,[4] took the virgin Truth, hewed her lovely form into a thousand pieces, and scattered them to the four winds. From that time ever since, the sad friends of Truth, such as durst appear, imitating the careful search that Isis made for the mangled body of Osiris, went up and down gathering up limb by limb, still as they could find them. We have not yet found them all, Lords and Commons, nor ever shall do, till her Master's second coming; he shall bring together every joint and member, and shall mold them into an immortal feature of loveliness and perfection. Suffer not these licensing prohibitions to stand at every place of opportunity, forbidding and disturbing them that continue seeking, that continue to do our obsequies to the torn body of our martyred saint. We boast our light; but if we look not wisely on the sun itself, it smites us into darkness. Who can discern those planets that are oft combust,[5] and those stars of brightest magnitude that rise and set with the sun, until the opposite motion of their orbs bring them to such a place in the firmament where they may be seen evening or morning? The light which we have gained was given us, not to be ever staring on, but by it to discover onward things more remote from our knowledge. It is not the unfrocking of a priest, the unmitering of a bishop, and the removing him from off the Presbyterian shoulders, that will make us a happy nation. No, if other things as great in the church, and in the rule of life both economical[6] and political, be not looked into and reformed, we have looked so long upon the blaze that Zwinglius[7] and Calvin hath beaconed up to us, that we are stark blind.

There be who perpetually complain of schisms and sects, and make it such a calamity that any man dissents from their maxims. 'Tis their own pride and ignorance which causes the disturbing, who neither will hear with meekness, nor can convince; yet all must be suppressed which is not found in their syntagma.[8] They are the

---

3. To set barriers in the way of fresh truths implies that a nation has all the truth it needs; but this, Milton argues, is far from the case. England has no grounds for smugness; the nation needs every bit of truth it can discover.
4. Plutarch tells, in his *Isis and Osiris*, of Typhon's scattering the fragments of his brother Osiris, and of Isis' efforts

to recover them.
5. Literally, burned up; in astrology. so close to the sun as not to be visible.
6. Domestic.
7. Zwingli and Calvin, both radical Swiss reformers, were mainstays of the Presbyterian cause, which Milton was already feeling to be a little narrow.
8. Compilation of beliefs, creed.

troublers, they are the dividers of unity, who neglect and permit not others to unite those dissevered pieces which are yet wanting to the body of Truth. To be still searching what we know not by what we know, still closing up truth to truth as we find it (for all her body is homogeneal and proportional), this is the golden rule in theology as well as in arithmetic, and makes up the best harmony in a church; not the forced and outward union of cold and neutral and inwardly divided minds.

Lords and Commons of England, consider what nation it is whereof ye are, and whereof ye are the governors: a nation not slow and dull, but of a quick, ingenious and piercing spirit, acute to invent, subtle and sinewy to discourse, not beneath the reach of any point, the highest that human capacity can soar to. Therefore the studies of learning in her deepest sciences have been so ancient and so eminent among us, that writers of good antiquity and ablest judgment have been persuaded that even the school of Pythagoras and the Persian wisdom took beginning from the old philosophy of this island.[9] And that wise and civil Roman, Julius Agricola, who governed once here for Caesar, preferred the natural wits of Britain before the labored studies of the French. Nor is it for nothing that the grave and frugal Transylvanian sends out yearly from as far as the mountainous borders of Russia, and beyond the Hercynian wilderness, not their youth, but their staid men, to learn our language and our theologic arts.

Yet that which is above all this, the favor and the love of heaven, we have great argument[1] to think in a peculiar manner propitious and propending towards us. Why else was this nation chosen before any other, that out of her, as out of Zion,[2] should be proclaimed and sounded forth the first tidings and trumpet of Reformation to all Europe? And had it not been the obstinate perverseness of our prelates against the divine and admirable spirit of Wycliffe, to suppress him as a schismatic and innovator, perhaps neither the Bohemian Huss and Jerome,[3] no, nor the name of Luther or of Calvin, had been ever known: the glory of reforming all our neighbors had been completely ours. But now, as our obdurate clergy have with violence demeaned[4] the matter, we are become hitherto the latest and backwardest scholars of whom God offered to have made us the teachers. Now once again by all concurrence of signs, and by the general instinct of holy and devout men, as they daily

9. So far as it concerns Pythagoras and the Persians, this sentence is better patriotism than it is intellectual history. Agricola's opinion of the British intellect (referred to next), is found in Tacitus' *Life of Agricola;* "civil" means "cultured, civilized." The Transylvanians, being Protestants, did sometimes come to England from "beyond the Hercynian wilderness" (the Harz mountains) to study.
1. Reason. "Propending": inclining, favorable.
2. Mt. Zion, in Jerusalem, the site of the temple, the holy of holies.
3. Jerome of Prague (martyred in 1416) was a follower of Huss and so of Wycliffe.
4. Conducted.

and solemnly express their thoughts, God is decreeing to begin some new and great period in his church, even to the reforming of Reformation itself; what does he then but reveal himself to his servants, and as his manner is, first to his Englishmen? I say, as his manner is, first to us, though we mark not the method of his counsels, and are unworthy. Behold now this vast city: a city of refuge, the mansion house of liberty, encompassed and surrounded with his protection; the shop of war hath not there more anvils and hammers waking, to fashion out the plates[5] and instruments of armed justice in defense of beleaguered truth, than there be pens and heads there, sitting by their studious lamps, musing, searching, revolving new notions and ideas wherewith to present, as with their homage and their fealty, the approaching Reformation: others as fast reading, trying all things, assenting to the force of reason and convincement.

What could a man require more from a nation so pliant and so prone to seek after knowledge? What wants there to such a towardly[6] and pregnant soil, but wise and faithful laborers, to make a knowing people, a nation of prophets, of sages, and of worthies? We reckon more than five months yet to harvest; there need not be five weeks; had we but eyes to lift up, the fields are white already.[7] Where there is much desire to learn, there of necessity will be much arguing, much writing, many opinions; for opinion in good men is but knowledge in the making. Under these fantastic terrors of sect and schism we wrong the earnest and zealous thirst after knowledge and understanding which God hath stirred up in this city.

What some lament of, we rather should rejoice at, should rather praise this pious forwardness among men, to reassume the ill-deputed care of their religion into their own hands again. A little generous prudence, a little forbearance of one another, and some grain of charity might win all these diligences to join, and unite into one general and brotherly search after truth; could we but forgo this prelatical tradition of crowding free consciences and Christian liberties into canons and precepts of men. I doubt not, if some great and worthy stranger should come among us, wise to discern the mold and temper of a people, and how to govern it, observing the high hopes and aims, the diligent alacrity of our extended thoughts and reasonings in the pursuance of truth and freedom, but that he would cry out as Pyrrhus did, admiring the Roman docility and courage: "If such were my Epirots, I would not despair the greatest design that could be attempted, to make a church or kingdom happy."[8] Yet these are the men cried out against for schismat-

---

5. Plate mail, armor plate.
6. Favorable.
7. Milton is paraphrasing Christ's words to the disciples (John iv.35).

8. Though King Pyrrhus of Epirus beat the Roman armies at Heraclea in 280 B.C., he was much impressed by their discipline.

ics and sectaries;[9] as if, while the temple of the Lord was building, some cutting, some squaring the marble, others hewing the cedars, there should be a sort of irrational men, who could not consider there must be many schisms and many dissections[1] made in the quarry and in the timber, ere the house of God can be built. And when every stone is laid artfully together, it cannot be united into a continuity, it can but be contiguous in this world; neither can every piece of the building be of one form; nay rather the perfection consists in this, that out of many moderate varieties and brotherly dissimilitudes that are not vastly disproportional, arises the goodly and the graceful symmetry that commends the whole pile and structure. Let us therefore be more considerate builders, more wise in spiritual architecture, when great reformation is expected. For now the time seems come, wherein Moses the great prophet may sit in heaven rejoicing to see that memorable and glorious wish of his fulfilled, when not only our seventy elders, but all the Lord's people, are become prophets.[2] * * *

Methinks I see in my mind a noble and puissant nation rousing herself like a strong man after sleep, and shaking her invincible locks: methinks I see her as an eagle mewing[3] her mighty youth, and kindling her undazzled eyes at the full midday beam; purging and unscaling her long-abused sight at the fountain itself of heavenly radiance; while the whole noise of timorous and flocking birds, with those also that love the twilight, flutter about, amazed at what she means, and in their envious gabble would prognosticate a year of sects and schisms.[4] * * *

1644

9. Sectarians, dividers of the church.
1. Milton puns on the literal meanings of "schisms" and "dissections" ("split" and "cut up") to press the image of the church as a temple built of believers.
2. In Numbers xi.29, Moses expressed the wish that all the Lord's people (not just the council of "seventy," or Sanhedrin) were prophets.
3. Molting, shaking off. Or the word may be "newing," i.e., renewing.
4. With this vigorous expression of idealistic optimism, Milton's argument subsides into a few last repetitions and afterthoughts. In practical terms, it was not a successful argument; the ordinance against which it protested was not repealed, though it was never effectively enforced, being, in effect, unenforceable. In time, Milton himself became, temporarily, a licenser of news sheets under Cromwell. But this biographical fact need not and must not be taken as a retraction or limitation of the position assumed in *Areopagitica*, which moves throughout on a plane of policy far removed from mundane considerations of practical politics.

Paradise Lost   The entry into *Paradise Lost* is easy—deceptively so. Carried along by the impetus of Satan's tremendous adventures, readers are apt to forget there is any other part to the poem. Indeed, while we are getting acclimated to the Miltonic world, there is no reason to hold back our sympathy with Satan, our admiration for his heroic energy. It is energy in a bad cause, clearly; but it is energy, it is heroically exercised, and there is as yet no source of virtuous power to oppose or offset it. With the appearance of Christ the Son, at the opening of Book III, we begin to see in heavenly Love the counterpoise of Satan's hellish Hate; and in Book IV, as we are introduced not only to Adam and Eve but to Paradise, our sympathies gradually shift. Satan is no longer a glamorous underdog, fighting his adventurous way through the universe against enormous odds; he is a menacing vulture, a cormorant, a toad, a snake. He is not only dangerous, he is dull; whatever richness and variety he discovers in the universe serve only to produce in him envious hatred and destructiveness. His sin is incestuous, as the allegory of Sin and Death points out; it breeds out of itself ever fresh occasions of sin. Adam and Eve, who are weaker, less active, and less spectacular in every way, finally outweigh Satan in our interest and sympathy simply because they can respond to life, and to the terrifying experience of guilt, more vigorously than Satan can.

Seen overall—from above, as it were—*Paradise Lost* is a vast but delicately balanced structure. The adventure of Satan in Books I–III balances the history of mankind in Books X–XII. Book IV, the entry of Satan (and the reader) into Paradise, balances Book IX, describing the loss of Paradise. Books V and VI, describing the destructive war in Heaven, balance as on a fulcrum against Books VII and VIII, which describe the Creation and deal with the problems of understanding it.

Within the poem's larger structure, there are all sorts of secondary balances which the knowing reader will recognize for himself. The consult in Hell (Book II) is paralleled by a consult in Heaven (Book III); the Heavenly Trinity of Father, Son, and Holy Ghost is paralleled by a diabolic trinity of Satan, Sin, and Death. Satan's fall parallels Adam's fall, and the parallel is prolonged into that extended series of falls and recoveries which is the history of mankind. Moloch contrasts with Mammon; the Son's mercy with the Father's justice; Raphael's affability with Michael's severity; and so on, almost without limit.

The structure of the poem is at once massive and delicate; its language is also both rich and strong. Milton's range of classical reference and gift for epithet are undoubtedly staggering at first view, and his long, complexly subordinated sentences are sometimes hard to follow. Footnotes, alas, provide the only proper solution to this problem. But one need not equal, or even follow, all Milton's learning in order to appreciate his poem, especially at a first reading. The poem progresses as through a garden of metaphor and reference which stretches away on either side of one, as far as the eye can see; on a first tour, it is enough to get the general prospect clear, without learning the name of each particular blossom. Ultimately, the reader who is experienced in the poem comes to appreciate its details—epic similes like Leviathan the seabeast (I.201), no less than the one-eyed Arimaspians and the gryphon (II.944)—its epithets and circumlocutions like Mulciber (I.740), who is Vulcan, and Amram's son (I.339) who is Moses—without sense of strain or strangeness. Milton himself moved securely through the literatures of half a dozen languages and as many cultures; it is one of the supreme rewards of literary study to be able to follow him with an equivalent security.

Paradise Lost is at once a deeply traditional and a boldly original poem. Milton takes pains to fulfill the traditional prescriptions of the epic form; he gives us love, war, supernatural characters, a descent into Hell, a catalogue of warriors, all the conventional items of epic machinery. Yet no poem in which the climax of the central action is a woman eating a piece of fruit can be a conventional epic. Similarly, Milton himself defined his own moral purpose as being to "justify the ways of God to man." This seems no more than conventionally meek. Yet we cannot even think of equating the message of Milton's poem with Pope's injunction to "submit" because "whatever is is right." The way of life which Adam and Eve take up as the poem ends is that of the Christian pilgrimage through this world. Paradise was no place or condition in which to exercise Christian heroism as Milton conceives it. Expelled from Eden, our first "grand parents" pick up the burdens of humanity as we know them, sustained by a faith which we also know, and go forth to seek a blessing which we do not know yet. They are to become wayfaring, warfaring Christians, like John Milton; and in this condition, with its weaknesses and strivings and inevitable defeats, there is a glory that no devil can ever understand. Thus Milton strikes, humanly as well as artistically, a grand resolving chord. It is the careful, triumphant balancing and tempering of this conclusion which makes Milton's poem the noble architecture it is; and which makes of the end a richer, if not a more exciting, experience than the beginning.

From PARADISE LOST

Book I

The Argument[1]

This first book proposes, first in brief, the whole subject, man's disobedience, and the loss thereupon of Paradise, wherein he was placed: then touches the prime cause of his fall, the serpent, or rather Satan in the serpent; who, revolting from God, and drawing to his side many legions of angels, was, by the command of God, driven out of Heaven, with all his crew, into the great deep. Which action passed over, the poem hastens into the midst of things;[2] presenting Satan, with his angels, now fallen into Hell—described here not in the center (for heaven and earth may be supposed as yet not made, certainly not yet accursed), but in a place of utter darkness, fitliest called Chaos. Here Satan with his angels lying on the burning lake, thunderstruck and astonished, after a certain space recovers, as from confusion; calls up him who, next in order and dignity, lay by him: they confer of their miserable fall. Satan awakens all his legions, who lay till then in the same manner confounded. They rise: their numbers; array of battle; their

1. *Paradise Lost* appeared originally without any sort of prose aid to the reader; but, since many readers found the poem hard going, the printer asked Milton for some prose "Arguments" or summary explanations of the action in the various books, and prefixed them to later issues of the poem. We reprint those for the first three books and the ninth.
2. Adapted from Horace's prescription that the epic poet should start *"in medias res."*

chief leaders named, according to the idols known afterwards in
Canaan and the countries adjoining. To these Satan directs his
speech; comforts them with hope yet of regaining Heaven; but tells
them, lastly, of a new world and new kind of creature to be created,
according to an ancient prophecy, or report, in Heaven; for that
angels were long before this visible creation was the opinion of many
ancient fathers.[3] To find out the truth of this prophecy, and what
to determine[4] thereon, he refers to a full council. What his associates thence attempt. Pandemonium, the palace of Satan, rises,
suddenly built out of the deep: the infernal peers there sit in council.

    Of man's first disobedience, and the fruit[5]
Of that forbidden tree whose mortal[6] taste
Brought death into the world, and all our woe,
With loss of Eden, till one greater Man[7]
Restore us, and regain the blissful seat,   5
Sing, Heavenly Muse,[8] that, on the secret top
Of Oreb, or of Sinai, didst inspire
That shepherd who first taught the chosen seed
In the beginning how the Heavens and Earth
Rose out of Chaos: or, if Sion hill[9]   10
Delight thee more, and Siloa's brook that flowed
Fast[1] by the oracle of God, I thence
Invoke thy aid to my adventurous song,
That with no middle flight intends to soar
Above th' Aonian mount,[2] while it pursues   15
Things unattempted yet in prose or rhyme.
And chiefly thou, O Spirit,[3] that dost prefer
Before all temples th' upright heart and pure,
Instruct me, for thou know'st; thou from the first
Wast present, and, with mighty wings outspread,   20
Dovelike sat'st brooding[4] on the vast abyss,

3. I.e., Church Fathers, the Christian writers of the first three centuries of the church.
4. I.e., what action to take upon their information.
5. Eve's apple, of course; but also all the consequences of eating it.
6. Deadly; but also "to mortals" (i.e., human beings).
7. Christ, the second Adam.
8. In Greek mythology, Urania, Muse of astronomy and epic poetry; but here identified, by references to Oreb and Sinai, with the Holy Spirit of the Bible, which inspired Moses ("that shepherd") to write Genesis and the other four books of the Pentateuch for the instruction of the Jews ("the chosen seed").
9. The hill of Sion and the brook of Siloa are two features of the landscape around Jerusalem likely to appeal to a Muse, whose natural haunts are springs and mountains (see *Lycidas*,

line 15). Milton's aim is to show that poetry is everywhere recognized as an inspiration close to that of religion.
1. Close.
2. Helicon, home of the classical Muses; Milton is deliberately courting comparison with Homer and Virgil.
3. The Spirit is an impulse or voice of God, by which the Hebrew prophets were directly inspired.
4. A composite of phrases and ideas from Genesis i.2 ("And the earth was without form, and void; and darkness was upon the face of the deep. And the Spirit of God moved upon the face of the waters"); Matthew iii.16 ("and he saw the Spirit of God descending like a dove, and lighting upon him"); and Luke iii.22 ("and the Holy Ghost descended in a bodily shape like a dove upon him"). Milton's mind as he wrote was impregnated with expressions from the King James Bible, only a few of which can be indicated in the notes.

And mad'st it pregnant: what in me is dark
Illumine; what is low, raise and support;
That, to the height of this great argument,[5]
I may assert Eternal Providence,   25
And justify the ways of God to men.
    Say first (for Heaven hides nothing from thy view,
Nor the deep tract of Hell), say first what cause
Moved our grand[6] parents, in that happy state,
Favored of Heaven so highly, to fall off   30
From their Creator, and transgress his will
For[7] one restraint, lords of the world besides?[8]
Who first seduced them to that foul revolt?
    Th' infernal serpent; he it was, whose guile,
Stirred up with envy and revenge, deceived   35
The mother of mankind, what time[9] his pride
Had cast him out from Heaven, with all his host
Of rebel angels, by whose aid, aspiring
To set himself in glory above his peers,[1]
He trusted to have equaled the Most High,   40
If he opposed; and with ambitious aim
Against the throne and monarchy of God,
Raised impious war in Heaven and battle proud,
With vain attempt. Him the Almighty Power
Hurled headlong flaming from th' ethereal sky,   45
With hideous ruin and combustion, down
To bottomless perdition, there to dwell
In adamantine chains and penal fire,
Who durst defy th' Omnipotent to arms.
    Nine times the space that measures day and night   50
To mortal men, he with his horrid crew,
Lay vanquished, rolling in the fiery gulf,
Confounded though immortal. But his doom
Reserved him to more wrath; for now the thought
Both of lost happiness and lasting pain   55
Torments him; round he throws his baleful[2] eyes,
That witnessed huge affliction and dismay,
Mixed with obdúrate pride and steadfast hate.
At once, as far as angels ken,[3] he views
The dismal situation waste and wild: 60
A dungeon horrible, on all sides round,
As one great furnace flamed; yet from those flames
No light,[4] but rather darkness visible

5. Theme.
6. First in importance; by implication, in time also.
7. Because of.
8. In every other respect.
9. I.e., at the time when.
1. His equals. The sentence mimics Satan's action, piling clause loosely upon clause, and building ever higher, till "with vain attempt" (line 44) brings the whole structure crashing down. It is a dramatic entry into "the midst of things," where epics begin. Book VI will recount more largely the war in Heaven, in the full narrative form which Aeneas used to tell Dido of the last days of Troy.
2. Malignant, as well as suffering.
3. As far as angels can see.
4. Omitting the verb conveys abruptly the paradox: fire-without-light.

Served only to discover sights of woe,
Regions of sorrow, doleful shades, where peace   65
And rest can never dwell, hope never comes
That comes to all,[5] but torture without end
Still urges,[6] and a fiery deluge, fed
With ever-burning sulphur unconsumed.
Such place Eternal Justice had prepared   70
For those rebellious; here their prison ordained
In utter[7] darkness, and their portion set,
As far removed from God and light of Heaven
As from the center[8] thrice to th' utmost pole.
O how unlike the place from whence they fell!   75
There the companions of his fall, o'erwhelmed
With floods and whirlwinds of tempestuous fire,
He soon discerns; and, weltering by his side,
One next himself in power, and next in crime,
Long after known in Palestine, and named   80
Beëlzebub.[9] To whom th' arch-enemy,
And thence in Heaven called Satan,[1] with bold words
Breaking the horrid silence, thus began:
"If thou beëst he—but O how fallen! how changed
From him who, in the happy realms of light   85
Clothed with transcendent brightness, didst outshine
Myriads, though bright! if he whom mutual league,
United thoughts and counsels, equal hope
And hazard in the glorious enterprise,
Joined with me once, now misery hath joined   90
In equal ruin; into what pit thou seest[2]
From what height fallen, so much the stronger proved
He with his thunder:[3] and till then who knew
The force of those dire arms? Yet not for those,
Nor what the potent Victor in his rage   95
Can else inflict, do I repent, or change,
Though changed in outward luster, that fixed mind,
And high disdain from sense of injured merit,

5. The phrase echoes an expression in
Dante ("All hope abandon, ye who
enter here"), but Milton expresses it
as a logical absurdity. Hope comes to
"all" but not to Helldwellers; they are
not included in "all."
6. Afflicts.
7. "Complete" but also "outer."
8. The earth. Milton makes use in
Paradise Lost of two images of the
cosmos: (1) the earth is the center
of the *created* (Ptolemaic) cosmos of
nine concentric spheres; but (2) the
earth and the whole created cosmos are
a mere appendage, hanging from Heaven
by a golden chain, in the larger,
aboriginal, and less shapely cosmos.
In the present passage, the fall from
Heaven to Hell (through the aboriginal
universe) is described as thrice as far
as the distance (in the created universe)

from the center (earth) to the outermost sphere.
9. A Phoenician deity, or Baal (the
name means "Lord of flies"); traditionally, a prince of devils and enemy
of Jehovah. The Phoenician Baal, a
sun god, had many aspects and so
many names; most Baals were nature
deities. But in the poem's time scheme
all this lies in the future; Beelzebub's
angelic name, whatever it was, has been
erased from the Book of Life, and as he
has not yet got another one, he must
be called by the name he will have later
on.
1. In Hebrew, the name means "Adversary."
2. Satan's syntax, like that of a man
recovering from a stunning blow, is
not of the clearest.
3. God with his thunderbolts.

That with the Mightiest raised me to contend,
And to the fierce contentions brought along   100
Innumerable force of spirits armed,
That durst dislike his reign, and, me preferring,
His utmost power with adverse power opposed
In dubious battle on the plains of Heaven,
And shook his throne. What though the field be lost?   105
All is not lost: the unconquerable will,
And study⁴ of revenge, immortal hate,
And courage never to submit or yield:
And what is else not to be overcome?⁵
That glory never shall his wrath or might   110
Extort from me. To bow and sue for grace
With suppliant knee, and deify his power⁶
Who, from the terror of this arm, so late
Doubted his empire⁷—that were low indeed;
That were an ignominy and shame beneath   115
This downfall; since, by fate, the strength of gods,⁸
And this empyreal substance, cannot fail;
Since, through experience of this great event,
In arms not worse, in foresight much advanced,
We may with more successful hope resolve   120
To wage by force or guile eternal war,
Irreconcilable to our grand Foe,
Who now triúmphs, and in th' excess of joy
Sole reigning holds the tyranny⁹ of Heaven."
  So spake th' apostate angel, though in pain,   125
Vaunting aloud, but racked with deep despair;
And him thus answered soon his bold compeer:¹
  "O prince, O chief of many thronéd powers,
That led th' embattled seraphim² to war
Under thy conduct, and, in dreadful deeds   130
Fearless, endangered Heaven's perpetual King,
And put to proof his high supremacy,
Whether upheld by strength, or chance, or fate!³
Too well I see and rue the dire event⁴

4. Pursuit.
5. I.e., what else does it mean not to be beaten? "That glory" is the glory of hearing Satan confess himself overcome.
6. I.e., deify the power of him who. Milton sometimes writes English as if it were an inflected language.
7. I.e., doubted whether he could maintain his empire. In the next line, "ignominy" is pronounced "ignomy."
8. The essence of Satan's fault is his claim to the position of a god, subject to fate but to nothing else. His substance is "empyreal" (heavenly, from the empyrean), and cannot be destroyed; but, as he learns in the poem, it can be confounded by God's greater power and weakened by its own cor-

ruption and self-contradictions. "Fail": cease to exist.
9. The accusation is bold, but one of the aims of the poem is to show that Satan is a tyrant and God is not. The next two lines start this dramatic process by suggesting that Satan's brave exterior is merely a front.
1. Comrade and equal.
2. According to tradition, there were nine orders of angels—seraphim, cherubim, thrones, dominions, virtues, powers, principalities, archangels, and angels; but Milton does not use these systematic categories systematically.
3. The devils can conceive of any reason for God's continuing rule, except goodness and justice.
4. Outcome.

That with sad overthrow and foul defeat 135
Hath lost us Heaven, and all this mighty host
In horrible destruction laid thus low,
As far as gods and heavenly essences
Can perish: for the mind and spirit remains
Invincible, and vigor soon returns, 140
Though all our glory extinct, and happy state
Here swallowed up in endless misery.
But what if he our Conqueror, (whom I now
Of force[5] believe almighty, since no less
Than such could have o'erpowered such force as ours) 145
Have left us this our spirit and strength entire,
Strongly to suffer and support our pains,
That we may so suffice[6] his vengeful ire,
Or do him mightier service as his thralls
By right of war, whate'er his business be, 150
Here in the heart of Hell to work in fire,
Or do his errands in the gloomy deep?
What can it then avail though yet we feel
Strength undiminished, or eternal being
To undergo eternal punishment?" 155
    Whereto with speedy words th' arch-fiend[7] replied:
"Fallen cherub, to be weak is miserable,
Doing or suffering:[8] but of this be sure,
To do aught good never will be our task,
But ever to do ill our sole delight, 160
As being the contrary to his high will
Whom we resist. If then his providence
Out of our evil seek to bring forth good,
Our labor must be to pervert that end,
And out of good still to find means of evil; 165
Which oft times may succeed, so as perhaps
Shall grieve him, if I fail not,[9] and disturb
His inmost counsels from their destined aim.
But see! the angry Victor hath recalled
His ministers of vengeance and pursuit 170
Back to the gates of Heaven; the sulphurous hail,
Shot after us in storm, o'erblown hath laid
The fiery surge that from the precipice
Of Heaven received us falling; and the thunder,
Winged with red lightning and impetuous rage, 175
Perhaps hath spent his shafts, and ceases now
To bellow through the vast and boundless deep.
Let us not slip[1] th' occasion, whether scorn
Or satiate fury yield it from our Foe.
Seest thou yon dreary plain, forlorn and wild, 180
The seat of desolation, void of light,

5. Perforce, necessarily.
6. Satisfy.
7. A fiend is an enemy, one who hates; the word is an antonym of "friend."
8. Whether one is active or passive.
9. "Unless I'm mistaken" (direct from the Latin, *ne fallor*).
1. I.e., let slip.

Save what the glimmering of these livid flames
Casts pale and dreadful? Thither let us tend
From off the tossing of these fiery waves;
There rest, if any rest can harbor there;   185
And, reassembling our afflicted powers,[2]
Consult how we may henceforth most offend
Our enemy, our own loss how repair,
How overcome this dire calamity,
What reinforcement we may gain from hope,   190
If not, what resolution from despair."[3]
 Thus Satan, talking to his nearest mate,
With head uplift above the wave, and eyes
That sparkling blazed; his other parts besides,
Prone on the flood, extended long and large,   195
Lay floating many a rood,[4] in bulk as huge
As whom[5] the fables name of monstrous size,
Titanian or Earth-born, that warred on Jove,
Briareos or Typhon,[6] whom the den
By ancient Tarsus held, or that sea beast   200
Leviathan,[7] which God of all his works
Created hugest that swim th' ocean-stream.
Him, haply, slumbering on the Norway foam,
The pilot of some small night-foundered[8] skiff,
Deeming some island, oft, as seamen tell,   205
With fixéd anchor in his scaly rind,
Moors by his side under the lee, while night
Invests[9] the sea, and wishéd morn delays.
So stretched out huge in length the arch-fiend lay,
Chained on the burning lake; nor ever thence   210
Had risen or heaved his head, but that the will
And high permission of all-ruling Heaven
Left him at large to his own dark designs,
That with reiterated crimes he might
Heap on himself damnation, while he sought   215
Evil to others, and enraged might see
How all his malice served but to bring forth
Infinite goodness, grace, and mercy shown
On man by him seduced, but on himself

2. Stricken armies.
3. Of the last nine lines of Satan's speech, no less than five rhyme. Milton may have felt the need for something like the couplet with which blank-verse dramatists cut off their scenes.
4. An old unit of measure, between six and eight yards.
5. I.e., as those whom.
6. Both the Titans, led by Briareos, and the earth-born Giants, represented by Typhon (who lived in Cilicia near Tarsus), fought with Jove. Briareos was said to have a hundred hands, and Typhon a hundred heads; and both were said, by different authors, to have been punished for their rebellion (like Satan for his) by being thrown into the underworld. Briareos and Typhon are still heard grumbling from time to time under Mt. Etna.
7. The great sea monster of Isaiah xxvii.1 or Job xli; for Milton and us, simply a whale, but scaly (line 206).
8. Overtaken by darkness.
9. Wraps, covers. The story of sailors mooring to whales was an old one, but the reference to Norway suggests that Milton was thinking of a recently translated version by Olaus Magnus, the Swedish historian.

Treble confusion, wrath, and vengeance poured.   220
   Forthwith upright he rears from off the pool
His mighty stature; on each hand the flames
Driven backward slope their pointing spires,[1] and, rolled
In billows, leave i' th' midst a horrid[2] vale.
Then with expanded wings he steers his flight   225
Aloft, incumbent on[3] the dusky air,
That felt unusual weight; till on dry land
He lights, if it were land that ever burned
With solid, as the lake with liquid fire,
And such appeared in hue; as when the force   230
Of subterranean wind transports a hill
Torn from Pelorus,[4] or the shattered side
Of thundering Etna, whose combustible
And fueled entrails, thence conceiving fire,
Sublimed[5] with mineral fury, aid the winds,   235
And leave a singéd bottom all involved[6]
With stench and smoke. Such resting found the sole
Of unblest feet. Him followed his next mate,
Both glorying to have 'scaped the Stygian[7] flood
As gods, and by their own recovered strength,   240
Not by the sufferance[8] of supernal power.
   "Is this the region, this the soil, the clime,"
Said then the lost archangel, "this the seat
That we must change for Heaven? this mournful gloom
For that celestial light? Be it so, since he   245
Who now is sovereign can dispose and bid
What shall be right: farthest from him is best,
Whom reason hath equaled, force hath made supreme
Above his equals.[9] Farewell, happy fields,
Where joy forever dwells! Hail, horrors! hail,   250
Infernal world! and thou, profoundest Hell,
Receive thy new possessor, one who brings
A mind not to be changed by place or time.
The mind is its own place, and in itself
Can make a Heaven of Hell, a Hell of Heaven.[1]   255
What matter where, if I be still the same,
And what I should be, all but less[2] than he
Whom thunder hath made greater? Here at least
We shall be free; th' Almighty hath not built
Here for his envy, will not drive us hence: 260
Here we may reign secure; and, in my choice,

1. Points of flame.
2. Not simply "ghastly," but in the Latin sense, "bristling."
3. Resting upon.
4. Pelorus and Etna are volcanic mountains in Sicily, which Milton pictures as exploding under pressure of underground winds.
5. Vaporized.
6. Wrapped.
7. Of the river Styx, i.e., demonic, hellish.

8. Permission.
9. Satan likes to think that by "reason" he is God's equal; this only shows how far he is from "right reason."
1. Satan's heroic resolution here, where he is converting Hell into a kind of plastic Heaven, takes another turn when in Book IV we find him bringing the Hell of his own mind into Paradise.
2. Second only to. The expression "all but less than" telescopes "all but equal to" and "only less than."

To reign is worth ambition, though in Hell:
Better to reign in Hell than serve in Heaven.
But wherefore let we then our faithful friends,
Th' associates and copartners of our loss,   265
Lie thus astonished[3] on th' oblivious pool,
And call them not to share with us their part
In this unhappy mansion, or once more
With rallied arms to try what may be yet
Regained in Heaven, or what more lost in Hell?"   270
    So Satan spake; and him Beëlzebub
Thus answered: "Leader of those armies bright
Which, but th' Omnipotent, none could have foiled!
If once they hear that voice, their liveliest pledge
Of hope in fears and dangers, heard so oft   275
In worst extremes, and on the perilous edge[4]
Of battle, when it raged, in all assaults
Their surest signal, they will soon resume
New courage and revive, though now they lie
Groveling and prostrate on yon lake of fire,   280
As we erewhile, astounded and amazed;
No wonder, fallen such a pernicious height!"
    He scarce had ceased when the superior fiend
Was moving toward the shore; his ponderous shield,
Ethereal temper,[5] massy, large, and round,   285
Behind him cast. The broad circumference
Hung on his shoulders like the moon, whose orb
Through optic glass the Tuscan artist[6] views
At evening, from the top of Fesolè,
Or in Valdarno, to descry new lands,   290
Rivers, or mountains, in her spotty globe.
His spear, to equal which the tallest pine
Hewn on Norwegian hills, to be the mast
Of some great admiral,[7] were but a wand,
He walked with, to support uneasy steps   295
Over the burning marl,[8] not like those steps
On Heaven's azure; and the torrid clime
Smote on him sore besides, vaulted with fire.
Nathless[9] he so endured, till on the beach
Of that inflaméd[1] sea he stood, and called   300
His legions, angel forms, who lay entranced,
Thick as autumnal leaves that strow the brooks
In Vallombrosa,[2] where th' Etrurian shades

3. Stunned. The epithet "oblivious" is transferred from the fallen angels to the pool in which they have fallen.
4. Not the fringe of battle but the front line (Latin *acies*).
5. With the qualities of ether, which, being the fifth element, is not subject to change, corruption, or decay.
6. Galileo, who looked through a telescope ("optic glass") from the hill town of Fiesole outside Florence in the Val d'Arno, is the only contemporary men-

tioned by Milton in *Paradise Lost*.
7. Not the naval commander, but his flagship, usually the biggest of the fleet.
8. Soil.
9. A compressed, archaic form of "not the less."
1. Flaming, of course, but also fevered.
2. "Shady Valley," high in the Apennines about twenty miles from Florence. "Etruria" is Etruscan land, i.e., Tuscany.

High over-arched embower;[3] or scattered sedge
Afloat, when with fierce winds Orion armed   305
Hath vexed the Red-Sea coast, whose waves o'erthrew
Busiris and his Memphian chivalry,
While with perfidious hatred they pursued
The sojourners of Goshen, who beheld
From the safe shore their floating carcasses   310
And broken chariot wheels.[4] So thick bestrown,
Abject and lost, lay these, covering the flood,
Under amazement of their hideous change.
He called so loud that all the hollow deep
Of Hell resounded: "Princes, potentates,   315
Warriors, the flower of Heaven, once yours, now lost,
If such astonishment as this can seize
Eternal spirits! or have ye chosen this place
After the toil of battle to repose
Your wearied virtue,[5] for the ease you find   320
To slumber here, as in the vales of Heaven?
Or in this abject posture have ye sworn
To adore the Conqueror, who now beholds
Cherub and seraph rolling in the flood
With scattered arms and ensigns,[6] till anon   325
His swift pursuers from Heaven-gates discern
Th' advantage, and descending tread us down
Thus drooping, or with linkéd thunderbolts
Transfix us to the bottom of this gulf?
Awake, arise, or be forever fallen!"   330
      They heard, and were abashed, and up they sprung
Upon the wing, as when men wont to watch
On duty, sleeping found by whom they dread,
Rouse and bestir themselves ere well awake.
Nor did they not perceive[7] the evil plight   335
In which they were, or the fierce pains not feel;
Yet to their general's voice they soon obeyed
Innumerable. As when the potent rod
Of Amram's son,[8] in Egypt's evil day,
Waved round the coast, up called a pitchy cloud   340
Of locusts, warping[9] on the eastern wind,
That o'er the realm of impious Pharaoh hung
Like night, and darkened all the land of Nile;

3. I.e., form bowers by enclosing space.
4. Orion is a constellation, visible chiefly in late summer and autumn, hence associated with storms; in the Red Sea, where sedge grows thick, these storms result in much floating seaweed. This reminds Milton of how the sea must have looked after the Israelites ("sojourners of Goshen") passed through it while escaping from Egypt, when it was covered with the littered corpses of Pharaoh ("Busiris") and his pursuing horsemen ("Memphian chivalry").
5. Strength, but Satan's sarcasm makes use of the other connotation too.
6. Standards, battle flags.
7. The double negatives make a positive: they did indeed perceive both plight and pains. (Latin, *neque non*, "nor . . . not," "and.")
8. Moses, who drew down a plague of locusts on Egypt (Exodus x.12–15). Milton's learned locution is designed to keep Moses out of Hell, as well as from appearing too often in the poem (cf. above, 307–11).
9. Swarming (a technical term from bee-culture).

So numberless were those bad angels seen
Hovering on wing under the cope[1] of Hell, 345
'Twixt upper, nether, and surrounding fires;
Till, as a signal given, th' uplifted spear
Of their great sultan[2] waving to direct
Their course, in even balance down they light
On the firm brimstone, and fill all the plain: 350
A multitude like which the populous North[3]
Poured never from her frozen loins to pass
Rhene or the Danaw, when her barbarous sons
Came like a deluge on the South, and spread
Beneath Gibraltar to the Libyan sands. 355
Forthwith, from every squadron and each band,
The heads and leaders thither haste where stood
Their great commander; godlike shapes, and forms
Excelling human; princely dignities,
And powers that erst in Heaven sat on thrones, 360
Though of their names in Heavenly records now
Be no memorial, blotted out and rased[4]
By their rebellion from the Books of Life.
Nor had they yet among the sons of Eve
Got them new names, till, wandering o'er the Earth, 365
Through God's high sufferance for the trial of man,
By falsities and lies the greatest part
Of mankind they corrupted to forsake
God their Creator, and th' invisible
Glory of him that made them to transform 370
Oft to the image of a brute, adorned
With gay religions[5] full of pomp and gold,
And devils to adore for deities.
Then were they known to men by various names,
And various idols through the heathen world. 375
    Say, Muse, their names then known, who first, who last,[6]
Roused from the slumber on that fiery couch,
At their great emperor's call, as next in worth
Came singly[7] where he stood on the bare strand,
While the promiscuous crowd stood yet aloof. 380
    The chief were those who, from the pit of Hell
Roaming to seek their prey on Earth, durst fix
Their seats, long after, next the seat of God,[8]

---

1. Roof.
2. A first use of the image, which will be reinforced later, of Satan as an Oriental despot.
3. The barbarian invasions of falling Rome began with crossings of the Rhine ("Rhene") and Danube ("Danaw") Rivers, and spread across Spain, via Gibraltar, to North Africa.
4. Erased. See above, line 81. Though reluctant to state the view strongly, Milton believed all the pagan deities had been devils in disguise.

5. Ceremonies.
6. The catalogue of gods here is an epic convention; Homer catalogues ships, Virgil warriors.
7. One at a time. The diabolical aristocrats rally round Satan, while the "promiscuous crowd," the vulgar gods, stand apart.
8. The first group of devils come from the Near East, close neighbors and intimate enemies of Jehovah at Jerusalem.

Their altars by his altar, gods adored
Among the nations round, and durst abide   385
Jehovah thundering out of Sion, throned
Between the cherubim; yea, often placed
Within his sanctuary itself their shrines,
Abominations; and with cursèd things
His holy rites and solemn feasts profaned,   390
And with their darkness durst affront his light.
First, Moloch,[9] horrid king, besmeared with blood
Of human sacrifice, and parents' tears;
Though, for the noise of drums and timbrels loud,
Their children's cries unheard, that passed through fire   395
To his grim idol. Him the Ammonite[1]
Worshiped in Rabba and her watery plain,
In Argob and in Basan, to the stream
Of utmost Arnon. Nor content with such
Audacious neighborhood, the wisest heart   400
Of Solomon he led by fraud to build
His temple right against the temple of God
On that opprobrious hill,[2] and made his grove
The pleasant valley of Hinnom, Tophet thence
And black Gehenna called, the type of Hell.   405
Next Chemos,[3] th' obscene dread of Moab's sons,
From Aroar to Nebo and the wild
Of southmost Abarim; in Hesebon
And Horonaim, Seon's realm, beyond
The flowery dale of Sibma clad with vines,   410
And Elealè to th' Asphaltic pool:
Peor[4] his other name, when he enticed
Israel in Sittim, on their march from Nile,
To do him wanton rites, which cost them woe.
Yet thence his lustful orgies he enlarged   415
Even to that hill of scandal, by the grove
Of Moloch homicide,[5] lust hard by hate,
Till good Josiah drove them thence to Hell.
With these came they who, from the bordering flood
Of old Euphrates to the brook that parts   420

9. A sun god, sometimes represented as a roaring bull or with a calf's head, within whose brazen image living children were often burned as sacrifices (for a lurid fictional account, see Flaubert's *Salammbô*). "Timbrels": tambourines.
1. The Ammonites lived east of the Jordan, and Milton uses uncouth place names ("Rabba," "Argob," "Basan," "utmost Arnon") to suggest wildness.
2. The rites of Moloch on "that opprobrious hill" (the Mount of Olives) right opposite the Jewish temple, and in the valley of Hinnom, so polluted these places that they were turned into the refuse dump of Jerusalem. Thus they became "types" (analogies) of

Hell, under the names "Tophet" and "Gehenna."
3. Chemos or Chemosh was another name for Moloch, used in Moab, a nation lying south and east of the Dead Sea ("th' Asphaltic pool"). Many of the geographical names clustered here come from Isaiah xv–xvi.
4. For the story of how Peor seduced "Israel in Sittim," see Numbers xxv.
5. An epithet was often joined to a god's name as a surname (e.g., *Jupiter Tonans*, Jove the Thunderer); Milton's epithet involves almost a parody, Moloch the Mankiller. The story of "good Josiah" and his campaign against pagan gods is told in II Kings xxiii and in II Chronicles xxxiv.

Egypt from Syrian ground,[6] had general names
Of Baalim and Ashtaroth, those male,
These feminine.[7] For spirits, when they please,
Can either sex assume, or both; so soft
And uncompounded is their essence pure,   425
Not tied or manacled with joint or limb,
Nor founded on the brittle strength of bones,
Like cumbrous flesh; but, in what shape they choose,
Dilated or condensed, bright or obscure,
Can execute their airy purposes,   430
And works of love or enmity fulfill.
For those the race of Israel oft forsook
Their Living Strength,[8] and unfrequented left
His righteous altar, bowing lowly down
To bestial gods; for which their heads as low   435
Bowed down in battle, sunk before the spear
Of despicable foes. With these in troop
Came Astoreth, whom the Phoenicians called
Astartè, queen of heaven, with crescent horns;
To whose bright image nightly by the moon   440
Sidonian virgins[9] paid their vows and songs;
In Sion also not unsung, where stood
Her temple on th' offensive mountain,[1] built
By that uxorious king[2] whose heart, though large,
Beguiled by fair idolatresses, fell   445
To idols foul. Thammuz[3] came next behind,
Whose annual wound in Lebanon allured
The Syrian damsels to lament his fate
In amorous ditties all a summer's day,
While smooth Adonis[4] from his native rock   450
Ran purple to the sea, supposed with blood
Of Thammuz yearly wounded: the love tale
Infected Sion's daughters with like heat,
Whose wanton passions in the sacred porch
Ezekiel[5] saw, when, by the vision led,   455
His eye surveyed the dark idolatries
Of alienated Judah. Next came one
Who mourned in earnest, when the captive ark

6. Palestine lies between the Euphrates and "the brook Besor" (I Samuel xxx.10).
7. I.e., plural forms, masculine and feminine respectively, for Baal and Astarte. As Baals were aspects of the sun god, Astartes (Ishtars) were manifestations of the moon goddess.
8. The Jews lost battles, Milton says, when they neglected Jehovah.
9. Sidon and Tyre were the chief cities of Phoenicia.
1. The Mount of Olives again (see above, lines 403 and 416).
2. Solomon, who "loved many strange women" (I Kings xi.1–8).
3. A Syrian god, who was supposed to have been killed by a boar in Lebanon; annual festivals mourned his death and celebrated his revival, imitating the cycle of vegetable life. In his Greek form he was Adonis, god of the solar year.
4. A Lebanese river, named after the deity because every spring it turned blood-red with sedimentary mud.
5. Ezekiel complained that the Jewish women of his day were worshiping Thammuz (Ezekiel viii.14).

Maimed his brute image, head and hands lopped off,
In his own temple, on the grunsel-edge,[6]   460
Where he fell flat, and shamed his worshipers:
Dagon his name, sea monster, upward man
And downward fish; yet had his temple high
Reared in Azotus, dreaded through the coast
Of Palestine, in Gath and Ascalon,   465
And Accaron and Gaza's frontier bounds.[7]
Him followed Rimmon, whose delightful seat
Was fair Damascus, on the fertile banks
Of Abbana and Pharphar, lucid streams.
He also 'gainst the house of God was bold: 470
A leper once he lost, and gained a king,
Ahaz,[8] his sottish conqueror, whom he drew
God's altar to disparage and displace
For one of Syrian mode, whereon to burn
His odious offerings, and adore the gods   475
Whom he had vanquished. After these appeared
A crew who, under names of old renown,
Osiris, Isis, Orus,[9] and their train,
With monstrous shapes[1] and sorceries abused
Fanatic Egypt and her priests to seek   480
Their wandering gods disguised in brutish forms
Rather than human. Nor did Israel 'scape
Th' infection, when their borrowed gold composed
The calf in Oreb;[2] and the rebel king
Doubled that sin in Bethel and in Dan,   485
Likening his Maker to the grazèd ox[3]—
Jehovah, who, in one night, when he passed
From Egypt marching, equaled[4] with one stroke
Both her first-born and all her bleating gods.
Belial[5] came last; than whom a spirit more lewd   490
Fell not from Heaven, or more gross to love
Vice for itself. To him no temple stood
Or altar smoked; yet who more oft than he

6. When the Philistines stole the ark of God, they tried to store it in the temple of their sea god, Dagon; but in the morning the mutilated statue of Dagon was found on the threshold ("grunsel-edge"). See I Samuel v.1–5.
7. Milton names the five chief cities of the Philistines as places where Dagon was worshiped.
8. A Syrian general, Naaman, was cured of leprosy and converted from worship of Rimmon by the waters of the Jordan (II Kings v). King Ahaz, on the other hand, an Israelite monarch who conquered Damascus, was converted there to worship of Rimmon (II Kings xvi).
9. The second group of devils includes those from Egypt, driven in terror from heaven by the revolt of the giants (so Ovid tells us in *Metamorphoses* V), and forced to wander through Egypt in animal dis-

guises.
1. Monstrous, because often represented with animals' heads.
2. Aaron made a golden calf in the wilderness (Exodus xxxii); Milton thought it an idol of the Egyptian god Apis because the gold of which it was made had been borrowed from the Egyptians.
3. Jeroboam, "the rebel king," doubled Aaron's sin by making *two* golden calves (I Kings xii.28–30).
4. Leveled. See Exodus xii.12 for Jehovah's vengeance on the first-born of Egypt and their gods.
5. Belial was never worshiped as a god; his name was originally an abstract noun meaning "wickedness"; hence used mainly in set phrases like "sons of Belial." He comes last, because weak and slothful.

In temples and at altars, when the priest
Turns atheist, as did Eli's sons,[6] who filled
With lust and violence the house of God? 495
In courts and palaces he also reigns,
And in luxurious cities, where the noise
Of riot ascends above their loftiest towers,
And injury and outrage; and, when night 500
Darkens the streets, then wander forth the sons
Of Belial, flown[7] with insolence and wine.
Witness the streets of Sodom,[8] and that night
In Gibeah, when the hospitable door
Exposed a matron, to avoid worse rape. 505
    These were the prime in order and in might;
The rest were long to tell, though far renowned,
Th' Ionian gods, of Javan's issue held
Gods, yet confessed later than Heaven and Earth,
Their boasted parents;[9] Titan, Heaven's first-born, 510
With his enormous brood, and birthright seized
By younger Saturn; he from mightier Jove,
His own and Rhea's son, like measure found;
So Jove usurping reigned.[1] These, first in Crete
And Ida known, thence on the snowy top 515
Of cold Olympus ruled the middle air,
Their highest heaven; or on the Delphian cliff,
Or in Dodona, and through all the bounds
Of Doric land; or who with Saturn old
Fled over Adria to th' Hesperian fields, 520
And o'er the Celtic roamed the utmost isles.
    All these and more came flocking; but with looks
Downcast and damp,[2] yet such wherein appeared
Obscure some glimpse of joy, to have found their chief
Not in despair, to have found themselves not lost 525
In loss itself; which on his countenance cast
Like doubtful hue.[3] But he, his wonted pride
Soon recollecting, with high words, that bore
Semblance of worth, not substance, gently raised
Their fainting courage, and dispelled their fears: 530
Then straight commands that, at the warlike sound

---

6. The misdeeds of Eli's sons, and the epithet "sons of Belial" applied to them, will be found in I Samuel ii. 12–17.
7. Flushed.
8. In Sodom and Gibeah ancient outrages befell, described in Genesis xix and Judges xix.
9. Though considered ancient by the Greeks ("Javan's issue," i.e., offspring of Javan, son of Japhet, son of Noah) and worshiped as the first children of "Heaven" (Uranus) and "Earth" (Ge), the Titans, Milton says, were actually confessed to be of a later age.
1. Cronos or Saturn, one of the Titans, deposed his elder brother, married his

sister Rhea, and ruled until Zeus, who had been reared in secret on Mt. Ida in Crete, overthrew his own father and came to rule on Mt. Olympus. Zeus was also worshiped in Delphi, Dodona, and throughout the "Doric (Grecian) land." Meanwhile Saturn (lines 519–21), after his downfall, fled across the Adriatic Sea ("Adria") to Italy ("th' Hesperian fields"), crossed "the Celtic" (fields) of France, and finally reached Britain ("the utmost isles").
2. Depressed.
3. Their comfort is the chilly one of finding themselves not completely annihilated; and at first it is reflected in Satan's face.

Of trumpets loud and clarions,[4] be upreared
His mighty standard. That proud honor claimed
Azazel[5] as his right, a cherub tall:
Who forthwith from the glittering staff unfurled   535
Th' imperial ensign; which, full high advanced,
Shone like a meteor streaming to the wind,
With gems and golden luster rich emblazed,
Seraphic arms and trophies; all the while
Sonorous metal[6] blowing martial sounds·   540
At which the universal host up sent
A shout that tore Hell's concave,[7] and beyond
Frighted the reign of Chaos and old Night.[8]
All in a moment through the gloom were seen
Ten thousand banners rise into the air,   545
With orient[9] colors waving: with them rose
A forest huge of spears; and thronging helms
Appeared, and serried[1] shields in thick array
Of depth immeasurable. Anon they move
In perfect phalanx to the Dorian[2] mood   550
Of flutes and soft recorders; such as raised
To height of noblest temper heroes old
Arming to battle, and instead of rage
Deliberate valor breathed, firm, and unmoved
With dread of death to flight or foul retreat;   555
Nor wanting power to mitigate and swage[3]
With solemn touches troubled thoughts, and chase
Anguish and doubt and fear and sorrow and pain
From mortal or immortal minds. Thus they,
Breathing united force with fixéd thought,   560
Moved on in silence to soft pipes that charmed
Their painful steps o'er the burnt soil. And now
Advanced in view they stand, a horrid[4] front
Of dreadful length and dazzling arms, in guise
Of warriors old, with ordered spear and shield,   565
Awaiting what command their mighty chief
Had to impose. He through the arméd files
Darts his experienced eye, and soon traverse[5]
The whole battalion views, their order due,
Their visages and stature as of gods;   570
Their number last he sums. And now his heart
Distends with pride, and hardening in his strength
Glories; for never, since created man,[6]
Met such embodied force as, named with these,

4. Small, shrill, treble trumpets.
5. Among the historians of angels and devils, a traditional diabolic leader.
6. Reverberant trumpets.
7. Vault.
8. Disorder and darkness, the first materials of the cosmos, still maintain a kingdom between Heaven and Hell.
9. Lustrous, like the colors of a pearl.
1. Locked together.

2. Severe, simple. The shrill trumpet, which first roused the courage of the devils, now gives way to firm, martial tones, played on instruments of softer timbre, in the Spartan manner.
3. Assuage.
4. Bristling.
5. Across. Satan glances, like a reviewing officer, down the files and columns.
6. I.e., since the creation of man.

Could merit more than that small infantry 575
Warred on by cranes:[7] though all the giant brood
Of Phlegra with th' heroic race were joined
That fought at Thebes and Ilium, on each side
Mixed with auxiliar[8] gods; and what resounds
In fable or romance of Uther's son, 580
Begirt with British and Armoric knights;
And all who since, baptized or infidel,
Jousted in Aspramont, or Montalban,
Damasco, or Marocco, or Trebisond;
Or whom Biserta sent from Afric shore 585
When Charlemagne with all his peerage fell
By Fontarabbia.[9] Thus far these beyond
Compare of mortal prowess, yet observed[1]
Their dread commander. He, above the rest
In shape and gesture proudly eminent, 590
Stood like a tower. His form had yet not lost
All her[2] original brightness, nor appeared
Less than archangel ruined, and th' excess
Of glory obscured: as when the sun new-risen
Looks through the horizontal[3] misty air 595
Shorn of his beams, or from behind the moon,
In dim eclipse,[4] disastrous twilight sheds
On half the nations, and with fear of change
Perplexes monarchs. Darkened so, yet shone
Above them all th' archangel; but his face 600
Deep scars of thunder had entrenched, and care
Sat on his faded cheek, but under brows
Of dauntless courage, and considerate[5] pride
Waiting revenge. Cruel his eye, but cast
Signs of remorse and passion,[6] to behold 605
The fellows of his crime, the followers rather
(Far other once beheld in bliss), condemned
Forever now to have their lot in pain;
Millions of spirits for his fault amerced[7]
Of Heaven, and from eternal splendors flung 610

7. The pygmies had periodic fights with the cranes, which (according to Pliny) they won by riding to battle on pigs and goats. This would make them cavalry; but Milton wanted the pun on "infants." His idea is that, compared with the devils, all other armies that ever were would look puny.
8. Allied.
9. The Giants of Greek mythology were born at Phlegra (line 577); Milton imagines them joined with the Seven who fought against Thebes, and the whole Greek host that besieged Troy ("Ilium"), plus the various gods who helped on both sides. He even adds the knights "British or Armoric" (from Brittany) who fought with King Arthur ("Uther's son"), and includes a list of proper names taken from the cycles of romance and suggesting vast, remote armies. Fontarabbia, the best known, was reputed to be the scene of Roland's last stand in the *Chanson de Roland*; Milton thus mingles the fall of Charlemagne with that of his best-known knight.
1. Obeyed.
2. *Forma*, in Latin, is feminine; hence "her."
3. The rays of the sun, as it first rises over the horizon, are almost horizontal.
4. Time of ill omen. "Disastrous": threatening disaster.
5. Thoughtful, conscious.
6. Compassion.
7. Deprived.

For his revolt; yet faithful how they stood,
Their glory withered; as, when Heaven's fire
Hath scathed the forest oaks or mountain pines,
With singéd top their stately growth, though bare,
Stands on the blasted heath. He now prepared   615
To speak; whereat their doubled ranks they bend
From wing to wing, and half enclose him round
With all his peers: attention held them mute.
Thrice he essayed, and thrice, in spite of scorn,
Tears, such as angels weep, burst forth: at last   620
Words interwove with sighs found out their way:

   "O myriads of immortal spirits! O powers
Matchless, but with th' Almighty!—and that strife
Was not inglorious, though th' event[8] was dire,
As this place testifies, and this dire change,   625
Hateful to utter. But what power of mind,
Foreseeing or presaging, from the depth
Of knowledge past or present, could have feared
How such united force of gods, how such
As stood like these, could ever know repulse?   630
For who can yet believe, though after loss,
That all these puissant[9] legions, whose exile
Hath emptied Heaven, shall fail to reascend,
Self-raised, and repossess their native seat?
For me, be witness all the host of Heaven,   635
If counsels different,[1] or danger shunned
By me, have lost our hopes. But he who reigns
Monarch in Heaven, till then as one secure
Sat on his throne, upheld by old repute,
Consent or custom, and his regal state   640
Put forth at full, but still his strength concealed,
Which tempted our attempt,[2] and wrought our fall.
Henceforth his might we know, and know our own,
So as not either to provoke, or dread
New war provoked: our better part remains   645
To work in close design,[3] by fraud or guile,
What force effected not; that he no less
At length from us may find, who overcomes
By force hath overcome but half his foe.
Space may produce new worlds; whereof so rife   650
There went a fame[4] in Heaven that he ere long
Intended to create, and therein plant
A generation whom his choice regard
Should favor equal to the sons of Heaven.
Thither, if but to pry, shall be perhaps   655
Our first eruption—thither, or elsewhere;

---

8. Outcome, result.
9. Potent, powerful.
1. Contradictory or even selfish, but also, in an obsolete sense, delaying.
2. Satan is an inveterate punster and player on words.
3. I.e., our best choice is to achieve by secret schemes.
4. Rumor. "Rife": common.

For this infernal pit shall never hold
Celestial spirits in bondage, nor th' abyss
Long under darkness cover. But these thoughts
Full counsel must mature. Peace is despaired,   660
For who can think submission? War, then, war
Open or understood,[5] must be resolved."
    He spake; and, to confirm his words, outflew
Millions of flaming swords, drawn from the thighs
Of mighty cherubim; the sudden blaze   665
Far round illumined Hell. Highly they raged
Against the Highest, and fierce with graspéd arms
Clashed on their sounding shields the din of war,[6]
Hurling defiance toward the vault of Heaven.
    There stood a hill not far, whose grisly[7] top   670
Belched fire and rolling smoke; the rest entire
Shone with a glossy scurf,[8] undoubted sign
That in his womb was hid metallic ore,
The work of sulphur.[9] Thither, winged with speed,
A numerous brigade hastened: as when bands   675
Of pioneers,[1] with spade and pickax armed,
Forerun the royal camp, to trench a field,
Or cast a rampart. Mammon led them on,
Mammon, the least erected[2] spirit that fell
From Heaven; for even in Heaven his looks and thoughts   680
Were always downward bent, admiring more
The riches of Heaven's pavement, trodden gold,
Than aught divine or holy else enjoyed
In vision beatific. By him first
Men also, and by his suggestion taught,   685
Ransacked the center, and with impious hands
Rifled the bowels of their mother Earth
For treasures better hid. Soon had his crew
Opened into the hill a spacious wound,
And digged out ribs[3] of gold. Let none admire   690
That riches grow in Hell; that soil may best
Deserve the precious bane. And here let those
Who boast in mortal things, and wondering tell
Of Babel, and the works of Memphian kings,
Learn how their greatest monuments of fame   695
And strength, and art, are easily outdone
By spirits reprobate,[4] and in an hour
What in an age they, with incessant toil
And hands innumerable, scarce perform.

5. Agreed-upon, tacit, hence secret.
6. Like Roman legionaries, the fallen angels applaud by beating swords on shields.
7. Horrible.
8. Crust.
9. Sulphur and mercury were considered the basic substances of all metals.
1. Sappers, engineers.
2. Elevated. Mammon is not a god but an abstract word meaning "wealth"; cf. Belial.
3. Bars, of course, but also with a hit at Eve, who was a "precious bane" (sweet poison) dug out of Adam's side. "Admire": wonder.
4. The tower of Babel and the Pyramids of Egypt ("works of Memphian kings") are easily outdone by the devils ("spirits reprobate").

Nigh on the plain, in many cells prepared,   700
That underneath had veins of liquid fire
Sluiced from the lake, a second multitude
With wondrous art founded the massy ore,
Severing each kind, and scummed the bullion-dross.
A third as soon had formed within the ground   705
A various mold, and from the boiling cells
By strange conveyance filled each hollow nook;[5]
As in an organ, from one blast of wind,
To many a row of pipes the soundboard breathes.
Anon out of the earth a fabric huge   710
Rose like an exhalation, with the sound
Of dulcet symphonies and voices sweet,
Built like a temple, where pilasters[6] round
Were set, and Doric pillars[7] overlaid
With golden architrave; nor did there want   715
Cornice or frieze, with bossy[8] sculptures graven;
The roof was fretted[9] gold. Not Babylon
Nor great Alcairo such magnificence
Equaled in all their glories,[1] to enshrine
Belus or Serapis their gods, or seat   720
Their kings, when Egypt with Assyria strove
In wealth and luxury. Th' ascending pile
Stood fixed[2] her stately height; and straight the doors,
Opening their brazen folds, discover, wide
Within, her ample spaces o'er the smooth   725
And level pavement: from the archéd roof,
Pendent by subtle magic, many a row
Of starry lamps and blazing cressets,[3] fed
With naphtha and asphaltus, yielded light
As from a sky. The hasty multitude   730
Admiring entered; and the work some praise,
And some the architect. His hand was known
In Heaven by many a towered structure high,
Where sceptered angels held their residence,
And sat as princes, whom the súpreme King   735
Exalted to such power, and gave to rule,
Each in his hierarchy, the orders bright.
Nor was his name unheard or unadored
In ancient Greece; and in Ausonian land
Men called him Mulciber;[4] and how he fell   740

5. After melting the gold with fire from the lake and pouring it into molds, the devils cause their building to rise by a sort of spiritual-musical magic.
6. Columns set in a wall.
7. Doric pillars are severe and plain.
8. Embossed.
9. Patterned.
1. At Babylon in Assyria there were temples to "Belus" or Baal; at Alcairo (modern Cairo, ancient Memphis) in Egypt, they were to Osiris, one of whose names was Serapis (here, but not ordi-

narily, accented on the first syllable).
2. Complete; "straight": straightway.
3. Basketlike lamps, hung from the ceiling.
4. Hephaestus, or Vulcan, was sometimes known in "Ausonian land" (Italy) by the secondary epithet of "Mulciber." The story of Jove's tossing him out of Heaven is told, to the accompaniment of much Homeric laughter, in *Iliad* I. Milton calls him by a secondary name because he is a little uneasy at having to put a "good" Greek deity in Hell.

From Heaven they fabled, thrown by angry Jove
Sheer o'er the crystal battlements: from morn
To noon he fell, from noon to dewy eve,
A summer's day, and with the setting sun
Dropped from the zenith, like a falling star, 745
On Lemnos, th' Aegean isle. Thus they relate,
Erring;[5] for he with this rebellious rout
Fell long before; nor aught availed him now
To have built in Heaven high towers; nor did he 'scape
By all his engines, but was headlong sent, 750
With his industrious crew, to build in Hell.
   Meanwhile the wingéd heralds, by command
Of sovereign power, with awful ceremony
And trumpet's sound, throughout the host proclaim
A solemn council forthwith to be held 755
At Pandemonium,[6] the high capital
Of Satan and his peers.[7] Their summons called
From every band and squaréd regiment
By place or choice the worthiest; they anon
With hundreds and with thousands trooping came 760
Attended. All access was thronged, the gates
And porches wide, but chief the spacious hall
(Though like a covered field, where champions bold
Wont ride in armed, and at the soldan's[8] chair
Defied the best of paynim chivalry 765
To mortal combat, or career with lance),
Thick swarmed, both on the ground and in the air,
Brushed with the hiss of rustling wings. As bees
In springtime, when the sun with Taurus[9] rides,
Pour forth their populous youth about the hive 770
In clusters; they among fresh dews and flowers
Fly to and fro, or on the smoothéd plank,
The suburb of their straw-built citadel,
New rubbed with balm, expatiate, and confer[1]
Their state-affairs: so thick the airy crowd 775
Swarmed and were straitened; till, the signal given,
Behold a wonder! They but now who seemed
In bigness to surpass Earth's giant sons,
Now less than smallest dwarfs, in narrow room
Throng numberless—like that pygmean race 780
Beyond the Indian mount;[2] or faery elves,
Whose midnight revels, by a forest side
Or fountain, some belated peasant sees,

5. Milton tells the story, and gives it six lines of splendid poetry (740–46), but in the end condemns it as a corrupt version of the Biblical truth.
6. "Pandemonium" (a Miltonic coinage) means literally "All-Demons"; an inversion of Pantheon, "All-Gods."
7. Nobility.
8. Sultan's. "Paynim": pagan.

9. The sun is in the Zodiacal sign of Taurus from April 19 to May 20.
1. Spread out and discuss, bring together. The simile of bees prepares for the sudden contraction of the devils' size; they can shrink or dilate at will.
2. The pygmies were supposed to live beyond the Himalayas, "the Indian mount."

Or dreams he sees, while overhead the Moon
Sits arbitress,[3] and nearer to the Earth   785
Wheels her pale course; they, on their mirth and dance
Intent, with jocund[4] music charm his ear;
At once with joy and fear his heart rebounds.
Thus incorporeal spirits to smallest forms
Reduced their shapes immense, and were at large,   790
Though without number still, amidst the hall
Of that infernal court. But far within,
And in their own dimensions like themselves,
The great seraphic lords and cherubim
In close recess and secret conclave sat,   795
A thousand demigods on golden seats,
Frequent and full.[5] After short silence then,
And summons read, the great consult began.

Book II
The Argument

The consultation begun, Satan debates whether another battle be
to be hazarded for the recovery of Heaven: some advise it, others
dissuade. A third proposal is preferred, mentioned before by Satan
—to search the truth of that prophecy or tradition in Heaven concerning another world, and another kind of creature, equal or not
much inferior to themselves, about this time to be created. Their
doubt who shall be sent on this difficult search: Satan, their chief,
undertakes alone the voyage; is honored and applauded. The council thus ended, the rest betake them several ways and to several
employments, as their inclinations lead them, to entertain[1] the
time till Satan return. He passes on his journey to Hell-gates; finds
them shut, and who sat there to guard them; by whom at length
they are opened, and discover[2] to him the great gulf between Hell
and Heaven. With what difficulty he passes through, directed by
Chaos, the power of that place, to the sight of this new world
which he sought.

High on a throne of royal state, which far
Outshone the wealth of Ormus[3] and of Ind,
Or where the gorgeous East with richest hand
Showers on her kings barbaric pearl and gold,
Satan exalted sat, by merit raised   5
To that bad eminence; and, from despair

3. Witness.
4. Merry.
5. Crowded ("frequent") and in full
complement ("full"); all present and
accounted for.

1. Pass.
2. Disclose.
3. An island in the Persian Gulf, modern Hormuz, famous for pearls. "Ind":
India

Thus high uplifted beyond hope, aspires
Beyond thus high, insatiate to pursue
Vain war with Heaven; and, by success[4] untaught,
His proud imaginations thus displayed: 10
    "Powers and dominions, deities of Heaven!
For since no deep within her gulf can hold
Immortal vigor, though oppressed and fallen,
I give not Heaven for lost: from this descent
Celestial virtues rising will appear   15
More glorious and more dread than from no fall,
And trust themselves to fear no second fate.
Me though just right, and the fixed laws of Heaven
Did first create your leader, next, free choice,
With what besides, in council or in fight,   20
Hath been achieved of merit, yet this loss
Thus far at least recovered, hath much more
Established in a safe unenvied throne
Yielded with full consent.[5] The happier state
In Heaven, which follows dignity, might draw   25
Envy from each inferior; but who here
Will envy whom the highest place exposes
Foremost to stand against the Thunderer's aim,
Your bulwark, and condemns to greatest share
Of endless pain? Where there is then no good   30
For which to strive, no strife can grow up there
From faction; for none sure will claim in Hell
Precédence, none, whose portion is so small
Of present pain, that with ambitious mind
Will covet more. With this advantage then   35
To union, and firm faith, and firm accord,
More than can be in Heaven, we now return
To claim our just inheritance of old,
Surer to prosper than prosperity
Could have assured us;[6] and by what best way,   40
Whether of open war or covert guile,
We now debate; who can advise, may speak."
    He ceased, and next him Moloch, sceptered king,
Stood up, the strongest and the fiercest spirit
That fought in Heaven, now fiercer by despair.   45
His trust was with th' Eternal to be deemed
Equal in strength, and rather than be less
Cared not to be at all; with that care lost
Went all his fear: of God, or Hell, or worse
He recked[7] not, and these words thereafter spake: 50

1384 · *John Milton*

"My sentence[8] is for open war: of wiles,
More unexpert,[9] I boast not: them let those
Contrive who need, or when they need, not now.
For while they sit contriving, shall the rest,
Millions that stand in arms, and longing wait   55
The signal to ascend, sit lingering here
Heaven's fugitives, and for their dwelling place
Accept this dark opprobrious den of shame,
The prison of his tyranny who reigns
By our delay? No! let us rather choose,   60
Armed with Hell-flames and fury, all at once
O'er Heaven's high towers to force resistless way,
Turning our tortures into horrid arms
Against the Torturer; when to meet the noise
Of his almighty engine[1] he shall hear   65
Infernal thunder, and for lightning see
Black fire and horror shot with equal rage
Among his angels, and his throne itself
Mixed with Tartarean[2] sulphur, and strange fire,
His own invented torments. But perhaps   70
The way seems difficult and steep to scale
With upright wing against a higher foe.
Let such bethink them, if the sleepy drench[3]
Of that forgetful lake benumb not still,
That in our proper motion[4] we ascend   75
Up to our native seat; descent and fall
To us is adverse. Who but felt of late,
When the fierce foe hung on our broken rear
Insulting,[5] and pursued us through the deep,
With what compulsion and laborious flight   80
We sunk thus low? Th' ascent is easy then;
Th' event[6] is feared: should we again provoke
Our stronger,[7] some worse way his wrath may find
To our destruction; if there be in Hell
Fear to be worse destroyed! What can be worse   85
Than to dwell here, driven out from bliss, condemned
In this abhorréd deep to utter woe;
Where pain of unextinguishable fire
Must exercise us without hope of end,
The vassals[8] of his anger, when the scourge   90
Inexorably, and the torturing hour,
Calls us to penance? More destroyed than thus,
We should be quite abolished, and expire.
What fear we then? what[9] doubt we to incense

8. Judgment.
9. Inexperienced. Moloch never had to be clever, and is proud of it.
1. The thunderbolt.
2. Tartarus is a classical name for Hell.
3. A draught of physic, as for animals; hence, used contemptuously here.
4. Natural impulse.

5. With the Latin sense of stamping or dancing on.
6. Outcome.
7. The word "enemy" is understood.
8. Servants, underlings; but perhaps also—or alternatively—"vessels."
9. Why.

His utmost ire? Which, to the height enraged,   95
Will either quite consume us, and reduce
To nothing this essential,[1] happier far
Than miserable to have eternal being!
Or if our substance be indeed divine,
And cannot cease to be, we are at worst   100
On this side nothing;[2] and by proof we feel
Our power sufficient to disturb his Heaven,
And with perpetual inroads to alarm,
Though inaccessible, his fatal throne:
Which, if not victory, is yet revenge."   105
   He ended frowning, and his look denounced
Desperate revenge, and battle dangerous
To less than gods.[3] On th' other side up rose
Belial, in act more graceful and humane;
A fairer person lost not Heaven; he seemed   110
For dignity composed, and high exploit.
But all was false and hollow; though his tongue
Dropped manna,[4] and could make the worse appear
The better reason, to perplex and dash
Maturest counsels: for his thoughts were low,   115
To vice industrious, but to nobler deeds
Timorous and slothful: yet he pleased the ear,
And with persuasive accent thus began:
   "I should be much for open war, O peers,
As not behind in hate, if what was urged   120
Main reason to persuade immediate war,
Did not dissuade me most, and seem to cast
Ominous conjecture on the whole success;[5]
When he who most excels in fact of arms,
In what he counsels, and in what excels   125
Mistrustful, grounds his courage on despair
And utter dissolution, as the scope
Of all his aim, after some dire revenge.
First, what revenge? The towers of Heaven are filled
With arméd watch, that render all access   130
Impregnable; oft on the bordering deep
Encamp their legions, or with óbscure wing
Scout far and wide into the realm of Night,
Scorning surprise. Or could we break our way
By force, and at our heels all Hell should rise   135
With blackest insurrection, to confound
Heaven's purest light, yet our great enemy
All incorruptible would on his throne

---

1. Essence.
2. I.e., we are now as badly off as we can be without being nothing, and so need have no fear.
3. Only gods could have withstood Moloch.
4. His tongue was honeyed. To "make the worse appear / The better reason" was characteristic of Sophists—hollow, mercenary logic-choppers of ancient Greece. "Dash": confuse.
5. As above, line 9, outcome. "Fact": feat.

Sit unpolluted, and th' ethereal mold[6]
Incapable of stain would soon expel   140
Her mischief, and purge off the baser fire,
Victorious. Thus repulsed, our final hope
Is flat despair: we must exasperate
Th' almighty Victor to spend all his rage,
And that must end us, that must be our cure,   145
To be no more. Sad cure! for who would lose,
Though full of pain, this intellectual being,
Those thoughts that wander through eternity,
To perish rather, swallowed up and lost
In the wide womb of uncreated Night,   150
Devoid of sense and motion? And who knows,
Let this be good,[7] whether our angry Foe
Can give it, or will ever? How he can
Is doubtful; that he never will is sure.
Will he, so wise, let loose at once his ire,   155
Belike[8] through impotence, or unaware,
To give his enemies their wish, and end
Them in his anger, whom his anger saves
To punish endless? 'Wherefore cease we then?'
Say they who counsel war, 'we are decreed,   160
Reserved and destined to eternal woe;
Whatever doing, what can we suffer more,
What can we suffer worse?' Is this then worst,
Thus sitting, thus consulting, thus in arms?
What when we fled amain,[9] pursued and strook   165
With Heaven's afflicting thunder, and besought
The deep to shelter us? this Hell then seemed
A refuge from those wounds. Or when we lay
Chained on the burning lake? that sure was worse.
What if the breath that kindled those grim fires,   170
Awaked, should blow them into sevenfold rage,
And plunge us in the flames? or from above
Should intermitted[1] vengeance arm again
His red right hand to plague us? What if all
Her[2] stores were opened, and this firmament   175
Of Hell should spout her cataracts of fire,
Impendent[3] horrors, threatening hideous fall
One day upon our heads; while we perhaps
Designing or exhorting glorious war,
Caught in a fiery tempest shall be hurled,   180
Each on his rock transfixed, the sport and prey
Of racking whirlwinds, or forever sunk
Under yon boiling ocean, wrapped in chains;

---

6. Substance. "Ethereal" substance, derived from "ether," is thought to be incorruptible.
7. I.e., suppose it is good to be destroyed.
8. Ironically, in the sense of "I dare say."
9. Headlong. "Strook": struck.
1. Momentarily suspended.
2. Those of Hell.
3. In the Latin sense, hanging down, threatening.

There to converse with everlasting groans,
Unrespited, unpitied, unreprieved,   185
Ages of hopeless end! This would be worse.
War therefore, open or concealed, alike
My voice dissuades; for what can force or guile[4]
With him, or who deceive his mind, whose eye
Views all things at one view? He from Heaven's height   190
All these our motions[5] vain, sees and derides,
Not more almighty to resist our might
Than wise to frustrate all our plots and wiles.
Shall we then live thus vile, the race of Heaven
Thus trampled, thus expelled to suffer here   195
Chains and these torments? Better these than worse,
By my advice; since fate inevitable
Subdues us, and omnipotent decree,
The Victor's will. To suffer, as to do,
Our strength is equal,[6] nor the law unjust   200
That so ordains: this was at first resolved,
If we were wise, against so great a foe
Contending, and so doubtful what might fall.
I laugh, when those who at the spear are bold
And venturous, if that fail them, shrink and fear   205
What yet they know must follow, to endure
Exile, or ignominy, or bonds, or pain,
The sentence of their Conqueror. This is now
Our doom; which if we can sustain and bear,
Our súpreme Foe in time may much remit   210
His anger, and perhaps, thus far removed,
Not mind us not offending, satisfied
With what is punished;[7] whence these raging fires
Will slacken, if his breath stir not their flames.
Our purer essence then will overcome   215
Their noxious vapor, or inured[8] not feel,
Or changed at length, and to the place conformed
In temper and in nature, will receive
Familiar the fierce heat, and void of pain;
This horror will grow mild, this darkness light;   220
Besides what hope the never-ending flight
Of future days may bring, what chance, what change
Worth waiting, since our present lot appears
For happy though but ill, for ill not worst,[9]
If we procure not to ourselves more woe."   225
     Thus Belial, with words clothed in reason's garb,

---

4. The verb "accomplish" or "achieve" is omitted.

5. Proposals, plots.

6. I.e., passive endurance and active energy are both in the devils' power. Belial points out, with dangerous good sense, that they must have known from the beginning that they might have to exercise both (lines 201–3).

7. A Latinism, *quod punitum est;* God will be satisfied with the punishment that has been inflicted.

8. Accustomed.

9. I.e., from the point of view of happiness, the devils are but ill off; from the point of view of evil, they could be worse. This is diabolic relativism.

Counseled ignoble ease and peaceful sloth,
Not peace; and after him thus Mammon spake:
    "Either to disenthrone the King of Heaven
We war, if war be best, or to regain   230
Our own right lost: him to unthrone we then
May hope, when everlasting Fate shall yield
To fickle Chance, and Chaos judge the strife.
The former, vain to hope, argues[1] as vain
The latter; for what place can be for us   235
Within Heaven's bound, unless Heaven's Lord supreme
We overpower? Suppose he should relent
And publish grace to all, on promise made
Of new subjection; with what eyes could we
Stand in his presence humble, and receive   240
Strict laws imposed, to celebrate his throne
With warbled hymns, and to his Godhead sing
Forced Halleluiahs; while he lordly sits
Our envied Sovereign, and his altar breathes
Ambrosial odors and ambrosial flowers,   245
Our servile offerings? This must be our task
In Heaven, this our delight; how wearisome
Eternity so spent in worship paid
To whom we hate! Let us not then pursue,
By force impossible, by leave obtained   250
Unácceptable, though in Heaven, our state
Of spendid vassalage;[2] but rather seek
Our own good from ourselves, and from our own
Live to ourselves, though in this vast recess,
Free, and to none accountable, preferring   255
Hard liberty before the easy yoke
Of servile pomp. Our greatness will appear
Then most conspicuous, when great things of small,
Useful of hurtful, prosperous of adverse,
We can create, and in what place soe'er   260
Thrive under evil, and work ease out of pain
Through labor and endurance. This deep world
Of darkness do we dread? How oft amidst
Thick clouds and dark doth Heaven's all-ruling Sire
Choose to reside, his glory unobscured,   265
And with the majesty of darkness round
Covers his throne; from whence deep thunders roar,
Mustering their rage, and Heaven resembles Hell!
As he our darkness, cannot we his light
Imitate when we please? This desert soil   270
Wants[3] not her hidden luster, gems, and gold;
Nor want we skill or art, from whence to raise
Magnificence; and what can Heaven show more?

---

1. Proves.
2. Servitude.
3. Lacks. Mammon proposes a tawdry

imitation-Heaven in Hell; this is the
ultimate in diabolic degradation.

Our torments also may in length of time
Become our elements, these piercing fires   275
As soft as now severe, our temper changed
Into their temper; which must needs remove
The sensible[4] of pain. All things invite
To peaceful counsels, and the settled state
Of order, how in safety best we may   280
Compose our present evils, with regard
Of what we are and where, dismissing quite
All thoughts of war. Ye have what I advise."
    He scarce had finished, when such murmur filled
Th' assembly, as when hollow rocks retain   285
The sound of blustering winds, which all night long
Had roused the sea, now with hoarse cadence lull
Seafaring men o'erwatched,[5] whose bark by chance,
Or pinnace, anchors in a craggy bay
After the tempest: such applause was heard   290
As Mammon ended, and his sentence pleased,
Advising peace; for such another field
They dreaded worse than Hell; so much the fear
Of thunder and the sword of Michaël[6]
Wrought still within them; and no less desire   295
To found this nether empire, which might rise
By policy, and long process of time,
In emulation opposite to Heaven.
Which when Beëlzebub perceived, than whom,
Satan except, none higher sat, with grave   300
Aspect he rose, and in his rising seemed
A pillar of state; deep on his front[7] engraven
Deliberation sat and public care;
And princely counsel in his face yet shone,
Majestic though in ruin. Sage he stood   305
With Atlantean[8] shoulders fit to bear
The weight of mightiest monarchies; his look
Drew audience and attention still as night
Or summer's noontide air, while thus he spake:
    "Thrones and imperial powers, offspring of Heaven,   310
Ethereal virtues; or these titles now
Must we renounce, and, changing style, be called
Princes of Hell? For so the popular vote
Inclines, here to continue, and build up here
A growing empire—Doubtless! while we dream,   315
And know not that the King of Heaven hath doomed
This place our dungeon, not our safe retreat
Beyond his potent arm, to live exempt
From Heaven's high jurisdiction, in new league

4. Sense, sensation.
5. Tired out with watching.
6. The warrior angel, chief stay of the angelic armies.
7. Forehead, brow.

8. Worthy of Atlas, one of the Titans, who as a punishment for rebellion was condemned to stand in North Africa and hold up the heavens.

Banded against his throne, but to remain   320
In strictest bondage, though thus far removed,
Under th' inevitable curb, reserved
His captive multitude. For he, be sure,
In height or depth, still first and last will reign
Sole King, and of his kingdom lose no part   325
By our revolt, but over Hell extend
His empire, and with iron scepter rule
Us here, as with his golden those in Heaven.
What[9] sit we then projecting peace and war?
War hath determined us,[1] and foiled with loss   330
Irreparable; terms of peace yet none
Vouchsafed or sought; for what peace will be given
To us enslaved, but custody severe,
And stripes, and arbitrary punishment
Inflicted? and what peace can we return,   335
But, to our power,[2] hostility and hate,
Untamed reluctance,[3] and revenge, though slow,
Yet ever plotting how the Conqueror least
May reap his conquest, and may least rejoice
In doing what we most in suffering feel?[4]   340
Nor will occasion want, nor shall we need
With dangerous expedition to invade
Heaven, whose high walls fear no assault or siege,
Or ambush from the deep. What if we find
Some easier enterprise? There is a place   345
(If ancient and prophetic fame[5] in Heaven
Err not), another world, the happy seat
Of some new race called *Man*, about this time
To be created like to us,[6] though less
In power and excellence, but favored more   350
Of him who rules above; so was his will
Pronounced among the gods, and by an oath,
That shook Heaven's whole circumference, confirmed.
Thither let us bend all our thoughts, to learn
What creatures there inhabit, of what mold,   355
Or substance, how endued,[7] and what their power,
And where their weakness, how attempted[8] best,
By force or subtlety. Though Heaven be shut,
And Heaven's high Arbitrator sit secure
In his own strength, this place may lie exposed,   360
The utmost border of his kingdom, left
To their defense who hold it;[9] here, perhaps,

---

9. Why.
1. I.e., war has decided the question for (but also, limited) us.
2. I.e., to the best of our power.
3. Resistance (in the Latin sense, struggling back).
4. How God may get least pleasure from our pain—a devil's view of the deity.

5. Report, rumor.
6. The created (Ptolemaic) cosmos came into existence only after the fall of Satan, and the fallen angels, being otherwise occupied, could not know of it.
7. Endowed.
8. Attacked, but also "tempted."
9. To be defended by the occupants.

Some advantageous act may be achieved
By sudden onset: either with Hell-fire
To waste[1] his whole creation, or possess 365
All as our own, and drive, as we were driven,
The puny habitants; or if not drive,
Seduce them to our party, that their God
May prove their foe, and with repenting hand
Abolish his own works. This would surpass 370
Common revenge, and interrupt his joy
In our confusion, and our joy upraise
In his disturbance; when his darling sons,
Hurled headlong to partake with us, shall curse
Their frail original,[2] and faded bliss, 375
Faded so soon! Advise if this be worth
Attempting, or to sit in darkness here
Hatching vain empires." Thus Beëlzebub
Pleaded his devilish counsel, first devised
By Satan, and in part proposed; for whence, 380
But from the author of all ill could spring
So deep a malice, to confound[3] the race
Of mankind in one root, and Earth with Hell
To mingle and involve, done all to spite
The great Creator? But their spite still serves 385
His glory to augment. The bold design
Pleased highly those infernal states, and joy
Sparkled in all their eyes; with full assent
They vote: whereat his speech he thus renews:
"Well have ye judged, well ended long debate, 390
Synod of gods, and, like to what ye are,
Great things resolved; which from the lowest deep
Will once more lift us up, in spite of Fate,
Nearer our ancient seat; perhaps in view
Of those bright confines, whence with neighboring arms 395
And opportune excursion we may chance
Re-enter Heaven; or else in some mild zone
Dwell not unvisited of Heaven's fair light,
Secure, and at the brightening orient beam
Purge off this gloom; the soft delicious air, 400
To heal the scar of these corrosive fires,
Shall breathe her balm. But first, whom shall we send
In search of this new world? whom shall we find
Sufficient? who shall tempt[4] with wandering feet
The dark, unbottomed, infinite abyss, 405
And through the palpable obscure[5] find out
His uncouth way, or spread his airy flight
Upborn with indefatigable wings

1. Lay waste.
2. Originator, parent; or, perhaps, "their original condition."
3. Destroy, ruin. Adam, the first man, is the "root" of mankind.
4. Try, attempt (from Latin *temptare*).
5. Darkness so thick it can be felt. "Uncouth": strange, new.

Over the vast abrupt,[6] ere he arrive
The happy isle?[7] What strength, what art, can then   410
Suffice, or what evasion bear him safe
Through the strict senteries[8] and stations thick
Of angels watching round? Here he had need
All circumspection, and we now no less
Choice in our suffrage;[9] for on whom we send   415
The weight of all, and our last hope, relies."
    This said, he sat; and expectation held
His look suspense,[1] awaiting who appeared
To second, or oppose, or undertake
The perilous attempt; but all sat mute,   420
Pondering the danger with deep thoughts; and each
In others' countenance read his own dismay,
Astonished. None among the choice and prime
Of those Heaven-warring champions could be found
So hardy as to proffer or accept   425
Alone the dreadful voyage; till at last
Satan, whom now transcendent glory raised
Above his fellows, with monarchal pride
Conscious of highest worth, unmoved thus spake:
    "O progeny of Heaven, empyreal thrones!   430
With reason hath deep silence and demur[2]
Seized us, though undismayed. Long is the way
And hard, that out of Hell leads up to light;
Our prison strong, this huge convex[3] of fire,
Outrageous to devour, immures us round   435
Ninefold,[4] and gates of burning adamant,
Barred over us, prohibit all egress.
These passed, if any pass, the void profound
Of unessential[5] Night receives him next,
Wide gaping, and with utter loss of being   440
Threatens him, plunged in that abortive gulf.
If thence he 'scape into whatever world,
Or unknown region, what remains him less[6]
Than unknown dangers and as hard escape?
But I should ill become this throne, O peers,   445
And this imperial sovereignty, adorned
With splendor, armed with power, if aught proposed
And judged of public moment,[7] in the shape
Of difficulty or danger, could deter
Me from attempting. Wherefore do I assume   450

6. Chaos; a striking example of sound imitating sense.
7. Wherever man is (for the fallen angels do not yet know of Earth).
8. Old spelling of *sentries*, necessary here for the meter.
9. Care in our voting.
1. I.e., everyone sat waiting in suspense.
2. Delay.
3. Vault.

4. Walls **us** in with nine thicknesses. See below, lines 645 ff.
5. Without real being, darkness being merely the absence of light. The "abortive gulf" expresses again this completely negative quality of Chaos and Night.
6. I.e., what awaits him except.
7. Importance.

These royalties,[8] and not refuse to reign,
Refusing to accept as great a share
Of hazard as of honor, due alike
To him who reigns, and so much to him due
Of hazard more, as he above the rest
High honored sits?[9] Go therefore, mighty powers,   455
Terror of Heaven, though fallen; intend[1] at home,
While here shall be our home, what best may ease
The present misery, and render Hell
More tolerable; if there be cure or charm   460
To respite, or deceive, or slack the pain
Of this ill mansion; intermit no watch
Against a wakeful foe, while I abroad
Through all the coasts of dark destruction seek
Deliverance for us all: this enterprise   465
None shall partake with me." Thus saying, rose
The monarch, and prevented[2] all reply;
Prudent, lest, from his resolution raised,[3]
Others among the chief might offer now
(Certain to be refused) what erst they feared,   470
And, so refused, might in opinion stand
His rivals, winning cheap the high repute
Which he through hazard huge must earn. But they
Dreaded not more th' adventure than his voice
Forbidding; and at once with him they rose;   475
Their rising all at once was as the sound
Of thunder heard remote. Towards him they bend
With awful[4] reverence prone; and as a god
Extol him equal to the Highest in Heaven.
Nor failed they to express how much they praised,   480
That for the general safety he despised
His own; for neither do the spirits damned
Lose all their virtue; lest bad men should boast
Their specious deeds on Earth, which glory excites,
Or close ambition varnished o'er with zeal.[5]   485
    Thus they their doubtful consultations dark
Ended, rejoicing in their matchless chief:
As when from mountain tops the dusky clouds
Ascending, while the north wind sleeps, o'erspread
Heaven's cheerful face, the lowering element   490
Scowls o'er the darkened landscape snow or shower;
If chance the radiant sun with farewell sweet
Extend his evening beam, the fields revive,

---

8. Insignia of royalty. "Refusing": i.e., if I refuse.
9. Satan's argument, simple though entangled in rhetoric, is that rulers must share in the dangers as well as the rewards of an enterprise.
1. Undertake, endeavor.
2. Forestalled, anticipated.
3. After their courage had been raised by his resolution.
4. Full of respect and awe.
5. The sense is that damned spirits still retain some virtues; lest bad men boast of good deeds they have done out of glory and ambition, Milton has shown us that devils do just as much. "Specious": pretending virtue. "Close": secret.

The birds their notes renew, and bleating herds
Attest their joy, that hill and valley rings.   495
O shame to men! Devil with devil damned
Firm concord holds, men only disagree
Of creatures rational, though under hope
Of heavenly grace; and, God proclaiming peace,[6]
Yet live in hatred, enmity, and strife   500
Among themselves, and levy cruel wars,
Wasting the earth, each other to destroy:
As if (which might induce us to accord)
Man had not hellish foes enow[7] besides,
That day and night for his destruction wait!   505
　　The Stygian council thus dissolved; and forth
In order came the grand infernal peers.
Midst came their mighty paramount,[8] and seemed
Alone th' antagonist of Heaven, nor less
Than Hell's dread emperor, with pomp supreme,   510
And godlike imitated state; him round
A globe[9] of fiery seraphim enclosed
With bright emblazonry,[1] and horrent arms.
Then of their session ended they bid cry
With trumpets' regal sound the great result: 515
Toward the four winds four speedy cherubim
Put to their mouths the sounding alchemy[2]
By herald's voice explained; the hollow abyss
Heard far and wide, and all the host of Hell
With deafening shout, returned them loud acclaim.   520
Thence more at ease their minds and somewhat raised
By false presumptuous hope, the rangéd[3] powers
Disband; and, wandering, each his several way
Pursues, as inclination or sad choice
Leads him perplexed where he may likeliest find   525
Truce to his restless thoughts, and entertain
The irksome hours, till his great chief return.
Part on the plain, or in the air sublime,[4]
Upon the wing, or in swift race contend,
As at th' Olympian games or Pythian fields;[5]   530
Part curb their fiery steeds, or shun the goal
With rapid wheels, or fronted brigades form.
As when, to warn proud cities, war appears
Waged in the troubled sky, and armies rush
To battle in the clouds;[6] before each van   535
Prick forth the airy knights, and couch their spears

6. I.e., though God proclaims peace.
7. I.e., enough; the old plural emphatic form.
8. Champion, chief.
9. Band or crowd.
1. Decorated shields. "Horrent": bristling.
2. I.e., resonant trumpets (made of the alloy brass by a marriage of metals which Milton associates with alchemy).
3. Arrayed in ranks.
4. Aloft, uplifted (the adjective modifies the flyer, not the air).
5. The Olympic games were held at Olympia, the Pythian games at Delphi. To "shun the goal" is to drive a chariot as close as possible around a column without hitting it.
6. Warfare in the skies at night, portending trouble on earth. "Prick": spur.

Till thickest legions close; with feats of arms
From either end of Heaven the welkin[7] burns.
Others with vast Typhoean[8] rage more fell
Rend up both rocks and hills, and ride the air   540
In whirlwind; Hell scarce holds the wild uproar.
As when Alcides, from Oechalia crowned
With conquest, felt th' envenomed robe, and tore
Through pain up by the roots Thessalian pines,
And Lichas from the top of Oeta threw   545
Into th' Euboic sea.[9] Others more mild,
Retreated in a silent valley, sing
With notes angelical to many a harp
Their own heroic deeds and hapless fall
By doom of battle; and complain that Fate   550
Free Virtue should enthrall to Force or Chance.
Their song was partial,[1] but the harmony
(What could it less when spirits immortal sing?)
Suspended[2] Hell, and took with ravishment
The thronging audience. In discourse more sweet   555
(For eloquence the soul, song charms the sense)
Others apart sat on a hill retired,
In thoughts more elevate, and reasoned high
Of providence, foreknowledge, will, and fate,
Fixed fate, free will, foreknowledge absolute,   560
And found no end, in wandering mazes lost.
Of good and evil much they argued then,
Of happiness and final misery,
Passion and apathy,[3] and glory and shame,
Vain wisdom all, and false philosophy![4]   565
Yet with a pleasing sorcery could charm
Pain for a while or anguish, and excite
Fallacious hope, or arm th' obduréd[5] breast
With stubborn patience as with triple steel.
Another part, in squadrons and gross[6] bands,   570
On bold adventure to discover wide
That dismal world, if any clime perhaps
Might yield them easier habitation, bend
Four ways their flying march, along the banks
Of four infernal rivers that disgorge   575

---

7. Sky.
8. Like that of Typhon, the hundred-headed Titan. See above, I.199.
9. Hercules, returning in triumph from Oechalia, prepared to sacrifice to the gods on top of Mt. Oeta, and sent to his wife Dejanira for a new robe. She had been told by the dying Nessus, a centaur whom Hercules had killed, that centaur's blood would preserve her husband's love. So she sent Hercules a robe anointed with the blood of Nessus. The "envenomed robe" tortured him into a frenzy, and before he died, he threw Lichas, who had brought it, to-gether with a good part of Mt. Oeta itself, into the sea of Euboea.
1. Prejudiced.
2. Held in suspense.
3. Feeling and lack of feeling; the angels are dabbling in Stoicism.
4. Milton means, not that the subjects themselves are vain (he himself, in the present poem, has a good deal to say on these topics), but that the very premises with which devils start are bound to land them in error.
5. Hardened.
6. Solid, dense.

Into the burning lake their baleful streams:[7]
Abhorréd Styx, the flood of deadly hate;
Sad Acheron of sorrow, black and deep;
Cocytus, named of lamentation loud
Heard on the rueful stream; fierce Phlegethon   580
Whose waves of torrent fire inflame with rage.
Far off from these a slow and silent stream,
Lethe, the river of oblivion, rolls
Her watery labyrinth, whereof who drinks
Forthwith his former state and being forgets,   585
Forgets both joy and grief, pleasure and pain.
Beyond this flood a frozen continent
Lies dark and wild, beat with perpetual storms
Of whirlwind and dire hail, which on firm land
Thaws not, but gathers heap,[8] and ruin seems   590
Of ancient pile; all else deep snow and ice,
A gulf profound as that Serbonian bog[9]
Betwixt Damiata and Mount Casius old,
Where armies whole have sunk: the parching air
Burns frore,[1] and cold performs th' effect of fire. 595
Thither by harpy-footed[2] Furies haled,
At certain revolutions[3] all the damned
Are brought; and feel by turns the bitter change
Of fierce extremes, extremes by change more fierce,
From beds of raging fire to starve[4] in ice   600
Their soft ethereal warmth, and there to pine
Immovable, infixed, and frozen round
Periods of time; thence hurried back to fire.
They ferry over this Lethean sound
Both to and fro, their sorrow to augment,   605
And wish and struggle, as they pass, to reach
The tempting stream, with one small drop to lose
In sweet forgetfulness all pain and woe,
All in one moment, and so near the brink;
But Fate withstands, and to oppose th' attempt   610
Medusa[5] with Gorgonian terror guards
The ford, and of itself the water flies
All taste of living wight, as once it fled
The lips of Tantalus.[6] Thus roving on
In cónfused march forlorn, th' adventurous bands   615

7. The four rivers are traditional in hellish geography; Milton takes pains to distinguish them by the original meanings of their Greek names (Styx means "hateful," Acheron "woeful," etc.). Lethe is "far off" and very different from the others, oblivion being relatively a blessed state in hell.
8. In a heap, so that it looks like the ruin of an old building ("ancient pile").
9. Lake Serbonis, once famous for its quicksands but today dried up, used to lie on the coast of Egypt, just east of the Nile, between Damiata and Mt.

Cassius.
1. Frosty.
2. With hooked claws.
3. I.e., of time.
4. Benumb.
5. One of the three Gorgons, women with snaky hair, scaly bodies, and boar's tusks, the very sight of whose faces changed men to stone.
6. Tantalus, afflicted with a raging thirst, stood in the middle of a lake, the water of which always eluded his grasp (hence, "tantalize").

With shuddering horror pale, and eyes aghast
Viewed first their lamentable lot, and found
No rest. Through many a dark and dreary vale
They passed, and many a region dolorous,
O'er many a frozen, many a fiery alp,[7]   620
Rocks, caves, lakes, fens, bogs, dens, and shades of death,
A universe of death, which God by curse
Created evil, for evil only good,
Where all life dies, death lives, and Nature breeds,
Perverse, all monstrous, all prodigious things,   625
Abominable, unutterable, and worse
Than fables yet have feigned, or fear conceived,
Gorgons, and Hydras, and Chimeras[8] dire.
    Meanwhile the adversary of God and man,
Satan with thoughts inflamed of highest design,   630
Puts on swift wings,[9] and toward the gates of Hell
Explores his solitary flight; sometimes
He scours the right hand coast, sometimes the left;
Now shaves with level wing the deep, then soars
Up to the fiery concave[1] towering high.   635
As when far off at sea a fleet descried
Hangs in the clouds, by equinoctial winds
Close sailing from Bengala,[2] or the isles
Of Ternate and Tidore,[3] whence merchants bring
Their spicy drugs; they on the trading flood   640
Through the wide Ethiopian[4] to the Cape
Ply stemming nightly toward the pole: so seemed
Far off the flying fiend. At last appear
Hell bounds, high reaching to the horrid roof,
And thrice threefold the gates; three folds were brass,   645
Three iron, three of adamantine rock,
Impenetrable, impaled with circling fire,
Yet unconsumed. Before the gates there sat
On either side a formidable shape;[5]
The one seemed woman to the waist, and fair,   650
But ended foul in many a scaly fold
Voluminous and vast, a serpent armed
With mortal sting. About her middle round
A cry[6] of Hellhounds never-ceasing barked

---

7. A "fiery alp" is a volcano.
8. The Hydra was a serpent with nine heads, which was slain by Hercules; the Chimera was a fire-breathing creature, part lion, part dragon, part goat. They exemplify abominations of nature.
9. Satan does not fasten on his wings; he takes swiftly to wing.
1. Vault.
2. An old form of "Bengal."
3. Two of the Molucca or "Spice" Islands, modern Indonesia.
4. The Indian Ocean, east of Africa. "The Cape" is of course the Cape of Good Hope; "the pole," the South Pole.
5. The allegorical figures of Sin and Death are founded on James i.15: "Then when lust hath conceived, it bringeth forth sin: and sin, when it is finished, bringeth forth death." But the incestuous relations of Sin and Death are Milton's own invention. Physically, Sin is modeled on Virgil's or Ovid's, with some touches adopted from Spenser's Error; Death is a traditional figure, vague and vast.
6. Pack.

With wide Cerberean[7] mouths full loud, and rung 655
A hideous peal; yet, when they list, would creep,
If aught disturbed their noise, into her womb,
And kennel there, yet there still barked and howled
Within unseen. Far less abhorred than these
Vexed Scylla,[8] bathing in the sea that parts 660
Calabria from the hoarse Trinacrian shore;
Nor uglier follow the night-hag,[9] when, called
In secret, riding through the air she comes,
Lured with the smell of infant blood, to dance
With Lapland witches, while the laboring moon 665
Eclipses at their charms. The other shape,
If shape it might be called that shape had none
Distinguishable in member, joint, or limb,
Or substance might be called that shadow seemed,
For each seemed either; black it stood as night, 670
Fierce as ten Furies, terrible as Hell,
And shook a dreadful dart; what seemed his head
The likeness of a kingly crown had on.
Satan was now at hand, and from his seat
The monster moving onward came as fast, 675
With horrid strides; Hell trembled as he strode.
Th' undaunted fiend what this might be admired,[1]
Admired, not feared; God and his Son except,
Created thing nought valued he nor shunned;
And with disdainful look thus first began: 680
    "Whence and what art thou, execrable shape,
That dar'st, though grim and terrible, advance
Thy miscreated front[2] athwart my way
To yonder gates? Through them I mean to pass,
That be assured, without leave asked of thee. 685
Retire, or taste thy folly, and learn by proof,
Hell-born, not to contend with spirits of Heaven."
    To whom the goblin, full of wrath, replied:
"Art thou that traitor angel, art thou he,
Who first broke peace in Heaven, and faith, till then 690
Unbroken, and in proud rebellious arms
Drew after him the third part of Heaven's sons
Conjured[3] against the Highest, for which both thou
And they, outcast from God, are here condemned
To waste eternal days in woe and pain? 695
And reckon'st thou thyself with spirits of Heaven,
Hell-doomed, and breath'st defiance here and scorn,
Where I reign king, and, to enrage thee more,

7. Like Cerberus, the traditional hound
of Hell.
8. Circe out of jealousy threw poison
into the water where Scylla bathed, in
the straits between Calabria and Sicily
("Trinacria"); as a result of the poisons, Scylla developed a ring of barking, snapping dogs around her waist.

9. Hecate, goddess of sorcery. She attends the orgies of witches in the home
of all witchcraft, Lapland, whither she
is drawn by the blood of babies sacrificed for the occasion.
1. Wondered.
2. Misshapen forehead, or face.
3. Sworn together by an oath.

Thy king and lord? Back to thy punishment,
False fugitive, and to thy speed add wings,   700
Lest with a whip of scorpions I pursue
Thy ling'ring, or with one stroke of this dart
Strange horror seize thee, and pangs unfelt before."
    So spake the grisly terror, and in shape,
So speaking and so threatening, grew tenfold   705
More dreadful and deform. On th' other side,
Incensed with indignation, Satan stood
Unterrified, and like a comet burned
That fires the length of Ophiucus⁴ huge
In th' Arctic sky, and from his horrid hair   710
Shakes pestilence and war. Each at the head
Leveled his deadly aim; their fatal hands
No second stroke intend,⁵ and such a frown
Each cast at th' other, as when two black clouds,
With Heaven's artillery fraught,⁶ come rattling on   715
Over the Caspian,⁷ then stand front to front
Hovering a space, till winds the signal blow
To join their dark encounter in mid-air:
So frowned the mighty combatants, that Hell
Grew darker at their frown; so matched they stood;   720
For never but once more was either like
To meet so great a foe.⁸ And now great deeds
Had been achieved, whereof all Hell had rung,
Had not the snaky sorceress that sat
Fast by Hell-gate, and kept the fatal key,   725
Ris'n, and with hideous outcry rushed between.
    "O father, what intends thy hand," she cried,
"Against thy only son?⁹ What fury, O son,
Possesses thee to bend that mortal dart
Against thy father's head? and know'st for whom?   730
For Him who sits above and laughs the while
At thee ordained his drudge, to execute
Whate'er his wrath, which he calls Justice, bids;
His wrath which one day will destroy ye both!"
    She spake, and at her words the hellish pest   735
Forbore, then these to her Satan returned:
    "So strange thy outcry, and thy words so strange
Thou interposest, that my sudden hand,
Prevented,¹ spares to tell thee yet by deeds
What it intends, till first I know of thee,   740
What thing thou art, thus double-formed, and why,
In this infernal vale first met, thou call'st

---

4. A vast Northern constellation, "The Serpent-Holder" (also called "Serpentarius"). Satan will soon appear as a snake; and, like a comet, he portends "pestilence and war."
5. I.e., the first stroke will do the business.
6. Loaded with thunderbolts.

7. The Caspian is a particularly stormy area.
8. I.e., the Son of God.
9. Sin, Death, and Satan, in their various interrelations, parody obscenely the relations between God and the Son, Adam and Eve.
1. Forestalled.

Me father, and that phantasm call'st my son?
I know thee not, nor ever saw till now
Sight more detestable than him and thee."   745
   T' whom thus the portress of Hell-gate replied:
"Hast thou forgot me then, and do I seem
Now in thine eye so foul? once deemed so fair
In Heaven, when at th' assembly, and in sight
Of all the seraphim with thee combined   750
In bold conspiracy against Heaven's King,
All on a sudden miserable pain
Surprised thee; dim thine eyes, and dizzy swum
In darkness, while thy head flames thick and fast
Threw forth, till on the left side opening wide,   755
Likest to thee in shape and countenance bright,
Then shining heavenly-fair, a goddess armed
Out of thy head I sprung.² Amazement seized
All th' host of Heaven; back they recoiled afraid
At first, and called me *Sin*, and for a sign   760
Portentous held me; but, familiar grown,
I pleased, and with attractive graces won
The most averse, thee chiefly, who full oft
Thyself in me thy perfect image viewing
Becam'st enamored;³ and such joy thou took'st   765
With me in secret, that my womb conceived
A growing burden. Meanwhile war arose,
And fields were fought in Heaven; wherein remained
(For what could else?) to our almighty Foe
Clear victory, to our part loss and rout   770
Through all the empyrean. Down they fell,
Driven headlong from the pitch⁴ of Heaven, down
Into this deep, and in the general fall
I also; at which time this powerful key
Into my hand was given, with charge to keep   775
These gates forever shut, which none can pass
Without my opening. Pensive here I sat
Alone, but long I sat not, till my womb
Pregnant by thee, and now excessive grown,
Prodigious motion felt and rueful throes.   780
At last this odious offspring whom thou seest,
Thine own begotten, breaking violent way,
Tore through my entrails, that, with fear and pain
Distorted, all my nether shape thus grew
Transformed; but he, my inbred enemy,   785
Forth issued, brandishing his fatal dart,
Made to destroy. I fled, and cried out *Death!*
Hell trembled at the hideous name, and sighed
From all her caves, and back resounded *Death!*

---

2. As Athena sprang full-grown from the head of Zeus.
3. Sin looks attractive at first, being a lovely woman at the top of her body; but she is a serpent below, and ends in a "mortal sting," i.e., death. See James i.14, "when lust hath conceived, it bringeth forth sin, and sin, when it is finished, bringeth forth death."
4. Peak.

I fled; but he pursued (though more, it seems, 790
Inflamed with lust than rage) and, swifter far,
Me overtook, his mother, all dismayed,
And in embraces forcible and foul
Engendering with me, of that rape begot
These yelling monsters, that with ceaseless cry 795
Surround me, as thou sawest, hourly conceived
And hourly born, with sorrow infinite
To me; for when they list, into the womb
That bred them they return, and howl, and gnaw
My bowels, their repast; then, bursting forth 800
Afresh, with conscious terrors vex me round,
That rest or intermission none I find.
Before mine eyes in opposition sits
Grim Death, my son and foe, who sets them on,
And me his parent would full soon devour 805
For want of other prey, but that he knows
His end with mine involved; and knows that I
Should prove a bitter morsel, and his bane,
Whenever that shall be; so Fate pronounced.
But thou, O father, I forewarn thee, shun 810
His deadly arrow; neither vainly hope
To be invulnerable in those bright arms,
Though tempered heavenly; for that mortal dint,
Save he who reigns above, none can resist."5

    She finished, and the subtle fiend his lore 815
Soon learned, now milder, and thus answered smooth:
"Dear daughter, since thou claimest me for thy sire,
And my fair son here show'st me, the dear pledge
Of dalliance had with thee in Heaven, and joys
Then sweet, now sad to mention, through dire change 820
Befallen us unforeseen, unthought of; know
I come no enemy, but to set free
From out this dark and dismal house of pain,
Both him and thee, and all the Heavenly host
Of spirits that, in our just pretenses6 armed, 825
Fell with us from on high. From them I go
This uncouth errand sole,7 and one for all
Myself expose, with lonely steps to tread
Th' unfounded deep, and through the void immense
To search with wandering quest a place foretold 830
Should be, and, by concurring signs, ere now
Created vast and round, a place of bliss
In the purlieus8 of Heaven, and therein placed
A race of upstart creatures, to supply
Perhaps our vacant room, though more removed, 835
Lest Heaven, surcharged9 with potent multitude,

5. I.e., only God is immune to death.
6. Grievances.
7. Alone on a desolate journey.
8. Outskirts, suburbs.
9. Too full. "Broils": controversies.

Might hap to move new broils. Be this, or aught
Than this more secret, now designed, I haste
To know; and, this once known, shall soon return,
And bring ye to the place where thou and Death   840
Shall dwell at ease, and up and down unseen
Wing silently the buxom[1] air, embalmed
With odors: there ye shall be fed and filled
Immeasurably; all things shall be your prey."
He ceased, for both seemed highly pleased, and Death   845
Grinned horrible a ghastly smile, to hear
His famine[2] should be filled, and blessed his maw
Destined to that good hour. No less rejoiced
His mother bad, and thus bespake her sire:
        "The key of this infernal pit, by due   850
And by command of Heaven's all-powerful King
I keep, by him forbidden to unlock
These adamantine gates; against all force
Death ready stands to interpose his dart,
Fearless to be o'ermatched by living might.   855
But what owe I to his commands above
Who hates me, and hath hither thrust me down
Into this gloom of Tartarus profound,
To sit in hateful office here confined,
Inhabitant of Heaven and heavenly-born,   860
Here in perpetual agony and pain,
With terrors and with clamors compassed round
Of mine own brood that on my bowels feed?
Thou art my father, thou my author, thou
My being gav'st me; whom should I obey   865
But thee? whom follow? Thou wilt bring me soon
To that new world of light and bliss, among
The gods who live at ease, where I shall reign
At thy right hand voluptuous,[3] as beseems
Thy daughter and thy darling, without end."   870
        Thus saying, from her side the fatal key,
Sad instrument of all our woe, she took;
And, towards the gate rolling her bestial train,[4]
Forthwith the huge portcullis high up-drew,
Which but herself not all the Stygian powers[5]   875
Could once have moved; then in the keyhole turns
Th' intricate wards, and every bolt and bar
Of massy iron or solid rock with ease
Unfastens: on a sudden open fly
With impetuous recoil and jarring sound   880
Th' infernal doors, and on their hinges grate

1. Yielding. "Embalmed": made fragrant, but also with a thought of the
process associated with death.
2. Hunger, belly.
3. As the Son sits at God's right hand,
Sin will sit at Satan's; a blasphemous

parody of the Creed, showed up by the
word "voluptuous."
4. I.e., accompanied by her yelping offspring.
5. The powers of Hell.

Harsh thunder, that the lowest bottom shook
Of Erebus.[6] She opened, but to shut
Excelled[7] her power; the gates wide open stood,
That with extended wings a bannered host,   885
Under spread ensigns[8] marching, might pass through
With horse and chariots ranked in loose array;
So wide they stood, and like a furnace-mouth
Cast forth redounding[9] smoke and ruddy flame.
Before their eyes in sudden view appear   890
The secrets of the hoary deep, a dark
Illimitable ocean, without bound,
Without dimension; where length, breadth, and height,
And time and place are lost; where eldest Night
And Chaos, ancestors of Nature, hold   895
Eternal anarchy, amidst the noise
Of endless wars, and by confusion stand.
For Hot, Cold, Moist, and Dry, four champions fierce
Strive here for mastery, and to battle bring
Their embryon atoms;[1] they around the flag   900
Of each his faction, in their several clans,
Light-armed or heavy, sharp, smooth, swift, or slow,
Swarm populous, unnumbered as the sands
Of Barca or Cyrene's torrid soil,[2]
Levied to side with warring winds, and poise[3]   905
Their lighter wings. To whom these most adhere,
He rules a moment; Chaos[4] umpire sits,
And by decision more embroils the fray
By which he reigns: next him, high arbiter,
Chance governs all. Into this wild abyss,   910
The womb of Nature and perhaps her grave,
Of neither sea, nor shore, nor air, nor fire,
But all these in their pregnant causes[5] mixed
Confusedly, and which thus must ever fight,
Unless th' Almighty Maker them ordain   915
His dark materials to create more worlds,[6]
Into this wild abyss the wary fiend
Stood on the brink of Hell and looked awhile,
Pondering his voyage; for no narrow frith[7]
He had to cross. Nor was his ear less pealed[8]   920
With noises loud and ruinous (to compare
Great things with small) than when Bellona[9] storms,

6. Another classical name for Hell.
7. Exceeded. That Sin cannot shut Hell gate, though she can open it, is symbolical.
8. Standards, flags.
9. Billowing.
1. The four elements, fire, earth, water, and air, struggle endlessly in Chaos. "Embryon": embryo, unformed.
2. Barca and Cyrene were cities built on the shifting sands of North Africa.
3. Give weight to.

4. Chaos is both the place where confusion reigns and personified confusion itself.
5. Chaos is not organized to the point of being matter; it is the seeds of all forms of matter.
6. God must impose order on Chaos to create worlds from it.
7. Channel, firth.
8. Rung.
9. Goddess of war.

With all her battering engines bent to raze
Some capital city; or less than if this frame
Of Heaven were falling, and these elements   925
In mutiny had from her axle torn
The steadfast Earth. At last his sail-broad vans[1]
He spreads for flight, and in the surging smoke
Uplifted spurns the ground; thence many a league,
As in a cloudy chair ascending, rides   930
Audacious; but that seat soon failing, meets
A vast vacuity: all unawares,
Fluttering his pennons[2] vain, plumb down he drops
Ten thousand fathom deep, and to this hour
Down had been falling, had not by ill chance   935
The strong rebuff[3] of some tumultuous cloud,
Instinct[4] with fire and niter, hurried him
As many miles aloft; that fury stayed,
Quenched in a boggy Syrtis,[5] neither sea,
Nor good dry land, nigh foundered on he fares,   940
Treading the crude consistence, half on foot,
Half flying; behoves[6] him now both oar and sail.
As when a gryphon through the wilderness
With wingéd course o'er hill or moory dale,
Pursues the Arimaspian, who by stealth   945
Had from his wakeful custody purloined
The guarded gold:[7] so eagerly the fiend
O'er bog or steep, through strait, rough, dense, or rare,
With head, hands, wings, or feet pursues his way,
And swims, or sinks, or wades, or creeps, or flies.   950
At length a universal hubbub wild
Of stunning sounds and voices all confused
Borne through the hollow dark, assaults his ear
With loudest vehemence. Thither he plies
Undaunted, to meet there whatever power   955
Or spirit of the nethermost abyss
Might in that noise reside, of whom to ask
Which way the nearest coast of darkness lies
Bordering on light; when straight behold the throne
Of Chaos, and his dark pavilion spread   960
Wide on the wasteful deep! With him enthroned
Sat sable-vested Night, eldest of things,
The consort of his reign; and by them stood
Orcus and Ades,[8] and the dreaded name

1. Wings.
2. Pinions, from Latin *pennae*, "wings."
3. Puff or blast.
4. Filled. "Niter": saltpeter.
5. Quicksand, from the North African gulfs, famous for their shifting sandbars.
6. Befits.
7. Gryphons, fabulous creatures, halfeagle, half-dragon, lived in northern Europe, and were said to hoard gold. When it was stolen from them by the one-eyed Arimaspians, they pursued these curious malefactors, hopping, flapping, and squawking. The story is a piece of moralized natural history, directed against the love of money.
8. Latin and Greek names of Pluto, god of Hell.

Of Demogorgon;⁹ Rumor next and Chance, 965
And Tumult and Confusion all embroiled,
And Discord with a thousand various mouths.
 T' whom Satan, turning boldly, thus: "Ye powers
And spirits of this nethermost abyss,
Chaos and ancient Night, I come no spy, 970
With purpose to explore or to disturb
The secrets of your realm; but by constraint
Wandering this darksome desert, as my way
Lies through your spacious empire up to light,
Alone and without guide, half lost, I seek 975
What readiest path leads where your gloomy bounds
Confine with¹ Heaven; or if some other place
From your dominion won, th' Ethereal King
Possesses lately, thither to arrive
I travel this profound.² Direct my course: 980
Directed, no mean recompense it brings
To your behoof,³ if I that region lost,
All usurpation thence expelled, reduce
To their original darkness and your sway
(Which is my present journey⁴), and once more 985
Erect the standard there of ancient Night.
Yours be th' advantage all, mine the revenge!"
 Thus Satan; and him thus the anarch⁵ old,
With faltering speech and visage incomposed,⁶
Answered: "I know thee, stranger, who thou art, 990
That mighty leading angel, who of late
Made head against Heaven's King, though overthrown.
I saw and heard; for such a numerous host
Fled not in silence through the frighted deep
With ruin upon ruin, rout on rout, 995
Confusion worse confounded; and Heaven-gates
Poured out by millions her victorious bands,
Pursuing. I upon my frontiers here
Keep residence; if all I can will serve,
That little which is left so to defend 1000
Encroached on still through our intestine broils⁷
Weakening the scepter of old Night: first Hell,
Your dungeon, stretching far and wide beneath;
Now lately Heaven and Earth,⁸ another world
Hung o'er my realm, linked in a golden chain 1005
To that side Heaven from whence your legions fell.
If that way be your walk, you have not far;

9. A mysterious subdeity, stronger than Fate itself, first invented by Boccaccio. Cf. Shelley's *Prometheus Unbound.*
1. Border on.
2. Deep pit.
3. On your behalf.
4. I.e., the purpose of my present journey.
5. Chaos is not "monarch" of his realm, but "anarch," i.e., nonruler.

6. Disturbed.
7. I.e., our territory is continually shrinking because of our civil wars ("intestine broils").
8. Our human world and its sky have been carved out of Chaos. The sky is distinguished from "Heaven" as used in line 1006, meaning the abode of the blessed, the Empyrean.

So much the nearer danger. Go, and speed!
Havoc and spoil and ruin are my gain.''
    He ceased; and Satan stayed not to reply,   1010
But, glad that now his sea should find a shore,
With fresh alacrity and force renewed
Springs upward, like a pyramid of fire,
Into the wild expanse, and through the shock
Of fighting elements, on all sides round   1015
Environed, wins his way; harder beset
And more endangered, than when Argo[9] passed
Through Bosporus betwixt the jostling rocks;
Or when Ulysses on the larboard shunned
Charybdis, and by th' other whirlpool steered: 1020
So he with difficulty and labor hard
Moved on: with difficulty and labor he;
But, he once past, soon after when man fell,
Strange alteration! Sin and Death amain,[1]
Following his track (such was the will of Heaven),   1025
Paved after him a broad and beaten way
Over the dark abyss, whose boiling gulf
Tamely endured a bridge of wondrous length
From Hell continued reaching th' utmost orb[2]
Of this frail world; by which the spirits perverse   1030
With easy intercourse pass to and fro
To tempt or punish mortals, except whom
God and good angels guard by special grace.
But now at last the sacred influence
Of light appears, and from the walls of Heaven   1035
Shoots far into the bosom of dim Night
A glimmering dawn. Here Nature first begins
Her farthest verge,[3] and Chaos to retire,
As from her outmost works a broken foe
With tumult less and with less hostile din;   1040
That[4] Satan with less toil, and now with ease
Wafts on the calmer wave by dubious light,
And, like a weather-beaten vessel, holds[5]
Gladly the port, though shrouds and tackle torn;
Or in the emptier waste, resembling air,   1045
Weighs his spread wings, at leisure to behold
Far off th' empyreal Heaven, extended wide
In circuit, undetermined[6] square or round,

9. Jason and his fifty Argonauts, sailing through the Bosporus to the Black Sea in pursuit of the Golden Fleece, had to pass through the Symplegades, or clashing rocks. Ulysses also had a tight squeeze to pass between Scylla and Charybdis, where Italy almost touches Sicily. Charybdis was a whirlpool, but Scylla, the dog-monster who ate alive six of Ulysses' best men, is called by Milton "th' other whirlpool."
1. At full speed, vigorously.
2. The world is surrounded by nine spheres, the whole construction comprising the created universe. The bridge built by Sin and Death ends on the outermost of these spheres.
3. Threshold. The end of Chaos is the beginning of (created) Nature.
4. So that.
5. Makes for.
6. Heaven is so vast that simply by looking at it one cannot tell its shape. Of course it is really round, the circle being an emblem of perfection.

With opal towers and battlements adorned
Of living sapphire, once his native seat;   1050
And fast by, hanging in a golden chain,
This pendant world,[7] in bigness as a star
Of smallest magnitude close by the moon.
Thither, full fraught with mischievous revenge,
Accursed, and in a curséd hour, he hies.   1055

Book III

The Argument

God sitting on his throne sees Satan flying towards this world,
then newly created; shows him to the Son who sat at his right hand;
foretells the success of Satan in perverting mankind; clears his own
justice and wisdom from all imputation, having created man free
and able enough to have withstood his tempter; yet declares his
purpose of grace towards him, in regard he fell not of his own
malice, as did Satan, but by him seduced. The Son of God renders
praises to his Father for the manifestations of his gracious purpose
towards man; but God again declares, that Grace cannot be extended
towards man without the satisfaction of divine justice; man hath
offended the majesty of God by aspiring to godhead, and therefore
with all his progeny devoted to death must die, unless some one
can be found sufficient to answer for his offense, and undergo his
punishment. The Son of God freely offers himself a ransom for man:
the Father accepts him, ordains his incarnation, pronounces his
exaltation above all names in Heaven and earth; commands all the
angels to adore him; they obey, and hymning to their harps in full
choir, celebrate the Father and the Son. Meanwhile Satan alights
upon the bare convex of this world's outermost orb; where wandering he first finds a place since called the Limbo of Vanity; what
persons and things fly up thither; thence comes to the gate of
Heaven, described ascending by stairs, and the waters above the
firmament that flow about it: His passage thence to the orb of the
sun; he finds there Uriel the regent of that orb, but first changes
himself into the shape of a meaner angel; and pretending a zealous
desire to behold the new creation and man whom God placed here,
inquires of him the place of his habitation, and is directed; alights
first on mount Niphates.

Hail, holy Light, offspring of Heaven first-born!
Or of th' Eternal coeternal beam,
May I express thee unblamed?[1] since God is light,

---

7. Homer first showed the world as
hanging from Heaven by a golden chain
(*Iliad* VIII). As Milton uses the image,
it has a symbolic meaning as well;
earth is dependent on Heaven. The
world which hangs from Heaven is not
just our earth, but earth and all its
nine spheres, the created cosmos, as described by Ptolemy.
1. Milton feels some hesitation at calling Light coeternal with God himself;
his reasons follow.

And never but in unapproachéd light
Dwelt from eternity, dwelt then in thee, 5
Bright effluence of bright essence increate![2]
Or hear'st thou rather[3] pure ethereal stream,
Whose fountain who shall tell? Before the sun,
Before the heavens, thou wert, and at the voice
Of God, as with a mantle, didst invest[4] 10
The rising world of waters dark and deep,
Won from the void and formless infinite!
Thee I revisit now with bolder wing,
Escaped the Stygian pool, though long detained
In that obscure sojourn, while in my flight, 15
Through utter and through middle darkness[5] borne,
With other notes than to th' Orphean lyre[6]
I sung of Chaos and eternal Night;
Taught by the Heavenly Muse[7] to venture down
The dark descent, and up to reascend, 20
Though hard and rare. Thee I revisit safe,
And feel thy sovereign vital lamp; but thou
Revisit'st not these eyes, that roll in vain
To find thy piercing ray, and find no dawn;
So thick a drop serene[8] hath quenched their orbs, 25
Or dim suffusion veiled. Yet not the more
Cease I to wander where the Muses haunt
Clear spring, or shady grove, or sunny hill,
Smit with the love of sacred song;[9] but chief
Thee, Sion,[1] and the flowery brooks beneath, 30
That wash thy hallowed feet, and warbling flow,
Nightly I visit: nor sometimes forget[2]
Those other two equaled with me in fate,[3]
So were I equaled with them in renown,
Blind Thamyris and blind Maeonides, 35
And Tiresias and Phineus, prophets old:[4]
Then feed on thoughts that voluntary move
Harmonious numbers; as the wakeful bird[5]
Sings darkling, and, in shadiest covert hid,
Tunes her nocturnal note. Thus with the year 40

2. Uncreated, i.e., eternal.
3. I.e., would you rather be called. The construction is a Latinism.
4. Occupy.
5. Hell and Chaos.
6. One of the so-called Orphean Hymns is *To Night.* But Milton's darkness, being Christian, is deeper and wider.
7. Urania.
8. One medical theory about blindness attributed it to a *gutta serena,* another to a *suffusio nigra.*
9. The phrase is Virgilian, "*ingenti percussus amore*" (*Georgics* II.476), but the adjective "sacred" is Milton's own reservation.
1. The mountain of Scriptural inspiration, with its brooks Siloa and Kidron.
2. I.e., and never forget: therefore always remember.

3. Blind like me.
4. Thamyris was a blind Thracian poet, who lived before Homer. "Maeonides" is an epithet of Homer, either as a son of Maeon or as a native of Maeonia. Tiresias was the blind prophet of Thebes (cf. *Oedipus Rex*); Phineus was another blind prophet and soothsayer (*Aeneid* III). For Milton poetry and prophesy were intimately joined; blindness of the outer eye rendered more acute the sight of the inner eye; and the very thought of these matters moved him, as he says, spontaneously to verse.
5. The nightingale. "Darkling": at night.

Seasons return; but not to me returns
Day, or the sweet approach of even or morn,
Or sight of vernal bloom, or summer's rose,
Or flocks, or herds, or human face divine;
But cloud instead and ever-during dark   45
Surrounds me, from the cheerful ways of men
Cut off, and, for the book of knowledge fair,
Presented with a universal blank
Of Nature's works, to me expunged and rased,[6]
And wisdom at one entrance quite shut out.   50
So much the rather thou, Celestial Light,
Shine inward, and the mind through all her powers
Irradiate; there plant eyes; all mist from thence
Purge and disperse, that I may see and tell
Of things invisible to mortal sight.   55
   Now had th' Almighty Father from above,
From the pure empyrean where he sits
High throned above all height, bent down his eye,
His own works and their works at once to view:
About him all the sanctities of Heaven   60
Stood thick as stars, and from his sight[7] received
Beatitude past utterance; on his right
The radiant image of his glory sat,
His only Son. On Earth he first beheld
Our two first parents, yet the only two   65
Of mankind, in the happy garden placed,
Reaping immortal fruits of joy and love,
Uninterrupted joy, unrivaled love,
In blissful solitude. He then surveyed
Hell and the gulf between, and Satan there   70
Coasting the wall of Heaven on this side Night,
In the dun air sublime,[8] and ready now
To stoop, with wearied wings and willing feet,
On the bare outside of this world, that seemed
Firm land embosomed without firmament,   75
Uncertain which, in ocean or in air.
Him God beholding from his prospect high,
Wherein past, present, future, he beholds,
Thus to his only Son foreseeing spake:
   "Only-begotten Son, seest thou what rage   80
Transports our adversary? whom no bounds
Prescribed, no bars of Hell, nor all the chains
Heaped on him there, nor yet the main abyss
Wide interrupt,[9] can hold; so bent he seems
On desperate revenge, that shall redound   85

---

6. Shaved off (like a Roman tablet), erased.
7. From sight of him.
8. From the aspect of God's radiance the air is "dun," i.e., dusky; Satan is literally "sublime" in it, i.e., lifted up, aloft. But from where Satan hangs, outside the world's outer shell, he cannot be sure the world and its nine concentric spheres are not a single solid (line 75). The points of view are precisely distinguished.
9. Dividing, in between.

Upon his own rebellious head. And now,
Through all restraint broke loose, he wings his way
Not far off Heaven, in the precincts of light,
Directly towards the new-created world,
And man there placed, with purpose to essay   90
If him by force he can destroy, or, worse,
By some false guile pervert: and shall pervert;
For man will hearken to his glozing[1] lies,
And easily transgress the sole command,
Sole pledge of his obedience; so will fall   95
He and his faithless progeny. Whose fault?
Whose but his own? Ingrate, he had of me
All he could have; I made him just and right,
Sufficient to have stood, though free to fall.
Such I created all th' ethereal powers   100
And spirits, both them who stood and them who failed:
Freely they stood who stood, and fell who fell.
Not free, what proof could they have given sincere[2]
Of true allegiance, constant faith, or love,
Where only what they needs must do appeared,   105
Not what they would? What praise could they receive,
What pleasure I, from such obedience paid,
When Will and Reason (Reason also is Choice),
Useless and vain, of freedom both despoiled,
Made passive both, had served Necessity,   110
Not me? They, therefore, as to right belonged,
So were created, nor can justly accuse
Their Maker, or their making, or their fate,
As if predestination overruled
Their will, disposed by absolute decree   115
Or high foreknowledge. They themselves decreed
Their own revolt, not I. If I foreknew,
Foreknowledge had no influence on their fault,
Which had no less proved certain unforeknown[3]
So without least impulse or shadow of fate,   120
Or aught by me immutably foreseen,
They trespass, authors to themselves in all,
Both what they judge and what they choose; for so
I formed them free, and free they must remain
Till they enthrall themselves: I else must change   125
Their nature, and revoke the high decree
Unchangeable, eternal, which ordained
Their freedom; they themselves ordained their fall.
The first sort[4] by their own suggestion fell,
Self-tempted, self-depraved; man falls, deceived   130
By the other first: man, therefore, shall find grace;

---

1. Flattering.
2. The delayed modifer is a favorite stylistic device of Milton's. "Sincere" goes
with "proof."
3. I.e., if I had not foreknown it.
4. The bad angels, Satan and his crew.

The other, none. In mercy and justice both,[5]
Through Heaven and Earth, so shall my glory excel;
But mercy, first and last, shall brightest shine."
    Thus while God spake ambrosial fragrance filled   135
All Heaven, and in the blessed spirits elect
Sense of new joy ineffable diffused.
Beyond compare the Son of God was seen
Most glorious; in him all his Father shone
Substantially expressed;[6] and in his face   140
Divine compassion visibly appeared,
Love without end, and without measure grace;
Which uttering, thus he to his Father spake:
    "O Father, gracious was that word which closed
Thy sovereign sentence, that man should find grace;   145
For which both Heaven and Earth shall high extol
Thy praises, with th' innumerable sound
Of hymns and sacred songs, wherewith thy throne
Encompassed shall resound thee ever blest.
For, should man finally be lost, should man,   150
Thy creature late so loved, thy youngest son,
Fall circumvented thus by fraud, though joined
With his own folly? That be from thee far,
That far be from thee, Father, who art judge
Of all things made, and judgest only right!   155
Or shall the adversary[7] thus obtain
His end, and frustrate thine? shall he fulfill
His malice, and thy goodness bring to naught
Or proud return, though to his heavier doom,
Yet with revenge accomplished, and to Hell   160
Draw after him the whole race of mankind,
By him corrupted? Or wilt thou thyself
Abolish thy creation, and unmake,
For him, what for thy glory thou hast made?
So should thy goodness and thy greatness both   165
Be questioned and blasphemed without defense."
    To whom the great Creator thus replied:
"O Son, in whom my soul hath chief delight,
Son of my bosom, Son who art alone
My word, my wisdom, and effectual might,   170
All hast thou spoken as my thoughts are, all
As my eternal purpose hath decreed.[8]
Man shall not quite be lost, but saved who will;
Yet not of will in him, but grace in me
Freely vouchsafed. Once more I will renew   175

5. Mercy and justice are two key terms in the poem. Their personifications here are separate: God is justice (he claims to be merciful, but his speech does not have this tone at all), the Son is mercy; but by Book XII Milton intends to show their identity.

6. God himself cannot be directly apprehended, except through the Son.
7. "Satan" in Hebrew means "Adversary."
8. The Lord's speech is notably rhythmic and even rhymed.

His lapséd powers, though forfeit, and enthralled
By sin to foul exorbitant desires:
Upheld by me, yet once more he shall stand
On even ground against his mortal foe,
By me upheld,[9] that he may know how frail   180
His fallen condition is, and to me owe
All his deliverance, and to none but me.
Some I have chosen of peculiar grace,
Elect above the rest; so is my will:
The rest shall hear me call, and oft be warned   185
Their sinful state,[1] and to appease betimes
Th' incenséd Deity, while offered grace
Invites; for I will clear their senses dark
What may suffice,[2] and soften stony hearts
To pray, repent, and bring obedience due.   190
To prayer, repentance, and obedience due,
Though but endeavored with sincere intent,
Mine ear shall not be slow, mine eye not be shut.
And I will place within them as a guide
My umpire Conscience; whom if they will hear,   195
Light after light well used they shall attain,[3]
And to the end persisting, safe arrive.
This my long sufferance, and my day of grace,
They who neglect and scorn shall never taste;
But hard be hardened, blind be blinded more,   200
That they may stumble on, and deeper fall;
And none but such from mercy I exclude.
But yet all is not done. Man, disobeying,
Disloyal, breaks his fealty, and sins
Against the high supremacy of Heaven,   205
Affecting[4] godhead, and so, losing all,
To expiate his treason hath naught left,
But, to destruction sacred and devote,
He with his whole posterity must die;
Die he or Justice must; unless for him   210
Some other, able and as willing,[5] pay
The rigid satisfaction, death for death.
Say, heavenly powers, where shall we find such love?
Which of ye will be mortal, to redeem
Man's mortal crime,[6] and just, th' unjust to save?   215
Dwells in all Heaven charity so dear?"
　　　He asked, but all the heavenly choir stood mute,[7]

---

9. Note the ambiguity: the second "by me upheld" (line 180) may modify either "he" (line 178) or "his mortal foe" (line 179). Both divine and hellish energy are ultimately divine.
1. I.e., warned about their sinful state.
2. I.e., as much as need be.
3. By using light well, they will reach even more light, and, in the end, salvation.

4. Pretending to. "Devote": dedicated, given up to.
5. I.e., able to pay, and as willing as he is able.
6. Note that "mortal" means "human" (line 214) but "deadly" (line 215).
7. The silence of the good angels in face of a difficult task parallels that of the devils in the "great consult" (II. 420–26).

And silence was in Heaven: on man's behalf
Patron or intercessor none appeared,
Much less that durst upon his own head draw
The deadly forfeiture, and ransom set.   220
And now without redemption all mankind
Must have been lost, adjudged to Death and Hell
By doom severe, had not the Son of God,
In whom the fullness dwells of love divine,   225
His dearest mediation[8] thus renewed:
  "Father, thy word is passed, man shall find grace;
And shall Grace not find means, that finds her way,
The speediest of thy wingéd messengers,
To visit all thy creatures, and to all   230
Comes unprevented,[9] unimplored, unsought?
Happy for man, so coming! He her aid
Can never seek, once dead in sins and lost;
Atonement for himself, or offering meet,
Indebted and undone, hath none to bring.   235
Behold me, then: me for him, life for life,
I offer; on me let thine anger fall;
Account me man: I for his sake will leave
Thy bosom, and this glory next to thee
Freely put off, and for him lastly die   240
Well pleased; on me let Death wreak all his rage.
Under his gloomy power I shall not long
Lie vanquished. Thou hast given me to possess
Life in myself forever; by thee I live;
Though now to Death I yield, and am his due,   245
All that of me can die, yet, that debt paid,
Thou wilt not leave me in the loathsome grave
His prey, nor suffer my unspotted soul
Forever with corruption there to dwell;
But I shall rise victorious, and subdue   250
My vanquisher, spoiled of his vaunted spoil.
Death his death's wound shall then receive, and stoop[1]
Inglorious, of his mortal sting disarmed;
I through the ample air in triumph high
Shall lead Hell captive maugre[2] Hell, and show   255
The powers of darkness bound. Thou, at the sight
Pleased, out of Heaven shalt look down and smile,
While, by thee raised, I ruin[3] all my foes,
Death last, and with his carcass glut the grave;
Then, with the multitude of my redeemed,   260
Shall enter Heaven, long absent, and return,
Father, to see thy face, wherein no cloud
Of anger shall remain, but peace assured

8. Intercession.
9. Unforestalled.
1. Be humbled, fall.
2. In spite of (French, *malgré*). The
Son's triumph is represented in a series
of fantastic paradoxes—a vanquisher
vanquished, a spoiler spoiled, death
dead, Hell captured in all Hell's despite.
3. In the Latin sense, throw down.

And reconcilement: wrath shall be no more
Thenceforth, but in thy presence joy entire." 265
    His words here ended; but his meek aspéct
Silent yet spake, and breathed immortal love
To mortal men, above which only shone
Filial obedience: as a sacrifice
Glad to be offered, he attends the will 270
Of his great Father. Admiration[4] seized
All Heaven, what this might mean, and whither tend,
Wondering; but soon th' Almighty thus replied:
    "O thou in Heaven and Earth the only peace
Found out for mankind under wrath,[5] O thou 275
My sole complacence![6] well thou know'st how dear
To me are all my works; nor man the least,
Though last created, that for him I spare
Thee from my bosom and right hand, to save,
By losing thee a while, the whole race lost! 280
Thou, therefore, whom thou only canst redeem,
Their nature also to thy nature join;[7]
And be thyself man among men on Earth,
Made flesh, when time shall be, of virgin seed,
By wondrous birth; be thou in Adam's room 285
The head of all mankind, though Adam's son.[8]
As in him perish all men, so in thee,
As from a second root, shall be restored
As many as are restored; without thee, none.
His crime makes guilty all his sons;[9] thy merit, 290
Imputed, shall absolve them who renounce
Their own both righteous and unrighteous deeds,[1]
And live in thee transplanted, and from thee
Receive new life. So man, as is most just,
Shall satisfy for man, be judged and die, 295
And dying rise, and, rising, with him raise
His brethren, ransomed with his own dear life.
So heavenly love shall outdo hellish hate,
Giving to death, and dying to redeem,
So dearly to redeem, what hellish hate 300
So easily destroyed, and still destroys
In those who, when they may, accept not grace.

4. Wonder, curiosity.
5. The Lord is looking to the future, when mankind will be under his wrath.
6. Contentment.
7. I.e., join the nature of those people (mankind) whom you alone can save to your own nature; in other words, "Become a man and suffer the pains of mortality." The antecedent of "whom" is, loosely construed, the "their" which follows it.
8. Adam is, properly, the "Old Adam"; Christ is the Second Adam (there was an old tradition that the Forbidden Tree and the Cross of Christ stood on the same spot). The Son of God, who long antedates the creation of Adam, and who is actually the first created being (III.383), is historical Jesus Christ in one sense, an eternal spiritual principle in another.
9. The intense legalism of the Deity is apparent.
1. I.e., the merit of Christ, imputed to men, frees from original sin those who renounce their own deeds both good and bad and hope to be saved by faith.

Nor shalt thou, by descending to assume
Man's nature, lessen or degrade thine own.
Because thou hast, though throned in highest bliss   305
Equal to God, and equally enjoying
Godlike fruition,[2] quitted all to save
A world from utter loss, and hast been found
By merit more than birthright Son of God,[3]
Found worthiest to be so by being good,   310
Far more than great or high; because in thee
Love hath abounded more than glory abounds;
Therefore thy humiliation shall exalt
With thee thy manhood also to this throne:
Here shalt thou sit incarnate, here shalt reign   315
Both God and man, Son both of God and man,
Anointed[4] universal King. All power
I give thee; reign forever, and assume
Thy merits; under thee, as Head Supreme,
Thrones, princedoms, powers, dominions, I reduce: 320
All knees to thee shall bow of them that bide
In Heaven, or Earth, or under Earth in Hell.
When thou, attended gloriously from Heaven,
Shalt in the sky appear, and from thee send
The summoning archangels to proclaim   325
Thy dread tribunal, forthwith from all winds[5]
The living, and forthwith the cited dead
Of all past ages, to the general doom
Shall hasten; such a peal shall rouse their sleep.
Then, all thy saints assembled, thou shalt judge   330
Bad men and angels; they arraigned shall sink
Beneath thy sentence; Hell, her numbers full,
Thenceforth shall be forever shut. Meanwhile
The world shall burn, and from her ashes spring
New Heaven and Earth, wherein the just shall dwell,[6]   335
And, after all their tribulations long,
See golden days, fruitful of golden deeds,
With Joy and Love triúmphing, and fair Truth.
Then thou thy regal scepter shalt lay by;
For regal scepter then no more shall need;[7]   340
God shall be all in all. But all ye gods,[8]
Adore him who, to compass all this, dies;
Adore the Son, and honor him as me."
      No sooner had th' Almighty ceased, but all
The multitude of angels, with a shout   345

---

2. Godlike pleasures, rewards.
3. An audacious doctrine, that Christ was Son of God by merit. Satan, one notes, was sultan of Hell on the same principle.
4. "The Anointed," in Hebrew, is the Messiah.
5. From all directions. "Cited": summoned.
6. The burning of the earth is based on II Peter iii.12, 13.
7. Be needed.
8. In addressing the angels as gods, the Lord is merely indicating their share in his divinity; the word is not literal.

Loud as from numbers without number, sweet
As from blest voices, uttering joy, Heaven rung[9]
With jubilee, and loud hosannas filled
Th' eternal regions. Lowly reverent
Towards either throne[1] they bow, and to the ground   350
With solemn adoration down they cast
Their crowns, inwove with amarant[2] and gold;
Immortal amarant, a flower which once
In Paradise, fast by the Tree of Life,
Began to bloom, but soon for man's offense   355
To Heaven removed, where first it grew, there grows
And flowers aloft, shading the Fount of Life,
And where the River of Bliss through midst of Heaven
Rolls o'er Elysian[3] flowers her amber stream.
With these, that never fade, the spirits elect   360
Bind their resplendent locks, enwreathed with beams.
Now in loose garlands thick thrown off, the bright
Pavement, that like a sea of jasper shone,
Empurpled with celestial roses smiled.
Then, crowned again, their golden harps they took,   365
Harps ever tuned, that glittering by their side
Like quivers hung; and with preamble sweet
Of charming symphony they introduce
Their sacred song, and waken raptures high:
No voice exempt,[4] no voice but well could join   370
Melodious part; such concord is in Heaven.
    Thee, Father, first they sung, Omnipotent,
Immutable, Immortal, Infinite,[5]
Eternal King; thee, Author of all being,
Fountain of light, thyself invisible   375
Amidst the glorious brightness where thou sitt'st
Throned inaccessible, but when thou shad'st
The full blaze of thy beams, and through a cloud
Drawn round about thee like a radiant shrine
Dark with excessive bright thy skirts appear,[6]   380
Yet dazzle Heaven, that brightest seraphim
Approach not, but with both wings veil their eyes.
Thee next they sang, of all creation first,

9. "Multitude" (line 345) is subject of
the sentence, "rung" the verb, and
"Heaven" the object.
1. Those of God and the Son.
2. Or "amaranth"; in Greek, "unwither-
ing"—an unfading flower and hence a
type of immortality, which could not
continue on earth after man became
subject to death.
3. Milton draws freely, and with no
sense of incongruity, on pagan properties for his Christian Heaven. "Amber":
not "yellow," but "clear." Milton's

epithets are not always visually strong.
4. Abstaining.
5. Joshua Sylvester, in translating the
long, pedestrian poem of Du Bartas on
the creation, makes use of this line. It
is the only example, and not a very
striking one, of Milton's paralleling an
English predecessor for ten consecutive
syllables.
6. In this hymn, for the first time, we
get a sense of the majesty and mystery
of the Godhead; hitherto, he has been
rather querulous and legalistic.

Begotten Son, divine similitude,
In whose conspicuous countenance, without cloud   385
Made visible, th' Almighty Father shines,
Whom else⁷ no creature can behold: on thee
Impressed th' effulgence of his glory abides;
Transfused on thee his ample spirit rests.
He Heaven of Heavens, and all the powers therein,   390
By thee created; and by thee threw down
Th' aspiring dominations.⁸ Thou that day
Thy Father's dreadful thunder didst not spare,
Nor stop thy flaming chariot wheels, that shook
Heaven's everlasting frame, while o'er the necks   395
Thou drov'st of warring angels disarrayed.
Back from pursuit, thy powers with loud acclaim
Thee only extolled, Son of thy Father's might,
To execute fierce vengeance on his foes.
Not so on man: him, through their malice fallen,   400
Father of mercy and grace, thou didst not doom
So strictly, but much more to pity incline.
No sooner did thy dear and only Son
Perceive thee purposed not to doom frail man
So strictly, but much more to pity inclined,⁹   405
He, to appease thy wrath, and end the strife
Of mercy and justice in thy face discerned,
Regardless of the bliss wherein he sat
Second to thee, offered himself to die
For man's offense. O unexampled love!   410
Love nowhere to be found less than divine!
Hail, Son of God, Savior of men! Thy name
Shall be the copious matter of my¹ song
Henceforth, and never shall my harp thy praise
Forget, nor from thy Father's praise disjoin!   415
     Thus they in Heaven, above the starry sphere,
Their happy hours in joy and hymning spent.
Meanwhile, upon the firm opacous globe
Of this round world, whose first convex divides
The luminous inferior orbs, enclosed   420
From chaos and th' inroad of darkness old,
Satan alighted walks.² A globe far off
It seemed; now seems a boundless continent,

7. Except for whom (if it were not for the Son. no creature could see God).
8. I.e., the rebel angels.
9. A "than" or "but" is understood at the end of line 405. The repetition (lines 402, 405) suggests the choral nature of the psalm. Note in 407 the re-emphasis on a conflict of mercy and justice.
1. Either the angels are singing as a single chorus, or Milton wishes to asso-

ciate himself with them; possibly both. The change of pronoun is deliberate and striking.
2. Satan is not on the earth's surface but on the outermost of the nine concentric spheres that make up the created cosmos. This sphere is "opacous" (opaque) by contrast with the inner eight (containing seven planets and the fixed stars), which are crystalline and transparent.

Dark, waste, and wild, under the frown of night
Starless exposed, and ever-threatening storms   425
Of chaos blustering round, inclement sky,
Save on that side which from the wall of Heaven,
Though distant far, some small reflection gains
Of glimmering air less vexed with tempest loud.
Here walked the fiend at large in spacious field.   430
As when a vulture, on Imaus bred,
Whose snowy ridge the roving Tartar bounds,[3]
Dislodging from a region scarce of prey,
To gorge the flesh of lambs or yeanling[4] kids
On hills where flocks are fed, flies toward the springs   435
Of Ganges or Hydaspes, Indian streams,
But in his way lights on the barren plains
Of Sericana, where Chineses drive
With sails and wind their cany wagons light;[5]
So, on this windy sea of land, the fiend   440
Walked up and down alone, bent on his prey:
Alone, for other creature in this place,
Living or lifeless, to be found was none;—
None yet; but store hereafter from the earth
Up hither like aerial vapors flew   445
Of all things transitory and vain, when sin
With vanity had filled the works of men—
Both all things vain, and all who in vain things
Built their fond hopes of glory or lasting fame,
Or happiness in this or th' other life.[6]   450
All who have their reward on earth, the fruits
Of painful superstition and blind zeal,
Naught seeking but the praise of men, here find
Fit retribution, empty as their deeds;
All th' unaccomplished works of nature's hand,   455
Abortive, monstrous, or unkindly[7] mixed,
Dissolved on earth, fleet hither, and in vain,
Till final dissolution, wander here—
Not in the neighboring moon, as some have dreamed:
Those argent fields more likely habitants,[8]   460

---

3. Imaus, a ridge of mountains beyond the modern Himalayas, is described by Pliny (*Natural History*, VI.17), and shown in Mercator's *Atlas*, as running north through Asia from modern Afghanistan to the Arctic Circle.
4. Newborn.
5. Both the Ganges and Hydaspes (a tributary of the river Indus) rise from the mountains of northern India; Sericana is an area (known only vaguely to Milton through the *Pilgrimage* of Purchas the traveler) in what is now Sinkiang province, in China. Milton got his memory of wind-driven land-carts from Peter Heylyn's *Cosmography*.

6. Milton's Paradise of Fools (named in line 496) was probably inspired by Ariosto's equivalent valley on the moon (*Orlando Furioso*, Canto 34; see below, line 459); it serves much the same function as Dante's Limbo, to dispose of those who deserve neither salvation nor damnation. But, instead of indifferents, Milton's region is reserved for deluded victims of misplaced devotion, chiefly Roman Catholics.
7. Against "kind," against their own natures.
8. Argent: silver. The moon Milton imagines, though only briefly, as a kind of middle Paradise.

Translated saints, or middle spirits hold,
Betwixt th' angelical and human kind.
Hither, of ill-joined sons and daughters born,
First from the ancient world those giants came,
With many a vain exploit, though then renowned:[9]   465
The builders next of Babel on the plain
Of Sennaar,[1] and still with vain design
New Babels, had they wherewithal, would build:
Others came single; he who, to be deemed
A god, leaped fondly into Etna flames,   470
Empedocles, and he who, to enjoy
Plato's Elysium, leaped into the sea,
Cleombrotus;[2] and many more, too long,
Embryos and idiots, eremites and friars,
White, black, and gray, with all their trumpery.[3]   475
Here pilgrims roam, that strayed so far to seek
In Golgotha him dead who lives in Heaven;
And they who, to be sure of paradise,
Dying put on the weeds of Dominic,
Or in Franciscan think to pass disguised.[4]   480
They pass the planets seven, and pass the fixed,
And that crystálline sphere whose balance weighs
The trepidation talked, and that first moved;[5]
And now Saint Peter at heaven's wicket seems
To wait them with his keys, and now at foot   485
Of heaven's ascent they lift their feet, when, lo!
A violent cross wind from either coast
Blows them transverse ten thousand leagues awry,
Into the devious air. Then might ye see
Cowls, hoods, and habits, with their wearers, tossed   490
And fluttered into rags; then relics, beads,
Indulgences, dispenses, pardons, bulls,[6]
The sport of winds: all these, upwhirled aloft,
Fly o'er the backside of the world far off

---

9. The "giants in the earth," born of un-natural marriages between the sons of God and the daughters of men, are creatures "unkindly mixed," therefore sent to the Paradise of Fools, "though then re-nowned," as Genesis vi.4 tells us.
1. Shinär, the plain of Babel, as in Genesis xi. 2–9. Babel for Milton is an emblem of human pride and folly
2. Both Empedocles and Cleombrotus carried piety to the point of folly and suicide. Hell is reserved for the wilfully malicious, the Paradise of Fools for the merely misguided.
3. Unnatural mixtures produce embryos and idiots; Milton adds to them hermits and friars (the white are Carmelites, the black Dominicans, and the gray Franciscans); he thinks they exemplify unnatural piety, frustrated by its very nature.
4. Pilgrims also are unnatural in their

piety, since they worship the relic and forget the spirit; so are those who try to trick God into granting them salvation by wearing religious garb on their death-beds.
5. Milton follows their souls through the spheres of the seven then-known planets, that of the fixed stars, and through the outermost sphere responsible for what astronomers call "the trepidation," a periodic corrective shudder of the cosmos. This is, or is right next to, the prime mover, or *primum mobile*—the next step seems to be the pearly gates themselves.
6. All that Milton considered the "trumpery", that is, the exterior and legal manifestations, of ecclesiasticism, is here cast aside as vanity. Milton certainly means "backside" (line 494) to have its vulgar connotation.

Into a limbo large and broad, since called   495
The Paradise of Fools; to few unknown
Long after, now unpeopled and untrod.
    All this dark globe the fiend found as he passed;
And long he wandered, till at last a gleam
Of dawning light turned thitherward in haste   500
His traveled steps. Far distant he descries,
Ascending by degrees magnificent
Up the wall of Heaven, a structure high;
At top whereof, but far more rich, appeared
The work as of a kingly palace-gate,   505
With frontispiece[7] of diamond and gold
Embellished; thick with sparkling orient gems
The portal shone, inimitable on earth
By model, or by shading pencil drawn.
The stairs were such as whereon Jacob saw   510
Angels ascending and descending, bands
Of guardians bright, when he from Esau fled
To Padan-Aram, in the field of Luz
Dreaming by night under the open sky,
And waking cried, *This is the gate of Heaven*.   515
Each stair mysteriously was meant, nor stood
There always, but drawn up to heaven sometimes
Viewless;[8] and underneath a bright sea flowed
Of jasper, or of liquid pearl, whereon
Who after came from earth sailing arrived   520
Wafted by angels, or flew o'er the lake
Rapt in a chariot drawn by fiery steeds.
The stairs were then let down, whether to dare
The fiend by easy ascent, or aggravate
His sad exclusion from the doors of bliss.[9]   525
Direct against which opened from beneath,
Just o'er the blissful seat of paradise,
A passage down to th' earth—a passage wide;
Wider by far than that of after-times
Over Mount Sion, and, though that were large,   530
Over the promised land to God so dear,
By which, to visit oft those happy tribes,
On high behests his angels to and fro
Passed frequent,[1] and his eye with choice regard

7. Façade.
8. Invisible. The story of Jacob's vision is summarized from Genesis xxviii.1–19. The stairs of the ladder were meant "mysteriously"—each represented a stage of spiritual growth.
9. In either case, Milton implies, heavenly authorities were aware of Satan's approach.

1. The crystalline spheres would be impenetrable if there weren't passages, or holes, in them, through which heavenly —and, alas, diabolic—spirits could make their way. The visiting angels "act as" his eye and "keep a" close regard on the chosen people. Cf., below, lines 650 and 660.

From Paneas, the fount of Jordan's flood,   535
To Beërsaba, where the holy land
Borders on Egypt and the Arabian shore.[2]
So wide the opening seemed, where bounds were set
To darkness, such as bound the ocean wave.
Satan from hence, now on the lower stair,   540
That scaled by steps of gold to heaven-gate,
Looks down with wonder at the sudden view
Of all this world at once. As when a scout,
Through dark and desert ways with peril gone
All night, at last by break of cheerful dawn   545
Obtains the brow of some high-climbing hill,
Which to his eye discovers unaware
The goodly prospect of some foreign land
First seen, or some renowned metropolis
With glistering spires and pinnacles adorned,   550
Which now the rising sun gilds with his beams;
Such wonder seized, though after heaven seen,
The spirit malign, but much more envy seized,
At sight of all this world beheld so fair.
Round he surveys (and well might, where he stood   555
So high above the circling canopy
Of night's extended shade) from eastern point
Of Libra to the fleecy star that bears
Andromeda far off Atlantic seas[3]
Beyond th' horizon; then from pole to pole   560
He views in breadth,—and, without longer pause,
Down right into the world's first region throws
His flight precipitant, and winds with ease
Through the pure marble air his oblique way[4]
Amongst innumerable stars, that shone   565
Stars distant, but nigh-hand seemed other worlds.
Or other worlds they seemed, or happy isles,
Like those Hesperian gardens famed of old,
Fortunate fields, and groves, and flowery vales;[5]
Thrice happy isles! But who dwelt happy there   570
He stayed not to inquire: above them all
The golden sun, in splendor likest heaven,
Allured his eye. Thither his course he bends,
Through the calm firmament (but up or down,
By center or eccentric, hard to tell,   575

2. From Paneas (or Dan) in northern Palestine to Beersaba, or Beersheba, near the Egyptian border—the whole land.
3. In the zodiac, Libra or the Scales are diametrically opposite the Ram ("the fleecy star"), which seems to carry the constellation Andromeda on its back.

4. "Marble" derives from the Greek word for "shining", but there's also a sense of solidity in the adjective to contrast with Satan's "oblique" approach.
5. The gardens of the Hesperides and the "fortunate isles" of Greek mythology lay far out in the Atlantic, almost like separate miniature worlds.

Or longitude)[6] where the great luminary,
Aloof the vulgar constellations thick,
That from his lordly eye keep distance due,
Dispenses light from far. They, as they move
Their starry dance in numbers that compute   580
Days, months, and years, towards his all-cheering lamp
Turn swift their various motions, or are turned
By his magnetic beam, that gently warms
The universe, and to each inward part
With gentle penetration, though unseen,   585
Shoots invisible virtue even to the deep;[7]
So wondrously was set his station bright.
There lands the fiend, a spot like which perhaps
Astronomer in the sun's lucent orb
Through his glazed optic tube yet never saw.[8]   590
The place he found beyond expression bright,
Compared with aught on earth,[9] metal or stone—
Not all parts like, but all alike informed
With radiant light, as glowing iron with fire.
If metal, part seemed gold, part silver clear;   595
If stone, carbuncle most or chrysolite,
Ruby or topaz, to the twelve that shone
In Aaron's breast-plate,[1] and a stone besides,
Imagined rather oft than elsewhere seen—
That stone, or like to that, which here below   600
Philosophers in vain so long have sought;
In vain, though by their powerful art they bind
Volatile Hermes, and call up unbound
In various shapes old Proteus from the sea,
Drained through a limbec to his native form.[2]   605
What wonder then if fields and regions here
Breathe forth elixir pure, and rivers run
Potable gold, when, with one virtuous touch,
Th' arch-chemic sun, so far from us remote,

6. Milton is cautious about saying whether the sun or the earth is at the center of the created cosmos. Like any educated man of his day, he knew that the earth goes around the sun, not vice versa, but poetically it was better for him to leave the option open.
7. "Virtue" in the sense of "influence," "strength": it was commonly thought that the "influence" of the sun caused seeds of gold to grow in the depths of the earth (see below, lines 608–612).
8. Galileo had discovered sun-spots in 1609; the possibility that the telescope might lead to an actual sighting of devils or angels was not yet extinct in Milton's day.
9. Strictly speaking, Satan has not been to the earth yet, but Milton cannot lose sight of the reader, who's been nowhere else.
1. Exodus xxviii lists the twelve precious stones in the breastplate of Aaron, the high-priest; "to" means "comparable to" or "to the number of."
2. The philosopher's stone had been sought by "binding" or fixing mercury ("volatile Hermes," i.e., quicksilver) or calling up Proteus to catch him in a limbec (alembic) in order to reduce both changeable deities to their natural forms. "Proteus" here stands for the gold which alchemists supposed to be hidden, in dilute form, within all other matter; their art aimed at extracting it.

Produces, with terrestrial humor mixed, 610
Here in the dark so many precious things
Of color glorious and effect so rare?[3]
Here matter new to gaze the devil met
Undazzled. Far and wide his eye commands;
For sight no obstacle found here, nor shade, 615
But all sunshine, as when his beams at noon
Culminate from th' equator, as[4] they now
Shot upward still direct, whence no way round
Shadow from body opaque can fall; and the air,
Nowhere so clear, sharpened his visual ray 620
To objects distant far, whereby he soon
Saw within ken a glorious angel stand,
The same whom John saw also in the sun.[5]
His back was turned, but not his brightness hid;
Of beaming sunny rays a golden tiar[6] 625
Circled his head, nor less his locks behind
Illustrious[7] on his shoulders fledge with wings
Lay waving round: on some great charge employed
He seemed, or fixed in cogitation deep.
Glad was the spirit impure, as now in hope 630
To find who might direct his wandering flight
To paradise, the happy seat of man,
His journey's end, and our beginning woe.
But first he casts to change his proper shape,
Which else might work him danger or delay: 635
And now a stripling cherub he appears,
Not of the prime, yet such as in his face
Youth smiled celestial, and to every limb
Suitable grace diffused; so well he feigned.
Under a coronet his flowing hair 640
In curls on either cheek played; wings he wore
Of many a colored plume sprinkled with gold,
His habit fit for speed succinct,[8] and held
Before his decent steps a silver wand.
He drew not nigh unheard; the angel bright, 645
Ere he drew nigh, his radiant visage turned,
Admonished by his ear, and straight was known
Th' archangel Uriel—one of the seven
Who in God's presence, nearest to his throne,

---

3. Milton argues that if the sun can cause gold to grow in mines, it must be itself full of "virtue" (power) to produce chemical changes—it is the "arch-chemic."
4. The sense of the passage will be clearer if for this second "as" we read "so." Satan, standing in the sun itself, can neither cast a shadow nor see one.
5. John of Patmos, author of the book

of Revelation, saw an angel standing in the sun (xix.17).
6. Tiara, crown.
7. Lustrous and illuminated. "Fledge": fledged, feathered.
8. From the Latin *succingere*, "to draw in, tuck up." Satan, in disguise, wears some sort of light cloak that can be gathered up to leave his legs (and wings) free for speed.

Stand ready at command, and are his eyes   650
That run through all the heavens, or down to th' earth
Bear his swift errands over moist and dry,
O'er sea and land. Him Satan thus accosts:—
    "Uriel! for thou of those seven spirits that stand
In sight of God's high throne, gloriously bright,   655
The first art wont his great authentic will
Interpreter through highest heaven to bring,
Where all his sons thy embassy attend,
And here art likeliest by supreme decree
Like honor to obtain, and as his eye   660
To visit oft this new creation round—
Unspeakable desire to see and know
All these his wondrous works, but chiefly man,
His chief delight and favor, him for whom
All these his works so wondrous he ordained,   665
Hath brought me from the choirs of cherubim[9]
Alone thus wandering. Brightest seraph, tell
In which of all these shining orbs hath man
His fixéd seat—or fixéd seat hath none,
But all these shining orbs his choice to dwell—   670
That I may find him, and with secret gaze
Or open admiration him behold
On whom the great creator hath bestowed
Worlds, and on whom hath all these graces poured;
That both in him and all things, as is meet,   675
The universal maker we may praise;
Who justly hath driven out his rebel foes
To deepest hell, and, to repair that loss,
Created this new happy race of men
To serve him better: wise are all his ways!"   680
    So spake the false dissembler unperceived;
For neither man nor angel can discern
Hypocrisy, the only evil that walks
Invisible, except to God alone,
By his permissive will, through Heaven and earth;[1]   685
And oft, though wisdom wake, suspicion sleeps
At wisdom's gate, and to simplicity
Resigns her charge, while goodness thinks no ill
Where no ill seems: which now for once beguiled
Uriel, though regent of the sun, and held   690
The sharpest-sighted spirit of all in heaven;
Who to the fraudulent imposter foul,

---

9. Uriel is one of the seraphim, the first order of angelic beings; cherubim would be of the second rank.
1. God has two wills—one active, by which he does, perforce, only good things, the other permissive, by which he allows things to take their course, whether for good or for evil.

In his uprightness, answer thus returned:—
   "Fair angel, thy desire, which tends to know
The works of God, thereby to glorify   695
The great work-master, leads to no excess
That reaches blame, but rather merits praise
The more it seems excess, that led thee hither
From thy empyreal mansion thus alone,
To witness with thine eyes what some perhaps,   700
Contented with report, hear only in Heaven:
For wonderful indeed are all his works,
Pleasant to know, and worthiest to be all
Had in remembrance always with delight!
But what created mind can comprehend   705
Their number, or the wisdom infinite
That brought them forth, but hid their causes deep?
I saw when, at his word, the formless mass,
This world's material mould, came to a heap:
Confusion heard his voice, and wild uproar   710
Stood ruled, stood vast infinitude confined;
Till, at his second bidding, darkness fled,
Light shone, and order from disorder sprung.
Swift to their several quarters hasted then
The cumbrous elements—earth, flood, air, fire;   715
And this etheral quintessence of Heaven
Flew upward, spirited[2] with various forms,
That rolled orbicular, and turned to stars
Numberless, as thou seest, and how they move:
Each had his place appointed, each his course;   720
The rest in circuit walls this universe.[3]
Look downward on that globe, whose hither side
With light from hence, though but reflected, shines:
That place is earth, the seat of man; that light
His day, which else, as th' other hemisphere,   725
Night would invade, but there the neighboring moon
(So call that opposite fair star) her aid
Timely interposes and, her monthly round
Still ending, still renewing, through mid-heaven,
With borrowed light her countenance triform[4]   730
Hence fills and empties, to enlighten th' earth,
And in her pale dominion checks the night.
That spot to which I point is paradise,
Adam's abode; those lofty shades his bower.

2. Informed with spiritual energy.
3. The rest of the stars became fixed in the outermost sphere, that which walls off the created universe from the immensity of Chaos outside.
4. Though the moon's cycle is divided into quarters, there are, strictly, only three of them: crescent, full, and waning (the dark of the moon, when it's invisible, is the fourth quarter); in addition, the moon has three classical names—Luna, Diana, and Hecate.

1426 · *John Milton*

Thy way thou canst not miss; me mine requires."   735
    Thus said, he turned; and Satan, bowing low,
As to superior spirits is wont in Heaven,
Where honor due and reverence none neglects,
Took leave, and toward the coast of earth beneath,
Down from th' ecliptic, sped with hoped success,   740
Throws his steep flight in many an airy wheel,
Nor stayed, till on Niphates'[5] top he lights.

From Book IV

[*Satan's Entry into Paradise*]

    O for that warning voice, which he who saw
Th' Apocalypse heard cry in Heaven aloud,
Then when the dragon, put to second rout,
Came furious down to be revenged on men,
Woe to the inhabitants on Earth![1] that now,   5
While time was, our first parents had been warned
The coming of their secret foe, and scaped,
Haply so scaped, his mortal snare![2] For now
Satan, now first inflamed with rage, came down,
The tempter, ere th' accuser, of mankind,   10
To wreak on innocent frail man his loss
Of that first battle, and his flight to hell.
Yet not rejoicing in his speed, though bold
Far off and fearless, nor with cause to boast,
Begins his dire attempt; which, nigh the birth   15
Now rolling, boils in his tumultuous breast,
And like a devilish engine back recoils
Upon himself. Horror and doubt distract
His troubled thoughts, and from the bottom stir
The Hell within him; for within him Hell   20
He brings, and round about him, nor from Hell
One step, no more than from himself, can fly
By change of place.[3] Now conscience wakes despair
That slumbered; wakes the bitter memory
Of what he was, what is, and what must be   25
Worse; of worse deeds worse sufferings must ensue.

5. Mt. Niphates lies in the northwest corner of modern Iran, not far from the Turkish border—it was an ideal spot from which to spy on Paradise, which lay in the plain below, between the Tigris and Euphrates rivers.
1. John of Patmos, in Revelation xii, describes a war in heaven between dragon and angels, in the course of which a voice cries from heaven, "Woe to the inhabitants of the earth and of the sea!"
2. "Haply": by good luck, happily. "Mortal": deadly. "First" in line 9 refers back to "second" in line 3; Milton wants us to remember that his story was the first of all the Bible stories, and is, as it were, their root.
3. Satan's proud statement that "the mind is its own place" (I, 254) finds here its bitter ironic echo.

Sometimes towards Eden, which now in his view
Lay pleasant, his grieved look he fixes sad;
Sometimes towards heaven and the full-blazing sun,
Which now sat high in his meridian tower:[4]   30
Then, much revolving, thus in sighs began:—
    "O thou that, with surpassing glory crowned,
Look'st from thy sole dominion like the god
Of this new world—at whose sight all the stars
Hide their diminished heads—to thee I call,   35
But with no friendly voice, and add thy name,
O sun, to tell thee how I hate thy beams,
That bring to my remembrance from what state
I fell, how glorious once above thy sphere,
Till pride and worse ambition threw me down,   40
Warring in Heaven against Heaven's matchless king!
Ah, wherefore? He deserved no such return
From me, whom he created what I was
In that bright eminence, and with his good
Upbraided none;[5] nor was his service hard.   45
What could be less than to afford him praise,
The easiest recompense, and pay him thanks,
How due! Yet all his good proved ill in me,
And wrought but malice. Lifted up so high,
I 'sdained[6] subjection, and thought one step higher   50
Would set me highest, and in a moment quit
The debt immense of endless gratitude,
So burdensome, still paying, still to owe;
Forgetful what from him I still received;
And understood not that a grateful mind   55
By owing owes not, but still pays, at once
Indebted and discharged—what burden then?
Oh, had his powerful destiny ordained
Me some inferior angel, I had stood
Then happy; no unbounded hope had raised   60
Ambition. Yet why not? Some other power
As great might have aspired, and me, though mean,
Drawn to his part. But other powers as great
Fell not, but stand unshaken, from within
Or from without to all temptations armed!   65
Hadst thou[7] the same free will and power to stand?
Thou hadst. Whom hast thou then, or what, to accuse,
But Heaven's free love dealt equally to all?

4. Midday, the height of noon. Milton's nephew Edward Phillips tells us that the speech which follows was the first part of the poem that existed, when Milton still thought of making it into the drama of "Adam Unparadised."

5. Demanded no return for his benefits; the phrase echoes James i.5.
6. Disdained. "Quit": acquit, pay off.
7. Satan addresses himself directly, as Adam will do under parallel circumstances in Book X, line 758.

Be then his love accursed, since, love or hate,
To me alike it deals eternal woe.   70
Nay, cursed be thou; since against his thy will
Chose freely what it now so justly rues.
Me miserable![8] which way shall I fly
Infinite wrath and infinite despair?
Which way I fly is Hell; myself am Hell;   75
And, in the lowest deep, a lower deep
Still threatening to devour me opens wide,
To which the Hell I suffer seems a Heaven.
O, then, at last relent! Is there no place
Left for repentance, none for pardon left?   80
None left but by submission; and that word
Disdain forbids me, and my dread of shame
Among the spirits beneath, whom I seduced
With other promises and other vaunts
Than to submit, boasting I could subdue   85
Th' omnipotent. Ay me! they little know
How dearly I abide that boast so vain,
Under what torments inwardly I groan.
While they adore me on the throne of Hell,
With diadem and scepter high advanced,   90
The lower still I fall, only supreme
In misery: such joy ambition finds!
But say I could repent, and could obtain,
By act of grace,[9] my former state, how soon
Would height recall high thoughts, how soon unsay   95
What feigned submission swore! Ease would recant
Vows made in pain, as violent and void
For never can true reconcilement grow
Where wounds of deadly hate have pierced so deep;
Which would but lead me to a worse relapse   100
And heavier fall: so should I purchase dear
Short intermission, bought with double smart.
This knows my punisher; therefore as far
From granting he, as I from begging, peace.
All hope excluded thus, behold, instead   105
Of us, outcast, exiled, his new delight,
Mankind, created, and for him this world!
So farewell hope, and, with hope, farewell fear,
Farewell remorse! All good to me is lost;
Evil, be thou my good: by thee at least   110
Divided empire with Heaven's king I hold,
By thee, and more than half perhaps will reign;

---

8. "Me miserable!": an exact Latinism,
"me miserum!" "Myself am hell" makes
brilliantly clear what can be meant by

"The mind is its own place," I.254.
9. The correct technical term for a formal pardon is an "act of grace."

As man ere long, and this new world, shall know."
    Thus while he spake, each passion dimmed his face,
Thrice changed with pale—ire, envy, and despair;   115
Which marred his borrowed visage, and betrayed
Him counterfeit, if any eye beheld:
For heavenly minds from such distempers foul
Are ever clear. Whereof he soon aware
Each perturbation smoothed with outward calm,   120
Artificer of fraud; and was the first
That practiced falsehood under saintly show,
Deep malice to conceal, couched with revenge:
Yet not enough had practiced to deceive
Uriel, once warned; whose eye pursued him down   125
The way he went, and on th' Assyrian mount
Saw him disfigured, more than could befall
Spirit of happy sort: his gestures fierce
He marked and mad demeanor, then alone,
As he supposed, all unobserved, unseen.   130
    So on he fares, and to the border comes.
Of Eden, where delicious Paradise,
Now nearer, crowns with her enclosure green,
As with a rural mound, the champaign[1] head
Of a steep wilderness, whose hairy sides   135
With thicket overgrown, grotesque[2] and wild,
Access denied; and overhead up grew
Insuperable height of loftiest shade,
Cedar, and pine, and fir, and branching palm,
A sylvan scene, and, as the ranks ascend   140
Shade above shade, a woody theater[3]
Of stateliest view. Yet higher than their tops
The verdurous wall of Paradise up sprung;
Which to our general sire[4] gave prospect large
Into his nether empire neighboring round.   145
And higher than that wall a circling row
Of goodliest trees, laden with fairest fruit,
Blossoms and fruits at once of golden hue,
Appeared, with gay enameled colors mixed;
On which the sun more glad impressed his beams   150
Than in fair evening cloud, or humid bow,[5]
When God hath showered the earth: so lovely seemed
That landscape. And of pure now purer air[6]

---

1. From French *champs*, open country-side. Paradise is an open garden on top of a hill straddling a river in the east of Eden.
2. One of the earliest uses of the word in English to mean "romantic" or "picturesque."
3. As if in a Greek amphitheater, the trees are set row on row.

4. Adam.
5. The rainbow. There is a thick wall of trees around Paradise, which "access denied"; then above them, the shaggy sides of Paradise itself ("the verdurous wall"), and above it the garden of fruit trees.
6. After breathing pure air, Satan now breathes even purer.

Meets his approach, and to the heart inspires
Vernal delight and joy, able to drive[7]   155
All sadness but despair. Now gentle gales,
Fanning their odoriferous wings, dispense
Native perfumes, and whisper whence they stole
Those balmy spoils. As when to them who sail
Beyond the Cape of Hope, and now are past   160
Mozambic, off at sea northeast winds blow
Sabean odors from the spicy shore
Of Araby the Blest,[8] with such delay
Well pleased they slack their course, and many a league
Cheered with the grateful smell old Ocean smiles;   165
So entertained those odorous sweets the fiend
Who came their bane, though with them better pleased
Than Asmodëus with the fishy fume
That drove him, though enamored, from the spouse
Of Tobit's son,[9] and with a vengeance sent   170
From Media post to Egypt, there fast bound.
    Now to th' ascent of that steep savage[1] hill
Satan had journeyed on, pensive and slow;
But further way found none; so thick entwined,
As one continued brake, the undergrowth   175
Of shrubs and tangling bushes had perplexed
All path of man or beast that passed that way.
One gate there only was, and that looked east
On th' other side. Which when th' arch-felon saw,
Due entrance he disdained, and, in contempt,   180
At one slight bound high overleaped all bound[2]
Of hill or highest wall, and sheer within
Lights on his feet. As when a prowling wolf,
Whom hunger drives to seek new haunt for prey,
Watching where shepherds pen their flocks at eve,   185
In hurdled cotes[3] amid the field secure,
Leaps o'er the fence with ease into the fold;
Or as a thief, bent to unhoard the cash
Of some rich burgher, whose substantial doors,
Cross-barred and bolted fast, fear no assault,   190
In at the window climbs, or o'er the tiles;
So clomb[4] this first grand thief into God's fold:

---

7. Scatter.
8. Coasting up East Africa after doubling the Cape of Good Hope, Milton supposes off "Mozambic" (Mozambique) one might meet "Sabean" (i.e., as from Sheba) odors coming from "Araby the Blest" (Arabia Felix). This is the fantasy of a man who learned his geography from medieval atlases and Diodorus Siculus, for the distance between Mozambique and Arabia is close to 2,000 miles.
9. Milton retells briefly here the story of Tobias, Tobit's son, who married Sara and was saved from the fate of her seven previous husbands by the advice of Raphael, who showed him how to make a fishy smell that would drive away the devil Asmodeus. See the Book of Tobit among the Apocrypha.
1. Wooded, entangled (from Latin, *silvaticus*, through Italian *selvaggio*, and French *sauvage*).
2. Satan enters Paradise, not only illegally, but with a contemptuous pun.
3. Pens made of woven reeds.
4. Old past tense of "climb," but used with a special feeling of ungainly energy. The whole metaphor, of God as a rich citizen hoarding Adam and Eve from Satan the second-story-man, is

So since into his church lewd hirelings[5] climb.
Thence up he flew, and on the Tree of Life,
The middle tree and highest there that grew,   195
Sat like a cormorant; yet not true life
Thereby regained, but sat devising death
To them who lived; nor on the virtue thought
Of that life-giving plant, but only used
For prospect,[6] what, well used, had been the pledge   200
Of immortality. So little knows
Any, but God alone, to value right
The good before him, but perverts best things
To worst abuse, or to their meanest use.
    Beneath him, with new wonder, now he views,   205
To all delight of human sense exposed,
In narrow room Nature's whole wealth; yea, more,
A Heaven on Earth; for blissful Paradise
Of God the garden was, by him in the east
Of Eden planted. Eden stretched her line   210
From Auran eastward to the royal towers
Of great Seleucia, built by Grecian kings,
Or where the sons of Eden long before
Dwelt in Telassar.[7] In this pleasant soil
His far more pleasant garden God ordained.   215
Out of the fertile ground he caused to grow
All trees of noblest kind for sight, smell, taste;
And all amid them stood the Tree of Life,
High eminent, blooming ambrosial fruit
Of vegetable gold; and next to life,   220
Our death, the Tree of Knowledge, grew fast by—
Knowledge of good, bought dear by knowing ill.
Southward through Eden went a river large,
Nor changed his course, but through the shaggy hill
Passed underneath engulfed; for God had thrown   225
That mountain, as his garden-mold,[8] high raised
Upon the rapid current, which, through veins
Of porous earth with kindly[9] thirst up drawn,
Rose a fresh fountain, and with many a rill
Watered the garden; thence united fell   230
Down the steep glade, and met the nether flood,
Which from his darksome passage now appears,
And now, divided into four main streams,
Runs diverse, wandering many a famous realm

instinct with comic feeling. On the devil
as a thief, see John x.1.
5. Base men interested only in money;
Milton felt strongly that churchmen
should be unsalaried to insure the purity
of their motives.
6. Perspective, lookout.
7. By suggesting alternate boundaries
of Eden, Milton invokes a hazy sense
of the richness, vastness, and antiquity
of the Middle East. "Auran" is an
area in Syria, to the south of Damascus; "Seleucia" lies near modern Bag-
dad, a powerful city founded by one of
Alexander's generals (hence, "built by
Grecian kings"); and "Telassar" is
another Near Eastern kingdom, this
one probably on the east bank of the
Euphrates.
8. The mountain is God's topsoil, out
of which grows Paradise. The river
(traditionally Tigris) flowed under the
hill.
9. Natural.

And country, whereof here needs no account;[1]   235
But rather to tell how, if art could tell,
How, from that sapphire fount the crispéd[2] brooks,
Rolling on orient pearl and sands of gold,
With mazy error[3] under pendant shades
Ran nectar, visiting each plant, and fed   240
Flowers worthy of Paradise; which not nice[4] art
In beds and curious knots, but Nature boon[5]
Poured forth profuse on hill, and dale, and plain,
Both where the morning sun first warmly smote
The open field, and where the unpierced shade   245
Embrowned[6] the noontide bowers. Thus was this place,
A happy rural seat of various view:[7]
Groves whose rich trees wept odorous gums and balm;
Others whose fruit, burnished with golden rind,
Hung amiable[8]—Hesperian fables true,   250
If true, here only—and of delicious taste.
Betwixt them lawns, or level downs, and flocks
Grazing the tender herb, were interposed,
Or palmy hillock; or the flowery lap
Of some irriguous[9] valley spread her store,   255
Flowers of all hue, and without thorn the rose.[1]
Another side, umbrageous[2] grots and caves
Of cool recess, o'er which the mantling vine
Lays forth her purple grape, and gently creeps
Luxuriant; meanwhile murmuring waters fall   260
Down the slope hills dispersed, or in a lake,
That to the fringéd bank with myrtle crowned
Her crystal mirror holds, unite their streams.
The birds their choir apply;[3] airs, vernal airs,
Breathing the smell of field and grove, attune   265
The trembling leaves, while universal Pan,[4]
Knit with the Graces and the Hours in dance,
Led on th' eternal spring.[5] Not that fair field
Of Enna, where Proserpin gathering flowers,
Herself a fairer flower, by gloomy Dis   270
Was gathered, which cost Ceres all that pain
To seek her through the world; nor that sweet grove

1. Milton has in mind Genesis ii.10; but the expression "whereof here needs no account" dodges many questions about the correct translation of this passage.
2. Wavy, ruffled.
3. From Latin *errare*, "wandering."
4. Particular, careful.
5. Liberal, bounteous.
6. Darkened.
7. Aspect.
8. Lovely. These were real golden apples like those said to have existed in the Hesperides, fabulous islands of the Western Ocean; Paradise was the only place where the fable of the Hesperides was literally true.
9. Well-watered.
1. Figuratively and literally, there was no need for thorns in Paradise.
2. Shady.
3. Practice their song. "Airs" may be either "breezes" or "melodies," and probably are both.
4. The god of all nature. "Pan" in Greek means "all" but it is also the name of the goat-legged nature god.
5. The god of nature dances with the Graces and Hours, an image of perfect harmony.

Of Daphne,[6] by Orontes and th' inspired
Castalian spring, might with this Paradise
Of Eden strive; nor that Nyseian isle,   275
Girt with the river Triton, where old Cham,
Whom Gentiles Ammon call and Libyan Jove,
Hid Amalthea, and her florid son,
Young Bacchus, from his stepdame Rhea's eye;[7]
Nor, where Abassin kings their issue guard,   280
Mount Amara[8] (though this by some supposed
True Paradise) under the Ethiop line
By Nilus' head, enclosed with shining rock,
A whole day's journey high, but wide remote
From this Assyrian garden, where the fiend   285
Saw undelighted all delight, all kind
Of living creatures, new to sight and strange.
Two of far nobler shape, erect and tall,
Godlike erect,[9] with native honor clad
In naked majesty, seemed lords of all,   290
And worthy seemed; for in their looks divine,
The image of their glorious Maker, shone
Truth, wisdom, sanctitude severe and pure—
Severe, but in true filial freedom[1] placed,
Whence true authority in men; though both   295
Not equal, as their sex not equal seemed.
For contemplation he and valor formed,
For softness she and sweet attractive grace;
He for God only, she for God in him.[2]
His fair large front[3] and eye sublime declared   300
Absolute rule; and hyacinthine[4] locks
Round from his parted forelock manly hung

6. Milton is comparing Paradise with the famous beauty spots of antiquity. Enna in Sicily was a lovely meadow from which "Proserpin" was kidnapped by "gloomy Dis" (i.e., Pluto); her mother Ceres sought her throughout the world. The grove of Daphne, near Antioch and the Orontes river in the Near East, had a spring called "Castalia" in imitation of the Muses' fountain near Delphi.

7. The isle of Nysa in the river Triton in Tunisia was where Ammon hid Bacchus, his bastard child by Amalthea, from the eye of his wife Rhea. "Florid" (wine-flushed) Bacchus, when he grew up, received the name of Dionysus in honor of his birthplace. The identification of the Egyptian god Ammon or Hammon with Cham or Ham, the son of Noah, is a piece of comparative anthropology on Milton's part.

8. Finally, Paradise ("this Assyrian garden," line 285) is finer than the palaces atop Mt. Amara, where the "Abassin" (Abyssinian) kings had a splendid palace. Milton's authority for this exotic scene was Peter Heylyn (*Cosmographie* IV.lxiv), from whom he took several phrases direct. His passage then had a continuing influence on the names and phrasings of Coleridge's *Kubla Khan*.

9. By emphasizing the word "erect," Milton means to distinguish man from the beasts of the field, who went "prone."

1. Though almost a paradox, the phrase suggests Milton's idea that true freedom always involves respect for authority and hierarchy. Cf. Eve's foolish question, "For, inferior, who is free?" (IX.825).

2. Milton's ideas on the relations between the sexes were strict for his day, though not as strict as they now appear.

3. Forehead.

4. A classical metaphor, often applied to hair, and implying "brown" or perhaps "flowing," but actually not very definite in its import.

Clustering, but not beneath his shoulders broad:
She, as a veil down to the slender waist,
Her unadornéd golden tresses wore   305
Disheveled, but in wanton ringlets waved
As the vine curls her tendrils,[5] which implied
Subjection, but required with gentle sway,
And by her yielded, by him best received,
Yielded with coy[6] submission, modest pride,   310
And sweet, reluctant, amorous delay.
Nor those mysterious parts were then concealed;
Then was not guilty shame. Dishonest shame
Of Nature's works, honor dishonorable,
Sin-bred, how have ye troubled all mankind   315
With shows instead, mere shows of seeming pure,
And banished from man's life his happiest life,
Simplicity and spotless innocence!
So passed they naked on, nor shunned the sight
Of God or angel; for they thought no ill;   320
So hand in hand they passed, the loveliest pair
That ever since in love's embraces met:
Adam the goodliest man of men since born
His sons; the fairest of her daughters Eve.[7]
Under a tuft of shade that on a green   325
Stood whispering soft, by a fresh fountain-side,
They sat them down; and, after no more toil
Of their sweet gardening labor than sufficed
To recommend cool Zephyr,[8] and make ease
More easy, wholesome thirst and appetite   330
More grateful, to their supper fruits they fell,
Nectarine fruits, which the compliant boughs
Yielded them, sidelong as they sat recline
On the soft downy bank damasked with flowers.
The savory pulp they chew, and in the rind,   335
Still as they thirsted scoop the brimming stream;
Nor gentle purpose,[9] nor endearing smiles
Wanted, nor youthful dalliance, as beseems
Fair couple linked in happy nuptial league,
Alone as they. About them frisking played   340
All beasts of th' earth, since wild, and of all chase[1]
In wood or wilderness, forest or den.
Sporting the lion ramped,[2] and in his paw
Dandled the kid; bears, tigers, ounces, pards,[3]
Gamboled before them; th' unwieldly elephant,   345
To make them mirth, used all his might, and wreathed
His lithe proboscis; close the serpent sly,

---

5. Eve's hair is curly, abundant, uncontrolled; like the vegetation in Paradise, it clings seductively about a severe and masculine virtue.
6. Shy.
7. Logically these constructions are absurd; Adam was not born since his day, Eve was not one of her own daughters.

Milton combines comparative with superlative forms for emphatic effect.
8. I.e., to make a cool breeze welcome.
9. Conversation. "Wanted": lacked.
1. Who lurk in every sort of cover.
2. Reared up.
3. Lynxes and leopards.

Insinuating,[4] wove with Gordian twine
His braided train,[5] and of his fatal guile
Gave proof unheeded. Others on the grass   350
Couched and now filled with pasture, gazing sat,
Or bedward ruminating;[6] for the sun,
Declined, was hasting now with prone career
To th' ocean isles,[7] and in th' ascending scale
Of Heaven the stars that usher evening rose: 355
When Satan, still in gaze as first he stood,
Scarce thus at length failed speech recovered sad:[8]
     "O Hell! what do mine eyes with grief behold?
Into our room of bliss thus high advanced
Creatures of other mold, Earth-born perhaps,   360
Not spirits, yet to heavenly spirits bright
Little inferior; whom my thoughts pursue
With wonder, and could love; so lively shines
In them divine resemblance, and such grace
The hand that formed them on their shape hath poured.[9]   365
Ah! gentle pair, ye little think how nigh
Your change approaches, when all these delights
Will vanish, and deliver ye to woe,
More woe, the more your taste is now of joy:
Happy, but for so happy[1] ill secured   370
Long to continue, and this high seat, your Heaven,
Ill fenced for Heaven to keep out such a foe
As now is entered; yet no purposed foe
To you, whom I could pity thus forlorn,
Though I unpitied. League with you I seek,   375
And mutual amity, so strait, so close,
That I with you must dwell, or you with me,
Henceforth.[2] My dwelling, haply, may not please,
Like this fair Paradise, your sense; yet such
Accept your Maker's work; he gave it me,   380
Which I as freely give. Hell shall unfold,
To entertain you two, her widest gates,
And send forth all her kings; there will be room,
Not like these narrow limits, to receive
Your numerous offspring; if no better place,   385
Thank him who puts me, loath, to this revenge
On you, who wrong me not, for him who wronged.[3]

4. Writhing and twisting, but with a glance at the Tempter's rhetorical techniques.
5. Checkered body. "Gordian twine": knots, like the Gordian knot, cut by Alexander the Great.
6. The animals are chewing their cuds before bedtime; in Paradise, where the animal kingdom is not yet subject to death, they are perforce vegetarians.
7. The Azores.
8. The choked, laborious line mirrors Satan's heavy, congested mind.
9. Though Satan's moral values are topsy-turvy ("Evil, be thou my Good," he has said in the first part of Book IV), his aesthetic values are strictly orthodox.
1. Such happiness.
2. Though it starts in simple admiration, Satan's friendship for mankind is, at the end, rather grisly and sardonic. The turning point seems to be "though I unpitied" (line 375)—the reaction of a spoiled child.
3. I.e., it is not my fault; Satan's favorite phrase.

And, should I at your harmless innocence
Melt, as I do, yet public reason just—
Honor and empire with revenge enlarged   390
By conquering this new world—compels me now
To do what else, though damned, I should abhor."[4]
 So spake the fiend, and with necessity,
The tyrant's plea, excused his devilish deeds.
Then from his lofty stand on that high tree   395
Down he alights among the sportful herd
Of those four-footed kinds, himself now one,
Now other, as their shape served best his end
Nearer to view his prey, and unespied,
To mark what of their state he more might learn   400
By word or action marked. About them round
A lion now he stalks with fiery glare;
Then as a tiger, who by chance hath spied
In some purlieu[5] two gentle fawns at play,
Straight couches close; then, rising, changes oft   405
His couchant watch, as one who chose his ground,
Whence rushing he might surest seize them both
Griped in each paw * * *

4. Satan's final reason for destroying Adam and Eve is thoroughly Satanic; it is *ragione di stato*, reason of state, the public interest.

5. The outskirt of a forest. Note that Satan can and does enter any animal he wants; it is only for the special purposes of the temptation that he finds the serpent specially convenient.

Summary By eavesdropping on Adam and Eve, Satan learns of the prohibited Tree of Knowledge; this weakness he resolves to exploit. Meanwhile Uriel, rendered suspicious by Satan's fierce demeanor outside Paradise, reports to Gabriel, the angel specially assigned to guard mankind, that a diabolic intruder may be near. Gabriel promises to search him out. After Adam and Eve say their evening prayers and retire, Gabriel divides his night watch into groups, assigning Ithuriel and Zephon to guard closely the bower of Adam and Eve. They find Satan whispering in the ear of the sleeping Eve, and bring him before Gabriel. A battle impends, but is averted by a heavenly signal, and Satan flees out of Paradise.

Book V. Summary In the morning Eve is distressed by her dreams of the previous night, which she relates to Adam; he comforts her. Meanwhile God dispatches Raphael to warn man of the approaching danger. Raphael arrives about noon, and dines with Adam and Eve. He then warns his hosts of the need to remain obedient, and, to explain the risks they run, recounts the story of Satan's revolt and fall. He describes how Satan, pretending that God's creation of the Son was an offense to angelic dignity, persuaded a host of his fellow angels to withdraw their allegiance to God and set up a camp in the north. When open war on God was announced, however, one of these angels was able to repent. The seraph Abdiel, though scorned by his fellows, denounced the rebellion and returned, heroically alone, to the camp of God's followers.

Book VI. Summary   Continuing the story of the war in Heaven,
Raphael describes the assembling of the armies and a first skirmish in which
Satan is both insulted and wounded by Abdiel. After the first day's battle,
the evil angels retire discomfited; but overnight Satan invents cannon with
which, on the second day, the good angels are put to some disorder. In
the fury of the fight, however, they pull up mountains by the roots and
bury the cannon beneath them; thus the issue remains inconclusive. On
the third day, God withdraws all his armies and sends the Son alone into
battle; the Son drives his enemies irresistibly over the wall of Heaven, and
after falling nine days through Chaos they are swallowed up in Hell.

From Book VII

[*The Invocation*]¹

Descend from Heaven, Urania, by that name
If rightly thou art called,² whose voice divine
Following, above th' Olympian hill I soar,
Above the flight of Pegasean wing!³
The meaning, not the name I call: for thou   5
Nor of the Muses nine, nor on the top
Of old Olympus dwell'st, but heavenly born,
Before the hills appeared, or fountain flowed,
Thou with eternal Wisdom didst converse,
Wisdom thy sister, and with her didst play   10
In presence of th' Almighty Father,⁴ pleased
With thy celestial song. Up led by thee
Into the Heaven of Heavens I have presumed,
An earthly guest, and drawn empyreal air,
Thy tempering;⁵ with like safety guided down,   15
Return me to my native element:
Lest from this flying steed unreined (as once
Bellerophon,⁶ though from a lower clime),
Dismounted, on th' Aleian field I fall,
Erroneous⁷ there to wander and forlorn.   20

1. To start the second half of his
poem, Milton must counterbalance the
destruction of the war in Heaven with
the creation by God of a new universe,
centering on the Earth. Book VII is
devoted to this topic; and to approach
so vast a subject, Milton once more invokes his Muse.
2. Milton has only the names of classical Muses with which to invoke the
spiritual principles of Christian theology. Properly the Muse of astronomy,
Urania is also the symbol of heavenly
love and of divine wisdom; Milton here
renews the invocation he made in
Book I.
3. Pegasus, the flying horse of poetry,
suggests (in connection with Bellero-

phon, line 18) Milton's sense of his
own perilous audacity in writing so vast
a poem.
4. In Proverbs viii.30, Wisdom is made
to speak of "playing always before
God" previous even to the Creation.
Milton makes his Muse coeval with divine wisdom.
5. Tempered by thee.
6. Bellerophon tried to explore the
stars astride Pegasus the flying horse;
but Zeus sent a gadfly to sting Pegasus,
and his rider, after falling onto the
Aleian plain in Lycia, wandered about
there till he died.
7. From Latin *errare*, "to wander," as
well as "to be mistaken."

Half yet remains unsung, but narrower bound
Within the visible diurnal sphere;
Standing on Earth, not rapt above the pole,
More safe I sing with mortal voice, unchanged
To hoarse or mute, though fall'n on evil days,   25
On evil days though fall'n, and evil tongues;
In darkness, and with dangers compassed round,
And solitude; yet not alone, while thou
Visit'st my slumbers nightly, or when morn
Purples the east:[8] still govern thou my song,   30
Urania, and fit audience find, though few.
But drive far off the barbarous dissonance
Of Bacchus and his revelers, the race
Of that wild rout that tore the Thracian bard[9]
In Rhodope, where woods and rocks had ears   35
To rapture, till the savage clamor drowned
Both harp and voice; nor could the Muse defend
Her son. So fail not thou, who thee implores:
For thou art heavenly, she an empty dream.

8. Milton composed mostly at night or very early in the morning.
9. The Thracian Bacchantes, female worshipers of Bacchus, tore Orpheus to pieces in Rhodope, though even the rocks and trees were so impressed with his music that they refused to be used against the poet. See *Lycidas*, lines 58–63. Orpheus was son of Calliope, the epic Muse.

Summary At Adam's request, Raphael continues his narration and describes how God, to replace the fallen angels, created the world, its creatures, and finally man, in the course of six days; the story of the creation concludes, on the seventh day, with a chorus of thanksgiving by the angels.

Book VIII. Summary Adam asks Raphael why so many and such splendid stars seem to be at the service of the earth, which appears smaller and less noble than they; at this point Eve leaves her husband and his guest to continue the discussion alone. Raphael proposes various astronomical possibilities but gives no conclusive answer to Adam's question, urging him instead to confine his curiosity to more practical matters. Adam now, at Raphael's request, describes his own recollections of his creation, as well as his first meeting and marriage with Eve. In the course of the story, he shows a somewhat exaggerated deference for Eve, which the angel rebukes; Adam is to be the head of the family, and follow his own judgment, not his wife's. Repeating his admonitions to beware of temptation, Raphael departs.

Book IX

The Argument

Satan, having compassed the Earth, with meditated guile returns as a mist by night into Paradise; enters into the serpent sleeping. Adam and Eve in the morning go forth to their labors, which Eve proposes to divide in several places, each laboring apart: Adam consents not, alleging the danger lest that enemy of whom they were forewarned should attempt her found alone. Eve, loath to be thought not circumspect or firm enough, urges her going apart, the rather desirous to make trial of her strength; Adam at last yields. The serpent finds her alone: his subtle approach, first gazing, then speaking, with much flattery extolling Eve above all other creatures. Eve, wondering to hear the serpent speak, asks how he attained to human speech and such understanding not till now; the serpent answers that by tasting of a certain tree in the garden he attained both to speech and reason, till then void of both. Eve requires him to bring her to that tree, and finds it to be the Tree of Knowledge forbidden: the serpent, now grown bolder, with many wiles and arguments induces her at length to eat. She, pleased with the taste, deliberates a while whether to impart thereof to Adam or not; at last brings him of the fruit; relates what persuaded her to eat thereof. Adam, at first amazed, but perceiving her lost, resolves, through vehemence of love, to perish with her, and, extenuating[1] the trespass, eats also of the fruit. The effects thereof in them both; they seek to cover their nakedness; then fall to variance and accusation of one another.

> No more of talk where God[2] or angel guest
> With man, as with his friend, familiar used
> To sit indulgent, and with him partake
> Rural repast, permitting him the while
> Venial[3] discourse unblamed. I now must change   5
> Those notes to tragic; foul distrust, and breach
> Disloyal, on the part of man, revolt
> And disobedience; on the part of Heaven,
> Now alienated, distance and distaste,
> Anger and just rebuke, and judgment given,   10
> That brought into this world a world of woe,
> Sin and her shadow Death, and Misery,
> Death's harbinger. Sad task! yet argument
> Not less but more heroic than the wrath
> Of stern Achilles on his foe pursued   15
> Thrice fugitive about Troy wall; or rage
> Of Turnus for Lavinia disespoused;
> Or Neptune's ire, or Juno's, that so long
> Perplexed the Greek, and Cytherea's son:[4]

1. Not "diminishing" or "excusing" as in customary English usage, but carrying further, drawing out.
2. God, of course, has not been lunching with Adam; but since man is about to fall, the age is now over when such an occasion could be contemplated.
3. Permissible.
4. In the *Iliad* (XXII), Achilles pursues Hector three times around Troy wall before catching him. In the *Aeneid*, Aeneas must fight with Turnus for the hand of Lavinia. Neptune (or Poseidon) was unfriendly to Odysseus (the Greek); Juno (or Hera) to Aeneas, who was Cytherea's, i.e., Aphrodite's, son by Anchises.

If answerable style I can obtain   20
Of my celestial Patroness,[5] who deigns
Her nightly visitation unimplored,
And dictates to me slumbering, or inspires
Easy my unpremeditated verse,[6]
Since first this subject for heroic song   25
Pleased me, long choosing and beginning late,[7]
Not sedulous by nature to indite
Wars, hitherto the only argument
Heroic deemed, chief mastery to dissect[8]
With long and tedious havoc fabled knights   30
In battles feigned (the better fortitude
Of patience and heroic martyrdom
Unsung), or to describe races and games,
Or tilting furniture,[9] emblazoned shields,
Impresses quaint, caparisons and steeds,   35
Bases and tinsel trappings, gorgeous knights
At joust and tournament; then marshaled feast
Served up in hall with sewers and seneschals:[1]
The skill of artifice or office mean;
Not that which justly gives heroic name   40
To person or to poem. Me, of these
Nor skilled nor studious, higher argument
Remains,[2] sufficient of itself to raise
That name,[3] unless an age too late, or cold
Climate, or years, damp my intended wing   45
Depressed; and much they may if all be mine,
Not hers who brings it nightly to my ear.
   The sun was sunk, and after him the star
Of Hesperus, whose office is to bring
Twilight upon the Earth, short arbiter   50
'Twixt day and night, and now from end to end
Night's hemisphere had veiled the horizon round,
When Satan, who late fled before the threats
Of Gabriel out of Eden,[4] now improved
In meditated fraud and malice, bent   55
On man's destruction, mauger what might hap
Of heavier on himself,[5] fearless returned.

5. The muse, Urania.
6. Milton, we are told by his nephew
Edward Philips, used to wake up in the
morning with lines of poetry full-formed
in his head; he would then dictate them
to an amanuensis.
7. Milton's early plans for epics, preserved in manuscript, did center on national heroes; his choice of a sacred
subject is a novelty within the epic tradition. "Sedulous": eager.
8. I.e., in describing wars one's chief
task is to dissect; dissect, in its strict
Latin sense of "cut apart," but perhaps
also with a comic overtone from the
anatomy table.

9. The equipment of tournaments; "impresses quaint": elaborate devices on
shields; "bases": trappings for horses.
1. Waiters and stewards, who also dissect.
2. I.e., for me, when these things are
set aside which I neither can nor want
to do, there remains a higher argument.
3. I.e., the name heroic poet. "Age too
late": not Milton's age, but the age of
the world. Milton felt a "cold climate,"
by forcing people to keep their mouths
shut and mumble, was inimical to epic
poetry. "Damp": stupefy, benumb.
4. At the end of Book IV.
5. Despite the peril of heavier (punishments).

By night he fled, and at midnight returned
From compassing the Earth—cautious of day
Since Uriel, regent of the sun, descried   60
His entrance, and forewarned the Cherubim
That kept their watch.[6] Thence, full of anguish, driven,
The space of seven continued nights he rode
With darkness; thrice the equinoctial line[7]
He circled, four times crossed the car of Night   65
From pole to pole, traversing each colure;
On the eighth returned, and on the coast averse
From entrance or cherubic watch by stealth
Found unsuspected way. There was a place   70
(Now not, though sin, not time, first wrought the change)
Where Tigris, at the foot of Paradise,
Into a gulf shot under ground, till part
Rose up a fountain by the Tree of Life.
In with the river sunk, and with it rose,   75
Satan, involved in rising mist; then sought
Where to lie hid. Sea he had searched and land
From Eden over Pontus, and the pool
Maeotis, up beyond the river Ob;[8]
Downward as far antarctic; and, in length,   80
West from Orontes to the ocean barred
At Darien, thence to the land where flows
Ganges and Indus.[9] Thus the orb he roamed
With narrow search, and with inspection deep
Considered every creature, which of all   85
Most opportune might serve his wiles, and found
The serpent subtlest beast of all the field.[1]
Him, after long debate, irresolute
Of thoughts revolved,[2] his final sentence chose
Fit vessel, fittest imp[3] of fraud, in whom   90
To enter, and his dark suggestions hide
From sharpest sight; for in the wily snake
Whatever sleights none would suspicious mark,
As from his wit and native subtlety
Proceeding, which, in other beasts observed,   95
Doubt[4] might beget of diabolic power
Active within beyond the sense of brute.

6. At the beginning of Book IV. These connections with Book IV not only bridge the intervening narration, but emphasize a balancing of the whole epic; see the headnote.
7. The equator. The colures are the two great circles of the celestial sphere which intersect at the poles. By circling the globe, either from east to west or over the north and south poles, Satan can remain continually hidden in darkness.
8. Pontus is the Black Sea, the pool Maeotis the swamps of the Sea of Azov;
the river Ob flows north through Siberia into the Arctic Ocean.
9. Flying west from Orontes in Syria, Satan now crosses the Atlantic to the Isthmus of Panama (Darien), then crosses the Pacific and southeast Asia to India.
1. Genesis iii.1 describes the serpent as the subtlest beast of the field.
2. I.e., unable to decide among his revolving thoughts. "Sentence": decision.
3. Graft, offshoot.
4. Suspicion.

Thus he resolved, but first from inward grief
His bursting passion into plaints thus poured:
  "O Earth, how like to Heaven, if not preferred
More justly, seat worthier of Gods, as built   100
With second thought, reforming what was old!
For what God, after better, worse would build?
Terrestrial Heaven, danced round by other Heavens,
That shine, yet bear their bright officious lamps,
Light above light, for thee alone, as seems,   105
In thee concent'ring all their precious beams
Of sacred influence![5] As God in Heaven
Is center, yet extends to all, so thou
Cent'ring receiv'st from all those orbs; in thee,
Not in themselves, all their known virtue appears,   110
Productive in herb, plant, and nobler birth
Of creatures animate with gradual life
Of growth, sense, reason,[6] all summed up in man.
With what delight could I have walked thee round,
If I could joy in aught; sweet interchange   115
Of hill and valley, rivers, woods, and plains,
Now land, now sea, and shores with forest crowned,
Rocks, dens, and caves! But I in none of these
Find place or refuge; and the more I see
Pleasures about me, so much more I feel   120
Torment within me, as from the hateful siege[7]
Of contraries; all good to me becomes
Bane,[8] and in Heaven much worse would be my state.
But neither here seek I, no, nor in Heaven,
To dwell, unless by mastering Heaven's Supreme;   125
Nor hope to be myself less miserable
By what I seek, but others to make such
As I, though thereby worse to me redound.
For only in destroying I find ease
To my relentless thoughts, and him [9] destroyed,   130
Or won to what may work his utter loss,
For whom all this was made, all this [1] will soon
Follow, as to him linked in weal or woe:
In woe then, that destruction wide may range!
To me shall be the glory sole among   135
The infernal Powers, in one day to have marred
What he, Almighty styled, six nights and days
Continued making, and who knows how long
Before had been contriving? though perhaps
Not longer than since I in one night freed   140

5. Satan, like Adam in Book VIII, is impressed that so many heavenly bodies center on (and "serve") the earth—as the old Ptolemaic astronomy taught that they did. "Officious": dutiful.
6. Life on earth is gradual, or graduated, from the herb which merely grows, to the animal which grows and feels, to man, who grows, feels, and thinks.
7. Conflict.
8. Poison. This is exactly what he willed in IV.110.
9. I.e., man.
1. I.e., the created cosmos.

From servitude inglorious well-nigh half
Th' angelic name, and thinner left the throng
Of his adorers. He, to be avenged,
And to repair his numbers thus impaired,
Whether such virtue,[2] spent of old, now failed   145
More angels to create (if they at least
Are his created),[3] or to spite us more,
Determined to advance into our room
A creature formed of earth, and him endow,
Exalted from so base original,   150
With heavenly spoils, our spoils. What he decreed
He effected; man he made, and for him built
Magnificent this World, and Earth his seat,
Him lord pronounced, and, O indignity!
Subjected to his service angel-wings   155
And flaming ministers, to watch and tend
Their earthy charge. Of these the vigilance
I dread, and to elude, thus wrapt in mist
Of midnight vapor, glide obscure, and pry
In every bush and brake, where hap may find   160
The serpent sleeping, in whose mazy folds
To hide me, and the dark intent I bring.
O foul descent! that I, who erst contended
With Gods to sit the highest, am now constrained
Into a beast, and, mixed with bestial slime,   165
This essence to incarnate and imbrute,[4]
That to the height of deity aspired!
But what will not ambition and revenge
Descend to? Who aspires must down as low
As high he soared, obnoxious,[5] first or last,   170
To basest things. Revenge, at first though sweet,
Bitter ere long back on itself recoils.
Let it; I reck not, so it light well aimed,
Since higher I fall short, on him who next
Provokes my envy, this new favorite   175
Of Heaven, this man of clay, son of despite,
Whom, us the more to spite,[6] his Maker raised
From dust: spite then with spite is best repaid."
    So saying, through each thicket, dank or dry,
Like a black mist low-creeping, he held on   180
His midnight search, where soonest he might find
The serpent. Him fast sleeping soon he found,
In labyrinth of many a round self-rolled,
His head the midst, well stored with subtle wiles:
Not yet in horrid shade or dismal den,   185

2. Strength, energy.
3. Satan never raises this question, whether angels are created or independent beings, without hesitating over it.
4. Satan's incarnation in a snake is a grotesque parody of the Son of God's incarnation in Christ.
5. Subject to.
6. Satan sees God in his own image, as a spiteful creature.

Nor nocent [7] yet, but on the grassy herb,
Fearless, unfeared, he slept. In at his mouth
The devil entered, and his brutal sense,
In heart or head, possessing soon inspired
With act intelligential; but his sleep   190
Disturbed not, waiting close[8] th' approach of morn.
　　Now, whenas sacred light began to dawn
In Eden on the humid flowers, that breathed
Their morning incense, when all things that breathe
From th' Earth's great altar send up silent praise   195
To the Creator, and his nostrils fill
With grateful smell, forth came the human pair,
And joined their vocal worship to the choir
Of creatures wanting voice; that done, partake
The season,[9] prime for sweetest scents and airs;   200
Then cómmune how that day they best may ply
Their growing work; for much their work outgrew
The hands' dispatch of two gardening so wide:
And Eve first to her husband thus began:
　　"Adam, well may we labor still [1] to dress   205
This garden, still to tend plant, herb, and flower,
Our pleasant task enjoined; but, till more hands
Aid us, the work under our labor grows,
Luxurious by restraint: what we by day
Lop overgrown, or prune, or prop, or bind,   210
One night or two with wanton growth derides,
Tending to wild. Thou, therefore, now advise,
Or hear what to my mind first thoughts present.
Let us divide our labors; thou where choice
Leads thee, or where most needs, whether to wind   215
The woodbine round this arbor, or direct
The clasping ivy where to climb; while I
In yonder spring [2] of roses intermixed
With myrtle find what to redress till noon.
For, while so near each other thus all day   220
Our task we choose, what wonder if so near
Looks intervene and smiles, or objects new
Casual discourse draw on, which intermits
Our day's work, brought to little, though begun
Early, and th' hour of supper comes unearned!"   225
　　To whom mild answer Adam thus returned:
"Sole Eve, associate sole, to me beyond
Compare above all living creatures dear!
Well hast thou motioned,[3] well thy thoughts employed
How we might best fulfil the work which here   230
God hath assigned us, nor of me shalt pass

7. Harmful.　　　　　　　　　　　　1. Continually.
8. In secret.　　　　　　　　　　　　2. Growth.
9. I.e., go forth into the morning air.　3. Suggested.
"Prime": the best.

Unpraised; for nothing lovelier can be found
In woman than to study household good,
And good works in her husband to promote.[4]
Yet not so strictly hath our Lord imposed   235
Labor as to debar us when we need
Refreshment, whether food or talk between,
Food of the mind, or this sweet intercourse
Of looks and smiles; for smiles from reason flow,
To brute denied, and are of love the food,   240
Love, not the lowest end of human life.
For not to irksome toil, but to delight,
He made us, and delight to reason joined.
These paths and bowers doubt not but our joint hands
Will keep from wilderness with ease, as wide   245
As we need walk, till younger hands ere long
Assist us. But, if much converse perhaps
Thee satiate, to short absence I could yield;
For solitude sometimes is best society,
And short retirement urges sweet return.   250
But other doubt possesses me, lest harm
Befall thee, severed from me; for thou know'st
What hath been warned us, what malicious foe,
Envying our happiness, and of his own
Despairing, seeks to work us woe and shame   255
By sly assault, and somewhere nigh at hand
Watches, no doubt, with greedy hope to find
His wish and best advantage, us asunder,[5]
Hopeless to circumvent us joined, where each
To other speedy aid might lend at need.   260
Whether his first design be to withdraw
Our fealty from God, or to disturb
Conjugal love, than which perhaps no bliss
Enjoyed by us excites his envy more;
Or this, or·worse,[6] leave not the faithful side   265
That gave thee being, still shades thee and protects.
The wife, where danger or dishonor lurks,
Safest and seemliest by her husband stays,
Who guards her, or with her the worst endures."
    To whom the virgin [7] majesty of Eve,   270
As one who loves, and some unkindness meets,
With sweet austere composure thus replied:
    "Offspring of Heaven and Earth, and all Earth's lord!
That such an enemy we have, who seeks
Our ruin, both by thee informed I learn,   275
And from the parting angel overheard,

---

4. Proverbs xxxi is devoted to the praise of a good wife, and Milton doubtless had it in mind here.
5. I.e., to find us apart, which will answer his wishes and serve his advantage.
6. I.e., whether this or something worse be his intent.
7. Unspotted.

As in a shady nook I stood behind,
Just then returned at shut of evening flowers.
But that thou shouldst my firmness therefore doubt
To God or thee, because we have a foe   280
May tempt it, I expected not to hear.
His violence thou fear'st not, being such
As we, not capable of death or pain,
Can either not receive, or can repel.
His fraud is, then, thy fear; which plain infers   285
Thy equal fear that my firm faith and love
Can by his fraud be shaken or seduced:
Thoughts, which how found they harbor in thy breast,
Adam, misthought of her to thee so dear?" [8]

    To whom, with healing words, Adam replied: 290
"Daughter of God and man, immortal Eve,
For such thou art, from sin and blame entire; [9]
Not diffident of thee do I dissuade
Thy absence from my sight, but to avoid
Th' attempt itself, intended by our foe.   295
For he who tempts, though in vain, at least asperses [1]
The tempted with dishonor foul, supposed
Not incorruptible of faith, not proof
Against temptation. Thou thyself with scorn
And anger wouldst resent the offered wrong,   300
Though ineffectual found; misdeem not, then,
If such affront I labor to avert
From thee alone, which on us both at once
The enemy, though bold, will hardly dare;
Or, daring, first on me th' assault shall light.   305
Nor thou his malice and false guile contemn—
Subtle he needs must be who could seduce
Angels—nor think superfluous others' aid.
I from the influence of thy looks receive
Access [2] in every virtue; in thy sight   310
More wise, more watchful, stronger, if need were
Of outward strength; while shame, thou looking on,
Shame to be overcome or overreached, [3]
Would utmost vigor raise, and raised unite.
Why shouldst not thou like sense within thee feel   315
When I am present, and thy trial choose
With me, best witness of thy virtue tried?"
    So spake domestic Adam in his care
And matrimonial love; but Eve, who thought
Less [4] attributed to her faith sincere,   320

8. I.e., these thoughts were misthought of (misapplied to) her to thee so dear (me).

9. "Entire" is from Latin *integer*, untouched. "Diffident": the usual English meaning is "shy," "timid"; Milton emphasizes the Latin roots, *dis* + *fides* = mistrustful.

1. The word is from Latin *spargere*, to sprinkle, with overtones from English "aspersion," an ugly insinuation.

2. Extra strength.

3. Overpowered or outwitted.

4. Too little.

Thus her reply with accent sweet renewed:
  "If this be our condition, thus to dwell
In narrow circuit straitened by a foe,
Subtle or violent, we not endued
Single with like defence wherever met, 325
How are we happy, still in fear of harm?
But harm precedes not sin: only our foe
Tempting affronts us with his foul esteem
Of our integrity: his foul esteem
Sticks no dishonor on our front,[5] but turns 330
Foul on himself; then wherefore shunned or feared
By us, who rather double honor gain
From his surmise proved false, find peace within,
Favor from Heaven, our witness, from th' event?
And what is faith, love, virtue, unassayed 335
Alone, without exterior help sustained?
Let us not then suspect our happy state
Left so imperfect by the Maker wise
As not secure to single or combined.
Frail is our happiness, if this be so; 340
And Eden were no Eden, thus exposed."
  To whom thus Adam fervently replied:
"O woman, best are all things as the will
Of God ordained them; his creating hand
Nothing imperfect or deficient left 345
Of all that he created, much less man,
Or aught that might his happy state secure,
Secure from outward force. Within himself
The danger lies, yet lies within his power;
Against his will he can receive no harm. 350
But God left free the will; for what obeys
Reason is free; and reason he made right,
But bid her well beware, and still erect,[6]
Lest, by some fair appearing good surprised,
She dictate false, and misinform the will 355
To do what God expressly hath forbid.
Not then mistrust, but tender love, enjoins
That I should mind [7] thee oft; and mind thou me.
Firm we subsist, yet possible to swerve,
Since reason not impossibly may meet 360
Some specious object by the foe suborned,
And fall into deception unaware,
Not keeping strictest watch, as she was warned.
Seek not temptation, then, which to avoid
Were better, and most likely if from me 365

5. Forehead.
6. Remain alert.

7. Remind; in the next phrase, "mind" means "obey."

Thou sever not: trial will come unsought.
Wouldst thou approve thy constancy, approve [8]
First thy obedience; th' other who can know,
Not seeing thee attempted, who attest?
But if thou think trial unsought may find   370
Us both securer than thus warned thou seem'st,
Go; for thy stay, not free, absents thee more.
Go in thy native innocence; rely
On what thou hast of virtue; summon all;
For God towards thee hath done his part: do thine.'   375
    So spake the patriarch of mankind; but Eve
Persisted; yet submiss, though last, replied:
    "With thy permission,[9] then, and thus forewarned,
Chiefly by what thy own last reasoning words
Touched only, that our trial, when least sought,   380
May find us both perhaps far less prepared,
The willinger I go, nor much expect
A foe so proud will first the weaker seek;
So bent, the more shall shame him his repulse."
Thus saying, from her husband's hand her hand   385
Soft she withdrew, and like a wood nymph light,
Oread or dryad, or of Delia's train,[1]
Betook her to the groves, but Delia's self
In gait surpassed and goddesslike deport,
Though not as she with bow and quiver armed,   390
But with such gardening tools as art yet rude,
Guiltless of fire[2] had formed, or angels brought.
To Pales, or Pomona, thus adorned,
Likest she seemed, Pomona when she fled
Vertumnus, or to Ceres in her prime,   395
Yet virgin of Proserpina from Jove.[3]
Her long with ardent look his eye pursued
Delighted, but desiring more her stay.
Oft he to her his charge of quick return
Repeated; she to him as oft engaged   400
To be returned by noon amid the bower,
And all things in best order to invite
Noontide repast, or afternoon's repose.
O much deceived, much failing, hapless Eve,

8. Prove, give evidence of.
9. Eve takes a reluctant and extorted permission as free leave to do what she wants. Though apparently submissive, she gets the last word.
1. An "oread" is a nymph of the mountain, a "dryad" one of the wood. "Delia" is Diana or Artemis, goddess of the chase, who when she hunted was accompanied by a train of nymphs.
2. There was no need of fire in Paradise; but that fire is a possession which renders one guilty suggests an overtone of the Prometheus myth.
3. Pales is a Roman goddess of flocks, Pomona a Roman divinity of fruits and orchards. Pomona was wooed by Vertumnus, god of spring, who assumed all sorts of shapes to win her. Ceres, the Mother Nature of the ancients (hence, the word "cereal"), bore Proserpina to Jupiter. All three goddesses are patrons of agriculture, like Eve.

Of thy presumed return!⁴ Event perverse!   405
Thou never from that hour in Paradise
Found'st either sweet repast, or sound repose;
Such ambush hid among sweet flowers and shades
Waited with hellish rancor imminent⁵
To intercept thy way, or send thee back   410
Despoiled of innocence, of faith, of bliss.
For now, and since first break of dawn, the fiend,
Mere serpent in appearance, forth was come,
And on his quest, where likeliest he might find
The only two of mankind, but in them   415
The whole included race, his purposed prey.
In bower and field he sought, where any tuft
Of grove or garden-plot more pleasant lay,
Their tendance⁶ or plantation for delight;
By fountain or by shady rivulet   420
He sought them both, but wished his hap might find
Eve separate; he wished, but not with hope
Of what so seldom chanced; when to his wish,
Beyond his hope, Eve separate he spies,
Veiled in a cloud of fragrance, where she stood,   425
Half spied, so thick the roses bushing round
About her glowed, oft stooping to support
Each flower of slender stalk, whose head though gay
Carnation, purple, azure, or specked with gold,
Hung drooping unsustained, them she upstays   430
Gently with myrtle band, mindless the while
Herself, though fairest unsupported flower,
From her best prop so far, and storm so nigh.⁷
Nearer he drew, and many a walk traversed
Of stateliest covert, cedar, pine, or palm;   435
Then voluble⁸ and bold, now hid, now seen
Among thick-woven arborets⁹ and flowers
Embordered on each bank, the hand of Eve:
Spot more delicious than those gardens feigned
Or of revived Adonis,¹ or renowned   440
Alcinous, host of old Laertes' son,
Or that, not mystic, where the sapient king²
Held dalliance with his fair Egyptian spouse.
Much he the place admired, the person more.
As one who long in populous city pent,   445

4. "Much deceived" carries over; Eve was "much deceived of" (about) her "presumed return."
5. Threatening.
6. Object of their tending.
7. The conceit of the flower-gatherer who is herself gathered is repeated here from IV.270, where it was applied to Proserpina.
8. Rolling (a Latinism).
9. Bushes. "Hand": handiwork.
1. The garden of Adonis was a heavenly bower where Venus' lover was supposed still to lie in secret, recovering from his wound received on earth (Venus would not allow him to die). Alcinous was king of the Phaeacians. His garden, visited by Odysseus ("old Laertes' son"), is described in the *Odyssey*.
2. Solomon; his "fair Egyptian spouse" is Pharaoh's daughter: Milton is referring to the Song of Solomon vi.2. The fact that it is "not mystic" (i.e., not mythical) distinguishes the Scriptural garden from the "feigned" (line 439) ones of classical legend.

Where houses thick and sewers annoy[3] the air,
Forth issuing on a summer's morn to breathe
Among the pleasant villages and farms
Adjoined, from each thing met conceives delight,
The smell of grain, or tedded[4] grass, or kine,   450
Or dairy, each rural sight, each rural sound:
If chance with nymphlike step fair virgin pass,[5]
What pleasing seemed, for her now pleases more,
She most, and in her look sums all delight.[6]
Such pleasure took the serpent to behold   455
This flowery plat,[7] the sweet recess of Eve
Thus early, thus alone; her heavenly form
Angelic, but more soft, and feminine,
Her graceful innocence, her every air
Of gesture or least action overawed   460
His malice, and with rapine[8] sweet bereaved
His fierceness of the fierce intent it brought:
That space the evil one abstracted stood
From his own evil, and for the time remained
Stupidly good,[9] of enmity disarmed,   465
Of guile, of hate, of envy, of revenge.
But the hot Hell that always in him burns,
Though in mid Heaven, soon ended his delight,
And tortures him now more, the more he sees
Of pleasure not for him ordained: then soon   470
Fierce hate he recollects, and all his thoughts
Of mischief, gratulating,[1] thus excites:
    "Thoughts, whither have ye led me? with what sweet
Compulsion thus transported to forget
What hither brought us? hate, not love, nor hope   475
Of Paradise for Hell, hope here to taste
Of pleasure, but all pleasure to destroy,
Save what is in destroying;[2] other joy
To me is lost. Then let me not let pass
Occasion which now smiles; behold alone   480
The woman, opportune to all attempts,
Her husband, for I view far round, not nigh,
Whose higher intellectual more I shun,
And strength, of courage haughty, and of limb
Heroic built, though of terrestrial mold;[3]   485
Foe not informidable, exempt from wound,[4]
I not; so much hath Hell debased, and pain

3. Make noisome, befoul.
4. Tossed and drying in the sun.
5. I.e., if it chance that with nymph-like step a fair virgin should pass.
6. I.e., in her look sums up, or epitomizes, all delight.
7. Plot.
8. It is a deliberate paradox that her sweetness can ravish his malice; the word is deliberately overviolent.
9. Without his evil, Satan (like many wicked people) is quite dull and ordinary. But at the moment he is stunned.
1. Exulting.
2. What brought Satan to Paradise was not hope of pleasure, but the wish to destroy all pleasure except the pleasure of destruction itself.
3. Made of earth.
4. Adam in the state of innocence is invulnerable.

Enfeebled me, to what I was in Heaven.
She fair, divinely fair, fit love for gods,
Not terrible, though terror be in love   490
And beauty, not approached by stronger hate,
Hate stronger, under show of love well feigned,
The way which to her ruin now I tend."5
    So spake the enemy of mankind, enclosed
In serpent, inmate bad, and toward Eve   495
Addressed his way, not with indented wave,
Prone on the ground, as since, but on his rear,
Circular base of rising folds, that towered
Fold above fold a surging maze; his head
Crested aloft, and carbuncle6 his eyes;   500
With burnished neck of verdant gold, erect
Amidst his circling spires,7 that on the grass
Floated redundant. Pleasing was his shape,
And lovely; never since of serpent kind
Lovelier, not those that in Illyria changed   505
Hermione and Cadmus,8 or the god
In Epidaurus;9 nor to which transformed
Ammonian Jove, or Capitoline was seen,
He with Olympias, this with her who bore
Scipio, the height of Rome.1 With tract oblique   510
At first, as one who sought access, but feared
To interrupt, sidelong he works his way.
As when a ship by skillful steersman wrought
Nigh river's mouth or foreland, where the wind
Veers oft, as oft so steers, and shifts her sail: 515
So varied he, and of his tortuous train
Curled many a wanton wreath in sight of Eve,
To lure her eye: she busied heard the sound
Of rustling leaves, but minded not, as used
To such disport before her through the field,   520
From every beast, more duteous at her call,
Than at Circean call the herd disguised.2
He bolder now, uncalled before her stood:
But as in gaze admiring; oft he bowed
His turret crest, and sleek enameled neck,   525
Fawning, and licked the ground whereon she trod.
His gentle dumb expression turned at length

5. I.e., love and beauty are terrible unless counteracted by hate—as they are being counteracted in Satan, to the ruin of Eve.
6. Deep red, inflamed.
7. Coils. "Redundant": abundantly, to excess.
8. Ovid tells how Cadmus and Harmonia (Milton's "Hermione") were changed to serpents after they retired (in despair at the misfortunes of their children) to Illyria.
9. Aesculapius, god of medicine, had a temple at Epidaurus, from which he sometimes emerged in the form of a serpent.
1. Jupiter Ammon ("Ammonian Jove"), in the form of a snake, was said to have consorted with Olympias to beget Alexander the Great; and in the same way, the Jupiter of the Roman capitol (Jove "Capitoline") was thought to have begotten Scipio Africanus, the savior and leader ("height") of Rome.
2. Circe, who enchanted men into the shape of swine, was attended by an obedient herd in the *Odyssey*.

The eye of Eve to mark his play: he, glad
Of her attention gained, with serpent tongue
Organic, or impulse of vocal air,[3]   530
His fraudulent temptation thus began.
    "Wonder not, sovereign mistress, if perhaps
Thou canst, who art sole wonder; much less arm
Thy looks, the heaven of mildness, with disdain,
Displeased that I approach thee thus, and gaze   535
Insatiate, I thus single, nor have feared
Thy awful brow, more awful thus retired.
Fairest resemblance of thy Maker fair,
Thee all things living gaze on, all things thine
By gift, and thy celestial beauty adore   540
With ravishment beheld, there best beheld
Where universally admired: but here
In this enclosure wild, these beasts among,
Beholders rude, and shallow to discern
Half what in thee is fair, one man except,   545
Who sees thee?[4] (and what is one?) who shouldst be seen
A goddess among gods, adored and served
By angels numberless, thy daily train."
    So glozed[5] the tempter, and his proem tuned;
Into the heart of Eve his words made way,   550
Though at the voice much marveling: at length,
Not unamazed, she thus in answer spake.
"What may this mean? Language of man pronounced
By tongue of brute, and human sense expressed?
The first at least of these I thought denied   555
To beasts, whom God on their creation-day
Created mute to all articulate sound;
The latter I demur,[6] for in their looks
Much reason, and in their actions oft appears.
Thee, serpent, subtlest beast of all the field   560
I knew, but not with human voice endued:[7]
Redouble then this miracle, and say,
How cam'st thou speakable of mute,[8] and how
To me so friendly grown above the rest
Of brutal kind, that daily are in sight?   565
Say, for such wonder claims attention due."
    To whom the guileful tempter thus replied:
"Empress of this fair world, resplendent Eve!
Easy to me it is to tell thee all
What thou command'st and right thou shouldst be obeyed: 570
I was at first as other beasts that graze
The trodden herb, of abject thoughts and low,

3. I.e., Satan either used the actual tongue of the serpent or himself impressed the air with speech.
4. The beasts cannot see the beauty of Eve's soul, only Adam can. Satan's entire speech is couched in the extravagant phrases of the Petrarchan love convention.
5. Flattered. "Proem": introduction.
6. I.e., as to whether rational sense was denied to brutes, I am doubtful.
7. Endowed.
8. To have speech after being dumb.

As was my food, nor aught but food discerned
Or sex, and apprehended nothing high:
Till on a day, roving the field, I chanced   575
A goodly tree far distant to behold
Loaden with fruit of fairest colors mixed,
Ruddy and gold; I nearer drew to gaze;
When from the boughs a savory odor blown,
Grateful to appetite, more pleased my sense   580
Than smell of sweetest fennel,[9] or the teats
Of ewe or goat dropping with milk at even,
Unsucked of lamb or kid, that tend their play.
To satisfy the sharp desire I had
Of tasting those fair apples, I resolved   585
Not to defer: hunger and thirst at once,
Powerful persuaders, quickened at the scent
Of that alluring fruit, urged me so keen.
About the mossy trunk I wound me soon,
For, high from ground, the branches would require   590
Thy utmost reach, or Adam's: round the tree
All other beasts that saw, with like desire
Longing and envying stood, but could not reach.
Amid the tree now got, where plenty hung
Tempting so nigh, to pluck and eat my fill   595
I spared not;[1] for such pleasure till that hour
At feed or fountain never had I found.
Sated at length, ere long I might perceive
Strange alteration in me, to degree
Of reason in my inward powers, and speech   600
Wanted not long, though to this shape retained.[2]
Thenceforth to speculations high or deep
I turned my thoughts, and with capacious mind
Considered all things visible in Heaven,
Or Earth, or middle, all things fair and good: 605
But all that fair and good in thy divine
Semblance, and in thy beauty's heavenly ray
United I beheld: no fair[3] to thine
Equivalent or second, which compelled
Me thus, though importune perhaps, to come   610
And gaze, and worship thee of right declared
Sovereign of creatures, universal dame."
    So talked the spirited[4] sly snake: and Eve
Yet more amazed, unwary thus replied:
    "Serpent, thy overpraising leaves in doubt   615
The virtue of that fruit, in thee first proved.
But say, where grows the tree, from hence how far?

9. Milton learned probably from Pliny, the natural historian, that serpents were fond of fennel; popular superstition had it that they drank the milk of sheep and goats.
1. Refrained not.

2. His inward powers, his mental constitution and gift of speech, were changed; but he retained his exterior shape as before.
3. Beauty.
4. Possessed by a spirit, inspired.

For many are the trees of God that grow
In Paradise, and various, yet unknown
To us; in such abundance lies our choice,   620
As leaves a greater store of fruit untouched,
Still hanging incorruptible, till men
Grow up to their provision, and more hands
Help to disburden Nature of her bearth."[5]
    To whom the wily adder, blithe and glad: 625
"Empress, the way is ready, and not long,
Beyond a row of myrtles, on a flat,
Fast by a fountain, one small thicket past
Of blowing[6] myrrh and balm: if thou accept
My conduct, I can bring thee thither soon."   630
    "Lead then," said Eve. He leading swiftly rolled
In tangles, and made intricate seem straight,
To mischief swift.[7] Hope elevates, and joy
Brightens his crest; as when a wandering fire
Compact of unctuous vapor,[8] which the night   635
Condenses, and the cold environs round,
Kindled through agitation to a flame
(Which oft, they say, some evil spirit attends),
Hovering and blazing with delusive light,
Misleads th' amazed night-wanderer from his way   640
To bogs and mires, and oft through pond or pool,
There swallowed up and lost, from succor far:
So glistered the dire snake, and into fraud
Led Eve our credulous mother, to the tree
Of prohibition,[9] root of all our woe: 645
Which when she saw, thus to her guide she spake:
    "Serpent, we might have spared our coming hither,
Fruitless to me, though fruit be here to excess,
The credit of whose virtue rest with thee;[1]
Wondrous indeed, if cause of such effects!   650
But of this tree we may not taste nor touch:
God so commanded, and left that command
Sole daughter of his voice;[2] the rest, we live
Law to ourselves; our reason is our law."
    To whom the Tempter guilefully replied: 655
"Indeed? Hath God then said that of the fruit
Of all these garden trees ye shall not eat,
Yet lords declared of all in Earth or air?"
    To whom thus Eve, yet sinless: "Of the fruit
Of each tree in the garden we may eat,   660
But of the fruit of this fair tree amidst

---

5. So spelled to pun on the idea of trees bearing fruit and thus in a way giving birth to young.
6. Blooming.
7. Milton's physical descriptions of the serpent often have distinct moral overtones, as here.
8. Composed of oily vapor; Milton's theory of the *ignis fatuus*, or will-o'-the-wisp, is strikingly material and "scientific."
9. Prohibited tree (a Hebraism).
1. I.e., you must remain the only evidence of the fruit's power.
2. His one injunction (a literal Hebraism). "The rest": in everything else.

The garden, God hath said, 'Ye shall not eat
Thereof, nor shall ye touch it, lest ye die.'"
    She scarce had said, though brief, when now more bold,
The tempter, but with show of zeal and love   665
To man, and indignation at his wrong,
New part puts on, and as to passion moved,
Fluctuates disturbed, yet comely, and in act
Raised,[3] as of some great matter to begin.
As when of old some orator renowned   670
In Athens or free Rome, where eloquence
Flourished, since mute, to some great cause addressed,
Stood in himself collected, while each part,
Motion, each act, won audience ere the tongue,
Sometimes in height began, as no delay   675
Of preface brooking,[4] through his zeal of right.
So standing, moving, or to height upgrown
The tempter all impassioned thus began:
    "O sacred, wise, and wisdom-giving plant,
Mother of science![5] now I feel thy power   680
Within me clear, not only to discern
Things in their causes, but to trace the ways
Of highest agents, deemed however wise.
Queen of this universe! do not believe
Those rigid threats of death. Ye shall not die;   685
How should ye? By the fruit? it gives you life
To knowledge;[6] by the Threatener? look on me,
Me who have touched and tasted, yet both live,
And life more perfect have attained than Fate
Meant me, by venturing higher than my lot.   690
Shall that be shut to man, which to the beast
Is open? Or will God incense his ire
For such a petty trespass, and not praise
Rather your dauntless virtue, whom the pain
Of death denounced, whatever thing death be,   695
Deterred not from achieving what might lead
To happier life, knowledge of good and evil?
Of good, how just![7] Of evil, if what is evil
Be real, why not known, since easier shunned?
God therefore cannot hurt ye, and be just;   700
Not just, not God; not feared then, nor obeyed:
Your fear itself of death removes the fear.[8]
Why then was this forbid? Why but to awe,
Why but to keep ye low and ignorant,
His worshipers? He knows that in the day   705
Ye eat thereof, your eyes that seem so clear,

---

3. Poised in posture.
4. The orator, as if too much moved to be bothered with a preface, bursts into the middle of his speech.
5. Knowledge.
6. Life in addition to knowledge; or, life with which to enlarge your knowl-

edge.
7. I.e., how just to have knowledge of good!
8. I.e., your fear of death removes your fear of God; since if God inflicts death, he will not be just and hence not God. The serpent's sophism is visible.

Yet are but dim, shall perfectly be then
Opened and cleared, and ye shall be as gods,
Knowing both good and evil, as they know.
That ye should be as gods, since I as man,   710
Internal man,[9] is but proportion meet,
I, of brute, human; ye, of human, gods.
So ye shall die perhaps, by putting off
Human, to put on gods:[1] death to be wished,
Though threatened, which no worse than this can bring.   715
And what are gods that man may not become
As they, participating godlike food?
The gods are first, and that advantage use
On our belief, that all from them proceeds.
I question it; for this fair Earth I see,   720
Warmed by the sun, producing every kind,
Them nothing: If they all things,[2] who enclosed
Knowledge of good and evil in this tree,
That whoso eats thereof forthwith attains
Wisdom without their leave? And wherein lies   725
Th' offense, that man should thus attain to know?
What can your knowledge hurt him, or this tree
Impart against his will if all be his?
Or is it envy, and can envy dwell
In heavenly breasts?[3] These, these, and many more   730
Causes import your need of this fair fruit.
Goddess humane,[4] reach then, and freely taste!"

    He ended, and his words, replete with guile,
Into her heart too easy entrance won:
Fixed on the fruit she gazed, which to behold   735
Might tempt alone, and in her ears the sound
Yet rung of his persuasive words, impregned[5]
With reason, to her seeming, and with truth;
Meanwhile the hour of noon drew on, and waked
An eager appetite, raised by the smell   740
So savory of that fruit, which with desire,
Inclinable now grown to touch or taste,
Solicited her longing eye;[6] yet first
Pausing a while, thus to herself she mused:

    "Great are thy virtues, doubtless, best of fruits,   745
Though kept from man, and worthy to be admired,
Whose taste, too long forborn, at first essay
Gave elocution to the mute, and taught
The tongue not made for speech to speak thy praise:
Thy praise he also who forbids thy use,   750

---

9. Man in intellectual powers.
1. The devil can quote scripture to his purpose, and here he is perverting Saint Paul, who told the Colossians (iii. 9–10) to put off the old man and put on the new. "Participating" (line 717): sharing.
2. The verb "produced" is understood. Satan is telling now, not about "God," but "the gods."

3. Adapted from Virgil, *Aeneid* I.15. "Import": imply, suggest.
4. Not so much "human goddess" (a Satanic paradox) as "kindly," "gracious" goddess.
5. Impregnated.
6. The five senses of Eve—sight, hearing, smell, taste, and touch—are all solicited by the fruit.

Conceals not from us,[7] naming thee the Tree
Of Knowledge, knowledge both of good and evil;
Forbids us then to taste; but his forbidding
Commends thee more, while it infers the good
By thee communicated, and our want: 755
For good unknown, sure is not had, or had
And yet unknown, is as not had at all.[8]
In plain then, what forbids he but to know?
Forbids us good, forbids us to be wise!
Such prohibitions bind not. But if Death   760
Bind us with after-bands, what profits then
Our inward freedom? In the day we eat
Of this fair fruit, our doom is, we shall die.
How dies the serpent? He hath eaten and lives,
And knows, and speaks, and reasons, and discerns,   765
Irrational till then. For us alone
Was death invented? Or to us denied
This intellectual food, for beasts reserved?
For beasts it seems: yet that one beast which first
Hath tasted, envies not, but brings with joy   770
The good befallen him, author unsuspect,[9]
Friendly to man, far from deceit or guile.
What fear I then, rather what know to fear[1]
Under this ignorance of good and evil,
Of God or death, of law or penalty?   775
Here grows the cure of all, this fruit divine,
Fair to the eye, inviting to the taste,
Of virtue[2] to make wise: what hinders then
To reach, and feed at once both body and mind?"
    So saying, her rash hand in evil hour,   780
Forth reaching to the fruit, she plucked, she eat.[3]
Earth felt the wound, and Nature from her seat[4]
Sighing through all her works gave signs of woe,
That all was lost. Back to the thicket slunk
The guilty serpent, and well might, for Eve   785
Intent now wholly on her taste, naught else
Regarded; such delight till then, as seemed,
In fruit she never tasted, whether true
Or fancied so, through expectation high
Of knowledge; nor was godhead from her thought.[5]   790
Greedily she engorged without restraint,
And knew not eating death:[6] satiate at length,
And heightened as with wine, jocund and boon,[7]

---

7. God himself, by naming it, has called attention to the tree's magic powers.
8. An unknown good is like no good at all. "In plain": i.e., in plain language.
9. A witness beyond suspicion.
1. In her ignorance, Eve does not really know what to fear and what not to fear.
2. Power.
3. In the 17th century, an accepted past tense of "eat."
4. Wherever Nature is hidden, in the heart of things, she sighs.
5. She expected to achieve godhead immediately.
6. A grim pun. She is eating death and does not know it; but death is eating her too. Compare "eating cares" (*L'Allegro*, line 135).
7. Joyous and liberal.

Thus to herself she pleasingly began:
　　"O sovereign, virtuous, precious of all trees　　　795
In Paradise! of operation blest
To sapience,[8] hitherto obscured, infamed,
And thy fair fruit let hang, as to no end
Created; but henceforth my early care,
Not without song each morning, and due praise　　　800
Shall tend thee, and the fertile burden ease
Of thy full branches offered free to all;
Till dieted by thee I grow mature
In knowledge, as the gods who all things know;
Though others[9] envy what they cannot give:　　　805
For had the gift been theirs, it had not here
Thus grown. Experience, next to thee I owe,
Best guide; not following thee I had remained
In ignorance; thou open'st Wisdom's way,
And giv'st access, though secret she retire.　　　810
And I perhaps am secret; Heaven is high,
High and remote to see from thence distinct
Each thing on Earth; and other care perhaps
May have diverted from continual watch
Our great Forbidder,[1] safe with all his spies　　　815
About him. But to Adam in what sort[2]
Shall I appear? Shall I to him make known
As yet my change, and give him to partake
Full happiness with me, or rather not,
But keep the odds[3] of knowledge in my power　　　820
Without copartner? so to add what wants
In female sex, the more to draw his love,
And render me more equal, and perhaps,
A thing not undesirable, sometime
Superior: for, inferior, who is free?[4]　　　825
This may be well: but what if God have seen
And death ensue? Then I shall be no more,
And Adam, wedded to another Eve,
Shall live with her enjoying, I extinct;
A death to think. Confirmed then I resolve,　　　830
Adam shall share with me in bliss or woe:
So dear I love him, that with him all deaths
I could endure, without him live no life."[5]
　　　So saying, from the tree her step she turned,
But first low reverence done,[6] as to the power　　　835

---

8. To wisdom, for the wise and those of good taste. (Latin *sapere*, to be wise, has its root in the verb "to taste.") "Infamed": without fear, but also defamed, i.e., maligned.
9. The gods, i.e., other gods. In saying that God did not give the tree, Eve is merely echoing a lesson learned from the serpent.
1. Now that Eve has fallen, God is a "great Forbidder," and all his gifts in Paradise are forgotten.
2. Guise.
3. Balance.
4. Eve's fatal foolishness implies that the only person in the world who can ever be free is an absolute tyrant.
5. Her affection is not unlike Satan's (IV.374–385) in its destructiveness.
6. Eve's first physical act after falling is idolatry.

That dwelt within, whose presence had infused
Into the plant sciental[7] sap, derived
From nectar, drink of gods. Adam the while
Waiting desirous her return, had wove
Of choicest flowers a garland to adorn   840
Her tresses, and her rural labors crown,
As reapers oft are wont their harvest queen.
Great joy he promised to his thoughts, and new
Solace in her return, so long delayed:
Yet oft his heart, divine[8] of something ill,   845
Misgave him; he the faltering measure[9] felt;
And forth to meet her went, the way she took
That morn when first they parted. By the Tree
Of Knowledge he must pass; there he her met,
Scarce from the tree returning; in her hand   850
A bough of fairest fruit that downy smiled,
New gathered, and ambrosial smell diffused.
To him she hastened, in her face excuse
Came prologue, and apology to prompt,[1]
Which with bland words at will she thus addressed: 855
   "Hast thou not wondered, Adam, at my stay?
Thee I have missed, and thought it long, deprived
Thy presence, agony of love till now
Not felt, nor shall be twice; for never more
Mean I to try, what rash untried I sought,   860
The pain of absence from thy sight. But strange
Hath been the cause, and wonderful to hear:
This tree is not as we are told, a tree
Of danger tasted,[2] nor to evil unknown
Opening the way, but of divine effect   865
To open eyes, and make them gods who taste;
And hath been tasted such. The serpent wise,
Or not restrained as we, or not obeying,
Hath eaten of the fruit, and is become,
Not dead, as we are threatened, but thenceforth   870
Endued with human voice and human sense,
Reasoning to admiration,[3] and with me
Persuasively hath so prevailed, that I
Have also tasted, and have also found
Th' effects to correspond, opener mine eyes   875
Dim erst, dilated spirits, ampler heart,
And growing up to godhead;[4] which for thee
Chiefly I sought, without thee can despise.
For bliss, as thou hast part, to me is bliss,
Tedious, unshared with thee, and odious soon.   880
Thou therefore also taste, that equal lot

7. Knowledge-giving.
8. Foreboding, suspicious.
9. I.e., of his pulse.
1. Her face had an excuse in it, as
prologue to an apology which followed
after.

2. If tasted.
3. Admirably. "Persuasively": by persuasion.
4. Everything that Eve says she feels
is what Satan has told her she will feel.

May join us, equal joy, as equal love;
Lest, thou not tasting, different degree⁵
Disjoin us, and I then too late renounce
Deity for thee, when Fate will not permit."⁶   885
    Thus Eve with countenance blithe her story told;
But in her cheek distemper⁷ flushing glowed.
On th' other side, Adam, soon as he heard
The fatal trespass done by Eve, amazed,
Astonied⁸ stood and blank, while horror chill   890
Ran through his veins, and all his joints relaxed;
From his slack hand the garland wreathed for Eve
Down dropped, and all the faded roses shed.
Speechless he stood and pale, till thus at length
First to himself he inward silence broke: 895
    "O fairest of creation, last and best
Of all God's works, creature in whom excelled
Whatever can to sight or thought be formed,
Holy, divine, good, amiable, or sweet!
How art thou lost, how on a sudden lost,   900
Defaced, deflowered, and now to death devote?⁹
Rather how hast thou yielded to transgress
The strict forbiddance, how to violate
The sacred fruit forbidden! Some cursèd fraud
Of enemy hath beguiled thee, yet unknown,¹   905
And me with thee hath ruined, for with thee
Certain my resolution is to die.
How can I live without thee, how forgo
Thy sweet converse and love so dearly joined,
To live again in these wild woods forlorn?²   910
Should God create another Eve, and I
Another rib afford, yet loss of thee
Would never from my heart; no, no! I feel
The link of nature draw me: flesh of flesh,
Bone of my bone thou art, and from thy state   915
Mine never shall be parted, bliss or woe."
    So having said, as one from sad dismay
Recomforted, and after thoughts disturbed
Submitting to what seemed remediless,
Thus in calm mood his words to Eve he turned: 920
    "Bold deed thou hast presumed, adventurous Eve
And peril great provoked, who thus hath dared
Had it been only coveting to eye
That sacred fruit, sacred³ to abstinence,
Much more to taste it, under ban to touch.   925

5. Differing rank in the hierarchy of creatures.
6. Contrast Eve's logic when she is alone (lines 817–825).
7. The proportion of Eve's humors—which, in the state of innocence, gave her perfect health—has been disturbed, and she is running a fever.
8. Astonished, perhaps even "petrified." "Blank": empty of mind.
9. Doomed.
1. "Yet unknown" modifies "enemy."
2. Without Eve, Paradise itself is wild and forlorn.
3. Devoted.

But past who can recall, or done undo?
Not God omnipotent, nor Fate! Yet so
Perhaps thou shalt not die, perhaps the fact[4]
Is not so heinous now, foretasted fruit,
Profaned first by the serpent, by him first   930
Made common and unhallowed ere our taste,
Nor yet on him found deadly; he yet lives,
Lives, as thou saidst, and gains to live as man
Higher degree of life: inducement strong
To us, as likely, tasting, to attain   935
Proportional ascent, which cannot be
But to be gods, or angels, demigods.[5]
Nor can I think that God, Creator wise,
Though threatening, will in earnest so destroy
Us his prime creatures, dignified so high,   940
Set over all his works, which in our fall,
For us created, needs with us must fail,
Dependent made; so God shall uncreate,
Be frustrate, do, undo, and labor lose;
Not well conceived of God,[6] who, though his power   945
Creation could repeat, yet would be loath
Us to abolish, lest the adversary
Triúmph and say: 'Fickle their state whom God
Most favors; who can please him long? Me first
He ruined, now mankind; whom will he next?'   950
Matter of scorn, not to be given the foe.
However, I with thee have fixed my lot,
Certain to undergo like doom: if death
Consort with thee, death is to me as life;
So forcible within my heart I feel   955
The bond of nature draw me to my own,
My own in thee, for what thou art is mine;
Our state cannot be severed; we are one,
One flesh; to lose thee were to lose myself."
     So Adam, and thus Eve to him replied: 960
"O glorious trial of exceeding love,
Illustrious evidence, example high!
Engaging me to emulate; but short
Of thy perfection, how shall I attain,
Adam? from whose dear side I boast me sprung,   965
And gladly of our union hear thee speak,
One heart, one soul in both; whereof good proof
This day affords, declaring thee resolved,
Rather than death or aught than death more dread
Shall separate us, linked in love so dear,   970
To undergo with me one guilt, one crime,
If any be, of tasting this fair fruit;

4. Act.
5. Note how Adam agrees first in Eve's harmless errors about the serpent, then in her sinful ambition to achieve
a higher form of life.
6. I.e., not a proper conception of God (as making his actions dependent on those of an inferior).

Whose virtue (for of good still good proceeds,
Direct, or by occasion[7]) hath presented
This happy trial of thy love, which else   975
So eminently never had been known.
Were it I thought death menaced would ensue[8]
This my attempt, I would sustain alone
The worst, and not persuade thee, rather die
Deserted, than oblige[9] thee with a fact   980
Pernicious to thy peace, chiefly assured
Remarkably so late of thy so true,
So faithful love unequaled;[1] but I feel
Far otherwise th' event;[2] not death, but life
Augmented, opened eyes, new hopes, new joys,   985
Taste so divine, that what of sweet before
Hath touched my sense, flat seems to this, and harsh.
On my experience, Adam, freely taste,
And fear of death deliver to the winds."
    So saying, she embraced him, and for joy   990
Tenderly wept, much won that he his love
Had so ennobled, as of choice to incur
Divine displeasure for her sake, or death.
In recompense (for such compliance bad
Such recompense best merits), from the bough   995
She gave him of that fair enticing fruit
With liberal hand; he scrupled not to eat,
Against his better knowledge, not deceived,
But fondly overcome with female charm.[3]
Earth trembled from her entrails, as again   1000
In pangs, and Nature gave a second groan,
Sky lowered, and muttering thunder, some sad drops
Wept at completing of the mortal sin
Original; while Adam took no thought,
Eating his fill, nor Eve to iterate   1005
Her former trespass feared, the more to soothe
Him with her loved society; that now
As with new wine intoxicated both,
They swim in mirth, and fancy that they feel
Divinity within them breeding wings   1010
Wherewith to scorn the Earth. But that false fruit
Far other operation first displayed,
Carnal desire inflaming; he on Eve
Began to cast lascivious eyes, she him
As wantonly repaid; in lust they burn,   1015
Till Adam thus 'gan Eve to dalliance move:
    "Eve, now I see thou art exact[4] of taste,

---

7. Indirectly.
8. Result from.
9. Render liable, involve.
1. Now that she knows Adam loves her, Eve has more misgivings than ever about involving him in her crime.

2. Result (of eating the apple).
3. See I Timothy ii.14: "And Adam was not deceived, but the woman being deceived was in the transgression."
4. Exacting, demanding.

And elegant, of sapience[5] no small part,
Since to each meaning savor we apply,
And palate call judicious. I the praise
Yield thee, so well this day thou hast purveyed.[6]   1020
Much pleasure we have lost, while we abstained
From this delightful fruit, nor known till now
True relish, tasting; if such pleasure be
In things to us forbidden, it might be wished,   1025
For this one tree had been forbidden ten.
But come; so well refreshed, now let us play,
As meet is, after such delicious fare;
For never did thy beauty, since the day
I saw thee first and wedded thee, adorned   1030
With all perfections, so enflame my sense
With ardor to enjoy thee, fairer now
Than ever, bounty of this virtuous tree."
    So said he, and forbore not glance or toy[7]
Of amorous intent, well understood   1035
Of[8] Eve, whose eye darted contagious fire.
Her hand he seized, and to a shady bank,
Thick overhead with verdant roof embowered
He led her, nothing loath; flowers were the couch,
Pansies, and violets, and asphodel,   1040
And hyacinth, Earth's freshest, softest lap.
There they their fill of love and love's disport
Took largely, of their mutual guilt the seal,
The solace of their sin, till dewy sleep
Oppressed them, wearied with their amorous play.   1045
    Soon as the force of that fallacious fruit,
That with exhilarating vapor bland
About their spirits had played, and inmost powers
Made err, was now exhaled, and grosser sleep
Bred of unkindly fumes,[9] with conscious dreams   1050
Encumbered, now had left them, up they rose
As from unrest, and each the other viewing,
Soon found their eyes how opened, and their minds
How darkened. Innocence, that as a veil
Had shadowed them from knowing ill, was gone;   1055
Just confidence, and native righteousness,
And honor from about them, naked left
To guilty Shame; he covered, but his robe
Uncovered more.[1] So rose the Danite strong,
Herculean Samson, from the harlot-lap   1060
Of Philistean Dalilah, and waked
Shorn of his strength;[2] they destitute and bare

---

5. Wisdom, but the word comes from Latin *sapere*, "to taste," which gives rise, via another etymology, to the word "savor." Adam's sentence plays rather heavily on these two meanings of *sapere*.
6. Provided for us, provisioned us.
7. Caress.
8. By.

9. Unnatural vapors.
1. They were covered with shame, which made them conscious of their nakedness as they had never been before.
2. See the story of Samson and Delilah, Judges xvi.4–20.

Of all their virtue. Silent, and in face
Confounded, long they sat, as strucken mute;
Till Adam, though not less than Eve abashed,   1065
At length gave utterance to these words constrained:
    "O Eve, in evil hour[3] thou didst give ear
To that false worm,[4] of whomsoever taught
To counterfeit man's voice, true in our fall,
False in our promised rising; since our eyes   1070
Opened we find indeed, and find we know
Both good and evil, good lost, and evil got:
Bad fruit of knowledge, if this be to know,
Which leaves us naked thus, of honor void,
Of innocence, of faith, of purity,   1075
Our wonted ornaments now soiled and stained,
And in our faces evident the signs
Of foul concupiscence; whence evil store,[5]
Even shame, the last of evils; of the first
Be sure then.[6] How shall I behold the face   1080
Henceforth of God or angel, erst with joy
And rapture so oft beheld? Those heavenly shapes
Will dazzle now this earthly[7] with their blaze
Insufferably bright. O might I here
In solitude live savage, in some glade   1085
Obscured, where highest woods, impenetrable
To star or sunlight, spread their umbrage broad,
And brown[8] as evening! Cover me, ye pines,
Ye cedars, with innumerable boughs
Hide me, where I may never see them more![9]   1090
But let us now, as in bad plight, devise
What best may for the present serve to hide
The parts of each from other, that seem most
To shame obnoxious,[1] and unseemliest seen;
Some tree whose broad smooth leaves together sewed,   1095
And girded on our loins, may cover round
Those middle parts, that this newcomer, Shame,
There sit not, and reproach us as unclean."
    So counseled he, and both together went
Into the thickest wood; there soon they chose   1100
The figtree,[2] not that kind for fruit renowned,
But such as at this day, to Indians known,
In Malabar or Deccan[3] spreads her arms

---

3. Even in his misery, Adam cannot resist the word-play on Eve-evil.
4. Serpent, with a connotation of disgust. "Of": by.
5. A store of evil.
6. I.e., since we now feel shame, the last and worst of evils, we shall soon experience the first and lesser ones.
7. The noun "nature" or "vision" is understood.
8. Dark.
9. Cf. Revelation vi.16: "And said to the mountains and rocks, Fall on us, and hide us from the face of him that sitteth on the throne, and from the wrath of the Lamb."
1. Vulnerable, liable.
2. The banyan, or Indian fig. It has, in fact, small leaves, but Milton's knowledge of it came from Gerard's *Herball*, where all the details of lines 1104–10 may be found.
3. Sections of southern India.

Branching so broad and long, that in the ground
The bended twigs take root, and daughters grow   1105
About the mother tree, a pillared shade
High overarched, and echoing walks between;
There oft the Indian herdsman, shunning heat,
Shelters in cool, and tends his pasturing herds
At loopholes cut through thickest shade. Those leaves   1110
They gathered, broad as Amazonian targe,[4]
And with what skill they had, together sewed,
To gird their waist; vain covering, if to hide
Their guilt and dreaded shame! O how unlike
To that first naked glory! Such of late   1115
Columbus found th' American, so girt
With feathered cincture,[5] naked else and wild
Among the trees on isles and woody shores.
Thus fenced, and, as they thought, their shame in part
Covered, but not at rest or ease of mind,   1120
They sat them down to weep; nor only tears
Rained at their eyes, but high winds worse within
Began to rise, high passions, anger, hate,
Mistrust, suspicion, discord, and shook sore
Their inward state of mind, calm region once   1125
And full of peace, now tossed and turbulent:
For Understanding ruled not, and the Will
Heard not her lore, both in subjection now
To sensual Appetite, who, from beneath
Usurping over sovereign Reason, claimed   1130
Superior sway.[6] From thus distempered breast,
Adam, estranged in look and altered style,
Speech intermitted thus to Eve renewed:
    "Would thou hadst hearkened to my words, and stayed
With me, as I besought thee, when that strange   1135
Desire of wandering, this unhappy morn,
I know not whence possessed thee! we had then
Remained still happy, not as now, despoiled
Of all our good, shamed, naked, miserable.
Let none henceforth seek needless cause to approve[7]   1140
The faith they owe; when earnestly they seek
Such proof, conclude, they then begin to fail."
    To whom, soon moved with touch of blame, thus Eve:
"What words have passed thy lips, Adam severe?
Imput'st thou that to my default, or will   1145
Of wandering, as thou call'st it, which who knows
But might as ill have happened, thou being by,
Or to thyself perhaps? Hadst thou been there,
Or here th' attempt, thou couldst not have discerned

---

4. Shield. The Amazons, mythical female warriors, carried large crescent-shaped shields.
5. Belt.
6. The psychology of the Fall is made explicit here. The higher faculties of reason, represented by the brain, are in subjection to the lower faculties of appetite, represented by sensuality. Moreover, Adam has lost his superiority over Eve.
7. Test, prove. "Owe": own.

Fraud in the serpent, speaking as he spake;   1150
No ground of enmity between us known,
Why he should mean me ill, or seek to harm?
Was I to have never parted from thy side?
As good have grown there still a lifeless rib.
Being as I am, why didst not thou, the head,[8]   1155
Command me absolutely not to go,
Going into such danger, as thou saidst?
Too facile[9] then, thou didst not much gainsay,
Nay, didst permit, approve, and fair dismiss.
Hadst thou been firm and fixed in thy dissent,   1160
Neither had I transgressed, nor thou with me."
    To whom, then first incensed, Adam replied:
"Is this the love, is this the recompense
Of mine to thee, ingrateful Eve, expressed
Immutable[1] when thou were lost, not I,   1165
Who might have lived and joyed immortal bliss,
Yet willingly chose rather death with thee?
And am I now upbraided as the cause
Of thy transgressing? not enough severe,
It seems, in thy restraint! What could I more?   1170
I warned thee, I admonished thee, foretold
The danger, and the lurking enemy
That lay in wait; beyond this had been force,
And force upon free will hath here no place.
But confidence then bore thee on, secure   1175
Either to meet no danger, or to find
Matter of glorious trial; and perhaps
I also erred in overmuch admiring
What seemed in thee so perfect, that I thought
No evil durst attempt thee! but I rue   1180
That error now, which is become my crime,
And thou th' accuser. Thus it shall befall
Him who, to worth in women overtrusting,
Lets her will rule; restraint she will not brook,[2]
And, left to herself, if evil thence ensue,   1185
She first his weak indulgence will accuse."
    Thus they in mutual accusation spent
The fruitless hours, but neither self-condemning;[3]
And of their vain contést appeared no end.

8. Head of the family, but also the rational director, as the head is to the rest of the body. Cf. I Corinthians xi.3, "the head of the woman is the man."
9. Easy, permissive.
1. Shown to be unchangeable.

2. Accept.
3. Sterile recrimination is an early fruit of the forbidden tree; only self-condemnation can turn the fall from a mind-closing to a mind-opening event.

From Book X

Summary When it is known in Heaven that man has fallen, God sends his Son to pass judgment on the sinners. Having found them in the garden, he hears their confession and passes instant sentence, cursing the serpent, condemning Eve to the pains of childbirth and Adam to those of daily toil; but in mercy he clothes the human couple both outwardly with the skins of beasts and inwardly with his righteousness. Meanwhile Sin and Death, sitting by Hell-gate, feel new strength, and pass across Chaos, leaving a great bridge behind them. On their way they meet with their parent, Satan, learn of his success on earth, and press eagerly forward in hopes of destroying man altogether. Satan, on the other hand, continues his flight back toward Hell, where he is to report to his constituents.

[*Consequences of the Fall*]

* * * Th' other way Satan went down
The causey[1] to Hell-gate; on either side   415
Disparted Chaos overbuilt exclaimed,
And with rebounding surge the bars assailed,
That scorned his indignation.[2] Through the gate,
Wide open and unguarded, Satan passed,
And all about found desolate; for those   420
Appointed to sit there[3] had left their charge,
Flown to the upper world; the rest were all
Far to the inland retired, about the walls
Of Pandemonium, city and proud seat
Of Lucifer, so by allusion called   425
Of that bright star to Satan paragoned.[4]
There kept their watch the legions, while the Grand
In council sat, solicitous what chance
Might intercept their emperor sent; so he
Departing gave command, and they observed.   430
As when the Tartar from his Russian foe,
By Astracan, over the snowy plains,
Retires, or Bactrian Sophi, from the horns
Of Turkish crescent, leaves all waste beyond
The realm of Aladule, in his retreat   435

1. Causeway.
2. Chaos, as the instinctive enemy of order, is hostile to the bridge built across its gulf by Sin and Death, even though it means an increase in the kingdom of Chaos itself.
3. I.e., Sin and Death.

4. Satan is called Lucifer, the light-bringer, because bright as the morning star (before he fell). The Grand (line 427) are the superior angels. "Grandee" was a new word in English, adapted from Spanish; it implied a man of large, undefined economic and social power.

To Tauris or Casbeen;[5] so these, the late
Heaven-banished host, left desert utmost Hell
Many a dark league, reduced in careful watch
Round their metropolis, and now expecting
Each hour their great adventurer from the search   440
Of foreign worlds. He through the midst unmarked,
In show plebeian angel militant[6]
Of lowest order, passed, and, from the door
Of that plutonian hall, invisible
Ascended his high throne, which, under state[7]   445
Of richest texture spread, at th' upper end
Was placed in regal luster. Down a while
He sat, and round about him saw, unseen.
At last, as from a cloud, his fulgent[8] head
And shape star-bright appeared, or brighter, clad   450
With what permissive glory since his fall
Was left him, or false glitter. All amazed
At that so sudden blaze, the Stygian throng
Bent their aspéct, and whom they wished beheld,
Their mighty chief returned: loud was th' acclaim.   455
Forth rushed in haste the great consulting peers,
Raised from their dark divan,[9] and with like joy
Congratulant approached him, who with hand
Silence, and with these words attention, won:
    "Thrones, Dominations, Princedoms, Virtues, Powers!   460
For in possession such, not only of right,[1]
I call ye, and declare ye now, returned,
Successful beyond hope, to lead ye forth
Triumphant out of this infernal pit
Abominable, accursed, the house of woe,   465
And dungeon of our tyrant! Now possess,
As lords, a spacious world, to our native Heaven
Little inferior, by my adventure hard
With peril great achieved. Long were to tell
What I have done, what suffered, with what pain   470
Voyaged th' unreal, vast, unbounded deep
Of horrible confusion, over which
By Sin and Death a broad way now is paved

---

5. The comparison is with the Persians and Tartars retreating across the Eastern wastes before the attacking Turks. "Bactrian": Persian, "Tauris," "Casbeen": Tabriz, Kazvin. Milton wants his simile to convey a mingled sense of barbaric Oriental splendor, cruelty, and desolation in Hell.

6. Literally, an angelic footsoldier or private, but with an ironic overtone from the phrase "church militant."

7. Canopy.

8. Glittering, refulgent.

9. The Turkish council of state; the Oriental theme continues.

1. Satan makes a distinction much in men's minds since the days of Cromwell and Charles I; a kingdom could be claimed either by right (in law, *de jure*) or in fact (by possession, *de facto*). The devils now have both claims to their titles. "Returned" (line 462) modifies "I" at the beginning of the line: "now that I have returned."

To expedite your glorious march; but I
Toiled out my uncouth passage, forced to ride   475
Th' untractable abyss, plunged in the womb
Of unoriginal[2] night and chaos wild,
That, jealous of their secrets, fiercely opposed
My journey strange, with clamorous uproar
Protesting fate supreme; thence how I found   480
The new-created world, which fame in Heaven
Long had foretold, a fabric wonderful,
Of absolute perfection; therein man
Placed in a paradise, by our exile
Made happy. Him by fraud I have seduced   485
From his creator, and, the more to increase
Your wonder, with an apple! He,[3] thereat
Offended—worth your laughter!—hath given up
Both his belovéd man and all his world
To Sin and Death a prey, and so to us,   490
Without our hazard, labor, or alarm,
To range in, and to dwell, and over man
To rule, as over all he should have ruled.
True is, me also he hath judged; or rather
Me not, but the brute serpent, in whose shape   495
Man I deceived. That which to me belongs
Is enmity, which he will put between
Me and mankind: I am to bruise his heel;
His seed (when, is not set) shall bruise my head.[4]
A world who would not purchase with a bruise,   500
Or much more grievous pain? Ye have th' account
Of my performance; what remains, ye gods,
But up and enter now into full bliss?"
    So having said, a while he stood, expecting
Their universal shout and high applause   505
To fill his ear; when, contrary, he hears,
On all sides, from innumerable tongues
A dismal universal hiss, the sound
Of public scorn. He wondered, but not long
Had leisure, wondering at himself now more.   510
His visage drawn he felt to sharp and spare,
His arms clung to his ribs, his legs entwining
Each other, till, supplanted,[5] down he fell,

2. Without source or origin, primeval.
3. God.
4. Satan seems to have overheard or understood the curse pronounced by God on the serpent, even though he was not present at the time.
5. The word is used with its Latin force of "tripped up by the heels." Ovid (*Metamorphosis* IV. 575 ff.), Lucan (*Pharsalia* IX. 700 ff.), and Dante (*Inferno* XXV) had made set pieces about people being transformed into serpents. This whole scene has been the occasion of much critical dispute. A. J. A. Waldock (*Paradise Lost and Its Critics*) denounced it as a "cartoon scene" in which Milton's editorial hand is much too heavily felt; various defenders have propounded alternative justifications.

A monstrous serpent on his belly prone,
Reluctant,[6] but in vain; a greater power   515
Now ruled him, punished in the shape he sinned,
According to his doom. He would have spoke,
But hiss for hiss returned with forkéd tongue
To forkéd tongue; for now were all transformed
Alike, to serpents all, as accessories   520
To his bold riot.[7] Dreadful was the din
Of hissing through the hall, thick-swarming now
With complicated monsters, head and tail—
Scorpion, and asp, and amphisbaena dire,[8]
Cerastes horned, hydrus, and ellops drear,   525
And dipsas (not so thick swarmed once the soil
Bedropped with blood of Gorgon, or the isle
Ophiusa); but still greatest he the midst,
Now dragon grown, larger than whom the sun
Engendered in the Pythian vale on slime,   530
Huge Python;[9] and his power no less he seemed
Above the rest still to retain. They all
Him followed, issuing forth to th' open field,
Where all yet left of that revolted rout,
Heaven-fallen, in station or just array,   535
Sublime[1] with expectation when to see
In triumph issuing forth their glorious chief.
They saw, but other sight instead, a crowd
Of ugly serpents. Horror on them fell,
And horrid sympathy; for what they saw   540
They felt themselves now changing. Down their arms,
Down fell both spear and shield; down they as fast,
And the dire hiss renewed, and the dire form
Catched by contagion, like in punishment
As in their crime. Thus was th' applause they meant   545
Turned to exploding hiss, triumph to shame
Cast on themselves from their own mouths. There stood
A grove hard by, sprung up with this their change,
His will who reigns above,[2] to aggravate
Their penance, laden with fair fruit, like that   550

6. The Latin sense is felt again, "struggling against the change."
7. Revolt.
8. "Complicated": again a Latinism, meaning "twined together." The "amphisbaena" was alleged to have a head at each end of its body; "cerastes" was a horned snake, "hydrus" a water-snake, "ellops" perhaps the swordfish, and "dipsas" a snake whose bite was supposed to create outrageous thirst. When Perseus flew over Libya with the head of the snaky-haired Gorgon, the drops of her blood fell to the ground and became serpents. The "isle Ophiusa" is Snake Island, in the Balearics.
9. Python was a gigantic mythological serpent engendered by Apollo, the sun god, from the slime left by Deucalion's flood, and slain by Apollo in a great contest.
1. On tiptoes. The ordinary devils are standing in ranks outside Pandemonium, trying to catch a glimpse of Satan.
2. "By the will of him who reigns above."

Which grew in paradise, the bait of Eve
Used by the tempter. On that prospect strange
Their earnest eyes they fixed, imagining
For one forbidden tree a multitude
Now risen, to work them further woe or shame;[3]   555
Yet, parched with scalding thirst and hunger fierce,
Though to delude them sent, could not abstain,
But on they rolled in heaps, and, up the trees
Climbing, sat thicker than the snaky locks
That curled Megaera.[4] Greedily they plucked   560
The fruitage fair to sight, like that which grew
Near that bituminous lake where Sodom flamed;[5]
This, more delusive, not the touch, but taste
Deceived; they, fondly[6] thinking to allay
Their appetite with gust, instead of fruit   565
Chewed bitter ashes, which th' offended taste
With spattering noise rejected. Oft they assayed,
Hunger and thirst constraining: drugged as oft,
With hatefulest disrelish writhed their jaws
With soot and cinders filled: so oft they fell   570
Into the same illusion, not as man
Whom they triúmphed once lapsed.[7] Thus were they plagued,
And worn with famine long, and ceaseless hiss,
Till their lost shape, permitted, they resumed—
Yearly enjoined, some say, to undergo   575
This annual humbling certain numbered days,
To dash their pride, and joy for man seduced.[8]
However, some tradition they dispersed
Among the heathen of their purchase got,
And fabled how the serpent, whom they called   580
Ophion, with Eurynome (the wide-
Encroaching Eve perhaps),[9] had first the rule
Of high Olympus, thence by Saturn driven
And Ops, ere yet Dictaean[1] Jove was born.

---

3. The punishment of the devils not only fits the crime, it *is* the crime (the eating of forbidden fruit) repeated again and again, in disgust and loathing.
4. Megaera, like her sister Furies, had snakes instead of hair on her head.
5. Sodom apples grew (legend had it) on the spot where that accursed city once stood; though good to look at, they dissolved into ashes when plucked.
6. Foolishly. "Gust": taste.
7. They fell again and again into delusion, though they had felt superior to man, who fell just once.
8. There are many folktales about fairies, devils, incubi, and the like, who are

forced periodically to take on the shape of some loathsome creature.
9. There is a mythological story about the Titan Ophion (the name means "snake") and his wife Eurynome ("the wide-reacher"), who ruled Olympus till Saturn and his wife Rhea (or Ops) drove them away. Milton feels this story may be a vague, pagan reminiscence of the real truth, the fall of Satan. But there is an unresolved suggestion here that Eve fell with Satan, becoming a kind of Proserpina to his role as Pluto, King of Hell.
1. Zeus was raised in a cave on Mount Dicte, in Crete; hence, "Dictaean Jove."

Summary   Sin and Death proceed without further interruption to the earth, and enter into possession of it. God sees their arrival and declines to interfere, but prophesies that their triumph will be only temporary; in due course they will be forced back to hell again, and forever. Meanwhile, the angels are ordered to twist the earth on its axis, disorder the planets so their influence will in future be bad as well as good, and rearrange the cosmos generally. In consequence, the temperate climate of Paradise at once gives way to extremes of heat and cold, and furious winds begin to blow across the ruined planet.

* * * Thus began

Outrage from lifeless things; but Discord, first
Daughter of Sin, among th' irrational,
Death introduced through fierce antipathy:[1]
Beast now with beast 'gan war, and fowl with fowl,
And fish with fish: to graze the herb[2] all leaving,
Devoured each other; nor stood much in awe
Of man, but fled him, or with countenance grim
Glared on him passing. These were from without
The growing miseries, which Adam saw   715
Already in part, though hid in gloomiest shade,
To sorrow abandoned, but worse felt within,
And in a troubled sea of passion tossed,
Thus to disburden sought with sad complaint:
    "O miserable of happy![3] Is this the end   720
Of this new glorious world, and me so late
The glory of that glory? who now, become
Accursed of blessed, hide me from the face
Of God, whom to behold was then my height
Of happiness! Yet well, if here would end   725
The misery; I deserved it, and would bear
My own deservings; but this will not serve.
All that I eat or drink, or shall beget,
Is propagated curse.[4] O voice, once heard
Delightfully, 'Increase and multiply,'   730
Now death to hear! for what can I increase
Or multiply, but curses on my head?
Who, of all ages to succeed, but, feeling
The evil on him brought by me, will curse
My head: "Ill fare our ancestor impure!   735
For this we may thank Adam!' but his thanks
Shall be the execration;[5] so, besides

1. "Discord" is the subject of the sentence, "Death" the object. "Th' irrational" are the beasts.
2. Grass.
3. I.e., change, to misery from happi-

4. Whatever prolongs life extends the curse.
5. The only thanks for Adam will be mankind's curses.

Mine own that bide upon me, all from me
Shall with a fierce reflux on me redound,
On me, as on their natural center, light   740
Heavy, though in their place.[6] O fleeting joys
Of Paradise, dear bought with lasting woes!
Did I request thee, Maker, from my clay
To mold me man? Did I solicit thee
From darkness to promote me, or here place   745
In this delicious garden? As my will
Concurred not to my being, it were but right
And equal[7] to reduce me to my dust,
Desirous to resign and render back
All I received, unable to perform   750
Thy terms too hard, by which I was to hold
The good I sought not. To the loss of that,
Sufficient penalty, why hast thou added
The sense of endless woes? Inexplicable
Thy justice seems; yet, to say truth, too late   755
I thus contest; then should have been refused
Those terms whatever, when they were proposed.
Thou[8] didst accept them; wilt thou enjoy the good,
Then cavil the conditions? And though God
Made thee without thy leave, what if thy son   760
Prove disobedient, and reproved, retort,
'Wherefore didst thou beget me? I sought it not.'
Wouldst thou admit for his contempt of thee
That proud excuse? Yet him not thy election,[9]
But natural necessity begot.   765
God made thee of choice his own, and of his own
To serve him; thy reward was of his grace;
Thy punishment then justly is at his will.
Be it so, for I submit; his doom is fair,
That dust I am and shall to dust return.   770
O welcome hour whenever! Why delays
His hand to execute what his decree
Fixed on this day? Why do I overlive?
Why am I mocked with death, and lengthened out
To deathless pain? How gladly would I meet   775
Mortality, my sentence, and be earth
Insensible! how glad would lay me down
As in my mother's lap![1] There I should rest
And sleep secure; his dreadful voice no more

6. Adam plays with the notion that natural objects have weight only as long as they are above their "natural" positions; so all curses will flow naturally to him, but they will still be heavy when they have lighted.
7. Just.

8. "Thou," which referred to God in lines 753 and 755, here shifts as Adam suddenly addresses himself.
9. Choice.
1. Adam's lamentations owe a good deal to the Book of Job iii.

Would thunder in my ears; no fear of worse   780
To me and to my offspring would torment me
With cruel expectation. Yet one doubt
Pursues me still, lest all I cannot die;[2]
Lest that pure breath of life, the spirit of man
Which God inspired, cannot together perish   785
With this corporeal clod; then, in the grave,
Or in some other dismal place, who knows
But I shall die a living death? O thought
Horrid, if true! Yet why? It was but breath
Of life that sinned; what dies but what had life   790
And sin? the body properly hath neither.
All of me then shall die: let this appease
The doubt, since human reach no further knows.[3]
For though the Lord of all be infinite,
Is his wrath also? Be it, man is not so,   795
But mortal doomed. How can he exercise
Wrath without end on man whom death must end?
Can he make deathless death? That were to make
Strange contradiction, which to God himself
Impossible is held, as argument   800
Of weakness, not of power.[4] Will he draw out,
For anger's sake, finite to infinite
In punished man, to satisfy his rigor
Satisfied never? That were to extend
His sentence beyond dust and Nature's law;   805
By which all causes else according still
To the reception of their matter act,
Not to th' extent of their own sphere.[5] But say
That death be not one stroke, as I supposed,
Bereaving[6] sense, but endless misery   810
From this day onward, which I feel begun
Both in me and without me, and so last
To perpetuity—Ay me! that fear
Comes thundering back with dreadful revolution
On my defenseless head! Both death and I   815
Am found eternal, and incorporate[7] both:
Nor I on my part single; in me all
Posterity stands cursed. Fair patrimony

2. Direct from Horace, *Odes* III.xxx.6: *non omnis moriar*.
3. Adam convinces himself, as Milton was apparently convinced, that both soul and body die at death; the corollary is that they are resurrected together.
4. For a man in a state of nature, Adam displays a fine command of medieval theology. He holds that if God contradicts himself, it is a sign of weakness.
5. A maxim of 17th-century physics; all agents (other than God) act according to the capacity of the object, not to the extent of their inherent powers.
6. Taking away.
7. In the same body. Adam is appalled to find that he has become death incarnate; the grammar ("both death and I / *Am*") displays his shock.

That I must leave ye, sons! O, were I able
To waste it all myself, and leave ye none! 820
So disinherited, how would ye bless
Me, now your curse! Ah, why should all mankind
For one man's fault thus guiltless be condemned,
If guiltless? But from me what can proceed,
But all corrupt, both mind and will depraved, 825
Not to do only, but to will the same
With me?[8] How can they then acquitted stand
In sight of God? Him, after all disputes,
Forced[9] I absolve. All my evasions vain
And reasonings, though through mazes, lead me still 830
But to my own conviction: first and last
On me, me only, as the source and spring
Of all corruption, all the blame lights due;[1]
So might the wrath! Fond[2] wish! Couldst thou support
That burden, heavier than the earth to bear; 835
Than all the world much heavier, though divided
With that bad woman? Thus, what thou desir'st,
And what thou fear'st, alike destroys all hope
Of refuge, and concludes thee miserable[3]
Beyond all past example and future; 840
To Satan only like, both crime and doom.
O Conscience! into what abyss of fears
And horrors hast thou driven me; out of which
I find no way, from deep to deeper plunged!"

 Thus Adam to himself lamented loud 845
Through the still night, not now, as ere man fell,
Wholesome and cool and mild, but with black air
Accompanied, with damps and dreadful gloom;
Which to his evil conscience represented
All things with double terror. On the ground 850
Outstretched he lay, on the cold ground, and oft
Cursed his creation; Death as oft accused
Of tardy execution, since denounced
The day of his offense. "Why comes not Death,"
Said he, "with one thrice-acceptable stroke 855
To end me? Shall Truth fail to keep her word,
Justice divine not hasten to be just?
But Death comes not at call; Justice divine
Mends not her slowest pace for prayers or cries.
O woods, O fountains, hillocks, dales, and bowers! 860

---

8. Not only will men repeat Adam's sin; their will is corrupted and they will *want* to be fallen like Adam.
9. Perforce.
1. In this discovery that he alone must accept the guilt of mankind, Adam has chosen crucially to be like Christ and unlike Satan—at the very moment when he feels exactly the opposite.
2. Foolish.
3. Shows thee to be miserable.

With other echo late I taught your shades
To answer, and resound far other song."
Whom thus afflicted when sad Eve beheld,
Desolate where she sat, approaching nigh,
Soft words to his fierce passion she essayed;   865
But her with stern regard he thus repelled:

"Out of my sight, thou serpent! that name best
Befits thee, with him leagued, thyself as false
And hateful: nothing wants, but that thy shape,
Like his, and color serpentine, may show   870
Thy inward fraud, to warn all creatures from thee
Henceforth; lest that too heavenly form, pretended[4]
To hellish falsehood, snare them. But for thee
I had persisted happy, had not thy pride
And wandering vanity, when least was safe,   875
Rejected my forewarning, and disdained
Not to be trusted, longing to be seen
Though by the devil himself, him overweening[5]
To overreach, but, with the serpent meeting,
Fooled and beguiled; by him thou, I by thee,   880
To trust thee from my side, imagined wise,
Constant, mature, proof against all assaults;
And understood not all was but a show
Rather than solid virtue, all but a rib
Crooked by nature—bent, as now appears,   885
More to the part sinister[6]—from me drawn;
Well if thrown out, as supernumerary
To my just number found![7] Oh, why did God,
Creator wise, that peopled highest Heaven
With spirits masculine, create at last   890
This novelty on earth, this fair defect
Of nature, and not fill the world at once
With men, as angels, without feminine;
Or find some other way to generate
Mankind?[8] This mischief had not then befallen,   895
And more that shall befall—innumerable
Disturbances on earth through female snares,
And strait conjunction[9] with this sex. For either
He never shall find out fit mate, but such
As some misfortune brings him, or mistake;   900
Or whom he wishes most shall seldom gain,
Through her perverseness, but shall see her gained
By a far worse, or, if she love, withheld
By parents, or his happiest choice too late

---

4. Serving as a mask.
5. Overconfident.
6. "On the left hand," as in Latin; also "unlucky."
7. Since men visibly have twelve ribs on both sides, it was supposed that Adam originally had thirteen ribs on

his left side, so that he could give up one and still have twelve, an even ("just") number.
8. Ancient traditions of antifeminist thought lie behind these ungenerous speculations.
9. Close connections, i.e., matrimony.

Shall meet, already linked and wedlock-bound   905
To a fell[1] adversary, his hate or shame:
Which infinite calamity shall cause
To human life, and household peace confound."
     He added not, and from her turned; but Eve,
Not so repulsed, with tears that ceased not flowing,   910
And tresses all disordered, at his feet
Fell humble, and, embracing them, besought
His peace, and thus proceeded in her plaint:
     "Forsake me not thus, Adam! witness Heaven
What love sincere and reverence in my heart   915
I bear thee, and unweeting[2] have offended,
Unhappily deceived! Thy suppliant[3]
I beg, and clasp thy knees; bereave me not,
Whereon I live, thy gentle looks, thy aid,
Thy counsel in this uttermost distress,   920
My only strength and stay: forlorn of thee,
Whither shall I betake me, where subsist?
While yet we live, scarce one short hour perhaps,
Between us two let there be peace; both joining,
As joined in injuries, one enmity   925
Against a foe by doom express assigned us,
That cruel serpent. On me exercise not
Thy hatred for this misery befallen;
On me already lost, me than thyself
More miserable. Both have sinned, but thou   930
Against God only; I against God and thee,
And to the place of judgement will return,
There with my cries importune Heaven, that all
The sentence, from thy head removed, may light
On me, sole cause to thee of all this woe,   935
Me, me only, just object of his ire."[4]
     She ended weeping; and her lowly plight,
Immovable till peace obtained from fault
Acknowledged and deplored,[5] in Adam wrought
Commiseration. Soon his heart relented   940
Towards her, his life so late and sole delight,
Now at his feet submissive in distress,
Creature so fair his reconcilement seeking,
His counsel, whom she had displeased, his aid;
As one disarmed, his anger all he lost,   945
And thus with peaceful words upraised her soon:
     "Unwary, and too desirous, as before,
So now, of what thou know'st not,[6] who desir'st

---

1. Bitter.
2. Unintentionally.
3. As a suppliant to thee.
4. Eve too now offers to accept the blame for the Fall; and the moral regeneration of man is henceforth possible.
5. Her suppliant posture ("lowly plight") would not be changed till she obtained forgiveness ("peace") from her admission of her fault, and repentance for it.
6. Adam's remark is rueful but affectionate; Eve is still looking for more trouble than she knows how to handle.

The punishment all on thyself! Alas!
Bear thine own first, ill able to sustain   950
His full wrath, whose thou feel'st as yet least part,[7]
And my displeasure bear'st so ill. If prayers
Could alter high decrees, I to that place
Would speed before thee, and be louder heard,
That on my head all might be visited,   955
Thy frailty and infirmer sex forgiven,
To me committed, and by me exposed.
But rise; let us no more contend, nor blame
Each other, blamed enough elsewhere, but strive
In offices of love, how we may lighten   960
Each other's burden in our share of woe;
Since this day's death denounced, if aught I see,
Will prove no sudden, but a slow-paced evil,
A long day's dying to augment our pain,
And to our seed (O hapless seed!) derived."[8]   965

7. I.e., ill able to sustain the full wrath   have felt only the least part.
of God—of whose wrath, so far, you   8. Handed down.

Summary   In her despair, Eve proposes to Adam that they refrain from having children, or commit suicide, in order to frustrate Sin and Death, but Adam persuades her to a better resolution. Book X ends with Adam and Eve reconciled to one another, partially reconciled to their fate, and praying forgiveness for their sins.

Book XI. Summary   The prayers of Adam and Eve prove acceptable to God. But while man may now hope for ultimate redemption, he may no longer dwell in Paradise; and Michael, the warrior archangel, is dispatched to explain the sentence, offer some hope for the future, and dismiss mankind from the happy garden. Adam is at first overcome with grief; but the angel encourages him, and while Eve is put in a trance, Adam is raised to the peak of a high hill and shown in a vision the future of the human race as far as the flood of Noah.

From Book XII

Summary   Continuing his instruction of Adam, Michael relates the history of the world from the time of Noah through the coming of Christ, whose ascent into Heaven and triumph over Death after the Crucifixion he describes. The Church which Christ and his apostles leave behind, however, will not be free from troubles caused by greedy and ambitious men; it will require reform. But the reformers will be persecuted and their road will be hard, until at length, in the Last Judgment, Satan and his kingdom will be dissolved, and new heavens and new earths created to exist in eternal bliss.

[*The Departure from Eden*]

So spake th' archangel Michaël; then paused,
As at the world's great period;[1] and our sire,
Replete with joy and wonder, thus replied:
"O goodness infinite, goodness immense!
That all this good of evil shall produce,   470
And evil turn to good; more wonderful
Than that which by creation first brought forth
Light out of darkness! Full of doubt I stand,
Whether I should repent me now of sin
By me done and occasioned, or rejoice   475
Much more that much more good thereof shall spring;
To God more glory, more good will to men
From God, and over wrath grace shall abound.
But say, if our Deliverer up to Heaven
Must reascend, what will betide the few,   480
His faithful, left among th' unfaithful herd,
The enemies of truth? Who then shall guide
His people, who defend? Will they not deal
Worse with his followers than with him they dealt?"

"Be sure they will," said th' angel; "but from Heaven   485
He to his own a Comforter will send,
The promise of the Father, who shall dwell,
His Spirit, within them, and the law of faith,
Working through love, upon their hearts shall write,
To guide them in all truth, and also arm   490
With spiritual armor, able to resist
Satan's assaults, and quench his fiery darts,
What[2] man can do against them, not afraid,
Though to the death; against such cruelties
With inward consolations recompensed,   495
And oft supported so as shall amaze
Their proudest persecutors.[3] For the Spirit,
Poured first on his Apostles, whom he sends
To evangelize the nations, then on all
Baptized, shall them with wondrous gifts endue[4]   500
To speak all tongues, and do all miracles,
As did their Lord before them. Thus they win
Great numbers of each nation to receive
With joy the tidings brought from Heaven: at length,
Their ministry performed, and race well run,   505
Their doctrine and their story written left,

1. Conclusion.
2. As much as.
3. Milton briefly summarizes here the
story of the Christian martyrs.
4. Endow.

They die; but in their room, as they forewarn,
Wolves shall succeed for teachers, grievous wolves,[5]
Who all the sacred mysteries of Heaven
To their own vile advantages shall turn   510
Of lucre and ambition, and the truth
With superstitions and traditions taint,
Left only in those written records pure,
Though not but by the Spirit understood.
Then shall they seek to avail themselves of names,   515
Places, and titles,[6] and with these to join
Secular power, though feigning still to act
By spiritual; to themselves appropriating
The Spirit of God, promised alike and given
To all believers; and, from that pretense,   520
Spiritual laws by carnal[7] power shall force
On every conscience, laws which none shall find
Left them enrolled, or what the Spirit within
Shall on the heart engrave.[8] What will they then,
But force the Spirit of Grace itself, and bind   525
His consort, Liberty? what but unbuild
His living temples,[9] built by faith to stand,
Their own faith, not another's? for, on Earth,
Who against faith and conscience can be heard
Infallible? Yet many will presume: 530
Whence heavy persecution shall arise
On all who in the worship persevere
Of Spirit and Truth; the rest, far greater part,
Will deem in outward rites and specious[1] forms
Religion satisfied; Truth shall retire   535
Bestuck with slanderous darts, and works of faith
Rarely be found. So shall the world go on,
To good malignant, to bad men benign,
Under her own weight groaning,[2] till the day
Appear of respiration[3] to the just   540
And vengeance to the wicked, at return
Of Him so lately promised to thy aid,
The Woman's Seed,[4] obscurely then foretold,
Now amplier known thy Savior and thy Lord;
Last in the clouds from Heaven to be revealed   545

5. To profit by religion was for Milton the lowest of crimes; he felt that priests should serve without pay. In addition, he regularly uses the wolf as an emblem of the Papacy; see *Lycidas,* line 128.
6. The name "Catholic," the place of court preacher, and the title of "bishop," for example.
7. Fleshly, i.e., secular, of this world.
8. I.e., the wolves will enforce laws which have no ancient authority or appeal to the conscience.
9. Individual believers. Milton's strict Protestant individualism speaks throughout this passage of protest against persecution.
1. Fair-seeming.
2. This passage, which in isolation appears to offer some justification for viewing the end of the poem as essentially pessimistic, should be set against Adam's earlier statement (lines 470–78) that the Fall was really a fortunate event, and gave rise to more good than evil.
3. Relief, refreshment.
4. Christ, whose Second Coming is here foreseen.

In glory of the Father, to dissolve
Satan with his perverted world; then raise
From the conflagrant mass,[5] purged and refined,
New Heavens, new Earth, ages of endless date
Founded in righteousness and peace and love,   550
To bring forth fruits, joy and eternal bliss."
    He ended, and thus Adam last replied:
"How soon hath thy prediction, seer blest,
Measured this transient world, the race of Time,
Till Time stand fixed! Beyond is all abyss,   555
Eternity, whose end no eye can reach.
Greatly instructed I shall hence depart,
Greatly in peace of thought, and have my fill
Of knowledge, what[6] this vessel can contain;
Beyond which was my folly to aspire.   560
Henceforth I learn that to obey is best,
And love with fear the only God, to walk
As in his presence, ever to observe
His providence, and on him sole depend,
Merciful over all his works, with good   565
Still overcoming evil, and by small
Accomplishing great things, by things deemed weak
Subverting worldly-strong, and worldly-wise
By simply meek; that suffering for truth's sake
Is fortitude to highest victory,   570
And to the faithful, death the gate of life;
Taught this by his example whom I now
Acknowledge my Redeemer ever blest."
    To whom thus also th' angel last replied:
"This having learned, thou hast attained the sum[7]   575
Of wisdom; hope no higher, though all the stars
Thou knew'st by name,[8] and all th' ethereal powers,
All secrets of the deep, all Nature's works,
Or works of God in heaven, air, earth, or sea,
And all the riches of this world enjoy'dst,   580
And all the rule, one empire. Only add
Deeds to thy knowledge answerable;[9] add faith,
Add virtue, patience, temperance; add love,
By name to come called charity, the soul
Of all the rest: then wilt thou not be loath   585
To leave this Paradise, but shalt possess
A Paradise within thee, happier far.
Let us descend now, therefore, from this top
Of speculation;[1] for the hour precise
Exacts[2] our parting hence; and, see! the guards,   590
By me encamped on yonder hill, expect

5. The burning world.
6. As much as.
7. Total.
8. Michael glances back at the rebuke administered by Raphael in Book VIII

to Adam's astronomical curiosity.
9. Corresponding.
1. Hill of vision.
2. Requires.

Their motion, at whose front[3] a flaming sword,
In signal of remove, waves fiercely round.
We may no longer stay. Go, waken Eve;
Her also I with gentle dreams have calmed, 595
Portending good, and all her spirits composed
To meek submission: thou, at season fit,
Let her with thee partake what thou hast heard;
Chiefly what may concern her faith to know,
The great deliverance by her seed to come 600
(For by the Woman's Seed) on all mankind;
That ye may live, which will be many days,[4]
Both in one faith unanimous; though sad
With cause for evils past, yet much more cheered
With meditation on the happy end." 605
   He ended, and they both descend the hill.
Descended, Adam to the bower where Eve
Lay sleeping ran before, but found her waked;
And thus with words not sad she him received:
   "Whence thou return'st and whither went'st, I know; 610
For God is also in sleep, and dreams advise,
Which he hath sent propitious, some great good
Presaging, since, with sorrow and heart's distress
Wearied, I fell asleep. But now lead on;
In me is no delay; with thee to go 615
Is to stay here; without thee here to stay
Is to go hence unwilling; thou to me
Art all things under Heaven, all places thou,
Who for my willful crime art banished hence.
This further consolation yet secure 620
I carry hence: though all by me is lost,
Such favor I unworthy am vouchsafed,
By me the Promised Seed shall all restore."
   So spake our mother Eve; and Adam heard
Well pleased, but answered not; for now too nigh 625
Th' archangel stood, and from the other hill
To their fixed station, all in bright array,
The cherubim descended; on the ground
Gliding meteorous, as evening mist
Risen from a river o'er the marish[5] glides, 630
And gathers ground fast at the laborer's heel
Homeward returning. High in front advanced,
The brandished sword of God before them blazed,
Fierce as a comet; which with torrid heat,
And vapor as the Libyan air adust,[6] 635
Began to parch that temperate clime; whereat
In either hand the hastening angel caught
Our lingering parents, and to th' eastern gate
Led them direct, and down the cliff as fast

3. Before whom.
4. Adam lived to be 930 (Genesis v.5).
5. Marsh (an old form).
6. The scorched climate of Libya, in North Africa, was proverbial.

To the subjected[7] plain; then disappeared.   640
They, looking back, all th' eastern side beheld
Of Paradise, so late their happy seat,[8]
Waved over by that flaming brand;[9] the gate
With dreadful faces thronged and fiery arms.
Some natural tears they dropped, but wiped them soon; 645
The world was all before them, where to choose
Their place of rest, and Providence their guide.
They, hand in hand, with wandering steps and slow,
Through Eden took their solitary way.

1662–67   1667, 1674

7. Low-lying.   9. "Sword," with the extra overtone
8. Home.   of "burning."

Samson Agonistes The figure of Samson, as one finds him in the Book of Judges, does not seem at first glance particularly adaptable to the elevated mode of tragedy. He is a promiscuous, violent fellow, given to riddles and practical jokes—the last of which puts a gruesome end to himself and his enemies. His long shaggy hair, his name (Samson, in Hebrew *Shimshun*), which includes the Hebrew word for "sun," and a persistent association with fire, all suggest a connection with some primitive solar cult, such as can be seen behind the equivalent figure of Hercules. A burly, truculent, and not-very-clever giant, in short; one would not easily see in him the dignified and purifying figure of the tragic sufferer.

But though Samson's rude vigor and vengeful nature appealed to Milton on one level; the story of his fall through the treachery of a woman on another; and the fact of his blindness on still another; there was a last level on which he could in fact be represented as the type and precursor of the Christian hero. He suffered for his people; in the very pit of despair he was rendered suddenly capable of God's revivifying grace; long exercised in physical warfare, he gave evidence in his last heroic action of having learned the principles of spiritual warfare.

Milton approached the idea of tragedy with hesitations and misgivings; for a Puritan of his day, the very idea of a stage play was instinct with moral danger. But the example of the Greeks and of his much-admired Tasso prevailed; he wrote a "closet drama," a drama intended not for the actual stage but for reading. As a play, Dr. Johnson proclaimed it deficient; it had, he said, a beginning and an end but no proper middle. Modern criticism, dissenting as usual from Dr. Johnson and stimulated as usual by his judgment, has exercised itself to find in Samson's spiritual progression during the successive visits of Manoa, Dalila, and Harapha ample psychological movement to sustain both action and interest. This is beyond doubt a useful exercise; but it is useful also to reflect that Samson acts in the end by direction of an inward spirit, a private, intimate inspiration; and that for the coming of this spirit there is no sufficient preparation. "The wind bloweth where it listeth, and thou hearest the sound thereof, but canst not tell whence it cometh, and whither it goeth: so is every one that is born of the Spirit" (John iii.8).

The story of Samson is told in Judges xiii-xvi. "Agonistes" means "in struggle" or "under trial"; it is a term derived from the Greek word for a wrestler and suggests not only that Samson is an athlete of the Lord but that he will wrestle with the pillars.

Samson Agonistes

A DRAMATIC POEM

Of That Sort of Dramatic Poem Which Is Called Tragedy

Tragedy, as it was anciently composed, hath been ever held the gravest, moralest, and most profitable of all other poems: therefore said by Aristotle to be of power, by raising pity and fear, or terror, to purge the mind of those and such-like passions, that is, to temper and reduce them to just measure with a kind of delight, stirred up by reading or seeing those passions well imitated.[1] Nor is Nature wanting in her own effects to make good his assertion; for so, in physic, things of melancholic hue and quality are used against melancholy, sour against sour, salt to remove salt humors.[2] Hence philosophers and other gravest writers, as Cicero, Plutarch, and others, frequently cite out of tragic poets, both to adorn and illustrate their discourse. The Apostle Paul himself thought it not unworthy to insert a verse of Euripides into the text of Holy Scripture, I Cor. xv. 33; and Paraeus, commenting on the Revelation, divides the whole book, as a tragedy, into acts, distinguished each by a chorus of heavenly harpings and song between.[3] Heretofore men in highest dignity have labored not a little to be thought able to compose a tragedy. Of that honor Dionysius the elder was no less ambitious than before of his attaining to the tyranny.[4] Augustus Caesar also had begun his *Ajax*, but unable to please his own judgment with what he had begun, left it unfinished. Seneca the philosopher is by some thought the author of those tragedies (at least the best of them) that go under that name. Gregory Nazianzen, a Father of the Church, thought it not unbeseeming the sanctity of his person to write a tragedy, which he entitled *Christ Suffering*.[5] This is mentioned to vindicate tragedy from the small esteem, or rather infamy, which in the account of many it undergoes at this

1. Milton is paraphrasing Aristotle's *Poetics* 6.
2. Italian critics like Minturno had applied notions of homeopathic medicine (like cures like) to tragedy; the idea is not Aristotelean. "Physic": medicine.
3. David Paraeus, a 17th-century German Calvinist.
4. Dionysius (4th century B.C.) won a prize at Athens for tragedy, after becoming tyrant of Syracuse.
5. Seneca the philosopher was indeed the author of tragedies; but Gregory Nazianzen, a Greek ecclesiastic of the 4th century, did not write the tragedy *Christ Suffering*, which scholarly opinion of Milton's day attributed to him.

day, with other common interludes—happening through the poet's error of intermixing comic stuff with tragic sadness and gravity, or introducing trivial and vulgar persons—which by all judicious hath been counted absurd, and brought in without discretion, corruptly to gratify the people. And, though ancient tragedy use no prologue,[6] yet using sometimes, in case of self-defense or explanation, that which Martial calls an epistle,[7] in behalf of this tragedy, coming forth after the ancient manner, much different from what among us passes for best, thus much beforehand may be epistled, that chorus is here introduced after the Greek manner, not ancient only, but modern, and still in use among the Italians.[8] In the modeling therefore of this poem, with good reason, the ancients and Italians are rather followed, as of much more authority and fame. The measure of verse used in the chorus is of all sorts, called by the Greeks *Monostrophic,*[9] or rather *Apolelymenon,*[1] without regard had to strophe, antistrophe, or epode, which were a kind of stanzas framed only for the music, then used with the chorus that sung; not essential to the poem, and therefore not material; or, being divided into stanzas or pauses, they may be called *alloeostropha.*[2] Division into act and scene, referring chiefly to the stage (to which this work never was intended), is here omitted.[3]

It suffices if the whole drama be found not produced[4] beyond the fifth act. Of the style and uniformity, and that commonly called the plot, whether intricate or explicit—which is nothing indeed but such economy, or disposition of the fable, as may stand best with verisimilitude and decorum[5]—they only will best judge who are not unacquainted with Aeschylus, Sophocles, and Euripides, the three tragic poets unequaled yet by any, and the best rule to all who endeavor to write tragedy. The circumscription of time wherein the whole drama begins and ends is, according to ancient rule and best example, within the space of twenty-four hours.[6]

6. Prologues and epilogues were frequent on the Restoration stage; Milton sets himself apart from contemporary styles.
7. Martial, the Roman epigrammatist of the 1st century A.D., prefixed an epistle to his book of epigrams.
8. Tasso's tragedy *Re Torrismondo* was modeled closely on classical examples.
9. Not divided into strophe, antistrophe, and epode.
1. Free from stanzaic patterns altogether.
2. With various forms of strophe, irregular.
3. The reader who cares will not find Milton's drama hard to divide into the customary five acts, each ending with a chorus: Act I (Samson and chorus) lines 1–325; II (Samson and Manoa) 326–709; III (Samson and Dalila) 710–1060; IV (Samson and Harapha) 1061–1296; V (Catastrophe) 1297–the end.
4. Led along, drawn out.
5. Decorum, for a Renaissance writer, is not simply solemn or sedate behavior but the use of appropriate and suitable style, depending on speaker, subject, setting, genre, and so on.
6. The so-called "unity of time," limiting dramatic action to 24 hours, was derived from Aristotle's *Poetics* by the Renaissance critic Castelvetro.

The Argument

Samson, made captive, blind, and now in the prison at Gaza,[7] there to labor as in a common workhouse, on a festival day, in the general cessation from labor, comes forth into the open air, to a place nigh, somewhat retired, there to sit a while and bemoan his condition. Where he happens at length to be visited by certain friends and equals of his tribe, which make the chorus, who seek to comfort him what they can; then by his old father, Manoa, who endeavors the like, and withal tells him his purpose to procure his liberty by ransom; lastly, that this feast was proclaimed by the Philistines as a day of thanksgiving for their deliverance from the hands of Samson—which yet more troubles him. Manoa then departs to prosecute his endeavor with the Philistian lords for Samson's redemption; who, in the meanwhile, is visited by other persons, and, lastly, by a public officer to require his coming to the feast before the lords and people, to play or show his strength in their presence. He at first refuses, dismissing the public officer with absolute denial to come; at length persuaded inwardly that this was from God, he yields to go along with him, who came now the second time with great threatenings to fetch him. The chorus yet remaining on the place, Manoa returns full of joyful hope to procure ere long his son's deliverance: in the midst of which discourse an Ebrew[8] comes in haste, confusedly at first, and afterwards more distinctly, relating the catastrophe—what Samson had done to the Philistines, and by accident to himself; wherewith the tragedy ends.

The Persons

SAMSON	HARAPHA *of Gath*
MANOA, *the father of*	*Public Officer*
Samson	*Messenger*
DALILA, *his wife*	*Chorus of Danites*[9]

The Scene, before the Prison in Gaza.

SAMSON. A little onward lend thy guiding hand
   To these dark steps, a little further on;
   For yonder bank hath choice of sun or shade.
   There I am wont to sit, when any chance
   Relieves me from my task of servile toil,   5
   Daily in the common prison else enjoined me,[1]

7. The Philistines, warlike and commercial, lived in Southwest Palestine (the southern coast of modern Israel between, approximately, Tel Aviv and Gaza) in five great cities splendidly named Ashdod, Eshkol, Gaza, Gath, and Ashkalon. They were a wholly urban people as against the largely rural Israelites.
8. Milton follows an old English tradi-

tion in transliterating the name "Ebrew."
9. Hebrews of the tribe of Dan, Samson's tribe. When the land of Canaan was divided among the twelve tribes, they received the southern portion, adjacent to the Philistines.
1. The metrical pattern of this line, with its many unaccented syllables and careful placement of the strong word "else," merits careful study.

Where I, a prisoner chained, scarce freely draw
The air, imprisoned also, close and damp,
Unwholesome draught. But here I feel amends—
The breath of heaven fresh blowing, pure and sweet,   10
With day-spring[2] born; here leave me to respire.
This day a solemn feast the people hold
To Dagon,[3] their sea-idol, and forbid
Laborious works. Unwillingly this rest
Their superstition yields me; hence, with leave   15
Retiring from the popular noise, I seek
This unfrequented place, to find some ease—
Ease to the body some, none to the mind
From restless thoughts, that, like a deadly swarm
Of hornets armed, no sooner found alone   20
But rush upon me thronging, and present
Times past, what once I was, and what am now.
Oh, wherefore was my birth from Heaven foretold
Twice by an angel,[4] who at last, in sight
Of both my parents, all in flames ascended   25
From off the altar where an offering burned,
As in a fiery column charioting
His godlike presence, and from some great act
Or benefit revealed to Abraham's race?
Why was my breeding ordered and prescribed   30
As of a person separate to God,
Designed for great exploits,[5] if I must die
Betrayed, captived, and both my eyes put out,
Made of my enemies the scorn and gaze,
To grind in brazen fetters under task   35
With this heaven-gifted strength? O glorious strength,
Put to the labor of a beast, debased
Lower than bondslave! Promise was that I
Should Israel from Philistian yoke deliver;
Ask for this great deliverer now, and find him   40
Eyeless in Gaza, at the mill with slaves,
Himself in bonds under Philistian yoke.
Yet stay; let me not rashly call in doubt
Divine prediction. What if all foretold
Had been fulfilled but through mine own default?   45
Whom have I to complain of but myself,
Who this high gift of strength committed to me,
In what part lodged, how easily bereft me,
Under the seal of silence could not keep,[6]

2. Break of day.
3. Dagon's name comes from *dag*, fish, and he seems to have had a fishy shape. His would thus be a marine cult to correspond with that of the many Baals, or land gods of the Philistines. See *Paradise Lost* I.457–66.
4. Before Samson was born an angel foretold that he would begin the delivery of Israel from the Philistines (Judges xiii.5).
5. Samson was a Nazarite, member of an ascetic group specially dedicated to the service of God. See Numbers vi.
6. I.e., who could not keep silent about the high gift of strength committed to me, or about where it was located, or about how easily it could be taken from me.

But weakly to a woman must reveal it,   50
O'ercome with importunity and tears?
O impotence of mind in body strong!
But what is strength without a double share
Of wisdom? Vast, unwieldy, burdensome,
Proudly secure,[7] yet liable to fall   55
By weakest subtleties; not made to rule,
But to subserve where wisdom bears command.
God, when he gave me strength, to show withal,
How slight the gift was, hung it in my hair.
But peace! I must not quarrel with the will   60
Of highest dispensation,[8] which herein
Haply had ends above my reach to know.
Suffices that to me strength is my bane,
And proves the source of all my miseries—
So many, and so huge, that each apart   65
Would ask a life to wail. But, chief of all,
O loss of sight, of thee I most complain!
Blind among enemies! O worse than chains,
Dungeon, or beggary, or decrepit age!
Light, the prime work of God,[9] to me is extinct,   70
And all her various objects of delight
Annulled, which might in part my grief have eased.
Inferior to the vilest now become
Of man or worm, the vilest here excel me:
They creep, yet see; I, dark in light, exposed   75
To daily fraud, contempt, abuse, and wrong,
Within doors, or without, still as a fool,
In power of others, never in my own—
Scarce half I seem to live, dead more than half.
O dark, dark, dark, amid the blaze of noon,   80
Irrecoverably dark, total eclipse
Without all hope of day!
O first-created beam, and thou great Word,
"Let there be light, and light was over all,"
Why am I thus bereaved thy prime decree? [1]   85
The sun to me is dark
And silent[2] as the moon,
When she deserts the night,
Hid in her vacant interlunar cave.[3]
Since light so necessary is to life,   90
And almost life itself, if it be true
That light is in the soul,
She all in every part,[4] why was the sight

7. Confident, free from care (Latin, *cura*).
8. Providence.
9. God's first ("prime") act in creating the world was to say "Let there be light" (Genesis i.3), a phrase Milton paraphrases below.
1. I.e., why am I thus deprived of the first-created (and most important) thing?
2. Unperceived.
3. Ancient astronomers supposed that during the daytime the moon hid in a cave.
4. A famous formula of Plotinus (*Ennead* IV.ii.1) describes the soul as "all in all and all in every part."

To such a tender ball as th' eye confined,
So obvious[5] and so easy to be quenched,   95
And not, as feeling, through all parts diffused,
That she might look at will through every pore?
Then had I not been thus exiled from light,
As in the land of darkness, yet in light,
To live a life half dead, a living death,   100
And buried; but, O yet more miserable!
Myself my sepulcher, a moving grave;
Buried, yet not exempt,
By privilege of death and burial,
From worst of other evils, pains, and wrongs;   105
But made hereby obnoxious[6] more
To all the miseries of life,
Life in captivity
Among inhuman foes.
But who are these? for with joint pace I hear   110
The tread of many feet steering this way;
Perhaps my enemies, who come to stare
At my affliction, and perhaps to insult,
Their daily practice to afflict me more.

CHORUS. This, this is he; softly a while;   115
　Let us not break in upon him.
　O change beyond report, thought, or belief!
　See how he lies at random, carelessly diffused,[7]
　With languished head unpropped,
　As one past hope, abandoned,   120
　And by himself given over,
　In slavish habit, ill-fitted weeds [8]
　O'er-worn and soiled.
　Or do my eyes misrepresent? Can this be he,
　That heroic, that renowned,   125
　Irresistible Samson? whom, unarmed,
　No strength of man, or fiercest wild beast, could withstand: [9]
　Who tore the lion as the lion tears the kid;
　Ran on embattled armies clad in iron,
　And, weaponless himself,   130
　Made arms ridiculous, useless the forgery[1]
　Of brazen shield and spear, the hammered cuirass,
　Chalybean-tempered[2] steel, and frock of mail
　Adamantean proof;
　But safest he who stood aloof,   135
　When insupportably[3] his foot advanced,
　In scorn of their proud arms and warlike tools,

5. Exposed.
6. Vulnerable, subject.
7. Literally, "poured forth," outstretched.
8. Rags.
9. Judges xiv.5–6 tells the story of Samson ripping apart a lion with his bare hands.

1. Weapons of forged steel, but also fraudulent, exterior protections.
2. The Chalybes lived on the Black Sea and were famous ironworkers. "Adamantean proof": hard as adamant, i.e., diamond.
3. Irresistibly.

Spurned them to death by troops. The bold Ascalonite[4]
Fled from his lion ramp; old warriors turned
Their plated backs under his heel,   140
Or groveling soiled their crested helmets in the dust.
Then with what trivial weapon came to hand,
The jaw of a dead ass, his sword of bone,
A thousand foreskins fell, the flower of Palestine,
In Ramath-lechi, famous to this day; [5]   145
Then by main force pulled up, and on his shoulders bore,
The gates of Azza, post and massy bar,
Up to the hill by Hebron, seat of giants old,
No journey of a Sabbath day, and loaded so,
Like whom the Gentiles feign to bear up Heaven.[6]   150
Which shall I first bewail,
Thy bondage or lost sight,
Prison within prison
Inseparably dark?
Thou art become (O worst imprisonment!)   155
The dungeon of thyself; thy soul
(Which men enjoying sight oft without cause complain),
Imprisoned now indeed,
In real darkness of the body dwells,
Shut up from outward light   160
To incorporate with gloomy night;
For inward light, alas!
Puts forth no visual beam.[7]
O mirror of our fickle state,
Since man on earth unparalleled! [8]   165
The rarer thy example stands,
By how much from the top of wondrous glory,
Strongest of mortal men,
To lowest pitch of abject fortune thou art fallen!
For him I reckon not in high estate   170
Whom long descent of birth,
Or the sphere[9] of fortune, raises;
But thee, whose strength, while virtue was her mate,
Might have subdued the Earth,

4. A man from Ascalon, or Ashkalon, one of the five great Philistine cities. "Lion ramp": a lion in the act of attacking its prey, rampant.
5. On one occasion Samson killed a thousand Philistines (i.e., "foreskins", uncircumcised warriors), using the jawbone of an ass (Judges xv.15–17). Judges xvi.3 tells how Samson, to escape his enemies, picked up and carried off the gates of Gaza (Azza).
6. In Greek (or, as Milton calls it, Gentile) mythology, Atlas supports the heavens. From Gaza to Hebron would be about forty miles—no journey for the day of rest.

7. Renaissance physiologists supposed the eye saw by sending forth a "visual beam" which it directed at various objects.
8. I.e., no such example (has been seen) since man (was) on earth. "Fickle": changeable.
9. "Sphere": wheel. Fortune was described as possessing a wheel which merely by rotating automatically interchanged the highest and lowest social positions. Milton's definition of "high estate" is interior and spiritual; he has no interest in the old "Fall of Princes" theme. In fact, the play exactly reverses that theme.

Universally crowned with highest praises.   175
SAMSON. I hear the sound of words; their sense the air
   Dissolves unjointed ere it reach my ear.
CHORUS. He speaks: let us draw nigh. Matchless in might,
   The glory late of Israel, now the grief!
   We come, thy friends and neighbors not unknown,   180
   From Eshtaol and Zora's fruitful vale,
   To visit or bewail thee; or, if better,
   Counsel or consolation we may bring,
   Salve to thy sores: apt words have power to swage[1]
   The tumors of a troubled mind,   185
   And are as balm to festered wounds.
SAMSON. Your coming, friends, revives me; for I learn
   Now of my own experience, not by talk,
   How counterfeit a coin they are who "friends"
   Bear in their superscription (of the most   190
   I would be understood). In prosperous days
   They swarm, but in adverse withdraw their head,
   Not to be found, though sought. Ye see, O friends,
   How many evils have enclosed me round;
   Yet that which was the worst now least afflicts me,   195
   Blindness; for, had I sight, confused with shame,
   How could I once look up, or heave[2] the head,
   Who, like a foolish pilot, have shipwrecked
   My vessel trusted to me from above,
   Gloriously rigged, and for a word, a tear,   200
   Fool! have divulged the secret gift of God
   To a deceitful woman? Tell me, friends,
   Am I not sung and proverbed for a fool
   In every street? Do they not say, "How well
   Are come upon him his deserts"? Yet why?   205
   Immeasurable strength they might behold
   In me; of wisdom nothing more than mean.[3]
   This with the other should at least have paired; [4]
   These two, proportioned ill, drove me transverse.[5]
CHORUS. Tax not divine disposal. Wisest men   210
   Have erred, and by bad women been deceived;
   And shall again, pretend they ne'er so wise.[6]
   Deject not, then, so overmuch thyself,
   Who hast of sorrow thy full load besides.
   Yet, truth to say, I oft have heard men wonder   215
   Why thou should'st wed Philistian women rather
   Than of thine own tribe fairer, or as fair,
   At least of thy own nation, and as noble.
SAMSON. The first I saw at Timna, and she pleased
   Me, not my parents, that I sought to wed   220

1. Assuage.
2. Lift.
3. Average.
4. Been equal.
5. Off the true course.
6. I.e., intend they never so wisely.

The daughter of an infidel.[7] They knew not
That what I motioned[8] was of God; I knew
From intimate impulse, and therefore urged
The marriage on, that, by occasion hence,[9]
I might begin Israel's deliverance—   225
The work to which I was divinely called.
She proving false, the next I took to wife
(O that I never had! fond wish too late!)
Was in the vale of Sorec, Dálila,[1]
That specious monster, my accomplished snare.   230
I thought it lawful from my former act
And the same end, still watching to oppress
Israel's oppressors. Of what now I suffer
She was not the prime cause, but I myself,
Who, vanquished with a peal of words (O weakness!),   235
Gave up my fort of silence to a woman.
CHORUS. In seeking just occasion to provoke
    The Philistine, thy country's enemy,
    Thou never wast remiss, I bear thee witness;
    Yet Israel still serves with all his sons.[2]   240
SAMSON. That fault I take not on me, but transfer
    On Israel's governors and heads of tribes,
    Who, seeing those great acts which God had done
    Singly by me against their conquerors,
    Acknowledged not, or not at all considered   245
    Deliverance offered. I, on th' other side,
    Used no ambition to commend my deeds;[3]
    The deeds themselves, though mute, spoke loud the doer.
    But they persisted deaf, and would not seem
    To count them things worth notice, till at length   250
    Their lords, the Philistines, with gathered powers,
    Entered Judea seeking me, who then
    Safe to the rock of Etham was retired,
    Not flying, but forecasting in what place
    To set upon them, what advantaged best.   255
    Meanwhile the men of Judah, to prevent
    The harass of their land, beset me round;
    I willingly on some conditions came
    Into their hands, and they as gladly yield me
    To the uncircumcised[4] a welcome prey,   260
    Bound with two cords. But cords to me were threads
    Touched with the flame: on their whole host I flew
    Unarmed, and with a trivial weapon felled
    Their choicest youth; they only lived who fled.[5]

7. Judges xiv.1–4 tells the story of Samson's first decision to marry outside his own tribe and nation.
8. Intended.
9. I.e., so that it might provide an occasion for me to begin Israel's deliverance.
1. Judges xvi.4.
2. I.e., Israel and the children of Israel are still in servitude.
3. I.e., sought for no testimonials to my actions.
4. Foreigners, the people outside the covenant of Abraham.
5. Judges xv.8–17 tells the tale of Samson's single-handed victory, using a "trivial weapon," the jawbone of an ass.

Had Judah that day joined, or one whole tribe, 265
They had by this[6] possessed the towers of Gath,
And lorded over them whom now they serve.
But what more oft, in nations grown corrupt,
And by their vices brought to servitude,
Than to love bondage more than liberty, 270
Bondage with ease than strenuous liberty,[7]
And to despise, or envy, or suspect,
Whom God hath of his special favor raised
As their deliverer? If he aught begin,
How frequent to desert him, and at last 275
To heap ingratitude on worthiest deeds!
CHORUS. Thy words to my remembrance bring
How Succoth and the fort of Penuel
Their great deliverer contemned,
The matchless Gideon, in pursuit 280
Of Madian, and her vanquished kings;[8]
And how ingrateful Ephraim
Had dealt with Jephtha, who by argument,
Not worse than by his shield and spear,
Defended Israel from the Ammonite, 285
Had not his prowess quelled their pride
In that sore battle when so many died
Without reprieve, adjudged to death
For want of well pronouncing *Shibboleth*.[9]
SAMSON. Of such examples add me to the roll. 290
Me easily indeed mine[1] may neglect,
But God's proposed deliverance not so.
CHORUS. Just are the ways of God,
And justifiable to men,
Unless there be who think not God at all. 295
If any be, they walk obscure;
For of such doctrine never was there school,
But the heart of the fool,
And no man therein doctor but himself.[2]
    Yet more there be who doubt his ways not just,
As to his own edicts found contradicting; 300
Then give the reins to wandering thought,
Regardless of his glory's diminution,
Till, by their own perplexities involved,
They ravel[3] more, still less resolved,
But never find self-satisfying solution. 305
As if they would confine th' Interminable,[4]
And tie him to his own prescript,

6. By this time.
7. Milton obviously has in mind, not only early Israel, but also contemporary England.
8. Judges viii: Succoth and Penuel refused aid to Gideon when he was pursuing the common foe, and he punished them.
9. Judges xi and xii.
1. My people.
2. Psalm xiv deals with the fool who says in his heart there is no God. "Doctor": teacher.
3. Become entangled.
4. Infinite.

Who made our laws to bind us, not himself,
And hath full right to exempt 310
Whomso it pleases him by choice
From national obstriction,[5] without taint
Of sin, or legal debt;
For with his own laws he can best dispense.
    He would not else, who never wanted means, 315
Nor in respect of the enemy just cause,
To set his people free,
Have prompted this heroic Nazarite,
Against his vow of strictest purity,
To seek in marriage that fallacious bride, 320
Unclean, unchaste.
    Down, Reason, then; at least, vain reasonings down;
Though Reason here aver
That moral verdict quits her of unclean:
Unchaste was subsequent; her stain, not his.[6] 325
But see! here comes thy reverend sire,
With careful step, locks white as down,[7]
Old Manoa: advise [8]
Forthwith how thou ought'st to receive him.

SAMSON. Ay me! another inward grief, awaked 330
  With mention of that name, renews th' assault.

MANOA. Brethren and men of Dan (for such ye seem,
  Though in this uncouth[9] place), if old respect,
  As I suppose, towards your once gloried friend,
  My son, now captive, hither hath informed[1] 335
  Your younger feet, while mine, cast back with age,
  Came lagging after, say if he be here.

CHORUS. As signal[2] now in low dejected state
  As erst in highest, behold him where he lies.

MANOA. O miserable change! Is this the man, 340
  That ínvincible Samson, far renowned,
  The dread of Israel's foes, who with a strength
  Equivalent to angels' walked their streets,
  None offering fight; who, single combatant,
  Dueled their armies ranked in proud array, 345
  Himself an army—now unequal match
  To save himself against a coward armed
  At one spear's length? O ever-failing trust
  In mortal strength! and, oh, what not in man
  Deceivable and vain? [3] Nay, what thing good 350

5. Obligation, i.e., the law against marrying Gentiles (Deuteronomy vii.3). The chorus here accepts Samson's argument that God had prompted him inexplicably to marry the woman of Timna.
6. The chorus, having accused the woman of Timna of being unclean (i.e., Gentile and taboo) and unchaste, now admits that since Samson married her at God's instigation she was not unclean to him; and that she was unchaste only after Samson left her. Reason is therefore puzzled.
7. "Careful": full of care; "down": swan's down.
8. Reflect, consider inwardly.
9. Unknown, unfamiliar.
1. Directed.
2. Notable, eminent.
3. I.e., what is there in man that is not deceivable and vain?

Prayed for, but often proves our woe, our bane?
I prayed for children, and thought barrenness
In wedlock a reproach; I gained a son,
And such a son as all men hailed me happy:
Who would be now a father in my stead?   355
Oh, wherefore did God grant me my request,
And as a blessing with such pomp adorned?
Why are his gifts desirable, to tempt
Our earnest prayers, then, given with solemn hand
As graces, draw a scorpion's tail behind?   360
For this did the angel twice descend?[4] for this
Ordained thy nurture holy, as of a plant
Select and sacred? glorious for a while,
The miracle of men; then in an hour
Ensnared, assaulted, overcome, led bound,   365
Thy foes' derision, captive, poor and blind,
Into a dungeon thrust, to work with slaves!
Alas! methinks whom God hath chosen once
To worthiest deeds, if he through frailty err,
He should not so o'erwhelm, and as a thrall   370
Subject him to so foul indignities,
Be it but for honor's sake of former deeds.

SAMSON. Appoint not heavenly disposition,[5] father.
Nothing of all these evils hath befallen me
But justly; I myself have brought them on;   375
Sole author I, sole cause.[6] If aught seem vile,
As vile hath been my folly, who have profaned
The mystery of God, given me under pledge
Of vow, and have betrayed it to a woman,
A Canaanite, my faithless enemy.   380
This well I knew, nor was at all surprised,
But warned by oft experience. Did not she
Of Timna first betray me, and reveal
The secret wrested from me in her height
Of nuptial love professed, carrying it straight   385
To them who had corrupted her, my spies
And rivals?[7] In this other was there found
More faith, who, also in her prime of love,
Spousal embraces, vitiated with gold,
Though offered only, by the scent conceived,   390
Her spurious first-born, treason against me?[8]
Thrice she assayed, with flattering prayers and sighs,
And amorous reproaches, to win from me

---

4. The angel who announced Samson's birth was sent a second time, in answer to Manoa's request, to give instructions concerning his education and training.
5. I.e., do not presume to control heaven's decisions.
6. Like Adam, *Paradise Lost* X, Samson proves his own resurgent virtue by accepting responsibility for his own faults.
7. Samson's first wife, the woman of Timna, revealed Samson's riddle to his enemies (Judges xiv.8–19).
8. At the mere scent of gold, Dalila conceived a bastard ("spurious") offspring for Samson—treason.

My capital secret,[9] in what part my strength
Lay stored, in what part summed, that she might know;   395
Thrice I deluded her, and turned to sport
Her importunity, each time perceiving
How openly and with what impudence
She purposed to betray me, and (which was worse
Than undissembled hate) with what contempt   400
She sought to make me traitor to myself.[1]
Yet, the fourth time, when, mustering all her wiles,
With blandished parleys, feminine assaults,
Tongue-batteries, she surceased[2] not day nor night
To storm me, over-watched and wearied out,   405
At times when men seek most repose and rest,
I yielded, and unlocked her all my heart,
Who, with a grain of manhood well resolved,
Might easily have shook off all her snares;
But foul effeminacy[3] held me yoked   410
Her bondslave. O indignity, O blot
To honor and religion! servile mind
Rewarded well with servile punishment!
The base degree to which I now am fallen,
These rags, this grinding, is not yet so base   415
As was my former servitude, ignoble,
Unmanly, ignominious, infamous,
True slavery; and that blindness worse than this,
That saw not how degenerately I served.
MANOA. I cannot praise thy marriage-choices, son,   420
Rather approved them not; but thou didst plead
Divine impulsion[4] prompting how thou might'st
Find some occasion to infest our foes.
I state not that; this I am sure, our foes
Found soon occasion thereby to make thee   425
Their captive, and their triumph; thou the sooner
Temptation found'st, or over-potent charms,
To violate the sacred trust of silence
Deposited within thee; which to have kept
Tacit was in thy power. True; and thou bear'st   430
Enough, and more, the burden of that fault;
Bitterly hast thou paid, and still art paying,
That rigid score.[5] A worse thing yet remains:
This day the Philistines a popular feast
Here celebrate in Gaza, and proclaim   435
Great pomp, and sacrifice, and praises loud,
To Dagon, as their god who hath delivered
Thee, Samson, bound and blind, into their hands—

---

9. The secret Dalila learned was of capital importance; also, it involved the hair on Samson's head (*caput*).
1. Judges xvi.5–20.
2. Forbore.
3. "Effeminacy": uxoriousness, over-

fondness, the fault of Adam.
4. Prudent Manoa mistrusts the inner impulse which is Samson's conscience and the first principle of his life. "Infest": attack.
5. Debt.

Them out of thine, who slew'st them many a slain.[6]
So Dagon shall be magnified,[7] and God,   440
Besides whom is no god, compared with idols,
Disglorified, blasphemed, and had in scorn
By th' idolatrous rout amidst their wine;
Which to have come to pass by means of thee,
Samson, of all thy sufferings think the heaviest,   445
Of all reproach the most with shame that ever
Could have befallen thee and thy father's house.
SAMSON. Father, I do acknowledge and confess
   That I this honor, I this pomp, have brought
   To Dagon, and advanced his praises high   450
   Among the heathen round; to God have brought
   Dishonor, obloquy, and oped the mouths
   Of idolists and atheists; have brought scandal
   To Israel, diffidence[8] of God, and doubt
   In feeble hearts, propense[9] enough before   455
   To waver, or fall off and join with idols:
   Which is my chief affliction, shame and sorrow,
   The anguish of my soul, that suffers not
   Mine eye to harbor sleep, or thoughts to rest.
   This only hope relieves me, that the strife   460
   With me hath end. All the contést is now
   'Twixt God and Dagon. Dagon hath presumed,
   Me overthrown, to enter lists[1] with God,
   His deity comparing and preferring
   Before the God of Abraham. He, be sure,   465
   Will not connive,[2] or linger, thus provoked,
   But will arise, and his great name assert.
   Dagon must stoop, and shall ere long receive
   Such a discomfit as shall quite despoil him
   Of all these boasted trophies won on me,   470
   And with confusion blank[3] his worshipers.
MANOA. With cause this hope relieves thee; and these words
   I as a prophecy receive; for God
   (Nothing more certain) will not long defer
   To vindicate the glory of his name   475
   Against all competition, nor will long
   Endure it doubtful whether God be Lord
   Or Dagon. But for thee what shall be done?
   Thou must not in the meanwhile, here forgot,
   Lie in this miserable loathsome plight   480
   Neglected. I already have made way
   To some Philistian lords, with whom to treat
   About thy ransom. Well they may by this[4]
   Have satisfied their utmost of revenge,

6. I.e., who slew many a one for them.
7. Glorified.
8. Mistrust.
9. Inclined.
1. Jousting courts as in medieval tour-neys.
2. Hesitate, palter.
3. Confound, turn pale.
4. By this time.

By pains and slaveries, worse than death, inflicted. 485
On thee, who now no more canst do them harm.
SAMSON. Spare that proposal, father; spare the trouble
Of that solicitation. Let me here,
As I deserve, pay on my punishment,
And expiate, if possible, my crime, 490
Shameful garrulity. To have revealed
Secrets of men, the secrets of a friend,
How heinous had the fact been, how deserving
Contempt and scorn of all; to be excluded
All friendship, and avoided as a blab, 495
The mark of fool set on his front! [5] But I
God's counsel have not kept, his holy secret
Presumptuously have published, impiously,
Weakly at least and shamefully: a sin
That Gentiles in their parables condemn 500
To their abyss and horrid pains confined.[6]
MANOA. Be penitent, and for thy fault contrite;
But act not in thy own affliction, son.
Repent the sin; but, if the punishment
Thou canst avoid, self-preservation bids; 505
Or th' execution leave to high disposal,
And let another hand, not thine, exact
Thy penal forfeit from thyself. Perhaps
God will relent, and quit [7] thee all his debt;
Who ever more approves and more accepts 510
(Best pleased with humble and filial submission)
Him who, imploring mercy, sues for life,
Than who, self-rigorous, chooses death as due; [8]
Which argues over-just, and self-displeased
For self-offense more than for God offended. 515
Reject not, then, what offered means who knows
But God hath set before us to return thee
Home to thy country and his sacred house,
Where thou may'st bring thy offerings, to avert
His further ire, with prayers and vows renewed. 520
SAMSON. His pardon I implore; but, as for life,
To what end should I seek it? When in strength
All mortals I excelled, and great in hopes,
With youthful courage, and magnanimous thoughts
Of birth from Heaven foretold and high exploits, 525
Full of divine instinct, after some proof
Of acts indeed heroic, far beyond
The sons of Anak,[9] famous now and blazed,
Fearless of danger, like a petty god

5. Forehead.
6. In classical legend, Tantalus was confined to hell and torment because he betrayed the secrets of the gods, and Prometheus was savagely punished for giving to mankind the secret of fire.
7. Cancel.
8. This is very similar to Adam's argument against suicide in *Paradise Lost* X.1013–30.
9. Giants, described in Numbers xiii.

I walked about, admired of all, and dreaded   530
On hostile ground, none daring my affront.
Then, swoll'n with pride, into the snare I fell
Of fair fallacious looks, venereal trains,[1]
Softened with pleasure and voluptuous life;
At length to lay my head and hallowed pledge   535
Of all my strength in the lascivious lap
Of a deceitful concubine, who shore me,
Like a tame wether,[2] all my precious fleece,
Then turned me out ridiculous, despoiled,
Shaven, and disarmed among my enemies.   540
CHORUS. Desire of wine and all delicious drinks,
Which many a famous warrior overturns,
Thou could'st repress; nor did the dancing ruby,
Sparkling out-poured, the flavor or the smell,
Or taste, that cheers the heart of gods and men,   545
Allure thee from the cool crystalline stream.
SAMSON. Wherever fountain or fresh current flowed
Against the eastern ray, translucent, pure
With touch ethereal of Heaven's fiery rod,[3]
I drank, from the clear milky juice allaying   550
Thirst, and refreshed; nor envied them the grape
Whose heads that turbulent liquor fills with fumes.
CHORUS. O madness! to think use of strongest wines
And strongest drinks our chief support of health,
When God with these forbidden made choice to rear   555
His mighty champion, strong above compare,
Whose drink was only from the liquid brook! [4]
SAMSON. But what availed this temperance, not complete
Against another object more enticing?
What boots it at one gate to make defense,   560
And at another to let in the foe,
Effeminately vanquished? by which means,
Now blind, disheartened, shamed, dishonored, quelled,
To what can I be useful? wherein serve
My nation, and the work from Heaven imposed?   565
But to sit idle on the household hearth,
A burdenous drone; to visitance a gaze,[5]
Or pitied object; these redundant [6] locks,
Robustious to no purpose, clustering down,
Vain monument of strength; till length of years   570
And sedentary numbness craze [7] my limbs
To a contemptible old age obscure.

1. Sensual, sexual lures.
2. A castrated male sheep.
3. The rays of the sun. Samson is saying that wherever water was purest and cleanest, he drank of it—never of wine; "rod" intimates a parallel with Moses, who like Samson brought forth a spring in the middle of the desert.
4. Samson's calling as a Nazarite forbade him the use of wine.
5. A spectacle for visitors.
6. In its Latin sense, "redundant" means "flowing," in the English sense "unnecessary," "unemployed." "Robustious": strong.
7. Weaken, twist.

Here rather let me drudge, and earn my bread,
Till vermin, or the draff of servile food,[8]
Consume me, and oft-invocated death   575
Hasten the welcome end of all my pains.

MANOA. Wilt thou then serve the Philistines with that gift
Which was expressly given thee to annoy them?
Better at home lie bed-rid, not only idle,
Inglorious, unemployed, with age outworn.   580
But God, who caused a fountain at thy prayer
From the dry ground to spring, thy thirst to allay
After the brunt of battle,[9] can as easy
Cause light again within thy eyes to spring,
Wherewith to serve him better than thou hast.   585
And I persuade me so. Why else this strength
Miraculous yet remaining in those locks?
His might continues in thee not for naught,
Nor shall his wondrous gifts be frustrate thus.

SAMSON. All otherwise to me my thoughts portend,   590
That these dark orbs no more shall treat with light,
Nor th' other light of life continue long,
But yield to double darkness nigh at hand;
So much I feel my genial spirits [1] droop,
My hopes all flat: Nature within me seems   595
In all her functions weary of herself;
My race of glory run, and race of shame,
And I shall shortly be with them that rest.

MANOA. Believe not these suggestions, which proceed
From anguish of the mind, and humors black   600
That mingle with thy fancy.[2] I, however,
Must not omit a father's timely care
To prosecute the means of thy deliverance
By ransom or how else: meanwhile be calm,
And healing words from these thy friends admit.   605

SAMSON. Oh, that torment should not be confined
To the body's wounds and sores,
With maladies innumerable
In heart, head, breast, and reins,
But must secret passage find   610
To th' inmost mind,
There exercise all his fierce accidents,[3]
And on her purest spirits prey,
As on entrails, joints, and limbs,
With answerable pains, but more intense,   615
Though void of corporal sense!

---

8. Garbage given to slaves as food.
9. The story of how Samson, with divine aid, created a spring in the desert after the battle with the ass's jawbone, is told in Judges xv.18–19.
1. Life forces, vital energy.

2. Black bile, the melancholy humor, was supposed to have specially ill effects on the imagination.
3. I.e., there put into effect all the fierce qualities (of torment).

My griefs not only pain me
As a lingering disease,
But, finding no redress, ferment and rage;
Nor less than wounds immedicable   620
Rankle, and fester, and gangrene,
To black mortification.[4]
Thoughts, my tormentors, armed with daily stings,
Mangle my apprehensive tenderest parts,
Exasperate, exulcerate, and raise   625
Dire inflammation, which no cooling herb
Or med'cinal liquor can assuage,
Nor breath of vernal air from snowy Alp.
Sleep hath forsook and given me o'er
To death's benumbing opium as my only cure;   630
Thence faintings, swoonings of despair,
And sense of Heaven's desertion.[5]
     I was his nursling once and choice delight,
His destined from the womb,
Promised by heavenly message [6] twice descending.   635
Under his special eye
Abstemious I grew up and thrived amain;
He led me on to mightiest deeds,
Above the nerve [7] of mortal arm,
Against the uncircumcised, our enemies: 640
But now hath cast me off as never known,
And to those cruel enemies,
Whom I by his appointment had provoked,
Left me, all helpless with th' irreparable loss
Of sight, reserved alive to be repeated [8]   645
The subject of their cruelty or scorn.
Nor am I in the list of them that hope;
Hopeless are all my evils, all remediless.
This one prayer yet remains, might I be heard,
No long petition—speedy death,   650
The close of all my miseries and the balm.
CHORUS. Many are the sayings of the wise,
In ancient and in modern books enrolled,
Extolling patience as the truest fortitude,
And to the bearing well of all calamities,   655
All chances incident to man's frail life,
Consolatories writ
With studied argument, and much persuasion sought,
Lenient [9] of grief and anxious thought.
But with th' afflicted in his pangs their sound   660
Little prevails, or rather seems a tune

---

4. A medical term for decay.
5. Samson comes close here to suggesting that religious despair is the symptom of a physical condition; cf. Burton's *Anatomy of Melancholy.*

6. Messenger.
7. Sinew, hence, strength.
8. Repeatedly, continually.
9. Soothing (from Latin, *leniens*).

Harsh, and of dissonant mood [1] from his complaint,
Unless he feel within
Some source of consolation from above,
Secret refreshings that repair his strength   665
And fainting spirits uphold.[2]
     God of our fathers! what is man,
That thou towards him with hand so various—
Or might I say contrarious?—
Temper'st thy providence through his short course: 670
Not evenly, as thou rul'st
The angelic orders, and inferior creatures mute,
Irrational and brute? [3]
Nor do I name of men the common rout,
That, wandering loose about,   675
Grow up and perish as the summer fly,
Heads without name, no more remembered;
But such as thou hast solemnly elected,
With gifts and graces eminently adorned,
To some great work, thy glory,   680
And people's safety, which in part they effect.
Yet toward these, thus dignified, thou oft,
Amidst their height of noon,
Changest thy countenance and thy hand, with no regard
Of highest favors past   685
From thee on them, or them to thee of service.[4]
     Nor only dost degrade them, or remit
To life obscured, which were a fair dismission,
But throw'st them lower than thou didst exalt them high,
Unseemly falls in human eye,   690
Too grievous for the trespass or omission;
Oft leav'st them to the hostile sword
Of heathen and profane, their carcasses
To dogs and fowls a prey, or else captíved,
Or to the unjust tribunals, under change of times,   695
And condemnation of the ingrateful multitude.[5]
If these they 'scape, perhaps in poverty
With sickness and disease thou bow'st them down,
Painful diseases and deformed,
In crude [6] old age;   700
Though not disordinate,[7] yet causeless suffering
The punishment of dissolute days. In fine,

1. The musical mode, or psychological mood, of the comforter jars on that of the sufferer.
2. Compare Job's answers to his comforters, especially xiv.
3. The chorus feels that the beings above and below man on the Great Chain of Being (the nine orders of angels above, the many mute beasts below) are ruled by a less capricious code than is man.
4. Manoa has already voiced this plaint, lines 368–72.

5. After the Restoration, many Puritan leaders were executed, jailed, or exiled, while even the corpses of some who were dead were exhumed, beheaded, and publicly exhibited.
6. Literally, "raw," but, figuratively, "premature."
7. I.e., though they have not been dissipated (disordinate). Milton resented having the gout, supposed to be a disease of the luxurious.

Just or unjust alike seem miserable,
For oft alike both come to evil end.
   So deal not with this once thy glorious champion, 705
The image of thy strength, and mighty minister.[8]
What do I beg? how hast thou dealt already!
Behold him in this state calamitous, and turn
His labors, for thou canst, to peaceful end.
   But who is this? what thing of sea or land— 710
Female of sex it seems—
That, so bedecked, ornate, and gay,
Comes this way sailing,
Like a stately ship
Of Tarsus, bound for th' isles 715
Of Javan or Gadire,[9]
With all her bravery on, and tackle trim,
Sails filled, and streamers waving,
Courted by all the winds that hold them play;
An amber [1] scent of odorous perfume 720
Her harbinger, a damsel train behind?
Some rich Philistian matron she may seem;
And now, at nearer view, no other certain
Than Dálila thy wife.[2]

SAMSON. My wife! my traitress! let her not come near me. 725

CHORUS. Yet on she moves; now stands and eyes thee fixed,
About t'have spoke; but now, with head declined,
Like a fair flower surcharged with dew, she weeps,
And words addressed seem into tears dissolved,
Wetting the borders of her silken veil. 730
But now again she makes address to speak.

DALILA. With doubtful feet and wavering resolution
I came, still dreading thy displeasure, Samson;
Which to have merited, without excuse,
I cannot but acknowledge. Yet, if tears 735
May expiate (though the fact more evil drew
In the perverse event than I foresaw),[3]
My penance hath not slackened, though my pardon
No way assured. But conjugal affection,
Prevailing over fear and timorous doubt, 740
Hath led me on, desirous to behold
Once more thy face, and know of thy estate,[4]
If aught in my ability may serve
To lighten what thou suffer'st, and appease
Thy mind with what amends is in my power— 745

---

8. Agent, but with a religious connotation as well.
9. Tarsus (the birthplace of St. Paul) is a trading city in modern Turkey; the isles of Javan are the isles of Greece, supposed to be populated by descendants of Javan, son of Noah's son Japhet. Gadire is modern Cadiz in Spain. Many of these geographical details are to be found an Isaiah II.lxvi, etc.
1. Ambergris.
2. The circling, mocking, derisive description of the chorus carefully holds Samson in suspense till the last minute.
3. I.e., my action turned out worse than I intended.
4. Condition.

Though late, yet in some part to recompense
My rash but more unfortunate misdeed.
SAMSON. Out, out, hyena! [5] These are thy wonted arts,
    And arts of every woman false like thee,
    To break all faith, all vows, deceive, betray;   750
    Then, as repentant, to submit, beseech,
    And reconcilement move with feigned remorse,
    Confess, and promise wonders in her change—
    Not truly penitent, but chief to try
    Her husband, how far urged his patience bears,   755
    His virtue or weakness which way to assail:
    Then, with more cautious and instructed skill,
    Again transgresses, and again submits;
    That wisest and best men, full oft beguiled,
    With goodness principled not to reject   760
    The penitent, but ever to forgive,
    Are drawn to wear out miserable days,
    Entangled with a poisonous bosom-snake,
    If not by quick destruction soon cut off,
    As I by thee, to ages an example.   765
DALILA. Yet hear me, Samson, not that I endeavor
    To lessen or extenuate my offense,
    But that, on th' other side, if it be weighed
    By itself, with aggravations not surcharged,
    Or else with just allowance counterpoised,   770
    I may, if possible, thy pardon find
    The easier towards me, or thy hatred less.
    First granting, as I do, it was a weakness
    In me, but incident to all our sex,
    Curiosity, inquisitive, importune   775
    Of secrets, then with like infirmity
    To publish them, both common female faults,
    Was it not weakness also to make known,
    For importunity, that is for naught,
    Wherein consisted all thy strength and safety?   780
    To what I did thou show'dst me first the way.
    But I to enemies revealed, and should not!
    Nor should'st thou have trusted that to woman's frailty: [6]
    Ere I to thee, thou to thyself wast cruel.
    Let weakness, then, with weakness come to parle,[7]   785
    So near related, or the same of kind;
    Thine forgive mine, that men may censure thine
    The gentler, if severely thou exact not
    More strength from me than in thyself was found.

---

5. Apart from being an animal of odious habits and appearance, the hyena was a traditional beast of hypocrisy, supposed to entice men to destruction by its power of imitating the human voice.
6. Like Eve, who wore down Adam with importunity, then blamed him for giving in (*Paradise Lost* IX.1155–61) Dalila blames Samson for doing what she herself has demanded.
7. Parley, agreement.

And what if love, which thou interpret'st hate,   790
The jealousy of love, powerful of sway
In human hearts, nor less in mine towards thee,
Caused what I did? I saw thee mutable
Of fancy; feared lest one day thou would'st leave me,
As her at Timna; sought by all means, therefore,   795
How to endear, and hold thee to me firmest:
No better way I saw than by importuning
To learn thy secrets, get into my power
Thy key of strength and safety. Thou wilt say,
"Why, then, revealed?" I was assured by those   800
Who tempted me that nothing was designed
Against thee but safe custody and hold.
That made for me; I knew that liberty
Would draw thee forth to perilous enterprises,
While I at home sat full of cares and fears,   805
Wailing thy absence in my widowed bed;
Here I should still enjoy thee, day and night,
Mine and love's prisoner, not the Philistines',
Whole to myself, unhazarded abroad,
Fearless at home of partners in my love.   810
These reasons in love's law have passed for good,
Though fond [8] and reasonless to some perhaps;
And love hath oft, well meaning, wrought much woe,
Yet always pity or pardon hath obtained.
Be not unlike all others, not austere   815
As thou art strong, inflexible as steel.
If thou in strength all mortals dost exceed,
In uncompassionate anger do not so.
SAMSON. How cunningly the sorceress displays
Her own transgressions, to upbraid me mine!   820
That malice, not repentance, brought thee hither,
By this appears. I gave, thou say'st, th' example,
I led the way—bitter reproach, but true;
I to myself was false ere thou to me.
Such pardon, therefore, as I give my folly   825
Take to thy wicked deed; which when thou seest
Impartial, self-severe, inexorable,
Thou wilt renounce thy seeking, and much rather
Confess it feigned. Weakness is thy excuse,
And I believe it, weakness to resist   830
Philistian gold. If weakness may excuse,
What murderer, what traitor, parricide,
Incestuous, sacrilegious, but may plead it?
All wickedness is weakness; that plea, therefore,
With God or man will gain thee no remission.   835
But love constrained thee! Call it furious rage
To satisfy thy lust. Love seeks to have love;

8. Foolish.

My love how could'st thou hope, who took'st the way
To raise in me inexpiable [9] hate,
Knowing, as needs I must, by thee betrayed?   840
In vain thou striv'st to cover shame with shame,
Or by evasions thy crime uncover'st more.
DALILA. Since thou determin'st weakness for no plea
In man or woman, though to thy own condemning,
Hear what assaults I had, what snares besides,   845
What sieges girt me round, ere I consented;
Which might have awed the best resolved of men,
The constantest, to have yielded without blame.
It was not gold, as to my charge thou lay'st,
That wrought with me.[1] Thou know'st the magistrates   850
And princes of my country came in person,
Solicited, commanded, threatened, urged,
Adjured by all the bonds of civil duty
And of religion—pressed how just it was,
How honorable, how glorious, to entrap   855
A common enemy, who had destroyed
Such numbers of our nation: and the priest
Was not behind, but ever at my ear,
Preaching how meritorious with the gods
It would be to ensnare an irreligious   860
Dishonorer of Dagon. What had I
To oppose against such powerful arguments?
Only my love of thee held long debate,
And combated in silence all these reasons
With hard contest. At length, that grounded maxim,   865
So rife and celebrated in the mouths
Of wisest men, that to the public good
Private respects must yield,[2] with grave authority
Took full possession of me, and prevailed;
Virtue, as I thought, truth, duty, so enjoining.   870
SAMSON. I thought where all thy circling wiles would end,
In feigned religion, smooth hypocrisy!
But, had thy love, still odiously pretended,
Been, as it ought, sincere, it would have taught thee
Far other reasonings, brought forth other deeds.   875
I, before all the daughters of my tribe
And of my nation, chose thee from among
My enemies, loved thee, as too well thou knew'st;
Too well; unbosomed all my secrets to thee,
Not out of levity, but overpowered   880
By thy request, who could deny thee nothing;
Yet now am judged an enemy. Why, then,

---

9. Inextinguishable.
1. Judges xvi is very explicit that Dalila betrayed Samson for money—eleven hundred pieces of silver offered her by each one of the Philistine lords.

2. Reason of state, political expediency, was in Milton's eyes the worst of all possible motives for an action. Cf. *Paradise Lost* IV. 393–94.

Didst thou at first receive me for thy husband,
Then, as since then, thy country's foe professed?
Being once a wife, for me thou wast to leave   885
Parents and country; nor was I their subject,
Nor under their protection, but my own;
Thou mine, not theirs.[3] If aught against my life
Thy country sought of thee, it sought unjustly,
Against the law of nature, law of nations;   890
No more thy country, but an impious crew
Of men conspiring to uphold their state
By worse than hostile deeds, violating the ends
For which our country is a name so dear;
Not therefore to be obeyed. But zeal moved thee;   895
To please thy gods thou didst it! Gods unable
To acquit themselves and prosecute their foes
But by ungodly deeds, the contradiction
Of their own deity, gods cannot be;
Less therefore to be pleased, obeyed, or feared.   900
These false pretexts and varnished colors failing,
Bare in thy guilt, how foul must thou appear!
DALILA. In argument with men a woman ever
      Goes by the worse,[4] whatever be her cause.
SAMSON. For want of words, no doubt, or lack of breath!   905
      Witness when I was worried with thy peals.
DALILA. I was a fool, too rash, and quite mistaken
      In what I thought would have succeeded best.
      Let me obtain forgiveness of thee, Samson;
      Afford me place to show what recompense   910
      Towards thee I intend for what I have misdone,
      Misguided. Only what remains past cure
      Bear not too sensibly,[5] nor still insist
      To afflict thyself in vain. Though sight be lost,
      Life yet hath many solaces, enjoyed   915
      Where other senses want not their delights—
      At home, in leisure and domestic ease,
      Exempt from many a care and chance to which
      Eyesight exposes, daily, men abroad.
      I to the lords will intercede, not doubting   920
      Their favorable ear, that I may fetch thee
      From forth this loathsome prison house, to abide
      With me, where my redoubled love and care,
      With nursing diligence, to me glad office,
      May ever tend about thee to old age,   925
      With all things grateful cheered, and so supplied
      That what by me thou hast lost thou least shalt miss.
SAMSON. No, no; of my condition take no care;

3. I.e., you were under my protection, not theirs.
4. Comes off second best.
5. "Too sensibly": with too great sensitivity.

It fits not; thou and I long since are twain;
Nor think me so unwary or accursed [6]   930
To bring my feet again into the snare
Where once I have been caught. I know thy trains,
Though dearly to my cost, thy gins, and toils.[7]
Thy fair enchanted cup, and warbling charms,
No more on me have power; their force is nulled;   935
So much of adder's wisdom I have learned,
To fence my ear against thy sorceries.[8]
If in my flower of youth and strength, when all men
Loved, honored, feared me, thou alone could hate me,
Thy husband, slight me, sell me, and forgo me,   940
How would'st thou use me now, blind, and thereby
Deceivable, in most things as a child
Helpless, thence easily contemned and scorned,
And last neglected! How would'st thou insult,
When I must live uxorious to thy will   945
In perfect thraldom! how again betray me,
Bearing my words and doings to the lords
To gloss upon, and, censuring, frown or smile! [9]
This jail I count the house of liberty
To thine, whose doors my feet shall never enter.   950
DALILA. Let me approach at least, and touch thy hand.
SAMSON. Not for thy life, lest fierce remembrance wake
My sudden rage to tear thee joint by joint.[1]
At distance I forgive thee, go with that;
Bewail thy falsehood, and the pious works   955
It hath brought forth to make thee memorable
Among illustrious women, faithful wives;
Cherish thy hastened widowhood with the gold
Of matrimonial treason: so farewell.
DALILA. I see thou art implacable, more deaf   960
To prayers than winds and seas. Yet winds to seas
Are reconciled at length, and sea to shore:
Thy anger, unappeasable, still rages,
Eternal tempest never to be calmed.
Why do I humble thus myself, and, suing   965
For peace, reap nothing but repulse and hate,
Bid go with evil omen,[2] and the brand
Of infamy upon my name denounced?
To mix with thy concernments I desist
Henceforth, nor too much disapprove my own.   970

---

6. I.e., so neglectful or bewitched.
7. "Trains": tricks; "gins": snares;
"toils": nets. The traditional images for
female wiles are heightened by reference
to an enchanting cup and warbled charms
reminiscent of Homer's Circe (*Odyssey*,
X).
8. Psalm lviii verses 4 and 5 describes
the "deaf adder that stoppeth her ear;
which will not hearken to the voice of

charmers, charming never so wisely."
9. Milton's libertarian hatred of censorship and managed liberty is very apparent.
1. What Samson might remember, at the touch of Dalila, which would lead him to tear her to pieces, is a problem in domestic psychology.
2. I.e., dismissed with threats of ill fame.

Fame, if not double-faced, is double-mouthed,
And with contrary blast proclaims most deeds; [3]
On both his wings, one black, th' other white,
Bears greatest names in his wild airy flight.
My name, perhaps, among the circumcised   975
In Dan, in Judah, and the bordering tribes,
To all posterity may stand defamed,
With malediction mentioned, and the blot
Of falsehood most unconjugal traduced.
But in my country, where I most desire,   980
In Ecron, Gaza, Asdod, and in Gath,
I shall be named among the famousest
Of women, sung at solemn festivals,
Living and dead recorded, who to save
Her country from a fierce destroyer chose   985
Above the faith of wedlock bands; my tomb
With odors [4] visited and annual flowers;
Not less renowned than in Mount Ephraim
Jael, who, with inhospitable guile,
Smote Sisera sleeping,[5] through the temples nailed.   990
Nor shall I count it heinous to enjoy
The public marks of honor and reward
Conferred upon me for the piety
Which to my country I was judged to have shown.
At this whoever envies or repines,   995
I leave him to his lot, and like my own.
CHORUS. She's gone, a manifest serpent by her sting
      Discovered in the end, till now concealed.
SAMSON. So let her go. God sent her to debase me,
      And aggravate my folly, who committed   1000
      To such a viper his most sacred trust
      Of secrecy, my safety, and my life.
CHORUS. Yet beauty, though injurious, hath strange power,
      After offense returning, to regain
      Love once possessed, nor can be easily   1005
      Repulsed, without much inward passion [6] felt,
      And secret sting of amorous remorse.
SAMSON. Love-quarrels oft in pleasing concord end;
      Not wedlock-treachery, endangering life.
CHORUS. It is not virtue, wisdom, valor, wit,   1010
      Strength, comeliness of shape, or amplest merit,
      That woman's love can win, or long inherit; [7]
      But what it is hard is to say,
      Harder to hit,

---

3. The figure of Fame, in Milton's youthful poem *On the Fifth of November*, does indeed have a double tongue, one for truth and one for lies. Fame or Rumor was a favorite grotesque allegorical figure in classical poets like Ovid (*Metamorphoses* XII.43 ff.) and Virgil (*Aeneid* IV.173 ff.).

4. Perfumes.
5. Jael lured Sisera, who saw in her the wife of his ally and friend, into a tent, and there drove a large nail into his head (Judges iv.17–21).
6. Suffering.
7. Possess.

Which way soever men refer it   1015
(Much like thy riddle, Samson),[8] in one day
Or seven though one should musing sit.
    If any of these, or all, the Timnian bride
Had not so soon preferred
Thy paranymph, worthless to thee compared,   1020
Successor in thy bed,[9]
Nor both so loosely disallied
Their nuptials,[1] nor this last so treacherously
Had shorn the fatal harvest of thy head.
Is it for that [2] such outward ornament   1025
Was lavished on their sex, that inward gifts
Were left for haste unfinished, judgment scant,
Capacity not raised to apprehend
Or value what is best
In choice, but oftest to affect [3] the wrong?   1030
Or was too much of self-love mixed,
Of constancy no root infixed,
That either they love nothing, or not long?
    Whate'er it be, to wisest men and best,
Seeming at first all heavenly under virgin veil,   1035
Soft, modest, meek, demure,
Once joined, the contrary she proves, a thorn
Intestine,[4] far within defensive arms
A cleaving [5] mischief, in his way to virtue
Adverse and turbulent; or by her charms   1040
Draws him awry, enslaved
With dotage, and his sense depraved
To folly and shameful deeds, which ruin ends.
What pilot so expert but needs must wreck,
Embarked with such a steers-mate at the helm?   1045
    Favored of Heaven who finds
One virtuous, rarely found,
That in domestic good combines:
Happy that house! his way to peace is smooth:
But virtue which breaks through all opposition,   1050
And all temptation can remove,
Most shines and most is acceptable above.
    Therefore God's universal law
Gave to the man despotic power
Over his female in due awe,   1055
Nor from that right to part an hour,
Smile she or lour:
So shall he least confusion draw
On his whole life, not swayed

8. Samson's riddle is propounded and answered in Judges xiv, verses 14 and 18.
9. I.e., if any of these ("virtue, . . . ," lines 1010–11) sufficed, Samson's wife (the Timnian bride) would not have preferred to marry his "paranymph" (best man). See Judges xiv.
1. I.e., nor would both your wives have been so careless about their marriage vows.
2. Because.
3. Desire.
4. An inward thorn, a viper in the bosom.
5. Clinging; a traditional emblem of marriage was the elm and the vine.

By female usurpation, nor dismayed.   1060
    But had we best retire? I see a storm.
SAMSON. Fair days have oft contracted [6] wind and rain.
CHORUS. But this another kind of tempest brings.
SAMSON. Be less abstruse; my riddling days are past.
CHORUS. Look now for no enchanting voice, nor fear   1065
    The bait of honeyed words; a rougher tongue
    Draws hitherward, I know him by his stride,
    The giant Harapha [7] of Gath, his look
    Haughty, as is his pile [8] high-built and proud.
    Comes he in peace? What wind hath blown him hither   1070
    I less conjecture than when first I saw
    The sumptuous Dalila floating this way: [9]
    His habit carries peace, his brow defiance.
SAMSON. Or peace or not, alike to me he comes.
CHORUS. His fraught [1] we soon shall know: he now arrives.   1075
HARAPHA. I come not, Samson, to condole thy chance,
    As these [2] perhaps, yet wish it had not been,
    Though for no friendly intent. I am of Gath;
    Men call me Harapha, of stock renowned
    As Og, or Anak, and the Emims old   1080
    That Kiriathaim held.[3] Thou know'st me now,
    If thou at all art known.[4] Much I have heard
    Of thy prodigious might and feats performed,
    Incredible to me, in this displeased,
    That I was never present on the place   1085
    Of those encounters, where we might have tried
    Each other's force in camp or listed field; [5]
    And now am come to see of whom such noise
    Hath walked about, and each limb to survey,
    If thy appearance answer loud report.   1090
SAMSON. The way to know were not to see, but taste.[6]
HARAPHA. Dost thou already single [7] me? I thought
    Gyves and the mill had tamed thee. O that fortune
    Had brought me to the field where thou art famed
    To have wrought such wonders with an ass's jaw!   1095
    I should have forced thee soon wish [8] other arms,

6. Drawn after them.
7. Harapha does not appear at all within the story told in the Book of Judges; Milton invented him with the help of some hints from the image of Goliath in I Samuel xvii and some other giants in II Samuel xxi. *Rapha* means giant in Hebrew.
8. Body; with the suggestion that he is tall as a tower.
9. That the various visitors of Samson are blown hither and yon by the winds of occasion serves to emphasize the deep steadiness of Samson's final resolution.
1. Intent.
2. The chorus of Danites, naturally sympathetic to Samson.
3. Og was a giant King of Bashan in Deuteronomy iii.11; Anak and his sons were giants in Numbers xiii.33; the Emims were giants in Deuteronomy ii. 10–11 and Genesis xiv.5.
4. I.e., you know me now if you know anything; but also "if you are anyone worth knowing." Compare Satan's brag to Zephon and Ithuriel, "Not to know me argues yourselves unknown." *Paradise Lost* IV.830.
5. "Camp": field of battle (from Latin, *campus*); "listed field": lists, tourney-ground.
6. Make a trial of.
7. Challenge; "gyves": chains.
8. Eighteenth-century editors changed "wish" to "with", easing the grammar at the expense of the sense.

Or left thy carcass where the ass lay thrown;
So had the glory of prowess been recovered
To Palestine, won by a Philistine
From the unforeskinned race, of whom thou bear'st   1100
The highest name for valiant acts. That honor,
Certain to have won by mortal duel from thee,
I lose, prevented by thy eyes put out.

SAMSON. Boast not of what thou would'st have done, but do
What then thou would'st; thou seest it in thy hand.   1105

HARAPHA. To combat with a blind man I disdain,
And thou hast need much washing to be touched.

SAMSON. Such usage as your honorable lords
Afford me, assassinated [9] and betrayed;
Who durst not with their whole united powers   1110
In fight withstand me single and unarmed,
Nor in the house with chamber ambushes [1]
Close-banded durst attack me, no, not sleeping,
Till they had hired a woman with their gold,
Breaking her marriage-faith, to circumvent me.   1115
Therefore, without feigned shifts, let be assigned
Some narrow place enclosed, where sight may give thee,
Or rather flight, no great advantage on me;
Then put on all thy gorgeous arms, thy helmet
And brigandine of brass, thy broad habergeon,   1120
Vant-brace and greaves and gauntlet; [2] add thy spear,
A weaver's beam, and seven-times-folded shield:
I only with an oaken staff will meet thee,
And raise such outcries on thy clattered iron,
Which long shall not withhold me from thy head,   1125
That in a little time, while breath remains thee,
Thou oft shalt wish thyself at Gath, to boast
Again in safety what thou would'st have done
To Samson, but shalt never see Gath more.

HARAPHA. Thou durst not thus disparage glorious arms,   1130
Which greatest heroes have in battle worn,
Their ornament and safety, had not spells
And black enchantments, some magician's art,
Armed thee or charmed thee strong, which thou from Heaven
Feign'dst at thy birth was given thee in thy hair,   1135
Where strength can least abide, though all thy hairs
Were bristles ranged like those that ridge the back
Of chafed wild boars or ruffled porcupines.

SAMSON. I know no spells, use no forbidden arts;
My trust is in the Living God, who gave me,   1140

---

9. Treacherously assailed.
1. Samson refers to the four occasions
on which Philistines hid in his bedroom
while Dalila tried unsuccessfully to betray him to them.
2. "Brigandine": a padded chest-protec-
tor, covered with iron scales or rings;
"habergeon": a coat of mail, a hauberk;

"vant-brace": a steel cuff for the fore-
arm; greaves protect the shins and
thighs, and gauntlets the hands. A
weaver's beam, emblem of weightiness,
is used to keep threads hanging tautly
in a loom. All these military details are
from the description of Goliath, I Samuel
xvii.4–7.

At my nativity, this strength, diffused
No less through all my sinews, joints, and bones,
Than thine, while I preserved these locks unshorn,
The pledge of my unviolated vow.
For proof hereof, if Dagon be thy god, 1145
Go to his temple, invocate his aid
With solemnest devotion, spread before him
How highly it concerns his glory now
To frustrate and dissolve these magic spells,
Which I to be the power of Israel's God 1150
Avow, and challenge Dagon to the test,
Offering to combat thee, his champion bold,
With th' utmost of his godhead seconded:
Then thou shalt see, or rather to thy sorrow
Soon feel, whose God is strongest, thine or mine. 1155
HARAPHA. Presume not on thy God. Whate'er he be,
Thee he regards not, owns not, hath cut off
Quite from his people, and delivered up
Into thy enemies' hand; permitted them
To put out both thine eyes, and fettered send thee 1160
Into the common prison, there to grind
Among the slaves and asses, thy comrádes,
As good for nothing else, no better service
With those thy boisterous locks; no worthy match
For valor to assail, nor by the sword 1165
Of noble warrior, so to stain his honor,
But by the barber's razor best subdued.
SAMSON. All these indignities, for such they are
From thine,[3] these evils I deserve and more,
Acknowledge them from God inflicted on me 1170
Justly, yet despair not of his final pardon,
Whose ear is ever open, and his eye
Gracious to re-admit the suppliant;
In confidence whereof I once again
Defy thee to the trial of mortal fight, 1175
By combat to decide whose god is God,
Thine, or whom I with Israel's sons adore.
HARAPHA. Fair honor that thou dost thy God, in trusting
He will accept thee to defend his cause,
A murderer, a revolter, and a robber! 1180
SAMSON. Tongue-doughty giant, how dost thou prove me these?
HARAPHA. Is not thy nation subject to our lords?
Their magistrates confessed it when they took thee
As a league-breaker, and delivered bound
Into our hands; [4] for hadst not committed 1185

3. Thy people.
4. Judges xiv.8–20 and xv.9–15 describe the episode. Samson when he came to Timna to be married proposed a riddle and a bet to the marriage guests; they got his intended bride to reveal the riddle, and in revenge he killed thirty of their people and left the lady to the "paranymph," or best man. Old Testament Samson is indeed a rude and savage figure; Milton, with characteristic confidence, undertakes his legal defense in everything.

Notorious murder on those thirty men
At Ascalon, who never did thee harm,
Then, like a robber, stripp'dst them of their robes?
The Philistines, when thou hadst broke the league,
Went up with arméd powers thee only seeking,   1190
To others did no violence nor spoil.
SAMSON. Among the daughters of the Philistines
   I chose a wife, which argued me no foe,
   And in your city held my nuptial feast;
   But your ill-meaning politician lords,   1195
   Under pretense of bridal friends and guests,
   Appointed to await me thirty spies,
   Who, threatening cruel death, constrained the bride
   To wring from me, and tell to them, my secret,
   That solved the riddle which I had proposed.   1200
   When I perceived all set on enmity,
   As on my enemies, wherever chanced,
   I used hostility, and took their spoil,
   To pay my underminers in their coin.
   My nation was subjected to your lords![5]   1205
   It was the force of conquest; force with force
   Is well ejected when the conquered can.
   But I, a private person, whom my country
   As a league-breaker gave up bound, presumed
   Single rebellion, and did hostile acts!   1210
   I was no private,[6] but a person raised,
   With strength sufficient, and command from Heaven,
   To free my country. If their servile minds
   Me, their deliverer sent, would not receive,
   But to their masters gave me up for nought,   1215
   Th' unworthier they; whence to this day they serve.
   I was to do my part from Heaven assigned,
   And had performed it if my known offense
   Had not disabled me, not all your force.
   These shifts refuted, answer thy appellant,[7]   1220
   Though by his blindness maimed for high attempts,
   Who now defies thee thrice to single fight,
   As a petty enterprise of small enforce.[8]
HARAPHA. With thee, a man condemned, a slave enrolled,
   Due by the law to capital punishment?   1225
   To fight with thee no man of arms will deign.
SAMSON. Cam'st thou for this, vain boaster, to survey me,
   To descant on my strength, and give thy verdict?
   Come nearer; part not hence so slight informed;
   But take good heed my hand survey not thee.   1230
HARAPHA. O Baal-zebub![9] can my ears unused

---

5. I.e., you argue that my nation was subjected to your lords.
6. Outlaw.
7. I.e., now that we've disposed of these dodges, answer your challenger. "Apel-lant": literally, caller, one who calls you out.
8. Difficulty.
9. Baal-zebub is Beelzebub, god of the flies.

Hear these dishonors, and not render death?

SAMSON. No man withholds thee; nothing from thy hand
    Fear I incurable; bring up thy van; [1]
    My heels are fettered, but my fist is free.   1235

HARAPHA. This insolence other kind of answer fits.

SAMSON. Go, baffled coward, lest I run upon thee,
    Though in these chains, bulk without spirit vast,
    And with one buffet lay thy structure low,
    Or swing thee in the air, then dash thee down,   1240
    To the hazard of thy brains and shattered sides.

HARAPHA. By Astaroth,[2] ere long thou shalt lament
    These braveries,[3] in irons loaden on thee.

CHORUS. His giantship is gone somewhat crestfallen,
    Stalking with less unconscionable [4] strides,   1245
    And lower looks, but in a sultry chafe.

SAMSON. I dread him not, nor all his giant brood,
    Though fame divulge him father of five sons,
    All of gigantic size, Goliath chief.[5]

CHORUS. He will directly to the lords, I fear,   1250
    And with malicious counsel stir them up
    Some way or other yet further to afflict thee.

SAMSON. He must allege some cause, and offered fight
    Will not dare mention, lest a question rise
    Whether he durst accept the offer or not;   1255
    And that he durst not plain enough appeared.
    Much more affliction than already felt
    They cannot well impose, nor I sustain,
    If they intend advantage of my labors,
    The work of many hands, which earns my keeping,   1260
    With no small profit daily to my owners.
    But come what will; my deadliest foe will prove
    My speediest friend, by death to rid me hence;
    The worst that he can give to me the best.
    Yet so it may fall out, because their end   1265
    Is hate, not help to me, it may with mine
    Draw their own ruin who attempt the deed.

CHORUS. O, how comely it is, and how reviving
    To the spirits of just men long oppressed,
    When God into the hands of their deliverer   1270
    Puts invincible might,
    To quell the mighty of the earth, th' oppressor,
    The brute and boisterous force of violent men,
    Hardy and industrious to support
    Tyrannic power, but raging to pursue   1275
    The righteous, and all such as honor truth!

---

1. The vanguard of an army was, naturally, the first group engaged. Samson invites Harapha to start the fight.
2. Moon-goddess of the Philistines, consort of Dagon. See *Paradise Lost* I.437–46.
3. Boasts.
4. Excessive.
5. II Samuel xxi describes four giants "born to the giant in Gath" and slain by David; Milton makes the identification with Harapha on his own.

He all their ammunition
And feats of war defeats,[6]
With plain heroic magnitude of mind
And celestial vigor armed;   1280
Their armories and magazines contemns,
Renders them useless, while
With wingéd expedition [7]
Swift as the lightning glance he executes
His errand on the wicked, who, surprised,   1285
Lose their defense, distracted and amazed.
    But patience is more oft the exercise
Of saints, the trial of their fortitude,
Making them each his own deliverer,
And victor over all   1290
That tyranny or fortune can inflict.
Either of these is in thy lot,[8]
Samson, with might endued
Above the sons of men; but sight bereaved
May chance to number thee with those   1295
Whom patience finally must crown.[9]
    This Idol's day hath been to thee no day of rest,
Laboring thy mind
More than the working day thy hands.
And yet, perhaps, more trouble is behind;   1300
For I descry this way
Some other tending; in his hand
A scepter or quaint [1] staff he bears,
Comes on amain, speed in his look.
By his habit I discern him now   1305
A public officer, and now at hand.
His message will be short and voluble.[2]
OFFICER. Ebrews, the prisoner Samson here I seek.
CHORUS. His manacles remark [3] him; there he sits.
OFFICER. Samson, to thee our lords thus bid me say: 1310
    This day to Dagon is a solemn feast,
    With sacrifices, triumph, pomp, and games;
    Thy strength they know surpassing human rate,
    And now some public proof thereof require
    To honor this great feast, and great assembly.   1315
    Rise, therefore, with all speed, and come along,
    Where I will see thee heartened and fresh clad,
    To appear as fits before th' illustrious lords.
SAMSON. Thou know'st I am an Ebrew; therefore tell them
    Our law forbids at their religious rites   1320
    My presence; for that cause I cannot come.

6. A touch of the pervasive Miltonic
punning.
7. Haste.
8. Fate.
9. The Christian tragedy, like the Christian epic, must center ultimately on an
act of passive, not active, fortitude. It
is the special achievement of Samson to
combine in a single action both qualities.
1. Ornamented.
2. To the point.
3. Distinguish.

OFFICER. This answer, be assured, will not content them.
SAMSON. Have they not sword-players, and every sort
 Of gymnic artists, wrestlers, riders, runners,
 Jugglers and dancers, antics, mummers, mimics,[4]   1325
 But they must pick me out, with shackles tired,
 And over-labored at their public mill,
 To make them sport with blind activity?
 Do they not seek occasion of new quarrels,
 On my refusal, to distress me more,   1330
 Or make a game of my calamities?
 Return the way thou cam'st; I will not come.
OFFICER. Regard thyself; this will offend them highly.
SAMSON. Myself? my conscience, and internal peace.
 Can they think me so broken, so debased   1335
 With corporal servitude, that my mind ever
 Will condescend to such absurd commands?
 Although their drudge, to be their fool or jester,
 And, in my midst of sorrow and heart-grief,
 To show them feats, and play before their god,   1340
 The worst of all indignities, yet on me
 Joined [5] with supreme contempt! I will not come.
OFFICER. My message was imposed on me with speed,
 Brooks no delay: is this thy resolution?
SAMSON. So take it with what speed thy message needs.   1345
OFFICER. I am sorry what this stoutness [6] will produce.
SAMSON. Perhaps thou shalt have cause to sorrow indeed.
CHORUS. Consider, Samson; matters now are strained
 Up to the height, whether to hold or break.
 He's gone, and who knows how he may report   1350
 Thy words by adding fuel to the flame?
 Expect another message, more imperious,
 More lordly thundering than thou well wilt bear.
SAMSON. Shall I abuse this consecrated gift
 Of strength, again returning with my hair   1355
 After my great transgression, so requite
 Favor renewed, and add a greater sin
 By prostituting holy things to idols,
 A Nazarite, in place abominable,
 Vaunting my strength in honor to their Dagon?   1360
 Besides how vile, contemptible, ridiculous,
 What act more execrably unclean,[7] profane?
CHORUS. Yet with this strength thou serv'st the Philistines,
 Idolatrous, uncircumcised, unclean.
SAMSON. Not in their idol-worship, but by labor   1365
 Honest and lawful to deserve my food
 Of those who have me in their civil power.
CHORUS. Where the heart joins not, outward acts defile not.

---

4. "Gymnic artists": gymnasts; "an-   6. Defiance.
tics": clowns; "mummers": actors.   7. Taboo.
5. Enjoined, ordered.

SAMSON. Where outward force constrains, the sentence holds: [8]
  But who constrains me to the temple of Dagon,   1370
  Not dragging? The Philistian lords command:
  Commands are no constraints. If I obey them,
  I do it freely, venturing to displease
  God for the fear of man, and man prefer,
  Set God behind; which, in his jealousy,   1375
  Shall never, unrepented, find forgiveness.
  Yet that he may dispense with me, or thee,
  Present in temples at idolatrous rites
  For some important cause,[9] thou need'st not doubt.
CHORUS. How thou wilt here come off surmounts my reach.   1380
SAMSON. Be of good courage; I begin to feel
  Some rousing motions in me, which dispose
  To something extraordinary my thoughts.
  I with this messenger will go along—
  Nothing to do, be sure, that may dishonor   1385
  Our Law, or stain my vow of Nazarite.
  If there be aught of presage in the mind,
  This day will be remarkable in my life
  By some great act, or of my days the last.[1]
CHORUS. In time thou hast resolved: the man returns.   1390
OFFICER. Samson, this second message from our lords
  To thee I am bid say: Art thou our slave,
  Our captive, at the public mill our drudge,
  And dar'st thou, at our sending and command,
  Dispute thy coming? Come without delay;   1395
  Or we shall find such engines to assail
  And hamper thee, as thou shalt come of force,
  Though thou wert firmlier fastened than a rock.
SAMSON. I could be well content to try their art,
  Which to no few of them would prove pernicious;   1400
  Yet, knowing their advantages too many,
  Because [2] they shall not trail me through their streets
  Like a wild beast, I am content to go.
  Masters' commands come with a power resistless
  To such as owe them absolute subjection;   1405
  And for a life who will not change his purpose?
  (So mutable are all the ways of men!)
  Yet this be sure, in nothing to comply
  Scandalous or forbidden in our Law.
OFFICER. I praise thy resolution.[3] Doff these links: 1410
  By this compliance thou wilt win the lords
  To favor, and perhaps to set thee free.

---

8. I.e., where outward force constrains, your motto may be right.
9. God will make a special dispensation for Samson to attend idolatrous ceremonies "for some important cause," which Samson cannot yet define but which he intuits.
1. By a classic device of dramatic irony, Samson proposes as alternatives two events which will both simultaneously come true. "Presage": premonition, presight
2. So that.
3. Decision. "Doff these links": take off these chains.

SAMSON. Brethren, farewell. Your company along
   I will not wish, lest it perhaps offend them
   To see me girt with friends; and how the sight   1415
   Of me, as of a common enemy,
   So dreaded once, may now exasperate them
   I know not. Lords are lordliest in their wine;
   And the well-feasted priest then soonest fired
   With zeal, if aught religion seem concerned; [4]   1420
   No less the people, on their holy-days,
   Impetuous, insolent, unquenchable.
   Happen what may, of me expect to hear
   Nothing dishonorable, impure, unworthy
   Our God, our Law, my nation, or myself;   1425
   The last of me or no I cannot warrant.
CHORUS. Go, and the Holy One
   Of Israel be thy guide
   To what may serve his glory best, and spread his name
   Great among the heathen round;   1430
   Send thee the angel of thy birth, to stand
   Fast by thy side, who from thy father's field
   Rode up in flames after his message told
   Of thy conception, and be now a shield
   Of fire; that Spirit that first rushed on thee   1435
   In the camp of Dan,
   Be efficacious in thee now at need! [5]
   For never was from Heaven imparted
   Measure of strength so great to mortal seed
   As in thy wondrous actions hath been seen.   1440
   But wherefore comes old Manoa in such haste
   With youthful steps? Much livelier than erewhile
   He seems: supposing here to find his son,
   Or of him bringing to us some glad news?
MANOA. Peace with you, brethren! My inducement hither   1445
   Was not at present here to find my son,
   By order of the lords new parted hence
   To come and play before them at their feast.
   I heard all as I came; the city rings,
   And numbers thither flock: I had no will,   1450
   Lest I should see him forced to things unseemly.
   But that which moved my coming now was chiefly
   To give ye part with me [6] what hope I have
   With good success to work his liberty.
CHORUS. That hope would much rejoice us to partake   1455
   With thee. Say, reverend sire; we thirst to hear.
MANOA. I have attempted, one by one, the lords,

4. Milton's animus against paid priests, whom he considers particularly likely to contaminate the Word of God with their own private interests and worldly desires, comes out plainly here.
5. Samson's angel, appearing before his birth and at various crises during his life (Judges xiv.6,19; xv.14) is here invoked almost as a tutelary spirit or guardian angel.
6. I.e., to impart to you.

Either at home, or through the high street passing,
With supplication prone and father's tears,
To accept of ransom for my son, their prisoner.   1460
Some much averse I found, and wondrous harsh,
Contemptuous, proud, set on revenge and spite;
That part most reverenced Dagon and his priests:
Others more moderate seeming, but their aim
Private reward, for which both God and State   1465
They easily would set to sale: a third
More generous far and civil, who confessed
They had enough revenged, having reduced
Their foe to misery beneath their fears;
The rest was magnanimity to remit,   1470
If some convenient ransom were proposed.[7]
What noise or shout was that? It tore the sky.

CHORUS. Doubtless the people shouting to behold
  Their once great dread, captive and blind before them,
  Or at some proof of strength before them shown.   1475

MANOA. His ransom, if my whole inheritance
  May compass it, shall willingly be paid
  And numbered down. Much rather I shall choose
  To live the poorest in my tribe, than richest
  And he in that calamitous prison left.   1480
  No, I am fixed not to part hence without him.
  For his redemption all my patrimony,
  If need be, I am ready to forgo
  And quit. Not wanting him, I shall want nothing.

CHORUS. Fathers are wont to lay up for their sons;   1485
  Thou for thy son art bent to lay out all:
  Sons wont to nurse their parents in old age;
  Thou in old age car'st how to nurse thy son,
  Made older than thy age through eyesight lost.

MANOA. It shall be my delight to tend his eyes,   1490
  And view him sitting in his house, ennobled
  With all those high exploits by him achieved,
  And on his shoulders waving down those locks
  That of a nation armed the strength contained.
  And I persuade me God hath not permitted   1495
  His strength again to grow up with his hair
  Garrisoned round about him like a camp
  Of faithful soldiery, were not his purpose
  To use him further yet in some great service—
  Not to sit idle with so great a gift   1500
  Useless, and thence ridiculous, about him.[8]
  And, since his strength with eyesight was not lost,

---

7. The three parties are in effect bigots, swindlers, and gentlemen—three types common enough in Restoration England, with whom Milton and the defeated Puritans must have had frequently to deal.
8. A good deal of the play deals with the concept of relevance and irrelevance; outward weapons and outward strength are often beside the point ("ridiculous") in the face of inward and spiritual powers.

God will restore him eyesight to [9] his strength.
CHORUS. Thy hopes are not ill founded, nor seem vain,
  Of his delivery, and thy joy thereon   1505
  Conceived, agreeable to a father's love;
  In both which we, as next,[1] participate.
MANOA. I know your friendly minds, and—O, what noise!
  Mercy of Heaven! what hideous noise was that?
  Horribly loud, unlike the former shout.   1510
CHORUS. Noise call you it, or universal groan,
  As if the whole inhabitation perished?
  Blood, death, and deathful deeds, are in that noise,
  Ruin,[2] destruction at the utmost point.
MANOA. Of ruin indeed methought I heard the noise.   1515
  Oh! it continues; they have slain my son.
CHORUS. Thy son is rather slaying them; that outcry
  From slaughter of one foe could not ascend.
MANOA. Some dismal accident it needs must be.
  What shall we do, stay here, or run and see?   1520
CHORUS. Best keep together here, lest, running thither,
  We unawares run into danger's mouth.
  This evil on the Philistines is fallen:
  From whom could else a general cry be heard?
  The sufferers then will scarce molest us here;   1525
  From other hands we need not much to fear.
  What if, his eyesight (for to Israel's God
  Nothing is hard) by miracle restored,
  He now be dealing dole [3] among his foes,
  And over heaps of slaughtered walk his way?   1530
MANOA. That were a joy presumptuous to be thought.
CHORUS. Yet God hath wrought things as incredible
  For his people of old; what hinders now?
MANOA. He can, I know, but doubt to think he will;
  Yet hope would fain subscribe, and tempts belief.   1535
  A little stay will bring some notice hither.
CHORUS. Of good or bad so great, of bad the sooner;
  For evil news rides post, while good news baits.[4]
  And to our wish I see one hither speeding—
  An Ebrew, as I guess, and of our tribe.   1540
MESSENGER.[5] O, whither shall I run, or which way fly
  The sight of this so horrid spectacle,
  Which erst [6] my eyes beheld, and yet behold?
  For dire imagination still pursues me.
  But providence or instinct of nature seems,   1545
  Or reason, though disturbed, and scarce consulted,
  To have guided me aright, I know not how,

9. To accompany.
1. "As next": as kinsmen.
2. From Latin *ruina*, downfall.
3. Wreaking havoc.
4. Pauses to renew (bait) the horses.
5. Greek tragedy forbade the representation on stage of actual bloodshed; a messenger is therefore a frequent figure at the end of the Greek tragedy, arriving posthaste from the scene of the final catastrophe, to deliver in a long set speech a descriptive report.
6. A moment ago.

To thee first, reverend Manoa, and to these
My countrymen, whom here I knew remaining,
As [7] at some distance from the place of horror,   1550
So in the sad event too much concerned.
MANOA. The accident was loud, and here before thee
With rueful cry; yet what it was we hear not.
No preface needs; thou seest we long to know.
MESSENGER. It would burst forth; but I recover breath,   1555
And sense distract, to know well what I utter.
MANOA. Tell us the sum; the circumstance defer.
MESSENGER. Gaza yet stands; but all her sons are fallen,
All in a moment overwhelmed and fallen.
MANOA. Sad, but thou know'st to Israelites not saddest   1560
The desolation of a hostile city.
MESSENGER. Feed on that first; there may in grief be surfeit.[8]
MANOA. Relate by whom.
MESSENGER.   By Samson.
MANOA.   That still lessens
The sorrow, and coverts it nigh to joy.
MESSENGER. Ah! Manoa, I refrain too suddenly   1565
To utter what will come at last too soon,
Lest evil tidings, with too rude irruption
Hitting thy agéd ear, should pierce too deep.
MANOA. Suspense in news is torture; speak them out.
MESSENGER. Then take the worst in brief: Samson is dead.   1570
MANOA. The worst indeed! O, all my hopes defeated
To free him hence! but Death, who sets all free,
Hath paid his ransom now and full discharge.
What windy [9] joy this day had I conceived,
Hopeful of his delivery, which now proves   1575
Abortive as the first-born bloom of spring
Nipped with the lagging rear of winter's frost!
Yet, ere I give the reins to grief, say first
How died he; death to life is crown or shame.
All by him fell, thou say'st; by whom fell he?   1580
What glorious hand gave Samson his death's wound?
MESSENGER. Unwounded of his enemies he fell.
MANOA. Wearied with slaughter, then, or how? explain.
MESSENGER. By his own hands.
MANOA.   Self-violence! What cause
Brought him so soon at variance with himself   1585
Among his foes?
MESENGER.   Inevitable cause
At once both to destroy and be destroyed.
The edifice, where all were met to see him,
Upon their heads and on his own he pulled.
MANOA. O lastly over-strong against thyself!   1590
A dreadful way thou took'st to thy revenge.

7. The construction "As . . . So . . ." is   to follow.
equivalent to a "Though . . . Yet . . .".   9. Empty and talky.
8. I.e., there may be all too much grief

More than enough we know; but, while things yet
Are in confusion, give us, if thou canst,
Eyewitness of what first or last was done,
Relation more particular and distinct.   1595
MESSENGER. Occasions drew me early to this city;
And, as the gates I entered with sunrise,
The morning trumpets festival proclaimed
Through each high street. Little I had dispatched,
When all abroad was rumored that this day   1600
Samson should be brought forth, to show the people
Proof of his mighty strength in feats and games.
I sorrowed at his captive state, but minded
Not to be absent at that spectacle.
The building was a spacious theater,   1605
Half round on two main pillars vaulted high,
With seats where all the lords, and each degree
Of sort,[1] might sit in order to behold;
The other side was open, where the throng
On banks and scaffolds under sky might stand:[2]   1610
I among these aloof obscurely stood.
The feast and noon grew high, and sacrifice
Had filled their hearts with mirth, high cheer, and wine,
When to their sports they turned. Immediately
Was Samson as a public servant brought,   1615
In their state livery clad: before him pipes
And timbrels;[3] on each side went arméd guards;
Both horse and foot before him and behind,
Archers and slingers, cataphracts[4] and spears.
At sight of him the people with a shout   1620
Rifted the air, clamoring their god with praise,
Who had made their dreadful enemy their thrall.
He patient, but undaunted, where they led him,
Came to the place; and what was set before him,
Which without help of eye might be assayed,[5]   1625
To heave, pull, draw, or break, he still performed
All with incredible, stupendious force,
None daring to appear antagonist.
At length, for intermission sake, they led him
Between the pillars; he his guide requested   1630
(For so from such as nearer stood we heard),
As over-tired, to let him lean a while
With both his arms on those two massy pillars,
That to the archéd roof gave main support.
He unsuspicious led him; which when Samson   1635
Felt in his arms, with head a while inclined,

---

1. Of rank.
2. The temple at Gaza comprised a covered pavilion or shell for the gentry, semi-circular in shape and supported at the center of the semi-circle by two pillars; on the open side, under the hot sun, and behind the stage, as it were, sat the common people.
3. Tambourines.
4. Armored horsemen on armored horses.
5. Attempted.

And eyes fast fixed, he stood, as one who prayed,
Or some great matter in his mind revolved:
At last, with head erect, thus cried aloud:
"Hitherto, Lords, what your commands imposed   1640
I have performed, as reason was, obeying,
Not without wonder or delight beheld;
Now, of my own accord,[6] such other trial
I mean to show you of my strength yet greater
As with amaze shall strike all who behold."   1645
This uttered, straining all his nerves,[7] he bowed;
As with the force of winds and waters pent
When mountains tremble,[8] those two massy pillars
With horrible convulsion to and fro
He tugged, he shook, till down they came, and drew   1650
The whole roof after them with burst of thunder
Upon the heads of all who sat beneath,
Lords, ladies, captains, counselors, or priests,
Their choice nobility and flower, not only
Of this, but each Philistian city round,   1655
Met from all parts to solemnize this feast.
Samson, with these immixed, inevitably
Pulled down the same destruction on himself;
The vulgar [9] only 'scaped, who stood without.
CHORUS. O dearly bought revenge, yet glorious!   1660
  Living or dying thou hast fulfilled
  The work for which thou wast foretold
  To Israel, and now li'st victorious
  Among thy slain self-killed;
  Not willingly, but tangled in the fold   1665
  Of dire Necessity,[1] whose law in death conjoined
  Thee with thy slaughtered foes, in number more
  Than all thy life had slain before.
SEMICHORUS. While their hearts were jocund and sublime,[2]
  Drunk with idolatry, drunk with wine   1670
  And fat regorged [3] of bulls and goats,
  Chaunting their idol, and preferring
  Before our living Dread, who dwells
  In Silo, his bright sanctuary,[4]
  Among them he a spirit of frenzy sent,   1675
  Who hurt their minds,
  And urged them on with mad desire
  To call in haste for their destroyer.
  They, only set on sport and play,

---

6. Latin, *mea sponte*, on spontaneous
impulse of conscience.
7. Muscles.
8. Earthquakes in Milton's day were
supposed to be the effect of escaping
winds and waters imprisoned (pent) beneath the earth.

9. The common people.
1. Samson must not be supposed guilty
of suicide. See above, lines 1586–87.
2. Joyous and exalted.
3. Greedily devoured.
4. Shiloh, where the Israelites established their tabernacle (Joshua xviii.1).

Unweetingly [5] importuned   1680
Their own destruction to come speedy upon them.
So fond are mortal men,
Fallen into wrath divine,
As their own ruin on themselves to invite,
Insensate left, or to sense reprobate,   1685
And with blindness internal [6] struck.
SEMICHORUS. But he, though blind of sight,
  Despised, and thought extinguished quite,
  With inward eyes illuminated,
  His fiery virtue roused   1690
From under ashes into sudden flame,
And as an evening dragon [7] came,
Assailant on the perchéd roosts
And nests in order ranged
Of tame villatic [8] fowl, but as an eagle   1695
His cloudless thunder bolted on their heads.
So Virtue, given for lost,[9]
Depressed and overthrown, as seemed,
Like that self-begotten bird,[1]
In the Arabian woods embossed,[2]   1700
That no second knows nor third,
And lay erewhile a holocaust,[3]
From out her ashy womb now teemed,
Revives, reflourishes, then vigorous most
When most unactive deemed;   1705
And, though her body die, her fame survives,
A secular [4] bird, ages of lives.
MANOA. Come, come; no time for lamentation now,
  Nor much more cause. Samson hath quit [5] himself
Like Samson, and heroicly hath finished   1710
A life heroic, on his enemies
Fully revenged; hath left them years of mourning
And lamentation to the sons of Caphtor [6]
Through all Philistian bounds; to Israel
Honor hath left and freedom, let but them   1715
Find courage to lay hold on this occasion;
To himself and father's house eternal fame;
And, which is best and happiest yet, all this
With God not parted from him, as was feared,
But favoring and assisting to the end.   1720
Nothing is here for tears, nothing to wail

5. Unwittingly.
6. The play accomplishes itself by showing the internal blindness of the Philistines at the very moment of Samson's
spiritual illumination.
7. Serpent (from Latin, *draco*).
8. Farmyard (from Latin, *villaticus*);
"bolted": cast as a thunderbolt.
9. "Given up for lost."
1. The mythical phoenix begets itself
out of its own ashes; it is unique, that

is, there is only one phoenix alive at
any one time, and it lives in the deserts
of Arabia.
2. Enclosed, hidden.
3. A sacrifice burned whole on the altar.
4. Living through the centuries (Latin,
saecula).
5. Acquitted.
6. In Amos ix.7 the Philistines are described as immigrants from Caphtor,
i.e. Crete.

Or knock the breast; no weakness, no contempt,
Dispraise, or blame; nothing but well and fair,
And what may quiet us in a death so noble.
Let us go find the body where it lies   1725
Soaked in his enemies' blood, and from the stream
With lavers [7] pure, and cleansing herbs, wash off
The clotted gore. I, with what speed the while [8]
(Gaza is not in plight to say us nay),
Will send for all my kindred, all my friends,   1730
To fetch him hence, and solemnly attend,
With silent obsequy and funeral train,
Home to his father's house. There will I build him
A monument, and plant it round with shade
Of laurel ever green and branching palm, [9]   1735
With all his trophies hung, and acts enrolled
In copious legend, or sweet lyric song.
Thither shall all the valiant youth resort,
And from his memory inflame their breasts
To matchless valor and adventures high;   1740
The virgins also shall, on feastful days,
Visit his tomb with flowers, only bewailing
His lot unfortunate in nuptial choice,
From whence captivity and loss of eyes.

CHORUS.[1] All is best, though we oft doubt   1745
    What th' unsearchable dispose [2]
    Of Highest Wisdom brings about,
    And ever best found in the close.
    Oft he seems to hide his face,
    But unexpectedly returns,   1750
    And to his faithful champion hath in place [3]
    Bore witness gloriously; whence Gaza mourns,
    And all that band them to resist
    His uncontrollable intent.
    His servants he, with new acquist [4]   1755
    Of true experience from this great event,
    With peace and consolation hath dismissed,
    And calm of mind, all passion spent.
                                                             1671

7. Basins.
8. I.e., with what speed (I may) in the meanwhile.
9. Leaves of laurel were worn by civic conquerors on triumphal occasions; wreaths of palm were given to victors in the Olympic games. Samson, as both an athletic victor in his *agon* and the favored of Heaven, gets both.
1. The final chorus of the play is cast in the form of a sonnet.
2. Appointment, disposition.
3. On this very spot, at this very instant.
4. Increase, acquisition.

Seventeenth-Century Lyrics

Although the early 17th century witnessed the death of several major art forms—the old English madrigal, the masque, the folk dance—it also experienced a brief revival in the art of lyric poetry. Literary historians conventionally divide the period between the "metaphysical" and "Cavalier" schools, but some poets (like Sir Robert Aytoun) do not fit either classification, and some (like Thomas Carew) obligingly fit both. Yet the tone of the English poetry does undergo a pervasive change some time after the turn of the century. The typical Jacobean or Caroline lyric is not exuberant and boisterous, as the lyrics of the Elizabethan age often were: rather, it is touched with a grave, half-melancholy beauty; its feelings are quiet and its techniques restrained. Typically, it is a rather elegant, even an artificial, performance; in this connection, we may note that the word "artificial" sometimes had, in those days, the force of a commendation. For a poem to be the product of artifice was altogether proper.

The lower levels of artifice border on the trifling; and not all the minor lyricists of the 17th century avoided this failing all the time. But even in flowery little tributes to Chloris, Flora, or Amaryllis, the poets often uncovered a true vein of feeling. And sometimes their limitations are themselves a matter of interest. For example, the student of literary modes can trace a notable line of decline in the "gentlemanly" poetry of the century. Measured against the elevated and serious courtier's verse which Sidney and Sir Edward Dyer produced during the 1580's, the "gentleman's verse" of the early 17th century seems increasingly slight. Courtly poets like Waller, Davenant, and Cleveland were all too often perfunctory and bloodless. In Sir John Suckling one sees a growing quality of willful triviality and conscious carelessness. The Cavalier heroics of Richard Lovelace flourish their gallantry in the wind like a flag, but cool, conscious, limited control was the ideal proposed and exemplified by John Denham in his famous apostrophe to the river Thames:

> Oh could I flow like thee, and make thy stream
> My great example, as it is my theme!
> Though deep, yet clear, though gentle, yet not dull,
> Strong without rage, without o'erflowing full.
>
> [*Cooper's Hill*, lines 46–49]

The Restoration lyric declined, in part as a consequence of this new habit of mind, the antithetical, balanced rationalism of Enlightened England, for which the perfect vehicle was the heroic couplet. The first great commander of this reasonable middle ground, who builds his poetry on the counterpoint of empirical fact and logical dialectic, is John Dryden; seen from this point of view, he belongs very properly among the writers of the early 18th century. But the versification he used had been sharpened and shaped by Ben Jonson and his "sons." The "refinement of our numbers [verses]" (it is Dryden's own phrase) was the work of men like Waller, Suckling, and Denham; what it implied was the development of an art of easy versification—orderly, unstrained, unpadded, fluent, not necessarily inspired—through which civilized communication could take place between polite folk. On one side of this central development, rakish, gentlemanly wit remained current, turning slowly toward cynicism and pornography. And on the other side, the tradition of devotional poetry flared up briefly, just before the century's end, in the private visionary verses of Thomas Traherne. Thus the poetry of the 17th century lingered on, till just about the end of the 17th century, even though a poetry which was essentially of the Enlightenment had grown up and taken command of the central areas of discourse well before the century actually turned.

SIR ROBERT AYTOUN

(1570–1638)

Scots by birth, Aytoun wrote a great deal of poetry in Latin, Greek, and French as well as English, but published little of it, and never laid formal claim to the title of a poet. When one of his descendants published the entire body of his writings, in 1844, it became clear that there were very good reasons for his modesty—except for this one poised and dignified poem, nothing else that he wrote has a trace of distinction. But this is an eloquent valediction.

To an Inconstant One

I loved thee once; I'll love no more—
  Thine be the grief as is the blame;
Thou art not what thou wast before,
  What reason I should be the same?
    He that can love unloved again,   5
    Hath better store of love than brain:
God send me love my debts to pay,
While unthrifts fool their love away!

Nothing could have my love o'erthrown
  If thou hadst still continued mine: 10
Yea, if thou hadst remained thine own,
  I might perchance have yet been thine.
    But thou thy freedom didst recall
    That it thou might elsewhere enthral:
And then how could I but disdain   15
A captive's captive to remain?

When new desires had conquered thee
  And changed the object of thy will,
It had been lethargy in me,
    Not constancy, to love thee still.   20
      Yea, it had been a sin to go
      And prostitute affection so:
Since we are taught no prayers to say
To such as must to others pray.

Yet do thou glory in thy choice,   25
  Thy choice of his good fortune boast;
I'll neither grieve nor yet rejoice
  To see him gain what I have lost.
    The height of my disdain shall be
      To laugh at him, to blush for thee;   30
To love thee still, but go no more
A-begging at a beggar's door.

1844

ROBERT HAYMAN

(ca. 1579–ca. 1631)

Robert Hayman was born in Devonshire, probably in Totnes, the little sea-side town where he saw Drake. After studying at Oxford and Lincoln's Inn, he was appointed governor "of the plantation of Harbour-Grace in Bristol-hope in Britaniola anciently called Newfoundland," and served there for seven years. One fruit of his study during the long winter nights was a little volume called *Quodlibets lately come over from New Britaniola anciently called Newfoundland, epigrams and other small parcels both moral and divine*, which he published in 1628, after his return. As poetry, it will prob-ably never win him any immortality; but as a human record of a meeting with a great man, it has the curious charm of a fly in amber.

Of the Great and Famous
Ever-To-Be-Honored Knight, Sir Francis Drake,
and of My Little-Little Self

The Dragon[1] that our seas did raise his crest
And brought back heaps of gold unto his nest,
Unto his foes more terrible than thunder,
Glory of his age, after-ages' wonder,
Excelling all those that excelled before—   5
It's feared we shall have none such any more—

---

1. The name "Drake" would normally turn to "Draco" in Spanish; that is Latin for "Dragon," and that is the way the Spanish sailors thought of Drake.

Effecting all, he sole did undertake,
Valiant, just, wise, mild, honest, godly Drake.
This man when I was little I did meet
As he was walking up Totnes' long street.   10
He asked me whose I was. I answered him.
He asked me if his good friend were within.
A fair red orange in his hand he had;
He gave it me, whereof I was right glad,
Takes and kissed me, and prays, "God bless my boy,"   15
Which I record with comfort to this day.
Could he on me have breathéd with his breath
His gifts, Elias-like,[2] after his death,
Then had I been enabled for to do
Many brave things I have a heart unto.   20
I have as great desire as e'er had he
To joy, annoy, friends, foes; but 'twill not be.

1628

2. Elijah was an Old-Testament prophet who ascended in a chariot to heaven, leaving his mantle and his prophetic spirit to his son Elisha (II Kings ii).

JOHN CLEVELAND

(1613–1658)

John Cleveland was a clever young contemporary of Milton's at Christ's College, Cambridge. In the civil wars he chose the royalist side, and became a bitter satirist of the parliamentarians. But though known in his own time chiefly as a wit and controversialist, he is best remembered now for his *Mark Antony*, a strange and uncharacteristically "deep" lyric piece.

Mark Antony[1]

Whenas the nightingale chanted her vespers,
And the wild forester[2] couched on the ground,
Venus invited me in th' evening whispers
Unto a fragrant field with roses crowned
Where she before had sent   5
My wishes' complement;
Unto my heart's content
Played with me on the green.
Never Mark Antony
Dallied more wantonly   10
With the fair Egyptian queen.

1. Cleveland's customary vein led him to metaphysical ingenuities almost as frigid as Cowley's, and rather more tortured. But *Mark Antony* is looser and more natural; its dancing dactyls balance beautifully across a strongly-felt caesura —as in the line,

Mystical grámmar of || ámorous glánces.

It is an odd metrical pattern in English, and especially in the 17th century, but very striking when one gets the swing of it.

2. A rough pony.

First on her cherry cheeks I mine eyes feasted,
Thence fear of surfeiting made me retire;
Next on her warmer lips, which when I tasted,
My duller spirits made active as fire.   15
  Then we began to dart
  Each at another's heart
  Arrows that knew no smart,
  Sweep lips and smiles between.
    Never Mark, &c.   20

Wanting a glass to plait her amber tresses,
Which like a bracelet rich deckéd mine arm,
Gaudier than Juno wears whenas she graces
Jove with embraces more stately than warm,
  Then did she peep in mine   25
  Eyes' humor crystalline;
  I in her eyes was seen
  As if we one had been.
    Never Mark, &c.

Mystical grammar of amorous glances,   30
Feeling of pulses, the physic of love,
Rhetorical courtings, and musical dances,
Numbering of kisses arithmetic prove.
  Eyes like astronomy;
  Straight-limbed geometry;   35
  In her art's ingeny[3]
  Our wits were sharp and keen.
    Never Mark Antony
    Dallied more wantonly
    With the fair Egyptian queen.   40

                                                  1647

3. Ingenuity, also exercise.

ABRAHAM COWLEY

(1618–1667)

An essentially mild and moderate man, Abraham Cowley began to write
poetry before he was into his teens, and under the metaphysical influence
persuaded himself not only that he should be, but that he actually was, a
poet of overpowering wit and rhapsodic genius. "The Muses' Hannibal"
was his favorite epithet for himself. During his lifetime, lofty odes and a
learned if heavy epic (*Davideis*) sustained his name; but after his death, he
quickly sank in public esteem. The *Ode to Mr. Hobbes* represents his real
intellectual vigor, as well as his mechanical style; *The Wish*, with its
modest scope and genuine appreciation of homely pleasures, suggests where
his tastes and talents really lay.

To Mr. Hobbes[1]

Vast bodies of philosophy
   I oft have seen and read,
   But all are bodies dead,
Or bodies by Art fashionéd;
I never yet the living soul could see   5
   But in thy books and thee.
   'Tis only God can know
Whether the fair idea thou dost show
Agree entirely with his own or no.
   This I dare boldly tell,   10
'Tis so like truth, 'twill serve our turn as well.
Just, as in nature, thy proportions be,
As full of concord their variety,
As firm the parts upon their center rest,
And all so solid are, that they, at least   15
As much as nature, emptiness detest.

Long did the mighty Stagirite[2] retain
The universal intellectual reign,
Saw his own country's short-lived leopard[3] slain;
The stronger Roman eagle did out-fly,   20
Oftener renewed his age, and saw that die.
Mecca itself, in spite of Mahomet possessed,
And chased by a wild deluge from the east,
His monarchy new planted in the west.[4]
But as in time each great imperial race   25
Degenerates, and gives some new one place,
   So did this noble empire waste,
   Sunk by degrees from glories past,
And in the school-men's[5] hands, it perished quite at last.
   Then nought but words it grew,   30
   And those all barbarous too.
   It perished and it vanished there,
The life and soul breathed out, became but empty air.

1. The poem is addressed to Thomas Hobbes, the Malmesbury philosopher, a friend of Cowley's; in form, it is a loose imitation of the Greek odes written by the Theban poet Pindar. Cowley understood these odes to be irregular and sublime (in which he was right), and that this was the character of his own genius (in which he was hopelessly wrong). His effort here to work up an artificial "sublime" is not very impressive; but his sense that a new world of philosophy is just opening before men is characteristic of his age. Cowley had an amateur's interest in science, and great admiration for the Royal Society; but the problem of accommodating scientific rationalism within a rhetoric of poetic enthusiasm was too hard for him to handle.
2. Aristotle (who came from the town of Stagira, in Greece).
3. Alexander the Great, Aristotle's pupil. Cowley is here tracing the history of Aristotelian philosophy through the ages.
4. Arabian thinkers like Avicenna and Averroes were largely responsible for transmitting Aristotle's work to the Western world. The "monarchy new planted in the west" is the Moorish regime in Spain.
5. Cowley's contempt for the scholastic philosophers (Scotus, Occam, Aquinas, and the rest) is unbounded.

The fields which answered well the ancients' plow,
Spent and outworn, return no harvest now;   35
In barren age wild and inglorious lie,
    And boast of past fertility,
The poor relief of present poverty.
  Food and fruit we now must want
    Unless new lands we plant.   40
We break up tombs with sacrilegious hands;
    Old rubbish we remove;
To walk in ruins, like vain ghosts, we love,
  And with fond divining wands,
    We search among the dead   45
    For treasures buriéd,
  Whilst still the liberal earth does hold
So many virgin mines of undiscovered gold.

The Baltic, Euxine, and the Caspian
And slender-limbed Mediterranean,   50
Seem narrow creeks to thee,[6] and only fit
For the poor wretched fisher-boats of wit.
Thy nobler vessel the vast ocean tries,
    And nothing sees but seas and skies,
    Till unknown regions it descries,   55
Thou great Columbus of the golden lands of new philosophies.
    Thy task was harder much than his,
    For thy learned America is
Not only found out first by thee,
And rudely left to future industry,   60
  But thy eloquence and thy wit
Has planted, peopled, built, and civilized it.

    I little thought before,
    (Nor, being my own self so poor,
    Could comprehend so vast a store)   65
  That all the wardrobe of rich eloquence
    Could have afforded half enough
    Of bright, of new and lasting stuff,
To clothe the mighty limbs of thy gigantic sense.
  Thy solid reason, like the shield from heaven   70
    To the Trojan hero given,[7]
Too strong to take a mark from any mortal dart,
Yet shines with gold and gems in every part,
And wonders on it graved by the learned hand of art,
    A shield that gives delight   75
    Even to the enemy's sight,
Then when they're sure to lose the combat by 't.

6. Hobbes himself. Cowley's conviction that the new philosophy of "things" rather than "words" represents a whole new world for exploration and discovery echoes the confident affirmations of Bacon.

7. In Book VIII of the *Aeneid*, Aeneas gets from his mother, Venus, a splendid shield made by her husband, Vulcan.

Nor can the snow which now cold age does shed
    Upon thy reverend head[8]
Quench or allay the noble fires within;   80
    But all which thou hast been,
    And all that youth can be thou 'rt yet,
    So fully still dost thou
Enjoy the manhood and the bloom of wit,
And all the natural heat, but not the fever too.   85
    So contraries on Etna's[9] top conspire,
Here hoary frosts, and by them breaks out fire.
A secure peace the faithful neighbors keep,
Th' emboldened snow next to the flame does sleep.
    And if we weigh, like thee,   90
    Nature and causes, we shall see
    That thus it needs must be;
To things immortal time can do no wrong,
And that which never is to die, forever must be young.

            1656

The Wish

    Well then; I now do plainly see,
This busy world and I shall ne'er agree;
The very honey of all earthly joy
    Does of all meats the soonest cloy;
    And they, methinks, deserve my pity   5
Who for it can endure the stings,
The crowd, and buzz, and murmurings
    Of this great hive, the city.

    Ah, yet, ere I descend to the grave
May I a small house and large garden have!   10
And a few friends, and many books, both true,
    Both wise, and both delightful too!
    And since love ne'er will from me flee,
A mistress moderately fair,
And good as guardian angels are,
    Only beloved, and loving me!   15

    O fountains, when in you shall I
Myself, eased of unpeaceful thoughts, espy?
O fields! O woods! when, when shall I be made
    The happy tenant of your shade?   20
    Here's the spring-head of pleasure's flood,
Here's wealthy Nature's treasury,
Where all the riches lie that she
    Has coined and stamped for good.

8. Hobbes was born in 1588, the year of the Spanish Armada; he was therefore 68 when Cowley's poem first appeared.

9. Mount Etna, a volcano in Sicily, is so high that in winter it is sometimes snow-capped.

Pride and ambition here   25
Only in farfetched metaphors appear;
Here naught but winds can hurtful murmurs scatter,
    And naught but Echo flatter.
    The gods, when they descended, hither
From heaven did always choose their way;   30
And therefore we may boldly say
    That 'tis the way, too, thither.

    How happy here should I
And one dear she live and, embracing, die!
She who is all the world, and can exclude   35
    In deserts, solitude.
    I should have then this only fear,
Lest men, when they my pleasures see,
Should hither throng to live like me,
    And so make a city here.
                                                                         40
                                                             1647

THOMAS CAREW

(ca. 1594–1640)

Bright, talented, and idle, Thomas Carew (pronounced *Carey*) carefully avoided serious work of all sorts; he hung around the court, amusing himself and other people, and died just in time to get out of the civil wars. Yet the poetry he wrote in his spare time is clean, chiseled, and amazingly perceptive. Most of it remained unpublished during his life; but the great *Elegy on Donne* appeared in the 1633 edition of Donne's poems, and in the following year he published one of the finest of court masques, *Coelum Britannicum*. His poetry was collected and printed in 1640, the year of his death.

An Elegy upon the Death of the Dean of Paul's, Dr. John Donne[1]

    Can we not force from widowed poetry,
    Now thou art dead, great Donne, one elegy
    To crown thy hearse? Why yet did we not trust,
    Though with unkneaded dough-baked prose, thy dust,
    Such as the unscissored[2] lect'rer from the flower   5
    Of fading rhetoric, short-lived as his hour,
    Dry as the sand that measures it,[3] should lay

1. First appearing in the 1633 edition of Donne's poems, this elegy was described as by "Mr. Tho: Carie." It was reprinted in the 1640 edition of Carew's poems, from which our text is taken.

2. I.e., with uncut hair. Whether from grief, poverty, or in imitation of Apollo is not clear.

3. The hourglass was used by preachers to keep track of time.

Upon the ashes on the funeral day?
Have we nor tune, nor voice? Didst thou dispense
Through all our language both words and sense?   10
'Tis sad truth. The pulpit may her plain
And sober Christian precepts still retain;
Doctrines it may, and wholesome uses, frame,
Grave homilies and lectures; but the flame
Of thy brave soul, that shot such heat and light   15
As burnt our earth and made our darkness bright,
Committed holy rapes upon our will,
Did through the eye the melting heart distil,
And the deep knowledge of dark truths so teach
As sense might judge what fancy could not reach,[4]   20
Must be desired forever. So the fire
That fills with spirit and heat the Delphic choir,[5]
Which, kindled first by thy Promethean[6] breath,
Glowed here a while, lies quenched now in thy death.
The Muses' garden, with pedantic weeds   25
O'erspread, was purged by thee; the lazy seeds
Of servile imitation thrown away,
And fresh invention planted; thou didst pay
The debts of our penurious bankrupt age—
Licentious thefts, that make poetic rage   30
A mimic fury, when our souls must be
Possessed, or with Anacreon's ecstasy,
Or Pindar's,[7] not their own. The subtle cheat
Of sly exchanges, and the juggling feat
Of two-edged words,[8] or whatsoever wrong   35
By ours was done the Greek or Latin tongue,
Thou hast redeemed, and opened us a mine
Of rich and pregnant fancy, drawn a line
Of masculine expression, which had good
Old Orpheus[9] seen, or all the ancient brood   40
Our superstitious fools admire, and hold
Their lead more precious than thy burnished gold,
Thou hadst been their exchequer, and no more
They in each other's dung had raked for ore.
Thou shalt yield no precedence, but of time   45
And the blind fate of language, whose tuned chime
More charms the outward sense; yet thou mayest claim

4. I.e., so that things too abstract and elevated even to be imagined might be made plain to sense. "Desired": missed.
5. The choir of poets, inspired by Apollo, whose oracle used to be at Delphi.
6. Donne stole fire from heaven, like Prometheus, and used it to fill with spirit and heat the choir of poets.
7. Anacreon (6th and 5th centuries B.C.) and Pindar (first half of the 5th century B.C.) were famous Greek lyric poets.

8. "Sly exchanges": Carew seems to refer to the habit, frequent in Jonsonian and Miltonic style, of using English words in their Latin senses, e.g., "horrid (bristling) spears." "Two-edged words" might be puns; but as these were a favorite device of Donne's, this cannot be the sense. Perhaps "two-edged words" are not far from "sly exchanges" in meaning.
9. Ancient Greek poet and prophet, so mythical that he is often used as the type of all poets.

From so great disadvantage greater fame,
Since to the awe of thy imperious wit
Our troublesome language bends, made only fit   50
With her tough thick-ribbed hoops, to gird about
Thy giant fancy, which had proved too stout
For their soft melting phrases. As in time
They had the start, so did they cull the prime
Buds of invention many a hundred year,   55
And left the rifled fields, besides the fear
To touch their harvest; yet from those bare lands
Of what is only thine, thy only hands
(And that their smallest work) have gleaned more
Than all those times and tongues could reap before.   60
    But thou art gone, and thy strict laws will be
Too hard for libertines in poetry.
They will repeal[1] the goodly exiled train
Of gods and goddesses, which in thy just reign
Were banished nobler poems; now with these   65
The silenced tales in the *Metamorphoses*[2]
Shall stuff their lines and swell the windy page,
Till verse, refined by thee in this last age,
Turn ballad-rhyme, or those old idols be
Adored again with new apostasy.   70
    O pardon me, that break with untuned verse
The reverend silence that attends thy hearse,
Whose awful[3] solemn murmurs were to thee,
More than these faint lines, a loud elegy,
That did proclaim in a dumb eloquence   75
The death of all the arts, whose influence,
Grown feeble, in these panting numbers lies
Gasping short-winded accents, and so dies:
So doth the swiftly turning wheel not stand
In th' instant we withdraw the moving hand,   80
But some small time retain a faint weak course
By virtue of the first impulsive force;
And so whilst I cast on thy funeral pile
Thy crown of bays,[4] oh, let it crack awhile
And spit disdain, till the devouring flashes   85
Suck all the moisture up; then turn to ashes.
    I will not draw the envy to engross
All thy perfections, or weep all the loss;
Those are too numerous for one elegy,
And this too great to be expressed by me.   90
Let others carve the rest; it shall suffice
I on thy grave this epitaph incise:

---

1. Recall, as from banishment.
2. Ovid's tales in the *Metamorphoses* had been a favorite stockpile of poetical properties for Renaissance poets; Donne forwent them, but soon they will return.
3. I.e., awed.
4. The poet's crown.

Here lies a king, that ruled as he thought fit
The universal monarchy of wit;
Here lie two flamens,[5] and both those the best: 95
Apollo's[6] first, at last the true God's priest.

1633, 1640

Disdain Returned

He that loves a rosy cheek,
    Or a coral lip admires,
Or from starlike eyes doth seek
    Fuel to maintain his fires;
As old Time makes these decay,   5
So his flames must waste away.

But a smooth and steadfast mind,
    Gentle thoughts and calm desires,
Hearts with equal love combined,
    Kindle never-dying fires.   10
Where these are not, I despise
Lovely cheeks, or lips, or eyes.

No tears, Celia, now shall win
    My resolved heart to return;
I have searched thy soul within,   15
    And find naught but pride and scorn;
I have learned thy arts, and now
    Can disdain as much as thou.
Some power, in my revenge convey
That love to her I cast away.[7]   20

1640

A Song

Ask me no more where Jove bestows,
When June is past, the fading rose;
For in your beauties orient deep,[8]
These flowers, as in their causes, sleep.[9]

---

5. Priests of the Roman religion.
6. I.e., of the god of poetry.
7. I.e., to a previous mistress.
8. The text permits two readings here: "in your beauties which are orient deep" or "in the orient depths of your beauty." In addition to its reference to the Far East, "orient" implies "pearly" or "lustrous."
9. Aristotelian philosophy suggested that objects often lay latent in their causes—e.g., that in the seed creating man there was a little man (*homunculus*). In Carew's compliment, the lady is a summation of last summer and cause of the next one.

Ask me no more whither do stray 5
The golden atoms of the day;
For in pure love heaven did prepare
Those powders to enrich your hair.

Ask me no more whither doth haste
The nightingale when May is past; 10
For in your sweet dividing[1] throat
She winters, and keeps warm her note.

Ask me no more where those stars light,
That downwards fall in dead of night;
For in your eyes they sit, and there 15
Fixéd become, as in their sphere.

Ask me no more if east or west
The phoenix builds her spicy nest;[2]
For unto you at last she flies,
And in your fragrant bosom dies. 20

1640

The Second Rapture[3]

No, worldling, no, 'tis not thy gold
Which thou dost use but to behold,
Nor fortune, honor, nor long life,
Children, or friends, nor a good wife
That makes thee happy; these things be 5
But shadows of felicity.
Give me a wench about thirteen,
Already voted[4] to the queen
Of lust and lovers, whose soft hair,
Fanned with the breath of gentle air, 10
O'erspreads her shoulders like a tent,
And is her veil and ornament:
Whose tender touch will make the blood
Wild in the aged and the good;
Whose kisses fastened to the mouth 15
Of threescore years' and longer sloth
Renew the age, and whose bright eye
Obscures those lesser lights of sky;
Whose snowy breasts (if we may call

---

1. Harmonious (from the "division," or musical trill).
2. The phoenix, an Arabian bird, builds her nest from spicy shrubs. She dies every thousand years and a new bird springs from her ashes.
3. Carew's *A Rapture*, in imitation of Donne's *Elegy XIX*, is an erotic fantasy involving a lady whose name ("Caelia")

and other attributes involve a great deal of Platonic idealization, as well as a strong streak of sensuality. The poet's second, and much shorter, rapture dispenses with most of the idealism to say bluntly and brutally what really pleases him.
4. Devoted.

That snow, that never melts at all)   20
Makes Jove invent a new disguise
In spite of Juno's jealousies;
Whose every part doth re-invite
The old decayed appetite;
And in whose sweet embraces I   25
May melt myself to lust, and die.
    This is true bliss, and I confess
    There is no other happiness.

                                    1640

EDMUND WALLER

(1606–1687)

In the course of a long, eventful, and fortunate life (he is said to have been the wealthiest of English poets), Edmund Waller managed to survive a lot of rough political water and turn out a number of smooth, effortless, lucid verses. *Sacharissa* was the half-imaginary lady to whom these graceful melodies were indited, and at their best they rise just a little above the synthetic.

Song

    Go, lovely rose!
Tell her that wastes her time and me
    That now she knows,
When I resemble[1] her to thee,
How sweet and fair she seems to be.   5

    Tell her that's young,
And shuns to have her graces spied,
    That hadst thou sprung
In deserts, where no men abide,
Thou must have uncommended died.   10

    Small is the worth
Of beauty from the light retired;
    Bid her come forth,
Suffer herself to be desired,
And not blush so to be admired.   15

    Then die! that she
The common fate of all things rare
    May read in thee;

1. Compare.

How small a part of time they share
That are so wondrous sweet and fair!

₂₀
1645

On a Girdle

That which her slender waist confined,
Shall now my joyful temples bind;
No monarch but would give his crown,
His arms might do what this has done.

It was my heaven's extremest sphere,[2]   5
The pale[3] which held that lovely deer;
My joy, my grief, my hope, my love
Did all within this circle move!

A narrow compass! and yet there
Dwelt all that's good, and all that's fair;   10
Give me but what this ribbon bound,
Take all the rest the sun goes round! [4]

1686

Of the Last Verses in the Book

When we for age could neither read nor write,
The subject made us able to indite;
The soul, with nobler resolutions decked,
The body stooping, does herself erect.
No mortal parts are requisite to raise   5
Her that, unbodied, can her Maker praise.
The seas are quiet when the winds give o'er;
So calm are we when passions are no more!
For then we know how vain it was to boast
Of fleeting things, so certain to be lost.   10
Clouds of affection[5] from our younger eyes
Conceal that emptiness which age descries.
The soul's dark cottage, battered and decayed,
Lets in new light through the chinks that time has made;
Stronger by weakness, wiser men become,   15
As they draw near to their eternal home.
Leaving the old, both worlds at once they view,
That stand upon the threshold of the new.

1686

---

2. The last of the nine concentric crystalline spheres which, according to Ptolemaic astronomy, made up the universe. Hence, the lady's outermost garment.
3. Fence encircling a park. There is, of course, a pun on "deer" in this line.

4. The version of this poem printed in 1645 substituted "Do" for "Did" in line 8, and gave the last couplet as: "Give me but what this ribbon tied, / Take all the sun goes round beside."
5. Passion.

SIR JOHN SUCKLING

(1609–1642)

"Natural, easy Suckling" says Millamant, rapturously, in *The Way of the World*; he is her ideal of a poet, one who doesn't take the business too seriously. Sir John himself declared, as a joke, but with a lot of truth in it, that he

> prized black eyes, or a lucky hit
> At bowls, above all the trophies of wit.

Most of his poems are more concerned with being careless and off-hand than with getting anything in particular said. Hardly anybody took him seriously during his lifetime, and when he tried to take part in the king's wars he made himself a laughingstock. (Rushing to the aid of his king with a picked body of horsemen, he was defeated with ludicrous ease by a band of dour, practical Scots.) But his gay trifles have remained current in the language, as some weightier structures have not; he is the prototype of the Cavalier playboy.

Song

Why so pale and wan, fond lover?
  Prithee, why so pale?
Will, when looking well can't move her,
  Looking ill prevail?
  Prithee, why so pale?   5

Why so dull and mute, young sinner?
  Prithee, why so mute?
Will, when speaking well can't win her,
  Saying nothing do't?
  Prithee, why so mute?   10

Quit, quit, for shame; this will not move,
  This cannot take her.
If of herself she will not love,
  Nothing can make her:
  The devil take her!   15

1638

A Ballad upon a Wedding[1]

I tell thee, Dick,[2] where I have been,
Where I the rarest things have seen,

---

1. This ballad is traditionally said to describe the wedding of Roger Boyle, Baron Broghill, to Lady Margaret Howard on January 27, 1641; it is part of the humor that the speaker is portrayed as a country bumpkin.

2. "Dick" may well refer to Richard Lovelace; though for the speaker, he is simply a country friend, like "George upon the Green" and "Vincent of the Crown" below.

Oh, things without compare!
Such sights again cannot be found
In any place on English ground,
    Be it at wake[3] or fair.   5

At Charing Cross,[4] hard by the way
Where we (thou know'st) do sell our hay,
    There is a house with stairs;
And there did I see coming down   10
Such folk as are not in our town,
    Forty, at least, in pairs.

Amongst the rest, one pest'lent fine
(His beard no bigger, though, than thine)
    Walked on before the rest.   15
Our landlord looks like nothing to him;
The king (God bless him!), 'twould undo[5] him
    Should he go still so dressed.

At course-a-park,[6] without all doubt,
He should have first been taken out   20
    By all the maids i' th' town,
Though lusty Roger there had been,
Or little George upon the Green,
    Or Vincent of the Crown.

But wot you what? the youth was going   25
To make an end of all his wooing;
    The parson for him stayed.
Yet by his leave, for all his haste,
He did not so much wish all past,
    Perchance, as did the maid.   30

The maid (and thereby hangs a tale),
For such a maid no Whitsun-ale[7]
    Could ever yet produce;
No grape, that's kindly[8] ripe, could be
So round, so plump, so soft as she,   35
    Nor half so full of juice.

Her finger was so small the ring
Would not stay on, which they did bring;
    It was too wide a peck:
And to say truth (for out it must),   40
It looked like the great collar (just)
    About our young colt's neck.

Her feet beneath her petticoat,
Like little mice, stole in and out,

3. Festival.
4. A suburban center in the 17th century, not far from Haymarket and the present site of Trafalgar Square.
5. I.e., bankrupt.
6. A country game, in which a girl asks a boy to chase her.
7. A rural feast held at Whitsuntide (fifty days after Easter).
8. Naturally, by nature; ripened on the vine.

As if they feared the light;   45
But oh, she dances such a way,
No sun upon an Easter day[9]
    Is half so fine a sight!

He would have kissed her once or twice,
But she would not, she was so nice,[1]   50
    She would not do 't in sight;
And then she looked as who should say,
I will do what I list today;
    And you shall do 't at night.

Her cheeks so rare a white was on,   55
No daisy makes comparison
    (Who sees them is undone),
For streaks of red were mingled there,
Such as are on a Catherine pear
    (The side that's next the sun).   60

Her lips were red, and one was thin
Compared to that was next her chin
    (Some bee had stung it newly);
But, Dick, her eyes so guard her face
I durst no more upon them gaze   65
    Than on the sun in July.

Her mouth so small, when she does speak,
Thou 'dst swear her teeth her words did break,
    That they might passage get;
But she so handled still the matter,   70
They came as good as ours, or better,
    And are not spent a whit.

If wishing should be any sin,
The parson himself had guilty been
    (She looked that day so purely);   75
And did the youth so oft the feat
At night, as some did in conceit,
    It would have spoiled him, surely.

Just in the nick the cook knocked thrice,
And all the waiters in a trice   80
    His summons did obey;
Each servingman, with dish in hand,
Marched boldly up, like our trained band,[2]
    Presented, and away.

When all the meat was on the table,   85
What man of knife or teeth was able
    To stay to be entreated?
And this the very reason was,
Before the parson could say grace,
    The company was seated.   90

9. The sun was often said to dance at
Easter in honor of the Resurrection.

1. Particular, delicate.
2. "Trained bands" were the militia.

The business of the kitchen's great,
For it is fit that men should eat;
    Nor was it there denied.
Passion o' me, how I run on!
There's that that would be thought upon,   95
    I trow, besides the bride.

Now hats fly off, and youths carouse;
Healths first go round, and then the house;
    The bride's came thick and thick:
And when 'twas named another's health,   100
Perhaps he made it hers by stealth;
    And who could help it, Dick?

O' th' sudden up they rise and dance;
Then sit again and sigh and glance;
    Then dance again and kiss.   105
Thus several ways the time did pass,
Till every woman wished her place,
    And every man wished his!

By this time all were stolen aside
To counsel and undress the bride,   110
    But that he must not know;
But yet 'twas thought he guessed her mind,
And did not mean to stay behind
    Above an hour or so.

When in he came, Dick, there she lay   115
Like new-fallen snow melting away
    ('Twas time, I trow, to part);
Kisses were now the only stay,[3]
Which soon she gave, as who would say,
    "God be with ye,[4] with all my heart."   120

But just as heaven would have to cross it,
In came the bridesmaids with the posset.[5]
    The bridegroom ate in spite,
For had he left the women to 't,
It would have cost two hours to do 't,   125
    Which were too much that night.

At length the candle's out, and now
All that they had not done, they do.
    What that is, who can tell?
But I believe it was no more   130
Than thou and I have done before
    With Bridget and with Nell.

ca. 1641   1646

3. Delay.
4. Some texts read "God b'w'y," i.e.,
"God be with ye"; others simply "Good
Boy!" which improves the meter at the
cost of the sense.
5. A drink compounded of hot milk,
liquor, and spices.

Out upon It!

Out upon it! I have loved
    Three whole days together;
And am like to love three more,
    If it prove fair weather.

Time shall molt away his wings,   5
    Ere he shall discover
In the whole wide world again
    Such a constant lover.

But the spite on 't is, no praise
    Is due at all to me: 10
Love with me had made no stays
    Had it any been but she.

Had it any been but she,
    And that very face,
There had been at least ere this   15
    A dozen dozen in her place.

1659

RICHARD LOVELACE
(1618–1657)

Of an old and wealthy Kentish family, Richard Lovelace was educated at Oxford; he was an attractive, handsome, and witty young man, the very model of a courtier. King Charles and Queen Henrietta Maria admired his demeanor so much, when they visited Oxford in 1636, that they had him created M.A. on the spot. During the wars, Lovelace stood firm for the king. In 1641, he presented a petition to the Long Parliament which earned him a prison term, after which he went abroad; in 1646 he was wounded at Dunkirk while serving with the French army against the Spaniards, and some time later he returned to England, where the Puritan government once more cast him into prison. In the course of this turbulent activity, his estates melted away, and he died in poverty at the early age of 39. Lovelace published *Lucasta* in 1649; and a posthumous volume appeared in 1659, with his remaining writings.

To Althea, from Prison

When Love with unconfinéd wings
Hovers within my gates,
And my divine Althea brings
To whisper at the grates;

When I lie tangled in her hair   5
And fettered to her eye,
The gods[1] that wanton in the air
Know no such liberty.

When flowing cups run swiftly round,
With no allaying Thames,[2]   10
Our careless heads with roses bound,
Our hearts with loyal flames;
When thirsty grief in wine we steep,
When healths and draughts go free,
Fishes, that tipple in the deep,   15
Know no such liberty.

When, like committed linnets,[3] I
With shriller throat shall sing
The sweetness, mercy, majesty,
And glories of my King;   20
When I shall voice aloud how good
He is, how great should be,
Enlargéd winds, that curl the flood,
Know no such liberty.

Stone walls do not a prison make,   25
Nor iron bars a cage;
Minds innocent and quiet take
That for an hermitage.
If I have freedom in my love,
And in my soul am free,   30
Angels alone, that soar above,
Enjoy such liberty.

                                                        1649

To Lucasta, Going to the Wars

Tell me not, Sweet, I am unkind
That from the nunnery
Of thy chaste breast and quiet mind,
To war and arms I fly.

True, a new mistress now I chase,   5
The first foe in the field;
And with a stronger faith embrace
A sword, a horse, a shield.

Yet this inconstancy is such
As you too shall adore;   10
I could not love thee, Dear, so much,
Loved I not honor more.

                                                        1649

---

1. Some versions read "birds" instead   2. No mixture of water in the wine.
of "gods."   3. Caged finches.

The Grasshopper

TO MY NOBLE FRIEND, MR. CHARLES COTTON[4]
Oh, thou that swing'st upon the waving hair
  Of some well-filled oaten beard,
Drunk every night with a delicious tear
  Dropped thee from heav'n, where now th' art reared,

The joys of earth and air are thine entire,   5
  That with thy feet and wings dost hop and fly;
And when thy poppy [5] works thou dost retire
  To thy carved acorn bed to lie.

Up with the day, the sun thou welcom'st then,
  Sport'st in the gilt-plats [6] of his beams,   10
And all these merry days mak'st merry men,
  Thyself, and melancholy streams.[7]

But ah, the sickle! golden ears are cropped,
  Ceres and Bacchus [8] bid goodnight;
Sharp frosty fingers all your flow'rs have topped,   15
  And what scythes spared, winds shave off quite.

Poor verdant fool! and now green ice! thy joys
  Large and as lasting as thy perch of grass,
Bid us lay in 'gainst winter rain, and poise
  Their floods with an o'erflowing glass.   20

Thou best of men and friends! we will create
  A genuine summer in each other's breast;
And spite of this cold time and frozen fate
  Thaw us a warm seat to our rest.

Our sacred hearths shall burn eternally   25
  As vestal flames; [9] the North wind, he
Shall strike his frost-stretched wings, dissolve, and fly
  This Etna in epitome.[1]

4. Lovelace's friend Mr. Charles Cotton, scholar, man of letters, and father of Montaigne's translator, may have appeared to the poet an industrious and prudent ant, compared with himself, the melodious and improvident grasshopper. (Lovelace lost his entire fortune in the Civil Wars.) The circumstances of the poem are evidently those of the interregnum, when a winter of Puritanism seemed to be settling over all civilized feeling in England. For a copious explication of the poem's backgrounds and overtones, see D. C. Allen's article in *Modern Language Quarterly*, XVIII (1957), 35–43.
5. Opiate, sleeping potion.
6. Golden meadows.
7. The three objects of "mak'st merry" are "men," "thyself," and "melancholy streams."
8. The grain and the grape.
9. The vestal virgins, in Rome, were responsible for tending an eternal flame.
1. Boreas, the North wind, "striking" (i.e., folding up) his wings, flees from the underground warmth of Etna, an emblem of the flame of friendship.

Dropping December shall come weeping in,
　Bewail th'usurping of his reign;   30
But when in showers of old Greek [2] we begin,
　Shall cry, he hath his crown again!

Night as clear Hesper [3] shall our tapers whip
　From the light casements where we play,
And the dark hag from her black mantle strip,   35
　And stick there everlasting day.

Thus richer than untempted kings are we,
　That asking nothing, nothing need:
Though lord of all that seas embrace, yet he
　That wants himself is poor indeed.   40

1649

2. Greek wine was especially favored in the classical world; drinkers, in classical times, often wore festive crowns at their carousals; and December "crowns," i.e., terminates the year.

3. The tapers are compared to Hesperus, the morning star, which whips night from the sky. Hecate, the dark hag, was sometimes described as the daughter of Night.

SIR WILLIAM DAVENANT

(1606–1668)

The chief literary importance of Sir William Davenant is that he kept alive the theatrical traditions of the pre-Commonwealth era, to be revived after the Restoration. In the process, he became the author of the first English opera, *The Siege of Rhodes* (1656). His *Song* is a parody of the traditional aubade, or song of the lover to his mistress at dawn: compare with Donne's *The Good Morrow* and *Break of Day*, above.

A Song

O thou that sleep'st like pig in straw,
　Thou lady dear, arise;
Open (to keep the sun in awe)
　Thy pretty pinking[1] eyes:
And, having stretched each leg and arm,   5
　Put on your clean white smock,
And then I pray, to keep you warm,
　A petticoat or dock.[2]
Arise, arise! Why should you sleep
　When you have slept enough?   10
Long since, French boys cried Chimney-sweep,
　And damsels Kitchen-stuff.

1. Blinking, but also wounding.   2. A kind of primitive bustle.

The shops were opened long before,
   And youngest prentice goes
To lay at's master's chamber-door   15
   His master's shining shoes.
Arise, arise! your breakfast stays,
   Good water-gruel warm,
Or sugar-sops, which Galen[3] says
   With mace, will do no harm.   20
Arise, arise! when you are up
   You'll find more to your cost,
For morning's draught in caudle-cup,[4]
   Good nutbrown ale, and toast.[5]

1673

3. Galen is the ancient Greek physician; sugar-sops are slices of bread with sugar and spice.
4. Gruel, served to invalids and for breakfast.

5. As a breakfast drink, the young person will find more to her cost (perhaps "taste") a cup of ale and a crust of bread.

ANONYMOUS

The Power of Money[1]

'Tis not the silver nor gold for itself
   That makes men adore it, but 'tis for its power:
For no man does dote upon pelf[2] because pelf,
   But all court the lady in hope of her dower:
The wonders that now in our days we behold,   5
Done by the irresistible power of gold,
Our zeal, and our love, and allegiance do hold.

This purchaseth kingdoms, kings, scepters, and crowns;
   Wins battles, and conquers the conquerors bold;
Takes bulwarks, and castles, and cities, and towns,   10
   And our prime laws are writ in letters of gold;
'Tis this that our Parliament calls and creates,
Turns kings into keepers, and kingdoms to states,
And peopledoms these into highdoms translates.[3]

* * *

1. When the Puritans marched off to war with the king, they tended to sing hymns of Sion; but their enemies, the Cavaliers, were more original in their versing. They made up satirical ballads about the Puritans and their Rump Parliament, which were collected under the title of "Rump Songs." From one of these we excerpt some verses distinguished as much for their truth as for their poetry. A song like this, set to a well-known tune and sung in taverns or on the march, accumulated stanzas as people thought of new applications—thus it exists in numerous different versions. (From *Rump: or an exact collection of the choicest Poems and Songs relating to the late times,* 1662.)
2. Goods; riches.
3. Money converts government by the people into government by high dignitaries, high councils, etc.

This, plots can devise, and discover what they are;   15
    This, makes the great felons the lesser condemn;
This, sets those on the bench, that should stand at the bar,
    Who judge such as by right ought to execute them;
Gives the boisterous clown his unsufferable pride,
Makes beggars, and fools, and usurpers to ride,   20
Whiles ruin'd proprietors run by their side.

                              *   *   *

This makes your blue aprons Right Worshipful;[4]
    And for this we stand bare, and before them do fall;
They leave their young heirs well fleeced with wool,
    Whom we must call squires, and then they pay all: 25
Who with beggarly souls, though their bodies be gaudy,
Court the pale chambermaid, and nickname her a lady,
And for want of good wit, they do swear and talk bawdy.

This marriages makes, 'tis a center of love,
    It draws on the man, and it pricks up the woman   30
Birth, virtue, and parts no affection can move,
    Whilst this makes a lord stoop to the brat of a broom-man;
This gives virtue and beauty to the lasses that you woo,
Makes women of all sorts and ages to do;
'Tis the soul of the world, and the worldling too.   35

This procures us whores, hawks, hounds and hares;
    'Tis this keeps your groom, and your groom keeps your gelding;
This built citizens wives, as well as wares;
    And this makes your coy lady so coming and yielding;
This buys us good sack, which revives like the spring,   40
'Tis this your poetical fancies do bring;
And this makes you as merry as we that do sing.

                                                        ca. 1650

4. Apprentices wore blue aprons; mayors were addressed as "Right Worshipful."

THOMAS TRAHERNE

(1637–1674)

Thomas Traherne did not become one of the English poets till the 20th century, when a manuscript volume of his poems fell into the hands of a perceptive bookseller, who published it. First guesses were that the author was Vaughan, and they were not bad guesses. But there is a freshness and visionary innocence in Traherne's lyrics, the like of which will not be seen again till Blake.

Wonder

How like an angel came I down!
    How bright are all things here!
When first among his works I did appear,
    O how their glory did me crown!
The world resembled his eternity,   5
    In which my soul did walk,
    And everything that I did see
        Did with me talk.

The skies in their magnificence,
    The lively, lovely air;   10
O how divine, how soft, how sweet, how fair!
    The stars did entertain my sense,
And all the works of God so bright and pure,
    So rich and great did seem,
    As if they ever must endure,   15
        In my esteem.

A native health and innocence
    Within my bones did grow,
And while my God did all his glories show,
    I felt a vigor in my sense   20
That was all SPIRIT. I within did flow
    With seas of life like wine;
    I nothing in the world did know
        But 'twas divine.

Harsh ragged objects were concealed,   25
    Oppression's tears and cries,
Sins, griefs, complaints, dissensions, weeping eyes,
    Were hid; and only things revealed
Which heavenly spirits and the angels prize.
    The state of innocence   30
    And bliss, not trades and poverties,
        Did fill my sense.

The streets were paved with golden stones,
    The boys and girls were mine,
O how did all their lovely faces shine!   35
    The sons of men were holy ones.
In joy and beauty then appeared to me
    And everything which here I found
    While like an angel I did see,
        Adorned the ground.   40

Rich diamond and pearl and gold
  In every place was seen;
Rare splendors, yellow, blue, red, white, and green,
  Mine eyes did everywhere behold.
Great wonders clothed with glory did appear,   45
  Amazement was my bliss.
That and my wealth was everywhere:
   No joy to this![1]

Cursed and devised proprieties,[2]
  With envy, avarice,   50
And fraud, those fiends that spoil even paradise,
  Fled from the splendor of mine eyes.
And so did hedges, ditches, limits, bounds,
  I dreamed not aught of those,
But wandered over all men's grounds,   55
  And found repose.

Proprieties themselves were mine,
  And hedges ornaments;
Walls, boxes, coffers, and their rich contents
  Did not divide my joys, but all combine.   60
Clothes, ribbons, jewels, laces, I esteemed
  My joys by others worn;
For me they all to wear them seemed
   When I was born.

              1903

1. Compared to this.
2. Properties. It is not simply private property, but more importantly the individual self from which Traherne in his vision has escaped.

Prose of the
Seventeenth Century

When Monsieur Jourdain (in Molière's comedy *The Bourgeois Gentleman*) consults with his newly acquired and very expensive tutor, he learns with surprise and pleasure that he has been talking prose all his life without knowing it. Everything else in the new life of a gentleman is hard and expensive, but prose, it seems, he already knows. In somewhat the same way, English writers discovered toward the end of Elizabeth's reign that they had somehow developed a common, workable prose style. A supple, secure English prose had seemed very remote indeed in the days of Henry VIII. Thomas More deliberately wrote his *Utopia* in Latin; among other reasons, he did so because English vocabulary was meager and English syntax unwieldy for the expression of complex ideas. Starting from that humble state, English prose had come a long way by the end of the century, the period of Hooker and Raleigh, Florio and North. It did so, on the whole, not through conscious experiment, but through practice and exercise in circumstances where style was at best a secondary consideration. Indeed, various experiments with learned or artful prose were undertaken, and these were not wholly without influence, especially in court circles, where intricate poetry also tended to flourish. Erudite Latinate importations known derisively as "inkhorn terms" did on occasion take root in the language; the flowers of rhetoric known collectively as "Euphuism" (from the Greek for "fine speech") contributed to an ornate style that was more than a fad. Particularly among the pulpit orators who addressed themselves to the learned and cultured audiences gathered at court and in the several "inns" where lawyers got their training, mental and stylistic ingenuity were developed to a high art. Rhetorical gymnasts like Lancelot Andrewes and John Donne were at the center of these occasions. But in the other direction, plain, practical discourse developed with no more erudite encouragement than could be had from the prose style of Seneca, the Roman moralist—a prose style marked by short, sententious phrases and abrupt transitions. In the long run, that was to be the great achievement of 17th-century prose: a simple, sinewy, versatile speech, as natural on the tongues of soldiers and ploughmen as of pedagogues and princes. Much more than poetry, prose responds to the demands of busy men, who have something to get said, and want to declare it as plainly and directly as possible. The narratives of seafarers and adventurers, the exhortations of controversialists and preachers, the books of botanists and translators, economists, diplomats, doctors, and biographers all contributed to the fullness and ease with which modern English started to root itself in the affairs of this world.

Two recurrent preoccupations of the century, which evoked some of its finest prose, were the direct exploration of human personality, and the search for a law, human or divine, natural or supernatural, by which men could agree to settle their differences. Naturally, these two themes were not exclusive concerns of the 17th century, nor did the 17th-century writers deliberately sit down to concentrate on them. But as they developed, these themes did come very close to defining the central problems of the age, and pointing toward the most striking and substantial developments of the age to come. The "solution" they reached united both preoccupations.

The crisis of the 17th century was first and foremost a human or personal crisis. Men felt stirring within themselves energies and potentialities which the old forms of life would not absorb. Puritans, with their prickly, demanding consciences, were a striking and novel example of this discontent; when they began migrating in numbers to the New World after 1620, they linked up with another and traditional form of Elizabethan restlessness —the explorer's urge. But outward exploration found its counterpart, for this age haunted by multiple worlds, in interior exploration. When frustrated and driven inward, Jacobean impatience and disgust with the social world found expression in the guise of that cosmic melancholy which so fascinated poets and playwrights of the age. A new inwardness is apparent in metaphysical poetry, a new self-questioning makes itself felt in the literature of religious devotion and moral casuistry. Among the arts of personality that come to the fore, we may number the work of the abnormal psychologist, the biographer and autobiographer, the character analyst, the diarist and spiritual self-questioner, even the personal essayist. Each of these new forms contributed to the effort at representing and understanding that various, elastic, multiform, and disorder-prone human nature which the Renaissance had encouraged man to find or create in himself.

The essay, for example, arose late as a literary form, and arose specifically as a form for self-discovery; its creator was Michel de Montaigne. The *Essais* which Montaigne started to write in 1571 and to publish in 1580 undertook to explore the only subject in the world on which Montaigne thought he was an authority, that is, himself. They tell us directly and personally a great many detailed and intimate things about their author—about his diet and digestion, his sleeping habits, his gall-bladder, his sex-life, and his toilet-training—as well as his reading; for he lived a retired life in his chateau near Bordeaux, literally immersed in books. Out of these books he built his essays, in successive editions, into immense cocoons of quotation, surrounding the little larva of his self. This concentration on self is not simply a matter of egotism or self-display; Montaigne thinks himself a fair specimen of the entire human race, and proposes that we can learn a good deal about man in general by studying one sample, even if a random sample, in depth. The result is one of the world's great open-stanced, undefensive self-explorations. John Florio translated Montaigne into salty, colloquial English about the turn of the century, and the book immediately became popular in England, as it had been in France. Bacon's essays, the first in English, are much less open and personal than Montaigne's, but they follow the same process of balancing ideas acquired from experience against those acquired from books, particularly classical moralists like Seneca. Of course Bacon's chief importance lies in the realm of philosophical thought, where he was a major exponent of what was to become the scientific method; but he also provides an introduction to the century's developing concern with the arts of personality.

THE ARTS OF PERSONALITY

The fact that men were now trying out their selves in "essays" (the word implies something tentative)—rather than taking their selves as defined once and for all by a social or theological structure—suggests a decline in the authority of theology. And this decline had indeed taken place; after Henry VIII, the church was not only weaker in its disciplinary powers, it was less coherent intellectually. But as the central framework of theology crumbled, a mass of rubble remained behind it, more fascinating and popular than ever. This is the body of material which became known as "curious lore." Its chief explorers in the 17th century were Robert Burton and Sir Thomas Browne, a psychologist and a meditative medical philosopher.

Essentially "curious lore" is a corpus of semi-religious, pseudo-scientific folk wisdom, embracing elements of pious legend, alchemy and natural magic, superstition, primitive science, and book learning. Over the ages, in the volumes of philosophers, theologians, magicians, doctors, moralists, and mythographers, the materials had been accumulated by thousands of "authorities," most of whom were simply copying from previous "authorities." Of course the age saw nothing wrong with that procedure. The older a piece of "lore" was, the more likely it was to be true. Curious lore could tell you anything you wanted to know about your astrological configuration, about basilisks or amphisbaenas, about the potent number 63, or about your psychological hangups and the reasons for them. If it had been pure nonsense, this lore would have been relatively easy to discard over the ages. But mixed up with the grotesque fables were all sorts of shrewd observations and practical formulas. Though the study of alchemy never led to the philosopher's stone, it led to interesting and occasionally useful observations; though the theory of "humors" was an illusion, a shrewd and experienced doctor could use it to make valid diagnoses and to perform effective cures. Thus, though much of this material was recognized as obsolete before the 17th century, it continued to be copied off and circulated. Scholars who had invested time in learning it repeated it (as scholars often do) because it was what they had learned. Out of affection, amusement, curiosity, and only partly because they hoped to understand and explain their ostensible subjects, Burton and Browne (like many of their predecessors in the study of "curious lore") delighted in wandering, in losing and then finding themselves, amid this wilderness of obsolete and fascinating material.

More direct assaults on the mystery of personality took place during the early 17th century, in the shape of a vogue for set "characters." The origin of the form lies in the work of Theophrastus, a pupil, associate, and successor of Aristotle. The *Characters* of Theophrastus express the classifying temper of Greece in the third century B.C.; they were short lists of things that people of a certain type did. Theophrastus wrote characters of "good" and "bad" people in separate lists; but by an accident of history, only the "bad" people have survived. Thus, even in its cradle, the set "character" had a didactic, even a satiric, purpose. It focused on types, not individuals, posed them in static rather than active situations, and made remarks about them from a moral and critical distance. English interest in the genre was stimulated when a classical scholar, Isaac Casaubon, in 1592 translated Theophrastus' little book from Greek into Latin. The form agreed happily with prevailing medical theories of "humors," according to which a man's personality was shaped by a single predominating humor or trait. A ruling passion could be traced in all the actions of a man's life, and to expose it to healthful ridicule was considered socially therapeutic as well as morally sound. Thus "characters" were written for a while, and circulated in little collections; but the critical, exterior stance of the author, and the total lack of motion or development, kept them from developing toward fiction.

Historians and biographers also had to wrestle with this problem of putting the character in action, making him move from the inside out. The chief historian of the period was Edward Earl of Clarendon. As plain Mr. Edward Hyde, he had stood loyally by Charles I through the thick of the civil wars; he knew well all the actors in the great story which he began to write in the middle of the events themselves, then finished years later (in exile and disgrace) under the title of *History of the Rebellion and Civil Wars in England*. Clarendon is a fine historian, or rather—for better and for worse—he is two fine historians. He can tell an active and vigorous story, fluently and with a great sense for the shape of events. He can also describe a character, setting forth the motivations and characteristics of his man with magisterial authority. But the subject in his characterizations must always be frozen into a formal, composed picture. The story stops, and Clarendon gives us a polished portrait, as if posed by one of the painters of the age, Sir Anthony Van Dyke, or Sir Peter Lely. Some historians have the art of making us feel that we are participating in the making of history, the forging of men; Clarendon gives us nothing but beautifully finished products. For the political theorist and historian of ideas, his majestic volumes have other fascinations as well. Clarendon was a major maker of the Tory philosophy of history (it emphasizes authority and order, but is capable of surprisingly liberal modifications in response to the general welfare), the adaptability of which is shown by the fact that it survives in full energy to this day. But the art of making men's souls speak in individual accents, as from the center of their being, he never mastered.

Izaak Walton, England's first major biographer, never attempted the high style or broad canvas of Clarendon; he was a quiet, modest man who deeply appreciated the traditional quiet and modesty of the Church of England. When the church to which he was devoted came under Puritan attack during the late 1630's, Walton sprang to its defense with the first of a series of biographies, clearly modeled on the saints' lives familiar from earlier days, but enriched and humanized, as far as possible, by personal details and intimate anecdotes. In all, he wrote five biographies: four of his subjects were churchmen, the other a great lay friend of the church. And over all these figures Walton shed the gentle, benevolent radiance of his own quiet spirit. What conflicted with this tonality he did not exactly suppress; but he minimized it. Holy Doctor Donne was much more to his purposes than randy Jack Donne, and the emphasis of his biography runs inevitably that way. All Walton's subjects tended to become the sort of sweet, cheerful person whom he described in his *Complete Angler*. He composed his "lives" in that key; and it's perhaps the fact that John Aubrey never composed his "Brief Lives" at all that gives them so much more of the gust of life, the sense of real presence.

Aubrey was a friend, agent, enemy, and employee of the Oxford historian Anthony à Wood, who toward the end of the century undertook to write capsule biographies of all the writers and bishops educated at the university over the past 200 years. Since Wood understood a "writer" to be anyone who had ever written anything, there was a lot of ground to cover. Aubrey thus became an investigator, that is, an official snoop. His notes were taken on scraps of miscellaneous paper; they are full of gaps, blanks, incoherencies, and indecencies. He never expected to publish them as they now exist; someone else, perhaps Wood, would fix them up, use them in a formal composition. But because this work was never done, the breath of life blows through Aubrey's work. This isn't altogether a matter of scandal and vulgarity. Aubrey admired his friend Thomas Hobbes the philosopher only this side idolatry. But he saw that the cause of biographical veracity would not be served by piety or false dignity. And he gives us, as a result, a portrait of his friend vivid and intimate beyond comparison with anything else in the 17th century.

Aubrey is a master of the quirks and idiosyncrasies of character, but the authentic voice of deep personal feeling is heard, more fully than ever before, through the accents of those Puritans who were impelled to account for their faith by way of a spiritual autobiography. In literature as such these Puritans were not much interested; they wanted to declare, as directly as possible, what the Christian experience had meant to them. But in doing so, they often found that the fullness of their experience could only be rendered by a certain sort of prose style. What they wanted to find out was that they had been blessed with a lively, personal, inward, saving faith. Reading Saint Augustine's exciting *Confessions*, and reflecting on the vicissitudes of their own personal existence, they found that man's life inevitably re-enacted the parable of the talents. God gave man at birth a soul to be saved; that soul must be either used in God's service, and so saved, or squandered, and so cast away; it could not lie neutral or inactive. Discovered only through agonized soul-searching, it must be tested against the world's snares, and used in the Lord's service down to the last scruple.

Thus the Puritans came to define life as a battle and a pilgrimage, in which their entire existence was at stake. In a string of famous phrases, they were wayfaring, warfaring Christians, wandering through the wilderness of this world, doing battle against Satan and his minions, on their way to the Heavenly City, the New Jerusalem. These powerful and dramatic images inspired Puritan preacher-teachers like John Bunyan; the directness, sincerity, and full-throated energy of his spiritual autobiography and his plain but passionate allegory, *The Pilgrim's Progress*, represent a new stage in the development of English prose style.

Bunyan was a soldier of the spirit, the type of man who made Cromwell's Ironsides invincible; but as the messianic dreams faded, and the practical workaday world impinged, English Puritanism began to develop new character-types—men who kept track of their spiritual state, and counted those favors that the Lord poured upon them, but who tended to measure those favors in material terms. In the early days of the Puritan movement, a man like Samuel Pepys would not have been thought a Puritan at all; apart from his personal habits, which included a bit of discreet libertinism, he actually attended the Anglican church. Yet the Puritan streak was in him —and it went beyond the fact that, as a very young man, he had approved of the execution of Charles I. Like Bunyan, he was a methodical and pains-taking keeper of accounts, material as well as spiritual accounts, which he managed to reconcile with a kind of cheerful complacency which still has its charm. The *Diary* is as complete a human document (in its own way) as Montaigne's *Essays*. Reading it, we sometimes smile at the snug way in which Christ and Mammon, snobbery, vulgarity, petty lust, petty malice, and a comfortable measure of devotion joggle together on its pages. But this was the triumph of Restoration Puritanism, to put back together in a new amalgam elements of human nature which the earlier part of the cen-tury had tried to dissect, attack, or question. From our modern point of view, we are apt to think of Puritanism as pure nay-saying and abstinence —"Thou shalt not" elevated to a creed in itself. In fact, it was an active, inspirational movement, which called on men to use their gifts, use their talents, fulfill themselves completely, in the service of a creed. Narrowly dogmatic in some of its earlier formulations, that creed grew rapidly more capacious and accommodating as the century advanced.

THE DISPUTE OVER NATURAL LAW

When Hooker appealed to natural law in his effort to answer the Calvinist argument that all human problems should be solved by reference to the law of God recorded in Holy Scriptures, he certainly seems in modern eyes to be laboring a commonplace. Beyond any doubt, we suppose, a government can make convenient rules for its citizens ("everybody drive on the same side of the road," for example) without finding authority for it in an ancient Hebrew book. But four hundred years ago, the issue was a serious one. Many men did think their eternal salvation depended on their giving evidence in everyday life of a saving Christian faith or zeal, best manifested by obeying scrupulously laws laid down in the Bible. To limit this rigid divine law, Hooker and those who followed him tried to formulate a "law of reason" or "law of nature." But however liberal their intentions, the "law of nature," precisely because it was a slippery, evasive concept, tended toward rigid and authoritarian definitions. James I, for example, was sure that the natural law supported his claim to govern, not only as he saw fit, but as only he saw fit. Indeed, for James, one law supporting his author-ity was by no means enough; he could not be satisfied with fewer than three, the law of God, the law of nature, and the law of the land, all insist-ing on the same thing. As he fancied himself a philosopher and a stylist (behind his back people sometimes referred to him as "the wisest fool in Christendom"), he wrote a book to argue the point. *The True Law of Free Monarchies* laid down the basic principles of royal absolutism, later to be known as "the divine right of kings." The essential point of this doctrine is that the king has been appointed by God and is responsible only to God; for subjects to call him to question is not only treasonable, it is blasphe-mous. James began his argument by citing the law of God out of I Samuel viii, where the Lord, speaking through Samuel the prophet, warns the Hebrew people that kings may be very harsh and demanding. If, therefore, the Jews insisted on a king (they did, and got Saul), they had no reason to complain of subsequent misfortunes, because they had been amply warned. And if they could not complain, then neither could anyone else, ever, under any circumstances, till the end of time.

This analogical rigidity, which proposed that a nation of 17th-century

Englishmen should submit abjectly to any royal decrees, however unreasonable—against morality, common sense, and self-interest, simply because the Hebrew people of 2,500 years ago were once stupid—served the interests of James very nicely. But it hardly won much general acceptance until the temper of the nation had been sharpened and hardened by years of civil war. The doctrine reached a climax of rigor and of absurdity in Sir Robert Filmer's *Patriarcha*, written about 1650 but only published thirty years later. Sir Robert, arguing that Adam was absolute ruler of his sons, went on to declare that every monarch, as absolute father of his people, is absolute ruler over them; hence, he declared that any sort of limit on absolute monarchy—any attempt even to reason with the king—is an open invitation to anarchy. Subjects have only one duty, to submit; even if ordered to commit a deadly sin, they are not to resist, only to endure the king's penalty.

The stiffness and pedantry of this thinking, which could only have flourished in an age of crisis, contrasts sharply with the gruff realism of Hobbes, who frankly makes the self-interest of people the basic principle of government. Hobbes believes in authority as much as any royalist; but it is authority serving the welfare of the people, not destructive of it. Hobbes doesn't deduce his laws of politics from Biblical or any other texts; he builds them on a conception of human nature itself. From Bacon (whose secretary he had been) he had learned to mistrust abuses of language, in the form of vague, undefined terms, and unquestioned assumptions; his treatises all begin with a set of strict definitions in which he reduces his terms, so far as possible, to distinct, concrete, specific meanings. In his most famous book, *Leviathan* (1651), he declares that the foundation of all political power lies in a purely human contract made by men with other men for their common advantage. God is conspicuously *not* a partner to this contract. Since it is made for a practical purpose (mutual security), there is some reason to think the contract valid only as long as it serves that purpose. In Chapter 15 of the book's first part, Hobbes actually goes out of his way to encounter a very tough-minded and intelligent "fool," who proposes to him that a reasonable man (whose name might just be "Cromwell") may very well break his oath of allegiance (as for example to a king named Charles I) in order to get a kingdom for himself; and that in so doing, he will act reasonably and virtuously, maybe even to the real advantage of those over whom he rules. Hobbes argues, a bit perfunctorily, that this reasonable man is really foolish, and wicked as well; but evidently he was unable to persuade himself, for shortly after *Leviathan* appeared, he returned to England and accepted the government of the usurper Cromwell.

Like his prose style, Hobbes's view of human nature was crusty, rational, structured and tempered with practicality; people, he proposed, should be guided and are guided by a long-term consideration of their material interests. But the revolution through which he was living could have taught him differently. It was led by men who cared far less about their material interests than about the fulfilment of a developing collective myth, a vision of the Christian life which flowered in—and out of—the vehement, vociferous imagery of prophetic imagination, as stimulated by a passionate reading of the Bible. The early Puritan movement had indeed based all its demands for reform on the idea of conforming, in every last detail, with the rule of Scripture as interpreted by John Calvin. But as the revolution widened and deepened, men of imperious and imaginative tempers came to the fore, who consulted their individual consciences more and the legalistic words of Scripture less. Agitators and enthusiasts sought their inspiration in the cloudier books of the Bible (Daniel and Revelation by preference); they also drew inspiration from the example of the Apostle Paul and from a tradition (dating back to Foxe's *Book of Martyrs* and the persecution of English Protestants by the Catholic Mary Tudor) that the English people were destined to be vessels of God's truth, as the Hebrews were in days gone by. Some even identified the English with one or several of the lost tribes, and spoke of themselves as English Israelites.

These Messianic hopes and expectations were shared by many, even by a learned man like Milton, during the days when revolutionary fervor was burning hot. But Milton, as he knew very well himself, was not at his best in prose, least of all in prose that was bound to appeal to a common, popular reader. The weight of an elaborate, Latinate syntax and a learned, Latinate vocabulary lay heavy on Milton's prose style; one can feel him struggling unsuccessfully to throw it off. Men less encumbered with learning reached the solution sooner. The language in which agitators like John Lilburne and Gerrard Winstanley put forward their extreme conceptions· of natural law and natural right represents something new in English political life. Lilburne—who was only one agitator out of hundreds—argues his case in the hoarse, colloquial accents of common sense. He is a man speaking his conscience before other men, and appealing for their sympathy. Contentious, theatrical, terribly in earnest, he is a perfect advocate, a tribute of the people. Winstanley's messianic, visionary diction flies higher than Lilburne's, and in its own time fell flatter—it will not find its echo until some of the prophetic writings of Blake. But both men represent an aroused, involved, conscientious concern, an active ethical interest in politics, which has at last found a voice. The participation of men like Lilburne and Winstanley points toward the formation of that vast, amorphous, intermittent force known to the modern world as "an aroused public opinion."

It was on the shifting sands of public opinion (not on any political or religious infallibility) that the 17th century finally settled its philosophical and political foundations. The man who, more than any other, formulated this compromise, was John Locke. A particular experience which lay behind Locke's famous *Essay Concerning Human Understanding* (1689) represents in capsule form the experience of the entire nation in the course of the entire century. A group of friends had gathered to discuss certain subjects, and found themselves in great and growing disagreement. To resolve these differences, they asked one of their number (Locke) to think about the nature of the human mind itself, in order to decide if it was capable of leading them to certainty on the original issues. Locke was a grave, supple, dispassionate man; he decided, after much quiet but weighty consideration, that if men will confine themselves to talking only about those things of which they can form clear and exact ideas, they can reach sufficient certainty for most practical purposes. All sorts of infallibilities after which the century had been striving thus went by the board. Farfetched analogies based on Scriptures, intricate notions of divine law inscribed upon men's consciences, all crumbled. Common sense (that plain sense common to all men) became the arbiter of those questions on which men can hope to reach agreement; and on matters where they cannot hope to reach agreement, each man is left to his own devices. It was a pragmatic conclusion; and it was phrased in a smooth, consecutive, and polished prose which seemed to carry immense weights of thought gracefully and without strain. Since clear ideas, according to Locke, all originate in sense experience, they are all subject to checking and verification; and Locke was perfectly blunt in asking every reader of the *Essay* to test its formulations against his own experience. So bold and yet so modest a book, so casual in its definition of its subject ("a few coarse thoughts") and so rigorous in following out its argument, had an influence on the thought of Europe which is impossible to calculate. For over a century, European philosophy (not simply the thought of professional philosophers, but the assumptions of everyday people) was dominated by Locke. In the depth and extent of its influence, Locke's *Essay* is surely one of the most important books ever written. For behind it lay, as we have seen, the experience of an entire era.

FRANCIS BACON

(1561–1626)

> 1597: First edition of the *Essays* (augmented and revised editions in 1612 and 1625).
> 1605: *The Advancement of Learning.*
> 1620: *Novum Organum.*
> 1621: Bacon's disgrace and retirement.

Francis Bacon, the younger son of a highly placed Elizabethan civil servant, studied law at Cambridge and Gray's Inn, entered the legal bureaucracy of Elizabeth, and rose steadily through it until, under James, he stood at the head of his profession, as Lord Chancellor of England. But after barely three years in this office, he fell from power and reputation, accused of taking bribes in office, and confessing himself guilty of corruption and neglect. The last five years of his life were spent in retirement.

In the field of the essay, Bacon's only predecessor was Montaigne; but Bacon's social and business position (which he had no intention of resigning, as Montaigne had done) kept him from following Montaigne's example in writing personal confessions. As a man with a judicial position to maintain, he was not out to discover himself or explore unknown thoughts. His training in law and his reading in the Roman moralists had given him the habit of thinking in axioms; and axioms of prudent, practical conduct were what he laid down. Montaigne, in titling his writings *Essais*, emphasized the tentative and exploratory nature of his thought; he didn't care about developing a consistent, defensible philosophy, only about tracing the quirky track of his changing moods. Bacon laid down the law like a magistrate or a Dutch uncle, and largely concealed his "self"—at least in the way Montaigne defined "self"—under the official robes of worldly wisdom.

Only the bookish side of Montaigne came out in Bacon's *Essays*; reading them, you would imagine that he was born at the age of thirty-eight, with a volume of moral epistles for one parent and a treatise of English law for the other. Neither do his *Essays* provide much of a guide to human nature; you would scarcely learn from them, any more than from the writings of Emerson, that the human race is divided into two sexes. What one could pick up are certain prudential, practical rules about the successful conduct of business life. Philadelphia lawyers were once famous for giving this kind of advice, and Bacon phrased it in crisp, compressed phrases, easy for a busy man to remember. Axioms and adages are the kernels of legal wisdom, and Bacon's essays often read like a string of walnut sayings, hard to crack, but meaty and nourishing enough, once one has got inside them.

Bacon's reticence—not to say inhibition—when writing personal essays contrasts strikingly with the sweep and boldness of his directly philosophical work. Here the importance of what he says and implies is almost impossible to overstate. He was not himself much of a practical scientist, and anyone who tries can comb from his works an amazing collection of superstitious and unfounded beliefs. But his vision of intellectual method was wide as well as deep, and its emphasis on verifiable experiment held immense promise for the future. In fact, simple emphasis on "experience" and "experiment" (the former word was sometimes used where we would employ the latter) was not a novel principle when Bacon put it forth. A man like Paracelsus, the Swiss alchemist of the 16th century, had insisted on following his own experience against the authority of the great Galen and other doctors of classical antiquity. That was why Paracelsus and his alchemical followers were called "empirics." But their observations were uncontrolled. They noted the effects of what they called occult sympathies (for example, the peculiar affinity of the sunflower for the sun), and generalized from that single observation by analogy. Bacon recommended controlled and repeated experiments, in which theory worked to direct and focus experience, and in which all experiments were coordinated with one another. And this vision, as most memorably outlined in *The New Atlantis,* represented the ideal of the future. If anything, the great chancellor did not give enough weight to the concept of the controlling hypothesis; a modern scientist would give more, reducing the role of experiment to simple verification. But in most other respects, Bacon was centuries ahead of his time.

Yet, before anything could be built out of scientific hypothesis and verification, there was a major work of demolition to be accomplished. That was simply the mass of things that men already knew, under the name of "science," which weren't so. Bacon attacked such errors and their causes in the *Novum Organum,* or "New Instrument of Knowledge," (1620), under the heading of "idols," or false images of the mind.

From ESSAYS
Of Truth

"What is truth?" said jesting Pilate; and would not stay for an answer.[1] Certainly there be that delight in giddiness,[2] and count it

---

1. See John xviii.38 for Pilate's idle query to Jesus.

2. Changeability, insecurity of ideas. "That": those who.

a bondage to fix a belief; affecting free-will in thinking, as well as in acting. And though the sects of philosophers of that kind[3] be gone, yet there remain certain discoursing wits, which are of the same veins, though there be not so much blood in them as was in those of the ancients. But it is not only the difficulty and labor which men take in finding out of truth; nor again, that when it is found, it imposeth upon[4] men's thoughts, that doth bring lies in favor; but a natural though corrupt love of the lie itself. One of the later school of the Grecians examineth the matter, and is at a stand to think what should be in it, that men should love lies; where neither they make for pleasure, as with poets; nor for advantage, as with the merchant, but for the lie's sake. But I cannot tell:[5] this same truth is a naked and open daylight, that doth not show the masks and mummeries and triumphs of the world half so stately and daintily as candle lights. Truth may perhaps come to the price of a pearl, that showeth best by day, but it will not rise to the price of a diamond or carbuncle,[6] that showeth best in varied lights. A mixture of a lie doth ever add pleasure. Doth any man doubt that if there were taken out of men's minds vain opinions, flattering hopes, false valuations, imaginations as one would, and the like, but it would leave the minds of a number of men poor shrunken things, full of melancholy and indisposition, and unpleasing to themselves? One of the fathers, in great severity, called poesy *vinum daemonum*,[7] because it filleth the imagination, and yet it is but with the shadow of a lie. But it is not the lie that passeth through the mind, but the lie that sinketh in, and settleth in it, that doth the hurt, such as we spake of before. But howsoever these things are thus in men's depraved judgments and affections, yet truth, which only doth judge itself, teacheth that the inquiry of truth, which is the love-making, or wooing of it, the knowledge of truth, which is the presence of it, and the belief of truth, which is the enjoying of it, is the sovereign good of human nature. The first creature[8] of God, in the works of the days, was the light of the sense; the last was the light of reason; and His sabbath work ever since is the illumination of His Spirit. First, He breathed light upon the face of the matter, or chaos; then He breathed light into the face of man; and still He breatheth and inspireth light into the face of His chosen. The poet that beautified the sect that was otherwise inferior to the rest[9] saith yet excellently well: "It is a pleasure to stand upon the shore, and to see ships tossed upon the sea: a pleasure to stand in the window of a castle,

---

3. The Greek Skeptics, who taught the uncertainty of all knowledge. "Discoursing wits": discursive minds.
4. Restricts, limits.
5. "I cannot tell," says Bacon, and tells.
6. Ruby.
7. The wine of devils; St. Augustine

is probably being cited.
8. Creation.
9. Lucretius' *On the Nature of Things* expressed the Epicurean creed, which Bacon thought inferior because it emphasized pleasure. The passage cited comprises the first words of Book I.

and to see a battle, and the adventures thereof below: but no pleasure is comparable to the standing upon the vantage ground of truth" (a hill not to be commanded,[1] and where the air is always clear and serene), "and to see the errors, and wanderings, and mists, and tempests, in the vale below": so always that this prospect[2] be with pity, and not with swelling or pride. Certainly, it is heaven upon earth to have a man's mind move in charity, rest in providence, and turn upon the poles of truth.

To pass from theological and philosophical truth to the truth of civil business; it will be acknowledged even by those that practice it not, that clear and round dealing[3] is the honor of man's nature, and that mixture of falsehood is like alloy in coin of gold and silver, which may make the metal work the better, but it embaseth[4] it. For these winding and crooked courses are the goings of the serpent; which goeth basely upon the belly, and not upon the feet. There is no vice that doth so cover a man with shame as to be found false and perfidious; and therefore Montaigne saith prettily, when he inquired the reason why the word of the lie should be such a disgrace, and such an odious charge, saith he, "If it be well weighed, to say that a man lieth is as much as to say that he is brave towards God and a coward towards men."[5] For a lie faces God, and shrinks from man. Surely the wickedness of falsehood and breach of faith cannot possibly be so highly expressed, as in that it shall be the last peal to call the judgments of God upon the generations of men, it being foretold that when Christ cometh, he shall not "find faith upon the earth."[6]

1625

Of Marriage and Single Life[1]

He that hath wife and children hath given hostages to fortune; for they are impediments to great enterprises, either of virtue or mischief. Certainly the best works, and of greatest merit for the public, have proceeded from the unmarried or childless men, which both in affection and means have married and endowed the public. Yet it were great reason that those that have children should have greatest care of future times, unto which they know they must transmit their dearest pledges. Some there are who, though they lead a single life, yet their thoughts do end with themselves, and account future times impertinences.[2] Nay, there are some other that account wife and children but as bills of charges. Nay more, there

---

1. Dominated.
2. I.e., provided always that this contemplation.
3. The dealing that Bacon calls "round" we should describe as "square."

4. Debases.
5. *Essays* II.18.
6. Luke xviii.8.
1. The text is that of the 1625 edition.
2. Irrelevant concerns.

are some foolish rich covetous men that take a pride in having no children, because they may be thought so much the richer. For perhaps they have heard some talk, "Such an one is a great rich man," and another except to it, "Yea, but he hath a great charge of children"; as if it were an abatement to his riches. But the most ordinary cause of a single life is liberty, especially in certain self-pleasing and humorous[3] minds, which are so sensible of every restraint, as they will go near to think their girdles and garters to be bonds and shackles. Unmarried men are best friends, best masters, best servants, but not always best subjects, for they are light to run away, and almost all fugitives are of that condition. A single life doth well with churchmen, for charity will hardly water the ground where it must first fill a pool. It is indifferent for judges and magistrates, for if they be facile[4] and corrupt, you shall have a servant five times worse than a wife. For soldiers, I find the generals commonly in their hortatives[5] put men in mind of their wives and children; and I think the despising of marriage amongst the Turks maketh the vulgar soldier more base. Certainly wife and children are a kind of discipline of humanity; and single men, though they be many times more charitable, because their means are less exhaust,[6] yet, on the other side, they are more cruel and hard-hearted (good to make severe inquisitors), because their tenderness is not so oft called upon. Grave natures, led by custom, and therefore constant, are commonly loving husbands, as was said of Ulysses, *Vetulam suam praetulit immortalitati.*[7] Chaste women are often proud and froward, as presuming upon the merit of their chastity. It is one of the best bonds, both of chastity and obedience, in the wife if she think her husband wise, which she will never do if she find him jealous. Wives are young men's mistresses, companions for middle age, and old men's nurses, so as a man may have a quarrel[8] to marry when he will. But yet he was reputed one of the wise men that made answer to the question when a man should marry: "A young man not yet, an elder man not at all."[9] It is often seen that bad husbands have very good wives; whether it be that it raiseth the price of their husbands' kindness when it comes, or that the wives take a pride in their patience. But this never fails, if the bad husbands were of their own choosing, against their friends' consent; for then they will be sure to make good their own folly.

1612, 1625

---

3. Unbalanced, whimsical.
4. Pliable.
5. Exhortations.
6. Exhausted, drained.
7. "He preferred his old wife to immortality." Ulysses might have had immortality in the company of the

nymph Calypso, but preferred to go back to Penelope.
8. Pretext.
9. Thales (6th century B.C.) was the confirmed bachelor who made this remark. He was one of the Seven Sages of Greece.

Of Studies[1]

Studies serve for delight, for ornament, and for ability. Their chief use for delight is in privateness[2] and retiring; for ornament, is in discourse; and for ability, is in the judgment and disposition of business. For expert men[3] can execute, and perhaps judge of particulars, one by one; but the general counsels, and the plots and marshaling of affairs, come best from those that are learned. To spend too much time in studies is sloth; to use them too much for ornament is affectation; to make judgment wholly by their rules is the humor[4] of a scholar. They perfect nature, and are perfected by experience; for natural abilities are like natural plants, that need pruning by study; and studies themselves do give forth directions too much at large, except they be bounded in by experience. Crafty men contemn studies, simple men admire them, and wise men use them, for they teach not their own use; but that is a wisdom without them, and above them, won by observation. Read not to contradict and confute, nor to believe and take for granted, nor to find talk and discourse, but to weigh and consider. Some books are to be tasted, others to be swallowed, and some few to be chewed and digested; that is, some books are to be read only in parts; others to be read, but not curiously;[5] and some few to be read wholly, and with diligence and attention. Some books also may be read by deputy and extracts made of them by others, but that would be only in the less important arguments and the meaner sort of books; else distilled books are like common distilled waters,[6] flashy things. Reading maketh a full man, conference[7] a ready man, and writing an exact man. And therefore, if a man write little, he had need have a great memory; if he confer little, he had need have a present wit;[8] and if he read little, he had need have more cunning, to seem to know that[9] he doth not. Histories make men wise; poets, witty;[1] the mathematics, subtle; natural philosophy, deep; moral, grave; logic and rhetoric, able to contend. *Abeunt studia in mores.*[2] Nay, there is no stond or impediment in the wit but may be wrought out by fit studies, like as diseases of the body may have appropriate exercises. Bowling is good for the stone and reins,[3] shooting for the lungs and breast, gentle walking for the stomach, riding for the head, and the like. So if a

---

1. The text is that of the 1625 edition.
2. Private life.
3. Men of experience, the English adjective being used in its Latin sense, *experti*.
4. Mannerism, implying absurd error.
5. Not with care.
6. Infusions of herbs, etc., used as home remedies.
7. Conversation, meetings.
8. Lively intelligence.
9. That which.
1. Imaginative, inventive.
2. "Studies culminate in manners" (Ovid, *Heroides*). "Stond": difficulty.
3. Gall bladder and kidneys.

man's wit be wandering, let him study the mathematics; for in demonstrations, if his wit be called away never so little, he must begin again. If his wit be not apt to distinguish or find differences, let him study the schoolmen,[4] for they are *Cymini sectores.* If he be not apt to beat over matters[5] and to call up one thing to prove and illustrate another, let him study the lawyer's cases. So every defect of the mind may have a special receipt.[6]

1597, 1625

Of Negotiating

It is generally better to deal by speech than by letter, and by the mediation of a third than by a man's self. Letters are good when a man would draw an answer by letter back again, or when it may serve for a man's justification afterwards to produce his own letter, or where it may be danger to be interrupted or heard by pieces. To deal in person is good when a man's face breedeth regard, as commonly with inferiors, or in tender[1] cases, where a man's eye upon the countenance of him with whom he speaketh may give him a direction how far to go; and generally, where a man will reserve to himself liberty either to disavow or to expound. In choice of instruments, it is better to choose men of a plainer sort, that are like to do that that is committed to them, and to report back again faithfully the success, than those that are cunning to contrive out of other men's business somewhat to grace themselves, and will help the matter in report for satisfaction sake. Use also such persons as affect[2] the business wherein they are employed, for that quickeneth much; and such as are fit for the matter, as bold men for expostulation, fair-spoken men for persuasion, crafty men for inquiry and observation, froward and absurd men for business that doth not well bear out itself.[3] Use also such as have been lucky, and prevailed before in things wherein you have employed them; for that breeds confidence, and they will strive to maintain their prescription.[4] It is better to sound a person with whom one deals afar off, than to fall upon the point at first, except you mean to surprise him by some short question. It is better dealing with men in appetite,[5] than with those that are where they would be. If a man deal with another upon conditions, the start or first performance is all,[6] which a man cannot reasonably demand, except either the

---

4. Medieval theologians. The Latin means "dividers of cuminseed," i.e., hairsplitters.
5. Discuss a subject thoroughly.
6. Cure, prescription.
1. Difficult, complex.
2. Like.
3. Bacon suggests that when you have

an unjust demand to make, you select a fool to make it.
4. Keep up their reputation.
5. Hungry men.
6. If you're arguing over details, they will have to be settled by reference to the basic agreement, or to some other power relationship.

nature of the thing be such which must go before, or else a man can persuade the other party that he shall still need him in some other thing, or else that he be counted the honester man. All practice is to discover or to work.[7] Men discover themselves in trust, in passion, at unawares, and of necessity, when they would have somewhat done and cannot find an apt pretext. If you would work any man, you must either know his nature and fashions, and so lead him; or his ends, and so persuade him; or his weakness and disadvantages, and so awe him; or those that have interest in him, and so govern him. In dealing with cunning persons, we must ever consider their ends, to interpret their speeches; and it is good to say little to them, and that which they least look for. In all negotiations of difficulty, a man may not look to sow and reap at once; but must prepare business, and so ripen it by degrees.

From Novum Organum[1]
[*The Idols*]

50

But by far the greatest hindrance and aberration of the human understanding proceeds from the dullness, incompetency, and deceptions of the senses; in that things which strike the sense outweigh things which do not immediately strike it, though they[2] be more important. Hence it is that speculation commonly ceases where sight ceases; insomuch that of things invisible there is little or no observation. Hence all the working of the spirits enclosed in tangible bodies lies hid and unobserved of men.[3] So also all the more subtle changes of form in the parts of coarser substances (which they commonly call alteration, though it is in truth local motion through exceedingly small spaces) is in like manner unobserved. And yet unless these two things just mentioned be searched

---

7. All sharp bargaining aims to find out what men are up to or to make use of them. "Discover": reveal.
1. *Novum Organum,* or "The New Instrument of Learning," does not properly represent a work of English literature, since it was written in Latin, for an international scholarly audience. (Bacon rather mistrusted the modern languages, thinking they would "wear away" in time; but Latin was safe.) Still, no history of English ideas can afford to ignore this book; for it was the keystone of Bacon's vast project to renovate the structure of human learning from the ground up. The translation is that of Spedding, Ellis, and Heath, from their edition of the *Works* (1860–64).
  Observation was the essential process of Bacon's new method; he felt that

only observation, long continued and carefully directed, was capable of producing certainty about the operations of nature. As against the true intellectual mean produced by careful observation and controlled experiment, he set the frivolity of the skeptics and the unwarranted confidence of the dogmatists. This argument rises to its height about halfway through the first (destructive) part of the book, in an extended account of the various Idols, or delusive ideas, which mislead and bewilder the human understanding.
2. The latter.
3. Though his views on scientific method were amazingly modern, Bacon's ideas about physical phenomena were those of his age; he believed in subtle spiritual principles which might lie concealed in physical objects, unobserved by men.

out and brought to light, nothing great can be achieved in nature, as far as the production of works is concerned. So again the essential nature of our common air, and of all bodies less dense than air (which are very many), is almost unknown. For the sense by itself is a thing infirm and erring; neither can instruments for enlarging or sharpening the senses do much; but all the truer kind of interpretation of nature is effected by instances and experiments fit and apposite; wherein the sense decides touching the experiment only, and the experiment touching the point in nature and the thing itself.

51

The human understanding is of its own nature prone to abstractions and gives a substance and reality to things which are fleeting. But to resolve nature into abstractions is less to our purpose than to dissect her into parts; as did the school of Democritus,[4] which went further into nature than the rest. Matter rather than forms should be the object of our attention, its configurations and changes of configuration, and simple action, and law of action or motion; for forms are figments of the human mind, unless you will call those laws of action forms.

52

Such then are the idols which I call *Idols of the Tribe*;[5] and which take their rise either from the homogeneity of the substance of the human spirit, or from its preoccupation, or from its narrowness, or from its restless motion, or from an infusion of the affections, or from the incompetency of the senses, or from the mode of impression.

53

The *Idols of the Cave* take their rise in the peculiar constitution, mental or bodily, of each individual; and also in education, habit, and accident. Of this kind there is a great number and variety; but I will instance those the pointing out of which contains the most important caution, and which have most effect in disturbing the clearness of the understanding.

54

Men become attached to certain particular sciences[6] and speculations, either because they fancy themselves the authors and inventors thereof, or because they have bestowed the greatest pains upon them and become most habituated to them. But men of this kind,

4. The school of Democritus, the "laughing philosopher" of ancient Greece (5th century B.C.), held that the world was composed of atoms. Democritus developed the atomic theory, of which Leucippus was the originator; Lucretius (four centuries later) became the great literary exponent of this school.

5. By "Idols" Bacon means delusive images of truth, leading men away from the exact knowledge of science. By "Idols of the Tribe" he denotes particularly generalizations based on inadequate facts—a fault to which all men are prone.
6. Ideas, bits of information.

if they betake themselves to philosophy and contemplations of a general character, distort and color them in obedience to their former fancies; a thing especially to be noticed in Aristotle, who made his natural philosophy a mere bondservant to his logic, thereby rendering it contentious and well nigh useless. The race of chemists[7] again out of a few experiments of the furnace have built up a fantastic philosophy, framed with reference to a few things; and Gilbert also, after he had employed himself most laboriously in the study and observation of the loadstone, proceeded at once to construct an entire system in accordance with his favorite subject.[8]

55

There is one principal and, as it were, radical distinction between different minds, in respect of philosophy and the sciences, which is this: that some minds are stronger and apter to mark the differences of things, others to mark their resemblances. The steady and acute mind can fix its contemplations and dwell and fasten on the subtlest distinctions: the lofty and discursive mind recognizes and puts together the finest and most general resemblances. Both kinds however easily err in excess, by catching the one at gradations, the other at shadows.

56

There are found some minds given to an extreme admiration of antiquity, others to an extreme love and appetite for novelty; but few so duly tempered that they can hold the mean, neither carping at what has been well laid down by the ancients, nor despising what is well introduced by the moderns. This however turns to the great injury of the sciences and philosophy; since these affectations of antiquity and novelty are the humors of partisans rather than judgments; and truth is to be sought for not in the felicity of any age, which is an unstable thing, but in the light of nature and experience, which is eternal. These factions therefore must be abjured, and care must be taken that the intellect be not hurried by them into assent.

57

Contemplations of nature and of bodies in their simple form break up and distract the understanding, while contemplations of nature and bodies in their composition and configuration overpower and dissolve the understanding:[9] a distinction well seen in the school of Leucippus and Democritus as compared with the other philosophies. For that school is so busied with the particles that it hardly attends to the structure; while the others are so lost in admiration of the structure that they do not penetrate to the simplicity of nature.

7. Alchemists.
8. William Gilbert, author of a famous treatise on the magnet (1600), serves Bacon (rather unfairly) as an example of dogmatism founded on a few limited experiments.
9. I.e., reducing nature to first principles is, intellectually, as dangerous as trying to observe all its particulars.

These kinds of contemplation should therefore be alternated and taken by turns; that so the understanding may be rendered at once penetrating and comprehensive, and the inconveniences above mentioned, with the idols which proceed from them, may be avoided.

58

Let such then be our provision and contemplative prudence for keeping off and dislodging the *Idols of the Cave*, which grow for the most part either out of the predominance of a favorite subject, or out of an excessive tendency to compare or to distinguish, or out of partiality for particular ages, or out of the largeness or minuteness of the objects contemplated. And generally let every student of nature take this as a rule—that whatever his mind seizes and dwells upon with peculiar satisfaction is to be held in suspicion, and that so much the more care is to be taken in dealing with such questions to keep the understanding even and clear.

59

But the *Idols of the Market-place* are the most troublesome of all: idols which have crept into the understanding through the alliances of words and names. For men believe that their reason governs words; but it is also true that words react on the understanding; and this it is that has rendered philosophy and the sciences sophistical and inactive. Now words, being commonly framed and applied according to the capacity of the vulgar, follow those lines of division which are most obvious to the vulgar understanding. And whenever an understanding of greater acuteness or a more diligent observation would alter those lines to suit the true divisions of nature, words stand in the way and resist the change. Whence it comes to pass that the high and formal discussions of learned men end oftentimes in disputes about words and names; with which (according to the use[1] and wisdom of the mathematicians) it would be more prudent to begin, and so by means of definitions reduce them to order. Yet even definitions cannot cure this evil in dealing with natural and material things; since the definitions themselves consist of words, and those words beget others: so that it is necessary to recur to individual instances, and those in due series and order; as I shall say presently when I come to the method and scheme for the formation of notions and axioms.[2]

60

The idols imposed by words on the understanding are of two kinds. They are either names of things which do not exist (for as there are things left unnamed through lack of observation, so likewise are there names which result from fantastic suppositions and

---

1. Custom.
2. Bacon's mistrust of words, evident here, led the Royal Society to cultivate a plain, stripped prose style for purposes of scientific communication.

to which nothing in reality responds), or they are names of things which exist, but yet confused and ill-defined, and hastily and irregularly derived from realities. Of the former kind are Fortune, the Prime Mover, Planetary Orbits, Element of Fire, and like fictions which owe their origin to false and idle theories.[3] And this class of idols is more easily expelled, because to get rid of them it is only necessary that all theories should be steadily rejected and dismissed as obsolete.[4]

But the other class, which springs out of a faulty and unskillful abstraction, is intricate and deeply rooted. Let us take for example such a word as *humid*; and see how far the several things which the word is used to signify agree with each other; and we shall find the word *humid* to be nothing else than a mark loosely and confusedly applied to denote a variety of actions which will not bear to be reduced to any constant meaning. For it both signifies that which easily spreads itself round any other body; and that which in itself is indeterminate and cannot solidize; and that which readily yields in every direction; and that which easily divides and scatters itself; and that which easily unites and collects itself; and that which readily flows and is put in motion; and that which readily clings to another body and wets it; and that which is easily reduced to a liquid, or being solid easily melts. Accordingly when you come to apply the word—if you take it in one sense, flame is humid; if in another, air is not humid; if in another, fine dust is humid; if in another, glass is humid. So that it is easy to see that the notion is taken by abstraction only from water and common and ordinary liquids, without any due verification.

There are however in words certain degrees of distortion and error. One of the least faulty kinds is that of names of substances, especially of lowest species and well-deduced (for the notion of *chalk* and of *mud* is good, of *earth* bad); a more faulty kind is that of actions, as *to generate, to corrupt, to alter*; the most faulty is of qualities (except such as are the immediate objects of the sense), as *heavy, light, rare, dense*, and the like. Yet in all these cases some notions are of necessity a little better than others, in proportion to the greater variety of subjects that fall within the range of the human sense.

3. The "Prime Mover" was a transparent sphere on the outside of the universe, supposed to move all the other spheres; the "Element of Fire" was an area of pure, invisible fire, supposed to exist above the atmosphere. In the nature of things, these concepts could be based on no observation. "Planetary Orbits," on the other hand, are very real; Bacon may be referring to the old notion of crystalline spheres in which the planets were supposed to be set.

4. Bacon does not really mean "theories" in the inclusive modern sense, but "abstractions loosely invoked to explain particular facts." He is actually restating William of Occam's famous 14th-century principle, known as "Occam's razor," to the effect that "essences must not be multiplied beyond necessity."

61

But the *Idols of the Theater*[5] are not innate, nor do they steal into the understanding secretly, but are plainly impressed and received into the mind from the play-books of philosophical systems and the perverted rules of demonstration. To attempt refutations in this case would be merely inconsistent with what I have already said: for since we agree neither upon principles nor upon demonstrations, there is no place for argument. And this is so far well, inasmuch as it leaves the honor of the ancients untouched. For they are no wise disparaged—the question between them and me being only as to the way. For as the saying is, the lame man who keeps the right road outstrips the runner who takes a wrong one. Nay, it is obvious that when a man runs the wrong way, the more active and swift he is the further he will go astray.

But the course I propose for the discovery of sciences is such as leaves but little to the acuteness and strength of wits, but places all wits and understandings nearly on a level. For as in the drawing of a straight line or a perfect circle, much depends on the steadiness and practice of the hand, if it be done by aim of hand only, but if with the aid of rule or compass, little or nothing; so is it exactly with my plan. But though particular confutations would be of no avail, yet touching the sects and general divisions of such systems I must say something; something also touching the external signs which show that they are unsound; and finally something touching the causes of such great infelicity and of such lasting and general agreement in error; that so the access to truth may be made less difficult, and the human understanding may the more willingly submit to its purgation and dismiss its idols.

62

Idols of the Theater, or of systems, are many, and there can be and perhaps will be yet many more. For were it not that now for many ages men's minds have been busied with religion and theology; and were it not that civil governments, especially monarchies, have been averse to such novelties, even in matters speculative; so that men labor therein to the peril and harming of their fortunes—not only unrewarded, but exposed also to contempt and envy; doubtless there would have arisen many other philosophical sects like to those which in great variety flourished once among the Greeks. For as on the phenomena of the heavens many hypotheses may be constructed, so likewise (and more also) many various dogmas may be set up

---

5. I.e., those derived from previous philosophical systems, which misrepresent life by overdramatizing it and mislead men by pretending to show them reality itself.

and established on the phenomena of philosophy. And in the plays of this philosophical theater you may observe the same thing which is found in the theater of the poets, that stories invented for the stage are more compact and elegant, and more as one would wish them to be, than true stories out of history.

In general, however, there is taken for the material of philosophy either a great deal out of a few things, or a very little out of many things; so that on both sides philosophy is based on too narrow a foundation of experiment and natural history, and decides on the authority of too few cases. For the rational school of philosophers snatches from experience a variety of common instances, neither duly ascertained nor diligently examined and weighed, and leaves all the rest to meditation and agitation of wit.[6]

There is also another class of philosophers, who having bestowed much diligent and careful labor on a few experiments, have thence made bold to educe and construct systems; wresting all other facts in a strange fashion to conformity therewith.

And there is yet a third class, consisting of those who out of faith and veneration mix their philosophy with theology and traditions; among whom the vanity of some has gone so far aside as to seek the origin of sciences among spirits and genii. So that this parent stock of errors—this false philosophy—is of three kinds; the sophistical, the empirical, and the superstitious. * * *

68

So much concerning the several classes of idols, and their equipage: all of which must be renounced and put away with a fixed and solemn determination, and the understanding thoroughly freed and cleansed; the entrance into the kingdom of man, founded on the sciences, being not much other than the entrance into the kingdom of heaven, whereinto none may enter except as a little child.

1620

6. Bacon's thought contained a concealed element of anti-intellectualism: his enthusiasm for experiment led him to denigrate the value of reason, as very few modern scientists would feel it necessary to do. What he is opposing here is an excessive concern with the forms of logic, as exemplified, he would say, in "the schoolmen."

From The New Atlantis[1]
[*Solomon's House*]

We came at our day and hour, and I was chosen by my fellows for the private access.[2] We found him in a fair chamber, richly hanged, and carpeted under foot, without any degrees to the state.[3] He was set upon a low throne richly adorned, and a rich cloth of state over his head, of blue satin embroidered. He was alone, save that he had two pages of honor, on either hand one, finely attired in white. His undergarments were the like that we saw him wear in the chariot; but instead of his gown, he had on him a mantle with a cape of the same fine black, fastened about him. When we came in, as we were taught, we bowed low at our first entrance, and when we were come near his chair, he stood up, holding forth his hand ungloved and in posture of blessing; and we every one of us stooped down, and kissed the hem of his tippet.[4] That done, the rest departed, and I remained. Then he warned the pages forth of the room, and caused me to sit down beside him, and spake to me thus in the Spanish tongue:

"God bless thee, my son; I will give thee the greatest jewel I have. For I will impart unto thee, for the love of God and men, a relation of the true state of Solomon's House. Son, to make you know the true state of Solomon's House, I will keep this order. First, I will set forth unto you the end of our foundation. Secondly, the preparations and instruments we have for our works. Thirdly, the several employments and functions whereto our fellows are assigned. And fourthly, the ordinances and rites which we observe.

"The end of our foundation is the knowledge of causes, and secret motions of things; and the enlarging of the bounds of human empire, to the effecting of all things possible.

"The preparations and instruments are these. We have large and deep caves of several depths: the deepest are sunk six hundred

1. Sir Thomas More's *Utopia* (1516) set a fashion for imaginary communities with ideal forms of government which was suddenly taken up in the early 17th century. The German Johann Andreae published in 1619 his *Christianopolis;* Thomas Campanella, languishing in a Neapolitan jail, wrote his *City of the Sun* in 1623. Bacon's contribution to the discussion, perhaps because he never completed it, is really tangential to the concept of an ideal commonwealth. His *New Atlantis* is in effect a research establishment which could exist in any society that would tolerate it. Perhaps for that reason, it had an immediate influence beyond that of most full-

fledged Utopias; and was largely realized, within thirty years of its publication, in the shape of the Philosophical Society which in 1662 became the Royal Society. Bacon begins by describing an imaginary voyage to the island of Bensalem, supposed to lie in the vicinity of the Bering Straits. Here, after learning about the miraculous diffusion of Christianity to the island, he is invited to visit their most interesting institution, Solomon's House.
2. Audience.
3. I.e., without stairs leading up to the dais.
4. Scarf.

fathoms; and some of them are digged and made under great hills and mountains; so that if you reckon together the depth of the hill, and the depth of the cave, they are, some of them, above three miles deep. For we find that the depth of a hill, and the depth of a cave from the flat, is the same thing; both remote alike from the sun and heaven's beams, and from the open air. These caves we call the lower region, and we use them for all coagulations, indurations,[5] refrigerations, and conservations of bodies. We use them likewise for the imitation of natural mines, and the producing also of new artificial metals, by compositions and materials which we use, and lay there for many years. We use them also sometimes (which may seem strange) for curing of some diseases, and for prolongation of life in some hermits that choose to live there, well accommodated of[6] all things necessary, and indeed live very long; by whom also we learn many things.

"We have burials in several earths, where we put divers cements,[7] as the Chinese do their porcelain. But we have them in greater variety, and some of them more fine. We also have great variety of composts[8] and soils, for the making of the earth fruitful.

"We have high towers, the highest about half a mile in height, and some of them likewise set upon high mountains, so that the vantage of the hill, with the tower, is in the highest of them three miles at least. And these places we call the upper region, accounting the air between the high places and the low as a middle region. We use these towers, according to their several heights and situations, for insolation,[9] refrigeration, conservation, and for the view of divers meteors—as winds, rain, snow, hail;[1] and some of the fiery meteors also. And upon them, in some places, are dwellings of hermits, whom we visit sometimes, and instruct what to observe.

"We have great lakes, both salt and fresh, whereof we have use for the fish and fowl. We use them also for burials of some natural bodies, for we find a difference in things buried in earth, or in air below the earth, and things buried in water. We have also pools, of which some do strain fresh water out of salt, and others by art do turn fresh water into salt. We have also some rocks in the midst of the sea, and some bays upon the shore, for some works wherein is required the air and vapor of the sea. We have likewise violent streams and cataracts, which serve us for many motions; and likewise engines for multiplying and enforcing[2] of winds to set also on going divers motions.

"We have also a number of artificial wells and fountains, made in imitation of the natural sources and baths, as tincted upon[3]

---

5. Hardenings.
6. Provided with.
7. Clays and pottery mixtures.
8. Manures.
9. Exposure to the sun.

1. Anything that fell from the sky was, in Renaissance terminology, a meteor.
2. Re-enforcing, strengthening.
3. Tinctured with.

vitriol, sulphur, steel, brass, lead, nitre, and other minerals; and again, we have little wells for infusions of many things, where the waters take the virtue[4] quicker and better than in vessels or basins. And amongst them we have a water, which we call Water of Paradise, being by that we do to it, made very sovereign[5] for health and prolongation of life.

"We have also great and spacious houses, where we imitate and demonstrate meteors—as snow, hail, rain, some artificial rains of bodies, and not of water, thunders, lightnings; also generations of bodies in air—as frogs, flies, and divers others.

"We have also certain chambers, which we call chambers of health, where we qualify[6] the air as we think good and proper for the cure of divers diseases, and preservation of health.

"We have also fair and large baths, of several mixtures, for the cure of diseases, and the restoring of a man's body from arefaction;[7] and others for the confirming of it in strength of sinews, vital parts, and the very juice and substance of the body.

"We have also large and various orchards and gardens, wherein we do not so much respect beauty as variety of ground and soil, proper for divers trees and herbs, and some very spacious, where trees and berries are set, whereof we make divers kinds of drinks, besides the vineyards. In these we practice likewise all conclusions[8] of grafting and inoculating, as well of wild-trees as fruit-trees, which produceth many effects. And we make (by art) in the same orchards and gardens trees and flowers to come earlier or later than their seasons, and to come up and bear more speedily than by their natural course they do. We make them also by art greater much than their nature; and their fruit greater and sweeter, and of differing taste, smell, color, and figure, from their nature. And many of them we so order as they become of medicinal use.

"We have also means to make divers plants rise by mixtures of earths without seeds, and likewise to make divers new plants, differing from the vulgar,[9] and to make one tree or plant turn into another.

"We have also parks, and enclosures of all sorts, of beasts and birds; which we use not only for view or rareness, but likewise for dissections and trials,[1] that thereby we may take light what may be wrought upon the body of man. Wherein we find many strange effects: as continuing life in them, though divers parts, which you account vital, be perished and taken forth; resuscitating of some that seem dead in appearance, and the like. We try also all poisons, and other medicines upon them, as well of chirurgery[2] as physic. By art

4. Property (of the substances put into water).
5. Efficacious.
6. Modify.
7. Drying up.

8. Theories.
9. Ordinary.
1. Experiments.
2. Surgery.

likewise, we make them greater or taller than their kind is, and contrariwise dwarf them and stay their growth; we make them more fruitful and bearing than their kind is, and contrariwise barren and not generative. Also we make them differ in color, shape, activity, many ways. We find means to make commixtures and copulations of divers kind, which have produced many new kinds,[3] and them not barren, as the general opinion is. We make a number of kinds of serpents, worms, fishes, flies, of putrefaction, whereof some are advanced (in effect) to be perfect creatures, like beasts or birds, and have sexes, and do propagate. Neither do we this by chance, but we know beforehand of what matter and commixture what kind of those creatures will arise.

"We have also particular pools where we make trials upon fishes, as we have said before of beasts and birds.

"We have also places for breed and generation of those kinds of worms and flies which are of special use; such as are with you your silkworms and bees.

"I will not hold you long with recounting of our brew-houses, bake-houses, and kitchens, where are made divers drinks, breads, and meats, rare and of special effects. Wines we have of grapes, and drinks of other juice of fruits, of grains, and of roots, and of mixtures with honey, sugar, manna, and fruits dried and decocted;[4] also of the tears or woundings of trees, and of the pulp of canes. And these drinks are of several ages, some to the age or last[5] of forty years. We have drinks also brewed with several herbs, and roots and spices; yea, with several fleshes and whitemeats;[6] whereof some of the drinks are such as they are in effect meat and drink both, so that divers, especially in age, do desire to live with them, with little or no meat or bread. And above all, we strive to have drinks of extreme thin parts, to insinuate into the body, and yet without all biting, sharpness, or fretting; insomuch as some of them, put upon the back of your hand, will with a little stay[7] pass through to the palm, and yet taste mild to the mouth. We have also waters, which we ripen in that fashion, as they become nourishing, so that they are indeed excellent drink, and many will use no other. Bread we have of several grains, roots, and kernels; yea, and some of flesh, and fish, dried; with divers kinds of leavenings and seasonings; so that some do extremely move appetites; some do nourish so, as divers do live of them, without any other meat, who live very long. So for meats, we have some of them so beaten, and made tender, and mortified,[8] yet without all corrupting, as a weak heat of the stomach will turn them into good chylus,[9] as well as a strong heat would meat other-

3. Species.
4. Dissolved in water, by boiling.
5. Duration.
6. Breast of chicken, fish, sometimes cheese.
7. Delay.

8. Softened.
9. Chyle, food in its emulsified and digestible form. Bacon thinks of the stomach as a furnace, which softens food by heat.

wise prepared. We have some meats also, and breads, and drinks, which taken by men, enable them to fast long after; and some other, that used[1] make the very flesh of men's bodies sensibly more hard and tough, and their strength far greater than otherwise it would be.

"We have dispensatories, or shops of medicines; wherein you may easily think, if we have such variety of plants and living creatures more than you have in Europe (for we know what you have), the simples,[2] drugs, and ingredients of medicines, must likewise be in so much the greater variety. We have them likewise of divers ages, and long fermentations. And for their preparations, we have not only all manner of exquisite distillations and separations, and especially by gentle heats, and percolations through divers strainers, yea, and substances; but also exact forms of composition,[3] whereby they incorporate almost as they were natural simples.

"We have also divers mechanical arts, which you have not; and stuffs made by them, as papers, linen, silks, tissues, dainty works of feathers of wonderful luster, excellent dyes, and many others. and shops likewise, as well for such as are not brought into vulgar use amongst us, as for those that are. For you must know, that of the things before recited, many of them are grown into use throughout the kingdom, but yet, if they did flow from our invention, we have of them also for patterns and principals.[4]

"We have also furnaces of great diversities, and that keep great diversity of heats: fierce and quick, strong and constant, soft and mild; blown, quiet; dry, moist; and the like. But above all we have heats, in imitations of the sun's and heavenly bodies' heats, that pass divers inequalities, and (as it were) orbs, progresses, and returns,[5] whereby we produce admirable effects. Besides, we have heats of dungs, and of bellies and maws of living creatures and of their bloods and bodies, and of hays and herbs laid up moist, of lime unquenched, and such like. Instruments also which generate heat only by motion. And farther, places for strong insolations; and again, places under the earth, which by nature or art yield heat. These divers heats we use as the nature of the operation which we intend requireth.

"We have also perspective houses,[6] where we make demonstrations of all lights and radiations, and of all colors; and out of things uncolored and transparent we can represent unto you all several colors, not in rainbows (as it is in gems and prisms), but of themselves single. We represent also all multiplications of light, which we carry to great distance, and make so sharp, as to discern small

1. The word "when" is understood here.
2. Herbs.
3. Ways of putting the ingredients of medicines together, making compounds.
4. Models.
5. I.e.. the furnaces produce various heats at will.
6. For optical experiments.

points and lines. Also all colorations of light; all delusions and deceits of the sight, in figures, magnitudes, motions, colors; all demonstrations of shadows. We find also divers means, yet unknown to you, of producing of light originally from divers bodies. We procure means of seeing objects afar off, as in the heaven and remote places; and represent things near as afar off, and things afar off as near, making feigned distances. We have also helps for the sight, far above spectacles and glasses in use. We have also glasses and means to see small and minute bodies, perfectly and distinctly; as the shapes and colors of small flies and worms, grains and flaws in gems which cannot otherwise be seen, observations in urine and blood not otherwise to be seen. We make artificial rainbows, halos, and circles about light. We represent also all manner of reflections, refractions, and multiplications of visual beams of objects.

"We have also precious stones of all kinds, many of them of great beauty and to you unknown; crystals likewise; and glasses of divers kinds; and amongst them some of metals vitrificated,[7] and other materials besides those of which you make glass. Also a number of fossils and imperfect minerals, which you have not. Likewise loadstones of prodigious virtue:[8] and other rare stones, both natural and artificial.

"We have also sound-houses, where we practice and demonstrate all sounds and their generation. We have harmonies which you have not, of quarter sounds and lesser slides of sounds. Divers instruments of music likewise to you unknown, some sweeter than any you have; together with bells and rings that are dainty and sweet. We represent small sounds as great and deep; likewise great sounds, extenuate[9] and sharp; we make divers tremblings and warblings of sounds, which in their original are entire.[1] We represent and imitate all articulate sounds and letters, and the voices and notes of beasts and birds. We have certain helps, which set to the ear do further the hearing greatly. We have also divers strange and artificial echoes, reflecting the voice many times, and as it were tossing it; and some that give back the voice louder than it came, some shriller and some deeper; yea, some rendering[2] the voice, differing in the letters or articulate sound from that they receive. We have also means to convey sounds in trunks[3] and pipes, in strange lines and distances.

"We have also perfume-houses, wherewith we join also practices of taste. We multiply smells, which may seem strange: we imitate smells, making all smells to breathe out of other mixtures than those that give them. We make divers imitations of taste likewise, so that they will deceive any man's taste. And in this house we contain also

7. Turned to glass.
8. Strength.
9. Drawn out thin.
1. I.e.. we can vary notes which in nature are single.
2. Transforming.
3. Tubes.

a confiture-house, where we make all sweetmeats, dry and moist, and divers pleasant wines, milks, broths, and salads, far in greater variety than you have.

"We have also engine-houses, where are prepared engines and instruments for all sorts of motions. There we imitate and practice to make swifter motions than any you have, either out of your muskets or any engine that you have; and to make them and multiply them more easily and with small force, by wheels and other means, and to make them stronger and more violent than yours are, exceeding your greatest cannons and basilisks.[4] We represent also ordnance and instruments of war and engines of all kinds; and likewise new mixtures and compositions of gunpowder, wildfires burning in water and unquenchable; also fireworks of all variety, both for pleasure and use. We imitate also flights of birds; we have some degrees of flying[5] in the air. We have ships and boats for going under water and brooking[6] of seas, also swimming girdles and supporters. We have divers curious clocks, and other like motions of return, and some perpetual motions. We imitate also motions of living creatures by images of men, beasts, birds, fishes, and serpents; we have also a great number of other various motions, strange for equality,[7] fineness, and subtlety.

"We have also a mathematical-house, where are represented all instruments, as well of geometry as astronomy, exquisitely made.

"We have also houses of deceits of the senses, where we represent all manners of feats of juggling, false apparitions, impostures and illusions, and their fallacies. And surely you will easily believe that we, that have so many things truly natural which induce admiration, could in a world of particulars deceive the senses if we would disguise those things, and labor to make them seem more miraculous. But we do hate all impostures and lies, insomuch as we have severely forbidden it to all our fellows, under pain of ignominy and fines, that they do not show any natural work or thing adorned or swelling, but only pure as it is, and without all affectation of strangeness.

"These are, my son, the riches of Solomon's House.

"For the several employments and offices of our fellows, we have twelve that sail into foreign countries under the names of other nations (for our own we conceal), who bring us the books and abstracts and patterns of experiments of all other parts. These we call Merchants of Light.

"We have three that collect the experiments which are in all books. These we call Depredators.

"We have three that collect the experiments of all mechanical arts, and also of liberal sciences, and also of practices which are not brought into arts. These we call Mystery-men.

4. Cannon, named after the fabulous beast that killed by a beam from its eye.
5. I.e., rudimentary forms of flying.
6. Withstanding.
7. Unusual for their evenness.

"We have three that try new experiments, such as themselves think good. These we call Pioneers or Miners.

"We have three that draw the experiments of the former four into titles and tables, to give the better light for the drawing of observations and axioms out of them. These we call Compilers.

"We have three that bend themselves, looking into the experiments of their fellows, and cast about how to draw out of them things of use and practice for man's life and knowledge, as well for works as for plain demonstration of causes, means of natural divinations, and the easy and clear discovery of the virtues and parts of bodies. These we call Dowry-men or Benefactors.

"Then after divers meetings and consults of our whole number, to consider of the former labors and collections, we have three that take care out of them to direct new experiments, of a higher light, more penetrating into Nature than the former. These we call Lamps.

"We have three others that do execute the experiments so directed, and report them. These we call Inoculators.

"Lastly, we have three that raise the former discoveries by experiments into greater observations, axioms, and aphorisms. These we call Interpreters of Nature.[8]

"We have also, as you must think, novices and apprentices, that the succession of the former employed men do not fail; besides a great number of servants and attendants, men and women. And this we do also: we have consultations, which of the inventions and experiences which we have discovered shall be published, and which not; and take all an oath of secrecy for the concealing of those which we think fit to keep secret; though some of those we do reveal sometimes to the State, and some not.[9]

"For our ordinances and rites, we have two very long and fair galleries: in one of these we place patterns and samples of all manner of the more rare and excellent inventions; in the other we place the statues of all principal inventors. There we have the statue of your Columbus, that discovered the West Indies; also the inventor of ships; your monk that was the inventor of ordnance and of gunpowder;[1] the inventor of music; the inventor of letters; the inventor of printing; the inventor of observations of astronomy; the inventor of works in metal; the inventor of glass; the inventor of silk of the worm; the inventor of wine; the inventor of corn and bread; the inventor of sugars; and all these by more certain tradition than you have. Then we have divers inventors of our own, of excellent works, which since you have not seen, it were too long to

8. The total staff of Solomon's House is 36; a generous allowance, by Bacon's estimate, for the project of understanding the natural cosmos. Modern researchers would want a little more staff.
9. Observe Bacon's suspicion of the body politic, and the freedom which he allows to Solomon's House from political pressure.
1. Tradition credits Roger Bacon, a 13th-century monk, with the discovery of gunpowder. Bacon tactfully avoids his name

make descriptions of them; and besides, in the right understanding of those descriptions you might easily err. For upon every invention of value we erect a statue to the inventor, and give him a liberal and honorable reward. These statues are some of brass, some of marble and touchstone,[2] some of cedar and other special woods gilt and adorned; some of iron, some of silver, some of gold.

"We have certain hymns and services, which we say daily of laud and thanks to God for His marvelous works. And forms of prayer, imploring His aid and blessing for the illumination of our labors, and the turning of them into good and holy uses.

"Lastly, we have circuits or visits, of divers principal cities of the kingdom; where, as it cometh to pass, we do publish such new profitable inventions as we think good. And we do also declare natural divinations of diseases, plagues, swarms of hurtful creatures, scarcity, tempests, earthquakes, great inundations, comets, temperature of the year, and divers other things; and we give counsel thereupon, what the people shall do for the prevention and remedy of them."

And when he had said this he stood up; and I, as I had been taught, kneeled down; and he laid his right hand upon my head, and said, "God bless thee, my son, and God bless this relation which I have made. I give thee leave to publish it, for the good of other nations; for we here are in God's bosom, a land unknown." And so he left me; having assigned a value of about two thousand ducats for a bounty to me and my fellows. For they give great largesses, where they come, upon all occasions.

The rest was not perfected.

1627

2. A hard basaltic-type rock.

The Arts of Personality

ROBERT BURTON

(1577–1640)

Robert Burton was a scholar at Christ Church, Oxford, where he matriculated in 1593 and stayed for the rest of his life. He never traveled, never married, never sought "success" or attained it; he existed exclusively among books—old, crabbed books by preference. All this absorption in books was supposed (according to the lore of traditional medicine and the theory of "humors" dating back to the Greeks) to throw his constitution out of balance and produce a "melancholy" temperament in which black bile predominated. And in Burton's case, sure enough, that was what happened. His cure for the desperate condition afflicting him was to write a book about his disease; this project occupied the rest of his life.

It wasn't altogether an eccentric project. There had been many books on melancholy before: because of their sedentary life, it was the favorite disease of scholars, and so got a lot of attention. And the age was interested in taking man apart, in finding out what makes him tick. Sir John Davies wrote a long poem on normal psychology, in 1599; it was called *Nosce Teipsum*, or "Know Thyself." Somewhat later, Phineas Fletcher expanded on some Spenserian hints, particularly the "House of Alma" passage in the *Faerie Queene* (Book II, Canto ix), to create an allegorical anatomy of man, called *The Purple Island*. (Man's body is an island, rather like England, floating in the purple sea of his own blood: James Joyce was fascinated with the poem, and used it in the composition of *Ulysses*.) Thus Burton was in good company when he began his *Anatomy*. But nobody ever put so much energy into the subject, or handled it in such an epic way. The first edition came out in 1621; later editions, each augmented over the previous one, appeared in 1624, 1628, 1632, and 1638. When he died, in 1640, Burton left behind materials for still another, and bigger edition: the book continued to grow, even after the author's death, as if it had acquired a queer, unnatural vitality of its own.

These cumulative additions do not generally deepen the thought of the book or advance its argument into new territory; they are verbal tags from Burton's immense reading, stuck into the text of the book, after Montaigne's fashion, wherever they seemed more or less appropriate. For though he was perfectly serious in trying to understand the disease of melancholy, Burton wrote like a man afflicted with logorrhea. He poured forth words, his own and other people's, as if he were using them to relieve an inner pressure, rather than to express something. He never used one word where fifty would do, never refrained from an erudite citation just because he had said the same thing three times already. He was a humorist and a bit of a buffoon; the role he assumes in his *Anatomy* is that of a mad scholar choked on his own erudition and in danger of exploding from its inner pressures. When he thinks of all things that can make a man melancholy (or, as we would say, "neurotic"), Burton envisages "a stupend, vast, infinite Ocean of incredible madness and folly: a Sea full of shelves and rocks, sands, gulfs, Euripuses [currents] and contrary tides, full of fearful monsters, uncouth shapes, roaring waves, tempests, and Siren calms, Halcyonian Seas, unspeakable misery, such absurd and ridiculous, feral and lamentable fits, that I know not whether they are more to be pitied or derided, or may be believed, but that we daily see the same practiced in our days, fresh examples, new news, fresh objects of misery and madness in this kind, that are still represented to us, abroad, at home, in the midst of us, in our bosoms."

All that seething turmoil in the bosom of a retiring Oxford scholar! To relieve the pressure of it, Burton prescribed (among many, many other things) exercise and study, more and more study, more and more books, difficult but not necessarily useful projects, in a word, distractions—projects like the very book we are reading. Hysteria is diverted by giving it a toy to play with, a trifle to agitate: the mechanism is that described later by Swift in *A Tale of a Tub*. Burton describes the remedy at such vociferous length that it's clear he is practicing what he preaches in the very act of preaching it. But at the end of our selection, the whole exercise is stood on its head when the recommended cure turns out to be nothing less than the disease itself. It is a joke worthy of Burton's great predecessor in the field of medical clowning, François Rabelais.

From The Anatomy of Melancholy

From *Exercise Rectified*[1]

But amongst those exercises or recreations of the mind within doors, there is none so general, so aptly to be applied to all sorts of men, so fit and proper to expel idleness and melancholy, as that of study: "Study is the delight of old age, the support of youth, the ornament of prosperity, the solace and refuge of adversity, the delight of the household," etc., find the rest in Tully, *Pro Archia Poeta*.[2] What so full of content as to read, walk, and see maps, pictures, statues, jewels, marbles, which some so much magnify, as those that Phidias made of old so exquisite and pleasing to be beheld, that, as Chrysostom thinketh, "if any man be sickly, troubled in mind, or that cannot sleep for grief, and shall but stand over against one of Phidias's images, he will forget all care, or whatsoever else may molest him, in an instant?"[3] There be those as much taken with Michael Angelo's, Raphael de Urbino's, Francesco Francia's pieces, and many of those Italian and Dutch painters, which were excellent in their ages; and esteem of it as a most pleasing sight to view those neat architectures, devices, escutcheons, coats of arms, read such books, to peruse old coins of several sorts in a fair gallery; artificial works, perspective glasses, old relics, Roman antiquities, variety of colors. A good picture is *falsa veritas et muta poesis*[4] and though (as Vives saith)[5] *artificia delectant, sed*

---

1. Part II, Sect. 2, Mem. 4. Burton's book is elaborately subdivided into Parts, Sections, and Members; these are more formal than real, since he clearly writes whatever occurs to him next.
2. Tully is Cicero, the oration that in behalf of Archias the poet. In general, the footnotes for this selection will make no effort to follow Burton through the incredible mazes of the Bodleian library and his own memory.
3. St. John Chrysostom, an early Christian saint famous for his eloquence; Burton cites from his 12th oration.
4. "False truth and silent poetry."
5. Juan Luis Vives, 16th-century Spanish humanist: Burton cites from his commentary on *De Anima*.

mox fastidimus, artificial toys please but for a time; yet who is he that will not be moved with them for the present?

* * * To most kind of men it is an extraordinary delight to study. For what a world of books offers itself, in all subjects, arts, and sciences, to the sweet content and capacity of the reader? In arithmetic, geometry, perspective, optics, astronomy, architecture, sculpture, painting, of which so many and such elaborate treatises are of late written; in mechanics and their mysteries, military matters, navigation, riding of horses, fencing, swimming, gardening, planting, great tomes of husbandry, cookery, falconry, hunting, fishing, fowling, &c., with exquisite pictures of all sports, games, and what not? In music, metaphysics, natural and moral philosophy, philology, in policy, heraldry, genealogy, chronology, &c., they afford great tomes, or those studies of antiquity, &c., *et quid subtilius Arithmeticis inventionibus, quid jucundius Musicis rationibus, quid divinius Astronomicis, quid rectius Geometricis demonstrationibus?*[6] What so sure, what so pleasant? He that shall but see that geometrical tower of Garezenda at Bologna in Italy, the steeple and clock at Strasburg, will admire the effects of art, or that engine of Archimedes, to remove the earth itself, if he had but a place to fasten his instrument; *Archimedis Cochlea,*[7] and the rare devices to corrivate waters, musical instruments, and trisyllable echoes again, again, and again repeated, with myriads of such. What vast tomes are extant in law, physic, and divinity for profit, pleasure, practice, speculation, in verse or prose, &c.! their names alone are the subject of great volumes, we have thousands of authors of all sorts, many great libraries full well furnished, like so many dishes of meat, served out for several palates; and he is a very block that is affected with none of them. Some take an infinite delight to study the very languages wherein these books are written, Hebrew, Greek, Syriac, Chaldee, Arabic, &c. Methinks it would please any man to look upon a geographical map, *suavi animum delectatione allicere, ob incredibilem rerum varietatem et jucunditatem, et ad pleniorem sui cognitionem excitare,*[8] chorographical, topographical delineations, to behold, as it were, all the remote provinces, towns, cities of the world, and never to go forth to the limits of his study, to measure by the scale and compass their extent, distance, examine their site.

6. "And what is subtler than arithmetical discoveries, what more pleasant than musical harmonies, what more divine than astronomical or more certain than geometrical demonstrations?" From Girolamo Cardano, 16th-century Italian physician-philosopher. The tower at Bologna and the steeple at Strasburg are about as real to Burton as the imaginary lever with which Archimedes said he could move the earth.
7. Archimedes' water screw.
8. "It allures the mind with profound pleasure, on account of the incredible variety and beauty of the subjects, and excites it to further knowledge." From the preface to Mercator's *Geography.*

Charles the Great, as Platina writes, had three fair silver tables, in one of which superficies was a large map of Constantinople, in the second, Rome neatly engraved, in the third an exquisite description of the whole world, and much delight he took in them. What greater pleasure can there now be, than to view those elaborate maps of Ortelius, Mercator, Hondius, &c.? To peruse those books of cities, put out by Braunus and Hogenbergius? To read those exquisite descriptions of Maginus, Munster, Herrera, Laet, Merula, Boterus, Leander, Albertus, Camden, Leo Afer, Adricomius, Nic. Gerbelius, &c.! Those famous expeditions of Christoph. Columbus, Americus Vespucius, Marcus Polus the Venetian, Lod. Vertomannus, Aloysius Cadamustus, &c.? Those accurate diaries of Portuguese, Hollanders, of Bartison, Oliver à Nort, &c., Hakluyt's Voyages, Pet. Martyr's Decades, Benzo, Lerius, Linschoten's relations, those Hodaeporicons of Jod. a Meggen, Brocard the monk, Bredenbachius, Jo. Dublinius, Sands, &c., to Jerusalem, Egypt, and other remote places of the world? Those pleasant itineraries of Paulus Hentzerus, Jodocus Sincerus, Dux Polonus, &c., to read Bellonius's observations, P. Gillius his surveys; those parts of America set out and curiously cut in pictures by Fratres a Bry. To see a well-cut herbal, herbs, trees, flowers, plants, all vegetables expressed in their proper colors to the life, as that of Matthiolus upon Dioscorides, Delacampius, Lobel, Bauhinus, and that last voluminous and mighty herbal of Beslar of Nuremberg, wherein almost every plant is to his own bigness. To see birds, beasts, and fishes of the sea, spiders, gnats, serpents, flies, &c., all creatures set out by the same art, and truly expressed in lively colors, with an exact description of their natures, qualities, &c., as hath been accurately performed by Aelian, Gesner, Ulysses Aldrovandus, Bellonius, Rondoletius, Hippolytus Salvianus, &c. * * *

King James, 1605, when he came to see our University of Oxford, and amongst other edifices now went to view that famous library renewed by Sir Thomas Bodley, in imitation of Alexander at his departure brake out into that noble speech, If I were not a king, I would be a university man; "and if it were so that I must be a prisoner, if I might have my wish, I would desire to have no other prison than that library, and to be chained together with so many good authors *et mortuis magistris* (and dead teachers)." So sweet is the delight of study, the more learning they have (as he that hath a dropsy. The more he drinks the thirstier he is), the more they covet to learn, and the last day is *prioris discipulus* (the student of the day before); harsh at first learning is, *radices amarae* (bitter roots), but *fructus dulces* (sweet fruits), according to that of Isocrates, pleasant at last; the longer they live, the more they are enamored with the Muses. Heinsius, the keeper of the library at Leyden in Holland, was mewed up in it all the year long; and that which to thy thinking should have bred a loathing caused in him a greater liking. "I no sooner (saith he) come into the library, but I bolt the door to me, excluding lust, ambition, avarice, and all such vices, whose nurse is idleness, the mother of ignorance, and melancholy herself, and in the very lap of eternity, amongst so many divine souls, I take my seat, with so lofty a spirit and sweet content, that I pity all our great ones, and rich men that know not this happiness."[9] * * *

Whosoever he is therefore that is overrun with solitariness, or carried away with pleasing melancholy and vain conceits, and for want of employment knows not how to spend his time, or crucified with worldly care, I can prescribe him no better remedy than this of study, to compose himself to the learning of some art or science. Provided always that this malady proceed not from overmuch study; for in such case he adds fuel to the fire, and nothing can be more pernicious; let him take heed he do not overstretch his wits, and make a skeleton of himself; or such inamoratos as read nothing but playbooks, idle poems, jests, Amadis de Gaul, the Knight of the Sun, the Seven Champions, Palmerin de Oliva, Huon of Bordeaux, &c. Such many times prove in the end as mad as Don Quixote. Study is only prescribed to those that are otherwise idle, troubled in mind, or carried headlong with vain thoughts and imaginations, to distract their cogitations (although variety of study, or some serious subject, would do the former no harm), and divert their continual meditations another way. Nothing in this case better than study. * * *

1621

9. From the letters of Daniel Heinsius. Burton in his last paragraph gets thoroughly entangled, for the people who can't be cured by study include not only those who've already studied too much, but those who haven't studied at all, who have read nothing but "playbooks, idle poems, jests." In short, study is a good cure for anyone who's cured by study, but not for anyone who isn't.

SIR THOMAS BROWNE

(1605–1682)

Though his life was long, Browne's biography contains few events. Born in London, he attended Oxford and then medical schools on the Continent— at Montpellier in France, Padua in Italy, and Leyden in Holland. Rubbing elbows with people of different religions encouraged Browne to reflect on his own religious stance, and shortly after his return to England (about 1635) he wrote a little essay called *Religio Medici* ("A Doctor's Faith"). Not being intended for publication, it wasn't published for several years, till a printer (prophetically named Andrew Crook) brought out a pirated edition in 1642. Browne had by then married and settled down to practice medicine at the remote little town of Norwich in the marshy countryside of Norfolk. His book was thought witty and ingenious, perhaps because it managed to talk at length about religion without ever discussing or even facing any of the great religious issues which were tearing the country apart. What fascinated Browne was a private game he was playing between faith and doubt; he would think of all the most intricate and perplexing questions that his "philosophy" could invent, and then solve them by means of his faith. Absorbed in this curious inner drama of his, Browne never entered the literary "world" (such as it was) of London, and never took active sides in the civil war. Like Thoreau, one of his later admirers, he did not need to move around because he was traveling widely in Norwich.

Some of his investigations were published in 1645 under the forbidding title of *Pseudodoxia Epidemica*, or "Vulgar Errors." They consisted of immense researches into all the foolish ideas entertained by mankind over the ages—superstitions and oddities of opinion, mythical animals, pious legends, hexes, hoaxes, assorted nonsense of every description. It was characteristic of Browne's mind that he was always more interested in what wasn't knowable than in what was. His thought instinctively moved toward the mysterious, the remote, the legendary; and though, for his day, he was an enlightened man, he accepted almost as many vulgar errors as he exposed. He enjoyed the mysteries of ancient wisdom; he enjoyed even more thinking about the unthinkable. Thus when some workmen near Norwich accidentally dug up some funeral urns dating back hundreds, and probably thousands of years, Doctor Browne took occasion to visit the site, inspect the find, and write (in 1658) a private meditation on death and burial practices. The subject might have produced a morbid (or, worse, a dull) document; but Browne's agile metaphysical wit, and gorgeous, polysyllabic rhetoric, gave an immense, resonant poetry to his treatise *Hydriotaphia, Urn-Burial*.

Whatever the ostensible topic of which he was treating, Browne always turned it toward that curious inward balance of faith and scepticism which fascinated him. "We carry with us," he wrote, "the wonders we seek without us: there is all Africa and her prodigies within us. We are that bold and adventurous piece of nature which he that studies wisely learns in a compendium what others labor at in a divided piece and endless volume." His focus was on himself, rarely on those areas of material, factual information where his age was learning, at a furious pace and with ruthless precision, to discriminate truth from falsehood. During his lifetime, the modern scientific outlook, the modern scientific method, established themselves beyond serious challenge at the center of intellectual life. Browne as a philosopher of the old school hardly gave the new developments a thought. What song the sirens sang, and what name Achilles assumed when he hid himself among women, were subjects more congenial for his speculative, inward mind. No doubt he knew that they were funny subjects to think about; the prose in which he discussed these matters, always polysyllabic and Latinate, sometimes gets so elaborate that one can't help suspecting self-mockery. But these were all essential ingredients in the alchemy of a personality, and it is the fascination of that personality—darker and more mysterious than Burton's, but just as much the deliberate creation of an artist—that has kept Browne's name and books alive over the centuries.

From Religio Medici[1]

* * *

40. I am naturally bashful, nor hath conversation, age, or travel been able to effront or enharden me; yet I have one part of modesty which I have seldom discovered in another; that is (to speak truly) I am not so much afraid of death as ashamed thereof. 'Tis the very disgrace and ignominy of our natures, that in a moment can so disfigure us that our nearest friends, wife, and children stand afraid and start at us. The birds and beasts of the field that before in a natural fear obeyed us, forgetting all allegiance begin to prey upon us. This very conceit hath in a tempest disposed and left me willing to be swallowed up in the abyss of waters, wherein I had perished unseen, unpitied, without wondering eyes, tears of pity, lectures of mortality, and none had said, *"Quantum mutatus ab illo!"*[2] Not

1. Browne wrote *Religio Medici* about 1635, when he was a little short of 30 years old (see Section 41); he had just returned from his medical studies on the continent, where he had been forced to worship—if he was to worship at all—with communities of different faiths. The essay was written as a form of personal stock-taking, in the shape of a letter to a friend; in 1642 it was printed without Browne's permission, and in 1643 reprinted in an authorized and corrected version. Our text follows the 1643 printing with a few additions, in brackets, from M. Jean-Jacques Denonain's edition based on manuscript copies (Cambridge, 1953).
The title means "A Doctor's Faith," and one might well ask why a doctor should have a special religion of his own, different from a lawyer's or a merchant's. By "faith," however, Browne does not simply mean "creed." He disposes, almost casually, of all the things his age usually meant by "faith"—doctrinal and dogmatic tenets, ceremonies and public observances, an ecclesiastical organization. Not that he is a doubter or a heretic; he accepts the establishment in every detail. But he is interested in something more mysterious and personal, which most of his essay is devoted to exploring; this is a relation to the Christian mystery of faith and resurrection, in which he believes, not because he can explain or defend it but because he cannot. Browne's position, known as "fideism," vigorously separates philosophy from faith and exempts faith from criticism by reason, while at the same time depriving it of reason's support. Previous speculators along these lines, like Montaigne, had explicitly recognized that "fideism" was a dangerous weapon of intellectual foilplay. But for Browne it answered a deep temperamental need.
2. "How greatly changed from what he was!" The phrase was used by Aeneas of Hector, *Aeneid* II.274; Browne may be referring to an occasion when he was shipwrecked between Ireland and England in 1630.

that I am ashamed of the anatomy of my parts or can accuse nature for playing the bungler in any part of me or my own vicious life for contracting any shameful disease up on me, whereby I might not call myself as wholesome a morsel for the worms as any.

41. Some, upon the courage of a fruitful issue[3] wherein, as in the truest chronicle, they seem to outlive themselves, can with greater patience away with death. This conceit and counterfeit subsisting in our progenies seems to me a mere fallacy, unworthy the desires of a man that can but conceive a thought of the next world; who, in a nobler ambition, should desire to live in his substance in heaven rather than his name and shadow in the earth. And therefore at my death I mean to take a total adieu of the world, not caring for a monument, history, or epitaph, not so much as the bare memory of my name to be found anywhere but in the universal register of God. I am not yet so cynical as to approve the testament of Diogenes,[4] nor do I altogether allow that *rodomontado* of Lucan—

> *Caelo tegitur, qui non habet urnam.*[5]
> He that unburied lies wants not his hearse,
> For unto him a tomb's the universe.

but commend in my calmer judgment those ingenuous intentions that desire to sleep by the urns of their fathers and strive to go the nearest way unto corruption. I do not envy the temper of crows and daws,[6] nor the numerous and weary days of our fathers before the flood. If there be any truth in astrology, I may outlive a jubilee;[7] as yet I have not seen one revolution of Saturn,[8] nor hath my pulse beat thirty years; and yet, excepting one, have seen the ashes and left underground all the kings of Europe, have been contemporary to three emperors, four Grand Seignieurs,[9] and as many popes. Methinks I have outlived myself and begin to be weary of the sun. I have shaken hands with delight in my warm blood and canicular days.[1] I perceive I do anticipate the vices of age. The world to me is but a dream or mock-show, and we all therein but pantaloons and antics[2] to my severer contemplations.

42. It is not, I confess, an unlawful prayer to desire to surpass the days of our Savior, or wish to outlive that age wherein He thought fittest to die; yet if (as divinity affirms) there shall be no gray hairs in heaven, but all shall rise in the perfect state of men, we do but outlive those perfections in this world to be recalled unto them by

3. Emboldened by having had children.
4. Diogenes asked his friends not to bury him but to hang him out for a scarecrow.
5. *Pharsalia* VII.819.
6. Traditionally long-lived creatures, linked here with patriarchs like Noah and Methuselah.
7. Fifty years. Browne lived to 77.

8. Browne was born under Saturn (October 19); he was saturnine (melancholy and philosophical) by temperament; and Saturn completes a heavenly cycle in a little less than thirty years.
9. Sultans of Turkey.
1. Dog days, of July and early August, when summer heat is often at its height.
2. Jokers and clowns.

a greater miracle in the next, and run on here but to be retrograde hereafter. Were there any hopes to outlive vice or a point to be superannuated from sin, it were worthy our knees to implore the days of Methuselah. But age doth not rectify but incurvate our natures, turning bad dispositions into worser habits, and, like diseases, brings on incurable vices. For every day as we grow weaker in age, we grow stronger in sin, and the number of our days doth but make our sins innumerable. The same vice committed at sixteen is not the same, though it agree in all other circumstances, at forty, but swells and doubles from the circumstance of our ages, wherein, besides the constant and inexcusable habit of transgressing, the maturity of our judgment cuts off pretence unto excuse or pardon.

Every sin, the oftener it is committed the more it acquireth in the quality of evil; as it succeeds in time, so it proceeds in degrees of badness, for as they proceed they ever multiply and, like figures in arithmetic, the last stands for more than all that went before it. [The course and order of my life would be a very death unto another. I use [3] myself to all diets, humors, airs, hunger, thirst, cold, heat, want, plenty, necessity, dangers, hazards. When I am cold I cure not myself by heat; when sick, not by physic. Those that know how I live may justly say I regard not life, nor stand in fear of death.] [4] And though I think no man can live well once but he that could live twice, yet for my own part I would not live over my hours past, or begin again the thread of my days—not upon Cicero's ground [5] because I have lived them well, but for fear I should live them worse. I find my growing judgment daily instructs me how to be better, but my untamed affections and confirmed vitiosity makes me daily do worse. I find in my confirmed age the same sins I discovered in my youth. I committed many then because I was a child, and because I commit them still I am yet an infant. Therefore, I perceive a man may be twice a child before the days of dotage, and stand in need of Aeson's bath [6] before threescore.

43. And truly there goes a great deal of providence to produce a man's life unto threescore. There is more required than an able temper for those years. Though the radical humor contain in it sufficient oil for seventy, yet I perceive in some it gives no light past thirty.[7] Men assign not all the causes of long life that write whole books thereof. They that found themselves[8] on the radical

---

3. Accustom.
4. This passage was substituted for most of section 42 and all of section 43 in the manuscript copies and unauthorized editions.
5. In *De Senectute* 23, Cicero supposes the philosopher will be ready to die because he has lived well.
6. A classical fountain of youth.

7. A man's "radical humor" is the basic constitution governing his disposition— phlegm, choler, and so on; Browne compares it to the oil feeding the lamp of life.
8. Base their judgments (as to a man's longevity). Abel, of course, failed to live as long as Adam because Cain killed him.

balsam or vital sulphur of the parts determine not why Abel lived not so long as Adam. There is, therefore, a secret gloom or bottom of our days. 'Twas His wisdom to determine them, but His perpetual and waking providence that fulfills and accomplishes them, wherein the spirits, ourselves, and all the creatures of God in a secret and disputed way do execute His will. Let them not therefore complain of immaturity that die about thirty; they fall but like the whole world, whose solid and well composed substance must not expect the duration and period of its constitution; when all things are completed in it, its age is accomplished, and the last and general fever may as naturally destroy it before six thousand as me before forty. There is therefore some other hand that twines the thread of life than that of nature. We are not only ignorant in antipathies and occult qualities, our ends are as obscure as our beginnings. The line of our days is drawn by night, and the various effects therein by a pencil that is invisible, wherein, though we confess our ignorance, I am sure we do not err if we say it is the hand of God.

44. I am much taken with two verses of Lucan since I have been able not only, as we do at school to construe, but understand them:

> *Victurosque Dei celant ut vivere durent,*
> *Felix esse mori.*[9]
> We're all deluded, vainly searching ways
> To make us happy by the length of days;
> For, cunningly to make's protract this breath
> The Gods conceal the happiness of death.

There be many excellent strains in that poet, wherewith his Stoical genius hath liberally supplied him; and truly there are singular pieces in the philosophy of Zeno and doctrine of the Stoics,[1] which, I perceive, delivered in a pulpit pass for current divinity. Yet herein are they in extremes that can allow a man to be his own assassin and so highly extol the end and suicide of Cato.[2] This is indeed not to fear death but yet to be afraid of life. It is a brave act of valor to contemn death; but where life is more terrible than death, it is then the truest valor to dare to live, and herein religion hath taught us a noble example. For, all the valiant acts of Curtius, Scevola, or Codrus[3] do not parallel or match that one of Job; and sure there is no torture to the rack of a disease, nor any poniards in death itself like those in the way or prologue unto it. *Emori nolo, sed me esse mortuum nihil curo*—"I would not die but care not if I am dead."[4]

Were I of Caesar's religion I should be of his desires, and wish rather to go off at one blow than to be sawed in pieces by the grat-

9. *Pharsalia* IV.519.
1. Zeno was the first of the Stoic philosophers, who taught avoidance of passion and submission to necessity.
2. The younger Cato ("of Utica" from the place of his death) committed sui-

cide (46 B.C.) rather than compromise with Caesar.
3. Curtius, Scevola, and Codrus all suffered (Curtius and Codrus death, Scevola mutilation) in behalf of their country.
4. Cicero, *Tusculan Disputations* I.8.

ing torture of a disease. Men that look no further than their outsides think health an appurtenance unto life, and quarrel with their constitutions for being sick. But I that have examined the parts of man and know upon what tender filaments that fabric hangs, do wonder that we are not always so; and, considering the thousand doors that lead to death, do thank my God that we can die but once. 'Tis not only the mischief of diseases and the villainy of poisons that make an end of us; we vainly accuse the fury of guns and the new inventions of death. 'Tis in the power of every hand to destroy us, and we are beholding unto every one we meet he doth not kill us. There is therefore but one comfort left, that, though it be in the power of the weakest arm to take away life, it is not in the strongest to deprive us of death. God would not exempt Himself from that; the misery of immortality in the flesh He undertook not That was in it immortal.[5] Certainly there is no happiness within this circle of flesh, nor is it in the optics of these eyes to behold felicity. The first day of our jubilee is death. The devil hath therefore failed of his desires: we are happier with death than we should have been without it. There is no misery but in himself, where there is no end of misery; and so indeed in his own sense the Stoic is in the right. He forgets that he can die who complains of misery: we are in the power of no calamity while death is in our own.

45. Now, besides this literal and positive kind of death, there are others whereof divines make mention, and those, I think, not merely metaphorical—as mortification, dying unto sin and the world. Therefore I say every man hath a double horoscope: one of his humanity, his birth; another of his Christianity, his baptism. And from this do I compute or calculate my nativity, not reckoning those *horae combustae*[6] and odd days, or esteeming myself anything before I was my Savior's and enrolled in the register of Christ. Whosoever enjoys not this life, I count him but an apparition, though he wear about him the sensible affections of flesh. In these moral acceptions, the way to be immortal is to die daily; nor can I think I have the true theory of death when I contemplate a skull or behold a skeleton with those vulgar imaginations it casts upon us. I have therefore enlarged that common *memento mori* into a more Christian memorandum: *memento quatuor novissima*,[7] those four inevitable points of us all—death, judgment, heaven, and hell. Neither did the contemplations of the heathens rest in their graves without a further thought of Rhadamanth[8] or some judicial proceeding after death, though in another way and upon suggestion of

5. Christ, who was an immortal in mortal garb, never undertook the burden of physical immortality.
6. Literally, burnt hours, hours when the moon is obscured by the sun; used here as a metaphor for the period between birth and baptism.
7. Remember the four last things. A *memento mori* is a reminder of death, generally a skull.
8. Greek judge of the underworld.

their natural reasons. I cannot but marvel from what sybil or oracle they stole the prophesy of the world's destruction by fire, or whence Lucan learned to say,

> *Communis mundo superest rogus, ossibus astra misturus*—[9]
> There yet remains to th' world one common fire
> Wherein our bones with stars shall make one pyre.

I believe the world grows near its end, yet is neither old nor decayed, nor will ever perish upon the ruins of its own principles. As the work of creation was above nature, so is its adversary, annihilation, without which the world hath not its end but its mutation. Now what fire should be able to consume it thus far without the breath of God, which is the truest consuming flame, my philosophy cannot inform me. Some believe there went not a minute to the world's creation, nor shall there go to its destruction; those six days, so punctually described, make not to them one moment but rather seem to manifest the method and idea of that great work in the intellect of God than the manner how He proceeded in its operation. I cannot dream that there should be at the last day any such judicial proceeding or calling to the bar as indeed the Scripture seems to imply and the literal commentators do conceive. For unspeakable mysteries in the Scripture are often delivered in a vulgar and illustrative way, and, being written unto man, are delivered not as they truly are but as they may be understood. Wherein, notwithstanding, the different interpretations according to different capacities may stand firm with our devotion, nor be any way prejudicial to each single edification.

46. Now, to determine the day and year of this inevitable time is not only convincible and statute-madness but also manifest impiety. How shall we interpret Elias' six thousand years [1] or imagine the secret communicated to a rabbi which God hath denied unto His angels? [2] It had been an excellent query to have posed the devil of Delphos, and must needs have forced him to some strange amphibology.[3] It hath not only mocked the predictions of sundry astrologers in ages past but the prophecies of many melancholy heads in these present, who, neither understanding reasonably things past or present, pretend a knowledge of things to come, heads ordained only to manifest the incredible effects of melancholy and to fulfill

---

9. *Pharsalia* VII.814.

1. According to Jewish tradition, Elijah (Elias) prophesied that 6,000 years would be the ultimate age of the world.
2. In Matthew xxiv.36, Christ says no man knows the hour of the Last Judgment; the "rabbi" is any rabbinical commentator, type of the esoteric exegete.

3. Pagan oracles like that at Delphos (Delphi) were often attributed by Christian writers to the work of daemons or devils; an amphibology is an ambiguous pronouncement, in which the oracles specialized.

old prophecies rather than be the authors of new. "In those days there shall come wars and rumors of wars" [4] to me seems no prophecy but a constant truth, in all times verified since it was pronounced. "There shall be signs in the moon and stars." [5] How comes He, then, like a thief in the night when He gives an item of his coming? That common sign drawn from the revelation of Antichrist is as obscure as any; in our common compute he hath been come these many years. But, for my own part, to speak freely, omitting those ridiculous anagrams, I am half of Paracelsus' opinion, and think that Antichrist is the philosopher's stone in divinity, [6] for the discovery and invention whereof, though there be prescribed rules and probable inductions, yet hath hardly any man attained the perfect discovery thereof. That general opinion that the world grows near its end hath possessed all ages past as nearly as ours. I am afraid that the souls that now depart cannot escape that lingering expostulation of the saints under the altar, *"Quousque Domine? How long, O Lord?"* [7] and groan in the expectation of the great jubilee.

* * *

50. I cannot tell how to say that fire is the essence of hell; I know not what to make of purgatory, or conceive a flame that can either prey upon or purify the substance of a soul. Those flames of sulphur mentioned in the Scriptures [8] I take not to be understood of this present hell but of that to come, where fire shall make up the complement of our tortures and have a body or subject wherein to manifest its tyranny. Some who have had the honor to be textuary in divinity are of opinion it shall be the same specifical fire with ours. This is hard to conceive, yet I can make good how even that may prey upon our bodies and yet not consume us; for in this material world there are bodies that persist invincible in the powerfullest flames, and though by the action of fire they fall into ignition and liquation, yet will they never suffer a destruction. I would gladly know how Moses with an actual fire calcined or burned the golden calf into powder, [9] for that mystical metal of gold, whose solary and celestial nature I admire, exposed unto the violence of fire, grows only hot and liquifies but consumeth not. So, when the

4. Matthew xxiv.6.
5. Luke xxi.25.
6. The coming of Antichrist was supposed to foreshadow the Last Judgment; Paracelsus was a doubter. Browne uses the "philosopher's stone" as an emblem of fantastic illusion. The "ridiculous anagrams" were arguments made from the names of the Popes, which, being translated into Greek or Hebrew (where every letter has a numerical value), were sometimes triumphantly added up to the number of the Beast in the Book of Revelation, i.e., 666.
7. Revelation vi.9–10.
8. Revelation xxi.8.
9. Exodus xxxii.20 says that Moses not only burnt the golden calf and ground it to powder, but strewed it on the water and made the children of Israel drink of it.

consumable and volatile pieces of our bodies shall be defined into a more impregnable and fixed temper like gold, though they suffer from the action of flames, they shall never perish but lie immortal in the arms of fire.

And surely if this frame must suffer only by the action of this element, there will many bodies escape, and not only heaven but earth will not be at an end but rather a beginning. For, at present it is not earth but a composition of fire, water, earth, and air; [1] but at that time, spoiled of these ingredients, it shall appear in a substance more like itself, its ashes. Philosophers that opinioned the world's destruction by fire did never dream of annihilation, which is beyond the power of sublunary causes, for the last and proper action of that element is but vitrification or a reduction of a body into glass. And therefore some of our chemists facetiously affirm, yea, and urge Scripture for it, that at the last fire all shall be crystallized and reverberated into glass, which is the utmost action of that element. Nor need we fear this term of annihilation or wonder that God will destroy the works of His creation. For, man subsisting, who is and will then truly appear a microcosm, the world cannot be said to be destroyed. For the eyes of God and perhaps also of our glorified selves shall as really behold and contemplate the world in its epitome or contracted essence, as now they do at large and in its dilated substance. In the seed of a plant, to the eyes of God and to the understanding of man, there exist, though in an invisible way, the perfect leaves, flowers, and fruit thereof; for things that are *in posse* [2] to the sense are actually existent to the understanding. Thus God beholds all things, Who contemplates as fully His works in their epitome as in their full volume, and beheld as amply the whole world in that little compendium of the sixth day [3] as in the scattered and dilated pieces of those five before.

51. Men commonly set forth the torments of hell by fire and the extremity of corporal afflictions, and describe hell in the same method that Mahomet doth heaven. This indeed makes a noise and drums in popular ears; but if this be the terrible piece thereof, it is not worthy to stand in diameter with heaven, whose happiness consists in that part that is best able to comprehend it, that immortal essence, that translated divinity and colony of God, the soul. Surely, though we place hell under earth, the devil's walk and purlieu is about it. Men speak too popularly who place it in those

---

1. The four Aristotelian elements.
2. A state of potential being.
3. Man was made on the sixth day as a summary (microcosm) of the work of the first five.

flaming mountains [4] which to grosser apprehensions represent hell. The heart of man is the place the devil dwells in. I feel sometimes a hell within myself; Lucifer keeps his court in my breast, Legion is revived in me.[5] There are as many hells as Anaxagoras' conceited worlds.[6] There was more than one hell in Magdalen when there were seven devils,[7] for every devil is an hell unto himself. He holds enough of torture in his own *ubi* [8] and needs not the misery of circumference to afflict him; and thus a distracted conscience here is a shadow or introduction unto hell hereafter. Who can but pity the merciful intention of those hands that do destroy themselves? The devil, were it in his power, would do the like; which being impossible, his miseries are endless, and he suffers most in that attribute wherein he is impassable,[9] his immortality.

52. I thank God, and with joy I mention it, I was never afraid of hell nor never grew pale at the description of that place. I have so fixed my contemplations on heaven that I have almost forgot the idea of hell, and am afraid rather to lose the joys of the one than endure the misery of the other. To be deprived of them is a perfect hell and needs, methinks, no addition to complete our afflictions. That terrible term hath never detained me from sin, nor do I owe any good action to the name thereof. I fear God, yet am not afraid of Him; His mercies make me ashamed of my sins before His judgments afraid thereof. These are the forced and secondary method of His wisdom, which He useth but as the last remedy and upon provocation; a course rather to deter the wicked than incite the virtuous to His worship. I can hardly think there was ever any scared into heaven. They go the fairest way to heaven that would serve God without a hell; other mercenaries that crouch unto Him in fear of hell, though they term themselves the servants, are indeed but the slaves of the Almighty.

53. And to be true and speak my soul, when I survey the occurrences of my life and call into account the finger of God, I can perceive nothing but an abyss and mass of mercies, either in general to mankind or in particular to myself. And, whether out of the prejudice of my affection or an inverting and partial conceit of His mercies, I know not, but those which others term crosses, afflictions,

---

4. Volcanoes.
5. Lucifer is the devil, Legion (from Mark v.9) the assembly of unclean spirits.
6. Browne has apparently confused Anaxagoras with Anaximander who "conceited" (i.e., imagined) an indefinite

number of worlds.
7. Luke viii.2 tells the story of Christ's driving seven devils out of Mary Magdalene.
8. Literally, in Latin, *where;* in context, his own self.
9. Inassailable.

judgments, misfortunes, to me, who enquire farther into them than their visible effects, they both appear and in event have ever proved the secret and dissembled favors of His affection. It is a singular piece of wisdom to apprehend truly and without passion the works of God, and so well to distinguish His justice from His mercy as not to miscall those noble attributes. Yet it is likewise an honest piece of logic so to dispute and argue the proceedings of God as to distinguish even His judgments into mercies. For God is merciful unto all because better to the worst than the best deserve, and to say He punisheth none in this world, though it be a paradox, is no absurdity. To one that hath committed murder, if the judge should only ordain a fine, it were a madness to call this a punishment and to repine at the sentence rather than admire the clemency of the judge. Thus, our offences being mortal, and deserving not only death but damnation, if the goodness of God be content to traverse and pass them over with a loss, misfortune, or disease, what frenzy were it to term this a punishment rather than an extremity of mercy, and to groan under the rod of His judgments rather than admire the scepter of His mercies!

Therefore to adore, honor, and admire Him is a debt of gratitude due from the obligation of our nature, states, and conditions; and with these thoughts, he that knows them best will not deny that I adore Him. That I obtain heaven and the bliss thereof is accidental and not the intended work of my devotion, it being a felicity I can neither think to deserve nor scarce in modesty to expect. For these two ends of us all, either as rewards or punishments, are mercifully ordained and disproportionally disposed unto our actions; the one being so far beyond our deserts, the other so infinitely below our demerits.

* * *

1635   1642 (*surreptitious*)
                                         1643 (*authentic*)

From Hydriotaphia, Urn-Burial
Chapter V

Now since these dead bones have already outlasted the living ones of Methuselah,[1] and in a yard under ground, and thin walls of clay, outworn all the strong and specious buildings above it, and quietly rested under the drums and tramplings of three conquests;[2]

1. Methuselah lived 969 years (Genesis v.27).

2. Roman, Saxon, and Norman. "Diuturnity": long life.

what prince can promise such diuturnity unto his relics, or might not gladly say,

Sic ego componi versus in ossa velim?[3]

Time, which antiquates antiquities, and hath an art to make dust of all things, hath yet spared these minor monuments.

In vain we hope to be known by open and visible conservatories, when to be unknown was the means of their continuation, and obscurity their protection. If they died by violent hands, and were thrust into their urns, these bones become considerable, and some old philosophers would honor them, whose souls they conceived most pure, which were thus snatched from their bodies, and to retain a stronger propension[4] unto them; whereas they weariedly left a languishing corpse, and with faint desires of reunion. If they fell by long and aged decay, yet wrapped up in the bundle of time, they fall into indistinction, and make but one blot with infants. If we begin to die when we live, and long life be but a prolongation of death, our life is a sad composition; we live with death, and die not in a moment. How many pulses made up the life of Methuselah, were work for Archimedes: common counters sum up the life of Moses his man.[5] Our days become considerable, like petty sums, by minute accumulations; where numerous fractions make up but small round numbers; and our days of a span long make not one little finger.[6]

If the nearness of our last necessity[7] brought a nearer conformity unto it, there were a happiness in hoary hairs, and no calamity in half-senses. But the long habit of living indisposeth us for dying; when avarice makes us the sport of death, when even David grew politicly cruel, and Solomon could hardly be said to be the wisest of men.[8] But many are too early old, and before the date of age. Adversity stretcheth our days, misery makes Alcmena's nights,[9] and time hath no wings unto it. But the most tedious being is that which can unwish itself, content to be nothing, or never to have been, which was beyond the malcontent of Job, who cursed not the day of his life, but his nativity:[1] content to have so far been as to have

3. "Thus I, when dead, should wish to go to rest" (Tibullus).
4. Attraction. "They" are the philosophers, who traditionally die in bed.
5. I.e., the ordinary man, alluded to in Psalm xc, supposed to be by Moses; it says (verse 10), "The days of our years are three-score years and ten."
6. In certain ancient arithmetics, Browne's note tells us, "the little finger of the right hand, contracted, signified an hundred."

7. I.e., death.
8. David suffered in his last years from the rebellion and death of his son Absalom; Solomon was seduced by fair idolatresses to the service of alien gods.
9. Sleeping with Alcmena to beget Hercules, Jove enjoyed himself so much that he forbade the sun to rise for one day; thus there were three nights in a row.
1. Job iii.

a title to future being; although he had lived here but in an hidden state of life, and as it were an abortion.

What song the Sirens sang, or what name Achilles assumed when he hid himself among women, though puzzling questions, are not beyond all conjecture.[2] What time the persons of these ossuaries entered the famous nations of the dead, and slept with princes and counselors, might admit a wide[3] solution. But who were the proprietaries of these bones, or what bodies these ashes made up, were a question above antiquarism; not to be resolved by man, nor easily perhaps by spirits, except we consult the provincial guardians, or tutelary observators.[4] Had they made as good provision for their names as they have done for their relics, they had not so grossly erred in the art of perpetuation. But to subsist in bones, and be but pyramidally extant,[5] is a fallacy in duration. Vain ashes, which in the oblivion of names, persons, times, and sexes, have found unto themselves a fruitless continuation, and only arise unto late posterity, as emblems of mortal vanities, antidotes against pride, vainglory, and madding vices. Pagan vainglories, which thought the world might last forever, had encouragement for ambition; and, finding no Atropos[6] unto the immortality of their names, were never damped with the necessity of oblivion. Even old ambitions had the advantage of ours, in the attempts of their vainglories, who, acting early and before the probable meridian[7] of time, have by this time found great accomplishment of their designs, whereby the ancient heroes have already outlasted their monuments and mechanical preservations. But in this latter scene of time, we cannot expect such mummies unto our memories, when ambition may fear the prophecy of Elias,[8] and Charles the Fifth can never hope to live within two Methuselahs of Hector.[9]

And therefore, restless inquietude for the diuturnity of our memories unto present considerations seems a vanity almost out of date, and superannuated piece of folly. We cannot hope to live so long in our names as some have done in their persons; one face of Janus[1] holds no proportion unto the other. 'Tis too late to be ambitious.

---

2. Suetonius (*Lives of the Twelve Caesars*) says that Tiberius went to the "silly and laughable extreme" of testing grammarians (whom he admired) with these questions.
3. Approximate.
4. Browne, who believed in witches, also believed in angelic protectors, both personal ("tutelary observators") and of more extended jurisdiction ("provincial guardians").
5. Like a pyramid, famous though the person buried within it is long forgotten.
6. Of the three Fates, Clotho, Lachesis, and Atropos, the last-named held the scissors. They cut the threads of mortal life.
7. Noon, midday.
8. "That the earth will last but 6,000 years" [Browne's note]. There is no warrant for this in the Bible.
9. Since Methuselah lived to be 969, Browne's estimate is conservative: Hector, the hero of Troy, had more than three "Methuselahs" head start on Charles V (1500–58).
1. Janus, Roman god of doorways and beginnings (hence "January"), had two heads facing in opposite directions, the past and the future.

The great mutations of the world are acted, or time may be too short for our designs. To extend our memories by monuments, whose death we daily pray for,[2] and whose duration we cannot hope, without injury to our expectations in the advent of the last day, were a contradiction to our beliefs. We whose generations are ordained in this setting part of time[3] are providentially taken off from such imaginations; and, being necessitated to eye the remaining particle of futurity, are naturally constituted unto thoughts of the next world, and cannot excusably decline the consideration of that duration, which maketh pyramids pillars of snow, and all that's past a moment.

Circles and right lines limit and close all bodies, and the mortal right-lined circle must conclude and shut up all.[4] There is no antidote against the opium of time, which temporally considereth all things: our fathers find their graves in our short memories, and sadly tell us how we may be buried in our survivors. Gravestones tell truth scarce forty years.[5] Generations pass while some trees stand, and old families last not three oaks. To be read by bare inscriptions like many in Gruter,[6] to hope for eternity by enigmatical epithets or first letters of our names, to be studied by antiquaries, who we were, and have new names given us like many of the mummies, are cold consolations unto the students of perpetuity, even by everlasting languages.

To be content that times to come should only know there was such a man, not caring whether they knew more of him, was a frigid ambition in Cardan;[7] disparaging his horoscopal inclination and judgment of himself. Who cares to subsist like Hippocrates' patients, or Achilles' horses in Homer, under naked nominations, without deserts and noble acts, which are the balsam of our memories, the *entelechia*[8] and soul of our subsistences? To be nameless in worthy deeds exceeds[9] an infamous history. The Canaanitish woman lives more happily without a name than Herodias with one. And who had not rather have been the good thief than Pilate?[1]

But the iniquity of oblivion blindly scattereth her poppy, and deals with the memory of men without distinction to merit of perpetuity. Who can but pity the founder of the pyramids? Herostratus

---

2. We pray for the "death" and destruction of our graves at the Last Judgment.
3. The image is from the sunset.
4. Θ (*theta*), the first letter of Θάνατος ("death"), symbolizes it.
5. Because old corpses are dug up and replaced with new; see *Hamlet* V.i; and Donne, *The Relic*, lines 3–4.
6. Jan Gruter (1560–1627) was a Dutch scholar who published a collection of Latin inscriptions.
7. Girolamo Cardano, a famous Italian

mathematician and occultist of the 16th century. Taking his own horoscope, he found himself destined to great things.
8. Essence, perfection.
9. Is better than.
1. The woman of Canaan had faith in Jesus; Herodias asked for the head of John the Baptist (Matthew xv.27–28; Mark vi.22–25). The good thief, crucified beside Christ, had his blessing; Pontius Pilate, the procurator of Judea, typifies the sanctimonious villain.

lives that burnt the temple of Diana;[2] he is almost lost that built it. Time hath spared the epitaph of Adrian's horse,[3] confounded that of himself. In vain we compute our felicities by the advantage of our good names, since bad have equal durations, and Thersites is like to live as long as Agamemnon.[4] Who knows whether the best of men be known, or whether there be not more remarkable persons forgot than any that stand remembered in the known account of time? Without the favor of the everlasting register, the first man had been as unknown as the last, and Methuselah's long life had been his only chronicle.

Oblivion is not to be hired: the greater part must be content to be as though they had not been, to be found in the register of God, not in the record of man. Twenty-seven names make up the first story, and the recorded names ever since contain not one living century.[5] The number of the dead long exceedeth all that shall live. The night of time far surpasseth the day, and who knows when was the equinox? Every hour adds unto that current arithmetic,[6] which scarce stands one moment. And since death must be the Lucina[7] of life, and even pagans could doubt whether thus to live were to die; since our longest sun sets at right descensions, and makes but winter arches, and therefore it cannot be long before we lie down in darkness, and have our light in ashes;[8] since the brother of death daily haunts us with dying mementos, and time that grows old in itself bids us hope no long duration; diuturnity is a dream and folly of expectation.

Darkness and light divide the course of time, and oblivion shares with memory a great part even of our living beings; we slightly remember our felicities, and the smartest strokes of affliction leave but short smart upon us. Sense endureth no extremities, and sorrows destroy us or themselves. To weep into stones are fables.[9] Afflictions induce callosities;[1] miseries are slippery, or fall like snow upon us, which notwithstanding is no unhappy stupidity. To be ignorant of evils to come, and forgetful of evils past, is a merciful provision in nature, whereby we digest the mixture of our few and evil days, and, our delivered senses not relapsing into cutting re-

2. Herostratus of Ephesus set fire to the great temple in that city simply in order to gain a stupid immortality.
3. Adrian (Hadrian) was emperor of Rome in the 2nd century A.D.
4. Thersites, the scurrilous scoffer of the *Iliad*, is contrasted with Agamemnon, the royal leader.
5. Genesis i–v tells the story of the human race from the creation to the flood in 27 names; of all the names since the flood, not 100 ("century")
are really living ones.
6. That continual addition.
7. Roman goddess of childbirth, hence, "the deliverance."
8. At funerals, Browne's note says, the Jews place a wax candle in a pot of ashes beside the corpse. The "brother of death" is sleep.
9. Like Niobe, whose grief turned her to stone.
1. Callouses, hardness, indifference.

membrances, our sorrows are not kept raw by the edge of repetitions. A great part of antiquity contented their hopes of subsistency with a transmigration of their souls: a good way to continue memories, while having the advantage of plural successions, they could not but act something remarkable in such variety of beings, and enjoying the fame of their passed selves, make accumulation of glory unto their last durations. Others, rather than be lost in the uncomfortable night of nothing, were content to recede into the common being, and make one particle of the public soul of all things, which was no more than to return into their unknown and divine original again. Egyptian ingenuity[2] was more unsatisfied, contriving their bodies in sweet consistencies, to attend the return of their souls. But all was vanity, feeding the wind, and folly. The Egyptian mummies, which Cambyses or time hath spared, avarice now consumeth.[3] Mummy is become merchandise, Mizraim cures wounds, and Pharaoh is sold for balsams.

In vain do individuals hope for immortality, or any patent[4] from oblivion, in preservations below the moon; men have been deceived even in their flatteries above the sun, and studied conceits to perpetuate their names in heaven. The various cosmography of that part hath already varied the names of contrived constellations: Nimrod is lost in Orion, and Osiris in the Dog Star.[5] While we look for incorruption in the heavens, we find they are but like the earth, durable in their main bodies, alterable in their parts: whereof beside comets and new stars, perspectives[6] begin to tell tales, and the spots that wander about the sun, with Phaethon's favor,[7] would make clear conviction.

There is nothing strictly immortal but immortality. Whatever hath no beginning may be confident of no end; all others have a dependent being and within the reach of destruction; which is the peculiar[8] of that necessary essence that cannot destroy itself; and the highest strain of omnipotency, to be so powerfully constituted as not to suffer even from the power of itself. But the sufficiency of Christian immortality frustrates all earthly glory, and the quality of either state after death makes a folly of posthumous memory.

2. The reference is to embalming practices.
3. The story of Cambyses ravaging Egypt is told in Herodotus, Book III. Powdered mummy was sold in the 17th century as medicine (see Donne, *Love's Alchemy*, line 24). "Mizraim": i.e., Egypt; Mizraim was a son of Ham (Genesis x.6–14).
4. Protection.
5. I.e., the names of the stars change —Osiris to Sirius, Nimrod the mighty hunter (Genesis x.9) to Orion.
6. Telescopes.
7. Phaethon was an unfortunate son of the Sun, who tried to drive his father's chariot and nearly set the universe on fire. His erratic course reminds Browne of spots which wander across the sun's face, and which had only recently been charted by astronomers, starting with Galileo.
8. Characteristic.

God, who can only[9] destroy our souls, and hath assured our resurrection, either of our bodies or names hath directly promised no duration. Wherein there is so much of chance that the boldest expectants have found unhappy frustration; and to hold long subsistence seems but a scape in oblivion.[1] But man is a noble animal, splendid in ashes, and pompous in the grave, solemnizing nativities and deaths with equal luster, nor omitting ceremonies of bravery[2] in the infamy of his nature.

Life is a pure flame, and we live by an invisible sun within us. A small fire sufficeth for life, great flames seemed too little after death, while men vainly affected precious pyres, and to burn like Sardanapalus;[3] but the wisdom of funeral laws found the folly of prodigal blazes, and reduced undoing fires unto the rule of sober obsequies, wherein few could be so mean as not to provide wood, pitch, a mourner, and an urn.

Five languages secured not the epitaph of Gordianus.[4] The man of God[5] lives longer without a tomb than any by one, invisibly interred by angels, and adjudged to obscurity, though not without some marks directing human discovery. Enoch and Elias,[6] without either tomb or burial, in an anomalous state of being, are the great examples of perpetuity, in their long and living memory, in strict account being still on this side death, and having a late part yet to act upon this stage of earth. If in the decretory term of the world[7] we shall not all die but be changed, according to received translation, the last day will make but few graves; at least quick resurrections will anticipate lasting sepultures; some graves will be opened before they be quite closed, and Lazarus be no wonder.[8] When many that feared to die shall groan that they can die but once, the dismal state is the second and living death, when life puts despair on the damned; when men shall wish the coverings of mountains, not of monuments, and annihilations shall be courted.[9]

While some have studied monuments, others have studiously declined them; and some have been so vainly boisterous that they durst not acknowledge their graves, wherein Alaricus[1] seems most

---

9. Who alone can.
1. Weak trick against forgetfulness.
2. Proud ceremonies.
3. Sardanapalus burned up a palace full of eunuchs, concubines, and treasures as his funeral pyre; later civilizations often forbade such lavish displays.
4. The epitaph of Gordianus, emperor of Rome (238–244), was written in five languages; but it was obliterated in all of them by his successor, Licinius.
5. Moses (see Deuteronomy xxxiv).
6. Enoch and "Elias" (Elijah) were translated straight to heaven (Genesis v.24; II Kings ii.11).
7. The Last Judgment.
8. Lazarus, the dead man raised by Christ (John xi).
9. The damned soul shrieking for mountains to shield him from the wrath of God was a figure beloved of preachers. See Luke xxiii.30 and Revelation vi.16.
1. Alaric, the Gothic invader, was buried in the bed of the river Busento (A.D. 410).

subtle, who had a river turned to hide his bones at the bottom. Even Sulla,[2] that thought himself safe in his urn, could not prevent revenging tongues, and stones thrown at his monument. Happy are they whom privacy makes innocent, who deal so with men in this world that they are not afraid to meet them in the next; who, when they die, make no commotion among the dead, and are not touched with that poetical taunt of Isaiah.[3]

Pyramids, arches, obelisks were but the irregularities of vainglory, and wild enormities of ancient magnanimity. But the most magnanimous resolution rests in the Christian religion, which trampleth upon pride, and sits on the neck of ambition, humbly pursuing that infallible perpetuity unto which all others must diminish their diameters, and be poorly seen in angles of contingency.[4]

Pious spirits who passed their days in raptures of futurity made little more of this world than the world that was before it, while they lay obscure in the chaos of pre-ordination, and night of their fore-beings. And if any have been so happy as truly to understand Christian annihilation, ecstasies, exolution,[5] liquefaction, transformation, the kiss of the spouse, gustation of God, and ingression into the divine shadow, they have already had an handsome anticipation of heaven; the glory of the world is surely over, and the earth in ashes unto them.

To subsist in lasting monuments, to live in their productions, to exist in their names and predicament of chimeras,[6] was large satisfaction unto old expectations, and made one part of their Elysiums.[7] But all this is nothing in the metaphysics of true belief. To live indeed is to be again ourselves, which being not only an hope but an evidence in noble believers, 'tis all one to lie in St. Innocent's churchyard,[8] as in the sands of Egypt: ready to be anything, in the ecstasy of being ever, and as content with six foot as the *moles* of Adrianus.[9]

> —*Tabesne cadavera solvat,*
> *An rogus, haud refert.*
> —LUCAN

1658

2. Roman politician and general, who died 78 B.C.

3. In Isaiah xiv the mighty ones of the earth are taunted with their approaching downfall into hell.

4. The angle of contingency is the smallest possible angle; Browne puns on the idea that all these lesser perpetuities are subject to accident ("contingency").

5. The loosening or freeing of the spirit from the bonds of the body.

6. In the condition of phantasms.

7. The pagan afterworld.

8. In Paris, where bodies soon consume; contrasted with the desert, where they last a long time.

9. Adrian's (Hadrian's) tomb, now Castel San Angelo in Rome, the type of a magnificent mausoleum. The Latin tag is translated, "By the swift funeral pyre or slow decay / (No matter which) the bodies pass away" (Lucan, *Pharsalia* VII.809).

JOSEPH HALL
(1574–1656)

SIR THOMAS OVERBURY *and* JOHN EARLE
(1581–1613)   (1600–1665)

The vogue for writing set "characters" which swept through English court-society during the second and third decades of the century caught up, if only momentarily, all sorts of men who had other careers to make. Joseph Hall and John Earle were churchmen who would ultimately become bishops; Sir Thomas Overbury was a politician who lost his life in a shadowy court-intrigue, and thus became a legend. All three were men who found in the "character" an opportunity to display their wit, their style, their worldly knowledge.

Hall, who claimed to be the first English satirist, was also one of the first character-writers. *Characters of Virtues and Vices,* published in 1608, has an obvious moral slant, and the portrait of a "malcontent" may be polemical as well, since the malcontent sounds much like a Puritan. Hall lived long enough to cross polemical swords, inconclusively of course, with the foremost Puritan man of letters, John Milton, who had been born in the very year when Hall's *Characters* were published.

Sir Thomas Overbury died young, poisoned in the Tower by the mistress of one of James Stuart's favorites; many rumors and innuendos surrounded the event. Overbury had himself written a few characters in verse and prose; but as a result of the mystery surrounding his death, numerous other "characters," by an assortment of hands, clustered around his name. The collection was first published in 1614, and was augmented in successive editions for nearly a decade thereafter.

John Earle was probably the most talented man who tried his hand at characters; he was also nearly the last. *Micro-cosmography* aims to present a portrait of the little world, i.e., humankind as a whole. It originally included 54 and ultimately grew to 78 characters. Earle himself, who was a fellow at Oxford when he first published the book (anonymously), went through the civil wars on the royalist side, and rose after the Restoration to be a power in the church. But he was always a quiet, peaceful man, with a little, acid wit, after the model of Hooker, whom he deeply admired.

JOSEPH HALL: The Malcontent

He is neither well full nor fasting; and though he abound with complaints, yet nothing dislikes[1] him but the present; for what he condemned while it was, once past, he magnifies and strives to recall

---

1. Displeases.

it out of the jaws of Time. What he hath he sees not, his eyes are so taken up with what he wants; and what he sees he cares not for, because he cares so much for that which is not. When his friend carves him the best morsel, he murmurs that it is a happy feast wherein each one may cut for himself. When a present is sent him, he asks, "Is this all?" and "What, no better?" and so accepts it as if he would have his friend know how much he is bound to him for vouchsafing to receive it. It is hard to entertain him with a proportionable[2] gift. If nothing, he cries out of unthankfulness; if little, that he is basely regarded; if much, he exclaims of flattery and expectation of a large requital. Every blessing hath somewhat to disparage and distaste it. Children bring cares, single life is wild and solitary; eminency is envious,[3] retiredness obscure; fasting painful, satiety unwieldy; religion nicely[4] severe, liberty is lawless; wealth burdensome, mediocrity contemptible. Everything faulteth either in too much or too little. This man is ever headstrong and self-willed, neither is he always tied to esteem or pronounce according to reason; some things he must dislike he knows not wherefore, but he likes them not; and otherwhere, rather than not censure, he will accuse a man of virtue. Everything he meddleth with he either findeth imperfect or maketh so; neither is there anything that soundeth so harsh in his ear as the commendation of another, whereto yet perhaps he fashionably[5] and coldly assenteth, but with such an after-clause of exception as doth more than mar his former allowance. And if he list not to give a verbal disgrace,[6] yet he shakes his head and smiles, as if his silence should say, "I could, and will not." And when himself is praised without excess, he complains that such imperfect kindness hath not done him right. If but an unseasonable shower cross his recreation, he is ready to fall out with heaven, and thinks he is wronged if God will not take his times when to rain, when to shine. He is a slave to envy and loseth flesh with fretting, not so much at his own infelicity, as at others' good; neither hath he leisure to joy in his own blessings whilst another prospereth.[7] Fain would he see some mutinies, but dare not raise them; and suffers his lawless tongue to walk through the dangerous paths of conceited alterations,[8] but so as in good manners he had rather thrust every man before him when it comes to acting. Nothing but fear keeps him from conspiracies, and no man is more cruel when he is not manacled with danger. He speaks nothing but satires and libels, and lodgeth no guests in his heart but rebels. The inconstant and he agree well in their felicity, which both place in change, but herein they differ: the inconstant man affects that which will be, the mal-

---

2. Appropriate.
3. Exposed to envy.
4. Fastidiously.
5. Conventionally.
6. Slight.

7. In this section of the character, Hall is glancing at the Puritans.
8. "Imaginary changes" in church government, proposed by the Puritans, were hateful to Hall.

content commonly that which was. Finally, he is a querulous cur, whom no horse can pass by without barking at;[9] yea, in the deep silence of night the very moonshine openeth his clamorous mouth; he is the wheel of a well-couched firework that flies out on all sides, not without scorching itself. Every ear was long ago weary of him, and he is now almost weary of himself. Give him but a little respite, and he will die alone, of no other death than others' welfare.

1608

9. Without his barking at it.

SIR THOMAS OVERBURY: A Puritan

Is a diseased piece of Apocrypha:[1] bind him to the Bible, and he corrupts the whole text; ignorance, and fat feed are his founders; his nurses, railing, rabies, and round breeches;[2] his life is but a borrowed blast of wind, for between two religions, as between two doors, he is ever whistling. Truly whose child he is, is yet unknown, for willingly his faith allows no father:[3] only thus far his pedigree is found, Bragger, and he flourished about a time first; his fiery zeal keeps him continually costive,[4] which withers him into his own translation, and till he eat a Schoolman,[5] he is hidebound; he ever prays against nonresidents,[6] but is himself the greatest discontinuer, for he never keeps near his text: anything that the law allows, but marriage, and March beer, he murmurs at; what it disallows and holds dangerous, makes him a discipline. Where the gate stands open, he is ever seeking a stile; and where his learning ought to climb, he creeps through; give him advice, you run into *traditions*, and urge a modest course, he cries out *councils*.[7] His greatest care is to contemn obedience, his last care to serve God handsomely and cleanly; he is now become so cross a kind of teaching, that should the church enjoin

1. The suspect or doubtful books of the Bible.
2. Abuse, madness, and gross fat—with, perhaps, a hit at the Dutch, who wore baggy trousers, and among whom the Protestant sects flourished. "Rabies" may also include a pun on "rabbis"—the text of the original reads "rabbies."
3. The Puritans were much opposed to historical traditions in the church, hence to those early writers known as "fathers of the church." "Bragger" is an imaginary figure of the first ages of history, on the model of Nimrod.
4. Constipated.
5. Puritan hatred of the medieval

Schoolmen (all Catholics, naturally) was proverbial. There seems to be a whole series of buried jokes in these opening lines on the Puritan as a book: "bind him to the Bible," "his own translation," and "hidebound" (i.e., bound in leather, but also scrawny, meager, and stubborn).
6. Preachers who do not live among their flock; the Puritan also departs from his duty, i.e., "his text."
7. "Councils" of the church were as odious to Puritans as historical "traditions"—both being ways of adulterating God's pure word with mere human prudence.

clean shirts, he were lousy; more sense than single prayers is not his, nor more in those than still the same petitions:[8] from which he either fears a learned faith, or doubts God understands not at first hearing. Show him a ring, he runs back like a bear; and hates square dealing as allied to caps;[9] a pair of organs blow him out of the parish and are the only clyster pipes[1] to cool him. Where the meat is best, there he confutes most, for his arguing is but the efficacy of his eating: good bits he holds breed good positions, and the Pope he best concludes against in plum broth. He is often drunk, but not as we are, temporally; nor can his sleep then cure him, for the fumes of his ambition make his very soul reel, and that small beer that should allay him (silence) keeps him more surfeited, and makes his heat break out in private houses;[2] women and lawyers are his best disciples; the one, next fruit,[3] longs for forbidden doctrine, the other to maintain forbidden titles, both which he sows amongst them. Honest he dare not be, for that loves order; yet if he can be brought to ceremony, and made but master of it, he is converted.

1614

SIR THOMAS OVERBURY: What a Character Is[4]

If I must speak the schoolmaster's language, I will confess that character comes of this infinite mood χαράξω, that signifieth to engrave, or make a deep impression. And for that cause, a letter (as A, B) is called a character.

Those elements which we learn first, leaving a strong seal in our memories.

Character is also taken from an Egyptian hieroglyphic, for an impress, or short emblem; in little comprehending much.

To square out a character by our English level, it is a picture (real or personal) quaintly drawn, in various colors, all of them heightened by one shadowing.

It is a quick and soft touch of many strings, all shutting up in one musical close; it is wit's descant[5] on any plain song.

1614

8. Puritans were notorious for long, repetitive sermons, but not for logical discourse.

9. The Puritan antipathy to the ceremony of the ring in marriage, compared with a bear's antipathy to the bear ring. "Square dealing" (i.e., honesty) is allied in Puritan eyes to square "caps" (i.e., learning; from the scholar's cap).

1. Enema tubes. The organ is added to the list of Puritan hates.

2. Drunk with ambition, as other men get drunk with ale, the Puritan breaks out in private houses as they do in public houses (taverns).

3. After forbidden fruit, women long for forbidden doctrine.

4. The last of Overbury's characters, this is really the character of a character

5. Variations.

JOHN EARLE: A Pretender to Learning

Is one that would make others more fools than himself; for though he knows nothing, he would not have the world know so much. He conceits nothing in learning but the opinion,[6] which he seeks to purchase without it, though he might with less labor cure his ignorance than hide it. He is indeed a kind of scholar-mountebank, and his art our delusion. He is tricked out in all the accoutrements of learning, and at the first encounter none passes better. He is oftener in his study than at his book, and you cannot pleasure him better than to deprehend him.[7] Yet he hears you not till the third knock, and then comes out very angry, as interrupted. You find him in his slippers and a pen in his ear, in which formality he was asleep. His table is spread wide with some classic folio, which is as constant to it as the carpet,[8] and hath laid open in the same page this half year. His candle is always a longer sitter-up than himself, and the boast of his window at midnight. He walks much alone in the posture of meditation, and has a book still before his face in the fields. His pocket is seldom without a Greek Testament or Hebrew Bible, which he opens only in the church, and that when some stander-by looks over. He has his sentences[9] for company, some scatterings of Seneca and Tacitus which are good upon all occasions. If he read anything in the morning, it comes up all at dinner; and as long as that lasts, the discourse is his. He is a great plagiary of tavern-wit; and comes to sermons only that he may talk of Austin.[1] His parcels are the mere scrapings from company, yet he complains at parting what time he has lost. He is wondrously capricious to seem a judgment,[2] and listens with a sour attention to what he understands not. He talks much of Scaliger and Casaubon[3] and the Jesuits, and prefers some unheard-of Dutch name before them all. He has verses to bring in upon these and these hints, and it shall go hard but he will wind in his opportunity. He is critical in a language he cannot construe, and speaks seldom under Arminius in divinity.[4] His business and retirement and caller-away is his

6. I.e., "the only thing he values in learning is the reputation of being learned."
7. I.e., "you cannot please him better than by taking him away from his study."
8. Not on the floor but on the table—a kind of dust-cloth.
9. Verbal formulas, sententious utterances.
1. St. Augustine; the "pretender" adapts himself to every occasion.

2. Eager to seem a man of judgment and insight.
3. Joseph Justus Scaliger and Isaac Casaubon were great Protestant scholars of the previous age, much opposed by the Jesuit order of the Roman church.
4. Arminius was a 16th-century Dutch theologian whose anti-Calvinist views involved him in many intricate arguments over predestination—an impressive authority.

study, and he protests no delight to it comparable. He is a great nomen-clator of authors, which he has read in general in the catalogue and in particular in the title,[5] and goes seldom so far as the dedication. He never talks of anything but learning, and learns all from talking. Three encounters with the same men pump him,[6] and then he only puts in or gravely says nothing. He has taken pains to be an ass, though not to be a scholar, and is at length discovered and laughed at.

1628

5. Having picked up authors' names from catalogues, he studies them at length—on their title-pages.
6. Exhaust him.

EDWARD HYDE, EARL OF CLARENDON
(1609–1674)

Edward Hyde was educated at Oxford and during the 1630's practiced law. From about 1641 onward, he was among the chief supporters and advisers of Charles I; he went into exile with the boy who was to become Charles II, and remained the center of the Stuart cause during the Interregnum. After the Restoration, he became Lord Chancellor and Prime Minister to Charles II, but was impeached in 1667 (owing partly to England's ill success in the Dutch War), and spent the last seven years of his life in France.

From The History of the Rebellion
[*The Character of John Hampden*]

He was a gentleman of a good family in Buckinghamshire, and born to a fair fortune, and of a most civil and affable deportment. In his entrance into the world, he indulged to himself all the license in sports and exercises and company, which was used by men of the most jolly conversation; afterwards he retired to a more reserved and melancholic society, yet preserving his own natural cheerfulness and vivacity, and above all a flowing courtesy to all men; though they who conversed nearly[1] with him found him growing into a dislike of the ecclesiastical government of the church, yet most believed it rather a dislike of some churchmen, and of some introducements[2] of theirs which he apprehended might disquiet the public peace. He was rather of reputation in his own country, than of public discourse or fame in the kingdom, before the business of

1. Intimately.   2. Novelties.

ship-money,[3] but then he grew the argument of all tongues, every man inquiring who and what he was, that durst at his own charge support the liberty and property of the kingdom, and rescue his country from being made a prey to the court; his carriage[4] throughout that agitation was with that rare temper and modesty, that they who watched him narrowly to find some advantage against his person to make him less resolute in his cause, were compelled to give him a just testimony: and the judgment that was given against him infinitely more advanced him, than the service for which it was given. When this Parliament began (being returned knight of the shire[5] for the county where he lived) the eyes of all men were fixed on him as their *Patriae Pater*,[6] and the pilot that must steer their vessel through the tempests and rocks which threatened it. And I am persuaded his power and interest at that time was greater, to do good or hurt, than any man's in the kingdom, or than any man of his rank hath had in any time; for his reputation of honesty was universal, and his affections seemed so publicly guided, that no corrupt or private ends could bias them.

He was of that rare affability and temper in debate, and of that seeming humility and submission of judgment, as if he brought no opinions with him, but a desire of information and instruction, yet he had so subtle a way of interrogating, and under the notion of doubts insinuating his objections, that he left his opinions with those, from whom he pretended to learn and receive them; and even with them, who were able to preserve themselves from his infusions,[7] and discerned those opinions to be fixed in him, with which they could not comply, he always left the character of an ingenious[8] and conscientious person. He was indeed a very wise man, and of great parts,[9] and possessed with the most absolute spirit of popularity, that is, the most absolute faculties to govern the people, of any man I ever knew. For the first year of the Parliament he seemed rather to moderate and soften the violent and distempered humors than to inflame them, but wise and dispassioned men plainly discerned that that moderation proceeded from prudence, and observation that the season was not ripe, rather than that he approved of the moderation, and that he begat many opinions and motions the education[1] whereof he committed to other men, so far disguising his own designs that he seemed seldom to wish more than was concluded, and in many gross conclusions which would hereafter contribute to designs not yet set on foot, when he

---

3. Charles I tried to collect a tax from the entire kingdom under an ancient law empowering him to tax the harbors of England to support a navy. Hampden legally resisted the third levy of ship-money, and so became the "argument" (subject) of discussion throughout the land.
4. Behavior.

5. The "knight of the shire" represented the whole county, not just a constituency.
6. Father of his country.
7. Insinuations.
8. Ingenuous (in the 17th century, the words were frequently interchanged).
9. Capacities.
1. Leading forward.

found them sufficiently backed by majority of voices, he would withdraw himself before the question, that he might seem not to consent to so much visible unreasonableness, which produced as great a doubt in some, as it did approbation in others of his integrity. What combination soever had been originally with the Scots for the invasion of England, and what farther was entered into afterwards, in favor of them, and to advance any alteration in Parliament, no man doubts was at least with the privity of this gentleman.[2]

After he was amongst those members accused by the King of high treason, he was much altered, his nature and carriage seeming much fiercer than it did before; and without question when he first drew his sword, he threw away the scabbard, for he passionately opposed the overture made by the King for a treaty from Nottingham, and as eminently any expedients that might have produced an accommodation in this[3] that was at Oxford, and was principally relied on to prevent any infusions which might be made into the Earl of Essex towards peace, or to render them ineffectual if they were made; and was indeed much more relied on by that party, than the General himself.[4] In the first entrance into the troubles he undertook the command of a regiment of foot, and performed the duty of a colonel on all occasions most punctually. He was very temperate in diet, and a supreme governor over all his passions and affections, and had thereby a great power over other men's. He was of an industry and vigilance not to be tired out, or wearied by the most laborious, and of parts not to be imposed upon by the most subtle or sharp, and of a personal courage equal to his best parts, so that he was an enemy not to be wished wherever he might have been made a friend, and as much to be apprehended where he was so, as any man could deserve to be, and therefore his death was no less congratulated on the one party than it was condoled on the other. In a word, what was said of Cinna might well be applied to him, *Erat illi consilium ad facinus aptum, consilio autem neque lingua neque manus deerat,* he had a head to contrive, and a tongue to persuade, and a hand to execute any mischief;[5] his death therefore seemed to be a great deliverance to the nation.

[The Character of Oliver Cromwell]

He was one of those men, *quos vituperare ne inimici quidem possent, nisi ut simul laudent,*[6] for he could never have done half that

---

2. The English Civil Wars were set off by a Scottish invasion which had actually been invited by the English Parliament. This was done with the "privity" of Hampden, i.e., with his knowledge.
3. I.e., this treaty.
4. The point is that Hampden was an uncompromising member of the Puri-

tan war-party, whereas the Earl of Essex, who was commander in chief of the Parliamentary armies, was too moderate a man for the war-party.
5. Clarendon quotes from memory; the words concern not Cinna but Catiline. They are from Cicero's third oration against Catiline.
6. "Whom not even his enemies could

mischief without great parts of courage and industry and judgment, and he must have had a wonderful understanding in the natures and humors of men, and as great a dexterity in applying them, who from a private and obscure birth (though of a good family), without interest of estate, alliance, or friendships, could raise himself to such a height, and compound and knead such opposite and contradictory tempers, humors, and interests into a consistence that contributed to his designs and to their own destruction, whilst himself grew insensibly powerful enough to cut off those by whom he had climbed in the instant that they projected to demolish their own building. What Velleius Paterculus said of Cinna may very justly be said of him, *Ausum eum quae nemo auderet bonus, perfecisse quae a nullo nisi fortissimo perfici possunt*.[7] Without doubt, no man with more wickedness ever attempted anything, or brought to pass what he desired more wickedly, more in the face and contempt of religion and moral honesty, yet wickedness as great as his could never have accomplished those trophies[8] without the assistance of a great spirit, an admirable circumspection and sagacity, and a most magnanimous resolution. When he appeared first in Parliament he seemed to have a person in no degree gracious, no ornament of discourse, none of those talents which use to reconcile the affections of the standers-by, yet as he grew into place and authority, his parts seemed to be renewed, as if he had concealed faculties till he had occasion to use them; and when he was to act the part of a great man, he did it without any indecency[9] through the want of custom. * * *

He was not a man of blood, and totally declined Machiavel's method,[1] which prescribes upon any alteration of a government, as a thing absolutely necessary, to cut off all the heads of those, and extirpate their families, who are friends to the old; and it was confidently reported that in the Council of Officers, it was more than once proposed that there might be a general massacre of all the royal party, but Cromwell would never consent to it, it may be out of too much contempt of his enemies. In a word, as he had all the wickednesses against which damnation is denounced and for which Hell-fire is prepared, so he had some virtues, which have caused the memory of some men in all ages to be celebrated, and he will be looked upon by posterity as a brave, bad man.

1702–4

blame unless at the same time they praised.' The tag has not proved traceable; Clarendon may have invented it.
7. "He dared to undertake things which no good man would have undertaken, and completed projects which only the strongest of men could have completed." Velleius Paterculus, who died ca. 30

A.D., wrote an indignant *History of Rome;* the quotation is from II.xxiv.
8. Great results.
9. Lack of decorum.
1. Machiavelli is cited in his usual role as an exponent of political ruthlessness.

IZAAK WALTON
(1593–1683)

Izaak Walton, who was by profession a London ironmonger, is remembered these days as the author of *The Complete Angler*. This is an early treatise on the art of angling, with interpolated passages of quaintly humorous dialogue; it is consulted nowadays not so much by people who want to catch fish as by people who want to think about fishing from the placid perspective of a library. But to his own generation, Izaak was essentially a pious biographer. A devout Anglican himself, he first turned to biography in the late 30's, just as the Civil Wars were looming; and all his biographical work was done at a time when the English church was under attack from the Puritans, or struggling to re-establish itself after the Restoration. The men whose lives he wrote were ideally suited to be saints and martyrs in a roster of Anglican worthies; or, if they were not ideally suited for the role, Izaak's happy imagination and faculty of forgetting inconvenient details did much to make them so. But if they are not models of scholarly objectivity—how could they be, in that age?—the biographies of Walton are warm and moving compositions of literary art. Certainly he has not been the last man to feel that a good cause justified a little liberty with exact truth.

From The Life of Dr. John Donne[1]
[*Donne Takes Holy Orders*]

I return from my account of the vision to tell the reader that both before Mr. Donne's going into France, at his being there, and after his return, many of the nobility and others that were powerful at court were watchful and solicitous to the king for some secular employment for him. The king had formerly both known and put a value upon his company, and had also given him some hopes of a state-employment; being always much pleased when Mr. Donne attended him, especially at his meals, where there were usually many deep discourses of general learning and very often friendly disputes or debates of religion betwixt His Majesty and those divines. whose places required their attendance on him at those times: particularly the Dean of the Chapel, who then was Bishop Montague (the publisher of the learned and eloquent works of His Majesty) and the

---

1. The present selection begins with Donne in middle life. Walton has broken his account of these middle years with a digression on second sight, occasioned by a vision which Donne is said to have had in France when his wife was ill at home. Izaak then picks up the thread of his narrative with Donne on the threshold of his career in the church. The text is from the fourth edition (1675); "Feb. 15, 1639," the date at the end of the *Life*, is misleading.

most Reverend Doctor Andrewes the late learned Bishop of Winchester, who then was the king's almoner.[2]

About this time there grew many disputes that concerned the Oath of Supremacy and Allegiance,[3] in which the king had appeared, and engaged himself by his public writings now extant: and His Majesty discoursing with Mr. Donne concerning many of the reasons which are usually urged against the taking of those oaths, apprehended such a validity and clearness in his stating the questions, and his answers to them, that His Majesty commanded him to bestow some time in drawing the arguments into a method, and then to write his answers to them; and, having done that, not to send, but be his own messenger and bring them to him. To this he presently and diligently applied himself, and within six weeks brought them to him under his own handwriting, as they be now printed; the book bearing the name of *Pseudo-Martyr*, printed *anno* 1610.

When the king had read and considered that book, he persuaded Mr. Donne to enter into the ministry; to which, at that time, he was, and appeared, very unwilling, apprehending it (such was his mistaking modesty) to be too weighty for his abilities: and though His Majesty had promised him a favor, and many persons of worth mediated with His Majesty for some secular employment for him (to which his education had apted[4] him), and particularly the Earl of Somerset[5] when in his greatest height of favor; who being then at Theobald's with the king, where one of the clerks of the council died that night, the Earl posted a messenger for Mr. Donne to come to him immediately, and at Mr. Donne's coming, said, "Mr. Donne, to testify the reality of my affection, and my purpose to prefer you, stay in this garden till I go up to the king, and bring you word that you are clerk of the council: doubt not my doing this, for I know the king loves you, and know the king will not deny

2. Donne's friends were Richard Montague, later Bishop of Chichester, and famous as an Anglican controversialist and historian; and Lancelot Andrewes, eminent divine, preacher, and translator of the Bible. Both were members of the High-Church, anti-Calvinist wing of the church; both were men of vast learning. As "king's almoner," Andrewes was his Majesty's official almsgiver; Montague, as the king's "publisher," prepared for the press the literary works of which James was so proud.
3. A requirement that they swear unequivocal allegiance to the Crown, under pain of fines and imprisonment, was troubling to the Roman Catholics of England, who claimed that they were

being persecuted for following their consciences in upholding Papal supremacy. The title of Donne's book, *Pseudo-Martyr*, shows the line he took with this argument.
4. Fitted.
5. Robert Carr, a handsome young page about court, had been raised by King James's favor to the rank of Earl of Somerset; and thus had reason to think the king would deny him nothing. He was later disgraced by the scandal surrounding the mysterious death of Sir Thomas Overbury. "Theobald's" was Lord Burghley's country house in Herts, acquired by James as a royal recreation-spot.

me." But the king gave a positive denial to all requests, and, having a discerning spirit, replied, "I know Mr. Donne is a learned man, has the abilities of a learned divine, and will prove a powerful preacher; and my desire is to prefer him that way, and in that way I will deny you nothing for him." After that time, as he professeth, "the king descended to a persuasion, almost to a solicitation, of him to enter into sacred orders":[6] which, although he then denied not, yet he deferred it for almost three years. All which time he applied himself to an incessant study of textual divinity, and to the attainment of a great perfection in the learned languages, Greek and Hebrew.

In the first and most blessed times of Christianity, when the clergy were looked upon with reverence, and deserved it, when they overcame their opposers by high examples of virtue, by a blessed patience and long suffering, those only were then judged worthy the ministry whose quiet and meek spirits did make them look upon that sacred calling with an humble adoration and fear to undertake it; which indeed requires such great degrees of humility, and labor, and care, that none but such were then thought worthy of that celestial dignity. And such only were then sought out and solicited to undertake it. This I have mentioned because forwardness and inconsideration could not in Mr. Donne, as in many others, be an argument of insufficiency or unfitness;[7] for he had considered long, and had many strifes within himself concerning the strictness of life and competency of learning required in such as enter into sacred orders; and doubtless, considering his own demerits, did humbly ask God with St. Paul, "Lord, who is sufficient for these things?" and with meek Moses, "Lord, who am I?"[8] And sure, if he had consulted with flesh and blood, he had not for these reasons put his hand to that holy plow. But God, who is able to prevail, wrestled with him, as the angel did with Jacob, and marked him; marked him for his own; marked him with a blessing, a blessing of obedience to the motions of his blessed spirit. And then, as he had formerly asked God with Moses, "Who am I?" so now, being inspired with an apprehension of God's particular mercy to him, in the king's and other solicitations of him, he came to ask King David's thankful question, "Lord, who am I, that thou art so mindful of me?"[9] So mindful of me as to lead me for more than forty years through this wilderness of the many temptations and various turnings of a dangerous life; so

6. A quotation from Donne himself, in the *Devotions upon Emergent Occasions.*

7. I.e., in many men, the fact that they sought a job eagerly might be evidence of their unfitness for it; but not in

Donne, for he did not seek it.

8. II Corinthians ii.16 and Exodus iii.11.

9. A paraphrase of Psalm viii.4. Donne's "soliloquy" is, naturally, the work of Walton's imagination—an ef-

merciful to me as to move the learnedest of kings to descend to move me to serve at the altar; so merciful to me as at last to move my heart to embrace this holy motion! Thy motions I will and do embrace: and I now say with the blessed Virgin, "Be it with thy servant as seemeth best in thy sight";[1] and so, blessed Jesus, I do take the cup of salvation and will call upon thy name and will preach thy gospel.

Such strifes as these St. Austin[2] had, when St. Ambrose endeavored his conversion to Christianity; with which he confesseth he acquainted his friend Alipius. Our learned author (a man fit to write after no mean copy) did the like. And declaring his intentions to his dear friend Dr. King,[3] then Bishop of London, a man famous in his generation and no stranger to Mr. Donne's abilities (for he had been chaplain to the Lord Chancellor at the time of Mr. Donne's being his lordship's secretary), that reverend man did receive the news with much gladness; and, after some expressions of joy, and a persuasion to be constant in his pious purpose, he proceeded with all convenient speed to ordain him first deacon, and then priest not long after.

Now the English Church had gained a second St. Austin; for I think none was so like him before his conversion, none so like St. Ambrose after it:[4] and if his youth had the infirmities of the one, his age had the excellencies of the other; the learning and holiness of both.

And now all his studies, which had been occasionally diffused, were all concentered in divinity. Now he had a new calling, new thoughts, and a new employment for his wit and eloquence. Now, all his earthly affections were changed into divine love; and all the faculties of his own soul were engaged in the conversion of others: in preaching the glad tidings of remission to repenting sinners and peace to each troubled soul. To these he applied himself with all care and diligence: and now such a change was wrought in him that he could say with David, "O how amiable are thy tabernacles, O Lord God of Hosts!"[5] Now he declared openly, "That when he required a temporal, God gave him a spiritual blessing." And that "he was now gladder to be a doorkeeper in the House of God, than he could be to enjoy the noblest of all temporal employments."

Presently after he entered into his holy profession, the king sent

fort to render vividly the character in conflict.
1. Cf. Luke i.38.
2. Augustine. The reference is to Augustine's conversion, described in the *Confessions*.
3. This is John King (father of Henry King, the poet); he was created bishop of London in 1611.
4. Augustine, though his literary gifts were never in question, was tainted in his youth with libertinism and the Manichaean heresy; St. Ambrose, bishop of Milan, though less eloquent, was a steady pillar of the church against heretics, particularly the Arians. These great prototypes from the 4th century A.D. were widely known and imitated as a result of Augustine's *Confessions*.
5. Cf. Psalm lxxxiv.1.

for him, and made him his Chaplain in Ordinary,[6] and promised to take a particular care for his preferment.

And though his long familiarity with scholars and persons of greatest quality was such as might have given some men boldness enough to have preached to any eminent auditory; yet his modesty in this employment was such that he could not be persuaded to it, but went, usually accompanied with some one friend, to preach privately in some village not far from London; his first sermon being preached at Paddington. This he did till His Majesty sent and appointed him a day to preach to him at Whitehall;[7] and, though much were expected from him, both by His Majesty and others, yet he was so happy (which few are) as to satisfy and exceed their expectations: preaching the Word so, as showed his own heart was possessed with those very thoughts and joys that he labored to distill into others: a preacher in earnest; weeping sometimes for his auditory, sometimes with them; always preaching to himself, like an angel from a cloud, but in none; carrying some, as St. Paul was, to heaven in holy raptures, and enticing others by a sacred art and courtship to amend their lives: here picturing a vice so as to make it ugly to those that practiced it; and a virtue so as to make it be beloved, even by those that loved it not; and all this with a most particular grace and an unexpressible addition of comeliness.[8]

[Donne on His Deathbed]

It is observed that a desire of glory or commendation is rooted in the very nature of man; and that those of the severest and most mortified lives, though they may become so humble as to banish self-flattery, and such weeds as naturally grow there; yet they have not been able to kill this desire of glory, but that like our radical heat,[9] it will both live and die with us; and many think it should do so; and we want not sacred examples to justify the desire of having our memory to outlive our lives; which I mention, because Dr. Donne, by the persuasion of Dr. Fox, easily yielded at this very time[1] to have a monument made for him; but Dr. Fox undertook not to persuade him how, or what monument it should be; that was left to Dr. Donne himself.

A monument being resolved upon, Dr. Donne sent for a carver to make for him in wood the figure of an urn, giving him directions for the compass and height of it; and to bring with it a board, of the just[2] height of his body. These being got, then without delay

---

6. One of the king's regular staff of chaplains.
7. At court.
8. Having described Donne's decision to take holy orders, Walton proceeds to represent him as a perfect priest—eloquent, laborious, patient, and cheerful. At last, however, he sickened and grew ill; the stage is set for a protracted deathbed scene, such as Donne, Walton, and the 17th century relished enthusiastically.
9. Bodily warmth.
1. Toward the end of his life, in 1631. Dr. Simeon Fox was Donne's physician.
2. Exact.

a choice painter was got to be in readiness to draw his picture, which was taken as followeth. Several charcoal fires being first made in his large study, he brought with him into that place his winding-sheet in his hand, and having put off all his clothes, had this sheet put on him, and so tied with knots at his head and feet, and his hands so placed as dead bodies are usually fitted to be shrouded and put into their coffin or grave. Upon this urn he thus stood with his eyes shut and with so much of the sheet turned aside as might show his lean, pale, and deathlike face, which was purposely turned towards the east, from whence he expected the second coming of his and our Saviour Jesus. In this posture he was drawn at his just height; and when the picture was fully finished, he caused it to be set by his bedside, where it continued and became his hourly object till his death, and was then given to his dearest friend and executor Dr. Henry King,[3] then chief residentiary of St. Paul's, who caused him to be thus carved in one entire piece of white marble, as it now stands in that church;[4] and by Dr. Donne's own appointment, these words were to be affixed to it as his epitaph:

JOHANNES DONNE
Sac. Theol. Profess.

Post varia studia quibus ab annis tenerrimis
fideliter, nec infeliciter incubuit,
instinctu et impulsu Sp. Sancti, monitu
et hortatu

REGIS JACOBI, *ordines sacros*
amplexus, anno sui Jesu, 1614, et suae aetatis 42,
decanatu hujus ecclesiae indutus 27
Novembris, 1621,

exutus morte ultimo die Martii, 1631,
hic licet in occiduo cinere aspicit eum
cujus nomen est Oriens.[5]

And now, having brought him through the many labyrinths and perplexities of a various life, even to the gates of death and the grave, my desire is, he may rest till I have told my reader that I have seen many pictures of him in several habits and at several ages and in several postures; and I now mention this, because I have seen one picture of him, drawn by a curious[6] hand, at his age of

---

3. This is the poet, son of the Bishop of London who had advised Donne to enter holy orders, and himself later Bishop of Chichester. A reproduction of the portrait may be found in Grierson's edition of the poems, Vol. I, opp. p. 369.
4. Donne's tomb was destroyed in the great fire of 1666; only the statue survived, and is still seen in St. Paul's.
5. "John Donne, Professor of Sacred Theology. After various studies, which he plied from his tenderest youth faithfully and not unsuccessfully, moved by the instinct and impulse of the Holy Spirit and the admonition and encouragement of King James, he took holy orders in the year of our Lord 1614 at the age of 42. On the 27th of November, 1621, he was made deacon of this church; and he died on the last day of March, 1631. Here in the decline and decay of ashes, may he look upon Him whose name is a Rising Sun."
6. Skillful.

eighteen, with his sword, and what other adornments might then suit with the present fashions of youth and the giddy gaieties of that age;[7] and his motto then was—

> How much shall I be changed,
> Before I am changed![8]

And if that young and his now dying picture were at this time set together, every beholder might say, "Lord! how much is Dr. Donne already changed, before he is changed!" And the view of them might give my reader occasion to ask himself with some amazement, "Lord! how much may I also, that am now in health, be changed before I am changed; before this vile, this changeable body shall put off mortality!" and therefore to prepare for it. But this is not writ so much for my reader's memento as to tell him that Dr. Donne would often in his private discourses, and often publicly in his sermons, mention the many changes both of his body and mind; especially of his mind from a vertiginous giddiness; and would as often say, "his great and most blessed change was from a temporal to a spiritual employment"; in which he was so happy, that he accounted the former part of his life to be lost; and the beginning of it to be from his first entering into sacred orders and serving his most merciful God at his altar.

Upon Monday, after the drawing this picture, he took his last leave of his beloved study; and, being sensible of his hourly decay, retired himself to his bedchamber; and that week sent at several[9] times for many of his most considerable friends, with whom he took a solemn and deliberate farewell, commending to their considerations some sentences useful for the regulation of their lives; and then dismissed them, as good Jacob did his sons, with a spiritual benediction. The Sunday following, he appointed his servants, that if there were any business yet undone that concerned him or themselves, it should be prepared against Saturday next; for after that day he would not mix his thoughts with anything that concerned this world; nor ever did; but, as Job, so he "waited for the appointed day of his dissolution."

And now he was so happy as to have nothing to do but to die, to do which he stood in need of no longer time; for he had studied it long and to so happy a perfection that in a former sickness he called God to witness, "he was that minute ready to deliver his soul into his hands, if that minute God would determine his dissolution."[1] In that sickness he begged of God the constancy to be preserved in that estate forever; and his patient expectation to have his immortal soul disrobed from her garment of mortality makes me confident that he now had a modest assurance that his prayers were then heard and his petition granted. He lay fifteen days ear-

7. See the portrait reproduced in Grierson, Vol. I, opp. p. 7.
8. Transformed (i.e., by death).
9. Separate.
1. Walton again quotes from the *Devotions*.

nestly expecting his hourly change; and in the last hour of his last day, as his body melted away and vapored into spirit, his soul having, I verily believe, some revelation of the beatifical vision, he said, "I were miserable if I might not die"; and after those words, closed many periods of his faint breath by saying often, "Thy kingdom come, thy will be done." His speech, which had long been his ready and faithful servant, left him not till the last minute of his life, and then forsook him, not to serve another master (for who speaks like him) but died before him; for that it was then become useless to him that now conversed with God on earth as angels are said to do in heaven, only by thoughts and looks. Being speechless, and seeing heaven by that illumination by which he saw it, he did, as St. Stephen, "look steadfastly into it, till he saw the Son of Man standing at the right hand of God his Father";[2] and being satisfied with this blessed sight, as his soul ascended and his last breath departed from him, he closed his own eyes; and then disposed his hands and body into such a posture as required not the least alteration by those that came to shroud him.

Thus variable, thus virtuous was the life: thus excellent, thus exemplary was the death of this memorable man.

He was buried in that place of St. Paul's Church which he had appointed for that use some years before his death; and by which he passed daily to pay his public devotions to Almighty God (who was then served twice a day by a public form of prayer and praises in that place):[3] but he was not buried privately, though he desired it; for, besides an unnumbered number of others, many persons of nobility, and of eminency for learning, who did love and honor him in his life, did show it at his death by a voluntary and sad attendance of his body to the grave, where nothing was so remarkable as a public sorrow.

To which place of his burial some mournful friends repaired, and, as Alexander the Great did to the grave of the famous Achilles, so they strewed his with an abundance of curious and costly flowers; which course, they (who were never yet known) continued morning and evening for many days, not ceasing, till the stones that were taken up in that church to give his body admission into the cold earth (now his bed of rest) were again by the mason's art so leveled and firmed as they had been formerly, and his place of burial undistinguishable to common view.

The next day after his burial, some unknown friend, some one of the many lovers and admirers of his virtue and learning, wrote this epitaph with a coal on the wall over his grave:

> Reader! I am to let thee know,
> Donne's body only lies below;

2. Cf. Acts vii.55.
3. This phrase clearly shows up as one of Walton's later additions to the *Life;*

Walton originally wrote when the forms of liturgy had not been changed.

> For, could the grave his soul comprise,
> Earth would be richer than the skies!

Nor was this all the honor done to his reverend ashes; for, as there be some persons that will not receive a reward for that for which God accounts himself a debtor, persons that dare trust God with their charity and without a witness; so there was by some grateful unknown friend that thought Dr. Donne's memory ought to be perpetuated, an hundred marks sent to his two faithful friends and executors,[4] towards the making of his monument. It was not for many years known by whom; but after the death of Dr. Fox, it was known that it was he that sent it; and he lived to see as lively a representation of his dead friend as marble can express: a statue indeed so like Dr. Donne, that (as his friend Sir Henry Wotton hath expressed himself) "it seems to breathe faintly, and posterity shall look upon it as a kind of artificial miracle."

He was of stature moderately tall; of a straight and equally proportioned body, to which all his words and actions gave an unexpressible addition of comeliness.

The melancholy and pleasant humor were in him so contempered that each gave advantage to the other, and made his company one of the delights of mankind.

His fancy was unimitably high, equaled only by his great wit; both being made useful by a commanding judgment.

His aspect was cheerful, and such as gave a silent testimony of a clear knowing soul, and of a conscience at peace with itself.

His melting eye showed that he had a soft heart, full of noble compassion; of too brave a soul to offer injuries and too much a Christian not to pardon them in others.

He did much contemplate (especially after he entered into his sacred calling) the mercies of Almighty God, the immortality of the soul, and the joys of heaven: and would often say in a kind of sacred ecstasy—"Blessed be God that he is God, only and divinely like himself."

He was by nature highly passionate, but more apt to reluct at[5] the excesses of it. A great lover of the offices of humanity, and of so merciful a spirit that he never beheld the miseries of mankind without pity and relief.

He was earnest and unwearied in the search of knowledge, with which his vigorous soul is now satisfied, and employed in a continual praise of that God that first breathed it into his active body: that body, which once was a temple of the Holy Ghost and is now become a small quantity of Christian dust:

But I shall see it reanimated.

Feb. 15, 1639.

I. W.

1639, 1675

4. "Dr. King and Dr. Monfort" [marginal note].   5. Oppose.

JOHN AUBREY

(1626–1697)

John Aubrey's *Life* of his friend Thomas Hobbes is far from a proper biography; it is a collection of random jottings on bits and scraps of paper, full of gaps and question marks and "low" details which Aubrey probably never intended to print. A modern editor of Aubrey's *Brief Lives*, Andrew Clark, has painstakingly assembled them in rough chronological or topical order, placing his own headings in italic type between caret-shaped brackets 〈 〉 to distinguish his words from Aubrey's. Occasionally, too, he will fill out Aubrey's initials or incomplete sentences with material which he encloses between the same sort of brackets. Scrappy as it seems to be, the account of Hobbes owes a great deal of what coherence it possesses to the labors of Clark, whose shuffling of the manuscripts bore fruit in two fascinating volumes, published by the Clarendon Press (Oxford, 1898 and 1931), from which the present selection is taken. In order to emphasize the rough, unfinished quality of Aubrey's work, the notes are reproduced here in their original spelling and their original gabble of tongues. Like most learned men of his day, Aubrey used Latin tags almost as if they were English. The most frequent are: *Quaere de hoc* = Look into this; *scilicet* or *scil.* = to wit; *vide* = see; *Quod N.B.* = note this well; and *inter nos* = between ourselves. Aubrey's spelling is about average for his day and circumstances —i.e., he was writing by hand and for himself; in a printed book, he might have been a bit more careful. Thus, one finds in the first few lines two uses of "house" and two of "howse" and throughout there is a very casual attitude toward consistency. Certain details are repeated, occasionally with variations; there are blanks and gaps everywhere. As for the style itself, it is just such speech as one may suppose Aubrey himself talked over a bottle of ale—crotchety, humorous, rambling, and incomparably rich in the sense of life.

From The Life of Thomas Hobbes

〈*Place and Date of His Birth*〉

Thomas Hobbes, Malmesburiensis, Philosophus, was borne at his father's house in Westport, being that extreme howse that pointes into, or faces, the Horse-fayre; the farthest howse on the left hand as you goe to Tedbury, leaving the church on your right. To prevent mistakes, and that hereafter may rise no doubt what house was famous for this famous man's birth; I doe here testifie that in April, 1659, his brother Edmond went with me into this house, and

into the chamber where he was borne. Now things begin to be antiquated, and I have heard some guesse it might be at the howse where his brother Edmond lived and dyed. But this is so, as I here deliver it. This house was given by Thomas, the vicar, to his
daughter† . . . . . whose daughter or grand-
† Quaere William Aubrey daughter possessed it, when I was there. It
if . . . Potluck.[1] is a firme house, stone-built and tiled, of one
roome (besides a buttery,[2] or the like, within) below, and two chambers above. 'Twas in the innermost where he first drew breath.

The day of his birth was April the fifth, Anno Domini 1588, on a Fryday morning, which that yeare was Good Fryday. His mother fell in labour with him upon the fright of the invasion of the Spaniards—

> [Fama ferebat enim, sparsitque per oppida nostra
> Extremum genti classe venire diem;
> Atque metum concepit tunc mea mater
> Ut pareret geminos meque metumque simul.][3]

—he told me himself between the houres of four and six: but by rectification his nativity is found to be at . . . † .

His horoscope is Taurus, having in it a
† See my collection of *satellitium* of 5 of the 7 planets. It is a
genitures, where I have maxime in astrologie—vide Ptol. Centil.—
it more exact from his
owne mouth, viz. 5ʰ.2' that a native that hath a *satellitium* in his
mane.[4] ascendent becomes more eminent in his life
then ordinary, e.g. divers which see in Origanus, etc., and Oliver Cromwell had so, etc.[5]

⟨*His School and College Life*⟩

At four years old he went to schoole in Westport church, till eight; by that time he could read well, and number four figures. Afterwards he went to schoole to Malmesbury, to Mr. Evans, the

1. Aubrey reminds himself to look up a proper genealogy of Hobbes because he remembers vaguely an aunt who married a man enchantingly named Potluck.
2. Pantry.
3. Hobbes wrote in Latin a metrical autobiography from which Aubrey is here quoting (the square brackets suggest that he left a space for his quote and filled it up later). The verses translate loosely: "For Fame now raised and scattered through the land / News that the day of judgment was at hand, / Which struck so horribly my mother's ear / That she gave birth to twins, myself and fear."
4. As all astrologers know, the exact hour and minute of one's birth are of the greatest importance: Hobbes was born at 5:02 in the morning.
5. In the finished biography, Hobbes' horoscope would have been filled out at length; here Aubrey simply sketches the outlines.

minister of the towne; and afterwards to Mr. Robert Latimer, a young man of about nineteen or twenty, newly come from the University, who then kept a private schoole in Westport, where the broad place (quaere nomen)[6] is, next dore north from the smyth's shop, opposite to the Three Cuppes (as I take it). He was a batchelour and delighted in his scholar, T. H.'s company, and used to instruct him, and two or three ingeniose youths more, in the evening till nine a clock. Here T. H. so well profited in his learning, that at fourteen yeares of age, he went away a good schoole-scholar to Magdalen-hall, in Oxford. It is not to be forgotten, that before he went to the University, he had turned Euripidis Medea out of Greeke into Latin Iambiques,[7] which he presented to his master. Mr. H. told me that he would faine have had them, to have seen how he did grow in . . . . . Twenty odde yeares agoe I searcht all old Mr. Latimer's papers, but could not find them; the good huswives had sacrificed them.

I have heard his brother Edmund and Mr. Wayte (his schoolefellowe) say that when he was a boy he was playsome enough, but withall he had even then a contemplative melancholinesse; he would gett him into a corner, and learne his lesson by heart presently. His haire was black, and his schoolfellows were wont to call him 'Crowe.'

This Mr. Latimer was a good Graecian, and the first that came into our parts hereabout since the Reformation. He was afterwards minister of Malmesbury, and from thence preferred to a better living of 100 *li.*[8] per annum, or +, at Leigh-de-la-mere within this hundred.

At Oxford Mr. T. H. used, in the summer time especially, to rise very early in the morning, and would tye the leaden-counters (which they used in those dayes at Christmas, at post and payre)[9] with pacthreds,[9] which he did besmere with birdlime, and bayte them with parings of cheese, and the jack-dawes would spye them a vast distance up in the aire†, and as far as Osney-abbey, and strike at the bayte, and so be harled in the string, which the wayte of the counter would make cling about their wings. He did not much care for logick, yet he learned it, and thought himselfe a good disputant. He tooke great delight there to goe to the booke-binders' shops, and lye gaping on mappes * * *

† This story he happened to tell me, discoursing of the Optiques, to instance such sharpnes of sight in so little an eie.

6. Look up the name.
7. Latin iambic verses. "Mr. H." is Hobbes himself, who was curious to see how his Latin had improved; the "huswives" or housewives tended to sacrifice old paper to line pie-plates or polish brass.
8. A hundred pounds; in modern money less than $250 a year, but worth at least 20 times as much in those days. "Hundred": a division of a county.
9. An ancient card game (but Aubrey doesn't explain why it was played at Christmas or how the lead weights were used). "Pacthreds": twine for tying bundles.

⟨His Mathematical Studies⟩

He was (vide his life) 40 yeares old before he looked on geometry; which happened accidentally. Being in a gentleman's library in . . . , Euclid's Elements lay open, and 'twas the 47 El. libri I.[1] He read the proposition. 'By† G——,' sayd he, 'this is impossible!' So he reads the demonstration of it, which referred him back to such a proposition; which proposition he read. That referred him back to another, which he also read. Et sic deinceps,[2] that at last he was demonstratively convinced of that trueth. This made him in love with geometry.

† He would now and then sweare, by way of emphasis.

I have heard Sir Jonas Moore (and others) say that 'twas a great pity he had not began the study of the mathematics sooner, for such a working head would have made great advancement in it. So had he donne, he would not have layn so open to his learned mathematicall antagonists.[3] But one may say of him, as one (quaere who) sayes of Jos. Scaliger, that where he erres, he erres so ingeniosely, that one had rather erre with him then hitt the mark with Clavius.[4] I have heard Mr. Hobbes say that he was wont to draw lines on his thigh and on the sheetes, abed, and also multiply and divide. He would often complain that algebra† (though of great use) was too much admired, and so followed after, that it made men not contemplate and consider so much the nature and power of lines, which was a great hinderance to the groweth of geometrie; for that though algebra did rarely well and quickly, and easily in right lines, yet 'twould not *bite* in *solid* (I thinke) geometrie. Quod N.B.

† Vide de hoc in his *De corpore*, and also in his 5 Dialogue. Quaere Dr. Blackburne.[5]

Memorandum—After he began to reflect on the interest of the king of England as touching his affaires between him and the parliament, for ten yeares together his thoughts were much, or almost altogether, unhinged from the mathematiques; but chiefly intent on his *De Cive*, and after that on his *Leviathan*: which was a great puttback to his mathematicall improvement—quod N.B.—for in ten yeares' (or better) discontinuance of that study (especially) one's mathematiques will become very rusty.

1. The 47th proposition of Euclid's first book.
2. And so back to the beginning.
3. Hobbes' greatest folly in mathematics was to announce a triumphant solution to the problem of squaring the circle; unhappily, he did not know enough mathematics to understand the argument which proves this impossible.

4. Scaliger and Clavius were classical scholars who debated the emendation of texts—an activity in which brilliant error may well be superior to stodgy correctness.
5. Hobbes' book *De corpore* (On Matter) develops his argument against algebra, which was one of the truly great mathematical discoveries of his age.

⟨*Acquaintance and Studies*⟩

Amongst other of his acquaintance I must not forget our common friend, Mr. Samuel Cowper, the prince of limners[6] of this last
age, who drew his picture† as like as art
could afford, and one of the best pieces that
ever he did: which his majesty, at his returne,
bought of him, and conserves as one of his
great rarities in his closet[7] at Whitehall.

† This picture intended to
be borrowed of his
majesty, for Mr. (David)
Loggan to engrave an
accurate piece by, which
will sell well both at
home and abroad. Mr.
Loggan is well acquainted.

1659. In 1659 his lord[8] was—and some
yeares before—at Little Salisbury-house
(now turned to the Middle-Exchange), where he wrot, among other
things, a poeme, in Latin hexameter and pentameter, of the encroachment of the clergie (both Roman and reformed) on the civil
power. I remember I saw then 500 + verses, for he numbered every
tenth as he wrote. I remember he did read Cluverius's *Historia Uni-
versalis,* and made-up his poeme from thence. His amanuensis remembers this poeme, for he wrote them out, but knows ⟨not what
became of it⟩.

His place of meditation was then in the portico in the garden.

* * *

There was a report† (and surely true)
that in parliament, not long after the king
was setled, some of the bishops made a motion to have the good old gentleman burn't
for a heretique. Which he hearing, feared that his papers might be
search't by their order, and he told me he had burn't part of them.—
I have received word from his amanuensis and executor that he 'remembers there were such verses for he wrote them out, but knowes
not what became of them, unless he presented them to Judge
Vaughan, or burned them as I did seeme to intimate.' ☞ But
I understand since by W. Crooke, that he can retrive a good
many of them. * * *

† Quaere the bishop of
Sarum de hoc, i.e. pro
tempore.

⟨*Secures the Protection of Charles II*⟩

1660. The winter-time of 1659 he spent in Derbyshire. In March
following was the dawning of the coming in of our gracious soveraigne, and in April the Aurora.[9]

* * *

It happened, about two or three dayes after his majestie's happy
returne, that, as he was passing in his coach through the Strand,

6. Artists.
7. Gallery.
8. During most of his life Hobbes was
in service—as tutor-adviser-retainer—to
the Cavendish family.

9. Aurora = the dawn. Aubrey has in
mind some fancy phrases about the Restoration, but gives up after a gesture at
them.

Mr. Hobbes was standing at Little Salisbury-house gate (where his lord then lived). The king espied him, putt of his hatt very kindly to him, and asked him how he did. About a weeke after he had orall conference with his majesty at Mr. S. Cowper's, where, as he sate for his picture, he was diverted by Mr. Hobbes's pleasant discourse. Here his majestie's favours were redintegrated to him, and order was given that he should have free accesse to his majesty, who was always much delighted in his witt and smart repartees.

The witts at Court were wont to bayte him. But he feared none of them, and would make his part good. The king would call him the beare†: 'Here comes the beare to be bayted!'

† This is *too low* witt to be published.

⟨Personal Characteristics⟩

Describe face, eyes, forehead, nose, mouth, eyebrows, figure of the face, complexion; stature of body; shape (slender, large, neat, or otherwise); figure of head and magnitude of head; shoulders (large, round, etc.) arms, legs, how?—

Mr. Hobbes' person, etc.:—hazel, quick eie, which continued to his last. He was a tall man, higher then I am by about halfe a head (scil. . . . feet), i.e. I could putt my hand between my head and his hatt.—When young he loved musique and practised on the lute. In his old age he used to sing prick-song[1] every night (when all were gonne and sure nobody could heare him) for his health, which he did beleeve would make him live two or three yeares longer.

In his youth unhealthy; of an ill yellowish complexion: wett in his feet, and trod both his shoes the same way.

His complexion. In his youth he was unhealthy, and of an ill complexion (yellowish).

His† lord, who was a waster, sent him up and downe to borrow money, and to gett gentlemen to be bound for him, being ashamed to speake him selfe: he tooke colds, being wett in his feet(then were no hackney coaches to stand in the streetes), and trod both his shoes aside the same way. Notwithstanding he was well-beloved: they lov'd his company for his pleasant facetiousness and good-nature.

† This only *inter nos.*

From forty, or better, he grew healthier, and then he had a fresh, ruddy, complexion. He was *sanguineo-melancholicus*;[2] which the physiologers say is the most ingeniose complexion. He would say that 'there might be good witts of all complexions; but good-natured, impossible,'

Head. In his old age he was very bald (which claymed a veneration); yet within dore, he used to study, and sitt, bare-headed, and

---

1. A generic term for vocal music with written (pricked-out) notes.

2. Ruddy and melancholy at once, a mixture of two opposed humors.

sayd he never tooke cold in his head, but that the greatest trouble was to keepe-off the flies from pitching on the baldness. His head was . . . inches in compasse (I have the measure), and of a mallet-forme (approved by the physiologers).

Skin. His skin was soft and of that kind which my Lord Chancellor Bacon in his *History of Life and Death* calles a goose-skin, i.e. of a wide texture:—

Crassa cutis, crassum cerebrum, crassum ingenium.[3]

Face not very great; ample forehead; whiskers yellowish-redish, which naturally turned up—which is a signe of a brisque witt, e.g. James Howell, Henry Jacob of Merton College.

⟨*Beard*.⟩ Belowe he was shaved close, except a little tip under his lip. Not but that nature could have afforded a venerable beard (Sapientem pascere barbam—Horat. Satyr. lib. 2),[4] but being naturally of a cheerfull and pleasant humour, he affected not at all austerity and gravity and to looke severe.—'Gravity and heavinesse of countenance are not so good marks of assurance of God's favour, as a chearfull, charitable, and upright behaviour, which are better signes of religion than the zealous maintaining of controverted doctrines.'[5] He desired not the reputation of his wisdome to be taken from the cutt of his beard, but from his reason—

Barba non facit philosophum. 'Il consiste tout en la pointe de sa barbe et en ses deux moustaches; et, par consequence, pour le diffaire il ne faut que trois coups de ciseau.'—Balzac, *Letters*, tom. 2, p. 242.[6]

Eie. He had a good eie, and that of a hazell colour, which was full of life and spirit, even to the last. When he was earnest in discourse, there shone (as it were) a bright live-coale within it. He had two kind of looks:—when he laugh't, was witty, and in a merry humour, one could scarce see his eies; by and by, when he was serious and positive, he open'd his eies round (i.e. his eie-lids). He had midling eies, not very big, nor very little (from Sir W⟨illiam⟩ P⟨etty⟩).

Stature. He was six foote high, and something better (quaere James Wh⟨eldon⟩), and went indifferently erect, or rather, considering his great age, very erect.

Sight; witt. His sight and witt continued to the last. He had a curious sharp sight, as he had a sharpe witt, which was also so sure and steady (and contrary to that men call bro⟨a⟩dwittednes) that I have heard him oftentimes say that in multiplying and dividing he never mistooke a figure: and so in other things.

3. "Fat skin, fat brain, fat wit."
4. "Raise a learned beard" (Horace, *Satires*, Book II).
5. The Puritans were particularly hostile to Hobbes, seeing his materialism as the very antithesis of their spiritual faith; Aubrey is quoting from a book written in rebuttal of their charges.

6. The beard doesn't make the philosopher. The French quotation is from Jean-Louis Balzac (1597–1654): "He consists entirely of a pointy beard and two moustaches; consequently, all one needs to wipe him from the face of the earth is three snips of a scissor."

⟨*Habits of Body and Mind*⟩

He thought much and with excellent method and stedinesse, which made him seldome make a false step.

☞ He had very few bookes. I never sawe (nor Sir William Petty) above halfe a dozen about him in his chamber. Homer and Virgil were commonly on his table; sometimes Xenophon, or some probable historie, and Greek Testament, or so.

Reading. He had read much, if one considers his long life; but his contemplation was much more then his reading. He was wont to say that if he had read as much as other men, he should have knowne no more then other men.

His physique.[7] He seldome used any physique (quaere Sir W⟨illiam⟩ P⟨etty⟩). What 'twas I have forgot, but will enquire of Mr. Shelbrooke his apothecary at the Black Spread-eagle in the Strand.

Memorandum—Mr. Hobbes was very sick and like to dye at Bristoll-house in Queene Street, about 1668.

He had a sickness, anno . . .[8]

He was wont to say that he had rather have the advice, or take physique from an experienced old woman, that had been at many sick people's bed-sides, then from the learnedst but unexperienced physitian.

'Tis not consistent with an harmonicall soule to be a woman-hater, neither had he an abhorrescence to good wine but . . .—this only *inter nos.*

Temperance and diet. He was, even in his youth, ⟨generally⟩ temperate, both as to wine and women, ⟨et tamen haec omnia mediocriter⟩—

Homo sum, humani nihil a me alienum puto.[9]

I have heard him say that he did beleeve he had been in excesse[1] in his life, a hundred times; which, considering his great age, did not amount to above once a yeare. When he did drinke, he would drinke to excesse to have the benefit of vomiting, which he did easily; by which benefit neither his witt was disturbt longer then he was spuing nor his stomach oppressed; but he never was, nor could not endure to be, habitually a good fellow, i.e. to drinke every day wine with company, which, though not to drunkennesse, spoiles the braine.

For his last 30 + yeares, his dyet, etc., was very moderate and regular. After sixty he dranke no wine, his stomach grew weak, and he did eate most fish, especially whitings, for he sayd he digested fish

---

7. Not his physical constitution, but his medications.
8. *Anno* (in the year) indicates that Aubrey meant to look up the date, but forgot.

9. The tag is from Terence: "I am a man and consider nothing human beyond my sympathy." "*Et tamen haec omnia mediocriter*": all these things too in moderation.

better then flesh. He rose about seven, had his breakfast of bread and butter; and tooke his walke, meditating till ten; then he did putt downe the minutes of his thoughts, which he penned in the afternoon.

He had an inch thick board about 16 inches square, whereon paper was pasted. On this board he drew his lines (schemes). When a line came into his head, he would, as he was walking, take a rude memorandum of it, to preserve it in his memory till he came to his chamber. ☞ He was never idle; his thoughts were always working.

His dinner was provided for him exactly by eleaven, for he could not now stay till his lord's howre—scil. about two: that his stomach could not beare.

After dinner he tooke a pipe of tobacco, and then threw himselfe immediately on his bed, with his band[2] off, and slept (tooke a nap of about halfe an howre).

In the afternoon he penned his morning thoughts.

Exercises. Besides his dayly walking, he did twice or thrice a yeare play at tennis† (at about 75 he did it); then went to bed there and was well rubbed.‡ This he did believe would make him live two or three yeares the longer.

† Quaere James Wheldon *de hoc*—how often, and to what age?
‡ Memorandum there was no bagnio[3] in his time. That in Newgate Street was built about the time of his death.

In the countrey, for want of a tennis-court, he would walke up-hill and downe-hill in the parke, till he was in a great sweat, and then give the servant some money to rubbe him.

* * *

1898

1. Overtaken in liquor, that is to say, drunk.
2. Collar.
3. Public bath.

SAMUEL PEPYS

(1633–1703)

Samuel Pepys (pronounced "Peeps") was a bureaucrat in the London office of the Royal Navy, docile if not very enthusiastic in his attachment to the church of England, energetic and ultimately very influential in his office. The spirit of Puritanism touched him only tangentially, but touch him it did, not on the revivalist side but on the sober, bookkeeping side of his functionary's soul. In 1660, when he was about 27 years old, married, and solidly settled in office, he started to keep a private diary of his daily life; and, being a methodical, persistent man, he kept it going in minute detail for nine years, covering the most colorful and turbulent period of the Restoration. For the social historian, it provides an unparalleled record of London life, its plays and plagues, vulgarities, executions, wars, fires, scandals and intrigues. It is also a great human document *à la* Montaigne; an epic of the ordinary. The hero is Mr. Pepys; the epic action is his rise in the world to affluence and influence.

Because he wrote in shorthand, only recently invented and not very widely known, Pepys felt safe in recording all the undignified and squalid episodes of his existence. As a result the *Diary* acquired, during the prudish 19th century, a false reputation for obscenity. Only recently has it been deciphered in its unexpurgated entirety, and revealed itself as a remarkably sane and full record of a man's life. Pepys recorded his life as it happened and completely because he was a truthful man, and because he wanted a record of his spiritual and material progress through this world. The *Diary* served him as an aid to navigation through life's ocean; Pepys used it to take recurrent fixes on his social latitude and longitude. A normal time for this review of things was year's end, when practicality and piety were apt to blend in a singular amalgam of complacency and good practical sense.

Our text is from *The Diary of Samuel Pepys*, transcribed and edited by Robert Latham and William Matthews (University of California Press, 1970).

From The Diary

January 28, 1661

At the office all morning. Dined at home. And after dinner to Fleet street with my sword to Mr. Brigden (lately made Captain of the Auxiliaries) to be refreshed.[1] And with him to an alehouse, where I met Mr. Damport; and after some talk of Cromwell, Ireton, and Bradshaw's bodies being taken out of their graves today,[2] I went to Mr. Crew's and thence to the theater, where I saw again *The Lost Lady*,[3] which doth now please me better than before. And here, I sitting behind in a dark place, a lady spat backward upon me by a mistake, not seeing me. But after seeing her to be a very pretty lady, I was not troubled at it at all. Thence to Mr. Crew's; and there met Mr. Moore, who came lately to town, and went with me to my father's and with him to Standing's—whither came to us Dr. Fairbrother,[4] who I took and my father to the Bear and gave a pint of sack and a pint of claret. He doth still continue his expressions of respect and love to me. And tells me my brother John will make a good scholar.

Thence to see the Doctor at his lodgings at Mr. Holden's, where I bought a hat, cost me 35s. So home by moonshine, and by the way was overtaken by the Comptroller's[5] coach; and so home to his

1. Pepys was evidently enrolled in some sort of militia, and had to renew his oath.
2. The bodies of Cromwell, Ireton, and Bradshaw, all men who had taken part in the execution of Charles I, were exhumed, hanged, and disgraced as traitors.
3. Pepys had seen this play, first acted in 1638, only nine days before. He did not like it at all the first time.
4. Dr. Fairbrother, of King's College, Cambridge, was in charge of the education of Pepys' younger brother, John.
5. The Comptroller of the Navy, Sir Robert Slingsby; as a high-level bureaucrat, he is riding in a coach, and picks up Pepys; within a few years, Pepys will have his own coach. Press: chest of drawers.

house with him. So home and to bed. This noon I had my press set up in my chamber for papers to be put in.

October 28, 1661

At the office all day, and dined at home; and so to Paul's church-yard to Hunt's, and there find my Therobo[6] done. Which pleases me very well, and costs me 26s. to the altering—but now he tells me it is as good a lute as any is in England, and is worth well 10l. Hither I sent for Captain Ferrers to me, who comes with a friend of his, and they and I to the theater and there saw *Argalus and Parthenia*;[7] where a woman acted Parthenia and came afterward on the stage in man's clothes, and had the best legs that ever I saw; and I was very well pleased with it. Thence to the Ringo ale house, and thither sent for a belt-maker and bought of him a handsome belt for second mourning,[8] which cost me 24s. and is very neat. So home and to bed.

December 31, 1662

Thus ended this year, with great mirth to me and my wife. Our condition being thus—we are at present spending a night or two at my Lord's[9] lodgings at Whitehall. Our home at the Navy office, which is and hath a pretty while been in good condition, finished and made very convenient. My purse is worth about 650l.—besides my goods of all sorts—which yet might have been more but for my late layings-out upon my house and public assessment, and yet would not have been so much if I had not lived a very orderly life all this year, by virtue of the oaths that God put into my heart to take against wine, plays, and other expenses, and to observe for these last twelve months—and which I am now going to renew, I under God owing my present content thereunto.[1] My family is myself and wife; William my clerk; Jane, my wife's upper-maid, but I think growing proud and negligent upon it, we must part, which troubles me; Susan our cook-maid, a pretty willing wench but no good cook; and Waynman my boy,[2] who I am now turning away

6. Theorbo, a kind of early guitar. Pepys was an enthusiastic amateur musician, not only singing and playing, but also composing an occasional song of his own. Shillings and pounds are represented in the *Diary* by *s.* and *l.*
7. This romantic pastoral play had been written and published during the 1630's, but was being revived during the Restoration, for lack of other dramatic fare. The appearance of women on the stage was still a novelty, female parts having previously been taken by boys.
8. Pepys' Uncle Robert had died three months earlier; second mourning was evidently less austere than first.
9. My Lord Sandwich, after whose de-

scendant the snack was named; as chief Lord of the Admiralty, he was Pepys's administrative superior, his patron, and on occasion his financial guide.
1. Pepys had found himself going to the theater too often in 1661, and getting drunk too often; he took great oaths, and reduced both habits sharply.
2. Waynman was a very bad boy indeed, though we know only a few of his specific faults. Pepys beat him savagely to reform his character, and when that did not work, had him shipped off to the Barbadoes. To be known as a bad boy could have thoroughly disagreeable consequences in those days.

for his naughty tricks. We have had from the beginning our healths to this day very well, blessed be God. Our late maid Sarah going from us (though put away by us) to live with Sir W. Penn[3] doth trouble me, though I love the wench—so that we do make ourselves a little strange to him and his family for it, and resolve to do so.

December 31, 1663

* * * And so home; and after a little while at my office, I home and supped; and so had a good fire in my chamber, and there sat till 4 o'clock in the morning, making up my accounts and writing this past Journal of the year. And first I bless God, I do, after a large expense, even this month by reason of Christmas and some payments to my father and other things extraordinary, find that I am worth in money, besides all my household stuff or anything of Brampton,[4] above 800*l*.; whereof, in my Lord Sandwich's hand, 700*l*., and the rest in my hand; so that there is not above 15*l*. of all my estate in money at this minute out of my hands and my Lord's —for which the good God be pleased to give me a thankful heart and a mind careful to preserve this and increase it.

I do live at my lodgings in the Navy Office—my family being, besides my wife and I, Jane Gentleman, Bess our excellent good-natured cook-maid, and Susan a little girl—having neither man nor boy, nor like to have again a good while—living now in most perfect content and quiet and very frugally also. My health pretty good, but only that I have been much troubled with a costiveness[5] which I am laboring to get away, and have hopes of doing it. At the office I am well, though envied to the devil by Sir W. Batten, who hates me to death but cannot hurt me. The rest either love or at least do not show otherwise, though I know Sir W. Penn to be a false knave touching me, though he seems fair.

December 31, 1664

At the office all morning, and after dinner there again; despatched first my letters, and then to my accounts, not of the month but of the whole year also, and was at it till past 12 at night—it being bitter cold; but yet I was well satisfied with my work and, above all, to find myself, by the great blessing of God, worth 1349*l*. —by which, as I have spent very largely, so I have laid up above 500*l*. this year above what I was worth this day twelvemonth. The Lord make me for ever thankful to his holy name for it.

Thence home to eat a little, and so to bed. As soon as ever the clock struck one, I kissed my wife in the kitchen by the fireside, wishing her a merry New Year, observing that I believe I was the

3. Sir W. Penn was the father of the Quaker leader.
4. Pepys had inherited some property at

Brampton near Huntingdon.
5. Constipation.

first proper wisher of it this year, for I did it as soon as ever the clock struck one.

So ends the old year, I bless God with great joy to me; not only from my having made so good a year of profit, as having spent 42*l.* and laid up 54*l.* and upward.

But I bless God, I have never been in so good plight as to my health in so very cold weather as this is, nor indeed in any hot weather these ten years, as I am at this day and have been these four or five months. But I am at a great loss to know whether it be my hare's foot,[6] or taking every morning of a pill of turpentine, or my having left off the wearing of a gown.

My family is my wife, in good health, and happy with her—her woman Mercer, a pretty modest quiet maid—her chambermaid Bess —her cook-maid Jane—the little girl Susan, and my boy which I have had about half a year, Tom Edwards, which I took from the King's chapel. And a pretty and loving quiet family I have as any man in England.

January 23, 1665

Thence to Jervas's,[7] my mind, God forgive me, running too much after sa fille,[8] but elle[9] not being within, I away by coach to the Change[1]—and thence home to dinner; and finding Mrs. Bagwell[2] waiting at the office after dinner, away elle and I to a cabaret where elle and I have été[3] before; and there I had her company toute l'après-dîner and had mon plein plaisir of elle[4]—but strange, to see how a woman, notwithstanding her greatest pretences of love à son mari[5] and religion, may be vaincue.[6] Thence to the Court of the Turkey Company at Sir Andr. Rickard's, to treat about carrying some men of ours to Tangiers,[7] and had there a very civil reception, though a denial of the thing, as not practicable with them, and I think so too. So to my office a little; but being minded to make an end of my pleasure today, that I might fallow[8] my business, I did take a coach and to Jervas's again, thinking to avoir recontré[9] Jane; mais elle n'était pas dedans.[1] So I back again and to my office, where I did with great content faire[2] a vow to mind my business and laisser aller les femmes[3] for a month; and am with all my heart

6. Pepys carried a hare's foot as a protection against colic.
7. An alehouse where Pepys knew from experience casual female companionship could easily be picked up. His French phrases are for extra security—though, as a matter of fact, his wife was French by birth, and knew the language perfectly.
8. Her daughter.
9. She.
1. The Exchange, where merchants met to transact business.
2. The wife of a ship's carpenter, with whom Pepys had earlier reached an understanding.

3. She and I have been.
4. The whole afternoon and I had my fill of pleasure with her.
5. To her husband.
6. Overcome.
7. Pepys, an official of the Navy, was shrewdly trying to arrange some cheap transportation for naval personnel to the base at Tangiers aboard the vessels of a private company.
8. Follow.
9. Have met.
1. But she was not in.
2. Make.
3. Leave women alone.

glad to find myself able to come to so good a resolution, that thereby I may fallow my business, which, and my honor thereby, lies a-bleeding. So home to supper and to bed.

December 31, 1666

* * * Thence to the New Exchange to clear my wife's score;[4] and so going back again, I met Doll Lane (Mrs. Martin's sister) with another young woman of the Hall, one Scott, and took them to the Half-Moon tavern and there drank some burned wine with them, without more pleasure; and so away home by coach,[5] and there to dinner and then to my accounts, wherein at last I find them clear and right; but to my great discontent, do find that my gettings this year have been 573*l.* less than my last—it being this year in all but 2986*l.*; whereas the last I got 3560*l.* And then again my spendings this year have exceeded my spendings the last by 644*l.*—my whole spendings last year being but 509*l.*; whereas this year it appears I have spent 1154*l.*—which is a sum not fit to be said that ever I should spend in one year, before I am master of a better estate than I am. Yet, blessed be God, and I pray God make me thankful for it, I do find myself worth in money, all good, above 6,200*l.*; which is above 1800*l.* more than I was the last year. This, I trust in God, will make me thankful for what I have, and careful to make up by care next year what by my negligence and prodigality I have lost and spent this year.

4. At the New Exchange one could buy fabrics, dress materials, laces, etc. Pepys was clearing up his wife's charge account at the end of the year.
5. The coach, to which Pepys has now

graduated, is doubtless one of the expenses that appall him. In earlier days, he walked: see entry for January 28, 1661, above.

The Dispute over Natural Law

KING JAMES I

(1566–1625)

James Stuart (the sixth king of that name in Scotland, the first in England) had an itch to be writing as well as governing. He wrote a good deal of Scots verse, a denunciation of tobacco, and an essay upholding belief in witches, besides a treatise on government. *The True Law of Free Monarchies* was composed just five years before he became heir to the English throne, by the death of his cousin Elizabeth Tudor. James's point in this treatise is clear and simple; he proposes that the king can do absolutely anything he wants, and nobody can criticize him. Naturally, this elegant argument is framed primarily in analogies and metaphors; naturally also, James slips, now and again, from regular English into a locution from his native Scots.

From The True Law of Free Monarchies

[The Natural Necessity of Absolute Obedience]

* * *

And the agreement of the law of nature in this our ground with the laws and constitutions of God and man already alleged will by two similitudes easily appear. The king towards his people is rightly compared to a father of children, and to a head of a body composed of divers members. For as fathers the good princes and magistrates of the people of God acknowledged themselves to their subjects. And for all other well-ruled commonwealths, the style of *Pater patriae* (father of his country) was ever and is commonly used to kings. And the proper office of a king towards his subjects agrees very well with the office of the head towards the body and all members thereof. For from the head, being the seat of judgment, proceedeth the care and foresight of guiding and preventing all evil that may come to the body or any part thereof. The head cares for the body, so doth the king for his people. As the discourse and direction flows from the head, and the execution according thereunto belongs to the rest of the members, every one according to their office: so is it betwixt a wise prince and his people. As the judgment coming from the head may not only employ the members, every one in their own office, as long as they are able for it; but likewise in case any of them affected with any infirmity must care and provide for their remedy, in case it be curable, and if otherwise gar[1] cut them off for fear of infecting the rest: even so is it betwixt the prince and his people. And as there is ever hope of curing any diseased member by the direction of the head, as long as it is whole; but by the contrary, if it be troubled, all the members are partakers of that pain, so is it betwixt the prince and his people.

And now first of the father's part (whose natural love to his children I described in the first part of this my discourse, speaking of the duty that kings owe to their subjects), consider, I pray you, what duty his children owe to him, and whether upon any pretext whatever it will not be thought monstrous and unnatural for his sons to rise up against him, to control him at their appetite, and when they think good to slay him, or to cut him off, and adopt to themselves any other they please in his room. Or can any pretense of wickedness or rigor on his part be a just excuse for his children to put hand into him? And although we see by the course of nature

1. Have someone (a Scots locution).

that love useth to descend more than to ascend, in case it were true that the father hated and wronged the children never so much, will any man endued with the least sponk[2] of reason think it lawful for them to meet him with the line? Yea, suppose the father were furiously following his sons with a drawn sword, is it lawful for them to turn and strike again, or make any resistance but by flight? I think surely if there were no more but the example of brute beasts and unreasonable creatures, it may serve well enough to qualify and prove this my argument. We read often the piety that the storks have to their old and decayed parents: and generally we know that there are many sorts of beasts and fowls that with violence and many bloody strokes will beat and banish their young ones from them, how soon they perceive them to be able to fend themselves; but we never read nor heard of any resistance on their part, except among the vipers; which proves such persons as ought to be reasonable creatures, and yet unnaturally follow this example, to be endued with their viperous nature.

And for the similitude of the head and the body, it may very well fall out that the head will be forced to gar cut off some rotten member (as I have already said) to keep the rest of the body in integrity: but what state the body can be in, if the head for any infirmity that can fall to it be cut off, I leave it to the reader's judgment.

So as (to conclude this part) if the children may upon any pretext that can be imagined lawfully rise up against their father, cut him off, and choose any other whom they please in his room; and if the body for the weal of it may for an infirmity that may be in the head strike it off, then I cannot deny that the people may rebel, control and displace, or cut off their king, at their own pleasure, and upon respects moving them. * * *

1598

2. Spunk, spark.

THOMAS HOBBES

(1588–1679)

Thomas Hobbes, the second great philosopher of the 17th century, was the acknowledged pupil of the first, Francis Bacon, and the unacknowledged instructor of the third, John Locke. Born in 1588 (Armada year), he had attended Oxford and then served as tutor and secretary to various noblemen, including several members of the Cavendish family, and Bacon. When the civil wars broke out in 1641 he took the Royalist side, though not very actively, and when the king's party was defeated, he went off to Paris with the royal court-in-exile. His plan as a philosopher was to publish one book on physical bodies, one on human nature, and one on the state; and in fact he wrote books under these three titles, both in English and Latin. But in reality his career is less symmetrical and orderly than that fact implies, because the English texts are often quite different from the Latin, and the book for which he is best known, *Leviathan*, does not fit into the scheme at all. *Leviathan* appeared in Paris in 1651, scandalizing Puritans by its frankly secular tone, and disturbing Royalists because it seemed to make no real distinction between a legal king and an established usurper. When Hobbes left Paris shortly after the book's publication, returned to England, and made his peace with Cromwell, the worst fears of the Royalists were realized. But their fury hit a peak after the Restoration, when Hobbes not only went unpunished for his "treason," but was pensioned by his old friend and former pupil, Charles II. Throughout the Restoration, his out-spoken materialism made him a cause of scandal around the court; but his caustic tongue made him feared, and the indolent, cynical king was fond of him. Toward the end of his life he began gathering disciples, some of whom he would just as gladly have done without; for lewd, swearing, scepti-cal fellows sometimes took delight in being known as "Hobbists," not because they had studied or understood his philosophy, but because it was a name of scandal. He had a deeper influence on his enemies. A whole gener-ation of theologians and moralists trained themselves by thundering against Hobbes. And in the meanwhile, the quiet, capacious mind of Locke absorbed what it wanted from the thought of Hobbes and, without getting involved in the Hobbist controversies, built a structure of incomparable solidity using many of the older philosopher's materials.

From Leviathan

Part I, Chapter 13. Of the Natural Condition of Mankind as Concerning Their Felicity and Misery

Nature hath made men so equal in the faculties of body and mind as that, though there be found one man sometimes manifestly stronger in body or of quicker mind than another, yet when all is reckoned together, the difference between man and man is not so considerable as that one man can thereupon claim to himself any benefit, to which another may not pretend as well as he. For as to the strength of body, the weakest has strength enough to kill the strongest, either by secret machination, or by confederacy with others that are in the same danger with himself.

And as to the faculties of the mind—setting aside the arts grounded upon words, and especially that skill of proceeding upon general and infallible rules, called science; which very few have, and but in few things; as being not a native faculty, born with us; nor attained, as prudence, while we look after somewhat else—I find yet a greater equality amongst men than that of strength. For prudence is but experience, which equal time equally bestows on all men, in those things they equally apply themselves unto. That which may perhaps make such equality incredible is but a vain conceit of one's own wisdom, which almost all men think they have in a greater degree than the vulgar—that is, than all men but themselves and a few others, whom by fame, or for concurring with themselves, they approve. For such is the nature of men, that howsoever they may acknowledge many others to be more witty, or more eloquent, or more learned, yet they will hardly believe there be many so wise as themselves; for they see their own wit at hand, and other men's at a distance. But this proveth rather that men are in that point equal, than unequal. For there is not ordinarily a greater sign of the equal distribution of anything than that every man is contented with his share.

From this equality of ability ariseth equality of hope in the attaining of our ends. And therefore if any two men desire the same thing, which nevertheless they cannot both enjoy, they become enemies; and in the way to their end (which is principally their own conservation, and sometimes their delectation only) endeavor to destroy or subdue one another. And from hence it comes to pass that where an invader hath no more to fear than another man's single power; if one plant, sow, build, or possess a convenient seat, others may probably be expected to come prepared with forces united, to dispossess and deprive him, not only of the fruit of his labor, but also of his life or liberty. And the invader again is in the like danger of another.

And from this diffidence[1] of one another, there is no way for any man to secure himself so reasonable as anticipation; that is, by force or wiles to master the persons of all men he can, so long, till he see no other power great enough to endanger him, and this is no more than his own conservation requireth, and is generally allowed. Also because there be some, that taking pleasure in contemplating their own power in the acts of conquest, which they pursue farther than their security requires; if others that otherwise would be glad to be at ease within modest bounds, should not by invasion increase their power, they would not be able long time, by standing only on their defense, to subsist. And by consequence, such augmentation of dominion over men being necessary to a man's conservation, it ought to be allowed him.

Again, men have no pleasure, but on the contrary a great deal of grief, in keeping company, where there is no power able to overawe them all. For every man looketh that his companion should value him at the same rate he sets upon himself; and upon all signs of

1. **Lack of faith, mistrust.**

contempt, or undervaluing, naturally endeavors, as far as he dares (which amongst them that have no common power to keep them in quiet, is far enough to make them destroy each other), to extort a greater value from his contemners by damage, and from others by the example.

So that in the nature of man, we find three principal causes of quarrel. First, competition; second, diffidence; thirdly, glory.

The first maketh men invade for gain; the second, for safety; and the third, for reputation. The first use violence to make themselves masters of other men's persons, wives, children, and cattle; the second, to defend them; the third, for trifles, as a word, a smile, a different opinion, and any other sign of undervalue, either direct in their persons, or by reflection in their kindred, their friends, their nation, their profession, or their name.

Hereby it is manifest that during the time men live without a common power to keep them all in awe, they are in that condition which is called war; and such a war as is of every man against every man. For war consisteth not in battle only, or the act of fighting, but in a tract of time wherein the will to contend by battle is sufficiently known, and therefore the notion of time is to be considered in the nature of war, as it is in the nature of weather. For as the nature of foul weather lieth not in a shower or two of rain, but in an inclination thereto of many days together; so the nature of war consisteth not in actual fighting, but in the known disposition thereto, during all the time there is no assurance to the contrary. All other time is peace.

Whatsoever therefore is consequent to a time of war, where every man is enemy to every man; the same is consequent to the time wherein men live without other security than what their own strength and their own invention shall furnish them withal. In such condition there is no place for industry, because the fruit thereof is uncertain, and consequently no culture of the earth; no navigation, nor use of the commodities that may be imported by sea; no commodious building; no instruments of moving, and removing, such things as require much force; no knowledge of the face of the earth; no account of time; no arts; no letters; no society; and which is worst of all, continual fear, and danger of violent death; and the life of man, solitary, poor, nasty, brutish, and short.

It may seem strange to some man that has not well weighed these things, that nature should thus dissociate, and render men apt to invade and destroy one another; and he may therefore, not trusting to this inference, made from the passions, desire perhaps to have the same confirmed by experience. Let him therefore consider with himself, when taking a journey, he arms himself and seeks to go well accompanied; when going to sleep, he locks his doors; when even in his house he locks his chests; and this when he knows there be laws, and public officers, armed, to revenge all injuries shall be done him; what opinion he has of his fellow subjects, when he rides armed; of his fellow citizens, when he locks his doors; and of his children, and servants, when he locks his chests. Does he not there as much accuse mankind by his actions, as I do by my words? But neither of us accuse man's nature in it. The desires and other passions of man are in themselves no sin. No more are the actions that proceed from those passions, till they know a law that forbids them, which, till laws be made, they cannot know; nor can any law be made, till they have agreed upon the person that shall make it.

It may peradventure be thought there was never such a time nor condition of war as this; and I believe it was never generally so, over all the world; but there are many places where they live so now. For the savage people in many places of America, except the government of small families, the concord whereof dependeth on natural lust, have no government at all and live at this day in that brutish manner, as I said before. Howsoever, it may be perceived what manner of life there would be, where there were no common power to fear; by the manner of life which men that have formerly lived under a peaceful government use to degenerate into in a civil war.[2]

But though there had never been any time wherein particular men were in a condition of war one against another; yet in all times, kings and persons of sovereign authority, because of their independency, are in continual jealousies, and in the state and posture of gladiators; having their weapons pointing, and their eyes fixed on one another; that is, their forts, garrisons, and guns upon the frontiers of their kingdoms; and continual spies upon their neighbors; which is a posture of war. But because they uphold thereby the industry of their subjects, there does not follow from it that misery which accompanies the liberty of particular men.

To this war of every man against every man, this also is consequent: that nothing can be unjust. The notions of right and wrong, justice and injustice, have there no place. Where there is no common power, there is no law; where no law, no injustice. Force and fraud are in war the two cardinal virtues. Justice and injustice are none of the faculties neither of the body nor mind. If they were, they might be in a man that were alone in the world, as well as his senses and passions. They are qualities that relate to men in society, not in solitude. It is consequent also to the same conditions that there be no propriety,[3] no dominion, no *mine* and *thine* distinct; but only that to be every man's, that he can get; and for so

---

2. Hobbes may well be thinking of such famous accounts of savage civil wars as that of Thucydides (whom he translated).

3. Property.

long as he can keep it. And thus much for the ill condition which man by mere nature is actually placed in; though with a possibility to come out of it, consisting partly in the passions, partly in his reason.

The passions that incline men to peace are fear of death, desire of such things as are necessary to commodious living, and a hope by their industry to obtain them. And reason suggesteth convenient articles of peace, upon which men may be drawn to agreement. These articles are they which otherwise are called the Laws of Nature whereof I shall speak more particularly in the two following chapters.

From *Part I, Chapter 14. Of the First and Second Natural Laws*

The Right of Nature, which writers commonly call *jus naturale,* is the liberty each man hath to use his own power as he will himself for the preservation of his own nature, that is to say, of his own life; and consequently of doing anything which in his own judgment and reason he shall conceive to be the aptest means thereunto.

By Liberty is understood, according to the proper signification of the word, the absence of external impediments, which impediments may oft take away part of a man's power to do what he would, but cannot hinder him from using the power left him according as his judgment and reason shall dictate to him.

A Law of Nature (*lex naturalis*) is a precept or general rule found out by reason, by which a man is forbidden to do that which is destructive of his life or taketh away the means of preserving the same; and to omit that by which he thinketh it may be best preserved. For though they that speak of this subject use to confound[4] *Jus* and *Lex*, *Right* and *Law*; yet they ought to be distinguished, because Right consisteth in liberty to do or to forbear, whereas Law determineth and bindeth to one of them: so that Law and Right differ as much as obligation and liberty, which in one and the same matter are inconsistent.

And because the condition of man (as hath been declared in the precedent chapter) is a condition of war of every one against every one, in which case every one is governed by his own reason, and there is nothing he can make use of that may not be a help unto him in preserving his life against his enemies: it followeth that in such a condition every man has a right to every thing, even to one another's body. And therefore as long as this natural right of every man to every thing endureth, there can be no security to any man (how strong or wise soever he be) of living out the time which

4. Customarily confuse.

nature ordinarily alloweth men to live. And consequently it is a precept, or general rule of reason, *That every man ought to endeavor peace as far as he has hope of obtaining it; and when he cannot obtain it, that he may seek and use all helps and advantages of war.* The first branch of which rule containeth the first and fundamental law of nature, which is *to seek peace and follow it.* The second, the sum of the right of nature, which is, *by all means we can to defend ourselves.*

From this fundamental law of nature, by which men are commanded to endeavor peace, is derived this second law: *That a man be willing, when others are so too, as far-forth as*[5] *for peace and defence of himself he shall think necessary, to lay down this right to all things, and be contented with so much liberty against other men as he would allow other men against himself.* For as long as any man holdeth this right of doing anything he liketh, so long are all men in the condition of war. But if other men will not lay down their right, as well as he, then there is no reason for anyone to divest himself of his. For that were to expose himself to prey (which no man is bound to) rather than to dispose himself to peace. This is that law of the Gospel: *Whatsoever you require that others should do to you, that do ye to them.*[6] * * *

From *Part I, Chapter 15. Of Other Laws of Nature*

From that law of nature by which we are obliged to transfer to another such rights as, being retained, hinder the peace of mankind, there followeth a third, which is this: *That men perform their covenants made.* Without which covenants are in vain, and but empty words; and, the right of all men to all things remaining, we are still in the condition of war.

And in this law of nature consisteth the fountain and original of Justice. For where no covenant hath preceded, there hath no right been transferred, and every man has right to every thing; and consequently no action can be unjust. But when a covenant is made, then to break it is unjust; and the definition of injustice is no other than *the not performance of covenant.* And whatsoever is not unjust is just.

But because covenants of mutual trust, where there is a fear of not performance on either part * * * are invalid; though the original of justice be the making of covenants, yet injustice actually there can be none, till the cause of such fear be taken away; which while men are in the natural condition of war, cannot be done. Therefore, before the names of just and unjust can have place, there must be some coercive power, to compel men equally to the performance of

5. Insofar as.
6. The golden rule: Matthew vii.12, Luke vi.31.

their covenants by the terror of some punishment greater than the benefit they expect by the breach of their covenant, and to make good that propriety[7] which by mutual contract men acquire in recompense of the universal right they abandon: and such power there is none before the erection of a commonwealth. And this is also to be gathered out of the ordinary definition of justice in the schools;[8] for they say that *Justice is the constant will of giving to every man his own.* And therefore where there is no *own,* that is, no propriety, there is no injustice; and where there is no coercive power erected, that is, where there is no commonwealth, there is no propriety, all men having right to all things. Therefore where there is no commonwealth, there nothing is unjust. So that the nature of justice consisteth in keeping of valid covenants; but the validity of covenants begins not but with the constitution of a civil power, sufficient to compel men to keep them. And then it is also that propriety begins.

The fool hath said in his heart, there is no such thing as justice, and sometimes also with his tongue;[9] seriously alleging that every man's conservation and contentment being committed to his own care, there could be no reason why every man might not do what he thought conduced thereunto: and therefore also, to make or not make, keep or not keep covenants was not against reason, when it conduced to one's benefit. He does not therein deny that there be covenants, and that they are sometimes broken, sometimes kept, and that such breach of them may be called injustice, and the observance of them, justice: but he questioneth whether injustice, taking away the fear of God (for the same fool hath said in his heart there is no God), may not sometimes stand with that reason which dictateth to every man his own good; and particularly then when it conduceth to such a benefit as shall put a man in a condition to neglect, not only the dispraise and revilings, but also the power of other men. The kingdom of God is gotten by violence; but what if it could be gotten by unjust violence? were it against reason so to get it, when it is impossible to receive hurt by it? and if it be not against reason, it is not against justice, or else justice is not to be approved for good. From such reasoning as this, successful wickedness hath obtained the name of virtue; and some that in all other things have disallowed the violation of faith, yet have allowed it when it is for the getting of a kingdom. And the heathen that believed that *Saturn* was deposed by his son *Jupiter* believed never-

---

7. Property, in the sense of right or privilege.
8. I.e., among the schoolmen, medieval Aristotelians like St. Thomas Aquinas.
9. It is by no means a common fool who speaks up at this point; what he is saying is that a man who breaks his covenant (as Cromwell broke his oath of allegiance to Charles I) does not act unreasonably, as long as he serves his own interest. Though Hobbes tries to answer this fool, it is not clear that he succeeds.

theless the same *Jupiter* to be the avenger of injustice:[1] somewhat like to a piece of law in Coke's commentaries on Littleton, where he says, if the right heir of the crown be attainted of treason, yet the crown shall descend to him, and *eo instante*[2] the attainder be void. From which instances a man will be very prone to infer that when the heir apparent of a kingdom shall kill him that is in possession, though his father; you may call it injustice or by what other name you will; yet it can never be against reason, seeing all the voluntary actions of men tend to the benefit of themselves, and those actions are most reasonable that conduce most to their ends. This specious reasoning is nevertheless most false.

For the question is not of promises mutual where there is no security of performance on either side, as when there is no civil power erected over the parties promising; for such promises are no covenants. But either where one of the parties has performed already, or where there is a power to make him perform: there is the question whether it be against reason, that is against the benefit of the other, to perform or not. And I say it is not against reason (to perform the promise). For the manifestation whereof, we are to consider: first, that when a man doth a thing which (notwithstanding anything that can be foreseen and reckoned on) tendeth to his own destruction, howsoever[3] some accident which he could not expect arriving may turn it to his benefit; yet such events do not make it reasonably or wisely done. Secondly, that in a condition of war, wherein every man to every man, for want of a common power to keep them all in awe, is an enemy, there is no man can hope by his own strength or wit to defend himself from destruction without the help of confederates; where everyone expects the same defence by the confederation that anyone else does. And therefore he which declares he thinks it reason to deceive those that help him can in reason expect no other means of safety than what can be had from his own single power. He therefore that breaketh his covenant, and subsequently declareth that he thinks he may with reason do so, cannot be received into any society that unite themselves for peace and defence, but by the error of them that receive him; nor when he is received be retained in it without seeing the danger of their error; which errors a man cannot reasonably reckon upon as the

1. In Greek mythology, Saturn was deposed by Zeus (Jupiter), his son; yet Zeus, though himself a usurper, became father of the gods and the spokesman of justice. In all this discussion, the parallel with Cromwell (a usurper, yet perhaps the creator of a new justice) is strongly felt. Compare Marvell's *Horatian Ode*.
2. In that very instant. The heir to a throne is a traitor when he conspires against his father; but the instant he is successful, the king is dead, he is the new king, he cannot commit treason against himself, so the attainder of treason is void. "Coke upon Littleton" (the commentaries of Sir Edward Coke on Sir Thomas Littleton's 15th-century law-treatise) is a famous legal authority.
3. Even though.

means of his security. And therefore if he be left or cast out of society, he perisheth; and if he live in society, it is by the errors of other men, which he could not foresee nor reckon upon; and consequently against the reason of his preservation; and so as all men that contribute not to his destruction forbear him only out of ignorance of what is good for themselves.

As for the instance of gaining the secure and perpetual felicity of heaven by any way, it is frivolous; there being but one way imaginable, and that is not breaking, but keeping of covenant.

And for the other instance of attaining sovereignty by rebellion, it is manifest that though the event follow, yet because it cannot reasonably be expected, but rather the contrary; and because by gaining it so others are taught to gain the same in like manner, the attempt thereof is against reason. Justice therefore, that is to say, keeping of covenant, is a rule of reason, by which we are forbidden to do anything destructive to our life, and consequently a law of nature. * * *

1651

JOHN LILBURNE

(1615?–1657)

The iron determination of the revolutionary often comes out most vividly in conflict with his fellow revolutionaries. John Lilburne was a natural-born agitator who had suffered for propagandizing against the bishops and had fought in the parliamentary army against the king, but who achieved perhaps his finest moment in a direct confrontation with Oliver Cromwell during the early months of 1649.

Charles I had just been executed (January 30, 1649), and Cromwell, with a picked council of army officers and trusted allies from the House of Commons, was trying to set up a new form of governmental authority. But his plan was simply to keep power in his own hands. Lilburne and the Levelers (a name given them originally in derision because of their democratic principles) wanted a radically new political deal. They wanted, for instance, free elections; by one device or another, they estimated, nineteen of every twenty potential voters were being disenfranchised. They wanted freedom of speech; they wanted the political, legal, and social rights for which, as they thought, the whole war had been fought. When they saw Cromwell moving the other way, toward a tight personal dictatorship, they protested violently. A pamphlet titled *England's New Chains Discovered* denounced the betrayal of the revolution in unmeasured terms, and determined Cromwell to suppress a movement which seemed to be making dangerous headway against him. Toward the end of March he ordered troops to arrest the four leading Levelers (Lilburne, Prince, Overton, and Walwyn), and bring them before his Council of State for examination.

The whole proceeding stood on very dubious legal ground. Cromwell was general of the parliamentary armies, but that fact gave him no right to arrest ordinary citizens. The Council of State existed on Cromwell's say-so; it had never been created legally by an official body. With the king dead, the House of Lords abolished, and the House of Commons reduced by purges to a fraction of its original size, the Levelers were quite justified in arguing that nothing could set up a stable legal authority in England except new elections.

Being arrested was therefore a great opportunity for Lilburne—a head-strong, fearless, melodramatic man with a strong sense of national pride. He saw at once that the tribunal before which he was forced to appear must itself be put on trial; and he lectured his judges unmercifully. He said he would not plead his great services to the parliamentary cause, and then referred to them constantly, for the rest of his speech. Thrown into jail by the Council, as he actually asked them to do, he and his fellow Levelers published a long and passionate pamphlet titled *The Picture of the Council of State*, in which they represented at length their own eloquence and logic, while contrasting it with the harsh and narrow behavior of their persecutors. Our excerpt begins at the moment when Lilburne has just been asked by Mr. John Bradshaw, President of the Council, what he has to say for himself.

From The Picture of the Council of State

* * *

"Well, then, Mr. Bradshaw," said I, "if it please you and these gentlemen to afford me the same liberty and privilege that the Cavaliers did at Oxford, when I was arraigned against them for my life, for levying war in the quarrel of the commonwealth against the late king and his party (which was liberty of speech, to speak my mind freely without interruption), I shall speak and go on; but without the grant of liberty of speech, I shall not say a word more to you."

To which he replied, "That is already granted to you, and therefore you may go on to speak what you can or will say for yourself, if you please; or if you will not, you may hold your peace and withdraw."

"Well, then," said I, "Mr. Bradshaw, with your favor, thus. I am an Englishman born, bred, and brought up, and England is a nation governed, bounded, and limited by laws and liberties: and for the liberties of England I have both fought and suffered much. But truly, sir, I judge it now infinitely below me, and the glory and excellency of my late actions, now to plead merit or desert unto you, as though I were forced to fly to the merit of my former actions, to lay in a counter-scale, to weigh down your indignation against me, for my pretended late offences. No, sir, I scorn it, I abhor it. And therefore, sir, I now stand before you upon the bare, naked, and single account of an Englishman, as though I had never said, done, or acted anything that tended to the preservation of the liberties thereof; but yet, have never done any act that did put me out of a legal capacity to claim the utmost punctilio, benefit, and privilege that the laws and liberties of England will afford to any of you here present, or any other man in the whole nation. And the laws and liberties of England are my inheritance and birthright.

"And in your late declaration, published about four or five days ago, wherein you lay down the grounds and reasons (as I remember) of your doing justice upon the late king, and why you have abolished kingly government and the House of Lords, you declare in effect the same, and promise to maintain the laws of England in reference to the people's liberties and freedoms. And amongst other things therein contained, you highly commend and extol the Petition of Right,[1] made in the third year of the late king, as one of the most excellent and glorious laws in reference to the people's liberties that ever was made in this nation; and you there very much blame and cry out upon the king for robbing and denying the people of England the benefit of that law. And sure I am (for I have read and studied it), there is one clause in it that saith expressly, That no freeman of England ought to be adjudged for life, limb, liberty, or estate but by the laws already in being established and declared. And truly, sir, if this be good and sound legal doctrine (as undoubtedly it is, or else your own declarations are false and lies), I wonder what you gentlemen are. For the declared and known laws of England know you not, neither by names nor qualifications, as persons endowed with any power either to imprison or try me, or the meanest freeman of England. And truly, were it not that I know the faces of divers of you, and honor the persons of some of you, as members of the House of Commons that have stood pretty firm in shaking times to the interest of the nation, I should wonder what you are, or before whom I am, and should not in the least honor or reverence you so much as with civil respect, especially considering the manner of my being brought before you, with armed men, and the manner of your close sitting, contrary to all courts of justice. * * *

"Sir, by the law of England, let me tell you, what the House [of Commons] votes, orders, and enacts within their walls is nothing to me, I am not at all bound by them, nor in law can take any cognizance of them as laws, although twenty members come out of the House and tell me such things are done, till they be published and declared by sound of trumpet, proclamation, or the like, by a public officer or magistrate, in the public and open places of the nation. But truly sir, I never saw any print or writing that declares your power so proclaimed or published. And therefore, sir, I know not

1. In the so-called Petition of Right (1628), Parliament drew up and presented to Charles I a formal statement of the rights and privileges to which they laid claim in the name of the people of England.

what more to make of you than a company of private men, being neither able to own you as a court of justice, because the law speaks nothing of you; nor as a council of state, till I see and read or hear your commission, which I desire (if you please) to be acquainted with." * * *

[After a great deal of haggling over whether the Council really exists in a legal sense, Mr. Bradshaw finally gets down to asking the question which is at the root of the whole affair.]

"Whether you made not this book, or were privy to the making of it, or no?"

And after some pause, and wondering at the strangeness of the question, I answered, and said: "Mr. Bradshaw, I cannot but stand amazed that you should ask me such a question as this, at this time of the day, considering what you first said unto me at my first being before you; and considering it is now about eight years ago since this very Parliament annihilated the court of Star Chamber, Council Board, and High Commission,[2] and that for such proceedings as these. And truly, sir, I have been a contestor and sufferer for the liberties of England these twelve years together, and I should now look upon myself as the basest fellow in the world if now in one moment I should undo all that I have been doing all this while, which I must of necessity do if I should answer to you questions against myself. For in the first place, by answering this question against myself, I should betray the liberties of England in acknowledging you to have a legal jurisdiction over me to try and ajudge me; which I have already proved to your faces you have not in the least. And if you have forgot what you said to me thereupon, yet I have not forgot what I said to you. And secondly, sir, if I should answer to questions against myself and to betray myself, I should do that which not only law but nature abhors. And therefore I cannot but wonder that you yourselves are not ashamed to demand so illegal and unworthy a thing of me as this is. And therefore in short were it that I owned your power (which I do not in the least) I would be hanged before I would do so base and un-Englishman-like an action, to betray my liberty, which I must of necessity do in answering questions to accuse myself. But, sir, this I will say to you, my late actions have not been done in a hole or a corner, but on the housetop in the face of the sun, before hundreds and some thousands of people. And therefore why ask you me any questions? Go to those that have heard me and seen me, and it is possible you may find some hundreds of witnesses to tell you what I have said and done. For I hate holes and corners. My late actions need no

---

2. These were all courts which had become infamous under the 11-year tyranny of Charles I. Star Chamber and High Commission were particularly hateful as ecclesiastical courts which reminded their victims of the Inquisition. Lilburne himself had suffered imprisonment and whipping at their hands.

covers nor hidings, they have been more honest than so, and I am not sorry for what I have done, for I did look well about me before I did what I did, and I am ready to lay down my life to justify what I have done. And so much in answer to your question.

"But now, sir, with your favor one word more, to mind you again of what I said before, in reference to my martial imprisonment. And truly, sir, I must tell you, circumstantials of my liberty at this time I shall not much dispute, but for the essentials of them I shall die. I am now in the soldiers' custody, where to continue in silence and patience is absolutely to betray my liberty. For they have nothing to do with me, nor the meanest freeman in England in this case. And besides, sir, they have no rules to walk by but their wills and their swords, which are two dangerous things. It may be I may be of an hasty, choleric temper, and not able or willing to bear their affronts; and peradventure,[3] they may be as willing to put them upon me as I am unwilling to bear them. And for you in this case to put fire and tinder together, to burn up one another, will not be much commendable, nor tend much to the accomplishment of your ends. But if for all this you shall send me back to the military sword again, either to Whitehall or any other such like garrisoned place in England, I do solemnly protest before the Eternal God of Heaven and Earth, I will fire it and burn it down to the ground, if possibly I can, although I be burnt to ashes with the flames thereof. For, sir, I say again, the soldiers have nothing to do to be my jailers; and besides, it is a maxim among the soldiers, that they must obey without dispute all the commands of their officers, be they right or wrong; and it is also the maxim amongst the officers, that if they do not do it, they must hang for it. Therefore if the officers command them to cut my throat, they must either do it or hang for it. And truly, sir (looking wishfully[4] upon Cromwell, that sat just against me), I must be plain with you, I have not found so much honor, honesty, justice, or conscience in any of the principal officers of the army as to trust my life under their protection or to think it can be safe under their immediate fingers. And therefore, not knowing nor very much caring what you will do with me, I earnestly entreat you, if you will again imprison me, send me to a civil jail that the law knows, as Newgate, the Fleet, or Gatehouse." * * *

[After being questioned by the Council, and uniformly refusing to answer, Lilburne and his three associates are shut in a room alongside the Council-room.]

So after we were all come out, and all four in a room close by them, all alone, I laid my ear to their door and heard Lieutenant General Cromwell (I am sure of it) very loud, thumping his fist upon the Council table till it rang again, and heard him speak in these very words or to this effect: "I tell you, sir, you have no other way to deal with these men but to break them in pieces." And thumping on the Council table again, he said: "Sir, let me tell you

3. Perhaps.   4. Intently.

that which is true, if you do not break them, they will break you; yea, and bring all the guilt of the blood and treasure shed and spent in this kingdom upon your head and shoulders; and frustrate and make void all that work that with so many years' industry, toil, and pains you have done, and so render you to all rational men in the world as the most contemptiblest generation of silly, low-spirited men in the earth, to be broken and routed by such a despicable contemptible generation of men as they are; and therefore, sir, I tell you again, you are necessitated to break them." . . . Upon which discourse of Cromwell's, the blood run up and down my veins, and I heartily wished myself in again amongst them (being scarce able to contain myself), that so I might have gone five or six stories higher than I did before. * * *

[Lilburne concludes his narration with a direct personal appeal to his reader and to his own religious conscience.]

I know they have an army at command, but if every hair on the head of that officer or soldier they have at command were a legion of men, I would fear them no more than so many straws, for the Lord Jehovah is my rock and defense, under the assured shelter of whose wings I am safe and secure, and therefore will sing and be merry; and do hereby sound an eternal trumpet of defiance to all the men and evils in earth and hell, but[5] only those men that have the image of God in them, and demonstrate it among men by their just, honest, merciful, and righteous actions. And as for all those vile actions their saint-like agents have fixed upon me[6] of late, I know before God that none is righteous, no, not one, but only he that is clothed with the glorious righteousness of Jesus Christ, which I assuredly know my soul hath been, and now is clothed with, in the strength of which I have walked for above twelve years together, and through the strength of which I have been able at any time in all that time to lay down my life on a quarter of an hour's warning. But as to man, I bid defiance to all my adversaries upon earth, to search my ways and goings with a candle and to lay any one base action to my charge in any kind whatsoever, since the first day that I visibly made profession of the fear of God, which is now above twelve years. Yes, I bid defiance to him or them to proclaim it upon the housetops, provided he will set his hand to it, and proclaim a public place where before indifferent men in the face of the sun his accusation may be scanned. Yea, I here declare that if any man or woman in England, either in reference to my public dealings, to the state's money, or in reference to my private dealings in the world, shall come in and prove against me that ever I defrauded him or her of twelvepence, and for every twelvepence that I have so done, I will make him or her twenty shillings worth of amends, so far as all the estate I have in the world will extend.

Courteous reader and dear countryman, excuse I beseech thee my

---

5. Except.   6. Attributed to me.

boasting and glorying, for I am necessitated to it, my adversaries' base and lying calumniations putting me upon it, and Paul and Samuel did it before me: and so I am thine, if thou art for the just freedoms and liberties of the land of thy nativity.

> JOHN LILBURNE, that never yet changed his princi-
> ples from better to worse, nor could never be threat-
> ened out of them, nor courted from them, that never
> feared the rich nor mighty, nor never despised the poor
> nor needy, but always hath, and hopes by God's good-
> ness to contine, *semper idem*.[7]

From the Tower of London, April 3, 1649

1649

7. Ever the same.

GERRARD WINSTANLEY

(1609?–?)

Gerrard Winstanley is generally taken to represent the high-water mark of the English Puritan revolution. His little movement of Diggers grew out of Lilburne's Levelers, complementing a program of political radicalism with one of economic radicalism. But it faded away as abruptly as it appeared. And so did Winstanley himself; we can hardly guess his birth-date or trace his career through a possible bankruptcy as far as the years 1649–51 when the notoriety of the Diggers brought him to public view. After that brief moment, he relapses again into obscurity, and we cannot tell where he lived or when he died.

What Winstanley propounded in that short crest of time was the repeal, not only of the Norman Conquest, but of Adam's fall. His first messianic manifestos attracted little notice, being unclear, though ardent, in their rhetoric. But then on April 1, 1649, Winstanley with a handful of followers appeared on George's Hill in Surrey, and began to dig there in preparation for planting. Everyone understood what *that* meant. The ground did not belong to the cultivators; one Francis Drake, as "Lord of the Manor," held title to it, and they did not have his permission to dig there. That was the point of the exercise. What Winstanley wanted to establish was what we would instantly recognize as a commune. While disclaiming all violence, the Diggers called on the common people of England to reassume the earth which was rightfully theirs and to live on it as a common inheritance. Violence was unnecessary, as Winstanley argued, because the defeat and execution of Charles I had cancelled not only the Norman Conquest, but the original contract by which the Jews took to themselves a monarch, King Saul. James I had been 25 years in his grave, and he would have sputtered with fury had he been able to read Winstanley's pamphlets; but their logic was his own, only turned against his son and successor.

Property owners near and far were naturally dismayed by Winstanley and his little band of 50 or 60 instant communists. Like threatened landowners everywhere, they resorted to counter-measures—law officers, lawsuits, vigilante assaults, trampling of the new crops. The Diggers were driven from George's Hill and the island made safe once again for private property. Within the last decade or so, people calling themselves Diggers and acting much like Diggers have begun appearing in America and elsewhere; they know about Winstanley and are trying to revive his ideas. It may be that these ideas will get a second trial.

From The True Leveler's Standard Advanced

[*The Freeing of the English Israelites*]

A DECLARATION TO THE POWERS OF ENGLAND, AND TO ALL THE POWERS OF THE WORLD, SHOWING THE CAUSE WHY THE COMMON PEOPLE OF ENGLAND HAVE BEGUN, AND GIVES CONSENT TO DIG UP, MANURE, AND SOW CORN UPON GEORGE-HILL IN SURREY; BY THOSE THAT HAVE SUBSCRIBED, AND THOUSANDS MORE THAT GIVES CONSENT.

In the beginning of time, the great Creator Reason[1] made the earth to be a common treasury, to preserve beasts, birds, fishes, and man, the lord that was to govern this creation; for man had domination given to him, over the beasts, birds, and fishes; but not one word was spoken in the beginning, that one branch of mankind should rule over another.

And the reason is this. Every single man, male and female, is a perfect creature of himself;[2] and the same spirit that made the globe dwells in man, to govern the globe; so that the flesh of man being subject to Reason, his Maker, hath him to be his teacher and ruler within himself, therefore needs not run abroad after any teacher and ruler without him, for he needs not that any man should teach him, for the same anointing that ruled in the son of man teacheth him all things.

But since human flesh (that king of beasts) began to delight himself in the objects of the creation, more than in the spirit of Reason and Righteousness, who manifests himself to be the indweller in the five senses, of hearing, seeing, tasting, smelling, feeling; then he fell into blindness of mind and weakness of heart, and runs abroad for a teacher and ruler: And so selfish imagination taking possession of the five senses and ruling as king in the room of reason therein, and working with covetousness, did set up one

1. Though his basic myth is obviously Biblical, Winstanley does not in this tract refer directly to God; "the great Creator Reason" perhaps seemed to him more general or more persuasive as a title.
2. The perfection of the human creature is an ancient heresy, sometimes known as Pelagianism. Winstanley's social Utopianism is rooted in theology.

man to teach and rule over another; and thereby the spirit was killed, and man was brought into bondage, and became a greater slave to such of his own kind than the beasts of the field were to him.

And hereupon the earth (which was made to be a common treasury of relief for all, both beasts and men) was hedged into enclosures[3] by the teachers and rulers, and the others were made servants and slaves: and that the earth, that is within this creation made a common storehouse for all, is bought and sold and kept in the hands of a few, whereby the great Creator is mightily dishonored, as if he were a respecter of persons, delighting in the comfortable livelihood of some and rejoicing in the miserable poverty and straits of others. From the beginning it was not so.

* * *

But this coming in of Bondage is called A-*dam* because this ruling and teaching power without doth *dam* up the spirit of peace and liberty;[4] first within the heart, by filling it with slavish fears of others. Secondly without, by giving the bodies of one to be imprisoned, punished, and oppressed by the outward power of another. And this evil was brought upon us through his own covetousness, whereby he is blinded and made weak and sees not the law of righteousness in his heart, which is the pure light of reason, but looks abroad for it, and thereby the creation is cast under bondage and curse, and the Creator is slighted. First by the teachers and rulers that set themselves down in the spirit's room to teach and rule, where he himself is only king. Secondly, by the other that refuses the spirit, to be taught and governed by fellow creatures, and this was called Israel's sin in casting off the Lord and choosing Saul, one like themselves to be their king. * * *

And thus Esau, the man of flesh, which is covetousness and pride, hath killed Jacob,[5] the spirit of meekness and righteous government in the light of reason, and rules over him. And so the earth that was made a common treasury for all to live comfortably upon, is become through man's unrighteous actions one over another, to be a place wherein one torments another.

And this elder son or man of bondage (Esau) hath held the earth in bondage to himself, not by a meek law of righteousness, but by subtle selfish counsels and by open and violent force. For wherefore is it that there is such wars and rumors of wars in the nations of the earth? and wherefore are men so mad to destroy one another? But only to uphold civil propriety[6] of honor, dominion,

---

3. Private property in land, signalized by fences and restrictions.
4. The naïve etymology evidently supposes that the ancient Hebrews spoke English.
5. Esau was a hunter, Jacob (his younger brother) a dweller in tents. Of course there was no such killing in the Bible; Winstanley is expressing his sense of the unnaturalness of the present social order—*as if* Esau had killed Jacob.
6. Property.

and riches one over another, which is the curse the creation groans under waiting for deliverance.

But when once the earth becomes a common treasury again, as it must, for all the prophecies of scriptures and reason are circled here in this community, and mankind must have the law of righteousness once more writ in his heart, and all must be made of one heart and one mind.

Then this enmity in all lands will cease, for none shall dare to seek a dominion over others, neither shall any dare to kill another, nor desire more of the earth than another; for he that will rule over, imprison, oppress, and kill his fellow creatures, under what pretence soever, is a destroyer of the creation and an actor of the curse, and walks contrary to the rule of righteousness. * * *

The work we are going about is this. To dig up George's Hill and the waste ground thereabouts,[7] and to sow corn and to eat our bread together by the sweat of our brows.

And the first reason is this, that we may work in righteousness and lay the foundation of making the earth a common treasury for all, both rich and poor, that every one that is born in the land may be fed by the earth his mother that brought him forth, according to the Reason that rules in the creation. Not enclosing any part into any particular hand, but all as one man working together and feeding together as sons of one father, members of one family; not one lording over another, but all looking upon each other as equals in the creation; so that our Maker may be glorified in the work of his own hands, and that everyone may see, he is no respecter of persons, but equally loves his whole creation, and hates nothing but the serpent, which is covetousness branching forth into selfish imagination, pride, envy, hypocrisy, uncleanness; all seeking the ease and honor of flesh, and fighting against the spirit Reason that made the Creation; for that is the corruption, the curse, the devil, the father of lies; death and bondage that serpent and dragon that the creation is to be delivered from. * * *

If you cast your eye a little backward, you shall see that this outward teaching and ruling power is the Babylonish yoke laid upon Israel of old, under Nebuchadnezzar:[8] and so successively from that time the conquering enemy have still laid these yokes upon Israel to keep Jacob down: and the last enslaving conquest which the enemy got over Israel was the Norman over England; and from that time,

---

7. "George" means "farmer," and St. George is patron saint of England; but the Diggers probably began their work on this hill in Surrey (not far from present Wimbledon) because it was near London.

8. With serpent, dragon, and Babylon in the background, we are not far from the stock apocalyptic imagery of the Book of Revelation. The Babylonian captivity of the Jews in the 6th century B.C., when they had to serve Nebuchadnezzar, gets into the story (anachronistically) as another piece of oppression.

kings, lords, judges, justices, bailiffs and the violent bitter people that are free-holders are and have been successively: the Norman Bastard William[9] himself, his colonels, captains, inferior officers, and common soldiers who still are from that time to this day in pursuit of that victory, imprisoning, robbing, and killing the poor enslaved English Israelites. * * *

1649

9. William the Conqueror was in fact illegitimate; but he would have been amazed to learn that the English whom he conquered would someday compare themselves to the Children of Israel, and him (consequently) to Nebuchadnezzar.

JOHN LOCKE

(1632–1704)

1667: Physician to the first Earl of Shaftesbury
1684: Expelled from Oxford post as part of intrigues against Shaftesbury
1689–90: Publication of the *Essay*, *Letter Concerning Toleration*, and *Treatise of Government*

Locke's *Essay Concerning Human Understanding*, which is a pretty formidable book of technical philosophy, drew some protests over its title, and others of a contrary tendency over its method. It seemed too heavy, hard, and long to be a mere essay. On the other hand, its basic material was described as too trifling to merit so much analysis. For all Mr. Locke proposed to do in 600 knotty pages was to analyze a few ideas that he found lying about in his own mind.

As usual, the philosopher, who was nothing if not a long-headed man, had considered these criticisms already and had devised a single answer for both. His book was an essay because, like that of Montaigne, it aimed to explore the mind of mankind in general through a discriminating analysis of one mind in particular. When Locke analyzed the ideas of his mind, the ways they were acquired and put together, he found they were clear when they were based on direct experience, and adequate when they were clear. Usually, it appeared, problems occurred when the basic ideas with which he was trying to calculate were blurred or confused or did not refer to anything determinate. Thus a critical analysis of the ideas in an individual mind could lead straight to a rule about adequate ideas in general and the sort of subject where adequate ideas were possible. On the basis of such a limitation, individuals might reach rational agreement with one another, and so set up an area of natural law, within which a common rule of understanding was available.

The clergy were naturally upset over Locke's new "way of ideas," which invited people to discard from their minds any ideas that they could not reduce to clear, distinct, i.e., determinate, form. "Mysteries of faith" were essential to the mental economy of churchmen. How could the Trinity or the doctrine of predestination be reduced to clear, distinct ideas? If they couldn't, must one then discard them? On this last point, Locke was polite but very firm. Yes, if one wanted to discourse reasonably and understandably, one really must discard any idea which could not be given a determinate shape and meaning. The philosopher had evidently performed this operation on any unclear and indistinct ideas he found in his own mind. What was left of Christianity when one got rid of all its "unreasonable" elements was a cool, general, undemanding creed, which did not commit one to much more than a belief in the existence of God, and was therefore known as "Deism." Locke did not like labels, but he was a kind of Deist. Though a scandalous idea in the late 17th century, Deism was a perfectly respectable creed by the time of Pope.

Like most philosophers, Locke had a minimum of personal history. His background and connections were all with the Puritan movement, but he was early disillusioned with the enthusiastic moods and dogmatic persecutions to which he found the Puritans prone. Having a small but steady private income, he became a student, chiefly at Oxford, learning enough medicine to act as a physician, holding an occasional appointive office, but never allowing any of these activities to limit his controlling passion, which was simply for thought. After 1667, he was personal physician and tutor in the household of a violent, crafty politician, the first Earl of Shaftesbury (Dryden's "Achitophel"). But Locke himself was always a grave, dispassionate man, almost frighteningly judicious. On one occasion, Shaftesbury's political enemies at Oxford had Locke watched for several years on end, during which he was not heard to say one word either critical of the government or favorable to it. When times are turbulent, so much discretion is suspicious in itself; and Locke found it convenient to go abroad for several years during the 1680's. He lived quietly in Holland, and pursued his thoughts. The Glorious Revolution and the accession of William III brought him back to England, and made possible the publication of the *Essay*, on which he had been working for many years. Its publication foreshadowed the coming Age of Reason, not only in the positive ideas that the book advanced, but in the quiet way it set aside as insoluble a range of problems about absolute authority and absolute assurance to which the 17th century had prodigally sacrificed its best resources of mind and heart.

From An Essay Concerning Human Understanding

From *The Epistle to the Reader*

Reader,

I here put into thy hands what has been the diversion of some of my idle and heavy hours; if it has the good-luck to prove so of any of thine, and thou hast but half so much pleasure in reading as I had in writing it, thou wilt as little think thy money, as I do my pains, ill bestowed. Mistake not this for a commendation of my work; nor conclude, because I was pleased with the doing of it, that therefore I am fondly taken with it now it is done. He that hawks at larks and sparrows, has no less sport, though a much less considerable quarry, than he that flies at nobler game: and he is little acquainted with the subject of this treatise, the Understanding, who does not know, that as it is the most elevated faculty of the soul, so it is employed with a greater and more constant delight than any of the other. Its searches after truth are a sort of hawking and hunting, wherein the very pursuit makes a great part of the pleasure. Every step the mind takes in its progress towards knowledge makes some discovery, which is not only new, but the best, too, for the time at least.

For the understanding, like the eye, judging of objects only by its own sight, cannot but be pleased with what it discovers, having less regret for what has escaped it, because it is unknown. Thus he who has raised himself above the alms-basket, and not content to live lazily on scraps of begged opinions, sets his own thoughts on work, to find and follow truth, will (whatever he lights on) not miss the hunter's satisfaction; every moment of his pursuit will reward his pains with some delight, and he will have reason to think his time not ill spent, even when he cannot much boast of any great acquisition.

This, reader, is the entertainment of those who let loose their own thoughts, and follow them in writing; which thou oughtest not to envy them, since they afford thee an opportunity of the like diversion, if thou wilt make use of thy own thoughts in reading. It is to them, if they are thy own, that I refer myself; but if they are taken upon trust from others, it is no great matter what they are, they not following truth, but some meaner consideration; and it is not worth while to be concerned what he says or thinks, who says or thinks only as he is directed by another. If thou judgest for thyself, I know thou wilt judge candidly; and then I shall not be harmed or offended, whatever be thy censure. For, though it be certain that there is nothing in this treatise of the truth whereof I am not fully persuaded, yet I consider myself as liable to mistakes as I can think thee; and know that this book must stand or fall with thee, not by any opinion I have of it, but thy own. If thou findest little in it new or instructive to thee, thou art not to blame me for it. It was not meant for those that had already mastered this subject, and made a thorough acquaintance with their own understandings, but for my own information, and the satisfaction of a few friends, who acknowledged themselves not to have sufficiently considered it. Were it fit to trouble thee with the history of this Essay, I should tell thee, that five or six friends, meeting at my chamber, and discoursing on a subject very remote from this, found themselves quickly at a stand by the difficulties that rose on every side. After

we had awhile puzzled ourselves, without coming any nearer a resolution of those doubts which perplexed us, it came into my
thoughts, that we took a wrong course; and that, before we set ourselves upon inquiries of that nature, it was necessary to examine our
own abilities, and see what objects our understandings were or were
not fitted to deal with. This I proposed to the company, who all
readily assented; and thereupon it was agreed, that this should be
our first inquiry. Some hasty and undigested thoughts, on a subject
I had never before considered, which I set down against our next
meeting, gave the first entrance into this discourse, which, having
been thus begun by chance, was continued by entreaty; written by
incoherent parcels; and, after long intervals of neglect, resumed
again, as my humor or occasions permitted; and at last, in a retirement, where an attendance on my health gave me leisure, it was
brought into that order thou now seest it.

This discontinued way of writing may have occasioned, besides
others, two contrary faults; viz., that too little and too much may be
said in it. If thou findest anything wanting, I shall be glad, that
what I have writ gives thee any desire that I should have gone farther: if it seems too much to thee, thou must blame the subject; for
when I first put pen to paper, I thought all I should have to say on
this matter would have been contained in one sheet of paper; but
the farther I went, the larger prospect I had: new discoveries led me
still on, and so it grew insensibly to the bulk it now appears in. I
will not deny but possibly it might be reduced to a narrower compass than it is; and that some parts of it might be contracted; the
way it has been writ in, by catches, and many long intervals of
interruption, being apt to cause some repetitions. But, to confess
the truth, I am now too lazy or too busy to make it shorter.

I am not ignorant how little I herein consult my own reputation,
when I knowingly let it go with a fault so apt to disgust the most
judicious, who are always the nicest[1] readers. But they who know
sloth is apt to content itself with any excuse, will pardon me, if
mine has prevailed on me where I think I have a very good one. I
will not, therefore, allege in my defense, that the same notion,
having different respects,[2] may be convenient or necessary to prove
or illustrate several parts of the same discourse; and that so it has
happened in many parts of this: but, waiving that, I shall frankly
avow, that I have sometimes dwelt long upon the same argument,
and expressed it different ways, with a quite different design. I pretend not to publish this Essay for the information of men of large
thoughts and quick apprehensions; to such masters of knowledge, I
profess myself a scholar, and therefore warn them beforehand not

---

1. Most critical.   2. Aspects.

to expect any thing here but what, being spun out of my own coarse thoughts,[3] is fitted to men of my own size, to whom, perhaps, it will not be unacceptable that I have taken some pains to make plain and familiar to their thoughts some truths, which established prejudice or the abstractness of the ideas themselves, might render difficult. Some objects had need be turned on every side; and when the notion is new, as I confess some of these are to me, or out of the ordinary road, as I suspect they will appear to others, it is not one simple view of it that will gain it admittance into every understanding, or fix it there with a clear and lasting impression. There are few, I believe, who have not observed in themselves or others, that what in one way of proposing was very obscure, another way of expressing it has made very clear and intelligible; though afterward the mind found little difference in the phrases, and wondered why one failed to be understood more than the other. But every thing does not hit alike upon every man's imagination. We have our understandings no less different than our palates; and he that thinks the same truth shall be equally relished by every one in the same dress, may as well hope to feast every one with the same sort of cookery; the meat may be the same and the nourishment good, yet every one not be able to receive it with that seasoning; and it must be dressed another way, if you will have it go down with some even of strong constitutions. The truth is, those who advised me to publish it, advised me, for this reason, to publish it as it is; and since I have been brought to let it go abroad, I desire it should be understood by whoever gives himself the pains to read it. I have so little affection to be in print, that if I were not flattered this Essay might be of some use to others, as I think it has been to me, I should have confined it to the view of some friends, who gave the first occasion to it. My appearing therefore in print being on purpose to be as useful as I may, I think it necessary to make what I have to say as easy and intelligible to all sorts of readers as I can. And I had much rather the speculative and quick-sighted should complain of my being in some parts tedious, than that anyone, not accustomed to abstract speculations, or prepossessed with different notions, should mistake or not comprehend my meaning.

It will possibly be censured as a great piece of vanity or insolence in me, to pretend to instruct this our knowing age, it amounting to little less when I own that I publish this Essay with hopes that it may be useful to others. But if it may be permitted to speak freely of those who, with a feigned modesty, condemn as useless what they themselves write, methinks it savors much more of vanity or insolence to publish a book for any other end; and he fails very

3. Locke's mock-modest confession that his philosophy had been "spun out of his own coarse thoughts" gave rise to a good deal of critical ridicule, echoes of which are heard in the debate between the spider and the bee in Swift's *Battle of the Books*.

much of that respect he owes the public, who prints, and consequently expects that men should read, that wherein he intends not
they should meet with any thing of use to themselves or others: and
should nothing else be found allowable in this treatise, yet my
design will not cease to be so; and the goodness of my intention
ought to be some excuse for the worthlessness of my present. It is
that chiefly which secures me from the fear of censure, which I
expect not to escape more than better writers. Men's principles,
notions, and relishes are so different, that it is hard to find a book
which pleases or displeases all men. I acknowledge the age we live
in is not the least knowing, and therefore not the most easy to be
satisfied. If I have not the good luck to please, yet nobody ought to
be offended with me. I plainly tell all my readers, except half a
dozen, this treatise was not at first intended for them; and therefore
they need not be at the trouble to be of that number. But yet if any
one thinks fit to be angry, and rail at it, he may do it securely; for I
shall find some better way of spending my time than in such kind
of conversation. I shall always have the satisfaction to have aimed
sincerely at truth and usefulness, though in one of the meanest
ways. The commonwealth of learning is not at this time without
master-builders, whose mighty designs in advancing the sciences will
leave lasting monuments to the admiration of posterity: but every
one must not hope to be a Boyle or a Sydenham; and in an age that
produces such masters as the great Huygenius, and the incomparable Mr. Newton, with some other of that strain,[4] it is ambition
enough to be employed as an under-laborer in clearing ground a
little, and removing some of the rubbish that lies in the way to
knowledge; which certainly had been very much more advanced in
the world, if the endeavors of ingenious and industrious men had
not been much cumbered with the learned but frivolous use of
uncouth, affected, or unintelligible terms introduced into the sciences, and there made an art of to that degree, that philosophy,
which is nothing but the true knowledge of things was thought
unfit or uncapable to be brought into well-bred company and polite
conversation.[5] Vague and insignificant forms of speech, and abuse
of language, have so long passed for mysteries of science; and hard
or misapplied words, with little or no meaning, have, by prescription, such a right to be mistaken for deep learning and height of

4. Robert Boyle is the great Anglo-Irish chemist and physicist; Thomas Syden-ham, a physician and authority on the cure of fevers; Christiaan Huygens was a Dutch mathematician and astronomer: and Newton is of course Sir Isaac. Locke's choice of scientists to illustrate the great minds of his time is certainly tendentious. A generation or two earlier a list of "great men" would have con-sisted largely of theologians and perhaps lawyers.

5. Locke was tutor to Anthony Ashley Cooper, third Earl of Shaftsbury, whose philosophical writings make of genteel social conversation and civilized good humor something like guides to ultimate truth. Whatever can't be spoken in a drawing room without exposing a gentle-man to ridicule—so Shaftesbury comes close to saying—is not likely to be true. Locke's basic hostility to cant and jar-gon has been extended by Shaftesbury, but its original source is apparent.

speculation; that it will not be easy to persuade either those who speak or those who hear them, that they are but the covers of ignorance, and hindrance of true knowledge. To break in upon the sanctuary of vanity and ignorance, will be, I suppose, some service to human understanding: though so few are apt to think they deceive or are deceived in the use of words, or that the language of the sect they are of has any faults in it which ought to be examined or corrected, that I hope I shall be pardoned if I have in the third book dwelt long on this subject; and endeavored to make it so plain, that neither the inveterateness of the mischief, nor the prevalency of the fashion, shall be any excuse for those who will not take care about the meaning of their own words, and will not suffer the significancy of their expressions to be inquired into. * * *

The booksellers, preparing for the fourth edition of my Essay, gave me notice of it, that I might, if I had leisure, make any additions or alterations I should think fit. Whereupon I thought it convenient to advertise the reader, that besides several corrections I had made here and there, there was one alteration which it was necessary to mention, because it ran through the whole book, and is of consequence to be rightly understood. What I thereupon said, was this:—

"Clear and distinct ideas" are terms which, though familiar and frequent in men's mouths, I have reason to think every one who uses does not perfectly understand. And possibly it is but here and there one who gives himself the trouble to consider them so far as to know what he himself or others precisely mean by them. I have therefore, in most places, chose to put "determinate" or "determined," instead of "clear" and "distinct," as more likely to direct men's thoughts to my meaning in this matter. By those denominations, I mean some object in the mind, and consequently determined, i.e., such as it is there seen and perceived to be. This, I think, may fitly be called a "determinate" or "determined" idea, when such as it is at any time objectively in the mind, and so determined there, it is annexed, and without variation determined, to a name or articulate sound which is to be steadily the sign of that very same object of the mind, or determinate idea.

To explain this a little more particularly: By "determinate," when applied to a simple idea, I mean that simple appearance which the mind has in its view, or perceives in itself, when that idea is said to be in it. By "determinate," when applied to a complex idea, I mean such an one as consists of a determinate number of certain simple or less complex ideas, joined in such a proportion and situation as the mind has before its view, and sees in itself, when that idea is present in it, or should be present in it when a man gives a name to it. I say "should be;" because it is not every one, nor perhaps any one, who is so careful of his language as to use no word till he views in his mind the precise determined idea which he resolves to make it the sign of. The want of this is the cause of no small obscurity and confusion in men's thoughts and discourses.

I know there are not words enough in any language to answer all the variety of ideas that enter into men's discourses and reasonings. But this hinders not but that when anyone uses any term, he may have in his mind a determined idea which he makes it the sign of, and to which he should keep it steadily annexed during that present discourse. Where he does not or cannot do this, he in vain pretends to clear or distinct ideas: it is plain his are not so; and therefore there can be expected nothing but obscurity and confusion, where such terms are made use of which have not such a precise determination.

Upon this ground I have thought "determined ideas" a way of speaking less liable to mistake than "clear and distinct"; and where men have got such determined ideas of all that they reason, inquire, or argue about, they will find a great part of their doubts and disputes at an end. The greatest part of the questions and controversies that perplex mankind, depending on the doubtful and uncertain use of words, or (which is the same) indetermined ideas, which they are made to stand for: I have made choice of these terms to signify, 1. Some immediate object of the mind, which it perceives and has before it, distinct from the sound it uses as a sign of it. 2. That this idea, thus determined, i.e., which the mind has in itself, and knows and sees there, be determined without any change to that name, and that name determined to that precise idea. If men had such determined ideas in their inquiries and discourses, they would both discern how far their own inquiries and discourses went, and avoid the greatest part of the disputes and wranglings they have with others.

1689

Topic in Seventeenth-Century Literature

THE UNICORN: END OF A LEGEND

Medieval natural histories, being primarily moral in their interests, loved to interpret allegorically the habits of the beasts. Because he never existed, the unicorn lent himself ideally to this purpose. The story of the virgin, who alone can capture (incarnate) him, and the story of his miraculous power against evil are clearly stages leading toward the identification of the unicorn with Christ himself. Unfortunately, scientific skepticism intervened; not only the existence of the unicorn, but the magical efficacy of his horn, was called into question. Finally, the gentlemen of the Royal Society performed a decisive and historic experiment. Under laboratory conditions, they placed a poisonous spider in a circle of powdered unicorn's horn, and proved, beyond a shadow of a doubt, that no mysterious antipathy between the virtuous horn and the evil poison would cause the spider to shrivel up and die. Indeed, only one major problem remained, after their experiment: where did they get the unicorn's horn with which they performed it?

Our materials include some miscellaneous unicorn lore. Early items in the unicorn's story are amusing as they show the slender foundations on which the later myth was built. On the other hand, the foolish and naïve treatise of Alexander Ross illustrates how late the superstitions of the Middle Ages survived, and what dominion they retained over credulous minds. Finally, in the dry, businesslike pages of Sprat's *History of the Royal Society*, the legend, unlike the spider, quietly expires. For all its comic overtones, the experiment with unicorn's horn is one of many which had to be performed in all sober seriousness, in order to clear the way for modern scientific empiricism.

1

He says too that wild asses are taken in its marshes,[1] which have a horn in their foreheads with which they fight like bulls, and not badly; and that the Indians make drinking-cups from this horn, which have such virtue that the man who drinks from one will for one whole day neither fall ill, nor feel pain if wounded, nor be burned by passing through fire, nor even be affected by poisons

1. The Hyphasis River.

which he could not swallow at any other time without harm. These cups are reserved for the king, and only the king may hunt these animals. Apollonius writes that he saw this beast and admired its appearance, and that when Damis asked him if he believed that story about the horn cups, he said: "I will believe it when I find that the king who rules this country never dies." * * *

[Philostratus (3rd century A.D.): from *Life of Apollonius of Tyana* III.ii]

2

Unicornis the Unicorn, which is also called Rhinoceros by the Greeks, is of the following nature.

He is a very small animal like a kid, excessively swift, with one horn in the middle of his forehead, and no hunter can catch him. But he can be trapped by the following stratagem.

A virgin girl is led to where he lurks, and there she is sent off by herself into the wood. He soon leaps into her lap when he sees her, and embraces her, and hence he gets caught.

Our Lord Jesus Christ is also a Unicorn spiritually, about whom it is said: "And he was beloved like the Son of the Unicorns." And in another psalm: "He hath raised up a horn of salvation for us in the house of his son David."

The fact that it has just one horn on its head means what he himself said: "I and the Father are One." Also, according to the Apostle: "The head of Christ is the Lord."

It says that he is very swift because neither Principalities, nor Powers, nor Thrones, nor Dominations could keep up with him, nor could Hell contain him, nor could the most subtle Devil prevail to catch or comprehend him; but, by the sole will of the Father, he came down into the virgin womb for our salvation.

It is described as a tiny animal on account of the lowliness of his incarnation, as he said himself: "Learn from me, because I am mild and lowly of heart."

It is like a kid or scapegoat because the Saviour himself was made in the likeness of sinful flesh, and from sin he condemned sin.

The Unicorn often fights with elephants, and conquers them by wounding them in the belly.

[From a 12th-century Latin bestiary, tr. T. H. White]

3

First, we understand by the word Licorn, a beast born in far distant lands, having a single horn in his forehead, which is taken as a miraculous influence against all poisons, and highly esteemed by

Kings, Princes, and great Lords, and even by the vulgar * * *
Some say that if one dips it in water, and with this water draws a
circle on a table, one may then put within it a scorpion or spider
or toad, and that these beasts will die rather than pass outside the
circle, indeed, that the toad will kill itself.

[Ambroise Paré: from *Discourse on the Licorn* (1582) I, XV]

4

Now let any Reader consider, and observe it as a Thing worthy
of Note, that the true *Unicorns-horn*, sophisticated by no fallacy,[2]
repels all Venom from it self, nor can it assume or draw to it self
any thing of Venom, as is manifest by Experience. Let a living
Spider be put in a Circle made of *Unicorns-horn*, and out of this
Circle it cannot go, or passe over the *Unicorns-horn*, for it shuns
whatsoever is adverse to Venom.

[Basil Valentine: from *Triumphant Chariot of Antimony*,
1400, 1678]

5

The unicorn is a beast that has one horn in its brow, and this
horn is good against poison and pestilential fevers. But one is to
observe that there is very little of the true horn to be found. * * *
I will take this occasion to describe a true test by which one may
know the genuine horn from the false. The test is this: place the
horn in a vessel of any sort of material you like, and with it three
or four live and large scorpions, keeping the vessel covered. If you
find four hours later that the scorpions are dead, or almost lifeless,
the alicorn is a good one, and there is not money enough in the
world to pay for it. Otherwise, it is false.

[David de Pomis: from *Dittionario Novo Hebraico* (1587), tr.
Odell Shepard]

6

As men, to try the precious unicorn's horn,
Make of the powder a preservative circle,
And in it put a spider. * * *

[John Webster: from *The White Devil* II.i]

7

These Beasts are very swift, and their legs have no Articles. They
keep for the most part in the deserts, and live solitary in the tops of
the mountains. There was nothing more horrible than the voice or

2. Adulterated by no inferior products.

braying of it, for the voice is strained above measure. It fighteth both with the mouth and with the heels, with the mouth biting like a Lion, and with the heels kicking like a Horse. It is a beast of an untamable nature, and therefore the Lord himself in *Job* saith, that he cannot be tied with any halter, nor yet accustomed to any cratch or stable. He feareth not Iron nor any iron instrument (as *Isidorus* writeth) and that which is most strange of all other, it fighteth with his own kind, yea with even the females unto death, except when it burneth in lust for procreation; but unto stranger-Beasts, with whom he hath no affinity in nature, he is more sociable and familiar, delighting in their company when they come willing unto him, never rising against them, but proud of their dependence and retinue, keepeth with them all quarters of league & truce, but with his female, when once his flesh is tickled with lust, he groweth tame, gregall and loving, and so continueth till she is filled and great with young, and then returneth to his former hostility. He is an enemy to the Lions, wherefore as soon as ever a Lion seeth a Unicorn, he runneth to a tree for succor, that so when the Unicorn maketh force at him, he may not only avoid his horn, but also destroy him; for the Unicorn in the swiftness of his course runneth against the tree wherein his sharp horn sticketh fast, then when the Lion seeth the Unicorn fastened by the horn without all danger, he falleth upon him and killeth him. These things are reported by the king of *Aethiopia* in an Haebrew Epistle unto the Bishop of Rome.

[Edward Topsell: from *The History of Four-Footed Beasts*, 1607]

8

* * * Lastly, Although we allow it an Antidotal efficacy, and such as the Ancients commended, yet are there some vertues ascribed thereto by Moderns not easily to be received; and it hath surely faln out in this, as other magnified[3] medicines, whose operations effectual in some diseases, are presently extended unto all. That some Antidotal quality it may have, we have no reason to deny; for since Elk's Hoofs and Horns are magnified for Epilepsies, since not only the bone in the heart,[4] but the Horn of a Deer is Alexipharmacal,[5] and ingredient into the confection of Hyacinth, and the Electuary of Maximilian;[6] we cannot without prejudice except against the efficacy of this. But when we affirm it is not only Antidotal to proper venoms, and substances destructive by qualities

---

3. Praised.
4. The roots of the arterial vein and chief artery of the deer, which harden with age and were sometimes likened

to a bone.
5. "Expulsive of poisons" [Browne's note].
6. Ancient medical compounds.

we cannot express; but that it resisteth also Sublimate, Arsenick, and poysons which kill by second qualities, that is, by corrosion of parts; I doubt we exceed the properties of its nature, and the promises of experiment will not secure the adventure. * * *

Since therefore there be many Unicorns;[7] since that whereto we appropriate a Horn is so variously described, that it seemeth either never to have been seen by two persons, or not to have been one animal; Since though they agreed in the description of the animal, yet is not the Horn we extol the same with that of the Ancients; Since what Horns soever they be that pass among us, they are not the Horns of one, but several animals: Since many in common use and high esteem are no Horns at all: Since if there were true Horns, yet might their vertues be questioned: Since though we allowed some vertues, yet were not others to be received; with what security a man may rely on this remedy, the mistress of fools[8] hath already instructed some, and to wisdom (which is never too wise to learn) it is not too late to consider. * * *

[Sir Thomas Browne: from *Pseudodoxia Epidemica* (1646) III. 23]

9

* * * If the Ancients adscribed no vertue to this horn, why was it of such account among them? Why did the *Indian* Princes drink out of them, and make Cups and Rings of them, which either they wore on their fingers, or applied to their breasts, but that they knew there was in them an antidotal vertue against poison, as Andreth Baccius (*l. de Unicor.*) sheweth, and the Doctor[9] denyeth not (an Antidotall efficacy, and such as the Ancients commended in this Horn) and yet two lines before, he denies that the Ancients adscribed any vertue to it. But sure it is apparent, that not only there is an occult quality in it against poison, as in the *Elks* Hoof against the falling sicknesse,[1] but also by manifest qualities it works; for *Baccius* proves it to be of an excessive drying quality, and therefore good against worms and putrefaction. And that *Riccius* the Physitian did use sometimes the weight of a scruple, sometimes of ten grains thereof in burning fevers with good successe. That it can resist Arsnick, the same *Baccius* proves, by the experiment which the Cardinal of *Trent* made upon two Pigeons, (*l. de Unic.*) to which he caused some Arsenick to be given: shortly after he gave som scrapings of his Unicorns horn to one of them, which after some symptoms recovered and lived, the other died two hours after it had eaten the Arsenick: The same Horn cured divers pestilential Fevers, and

7. Browne's many unicorns include rhinoceri, oryces, narwhals, and even "four kinds of nasicornous Beetles."
8. Experience is the mistress of fools.

9. I.e., Thomas Browne.
1. The value of elk's hoof against epilepsy was an article of Ross's faith, and even Browne conceded it.

such as were poisoned. Hence then it appears, that this Horn was both commended by the Ancients, namely by *Aelian, Philostrates,* and divers others, as also by modern Physitians, as *Ficinus, Brasavolus, Matthiolus, Mandella,* and many more. It is true that some might not find the vertue of it, either because it was not the true Horn, or the true dosis was not exhibited,[2] or due time was not observed, or else the malignancy of the disease would not yield. For *Interdum docta plus valet arte malum.*[3] But from hence to deny the Horn or its vertue, were all one as to deny Rhubarb, Agarick, Sena, or other Simples,[4] because they do not always produce the wished effect, or work upon all bodies at all times alike. The means to discriminate the true Unicorns horn from the false, are two, to wit; if it cause the liquor in which it is put, to bubble; and secondly, if it sweat when the poison is near it, as *Baccius* tells us. * * *

[Alexander Ross: from *Arcana Microcosmi* (1652)]

10

* * * Experiments[5] of destroying *Mites* by several Fumes: of the equivocal *Generation* of *Insects:* of feeding a *Carp* in the Air: of making Insects with Cheese, and Sack: of killing Water-Newts, Toads, and Sloworms with several Salts: of killing Frogs by touching their skin, with Vinegar, Pitch, or Mercury: of a Spiders not being Inchanted by a Circle of *Unicorns-horn,* or *Irish Earth,*[6] laid round about it. * * *

[Thomas Sprat: from *The History of the Royal Society,* 1667]

2. It was given in wrong amounts.
3. "Sometimes a sickness is stronger than learned art."
4. Herbs.
5. In this extract, Sprat is describing experiments conducted by the Royal Society.

6. The absence of reptiles from Ireland gave rise to superstitions about the magic properties of Irish earth, as early as Giraldus Cambrensis (ca. 1146–ca. 1220); but this is another story and another set of experiments.

The Restoration and the Eighteenth Century

(1660-1798)

1660:   Charles II restored to the English throne.

1688–89: The Glorious Revolution: deposition of James II and accession of William of Orange.

1700:   Death of John Dryden.

1707:   Act of Union unites Scotland and England, which thus become "Great Britain."

1714:   Rule by house of Hanover begins with accession of George I.

1744–45: Deaths of Pope and Swift.

1784:   Death of Samuel Johnson.

1789:   The French Revolution begins.

The England to which Charles Stuart returned in 1660 was a nation divided against itself, exhausted by twenty years of civil war and revolution. Early in Charles's reign, the people were visited by two frightful calamities that seemed to the superstitious to be the work of a divine Providence outraged by rebellion and regicide: the plague of 1665, ravaging the country, carried off over 70,000 souls in London alone; and in September, 1666, a fire which raged for five days destroyed a large part of the City (more than 13,000 houses), leaving about two-thirds of the population homeless. Yet the nation rose from its ashes, in the century that followed, to become an empire. Within two decades of the king's return, the Royal Navy had defeated the navy of Holland, England's greatest maritime and commercial rival; and, in a series of wars fought between 1689 and 1763 against France, the British acquired dominions that stretched around the world, from Canada in the west to India in the east. Internally, moreover, the nation became whole again. The Glorious Revolution of 1689 established a rule of law, and the Act of Union of 1707 a political alliance, under which England was transformed into Great Britain in fact as well as name—a larger country to which men of widely differing backgrounds and origins felt they owed allegiance. Many of the great British writers of the 18th century came from Ireland, like Swift, Burke, Sheridan, and Goldsmith; many came from

Scotland, like Thomson, Boswell, and Hume. Strengthened from without and from within, Great Britain was able to endure the loss of her thirteen American colonies and to enter the final struggle with Revolutionary and Napoleonic France as a world power.

RELIGION AND POLITICS

Charles came home to the almost universal satisfaction of his subjects, for after the abdication of Richard Cromwell in 1659 the country had seemed at the brink of chaos, and Britons were eager to believe that the king would bring order, peace, freedom under law, and a spirit of mildness back into the national life. But no political settlement could be stable until the religious issues of the age had been resolved. The restoration of the monarchy meant, inevitably, the restoration of the Established Church; and though Charles had promised mildness toward all but a few of his late father's enemies, the bishops and Anglican clergy felt anything but Christian charity toward their Dissenting brothers. In 1662 Parliament reimposed the Book of Common Prayer on all ministers and congregations, and in 1664 religious meetings in which the forms of the Established Church were not followed were declared illegal. Thousands of clergymen resigned their livings, and the jails were filled with Nonconformist preachers who, like John Bunyan, refused to be silenced. In 1673 the triumph of the Establishment was completed by the Test Act, which required all holders of civil and military offices to receive the sacrament according to the Anglican rite and to declare their disbelief in transubstantiation. Thus the two adversaries of the Anglican Church, Protestant Dissenters and Roman Catholics, were alike excluded from public life, though the practice of occasional conformity (i.e., receiving the sacrament in an Anglican church at rare intervals) enabled many Dissenters to comply with the law. Throughout the closing decades of the 17th century, Anglicans associated Nonconformity with revolution, regicide, republicanism, and the rule of the Puritan Saints—hence, with subversion; and with excessive zeal, "enthusiasm" (i.e., belief in private revelation), and irrationality—hence, with absurdity. The scorn and detestation in which Dissenters were held may be measured by the delight that readers took in Samuel Butler's caricature of Presbyterians and Independents in *Hudibras* (1663), an attitude that persisted unchanged for the rest of the century, as Jonathan Swift's *Tale of a Tub*, written about 1697, makes clear. As for the English Catholics, they appeared always as potential traitors of whom anything evil could be believed. Few doubted, for example, that the Great Fire of 1666 had been set by Catholics.

Although ecclesiastical problems seemed to have been quickly and effectively solved, the constitutional issues which had divided Charles I and Parliament were not so readily settled. Charles II had promised to govern through Parliament, but like other members of his family he held strong views on the power and prerogatives of the Crown. Nevertheless, he was content to avoid crises whenever he could, and since he was an astute politician he frequently could. He concealed from his subjects his Catholic sympathies (on his deathbed he received the last rites of the Roman Church), for he had no wish "to go on his travels" again. The one great religious and constitutional crisis of his reign was the Popish Plot and its political consequences (1678–81)—the unsuccessful attempt of a faction in

Parliament to force Charles to accept a bill excluding his Catholic brother, James, Duke of York, from the succession. Except in this instance, where he was successful because of his courage, duplicity, and political skill, Charles allowed no opportunity for a test of strength between Crown and Parliament.

One important result of the political and religious turmoils of the decade following the Popish Plot was the emergence of two clearly defined political parties, Whig and Tory. The party of the court, which supported the king in 1681, came to be called Tories; the king's opponents, Whigs. By the end of the century the two parties had developed opposed attitudes on other important issues. The Tories drew their strength largely from the landed gentry and the country clergy. They were the conservatives of the period: strong supporters of the Crown and of the Established Church as the two great sources of political and social stability, they bitterly (though futilely) opposed toleration of Dissenters and successfully supported the Test Act. They were hostile to the new moneyed interests, whether among the newer nobility or the increasingly well-to-do middle class, for they held that landed wealth is the only responsible wealth. The Whigs were a less homogeneous group: many powerful nobles, jealous of the powers of the Crown, the merchants and financiers of London, a number of bishops and Low Church clergymen, and the Dissenters; these varied groups were united by their policies of toleration and support of commerce.

After James II came to the throne in 1685, determined to advance the cause of the Roman Church in England, an atmosphere of crisis rapidly developed. Claiming the right to set aside laws and to overrule Parliament, he issued in 1687 a Declaration of Indulgence, suspending the Tests and penal laws against both Catholics and Dissenters, and he began to fill the army and government—not to mention the universities—with his core-ligionists. Matters came to a crisis in the summer of 1688, when a son was born to the queen and the prospect of a succession of Catholic monarchs confronted the nation. Secret negotiations paved the way for the arrival in England of the Dutchman William of Orange at the head of a small armed force. He was the leading champion of Protestantism on the Continent and the husband of James's Protestant daughter Mary. Finding resistance to his hostile subjects impossible, James, after sending his wife and the infant prince out of the country, fled to France on December 11. There he was cordially received by Louis XIV, granted a subsidy, and established with his court at St. Germain. For over half a century the possibility of invasion and the forcible restoration first of James, later of his son "the Old Pretender," and finally of his grandson Prince Charles Edward, was a source of anxiety to the English government. Adherents of the exiled family are called Jacobites (from the Latin *Jacobus*, James). Many Englishmen and a great many more Scots remained loyal to the house of Stuart until there was nothing left of the Jacobite cause but a pleasant sentiment. Two serious Jacobite rebellions actually occurred: in 1715, when the Old Pretender arrived in Scotland to support an uprising against the newly crowned Hanoverian, George I, and more threateningly in 1745, when Prince Charles Edward (the "Bonnie Prince Charlie" of romantic story) came dangerously close to success in his invasion of England, an event which affects the fortunes of the hero in Henry Fielding's novel *Tom Jones*.

It was only with the flight of James that England could begin to bury the past and to turn toward her destiny in the next age. The coming in of William and Mary and the settlement achieved in 1689 were known as the Glorious or Bloodless Revolution, all the more glorious for being bloodless. A more tolerant era was opening, as was made apparent in important acts passed by Parliament in the first year of the new reign. Since the Revolution had been largely achieved by Whigs, Whig principles prevailed during William's reign. In 1689 the Bill of Rights limited the powers of the Crown, reaffirmed the supremacy of Parliament, and guaranteed important legal rights to individuals. Moreover, the Toleration Act, although it did not repeal the Test, did grant freedom of worship to Dissenters. A number of the conflicting elements in the national life were thus reconciled through what proved to be a workable compromise; and with the passage of the Act of Settlement in 1701, settling the succession to the throne upon Sophia, Electress of Hanover, and her descendants (as the granddaughter of James I, she was the closest Protestant relative of the Princess Anne, James II's younger daughter, whose sole surviving child died in that year), the difficult problems that had so long divided England seemed resolved. The principles established in 1689 brought stability and order into English life and endured unaltered in essentials until the Reform Bill of 1832.

During the reign of Anne, the last Stuart monarch (1702–14), a renewal of tension embittered the political atmosphere. On the Continent England led her allies, Holland, Austria, and Bavaria, to victory in the War of the Spanish Succession against France and Spain (1702–13). The hero of the war was the brilliant Captain-General John Churchill, Duke of Marlborough, who, with his duchess, dominated the queen until 1710. The war was a Whig war, supported by powerful Whig lords and the Whig merchants of London, who grew increasingly rich on war profits and who stood to gain by any weakening of the power of France and Spain. The Whigs were anxious to reward the Dissenters for their loyalty by removing the Test. Unfortunately for them, Anne was especially devoted to the church, and when, in 1710, they were made to appear to threaten the health of the Establishment, she dismissed her Whig ministers and called in Robert Harley as Lord Treasurer and the brilliant young Henry St. John as Secretary of State (in charge of foreign relations) to form the Tory ministry which governed England during the last four years of her reign. The Marlboroughs were dismissed, the duke even losing his command in 1711, but not before the royal favor and a grateful nation had made him immensely rich and had given him the land on which he built his famous palace, Blenheim (pronounced *Blen'm*) in memory of the most brilliant victory (pronounced *Blén-hime*) of the war.

It was these Tory ministers whom Defoe and Swift served in their different ways; it was for them that Matthew Prior negotiated the Peace of Utrecht, ratified in 1713. To Swift's despair, a bitter rivalry developed between Harley (then Earl of Oxford) and St. John (then Viscount Bolingbroke) during 1713–14, and as the queen's life faded in the summer of 1714, Bolingbroke succeeded in ousting Oxford, only to have his own ambitions thwarted by the death of Anne and the return to power of the vindictive Whigs with the accession of George I, son of the late Sophia, Electress of Hanover. For a moment it seemed as if this event might not occur without bloodshed, but the crisis quickly passed, the Protestant succession was not immediately opposed by Jacobites, and the Whigs turned happily to investigating the conduct of the former ministers. Harley was imprisoned in the Tower of London (where he remained until 1717), and Bolingbroke, charged with treasonable correspondence with the Pretender, fled to France, where he actually became, for a while, Secretary of State to the Jacobite court. Pardoned in 1723, but denied his seat in the House of Lords, he returned to England and directed the opposition to Robert Walpole, while seeing much of Pope and playing the gentleman-farmer-philosopher at Dawley Farm.

The three Georges who occupied the throne during the rest of the century presided over a nation that grew increasingly prosperous through war, trade, and the beginnings of industrialism. George I (reigned 1714–27) and George II (reigned 1727–60) spoke broken English, had little interest in the affairs of the country. In their hearts they remained petty German princelings even when they were kings of Great Britain, spending as much time as possible in Hanover. Under such circumstances it was inevitable that ministers should become more important and more independent of the Crown than they had been under stronger and more intelligent monarchs. Through the indifference of two kings and the ambition and great abilities of the Whig Prime Minister Sir Robert Walpole, the modern system of ministerial government began to develop. This was the last important contribution of the age to British political institutions. Walpole's long ascendency (1721–42) brought a period of peace and prosperity and of capable government based, paradoxically, on flagrant political corruption. Although Walpole strengthened the importance of the House of Commons in British politics, he nonetheless continued, if he did not increase, the corruption of its members through bribery. He was a practical man and cared little for literature, preferring to spend money on useful journalists and voting Members of Parliament rather than on poets. Thus with two kings who knew nothing of literature and a prime minister who was indifferent to it, English writers could not expect the shower of offices and government sinecures that had made the age of Anne the great age of patronage: Congreve, Steele, Addison, Prior, Swift had expected and obtained such rewards both for their literary eminence and for their service to party. But after 1715, as patronage declined, authors found that they must turn to the publishers, who could pay them well because of the growing reading public. Indeed, Johnson was accustomed to declare that the booksellers of the midcentury had become the patrons of literature.

The long reign of George III (1760–1820), the first Hanoverian monarch born in England, somewhat retarded the development of government through parties and responsible ministers, for the king was determined to rule personally, and he succeeded in doing so to a remarkable degree. This was a dangerous policy for a man who, as a politician, was neither wise nor liberal. He brought the Tories back into power after they had been excluded from office for 46 years, and he did all that he could to crush the long-powerful Whig oligarchy.

INTELLECTUAL BACKGROUND

The political turbulence of the 17th century subsided only gradually during the last decades of the century, and the "peace of the Augustans" did not settle over England until the Protestant succession had been safely accomplished. Analogously, the literature of the Restoration period (1660–1700) did not at once attain the measured pace and disciplined order that we associate with "classic" art. John Dryden himself, the principal writer of the period, delighted, as Johnson remarked, "in wild and daring sallies of sentiment, in the irregular and eccentric violence of wit." The period is remarkable for variety: Milton's major poems, relics of an earlier age, appeared in 1667 (*Paradise Lost*) and 1671 (*Paradise Regained* and *Samson Agonistes*). The age that produced Bunyan's *Pilgrim's Progress*, perhaps the greatest literary expression of the Nonconformist conscience, produced also the libertine poems of such court wits as Rochester, Sedley, and Etherege, savage satire like Butler's, the brilliant depiction of the dissolute but elegant manners of the upper classes in the comedies of Etherege, Wycherley, and Congreve, and the rant and bombast of Dryden's rhymed heroic plays. But the general drift was toward classic restraint and good sense; and both Dryden's example, in the works of his maturity, and his numerous critical essays helped to formulate standards and to make the period the foundation on which the neoclassical art of the next century was erected.

Perhaps most people think of the Restoration as a period wholly given over to frivolity and debauchery. It is true that Puritan rigidities (never enforced quite as rigorously as sometimes has been made out) were quickly repudiated by the upper classes. It is true that the king was easy-going, pleasure-loving, and amorous, more fond of the society of boon companions —and mistresses—than he was of business of state. It is true that the court itself was luxurious, immoral, full of intrigue. It is true that all this is vividly reflected in lampoons, satires, and comedies. But the ordinary life of the nation did not radically change. Rural manners, then as now, were conservative and old-fashioned. The London citizens, middle-class and respectable, cherishing much of the independence and piety of Dissent, were scandalized by the behavior of such lewd young men as Rochester and Etherege, who regarded them with contempt and considered their wives and daughters fair game. Even good royalists like John Evelyn and Samuel Pepys often speak anxiously in their diaries of the moral laxness of the court and the danger to the country of the king's example.

Charles himself had serious intellectual interests and was a patron of the arts. He dabbled in chemistry and was interested in the progress of science. A characteristic act was his chartering in 1662 the Royal Society of London for the Improving of Natural Knowledge, thus giving official approval to the scientific movement that Francis Bacon had initiated early in the century and that was just then coming to maturity. The king's love of music and painting led him to import from the Continent composers, musicians, new musical instruments, the French and Italian opera, and painting and painters largely from the Low Countries. His interest in the theater was demonstrated by the chartering of two companies of actors in 1660, both under royal patronage, the King's Players, and the Duke's—the Duke being James, Duke of York.

It is natural, therefore, that the most characteristic art of the period reflected the interests and tastes of those who supported it, as is the case today. Artists addressed themselves to court and "town," the western suburbs which were the center of fashion. The middle-class tradesmen who lodged over their shops in the City (i.e., that part of greater London which was once within the city walls and which was then thickly populated) were scorned as tasteless barbarians. Except in the theater, literature was not in itself a gainful profession (as it was to become in the 18th century), and writers looked for patronage from the court and the great nobles. Milton, for example, received only £10 for the first edition of *Paradise Lost*. By the end of the century, however, thanks to the enterprise of the bookseller Jacob Tonson and the new device of publishing books through subscription (i.e., soliciting payment in advance for de luxe copies of a work, in addition to publishing a regular trade edition), Dryden was able to earn between £1000 and £1200 by his translation of the works of Virgil (1697). And Pope's Homer, similarly published between 1715 and 1726, was to prove even more profitable.

Perhaps the most important aspect of the Restoration period is the increasing challenge of various forms of secular thought to the old religious orthodoxies which had been matters of life and death since the Reformation. As the contentious voices of Roman, Anglican, and Dissenter grew more and more subdued, other interests attracted adventurous minds. Thomas Hobbes, in *Leviathan* (1651), had taught a philosophic materialism and advocated an absolute government as the most efficacious check to human nature, which he described as wholly driven by egoistic and predatory passions. Detested by the church and attacked on all sides, these ideas nonetheless played their role in the lives and writings of some of the more advanced young men, and they provoked by way of reaction in the next century an optimistic insistence on the natural goodness of man. A soberer and more ancient tradition was philosophic skepticism. Originating in ancient Greece, skepticism had found its most persuasive recent statement in the essays of the Frenchman Michel de Montaigne (1533–92), whose influence was widespread throughout 17th-century Europe. The skeptic argued that all our knowledge is derived from our senses, but that our senses do not report the world around us accurately, and that therefore reliable knowledge is an impossibility. The safest course is to affirm nothing as absolutely true, to remember that most beliefs are mere opinions, and, where possible, to be guided by the traditional in matters intellectual, political, and ethical. Butler, Dryden, and Rochester, among others, more or less adhered to this doctrine. But though the skeptic remained in doubt about the results of human reasoning, he was not precluded from religious beliefs, for he could assert (as did Dryden after his conversion to Catholicism) that faith alone is necessary for accepting the mysteries of the Christian religion.

The new science, advanced by members of the Royal Society, was rapidly altering men's view of nature. Science in the 17th century was principally concerned with the physical sciences—with astronomy, physics, and, to a lesser degree, chemistry; and the discoveries in these sciences were reassuring in their revelation of universal and immutable law and order, clear revelations of the wisdom and goodness of God in His creation. Such laws of nature as Boyle's law of the behavior of gases under pressure or Newton's law of gravitation seemed obviously to support the idea that a beneficent, divine intelligence created and directs the universe. The whole creation appeared a revelation of the mind, intent, and nature of the Creator. The truest truths proved to be the clearest, the simplest, the most general. Such truths, while they confirmed the existence of a Deity, seemed at the same time to render unnecessary, even preposterous, the intricate a priori reasoning of Scholastic philosophy, and to promise a time, not remote, when mystery would be banished entirely from nature. Indeed, the new religion, Deism or Natural Religion, which had an increasingly wide appeal to "enlightened" minds, deduced its simple rationalistic creed from the Book of Nature, God's first and, to many 18th-century men, only valid revelation. The Deists deduced the existence of a Supreme Being or First Cause from the existence of the universe: a creature presupposes a Creator. The laws of nature, the structure of the universe—its regularity, order, and purposefulness—sufficiently proved the reasonableness, goodness, and wisdom of this Creator. Him we can and must revere; but, good though He is, it is demonstrable that He does not punish vice and reward virtue in this life; and therefore, being good and just, He must do so in some future life: hence, we must believe in immortality. Meanwhile, here on earth, it is our duty to co-operate with Nature and the Deity, cultivating as best we can wisdom, virtue, and benevolence. This creed is as simple and as rational as one of Newton's laws; but its complete omission of the "second revelation" of the Scriptures, the scheme of salvation through the vicarious atonement, made it unacceptable to many Christians, although many found it possible to accept both Natural Religion and revealed Christianity.

As the 17th century drew to a close, its temper became more secular, tolerant, and moderate. If it is not quite possible to talk sensibly of an "Age of Reason" in England, it is possible to think of the early decades of the 18th century as a period of good sense, restraint, and reasonableness. "Enthusiasm," that state of mind which asserted the validity of private inspiration and which had fostered a dangerous zeal among the Saints of Dissent, was decried. The new age was willing to settle for the possible within the limits of human intelligence and of the material world. Its temper was expressed by its most influential philosopher, John Locke (1632–1704), in his *Essay Concerning Human Understanding* (1690):

> If by this inquiry into the nature of the understanding, I can discover the powers thereof; how far they reach; to what things they are in any degree proportionate; and where they fail us, I suppose it may be of use to prevail with the busy mind of man to be more cautious in meddling with things exceeding its comprehension; to stop when it is at the utmost extent of its tether; and to sit down in a quiet ignorance of those things which, upon examination, are found to be beyond the reach of our capacities. * * * Our business here is not to know all things, but those which concern our conduct.

These words might be taken as the creed of 18th-century England. Such a position is Swift's, when he inveighs against metaphysics, abstract logical deductions, and theoretical science; it is similar to Pope's in the *Essay on Man*; it prompts Dr. Johnson to talk of "the business of living"; it helps to account for the emphasis that the Anglican clergy put on good works, rather than faith, as the way to salvation, and for their dislike of emotion and "enthusiasm" in religion.

But if the 18th century brought a recognition of the limitations of man, it also took an optimistic view of his moral nature. Rejecting Hobbes, 18th-century philosophers asserted that man is naturally good and that he finds his highest happiness in the exercise of virtue and benevolence. Such a view of human nature we describe as "sentimental." It found the source of virtue in men's instinctive and social impulses rather than in a code of conduct sanctioned by divine law. And men began to feel—or to fancy that they felt—exquisite pleasure in the exercise of benevolent impulses. Sentimentalism fostered a benevolism that led to social reforms seldom envisioned in earlier times—to the improvement of jails, to the relief of imprisoned debtors, to the establishment of foundling hospitals and of homes for penitent prostitutes, and ultimately to the abolition of the slave trade; but it also encouraged a ready flow of feeling and tears and a capacity to respond to the joys and sorrows of others. The doctrine of the natural goodness of man seemed to many to suggest that it is civilization which corrupts us and that primitive men, "noble savages" who live according to nature, are models of innocence and virtue. Such notions encouraged an interest in primitive societies and even helped to prepare for the enthusiastic reception given the peasant poet Robert Burns, an "original genius," as well as for William Wordsworth's interest in children and in simple, rural people.

As the wave of sentimentalism mounted, a parallel rise of religious feeling occurred after about 1740. The great religious revival known as Methodism was lead by John Wesley (1703–91), his brother Charles (1707–88), and George Whitefield (1714–70), all Oxford graduates. The Methodists took their gospel to the common people, preaching the necessity of a conviction of sin, and of conversion, and the joy of the "blessed assurance" of being saved. Often denied the privilege of preaching in village churches, they preached to thousands in the open fields and in barns. The somnolent Anglican Church and the self-assured upper classes were repelled by the emotionalism aroused by Methodist preachers among the lower orders. It seemed as if the irrationality, zeal, and enthusiasm of the Puritan sects were being revived. But the religious awakening persisted, and affected many clergymen and laymen within the Establishment, who, as "Evangelicals," reanimated the church and promoted unworldliness and piety. And yet the insistence of Methodists on faith over works as the way to salvation did not prevent them or their Anglican counterparts from playing important roles in many of the social reforms of the time, especially in helping to abolish slavery and the slave trade.

NEOCLASSICAL LITERARY THEORY

The literature of the period between 1660 and 1785 can conveniently, though perhaps too schematically, be considered as falling into three lesser periods of about forty years each: the first, extending to the death of Dryden in 1700, may be thought of as the period in which English "neoclassical" literature came into being and its critical principles were formulated; the second, ending with the death of Pope in 1744 and of Swift in 1745, brought to its culmination the literary movement initiated by Dryden and his generation; the third, concluding with the death of Johnson in 1784 and the publication of William Cowper's *The Task* in 1785, was a period in which neoclassical principles were confronted by new ideas which contained within themselves the origins of the Romantic movement of the early 19th century.

Apparently a sudden change of taste took place about 1660; but the change was not so sudden as it appears. Like the English Renaissance, it was part of a general movement in European culture, seen perhaps at its most impressive in 17th-century France. Described most simply, it was a reaction against the intricacy and occasional obscurity, boldness, and extravagance of European literature of the late Renaissance, in favor of greater simplicity, clarity, restraint, regularity, and good sense. This tendency is most readily to be observed in the preference of Dryden and his contemporaries for "easy, natural" wit, which aims to surprise rather than to shock. It accompanied, though it was not necessarily caused by, the development of certain rationalistic philosophies and the rise of experimental science, as well as a desire for peace and order after an era of violent extremism.

This movement produced in France the impressive body of classical literature that distinguished the age of Louis XIV. In England it produced a literature that we term "neoclassical," or "Augustan," because it was strongly influenced by the writers of the reign of the first Roman emperor, Augustus Caesar, just before the beginning of the Christian era. Rome's Augustan Age was a period of stability and peace after the civil war that followed the death of Julius Caesar. Its chief poets, Virgil, Horace, and Ovid, addressed their carefully ordered, disciplined, and polished works to a sophisticated aristocracy, among whom they found generous patrons. Dryden's generation was aware of an analogy between the situations of post-Civil War England and Augustan Rome. Charles seemed in 1660 a kind of Augustus, bringing to England civilized order and enlightened patronage of the arts, a self-consciously Augustan age.

Charles and his followers inevitably brought back from France an admiration of contemporary French literature as well as of French fashions and elegance. But it is a mistake to regard the Restoration, as many historians have done, as a period in which the court and its poets betrayed English genius to French rules and taste. The French critics were of course known and studied in England, and the theories of such writers as Pierre Corneille, René Rapin, and Nicolas Boileau were influential. But English literature remained stubbornly English: English writers took what they required from France, but used it for their own ends. It was not Dryden's aim merely to imitate the French poets or for that matter the Latin, but to produce in England works that would be worthy to stand beside theirs. He knew that this could be done only if English literature remained true to its living tradition: Chaucer, Spenser, Shakespeare, Jonson, Donne entered into his literary consciousness as well as Virgil, Horace, Longinus, or Corneille.

It is likely that, had Charles never lived abroad, the English neoclassical period would have come into existence pretty much in the form that it actually assumed. Ben Jonson's poems and criticism brought the classicizing tendencies of the English Renaissance to a focus. His closed heroic couplets are the model for those of Edmund Waller and Sir John Denham, whom Dryden considered the principal "refiners" of English metrics. One of the lesser "Sons of Ben," Sir John Beaumont, at least as early as 1625—and incidentally in couplets that might have been the very pattern of those of Dryden and Pope—proposed critical standards that became dominant after 1660:

> Pure phrase, fit epithets, a sober care
> Of metaphors, descriptions clear, yet rare,
> Similitudes contracted, smooth and round,
> Not vexed by learning, but with Nature crowned:
> Strong figures drawn from deep inventions, springs,
> Consisting less in words, and more in things:
> A language not affecting ancient times,
> Nor Latin shreds, by which the pedant climbs.
>
> [*To His Late Majesty, Concerning the True Form
> of English Poetry*]

Such standards, alien to the poetry of Donne, Crashaw, or Milton, prefigure the poetry of the Augustans, and make evident the fact that a native "classicism" existed side by side with metaphysical poetry. The emphasis on the correct ("pure"), the appropriate ("fit"), restraint and discipline ("sober care"), clarity, the fresh and surprising ("rare"), Nature, strength, freedom from pedantry—these indicate exactly the direction English literature was to take after the Restoration.

What was the prevalent idea of the nature of the poet? He must, of course, be a genius, for all agreed with Horace that the poet is born, not made. But even genius must be trained and disciplined if it is to produce art. The word *poet* is derived from a Greek word meaning "maker," and this notion dominated the Augustans' idea of the poet: he is the maker of an object, a poem. He must have "invention," the gift of finding materials for his poems—fictional, but representative, images of human actions and of the world in which those actions take place; and he must so vivify, heighten, and order those materials that they seem true pictures of what is, or might or ought to be, or of the evil and folly that we should avoid. For the poet makes this image of life in order to teach, not so much by precept and moral sentences as by examples that move our love and admiration or evoke our fear and detestation. And to teach effectively he must please us by his fictions and by all the ornaments of language, metrics, and rhetoric that belong to his craft.

The materials of poetry must derive from, conform to, and recognizably represent "Nature," a word of many meanings in the neoclassic or any age. The Augustans were especially conscious of one meaning: Nature as the universal, permanent, and representative elements in the moral and intellectual experience of men. External nature—the landscape—both as a source of aesthetic pleasure and as an object of scientific inquiry or religious contemplation attracted the attention of Englishmen throughout the 18th century. But Pope's injunction to the critic, "First follow Nature," has primarily *human* nature and *human* experience in view. Nature is truth in the sense that it includes the permanent, enduring, general truths which have been, are, and will be true for all men, in all times, everywhere. The poet exists not to take us on long voyages to discover the new and unique, but to reveal the permanent and the representative in human experience through what becomes for us an act of recognition. Johnson, in Chapter X of *Rasselas*, says that the poet is to examine "not the individual, but the species; to remark general properties and large appearances * * * to exhibit in his portraits of nature such prominent and striking features as recall the original to every mind." Historians during this period studied the particulars of history in order to observe the universal human nature which those particulars reveal; and scientists formulated, after experiment and observation of particulars, universal and permanent laws of nature. Indeed, Sir Isaac Newton's *Principia* (1687) did much to reinforce scientifically the idea of Nature as order, which underlies such a typical 18th-century work as Pope's *Essay on Man*.

But it would be erroneous to assume that this emphasis on the general and the representative excluded the particular from the arts and reduced their material to the merely obvious, typical, and familiar. If human nature was held to be uniform, men were known to be infinitely varied; and the task of the artist was so to treat the particular as to render it representative. Thus Pope, after praising the characters of Shakespeare because they are "Nature herself," continued: "But every single character in Shakespeare is as much an individual as those in life itself; it is * * * impossible to find any two alike * * * " And Johnson praised the poet James Thompson because he looked on external nature "with a mind that at once comprehends the vast, and attends to the minute."

But although Nature was "at once the source, and end, and test of art," the poet could learn much from the ancients—the great writers, philosophers, critics, sculptors, and architects of Greece and especially of Rome. They were useful guides not because they were ancient, but because they had so truly expressed Nature that, despite changes as radical as those wrought by the establishment of Christianity in Europe, they had lost none of their relevance to the experience of modern men. As Pope said, Homer and Nature were the same; and both Pope and his readers found Horace's satires on Roman society thoroughly applicable to their own world, for Horace had followed Nature, "one clear, unchanged, and universal light."

And how did a poet come to know Nature? Not, certainly, by a life of solitude or rural retirement, or by the intermittent light of visionary gleams. The poet was to be a member of society, an important and functional part of a civilized community that would not be civilized without his presence. Only by living among men and by ceaseless and sympathetic observation of them could he gain the knowledge of Nature required of him as a poet. He was also to supplement his own inevitably limited experience by the wisdom of the past, by studying Nature wherever truthfully represented: in Homer, Virgil, Horace, or Shakespeare.

He could learn also from the ancients how to practice his craft. If a poem is an object to be made, the maker, like an architect or a cabinet-maker, must follow sound principles or botch the job. The ancients—Aristotle in his *Poetics*, Horace in his *Ars Poetica*, Quintilian in his *Institutio Oratoria*, for instance—had left more or less systematized principles (or to use the word current among the Augustans, "rules") by which to order "Nature"—the material of art—into an epic, a tragedy, a dramatic character, an oration. They had deduced these rules from the practice of earlier masters—Homer, Sophocles, the Greek and Roman orators. Italian and French critics during the 16th and 17th centuries invented new rules of their own and refined on and further codified those of the ancients. The rules directed the planning and executing of one or another of the literary "kinds," or genres: epic, tragedy, comedy, pastoral, satire, ode; the choice of language, which must differ from genre to genre; the use of figures and tropes; tone, style, characters. They could serve as a short cut to Nature, for as Pope said, they "are Nature methodized."

In England, actually, the rules were followed in rather a casual way. Most readers were prepared to admit that mere correctness could not recommend a poem which was commonplace in thought and sentiment and unanimated by the vital force of genius. Almost everyone acknowledged that Shakespeare had written the greatest body of drama in modern literature without following the rules of the ancients or the moderns. Indeed, the presence of Shakespeare and the native English suspicion of mere theory prevented English neoclassical literature from being shackled by pedantic critics. In 1765 Samuel Johnson was to brush aside in the name of Shakespeare and good sense two hundred years of critical reverence for the three unities of action, place, and time, a reverence which had not, however, much affected the plotting of English plays during that period.

The idea that each of the literary kinds is distinct and has its own proper material, characters, language, and style, was influential throughout our period. Epic and tragedy, the loftiest and most serious of the kinds, demand noble English, stately verse, heightened diction, splendor of figures and ornaments. (This can be readily understood by examining a few pages of *Paradise Lost*.) Comedy, on the other hand, since it deals with ordinary people in daily life, calls for a lower style and natural, unadorned language. This principle was known as the principle of "decorum" or the appropriate; it determined Dryden's definition of wit as "a propriety of thoughts and words; or, in other terms, thoughts and words elegantly adapted to the subject."

Examining the psychological faculties that distinguish the artist from other men, critics fixed upon "wit" as his most important and characteristic endowment. "Wit," like "Nature," is a complicated word of many meanings. Here it implies quickness and liveliness of mind, inventiveness, a readiness to perceive resemblances between things apparently unlike and so to enliven literary discourse with appropriate images, similes, and metaphors. This faculty was often identified with "fancy" or "imagination," and was thought to be irregular, wayward, extravagant, unless curbed and disciplined by another and soberer faculty, "judgment." An excess of imagination was considered dangerous to sanity, and in literature to lead away from Nature and truth to falsehood and such violent and farfetched conceits as we find in the poetry of Donne or Crashaw at their boldest. One task of the age was to tame what seemed the wildness of metaphysical wit into the more reasonable and decorous wit that Dryden described in the passage quoted above. So Pope insists in the *Essay on Criticism*, lines 80–83, on the necessity of a harmonious union of judgment and fancy (which he calls "wit") in a work of literature. Though judgment was to tame, it was not to suppress passion, energy, or originality, but to make them more effective through discipline: "The winged courser, like a generous horse, / Shows most true mettle when you check his course."

Two more general observations must be made. When Wordsworth, in the Preface to *Lyrical Ballads* (1800), declared that the poems were written "in a selection of the language really used by men," he went on to attack 18th-century poets for their use of an artificial and stock "diction." Coleridge, in *Biographia Literaria* (1817), also had a good deal to say on the subject. Although the bulk of good poetry in the 18th century, as in other times, is written in "a selection of the language really used by men," the special and stylized diction to which the two early Romantics objected did exist, especially in heroic, descriptive, pastoral, and lyric poetry. It is characterized by periphrasis (a roundabout and elegant way of avoiding homely words: "finny tribe" for "fish," or "household feathery people" for "chickens"); frequently used stock phrases, such as "shining sword," "verdant mead," "bounding main," "checkered shade"; words used in their original Latin sense, such as "genial," "gelid," "horrid"; and a fondness for adjectives ending in *y*. This language originated in the attempt of Renaissance poets all over Europe to rival the elegant and golden diction of Virgil and other Roman writers. Milton depended on it to help him obtain "answerable style" for the lofty theme of *Paradise Lost*. Dryden used it in his translation of Virgil. Thomson found it suitable in passages of generalized description in *The Seasons*, and Pope employed it, not always happily, in his versions of Homer. Used with discretion it could be both subtle and expressive; but when it became a mannerism, or a dead and conventional language used mechanically, as it did with scores of mere versifiers, it properly became an object of contempt. "Hay and straw were burned in the fields of Thessaly," for instance, was translated into poetic diction:

> There at his words devouring Vulcan feasts
> On all the tribute which Thessalian meads
> Yield to the scythe, and riots on the heaps
> Of Ceres, emptied of the ripened grain.

> [Glover's *Leonidas*, 1737]

But such extremes of mannerism are seldom to be found in the works of the good poets of the century.

Finally, there is the matter of versification. Everyone associates the neoclassical period with the "closed" heroic couplet—i.e., a pentameter couplet which more often than not contains within itself a complete statement and so is closed by a semicolon, period, question mark, or exclamation point. Within these two lines it was possible to attain certain rhetorical or witty effects by the use of parallelism, balance, or antithesis within the couplet as a whole or the individual line. The second line of the couplet might be made closely parallel in structure and meaning to the first, or the two could be played off against each other in antithesis; taking advantage of the fact that normally a pentameter line of English verse contains at some point a slight pause called a "caesura," one part of a line so divided can be made parallel with or antithetical to the other or even to one of the two parts of the following line. This can be illustrated by a passage from Sir John Denham's *Cooper Hill* (1642), which was quoted and parodied *ad nauseam* for many years. The poem addresses the Thames and builds up a witty comparison between the flow of a river and the flow of verse (italics are ours, to illustrate the rhetorical effects):

	O could I flow like thee, | | and make thy stream
Parallelism:	*My great example,* | | as it is *my theme!*
Double balance:	*Though deep, yet clear,* | | *though gentle,* yet not *dull,*
Double balance:	*Strong* without *rage,* | | without *o'erflowing, full.*

It only remained for Dryden and Pope to bind such passages more tightly together with alliteration and assonance, and the typical metrical-rhetorical wit of the new age had been perfected.

Shortly after the beginning of the 18th century began the vogue of blank verse—the other metrical form most favored by the age. Philosophical poems, descriptive poems, meditative poems, and original or translated epics employed blank verse of one sort or another from Thomson's *Seasons* (1726–30) to Cowper's *The Task* (1785); and the tradition determined Wordsworth's use of the form in *Tintern Abbey* and *The Prelude*. The two chief patterns of blank verse available to the age were the blank verse of Milton in *Paradise Lost* and the dramatic blank verse of Dryden and other Restoration tragic poets. The influence of Milton is easily detected, not by the success with which his manner was imitated, but by the amateur performance of most of those who try to play on his instrument. The dramatic blank verse of the Restoration too often led in 18th-century poetry to a rather disagreeably declamatory and rhetorical manner. But gradually a more lyrical blank verse developed, of which William Cowper is the master; and this more plastic metrical line had a formative influence on the blank verse of William Wordsworth.

RESTORATION LITERATURE, 1660–1700

The period between 1660 and 1700 was remarkably varied and vigorous. Dryden was the dominant figure, of course, writing in all the important contemporary forms—occasional verse, comedy, tragedy, heroic play, ode, satire, translation, and critical essay—and the variety of Dryden suggests the variety of his age. Both his example and his precepts had great infleunce, but that influence did not enforce a sterile and pedantic conformity to the rules of critics, but instead gave to the England of his day a *modern* literature, cosmopolitan, to be sure, but possessing the richness and variety that he admired in the Elizabethans, the "God's plenty" that he praised in Chaucer's *Canterbury Tales.*

The prose of the Restoration is a clear indication of the direction in which literature was moving. The styles of Donne's sermons, of Milton's pamphlets, of Sir Thomas Browne's writings, and of the character books (to select four different kinds of earlier 17th-century prose) were quite unsuitable to serve the ends of the new age. They were too elaborate, too involved, too ornate, too insistently musical, or too wittily rhetorical and pointed for mere exposition or social intercourse. The Royal Society decreed that its members must employ only a plain, concise, and utilitarian prose style suitable to the clear communication of scientific truths. Metaphors, similes, and rhetorical flourishes were disapproved because they engaged the emotions, not the reason, and though they were tolerable in poetry, they had no place in rational discourse. Similarly the learned, often pedantic language, the rhetoric and imagery and emotional intensity of earlier 17th-century pulpit oratory gradually gave way to a simplicity and plainness of diction and style entirely appropriate to sermons which sought mainly to inculcate in both the ignorant and the learned a rational morality in the conduct of life, and to avoid anything smacking of religious "enthusiasm." In polite literature, thanks to the example of such writers as Abraham Cowley, Dryden, and Sir William Temple, the ideal of good prose came to be a clear, simple, and natural style which has the ease and poise of well-bred urbane conversation. This is a social prose, designed for a social age. Later, it was available to the writers of periodical essays, such as Addison or Steele, to the novelists of the 18th century, and to the many practitioners of the delightful art of letter-writing, one of the minor literary achievements of the 18th century; the brilliant but intimate letters of Horace Walpole, and of the poets Thomas Gray and William Cowper, have never been surpassed. This movement toward clarity and simplicity in prose accompanied a similar movement away from the intricacies of metaphysical wit in verse, which found an early statement in Dryden's *Essay of Dramatic Poesy*.

But if prose was simplified and wit was tamed, the Restoration did not break wholly with the immediate past. It retained the Renaissance admiration for the typically aristocratic heroic ideal as expressed in the "heroic poem" or epic. *Paradise Lost*, carefully modeled though it is on the structure and conventions of ancient epic poetry, did not meet the expectations of most Restoration readers, who associated the heroic poem with "fierce wars and faithful loves" and expected it to offer patterns of ideal virtue and heroism for the emulation of princes and generals. General enthusiasm for Milton's epic did not develop until the early 18th century. The romantic idealism of the heroic mode was most characteristically expressed during the Restoration not in the heroic poem (except for Dryden's translations of the *Aeneid* and of Chaucer's *Knight's Tale*), but in the heroic play, which Dryden, its foremost practitioner, defined as "a heroic poem in little." The theme of these plays (their vogue lasted from about 1664 to about 1675) was the conflict between love and honor in the hearts of impossibly valorous heroes and impossibly high-minded and attractive ladies.

Dryden's one undoubted masterpiece in serious drama is his blank verse tragedy *All for Love* (produced 1677), based on the story of Antony and Cleopatra. In this play we can observe the effect of neoclassic taste on the drama: Dryden kept the three unities of action, place, and time more exactly, as he remarked, than "the English theater requires." Instead of Shakespeare's world-wide panorama, his rapid shifts of scene, his complex characters, we have the last hours of the tragic lovers presented in a static though grand manner and in a plot that is almost too neatly symmetrical. But though not Shakespeare, *All for Love* is a noble tragedy. The two other eminent tragic poets of the period were Nathaniel Lee (ca. 1649–92), known for violent plots, the wild emotions of his characters, and the extravagance of his rhetoric; and Thomas Otway (1652–85), who excelled in pathos. Not one enduring tragedy was written during the 18th century. Addison's *Cato* (produced in 1713) is a museum piece, illustrating the frigidity of "correct" and rule-bound tragedy. The long succession of verse tragedy thereafter was cursed by hollow rhetoric, stilted declamation, forced emotion, and conventional diction. George Lillo's *London Merchant* (produced in 1731) in prose, dealing with commonplace characters in mercantile life, took a feeble step in the direction of the sort of realistic, middle-class tragedy with which we are familiar today.

The real distinction of Restoration drama was comedy, which, like its cousin satire, is concerned with criticism of man as a moral and social being. Although Dryden had no great talent for the comic, he produced a number of successful comedies, the best of which have well-constructed plots and amusing dialogue, spiced with quick repartee between gay and emancipated rakes, male and female (as in *Marriage à la Mode*, produced ca. 1672). Thomas Shadwell (ca. 1642–92), later the unhappy object of Dryden's satire, specialized in comedies of humor, following his master Ben Jonson in his own rather clumsy but not incompetent way. But the finest comedies of the period are those of Sir George Etherege (ca. 1635–91), William Wycherley (ca. 1640–1716), William Congreve, and the less accomplished but witty Sir John Vanbrugh (pronounced Vánbroo or Van-bróok, 1664–1726) and George Farquhar (ca. 1677–1707). These writers excelled in representing—and critically evaluating—the social behavior of the fashionable upper classes of the town, though of course their version of that life is heightened and stylized, not a literal transcript. This sort of comedy—brilliantly witty, cynical in its view of the nature of man, whom it shows to be sensual, egoistic, and predatory—is known as "the comedy of manners," since its concern is to bring the moral and social behavior of its familiar social types to the test of comic laughter. The principal male character is a hero who lives not for military glory but for pleasure and the conquests that he can achieve in his amorous campaigns. The object of his very practical game of sexual intrigue is a beautiful, witty, pleasure-loving, and emancipated lady, every bit his equal in the strategies of love. The two are distinguished not for virtue, but for the good taste, aristocratic good breeding, true wit, sophisticated charm, and well-bred grace with which they conduct the often complicated intrigue that makes up the plot of such comedies. The best examples of the comedy of manners before William Congreve's *The Way of the World* (produced in 1700) are Etherege's *The Man of Mode* (produced in 1676), William Wycherley's *The Country Wife* (produced ca. 1672–74), and Congreve's earlier *Love for Love* (produced in 1695).

During the 1690's a considerable demand arose for moral reform in both literature and daily life, partly because of the nature of Restoration comedy. "Societies for the Reformation of Manners" were founded with the support of the soberer Anglicans and the resurgent Nonconformists. Their members served not only as propagandists of moral respectability, but also less pleasingly as spies and informers who brought offenders to trial for blasphemy, obscenity, and sexual immorality. The most effective attack on the indecencies of language and situation in comedy was made by the Anglican clergyman Jeremy Collier, whose *Short View of the Immortality and Profaneness of the English Stage* (1698) bore hard on Dryden and Congreve, among others. Collier spoke for the outraged moral sense of the godly middle classes as well as for the church, and his attack helped to discredit "wit" and the wits as subversive of religion and morals. One of the tasks that Steele and Addison undertook in the *Tatler* and *Spectator* and Pope in his *Essay on Criticism*, early in the next century, was to rehabilitate "wit" by making it the servant of social and moral decorum. When Dryden died, a better ordered and more respectable (if not actually more virtuous) society was coming into being.

The literary life of Restoration and 18th-century London differs from that of our own time in no more striking way than in its semipublic and social character. From 1652 and increasingly during the first half of the 18th century, the coffeehouses of London served as informal meeting places for men of all classes, and their popularity did much to promote conversation and the exchange of opinion. At the coffeehouses men could smoke, drink chocolate or coffee, read the newspapers, write and receive letters, exchange news, gossip, and opinions, and observe the oddities of character that the English have always been happy to cultivate. Like-minded men tended to congregate at certain coffeehouses: literary men at Will's in Covent Garden, where Dryden ruled during most of his life in London; scholars and the learned professions at the Grecian; Whigs at St. James's, and so on. Thus the clubs which played an important role in English masculine society came into being, from Addison's imaginary Spectator Club to the brilliant men who formed Johnson's famous Club. The men who frequented the coffeehouses formed an influential element among the reading public and helped to determine the tone of literature, the critical reputation of writers, the success or failure of plays, and the character of such periodicals as the *Tatler* and the *Spectator*. After the middle of the century, certain literary ladies known as bluestockings, led by the wealthy Mrs. Elizabeth Montague, established the salon and the evening *conversazione* as a means of encouraging literary conversation between the sexes.

EIGHTEENTH-CENTURY LITERATURE, 1700-1745

During the 45 years between the deaths of Dryden and Swift, the literature that Dryden and his contemporaries had created attained full maturity. A new and brilliant group of writers took the stage: Swift, with A *Tale of a Tub* (1704-10); Addison, with his overpraised and vastly popular poetic celebration of Marlborough's victory at Blenheim, *The Campaign* (1705); Prior, with *Poems on Several Occasions* (1707); Steele, with the *Tatler* (1709); and the youthful Pope, in the same year, with his *Pastorals*. On the whole, the literature of this period is chiefly a literature of wit, concerned with civilization, with man in his social relationships; and consequently it is critical and in some degree moral or satiric. It preserves the earlier period's interest in the heroic, but apart from Pope's translations of Homer, no writer succeeded in heroic poetry. It is revealing and characteristic that on the other hand some of the finest works of the period are mock-heroic (individual passages in Swift's *Battle of the Books* and A *Description of a City Shower* and Pope's *Rape of the Lock* and *The Dunciad*) or humorous burlesques of serious classic or modern modes (John

Gay's delightful town mock-Georgic, *Trivia, or the Art of Walking the Streets of London*, 1716, or his burlesque of the heroics of Italian opera, *The Beggar's Opera*, produced in 1728). Such literature is addressed to highly sophisticated and cultivated readers, and it reminds us that earlier 18th-century literature retained the aristocratic bias that had marked the literature of the 17th century.

Nevertheless a body of writing that reached a wider audience was coming into being. The reading public expanded steadily throughout the 18th century, and its new recruits were upper-class women and the increasingly numerous rich and leisured people of both sexes in the trading middle class. The popular press flourished, producing a succession of newspapers, literary periodicals in the manner of the *Tatler*, miscellanies of various sorts, and finally, in 1731, the first magazine in the modern sense, the *Gentleman's Magazine*, which was to be followed not only by imitations but also by the appearance of such successful literary reviews as the *Monthly Review* (1749) and the *Critical Review* (1756). The new journalism satisfied the hunger of the less well-educated among the literate for all sorts of information about politics, science, philosophy, literature, as well as for such less edifying materials as scandal and gossip. It also created a demand for writers —not necessarily for geniuses—and, though often on harsh terms, men began to subsist as hack writers and compilers in a milieu that came to be called Grub Street, from the name of an actual street, just as we can speak of the whole sphere of speculative finance and banking as Wall Street. To such writers as Pope and Swift, Grub Street with all its denizens (it was to gain the services of both Johnson and Oliver Goldsmith!) represented a serious threat to humanistic learning, urbane enlightenment, and good taste. But literature became in this period of expanding publication and increasingly numerous readers a gainful profession. Something will shortly be said of the novel, but it may be remarked here that the novel as we know it—a long prose narrative concerned with the actual world and the men and women who inhabit it—very probably could not have come into existence had not these new readers existed. The 18th-century novel supplied the place in the life of the common reader that the heroic poem had occupied in the life of the courtly reader of the past.

During this period certain literary kinds changed very much for the worse. The lyric, one of the glories of the Elizabethan age and the first half of the 17th century, had become in the Restoration a minor and graceful mode, appropriate to a song or a "paper of verses" addressed to a mistress. The wits of Charles II's court could turn out accomplished, conventional poems of this sort which do not lack distinction; and Matthew Prior was their counterpart in the time of William of Orange and Queen Anne. But between 1700 and 1740 lyric poetry became increasingly trivial and empty. Comedy, too, underwent a deplorable change. The moral reform of the 1690's, together with the increasingly optimistic and flattering view of human nature, made the rakes of Restoration comedy seem distasteful libels on humanity. A new sort of comedy, "sentimental comedy," began to replace the old comedy of manners; not only because it is based on the sentimental notion that man is naturally good and that, given a chance, his virtuous feelings and his good heart will triumph over his accidentally acquired

vices and follies, but also because its dialogue deals in high moral sentiments rather than wit, and because its virtuous heroines and virtuous (or
penitent) heroes suffer misfortunes which move the audience not to laughter, but to tears. One of the pleasures invented in 18th-century Europe was
the delicious pleasure of weeping, and sentimental comedy (or, as the
French phrased it, *la comédie larmoyante*, "weeping comedy") brought
that pleasure to playgoers through many decades. As tragedy froze into rhetoric, comedy dissolved in tears. And the successes enjoyed by John Gay's
comic ballad opera *The Beggar's Opera* (1728), or the laughing comedies of Goldsmith and Sheridan later in the century, could not eradicate
the taste for sentimentality. It is a curious fact that although during the
18th century the *theater* prospered and the stage was adorned by a succession of great actors and actresses (the finest being Johnson's pupil and
friend, David Garrick), the *drama* declined into a depressing nullity.

On the other hand, of course, satire flourished, its most distinguished
practitioners being Pope and Swift, though they are only two among many
effective writers. The satirist is usually a conservative, who uses his weapon
against those deviations from norms of conduct which threaten to undermine traditional and socially approved behavior. Both Pope and Swift wrote
their major satires as Tories, at a time when Britain was dominated by the
Whig party. The Tories resisted, but resisted futilely, the social and economic changes which were taking place as England grew from an island
kingdom into a world power, and transformed its agrarian into a mercantile
economy. They looked with gloomy forebodings on the rising tide of popular taste, on what they considered the invasion and debasement of the
polite world by the barbarians from the middle classes and by vulgar and
luxurious rich and noble families, and on the increase of corruption in
public life. The satire of both Swift and Pope is great because it was animated by moral urgency and heightened by a tragic sense of doom. Pope
saw the issue as a struggle between Darkness and Light, Chaos and Order,
Barbarism and Civilization: a vision which he expressed in his greatest
work, *The Dunciad*. For Swift the issue was one between "right reason"
and "madness"—not clinical insanity, of course, but a blindness to anything
but one's own private illusions, which is an abandonment of practical reality.

But the great age of satire also produced a wholly different sort of poetry
from that which Pope was writing in the 1730's. After 1726, when James
Thomson published the first of his nature poems, *Winter*, the poetry of
natural description flourished and the characteristic 18th-century English
taste for natural and picturesque beauty found expression—not only in
poetry, but also in that typical Georgian art, landscape gardening, and
finally in the beginning of the art of landscape in water color or oils, which
has been England's principal achievement in painting. Nothing could be
further from the truth than the assumption of most 19th-century critics
and literary historians that a love of external nature was unknown to English literature until the coming of the Romantic poets, a view encouraged
by some not disinterested remarks of Coleridge and Wordsworth. But
Wordsworth was the heir of 18th-century nature poets: *Tintern Abbey*

(1798) not only was written *within* the century, but in most respects is very much a poem *of* the century.

In the course of the century, Englishmen not only admired tamed and ordered nature, in large landscape gardens or cultivated fields, but also early learned to enjoy the more thrilling, emotional pleasure which they began to feel in the presence of what they called "the sublime" in nature: vast spaces, mountainous country, wild and untamed landscape. Whether the enthusiast of nature went to landscape for evidence of the presence of the Deity or merely to enjoy natural beauty, he inevitably learned to feel emotions in the presence of external nature and to examine the quality of his feelings. Before the death of Pope and Swift, in the poetry of Thomson and others, a literature of feeling had come into existence alongside the dominant literature of wit. The development of such a literature of sentiment is perhaps the crucial fact in the literary history of the century after the deaths of Pope and Swift.

THE EMERGENCE OF NEW LITERARY THEMES AND MODES, 1740–1785

When Matthew Arnold, speaking for Victorian taste, called the 18th century an "Age of Prose," he meant to cast doubt upon its poetry; but the later part of the century might indeed be honored as an age of prose. Never before nor since have so many great writers of prose flourished at once, nor so many kinds of intellectual prose been perfected: literary criticism, with Samuel Johnson; biography, James Boswell; philosophy, David Hume; politics, Edmund Burke; history, Edward Gibbon; aesthetics, Sir Joshua Reynolds; economics, Adam Smith; natural history, Gilbert White. Each of these authors is a master stylist, whose effort to express himself clearly and fully creates an art as difficult to achieve, and as precise, as poetry. Indeed, the prose style of the period often seems to build upon the principles of neoclassical verse: its elaborately balanced use of parallels and antitheses, its elegant allusions to classical literature, its public, rhetorical manner, its craving for generality. At its best, however, such prose depends less on formal virtues than on its weight of thought. Unlike the earlier masters of simplicity in prose—Addison, Swift, Defoe—the authors of the Age of Johnson have little confidence in plain speaking. Readers will not be convinced of the truth, they suspect, merely by having the facts laid before them; they must be offered scientific demonstration or passionate eloquence. Some comments by Johnson on the prose of Swift make the point by example as well as precept:

> His style was well suited to his thoughts, which are never subtilized by nice disquisitions, decorated by sparkling conceits, elevated by ambitious sentences, or variegated by far-sought learning. He pays no court to the passions, he excites neither surprise nor admiration; he always understands himself, and his readers always understand him. * * * This easy and safe conveyance of meaning it was Swift's desire to attain, and for having attained he deserves praise, though perhaps not the highest praise. For purposes merely didactic, when something is to be told that was not known before, it is the best mode; but against that inattention by which known truths are suffered to lie neglected, it makes no provision; it instructs, but does not persuade.

Johnson's prose bristles with long words, qualifications of thought, and "ambitious sentences" that are the very opposite of the style he describes; he attempts not merely to be understood, not merely to instruct, but to persuade. And similar ambitions motivate many of the authors of his time. An unprecedented effort to formulate the first principles of philosophy, history, psychology, and art required a whole new language of persuasion, more subtle, logical, and accurate than English had ever been before.

An age of great prose, however, can put a burden on its poets. Many of the generation of talented young poets who emerged about the time of Pope's death, a group that includes William Collins, Thomas Gray, and the brothers Joseph and Thomas Warton, are haunted by the fear that the spirit of poetry may have passed away—driven out by the spirit of prose, by an ideal of mere "correctness," by the end of superstitions that had once peopled the landscape with fairies and demons, the stuff of poetry. In an age barren of magic, they ask, where is poetry to be found? That question becomes obsessive in many poems of the period, suffusing them with melancholy. Indeed, more and more poetry itself was associated with melancholy, a sweet sadness, a yearning for another time and place. The prototype of the mid-18th-century melancholy poet was Milton's *Il Penseroso*, a night-loving solitary, who sucks pensive sadness from the "far-off curfew" or the swelling organ in the twilight of a Gothic church. Such a figure is most unlike the Augustan poet, a social being, living in a crowded world and little given to the impropriety of the public confession of private feelings. He is rather a not very remote ancestor of such typically Romantic figures as Wordsworth, wandering "lonely as a cloud," of Byron's Childe Harold, brooding over the ruins of Rome, or of the speaker of Keats's sonnet, who, contemplating his own mortal day and the transitoriness of love and beauty, exclaims:

> on the shore
> Of the wide world I stand alone and think,
> Till love and fame to nothingness do sink.

The "pilgrim" in William Collins' *Ode to Evening* and the speaker in Thomas Gray's *Elegy Written in a Country Churchyard* are typical 18th-century Penserosos. The idea of the poet was changing from that of a maker to that of an introspective, brooding confessor; the materials of poetry were becoming rather the inner life and private vision of the poet than the public, social affairs of men.

Poets who brood in silence are never far from thoughts of death; and an often morbid fascination with death, suicide, and the grave preoccupies the poets of midcentury. The clergyman Edward Young (1683–1765) wrote an immensely long and popular poem in blank verse, *The Complaint: or Night Thoughts on Life, Death, and Immortality* (1742–46), to supplement the Christian optimism of Pope's *Essay on Man* with a darker view of Christianity based on fear of the life to come. But the "graveyard school" is less concerned with religion than with horror and decay. Within an elaborate stage-setting of medieval ruins and fleshless bodies, the soul of the graveyard poet self-consciously acts out its secret fears. The revival of

Gothic architectural styles, most famously Horace Walpole's tiny and precious pseudo-Gothic castle, Strawberry Hill, helped influence literary styles as well. The Gothic vogue, like a similar vogue for Chinese decor, seemed to suggest that old-fashioned canons of taste—proportion, balance, simplicity, and harmony—might count for less in art than the pleasures of fancy and extravagance—intricacy, asymmetry, a willful excess. Poets began to cultivate archaic language and dead literary forms; especially, after Thomas Percy's edition of *Reliques of Ancient English Poetry* (1765), the ballad. Thus Thomas Chatterton (1752–1770), whom the Romantics later idolized for his precocious genius and his tragic early death, composed sham medieval ballads he pretended to have found in an old manuscript. The most remarkable literary consequence of such medievalizing, however, was the invention of the Gothic romance. Horace Walpole's *Castle of Otranto* (1765), a dreamlike tale of terror inspired by the physical appearance of Strawberry Hill, created a mode of fiction that retains its popularity to the present day. In the typical Gothic romance, set amidst the glooms and intricacies of a medieval castle, the laws of nightmare replace the laws of probability. Forbidden themes—incest, murder, necrophilia, atheism, the torments of sexual desire—are allowed free play; repressed feelings, morbid fears rise to the surface of the narrative. Although most such romances, like William Beckford's *Vathek* (1786) and Matthew Lewis's *The Monk* (1796), depend on sensationalism and the grotesque, Gothicism also influenced serious novels of social purpose, like William Godwin's *Caleb Williams* (1794); and Godwin's daughter, Mary Shelley, eventually composed a romantic nightmare, *Frankenstein* (1816), that continues to haunt our dreams.

Ultimately, it was not to a medieval revival that poets looked for a renewal of poetry, but to their own imaginations and feelings. In his *Ode to Fancy* (1746), Joseph Warton associated "fancy" with the natural, the wild and spontaneous, with solitude, and with enthusiasm and the passions. Such a concept of the fancy or imagination emphasizes not rules and crafts of the maker, but original genius, the poet as the seer, as nature's priest. True poets, Warton suggests, should not be conversationalists or orators but singers. A sublime excess, a visionary fervor, became the mark of poetry. "The public has seen all that art can do," William Shenstone wrote in 1761, welcoming James Macpherson's bardic *Ossian*, "and they want the more striking efforts of wild, original, enthusiastic genius." But genius is easier to call for than to recognize; when it does come, people are apt to call it madness. Many of the best poets of the period—Collins, Christopher Smart, later William Cowper—suffered from mental illness, and others, like Chatterton, were scorned by society. Nor did many readers so much as notice the extraordinary work of Smart, or later of William Blake. The apocalyptic strain of poetry, bursting the bonds of logical transition, of grammar, and even of the natural world, proved difficult to approach. Cowper, the most popular poet of the latter part of the century, won his readers with a more modest, intimate kind of verse, never departing far from the accents of friendly conversation. Nevertheless, it was to visionary poetry, and to genius, that the future belonged. "The road of excess," Blake notes in a Proverb of Hell, "leads to the palace of wisdom." As the

18th century drew to an end amid revolutions in society and thought, poets began to travel that road.

THE BEGINNING OF THE NOVEL

To say that the modern novel came into existence in the 18th century is not to say that there was no prose fiction before 1700. There were the ancient Greek romances and their modern European imitators; the courtly *Arcadia* of Sidney and the humbler fiction of Deloney and Nashe and other Elizabethans; the interminable French romances of the 17th century and their English translations and imitations, loosely constructed, blending aristocratic refinement, chivalric adventure, and courtly love; the tales of the adventures of rogues and the careers of famous criminals; and, in a world apart, Bunyan's vivid allegories of the spiritual adventures of wayfaring and militant Christians and their adversaries. But it remains true that, if we except Daniel Defoe, the creator of the modern novel was Samuel Richardson (1689–1761). It is interesting to observe that both Defoe and Richardson belonged to the middle class and expressed in their works middle-class interests and attitudes. Defoe simply ignored the sentimental and aristocratic refinements of the earlier romances and was content to show his readers not a world as it might be, a heroic world, but their world as it was, populated with believable people who were motivated by the practical concerns that dominate our daily lives. He did not seek—and except through *Robinson Crusoe* (1719) did not often find—readers among the upper classes. He was content to interest shopkeepers, apprentices, and servants, who were already avid readers of tales of crime and adventure, usually heavily laced with pious moral observations.

Richardson, however, caught the attention of all literate Europe. In *Pamela, or Virtue Rewarded* (1740), he once for all established the novel as we know it, as a solid and enduring object in the literary landscape. He brought to the writing of his novels a conventional moral code, a touch of middle-class snobbery, and a surprising insight into the sensibilities of women. His three novels were strikingly new in their minute and subtle analysis of emotions and states of mind. It was while he was compiling a little book of model letters to serve as a guide to the less well-educated that he conceived the idea of telling in a series of letters written by his heroine, Pamela, to her parents, the story of a virtuous servant girl—Pamela herself—in the household of a bachelor, Mr. B——, who resists her master's base designs on her virtue and eventually wins her would-be seducer as her husband. The epistolary method (which he used in all his novels) creates palpable improbabilities; nonetheless, Richardson found that by using it he was able to reveal the thoughts and emotions of his characters more vividly than any of his predecessors had done. Pamela's virtue seems as bogus to the modern reader as it did to Richardson's contemporary Henry Fielding; but there is no denying that Richardson's narrative method allows the reader to share his heroine's experiences to a degree which was quite new in fiction. Richardson's masterpiece is the more involved and gloomy *Clarissa* (1747–48). His third and final novel, *Sir Charles Grandison* (1753–54), is less impressive.

Henry Fielding (1707–54), who loved virtue as much as Richardson did, but to whom goodness was a matter of spontaneity and lack of calculation, not of more propriety or conformity to a code, considered Pamela a misleading image of virtue; therefore, in 1742, he published *Joseph Andrews,* which begins as an hilarious burlesque of *Pamela* by describing the staunch resistance offered to the lewd advances of Lady Booby by her servant, the virtuous Joseph, brother of Pamela. Expelled for his chastity from Lady Booby's household, he takes to the road, joining the guileless Parson Adams, who is walking to London to try to sell a bundle of his sermons to a publisher. Their adventures make up what Fielding called "a comic epic in prose." His great novel is *The History of Tom Jones, A Foundling* (1749). The protagonist became the pattern of the sentimental hero of the age: a young man of manly virtues, generous, high-spirited, loyal, and courageous, but impulsive, unreflecting, full of animal spirits and sensuality. The novel is crowded with incident and with varied types of men and women; and critics have agreed with Coleridge's praise of its brilliantly constructed plot. Fielding's sentimentality is not the sentimentality of Richardson, whose dying heroine Clarissa gives full expression to every shade of feeling as she writes her letters, using her coffin as an escritoire; rather it is the sentimentality of a man—of most English men and women of his time—who accepted the curious doctrine that men are naturally good and that our innate love of truth and virtue can in the end save us from our baser selves. Fielding's other important novel, *Amelia* (1751), having as its heroine a long-suffering woman, almost wholly passive, is an example of pathos rather than of Fielding's comic vigor and healthy gusto.

Two other novelists must be mentioned: Tobias Smollett (1721–71) and Laurence Sterne (1713–68). Smollett was a gifted caricaturist, a dealer in grotesque humor and rather strongly flavored comedy. He delighted to depict the seamier side of 18th-century life, its brutality, coarse practical jokes, and strong odors. *Roderick Random* (1748), *Peregrine Pickle* (1751), and *Ferdinand, Count Fathom* (1753), owe something to the picaresque tradition, as, of course, did Fielding's first two novels. Smollett's one masterpiece is an epistolary novel, *Humphry Clinker* (1771), which recounts, through letters written by several members of a traveling party, the comic incidents of a journey through England and Scotland, from the differing points of view of the travelers, some of them "originals" in a high degree.

Sterne, an unclerical clergyman, a humorist, a wit, a consumptive whose disease gave a hectic, heightened quality to his senses and emotions, a masterly recorder of the refinements of sensation, feeling, and thought, produced between 1760 and 1767 his long, brilliant, sentimental-comic, and eccentric novel, *The Life and Opinions of Tristram Shandy.* He deliberately frustrated all the stock expectations of his readers. The plot has not the logical order of a beginning, a middle, and an end; instead it abandons clock time for psychological time, interrupts scenes in order to digress or to recount past or future events, follows whimsically any apparently chance association, digresses for several chapters—in fact, it is designed as an elaborate joke at the reader's expense. And yet the method gets us inside the consciousness of the narrator and the other characters, and into a world peopled by the most engaging of comic characters.

Fielding, Smollett, and Sterne gave to English literature not only vivid scenes from the life of their times, but a gallery of eccentric and original characters that illustrate the interest of the age not only in the ideal and the general, but also in the individual and the unique. The novels of Dickens and of Thackeray in the 19th century owe much to their forerunners in the 18th.

THE CONTINUITY OF THE AUGUSTAN TRADITION

Despite the emergence of new literary forms, materials, and methods after the death of Pope and Swift, the Augustan line continued vigorously throughout the last half of the 18th and even into the 19th century. If the years between 1745 and 1784 were years of change and experiment, they were also the period of Samuel Johnson's greatest achievement and influence. A conservative in literature as in politics and religion, Johnson defended in conversation and in his critical writings the humanistic neoclassicism which he had inherited from the older generation. His two major poems, *London* (1738) and *The Vanity of Human Wishes* (1749), are satirical and ethical and show no influence of the new sensibility of the midcentury. He was loyal to the heroic couplet and to the use of generalized diction. His *Dictionary* (1755) was designed not to fix our language permanently but certainly to retard the process of change and to expel words which he considered superfluous. His critical writings sufficiently reveal his devotion to the standards of Dryden and Pope, though his judgments of particular writers and works were often personal, even idiosyncratic. But his conservatism was saved from pedantry by the empirical bent of his mind and his broad and humanistic learning.

If Johnson speaks for his age, the reason is partly that he shares a faith, with many of his contemporaries, in common sense and the common reader. "By the common sense of readers uncorrupted with literary prejudices," he wrote in the last of his great *Lives of the Poets* (1780), " * * * must be finally decided all claim to poetical honors." A similar respect for common sense, and for standards of taste and behavior based upon universal principles of mind that all men share, marks many of the grandest achievements of the century; for instance, the political writings of Edmund Burke, the great Whig statesman and orator, or the *Discourses on Art* (1769–90) of Sir Joshua Reynolds, who drew the best aesthetic theory of his day into an elegant whole. Moreover, the poets whom everyone read relied less upon apocalyptic visions than upon a verse that could do justice to the ordinary feelings of ordinary people. Gray's *Elegy*, Goldsmith's *The Deserted Village*, Crabbe's *The Village*, and the lyrics of Robert Burns are only a few of the poems that strive to make poetry from and for the lives of the common man. Nor did Goldsmith, Crabbe, and Burns, for all their attachment to the growing wave of sentimentalism, desert the verse forms—the careful craftsmanship, the rhyming couplets—developed by the earlier Augustan masters. Even Cowper's *The Task* (1785), which brings us to the threshold of the Romantic movement, belongs most definitely in the 18th century. Indeed, the Augustan age did not die on that day in 1798 when a small and unsuccessful volume of poems, *Lyrical Ballads*, was published by Wordsworth and Coleridge. We hear the accents of that age from time to time in the poems of both Wordsworth and Coleridge, in many of the poems of Byron, and in Byron's ardent defense of Pope and Dryden, when the new age finally brought those masters to judgment. And we hear its old verities expressed in its own vocabulary in the criticism of that arch-enemy of the Romantic movement, Francis Jeffrey, editor of the *Edinburgh Review*, as when, for example, in a review (1808) of a volume of poems by George Crabbe, he paused to rebuke the (as he believed) affectedly eccentric poet Wordsworth for having written *The Thorn* and one of the Lucy poems:

Now we leave it to any reader of common candor and discernment to say whether these representations of character and sentiment are drawn from the eternal and universal standard of truth and nature, which every one is knowing enough to recognize, and no one great enough to depart from with impunity; or whether they are not formed * * * upon certain fantastic and affected peculiarities in the mind or fancy of the author, into which it is most improbable that many of his readers will enter, and which cannot, in some cases, be comprehended without much effort and explanation.

JOHN DRYDEN
(1631–1700)

1668:   Made poet laureate.
1681:   *Absalom and Achitophel.*
ca. 1686: Conversion to Catholicism.
1689:   Loss of court offices upon accession of William and
           Mary.
1697:   Translation of Virgil.

Although John Dryden's parents seem to have sided with Parliament against the king, there is no evidence that the poet grew up in a strict Puritan family. His father, a country gentleman of moderate fortune, gave his son a gentleman's education at Westminster School, under the renowned Dr. Richard Busby, who used the rod as a pedagogical aid in imparting a sound knowledge of the learned languages and literatures to his charges (among others John Locke and Matthew Prior). From Westminster, Dryden went to Trinity College, Cambridge, where he took his A.B. in 1654. He probably held a minor post in Cromwell's government, and if he did so, it was obtained through the influence of his cousin Sir Gilbert Pickering, a member of the Protector's Council. His first important and impressive poem, *Heroic Stanzas* (1659), was written to commemorate the death of Cromwell. It was followed in the next year by *Astraea Redux*, celebrating the return of Charles II to his throne. Years later Dryden's political and religious enemies taunted him with this sudden change of position, as if he had been a political turncoat, ready to change sides whenever he could serve his own interests. The charge has often been repeated, but it is both malicious and stupid: as Dr. Johnson long ago said, "if he changed, he changed with the nation," for in 1660 most Englishmen enthusiastically welcomed the Restoration. During the rest of his life Dryden was to remain entirely loyal to Charles and to his successor James II.

Dryden is the commanding literary figure of the last four decades of the 17th century. He is that rare phenomenon, the man of letters in whose work the image of an age can be discerned. Every important aspect of the life of his times—political, religious, philosophical, artistic—finds expression somewhere in his writings. Dryden is the least personal of our poets. He is not at all the solitary, subjective poet listening to the murmur of his own voice and preoccupied with his own personal view of experience, but rather a citizen of the world commenting publicly on matters of public concern.

From the beginning to the end of his literary career, Dryden's original nondramatic poems are most typically occasional poems, i.e., poems which celebrate particular events of a public character—a coronation, a military victory, a death, a political crisis. Such poems are social and ceremonial, and they demand of the writer tact as well as talent. They are public and formal, blending poetry with rhetoric and oratory, and their tone is that of the forum, not of intimate conversation or private meditation. In varying degrees Dryden's occasional poems have these qualities. His earliest published poem, to be sure, *Upon the Death of Lord Hastings* (1649), belongs stylistically to the tradition of metaphysical poetry, but ten years later, when his next ambitious poem appeared, the *Heroic Stanzas* on the death of Cromwell, he had mastered the tone, language, and manner of grave public speech. His principal achievements in this form are the two poems on the king's return and his coronation; *Annus Mirabilis* (1667), which celebrates the English naval victory over the Dutch and the fortitude of the people of London and the king during the Great Fire, both events of that "wonderful year," 1666; the political poems, the lines on the death of Oldham (1684), the odes, and the masque printed below.

Between 1664 and 1681, however, Dryden was mainly and most seriously a playwright. The newly chartered theaters needed a modern repertory, and Dryden was foremost among those who set vigorously about supplying the need. As his *Essay of Dramatic Poesy* (1668) shows, he studied the works of the great playwrights of Greece and Rome, of the English Renaissance, and of contemporary France, seeking sound theoretical principles on which to construct the new drama that the age demanded. Indeed his fine critical intelligence always supported his creative powers, and because he took literature seriously and enjoyed discussing it, he became, it appears almost casually, what Dr. Johnson called him: "the father of English criticism." His abilities as both poet and dramatist brought him to the attention of the king, who in 1668 made him poet laureate. Two years later the post of Historiographer Royal was added to the laureateship at a combined stipend of £200, well over £2000 in modern money.

Dryden is not a great playwright, but he was influential in his own time. He wrote his plays, as he frankly confessed, to please his audiences, which were not heterogeneous, like Shakespeare's, but were largely drawn from the court and from the fashionable world that took its standard from the court. He followed rather than formed the taste of his audiences, producing rhymed heroic plays, in which incredibly noble heroes and heroines face incredibly difficult choices between their mutual love and the claims of honor, and the dialogue is conducted in a boldly rhetorical style; comedies of busy intrigue and bright, witty repartee, especially between a male and female rake; and, later, libretti for the newly introduced dramatic form, the opera. His one great tragedy—on Antony and Cleopatra—is *All for Love* (1677), in blank verse, written more in emulation than in imitation of Shakespeare.

Between 1678 and 1681, when he was nearing 50, Dryden discovered his great gift for writing formal verse satire. A quarrel with Thomas Shadwell, a playwright of some talent, prompted the mock-heroic episode *Mac Flecknoe*, which was probably written about 1678 but which was not published until 1682. Out of the stresses occasioned by the Popish Plot (1678) and its political aftermath came his major political satires, *Absalom and Achitophel* (1681), and *The Medal* (1682), his final attack on the villain of *Absalom and Achitophel*, the Earl of Shaftesbury. Twenty years' experience as poet and playwright had prepared him technically for the triumphant achievement that *Absalom and Achitophel* undoubtedly is. He had completely mastered the heroic couplet, having fashioned it into an instrument suitable in his hands for every sort of discourse from the thrust and parry of quick logical argument, to lyric feeling, rapid narrative, or forensic declamation. And he had fashioned a noble, resonant, and malleable language as well. Thanks to this long discipline, he was able in one stride to assume his proper place beside the masters of verse satire: Horace, Juvenal, Persius, in ancient Rome, and Boileau, his French contemporary.

The consideration of religious and political questions that the events of 1678–81 forced on Dryden brought a new seriousness to his mind and works. In 1682 he published *Religio Laici*, a poem in which he examined the grounds of his religious faith and defended the *via media* of the Anglican Church against the rationalism of Deism on the one hand and the authoritarianism of Rome on the other. But he had moved closer to Rome than he perhaps realized when he wrote the poem. Charles II died in 1685 and was succeeded by his Catholic brother, James II. Within less than a year Dryden and his two sons were converted to Catholicism. Just when, by whom, and under what circumstances the poet was converted we do not know, but once again his enemies were loud in denouncing his apparent venality. Again the accusation does not survive serious scrutiny. Dryden's court appointments had been renewed promptly on the accession of James, certainly before his conversion. Moreover, as Louis Bredvold has shown, Dryden's early philosophic skepticism (the conviction that the human reason cannot arrive at truth) gave way to fideism (the acceptance by faith alone of Christian mysteries as interpreted by some valid tradition). The development was slow and consistent, and his sincerity is borne out by his steadfast loyalty to the Roman Church after James abdicated and the Protestant William and Mary came in; as a result he was to lose his offices and their much-needed stipends. From his new position as a Roman Catholic, Dryden wrote in 1687 *The Hind and the Panther*, in which he defended the doctrines of his church and the policies (which he knew to be ruinous for the king and his coreligionists) that James was pursuing. Though full of splendid passages, this poem is a rather odd performance. The various religious sects of England are represented by appropriate animals, and, surprisingly enough, we listen to a prolonged theological debate between two of them, the milk-white Hind (the Roman Church) and the spotted Panther (the Anglican Church).

Dryden was now nearing 60, with a family to support on a much-diminished income. With quiet dignity he once more undertook to earn his living. He easily resumed his career as a playwright, producing five more plays before his death. He had occasionally practiced translation in the past and to this minor but, in his time, highly esteemed art he now returned. In 1693 appeared his translations from Juvenal and Persius, with the long dedicatory epistle on satire; and in 1697, his greatest achievement in this mode, the magnificent folio, illustrated, of the works of Virgil. At the very end, two months before his death, came the *Fables Ancient and Modern*, prefaced by one of the finest of his critical essays and made up of superb translations from Ovid, Boccaccio, and Chaucer.

What was the nature of Dryden's achievement? His drama, by and large, belongs entirely to his age, though its influence persisted into the next century. His critical writings established canons of taste and theoretical principles that determined the character of neoclassic literature in the next century. He helped establish a new sort of prose—easy, lucid, plain, and shaped to the cadences of natural speech. This is the prose that we like to think of as "modern," although it is not everywhere evident in our modern age. Johnson praised it for its informality and apparent artlessness:

* * * every word seems to drop by chance, though it falls into its proper place. Nothing is cold or languid; the whole is airy, animated, and vigorous * * * though all is easy, nothing is feeble; though all seems careless, there is nothing harsh * * *

His satire, as vital today as it was nearly 300 years ago, exerted a fruitful influence on the most brilliant verse satirist of the next century, Alexander Pope. The vigor and variety of his metrics made inevitable the long-enduring vogue of the heroic couplet among his successors. At the same time, he created a poetic language that remained the basic language of poetry until the early 19th century and that even the Romantic movement did not wholly destroy. This is not to say that he created the stock "poetic diction" to which Wordsworth and Coleridge justly objected later on, though he added to it and used it judiciously. His language is the superbly civilized language of the Augustan style at its best: dignified, unaffected, precise and always musical—a noble instrument of public speech. Johnson's final estimate remains valid:

By him we were taught *sapere et fari*, to think naturally and express forcibly * * * What was said of Rome, adorned by Augustus, may be applied by an easy metaphor to English poetry embellished by Dryden, *lateritiam invenit, marmoream reliquit*, he found it brick, and he left it marble.

From Annus Mirabilis[1]

[London Reborn]

Yet London, empress of the northern clime,   845
       By an high fate thou greatly didst expire;
Great as the world's, which at the death of time
       Must fall, and rise a nobler frame by fire.[2]

As when some dire usurper Heaven provides,
       To scourge his country with a lawless sway:[3]   850
His birth, perhaps, some petty village hides,
       And sets his cradle out of fortune's way:

1. 1666 was a "year of wonders" (*annus mirabilis*): war, plague, the great fire of London. According to the enemies of Charles II, God was visiting His wrath upon the English people to signify that the reign of an unholy king would soon come to an end. Dryden's long "historical poem" *Annus Mirabilis*, written the same year, interprets the wonders differently: as trials sent by God to punish rebellious spirits and to bind the king and his people together. "Never had prince or people more mutual reason to love each other," Dryden wrote, "if suffering for each other can endear affection." Charles had endured rejection and exile, England had been torn by civil war. Dryden views these sufferings as a covenant, pledge of better times to come. Out of Charles' troubles, he predicts in heroic stanzas modeled on Virgil, the king shall arise like a new Augustus, the ruler of a great empire; and out of fire London shall arise like the phoenix, ready to take her place as trade center for the world, in the glory of a new Augustan age.
2. Ovid, whom Dryden quotes, foretells, in Book I of *The Metamorphoses*, that the world will be purged by fire.
3. Probably a reference to Oliver Cromwell.

Till fully ripe his swelling fate breaks out,
    And hurries him to mighty mischiefs on:
His Prince, surprised at first, no ill could doubt,[4]   855
    And wants the power to meet it when 'tis known:

Such was the rise of this prodigious fire,
    Which in mean buildings first obscurely bred,
From thence did soon to open streets aspire,
    And straight to palaces and temples spread.   860

              * * *

Me-thinks already, from this chymic[5] flame,
    I see a city of more precious mold: 1170
Rich as the town which gives the Indies name,[6]
    With silver paved, and all divine with gold.

Already, laboring with a mighty fate,
    She shakes the rubbish from her mounting brow,
And seems to have renewed her charter's date,   1175
    Which Heaven will to the death of time allow.

More great than human, now, and more August,[7]
    New deified she from her fires does rise:
Her widening streets on new foundations trust,
    And, opening, into larger parts she flies.   1180

Before, she like some shepherdess did show,
    Who sat to bathe her by a river's side:
Not answering to her fame, but rude and low,
    Nor taught the beauteous arts of modern pride.

Now, like a Maiden Queen, she will behold,   1185
    From her high turrets, hourly suitors come:
The East with incense, and the West with gold,
    Will stand, like suppliants, to receive her doom.[8]

The silver Thames, her own domestic flood,
    Shall bear her vessels like a sweeping train;   1190
And often wind (as of his mistress proud)
    With longing eyes to meet her face again.

The wealthy Tagus, and the wealthier Rhine,
    The glory of their towns no more shall boast;
And Seine, that would with Belgian rivers join,[9]   1195
    Shall find her luster stained, and traffic lost.

The venturous merchant, who designed[1] more far,
    And touches on our hospitable shore,

4. Fear.
5. Alchemic or transmuting. The fire of London, which utterly consumed the central city, burned for four days, September 2–6. By September 10 Christopher Wren had already submitted a plan, much of it later adopted, for rebuilding the city on a grander scale.
6. Mexico.

7. Augusta, the old name of London [Dryden's note].
8. Judgment, decree.
9. France and Holland (which then included Belgium) had made an alliance for trade, as well as war, against England. The river Tagus flows into the Atlantic at Lisbon.
1. Intended to go.

Charmed with the splendor of this northern star,
    Shall here unlade him, and depart no more.   1200

Our powerful navy shall no longer meet,
    The wealth of France or Holland to invade;
The beauty of this Town, without a fleet,
    From all the world shall vindicate² her trade.

And while this famed emporium we prepare,   1205
    The British ocean shall such triumphs boast,
That those who now disdain our trade to share,
    Shall rob like pirates on our wealthy coast.

Already we have conquered half the war,
    And the less dangerous part is left behind: 1210
Our trouble now is but to make them dare,
    And not so great to vanquish as to find.

Thus to the eastern wealth through storms we go,
    But now, the Cape once doubled,³ fear no more;
A constant trade-wind will securely blow,   1215
    And gently lay us on the spicy shore.
1666   1667

Prologue to *The Tempest*¹

OR THE ENCHANTED ISLAND

As, when a tree's cut down, the secret root
Lives underground, and thence new branches shoot;
So from old Shakespeare's honored dust, this day
Springs up and buds a new reviving play:
Shakespeare, who (taught by none)² did first impart   5
To Fletcher³ wit, to laboring Jonson art.
He, monarch-like, gave those, his subjects, law;
And is that nature which they paint and draw.
Fletcher reached that which on his heights did grow,
Whilst Jonson crept, and gathered all below.   10
This did his love, and this his mirth digest:
One imitates him most, the other best.
If they have since outwrit all other men,
'Tis with the drops which fell from Shakespeare's pen.
The storm which vanished on the neighboring shore,   15
Was taught by Shakespeare's *Tempest* first to roar.⁴

2. Defend, protect.
3. Sailed around.
1. In 1667 Dryden collaborated with the poet laureate, Sir William Davenant, in adapting Shakespeare's *Tempest* to the Restoration stage and the tastes of Restoration audiences.
2. The view of Shakespeare as a natural genius, writing without the advantages of classical learning, was a critical commonplace. Compare Jonson's *To the Memory of * * * Shakespeare*, line 31, Milton's *L'Allegro*, lines 131–34, and Dryden's *Essay of Dramatic Poesy*.
3. John Fletcher (1579–1625), who collaborated with Francis Beaumont (ca. 1584–1616) in writing plays. During the early years of the Restoration period, their dramas were the most frequently revived plays "of the last age."
4. Details of the plot of *The Sea-Voyage* (1622), by Fletcher and Philip Massinger, suggest *The Tempest*.

That innocence and beauty which did smile
In Fletcher, grew on this *Enchanted Isle.*
But Shakespeare's magic could not copied be;
Within that circle none durst walk but he.   20
I must confess 'twas bold, nor would you now
That liberty to vulgar wits[5] allow,
Which works by magic supernatural things;
But Shakespeare's power is sacred as a king's.
Those legends from old priesthood were received,   25
And he then writ, as people then believed.
But if for Shakespeare we your grace implore,
We for our theater shall want it more:
Who by our dearth of youths are forced to employ
One of our women to present a boy;   30
And that's a transformation, you will say,
Exceeding all the magic in the play.
Let none expect in the last act to find
Her sex transformed from man to womankind.
Whate'er she was before the play began,   35
All you shall see of her is perfect man.
Or if your fancy will be farther led
To find her woman, it must be abed.

1667   1670

Epilogue to *Tyrannic Love*

SPOKEN BY MRS. ELLEN,[1] WHEN SHE WAS TO BE
CARRIED OFF DEAD BY THE BEARERS

[*To the Bearer.*] Hold, are you mad? you damned confounded
    dog,
I am to rise, and speak the epilogue.
[*To the Audience.*] I come, kind gentlemen, strange news to tell
    ye,
I am the ghost of poor departed Nelly.
Sweet ladies, be not frighted, I'll be civil;   5
I'm what I was, a little harmless devil:
For after death, we sprites have just such natures
We had for all the world, when human creatures;[2]
And therefore, I that was an actress here,
Play all my tricks in hell, a goblin there.   10
Gallants, look to it, you say there are no sprites;
But I'll come dance about your beds at nights.
And faith you'll be in a sweet kind of taking,
When I surprise you between sleep and waking.

5. The common run of poets.
1. The famous actress Nell Gwynn
("Mrs."—i.e., "Mistress"—was the title given all young unmarried women);
her beauty and wit made her not only
a favorite of London audiences, but
eventually a mistress of Charles II. As
he lay dying he was heard to say,
"Don't let poor Nelly starve." Her
great roles were comic parts, but in

Tyrannic Love she acted Valeria, the
daughter of the wicked Roman Emperor Maximin, who puts to death St.
Catharine of Alexandria. Valeria is
killed in the general slaughter which
ends the play.
2. Pope develops this idea brilliantly in
the sylphs and gnomes of *The Rape of
the Lock.*

To tell you true, I walk because I die   15
Out of my calling in a tragedy.
O poet, damned dull poet, who could prove
So senseless! to make Nelly die for love!
Nay, what's yet worse, to kill me in the prime
Of Easter term,[3] in tart and cheese-cake time!   20
I'll fit[4] the fop, for I'll not one word say
To excuse his godly out-of-fashion play:
A play, which if you dare but twice sit out,
You'll all be slandered, and be thought devout.
But farewell, gentlemen, make haste to me;   25
I'm sure ere long to have your company.
As for my epitaph, when I am gone,
I'll trust no poet, but will write my own:

Here Nelly lies, who, though she lived a slattern,
Yet died a princess, acting in St. Cathar'n.[5]
1669   30
                                                                        1670

Song from *Marriage à la Mode*

1

Why should a foolish marriage vow,
    Which long ago was made,
Oblige us to each other now,
    When passion is decayed?
We loved, and we loved, as long as we could,   5
    Till our love was loved out in us both;
But our marriage is dead when the pleasure is fled:
    'Twas pleasure first made it an oath.

2

If I have pleasures for a friend,
    And farther love in store,   10
What wrong has he whose joys did end,
    And who could give no more?
'Tis a madness that he should be jealous of me,
    Or that I should bar him of another:
For all we can gain is to give ourselves pain,   15
    When neither can hinder the other.
ca. 1672
                                                         1673

Absalom and Achitophel

In 1678 a dangerous crisis, both religious and political, threatened to undo the Restoration settlement and to precipitate England once again into civil war. The Popish Plot and its aftermath not only whipped up extreme anti-Catholic passions, but led between 1679 and 1681 to a bitter political struggle between Charles II (whose adherents came to be called Tories) and the Earl of Shaftesbury (whose followers were termed Whigs). The issues were nothing less than

---

3. One of the four periods of the year when the law courts sit.
4. Punish.

5. The normal pronunciation of *Catharine* at the time.

the prerogatives of the Crown and the possible exclusion of the king's Catholic brother, James, Duke of York, from his rightful position as heir-presumptive to the throne. Charles's cool courage and brilliant, if un-scrupulous, political genius saved the throne for his brother and gave at least temporary peace to his people.

Charles was a Catholic at heart—he received the last rites of that Church on his deathbed—and was eager to do what he could do discreetly for the relief of his Catholic subjects, who suffered severe civil and re-ligious disabilities imposed by their numerically superior Protestant country-men. James openly professed the Catholic religion, an awkward fact po-litically, for he was next in line of succession since Charles had no legiti-mate children. The household of the duke, as well as that of Charles's neglected queen, Catherine of Braganza, inevitably became the center of Catholic life and intrigue at court and consequently of Protestant preju-dice and suspicion.

No one understood, however, that the situation was explosive until 1678, when Titus Oates (a renegade Catholic convert and a man of the most infamous character) offered sworn testimony of the existence of a Jesuit plot to assassinate the king, burn London, massacre Protestants, and re-establish the Roman Church.

The country might have kept its head and come to realize (what no historian has doubted) that Oates and his confederates were perjured rascals, as Charles himself quickly perceived. But panic was created by the discovery of the murdered body of a prominent London Justice of the Peace, Sir Edmund Berry Godfrey, who a few days before had received for safekeeping a copy of Oates's testimony. The crime, immediately ascribed to the Catholics, has never been solved. Fear and indignation reached a hysterical pitch when the seizure of the papers of the Duke of York's secretary revealed that he had been in correspondence with the confessor of Louis XIV regarding the re-establishment of the Roman Church in England. Before the terror subsided many innocent men were executed on the increasingly bold and always false evidence of Oates and his fellows.

The Earl of Shaftesbury, the Duke of Buckingham, and others quickly took advantage of the situation. With the support of the Commons and the City of London, they moved to exclude the Duke of York from the succession. Between 1679 and 1681 Charles and Shaftesbury were en-gaged in a mighty struggle. The Whigs found a candidate of their own in the king's favorite illegitimate son, the handsome and engaging Duke of Monmouth, whom they advanced as a proper successor to his father. They urged Charles to legitimize him, and when he refused they whis-pered that there was proof that the king had secretly married Monmouth's mother. The young man allowed himself to be used against his father. He was sent on a triumphant progress through western England, where he was enthusiastically received. Twice an Exclusion Bill nearly passed both Houses. But by early 1681 Charles had secured his own position by secretly accepting from Louis XIV a three-year subsidy that made him independent of Parliament, which had tried to force his hand by refusing to vote him funds. He summoned Parliament to meet at Oxford in the spring of 1681, and, a few moments after the Commons had passed the Exclusion Bill, in a bold stroke he abruptly dissolved Parliament, which never met again during his reign. Already, as Charles was aware, a reaction had set in

1712 · John Dryden

against the violence of the Whigs. In midsummer, when he felt it safe to move against his enemies, Shaftesbury was sent to the Tower, charged with high treason. In November the Grand Jury, packed with Whigs, threw out the indictment, and the earl was free; but his power was broken, and he lived only two more years.

Shortly before the Grand Jury acted, Dryden published anonymously the first part of *Absalom and Achitophel*, apparently hoping to influence their verdict. It is worthy of the occasion which produced it. The issues in question were grave; the chief actors, the most important men in the realm. Dryden, therefore, could not use burlesque and caricature as had Butler, or the mock-heroic as he himself had done in *Mac Flecknoe*. Only a heroic style and manner were appropriate to his weighty material, and the poem is most original in its blending of the heroic and the satiric. Dryden's task called for all his tact and literary skill; he had to mention, but to gloss over, the king's faults: his indolence and love of pleasure; his neglect of his wife and his devotion to his mistresses—conduct which had left him with many children, but no heir except his Catholic brother. He had to deal gently with Monmouth, whom Charles still loved. And he had to present, or appear to present, the king's case objectively.

The remarkable parallels between the rebellion of Absalom against his father King David (II Samuel xiii–xviii) had already been remarked in sermons, satires, and pamphlets. Dryden took the hint and gave contemporary events a due distance and additional dignity by approaching them indirectly through their Biblical analogues. The poem is famous for its brilliant portraits of the king's enemies and friends; but equally admirable are the temptation scene (which, like other passages, is indebted to *Paradise Lost*) and the remarkably astute analysis of the Popish Plot itself.

A second part of *Absalom and Achitophel* appeared in 1682. Most of it is the work of Nahum Tate, but lines 310–509, which include the devastating portraits of Doeg and Og (two Whig poets, Elkanah Settle and Thomas Shadwell) are certainly by Dryden.

Absalom and Achitophel: A Poem

In pious times, ere priestcraft did begin,
Before polygamy was made a sin;
When man on many multiplied his kind,
Ere one to one was cursedly confined;
When nature prompted and no law denied   5
Promiscuous use of concubine and bride;
Then Israel's monarch after Heaven's own heart,[1]
His vigorous warmth did variously impart
To wives and slaves; and, wide as his command,
Scattered his Maker's image through the land.   10
Michal,[2] of royal blood, the crown did wear,
A soil ungrateful to the tiller's care:
Not so the rest; for several mothers bore
To godlike David several sons before.
But since like slaves his bed they did ascend,   15
No true succession could their seed attend.

1. David ("a man after [God's] own heart," according to Acts xiii.22) represents Charles II.

2. "Michal," one of David's wives, represents the childless queen, Catherine of Braganza.

Of all this numerous progeny was none
So beautiful, so brave, as Absalom:[3]
Whether, inspired by some diviner lust,
His father got him with a greater gust,[4]   20
Or that his conscious destiny made way,
By manly beauty, to imperial sway.
Early in foreign fields he won renown,
With kings and states allied to Israel's crown:[5]
In peace the thoughts of war he could remove,   25
And seemed as he were only born for love.
Whate'er he did, was done with so much ease,
In him alone 'twas natural to please;
His motions all accompanied with grace;
And paradise was opened in his face.   30
With secret joy indulgent David viewed
His youthful image in his son renewed:
To all his wishes nothing he denied;
And made the charming Annabel[6] his bride.
What faults he had (for who from faults is free?) 35
His father could not, or he would not see.
Some warm excesses which the law forbore,
Were construed youth that purged by boiling o'er:
And Amnon's murther,[7] by a specious name,
Was called a just revenge for injured fame.   40
Thus praised and loved the noble youth remained,
While David, undisturbed, in Sion[8] reigned.
But life can never be sincerely[9] blest;
Heaven punishes the bad, and proves[1] the best.
The Jews,[2] a headstrong, moody, murmuring race, 45
As ever tried the extent and stretch of grace;
God's pampered people, whom, debauched with ease,
No king could govern, nor no God could please
(Gods they had tried of every shape and size
That god-smiths could produce, or priests devise);[3] 50
These Adam-wits,[4] too fortunately free,
Began to dream they wanted liberty;
And when no rule, no precedent was found,
Of men by laws less circumscribed and bound,
They led their wild desires to woods and caves,   55
And thought that all but savages were slaves.
They who, when Saul[5] was dead, without a blow,

3. James Scott, Duke of Monmouth (1649–85).
4. Relish, pleasure.
5. Monmouth had won repute as a soldier fighting for France against Holland and for Holland against France.
6. Anne Scott, Duchess of Buccleuch (pronounced *Bue-cloo*), a beauty and a great heiress.
7. Absalom killed his half-brother Amnon, who had raped Absalom's sister Tamar (II Samuel xiii.28–29). The parallel with Monmouth is vague. He is known to have committed acts of violence in his youth, but certainly not fratricide.
8. London.
9. Wholly.
1. Tests.
2. The English.
3. Dryden recalls the political and religious controversies which, since the Reformation, had divided England and finally caused civil war.
4. Adam rebelled because he felt that he lacked ("wanted") liberty, since he was forbidden to eat the fruit of one tree.
5. Oliver Cromwell. "Ishbosheth": Saul's son; he stands for Richard Cromwell, who succeeded his father as Lord Protector.

Made foolish Ishbosheth the crown forgo;
Who banished David did from Hebron[6] bring,
And with a general shout proclaimed him king: 60
Those very Jews, who, at their very best,
Their humor[7] more than loyalty expressed,
Now wondered why so long they had obeyed
An idol monarch, which their hands had made;
Thought they might ruin him they could create,   65
Or melt him to that golden calf,[8] a state.
But these were random bolts;[9] no formed design
Nor interest made the factious crowd to join:
The sober part of Israel, free from stain,
Well knew the value of a peaceful reign;   70
And, looking backward with a wise affright,
Saw seams of wounds, dishonest[1] to the sight:
In contemplation of whose ugly scars
They cursed the memory of civil wars.
The moderate sort of men, thus qualified,[2]   75
Inclined the balance to the better side;
And David's mildness managed it so well,
The bad found no occasion to rebel.
But when to sin our biased[3] nature leans,
The careful Devil is still at hand with means;   80
And providently pimps for ill desires:
The Good Old Cause[4] revived, a plot requires.
Plots, true or false, are necessary things,
To raise up commonwealths and ruin kings.
    The inhabitants of old Jerusalem   85
Were Jebusites;[5] the town so called from them;
And theirs the native right.
But when the chosen people[6] grew more strong,
The rightful cause at length became the wrong;
And every loss the men of Jebus bore,   90
They still were thought God's enemies the more.
Thus worn and weakened, well or ill content,
Submit they must to David's government:
Impoverished and deprived of all command,
Their taxes doubled as they lost their land;   95
And, what was harder yet to flesh and blood,
Their gods disgraced, and burnt like common wood.[7]
This set the heathen priesthood[8] in a flame;
For priests of all religions are the same:
Of whatsoe'er descent their godhead be,   100

6. Where David reigned over Judah after the death of Saul and before he became king of Israel (II Samuel i–v). Charles had been crowned in Scotland in 1651.
7. Caprice.
8. The image worshiped by the Children of Israel during the period that Moses spent on Mt. Sinai, receiving the law from God. "A state": a republic.
9. Shots.
1. Disgraceful.
2. Assuaged.
3. Inclined. Cf. *Mac Flecknoe*, line 189 and note.
4. The Commonwealth. Dryden stigmatizes the Whigs by associating them with subversion.
5. Roman Catholics. The original name of Jerusalem (here, London) was Jebus.
6. Protestants.
7. Such oppressive laws against Roman Catholics date from the time of Elizabeth I.
8. Roman Catholic clergy.

Stock, stone, or other homely pedigree,
In his defense his servants are as bold,
As if he had been born of beaten gold.
The Jewish rabbins,[9] though their enemies,
In this conclude them honest men and wise: 105
For 'twas their duty, all the learned think,
To espouse his cause, by whom they eat and drink.
From hence began that Plot, the nation's curse,
Bad in itself, but represented worse;
Raised in extremes, and in extremes decried;   110
With oaths affirmed, with dying vows denied;
Not weighed or winnowed by the multitude;
But swallowed in the mass, unchewed and crude.
Some truth there was, but dashed[1] and brewed with lies,
To please the fools, and puzzle all the wise.   115
Succeeding times did equal folly call,
Believing nothing, or believing all.
The Egyptian[2] rites the Jebusites embraced,
Where gods were recommended by their taste.
Such savory deities must needs be good,   120
As served at once for worship and for food.
By force they could not introduce these gods,
For ten to one in former days was odds;
So fraud was used (the sacrificer's trade):
Fools are more hard to conquer than persuade.   125
Their busy teachers mingled with the Jews,
And raked for converts even the court and stews:[3]
Which Hebrew priests the more unkindly took,
Because the fleece accompanies the flock.[4]
Some thought they God's anointed [4a] meant to slay   130
By guns, invented since full many a day:
Our author swears it not; but who can know
How far the Devil and Jebusites may go?
This Plot, which failed for want of common sense,
Had yet a deep and dangerous consequence: 135
For, as when raging fevers boil the blood,
The standing lake soon floats into a flood,
And every hostile humor, which before
Slept quiet in its channels, bubbles o'er;
So several factions from this first ferment   140
Work up to foam, and threat the government.
Some by their friends, more by themselves thought wise,
Opposed the power to which they could not rise.
Some had in courts been great, and thrown from thence,
Like fiends were hardened in impenitence;   145
Some, by their monarch's fatal mercy, grown
From pardoned rebels kinsmen to the throne,
Were raised in power and public office high;

9. Anglican clergy.
1. Adulterated.
2. French, therefore Catholic. In the next line Dryden sneers at the doctrine of transubstantiation.
3. Brothels.
4. Dryden charges that the Anglican clergy ("Hebrew priests") resented proselytizing by Catholics chiefly because they stood to lose their tithes ("fleece").
4a. The King.

Strong bands, if bands ungrateful men could tie.
    Of these the false Achitophel[5] was first;   150
A name to all succeeding ages cursed:
For close designs, and crooked counsels fit;
Sagacious, bold, and turbulent of wit;[6]
Restless, unfixed in principles and place;
In power unpleased, impatient of disgrace: 155
A fiery soul, which, working out its way,
Fretted the pygmy body to decay,
And o'er-informed the tenement of clay.[7]
A daring pilot in extremity;
Pleased with the danger, when the waves went high,   160
He sought the storms; but, for a calm unfit,
Would steer too nigh the sands, to boast his wit.
Great wits[8] are sure to madness near allied,
And thin partitions do their bounds divide;
Else why should he, with wealth and honor blest,   165
Refuse his age the needful hours of rest?
Punish a body which he could not please;
Bankrupt of life, yet prodigal of ease?
And all to leave what with his toil he won,
To that unfeathered two-legged thing,[9] a son;   170
Got, while his soul did huddled[1] notions try;
And born a shapeless lump, like anarchy.
In friendship false, implacable in hate,
Resolved to ruin or to rule the state.
To compass this the triple bond[2] he broke,   175
The pillars of the public safety shook,
And fitted Israel for a foreign yoke;
Then seized with fear, yet still affecting fame,
Usurped a patriot's all-atoning name.
So easy still it proves in factious times,   180
With public zeal to cancel private crimes.
How safe is treason, and how sacred ill,
Where none can sin against the people's will!
Where crowds can wink, and no offense be known,
Since in another's guilt they find their own!   185
Yet fame deserved, no enemy can grudge;
The statesman we abhor, but praise the judge.
In Israel's courts ne'er sat an Abbethdin[3]

5. Anthony Ashley Cooper, 1st Earl of Shaftesbury (1621–83). He had served in the Parliamentary army and been a member of Cromwell's Council of State. He later helped bring back Charles, and in 1670 was made a member of the notorious Cabal Ministry, which formed an alliance with Louis XIV in which England betrayed her ally, Holland, and joined France in war against that country. In 1672 he became Lord Chancellor, but with the dissolulution of the Cabal in 1673 he was removed from office. Lines 146–49 apply perfectly to him.
6. Unruly imagination.
7. The soul is thought of as the animat-

ing principle, the force that puts the body in motion. Shaftesbury's body seemed too small to house his fiery, energetic soul.
8. Men of genius. That genius and madness are akin is a very old idea.
9. Cf. Plato's definition of man: "a featherless biped."
1. Confused, hurried.
2. The Triple Alliance of England, Sweden, and Holland against France, 1668. Shaftesbury helped to bring about the war against Holland in 1672.
3. The chief of the seventy elders who composed the Jewish supreme court. The allusion is to Shaftesbury's serving as Lord Chancellor in 1672–73. Dry-

With more discerning eyes, or hands more clean;
Unbribed, unsought, the wretched to redress;   190
Swift of dispatch, and easy of access.
Oh, had he been content to serve the crown,
With virtues only proper to the gown;
Or had the rankness of the soil been freed
From cockle, that oppressed the noble seed;   195
David for him his tuneful harp had strung,
And Heaven had wanted one immortal song.[4]
But wild Ambition loves to slide, not stand,
And Fortune's ice prefers to Virtue's land.
Achitophel, grown weary to possess   200
A lawful fame, and lazy happiness,
Disdained the golden fruit to gather free,
And lent the crowd his arm to shake the tree.
Now, manifest of[5] crimes contrived long since,
He stood at bold defiance with his prince;   205
Held up the buckler of the people's cause
Against the crown, and skulked behind the laws.
The wished occasion of the Plot he takes;
Some circumstances finds, but more he makes.
By buzzing emissaries fills the ears   210
Of listening crowds with jealousies[6] and fears
Of arbitrary counsels brought to light,
And proves the king himself a Jebusite.
Weak arguments! which yet he knew full well
Were strong with people easy to rebel.   215
For, governed by the moon, the giddy Jews
Tread the same track when she the prime renews;[7]
And once in twenty years, their scribes record,
By natural instinct they change their lord.
Achitophel still wants a chief, and none   220
Was found so fit as warlike Absalom:
Not that he wished his greatness to create
(For politicians neither love nor hate),
But, for he knew his title not allowed,
Would keep him still depending on the crowd,   225
That kingly power, thus ebbing out, might be
Drawn to the dregs of a democracy.[8]
Him he attempts with studied arts to please,
And sheds his venom in such words as these:
    "Auspicious prince, at whose nativity   230
Some royal planet[9] ruled the southern sky;
Thy longing country's darling and desire;

den's praise of Shaftesbury's integrity in this office, by suggesting a balanced judgment, makes his condemnation of the statesman more effective than it might otherwise have been.

4. I.e., David would have had occasion to write one less song of praise to Heaven. The reference may be to II Samuel xxii or to Psalm iv.
5. Detected in.
6. Suspicions.
7. The moon "renews her prime" when her several phases recur on the same day of the solar calendar—i.e., complete a cycle—as happens approximately every twenty years. The crisis between Charles I and Parliament began to grow acute about 1640; Charles II returned in 1660; it is now 1680 and a full cycle has been completed.
8. To Dryden, "democracy" meant popular government. The "dregs of a democracy" would be mob rule.
9. A planet whose influence destines him to kingship.

Their cloudy pillar and their guardian fire:[1]
Their second Moses, whose extended wand
Divides the seas, and shows the promised land;   235
Whose dawning day in every distant age
Has exercised the sacred prophet's rage:
The people's prayer, the glad diviners' theme,
The young men's vision, and the old men's dream![2]
Thee, savior, thee, the nation's vows[3] confess,   240
And, never satisfied with seeing, bless:
Swift unbespoken pomps thy steps proclaim,
And stammering babes are taught to lisp thy name.
How long wilt thou the general joy detain,
Starve and defraud the people of thy reign?   245
Content ingloriously to pass thy days
Like one of Virtue's fools that feeds on praise;
Till thy fresh glories, which now shine so bright,
Grow stale and tarnish with our daily sight.
Believe me, royal youth, thy fruit must be   250
Or gathered ripe, or rot upon the tree.
Heaven has to all allotted, soon or late,
Some lucky revolution of their fate;
Whose motions if we watch and guide with skill
(For human good depends on human will),   255
Our Fortune rolls as from a smooth descent,
And from the first impression takes the bent;
But, if unseized, she glides away like wind,
And leaves repenting Folly far behind.
Now, now she meets you with a glorious prize,   260
And spreads her locks before her as she flies.[4]
Had thus old David, from whose loins you spring,
Not dared, when Fortune called him, to be king,
At Gath[5] an exile he might still remain,
And heaven's anointing[6] oil had been in vain.   265
Let his successful youth your hopes engage;
But shun the example of declining age;
Behold him setting in his western skies,
The shadows lengthening as the vapors rise.
He is not now, as when on Jordan's sand[7]   270
The joyful people thronged to see him land,
Covering the beach, and blackening all the strand;
But, like the Prince of Angels, from his height
Comes tumbling downward with diminished light;[8]

1. After their exodus from Egypt under the leadership of Moses, whose "extended wand" separated the waters of the Red Sea so that they crossed over on dry land, the Israelites were led in their forty-year wandering in the wilderness by a pillar of cloud by day and a pillar of fire by night. See Exodus xiii–xiv.
2. Cf. Joel ii.28.
3. Solemn promises of fidelity.
4. Achitophel gives to Fortune the traditional attributes of the allegorical personification of Opportunity: bald except for a forelock, she can be seized only as she approaches.
5. Brussels, where Charles spent his last years in exile. David took refuge from Saul in Gath (I Samuel xxvii.4).
6. After God rejected Saul, He sent Samuel to anoint the boy David, as a token that he should finally come to the throne (I Samuel xvi.1–13).
7. The seashore at Dover, where Charles landed (May 25, 1660).
8. Cf. the fall of Satan in *Paradise Lost*, which dims the brightness of the archangel. The choice of the undignified word "tumbling" is deliberate.

Betrayed by one poor plot to public scorn   275
(Our only blessing since his cursed return),
Those heaps of people which one sheaf did bind,
Blown off and scattered by a puff of wind.
What strength can he to your designs oppose,
Naked of friends, and round beset with foes?   280
If Pharaoh's[9] doubtful succor he should use,
A foreign aid would more incense the Jews:
Proud Egypt would dissembled friendship bring;
Foment the war, but not support the king:
Nor would the royal party e'er unite   285
With Pharaoh's arms to assist the Jebusite;
Or if they should, their interest soon would break,
And with such odious aid make David weak.
All sorts of men by my successful arts,
Abhorring kings, estrange their altered hearts   290
From David's rule: and 'tis the general cry,
'Religion, commonwealth, and liberty.'[1]
If you, as champion of the public good,
Add to their arms a chief of royal blood,
What may not Israel hope, and what applause   295
Might such a general gain by such a cause?
Not barren praise alone, that gaudy flower
Fair only to the sight, but solid power;
And nobler is a limited command,
Given by the love of all your native land,   300
Than a successive title,[2] long and dark,
Drawn from the moldy rolls of Noah's ark."
　　What cannot praise effect in mighty minds,
When flattery soothes, and when ambition blinds!
Desire of power, on earth a vicious weed,   305
Yet, sprung from high, is of celestial seed:
In God 'tis glory; and when men aspire,
'Tis but a spark too much of heavenly fire.
The ambitious youth, too covetous of fame,
Too full of angels' metal[3] in his frame,   310
Unwarily was led from virtue's ways,
Made drunk with honor, and debauched with praise.
Half loath, and half consenting to the ill
(For loyal blood within him struggled still),
He thus replied: "And what pretense have I   315
To take up arms for public liberty?
My father governs with unquestioned right;
The faith's defender, and mankind's delight,
Good, gracious, just, observant of the laws:
And heaven by wonders has espoused his cause.   320
Whom has he wronged in all his peaceful reign?
Who sues for justice to his throne in vain?
What millions has he pardoned of his foes,

9. Louis XIV of France.
1. Cf. line 82 and note.
2. A title to the crown based on succession.
3. An alternative spelling of *mettle*, (i.e., spirit). But a pun on "metal" is intended, as is obvious from the pun "angel" (a purely intellectual being and a coin). Ambition caused the revolt of the angels in heaven.

Whom just revenge did to his wrath expose?
Mild, easy, humble, studious of our good,   325
Inclined to mercy, and averse from blood;
If mildness ill with stubborn Israel suit,
His crime is God's beloved attribute.
What could he gain, his people to betray,
Or change his right for arbitrary sway?   330
Let haughty Pharaoh curse with such a reign
His fruitful Nile, and yoke a servile train.
If David's rule Jerusalem displease,
The Dog Star[4] heats their brains to this disease.
Why then should I, encouraging the bad,   335
Turn rebel and run popularly mad?
Were he a tyrant, who, by lawless might
Oppressed the Jews, and raised the Jebusite,
Well might I mourn; but nature's holy bands
Would curb my spirits and restrain my hands: 340
The people might assert[5] their liberty,
But what was right in them were crime in me.
His favor leaves me nothing to require,
Prevents my wishes, and outruns desire.
What more can I expect while David lives?   345
All but his kingly diadem he gives:
And that"— But there he paused; then sighing, said—
"Is justly destined for a worthier head.
For when my father from his toils shall rest
And late augment the number of the blest,   350
His lawful issue shall the throne ascend,
Or the collateral line,[6] where that shall end.
His brother, though oppressed with vulgar spite,
Yet dauntless, and secure of native right,
Of every royal virtue stands possessed;   355
Still dear to all the bravest and the best.
His courage foes, his friends his truth proclaim;
His loyalty the king, the world his fame.
His mercy even the offending crowd will find,
For sure he comes of a forgiving kind.[7]   360
Why should I then repine at heaven's decree,
Which gives me no pretense to royalty?
Yet O that fate, propitiously inclined,
Had raised my birth, or had debased my mind;
To my large soul not all her treasure lent,   365
And then betrayed it to a mean descent!
I find, I find my mounting spirits bold,
And David's part disdains my mother's mold.
Why am I scanted by a niggard birth?[8]

4. Sirius, which in midsummer rises and sets with the sun and is thus associated with the maddening heat of the "dog days."
5. Claim.
6. In the event of Charles's dying without legitimate issue, the throne would constitutionally pass to his brother James, or his descendants, the "collateral line."
7. Race, in the sense of family.
8. I.e., why am I limited by a sordid birth?

My soul disclaims the kindred of her earth; 370
And, made for empire, whispers me within,
'Desire of greatness is a godlike sin.' "
    Him staggering so when hell's dire agent found,[9]
While fainting Virtue scarce maintained her ground,
He pours fresh forces in, and thus replies: 375
    "The eternal God, supremely good and wise,
Imparts not these prodigious gifts in vain:
What wonders are reserved to bless your reign!
Against your will, your arguments have shown,
Such virtue's only given to guide a throne. 380
Not that your father's mildness I contemn,
But manly force becomes the diadem.
'Tis true he grants the people all they crave;
And more, perhaps, than subjects ought to have:
For lavish grants suppose a monarch tame, 385
And more his goodness than his wit[1] proclaim.
But when should people strive their bonds to break,
If not when kings are negligent or weak?
Let him give on till he can give no more,
The thrifty Sanhedrin[2] shall keep him poor; 390
And every shekel which he can receive,
Shall cost a limb of his prerogative.[3]
To ply him with new plots shall be my care;
Or plunge him deep in some expensive war;
Which when his treasure can no more supply, 395
He must, with the remains of kingship, buy.
His faithful friends our jealousies and fears
Call Jebusites, and Pharaoh's pensioners;
Whom when our fury from his aid has torn,
He shall be naked left to public scorn. 400
The next successor, whom I fear and hate,
My arts have made obnoxious to the state;
Turned all his virtues to his overthrow,
And gained our elders[4] to pronounce a foe.
His right, for sums of necessary gold, 405
Shall first be pawned, and afterward be sold;
Till time shall ever-wanting David draw,
To pass your doubtful title into law:
If not, the people have a right supreme
To make their kings; for kings are made for them. 410
All empire is no more than power in trust,
Which, when resumed, can be no longer just.
Succession, for the general good designed,
In its own wrong a nation cannot bind;
If altering that the people can relieve, 415
Better one suffer than a nation grieve.

9. Observe the Miltonic inversion, which helps to maintain the epic tone.
1. Intelligence.
2. The highest judicial counsel of the Jews; here, Parliament.
3. The Whigs hoped to limit the special privileges of the Crown (the royal "prerogative") by refusing to vote money to Charles. He circumvented them by living on French subsidies and refusing to summon Parliament.
4. The chief magistrates and rulers of the Jews. Shaftesbury had won over ("gained") country gentlemen and nobles to his hostile view of James.

The Jews well know their power: ere Saul they chose,[5]
God was their king, and God they durst depose.
Urge now your piety,[6] your filial name,
A father's right, and fear of future fame;   420
The public good, that universal call,
To which even heaven submitted, answers all.
Nor let his love enchant your generous mind;
'Tis Nature's trick to propagate her kind.
Our fond begetters, who would never die,   425
Love but themselves in their posterity.
Or let his kindness by the effects be tried,
Or let him lay his vain pretense aside.
God said he loved your father; could he bring
A better proof than to anoint him king?   430
It surely showed he loved the shepherd well,
Who gave so fair a flock as Israel.
Would David have you thought his darling son?
What means he then, to alienate[7] the crown?
The name of godly he may blush to bear: 435
'Tis after God's own heart[8] to cheat his heir.
He to his brother gives supreme command;
To you a legacy of barren land,[8a]
Perhaps the old harp, on which he thrums his lays,
Or some dull Hebrew ballad in your praise.   440
Then the next heir, a prince severe and wise,
Already looks on you with jealous eyes;
Sees through the thin disguises of your arts,
And marks your progress in the people's hearts.
Though now his mighty soul its grief contains,   445
He meditates revenge who least complains;
And, like a lion, slumbering in the way,
Or sleep dissembling, while he waits his prey,
His fearless foes within his distance draws,
Constrains his roaring, and contracts his paws;   450
Till at the last, his time for fury found,
He shoots with sudden vengeance from the ground;
The prostrate vulgar[9] passes o'er and spares,
But with a lordly rage his hunters tears.
Your case no tame expedients will afford: 455
Resolve on death, or conquest by the sword,
Which for no less a stake than life you draw;
And self-defense is nature's eldest law.
Leave the warm people no considering time;
For then rebellion may be thought a crime.   460
Prevail yourself of what occasion gives,
But try your title while your father lives;
And that your arms may have a fair pretense,[1]

5. Before Saul, the first king of Israel, came to the throne, the Jews were governed by judges. Similarly Oliver Cromwell ("Saul") as Lord Protector took over the reins of government, after he had dissolved the Rump Parliament in 1653.
6. Dutifulness to a parent.

7. In law, to convey the title to property to another person.
8. An irony: cf. line 7, note.
8a. James was given the title of generalissimo in 1678. In 1679 Monmouth was banished and withdrew to Holland.
9. Common people.
1. Pretext.

Proclaim you take them in the king's defense;
Whose sacred life each minute would expose   465
To plots, from seeming friends, and secret foes.
And who can sound the depth of David's soul?
Perhaps his fear his kindness may control.
He fears his brother, though he loves his son,
For plighted vows too late to be undone.   470
If so, by force he wishes to be gained,
Like women's lechery, to seem constrained.[2]
Doubt not; but when he most affects the frown,
Commit a pleasing rape upon the crown.
Secure his person to secure your cause: 475
They who possess the prince, possess the laws."
    He said, and this advice above the rest
With Absalom's mild nature suited best:
Unblamed of life (ambition set aside),
Not stained with cruelty, nor puffed with pride,   480
How happy had he been, if destiny
Had higher placed his birth, or not so high!
His kingly virtues might have claimed a throne,
And blest all other countries but his own.
But charming greatness since so few refuse,   485
'Tis juster to lament him than accuse.
Strong were his hopes a rival to remove,
With blandishments to gain the public love;
To head the faction while their zeal was hot,
And popularly prosecute the Plot.   490
To further this, Achitophel unites
The malcontents of all the Israelites;
Whose differing parties he could wisely join,
For several ends, to serve the same design:
The best (and of the princes some were such),   495
Who thought the power of monarchy too much;
Mistaken men, and patriots in their hearts;
Not wicked, but seduced by impious arts.
By these the springs of property were bent,
And wound so high, they cracked the government.   500
The next for interest sought to embroil the state,
To sell their duty at a dearer rate;
And make their Jewish markets of the throne,
Pretending public good, to serve their own.
Others thought kings an useless heavy load,   505
Who cost too much, and did too little good.
These were for laying honest David by,
On principles of pure good husbandry.[3]
With them joined all the haranguers of the throng,
That thought to get preferment by the tongue.   510
Who follow next, a double danger bring,
Not only hating David, but the king:
The Solymaean rout,[4] well-versed of old
In godly faction, and in treason bold;

2. Forced.
3. Economy.
4. I.e., London rabble. Solyma was a name for Jerusalem.

Cowering and quaking at a conqueror's sword,   515
But lofty to a lawful prince restored;
Saw with disdain an ethnic[5] plot begun,
And scorned by Jebusites to be outdone.
Hot Levites[6] headed these; who, pulled before
From the ark, which in the Judges' days they bore,   520
Resumed their cant, and with a zealous cry
Pursued their old beloved theocracy:
Where Sanhedrin and priest enslaved the nation,
And justified their spoils by inspiration:[7]
For who so fit for reign as Aaron's race,[8]   525
If once dominion they could found in grace?
These led the pack; though not of surest scent,
Yet deepest-mouthed[9] against the government.
A numerous host of dreaming saints[1] succeed,
Of the true old enthusiastic breed: 530
'Gainst form and order they their power employ,
Nothing to build, and all things to destroy.
But far more numerous was the herd of such,
Who think too little, and who talk too much.
These out of mere instinct, they knew not why,   535
Adored their fathers' God and property;
And, by the same blind benefit of fate,
The Devil and the Jebusite did hate:
Born to be saved, even in their own despite,
Because they could not help believing right.   540
Such were the tools; but a whole Hydra more
Remains, of sprouting heads too long to score.
Some of their chiefs were princes of the land:
In the first rank of these did Zimri[2] stand;
A man so various, that he seemed to be   545
Not one, but all mankind's epitome:
Stiff in opinions, always in the wrong;

5. Gentile; here, Roman Catholic.

6. I.e., Presbyterian clergymen. The tribe of Levi, assigned to duties in the tabernacle, carried the ark of the covenant during the forty-year sojourn in the wilderness (Numbers iv). Under the Commonwealth ("in the Judges' days") Presbyterianism became the state religion, and its clergy therefore "bore the ark." The Act of Uniformity (1662) forced the Presbyterian clergy out of their livings: in short, before the Popish Plot, they had been "pulled from the ark." They are represented here as joining the Whigs in the hope of restoring the Commonwealth, "their old beloved theocracy."

7. Observe in these lines the cluster of disparaging words: "cant," "zealous," "inspiration." Dryden shared Samuel Butler's contempt for the irrationality of Dissenters.

8. Priests had to be descendants of Aaron (Exodus xxviii.1; Numbers xviii.7).

9. Loudest. The phrase is applied to hunting dogs. "Pack" and "scent" sustain the image.

1. A term used by certain Dissenters for those elected to salvation. The extreme fanaticism of the "saints" and their claims to inspiration are characterized as a form of religious madness ("enthusiastic").

2. George Villiers, 2nd Duke of Buckingham (1628–87), wealthy, brilliant, dissolute, unstable. He had been an influential member of the Cabal, but after 1673 had joined Shaftesbury in opposition to the Court party. This is the least political of the satirical portraits in the poem. Buckingham had been the chief author of *The Rehearsal* (1671), the play which satirized the heroic play and ridiculed Dryden in the character of Mr. Bayes. Politics gave Dryden an opportunity to retaliate. He comments on this portrait in his *Discourse Concerning the Original and Progress of Satire.* Dryden had two Biblical Zimris in mind: the Zimri destroyed for his lustfulness and blasphemy (Numbers xxv) and the conspirator and regicide of I Kings xvi.8–20 and II Kings ix.31.

Was everything by starts, and nothing long;
But, in the course of one revolving moon,
Was chymist,[3] fiddler, statesman, and buffoon: 550
Then all for women, painting, rhyming, drinking,
Besides ten thousand freaks that died in thinking.
Blest madman, who could every hour employ,
With something new to wish, or to enjoy!
Railing[4] and praising were his usual themes;   555
And both (to show his judgment) in extremes:
So over-violent, or over-civil,
That every man, with him, was God or Devil.
In squandering wealth was his peculiar art:
Nothing went unrewarded but desert.   560
Beggared by fools, whom still he found[5] too late,
He had his jest, and they had his estate.
He laughed himself from court; then sought relief
By forming parties, but could ne'er be chief;
For, spite of him, the weight of business fell   565
On Absalom and wise Achitophel:
Thus, wicked but in will, of means bereft,
He left not faction, but of that was left.
    Titles and names 'twere tedious to rehearse
Of lords, below the dignity of verse.   570
Wits, warriors, Commonwealth's men, were the best;
Kind husbands, and mere nobles, all the rest.
And therefore, in the name of dullness, be
The well-hung Balaam and cold Caleb, free;
And canting Nadab[6] let oblivion damn,   575
Who made new porridge for the paschal lamb.
Let friendship's holy band some names assure;
Some their own worth, and some let scorn secure.
Nor shall the rascal rabble here have place,
Whom kings no titles gave, and God no grace: 580
Not bull-faced Jonas,[7] who could statutes draw
To mean rebellion, and make treason law.
But he, though bad, is followed by a worse,
The wretch who heaven's anointed dared to curse:
Shimei,[8] whose youth did early promise bring   585
Of zeal to God and hatred to his king,
Did wisely from expensive sins refrain,

3. Chemist.
4. Reviling, abusing.
5. **Found out; "still": constantly.**
6. The identities of Balaam, Caleb, and Nadab have not been certainly established, although various Whig nobles have been suggested. For Balaam see Numbers xxii–xxiv; for Caleb, Numbers xiii–xiv; for Nadab, Leviticus x.1–2. "Well-hung" may mean "fluent of speech" or "sexually potent" or both; "cold" would contrast with the second meaning of "well-hung." "Canting" points to a Nonconformist, as does the obscure line 576, for Dissenters referred to the Book of Common Prayer contemptuously as "porridge," a hodgepodge, unsubstantial stuff. The "paschal lamb," the lamb slain at the Passover, is Christ.
7. Sir William Jones, Attorney General, had been largely responsible for the passage of the first Exclusion Bill by the House of Commons. He prosecuted the accused in the Popish Plot.
8. Shimei cursed and stoned David when he fled into the wilderness during Absalom's revolt (II Samuel xvi.5–14); his name is used here for one of the two sheriffs of London, Slingsby Bethel, a Whig, former republican, and virulent enemy of Charles. He packed juries with Whigs and so secured the acquittal of enemies of the court, among them Shaftesbury himself.

And never broke the Sabbath, but for gain;
Nor ever was he known an oath to vent,
Or curse, unless against the government.   590
Thus heaping wealth, by the most ready way
Among the Jews, which was to cheat and pray,
The city, to reward his pious hate
Against his master, chose him magistrate.
His hand a vare[9] of justice did uphold;   595
His neck was loaded with a chain of gold.
During his office, treason was no crime;
The sons of Belial[1] had a glorious time;
For Shimei, though not prodigal of pelf,
Yet loved his wicked neighbor as himself.   600
When two or three were gathered to declaim ⎫
Against the monarch of Jerusalem,   ⎬
Shimei was always in the midst of them;   ⎭
And if they cursed the king when he was by,
Would rather curse than break good company.   605
If any durst his factious friends accuse,
He packed a jury of dissenting Jews;
Whose fellow-feeling in the godly cause
Would free the suffering saint from human laws.
For laws are only made to punish those   610
Who serve the king, and to protect his foes.
If any leisure time he had from power
(Because 'tis sin to misemploy an hour),
His business was, by writing, to persuade
That kings were useless, and a clog to trade;   615
And, that his noble style he might refine,
No Rechabite[2] more shunned the fumes of wine.
Chaste were his cellars, and his shrieval board[3]
The grossness of a city feast abhorred:
His cooks, with long disuse, their trade forgot;   620
Cool was his kitchen, though his brains were hot.
Such frugal virtue malice may accuse,
But sure 'twas necessary to the Jews:
For towns once burnt[4] such magistrates require
As dare not tempt God's providence by fire.   625
With spiritual food he fed his servants well,
But free from flesh that made the Jews rebel;
And Moses' laws he held in more account,
For forty days of fasting in the mount.[5]
To speak the rest, who better are forgot,   630
Would tire a well-breathed witness of the Plot.
    Yet, Corah,[6] thou shalt from oblivion pass:

9. Staff.
1. Sons of wickedness. Cf. Milton, *Paradise Lost* I.490–505. Dryden probably intended a pun on Balliol, the Oxford college in which leading Whigs stayed during the brief and fateful meeting of Parliament at Oxford in 1681.
2. An austere Jewish sect that drank

no wine (Jeremiah xxxv.2–19).
3. Sheriff's dinner table.
4. London burned in 1666.
5. Mt. Sinai, where, during a fast of forty days, Moses received the law (Exodus xxxiv.28).
6. Or Korah, a rebellious Levite, swallowed up by the earth because of his

Erect thyself, thou monumental brass,
High as the serpent of thy metal made,[7]
While nations stand secure beneath thy shade.   635
What though his birth were base, yet comets rise
From earthy vapors, ere they shine in skies.
Prodigious actions may as well be done
By weaver's issue,[8] as by prince's son.
This arch-attestor for the public good   640
By that one deed ennobles all his blood.
Who ever asked the witnesses' high race
Whose oath with martyrdom did Stephen grace?[9]
Ours was a Levite, and as times went then,
His tribe were God Almighty's gentlemen.   645
Sunk were his eyes, his voice was harsh and loud,
Sure signs he neither choleric[1] was nor proud:
His long chin proved his wit; his saintlike grace
A church vermilion, and a Moses' face.[2]
His memory, miraculously great,   650
Could plots, exceeding man's belief, repeat;
Which therefore cannot be accounted lies,
For human wit could never such devise.
Some future truths are mingled in his book;
But where the witness failed, the prophet spoke: 655
Some things like visionary flights appear;
The spirit caught him up, the Lord knows where,
And gave him his rabbinical degree,
Unknown to foreign university.[3]
His judgment yet his memory did excel;   660
Which pieced his wondrous evidence so well,
And suited to the temper of the times,
Then groaning under Jebusitic crimes.
Let Israel's foes suspect his heavenly call,
And rashly judge his writ apocryphal;[4]   665
Our laws for such affronts have forfeits made:
He takes his life, who takes away his trade.
Were I myself in witness Corah's place,
The wretch who did me such a dire disgrace
Should whet my memory, though once forgot,   670
To make him an appendix of my plot.
His zeal to heaven made him his prince despise,
And load his person with indignities;

crimes (Numbers xvi). Corah is Titus
Oates, the self-appointed, perjured, and
"well-breathed" (long-winded) witness
of the Plot.
7. Moses erected a brazen serpent to
heal the Jews bitten by fiery serpents
(Numbers xxi.4–9). "Brass" also means
"impudence" or "shamelessness."
8. Oates's father, a clergyman, belonged
to an obscure family of ribbon weavers.
9. The first Christian martyr, accused
by false witnesses (Acts vi–vii).

1. Prone to anger.
2. Moses' face shone when he came
down from Mt. Sinai with the tables of
the law (Exodus xxxiv.29–30). Oates's
face suggests high living, not spiritual
illumination.
3. Oates falsely claimed to be a Doctor
of Divinity in the University of Sala-
manca.
4. Not inspired, and hence excluded
from Holy Writ.

But zeal peculiar privilege affords,
Indulging latitude to deeds and words;   675
And Corah might for Agag's murder [5] call,
In terms as coarse as Samuel used to Saul.
What others in his evidence did join
(The best that could be had for love or coin),
In Corah's own predicament will fall;   680
For *witness* is a common name to all.

   Surrounded thus with friends of every sort,
Deluded Absalom forsakes the court:
Impatient of high hopes, urged with renown,
And fired with near possession of a crown.   685
The admiring crowd are dazzled with surprise,
And on his goodly person feed their eyes:
His joy concealed, he sets himself to show,
On each side bowing popularly [6] low;
His looks, his gestures, and his words he frames,   690
And with familiar ease repeats their names.
Thus formed by nature, furnished out with arts,
He glides unfelt into their secret hearts.
Then, with a kind compassionating look,
And sighs, bespeaking pity ere he spoke,   695
Few words he said; but easy those and fit,
More slow than Hybla-drops,[7] and far more sweet.

   "I mourn, my countrymen, your lost estate;
Though far unable to prevent your fate:
Behold a banished man, for your dear cause   700
Exposed a prey to arbitrary laws!
Yet oh! that I alone could be undone,
Cut off from empire, and no more a son!
Now all your liberties a spoil are made; ⎤
Egypt and Tyrus [8] intercept your trade, ⎬   705
And Jebusites your sacred rites invade. ⎦
My father, whom with reverence yet I name,
Charmed into ease, is careless of his fame;
And, bribed with petty sums of foreign gold,
Is grown in Bathsheba's [9] embraces old;   710
Exalts his enemies, his friends destroys;
And all his power against himself employs.
He gives, and let him give, my right away;
But why should he his own, and yours betray?
He only, he can make the nation bleed,   715
And he alone from my revenge is freed.
Take then my tears (with that he wiped his eyes),

---

5. Agag is probably one of the five Catholic peers executed for the Popish Plot in 1680, most likely Lord Stafford, against whom Oates fabricated testimony; almost certainly not, as is usually suggested, Sir Edmund Berry Godfrey (cf. title note). For "Agag's murder" and Samuel's coarse terms to Saul, see I Samuel xv.

6. "So as to please the crowd" (Johnson's *Dictionary*).
7. The famous honey of Hybla in Sicily.
8. France and Holland.
9. With whom David committed adultery (II Samuel xi); here, Charles II's French mistress, Louise de Keroualle, Duchess of Portsmouth.

'Tis all the aid my present power supplies:
No court-informer can these arms accuse;
These arms may sons against their fathers use: 720
And 'tis my wish, the next successor's reign
May make no other Israelite complain."
    Youth, beauty, graceful action seldom fail;
But common interest always will prevail;
And pity never ceases to be shown   725
To him who makes the people's wrongs his own.
The crowd (that still believe their kings oppress),
With lifted hands their young Messiah bless:
Who now begins his progress to ordain
With chariots, horsemen, and a numerous train;   730
From east to west his glories he displays,[1]
And, like the sun, the promised land surveys.
Fame runs before him as the morning star,
And shouts of joy salute him from afar:
Each house receives him as a guardian god,   735
And consecrates the place of his abode:
But hospitable treats did most commend
Wise Issachar,[2] his wealthy western friend.
This moving court, that caught the people's eyes,
And seemed but pomp, did other ends disguise: 740
Achitophel had formed it, with intent
To sound the depths, and fathom where it went,
The people's hearts; distinguish friends from foes,
And try their strength, before they came to blows.
Yet all was colored with a smooth pretense   745
Of specious love, and duty to their prince.
Religion, and redress of grievances,
Two names that always cheat and always please,
Are often urged; and good King David's life
Endangered by a brother and a wife.[3]   750
Thus, in a pageant show, a plot is made,
And peace itself is war in masquerade.
O foolish Israel! never warned by ill,
Still the same bait, and circumvented still!
Did ever men forsake their present ease,   755
In midst of health imagine a disease;
Take pains contingent mischiefs to foresee,
Make heirs for monarchs, and for God decree?
What shall we think! [4] Can people give away
Both for themselves and sons, their native sway?   760
Then they are left defenseless to the sword
Of each unbounded, arbitrary lord:

1. In 1680 Monmouth made a progress through the west of England, seeking popular support for his cause.
2. Thomas Thynne of Longleat. He entertained Monmouth on his journey in the west. "Wise" is, of course, ironic.
3. Titus Oates had sworn that both James, Duke of York, and the Queen were involved in a plot to poison Charles II.
4. In the passage that follows, Dryden states his political philosophy. He bases the royal authority on a covenant entered into by the governor and the governed.

And laws are vain, by which we right enjoy,
If kings unquestioned can those laws destroy.
Yet if the crowd be judge of fit and just,   765
And kings are only officers in trust,
Then this resuming covenant was declared
When kings were made, or is forever barred.
If those who gave the scepter could not tie
By their own deed their own posterity,   770
How then could Adam bind his future race?
How could his forfeit on mankind take place?
Or how could heavenly justice damn us all,
Who ne'er consented to our father's fall?
Then kings are slaves to those whom they command,   775
And tenants to their people's pleasure stand.
Add, that the power for property allowed
Is mischievously seated in the crowd;
For who can be secure of private right,
If sovereign sway may be dissolved by might?   780
Nor is the people's judgment always true:
The most may err as grossly as the few;
And faultless kings run down, by common cry,
For vice, oppression, and for tyranny.
What standard is there in a fickle rout,   785
Which, flowing to the mark,[5] runs faster out?
Nor only crowds, but Sanhedrins may be
Infected with this public lunacy,
And share the madness of rebellious times,
To murder monarchs for imagined crimes.[6]   790
If they may give and take whene'er they please,
Not kings alone (the Godhead's images),
But government itself at length must fall
To nature's state, where all have right to all.
Yet, grant our lords the people kings can make,   795
What prudent men a settled throne would shake?
For whatsoe'er their sufferings were before,
That change they covet makes them suffer more.
All other errors but disturb a state,
But innovation is the blow of fate.   800
If ancient fabrics nod, and threat to fall,
To patch the flaws, and buttress up the wall,
Thus far 'tis duty; but here fix the mark;
For all beyond it is to touch our ark.[7]
To change foundations, cast the frame anew,   805
Is work for rebels, who base ends pursue,
At once divine and human laws control,
And mend the parts by ruin of the whole.

---

5. An obscure couplet, rare in Dryden.
George R. Noyes paraphrases it thus:
"The fickle crowd is apparently compared to water, which, after rising to the
mark, or boundary, it was intended to
reach, overflows all the faster."

6. An allusion to the execution of
Charles I.
7. Uzzah was struck dead because he
sacrilegiously touched the Ark of the
Covenant. II Samuel vi. 6–7.

The tampering world is subject to this curse,
To physic their disease into a worse.   810
    Now what relief can righteous David bring?
How fatal 'tis to be too good a king!
Friends he has few, so high the madness grows:
Who dare be such, must be the people's foes:
Yet some there were, even in the worst of days;   815
Some let me name, and naming is to praise.
    In this short file Barzillai [8] first appears;
Barzillai, crowned with honor and with years:
Long since, the rising rebels he withstood
In regions waste, beyond the Jordan's flood: 820
Unfortunately brave to buoy the State;
But sinking underneath his master's fate:
In exile with his godlike prince he mourned;
For him he suffered, and with him returned.
The court he practiced, not the courtier's art: 825
Large was his wealth, but larger was his heart:
Which well the noblest objects knew to choose,
The fighting warrior, and recording Muse.
His bed could once a fruitful issue boast;
Now more than half a father's name is lost.   830
His eldest hope,[9] with every grace adorned,
By me (so Heaven will have it) always mourned,
And always honored, snatched in manhood's prime
By unequal fates, and Providence's crime:
Yet not before the goal of honor won,   ⎫   835
All parts fulfilled of subject and of son;   ⎬
Swift was the race, but short the time to run. ⎭
O narrow circle, but of power divine,
Scanted in space, but perfect in thy line!
By sea, by land, thy matchless worth was known,   840
Arms thy delight, and war was all thy own:
Thy force, infused, the fainting Tyrians [1] propped;
And haughty Pharaoh found his fortune stopped.
Oh ancient honor! Oh unconquered hand,
Whom foes unpunished never could withstand!   845
But Israel was unworthy of thy name:
Short is the date of all immoderate fame.
It looks as Heaven our ruin had designed,
And durst not trust thy fortune and thy mind.
Now, free from earth, thy disencumbered soul   850
Mounts up, and leaves behind the clouds and starry pole:
From thence thy kindred legions mayst thou bring,
To aid the guardian angel of thy king.
Here stop my Muse, here cease thy painful flight;

8. James Butler, Duke of Ormond (1610–88). He was famous for his loyalty to the Stuart cause. He fought for Charles I in Ireland, and when that cause was hopeless, he joined Charles II in his exile abroad. He spent a large fortune in behalf of the King and continued to serve him loyally after the Restoration.
9. Ormond's son, Thomas, Earl of Ossory (1634–80), a famous soldier, and like his father devoted to Charles II.
1. The Dutch.

No pinions can pursue immortal height;   855
Tell good Barzillai thou canst sing no more,
And tell thy soul she should have fled before:
Or fled she with his life, and left this verse
To hang on her departed patron's hearse?
Now take thy steepy flight from heaven, and see   860
If thou canst find on earth another *he*:
Another *he* would be too hard to find;
See then whom thou canst see not far behind.
Zadoc the priest,[2] whom, shunning power and place,
His lowly mind advanced to David's grace: 865
With him the Sagan of Jerusalem,
Of hospitable soul, and noble stem;
Him of the western dome, whose weighty sense
Flows in fit words and heavenly eloquence.
The prophets' sons, by such example led,   870
To learning and to loyalty were bred:
For colleges on bounteous kinds depend,
And never rebel was to arts a friend.
To these succeed the pillars of the laws,
Who best could plead, and best can judge a cause.   875
Next them a train of loyal peers ascend;
Sharp-judging Adriel, the Muses' friend,
Himself a Muse—in Sanhedrin's debate
True to his prince, but not a slave of state:
Whom David's love with honors did adorn,   880
That from his disobedient son were torn.
Jotham of piercing wit, and pregnant thought,
Indued by nature, and by learning taught
To move assemblies, who but only tried
The worse a while, then chose the better side;   885
Nor chose alone, but turned the balance too;
So much the weight of one brave man can do.
Hushai, the friend of David in distress,
In public storms, of manly steadfastness:
By foreign treaties he informed his youth,   890
And joined experience to his native truth.
His frugal care supplied the wanting throne,
Frugal for that, but bounteous of his own:
'Tis easy conduct when exchequers flow,
But hard the task to manage well the low;   895
For sovereign power is too depressed or high,
When kings are forced to sell, or crowds to buy.
Indulge one labor more, my weary Muse,
For Amiel: who can Amiel's praise refuse?
Of ancient race by birth, but nobler yet   900

2. William Sancroft, Archbishop of Canterbury; the Sagan is Henry Compton, Bishop of London; "Him of the western dome" is John Dolben, Dean of Westminster; "The prophets' sons" are the boys of Westminster School, which Dryden had attended; Adriel is John Sheffield, Earl of Mulgrave; Jotham, George Savile, Marquis of Halifax; Hushai, Laurence Hyde, Earl of Rochester; and Amiel is Edward Seymour, Speaker of the House of Commons.

In his own worth, and without title great:
The Sanhedrin long time as chief he ruled,
Their reason guided, and their passion cooled:
So dexterous was he in the crown's defence,
So formed to speak a loyal nation's sense,   905
That, as their band was Israel's tribes in small,
So fit was he to represent them all.
Now rasher charioteers the seat ascend,
Whose loose careers his steady skill commend:
They like the unequal ruler of the day,   910
Misguide the seasons, and mistake the way;
While he withdrawn at their mad labor smiles,
And safe enjoys the sabbath of his toils.
   These were the chief, a small but faithful band ⎫
Of worthies, in the breach who dared to stand, ⎬   915
And tempt the united fury of the land.   ⎭
With grief they viewed such powerful engines bent,
To batter down the lawful government:
A numerous faction, with pretended frights,
In Sanhedrins to plume the regal rights;   920
The true successor from the court removed: [3]
The Plot, by hireling witnesses, improved.
These ills they saw, and, as their duty bound,
They showed the king the danger of the wound:
That no concessions from the throne would please,   925
But lenitives [4] fomented the disease;
That Absalom, ambitious of the crown,
Was made the lure to draw the people down;
That false Achitophel's pernicious hate
Had turned the Plot to ruin Church and State: 930
The council violent, the rabble worse;
That Shimei taught Jerusalem to curse.
   With all these loads of injuries oppressed,
And long revolving in his careful breast,
The event of things, at last, his patience tired,   935
Thus from his royal throne, by Heaven inspired,
The godlike David spoke: with awful fear
His train their Maker in their master hear.
   "Thus long have I, by native mercy swayed,
My wrongs dissembled, my revenge delayed: 940
So willing to forgive the offending age,
So much the father did the king assuage.
But now so far my clemency they slight,
The offenders question my forgiving right.
That one was made for many, they contend;   945
But 'tis to rule; for that's a monarch's end.
They call my tenderness of blood, my fear;
Though manly tempers can the longest bear.
Yet, since they will divert my native course,

3. The Duke of York had been banished   4. Any medicine that relieves pain.
from England.

'Tis time to show I am not good by force.   950
Those heaped affronts that haughty subjects bring,
Are burdens for a camel, not a king:
Kings are the public pillars of the State,
Born to sustain and prop the nation's weight:
If my young Samson will pretend a call   955
To shake the column, let him share the fall: [5]
But, oh, that yet he would repent and live!
How easy 'tis for parents to forgive!
With how few tears a pardon might be won
From nature, pleading for a darling son!   960
Poor pitied youth, by my paternal care
Raised up to all the height his frame could bear:
Had God ordained his fate for empire born,
He would have given his soul another turn:
Gulled [6] with a patriot's name, whose modern sense
Is one that would by law supplant his prince: 965
The people's brave, the politician's tool;
Never was patriot yet, but was a fool.
Whence comes it that religion and the laws
Should more be Absalom's than David's cause?   970
His old instructor, ere he lost his place,
Was never thought indued with so much grace.[7]
Good heavens, how faction can a patriot paint!
My rebel ever proves my people's saint:
Would *they* impose an heir upon the throne?   975
Let Sanhedrins be taught to give their own.
A king's at least a part of government,
And mine as requisite as their consent;
Without my leave a future king to choose,
Infers a right the present to depose: 980
True, they petition me to approve their choice;
But Esau's hands suit ill with Jacob's voice.[8]
My pious subjects for my safety pray,
Which to secure, they take my power away.
From plots and treasons Heaven preserve my years,   985
But save me most from my petitioners.
Unsatiate as the barren womb or grave;
God cannot grant so much as they can crave.
What then is left but with a jealous eye
To guard the small remains of royalty?   990
The law shall still direct my peaceful sway,
And the same law teach rebels to obey:
Votes shall no more established power control—
Such votes as make a part exceed the whole:
No groundless clamors shall my friends remove,   995
Nor crowds have power to punish ere they prove:
For gods and godlike kings, their care express,
Still to defend their servants in distress.

5. Judges xvi.   7. The Earl of Shaftesbury.
6. Deceived.   8. Genesis xxvii. 22.

O that my power to saving were confined:
Why am I forced, like Heaven, against my mind,
To make examples of another kind?
Must I at length the sword of justice draw?
O curst effects of necessary law!
How ill my fear they by my mercy scan!
Beware the fury of a patient man.   1005
Law they require, let Law then show her face;
They could not be content to look on Grace,
Her hinder parts, but with a daring eye
To tempt the terror of her front and die.[9]
By their own arts, 'tis righteously decreed,   1010
Those dire artificers of death shall bleed.
Against themselves their witnesses will swear,
Till viper-like their mother Plot they tear:
And suck for nutriment that bloody gore,
Which was their principle of life before.   1015
Their Belial with their Belzebub [10] will fight;
Thus on my foes, my foes shall do me right:
Nor doubt the event; for factious crowds engage,
In their first onset, all their brutal rage.
Then let 'em take an unresisted course,   1020
Retire and traverse, and delude their force:
But when they stand all breathless, urge the fight,
And rise upon 'em with redoubled might:
For lawful power is still superior found,
When long driven back, at length it stands the ground."   1025
    He said. The Almighty, nodding, gave consent;
And peals of thunder shook the firmament.
Henceforth a series of new time began,
The mighty years in long procession ran:
Once more the godlike David was restored,   1030
And willing nations knew their lawful lord.

1681

Mac Flecknoe[1]

OR A SATIRE UPON THE TRUE-BLUE-PROTESTANT POET, T. S.

All human things are subject to decay,
And when fate summons, monarchs must obey.

9. Moses was not allowed to see the countenance of Jehovah. Exodus xxxiii. 20–23.

10. Belial, the incarnation of all evil; Beelzebub, a god of the Philistines.

1. The victim of this superb satire, which is cast in the form of a mock-heroic episode, is Thomas Shadwell (1640–92), the playwright, with whom Dryden had been on good terms for a number of years, certainly as late as March, 1678. Shadwell considered himself the successor of Ben Jonson and

the champion of the type of comedy that Jonson had written, the "comedy of humors," in which each character is presented under the domination of a single psychological trait or eccentricity, his humor. His plays are not without merit, but they are often clumsy and prolix, and certainly much inferior to Jonson's. For many years he had conducted a public argument with Dryden on the merits of Jonson's comedies, which he thought Dryden undervalued. Exactly what moved Dry-

This Flecknoe found, who, like Augustus,[2] young
Was called to empire, and had governed long;
In prose and verse, was owned, without dispute,
Through all the realms of Nonsense, absolute.   5
This aged prince, now flourishing in peace,
And blest with issue of a large increase,
Worn out with business, did at length debate
To settle the succession of the state;   10
And, pondering which of all his sons was fit
To reign, and wage immortal war with wit,
Cried: " 'Tis resolved; for nature pleads that he
Should only rule, who most resembles me.
Sh——[3] alone my perfect image bears,   15
Mature in dullness from his tender years:
Sh—— alone, of all my sons, is he
Who stands confirmed in full stupidity.
The rest to some faint meaning make pretense,
But Sh—— never deviates into sense.   20
Some beams of wit on other souls may fall,
Strike through, and make a lucid interval;
But Sh——'s genuine night admits no ray,
His rising fogs prevail upon the day.
Besides, his goodly fabric[4] fills the eye,   25
And seems designed for thoughtless majesty:
Thoughtless as monarch oaks that shade the plain,
And, spread in solemn state, supinely reign.

den to attack him is a matter of conjecture: he may simply have grown progressively bored and irritated by Shadwell and his tedious argument. The poem seems to have been written in late 1678 or 1679 and to have circulated only in manuscript, until it was printed in 1682 in a pirated edition by an obscure publisher. By that time, the two playwrights were alienated by politics as well as by literary quarrels. Shadwell was a violent Whig and the reputed author of a sharp attack on Dryden as the Tory author of *Absalom and Achitophel* and *The Medal*. It was probably for this reason that the printer added the subtitle referring to Shadwell's Whiggism in the phrase "true-blue-Protestant poet." Political passions were running high and sales would be helped if the poem seemed to refer to the events of the day.

Whereas Butler had debased and degraded his victims by using burlesque, caricature, and the grotesque, Dryden exposed Shadwell to ridicule by using the devices of mock-epic, which treats the low, mean, or absurd in the grand language, lofty style, and solemn tone of epic poetry. The obvious disparity between subject and style makes the satiric point. In 1678 an execrable Irish poet and playwright, Richard Flecknoe, died. Dryden conceived the idea of presenting Shadwell (the self-proclaimed heir of Ben Jonson, the laureate) as the son and successor of Flecknoe—hence *Mac* (i.e., son of) *Flecknoe*—from whom he interits the throne of dullness. Flecknoe in the triple role of king, priest, and poet hails his successor, pronounces a panegyric on his perfect fitness for the throne, anoints and crowns him, foretells his glorious reign, and, as he sinks (leaden dullness cannot soar), leaves his mantle to fall symbolically upon Shadwell's shoulders. The poem abounds in literary allusions—to Roman legend and history and to the *Aeneid;* to Cowley's fragmentary epic, *The Davideis,* and to *Paradise Lost;* and to Shadwell's own plays. Biblical allusions add an unexpected dimension of incongruous dignity to the low scene. The coronation takes place in the City, to the plaudits of the citizens, who are fit to admire only what is dull. In 217 lines Dryden created an image of Shadwell which has fixed his reputation to this day.

2. In 31 B.C. Octavian became the first Roman emperor at the age of 32. He assumed the title Augustus in 27 B.C.
3. Thomas Shadwell. The initial and second letter of the name followed by a dash give the appearance, but only the appearance, of protecting Dryden's victim by concealing his name. A common device in the satire of the period.
4. His body. Shadwell was a corpulent man.

Heywood and Shirley[5] were but types of thee,
Thou last great prophet of tautology.[6]
Even I, a dunce of more renown than they,   30
Was sent before but to prepare thy way;
And, coarsely clad in Norwich drugget,[7] came
To teach the nations in thy greater name.[8]
My warbling lute, the lute I whilom[9] strung,   35
When to King John of Portugal I sung,
Was but the prelude to that glorious day,
When thou on silver Thames didst cut thy way,
With well-timed oars before the royal barge,
Swelled with the pride of thy celestial charge;   40
And big with hymn, commander of a host,
The like was ne'er in Epsom blankets tossed.[1]
Methinks I see the new Arion[2] sail,
The lute still trembling underneath thy nail.
At thy well-sharpened thumb from shore to shore   45
The treble squeaks for fear, the basses roar;
Echoes from Pissing Alley Sh—— call,
And Sh—— they resound from Aston Hall.
About thy boat the little fishes throng,
As at the morning toast[3] that floats along.   50
Sometimes, as prince of thy harmonious band,
Thou wield'st thy papers in thy threshing hand.
St. André's[4] feet ne'er kept more equal time,
Not ev'n the feet of thy own *Psyche's* rhyme;
Though they in number as in sense excel: 55
So just, so like tautology, they fell,
That, pale with envy, Singleton[5] forswore ⎫
The lute and sword, which he in triumph bore, ⎬
And vowed he ne'er would act Villerius[6] more." ⎭
Here stopped the good old sire, and wept for joy   60
In silent raptures of the hopeful boy.
All arguments, but most his plays, persuade,
That for anointed[7] dullness he was made.

5. Thomas Heywood (ca. 1570–1641) and James Shirley (1596–1666), playwrights popular before the closing of the theaters in 1642 but now out of fashion. They are introduced here as "types" (i.e., prefigurings) of Shadwell, in the sense that Solomon was regarded as an Old Testament prefiguring of Christ, the "last [final] great prophet."
6. Unnecessary repetition of meaning in different words.
7. A coarse woolen cloth.
8. The parallel between Flecknoe, as forerunner of Shadwell, and John the Baptist, as forerunner of Jesus, is made plain in lines 32–34 by the use of details and even words taken from Matthew iii.3–4 and John i.23.
9. Formerly. Flecknoe boasted of the patronage of the Portuguese king.
1. A reference to Shadwell's comedy *Epsom Wells* and to the farcical scene

in his *Virtuoso,* in which Sir Samuel Hearty is tossed in a blanket.
2. A legendary Greek poet. Returning home by sea, he was robbed and thrown overboard by the sailors, but was saved by a dolphin which had been charmed by his music.
3. Sewage.
4. A French dancer who designed the choreography of Shadwell's opera *Psyche* (1675). Dryden's sneer in the next line at the mechanical metrics of the songs in *Psyche* is justified.
5. John Singleton (d. 1686), a musician at the Theatre Royal.
6. A character in Sir William Davenant's *Siege of Rhodes* (1656), the first English opera.
7. The anticipated phrase is "anointed *majesty.*" English kings are anointed with oil at their coronations.

Close to the walls which fair Augusta[8] bind
(The fair Augusta much to fears inclined),   65
An ancient fabric[9] raised to inform the sight,
There stood of yore, and Barbican it hight:
A watchtower once; but now, so fate ordains,
Of all the pile an empty name remains.
From its old ruins brothel houses rise,   70
Scenes of lewd loves, and of polluted joys,
Where their vast courts the mother-strumpets keep,
And, undisturbed by watch, in silence sleep.
Near these a Nursery[1] erects its head,
Where queens are formed, and future heroes bred;   75
Where unfledged actors learn to laugh and cry, ⎫
Where infant punks[2] their tender voices try, ⎬
And little Maximins[3] the gods defy.   ⎭

Great Fletcher[4] never treads in buskins here,
Nor greater Jonson dares in socks appear;   80
But gentle Simkin[5] just reception finds
Amidst this monument of vanished minds:
Pure clinches[6] the suburbian Muse affords,
And Panton[7] waging harmless war with words.
Here Flecknoe, as a place to fame well known,   85
Ambitiously design'd his Sh——'s throne;
For ancient Dekker[8] prophesied long since,   ⎫
That in this pile would reign a mighty prince, ⎬
Born for a scourge of wit, and flail of sense; ⎭
To whom true dullness should some *Psyches* owe,   90
But worlds of *Misers* from his pen should flow;
Humorists and *Hypocrites*[9] it should produce,
Whole Raymond families, and tribes of Bruce.
   Now Empress Fame had published the renown
Of Sh——'s coronation through the town.   95
Roused by report of Fame, the nations meet,
From near Bunhill, and distant Watling Street.[1]
No Persian carpets spread the imperial way,
But scattered limbs of mangled poets lay;
From dusty shops neglected authors come,   100
Martyrs of pies, and relics of the bum.[2]

8. London. The next line alludes to
the fears excited by the Popish Plot
(cf. *Absalom and Achitophel*).
9. Building.
1. The name of a training school for
young actors.
2. Prostitutes.
3. Maximin is the cruel emperor in
Dryden's *Tyrannic Love* (1669), notorious for his bombast.
4. John Fletcher (1579–1625), the
playwright and collaborator with Francis Beaumont (ca. 1584–1616). "Buskins" and "socks" were the symbols of
tragedy and comedy.
5. A popular character in low farces.
6. Puns.
7. Said to have been a celebrated punster.

8. Thomas Dekker (ca. 1572–1632),
the playwright, whom Jonson had satirized in *The Poetaster*.
9. Three of Shadwell's plays; *The Hypocrite,* a failure, was not published.
"Raymond" and "Bruce" (line 94) are
characters in *The Humorists* and *The
Virtuoso* respectively.
1. Since Bunhill is about a quarter of
a mile and Watling Street little more
than half a mile from the site of the
Nursery, where the coronation is held,
Shadwell's fame is narrowly circumscribed. Moreover, his subjects live in
the heart of the City, regarded by men
of wit and fashion as the abode of bad
taste and middle-class vulgarity.
2. Unsold books eventually went to
bakers' shops and privies.

Much Heywood, Shirley, Ogilby[3] there lay,
But loads of Sh—— almost choked the way.
Bilked stationers[4] for yeomen stood prepared,
And Herringman was captain of the guard.   105
The hoary prince in majesty appeared,
High on a throne of his own labors reared.
At his right hand our young Ascanius[5] sate,
Rome's other hope, and pillar of the state.
His brows thick fogs, instead of glories, grace,   110
And lambent dullness played around his face.
As Hannibal did to the altars come,
Sworn by his sire a mortal foe to Rome,[6]
So Sh—— swore, nor should his vow be vain,
That he till death true dullness would maintain;   115
And, in his father's right, and realm's defense,
Ne'er to have peace with wit, nor truce with sense.
The king himself the sacred unction[7] made,
As king by office, and as priest by trade.
In his sinister[8] hand, instead of ball,   120
He placed a mighty mug of potent ale;
Love's Kingdom to his right he did convey,
At once his scepter, and his rule of sway;
Whose righteous lore the prince had practiced young,
And from whose loins recorded *Psyche* sprung.   125
His temples, last, with poppies were o'erspread,
That nodding seemed to consecrate his head.
Just at that point of time, if fame not lie,
On his left hand twelve reverend owls did fly.[9]
So Romulus, 'tis sung, by Tiber's brook,   130
Presage of sway from twice six vultures took.
The admiring throng loud acclamations make,
And omens of his future empire take.
The sire then shook the honors[1] of his head,
And from his brows damps of oblivion shed   135
Full on the filial dullness: long he stood,
Repelling from his breast the raging god;
At length burst out in this prophetic mood:

3. John Ogilby, a translator of Homer and Virgil, ridiculed by both Dryden and Pope as a bad poet.
4. Cheated publishers, who acted as "yeomen" of the guard, led by Henry Herringman, who until 1679 was the publisher of both Shadwell and Dryden.
5. Or Iulus, son of Aeneas; Virgil referred to him as "*spes altera Romae*" ("Rome's other hope"; *Aeneid* XII. 168). As Troy fell, he was marked as favored by the gods when a flickering ("lambent") flame played round his head (*Aeneid* II.680–84).
6. Hannibal, who almost conquered Rome in 216 B.C., during the 2nd Punic War, took this oath at the age of 9 (Livy xxi.1).
7. The sacramental oil, used in the coronation.
8. Left. During his coronation a British monarch holds two symbols of kingship: a globe ("ball") representing the world in his left hand, a scepter in his right. In lines 121–27, Shadwell's symbols of monarchy—a mug of ale; Flecknoe's dreary play, *Love's Kingdom;* a crown of poppies—suggest heaviness, dullness, drowsiness. The poppies also refer obliquely to Shadwell's addiction to opium.
9. Birds of night, appropriate substitutes for the twelve vultures whose flight confirmed to Romulus the destined site of Rome, of which he was founder and king.
1. Ornaments, hence locks.

"Heavens bless my son, from Ireland let him reign
To far Barbadoes on the western main;[2]   140
Of his dominion may no end be known,
And greater than his father's be his throne;
Beyond *Love's Kingdom* let him stretch his pen!"
He paused, and all the people cried, "Amen."
Then thus continued he: "My son, advance   145
Still in new impudence, new ignorance.
Success let others teach, learn thou from me
Pangs without birth, and fruitless industry.
Let *Virtuosos* in five years be writ;
Yet not one thought accuse thy toil of wit.   150
Let gentle George[3] in triumph tread the stage,
Make Dorimant betray, and Loveit rage;
Let Cully, Cockwood, Fopling, charm the pit,
And in their folly show the writer's wit.
Yet still thy fools shall stand in thy defense,   155
And justify their author's want of sense.
Let 'em be all by thy own model made
Of dullness, and desire no foreign aid;
That they to future ages may be known,
Not copies drawn, but issue of thy own.   160
Nay, let thy men of wit too be the same,
All full of thee, and differing but in name.
But let no alien S—dl—y[4] interpose,
To lard with wit[5] thy hungry *Epsom* prose.
And when false flowers of rhetoric thou wouldst cull,   165
Trust nature, do not labor to be dull;
But write thy best, and top; and, in each line,
Sir Formal's[6] oratory will be thine:
Sir Formal, though unsought, attends thy quill,
And does thy northern dedications[7] fill.   170
Nor let false friends seduce thy mind to fame,
By arrogating Jonson's hostile name.
Let father Flecknoe fire thy mind with praise,
And uncle Ogilby thy envy raise.
Thou art my blood, where Jonson has no part: 175
What share have we in nature, or in art?
Where did his wit on learning fix a brand,
And rail at arts he did not understand?
Where made he love in Prince Nicander's vein,[8]
Or swept the dust in *Psyche's* humble strain?   180

2. Shadwell's empire is vast but empty.
3. Sir George Etherege (ca. 1635–91), a writer of brilliant comedies. In the next couplet Dryden names characters from his plays.
4. Sir Charles Sedley (1638–1701), wit, rake, poet, playwright. Dryden hints that he contributed more than the prologue to Shadwell's *Epsom Wells*.
5. The phrase "lard with wit" recalls a sentence in Burton's *Anatomy of Melancholy:* "They lard their lean books with the fat of others' works * * * "
6. Sir Formal Trifle, the ridiculous and vapid orator in *The Virtuoso.*
7. Shadwell frequently dedicated his works to the Duke of Newcastle and members of his family.
8. In *Psyche.*

Where sold he bargains,[9] 'whip-stitch, kiss my arse,'
Promised a play and dwindled to a farce?[1]
When did his Muse from Fletcher scenes purloin,
As thou whole Eth'rege dost transfuse to thine?
But so transfused, as oil on water's flow,   185
His always floats above, thine sinks below.
This is thy province, this thy wondrous way,
New humors to invent for each new play:
This is that boasted bias[2] of thy mind,
By which one way, to dullness, 'tis inclined;   190
Which makes thy writings lean on one side still,
And, in all changes, that way bends thy will.
Nor let thy mountain-belly make pretense
Of likeness; thine's a tympany[3] of sense.
A tun[4] of man in thy large bulk is writ,   195
But sure thou'rt but a kilderkin of wit.
Like mine, thy gentle numbers feebly creep;
Thy tragic Muse gives smiles, thy comic sleep.
With whate'er gall thou sett'st thyself to write,
Thy inoffensive satires never bite.   200
In thy felonious heart though venom lies,
It does but touch thy Irish pen,[5] and dies.
Thy genius calls thee not to purchase fame
In keen iambics,[6] but mild anagram.
Leave writing plays, and choose for thy command   205
Some peaceful province in acrostic land.
There thou may'st wings display and altars raise,
And torture one poor word ten thousand ways.[7]
Or, if thou wouldst thy different talent suit,
Set thy own songs, and sing them to thy lute."   210
   He said: but his last words were scarcely heard ⎤
For Bruce and Longville had a trap prepared,   ⎬
And down they sent the yet declaiming bard.[8]   ⎦
Sinking he left his drugget robe behind,
Borne upwards by a subterranean wind.   215

9. To "sell bargains" is to answer an innocent question with a coarse or indecent phrase as in this line. "Whip-stitch" is a nonsense word frequently used by Sir Samuel Hearty in *The Virtuoso*.
1. Low comedy which depends largely on situation rather than wit, consistently condemned by Dryden and other serious playwrights.
2. In bowling, the spin given to the bowl that causes it to swerve. Dryden closely parodies a passage in Shadwell's epilogue to *The Humorists*.
3. A swelling in some part of the body caused by wind.
4. A large wine cask. "Kilderkin": a very small cask.
5. Flecknoe was Irish, and so his son must be Irish. Ireland suggested only poverty, superstition, and barbarity to 17th-century Londoners.
6. Sharp satire.
7. "Anagram": the transposition of letters in a word so as to make a new one; "acrostic": a poem in which the first letter of each line, read downward, makes up the name of the person or thing that is the subject of the poem; "wings" and "altars" refer to poems in the shape of these objects as in George Herbert's *Easter Wings* and *The Altar*. Dryden is citing instances of triviality and overingenuity in literature.
8. In *The Virtuoso*, Bruce and Longville play this trick on Sir Formal Trifle while he makes a speech.

The mantle fell to the young prophet's part,[9]
With double portion of his father's art.

ca. 1679   1682

To the Memory of Mr. Oldham[1]

Farewell, too little, and too lately known,
Whom I began to think and call my own:
For sure our souls were near allied, and thine
Cast in the same poetic mold with mine.
One common note on either lyre did strike,
And knaves and fools[2] we both abhorred alike.   5
To the same goal did both our studies drive;
The last set out the soonest did arrive.
Thus Nisus[3] fell upon the slippery place,
While his young friend performed and won the race.   10
O early ripe! to thy abundant store
What could advancing age have added more?
It might (what nature never gives the young)
Have taught the numbers[4] of thy native tongue.
But satire needs not those, and wit will shine   15
Through the harsh cadence of a rugged line:[5]
A noble error, and but seldom made,
When poets are by too much force betrayed.
Thy generous fruits, though gathered ere their prime,
Still showed a quickness;[6] and maturing time   20
But mellows what we write to the dull sweets of rhyme.
Once more, hail and farewell;[7] farewell, thou young,
But ah too short, Marcellus[8] of our tongue;
Thy brows with ivy, and with laurels bound;[9]
But fate and gloomy night encompass thee around.   25

1684

9. When the prophet Elijah was carried to heaven in a chariot of fire borne on a whirlwind, his mantle fell on his successor, the younger prophet Elisha (II Kings.ii.8–14). Flecknoe, prophet of dullness, naturally cannot ascend, but must sink.
1. John Oldham (1653–83), the young poet whose *Satires upon the Jesuits* (1681) won Dryden's admiration. This elegy was published in Oldham's *Remains in Verse and Prose* (1684).
2. The objects of satire.
3. Nisus, on the point of winning a foot race, slipped in a pool of blood; his "young friend" was Euryalus (Virgil, *Aeneid* V.315–39).
4. Metrics, verse.
5. Dryden repeats the Renaissance idea

that the satirist should avoid smoothness and affect rough meters ("harsh cadence").
6. Sharpness of flavor.
7. Dryden echoes the famous words that conclude Catullus' elegy to his brother: "*Atque in perpetuum, frater, ave atque vale*" ("And forever, brother, hail and farewell!").
8. The nephew of Augustus, adopted by him as his successor. After winning military fame as a youth, he died at the age of 20. Virgil celebrated him in the *Aeneid* VI.854–86; the last line of Dryden's poem is a reminiscence of *Aeneid* VI.866.
9. The poet's wreath. Cf. Milton's *Lycidas*, lines 1–2.

To the Pious Memory of the Accomplished Young Lady Mrs.[1] Anne Killigrew

EXCELLENT IN THE TWO SISTER ARTS OF POESY AND PAINTING.

AN ODE [1a]

1

Thou youngest virgin-daughter of the skies,
Made in the last promotion of the blest,
Whose palms,[2] new plucked from paradise,

---

1. "Mrs." means "Mistress," used at this time for our "Miss."

1a. Like Milton's *Lycidas*, Dryden's ode to Anne Killigrew is not so much the expression of private grief as it is a decorous ceremonial gesture dignifying a public occasion. In both poems the death of an individual becomes the point of departure for the treatment of larger topics. The fact that Mrs. Killigrew was not a distinguished poet or painter is irrelevant: her death prompted the poet to consider the arts themselves, their present state in a corrupt age, their central role in civilization, their service to virtue and religion. In the course of the poem, the dead woman is transformed into a symbol of the sister arts themselves, what they are, and what, on earth, they might become. *Lycidas* is an elegy; Dryden's ode combines the elegiac with the lyric and the heroic. Although *Lycidas* is cast in the traditional mode of the pastoral lament, and *Anne Killigrew* in the form of a eulogistic memorial, both poems develop classical and Christian themes which had become conventions of the funeral poem: the death of the young and promising, the praise of his genius and virtues, a lament for the times which suffer such loss, and a consolation, offered by describing the reception of the soul of the dead into heaven.

Dryden's poem, in form, is an irregular ode, a lyric poem which develops a serious theme in a dignified or exalted manner. Two kinds of ode were recognized during the 18th century. To quote Johnson: " * * * the ode is either of the greater or less kind. The less is characterized by sweetness and ease; the greater by sublimity, rapture, and quickness of transition." The greater ode, of which this is the finest example in 17th-century poetry, was associated with the odes of Pindar, the lyric poet of 5th-century Greece, whose intricate metrics, bold imagery, and intense and energetic power were aspired to (seldom with success) by English poets throughout our period. Pindar's odes were rigorously constructed: each

was divided into long stanzas, which in turn were subdivided into three parts—called in Greek strophe, antistrophe, and epode—whose metrical structure was repeated throughout the whole poem. Strophes and antistrophes were identical but the epodes followed a different metrical pattern. Such symmetry is not easily attained in English verse because of the paucity of rhymes in our language, but Ben Jonson's *To the Immortal Memory * * * of * * * Sir Lucius Cary and Sir Henry Morison* is strictly Pindaric, as are Thomas Gray's *The Progress of Poesy* and *The Bard* (1757).

In 1656 Abraham Cowley published loose paraphrases of two of Pindar's odes in which he abandoned the formal structure of the originals in favor of irregular meters and irregularly constructed stanzas, while trying to preserve Pindar's rapture, boldness, and sublimity. Thanks to Cowley's popularity, his irregular Pindarics became the standard of what the age considered the loftiest sort of lyric poetry. It was a tempting form for poets who wished to achieve (or to simulate) the loftiest lyric rapture, for the apparent structural disorder could suggest inspired improvisation. The result was a plague of turgid rhetoric in uninteresting irregular meter.

Dryden declared that Cowley's Pindarics lacked "somewhat of a finer turn and more lyrical verse" and that such odes should consist in "the warmth and vigor of fancy, the masterly figures, and the copiousness of imagination" (Ker, *Essays* I.267–268). His superb ear and gift for melodious eloquence enabled him in this poem to raise the greater ode to heights not to be equaled again until Wordsworth wrote his *Ode: Intimations of Immortality*.

The lesser ode, often in this period associated with the odes of Horace, is more quiet and contemplative, more lyrical in mood, and it usually employs an uncomplicated, rather short stanza.

2. The symbol of victory (cf. Revelation vii.9).

In spreading branches more sublimely rise,
Rich with immortal green above the rest;   5
Whether, adopted to some neighboring star,
Thou roll'st above us in thy wandering race,
    Or in procession fixed and regular,
    Moved with the heavens' majestic pace,
    Or called to more superior bliss,   10
Thou tread'st with seraphims the vast abyss:[3]
Whatever happy region is thy place,
Cease thy celestial song a little space;
Thou wilt have time enough for hymns divine,
    Since heaven's eternal year is thine.   15
Hear then a mortal Muse thy praise rehearse,
        In no ignoble verse;
But such as thy own voice did practice here,
When thy first fruits of poesy were given,
To make thyself a welcome inmate there,   20
        While yet a young probationer,
        And candidate of heaven.

                        2
        If by traduction came thy mind,
        Our wonder is the less to find
A soul so charming from a stock so good;   25
Thy father was transfused into thy blood:[4]
So wert thou born into the tuneful strain
(An early, rich, and inexhausted vein).
        But if thy pre-existing soul
        Was formed at first with myriads more,   30
It did through all the mighty poets roll
        Who Greek or Latin laurels wore,
And was that Sappho last, which once it was before.[5]
        If so, then cease thy flight, O heaven-born mind!
Thou hast no dross to purge from thy rich ore;   35
Nor can thy soul a fairer mansion find   ⎫
Than was the beauteous frame she left behind: ⎬
Return, to fill or mend the choir of thy celestial kind. ⎭

                        3
        May we presume to say that at thy birth
New joy was sprung in heaven, as well as here on earth?   40
        For sure the milder planets did combine   ⎫

3. Dryden is speculating on where the soul of the dead poetess has come to rest: is she the tutelary deity of a planet ("neighboring star")? or of one of the remote "fixed" stars? or does she enjoy the higher ("superior") bliss of having joined the "seraphim," the guardians of the throne of God? (cf. Isaiah vi). Like Milton, Dryden makes use of the Ptolemaic universe of concentric spheres moving around the earth "in procession fixed and regular."
4. The idea that the soul is transmitted by the father at the moment of conception. Since Henry Killigrew had written a tragedy, his daughter is said to have inherited a poet's soul from him. In lines 29–32, Dryden proposes the theory that the soul exists before birth, and less seriously that through the ages it transmigrates from body to body.
5. Mrs. Killigrew is said to have been Sappho (the Greek lyric poetess of the 7th century B.C.) twice: "once before," when her soul transmigrated into Sappho's body, and most recently ("last"), when it inhabited the body of the modern Sappho, Anne Killigrew.

On thy auspicious horoscope to shine,[6]
And even the most malicious were in trine.
Thy brother-angels at thy birth
    Strung each his lyre, and tuned it high,   45
    That all the people of the sky
Might know a poetess was born on earth.
    And then, if ever, mortal ears
    Had heard the music of the spheres!
And if no clustering swarm of bees   50
On thy sweet mouth distilled their golden dew,[7]
    'Twas that such vulgar miracles
    Heaven had not leisure to renew:
For all the blest fraternity of love
Solemnized there thy birth, and kept thy holiday above.   55

4

O gracious God! how far have we
Profaned thy heavenly gift of poesy!
Made prostitute and profligate the Muse,
Debased to each obscene and impious use,
Whose harmony was first ordained above   60
For tongues of angels, and for hymns of love!
O wretched we! why were we hurried down
    This lubric and adulterate[8] age
(Nay, added fat pollutions of our own)
    To increase the steaming ordures of the stage?   65
What can we say to excuse our second fall?
Let this thy vestal,[9] Heaven, atone for all:
Her Arethusan stream remains unsoiled,
Unmixed with foreign filth, and undefiled;
Her wit was more than man, her innocence a child!   70

5

Art she had none, yet wanted none,
    For nature did that want supply;
    So rich in treasures of her own,
    She might our boasted stores defy:
Such noble vigor did her verse adorn   75
That it seemed borrowed where 'twas only born.
Her morals too were in her bosom bred,
    By great examples daily fed,
What in the best of books, her father's life, she read.
And to be read herself she need not fear;   80
Each test and every light her Muse will bear,

6. The familiar idea that character and destiny are determined by the position of the planets at the moment of birth ("horoscope"). Mrs. Killigrew's horoscope was fortunate ("auspicious"): even those planets that are usually baleful ("malicious") were "in trine" —120 degrees apart and hence favorable in their influence.

7. It was said that bees clustered on the lips of the infant Pindar, thus foretelling his greatness as a lyric poet.
8. Lewd and corrupted.
9. I.e., thy virgin. The Roman "vestal" virgins guarded the fire in the Temple of Vesta, goddess of the hearth. For "Arethusan stream," cf. Milton's *Lycidas*, line 85.

Though Epictetus with his lamp were there.[1]
Even love (for love sometimes her Muse expressed)
Was but a lambent flame[2] which played about her breast,
Light as the vapors of a morning dream; 85
So cold herself, whilst she such warmth expressed,
'Twas Cupid bathing in Diana's stream.

6

Born to the spacious empire of the Nine,[3]
One would have thought she should have been content
To manage well that mighty government; 90
But what can young ambitious souls confine?
    To the next realm she stretched her sway,
    For Painture[4] near adjoining lay,
A plenteous province, and alluring prey.
A chamber of dependences[5] was framed 95
(As conquerors will never want pretense,
    When armed, to justify the offense)
And the whole fief in right of Poetry she claimed.
The country open lay without defense;
For poets frequent inroads there had made, 100
    And perfectly could represent
    The shape, the face, with every lineament;
And all the large demains[6] which the dumb Sister swayed,
    All bowed beneath her government,
    Received in triumph wheresoe'er she went. 105
Her pencil[7] drew whate'er her soul designed,
And oft the happy draft surpassed the image in her mind.
    The sylvan scenes[8] of herds and flocks
    And fruitful plains and barren rocks;
    Of shallow brooks that flowed so clear 110
    The bottom did the top appear;
    Of deeper too and ampler floods,
    Which, as in mirrors, showed the woods;
    Of lofty trees, with sacred shades
    And pérspectives[9] of pleasant glades, 115
    Where nymphs of brightest form appear,
    And shaggy satyrs standing near,
    Which them at once admire and fear;

1. A collector is said to have paid a large sum for the lamp of the philosopher Epictetus in the faith that owning it would make him wise. Dryden merely means that Anne Killigrew's poems would appear pure even if judged in the light of the most severe Stoic ethical standards.
2. I.e., "a flickering flame." Cf. Dryden's *Mac Flecknoe*, line 111 and note on line 108.
3. The nine Muses, who preside over the arts of literature, the dance, music, and astronomy.
4. The art of painting (a Gallicism).
5. In the elaborate figure that dominates lines 95–98, Dryden alludes to recent peaceful annexations by Louis XIV of France, who in 1679 added most of Alsace, Lorraine, and Luxembourg to his realm through his policy of *"réunions,"* by setting up *"Chambres de Réunions."* These chambers by quasi-legal means awarded to Louis, as overlord, towns, cities, and estates with all their "dependences" or fiefs, i.e., estates held under the feudal system from overlords, to whom the holders owed services and rents.
6. I.e.. an estate held in one's own right, as opposed to "fief" (line 98). The "dumb Sister" is the Muse of painting.
7. Painter's brush.
8. Cf. Milton, *Paradise Lost* IV.140.
9. Vistas.

The ruins, too, of some majestic piece,
Boasting the power of ancient Rome or Greece,   120
Whose statues, friezes, columns broken lie,
And, though defaced, the wonder of the eye:[1]
What nature, art, bold fiction e'er durst frame,
Her forming hand gave feature to the name.
So strange a concourse ne'er was seen before   125
But when the peopled ark the whole creation bore.[2]

7

The scene then changed: with bold erected look
Our martial king[3] the sight with reverence strook;
For, not content to express his outward part,
Her hand called out the image of his heart: 130
His warlike mind, his soul devoid of fear,   ⎫
His high-designing thoughts were figured there, ⎬
As when by magic, ghosts are made appear.   ⎭
Our phoenix queen[4] was portrayed, too, so bright,
Beauty alone could beauty take[5] so right: 135
Her dress, her shape, her matchless grace
Were all observed, as well as heavenly face.
With such a peerless majesty she stands
As in that day she took the crown from sacred hands;[6]
Before a train of heroines was seen,   140
In beauty foremost, as in rank the queen.
Thus nothing to her genius was denied,
    But like a ball of fire, the further thrown,
    Still with a greater blaze she shone,
And her bright soul broke out on every side.   145
What next she had designed, heaven only knows;[7] ⎫
To such immoderate growth her conquest rose   ⎬
That fate alone its progress could oppose.   ⎭

8

Now all those charms, that blooming grace,
The well-proportioned shape, and beauteous face,   150
Shall never more be seen by mortal eyes:
In earth the much-lamented virgin lies!
    Not wit nor piety could fate prevent;
    Nor was the cruel destiny content
    To finish all the murder at a blow,   155
    To sweep at once her life and beauty too;
But, like a hardened felon, took a pride

1. Mrs. Killigrew's landscapes are typical of the ideal classical landscape of 17th-century Italian painters: contrasts of fruitful plains and barren rocks, water that reflects trees, vistas, classical ruins, and mythological figures.
2. Noah's ark, which contained all that survived of created beings.
3. James II, who, as Duke of York, had won a reputation for courage and skill while fighting as a soldier with the French armies in the 1650's and serving as an admiral during the English-Dutch wars of the 1660's.
4. Mary of Modena, wife of James II, whose unique beauty is expressed by the reference to the "phoenix," the fabulous bird, only one of which exists during each thousand years.
5. I.e., take the likeness of.
6. The queen was crowned by the "sacred hands" of the Archbishop of Canterbury.
7. God alone knows.

To work more mischievously slow,
And plundered first, and then destroyed.
O double sacrilege on things divine,   160
To rob the relic, and deface the shrine!
   But thus Orinda died:[8]
Heaven, by the same disease, did both translate;
As equal were their souls, so equal was their fate.

9

   Meantime her warlike brother[9] on the seas   165
   His waving streamers to the winds displays,
And vows for his return with vain devotion pays.
   Ah, generous youth, that wish forbear;
   The winds too soon will waft thee here!
   Slack all thy sails, and fear to come,   170
Alas, thou know'st not thou art wrecked at home!
No more shalt thou behold thy sister's face;
Thou hast already had her last embrace.
But look aloft, and if thou kenn'st[1] from far,
Among the Pleiads,[2] a new-kindled star,   175
If any sparkles than the rest more bright,
'Tis she that shines in that propitious light.

10

   When in mid-air the golden trump shall sound,
   To raise the nations under ground;
   When in the Valley of Jehosaphat[3]   180
The judging God shall close the book of fate,
   And there the last assizes[4] keep
   For those who wake and those who sleep;
   When rattling bones together fly
   From the four corners of the sky;   185
When sinews o'er the skeletons are spread,
Those clothed with flesh, and life inspires the dead;
The sacred poets first shall hear the sound,   ⎤
And foremost from the tomb shall bound,   ⎬
For they are covered with the lightest ground,   ⎦   190
And straight, with inborn vigor, on the wing,
Like mounting larks, to the new morning sing.
There thou, sweet saint, before the choir shalt go,   ⎤
As harbinger[5] of heaven, the way to show,   ⎬
The way which thou so well hast learned below.   ⎦   195

1686

---

8. The poetess Katharine Philips (1631–
64), fancifully referred to by her admirers as "the matchless Orinda," who,
like Anne Killigrew, died of the dis-
figuring disease, smallpox.
9. Henry Killigrew, an officer in the
Royal Navy. Pennons ("streamers") fly
from the mast of his ship.
1. Perceivest.
2. The Pleiades, a cluster of stars (six
are visible to the unaided eye) in the
constellation Taurus.
3. Joel iii.12; Ezekial xxxvii.
4. Periodical sessions of superior courts
held in each county in England; here,
of course, the Last Judgment—at which
some will be alive on earth ("wake")
and many will have already died
("sleep").
5. One who goes ahead to provide a
lodging.

A Song for St. Cecilia's Day[1]

1

From harmony, from heavenly harmony
    This universal frame began:
    When Nature[2] underneath a heap
      Of jarring atoms lay,
      And could not heave her head,   5
The tuneful voice was heard from high:
    "Arise, ye more than dead."
Then cold, and hot, and moist, and dry,
In order to their stations leap,
      And Music's power obey.   10
From harmony, from heavenly harmony
    This universal frame began:
    From harmony to harmony
Through all the compass of the notes it ran,
The diapason[3] closing full in man.   15

2

What passion cannot Music raise and quell![4]
    When Jubal[5] struck the corded shell,
    His listening brethren stood around,
    And, wondering, on their faces fell
    To worship that celestial sound.   20
Less than a god they thought there could not dwell
    Within the hollow of that shell
    That spoke so sweetly and so well.
What passion cannot Music raise and quell!

1. St. Cecilia, a Roman lady, was an early Christian martyr. She has long been regarded as the patroness of music and the supposed inventor of the organ. Celebrations of her festival day (November 22) in England were usually devoted to music and the praise of music, and from about 1683 to 1703 a "Musical Society" in London annually commemorated it with a religious service and a public concert. This concert always included an ode written and set to music for the occasion, of which the two by Dryden (*A Song for St. Cecilia's Day*, 1687, and *Alexander's Feast*, 1697) are the most distinguished. G. B. Draghi, an Italian brought to England by Charles II, set this ode to music, but Handel's fine score, composed in 1739, has completely obscured the original setting. Like the ode to Mrs. Killigrew, this is an irregular ode in the manner of Cowley. In stanzas 3–6 Dryden boldly attempted to suggest in the sounds of his words the characteristic tones of the instruments mentioned.
2. Created nature, ordered by the Divine Wisdom out of chaos, which Dryden, adopting the physics of the Greek philosopher Epicurus, describes as composed of the warring and discordant ("jarring") atoms of the four elements: earth, fire, water, air ("cold," "hot," "moist," "dry").
3. The entire compass of tones in the scale. Dryden is thinking of the Chain of Being, the ordered creation from inanimate nature up to man, God's latest and final work. The just gradations of notes in a scale is analogous to the equally just gradations in the ascending scale of created beings. Both are the result of harmony.
4. The power of music to describe, evoke, or subdue emotion ("passion") is a frequent theme in 17th-century literature. In stanzas 2–6 the poet considers music as awakening religious awe, warlike courage, sorrow for unrequited love, jealousy and fury, and the impulse to worship God.
5. According to Genesis iv.21, the inventor of the harp and the organ. Dryden imagines Jubal's harp to have been made of a tortoise shell ("corded shell").

3

The trumpet's loud clangor   25
   Excites us to arms,
With shrill notes of anger,
   And mortal alarms.
The double double double beat
   Of the thundering drum   30
Cries: "Hark! the foes come;
Charge, charge, 'tis too late to retreat."

4

The soft complaining flute
In dying notes discovers
The woes of hopeless lovers,
Whose dirge is whispered by the warbling lute.   35

5

   Sharp violins[6] proclaim
Their jealous pangs, and desperation,
Fury, frantic indignation,
Depth of pains, and height of passion,   40
   For the fair, disdainful dame.

6

   But O! what art can teach,
   What human voice can reach,
   The sacred organ's praise?
   Notes inspiring holy love,   45
Notes that wing their heavenly ways
   To mend the choirs above.

7

Orpheus[7] could lead the savage race;
And trees unrooted left their place,
   Sequacious of the lyre;
But bright Cecilia raised the wonder higher: 50
When to her organ vocal breath was given,
An angel heard, and straight appeared,[8]
   Mistaking earth for heaven.

GRAND CHORUS

As from the power of sacred lays
   The spheres began to move,[9]   55
And sung the great Creator's praise
   To all the blest above;
So, when the last and dreadful hour

6. A reference to the bright tone of the modern violin, introduced into England at the Restoration. The tone of the old-fashioned viol is much duller (Bronson).

7. A legendary poet, son of one of the Muses, who played so wonderfully on the lyre that wild beasts ("the savage race") grew tame and followed him, as did even rocks and trees. "Sequacious of": following.

8. According to the legend, it was Cecilia's piety, not her music, that brought an angel to visit her.

9. As it was harmony which ordered the universe, so it was angelic song ("sacred lays") which put the celestial bodies ("spheres") in motion. The harmonious chord which results from the traditional "music of the spheres" is a hymn of "praise" sung by created nature to its "Creator."

This crumbling pageant[1] shall devour,   60
The trumpet shall be heard on high,[2] ⎫
The dead shall live, the living die,   ⎬
And Music shall untune the sky.   ⎭

1687

Epigram on Milton[3]

Three poets, in three distant ages born,
Greece, Italy, and England did adorn.
The first in loftiness of thought surpassed,
The next in majesty, in both the last:
The force of Nature could no farther go;   5
To make a third, she joined the former two.

1688

Alexander's Feast[1]

OR THE POWER OF MUSIC; AN ODE IN HONOR OF
ST. CECILIA'S DAY

1

'Twas at the royal feast, for Persia won
    By Philip's[2] warlike son:
    Aloft in awful state
    The godlike hero sate
        On his imperial throne;   5
His valiant peers were placed around;
Their brows with roses and with myrtles[3] bound:
    (So should desert in arms be crowned).
The lovely Thaïs, by his side,
Sate like a blooming Eastern bride   10
In flower of youth and beauty's pride.
    Happy, happy, happy pair!
    None but the brave,
    None but the brave,
    None but the brave deserves the fair.   15

1. The universe: the stage on which the drama of man's salvation has been acted out.
2. The "last trump" of I Corinthians xv.52, which will announce the Resurrection and the Last Judgment. Dryden develops his theme of harmony as order in such a way as to give full emphasis of the splendid paradox ("Music shall *untune*") in the final line of the ode.
3. Engraved beneath the portrait of Milton in Jacob Tonson's edition of *Paradise Lost* (1688). The "three poets" are Homer, Virgil, Milton.
1. In Dryden's earlier poem for St. Cecilia's Day, music was celebrated primarily as harmony and order, though its power over the passions was also praised. *Alexander's Feast* is devoted entirely to the second theme. It is based upon a well-known episode in the life of Alexander the Great. After the de-

feat of the Persian Emperor Darius III and the fall of the Persian capital, Persepolis (331 B.C.), Alexander held a great feast for his officers. Thaïs, his Athenian mistress, persuaded him to set fire to the palace in revenge for the burning of Athens by the Persians under Xerxes in 480 B.C. According to Plutarch, Alexander was moved by love and wine, not by music; but Dryden, perhaps altering an old tradition that Alexander's musician Timotheus once caused the hero by his flute-playing to start up and arm himself, attributes the burning of Persepolis to the power of music. The original music was by Jeremiah Clarke, but Handel's score of 1736 is better known.
2. King Philip II of Macedonia, father of Alexander the Great.
3. The Greeks and Romans wore wreaths of flowers at banquets. Roses and myrtles are emblems of love.

CHORUS

Happy, happy, happy pair!
None but the brave,
None but the brave,
None but the brave deserves the fair.

2

Timotheus, placed on high   20
  Amid the tuneful choir,
    With flying fingers touched the lyre:
The trembling notes ascend the sky,
      And heavenly joys inspire.
The song began from Jove,   25
Who left his blissful seats above
(Such is the power of mighty love).[4]
A dragon's fiery form belied the god:
Sublime on radiant spires[5] he rode,
    When he to fair Olympia pressed;   30
    And while he sought her snowy breast:
Then, round her slender waist he curled,
And stamped an image of himself, a sovereign of the world.
The listening crowd admire[6] the lofty sound:
"A present deity," they shout around;   35
"A present deity," the vaulted roofs rebound.
      With ravished ears
      The monarch hears,
      Assumes the god,
      Affects to nod,   40
And seems to shake the spheres.[7]

CHORUS

*   With ravished ears*
*   The monarch hears,*
*   Assumes the god,*
*   Affects to nod,*   45
And seems to shake the spheres.

3

The praise of Bacchus[8] then the sweet musician sung,
  Of Bacchus ever fair and ever young:
    The jolly god in triumph comes;
    Sound the trumpets; beat the drums;
      Flushed with a purple grace   50
      He shows his honest face:
Now give the hautboys[9] breath; he comes, he comes!
    Bacchus, ever fair and young
      Drinking joys did first ordain;   55

4. An oracle had declared that Alexander was the son of Zeus ("Jove") by Philip's wife Olympias (not, as Dryden calls her in line 30, "Olympia"), thus conferring on him that semi-divinity often claimed by heroes. Zeus habitually conducted his amours with mortals in the guise of an animal: in this case a dragon.
5. High on shining coils ("radiant spires"). "Spires" for the coils of a serpent is derived from the Latin word *spira*, which Virgil uses in this sense, *Aeneid* II.217. Cf. *Paradise Lost* IX.502.
6. Wonder at.
7. According to Virgil (*Aeneid* X.115) the nod of Jove causes earthquakes.
8. The god of wine.
9. Oboes.

Bacchus' blessings are a treasure,
Drinking is a soldier's pleasure;
 Rich the treasure,
 Sweet the pleasure,
Sweet is pleasure after pain.   60

CHORUS

Bacchus' blessings are a treasure,
Drinking is the soldier's pleasure;
 Rich the treasure,
 Sweet the pleasure,
Sweet is pleasure after pain.   65

4

Soothed with the sound, the king grew vain;
 Fought all his battles o'er again,
And thrice he routed all his foes, and thrice he slew the slain.
The master saw the madness rise,
His glowing cheeks, his ardent eyes;   70
And, while he[1] heaven and earth defied,
Changed his hand, and checked his pride.
 He chose a mournful Muse,
  Soft pity to infuse:
He sung Darius great and good,   75
  By too severe a fate
Fallen, fallen, fallen, fallen,
  Fallen from his high estate,
   And weltering in his blood;
Deserted at his utmost need   80
By those his former bounty fed;
On the bare earth exposed he lies,
With not a friend to close his eyes.[2]
With downcast looks the joyless victor sate,
 Revolving[3] in his altered soul   85
  The various turns of chance below;
 And, now and then, a sigh he stole,
  And tears began to flow.

CHORUS

Revolving in his altered soul
 The various turns of chance below;   90
And, now and then, a sigh he stole,
 And tears began to flow.

5

The mighty master smiled to see
That love was in the next degree;
'Twas but[4] a kindred sound to move,   95
For pity melts the mind to love.
 Softly sweet, in Lydian[5] measures,

1. Alexander; in line 72, "his hand" is the hand of Timotheus, "his pride," the pride of Alexander.
2. After his final defeat by Alexander, Darius was assassinated by his own followers.
3. Pondering.
4. I.e., it was necessary only.
5. In Greek music the Lydian mode expressed the plaintive and the sad.

Soon he soothed his soul to pleasures.
"War," he sung, "is toil and trouble;
Honor, but an empty bubble.
   Never ending, still beginning,   100
Fighting still, and still destroying:
   If the world be worth thy winning,
Think, O think it worth enjoying.
     Lovely Thais sits beside thee,   105
     Take the good the gods provide thee."
The many[6] rend the skies with loud applause;
So Love was crowned, but Music won the cause.
   The prince, unable to conceal his pain,
      Gazed on the fair   110
      Who caused his care,
   And sighed and looked, sighed and looked,
Sighed and looked, and sighed again:
At length, with love and wine at once oppressed,
The vanquished victor sunk upon her breast.   115

CHORUS

*   The prince, unable to conceal his pain,*
*   Gazed on the fair*
*   Who caused his care,*
*   And sighed and looked, sighed and looked,*
Sighed and looked, and sighed again: 120
At length, with love and wine at once oppressed,
The vanquished victor sunk upon her breast.

6

Now strike the golden lyre again:
A louder yet, and yet a louder strain.
Break his bands of sleep asunder,   125
And rouse him, like a rattling peal of thunder.
      Hark, hark, the horrid[7] sound
       Has raised up his head:
       As waked from the dead,
      And amazed, he stares around.   130
"Revenge, revenge!" Timotheus cries,
    "See the Furies[8] arise!
   See the snakes that they rear,
   How they hiss in their hair,
And the sparkles that flash from their eyes!
     Behold a ghastly band,   135
     Each a torch in his hand!
Those are Grecian ghosts, that in battle were slain,
     And unburied remain[9]
     Inglorious on the plain: 140

6. As G. R. Noyes points out, "many" means *meiny,* "a retinue," a spelling that Dryden used elsewhere in his work.
7. Rough, from Latin *horridus.*
8. The Erinyes of the Greeks, avengers of crimes against the natural and the social orders. They are described as women with snakes in their hair and around their waists and arms.
9. According to Greek beliefs, the shades of the dead could not rest until their bodies were buried.

> Give the vengeance due
> To the valiant crew.
> Behold how they toss their torches on high,
> How they point to the Persian abodes,
> And glittering temples of their hostile gods!" 145
> The princes applaud, with a furious joy;
> And the king seized a flambeau[1] with zeal to destroy;
> Thaïs led the way,
> To light him to his prey,
> And, like another Helen, fired another Troy.[2] 150

CHORUS

> *And the king seized a flambeau with zeal to destroy;*
> *Thaïs led the way,*
> *To light him to his prey,*
> *And, like another Helen, fired another Troy.*

7

> Thus long ago, 155
> Ere heaving bellows learned to blow,
> While organs yet were mute;
> Timotheus, to his breathing flute,
> And sounding lyre,
> Could swell the soul to rage, or kindle soft desire. 160
> At last, divine Cecilia came,
> Inventress of the vocal frame;[3]
> The sweet enthusiast,[4] from her sacred store,
> Enlarged the former narrow bounds,
> And added length to solemn sounds, 165
> With nature's mother wit, and arts unknown before.
> Let old Timotheus yield the prize,
> Or both divide the crown:
> He raised a mortal to the skies;
> She drew an angel down. 170

GRAND CHORUS

> *At last, divine Cecilia came,*
> *Inventress of the vocal frame;*
> *The sweet enthusiast, from her sacred store,*
> *Enlarged the former narrow bounds,*
> *And added length to solemn sounds,* 175
> *With nature's mother wit, and arts unknown before.*
> *Let old Timotheus yield the prize,*
> *Or both divide the crown:*
> *He raised a mortal to the skies;*
> *She drew an angel down.* 180

1697

1. Torch.
2. Helen's elopement to Troy with Paris brought on the Trojan War and the ultimate destruction of the city by the Greeks.
3. Organ.
4. Usually at this time a disparaging word, frequently, though not always, applied to a religious zealot or fanatic. Here it is used approvingly and in its literal sense, "possessed by a god," an allusion to Cecilia's angelic companion referred to in line 170. But see note on *Song for St. Cecilia's Day*, line 53.

The Secular Masque[1]

[*Enter* JANUS.[2]]

JANUS.   Chronos,[3] Chronos, mend thy pace;
                An hundred times the rolling sun
                Around the radiant belt[4] has run
           In his revolving race.
           Behold, behold, the goal in sight;   5
           Spread thy fans,[5] and wing thy flight.

[*Enter* CHRONOS, *with a scythe in his hand, and a great globe on his back, which he sets down at his entrance.*]

CHRONOS.   Weary, weary of my weight,
           Let me, let me drop my freight,
           And leave the world behind.
           I could not bear   10
           Another year
                The load of humankind.

[*Enter* MOMUS,[6] *laughing.*]

MOMUS.   Ha! ha! ha! ha! ha! ha! well hast thou done
                To lay down thy pack,
                And lighten thy back;   15
           The world was a fool, e'er since it begun,
           And since neither Janus, nor Chronos, nor I
                Can hinder the crimes,
                Or mend the bad times,
           'Tis better to laugh than to cry.   20

CHORUS OF ALL THREE.
           'Tis better to laugh than to cry.

JANUS.   Since Momus comes to laugh below,
                Old Time, begin the show,
                That he may see, in every scene,
           What changes in this age have been.   25

CHRONOS.   Then, goddess of the silver bow,[7] begin.

[*Horns, or hunting music within.*]
[*Enter* DIANA.]

DIANA.   With horns and with hounds I waken the day,

1. A masque is a dramatic performance, usually mythological in character,
that combines poetry, music, dance, and
spectacle. Distinctly a courtly form of
art, it flourished at the courts of James
I and Charles I. This masque, however,
was written for public performance as
an afterpiece to the revival of Fletcher's
The Pilgrim, revised by Sir John Vanbrugh, and produced for the financial
benefit of Dryden himself. It is a "secular masque" because it celebrates the
end of the century, "secular" being derived from the Latin *saeculares*, applied to the games, plays, and shows
celebrated in Rome once an "age,"
a period of 120 years. It is not certain
that Dryden lived to see his masque
performed.
2. The god of beginnings, who here
presides over the opening of the new
century.
3. God of time.
4. The sun, in the course of a year,
passes through all twelve signs of the
zodiac ("the radiant belt").
5. Wings.
6. God of mockery and faultfinding.
7. Diana, the virgin goddess of the
moon, a huntress. She symbolizes England before the Civil War, an allusion
to James I's passion for the chase.

And hie to my woodland walks away;
I tuck up my robe, and am buskined[8] soon,
And tie to my forehead a wexing[9] moon.   30
I course the fleet stag, unkennel the fox,
And chase the wild goats o'er summits of rocks;
With shouting and hooting we pierce through the sky,
And Echo turns hunter, and doubles the cry.

CHORUS OF ALL.
With shouting and hooting we pierce through the sky, 35
And Echo turns hunter, and doubles the cry.

JANUS.   Then our age was in its prime:
CHRONOS.   Free from rage:
DIANA.   And free from crime:
MOMUS.   A very merry, dancing, drinking,
Laughing, quaffing, and unthinking time.   40

CHORUS OF ALL.
Then our age was in its prime,
Free from rage, and free from crime;
A very merry, dancing, drinking,
Laughing, quaffing, and unthinking time.
[*Dance of* DIANA'S *attendants.*]
[*Enter* MARS.[1]]

MARS.   Inspire[2] the vocal brass, inspire;   45
The world is past its infant age:
Arms and honor,
Arms and honor,
Set the martial mind on fire,
And kindle manly rage.   50
Mars has looked the sky to red;
And Peace, the lazy good, is fled.
Plenty, Peace, and Pleasure fly;
The sprightly green
In woodland walks no more is seen;   55
The sprightly green has drunk the Tyrian dye.[3]

CHORUS OF ALL.
Plenty, Peace, etc.

MARS.   Sound the trumpet, beat the drum;
Through all the world around,
Sound a reveille, sound, sound,   60
The warrior god is come.

CHORUS OF ALL.
Sound the trumpet, etc.

MOMUS.   Thy sword within the scabbard keep,
And let mankind agree;
Better the world were fast asleep,   65

8. Wearing hunting boots.
9. Waxing (i.e., increasing, because in the first quarter).
1. God of war, who represents the period of the Civil War and the Commonwealth.

2. Breathe into.
3. I.e., the costume has changed from the green of the hunter to the crimson of the soldier (at once the color of blood and of "Tyrian dye," known to the ancients as "purple").

Than kept awake by thee.
The fools are only thinner,
With all our cost and care;
But neither side a winner,
For things are as they were.   70

CHORUS OF ALL.
The fools are only, etc.
[*Enter* VENUS.[4]]

VENUS.   Calms appear when storms are past,
Love will have his hour at last:
Nature is my kindly care;
Mars destroys, and I repair;   75
Take me, take me, while you may;
Venus comes not every day.

CHORUS OF ALL.
Take her, take her, etc.

CHRONOS.   The world was then so light,
I scarcely felt the weight;   80
Joy ruled the day, and Love the night.
But since the Queen of Pleasure left the ground,[5]
I faint, I lag,
And feebly drag
The ponderous orb around.   85

MOMUS.   All, all of a piece throughout:
[*Pointing to* DIANA.]
Thy chase had a beast in view;
[*To* MARS.]
Thy wars brought nothing about;
[*To* VENUS.]
Thy lovers were all untrue.

JANUS.   'Tis well an old age is out: 90
CHRONOS.   And time to begin a new.

CHORUS OF ALL.
All, all of a piece throughout:
Thy chase had a beast in view;
Thy wars brought nothing about;
Thy lovers were all untrue.   95
'Tis well an old age is out,
And time to begin a new.

[*Dance of huntsmen, nymphs, warriors, and lovers.*]

1700

4. Goddess of love and beauty, representing the licentious reigns of Charles
II and James II.

5. Sir Walter Scott suggested that this
line refers to the exiled Queen Mary
of Modena, wife of James II.

Criticism   Because Dryden liked to talk about literature, he became
a critic, indeed the first comprehensive critic in England. The Elizabethans, largely impelled by the example of Italian humanists, had produced an interesting and unsystematic body of critical writings. Dryden
could look back to such pioneer works as George Puttenham's *Art of
English Poesy* (1589), Sir Philip Sidney's *Apology for Poetry* (1595),
Samuel Daniel's *Defense of Rhyme* (ca. 1603), and Ben Jonson's *Timber,
or Discoveries* (1641), which is more Jonson's commonplace book than a
collection of critical essays. These and later writings Dryden knew, as he
knew the ancient critics, especially Aristotle, Horace, Quintilian, and
Longinus, and the important contemporary French critics, notably Corneille, Rapin, and Boileau. Taken as a whole, his critical prefaces and
dedications, which appeared between 1664 and 1700, are the work of a
man of independent mind who has made his own synthesis of critical
canons from wide reading, a great deal of thinking, and the constant practice of the art of writing. As a critic he is no man's disciple, and he has
the saving grace of being always willing to change his mind. This unwillingness to construct a rigid and dogmatic critical system has been regarded
by many as mere inconsistency, but recent students of Dryden have held
that it is actually the sign of a lively mind, always capable of growth.

  All but a very few of Dryden's critical works (most notably the *Essay of
Dramatic Poesy*) grew out of the works to which they served as prefaces:
comedies, heroic plays, tragedies, translations, poems of various sorts. Each
work posed problems which Dryden was eager to discuss with his readers,
and the topics that he treated proved to be important in the development
of the new literature of which he was the principal apologist. Little that
was pertinent escaped his attention: the processes of literary creation fascinated him and led him to talk of wit, fancy, imagination, and judgment;
the question of the relation of the poet to tradition prompted him to explore earlier literatures in search of safe guides and models; the problems
posed by the new theater and the new drama made it desirable that he,
as a playwright, should reassess the achievement of Shakespeare's generation and should theorize about the nature of the forms of modern drama
from tragedy down to farce; his interest in poetry as a craft started discussions of metrics, language, imagery, metaphors, poetic license, methods
of translation, the literary kinds, the decorum of styles; and always his
ready enthusiasm for great writers evoked warm and generous characterizations of the genius of other poets: Shakespeare, Jonson, Chaucer, Juvenal,
Horace, Homer, Virgil. For nearly forty years this voice was heard in
the land, and when it was finally silenced, a set of critical standards had
come into existence and the Augustan age was approaching maturity. The
representative selections below may give some insight into how Dryden
helped to order taste and critical standards, while he sacrificed nothing
of that freedom without which the English literary genius could not
function.

From An Essay of Dramatic Poesy[1]
[*Two Sorts of Bad Poetry*]

" * * * I have a mortal apprehension of two poets,[2] whom this victory, with the help of both her wings, will never be able to escape." " 'Tis easy to guess whom you intend," said Lisideius; "and without naming them, I ask you if one of them does not perpetually pay us with clenches[3] upon words, and a certain clownish kind of raillery?[4] if now and then he does not offer at a catachresis[5] or Clevelandism, wresting and torturing a word into another meaning: in fine, if he be not one of those whom the French would call *un mauvais buffon;*[6] one who is so much a well-willer to the satire, that he spares no man; and though he cannot strike a blow to hurt any, yet ought to be punished for the malice of the action, as our witches are justly hanged, because they think themselves so, and suffer deservedly for believing they did mischief, because they meant it." "You have described him," said Crites, "so exactly that I am afraid to come after you with my other extremity of poetry. He is one of those who, having had some advantage of education and converse, knows better than the other what a poet should be,

1. With the reopening of the theaters in 1660, older plays were revived, but, despite their power and charm, they seemed old-fashioned. Although new playwrights, ambitious to create a modern English drama, soon appeared, they were uncertain of their direction. What, if anything, useful could they learn from the dramatic practice of the ancients? Should they ignore the English dramatists of the late 16th and early 17th centuries? Should they make their example the vigorous contemporary drama of France? Dryden addresses himself to these and other problems in this essay, his first extended piece of criticism. Its purpose, he tells us, was "chiefly to vindicate the honor of our English writers from the censure of those who unjustly prefer the French before them." Its method is skeptical: Dryden presents several points of view, but imposes none. The form is a dialogue among friends, like the *Tusculan Disputations* or the *Brutus* of Cicero. Crites praises the drama of the ancients; Eugenius protests against their authority and argues for the idea of progress in the arts; Lisideius urges the excellence of French plays; Neander, speaking in the climactic position, defends the native tradition and the greatness of Shakespeare, Fletcher, and Jonson. The dialogue takes place on June 3, 1665, in a boat on the Thames. The four friends are rowed downstream to listen to the cannonading of the English and Dutch fleets, engaged in battle off the Suffolk coast. As the gunfire recedes they are assured of victory and order their boatman to return to London, and naturally enough they fall to discussing the number of bad poems that the victory will evoke.

2. Probably Robert Wilde and possibly Richard Flecknoe, whom Dryden later ridiculed in *Mac Flecknoe*. Their actual identity is unimportant, for they merely represent two extremes in poetry, both deplorable: the fantastic and extravagant manner of decadent metaphysical wit and its opposite, the flat and the dull. The new poetry was to seek a mean between these extremes. Cf. Pope, *Essay on Criticism* II.239–42 and 289–300.

3. Puns.

4. Boorish banter.

5. The use of a word in a sense remote from its normal meaning: a legitimate figure of speech used by all poets, it had been abused by John Cleveland (1613–58), who was at first admired for his ingenuity, but whose reputation declined rapidly after the Restoration. A Clevelandism: "The marigold, whose courtier's face / *Echoes* the sun * * * "

6. A malicious jester.

but puts it into practice more unluckily than any man; his style and matter are everywhere alike: he is the most calm, peaceable writer you ever read: he never disquiets your passions[7] with the least concernment, but still[8] leaves you in as even a temper as he found you; he is a very Leveler[9] in poetry: he creeps along with ten little words in every line, and helps out his numbers with *for to,* and *unto,* and all the pretty expletives[1] he can find, till he drags them to the end of another line; while the sense is left tired half-way behind it: he doubly starves all his verses, first for want of thought, and then of expression; his poetry neither has wit in it, nor seems to have it; like him in Martial:

> *Pauper videri Cinna vult, et est pauper.*[2]

"He affects plainness, to cover his want of imagination: when he writes the serious way, the highest flight of his fancy is some miserable antithesis, or seeming contradiction; and in the comic he is still reaching at some thin conceit, the ghost of a jest, and that too flies before him, never to be caught; these swallows which we see before us on the Thames are the just resemblance of his wit: you may observe how near the water they stoop, how many proffers they make to dip, and yet how seldom they touch it; and when they do, it is but the surface: they skim over it but to catch a gnat, and then mount into the air and leave it."

[The Wit of the Ancients: The Universal]

" * * * A thing well said will be wit in all languages; and though it may lose something in the translation, yet to him who reads it in the original, 'tis still the same: he has an idea of its excellency, though it cannot pass from his mind into any other expression or words than those in which he finds it. When Phaedria, in the *Eunuch,*[3] had a command from his mistress to be absent two days, and, encouraging himself to go through with it, said, '*Tandem ego non illa caream, si sit opus, vel totum triduum?*'[4]—Parmeno, to mock the softness of his master, lifting up his hands and eyes, cries out, as it were in admiration,[5] '*Hui! universum triduum!*' the elegancy of which *universum,* though it cannot be rendered in our language, yet leaves an impression on our souls: but this happens seldom in him; in Plautus[6] oftener, who is infinitely too bold

7. Emotions.
8. Always.
9. The Levelers were radical egalitarians and republicans, a powerful political force in the Puritan Army about 1648. They were suppressed by Cromwell.
1. Words used merely to fill out a line of verse. Cf. Pope, *Essay on Criticism* II.346–47.
2. "Cinna wishes to seem poor, and he is poor" (*Epigrams* VIII.xix).

3. A comedy by the Roman poet Terence (ca. 185–159 B.C.).
4. "Shall I not then do without her, if need be, for three whole days?"
5. Wonder. The wit of Parmeno's exclamation, "Oh, three entire days," depends on *universum,* which suggests that a lover may regard three days as an eternity.
6. Titus Maccus Plautus, Roman comic poet (ca. 254–184 B.C.).

in his metaphors and coining words, out of which many times his wit is nothing; which questionless was one reason why Horace falls upon him so severely in those verses:

> Sed proavi nostri Plautinos et numeros et
> Laudavere sales, nimium patienter utrumque,
> Ne dicam stolide.[7]

For Horace himself was cautious to obtrude a new word on his readers, and makes custom and common use the best measure of receiving it into our writings:

> Multa renascentur quae nunc cecidere, cadentque
> Quae nunc sunt in honore vocabula, si volet usus,
> Quem penes arbitrium est, et jus, et norma loquendi.[8]

"The not observing this rule is that which the world has blamed in our satirist, Cleveland: to express a thing hard and unnaturally is his new way of elocution. 'Tis true no poet but may sometimes use a catachresis: Virgil does it—

> Mistaque ridenti colocasia fundet acantho[9]—

in his eclogue of Pollio; and in his seventh *Aeneid*:

> mirantur et undae,
> Miratur nemus insuetum fulgentia longe
> Scuta virum fluvio pictasque innare carinas.[1]

And Ovid once so modestly that he asks leave to do it:

> quem, si verbo audacia detur,
> Haud metuam summi dixisse Palatia caeli.[2]

calling the court of Jupiter by the name of Augustus his palace; though in another place he is more bold, where he says, 'et longas visent Capitolia pompas.'[3] But to do this always, and never be able to write a line without it, though it may be admired by some few pedants, will not pass upon those who know that wit is best conveyed to us in the most easy language; and is most to be admired when a great thought comes dressed in words so commonly received that it is understood by the meanest apprehensions, as the

---

7. "But our ancestors too tolerantly (I do not say foolishly) praised both the verse and the wit of Plautus" (*Ars Poetica*, lines 270–72). Dryden misquotes slightly.
8. "Many words that have perished will be born again, and those shall perish that are now esteemed, if usage wills it, in whose power are the judgment, the law, and the pattern of speech" (*Ars Poetica*, lines 70–72).
9. "[The earth] shall give forth the Egyptian bean, mingled with the smiling acanthus" (*Eclogues* IV.20). "Smil-

ing acanthus" is a catachresis.
1. Actually *Aeneid* VIII.91–93. Dryden's paraphrase makes the point clearly: "The woods and waters wonder at the gleam / Of shields and painted ships that stem the stream" (*Aeneis* VIII.125–26). "Wonder" is a catachresis.
2. "[This is the place] which, if boldness of expression be permitted, I shall not hesitate to call the Palace of high heaven" (*Metamorphoses* I.175–76).
3. "And the Capitol shall see the long processions" (*Metamorphoses* I.561).

best meat is the most easily digested: but we cannot read a verse of Cleveland's without making a face at it, as if every word were a pill to swallow: he gives us many times a hard nut to break our teeth, without a kernel for our pains. So that there is this difference betwixt his satires and Doctor Donne's; that the one gives us deep thoughts in common language, though rough cadence; the other gives us common thoughts in abstruse words: 'tis true in some places his wit is independent of his words, as in that of the *Rebel Scot*:

> Had Cain been Scot, God would have changed his doom;
> Not forced him wander, but confined him home.[4]

"*Si sic omnia dixisset!*[5] This is wit in all languages: it is like mercury, never to be lost or killed:[6] and so that other—

> For beauty, like white powder, makes no noise,
> And yet the silent hypocrite destroys.

You see the last line is highly metaphorical, but it is so soft and gentle that it does not shock us as we read it."

[Shakespeare and Ben Jonson Compared]

"To begin, then, with Shakespeare. He was the man who of all modern, and perhaps ancient poets, had the largest and most comprehensive soul. All the images of Nature were still present to him, and he drew them, not laboriously, but luckily; when he describes anything, you more than see it, you feel it too. Those who accuse him to have wanted learning, give him the greater commendation: he was naturally learned; he needed not the spectacles of books to read Nature; he looked inwards, and found her there. I cannot say he is everywhere alike; were he so, I should do him injury to compare him with the greatest of mankind. He is many times flat, insipid; his comic wit degenerating into clenches, his serious swelling into bombast. But he is always great when some great occasion is presented to him; no man can say he ever had a fit subject for his wit and did not then raise himself as high above the rest of poets,

Quantum lenta solent inter viburna cupressi[7]

The consideration of this made Mr. Hales of Eton[8] say that there was no subject of which any poet ever writ, but he would produce it much better treated of in Shakespeare; and however others are now generally preferred before him, yet the age wherein he lived,

---

4. Lines 63–64.
5. "Had he said everything thus!" (Juvenal, *Satires* X.123–24).
6. Mercury is said to be "killed" if its fluidity is destroyed. The couplet quoted below is from *Rupertismus*,

lines 39–40.
7. "As do cypresses among the bending shrubs" (Virgil, *Eclogues* I.25).
8. The learned John Hales (1584–1656), provost of Eton. He is reputed to have said this to Jonson himself.

which had contemporaries with him Fletcher and Jonson, never equaled them to him in their esteem: and in the last king's[9] court, when Ben's reputation was at highest, Sir John Suckling,[1] and with him the greater part of the courtiers, set our Shakespeare far above him. * * *

"As for Jonson, to whose character I am now arrived, if we look upon him while he was himself (for his last plays were but his dotages), I think him the most learned and judicious writer which any theater ever had. He was a most severe judge of himself, as well as others. One cannot say he wanted wit, but rather that he was frugal of it. In his works you find little to retrench[2] or alter. Wit, and language, and humor also in some measure, we had before him; but something of art[3] was wanting to the drama till he came. He managed his strength to more advantage than any who preceded him. You seldom find him making love in any of his scenes or endeavoring to move the passions; his genius was too sullen and saturnine[4] to do it gracefully, especially when he knew he came after those who had performed both to such an height. Humor was his proper sphere:[5] and in that he delighted most to represent mechanic people.[6] He was deeply conversant in the ancients, both Greek and Latin, and he borrowed boldly from them: there is scarce a poet or historian among the Roman authors of those times whom he has not translated in *Sejanus* and *Catiline*.[7] But he has done his robberies so openly, that one may see he fears not to be taxed by any law. He invades authors like a monarch; and what would be theft in other poets is only victory in him. With the spoils of these writers he so represents old Rome to us, in its rites, ceremonies, and customs, that if one of their poets had written either of his tragedies, we had seen less of it than in him. If there was any fault in his language, 'twas that he weaved it too closely and laboriously, in his serious plays:[8] perhaps, too, he did a little too much Romanize our tongue, leaving the words which he translated almost as much Latin as he found them: wherein, though he learnedly followed the idiom of their language, he did not enough comply with the idiom of ours. If I would compare him with Shakespeare, I must acknowledge him the more correct poet, but Shakespeare the greater wit.[9] Shakespeare was the Homer, or father of our dramatic poets; Jonson was the Virgil, the pattern of elaborate writing; I admire him, but I love Shakespeare. To

9. Charles I.
1. Courtier, poet, playwright, much admired in Dryden's time for his wit and the easy naturalness of his style.
2. Delete.
3. Craftsmanship.
4. Heavy.
5. In Jonson's comedies the characters are seen under the domination of some psychological trait, ruling passion, or affectation—i.e., some "humor"—which makes them unique and ridiculous.
6. I.e., artisans.
7. Jonson's two Roman plays, dated 1605 and 1611 respectively.
8. This is the reading of the first edition. Curiously enough, in the second edition Dryden altered the phrase to "in his comedies especially."
9. Genius.

conclude of him; as he has given us the most correct plays, so in the precepts which he has laid down in his *Discoveries*, we have as many and profitable rules for perfecting the stage, as any wherewith the French can furnish us."

1668

From The Author's Apology for Heroic Poetry and Heroic License[1]

[*"Boldness" of Figures and Tropes Defended: The Appeal to "Nature"*]

* * * They, who would combat general authority with particular opinion, must first establish themselves a reputation of understanding better than other men. Are all the flights of heroic poetry to be concluded bombast, unnatural, and mere madness, because they are not affected with their excellencies? It is just as reasonable as to conclude there is no day, because a blind man cannot distinguish of light and colors. Ought they not rather, in modesty, to doubt of their own judgments, when they think this or that expression in Homer, Virgil, Tasso, or Milton's *Paradise* to be too far strained, than positively to conclude that 'tis all fustian and mere nonsense? 'Tis true there are limits to be set betwixt the boldness and rashness of a poet; but he must understand those limits who pretends to judge as well as he who undertakes to write: and he who has no liking to the whole ought, in reason, to be excluded from censuring of the parts. He must be a lawyer before he mounts the tribunal; and the judicature of one court, too, does not qualify a man to preside in another. He may be an excellent pleader in the Chancery, who is not fit to rule the Common Pleas. But I will presume for once to tell them that the boldest strokes of poetry, when they are managed artfully, are those which most delight the reader.

Virgil and Horace, the severest writers of the severest age, have made frequent use of the hardest metaphors and of the strongest hyperboles; and in this case the best authority is the best argument, for generally to have pleased, and through all ages, must bear the force of universal tradition. And if you would appeal from thence to right reason, you will gain no more by it in effect than,

1. This essay was prefixed to Dryden's *State of Innocence*, the libretto for an opera (never produced), based on *Paradise Lost*. Dryden had been ridiculed for the extravagant and bold imagery and rhetorical figures that are typical of the style of his rhymed heroic plays. This preface is a defense not only of his own predilection for what Samuel Johnson described as "wild and daring sallies of sentiment, in the irregular and eccentric violence of wit," but also of the theory that heroic and idealized materials should be treated in lofty and boldly metaphorical style; hence his definition of "wit" as propriety.

first, to set up your reason against those authors, and, secondly, against all those who have admired them. You must prove why that ought not to have pleased which has pleased the most learned and the most judicious; and, to be thought knowing, you must first put the fool upon all mankind. If you can enter more deeply than they have done into the causes and resorts[2] of that which moves pleasure in a reader, the field is open, you may be heard: but those springs of human nature are not so easily discovered by every superficial judge: it requires philosophy, as well as poetry, to sound the depth of all the passions, what they are in themselves, and how they are to be provoked; and in this science the best poets have excelled. * * * From hence have sprung the tropes[3] and figures, for which they wanted a name who first practiced them and succeeded in them. Thus I grant you that the knowledge of Nature was the original rule, and that all poets ought to study her, as well as Aristotle and Horace, her interpreters.[4] But then this also undeniably follows, that those things which delight all ages must have been an imitation of Nature—which is all I contend. Therefore is rhetoric made an art; therefore the names of so many tropes and figures were invented, because it was observed they had such and such effect upon the audience. Therefore catachreses and hyperboles[5] have found their place amongst them; not that they were to be avoided, but to be used judiciously and placed in poetry as heightenings and shadows are in painting, to make the figure bolder, and cause it to stand off to sight. * * *

[Wit as "Propriety"]

* * * [Wit] is a propriety of thoughts and words; or, in other terms, thought and words elegantly adapted to the subject. If our critics will join issue on this definition, that we may *convenire in aliquo tertio;*[6] if they will take it as a granted principle, it will be easy to put an end to this dispute. No man will disagree from another's judgment concerning the dignity of style in heroic poetry; but all reasonable men will conclude it necessary that sublime subjects ought to be adorned with the sublimest, and, consequently, often with the most figurative expressions. * * *

1677

2. Mechanical springs which set something in motion.
3. The use of a word in a figurative sense; "figures," in this phrase, means such figures of speech as metaphors and similes.
4. In the words of the French critic René Rapin, the rules (largely derived from Aristotle's *Poetics* and Horace's *Ars Poetica*) were made in order to

"reduce Nature to method." Cf. Pope, *Essay on Criticism* I.88–89.
5. "Catachresis" is the use of a word in a sense remote from its normal meaning; "hyperbole," deliberate overstatement or exaggeration.
6. "To find some means of agreement, in a third term, between the two opposites" [W. P. Ker's note].

From A Discourse Concerning the Original and Progress of Satire[1]
[*The Art of Satire*]

* * * How easy is it to call rogue and villain, and that wittily! But how hard to make a man appear a fool, a blockhead, or a knave without using any of those opprobrious terms! To spare the grossness of the names, and to do the thing yet more severely, is to draw a full face, and to make the nose and cheeks stand out, and yet not to employ any depth of shadowing.[2] This is the mystery of that noble trade, which yet no master can teach to his apprentice; he may give the rules, but the scholar is never the nearer in his practice. Neither is it true that this fineness of raillery[3] is offensive. A witty man is tickled while he is hurt in this manner, and a fool feels it not. The occasion of an offense may possibly be given, but he cannot take it. If it be granted that in effect this way does more mischief; that a man is secretly wounded, and though he be not sensible himself, yet the malicious world will find it out for him; yet there is still a vast difference betwixt the slovenly butchering of a man, and the fineness of a stroke that separates the head from the body, and leaves it standing in its place. A man may be capable, as Jack Ketch's[4] wife said of his servant, of a plain piece of work, a bare hanging; but to make a malefactor die sweetly was only belonging to her husband. I wish I could apply it to myself, if the reader would be kind enough to think it belongs to me. The character of Zimri in my *Absalom*[5] is, in my opinion, worth the whole poem: it is not bloody, but it is ridiculous enough; and he, for whom it was intended, was too witty to resent it as an injury. If I had railed,[6] I might have suffered for it justly; but I managed my own work more happily, perhaps more dexterously. I avoided the mention of great crimes, and applied myself to the representing of blindsides, and little extravagancies; to which, the wittier a man is, he is generally the more obnoxious.[7] It succeeded as I

1. This passage is an excerpt from the long and rambling preface which served as the dedication of a translation of the satires of the Roman satirists Juvenal and Persius to Charles Sackville, 6th Earl of Dorset. The translations were made by Dryden and other writers, among them William Congreve. Dryden traces the origin and development of verse satire in Rome, and in a very fine passage contrasts Horace and Juvenal as satiric poets. It is plain that he prefers the "tragic" satire of Juvenal to the urbane and laughing satire of Horace. But in the passage printed here he praises his own satiric character of Zimri (the Duke of Buckingham) in *Absalom and Achitophel* for the very

reason that it is modeled on Horatian "raillery," not Juvenalian invective.
2. Early English miniaturists prided themselves on the art of giving roundness to the full face without painting in shadows.
3. Satirical mirth, good-natured satire.
4. A notorious public executioner of Dryden's time (d. 1686). His name later became a generic term for all members of his profession.
5. See *Absalom and Achitophel* I.544–68.
6. Reviled, abused. Observe that the verb differed in meaning from its noun, defined above.
7. Liable.

wished; the jest went round, and he was laughed at in his turn who began the frolic. * * *

1693

From The Preface to *Fables Ancient and Modern*[1]
[In Praise of Chaucer]

In the first place, as he is the father of English poetry, I hold him in the same degree of veneration as the Grecians held Homer, or the Romans Virgil. He is a perpetual fountain of good sense; learned in all sciences;[2] and, therefore, speaks properly on all subjects. As he knew what to say, so he knows also when to leave off; a continence which is practiced by few writers, and scarcely by any of the ancients, excepting Virgil and Horace. * * *

Chaucer followed Nature everywhere, but was never so bold to go beyond her; and there is a great difference of being *poeta* and *nimis poeta*,[3] if we may believe Catullus, as much as betwixt a modest behavior and affectation. The verse of Chaucer, I confess, is not harmonious to us; but 'tis like the eloquence of one whom Tacitus commends, it was *auribus istius temporis accommodata:*[4] they who lived with him, and some time after him, thought it musical; and it continues so, even in our judgment, if compared with the numbers[5] of Lydgate and Gower, his contemporaries; there is the rude sweetness of a Scotch tune in it, which is natural and pleasing, though not perfect. 'Tis true I cannot go so far as he who published the last edition of him;[6] for he would make us believe the fault is in our ears, and that there were really ten syllables in a verse where we find but nine; but this opinion is not worth confuting; 'tis so gross and obvious an error that common sense (which is a rule in everything but matters of faith and revelation) must convince the reader that equality of numbers in every verse which we call heroic[7] was either not known, or not always practiced in Chaucer's age. It were an easy matter to produce some thousands

1. Dryden's final work, published in the year of his death, was a collection of translations from Homer, Ovid, Boccaccio, and Chaucer, and one or two other pieces. The Preface, in many ways, is Dryden's ripest and finest critical essay. In it, he is not concerned with critical theory or with a formalistic approach to literature; he is simply a man, grown old in the reading and writing of poetry, who is eager to talk informally with his readers about some of his favorite authors. His praise of Chaucer (unusually sympathetic and perceptive for 1700) is animated by that love of great literature which is manifest in everything that Dryden wrote.
2. Branches of learning.
3. A poet (*"poeta"*) and too much of

a poet (*"nimis poeta"*). The phrase is not from Catullus but from Martial (*Epigrams* III.44).
4. "Suitable to the ears of that time." Tacitus was a Roman historian and writer on oratory (A.D. ca. 55–ca. 117).
5. Versification. John Lydgate (ca. 1370–ca. 1449) wrote poetry which shows the influence of Chaucer. John Gower (d. 1408), poet and friend of Chaucer.
6. Thomas Speght's Chaucer, which Dryden used, was first published in 1598; the second edition, published in 1602, was reprinted in 1687.
7. The pentameter line. In Dryden's time few readers knew how to pronounce Middle English, especially the syllabic *e*. Moreover, Chaucer's works were

of his verses which are lame for want of half a foot, and sometimes
a whole one, and which no pronunciation can make otherwise.
We can only say that he lived in the infancy of our poetry, and that
nothing is brought to perfection at the first. * * *

He must have been a man of a most wonderful comprehensive
nature, because, as it has been truly observed of him, he has taken
into the compass of his *Canterbury Tales* the various manners and
humors (as we now call them) of the whole English nation in his
age. Not a single character has escaped him. All his pilgrims are
severally distinguished from each other; and not only in their inclinations but in their very physiognomies and persons. Baptista
Porta[8] could not have described their natures better than by the
marks which the poet gives them. The matter and manner of their
tales, and of their telling, are so suited to their different educations,
humors, and callings that each of them would be improper in any
other mouth. Even the grave and serious characters are distinguished by their several sorts of gravity: their discourses are such
as belong to their age, their calling, and their breeding; such as are
becoming of them, and of them only. Some of his persons are vicious, and some virtuous; some are unlearned, or (as Chaucer calls
them) lewd, and some are learned. Even the ribaldry of the low characters is different: the Reeve, the Miller, and the Cook are several[9]
men, and distinguished from each other as much as the mincing
Lady Prioress and the broad-speaking, gap-toothed Wife of Bath.
But enough of this; there is such a variety of game springing up
before me that I am distracted in my choice, and know not which
to follow. 'Tis sufficient to say, according to the proverb, that here
is God's plenty. * * *

1700

known only in corrupt printed texts. As
a consequence Chaucer's verse seemed
rough and irregular.
8. Giambattista della Porta (ca. 1535–

1615), author of a Latin treatise on
physiognomy.
9. Different.

JOHN BUNYAN
(1628–1688)

1653:　　　Conversion.
1660–72: Imprisoned in Bedford jail.
1675:　　　Second imprisonment in Bedford jail; *The Pilgrim's
　　　　　　　Progress* composed.

Bunyan is one of the most remarkable figures in 17th-century literature.
The son of a poor Bedfordshire tinker (a maker and mender of metal
pots), he received only meager schooling and then learned his father's
craft. Nothing in the circumstances of his early life could have suggested

that he would become a writer known the world over in translations too numerous to reckon, many of them in languages and dialects of which he had never heard.

His inner life is fully chronicled in his spiritual autobiography, *Grace Abounding to the Chief of Sinners* (1666). Here we learn of his humble parentage, his marriage to a woman (he does not tell us her name) whose dowry consisted only of two pious tracts, and of his military service—in the Parliamentary army (though he neglects to say so). But such details scarcely interest him except as he can use them to reveal the purposes of Divine Providence. *Grace Abounding* was written to show the way by which a man, convinced of his sins, is led by God's grace through the agonies of spiritual crises to a new birth and the assurance of salvation; and to record how the obscure and sinful tinker was transformed into the eloquent and fearless preacher. Such books abounded in Puritan England and followed a conventional formula; but Bunyan's psychological insight and vivid narrative gifts make *Grace Abounding* one of the most enthralling autobiographies in the language.

As a result of his spiritual struggle and triumph, he joined one of the several groups of Baptists and began his career as a preacher and religious writer. Preachers, both male and female, often even less educated than Bunyan, were common phenomena among the sects during the Commonwealth. They wished no ordination but the "call," and they could dispense with learning since they abounded in inspiration, inner light, and the gifts conferred by the Holy Spirit. In November, 1660, despite Charles II's promised policy of mildness, the Anglican Church began to persecute and silence the Dissenting sects. Jails filled with unlicensed Nonconformist preachers, and John Bunyan was one of the prisoners. Refusing to keep silent, he chose imprisonment and so for twelve years remained in Bedford jail, preaching to his fellow prisoners and writing religious books. Upon his release, he was called to the pastorate of a Nonconformist group in Bedford. It was during a second imprisonment, in 1675, when the Test Act was once again rigorously enforced against Nonconformists, that he wrote his greatest work, *The Pilgrim's Progress from This World to That Which Is to Come* (1678), revised and augmented in the third edition (1679). Bunyan was a prolific writer: Part II of *The Pilgrim's Progress*, dealing with the journey of Christian's wife and children, appeared in 1684; *The Life and Death of Mr. Badman*, in 1680; *The Holy War*, in 1682. But these major works form only a small part of all his writings.

The Pilgrim's Progress is the most successful allegory in our literature. Its basic metaphor—life is a journey—is simple and familiar; the objects that the pilgrim Christian meets are homely and commonplace: a quagmire, the highway, the bypaths and short cuts through pleasant meadows; the inn, the steep hill, the town fair on market day; the river that must be forded—such objects were familiar then, and *mutatis mutandis*, are familiar even in our automotive age. They have the immediacy of daily experience, a quality that recalls the equally homely parables of Jesus, but Bunyan's allegorizing of these details charges them with spiritual significance. Moreover, Bunyan is a superb storyteller: this is, after all, a tale of adventure; he knows how to keep his reader in suspense, and because he was of the folk, how to mingle the romantic and the strange with the familiar. If the road that Christian travels is the King's Highway, it is also a perilous path along which we encounter giants, wild beasts, hobgoblins, and the terrible Apollyon, "the angel of the bottomless pit," with whom Christian must fight. Bunyan's knowledge of human nature keeps the tale firmly based on universal experience—whether in the brilliant and some-times humorous characterization of other travelers along the way (who represent states of the soul and intellectual or moral attitudes) or in the inevitably right arrangement of Christian's own experiences, from the un-forgettable first sight that we catch of him as his reading in the book convinces him of his sins and evokes his cry of terror, to the moving ac-count of his death with Hopeful in the river. Finally, Bunyan's style, modeled on the prose of the English Bible, together with his concrete and living language and carefully observed and vividly rendered details, enable even the simplest reader to share the experiences of the characters. What could be better than the following sentence? "Some cry out against sin even as the mother cries out against her child in her lap, when she calleth it slut and naughty girl, and then falls to hugging and kissing it." Even the conversations on doctrinal matters, tedious though they are, can-not seriously damage so human and dramatic a tale. In a secular age like the present, *The Pilgrim's Progress* is no longer a household book; but it survives in the speech of men who have never read it, for it gave to our language phrases that will doubtless always live: "the slough of despond," "the house beautiful," "Mr. Worldly-Wiseman," "Vanity Fair." And it lives again for anyone who reads beyond the first page.

From Grace Abounding to the Chief of Sinners

It would be too long for me here to stay, to tell you in particu-lar how God did set me down in all the things of Christ, and how he did, that he might so do, lead me into his words, yea and also how he did open them unto me, make them shine before me, and cause them to dwell with me and comfort me over and over, both of his own being, and the being of his Son, and Spirit, and Word, and Gospel.

Only this, as I said before I will say unto you again, that in gen-eral he was pleased to take this course with me, first, to suffer me to be afflicted with temptation concerning them, and then reveal them to me; as sometimes I should lie under great guilt for sin, even crushed to the ground therewith, and then the Lord would shew me the death of Christ, yea and so sprinkle my Conscience with his Blood, that I should find, and that before I was aware, that in that Conscience where but just now did reign and rage the Law, even there would rest and abide the Peace and Love of *God* through Christ.

Now had I an evidence, as I thought, of my salvation from Heaven, with many golden Seals thereon, all hanging in my sight; now could I remember this manifestation, and the other discovery of grace with comfort; and should often long and desire that the last day were come, that I might forever be inflamed with the sight, and joy, and communion of him, whose Head was crowned with Thorns, whose Face was spit on, and Body broken, and Soul made an offering for my sins: for whereas before I lay continually trembling at the mouth of Hell; now me thought I was got so far therefrom, that I could not, when I looked back, scarce discern it; and O thought I, that I were fourscore years old now, that I might die quickly, that my soul might be gone to rest.

But before I had got thus far out of these my temptations, I did greatly long to see some ancient Godly man's Experience, who had writ some hundred of years before I was born; for, for those who had writ in our days, I thought (but I desire them now to pardon me) that they had Writ only that which others felt, or else had, through the strength of their Wits and Parts, studied to answer such Objections as they perceived others were perplexed with, without going down themselves into the deep. Well, after many such longings in my mind, the God in whose hands are all our days and ways, did cast into my hand, one day, a book of *Martin Luther*, his comment on the *Galathians*, so old that it was ready to fall piece from piece, if I did but turn it over. Now I was pleased much that such an old book had fallen into my hand; the which, when I had but a little way perused, I found my condition in his experience, so largely and profoundly handled, as if his Book had been written out of my heart; this made me marvel: for thus thought I, this man could not know anything of the state of Christians now, but must needs write and speak of the Experience of former days.

Besides, he doth most gravely also, in that book debate of the rise of these temptations, namely, Blasphemy, Desperation, and the like, shewing that the law of *Moses*, as well as the Devil, Death, and Hell, hath a very great hand therein; the which at first was very strange to me, but considering and watching, I found it so indeed. But of Particulars here I intend nothing, only this methinks I must let fall before all men, I do prefer this book of Mr. *Luther* upon the *Galathians*, (excepting the Holy Bible) before all the books that ever I have seen, as most fit for a wounded Conscience.

* * *

And now I found, as I thought, that I loved Christ dearly. O me thought my soul cleaved unto him, my affections cleaved unto him. I felt love to him as hot as fire, and now, as Job said, I thought I should die in my nest; but I did quickly find that my great love was but little, and that I, who had as I thought such burning love to Jesus Christ, could let him go again for a trifle. God can tell how to abase us, and can hide pride from man. Quickly after this my love was tried to purpose.

For after the Lord had in this manner thus graciously delivered me from this great and sore temptation, and had set me down so sweetly in the faith of his holy gospel, and had given me such strong consolation and blessed evidence from heaven touching my interest in his love through Christ; the Tempter came upon me again, and that with a more grievous and dreadful temptation than before.

And that was to sell and part with this most blessed Christ, to exchange him for the things of this life, for any thing: the temptation lay upon me for the space of a year, and did follow me so continally that I was not rid of it one day in a month, no not sometimes one hour in many days together, unless I was asleep.

And though in my judgment I was persuaded that those who were once effectually in Christ (as I hoped, through his grace, I had seen myself) could never lose him forever . . . yet it was a continual vexation to me to think I should have so much as one such thought within me against a Christ, a Jesus, that had done for me as he had done; and yet then I had almost none others, but such blasphemous ones.

But it was neither my dislike of the thought, nor yet any desire and endeavor to resist it, that in the least did shake or abate the continuation or force and strength thereof; for it did always in almost whatever I thought intermix itself therewith, in such sort that I could neither eat my food, stoop for a pin, chop a stick, or cast mine eye to look on this or that, but still the temptation would come, *Sell Christ for this, or sell Christ for that; sell him, sell him.*

Sometimes it would run in my thoughts not so little as a hundred times together, Sell him, sell him, sell him; against which, I may say, for whole hours together, I have been forced to stand as continually leaning and forcing my spirit against it, lest haply before I were aware, some wicked thought might arise in my heart that might consent thereto; and sometimes also the Tempter would make me believe I had consented to it, then should I be as tortured on a rack for whole days together.

This temptation did put me to such scares lest I should sometimes, I say, consent thereto and be overcome therewith, that by the very force of my mind in laboring to gainsay and resist this wickedness, my very body also would be put into action or motion, by way of pushing or thrusting with my hands or elbows; still answering, as fast as the destroyer said *Sell him:* I will not, I will not, I will not, I will not, no, not for thousands, thousands, thousands of worlds, thus reckoning lest I should in the midst of these assaults set too low a value of him, even until I scarce well knew where I was, or how to be composed again.

At these seasons he would not let me eat my food at quiet, but forsooth when I was set at the table at my meat, I must go hence to pray, I must leave my food now, just now, so counterfeit holy would this Devil be. When I was thus tempted, I should say in myself, *Now I am at my meat, let me make an end.* No, said he, *you must do it now, or you will displease God and despise Christ.* Wherefore

I was much afflicted with these things; and because of the sinfulness of my nature (imagining that these things were impulses from God), I should deny to do it as if I denied God; and then should I be as guilty because I did not obey a temptation of the Devil, as if I had broken the law of God indeed.

But to be brief, one morning, as I did lie in my bed, I was, as at other times, most fiercely assaulted with this temptation, to *sell and part with Christ*; the wicked suggestion still running in my mind, *Sell him, sell him, sell him*, as fast as a man could speak; against which also in my mind, as at other times, I answered, No, no, not for thousands, thousands, thousands, at least twenty times together; but at last, after much striving, even until I was almost out of breath, I felt this thought pass through my heart, *Let him go if he will!* and I thought also that I felt my heart freely consent thereto. Oh, the diligence of Satan! Oh, the desperateness of man's heart!

Now was the battle won, and down I fell, as a bird that is shot from the top of a tree, into great guilt and fearful despair; thus getting out of my bed, I went moping into the field; but God knows with as heavy a heart as mortal man, I think, could bear; where for the space of two hours, I was like a man bereft of life, and as now past all recovery, and bound over to eternal punishment.

* * *

Now was I as one bound, I felt myself shut up unto the judgment to come; nothing now for two years together would abide with me but damnation and an expectation of damnation: I say nothing now would abide with me but this, save some few moments for relief, as in the sequel you will see.

These words were to my soul like fetters of brass to my legs, in the continual sound of which I went for several months together. But about ten or eleven a clock one day, as I was walking under a hedge, full of sorrow and guilt, God knows, and bemoaning myself for this hard hap, that such a thought should arise within me, suddenly this sentence bolted in upon me, *The blood of Christ remits all guilt*; at this I made a stand in my spirit: with that, this word took hold upon me, *The blood of Jesus Christ his son cleanseth us from all sin.*

Now I began to conceive peace in my soul, and methought I saw as if the tempter did leer and steal away from me, as being ashamed of what he had done. At the same time also I had my sin and the blood of Christ thus represented to me, That my sin when compared to the blood of Christ was no more to it than this little clot or stone before me is to this vast and wide field that here I see. This gave me good encouragement for the space of two or three hours, in which time also methought I saw by faith the son of God as suffering for my sins. But because it tarried not, I therefore sunk in my spirit under exceeding guilt again.

* * *

And now I was both a burden and a terror to myself, nor did I ever so know, as now, what it was to be weary of my life and yet afraid to die. Oh, how gladly now would I have been anybody but myself! Anything but a man! and in any condition but mine own! for there was nothing did pass more frequently over my mind, than that it was impossible for me to be forgiven my transgression, and to be saved from the wrath to come.

* * *

Once as I was walking to and fro in a good man's shop, bemoaning to myself in my sad and doleful state, afflicting myself with self-abhorrence for this wicked and ungodly thought, lamenting also for this hard hap of mine, for that I should commit so great a sin, greatly fearing I should not be pardoned; praying also in my heart, That if this sin of mine did differ from that against the Holy Ghost, the Lord would show it to me: and being now ready to sink with fear, suddenly there was as if there had rushed in at the window the noise of wind upon me, but very pleasant, and as if I had heard a voice speaking, *Didst ever refuse to be justified by the blood of Christ?* and withal my whole life of profession[1] past was in a moment opened to me, wherein I was made to see that designedly I had not; so my heart answered groaningly, No. Then fell with power that word of God upon me, *See that ye refuse not him that speaketh* (Hebrews 12.25). This made a strange seizure upon my spirit; it brought light with it, and commanded a silence in my heart of all those tumultuous thoughts that before did use, like masterless hellhounds to roar and bellow and make a hideous noise within me. It showed me also that Jesus Christ had yet a work of grace and mercy for me, that he had not, as I had feared, quite forsaken and cast off my soul; yea, this was a kind of chide for my proneness to desperation; a kind of threatening me if I did not, notwithstanding my sins and the heinousness of them, venture my salvation upon the son of God. * * * This lasted in the savor of it, for about three or four days, and then I began to mistrust and to despair again.

* * *

At another time I remember I was again much under the question, Whether the blood of Christ was sufficient to save my soul? In which doubt I continued from morning till about seven or eight at night; and at last when I was, as it were, quite worn out with fear lest it should not lay hold on me, these words did sound suddenly within me, *He is able*: but me thought this word *able* was spoke so loud unto me, it showed such a *great* word, it seemed to be writ in *great* letters, and gave such a justle to my fear and doubt (I mean for the time it tarried with me, which was about a day) as I never

1. My life as a believing (professing) Christian.

had from that, all my life either before or after that.

But one morning when I was again at prayer and trembling under the fear of this, that no word of God could help me, that piece of a sentence darted in upon me, *My grace is sufficient.* At this me thought I felt some stay, as if there might be hopes. But O how good a thing is it for God to send his word! for about a fortnight before, I was looking on this very place, and then I thought it could not come near my soul with comfort, and threw down my book in a pet. Then I thought it was not large enough for me; no, not large enough; but now it was as if it had arms of grace so wide that it could not only enclose me, but many more besides.

By these words I was sustained, yet not without exceeding conflicts, for the space of seven or eight weeks: for my peace would be in and out sometimes twenty times a day. Comfort now and trouble presently; peace now, and before I could go a furlong, as full of fear and guilt as ever heart could hold. And this was not only now and then, but my whole seven weeks' experience; for this about the sufficiency of grace and that of Esau's parting with his birthright[2] would be like a pair of scales within my mind, sometimes one end would be uppermost and sometimes again the other, according to which would be my peace or trouble.

1666

From The Pilgrim's Progress
FROM THIS WORLD TO THAT WHICH IS TO COME:
DELIVERED UNDER THE SIMILITUDE OF A DREAM

[Christian Sets out for the Celestial City]

As I walked through the wilderness of this world, I lighted on a certain place where was a Den, and I laid me down in that place to sleep; and, as I slept, I dreamed a dream. I dreamed, and behold I saw a man clothed with rags, standing in a certain place, with his face from his own house, a book in his hand, and a great burden upon his back (*Isaiah lxiv.6; Luke xiv.33; Psalms xxxviii.4; Habakkuk ii.2; Acts xvi.31*). I looked and saw him open the book and read therein; and, as he read, he wept, and trembled; and not being able longer to contain, he brake out with a lamentable cry, saying, "What shall I do?" (*Acts ii.37*).

In this plight, therefore, he went home and refrained himself as long as he could, that his wife and children should not perceive his distress; but he could not be silent long, because that his trouble increased. Wherefore at length he brake his mind to his wife

2. Bunyan believed that when the fatal phrase about "letting Christ go if he would" flashed through his mind, all power to share in the Christian blessing was eternally lost to him, as Esau sold his birthright irrevocably, irretrievably, forever.

and children; and thus he began to talk to them. O my dear wife, said he, and you the children of my bowels, I your dear friend am in myself undone by reason of a burden that lieth hard upon me; moreover, I am for certain informed that this our city will be burned with fire from heaven, in which fearful overthrow both myself, with thee, my wife, and you, my sweet babes, shall miserably come to ruin, except (the which yet I see not) some way of escape can be found, whereby we may be delivered. At this his relations were sore amazed; not for that they believed that what he had said to them was true, but because they thought that some frenzy distemper[1] had got into his head; therefore, it drawing towards night, and they hoping that sleep might settle his brains, with all haste they got him to bed; but the night was as troublesome to him as the day; wherefore, instead of sleeping, he spent it in sighs and tears. So when the morning was come, they would know how he did. He told them, Worse and worse; he also set to talking to them again, but they began to be hardened. They also thought to drive away his distemper by harsh and surly carriages[2] to him: sometimes they would deride, sometimes they would chide, and sometimes they would quite neglect him. Wherefore he began to retire himself to his chamber, to pray for and pity them, and also to condole his own misery; he would also walk solitarily in the fields, sometimes reading, and sometimes praying; and thus for some days he spent his time.

Now I saw, upon a time, when he was walking in the fields, that he was (as he was wont) reading in this book, and greatly distressed in his mind; and as he read, he burst out, as he had done before, crying, "What shall I do to be saved?"

I saw also that he looked this way and that way, as if he would run; yet he stood still, because (as I perceived) he could not tell which way to go. I looked then, and saw a man named Evangelist[3] coming to him, who asked, Wherefore dost thou cry? (*Job xxxiii.23*). He answered, Sir, I perceive by the book in my hand that I am condemned to die, and after that to come to judgment (*Hebrews ix.27*), and I find that I am not willing to do the first (*Job xvi.21*), nor able to do the second (*Ezekiel xxii.14*). * * *

Then said Evangelist, Why not willing to die, since this life is attended with so many evils? The man answered, Because I fear that this burden that is upon my back will sink me lower than the grave, and I shall fall into Tophet[4] (*Isaiah xxx.33*). And, sir, if I be not fit to go to prison, I am not fit to go to judgment, and from thence to execution; and the thoughts of these things make me cry.[5]

1. A malady causing madness; the use of "frenzy" as an adjective was not uncommon in the 17th century.
2. Behavior.
3. A preacher of the Gospel; literally, a bearer of good news.
4. The place near Jerusalem where bodies and filth were burned; hence, by association, a name for hell.
5. Cry out.

Then said Evangelist, If this be thy condition, why standest thou still? He answered, Because I know not whither to go. Then he gave him a parchment roll, and there was written within, "Fly from the wrath to come" (*Matthew iii.7*).

The man therefore read it, and looking upon Evangelist very carefully,[6] said, Whither must I fly? Then said Evangelist, pointing with his finger over a very wide field, Do you see yonder wicket-gate?[7] (*Matthew vii.13, 14.*) The man said, No. Then said the other, Do you see yonder shining light? (*Psalms cxix.105; II Peter i.19.*) He said, I think I do. Then said Evangelist, Keep that light in your eye, and go up directly thereto; so shalt thou see the gate; at which when thou knockest it shall be told thee what thou shalt do.

So I saw in my dream that the man began to run. Now, he had not run far from his own door, but his wife and children perceiving it, began to cry after him to return; but the man put his fingers in his ears, and ran on, crying, Life! life! eternal life! (*Luke xiv.26.*) So he looked not behind him, but fled towards the middle of the plain (*Genesis xix.17*).

The neighbors also came out to see him run (*Jeremiah xx.10*); and as he ran some mocked, others threatened, and some cried after him to return; and, among those that did so, there were two that resolved to fetch him back by force. The name of the one was Obstinate, and the name of the other Pliable. Now by this time the man was got a good distance from them; but, however, they were resolved to pursue him, which they did, and in a little time they overtook him. Then said the man, Neighbors, wherefore are ye come? They said, To persuade you to go back with us. But he said, That can by no means be; you dwell, said he, in the City of Destruction (the place also where I was born) I see it to be so; and, dying there, sooner or later, you will sink lower than the grave, into a place that burns with fire and brimstone; be content, good neighbors, and go along with me.

OBST. What! said Obstinate, and leave our friends and our comforts behind us?

CHR. Yes, said Christian (for that was his name), because that ALL which you shall forsake is not worthy to be compared with a little of that which I am seeking to enjoy (*II Corinthians v.17*); and, if you will go along with me, and hold it, you shall fare as I myself; for there, where I go, is enough and to spare (*Luke xv.17*). Come away, and prove my words.

OBST. What are the things you seek, since you leave all the world to find them?

CHR. I seek an inheritance incorruptible, undefiled, and that fad-

6. Sorrowfully.
7. A small gate in or beside a larger gate.

eth not away (*I Peter i.4*), and it is laid up in heaven, and safe there (*Hebrews xi.16*), to be bestowed, at the time appointed, on them that diligently seek it. Read it so, if you will, in my book.

OBST. Tush! said Obstinate, away with your book; will you go back with us or no?

CHR. No, not I, said the other, because I have laid my hand to the plow (*Luke ix.62*).

OBST. Come, then, neighbor Pliable, let us turn again, and go home without him; there is a company of these crazed-headed cox-combs,[8] that, when they take a fancy by the end, are wiser in their own eyes than seven men that can render a reason (*Proverbs xxvi.16*).

PLI. Then said Pliable, Don't revile; if what the good Christian says is true, the things he looks after are better than ours; my heart inclines to go with my neighbor.

OBST. What! more fools still? Be ruled by me, go back; who knows whither such a brain-sick fellow will lead you? Go back, go back, and be wise.

CHR. Nay, but do thou come with thy neighbor, Pliable; there are such things to be had which I spoke of, and many more glories besides. If you believe not me, read here in this book; and for the truth of what is expressed therein, behold, all is confirmed by the blood of Him that made it (*Hebrews ix.17–22; xiii.20*).

PLI. Well, neighbour Obstinate, said Pliable, I begin to come to a point,[9] I intend to go along with this good man, and to cast in my lot with him: but, my good companion, do you know the way to this desired place?

CHR. I am directed by a man, whose name is Evangelist, to speed me to a little gate that is before us, where we shall receive instructions about the way.

PLI. Come, then, good neighbor, let us be going. Then they went both together. * * *

[The Slough of Despond]

Now I saw in my dream, that just as they had ended this talk they drew near to a very miry slough,[1] that was in the midst of the plain; and they, being heedless, did both fall suddenly into the bog. The name of the slough was Despond. Here, therefore, they wallowed for a time, being grievously bedaubed with dirt; and Christian, because of the burden that was on his back, began to sink in the mire.

PLI. Then said Pliable, Ah, neighbor Christian, where are you now?

CHR. Truly, said Christian, I do not know.

PLI. At that Pliable began to be offended, and angrily said to his

---

8. Fools: "fancy": delusion.
9. Decision.

1. Pronounce to rhyme with *now*.

fellow, Is this the happiness you have told me all this while of? If we have such ill speed at our first setting out, what may we expect 'twixt this and our journey's end? May I get out again with my life, you shall possess the brave country alone for me. And, with that, he gave a desperate struggle or two, and got out of the mire on that side of the slough which was next[2] to his own house: so away he went, and Christian saw him no more.

Wherefore Christian was left to tumble in the Slough of Despond alone: but still he endeavored to struggle to that side of the slough that was further from his own house, and next to the wicket-gate; the which he did, but could not get out, because of the burden that was upon his back: but I beheld in my dream, that a man came to him, whose name was Help, and asked him what he did there?

CHR. Sir, said Christian, I was bid go this way by a man called Evangelist, who directed me also to yonder gate, that I might escape the wrath to come; and as I was going thither I fell in here.

HELP. But why did not you look for the steps?

CHR. Fear followed me so hard that I fled the next way, and fell in.

HELP. Then said he, Give me thy hand; so he gave him his hand, and he drew him out, and set him upon sound ground, and bid him go on his way.

Then I stepped to him that plucked him out, and said, Sir, wherefore, since over this place is the way from the City of Destruction to yonder gate, is it that this plat[3] is not mended, that poor travelers might go thither with more security? And he said unto me, This miry slough is such a place as cannot be mended; it is the descent whither the scum and filth that attends conviction for sin doth continually run, and therefore it was called the Slough of Despond; for still, as the sinner is awakened about his lost condition, there ariseth in his soul many fears, and doubts, and discouraging apprehensions, which all of them get together, and settle in this place. And this is the reason of the badness of this ground. * * *

[Vanity Fair][4]

Then I saw in my dream, that when they were got out of the wilderness, they presently saw a town before them, and the name

2. Nearest.
3. A plot of ground.
4. In this, perhaps the best-known episode in the book, Bunyan characteristically turns one of the most familiar institutions in contemporary England —annual fairs—into an allegory of universal spiritual significance. Christian and his companion Faithful pass through the town of Vanity at the season of the local fair. "Vanity" means "emptiness" or "worthlessness," and hence the fair is an allegory of worldliness and the corruption of the religious life through the attractions of the world. From earliest times numerous fairs were held for stated periods throughout Britain; to them the most important merchants from all over Europe brought their wares. The serious business of buying and selling was accompanied by all sorts of diversions —eating, drinking, and other fleshly pleasures, as well as spectacles of strange animals, acrobats, and other wonders.

of that town is Vanity; and at the town there is a fair kept, called Vanity Fair; it is kept all the year long; it beareth the name of Vanity Fair because the town where it is kept is lighter than vanity; and also because all that is there sold, or that cometh thither, is vanity. As is the saying of the wise, "All that cometh is vanity" (*Ecclesiastes i.2, 14; ii.11, 17; xi.8; Isaiah xl.17*).

This fair is no new-erected business, but a thing of ancient standing; I will show you the original of it.

Almost five thousand years agone, there were pilgrims walking to the Celestial City, as these two honest persons are; and Beelzebub, Apollyon, and Legion,[5] with their companions, perceiving by the path that the pilgrims made, that their way to the city lay through this town of Vanity, they contrived here to set up a fair; a fair wherein should be sold all sorts of vanity, and that it should last all the year long. Therefore at this fair are all such merchandise sold, as houses, lands, trades, places, honors, preferments,[6] titles, countries, kingdoms, lusts, pleasures, and delights of all sorts, as whores, bawds, wives, husbands, children, masters, servants, lives, blood, bodies, souls, silver, gold, pearls, precious stones, and what not.

And, moreover, at this fair there is at all times to be seen jugglings, cheats, games, plays, fools, apes, knaves, and rogues, and that of every kind.

Here are to be seen, too, and that for nothing, thefts, murders, adulteries, false swearers, and that of a blood-red color.

And as in other fairs of less moment, there are the several rows and streets, under their proper names, where such and such wares are vended; so here likewise you have the proper places, rows, streets (viz., countries and kingdoms), where the wares of this fair are soonest to be found. Here is the Britain Row, the French Row, the Italian Row, the Spanish Row, the German Row, where several sorts of vanities are to be sold. But, as in other fairs, some one commodity is as the chief of all the fair, so the ware of Rome and her merchandise[7] is greatly promoted in this fair; only our English nation, with some others, have taken a dislike thereat.

Now, as I said, the way to the Celestial City lies just through this town where this lusty[8] fair is kept; and he that will go to the City, and yet not go through this town, must needs "go out of the world" (*I Corinthians v.10*). The Prince of princes himself, when here, went through this town to his own country, and that upon a fairday too;[9] yea, and as I think, it was Beelzebub, the chief lord of this fair, that invited him to buy of his vanities; yea, would have

5. Beelzebub, prince of the devils (Matthew xii.24); Apollyon, the Destroyer, "the Angel of the bottomless pit" (Revelation ix.11); Legion, the "unclean spirit" sent by Jesus into the Gadarene swine (Mark v.9).
6. Appointments and promotions to political or ecclesiastical positions.
7. The usages and the temporal power of the Roman Catholic Church.
8. Merry.
9. The temptation of Jesus in the wilderness (Matthew iv.1–11).

made him lord of the fair, would he but have done him reverence as he went through the town. (*Matthew iv.8; Luke iv.5–7.*) Yea, because he was such a person of honor, Beelzebub had him from street to street, and showed him all the kingdoms of the world in a little time, that he might, if possible, allure the Blessed One to cheapen[1] and buy some of his vanities; but he had no mind to the merchandise, and therefore left the town, without laying out so much as one farthing upon these vanities. This fair, therefore, is an ancient thing, of long standing, and a very great fair.

Now these pilgrims, as I said, must needs go through this fair. Well, so they did; but, behold, even as they entered into the fair, all the people in the fair were moved, and the town itself as it were in a hubbub about them; and that for several reasons: for

First, The pilgrims were clothed with such kind of raiment as was diverse from the raiment of any that traded in that fair. The people, therefore, of the fair, made a great gazing upon them: some said they were fools, some they were bedlams,[2] and some they are outlandish men. (*I Corinthians ii.7, 8.*)

Secondly, And as they wondered at their apparel, so they did likewise at their speech; for few could understand what they said; they naturally spoke the language of Canaan,[3] but they that kept the fair were the men of this world; so that, from one end of the fair to the other, they seemed barbarians[4] each to the other.

Thirdly, But that which did not a little amuse the merchandisers was that these pilgrims set very light by all their wares; they cared not so much as to look upon them; and if they called upon them to buy, they would put their fingers in their ears, and cry, "Turn away mine eyes from beholding vanity," and look upwards, signifying that their trade and traffic was in heaven. (*Psalms cxix.37; Philippians iii.19, 20.*)

One chanced mockingly, beholding the carriages of the men, to say unto them, What will ye buy? But they, looking gravely upon him, said, "We buy the truth" (*Proverbs xxiii.23*). At that there was an occasion taken to despise the men the more; some mocking, some taunting, some speaking reproachfully, and some calling upon others to smite them. At last things came to an hubbub and great stir in the fair, insomuch that all order was confounded. Now was word presently brought to the great one of the fair, who quickly came down, and deputed some of his most trusty friends to take these men into examination, about whom the fair was almost overturned. So the men were brought to examination; and they that sat

1. Ask the price of.
2. Lunatics from Bethlehem Hospital, the insane asylum in London. "Outlandish": foreign.
3. The Promised Land, ultimately conquered by the Children of Israel (Joshua iv) and settled by them: hence

the pilgrims speak the language of the Bible and of the true religion. Dissenters were notorious for their habitual use of Biblical language.
4. The Greeks and Romans so designated all those who spoke a foreign tongue.

upon them[5] asked them whence they came, whither they went, and what they did there, in such an unusual garb? The men told them that they were pilgrims and strangers in the world, and that they were going to their own country, which was the Heavenly Jerusalem (*Hebrews xi.13–16*); and that they had given no occasion to the men of the town, nor yet to the merchandisers, thus to abuse them, and to let[6] them in their journey, except it was for that, when one asked them what they would buy, they said they would buy the truth. But they that were appointed to examine them did not believe them to be any other than bedlams and mad, or else such as came to put all things into a confusion in the fair. Therefore they took them and beat them, and besmeared them with dirt, and then put them into the cage, that they might be made a spectacle to all the men of the fair. * * *

[The River of Death and the Celestial City]

So I saw that when they[7] awoke, they addressed themselves to go up to the City; but, as I said, the reflection of the sun upon the City (for the City was pure gold, *Revelation xxi.18*) was so extremely glorious, that they could not, as yet, with open face behold it, but through an instrument made for that purpose. (*II Corinthians iii.18.*) So I saw that as I went on, there met them two men, in raiment that shone like gold; also their faces shone as the light.

These men asked the pilgrims whence they came; and they told them. They also asked them where they had lodged, what difficulties and dangers, what comforts and pleasures they had met in the way; and they told them. Then said the men that met them, You have but two difficulties more to meet with, and then you are in the City.

Christian then and his companion asked the men to go along with them; so they told them they would. But, said they, you must obtain it by your own faith. So I saw in my dream that they went on together till they came in sight of the gate.

Now I further saw that betwixt them and the gate was a river, but there was no bridge to go over; the river was very deep. At the sight, therefore, of this river, the pilgrims were much stunned;[8] but the men that went with them said, You must go through, or you cannot come at the gate.

The pilgrims then began to inquire if there was no other way to the gate; to which they answered, Yes; but there hath not any, save two, to wit, Enoch and Elijah,[9] been permitted to tread that path, since the foundation of the world, nor shall, until the last

---

5. Interrogated and tried them.
6. Hinder.
7. Christian and his companion, Hopeful. Ignorance, who appears tragically in the final paragraph, had tried to accompany the two pilgrims, but had dropped behind because of his hobbling gait.
8. Amazed.
9. Both were "translated" alive to heaven (Genesis v.24, Hebrews xi.5, II Kings ii.11–12).

trumpet shall sound. (*I Corinthians xv.51, 52.*) The pilgrims then, especially Christian, began to despond in his mind, and looked this way and that, but no way could be found by them by which they might escape the river. Then they asked the men if the waters were all of a depth. They said no; yet they could not help them in that case; for, said they, you shall find it deeper or shallower, as you believe in the King of the place.

They then addressed themselves to the water; and entering, Christian began to sink, and crying out to his good friend Hopeful, he said, I sink in deep waters; the billows go over my head, all his waves go over me! Selah.[1]

Then said the other, Be of good cheer, my brother, I feel the bottom, and it is good. Then said Christian, Ah, my friend, the sorrows of death have compassed me about; I shall not see the land that flows with milk and honey. And with that a great darkness and horror fell upon Christian, so that he could not see before him. Also here he in great measure lost his senses, so that he could neither remember nor orderly talk of any of those sweet refreshments that he had met with in the way of his pilgrimage. But all the words that he spake still tended to discover that he had horror of mind, and heart-fears that he should die in that river, and never obtain entrance in at the gate. Here also, as they that stood by perceived, he was much in the troublesome thoughts of the sins that he had committed, both since and before he began to be a pilgrim. 'Twas also observed that he was troubled with apparitions of hobgoblins and evil spirits; for ever and anon he would intimate so much by words. Hopeful, therefore, here had much ado to keep his brother's head above water; yea, sometimes he would be quite gone down, and then, ere a while, he would rise up again half dead. Hopeful also would endeavor to comfort him, saying, Brother, I see the gate and men standing by to receive us; but Christian would answer, 'Tis you, 'tis you they wait for; you have been Hopeful ever since I knew you. And so have you, said he to Christian. Ah, brother, said he, surely if I was right he would now arise to help me; but for my sins he hath brought me into the snare, and hath left me. Then said Hopeful, My brother, you have quite forgot the text, where it is said of the wicked, "There are no bands in their death, but their strength is firm. They are not in trouble as other men, neither are they plagued like other men" (*Psalms lxxiii.4, 5*). These troubles and distresses that you go through in these waters are no sign that God hath forsaken you, but are sent to try you, whether you will call to mind that which heretofore you have received of his goodness, and live upon him in your distresses.

Then I saw in my dream that Christian was as in a muse[2] a

1. A word of uncertain meaning that occurs frequently at the end of a verse in the Psalms. Bunyan may have sup- posed it to signify the end.
2. A deep meditation.

while, to whom also Hopeful added this word, Be of good cheer. Jesus Christ maketh thee whole. And with that Christian brake out with a loud voice, Oh, I see him again! and he tells me, "When thou passest through the waters, I will be with thee; and through the rivers, they shall not overflow thee" (*Isaiah xliii.2*). Then they both took courage, and the Enemy was after that as still as a stone, until they were gone over. Christian therefore presently found ground to stand upon, and so it followed that the rest of the river was but shallow. Thus they got over. Now, upon the bank of the river on the other side, they saw the two Shining Men again, who there waited for them. Wherefore, being come out of the river, they saluted them saying, We are ministering spirits, sent forth to minister for those that shall be heirs of salvation. Thus they went along towards the gate. * * *

Now when they were come up to the gate, there was written over it in letters of gold, "Blessed are they that do his commandments, that they may have right to the tree of life, and may enter in through the gates into the city" (*Revelation xxii.14*).

Then I saw in my dream, that the Shining Men bid them call at the gate; the which, when they did, some from above looked over the gate, to wit, Enoch, Moses, and Elijah, etc., to whom it was said, These pilgrims are come from the City of Destruction, for the love that they bear to the King of this place; and then the pilgrims gave in unto them each man his certificate, which they had received in the beginning; those, therefore, were carried in to the King, who, when he had read them, said, Where are the men? To whom it was answered, They are standing without the gate. The King then commanded to open the gate, "That the righteous nation," said he, "which keepeth the truth, may enter in" (*Isaiah xxvi.2*).

Now I saw in my dream that these two men went in at the gate; and lo, as they entered, they were transfigured, and they had raiment put on that shone like gold. There was also that met them with harps and crowns, and gave them to them: the harps to praise withal, and the crowns in token of honor. Then I heard in my dream that all the bells in the city rang again for joy, and that it was said unto them, "ENTER YE INTO THE JOY OF OUR LORD" (*Matthew xxv.21*). I also heard the men themselves, that they sang with a loud voice, saying, "BLESSING AND HONOR, GLORY AND POWER, BE TO HIM THAT SITTETH UPON THE THRONE, AND TO THE LAMB FOREVER AND EVER" (*Revelation v.13*).

Now just as the gates were opened to let in the men, I looked in after them, and, behold, the City shone like the sun; the streets also were paved with gold, and in them walked many men, with crowns on their heads, palms in their hands, and golden harps to sing praises withal.

There were also of them that had wings, and they answered one another without intermission, saying, "Holy, holy, holy is the Lord" (*Revelation iv*.8). And after that they shut up the gates, which when I had seen I wished myself among them.

Now while I was gazing upon all these things, I turned my head to look back, and saw Ignorance come up to the riverside; but he soon got over, and that without half that difficulty which the other two men met with. For it happened that there was then in that place one Vain-hope, a ferryman, that with his boat helped him over; so he, as the other, I saw, did ascend the hill to come up to the gate, only he came alone; neither did any man meet him with the least encouragement. When he was come up to the gate, he looked up to the writing that was above, and then began to knock, supposing that entrance should have been quickly administered to him; but he was asked by the men that looked over the top of the gate, Whence came you? and what would you have? He answered, I have eat and drank in the presence of the King, and he has taught in our streets. Then they asked him for his certificate, that they might go in and show it to the King; so he fumbled in his bosom for one, and found none. Then said they, Have you none? But the man answered never a word. So they told the King, but he would not come down to see him, but commanded the two Shining Ones that conducted Christian and Hopeful to the City, to go out and take Ignorance, and bind him hand and foot, and have him away. Then they took him up, and carried him through the air, to the door that I saw in the side of the hill, and put him in there. Then I saw that there was a way to hell, even from the gates of heaven, as well as from the City of Destruction. So I awoke, and behold it was a dream. 1678

WILLIAM CONGREVE
(1670–1729)

1693: First play, *The Old Bachelor*, produced.
1695: *Love for Love*, a successful comedy.
1700: Failure of *The Way of the World*; Congreve retires from the stage.

On both sides of his family Congreve was descended from well-to-do and prominent county families. His father, a younger son, obtained a commission as lieutenant in the army and removed with his family to Ireland in 1674. There the future playwright was educated at Kilkenny School and Trinity College, Dublin; at both places he was a younger contemporary of Swift, with whom he was always on friendly terms. In 1691 he took rooms in the Middle Temple and began to study law, but like other Templars of fact and fiction he preferred the wit of the coffeehouses and the theater to the aridity of the law. Within a year he had so distinguished himself at Will's Coffeehouse that he had become intimate with the great Dryden himself; and his brief career as a dramatist began shortly thereafter.

The success of *The Old Bachelor* (produced in 1693) immediately established him as the most promising young dramatist in London. It had the then phenomenally long run of fourteen days, and Dryden declared it the best first play he had ever read. *The Double Dealer* (produced in 1693) was a near failure, though it evoked one of Dryden's most graceful and gracious poems, in which he praised Congreve as the superior of Jonson and Fletcher and the equal of Shakespeare. *Love for Love* (produced in 1695) was an unqualified success and remains Congreve's most frequently revived play. In 1697 he brought out a tragedy, *The Mourning Bride*, which enjoyed great popular esteem. But in 1700 Congreve's greatest work, *The Way of the World*, despite a brilliant cast, was a failure. Subsequently, Congreve gave up the stage. He held a minor government post, which, though a Whig, he was allowed to keep during the Tory ministry of Oxford and Bolingbroke; after the accession of George I he was given a more lucrative government sinecure. Despite the political animosities of the first two decades of the century, he managed to remain on friendly terms with Swift and Pope, and Pope dedicated to him his translation of the *Iliad*. His final years were perplexed by poor health, but were made bearable by the love of Henrietta, Duchess of Marlborough, whose last child, a daughter, was in all probability the playwright's.

Although *The Way of the World* has never been remarkably successful on the stage, it remains in the judgment of most critics the finest example of the comedy of manners; it has, then, been esteemed as literature rather than as a stage play. The reasons for its unsuccess in the theater are obvious: the plot is extremely involved and not easy to follow on the stage, while the dialogue, phrased in fastidiously exact and melodious language and subtle cadences, is swift, compact, allusive, poetically rich, and dazzlingly witty, and thus beyond the immediate comprehension of an audience, though utterly delightful to readers who can take their time. In short, Congreve's virtues as a writer, when brought to full maturity, served to frustrate his designs as a dramatist. One unusual quality in this comedy is its serious moral point of view. The characters of the hero and heroine, Mirabell and Millamant, and of the two villains, Fainall and Mrs. Marwood, have a moral complexity which the gay couples and dissolute male and female wits of more typical comedies of the period usually lacked. The play is not simply a frivolous examination of manners in the beau monde. It is informed with a moral insight into the nature of illicit and married love, and though it is no sermon, it seriously examines sexual morality.

The central four, whose complex interrelationships provide the groundwork of the plot, are surrounded by characters who serve in one way or another as foils: Witwoud, the would-be wit, with whom we contrast the true wit of Mirabell and Millamant; Petulant, a "humor" character, who affects bluff candor and cynical realism, but succeeds only in being offensive; and Sir Wilfull Witwoud, the booby squire from the country, who serves with Petulant to throw into relief the high good breeding and fineness of nature of the hero and heroine. Finally there is one of Congreve's finest creations, Lady Wishfort ("wish for it"), who though aging and ugly still longs for love, gallantry, and courtship and who is led by her appetites into the trap that Mirabell lays for her.

Because of the complexity of the plot, a summary of the situation at the rise of the curtain will prove helpful. Mirabell (a reformed rake) is sincerely in love with and wishes to marry Millamant, who, though a coquette and a highly sophisticated wit, is a virtuous woman. Mirabell some time before has married off his former mistress, the daughter of Lady Wishfort, to his friend Fainall. Fainall has grown tired of his wife and has been squandering her money on his mistress, Mrs. Marwood. In order to gain access to Millamant, Mirabell has pretended to pay court to the elderly and amorous Lady Wishfort, who is the guardian of Millamant and as such controls half her fortune. But his game has been spoiled by Mrs. Marwood, who nourishes a secret love for Mirabell, and in order to separate him from Millamant has made Lady Wishfort aware of Mirabell's duplicity. Lady Wishfort now loathes Mirabell for making a fool of her —an awkward situation, since if Millamant should marry without her guardian's consent she would lose half her fortune, and Mirabell cannot afford to marry any but a rich wife. It is at this point that the action begins. Mirabell perfects a plot to get such power over Lady Wishfort as to force her to agree to the marriage, while Millamant continues to doubt whether she wishes to marry at all.

The Way of the World

Dramatis Personae[1]
Men

FAINALL, *in love with* MRS. MARWOOD
MIRABELL, *in love with* MRS. MILLAMANT
WITWOUD ⎱ *followers of* MRS. MILLAMANT
PETULANT ⎰
SIR WILFULL WITWOUD, *half brother to* WITWOUD, *and nephew to* LADY WISHFORT
WAITWELL, *servant to* MIRABELL

1. The names of the principal characters reveal their dominant traits: for example, Fainall would *fain* have *all*, with perhaps also the suggestion that he is the complete hypocrite, who *feigns;* Witwoud is the *would-be wit;* Wishfort suggests *wish for it;* Millamant is the lady with a thousand lovers (*mille amants*); Marwood *would* willingly *mar* (injure) the lovers; Mincing has an air of affected gentility (i.e., she *minces*), which sorts ill with her vulgar English. "Mrs." is "Mistresss," a title then used by young unmarried ladies as well as by the married Mrs. Fainall.

Women

LADY WISHFORT, *enemy to* MIRABELL, *for having falsely pretended love to her*

MRS. MILLAMANT, *a fine lady, niece to* LADY WISHFORT, *and loves* MIRABELL

MRS. MARWOOD, *friend to* MR. FAINALL, *and likes* MIRABELL

MRS. FAINALL, *daughter to* LADY WISHFORT, *and wife to* FAINALL, *formerly friend to* MIRABELL

FOIBLE, *woman to* LADY WISHFORT

MINCING, *woman to* MRS. MILLAMANT

BETTY, *waitress at the chocolate house*

PEG, *under-servant to* LADY WISHFORT

DANCERS, FOOTMEN, *and* ATTENDANTS

SCENE—*London.*

Prologue

SPOKEN BY MR. BETTERTON[2]

Of those few fools, who with ill stars are cursed,
Sure scribbling fools, called poets, fare the worst:
For they're a sort of fools which Fortune makes,
And after she has made 'em fools, forsakes.
With nature's oafs 'tis quite a different case,   5
For Fortune favors all her idiot race.
In her own nest the cuckoo eggs we find,
O'er which she broods to hatch the changeling kind.[3]
No portion for her own she has to spare,
So much she dotes on her adopted care.   10
   Poets are bubbles,[4] by the town drawn in,
Suffered at first some trifling stakes to win:
But what unequal hazards do they run!
Each time they write they venture all they've won:
The squire that's buttered still,[5] is sure to be undone.   15
This author, heretofore, has found your favor,
But pleads no merit from his past behavior;
To build on that might prove a vain presumption,
Should grants to poets made, admit resumption:[6]
And in Parnassus he must lose his seat,   20
If that be found a forfeited estate.[7]
   He owns, with toil, he wrought the following scenes,
But if they're naught ne'er spare him for his pains:
Damn him the more; have no commiseration

---

2. Thomas Betterton (ca. 1635–1710), the greatest actor of the period, played Fainall in the original production of this play.
3. Simpletons; children supposed to have been secretly exchanged in infancy for others. The analogy to the "cuckoo," which lays its eggs in the nests of other birds, is obvious.

4. Dupes.
5. Constantly flattered.
6. The crown could both grant and take back ("resume") estates.
7. *Seat* rhymed with *estate;* in the next couplet, *scenes* and *pains* rhymed. A few lines later *scene* is similarly pronounced to rhyme with *maintain,* and *fault* (the *l* being silent) is rhymed with *thought.*

For dullness on mature deliberation. 25
He swears he'll not resent one hissed-off scene ⎤
Nor, like those peevish wits, his play maintain, ⎬
Who, to assert their sense, your taste arraign. ⎦
Some plot we think he has, and some new thought;
Some humor too, no farce; but that's a fault. 30
Satire, he thinks, you ought not to expect,
For so reformed a town,[8] who dares correct?
To please, this time, has been his sole pretense,
He'll not instruct, lest it should give offense.
Should he by chance a knave or fool expose, 35
That hurts none here; sure here are none of those.
In short, our play shall (with your leave to show it)
Give you one instance of a passive poet
Who to your judgments yields all resignation;
So save or damn after your own discretion. 40

Act I—A chocolate house.

SCENE 1

Mirabell and Fainall rising from cards, Betty waiting.

MIRA. You are a fortunate man, Mr. Fainall.

FAIN. Have we done?

MIRA. What you please. I'll play on to entertain you.

FAIN. No, I'll give you your revenge another time, when you are not so indifferent; you are thinking of something else now, and play too negligently. The coldness of a losing gamester lessens the pleasure of the winner. I'd no more play with a man that slighted his ill fortune than I'd make love to a woman who undervalued the loss of her reputation.

MIRA. You have a taste extremely delicate, and are for refining on your pleasures.

FAIN. Prithee, why so reserved? Something has put you out of humor.

MIRA. Not at all. I happen to be grave today, and you are gay; that's all.

FAIN. Confess, Millamant and you quarreled last night after I left you; my fair cousin has some humors that would tempt the patience of a stoic. What, some coxcomb came in, and was well received by her, while you were by?

MIRA. Witwoud and Petulant; and what was worse, her aunt, your wife's mother, my evil genius; or to sum up all in her own name, my old Lady Wishfort came in.

FAIN. O, there it is then—she has a lasting passion for you, and with reason. What, then my wife was there?

MIRA. Yes, and Mrs. Marwood and three or four more, whom I

---

8. A sarcasm, directed against the general movement to reform manners and morals and, more particularly, against Jeremy Collier's attack on actors and playwrights in his *Short View of the Profaneness and Immorality of the English Stage* (1698).

never saw before. Seeing me, they all put on their grave faces, whispered one another; then complained aloud of the vapors,[9] and after fell into a profound silence.

FAIN. They had a mind to be rid of you.

MIRA. For which good reason I resolved not to stir. At last the good old lady broke through her painful taciturnity, with an invective against long visits. I would not have understood her, but Millamant joining in the argument, I rose and with a constrained smile told her I thought nothing was so easy as to know when a visit began to be troublesome. She reddened and I withdrew, without expecting[1] her reply.

FAIN. You were to blame to resent what she spoke only in compliance with her aunt.

MIRA. She is more mistress of herself than to be under the necessity of such a resignation.

FAIN. What? though half her fortune depends upon her marrying with my lady's approbation?

MIRA. I was then in such a humor that I should have been better pleased if she had been less discreet.

FAIN. Now I remember, I wonder not they were weary of you: last night was one of their cabal[2] nights; they have 'em three times a week, and meet by turns, at one another's apartments, where they come together like the coroner's inquest, to sit upon the murdered reputations of the week. You and I are excluded; and it was once proposed that all the male sex should be excepted; but somebody moved that to avoid scandal there might be one man of the community; upon which Witwoud and Petulant were enrolled members.

MIRA. And who may have been the foundress of this sect? My Lady Wishfort, I warrant, who publishes her detestation of mankind, and full of the vigor of fifty-five, declares for a friend and ratafia;[3] and let posterity shift for itself, she'll breed no more.

FAIN. The discovery of your sham addresses to her, to conceal your love to her niece, has provoked this separation. Had you dissembled better, things might have continued in the state of nature.

MIRA. I did as much as man could, with any reasonable conscience: I proceeded to the very last act of flattery with her, and was guilty of a song in her commendation. Nay, I got a friend to put her into a lampoon and compliment her with the imputation of an affair with a young fellow, which I carried so far that I told her the malicious town took notice that she was grown fat of a sudden; and when she lay in of a dropsy, persuaded her she was reported to be in labor. The devil's in't, if an old woman is to be flattered further, unless a man should endeavor downright personally to debauch her; and that my virtue forbade me. But for the discovery of this amour, I am indebted to your friend, or your wife's friend, Mrs. Marwood.

FAIN. What should provoke her to be your enemy, unless she has

9. Melancholy, the blues.
1. Awaiting.
2. Secret organization designed for in-

trigue.
3. A liqueur flavored with fruit kernels (pronounced *rat-a-fé-a*).

made you advances, which you have slighted? Women do not easily forgive omissions of that nature.

MIRA. She was always civil to me, till of late. I confess I am not one of those coxcombs who are apt to interpret a woman's good manners to her prejudice, and think that she who does not refuse 'em everything, can refuse 'em nothing.

FAIN. You are a gallant man, Mirabell; and though you may have cruelty enough not to satisfy a lady's longing, you have too much generosity not to be tender of her honor. Yet you speak with an indifference which seems to be affected, and confesses you are conscious of a negligence.

MIRA. You pursue the argument with a distrust that seems to be unaffected, and confesses you are conscious of a concern for which the lady is more indebted to you than is your wife.

FAIN. Fie, fie, friend, if you grow censorious I must leave you.—I'll look upon the gamesters in the next room.

MIRA. Who are they?

FAIN. Petulant and Witwoud.—Bring me some chocolate.

MIRA. Betty, what says your clock?

BET. Turned of the last canonical hour,[4] sir.

MIRA. How pertinently the jade answers me! Ha? almost one a clock! [looking on his watch]—O, y'are come—

SCENE 2

Mirabell and Footman.

MIRA. Well, is the grand affair over? You have been something tedious.

FOOT. Sir, there's such coupling at Pancras[5] that they stand behind one another, as 'twere in a country dance. Ours was the last couple to lead up; and no hopes appearing of dispatch, besides, the parson growing hoarse, we were afraid his lungs would have failed before it came to our turn; so we drove around to Duke's Place, and there they were riveted in a trice.

MIRA. So, so, you are sure they are married?

FOOT. Married and bedded, sir. I am witness.

MIRA. Have you the certificate?

FOOT. Here it is, sir.

MIRA. Has the tailor brought Waitwell's clothes home, and the new liveries?

FOOT. Yes, sir.

MIRA. That's well. Do you go home again, d'ye hear, and adjourn the consummation till farther order. Bid Waitwell shake his ears, and Dame Partlet[6] rustle up her feathers, and meet me at one a clock by Rosamond's Pond, that I may see her before she returns to her lady: and as you tender your ears, be secret.

---

4. The hours in which marriage can legally be performed in the Anglican Church, then 8–12 noon.
5. The Church of St. Pancras, like that of St. James in Duke's Place (referred to later in the same speech), was noto-rious for a thriving trade in unlicensed marriages.
6. Pertelote, the hen-wife of the cock Chauntecleer in Chaucer's Nun's Priest's Tale. Rosamond's Pond was in St. James's Park.

SCENE 3

Mirabell, Fainall, Betty.

FAIN. Joy of your success, Mirabell; you look pleased.

MIRA. Aye, I have been engaged in a matter of some sort of mirth, which is not yet ripe for discovery. I am glad this is not a cabal night. I wonder, Fainall, that you who are married, and of consequence should be discreet, will suffer your wife to be of such a party.

FAIN. Faith, I am not jealous. Besides, most who are engaged are women and relations; and for the men, they are of a kind too contemptible to give scandal.

MIRA. I am of another opinion. The greater the coxcomb, always the more the scandal: for a woman who is not a fool can have but one reason for associating with a man who is one.

FAIN. Are you jealous as often as you see Witwoud entertained by Millamant?

MIRA. Of her understanding I am, if not of her person.

FAIN. You do her wrong; for to give her her due, she has wit.

MIRA. She has beauty enough to make any man think so; and complaisance enough not to contradict him who shall tell her so.

FAIN. For a passionate lover, methinks you are a man somewhat too discerning in the failings of your mistress.

MIRA. And for a discerning man, somewhat too passionate a lover; for I like her with all her faults, nay, like her for her faults. Her follies are so natural, are so artful, that they become her, and those affectations which in another woman would be odious, serve but to make her more agreeable. I'll tell thee, Fainall, she once used me with that insolence that in revenge I took her to pieces; sifted her, and separated her failings; I studied 'em, and got 'em by rote. The catalogue was so large that I was not without hopes, one day or other, to hate her heartily: to which end I so used myself to think of 'em that at length, contrary to my design and expectation, they gave me every hour less and less disturbance, till in a few days it became habitual to me to remember 'em without being displeased. They are now grown as familiar to me as my own frailties, and in all probability in a little time longer I shall like 'em as well.

FAIN. Marry her, marry her; be half as well acquainted with her charms as you are with her defects, and my life on't, you are your own man again.

MIRA. Say you so?

FAIN. Aye, aye, I have experience; I have a wife, and so forth.

SCENE 4

[*To them*] *Messenger.*

MESS. Is one Squire Witwoud here?

BET. Yes. What's your business?

MESS. I have a letter for him, from his brother Sir Wilfull, which I am charged to deliver into his own hands.

BET. He's in the next room, friend—that way.

SCENE 5

Mirabell, Fainall, Betty.

MIRA. What, is the chief of that noble family in town, Sir Wilfull Witwoud?

FAIN. He is expected today. Do you know him?

MIRA. I have seen him. He promises to be an extraordinary person; I think you have the honor to be related to him.

FAIN. Yes; he is half brother to this Witwoud by a former wife, who was sister to my Lady Wishfort, my wife's mother. If you marry Millamant, you must call cousins too.

MIRA. I had rather be his relation than his acquaintance.

FAIN. He comes to town in order to equip himself for travel.

MIRA. For travel! Why the man that I mean is above forty.[7]

FAIN. No matter for that; 'tis for the honor of England that all Europe should know that we have blockheads of all ages.

MIRA. I wonder there is not an Act of Parliament to save the credit of the nation, and prohibit the exportation of fools.

FAIN. By no means, 'tis better as 'tis; 'tis better to trade with a little loss than to be quite eaten up with being overstocked.

MIRA. Pray, are the follies of this knight-errant, and those of the squire his brother, anything related?

FAIN. Not at all. Witwoud grows by the knight, like a medlar[8] grafted on a crab. One will melt in your mouth, and t'other set your teeth on edge; one is all pulp, and the other all core.

MIRA. So one will be rotten before he be ripe, and the other will be rotten without ever being ripe at all.

FAIN. Sir Wilfull is an odd mixture of bashfulness and obstinacy. But when he's drunk, he's as loving as the monster in the *Tempest*;[9] and much after the same manner. To give t'other his due, he has something of good nature, and does not always want wit.

MIRA. Not always; but as often as his memory fails him, and his commonplace of comparisons.[1] He is a fool with a good memory, and some few scraps of other folks' wit. He is one whose conversation can never be approved, yet it is now and then to be endured. He has indeed one good quality, he is not exceptious,[2]

7. The grand tour of the Continent was rapidly becoming a part of the education of gentlemen, but it was usually made in company with a tutor after a young man had graduated from a university, not after a man had passed the age of forty.

8. A fruit eaten when it is overripe. "Crab": crab apple.

9. Trinculo, in the adaptation of Shakespeare's *Tempest* by Sir William Davenant and Dryden (1667), having made Caliban drunk, says: "The poor monster is loving in his drink" (II.2).

1. One recognized sign of wit was the ability to discover quickly resemblances between objects apparently unlike. Witwoud specializes in this kind of wit, but Mirabell suggests that they are all obvious and collected from others, like observations copied in a notebook, or "commonplace" book.

2. Quarrelsome.

for he so passionately affects the reputation of understanding raillery that he will construe an affront into a jest; and call downright rudeness and ill language, satire and fire.

FAIN. If you have a mind to finish his picture, you have an opportunity to do it at full length. Behold the original.

SCENE 6

[To them] Witwoud.

WIT. Afford me your compassion, my dears; pity me, Fainall, Mirabell, pity me.

MIRA. I do from my soul.

FAIN. Why, what's the matter?

WIT. No letters for me, Betty?

BET. Did not a messenger bring you one but now, sir?

WIT. Aye, but no other?

BET. No, sir.

WIT. That's hard, that's very hard. A messenger, a mule, a beast of burden, he has brought me a letter from the fool my brother, as heavy as a panegyric in a funeral sermon, or a copy of commendatory verses from one poet to another. And what's worse, 'tis as sure a forerunner of the author as an epistle dedicatory.

MIRA. A fool, and your brother, Witwoud!

WIT. Aye, aye, my half brother. My half brother he is, no nearer upon honor.

MIRA. Then 'tis possible he may be but half a fool.

WIT. Good, good, Mirabell, *le drôle!*[3] Good, good. Hang him, don't let's talk of him. Fainall, how does your lady? Gad. I say anything in the world to get this fellow out of my head. I beg pardon that I should ask a man of pleasure and the town a question at once so foreign and domestic. But I talk like an old maid at a marriage, I don't know what I say: but she's the best woman in the world.

FAIN. 'Tis well you don't know what you say, or else your commendation would go near to make me either vain or jealous.

WIT. No man in town lives well with a wife but Fainall. Your judgment, Mirabell?

MIRA. You had better step and ask his wife, if you would be credibly informed.

WIT. Mirabell.

MIRA. Aye.

WIT. My dear, I ask ten thousand pardons—gad, I have forgot what I was going to say to you.

MIRA. I thank you heartily, heartily.

WIT. No, but prithee excuse me—my memory is such a memory.

MIRA. Have a care of such apologies, Witwoud—for I never knew a fool but he affected to complain, either of the spleen or his memory.

FAIN. What have you done with Petulant?

3. The witty fellow.

WIT. He's reckoning his money—my money it was.—I have no luck today.

FAIN. You may allow him to win of you at play—for you are sure to be too hard for him at repartee. Since you monopolize the wit that is between you, the fortune must be his of course.

MIRA. I don't find that Petulant confesses the superiority of wit to be your talent, Witwoud.

WIT. Come, come, you are malicious now, and would breed debates.
—Petulant's my friend, and a very honest fellow, and a very pretty fellow, and has a smattering—faith and troth a pretty deal of an odd sort of a small wit: nay, I'll do him justice. I'm his friend, I won't wrong him.—And if he had any judgment in the world—he would not be altogether contemptible. Come, come, don't detract from the merits of my friend.

FAIN. You don't take your friend to be over-nicely bred.

WIT. No, no, hang him, the rogue has no manners at all, that I must own—no more breeding than a bum-bailey,[4] that I grant you.—'Tis pity; the fellow has fire and life.

MIRA. What, courage?

WIT. Hum, faith I don't know as to that—I can't say as to that.—Yes, faith, in a controversy he'll contradict anybody.

MIRA. Though 'twere a man whom he feared, or a woman whom he loved.

WIT. Well, well, he does not always think before he speaks—we have all our failings; you are too hard upon him, you are, faith. Let me excuse him—I can defend most of his faults, except one or two. One he has, that's the truth on't, if he were my brother, I could not acquit him.—That indeed I could wish were otherwise.

MIRA. Aye marry, what's that, Witwoud?

WIT. O, pardon me—expose the infirmities of my friend?—No, my dear, excuse me there.

FAIN. What, I warrant he's unsincere, or 'tis some such trifle.

WIT. No, no, what if he be? 'Tis no matter for that, his wit will excuse that. A wit should no more be sincere than a woman constant; one argues a decay of parts, as t'other of beauty.

MIRA. Maybe you think him too positive?

WIT. No, no, his being positive is an incentive to argument, and keeps up conversation.

FAIN. Too illiterate.

WIT. That! that's his happiness.—His want of learning gives him the more opportunities to show his natural parts.

MIRA. He wants words.

WIT. Aye; but I like him for that now; for his want of words gives me the pleasure very often to explain his meaning.

FAIN. He's impudent.

WIT. No, that's not it.

MIRA. Vain.

WIT. No.

4. Bumbailiff, the lowest kind of arresting officer.

MIRA. What, he speaks unseasonable truths sometimes, because he
has not wit enough to invent an evasion.

WIT. Truths! Ha, ha, ha! No, no, since you will have it—I mean,
he never speaks truth at all—that's all. He will lie like a chambermaid, or a woman of quality's porter. Now that is a fault.

SCENE 7

[To them] Coachman.

COACH. Is Master Petulant here, mistress?

BET. Yes.

COACH. Three gentlewomen in a coach would speak with him.

FAIN. O brave Petulant, three!

BET. I'll tell him.

COACH. You must bring two dishes of chocolate and a glass of
cinnamon water.

SCENE 8

Mirabell, Fainall, Witwoud.

WIT. That should be for two fasting strumpets, and a bawd troubled
with wind. Now you may know what the three are.

MIRA. You are free with your friend's acquaintance.

WIT. Aye, aye, friendship without freedom is as dull as love without
enjoyment, or wine without toasting; but to tell you a secret,
these are trulls whom he allows coach-hire, and something more
by the week, to call on him once a day at public places.

MIRA. How!

WIT. You shall see he won't go to 'em because there's no more
company here to take notice of him.—Why this is nothing to
what he used to do, before he found out this way, I have known
him call for himself.—

FAIN. Call for himself? What dost thou mean?

WIT. Mean? Why he would slip you out of this chocolate house,
just when you had been talking to him.—As soon as your back
was turned—whip he was gone—then trip to his lodging, clap
on a hood and scarf, and a mask, slap into a hackney coach, and
drive hither to the door again in a trice; where he would send
in for himself, that I mean, call for himself, wait for himself, nay
and what's more, not finding himself, sometimes leave a letter
for himself.

MIRA. I confess this is something extraordinary.—I believe he waits
for himself now, he is so long a-coming. O, I ask his pardon.

SCENE 9

Petulant, Mirabell, Fainall, Witwoud, Betty.

BET. Sir, the coach stays.

PET. Well, well; I come.—'Sbud,[5] a man had as good be a pro-

5. God's body.

fessed midwife, as a professed whoremaster, at this rate; to be knocked up and raised at all hours, and in all places. Pox on 'em, I won't come.—D'ye hear, tell 'em I won't come.—Let 'em snivel and cry their hearts out.

FAIN. You are very cruel, Petulant.

PET. All's one, let it pass—I have a humor to be cruel.

MIRA. I hope they are not persons of condition that you use at this rate.

PET. Condition, condition's a dried fig, if I am not in humor.— By this hand, if they were your—a—a—your what-dee-call-'ems themselves, they must wait or rub off,[6] if I want appetite.

MIRA. What-de-call-'ems! What are they, Witwoud?

WIT. Empresses,[7] my dear.—By your what-dee-call-'ems he means sultana queens.

PET. Aye, Roxolanas.

MIRA. Cry you mercy.

FAIN. Witwoud says they are—

PET. What does he say th' are?

WIT. I? Fine ladies I say.

PET. Pass on, Witwoud.—Harkee, by this light his relations—two co-heiresses his cousins, and an old aunt, who loves caterwauling better than a conventicle.[8]

WIT. Ha, ha, ha; I had a mind to see how the rogue would come off.—Ha, ha, ha; gad, I can't be angry with him, if he had said they were my mother and my sisters.

MIRA. No!

WIT. No; the rogue's wit and readiness of invention charm me, dear Petulant.

BET. They are gone, sir, in great anger.

PET. Enough, let 'em trundle. Anger helps complexion, saves paint.

FAIN. This continence is all dissembled; this is in order to have something to brag of the next time he makes court to Millamant, and swear he has abandoned the whole sex for her sake.

MIRA. Have you not left off your impudent pretensions there yet? I shall cut your throat, sometime or other, Petulant, about that business.

PET. Aye, aye, let that pass.—There are other throats to be cut.—

MIRA. Meaning mine, sir?

PET. Not I—I mean nobody.—I know nothing. But there are uncles and nephews in the world—and they may be rivals—What then? All's one for that—

MIRA. How! Harkee, Petulant, come hither—explain, or I shall call your interpreter.

PET. Explain? I know nothing.—Why, you have an uncle, have you not, lately come to town, and lodges by my Lady Wishfort's?

MIRA. True.

PET. Why, that's enough.—You and he are not friends; and if he

---

6. Make off.

7. "Empresses," like "sultana queens" and "Roxolanas," were terms for prostitutes. Roxolana is the wife of the Sul-

tan in Davenant's *Siege of Rhodes* (1656).

8. Nonconformist religious meeting.

should marry and have a child, you may be disinherited, ha?

MIRA. Where hast thou stumbled upon all this truth?

PET. All's one for that; why, then, say I know something.

MIRA. Come, thou art an honest fellow, Petulant, and shalt make love to my mistress, thou sha't, faith. What hast thou heard of my uncle?

PET. I, nothing, I. If throats are to be cut, let swords clash; snug's the word, I shrug and am silent.

MIRA. O raillery, raillery. Come, I know thou art in the women's secrets.—What, you're a cabalist. I know you stayed at Millamant's last night, after I went. Was there any mention made of my uncle or me? Tell me; if thou hadst but good nature equal to thy wit, Petulant, Tony Witwoud, who is now thy competitor in fame, would show as dim by thee as a dead whiting's eye by a pearl of Orient. He would no more be seen by thee than Mercury is by the sun: come, I'm sure thou wo't tell me.

PET. If I do, will you grant me common sense then, for the future?

MIRA. Faith, I'll do what I can for thee, and I'll pray that Heaven may grant it thee in the meantime.

PET. Well, harkee.

FAIN. Petulant and you both will find Mirabell as warm a rival as a lover.

WIT. Pshaw, pshaw, that she laughs at Petulant is plain. And for my part—but that it is almost a fashion to admire her, I should —harkee—to tell you a secret, but let it go no further—between friends, I shall never break my heart for her.

FAIN. How!

WIT. She's handsome; but she's a sort of an uncertain woman.

FAIN. I thought you had died for her.

WIT. Umh—no—

FAIN. She has wit.

WIT. 'Tis what she will hardly allow anybody else.—Now, demme, I should hate that, if she were as handsome as Cleopatra. Mirabell is not so sure of her as he thinks for.

FAIN. Why do you think so?

WIT. We stayed pretty late there last night, and heard something of an uncle to Mirabell, who is lately come to town—and is between him and the best part of his estate. Mirabell and he are at some distance, as my Lady Wishfort has been told; and you know she hates Mirabell, worse than a Quaker hates a parrot, or than a fishmonger hates a hard frost. Whether this uncle has seen Mrs. Millamant or not, I cannot say; but there were items of such a treaty being in embryo; and if it should come to life, poor Mirabell would be in some sort unfortunately fobbed[9] i' faith.

FAIN. 'Tis impossible Millamant should harken to it.

WIT. Faith, my dear, I can't tell; she's a woman and a kind of a humorist.[1]

MIRA. And this is the sum of what you could collect last night.

PET. The quintessence. Maybe Witwoud knows more, he stayed

9. Tricked.   1. A capricious person.

longer.—Besides they never mind him; they say anything before him.

MIRA. I thought you had been the greatest favorite.

PET. Aye, *tête à tête;*[2] but not in public, because I make remarks.

MIRA. You do?

PET. Aye, aye, pox, I'm malicious, man. Now he's soft, you know, they are not in awe of him.—The fellow's well bred, he's what you call a—what-d'ye-call-'em. A fine gentleman, but he's silly withal.

MIRA. I thank you, I know as much as my curiosity requires. Fainall, are you for the Mall?[3]

FAIN. Aye, I'll take a turn before dinner.

WIT. Aye, we'll all walk in the park, the ladies talked of being there.

MIRA. I thought you were obliged to watch for your brother Sir Wilfull's arrival.

WIT. No, no, he's come to his aunt's, my Lady Wishfort. Pox on him, I shall be troubled with him too. What shall I do with the fool?

PET. Beg him for his estate, that I may beg you afterwards, and so have but one trouble with you both.

WIT. O rare Petulant; thou art as quick as fire in a frosty morning; thou shalt to the Mall with us; and we'll be very severe.

PET. Enough, I'm in a humor to be severe.

MIRA. Are you? Pray then walk by yourselves.—Let not us be accessory to your putting the ladies out of countenance with your senseless ribaldry, which you roar out aloud as often as they pass by you; and when you have made a handsome woman blush, then you think you have been severe.

PET. What, what? Then let 'em either show their innocence by not understanding what they hear, or else show their discretion by not hearing what they would not be thought to understand.

MIRA. But hast not thou then sense enough to know that thou ought'st to be most ashamed thyself, when thou hast put another out by countenance?

PET. Not I, by this hand.—I always take blushing either for a sign of guilt, or ill breeding.

MIRA. I confess you ought to think so. You are in the right, that you may plead the error of your judgment in defense of your practice.

> Where modesty's ill manners, 'tis but fit
> That impudence and malice pass for wit.

Act II—St. James's Park.

SCENE 1

Mrs. Fainall and Mrs. Marwood.

MRS. FAIN. Aye, aye, dear Marwood, if we will be happy, we must find the means in ourselves, and among ourselves. Men are ever

---

2. Face to face, i.e., in private.   3. A walk in St. James's Park, one of the fashionable resorts of the day.

in extremes; either doting or averse. While they are lovers, if they have fire and sense, their jealousies are insupportable: and when they cease to love (we ought to think at least) they loathe. They look upon us with horror and distaste; they meet us like the ghosts of what we were, and as from such, fly from us.

MRS. MAR. True, 'tis an unhappy circumstance of life that love should ever die before us; and that the man so often should out-live the lover. But say what you will, 'tis better to be left than never to have been loved. To pass over youth in dull indifference, to refuse the sweets of life because they once must leave us, is as preposterous as to wish to have been born old, because we one day must be old. For my part, my youth may wear and waste, but it shall never rust in my possession.

MRS. FAIN. Then it seems you dissemble an aversion to mankind only in compliance to my mother's humor.

MRS. MAR. Certainly. To be free, I have no taste of those insipid dry discourses with which our sex of force must entertain them-selves apart from men. We may affect endearments to each other, profess eternal friendships, and seem to dote like lovers; but 'tis not in our natures long to persevere. Love will resume his empire in our breasts, and every heart, or soon or late, receive and readmit him as its lawful tyrant.

MRS. FAIN. Bless me, how have I been deceived! Why, you profess a libertine.

MRS. MAR. You see my friendship by my freedom. Come, be as sincere, acknowledge that your sentiments agree with mine.

MRS. FAIN. Never.

MRS. MAR. You hate mankind?

MRS. FAIN. Heartily, inveterately.

MRS. MAR. Your husband?

MRS. FAIN. Most transcendently; aye, though I say it, meritoriously.

MRS. MAR. Give me your hand upon it.

MRS. FAIN. There.

MRS. MAR. I join with you. What I have said has been to try you.

MRS. FAIN. Is it possible? Dost thou hate those vipers men?

MRS. MAR. I have done hating 'em, and am now come to despise 'em; the next thing I have to do is eternally to forget 'em.

MRS. FAIN. There spoke the spirit of an Amazon, a Penthesilea.[4]

MRS. MAR. And yet I am thinking sometimes to carry my aversion further.

MRS. FAIN. How?

MRS. MAR. Faith, by marrying. If I could but find one that loved me very well, and would be thoroughly sensible of ill usage, I think I should do myself the violence of undergoing the cere-mony.

MRS. FAIN. You would not make him a cuckold?

MRS. MAR. No; but I'd make him believe I did, and that's as bad.

MRS. FAIN. Why had not you as good do it?

MRS. MAR. O, if he should ever discover it, he would then know

4. Queen of the Amazons (a legendary nation of women warriors).

the worst, and be out of his pain; but I would have him ever to continue upon the rack of fear and jealousy.

MRS. FAIN. Ingenious mischief! Would thou wert married to Mirabell.

MRS. MAR. Would I were.

MRS. FAIN. You change color.

MRS. MAR. Because I hate him.

MRS. FAIN. So do I; but I can hear him named. But what reason have you to hate him in particular?

MRS. MAR. I never loved him; he is and always was insufferably proud.

MRS. FAIN. By the reason you give for your aversion, one would think it dissembled; for you have laid a fault to his charge of which his enemies must acquit him.

MRS. MAR. O then it seems you are one of his favorable enemies. Methinks you look a little pale, and now you flush again.

MRS. FAIN. Do I? I think I am a little sick o' the sudden.

MRS. MAR. What ails you?

MRS. FAIN. My husband. Don't you see him? He turned short upon me unawares, and has almost overcome me.

SCENE 2

[To them] Fainall and Mirabell.

MRS. MAR. Ha, ha, ha; he comes opportunely for you.

MRS. FAIN. For you, for he has brought Mirabell with him.

FAIN. My dear.

MRS. FAIN. My soul.

FAIN. You don't look well today, child.

MRS. FAIN. D'ye think so?

MIRA. He is the only man that does, madam.

MRS. FAIN. The only man that would tell me so at least; and the only man from whom I could hear it without mortification.

FAIN. O my dear, I am satisfied of your tenderness; I know you cannot resent anything from me, especially what is an effect of my concern.

MRS. FAIN. Mr. Mirabell, my mother interrupted you in a pleasant relation last night. I would fain hear it out.

MIRA. The persons concerned in that affair have yet a tolerable reputation.—I am afraid Mr. Fainall will be censorious.

MRS. FAIN. He has a humor more prevailing than his curiosity, and will willingly dispense with the hearing of one scandalous story to avoid giving an occasion to make another by being seen to walk with his wife. This way, Mr. Mirabell, and I dare promise you will oblige us both.

SCENE 3

Fainall, Mrs. Marwood.

FAIN. Excellent creature! Well, sure if I should live to be rid of my wife, I should be a miserable man.

MRS. MAR. Aye!

FAIN. For having only that one hope, the accomplishment of it of consequence must put an end to all my hopes; and what a wretch is he who must survive his hopes! Nothing remains when that day comes but to sit down and weep like Alexander, when he wanted other worlds to conquer.

MRS. MAR. Will you not follow 'em?

FAIN. Faith, I think not.

MRS. MAR. Pray let us; I have a reason.

FAIN. You are not jealous?

MRS. MAR. Of whom?

FAIN. Of Mirabell.

MRS. MAR. If I am, is it inconsistent with my love to you that I am tender of your honor?

FAIN. You would intimate then, as if there were a fellow-feeling between my wife and him.

MRS. MAR. I think she does not hate him to that degree she would be thought.

FAIN. But he, I fear, is too insensible.

MRS. MAR. It may be you are deceived.

FAIN. It may be so. I do now begin to apprehend it.

MRS. MAR. What?

FAIN. That I have been deceived, Madam, and you are false.

MRS. MAR. That I am false! What mean you?

FAIN. To let you know I see through all your little arts.—Come, you both love him; and both have equally dissembled your aversion. Your mutual jealousies of one another have made you clash till you have both struck fire. I have seen the warm confession reddening on your cheeks, and sparkling from your eyes.

MRS. MAR. You do me wrong.

FAIN. I do not.—'Twas for my ease to oversee[5] and willfully neglect the gross advances made him by my wife; that by permitting her to be engaged I might continue unsuspected in my pleasures; and take you oftener to my arms in full security. But could you think, because the nodding husband would not wake, that e'er the watchful lover slept?

MRS. MAR. And wherewithal can you reproach me?

FAIN. With infidelity, with loving another, with love of Mirabell.

MRS. MAR. 'Tis false. I challenge you to show an instance that can confirm your groundless accusation. I hate him.

FAIN. And wherefore do you hate him? He is insensible, and your resentment follows his neglect. An instance! The injuries you have done him are a proof: your interposing in his love. What cause had you to make discoveries of his pretended passion? To undeceive the credulous aunt, and be the officious obstacle of his match with Millamant?

MRS. MAR. My obligations to my lady urged me. I had professed a friendship to her, and could not see her easy nature so abused by that dissembler.

5. Overlook.

FAIN. What, was it conscience then? Professed a friendship! O the pious friendships of the female sex!

MRS. MAR. More tender, more sincere, and more enduring than all the vain and empty vows of men, whether professing love to us, or mutual faith to one another.

FAIN. Ha, ha, ha; you are my wife's friend too.

MRS. MAR. Shame and ingratitude! Do you reproach me? You, you upbraid me! Have I been false to her, through strict fidelity to you, and sacrificed my friendship to keep my love inviolate? And have you the baseness to charge me with the guilt, unmindful of the merit! To you it should be meritorious that I have been vicious: and do you reflect that guilt upon me, which should lie buried in your bosom?

FAIN. You misinterpret my reproof. I meant but to remind you of the slight account you once could make of strictest ties, when set in competition with your love to me.

MRS. MAR. 'Tis false, you urged it with deliberate malice.—'Twas spoke in scorn, and I never will forgive it.

FAIN. Your guilt, not your resentment, begets your rage. If yet you loved, you could forgive a jealousy, but you are stung to find you are discovered.

MRS. MAR. It shall be all discovered. You too shall be discovered; be sure you shall. I can but be exposed.—If I do it myself, I shall prevent[6] your baseness.

FAIN. Why, what will you do?

MRS. MAR. Disclose it to your wife; own what has passed between us.

FAIN. Frenzy!

MRS. MAR. By all my wrongs I'll do't—I'll publish to the world the injuries you have done me, both in my fame and fortune: with both I trusted you, you bankrupt in honor, as indigent of wealth.

FAIN. Your fame[7] I have preserved. Your fortune has been bestowed as the prodigality of your love would have it, in pleasures which we both have shared. Yet, had not you been false, I had e'er this repaid it.—'Tis true—had you permitted Mirabell with Millamant to have stolen their marriage, my lady had been incensed beyond all means of reconcilement: Millamant had forfeited the moiety[8] of her fortune, which then would have descended to my wife—and wherefore did I marry, but to make lawful prize 'of a rich widow's wealth, and squander it on love and you?

MRS. MAR. Deceit and frivolous pretense.

FAIN. Death, am I not married? What's pretense? Am I not imprisoned, fettered? Have I not a wife? Nay, a wife that was a widow, a young widow, a handsome widow; and would be again a widow, but that I have a heart of proof, and something of a constitution to bustle through the ways of wedlock and this

6. Anticipate.
7. Good name.

8. Half.

world. Will you yet be reconciled to truth and me?

MRS. MAR. Impossible. Truth and you are inconsistent—I hate you, and shall forever.

FAIN. For loving you?

MRS. MAR. I loathe the name of love after such usage; and next to the guilt with which you would asperse me, I scorn you most. Farewell.

FAIN. Nay, we must not part thus.

MRS. MAR. Let me go.

FAIN. Come, I'm sorry.

MRS. MAR. I care not.—Let me go.—Break my hands, do—I'd leave 'em to get loose.

FAIN. I would not hurt you for the world. Have I no other hold to keep you here?

MRS. MAR. Well, I have deserved it all.

FAIN. You know I love you.

MRS. MAR. Poor dissembling!—O that—Well, it is not yet—

FAIN. What? What is it not? What is it not yet? It is not yet too late—

MRS. MAR. No, it is not yet too late—I have that comfort.

FAIN. It is, to love another.

MRS. MAR. But not to loathe, detest, abhor mankind, myself, and the whole treacherous world.

FAIN. Nay, this is extravagance.—Come, I ask your pardon.—No tears.—I was to blame. I could not love you and be easy in my doubts.—Pray forbear.—I believe you; I'm convinced I've done you wrong; and any way, every way will make amends.—I'll hate my wife yet more, damn her, I'll part with her, rob her of all she's worth, and we'll retire somewhere, anywhere, to another world. I'll marry thee.—Be pacified.—'Sdeath, they come, hide your face, your tears.—You have a mask,[9] wear it a moment. This way, this way, be persuaded.

SCENE 4

Mirabell and Mrs. Fainall.

MRS. FAIN. They are here yet.

MIRA. They are turning into the other walk.

MRS. FAIN. While I only hated my husband, I could bear to see him, but since I have despised him, he's too offensive.

MIRA. O, you should hate with prudence.

MRS. FAIN. Yes, for I have loved with indiscretion.

MIRA. You should have just so much disgust for your husband as may be sufficient to make you relish your lover.

MRS. FAIN. You have been the cause that I have loved without bounds, and would you set limits to that aversion, of which you have been the occasion? Why did you make me marry this man?

MIRA. Why do we daily commit disagreeable and dangerous ac-

9. Often worn in public places by fashionable women of the time in order to preserve their complexions; they were also useful to disguise a woman and so to protect her reputation when she was carrying on an illicit affair.

tions? To save that idol, reputation. If the familiarities of our loves had produced that consequence, of which you were apprehensive, where could you have fixed a father's name with credit, but on a husband? I knew Fainall to be a man lavish of his morals, an interested and professing friend, a false and a designing lover; yet one whose wit and outward fair behavior have gained a reputation with the town, enough to make that woman stand excused who has suffered herself to be won by his addresses. A better man ought not to have been sacrificed to the occasion; a worse had not answered to the purpose. When you are weary of him, you know your remedy.

MRS. FAIN. I ought to stand in some degree of credit with you, Mirabell.

MIRA. In justice to you, I have made you privy to my whole design, and put it in your power to ruin or advance my fortune.

MRS. FAIN. Whom have you instructed to represent your pretended uncle?

MIRA. Waitwell, my servant.

MRS. FAIN. He is an humble servant to Foible,[1] my mother's woman, and may win her to your interest.

MIRA. Care is taken for that.—She is won and worn by this time. They were married this morning.

MRS. FAIN. Who?

MIRA. Waitwell and Foible. I would not tempt my servant to betray me by trusting him too far. If your mother, in hopes to ruin me, should consent to marry my pretended uncle, he might, like Mosca in *The Fox*,[2] stand upon terms; so I made him sure beforehand.

MRS. FAIN. So, if my poor mother is caught in a contract, you will discover the imposture betimes; and release her by producing a certificate of her gallant's former marriage.

MIRA. Yes, upon condition that she consent to my marriage with her niece, and surrender the moiety of her fortune in her possession.

MRS. FAIN. She talked last night of endeavoring at a match between Millamant and your uncle.

MIRA. That was by Foible's direction, and my instruction, that she might seem to carry it more privately.

MRS. FAIN. Well, I have an opinion of your success, for I believe my lady will do anything to get an husband; and when she has this, which you have provided for her, I suppose she will submit to anything to get rid of him.

MIRA. Yes, I think the good lady would marry anything that resembled a man, though 'twere no more than what a butler could pinch out of a napkin.

MRS. FAIN. Female frailty! We must all come to it, if we live to be old, and feel the craving of a false appetite when the true is decayed.

1. I.e., he is Foible's lover.
2. The scheming parasite in Ben Jonson's *Volpone*, who in the end tries to blackmail Volpone. "To stand upon terms" means to insist upon conditions —hence, here, to blackmail.

MIRA. An old woman's appetite is depraved like that of a girl—'tis the greensickness[3] of a second childhood; and like the faint offer of a latter spring, serves but to usher in the fall and withers in an affected bloom.

MRS. FAIN. Here's your mistress.

SCENE 5

[To them] Mrs. Millamant, Witwoud, Mincing.

MIRA. Here she comes, i'faith, full sail, with her fan spread and streamers out, and a shoal of fools for tenders.—Ha, no, I cry her mercy.

MRS. FAIN. I see but one poor empty sculler, and he tows her woman after him.

MIRA. You seem to be unattended, madam.—You used to have the *beau monde*[4] throng after you; and a flock of gay fine perukes hovering round you.

WIT. Like moths about a candle—I had like to have lost my comparison for want of breath.

MILLA. O, I have denied myself airs today. I have walked as fast through the crowd—

WIT. As a favorite just disgraced; and with as few followers.

MILLA. Dear Mr. Witwoud, truce with your similitudes: For I am as sick of 'em—

WIT. As a physician of a good air—I cannot help it, madam, though 'tis against myself.

MILLA. Yet again! Mincing, stand between me and his wit.

WIT. Do, Mrs. Mincing, like a screen before a great fire. I confess I do blaze today, I am too bright.

MRS. FAIN. But dear Millamant, why were you so long?

MILLA. Long! Lord, have I not made violent haste? I have asked every living thing I met for you; I have inquired after you, as after a new fashion.

WIT. Madam, truce with your similitudes.—No, you met her husband, and did not ask him for her.

MIRA. By your leave, Witwoud, that were like inquiring after an old fashion, to ask a husband for his wife.

WIT. Hum, a hit, a hit, a palpable hit,[5] I confess it.

MRS. FAIN. You were dressed before I came abroad.

MILLA. Aye, that's true.—O, but then I had—Mincing, what had I? Why was I so long?

MINC. O mem, your la'ship stayed to peruse a packet of letters.

MILLA. O, aye, letters—I had letters—I am persecuted with letters —I hate letters.—Nobody knows how to write letters; and yet one has 'em, one does not know why.—They serve one to pin up one's hair.

WIT. Is that the way? Pray, madam, do you pin up your hair with

3. The anemia that sometimes affects girls at puberty.
4. Fashionable world. "Perukes": periwigs, worn by fashionable men. Cf. Pope's *Rape of the Lock* I.101.
5. An allusion to the dueling scene in *Hamlet* V.ii.

all your letters? I find I must keep copies.

MILLA. Only with those in verse, Mr. Witwoud. I never pin up my hair with prose. I think I tried once, Mincing.

MINC. O mem, I shall never forget it.

MILLA. Aye, poor Mincing tiffed[6] and tiffed all the morning.

MINC. Till I had the cramp in my fingers, I'll vow, mem. And all to no purpose. But when your la'ship pins it up with poetry, it sits so pleasant the next day as anything, and is so pure and so crips.[7]

WIT. Indeed, so crips?

MINC. You're such a critic, Mr. Witwoud.

MILLA. Mirabell, did you take exceptions last night? O, aye, and went away.—Now I think on't I'm angry.—No, now I think on't I'm pleased—for I believe I gave you some pain.

MIRA. Does that please you?

MILLA. Infinitely; I love to give pain.

MIRA. You would affect a cruelty which is not in your nature; your true vanity is in the power of pleasing.

MILLA. O, I ask your pardon for that—one's cruelty is one's power, and when one parts with one's cruelty, one parts with one's power; and when one has parted with that, I fancy one's old and ugly.

MIRA. Aye, aye, suffer your cruelty to ruin the object of your power, to destroy your lover.—And then how vain, how lost a thing you'll be? Nay, 'tis true: you are no longer handsome when you've lost your lover; your beauty dies upon the instant: for beauty is the lover's gift; 'tis he bestows your charms—your glass is all a cheat. The ugly and the old, whom the looking glass mortifies, yet after commendation can be flattered by it, and discover beauties in it: for that reflects our praises, rather than your face.

MILLA. O, the vanity of these men! Fainall, d'ye hear him? If they did not commend us, we were not handsome! Now you must know they could not commend one, if one was not handsome. Beauty the lover's gift?—Lord, what is a lover, that it can give? Why, one makes lovers as fast as one pleases, and they live as long as one pleases, and they die as soon as one pleases: and then if one pleases one makes more.

WIT. Very pretty. Why, you make no more of making of lovers, madam, than of making so many card-matches.[8]

MILLA. One no more owes one's beauty to a lover than one's wit to an echo.—They can but reflect what we look and say; vain empty things if we are silent or unseen, and want a being.

MIRA. Yet, to those two vain empty things, you owe two of the greatest pleasures of your life.

MILLA. How so?

MIRA. To your lover you owe the pleasure of hearing yourselves praised; and to an echo the pleasure of hearing yourselves talk.

WIT. But I know a lady that loves talking so incessantly she won't

---

6. Dressed the hair.
7. A dialectal form of "crisp," curly.

8. Matches made by dipping pieces of card in melted sulphur.

give an echo fair play; she has that everlasting rotation of tongue, that an echo must wait till she dies before it can catch her last words.

MILLA. O, fiction; Fainall, let us leave these men.

MIRA. [*aside to* MRS. FAINALL] Draw off Witwoud.

MRS. FAIN. Immediately; I have a word or two for Mr. Witwoud.

SCENE 5

Millamant, Mirabell, Mincing.

MIRA. I would beg a little private audience too.—You had the tyranny to deny me last night, though you knew I came to impart a secret to you that concerned my love.

MILLA. You saw I was engaged.

MIRA. Unkind. You had the leisure to entertain a herd of fools, things who visit you from their excessive idleness, bestowing on your easiness that time, which is the encumbrance of their lives. How can you find delight in such society? It is impossible they should admire you, they are not capable: or if they were, it should be to you as a mortification; for sure to please a fool is some degree of folly.

MILLA. I please myself—besides, sometimes to converse with fools is for my health.

MIRA. Your health! Is there a worse disease than the conversation of fools?

MILLA. Yes, the vapors; fools are physic for it, next to asafetida.[9]

MIRA. You are not in a course of fools?

MILLA. Mirabell, if you persist in this offensive freedom, you'll displease me. I think I must resolve after all not to have you.— We shan't agree.

MIRA. Not in our physic, it may be.

MILLA. And yet our distemper in all likelihood will be the same, for we shall be sick of one another. I shan't endure to be reprimanded nor instructed; 'tis so dull to act always by advice, and so tedious to be told of one's faults.—I can't bear it. Well, I won't have you, Mirabell—I'm resolved—I think—you may go— ha, ha, ha. What would you give that you could help loving me?

MIRA. I would give something that you did not know I could not help it.

MILLA. Come, don't look grave then. Well, what do you say to me?

MIRA. I say that a man may as soon make a friend by his wit, or a fortune by his honesty, as win a woman with plain-dealing and sincerity.

MILLA. Sententious Mirabell! prithee don't look with that violent and inflexible wise face, like Solomon at the dividing of the child in an old tapestry hanging.[1]

MIRA. You are merry, madam, but I would persuade you for a moment to be serious.

9. An evil-smelling drug.

1. The Judgment of Solomon (I Kings iii.16–27) was a favorite subject in painting and tapestry.

MILLA. What, with that face? No, if you keep your countenance, 'tis impossible I should hold mine. Well, after all, there is something very moving in a lovesick face. Ha, ha, ha.—Well I won't laugh, don't be peevish—heigho! Now I'll be melancholy, as melancholy as a watchlight. Well, Mirabell, if ever you will win me, woo me now. Nay, if you are so tedious, fare you well; I see they are walking away.

MIRA. Can you not find in the variety of your disposition one moment—

MILLA. To hear you tell me Foible's married and your plot like to speed.—No.

MIRA. But how you came to know it—

MILLA. Without the help of the devil, you can't imagine; unless she should tell me herself. Which of the two it may have been, I will leave you to consider; and when you have done thinking of that, think of me.

SCENE 7

Mirabell alone.

MIRA. I have something more.—Gone!—Think of you! To think of a whirlwind, though 'twere in a whirlwind, were a case of more steady contemplation, a very tranquility of mind and mansion. A fellow that lives in a windmill has not a more whimsical dwelling than the heart of a man that is lodged in a woman. There is no point of the compass to which they cannot turn, and by which they are not turned; and by one as well as another, for motion, not method, is their occupation. To know this, and yet continue to be in love, is to be made wise from the dictates of reason, and yet persevere to play the fool by the force of instinct. O, here come my pair of turtles[2]—what, billing so sweetly! Is not Valentine's Day over with you yet?

SCENE 8

[To him] Waitwell, Foible.

MIRA. Sirrah Waitwell, why sure you think you were married for your own recreation and not for my conveniency.

WAIT. Your pardon, sir. With submission, we have indeed been solacing in lawful delights, but still with an eye to business, sir. I have instructed her as well as I could. If she can take your directions as readily as my instructions, sir, your affairs are in a prosperous way.

MIRA. Give you joy, Mrs. Foible.

FOIB. O-las, sir, I'm so ashamed—I'm afraid my lady has been in a thousand inquietudes for me. But I protest, sir, I made as much haste as I could.

WAIT. That she did indeed, sir. It was my fault that she did not

2. Turtledoves, remarkable for their affectionate billing and cooing. Birds were popularly supposed to choose their mates on St. Valentine's Day.

make more.

MIRA. That I believe.

FOIB. But I told my lady as you instructed me, sir. That I had a prospect of seeing Sir Rowland your uncle, and that I would put her ladyship's picture in my pocket to show him; which I'll be sure to say has made him so enamored of her beauty that he burns with impatience to lie at her ladyship's feet and worship the original.

MIRA. Excellent, Foible! Matrimony has made you eloquent in love.

WAIT. I think she has profited, sir. I think so.

FOIB. You have seen Madam Millamant, sir?

MIRA. Yes.

FOIB. I told her, sir, because I did not know that you might find an opportunity; she had so much company last night.

MIRA. Your diligence will merit more—in the meantime—

[*Gives money.*]

FOIB. O dear sir, your humble servant.

WAIT. Spouse.

MIRA. Stand off, sir, not a penny. Go on and prosper, Foible. The lease shall be made good and the farm stocked if we succeed.

FOIB. I don't question your generosity, sir. And you need not doubt of success. If you have no more commands, sir, I'll be gone; I'm sure my lady is at her toilet, and can't dress till I come. O dear, I'm sure that [*looking out*] was Mrs. Marwood that went by in a mask; if she has seen me with you I'm sure she'll tell my lady. I'll make haste home and prevent her.[3] Your servant, sir. B'w'y, Waitwell.

SCENE 9

Mirabell, Waitwell.

WAIT. Sir Rowland, if you please. The jade's so pert upon her preferment she forgets herself.

MIRA. Come, sir, will you endeavor to forget yourself—and transform into Sir Rowland.

WAIT. Why, sir, it will be impossible I should remember myself—married, knighted, and attended all in one day! 'Tis enough to make any man forget himself. The difficulty will be how to recover my acquaintance and familiarity with my former self; and fall from my transformation to a reformation into Waitwell. Nay, I shan't be quite the same Waitwell neither—for now I remember me, I'm married and can't be my own man again.

Aye, there's my grief; that's the sad change of life;
To lose my title, and yet keep my wife.

---

3. Arrive before she does. "B'w'y" is a shortened form of "God be with you" (our word "goodbye").

Act III—A room in Lady Wishfort's house.

SCENE 1

Lady Wishfort at her toilet, Peg waiting.

LADY. Merciful, no news of Foible yet?

PEG. No, madam.

LADY. I have no more patience. If I have not fretted myself till I am pale again, there's no veracity in me. Fetch me the red—the red, do you hear, sweetheart? An errant ash color, as I'm a person. Look you how this wench stirs! Why dost thou not fetch me a little red? Didst thou not hear me, mopus?[4]

PEG. The red ratafia does your ladyship mean, or the cherry brandy?

LADY. Ratafia, fool. No, fool. Not the ratafia, fool. Grant me patience! I mean the Spanish paper,[5] idiot—complexion, darling. Paint, paint, paint, dost thou understand that, changeling, dangling thy hands like bobbins before thee? Why dost thou not stir, puppet? Thou wooden thing upon wires.

PEG. Lord, madam, your ladyship is so impatient.—I cannot come at the paint, madam. Mrs. Foible has locked it up and carried the key with her.

LADY. A pox take you both!—Fetch me the cherry brandy then.

SCENE 2

Lady Wishfort.

I'm as pale and as faint, I look like Mrs. Qualmsick, the curate's wife, that's always breeding. Wench, come, come, wench, what art thou doing? Sipping? Tasting? Save thee, dost thou not know the bottle?

SCENE 3

Lady Wishfort, Peg with a bottle and china cup.

PEG. Madam, I was looking for a cup.

LADY. A cup, save thee, and what a cup hast thou brought! Dost thou take me for a fairy, to drink out of an acorn? Why didst thou not bring thy thimble? Hast thou ne'er a brass thimble clinking in thy pocket with a bit of nutmeg? I warrant thee. Come, fill, fill.—So—again. See who that is.—[*One knocks.*]— Set down the bottle first. Here, here, under the table.—What, wouldst thou go with the bottle in thy hand like a tapster? As I'm a person, this wench has lived in an inn upon the road before she came to me, like Maritornes the Asturian[6] in *Don Quixote.* No Foible yet?

PEG. No, madam, Mrs. Marwood.

LADY. O Marwood, let her come in. Come in, good Marwood.

---

4. Dull, stupid person.
5. Rouge.

6. The servant at the inn where the Don and Sancho Panza are succored.

SCENE 4

[To them] *Mrs. Marwood.*

MRS. MAR. I'm surprised to find your ladyship in *deshabillé*[7] at this time of day.

LADY. Foible's a lost thing; has been abroad since morning, and never heard of since.

MRS. MAR. I saw her but now, as I came masked through the park, in conference with Mirabell.

LADY. With Mirabell! You call my blood into my face, with mentioning that traitor. She durst not have the confidence. I sent her to negotiate an affair, in which if I'm detected I'm undone. If that wheedling villain has wrought upon Foible to detect me, I'm ruined. O my dear friend, I'm a wretch of wretches if I'm detected.

MRS. MAR. O madam, you cannot suspect Mrs. Foible's integrity.

LADY. O, he carries poison in his tongue that would corrupt integrity itself. If she has given him an opportunity, she has as good as put her integrity into his hands. Ah dear Marwood, what's integrity to an opportunity? Hark! I hear her—dear friend, retire into my closet,[8] that I may examine her with more freedom. You'll pardon me, dear friend, I can make bold with you. There are books over the chimney—Quarles and Prynne, and the *Short View of the Stage*, with Bunyan's works to entertain you.[9] *[to* PEG*]* Go, you thing, and send her in.

SCENE 5

Lady Wishfort, Foible.

LADY. O Foible, where hast thou been? What hast thou been doing?

FOIB. Madam, I have seen the party.

LADY. But what hast thou done?

FOIB. Nay, 'tis your ladyship has done, and are to do; I have only promised. But a man so enamored—so transported! Well, if worshiping of pictures be a sin—poor Sir Rowland, I say.

LADY. The miniature has been counted like[1]—but hast thou not betrayed me, Foible? Hast thou not detected me to that faithless Mirabell?—What hadst thou to do with him in the park? Answer me, has he got nothing out of thee?

FOIB. *[aside]* So, the devil has been beforehand with me. What shall I say?—Alas, madam, could I help it if I met that confident thing? Was I in fault? If you had heard how he used me, and

7. In negligee.
8. Private retiring room.
9. Francis Quarles (1592–1644), a religious poet, by 1700 regarded with contempt, but formerly greatly admired, especially among the Puritans; William Prynne (1600–69), Puritan pamphleteer, author of *Histriomastix* (1632), a violent attack on the stage. For Jeremy Collier's *Short View*, see the Prologue of this play: Congreve, who had been the object of much of Collier's vituperation, slyly identifies his enemy with Puritans and Nonconformists, whom Collier, an ardent high churchman, despised.
1. Considered a likeness.

all upon your ladyship's account, I'm sure you would not suspect my fidelity. Nay, if that had been the worst I could have borne; but he had a fling at your ladyship too; and then I could not hold; but i'faith I gave him his own.

LADY. Me? What did the filthy fellow say?

FOIB. O madam; 'tis a shame to say what he said—with his taunts and his fleers, tossing up his nose. Humh (says he) what, you are a-hatching some plot (says he) you are so early abroad, or catering[2] (says he), ferreting for some disbanded officer, I warrant—half pay is but thin subsistence (says he).—Well, what pension does your lady propose? Let me see (says he) what, she must come down pretty deep now, she's superannuated (says he) and—

LADY. Ods my life, I'll have him—I'll have him murdered. I'll have him poisoned. Where does he eat? I'll marry a drawer[3] to have him poisoned in his wine. I'll send for Robin from Locket's —immediately.

FOIB. Poison him? Poisoning's too good for him. Starve him, madam, starve him; marry Sir Rowland, and get him disinherited. O, you would bless yourself, to hear what he said.

LADY. A villain!—superannuated!

FOIB. Humh (says he) I hear you are laying designs against me too (says he) and Mrs. Millamant is to marry my uncle; (he does not suspect a word of your ladyship) but (says he) I'll fit you for that, I warrant you (says he) I'll hamper you for that (says he) you and your old frippery[4] too (says he). I'll handle you—

LADY. Audacious villain! handle me, would he durst—frippery? old frippery! Was there ever such a foul-mouthed fellow? I'll be married tomorrow, I'll be contracted tonight.

FOIB. The sooner the better, madam.

LADY. Will Sir Rowland be here, say'st thou? When, Foible?

FOIB. Incontinently, madam. No new sheriff's wife expects the return of her husband after knighthood, with that impatience in which Sir Rowland burns for the dear hour of kissing your ladyship's hand after dinner.

LADY. Frippery! Superannuated frippery! I'll frippery the villain, I'll reduce him to frippery and rags. A tatterdemalion—I hope to see him hung with tatters, like a Long Lane penthouse,[5] or a gibbet-thief. A slander-mouthed railer—I warrant the spendthrift prodigal's in debt as much as the million lottery, or the whole court upon a birthday. I'll spoil his credit with his tailor. Yes, he shall have my niece with her fortune, he shall.

FOIB. He! I hope to see him lodge in Ludgate first, and angle into Blackfriars for brass farthings with an old mitten.[6]

2. Procuring (i.e., pimping for Lady Wishfort). When a regiment was "disbanded," its officers went on half pay, often for life.
3. One who draws wine from casks and serves it. Locket's was a fashionable tavern near Charing Cross.
4. Old, cast-off clothes; an insulting

metaphor to apply to Lady Wishfort.
5. "Tatterdemalion": ragamuffin. Long Lane was a street where old clothes were sold; "penthouse": a shed, supported by the wall toward which it is inclined.
6. Ludgate was a debtor's prison, adjoined the district of Blackfriars in London. Prisoners begged by letting down

LADY. Aye, dear Foible; thank thee for that, dear Foible. He has put me out of all patience. I shall never recompose my features to receive Sir Rowland with any economy of face. This wretch has fretted me that I am absolutely decayed. Look, Foible.

FOIB. Your ladyship has frowned a little too rashly, indeed, madam. There are some cracks discernible in the white varnish.

LADY. Let me see the glass.—Cracks, say'st thou? Why I am arrantly flayed—I look like an old peeled wall. Thou must repair me, Foible, before Sir Rowland comes, or I shall never keep up to my picture.

FOIB. I warrant you, madam; a little art once made your picture like you and now a little of the same art must make you like your picture. Your picture must sit for you, madam.

LADY. But art thou sure Sir Rowland will not fail to come? Or will a' not fail[7] when he does come? Will he be importunate, Foible, and push? For if he should not be importunate—I shall never break decorums.—I shall die with confusion, if I am forced to advance.—Oh, no, I can never advance.—I shall swoon if he should expect advances. No, I hope Sir Rowland is better bred than to put a lady to the necessity of breaking her forms. I won't be too coy neither—I won't give him despair—but a little disdain is not amiss; a little scorn is alluring.

FOIB. A little scorn becomes your ladyship.

LADY. Yes, but tenderness becomes me best.—A sort of dyingness —You see that picture has a sort of a—Ha, Foible? A swimming-ness in the eyes—Yes, I'll look so—my niece affects it; but she wants features. Is Sir Rowland handsome? Let my toilet be removed—I'll dress above. I'll receive Sir Rowland here. Is he handsome? Don't answer me. I won't know: I'll be surprised. I'll be taken by surprise.

FOIB. By storm, madam. Sir Rowland's a brisk man.

LADY. Is he! O, then he'll importune, if he's a brisk man. I shall save decorums if Sir Rowland importunes. I have a mortal terror at the apprehension of offending against decorums. O, I'm glad he's a brisk man. Let my things be removed, good Foible.

SCENE 6

Mrs. Fainall, Foible.

MRS. FAIN. O Foible, I have been in a fright, lest I should come too late. That devil Marwood saw you in the park with Mirabell, and I'm afraid will discover it to my lady.

FOIB. Discover what, madam?

MRS. FAIN. Nay, nay, put not on that strange face. I am privy to the whole design and know Waitwell, to whom thou wert this morning married, is to personate Mirabell's uncle, and as such, winning my lady, to involve her in those difficulties from which Mirabell only must release her, by his making his conditions to

a mitten on a string; passers-by dropped   7. I.e., will *he* not fail?
coins into it.

have my cousin and her fortune left to her own disposal.

FOIB. O dear madam, I beg your pardon. It was not my confidence in your ladyship that was deficient, but I thought the former good correspondence between your ladyship and Mr. Mirabell might have hindered his communicating this secret.

MRS. FAIN. Dear Foible, forget that.

FOIB. O dear madam, Mr. Mirabell is such a sweet winning gentleman—but your ladyship is the pattern of generosity. Sweet lady, to be so good! Mr. Mirabell cannot choose but to be grateful. I find your ladyship has his heart still. Now, madam, I can safely tell your ladyship our success. Mrs. Marwood had told my lady; but I warrant I managed myself. I turned it all for the better. I told my lady that Mr. Mirabell railed at her. I laid horrid things to his charge, I'll vow; and my lady is so incensed that she'll be contracted to Sir Rowland tonight, she says—I warrant I worked her up, that he may have her for asking for, as they say of a Welsh maidenhead.

MRS. FAIN. O rare Foible!

FOIB. Madam, I beg your ladyship to acquaint Mr. Mirabell of his success. I would be seen as little as possible to speak to him—besides, I believe Madam Marwood watches me. She has a month's mind;[8] but I know Mr. Mirabell can't abide her.—[Calls.]—John—remove my lady's toilet. Madam, your servant. My lady is so impatient, I fear she'll come for me if I stay.

MRS. FAIN. I'll go with you up the back stairs, lest I should meet her.

SCENE 7

Mrs. Marwood alone.

MRS. MAR. Indeed, Mrs. Engine,[9] is it thus with you? Are you become a go-between of this importance? Yes, I shall watch you. Why, this wench is the *passe-partout*, a very master key to everybody's strongbox. My friend Fainall,[1] have you carried it so swimmingly? I thought there was something in it; but it seems it's over with you. Your loathing is not from a want of appetite, then, but from a surfeit. Else you could never be so cool to fall from a principal to be an assistant; to procure for him! A pattern of generosity, that I confess. Well, Mr. Fainall, you have met with your match. O, man, man! Woman, woman! The devil's an ass: If I were a painter, I would draw him like an idiot, a driveler with a bib and bells. Man should have his head and horns, and woman the rest of him. Poor simple fiend! Madam Marwood has a month's mind, but he can't abide her.—'Twere better for him you had not been his confessor in that affair without you could have kept his counsel closer. I shall not prove another pattern of generosity.—He has not obliged me to that with those excesses of himself; and now I'll have none of him. Here

8. An inclination (toward Mirabell).
9. A person who serves as an instru-

ment or tool of others in an intrigue.
1. I.e., Mrs. Fainall.

comes the good lady, panting ripe, with a heart full of hope and a head full of care, like any chemist upon the day of projection.[2]

SCENE 8

[To her] Lady Wishfort.

LADY. O dear Marwood, what shall I say for this rude forgetfulness —but my dear friend is all goodness.

MRS. MAR. No apologies, dear madam. I have been very well entertained.

LADY. As I'm a person I am in a very chaos to think I should so forget myself—but I have such an olio[3] of affairs really I know not what to do—[*Calls.*]—Foible—I expect my nephew Sir Wilfull every moment too.—Why, Foible!—He means to travel for improvement.

MRS. MAR. Methinks Sir Wilfull should rather think of marrying than traveling at his years. I hear he is turned of forty.

LADY. O, he's in less danger of being spoiled by his travels.—I am against my nephew's marrying too young. It will be time enough when he comes back and has acquired discretion to choose for himself.

MRS. MAR. Methinks Mrs. Millamant and he would make a very fit match. He may travel afterwards. 'Tis a thing very usual with young gentlemen.

LADY. I promise you I have thought on't—and since 'tis your judgment, I'll think on't again. I assure you I will; I value your judgment extremely. On my word I'll propose it.

SCENE 9

[To them] Foible.

LADY. Come, come Foible—I had forgot my nephew will be here before dinner.—I must make haste.

FOIB. Mr. Witwoud and Mr. Petulant are come to dine with your ladyship.

LADY. O dear, I can't appear till I am dressed. Dear Marwood, shall I be free with you again and beg you to entertain 'em? I'll make all imaginable haste. Dear friend, excuse me.

SCENE 10

Mrs. Marwood, Mrs. Millamant, Mincing.

MILLA. Sure never anything was so unbred as that odious man.— Marwood, your servant.

MRS. MAR. You have a color.What's the matter?

MILLA. That horrid fellow Petulant has provoked me into a flame —I have broke my fan.—Mincing, lend me yours; is not all the powder out of my hair?

---

2. An alchemical term denoting the final step in the transmutation of baser metals into gold.
3. Hodgepodge.

MRS. MAR. No. What has he done?

MILLA. Nay, he has done nothing; he has only talked.—Nay, he has said nothing neither; but he has contradicted everything that has been said. For my part, I thought Witwoud and he would have quarreled.

MINC. I vow, mem, I thought once they would have fitt.

MILLA. Well, 'tis a lamentable thing, I swear, that one has not the liberty of choosing one's acquaintance as one does one's clothes.

MRS. MAR. If we had that liberty, we should be as weary of one set of acquaintance, though never so good, as we are of one suit, though never so fine. A fool and a doily stuff[4] would now and then find days of grace, and be worn for variety.

MILLA. I could consent to wear 'em, if they would wear alike; but fools never wear out—they are such drap-de-Berry[5] things! Without one could give 'em to one's chambermaid after a day or two.

MRS. MAR. 'Twere better so indeed. Or what think you of the play house? A fine gay glossy fool should be given there, like a new masking habit after the masquerade is over,[6] and we have done with the disguise. For a fool's visit is always a disguise, and never admitted by a woman of wit, but to blind her affair with a lover of sense. If you would but appear barefaced now and own Mirabell, you might as easily put off Petulant and Witwoud as your hood and scarf. And indeed 'tis time, for the town has found it: the secret is grown too big for the pretense: 'tis like Mrs. Primly's great belly; she may lace it down before, but it burnishes[7] on her hips. Indeed, Millamant, you can no more conceal it than my Lady Strammel can her face, that goodly face, which in defiance of her Rhenish-wine tea will not be comprehended in a mask.[8]

MILLA. I'll take my death, Marwood, you are more censorious than a decayed beauty, or a discarded toast.[9] Mincing, tell the men they may come up. My aunt is not dressing here; their folly is less provoking than your malice.

SCENE 11

Millamant, Marwood.

MILLA. "The town has found it." What has it found? That Mirabell loves me is no more a secret than it is a secret that you discovered it to my aunt, or than the reason why you discovered it is a secret.

MRS. MAR. You are nettled.

MILLA. You're mistaken. Ridiculous!

MRS. MAR. Indeed, my dear, you'll tear another fan if you don't mitigate those violent airs.

4. A woolen cloth.
5. Coarse woolen cloth, made in the Berry district of France.
6. Fine gentlemen and ladies sometimes donated their old clothes to the playhouses.
7. Spreads out.

8. Lady Strammel (the name means "a lean, ill-favored person") reduces by drinking Rhenish wine, but still her face is too large to be contained ("comprehended") in a mask.
9. A lady to whom toasts are no longer drunk.

MILLA. O silly! Ha, ha, ha. I could laugh immoderately. Poor Mirabell! His constancy to me has quite destroyed his complaisance for all the world beside. I swear, I never enjoined it him, to be so coy.—If I had the vanity to think he would obey me, I would command him to show more gallantry.—'Tis hardly well bred to be so particular on one hand and so insensible on the other. But I despair to prevail, and so let him follow his own way. Ha, ha, ha. Pardon me, dear creature, I must laugh, ha, ha, ha; though I grant you 'tis a little barbarous, ha, ha, ha.

MRS. MAR. What pity 'tis, so much fine raillery, and delivered with so significant gesture, should be so unhappily directed to miscarry.

MILLA. Hae? Dear creature, I ask your pardon—I swear I did not mind you.

MRS. MAR. Mr. Mirabell and you both may think it a thing impossible, when I shall tell him by telling you—

MILLA. O dear, what? For it is the same thing, if I hear it—Ha, ha, ha.

MRS. MAR. That I detest him, hate him, madam.

MILLA. O madam, why so do I—and yet the creature loves me, ha, ha, ha. How can one forbear laughing to think of it?—I am a sibyl[1] if I am not amazed to think what he can see in me. I'll take my death, I think you are handsomer—and within a year or two as young. If you could but stay for me, I should overtake you.—But that cannot be.—Well, that thought makes me melancholy.—Now I'll be sad.

MRS. MAR. Your merry note may be changed sooner than you think.

MILLA. D'ye say so? Then I'm resolved I'll have a song to keep up my spirits.

SCENE 12.

[To them] Mincing.

MINC. The gentlemen stay but to comb,[2] madam, and will wait on you.

MILLA. Desire Mrs. ———[3] that is in the next room to sing the song I would have learnt yesterday. You shall hear it, madam—not that there's any great matter in it—But 'tis agreeable to my humor.

Song. Set by Mr. John Eccles

1

Love's but the frailty of the mind,
    When 'tis not with ambition joined;
A sickly flame, which if not fed expires;
And feeding, wastes in self-consuming fires.

2

'Tis not to wound a wanton boy
    Or amorous youth, that gives the joy;

---

1. A prophetess.
2. I.e., to comb their periwigs.
3. The name of the singer was to be in-

serted. The music was by John Eccles (d. 1735), a popular composer for the theater.

But 'tis the glory to have pierced a swain,
For whom inferior beauties sighed in vain.

3

Then I alone the conquest prize,
    When I insult a rival's eyes:
If there's delight in love, 'tis when I see
That heart which others bleed for, bleed for me.

SCENE 13

[To them] Petulant, Witwoud.

MILLA. Is your animosity composed, gentlemen?

WIT. Raillery, raillery, madam, we have no animosity. We hit off
a little wit now and then, but no animosity. The falling out of
wits is like the falling out of lovers—we agree in the main, like
treble and bass. Ha, Petulant!

PET. Aye, in the main. But when I have a humor to contradict—

WIT. Aye, when he has a humor to contradict, then I contradict too.
What, I know my cue. Then we contradict one another like two
battledores;[4] for contradictions beget one another like Jews.

PET. If he says black's black—if I have a humor to say 'tis blue—
let that pass.—All's one for that. If I have a humor to prove it,
it must be granted.

WIT. Not positively must—but it may—it may.

PET. Yes, it positively must, upon proof positive.

WIT. Aye, upon proof positive it must; but upon proof presumptive
it only may. That's a logical distinction now, madam.

MRS. MAR. I perceive your debates are of importance and very learnedly handled.

PET. Importance is one thing, and learning's another; but a debate's
a debate, that I assert.

WIT. Petulant's an enemy to learning; he relies altogether on his
parts.[5]

PET. No, I'm no enemy to learning; it hurts not me.

MRS. MAR. That's a sign indeed it's no enemy to you.

PET. No, no, it's no enemy to anybody but them that have it.

MILLA. Well, an illiterate man's my aversion. I wonder at the impudence of any illiterate man, to offer to make love.

WIT. That I confess I wonder at too.

MILLA. Ah! to marry an ignorant! that can hardly read or write.

PET. Why should a man be any further from being married though
he can't read than he is from being hanged. The ordinary's[6] paid
for setting the Psalm, and the parish priest for reading the ceremony. And for the rest which is to follow in both cases, a man
may do it without book.—So all's one for that.

MILLA. D'ye hear the creature? Lord, here's company, I'll be gone.

---

4. Rackets used to strike the shuttle-
cock, or bird, in the old game from
which badminton is descended.

5. Native abilities.
6. The clergyman appointed to prepare
condemned prisoners for death.

SCENE 14

Sir Wilfull Witwoud in a riding dress, Mrs. Marwood,
Petulant, Witwoud, Footman.

WIT. In the name of Bartlemew and his Fair,[7] what have we here?

MRS. MAR. 'Tis your brother, I fancy. Don't you know him?

WIT. Not I.—Yes, I think it is he—I've almost forgot him; I have
not seen him since the Revolution.[8]

FOOT. Sir, my lady's dressing. Here's company; if you please to
walk in, in the meantime.

SIR WIL. Dressing! What, it's but morning here, I warrant, with
you in London; we should count it towards afternoon in our
parts, down in Shropshire. Why, then belike my aunt han't dined
yet—ha, friend?

FOOT. Your aunt, Sir?

SIR WIL. My aunt, sir, yes, my aunt, sir, and your lady, sir; your
lady is my aunt, sir.—Why, what do'st thou not know me, friend?
Why, then send somebody hither that does. How long hast thou
lived with thy lady, fellow, ha?

FOOT. A week, sir; longer than anybody in the house, except my
lady's woman.

SIR WIL. Why, then belike thou dost not know thy lady, if thou
see'st her, ha, friend?

FOOT. Why truly, sir, I cannot safely swear to her face in a morning, before she is dressed. 'Tis like I may give a shrewd guess at
her by this time.

SIR WIL. Well, prithee try what thou canst do; if thou canst not
guess, inquire her out, do'st hear, fellow? And tell her her
nephew, Sir Wilfull Witwoud, is in the house.

FOOT. I shall, sir.

SIR WIL. Hold ye, hear me, friend; a word with you in your ear.
Prithee who are these gallants?

FOOT. Really, sir, I can't tell; there come so many here, 'tis hard to
know 'em all.

SCENE 15

Sir Wilfull Witwoud, Petulant, Witwoud, Mrs. Marwood.

SIR WIL. Oons,[9] this fellow knows less than a starling; I don't think
a'knows his own name.

MRS. MAR. Mr. Witwoud, your brother is not behind hand in forgetfulness—I fancy he has forgot you too.

WIT. I hope so.—The devil take him that remembers first, I say.

SIR WIL. Save you, gentlemen and lady.

MRS. MAR. For shame, Mr. Witwoud; why don't you speak to him?
—And you, sir.

7. A feature of St. Bartholomew's Fair,
held during August in Smithfield, London, was the exhibition of monsters and
freaks of nature.

8. The "Glorious" Revolution of 1688
that forced the abdication of James II.
9. An uncouth oath: "God's wounds."

wit. Petulant, speak.

pet. And you, sir.

sir wil. [*Salutes* marwood.] No offense, I hope.

mrs. mar. No sure, sir.

wit. This is a vile dog, I see that already. No offense! Ha, ha, ha, to him; to him, Petulant, smoke him.[1]

pet. [*surveying him round*] It seems as if you had come a journey, sir. Hem, hem.

sir wil. Very likely, sir, that it may seem so.

pet. No offense, I hope, sir.

wit. Smoke the boots, the boots, Petulant, the boots. Ha, ha, ha.

sir wil. Maybe not, sir; thereafter as 'tis meant, sir.

pet. Sir, I presume upon the information of your boots.

sir wil. Why, 'tis like you may, sir: If you are not satisfied with the information of my boots, sir, if you will step to the stable, you may inquire further of my horse, sir.

pet. Your horse, sir! Your horse is an ass, sir!

sir wil. Do you speak by way of offense, sir?

mrs. mar. The gentleman's merry, that's all, sir.—[*aside*] 'Slife,[2] we shall have a quarrel betwixt an horse and an ass, before they find one another out. [*aloud*] You must not take anything amiss from your friends, sir. You are among your friends, here, though it may be you don't know it.—If I am not mistaken, you are Sir Wilfull Witwoud.

sir wil. Right, lady; I am Sir Wilfull Witwoud, so I write myself; no offense to anybody, I hope; and nephew to the Lady Wishfort of this mansion.

mrs. mar. Don't you know this gentleman, sir?

sir wil. Hum! What, sure, 'tis not—yea by'r Lady, but 'tis—'sheart,[3] I know not whether 'tis or no.—Yea but 'tis, by the Wrekin.[4] Brother Antony! What, Tony, i'faith! What, do'st thou not know me? By'r Lady, nor I thee, thou art so becravated and so beperriwigged—'sheart, why do'st not speak? Art thou o'erjoyed?

wit. Odso, brother, is it you? Your servant, brother.

sir wil. Your servant! Why, yours, sir. Your servant again—'sheart, and your friend and servant to that—and a—[*Puff.*]—and a flapdragon[5] for your service, sir: and a hare's foot, and a hare's scut[6] for your service, sir; an you be so cold and so courtly!

wit. No offense, I hope, brother.

sir wil. 'Sheart, sir, but there is, and much offense. A pox, is this your Inns o' Court[7] breeding, not to know your friends and your relations, your elders and your betters?

wit. Why, Brother Wilfull of Salop,[8] you may be as short as a

1. Make fun of him.
2. "God's life."
3. "God's heart."
4. A solitary mountain peak in Shropshire, near the Welsh border.
5. Something worthless.
6. Rabbit's tail.
7. The buildings—Gray's Inn, Lincoln's Inn, the Inner Temple, the Middle Temple—housing the four legal societies that have the sole right to admit persons to the practice of law.
8. An ancient name of Shropshire. A "Shrewsbury cake" was a "short" cake, in the modern meaning of the term. Witwould puns, using "short" also in the sense of "abrupt."

Shrewsbury cake, if you please. But I tell you 'tis not modish to know relations in town. You think you're in the country, where great lubberly brothers slabber and kiss one another when they meet, like a call of sergeants.[9]—'Tis not the fashion here; 'tis not inded, dear brother.

SIR WIL. The fashion's a fool; and you're a fop, dear brother. 'Sheart, I've suspected this—by'r Lady, I conjectured you were a fop, since you began to change the style of your letters and write in a scrap of paper gilt round the edges, no bigger than a subpoena. I might expect this when you left off "Honored Brother" and "hoping you are in good health," and so forth—to begin with a "Rat me, knight, I'm so sick of a last night's debauch"— 'od's heart, and then tell a familiar tale of a cock and bull, and a whore and a bottle, and so conclude—You could write news before you were out of your time,[1] when you lived with honest Pumple-Nose, the attorney of Furnival's Inn—You could entreat to be remembered then to your friends round the Wrekin. We could have gazettes[2] then, and Dawks's *Letter*, and the Weekly Bill, till of late days.

PET. 'Slife, Witwoud, were you ever an attorney's clerk? Of the family of the Furnivals. Ha, ha, ha!

WIT. Aye, aye, but that was but for a while. Not long, not long; pshaw, I was not in my own power then. An orphan, and this fellow was my guardian; aye, aye, I was glad to consent to that man to come to London. He had the disposal of me then. If I had not agreed to that, I might have been bound 'prentice to a felt-maker in Shrewsbury; this fellow would have bound me to a maker of felts.

SIR WIL. 'Sheart, and better than to be bound to a maker of fops; where, I suppose, you have served your time; and now you may set up for yourself.

MRS. MAR. You intend to travel, sir, as I'm informed.

SIR WIL. Belike I may, madam. I may chance to sail upon the salt seas, if my mind hold.

PET. And the wind serve.

SIR WIL. Serve or not serve, I shan't ask license of you, sir; nor the weather-cock your companion. I direct my discourse to the lady, sir. 'Tis like my aunt may have told you, madam—Yes, I have settled my concerns, I may say now, and am minded to see foreign parts. If an' how that the peace[3] holds, whereby, that is, taxes abate.

---

9. Witwoud refers to the mutual greetings and felicitations of a group of barristers ("sergeants") newly admitted to the bar.
1. Before he had served out his apprenticeship. Furnival's Inn was one of the Inns of Chancery, attached to Lincoln's Inn. Attorneys were looked down on socially; hence Petulant's ill-natured mirth in his next speech.
2. Newspapers. Dawks's *News-Letter* was a popular source of news in the

country. The Weekly Bill was the official list of the deaths occurring in London.
3. The peace established by the Treaty of Ryswick in 1697, which concluded the war against France waged under the leadership of William III by England, the Empire, Spain, and Holland. It endured until the spring of 1702, when the War of the Spanish Succession began.

MRS. MAR. I thought you had designed for France at all adventures.

SIR WIL. I can't tell that; 'tis like I may and 'tis like I may not. I am somewhat dainty[4] in making a resolution, because when I make it I keep it, I don't stand shill I, shall I,[5] then; if I say't, I'll do't. But I have thoughts to tarry a small matter in town, to learn somewhat of your lingo first, before I cross the seas. I'd gladly have a spice of your French as they say, whereby to hold discourse in foreign countries.

MRS. MAR. Here's an academy in town for that use.

SIR WIL. There is? 'Tis like there may.

MRS. MAR. No doubt you will return very much improved.

WIT. Yes, refined like a Dutch skipper from a whale-fishing.

SCENE 16

[To them] Lady Wishfort and Fainall.

LADY. Nephew, you are welcome.

SIR WIL. Aunt, your servant.

FAIN. Sir Wilfull, your most faithful servant.

SIR WIL. Cousin Fainall, give me your hand.

LADY. Cousin Witwoud, your servant; Mr. Petulant, your servant. —Nephew, you are welcome again. Will you drink anything after your journey, nephew, before you eat? Dinner's almost ready.

SIR WIL. I'm very well, I thank you, aunt. However, I thank you for your courteous offer. 'Sheart, I was afraid you would have been in the fashion too, and have remembered to have forgot your relations. Here's your cousin Tony, belike, I mayn't call him brother for fear of offense.

LADY. O, he's a rallier, nephew—my cousin's a wit; and your great wits always rally their best friends to choose.[6] When you have been abroad, nephew, you'll understand raillery better.

[FAIN. *and* MRS. MARWOOD *talk apart.*]

SIR WIL. Why then let him hold his tongue in the meantime, and rail when that day comes.

SCENE 17

[To them] Mincing.

MINC. Mem, I come to acquaint your la'ship that dinner is impatient.

SIR WIL. Impatient? Why then belike it won't stay till I pull off my boots. Sweetheart, can you help me to a pair of slippers?— My man's with his horses, I warrant.

LADY. Fie, fie, nephew, you would not pull off your boots here. Go down into the hall.—Dinner shall stay for you. My nephew's a little unbred; you'll pardon him, madam.—Gentlemen, will you walk? Marwood?

MRS. MAR. I'll follow you, madam—before Sir Wilfull is ready.

4. Scrupulous, cautious.
5. Shilly-shally.
6. By choice.

SCENE 18

Marwood, Fainall.

FAIN. Why then Foible's a bawd, an errant, rank, match-making bawd. And I it seems am a husband, a rank husband; and my wife a very errant, rank wife—all in the way of the world. 'Sdeath, to be a cuckold by anticipation, a cuckold in embryo? Sure I was born with budding antlers like a young satyr, or a citizen's child.[7] 'Sdeath, to be outwitted, to be outjilted—outmatrimonied. If I had kept my speed like a stag, 'twere somewhat, but to crawl after, with my horns like a snail, and be outstripped by my wife 'tis scurvy wedlock.

MRS. MAR. Then shake it off. You have often wished for an opportunity to part, and now you have it. But first prevent their plot.—The half of Millamant's fortune is too considerable to be parted with to a foe, to Mirabell.

FAIN. Damn him, that had been mine—had you not made that fond[8] discovery.—That had been forfeited, had they been married. My wife had added luster to my horns. By that increase of fortune, I could have worn 'em tipped with gold, though my forehead had been furnished like a Deputy-Lieutenant's hall.[9]

MRS. MAR. They may prove a cap of maintenance[1] to you still, if you can away with your wife. And she's no worse than when you had her—I dare swear she had given up her game, before she was married.

FAIN. Hum! That may be—

MRS. MAR. You married her to keep you, and if you can contrive to have her keep you better than you expected, why should you not keep her longer than you intended?

FAIN. The means, the means.

MRS. MAR. Discover to my lady your wife's conduct; threaten to part with her.—My lady loves her and will come to any composition to save her reputation. Take the opportunity of breaking it, just upon the discovery of this imposture. My lady will be enraged beyond bounds and sacrifice niece and fortune and all at that conjuncture. And let me alone to keep her warm; if she should flag in her part, I will not fail to prompt her.

FAIN. Faith, this has an appearance.

MRS. MAR. I'm sorry I hinted to my lady to endeavor a match between Millamant and Sir Wilfull. That may be an obstacle.

FAIN. O, for that matter leave me to manage him; I'll disable him for that; he will drink like a Dane; after dinner, I'll set his hand in.

---

7. "Satyr": a sylvan deity, usually represented with a goat's legs and horns. A cuckold is said to wear horns. Since the wives of "citizens" (merchants living in the old city of London, not the fashionable suburbs) were regarded by the rakes as their natural and easy prey, a "citizen's child" was born to be cuckolded.

8. Foolish.

9. I.e., the great hall in the house of the Deputy Lieutenant of a shire. Fainall imagines it ornamented with numerous antlers taken from deer slain in the hunt. The allusion, of course, is to the horns of a cuckold.

1. In heraldry, a cap with two points like horns.

MRS. MAR. Well, how do you stand affected towards your lady?

FAIN. Why, faith, I'm thinking of it. Let me see—I am married already; so that's over. My wife has played the jade with me—well, that's over too. I never loved her, or if I had, why that would have been over too by this time. Jealous of her I cannot be, for I am certain; so there's an end of jealousy. Weary of her I am and shall be—no, there's no end of that; no, no, that were too much to hope. Thus far concerning my repose. Now for my reputation. As to my own, I married not for it; so that's out of the question. And as to my part in my wife's—why, she had parted with hers before; so bringing none to me, she can take none from me; 'tis against all rule of play that I should lose to one who has not wherewithal to stake.

MRS. MAR. Besides you forget, marriage is honorable.

FAIN. Hum! Faith, and that's well thought on; marriage is honorable, as you say; and if so, wherefore should cuckoldom be a discredit, being derived from so honorable a root?

MRS. MAR. Nay, I know not; if the root be honorable, why not the branches?[2]

FAIN. So, so, why this point's clear. Well, how do we proceed?

MRS. MAR. I will contrive a letter which shall be delivered to my lady at the time when that rascal who is to act Sir Rowland is with her. It shall come as from an unknown hand—for the less I appear to know of the truth, the better I can play the incendiary. Besides, I would not have Foible provoked if I could help it, because you know she knows some passages—nay, I expect all will come out. But let the mine be sprung first, and then I care not if I am discovered.

FAIN. If the worst come to the worst, I'll turn my wife to grass—I have already a deed of settlement of the best part of her estate; which I wheedled out of her; and that you shall partake at least.

MRS. MAR. I hope you are convinced that I hate Mirabell now: you'll be no more jealous?

FAIN. Jealous, no—by this kiss.—Let husbands be jealous; but let the lover still believe: or if he doubt; let it be only to endear his pleasure, and prepare the joy that follows, when he proves his mistress true. But let husbands' doubts convert to endless jealousy; or if they have belief, let it corrupt to superstition and blind credulity. I am single, and will herd no more with 'em. True, I wear the badge, but I'll disown the order. And since I take my leave of 'em, I care not if I leave 'em a common motto to their common crest.

> All husbands must, or pain, or shame, endure;
> The wise too jealous are, fools too secure.

2. I.e., of the cuckold's horns.

Act IV—Scene continues.

SCENE 1

Lady Wishfort and Foible.

LADY. Is Sir Rowland coming, say'st thou, Foible? and are things in order?

FOIB. Yes, madam. I have put wax lights in the sconces, and placed the footmen in a row in the hall, in their best liveries, with the coachman and postilion to fill up the equipage.

LADY. Have you pulvilled[3] the coachman and postilion, that they may not stink of the stable, when Sir Rowland comes by?

FOIB. Yes, madam.

LADY. And are the dancers and the music ready, that he may be entertained in all points with correspondence to his passion?

FOIB. All is ready, madam.

LADY. And—well—and how do I look, Foible?

FOIB. Most killing well, madam.

LADY. Well, and how shall I receive him? In what figure shall I give his heart the first impression? There is a great deal in the first impression. Shall I sit?—No, I won't sit—I'll walk.—Aye, I'll walk from the door upon his entrance; and then turn full upon him.—No, that will be too sudden. I'll lie—aye, I'll lie down— I'll receive him in my little dressing-room, there's a couch.—Yes, yes, I'll give the first impression on a couch.—I won't lie neither, but loll and lean upon one elbow; with one foot a little dangling off, jogging in a thoughtful way—yes—and then as soon as he appears, start, aye, start and be surprised, and rise to meet him in a pretty disorder—yes. O, nothing is more alluring than a levee[4] from a couch in some confusion. It shows the foot to advantage and furnishes with blushes and recomposing airs beyond comparison. Hark! There's a coach.

FOIB. 'Tis he, madam.

LADY. O dear, has my nephew made his addresses to Millamant? I ordered him.

FOIB. Sir Wilfull is set in to drinking, madam, in the parlor.

LADY. 'Ods my life, I'll send him to her. Call her down, Foible; bring her hither. I'll send him as I go.—When they are together, then come to me, Foible, that I may not be too long alone with Sir Rowland.

SCENE 2

Mrs. Millamant, Mrs. Fainall, Foible.

FOIB. Madam, I stayed here to tell your ladyship that Mr. Mirabell has waited this half hour for an opportunity to talk with you. Though my lady's orders were to leave you and Sir Wilfull together. Shall I tell Mr. Mirabell that you are at leisure?

---

3. Sprinkled with perfumed powder.   4. A rising.

MILLA. No—What would the dear man have? I am thoughtful and would amuse myself.—Bid him come another time.

> There never yet was woman made,
> Nor shall, but to be cursed.[5]
>
> [*Repeating and walking about.*]

That's hard!

MRS. FAIN. You are very fond of Sir John Suckling today, Millamant, and the poets.

MILLA. He? Aye and filthy verses—so I am.

FOIB. Sir Wilfull is coming, madam. Shall I send Mr. Mirabell away?

MILLA. Aye, if you please, Foible, send him away—or send him hither, just as you will, dear Foible. I think I'll see him—Shall I? Aye, let the wretch come.

> Thyrsis, a youth of the inspiréd train.[6]
>
> [*Repeating.*]

Dear Fainall, entertain Sir Wilfull.—Thou hast philosophy to undergo a fool, thou art married and hast patience.—I would confer with my own thoughts.

MRS. FAIN. I am obliged to you that you would make me your proxy in this affair, but I have business of my own.

SCENE 3
[*To them*] Sir Wilfull.

MRS. FAIN. O Sir Wilfull; you are come at the critical instant. There's your mistress up to the ears in love and contemplation. Pursue your point, now or never.

SIR WIL. Yes; my aunt will have it so.—I would gladly have been encouraged with a bottle or two, because I'm somewhat wary at first, before I am acquainted; [*This while* MILLA. *walks about repeating to herself.*]—but I hope, after a time, I shall break my mind—that is upon further acquaintance.—So for the present, cousin, I'll take my leave.—If so be you'll be so kind to make my excuse, I'll return to my company.—

MRS. FAIN. O fie, Sir Wilfull! What, you must not be daunted.

SIR WIL. Daunted, no, that's not it; it is not so much for that—for if so be that I set on't, I'll do't. But only for the present, 'tis sufficient till further acquaintance, that's all.—Your servant.

MRS. FAIN. Nay, I'll swear you shall never lose so favorable an opportunity if I can help it. I'll leave you together and lock the door.

---

5. The opening lines of a poem by Sir John Suckling. Impelled by her love to accept Mirabell, but reluctant to give herself, Millamant broods over poems that speak of the brief happiness of lovers and the falseness of men.

6. The first line of Edmund Waller's *Story of Phoebus and Daphne Applied.* In the flight of the virgin nymph from the embraces of the amorous god, Millamant finds an emblem of her relations with Mirabell.

SCENE 4

Sir Wilfull, Millamant.

SIR WIL. Nay, nay, cousin—I have forgot my gloves.—What d'ye do? 'Sheart, a'has locked the door indeed, I think.—Nay, cousin Fainall, open the door.—Pshaw, what a vixen trick is this? Nay, now a'has seen me too.—Cousin, I made bold to pass through, as it were.—I think this door's enchanted.—

MILLA. [*repeating*]

> I prithee spare me, gentle boy,
> Press me no more for that slight toy.[7]

SIR WIL. Anan?[8] Cousin, your servant.

MILLA.—"That foolish trifle of a heart"—Sir Wilfull!

SIR WIL. Yes—your servant. No offense I hope, cousin.

MILLA. [*repeating*]

> I swear it will not do its part,
> Though thou dost thine, employ'st thy power and art.

Natural, easy Suckling!

SIR WIL. Anan? Suckling? No such suckling neither, cousin, nor stripling: I thank heaven I'm no minor.

MILLA. Ah rustic, ruder than Gothic.[9]

SIR WIL. Well, well, I shall understand your lingo one of these days, cousin. In the meanwhile I must answer in plain English.

MILLA. Have you any business with me, Sir Wilfull?

SIR WIL. Not at present, cousin.—Yes, I made bold to see, to come and know if that how you were disposed to fetch a walk this evening, if so be that I might not be troublesome, I would have sought a walk with you.

MILLA. A walk? What then?

SIR WIL. Nay nothing—only for the walk's sake, that's all—

MILLA. I nauseate walking; 'tis a country diversion. I loathe the country and everything that relates to it.

SIR WIL. Indeed! Hah! Look ye, look ye, you do? Nay, 'tis like you may.—Here are choice of pastimes here in town, as plays and the like; that must be confessed indeed.—

MILLA. Ah, *l'étourdi*.[1] I hate the town too.

SIR WIL. Dear heart, that's much—Hah! that you should hate 'em both! Hah! 'tis like you may; there are some can't relish the town, and others can't away with the country—'tis like you may be one of those, cousin.

MILLA. Ha, ha, ha. Yes, 'tis like I may. You have nothing further to say to me?

SIR WIL. Not at present, cousin. 'Tis like when I have an oppor-

---

7. The first lines of a song by Suckling.
8. "How's that?"
9. To the new age with its classical taste, medieval art, especially architec-

ture, seemed crude ("rude").
1. I.e., "Oh, the silly fellow!" The French phrase forms the title of a comedy by Molière.

tunity to be more private, I may break my mind in some measure.—I conjecture you partly guess—however, that's as time
shall try; but spare to speak and spare to speed, as they say.

MILLA. If it is of no great importance, Sir Wilfull, you will oblige
me to leave me. I have just now a little business.

SIR WIL. Enough, enough, cousin. Yes, yes, all a case—when you're
disposed, when you're disposed. Now's as well as another time;
and another time as well as now. All's one for that.—Yes, yes, if
your concerns call you, there's no haste; it will keep cold as they
say.—Cousin, your servant. I think this door's locked.

MILLA. You may go this way, sir.

SIR WIL. Your servant—then with your leave I'll return to my company.

MILLA. Aye, aye. Ha, ha, ha.

Like Phoebus sung the no less amorous Boy.[2]

SCENE 5
Millamant, Mirabell.

MIRA.
Like Daphne she, as lovely and as coy.

Do you lock yourself up from me, to make my search more curious?[3] Or is this pretty artifice contrived to signify that here the
chase must end, and my pursuit be crowned, for you can fly no
further?

MILLA. Vanity! No—I'll fly and be followed to the last moment.
Though I am upon the very verge of matrimony, I expect you
should solicit me as much as if I were wavering at the grate of a
monastery,[4] with one foot over the threshold. I'll be solicited
to the very last, nay and afterwards.

MIRA. What, after the last?

MILLA. O, I should think I was poor and had nothing to bestow, if
I were reduced to an inglorious ease; and freed from the agreeable fatigues of solicitation.

MIRA. But do not you know that when favors are conferred upon
instant and tedious solicitation, that they diminish in their value
and that both the giver loses the grace, and the receiver lessens
his pleasure?

MILLA. It may be in things of common application, but never sure
in love. O, I hate a lover that can dare to think he draws a moment's air, independent on the bounty of his mistress. There is
not so impudent a thing in nature as the saucy look of an assured
man, confident of success. The pedantic arrogance of a very husband has not so pragmatical[5] an air. Ah! I'll never marry, unless I am first made sure of my will and pleasure.

MIRA. Would you have 'em both before marriage? Or will you be

2. This, and the line that Mirabell caps it with, are from Waller's poem mentioned in note 6 (above).
3. Intricate, laborious.
4. The grated door of a convent.
5. Self-assured, conceited.

contented with the first now, and stay for the other till after grace?

MILLA. Ah, don't be impertinent.—My dear liberty, shall I leave thee? My faithful solitude, my darling contemplation, must I bid you then adieu? Ay-h adieu—My morning thoughts, agreeable wakings, indolent slumbers, all ye *douceurs,* ye *sommeils du matin,*[6] adieu.—I can't do't, 'tis more than impossible.—Positively, Mirabell, I'll lie abed in a morning as long as I please.

MIRA. Then I'll get up in a morning as early as I please.

MILLA. Ah, idle creature, get up when you will.—and d'ye hear? I won't be called names after I'm married; positively I won't be called names.

MIRA. Names!

MILLA. Aye, as wife, spouse, my dear, joy, jewel, love, sweetheart, and the rest of that nauseous cant, in which men and their wives are so fulsomely familiar—I shall never bear that.—Good Mirabell, don't let us be familiar or fond, nor kiss before folks, like my Lady Fadler[7] and Sir Francis; nor go to Hyde Park together the first Sunday in a new chariot, to provoke eyes and whispers; and then never be seen there together again, as if we were proud of one another the first week, and ashamed of one another ever after. Let us never visit together, nor go to a play together, but let us be very strange[8] and well bred; let us be as strange as if we had been married a great while; and as well bred as if we were not married at all.

MIRA. Have you any more conditions to offer? Hitherto your demands are pretty reasonable.

MILLA. Trifles—as liberty to pay and receive visits to and from whom I please; to write and receive letters, without interrogatories or wry faces on your part; to wear what I please; and choose conversation with regard only to my own taste; to have no obligation upon me to converse with wits that I don't like, because they are your acquaintance; or to be intimate with fools, because they may be your relations. Come to dinner when I please, dine in my dressing room when I'm out of humor, without giving a reason. To have my closet inviolate; to be sole empress of my tea table, which you must never presume to approach without first asking leave. And lastly, wherever I am, you shall always knock at the door before you come in. These articles subscribed, if I continue to endure you a little longer, I may by degrees dwindle into a wife.

MIRA. Your bill of fare is something advanced in this latter account. Well, have I liberty to offer conditions—that when you are dwindled into a wife, I may not be beyond measure enlarged into a husband?

MILLA. You have free leave, propose your utmost, speak and spare not.

MIRA. I thank you. *Imprimis*[9] then, I covenant that your acquaint-

6. I.e., soft (pleasures) and morning naps.
7. "Fondler."
8. Reserved.
9. In the first place, as in legal documents.

ance be general; that you admit no sworn confidante or intimate of your own sex; no she-friend to screen her affairs under your countenance and tempt you to make trial of a mutual secrecy. No decoy duck to wheedle you a fop—scrambling to the play in a mask—then bring you home in a pretended fright, when you think you shall be found out—and rail at me for missing the play, and disappointing the frolic which you had to pick me up and prove my constancy.

MILLA. Detestable *imprimis!* I go to the play in a mask!

MIRA. *Item,*[1] I article, that you continue to like your own face as long as I shall; and while it passes current with me, that you endeavor not to new coin it. To which end, together with all vizards[2] for the day, I prohibit all masks for the night, made of oiled-skins and I know not what—hog's bones, hare's gall, pig water, and the marrow of a roasted cat. In short, I forbid all commerce with the gentlewoman in what-d'ye-call-it court. *Item,* I shut my doors against all bawds with baskets, and pennyworths of muslin, china, fans, atlases,[3] etc. *Item,* when you shall be breeding—

MILLA. Ah! Name it not.

MIRA. Which may be presumed, with a blessing on our endeavors—

MILLA. Odious endeavors!

MIRA. I denounce against all strait lacing, squeezing for a shape, till you mold my boy's head like a sugar loaf; and instead of a man-child, make me father to a crooked billet.[4] Lastly, to the dominion of the tea table I submit.—But with proviso that you exceed not in your province; but restrain yourself to native and simple tea-table drinks, as tea, chocolate, and coffee. As likewise to genuine and authorized tea-table talk—such as mending of fashions, spoiling reputations, railing at absent friends, and so forth—but that on no account you encroach upon the men's prerogative, and presume to drink healths, or toast fellows; for prevention of which, I banish all foreign forces, all auxiliaries to the tea table, as orange brandy, all aniseed, cinnamon, citron and Barbados waters,[5] together with ratafia and the most noble spirit of clary.—But for cowslip-wine, poppy water, and all dormitives,[6] those I allow. These provisos admitted, in other things I may prove a tractable and complying husband.

MILLA. O, horrid provisos! filthy strong waters! I toast fellows, odious men! I hate your odious provisos.

MIRA. Then we're agreed. Shall I kiss your hand upon the contract? And here comes one to be a witness to the sealing of the deed.

---

1. Used to introduce each item in a list. "I article": I stipulate.
2. Masks. Cosmetics were made of materials as repulsive as those that Mirabell names.
3. Rich silk fabrics.

4. I.e., a crooked piece of firewood.
5. All of these "waters" are alcoholic drinks. "Clary": a sweet liqueur made of wine, honey, and spices.
6. Sleeping draughts.

SCENE 6

[*To them*] *Mrs. Fainall.*

MILLA. Fainall, what shall I do? Shall I have him? I think I must
have him.

MRS. FAIN. Aye, aye, take him, take him. What should you do?

MILLA. Well then—I'll take my death I'm in a horrid fright—
Fainall, I shall never say it—well—I think—I'll endure you.

MRS. FAIN. Fy, fy, have him, have him, and tell him so in plain
terms: for I am sure you have a mind to him.

MILLA. Are you? I think I have—and the horrid man looks as if
he thought so too.—Well, you ridiculous thing you, I'll have
you.—I won't be kissed, nor I won't be thanked.—Here kiss my
hand though.—So, hold your tongue now, don't say a word.

MRS. FAIN. Mirabell, there's a necessity for your obedience—you
have neither time to talk nor stay. My mother is coming; and in
my conscience if she should see you, would fall into fits, and
maybe not recover, time enough to return to Sir Rowland; who,
as Foible tells me, is in a fair way to succeed. Therefore spare
your ectasies for another occasion, and slip down the back stairs,
where Foible waits to consult you.

MILLA. Aye, go, go. In the meantime I suppose you have said something to please me.

MIRA. I am all obedience.

SCENE 7

Millamant, Mrs. Fainall.

MRS. FAIN. Yonder Sir Wilfull's drunk, and so noisy that my mother
has been forced to leave Sir Rowland to appease him; but he
answers her only with singing and drinking.—What they may
have done by this time I know not, but Petulant and he were
upon quarreling as I came by.

MILLA. Well, if Mirabell should not make a good husband, I am
a lost thing; for I find I love him violently.

MRS. FAIN. So it seems, for you mind not what's said to you.—If
you doubt him, you had best take up with Sir Wilfull.

MILLA. How can you name that superannuated lubber? foh!

SCENE 8

[*To them*] *Witwoud from drinking.*

MRS. FAIN. So, is the fray made up, that you have left 'em?

WIT. Left 'em? I could stay no longer—I have laughed like ten
christenings—I am tipsy with laughing.—If I had stayed any
longer, I should have burst—I must have been let out and pieced
in the sides like an unsized camlet.[7]—Yes, yes, the fray is composed; my lady came in like a *nolle prosequi*[8] and stopped the

---

7. A fabric made by mixing wool and
silk; "unsized" because not stiffened
with some glutinous substance.

8. A phrase indicating the withdrawal
of a lawsuit.

proceedings.

MILLA. What was the dispute?

WIT. That's the jest; there was no dispute. They could neither of 'em speak for rage; and so fell a-sputtering at one another like two roasting apples.

SCENE 9

[To them] Petulant drunk.

WIT. Now, Petulant? All's over, all's well? Gad, my head begins to whim it about.—Why dost thou not speak? Thou art both as drunk and as mute as a fish.

PET. Look you, Mrs. Millamant—if you can love me, dear nymph —say it—and that's the conclusion—pass on, or pass off—that's all.

WIT. Thou hast uttered volumes, folios, in less than decimo sexto,[9] my dear Lacedemonian. Sirrah Petulant, thou art an epitomizer of words.

PET. Witwoud—You are an annihilator of sense.

WIT. Thou art a retailer of phrases, and dost deal in remnants of remnants, like a maker of pincushions. Thou art in truth (metaphorically speaking) a speaker of shorthand.

PET. Thou art (without a figure) just one-half of an ass, and Baldwin[1] yonder, thy half brother, is the rest.—A Gemini of asses split, would make just four of you.

WIT. Thou dost bite, my dear mustard-seed; kiss me for that.

PET. Stand off—I'll kiss no more males.—I have kissed your twin yonder in a humor of reconciliation, till he—[*hiccup*]—rises upon my stomach like a radish.

MILLA. Eh! filthy creature.—What was the quarrel?

PET. There was no quarrel—there might have been a quarrel.

WIT. If there had been words enow between 'em to have expressed provocation, they had gone together by the ears like a pair of castanets.

PET. You were the quarrel.

MILLA. Me!

PET. If I have a humor to quarrel, I can make less matters conclude premises.—If you are not handsome, what then, if I have a humor to prove it?—If I shall have my reward, say so; if not, fight for your face the next time yourself.—I'll go sleep.

WIT. Do, wrap thyself up like a woodlouse, and dream revenge—and hear me, if thou canst learn to write by tomorrow morning, pen me a challenge.—I'll carry it for thee.

PET. Carry your mistress's monkey a spider[2]—go flea dogs, and read

9. "Folios" are books of the largest size, as "decimo sexto" means a book of the smallest size. The Spartans ("Lacedemonians") were men of few words.
1. The name of the ass in the beast epic, *Reynard the Fox.* "Gemini," the twin Roman deities, Castor and Pollux, for whom one of the signs of the zodiac is named.
2. Monkeys were supposed to eat spiders. Petulant scornfully contrasts what he imagines to be Witwoud's technique with his lady and his own more vigorous and direct program for the rest of the evening.

romances—I'll go to bed to my maid.

MRS. FAIN. He's horridly drunk—how came you all in this pickle?

WIT. A plot, a plot, to get rid of the knight—your husband's advice; but he sneaked off.

SCENE 10

Sir Wilfull drunk, Lady Wishfort, Witwoud,
Millamant, Mrs. Fainall.

LADY. Out upon't, out upon't! At years of discretion, and comport yourself at this rantipole[3] rate!

SIR WIL. No offense, aunt.

LADY. Offense? As I'm a person, I'm ashamed of you.—Fogh! how you stink of wine! D'ye think my niece will ever endure such a borachio![4] you're an absolute borachio.

SIR WIL. Borachio!

LADY. At a time when you should commence an amour, and put your best foot foremost—

SIR WIL. 'Sheart, an you grutch[5] me your liquor, make a bill.—Give me more drink, and take my purse.

[*Sings.*]   Prithee fill me the glass
           'Till it laugh in my face,
        With ale that is potent and mellow;
           He that whines for a lass
           Is an ignorant ass,
        For a bumper[6] has not its fellow.

But if you would have me marry my cousin—say the word and I'll do't—Wilfull will do't, that's the word—Wilfull will do't, that's my crest—my motto I have forgot.[6a]

LADY. My nephew's a little overtaken, cousin—but 'tis with drinking your health—O' my word you are obliged to him—

SIR WIL. *In vino veritas*,[7] aunt.—If I drunk your health today, cousin—I am a borachio. But if you have a mind to be married, say the word, and send for the piper; Wilfull will do't. If not, dust it away, and let's have t'other round.—Tony, 'ods heart, where's Tony?—Tony's an honest fellow, but he spits after a bumper, and that's a fault—

[*Sings.*]   We'll drink and we'll never ha' done, boys,
           Put the glass then around with the sun, boys,
        Let Apollo's example invite us;
           For he's drunk every night,
           And that makes him so bright,
        That he's able next morning to light us.

The sun's a good pimple,[8] an honest soaker, he has a cellar at your Antipodes. If I travel, aunt, I touch at your Antipodes.—

3. Rakish.
4. Drunkard. The word is Spanish.
5. Grudge.
6. A wineglass filled to the brim; the word comes from the custom of touching (bumping) glasses when drinking toasts.

6a. A coat of arms had a crest—a helmet surmounting the shield—and a motto. In his drunkenness, Sir Wilfull confuses the two.
7. "In wine [there is] truth."
8. Boon companion.

Your Antipodes are a good rascally sort of topsy-turvy fellows.—
If I had a bumper, I'd stand upon my head and drink a health to
'em.—A match or no match, cousin, with the hard name?—aunt,
Wilfull will do't. If she has her maidenhead, let her look to't;
if she has not, let her keep her own counsel in the meantime, and
cry out at the nine months' end.

MILLA. Your pardon, madam, I can stay no longer—Sir Wilfull
grows very powerful. Egh! how he smells! I shall be overcome if
I stay. Come, cousin.

SCENE 11

Lady Wishfort, Sir Wilfull Witwoud, Mr. Witwoud, Foible.

LADY. Smells! he would poison a tallow-chandler and his family.
Beastly creature, I know not what to do with him. Travel, quoth
a'; aye, travel, travel, get thee gone, get thee but far enough, to
the Saracens, or the Tartars, or the Turks—for thou art not fit
to live in a Christian commonwealth, thou beastly pagan.

SIR WIL. Turks, no; no Turks, aunt. Your Turks are infidels, and
believe not in the grape. Your Mahometan, your Mussulman is
a dry stinkard.—No offense, aunt. My map says that your Turk is
not so honest a man as your Christian.—I cannot find by the
map that your Mufti[9] is orthodox—whereby it is a plain case,
that orthodox is a hard word, aunt, and—[*hiccup*]—Greek for
claret.

[*Sings.*]   To drink is a Christian diversion,
         Unknown to the Turk or the Persian:
            Let Mahometan fools
            Live by heathenish rules,
       And be damned over tea cups and coffee.
            But let British lads sing,
            Crown a health to the king,
       And a fig for your sultan and sophy.[1]

Ah, Tony!

[FOIBLE *whispers* LADY W.]

LADY. Sir Rowland impatient? Good lack! what shall I do with this
beastly tumbrel?[2]—Go lie down and sleep, you sot—or as I'm
a person, I'll have you bastinadoed with broomsticks. Call up
the wenches with broomsticks.

SIR WIL. Ahay? Wenches, where are the wenches?

LADY. Dear cousin Witwoud, get him away, and you will bind me
to you inviolably. I have an affair of moment that invades me
with some precipitation—you will oblige me to all futurity.

WIT. Come, knight.—Pox on him, I don't know what to say to
him.—Will you go to a cockmatch?

SIR WIL. With a wench, Tony? Is she a shakebag,[3] sirrah? Let me
bite your cheek for that.

9. The Grand Mufti, head of the state
religion of Turkey. Moslems do not use
alcohol.
1. The Shah of Persia.

2. Dung cart. "To bastinado" is to punish by beating the soles of the feet.
3. Gamecock.

WIT. Horrible! He has a breath like a bagpipe.—Aye, aye, come, will you march, my Salopian?[4]

SIR WIL. Lead on, little Tony—I'll follow thee, my Anthony, my Tantony. Sirrah, thou shalt be my Tantony, and I'll be thy pig.[5]

—And a fig for your sultan and sophy.

LADY. This will never do. It will never make a match—at least before he has been abroad.

SCENE 12

Lady Wishfort, Waitwell disguised as for Sir Rowland.

LADY. Dear Sir Rowland, I am confounded with confusion at the retrospection of my own rudeness—I have more pardons to ask than the Pope distributes in the Year of Jubilee. But I hope where there is likely to be so near an alliance—we may unbend the severity of decorum—and dispense with a little ceremony.

WAIT. My impatience, madam, is the effect of my transport—and till I have the possession of your adorable person, I am tantalized on the rack;[5a] and do but hang, madam, on the tenter[6] of expectation.

LADY. You have excess of gallantry, Sir Rowland; and press things to a conclusion, with a most prevailing vehemence.—But a day or two for decency of marriage.—

WAIT. For decency of funeral, madam. The delay will break my heart—or if that should fail, I shall be poisoned. My nephew will get an inkling of my designs, and poison me—and I would willingly starve him before I die—I would gladly go out of the world with that satisfaction.—That would be some comfort to me, if I could but live so long as to be revenged on that unnatural viper.

LADY. Is he so unnatural, say you? Truly I would contribute much both to the saving of your life, and the accomplishment of your revenge—Not that I respect[7] myself; though he has been a perfidious wretch to me.

WAIT. Perfidious to you!

LADY. O Sir Rowland, the hours that he has died away at my feet, the tears that he has shed, the oaths that he has sworn, the palpitations that he has felt, the trances and the tremblings, the ardors and the ecstasies, the kneelings, and the risings, the heart-heavings and the hand-gripings, the pangs and the pathetic regards of his protesting eyes! Oh, no memory can register.

WAIT. What, my rival! Is the rebel my rival? a'dies.

LADY. No, don't kill him at once, Sir Rowland, starve him gradually inch by inch.

---

4. Inhabitant of Shropshire.
5. St. Anthony (hence "Tantony"), the patron of swineherds, was represented accompanied by a pig.
5a. Waitwell mixes his metaphors. Tantalus, from whose name we derive the word *tantalize*, was not tortured on the rack. In Hades he was placed in a pool of water that receded from his lips when he tried to drink and under fruit trees whose boughs blew out of his reach when he tried to pluck the fruit.
6. A frame for stretching cloth on hooks so that it may dry without losing its original shape (cf. the phrase "to be on tenterhooks").
7. Consider.

WAIT. I'll do't. In three weeks he shall be barefoot; in a month out at knees with begging an alms—he shall starve upward and upward, till he has nothing living but his head, and then go out in a stink like a candle's end upon a saveall.[8]

LADY. Well, Sir Rowland, you have the way.—You are no novice in the labyrinth of love—you have the clue—but as I am a person, Sir Rowland, you must not attribute my yielding to any sinister appetite, or indigestion of widowhood; nor impute my complacency to any lethargy of continence.—I hope you do not think me prone to any iteration of nuptials.—

WAIT. Far be it from me—

LADY. If you do, I protest I must recede—or think that I have made a prostitution of decorums, but in the vehemence of compassion, and to save the life of a person of so much importance—

WAIT. I esteem it so—

LADY. Or else you wrong my condescension—

WAIT. I do not, I do not—

LADY. Indeed you do.

WAIT. I do not, fair shrine of virtue.

LADY. If you think the least scruple of carnality was an ingredient—

WAIT. Dear madam, no. You are all camphire[9] and frankincense, all chastity and odor.

LADY. Or that—

SCENE 13

[*To them*] *Foible.*

FOIB. Madam, the dancers are ready, and there's one with a letter, who must deliver it into your own hands.

LADY. Sir Rowland, will you give me leave? Think favorably, judge candidly, and conclude you have found a person who would suffer racks in honor's cause, dear Sir Rowland, and will wait on you incessantly.[1]

SCENE 14

Waitwell, Foible.

WAIT. Fie, fie!—What a slavery have I undergone; spouse, hast thou any cordial? I want spirits.

FOIB. What a washy rogue art thou, to pant thus for a quarter of an hour's lying and swearing to a fine lady?

WAIT. O, she is the antidote to desire. Spouse, thou wilt fare the worse for't—I shall have no appetite for iteration of nuptials—this eight and forty hours—by this hand I'd rather be a chairman in the dog days[2]—than act Sir Rowland till this time tomorrow.

---

8. A small pan inserted into a candlestick to catch the drippings of the candle.
9. Camphor was considered an effective antidote to sexual desire.
1. Immediately.

2. I.e., one who carries a sedan chair during the hottest part of the summer. July and August were called the "dog days" because during these months the Dog Star, Sirius, rises and sets with the sun.

SCENE 15

[To them] Lady with a letter.

LADY. Call in the dancers.—Sir Rowland, we'll sit, if you please, and see the entertainment.

[*Dance.*]

Now with your permission, Sir Rowland, I will peruse my letter. —I would open it in your presence, because I would not make you uneasy. If it should make you uneasy, I would burn it—speak if it does—but you may see, the superscription is like a woman's hand.

FOIB. [*to him*] By heaven! Mrs. Marwood's, I know it—my heart aches—get it from her.—

WAIT. A woman's hand? No, madam, that's no woman's hand, I see that already. That's somebody whose throat must be cut.

LADY. Nay, Sir Rowland, since you give me a proof of your passion by your jealousy, I promise you I'll make a return, by a frank communication—you shall see it—we'll open it together—look you here.—[*Reads.*]—*Madam, though unknown to you* (Look you there, 'tis from nobody that I know.)—*I have that honor for your character, that I think myself obliged to let you know you are abused. He who pretends to be Sir Rowland is a cheat and a rascal*—O Heavens! what's this?

FOIB. Unfortunate, all's ruined.

WAIT. How, how, let me see, let me see—[*Reads.*]—*A rascal and disguised, and suborned for that imposture*—O villainy! O villainy!—*by the contrivance of*—

LADY. I shall faint, I shall die, oh!

FOIB. [*to him*] Say, 'tis your nephew's hand.—Quickly, his plot, swear, swear it.—

WAIT. Here's a villain! Madam, don't you perceive it, don't you see it?

LADY. Too well, too well. I have seen too much.

WAIT. I told you at first I knew the hand—A woman's hand? The rascal writes a sort of a large hand, your Roman hand—I saw there was a throat to be cut presently. If he were my son, as he is my nephew, I'd pistol him—

FOIB. O treachery! But are you sure, Sir Rowland, it is his writing?

WAIT. Sure? Am I here? Do I live? Do I love this pearl of India? I have twenty letters in my pocket from him in the same character.

LADY. How!

FOIB. O, what luck it is, Sir Rowland, that you were present at this juncture! This was the business that brought Mr. Mirabell disguised to Madam Millamant this afternoon. I thought something was contriving, when he stole by me and would have hid his face.

LADY. How, how!—I heard the villain was in the house indeed; and now I remember, my niece went away abruptly, when Sir Wilfull was to have made his addresses.

FOIB. Then, then, madam, Mr. Mirabell waited for her in her chamber; but I would not tell your ladyship to discompose you when you were to receive Sir Rowland.

WAIT. Enough, his date is short.

FOIB. No, good Sir Rowland, don't incur the law.

WAIT. Law! I care not for law. I can but die, and 'tis in a good cause—my lady shall be satisfied of my truth and innocence, though it cost me my life.

LADY. No, dear Sir Rowland, don't fight. If you should be killed I must never show my face—or be hanged—O, consider my reputation, Sir Rowland—no, you shan't fight—I'll go and examine my niece; I'll make her confess. I conjure you, Sir Rowland, by all your love not to fight.

WAIT. I am charmed, madam, I obey. But some proof you must let me give you—I'll go for a black box, which contains the writings of my whole estate, and deliver that into your hands.

LADY. Aye, dear Sir Rowland, that will be some comfort. Bring the black box.

WAIT. And may I presume to bring a contract to be signed this night? May I hope so far?

LADY. Bring what you will; but come alive, pray come alive. O, this is a happy discovery.

WAIT. Dead or alive I'll come—and married we will be in spite of treachery; aye, and get an heir that shall defeat the last remaining glimpse of hope in my abandoned nephew. Come, my buxom widow:

> E'er long you shall substantial proof receive
> That I'm an arrant[3] knight——

FOIB.   Or arrant knave.

Act V—Scene continues.

SCENE 1

Lady Wishfort and Foible.

LADY. Out of my house, out of my house, thou viper, thou serpent, that I have fostered; thou bosom traitress, that I raised from nothing.—Begone, begone, begone, go, go—that I took from washing of old gauze and weaving of dead hair,[4] with a bleak blue nose over a chafing dish of starved embers, and dining behind a traverse rag,[5] in a shop no bigger than a bird cage—go, go, starve again, do, do.

FOIB. Dear madam, I'll beg pardon on my knees.

---

3. The two words *errant* ("wandering," as in "knight-errant") and *arrant* ("thorough-going," "notorious") were originally the same and were still pronounced alike. This makes possible

Foible's pun.
4. Foible had been a wigmaker.
5. A worn cloth, used to curtain off part of a room.

LADY. Away, out, out, go set up for yourself again.—Do, drive a trade, do, with your three-pennyworth of small ware, flaunting upon a packthread, under a brandy-seller's bulk or against a dead wall by a ballad-monger. Go, hang out an old frisoneer-gorget,[6] with a yard of yellow colberteen again; do; an old gnawed mask, two rows of pins and a child's fiddle; a glass necklace with the beads broken, and a quilted nightcap with one ear. Go, go, drive a trade—these were your commodities, you treacherous trull, this was the merchandise you dealt in when I took you into my house, placed you next myself, and made you governante[7] of my whole family. You have forgot this, have you, now you have feathered your nest?

FOIB. No, no, dear madam. Do but hear me, have but a moment's patience—I'll confess all. Mr. Mirabell seduced me; I am not the first that he has wheedled with his dissembling tongue. Your ladyship's own wisdom has been deluded by him, then how should I, a poor ignorant, defend myself? O madam, if you knew but what he promised me, and how he assured me your ladyship should come to no damage—or else the wealth of the Indies should not have bribed me to conspire against so good, so sweet, so kind a lady as you have been to me.

LADY. No damage? What, to betray me, to marry me to a cast[8] servingman; to make me a receptacle, an hospital for a decayed pimp? No damage? O, thou frontless[9] impudence, more than a big-bellied actress.

FOIB. Pray do but hear me, madam. He could not marry your ladyship, madam.—No, indeed, his marriage was to have been void in law; for he was married to me first, to secure your ladyship. He could not have bedded your ladyship; for if he had consummated with your ladyship, he must have run the risk of the law, and been put upon his clergy.[1]—Yes, indeed, I inquired of the law in that case before I would meddle or make.[2]

LADY. What, then I have been your property, have I? I have been convenient to you, it seems.—While you were catering for Mirabell, I have been broker for you? What, have you made a passive bawd of me?—This exceeds all precedent; I am brought to fine uses, to become a botcher[3] of second-hand marriages between Abigails and Andrews! I'll couple you. Yes, I'll baste you together, you and your philander.[4] I'll Duke's-Place you, as I'm a person. Your turtle is in custody already: you shall coo in the same cage, if there be constable or warrant in the parish.

6. A woolen garment that covers the neck and breast. "Colberteen": a French imitation of Italian lace.
7. Housekeeper.
8. Cast off, discharged.
9. Shameless.
1. I.e., pleaded "benefit of clergy," originally the privilege of the clergy to be tried for felony before ecclesiastical, not secular, courts; by Congreve's time it had become the privilege to plead exemption from a penal sentence granted a person who could read and was a first offender.
2. A dialectal phrase; the two words mean approximately the same thing.
3. A mender of old clothes; Lady Wishfort means something like "a patcher-up of marriages." "Abigail" and "Andrew" were generic names for maidservants and servingmen.
4. Lover. For "Duke's Place," see Act I, Scene 2, note 5.

FOIB. O, that ever I was born, O, that I was ever married.—A bride, aye, I shall be a Bridewell-bride.[5] Oh!

SCENE 2

Mrs. Fainall, Foible.

MRS. FAIN. Poor Foible, what's the matter?

FOIB. O madam, my lady's gone for a constable. I shall be had to a justice, and put to Bridewell to beat hemp; poor Waitwell's gone to prison already.

MRS. FAIN. Have a good heart, Foible. Mirabell's gone to give security for him. This is all Marwood's and my husband's doing.

FOIB. Yes, yes, I know it, madam; she was in my lady's closet, and overheard all that you said to me before dinner. She sent the letter to my lady; and that missing effect, Mr. Fainall laid this plot to arrest Waitwell, when he pretended to go for the papers; and in the meantime Mrs. Marwood declared all to my lady.

MRS. FAIN. Was there no mention made of me in the letter?—My mother does not suspect my being in the confederacy? I fancy Marwood has not told her, though she has told my husband.

FOIB. Yes, madam; but my lady did not see that part. We stifled the letter before she read so far. Has that mischievous devil told Mr. Fainall of your ladyship then?

MRS. FAIN. Aye, all's out, my affair with Mirabell, everything discovered. This is the last day of our living together, that's my comfort.

FOIB. Indeed, madam, and so 'tis a comfort if you knew all.—He has been even with your ladyship; which I could have told you long enough since, but I love to keep peace and quietness by my good will. I had rather bring friends together than set 'em at distance. But Mrs. Marwood and he are nearer related than ever their parents thought for!

MRS. FAIN. Say'st thou so, Foible? Canst thou prove this?

FOIB. I can take my oath of it, madam. So can Mrs. Mincing; we have had many a fair word from Madam Marwood, to conceal something that passed in our chamber one evening when you were at Hyde Park—and we were thought to have gone a-walking; but we went up unawares—though we were sworn to secrecy too; Madam Marwood took a book and swore us upon it, but it was but a book of poems.—So long as it was not a Bible-oath, we may break it with a safe conscience.

MRS. FAIN. This discovery is the most opportune thing I could wish. Now, Mincing?

SCENE 3

[To them] Mincing.

MINC. My lady would speak with Mrs. Foible, mem. Mr. Mirabell is with her; he has set your spouse at liberty, Mrs. Foible, and

5. Bridewell was the house of correction for women in London.

What, a whore? And thought it excommunication to set her foot within the door of a playhouse? O dear friend, I can't believe it, no, no; as she says, let him prove it, let him prove it.

MRS. MAR. Prove it, madam? What, and have your name prostituted in a public court; yours and your daughter's reputation worried at the bar by a pack of bawling lawyers? To be ushered in with an O *Yes*[2] of scandal; and have your case opened by an old fumbler lecher in a quoif[3] like a man midwife, to bring your daughter's infamy to light; to be a theme for legal punsters, and quibblers by the statute; and become a jest, against a rule of court, where there is no precedent for a jest in any record; not even in Doomsday Book;[4] to discompose the gravity of the bench, and provoke naughty naughty interrogatories in more naughty law-Latin; while the good judge, tickled with the proceeding, simpers under a gray beard, and figes off and on his cushion as if he had swallowed cantharides, or sate upon cowhage.[5]

LADY. O, 'tis very hard!

MRS. MAR. And then to have my young revelers of the Temple[6] take notes, like 'prentices at a conventicle; and after talk it over again in commons, or before drawers in an eating house.

LADY. Worse and worse.

MRS. MAR. Nay, this is nothing; if it would end here 'twere well. But it must after this be consigned by the shorthand writers to the public press; and from thence be transferred to the hands, nay into the throats and lungs of hawkers, with voices more licentious than the loud flounderman's;[7] and this you must hear till you are stunned; nay, you must hear nothing else for some days.

LADY. O, 'tis insupportable. No, no, dear friend, make it up, make it up; aye, aye, I'll compound. I'll give up all, myself and my all, my niece and her all—anything, everything for composition.

MRS. MAR. Nay, madam, I advise nothing; I only lay before you, as a friend, the inconveniencies which perhaps you have overseen.[8] Here comes Mr. Fainall. If he will be satisfied to huddle up all in silence, I shall be glad. You must think I would rather congratulate than condole with you.

SCENE 6

Fainall, Lady Wishfort, Mrs. Marwood.

LADY. Aye, aye, I do not doubt it, dear Marwood. No, no, I do not doubt it.

FAIN. Well, madam; I have suffered myself to be overcome by the importunity of this lady, your friend, and am content you shall enjoy your own proper estate during life; on condition you oblige

2. The formula for opening court, a variant of Old French *Oyez*, "Hear ye."
3. The cap of a sergeant-at-law.
4. Or Domesday Book, the survey of England made in 1085–86 by William the Conqueror.
5. "Figes": fidgets; "cantharides" (or Spanish fly) is an irritant; "cowhage": a plant that causes intolerable itching.
6. The law students at the Temple, one of the Inns of Court.
7. A seller of flounders, well known throughout London for his loud voice.
8. Overlooked.

yourself never to marry, under such penalty as I think convenient.

LADY. Never to marry?

FAIN. No more Sir Rowlands—the next imposture may not be so timely detected.

MRS. MAR. That condition, I dare answer, my lady will consent to, without difficulty; she has already but too much experienced the perfidiousness of men. Besides, madam, when we retire to our pastoral solitude we shall bid adieu to all other thoughts.

LADY. Aye, that's true; but in case of necessity; as of health, or some such emergency—

FAIN. O, if you are prescribed marriage, you shall be considered; I will only reserve to myself the power to choose for you. If your physic be wholesome, it matters not who is your apothecary. Next, my wife shall settle on me the remainder of her fortune, not made over already; and for her maintenance depend entirely on my discretion.

LADY. This is most inhumanly savage; exceeding the barbarity of a Muscovite husband.

FAIN. I learned it from His Czarish Majesty's retinue,[9] in a winter evening's conference over brandy and pepper, amongst other secrets of matrimony and policy, as they are at present practiced in the northern hemisphere. But this must be agreed unto, and that positively. Lastly, I will be endowed, in right of my wife, with that six thousand pound, which is the moiety of Mrs. Millamant's fortune in your possession; and which she has forfeited (as will appear by the last will and testament of your deceased husband, Sir Jonathan Wishfort) by her disobedience in contracting herself against your consent or knowledge; and by refusing the offered match with Sir Wilfull Witwoud, which you, like a careful aunt, had provided for her.

LADY. My nephew was *non compos*,[1] and could not make his addresses.

FAIN. I come to make demands—I'll hear no objections.

LADY. You will grant me time to consider?

FAIN. Yes, while the instrument is drawing, to which you must set your hand till more sufficient deeds can be perfected: which I will take care shall be done with all possible speed. In the meanwhile I will go for the said instrument, and till my return you may balance this matter in your own discretion.

SCENE 7

Lady Wishfort, Mrs. Marwood.

LADY. This insolence is beyond all precedent, all parallel; must I be subject to this merciless villain?

MRS. MAR. 'Tis severe indeed, madam, that you should smart for your daughter's wantonness.

LADY. 'Twas against my consent that she married this barbarian,

9. Peter the Great of Russia visited London in 1698.

1. I.e., *non compos mentis*, "of unsound mind."

but she would have him, though her year was not out.[2]—Ah! her first husband, my son Languish, would not have carried it thus. Well, that was my choice, this is hers; she is matched now with a witness[3]—I shall be mad, dear friend. Is there no comfort for me? Must I live to be confiscated at this rebel-rate?— Here comes two more of my Egyptian plagues,[4] too.

SCENE 8

[To them] Millamant, Sir Wilfull.

SIR WIL. Aunt, your servant.

LADY. Out, caterpillar, call not me aunt; I know thee not.

SIR WIL. I confess I have been a little in disguise,[5] as they say— 'Sheart! and I'm sorry for't. What would you have? I hope I committed no offense, aunt—and if I did, I am willing to make satisfaction; and what can a man say fairer? If I have broke anything, I'll pay for't, and it cost a pound. And so let that content for what's past, and make no more words. For what's to come, to pleasure you I'm willing to marry my cousin. So, pray, let's all be friends. She and I are agreed upon the matter before a witness.

LADY. How's this, dear niece? Have I any comfort? Can this be true?

MILLA. I am content to be a sacrifice to your repose, madam; and to convince you that I had no hand in the plot, as you were misinformed, I have laid my commands on Mirabell to come in person, and be a witness that I give my hand to this flower of knighthood; and for the contract that passed between Mirabell and me, I have obliged him to make a resignation of it in your ladyship's presence.—He is without, and waits your leave for admittance.

LADY. Well, I'll swear I am something revived at this testimony of your obedience; but I cannot admit that traitor—I fear I cannot fortify myself to support his appearance. He is as terrible to me as a Gorgon;[6] if I see him, I fear I shall turn to stone, petrify incessantly.

MILLA. If you disoblige him, he may resent your refusal, and insist upon the contract still. Then 'tis the last time he will be offensive to you.

LADY. Are you sure it will be the last time?—If I were sure of that —Shall I never see him again?

MILLA. Sir Wilfull, you and he are to travel together, are you not?

SIR WIL. 'Sheart, the gentleman's a civil gentleman, aunt, let him come in; why, we are sworn brothers and fellow travelers. We are to be Pylades[7] and Orestes, he and I. He is to be my inter-

2. The conventional period of mourning for a widow was one year.
3. With a vengeance.
4. The plagues visited by Moses on Pharaoh until he agreed to release the Israelites from bondage (Exodus vii–xii).
5. Drunk.
6. In Greek mythology, a hideous monster with snakes in her hair. Her glance turned men to stone.
7. The constant friend who journeyed with Orestes, the son and avenger of the murdered King Agamemnon.

preter in foreign parts. He has been overseas once already; and with proviso that I marry my cousin, will cross 'em once again, only to bear me company.—'Sheart, I'll call him in—an I set on't once, he shall come in; and see who'll hinder him.

[*Goes to the door and hems.*]

MRS. MAR. This is precious fooling, if it would pass; but I'll know the bottom of it.

LADY. O dear Marwood, you are not going?

MAR. Not far, madam; I'll return immediately.

SCENE 9

Lady Wishfort, Millamant, Sir Wilfull, Mirabell.

SIR WIL. [*aside*] Look up, man, I'll stand by you. 'Sbud an she do frown, she can't kill you—besides—harkee, she dare not frown desperately, because her face is none of her own. 'Sheart, an she should her forehead would wrinkle like the coat of a cream cheese; but mum for that, fellow traveler.

MIRA. If a deep sense of the many injuries I have offered to so good a lady, with a sincere remorse, and a hearty contrition, can but obtain the least glance of compassion, I am too happy—Ah madam, there was a time—but let it be forgotten—I confess I have deservedly forfeited the high place I once held of sighing at your feet. Nay kill me not by turning from me in disdain—I come not to plead for favor—nay not for pardon. I am a suppliant only for pity—I am going where I never shall behold you more—

SIR WIL. [*aside*] How, fellow traveler!—You shall go by yourself then.

MIRA. Let me be pitied first, and afterwards forgotten—I ask no more.

SIR WIL. By'r Lady a very reasonable request, and will cost you nothing, aunt.—Come, come, forgive and forget, aunt. Why you must, an you are a Christian.

MIRA. Consider, madam, in reality you could not receive much prejudice; it was an innocent device, though I confess it had a face of guiltiness.—It was at most an artifice which love contrived—and errors which love produces have ever been accounted venial. At least think it is punishment enough that I have lost what in my heart I hold most dear, that to your cruel indignation, I have offered up this beauty, and with her my peace and quiet; nay, all my hopes of future comfort.

SIR WIL. An he does not move me, would I may never be o' the quorum[8]—An it were not as good a deed as to drink, to give her to him again—I would I might never take shipping.—Aunt, if you don't forgive quickly I shall melt, I can tell you that. My contract went no farther than a little mouth glue,[9] and that's

8. Justices of the peace, who were required to be present at the sessions of a court.
9. Literally, glue to be used by moisten-ing with the tongue, but here the meaning is "glue made of mere words" and therefore not binding.

hardly dry.—One doleful sigh more from my fellow traveler and
'tis dissolved.

LADY. Well, nephew, upon your account—Ah, he has a false insinuating tongue.—Well, sir, I will stifle my just resentment at
my nephew's request. I will endeavor what I can to forget—but
on proviso that you resign the contract with my niece immediately.

MIRA. It is in writing and with papers of concern, but I have sent
my servant for it and will deliver it to you, with all acknowledgments for your transcendent goodness.

LADY. [*aside*] O, he has witchcraft in his eyes and tongue; when I
did not see him I could have bribed a villain to his assassination;
but his appearance rakes the embers which have so long lain
smothered in my breast.—

SCENE 10

[*To them*] Fainall, Mrs. Marwood.

FAIN. Your date of deliberation, madam, is expired. Here is the instrument; are you prepared to sign?

LADY. If I were prepared, I am not empowered. My niece exerts
a lawful claim, having matched herself by my direction to Sir
Wilfull.

FAIN. That sham is too gross to pass on me—though 'tis imposed
on you, madam.

MILLA. Sir, I have given my consent.

MIRA. And, sir, I have resigned my pretensions.

SIR WIL. And, sir, I assert my right; and will maintain it in defiance
of you, sir, and of your instrument. 'Sheart, an you talk of an
instrument, sir, I have an old fox[1] by my thigh shall hack your
instrument of ram vellum to shreds, sir. It shall not be sufficient
for a *mittimus*[2] or a tailor's measure; therefore withdraw your
instrument, sir, or by'r Lady I shall draw mine.

LADY. Hold, nephew, hold.

MILLA. Good Sir Wilfull, respite your valor.

FAIN. Indeed? Are you provided of your guard, with your single
beefeater[3] there? But I'm prepared for you; and insist upon my
first proposal. You shall submit your own estate to my management and absolutely make over my wife's to my sole use, as pursuant to the purport and tenor of this other covenant. I suppose,
madam, your consent is not requisite in this case; nor, Mr. Mirabell, your resignation; nor, Sir Wilfull, your right—You may
draw your fox if you please, sir, and make a bear garden[4] flourish
somewhere else: for here it will not avail. This, my Lady Wishfort, must be subscribed, or your darling daughter's turned adrift,
like a leaky hulk to sink or swim, as she and the current of this
lewd town can agree.

---

1. A kind of sword. "Ram vellum": the
legal instrument to be signed is written
on vellum.
2. A warrant, committing a felon to
jail.
3. Yeoman of the guard.
4. The place for bearbaiting, frequented
by a vulgar and unruly crowd.

LADY. Is there no means, no remedy, to stop my ruin? Ungrateful
wretch! Dost thou not owe thy being, thy subsistance to my
daughter's fortune?

FAIN. I'll answer you when I have the rest of it in my possession.

MIRA. But that you would not accept of a remedy from my hands
—I own I have not deserved you should owe any obligation to
me; or else perhaps I could advise—

LADY. O, what? what? to save me and my child from ruin, from
want, I'll forgive all that's past; nay, I'll consent to anything to
come, to be delivered from this tyranny.

MIRA. Aye, madam, but that is too late; my reward is intercepted.
You have disposed of her who only could have made me a com-
pensation for all my services; but be it as it may, I am resolved
I'll serve you. You shall not be wronged in this savage manner.

LADY. How! Dear Mr. Mirabell, can you be so generous at last!
But it is not possible. Harkee, I'll break my nephew's match, you
shall have my niece yet, and all her fortune, if you can but save
me from this imminent danger.

MIRA. Will you? I take you at your word. I ask no more. I must
have leave for two criminals to appear.

LADY. Aye, aye, anybody, anybody.

MIRA. Foible is one, and a penitent.

SCENE 11

[To them] Mrs. Fainall, Foible, Mincing.

MRS. MAR. O, my shame! These corrupt things are brought hither
to expose me.

[MIRA. *and* LADY *go to* MRS. FAIN. *and* FOIB.]

FAIN. If it must all come out, why let 'em know it, 'tis but *the way
of the world*. That shall not urge me to relinquish or abate one
tittle of my terms, no, I will insist the more.

FOIB. Yes indeed, madam, I'll take my Bible-oath of it.

MINC. And so will I, mem.

LADY. O Marwood, Marwood, art thou false? My friend deceive
me? Hast thou been a wicked accomplice with that profligate
man?

MRS. MAR. Have you so much ingratitude and injustice, to give
credit against your friend to the aspersions of two such mercenary
trulls?

MINC. Mercenary, mem? I scorn your words. 'Tis true we found you
and Mr. Fainall in the blue garret; by the same token, you swore
us to secrecy upon Messalina's[5] poems. Mercenary? No, if we
would have been mercenary, we should have held our tongues;
you would have bribed us sufficiently.

FAIN. Go, you are an insignificant thing. Well, what are you the
better for this! Is this Mr. Mirabell's expedient? I'll be put off

---

5. Mincing means "Miscellany," a collection of poems by various writers, such
as Dryden's popular *Miscellanies*. Messalina was the viciously debauched wife
of the Roman Emperor Claudius.

no longer. You, thing that was a wife, shall smart for this. I will not leave thee wherewithal to hide thy shame: your body shall be naked as your reputation.

MRS. FAIN. I despise you and defy your malice.—You have aspersed me wrongfully.—I have proved your falsehood.—Go, you and your treacherous—I will not name it, but starve together—perish.

FAIN. Not while you are worth a groat, indeed, my dear. Madam, I'll be fooled no longer.

LADY. Ah, Mr. Mirabell, this is small comfort, the detection of this affair.

MIRA. O, in good time—Your leave for the other offender and penitent to appear, madam.

SCENE 12

[To them] Waitwell with a box of writings.

LADY. O Sir Rowland—Well, rascal.

WAIT. What your ladyship pleases—I have brought the black box at last, madam.

MIRA. Give it me. Madam, you remember your promise.

LADY. Aye, dear sir.

MIRA. Where are the gentlemen?

WAIT. At hand, sir, rubbing their eyes, just risen from sleep.

FAIN. 'Sdeath, what's this to me? I'll not wait your private concerns.

SCENE 13

[To them] Petulant, Witwoud.

PET. How now? What's the matter? Who's hand's out?

WIT. Heyday! What, are you all got together, like players at the end of the last act?

MIRA. You may remember, gentlemen, I once requested your hands as witnesses to a certain parchment.

WIT. Aye, I do, my hand I remember—Petulant set his mark.

MIRA. You wrong him, his name is fairly written, as shall appear. You do not remember, gentlemen, anything of what that parchment contained—   [*Undoing the box.*]

WIT. No.

PET. Not I. I writ, I read nothing.

MIRA. Very well, now you shall know. Madam, your promise.

LADY. Aye, aye, sir, upon my honor.

MIRA. Mr. Fainall, it is now time that you should know that your lady, while she was at her own disposal, and before you had by your insinuations wheedled her out of a pretended settlement of the greatest part of her fortune—

FAIN. Sir! Pretended!

MIRA. Yes, sir. I say that this lady while a widow, having, it seems, received some cautions respecting your inconstancy and tyranny of temper, which from her own partial opinion and fondness of you she could never have suspected—she did, I say, by the wholesome advice of friends and of sages learned in the laws of this land, deliver this same as her act and deed to me in trust, and to the uses within mentioned. You may read if you please— [*Holding out the parchment*]—though perhaps what is written on the back may serve your occasions.

FAIN. Very likely, sir. What's here? Damnation?—[*Reads.*] A *deed of conveyance of the whole estate real of Arabella Languish, widow, in trust to Edward Mirabell.* Confusion!

MIRA. Even so, sir, 'tis the way of the world, sir; of the widows of the world. I suppose this deed may bear an elder date than what you have obtained from your lady.

FAIN. Perfidious fiend! Then thus I'll be revenged.

[*Offers to run at* MRS. FAIN.]

SIR WIL. Hold, sir, now you may make your bear garden flourish somewhere else, sir.

FAIN. Mirabell, you shall hear of this, sir, be sure you shall. Let me pass, oaf.

MRS. FAIN. Madam, you seem to stifle your resentment: you had better give it vent.

MRS. MAR. Yes, it shall have vent—and to your confusion, or I'll perish in the attempt.

SCENE THE LAST

Lady Wishfort, Millamant, Mirabell, Mrs. Fainall, Sir Wilfull, Petulant, Witwoud, Foible, Mincing, Waitwell.

LADY. O daughter, daughter, 'tis plain thou hast inherited thy mother's prudence.

MRS. FAIN. Thank Mr. Mirabell, a cautious friend, to whose advice all is owing.

LADY. Well, Mr. Mirabell, you have kept your promise and I must perform mine. First I pardon for your sake Sir Rowland there and Foible.—The next thing is to break the matter to my nephew —and how to do that—

MIRA. For that, madam, give yourself no trouble—let me have your consent.—Sir Wilfull is my friend; he has had compassion upon lovers, and generously engaged a volunteer in this action, for our service; and now designs to prosecute his travels.

SIR WIL. 'Sheart, aunt, I have no mind to marry. My cousin's a fine lady, and the gentleman loves her, and she loves him, and they deserve one another. My resolution is to see foreign parts—I have set on't—and when I'm set on't, I must do't. And if these two gentlemen would travel too, I think they may be spared.

PET. For my part, I say little—I think things are best off or on.

WIT. Igad, I understand nothing of the matter—I'm in a maze yet, like a dog in a dancing school.

LADY. Well, sir, take her, and with her all the joy I can give you.

MILLA. Why does not the man take me? Would you have me give myself to you over again?

MIRA. Aye, and over and over again—[*Kisses her hand.*]—I would have you as often as possibly I can. Well, Heaven grant I love you not too well, that's all my fear.[5a]

SIR WIL. 'Sheart, you'll have time enough to toy after you're married; or if you will toy now, let us have a dance in the meantime; that we who are not lovers may have some other employment, besides looking on.

MIRA. With all my heart, dear Sir Wilfull. What shall we do for music?

FOIB. O, sir, some that were provided for Sir Rowland's entertainment are yet within call.

[*A dance.*]

LADY. As I am a person I can hold out no longer.—I have wasted my spirits so today already, that I am ready to sink under the fatigue; and I cannot but have some fears upon me yet, that my son Fainall will pursue some desperate course.

MIRA. Madam, disquiet not yourself on that account; to my knowledge his circumstances are such, he must of force comply. For my part, I will contribute all that in me lies to a reunion: in the meantime, madam—[*to* MRS. FAIN.]—let me before these witnesses restore to you this deed of trust; it may be a means, well managed, to make you live easily together.

> From hence let those be warned, who mean to wed;
> Lest mutual falsehood stain the bridal bed:
> For each deceiver to his cost may find,
> That marriage frauds too oft are paid in kind.

[*Exeunt omnes.*]

Epilogue

SPOKEN BY MRS. BRACEGIRDLE[6]

> After our Epilogue this crowd dismisses,
> I'm thinking how this play'll be pulled to pieces.
> But pray consider, e'er you doom its fall,
> How hard a thing 'twould be to please you all.
> There are some critics so with spleen diseased,   5
> They scarcely come inclining to be pleased;
> And sure he must have more than mortal skill,
> Who pleases anyone against his will.
> Then, all bad poets we are sure are foes,
> And how their number's swelled the town well knows: 10
> In shoals, I've marked 'em judging in the pit;   ⎫
> Though they're on no pretence for judgment fit,   ⎬
> But that they have been damned for want of wit.   ⎭
> Since when, they by their own offenses taught.

5a. Mirabell alludes to Othello's last speech, in which he speaks of having loved Desdemona "not wisely but too well."

6. Anne Bracegirdle (ca. 1663–1748), the most brilliant actress of her generation. She created the role of Millamant. Congreve loved her, and it was rumored that they were secretly married.

Set up for spies on plays, and finding fault.　　　　　　15
Others there are whose malice we'd prevent; ⎫
Such, who watch plays, with scurrilous intent ⎬
To mark out who by characters are meant. ⎭
And though no perfect likeness they can trace,
Yet each pretends to know the copied face.　　　　　　20
These, with false glosses feed their own ill-nature,
And turn to libel, what was meant a *satire*.[7]
May such malicious fops this fortune find,
To think themselves alone the fools designed:
If any are so arrogantly vain, ⎫　　　　　　25
To think they singly can support a scene, ⎬
And furnish fool enough to entertain. ⎭
For well the learn'd and the judicious know, ⎫
That satire scorns to stoop so meanly low, ⎬
As any one abstracted fop to show. ⎭　　　　　30
For, as when painters form a matchless face,
They from each fair one catch some different grace,
And shining features in one portrait blend,
To which no single beauty must pretend:
So poets oft do in one piece expose　　　　　　35
Whole *belles assemblées* of coquettes and beaux.

　　　　　　　　　　　　　　　　　　　　　1700

7. Pronounce *nā-ter* and *sā-ter*.

DANIEL DEFOE

(ca. 1660–1731)

1703:　　Pilloried and jailed for political pamphleteering.
1704–13: Editor of the *Review*.
1719:　　*Robinson Crusoe*, first of his adventure tales.

By birth, education, and occupations Daniel Defoe was a stranger to the
sphere of refined tastes and classical learning that determined the course
of English literature during his lifetime. Middle-class in his birth, Presbyterian in his religion, he belonged to the vigorous and durable group of
Nonconformist tradesmen who, after the Restoration, slowly increased
their wealth and toward the end of the 17th century began to achieve
political importance.

　　He began life as a small merchant and for a while prospered; but he was
not overscrupulous in his dealings, and in 1692 he found himself bankrupt, with debts amounting to £17,000. This was the first of his many
financial crises, crises which drove him to make his way, like his own heroes
and heroines, by whatever means presented themselves to his clever
mind and abundant energy. And however double his dealings, he seems
always to have found the way to reconcile them with his genuine Non-

conformist piety. His restless mind was fertile in "projects," both for himself and for the country; and his itch for politics made the role of passive observer impossible for him.

An ardent Whig, he first gained notoriety by political verses and pamphlets, and for one of them, in which he ironically defended the Anglican's hostility to the Dissenter, *The Shortest Way with the Dissenters*, he stood in the pillory three times and was sentenced to jail. He was released through the influence of that astute politician, Robert Harley (later Earl of Oxford), who recognized in Defoe, as he was to do in Swift, a useful ally. For the next eleven years Defoe served his benefactor secretly as a political spy and confidential agent, traveling throughout England and Scotland, reporting and perhaps influencing opinion. As founder and editor of the *Review*, his job was to gain support for Harley's policies, and his Whiggism did not seem to make it difficult for him to follow Harley's lead, even when, in 1710, his master became head of a Tory ministry. It is characteristic of Defoe that, after the fall of the Tories in 1714, he went over to the triumphant Whigs and served them as loyally as he had their enemy.

When he was nearly 60, Defoe's energy and inventiveness enabled him to break new ground, indeed to begin a new career. One of the few books of the century that belong to world literature is *Robinson Crusoe*, which appeared in 1719. It is the first of a series of tales of adventure for which Defoe is now admired, but which brought him little esteem from the polite world, however much they gratified the less cultivated readers in the City or the servants' hall. In this and other tales which followed, Defoe was able to use all his greatest gifts: the ability to re-create a milieu vividly, through the cumulative effect of carefully observed, often petty details; a special skill in writing relaxed and careless prose which seems to reveal the consciousness of the first-person narrator and which comes alive because the language is the language of actual speech; his wide knowledge of the society in which he lived, both the trading bourgeoisie and the rogues who preyed on them; and his absorption in the spectacle of the lonely human being, whether Crusoe on his island or Moll Flanders in England and Virginia, somehow bending a stubborn and indifferent environment to his own ends of survival or profits. He was interested in the mere processes of living, and there is something of himself in all his protagonists: enormous vitality, ultimate humanity, a scheming and not always edifying ingenuity. In these fictitious autobiographies of adventurers or rogues—*Captain Singleton* (1720), *Moll Flanders* (1722), *Colonel Jack* (1722), and *Roxana* (1724)—Defoe spoke for and to the members of his own class. Like them, he was engrossed by property and success; and his way of writing made all he touched seem true.

The Apparition of Mrs. Veal (1706) is similarly "true." Once thought pure fiction, an early example of the ghost story, it is now known to be based on fact. There was a Mrs. Bargrave, and there was—or had been, at least until September 7, 1705—a Mrs. Veal. Like the later *Journal of the Plague Year* (1722), however, Defoe's account of the apparition is a remarkable example of reporting transformed by art. To make the story credible, he calls upon most of the techniques his novels were to develop: the authority of the first-person narrator, the swiftness and suspense of the action, the matter-of-fact style. Defoe himself was willing to believe in ghosts—he later wrote an essay on *The History and Reality of Apparitions* (1727)—and he induces us to suspend any disbelief of our own. Most of all, he directs us to the facts. The apparition of Mrs. Veal walks through a world of concrete details; an elbow chair, a scoured silk gown, an averted kiss, the striking of a clock. It is these details, not the world of spirits, that absorb our interest. Modestly but irresistibly, with the magic of the storyteller's art, they revive the sense of a place, a moment of time, people we can touch.

A True Relation
of the
Apparition of One Mrs. Veal,
THE NEXT DAY AFTER HER DEATH:
TO ONE MRS. BARGRAVE
AT CANTERBURY. THE 8TH OF SEPTEMBER, 1705.

The Preface

This relation is matter of fact, and attended with such circumstances as may induce any reasonable man to believe it. It was sent by a gentleman, a justice of peace at Maidstone in Kent, and a very intelligent person, to his friend in London, as it is here worded;[1] which discourse is attested by a very sober and understanding gentlewoman, a kinswoman of the said gentleman's, who lives in Canterbury, within a few doors of the house in which the within-named Mrs. Bargrave lives; who believes his kinswoman to be of so discerning a spirit, as not to be put upon by any fallacy, and who positively assured him that the whole matter, as it is here related and laid down, is what is really true, and what she herself had in the same words (as near as may be) from Mrs. Bargrave's own mouth, who she knows had no reason to invent and publish such a story, nor any design to forge and tell a lie, being a woman of much honesty and virtue, and her whole life a course, as it were, of piety. The use which we ought to make of it is to consider that there is a life to come after this, and a just God who will retribute to every one according to the deeds done in the body; and therefore to reflect upon our past course of life we have led in the world, that our time is short and uncertain, and that if we would escape the punishment of the ungodly and receive the reward of the righteous, which is the laying hold of eternal life, we ought, for the time to come, to return to God by a speedy repentance, ceasing to do evil and learning to do well; to seek after God early, if happily he may be found of us,

---

1. No source has been found for Defoe's "relation," though several earlier accounts of the apparition were available to him.

and lead such lives for the future as may be well pleasing in his sight.

A Relation of the Apparition of Mrs. Veal

This thing is so rare in all its circumstances, and on so good authority, that my reading and conversation has not given me anything like it. It is fit to gratify the most ingenious and serious inquirer. Mrs. Bargrave is the person to whom Mrs. Veal appeared after her death; she is my intimate friend, and I can avouch for her reputation, for these last fifteen or sixteen years, on my own knowledge; and I can confirm the good character she had from her youth to the time of my acquaintance. Though since this relation she is calumniated by some people that are friends to the brother of Mrs. Veal who appeared; who think the relation of this appearance to be a reflection, and endeavor what they can to blast Mrs. Bargrave's reputation, and to laugh the story out of countenance. But the circumstances thereof, and the cheerful disposition of Mrs. Bargrave, notwithstanding the unheard-of ill usage of a very wicked husband, there is not the least sign of dejection in her face; nor did I ever hear her let fall a desponding or murmuring expression; nay, not when actually under her husband's barbarity; which I have been witness to, and several other persons of undoubted reputation.

Now you must know, that Mrs.[2] Veal was a maiden gentlewoman of about thirty years of age, and for some years last past had been troubled with fits, which were perceived coming on her by her going off from her discourse very abruptly, to some impertinence.[3] She was maintained by an only brother, and kept his house in Dover. She was a very pious woman, and her brother a very sober man, to all appearance; but now he does all he can to null or quash the story. Mrs. Veal was intimately acquainted with Mrs. Bargrave from her childhood. Mrs. Veal's circumstances were then mean; her father did not take care of his children as he ought, so that they were exposed to hardships; and Mrs. Bargrave in those days had as unkind a father, though she wanted for neither food nor clothing, whilst Mrs. Veal wanted for both; so that it was in the power of Mrs. Bargrave to be very much her friend in several instances, which mightily endeared Mrs. Veal; insomuch that she would often say, "Mrs. Bargrave, you are not only the best, but the only friend I have in the world; and no circumstances of life shall ever dissolve my friendship." They would often condole each other's adverse fortune, and read together *Drelincourt upon Death*,[4] and other good

---

2. "Mrs."—pronounced "Mistress"—designated any woman, married or unmarried, with no superior title.
3. Irrelevancy.
4. *The Christian's Consolations Against* *the Fears of Death*. Defoe's story, which mentions Drelincourt's popular book several times, was regularly printed as a foreword to it in the 18th century.

books; and so, like two Christian friends, they comforted each other under their sorrow.

Sometime after, Mr. Veal's friends got him a place in the custom-house at Dover, which occasioned Mrs. Veal, by little and little, to fall off from her intimacy with Mrs. Bargrave, though there was never any such thing as a quarrel; but an indifferency came on by degrees, till at last Mrs. Bargrave had not seen her in two years and a half, though above a twelvemonth of the time Mrs. Bargrave had been absent from Dover, and this last half-year has been in Canterbury about two months of the time, dwelling in a house of her own.

In this house, on the eighth of September last, *viz.* 1705, she was sitting alone in the forenoon, thinking over her unfortunate life, and arguing herself into a due resignation to Providence, though her condition seemed hard. "And," said she, "I have been provided for hitherto, and doubt not but I shall be still; and am well satisfied that my afflictions shall end, when it is most fit for me"; and then took up her sewing-work, which she had no sooner done but she hears a knocking at the door; she went to see who it was there, and this proved to be Mrs. Veal, her old friend, who was in a riding-habit: at that moment of time the clock struck twelve at noon.

"Madam," says Mrs. Bargrave, "I am surprised to see you, you have been so long a stranger," but told her she was glad to see her and offered to salute[5] her, which Mrs. Veal complied with, till their lips almost touched, and then Mrs. Veal drew her hand across her own eyes and said, "I am not very well," and so waived it. She told Mrs. Bargrave she was going a journey, and had a great mind to see her first. "But," says Mrs. Bargrave, "how came you to take a journey alone? I am amazed at it, because I know you have so fond a brother." "O!" says Mrs. Veal, "I gave my brother the slip, and came away, because I had so great a mind to see you before I took my journey." So Mrs. Bargrave went in with her, into another room within the first, and Mrs. Veal sat herself down in an elbow-chair, in which Mrs. Bargrave was sitting when she heard Mrs. Veal knock. Then says Mrs. Veal, "My dear friend, I am come to renew our old friendship again, and to beg your pardon for my breach of it, and if you can forgive me you are one of the best of women." "O!" says Mrs. Bargrave, "don't mention such a thing, I have not had an uneasy thought about it, I can easily forgive it." "What did you think of me?" says Mrs. Veal. Says Mrs. Bargrave, "I thought you were like the rest of the world, and that prosperity had made you forget yourself and me." Then Mrs. Veal reminded Mrs. Bargrave of the many friendly offices she did her in former days, and

5. Tried to kiss.

much of the conversation they had with each other in the time of their adversity; what books they read, and what comfort in particular they received from Drelincourt's *Book of Death*, which was the best, she said, on that subject, was ever wrote. She also mentioned Dr. Sherlock,[6] and two Dutch books which were translated, wrote upon death, and several others: but Drelincourt, she said, had the clearest notions of death, and of the future state, of any who have handled that subject. Then she asked Mrs. Bargrave whether she had Drelincourt; she said yes. Says Mrs. Veal, "Fetch it," and so Mrs. Bargrave goes upstairs, and brings it down. Says Mrs. Veal, "Dear Mrs. Bargrave, if the eyes of our faith were as open as the eyes of our body, we should see numbers of angels about us for our guard. The notions we have of heaven now are nothing like what it is, as Drelincourt says. Therefore be comforted under your afflictions, and believe that the Almighty has a particular regard to you, and that your afflictions are marks of God's favor; and when they have done the business they were sent for, they shall be removed from you. And believe me, my dear friend, believe what I say to you, one minute of future happiness will infinitely reward you for all your sufferings. For I can never believe" (and claps her hand upon her knee with a great deal of earnestness, which indeed ran through all her discourse) "that ever God will suffer you to spend all your days in this afflicted state; but be assured that your afflictions shall leave you, or you them in a short time." She spake in that pathetical and heavenly manner, that Mrs. Bargrave wept several times, she was so deeply affected with it. Then Mrs. Veal mentioned Dr. Horneck's *Ascetick*,[7] at the end of which he gives an account of the lives of the primitive Christians. Their pattern she recommended to our imitation; and said, "their conversation was not like this of our age. For now" (says she) "there is nothing but frothy vain discourse, which is far different from theirs. Theirs was to edification, and to build one another up in the faith: so that they were not as we are, nor are we as they are; but," said she, "we might do as they did. There was a hearty friendship among them, but where is it now to be found?" Says Mrs. Bargrave, " 'Tis hard indeed to find a true friend in these days." Says Mrs. Veal, "Mr. Norris has a fine copy of verses, called 'Friendship in Perfection,' which I wonderfully admire, have you seen the book?" says Mrs. Veal. "No," says Mrs. Bargrave, "but I have the verses of my own writing out." "Have you?" says Mrs. Veal, "then fetch them"; which she did from above stairs, and offered them to Mrs. Veal to read, who refused, and waived the thing, saying holding down her

6. William Sherlock, *A Practical Discourse Concerning Death* (1689).

7. Anthony Horneck, *The Happy Ascetick* (1681).

head would make it ache, and then desired Mrs. Bargrave to read
them to her, which she did. As they were admiring Friendship, Mrs.
Veal said, "Dear Mrs. Bargrave, I shall love you forever."[8] In the
verses there is twice used the word "Elysium." "Ah!" says Mrs.
Veal, "these poets have such names for heaven." She would often
draw her hand cross her own eyes; and say, "Mrs. Bargrave, don't you
think I am mightily impaired by my fits?" "No," says Mrs. Bargrave, "I think you look as well as ever I knew you."

After all this discourse, which the apparition put in words much
finer than Mrs. Bargrave said she could pretend to, and was much
more than she can remember (for it cannot be thought that an
hour and three-quarters' conversation could all be retained, though
the main of it, she thinks she does), she said to Mrs. Bargrave, she
would have her write a letter to her brother, and tell him, she
would have him give rings to such and such; and that there was a
purse of gold in her cabinet, and that she would have two broad
pieces given to her cousin Watson. Talking at this rate, Mrs. Bargrave thought that a fit was coming upon her, and so placed herself
in a chair just before her knees, to keep her from falling to the
ground, if her fits should occasion it; for the elbow chair, she
thought, would keep her from falling on either side. And to divert
Mrs. Veal, as she thought, she took hold of her gown sleeve several
times, and commended it. Mrs. Veal told her it was a scoured silk,
and newly made up. But for all this Mrs. Veal persisted in her
request, and told Mrs. Bargrave she must not deny her; and she
would have her tell her brother all their conversation, when she had
an opportunity. "Dear Mrs. Veal," says Mrs. Bargrave, "this seems
so impertinent that I cannot tell how to comply with it; and what a
mortifying story will our conversation be to a young gentleman?"
"Well," says Mrs. Veal, "I must not be denied." "Why," says Mrs.
Bargrave, " 'tis much better methinks to do it yourself." "No," says
Mrs. Veal, "though it seems impertinent to you now, you will see
more reason for it hereafter." Mrs. Bargrave then, to satisfy her
importunity, was going to fetch a pen and ink; but Mrs. Veal said,
"Let it alone now, and do it when I am gone; but you must be sure
to do it"; which was one of the last things she enjoined her at parting; and so she promised her.

Then Mrs. Veal asked for Mrs. Bargrave's daughter. She said she
was not at home, "but if you have a mind to see her," says Mrs.
Bargrave, "I'll send for her." "Do," says Mrs. Veal. On which she
left her, and went to a neighbor's, to send for her; and by the time
Mrs. Bargrave was returning, Mrs. Veal was got without the door in

8. In John Norris' poem (1687), Damon
assures Pythias that even death will not
sever their friendship:

"I then will be
Your friend and guardian angel too.
And though with more refined society
I'll leave Elysium to converse with you."

the street, in the face of the beast-market on a Saturday (which is market day) and stood ready to part as soon as Mrs. Bargrave came to her. She asked her, why she was in such haste? She said, she must be going, though perhaps she might not go her journey till Monday. And told Mrs. Bargave she hoped she should see her again at her cousin Watson's before she went whither she was agoing. Then she said, she would not take her leave of her, and walked from Mrs. Bargrave in her view, till a turning interrupted the sight of her, which was three-quarters after one in the afternoon.

Mrs. Veal died the 7th of September, at twelve o'clock at noon, of her fits, and had not above four hours' senses before her death, in which time she received the sacrament. The next day after Mrs. Veal's appearing, being Sunday, Mrs. Bargrave was mightily indisposed with a cold and a sore throat, that she could not go out that day; but on Monday morning she sends a person to Captain Watson's to know if Mrs. Veal were there. They wondered at Mrs. Bargrave's inquiry, and sent her word that she was not there, nor was expected. At this answer Mrs. Bargrave told the maid she had certainly mistook the name, or made some blunder. And though she was ill, she put on her hood, and went herself to Captain Watson's, though she knew none of the family, to see if Mrs. Veal was there or not. They said, they wondered at her asking, for that she had not been in town; they were sure, if she had, she would have been there. Says Mrs. Bargrave, "I am sure she was with me on Saturday almost two hours." They said it was impossible, for they must have seen her if she had. In comes Captain Watson, while they were in dispute, and said that Mrs. Veal was certainly dead, and her escutcheons[9] were making. This strangely surprised Mrs. Bargrave, who went to the person immediately who had the care of them, and found it true. Then she related the whole story to Captain Watson's family, and what gown she had on, and how striped. And that Mrs. Veal told her it was scoured. Then Mrs. Watson cried out, "You have seen her indeed, for none knew but Mrs. Veal and myself, that the gown was scoured"; and Mrs. Watson owned that she described the gown exactly; "for," said she, "I helped her to make it up." This Mrs. Watson blazed all about the town, and avouched the demonstration of the truth of Mrs. Bargrave's seeing Mrs. Veal's apparition. And Captain Watson carried two gentlemen immediately to Mrs. Bargrave's house, to hear the relation from her own mouth. And then it spread so fast that gentlemen and persons of quality, the judicious and skeptical part of the world, flocked in upon her, which at last became such a task, that she was forced to go out of the way. For they were in general extremely satisfied of

---

9. An armorial panel placed on the house of a dead person.

the truth of the thing; and plainly saw that Mrs. Bargrave was no hypochondriac,[1] for she always appears with such a cheerful air, and pleasing mien, that she has gained the favor and esteem of all the gentry. And it's thought a great favor if they can but get the relation from her own mouth. I should have told you before, that Mrs. Veal told Mrs. Bargrave that her sister and brother-in-law were just come down from London to see her. Says Mrs. Bargrave, "How came you to order things so strangely?" "It could not be helped," said Mrs. Veal; and her sister and brother did come to see her, and entered the town of Dover just as Mrs. Veal was expiring. Mrs. Bargrave asked her whether she would not drink some tea. Says Mrs. Veal, "I do not care if I do; but I'll warrant this mad fellow" (meaning Mrs. Bargrave's husband) "has broke all your trinkets."[2] "But," says Mrs. Bargrave, "I'll get something to drink in for all that"; but Mrs. Veal waived it, and said, "It is no matter, let it alone," and so it passed.

All the time I sat with Mrs. Bargrave, which was some hours, she recollected fresh sayings of Mrs. Veal. And one material thing more she told Mrs. Bargrave, that old Mr. Breton allowed Mrs. Veal ten pounds a year, which was a secret, and unknown to Mrs. Bargrave, till Mrs. Veal told it her. Mrs. Bargrave never varies in her story, which puzzles those who doubt of the truth, or are unwilling to believe it. A servant in a neighbor's yard adjoining to Mrs. Bargrave's house heard her talking to somebody, an hour of the time Mrs. Veal was with her. Mrs. Bargrave went out to her next neighbor's the very moment she parted with Mrs. Veal, and told what ravishing conversation she had with an old friend, and told the whole of it. Drelincourt's *Book of Death* is, since this happened, bought up strangely. And it is to be observed, that notwithstanding all this trouble and fatigue Mrs. Bargrave has undergone upon this account, she never took the value of a farthing, nor suffered her daughter to take anything of anybody, and therefore can have no interest[3] in telling the story.

But Mr. Veal does what he can to stifle the matter, and said he would see Mrs. Bargrave; but yet it is certain matter of fact that he has been at Captain Watson's since the death of his sister, and yet never went near Mrs. Bargrave; and some of his friends report her to be a great liar, and that she knew of Mr. Breton's ten pounds a year. But the person who pretends to say so has the reputation of a notorious liar, among persons which I know to be of undoubted repute. Now Mr. Veal is more a gentleman than to say she lies; but says a bad husband has crazed her. But she needs only to present herself, and it will effectually confute that pretense. Mr. Veal says

1. Someone given to melancholy and fantasies.
2. That is, her tea-set.
3. Financial advantage or profit.

he asked his sister on her deathbed whether she had a mind to dispose of anything, and she said no. Now the things which Mrs. Veal's apparition would have disposed of were so trifling, and nothing of justice aimed at in their disposal, that the design of it appears to me to be only in order to make Mrs. Bargrave so to demonstrate the truth of her appearance, as to satisfy the world of the reality thereof, as to what she had seen and heard; and to secure her reputation among the reasonable and understanding part of mankind. And then again, Mr. Veal owns that there was a purse of gold; but it was not found in her cabinet, but in a comb-box. This looks improbable, for that Mrs. Watson owned that Mrs. Veal was so very careful of the key of her cabinet, that she would trust nobody with it. And if so, no doubt she would not trust her gold out of it. And Mrs. Veal's often drawing her hand over her eyes, and asking Mrs. Bargrave whether her fits had not impaired her, looks to me as if she did it on purpose to remind Mrs. Bargrave of her fits, to prepare her not to think it strange that she should put her upon writing to her brother to dispose of rings and gold, which looked so much like a dying person's bequest; and it took accordingly with Mrs. Bargrave, as the effect of her fits coming upon her; and was one of the many instances of her wonderful love to her, and care of her, that she should not be affrighted: which indeed appears in her whole management; particularly in her coming to her in the daytime, waiving the salutation, and when she was alone; and then the manner of her parting, to prevent a second attempt to salute her.

Now, why Mr. Veal should think this relation a reflection (as 'tis plain he does by his endeavoring to stifle it) I can't imagine, because the generality believe her to be a good spirit, her discourse was so heavenly. Her two great errands were to comfort Mrs. Bargrave in her affliction, and to ask her forgiveness for her breach of friendship, and with a pious discourse to encourage her. So that after all, to suppose that Mrs. Bargrave could hatch such an invention as this from Friday noon till Saturday noon (supposing that she knew of Mrs. Veal's death the very first moment) without jumbling circumstances, and without any interest too, she must be more witty, fortunate, and wicked too, than any indifferent person, I dare say, will allow. I asked Mrs. Bargrave several times if she was sure she felt the gown. She answered modestly, "If my senses be to be relied on, I am sure of it." I asked her if she heard a sound, when she clapped her hand upon her knee. She said, she did not remember she did; and she said, "She appeared to be as much a substance as I did, who talked with her. And I may," said she, "be as soon persuaded that your apparition is talking to me now, as that I did not really see her; for I was under no manner of fear. I received her as a friend, and parted with her as such. I would not," says she, "give one farthing to make anyone believe it, I have no interest in it; nothing but trouble is entailed upon me for a long time, for aught that I know; and had it not come to light by accident, it would never have been made public." But now, she says, she will make her own private use of it, and keep herself out of the way as much as she can. And so she has done since. She says, she had a gentleman who came thirty miles to her to hear the relation; and that she had told it to a room full of people at a time. Several particular gentlemen have had the story from Mrs. Bargrave's own mouth.

This thing has very much affected me, and I am as well satisfied as I am of the best grounded matter of fact. And why we should dispute matter of fact because we cannot solve things of which we have no certain or demonstrative notions, seems strange to me. Mrs. Bargrave's authority and sincerity alone would have been undoubted in any other case.

1706

Poetry: The Augustan Mode

SAMUEL BUTLER
(1612–1680)

Butler passed his middle years during the "fury" of the Civil War and
under the Commonwealth, sardonically observing the behavior and lovingly memorizing the faults of the Puritan rulers. He despised them and
found relief for his feelings by satirizing them, though, naturally enough,
he could not publish while they were in power. He served as clerk to
several Puritan justices of the peace in the west of England, one of whom,
according to tradition, was the original of Sir Hudibras (the *s* is pronounced). To Butler these men were fanatics, rapacious rascals, and hypocrites, inhabiting a world populated by only two classes: knaves and their
preordained victims, fools.

Hudibras, Part I, was published late in 1662 (the edition bears the
date 1663) and pleased the triumphant Royalists. King Charles II admired
and often quoted the poem and rewarded its author with a gift of £300;
it was, after all, a relief to laugh at what he had earlier hated and feared.
The first part, attacking Presbyterians and Independents, proved more
vigorous and effective than Parts II and III, which followed in 1664 and
1678 respectively, and which are less unified, since they aim at several
different objects: romantic love, sex, astrology, and the new science, among
others. After his initial success, Butler was neglected by the men he had
pleased. He died in poverty, and not until 1721 was a monument erected
in Westminster Abbey to his memory.

Hudibras is a travesty, or burlesque, i.e., it takes a serious subject and
debases it by using a low style or distorts it by grotesque exaggeration.
Butler carried this mode even into his verse, for he reduced the iambic
tetrameter line (used subtly and seriously by such 17th-century poets as
John Donne, John Milton, and Andrew Marvell) to something approaching doggerel, and his boldly comic rhymes add to the effect of broad
comedy which he sought to create. Burlesque was a popular form of satire
during the 17th century, especially after the French poet Paul Scarron
published his *Virgile Travesti* (1648), which provoked mirth by retelling
the heroic fable of the *Aeneid* in the most vulgar terms. Butler's use of
burlesque expresses his contempt for the Puritans and their Commonwealth. Their theology he reduced to absurdity, their religious practices
to pretense and self-deception, their morality to imposture and hypocrisy.
In short, the history of England from 1642 to 1660 is made to appear
mere sound and fury.

Butler took his hero's name from Spenser's *Faerie Queene*, II.ii, where

Sir Huddibras appears briefly as the lover of Elissa, who represents sullenness as opposed to high spirits. To a mind like Butler's, chivalric romance seemed contemptibly absurd, and therefore a suitable vehicle for his satiric narrative: Hudibras, the pedantic Presbyterian and his squire Ralph, the Independent, who relies on inner light and inspiration and who talks a deal of mystical nonsense, move in a romantic and hence an irrational world. The questing knight of chivalric romance is degraded into the meddling, hypocritical busybody Hudibras, who goes out, like an officer in Cromwell's army, "a-coloneling" against the popular sport of bearbaiting. The knight and the squire suggest Don Quixote and Sancho Panza, but the temper of Butler's mind is as remote from Cervantes' warm humanity as it is from Spenser's ardent idealism.

Butler had no illusions; he was skeptical in philosophy and conservative in politics, distrusting theoretical reasoning and the new science, disdainful of claims of inspiration and illumination, contemptuous of Catholicism and dubious of bishops, Anglican no less than Roman. It is difficult to think of anything which he approved unless it was peace, common sense, and the wisdom that emerges from the experience of mankind through the ages.

From Hudibras
From *Part I, Canto I*

THE ARGUMENT

Sir Hudibras, his passing worth,
The manner how he sallied forth,
His arms and equipage are shown,
His horse's virtues and his own:
The adventure of the Bear and Fiddle
Is sung, but breaks off in the middle.

When civil fury[1] first grew high,
And men fell out, they knew not why;
When hard words, jealousies, and fears
Set folks together by the ears
And made them fight, like mad or drunk,   5
For Dame Religion as for punk,[2]
Whose honesty they all durst swear for,
Though not a man of them knew wherefore;
When gospel-trumpeter,[3] surrounded
With long-eared rout, to battle sounded,   10
And pulpit, drum ecclesiastic,[4]

1. The Civil War between Royalists and Parliamentarians (1642–1649).
2. I.e., a prostitute.
3. A Presbyterian minister, vehemently preaching rebellion. The "long-eared rout" is a mob of Puritans or Roundheads, so called because they wore their hair short instead of in flowing curls

and thus exposed their ears, which to many satirists suggested the long ears of the ass.
4. The Presbyterian clergy were said to have preached the country into civil war. Hence, in pounding their pulpits with their fists, they are said to beat their ecclesiastical drums.

Was beat with fist instead of a stick;
Then did Sir Knight abandon dwelling,
And out he rode a-coloneling.[5]
    A wight he was whose very sight would   15
Entitle him Mirror of Knighthood;
That never bent his stubborn knee
To anything but chivalry,
Nor put up blow but that which laid
Right worshipful on shoulder blade;[6]   20
Chief of domestic knights and errant,
Either for chartel or for warrant;[7]
Great on the bench, great in the saddle,
That could as well bind o'er as swaddle.[8]
Mighty he was at both of these,   25
And styled of war as well as peace.
(So some rats of amphibious nature
Are either for the land or water.)
But here our authors make a doubt
Whether he were more wise or stout.   30
Some hold the one and some the other;
But howsoe'er they make a pother,
The difference was so small his brain
Outweighed his rage but half a grain;
Which made some take him for a tool   35
That knaves do work with, called a fool,
And offer to lay wagers that,
As Montaigne, playing with his cat,
Complains she thought him but an ass,[9]
Much more she would Sir Hudibras   40
(For that's the name our valiant knight
To all his challenges did write).
But they're mistaken very much,
'Tis plain enough he was no such.
We grant, although he had much wit,   45
He was very shy of using it;
As being loath to wear it out,
And therefore bore it not about,
Unless on holidays, or so,
As men their best apparel do.   50
Beside, 'tis known he could speak Greek

5. Here pronounced *có-lo-nel-ing.* "Wight:" a creature.
6. When a man is knighted he kneels and is tapped on the shoulder by his overlord's sword.
7. "Chartel," a written challenge to combat, such as a knight errant sends. But Hudibras, as Justice of the Peace ("domestic knight"), could also issue a "warrant" (a writ authorizing an arrest, a seizure, or a search). Hence he is satirically called "great on the [Justice's] bench" as well as in the saddle. "Errant" was spelled and pronounced *arrant.*
8. Both Justice of the Peace and soldier, he is equally able to "bind over" a malefactor to be tried at the next sessions or in his role of colonel, to beat ("swaddle") him.
9. In his *Apology for Raymond Sebond,* Michel de Montaigne (1533–92), French skeptic and essayist, wondered whether he played with his cat or his cat played with him.

As naturally as pigs squeak;
That Latin was no more difficile
Than to a blackbird 'tis to whistle.
Being rich in both, he never scanted   55
His bounty unto such as wanted,
But much of either would afford
To many that had not one word.
For Hebrew roots, although they're found
To flourish most in barren ground,[1]   60
He had such plenty as sufficed
To make some think him circumcised;
And truly so perhaps he was,
'Tis many a pious Christian's case.
    He was in logic a great critic,   65
Profoundly skilled in analytic.
He could distinguish and divide
A hair 'twixt south and southwest side;
On either which he would dispute,
Confute, change hands, and still confute.   70
He'd undertake to prove, by force
Of argument, a man's no horse;
He'd prove a buzzard is no fowl,
And that a lord may be an owl,
A calf an alderman, a goose a justice,   75
And rooks committee-men and trustees.[2]
He'd run in debt by disputation,
And pay with ratiocination.
All this by syllogism true,
In mood and figure,[3] he would do.   80
    For rhetoric, he could not ope
His mouth but out there flew a trope;[4]
And when he happened to break off
In the middle of his speech, or cough,[5]
He had hard words ready to show why,   85
And tell what rules he did it by.
Else, when with greatest art he spoke,
You'd think he talked like other folk;
For all a rhetorician's rules
Teach nothing but to name his tools.   90
His ordinary rate of speech
In loftiness of sound was rich,
A Babylonish dialect,[6]

1. Hebrew, the language of Adam, was thought of as the primitive language, the one which men in a state of nature would naturally speak.
2. Committees were set up in the counties by Parliament and given authority to imprison Royalists and to sequestrate their estates. "Rooks": a kind of blackbird; slang for "cheats."
3. "Mood" is the form of an argument. The "figure" of a syllogism is "the proper disposition of the middle term with the parts of the question."
4. Figure of speech.
5. Some pulpit orators regarded hemming and coughing as ornaments of speech.
6. Pedants affected the use of foreign words. The allusion is to the Tower of Babel (Genesis xi.4–9).

Which learned pedants much affect.
It was a parti-colored dress   95
Of patched and piebald languages;
'Twas English cut on Greek and Latin,
Like fustian heretofore on satin.[7]
It had an odd promiscuous tone,
As if he had talked three parts in one;   100
Which made some think, when he did gabble,
They had heard three laborers of Babel,
Or Cerberus himself pronounce
A leash of languages at once.[8]
This he as volubly would vent   105
As if his stock would ne'er be spent;
And truly, to support that charge,
He had supplies as vast and large.
For he could coin or counterfeit
New words with little or no wit;[9]   110
Words so debased and hard no stone
Was hard enough to touch them on.
And when with hasty noise he spoke 'em,
The ignorant for current took 'em;
That had the orator, who once   115
Did fill his mouth with pebble-stones
When he harangued,[1] but known his phrase,
He would have used no other ways.
   In mathematics he was greater
Than Tycho Brahe,[2] or Erra Pater: 120
For he, by geometric scale,
Could take the size of pots of ale;
Resolve by sines and tangents straight,
If bread or butter wanted weight;
And wisely tell what hour o' the day   125
The clock does strike, by algebra.
   Beside, he was a shrewd philosopher,
And had read every text and gloss over;
Whate'er the crabbed'st author hath,
He understood by implicit faith;   130
Whatever skeptic could inquire for,
For every *why* he had a *wherefore;*
Knew more than forty of them do,
As far as words and terms could go,
All which he understood by rote   135

---

7. Clothes made of coarse cloth ("fustian") were slashed so as to display the richer satin lining.
8. The sporting term "leash" denotes a group of three dogs, hawks, deer, etc.; hence, *three* in general. Cerberus was the three-headed dog that guarded the entrance to Hades.
9. The Presbyterians and other sects invented a special religious vocabulary, much ridiculed by Anglicans: "outgoings," "workings-out," "gospel-walking-times," etc.
1. Demosthenes cured a stutter by speaking with pebbles in his mouth.
2. A Danish astronomer (1546–1601). "Erra Pater": Butler's contemptuous name for the popular astrologer William Lilly (1602–81).

And, as occasion served, would quote,
No matter whether right or wrong;
They might be either said or sung.
His notions fitted things so well
That which was which he could not tell,   140
But oftentimes mistook the one
For the other, as great clerks have done.[3]
He could reduce all things to acts,
And knew their natures by abstracts;
Where entity and quiddity,[4]   145
The ghosts of defunct bodies, fly;
Where truth in person does appear,
Like words congealed in northern air.[5]
He knew what's what, and that's as high
As metaphysic wit can fly.   150
    In school-divinity[6] as able
As he that hight Irrefragable;[7]
Profound in all the nominal
And real ways beyond them all;
And with as delicate a hand   155
Could twist as tough a rope of sand.
And weave fine cobwebs, fit for skull
That's empty when the moon is full;[8]
Such as take lodgings in a head
That's to be let unfurnishéd   160
He could raise scruples dark and nice,[9]
And after solve 'em in a trice;
As if divinity had catched
The itch on purpose to be scratched,
Or, like a mountebank,[1] did wound   165
And stab herself with doubts profound,
Only to show with how small pain
The sores of faith are cured again;
Although by woeful proof we find
They always leave a scar behind.   170
    He knew the seat of paradise,[2]

3. Elsewhere Butler wrote: "Notions are but pictures of things in the imagination of man, and if they agree with their originals in nature, they are true, and if not, false." "Clerks": scholars.
4. In the hair-splitting logic of medieval Scholastic philosophy, a distinction was drawn between the "entity" or *being* and the "quiddity" or *essence* of bodies. Butler calls entity and quiddity "ghosts" because they were held to be independent realities and so to survive the bodies in which they lodge.
5. The notion, as old as the Greek wit Lucian, that in arctic regions words freeze as they are uttered and become audible only when they thaw.
6. Scholastic theology.
7. Alexander of Hales (d. 1245) was called "Irrefragable," i.e., unanswer-

able, because his system seemed incontrovertible. The next couplet refers to the debate, continuous throughout the Middle Ages, as to whether the objects of our concepts exist in nature or are mere intellectual abstractions. The "nominalists" denied their objective reality, the "realists" affirmed it.
8. The frenzies of madmen were supposed to wax and wane with the moon (hence "lunatic").
9. Obscure ("dark") and subtle ("nice") intellectual perplexities ("scruples").
1. A seller of quack medicines.
2. The problem of the precise location of the Garden of Eden and the similar problems listed in the ensuing dozen lines had all been the subject of controversy among theologians.

Could tell in what degree it lies;
And, as he was disposed, could prove it
Below the moon, or else above it;
What Adam dreamt of when his bride   175
Came from her closet in his side;
Whether the devil tempted her
By a High Dutch interpreter;
If either of them had a navel;
Who first made music malleable; [2a]   180
Whether the serpent at the fall
Had cloven feet or none at all:
All this without a gloss or comment
He could unriddle in a moment,
In proper terms, such as men smatter   185
When they throw out and miss the matter.
    For his religion, it was fit
To match his learning and his wit:
'Twas Presbyterian true blue,[3]
For he was of that stubborn crew   190
Of errant[4] saints whom all men grant
To be the true church militant,
Such as do build their faith upon
The holy text of pike and gun;
Decide all controversies by   195
Infallible artillery,
And prove their doctrine orthodox
By apostolic blows and knocks;
Call fire, and sword, and desolation
A godly, thorough reformation,   200
Which always must be carried on
And still be doing, never done;
As if religion were intended
For nothing else but to be mended.
A sect whose chief devotion lies   205
In odd, perverse antipathies;[5]
In falling out with that or this,
And finding somewhat still amiss;
More peevish, cross, and splénetic
Than dog distract or monkey sick;   210

2a. Capable of being fashioned into form. Pythagoras is said to have organized sounds into the musical scale.
3. The Scotch Covenanters adopted blue as their color, in contrast to the Royalist red. Blue is the color of constancy; hence, "true blue," staunch, unwavering. This and the next five couplets bitterly recall the violence and fanaticism of the Parliamentary armies in attempting to reform the Anglican Church.
4. A pun: "arrant," meaning "un- mitigated," and "errant," meaning "wandering," were both spelled and pronounced *arrant*. The Puritans frequently called themselves "saints."
5. The hostility of the sects to everything Anglican or Roman Catholic laid them open to the charge of opposing innocent practices out of mere perverse antipathy. Some extreme Presbyterians fasted at Christmas, instead of following the old custom of feasting and rejoicing. Cf. lines 211–12.

That with more care keep holiday
The wrong, than others the right way;
Compound for sins they are inclined to
By damning those they have no mind to;
Still so perverse and opposite   215
As if they worshiped God for spite.
The selfsame thing they will abhor
One way and long another for.
Free-will they one way disavow,[6]
Another, nothing else allow: 220
All piety consists therein
In them, in other men all sin.
Rather than fail, they will defy
That which they love most tenderly;
Quarrel with minced pies and disparage   225
Their best and dearest friend, plum-porridge;
Fat pig and goose itself oppose,
And blaspheme custard through the nose.[7]

* * *

1663

6. By the doctrine of predestination.   7. A reference to the nasal whine of
the pious sectarians.

JOHN WILMOT,
SECOND EARL OF ROCHESTER

(1647–1680)

John Wilmot, Second Earl of Rochester, was the precocious son of one of
Charles II's most loyal followers in exile. He won the king's favor at the
Restoration and, in 1664, after education at Oxford and on the continent,
took a place at court, at the age of seventeen. There he soon distinguished
himself as "the man who has the most wit and the least honor in England." For one escapade, the abduction of Elizabeth Malet, an heiress, he
was imprisoned in the Tower. But he regained his position by courageous
service in the naval war against the Dutch; and in 1667 he married Miss
Malet. The rest of his career was no less stormy. His satiric wit, directed
not only at ordinary mortals but at Dryden and Charles II himself,
embroiled him in constant quarrels and exiles; his practical jokes, his affairs,
his dissipation were legendary. He told his biographer, Gilbert Burnet, that
"for five years together he was continually drunk." Just before his death,
however, Burnet converted him to Christian repentance; and for posterity
Rochester became a favorite moral topic: the libertine who had seen the
error of his ways.

"Wit," in the Restoration, meant not only a clever turn of phrase but
mental capacity, intellectual power. Rochester was famous for both kinds of
wit. His fierce intelligence, impatient of sham and convention, helped
design a way of life based on style, cleverness, self-interest—a way of life
observable in Restoration plays (Dorimant, in Etherege's *The Man of*

Mode, strongly resembles Rochester). Philosophically, such behavior may be seen as an experiment in living the life of a "natural man," in accord with Hobbes's doctrine that all laws, even our notions of good and evil, are artificial social checks upon natural human desires. *The Disabled Debauchee*, composed in "heroic stanzas" like those of Dryden's *Annus Mirabilis*, subverts the very notion of heroism by turning conventions upside-down. Yet everything is kept plausible by Rochester's special gift for impersonation, the same talent, according to one enemy, that made him a dangerous seducer—"He enters into all your tastes and your feelings, and makes you believe everything he says, though not a single word is sincere."

The Disabled Debauchee

As some brave admiral, in former war
    Deprived of force, but pressed with courage still,
Two rival fleets appearing from afar,
    Crawls to the top of an adjacent hill;

From whence, with thoughts full of concern, he views   5
    The wise and daring conduct of the fight,
Whilst each bold action to his mind renews
    His present glory and his past delight;

From his fierce eyes flashes of fire he throws,
    As from black clouds when lightning breaks away;   10
Transported, thinks himself amidst the foes,
    And absent, yet enjoys the bloody day;

So, when my days of impotence approach,
    And I'm by pox[1] and wine's unlucky chance
Forced from the pleasing billows of debauch   15
    On the dull shore of lazy temperance,

My pains at least some respite shall afford
    While I behold the battle you maintain
When fleets of glasses sail about the board,[2]
    From whose broadsides[3] volleys of wit shall rain.   20

Nor let the sight of honorable scars,
    Which my too forward valor did procure,
Frighten new-listed[4] soldiers from the wars:
    Past joys have more than paid what I endure.

Should any youth (worth being drunk) prove nice,[5]   25
    And from his fair inviter meanly shrink,

1. Venereal disease.
2. Table.
3. The sides of the table; artillery on a ship; sheets on which satirical verses were printed.
4. Newly enlisted.
5. Coy, fastidious.

'Twill please the ghost of my departed vice
    If, at my counsel, he repent and drink.

Or should some cold-complexioned sot forbid,
    With his dull morals, our bold night-alarms,   30
I'll fire his blood by telling what I did
    When I was strong and able to bear arms.

I'll tell of whores attacked, their lords at home;
    Bawds' quarters beaten up, and fortress won;
Windows demolished, watches[6] overcome;   35
    And handsome ills by my contrivance done.

Nor shall our love-fits, Chloris, be forgot,
    When each the well-looked linkboy[7] strove t' enjoy,
And the best kiss was the deciding lot
    Whether the boy used you, or I the boy.   40

With tales like these I will such thoughts inspire
    As to important mischief shall incline:
I'll make him long some ancient church to fire,
    And fear no lewdness he's called to by wine.

Thus, statesmanlike, I'll saucily impose,   45
    And safe from action, valiantly advise;
Sheltered in impotence, urge you to blows,
    And being good for nothing else, be wise.

    1680

6. Watchmen.
7. Good-looking boy employed to light the way with a link or torch.

ANNE FINCH,
COUNTESS OF WINCHILSEA

(1661–1720)

Born into an ancient country family, Anne Kingsmill became a maid of honor at the court of Charles II. There she met Colonel Heneage Finch, Lord Winchilsea's eldest son; in 1684 they married. During the short reign of James II they prospered at court, but at the king's fall in 1688 they were forced to retire, eventually settling on a beautiful family estate at Eastwell, in Kent, near the south coast of England. Here Lady Winchilsea wrote most of her poems, influenced, she said, by "the solitude & security of the country," and by "objects naturally inspiring soft and poetical imaginations." Her *Miscellany Poems on Several Occasions, Written by a Lady* were published in 1713; one poem, *The Spleen*, a description of the mysterious melancholic illness from which she and many other fashionable people suffered, achieved some fame. But her larger reputation only began a century later, when Wordsworth praised her for keeping her eye upon external nature, and for a style "often admirable, chaste, tender, and vigorous."

Three things conspired to keep Lady Winchilsea's poems in the shade: she was an aristocrat; her nature was retiring; and she was a woman. Any one of these might have made her shrink from exposing herself to the jeers that still, at the turn of the century, greeted any effort by a "scribbling lady." Many of her best poems, for instance *The Petition for an Absolute Retreat*, celebrate the joys of solitude. Nevertheless, remarkably, she chose to publish. The reason may be found in her contempt for the notion that women are fit for nothing but trivial pursuits. "Women are education's and not nature's fools," she once wrote. Lady Winchilsea, like the blue-stockings who became so prominent later in the century, is a serious woman, and proud of it. Against the scoffers, she offers herself as an example of what a woman can be: thoughtful, sensitive, observant; able to find strength in her own mind and quiet joy in her musings in the night.

On Myself

Good heaven, I thank thee, since it was designed
I should be framed but of the weaker kind,
That yet my soul is rescued from the love
Of all those trifles, which their[1] passions move.
Pleasures, and praise, and plenty have with me   5
But their just value. If allowed they be,
Freely and thankfully as much I taste,
As will not reason or religion waste.[2]
If they're denied, I on my self can live,
And slight those aids unequal chance does give.   10
When in the sun, my wings can be displayed,
And in retirement, I can bless the shade.

1713

A Nocturnal Reverie

In such a night,[3] when every louder wind
Is to its distant cavern safe confined;
And only gentle Zephyr fans his wings,
And lonely Philomel,[4] still waking, sings;
Or from some tree, famed for the owl's delight,   5
She, hollowing clear, directs the wanderer right:
In such a night, when passing clouds give place,

1. I.e., most women's.
2. As will not destroy reason or religion.
3. This phrase, repeated twice below, echoes the same repeated phrase in the
night-piece that opens Act V of *The Merchant of Venice*.
4. The nightingale.

Or thinly veil the heavens' mysterious face;
When in some river, overhung with green,
The waving moon and trembling leaves are seen;　　　　10
When freshened grass now bears itself upright,
And makes cool banks to pleasing rest invite,
Whence springs the woodbind, and the bramble-rose,
And where the sleepy cowslip sheltered grows;
Whilst now a paler hue the foxglove takes,　　　　　15
Yet checkers still with red the dusky brakes:
When scattered glow-worms, but in twilight fine,
Show trivial beauties watch their hour to shine;
Whilst Salisbury[5] stands the test of every light,
In perfect charms, and perfect virtue bright:　　　　20
When odors, which declined repelling day,
Through temperate air uninterrupted stray;
When darkened groves their softest shadows wear,
And falling waters we distinctly hear;
When through the gloom more venerable shows　　　25
Some ancient fabric,[6] awful in repose,
While sunburnt hills their swarthy looks conceal,
And swelling haycocks thicken up the vale:
When the loosed horse now, as his pasture leads,
Comes slowly grazing through the adjoining meads,　　30
Whose stealing pace, and lengthened shade we fear,
Till torn-up forage in his teeth we hear:
When nibbling sheep at large pursue their food,
And unmolested kine rechew the cud;
When curlews cry beneath the village walls,　　　　35
And to her straggling brood the partridge calls;
Their shortlived jubilee the creatures keep,
Which but endures, whilst tyrant man does sleep;
When a sedate content the spirit feels,
And no fierce light disturbs, whilst it reveals;　　　40
But silent musings urge the mind to seek
Something, too high for syllables to speak;
Till the free soul to a composedness charmed,
Finding the elements of rage disarmed,
O'er all below a solemn quiet grown,　　　　　　45
Joys in the inferior world,[7] and thinks it like her own:
In such a night let me abroad remain,
Till morning breaks, and all's confused again;
Our cares, our toils, our clamors are renewed,
Or pleasures, seldom reached, again pursued.　　　　50

　　　　　　　　　　　　　　　　　　　　1713

5. Probably Lady Salisbury, the daughter of a friend. The sense is that this lady differs from others more trivial, who like glow-worms look fine only one hour a day.
6. Edifice.
7. The world of nature (compared to the world of the soul).

MATTHEW PRIOR
(1664–1721)

Prior's distinguished diplomatic achievements cannot concern us here. He became a diplomat through the patronage of Dryden's friend the Earl of Dorset, wit, courtier, and poet, when he was appointed secretary to the embassy at The Hague. His public career culminated in his negotiating for Oxford's Tory ministry the Treaty of Utrecht (1713), which ended the War of the Spanish Succession; but after the fall of the Tories in 1714, Prior was recalled from Paris, placed under house arrest for over a year, and frequently interrogated in the hope that his evidence could be used to bring Oxford to trial as a traitor. Upon his release he found himself out of place and broken in fortune. But the extraordinary success of such friends as Swift and Pope in supporting the publication by subscription of his *Poems on Several Occasions* (1718) secured him a profit of 4,000 guineas, a very large sum at that time, which enabled him to end his life in comfort.

Prior was a representative man of his time: philosophically a skeptic; in public life ambitious and self-seeking, but not corruptible; a wit who entertained no illusions about life and who accepted its darker side and the fallibility of man with grace and irony. In his own words:

> Now in equipage stately, now humbly on foot,
>   Both fortunes he tried, but to neither would trust,
> And whirled in the round, as the wheel turned about,
>   He found riches had wings, and knew man was but dust.

His poetry was the by-product of a busy life—"the fruits of [his] vacant hours," as he once wrote. This pose of being the gentleman amateur he inherited from the Restoration court poets—naturally enough, considering his early association with Dorset and others. And indeed as a lyric poet he stands at the end of the long tradition of *vers de société*, such as was written by the "mob of gentlemen who wrote with ease" at the courts of Charles and James. But Prior was no careless writer: his grace and colloquial simplicity of language are the effects of studied art. His finest pieces are his lyrics, not his official odes and panegyrics. Of his two philosophical poems it is not the serious *Solomon* in weighty language and heroic couplets that attracts readers today, but rather the skeptical and delightfully witty *Alma* (written during his arrest in 1715) in deft octosyllabic couplets and homely conversational language that suggest Swift at his best. William Cowper admired Prior's ability to "make verse speak the language of prose, without being prosaic—to marshal the words of it in such an order as they might naturally take in falling from the lips of an extemporary speaker, yet without meanness, harmoniously, elegantly, and without seeming to displace a syllable for the sake of the rhyme * * * "

No poems were more popular, in the 17th and 18th centuries, than those which praised the virtues of a modest, retired life, sequestered from the ambitions of city and court. According to Dr. Johnson, "Perhaps no composition in our language has been oftener perused than Pomfret's *Choice*" (1700), which chooses the Golden Mean: a small estate, old books and wines, a few friends, a prudent wife, a peaceful death. Yet Prior, who knew well enough the disappointments of public life, also knew that simple country living did not guarantee virtue. *An Epitaph* satirizes not the quiet but the unexamined life. For an epigraph, Prior took a chorus from Seneca's *Thyestes*—"All I seek is to lie still"—to which we might add Tolstoy's judgment of Ivan Ilych, whose "life was most ordinary and most simple and therefore most terrible."

An Epitaph

Interred beneath this marble stone
Lie sauntering Jack and idle Joan.
While rolling threescore years and one
Did round this globe their courses run;
If human things went ill or well;   5
If changing empires rose or fell;
The morning passed, the evening came,
And found this couple still the same.
They walked and ate, good folks: what then?
Why then they walked and ate again.   10
They soundly slept the night away;
They did just nothing all the day;
And having buried children four,
Would not take pains to try for more.
Nor sister either had, nor brother: 15
They seemed just tallied for each other.
   Their moral and economy[1]
Most perfectly they made agree:
Each virtue kept its proper bound,
Nor trespassed on the other's ground.   20
Nor fame, nor censure they regarded:
They neither punished, nor rewarded.
He cared not what the footmen did;
Her maids she neither praised, nor chid:
So every servant took his course;   25
And bad at first, they all grew worse.
Slothful disorder filled his stable,
And sluttish plenty decked her table.
Their beer was strong; their wine was port;
Their meal was large; their grace was short.   30
They gave the poor the remnant-meat
Just when it grew not fit to eat.
   They paid the church and parish rate,[2]
And took, but read not the receipt;

---

1. Morality and household management.   2. Tax.

For which they claimed their Sunday's due   35
Of slumbering in an upper pew.
     No man's defects sought they to know,
So never made themselves a foe.
No man's good deeds did they commend,
So never raised themselves a friend.   40
Nor cherished they relations poor:
That might decrease their present store;
Nor barn nor house did they repair:
That might oblige their future heir.
     They neither added, nor confounded;[3]   45
They neither wanted, nor abounded.
Each Christmas they accompts[4] did clear;
And wound their bottom[5] round the year.
Nor tear nor smile did they employ
At news of public grief or joy.   50
When bells were rung and bonfires made,
If asked, they ne'er denied their aid:
Their jug was to the ringers carried,
Whoever either died, or married.
Their billet[6] at the fire was found,   55
Whoever was deposed, or crowned.
     Nor good, nor bad, nor fools, nor wise;
They would not learn, nor could advise;
Without love, hatred, joy, or fear,
They led—a kind of—as it were;   60
Nor wished, nor cared, nor laughed, nor cried:
And so they lived; and so they died.
                                              1718

3. Wasted.   is, they set the year nicely to rights.
4. Accounts.   6. Firewood.
5. Wound up their skein of thread; that

JOHN GAY

(1685–1732)

The career of John Gay encompasses most of the ways that a talented but indigent author of the early 18th century could try to make a living: publication, patronage, odd jobs at court, the theater. Having been well educated at school in Devon, he came to London at seventeen to try his luck as apprentice to a silk mercer. Five years later he became secretary to his friend Aaron Hill, who introduced him to the publishing world and literary circles. Eventually most of the leading authors in London adopted him as a favorite; with Pope, Swift, and Arbuthnot he helped found the Scriblerus Club, famous for its literary satires and practical jokes. Through the offices of friends like these he obtained the patrons and political appointments that supported him. The same Scriblerian influence may be

discerned in his first successful poem, *The Shepherd's Week* (1714), a burlesque pastoral. Two years later a mock-georgic, *Trivia, or the Art of Walking the Streets of London*, showed that the town could be as rough as, and
more corrupting than, the country. Gay's popularity and financial security,
however, were confirmed only by later works: two sets of verse *Fables*, published in 1727 and 1738; and above all *The Beggar's Opera* (1728). This
ballad-opera, suggested by Swift—"what think you of a Newgate pastoral,
among the thieves and whores there?"—satirized political corruption and
Italian opera; the vitality of its raffish characters, and of its theme that vice
is the same in high places as in low, maintains its popularity.

Gay seldom seems to take his verse seriously, yet few poets have looked
with deeper irony upon the social fabric; life, not as poets would gild it, but
as it is. The playfulness of his mock forms and literary parodies, as in *The
Birth of the Squire*, exposes the disparity between high poetic expectations
and coarse human reality. The squire, expected to bring about a new
Golden Age, will waste his life in hunting and drink. For all his lightness
of touch, Gay views society with a clarity and a complexity that many
greater poets might envy.

Pope's epitaph on Gay, inscribed in Westminster Abbey, begins this
way:

> Of manners gentle, of affections mild;
> In wit, a man; simplicity, a child;
> With native humor tempering virtuous rage,
> Formed to delight at once and lash the age.

But Gay wrote an epitaph of his own.

> Life is a jest, and all things show it;
> I thought so once, but now I know it.

The Birth of the Squire. An Eclogue

IN IMITATION OF THE POLLIO OF VIRGIL[1]

Ye sylvan Muses, loftier strains recite,
Not all in shades and humble cots[2] delight.
Hark! the bells ring; along the distant grounds
The driving gales convey the swelling sounds;
Th' attentive swain, forgetful of his work,   5
With gaping wonder leans upon his fork.
What sudden news alarms the waking morn?
To the glad squire a hopeful heir is born.
Mourn, mourn, ye stags, and all ye beasts of chase,
This hour destruction brings on all your race.   10
See the pleased tenants duteous offerings bear,
Turkeys, and geese, and grocer's sweetest ware;

1. Virgil's famous Fourth Eclogue (dedicated to Consul Pollio) foretells the
birth of a marvelous child, the hope of
Rome. In the Middle Ages it was assumed that the poet had foreseen the
birth of Christ, and he became known as
a great magician.
2. Cottages.

With the new health[3] the ponderous tankard flows,
And old October[4] reddens every nose.
Beagles and spaniels round his cradle stand,   15
Kiss his moist lip and gently lick his hand.
He joys to hear the shrill horn's echoing sounds,
And learns to lisp the names of all the hounds.
With frothy ale to make his cup o'erflow,
Barley shall in paternal acres grow;   20
The bee shall sip the fragrant dew from flowers,
To give metheglin[5] for his morning hours;
For him the clustering hop shall climb the poles,
And his own orchard sparkle in his bowls.

His sire's exploits he now with wonder hears,   25
The monstrous tales indulge his greedy ears:
How when youth strung his nerves and warmed his veins,
He rode, the mighty Nimrod[6] of the plains.
He leads the staring infant through the hall,
Points out the horny spoils that grace the wall;   30
Tells how this stag through three whole counties fled,
What rivers swam, where bayed, and where he bled.
Now he the wonders of the fox repeats,
Describes the desperate chase, and all his cheats;
How in one day, beneath his furious speed,   35
He tired seven coursers of the fleetest breed;
How high the pale he leapt, how wide the ditch,
When the hound tore the haunches of the witch![7]
These stories, which descend from son to son,
The forward boy shall one day make his own.   40

Ah, too fond mother, think the time draws nigh
That calls the darling from thy tender eye;
How shall his spirit brook the rigid rules,
And the long tyranny of grammar schools?
Let younger brothers o'er dull authors plod,   45
Lashed into Latin by the tingling rod;
No, let him never feel that smart disgrace:
Why should he wiser prove than all his race?

When ripening youth with down o'ershades his chin,
And every female eye incites to sin,   50
The milkmaid (thoughtless of her future shame)
With smacking lip shall raise his guilty flame;
The dairy, barn, the hayloft, and the grove
Shall oft be conscious of their stolen love.
But think, Priscilla, on that dreadful time   55
When pangs and watery qualms shall own[8] thy crime;

3. Toast.
4. Ale.
5. Mead (made from honey).
6. A great hunter (*Genesis* 10.9).

7. "The most common accident to sports-
men; to hunt a witch in the shape of a
hare "[Gay's note].
8. Confess.

How wilt thou tremble when thy nipple's pressed
To see the white drops bathe thy swelling breast!
Nine moons shall publicly divulge her shame,
And the young squire forestall a father's name.   60

    When twice twelve times the reaper's sweeping hand
With leveled harvests has bestrewn the land,
On famed St. Hubert's feast[9] his winding horn
Shall cheer the joyful hound and wake the morn.
This memorable day his eager speed   65
Shall urge with bloody heel the rising steed.
O check the foamy bit, nor tempt thy fate;
Think on the murders of a five-bar gate!
Yet prodigal of life, the leap he tries,
Low in the dust his groveling honor lies,   70
Headlong he falls, and on the rugged stone
Distorts[1] his neck, and cracks the collarbone.
O venturous youth, thy thirst of game allay;
May'st thou survive the perils of this day!
He shall survive; and in late years be sent   75
To snore away debates in Parliament.

    The time shall come, when his more solid sense
With nod important shall the laws dispense;
A justice, with grave justices shall sit,
He praise their wisdom, they admire his wit.   80
No greyhound shall attend the tenant's pace,
No rusty gun the farmer's chimney grace;
Salmons shall leave their covers void of fear,
Nor dread the thievish net or triple spear;
Poachers shall tremble at his awful name,   85
Whom vengeance now o'ertakes for murdered game.

    Assist me, Bacchus, and ye drunken powers,
To sing his friendships and his midnight hours!

    Why dost thou glory in thy strength of beer,
Firm-corked and mellowed till the twentieth year;   90
Brewed or when Phoebus warms the fleecy sign
Or when his languid rays in Scorpio shine?[2]
Think on the mischiefs which from hence have sprung!
It arms with curses dire the wrathful tongue;
Foul scandal to the lying lip affords,   95
And prompts the memory with injurious words.
O where is wisdom, when by this o'erpowered?
The state is censured, and the maid deflowered!
And wilt thou still, O squire, brew ale so strong?
Hear then the dictates of prophetic song.   100

9. November 3, which opens the hunting   2. Either in spring (Aries) or fall (Scor-
season.   pio).
1. Wrenches.

Methinks I see him in his hall appear,
Where the long table floats in clammy beer,
'Midst mugs and glasses shattered o'er the floor,
Dead-drunk, his servile crew supinely snore;
Triumphant, o'er the prostrate brutes he stands,   105
The mighty bumper trembles in his hands;
Boldly he drinks, and like his glorious sires,
In copious gulps of potent ale expires.

1720

JONATHAN SWIFT
(1667–1745)

1704:   A *Tale of a Tub* and *The Battle of the Books.*
1710–14: Alignment with Tories; political writings in defense
            of the Tory ministry.
1713:   Made Dean of St. Patrick's Cathedral, Dublin.
1726:   Publication of *Gulliver's Travels.*

Swift—a posthumous child—was born of English parents in Dublin.
Through the generosity of an uncle he was educated at Kilkenny School
and Trinity College, Dublin; but before he could fix on a career, the
troubles that followed upon James II's abdication and his subsequent invasion of Ireland drove him along with other Anglo-Irish to England. Between 1689 and 1699 he was more or less continuously a member of the
household of his kinsman Sir William Temple, an urbane, civilized man,
a retired diplomat, and a friend of King William. During these years Swift
read widely; rather reluctantly decided on the church as a career and so
took orders; and discovered his astonishing gifts as a satirist. About 1696–
97 he wrote his powerful satires on corruptions in religion and learning, *A
Tale of a Tub* and *The Battle of the Books,* which were published in 1704
and reached their final form only in the fifth edition of 1710. These were
the years in which he slowly came to maturity. When at the age of 32,
he returned to Ireland as chaplain to the Lord Justice, the Earl of Berkeley,
he had a clear sense of his genius.
     It was at Temple's that Swift met and learned to love the woman whose
role in his life has been the cause of much conjecture. Esther Johnson
(Swift's "Stella") was the daughter of Temple's steward, and when Swift
first knew her she was little more than a child. He educated her, formed
her character, and came to love her as he was to love no other person. After
Temple's death she removed (at Swift's suggestion) with her lifelong companion, Rebecca Dingley, to Dublin, where she and Swift met constantly,
but never alone. To her he wrote the famous journal-letters, later published (1766) as *The Journal to Stella,* during his four-year residence
in London when he was working with the Tories; and to her he wrote
charming poems. Whether they were secretly married or whether they
never married—and in either case why—has been often debated. A marriage of any sort seems most unlikely; and however perplexing their relationship was to others, it was obviously satisfying to each of them. Not even
the violent passion that Swift awakened, no doubt unwittingly, in a much
younger woman, Hester Vanhomrigh (pronounced V*an-úm-mer-y*), her
pleadings and reproaches and early death, could unsettle his devotion to
Stella. An enigmatic account of his relations with "Vanessa," as he called
Miss Vanhomrigh, is given in his poem *Cadenus and Vanessa.*
     The man who gained the lifelong devotion of Stella and evoked the

romantic passion of Vanessa was also admired and loved by many of the distinguished men of his time. His friendships with Addison, Pope, Dr. Arbuthnot, John Gay, Prior, Oxford, Bolingbroke, not to mention those with his less brilliant, but pleasant, Irish circle, bear witness to his moral integrity and social charm. The dark side of Swift's nature has been exaggerated at the cost of neglecting the wit and gaiety, the playful humor, and the consciously assumed eccentricities which marked his social behavior. Nor is it tenable that his satires are the product of a diseased mind which was gradually disintegrating throughout his life. Swift suffered most of his adult life from what we now recognize as Ménière's syndrome, which affects the inner ear, causing dizziness, nausea, and deafness. By all these ills he was greatly afflicted, but he was never in any sense insane. After 1739, when he was 72 years old, his infirmities and deafness cut him off from social life and his duties as Dean, and from then on senility advanced inexorably. In 1742 guardians were appointed to administer his affairs, and his last three years were spent in gloom and lethargy. But the writer of the satires was a man in full control of very great intellectual powers.

Because Swift was a clergyman, a spirited controversialist, and a devoted supporter of the Anglican Church as an institution no less important than the Crown itself, he was drawn into politics in both England and Ireland. He was hostile to all who seemed to threaten the Established Church— Deists, freethinkers, Roman Catholics, Nonconformists, or merely Whig politicians. In 1710 he abandoned his old party, the Whig, because he disapproved of its indifference to the welfare of the Anglican Church in Ireland and of its desire to repeal the Test Act, which required all holders of offices of state to take the Sacrament according to the Anglican rites, thus excluding Roman Catholics and Dissenters. Welcomed by the Tories, he became the most brilliant political journalist of the day, serving the government of Oxford and Bolingbroke as editor of the party organ, the *Examiner*, and as author of its most powerful articles, as well as writing longer pamphlets in support of important policies, such as that favoring the Peace of Utrecht (1713). He was greatly valued by the two ministers, who admitted him to social intimacy, though never to their counsels. The reward of his services was not the English bishopric which he had a right to expect, but the Deanship of St. Patrick's Cathedral in Dublin, which came to him in 1713, a year before the death of Queen Anne and the fall of the Tories put an end to all his hopes of preferment in England.

In Ireland, where he lived unwillingly, he became not only an efficient ecclesiastical administrator, but also, in 1724, the leader of Irish resistance to English oppression. Under the pseudonym of "M. B., Drapier," he published the famous series of public letters that aroused the country to refuse to accept £100,000 in new copper coins (minted in England by William Wood, who had obtained his patent through court corruption) which, it was feared, would further debase the coinage of the already poverty-stricken kingdom. Although his authorship of the letters was known to all Dublin, no one could be found to earn the £300 offered by the government for information as to the identity of the Drapier. Swift is still venerated in Ireland as a national hero. He earned the right to refer to himself in the epitaph that he wrote for his tomb as a vigorous defender of liberty.

For all his involvement in public affairs, Swift seems to stand apart from his contemporaries—a striking figure even among the statesmen of the time, a man who towered above other writers by reason of his more profound imagination, mordant wit, and emotional intensity. He has been called a misanthrope, a hater of mankind; and *Gulliver's Travels* has been considered an expression of savage misanthropy. It is true that Swift proclaimed himself a misanthrope in a letter to Pope, declaring that though he loved individuals, he hated mankind in general, and offering a new definition of man as not *animal rationale* ("a rational animal"), but as merely *animal rationis capax* ("an animal *capable* of reason"). This, he declared, is the "great foundation" upon which his "misanthropy" was erected. Swift was stating not his hatred of his fellowmen, but his antagonism to the current optimistic view that human nature is essentially good. To the "philanthropic" flattery that sentimentalism and Deistic rationalism were paying to human nature, Swift opposed a more ancient and plausible view: that human nature is deeply and permanently flawed, and that we can do nothing with or for the human race until we recognize its moral and intellectual limitations. This attitude he was pleased to call "misanthropy." In his epitaph he spoke of the "fierce indignation" which had torn his heart, an indignation that found superb expression in his greatest satires. It was provoked by the constant spectacle of creatures capable of reason, and therefore of reasonable conduct, steadfastly refusing to live up to their capabilities.

Swift is one of our greatest writers of prose. He defined a good style as "proper words in proper places," a more complex and difficult saying than at first appears. Clear, simple, concrete diction, uncomplicated syntax, economy and conciseness of language mark all of his writings. His is a style that shuns ornaments and singularity of all kinds, a style that grows more tense and controlled the more fierce the indignation that it is called upon to express. The virtues of his prose are those of his poetry, which only lately has come to be much valued. It is unpoetic poetry, devoid of, indeed as often as not mocking at, inspiration, romantic love, easily assumed literary attitudes, and conventional poetic language. Like the prose it is predominantly satiric in purpose, but not without its moments of comedy and light-heartedness, though written most often not so much to divert as to reform mankind.

A Description of a City Shower

Careful observers may foretell the hour
(By sure prognostics) when to dread a shower:
While rain depends,[1] the pensive cat gives o'er
Her frolics, and pursues her tail no more.
Returning home at night, you'll find the sink[2]   5
Strike your offended sense with double stink.
If you be wise, then go not far to dine;
You'll spend in coach hire more than save in wine.

---

1. Impends, is imminent. An example of elevated diction used frequently throughout the poem in order to gain a mock dignity, comically inappropriate to the homely and realistic subject.
2. Sewer.

A coming shower your shooting corns presage,
Old achés throb, your hollow tooth will rage.   10
Sauntering in coffeehouse is Dulman[3] seen;
He damns the climate and complains of spleen.

   Meanwhile the South, rising with dabbled wings,
A sable cloud athwart the welkin flings,
That swilled more liquor than it could contain,   15
And, like a drunkard, gives it up again.
Brisk Susan whips her linen from the rope,
While the first drizzling shower is borne aslope:
Such is that sprinkling which some careless quean[4]
Flirts on you from her mop, but not so clean: 20
You fly, invoke the gods; then turning, stop
To rail; she singing, still whirls on her mop.
Not yet the dust had shunned the unequal strife,
But, aided by the wind, fought still for life,
And wafted with its foe by violent gust,   25
'Twas doubtful which was rain and which was dust.
Ah! where must needy poet seek for aid,
When dust and rain at once his coat invade?
Sole coat, where dust cemented by the rain
Erects the nap, and leaves a mingled stain.   30

   Now in contiguous drops the flood comes down,
Threatening with deluge this devoted town.
To shops in crowds the daggled[5] females fly,
Pretend to cheapen goods, but nothing buy.
The Templar[6] spruce, while every spout's abroach,   35
Stays till 'tis fair, yet seems to call a coach.
The tucked-up sempstress walks with hasty strides,
While streams run down her oiled umbrella's sides.
Here various kinds, by various fortunes led,
Commence acquaintance underneath a shed.   40
Triumphant Tories and desponding Whigs
Forget their feuds,[7] and join to save their wigs.
Boxed in a chair[8] the beau impatient sits,
While spouts run clattering o'er the roof by fits,
And ever and anon with frightful din   45
The leather sounds;[9] he trembles from within.
So when Troy chairmen bore the wooden steed,
Pregnant with Greeks impatient to be freed
(Those bully Greeks, who, as the moderns do,

3. A type name (from "dull man"), like Congreve's "Petulant" or "Witwoud." It was commonly believed at this time that the Englishman's tendency to melancholy ("the spleen") was attributable to the rainy climate.
4. Wench, slut.
5. Spattered with mud. "To cheapen": to bargain for.
6. A young man engaged in studying law. In the literature of the period the Templar is usually depicted as neglecting his professional studies for the sake of dissipation and the pursuit of literature. Cf. the Member of the Inner Temple in *Spectator* 2. "Abroach": pouring out water.
7. The Whig ministry had just fallen and the Tories, led by Harley and St. John, were forming the government with which Swift was to be closely associated until the death of the Queen in 1714.
8. Sedan chair.
9. The roof of the sedan chair was made of leather.

Instead of paying chairmen, run them through[1]),   50
Laocoön struck the outside with his spear,
And each imprisoned hero quaked for fear.[2]
  Now from all parts the swelling kennels[3] flow,
And bear their trophies with them as they go:
Filth of all hues and odors seem to tell   55
What street they sailed from, by their sight and smell.
They, as each torrent drives with rapid force,
From Smithfield or St. Pulchre's shape their course,
And in huge confluence joined at Snow Hill ridge,
Fall from the conduit prone to Holborn Bridge.[4]   60
Sweepings from butchers' stalls, dung, guts, and blood, ⎤
Drowned puppies, stinking sprats,[5] all drenched in mud, ⎬
Dead cats, and turnip tops, come tumbling down the flood.[6] ⎦

                                                  1710

Verses on the Death of Dr. Swift

OCCASIONED BY READING A MAXIM IN ROCHEFOUCAULD [1]

*Dans l'adversité de nos meilleurs amis nous trouvons toujours quelque chose,
qui ne nous déplaît pas.*[2]

        As Rochefoucauld his maxims drew
        From nature, I believe 'em true:
        They argue no corrupted mind
        In him; the fault is in mankind.
          This maxim more than all the rest   5
        Is thought too base for human breast:
        "In all distresses of our friends
        We first consult our private ends,
        While Nature, kindly bent to ease us,
        Points out some circumstance to please us."   10
          If this perhaps your patience move,
        Let reason and experience prove.

1. Run them through with their swords. The bully, always prone to violence, was a familiar figure in London streets and places of amusement.
2. *Aeneid* II.40–53.
3. The open gutters in the middle of the street.
4. An accurate description of the drainage system of this part of London—the eastern edge of Holborn and West Smithfield, which lie outside the old walls west and east of Newgate. The great cattle and sheep markets were in Smithfield. The church of St. Sepulchre ("St. Pulchre's") stood opposite Newgate Prison. Holborn Conduit was at the foot of Snow Hill. It drained into Fleet Ditch, an evil-smelling open sewer, at Holborn Bridge.
5. Small herrings.

6. In Falkner's edition of Swift's *Works* (Dublin, 1735) a note almost certainly suggested by Swift points to the concluding triplet, with its resonant final Alexandrine, as a burlesque of a mannerism of Dryden and other Restoration poets, and claims that Swift's ridicule banished the triplet from contemporary poetry.
1. François de La Rochefoucauld (1613–80), writer of witty, cynical maxims. Writing to Pope (November 26, 1725), Swift, opposing the optimistic philosophy that Pope and Bolingbroke were at that time developing, professed to have founded his whole character on these maxims.
2. "In the misfortune of our best friends we always find something that does not displease us."

We all behold with envious eyes
Our equal raised above our size.
Who would not at a crowded show   15
Stand high himself, keep others low?
I love my friend as well as you,
But why should he obstruct my view?
Then let me have the higher post;
Suppose it but an inch at most.   20
    If in a battle you should find
One, whom you love of all mankind,
Had some heroic action done,
A champion killed, or trophy won;
Rather than thus be overtopped,   25
Would you not wish his laurels cropped?
    Dear honest Ned is in the gout,
Lies racked with pain, and you without:
How patiently you hear him groan!
How glad the case is not your own!   30
    What poet would not grieve to see
His brethren write as well as he?
But rather than they should excel,
He'd wish his rivals all in hell.
    Her end when Emulation misses,   35
She turns to envy, stings, and hisses:
The strongest friendship yields to pride,
Unless the odds be on our side.
    Vain humankind! fantastic race!
Thy various follies who can trace?   40
Self-love, ambition, envy, pride,
Their empire in our hearts divide.
Give others riches, power, and station;
'Tis all on me an usurpation;
I have no title to aspire,   45
Yet, when you sink, I seem the higher.
In Pope I cannot read a line,
But with a sigh I wish it mine:
When he can in one couplet fix
More sense than I can do in six,   50
It gives me such a jealous fit,
I cry, "Pox take him and his wit!"
    I grieve to be outdone by Gay [3]
In my own humorous biting way.
Arbuthnot [4] is no more my friend,   55
Who dares to irony pretend,
Which I was born to introduce,

---

3. John Gay (1685–1732), author of
the famous *Beggar's Opera* (1728), intimate friend of Swift and Pope. His
*Trivia, or the Art of Walking the
Streets of London* (1716) owes something to Swift's *City Shower*.
4. Dr. John Arbuthnot, physician and
wit, friend of Swift and Pope. See
Pope's *Epistle to Dr. Arbuthnot*.

Refined it first, and showed its use.
St. John,[5] as well as Pulteney, knows
That I had some repute for prose;   60
And, till they drove me out of date,
Could maul a minister of state.
If they have mortified my pride,
And made me throw my pen aside;
If with such talents Heaven hath blessed 'em,   65
Have I not reason to detest 'em?

   To all my foes, dear Fortune, send
Thy gifts, but never to my friend:
I tamely can endure the first,
But this with envy makes me burst.   70

   Thus much may serve by way of proem;
Proceed we therefore to our poem.

   The time is not remote, when I
Must by the course of nature die;
When, I foresee, my special friends   75
Will try to find their private ends:
Though it is hardly understood
Which way my death can do them good;
Yet thus, methinks, I hear 'em speak:
"See how the Dean begins to break!   80
Poor gentleman! he droops apace!
You plainly find it in his face.
That old vertigo [6] in his head
Will never leave him till he's dead.
Besides, his memory decays;   85
He recollects not what he says;
He cannot call his friends to mind;
Forgets the place where last he dined;
Plies you with stories o'er and o'er,
He told them fifty times before.   90
How does he fancy we can sit
To hear his out-of-fashion wit?
But he takes up with younger folks,
Who for his wine will bear his jokes.
Faith, he must make his stories shorter,   95
Or change his comrades once a quarter;
In half the time he talks them round,
There must another set be found.

   "For poetry, he's past his prime;
He takes an hour to find a rhyme;   100
His fire is out, his wit decayed,
His fancy sunk, his Muse a jade.[7]

---

5. Henry St. John, Lord Bolingbroke
(see note, Pope's *Essay on Man.* I.1),
though debarred from the House of
Lords and from public office, had become the center of a group of Tories
and discontented young Whigs (of
whom William Pulteney was one) who
united in opposing Sir Robert Walpole,
the chief minister. They published a
political periodical, the *Craftsman*, thus
rivaling Swift in his role of political
pamphleteer and enemy of Sir Robert.
6. Johnson in his *Dictionary* authorizes
Swift's pronunciation: *ver-ti-go*.
7. A worn-out horse, in contrast to
Pegasus, the winged horse of Greek
mythology, emblem of poetic inspiration.

I'd have him throw away his pen—
But there's no talking to some men."
   And then their tenderness appears   105
By adding largely to my years:
"He's older than he would be reckoned,
And well remembers Charles the Second.
He hardly drinks a pint of wine;
And that, I doubt, is no good sign.   110
His stomach, too, begins to fail;
Last year we thought him strong and hale;
But now he's quite another thing;
I wish he may hold out till spring."
They hug themselves, and reason thus: 115
"It is not yet so bad with us."
   In such a case they talk in tropes,[8]
And by their fears express their hopes.
Some great misfortune to portend
No enemy can match a friend.   120
With all the kindness they profess,
The merit of a lucky guess
(When daily how-d'ye's come of course,
And servants answer, "Worse and worse!")
Would please 'em better, than to tell   125
That God be praised! the Dean is well.
Then he who prophesied the best,
Approves his foresight to the rest:
"You know I always feared the worst,
And often told you so at first."   130
He'd rather choose that I should die,
Than his prediction prove a lie.
Not one foretells I shall recover,
But all agree to give me over.
   Yet, should some neighbor feel a pain   135
Just in the parts where I complain,
How many a message would he send!
What hearty prayers that I should mend!
Inquire what regimen I kept;
What gave me ease, and how I slept,   140
And more lament, when I was dead,
Then all the snivelers round my bed.
   My good companions, never fear;
For though you may mistake a year,
Though your prognostics run too fast,   145
They must be verified at last.
   Behold the fatal day arrive!
   "How is the Dean?"—"He's just alive."
Now the departing prayer is read.
"He hardly breathes"—"The Dean is dead."   150
Before the passing bell begun,

8. Figures of speech.

The news through half the town has run.
"Oh! may we all for death prepare!
What has he left? and who's his heir?"
"I know no more than what the news is;   155
'Tis all bequeathed to public uses."
"To public use! a perfect whim!
What had the public done for him?
Mere envy, avarice, and pride:
He gave it all—but first he died.   160
And had the Dean in all the nation
No worthy friend, no poor relation?
So ready to do strangers good,
Forgetting his own flesh and blood?"
Now Grub Street [9] wits are all employed;   165
With elegies the town is cloyed;
Some paragraph in every paper
To curse the Dean, or bless the Drapier.[1]

   The doctors, tender of their fame,
Wisely on me lay all the blame.   170
"We must confess his case was nice;[2]
But he would never take advice.
Had he been ruled, for aught appears,
He might have lived these twenty years:
For, when we opened him, we found,   175
That all his vital parts were sound."

   From Dublin soon to London spread,
'Tis told at court, "The Dean is dead."
Kind Lady Suffolk,[3] in the spleen,
Runs laughing up to tell the Queen.   180
The Queen, so gracious, mild and good,
Cries, "Is he gone? 'tis time he should.
He's dead, you say; why, let him rot:
I'm glad the medals were forgot.[4]
I promised him, I own; but when?   185
I only was the Princess then;
But now, as consort of the King,
You know, 'tis quite a different thing."

   Now Chartres,[5] at Sir Robert's levee,
Tells with a sneer the tidings heavy: 190
"Why, is he dead without his shoes?"
Cries Bob, "I'm sorry for the news:
Oh, were the wretch but living still,
And in his place my good friend Will! [6]

9. Originally a street in London largely inhabited by hack writers; later, a generic term applied to all such writers.
1. It was in the character of "M. B.," a Dublin drapier, that Swift aroused the Irish people to resistance against the importation of Wood's halfpence. See biographical introduction.
2. Delicate; hence demanding careful diagnosis and treatment.
3. George II's mistress, with whom Swift became friendly during his visit to Pope in 1726. "In the spleen": in low spirits. The phrase is ironic, as "laughing" in the next line makes clear.
4. Queen Caroline had promised Swift some medals when she was Princess of Wales during the same year.
5. Col. Francis Chartres, a debauchee often satirized by Pope; Sir Robert Walpole.
6. William Pulteney (see line 59 and its note.)

Or had a miter on his head,   195
Provided Bolingbroke were dead!"
    Now Curll his shop from rubbish drains: [7]
Three genuine tomes of Swift's remains!
And then, to make them pass the glibber,
Revised by Tibbalds, Moore, and Cibber.[8]   200
He'll treat me as he does my betters,
Publish my will, my life, my letters;
Revive the libels born to die,
Which Pope must bear, as well as I.
    Here shift the scene, to represent   205
How those I love my death lament.
Poor Pope will grieve a month, and Gay
A week, and Arbuthnot a day.
    St. John himself will scarce forbear
To bite his pen, and drop a tear.   210
The rest will give a shrug, and cry,
"I'm sorry—but we all must die!"
    Indifference clad in wisdom's guise
All fortitude of mind supplies:
For how can stony bowels melt   215
In those who never pity felt?
When *we* are lashed, *they* kiss the rod,
Resigning to the will of God.
    The fools, my juniors by a year,
Are tortured with suspense and fear;   220
Who wisely thought my age a screen,
When death approached, to stand between:
The screen removed, their hearts are trembling;
They mourn for me without dissembling.
    My female friends, whose tender hearts   225
Have better learned to act their parts,
Receive the news in doleful dumps:
"The Dean is dead (and what is trumps?)
Then, Lord have mercy on his soul!
(Ladies, I'll venture for the vole.[9])   230
Six deans, they say, must bear the pall.
(I wish I knew what king to call.)
Madam, your husband will attend
The funeral of so good a friend?"
"No, madam, 'tis a shocking sight;   235
And he's engaged tomorrow night:
My Lady Club would take it ill,
If he should fail her at quadrille.
He loved the Dean—(I lead a heart)

7. Edmund Curll, shrewd and disreputable bookseller, published pirated works, scandalous biographies, and works falsely ascribed to notable writers of the time.
8. Lewis Theobald (1688–1744), Shakespeare scholar and editor, already enthroned as King of the Dunces in Pope's *Dunciad* (1728). Like Pope, Swift spells the name phonetically. James Moore-Smyth, poetaster and playwright, an enemy of Pope. Colley Cibber (1671–1757), comic actor, playwright, and supremely untalented poet laureate. He succeeded Theobald as King of the Dunces in the *Dunciad* of 1743.
9. The equivalent in the card game quadrille of bidding a grand slam in bridge.

But dearest friends, they say, must part. 240
His time was come; he ran his race;
We hope he's in a better place."
    Why do we grieve that friends should die?
No loss more easy to supply.
One year is past; a different scene! 245
No further mention of the Dean,
Who now, alas! no more is missed,
Than if he never did exist.
Where's now this favorite of Apollo?
Departed—and his works must follow, 250
Must undergo the common fate;
His kind of wit is out of date.
    Some country squire to Lintot [1] goes,
Inquires for Swift in verse and prose.
Says Lintot, "I have heard the name; 255
He died a year ago."—"The same."
He searches all the shop in vain.
"Sir, you my find them in Duck Lane: [2]
I sent them, with a load of books,
Last Monday to the pastry-cook's.[3] 260
To fancy they could live a year!
I find you're but a stranger here.
The Dean was famous in his time,
And had a kind of knack at rhyme.
His way of writing now is past: 265
The town has got a better taste.
I keep no antiquated stuff;
But spick and span I have enough.
Pray do but give me leave to show 'em:
Here's Colley Cibber's birthday poem. 270
This ode you never yet have seen
By Stephen Duck [4] upon the Queen.
Then here's a letter finely penned
Against the *Craftsman* [5] and his friend;
It clearly shows that all reflection 275
On ministers is disaffection.
Next, here's Sir Robert's vindication,[6]
    And Mr. Henley's last oration.[7]
The hawkers have not got them yet:
Your honor please to buy a set? 280
    "Here's Woolston's tracts,[8] the twelfth edition;

---

1. Bernard Lintot, the publisher of Pope's Homer and some of his early poems.
2. London street where second-hand books and publishers' "remainders" were sold.
3. To be used as waste paper for lining baking dishes and wrapping parcels.
4. Stephen Duck, "the thresher poet," an agricultural laborer, whose mild poetic gifts brought him to the notice and patronage of Queen Caroline.

5. See line 59 and its note.
6. "Walpole hires a string of party scribblers who do nothing else but write in his defense" [Swift's note].
7. "Orator" John Henley, an Independent preacher, who dazzled unlearned audiences with his oratory and who wrote treatises on elocution.
8. Thomas Woolston (1670–1733), a freethinker, whose *Discourses on the Miracles of Our Saviour* had recently earned him notoriety.

'Tis read by every politician:
The country members, when in town,
To all their boroughs send them down;
You never met a thing so smart;   285
The courtiers have them all by heart;
Those maids of honor (who can read)
Are taught to use them for their creed.
The reverend author's good intention
Has been rewarded with a pension.   290
He does an honor to his gown,
By bravely running priestcraft down;
He shows, as sure as God's in Gloucester,
That Jesus was a grand impostor;
That all his miracles were cheats,   295
Performed as jugglers do their feats:
The Church had never such a writer;
A shame he has not got a miter!"
    Suppose me dead; and then suppose
A club assembled at the Rose;   300
Where, from discourse of this and that,
I grow the subject of their chat.
And while they toss my name about,
With favor some, and some without,
One, quite indifferent in the cause,   305
My character impartial draws:
    "The Dean, if we believe report,
Was never ill received at court.
As for his works in verse and prose,
I own myself no judge of those;   310
Nor can I tell what critics thought 'em:
But this I know, all people bought 'em,
As with a moral view designed
To cure the vices of mankind.
    "His vein, ironically grave,   315
Exposed the fool and lashed the knave,
To steal a hint was never known,
But what he writ was all his own.
    "He never thought an honor done him,
Because a duke was proud to own him,   320
Would rather slip aside and choose
To talk with wits in dirty shoes;
Despised the fools with stars and garters,
So often seen caressing Chartres.
He never courted men in station,   325
Nor persons held in admiration;
Of no man's greatness was afraid,
Because he sought for no man's aid.
Though trusted long in great affairs,
He gave himself no haughty airs;   330
Without regarding private ends,
Spent all his credit for his friends;

And only chose the wise and good;
No flatterers, no allies in blood;
But succored virtue in distress,   335
And seldom failed of good success;
As numbers in their hearts must own,
Who, but for him, had been unknown.
    "With princes kept a due decorum,
But never stood in awe before 'em.   340
He followed David's lesson just;
In princes never put thy trust:[9]
And would you make him truly sour,
Provoke him with a slave in power.
The Irish senate if you named,   345
With what impatience he declaimed!
Fair Liberty was all his cry,
For her he stood prepared to die;
For her he boldly stood alone;
For her he oft exposed his own.   350
Two kingdoms, just as faction led,
Had set a price upon his head,
But not a traitor could be found,
To sell him for six hundred pound.[1]
    "Had he but spared his tongue and pen,   355
He might have rose like other men;
But power was never in his thought,
And wealth he valued not a groat:
Ingratitude he often found,
And pitied those who meant the wound;   360
But kept the tenor of his mind,
To merit well of human kind:
Nor made a sacrifice of those
Who still were true, to please his foes.
He labored many a fruitless hour,   365
To reconcile his friends in power;
Saw mischief by a faction brewing,
While they pursued each other's ruin.
But finding vain was all his care,
He left the court in mere despair.[2]   370
    "And, oh! how short are human schemes!
Here ended all our golden dreams.
What St. John's skill in state affairs,

9. Psalm cxlvi.3.
1. In 1714 the government offered £300 for the discovery of the author of Swift's *Public Spirit of the Whigs,* and in 1724 the Irish government offered a similar amount for the discovery of the author of the fourth of Swift's *Drapier's Letters.*
2. The antagonism between the two chief ministers (his dear friends), Robert Harley, Earl of Oxford, and Bolingbroke paralyzed the Tory ministry in the crucial last months of Queen Anne's life and drove Swift to retirement in Ireland, whence he returned in 1714 to make a final effort to heal the breach and save the government. He failed and retired to the country in despair. There he received the news of Anne's death on August 1. The Hanoverian succession brought the Whigs back in triumph, ruined Swift's friends, and brought Swift's public life to a close.

What Ormonde's [3] valor, Oxford's cares,
To save their sinking country lent,   375
Was all destroyed by one event.[4]
Too soon that precious life was ended,
On which alone our weal depended.
When up a dangerous faction starts,[5]
With wrath and vengeance in their hearts;   380
By solemn League and Covenant bound,
To ruin, slaughter, and confound;
To turn religion to a fable,
And make the government a Babel;
Pervert the laws, disgrace the gown,   385
Corrupt the senate, rob the crown;
To sacrifice old England's glory,
And make her infamous in story:
When such a tempest shook the land,
How could unguarded Virtue stand?   390
With horror, grief, despair, the Dean
Beheld the dire destructive scene:
His friends in exile, or the Tower,[6]
Himself within the frown of power,
Pursued by base envenomed pens,   395
Far to the land of slaves and fens;[7]
A servile race in folly nursed,
Who truckle most, when treated worst.
    "By innocence and resolution,
He bore continual persecution;   400
While numbers to preferment rose,
Whose merits were to be his foes;
When even his own familiar friends,
Intent upon their private ends,
Like renegadoes now he feels,   405
Against him lifting up their heels.
    "The Dean did, by his pen, defeat
An infamous destructive cheat;[8]
Taught fools their interest how to know,
And gave them arms to ward the blow.   410
Envy has owned it was his doing,
To save that hapless land from ruin;
While they who at the steerage [9] stood,
And reaped the profit, sought his blood.
    "To save them from their evil fate,   415

3. James Butler, Duke of Ormonde, who succeeded to the command of the English armies on the Continent, when, in 1711, the Duke of Marlborough was stripped of his offices by Anne. He went into exile in 1714 and was active in Jacobite intrigue.
4. The death of Queen Anne.
5. Swift's view of the policies of the "dangerous faction" (the Whig party) is hardly impartial. He feared it espe-cially because of its toleration of Dis-senters, and so as an enemy of the Church of England.
6. Bolingbroke was in exile; Oxford was sent to the Tower by the Whigs.
7. Ireland.
8. The scheme to introduce Wood's cop-per halfpence into Ireland in 1723–24.
9. Literally the steering of a ship. Here the direction and management of public affairs in Ireland.

name of madness or frenzy. For, if we take a survey of the greatest
actions that have been performed in the world, under the influence
of single men, which are the establishment of new empires by conquest, the advance and progress of new schemes in philosophy, and
the contriving, as well as the propagating, of new religions, we shall
find the authors of them all to have been persons whose natural
reason had admitted great revolutions from their diet, their education, the prevalency of some certain temper, together with the particular influence of air and climate. Besides, there is something individual in human minds, that easily kindles at the accidental
approach and collision of certain circumstances, which, though of
paltry and mean appearance, do often flame out into the greatest
emergencies of life. For great turns are not always given by strong
hands, but by lucky adaption, and at proper seasons; and it is of no
import where the fire was kindled, if the vapor has once got up into
the brain. For the upper region of man is furnished like the middle
region of the air; the materials are formed from causes of the widest
difference, yet produce at last the same substance and effect. Mists
arise from the earth, steams from dunghills, exhalations from the
sea, and smoke from fire; yet all clouds are the same in composition
as well as consequences, and the fumes issuing from a jakes[3] will
furnish as comely and useful a vapor as incense from an altar. Thus
far, I suppose, will easily be granted me; and then it will follow,
that as the face of nature never produces rain but when it is overcast and disturbed, so human understanding, seated in the brain,
must be troubled and overspread by vapors, ascending from the
lower faculties to water the invention and render it fruitful. Now,
although these vapors, (as it hath been already said) are of as various original as those of the skies, yet the crop they produce differs
both in kind and degree, merely according to the soil. I will produce
two instances to prove and explain what I am now advancing.

A certain great prince[4] raised a mighty army, filled his coffers
with infinite treasures, provided an invincible fleet, and all this
without giving the least part of his design to his greatest ministers
or his nearest favorites. Immediately the whole world was alarmed;
the neighboring crowns in trembling expectation towards what
point the storm would burst; the small politicians everywhere forming profound conjectures. Some believed he had laid a scheme for
universal monarchy; others, after much insight, determined the
matter to be a project for pulling down the Pope, and setting up
the reformed religion, which had once been his own. Some again, of
a deeper sagacity, sent him into Asia to subdue the Turk, and
recover Palestine. In the midst of all these projects and prepara-

3. Latrine.
4. "This was Harry the Great of
France" [Swift's note]. Henry IV
(1553–1610), infatuated with the Princesse de Condé, whose husband had removed her to the Spanish Netherlands,
prepared an expedition to bring her
back.

tions, a certain state-surgeon,[5] gathering the nature of the disease by these symptoms, attempted the cure, at one blow performed the operation, broke the bag, and out flew the vapor; nor did anything want to render it a complete remedy, only that the prince unfortunately happened to die in the performance. Now, is the reader exceeding curious to learn whence this vapor took its rise, which had so long set the nations at a gaze? What secret wheel, what hidden spring, could put into motion so wonderful an engine? It was afterwards discovered that the movement of this whole machine had been directed by an absent female, whose eyes had raised a protuberancy, and before emission, she was removed into an enemy's country. What should an unhappy prince do in such ticklish circumstances as these? He tried in vain the poet's never-failing receipt of *corpora quaeque*;[6] for,

> *Idque petit corpus mens unde est saucia amore:*
> *Unde feritur, eo tendit, gestitque coire.*—LUCRETIUS[7]

Having to no purpose used all peaceable endeavors, the collected part of the semen, raised and inflamed, became adust, converted to choler, turned head upon the spinal duct, and ascended to the brain. The very same principle that influences a bully to break the windows of a whore who has jilted him, naturally stirs up a great prince to raise mighty armies, and dream of nothing but sieges, battles, and victories.

> ——*Teterrima belli*
> *Causa*——[8]

The other instance is what I have read somewhere in a very ancient author, of a mighty king,[9] who, for the space of above thirty years, amused himself to take and lose towns, beat armies, and be beaten, drive princes out of their dominions; fright children from their bread and butter; burn, lay waste, plunder, dragoon, massacre subject and stranger, friend and foe, male and female. 'Tis recorded, that the philosophers of each country were in grave dispute upon causes natural, moral, and political, to find out where they should assign an original solution of this phenomenon. At last the vapor or spirit, which animated the hero's brain, being in perpetual circulation, seized upon that region of the human body, so renowned for furnishing the *zibeta occidentalis*,[1] and gathering

---

5. "Ravillac, who stabbed Henry the Great in his coach" [Swift's note].
6. "Any available bodies."
7. "The body strives for that which sickens the mind with love. . . . Stretches out toward that which smites it, and yearns to couple" (*De Rerum Natura* IV. 1048 ff.).
8. "The most abominable cause of war" in olden days, according to Horace, *Sat-*

ires I. iii. 107–8, was a whore.
9. "This is meant of the present French king" [Louis XIV] [Swift's note].
1. "Paracelsus, who was so famous for chemistry, tried an experiment upon human excrement, to make a perfume of it, which when he had brought to perfection, he called *zibeta occidentalis*, or western-civet, the back parts of man . . . being the west" [Swift's note].

there into a tumor, left the rest of the world for that time in peace. Of such mighty consequence it is where those exhalations fix, and of so little from whence they proceed. The same spirits which, in their superior progress, would conquer a kingdom, descending upon the anus, conclude in a fistula.[2]

Let us next examine the great introducers of new schemes in philosophy, and search till we can find from what faculty of the soul the disposition arises in mortal man, of taking it into his head to advance new systems with such an eager zeal, in things agreed on all hands impossible to be known; from what seeds this disposition springs, and to what quality of human nature these grand innovators have been indebted for their number of disciples. Because it is plain, that several of the chief among them, both ancient and modern, were usually mistaken by their adversaries, and indeed by all except their own followers, to have been persons crazed, or out of their wits; having generally proceeded, in the common course of their words and actions, by a method very different from the vulgar dictates of unrefined reason; agreeing for the most part in their several models, with their present undoubted successors in the academy of modern Bedlam[3] (whose merits and principles I shall farther examine in due place). Of this kind were *Epicurus, Diogenes, Apollonius, Lucretius, Paracelsus, Descartes,*[4] and others, who, if they were now in the world, tied fast, and separate from their followers, would, in this our undistinguishing age, incur manifest danger of phlebotomy,[5] and whips, and chains, and dark chambers, and straw. For what man, in the natural state or course of thinking, did ever conceive it in his power to reduce the notions of all mankind exactly to the same length, and breadth, and height of his own? Yet this is the first humble and civil design of all innovators in the empire of reason. Epicurus modestly hoped, that one time or other a certain fortuitous concourse of all men's opinions, after perpetual justlings, the sharp with the smooth, the light and the heavy, the round and the square, would by certain *clinamina*[6] unite in the notions of atoms and void, as these did in the originals of all things. Cartesius reckoned to see, before he died, the sentiments of all philosophers, like so many lesser stars in his romantic system, wrapped and drawn within his own vortex.[7] Now, I would gladly be informed, how it is possible to account for such imaginations as

---

2. Ulcer shaped like a pipe.
3. Bethlehem hospital, London's lunatic asylum.
4. Each of these famous speculative thinkers was known as a materialist, hence suspected by Swift of encouraging atheism.
5. Medical blood-letting.
6. Swerves. The Greek philosopher Epi-

curus held that the universe was formed by atoms swerving together; Swift implies that a similar miracle would be required for men to join in agreement with Epicurus.
7. The physics of René Descartes (1596–1650) is based on a theory of vortices; Swift considered the theory pure romance.

these in particular men without recourse to my phenomenon of vapors, ascending from the lower faculties to overshadow the brain, and there distilling into conceptions for which the narrowness of our mother-tongue has not yet assigned any other name beside that of madness or frenzy. Let us therefore now conjecture how it comes to pass, that none of these great prescribers do ever fail providing themselves and their notions with a number of implicit disciples. And, I think, the reason is easy to be assigned: for there is a peculiar string in the harmony of human understanding, which in several individuals is exactly of the same tuning. This, if you can dexterously screw up to its right key, and then strike gently upon it, whenever you have the good fortune to light among those of the same pitch, they will, by a secret necessary sympathy, strike exactly at the same time. And in this one circumstance lies all the skill or luck of the matter; for if you chance to jar the string among those who are either above or below your own height, instead of subscribing to your doctrine, they will tie you fast, call you mad, and feed you with bread and water. It is therefore a point of the nicest conduct to distinguish and adapt this noble talent, with respect to the differences of persons and of times. Cicero understood this very well, when writing to a friend in England, with a caution, among other matters, to beware of being cheated by our hackney-coachmen (who, it seems, in those days were as arrant rascals as they are now), has these remarkable words: *Est quod gaudeas te in ista loca venisse, ubi aliquid sapere viderere.*[8] For, to speak a bold truth, it is a fatal miscarriage so ill to order affairs, as to pass for a fool in one company, when in another you might be treated as a philosopher. Which I desire some certain gentlemen of my acquaintance to lay up in their hearts, as a very seasonable *innuendo.*

This, indeed, was the fatal mistake of that worthy gentleman, my most ingenious friend, Mr. W—tt—n,[9] a person, in appearance, ordained for great designs, as well as performances; whether you will consider his notions or his looks. Surely no man ever advanced into the public with fitter qualifications of body and mind, for the propagation of a new religion. Oh, had those happy talents, misapplied to vain philosophy, been turned into their proper channels of dreams and visions, where distortion of mind and countenance are of such sovereign use, the base detracting world would not then have dared to report that something is amiss, that his brain has undergone an unlucky shake; which even his brother modernists

8. "It is ground for rejoicing that you have come to such places, where anyone can seem wise" (Cicero, *Familiar Epistles* vii. 10).
9. William Wotton (who had championed ancient authors against Swift's patron, Sir William Temple, a spokesman for the moderns) is ridiculed in Swift's *Battle of the Books*, published in the same volume as *A Tale of a Tub* (1704).

themselves, like ungrates, do whisper so loud, that it reaches up to the very garret I am now writing in.

Lastly, whosoever pleases to look into the fountains of enthusiasm,[1] from whence, in all ages, have eternally proceeded such fattening streams, will find the springhead to have been as troubled and muddy as the current. Of such great emolument is a tincture of this vapor, which the world calls madness, that without its help, the world would not only be deprived of those two great blessings, conquests and systems, but even all mankind would unhappily be reduced to the same belief in things invisible. Now, the former *postulatum* being held, that it is of no import from what originals this vapor proceeds, but either in what angles it strikes and spreads over the understanding, or upon what species of brain it ascends; it will be a very delicate point to cut the feather, and divide the several reasons to a nice and curious reader, how this numerical difference in the brain can produce effects of so vast a difference from the same vapor, as to be the sole point of individuation between Alexander the Great, Jack of Leyden[2] and Monsieur Descartes. The present argument is the most abstracted that ever I engaged in; it strains my faculties to their highest stretch; and I desire the reader to attend with utmost perpensity; for I now proceed to unravel this knotty point.

There is in mankind a certain[3]   *   *   *   *   *
*   *   *   *   *   *   *   *   *
Hic multa   *   *   *   *   *   *
desiderantur.   *   *   *   *   *   *
*   *   *   *   *   And this I take to be a clear solution of the matter.

Having therefore so narrowly passed through this intricate difficulty, the reader will, I am sure, agree with me in the conclusion, that if the moderns mean by madness, only a disturbance or transposition of the brain, by force of certain vapors issuing up from the lower faculties, then has this madness been the parent of all those mighty revolutions that have happened in empire, in philosophy, and in religion. For the brain, in its natural position and state of serenity, disposeth its owner to pass his life in the common forms, without any thought of subduing multitudes to his own power, his reasons, or his visions; and the more he shapes his under-

---

1. For much of the 18th century the word "enthusiasm" (literally, "possessed by a god") signified a deluded belief in personal revelation.
2. John of Leyden, a tailor and prophet, briefly established a revolutionary Anabaptist community, the "New Jerusalem," in the city of Münster early in the 16th century.
3. "Here is another defect in the manuscript, but I think the author did wisely, and that the matter which thus strained his faculties, was not worth a solution; and it were well if all metaphysical cobweb problems were no otherwise answered" [Swift's note]. The Latin phrase ("Much is missing here") indicates a gap in the text Swift pretends to be "editing."

standing by the pattern of human learning, the less he is inclined to form parties after his particular notions, because that instructs him in his private infirmities, as well as in the stubborn ignorance of the people. But when a man's fancy gets astride on his reason, when imagination is at cuffs with the senses, and common understanding, as well as common sense, is kicked out of doors, the first proselyte he makes is himself; and when that is once compassed, the difficulty is not so great in bringing over others; a strong delusion always operating from without as vigorously as from within. For cant[4] and vision are to the ear and the eye, the same that tickling is to the touch. Those entertainments and pleasures we most value in life, are such as dupe and play the wag with the senses. For, if we take an examination of what is generally understood by happiness, as it has respect either to the understanding or the senses, we shall find all its properties and adjuncts will herd under this short definition, that it is a perpetual possession of being well deceived. And first, with relation to the mind or understanding, 'tis manifest what mighty advantages fiction has over truth; and the reason is just at our elbow, because imagination can build nobler scenes, and produce more wonderful revolutions, than fortune or nature will be at expense to furnish. Nor is mankind so much to blame in his choice thus determining him, if we consider that the debate merely lies between things past and things conceived; and so the question is only this: whether things that have place in the imagination, may not as properly be said to exist, as those that are seated in the memory; which may be justly held in the affirmative, and very much to the advantage of the former, since this is acknowledged to be the womb of things, and the other allowed to be no more than the grave. Again, if we take this definition of happiness, and examine it with reference to the senses, it will be acknowledged wonderfully adapt. How fading and insipid do all objects accost us, that are not conveyed in the vehicle of delusion! How shrunk is everything, as it appears in the glass of nature! So that if it were not for the assistance of artificial mediums, false lights, refracted angles, varnish, and tinsel, there would be a mighty level in the felicity and enjoyments of mortal men. If this were seriously considered by the world, as I have a certain reason to suspect it hardly will, men would no longer reckon among their high points of wisdom, the art of exposing weak sides, and publishing infirmities; an employment, in my opinion, neither better nor worse than that of unmasking, which, I think, has never been allowed[5] fair usage, either in the world, or the playhouse.

In the proportion that credulity is a more peaceful possession of

4. "Sudden exclamations, whining, unusual tones, and in fine all praying and preaching like the unlearned of the Presbyterians" (*Spectator* 147).
5. Admitted to be.

the mind than curiosity, so far preferable is that wisdom, which converses about the surface, to that pretended philosophy which enters into the depth of things, and then comes gravely back with informations and discoveries, that in the inside they are good for nothing. The two senses, to which all objects first address themselves, are the sight and the touch; these never examine farther than the color, the shape, the size, and whatever other qualities dwell, or are drawn by art upon the outward of bodies; and then comes reason officiously with tools for cutting, and opening, and mangling, and piercing, offering to demonstrate, that they are not of the same consistence quite through. Now I take all this to be the last degree of perverting nature; one of whose eternal laws it is, to put her best furniture forward. And therefore, in order to save the charges of all such expensive anatomy for the time to come, I do here think fit to inform the reader, that in such conclusions as these, reason is certainly in the right, and that in most corporeal beings, which have fallen under my cognizance, the outside has been infinitely preferable to the in; whereof I have been farther convinced from some late experiments. Last week I saw a woman flayed, and you will hardly believe how much it altered her person for the worse. Yesterday I ordered the carcass of a beau to be stripped in my presence; when we were all amazed to find so many unsuspected faults under one suit of clothes. Then I laid open his brain, his heart, and his spleen; but I plainly perceived at every operation, that the farther we proceeded, we found the defects increase upon us in number and bulk; from all which, I justly formed this conclusion to myself: that whatever philosopher or projector[6] can find out an art to solder and patch up the flaws and imperfections of nature, will deserve much better of mankind, and teach us a more useful science, than that so much in present esteem, of widening and exposing them (like him who held anatomy to be the ultimate end of physic).[7] And he, whose fortunes and dispositions have placed him in a convenient station to enjoy the fruits of this noble art; he that can with Epicurus content his ideas with the films and images that fly off upon his senses from the superficies[8] of things; such a man, truly wise, creams off nature, leaving the sour and the dregs for philosophy and reason to lap up. This is the sublime and refined point of felicity, called the possession of being well deceived; the serene peaceful state of being a fool among knaves.

But to return to madness. It is certain, that according to the system I have above deduced, every species thereof proceeds from a redundancy of vapors; therefore, as some kinds of frenzy give double strength to the sinews, so there are of other species, which add

---

6. Someone given to speculative experiments.
7. Medical practice.

8. Surfaces. Epicurus considered the senses, directly affected by objects, more trustworthy than reason.

vigor, and life, and spirit to the brain. Now, it usually happens, that these active spirits, getting possession of the brain, resemble those that haunt other waste and empty dwellings, which for want of business, either vanish, and carry away a piece of the house, or else stay at home and fling it all out of the windows. By which are mystically displayed the two principal branches of madness, and which some philosophers, not considering so well as I, have mistaken to be different in their causes, over-hastily assigning the first to deficiency, and the other to redundance.

I think it therefore manifest, from what I have here advanced, that the main point of skill and address is to furnish employment for this redundancy of vapor, and prudently to adjust the season of it; by which means it may certainly become of cardinal and catholic emolument, in a commonwealth. Thus one man, choosing a proper juncture, leaps into a gulf, from thence proceeds a hero, and is called the saver of his country; another achieves the same enterprise, but unluckily timing it, has left the brand of madness fixed as a reproach upon his memory; upon so nice a distinction, are we taught to repeat the name of Curtius[9] with reverence and love, that of Empedocles with hatred and contempt. Thus also it is usually conceived, that the elder Brutus only personated the fool and madman for the good of the public; but this was nothing else than a redundancy of the same vapor long misapplied, called by the Latins, *ingenium par negotiis;*[1] or (to translate it as nearly as I can) a sort of frenzy, never in its right element, till you take it up in business of the state.

Upon all which, and many other reasons of equal weight, though not equally curious, I do here gladly embrace an opportunity I have long sought for, of recommending it as a very noble undertaking to Sir Edward Seymour, Sir Christopher Musgrave, Sir John Bowls, John How, Esq.,[2] and other patriots concerned, that they would move for leave to bring in a bill for appointing commissioners to inspect into Bedlam, and the parts adjacent; who shall be empowered to send for persons, papers, and records, to examine into the merits and qualifications of every student and professor, to observe with utmost exactness their several dispositions and behavior, by which means, duly distinguishing and adapting their talents, they might produce admirable instruments for the several offices in a state, * * * * *,[3] civil, and military, proceeding in such methods as I shall here humbly propose. And I hope the gentle reader will give some allowance to my great solicitudes in this important affair,

---

9. The Roman hero Marcus Curtius appeased the gods by hurling himself into an ominous crack in the earth of the Forum; Empedocles committed suicide by leaping into the crater of Mount Etna.
1. "A talent for business." Lucius Junius

Brutus, like Hamlet, pretended madness to deceive his murderous uncle, Tarquin the Proud.
2. Members of Parliament.
3. Swift omits the third office, Ecclesiastical. "Instruments": useful persons.

upon account of the high esteem I have borne that honorable
society, whereof I had some time the happiness to be an unworthy
member.

Is any student tearing his straw in piece-meal, swearing and blaspheming, biting his grate, foaming at the mouth, and emptying his
piss-pot in the spectators' faces? Let the right worshipful the commissioners of inspection give him a regiment of dragoons, and send
him into Flanders among the rest. Is another eternally talking, sput-
tering, gaping, bawling in a sound without period or article? What
wonderful talents are here mislaid! Let him be furnished immediately with a green bag and papers, and threepence in his pocket,[4]
and away with him to Westminster Hall. You will find a third
gravely taking the dimensions of his kennel, a person of foresight
and insight, though kept quite in the dark; for why, like Moses,
ecce cornuta erat ejus facies.[5] He walks duly in one pace, entreats
your penny with due gravity and ceremony, talks much of hard
times, and taxes, and the whore of Babylon, bars up the wooden
window of his cell constantly at eight o'clock, dreams of fire, and
shoplifters, and court-customers, and privileged places. Now, what a
figure would all these acquirements amount to, if the owner were
sent into the city[6] among his brethren! Behold a fourth, in much
and deep conversation with himself, biting his thumbs at proper
junctures, his countenance checkered with business and design,
sometimes walking very fast, with his eyes nailed to a paper that he
holds in his hands; a great saver of time, somewhat thick of hearing,
very short of sight, but more of memory; a man ever in haste, a
great hatcher and breeder of business, and excellent at the famous
art of whispering nothing; a huge idolator of monosyllables and pro-
crastination, so ready to give his word to everybody, that he never
keeps it; one that has forgot the common meaning of words, but an
admirable retainer of the sound; extremely subject to the looseness,[7]
for his occasions are perpetually calling him away. If you approach
his grate in his familiar intervals, "Sir," says he, "give me a penny,
and I'll sing you a song; but give me the penny first." (Hence
comes the common saying, and commoner practice, of parting with
money for a song.) What a complete system of court skill is here
described in every branch of it, and all utterly lost with wrong application! Accost the hole of another kennel, first stopping your nose,
you will behold a surly, gloomy, nasty, slovenly mortal, raking in his
own dung, and dabbling in his urine. The best part of his diet is
the reversion of his own ordure, which expiring into steams, whirls

---

4. "A lawyers coach-hire" [Swift's note]
from the Inns of Court to Westminster.
Most lawyers carried green bags.
5. "Cornutus is either horned or shining,
and by this term, Moses is described in
the vulgar Latin of the Bible" [Swift's

note]. Swift puns on the Latin phrase
("Behold his face was shining") by suggesting someone kept in the dark
through being "horned," i. e., a cuckold.
6. The commercial center of London.
7. Diarrhea.

perpetually about, and at last re-infunds. His complexion is of a dirty yellow, with a thin scattered beard, exactly agreeable to that of his diet upon its first declination, like other insects, who having their birth and education in an excrement, from thence borrow their color and their smell. The student of this apartment is very sparing of his words, but somewhat over-liberal of his breath; he holds his hand out ready to receive your penny, and immediately upon receipt withdraws to his former occupations. Now, is it not amazing to think, the society of Warwick-lane[8] should have no more concern for the recovery of so useful a member, who, if one may judge from these appearances, would become the greatest ornament to that illustrious body? Another student struts up fiercely to your teeth, puffing with his lips, half squeezing out his eyes, and very graciously holds you out his hand to kiss. The keeper desires you not to be afraid of this professor, for he will do you no hurt; to him alone is allowed the liberty of the antechamber, and the orator of the place gives you to understand, that this solemn person is a tailor run mad with pride. This considerable student is adorned with many other qualities, upon which at present I shall not farther enlarge.------*Hark in your ear*[9]------I am strangely mistaken, if all his address, his motions, and his airs, would not then be very natural, and in their proper element.

I shall not descend so minutely, as to insist upon the vast number of beaux, fiddlers, poets, and politicians, that the world might recover by such a reformation; but what is more material, besides the clear gain redounding to the commonwealth, by so large an acquisition of persons to employ, whose talents and acquirements, if I may be so bold as to affirm it, are now buried, or at least misapplied; it would be a mighty advantage accruing to the public from this inquiry, that all these would very much excel, and arrive at great perfection in their several kinds; which, I think, is manifest from what I have already shown, and shall enforce by this one plain instance: that even I myself, the author of these momentous truths, am a person, whose imaginations are hard-mouthed,[1] and exceedingly disposed to run away with his reason, which I have observed from long experience to be a very light rider, and easily shook off; upon which account, my friends will never trust me alone, without a solemn promise to vent my speculations in this, or the like manner, for the universal benefit of human kind; which perhaps the gentle, courteous, and candid reader, brimful of that modern charity and tenderness usually annexed to his office, will be very hardly persuaded to believe.

1704

8. Royal College of Physicians.
9. "I cannot conjecture what the author means here, or how this chasm could be filled, though it is capable of more than one interpretation" [Swift's note].
1. (Of a horse) apt to reject control by the bit.

1910 · *Jonathan Swift*

Was Swift an Anglican priest?

reductio ad absurdum?

AN ARGUMENT TO PROVE THAT THE

Abolishing of Christianity in England

MAY, AS THINGS NOW STAND, BE ATTENDED WITH
SOME INCONVENIENCES, AND PERHAPS NOT
PRODUCE THOSE MANY GOOD EFFECTS PRO-
POSED THEREBY.[1]

I am very sensible what a weakness and presumption it is, to reason against the general humor and disposition of the world. I remember it was with great justice, and a due regard to the freedom both of the public and the press, forbidden upon several penalties to write, or discourse, or lay wagers against the Union,[2] even before it was confirmed by Parliament, because that was looked upon as a design to oppose the current of the people, which, besides the folly of it, is a manifest breach of the fundamental law that makes this majority of opinion the voice of God. In like manner, and for the very same reasons, it may perhaps be neither safe nor prudent to argue against the abolishing of Christianity at a juncture when all parties appear so unanimously determined upon the point, as we cannot but allow from their actions, their discourses, and their writings. However, I know not how, whether from the affectation of singularity, or the perverseness of human nature, but so it unhappily falls out that I cannot be entirely of this opinion. Nay, though I were sure an order were issued for my immediate prosecution by the attorney-general, I should still confess that in the present posture of our affairs at home or abroad, I do not yet see the absolute necessity of extirpating the Christian religion from among us.

This perhaps may appear too great a paradox even for our wise and paradoxical age to endure: therefore I shall handle it with all tenderness, and with the utmost deference to that great and profound majority which is of another sentiment.

And yet the curious may please to observe how much the genius of a nation is liable to alter in half an age: I have heard it affirmed for certain by some very old people that the contrary opin-

---

1. The Test Act of 1673 required all holders of public office to take the sacrament of the Lord's Supper according to the usage of the Church of England; it was directed against Dissenters and Roman Catholics. In 1708 the Whigs (with whom Swift was then allied) were seeking to repeal the Test in Ireland and eventually in England, in an effort to consolidate the support of the Dissenters. Swift believed that repeal would do great harm to the Established Church, and as a good Anglican priest he opposed it with this essay.

Swift's technique is to assume blandly that to argue against the Test Act is to argue against Christianity and the Church, and he constructs his essay accordingly. The basic satiric principle is therefore that of the *reductio ad absurdum*, but this device is surrounded by a host of other ironies.

2. The union of Scotland and England under one crown in 1707.

human society is unsteady

ion was even in their memories as much in vogue as the other is now; and that a project for the abolishing of Christianity would then have appeared as singular, and been thought as absurd, as it would be at this time to write or discourse in its defense.

Therefore I freely own that all appearances are against me. The system of the Gospel, after the fate of other systems, is generally antiquated and exploded; and the mass or body of the common people, among whom it seems to have had its latest credit, are now grown as much ashamed of it as their betters; opinions, like fashions, always descending from those of quality to the middle sort, and thence to the vulgar, where at length they are dropped and vanish.

But here I would not be mistaken, and must therefore be so bold as to borrow a distinction from the writers on the other side, when they make a difference between nominal and real Trinitarians. I hope no reader imagines me so weak to stand up in the defense of real Christianity, such as used in primitive times (if we may believe the authors of those ages) to have an influence upon men's belief and actions: to offer at the restoring of that would indeed be a wild project; it would be to dig up foundations; to destroy at one blow all the wit, and half the learning of the kingdom; to break the entire frame and constitution of things; to ruin trade, extinguish arts and sciences with the professors of them; in short, to turn our courts, exchanges, and shops into deserts; and would be full as absurd as the proposal of Horace,[3] where he advises the Romans all in a body to leave their city and seek a new seat in some remote part of the world, by way of cure for the corruption of their manners.

Therefore I think this caution was in itself altogether unnecessary (which I have inserted only to prevent all possibility of caviling), since every candid reader will easily understand my discourse to be intended only in defense of nominal Christianity, the other having been for some time wholly laid aside by general consent as utterly inconsistent with all other present schemes of wealth and power. *Sounds rather hypocritical*

But why we should therefore cast off the name and title of Christians, although the general opinion and resolution be so violent for it, I confess I cannot (with submission) apprehend the consequence necessary. However, since the undertakers propose such wonderful advantages to the nation by this project, and advance many plausible objections against the system of Christianity, I shall briefly consider the strength of both, fairly allow them their greatest weight, and offer such answers as I think most reasonable. After which I will beg leave to show what inconveniences may possibly happen by such an innovation, in the present posture of our affairs.

3. **Epode** xvi.   *Seems to be for tradition*

is to destroy culture

"Christianity"

to go back to primitive

quibble

in name only

First, one great advantage proposed by the abolishing of Christianity is that it would very much enlarge and establish liberty of conscience, that great bulwark of our nation, and of the protestant religion, which is still too much limited by priestcraft, notwithstanding all the good intentions of the legislature, as we have lately found by a severe instance. For it is confidently reported that two *who?* young gentlemen of real hopes, bright wit, and profound judgment, who upon a thorough examination of causes and effects, and by the mere force of natural abilities, without the least tincture of learning, having made a discovery that there was no God, and generously communicating their thoughts for the good of the public, were some time ago, by an unparalleled severity, and upon I know not what obsolete law, broke only for blasphemy. And as it hath been wisely observed, if persecution once begins, no man alive knows how far it may reach, or where it will end.

In answer to all which, with deference to wiser judgments, I think this rather shows the necessity of a nominal religion among us. Great wits love to be free with the highest objects; and if they cannot be allowed a God to revile or renounce, they will speak evil of dignities, abuse the government, and reflect upon the ministry; which I am sure few will deny to be of much more pernicious consequence, according to the saying of Tiberius, *Deorum offensa diis curae*.[4] As to the particular fact related, I think it is not fair to argue from one instance; perhaps another cannot be produced; yet (to the comfort of all those who may be apprehensive of persecution) blasphemy we know is freely spoken a million of times in every coffeehouse and tavern, or wherever else good company meet. It must be allowed indeed, that to break an English freeborn officer only for blasphemy, was, to speak the gentlest of such an action, a very high strain of absolute power. Little can be said in excuse for the general; perhaps he was afraid it might give offense to the allies [5] among whom, for aught we know, it may be the custom of the country to believe a God. But if he argued, as some have done, upon a mistaken principle, that an officer who is guilty of speaking blasphemy may some time or other proceed so far as to raise a mutiny, the consequence is by no means to be admitted: for, surely the commander of an English army is likely to be but ill obeyed whose soldiers fear and reverence him as little as they do a deity.

It is further objected against the gospel system that it obliges men to the belief of things too difficult for freethinkers, and such who have shaken off the prejudices that usually cling to a confined

4. "Offenses against the gods are the concern of the gods" (Tacitus, *Annals* I.lxxiii).
5. England's principal allies against France in the War of the Spanish Succession were Holland, Austria, Prussia, Portugal, and Savoy.

education. To which I answer that men should be cautious how they raise objections which reflect upon the wisdom of the nation. Is not everybody freely allowed to believe whatever he pleases, and to publish his belief to the world whenever he thinks fit, especially if it serves to strengthen the party which is in the right? Would any indifferent foreigner who should read the trumpery lately written by Asgil, Tindal, Toland, Coward,[6] and forty more, imagine the Gospel to be our rule of faith, and confirmed by parliaments? Does any man either believe, or say he believes, or desire to have it thought that he says he believes one syllable of the matter? And is any man worse received upon that score, or does he find his want of nominal faith a disadvantage to him in the pursuit of any civil or military employment? What if there be an old dormant statute or two against him? Are they not now obsolete to a degree that Empson and Dudley [7] themselves, if they were now alive, would find it impossible to put them in execution?

Practicality?

It is likewise urged that there are by computation in this kingdom above ten thousand parsons whose revenues, added to those of my lords the bishops, would suffice to maintain at least two hundred young gentlemen of wit and pleasure, and freethinking enemies to priestcraft, narrow principles, pedantry, and prejudices; who might be an ornament to the court and town. And then again, so great a number of able (-bodied) divines might be a recruit to our fleet and armies. This indeed appears to be a consideration of some weight; but then, on the other side, several things deserve to be considered likewise: as, first, whether it may not be thought necessary that in certain tracts of country, like what we call parishes, there shall be one man at least of abilities to read and write. Then it seems a wrong computation that the revenues of the Church throughout this island would be large enough to maintain two hundred young gentlemen, or even half that number, after the present refined way of living; that is, to allow each of them such a rent [8] as, in the modern form of speech, would make them easy. But still there is in this project a greater mischief behind; and we ought to beware of the woman's folly who killed the hen that every morning laid her a golden egg. For, pray, what would become of the race of men in the next age if we had nothing to trust to beside the scrofulous, consumptive productions, furnished by our men of wit and pleasure, when, having squandered away their vigor, health, and estates, they are forced by some disagreeable marriage to piece up their broken fortunes, and entail rottenness and politeness on their posterity? Now here are ten thousand persons reduced by the wise

6. Deistic writers.
7. Two corrupt ministers of Henry VII, notorious for reviving obsolete statutes in subservience to that king's greed.
8. Income.

regulations of Henry the Eighth to the necessity of a low diet and moderate exercise,[9] who are the only great restorers of our breed, without which the nation would in an age or two become one great hospital.

Another advantage proposed by the abolishing of Christianity is the clear gain of one day in seven, which is now entirely lost, and consequently the kingdom one-seventh less considerable in trade, business, and pleasure; besides the loss to the public of so many stately structures now in the hands of the clergy, which might be converted into playhouses, exchanges, markethouses, common dormitories, and other public edifices.

I hope I shall be forgiven a hard word, if I call this a perfect cavil. I readily own there hath been an old custom, time out of mind, for people to assemble in the churches every Sunday, and that shops are still frequently shut, in order, as it is conceived, to preserve the memory of that ancient practice; but how this can prove a hindrance to business or pleasure is hard to imagine. What if the men of pleasure are forced, one day in the week, to game at home instead of the chocolatehouse? Are not the taverns and coffeehouses open? Can there be a more convenient season for taking a dose of physic? Are fewer claps got upon Sundays than other days? Is not that the chief day for traders to sum up the accounts of the week and for lawyers to prepare their briefs? But I would fain know how it can be pretended that the churches are misapplied? Where are more appointments and rendezvouses of gallantry? Where more care to appear in the foremost box with greater advantage of dress? Where more meetings for business? Where more bargains driven of all sorts? And where so many conveniences or incitements to sleep?

There is one advantage greater than any of the foregoing proposed by the abolishing of Christianity: that it will utterly extinguish parties among us by removing those factious distinctions of High and Low Church, of Whig and Tory, Presbyterian and Church of England, which are now so many mutual clogs upon public proceedings, and dispose men to prefer the gratifying themselves, or depressing their adversaries, before the most important interest of the state.

I confess, if it were certain that so great an advantage would redound to the nation by this expedient, I would submit and be silent: but will any man say that if the words *whoring, drinking, cheating, lying, stealing,* were by act of Parliament ejected out of the English tongue and dictionaries, we should all awake next morn-

9. Swift refers ironically to Henry VIII's expropriation of church lands at the time of the Reformation. Instead of giving them to the church for the support of the clergy, as Swift thought he should have done, he bestowed them on laymen, thus impoverishing the lower clergy, who were deprived of the tithes that would otherwise have been their due.

ing chaste and temperate, honest and just, and lovers of truth? Is this a fair consequence? Or, if the physicians would forbid us to pronounce the words *pox, gout, rheumatism,* and *stone,* would that expedient serve like so many talismans to destroy the diseases themselves? Are party and faction rooted in men's hearts no deeper than phrases borrowed from religion, or founded upon no firmer principles? And is our language so poor that we cannot find other terms to express them? Are *envy, pride, avarice,* and *ambition* such ill nomenclators that they cannot furnish appellations for their owners? Will not *heydukes* and *mamalukes, mandarins* and *patshaws,* or any other words formed at pleasure, serve to distinguish those who are in the ministry from others who would be in it if they could? What, for instance, is easier than to vary the form of speech, and instead of the *church,* make it a question in politics whether the Monument [1] be in danger? Because religion was nearest at hand to furnish a few convenient phrases, is our invention so barren we can find no others? Suppose, for argument sake, that the Tories favored Margarita, the Whigs Mrs. Tofts, and the Trimmers Valentini,[2] would not *Margaritians, Toftians,* and *Valentinians* be very tolerable marks of distinction? The *Prasini* and *Veniti,*[3] two most virulent factions in Italy, began (if I remember right) by a distinction of colors in ribbons, which we might do with as good a grace about the dignity of the blue and the green, and would serve as properly to divide the court, the Parliament, and the kingdom between them, as any terms of art whatsoever borrowed from religion. Therefore I think there is little force in this objection against Christianity, or prospect of so great an advantage as is proposed in the abolishing of it.

'Tis again objected as a very absurd, ridiculous custom that a set of men should be suffered, much less employed and hired, to bawl one day in seven against the lawfulness of those methods most in use toward the pursuit of greatness, riches, and pleasure, which are the constant practice of all men alive on the other six. But this objection is, I think, a little unworthy so refined an age as ours. Let us argue this matter calmly; I appeal to the breast of any polite freethinker whether in the pursuit of gratifying a predominant passion he hath not always felt a wonderful incitement, by reflecting it was a thing forbidden; and therefore we see, in order to cultivate this taste, the wisdom of the nation hath taken special care that the ladies should be furnished with prohibited silks and the men with prohibited wine. And indeed, it were to be wished that some other prohibitions were promoted in order to improve the pleasures of the town; which, for want of such expedients begin already, as I am

---

1. The column that commemorates the great fire of London, 1666.
2. Singers in the popular Italian opera.

3. Rival factions in the Roman chariot races, violently supported by the populace.

told, to flag and grow languid, giving way daily to cruel inroads from the spleen.[4]

'Tis likewise proposed as a great advantage to the public that if we once discard the system of the Gospel, all religion will of course be banished for ever; and consequently, along with it, those grievous prejudices of education, which under the names of *virtue, conscience, honor, justice*, and the like, are so apt to disturb the peace of human minds, and the notions whereof are so hard to be eradicated by right reason or freethinking, sometimes during the whole course of our lives.

Here first I observe how difficult it is to get rid of a phrase which the world is once grown fond of, though the occasion that first produced it be entirely taken away. For several years past, if a man had but an ill-favored nose, the deep thinkers of the age would some way or other contrive to impute the cause to the prejudice of his education. From this fountain were said to be derived all our foolish notions of justice, piety, love of our country, all our opinions of God, or a future state, heaven, hell, and the like: and there might formerly perhaps have been some pretense for this charge. But so effectual care hath been since taken to remove those prejudices by an entire change in the methods of education that (with honor I mention it to our polite innovators) the young gentlemen who are now on the scene, seem to have not the least tincture of those infusions, or string of those weeds; and, by consequence, the reason for abolishing nominal Christianity upon that pretext is wholly ceased.

For the rest, it may perhaps admit a controversy whether the banishing of all notions of religion whatsoever would be convenient for the vulgar. Not that I am in the least of opinion with those who hold religion to have been the invention of politicians to keep the lower part of the world in awe by the fear of invisible powers; unless mankind were then very different from what it is now: for I look upon the mass or body of our people here in England to be as freethinkers, that is to say, as staunch unbelievers, as any of the highest rank. But I conceive some scattered notions about a superior power to be of singular use for the common people, as furnishing excellent materials to keep children quiet when they grow peevish, and providing topics of amusement in a tedious winter night.

Lastly, it is proposed as a singular advantage that the abolishing of Christianity will very much contribute to the uniting of Protestants, by enlarging the terms of communion so as to take in all sorts of Dissenters, who are now shut out of the pale upon account of a few ceremonies which all sides confess to be things indifferent;

4. Melancholy; often a real affliction, but as often affected as a fashionable ailment.

that this alone will effectually answer the great ends of a scheme for comprehension, by opening a large noble gate, at which all bodies may enter: whereas the chaffering with Dissenters, and dodging about this or t'other ceremony, is but like opening a few wickets [5] and leaving them at jar, by which no more than one can get in at a time, and that, not without stooping, and sideling, and squeezing his body. *religion as outlet for anxieties*

To all this I answer that there is one darling inclination of mankind, which usually affects to be a retainer to religion, though she be neither its parent, its godmother, or its friend; I mean the spirit of opposition, that lived long before Christianity, and can easily subsist without it. Let us, for instance, examine wherein the opposition of sectaries [6] among us consists; we shall find Christianity to have no share in it at all. Does the Gospel any where prescribe a starched, squeezed countenance, a stiff, formal gait, a singularity of manners and habit, or any affected modes of speech different from the reasonable part of mankind? Yet, if Christianity did not lend its name to stand in the gap, and to employ or divert these humors, they must of necessity be spent in contraventions to the laws of the land, and disturbance of the public peace. There is a portion of enthusiasm assigned to every nation, which, if it hath not proper objects to work on, will burst out, and set all in a flame. If the quiet of state can be bought by only flinging men a few ceremonies to devour, it is a purchase no wise man would refuse. Let the mastiffs amuse themselves about a sheepskin stuffed with hay, provided it will keep them from worrying the flock. The institution of convents abroad seems in one point a strain of great wisdom, there being few irregularities in human passions that may not have recourse to vent themselves in some of those orders, which are so many retreats for the speculative, the melancholy, the proud, the silent, the politic and the morose, to spend themselves, and evaporate the noxious particles; for each of whom we in this island are forced to provide a several sect of religion, to keep them quiet. And whenever Christianity shall be abolished, the legislature must find some other expedient to employ and entertain them. For what imports it how large a gate you open if there will be always left a number who place a pride and merit in refusing to enter?

Having thus considered the most important objections against Christianity and the chief advantages proposed by the abolishing thereof, I shall now with equal deference and submission to wiser judgments as before, proceed to mention a few inconveniences that may happen if the Gospel should be repealed; which perhaps the projectors may not have sufficiently considered.

And first, I am very sensible how much the gentlemen of wit and

---

5. Small gates.   6. Adherents of one of the dissenting sects.

pleasure are apt to murmur, and be choked at the sight of so many daggled-tail parsons who happen to fall in their way, and offend their eyes. But at the same time, these wise reformers do not consider what an advantage and felicity it is for great wits to be always provided with objects of scorn and contempt, in order to exercise and improve their talents, and divert their spleen from falling on each other or on themselves; especially when all this may be done without the least imaginable danger to their persons.

And to urge another argument of a parallel nature: if Christianity were once abolished, how could the freethinkers, the strong reasoners, and the men of profound learning, be able to find another subject so calculated in all points whereon to display their abilities? What wonderful productions of wit should we be deprived of from those whose genius by continual practice hath been wholly turned upon raillery and invectives against religion, and would therefore never be able to shine or distinguish themselves upon any other subject! We are daily complaining of the great decline of wit among us, and would we take away the greatest, perhaps the only, topic we have left? Who would ever have suspected Asgil for a wit, or Toland for a philosopher, if the inexhaustible stock of Christianity had not been at hand to provide them with materials? What other subject, through all art or nature, could have produced Tindal for a profound author, or furnished him with readers? It is the wise choice of the subject that alone adorns and distinguishes the writer. For had a hundred such pens as these been employed on the side of religion, they would have immediately sunk into silence and oblivion.

Nor do I think it wholly groundless, or my fears altogether imaginary, that the abolishing of Christianity may perhaps bring the Church in danger, or at least put the senate to the trouble of another securing vote. I desire I may not be mistaken; I am far from presuming to affirm or think that the Church is in danger at present, or as things now stand; but we know not how soon it may be so when the Christian religion is repealed. As plausible as this project seems, there may a dangerous design lurk under it. Nothing can be more notorious than that the atheists, deists, Socinians,[7] Antitrinitarians, and other subdivisions of freethinkers are persons of little zeal for the present ecclesiastical establishment: their declared opinion is for repealing the Sacramental Test; they are very indifferent with regard to ceremonies; nor do they hold the *jus divinum* of Episcopacy.[8] Therefore this may be intended as one politic step toward altering the constitution of the Church estab-

---

7. The Socinians denied the divinity of Jesus.
8. The divine authority of Anglican bishops, derived from apostolic succession.

lished, and setting up Presbytery [9] in the stead, which I leave to be further considered by those at the helm.

In the last place, I think nothing can be more plain than that by this expedient, we shall run into the evil we chiefly pretend to avoid; and that the abolishment of the Christian religion will be the readiest course we can take to introduce popery. And I am the more inclined to this opinion because we know it has been the constant practice of the Jesuits to send over emissaries with instructions to personate themselves members of the several prevailing sects among us. So it is recorded that they have at sundry times appeared in the guise of Presbyterians, Anabaptists, Independents, and Quakers, according as any of these were most in credit; so, since the fashion hath been taken up of exploding religion, the popish missionaries have not been wanting to mix with the freethinkers; among whom, Toland, the great oracle of the Antichristians, is an Irish priest, the son of an Irish priest; and the most learned and ingenious author of a book called *The Rights of the Christian Church*, was in a proper juncture reconciled to the Romish faith, whose true son, as appears by an hundred passages in his treatise, he still continues. Perhaps I could add some others to the number; but the fact is beyond dispute, and the reasoning they proceed by is right: for, supposing Christianity to be extinguished, the people will never be at ease till they find out some other method of worship; which will as infallibly produce superstition as this will end in popery.

And therefore, if notwithstanding all I have said, it still be thought necessary to have a bill brought in for repealing Christianity, I would humbly offer an amendment; that instead of the word *Christianity* may be put *religion* in general; which I conceive will much better answer all the good ends proposed by the projectors of it. For, as long as we leave in being a God and his providence, with all the necessary consequences which curious and inquisitive men will be apt to draw from such premises, we do not strike at the root of the evil, though we should ever so effectually annihilate the present scheme of the Gospel. For of what use is freedom of thought, if it will not produce freedom of action, which is the sole end, how remote soever in appearance, of all objections against Christianity? And, therefore, the freethinkers consider it as a sort of edifice wherein all the parts have such a mutual dependence on each other that if you happen to pull out one single nail, the whole fabric must fall to the ground. This was happily expressed by him who had heard of a text brought for proof of the Trinity, which in an ancient manuscript was differently read; he thereupon immedi-

---

9. The Presbyterians opposed episcopacy and set up a democratic form of church government.

ately took the hint, and by a sudden deduction of a long *sorites*, [1] most logically concluded, "Why, if it be as you say, I may safely whore and drink on, and defy the parson." From which, and many the like instances easy to be produced, I think nothing can be more manifest than that the quarrel is not against any particular points of hard digestion in the Christian system, but against religion in general; which, by laying restraints on human nature, is supposed the great enemy to the freedom of thought and action.

Upon the whole, if it shall still be thought for the benefit of Church and State that Christianity be abolished, I conceive, however, it may be more convenient to defer the execution to a time of peace, and not venture in this conjuncture to disoblige our allies, who, as it falls out, are all Christians; and many of them, by the prejudices of their education, so bigoted as to place a sort of pride in the appellation. If upon being rejected by them, we are to trust to an alliance with the Turk, we shall find ourselves much deceived: for, as he is too remote, and generally engaged in war with the Persian emperor, so his people would be more scandalized at our infidelity than our Christian neighbors. Because the Turks are not only strict observers of religious worship, but what is worse, believe a God; which is more than is required of us even while we preserve the name of Christians.

To conclude: whatever some may think of the great advantages to trade by this favorite scheme, I do very much apprehend that in six months time after the act is passed for the extirpation of the Gospel, the Bank and East-India Stock may fall at least one per cent. And since that is fifty times more than ever the wisdom of our age thought fit to venture for the preservation of Christianity, there is no reason we should be at so great a loss merely for the sake of destroying it.

1708   1711

Gulliver's Travels

Gulliver's Travels is Swift's most universal satire. Although it is full of allusions to recent and contemporary historical events, it is as valid today as it was in 1726, for its objects are man's moral nature and the defective political, economic, and social institutions which, because of his imperfections, he creates. Swift adopts an ancient satirical device: the imaginary voyage. Lemuel Gulliver, the narrator, is a ship's surgeon, a reasonably well-educated man, kindly, resourceful, cheerful, inquiring, patriotic, truthful, and rather unimaginative. He is, in short, a reasonably decent example of humanity, with whom we identify ourselves readily enough. He undertakes four voyages, all of which end disastrously among "several remote nations of the world." In the first, Gulliver is shipwrecked in the

1. "An argument when one proposition is accumulated on another" (Johnson's *Dictionary*).

empire of Lilliput, where he finds himself a giant among a diminutive people, charmed by their miniature city and amused by their toylike prettiness. But in the end they prove to be treacherous, malicious, ambitious, vengeful, and cruel. As we read we grow disenchanted with the inhabitants of this fanciful kingdom, and then gradually we begin to recognize our likeness to them, especially in the disproportion between our natural pettiness and our boundless and destructive passions. In the second voyage, Gulliver is abandoned by his shipmates in Brobdingnag, a land of giants, creatures ten times as large as Europeans. Naturally enough, he assumes that such monsters must be brutes, but the reverse proves to be the case. Brobdingnag is something of a utopia, governed by a humane and enlightened prince who is the embodiment of moral and political wisdom. In the long interview in which Gulliver pridefully enlarges on the glories of England and her political institutions, the King reduces him to resentful silence by asking questions which reveal the difference between what is and what ought to be in human, especially British, institutions. In Brobdingnag, Gulliver finds himself a Lilliputian, his pride humbled by his helpless state and his human vanity diminished by the realization that his body must have seemed as disgusting to the Lilliputians as do the bodies of the Brobdingnagians to him.

In the third voyage, to Laputa, Swift is chiefly concerned with attacking extremes of theoretical and speculative reasoning, whether in science, politics, or economics. Much of this voyage is an allegory of political life under the administration of the Whig minister, Sir Robert Walpole. The final voyage sets Gulliver between a race of horses, Houyhnhnms (pronounced *Hwín-ims*), who live entirely by reason except for a few well-controlled and muted social affections, and their slaves, the Yahoos, whose bodies are obscene caricatures of the human body, and who have no glimmer of reason, but are mere creatures of appetite and passion.

When *Gulliver's Travels* first appeared, everyone read it—children for the story, politicians for the satire of current affairs—and ever since it has retained a hold on readers of every kind. Almost unique in world literature, it is simple enough for a child, complex enough to carry an adult beyond his depth. Swift's art works on many levels. First of all, there is the sheer playfulness of the narrative. Through Gulliver's eyes, we gaze on marvel after marvel: a tiny girl who threads an invisible needle with invisible silk, or a white mare who threads a needle between pastern and hoof. The travels, like a fairy story, transport us to imaginary worlds that function with a perfect, fantastic logic different from our own; Swift exercises our sense of vision. But beyond that, he exercises our perceptions of meaning. In *Gulliver's Travels*, things are seldom what they seem; irony, probing or corrosive, underlies almost every word. During the last chapter, Gulliver insists that the example of the Houyhnhnms has made him incapable of telling a lie— but the oath he swears is quoted from Sinon, whose lies to the Trojans persuaded them to accept the Trojan *horse*. Swift trains us to read alertly, to look beneath the surface. Yet on its deepest level, the book does not offer final meanings, but a question: what sort of thing is man? Voyaging through imaginary worlds, we try to find ourselves. Are we prideful insects, or lords of creation? brutes, or reasonable beings? In the last voyage, Swift pushes such questions, and Gulliver himself, almost beyond endurance; hating his own humanity, Gulliver forgets who he is. For the reader, however, the outcome cannot be so clear. Swift does not set out to satisfy our minds, but to vex and unsettle them. And he leaves us at the moment when the mixed face of humanity—the pettiness of the Lilliputians, the savagery of the Yahoos, the innocence of Gulliver himself—begins to look strangely familiar, like our own faces in a mirror.

From Gulliver's Travels[1]

A *Letter from Captain Gulliver to His Cousin Sympson*

I hope you will be ready to own publicly, whenever you shall be called to it, that by your great and frequent urgency you prevailed on me to publish a very loose and uncorrect account of my travels; with direction to hire some young gentlemen of either University to put them in order, and correct the style, as my Cousin Dampier[2] did by my advice, in his book called *A Voyage round the World*. But I do not remember I gave you power to consent that anything should be omitted, and much less that anything should be inserted: therefore, as to the latter, I do here renounce everything of that kind; particularly a paragraph about her Majesty the late Queen Anne, of most pious and glorious memory; although I did reverence and esteem her more than any of human species. But you, or your interpolator, ought to have considered that as it was not my inclination, so was it not decent to praise any animal of our composition before my master Houyhnhnm; and besides, the fact was altogether false; for to my knowledge, being in England during some part of her Majesty's reign, she did govern by a chief Minister; nay, even by two successively; the first whereof was the Lord of Godolphin, and the second the Lord of Oxford; so that you have made me *say the thing that was not*. Likewise, in the account of the Academy of Projectors, and several passages of my discourse to my master Houyhnhnm, you have either omitted some material circumstances, or minced or changed them in such a manner, that I do hardly know mine own work. When I formerly hinted to you some-

1. Swift's full title for this work was *Travels into Several Remote Nations of the World. In Four Parts. By Lemuel Gulliver, First a Surgeon, and then a Captain of several Ships.* In the first edition (1726), either the bookseller or Swift's friends Charles Ford, Pope, and others, who were concerned in getting the book anonymously into print, altered and omitted so much of the original manuscript (because of its dangerous political implications) that Swift was seriously annoyed. When, in 1735, the Dublin bookseller George Faulkner brought out an edition of Swift's works, the Dean seems to have taken pains, surreptitiously, to see that a more authentic version of the work was published. This text is the basis of modern editions.

In this letter, first published in 1735, Swift complains, among other matters, of the alterations in his original text made by the publisher, Benjamin Motte, in the interest of what he considered political discretion.
2. William Dampier (1652–1715), the explorer, whose account of his circumnavigation of the globe Swift had read.

thing of this in a letter, you were pleased to answer that you were afraid of giving offense; that people in power were very watchful over the press; and apt not only to interpret, but to punish everything which looked like an *inuendo* (as I think you called it). But pray, how could that which I spoke so many years ago, and at above five thousand leagues distance, in another reign, be applied to any of the Yahoos, who now are said to govern the herd; especially, at a time when I little thought on or feared the unhappiness of living under them. Have not I the most reason to complain, when I see these very Yahoos carried by Houyhnhnms in a vehicle, as if these were brutes, and those the rational creatures? And, indeed, to avoid so monstrous and detestable a sight was one principal motive of my retirement hither.[3]

Thus much I thought proper to tell you in relation to yourself, and to the trust I reposed in you.

I do in the next place complain of my own great want of judgment, in being prevailed upon by the intreaties and false reasonings of you and some others, very much against mine own opinion, to suffer my travels to be published. Pray bring to your mind how often I desired you to consider, when you insisted on the motive of public good, that the Yahoos were a species of animals utterly incapable of amendment by precepts or examples; and so it hath proved; for instead of seeing a full stop put to all abuses and corruptions, at least in this little island, as I had reason to expect, behold, after above six months warning. I cannot learn that my book hath produced one single effect according to mine intentions; I desired you would let me know by a letter, when party and faction were extinguished; judges learned and upright; pleaders honest and modest, with some tincture of common sense; and Smithfield [4] blazing with pyramids of law books; the young nobility's education entirely changed; the physicians banished; the female Yahoos abounding in virtue, honor, truth, and good sense; courts and levees of great ministers thoroughly weeded and swept; wit, merit, and learning rewarded; all disgracers of the press in prose and verse, condemned to eat nothing but their own cotton,[5] and quench their thirst with their own ink. These, and a thousand other reformations, I firmly counted upon by your encouragement; as indeed they were plainly deducible from the precepts delivered in my book. And, it must be owned that seven months were a sufficient time to correct every vice and folly to which Yahoos are subject; if their natures had been capable of the least disposition to virtue or wisdom; yet so far have you been from answering mine expectation in any of your letters, that on the contrary, you are loading our carrier every week with libels, and keys, and reflections, and memoirs, and second

3. To Nottinghamshire.
4. A part of London containing many
bookshops.
5. Presumably their paper.

parts; wherein I see myself accused of reflecting upon great states-folk; of degrading human nature (for so they have still the con-fidence to style it) and of abusing the female sex. I find likewise, that the writers of those bundles are not agreed among themselves; for some of them will not allow me to be author of mine own travels; and others make me author of books to which I am wholly a stranger.

I find likewise that your printer hath been so careless as to con-found the times, and mistake the dates of my several voyages and returns; neither assigning the true year, or the true month, or day of the month; and I hear the original manuscript is all destroyed, since the publication of my book. Neither have I any copy left; however, I have sent you some corrections, which you may insert, if ever there should be a second edition; and yet I cannot stand to them, but shall leave that matter to my judicious and candid readers, to adjust it as they please.

I hear some of our sea Yahoos find fault with my sea language, as not proper in many parts, nor now in use. I cannot help it. In my first voyages, while I was young, I was instructed by the oldest mariners, and learned to speak as they did. But I have since found that the sea Yahoos are apt, like the land ones, to become new fangled in their words; which the latter change every year; inso-much, as I remember upon each return to mine own country, their old dialect was so altered, that I could hardly understand the new. And I observe, when any Yahoo comes from London out of curiosity to visit me at mine own house, we neither of us are able to deliver our conceptions in a manner intelligible to the other.[6]

If the censure of Yahoos could any way affect me, I should have great reason to complain that some of them are so bold as to think my book of travels a mere fiction out of mine own brain; and have gone so far as to drop hints that the Houyhnhnms, and Yahoos have no more existence than the inhabitants of Utopia.

Indeed I must confess that as to the people of Lilliput, Brob-dingrag (for so the word should have been spelled, and not errone-ously Brobdingnag) and Laputa, I have never yet heard of any Yahoo so presumptuous as to dispute their being, or the facts I have related concerning them; because the truth immediately strikes every reader with conviction. And, is there less probability in my account of the Houyhnhnms or Yahoos, when it is manifest as to the latter, there are so many thousands even in this city, who only differ from their brother brutes in Houyhnhnmland, because they use a sort of a jabber, and do not go naked. I wrote for their amend-ment, and not their approbation. The united praise of the whole race would be of less consequence to me, than the neighing of those two degenerate Houyhnhnms I keep in my stable; because, from

6. Swift was the inveterate enemy of slang.

these, degenerate as they are, I still improve in some virtues, without any mixture of vice.

Do these miserable animals presume to think that I am so far degenerated as to defend my veracity; Yahoo as I am, it is well known through all Houyhnhnmland, that by the instructions and example of my illustrious master, I was able in the compass of two years (although I confess with the utmost difficulty) to remove that infernal habit of lying, shuffling, deceiving, and equivocating, so deeply rooted in the very souls of all my species; especially the Europeans.

I have other complaints to make upon this vexatious occasion; but I forbear troubling myself or you any further. I must freely confess that since my last return, some corruptions of my Yahoo nature have revived in me by conversing with a few of your species, and particularly those of mine own family, by an unavoidable necessity; else I should never have attempted so absurd a project as that of reforming the Yahoo race in this kingdom; but I have now done with all such visionary schemes for ever.

1727?

1735

The Publisher to the Reader

The author of these travels, Mr. Lemuel Gulliver, is my ancient and intimate friend; there is likewise some relation between us by the mother's side. About three years ago Mr. Gulliver, growing weary of the concourse of curious people coming to him at his house in Redriff,[1] made a small purchase of land, with a convenient house, near Newark, in Nottinghamshire, his native country; where he now lives retired, yet in good esteem among his neighbors.

Although Mr. Gulliver were born in Nottinghamshire, where his father dwelt, yet I have heard him say his family came from Oxfordshire; to confirm which, I have observed in the churchyard at Banbury, in that county, several tombs and monuments of the Gullivers.

Before he quitted Redriff, he left the custody of the following papers in my hands, with the liberty to dispose of them as I should think fit. I have carefully perused them three times; the style is very plain and simple; and the only fault I find is that the author, after the manner of travelers, is a little too circumstantial. There is an air of truth apparent through the whole; and indeed the author was so distinguished for his veracity, that it became a sort of proverb among his neighbors at Redriff, when anyone affirmed a thing, to say, it was as true as if Mr. Gulliver had spoke it.

---

1. Rotherhithe, a district in southern London, below Tower Bridge, then frequented by sailors.

By the advice of several worthy persons, to whom, with the author's permission, I communicated these papers, I now venture to send them into the world; hoping they may be, at least for some time, a better entertainment to our young noblemen, than the common scribbles of politics and party.

This volume would have been at least twice as large, if I had not made bold to strike out innumerable passages relating to the winds and tides, as well as to the variations and bearings in the several voyages; together with the minute descriptions of the management of the ship in storms, in the style of sailors; likewise the account of the longitudes and latitudes, wherein I have reason to apprehend that Mr. Gulliver may be a little dissatisfied; but I was resolved to fit the work as much as possible to the general capacity of readers. However, if my own ignorance in sea affairs shall have led me to commit some mistakes, I alone am answerable for them; and if any traveler hath a curiosity to see the whole work at large, as it came from the hand of the author, I will be ready to gratify him.

As for any further particulars relating to the author, the reader will receive satisfaction from the first pages of the book.

RICHARD SYMPSON

Part I. A Voyage to Lilliput

CHAPTER I. *The author gives some account of himself and family; his first inducements to travel. He is shipwrecked, and swims for his life; gets safe on shore in the country of Lilliput; is made a prisoner, and carried up the country.*

My father had a small estate in Nottinghamshire; I was the third of five sons. He sent me to Emanuel College in Cambridge, at fourteen years old, where I resided three years, and applied myself close to my studies: but the charge of maintaining me (although I had a very scanty allowance) being too great for a narrow fortune, I was bound apprentice to Mr. James Bates, an eminent surgeon in London, with whom I continued four years; and my father now and then sending me small sums of money, I laid them out in learning navigation, and other parts of the mathematics, useful to those who intend to travel, as I always believed it would be some time or other my fortune to do. When I left Mr. Bates, I went down to my father; where, by the assistance of him and my uncle John, and some other relations, I got forty pounds, and a promise of thirty pounds a year to maintain me at Leyden:[1] there I studied physic two years and seven months, knowing it would be useful in long voyages.

1. The University of Leyden, in Holland, a center for the study of "physic" (medicine).

Soon after my return from Leyden, I was recommended by my good master Mr. Bates, to be surgeon to the *Swallow*, Captain Abraham Pannell commander; with whom I continued three years and a half, making a voyage or two into the Levant[2] and some other parts. When I came back, I resolved to settle in London, to which Mr. Bates, my master, encouraged me; and by him I was recommended to several patients. I took part of a small house in the Old Jury; and being advised to alter my condition, I married Mrs.[3] Mary Burton, second daughter to Mr. Edmond Burton, hosier, in Newgate Street, with whom I received four hundred pounds for a portion.

But, my good master Bates dying in two years after, and I having few friends, my business began to fail; for my conscience would not suffer me to imitate the bad practice of too many among my brethren. Having therefore consulted with my wife, and some of my acquaintance, I determined to go again to sea. I was surgeon successively in two ships, and made several voyages, for six years, to the East and West Indies; by which I got some addition to my fortune. My hours of leisure I spent in reading the best authors, ancient and modern, being always provided with a good number of books; and when I was ashore, in observing the manners and dispositions of the people, as well as learning their language; wherein I had a great facility by the strength of my memory.

The last of these voyages not proving very fortunate, I grew weary of the sea, and intended to stay at home with my wife and family. I removed from the Old Jury to Fetter Lane, and from thence to Wapping, hoping to get business among the sailors; but it would not turn to account. After three years' expectation that things would mend, I accepted an advantageous offer from Captain William Prichard, master of the *Antelope*, who was making a voyage to the South Sea. We set sail from Bristol, May 4th, 1699, and our voyage at first was very prosperous.

It would not be proper, for some reasons, to trouble the reader with the particulars of our adventures in those seas: let it suffice to inform him, that in our passage from thence to the East Indies we were driven by a violent storm to the northwest of Van Diemen's Land.[4] By an observation, we found ourselves in the latitude of 30 degrees 2 minutes south. Twelve of our crew were dead by immoderate labor, and ill food, the rest were in a very weak condition. On the fifth of November, which was the beginning of summer in those parts, the weather being very hazy, the seamen spied a rock, within half a cable's length of the ship; but the wind was so strong, that we were driven directly upon it, and immediately split. Six of the

2. The eastern Mediterranean.
3. "Mrs." (pronounced "Mistress") designated any woman, married or unmar- ried. "Old Jury": a street (once "Old Jewry") in the City of London.
4. Tasmania.

crew, of whom I was one, having let down the boat into the sea, made a shift to get clear of the ship, and the rock.We rowed by my computation about three leagues, till we were able to work no longer, being already spent with labor while we were in the ship. We therefore trusted ourselves to the mercy of the waves; and in about half an hour the boat was overset by a sudden flurry from the north. What became of my companions in the boat, as well as of those who escaped on the rock, or were left in the vessel, I cannot tell; but conclude they were all lost. For my own part, I swam as fortune directed me, and was pushed forward by wind and tide. I often let my legs drop, and could feel no bottom; but when I was almost gone, and able to struggle no longer, I found myself within my depth; and by this time the storm was much abated. The declivity was so small, that I walked near a mile before I got to the shore, which I conjectured was about eight o'clock in the evening. I then advanced forward near half a mile, but could not discover any sign of houses or inhabitants; at least I was in so weak a condition, that I did not observe them. I was extremely tired, and with that, and the heat of the weather, and about half a pint of brandy that I drank as I left the ship, I found myself much inclined to sleep. I lay down on the grass, which was very short and soft, where I slept sounder than ever I remember to have done in my life, and as I reckoned, above nine hours; for when I awaked, it was just daylight. I attempted to rise, but was not able to stir: for as I happened to lie on my back, I found my arms and legs were strongly fastened on each side to the ground; and my hair, which was long and thick, tied down in the same manner. I likewise felt several slender ligatures across my body, from my armpits to my thighs. I could only look upwards; the sun began to grow hot, and the light offended my eyes. I heard a confused noise about me, but in the posture I lay, could see nothing except the sky. In a little time I felt something alive moving on my left leg, which advancing gently forward over my breast, came almost up to my chin; when bending my eyes downwards as much as I could, I perceived it to be a human creature not six inches high,[5] with a bow and arrow in his hands, and a quiver at his back. In the meantime, I felt at least forty more of the same kind (as I conjectured) following the first. I was in the utmost astonishment, and roared so loud, that they all ran back in a fright; and some of them, as I was afterwards told, were hurt with the falls they got by leaping from my sides upon the ground. However, they soon returned; and one of them, who ventured so far as to get a full sight of my face, lifting up his hands and eyes by way of admiration,[6] cried out in a shrill, but distinct voice, *Hekinah*

5. Lilliput is scaled, fairly consistently, at one-twelfth of Gulliver's world.

6. Wonderment.

Degul: the others repeated the same words several times, but I then knew not what they meant. I lay all this while, as the reader may believe, in great uneasiness; at length, struggling to get loose, I had the fortune to break the strings, and wrench out the pegs that fastened my left arm to the ground; for, by lifting it up to my face, I discovered the methods they had taken to bind me; and, at the same time, with a violent pull, which gave me excessive pain, I a little loosened the strings that tied down my hair on the left side; so that I was just able to turn my head about two inches. But the creatures ran off a second time, before I could seize them; whereupon there was a great shout in a very shrill accent; and after it ceased, I heard one of them cry aloud, *Tolgo phonac;* when in an instant I felt above an hundred arrows discharged on my left hand, which pricked me like so many needles; and besides they shot another flight into the air, as we do bombs in Europe, whereof many, I suppose, fell on my body (though I felt them not) and some on my face, which I immediately covered with my left hand. When this shower of arrows was over, I fell a groaning with grief and pain; and then striving again to get loose, they discharged another volley larger than the first, and some of them attempted with spears to stick me in the sides; but, by good luck, I had on me a buff jerkin,[7] which they could not pierce. I thought it the most prudent method to lie still; and my design was to continue so till night, when, my left hand being already loose, I could easily free myself: and as for the inhabitants, I had reason to believe I might be a match for the greatest armies they could bring against me, if they were all of the same size with him that I saw. But fortune disposed otherwise of me. When the people observed I was quiet, they discharged no more arrows: but by the noise increasing, I knew their numbers were greater; and about four yards from me, over-against my right ear, I heard a knocking for above an hour, like people at work; when turning my head that way, as well as the pegs and strings would permit me, I saw a stage erected about a foot and a half from the ground, capable of holding four of the inhabitants, with two or three ladders to mount it: from whence one of them, who seemed to be a person of quality, made me a long speech, whereof I understood not one syllable. But I should have mentioned, that before the principal person began his oration, he cried out three times, *Langro Dehul san:* (these words and the former were afterwards repeated and explained to me). Whereupon immediately about fifty of the inhabitants came, and cut the strings that fastened the left side of my head, which gave me the liberty of turning it to the right, and of observing the person and gesture of him who was to speak. He appeared to be of a middle age, and taller than any of

7. Leather jacket.

the other three who attended him; whereof one was a page who held up his train, and seemed to be somewhat longer than my middle finger; the other two stood one on each side to support him. He acted every part of an orator, and I could observe many periods[8] of threatenings, and others of promises, pity and kindness. I answered in a few words, but in the most submissive manner, lifting up my left hand and both my eyes to the sun, as calling him for a witness; and being almost famished with hunger, having not eaten a morsel for some hours before I left the ship, I found the demands of nature so strong upon me, that I could not forbear showing my impatience (perhaps against the strict rules of decency) by putting my finger frequently on my mouth, to signify that I wanted food. The Hurgo (for so they call a great lord, as I afterwards learned) understood me very well. He descended from the stage, and commanded that several ladders should be applied to my sides, on which above an hundred of the inhabitants mounted, and walked towards my mouth, laden with baskets full of meat, which had been provided and sent thither by the King's orders upon the first intelligence he received of me. I observed there was the flesh of several animals, but could not distinguish them by the taste. There were shoulders, legs, and loins shaped like those of mutton, and very well dressed, but smaller than the wings of a lark. I eat them by two or three at a mouthful, and took three loaves at a time, about the bigness of musket bullets. They supplied me as fast as they could, showing a thousand marks of wonder and astonishment at my bulk and appetite. I then made another sign that I wanted drink. They found by my eating that a small quantity would not suffice me; and being a most ingenious people, they slung up with great dexterity one of their largest hogsheads; then rolled it towards my hand, and beat out the top; I drank it off at a draught, which I might well do, for it hardly held half a pint, and tasted like a small wine of Burgundy, but much more delicious. They brought me a second hogshead, which I drank in the same manner, and made signs for more, but they had none to give me. When I had performed these wonders, they shouted for joy, and danced upon my breast, repeating several times as they did at first, *Hekinah Degul*. They made me a sign that I should throw down the two hogsheads, but first warned the people below to stand out of the way, crying aloud, *Borach Mivola*, and when they saw the vessels in the air, there was an universal shout of *Hekinah Degul*. I confess I was often tempted, while they were passing backwards and forwards on my body, to seize forty or fifty of the first that came in my reach, and dash them against the ground. But the remembrance of what I had felt, which probably might not be the worst they could do; and the promise of

---

8. In rhetoric, complete, well-constructed sentences.

honor I made them, for so I interpreted my submissive behavior, soon drove out those imaginations. Besides, I now considered myself as bound by the laws of hospitality to a people who had treated me with so much expense and magnificence. However, in my thoughts I could not sufficiently wonder at the intrepidity of these diminutive mortals, who durst venture to mount and walk on my body, while one of my hands was at liberty, without trembling at the very sight of so prodigious a creature as I must appear to them. After some time, when they observed that I made no more demands for meat, there appeared before me a person of high rank from his Imperial Majesty. His Excellency, having mounted on the small of my right leg, advanced forwards up to my face, with about a dozen of his retinue. And producing his credentials under the Signet Royal, which he applied[9] close to my eyes, spoke about ten minutes, without any signs of anger, but with a kind of determinate resolution; often pointing forwards, which, as I afterwards found, was towards the capital city, about half a mile distant, whither it was agreed by his Majesty in council that I must be conveyed. I answered in a few words, but to no purpose, and made a sign with my hand that was loose, putting it to the other (but over his Excellency's head, for fear of hurting him or his train) and then to my own head and body, to signify that I desired my liberty. It appeared that he understood me well enough; for he shook his head by way of disapprobation, and held his hand in a posture to show that I must be carried as a prisoner. However, he made other signs to let me understand that I should have meat and drink enough, and very good treatment. Whereupon I once more thought of attempting to break my bonds; but again, when I felt the smart of their arrows upon my face and hands, which were all in blisters, and many of the darts still sticking in them; and observing likewise that the number of my enemies increased; I gave tokens to let them know that they might do with me what they pleased. Upon this the *Hurgo* and his train withdrew, with much civility and cheerful countenances. Soon after I heard a general shout, with frequent repetitions of the words, *Peplom Selan,* and I felt great numbers of the people on my left side relaxing the cords to such a degree, that I was able to turn upon my right, and to ease myself with making water; which I very plentifully did, to the great astonishment of the people, who conjecturing by my motions what I was going to do, immediately opened to the right and left on that side, to avoid the torrent which fell with such noise and violence from me. But before this, they had daubed my face and both my hands with a sort of ointment very pleasant to the smell, which in a few minutes removed all the smart of their arrows. These circumstances, added

9. Brought.

to the refreshment I had received by their victuals and drink, which were very nourishing, disposed me to sleep. I slept about eight hours, as I was afterwards assured; and it was no wonder; for the physicians, by the Emperor's order, had mingled a sleeping potion in the hogsheads of wine.

It seems that upon the first moment I was discovered sleeping on the ground after my landing, the Emperor had early notice of it by an express; and determined in council that I should be tied in the manner I have related (which was done in the night while I slept), that plenty of meat and drink should be sent me, and a machine prepared to carry me to the capital city.

This resolution perhaps may appear very bold and dangerous, and I am confident would not be imitated by any prince in Europe on the like occasion; however, in my opinion it was extremely prudent as well as generous. For supposing these people had endeavored to kill me with their spears and arrows while I was asleep; I should certainly have awaked with the first sense of smart, which might so far have roused my rage and strength, as to enable me to break the strings wherewith I was tied; after which, as they were not able to make resistance, so they could expect no mercy.

These people are most excellent mathematicians, and arrived to a great perfection in mechanics by the countenance and encouragement of the Emperor, who is a renowned patron of learning. This prince hath several machines fixed on wheels, for the carriage of trees and other great weights. He often builds his largest men of war, whereof some are nine foot long, in the woods where the timber grows, and has them carried on these engines[1] three or four hundred yards to the sea. Five hundred carpenters and engineers were immediately set at work to prepare the greatest engine they had. It was a frame of wood raised three inches from the ground, about seven foot long and four wide, moving upon twenty-two wheels. The shout I heard was upon the arrival of this engine, which it seems set out in four hours after my landing. It was brought parallel to me as I lay. But the principal difficulty was to raise and place me in this vehicle. Eighty poles, each of one foot high, were erected for this purpose, and very strong cords of the bigness of packthread were fastened by hooks to many bandages, which the workmen had girt round my neck, my hands, my body, and my legs. Nine hundred of the strongest men were employed to draw up these cords by many pulleys fastened on the poles; and thus, in less than three hours, I was raised and slung into the engine, and there tied fast. All this I was told, for while the whole operation was performing, I lay in a profound sleep, by the force of that soporiferous[2] medicine infused into my liquor. Fifteen hundred of

---

1. Contrivances.   2. Inducing unnatural sleep.

the Emperor's largest horses, each about four inches and a half high, were employed to draw me towards the metropolis, which, as I said, was half a mile distant.

About four hours after we began our journey, I awaked by a very ridiculous accident; for, the carriage being stopped a while to adjust something that was out of order, two or three of the young natives had the curiosity to see how I looked when I was asleep; they climbed up into the engine, and advancing very softly to my face, one of them, an officer in the guards, put the sharp end of his half-pike a good way up into my left nostril, which tickled my nose like a straw, and made me sneeze violently: whereupon they stole off unperceived, and it was three weeks before I knew the cause of my awaking so suddenly. We made a long march the remaining part of the day, and rested at night with five hundred guards on each side of me, half with torches, and half with bows and arrows, ready to shoot me if I should offer to stir. The next morning at sunrise we continued our march, and arrived within two hundred yards of the city gates about noon. The Emperor and all his court came out to meet us, but his great officers would by no means suffer his Majesty to endanger his person by mounting on my body.

At the place where the carriage stopped, there stood an ancient temple, esteemed to be the largest in the whole kingdom, which having been polluted some years before by an unnatural murder,[3] was, according to the zeal of those people, looked on as profane, and therefore had been applied to common use, and all the ornaments and furniture carried away. In this edifice it was determined I should lodge. The great gate fronting to the north was about four foot high, and almost two foot wide, through which I could easily creep. On each side of the gate was a small window not above six inches from the ground: into that on the left side, the King's smiths conveyed fourscore and eleven chains, like those that hang to a lady's watch in Europe, and almost as large, which were locked to my left leg with six and thirty padlocks. Over against this temple, on the other side of the great highway, at twenty foot distance, there was a turret at least five foot high. Here the Emperor ascended with many principal lords of his court, to have an opportunity of viewing me, as I was told, for I could not see them. It was reckoned that above an hundred thousand inhabitants came out of the town upon the same errand; and in spite of my guards, I believe there could not be fewer than ten thousand, at several times, who mounted upon my body by the help of ladders. But a proclamation was soon issued to forbid it upon pain of death. When the workmen found it was impossible for me to break loose, they cut all the strings that bound me; whereupon I rose up with as melancholy a

3. Presumably a reference to the execution of Charles I, who was sentenced in   Westminster Hall.

disposition as ever I had in my life. But the noise and astonishment of the people at seeing me rise and walk are not to be expressed. The chains that held my left leg were about two yards long, and gave me not only the liberty of walking backwards and forwards in a semicircle; but, being fixed within four inches of the gate, allowed me to creep in, and lie at my full length in the temple.

CHAPTER II. *The Emperor of Lilliput, attended by several of the nobility, comes to see the author in his confinement. The Emperor's person and habit described. Learned men appointed to teach the author their language. He gains favor by his mild disposition. His pockets are searched, and his sword and pistols taken from him.*

When I found myself on my feet, I looked about me, and must confess I never beheld a more entertaining prospect. The country round appeared like a continued garden, and the inclosed fields, which were generally forty foot square, resembled so many beds of flowers. These fields were intermingled with woods of half a stang,[4] and the tallest trees, as I could judge, appeared to be seven foot high. I viewed the town on my left hand, which looked like the painted scene of a city in a theater.

I had been for some hours extremely pressed by the necessities of nature; which was no wonder, it being almost two days since I had last disburthened myself. I was under great difficulties between urgency and shame. The best expedient I could think on, was to creep into my house, which I accordingly did; and shutting the gate after me, I went as far as the length of my chain would suffer; and discharged my body of that uneasy load. But this was the only time I was ever guilty of so uncleanly an action; for which I cannot but hope the candid reader will give some allowance, after he hath maturely and impartially considered my case, and the distress I was in. From this time my constant practice was, as soon as I rose, to perform that business in open air, at the full extent of my chain, and due care was taken every morning before company came, that the offensive matter should be carried off in wheelbarrows by two servants appointed for that purpose. I would not have dwelt so long upon a circumstance, that perhaps at first sight may appear not very momentous, if I had not thought it necessary to justify my character in point of cleanliness to the world; which I am told some of my maligners have been pleased, upon this and other occasions, to call in question.

When this adventure was at an end, I came back out of my house, having occasion for fresh air. The Emperor was already descended from the tower, and advancing on horseback towards me, which had like to have cost him dear; for the beast, although very

4. A quarter of an acre.

well trained, yet wholly unused to such a sight, which appeared as if a mountain moved before him, reared up on his hinder feet: but that prince, who is an excellent horseman, kept his seat, until his attendants ran in, and held the bridle, while his Majesty had time to dismount. When he alighted, he surveyed me round with great admiration, but kept beyond the length of my chains. He ordered his cooks and butlers, who were already prepared, to give me victuals and drink, which they pushed forward in a sort of vehicles upon wheels until I could reach them. I took these vehicles, and soon emptied them all; twenty of them were filled with meat, and ten with liquor; each of the former afforded me two or three good mouthfuls, and I emptied the liquor of ten vessels, which was contained in earthen vials, into one vehicle, drinking it off at a draught; and so I did with the rest. The Empress, and young princes of the blood, of both sexes, attended by many ladies, sat at some distance in their chairs; but upon the accident that happened to the Emperor's horse, they alighted, and came near his person; which I am now going to describe. He is taller, by almost the breadth of my nail, than any of his court, which alone is enough to strike an awe into the beholders. His features are strong and masculine, with an Austrian lip, and arched nose, his complexion olive, his countenance[5] erect, his body and limbs well proportioned, all his motions graceful, and his deportment majestic. He was then past his prime, being twenty-eight years and three quarters old, of which he had reigned about seven, in great felicity, and generally victorious. For the better convenience of beholding him, I lay on my side, so that my face was parallel to his, and he stood but three yards off: however, I have had him since many times in my hand, and therefore cannot be deceived in the description. His dress was very plain and simple, the fashion of it between the Asiatic and the European; but he had on his head a light helmet of gold, adorned with jewels, and a plume on the crest. He held his sword drawn in his hand, to defend himself, if I should happen to break loose; it was almost three inches long, the hilt and scabbard were gold enriched with diamonds. His voice was shrill, but very clear and articulate, and I could distinctly hear it when I stood up. The ladies and courtiers were all most magnificently clad, so that the spot they stood upon seemed to resemble a petticoat spread on the ground, embroidered with figures of gold and silver. His Imperial Majesty spoke often to me, and I returned answers, but neither of us could understand a syllable. There were several of his priests and lawyers present (as I conjectured by their habits) who were commanded to address themselves to me, and I spoke to them in as many languages as I had the least smattering of, which were High and Low

5. **Bearing, appearance. Swift is satirically idealizing George I, whom most of** the British thought gross.

Dutch,[6] Latin, French, Spanish, Italian, and Lingua Franca; but all to no purpose. After about two hours the court retired, and I was left with a strong guard, to prevent the impertinence, and probably the malice of the rabble, who were very impatient to crowd about me as near as they durst; and some of them had the impudence to shoot their arrows at me as I sat on the ground by the door of my house, whereof one very narrowly missed my left eye. But the colonel ordered six of the ringleaders to be seized, and thought no punishment so proper as to deliver them bound into my hands, which some of his soldiers accordingly did, pushing them forwards with the butt-ends of their pikes into my reach; I took them all in my right hand, put five of them into my coat-pocket; and as to the sixth, I made a countenance as if I would eat him alive. The poor man squalled terribly, and the colonel and his officers were in much pain, especially when they saw me take out my penknife: but I soon put them out of fear; for, looking mildly, and immediately cutting the strings he was bound with, I set him gently on the ground, and away he ran. I treated the rest in the same manner, taking them one by one out of my pocket, and I observed both the soldiers and people were highly obliged at this mark of my clemency, which was represented very much to my advantage at court.

Towards night I got with some difficulty into my house, where I lay on the ground, and continued to do so about a fortnight; during which time the Emperor gave orders to have a bed prepared for me. Six hundred beds of the common measure were brought in carriages, and worked up in my house; an hundred and fifty of their beds sewn together made up the breadth and length, and these were four double, which however kept me but very indifferently from the hardness of the floor, that was of smooth stone. By the same computation they provided me with sheets, blankets, and coverlets, tolerable enough for one who had been so long enured to hardships as I.

As the news of my arrival spread through the kingdom, it brought prodigious numbers of rich, idle, and curious people to see me; so that the villages were almost emptied, and great neglect of tillage and household affairs must have ensued, if his Imperial Majesty had not provided by several proclamations and orders of state against this inconveniency. He directed that those who had already beheld me should return home, and not presume to come within fifty yards of my house without license from court; whereby the secretaries of state got considerable fees.

In the mean time, the Emperor held frequent councils to debate what course should be taken with me; and I was afterwards assured by a particular friend, a person of great quality, who was as much in

6. German and Dutch; "lingua franca": a jargon, based on Italian, used by traders in the Mediterranean.

the secret as any, that the court was under many difficulties concerning me. They apprehended[7] my breaking loose, that my diet
would be very expensive, and might cause a famine. Sometimes they
determined to starve me, or at least to shoot me in the face and
hands with poisoned arrows, which would soon dispatch me: but
again they considered, that the stench of so large a carcass might
produce a plague in the metropolis, and probably spread through
the whole kingdom. In the midst of these consultations, several
officers of the army went to the door of the great council chamber;
and two of them being admitted, gave an account of my behavior
to the six criminals above-mentioned; which made so favorable an
impression in the breast of his Majesty, and the whole board, in my
behalf, that an imperial commission was issued out, obliging all the
villages nine hundred yards round the city to deliver in every morning six beeves, forty sheep, and other victuals for my sustenance;
together with a proportionable quantity of bread and wine, and
other liquors: for the due payment of which his Majesty gave
assignments[8] upon his treasury. For this prince lives chiefly upon
his own demesnes; seldom except upon great occasions raising any
subsidies upon his subjects, who are bound to attend him in his
wars at their own expense. An establishment was also made of six
hundred persons to be my domestics, who had board-wages allowed
for their maintenance, and tents built for them very conveniently
on each side of my door. It was likewise ordered, that three
hundred tailors should make me a suit of clothes after the fashion
of the country: that six of his Majesty's greatest scholars should be
employed to instruct me in their language: and, lastly, that the
Emperor's horses, and those of the nobility, and troops of guards,
should be exercised in my sight, to accustom themselves to me. All
these orders were duly put in execution; and in about three weeks I
made a great progress in learning their language; during which time
the Emperor frequently honored me with his visits, and was pleased
to assist my masters in teaching me. We began already to converse
together in some sort; and the first words I learned, were to express
my desire that he would please to give me my liberty; which I every
day repeated on my knees.[9] His answer, as I could apprehend, was,
that this must be a work of time, not to be thought on without the
advice of his council; and that first I must *Lumos kelmin pesso
desmar lon emposo*; that is, swear a peace with him and his kingdom. However, that I should be used with all kindness; and he
advised me to acquire by my patience and discreet behavior, the
good opinion of himself and his subjects. He desired I would not

7. Anticipated with fear.
8. Formal mandates of revenue.
9. Gulliver's plea for liberty, and the
threat of starvation or rebellion he represents to his captors, suggest the situation of Ireland with respect to England.

take it ill, if he gave orders to certain proper officers to search me;
for probably I might carry about me several weapons, which must
needs be dangerous things, if they answered the bulk of so prodigious a person.[1] I said, his Majesty should be satisfied, for I was
ready to strip myself, and turn up my pockets before him. This I
delivered part in words, and part in signs. He replied, that by the
laws of the kingdom, I must be searched by two of his officers; that
he knew this could not be done without my consent and assistance;
that he had so good an opinion of my generosity and justice, as to
trust their persons in my hands; that whatever they took from me
should be returned when I left the country, or paid for at the rate
which I would set upon them. I took up the two officers in my
hands, put them first into my coat-pockets, and then into every
other pocket about me, except my two fobs, and another secret
pocket which I had no mind should be searched, wherein I had
some little necessaries of no consequence to any but myself. In one
of my fobs there was a silver watch, and in the other a small quantity of gold in a purse. These gentlemen, having pen, ink, and paper
about them, made an exact inventory of every thing they saw; and
when they had done, desired I would set them down, that they
might deliver it to the Emperor. This inventory I afterwards translated into English, and is word for word as follows.

Imprimis, In the right coat-pocket of the Great Man-Mountain
(for so I interpret the words *Quinbus Flestrin*) after the strictest
search, we found only one great piece of coarse cloth, large
enough to be a foot-cloth for your Majesty's chief room of state.
In the left pocket, we saw a huge silver chest, with a cover of the
same metal, which we the searchers were not able to lift. We
desired it should be opened; and one of us, stepping into it,
found himself up to the mid leg in a sort of dust, some part
whereof flying up to our faces, set us both a sneezing for several
times together. In his right waistcoat-pocket, we found a prodigious bundle of white thin substances, folded one over another,
about the bigness of three men, tied with a strong cable, and
marked with black figures; which we humbly conceive to be writings; every letter almost half as large as the palm of our hands. In
the left there was a sort of engine, from the back of which were
extended twenty long poles, resembling the palisados[2] before
your Majesty's court; wherewith we conjecture the Man-Mountain combs his head; for we did not always trouble him with
questions, because we found it a great difficulty to make him
understand us. In the large pocket on the right side of his middle
cover (so I translate the word *ranfu-lo*, by which they meant my

---

1. When the Whigs came into power in
1715, the leading Tories, who included
Swift's friends Oxford and Bolingbroke
(Robert Harley and Henry St. John) as
well as Swift himself, were investigated
by a Committee of Secrecy.
2. Fences of stakes.

breeches) we saw a hollow pillar of iron, about the length of a man, fastened to a strong piece of timber, larger than the pillar; and upon one side of the pillar were huge pieces of iron sticking out, cut into strange figures; which we know not what to make of. In the left pocket, another engine of the same kind. In the smaller pocket on the right side, were several round flat pieces of white and red metal, of different bulk; some of the white, which seemed to be silver, were so large and heavy, that my comrade and I could hardly lift them. In the left pocket were two black pillars irregularly shaped: we could not, without difficulty, reach the top of them as we stood at the bottom of his pocket. One of them was covered, and seemed all of a piece; but at the upper end of the other, there appeared a white round substance, about twice the bigness of our heads. Within each of these was inclosed a prodigious plate of steel; which, by our orders, we obliged him to show us, because we apprehended they might be dangerous engines. He took them out of their cases, and told us, that in his own country his practice was to shave his beard with one of these, and to cut his meat with the other. There were two pockets which we could not enter: these he called his fobs; they were two large slits cut into the top of his middle cover, but squeezed close by the pressure of his belly. Out of the right fob hung a great silver chain, with a wonderful kind of engine at the bottom. We directed him to draw out whatever was at the end of the chain, which appeared to be a globe, half silver, and half of some transparent metal: for on the transparent side we saw certain strange figures circularly drawn, and thought we could touch them, until we found our fingers stopped with that lucid substance. He put this engine to our ears, which made an incessant noise like that of a watermill. And we conjecture it is either some unknown animal, or the god that he worships: but we are more inclined to the latter opinion, because he assured us (if we understood him right, for he expressed himself very imperfectly), that he seldom did any thing without consulting it. He called it his oracle, and said it pointed out the time for every action of his life. From the left fob he took out a net almost large enough for a fisherman, but contrived to open and shut like a purse, and served him for the same use: we found therein several massy pieces of yellow metal, which if they be of real gold, must be of immense value.

Having thus, in obedience to your Majesty's commands, diligently searched all his pockets, we observed a girdle[3] about his waist made of the hide of some prodigious animal; from which, on the left side, hung a sword of the length of five men; and on the right, a bag or pouch divided into two cells; each cell capable of holding three of your Majesty's subjects. In one of these cells were several globes or balls of a most ponderous metal, about the bigness of our heads, and required a strong hand to lift them: the

3. Belt.

other cell contained a heap of certain black grains, but of no great bulk or weight, for we could hold above fifty of them in the palms of our hands.

This is an exact inventory of what we found about the body of the Man-Mountain; who used us with great civility, and due respect to your Majesty's commission. Signed and sealed on the fourth day of the eighty-ninth moon of your Majesty's auspicious reign.

CLEFREN FRELOCK, MARSI FRELOCK.

When this inventory was read over to the Emperor, he directed me to deliver up the several particulars. He first called for my scimitar, which I took out, scabbard and all. In the meantime he ordered three thousand of his choicest troops (who then attended him) to surround me at a distance, with their bows and arrows just ready to discharge: but I did not observe it; for my eyes were wholly fixed upon his Majesty. He then desired me to draw my scimitar, which, although it had got some rust by the sea water, was in most parts exceeding bright. I did so, and immediately all the troops gave a shout between terror and surprise; for the sun shone clear, and the reflection dazzled their eyes, as I waved the scimitar to and fro in my hand. His Majesty, who is a most magnanimous[4] prince, was less daunted than I could expect; he ordered me to return it into the scabbard, and cast it on the ground as gently as I could, about six foot from the end of my chain. The next thing he demanded was one of the hollow iron pillars, by which he meant my pocket-pistols. I drew it out, and at his desire, as well as I could, expressed to him the use of it, and charging it only with powder, which by the closeness of my pouch happened to escape wetting in the sea (an inconvenience that all prudent mariners take special care to provide against), I first cautioned the Emperor not to be afraid; and then I let it off in the air. The astonishment here was much greater than at the sight of my scimitar. Hundreds fell down as if they had been struck dead; and even the Emperor, although he stood his ground, could not recover himself in some time. I delivered up both my pistols in the same manner as I had done my scimitar, and then my pouch of powder and bullets; begging him that the former might be kept from fire; for it would kindle with the smallest spark, and blow up his imperial palace into the air. I likewise delivered up my watch, which the Emperor was very curious to see; and commanded two of his tallest yeomen of the guards to bear it on a pole upon their shoulders, as draymen in England do a barrel of ale. He was amazed at the continual noise it made, and the motion of the minute-hand, which he could easily discern; for their sight is much

---

4. Courageous, great-spirited. Magnanimity, the relation (direct or inverse) between the size of the body and the soul, is a central concern of the first two parts of the *Travels*.

more acute than ours: he asked the opinions of his learned men about him, which were various and remote, as the reader may well imagine without my repeating; although indeed I could not very perfectly understand them. I then gave up my silver and copper money, my purse with nine large pieces of gold, and some smaller ones; my knife and razor, my comb and silver snuffbox, my handkerchief and journal book. My scimitar, pistols, and pouch, were conveyed in carriages to his Majesty's stores; but the rest of my goods were returned me.

I had, as I before observed, one private pocket which escaped their search, wherein there was a pair of spectacles (which I sometimes use for the weakness of my eyes), a pocket perspective,[5] and several other little conveniences; which, being of no consequence to the Emperor, I did not think myself bound in honor to discover, and I apprehended they might be lost or spoiled if I ventured them out of my possession.

CHAPTER III. *The author diverts the Emperor and his nobility of both sexes in a very uncommon manner. The diversions of the court of Lilliput described. The author hath his liberty granted him upon certain conditions.*

My gentleness and good behavior had gained so far on the Emperor and his court, and indeed upon the army and people in general, that I began to conceive hopes of getting my liberty in a short time. I took all possible methods to cultivate this favorable disposition. The natives came by degrees to be less apprehensive of any danger from me. I would sometimes lie down, and let five or six of them dance on my hand. And at last the boys and girls would venture to come and play at hide-and-seek in my hair. I had now made a good progress in understanding and speaking their language. The Emperor had a mind one day to entertain me with several of the country shows; wherein they exceed all nations I have known, both for dexterity and magnificence. I was diverted with none so much as that of the rope-dancers, performed upon a slender white thread, extended about two foot, and twelve inches from the ground. Upon which I shall desire liberty, with the reader's patience, to enlarge a little.

This diversion is only practiced by those persons who are candidates for great employments, and high favor, at court. They are trained in this art from their youth, and are not always of noble birth, or liberal education. When a great office is vacant either by death or disgrace (which often happens) five or six of those candidates petition the Emperor to entertain his Majesty and the court

5. Telescope.

with a dance on the rope; and whoever jumps the highest without falling, succeeds in the office. Very often the chief ministers themselves are commanded to show their skill, and to convince the Emperor that they have not lost their faculty. Flimnap,[6] the Treasurer, is allowed to cut a caper on the strait rope, at least an inch higher than any other lord in the whole empire. I have seen him do the summerset several times together upon a trencher[7] fixed on the rope, which is no thicker than a common packthread in England. My friend Reldresal, Principal Secretary for Private Affairs, is, in my opinion, if I am not partial, the second after the Treasurer; the rest of the great officers are much upon a par.

These diversions are often attended with fatal accidents, whereof great numbers are on record. I myself have seen two or three candidates break a limb. But the danger is much greater when the ministers themselves are commanded to show their dexterity; for, by contending to excel themselves and their fellows, they strain so far, that there is hardly one of them who hath not received a fall; and some of them two or three. I was assured, that a year or two before my arrival, Flimnap would have infallibly broke his neck, if one of the King's cushions,[8] that accidentally lay on the ground, had not weakened the force of his fall.

There is likewise another diversion, which is only shown before the Emperor and Empress, and first minister, upon particular occasions. The Emperor lays on a table three fine silken threads of six inches long. One is blue, the other red, and the third green.[9] These threads are proposed as prizes for those persons whom the Emperor hath a mind to distinguish by a peculiar mark of his favor. The ceremony is performed in his Majesty's great chamber of state; where the candidates are to undergo a trial of dexterity very different from the former, and such as I have not observed the least resemblance of in any other country of the old or the new world. The Emperor holds a stick in his hands, both ends parallel to the horizon, while the candidates, advancing one by one, sometimes leap over the stick, sometimes creep under it backwards and forwards several times, according as the stick is advanced or depressed. Sometimes the Emperor holds one end of the stick, and his first minister the other; sometimes the minister has it entirely to himself. Whoever performs his part with most agility, and holds out the longest in *leaping* and *creeping*, is rewarded with the blue-colored silk; the red is given to the next, and the green to the third, which they all wear girt twice round about the middle; and you see few great persons about this court who are not adorned with one of these girdles.

---

6. Sir Robert Walpole, the Whig head of the government, notorious in Swift's circle for his political acrobatics.
7. Plate; "summerset": somersault.
8. A mistress of George I was supposed to have helped restore Walpole to office in 1721.
9. The Orders of the Garter, the Bath, and the Thistle, conferred for services to the King.

The horses of the army, and those of the royal stables, having been daily led before me, were no longer shy, but would come up to my very feet, without starting. The riders would leap them over my hand as I held it on the ground; and one of the Emperor's huntsmen, upon a large courser, took[1] my foot, shoe and all; which was indeed a prodigious leap. I had the good fortune to divert the Emperor one day after a very extraordinary manner. I desired he would order several sticks of two foot high, and the thickness of an ordinary cane, to be brought me; whereupon his Majesty commanded the master of his woods to give directions accordingly; and the next morning six woodmen arrived with as many carriages, drawn by eight horses to each. I took nine of these sticks, and fixing them firmly in the ground in a quadrangular figure, two foot and a half square, I took four other sticks, and tied them parallel at each corner, about two foot from the ground; then I fastened my handkerchief to the nine sticks that stood erect, and extended it on all sides till it was as tight as the top of a drum; and the four parallel sticks, rising about five inches higher than the handkerchief, served as ledges on each side. When I had finished my work, I desired the Emperor to let a troop of his best horse, twenty-four in number, come and exercise upon this plain. His Majesty approved of the proposal, and I took them up one by one in my hands, ready mounted and armed, with the proper officers to exercise them. As soon as they got into order, they divided into two parties, performed mock skirmishes, discharged blunt arrows, drew their swords, fled and pursued, attacked and retired; and in short discovered the best military discipline I ever beheld. The parallel sticks secured them and their horses from falling over the stage; and the Emperor was so much delighted, that he ordered this entertainment to be repeated several days; and once was pleased to be lifted up, and give the word of command; and, with great difficulty, persuaded even the Empress herself to let me hold her in her close chair[2] within two yards of the stage, from whence she was able to take a full view of the whole performance. It was my good fortune that no ill accident happened in these entertainments, only once a fiery horse that belonged to one of the captains pawing with his hoof struck a hole in my handkerchief, and his foot slipping, he overthrew his rider and himself; but I immediately relieved them both; for covering the hole with one hand, I set down the troop with the other, in the same manner as I took them up. The horse that fell was strained in the left shoulder, but the rider got no hurt, and I repaired my handkerchief as well as I could; however, I would not trust to the strength of it any more in such dangerous enterprises.

About two or three days before I was set at liberty, as I was enter-

1. Jumped over.   2. An enclosed or sedan chair.

taining the court with these kinds of feats, there arrived an express to inform his Majesty that some of his subjects, riding near the place where I was first taken up, had seen a great black substance lying on the ground, very oddly shaped, extending its edges round as wide as his Majesty's bedchamber, and rising up in the middle as high as a man; that it was no living creature, as they at first apprehended, for it lay on the grass without motion, and some of them had walked round it several times; that by mounting upon each others' shoulders, they had got to the top, which was flat and even; and stamping upon it they found it was hollow within; that they humbly conceived it might be something belonging to the Man-Mountain, and if his Majesty pleased, they would undertake to bring it with only five horses. I presently[3] knew what they meant; and was glad at heart to receive this intelligence. It seems upon my first reaching the shore after our shipwreck, I was in such confusion, that before I came to the place where I went to sleep, my hat, which I had fastened with a string to my head while I was rowing, and had stuck on all the time I was swimming, fell off after I came to land; the string, as I conjecture, breaking by some accident which I never observed, but thought my hat had been lost at sea. I intreated his Imperial Majesty to give orders it might be brought to me as soon as possible, describing to him the use and the nature of it: and the next day the wagoners arrived with it, but not in a very good condition; they had bored two holes in the brim, within an inch and half of the edge, and fastened two hooks in the holes; these hooks were tied by a long cord to the harness, and thus my hat was dragged along for above half an English mile: but the ground in that country being extremely smooth and level, it received less damage than I expected.

Two days after this adventure, the Emperor, having ordered that part of his army which quarters in and about his metropolis to be in a readiness, took a fancy of diverting himself in a very singular manner. He desired I would stand like a colossus, with my legs as far asunder as I conveniently could. He then commanded his general (who was an old experienced leader, and a great patron of mine) to draw up the troops in close order, and march them under me; the foot[4] by twenty-four in a breast, and the horse by sixteen, with drums beating, colors flying, and pikes advanced. This body consisted of three thousand foot, and a thousand horse. His Majesty gave orders, upon pain of death, that every soldier in his march should observe the strictest decency with regard to my person; which, however, could not prevent some of the younger officers from turning up their eyes as they passed under me. And, to confess

---

3. Immediately.   4. Foot-soldiers or infantry.

<u>the truth, my breeches were at that time in so ill a condition, that they afforded some opportunities for laughter and admiration</u>.

I had sent so many memorials and petitions for my liberty, that his Majesty at length mentioned the matter first in the cabinet, and then in a full council; where it was opposed by none, except Skyresh Bolgolam,[5] who was pleased, without any provocation, to be my mortal enemy. But it was carried against him by the whole board, and confirmed by the Emperor. That minister was *Galbet*, or Admiral of the Realm; very much in his master's confidence, and a person well versed in affairs, but of a morose and sour complexion.[6] However, he was at length persuaded to comply; but prevailed that the articles and conditions upon which I should be set free, and to which I must swear, should be drawn up by himself. These articles were brought to me by Skyresh Bolgolam in person, attended by two under-secretaries, and several persons of distinction. After they were read, I was demanded to swear to the performance of them; first in the manner of my own country, and afterwards in the method prescribed by their laws; which was to hold my right foot in my left hand, to place the middle finger of my right hand on the crown of my head, and my thumb on the tip of my right ear. But because the reader may perhaps be curious to have some idea of the style and manner of expression peculiar to that people, as well as to know the articles upon which I recovered my liberty, I have made a translation of the whole instrument,[7] word for word, as near as I was able; which I here offer to the public.

GOLBASTO MOMAREN EVLAME GURDILO SHEFIN MULLY ULLY GUE, most mighty Emperor of Lilliput, delight and terror of the universe, whose dominions extend five thousand *blustrugs* (about twelve miles in circumference) to the extremities of the globe; Monarch of all Monarchs; taller than the sons of men; whose feet press down to the center, and whose head strikes against the sun; at whose nod the princes of the earth shake their knees; pleasant as the spring, comfortable as the summer, fruitful as autumn, dreadful as winter. His most sublime Majesty proposeth to the Man-Mountain, lately arrived at our celestial dominions, the following articles, which by a solemn oath he shall be obliged to perform.

First, The Man-Mountain shall not depart from our dominions, without our license under our great seal.

Secondly, He shall not presume to come into our metropolis, without our express order; at which time the inhabitants shall have two hours warning, to keep within their doors.

Thirdly, The said Man-Mountain shall confine his walks to our

---

5. The Earl of Nottingham, an enemy of Swift.

6. Disposition.

7. A formal legal document.

principal high roads; and not offer to walk or lie down in a meadow, or field of corn.

Fourthly, As he walks the said roads, he shall take the utmost care not to trample upon the bodies of any of our loving subjects, their horses, or carriages, nor take any of our said subjects into his hands, without their own consent.

Fifthly, If an express require extraordinary dispatch, the Man-Mountain shall be obliged to carry in his pocket the messenger and horse, a six days' journey once in every moon, and return the said messenger back (if so required) safe to our Imperial Presence.

Sixthly, He shall be our ally against our enemies in the island of Blefuscu, and do his utmost to destroy their fleet, which is now preparing to invade us.

Seventhly, That the said Man-Mountain shall, at his times of leisure, be aiding and assisting to our workmen, in helping to raise certain great stones, towards covering the wall of the principal park, and other our royal buildings.

Eighthly, That the said Man-Mountain shall, in two moons' time, deliver in an exact survey of the circumference of our dominions by a computation of his own paces round the coast.

Lastly, That upon his solemn oath to observe all the above articles, the said Man-Mountain shall have a daily allowance of meat and drink sufficient for the support of 1,728 of our subjects; with free access to our Royal Person, and other marks of our favor. Given at our palace at Belfaborac the twelfth day of the ninety-first moon of our reign.

I swore and subscribed to these articles with great cheerfulness and content, although some of them were not so honorable as I could have wished; which proceeded wholly from the malice of Skyresh Bolgolam the High Admiral: whereupon my chains were immediately unlocked, and I was at full liberty: the Emperor himself in person did me the honor to be by at the whole ceremony. I made my acknowledgements by prostrating myself at his Majesty's feet: but he commanded me to rise; and after many gracious expressions, which, to avoid the censure of vanity, I shall not repeat, he added, that he hoped I should prove a useful servant, and well deserve all the favors he had already conferred upon me, or might do for the future.

The reader may please to observe, that in the last article for the recovery of my liberty, the Emperor stipulates to allow me a quantity of meat and drink, sufficient for the support of 1,728 Lilliputians. Some time after, asking a friend at court how they came to fix on that determinate number, he told me, that his Majesty's mathematicians, having taken the height of my body by the help of a quadrant, and finding it to exceed theirs in the proportion of twelve to one, they concluded from the similarity of their bodies, that mine must contain at least 1,728 of theirs, and consequently would require as much food as was necessary to support that number of Lilliputians. By which, the reader may conceive an idea of the inge-nuity of that people, as well as the prudent and exact economy of so great a prince.

CHAPTER IV. *Mildendo, the metropolis of Lilliput, described, together with the Emperor's palace. A conversation between the author and a principal secretary, concerning the affairs of that empire; the author's offers to serve the Emperor in his wars.*

The first request I made after I had obtained my liberty, was, that I might have license to see Mildendo, the metropolis; which the Emperor easily granted me, but with a special charge to do no hurt, either to the inhabitants, or their houses. The people had notice by proclamation of my design to visit the town. The wall which encompassed it is two foot and an half high, and at least eleven inches broad, so that a coach and horses may be driven very safely round it; and it is flanked with strong towers at ten foot dis-tance. I stepped over the great western gate, and passed very gently, and sideling[8] through the two principal streets, only in my short waistcoat, for fear of damaging the roofs and eaves of the houses with the skirts of my coat. I walked with the utmost circumspec-tion, to avoid treading on any stragglers, who might remain in the streets, although the orders were very strict, that all people should keep in their houses, at their own peril. The garret windows and tops of houses were so crowded with spectators, that I thought in all my travels I had not seen a more populous place. The city is an exact square, each side of the wall being five hundred foot long. The two great streets, which run cross and divide it into four quar-ters, are five foot wide. The lanes and alleys, which I could not enter, but only viewed them as I passed, are from twelve to eighteen inches. The town is capable of holding five hundred thousand souls. The houses are from three to five stories. The shops and markets well provided.

The Emperor's palace is in the center of the city, where the two great streets meet. It is enclosed by a wall of two foot high, and twenty foot distant from the buildings. I had his Majesty's permis-sion to step over this wall; and the space being so wide between that and the palace, I could easily view it on every side. The out-ward court is a square of forty foot, and includes two other courts: in the inmost are the royal apartments, which I was very desirous to see, but found it extremely difficult; for the great gates, from one square into another, were but eighteen inches high, and seven inches wide. Now the buildings of the outer court were at least five foot high; and it was impossible for me to stride over them, without

8. Sideways.

infinite damage to the pile, although the walls were strongly built of hewn stone, and four inches thick. At the same time the Emperor had a great desire that I should see the magnificence of his palace; but this I was not able to do till three days after, which I spent in cutting down with my knife some of the largest trees in the royal park, about an hundred yards distant from the city. Of these trees I made two stools, each about three foot high, and strong enough to bear my weight. The people having received notice a second time, I went again through the city to the palace, with my two stools in my hands. When I came to the side of the outer court, I stood upon one stool, and took the other in my hand: this I lifted over the roof, and gently set it down on the space between the first and second court, which was eight foot wide. I then stepped over the buildings very conveniently from one stool to the other, and drew up the first after me with a hooked stick. By this contrivance I got into the inmost court; and lying down upon my side, I applied my face to the windows of the middle stories, which were left open on purpose, and discovered the most splendid apartments that can be imagined. There I saw the Empress, and the young princes in their several lodgings, with their chief attendants about them. Her Imperial Majesty was pleased to smile very graciously upon me and gave me out of the window her hand to kiss.

But I shall not anticipate the reader with farther descriptions of this kind, because I reserve them for a greater work, which is now almost ready for the press; containing a general description of this empire, from its first erection, through a long series of princes, with a particular account of their wars and politics, laws, learning, and religion; their plants and animals, their peculiar manners and customs, with other matters very curious and useful; my chief design at present being only to relate such events and transactions as happened to the public, or to myself, during a residence of about nine months in that empire.

One morning, about a fortnight after I had obtained my liberty, Reldresal, Principal Secretary (as they style him) of Private Affairs, came to my house, attended only by one servant. He ordered his coach to wait at a distance, and desired I would give him an hour's audience; which I readily consented to, on account of his quality, and personal merits, as well as of the many good offices he had done me during my solicitations at court. I offered to lie down, that he might the more conveniently reach my ear; but he chose rather to let me hold him in my hand during our conversation. He began with compliments on my liberty, said he might pretend to some merit in it; but, however, added, that if it had not been for the present situation of things at court, perhaps I might not have obtained it so soon. For, said he, as flourishing a condition as we appear to be in to foreigners, we labor under two mighty evils; a violent faction at home, and the danger of an invasion by a most potent enemy from abroad. As to the first, you are to understand, that for above seventy moons past, there have been two struggling parties in the empire, under the names of *Tramecksan*, and *Slamecksan*,[9] from the high and low heels on their shoes, by which they distinguish themselves.

It is alleged indeed, that the high heels are most agreeable to our ancient constitution: but however this be, his Majesty hath determined to make use of only low heels in the administration of the government and all offices in the gift of the crown; as you cannot but observe; and particularly, that his Majesty's imperial heels are lower at least by a *drurr* than any of his court; (*drurr* is a measure about the fourteenth part of an inch). The animosities between these two parties run so high, that they will neither eat nor drink, nor talk with each other. We compute the *Tramecksan*, or High-Heels, to exceed us in number; but the power is wholly on our side. We apprehend his Imperial Highness, the heir to the crown, to have some tendency towards the High-Heels; at least we can plainly discover one of his heels higher than the other, which gives him a hobble in his gait.[1] Now, in the midst of these intestine disquiets, we are threatened with an invasion from the island of Blefuscu,[2] which is the other great empire of the universe, almost as large and powerful as this of his Majesty. For as to what we have heard you affirm, that there are other kingdoms and states in the world, inhabited by human creatures as large as yourself, our philosophers are in much doubt; and would rather conjecture that you dropped from the moon, or one of the stars; because it is certain, that an hundred mortals of your bulk would, in a short time, destroy all the fruits and cattle of his Majesty's dominions. Besides, our histories of six thousand moons make no mention of any other regions, than the two great empires of Lilliput and Blefuscu. Which two mighty powers have, as I was going to tell you, been engaged in a most obstinate war for six and thirty moons past. It began upon the following occasion. It is allowed on all hands, that the primitive way of breaking eggs before we eat them, was upon the larger end: but his present Majesty's grandfather, while he was a boy, going to eat an egg, and breaking it according to the ancient practice, happened to cut one of his fingers. Whereupon the Emperor his father published an edict, commanding all his subjects, upon great penalties, to break the smaller end of their eggs. The people so highly resented this law, that our histories tell us there have been six rebellions raised on that account; wherein one emperor lost his life, and another his crown.[3] These civil commotions were constantly

---

9. Tory (High Church) and Whig (Low Church).
1. The Prince of Wales (later George II) had friends in both parties.
2. France.
3. Swift's satirical allegory of the strife between Catholics (Big-Endians) and Protestants (Little-Endians) touches on Henry VIII (who "broke" with the Pope), Charles I (who lost his life), and James II (who lost his crown).

fomented by the monarchs of Blefuscu; and when they were quelled, the exiles always fled for refuge to that empire. It is computed, that eleven thousand persons have, at several times, suffered death, rather than submit to break their eggs at the smaller end. Many hundred large volumes have been published upon this controversy: but the books of the Big-Endians have been long forbidden, and the whole party rendered incapable by law of holding employments.[4] During the course of these troubles, the emperors of Blefuscu did frequently expostulate by their ambassadors, accusing us of making a schism in religion, by offending against a fundamental doctrine of our great prophet Lustrog, in the fifty-fourth chapter of the *Brundecral* (which is their Alcoran). This, however, is thought to be a mere strain upon the text: for the words are these; *That all true believers shall break their eggs at the convenient end*: and which is the convenient end, seems, in my humble opinion, to be left to every man's conscience, or at least in the power of the chief magistrate[5] to determine. Now the Big-Endian exiles have found so much credit in the Emperor of Blefuscu's court, and so much private assistance and encouragement from their party here at home, that a bloody war hath been carried on between the two empires for six and thirty moons with various success;[6] during which time we have lost forty capital ships, and a much greater number of smaller vessels, together with thirty thousand of our best seamen and soldiers; and the damage received by the enemy is reckoned to be somewhat greater than ours. However, they have now equipped a numerous fleet, and are just preparing to make a descent upon us; and his Imperial Majesty, placing great confidence in your valor and strength, hath commanded me to lay this account of his affairs before you.

I desired the Secretary to present my humble duty to the Emperor, and to let him know, that I thought it would not become me, who was a foreigner, to interfere with parties; but I was ready, with the hazard of my life, to defend his person and state against all invaders.

CHAPTER V. *The author by an extraordinary stratagem prevents an invasion. A high title of honor is conferred upon him. Ambassadors arrive from the Emperor of Blefuscu, and sue for peace. The Empress's apartment on fire by an accident; the author instrumental in saving the rest of the palace.*

The empire of Blefuscu is an island situated to the north northeast side of Lilliput, from whence it is parted only by a channel of

4. The Test Act (1673) prevented Catholics and Nonconformists from holding office unless they accepted the Anglican sacrament.
5. Ruler, sovereign. Swift himself ac-

cepted the right of the king to determine religious observances.
6. Reminiscent of the War of the Spanish Succession (1701–1713).

eight hundred yards wide. I had not yet seen it, and upon this notice of an intended invasion, I avoided appearing on that side of the coast, for fear of being discovered by some of the enemy's ships, who had received no intelligence of me; all intercourse between the two empires having been strictly forbidden during the war, upon pain of death; and an embargo laid by our Emperor upon all vessels whatsoever. I communicated to his Majesty a project I had formed of seizing the enemy's whole fleet; which, as our scouts assured us, lay at anchor in the harbor ready to sail with the first fair wind. I consulted the most experienced seamen upon the depth of the channel, which they had often plumbed; who told me, that in the middle at high water it was seventy *glumgluffs* deep, which is about six foot of European measure; and the rest of it fifty *glumgluffs* at most. I walked to the northeast coast over against Blefuscu; where, lying down behind a hillock, I took out my small pocket perspective glass, and viewed the enemy's fleet at anchor, consisting of about fifty men of war, and a great number of transports: I then came back to my house, and gave order (for which I had a warrant) for a great quantity of the strongest cable and bars of iron. The cable was about as thick as packthread, and the bars of the length and size of a knitting-needle. I trebled the cable to make it stronger, and for the same reason I twisted three of the iron bars together, bending the extremities into a hook. Having thus fixed fifty hooks to as many cables, I went back to the northeast coast, and putting off my coat, shoes, and stockings, walked into the sea in my leathern jerkin, about half an hour before high water. I waded with what haste I could, and swam in the middle about thirty yards until I felt the ground; I arrived at the fleet in less than half an hour. The enemy was so frighted when they saw me, that they leaped out of their ships, and swam to shore, where there could not be fewer than thirty thousand souls. I then took my tackling, and fastening a hook to the hole at the prow of each, I tied all the cords together at the end. While I was thus employed, the enemy discharged several thousand arrows, many of which stuck in my hands and face; and besides the excessive smart, gave me much disturbance in my work. My greatest apprehension was for my eyes, which I should have infallibly lost, if I had not suddenly thought of an expedient. I kept, among other little necessaries, a pair of spectacles in a private pocket, which, as I observed before, had escaped the Emperor's searchers. These I took out, and fastened as strongly as I could upon my nose; and thus armed went on boldly with my work in spite of the enemy's arrows; many of which struck against the glasses of my spectacles, but without any other effect, further than a little to discompose them. I had now fastened all the hooks, and taking the knot in my hand, began to pull; but not a ship would stir, for they were all too fast by their anchors, so that the boldest part of my enterprise remained. I therefore let go the cord, and leaving the hooks fixed to the ships, I resolutely cut with my knife the cables that fastened the anchors, receiving above two hundred shots in my face and hands; then I took up the knotted end of the cables to which my hooks were tied; and with great ease drew fifty of the enemy's largest men-of-war after me.

The Blefuscudians, who had not the least imagination of what I intended, were at first confounded with astonishment. They had seen me cut the cables, and thought my design was only to let the ships run adrift, or fall foul on each other: but when they perceived the whole fleet moving in order, and saw me pulling at the end, they set up such a scream of grief and despair, that it is almost impossible to describe or conceive. When I had got out of danger, I stopped a while to pick out the arrows that stuck in my hands and face, and rubbed on some of the same ointment that was given me at my first arrival, as I have formerly mentioned. I then took off my spectacles, and waiting about an hour until the tide was a little fallen, I waded through the middle with my cargo, and arrived safe at the royal port of Lilliput.

The Emperor and his whole court stood on the shore, expecting the issue of this great adventure. They saw the ships move forward in a large half-moon, but could not discern me, who was up to my breast in water. When I advanced to the middle of the channel, they were yet more in pain, because I was under water to my neck. The Emperor concluded me to be drowned, and that the enemy's fleet was approaching in a hostile manner: but he was soon eased of his fears, for the channel growing shallower every step I made, I came in a short time within hearing; and holding up the end of the cable by which the fleet was fastened, I cried in a loud voice, Long live the most puissant Emperor of Lilliput! This great prince received me at my landing with all possible encomiums, and created me a *Nardac* upon the spot, which is the highest title of honor among them.

His Majesty desired I would take some other opportunity of bringing all the rest of his enemy's ships into his ports. And so unmeasurable is the ambition of princes, that he seemed to think of nothing less than reducing the whole empire of Blefuscu into a province, and governing it by a viceroy; of destroying the Big-Endian exiles, and compelling that people to break the smaller end of their eggs, by which he would remain sole monarch of the whole world. But I endeavored to divert him from this design, by many arguments drawn from the topics of policy as well as justice: and I plainly protested, that I would never be an instrument of bringing a free and brave people into slavery. And when the matter was debated in council, the wisest part of the ministry were of my opinion.

This open bold declaration of mine was so opposite to the

schemes and politics of his Imperial Majesty, that he could never forgive me; he mentioned it in a very artful manner at council, where I was told that some of the wisest appeared, at least by their silence, to be of my opinion; but others, who were my secret enemies, could not forbear some expressions, which by a side-wind[7] reflected on me. And from this time began an intrigue between his Majesty and a junta of ministers maliciously bent against me, which broke out in less than two months, and had like to have ended in my utter destruction. Of so little weight are the greatest services to princes, when put into the balance with a refusal to gratify their passions.[8]

About three weeks after this exploit, there arrived a solemn embassy frrom Blefuscu, with humble offers of a peace; which was soon concluded upon conditions very advantageous to our Emperor; wherewith I shall not trouble the reader. There were six ambassadors, with a train of about five hundred persons; and their entry was very magnificent, suitable to the grandeur of their master, and the importance of their business. When their treaty was finished, wherein I did them several good offices by the credit I now had, or at least appeared to have at court, their Excellencies, who were privately told how much I had been their friend, made me a visit in form. They began with many compliments upon my valor and generosity; invited me to that kingdom in the Emperor their master's name; and desired me to show them some proofs of my prodigious strength, of which they had heard so many wonders; wherein I readily obliged them, but shall not interrupt the reader with the particulars.

When I had for some time entertained their Excellencies to their infinite satisfaction and surprise, I desired they would do me the honor to present my most humble respects to the Emperor their master, the renown of whose virtues had so justly filled the whole world with admiration, and whose royal person I resolved to attend before I returned to my own country. Accordingly, the next time I had the honor to see our Emperor, I desired his general license to wait on the Blefuscudian monarch, which he was pleased to grant me, as I could plainly perceive, in a very cold manner; but could not guess the reason, till I had a whisper from a certain person, that Flimnap and Bolgolam had represented my intercourse with those ambassadors as a mark of disaffection, from which I am sure my heart was wholly free. And this was the first time I began to conceive some imperfect idea of courts and ministers.

It is to be observed, that these ambassadors spoke to me by an interpreter; the languages of both empires differing as much as from

7. Indirectly.
8. After a series of British naval victories, the Treaty of Utrecht (1713) had ended the war with France, but the Tory ministers who engineered the peace were subsequently accused of having sold out to the enemy.

each other as any two in Europe, and each nation priding itself upon the antiquity, beauty, and energy of their own tongues, with an avowed contempt for that of their neighbor; yet our Emperor, standing upon the advantage he had got by the seizure of their fleet, obliged them to deliver their credentials, and make their speech, in the Lilliputian tongue. And it must be confessed, that from the great intercourse of trade and commerce between both realms, from the continual reception of exiles, which is mutual among them, and from the custom in each empire to send their young nobility and richer gentry to the other, in order to polish themselves, by seeing the world, and understanding men and manners, there are few persons of distinction, or merchants, or seamen, who dwell in the maritime parts, but what can hold conversation in both tongues; as I found some weeks after, when I went to pay my respects to the Emperor of Blefuscu, which in the midst of great misfortunes, through the malice of my enemies, proved a very happy adventure to me, as I shall relate in its proper place.

The reader may remember, that when I signed those articles upon which I recovered my liberty, there were some which I disliked upon account of their being too servile, neither could any thing but an extreme necessity have forced me to submit. But being now a *Nardac*, of the highest rank in that empire, such offices[9] were looked upon as below my dignity, and the Emperor (to do him justice) never once mentioned them to me. However, it was not long before I had an opportunity of doing his Majesty, at least as I then thought, a most signal service. I was alarmed at midnight with the cries of many hundred people at my door; by which being suddenly awaked, I was in some kind of terror. I heard the word *burglum* repeated incessantly; several of the Emperor's court, making their way through the crowd, intreated me to come immediately to the palace, where her Imperial Majesty's apartment was on fire, by the carelessness of a maid of honor, who fell asleep while she was reading a romance. I got up in an instant; and orders being given to clear the way before me, and it being likewise a moonshine night, I made a shift to get to the palace without trampling on any of the people. I found they had already applied ladders to the walls of the apartment, and were well provided with buckets, but the water was at some distance. These buckets were about the size of a large thimble, and the poor people supplied me with them as fast as they could; but the flame was so violent, that they did little good. I might easily have stifled it with my coat, which I unfortunately left behind me for haste, and came away only in my leathern jerkin. The case seemed wholly desperate and deplorable; and this magnificent palace would have infallibly been burnt down to the ground, if, by a presence of mind, unusual to me, I had not suddenly thought of an expedient. I had the evening before drank plentifully

9. Duties.

of a most delicious wine, called *glimigrim* (the Blefuscudians call it *flunec*, but ours is esteemed the better sort), which is very diuretic. By the luckiest chance in the world, I had not discharged myself of any part of it. The heat I had contracted by coming very near the flames, and by my laboring to quench them, made the wine begin to operate by urine; which I voided in such a quantity, and applied so well to the proper places, that in three minutes the fire was wholly extinguished; and the rest of that noble pile, which had cost so many ages in erecting, preserved from destruction.

It was now daylight, and I returned to my house, without waiting to congratulate with the Emperor; because, although I had done a very eminent piece of service, yet I could not tell how his Majesty might resent the manner by which I had performed it: for, by the fundamental laws of the realm, it is capital[1] in any person, of what quality soever, to make water within the precincts of the palace. But I was a little comforted by a message from his Majesty, that he would give orders to the Grand Justiciary for passing my pardon in form; which, however, I could not obtain. And I was privately assured, that the Empress, conceiving the greatest abhorrence of what I had done,[2] removed to the most distant side of the court, firmly resolved that those buildings should never be repaired for her use; and, in the presence of her chief confidents, could not forbear vowing revenge.

CHAPTER VI. *Of the inhabitants of Lilliput; their learning, laws, and customs, the manner of educating their children. The author's way of living in that country. His vindication of a great lady.*

Although I intend to leave the description of this empire to a particular treatise, yet in the mean time I am content to gratify the curious reader with some general ideas. As the common size of the natives is somewhat under six inches, so there is an exact proportion in all other animals, as well as plants and trees: for instance, the tallest horses and oxen are between four and five inches in height, the sheep an inch and a half, more or less; their geese about the bigness of a sparrow; and so the several gradations downwards, till you come to the smallest, which, to my sight, were almost invisible; but nature hath adapted the eyes of the Lilliputians to all objects proper for their view: they see with great exactness, but at no great distance. And to show the sharpness of their sight towards objects that are near, I have been much pleased with observing a cook pulling[3] a lark, which was not so large as a common fly; and a young girl threading an invisible needle with invisible silk. Their tallest trees are about seven foot high; I mean some of those in the great royal park, the tops whereof I could but just reach with my

1. Punishable by death.
2. Queen Anne, whom Swift called "a royal prude," strongly objected to the coarseness of *A Tale of a Tub.*
3. Plucking.

fist clinched. The other vegetables[4] are in the same proportion; but this I leave to the reader's imagination.

I shall say but little at present of their learning, which for many ages hath flourished in all its branches among them: but their manner of writing is very peculiar; being neither from the left to the right, like the Europeans; nor from the right to the left, like the Arabians; nor from up to down, like the Chinese; nor from down to up, like the Cascagians;[5] but aslant from one corner of the paper to the other, like ladies in England.

They bury their dead with their heads directly downwards; because they hold an opinion that in eleven thousand moons they are all to rise again; in which period, the earth (which they conceive to be flat) will turn upside down, and by this means they shall, at their resurrection, be found ready standing on their feet. The learned among them confess the absurdity of this doctrine; but the practice still continues, in compliance to the vulgar.

There are some laws and customs in this empire very peculiar; and if they were not so directly contrary to those of my own dear country, I should be tempted to say a little in their justification. It is only to be wished, that they were as well executed. The first I shall mention relateth to informers. All crimes against the state are punished here with the utmost severity; but if the person accused make his innocence plainly to appear upon his trial, the accuser is immediately put to an ignominious death; and out of his goods or lands, the innocent person is quadruply recompensed for the loss of his time, for the danger he underwent, for the hardship of his imprisonment, and for all the charges he hath been at in making his defense. Or, if that fund be deficient, it is largely[6] supplied by the crown. The Emperor doth also confer on him some public mark of his favor; and proclamation is made of his innocence through the whole city.

They look upon fraud as a greater crime than theft, and therefore seldom fail to punish it with death; for they allege, that care and vigilance, with a very common understanding, may preserve a man's goods from thieves; but honesty hath no fence against superior cunning: and since it is necessary that there should be a perpetual intercourse of buying and selling, and dealing upon credit, where fraud is permitted or connived at, or hath no law to punish it, the honest dealer is always undone, and the knave gets the advantage. I remember when I was once interceding with the King for a criminal who had wronged his master of a great sum of money, which he had received by order, and ran away with; and happening to tell his Majesty, by way of extenuation, that it was only a breach of trust, the Emperor thought it monstrous in me to offer, as a defense, the greatest aggravation of the crime: and truly, I had little to say in

4. Plants.   6. Fully.
5. Swift's invention.

return, farther than the common answer, that different nations had different customs; for, I confess, I was heartily ashamed.

Although we usually call reward and punishment the two hinges upon which all government turns, yet I could never observe this maxim to be put in practice by any nation, except that of Lilliput. Whoever can there bring sufficient proof that he hath strictly observed the laws of his country for seventy-three moons, hath a claim to certain privileges, according to his quality[7] and condition of life, with a proportionable sum of money out of a fund appropri-ated for that use: he likewise acquires the title of *Snilpall*, or *Legal*, which is added to his name, but doth not descend to his posterity. And these people thought it a prodigious defect of policy among us, when I told them that our laws were enforced only by penalties, without any mention of reward. It is upon this account that the image of Justice, in their courts of judicature, is formed with six eyes, two before, as many behind, and on each side one, to signify circumspection; with a bag of gold open in her right hand, and a sword sheathed in her left, to show she is more disposed to reward than to punish.

In choosing persons for all employments, they have more regard to good morals than to great abilities; for, since government is nec-essary to mankind, they believe that the common size of human understandings is fitted to some station or other; and that Provid-ence never intended to make the management of public affairs a mystery, to be comprehended only by a few persons of sublime genius, of which there seldom are three born in an age: but they suppose truth, justice, temperance, and the like, to be in every man's power; the practice of which virtues, assisted by experience and a good intention, would qualify any man for the service of his country, except where a course of study is required. But they thought the want of moral virtues was so far from being supplied by superior endowments of the mind, that employments could never be put into such dangerous hands as those of persons so qualified; and at least, that the mistakes committed by ignorance in a virtuous disposition would never be of such fatal consequence to the public weal, as the practices of a man whose inclinations led him to be cor-rupt, and had great abilities to manage, to multiply, and defend his corruptions.

In like manner, the disbelief of a divine Providence renders a man uncapable of holding any public station; for since kings avow themselves to be the deputies of Providence, the Lilliputians think nothing can be more absurd than for a prince to employ such men as disown the authority under which he acteth.

In relating these and the following laws, I would only be under-stood to mean the original institutions, and not the most scandalous

7. Social position.

corruptions into which these people are fallen by the degenerate nature of man. For as to that infamous practice of acquiring great employments by dancing on the ropes, or badges of favor and distinction by leaping over sticks, and creeping under them, the reader is to observe, that they were first introduced by the grandfather of the Emperor now reigning; and grew to the present height by the gradual increase of party and faction.

Ingratitude is among them a capital crime, as we read it to have been in some other countries; for they reason thus, that whoever makes ill returns to his benefactor, must needs be a common enemy to the rest of mankind, from whom he hath received no obligation; and therefore such a man is not fit to live.

Their notions relating to the duties of parents and children differ extremely from ours. For, since the conjunction of male and female is founded upon the great law of nature, in order to propagate and continue the species, the Lilliputians will needs have it, that men and women are joined together like other animals, by the motives of concupiscence; and that their tenderness towards their young proceedeth from the like natural principle: for which reason they will never allow, that a child is under any obligation to his father for begetting him, or to his mother for bringing him into the world; which, considering the miseries of human life, was neither a benefit in itself, nor intended so by his parents, whose thoughts in their love-encounters were otherwise employed. Upon these, and the like reasonings, their opinion is, that parents are the last of all others to be trusted with the education of their own children: and therefore they have in every town public nurseries, where all parents, except cottagers[8] and laborers, are obliged to send their infants of both sexes to be reared and educated when they come to the age of twenty moons; at which time they are supposed to have some rudiments of docility. These schools are of several kinds, suited to different qualities, and to both sexes. They have certain professors[9] well skilled in preparing children for such a condition of life as befits the rank of their parents, and their own capacities as well as inclinations. I shall first say something of the male nurseries, and then of the female.

The nurseries for males of noble or eminent birth are provided with grave and learned professors, and their several deputies. The clothes and food of the children are plain and simple. They are bred up in the principles of honor, justice, courage, modesty, clemency, religion, and love of their country; they are always employed in some business, except in the times of eating and sleeping, which are very short, and two hours for diversions, consisting of bodily exercises.[1] They are dressed by men until four years of age, and then are obliged to dress themselves, although their quality be ever so great; and the women attendants, who are aged proportionably to

8. Agricultural workers, peasants.
9. Professional teachers.

1. Activities.

ours at fifty, perform only the most menial offices. They are never suffered to converse with servants, but go together in small or greater numbers to take their diversions, and always in the presence of a professor, or one of his deputies; whereby they avoid those early bad impressions of folly and vice to which our children are subject. Their parents are suffered to see them only twice a year; the visit is not to last above an hour; they are allowed to kiss the child at meeting and parting; but a professor, who always standeth by on those occasions, will not suffer them to whisper, or use any fondling expressions, or bring any presents of toys, sweetmeats, and the like.

The pension from each family for the education and entertainment[2] of a child, upon failure of due payment, is levied by the Emperor's officers.

The nurseries for children of ordinary gentlemen, merchants, traders, and handicrafts, are managed proportionably after the same manner; only those designed for trades are put out apprentices at seven years old; whereas those of persons of quality continue in their exercises until fifteen, which answers to one and twenty with us: but the confinement is gradually lessened for the last three years.

In the famale nurseries, the young girls of quality are educated much like the males, only they are dressed by orderly servants of their own sex, but always in the presence of a professor or deputy, until they come to dress themselves, which is at five years old. And if it be found that these nurses ever presume to entertain the girls with frightful or foolish stories, or the common follies practiced by chambermaids among us, they are publicly whipped thrice about the city, imprisoned for a year, and banished for life to the most desolate parts of the country. Thus the young ladies there are as much ashamed of being cowards and fools as the men; and despise all personal ornaments beyond decency and cleanliness: neither did I perceive any difference in their education, made by their difference of sex, only that the exercises of the females were not altogether so robust; and that some rules were given them relating to domestic life, and a smaller compass of learning was enjoined them: for their maxim is, that among people of quality, a wife should be always a reasonable and agreeable companion, because she cannot always be young. When the girls are twelve years old, which among them is the marriageable age, their parents or guardians take them home, with great expressions of gratitude to the professors, and seldom without tears of the young lady and her companions.

In the nurseries of females of the meaner sort, the children are instructed in all kinds of works proper for their sex, and their several degrees:[3] those intended for apprentices are dismissed at seven years old, the rest are kept to eleven.

The meaner families who have children at these nurseries are

---

2. Sustenance.   3. Various social ranks.

obliged, besides their annual pension, which is as low as possible, to return to the steward of the nursery a small monthly share of their gettings, to be a portion for the child; and therefore all parents are limited in their expenses by the law. For the Lilliputians think nothing can be more unjust, than that people, in subservience to their own appetites, should bring children into the world, and leave the burthen of supporting them on the public. As to persons of quality, they give security to appropriate a certain sum for each child, suitable to their condition; and these funds are always managed with good husbandry, and the most exact justice.

The cottagers and laborers keep their children at home, their business being only to till and cultivate the earth; and therefore their education is of little consequence to the public; but the old and diseased among them are supported by hospitals: for begging is a trade unknown in this empire.

And here it may perhaps divert the curious reader, to give some account of my domestic,[4] and my manner of living in this country, during a residence of nine months and thirteen days. Having a head mechanically turned, and being likewise forced by necessity, I had made for myself a table and chair convenient enough, out of the largest trees in the royal park. Two hundred sempstresses were employed to make me shirts, and linen for my bed and table, all of the strongest and coarsest kind they could get; which, however, they were forced to quilt together in several folds; for the thickest was some degrees finer than lawn. Their linen is usually three inches wide, and three foot make a piece. The sempstresses took my measure as I lay on the ground, one standing at my neck, and another at my mid-leg, with a strong cord extended, that each held by the end, while the third measured the length of the cord with a rule of an inch long. Then they measured my right thumb, and desired no more; for by a mathematical computation, that twice round the thumb is one round the wrist, and so on to the neck and the waist; and by the help of my old shirt, which I displayed on the ground before them for a pattern, they fitted me exactly. Three hundred tailors were employed in the same manner to make me clothes; but they had another contrivance for taking my measure. I kneeled down, and they raised a ladder from the ground to my neck; upon this ladder one of them mounted, and let fall a plumb-line from my collar to the floor, which just answered the length of my coat; but my waist and arms I measured myself. When my clothes were finished, which was done in my house (for the largest of theirs would not have been able to hold them), they looked like the patchwork made by the ladies in England, only that mine were all of a color.

I had three hundred cooks to dress my victuals, in little convenient huts built about my house, where they and their families lived,

---

4. Household.

and prepared me two dishes apiece. I took up twenty waiters in my hand, and placed them on the table; an hundred more attended below on the ground, some with dishes of meat, and some with barrels of wine, and other liquors, slung on their shoulders; all which the waiters above drew up as I wanted, in a very ingenious manner, by certain cords, as we draw the bucket up a well in Europe. A dish of their meat was a good mouthful, and a barrel of their liquor a reasonable draught. Their mutton yields to ours, but their beef is excellent. I have had a sirloin so large, that I have been forced to make three bites of it; but this is rare. My servants were astonished to see me eat it bones and all, as in our country we do the leg of a lark. Their geese and turkeys I usually eat at a mouthful, and I must confess they far exceed ours. Of their smaller fowl I could take up twenty or thirty at the end of my knife.

One day his Imperial Majesty, being informed of my way of living, desired that himself and his royal consort, with the young princes of the blood of both sexes, might have the happiness (as he was pleased to call it) of dining with me. They came accordingly, and I placed them upon chairs of state on my table, just over against me, with their guards about them. Flimnap the Lord High Treasurer attended there likewise, with his white staff; and I observed he often looked on me with a sour countenance, which I would not seem to regard, but eat more than usual, in honor to my dear country, as well as to fill the court with admiration. I have some private reasons to believe, that this visit from his Majesty gave Flimnap an opportunity of doing me ill offices to his master. That minister had always been my secret enemy, although he outwardly caressed me more than was usual to the moroseness of his nature. He represented to the Emperor the low condition of his treasury; that he was forced to take up money at great discount; that exchequer bills[5] would not circulate under nine per cent below par; that I had cost his Majesty above a million and a half of *sprugs* (their greatest gold coin, about the bigness of a spangle); and upon the whole, that it would be advisable in the Emperor to take the first fair occasion of dismissing me.

I am here obliged to vindicate the reputation of an excellent lady, who was an innocent sufferer upon my account. The Treasurer took a fancy to be jealous of his wife, from the malice of some evil tongues, who informed him that her Grace had taken a violent affection for my person; and the court-scandal ran for some time that she once came privately to my lodging. This I solemnly declare to be a most infamous falsehood, without any grounds, farther than that her Grace was pleased to treat me with all innocent marks of freedom and friendship. I own she came often to my house, but always publicly, nor ever without three more in the coach, who were usually her sister and young daughter, and some particular acquaint-

5. Government bills of credit. Walpole was noted as a canny financier.

ance; but this was common to many other ladies of the court. And I still appeal to my servants round, whether they at any time saw a coach at my door without knowing what persons were in it. On those occasions, when a servant had given me notice, my custom was to go immediately to the door; and, after paying my respects, to take up the coach and two horses very carefully in my hands (for if there were six horses, the postillion always unharnessed four) and place them on a table, where I had fixed a moveable rim quite round, of five inches high, to prevent accidents. And I have often had four coaches and horses at once on my table full of company, while I sat in my chair leaning my face towards them; and when I was engaged with one set, the coachmen would gently drive the others round my table. I have passed many an afternoon very agreeably in these conversations. But I defy the Treasurer, or his two informers (I will name them, and let them make their best of it) Clustril and Drunlo, to prove that any person ever came to me *incognito*, except the Secretary Reldresal, who was sent by express command of his Imperial Majesty, as I have before related. I should not have dwelt so long upon this particular, if it had not been a point wherein the reputation of a great lady is so nearly concerned, to say nothing of my own; although I had the honor to be a *Nardac*, which the Treasurer himself is not; for all the world knows he is only a *Clumglum*, a title inferior by one degree, as that of a marquis is to a duke in England; yet I allow he preceded me in right of his post. These false informations, which I afterwards came to the knowledge of, by an accident not proper to mention, made the Treasurer show his lady for some time an ill countenance, and me a worse; for although he was at last undeceived and reconciled to her, yet I lost all credit with him; and found my interest decline very fast with the Emperor himself, who was indeed too much governed by that favorite.

CHAPTER VII. *The author, being informed of a design to accuse him of high treason, makes his escape to Blefuscu. His reception there.*

Before I proceed to give an account of my leaving this kingdom, it may be proper to inform the reader of a private intrigue which had been for two months forming against me.

I had been hitherto all my life a stranger to courts, for which I was unqualified by the meanness of my condition. I had indeed heard and read enough of the dispositions of great princes and ministers; but never expected to have found such terrible effects of them in so remote a country, governed, as I thought, by very different maxims from those in Europe.

When I was just preparing to pay my attendance on the Emperor of Blefuscu, a considerable person at court (to whom I had been very serviceable at a time when he lay under the highest displeasure of his Imperial Majesty) came to my house very privately at night in a close chair, and without sending his name, desired admittance. The chairmen were dismissed; I put the chair, with his Lordship in it, into my coat-pocket; and giving orders to a trusty servant to say I was indisposed and gone to sleep, I fastened the door of my house, placed the chair on the table, according to my usual custom, and sat down by it. After the common salutations were over, observing his Lordship's countenance full of concern, and enquiring into the reason, he desired I would hear him with patience, in a matter that highly concerned my honor and my life. His speech was to the following effect, for I took notes of it as soon as he left me.

You are to know, said he, that several committees of council have been lately called in the most private manner on your account: and it is but two days since his Majesty came to a full resolution.

You are very sensible that Skyresh Bolgolam (*Galbet*, or High Admiral) hath been your mortal enemy almost ever since your arrival. His original reasons I know not; but his hatred is much increased since your great success against Blefuscu, by which his glory, as Admiral, is obscured. This lord, in conjunction with Flimnap the High Treasurer, whose enmity against you is notorious on account of his lady, Limtoc the General, Lalcon the Chamberlain, and Balmuff the Grand Justiciary, have prepared articles of impeachment against you, for treason, and other capital crimes.[6]

This preface made me so impatient, being conscious of my own merits and innocence, that I was going to interrupt; when he entreated me to be silent, and thus proceeded.

Out of gratitude for the favors you have done me, I procured information of the whole proceedings, and a copy of the articles, wherein I venture my head for your service.

Articles of Impeachment against Quinbus Flestrin
(*the* Man-Mountain).

ARTICLE I

Whereas, by a statute made in the reign of his Imperial Majesty Calin Deffar Plune, it is enacted, that whoever shall make water within the precincts of the royal palace shall be liable to the pains and penalties of high treason: notwithstanding, the said Quinbus Flestrin, in open breach of the said law, under color of extinguishing the fire kindled in the apartment of his Majesty's most dear imperial consort, did maliciously, traitorously, and devilishly, by discharge of his urine, put out the said fire kindled in the said apartment, lying and being within the precincts of the said royal palace; against the statute in that case provided, etc., against the duty, etc.

6. After the Whigs had investigated Oxford and Bolingbroke, both were impeached for high treason, on charges of being sympathetic to the Jacobites and the French.

ARTICLE II

That the said Quinbus Flestrin, having brought the imperial fleet of Blefuscu into the royal port, and being afterwards commanded by his Imperial Majesty to seize all the other ships of the said empire of Blefuscu, and reduce that empire to a province, to be governed by a viceroy from hence; and to destroy and put to death not only all the Big-Endian exiles, but likewise all the people of that empire who would not immediately forsake the Big-Endian heresy: he, the said Flestrin, like a false traitor against his most auspicious, serene, Imperial Majesty, did petition to be excused from the said service, upon pretense of unwillingness to force the consciences, or destroy the liberties and lives of an innocent people.

ARTICLE III

That, whereas certain ambassadors arrived from the court of Blefuscu to sue for peace in his Majesty's court: he the said Flestrin did, like a false traitor, aid, abet, comfort, and divert the said ambassadors; although he knew them to be servants to a prince who was lately an open enemy to his Imperial Majesty, and in open war against his said Majesty.

ARTICLE IV

That the said Quinbus Flestrin, contrary to the duty of a faithful subject, is now preparing to make a voyage to the court and empire of Blefuscu, for which he hath received only verbal license from his Imperial Majesty; and under color of the said license, doth falsely and traitorously intend to take the said voyage, and thereby to aid, comfort, and abet the Emperor of Blefuscu, so late an enemy, and in open war with his Imperial Majesty aforesaid.

There are some other articles, but these are the most important, of which I have read you an abstract.

In the several debates upon this impeachment, it must be confessed that his Majesty gave many marks of his great *lenity*; often urging the services you had done him, and endeavoring to extenuate your crimes. The Treasurer and Admiral insisted that you should be put to the most painful and ignominious death, by setting fire on your house at night; and the General was to attend with twenty thousand men armed with poisoned arrows, to shoot you on the face and hands. Some of your servants were to have private orders to strew a poisonous juice on your shirts and sheets, which would soon make you tear your own flesh, and die in the utmost torture. The General came into the same opinion; so that for a long time there was a majority against you. But his Majesty resolving, if possible, to spare your life, at last brought off[7] the Chamberlain.

Upon this incident, Reldresal, Principal Secretary for Private

---

7. Won over.

Affairs, who always approved[8] himself your true friend, was commanded by the Emperor to deliver his opinion, which he accordingly did; and therein justified the good thoughts you have of him. He allowed your crimes to be great; but that still there was room for mercy, the most commendable virtue in a prince, and for which his Majesty was so justly celebrated. He said, the friendship between you and him was so well known to the world, that perhaps the most honorable board might think him partial: however, in obedience to the command he had received, he would freely offer his sentiments. That if his Majesty, in consideration of your services, and pursuant to his own merciful disposition, would please to spare your life, and only give order to put out both your eyes, he humbly conceived, that by this expedient justice might in some measure be satisfied, and all the world would applaud the *lenity* of the Emperor, as well as the fair and generous proceedings of those who have the honor to be his counselors. That the loss of your eyes would be no impediment to your bodily strength, by which you might still be useful to his Majesty. That blindness is an addition to courage, by concealing dangers from us; that the fear you had for your eyes was the greatest difficulty in bringing over the enemy's fleet; and it would be sufficient for you to see by the eyes of the ministers, since the greatest princes do no more.

This proposal was received with the utmost disapprobation by the whole board. Bolgolam, the Admiral, could not preserve his temper; but rising up in fury, said, he wondered how the Secretary durst presume to give his opinion for preserving the life of a traitor: that the services you had performed were, by all true reasons of state, the great aggravation of your crimes; that you, who were able to extinguish the fire by discharge of urine in her Majesty's apartment (which he mentioned with horror), might, at another time, raise an inundation by the same means, to drown the whole palace; and the same strength which enabled you to bring over the enemy's fleet might serve, upon the first discontent, to carry it back: that he had good reasons to think you were a Big-Endian in your heart; and as treason begins in the heart before it appears in overt acts, so he accused you as a traitor on that account, and therefore insisted you should be put to death.

The Treasurer was of the same opinion; he showed to what straits his Majesty's revenue was reduced by the charge of maintaining you, which would soon grow insupportable: that the Secretary's expedient of putting out your eyes was so far from being a remedy against this evil, that it would probably increase it; as it is manifest from the common practice of blinding some kind of fowl, after which they fed the faster, and grew sooner fat: that his sacred Majesty, and the council, who are your judges, were in their own consciences fully convinced of your guilt; which was a sufficient argu-

8. Proved.

ment to condemn you to death, without the formal proofs required by the strict letter of the law.

But his Imperial Majesty, fully determined against capital punishment, was graciously pleased to say, that since the council thought the loss of your eyes too easy a censure, some other may be inflicted hereafter. And your friend the Secretary humbly desiring to be heard again, in answer to what the Treasurer had objected concerning the great charge his Majesty was at in maintaining you, said, that his Excellency, who had the sole disposal of the Emperor's revenue, might easily provide against this evil, by gradually lessening your establishment; by which, for want of sufficient food, you would grow weak and faint, and lose your appetite, and consequently decay and consume in a few months; neither would the stench of your carcass be then so dangerous, when it should become more than half diminished; and immediately upon your death, five or six thousand of his Majesty's subjects might, in two or three days, cut your flesh from your bones, take it away by cart-loads, and bury it in distant parts to prevent infection; leaving the skeleton as a monument of admiration to posterity.

Thus by the great friendship of the Secretary, the whole affair was compromised. It was strictly enjoined, that the project of starving you by degrees should be kept a secret; but the sentence of putting out your eyes was entered on the books; none dissenting except Bolgolam the Admiral, who being a creature of the Empress, was perpetually instigated by her Majesty to insist upon your death; she having borne perpetual malice against you, on account of that infamous and illegal method you took to extinguish the fire in her apartment.

In three days your friend the Secretary will be directed to come to your house, and read before you the articles of impeachment; and then to signify the great lenity and favor of his Majesty and council; whereby you are only condemned to the loss of your eyes, which his Majesty doth not question you will gratefully and humbly submit to; and twenty of his Majesty's surgeons will attend, in order to see the operation well performed, by discharging very sharp-pointed arrows into the balls of your eyes, as you lie on the ground.

I leave to your prudence what measures you will take; and to avoid suspicion, I must immediately return in as private a manner as I came.

His Lordship did so, and I remained alone, under many doubts and perplexities of mind.

It was a custom introduced by this prince and his ministry (very different, as I have been assured, from the practices of former times), that after the court had decreed any cruel execution, either to gratify the monarch's resentment, or the malice of a favorite, the Emperor always made a speech to his whole council, expressing his great lenity and tenderness, as qualities known and confessed by all the world. This speech was immediately published through the kingdom; nor did any thing terrify the people so much as those encomiums on his Majesty's mercy; because it was observed, that the more these praises were enlarged and insisted on, the more inhuman was the punishment, and the sufferer more innocent. Yet as to myself, I must confess, having never been designed for a courtier, either by my birth or education, I was so ill a judge of things, that I could not discover the lenity and favor of this sentence, but conceived it (perhaps erroneously) rather to be rigorous than gentle. I sometimes thought of standing my trial; for although I could not deny the facts alleged in the several articles, yet I hoped they would admit of some extenuations. But having in my life perused many state trials, which I ever observed to terminate as the judges thought fit to direct, I durst not rely on so dangerous a decision, in so critical a juncture, and against such powerful enemies. Once I was strongly bent upon resistance: for while I had liberty, the whole strength of that empire could hardly subdue me, and I might easily with stones pelt the metropolis to pieces; but I soon rejected that project with horror, by remembering the oath I had made to the Emperor, the favors I received from him, and the high title of *Nardac* he conferred upon me. Neither had I so soon learned the gratitude of courtiers, to persuade myself that his Majesty's present severities acquitted me of all past obligations.

At last I fixed upon a resolution, for which it is probable I may incur some censure, and not unjustly; for I confess I owe the preserving my eyes, and consequently my liberty, to my own great rashness and want of experience: because if I had then known the nature of princes and ministers, which I have since observed in many other courts, and their methods of treating criminals less obnoxious than myself, I should with great alacrity and readiness have submitted to so *easy* a punishment. But hurried on by the precipitancy of youth, and having his Imperial Majesty's license to pay my attendance upon the Emperor of Blefuscu, I took this opportunity, before the three days were elapsed, to send a letter to my friend the Secretary, signifying my resolution of setting out that morning for Blefuscu,[9] pursuant to the leave I had got; and without waiting for an answer, I went to that side of the island where our fleet lay. I seized a large man of war, tied a cable to the prow, and lifting up the anchors, I stripped myself, put my clothes (together with my coverlet, which I carried under my arm) into the vessel; and drawing it after me, between wading and swimming, arrived at the royal port of Blefuscu, where the people had long expected me. They lent me two guides to direct me to the capital city, which is

9. Before his trial for treason could be held, Bolingbroke had escaped to France.

of the same name; I held them in my hands until I came within two hundred yards of the gate; and desired them to signify my arrival to one of the secretaries, and let him know, I there waited his Majesty's commands. I had an answer in about an hour, that his Majesty, attended by the royal family, and great officers of the court, was coming out to receive me. I advanced a hundred yards; the Emperor, and his train, alighted from their horses, the Empress and ladies from their coaches; and I did not perceive they were in any fright or concern. I lay on the ground to kiss his Majesty's and the Empress's hand. I told his Majesty that I was come according to my promise, and with the license of the Emperor my master, to have the honor of seeing so mighty a monarch, and to offer him any service in my power, consistent with my duty to my own prince; not mentioning a word of my disgrace, because I had hitherto no regular information of it, and might suppose myself wholly ignorant of any such design; neither could I reasonably conceive that the Emperor would discover the secret while I was out of his power: wherein, however, it soon appeared I was deceived.

I shall not trouble the reader with the particular account of my reception at this court, which was suitable to the generosity of so great a prince; nor of the difficulties I was in for want of a house and bed, being forced to lie on the ground, wrapped up in my coverlet.

CHAPTER VIII. *The author, by a lucky accident, finds means to leave Blefuscu; and, after some difficulties, returns safe to his native country.*

Three days after my arrival, walking out of curiosity to the northeast coast of the island, I observed, about half a league off, in the sea, somewhat that looked like a boat overturned. I pulled off my shoes and stockings, and wading two or three hundred yards, I found the object to approach nearer by force of the tide; and then plainly saw it to be a real boat, which I supposed might, by some tempest, have been driven from a ship. Whereupon I returned immediately towards the city, and desired his Imperial Majesty to lend me twenty of the tallest vessels he had left after the loss of his fleet, and three thousand seamen under the command of his Vice Admiral. This fleet sailed round, while I went back the shortest way to the coast where I first discovered the boat; I found the tide had driven it still nearer; the seamen were all provided with cordage, which I had beforehand twisted to a sufficient strength. When the ships came up, I stripped myself, and waded till I came within an hundred yards of the boat; after which I was forced to swim till I got up to it. The seamen threw me the end of the cord, which I fastened to a hole in the fore-part of the boat, and the other end to a man of war: but I found all my labor to little purpose; for being out of my depth, I was not able to work. In this necessity, I was forced to swim behind, and push the boat forwards as often as I could, with one of my hands; and the tide favoring me, I advanced so far, that I could just hold up my chin and feel the ground. I rested two or three minutes, and then gave the boat another shove, and so on till the sea was no higher than my armpits. And now the most laborious part being over, I took out my other cables which were stowed in one of the ships, and fastening them first to the boat, and then to nine of the vessels which attended me, the wind being favorable, the seamen towed, and I shoved till we arrived within forty yards of the shore; and waiting till the tide was out, I got dry to the boat, and by the assistance of two thousand men, with ropes and engines,[1] I made a shift to turn it on its bottom, and found it was but little damaged.

I shall not trouble the reader with the difficulties I was under by the help of certain paddles, which cost me ten days making, to get my boat to the royal port of Blefuscu; where a mighty concourse of people appeared upon my arrival, full of wonder at the sight of so prodigious a vessel. I told the Emperor that my good fortune had thrown this boat in my way, to carry me to some place from whence I might return into my native country; and begged his Majesty's orders for getting materials to fit it up, together with license to depart; which, after some kind expostulations, he was pleased to grant.

I did very much wonder, in all this time, not to have heard of any express relating to me from our Emperor to the court of Blefuscu. But I was afterwards given privately to understand, that his Imperial Majesty, never imagining I had the least notice of his designs, believed I was only gone to Blefuscu in performance of my promise, according to the license he had given me, which was well known at our court; and would return in a few days when that ceremony was ended. But he was at last in pain at my long absence; and, after consulting with the Treasurer, and the rest of that cabal, a person of quality was dispatched with the copy of the articles against me. This envoy had instructions to represent to the monarch of Blefuscu the great lenity of his master, who was content to punish me no further than with the loss of my eyes; that I had fled from justice, and if I did not return in two hours, I should be deprived of my title of *Nardac*, and declared a traitor. The envoy further added, that in order to maintain the peace and amity between both empires, his master expected, that his brother of Blefuscu would give orders to have me sent back to Lilliput, bound hand and foot, to be punished as a traitor.

The Emperor of Blefuscu, having taken three days to consult, returned an answer consisting of many civilities and excuses. He

---

1. Mechanical contrivances.

said, that as for sending me bound, his brother knew it was impossible; that although I had deprived him of his fleet, yet he owed great obligations to me for many good offices I had done him in making the peace. That however, both their Majesties would soon be made easy; for I had found a prodigious vessel on the shore, able to carry me on the sea, which he had given order to fit up with my own assistance and direction; and he hoped in a few weeks both empires would be freed from so insupportable an incumbrance.

With this answer the envoy returned to Lilliput, and the monarch of Blefuscu related to me all that had passed, offering me at the same time (but under the strictest confidence) his gracious protection, if I would continue in his service; wherein although I believed him sincere, yet I resolved never more to put any confidence in princes or ministers, where I could possibly avoid it; and therefore, with all due acknowledgements for his favorable intentions, I humbly begged to be excused. I told him, that since fortune, whether good or evil, had thrown a vessel in my way, I was resolved to venture myself in the ocean, rather than be an occasion of difference between two such mighty monarchs. Neither did I find the Emperor at all displeased; and I discovered by a certain accident, that he was very glad of my resolution, and so were most of his ministers.

These considerations moved me to hasten my departure somewhat sooner than I intended; to which the court, impatient to have me gone, very readily contributed. Five hundred workmen were employed to make two sails to my boat, according to my directions, by quilting thirteen fold of their strongest linen together. I was at the pains of making ropes and cables, by twisting ten, twenty or thirty of the thickest and strongest of theirs. A great stone that I happened to find, after a long search by the seashore, served me for an anchor. I had the tallow of three hundred cows for greasing my boat, and other uses. I was at incredible pains in cutting down some of the largest timber trees for oars and masts, wherein I was, however, much assisted by his Majesty's ship-carpenters, who helped me in smoothing them, after I had done the rough work.

In about a month, when all was prepared, I sent to receive his Majesty's commands, and to take my leave. The Emperor and royal family came out of the palace; I lay down on my face to kiss his hand, which he very graciously gave me: so did the Empress, and young princes of the blood. His Majesty presented me with fifty purses of two hundred *sprugs* apiece, together with his picture at full length, which I put immediately into one of my gloves, to keep it from being hurt. The ceremonies at my departure were too many to trouble the reader with at this time.

I stored the boat with the carcasses of an hundred oxen, and three hundred sheep, with bread and drink proportionable, and as much meat ready dressed as four hundred cooks could provide. I took with me six cows and two bulls alive, with as many ewes and rams, intending to carry them into my own country, and propagate the breed. And to feed them on board, I had a good bundle of hay, and a bag of corn.[2] I would gladly have taken a dozen of the natives; but this was a thing the Emperor would by no means permit; and besides a diligent search into my pockets, his Majesty engaged my honor not to carry away any of his subjects, although with their own consent and desire.

Having thus prepared all things as well as I was able, I set sail on the twenty-fourth day of September, 1701, at six in the morning; and when I had gone about four leagues to the northward, the wind being at southeast, at six in the evening, I descried a small island about half a league to the northwest. I advanced forward, and cast anchor on the lee-side of the island, which seemed to be uninhabited. I then took some refreshment, and went to my rest. I slept well, and as I conjecture at least six hours; for I found the day broke in two hours after I awaked. It was a clear night; I eat my breakfast before the sun was up; and heaving anchor, the wind being favorable, I steered the same course that I had done the day before, wherein I was directed by my pocket compass. My intention was to reach, if possible, one of those islands which I had reason to believe lay to the northeast of Van Diemen's Land. I discovered nothing all that day; but upon the next, about three in the afternoon, when I had by my computation made twenty-four leagues from Blefuscu, I descried a sail steering to the southeast; my course was due east. I hailed her, but could get no answer; yet I found I gained upon her, for the wind slackened. I made all the sail I could, and in half an hour she spied me, then hung out her ancient,[3] and discharged a gun. It is not easy to express the joy I was in upon the unexpected hope of once more seeing my beloved country, and the dear pledges[4] I had left in it. The ship slackened her sails, and I came up with her between five and six in the evening, September 26; but my heart leapt within me to see her English colors. I put my cows and sheep into my coat-pockets and got on board with all my little cargo of provisions. The vessel was an English merchant-man, returning from Japan by the North and South Seas;[5] the captain, Mr. John Biddel of Deptford, a very civil man, and an excellent sailor. We were now in the latitude of 30 degrees south; there were about fifty men in the ship; and here I met an old comrade of mine, one Peter Williams, who gave me a good character to the captain. This gentleman treated me with kindness, and desired I

2. Wheat.
3. Flag.

4. Hostages (i.e., his family).
5. North and South Pacific.

would let him know what place I came from last, and whither I was bound; which I did in few words; but he thought I was raving, and that the dangers I underwent had disturbed my head; whereupon I took my black cattle and sheep out of my pocket, which, after great astonishment, clearly convinced him of my veracity. I then showed him the gold given me by the Emperor of Blefuscu, together with his Majesty's picture at full length, and some other rarities of that country. I gave him two purses of two hundred *sprugs* each, and promised, when we arrived in England, to make him a present of a cow and a sheep big with young.

I shall not trouble the reader with a particular account of this voyage; which was very prosperous for the most part. We arrived in the Downs[6] on the 13th of April, 1702. I had only one misfortune, that the rats on board carried away one of my sheep; I found her bones in a hole, picked clean from the flesh. The rest of my cattle I got safe on shore, and set them a grazing in a bowling-green at Greenwich, where the fineness of the grass made them feed very heartily, though I had always feared the contrary; neither could I possibly have preserved them in so long a voyage, if the captain had not allowed me some of his best biscuit, which rubbed to powder, and mingled with water, was their constant food. The short time I continued in England, I made a considerable profit by showing my cattle to many persons of quality, and others: and before I began my second voyage, I sold them for six hundred pounds. Since my last return, I find the breed is considerably increased, especially the sheep; which I hope will prove much to the advantage of the woolen manufacture, by the fineness of the fleeces.

I stayed but two months with my wife and family; for my insatiable desire of seeing foreign countries would suffer me to continue no longer. I left fifteen hundred pounds with my wife, and fixed her in a good house at Redriff. My remaining stock I carried with me, part in money, and part in goods, in hopes to improve my fortunes. My eldest uncle, John, had left me an estate in land, near Epping, of about thirty pounds a year; and I had a long lease of the Black Bull in Fetter Lane, which yielded me as much more: so that I was not in any danger of leaving my family upon the parish.[7] My son Johnny, named so after his uncle, was at the grammar school, and a towardly[8] child. My daughter Betty (who is now well married, and has children) was then at her needlework. I took leave of my wife, and boy and girl, with tears on both sides; and went on board the *Adventure*, a merchant-ship of three hundred tons, bound for Surat, Captain John Nicholas of Liverpool, Commander. But my account of this voyage must be referred to the second part of my *Travels*.

---

6. A rendezvous for ships off the south-east coast of England.
7. On welfare (living on charity given by the parish).
8. Promising.

Part II. A Voyage to Brobdingnag

CHAPTER I. *A great storm described. The longboat[1] sent to fetch water; the Author goes with it to discover the country. He is left on shore, is seized by one of the natives, and carried to a farmer's house. His reception there, with several accidents that happened there. A description of the inhabitants.*

Having been condemned by nature and fortune to an active and restless life, in ten months after my return I again left my native country, and took shipping in the Downs on the 20th day of June, 1702, in the *Adventure,* Captain John Nicholas, a Cornish man, Commander, bound for Surat.[2] We had a very prosperous gale till we arrived at the Cape of Good Hope, where we landed for fresh water, but discovering a leak we unshipped our goods and wintered there; for the Captain falling sick of an ague, we could not leave the Cape till the end of March. We then set sail, and had a good voyage till we passed the Straits of Madagascar; but having got northward of that island, and to about five degrees south latitude, the winds, which in those seas are observed to blow a constant equal gale between the north and west from the beginning of December to the beginning of May, on the 19th of April began to blow with much greater violence and more westerly than usual, continuing so for twenty days together, during which time we were driven a little to the east of the Molucca Islands and about three degrees northward of the Line, as our Captain found by an observation he took the 2nd of May, at which time the wind ceased, and it was a perfect calm, whereat I was not a little rejoiced. But he, being a man well experienced in the navigation of those seas, bid us all prepare against a storm, which accordingly happened the day following: for a southern wind, called the southern monsoon, began to set in.

Finding it was likely to overblow,[3] we took in our spritsail, and stood by to hand the foresail; but making foul weather, we looked the guns were all fast, and handed the mizzen. The ship lay very broad off, so we thought it better spooning before the sea, than trying or hulling. We reefed the foresail and set him, we hauled aft the foresheet; the helm was hard aweather. The ship wore bravely. We belayed the fore-downhaul; but the sail was split, and we hauled down the yard and got the sail into the ship, and unbound all the things clear of it. It was a very fierce storm; the sea broke

---

1. The largest boat carried by a merchant sailing vessel.
2. In India. The geography of the voyage is simple: The *Adventure,* after sailing up the east coast of Africa to about 5° south of the equator (the "Line"), is blown past India into the Malay Archipelago, north of the islands of Buru and Ceram. The storm then drives the ship northward and eastward, away from the coast of Siberia ("Great Tartary") into the northeast Pacific, at that time unexplored. Brobdingnag lies somewhere in the vicinity of Alaska.
3. This paragraph is taken almost literally from Samuel Sturmy's *Mariner's Magazine* (1669). Swift is ridiculing the use of technical terms by writers of popular voyages.

strange and dangerous. We hauled off upon the lanyard of the whip-staff, and helped the man at helm. We would not get down our topmast, but let all stand, because she scudded before the sea very well, and we knew that the topmast being aloft, the ship was the wholesomer, and made better way through the sea, seeing we had searoom. When the storm was over, we set foresail and mainsail, and brought the ship to. Then we set the mizzen, main topsail and the fore topsail. Our course was east-northeast, the wind was at southwest. We got the starboard tacks aboard, we cast off our weather braces and lifts; we set in the lee braces, and hauled forward by the weather bowlings, and hauled them tight, and belayed them, and hauled over the mizzen tack to windward, and kept her full and by as near as she would lie.

During this storm, which was followed by a strong wind west-southwest, we were carried by my computation about five hundred leagues to the east, so that the oldest sailor on board could not tell in what part of the world we were. Our provisions held out well, our ship was stanch, and our crew all in good health; but we lay in the utmost distress for water. We thought it best to hold on the same course rather than turn more northerly, which might have brought us to the northwest parts of Great Tartary, and into the frozen sea.

On the 16th day of June, 1703, a boy on the topmast discovered land. On the 17th we came in full view of a great island or continent (for we knew not whether) on the south side whereof was a small neck of land jutting out into the sea, and a creek[4] too shallow to hold a ship of above one hundred tons. We cast anchor within a league of this creek, and our Captain sent a dozen of his men well armed in the longboat, with vessels for water if any could be found. I desired his leave to go with them that I might see the country and make what discoveries I could. When we came to land we saw no river or spring, nor any sign of inhabitants. Our men therefore wandered on the shore to find out some fresh water near the sea, and I walked alone about a mile on the other side, where I observed the country all barren and rocky. I now began to be weary, and seeing nothing to entertain my curiosity, I returned gently down towards the creek; and the sea being full in my view, I saw our men already got into the boat, and rowing for life to the ship. I was going to hollow after them, although it had been to little purpose, when I observed a huge creature walking after them in the sea as fast as he could; he waded not much deeper than his knees and took prodigious strides, but our men had the start of him half a league, and the sea thereabouts being full of sharp-pointed rocks, the monster was not able to overtake the boat. This I was afterwards told, for I durst not stay to see the issue of that adventure, but ran as fast as I could the way I first went, and

4. A small bay or cove, affording anchorage.

then climbed up a steep hill, which gave me some prospect of the country. I found it fully cultivated; but that which first surprised me was the length of the grass, which, in those grounds that seemed to be kept for hay, was about twenty foot high.[5]

I fell into a highroad, for so I took it to be, although it served to the inhabitants only as a footpath through a field of barley. Here I walked on for some time, but could see little on either side, it being now near harvest, and the corn[6] rising at least forty foot. I was an hour walking to the end of this field, which was fenced in with a hedge of at least one hundred and twenty foot high, and the trees so lofty that I could make no computation of their altitude. There was a stile to pass from this field into the next: it had four steps, and a stone to cross over when you came to the utmost. It was impossible for me to climb this stile, because every step was six foot high, and the upper stone above twenty. I was endeavoring to find some gap in the hedge when I discovered one of the inhabitants in the next field advancing towards the stile, of the same size with him whom I saw in the sea pursuing our boat. He appeared as tall as an ordinary spire-steeple, and took about ten yards at every stride, as near as I could guess. I was struck with the utmost fear and astonishment, and ran to hide myself in the corn, from whence I saw him at the top of the stile, looking back into the next field on the right hand; and heard him call in a voice many degrees louder than a speaking trumpet; but the noise was so high in the air that at first I certainly thought it was thunder. Whereupon seven monsters like himself came towards him with reaping hooks in their hands, each hook about the largeness of six scythes. These people were not so well clad as the first, whose servants or laborers they seemed to be. For, upon some words he spoke, they went to reap the corn in the field where I lay. I kept from them at as great a distance as I could, but was forced to move with extreme difficulty, for the stalks of the corn were sometimes not above a foot distant, so that I could hardly squeeze my body betwixt them. However, I made a shift to go forward till I came to a part of the field where the corn had been laid by the rain and wind; here it was impossible for me to advance a step, for the stalks were so interwoven that I could not creep through, and the beards of the fallen ears so strong and pointed that they pierced through my clothes into my flesh. At the same time I heard the reapers not above an hundred yards behind me. Being quite dispirited with toil, and wholly overcome by grief and despair, I lay down between two ridges and heartily wished I might there end my days. I bemoaned my desolate widow and fatherless children; I lamented my own folly and willfulness in attempting a second voyage against the advice of all my friends and relations. In this terrible agitation of mind, I could not forbear thinking of Lilliput, whose inhabitants looked upon me as the

5. Swift's intention, not always carried out accurately, is that everything in Brobdingnag should be, in relation to our familiar world, on a scale of ten to one.

6. Wheat, not maize.

greatest prodigy that ever appeared in the world; where I was able
to draw an imperial fleet in my hand, and perform those other actions which will be recorded forever in the chronicles of that empire, while posterity shall hardly believe them, although attested by
millions. I reflected what a mortification it must prove to me to
appear as inconsiderable in this nation as one single Lilliputian
would be among us. But this I conceived was to be the least of my
misfortunes; for as human creatures are observed to be more savage
and cruel in proportion to their bulk, what could I expect but to
be a morsel in the mouth of the first among these enormous barbarians who should happen to seize me? Undoubtedly philosophers
are in the right when they tell us that nothing is great or little
otherwise than by comparison. It might have pleased fortune to
let the Lilliputians find some nation where the people were as diminutive with respect to them as they were to me. And who knows
but that even this prodigious race of mortals might be equally overmatched in some distant part of the world, whereof we have yet no
discovery?

Scared and confounded as I was, I could not forbear going on
with these reflections; when one of the reapers approaching within
ten yards of the ridge where I lay, made me apprehend that with
the next step I should be squashed to death under his foot, or cut
in two with his reaping hook. And therefore when he was again
about to move, I screamed as loud as fear could make me. Whereupon the huge creature trod short, and looking round about under
him for some time, at last espied me as I lay on the ground. He
considered a while with the caution of one who endeavors to lay
hold on a small dangerous animal in such a manner that it shall
not be able either to scratch or to bite him, as I myself have sometimes done with a weasel in England. At length he ventured to take
me up behind by the middle between his forefinger and thumb,
and brought me within three yards of his eyes, that he might behold my shape more perfectly. I guessed his meaning, and my good
fortune gave me so much presence of mind that I resolved not to
struggle in the least as he held me in the air about sixty foot from
the ground, although he grievously pinched my sides, for fear I
should slip through his fingers. All I ventured was to raise mine
eyes towards the sun, and place my hands together in a supplicating posture, and to speak some words in an humble melancholy
tone, suitable to the condition I then was in. For I apprehended
every moment that he would dash me against the ground, as we
usually do any little hateful animal which we have a mind to destroy. But my good star would have it that he appeared pleased with
my voice and gestures, and began to look upon me as a curiosity,
much wondering to hear me pronounce articulate words, although
he could not understand them. In the meantime I was not able to
forbear groaning and shedding tears and turning my head towards

my sides, letting him know, as well as I could, how cruelly I was hurt by the pressure of his thumb and finger. He seemed to apprehend my meaning; for, lifting up the lappet[7] of his coat, he put me gently into it, and immediately ran along with me to his master, who was a substantial farmer, and the same person I had first seen in the field.

The farmer having (as I supposed by their talk) received such an account of me as his servant could give him, took a piece of a small straw about the size of a walking staff, and therewith lifted up the lappets of my coat, which it seems he thought to be some kind of covering that nature had given me. He blew my hairs aside to take a better view of my face. He called his hinds[8] about him, and asked them (as I afterwards learned) whether they had ever seen in the fields any little creature that resembled me. He then placed me softly on the ground upon all four; but I got immediately up, and walked slowly backwards and forwards, to let those people see I had no intent to run away. They all sat down in a circle about me, the better to observe my motions. I pulled off my hat, and made a low bow towards the farmer; I fell on my knees, and lifted up my hands and eyes, and spoke several words as loud as I could; I took a purse of gold out of my pocket, and humbly presented it to him. He received it on the palm of his hand, then applied it close to his eye to see what it was, and afterwards turned it several times with the point of a pin (which he took out of his sleeve), but could make nothing of it. Whereupon I made a sign that he should place his hand on the ground; I then took the purse, and opening it, poured all the gold into his palm. There were six Spanish pieces of four pistoles each, beside twenty or thirty smaller coins. I saw him wet the tip of his little finger upon his tongue, and take up one of my largest pieces, and then another; but he seemed to be wholly ignorant what they were. He made me a sign to put them again into my purse, and the purse again into my pocket, which after offering to him several times, I thought it best to do.

The farmer by this time was convinced I must be a rational creature. He spoke often to me, but the sound of his voice pierced my ears like that of a water mill, yet his words were articulate enough. I answered as loud as I could in several languages, and he often laid his ear within two yards of me, but all in vain, for we were wholly unintelligible to each other. He then sent his servants to their work, and taking his handkerchief out of his pocket, he doubled and spread it on his hand, which he placed flat on the ground with the palm upwards, making me a sign to step into it, as I could easily do, for it was not above a foot in thickness. I thought it my part to obey, and for fear of falling, laid myself at full length upon the handkerchief, with the remainder of which

7. Flap or fold.   8. Farm servants.

he lapped me up to the head for further security, and in this manner carried me home to his house. There he called his wife, and showed me to her; but she screamed and ran back as women in England do at the sight of a toad or a spider. However, when she had a while seen my behavior, and how well I observed the signs her husband made, she was soon reconciled, and by degrees grew extremely tender of me.

It was about twelve at noon, and a servant brought in dinner. It was only one substantial dish of meat (fit for the plain condition of an husbandman) in a dish of about four-and-twenty foot diameter. The company were the farmer and his wife, three children, and an old grandmother. When they were sat down, the farmer placed me at some distance from him on the table, which was thirty foot high from the floor. I was in a terrible fright, and kept as far as I could from the edge, for fear of falling. The wife minced a bit of meat, then crumbled some bread on a trencher,[9] and placed it before me. I made her a low bow, took out my knife and fork, and fell to eat; which gave them exceeding delight. The mistress sent her maid for a small dram cup, which held about two gallons, and filled it with drink; I took up the vessel with much difficulty in both hands, and in a most respectful manner drank to her ladyship's health, expressing the words as loud as I could in English; which made the company laugh so heartily that I was almost deafened with the noise. This liquor tasted like a small cider,[1] and was not unpleasant. Then the master made me a sign to come to his trencher side; but as I walked on the table, being in great surprise all the time, as the indulgent reader will easily conceive and excuse, I happened to stumble against a crust, and fell flat on my face, but received no hurt. I got up immediately, and observing the good people to be in much concern, I took my hat (which I held under my arm out of good manners) and waving it over my head, made three huzzas to show I had got no mischief by my fall. But advancing forwards toward my master (as I shall henceforth call him), his youngest son who sat next him, an arch[2] boy of about ten years old, took me up by the legs, and held me so high in the air that I trembled every limb; but his father snatched me from him, and at the same time gave him such a box on the left ear as would have felled an European troop of horse to the earth, ordering him to be taken from the table. But being afraid the boy might owe me a spite, and well remembering how mischievous all children among us naturally are to sparrows, rabbits, young kittens, and puppy dogs, I fell on my knees, and pointing to the boy, made my master to understand, as well as I could, that I desired his son might be pardoned. The father complied, and the lad took his seat again; whereupon I went to him and kissed his hand, which my master took, and made him stroke me gently with it.

9. A platter.
1. I.e., weak cider.

2. Mischievous.

In the midst of dinner, my mistress's favorite cat leaped into her lap. I heard a noise behind me like that of a dozen stocking weavers at work; and turning my head, I found it proceeded from the purring of this animal, who seemed to be three times larger than an ox, as I computed by the view of her head and one of her paws, while her mistress was feeding and stroking her. The fierceness of this creature's countenance altogether discomposed me, although I stood at the farther end of the table, above fifty foot off, and although my mistress held her fast for fear she might give a spring and seize me in her talons. But it happened there was no danger, for the cat took not the least notice of me when my master placed me within three yards of her. And as I have been always told, and found true by experience in my travels, that flying or discovering[3] fear before a fierce animal is a certain way to make it pursue or attack you, so I resolved in this dangerous juncture to show no manner of concern. I walked with intrepidity five or six times before the very head of the cat, and came within half a yard of her; whereupon she drew herself back, as if she were more afraid of me; I had less apprehension concerning the dogs, whereof three or four came into the room, as it is usual in farmers' houses; one of which was a mastiff, equal in bulk to four elephants, and a greyhound, somewhat taller than the mastiff, but not so large.

When dinner was almost done, the nurse came in with a child of a year old in her arms, who immediately spied me, and began a squall that you might have heard from London Bridge to Chelsea, after the usual oratory of infants, to get me for a plaything. The mother out of pure indulgence took me up, and put me towards the child, who presently seized me by the middle, and got my head in his mouth, where I roared so loud that the urchin was frighted and let me drop; and I should infallibly have broke my neck if the mother had not held her apron under me. The nurse to quiet her babe made use of a rattle, which was a kind of hollow vessel filled with great stones, and fastened by a cable to the child's waist: but all in vain, so that she was forced to apply the last remedy by giving it suck. I must confess no object ever disgusted me so much as the sight of her monstrous breast, which I cannot tell what to compare with so as to give the curious reader an idea of its bulk, shape, and color. It stood prominent six foot, and could not be less than sixteen in circumference. The nipple was about half the bigness of my head, and the hue both of that and the dug so varified with spots, pimples, and freckles that nothing could appear more nauseous: for I had a near sight of her, she sitting down the more conveniently to give suck, and I standing on the table. This made me reflect upon the fair skins of our English ladies, who appear so beautiful to us, only because they are of our own size, and their defects not to be seen but through a magnifying glass, where

3. Revealing.

we find by experiment that the smoothest and whitest skins look rough and coarse and ill colored.

I remember when I was at Lilliput, the complexion of those diminutive people appeared to me the fairest in the world; and talking upon this subject with a person of learning there, who was an intimate friend of mine, he said that my face appeared much fairer and smoother when he looked on me from the ground than it did upon a nearer view when I took him up in my hand and brought him close, which he confessed was at first a very shocking sight. He said he could discover great holes in my skin; that the stumps of my beard were ten times stronger than the bristles of a boar, and my complexion made up of several colors altogether disagreeable: although I must beg leave to say for myself that I am as fair as most of my sex and country and very little sunburnt by all my travels. On the other side, discoursing of the ladies in that Emperor's court, he used to tell me one had freckles, another too wide a mouth, a third too large a nose; nothing of which I was able to distinguish. I confess this reflection was obvious enough; which however I could not forbear, lest the reader might think those vast creatures were actually deformed: for I must do them justice to say they are a comely race of people; and particularly the features of my master's countenance, although he were but a farmer, when I beheld him from the height of sixty foot, appeared very well proportioned.

When dinner was done, my master went out to his laborers; and as I could discover by his voice and gesture, gave his wife a strict charge to take care of me. I was very much tired and disposed to sleep, which my mistress perceiving, she put me on her own bed, and covered me with a clean white handkerchief, but larger and coarser than the mainsail of a man-of-war.

I slept about two hours, and dreamed I was at home with my wife and children, which aggravated my sorrows when I awaked and found myself alone in a vast room, between two and three hundred foot wide, and above two hundred high, lying in a bed twenty yards wide. My mistress was gone about her household affairs, and had locked me in. The bed was eight yards from the floor. Some natural necessities required me to get down; I durst not presume to call, and if I had, it would have been in vain with such a voice as mine at so great a distance from the room where I lay to the kitchen where the family kept. While I was under these circumstances, two rats crept up the curtains, and ran smelling backwards and forwards on the bed. One of them came up almost to my face; whereupon I rose in a fright, and drew out my hanger[4] to defend myself. These horrible animals had the boldness to attack me on both sides, and one of them held his forefeet at my collar; but I had the good fortune to rip up his belly before he

4. A short, broad sword.

could do me any mischief. He fell down at my feet; and the other seeing the fate of his comrade, made his escape, but not without one good wound on the back, which I gave him as he fled, and made the blood run trickling from him. After this exploit I walked gently to and fro on the bed, to recover my breath and loss of spirits. These creatures were of the size of a large mastiff, but infinitely more nimble and fierce; so that if I had taken off my belt before I went to sleep, I must have infallibly been torn to pieces and devoured. I measured the tail of the dead rat, and found it to be two yards long, wanting an inch; but it went against my stomach to drag the carcass off the bed, where it lay still bleeding; I observed it had yet some life, but with a strong slash cross the neck, I thoroughly dispatched it.

Soon after, my mistress came into the room, who seeing me all bloody, ran and took me up in her hand. I pointed to the dead rat, smiling and making other signs to show I was not hurt, whereat she was extremely rejoiced, calling the maid to take up the dead rat with a pair of tongs, and throw it out of the window. Then she set me on a table, where I showed her my hanger all bloody, and wiping it on the lappet of my coat, returned it to the scabbard. I was pressed to do more than one thing, which another could not do for me, and therefore endeavored to make my mistress understand that I desired to be set down on the floor; which after she had done, my bashfulness would not suffer me to express myself farther than by pointing to the door, and bowing several times. The good woman with much difficulty at last perceived what I would be at, and taking me up again in her hand, walked into the garden, where she set me down. I went on one side about two hundred yards; and beckoning to her not to look or to follow me, I hid myself between two leaves of sorrel, and there discharged the necessities of nature.

I hope the gentle reader will excuse me for dwelling on these and the like particulars, which however insignificant they may appear to groveling vulgar[5] minds, yet will certainly help a philosopher to enlarge his thoughts and imagination, and apply them to the benefit of public as well as private life, which was my sole design in presenting this and other accounts of my travels to the world; wherein I have been chiefly studious of truth, without affecting any ornaments of learning or of style. But the whole scene of this voyage made so strong an impression on my mind, and is so deeply fixed in my memory, that in committing it to paper I did not omit one material circumstance; however, upon a strict review, I blotted out several passages of less moment which were in my first copy, for fear of being censured as tedious and trifling, whereof travelers are often, perhaps not without justice, accused.

5. Commonplace, uncultivated, in contrast to the scientist ("philosopher"); an irony.

CHAPTER II. *A description of the farmer's daughter. The Author carried to a market town, and then to the metropolis. The particulars of his journey.*

My mistress had a daughter of nine years old, a child of towardly parts for her age, very dexterous at her needle, and skillful in dressing her baby.[6] Her mother and she contrived to fit up the baby's cradle for me against night: the cradle was put into a small drawer of a cabinet, and the drawer placed upon a hanging shelf for fear of the rats. This was my bed all the time I stayed with those people, although made more convenient by degrees as I began to learn their language, and make my wants known. This young girl was so handy, that after I had once or twice pulled off my clothes before her, she was able to dress and undress me, although I never gave her that trouble when she would let me do either myself. She made me seven shirts, and some other linen of as fine cloth as could be got, which indeed was coarser than sackcloth, and these she constantly washed for me with her own hands. She was likewise my schoolmistress to teach me the language: when I pointed to anything, she told me the name of it in her own tongue, so that in a few days I was able to call for whatever I had a mind to. She was very good-natured, and not above forty foot high, being little for her age. She gave me the name of *Grildrig*, which the family took up, and afterwards the whole kingdom. The word imports what the Latins call *nanunculus*, the Italian *homunceletino*,[7] and the English *mannikin*. To her I chiefly owe my preservation in that country: we never parted while I was there; I called her my *Glumdalclitch*, or little nurse: and I should be guilty of great ingratitude if I omitted this honorable mention of her care and affection towards me, which I heartily wish it lay in my power to requite as she deserves, instead of being the innocent but unhappy instrument of her disgrace, as I have too much reason to fear.

It now began to be known and talked of in the neighborhood that my master had found a strange animal in the field, about the bigness of a *splacknuck*, but exactly shaped in every part like a human creature, which it likewise imitated in all its actions: seemed to speak in a little language of its own, had already learned several words of theirs, went erect upon two legs, was tame and gentle, would come when it was called, do whatever it was bid, had the finest limbs in the world, and a complexion fairer than a nobleman's daughter of three years old. Another farmer who lived hard by, and was a particular friend of my master, came on a visit on purpose to inquire into the truth of this story. I was immediately produced, and placed upon a table, where I walked as I was commanded, drew my hanger, put it up again, made my reverence to my master's

6. Doll.
7. The Latin and Italian words are Swift's own coinages, as, of course, are the various words from the Brobdingnagian language.

guest, asked him in his own language how he did, and told him he was welcome, just as my little nurse had instructed me. This man, who was old and dimsighted, put on his spectacles to behold me better, at which I could not forbear laughing very heartily, for his eyes appeared like the full moon shining into a chamber at two windows. Our people, who discovered the cause of my mirth, bore me company in laughing, at which the old fellow was fool enough to be angry and out of countenance. He had the character of a great miser, and to my misfortune he well deserved it by the cursed advice he gave my master to show me as a sight upon a market day in the next town, which was half an hour's riding, about two and twenty miles from our house. I guessed there was some mischief contriving when I observed my master and his friend whispering long together, sometimes pointing at me; and my fears made me fancy that I overheard and understood some of their words. But the next morning Glumdalclitch, my little nurse, told me the whole matter, which she had cunningly picked out from her mother. The poor girl laid me on her bosom, and fell a weeping with shame and grief. She apprehended some mischief would happen to me from rude vulgar folks, who might squeeze me to death, or break one of my limbs by taking me in their hands. She had also observed how modest I was in my nature, how nicely I regarded my honor, and what an indignity I should conceive it to be exposed for money as a public spectacle to the meanest of the people. She said her papa and mamma had promised that Grildrig should be hers; but now she found they meant to serve her as they did last year, when they pretended to give her a lamb, and yet, as soon as it was fat, sold it to a butcher. For my own part, I may truly affirm that I was less concerned than my nurse. I had a strong hope, which never left me, that I should one day recover my liberty; and as to the ignominy of being carried about for a monster, I considered myself to be a perfect stranger in the country, and that such a misfortune could never be charged upon me as a reproach, if ever I should return to England; since the King of Great Britain himself, in my condition, must have undergone the same distress.

My master, pursuant to the advice of his friend, carried me in a box the next market day to the neighboring town, and took along with him his little daughter, my nurse, upon a pillion[8] behind him. The box was close on every side, with a little door for me to go in and out, and a few gimlet holes to let in air. The girl had been so careful to put the quilt of her baby's bed into it, for me to lie down on. However, I was terribly shaken and discomposed in this journey, although it were but of half an hour. For the horse went about forty foot at every step, and trotted so high that the agitation was equal to the rising and falling of a ship in a great storm, but much more frequent. Our journey was somewhat further than

8. A pad attached to the hinder part of a saddle, on which a second person, usually a woman, could ride.

from London to St. Albans. My master alighted at an inn which he used to frequent; and after consulting a while with the innkeeper, and making some necessary preparations, he hired the *Grultrud,* or crier, to give notice through the town of a strange creature to be seen at the Sign of the Green Eagle, not so big as a *splacknuck* (an animal in that country very finely shaped, about six foot long), and in every part of the body resembling an human creature, could speak several words and perform an hundred diverting tricks.

I was placed upon a table in the largest room of the inn, which might be near three hundred foot square. My little nurse stood on a low stool close to the table, to take care of me, and direct what I should do. My master, to avoid a crowd, would suffer only thirty people at a time to see me. I walked about on the table as the girl commanded; she asked me questions as far as she knew my understanding of the language reached, and I answered them as loud as I could. I turned about several times to the company, paid my humble respects, said they were welcome, and used some other speeches I had been taught. I took up a thimble filled with liquor, which Glumdalclitch had given me for a cup, and drank their health. I drew out my hanger, and flourished with it after the manner of fencers in England. My nurse gave me part of a straw, which I exercised as a pike, having learned the art in my youth. I was that day shown to twelve sets of company, and as often forced to go over again with the same fopperies, till I was half dead with weariness and vexation. For those who had seen me made such wonderful reports that the people were ready to break down the doors to come in. My master for his own interest would not suffer anyone to touch me except my nurse; and, to prevent danger, benches were set round the table at such a distance as put me out of everybody's reach. However, an unlucky schoolboy aimed a hazelnut directly at my head, which very narrowly missed me; otherwise, it came with so much violence that it would have infallibly knocked out my brains, for it was almost as large as a small pumpion:[9] but I had the satisfaction to see the young rogue well beaten, and turned out of the room.

My master gave public notice that he would show me again the next market day, and in the meantime he prepared a more convenient vehicle for me, which he had reason enough to do; for I was so tired with my first journey, and with entertaining company for eight hours together, that I could hardly stand upon my legs or speak a word. It was at least three days before I recovered my strength; and that I might have no rest at home, all the neighboring gentlemen from an hundred miles round, hearing of my fame, came to see me at my master's own house. There could not be fewer than thirty persons with their wives and children (for the country is very populous); and my master demanded the rate of a

9. Pumpkin.

full room whenever he showed me at home, although it were only to a single family. So that for some time I had but little ease every day of the week (except Wednesday, which is their Sabbath) although I were not carried to the town.

My master finding how profitable I was like to be, resolved to carry me to the most considerable cities of the kingdom. Having therefore provided himself with all things necessary for a long journey, and settled his affairs at home, he took leave of his wife; and upon the 17th of August, 1703, about two months after my arrival, we set out for the metropolis, situated near the middle of that empire, and about three thousand miles distance from our house. My master made his daughter Glumdalclitch ride behind him. She carried me on her lap in a box tied about her waist. The girl had lined it on all sides with the softest cloth she could get, well quilted underneath, furnished it with her baby's bed, provided me with linen and other necessaries, and made everything as convenient as she could. We had no other company but a boy of the house, who rode after us with the luggage.

My master's design was to show me in all the towns by the way, and to step out of the road for fifty or an hundred miles to any village or person of quality's house where he might expect custom. We made easy journeys of not above seven or eight score miles a day: for Glumdalclitch, on purpose to spare me, complained she was tired with the trotting of the horse. She often took me out of my box at my own desire, to give me air and show me the country, but always held me fast by leading strings. We passed over five or six rivers many degrees broader and deeper than the Nile or the Ganges; and there was hardly a rivulet so small as the Thames at London Bridge. We were ten weeks in our journey, and I was shown in eighteen large towns, besides many large villages and private families.

On the 26th day of October, we arrived at the metropolis, called in their language *Lorbrulgrud*, or Pride of the Universe. My master took a lodging in the principal street of the city, not far from the royal palace, and put out bills in the usual form, containing an exact description of my person and parts. He hired a large room between three and four hundred foot wide. He provided a table sixty foot in diameter, upon which I was to act my part, and palisadoed it round three foot from the edge, and as many high, to prevent my falling over. I was shown ten times a day to the wonder and satisfaction of all people. I could now speak the language tolerably well, and perfectly understood every word that was spoken to me. Besides, I had learned their alphabet, and could make a shift to explain a sentence here and there; for Glumdalclitch had been my instructor while we were at home, and at leisure hours during our journey. She carried a little book in her pocket, not much larger than a Sanson's *Atlas;*[1] it was a common treatise for the use of young girls, giving a short account of their religion: out of this she taught me my letters, and interpreted the words.

CHAPTER III. *The Author sent for to Court. The Queen buys him of his master, the farmer, and presents him to the King. He disputes with his Majesty's great scholars. An apartment at Court provided for the Author. He is in high favor with the Queen. He stands up for the honor of his own country. His quarrels with the Queen's dwarf.*

The frequent labors I underwent every day made in a few weeks a very considerable change in my health: the more my master got by me, the more unsatiable he grew. I had quite lost my stomach, and was almost reduced to a skeleton. The farmer observed it, and concluding I soon must die, resolved to make as good a hand of me as he could. While he was thus reasoning and resolving with himself, a *Slardral,* or Gentleman Usher, came from Court, commanding my master to carry me immediately thither for the diversion of the Queen and her ladies. Some of the latter had already been to see me and reported strange things of my beauty, behavior, and good sense. Her Majesty and those who attended her were beyond measure delighted with my demeanor. I fell on my knees and begged the honor of kissing her Imperial foot; but this gracious princess held out her little finger towards me (after I was set on a table), which I embraced in both my arms, and put the tip of it, with the utmost respect, to my lip. She made me some general questions about my country and my travels, which I answered as distinctly and in as few words as I could. She asked whether I would be content to live at Court. I bowed down to the board of the table, and humbly answered that I was my master's slave, but if I were at my own disposal, I should be proud to devote my life to her Majesty's service. She then asked my master whether he were willing to sell me at a good price. He, who apprehended I could not live a month, was ready enough to part with me, and demanded a thousand pieces of gold, which were ordered him on the spot, each piece being about the bigness of eight hundred moidores;[2] but, allowing for the proportion of all things between that country and Europe, and the high price of gold among them, was hardly so great a sum as a thousand guineas would be in England. I then said to the Queen, since I was now her Majesty's most humble creature and vassal, I must beg the favor that Glumdalclitch, who had always tended me with so much care and kindness, and understood to do it so well, might be admitted into her service, and continue to be my nurse and instructor. Her Majesty agreed to my petition, and easily got the farmer's consent, who was glad enough to have his daughter preferred at Court; and the poor girl herself was not able to hide her

1. I.e., over two feet long and about two feet wide.   2. Portuguese coins.

joy. My late master withdrew, bidding me farewell, and saying he had left me in a good service; to which I replied not a word, only making him a slight bow.

The Queen observed my coldness, and when the farmer was gone out of the apartment, asked me the reason. I made bold to tell her Majesty that I owed no other obligation to my late master than his not dashing out the brains of a poor harmless creature found by chance in his field; which obligation was amply recompensed by the gain he had made in showing me through half the kingdom, and the price he had now sold me for. That the life I had since led was laborious enough to kill an animal of ten times my strength. That my health was much impaired by the continual drudgery of entertaining the rabble every hour of the day; and that if my master had not thought my life in danger, her Majesty would not have got so cheap a bargain. But as I was out of all fear of being ill treated under the protection of so great and good an Empress, the Ornament of Nature, the Darling of the World, the Delight of her Subjects, the Phoenix of the Creation; so I hoped my late master's apprehensions would appear to be groundless, for I already found my spirits to revive by the influence of her most august presence.

This was the sum of my speech, delivered with great improprieties and hesitation; the latter part was altogether framed in the style peculiar to that people, whereof I learned some phrases from Glumdalclitch, while she was carrying me to Court.

The Queen, giving great allowance for my defectiveness in speaking, was however surprised at so much wit and good sense in so diminutive an animal. She took me in her own hand, and carried me to the King, who was then retired to his cabinet.[3] His Majesty, a prince of much gravity, and austere countenance, not well observing my shape at first view, asked the Queen after a cold manner how long it was since she grew fond of a *splacknuck;* for such it seems he took me to be, as I lay upon my breast in her Majesty's right hand. But this princess, who hath an infinite deal of wit and humor, set me gently on my feet upon the scrutore,[4] and commanded me to give his Majesty an account of myself, which I did in a very few words; and Glumdalclitch, who attended at the cabinet door, and could not endure I should be out of her sight, being admitted, confirmed all that had passed from my arrival at her father's house.

The King, although he be as learned a person as any in his dominions, had been educated in the study of philosophy and particularly mathematics; yet when he observed my shape exactly, and saw me walk erect, before I began to speak, conceived I might be a piece of clockwork (which is in that country arrived to a very great perfection) contrived by some ingenious artist. But when he heard my voice, and found what I delivered to be regular and ra-

3. A private apartment.   4. Writing desk.

tional, he could not conceal his astonishment. He was by no means satisfied with the relation I gave him of the manner I came into his kingdom, but thought it a story concerted between Glumdalclitch and her father, who had taught me a set of words to make me sell at a higher price. Upon this imagination he put several other questions to me, and still received rational answers, no otherwise defective than by a foreign accent, and an imperfect knowledge in the language, with some rustic phrases which I had learned at the farmer's house, and did not suit the polite style of a court.

His Majesty sent for three great scholars who were then in their weekly waiting (according to the custom in that country). These gentlemen, after they had a while examined my shape with much nicety, were of different opinions concerning me. They all agreed that I could not be produced according to the regular laws of nature, because I was not framed with a capacity of preserving my life, either by swiftness, or climbing of trees, or digging holes in the earth. They observed by my teeth, which they viewed with great exactness, that I was a carnivorous animal; yet most quadrupeds being an overmatch for me, and field mice, with some others, too nimble, they could not imagine how I should be able to support myself, unless I fed upon snails and other insects; which they offered, by many learned arguments, to evince that I could not possibly do. One of them seemed to think that I might be an embryo, or abortive birth. But this opinion was rejected by the other two, who observed my limbs to be perfect and finished, and that I had lived several years, as it was manifest from my beard, the stumps whereof they plainly discovered through a magnifying glass. They would not allow me to be a dwarf, because my littleness was beyond all degrees of comparison; for the Queen's favorite dwarf, the smallest ever known in that kingdom, was nearly thirty foot high. After much debate, they concluded unanimously that I was only *relplum scalcath*, which is interpreted literally, *lusus naturae*;[5] a determination exactly agreeable to the modern philosophy of Europe, whose professors, disdaining the old evasion of *occult causes*, whereby the followers of Aristotle endeavor in vain to disguise their ignorance, have invented this wonderful solution of all difficulties, to the unspeakable advancement of human knowledge.

After this decisive conclusion, I entreated to be heard a word or two. I applied myself to the King, and assured his Majesty that I came from a country which abounded with several millions of both sexes, and of my own stature, where the animals, trees, and houses were all in proportion, and where by consequence I might be as able to defend myself, and to find sustenance, as any of his Majesty's subjects could do here; which I took for a full answer to

5. One of nature's sports, or, roughly, freaks. Swift had contempt for both the medieval schoolmen, who discussed "occult causes," the unknown causes of observable effects, and modern scientists, who, he believed, often concealed their ignorance by using equally meaningless terms.

those gentlemen's arguments. To this they only replied with a smile of contempt, saying that the farmer had instructed me very well in my lesson. The King, who had a much better understanding, dismissing his learned men, sent for the farmer, who by good fortune was not yet gone out of town; having therefore first examined him privately, and then confronted him with me and the young girl, his Majesty began to think that what we told him might possibly be true. He desired the Queen to order that a particular care should be taken of me, and was of opinion that Glumdalclitch should still continue in her office of tending me, because he observed we had a great affection for each other. A convenient apartment was provided for her at Court; she had a sort of governess appointed to take care of her education, a maid to dress her, and two other servants for menial offices; but the care of me was wholly appropriated to herself. The Queen commanded her own cabinet-maker to contrive a box that might serve me for a bedchamber, after the model that Glumdalclitch and I should agree upon. This man was a most ingenious artist, and according to my directions, in three weeks finished for me a wooden chamber of sixteen foot square and twelve high, with sash windows, a door, and two closets, like a London bedchamber. The board that made the ceiling was to be lifted up and down by two hinges, to put in a bed ready furnished by her Majesty's upholsterer, which Glumdalclitch took out every day to air, made it with her own hands, and letting it down at night, locked up the roof over me. A nice[6] workman, who was famous for little curiosities, undertook to make me two chairs, with backs and frames, of a substance not unlike ivory, and two tables, with a cabinet to put my things in. The room was quilted on all sides, as well as the floor and the ceiling, to prevent any accident from the carelessness of those who carried me, and to break the force of a jolt when I went in a coach. I desired a lock for my door to prevent rats and mice from coming in: the smith, after several attempts, made the smallest that ever was seen among them, for I have known a larger at the gate of a gentleman's house in England. I made a shift[7] to keep the key in a pocket of my own, fearing Glumdalclitch might lose it. The Queen likewise ordered the thinnest silks that could be gotten, to make me clothes, not much thicker than an English blanket, very cumbersome till I was accustomed to them. They were after the fashion of the kingdom, partly resembling the Persian, and partly the Chinese, and are a very grave, decent habit.

The Queen became so fond of my company that she could not dine without me. I had a table placed upon the same at which her Majesty ate, just at her left elbow, and a chair to sit on. Glumdalclitch stood upon a stool on the floor, near my table, to assist and take care of me. I had an entire set of silver dishes and plates, and

6. Exact. 7. Contrived.

other necessaries, which, in proportion to those of the Queen, were not much bigger than what I have seen of the same kind in a London toyshop,[8] for the furniture of a baby-house: these my little nurse kept in her pocket in a silver box and gave me at meals as I wanted them, always cleaning them herself. No person dined with the Queen but the two Princesses Royal, the elder sixteen years old, and the younger at that time thirteen and a month. Her Majesty used to put a bit of meat upon one of my dishes, out of which I carved for myself; and her diversion was to see me eat in miniature. For the Queen (who had indeed but a weak stomach) took up at one mouthful as much as a dozen English farmers could eat at a meal, which to me was for some time a very nauseous sight. She would craunch the wing of a lark, bones and all, between her teeth, although it were nine times as large as that of a full-grown turkey; and put a bit of bread into her mouth as big as two twelve-penny loaves. She drank out of a golden cup, above a hogshead at a draught. Her knives were twice as long as a scythe set straight upon the handle. The spoons, forks, and other instruments were all in the same proportion. I remember when Glumdalclitch carried me out of curiosity to see some of the tables at Court, where ten or a dozen of these enormous knives and forks were lifted up together, I thought I had never till then beheld so terrible a sight.

It is the custom that every Wednesday (which, as I have before observed, was their Sabbath) the King and Queen, with the royal issue of both sexes, dine together in the apartment of his Majesty, to whom I was now become a favorite; and at these times my little chair and table were placed at his left hand, before one of the salt-cellars. This prince took a pleasure in conversing with me, inquiring into the manners, religion, laws, government, and learning of Europe; wherein I gave him the best account I was able. His apprehension was so clear, and his judgment so exact, that he made very wise reflections and observations upon all I said. But I confess that after I had been a little too copious in talking of my own beloved country, of our trade and wars by sea and land, of our schisms in religion and parties in the state, the prejudices of his education prevailed so far that he could not forbear taking me up in his right hand, and stroking me gently with the other, after an hearty fit of laughing, asked me whether I were a Whig or a Tory. Then turning to his first minister, who waited behind him with a white staff, near as tall as the mainmast of the *Royal Sovereign*,[9] he observed how contemptible a thing was human grandeur, which could be mimicked by such diminutive insects as I: "and yet," said he, "I dare engage, these creatures have their titles and distinctions of honor; they contrive little nests and burrows, that they call houses and cities; they make a figure in dress and equipage;[1] they love, they

8. A shop for selling knickknacks.
9. At the English court the Lord Treasurer bore a white staff as the symbol of his office. The *Royal Sover-* *eign* was one of the largest ships in the Royal Navy.
1. A carriage and horses, with attendant footmen.

fight, they dispute, they cheat, they betray." And thus he continued on, while my color came and went several times with indignation to hear our noble country, the mistress of arts and arms, the scourge of France, the arbitress of Europe, the seat of virtue, piety, honor, and truth, the pride and envy of the world, so contemptuously treated.

But as I was not in a condition to resent injuries, so, upon mature thoughts, I began to doubt whether I were injured or no. For, after having been accustomed several months to the sight and converse of this people, and observed every object upon which I cast my eyes to be of proportionable magnitude, the horror I had first conceived from their bulk and aspect was so far worn off that if I had then beheld a company of English lords and ladies in their finery and birthday clothes,[2] acting their several parts in the most courtly manner of strutting and bowing and prating, to say the truth, I should have been strongly tempted to laugh as much at them as this King and his grandees did at me. Neither indeed could I forbear smiling at myself when the Queen used to place me upon her hand towards a looking glass, by which both our persons appeared before me in full view together; and there could be nothing more ridiculous than the comparison; so that I really began to imagine myself dwindled many degrees below my usual size.

Nothing angered and mortified me so much as the Queen's dwarf, who being of the lowest stature that was ever in that country (for I verily think he was not full thirty foot high) became so insolent at seeing a creature so much beneath him that he would always affect to swagger and look big as he passed by me in the Queen's antechamber, while I was standing on some table talking with the lords or ladies of the court; and he seldom failed of a smart word or two upon my littleness, against which I could only revenge myself by calling him brother, challenging him to wrestle, and such repartees as are usual in the mouths of Court pages. One day at dinner this malicious little cub was so nettled with something I had said to him that, raising himself upon the frame of Her Majesty's chair, he took me up by the middle, as I was sitting down, not thinking any harm, and let me drop into a large silver bowl of cream, and then ran away as fast as he could. I fell over head and ears, and if I had not been a good swimmer, it might have gone very hard with me; for Glumdalclitch in that instant happened to be at the other end of the room, and the Queen was in such a fright that she wanted presence of mind to assist me. But my little nurse ran to my relief, and took me out, after I had swallowed above a quart of cream. I was put to bed; however, I received no other damage than the loss of a suit of clothes, which was utterly spoiled. The dwarf was soundly whipped, and as a further punishment, forced to drink up the bowl of cream into which he had

2. Courtiers dressed with especial splendor on the monarch's birthday.

thrown me; neither was he ever restored to favor: for soon after the Queen bestowed him to a lady of high quality, so that I saw him no more, to my very great satisfaction; for I could not tell to what extremity such a malicious urchin might have carried his resentment.

He had before served me a scurvy trick, which set the Queen a laughing, although at the same time she were heartily vexed, and would have immediately cashiered him,[3] if I had not been so generous as to intercede. Her Majesty had taken a marrow bone upon her plate, and after knocking out the marrow, placed the bone again in the dish, erect as it stood before; the dwarf watching his opportunity, while Glumdalclitch was gone to the sideboard, mounted upon the stool she stood on to take care of me at meals, took me up in both hands, and squeezing my legs together, wedged them into the marrow bone above my waist, where I stuck for some time, and made a very ridiculous figure. I believe it was near a minute before anyone knew what was become of me, for I thought it below me to cry out. But, as princes seldom get their meat hot, my legs were not scalded, only my stockings and breeches in a sad condition. The dwarf at my entreaty had no other punishment than a sound whipping.

I was frequently rallied by the Queen upon account of my fearfulness, and she used to ask me whether the people of my country were as great cowards as myself. The occasion was this. The kingdom is much pestered with flies in summer, and these odious insects, each of them as big as a Dunstable lark, hardly gave me any rest while I sat at dinner, with their continual humming and buzzing about my ears. They would sometimes alight upon my victuals, and leave their loathsome excrement or spawn behind, which to me was very visible, although not to the natives of that country, whose large optics were not so acute as mine in viewing smaller objects. Sometimes they would fix upon my nose or forehead, where they stung me to the quick, smelling very offensively; and I could easily trace that viscous matter, which our naturalists tell us enables those creatures to walk with their feet upwards upon a ceiling. I had much ado to defend myself against these destable animals, and could not forbear starting when they came on my face. It was the common practice of the dwarf to catch a number of these insects in his hand, as schoolboys do among us, and let them out suddenly under my nose, on purpose to frighten me, and divert the Queen. My remedy was to cut them in pieces with my knife as they flew in the air, wherein my dexterity was much admired.

I remember one morning when Glumdalclitch had set me in my box upon a window, as she usually did in fair days to give me air (for I durst not venture to let the box be hung on a nail out of the window, as we do with cages in England), after I had lifted up one

3. Dismissed him.

of my sashes, and sat down at my table to eat a piece of sweet cake for my breakfast, above twenty wasps, allured by the smell, came flying into the room, humming louder than the drones of as many bagpipes. Some of them seized my cake, and carried it piecemeal away; others flew about my head and face, confounding me with the noise, and putting me in the utmost terror of their stings. However, I had the courage to rise and draw my hanger, and attack them in the air. I dispatched four of them, but the rest got away, and I presently shut my window. These insects were as large as partridges; I took out their stings, found them an inch and a half long, and as sharp as needles. I carefully preserved them all, and having since shown them with some other curiosities in several parts of Europe, upon my return to England I gave three of them to Gresham College,[4] and kept the fourth for myself.

CHAPTER IV. *The country described. A proposal for correcting modern maps. The King's palace, and some account of the metropolis. The Author's way of traveling. The chief temple described.*

I now intend to give the reader a short description of this country, as far as I have traveled in it, which was not above two thousand miles round Lorbrulgrud the metropolis. For the Queen, whom I always attended, never went further when she accompanied the King in his progresses, and there stayed till his Majesty returned from viewing his frontiers. The whole extent of this prince's dominions reacheth about six thousand miles in length, and from three to five in breadth. From whence I cannot but conclude that our geographers of Europe are in a great error by supposing nothing but sea between Japan and California: for it was ever my opinion that there must be a balance of earth to counterpoise the great continent of Tartary; and therefore they ought to correct their maps and charts by joining this vast tract of land to the northwest parts of America, wherein I shall be ready to lend them my assistance.

The kingdom is a peninsula, terminated to the northeast by a ridge of mountains thirty miles high, which are altogether impassable by reason of the volcanoes upon the tops. Neither do the most learned know what sort of mortals inhabit beyond those mountains, or whether they be inhabited at all. On the three other sides it is bounded by the ocean. There is not one seaport in the whole kingdom; and those parts of the coasts into which the rivers issue are so full of pointed rocks, and the sea generally so rough, that there is no venturing with the smallest of their boats; so that these people are wholly excluded from any commerce with the rest of the world. But the large rivers are full of vessels, and abound with excellent fish, for they seldom get any from the sea, because the sea fish are of the same size with those in Europe, and consequently

4. The Royal Society, in its earliest years, met in Gresham College.

not worth catching; whereby it is manifest that nature, in the production of plants and animals of so extraordinary a bulk, is wholly confined to this continent, of which I leave the reasons to be determined by philosophers. However, now and then they take a whale that happens to be dashed against the rocks, which the common people feed on heartily. These whales I have known so large that a man could hardly carry one upon his shoulders; and sometimes for curiosity they are brought in hampers to Lorbrulgrud: I saw one of them in a dish at the King's table, which passed for a rarity, but I did not observe he was fond of it; for I think indeed the bigness disgusted him, although I have seen one somewhat larger in Greenland.

The country is well inhabited, for it contains fifty-one cities, near an hundred walled towns, and a great number of villages. To satisfy my curious reader, it may be sufficient to describe Lorbrulgrud. This city stand upon almost two equal parts on each side the river that passes through. It contains above eighty thousand houses, and about six hundred thousand inhabitants. It is in length three *glongluns* (which make about fifty-four English miles) and two and a half in breadth, as I measured it myself in the royal map made by the King's order, which was laid on the ground on purpose for me, and extended an hundred feet; I paced the diameter and circumference several times barefoot, and computing by the scale, measured it pretty exactly.

The King's palace is no regular edifice, but an heap of buildings about seven miles round: the chief rooms are generally two hundred and forty foot high, and broad and long in proportion. A coach was allowed to Glumdalclitch and me, wherein her governess frequently took her out to see the town, or go among the shops; and I was always of the party, carried in my box, although the girl at my own desire would often take me out, and hold me in her hand, that I might more conveniently view the houses and the people as we passed along the streets. I reckoned our coach to be about a square of Westminster Hall,[5] but not altogether so high; however, I cannot be very exact. One day the governess ordered our coachman to stop at several shops, where the beggars, watching their opportunity, crowded to the sides of the coach, and gave me the most horrible spectacles that ever an English eye beheld. There was a woman with a cancer in her breast, swelled to a monstrous size, full of holes, in two or three of which I could have easily crept, and covered my whole body. There was a fellow with a wen in his neck, larger than five woolpacks, and another with a couple of wooden legs, each about twenty foot high. But the most hateful sight of all was the lice crawling on their clothes. I could see distinctly the limbs of these vermin with my naked eye, much better than those

5. The ancient hall, now incorporated into the Houses of Parliament, where the Law Courts then sat. Swift presum- ably means the square of its breadth (just under 68 feet).

of an European louse through a microscope, and their snouts with
which they rooted like swine. They were the first I had ever beheld;
and I should have been curious enough to dissect one of them if I
had proper instruments (which I unluckily left behind me in the
ship), although indeed the sight was so nauseous that it perfectly
turned my stomach.

Besides the large box in which I was usually carried, the Queen
ordered a smaller one to be made for me, of about twelve foot
square and ten high, for the convenience of traveling, because the
other was somewhat too large for Glumdalclitch's lap, and cumbersome in the coach; it was made by the same artist, whom I directed
in the whole contrivance. This traveling closet was an exact square
with a window in the middle of three of the squares, and each window was latticed with iron wire on the outside, to prevent accidents
in long journeys. On the fourth side, which had no window, two
strong staples were fixed, through which the person that carried me,
when I had a mind to be on horseback, put in a leathern belt, and
buckled it about his waist. This was always the office of some grave
trusty servant in whom I could confide, whether I attended the
King and Queen in their progresses, or were disposed to see the
gardens, or pay a visit to some great lady or minister of state in
the court, when Glumdalclitch happened to be out of order: for
I soon began to be known and esteemed among the greatest officers,
I suppose more upon account of their Majesties' favor than any
merit of my own. In journeys, when I was weary of the coach, a
servant on horseback would buckle my box, and place it on a cushion
before him; and there I had a full prospect of the country on three
sides from my three windows. I had in this closet a field bed and a
hammock hung from the ceiling, two chairs and a table, neatly
screwed to the floor to prevent being tossed about by the agitation
of the horse or the coach. And having been long used to sea voyages,
those motions, although sometimes very violent, did not much discompose me.

When I had a mind to see the town, it was always in my traveling
closet, which Glumdalclitch held in her lap in a kind of open sedan,
after the fashion of the country, borne by four men, and attended by
two others in the Queen's livery. The people, who had often heard
of me, were very curious to crowd about the sedan; and the girl was
complaisant enough to make the bearers stop, and to take me in
her hand that I might be more conveniently seen.

I was very desirous to see the chief temple, and particularly the
tower belonging to it, which is reckoned the highest in the kingdom. Accordingly one day my nurse carried me thither, but I may
truly say I came back disappointed; for the height is not above
three thousand foot, reckoning from the ground to the highest
pinnacle top; which, allowing for the difference between the size
of those people and us in Europe, is no great matter for admiration,

nor at all equal in proportion (if I rightly remember) to Salisbury steeple.[6] But, not to detract from a nation to which during my life I shall acknowledge myself extremely obliged, it must be allowed that whatever this famous tower wants in height is amply made up in beauty and strength. For the walls are near an hundred foot thick, built of hewn stone, whereof each is about forty foot square, and adorned on all sides with statues of gods and emperors cut in marble larger than the life, placed in their several niches. I measured a little finger which had fallen down from one of these statues, and lay unperceived among some rubbish, and found it exactly four foot and an inch in length. Glumdalclitch wrapped it up in a handkerchief, and carried it home in her pocket to keep among other trinkets, of which the girl was very fond, as children at her age usually are.

The King's kitchen is indeed a noble building, vaulted at top, and about six hundred foot high. The great oven is not so wide by ten paces as the cupola at St. Paul's:[7] for I measured the latter on purpose after my return. But if I should describe the kitchen grate, the prodigious pots and kettles, the joints of meat turning on the spits, with many other particulars, perhaps I should be hardly believed; at least a severe critic would be apt to think I enlarged a little, as travelers are often suspected to do. To avoid which censure, I fear I have run too much into the other extreme, and that if this treatise should happen to be translated into the language of Brobdingnag (which is the general name of that kingdom) and transmitted thither, the King and his people would have reason to complain that I had done them an injury by a false and diminutive representation.

His Majesty seldom keeps above six hundred horses in his stables: they are generally from fifty-four to sixty foot high. But when he goes abroad on solemn days, he is attended for state by a militia guard of five hundred horse, which indeed I thought was the most splendid sight that could be ever beheld, till I saw part of his army in battalia;[8] whereof I shall find another occasion to speak.

CHAPTER V. *Several adventures that happened to the Author. The execution of a criminal. The Author shows his skill in navigation.*

I should have lived happy enough in that country if my littleness had not exposed me to several ridiculous and troublesome accidents, some of which I shall venture to relate. Glumdalclitch often carried me into the gardens of the court in my smaller box, and would sometimes take me out of it and hold me in her hand, or set me down to walk. I remember, before the dwarf left the Queen, he followed us one day into those gardens; and my nurse having set me down, he and I being close together near some dwarf apple

6. One of the most beautiful Gothic steeples in England is that of Salisbury Cathedral, 404 feet high.

7. The cupola of St. Paul's Cathedral in London is 108 feet in diameter.

8. Battle array.

trees, I must needs show my wit by a silly allusion between him and the trees, which happens to hold in their language as it doth in ours. Whereupon, the malicious rogue watching his opportunity, when I was walking under one of them, shook it directly over my head, by which a dozen apples, each of them near as large as a Bristol barrel, came tumbling about my ears; one of them hit me on the back as I chanced to stoop, and knocked me down flat on my face, but I received no other hurt; and the dwarf was pardoned at my desire, because I had given the provocation.

Another day Glumdalclitch left me on a smooth grassplot to divert myself while she walked at some distance with her governess. In the meantime there suddenly fell such a violent shower of hail that I was immediately by the force of it struck to the ground: and when I was down, the hailstones gave me such cruel bangs all over the body as if I had been pelted with tennis balls;[9] however I made a shift to creep on all four, and shelter myself by lying on my face on the lee side of a border of lemon thyme, but so bruised from head to foot that I could not go abroad in ten days. Neither is this at all to be wondered at, because nature in that country observing the same proportion through all her operations, a hailstone is near eighteen hundred times as large as one in Europe; which I can assert upon experience, having been so curious to weigh and measure them.

But a more dangerous accident happened to me in the same garden when my little nurse, believing she had put me in a secure place, which I often entreated her to do that I might enjoy my own thoughts, and having left my box at home to avoid the trouble of carrying it, went to another part of the garden with her governess and some ladies of her acquaintance. While she was absent and out of hearing, a small white spaniel belonging to one of the chief gardeners, having got by accident into the garden, happened to range near the place where I lay. The dog following the scent, came directly up, and taking me in his mouth, ran straight to his master, wagging his tail, and set me gently on the ground. By good fortune he had been so well taught that I was carried between his teeth without the least hurt, or even tearing my clothes. But the poor gardener, who knew me well, and had a great kindness for me, was in a terrible fright. He gently took me up in both his hands, and asked me how I did; but I was so amazed and out of breath that I could not speak a word. In a few minutes I came to myself, and he carried me safe to my little nurse, who by this time had returned to the place where she left me, and was in cruel agonies when I did not appear nor answer when she called; she severely reprimanded the gardener on account of his dog. But the thing was hushed up and never known at court; for the girl was afraid of the Queen's anger; and truly, as to myself, I thought it

9. 18th-century tennis balls, unlike the modern, were very hard.

would not be for my reputation that such a story should go about.

This accident absolutely determined Glumdalclitch never to trust me abroad for the future out of her sight. I had been long afraid of this resolution, and therefore concealed from her some little unlucky adventures that happened in those times when I was left by myself. Once a kite[1] hovering over the garden made a swoop at me, and if I had not resolutely drawn my hanger, and run under a thick espalier,[2] he would have certainly carried me away in his talons. Another time walking to the top of a fresh molehill, I fell to my neck in the hole through which that animal had cast up the earth, and coined some lie, not worth remembering, to excuse myself for spoiling my clothes. I likewise broke my right shin against the shell of a snail, which I happened to stumble over, as I was walking alone, and thinking on poor England.

I cannot tell whether I were more pleased or mortified to observe in those solitary walks that the smaller birds did not appear to be at all afraid of me; but would hop about within a yard distance, looking for worms and other food with as much indifference and security as if no creature at all were near them. I remember a thrush had the confidence to snatch out of my hand with his bill a piece of cake that Glumdalclitch had just given me for my breakfast. When I attempted to catch any of these birds, they would boldly turn against me, endeavoring to pick my fingers, which I durst not venture within their reach; and then they would hop back unconcerned to hunt for worms or snails, as they did before. But one day I took a thick cudgel, and threw it with all my strength so luckily at a linnet that I knocked him down, and seizing him by the neck with both my hands, ran with him in triumph to my nurse. However, the bird, who had only been stunned, recovering himself, gave me so many boxes with his wings on both sides of my head and body, though I held him at arm's length, and was out of the reach of his claws, that I was twenty times thinking to let him go. But I was soon relieved by one of our servants, who wrung off the bird's neck, and I had him next day for dinner, by the Queen's command. This linnet, as near as I can remember, seemed to be somewhat larger than an English swan.

The Maids of Honor often invited Glumdalclitch to their apartments, and desired she would bring me along with her, on purpose to have the pleasure of seeing and touching me. They would often strip me naked from top to toe and lay me at full length in their bosoms; wherewith I was much disgusted, because, to say the truth, a very offensive smell came from their skins, which I do not mention or intend to the disadvantage of those excellent ladies, for whom I have all manner of respect; but I conceive that my sense was more acute in proportion to my littleness, and that those illus-

---

1. A bird of prey.   2. A trellis on which fruit trees are trained.

trious persons were no more disagreeable to their lovers, or to each other, than people of the same quality are with us in England. And, after all, I found their natural smell was much more supportable than when they used perfumes, under which I immediately swooned away. I cannot forget that an intimate friend of mine in Lilliput took the freedom in a warm day, when I had used a good deal of exercise, to complain of a strong smell about me, although I am as little faulty that way as most of my sex: but I suppose his faculty of smelling was as nice with regard to me as mine was to that of this people. Upon this point, I cannot forbear doing justice to the Queen, my mistress, and Glumdalclitch, my nurse, whose persons were as sweet as those of any lady in England.

That which gave me most uneasiness among these Maids of Honor, when my nurse carried me to visit them, was to see them use me without any manner of ceremony, like a creature who had no sort of consequence. For they would strip themselves to the skin and put on their smocks in my presence, while I was placed on their toilet[3] directly before their naked bodies; which, I am sure, to me was very far from being a tempting sight, or from giving me any other emotions than those of horror and disgust. Their skins appeared so coarse and uneven, so variously colored, when I saw them near, with a mole here and there as broad as a trencher, and hairs hanging from it thicker than pack-threads, to say nothing further concerning the rest of their persons. Neither did they at all scruple, while I was by, to discharge what they had drunk, to the quantity of at least two hogsheads, in a vessel that held above three tuns. The handsomest among these Maids of Honor, a pleasant frolicsome girl of sixteen, would sometimes set me astride upon one of her nipples, with many other tricks, wherein the reader will excuse me for not being over particular. But I was so much displeased that I entreated Glumdalclitch to contrive some excuse for not seeing that young lady any more.

One day a young gentleman, who was nephew to my nurse's governess, came and pressed them both to see an execution. It was of a man who had murdered one of that gentleman's intimate acquaintance. Glumdalclitch was prevailed on to be of the company, very much against her inclination, for she was naturally tender-hearted: and as for myself, although I abhorred such kind of spectacles, yet my curiosity tempted me to see something that I thought must be extraordinary. The malefactor was fixed in a chair upon a scaffold erected for the purpose, and his head cut off at a blow with a sword of about forty foot long. The veins and arteries spouted up such a prodigious quantity of blood, and so high in the air, that the great *jet d'eau*[4] at Versailles was not equal for the time it lasted; and the head, when it fell on the scaffold floor, gave such a bounce,[5]

3. Toilet table.
4. This fountain rose over forty feet in the air.
5. A sudden noise.

as made me start, although I were at least half an English mile distant.

The Queen, who often used to hear me talk of my sea voyages, and took all occasions to divert me when I was melancholy, asked me whether I understood how to handle a sail or an oar, and whether a little exercise of rowing might not be convenient for my health. I answered that I understood both very well. For although my proper employment had been to be surgeon or doctor to the ship, yet often, upon a pinch, I was forced to work like a common mariner. But I could not see how this could be done in their country, where the smallest wherry was equal to a first-rate man-of-war among us, and such a boat as I could manage would never live in any of their rivers. Her Majesty said, if I would contrive a boat, her own joiner[6] should make it, and she would provide a place for me to sail in. The fellow was an ingenious workman and, by my instructions, in ten days finished a pleasure boat with all its tackling, able conveniently to hold eight Europeans. When it was finished, the Queen was so delighted that she ran with it in her lap to the King, who ordered it to be put in a cistern full of water, with me in it, by way of trial; where I could not manage my two sculls, or little oars, for want of room. But the Queen had before contrived another project. She ordered the joiner to make a wooden trough of three hundred foot long, fifty broad, and eight deep; which being well pitched to prevent leaking, was placed on the floor along the wall in an outer room of the palace. It had a cock near the bottom to let out the water when it began to grow stale, and two servants could easily fill it in half an hour. Here I often used to row for my own diversion, as well as that of the Queen and her ladies, who thought themselves well entertained with my skill and agility. Sometimes I would put up my sail, and then my business was only to steer, while the ladies gave me a gale with their fans; and when they were weary, some of the pages would blow my sail forward with their breath, while I showed my art by steering starboard or larboard as I pleased. When I had done, Glumdalclitch always carried my boat into her closet, and hung it on a nail to dry.

In this exercise I once met an accident which had like to have cost me my life. For one of the pages having put my boat into the trough, the governess who attended Glumdalclitch very officiously[7] lifted me up to place me in the boat; but I happened to slip through her fingers, and should have infallibly fallen down forty feet upon the floor, if by the luckiest chance in the world I had not been stopped by a corking-pin[8] that stuck in the good gentlewoman's stomacher; the head of the pin passed between my shirt and the waistband of my breeches, and thus I was held by the middle in the air until Glumdalclitch ran to my relief.

6. A skilled woodworker.
7. Kindly, dutifully.
8. A pin of the largest size. "Stom-

acher": an ornamental covering for the front and upper part of the body.

Another time, one of the servants, whose office it was to fill my trough every third day with fresh water, was so careless to let a huge frog (not perceiving it) slip out of his pail. The frog lay concealed till I was put into my boat, but then seeing a resting place, climbed up, and made it lean so much on one side that I was forced to balance it with all my weight on the other, to prevent overturning. When the frog was got in, it hopped at once half the length of the boat, and then over my head, backwards and forwards, daubing my face and clothes with its odious slime. The largeness of its features made it appear the most deformed animal that can be conceived. However, I desired Glumdalclitch to let me deal with it alone. I banged it a good while with one of my sculls, and at last forced it to leap out of the boat.

But the greatest danger I ever underwent in that kingdom was from a monkey, who belonged to one of the clerks of the kitchen. Glumdalclitch had locked me up in her closet, while she went somewhere upon business or a visit. The weather being very warm, the closet window was left open, as well as the windows in the door of my bigger box, in which I usually lived, because of its largeness and conveniency. As I sat quietly meditating at my table, I heard something bounce in at the closet window, and skip about from one side to the other, whereat, although I was much alarmed, yet I ventured to look out, but stirred not from my seat; and then I saw this frolicsome animal, frisking and leaping up and down, till at last he came to my box, which he seemed to view with great pleasure and curiosity, peeping in at the door and every window. I retreated to the farther corner of my room, or box, but the monkey looking in at every side, put me into such a fright that I wanted presence of mind to conceal myself under the bed, as I might easily have done. After some time spent in peeping, grinning, and chattering, he at last espied me, and reaching one of his paws in at the door, as a cat does when she plays with a mouse, although I often shifted place to avoid him, he at length seized the lappet of my coat (which, being made of that country cloth, was very thick and strong) and dragged me out. He took me up in his right forefoot, and held me as a nurse does a child she is going to suckle, just as I have seen the same sort of creature do with a kitten in Europe: and when I offered to struggle, he squeezed me so hard that I thought it more prudent to submit. I have good reason to believe that he took me for a young one of his own species, by his often stroking my face very gently with his other paw. In these diversions he was interrupted by a noise at the closet door, as if somebody were opening it, whereupon he suddenly leaped up to the window at which he had come in, and thence upon the leads and gutters, walking upon three legs, and holding me in the fourth, till he clambered up to a roof that was next to ours. I heard Glumdalclitch give a shriek at the moment he was carrying me out. The poor girl was almost distracted: that quarter of the palace was all in an uproar; the servants ran for ladders; the monkey was seen by hundreds in the court, sitting upon the ridge of a building, holding me like a baby in one of his forepaws and feeding me with the other, by cramming into my mouth some victuals he had squeezed out of the bag on one side of his chaps, and patting me when I would not eat; whereat many of the rabble below could not forbear laughing; neither do I think they justly ought to be blamed, for without question the sight was ridiculous enough to everybody but myself. Some of the people threw up stones, hoping to drive the monkey down; but this was strictly forbidden, or else very probably my brains had been dashed out.

The ladders were now applied, and mounted by several men; which the monkey observing, and finding himself almost encompassed, not being able to make speed enough with his three legs, let me drop on a ridge tile, and made his escape. Here I sat for some time three hundred yards from the ground, expecting every moment to be blown down by the wind, or to fall by my own giddiness, and come tumbling over and over from the ridge to the eaves. But an honest lad, one of my nurse's footmen, climbed up, and putting me into his breeches pocket, brought me down safe.

I was almost choked with the filthy stuff the monkey had crammed down my throat; but my dear little nurse picked it out of my mouth with a small needle, and then I fell a vomiting, which gave me great relief. Yet I was so weak and bruised in the sides with the squeezes given me by this odious animal that I was forced to keep my bed a fortnight. The King, Queen, and all the Court sent every day to inquire after my health, and her Majesty made me several visits during my sickness. The monkey was killed, and an order made that no such animal should be kept about the palace.

When I attended the King after my recovery, to return him thanks for his favors, he was pleased to rally me a good deal upon this adventure. He asked me what my thoughts and speculations were while I lay in the monkey's paw, how I liked the victuals he gave me, his manner of feeding, and whether the fresh air on the roof had sharpened my stomach. He desired to know what I would have done upon such an occasion in my own country. I told his Majesty that in Europe we had no monkeys, except such as were brought for curiosities from other places, and so small that I could deal with a dozen of them together, if they presumed to attack me. And as for that monstrous animal with whom I was so lately engaged (it was indeed as large as an elephant), if my fears had suffered me to think so far as to make use of my hanger (looking fiercely and clapping my hand upon the hilt as I spoke) when he poked his paw into my chamber, perhaps I should have given him such a wound as would have made him glad to withdraw it with more haste than he put it in. This I delivered in a firm tone, like a person who was jealous lest his courage should be called in question. However, my speech produced nothing else besides a loud laughter, which all the respect due to his Majesty from those about him could not make them contain. This made me reflect how vain an attempt it is for a man to endeavor doing himself honor among those who are out of all degree of equality or comparison with him. And yet I have seen the moral of my own behavior very frequent in England since my return, where a little contemptible varlet, without the least title to birth, person, wit, or common sense, shall presume to look with importance, and put himself upon a foot with the greatest persons of the kingdom.

I was every day furnishing the court with some ridiculous story; and Glumdalclitch, although she loved me to excess, yet was arch enough to inform the Queen whenever I committed any folly that she thought would be diverting to her Majesty. The girl, who had been out of order, was carried by her governess to take the air about an hour's distance, or thirty miles from town. They alighted out of the coach near a small footpath in a field, and Glumdalclitch setting down my traveling box, I went out of it to walk. There was a cow dung in the patch, and I must needs try my activity by attempting to leap over it. I took a run, but unfortunately jumped short, and found myself just in the middle up to my knees. I waded through with some difficulty, and one of the footmen wiped me as clean as he could with his handkerchief; for I was filthily bemired, and my nurse confined me to my box till we returned home, where the Queen was soon informed of what had passed and the footmen spread it about the Court, so that all the mirth, for some days, was at my expense.

CHAPTER VI. *Several contrivances of the Author to please the King and Queen. He shows his skill in music. The King inquires into the state of Europe, which the Author relates to him. The King's observations thereon.*

I used to attend the King's levee[9] once or twice a week, and had often seen him under the barber's hand, which indeed was at first very terrible to behold. For the razor was almost twice as long as an ordinary scythe. His Majesty, according to the custom of the country, was only shaved twice a week. I once prevailed on the barber to give me some of the suds or lather, out of which I picked forty or fifty of the strongest stumps of hair. I then took a piece of fine wood, and cut it like the back of a comb, making several holes in it at equal distance with as small a needle as I could get from Glumdalclitch. I fixed in the stumps so artificially,[1] scraping

9. A morning reception held by a prince or nobleman, sometimes while dressing for the day.
1. Skillfully.

and sloping them with my knife towards the points, that I made a very tolerable comb; which was a seasonable supply, my own being so much broken in the teeth that it was almost useless; neither did I know any artist in that country so nice and exact as would undertake to make me another.

And this puts me in mind of an amusement wherein I spent many of my leisure hours. I desired the Queen's woman to save for me the combings of her Majesty's hair, whereof in time I got a good quantity; and consulting with my friend the cabinetmaker, who had received general orders to do little jobs for me, I directed him to make two chair frames, no larger than those I had in my box, and then to bore little holes with a fine awl round those parts where I designed the backs and seats; through these holes I wove the strongest hairs I could pick out, just after the manner of cane chairs in England. When they were finished, I made a present of them to her Majesty, who kept them in her cabinet, and used to show them for curiosities, as indeed they were the wonder of every one that beheld them. The Queen would have made me sit upon one of these chairs, but I absolutely refused to obey her, protesting I would rather die a thousand deaths than place a dishonorable part of my body on those precious hairs that once adorned her Majesty's head. Of these hairs (as I had always a mechanical genius) I likewise made a neat little purse above five foot long, with her Majesty's name deciphered in gold letters, which I gave to Glumdalclitch by the Queen's consent. To say the truth, it was more for show than use, being not of strength to bear the weight of the larger coins; and therefore she kept nothing in it but some little toys[2] that girls are fond of.

The King, who delighted in music, had frequent consorts[3] at court, to which I was sometimes carried, and set in my box on a table to hear them; but the noise was so great that I could hardly distinguish the tunes. I am confident that all the drums and trumpets of a royal army, beating and sounding together just at your ears, could not equal it. My practice was to have my box removed from the places where the performers sat, as far as I could, then to shut the doors and windows of it, and draw the window curtains, after which I found their music not disagreeable.

I had learned in my youth to play a little upon the spinet. Glumdalclitch kept one in her chamber, and a master attended twice a week to teach her: I call it a spinet, because it somewhat resembled that instrument, and was played upon in the same manner. A fancy came into my head that I would entertain the King and Queen with an English tune upon this instrument. But this appeared extremely difficult: for the spinet was near sixty foot long, each key being almost a foot wide; so that, with my arms extended, I could

2. Trifles.   3. Concerts.

not reach to above five keys, and to press them down required a good smart stroke with my fist, which would be too great a labor and to no purpose. The method I contrived was this: I prepared two round sticks about the bigness of common cudgels; they were thicker at one end than the other, and I covered the thicker ends with a piece of a mouse's skin, that by rapping on them I might neither damage the tops of the keys, nor interrupt the sound. Before the spinet a bench was placed, about four foot below the keys, and I was put upon the bench. I ran sideling upon it that way and this, as fast as I could, banging the proper keys with my two sticks; and made a shift to play a jig, to the great satisfaction of both their Majesties: but it was the most violent exercise I ever underwent, and yet I could not strike above sixteen keys, nor, consequently, play the bass and treble together, as other artists do; which was a great disadvantage to my performance.

The King, who, as I before observed, was a prince of excellent understanding, would frequently order that I should be brought in my box and set upon the table in his closet. He would then command me to bring one of my chairs out of the box, and sit down within three yards distance upon the top of the cabinet, which brought me almost to a level with his face. In this manner I had several conversations with him. I one day took the freedom to tell his Majesty that the contempt he discovered towards Europe, and the rest of the world, did not seem answerable to those excellent qualities of mind that he was master of. That reason did not extend itself with the bulk of the body: on the contrary, we observed in our country that the tallest persons were usually least provided with it. That among other animals, bees and ants had the reputation of more industry, art, and sagacity than many of the larger kinds; and that, as inconsiderable as he took me to be, I hoped I might live to do his Majesty some signal service. The King heard me with attention, and began to conceive a much better opinion of me than he had before. He desired I would give him as exact an account of the government of England as I possibly could; because, as fond as princes commonly are of their own customs (for so he conjectured of other monarchs, by my former discourses), he should be glad to hear of anything that might deserve imitation.

Imagine with thyself, courteous reader, how often I then wished for the tongue of Demosthenes or Cicero, that might have enabled me to celebrate the praise of my own dear native country in a style equal to its merits and felicity.

I began my discourse by informing his Majesty that our dominions consisted of two islands, which composed three mighty kingdoms under one sovereign, beside our plantations in America. I dwelt long upon the fertility of our soil, and the temperature[4] of

4. Temperateness.

our climate. I then spoke at large upon the constitution of an English Parliament, partly made up of an illustrious body called the House of Peers, persons of the noblest blood, and of the most ancient and ample patrimonies. I described that extraordinary care always taken of their education in arts and arms, to qualify them for being counselors born to the king and kingdom; to have a share in the legislature, to be members of the highest Court of Judicature, from whence there could be no appeal; and to be champions always ready for the defense of their prince and country, by their valor, conduct, and fidelity. That these were the ornament and bulwark of the kingdom, worthy followers of their most renowned ancestors, whose honor had been the reward of their virtue, from which their posterity were never once known to degenerate. To these were joined several holy persons, as part of that assembly, under the title of Bishops, whose peculiar business it is to take care of religion, and of those who instruct the people therein. These were searched and sought out through the whole nation, by the prince and his wisest counselors, among such of the priesthood as were most deservedly distinguished by the sanctity of their lives and the depth of their erudition, who were indeed the spiritual fathers of the clergy and the people.

That the other part of the Parliament consisted of an assembly called the House of Commons, who were all principal gentlemen, freely picked and culled out by the people themselves, for their great abilities and love of their country, to represent the wisdom of the whole nation. And these two bodies make up the most august assembly in Europe, to whom, in conjunction with the prince, the whole legislature is committed.

I then descended to the Courts of Justice, over which the Judges, those venerable sages and interpreters of the law, presided, for determining the disputed rights and properties of men, as well as for the punishment of vice, and protection of innocence. I mentioned the prudent management of our treasury, the valor and achievements of our forces by sea and land. I computed the number of our people, by reckoning how many millions there might be of each religious sect, or political party among us. I did not omit even our sports and pastimes, or any other particular which I thought might redound to the honor of my country. And I finished all with a brief historical account of affairs and events in England for about an hundred years past.

This conversation was not ended under five audiences, each of several hours, and the King heard the whole with great attention, frequently taking notes of what I spoke, as well as memorandums of several questions he intended to ask me.

When I had put an end to these long discourses, his Majesty in a sixth audience consulting his notes, proposed many doubts, queries, and objections, upon every article. He asked what methods were used to cultivate the minds and bodies of our young nobility, and in what kind of business they commonly spent the first and teachable part of their lives. What course was taken to supply that assembly when any noble family became extinct. What qualifications were necessary in those who were to be created new lords. Whether the humor[5] of the prince, a sum of money to a Court lady or a prime minister, or a design of strengthening a party opposite to the public interest, ever happened to be motives in those advancements. What share of knowledge these lords had in the laws of their country, and how they came by it, so as to enable them to decide the properties of their fellow subjects in the last resort. Whether they were always so free from avarice, partialities, or want that a bribe or some other sinister view could have no place among them. Whether those holy lords I spoke of were constantly promoted to that rank upon account of their knowledge in religious matters, and the sanctity of their lives, had never been compliers with the times while they were common priests, or slavish prostitute chaplains to some nobleman, whose opinions they continued servilely to follow after they were admitted into that assembly.

He then desired to know what arts were practiced in electing those whom I called Commoners. Whether a stranger with a strong purse might not influence the vulgar voters to choose him before their own landlord or the most considerable gentleman in the neighborhood. How it came to pass that people were so violently bent upon getting into this assembly, which I allowed to be a great trouble and expense, often to the ruin of their families, without any salary or pension: because this appeared such an exalted strain of virtue and public spirit that his Majesty seemed to doubt it might possibly not be always sincere; and he desired to know whether such zealous gentlemen could have any views of refunding themselves for the charges and trouble they were at, by sacrificing the public good to the designs of a weak and vicious prince in conjunction with a corrupted ministry. He multiplied his questions, and sifted me thoroughly upon every part of this head, proposing numberless inquiries and objections, which I think it not prudent or convenient to repeat.

Upon what I said in relation to our Courts of Justice, his Majesty desired to be satisfied in several points: and this I was the better able to do, having been formerly almost ruined by a long suit in chancery, which was decreed for me with costs. He asked what time was usually spent in determining between right and wrong, and what degree of expense. Whether advocates and orators had liberty to plead in causes manifestly known to be unjust, vexatious, or oppressive. Whether party in religion or politics were observed

5. Whim.

to be of any weight in the scale of justice. Whether those pleading orators were persons educated in the general knowledge of equity, or only in provincial, national, and other local customs. Whether they or their judges had any part in penning those laws which they assumed the liberty of interpreting and glossing upon at their pleasure. Whether they had ever at different times pleaded for and against the same cause, and cited precedents to prove contrary opinions. Whether they were a rich or a poor corporation. Whether they received any pecuniary reward for pleading or delivering their opinions. And particularly whether they were ever admitted as members in the lower senate.

He fell next upon the management of our treasury, and said he thought my memory had failed me, because I computed our taxes at about five or six millions a year, and when I came to mention the issues,[6] he found they sometimes amounted to more than double, for the notes he had taken were very particular in this point; because he hoped, as he told me, that the knowledge of our conduct might be useful to him, and he could not be deceived in his calculations. But if what I told him were true, he was still at a loss how a kingdom could run out of its estate like a private person. He asked me, who were our creditors? and where we should find money to pay them? He wondered to hear me talk of such chargeable and extensive wars; that certainly we must be a quarrelsome people, or live among very bad neighbors, and that our generals must needs be richer than our kings.[7] He asked what business we had out of our own islands, unless upon the score of[8] trade or treaty or to defend the coasts with our fleet. Above all, he was amazed to hear me talk of a mercenary standing army[9] in the midst of peace, and among a free people. He said if we were governed by our own consent in the persons of our representatives, he could not imagine of whom we were afraid, or against whom we were to fight; and would hear my opinion whether a private man's house might not better be defended by himself, his children, and family, than by half a dozen rascals picked up at a venture[1] in the streets for small wages, who might get an hundred times more by cutting their throats.

He laughed at my odd kind of arithmetic (as he was pleased to call it) in reckoning the numbers of our people by a computation drawn from the several sects among us in religion and politics. He said he knew no reason why those who entertain opinions prejudicial to the public should be obliged to change, or should not be obliged

6. Expenditures.
7. An allusion to the enormous fortune gained by the Duke of Marlborough, formerly Captain-General of the army, whom Swift detested.
8. For the sake of.
9. Since the declaration of the Bill of Rights (1689), a standing army without authorization by Parliament had been illegal. Swift and the Tories in general were vigilant in their opposition to such an army.
1. By chance.

to conceal them. And as it was tyranny in any government to require the first, so it was weakness not to enforce the second: for a man may be allowed to keep poisons in his closet, but not to vend them about for cordials.[2]

He observed that among the diversions of our nobility and gentry I had mentioned gaming.[3] He desired to know at what age this entertainment was usually taken up, and when it was laid down; how much of their time it employed; whether it ever went so high as to affect their fortunes; whether mean, vicious people, by their dexterity in that art, might not arrive at great riches, and sometimes keep our very nobles in dependence, as well as habituate them to vile companions, wholly take them from the improvement of their minds, and force them, by the losses they have received, to learn and practice that infamous dexterity upon others.

He was perfectly astonished with the historical account I gave him of our affairs during the last century, protesting it was only an heap of conspiracies, rebellions, murders, massacres, revolutions, banishments, the very worst effects that avarice, faction, hypocrisy, perfidiousness, cruelty, rage, madness, hatred, envy, lust, malice, or ambition could produce.

His Majesty in another audience was at the pains to recapitulate the sum of all I had spoken; compared the questions he made with the answers I had given; then taking me into his hands, and stroking me gently, delivered himself in these words, which I shall never forget nor the manner he spoke them in. "My little friend Grildrig, you have made a most admirable panegyric[4] upon your country. You have clearly proved that ignorance, idleness, and vice are the proper ingredients for qualifying a legislator. That laws are best explained, interpreted, and applied by those whose interests and abilities lie in perverting, confounding, and eluding them. I observe among you some lines of an institution which in its original might have been tolerable; but these half erased, and the rest wholly blurred and blotted by corruptions. It doth not appear from all you have said how any one virtue is required towards the procurement of any one station among you; much less that men are ennobled on account of their virtue, that priests are advanced for their piety or learning, soldiers for their conduct or valor, judges for their integrity, senators for the love of their country, or counselors for their wisdom. As for yourself," continued the King, "who have spent the greatest part of your life in traveling, I am well disposed to hope you may hitherto have escaped many vices of your country. But by what I have gathered from your own relation, and the answers I have with much pains wringed and extorted from you, I cannot but conclude the bulk of your natives to be the most pernicious race

2. Medicines to stimulate the heart, or, equally commonly, liqueurs.
3. Gambling.

4. A formal oration in praise of someone or something.

of little odious vermin that nature ever suffered to crawl upon the surface of the earth."

CHAPTER VII. *The Author's love of his country. He makes a proposal of much advantage to the King; which is rejected. The King's great ignorance in politics. The learning of that country very imperfect and confined. Their laws, and military affairs, and parties in the State.*

Nothing but an extreme love of truth could have hindered me from concealing this part of my story. It was in vain to discover my resentments, which were always turned into ridicule: and I was forced to rest with patience while my noble and most beloved country was so injuriously treated. I am heartily sorry as any of my readers can possibly be that such an occasion was given, but this prince happened to be so curious and inquisitive upon every particular that it could not consist either with gratitude or good manners to refuse giving him what satisfaction I was able. Yet thus much I may be allowed to say in my own vindication: that I artfully eluded many of his questions, and gave to every point a more favorable turn by many degrees than the strictness of truth would allow. For I have always borne that laudable partiality to my own country, which Dionysius Halicarnassensis[5] with so much justice recommends to an historian. I would hide the frailties and deformities of my political mother, and place her virtues and beauties in the most advantageous light. This was my sincere endeavor in those many discourses I had with that mighty monarch, although it unfortunately failed of success.

But great allowances should be given to a King who lives wholly secluded from the rest of the world, and must therefore be altogether unacquainted with the manners and customs that most prevail in other nations: the want of which knowledge will ever produce many *prejudices*, and a certain *narrowness of thinking*, from which we and the politer countries of Europe are wholly exempted. And it would be hard indeed if so remote a prince's notions of virtue and vice were to be offered as a standard for all mankind.

To confirm what I have now said, and further, to show the miserable effects of a *confined education*, I shall here insert a passage which will hardly obtain belief. In hopes to ingratiate myself farther into his Majesty's favor, I told him of an invention discovered between three and four hundred years ago, to make a certain powder, into an heap of which the smallest spark of fire falling would kindle the whole in a moment, although it were as big as a mountain, and make it all fly up in the air together, with a noise and agitation

5. A Greek rhetorician and historian, who flourished ca. 25 B.C. His history of Rome was written to reconcile the Greeks to their Roman masters.

greater than thunder. That a proper quantity of this powder rammed into an hollow tube of brass or iron, according to its bigness, would drive a ball of iron or lead with such violence and speed as nothing was able to sustain its force. That the largest balls thus discharged would not only destroy whole ranks of an army at once, but batter the strongest walls to the ground; sink down ships with a thousand men in each, to the bottom of the sea; and, when linked together by a chain, would cut through masts and rigging; divide hundreds of bodies in the middle, and lay all waste before them. That we often put this powder into large hollow balls of iron, and discharged them by an engine into some city we were besieging; which would rip up the pavements, tear the houses to pieces, burst and throw splinters on every side, dashing out the brains of all who came near. That I knew the ingredients very well, which were cheap and common; I understood the manner of compounding them, and could direct his workmen how to make those tubes of a size proportionable to all other things in his Majesty's kingdom, and the largest need not be above two hundred foot long; twenty or thirty of which tubes, charged with the proper quantity of powder and balls, would batter down the walls of the strongest town in his dominions in a few hours; or destroy the whole metropolis, if ever it should pretend to dispute his absolute commands. This I humbly offered to his Majesty as a small tribute of acknowledgment in return of so many marks that I had received of his royal favor and protection.

The King was struck with horror at the description I had given of those terrible engines and the proposal I had made. He was amazed how so impotent and groveling an insect as I (these were his expressions) could entertain such inhuman ideas, and in so familiar a manner as to appear wholly unmoved at all the scenes of blood and desolation which I had painted as the common effects of those destructive machines; whereof he said some evil genius, enemy to mankind, must have been the first contriver. As for himself, he protested that although few things delighted him so much as new discoveries in art or in nature, yet he would rather lose half his kingdom than be privy[6] to such a secret, which he commanded me, as I valued my life, never to mention any more.

A strange effect of *narrow principles* and *short views!* that a prince possessed of every quality which procures veneration, love, and esteem; of strong parts, great wisdom, and profound learning; endued with admirable talents for government, and almost adored by his subjects; should from a *nice, unnecessary scruple,* whereof in Europe we can have no conception, let slip an opportunity put into his hands that would have made him absolute master of the lives, the liberties, and the fortunes of his people. Neither do I say this with the least intention to detract from the many virtues of that

6. To share secret knowledge.

excellent King, whose character I am sensible will on this account
be very much lessened in the opinion of an English reader: but I
take this defect among them to have risen from their ignorance;
they not having hitherto reduced politics into a science, as the
more acute wits of Europe have done. For I remember very well,
in a discourse one day with the King, when I happened to say there
were several thousand books among us written upon the art of
government, it gave him (directly contrary to my intention) a
very mean opinion of our understandings. He professed both to
abominate and despise all *mystery, refinement,* and *intrigue,* either
in a prince or a minister. He could not tell what I meant by *secrets
of state,* where an enemy or some rival nation were not in the case.
He confined the knowledge of governing within very *narrow bounds:*
to common sense and reason, to justice and lenity,[7] to the speedy
determination of civil and criminal causes, with some other obvious topics which are not worth considering. And he gave it for
his opinion that whoever could make two ears of corn or two
blades of grass to grow upon a spot of ground where only one grew
before would deserve better of mankind and do more essential service to his country than the whole race of politicians [7a] put together.

The learning of this people is very defective, consisting only in
morality, history, poetry, and mathematics; wherein they must
be allowed to excel. But the last of these is wholly applied to what
may be useful in life, to the improvement of agriculture and all
mechanical arts; so that among us it would be little esteemed. And
as to ideas, entities, abstractions, and transcendentals,[8] I could
never drive the least conception into their heads.

No law of that country must exceed in words the number of
letters in their alphabet, which consists only in two and twenty.
But indeed few of them extend even to that length. They are
expressed in the most plain and simple terms, wherein those people
are not mercurial[9] enough to discover above one interpretation.
And to write a comment upon any law is a capital crime. As to
the decision of civil causes, or proceedings against criminals, their
precedents[1] are so few that they have little reason to boast of any
extraordinary skill in either.

They have had the art of printing as well as the Chinese, time
out of mind. But their libraries are not very large; for that of the
King's, which is reckoned the biggest, doth not amount to above
a thousand volumes, placed in a gallery of twelve hundred foot long,
from whence I had liberty to borrow what books I pleased. The

7. Mildness.
7a. By "politicians" Swift means something like our modern "political scientists"—theorists.
8. In Swift's time, "transcendental"
was practically synonymous with "metaphysical."
9. Changeable.

1. A legal decision or a course of action
which comes to serve as a rule in determining similar cases in the future.
In the Fourth Voyage of *Gulliver's
Travels,* Gulliver is made to say: "It is
a maxim among these lawyers that
whatever hath been done before may
legally be done again. * * * "

Queen's joiner had contrived in one of the Glumdalclitch's rooms a kind of wooden machine five and twenty foot high, formed like a standing ladder; the steps were each fifty foot long. It was indeed a movable pair of stairs, the lowest end placed at ten foot distance from the wall of the chamber. The book I had a mind to read was put up leaning against the wall. I first mounted to the upper step of the ladder, and turning my face towards the book, began at the top of the page, and so walking to the right and left about eight or ten paces according to the length of the lines, till I had gotten a little below the level of mine eyes, and then descending gradually till I came to the bottom: after which I mounted again, and began the other page in the same manner, and so turned over the leaf, which I could easily do with both my hands, for it was as thick and stiff as a pasteboard, and in the largest folios[2] not above eighteen or twenty foot long.

Their style is clear, masculine, and smooth, but not florid; for they avoid nothing more than multiplying unnecessary words or using various expressions. I have perused many of their books, especially those in history and morality. Among the rest, I was much diverted with a little old treatise, which always lay in Glumdalclitch's bedchamber, and belonged to her governess, a grave elderly gentlewoman, who dealt in writings of morality and devotion. The book treats of the weakness of human kind, and is in little esteem, except among the women and the vulgar. However, I was curious to see what an author of that country could say upon such a subject. This writer went through all the usual topics of European moralists: showing how diminutive, contemptible, and helpless an animal was man in his own nature; how unable to defend himself from the inclemencies of the air, or the fury of wild beasts; how much he was excelled by one creature in strength, by another in speed, by a third in foresight, by a fourth in industry. He added that nature was degenerated in these latter declining ages of the world, and could now produce only small abortive births in comparison of those in ancient times. He said it was very reasonable to think, not only that the species of men were originally much larger, but also that there must have been giants in former ages; which, as it is asserted by history and tradition, so it hath been confirmed by huge bones and skulls casually dug up in several parts of the kingdom, far exceeding the common dwindled race of man in our days. He argued that the very laws of nature absolutely required we should have been made in the beginning of a size more large and robust, not so liable to destruction from every little accident of a tile falling from a house, or a stone cast from the hand of a boy, or of being drowned in a little brook. From this way of reasoning, the author drew several moral applications useful in the

2. A book of the largest size.

conduct of life, but needless here to repeat. For my own part, I could not avoid reflecting how universally this talent was spread, of drawing lectures in morality, or indeed rather matter of discontent and repining, from the quarrels we raise with nature. And I believe, upon a strict inquiry, those quarrels might be shown as ill grounded among us as they are among that people.

As to their military affairs, they boast that the King's army consists of an hundred and seventy-six thousand foot and thirty-two thousand horse: if that may be called an army which is made up of tradesmen in the several cities, and farmers in the country, whose commanders are only the nobility and gentry, without pay or reward. They are indeed perfect enough in their exercises, and under very good discipline, wherein I saw no great merit; for how should it be otherwise, where every farmer is under the command of his own landlord, and every citizen under that of the principal men in his own city, chosen after the manner of Venice by ballot?

I have often seen the militia of Lorbrulgrud drawn out to exercise in a great field near the city, of twenty miles square. They were in all not above twenty-five thousand foot, and six thousand horse; but it was impossible for me to compute their number, considering the space of ground they took up. A cavalier mounted on a large steed might be about an hundred foot high. I have seen this whole body of horse, upon a word of command, draw their swords at once, and brandish them in the air. Imagination can figure nothing so grand, so surprising, and so astonishing. It looked as if ten thousand flashes of lightning were darting at the same time from every quarter of the sky.

I was curious to know how this prince, to whose dominions there is no access from any other country, came to think of armies, or to teach his people the practice of military discipline. But I was soon informed, both by conversation and reading their histories. For in the course of many ages they have been troubled with the same disease to which the whole race of mankind is subject: the nobility often contending for power, the people for liberty, and the King for absolute dominion. All which, however happily tempered by the laws of the kingdom, have been sometimes violated by each of the three parties, and have more than once occasioned civil wars, the last whereof was happily put an end to by this prince's grandfather in a general composition;[3] and the militia, then settled with common consent, hath been ever since kept in the strictest duty.

CHAPTER VIII. *The King and Queen make a progress to the frontiers. The Author attends them. The manner in which he leaves the country very particularly related. He returns to England.*

3. A political settlement based upon general agreement of all parties.

I had always a strong impulse that I should some time recover my liberty, though it were impossible to conjecture by what means, or to form any project with the least hope of succeeding. The ship in which I sailed was the first ever known to be driven within sight of that coast; and the King had given strict orders that if at any time another appeared, it should be taken ashore, and with all its crew and passengers brought in a tumbrel[4] to Lorbrulgrud. He was strongly bent to get me a woman of my own size, by whom I might propagate the breed: but I think I should rather have died than undergone the disgrace of leaving a posterity to be kept in cages like tame canary birds, and perhaps in time sold about the kingdom to persons of quality for curiosities. I was indeed treated with much kindness: I was the favorite of a great King and Queen, and the delight of the whole Court, but it was upon such a foot as ill became the dignity of human kind. I could never forget those domestic pledges[5] I had left behind me. I wanted to be among people with whom I could converse upon even terms, and walk about the streets and fields without fear of being trod to death like a frog or a young puppy. But my deliverance came sooner than I expected, and in a manner not very common; the whole story and circumstances of which I shall faithfully relate.

I had now been two years in this country; and about the beginning of the third, Glumdalclitch and I attended the King and Queen in progress to the south coast of the kingdom. I was carried as usual in my traveling box, which, as I have already described, was a very convenient closet of twelve foot wide. I had ordered a hammock to be fixed by silken ropes from the four corners at the top, to break the jolts when a servant carried me before him on horseback, as I sometimes desired; and would often sleep in my hammock while we were upon the road. On the roof of my closet, set not directly over the middle of the hammock, I ordered the joiner to cut out a hole of a foot square to give me air in hot weather as I slept, which hole I shut at pleasure with a board that drew backwards and forwards through a groove.

When we came to our journey's end, the King thought proper to pass a few days at a palace he hath near Flanflasnic, a city within eighteen English miles of the seaside. Glumdalclitch and I were much fatigued; I had gotten a small cold, but the poor girl was so ill as to be confined to her chamber. I longed to see the ocean, which must be the only scene of my escape, if ever it should happen. I pretended to be worse than I really was, and desired leave to take the fresh air of the sea with a page whom I was very fond of, and who had sometimes been trusted with me. I shall never forget with what unwillingness Glumdalclitch consented, nor the strict charge she gave the page to be careful of me, bursting at the

4. A farm wagon.　　　　5. His wife and children.

same time into a flood of tears, as if she had some foreboding of what was to happen. The boy took me out in my box about half an hour's walk from the palace, towards the rocks on the seashore. I ordered him to set me down, and lifting up one of my sashes, cast many a wistful melancholy look towards the sea. I found myself not very well, and told the page that I had a mind to take a nap in my hammock, which I hoped would do me good. I got in, and the boy shut the window close down, to keep out the cold. I soon fell asleep: and all I can conjecture is that while I slept, the page, thinking no danger could happen, went among the rocks to look for birds' eggs; having before observed him from my window searching about, and picking up one or two in the clefts. Be that as it will, I found myself suddenly awaked with a violent pull upon the ring which was fastened at the top of my box for the conveniency of carriage. I felt my box raised very high in the air, and then borne forward with prodigious speed. The first jolt had like to have shaken me out of my hammock, but afterwards the motion was easy enough. I called out several times as loud as I could raise my voice, but all to no purpose. I looked towards my windows, and could see nothing but the clouds and sky. I heard a noise just over my head like the clapping of wings, and then began to perceive the woeful condition I was in; that some eagle had got the ring of my box in his beak, with an intent to let it fall on a rock, like a tortoise in a shell, and then pick out my body and devour it. For the sagacity and smell of this bird enable him to discover his quarry at a great distance, although better concealed than I could be within a two-inch board.

In a little time I observed the noise and flutter of wings to increase very fast, and my box was tossed up and down like a sign-post in a windy day. I heard several bangs or buffets, as I thought, given to the eagle (for such I am certain it must have been that held the ring of my box in his beak), and then all on a sudden felt myself falling perpendicularly down for above a minute, but with such incredible swiftness that I almost lost my breath. My fall was topped by a terrible squash, that sounded louder to mine ears than the cataract of Niagara; after which I was quite in the dark for another minute, and then my box began to rise so high that I could see light from the tops of my windows. I now perceived that I was fallen into the sea. My box, by the weight of my body, the goods that were in, and the broad plates of iron fixed for strength at the four corners of the top and bottom, floated about five foot deep in water. I did then and do now suppose that the eagle which flew away with my box was pursued by two or three others, and forced to let me drop while he was defending himself against the rest, who hoped to share in the prey. The plates of iron fastened at the bottom of the box (for those were the strongest) preserved the balance while it fell, and hindered it from being broken on the surface of the water. Every joint of it was well grooved, and the door did not move on hinges, but up and down like a sash; which kept my closet so tight that very little water came in. I got with much difficulty out of my hammock, having first ventured to draw back the slip-board on the roof already mentioned, contrived on purpose to let in air, for want of which I found myself almost stifled.

How often did I then wish myself with my dear Glumdalclitch, from whom one single hour had so far divided me! And I may say with truth that in the midst of my own misfortune, I could not forbear lamenting my poor nurse, the grief she would suffer for my loss, the displeasure of the Queen, and the ruin of her fortune. Perhaps many travelers have not been under greater difficulties and distress than I was at this juncture, expecting every moment to see my box dashed in pieces, or at least overset by the first violent blast or a rising wave. A breach in one single pane of glass would have been immediate death, nor could anything have preserved the windows but the strong lattice wires placed on the outside against accidents in traveling. I saw the water ooze in at several crannies, although the leaks were not considerable, and I endeavored to stop them as well as I could. I was not able to lift up the roof of my closet, which otherwise I certainly should have done, and sat on the top of it, where I might at least preserve myself from being shut up, as I may call it, in the hold. Or, if I escaped these dangers for a day or two, what could I expect but a miserable death of cold and hunger! I was four hours under these circumstances, expecting and indeed wishing every moment to be my last.

I have already told the reader that there were two strong staples fixed upon that side of my box which had no window and into which the servant, who used to carry me on horseback, would put a leathern belt, and buckle it about his waist. Being in this disconsolate state, I heard, or at least thought I heard, some kind of grating noise on that side of my box where the staples were fixed; and soon after I began to fancy that the box was pulled or towed along in the sea; for I now and then felt a sort of tugging, which made the waves rise near the tops of my windows, leaving me almost in the dark. This gave me some faint hopes of relief, although I was not able to imagine how it could be brought about. I ventured to unscrew one of my chairs, which were always fastened to the floor; and having made a hard shift to screw it down again directly under the slipping-board that I had lately opened, I mounted on the chair, and putting my mouth as near as I could to the hole, I called for help in a loud voice, and in all the languages I understood. I then fastened my handkerchief to a stick I usually carried, and thrusting it up the hole, waved it several times in the air, that if any boat or ship were near, the seamen might conjecture some unhappy mortal to be shut up in the box.

I found no effect from all I could do, but plainly perceived my closet to be moved along; and in the space of an hour or better, that side of the box where the staples were, and had no window, struck against something that was hard. I apprehended it to be a rock, and found myself tossed more than ever. I plainly heard a noise upon the cover of my closet, like that of a cable, and the grating of it as it passed through the ring. I then found myself hoisted up by degrees at least three foot higher than I was before. Whereupon I again thrust up my stick and handkerchief, calling for help till I was almost hoarse. In return to which, I heard a great shout repeated three time, giving me such transports of joy as are not to be conceived but by those who feel them. I now heard a trampling over my head, and somebody calling through the hole with a loud voice in the English tongue: "If there be anybody below, let them speak." I answered, I was an Englishman, drawn by ill fortune into the greatest calamity that ever any creature underwent, and begged, by all that was moving, to be delivered out of the dungeon I was in. The voice replied, I was safe, for my box was fastened to their ship; and the carpenter should immediately come and saw an hole in the cover, large enough to pull me out. I answered, that was needless and would take up too much time, for there was no more to be done but let one of the crew put his finger into the ring, and take the box out of the sea into the ship, and so into the captain's cabin. Some of them, upon hearing me talk so wildly, thought I was mad; others laughed; for indeed it never came into my head that I was now got among people of my own stature and strength. The carpenter came, and in a few minutes sawed a passage about four foot square; then let down a small ladder, upon which I mounted, and from thence was taken into the ship in a very weak condition.

The sailors were all in amazement, and asked me a thousand questions, which I had no inclination to answer. I was equally confounded at the sight of so many pygmies, for such I took them to be, after having so long accustomed my eyes to the monstrous objects I had left. But the Captain, Mr. Thomas Wilcocks, an honest, worthy Shropshire man, observing I was ready to faint, took me into his cabin, gave me a cordial to comfort me, and made me turn in upon his own bed, advising me to take a little rest, of which I had great need. Before I went to sleep I gave him to understand that I had some valuable furniture in my box, too good to be lost, a fine hammock, an handsome field bed, two chairs, a table, and a cabinet; that my closet was hung on all sides, or rather quilted with silk and cotton; that if he would let one of the crew bring my closet into his cabin, I would open it before him and show him my goods. The Captain, hearing me utter these absurdities, concluded I was raving; however (I suppose to pacify me), he promised to give order as I desired, and going upon deck, sent some of his men down into my closet, from whence (as I afterwards found) they drew up all my goods and stripped off the quilting; but the chairs, cabinet, and bedstead, being screwed to the floor, were much damaged by the ignorance of the seamen, who tore them up by force. Then they knocked off some of the boards for the use of the ship; and when they had got all they had a mind for, let the hulk drop into the sea, which, by reason of many breaches made in the bottom and sides, sunk to rights.[6] And indeed I was glad not to have been a spectator of the havoc they made, because I am confident it would have sensibly touched me, by bringing former passages into my mind, which I had rather forget.

I slept some hours, but perpetually disturbed with dreams of the place I had left, and the dangers I had escaped. However, upon waking, I found myself much recovered. It was now about eight o'clock at night, and the Captain ordered supper immediately, thinking I had already fasted too long. He entertained me with great kindness, observing me not to look wildly, or talk inconsistently; and when we were left alone, desired I would give him a relation of my travels, and by what accident I came to be set adrift in that monstrous wooden chest. He said that about twelve o'clock at noon, as he was looking through his glass, he spied it at a distance, and thought it was a sail, which he had a mind to make,[7] being not much out of his course, in hopes of buying some biscuit, his own beginning to fall short. That, upon coming nearer, and finding his error, he sent out his longboat to discover what I was; that his men came back in a fright, swearing they had seen a swimming house. That he laughed at their folly, and went himself in the boat, ordering his men to take a strong cable along with them. That the weather being calm, he rowed round me several times, observed my windows, and the wire lattices that defended them. That he discovered two staples upon one side, which was all of boards, without any passage for light. He then commanded his men to row up to that side, and fastening a cable to one of the staples, ordered his men to tow my chest (as he called it) towards the ship. When it was there, he gave directions to fasten another cable to the ring fixed in the cover, and to raise up my chest with pulleys, which all the sailors were not able to do above two or three foot. He said they saw my stick and handkerchief thrust out of the hole, and concluded that some unhappy man must be shut up in the cavity. I asked whether he or the crew had seen any prodigious birds in the air about the time he first discovered me. To which he answered that, discoursing this matter with the sailors while I was asleep, one of them said he had observed three eagles flying towards the

6. At once; altogether.   7. Overtake.

north, but remarked nothing of their being larger than the usual size (which I suppose must be imputed to the great height they were at), and he could not guess the reason of my question. I then asked the Captain how far he reckoned we might be from land; he said, by the best computation he could make, we were at least an hundred leagues. I assured him that he must be mistaken by almost half; for I had not left the country from whence I came above two hours before I dropped into the sea. Whereupon he began again to think that my brain was disturbed, of which he gave me a hint, and advised me to go to bed in a cabin he had provided. I assured him I was well refreshed with his good entertainment and company, and as much in my senses as ever I was in my life. He then grew serious and desired to ask me freely whether I were not troubled in mind by the consciousness of some enormous crime, for which I was punished at the command of some prince, by exposing me in that chest, as great criminals in other countries have been forced to sea in a leaky vessel without provisions; for although he should be sorry to have taken so ill[8] a man into his ship, yet he would engage his word to set me safe on shore in the first port where we arrived. He added that his suspicions were much increased by some very absurd speeches I had delivered at first to the sailors, and afterwards to himself, in relation to my closet or chest, as well as by my odd looks and behavior while I was at supper.

I begged his patience to hear me tell my story, which I faithfully did from the last time I left England to the moment he first discovered me. And as truth always forceth its way into rational minds, so this honest, worthy gentleman, who had some tincture of learning, and very good sense, was immediately convinced of my candor and veracity. But further to confirm all I had said, I entreated him to give order that my cabinet should be brought, of which I kept the key in my pocket (for he had already informed me how the seamen disposed of my closet). I opened it in his presence and showed him the small collection of rarities I made in the country from whence I had been so strangely delivered. There was the comb I had contrived out of the stumps of the King's beard, and another of the same materials, but fixed into a paring of her Majesty's thumbnail, which served for the back. There was a collection of needles and pins from a foot to half a yard long; four wasp-stings, like joiners' tacks; some combings of the Queen's hair; a gold ring which one day she made me a present of in a most obliging manner, taking it from her little finger, and throwing it over my head like a collar. I desired the Captain would please to accept this ring in return for his civilities, which he absolutely refused. I showed him a corn that I had cut off with my own hand from a Maid of Honor's toe; it was about the bigness of a Kentish pippin,[9] and grown so

8. Evil.   9. Apple.

hard that, when I returned to England, I got it hollowed into a cup and set in silver. Lastly, I desired him to see the breeches I had then on, which were made of a mouse's skin.

I could force nothing on him but a footman's tooth, which I observed him to examine with great curiosity, and found he had a fancy for it. He received it with abundance of thanks, more than such a trifle could deserve. It was drawn by an unskillful surgeon in a mistake from one of Glumdalclitch's men, who was afflicted with the toothache; but it was as sound as any in his head. I got it cleaned, and put it into my cabinet. It was about a foot long, and four inches in diameter.

The Captain was very well satisfied with this plain relation I had given him, and said he hoped when we returned to England I would oblige the world by putting it in paper and making it public. My answer was that I thought we were already overstocked with books of travels; that nothing could now pass which was not extraordinary; wherein I doubted some authors less consulted truth than their own vanity or interest, or the diversion of ignorant readers. That my story could contain little besides common events, without those ornamental descriptions of strange plants, trees, birds, and other animals, or the barbarous customs and idolatry of savage people, with which most writers abound. However, I thanked him for his good opinion, and promised to take the matter into my thoughts.

He said he wondered at one thing very much, which was to hear me speak so loud, asking me whether the King or Queen of that country were thick of hearing. I told him it was what I had been used to for above two years past, and that I admired[1] as much at the voices of him and his men, who seemed to me only to whisper, and yet I could hear them well enough. But, when I spoke in that country, it was like a man talking in the street to another looking out from the top of a steeple, unless when I was placed on a table, or held in any person's hand. I told him I had likewise observed another thing: that when I first got into the ship, and the sailors stood all about me, I thought they were the most little contemptible creatures I had ever beheld. For indeed while I was in that prince's country, I could never endure to look in a glass after mine eyes had been accustomed to such prodigious objects, because the comparison gave me so despicable a conceit[2] of myself. The Captain said that while we were at supper he observed me to look at everything with a sort of wonder, and that I often seemed hardly able to contain my laughter; which he knew not well how to take, but imputed it to some disorder in my brain. I answered, it was very true; and I wondered how I could forbear, when I saw his dishes of the size of a silver threepence, a leg of pork hardly a

---

1. Wondered at.   2. Notion.

mouthful, a cup not so big as a nutshell; and so I went on, describing the rest of his household stuff and provisions after the same manner. For, although the Queen had ordered a little equipage[3] of all things necessary for me while I was in her service, yet my ideas were wholly taken up with what I saw on every side of me, and I winked at my own littleness, as people do at their own faults. The Captain understood my raillery very well, and merrily replied with the old English proverb, that he doubted[4] mine eyes were bigger than my belly, for he did not observe my stomach so good, although I had fasted all day; and continuing in his mirth, protested he would have gladly given an hundred pounds to have seen my closet in the eagle's bill, and afterwards in its fall from so great an height into the sea; which would certainly have been a most astonishing object, worthy to have the description of it transmitted to future ages: and the comparison of Phaeton[5] was so obvious, that he could not forbear applying it, although I did not much admire the conceit.

The Captain having been at Tonquin,[6] was in his return to England driven northeastward to the latitude of 44 degrees, and of longitude 143. But meeting a trade wind two days after I came on board him, we sailed southward a long time, and coasting New Holland[7] kept our course west-southwest, and then south-southwest till we doubled the Cape of Good Hope. Our voyage was very prosperous, but I shall not trouble the reader with a journal of it. The Captain called in at one or two ports, and sent in his longboat for provisions and fresh water; but I never went out of the ship till we came into the Downs,[8] which was on the third day of June, 1706, about nine months after my escape. I offered to leave my goods in security for payment of my freight; but the Captain protested he would not receive one farthing. We took kind leave of each other, and I made him promise he would come to see me at my house in Redriff.[9] I hired a horse and guide for five shillings, which I borrowed of the Captain.

As I was on the road, observing the littleness of the houses, the trees, the cattle, and the people, I began to think myself in Lilliput. I was afraid of trampling on every traveler I met, and often called aloud to have them stand out of the way, so that I had like to have gotten one or two broken heads for my impertinence.

When I came to my own house, for which I was forced to inquire, one of the servants opening the door, I bent down to go in

3. Furnishings.
4. Feared.
5. The son of Apollo, whose unsuccessful attempt to drive the chariot of the sun god resulted in his death, when he was hurled by Zeus from the sky and fell into the river Eridanus, where he drowned.

6. Tonkin, in Indo-China.
7. Australia.
8. The sheltered anchorage between Goodwin Sands and the coast of Kent, near Deal.
9. Rotherhithe, on the south bank of the Thames, slightly below the City.

(like a goose under a gate) for fear of striking my head. My wife ran out to embrace me, but I stooped lower than her knees, thinking she could otherwise never be able to reach my mouth. My daughter kneeled to ask my blessing, but I could not see her till she arose, having been so long used to stand with my head and eyes erect to above sixty foot; and then I went to take her up with one hand by the waist. I looked down upon the servants and one or two friends who were in the house, as if they had been pygmies and I a giant. I told my wife she had been too thrifty; for I found she had starved herself and her daughter to nothing. In short, I behaved myself so unaccountably that they were all of the Captain's opinion when he first saw me, and concluded I had lost my wits. This I mention as an instance of the great power of habit and prejudice.

In a little time I and my family and friends came to a right understanding; but my wife protested I should never go to sea any more, although my evil destiny so ordered that she had not power to hinder me; as the reader may know hereafter. In the meantime I here conclude the second part of my unfortunate voyages.

From *Part III. A Voyage to Laputa, Balnibarbi, Glubbdubdrib, Luggnagg, and Japan*

[*The Flying Island of Laputa*]

CHAPTER I. *The author sets out on his third voyage. Is taken by pirates. The malice of a Dutchman. His arrival at an island. He is received into Laputa.*

I had not been at home above ten days, when Captain William Robinson, a Cornish man, commander of the *Hopewell*, a stout ship of three hundred tons, came to my house. I had formerly been surgeon of another ship where he was master, and a fourth part owner, in a voyage to the Levant. He had always treated me more like a brother than an inferior officer; and hearing of my arrival made me a visit, as I apprehended, only out of friendship, for nothing passed more than what is usual after long absence. But repeating his visits often, expressing his joy to find me in good health, asking whether I were now settled for life, adding that he intended a voyage to the East Indies, in two months, at last he plainly invited me, although with some apologies, to be surgeon of the ship; that I should have another surgeon under me, besides our two mates; that my salary should be double to the usual pay; and that having experienced my knowledge in sea-affairs to be at least equal to his, he would enter into any engagement to follow my advice, as much as if I had share in the command.

He said so many other obliging things, and I knew him to be so honest a man, that I could not reject his proposal; the thirst I had of seeing the world, notwithstanding my past misfortunes, continuing as violent as ever. The only difficulty that remained, was to persuade my wife, whose consent however I at last obtained, by the prospect of advantage she proposed to her children.

We set out the 5th day of August, 1706, and arrived at Fort St. George,[1] the 11th day of April, 1707. We stayed there three weeks to refresh our crew, many of whom were sick. From thence we went to Tonquin, where the captain resolved to continue some time, because many of the goods he intended to buy were not ready, nor could he expect to be dispatched in several months. Therefore in hopes to defray some of the charges he must be at, he bought a sloop, loaded it with several sorts of goods, wherewith the Tonquinese usually trade to the neighboring islands; and putting fourteen men on board, whereof three were of the country, he appointed me master of the sloop, and gave me power to traffic, while he transacted his affairs at Tonquin.

We had not sailed above three days, when a great storm arising, we were driven five days to the north-northeast, and then to the east; after which we had fair weather, but still with a pretty strong gale from the west. Upon the tenth day we were chased by two pirates, who soon overtook us; for my sloop was so deep loaden, that she sailed very slow; neither were we in a condition to defend ourselves.

We were boarded about the same time by both the pirates, who entered furiously at the head of their men; but finding us all prostrate upon our faces (for so I gave order), they pinioned us with strong ropes, and setting a guard upon us, went to search the sloop.

I observed among them a Dutchman, who seemed to be of some authority, although he was not commander of either ship. He knew us by our countenances to be Englishmen, and jabbering to us in his own language, swore we should be tied back to back, and thrown into the sea. I spoke Dutch tolerably well; I told him who we were, and begged him in consideration of our being Christians and Protestants, of neighboring countries, in strict alliance, that he would move the captains to take some pity on us. This inflamed his rage; he repeated his threatenings, and turning to his companions, spoke with great vehemence, in the Japanese language, as I suppose; often using the word *Christianos.*[2]

The largest of the two pirate ships was commanded by a Japanese captain, who spoke a little Dutch, but very imperfectly. He came up to me, and after several questions, which I answered in great humility, he said we should not die. I made the captain a very low bow, and then turning to the Dutchman, said, I was sorry to find more

---

1. Madras, in India.
2. Swift was prejudiced against Holland: as a republic that practiced religious toleration, it represented an alternative to England's establishment of Church and state. Though military allies against France, in 1707, the two countries remained commercial rivals.

mercy in a heathen, than in a brother Christian. But I had soon reason to repent those foolish words; for the malicious reprobate, having often endeavored in vain to persuade both the captains that I might be thrown into the sea (which they would not yield to after the promise made me, that I should not die), however prevailed so far as to have a punishment inflicted on me, worse in all human appearance than death itself. My men were sent by an equal division into both the pirate ships, and my sloop new manned. As to myself, it was determined that I should be set adrift in a small canoe, with paddles and a sail, and four days' provisions; which last the Japanese captain was so kind to double out of his own stores, and would permit no man to search me. I got down into the canoe, while the Dutchman, standing upon the deck, loaded me with all the curses and injurious terms his language could afford.

About an hour before we saw the pirates, I had taken an observation, and found we were in the latitude of 46 N. and of longitude 183. When I was at some distance from the pirates, I discovered by my pocket-glass several islands to the southeast. I set up my sail, the wind being fair, with a design to reach the nearest of those islands, which I made a shift to do in about three hours. It was all rocky; however I got many birds' eggs, and striking fire I kindled some heath and dry seaweed, by which I roasted my eggs. I eat no other supper, being resolved to spare my provisions as much as I could. I passed the night under the shelter of a rock, strowing some heath under me, and slept pretty well.

The next day I sailed to another island, and thence to a third and fourth, sometimes using my sail, and sometimes my paddles. But not to trouble the reader with a particular account of my distresses, let it suffice that on the 5th day I arrived at the last island in my sight, which lay south-southeast to the former.

This island was at a greater distance than I expected, and I did not reach it in less than five hours. I encompassed it almost round before I could find a convenient place to land in, which was a small creek, about three times the wideness of my canoe. I found the island to be all rocky, only a little intermingled with tufts of grass, and sweet-smelling herbs. I took out my small provisions, and after having refreshed myself, I secured the remainder in a cave, whereof there were great numbers. I gathered plenty of eggs upon the rocks, and got a quantity of dry seaweed, and parched grass, which I designed to kindle the next day, and roast my eggs as well as I could. (For I had about me my flint, steel, match, and burning glass.) I lay all night in the cave where I had lodged my provisions. My bed was the same dry grass and seaweed which I intended for fuel. I slept very little, for the disquiets of my mind prevailed over my weariness, and kept me awake. I considered how impossible it was to preserve my life in so desolate a place; and how miserable my end must be. Yet I found my self so listless and desponding, that I had not the heart to rise; and before I could get spirits enough to creep out of my cave, the day was far advanced. I walked a while among the rocks; the sky was perfectly clear, and the sun so hot, that I was forced to turn my face from it: when all on a sudden it became obscured, as I thought, in a manner very different from what happens by the interposition of a cloud. I turned back, and perceived a vast opaque body between me and the sun, moving forwards towards the island: it seemed to be about two miles high, and hid the sun six or seven minutes, but I did not observe the air to be much colder, or the sky more darkened, than if I had stood under the shade of a mountain. As it approached nearer over the place where I was, it appeared to be a firm substance, the bottom flat, smooth, and shining very bright from the reflection of the sea below. I stood upon a height about two hundred yards from the shore, and saw this vast body descending almost to a parallel with me, at less than an English mile distance. I took out my pocket perspective, and could plainly discover numbers of people moving up and down the sides of it, which appeared to be sloping, but what those people were doing I was not able to distinguish.

The natural love of life gave me some inward motions of joy, and I was ready to entertain a hope, that this adventure might some way or other help to deliver me from the desolate place and condition I was in. But at the same time, the reader can hardly conceive my astonishment, to behold an island in the air, inhabited by men, who were able (as it should seem) to raise, or sink, or put it into a progressive motion, as they pleased. But not being, at that time, in a disposition to philosophize upon this phenomenon, I rather chose to observe what course the island would take; because it seemed for a while to stand still. Yet soon after it advanced nearer; and I could see the sides of it, encompassed with several gradations of galleries and stairs, at certain intervals, to descend from one to the other. In the lowest gallery, I beheld some people fishing with long angling rods, and others looking on. I waved my cap (for my hat was long since worn out) and my handkerchief towards the island; and upon its nearer approach, I called and shouted with the utmost strength of my voice; and then looking circumspectly,[3] I beheld a crowd gathered to that side which was most in my view. I found by their pointing towards me and to each other, that they plainly discovered me, although they made no return to my shouting. But I could see four or five men running in great haste up the stairs to the top of the island, who then disappeared. I happened rightly to conjecture, that these were sent for orders to some person in authority upon this occasion.

The number of people increased, and in less than half an hour the island was moved and raised in such a manner, that the lowest gallery appeared in a parallel of less than an hundred yards' distance

3. Attentively around.

from the height where I stood. I then put myself into the most supplicating postures, and spoke in the humblest accent, but received no answer. Those who stood nearest over against me seemed to be persons of distinction, as I supposed by their habit. They conferred earnestly with each other, looking often upon me. At length one of them called out in a clear, polite, smooth dialect, not unlike in sound to Italian; and therefore I returned an answer in that language, hoping at least that the cadence might be more agreeable to his ears. Although neither of us understood the other, yet my meaning was easily known, for the people saw the distress I was in.

They made signs for me to come down from the rock, and go towards the shore, which I accordingly did; and the flying island being raised to a convenient height, the verge directly over me, a chain was let down from the lowest gallery, with a seat fastened to the bottom, to which I fixed myself, and was drawn up by pulleys.

CHAPTER II. *The humors and dispositions of the Laputans described. An account of their learning. Of the King and his court. The author's reception there. The inhabitants subject to fears and disquietudes. An account of the women.*

At my alighting I was surrounded by a crowd of people, but those who stood nearest seemed to be of better quality. They beheld me with all the marks and circumstances of wonder; neither indeed was I much in their debt, having never till then seen a race of mortals so singular in their shapes, habits, and countenances. Their heads were all reclined to the right, or the left; one of their eyes turned inward, and the other directly up to the zenith. Their outward garments were adorned with the figures of suns, moons, and stars, interwoven with those of fiddles, flutes, harps, trumpets, guitars, harpsichords, and many more instruments of music, unknown to us in Europe.[4] I observed here and there many in the habits of servants, with a blown bladder fastened like a flail to the end of a short stick, which they carried in their hands. In each bladder was a small quantity of dried pease or little pebbles (as I was afterwards informed). With these bladders they now and then flapped the mouths and ears of those who stood near them, of which practice I could not then conceive the meaning. It seems, the minds of these people are so taken up with intense speculations, that they neither can speak, or attend to the discourses of others, without being roused by some external taction[5] upon the organs of speech and hearing; for which reason those persons who are able to afford it always keep a flapper (the original is *climenole*) in their family, as one of their domestics; nor ever walk abroad or make visits without him. And the business of this officer is, when two or more persons

4. The Laputans represent contemporary speculation, deplored by Swift, about abstract theories of science, mathematics, and music. Both the Royal Society and Sir Isaac Newton took an interest in the mathematical basis of music.
5. Touch.

are in company, gently to strike with his bladder the mouth of him who is to speak, and the right ear of him or them to whom the speaker addresseth himself. This flapper is likewise employed diligently to attend his master in his walks, and upon occasion to give him a soft flap on his eyes, because he is always so wrapped up in cogitation, that he is in manifest danger of falling down every precipice, and bouncing his head against every post; and in the streets, of jostling others, or being jostled himself into the kennel.[6]

It was necessary to give the reader this information, without which he would be at the same loss with me, to understand the proceedings of these people, as they conducted me up the stairs to the top of the island, and from thence to the royal palace. While we were ascending, they forgot several times what they were about, and left me to myself, till their memories were again roused by their flappers; for they appeared altogether unmoved by the sight of my foreign habit and countenance, and by the shouts of the vulgar, whose thoughts and minds were more disengaged.

At last we entered the palace, and proceeded into the chamber of presence; where I saw the King seated on his throne, attended on each side by persons of prime quality. Before the throne was a large table filled with globes and spheres, and mathematical instruments of all kinds. His Majesty took not the least notice of us, although our entrance was not without sufficient noise, by the concourse of all persons belonging to the court. But he was then deep in a problem, and we attended at least an hour before he could solve it. There stood by him on each side a young page, with flaps in their hands, and when they saw he was at leisure, one of them gently struck his mouth, and the other his right ear; at which he started like one awaked on the sudden, and looking towards me, and the company I was in, recollected the occasion of our coming, whereof he had been informed before. He spoke some words, whereupon immediately a young man with a flap came up to my side, and flapped me gently on the right ear; but I made signs as well as I could, that I had no occasion for such an instrument; which as I afterwards found gave his Majesty and the whole court a very mean opinion of my understanding. The King, as far as I could conjecture, asked me several questions, and I addressed myself to him in all the languages I had. When it was found that I could neither understand nor be understood, I was conducted by his order to an apartment in his palace (this prince being distinguished above all his predecessors for his hospitality to strangers),[7] where two servants were appointed to attend me. My dinner was brought, and four persons of quality, whom I remembered to have seen very near the King's person, did me the honor to dine with me. We had two courses, of three dishes each. In the first course there was a shoul-

6. Gutter.
7. George I, a patron of music and science, had filled his court with Hanoverians when he came to England in 1714.

der of mutton, cut into an equilateral triangle; a piece of beef into a rhomboid; and a pudding into a cycloid. The second course was two ducks, trussed up into the form of fiddles; sausages and pudding resembling flutes and hautboys,[8] and a breast of veal in the shape of a harp. The servants cut our bread into cones, cylinders, parallelograms, and several other mathematical figures.

While we were at dinner, I made bold to ask the names of several things in their language, and those noble persons, by the assistance of their flappers, delighted to give me answers, hoping to raise my admiration of their great abilities, if I could be brought to converse with them. I was soon able to call for bread and drink, or whatever else I wanted.

After dinner my company withdrew, and a person was sent to me by the King's order, attended by a flapper. He brought with him pen, ink, and paper, and three or four books; giving me to understand by signs, that he was sent to teach me the language. We sat together four hours, in which time I wrote down a great number of words in columns, with the translations over against them. I likewise made a shift to learn several short sentences. For my tutor would order one of my servants to fetch something, to turn about, to make a bow, to sit, or stand, or walk, and the like. Then I took down the sentence in writing. He showed me also in one of his books the figures of the sun, moon, and stars, the zodiac, the tropics and polar circles, together with the denominations of many figures of planes and solids. He gave me the names and descriptions of all the musical instruments, and the general terms of art in playing on each of them. After he had left me, I placed all my words with their interpretations in alphabetical order. And thus in a few days, by the help of a very faithful memory, I got some insight into their language.

The word, which I interpret the *Flying* or *Floating Island*, is in the original *Laputa*; whereof I could never learn the true etymology. *Lap* in the old obsolete language signifieth *high*, and *untuh* a *governor*; from which they say by corruption was derived *Laputa*, from *Lapuntuh*. But I do not approve of this derivation, which seems to be a little strained. I ventured to offer to the learned among them a conjecture of my own, that *Laputa* was *quasi Lap outed*; *Lap* signifying properly the dancing of the sunbeams in the sea, and *outed* a wing, which however I shall not obtrude, but submit to the judicious reader.[9]

Those to whom the King had entrusted me, observing how ill I was clad, ordered a tailor to come next morning, and take my measure for a suit of clothes. This operator did his office after a different manner from those of his trade in Europe. He first took my altitude by a quadrant, and then, with rule and compasses, described the

8. Oboes.
9. Gulliver overlooks a likelier etymol-ogy: Spanish *la puta*, "the whore".

dimensions and outlines of my whole body; all which he entered upon paper, and in six days brought my clothes very ill made, and quite out of shape, by happening to mistake a figure in the calculation. But my comfort was, that I observed such accidents very frequent, and little regarded.

During my confinement for want of clothes, and by an indisposition that held me some days longer, I much enlarged my dictionary; and when I went next to court, was able to understand many things the King spoke, and to return him some kind of answers. His Majesty had given orders that the island should move northeast and by east, to the vertical point over Lagado, the metropolis of the whole kingdom, below upon the firm earth. It was about ninety leagues distant, and our voyage lasted four days and a half. I was not in the least sensible of the progressive motion made in the air by the island. On the second morning, about eleven o'clock, the King himself in person, attended by his nobility, courtiers, and officers, having prepared all their musical instruments, played on them for three hours without intermission, so that I was quite stunned with the noise; neither could I possibly guess the meaning, till my tutor informed me. He said, that the people of their island had their ears adapted to hear the music of the spheres, which always played at certain periods; and the court was now prepared to bear their part in whatever instrument they most excelled.

In our journey towards Lagado, the capital city, his Majesty ordered that the island should stop over certain towns and villages, from whence he might receive the petitions of his subjects. And to this purpose, several packthreads were let down with small weights at the bottom. On these packthreads the people strung their petitions, which mounted up directly like the scraps of paper fastened by schoolboys at the end of the string that holds their kite.[1] Sometimes we received wine and victuals from below, which were drawn up by pulleys.

The knowledge I had in mathematics gave me great assistance in acquiring their phraseology, which depended much upon that science and music; and in the latter I was not unskilled. Their ideas are perpetually conversant in lines and figures. If they would, for example, praise the beauty of a woman, or any other animal, they describe it by rhombs, circles, parallelograms, ellipses, and other geometrical terms; or else by words of art drawn from music, needless here to repeat. I observed in the King's kitchen all sorts of mathematical and musical instruments, after the figures of which they cut up the joints that were served to his Majesty's table.

Their houses are very ill built, the walls bevil, without one right angle in any apartment; and this defect ariseth from the contempt they bear for practical geometry; which they despise as vulgar and

1. Petitioners, that is, might as well go fly a kite. Throughout this section Swift satirizes the "distance" of George I (who spent much of his time in Hanover) from his English subjects.

mechanic, those instructions they give being too refined for the intellectuals of their workmen; which occasions perpetual mistakes. And although they are dextrous enough upon a piece of paper, in the management of the rule, the pencil, and the divider, yet in the common actions and behavior of life I have not seen a more clumsy, awkward, and unhandy people, nor so slow and perplexed in their conceptions upon all other subjects, except those of mathematics and music. They are very bad reasoners, and vehemently given to opposition, unless when they happen to be of the right opinion, which is seldom their case. Imagination, fancy, and invention, they are wholly strangers to, nor have any words in their language by which those ideas can be expressed; the whole compass of their thoughts and mind being shut up within the two forementioned sciences.

Most of them, and especially those who deal in the astronomical part, have great faith in judicial astrology, although they are ashamed to own it publicly. But what I chiefly admired,[2] and thought altogether unaccountable, was the strong disposition I observed in them towards news and politics; perpetually enquiring into public affairs, giving their judgments in matters of state; and passionately disputing every inch of a party opinion. I have indeed observed the same disposition among most of the mathematicians I have known in Europe; although I could never discover the least analogy between the two sciences; unless those people suppose, that because the smallest circle hath as many degrees as the largest, therefore the regulation and management of the world require no more abilities than the handling and turning of a globe. But I rather take this quality to spring from a very common infirmity of human nature, inclining us to be more curious and conceited in matters where we have least concern, and for which we are least adapted either by study or nature.

These people are under continual disquietudes, never enjoying a minute's peace of mind; and their disturbances proceed from causes which very little affect the rest of mortals. Their apprehensions arise from several changes they dread in the celestial bodies. For instance; that the earth, by the continual approaches of the sun towards it, must in course of time be absorbed or swallowed up. That the face of the sun will by degrees be encrusted with its own effluvia,[3] and give no more light to the world. That the earth very narrowly escaped a brush from the tail of the last comet, which would have infallibly reduced it to ashes; and that the next, which they have calculated for one and thirty years hence, will probably destroy us.[4] For, if in its perihelion it should approach within a certain degree of the sun (as by their calculations they have reason to

---

2. Wondered at.
3. Sunspots.
4. Halley's comet, some astronomers had feared, might strike the earth on its next

appearance (1758). All the disasters that disquiet the Laputans had occurred to English scientists as possible implications of Newtonian theory.

dread), it will conceive a degree of heat ten thousand times more intense than that of red-hot glowing iron; and in its absence from the sun, carry a blazing tail ten hundred thousand and fourteen miles long; through which if the earth should pass at the distance of one hundred thousand miles from the nucleus, or main body of the comet, it must in its passage be set on fire, and reduced to ashes. That the sun daily spending its rays without any nutriment to supply them, will at last be wholly consumed and annihilated; which must be attended with the destruction of this earth, and of all the planets that receive their light from it.

They are so perpetually alarmed with the apprehensions of these and the like impending dangers, that they can neither sleep quietly in their beds, nor have any relish for the common pleasures or amusements of life. When they meet an acquaintance in the morning, the first question is about the sun's health, how he looked at his setting and rising, and what hopes they have to avoid the stroke of the approaching comet. This conversation they are apt to run into with the same temper that boys discover in delighting to hear terrible stories of sprites and hobgoblins, which they greedily listen to, and dare not go to bed for fear.

The women of the island have abundance of vivacity; they contemn their husbands, and are exceedingly fond of strangers, whereof there is always a considerable number from the continent below, attending at court, either upon affairs of the several towns and corporations, or their own particular occasions; but are much despised, because they want the same endowments. Among these the ladies choose their gallants: but the vexation is, that they act with too much ease and security; for the husband is always so rapt in speculation, that the mistress and lover may proceed to the greatest familiarities before his face, if he be but provided with paper and implements, and without his flapper at his side.

The wives and daughters lament their confinement to the island, although I think it the most delicious spot of ground in the world; and although they live here in the greatest plenty and magnificence, and are allowed to do whatever they please, they long to see the world, and take the diversions of the metropolis, which they are not allowed to do without a particular license from the King; and this is not easy to be obtained, because the people of quality have found by frequent experience, how hard it is to persuade their women to return from below. I was told that a great court lady, who had several children, is married to the prime minister, the richest subject in the kingdom, a very graceful person, extremely fond of her, and lives in the finest palace of the island, went down to Lagado, on the pretense of health, there hid herself for several months, till the King sent a warrant to search for her, and she was found in an obscure eating-house all in rags, having pawned her clothes to maintain an old deformed footman, who beat her every day, and in whose company she was taken much against her will. And although her husband received her with all possible kindness, and without the least reproach, she soon after contrived to steal down again with all her jewels, to the same gallant, and hath not been heard of since.

This may perhaps pass with the reader rather for an European or English story, than for one of a country so remote. But he may please to consider, that the caprices of womankind are not limited by any climate or nation; and that they are much more uniform than can be easily imagined.

In about a month's time I had made a tolerable proficiency in their language, and was able to answer most of the King's questions, when I had the honor to attend him. His Majesty discovered not the least curiosity to enquire into the laws, government, history, religion, or manners of the countries where I had been; but confined his questions to the state of mathematics, and received the account I gave him with great contempt and indifference, though often roused by his flapper on each side.

[The Struldbruggs]

CHAPTER X. *The Luggnaggians commended. A particular description of the struldbruggs, with many conversations between the author and some eminent persons upon that subject.*

The Luggnaggians are a polite[1] and generous people, and although they are not without some share of that pride which is peculiar to all eastern countries, yet they show themselves courteous to strangers, especially such who are countenanced by the court. I had many acquaintance among persons of the best fashion, and being always attended by my interpreter, the conversation we had was not disagreeable.

One day in much good company, I was asked by a person of quality, whether I had seen any of their *struldbruggs* or *immortals*. I said I had not; and desired he would explain to me what he meant by such an appellation, applied to a mortal creature. He told me, that sometimes, although very rarely, a child happened to be born in a family with a red circular spot in the forehead, directly over the left eyebrow, which was an infallible mark that it should never die. The spot, as he described it, was about the compass of a silver threepence, but in the course of time grew larger, and changed its color; for at twelve years old it became green, so continued till five and twenty, then turned to a deep blue; at five and forty it grew coal black, and as large as an English shilling; but never admitted any farther alteration. He said these births were so rare, that he did not believe there could be above eleven hundred *struldbruggs* of

1. Refined, cultivated.

both sexes in the whole kingdom, of which he computed about fifty in the metropolis, and among the rest a young girl born about three years ago. That these productions were not peculiar to any family, but a mere effect of chance; and the children of the *struldbruggs* themselves were equally mortal with the rest of the people.

I freely own myself to have been struck with inexpressible delight upon hearing this account: and the person who gave it me happening to understand the Balnibarbian language, which I spoke very well, I could not forbear breaking out into expressions perhaps a little too extravagant. I cried out as in a rapture: Happy nation, where every child hath at least a chance for being immortal! Happy people who enjoy so many living examples of ancient virtue, and have masters ready to instruct them in the wisdom of all former ages! But happiest beyond all comparison are those excellent *struldbruggs*, who being born exempt from that universal calamity of human nature, have their minds free and disengaged, without the weight and depression of spirits caused by the continual apprehension of death. I discovered my admiration[2] that I had not observed any of these illustrious persons at court; the black spot on the forehead being so remarkable a distinction, that I could not have easily overlooked it; and it was impossible that his Majesty, a most judicious prince, should not provide himself with a good number of such wise and able counselors. Yet perhaps the virtue of those reverend sages was too strict for the corrupt and libertine manners of a court. And we often find by experience that young men are too opinionative[3] and volatile to be guided by the sober dictates of their seniors. However, since the King was pleased to allow me access to his royal person, I was resolved upon the very first occasion to deliver my opinion to him on this matter freely, and at large by the help of my interpreter; and whether he would please to take my advice or no, yet in one thing I was determined, that his Majesty having frequently offered me an establishment in this country, I would with great thankfulness accept the favor, and pass my life here in the conversation of those superior beings the *struldbruggs*, if they would please to admit me.

The gentleman to whom I addressed my discourse, because (as I have already observed) he spoke the language of Balnibarbi, said to me with a sort of a smile, which usually ariseth from pity to the ignorant, that he was glad of any occasion to keep me among them, and desired my permission to explain to the company what I had spoke. He did so; and they talked together for some time in their own language, whereof I understood not a syllable, neither could I observe by their countenances what impression my discourse had made on them. After a short silence the same person told me, that his friends and mine (so he thought fit to express himself) were

2. Wonder.
3. Speculative, impractical. Note, in the next sentence, Gulliver's own resolve to deliver his opinion.

very much pleased with the judicious remarks I had made on the great happiness and advantages of immortal life; and they were desirous to know in a particular manner, what scheme of living I should have formed to myself, if it had fallen to my lot to have been born a *struldbrugg*.

I answered, it was easy to be eloquent on so copious and delightful a subject, especially to me who have been often apt to amuse myself with visions of what I should do if I were a king, a general, or a great lord; and upon this very case I had frequently run over the whole system how I should employ myself, and pass the time if I were sure to live forever.

That, if it had been my good fortune to come into the world a *struldbrugg*, as soon as I could discover my own happiness by understanding the difference between life and death, I would first resolve by all arts and methods whatsoever to procure myself riches: in the pursuit of which, by thrift and management, I might reasonably expect in about two hundred years to be the wealthiest man in the kingdom. In the second place, I would from my earliest youth apply myself to the study of arts and sciences, by which I should arrive in time to excel all others in learning. Lastly, I would carefully record every action and event of consequence that happened in the public, impartially draw the characters of the several successions of princes, and great ministers of state; with my own observations on every point. I would exactly set down the several changes in customs, languages, fashions of dress, diet and diversions. By all which acquirements, I should be a living treasury of knowledge and wisdom, and certainly become the oracle of the nation.

I would never marry after threescore, but live in an hospitable manner, yet still on the saving side. I would entertain myself in forming and directing the minds of hopeful young men, by convincing them from my own remembrance, experience and observation, fortified by numerous examples, of the usefulness of virtue in public and private life. But my choice and constant companions should be a set of my own immortal brotherhood, among whom I would elect a dozen from the most ancient down to my own contemporaries. Where any of these wanted fortunes, I would provide them with convenient lodges round my own estate, and have some of them always at my table, only mingling a few of the most valuable among you mortals, whom length of time would harden me to lose with little or no reluctance, and treat your posterity after the same manner; just as a man diverts himself with the annual succession of pinks and tulips in his garden, without regretting the loss of those which withered the preceding year.

These *struldbruggs* and I would mutually communicate our observations and memorials[4] through the course of time; remark the several gradations by which corruption steals into the world, and

4. Memories.

oppose it in every step, by giving perpetual warning and instruction to mankind; which, added to the strong influence of our own example, would probably prevent that continual degeneracy of human nature, so justly complained of in all ages.

Add to all this, the pleasure of seeing the various revolutions of states and empires; the changes in the lower and upper world;[5] ancient cities in ruins; and obscure villages become the seats of kings. Famous rivers lessening into shallow brooks; the ocean leaving one coast dry, and overwhelming another; the discovery of many countries yet unknown. Barbarity overrunning the politest nations, and the most barbarous becoming civilized. I should then see the discovery of the longitude, the perpetual motion, the universal medicine,[6] and many other great inventions brought to the utmost perfection.

What wonderful discoveries should we make in astronomy, by outliving and confirming our own predictions, by observing the progress and returns of comets, with the changes of motion in the sun, moon and stars.

I enlarged upon many other topics, which the natural desire of endless life and sublunary happiness could easily furnish me with. When I had ended, and the sum of my discourse had been interpreted as before to the rest of the company, there was a good deal of talk among them in the language of the country, not without some laughter at my expense. At last the same gentleman who had been my interpreter said, he was desired by the rest to set me right in a few mistakes, which I had fallen into through the common imbecility[7] of human nature, and upon that allowance was less answerable for them. That this breed of *struldbruggs* was peculiar to their country, for there were no such people either in Balnibarbi or Japan, where he had the honor to be ambassador from his Majesty, and found the natives in both those kingdoms very hard to believe that the fact was possible; and it appeared from my astonishment when he first mentioned the matter to me, that I received it as a thing wholly new, and scarcely to be credited. That in the two kingdoms above mentioned, where during his residence he had conversed very much, he observed long life to be the universal desire and wish of mankind. That whoever had one foot in the grave was sure to hold back the other as strongly as he could. That the oldest had still hopes of living one day longer, and looked on death as the greatest evil, from which nature always prompted him to retreat; only in this island of Luggnagg the appetite for living was not so eager, from the continual example of the *struldbruggs* before their eyes.

5. Earth and heaven; figuratively, common people and the ruling class. "Revolutions": cycles.
6. The *elixir vitae*, an alchemical formula to preserve life forever, was considered by Swift an impossible dream, like a method for caluclating longitude at sea, or a perpetual motion machine.
7. Weakness.

That the system of living contrived by me was unreasonable and unjust, because it supposed a perpetuity of youth, health, and vigor, which no man could be so foolish to hope, however extravagant he might be in his wishes. That the question therefore was not whether a man would choose to be always in the prime of youth, attended with prosperity and health; but how he would pass a perpetual life under all the usual disadvantages which old age brings along with it. For although few men will avow their desires of being immortal upon such hard conditions, yet in the two kingdoms before mentioned of Balnibarbi and Japan, he observed that every man desired to put off death for some time longer, let it approach ever so late; and he rarely heard of any man who died willingly, except he were incited by the extremity of grief or torture. And he appealed to me whether in those countries I had traveled, as well as my own, I had not observed the same general disposition.

After this preface he gave me a particular account of the *struld-bruggs* among them. He said they commonly acted like mortals, till about thirty years old, after which by degrees they grew melancholy and dejected, increasing in both till they came to fourscore. This he learned from their own confession; for otherwise there not being above two or three of that species born in an age, they were too few to form a general observation by. When they came to fourscore years, which is reckoned the extremity of living in this country, they had not only all the follies and infirmities of other old men, but many more which arose from the dreadful prospect of never dying. They were not only opinionative, peevish, covetous, morose, vain, talkative; but uncapable of friendship, and dead to all natural affection, which never descended below their grandchildren. Envy and impotent desires are their prevailing passions. But those objects against which their envy seems principally directed, are the vices of the younger sort, and the deaths of the old. By reflecting on the former, they find themselves cut off from all possibility of pleasure; and whenever they see a funeral, they lament and repine that others are gone to an harbor of rest, to which they themselves never can hope to arrive. They have no remembrance of anything but what they learned and observed in their youth and middle age, and even that is very imperfect. And for the truth or particulars of any fact, it is safer to depend on common traditions than upon their best recollections. The least miserable among them appear to be those who turn to dotage, and entirely lose their memories; these meet with more pity and assistance, because they want[8] many bad qualities which abound in others.

If a *struldbrugg* happen to marry one of his own kind, the marriage is dissolved of course by the courtesy of the kingdom, as soon as the younger of the two comes to be fourscore. For the law thinks it a reasonable indulgence, that those who are condemned without

8. Lack.

any fault of their own to a perpetual continuance in the world, should not have their misery doubled by the load of a wife.

As soon as they have completed the term of eighty years, they are looked on as dead in law; their heirs immediately succeed to their estates, only a small pittance is reserved for their support; and the poor ones are maintained at the public charge. After that period they are held incapable of any employment of trust or profit; they cannot purchase lands, or take leases, neither are they allowed to be witnesses in any cause, either civil or criminal, not even for the decision of meers[9] and bounds.

At ninety they lose their teeth and hair; they have at that age no distinction of taste, but eat and drink whatever they can get, without relish or appetite. The diseases they were subject to still continue without increasing or diminishing. In talking they forget the common appellation of things, and the names of persons, even of those who are their nearest friends and relations. For the same reason they never can amuse themselves with reading, because their memory will not serve to carry them from the beginning of a sentence to the end, and by this defect they are deprived of the only entertainment whereof they might otherwise be capable.

The language of this country being always upon the flux, the *struldbruggs* of one age do not understand those of another; neither are they able after two hundred years to hold any conversation (farther than by a few general words) with their neighbors the mortals; and thus they lie under the disadvantage of living like foreigners in their own country.

This was the account given me of the *struldbruggs*, as near as I can remember. I afterwards saw five or six of different ages, the youngest not above two hundred years old, who were brought to me at several times by some of my friends; but although they were told that I was a great traveler, and had seen all the world, they had not the least curiosity to ask me a question; only desired I would give them *slumskudask*, or a token of remembrance; which is a modest way of begging, to avoid the law that strictly forbids it, because they are provided for by the public, although indeed with a very scanty allowance.

They are despised and hated by all sorts of people; when one of them is born, it is reckoned ominous, and their birth is recorded very particularly; so that you may know their age by consulting the registry, which however hath not been kept above a thousand years past, or at least hath been destroyed by time or public disturbances. But the usual way of computing how old they are, is by asking them what kings or great persons they can remember, and then consulting history; for infallibly the last prince in their mind did not begin his reign after they were fourscore years old.

They were the most mortifying sight I ever beheld; and the

9. Boundaries.

women more horrible than the men. Besides the usual deformities in extreme old age, they acquired an additional ghastliness in proportion to their number of years, which is not to be described; and among half a dozen I soon distinguished which was the oldest, although there were not above a century or two between them.

The reader will easily believe, that from what I had heard and seen, my keen appetite for perpetuity of life was much abated. I grew heartily ashamed of the pleasing visions I had formed; and thought no tyrant could invent a death into which I would not run with pleasure from such a life. The King heard of all that had passed between me and my friends upon this occasion, and rallied[1] me very pleasantly; wishing I would send a couple of *struldbruggs* to my own country, to arm our people against the fear of death; but this it seems is forbidden by the fundamental laws of the kingdom; or else I should have been well content with the trouble and expense of transporting them.

I could not but agree, that the laws of this kingdom relating to the *struldbruggs*, were founded upon the strongest reasons, and such as any other country would be under the necessity of enacting in the like circumstances. Otherwise, as avarice is the necessary consequent of old age, those immortals would in time become proprietors of the whole nation, and engross[2] the civil power; which, for want of abilities to manage, must end in the ruin of the public.

Part IV. A Voyage to the Country of the Houyhnhnms [1]

CHAPTER I. *The Author sets out as Captain of a ship. His men conspire against him, confine him a long time to his cabin, set him on shore in an unknown land. He travels up into the country. The Yahoos, a strange sort of animal, described. The Author meets two Houyhnhnms.*

I continued at home with my wife and children about five months in a very happy condition, if I could have learned the lesson of knowing when I was well. I left my poor wife big with child, and accepted an advantageous offer made me to be Captain of the *Adventure*, a stout merchantman of 350 tons; for I understood navigation well, and being grown weary of a surgeon's employment at sea, which however I could exercise upon occasion, I took a skillful young man of that calling, one Robert Purefoy, into my ship. We set sail from Portsmouth upon the 7th day of September, 1710; on the 14th we met with Captain Pocock of Bristol, at Tenariff,[2] who was going to the Bay of Campeachy[3] to cut logwood. On the 16th he was parted from us by a storm; I heard since my return that his ship foundered and none escaped, but one

1. Ridiculed.
2. Absorb, monopolize.
1. Pronounced Hwín-ims. The word sug-

gests the neigh characteristic of a horse.
2. Teneriffe, one of the Canary Islands.
3. In the Gulf of Mexico.

cabin boy. He was an honest man and a good sailor, but a little too positive in his own opinions, which was the cause of his destruction, as it hath been of several others. For if he had followed my advice, he might at this time have been safe at home with his family as well as myself.

I had several men died in my ship of calentures,[4] so that I was forced to get recruits out of Barbadoes and the Leeward Islands, where I touched by the direction of the merchants who employed me; which I had soon too much cause to repent, for I found afterwards that most of them had been buccaneers. I had fifty hands on board; and my orders were that I should trade with the Indians in the South Sea, and make what discoveries I could. These rogues whom I had picked up debauched my other men, and they all formed a conspiracy to seize the ship and secure me; which they did one morning, rushing into my cabin, and binding me hand and foot, threatening to throw me overboard, if I offered to stir. I told them I was their prisoner, and would submit. This they made me swear to do, and then unbound me, only fastening one of my legs with a chain near my bed, and placed a sentry at my door with his piece charged, who was commanded to shoot me dead if I attempted my liberty. They sent me down victuals and drink, and took the government of the ship to themselves. Their design was to turn pirates and plunder the Spaniards, which they could not do, till they got more men. But first they resolved to sell the goods in the ship, and then go to Madagascar for recruits, several among them having died since my confinement. They sailed many weeks, and traded with the Indians; but I knew not what course they took, being kept close prisoner in my cabin, and expecting nothing less than to be murdered, as they often threatened me.

Upon the 9th day of May, 1711, one James Welch came down to my cabin; and said he had orders from the Captain to set me ashore. I expostulated with him, but in vain; neither would he so much as tell me who their new Captain was. They forced me into the longboat, letting me put on my best suit of clothes, which were as good as new, and a small bundle of linen, but no arms except my hanger; and they were so civil as not to search my pockets, into which I conveyed what money I had, with some other little necessaries. They rowed about a league, and then set me down on a strand. I desired them to tell me what country it was; they all swore, they knew no more than myself, but said that the Captain (as they called him) was resolved, after they had sold the lading, to get rid of me in the first place where they discovered land. They pushed off immediately, advising me to make haste, for fear of being overtaken by the tide, and bade me farewell.

In this desolate condition I advanced forward, and soon got upon

4. "A distemper peculiar to sailors, in hot climates; wherein they imagine the sea to be green fields, and will throw themselves into it, if not restrained" (Johnson's *Dictionary*).

firm ground, where I sat down on a bank to rest myself, and consider what I had best to do. When I was a little refreshed, I went up into the country, resolving to deliver myself to the first savages I should meet, and purchase my life from them by some bracelets, glass rings, and other toys, which sailors usually provide themselves with in those voyages, and whereof I had some about me. The land was divided by long rows of trees, not regularly planted, but naturally growing; there was great plenty of grass, and several fields of oats. I walked very circumspectly for fear of being surprised, or suddenly shot with an arrow from behind, or on either side. I fell into a beaten road, where I saw many tracks of human feet, and some of cows, but most of horses. At last I beheld several animals in a field, and one or two of the same kind sitting in trees. Their shape was very singular, and deformed, which a little discomposed me, so that I lay down behind a thicket to observe them better. Some of them coming forward near the place where I lay, gave me an opportunity of distinctly marking their form. Their heads and breasts were covered with a thick hair, some frizzled and others lank; they had beards like goats, and a long ridge of hair down their backs, and the fore parts of their legs and feet; but the rest of their bodies were bare, so that I might see their skins, which were of a brown buff color. They had no tails, nor any hair at all on their buttocks, except about the anus; which, I presume Nature had placed there to defend them as they sat on the ground; for this posture they used, as well as lying down, and often stood on their hind feet. They climbed high trees, as nimbly as a squirrel, for they had strong extended claws before and behind, terminating in sharp points, and hooked. They would often spring, and bound, and leap with prodigious agility. The females were not so large as the males; they had long lank hair on their heads, and only a sort of down on the rest of their bodies, except about the anus, and pudenda. Their dugs hung between their forefeet, and often reached almost to the ground as they walked. The hair of both sexes was of several colors, brown, red, black, and yellow. Upon the whole, I never beheld in all my travels so disagreeable an animal, or one against which I naturally conceived so strong an antipathy. So that thinking I had seen enough, full of contempt and aversion, I got up and pursued the beaten road, hoping it might direct me to the cabin of some Indian: I had not gone far when I met one of these creatures full in my way, and coming up directly to me. The ugly monster, when he saw me, distorted several ways every feature of his visage, and stared as at an object he had never seen before; then approaching nearer, lifted up his forepaw, whether out of curiosity or mischief, I could not tell; but I drew my hanger, and gave him a good blow with the flat side of it; for I durst not strike him with the edge, fearing the inhabitants might be provoked against me, if they should come to know that I had killed or maimed any of their cattle. When the beast felt the smart, he drew back, and roared so loud, that a herd of at least forty came flocking about me from the next field, howling and making odious faces; but I ran to the body of a tree, and leaning my back against it, kept them off, by waving my hanger. Several of this cursed brood getting hold of the branches behind, leaped up into the tree, from whence they began to discharge their excrements on my head; however, I escaped pretty well, by sticking close to the stem of the tree, but was almost stifled with the filth, which fell about me on every side.

In the midst of this distress, I observed them all to run away on a sudden as fast as they could; at which I ventured to leave the tree, and pursue the road, wondering what it was that could put them into this fright. But looking on my left hand, I saw a horse walking softly in the field; which my persecutors having sooner discovered, was the cause of their flight. The horse started a little when he came near me, but soon recovering himself, looked full in my face with manifest tokens of wonder; he viewed my hands and feet, walking round me several times. I would have pursued my journey, but he placed himself directly in the way, yet looking with a very mild aspect, never offering the least violence. We stood gazing at each other for some time; at last I took the boldness, to reach my hand towards his neck, with a design to stroke it; using the common style and whistle of jockies when they are going to handle a strange horse. But, this animal seeming to receive my civilities with disdain, shook his head, and bent his brows, softly raising up his left forefoot to remove my hand. Then he neighed three or four times, but in so different a cadence, that I almost began to think he was speaking to himself in some language of his own.

While he and I were thus employed, another horse came up; who applying himself to the first in a very formal manner, they gently struck each others right hoof before, neighing several times by turns, and varying the sound, which seemed to be almost articulate. They went some paces off, as if it were to confer together, walking side by side, backward and forward, like persons deliberating upon some affair of weight; but often turning their eyes towards me, as it were to watch that I might not escape. I was amazed to see such actions and behavior in brute beasts; and concluded with myself that if the inhabitants of this country were endued with a proportionable degree of reason, they must needs be the wisest people upon earth. This thought gave me so much comfort, that I resolved to go forward until I could discover some house or village, or meet with any of the natives, leaving the two horses to discourse together as they pleased. But the first, who was a dapple grey, observing me to steal off, neighed after me in so expressive a tone that I fancied myself to understand what he meant; whereupon I turned back, and came near him, to expect his farther commands; but concealing my fear as much as I could; for I began to be in some pain, how this adventure might terminate; and the reader will easily believe I did not much like my present situation.

The two horses came up close to me, looking with great earnestness upon my face and hands. The grey steed rubbed my hat all round with his right fore hoof, and discomposed it so much that I was forced to adjust it better, by taking it off, and settling it again; whereat both he and his companion (who was a brown bay) appeared to be much surprised; the latter felt the lappet of my coat, and finding it to hang loose about me, they both looked with new signs of wonder. He stroked my right hand, seeming to admire the softness, and color; but he squeezed it so hard between his hoof and his pastern, that I was forced to roar; after which they both touched me with all possible tenderness. They were under great perplexity about my shoes and stockings, which they felt very often, neighing to each other, and using various gestures, not unlike those of a philosopher, when he would attempt to solve some new and difficult phenomenon.

Upon the whole, the behavior of these animals was so orderly and rational, so acute and judicious, that I at last concluded, they must needs be magicians, who had thus metamorphosed themselves upon some design; and seeing a stranger in the way, were resolved to divert themselves with him; or perhaps were really amazed at the sight of a man so very different in habit, feature, and complexion from those who might probably live in so remote a climate. Upon the strength of this reasoning, I ventured to address them in the following manner: "Gentlemen, if you be conjurers, as I have good cause to believe, you can understand any language; therefore I make bold to let your worships know that I am a poor distressed Englishman, driven by his misfortunes upon your coast; and I entreat one of you, to let me ride upon his back, as if he were a real horse, to some house or village, where I can be relieved. In return of which favor, I will make you a present of this knife and bracelet" (taking them out of my pocket). The two creatures stood silent while I spoke, seeming to listen with great attention; and when I had ended, they neighed frequently towards each other, as if they were engaged in serious conversation. I plainly observed, that their language expressed the passions very well, and the words might with little pains be resolved into an alphabet more easily than the Chinese.

I could frequently distinguish the word Yahoo,[5] which was repeated by each of them several times; and although it were impossible for me to conjecture what it meant, yet while the two horses were busy in conversation, I endeavored to practice this word upon my tongue; and as soon as they were silent, I boldly pronounced "Yahoo" in a loud voice, imitating, at the same time, as near as I could, the neighing of a horse; at which they were both visibly sur-

---

5. Morley suggested that *Yahoo* was compounded from two expressions of disgust, *yah* and *ugh* (or *hoo*) common in the 18th century [Case's note].

prised, and the grey repeated the same word twice, as if he meant to teach me the right accent, wherein I spoke after him as well as I could, and found myself perceivably to improve every time, although very far from any degree of perfection. Then the bay tried me with a second word, much harder to be pronounced; but reducing it to the English orthography, may be spelt thus, *Houyhnhnm*. I did not succeed in this so well as the former, but after two or three farther trials, I had better fortune; and they both appeared amazed at my capacity.

After some farther discourse, which I then conjectured might relate to me, the two friends took their leaves, with the same compliment of striking each other's hoof; and the grey made me signs that I should walk before him; wherein I thought it prudent to comply, till I could find a better director. When I offered to slacken my pace, he would cry, "Hhuun, Hhuun"; I guessed his meaning, and gave him to understand, as well as I could that I was weary, and not able to walk faster; upon which, he would stand a while to let me rest.

CHAPTER II. *The Author conducted by a Houyhnhnm to his house. The house described. The Author's reception. The food of the Houyhnhnms. The Author in distress for want of meat is at last relieved. His manner of feeding in that country.*

Having traveled about three miles, we came to a long kind of building, made of timber, stuck in the ground, and wattled across; the roof was low, and covered with straw. I now began to be a little comforted, and took out some toys, which travelers usually carry for presents to the savage Indians of America and other parts, in hopes the people of the house would be thereby encouraged to receive me kindly. The horse made me a sign to go in first; it was a large room with a smooth clay floor, and a rack and manger extending the whole length on one side. There were three nags, and two mares, not eating, but some of them sitting down upon their hams, which I very much wondered at; but wondered more to see the rest employed in domestic business; the last seemed but ordinary cattle; however this confirmed my first opinion, that a people who could so far civilize brute animals must needs excel in wisdom all the nations of the world. The grey came in just after, and thereby prevented any ill treatment, which the others might have given me. He neighed to them several times in a style of authority, and received answers.

Beyond this room there were three others, reaching the length of the house, to which you passed through three doors, opposite to each other, in the manner of a vista; we went through the second room towards the third; here the grey walked in first, beckoning me to attend; [6] I waited in the second room, and got ready my presents,

6. To wait.

for the master and mistress of the house; they were two knives, three bracelets of false pearl, a small looking glass and a bead necklace. The horse neighed three or four times, and I waited to hear some answers in a human voice, but I heard no other returns than in the same dialect, only one or two a little shriller than his. I began to think that this house must belong to some person of great note among them, because there appeared so much ceremony before I could gain admittance. But, that a man of quality should be served all by horses, was beyond my comprehension. I feared my brain was disturbed by my sufferings and misfortunes; I roused myself, and looked about me in the room where I was left alone; this was furnished as the first, only after a more elegant manner. I rubbed my eyes often, but the same objects still occurred. I pinched my arms and sides, to awake myself, hoping I might be in a dream. I then absolutely concluded that all these appearances could be nothing else but necromancy and magic. But I had no time to pursue these reflections; for the grey horse came to the door, and made me a sign to follow him into the third room; where I saw a very comely mare, together with a colt and foal, sitting on their haunches, upon mats of straw, not unartfully made, and perfectly neat and clean.

The mare soon after my entrance, rose from her mat, and coming up close, after having nicely observed my hands and face, gave me a most contemptuous look; then turning to the horse, I heard the word Yahoo often repeated betwixt them; the meaning of which word I could not then comprehend, although it were the first I had learned to pronounce; but I was soon better informed, to my everlasting mortification: for the horse beckoning to me with his head, and repeating the word, "Hhuun, Hhuun," as he did upon the road, which I understood was to attend him, led me out into a kind of court, where was another building at some distance from the house. Here we entered, and I saw three of those detestable creatures, which I first met after my landing, feeding upon roots, and the flesh of some animals, which I afterwards found to be that of asses and dogs, and now and then a cow dead by accident or disease. They were all tied by the neck with strong withes, fastened to a beam; they held their food between the claws of their forefeet, and tore it with their teeth.

The master horse ordered a sorrel nag, one of his servants, to untie the largest of these animals, and take him into a yard. The beast and I were brought close together; and our countenances diligently compared, both by master and servant, who thereupon repeated several times the word "Yahoo." My horror and astonishment are not to be described, when I observed, in this abominable animal, a perfect human figure; the face of it indeed was flat and broad, the nose depressed, the lips large, and the mouth wide; but these differences are common to all savage nations, where the lineaments of the countenance are distorted by the natives suffering their infants to lie groveling on the earth, or by carrying them on their backs, nuzzling with their face against the mother's shoulders. The forefeet of the Yahoo differed from my hands in nothing else but the length of the nails, the coarseness and brownness of the palms, and the hairiness on the backs. There was the same resemblance between our feet, with the same differences, which I knew very well, although the horses did not, because of my shoes and stockings; the same in every part of our bodies, except as to hairiness and color, which I have already described.

The great difficulty that seemed to stick with the two horses was to see the rest of my body so very different from that of a Yahoo, for which I was obliged to my clothes, whereof they had no conception; the sorrel nag offered me a root, which he held (after their manner, as we shall describe in its proper place) between his hoof and pastern; I took it in my hand, and having smelled it, returned it to him again as civilly as I could. He brought out of the Yahoo's kennel a piece of ass's flesh, but it smelled so offensively that I turned from it with loathing; he then threw it to the Yahoo, by whom it was greedily devoured. He afterwards showed me a wisp of hay, and a fetlock full of oats; but I shook my head, to signify that neither of these were food for me. And indeed, I now apprehended that I must absolutely starve, if I did not get to some of my own species; for as to those filthy Yahoos, although there were few greater lovers of mankind, at that time, than myself, yet I confess I never saw any sensitive being so detestable on all accounts; and the more I came near them, the more hateful they grew, while I stayed in that country. This the master horse observed by my behavior, and therefore sent the Yahoo back to his kennel. He then put his forehoof to his mouth, at which I was much surprised, although he did it with ease, and with a motion that appeared perfectly natural; and made other signs to know what I would eat; but I could not return him such an answer as he was able to apprehend; and if he had understood me, I did not see how it was possible to contrive any way for finding myself nourishment. While we were thus engaged, I observed a cow passing by; whereupon I pointed to her, and expressed a desire to let me go and milk her. This had its effect; for he led me back into the house, and ordered a mare-servant to open a room, where a good store of milk lay in earthen and wooden vessels, after a very orderly and cleanly manner. She gave me a large bowl full, of which I drank very heartily, and found myself well refreshed.

About noon I saw coming towards the house a kind of vehicle, drawn like a sledge by four Yahoos. There was in it an old steed, who seemed to be of quality; he alighted with his hind feet forward, having by accident got a hurt in his left forefoot. He came to dine with our horse, who received him with great civility. They dined in the best room, and had oats boiled in milk for the second course, which the old horse eat warm, but the rest cold. Their mangers were placed circular in the middle of the room, and divided into several partitions, round which they sat on their haunches upon bosses of straw. In the middle was a large rack with angles answering to every partition of the manger. So that each horse and mare eat their own hay, and their own mash of oats and milk, with much decency and regularity. The behavior of the young colt and foal appeared very modest; and that of the master and mistress extremely cheerful and complaisant to their guest. The grey ordered me to stand by him; and much discourse passed between him and his friend concerning me, as I found by the stranger's often looking on me, and the frequent repetition of the word Yahoo.

I happened to wear my gloves; which the master grey observing, seemed perplexed; discovering signs of wonder what I had done to my forefeet; he put his hoof three or four times to them, as if he would signify, that I should reduce them to their former shape, which I presently did, pulling off both my gloves, and putting them into my pocket. This occasioned farther talk, and I saw the company was pleased with my behavior, whereof I soon found the good effects. I was ordered to speak the few words I understood; and while they were at dinner, the master taught me the names for oats, milk, fire, water, and some others which I could readily pronounce after him, having from my youth a great facility in learning languages.

When dinner was done, the master horse took me aside, and by signs and words made me understand the concern he was in that I had nothing to eat. Oats in their tongue are called *hlunnh*. This word I pronounced two or three times; for although I had refused them at first, yet upon second thoughts, I considered that I could contrive to make a kind of bread, which might be sufficient with milk to keep me alive, till I could make my escape to some other country, and to creatures of my own species. The horse immediately ordered a white mare-servant of his family to bring me a good quantity of oats in a sort of wooden tray. These I heated before the fire as well as I could, and rubbed them till the husks came off, which I made a shift to winnow from the grain; I ground and beat them between two stones, then took water, and made them into a paste or cake, which I toasted at the fire, and eat warm with milk. It was at first a very insipid diet, although common enough in many parts of Europe, but grew tolerable by time; and having been often reduced to hard fare in my life, this was not the first experiment I had made how easily nature is satisfied. And I cannot but observe that I never had one hour's sickness, while I staid in this island. It is true, I sometimes made a shift to catch a rabbit, or bird, by springes [7] made of Yahoos' hairs; and I often gathered wholesome herbs, which I boiled, or eat as salads with my bread; and now and then, for a rarity, I made a little butter, and drank the whey. I was

7. Snares.

at first at a great loss for salt; but custom soon reconciled the want of it; and I am confident that the frequent use of salt among us is an effect of luxury, and was first introduced only as a provocative to drink; except where it is necessary for preserving of flesh in long voyages, or in places remote from great markets. For we observe no animal to be fond of it but man; [8] and as to myself, when I left this country, it was a great while before I could endure the taste of it in anything that I eat.

This is enough to say upon the subject of my diet, wherewith other travelers fill their books, as if the readers were personally concerned whether we fare well or ill. However, it was necessary to mention this matter, lest the world should think it impossible that I could find sustenance for three years in such a country, and among such inhabitants.

When it grew towards evening, the master horse ordered a place for me to lodge in; it was but six yards from the house, and separated from the stable of the Yahoos. Here I got some straw, and covering myself with my own clothes, slept very sound. But I was in a short time better accommodated, as the reader shall know hereafter, when I come to treat more particularly about my way of living.

CHAPTER III. *The Author studious to learn the language, the Houyhnhnm his master assists in teaching him. The language described. Several Houyhnhnms of quality come out of curiosity to see the Author. He gives his master a short account of his voyage.*

My principal endeavor was to learn the language, which my master (for so I shall henceforth call him) and his children, and every servant of his house were desirous to teach me. For they looked upon it as a prodigy, that a brute animal should discover such marks of a rational creature. I pointed to everything, and enquired the name of it, which I wrote down in my journal book when I was alone, and corrected my bad accent, by desiring those of the family to pronounce it often. In this employment, a sorrel nag, one of the under servants, was very ready to assist me.

In speaking, they pronounce through the nose and throat, and their language approaches nearest to the High Dutch or German, of any I know in Europe; but is much more graceful and significant. The Emperor Charles V made almost the same observation, when he said, that if he were to speak to his horse, it should be in High Dutch.[9]

The curiosity and impatience of my master were so great, that he spent many hours of his leisure to instruct me. He was convinced (as he afterwards told me) that I must be a Yahoo, but my

8. Gulliver is, of course, in error. Many animals require salt.
9. The Emperor is supposed to have said that he would speak to his God in Spanish, to his mistress in Italian, and to his horse in German.

teachableness, civility, and cleanliness astonished him; which were qualities altogether so opposite to those animals. He was most perplexed about my clothes, reasoning sometimes with himself whether they were a part of my body; for I never pulled them off till the family were asleep, and got them on before they waked in the morning. My master was eager to learn from whence I came; how I acquired those appearances of reason, which I discovered in all my actions; and to know my story from my own mouth, which he hoped he should soon do by the great proficiency I made in learning and pronouncing their words and sentences. To help my memory, I formed all I learned into the English alphabet, and writ the words down with the translations. This last, after some time, I ventured to do in my master's presence. It cost me much trouble to explain to him what I was doing; for the inhabitants have not the least idea of books or literature.

In about ten weeks time I was able to understand most of his questions; and in three months could give him some tolerable answers. He was extremely curious to know from what part of the country I came, and how I was taught to imitate a rational creature; because the Yahoos (whom he saw I exactly resembled in my head, hands, and face, that were only visible) with some appearance of cunning, and the strongest disposition to mischief, were observed to be the most unteachable of all brutes. I answered that I came over the sea, from a far place, with many others of my own kind, in a great hollow vessel made of the bodies of trees; that my companions forced me to land on this coast, and then left me to shift for myself. It was with some difficulty, and by the help of many signs, that I brought him to understand me. He replied that I must needs be mistaken, or that I *said the thing which was not.* (For they have no word in their language to express lying or falsehood.) He knew it was impossible that there could be a country beyond the sea, or that a parcel of brutes could move a wooden vessel whither they pleased upon water. He was sure no Houyhnhnm alive could make such a vessel, or would trust Yahoos to manage it.

The word Houyhnhnm, in their tongue, signifies a Horse; and in its etymology, the Perfection of Nature. I told my master that I was at a loss for expression, but would improve as fast as I could; and hoped in a short time I should be able to tell him wonders; he was pleased to direct his own mare, his colt, and foal, and the servants of the family to take all opportunities of instructing me; and every day for two or three hours, he was at the same pains himself; several horses and mares of quality in the neighborhood came often to our house, upon the report spread of a wonderful Yahoo, that could speak like a Houyhnhnm, and seemed in his words and actions to discover some glimmerings of reason. These delighted to converse with me; they put many questions, and received such answers as I was able to return. By all which advantages,

I made so great a progress, that in five months from my arrival, I understood whatever was spoke, and could express myself tolerably well.

The Houyhnhnms who came to visit my master, out of a design of seeing and talking with me, could hardly believe me to be a right Yahoo, because my body had a different covering from others of my kind. They were astonished to observe me without the usual hair or skin, except on my head, face, and hands; but I discovered that secret to my master, upon an accident, which happened about a fortnight before.

I have already told the reader, that every night when the family were gone to bed, it was my custom to strip and cover myself with my clothes; it happened one morning early, that my master sent for me, by the sorrel nag, who was his valet; when he came, I was fast asleep, my clothes fallen off on one side, and my shirt above my waist. I awaked at the noise he made, and observed him to deliver his message in some disorder; after which he went to my master, and in a great fright gave him a very confused account of what he had seen; this I presently discovered; for going as soon as I was dressed, to pay my attendance upon his honor, he asked me the meaning of what his servant had reported; that I was not the same thing when I slept as I appeared to be at other times; that his valet assured him, some part of me was white, some yellow, at least not so white, and some brown.

I had hitherto concealed the secret of my dress, in order to distinguish myself as much as possible, from that cursed race of Yahoos; but now I found it in vain to do so any longer. Besides, I considered that my clothes and shoes would soon wear out, which already were in a declining condition, and must be supplied by some contrivance from the hides of Yahoos, or other brutes; whereby the whole secret would be known. I therefore told my master, that in the country from whence I came, those of my kind always covered their bodies with the hairs of certain animals prepared by art, as well for decency, as to avoid inclemencies of air both hot and cold; of which, as to my own person I would give him immediate conviction, if he pleased to command me; only desiring his excuse, if I did not expose those parts that nature taught us to conceal. He said, my discourse was all very strange, but especially the last part; for he could not understand why Nature should teach us to conceal what Nature had given. That neither himself nor family were ashamed of any parts of their bodies; but however I might do as I pleased. Whereupon, I first unbuttoned my coat, and pulled it off. I did the same with my waistcoat; I drew off my shoes, stockings, and breeches. I let my shirt down to my waist, and drew up the bottom, fastening it like a girdle about my middle to hide my nakedness.

My master observed the whole performance with great signs of curiosity and admiration. He took up all my clothes in his pastern, one piece after another, and examined them diligently; he then stroked my body very gently, and looked round me several times; after which he said, it was plain I must be a perfect Yahoo; but that I differed very much from the rest of my species, in the whiteness and smoothness of my skin, my want of hair in several parts of my body, the shape and shortness of my claws behind and before, and my affectation of walking continually on my two hinder feet. He desired to see no more; and gave me leave to put on my clothes again, for I was shuddering with cold.

I expressed my uneasiness at his giving me so often the appellation of Yahoo, an odious animal, for which I had so utter an hatred and contempt. I begged he would forbear applying that word to me, and take the same order in his family, and among his friends whom he suffered to see me. I requested likewise, that the secret of my having a false covering to my body might be known to none but himself, at least as long as my present clothing should last; for as to what the sorrel nag his valet had observed, his honor might command him to conceal it.

All this my master very graciously consented to; and thus the secret was kept till my clothes began to wear out, which I was forced to supply by several contrivances, that shall hereafter be mentioned. In the meantime, he desired I would go on with my utmost diligence to learn their language, because he was more astonished at my capacity for speech and reason, than at the figure of my body, whether it were covered or no; adding that he waited with some impatience to hear the wonders which I promised to tell him.

From thenceforward he doubled the pains he had been at to instruct me; he brought me into all company, and made them treat me with civility, because, as he told them privately, this would put me into good humor, and make me more diverting.

Every day when I waited on him, beside the trouble he was at in teaching, he would ask me several questions concerning myself, which I answered as well as I could; and by those means he had already received some general ideas, although very imperfect. It would be tedious to relate the several steps, by which I advanced to a more regular conversation, but the first account I gave of myself in any order and length was to this purpose:

That, I came from a very far country, as I already had attempted to tell him, with about fifty more of my own species; that we traveled upon the seas, in a great hollow vessel made of wood, and larger than his honor's house. I described the ship to him in the best terms I could; and explained by the help of my handkerchief displayed, how it was driven forward by the wind. That, upon a quarrel among us, I was set on shore on this coast, where I walked forward without knowing whither, till he delivered me from the persecution of those execrable Yahoos. He asked me who made the ship, and how it was possible that the Houyhnhnms of my country would leave it to the management of brutes? My answer was that I durst proceed no farther in my relation, unless he would give me his word and honor that he would not be offended; and then I would tell him the wonders I had so often promised. He agreed; and I went on by assuring him, that the ship was made by creatures like myself, who in all the countries I had traveled, as well as in my own, were the only governing, rational animals; and that upon my arrival hither, I was as much astonished to see the Houyhnhnms act like rational beings, as he or his friends could be in finding some marks of reason in a creature he was pleased to call a Yahoo; to which I owned my resemblance in every part, but could not account for their degenerate and brutal nature. I said farther, that if good fortune ever restored me to my native country, to relate my travels hither, as I resolved to do; everybody would believe that I *said the thing which was not*; that I invented the story out of my own head; and with all possible respect to himself, his family, and friends, and under his promise of not being offended, our countrymen would hardly think it probable, that a Houyhnhnm should be the presiding creature of a nation, and a Yahoo the brute.

CHAPTER IV. *The Houyhnhnms' notion of truth and falsehood. The author's discourse disapproved by his master. The author gives a more particular account of himself, and the accidents of his voyage.*

My master heard me with great appearances of uneasiness in his countenance; because *doubting* or *not believing* are so little known in this country, that the inhabitants cannot tell how to behave themselves under such circumstances. And I remember in frequent discourses with my master concerning the nature of manhood, in other parts of the world, having occasion to talk of *lying* and *false representation*, it was with much difficulty that he comprehended what I meant; although he had otherwise a most acute judgment. For he argued thus: that the use of speech was to make us understand one another, and to receive information of facts; now if anyone *said the thing which was not*, these ends were defeated; because I cannot properly be said to understand him; and I am so far from receiving information, that he leaves me worse than in ignorance; for I am led to believe a thing *black* when it is *white*, and *short* when it is *long*. And these were all the notions he had concerning that faculty of *lying*, so perfectly well understood, and so universally practiced among human creatures.

To return from this digression; when I asserted that the Yahoos were the only governing animals in my country, which my master said was altogether past his conception, he desired to know, whether we had Houyhnhnms among us, and what was their employment; I told him we had great numbers; that in summer they grazed in the fields, and in winter were kept in houses, with hay and oats, where Yahoo servants were employed to rub their skins smooth, comb their manes, pick their feet, serve them with food, and make their beds. "I understand you well," said my master; "it is now very plain from all you have spoken, that whatever share of reason the Yahoos pretend to, the Houyhnhnms are your masters; I heartily wish our Yahoos would be so tractable." I begged his honor would please to excuse me from proceeding any farther, because I was very certain that the account he expected from me would be highly displeasing. But he insisted in commanding me to let him know the best and the worst; I told him he should be obeyed. I owned that the Houyhnhnms among us, whom we called Horses, were the most generous [1] and comely animal we had; that they excelled in strength and swiftness; and when they belonged to persons of quality, employed in traveling, racing, and drawing chariots, they were treated with much kindness and care, till they fell into diseases, or became foundered in the feet; but then they were sold, and used to all kind of drudgery till they died; after which their skins were stripped and sold for what they were worth, and their bodies left to be devoured by dogs and birds of prey. But the common race of horses had not so good fortune, being kept by farmers and carriers, and other mean people, who put them to greater labor, and feed them worse. I described as well as I could, our way of riding; the shape and use of a bridle, a saddle, a spur, and a whip; of harness and wheels. I added, that we fastened plates of a certain hard substance called iron at the bottom of their feet, to preserve their hoofs from being broken by the stony ways on which we often traveled.

My master, after some expressions of great indignation, wondered how we dared to venture upon a Houyhnhnm's back; for he was sure, that the weakest servant in his house would be able to shake off the strongest Yahoo; or by lying down, and rolling upon his back, squeeze the brute to death. I answered that our horses were trained up from three or four years old to the several uses we intended them for; that if any of them proved intolerably vicious, they were employed for carriages; that they were severely beaten while they were young for any mischievous tricks; that the males, designed for the common use of riding or draught, were generally castrated about two years after their birth, to take down their spirits, and make them more tame and gentle; that they were indeed sensible of rewards and punishments; but his honor would please to consider that they had not the least tincture of reason any more than the Yahoos in this country.

It put me to the pains of many circumlocutions to give my master a right idea of what I spoke; for their language doth not abound in variety of words, because their wants and passions are fewer than

1. Noble.

among us. But it is impossible to express his noble resentment at our savage treatment of the Houyhnhnm race; particularly after I had explained the manner and use of castrating horses among us, to hinder them from propagating their kind, and to render them more servile. He said, if it were possible there could be any country where Yahoos alone were endued with reason, they certainly must be the governing animal, because reason will in time always prevail against brutal strength. But, considering the frame of our bodies, and especially of mine, he thought no creature of equal bulk was so ill-contrived for employing that reason in the common offices of life; whereupon he desired to know whether those among whom I lived resembled me or the Yahoos of his country. I assured him that I was as well shaped as most of my age; but the younger and the females were much more soft and tender, and the skins of the latter generally as white as milk. He said I differed indeed from other Yahoos, being much more cleanly, and not altogether so deformed; but in point of real advantage, he thought I differed for the worse. That my nails were of no use either to my fore or hinder feet; as to my forefeet, he could not properly call them by that name, for he never observed me to walk upon them; that they were too soft to bear the ground; that I generally went with them uncovered, neither was the covering I sometimes wore on them of the same shape, or so strong as that on my feet behind. That I could not walk with any security; for if either of my hinder feet slipped, I must inevitably fall. He then began to find fault with other parts of my body; the flatness of my face, the prominence of my nose, my eyes placed directly in front, so that I could not look on either side without turning my head; that I was not able to feed myself without lifting one of my forefeet to my mouth; and therefore nature had placed those joints to answer that necessity. He knew not what could be the use of those several clefts and divisions in my feet behind; that these were too soft to bear the hardness and sharpness of stones without a covering made from the skin of some other brute; that my whole body wanted a fence against heat and cold, which I was forced to put on and off every day with tediousness and trouble. And lastly, that he observed every animal in his country naturally to abhor the Yahoos, whom the weaker avoided, and the stronger drove from them. So that supposing us to have the gift of reason, he could not see how it were possible to cure that natural antipathy which every creature discovered against us; nor consequently, how we could tame and render them serviceable. However, he would (as he said) debate the matter no farther, because he was more desirous to know my own story, the country where I was born, and the several actions and events of my life before I came hither.

I assured him how extremely desirous I was that he should be satisfied in every point; but I doubted much whether it would be possible for me to explain myself on several subjects whereof his honor could have no conception, because I saw nothing in his country to which I could resemble them. That however, I would do my best, and strive to express myself by similitudes, humbly desiring his assistance when I wanted proper words; which he was pleased to promise me.

I said, my birth was of honest parents, in an island called England, which was remote from this country, as many days journey as the strongest of his honor's servants could travel in the annual course of the sun. That I was bred a surgeon, whose trade it is to cure wounds and hurts in the body, got by accident or violence. That my country was governed by a female man, whom we called a queen. That I left it to get riches, whereby I might maintain myself and family when I should return. That in my last voyage, I was Commander of the ship and had about fifty Yahoos under me, many of which died at sea, and I was forced to supply them by others picked out from several nations. That our ship was twice in danger of being sunk; the first time by a great storm, and the second, by striking against a rock. Here my master interposed, by asking me, how I could persuade strangers out of different countries to venture with me, after the losses I had sustained, and the hazards I had run. I said, they were fellows of desperate fortunes, forced to fly from the places of their birth, on account of their poverty or their crimes. Some were undone by lawsuits; others spent all they had in drinking, whoring, and gaming; others fled for treason; many for murder, theft, poisoning, robbery, perjury, forgery, coining false money; for committing rapes or sodomy; for flying from their colors, or deserting to the enemy; and most of them had broken prison. None of these durst return to their native countries for fear of being hanged, or of starving in a jail; and therefore were under a necessity of seeking a livelihood in other places.

During this discourse, my master was pleased often to interrupt me. I had made use of many circumlocutions in describing to him the nature of the several crimes, for which most of our crew had been forced to fly their country. This labor took up several days conversation before he was able to comprehend me. He was wholly at a loss to know what could be the use or necessity of practicing those vices. To clear up which I endeavored to give him some ideas of the desire of power and riches; of the terrible effects of lust, intemperance, malice, and envy. All this I was forced to define and describe by putting of cases, and making suppositions. After which, like one whose imagination was struck with something never seen or heard of before, he would lift up his eyes with amazement and indignation. Power, government, war, law, punishment, and a thousand other things had no terms, wherein that language could express them; which made the difficulty almost insuperable to give my master any conception of what I meant; but being of an excellent understanding, much improved by contemplation and converse, he at last arrived at a competent knowledge of what human nature in our parts of the world is capable to perform; and desired I would give him some particular account of that land, which we call Europe, especially, of my own country.

CHAPTER V. *The Author, at his master's commands, informs him of the state of England. The causes of war among the princes of Europe. The Author begins to explain the English Constitution.*

The reader may please to observe that the following extract of many conversations I had with my master contains a summary of the most material points, which were discoursed at several times for above two years; his honor often desiring fuller satisfaction as I farther improved in the Houyhnhnm tongue. I laid before him, as well as I could, the whole state of Europe; I discoursed of trade and manufactures, of arts and sciences; and the answers I gave to all the questions he made, as they arose upon several subjects, were a fund of conversation not to be exhausted. But I shall here only set down the substance of what passed between us concerning my own country, reducing it into order as well as I can, without any regard to time or other circumstances, while I strictly adhere to truth. My only concern is that I shall hardly be able to do justice to my master's arguments and expressions; which must needs suffer by my want of capacity, as well as by a translation into our barbarous English.

In obedience therefore to his honor's commands, I related to him the Revolution under the Prince of Orange; the long war with France entered into by the said Prince, and renewed by his successor the present queen; wherein the greatest powers of Christendom were engaged, and which still continued. I computed at his request, that about a million of Yahoos might have been killed in the whole progress of it; and perhaps a hundred or more cities taken, and five times as many ships burned or sunk.[2]

He asked me what were the usual causes or motives that made one country to go to war with another. I answered, they were innumerable; but I should only mention a few of the chief. Sometimes the ambition of princes, who never think they have land or people enough to govern; sometimes the corruption of ministers, who engage their master in a war in order to stifle or divert the clamor of the subjects against their evil administration. Difference in opinions hath cost many millions of lives; for instance, whether flesh be bread, or bread be flesh; whether the juice of a certain berry be blood or wine; whether whistling be a vice or a virtue; whether it be better to kiss a post, or throw it into the fire; what is the best color for a coat, whether black, white, red, or grey; and

2. Gulliver relates recent English history: the Glorious Revolution of 1688 and the War of Spanish Succession (1703–13). He greatly exaggerates the casualties in the war.

whether it should be long or short, narrow or wide, dirty or clean; [3] with many more. Neither are any wars so furious and bloody, or of so long continuance, as those occasioned by difference in opinion, especially if it be in things indifferent.[4]

Sometimes the quarrel between two princes is to decide which of them shall dispossess a third of his dominions, where neither of them pretend to any right. Sometimes one prince quarreleth with another, for fear the other should quarrel with him. Sometimes a war is entered upon, because the enemy is too strong, and sometimes because he is too weak. Sometimes our neighbors want the things which we have, or have the things which we want; and we both fight, till they take ours or give us theirs. It is a very justifiable cause of war to invade a country after the people have been wasted by famine, destroyed by pestilence, or embroiled by factions amongst themselves. It is justifiable to enter into a war against our nearest ally, when one of his towns lies convenient for us, or a territory of land, that would render our dominions round and compact. If a prince send forces into a nation, where the people are poor and ignorant, he may lawfully put half of them to death, and make slaves of the rest, in order to civilize and reduce them from their barbarous way of living. It is a very kingly, honorable, and frequent practice, when one prince desires the assistance of another to secure him against an invasion, that the assistant, when he hath driven out the invader, should seize on the dominions himself, and kill, imprison, or banish the prince he came to relieve. Alliance by blood or marriage is a sufficient cause of war between princes; and the nearer the kindred is, the greater is their disposition to quarrel; poor nations are hungry, and rich nations are proud; and pride and hunger will ever be at variance. For these reasons, the trade of a soldier is held the most honorable of all others: because a soldier is a Yahoo hired to kill in cold blood as many of his own species, who have never offended him, as possibly he can.

There is likewise a kind of beggarly princes in Europe, not able to make war by themselves, who hire out their troops to richer nations for so much a day to each man; of which they keep three fourths to themselves, and it is the best part of their maintenance; such are those in many northern parts of Europe.[5]

"What you have told me," said my master, "upon the subject of war, doth indeed discover most admirably the effects of that reason you pretend to; however, it is happy that the shame is greater than the danger; and that Nature hath left you utterly uncapable of doing much mischief; for your mouths lying flat with your faces, you can hardly bite each other to any purpose, unless by

3. Gulliver refers to the religious controversies of the Reformation and Counter Reformation: the doctrine of transubstantiation, the use of music in church services, the veneration of the crucifix, and the wearing of priestly vestments.
4. Of little consequence.
5. A satiric glance at George I, who, as Elector of Hanover, had dealt in this trade.

consent. Then, as to the claws upon your feet before and behind, they are so short and tender, that one of our Yahoos would drive a dozen of yours before him. And therefore in recounting the numbers of those who have been killed in battle, I cannot but think that you have *said the thing which is not.*"

I could not forbear shaking my head and smiling a little at his ignorance. And, being no stranger to the art of war, I gave him a description of cannons, culverins, muskets, carabines, pistols, bullets, powder, swords, bayonets, battles, sieges, retreats, attacks, undermines, countermines, bombardments, sea fights; ships sunk with a thousand men; twenty thousand killed on each side; dying groans, limbs flying in the air; smoke, noise, confusion, trampling to death under horses' feet; flight, pursuit, victory; fields strewed with carcasses left for food to dogs, and wolves, and birds of prey; plundering, stripping, ravishing, burning, and destroying. And, to set forth the valor of my own dear countrymen, I assured him that I had seen them blow up a hundred enemies at once in a siege, and as many in a ship; and beheld the dead bodies drop down in pieces from the clouds, to the great diversion of all the spectators.

I was going on to more particulars, when my master commanded me silence. He said, whoever understood the nature of Yahoos might easily believe it possible for so vile an animal, to be capable of every action I had named, if their strength and cunning equaled their malice. But, as my discourse had increased his abhorrence of the whole species, so he found it gave him a disturbance in his mind, to which he was wholly a stranger before. He thought his ears being used to such abominable words, might by degrees admit them with less detestation. That, although he hated the Yahoos of this country, yet he no more blamed them for their odious qualities, than he did a *gnnayh* (a bird of prey) for its cruelty, or a sharp stone for cutting his hoof. But, when a creature pretending to reason could be capable of such enormities, he dreaded lest the corruption of that faculty might be worse than brutality itself. He seemed therefore confident, that instead of reason, we were only possessed of some quality fitted to increase our natural vices; as the reflection from a troubled stream returns the image of an ill-shapen body, not only larger, but more distorted.

He added that he had heard too much upon the subject of war, both in this and some former discourses. There was another point which a little perplexed him at present. I had said that some of our crew left their country on account of being ruined by law: that I had already explained the meaning of the word; but he was at a loss how it should come to pass, that the law which was intended for every man's preservation, should be any man's ruin. Therefore he desired to be farther satisfied what I meant by law, and the dispensers thereof, according to the present practice in my own country; because he thought nature and reason were sufficient guides for a reasonable animal, as we pretended to be, in showing us what we ought to do, and what to avoid.

I assured his honor that law was a science wherein I had not much conversed, further than by employing advocates, in vain, upon some injustices that had been done me. However, I would give him all the satisfaction I was able.

I said there was a society of men among us, bred up from their youth in the art of proving by words multiplied for the purpose, that white is black, and black is white, according as they are paid. To this society all the rest of the people are slaves.

"For example. If my neighbor hath a mind to my cow, he hires a lawyer to prove that he ought to have my cow from me. I must then hire another to defend my right; it being against all rules of law that any man should be allowed to speak for himself. Now in this case, I who am the true owner lie under two great disadvantages. First, my lawyer being practiced almost from his cradle in defending falsehood is quite out of his element when he would be an advocate for justice, which as an office unnatural, he always attempts with great awkwardness, if not with ill-will. The second disadvantage is that my lawyer must proceed with great caution, or else he will be reprimanded by the judges, and abhorred by his brethren, as one who would lessen the practice of the law. And therefore I have but two methods to preserve my cow. The first is to gain over my adversary's lawyer with a double fee; who will then betray his client, by insinuating that he hath justice on his side. The second way is for my lawyer to make my cause appear as unjust as he can; by allowing the cow to belong to my adversary; and this if it be skillfully done, will certainly bespeak the favor of the bench.

"Now, your honor is to know that these judges are persons appointed to decide all controversies of property, as well as for the trial of criminals; and picked out from the most dextrous lawyers who are grown old or lazy; and having been biased all their lives against truth and equity, lie under such a fatal necessity of favoring fraud, perjury, and oppression, that I have known some of them to have refused a large bribe from the side where justice lay, rather than injure the faculty,[6] by doing anything unbecoming their nature or their office.

"It is a maxim among these lawyers, that whatever hath been done before may legally be done again; and therefore they take special care to record all the decisions formerly made against common justice and the general reason of mankind. These, under the name of *precedents*, they produce as authorities to justify the most iniquitous opinions; and the judges never fail of directing accordingly.

6. Profession.

"In pleading, they studiously avoid entering into the merits of the cause; but are loud, violent, and tedious in dwelling upon all circumstances which are not to the purpose. For instance, in the case already mentioned, they never desire to know what claim or title my adversary hath to my cow; but whether the said cow were red or black; her horns long or short; whether the field I graze her in be round or square; whether she were milked at home or abroad; what diseases she is subject to, and the like. After which they consult precedents, adjourn the cause, from time to time, and in ten, twenty, or thirty years come to an issue.

"It is likewise to be observed, that this society hath a peculiar cant and jargon of their own, that no other mortal can understand, and wherein all their laws are written, which they take special care to multiply; whereby they have wholly confounded the very essence of truth and falsehood, of right and wrong; so that it will take thirty years to decide whether the field, left me by my ancestors for six generations, belong to me, or to a stranger three hundred miles off.

"In the trial of persons accused for crimes against the state, the method is much more short and commendable: the judge first sends to sound the disposition of those in power; after which he can easily hang or save the criminal, strictly preserving all the forms of law."

Here my master interposing said it was a pity that creatures endowed with such prodigious abilities of mind as these lawyers, by the description I gave of them must certainly be, were not rather encouraged to be instructors of others in wisdom and knowledge. In answer to which, I assured his honor that in all points out of their own trade, they were usually the most ignorant and stupid generation among us, the most despicable in common conversation, avowed enemies to all knowledge and learning; and equally disposed to pervert the general reason of mankind, in every other subject of discourse as in that of their own profession.

CHAPTER VI. *A continuation of the state of England, under Queen Anne. The character of a first minister in the courts of Europe.*

My master was yet wholly at a loss to understand what motives could incite this race of lawyers to perplex, disquiet, and weary themselves by engaging in a confederacy of injustice, merely for the sake of injuring their fellow animals; neither could he comprehend what I meant in saying they did it for hire. Whereupon I was at much pains to describe to him the use of money, the materials it was made of, and the value of the metals; that when a Yahoo had got a great store of his precious substance, he was able to purchase whatever he had a mind to; the finest clothing, the noblest houses, great tracts of land, the most costly meats and drinks; and have his choice of the most beautiful females. Therefore since money alone was able to perform all these feats, our Yahoos thought they could never have enough of it to spend or to save, as they found themselves inclined from their natural bent either to profusion or avarice. That the rich man enjoyed the fruit of the poor man's labor, and the latter were a thousand to one in proportion to the former. That the bulk of our people was forced to live miserably, by laboring every day for small wages to make a few live plentifully. I enlarged myself much on these and many other particulars to the same purpose, but his honor was still to seek,[7] for he went upon a supposition that all animals had a title to their share in the productions of the earth; and especially those who presided over the rest. Therefore he desired I would let him know what these costly meats were, and how any of us happened to want [8] them. Whereupon I enumerated as many sorts as came into my head, with the various methods of dressing them, which could not be done without sending vessels by sea to every part of the world, as well for liquors to drink, as for sauces, and innumerable other conveniencies. I assured him, that this whole globe of earth must be at least three times gone round, before one of our better female Yahoos could get her breakfast, or a cup to put it in. He said, "That must needs be a miserable country which cannot furnish food for its own inhabitants." But what he chiefly wondered at, was how such vast tracts of ground as I described, should be wholly without fresh water, and the people put to the necessity of sending over the sea for drink. I replied that England (the dear place of my nativity) was computed to produce three times the quantity of food, more than its inhabitants are able to consume, as well as liquors extracted from grain, or pressed out of the fruit of certain trees, which made excellent drink; and the same proportion in every other convenience of life. But, in order to feed the luxury and intemperance of the males, and the vanity of the females, we sent away the greatest part of our necessary things to other countries, from whence in return we brought the materials of diseases, folly, and vice, to spend among ourselves. Hence it follows of necessity, that vast numbers of our people are compelled to seek their livelihood by begging, robbing, stealing, cheating, pimping, forswearing, flattering, suborning, forging, gaming, lying, fawning, hectoring, voting, scribbling, star gazing, poisoning, whoring, canting, libeling, freethinking, and the like occupations; every one of which terms, I was at much pains to make him understand.

That, wine was not imported among us from foreign countries, to supply the want of water or other drinks, but because it was a sort of liquid which made us merry, by putting us out of our senses; diverted all melancholy thoughts, begat wild extravagant imaginations in the brain, raised our hopes, and banished our

7. Still did not understand.   8. Lack.

fears; suspended every office of reason for a time, and deprived us of the use of our limbs, until we fell into a profound sleep; although it must be confessed, that we always awaked sick and dispirited; and that the use of this liquor filled us with diseases, which made our lives uncomfortable and short.

But beside all this, the bulk of our people supported themselves by furnishing the necessities or conveniencies of life to the rich, and to each other. For instance, when I am at home and dressed as I ought to be, I carry on my body the workmanship of an hundred tradesmen; the building and furniture of my house employ as many more; and five times the number to adorn my wife.

I was going on to tell him of another sort of people, who get their livelihood by attending the sick; having upon some occasions informed his honor that many of my crew had died of diseases. But here it was with the utmost difficulty that I brought him to apprehend what I meant. He could easily conceive that a Houyhnhnm grew weak and heavy a few days before his death; or by some accident might hurt a limb. But that nature, who worketh all things to perfection, should suffer any pains to breed in our bodies, he thought impossible; and desired to know the reason of so unaccountable an evil. I told him, we fed on a thousand things which operated contrary to each other; that we eat when we were not hungry, and drank without the provocation of thirst; that we sat whole nights drinking strong liquors without eating a bit, which disposed us to sloth, inflamed our bodies, and precipitated or prevented digestion. That, prostitute female Yahoos acquired a certain malady, which bred rottenness in the bones of those who fell into their embraces; that this and many other diseases were propagated from father to son; so that great numbers come into the world with complicated maladies upon them; that it would be endless to give him a catalogue of all diseases incident to human bodies; for they could not be fewer than five or six hundred, spread over every limb, and joint; in short, every part, external and intestine, having diseases appropriated to each. To remedy which, there was a sort of people bred up among us, in the profession or pretense of curing the sick. And because I had some skill in the faculty, I would in gratitude to his honor let him know the whole mystery and method by which they proceed.

Their fundamental is that all diseases arise from repletion; from whence they conclude, that a great evacuation of the body is necessary, either through the natural passage, or upwards at the mouth. Their next business is, from herbs, minerals, gums, oils, shells, salts, juices, seaweed, excrements, barks of trees, serpents, toads, frogs, spiders, dead men's flesh and bones, birds, beasts and fishes, to form a composition for smell and taste the most abominable, nauseous, and detestable, that they can possibly contrive, which the stomach immediately rejects with loathing, and this they call a vomit. Or else from the same storehouse, with some other poisonous additions, they command us to take in at the orifice above or below (just as the physician then happens to be disposed) a medicine equally annoying and disgustful to the bowels; which relaxing the belly, drives down all before it; and this they call a purge, or a clyster. For nature (as the physicians allege) having intended the superior anterior orifice only for the intromission of solids and liquids, and the inferior posterior for ejection, these artists ingeniously considering that in all diseases nature is forced out of her seat; therefore to replace her in it, the body must be treated in a manner directly contrary, but interchanging the use of each orifice; forcing solids and liquids in at the anus, and making evacuations at the mouth.

But, besides real diseases, we are subject to many that are only imaginary, for which the physicians have invented imaginary cures; these have their several names, and so have the drugs that are proper for them; and with these our female Yahoos are always infested.

One great excellency in this tribe is their skill at prognostics, wherein they seldom fail; their predictions in real diseases, when they rise to any degree of malignity, generally portending death, which is always in their power, when recovery is not, and therefore, upon any unexpected signs of amendment, after they have pronounced their sentence rather than be accused as false prophets, they know how to approve [9] their sagacity to the world by a seasonable dose.

They are likewise of special use to husbands and wives, who are grown weary of their mates; to eldest sons, to great ministers of state, and often to princes.

I had formerly upon occasion discoursed with my master upon the nature of government in general, and particularly of our own excellent constitution, deservedly the wonder and envy of the whole world. But having here accidently mentioned a minister of state, he commanded me some time after to inform him what species of Yahoo I particularly meant by that appellation.

I told him that a first or chief minister of state, whom I intended to describe, was a creature wholly exempt from joy and grief, love and hatred, pity and anger; at least makes use of no other passions but a violent desire of wealth, power, and titles; that he applies his words to all uses, except to the indication of his mind; that he never tells a truth, but with an intent that you should take it for a lie; nor a lie, but with a design that you should take it for a truth; that those he speaks worst of behind their backs are in the surest way to preferment; and whenever he begins to praise you to others or to yourself, you are from that day forlorn. The worst mark you can receive is a promise, especially when it is confirmed

9. Prove.

2064 · *Jonathan Swift*

with an oath; after which every wise man retires, and gives over all hopes.

There are three methods by which a man may rise to be chief minister: the first is by knowing how with prudence to dispose of a wife, a daughter, or a sister; the second, by betraying or undermining his predecessor; and the third is by a furious zeal in public assemblies against the corruptions of the court. But a wise prince would rather choose to employ those who practice the last of these methods; because such zealots prove always the most obsequious and subservient to the will and passions of their master. That, these ministers having all employments at their disposal, preserve themselves in power by bribing the majority of a senate or great council; and at last by an expedient called an Act of Indemnity [1] (whereof I described the nature to him) they secure themselves from after reckonings, and retire from the public, laden with the spoils of the nation.

The palace of a chief minister is a seminary to breed up others in his own trade; the pages, lackies, and porter, by imitating their master, become ministers of state in their several districts, and learn to excel in the three principal ingredients, of insolence, lying, and bribery. Accordingly, they have a subaltern court paid to them by persons of the best rank; and sometimes by the force of dexterity and impudence, arrive through several gradations to be successors to their lord.

He is usually governed by a decayed wench, or favorite footman, who are the tunnels through which all graces are conveyed, and may properly be called, in the last resort, the governors of the kingdom.

One day, my master, having heard me mention the nobility of my country, was pleased to make me a compliment which I could not pretend to deserve: that, he was sure, I must have been born of some noble family, because I far exceeded in shape, color, and cleanliness, all the Yahoos of his nation, although I seemed to fail in strength, and agility, which must be imputed to my different way of living from those other brutes; and besides, I was not only endowed with the faculty of speech, but likewise with some rudiments of reason, to a degree, that with all his acquaintance I passed for a prodigy.

He made me observe, that among the Houyhnhnms, the white, the sorrel, and the iron grey were not so exactly shaped as the bay, the dapple grey, and the black; nor born with equal talents of mind, or a capacity to improve them; and therefore continued always in the condition of servants, without ever aspiring to match out of their own race, which in that country would be reckoned monstrous and unnatural.

1. An act passed at each session of Parliament to protect ministers of state who in good faith might have acted illegally.

I made his honor my most humble acknowledgments for the good opinion he was pleased to conceive of me; but assured him at the same time, that my birth was of the lower sort, having been born of plain, honest parents, who were just able to give me a tolerable education; that, nobility among us was altogether a different thing from the idea he had of it; that, our young noblemen are bred from their childhood in idleness and luxury; that, as soon as years will permit, they consume their vigor, and contract odious diseases among lewd females; and when their fortunes are almost ruined, they marry some woman of mean birth, disagreeable person, and unsound constitution, merely for the sake of money, whom they hate and despise. That, the productions of such marriages are generally scrofulous, rickety or deformed children; by which means the family seldom continues above three generations, unless the wife take care to provide a healthy father among her neighbors, or domestics, in order to improve and continue the breed. That a weak diseased body, a meager countenance, and sallow complexion are the true marks of noble blood; and a healthy robust appearance is so disgraceful in a man of quality, that the world concludes his real father to have been a groom or a coachman. The imperfections of his mind run parallel with those of his body; being a composition of spleen, dullness, ignorance, caprice, sensuality, and pride.

Without the consent of this illustrious body, no law can be enacted, repealed, or altered, and these nobles have likewise the decision of all our possessions without appeal.

CHAPTER VII. *The Author's great love of his native country. His master's observations upon the constitution and administration of England, as described by the Author, with parallel cases and comparisons. His master's observations upon human nature.*

The reader may be disposed to wonder how I could prevail on myself to give so free a representation of my own species, among a race of mortals who were already too apt to conceive the vilest opinion of humankind, from that entire congruity betwixt me and their Yahoos. But I must freely confess that the many virtues of those excellent quadrupeds placed in opposite view to human corruptions had so far opened my eyes, and enlarged my understanding, that I began to view the actions and passions of man in a very different light; and to think the honor of my own kind not worth managing;[2] which, besides, it was impossible for me to do before a person of so acute a judgment as my master, who daily convinced me of a thousand faults in myself, whereof I had not the least perception before, and which with us would never be numbered even among human infirmities. I had likewise learned from his example an utter detestation of all falsehood or disguise; and

2. Taking care of.

truth appeared so amiable to me, that I determined upon sacrificing everything to it.

Let me deal so candidly with the reader as to confess that there was yet a much stronger motive for the freedom I took in my representation of things. I had not been a year in this country, before I contracted such a love and veneration for the inhabitants, that I entered on a firm resolution never to return to humankind, but to pass the rest of my life among these admirable Houyhnhnms in the contemplation and practice of every virtue; where I could have no example or incitement to vice. But it was decreed by fortune, my perpetual enemy, that so great a felicity should not fall to my share. However, it is now some comfort to reflect that in what I said of my countrymen, I extenuated their faults as much as I durst before so strict an examiner; and upon every article, gave as favorable a turn as the matter would bear. For, indeed, who is there alive that will not be swayed by his bias and partiality to the place of his birth?

I have related the substance of several conversations I had with my master, during the greatest part of the time I had the honor to be in his service; but have indeed for brevity sake omitted much more than is here set down.

When I had answered all his questions, and his curiosity seemed to be fully satisfied; he sent for me one morning early, and commanding me to sit down at some distance (an honor which he had never before conferred upon me), he said he had been very seriously considering my whole story, as far as it related both to myself and my country; that, he looked upon us as a sort of animals to whose share, by what accident he could not conjecture, some small pittance of reason had fallen, whereof we made no other use than by its assistance to aggravate our natural corruptions, and to acquire new ones which nature had not given us. That we disarmed ourselves of the few abilities she had bestowed; had been very successful in multiplying our original wants, and seemed to spend our whole lives in vain endeavors to supply them by our own inventions. That, as to myself, it was manifest I had neither the strength or agility of a common Yahoo; that I walked infirmly on my hinder feet; had found out a contrivance to make my claws of no use or defense, and to remove the hair from my chin, which was intended as a shelter from the sun and the weather. Lastly, that I could neither run with speed, nor climb trees like my brethren (as he called them) the Yahoos in this country.

That our institutions of government and law were plainly owing to our gross defects in reason, and by consequence, in virtue; because reason alone is sufficient to govern a rational creature; which was therefore a character we had no pretense to challenge, even from the account I had given of my own people; although he manifestly perceived, that in order to favor them, I had concealed many particulars, and often *said the thing which was not.*

He was the more confirmed in this opinion, because he observed that I agreed in every feature of my body with other Yahoos, except where it was to my real disadvantage in point of strength, speed, and activity, the shortness of my claws, and some other particulars where nature had no part; so, from the representation I had given him of our lives, our manners, and our actions, he found as near a resemblance in the disposition of our minds. He said the Yahoos were known to hate one another more than they did any different species of animals; and the reason usually assigned was the odiousness of their own shapes, which all could see in the rest, but not in themselves. He had therefore begun to think it not unwise in us to cover our bodies, and by that invention, conceal many of our deformities from each other, which would else be hardly supportable. But he now found he had been mistaken; and that the dissentions of those brutes in his country were owing to the same cause with ours, as I had described them. For, if (said he) you throw among five Yahoos as much food as would be sufficient for fifty, they will, instead of eating peaceably, fall together by the ears, each single one impatient to have all to itself; and therefore a servant was usually employed to stand by while they were feeding abroad, and those kept at home were tied at a distance from each other. That, if a cow died of age or accident, before a Houyhnhnm could secure it for his own Yahoos, those in the neighborhood would come in herds to seize it, and then would ensue such a battle as I had described, with terrible wounds made by their claws on both sides, although they seldom were able to kill one another, for want of such convenient instruments of death as we had invented. At other times the like battles have been fought between the Yahoos of several neighborhoods without any visible cause; those of one district watching all opportunities to surprise the next before they are prepared. But if they find their project hath miscarried, they return home, and for want of enemies, engage in what I call a civil war among themselves.

That, in some fields of his country, there are certain shining stones of several colors, whereof the Yahoos are violently fond; and when part of these stones are fixed in the earth, as it sometimes happeneth, they will dig with their claws for whole days to get them out, and carry them away, and hide them by heaps in their kennels; but still looking round with great caution, for fear their comrades should find out their treasure. My master said he could never discover the reason of this unnatural appetite, or how these stones could be of any use to a Yahoo; but now he believed it might proceed from the same principle of avarice, which I had ascribed to mankind. That he had once, by way of experiment, privately removed a heap of these stones from the place where one of his Yahoos had buried it, whereupon, the sordid animal missing his treasure, by his loud lamenting brought the whole herd to the place, there miserably howled, then fell to biting and tearing the rest; began to pine away, would neither eat nor sleep, nor work, till he ordered a servant privately to convey the stones into the same hole, and hide them as before; which when his Yahoo had found, he presently recovered his spirits and good humor; but took care to remove them to a better hiding place; and hath ever since been a very serviceable brute.

My master farther assured me, which I also observed myself; that in the fields where these shining stones abound, the fiercest and most frequent battles are fought, occasioned by perpetual inroads of the neighboring Yahoos.

He said it was common when two Yahoos discovered such a stone in a field, and were contending which of them should be the proprietor, a third would take the advantage, and carry it away from them both; which my master would needs contend to have some resemblance with our suits at law; wherein I thought it for our credit not to undeceive him; since the decision he mentioned was much more equitable than many decrees among us; because the plaintiff and defendant there lost nothing beside the stone they contended for; whereas our courts of equity would never have dismissed the cause while either of them had anything left.

My master continuing his discourse said there was nothing that rendered the Yahoos more odious, than their undistinguished appetite to devour everything that came in their way, whether herbs, roots, berries, corrupted flesh of animals, or all mingled together; and it was peculiar in their temper, that they were fonder of what they could get by rapine or stealth at a greater distance, than much better food provided for them at home. If their prey held out, they would eat till they were ready to burst, after which nature had pointed out to them a certain root that gave them a general evacuation.

There was also another kind of root very juicy, but something rare and difficult to be found, which the Yahoos fought for with much eagerness, and would suck it with great delight; it produced the same effects that wine hath upon us. It would make them sometimes hug, and sometimes tear one another; they would howl and grin, and chatter, and reel, and tumble, and then fall asleep in the mud.

I did indeed observe that the Yahoos were the only animals in this country subject to any diseases; which however, were much fewer than horses have among us, and contracted not by any ill treatment they meet with, but by the nastiness and greediness of that sordid brute. Neither has their language any more than a general appellation for those maladies; which is borrowed from the name of the beast, and called *Hnea Yahoo,* or the Yahoo's Evil; and the cure prescribed is a mixture of their own dung and urine, forcibly put down the Yahoo's throat. This I have since often known to have been taken with success, and do here freely recommend it to my countrymen, for the public good, as an admirable specific against all diseases produced by repletion.

As to learning, government, arts, manufactures, and the like, my master confessed he could find little or no resemblance between the Yahoos of that country and those in ours. For he only meant to observe what parity there was in our natures. He had heard indeed some curious Houyhnhnms observe that in most herds there was a sort of ruling Yahoo (as among us there is generally some leading or principal stag in a park) who was always more deformed in body, and mischievous in disposition, than any of the rest. That this leader had usually a favorite as like himself as he could get, whose employment was to lick his master's feet and posteriors, and drive the female Yahoos to his kennel; for which he was now and then rewarded with a piece of ass's flesh. This favorite is hated by the whole herd; and therefore to protect himself, keeps always near the person of his leader. He usually continues in office till a worse can be found; but the very moment he is discarded, his successor, at the head of all the Yahoos in that district, young and old, male and female, come in a body, and discharge their excrements upon him from head to foot. But how far this might be applicable to our courts and favorites, and ministers of state, my master said I could best determine.

I durst make no return to this malicious insinuation, which debased human understanding below the sagacity of a common hound, who hath judgment enough to distinguish and follow the cry of the ablest dog in the pack, without being ever mistaken.

My master told me there were some qualities remarkable in the Yahoos, which he had not observed me to mention, or at least very slightly, in the accounts I had given him of humankind. He said, those animals, like other brutes, had their females in common; but in this they differed, that the she-Yahoo would admit the male while she was pregnant; and that the hes would quarrel and fight with the females as fiercely as with each other. Both which practices were such degrees of infamous brutality, that no other sensitive creature ever arrived at.

Another thing he wondered at in the Yahoos was their strange disposition to nastiness and dirt; whereas there appears to be a natural love of cleanliness in all other animals. As to the two former accusations, I was glad to let them pass without any reply, because I had not a word to offer upon them in defense of my species, which otherwise I certainly had done from my own inclinations. But I could have easily vindicated humankind from the imputation of singularity upon the last article, if there had been any swine in that country (as unluckily for me there were not) which although it may be a sweeter quadruped than a Yahoo, cannot I humbly conceive in justice pretend to more cleanliness; and so his honor himself must have owned, if he had seen their filthy way of feeding, and their custom of wallowing and sleeping in the mud.

My master likewise mentioned another quality, which his servants had discovered in several Yahoos, and to him was wholly unaccountable. He said, a fancy would sometimes take a Yahoo, to retire into a corner, to lie down and howl, and groan, and spurn away all that came near him, although he were young and fat, and wanted neither food nor water; nor did the servants imagine what could possibly ail him. And the only remedy they found was to set him to hard work, after which he would infallibly come to himself. To this I was silent out of partiality to my own kind; yet here I could plainly discover the true seeds of spleen,[3] which only seizeth on the lazy, the luxurious, and the rich; who, if they were forced to undergo the same regimen, I would undertake for the cure.

His Honor had farther observed, that a female Yahoo would often stand behind a bank or a bush, to gaze on the young males passing by, and then appear, and hide, using many antic gestures and grimaces; at which time it was observed, that she had a most offensive smell; and when any of the males advanced, would slowly retire, looking back, and with a counterfeit show of fear, run off into some convenient place where she knew the male would follow her.

At other times, if a female stranger came among them, three or four of her own sex would get about her, and stare and chatter, and grin, and smell her all over; and then turn off with gestures that seemed to express contempt and disdain.

Perhaps my master might refine a little in these speculations, which he had drawn from what he observed himself, or had been told by others; however, I could not reflect without some amazement, and much sorrow, that the rudiments of lewdness, coquetry, censure, and scandal, should have place by instinct in womankind.

I expected every moment that my master would accuse the Yahoos of those unnatural appetites in both sexes, so common among us. But nature it seems hath not been so expert a schoolmistress; and these politer pleasures are entirely the productions of art and reason, on our side of the globe.

CHAPTER VIII. *The Author relateth several particulars of the Yahoos. The great virtues of the Houyhnhnms. The education and exercises of their youth. Their general assembly.*

As I ought to have understood human nature much better than I supposed it possible for my master to do, so it was easy to apply

3. **Hypochondria.**

the character he gave of the Yahoos to myself and my countrymen; and I believed I could yet make farther discoveries from my own observation. I therefore often begged his honor to let me go among the herds of Yahoos in the neighborhood; to which he always very graciously consented, being perfectly convinced that the hatred I bore those brutes would never suffer me to be corrupted by them; and his honor ordered one of his servants, a strong sorrel nag, very honest and good-natured, to be my guard; without whose protection I durst not undertake such adventures. For I have already told the reader how much I was pestered by those odious animals upon my first arrival. I afterwards failed very narrowly three or four times of falling into their clutches, when I happened to stray at any distance without my hanger. And I have reason to believe, they had some imagination that I was of their own species, which I often assisted myself, by stripping up my sleeves, and shewing my naked arms and breast in their sight, when my protector was with me; at which times they would approach as near as they durst, and imitate my actions after the manner of monkeys, but ever with great signs of hatred; as a tame jackdaw with cap and stockings is always persecuted by the wild ones, when he happens to be got among them.

They are prodigiously nimble from their infancy; however, I once caught a young male of three years old, and endeavored by all marks of tenderness to make it quiet; but the little imp fell a squalling, scratching, and biting with such violence, that I was forced to let it go; and it was high time, for a whole troop of old ones came about us at the noise; but finding the cub was safe (for away it ran) and my sorrel nag being by, they durst not venture near us. I observed the young animal's flesh to smell very rank, and the stink was somewhat between a weasel and a fox, but much more disagreeable. I forgot another circumstance (and perhaps I might have the reader's pardon, if it were wholly omitted) that while I held the odious vermin in my hands, it voided its filthy excrements of a yellow liquid substance, all over my clothes; but by good fortune there was a small brook hard by, where I washed myself as clean as I could; although I durst not come into my master's presence until I were sufficiently aired.

By what I could discover, the Yahoos appear to be the most unteachable of all animals, their capacities never reaching higher than to draw or carry burdens. Yet I am of opinion, this defect ariseth chiefly from a perverse, restive disposition. For they are cunning, malicious, treacherous and revengeful. They are strong and hardy, but of a cowardly spirit, and by consequence insolent, abject, and cruel. It is observed that the red-haired of both sexes are more libidinous and mischievous than the rest, whom yet they much exceed in strength and activity.

The Houyhnhnms keep the Yahoos for present use in huts not far from the house; but the rest are sent abroad to certain fields, where they dig up roots, eat several kinds of herbs, and search about for carrion, or sometimes catch weasels and *luhimuhs* (a sort of wild rat) which they greedily devour. Nature hath taught them to dig deep holes with their nails on the side of a rising ground, wherein they lie by themselves; only the kennels of the females are larger, sufficient to hold two or three cubs.

They swim from their infancy like frogs, and are able to continue long under water, where they often take fish, which the females carry home to their young. And upon this occasion, I hope the reader will pardon my relating an odd adventure.

Being one day abroad with my protector the sorrel nag, and the weather exceeding hot, I entreated him to let me bathe in a river that was near. He consented, and I immediately stripped myself stark naked, and went down softly into the stream. It happened that a young female Yahoo standing behind a bank, saw the whole proceeding; and inflamed by desire, as the nag and I conjectured, came running with all speed, and leaped into the water within five yards of the place where I bathed. I was never in my life so terribly frighted; the nag was grazing at some distance, not suspecting any harm; she embraced me after a most fulsome manner; I roared as loud as I could, and the nag came galloping towards me, whereupon she quitted her grasp, with the utmost reluctancy, and leaped upon the opposite bank, where she stood gazing and howling all the time I was putting on my clothes.

This was matter of diversion to my master and his family, as well as of mortification to myself. For now I could no longer deny that I was a real Yahoo, in every limb and feature, since the females had a natural propensity to me as one of their own species; neither was the hair of this brute of a red color (which might have been some excuse for an appetite a little irregular) but black as a sloe, and her countenance did not make an appearance altogether so hideous as the rest of the kind; for I think, she could not be above eleven years old.

Having already lived three years in this country, the reader I suppose will expect that I should, like other travelers, give him some account of the manners and customs of its inhabitants, which it was indeed my principal study to learn.

As these noble Houyhnhnms are endowed by Nature with a general disposition to all virtues, and have no conceptions or ideas of what is evil in a rational creature; so their grand maxim is to cultivate reason, and to be wholly governed by it. Neither is reason among them a point problematical as with us, where men can argue with plausibility on both sides of a question; but strikes you with immediate conviction; as it must needs do where it is not mingled, obscured, or discolored by passion and interest. I remember it was with extreme difficulty that I could bring my master to understand the meaning of the word "opinion," or how a point could be disputable; because reason taught us to affirm or deny only where we are certain; and beyond our knowledge we cannot do either. So that controversies, wranglings, disputes, and positiveness in false or dubious propositions are evils unknown among the Houyhnhnms. In the like manner when I used to explain to him our several systems of natural philosophy, he would laugh that a creature pretending to reason should value itself upon the knowledge of other people's conjectures, and in things, where that knowledge, if it were certain, could be of no use. Wherein he agreed entirely with the sentiments of Socrates, as Plato delivers them, which I mention as the highest honor I can do that prince of philosophers. I have often since reflected what destruction such a doctrine would make in the libraries of Europe; and how many paths to fame would be then shut up in the learned world.

Friendship and benevolence are the two principal virtues among the Houyhnhnms; and these not confined to particular objects, but universal to the whole race. For a stranger from the remotest part is equally treated with the nearest neighbor, and wherever he goes, looks upon himself as at home. They preserve decency and civility in the highest degrees, but are altogether ignorant of ceremony. They have no fondness for their colts or foals; but the care they take in educating them proceedeth entirely from the dictates of reason. And I observed my master to show the same affection to his neighbor's issue that he had for his own. They will have it that nature teaches them to love the whole species, and it is reason only that maketh a distinction of persons, where there is a superior degree of virtue.

When the matron Houyhnhnms have produced one of each sex, they no longer accompany with their consorts, except they lose one of their issue by some casualty, which very seldom happens; but in such a case they meet again; or when the like accident befalls a person whose wife is past bearing, some other couple bestows on him one of their own colts, and then go together a second time, until the mother be pregnant. This caution is necessary to prevent the country from being overburdened with numbers. But the race of inferior Houyhnhnms bred up to be servants is not so strictly limited upon this article; these are allowed to produce three of each sex, to be domestics in the noble families.

In their marriages they are exactly careful to choose such colors as will not make any disagreeable mixture in the breed. Strength is chiefly valued in the male, and comeliness in the female; not upon the account of love, but to preserve the race from degenerating; for, where a female happens to excel in strength, a consort is

chosen with regard to comeliness. Courtship, love, presents, join-
tures, settlements, have no place in their thoughts, or terms
whereby to express them in their language. The young couple meet
and are joined, merely because it is the determination of their
parents and friends; it is what they see done every day; and they
look upon it as one of the necessary actions in a reasonable being.
But the violation of marriage, or any other unchastity, was never
heard of; and the married pair pass their lives with the same
friendship and mutual benevolence that they bear to all others of
the same species who come in their way, without jealousy, fondness, quarreling, or discontent.

In educating the youth of both sexes, their method is admirable,
and highly deserveth our imitation. These are not suffered to taste
a grain of oats, except upon certain days, till eighteen years old;
nor milk, but very rarely; and in summer they graze two hours in
the morning, and as many in the evening, which their parents
likewise observe; but the servants are not allowed above half that
time; and a great part of the grass is brought home, which they eat
at the most convenient hours, when they can be best spared from
work.

Temperance, industry, exercise, and cleanliness are the lessons
equally enjoined to the young ones of both sexes; and my master
thought it monstrous in us to give the females a different kind of
education from the males, except in some articles of domestic
management; whereby, as he truly observed, one half of our natives
were good for nothing but bringing children into the world; and
to trust the care of their children to such useless animals, he said
was yet a greater instance of brutality.

But the Houyhnhnms train up their youth to strength, speed,
and hardiness, by exercising them in running races up and down
steep hills, or over hard stony grounds; and when they are all in a
sweat, they are ordered to leap over head and ears into a pond or a
river. Four times a year the youth of certain districts meet to show
their proficiency in running, and leaping, and other feats of
strength or agility; where the victor is rewarded with a song made in
his or her praise. On this festival the servants drive a herd of Yahoos
into the field, laden with hay, and oats, and milk for a repast to the
Houyhnhnms; after which these brutes are immediately driven
back again, for fear of being noisome to the assembly.

Every fourth year, at the vernal equinox, there is a representative
council of the whole nation, which meets in a plain about twenty
miles from our house, and continueth about five or six days. Here
they inquire into the state and condition of the several districts;
whether they abound or be deficient in hay or oats, or cows or
Yahoos? And wherever there is any want (which is but seldom) it
is immediately supplied by unanimous consent and contribution.
Here likewise the regulation of children is settled: as for instance,

if a Houyhnhnm hath two males, he changeth one of them with another who hath two females, and when a child hath been lost by any casualty, where the mother is past breeding, it is determined what family in the district shall breed another to supply the loss.

CHAPTER IX. *A grand debate at the general assembly of the Houyhnhnms, and how it was determined. The learning of the Houyhnhnms. Their buildings. Their manner of burials. The defectiveness of their language.*

One of these grand assemblies was held in my time, about three months before my departure, whither my master went as the representative of our district. In this council was resumed their old debate, and indeed, the only debate that ever happened in their country; whereof my master after his return gave me a very particular account.

The question to be debated was whether the Yahoos should be exterminated from the face of the earth. One of the members for the affirmative offered several arguments of great strength and weight, alleging that, as the Yahoos were the most filthy, noisome, and deformed animal which nature ever produced, so they were the most restive and indocible, mischievous, and malicious; they would privately suck the teats of the Houyhnhnms' cows; kill and devour their cats, trample down their oats and grass, if they were not continually watched; and commit a thousand other extravagancies. He took notice of a general tradition, that Yahoos had not been always in their country, but that many ages ago, two of these brutes appeared together upon a mountain; whether produced by the heat of the sun upon corrupted mud and slime, or from the ooze and froth of the sea, was never known. That these Yahoos engendered, and their brood in a short time grew so numerous as to overrun and infest the whole nation. That the Houyhnhnms to get rid of this evil, made a general hunting, and at last enclosed the whole herd; and destroying the older, every Houyhnhnm kept two young ones in a kennel, and brought them to such a degree of tameness as an animal so savage by nature can be capable of acquiring, using them for draft and carriage. That there seemed to be much truth in this tradition, and that those creatures could not be *ylnhniamshy* (or aborigines of the land) because of the violent hatred the Houyhnhnms as well as all other animals bore them; which although their evil disposition sufficiently deserved, could never have arrived at so high a degree, if they had been aborigines, or else they would have long since been rooted out. That the inhabitants taking a fancy to use the service of the Yahoos, had very imprudently neglected to cultivate the breed of asses, which were a comely animal, easily kept, more tame and orderly, without any offensive smell, strong enough for labor, although they yield to the other in agility of body; and if their braying be no agreeable sound, it is far preferable to the horrible howlings of the Yahoos.

Several others declared their sentiments to the same purpose, when my master proposed an expedient to the assembly, whereof he had indeed borrowed the hint from me. He approved of the tradition, mentioned by the honorable member, who spoke before; and affirmed, that the two Yahoos said to be first seen among them, had been driven thither over the sea; that coming to land, and being forsaken by their companions, they retired to the mountains, and degenerating by degrees, became in process of time much more savage than those of their own species in the country from whence these two originals came. The reason of his assertion was that he had now in his possession a certain wonderful Yahoo (meaning myself) which most of them had heard of, and many of them had seen. He then related to them how he first found me; that my body was all covered with an artificial composure of the skins and hairs of other animals; that I spoke in a language of my own, and had thoroughly learned theirs; that I had related to him the accidents which brought me thither; that when he saw me without my covering, I was an exact Yahoo in every part, only of a whiter color, less hairy and with shorter claws. He added how I had endeavored to persuade him that in my own and other countries the Yahoos acted as the governing, rational animal, and held the Houyhnhnms in servitude; that he observed in me all the qualities of a Yahoo, only a little more civilized by some tincture of reason, which however was in a degree as far inferior to the Houyhnhnm race as the Yahoos of their country were to me; that among other things, I mentioned a custom we had of castrating Houyhnhnms when they were young, in order to render them tame; that the operation was easy and safe; that it was no shame to learn wisdom from brutes, as industry is taught by the ant, and building by the swallow (for so I translate the world *lyhannh*, although it be a much larger fowl). That this invention might be practiced upon the younger Yahoos here, which, besides rendering them tractable and fitter for use, would in an age put an end to the whole species without destroying life. That in the meantime the Houyhnhnms should be exhorted to cultivate the breed of asses, which, as they are in all respects more valuable brutes, so they have this advantage, to be fit for service at five years old, which the others are not till twelve.

This was all my master thought fit to tell me at that time, of what passed in the grand council. But he was pleased to conceal one particular, which related personally to myself, whereof I soon felt the unhappy effect, as the reader will know in its proper place, and from whence I date all the succeeding misfortunes of my life.

The Houyhnhnms have no letters, and consequently, their knowledge is all traditional. But there happening few events of any moment among a people so well united, naturally disposed to every virtue, wholly governed by reason, and cut off from all commerce with other nations, the historical part is easily preserved without burdening their memories. I have already observed that they are subject to no diseases, and therefore can have no need of physicians. However, they have excellent medicines composed of herbs, to cure accidental bruises and cuts in the pastern or frog of the foot by sharp stones, as well as other maims and hurts in the several parts of the body.

They calculate the year by the revolution of the sun and the moon, but use no subdivisions into weeks. They are well enough acquainted with the motions of those two luminaries, and understand the nature of eclipses; and this is the utmost progress of their astronomy.

In poetry they must be allowed to excell all other mortals; wherein the justness of their similes, and the minuteness, as well as exactness of their descriptions, are indeed inimitable. Their verses abound very much in both of these, and usually contain either some exalted notions of friendship and benevolence, or the praises of those who were victors in races and other bodily exercises. Their buildings, although very rude and simple, are not inconvenient, but well contrived to defend them from all injuries of cold and heat. They have a kind of tree, which at forty years old loosens in the root, and falls with the first storm; it grows very straight, and being pointed like stakes with a sharp stone (for the Houyhnhnms know not the use of iron), they stick them erect in the ground about ten inches asunder, and then weave in oat straw, or sometimes wattles, betwixt them. The roof is made after the same manner, and so are the doors.

The Houyhnhnms use the hollow part between the pastern and the hoof of their forefeet as we do our hands, and this with greater dexterity than I could at first imagine. I have seen a white mare of our family thread a needle (which I lent her on purpose) with that joint. They milk their cows, reap their oats, and do all the work which requires hands in the same manner. They have a kind of hard flints, which by grinding against other stones they form into instruments that serve instead of wedges, axes, and hammers. With tools made of these flints, they likewise cut their hay, and reap their oats, which there groweth naturally in several fields; the Yahoos draw home the sheaves in carriages, and the servants tread them in certain covered huts, to get out the grain, which is kept in stores. They make a rude kind of earthen and wooden vessels, and bake the former in the sun.

If they can avoid casualties, they die only of old age, and are buried in the obscurest places that can be found, their friends and relations expressing neither joy nor grief at their departure; nor does the dying person discover the least regret that he is leaving the world, any more than if he were upon returning home from a visit to one of his neighbors; I remember my master having once made an appointment with a friend and his family to come to his house upon some affair of importance; on the day fixed, the mistress and her two children came very late; she made two excuses, first for her husband, who, as she said, happened that very morning to *lhnuwnh*. The word is strongly expressive in their language, but not easily rendered into English; it signifies, *to retire to his first Mother*. Her excuse for not coming sooner was that her husband dying late in the morning, she was a good while consulting her servants about a convenient place where his body should be laid; and I observed she behaved herself at our house, as cheerfully as the rest; she died about three months after.

They live generally to seventy or seventy-five years, very seldom to fourscore; some weeks before their death they feel a gradual decay, but without pain. During this time they are much visited by their friends, because they cannot go abroad with their usual ease and satisfaction. However, about ten days before their death, which they seldom fail in computing, they return the visits that have been made by those who are nearest in the neighborhood, being carried in a convenient sledge drawn by Yahoos; which vehicle they use, not only upon this occasion, but when they grow old, upon long journeys, or when they are lamed by any accident. And therefore when the dying Houyhnhnms return those visits, they take a solemn leave of their friends, as if they were going to some remote part of the country, where they designed to pass the rest of their lives.

I know not whether it may be worth observing, that the Houyhnhnms have no word in their language to express anything that is evil, except what they borrow from the deformities or ill qualities of the Yahoos. Thus they denote the folly of a servant, an omission of a child, a stone that cuts their feet, a continuance of foul or unseasonable weather, and the like, by adding to each the epithet of Yahoo. For instance, *hhnm Yahoo, whnaholm Yahoo, ynlhmndwihlma Yahoo*, and an ill-contrived house, *ynholmhnmrohlnw Yahoo*.

I could with great pleasure enlarge farther upon the manners and virtues of this excellent people; but intending in a short time to publish a volume by itself expressly upon that subject, I refer the reader thither. And in the meantime, proceed to relate my own sad catastrophe.

CHAPTER X. *The Author's economy, and happy life among the Houyhnhnms. His great improvement in virtue, by conversing with them. Their conversations. The Author hath notice given him by his master that he must depart from the country. He falls into a swoon for grief, but submits. He contrives and finishes a canoe, by the help of a fellow servant, and puts to sea at a venture.*

I had settled my little economy to my own heart's content. My master had ordered a room to be made for me after their manner, about six yards from the house; the sides and floors of which I plastered with clay, and covered with rush mats of my own contriving; I had beaten hemp, which there grows wild, and made of it a sort of ticking; this I filled with the feathers of several birds I had taken with springes made of Yahoos' hairs, and were excellent food. I had worked two chairs with my knife, the sorrel nag helping me in the grosser and more laborious part. When my clothes were worn to rags, I made myself others with the skins of rabbits, and of a certain beautiful animal about the same size, called *nnuhnoh*, the skin of which is covered with a fine down. Of these I likewise made very tolerable stockings. I soled my shoes with wood which I cut from a tree, and fitted to the upper leather, and when this was worn out, I supplied it with the skins of Yahoos, dried in the sun. I often got honey out of hollow trees, which I mingled with water, or eat it with my bread. No man could more verify the truth of these two maxims, that *Nature is very easily satisfied*; and, that *Necessity is the mother of invention*. I enjoyed perfect health of body, and tranquility of mind; I did not feel the treachery or inconstancy of a friend, nor the inquiries of a secret or open enemy. I had no occasion of bribing, flattering, or pimping to procure the favor of any great man, or of his minion. I wanted no fence against fraud or oppression; here was neither physician to destroy my body, nor lawyer to ruin my fortune; no informer to watch my words and actions, or forge accusations against me for hire; here were no gibers, censurers, backbiters, pickpockets, highwaymen, housebreakers, attorneys, bawds, buffoons, gamesters, politicians, wits, splenetics, tedious talkers, controvertists, ravishers, murderers, robbers, virtuosos; no leaders or followers of party and faction; no encouragers to vice, by seducement or examples; no dungeons, axes, gibbets, whipping posts, or pillories; no cheating shopkeepers or mechanics; no pride, vanity or affectation; no fops, bullies, drunkards, strolling whores, or poxes; no ranting, lewd, expensive wives; no stupid, proud pedants; no importunate, overbearing, quarrelsome, noisy, roaring, empty, conceited, swearing companions; no scoundrels raised from the dust upon the merit of their vices; or nobility thrown into it on account of their virtues; no lords, fiddlers, judges, or dancing masters.

I had the favor of being admitted to several Houyhnhnms, who came to visit or dine with my master; where his honor graciously suffered me to wait in the room, and listen to their discourse. Both he and his company would often descend to ask me questions, and receive my answers. I had also sometimes the honor of attending my master in his visits to others. I never presumed to speak, except in answer to a question; and then I did it with inward regret, because it was a loss of so much time for improving myself; but I was infinitely delighted with the station of an humble auditor in such conversations, where nothing passed but what was useful, expressed in the fewest and most significant words; where (as I have already said) the greatest decency was observed, without the least degree of ceremony; where no person spoke without being pleased himself, and pleasing his companions; where there was no interruption, tediousness, heat, or difference of sentiments. They have a notion, that when people are met together, a short silence doth much improve conversation; this I found to be true; for during those little intermissions of talk, new ideas would arise in their minds, which very much enlivened the discourse. Their subjects are generally on friendship and benevolence; on order and economy; sometimes upon the visible operations of nature, or ancient traditions; upon the bounds and limits of virtue; upon the unerring rules of reason; or upon some determinations, to be taken at the next great assembly; and often upon the various excellencies of poetry. I may add, without vanity, that my presence often gave them sufficient matter for discourse, because it afforded my master an occasion of letting his friends into the history of me and my country, upon which they were all pleased to discant in a manner not very advantageous to human kind; and for that reason I shall not repeat what they said; only I may be allowed to observe that his honor, to my great admiration, appeared to understand the nature of Yahoos much better than myself. He went through all our vices and follies, and discovered many which I had never mentioned to him; by only supposing what qualities a Yahoo of their country, with a small proportion of reason, might be capable of exerting; and concluded, with too much probability, how vile as well as miserable such a creature must be.

I freely confess, that all the little knowledge I have of any value was acquired by the lectures I received from my master, and from hearing the discourses of him and his friends; to which I should be prouder to listen, than to dictate to the greatest and wisest assembly in Europe. I admired the strength, comeliness, and speed of the inhabitants; and such a constellation of virtues in such amiable persons produced in me the highest veneration. At first, indeed, I did not feel that natural awe which the Yahoos and all other animals bear towards them; but it grew upon me by degrees, much sooner than I imagined, and was mingled with a respectful love and gratitude, that they would condescend to distinguish me from the rest of my species.

When I thought of my family, my friends, my countrymen, or human race in general, I considered them as they really were, Yahoos in shape and disposition, perhaps a little more civilized, and qualified with the gift of speech; but making no other use of reason than to improve and multiply those vices, whereof their brethren in this country had only the share that nature allotted them. When I happened to behold the reflection of my own form in a lake or fountain, I turned away my face in horror and detestation of myself, and could better endure the sight of a common Yahoo than of my own person. By conversing with the Houyhnhnms, and looking upon them with delight, I fell to imitate their gait and gesture, which is now grown into a habit; and my friends often tell me in a blunt way, that I trot like a horse; which, however, I take for a great compliment; neither shall I disown, that in speaking I am apt to fall into the voice and manner of the Houyhnhnms, and hear myself ridiculed on that account without the least mortification.

In the midst of this happiness, when I looked upon myself to be fully settled for life, my master sent for me one morning a little earlier than his usual hour. I observed by his countenance that he was in some perplexity, and at a loss how to begin what he had to speak. After a short silence, he told me, he did not know how I would take what he was going to say; that, in the last general assembly, when the affair of the Yahoos was entered upon, the representatives had taken offense at his keeping a Yahoo (meaning myself) in his family more like a Houyhnhnm than a brute animal. That he was known frequently to converse with me, as if he could receive some advantage of pleasure in my company; that such a practice was not agreeable to reason or nature, or a thing ever heard of before among them. The assembly did therefore exhort him, either to employ me like the rest of my species, or command me to swim back to the place from whence I came. That the first of these expedients was utterly rejected by all the Houyhnhnms who had ever seen me at his house or their own; for, they alleged, that because I had some rudiments of reason, added to the natural pravity of those animals, it was to be feared, I might be able to seduce them into the woody and mountainous parts of the country, and bring them in troops by night to destroy the Houyhnhnms' cattle, as being naturally of the ravenous kind, and averse from labor.

My master added that he was daily pressed by the Houyhnhnms of the neighborhood to have the assembly's exhortation executed, which he could not put off much longer. He doubted it would be impossible for me to swim to another country; and therefore wished I would contrive some sort of vehicle resembling those I had described to him, that might carry me on the sea; in which work I should have the assistance of his own servants, as well as those of his neighbors. He concluded that for his own part he could have been content to keep me in his service as long as I lived; because he found I had cured myself of some bad habits and dispositions, by endeavoring, as far as my inferior nature was capable, to imitate the Houyhnhnms.

I should here observe to the reader, that a decree of the general assembly in this country is expressed by the word *hnhloayn*, which

signifies an exhortation, as near as I can render it; for they have no
conception how a rational creature can be compelled, but only advised, or exhorted; because no person can disobey reason without
giving up his claim to be a rational creature.

I was struck with the utmost grief and despair at my master's
discourse; and being unable to support the agonies I was under, I
fell into a swoon at his feet; when I came to myself, he told me
that he concluded I had been dead (for these people are subject to
no such imbecilities of nature). I answered, in a faint voice, that
death would have been too great an happiness; that although I
could not blame the assembly's exhortation, or the urgency of his
friends; yet in my weak and corrupt judgment, I thought it might
consist with reason to have been less rigorous. That I could not
swim a league, and probably the nearest land to theirs might be
distant above an hundred; that many materials, necessary for making a small vessel to carry me off, were wholly wanting in this country, which, however, I would attempt in obedience and gratitude
to his honor, although I concluded the thing to be impossible, and
therefore looked on myself as already devoted [4] to destruction.
That the certain prospect of an unnatural death was the least of
my evils; for, supposing I should escape with life by some strange
adventure, how could I think with temper [5] of passing my days
among Yahoos, and relapsing into my old corruptions, for want of
examples to lead and keep me within the paths of virtue. That I
knew too well upon what solid reasons all the determinations of
the wise Houyhnhnms were founded, not to be shaken by arguments of mine, a miserable Yahoo; and therefore after presenting
him with my humble thanks for the offer of his servants' assistance
in making a vessel, and desiring a reasonable time for so difficult a
work, I told him I would endeavor to preserve a wretched being;
and, if ever I returned to England, was not without hopes of being
useful to my own species by celebrating the praises of the renowned
Houyhnhnms, and proposing their virtues to the imitation of mankind.

My master in a few words made me a very gracious reply, allowed me the space of two months to finish my boat, and ordered
the sorrel nag, my fellow servant (for so at this distance I may presume to call him), to follow my instructions, because I told my
master that his help would be sufficient, and I knew he had a
tenderness for me.

In his company my first business was to go to that part of the
coast where my rebellious crew had ordered me to be set on shore.
I got upon a height, and looking on every side into the sea, fancied I
saw a small island towards the northeast; I took out my pocket glass,
and could then clearly distinguish it about five leagues off, as I
computed; but it appeared to the sorrel nag to be only a blue cloud;
for, as he had no conception of any country besides his own, so he

4. Doomed.   5. Equanimity.

could not be as expert in distinguishing remote objects at sea, as we who so much converse in that element.

After I had discovered this island, I considered no farther; but resolved, it should, if possible, be the first place of my banishment, leaving the consequence to fortune.

I returned home, and consulting with the sorrel nag, we went into a copse at some distance, where I with my knife, and he with a sharp flint fastened very artificially,[6] after their manner, to a wooden handle, cut down several oak wattles about the thickness of a walking staff, and some larger pieces. But I shall not trouble the reader with a particular description of my own mechanics; let it suffice to say, that in six weeks time, with the help of the sorrel nag, who performed the parts that required most labor, I finished a sort of Indian canoe; but much larger, covering it with the skins of Yahoos, well stitched together, with hempen threads of my own making. My sail was likewise composed of the skins of the same animal; but I made use of the youngest I could get, the older being too tough and thick; and I likewise provided myself with four paddles. I laid in a stock of boiled flesh, of rabbits and fowls; and took with me two vessels, one filled with milk, and the other with water.

I tried my canoe in a large pond near my master's house, and then corrected in it what was amiss, stopping all the chinks with Yahoo's tallow, till I found it staunch, and able to bear me and my freight. And when it was as complete as I could possibly make it, I had it drawn on a carriage very gently by Yahoos, to the seaside, under the conduct of the sorrel nag and another servant.

When all was ready, and the day came for my departure, I took leave of my master and lady, and the whole family, my eyes flowing with tears and my heart quite sunk with grief. But his honor, out of curiosity, and perhaps (if I may speak it without vanity) partly out of kindness, was determined to see me in my canoe; and got several of his neighboring friends to accompany him. I was forced to wait above an hour for the tide, and then observing the wind very fortunately bearing towards the island to which I intended to steer my course, I took a second leave of my master; but as I was going to prostrate myself to kiss his hoof, he did me the honor to raise it gently to my mouth. I am not ignorant how much I have been censured for mentioning this last particular. Detractors are pleased to think it improbable that so illustrious a person should descend to give so great a mark of distinction to a creature so inferior as I. Neither have I forgot how apt some travelers are to boast of extraordinary favors they have received. But, if these censurers were better acquainted with the noble and courteous disposition of the Houyhnhnms, they would soon change their opinion. I paid my respects to the rest of the Houyhnhnms in his honor's company; then getting into my canoe, I pushed off from shore.

6. Artfully.

CHAPTER XI. *The Author's dangerous voyage. He arrives at New Holland, hoping to settle there. Is wounded with an arrow by one of the natives. Is seized and carried by force into a Portuguese ship. The great civilities of the Captain. The Author arrives at England.*

I began this desperate voyage on February 15, 1714/5,[7] at 9 o'clock in the morning. The wind was very favorable; however, I made use at first only of my paddles; but considering I should soon be weary, and that the wind might probably chop about, I ventured to set up my little sail; and thus, with the help of the tide, I went at the rate of a league and a half an hour, as near as I could guess. My master and his friends continued on the shore, till I was almost out of sight; and I often heard the sorrel nag (who always loved me) crying out, "*Hnuy illa nyha maiah Yahoo,*" ("Take care of thyself, gentle Yahoo").

My design was, if possible, to discover some small island uninhabited, yet sufficient by my labor to furnish me with necessaries of life, which I would have thought a greater happiness than to be first minister in the politest court of Europe, so horrible was the idea I conceived of returning to live in the society and under the government of Yahoos. For in such a solitude as I desired, I could at least enjoy my own thoughts, and reflect with delight on the virtues of those inimitable Houyhnhnms, without any opportunity of degenerating into the vices and corruptions of my own species.

The reader may remember what I related when my crew conspired against me, and confined me to my cabin, how I continued there several weeks, without knowing what course we took; and when I was put ashore in the longboat, how the sailors told me with oaths, whether true or false, that they knew not in what part of the world we were. However, I did then believe us to be about 10 degrees southward of the Cape of Good Hope, or about 45 degrees southern latitude, as I gathered from some general words I overheard among them, being I supposed to the southeast in their intended voyage to Madagascar. And although this were but little better than conjecture, yet I resolved to steer my course eastward, hoping to reach the southwest coast of New Holland, and perhaps some such island as I desired, lying westward of it. The wind was full west, and by six in the evening I computed I had gone eastward at least eighteen leagues; when I spied a very small island about half a league off, which I soon reached. It was nothing but a rock with one creek,[8] naturally arched by the force of tempests. Here I put in my canoe, and climbing a part of the rock, I could plainly discover land to the east, extending from south to north. I lay all night in my canoe; and repeating my voyage early in the morning, I arrived in seven hours to the southeast point of New Holland. This confirmed me in the opinion I have long entertained, that the maps and charts place this country at least three degrees more to the east than it really is; which thought I communicated many years ago to my worthy friend Mr. Herman Moll,[9] and gave him my reasons for it, although he hath rather chosen to follow other authors.

I saw no inhabitants in the place where I landed; and being un-armed, I was afraid of venturing far into the country. I found some shellfish on the shore, and eat them raw, not daring to kindle a fire, for fear of being discovered by the natives. I continued three days feeding on oysters and limpets, to save my own provisions; and I fortunately found a brook of excellent water, which gave me great relief.

On the fourth day, venturing out early a little too far, I saw twenty or thirty natives upon a height, not above five hundred yards from me. They were stark naked, men, women, and children round a fire, as I could discover by the smoke. One of them spied me, and gave notice to the rest; five of them advanced towards me, leaving the women and children at the fire. I made what haste I could to the shore, and getting into my canoe, shoved off; the sav-ages observing me retreat, ran after me; and before I could get far enough into the sea, discharged an arrow, which wounded me deeply on the inside of my left knee. (I shall carry the mark to my grave.) I apprehended the arrow might be poisoned; and paddling out of the reach of their darts (being a calm day) I made a shift to suck the wound, and dress it as well as I could.

I was at a loss what to do, for I durst not return to the same land-ing place, but stood to the north, and was forced to paddle; for the wind, although very gentle, was against me, blowing northwest. As I was looking about for a secure landing place, I saw a sail to the north northeast, which appearing every minute more visible, I was in some doubt whether I should wait for them or no; but at last my detestation of the Yahoo race prevailed; and turning my canoe, I sailed and paddled together to the south, and got into the same creek from whence I set out in the morning, choosing rather to trust myself among these barbarians than live with European Yahoos. I drew up my canoe as close as I could to the shore, and hid myself behind a stone by the little brook, which, as I have already said, was excellent water.

The ship came within half a league of this creek, and sent out her longboat with vessels to take in fresh water (for the place it seems was very well known), but I did not observe it until the boat was almost on shore; and it was too late to seek another hiding place. The seamen at their landing observed my canoe, and rum-maging it all over, easily conjectured that the owner could not be far off. Four of them well armed searched every cranny and lurking hole, till at last they found me flat on my face behind the stone. They gazed a while in admiration [1] at my strange uncouth dress;

9. A famous contemporary map maker.   1. Wonder.

my coat made of skins, my wooden-soled shoes, and my furred stockings; from whence, however, they concluded I was not a native of
the place, who all go naked. One of the seamen in Portuguese bid me
rise, and asked who I was. I understood that language very well, and
getting upon my feet, said I was a poor Yahoo, banished from the
Houyhnhnms, and desired they would please to let me depart. They
admired to hear me answer them in their own tongue, and saw by
my complexion I must be an European; but were at a loss to know
what I meant by Yahoos and Houyhnhnms, and at the same time
fell a laughing at my strange tone in speaking, which resembled the
neighing of a horse. I trembled all the while betwixt fear and
hatred; I again desired leave to depart, and was gently moving to
my canoe; but they laid hold on me, desiring to know what country
I was of? whence I came? with many other questions. I told them I
was born in England, from whence I came about five years ago,
and then their country and ours was at peace. I therefore hoped
they would not treat me as an enemy, since I meant them no harm,
but was a poor Yahoo, seeking some desolate place where to pass the
remainder of his unfortunate life.

When they began to talk, I thought I never heard or saw any
thing so unnatural; for it appeared to me as monstrous as if a dog or
a cow should speak in England, or a Yahoo in Houyhnhnmland. The
honest Portuguese were equally amazed at my strange dress, and
the odd manner of delivering my words, which however they understood very well. They spoke to me with great humanity, and said
they were sure their Captain would carry me *gratis* to Lisbon, from
whence I might return to my own country; that two of the seamen
would go back to the ship, to inform the Captain of what they had
seen, and receive his orders; in the meantime, unless I would give
my solemn oath not to fly, they would secure me by force. I thought
it best to comply with their proposal. They were very curious to
know my story, but I gave them very little satisfaction; and they all
conjectured, that my misfortunes had impaired my reason. In two
hours the boat, which went laden with vessels of water, returned
with the Captain's commands to fetch me on board. I fell on my
knees to preserve my liberty; but all was in vain, and the men having
tied me with cords, heaved me into the boat, from whence I was
taken into the ship, and from thence into the Captain's cabin.

His name was Pedro de Mendez; he was a very courteous and
generous person; he entreated me to give some account of myself,
and desired to know what I would eat or drink; said I should be
used as well as himself, and spoke so many obliging things, that I
wondered to find such civilities from a Yahoo. However, I remained
silent and sullen; I was ready to faint at the very smell of him and
his men. At last I desired something to eat out of my own canoe;
but he ordered me a chicken and some excellent wine, and then directed that I should be put to bed in a very clean cabin. I would not

undress myself, but lay on the bedclothes; and in half an hour stole out, when I thought the crew was at dinner; and getting to the side of the ship, was going to leap into the sea, and swim for my life, rather than continue among Yahoos. But one of the seamen prevented me, and having informed the Captain, I was chained to my cabin.

After dinner Don Pedro came to me, and desired to know my reason for so desperate an attempt; assured me he only meant to do me all the service he was able; and spoke so very movingly, that at last I descended to treat him like an animal which had some little portion of reason. I gave him a very short relation of my voyage; of the conspiracy against me by my own men; of the country where they set me on shore, and of my five years residence there. All which he looked upon as if it were a dream or a vision; whereat I took great offense; for I had quite forgot the faculty of lying, so peculiar to Yahoos in all countries where they preside, and consequently the disposition of suspecting truth in others of their own species. I asked him whether it were the custom of his country to *say the thing that was not?* I assured him I had almost forgot what he meant by falsehood; and if I had lived a thousand years in Houyhnhnmland, I should never have heard a lie from the meanest servant. That I was altogether indifferent whether he believed me or no; but however, in return for his favors, I would give so much allowance to the corruption of his nature, as to answer any objection he would please to make; and he might easily discover the truth.

The Captain, a wise man, after many endeavors to catch me tripping in some part of my story, at last began to have a better opinion of my veracity. But he added that since I professed so inviolable an attachment to truth, I must give him my word of honor to bear him company in this voyage without attempting anything against my life; or else he would continue me a prisoner till we arrived at Lisbon. I gave him the promise he required; but at the same time protested that I would suffer the greatest hardships rather than return to live among Yahoos.

Our voyage passed without any considerable accident. In gratitude to the Captain I sometimes sat with him at his earnest request, and strove to conceal my antipathy against humankind, although it often broke out; which he suffered to pass without observation. But the greatest part of the day, I confined myself to my cabin, to avoid seeing any of the crew. The Captain had often entreated me to strip myself of my savage dress, and offered to lend me the best suit of clothes he had. This I would not be prevailed on to accept, abhorring to cover myself with anything that had been on the back of a Yahoo. I only desired he would lend me two clean shirts, which having been washed since he wore them, I believed would not so much defile me. These I changed every second day, and washed them myself.

We arrived at Lisbon, Nov. 5, 1715. At our landing, the Captain forced me to cover myself with his cloak, to prevent the rabble from crowding about me. I was conveyed to his own house; and at my earnest request, he led me up to the highest room backwards.[2] I conjured him to conceal from all persons what I had told him of the Houyhnhnms; because the least hint of such a story would not only draw numbers of people to see me, but probably put me in danger of being imprisoned, or burned by the Inquisition. The Captain persuaded me to accept a suit of clothes newly made; but I would not suffer the tailor to take my measure; however, Don Pedro being almost of my size, they fitted me well enough. He accoutred me with other necessaries, all new, which I aired for twenty-four hours before I would use them.

The Captain had no wife, nor above three servants, none of which were suffered to attend at meals; and his whole deportment was so obliging, added to very good human understanding, that I really began to tolerate his company. He gained so far upon me, that I ventured to look out of the back window. By degrees I was brought into another room, from whence I peeped into the street, but drew my head back in a fright. In a week's time he seduced me down to the door. I found my terror gradually lessened, but my hatred and contempt seemed to increase. I was at last bold enough to walk the street in his company, but kept my nose well stopped with rue, or sometimes with tobacco.

In ten days, Don Pedro, to whom I had given some account of my domestic affairs, put it upon me as a point of honor and conscience that I ought to return to my native country, and live at home with my wife and children. He told me there was an English ship in the port just ready to sail, and he would furnish me with all things necessary. It would be tedious to repeat his arguments, and my contradictions. He said it was altogether impossible to find such a solitary island as I had desired to live in; but I might command in my own house, and pass my time in a manner as recluse as I pleased.

I complied at last, finding I could not do better. I left Lisbon the 24th day of November, in an English merchantman, but who was the Master I never inquired. Don Pedro accompanied me to the ship, and lent me twenty pounds. He took kind leave of me, and embraced me at parting; which I bore as well as I could. During this last voyage I had no commerce with the Master, or any of his men; but pretending I was sick kept close in my cabin. On the fifth of December, 1715, we cast anchor in the Downs about nine in the morning, and at three in the afternoon I got safe to my house at Redriff.

My wife and family received me with great surprise and joy, because they concluded me certainly dead; but I must freely confess, the sight of them filled me only with hatred, disgust, and con-

2. At the rear.

tempt; and the more, by reflecting on the near alliance I had to them. For, although since my unfortunate exile from the Houyhn-hnm country, I had compelled myself to tolerate the sight of Yahoos, and to converse with Don Pedro de Mendez; yet my memory and imaginations were perpetually filled with the virtues and ideas of those exalted Houyhnhnms. And when I began to consider that by copulating with one of the Yahoo species, I had become a parent of more, it struck me with the utmost shame, confusion, and horror.

As soon as I entered the house, my wife took me in her arms, and kissed me; at which, having not been used to the touch of that odious animal for so many years, I fell in a swoon for almost an hour. At the time I am writing, it is five years since my last return to England; during the first year I could not endure my wife or children in my presence, the very smell of them was intolerable; much less could I suffer them to eat in the same room. To this hour they dare not presume to touch my bread, or drink out of the same cup; neither was I ever able to let one of them take me by the hand. The first money I laid out was to buy two young stone-horses,[3] which I keep in a good stable, and next to them the groom is my greatest favorite; for I feel my spirits revived by the smell he contracts in the stable. My horses understand me tolerably well; I converse with them at least four hours every day. They are strangers to bridle or saddle; they live in great amity with me, and friendship to each other.

CHAPTER XII. *The Author's veracity. His design in publishing this work. His censure of those travelers who swerve from the truth. The Author clears himself from any sinister ends in writing. An objection answered. The method of planting colonies. His native country commended. The right of the crown to those countries described by the Author is justified. The difficulty of conquering them. The Author takes his last leave of the reader; proposeth his manner of living for the future; gives good advice, and concludeth.*

Thus, gentle reader, I have given thee a faithful history of my travels for sixteen years, and above seven months; wherein I have not been so studious of ornament as of truth. I could perhaps like others have astonished thee with strange improbable tales; but I rather chose to relate plain matter of fact in the simplest manner and style; because my principal design was to inform, and not to amuse thee.

It is easy for us who travel into remote countries, which are seldom visited by Englishmen or other Europeans, to form descriptions of wonderful animals both at sea and land. Whereas a traveler's chief aim should be to make men wiser and better, and to improve their minds by the bad as well as good example of

3. Stallions.

what they deliver concerning foreign places.

I could heartily wish a law were enacted, that every traveler, before he were permitted to publish his voyages, should be obliged to make oath before the Lord High Chancellor that all he intended to print was absolutely true to the best of his knowledge; for then the world would no longer be deceived as it usually is, while some writers, to make their works pass the better upon the public, impose the grossest falsities on the unwary reader. I have perused several books of travels with great delight in my younger days; but, having since gone over most parts of the globe, and been able to contradict many fabulous accounts from my own observation, it hath given me a great disgust against this part of reading, and some indignation to see the credulity of mankind so impudently abused. Therefore, since my acquaintance were pleased to think my poor endeavors might not be unacceptable to my country; I imposed on myself as a maxim, never to be swerved from, that I would *strictly adhere to truth*; neither indeed can I be ever under the least temptation to vary from it, while I retain in my mind the lectures and example of my noble master, and the other illustrious Houyhnhnms, of whom I had so long the honor to be an humble hearer.

> ——*Nec si miserum Fortuna Sinonem*
> *Finxit, vanum etiam, mendacemque improba finget.*[4]

I know very well how little reputation is to be got by writings which require neither genius nor learning, nor indeed any other talent, except a good memory, or an exact *Journal*. I know likewise, that writers of travels, like dictionary-makers, are sunk into oblivion by the weight and bulk of those who come last, and therefore lie uppermost. And it is highly probable that such travelers who shall hereafter visit the countries described in this work of mine, may be detecting my errors (if there be any) and adding many new discoveries of their own, jostle me out of vogue, and stand in my place, making the world forget that ever I was an author. This indeed would be too great a mortification if I wrote for fame; but, as my sole intention was the PUBLIC GOOD, I cannot be altogether disappointed. For, who can read the virtues I have mentioned in the glorious Houyhnhnms, without being ashamed of his own vices, when he considers himself as the reasoning, governing animal of his country? I shall say nothing of those remote nations where Yahoos preside; amongst which the least corrupted are the Brobdingnagians, whose wise maxims in morality and government it would be our happiness to observe. But I forbear descanting further, and rather leave the judicious reader to his own remarks and applications.

---

4. Virgil, *Aeneid*, II, 79–80. "* * * nor if Fortune had moulded Sinon for misery, will she also in spite mould him as false and lying."

I am not a little pleased that this work of mine can possibly meet with no censurers; for what objections can be made against a writer who relates only plain facts that happened in such distant countries, where we have not the least interest with respect either to trade or negotiations? I have carefully avoided every fault with which common writers of travels are often too justly charged. Besides, I meddle not the least with any party, but write without passion, prejudice, or ill-will against any man or number of men whatsoever. I write for the noblest end, to inform and instruct mankind, over whom I may, without breach of modesty, pretend to some superiority, from the advantages I received by conversing so long among the most accomplished Houyhnhnms. I write without any view towards profit or praise. I never suffer a word to pass that may look like reflection, or possibly give the least offense even to those who are most ready to take it. So that, I hope, I may with justice pronounce myself an Author perfectly blameless; against whom the tribes of answerers, considerers, observers, reflectors, detecters, remarkers will never be able to find matter for exercising their talents.

I confess it was whispered to me that I was bound in duty as a subject of England, to have given in a memorial to a secretary of state, at my first coming over; because, whatever lands are discovered by a subject, belong to the Crown. But I doubt whether our conquests in the countries I treat of would be as easy as those of Ferdinando Cortez over the naked Americans. The Lilliputians, I think, are hardly worth the charge of a fleet and army to reduce them; and I question whether it might be prudent or safe to attempt the Brobdingnagians; or, whether an English army would be much at their ease with the Flying Island over their heads. The Houyhnhnms, indeed, appear not to be so well prepared for war, a science to which they are perfect strangers, and especially against missive weapons. However, supposing myself to be a minister of state, I could never give my advice for invading them. Their prudence, unanimity, unacquaintedness with fear, and their love of their country would amply supply all defects in the military art. Imagine twenty thousand of them breaking into the midst of an European army, confounding the ranks, overturning the carriages, battering the warriors' faces into mummy,[5] by terrible yerks [6] from their hinder hoofs: for they would well deserve the character given to Augustus, *Recalcitrat undique tutus*.[7] But instead of proposals for conquering that magnanimous nation, I rather wish they were in a capacity or disposition to send a sufficient number of their inhabitants for civilizing Europe; by teaching us the first principles of Honor, Justice, Truth, Temperance,

---

5. Pulp.
6. Kicks.
7. Horace, *Satires* II.i.20. "* * * he

kicks backward, at every point on his guard."

public Spirit, Fortitude, Chastity, Friendship, Benevolence, and Fidelity. The names of all which Virtues are still retained among us in most languages, and are to be met with in modern as well as ancient authors, which I am able to assert from my own small reading.

But I had another reason which made me less forward to enlarge his majesty's dominions by my discoveries: to say the truth, I had conceived a few scruples with relation to the distributive justice of princes upon those occasions. For instance, a crew of pirates are driven by a storm they know not whither; at length a boy discovers land from the topmast; they go on shore to rob and plunder; they see an harmless people, are entertained with kindness, they give the country a new name, they take formal possession of it for the king, they set up a rotten plank or a stone for a memorial, they murder two or three dozen of the natives, bring away a couple more by force for a sample, return home, and get their pardon. Here commences a new dominion acquired with a title by Divine Right. Ships are sent with the first opportunity; the natives driven out or destroyed, their princes tortured to discover their gold; a free license given to all acts of inhumanity and lust; the earth reeking with the blood of its inhabitants: and this execrable crew of butchers employed in so pious an expedition is a *modern colony* sent to convert and civilize an idolatrous and barbarous people.

But this description, I confess, doth by no means affect the British nation, who may be an example to the whole world for their wisdom, care, and justice in planting colonies; their liberal endowments for the advancement of religion and learning; their choice of devout and able pastors to propagate Christianity; their caution in stocking their provinces with people of sober lives and conversations from this the Mother Kingdom; their strict regard to the distribution of justice, in supplying the civil administration through all their colonies with officers of the greatest abilities, utter strangers to corruption: and to crown all, by sending the most vigilant and virtuous governors, who have no other views than the happiness of the people over whom they preside, and the honor of the king their master.

But, as those countries which I have described do not appear to have any desire of being conquered, and enslaved, murdered, or driven out by colonies, nor abound either in gold, silver, sugar, or tobacco, I did humbly conceive they were by no means proper objects of our zeal, our valor, or our interest. However, if those whom it may concern, think fit to be of another opinion, I am ready to depose, when I shall be lawfully called, that no European did ever visit these countries before me. I mean, if the inhabitants ought to be believed.

But, as to the formality of taking possession in my sovereign's name, it never came once into my thoughts; and if it had, yet as my affairs then stood, I should perhaps in point of prudence and self-preservation have put it off to a better opportunity.

Having thus answered the only objection that can be raised against me as a traveler, I here take a final leave of my courteous readers, and return to enjoy my own speculations in my little garden at Redriff; to apply those excellent lessons of virtue which I learned among the Houyhnhnms; to instruct the Yahoos of my own family as far as I shall find them docible animals; to behold my figure often in a glass, and thus if possible habituate myself by time to tolerate the sight of a human creature; to lament the brutality of Houyhnhnms in my own country, but always treat their persons with respect, for the sake of my noble master, his family, his friends, and the whole Houyhnhnm race, whom these of ours have the honor to resemble in all their lineaments, however their intellectuals came to degenerate.

I began last week to permit my wife to sit at dinner with me, at the farthest end of a long table; and to answer (but with the utmost brevity) the few questions I ask her. Yet the smell of a Yahoo continuing very offensive, I always keep my nose well stopped with rue, lavender, or tobacco leaves. And although it be hard for a man late in life to remove old habits, I am not altogether out of hopes in some time to suffer a neighbor Yahoo in my company, without the apprehensions I am yet under of his teeth or his claws.

My reconcilement to the Yahoo kind in general might not be so difficult, if they would be content with those vices and follies only which nature hath entitled them to. I am not in the least provoked at the sight of a lawyer, a pickpocket, a colonel, a fool, a lord, a gamester, a politician, a whoremonger, a physician, an evidence, a suborner, an attorney, a traitor, or the like: this is all according to the due course of things. But when I behold a lump of deformity, and diseases both in body and mind, smitten with pride, it immediately breaks all the measures of my patience; neither shall I be ever able to comprehend how such an animal and such a vice could tally together. The wise and virtuous Houyhnhnms, who abound in all excellencies that can adorn a rational creature, have no name for this vice in their language, which hath no terms to express anything that is evil, except those whereby they describe the detestable qualities of their Yahoos, among which they were not able to distinguish this of pride, for want of thoroughly understanding human nature, as it showeth itself in other countries, where that animal presides. But I, who had more experience, could plainly observe some rudiments of it among the wild Yahoos.

But the Houyhnhnms, who live under the government of reason, are no more proud of the good qualities they possess, than I should be for not wanting a leg or an arm, which no man in his wits would boast of, although he must be miserable without them. I dwell the longer upon this subject from the desire I have to make the society of an English Yahoo by any means not insupportable; and therefore I here entreat those who have any tincture of this absurd vice, that they will not presume to appear in my sight.

1726, 1735

A Modest Proposal[1]

For Preventing the Children of Poor People in Ireland from Being a Burden to Their Parents or Country, and for Making Them Beneficial to the Public

It is a melancholy object to those who walk through this great town[2] or travel in the country, when they see the streets, the roads, and cabin doors, crowded with beggars of the female sex, followed by three, four, or six children, all in rags and importuning every passenger for an alms. These mothers, instead of being able to work for their honest livelihood, are forced to employ all their time in strolling to beg sustenance for their helpless infants, who, as they grow up, either turn thieves for want of work, or leave their dear native country to fight for the Pretender in Spain, or sell themselves to the Barbadoes.[3]

I think it is agreed by all parties that this prodigious number of children in the arms, or on the backs, or at the heels of their mothers, and frequently of their fathers, is in the present deplor-

1. *A Modest Proposal* is an example of Swift's favorite satiric devices used with superb effect. Irony (from the deceptive adjective "modest" in the title to the very last sentence) pervades the piece. A rigorous logic deduces ghastly arguments from a shocking premise so quietly assumed that the reader assents before he is aware of what his assent implies. Parody, at which Swift is adept, allows him to glance sardonically at the by then familiar figure of the benevolent humanitarian (forerunner of the modern sociologist, social worker, economic planner) concerned to correct a social evil by means of a theoretically conceived plan. The proposer, as naïve as he is apparently logical and kindly, ignores and therefore emphasizes for the reader the enormity of his plan. The whole is an elaboration of a rather trite metaphor: "The English are devouring the Irish." But there is nothing trite about the pamphlet, which expresses in Swift's most controlled style his pity for the oppressed, ignorant, populous, and hungry Catholic peasants of Ireland, and his anger at the rapacious English absentee landlords, who were bleeding the country white with the silent approbation of Parliament, ministers, and the Crown.
2. Dublin.
3. James Francis Edward Stuart (1688–1766), the son of James II, was claimant ("Pretender") to the throne of England from which the Glorious Revolution had barred his succession. Catholic Ireland was loyal to him, and Irishmen joined him in his exile on the Continent. Because of the poverty in Ireland, many Irishmen emigrated to the West Indies and other British colonies in America; they paid their passage by binding themselves to work for a stated period for one of the planters.

able state of the kingdom a very great additional grievance; and therefore whoever could find out a fair, cheap, and easy method of making these children sound, useful members of the commonwealth would deserve so well of the public as to have his statue set up for a preserver of the nation.

But my intention is very far from being confined to provide only for the children of professed beggars; it is of a much greater extent, and shall take in the whole number of infants at a certain age who are born of parents in effect as little able to support them as those who demand our charity in the streets.

As to my own part, having turned my thoughts for many years upon this important subject, and maturely weighed the several schemes of other projectors,[4] I have always found them grossly mistaken in their computation. It is true, a child just dropped from its dam may be supported by her milk for a solar year, with little other nourishment; at most not above the value of two shillings, which the mother may certainly get, or the value in scraps, by her lawful occupation of begging; and it is exactly at one year old that I propose to provide for them in such a manner as instead of being a charge upon their parents or the parish, or wanting food and raiment for the rest of their lives, they shall on the contrary contribute to the feeding, and partly to the clothing, of many thousands.

There is likewise another great advantage in my scheme, that it will prevent those voluntary abortions, and that horrid practice of women murdering their bastard children, alas, too frequent among us, sacrificing the poor innocent babes, I doubt, more to avoid the expense than the shame, which would move tears and pity in the most savage and inhuman breast.

The number of souls in this kingdom[5] being usually reckoned one million and a half, of these I calculate there may be about two hundred thousand couple whose wives are breeders; from which number I subtract thirty thousand couples who are able to maintain their own children, although I apprehend there cannot be so many under the present distresses of the kingdom; but this being granted, there will remain an hundred and seventy thousand breeders. I again subtract fifty thousand for those women who miscarry, or whose children die by accident or disease within the year. There only remain an hundred and twenty thousand children of poor parents annually born. The question therefore is, how this number shall be reared and provided for, which, as I have already said, under the present situation of affairs, is utterly impossible by all the methods hitherto proposed. For we can neither employ them in handicraft or agriculture; we neither build houses (I mean in the country) nor cultivate land. They can very seldom pick up a livelihood

4. Devisers of schemes.   5. Ireland.

by stealing till they arrive at six years old, except where they are of towardly[6] parts; although I confess they learn the rudiments much earlier, during which time they can however be looked upon only as probationers, as I have been informed by a principal gentleman in the county of Cavan, who protested to me that he never knew above one or two instances under the age of six, even in a part of the kingdom so renowned for the quickest proficiency in that art.

I am assured by our merchants that a boy or a girl before twelve years old is no salable commodity; and even when they come to this age they will not yield above three pounds, or three pounds and half a crown at most on the Exchange; which cannot turn to account either to the parents or the kingdom, the charge of nutriment and rags having been at least four times that value.

I shall now therefore humbly propose my own thoughts, which I hope will not be liable to the least objection.

I have been assured by a very knowing American of my acquaintance in London, that a young healthy child well nursed is at a year old a most delicious, nourishing, and wholesome food, whether stewed, roasted, baked, or boiled; and I make no doubt that it will equally serve in a fricassee or a ragout.[7]

I do therefore humbly offer it to public consideration that of the hundred and twenty thousand children, already computed, twenty thousand may be reserved for breed, whereof only one fourth part to be males, which is more than we allow to sheep, black cattle, or swine; and my reason is that these children are seldom the fruits of marriage, a circumstance not much regarded by our savages, therefore one male will be sufficient to serve four females. That the remaining hundred thousand may at a year old be offered in sale to the persons of quality and fortune through the kingdom, always advising the mother to let them suck plentifully in the last month, so as to render them plump and fat for a good table. A child will make two dishes at an entertainment for friends; and when the family dines alone, the fore or hind quarter will make a reasonable dish, and seasoned with a little pepper or salt will be very good boiled on the fourth day, especially in winter.

I have reckoned upon a medium that a child just born will weigh twelve pounds, and in a solar year if tolerably nursed increaseth to twenty-eight pounds.

I grant this food will be somewhat dear, and therefore very proper for landlords, who, as they have already devoured most of the parents, seem to have the best title to the children.

Infant's flesh will be in season throughout the year, but more plentiful in March, and a little before and after. For we are told by a grave author, an eminent French physician,[8] that fish being

6. Dutiful, tractable.
7. A highly seasoned meat stew.
8. François Rabelais (ca. 1494–1553), a humorist and a satirist, by no means grave.

a prolific diet, there are more children born in Roman Catholic countries about nine months after Lent than at any other season; therefore, reckoning a year after Lent, the markets will be more glutted than usual, because the number of popish infants is at least three to one in this kingdom; and therefore it will have one other collateral advantage, by lessening the number of Papists among us.

I have already computed the charge of nursing a beggar's child (in which list I reckon all cottagers, laborers, and four fifths of the farmers) to be about two shillings per annum, rags included; and I believe no gentleman would repine to give ten shillings for the carcass of a good fat child, which, as I have said, will make four dishes of excellent nutritive meat, when he hath only some particular friend or his own family to dine with him. Thus the squire will learn to be a good landlord, and grow popular among the tenants; the mother will have eight shillings net profit, and be fit for work till she produces another child.

Those who are more thrifty (as I must confess the times require) may flay the carcass; the skin of which artificially[9] dressed will make admirable gloves for ladies, and summer boots for fine gentlemen.

As to our city of Dublin, shambles[1] may be appointed for this purpose in the most convenient parts of it, and butchers we may be assured will not be wanting; although I rather recommend buying the children alive, and dressing them hot from the knife as we do roasting pigs.

A very worthy person, a true lover of his country, and whose virtues I highly esteem, was lately pleased in discoursing on this matter to offer a refinement upon my scheme. He said that many gentlemen of this kingdom, having of late destroyed their deer, he conceived that the want of venison might be well supplied by the bodies of young lads and maidens, not exceeding fourteen years of age nor under twelve, so great a number of both sexes in every county being now ready to starve for want of work and service; and these to be disposed of by their parents, if alive, or otherwise by their nearest relations. But with due deference to so excellent a friend and so deserving a patriot, I cannot be altogether in his sentiments; for as to the males, my American acquaintance assured me from frequent experience that their flesh was generally tough and lean, like that of our schoolboys, by continual exercise, and their taste disagreeable; and to fatten them would not answer the charge. Then as to the females, it would, I think with humble submission, be a loss to the public, because they soon would become breeders themselves: and besides, it is not improbable that some scrupulous people might be apt to censure such a practice (although indeed very unjustly) as a little bordering upon cruelty;

9. Skillfully.   1. Slaughterhouses.

which, I confess, hath always been with me the strongest objection against any project, how well soever intended.

But in order to justify my friend, he confessed that this expedient was put into his head by the famous Psalmanazar,[2] a native of the island Formosa, who came from thence to London above twenty years ago, and in conversation told my friend that in his country when any young person happened to be put to death, the executioner sold the carcass to persons of quality as a prime dainty; and that in his time the body of a plump girl of fifteen, who was crucified for an attempt to poison the emperor, was sold to his Imperial Majesty's prime minister of state, and other great mandarins of the court, in joints from the gibbet, at four hundred crowns. Neither indeed can I deny that if the same use were made of several plump young girls in this town, who without one single groat to their fortunes cannot stir abroad without a chair, and appear at the playhouse and assemblies in foreign fineries which they never will pay for, the kingdom would not be the worse.

Some persons of a desponding spirit are in great concern about that vast number of poor people who are aged, diseased, or maimed, and I have been desired to employ my thoughts what course may be taken to ease the nation of so grievous an encumbrance. But I am not in the least pain upon that matter, because it is very well known that they are every day dying and rotting by cold and famine, and filth and vermin, as fast as can be reasonably expected. And as to the younger laborers, they are now in almost as hopeful a condition. They cannot get work, and consequently pine away for want of nourishment to a degree that if at any time they are accidentally hired to common labor, they have not strength to perform it; and thus the country and themselves are happily delivered from the evils to come.

I have too long digressed, and therefore shall return to my subject. I think the advantages by the proposal which I have made are obvious and many, as well as of the highest importance.

For first, as I have already observed, it would greatly lessen the number of Papists, with whom we are yearly overrun, being the principal breeders of the nation as well as our most dangerous enemies; and who stay at home on purpose to deliver the kingdom to the Pretender, hoping to take their advantage by the absence of so many good Protestants, who have chosen rather to leave their country than stay at home and pay tithes against their conscience to an Episcopal curate.

Secondly, the poorer tenants will have something valuable of their own, which by law may be made liable to distress,[3] and help

2. George Psalmanazar (ca. 1679–1763), a famous imposter. A Frenchman, he imposed himself on English bishops, noblemen, and scientists as a Formosan. He wrote an entirely fictitious account of Formosa, in which he described human sacrifices and cannibalism.

3. Distraint, i.e., the seizing, through legal action, of property for the payment of debts and other obligations.

to pay their landlord's rent, their corn and cattle being already seized and money a thing unknown.

Thirdly, whereas the maintenance of an hundred thousand children, from two years old and upwards, cannot be computed at less than ten shillings a piece per annum, the nation's stock will be thereby increased fifty thousand pounds per annum, besides the profit of a new dish introduced to the tables of all gentlemen of fortune in the kingdom who have any refinement in taste. And the money will circulate among ourselves, the goods being entirely of our own growth and manufacture.

Fourthly, the constant breeders, besides the gain of eight shillings sterling per annum by the sale of their children, will be rid of the charge of maintaining them after the first year.

Fifthly, this food would likewise bring great custom to taverns, where the vintners will certainly be so prudent as to procure the best receipts for dressing it to perfection, and consequently have their houses frequented by all the fine gentlemen, who justly value themselves upon their knowledge in good eating; and a skillful cook, who understands how to oblige his guests, will contrive to make it as expensive as they please.

Sixthly, this would be a great inducement to marriage, which all wise nations have either encouraged by rewards or enforced by laws and penalties. It would increase the care and tenderness of mothers toward their children, when they were sure of a settlement for life to the poor babes, provided in some sort by the public, to their annual profit instead of expense. We should see an honest emulation among the married women, which of them could bring the fattest child to the market. Men would become as fond of their wives during the time of their pregnancy as they are now of their mares in foal, their cows in calf, or sows when they are ready to farrow; nor offer to beat or kick them (as is too frequent a practice) for fear of a miscarriage.

Many other advantages might be enumerated. For instance, the addition of some thousand carcasses in our exportation of barreled beef, the propagation of swine's flesh, and improvement in the art of making good bacon, so much wanted among us by the great destruction of pigs, too frequent at our tables, which are no way comparable in taste or magnificence to a well-grown, fat, yearling child, which roasted whole will make a considerable figure at a lord mayor's feast or any other public entertainment. But this and many others I omit, being studious of brevity.

Supposing that one thousand families in this city would be constant customers for infants' flesh, besides others who might have it at merry meetings, particularly weddings and christenings, I compute that Dublin would take off annually about twenty thousand carcasses, and the rest of the kingdom (where probably they will be sold somewhat cheaper) the remaining eighty thousand.

I can think of no one objection that will possibly be raised against this proposal, unless it should be urged that the number of people will be thereby much lessened in the kingdom. This I freely own, and it was indeed one principal design in offering it to the world. I desire the reader will observe, that I calculate my remedy for this one individual kingdom of Ireland and for no other that ever was, is, or I think ever can be upon earth. Therefore let no man talk to me of other expedients: of taxing our absentees at five shillings a pound: of using neither clothes nor household furniture except what is of our own growth and manufacture: of utterly rejecting the materials and instruments that promote foreign luxury: of curing the expensiveness of pride, vanity, idleness, and gaming in our women: of introducing a vein of parsimony, prudence, and temperance: of learning to love our country, in the want of which we differ even from Laplanders and the inhabitants of Topinamboo:[4] of quitting our animosities and factions, nor acting any longer like the Jews, who were murdering one another at the very moment their city was taken:[5] of being a little cautious not to sell our country and conscience for nothing: of teaching landlords to have at least one degree of mercy toward their tenants: lastly, of putting a spirit of honesty, industry, and skill into our shopkeepers; who, if a resolution could now be taken to buy only our native goods, would immediately unite to cheat and exact upon us in the price, the measure, and the goodness, nor could ever yet be brought to make one fair proposal of just dealing, though often and earnestly invited to it.[6]

Therefore I repeat, let no man talk to me of these and the like expedients, till he hath at least some glimpse of hope that there will ever be some hearty and sincere attempt to put them in practice.

But as to myself, having been wearied out for many years with offering vain, idle, visionary thoughts, and at length utterly despairing of success, I fortunately fell upon this proposal, which, as it is wholly new, so it hath something solid and real, of no expense and little trouble, full in our own power, and whereby we can incur no danger in disobliging England. For this kind of commodity will not bear exportation, the flesh being of too tender a consistence to admit a long continuance in salt, although perhaps I could name a country which would be glad to eat up our whole nation without it.[7]

After all, I am not so violently bent upon my own opinion as

4. I.e., even Laplanders love their frozen, infertile country and the savage tribes of Brazil their jungle more than the Anglo-Irish love Ireland.
5. During the siege of Jerusalem by the Roman Emperor Titus, who captured and destroyed the city in A.D. 70, the city was torn by bloody fights between factions of fanatics.
6. Swift himself had made all these proposals in various pamphlets. In editions printed during his lifetime the various proposals were italicized to indicate that Swift is no longer being ironic.
7. I.e., England.

to reject any offer proposed by wise men, which shall be found equally innocent, cheap, easy, and effectual. But before something of that kind shall be advanced in contradiction to my scheme, and offering a better, I desire the author or authors will be pleased maturely to consider two points. First, as things now stand, how they will be able to find food and raiment for an hundred thousand useless mouths and backs. And secondly, there being a round million of creatures in human figure throughout this kingdom, whose sole subsistence put into a common stock would leave them in debt two millions of pounds sterling, adding those who are beggars by profession to the bulk of farmers, cottagers, and laborers, with their wives and children who are beggars in effect; I desire those politicians who dislike my overture, and may perhaps be so bold to attempt an answer, that they will first ask the parents of these mortals whether they would not at this day think it a great happiness to have been sold for food at a year old in the manner I prescribe, and thereby have avoided such a perpetual scene of misfortunes as they have since gone through by the oppression of landlords, the impossibility of paying rent without money or trade, the want of common sustenance, with neither house nor clothes to cover them from the inclemencies of the weather, and the most inevitable prospect of entailing the like or greater miseries upon their breed forever.

I profess, in the sincerity of my heart, that I have not the least personal interest in endeavoring to promote this necessary work, having no other motive than the public good of my country, by advancing our trade, providing for infants, relieving the poor, and giving some pleasure to the rich. I have no children by which I can propose to get a single penny; the youngest being nine years old, and my wife past childbearing.

1729

JOSEPH ADDISON *and* SIR RICHARD STEELE
(1672–1719)   (1672–1729)

> 1709–11: *Tatler* published.
> 1711–12: *Spectator* published.
> 1714:   *Spectator* resumed (for 80 numbers).

The friendship of Joseph Addison and Richard Steele began when they were schoolboys together at the Charterhouse in London. Their careers ran parallel courses and brought them for a while into fruitful collaboration. Addison, though a man of infinite charm among intimates, was by nature reserved, rather chilly, calculating, ungenerous, and prudent. Steele was impulsive and rakish when young (but ardently devoted to his beautiful wife), imprudent to a degree, and consequently in frequent financial distress. Addison never stumbled in his progress to financial competence, a late marriage to a dowager countess, and a successful political career; walking less surely, Steele experienced many vicissitudes and faced serious financial problems during his last years.

Both men attended Oxford, where Addison took his degree, won a fellowship, and earned a reputation for Latin verse; the less scholarly Steele, however, had only moderate academic success and did not stay for a degree, but left the University to take a commission in the army. For a while he cut a dashing figure in London, even, to his horror, seriously wounding a man in a duel. Both men enjoyed the patronage of the great Whig magnates, and except during the last four years of Queen Anne's reign, when the Tories were in the ascendency, they were generously treated. Steele became editor of the *London Gazette*, an official newspaper that appeared twice a week during the greater part of his editorship, listing government appointments and reporting domestic and foreign news—in short, the first newspaper in the modern sense, for it was very much unlike the news pamphlets or the news letters, written by hand and sent out to subscribers, that one finds in the previous century. Much later, Steele became manager of the Theatre Royal, Drury Lane. Meanwhile he had served in Parliament and been knighted by George I. Addison held more important positions: he was secretary to the Lord Lieutenant of Ireland, and later an Under-Secretary of State; finally, toward the end of his life, he became Secretary of State. Both men wrote plays: Addison's *Cato*, a frigid and very "correct" tragedy, had great success in 1713 because it was received by the town as a political play; and Steele's later plays at Drury Lane (*The Conscious Lovers*, 1722, for instance) were instrumental in establishing the popularity of sentimental comedy throughout the 18th century.

Steele's debts and Addison's loss of office in 1710 were the efficient causes of their journalistic enterprises, through which they developed one of the most characteristic types of 18th-century literature, the periodical essay. Steele's experience as gazetteer had involved him in journalism, and in 1709, when in need of money, he launched the *Tatler* under the pseudonym Isaac Bickerstaff. He sought to attract the largest possible audience: the title was a bid for female readers, and the early fivefold division of each number into departments (dated from four appropriate coffeehouses and the editor's own apartment) dealing respectively with "gallantry, pleasure and entertainment," poetry, learning, news, and personal reflections gave the paper a wide appeal among men. The fifth department soon swallowed up the other four, as the lucubrations of Squire Bickerstaff won readers in coffeehouses and at breakfast tables. The paper appeared thrice weekly from April, 1709, to January, 1711. Steele wrote by far the greater number of *Tatlers*, but Addison contributed helpfully, as did other friends. The *Spectator*, which appeared daily except Sunday from March, 1711, to December, 1712 (and was briefly resumed by Addison in 1714), was the joint undertaking of the two friends, though it was dominated by Addison. The papers had many imitators in their own day and throughout the rest of the century; Johnson's *Rambler* and *Idler* and Goldsmith's brief *Bee* are distinguished instances.

The periodical essay as developed in these two papers admits of no

strict definition. It is less formal and purely didactic than the essays of
Bacon, less personal than those of Charles Lamb and William Hazlitt in
the next century. It deals with the widest possible variety of topics: manners and morals, literature and philosophical ideas, types and characters,
fads, fashions, foibles; and these it was necessary to treat lightly and in
an agreeable manner. But one topic of the times was wisely avoided in
both papers—politics.

Both Steele and Addison were conscious moralists and did not disguise
their intention of improving the minds, morals, and manners of their
readers. Moral reform had been in the air since the 1690's, and the new
society that was coming into existence (and was certainly in some degree
the creation of Addison and Steele) was attaining a balance between the
morality and respectability of the old, rather Puritan middle class (which
was too often narrowly Philistine in taste and outlook) and the wit,
grace, and enlightenment of the older aristocratic and fashionable class
(which, in the previous century, had too often been libertine in morals
and thought). The new social ideal, which the two essayists themselves
fostered, stressed moderation, reasonableness, self-control, urbanity, and
good taste. Steele's *Tatler* essays on marriage and domestic life held up
an ideal which would have provoked the wits of Charles's day to contemptuous laughter. He wrote on any topic that suggested itself as pleasing or useful: the theater, true breeding as against vulgar manners, education, simplicity in dress, the proper use of Sunday, and so on; and he
lightly ridiculed common social types such as the prude, the coquette,
the "pretty fellow," and the rake. Addison's best *Tatler* essays initiated
his study of eccentric or affected characters (to be continued in the *Spectator*), cleverly observed and described with agreeable humor. These essays
on social types were a development of the "characters" of the 17th century. The *Tatler* papers quickly won an appreciative audience, and when
published in book form, they continued (like those of the *Spectator*) to
sell throughout the century. Steele's style is informal, even careless, but
for that very reason intimate and engaging. His generous, even sentimental,
warmth imparts itself to his style and animates his subject when, as is
most often the case, he writes from his heart. It was, he says, "a most
exquisite pleasure * * * to trace human life through all its mazes and
recesses, and to show much shorter methods than men ordinarily practice
to be happy, agreeable, and great." Shortly after Steele discontinued the
Tatler, John Gay in a pamphlet, *The Present State of Wit*, praised him
for banishing or checking follies and persuading the town to virtue, religion, and learning. "In the dress he gives it [learning] 'tis a most welcome
guest at tea tables and assemblies, and is relished and caressed by the
merchants on the 'Change * * * "

The readers whom Steele had reached and influenced were at hand
when the *Spectator* began to appear two months after the last *Tatler*.
Steele played a more important role in the paper than Addison had in
the *Tatler*, but the *Spectator* is throughout Addisonian. In the second
number Steele introduces us to the members of Mr. Spectator's Club
(male social life was dominated by clubs during the reign of Queen
Anne), who prove to be a man about town, a student of law and literature,
a churchman, a soldier, a Tory country squire, and, interestingly enough,
a London merchant. These men suggest the readers (other than women)

to whom the paper was primarily addressed. As a Whig, Steele was ardently sympathetic with the new moneyed class in the City, and it was evidently his intention to pit the merchant, Sir Andrew Freeport, the representative of the new order, against the Tory Sir Roger de Coverley, who is presented as belonging to a vanishing order. Addison, however, preferred to present Sir Roger in episodes set in town and in the country as an endearing, eccentric character, often absurd but always amiable and innocent. He is a prominent ancestor of a long line of similar characters in fiction during the next two centuries. The social criticism continued, with more wit and raillery than the *Tatler* had usually commanded. Addison's scholarly interests broadened the material to include the popularization of current philosophical notions about man and nature; and he wrote several important series of critical papers: among others, two recommending the ballad of *Chevy Chase* (old ballads had not yet come into fashion), a group distinguishing true and false wit, an extended series of Saturday essays evaluating *Paradise Lost*, and finally, an influential series on "the pleasures of the imagination" which treated the aesthetics of visual beauty in nature and art. Altogether, the *Spectator* fulfilled his ambition (see *Spectator* 10, below) to be considered a modern Socrates. Addison's contributions to the paper are the finest among the vast numbers of 18th-century periodical essays. If his tone is a little superior and his style a bit more fussy than we like today, his keen observation of the life around him, the graceful ease of his learning, his never cruel wit, and, despite the commonplaceness of most of his moral and philosophical reflections, his genuine if occasional originality made him the most agreeable, and consequently the most persuasive, instructor the age could have found.

The best description of Addison's prose is Dr. Johnson's in his *Life of Addison*: "His prose is the model of the middle style; on grave subjects not formal, on light occasions not groveling; pure without scrupulosity, and exact without apparent elaboration; always equable, and always easy, without glowing words or pointed sentences." And he concludes: "Whoever wishes to attain an English style, familiar but not coarse, and elegant but not ostentatious, must give his days and nights to the volumes of Addison," a course of study which a good many aspiring writers during the century seem to have undertaken with some success.

THE PERIODICAL ESSAY: MANNERS
STEELE: [The Gentleman; The Pretty Fellow]
From *The Tatler*, No. 21, Saturday, May 28, 1709

> *Quidquid agunt homines——*
> *——nostri est farrago libelli.*[1]
> —JUVENAL, *Satire* I.85–86

White's Chocolate House,[2] May 26

A gentleman has writ to me out of the country a very civil letter, and said things which I suppress with great violence to my vanity.

1. "Whatever men do * * * shall form the motley subject of my book." Steele used this epigraph for all but a very few of the first 62 *Tatlers*.
2. One of the fashionable chocolate houses, from which Steele, in the earlier numbers of the *Tatler*, dated "accounts of gallantry, pleasure, and entertainment."

There are many terms in my narratives which he complains want explaining, and has therefore desired that, for the benefit of my country readers, I would let him know what I mean by a Gentleman, a Pretty Fellow, a Toast, a Coquette, a Critic, a Wit, and all other appellations of those now in the gayer world, who are in possession of these several characters; together with an account of those who unfortunately pretend to them. I shall begin with him we usually call a Gentleman, or man of conversation.

It is generally thought that warmth of imagination, quick relish of pleasure, and a manner of becoming it, are the most essential qualities for forming this sort of man. But anyone that is much in company will observe that the height of good breeding is shown rather in never giving offense, than in doing obliging things. Thus, he that never shocks you, though he is seldom entertaining, is more likely to keep your favor than he who often entertains, and sometimes displeases you. The most necessary talent therefore in a man of conversation, which is what we ordinarily intend by a fine gentleman, is a good judgment. He that has this in perfection is master of his companion, without letting him see it; and has the same advantage over men of any other qualifications whatsoever, as one that can see would have over a blind man of ten times his strength.

This is what makes Sophronius the darling of all who converse with him, and the most powerful with his acquaintance of any man in town. By the light of this faculty, he acts with great ease and freedom among the men of pleasure, and acquits himself with skill and dispatch among the men of business. All which he performs with so much success that, with as much discretion in life as any man ever had, he neither is, nor appears, cunning. But as he does a good office, if he ever does it, with readiness and alacrity, so he denies what he does not care to engage in, in a manner that convinces you that you ought not to have asked it. His judgment is so good and unerring, and accompanied with so cheerful a spirit, that his conversation is a continual feast, at which he helps some, and is helped by others, in such a manner that the equality of society is perfectly kept up, and every man obliges as much as he is obliged: for it is the greatest and justest skill in a man of superior understanding, to know how to be on a level with his companions. This sweet disposition runs through all the actions of Sophronius, and makes his company desired by women, without being envied by men. Sophronius would be as just as he is, if there were no law; and would be as discreet as he is, if there were no such thing as calumny.

In imitation of this agreeable being, is made that animal we call a Pretty Fellow; who being just able to find out that what makes Sophronius acceptable is a natural behavior, in order to the same reputation, makes his own an artificial one. Jack Dimple is his perfect mimic, whereby he is of course the most unlike him of all men living. Sophronius just now passed into the inner room directly forward: Jack comes as fast after as he can for the right and left looking glass, in which he had but just approved himself by a nod at each, and marched on. He will meditate within for half an hour, till he thinks he is not careless enough in his air, and come back to the mirror to recollect his forgetfulness. * * *

STEELE: [Dueling]

From *The Tatler, No. 25, Tuesday, June 7, 1709*

Quidquid agunt homines——
——nostri est farrago libelli.
—JUVENAL, *Satire* I.85–86

White's Chocolate House, June 6

A letter from a young lady, written in the most passionate terms, wherein she laments the misfortune of a gentleman, her lover, who was lately wounded in a duel, has turned my thoughts to that subject, and inclined me to examine into the causes which precipitate men into so fatal a folly. And as it has been proposed to treat of subjects of gallantry in the article from hence, and no one point in nature is more proper to be considered by the company who frequent this place than that of duels, it is worth our consideration to examine into this chimerical groundless humor, and to lay every other thought aside, until we have stripped it of all its false pretenses to credit and reputation amongst men.

But I must confess, when I consider what I am going about, and run over in my imagination all the endless crowd of men of honor who will be offended at such a discourse, I am undertaking, methinks, a work worthy an invulnerable hero in romance, rather than a private gentleman with a single rapier; but as I am pretty well acquainted by great opportunities with the nature of man, and know of a truth that all men fight against their will, the danger vanishes, and resolution rises upon this subject. For this reason, I shall talk very freely on a custom which all men wish exploded, though no man has courage enough to resist it.

But there is one unintelligible word, which I fear will extremely perplex my dissertation, and I confess to you I find very hard to explain, which is the term "satisfaction." An honest country gentleman had the misfortune to fall into company with two or three modern men of honor, where he happened to be very ill treated; and one of the company, being conscious of his offense, sends a note to him in the morning, and tells him he was ready to give him satisfaction. "This is fine doing," says the plain fellow; "last night he sent me away cursedly out of humor, and this morning he fancies it would be a satisfaction to be run through the body."

As the matter at present stands, it is not to do handsome actions denominates a man of honor; it is enough if he dares to defend ill ones. Thus you often see a common sharper in competition with a gentleman of the first rank; though all mankind is convinced that a fighting gamester is only a pickpocket with the courage of an highwayman. One cannot with any patience reflect on the unaccountable jumble of persons and things in this town and nation, which occasions very frequently that a brave man falls by a hand below that of a common hangman, and yet his executioner escapes the clutches of the hangman for doing it. I shall therefore hereafter consider how the bravest men in other ages and nations have behaved themselves upon such incidents as we decide by combat; and show, from their practice, that this resentment neither has its foundation from true reason or solid fame; but is an imposture, made of cowardice, falsehood, and want of understanding. For this work, a good history of quarrels would be very edifying to the public, and I apply myself to the town for particulars and circumstances within their knowledge, which may serve to embellish the dissertation with proper cuts.[1] Most of the quarrels I have ever known have proceeded from some valiant coxcomb's persisting in the wrong, to defend some prevailing folly, and preserve himself from the ingenuity[2] of owning a mistake.

By this means it is called "giving a man satisfaction" to urge your offense against him with your sword; which puts me in mind of Peter's order to the keeper, in *The Tale of a Tub*:[3] "If you neglect to do all this, damn you and your generation forever: and so we bid you heartily farewell." If the contradiction in the very terms of one of our challenges were as well explained and turned into downright English, would it not run after this manner?

"Sir,

"Your extraordinary behavior last night, and the liberty you were pleased to take with me, makes me this morning give you this, to tell you, because you are an ill-bred puppy, I will meet you in Hyde Park an hour hence; and because you want both breeding and humanity, I desire you would come with a pistol in your hand, on horseback, and endeavor to shoot me through the head to teach you more manners. If you fail of doing me this pleasure, I shall say you are a rascal, on every post in town: and so, sir, if you will not injure me more, I shall never forgive what you have done already. Pray, sir, do not fail of getting everything ready; and you will infinitely oblige, sir, your most obedient humble servant, etc." * * *

1. Either woodcuts or engravings on copper plates.
2. Honorable candor.
3. In Swift's satire, the Roman Church is attacked in the character of Peter. The passage (slightly misquoted) satirizes the Pope's practice of issuing indulgences.

STEELE: [The Spectator's Club]

The Spectator, No. 2, Friday, March 2, 1711

——*Haec alii sex*
Vel plures uno conclamant ore.[1]
—JUVENAL, *Satire* VII.166–67

The first of our society is a gentleman of Worcestershire, of ancient descent, a baronet, his name Sir Roger de Coverley. His great-grandfather was inventor of that famous country-dance which is called after him. All who know that shire are very well acquainted with the parts and merits of Sir Roger. He is a gentleman that is very singular in his behavior, but his singularities proceed from his good sense, and are contradictions to the manners of the world only as he thinks the world is in the wrong. However, this humor creates him no enemies, for he does nothing with sourness or obstinacy; and his being unconfined to modes and forms makes him but the readier and more capable to please and oblige all who know him. When he is in town, he lives in Soho Square. It is said he keeps himself a bachelor by reason he was crossed in love by a perverse, beautiful widow of the next county to him. Before this disappointment, Sir Roger was what you call a fine gentleman, had often supped with my Lord Rochester and Sir George Etherege, fought a duel upon his first coming to town, and kicked Bully Dawson in a public coffeehouse for calling him "youngster."[2] But being ill used by the above-mentioned widow, he was very serious for a year and a half; and though, his temper being naturally jovial, he at last got over it, he grew careless of himself, and never dressed afterward. He continues to wear a coat and doublet of the same cut that were in fashion at the time of his repulse, which, in his merry humors, he tells us, has been in and out twelve times since he first wore it. 'Tis said Sir Roger grew humble in his desires after he had forgot this cruel beauty, insomuch that it is reported he has frequently offended in point of chastity with beggars and gypsies; but this is looked upon by his friends rather as matter of raillery than truth. He is now in his fifty-sixth year, cheerful, gay, and hearty; keeps a good house both in town and country; a great lover of mankind; but there is such a mirthful cast in his behavior that he is rather beloved than esteemed. His tenants grow rich, his servants look satisfied, all the young women profess love to him, and the young men are glad of his company; when he comes into a house he calls the servants by their names, and talks all the way upstairs to a visit. I must not omit that Sir Roger is a justice of the quorum;[3] that he fills the chair at a quarter-session with great abil-

1. "Six more at least join their consenting voice."
2. John Wilmot, Earl of Rochester (1647–80), the poet and rake, an intimate of Charles II; Sir George Etherege (ca. 1634–91), playwright, rake, and boon companion of the king and Rochester. Bully Dawson was a notorious sharper of the period.
3. A county justice of the peace, presiding over quarterly sessions of the court.

ities; and, three months ago, gained universal applause by explaining a passage in the Game Act.

The gentleman next in esteem and authority among us is another bachelor, who is a member of the Inner Temple;[4] a man of great probity, wit, and understanding; but he has chosen his place of residence rather to obey the direction of an old humorsome[5] father, than in pursuit of his own inclinations. He was placed there to study the laws of the land, and is the most learned of any of the house in those of the stage. Aristotle and Longinus are much better understood by him than Littleton or Coke.[6] The father sends up, every post, questions relating to marriage articles, leases, and tenures, in the neighborhood; all which questions he agrees with an attorney to answer and take care of in the lump. He is studying the passions themselves, when he should be inquiring into the debates among men which arise from them. He knows the argument of each of the orations of Demosthenes and Tully,[7] but not one case in the reports of our own courts. No one ever took him for a fool, but none, except his intimate friends, know he has a great deal of wit. This turn makes him at once both disinterested and agreeable; as few of his thoughts are drawn from business, they are most of them fit for conversation. His taste of books is a little too just[8] for the age he lives in; he has read all, but approves of very few. His familiarity with the customs, manners, actions, and writings of the ancients makes him a very delicate observer of what occurs to him in the present world. He is an excellent critic, and the time of the play is his hour of business; exactly at five he passes through New Inn, crosses through Russell Court, and takes a turn at Will's[9] till the play begins; he has his shoes rubbed and his periwig powdered at the barber's as you go into the Rose.[1] It is for the good of the audience when he is at a play, for the actors have an ambition to please him.

The person of next consideration is Sir Andrew Freeport, a merchant of great eminence in the city of London, a person of indefatigable industry, strong reason, and great experience. His notions of trade are noble and generous, and (as every rich man has usually some sly way of jesting which would make no great figure were he not a rich man) he calls the sea the British Common. He is acquainted with commerce in all its parts, and will tell you that it

4. One of the Inns of Court, where lawyers resided or had their offices and where students studied law.
5. Full of crotchets.
6. In other words, he is more familiar with the laws of literature than those of England. The *Poetics* of Aristotle and the Greek treatise *On the Sublime* (reputedly by Longinus) were in high favor among the critics of the time. Sir Thomas Littleton, 15th-century jurist, was author of a renowned treatise on *Tenures;* Sir Edward Coke (1552–

1634) was the judge and writer whose *Reports* and *Institutes of the Laws of England* (known as *Coke upon Littleton*) have exerted a great influence on the interpretation of English law.
7. Marcus Tullius Cicero.
8. Exact.
9. The coffeehouse in Covent Garden associated with literature and criticism since Dryden had begun to frequent it in the 1660's.
1. A tavern near Drury Lane.

is a stupid and barbarous way to extend dominion by arms; for true power is to be got by arts and industry. He will often argue that if this part of our trade were well cultivated, we should gain from one nation; and if another, from another. I have heard him prove that diligence makes more lasting acquisitions than valor, and that sloth has ruined more nations than the sword. He abounds in several frugal maxims, among which the greatest favorite is, "A penny saved is a penny got." A general trader of good sense is pleasanter company than a general scholar; and Sir Andrew having a natural unaffected eloquence, the perspicuity of his discourse gives the same pleasure that wit would in another man. He has made his fortunes himself, and says that England may be richer than other kingdoms by as plain methods as he himself is richer than other men; though at the same time I can say this of him, that there is not a point in the compass but blows home a ship in which he is an owner.

Next to Sir Andrew in the clubroom sits Captain Sentry, a gentleman of great courage, good understanding, but invincible modesty. He is one of those that deserve very well, but are very awkward at putting their talents within the observation of such as should take notice of them. He was some years a captain, and behaved himself with great gallantry in several engagements and at several sieges; but having a small estate of his own, and being next heir to Sir Roger, he has quitted a way of life in which no man can rise suitably to his merit who is not something of a courtier as well as a soldier. I have heard him often lament that in a profession where merit is placed in so conspicuous a view, impudence should get the better of modesty. When he has talked to this purpose I never heard him make a sour expression, but frankly confess that he left the world because he was not fit for it. A strict honesty and an even, regular behavior are in themselves obstacles to him that must press through crowds who endeavor at the same end with himself —the favor of a commander. He will, however, in his way of talk, excuse generals for not disposing according to men's desert, or inquiring into it, "for," says he, "that great man who has a mind to help me, has as many to break through to come at me as I have to come at him"; therefore he will conclude that the man who would make a figure, especially in a military way, must get over all false modesty, and assist his patron against the importunity of other pretenders by a proper assurance in his own vindication. He says it is a civil cowardice to be backward in asserting[2] what you ought to expect, as it is a military fear to be slow in attacking when it is your duty. With this candor does the gentleman speak of himself and others. The same frankness runs through all his conversation. The military part of his life has furnished him with many adventures, in the relation of which he is very agreeable to the company; for he is never overbearing, though accustomed to command men

2. Claiming.

in the utmost degree below him; nor ever too obsequious from an habit of obeying men highly above him.

But that our society may not appear a set of humorists[3] unacquainted with the gallantries and pleasures of the age, we have among us the gallant Will Honeycomb, a gentleman who, according to his years, should be in the decline of his life, but having ever been very careful of his person, and always had a very easy fortune, time has made but very little impression either by wrinkles on his forehead or traces in his brain. His person is well turned and of a good height. He is very ready at that sort of discourse with which men usually entertain women. He has all his life dressed very well, and remembers habits[4] as others do men. He can smile when one speaks to him, and laughs easily. He knows the history of every mode, and can inform you from which of the French king's wenches our wives and daughters had this manner of curling their hair, that way of placing their hoods; whose frailty was covered by such a sort of petticoat, and whose vanity to show her foot made that part of the dress so short in such a year. In a word, all his conversation and knowledge has been in the female world. As other men of his age will take notice to you what such a minister said upon such and such an occasion, he will tell you when the Duke of Monmouth[5] danced at court such a woman was then smitten, another was taken with him at the head of his troop in the Park. In all these important relations, he has ever about the same time received a kind glance or a blow of a fan from some celebrated beauty, mother of the present Lord Such-a-one. If you speak of a young commoner that said a lively thing in the House, he starts up: "He has good blood in his veins; Tom Mirabell begot him. The rogue cheated me in that affair; that young fellow's mother used me more like a dog than any woman I ever made advances to." This way of talking of his very much enlivens the conversation among us of a more sedate turn; and I find there is not one of the company but myself, who rarely speak at all, but speaks of him as of that sort of man who is usually called a well-bred, fine gentleman. To conclude his character, where women are not concerned he is an honest, worthy man.

I cannot tell whether I am to account him whom I am next to speak of as one of our company, for he visits us but seldom; but when he does, it adds to every man else a new enjoyment of himself. He is a clergyman, a very philosophic man, of general learning, great sanctity of life, and the most exact good breeding. He has the misfortune to be of a very weak constitution, and consequently cannot accept of such cares and business as preferments in his function would oblige him to; he is therefore among divines what a chamber-counselor is among lawyers. The probity of his mind and the integrity of his life create him followers, as being eloquent or

3. Eccentrics.
4. Clothes.
5. The illegitimate son of Charles II, the ill-fated Absalom of Dryden's *Absalom and Achitophel.*

loud advances others. He seldom introduces the subject he speaks upon; but we are so far gone in years that he observes, when he is among us, an earnestness to have him fall on some divine topic, which he always treats with much authority, as one who has no interest in this world, as one who is hastening to the object of all his wishes and conceives hope from his decays and infirmities. These are my ordinary companions.

ADDISON: [Party Patches]

The Spectator, No. 81, Saturday, June 2, 1711

Qualis ubi audio venantum murmure tigris
Horruit in maculas [1]———
—STATIUS, *Thebaid* II.128

About the middle of last winter I went to see an opera at the theater in the Haymarket, where I could not but take notice of two parties of very fine women that had placed themselves in the opposite side boxes, and seemed drawn up in a kind of battle array one against another. After a short survey of them, I found they were *patched* differently; the faces, on one hand, being spotted on the right side of the forehead, and those upon the other on the left. I quickly perceived that they cast hostile glances upon one another; and that their patches were placed in those different situations as party signals to distinguish friends from foes. In the middle boxes, between these two opposite bodies, were several ladies who patched indifferently on both sides of their faces, and seemed to sit there with no other intention but to see the opera. Upon inquiry I found, that the body of Amazons on my right hand were Whigs; and those on my left, Tories; and that those who had placed themselves in the middle boxes were a neutral party, whose faces had not yet declared themselves. These last, however, as I afterwards found, diminished daily, and took their party with one side or the other; insomuch that I observed in several of them the patches, which were before dispersed equally, are now all gone over to the Whig or Tory side of the face. The censorious say that the men whose hearts are aimed at are very often the occasions that one part of the face is thus dishonored and lies under a kind of disgrace, while the other is so much set off and adorned by the owner; and that the patches turn to the right or to the left, according to the principles of the man who is most in favor. But whatever may be the motives of a few fantastical coquettes, who do not patch for the public good, so much as for their own private advantage, it is certain that there are several women of honor who patch out of principle, and with an eye to the interest of their country. Nay, I am informed that some of them adhere so steadfastly to their party, and are so far from sacrificing their zeal for the public to their

1. Cowley's translation of these lines is quoted in the body of the essay.

passion for any particular person, that in a late draft of marriage articles a lady has stipulated with her husband that, whatever his opinions are, she shall be at liberty to patch on which side she pleases.

I must here take notice, that Rosalinda, a famous Whig partisan, has most unfortunately a very beautiful mole on the Tory part of her forehead; which, being very conspicuous, has occasioned many mistakes, and given an handle to her enemies to misrepresent her face, as though it had revolted from the Whig interest. But whatever this natural patch may seem to intimate, it is well known that her notions of government are still the same. This unlucky mole, however, has misled several coxcombs; and, like the hanging out of false colors, made some of them converse with Rosalinda in what they though the spirit of her party, when on a sudden she has given them an unexpected fire, that has sunk them all at once. If Rosalinda is unfortunate in her mole, Nigranilla is as unhappy in a pimple, which forces her, against her inclinations, to patch on the Whig side.

I am told that many virtuous matrons, who formerly have been taught to believe that this artificial spotting of the face was unlawful, are now reconciled by a zeal for their cause, to what they could not be prompted by a concern for their beauty. This way of declaring war upon one another puts me in mind of what is reported of the tigress, that several spots rise in her skin when she is angry; or as Mr. Cowley has imitated the verses that stand as the motto of this paper,

> ——She swells with angry pride,
> And calls forth all her spots on every side.

When I was in the theater the time above-mentioned, I had the curiosity to count the patches on both sides, and found the Tory patches to be about twenty stronger than the Whig; but to make amends for this small inequality, I the next morning found the whole puppet show filled with faces spotted after the Whiggish manner. Whether or no the ladies had retreated hither in order to rally their forces I cannot tell; but the next night they came in so great a body to the opera that they outnumbered the enemy.

This account of party patches will, I am afraid, appear improbable to those who live at a distance from the fashionable world; but as it is a distinction of a very singular nature, and what perhaps may never meet with a parallel, I think I should not have discharged the office of a faithful Spectator had I not recorded it.

I have, in former papers, endeavored to expose this party rage in women, as it only serves to aggravate the hatreds and animosities that reign among men, and in a great measure deprives the fair sex of those peculiar charms with which nature has endowed them.

When the Romans and Sabines were at war, and just upon the point of giving battle, the women, who were allied to both of them,[2] interposed with so many tears and entreaties that they prevented the mutual slaughter which threatened both parties, and united them together in a firm and lasting peace.

I would recommend this noble example to our British ladies, at a time when their country is torn with so many unnatural divisions that if they continue it will be a misfortune to be born in it. The Greeks thought it so improper for women to interest themselves in competitions and contentions that for this reason, among others, they forbade them, under pain of death, to be present at the Olympic games, notwithstanding these were the public diversions of all Greece.

As our English women excel those of all nations in beauty, they should endeavor to outshine them in all other accomplishments proper to the sex, and to distinguish themselves as tender mothers and faithful wives, rather than as furious partisans. Female virtues are of a domestic turn. The family is the proper province for private women to shine in. If they must be showing their zeal for the public, let it not be against those who are perhaps of the same family, or at least of the same religion or nation, but against those who are the open, professed, undoubted enemies of their faith, liberty, and country. When the Romans were pressed with a foreign enemy, the ladies voluntarily contributed all their rings and jewels to assist the government under a public exigence; which appeared so laudable an action in the eyes of their countrymen, that from thenceforth it was permitted by a law to pronounce public orations at the funeral of a woman in praise of the deceased person, which till that time was peculiar to men. Would our English ladies, instead of sticking on a patch against those of their own country, show themselves so truly public-spirited as to sacrifice every one her necklace against the common enemy, what decrees ought not to be made in favor of them?

Since I am recollecting upon this subject such passages as occur to my memory out of ancient authors, I cannot omit a sentence in the celebrated funeral oration of Pericles, which he made in honor of those brave Athenians that were slain in a fight with the Lacedemonians.[3] After having addressed himself to the several ranks and orders of his countrymen, and shown them how they should behave themselves in the public cause, he turns to the female part of his audience: "And as for you," says he, "I shall advise you in very few words. Aspire only to those virtues that are peculiar to your sex; follow your natural modesty, and think it your greatest commendation not to be talked of one way or other."

2. The Romans had provided themselves with wives by treacherously seizing a number of Sabine women, who were consequently allied by blood to the one side and by marriage to the other.

3. Spartans.

ADDISON: [Sir Roger at Church]

The Spectator, No. 112, *Monday, July* 9, 1711

Ἀθανάτους μὲν πρῶτα θεοὺς, νόμῳ ὡς διάκειται,
Τίμα.[1]

—PYTHAGORAS

I am always very well pleased with a country Sunday, and think, if keeping holy the seventh day were only a human institution, it would be the best method that could have been thought of for the polishing and civilizing of mankind. It is certain the country people would soon degenerate into a kind of savages and barbarians were there not such frequent returns of a stated time, in which the whole village meet together with their best faces, and in their cleanliest habits, to converse with one another upon indifferent subjects, hear their duties explained to them, and join together in adoration of the Supreme Being. Sunday clears away the rust of the whole week, not only as it refreshes in their minds the notions of religion, but as it puts both the sexes upon appearing in their most agreeable forms, and exerting all such qualities are apt to give them a figure in the eye of the village. A country fellow distinguishes himself as much in the churchyard as a citizen[2] does upon the 'Change, the whole parish politics being generally discussed in that place either after sermon or before the bell rings.

My friend Sir Roger, being a good churchman, has beautified the inside of his church with several texts of his own choosing; he has likewise given a handsome pulpit cloth, and railed in the communion table at his own expense. He has often told me that, at his coming to his estate, he found his parishioners very irregular; and that, in order to make them kneel and join in the responses, he gave every one of them a hassock and a Common Prayer book, and at the same time employed an itinerant singing master, who goes about the country for that purpose, to instruct them rightly in the tunes of the Psalms; upon which they now very much value themselves, and indeed outdo most of the country churches that I have ever heard.

As Sir Roger is landlord to the whole congregation, he keeps them in very good order, and will suffer nobody to sleep in it besides himself; for if by chance he has been surprised into a short nap at sermon, upon recovering out of it he stands up and looks about him, and if he sees anybody else nodding, either wakes them himself, or sends his servant to them. Several other of the old

1. "First worship the immortal gods as custom decrees." The first of the so-called Golden Verses of Pythagoras.
2. A citizen of the City of London, hence commonly a merchant. The " 'Change" is the Exchange in London, where merchants met to transact business.

knight's particularities break out upon these occasions; sometimes he will be lengthening out a verse in the Singing-Psalms half a minute after the rest of the congregation have done with it; sometimes, when he is pleased with the matter of his devotion, he pronounces "Amen" three or four times to the same prayer; and sometimes stands up when everybody else is upon their knees, to count the congregation, or see if any of his tenants are missing.

I was yesterday very much surprised to hear my old friend, in the midst of the service, calling out to one John Matthews to mind what he was about, and not disturb the congregation. This John Matthews, it seems, is remarkable for being an idle fellow, and at that time was kicking his heels for his diversion. This authority of the knight, though exerted in that odd manner which accompanies him in all circumstances of life, has a very good effect upon the parish, who are not polite[3] enough to see anything ridiculous in his behavior; besides that the general good sense and worthiness of his character makes his friends observe these little singularities as foils that rather set off than blemish his good qualities.

As soon as the sermon is finished, nobody presumes to stir till Sir Roger is gone out of the church. The knight walks down from his seat in the chancel between a double row of his tenants, that stand bowing to him on each side, and every now and then inquires how such an one's wife, or mother, or son, or father do, whom he does not see at church—which is understood as a secret reprimand to the person that is absent.

The chaplain has often told me that upon a catechizing day, when Sir Roger has been pleased with a boy that answers well, he has ordered a Bible to be given him next day for his encouragement, and sometimes accompanies it with a flitch of bacon to his mother. Sir Roger has likewise added five pounds a year to the clerk's place; and, that he may encourage the young fellows to make themselves perfect in the church service, has promised, upon the death of the present incumbent, who is very old, to bestow it according to merit.

The fair understanding between Sir Roger and his chaplain, and their mutual concurrence in doing good, is the more remarkable because the very next village is famous for the differences and contentions that rise between the parson and the squire, who live in a perpetual state of war. The parson is always preaching at the squire, and the squire, to be revenged on the parson, never comes to church. The squire has made all his tenants atheists and tithe-stealers;[4] while the parson instructs them every Sunday in the dignity of his order, and insinuates to them almost in every sermon that he is a better man than his patron. In short, matters are come to such an extremity that the squire has not said his prayers either in pub-

3. Refined.
4. Farmers who cheat the parson to whom they are bound to pay annual tithes (i.e., a tenth of the produce of their farms).

lic or private this half year; and that the parson threatens him, if
he does not mend his manners, to pray for him in the face of the
whole congregation.

Feuds of this nature, though too frequent in the country, are
very fatal to the ordinary people, who are so used to be dazzled
with riches that they pay as much deference to the understanding
of a man of an estate as of a man of learning; and are very hardly
brought to regard any truth, how important soever it may be, that
is preached to them, when they know there are several men of five
hundred a year who do not believe it.

ADDISON: [Sir Roger at the Assizes[1]]
The Spectator, No. 122, Friday, July 20, 1711

Comes jucundus in via pro vehiculo est.[2]
—PUBLILIUS SYRUS, *Fragments*

A man's first care should be to avoid the reproaches of his own
heart; his next, to escape the censures of the world. If the last interferes with the former, it ought to be entirely neglected; but otherwise there cannot be a greater satisfaction to an honest mind than
to see those approbations which it gives itself seconded by the ap-
plauses of the public. A man is more sure of his conduct when the
verdict which he passes upon his own behavior is thus warranted
and confirmed by the opinion of all that know him.

My worthy friend Sir Roger is one of those who is not only at
peace within himself but beloved and esteemed by all about him.
He receives a suitable tribute for his universal benevolence to mankind in the returns of affection and good will which are paid him
by everyone that lives within his neighborhood. I lately met with
two or three odd instances of that general respect which is shown
to the good old knight. He would needs carry Will Wimble[3] and
myself with him to the county assizes. As we were upon the road,
Will Wimble joined a couple of plain men who rid before us, and
conversed with them for some time, during which my friend Sir
Roger acquainted me with their characters.

"The first of them," says he, "that has a spaniel by his side, is
a yeoman[4] of about an hundred pounds a year, an honest man.
He is just within the Game Act,[5] and qualified to kill an hare or

1. Periodic sessions of superior courts
held by visiting judges throughout England.
2. "An agreeable companion upon the
road is as good as a coach." Addison
substituted *jucundus* for the original's
facundus ("eloquent").
3. A character used by Addison to
illustrate the injury done to younger

sons of gentlemen by not educating them
for a profession or to trade.
4. A man who owns and cultivates a
small estate. His rank is just below that
of gentleman.
5. This law restricted the right to kill
game to owners of land whose annual
income was £100 or more.

a pheasant. He knocks down a dinner with his gun twice or thrice a week; and by that means lives much cheaper than those who have not so good an estate as himself. He would be a good neighbor if he did not destroy so many partridges; in short he is a very sensible man, shoots flying,[6] and has been several times foreman of the petty jury.[7]

"The other that rides along with him is Tom Touchy, a fellow famous for taking the law of everybody. There is not one in the town where he lives that he has not sued at a quarter sessions. The rogue had once the impudence to go to law with the widow.[8] His head is full of costs, damages, and ejectments; he plagued a couple of honest gentlemen so long for a trespass in breaking one of his hedges, till he was forced to sell the ground it enclosed to defray the charges of the prosecution. His father left him fourscore pounds a year, but he has cast[9] and been cast so often that he is not now worth thirty. I suppose he is going upon the old business of the willow tree."

As Sir Roger was giving me this account of Tom Touchy, Will Wimble and his two companions stopped short till we came up to them. After having paid their respects to Sir Roger, Will told him that Mr. Touchy and he must appeal to him upon a dispute that arose between them. Will, it seems, had been giving his fellow travelers an account of his angling one day in such a hole; when Tom Touchy, instead of hearing out his story, told him that Mr. Such-an-one, if he pleased, might take the law of him for fishing in that part of the river. My friend Sir Roger heard them both, upon a round trot;[1] and after having paused some time, told them, with an air of a man who would not give his judgment rashly, "that much might be said on both sides." They were neither of them dissatisfied with the knight's determination, because neither of them found himself in the wrong by it. Upon which we made the best of our way to the assizes.

The court was sat before Sir Roger came; but notwithstanding all the justices had taken their places upon the bench, they made room for the old knight at the head of them; who, for his reputation in the country, took occasion to whisper in the judge's ear that he was glad his lordship had met with so much good weather in his circuit. I was listening to the proceedings of the court with much attention, and infinitely pleased with that great appearance and solemnity which so properly accompanies such a public administration of our laws, when, after about an hour's sitting, I observed to my great surprise, in the midst of a trial, that my friend Sir Roger

---

6. A true sportsman, he shoots birds only when they are on the wing.
7. The trial jury of twelve in an ordinary civil or criminal case.
8. The woman whom Sir Roger had loved in his youth. She is frequently mentioned in essays that deal with the old knight.
9. Defeated in a lawsuit.
1. While trotting briskly.

was getting up to speak. I was in some pain for him, till I found he had acquitted himself of two or three sentences, with a look of much business and great intrepidity.

Upon his first rising the court was hushed, and a general whisper ran among the country people that Sir Roger was up. The speech he made was so little to the purpose that I shall not trouble my readers with an account of it; and I believe was not so much designed by the knight himself to inform the court, as to give him a figure in my eye, and keep up his credit in the country.

I was highly delighted, when the court rose, to see the gentlemen of the country gathering about my old friend, and striving who should compliment him most; at the same time that the ordinary people gazed upon him at a distance, not a little admiring his courage that was not afraid to speak to the judge.

In our return home we met with a very odd accident which I cannot forbear relating, because it shows how desirous all who know Sir Roger are of giving him marks of their esteem. When we were arrived upon the verge of his estate, we stopped at a little inn to rest ourselves and our horses. The man of the house had, it seems, been formerly a servant in the knight's family; and to do honor to his old master, had some time since, unknown to Sir Roger, put him up in a signpost before the door; so that the knight's head had hung out upon the road about a week before he himself knew anything of the matter. As soon as Sir Roger was acquainted with it, finding that his servant's indiscretion proceeded wholly from affection and good will, he only told him that he had made him too high a compliment; and when the fellow seemed to think that could hardly be, added, with a more decisive look, that it was too great an honor for any man under a duke; but told him at the same time that it might be altered with a very few touches, and that he himself would be at the charge of it. Accordingly they got a painter, by the knight's directions, to add a pair of whiskers to the face, and by a little aggravation of the features to change it into the Saracen's Head. I should not have known this story had not the innkeeper, upon Sir Roger's alighting, told him in my hearing that his honor's head was brought back last night with the alterations that he had ordered to be made in it. Upon this my friend, with his usual cheerfulness, related the particulars above-mentioned, and ordered the head to be brought into the room. I could not forbear discovering greater expressions of mirth than ordinary upon the appearance of this monstrous face, under which, notwithstanding it was made to frown and stare in a most extraordinary manner, I could still discover a distant resemblance of my old friend. Sir Roger, upon seeing me laugh, desired me to tell him truly if I thought it possible for people to know him in that disguise. I at first kept my usual silence; but upon the knight's conjuring me to tell him whether it was not still more like himself than a Saracen, I composed my countenance in the best manner I could, and replied that much might be said on both sides.

These several adventures, with the knight's behavior in them, gave me as pleasant a day as ever I met with in any of my travels.

THE PERIODICAL ESSAY: IDEAS

ADDISON: [The Aims of the Spectator]

The Spectator, No. 10, Monday, March 12, 1711

Non aliter quam qui adverso vix flumine lembum
Remigiis subigit, si bracchia forte remisit,
Atque illum in præceps prono rapit alveus amni.[1]
—VIRGIL, *Georgics* I.201–3

It is with much satisfaction that I hear this great city inquiring day by day after these my papers, and receiving my morning lectures with a becoming seriousness and attention. My publisher tells me that there are already three thousand of them distributed every day. So that if I allow twenty readers to every paper, which I look upon as a modest computation, I may reckon about three-score thousand disciples in London and Westminster, who I hope will take care to distinguish themselves from the thoughtless herd of their ignorant and unattentive brethren. Since I have raised to myself so great an audience, I shall spare no pains to make their instruction agreeable, and their diversion useful. For which reasons I shall endeavor to enliven morality with wit, and to temper wit with morality, that my readers may, if possible, both ways find their account in the speculation of the day. And to the end that their virtue and discretion may not be short, transient, intermitting starts of thought, I have resolved to refresh their memories from day to day, till I have recovered them out of that desperate state of vice and folly into which the age is fallen. The mind that lies fallow but a single day sprouts up in follies that are only to be killed by a constant and assiduous culture. It was said of Socrates that he brought philosophy down from heaven, to inhabit among men; and I shall be ambitious to have it said of me that I have brought philosophy out of closets and libraries, schools and colleges, to dwell in clubs and assemblies, at tea tables and in coffeehouses.

I would therefore in a very particular manner recommend these my speculations to all well-regulated families that set apart an hour in every morning for tea and bread and butter; and would earnestly advise them for their good to order this paper to be punctually

---

1. "Like him whose oars can hardly force his boat against the current, if by chance he relaxes his arms, the boat sweeps him headlong down the steam."

served up, and to be looked upon as a part of the tea equipage.

Sir Francis Bacon observes that a well-written book, compared with its rivals and antagonists, is like Moses' serpent, that immediately swallowed up and devoured those of the Egyptians.[2] I shall not be so vain as to think that where *The Spectator* appears the other public prints will vanish; but shall leave it to my reader's consideration whether is it not much better to be let into the knowledge of one's self, than to hear what passes in Muscovy or Poland; and to amuse ourselves with such writings as tend to the wearing out of ignorance, passion, and prejudice, than such as naturally conduce to inflame hatreds, and make enmities irreconcilable?

In the next place, I would recommend this paper to the daily perusal of those gentlemen whom I cannot but consider as my good brothers and allies, I mean the fraternity of spectators, who live in the world without having anything to do in it; and either by the affluence of their fortunes or laziness of their dispositions have no other business with the rest of mankind but to look upon them. Under this class of men are comprehended all contemplative tradesmen, titular physicians, fellows of the Royal Society, Templars[3] that are not given to be contentious, and statesmen that are out of business; in short, everyone that considers the world as a theater, and desires to form a right judgment of those who are the actors on it.

There is another set of men that I must likewise lay a claim to, whom I have lately called the blanks of society, as being altogether unfurnished with ideas, till the business and conversation of the day has supplied them. I have often considered these poor souls with an eye of great commiseration, when I have heard them asking the first man they have met with, whether there was any news stirring? and by that means gathering together materials for thinking. These needy persons do not know what to talk of till about twelve o'clock in the morning; for by that time they are pretty good judges of the weather, know which way the wind sits, and whether the Dutch mail be come in.[4] As they lie at the mercy of the first man they meet, and are grave or impertinent all the day long, according to the notions which they have imbibed in the morning, I would earnestly entreat them not to stir out of their chambers till they have read this paper, and do promise them that I will daily instil into them such sound and wholesome sentiments as shall have a good effect on their conversation for the ensuing twelve hours.

But there are none to whom this paper will be more useful than

2. In *The Advancement of Learning*, II, "To the King." But it was the rod of Aaron, not of Moses, that turned into a devouring serpent (Exodus vii. 10–12).

3. Lawyers or students of the law who live or have their offices ("chambers") in the Middle or Inner Temple, one of the Inns of Court.

4. Bringing the latest war news.

to the female world. I have often thought there has not been sufficient pains taken in finding out proper employments and diversions for the fair ones. Their amusements seem contrived for them, rather as they are women, than as they are reasonable creatures; and are more adapted to the sex than to the species. The toilet is their great scene of business, and the right adjusting of their hair the principal employment of their lives. The sorting of a suit of ribbons[5] is reckoned a very good morning's work; and if they make an excursion to a mercer's[6] or a toyshop, so great a fatigue makes them unfit for anything else all the day after. Their more serious occupations are sewing and embroidery, and their greatest drudgery the preparation of jellies and sweetmeats. This, I say, is the state of ordinary women; though I know there are multitudes of those of a more elevated life and conversation, that move in an exalted sphere of knowledge and virtue, that join all the beauties of the mind to the ornaments of dress, and inspire a kind of awe and respect, as well as love, into their male beholders. I hope to increase the number of these by publishing this daily paper, which I shall always endeavor to make an innocent if not an improving entertainment, and by that means at least divert the minds of my female readers from greater trifles. At the same time, as I would fain give some finishing touches to those which are already the most beautiful pieces in human nature, I shall endeavor to point all those imperfections that are the blemishes, as well as those virtues which are the embellishments, of the sex. In the meanwhile I hope these my gentle readers, who have so much time on their hands, will not grudge throwing away a quarter of an hour in a day on this paper, since they may do it without any hindrance to business.

I know several of my friends and well-wishers are in great pain for me, lest I should not be able to keep up the spirit of a paper which I oblige myself to furnish every day: but to make them easy in this particular, I will promise them faithfully to give it over as soon as I grow dull. This I know will be matter of great raillery to the small wits; who will frequently put me in mind of my promise, desire me to keep my word, assure me that it is high time to give over, with many other little pleasantries of the like nature, which men of a little smart genius cannot forbear throwing out against their best friends, when they have such a handle given them of being witty. But let them remember that I do hereby enter my caveat against this piece of raillery.

---

5. A set of ribbons to be worn together.
6. A seller of such small-wares as tape, ribbon, fringe. A "toyshop" is a shop where baubles and trifles are sold.

ADDISON: [Wit: True, False, Mixed]

The Spectator, No. 62, Friday, May 11, 1711

Scribendi recte sapere est et principium et fons.[1]
—HORACE, *Ars Poetica* 309

Mr. Locke has an admirable reflection upon the difference of wit and judgment, whereby he endeavors to show the reason why they are not always the talents of the same person. His words are as follow: "And hence, perhaps, may be given some reason of that common observation, that men who have a great deal of wit and prompt memories, have not always the clearest judgment, or deepest reason. For wit lying most in the assemblage of ideas, and putting those together with quickness and variety, wherein can be found any resemblance or congruity, thereby to make up pleasant pictures and agreeable visions in the fancy; judgment, on the contrary, lies quite on the other side, in separating carefully one from another, ideas wherein can be found the least difference, thereby to avoid being misled by similitude, and by affinity to take one thing for another. This is a way of proceeding quite contrary to metaphor and allusion; wherein, for the most part, lies that entertainment and pleasantry of wit which strikes so lively on the fancy, and is therefore so acceptable to all people."[2]

This is, I think, the best and most philosophical account that I have ever met with of wit, which generally, though not always, consists in such a resemblance and congruity of ideas as this author mentions. I shall only add to it, by way of explanation, that every resemblance of ideas is not that which we call wit, unless it be such an one that gives delight and surprise to the reader. These two properties seem essential to wit, more particularly the last of them. In order therefore that the resemblance in the ideas be wit, it is necessary that the ideas should not lie too near one another in the nature of things; for where the likeness is obvious, it gives no surprise. To compare one man's singing to that of another, or to represent the whiteness of any object by that of milk and snow, or the variety of its colors by those of the rainbow, cannot be called wit, unless, besides this obvious resemblance, there be some further congruity discovered in the two ideas that is capable of giving the reader some surprise. Thus when a poet tells us, the bosom of his mistress is as white as snow, there is no wit in the comparison; but when he adds, with a sigh, that it is as cold too, it then grows into wit. Every reader's memory may supply him with innumerable

---

1. "Discernment is the source and fount of writing well."

2. John Locke, *Essay Concerning Human Understanding* (1690) II. 2.

instances of the same nature. For this reason, the similitudes in heroic poets, who endeavor rather to fill the mind with great conceptions, than to divert it with such as are new and surprising, have seldom anything in them that can be called wit. Mr. Locke's account of wit, with this short explanation, comprehends most of the species of wit, as metaphors, similitudes, allegories, enigmas, mottoes, parables, fables, dreams, visions, dramatic writings, burlesque, and all the methods of allusion:[3] as there are many other pieces of wit (how remote soever they may appear at first sight from the foregoing description) which upon examination will be found to agree with it.

As true wit generally consists in this resemblance and congruity of ideas, false wit chiefly consists in the resemblance and congruity sometimes of single letters, as in anagrams, chronograms,[4] lipograms, and acrostics; sometimes of syllables, as in echoes and doggerel rhymes; sometimes of words, as in puns and quibbles; and sometimes of whole sentences or poems, cast into the figures of eggs, axes, or altars:[5] nay, some carry the notion of wit so far, as to ascribe it even to external mimicry; and to look upon a man as an ingenious person, that can resemble the tone, posture, or face of another.

As true wit consists in the resemblance of ideas, and false wit in the resemblance of words, according to the foregoing instances; there is another kind of wit which consists partly in the resemblance of ideas, and partly in the resemblance of words; which for distinction's sake I shall call mixed wit. This kind of wit is that which abounds in Cowley, more than in any author that ever wrote. Mr. Waller has likewise a great deal of it. Mr. Dryden is very sparing in it. Milton had a genius much above it. Spenser is in the same class with Milton. The Italians, even in their epic poetry, are full of it. Monsieur Boileau, who formed himself upon the ancient poets, has everywhere rejected it with scorn. If we look after mixed wit among the Greek writers, we shall find it nowhere but in the epigrammatists. There are indeed some strokes of it in the little poem ascribed to Musaeus,[6] which by that, as well as many other marks, betrays itself to be a modern composition. If we look into the Latin writers, we find none of this mixed wit in Virgil, Lucretius, or Catullus; very little in Horace, but a great deal of it in Ovid, and scarce anything else in Martial.

Out of the innumerable branches of mixed wit, I shall choose one instance which may be met with in all the writers of this class. The passion of love in its nature has been thought to resemble fire; for which reason the words fire and flame are made use of to signify

3. Word-play; more broadly, any covert or symbolic use of language.
4. Phrase in which certain letters express a date; e.g., "LorD HaVe MerCIe Vpon Vs": the capital letters, in Roman numerals, add up to 1666, the *annus mirabilis* of fire, plague, and war. "Lipogram": a composition omitting all words that contain a certain letter or letters.
5. See *The Altar* and *Easter Wings* by George Herbert.
6. A poem called *Hero and Leander*, attributed to Musaeus, an ancient Greek poet, was first published in 1635.

love. The witty poets therefore have taken an advantage from the doubtful meaning of the word fire, to make an infinite number of witticisms. Cowley observing the cold regard of his mistress's eyes,[7] and at the same time their power of producing love in him, considers them as burning-glasses made of ice; and finding himself able to live in the greatest extremities of love, concludes the torrid zone to be habitable. When his mistress has read his letter written in juice of lemon by holding it to the fire, he desires her to read it over a second time by love's flames. When she weeps, he wishes it were inward heat that distilled those drops from the limbec.[8] When she is absent he is beyond eighty, that is, thirty degrees nearer the pole than when she is with him. His ambitious love is a fire that naturally mounts upwards; his happy love is the beams of heaven, and his unhappy love flames of hell. When it does not let him sleep, it is a flame that sends up no smoke; when it is opposed by counsel and advice, it is a fire that rages the more by the wind's blowing upon it. Upon the dying of a tree in which he had cut his loves, he observes that his written flames had burned up and withered the tree. When he resolves to give over his passion, he tells us that one burnt like him for ever dreads the fire. His heart is an Aetna, that instead of Vulcan's shop[9] encloses Cupid's forge in it. His endeavoring to drown his love in wine, is throwing oil upon the fire. He would insinuate to his mistress, that the fire of love, like that of the sun (which produces so many living creatures) should not only warm but beget. Love in another place cooks pleasure at his fire. Sometimes the poet's heart is frozen in every breast, and sometimes scorched in every eye. Sometimes he is drowned in tears, and burnt in love, like a ship set on fire in the middle of the sea.

The reader may observe in every one of these instances, that the poet mixes the qualities of fire with those of love; and in the same sentence speaking of it both as a passion, and as real fire, surprises the reader with those seeming resemblances or contradictions that make up all the wit in this kind of writing. Mixed wit therefore is a composition of pun and true wit, and is more or less perfect as the resemblance lies in the ideas or in the words: its foundations are laid partly in falsehood and partly in truth: reason puts in her claim for one half of it, and extravagance for the other. The only province therefore for this kind of wit, is epigram, or those little occasional poems that in their own nature are nothing else but a tissue of epigrams. I cannot conclude this head of mixed wit, without owning that the admirable poet out of whom I have taken the examples of it, had as much true wit as any author that ever writ; and indeed all other talents of an extraordinary genius.

It may be expected, since I am upon this subject, that I should

7. In *The Mistress, or Several Copies of Love-Verses* (1647).
8. Alembic, an apparatus used in distilling.

9. Mount Etna was supposed to be the workshop of Vulcan, the Roman god of fire and metal-working.

take notice of Mr. Dryden's definition of wit; which, with all the deference that is due to the judgment of so great a man, is not so properly a definition of wit, as of good writing in general. Wit, as he defines it, is "a propriety of words and thoughts adapted to the subject."[1] If this be a true definition of wit, I am apt to think that Euclid[2] was the greatest wit that ever set pen to paper: it is certain there never was a greater propriety of words and thoughts adapted to the subject, than what that author has made use of in his elements. I shall only appeal to my reader, if this definition agrees with any notion he has of wit: if it be a true one, I am sure Mr. Dryden was not only a better poet, but a greater wit than Mr. Cowley; and Virgil a much more facetious man than either Ovid or Martial.

Bouhours,[3] whom I look upon to be the most penetrating of all the French critics, has taken pains to show that it is impossible for any thought to be beautiful which is not just, and has not its foundation in the nature of things; that the basis of all wit is truth; and that no thought can be valuable, of which good sense is not the groundwork. Boileau[4] has endeavored to inculcate the same notion in several parts of his writings, both in prose and verse. This is that natural way of writing, that beautiful simplicity, which we so much admire in the compositions of the ancients; and which nobody deviates from, but those who want strength of genius to make a thought shine in its own natural beauties. Poets who want this strength of genius to give that majestic simplicity to nature, which we so much admire in the works of the ancients, are forced to hunt after foreign ornaments, and not to let any piece of wit of what kind soever escape them. I look upon these writers as Goths in poetry, who, like those in architecture, not being able to come up to the beautiful simplicity of the old Greeks and Romans, have endeavored to supply its place with all the extravagances of an irregular fancy. Mr. Dryden makes a very handsome observation on Ovid's writing a letter from Dido to Aeneas, in the following words:[5] "Ovid" (says he, speaking of Virgil's fiction of Dido and Aeneas) "takes it up after him, even in the same age, and makes an ancient heroine of Virgil's new-created Dido; dictates a letter for her just before her death to the ungrateful fugitive; and, very unluckily for himself, is for measuring a sword with a man so much superior in force to him, on the same subject. I think I may be judge of this, because I have translated both. The famous author of the Art of Love[6] has nothing of his own; he borrows all from a greater master

---

1. Adapted from Dryden's *Apology for Heroic Poetry* (1677).
2. Hellenic mathematician (ca. 300 B.C.)
3. Dominique Bouhours (1628–1702), who wrote an *Art of Criticism*.
4. Nicholas Boileau (1636–1711), a fa-

mous French neoclassicist, wrote a verse *Art of Poetry* (1674) translated by Dryden.
5. From Dryden's Dedication to his translation of the *Aeneid* (1697).
6. Ovid.

in his own profession, and, which is worse, improves nothing which he finds: nature fails him, and being forced to his old shift, he has recourse to witticism. This passes indeed with his soft admirers, and gives him the preference to Virgil in their esteem."

Were not I supported by so great an authority as that of Mr. Dryden, I should not venture to observe, that the taste of most of our English poets, as well as readers, is extremely Gothic. He quotes Monsieur Segrais[7] for a threefold distinction of the readers of poetry: in the first of which he comprehends the rabble of readers, whom he does not treat as such with regard to their quality,[8] but to their numbers and the coarseness of their taste. His words are as follow: "Segrais has distinguished the readers of poetry, according to their capacity of judging, into three classes. [He might have said the same of writers too, if he had pleased.] In the lowest form he places those whom he calls *les petits esprits*,[9] such things as are our upper-gallery audience in a play-house; who like nothing but the husk and rind of wit, prefer a quibble, a conceit, an epigram, before solid sense and elegant expression: these are mob-readers. If Virgil and Martial stood for parliament-men, we know already who would carry it.[1] But though they make the greatest appearance in the field, and cry the loudest, the best on 't is they are but a sort of French Huguenots, or Dutch boors,[2] brought over in herds, but not naturalized; who have not lands of two pounds per annum in Parnassus, and therefore are not privileged to poll.[3] Their authors are of the same level, fit to represent them on a mountebank's stage, or to be masters of the ceremonies in a bear-garden: yet these are they who have the most admirers. But it often happens, to their mortification, that as their readers improve their stock of sense (as they may by reading better books, and by conversation with men of judgment), they soon forsake them."

I must not dismiss this subject without observing, that as Mr. Locke in the passage above-mentioned has discovered the most fruitful source of wit, so there is another of a quite contrary nature to it, which does likewise branch itself out into several kinds. For not only the resemblance but the opposition of ideas does very often produce wit; as I could show in several little points, turns, and antitheses, that I may possibly enlarge upon in some future speculation.[4]

---

7. Jean Regnauld de Segrais (1624-1701), who had translated Virgil into French, is quoted extensively by Dryden.
8. Social standing.
9. The small-minded.
1. That is, the witty Martial would easily defeat the weighty Virgil in an election.
2. Peasants. Huguenots and the Dutch were the largest class of immigrants in England. "On 't": that one can say.
3. Vote. Only freeholders worth two pounds a year could go to the polls; and these readers of little taste hold no land in Parnassus (where the Muses live).
4. For such an "enlargement," see Samuel Johnson's remarks on wit in the *Life of Cowley*.

ADDISON: [*Paradise Lost*: General Critical
Remarks]

The Spectator, No. 267, *Saturday, January 5, 1712*

Cedite Romani scriptores, cedite Graii.[1]
—PROPERTIUS, *Elegies* II.xxxiv.65

There is nothing in nature so irksome as general discourses,
especially when they turn chiefly upon words. For this reason I
shall waive the discussion of that point which was started some
years since, Whether Milton's *Paradise Lost* may be called an
heroic poem? Those who will not give it that title may call it (if
they please) a *divine poem*. It will be sufficient to its perfection,
if it has in it all the beauties of the highest kind of poetry; and as
for those who allege it is not an heroic poem, they advance no more
to the diminution of it, than if they should say Adam is not Aeneas,
nor Eve Helen.

I shall therefore examine it by the rules of epic poetry,[2] and see
whether it falls short of the *Iliad* or *Aeneid*, in the beauties which
are essential to that kind of writing. The first thing to be considered
in an epic poem is the fable,[3] which is perfect or imperfect, according as the action which it relates is more or less so. This action
should have three qualifications in it. First, it should be but one
action. Secondly, it should be an entire action; and thirdly, it
should be a great action. To consider the action of the *Iliad*, *Aeneid*,
and *Paradise Lost*, in these three several lights. Homer to preserve
the unity of his action hastens into the midst of things, as Horace
has observed:[4] had he gone up to Leda's egg, or begun much later,
even at the rape of Helen, or the investing of Troy, it is manifest
that the story of the poem would have been a series of several actions. He therefore opens his poem with the discord of his princes,
and with great art interweaves in the several succeeding parts of it,
an account of everything material which relates to them and had
passed before that fatal dissension. After the same manner Aeneas
makes his first appearance in the Tyrrhene seas,[5] and within sight
of Italy, because the action proposed to be celebrated was that of

1. "Yield place, ye Roman and ye
Grecian writers, yield."
2. The rules for the conduct of an epic
poem, derived out of the poems of
Homer and Virgil, the *Poetics* of
Aristotle, and the *Ars Poetica* of Horace, had been given their most systematic and complete statement in Père
René Le Bossu's *Traité du poème
épique* (1675), which was immediately
absorbed into English critical thought.
Addison writes of *Paradise Lost* with

Le Bossu well in sight, but he is no
slavish disciple.
3. The plot of a drama or poem.
4. *Ars Poetica*, 147–49. Helen, whose
abduction from her husband Menelaus
by the Trojan prince Paris brought on
the Trojan War, was the daughter of
Leda, who was visited by Zeus in the
guise of a swan.
5. That part of the Mediterranean Sea
west of Italy, bounded by the islands of
Sicily, Sardinia, and Corsica.

his settling himself in Latium.[6] But because it was necessary for the reader to know what had happened to him in the taking of Troy, and in the preceding parts of his voyage, Virgil makes his hero relate it by way of episode[7] in the second and third books of the *Aeneid*. The contents of both which books come before those of the first book in the thread of the story, though for preserving of this unity of action, they follow them in the disposition of the poem. Milton, in imitation of these two great poets, opens his *Paradise Lost* with an infernal council plotting the fall of man, which is the action he proposed to celebrate; and as for those great action which preceded, in point of time, the battle of the angels, and the creation of the world (which would have entirely destroyed the unity of his principal action, had he related them in the same order that they happened), he cast them into the fifth, sixth, and seventh books, by way of episode to this noble poem.

Aristotle himself allows that Homer has nothing to boast of as to the unity of his fable, though at the same time that great critic and philosopher endeavors to palliate this imperfection in the Greek poet, by imputing it in some measure to the very nature of an epic poem. Some have been of opinion that the *Aeneid* labors also in this particular, and has episodes which may be looked upon as excrescences rather than as parts of the action. On the contrary, the poem which we have now under our consideration hath no other episodes than such as naturally arise from the subject, and yet is filled with such a multitude of astonishing incidents that it gives us at the same time a pleasure of the greatest variety, and of the greatest simplicity.

I must observe also that as Virgil, in the poem which was designed to celebrate the original of the Roman Empire, has described the birth of its great rival, the Carthaginian commonwealth, Milton with the like art in his poem on the Fall of Man, has related the fall of those angels who are his professed enemies. Besides the many other beauties in such an episode, its running parallel with the great action of the poem hinders it from breaking the unity so much as another episode would have done that had not so great an affinity with the principal subject. In short, this is the same kind of beauty which the critics admire in the *Spanish Friar, or The Double Discovery*,[8] where the two different plots look like counterparts and copies of one another.

The second qualification required in the action of an epic poem is, that it should be an *entire* action. An action is entire when it is complete in all its parts; or as Aristotle describes it, when it con-

---

6. The kingdom of the Latini, where Aeneas was hospitably received when he landed at the mouth of the Tiber. He married Lavinia, the daughter of King Latinus, and later ruled the kingdom.

7. An incidental narration or digression in an epic which arises naturally from the subject but is separable from the main action.

8. A comedy by Dryden.

sists of a beginning, a middle, and an end. Nothing should go before it, be intermixed with it, or follow after it, that is not related to it. As on the contrary, no single step should be omitted in that just and regular process which it must be supposed to take from its original to its consummation. Thus we see the anger of Achilles in its birth, its continuance, and effects; and Aeneas's settlement in Italy, carried on through all the oppositions in his way to it both by sea and land. The action in Milton excels (I think) both the former in this particular: we see it contrived in hell, executed upon earth, and punished by heaven. The parts of it are told in the most distinct manner, and grow out of one another in the most natural method.

The third qualification of an epic poem is its *greatness*. The anger of Achilles was of such consequence that it embroiled the kings of Greece, destroyed the heroes of Troy, and engaged all the gods in factions. Aeneas's settlement in Italy produced the Caesars, and gave birth to the Roman Empire. Milton's subject was still greater than either of the former; it does not determine the fate of single persons or nations, but of a whole species. The united powers of hell are joined together for the destruction of mankind, which they effected in part, and would have completed, had not Omnipotence itself interposed. The principal actors are man in his greatest perfection, and woman in her highest beauty. Their enemies are the fallen angels: the Messiah their friend, and the Almighty their protector. In short, everything that is great in the whole circle of being, whether within the verge of nature, or out of it, has a proper part assigned it in this noble poem.

In poetry, as in architecture, not only the whole, but the principal members, and every part of them, should be great. I will not presume to say, that the book of games in the *Aeneid*, or that in the *Iliad*, are not of this nature, nor to reprehend Virgil's simile of the top, and many other of the same nature in the *Iliad*, as liable to any censure in this particular; but I think we may say, without derogating from those wonderful performances, that there is an unquestionable magnificence in every part of *Paradise Lost*, and indeed a much greater than could have been formed upon any pagan system.

But Aristotle, by the greatness of the action, does not only mean that it should be great in its nature, but also in its duration, or in other words, that it should have a due length in it, as well as what we properly call greatness. The just measure of the kind of magnitude, he explains by the following similitude. An animal, no bigger than a mite, cannot appear perfect to the eye, because the sight takes it in at once, and has only a confused idea of the whole, and not a distinct idea of all its parts: if on the contrary you should suppose an animal of ten thousand furlongs in length, the eye would be so filled with a single part of it, that it could not give the mind an idea of the whole. What these animals are to the eye, a very short or a very long action would be to the memory. The first would be, as it were, lost and swallowed up by it, and the other difficult to be contained in it. Homer and Virgil have shown their principal art in this particular; the action of the *Iliad*, and that of the *Aeneid*, were in themselves exceeding short, but are so beautifully extended and diversified by the invention of episodes, and the machinery[9] of gods, with the like poetical ornaments, that they make up an agreeable story sufficient to employ the memory without overcharging it. Milton's action is enriched with such a variety of circumstances that I have taken as much pleasure in reading the contents of his books as in the best invented story I ever met with. It is possible that the traditions on which the *Iliad* and *Aeneid* were built had more circumstances in them than the history of the Fall of Man, as it is related in Scripture. Besides it was easier for Homer and Virgil to dash the truth with fiction, as they were in no danger of offending the religion of their country by it. But as for Milton, he had not only a very few circumstances upon which to raise his poem, but was also obliged to proceed with the greatest caution in everything that he added out of his own invention. And, indeed, notwithstanding all the restraints he was under, he has filled his story with so many surprising incidents, which bear so close an analogy with what is delivered in Holy Writ, that it is capable of pleasing the most delicate reader, without giving offense to the most scrupulous.

The modern critics have collected from several hints in the *Iliad* and *Aeneid* the space of time which is taken up by the action of each of those poems; but as a great part of Milton's story was transacted in regions that lie out of the reach of the sun and the sphere of day, it is impossible to gratify the reader with such a calculation, which indeed would be more curious than instructive; none of the critics, either ancient or modern, having laid down rules to circumscribe the action of an epic poem with any determined number of years, days, or hours.

This Piece of Criticism on Milton's Paradise Lost *shall be carried on in the following Saturdays' papers.*[1]

9. The technical term (from *deus ex machina*) in critical theory for the supernatural beings who oversee and intervene in the affairs of the characters in epic poems.
1. The series on *Paradise Lost* contains eighteen essays.

ADDISON: [On the Scale of Being]

The Spectator, No. 519, October 25, 1712

inde hominum pecudumque genus, vitaeque volantum,
et quae marmoreo fert monstra sub aequore pontus.[1]
—VIRGIL, *Aeneid* VI.728–29

Though there is a great deal of pleasure in contemplating the material world, by which I mean that system of bodies into which nature has so curiously wrought the mass of dead matter, with the several relations which those bodies bear to one another, there is still, methinks, something more wonderful and surprising in contemplations on the world of life, by which I mean all those animals with which every part of the universe is furnished. The material world is only the shell of the universe: the world of life are its inhabitants.

If we consider those parts of the material world which lie the nearest to us and are, therefore, subject to our observations and inquiries, it is amazing to consider the infinity of animals with which it is stocked. Every part of matter is peopled. Every green leaf swarms with inhabitants. There is scarce a single humor in the body of a man, or of any other animal, in which our glasses do not discover myriads of living creatures. The surface of animals is also covered with other animals which are, in the same manner, the basis of other animals that live upon it; nay, we find in the most solid bodies, as in marble itself, innumerable cells and cavities that are crowded with such imperceptible inhabitants as are too little for the naked eye to discover. On the other hand if we look into the more bulky parts of nature, we see the seas, lakes, and rivers teeming with numberless kinds of living creatures. We find every mountain and marsh, wilderness and wood, plentifully stocked with birds and beasts, and every part of matter affording proper necessaries and conveniences for the livelihood of multitudes which inhabit it.

The author of *The Plurality of Worlds*[2] draws a very good argument upon this consideration for the peopling of every planet, as indeed it seems very probable from the analogy of reason that, if no part of matter which we are acquainted with lies waste and useless, those great bodies, which are at such a distance from us, should not be desert and unpeopled, but rather that they should be furnished with beings adapted to their respective situations.

Existence is a blessing to those beings only which are endowed

1. "Thence the race of men and beasts, the life of flying creatures, and the monsters that ocean bears beneath her smooth surface."
2. Bernard de Fontenelle (1657–1757). This delightful book, a series of dialogues between a scientist and a countess concerning the possibility of other inhabited planets and the new astrophysics in general, was published in 1686 in France and beautifully translated by Joseph Glanvill in 1688.

with perception and is, in a manner, thrown away upon dead matter any further than as it is subservient to beings which are conscious of their existence. Accordingly we find from the bodies which lie under observation that matter is only made as the basis and support of animals and that there is no more of the one than what is necessary for the existence of the other.

Infinite Goodness is of so communicative a nature that it seems to delight in the conferring of existence upon every degree of perceptive being. As this is a speculation which I have often pursued with great pleasure to myself, I shall enlarge farther upon it, by considering that part of the scale of beings which comes within our knowledge.

There are some living creatures which are raised but just above dead matter. To mention only that species of shellfish, which are formed in the fashion of a cone, that grow to the surface of several rocks and immediately die upon their being severed from the place where they grow. There are many other creatures but one remove from these, which have no other sense besides that of feeling and taste. Others have still an additional one of hearing; others of smell, and others of sight. It is wonderful to observe by what a gradual progress the world of life advances through a prodigious variety of species before a creature is formed that is complete in all its senses; and, even among these, there is such a different degree of perfection in the sense which one animal enjoys, beyond what appears in another, that, though the sense in different animals be distinguished by the same common denomination, it seems almost of a different nature. If after this we look into the several inward perfections of cunning and sagacity, or what we generally call instinct, we find them rising after the same manner, imperceptibly, one above another, and receiving additional improvements, according to the species in which they are implanted. This progress in nature is so very gradual that the most perfect of an inferior species comes very near to the most imperfect of that which is immediately above it.

The exuberant and overflowing goodness of the Supreme Being, whose mercy extends to all his works, is plainly seen, as I have before hinted, from his having made so very little matter, at least what falls within our knowledge, that does not swarm with life. Nor is his goodness less seen in the diversity than in the multitude of living creatures. Had he only made one species of animals, none of the rest would have enjoyed the happiness of existence; he has, therefore, *specified* in his creation every degree of life, every capacity of being. The whole chasm in nature, from a plant to a man, is filled up with diverse kinds of creatures, rising one over another by such a gentle and easy ascent that the little transitions and deviations from one species to another are almost insensible.

This intermediate space is so well husbanded and managed that there is scarce a degree of perception which does not appear in some one part of the world of life. Is the goodness or wisdom of the Divine Being more manifested in this his proceeding?

There is a consequence, besides those I have already mentioned, which seems very naturally deducible from the foregoing considerations. If the scale of being rises by such a regular progress so high as man, we may by a parity of reason suppose that it still proceeds gradually through those beings which are of a superior nature to him, since there is an infinitely greater space and room for different degrees of perfection between the Supreme Being and man than between man and the most despicable insect. This consequence of so great a variety of beings which are superior to us, from that variety which is inferior to us, is made by Mr. Locke[3] in a passage which I shall here set down after having premised that, notwithstanding there is such infinite room between man and his Maker for the creative power to exert itself in, it is impossible that it should ever be filled up, since there will be still an infinite gap or distance between the highest created being and the Power which produced him:

"That there should be more species of intelligent creatures above us than there are of sensible and material below, is probable to me from hence: That in all the visible corporeal world we see no chasms or no gaps. All quite down from us, the descent is by easy steps and a continued series of things that, in each remove, differ very little from the other. There are fishes that have wings and are not strangers to the airy region; and there are some birds that are inhabitants of the water, whose blood is cold as fishes and their flesh so like in taste that the scrupulous are allowed them on fish days. There are animals so near of kin both to birds and beasts that they are in the middle between both: amphibious animals link the terrestrial and aquatic together; seals live at land and at sea, and porpoises have the warm blood and entrails of a hog, not to mention what is confidently reported of mermaids or seamen. There are some brutes that seem to have as much knowledge and reason as some that are called men; and the animal and vegetable kingdoms are so nearly joined that, if you will take the lowest of one and the highest of the other, there will scarce be perceived any great difference between them; and so on, till we come to the lowest and the most inorganical parts of matter, we shall find everywhere that the several species are linked together and differ but in almost insensible degrees. And when we consider the infinite power and wisdom of the Maker, we have reason to think that it is suitable to the magnificent harmony of the universe and the great design and infinite goodness of the Architect, that the species of creatures should also, by gentle degrees, ascend upward from us

3. John Locke, in his *Essay Concerning Human Understanding* (1690) III.vi. 12.

toward his infinite perfection, as we see they gradually descend from us downward; which, if it be probable, we have reason to be persuaded that there are far more species of creatures above us than there are beneath, we being in degrees of perfection much more remote from the infinite being of God than we are from the lowest state of being and that which approaches nearest to nothing. And yet of all those distinct species we have no clear distinct ideas."

In this system of being, there is no creature so wonderful in its nature, and which so much deserves our particular attention, as man, who fills up the middle space between the animal and intellectual nature, the visible and invisible world, and is that link in the chain of beings which has been often termed the *nexus utriusque mundi.*[4] So that he who, in one respect, is associated with angels and archangels, may look upon a Being of infinite perfection as his father, and the highest order of spirits as his brethren, and may, in another respect, say to corruption, "Thou art my father," and to the worm, "Thou art my mother and my sister."[5]

4. "The binding together of both 5. Job xvii.14.
worlds."

ALEXANDER POPE
(1688–1744)

1711:   *Essay on Criticism.*
1712:   First version of *The Rape of the Lock.*
1713–26: Translating Homer, editing Shakespeare.
1728:   The *Dunciad* begins Pope's career as major verse satirist.
1733–34: The *Essay on Man* begins Pope's career as ethical and philosophical poet.

Pope is the only important writer of his generation who was solely a man of letters. Since he could not, as a Roman Catholic, attend a university, vote, or hold public office, he was excluded from the sort of patronage which was freely bestowed by statesmen on most writers during the reign of Anne. This disadvantage he turned into a positive good, for the translation of Homer's *Iliad* and *Odyssey*, which he undertook for profit as well as for fame, gave him ample means to live the life of an independent suburban gentleman. After 1718 he lived hospitably in his villa by the Thames at Twickenham (then pronounced *Twit'nam*), entertaining his friends and converting his five acres of land into a diminutive landscape garden. Almost exactly a century earlier, Shakespeare had earned enough to retire to a country estate at Stratford—but he had been an actor-manager as well as a playwright; Pope, therefore, was the first writer to demonstrate that literature alone could be a gainful profession.

Ill health plagued Pope almost from birth. Delicate as a child, he was early stunted and deformed by tuberculosis of the spine. His father, a well-to-do London merchant, retired from business in the year of the poet's birth, and about 1700 acquired a small property at Binfield in Windsor Forest. In rural surroundings, as the boy's health improved, he early acquired his lifelong taste for natural beauty and for gardening. There he completed by wide reading the desultory schooling that both his ill health and his religion had made inevitable, and, encouraged by his father, he began also to develop his precocious talent for poetry. The removal to Binfield, then, was in every way advantageous. But Pope was never to enjoy good health: in later life he was troubled by violent head-aches, and he suffered from easily exacerbated nerves. This neurotic ir-ritability was a price he had to pay for the sensitive and ardent tempera-ment that helped make him one of our greatest poets. Because of it, he both hated and loved intensely; because of it his responsiveness to beauty in all its forms was unusually acute.

Pope's first striking success as a poet was the *Essay on Criticism* (1711), which earned him the fame of Addison's approval and the notoriety of an intemperate personal attack from the critic John Dennis, who was angered by a casual reference to himself in the poem. *The Rape of the Lock*, both in its original shorter version of 1712 and in its more elaborate version of 1714, established the author of the *Essay on Criticism* as a master not only of metrics and of language, but also of witty, urbane satire. In the earlier work, Pope had excelled all his predecessors in writing a didactic poem after the example of Horace; in the later, he had written the most brilliant mock epic in the language. But there was another vein in Pope's youthful poetry, much of which, concerned as it is with natural beauty and love, reveals a temperament that in a later poet might have been called "Romantic." The *Pastorals* (1709), Pope's first publication, and *Windsor Forest* (1713; much of it was written earlier) are essentially nature poems, abounding in visual imagery and descriptive passages of ideally ordered nature. They remind us that Pope was an amateur painter who delighted in the beauty of external nature, as well as in the artificial beauty of the world of *The Rape of the Lock*. The *Elegy to the Memory of an Unfortunate Lady*, published in the collected poems of 1717, presents the high heroics of romantic love. Looking back to his early poems, Pope said that he had wandered "in Fancy's maze." And even the long task of translating Homer, the "dull duty" of editing Shakespeare, and, in middle age, his preoccupation with ethical and satirical poetry did not extinguish this side of Pope's nature and art. He learned to subordinate, but he did not cease to use, this sensitive awareness of visual beauty in his later poetry.

Pope's early poetry brought him to the attention of literary men, with whom he began to associate in the masculine world of coffeehouse and tavern. His fragile health never permitted him to live the rakish life that he would have liked, but it did not prevent his enjoying the company of some of the most distinguished men of letters of the time. Between 1706 and 1711 he came to know, among many others, William Congreve, William Walsh, the critic and poet, and Richard Steele and Joseph Ad-dison, who, after 1709, were two of the most admired writers of the day. As it happened, all these men were Whigs. Pope was probably indifferent to politics at this time, or at least he could readily ignore politics in the excitement of taking his place among the leading wits of the town. But after the fall of the Whigs in 1710, and the formation of the Tory government under Robert Harley (later Earl of Oxford) and Henry St. John (later Viscount Bolingbroke) party loyalties bred bitterness among the wits as among the politicians.

By 1712 Pope had made the acquaintance of another group of writers, all Tories, who soon became his intimate friends: Jonathan Swift, by then the close associate of Harley and St. John and the principal propagandist for their policies; Dr. John Arbuthnot, physician to the queen, a learned scientist, a wit of the first quality, and a man of deep humanity and utter integrity; John Gay, the poet, who in 1728 was to produce the *Beggar's Opera*, the greatest theatrical success of the century; and Thomas Parnell, a poet of some distinction, who died prematurely in 1718. It was among these men that Pope was to find his lifelong friends; and it was through them that he became the friend and admirer of Oxford, and later the intimate of Bolingbroke. As he grew more intimate with his new circle, he began to drift away from Addison and his earlier friends.

In 1714 this group, at the instigation of Pope, formed a club which was to cooperate in a scheme for satirizing all sorts of false learning and pedantry in philosophy, science, and other branches of knowledge. They were joined by the Earl of Oxford, who attended as often as business permitted. The friends proposed to write jointly the biography of a learned fool whom they named Martinus Scriblerus (Martin the Scribbler), whose life and opinions would be a running commentary on whatever they considered the abuses of learning and the follies of the learned. The death of the queen in August, 1714, brought the venture to a premature end, but not before some amusing episodes had been invented, as the published (probably very much rewritten) version of the *Memoirs of Martinus Scriblerus* (1741), makes plain. The real importance of the club, however, is that it fostered a satiric temper which was to find unexpected expression in such mature works of the friends as *Gulliver's Travels*, the *Dunciad*, and even, perhaps, the *Beggar's Opera*.

"The life of a wit is a warfare on earth," said Pope, generalizing from his own experience. His very success as a poet (and his astonishing precocity brought him success very early) made enemies among the less talented and consequently envious writers, who were to plague him in pamphlets, verse satires, and squibs in the journals throughout his entire literary career. He was to be attacked for his writings, his religion, and his physical deformity. Though he smarted under the jibes of his detractors, he was a fighter who struck back, always giving better than he got. The common notion that he was a malicious, treacherous, venomous man, motivated merely by personal vanity and malice, is the creation of his enemies, and can be accepted by no one who reads the vicious attacks on him published from 1711 to the end of his life. Usually he was not the aggressor, but he never forgot an insult or forgave an injury, and sooner or later he took his revenge—sometimes, it must be admitted, in rather unsavory ways. But he was loved and trusted by many of the most honorable, eminent, and gifted men of his time, and with only a few exceptions (aside from politicians), the objects of his satire are people who would be forgotten today had they not been so humiliatingly preserved to posterity.

Pope's literary warfare began in 1713, when he announced his intention of translating the *Iliad* and sought, with the support of his friends, subscribers to a de luxe edition of the work. Subscribers came in droves, but Pope had enemies as well. The Whig writers who surrounded Addison at Button's Coffee House did all they could through anonymous attacks to hinder the success of the venture, and even (with Addison's knowledge and perhaps encouragement) announced a rival translation by Thomas Tickell, one of Addison's Oxford friends. The eventual success of the first published installment of his *Iliad* in 1715 did not obliterate Pope's just resentment against Addison and his "little senate"; and this resentment found expression in the damaging portrait of Addison (under the name of Atticus), which, years after it was written, was included in Pope's *Epistle to Dr. Arbuthnot* (1735), lines 193–214. The not unjustified attacks on Pope's edition of Shakespeare (1725), especially those by the learned Shakespeare scholar Lewis Theobald (Pope always spelled and pronounced the name "Tibbald" in his satires), led to Theobald's appearance as king of the dunces in the *Dunciad* (1728). In this impressive poem Pope stigmatized his literary enemies as agents of all that he disliked and feared in the literary tendencies of his time—the vulgarization of taste and the arts consequent on the rapid growth of the reading public, the development of journalism, magazines, and other popular and cheap publications, which spread scandal, sensationalism, and political partisanship—in short the new commercial spirit of the nation, which was corrupting not only the arts, but, as Pope saw it, the national life itself.

In the 1730's Pope moved on to philosophical, ethical, and political subjects in the *Essay on Man*, the *Epistles to Several Persons*, and the *Imitations of Horace*. The reigns of George I and George II appeared to him, as to Swift and other Tories, a period of rapid moral, political, and cultural deterioration. The agents of decay seemed in one way or another related to the spread of moneyed (as opposed to landed) wealth, which accounted for the political corruption encouraged by Sir Robert Walpole and the court party, and the increasing influence in all aspects of the national life of a vulgar class of *nouveaux riches*. Pope assumed the role of the champion of traditional civilization: of right reason, humanistic learning, sound art, good taste, and public virtue. For him the supreme value was order —cosmic, political, social, aesthetic—which he saw (or believed he saw) threatened on all sides. It was fortunate that most of his enemies seem to have been designed by nature to illustrate various degrees of unreason, pedantry, bad art, vulgar taste, and, at best, indifferent morals. Personal malice edged his satire, but his art elevated his unhappy victims into symbols of Georgian barbarism.

The principal obstacle between the modern reader and Pope's satires is that they seem to require a vast amount of particular knowledge about a long-vanished age. This is not entirely the case. Although a certain amount of social and political history is helpful, the whole body of Pope's satire can be read and enjoyed without much biographical information. The satirist traditionally deals in generally prevalent evils and generally observable human types, and this is true of Pope, even when he named actual individuals. Usually in the late satires, as in the earlier *Rape*, he used fictional or type names, although he most often had an individual in mind —Sappho, Atossa, Atticus, Sporus; and when he named individuals (as he consistently did in the *Dunciad* and occasionally elsewhere), his purpose was to raise his victims to the bad eminence of typifying some sort of obliquity. Nor need we be concerned with whether or not the moral character of the speaker of the satires is identical with that of Alexander Pope of Twickenham. Pope created a clearly defined person (the "I" of the satires) with the character and personality of one who could freely censure the age. This fictional or semi-fictional figure is the detached observer, somewhat removed from City, town, and court, the centers of corruption; he is the friend of virtuous men, whose friendship for him testifies to his integrity; he is fond of peace, country life, the arts, morality, and truth, and he detests their opposites which flourish in the great world. In such an age, Pope implies, it is impossible for such a man—honest, truthful, blunt—not to write satire. Where even political power and law are subject to the corruptor wealth, no weapon remains to the guardian of the public weal but the "sacred weapon" of satire. This is the satirist whom Pope creates, and to move from him to the private character of Pope is to move away from the poems.

Something must be said about Pope's versification, and the varied styles of his poems. It takes only a little familiarity with his writings to discover how wrong has been the conventional judgment that they are artificial, mechanical, and monotonous. From first to last, the permanent elements of Pope's poetic style are his remarkable rhythmic variety, despite the apparently rigid metrical unit—the heroic couplet—in which he wrote; the precision of meaning and the harmony (or the expressive disharmony, when necessary) of his language; and his superb discipline, which enables him at his characteristic best to achieve maximum conciseness together with maximum complexity. Something of Pope's metrical variety and verbal harmony can be observed in even so short a passage as lines 71–76 of the pastoral *Summer* (1709), lines so lyrical that Handel set them to music. In the passage quoted below (as also in the following quotation), only those rhetorical stresses which distort the normal iambic flow of the verse have been marked; internal pauses within the line are indicated by single and double bars, alliteration and assonance by italics.

> Óh déign to visit our *forsaken seats,*
> The mossy *fountains* || and the *green retreats!*
> Where'er you wálk || cóol gáles shall *fan* the *glade,*
> Tréés where you sít || shall crowd into a shade:
> Where'er you tréad || the blushing *flowers* shall rise,
> And all things *flourish* where you túrn your eyes.

Pope has attained metrical variety here by the free substitution of trochees and spondees for the normal iambs; he has achieved rhythmic variety by arranging phrases and clauses (units of syntax and logic) of different lengths within single lines and couplets, so that the passage moves with the sinuous fluency of thought and feeling, not the mechanical regularity of a metronome; and he has not only chosen musical combinations of words, but has also subtly modulated the harmony of the passage by unobtrusive patterns of alliteration and assonance.

Contrast with this pastoral passage lines 16–25 of the *Epilogue to the Satires, Dialogue II* (1738), in which Pope is not making music, but is imitating actual conversation so realistically that the metrical pattern and the integrity of the couplet and individual line seem to be destroyed (though in fact they are very much present). The poet-satirist is engaged in a dialogue with a friend who warns him that his satire is too personal, indeed mere libel. The poet is speaking:

> Yé státesmen, | priests of one religion all!
> Yé trádesmen vile || in army, court, or hall!
> Yé réverend atheists. || F. Scandal! | name them, | Who?
>   P. Why that's the thing you bid me not to do.
> Who stárved a sister, || who foreswore a debt,
> Í never named; || the town's inquiring yet.
> The poisoning dame— | F. Yóu méan— | P. I don't— | F. Yóu dó.
>   P. Sée, nów I kéep the secret, || and nót yóu!
> The bribing statesman— | F. Hóld, || tóo high you go.
>   P. The bribed electŏr— || F. There you stoop tóo lów.

In such a passage the language and rhythms of poetry merge with the language and rhythms of impassioned living speech.

A fine example of Pope's ability to derive the maximum of meaning from the most economic use of language and image is the description of the manor house in which lives old Cotta, the miser (*Epistle to Lord Bathurst*, lines 187–196):

> Like some lone Chartreuse stands the good old Hall,
> Silence without, and fasts within the wall;
> No raftered roofs with dance and tabor sound,
> No noontide bell invites the country round;
> Tenants with sighs the smokeless towers survey,
> And turn the unwilling steeds another way;
> Benighted wanderers, the forest o'er,
> Curse the saved candle and unopening door;
> While the gaunt mastiff growling at the gate,
> Affrights the beggar whom he longs to eat.

The first couplet of this passage, which associates the "Hall," symbol of English rural hospitality, with the Grande Chartreuse, the monastery in the French Alps, which, though a place of "silence" and "fasts" for the monks, afforded food and shelter to all travelers, clashes forcefully with the dismal details of Cotta's miserly dwelling; and the meaning of the scene is concentrated in the grotesque image of the last couplet: the half-starved watchdog and the frightened beggar confronting each other in mutual hunger.

But there is another sort of variety within Pope's work as a whole which derives from the poet's respect for the idea that the different kinds of literature have their different and appropriate styles. Thus the *Essay on Criticism*, an informal discussion of literary theory, is written, like Horace's *Ars Poetica*, a similarly didactic poem, in a plain style, relatively devoid of imagery and eloquence, and in the easy language of well-bred talk. *The Rape of the Lock*, being "a heroi-comical poem" (that is, a comic poem that treats trivial material in an epic style), employs the lofty heroic language that Dryden had perfected in his translation of Virgil, and introduces amusing parodies of passages in *Paradise Lost*; parodies raised to truly Miltonic sublimity and complexity by the conclusion of the *Dunciad*. *Eloisa to Abelard* renders the brooding, passionate voice of its heroine in a declamatory language, given to sudden outbursts and shifts of tone, that recalls the stage. The grave epistles that make up the *Essay on Man*, a philosophical discussion of such majestic themes as the Creator and his creation, the universe, and the nature of man, of human society, and of happiness, are written in a stately forensic language and tone and constantly employ the traditional rhetoric figures. The *Imitations of Horace*, and, above all, the *Epistle to Dr. Arbuthnot*, his finest poem "in the Horatian way," reveal Pope's final mastery of the plain style of Horace's epistles and satires and justify his image of himself as the heir of the Roman poet. In short no other poet of the century can equal Pope in the range of his materials, the diversity of his poetic styles, and the sheer mastery of the poet's craft.

From An Essay on Criticism[1]

Part I

'Tis hard to say, if greater want of skill
Appear in writing or in judging ill;
But of the two less dangerous is the offense
To tire our patience than mislead our sense.
Some few in that, but numbers err in this,
Ten censure[1a] wrong for one who writes amiss;   5

1. There is no pleasanter introduction to the canons of taste in the English Augustan age than Pope's *Essay on Criticism*. As Addison said in his review in *Spectator* 253, it assembles the "most known and most received observations on the subject of literature and criticism." Pope was attempting to do for his time what Horace, in his *Ars Poetica*, and what Nicolas Boileau (French poet of the age of Louis XIV), in his *L'Art Poëtique*, had done for theirs. Horace is not only one of Pope's instructors in the principles of criticism; he is also Pope's model in this poem, especially in the simple, conversational language, the tone of well-bred ease, and the deliberately plain style of the *Ars Poetica*—all of which qualities Pope reproduces.

In framing his critical creed, Pope did not try for novelty: he drew from the standard writings of classical antiquity, especially from the *Ars Poetica*, and the *Institutio Oratoria* of the Roman rhetorician Quintilian; from French critical theory of the preceding century; and from Ben Jonson's *Timber, or Discoveries* and the prefaces of John Dryden. He wished merely to give to generally accepted doctrines pleasing and memorable expression. Here one meets the key words of neoclassical criticism: *wit*, *Nature*, *ancients*, *rules*, *genius*. *Wit* in the poem is a word of many meanings—a clever remark, or the man who makes it; a conceit; liveliness of mind; inventiveness; fancy; genius; a genius; poetry itself, among

others. *Nature* is an equally ambiguous word, meaning not "things out there," or "the outdoors," but most importantly that which is representative, universal, permanent in human experience as opposed to the idiosyncratic, the individual, the temporary. In line 21, the word comes close to meaning "intuitive knowledge." In line 52, it means that half-personified power manifested in the cosmic order, which in its modes of working is a model for art. The reverence felt by most Augustans for the works of the great writers of ancient Greece and Rome raised the question how far the authority of these *ancients* extended. Were their works to be received as models to be conscientiously imitated? Were the *rules* received from them or deducible from their works to be accepted as prescriptive laws or merely convenient guides? Was individual *genius* to be bound by what has been conventionally held to be *Nature*, by the authority of the *ancients*, and by the legalistic pedantry of *rules*? Or could it go its own way?

In Part I of the *Essay* Pope constructs a harmonious system in which he effects a compromise among all these conflicting forces—a compromise which is typically 18th century in spirit. Part II analyzes the causes of faulty criticism. Part III (not printed here) characterizes the good critic and praises the great critics of the past.
1a. Judge.

A fool might once himself alone expose,
Now one in verse makes many more in prose.
    'Tis with our judgments as our watches, none
Go just alike, yet each believes his own.   10
In poets as true genius is but rare,
True taste as seldom is the critic's share;
Both must alike from Heaven derive their light,
These born to judge, as well as those to write.
Let such teach others who themselves excel,   15
And censure freely who have written well.
Authors are partial to their wit, 'tis true,
But are not critics to their judgment too?
    Yet if we look more closely, we shall find
Most have the seeds of judgment in their mind: 20
Nature affords at least a glimmering light;
The lines, though touched but faintly, are drawn right.
But as the slightest sketch, if justly traced,   ⎤
Is by ill coloring but the more disgraced,   ⎬
So by false learning is good sense defaced: ⎦   25
Some are bewildered in the maze of schools,
And some made coxcombs[2] Nature meant but fools.
In search of wit these lose their common sense,
And then turn critics in their own defense:
Each burns alike, who can, or cannot write,   30
Or with a rival's or an eunuch's spite.
All fools have still an itching to deride,
And fain would be upon the laughing side.
If Maevius[3] scribble in Apollo's spite,
There are who judge still worse than he can write.   35
    Some have at first for wits, then poets passed,
Turned critics next, and proved plain fools at last.
Some neither can for wits nor critics pass,
As heavy mules are neither horse nor ass.
Those half-learn'd witlings, numerous in our isle,   40
As half-formed insects on the banks of Nile;[4]
Unfinished things, one knows not what to call,
Their generation's so equivocal:
To tell[5] them would a hundred tongues require,
Or one vain wit's, that might a hundred tire.   45
    But you who seek to give and merit fame,
And justly bear a critic's noble name,
Be sure yourself and your own reach to know,
How far your genius, taste, and learning go;
Launch not beyond your depth, but be discreet,   50
And mark that point where sense and dullness meet.
    Nature to all things fixed the limits fit,
And wisely curbed proud man's pretending wit.
As on the land while here the ocean gains,

---

2. Superficial pretenders to learning.
3. A silly poet alluded to contemptuously by Virgil in *Eclogue III* and by
Horace in *Epode X*.
4. The ancients believed that many
forms of life were spontaneously generated in the fertile mud of the Nile.
5. Reckon, count.

In other parts it leaves wide sandy plains; 55
Thus in the soul while memory prevails,
The solid power of understanding fails;
Where beams of warm imagination play,
The memory's soft figures melt away.
One science[6] only will one genius fit, 60
So vast is art, so narrow human wit.
Not only bounded to peculiar arts,
But oft in those confined to single parts.
Like kings we lose the conquests gained before,
By vain ambition still to make them more; 65
Each might his several province well command,
Would all but stoop to what they understand.
    First follow Nature, and your judgment frame
By her just standard, which is still the same;
Unerring Nature, still divinely bright, 70
One clear, unchanged, and universal light,
Life, force, and beauty must to all impart,
At once the source, and end, and test of art.
Art from that fund each just supply provides,
Works without show, and without pomp presides. 75
In some fair body thus the informing soul
With spirits feeds, with vigor fills the whole,
Each motion guides, and every nerve sustains;
Itself unseen, but in the effects remains.
Some, to whom Heaven in wit has been profuse, 80
Want as much more to turn it to its use;
For wit and judgment often are at strife,
Though meant each other's aid, like man and wife.
'Tis more to guide than spur the Muse's steed,
Restrain his fury than provoke his speed; 85
The wingéd courser,[7] like a generous horse,
Shows most true mettle when you check his course.
    Those rules of old discovered, not devised,
Are Nature still, but Nature methodized;
Nature, like liberty, is but restrained 90
By the same laws which first herself ordained.
    Hear how learn'd Greece her useful rules indites,
When to repress and when indulge our flights:
High on Parnassus' top her sons she showed,
And pointed out those arduous paths they trod; 95
Held from afar, aloft, the immortal prize,
And urged the rest by equal steps to rise.
Just precepts thus from great examples given,
She drew from them what they derived from Heaven.
The generous critic fanned the poet's fire, 100
And taught the world with reason to admire.
Then criticism the Muse's handmaid proved,

---

6. Branch of learning.
7. Pegasus, associated with the Muses and poetic inspiration; "generous": spirited, highly bred.

To dress her charms, and make her more beloved:
But following wits from that intention strayed,
Who could not win the mistress, wooed the maid;   105
Against the poets their own arms they turned,
Sure to hate most the men from whom they learned.
So modern 'pothecaries, taught the art
By doctors' bills[8] to play the doctor's part,
Bold in the practice of mistaken rules,   110
Prescribe, apply, and call their masters fools.
Some on the leaves of ancient authors prey,
Nor time nor moths e'er spoiled so much as they.
Some dryly plain, without invention's aid,
Write dull receipts[9] how poems may be made.   115
These leave the sense their learning to display,
And those explain the meaning quite away.
        You then whose judgment the right course would steer,
Know well each ancient's proper character;
His fable,[1] subject, scope in every page;   120
Religion, country, genius of his age:
Without all these at once before your eyes,
Cavil you may, but never criticize.
Be Homer's works your study and delight,
Read them by day, and meditate by night;   125
Thence form your judgment, thence your maxims bring,
And trace the Muses upward to their spring.
Still with itself compared, his text peruse;
And let your comment be the Mantuan Muse.[2]
        When first young Maro in his boundless mind   130
A work to outlast immortal Rome designed,
Perhaps he seemed above the critic's law,
And but from Nature's fountains scorned to draw;
But when to examine every part he came,
Nature and Homer were, he found, the same.   135
Convinced, amazed, he checks the bold design, ⎫
And rules as strict his labored work confine   ⎬
As if the Stagirite[3] o'erlooked each line.   ⎭
Learn hence for ancient rules a just esteem;
To copy Nature is to copy them.   140
        Some beauties yet no precepts can declare,
For there's a happiness as well as care.[4]

---

8. Prescriptions.
9. Formulas for preparing a dish; recipes. Pope himself wrote an amusing burlesque *Receipt to Make an Epic Poem*, first published in the *Guardian* 78 (1713).
1. Plot or story of a play or poem.
2. Virgil, the "young Maro" of the following line, was born in a village adjacent to Mantua in Italy; hence "Mantuan Muse." His epic, the *Aeneid*, was modeled on Homer's *Iliad* and *Odyssey* and was considered to be a refinement on the Greek poems. Thus it could be thought of as a commentary ("comment") on Homer's poems.
3. Aristotle, native of Stagira, from whose *Poetics* later critics formulated strict rules for writing tragedy and the epic.
4. I.e., no rules ("precepts") can explain ("declare") some beautiful effects in a work of art which can be the result only of inspiration or good luck ("happiness"), not of painstaking labor ("care").

Music resembles poetry, in each ⎫
Are nameless graces which no methods teach, ⎬
And which a master hand alone can reach. ⎭ 145
If, where the rules not far enough extend
(Since rules were made but to promote their end)
Some lucky license answer to the full
The intent proposed, that license is a rule.
Thus Pegasus, a nearer way to take, 150
May boldly deviate from the common track.
From vulgar bounds with brave disorder part,
And snatch a grace beyond the reach of art,
Which without passing through the judgment, gains
The heart, and all its end at once attains. 155
In prospects thus, some objects please our eyes, ⎫
Which out of Nature's common order rise, ⎬
The shapeless rock, or hanging precipice. ⎭
Great wits sometimes may gloriously offend,
And rise to faults true critics dare not mend; 160
But though the ancients thus their rules invade
(As kings dispense with laws themselves have made)
Moderns, beware! or if you must offend
Against the precept, ne'er transgress its end;
Let it be seldom, and compelled by need; 165
And have at least their precedent to plead.
The critic else proceeds without remorse,
Seizes your fame, and puts his laws in force.
    I know there are, to whose presumptuous thoughts
Those freer beauties, even in them, seem faults.[5] 170
Some figures monstrous and misshaped appear,
Considered singly, or beheld too near,
Which, but proportioned to their light or place,
Due distance reconciles to form and grace.
A prudent chief not always must display 175
His powers in equal ranks and fair array,
But with the occasion and the place comply,
Conceal his force, nay seem sometimes to fly.
Those oft are stratagems which errors seem,
Nor is it Homer nods, but we that dream. 180
    Still green with bays each ancient altar stands
Above the reach of sacrilegious hands,
Secure from flames, from envy's fiercer rage,
Destructive war, and all-involving age.
See, from each clime the learn'd their incense bring! 185
Here in all tongues consenting[6] paeans ring!
In praise so just let every voice be joined,[7]
And fill the general chorus of mankind.
Hail, bards triumphant! born in happier days,
Immortal heirs of universal praise! 190

5. Pronounced *fawts*.   7. Pronounced *jined*.
6. Agreeing, concurring.

Whose honors with increase of ages grow,
As streams roll down, enlarging as they flow;
Nations unborn your mighty names shall sound,
And worlds applaud that must not yet be found!
Oh, may some spark of your celestial fire,   195
The last, the meanest of your sons inspire
(That on weak wings, from far, pursues your flights,
Glows while he reads, but trembles as he writes)
To teach vain wits a science little known,
To admire superior sense, and doubt their own!   200

Part II

Of all the causes which conspire to blind
Man's erring judgment, and misguide the mind,
What the weak head with strongest bias rules,
Is pride, the never-failing vice of fools.
Whatever Nature has in worth denied,   205
She gives in large recruits[8] of needful pride;
For as in bodies, thus in souls, we find
What wants in blood and spirits swelled with wind:
Pride, where wit fails, steps in to our defense,
And fills up all the mighty void of sense.   210
If once right reason drives that cloud away,
Truth breaks upon us with resistless day.
Trust not yourself: but your defects to know,
Make use of every friend—and every foe.
A little learning is a dangerous thing;   215
Drink deep, or taste not the Pierian spring.[9]
There shallow draughts intoxicate the brain,
And drinking largely sobers us again.
Fired at first sight with what the Muse imparts,
In fearless youth we tempt[1] the heights of arts,   220
While from the bounded level of our mind
Short views we take, nor see the lengths behind;
But more advanced, behold with strange surprise
New distant scenes of endless science rise!
So pleased at first the towering Alps we try,   225
Mount o'er the vales, and seem to tread the sky,
The eternal snows appear already past,
And the first clouds and mountains seem the last;
But, those attained, we tremble to survey
The growing labors of the lengthened way,   230
The increasing prospect tires our wandering eyes,
Hills peep o'er hills, and Alps on Alps arise!
A perfect judge will read each work of wit
With the same spirit that its author writ:
Survey the whole, nor seek slight faults to find   235
Where Nature moves, and rapture warms the mind;

8. Supplies.   sacred to the Muses.
9. The spring in Pieria on Mt. Olympus,   1. Attempt.

Nor lose, for that malignant dull delight,
The generous pleasure to be charmed with wit.
But in such lays as neither ebb nor flow,
Correctly cold, and regularly low,   240
That, shunning faults, one quiet tenor keep,
We cannot blame indeed—but we may sleep.
In wit, as nature, what affects our hearts
Is not the exactness of peculiar parts;
'Tis not a lip, or eye, we beauty call,   245
But the joint force and full result of all.
Thus when we view some well-proportioned dome
(The world's just wonder, and even thine, O Rome![2]),
No single parts unequally surprise,
All comes united to the admiring eyes: 250
No monstrous height, or breadth, or length appear;
The whole at once is bold and regular.
    Whoever thinks a faultless piece to see,
Thinks what ne'er was, nor is, nor e'er shall be.
In every work regard the writer's end,   255
Since none can compass more than they intend;
And if the means be just, the conduct true,
Applause, in spite of trivial faults, is due.
As men of breeding, sometimes men of wit,
To avoid great errors must the less commit,   260
Neglect the rules each verbal critic lays,
For not to know some trifles is a praise.
Most critics, fond of some subservient art,
Still make the whole depend upon a part:
They talk of principles, but notions prize,   265
And all to one loved folly sacrifice.
    Once on a time La Mancha's knight,[3] they say,
A certain bard encountering on the way,
Discoursed in terms as just, with looks as sage,
As e'er could Dennis,[4] of the Grecian stage;   270
Concluding all were desperate sots and fools
Who durst depart from Aristotle's rules.
Our author, happy in a judge so nice,
Produced his play, and begged the knight's advice;
Made him observe the subject and the plot,   275
The manners, passions, unities; what not?
All which exact to rule were brought about,
Were but a combat in the lists left out.
"What! leave the combat out?" exclaims the knight.
"Yes, or we must renounce the Stagirite."   280
"Not so, by Heaven!" he answers in a rage,

2. The dome of St. Peter's, designed by Michelangelo.
3. Don Quixote. The story comes not from Cervantes' novel, but from a spurious sequel to it by Don Alonzo Fernandez de Avellaneda.
4. John Dennis (1657–1734), though one of the leading critics of the time. was frequently ridiculed by the wits for his irascibility and his rather solemn pomposity. Pope apparently did not know Dennis personally, but his jibe at him in Part III of this poem incurred the critic's lasting animosity.

"Knights, squires, and steeds must enter on the stage."
"So vast a throng the stage can ne'er contain."
"Then build a new, or act it in a plain."
    Thus critics of less judgment than caprice,   285
Curious,[5] not knowing, not exact, but nice,
Form short ideas, and offend in arts
(As most in manners), by a love to parts.
    Some to conceit[6] alone their taste confine,
And glittering thoughts struck out at every line;   290
Pleased with a work where nothing's just or fit,
One glaring chaos and wild heap of wit.
Poets, like painters, thus unskilled to trace
The naked nature and the living grace,
With gold and jewels cover every part,   295
And hide with ornaments their want of art.
    True wit is Nature to advantage dressed,
What oft was thought, but ne'er so well expressed;
Something whose truth convinced at sight we find,
That gives us back the image of our mind.   300
As shades more sweetly recommend the light,
So modest plainness sets off sprightly wit;
For works may have more wit than does them good,
As bodies perish through excess of blood.
    Others for language all their care express,   305
And value books, as women men, for dress.
Their praise is still—the style is excellent;
The sense they humbly take upon contént.[7]
Words are like leaves; and where they most abound,
Much fruit of sense beneath is rarely found.   310
False eloquence, like the prismatic glass,
Its gaudy colors spreads on every place;[8]
The face of Nature we no more survey,
All glares alike, without distinction gay.
But true expression, like the unchanging sun,   315
Clears and improves whate'er it shines upon;
It gilds all objects, but it alters none.
Expression is the dress of thought, and still
Appears more decent as more suitable.
A vile conceit in pompous words expressed   320
Is like a clown[9] in regal purple dressed:
For different styles with different subjects sort,
As several garbs with country, town, and court.
Some by old words to fame have made pretense,
Ancients in phrase, mere moderns in their sense.   325
Such labored nothings, in so strange a style,
Amaze the unlearn'd, and make the learned smile;

---

5. Laboriously careful. "Nice": minutely accurate, over refined.
6. Pointed wit, ingenuity and extravagance, or affectation in the use of figures, especially similes and metaphors.
7. Mere acquiescence.

8. A very up-to-date scientific reference. Newton's *Optics*, which treated of the prism and the spectrum, had been published in 1704, though his theories had been known earlier.
9. Rustic, boor.

Unlucky as Fungoso[1] in the play,
These sparks with awkward vanity display
What the fine gentleman wore yesterday; 330
And but so mimic ancient wits at best,
As apes our grandsires in their doublets dressed.
In words as fashions the same rule will hold,
Alike fantastic if too new or old:
Be not the first by whom the new are tried, 335
Nor yet the last to lay the old aside.
    But most by numbers[2] judge a poet's song,
And smooth or rough with them is right or wrong.
In the bright Muse though thousand charms conspire,
Her voice is all these tuneful fools admire, 340
Who haunt Parnassus but to please their ear,
Not mend their minds; as some to church repair,
Not for the doctrine, but the music there.
These equal syllables alone require,
Though oft the ear the open vowels tire,[3] 345
While expletives[4] their feeble aid do join,
And ten low words oft creep in one dull line:
While they ring round the same unvaried chimes,
With sure returns of still expected rhymes;
Where'er you find "the cooling western breeze," 350
In the next line, it "whispers through the trees";
If crystal streams "with pleasing murmurs creep,"
The reader's threatened (not in vain) with "sleep";
Then, at the last and only couplet fraught
With some unmeaning thing they call a thought, 355
A needless Alexandrine[5] ends the song
That, like a wounded snake, drags its slow length along.
Leave such to tune their own dull rhymes, and know
What's roundly smooth or languishingly slow;
And praise the easy vigor of a line 360
Where Denham's strength and Waller's sweetness join.[6]
True ease in writing comes from art, not chance,
As those move easiest who have learned to dance.
'Tis not enough no harshness gives offense,
The sound must seem an echo to the sense. 365
Soft is the strain when Zephyr gently blows,
And the smooth stream in smoother numbers flows;
But when loud surges lash the sounding shore,
The hoarse, rough verse should like the torrent roar.
When Ajax strives some rock's vast weight to throw, 370

1. A character in Ben Jonson's comedy *Every Man out of His Humor* (1599).
2. Versification.
3. In lines 345–57 Pope cleverly contrives to make his own metrics or diction illustrate the faults that he is exposing.
4. Words used merely to achieve the necessary number of feet in a line of verse.
5. A line of verse containing six iambic feet; it is illustrated in the next line.
6. Dryden, whom Pope echoes here, considered Sir John Denham (1615–69) and Edmund Waller (1606–87) to have been the principal shapers of the closed pentameter couplet. He had distinguished the "strength" of the one and the "sweetness" of the other.

The line too labors, and the words move slow;
Not so when swift Camilla scours the plain,
Flies o'er the unbending corn, and skims along the main.
Hear how Timotheus'[7] varied lays surprise,
And bid alternate passions fall and rise!   375
While at each change the son of Libyan Jove[8]
Now burns with glory, and then melts with love;
Now his fierce eyes with sparkling fury glow,
Now sighs steal out, and tears begin to flow:
Persians and Greeks like turns of nature[9] found   380
And the world's victor stood subdued by sound!
The power of music all our hearts allow,
And what Timotheus was is Dryden now.
    Avoid extremes; and shun the fault of such
Who still are pleased too little or too much.   385
At every trifle scorn to take offense:
That always shows great pride, or little sense.
Those heads, as stomachs, are not sure the best,
Which nauseate all, and nothing can digest.
Yet let not each gay turn thy rapture move;   390
For fools admire,[1] but men of sense approve:
As things seem large which we through mists descry,
Dullness is ever apt to magnify.
    Some foreign writers, some our own despise;
The ancients only, or the moderns prize.   395
Thus wit, like faith, by each man is applied
To one small sect, and all are damned beside.
Meanly they seek the blessing to confine,
And force that sun but on a part to shine,
Which not alone the southern wit sublimes,   400
But ripens spirits in cold northern climes;
Which from the first has shone on ages past,
Enlights the present, and shall warm the last;
Though each may feel increases and decays,
And see now clearer and now darker days.   405
Regard not then if wit be old or new,
But blame the false and value still the true.
    Some ne'er advance a judgment of their own,
But catch the spreading notion of the town;
They reason and conclude by precedent,   410
And own stale nonsense which they ne'er invent.
Some judge of authors' names, not works, and then
Nor praise nor blame the writings, but the men.
Of all this servile herd the worst is he
That in proud dullness joins with quality,   415
A constant critic at the great man's board,
To fetch and carry nonsense for my lord.

7. The musician in Dryden's *Alexander's Feast*. Pope retells the story of
that poem in the following lines.
8. Alexander the Great.

9. Alternations of feelings.
1. Wonder. "Approve": judge favorably
only after due deliberation.

What woeful stuff this madrigal would be
In some starved hackney sonneteer or me!
But let a lord once own the happy lines, 420
How the wit brightens! how the style refines!
Before his sacred name flies every fault,
And each exalted stanza teems with thought!
    The vulgar thus through imitation err;
As oft the learn'd by being singular; 425
So much they scorn the crowd, that if the throng
By chance go right, they purposely go wrong.
So schismatics[2] the plain believers quit,
And are but damned for having too much wit.
Some praise at morning what they blame at night, 430
But always think the last opinion right.
A Muse by these is like a mistress used,
This hour she's idolized, the next abused;
While their weak heads like towns unfortified,
'Twixt sense and nonsense daily change their side. 435
Ask them the cause; they're wiser still, they say;
And still tomorrow's wiser than today.
We think our fathers fools, so wise we grow;
Our wiser sons, no doubt, will think us so.
Once school divines[3] this zealous isle o'erspread; 440
Who knew most sentences was deepest read.
Faith, Gospel, all seemed made to be disputed,
And none had sense enough to be confuted.
Scotists and Thomists now in peace remain
Amidst their kindred cobwebs in Duck Lane.[4] 445
If faith itself has different dresses worn,
What wonder modes in wit should take their turn?
Oft, leaving what is natural and fit,
The current folly proves the ready wit;
And authors think their reputation safe, 450
Which lives as long as fools are pleased to laugh.
    Some valuing those of their own side or mind,
Still make themselves the measure of mankind:
Fondly[5] we think we honor merit then,
When we but praise ourselves in other men. 455
Parties in wit attend on those of state,
And public faction doubles private hate.
Pride, Malice, Folly against Dryden rose,
In various shapes of parsons, critics, beaux;
But sense survived, when merry jests were past; 460
For rising merit will buoy up at last.

2. Those who have divided the church on points of theology. Pope stressed the first syllable, the pronunciation approved by Johnson in his *Dictionary*.
3. The medieval theologians, such as the followers of Duns Scotus and St. Thomas Aquinas mentioned in line 444;

"sentences" alludes to Peter Lombard's *Book of Sentences*, a book esteemed by Scholastic philosophers.
4. Street where publishers' remainders and second-hand books were sold.
5. Foolishly.

Might he return and bless once more our eyes,
New Blackmores and new Milbourns must arise.[6]
Nay, should great Homer lift his awful head,
Zoilus[7] again would start up from the dead.   465
Envy will merit, as its shade, pursue,
But like a shadow, proves the substance true;
For envied wit, like Sol eclipsed, makes known
The opposing body's grossness, not its own.
When first that sun too powerful beams displays,   470
It draws up vapors which obscure its rays,
But even those clouds at last adorn its way,
Reflect new glories, and augment the day.
    Be thou the first true merit to befriend;
His praise is lost who stays till all commend.   475
Short is the date, alas! of modern rhymes,
And 'tis but just to let them live betimes.
No longer now that golden age appears,
When patriarch wits survived a thousand years:
Now length of fame (our second life) is lost,   480
And bare threescore is all even that can boast;
Our sons their fathers' failing language see,
And such as Chaucer is shall Dryden be.[8]
So when the faithful pencil has designed
Some bright idea of the master's mind,   485
Where a new world leaps out at his command,
And ready Nature waits upon his hand;
When the ripe colors soften and unite,
And sweetly melt into just shade and light;
When mellowing years their full perfection give,   490
And each bold figure just begins to live,
The treacherous colors the fair art betray,
And all the bright creation fades away!
    Unhappy wit, like most mistaken things,
Atones not for that envy which it brings.   495
In youth alone its empty praise we boast,
But soon the short-lived vanity is lost;
Like some fair flower the early spring supplies,
That gaily blooms, but even in blooming dies,
What is this wit, which must our cares employ?   500
The owner's wife, that other men enjoy;
Then most our trouble still when most admired,
And still the more we give, the more required;
Whose fame with pains we guard, but lose with ease,
Sure some to vex, but never all to please;   505

---

6. Sir Richard Blackmore, physician and poet, had attacked Dryden for the immorality of his plays; the Rev. Luke Milbourn had attacked his translation of Virgil.
7. A Greek critic of the 4th century B.C., who wrote a book of carping criticism of Homer.

8. The radical changes that took place in the English language between the death of Chaucer in 1400 and the death of Dryden in 1700 suggested that in another 300 years Dryden would be unintelligible. Latin seemed the only means of attaining enduring fame.

'Tis what the vicious fear, the virtuous shun,
By fools 'tis hated, and by knaves undone!
　If wit so much from ignorance undergo,
Ah, let not learning too commence its foe!
Of old those met rewards who could excel, 510
And such were praised who but endeavored well;
Though triumphs were to generals only due,
Crowns were reserved to grace the soldiers too.
Now they who reach Parnassus' lofty crown
Employ their pains to spurn some others down; 515
And while self-love each jealous writer rules,
Contending wits become the sport of fools;
But still the worst with most regret commend,
For each ill author is as bad a friend.
To what base ends, and by what abject ways, 520
Are morals urged through sacred[9] lust of praise!
Ah, ne'er so dire a thirst of glory boast,
Nor in the critic let the man be lost!
Good nature and good sense must ever join;
To err is human, to forgive divine. 525
　But if in noble minds some dregs remain
Nor yet purged off, of spleen and sour disdain,
Discharge that rage on more provoking crimes,
Nor fear a dearth in these flagitious[1] times.
No pardon vile obscenity should find, 530
Though wit and art conspire to move your mind;
But dullness with obscenity must prove
As shameful sure as impotence in love.
In the fat age of pleasure, wealth, and ease
Sprung the rank weed, and thrived with large increase: 535
When love was all an easy monarch's[2] care,
Seldom at council, never in a war;
Jilts ruled the state, and statesmen farces writ;
Nay, wits had pensions, and young lords had wit;
The fair sat panting at a courtier's play, 540
And not a mask[3] went unimproved away;
The modest fan was lifted up no more,
And virgins smiled at what they blushed before.
The following license of a foreign reign
Did all the dregs of bold Socinus drain;[4] 545
Then unbelieving priests reformed the nation,
And taught more pleasant methods of salvation;
Where Heaven's free subjects might their rights dispute,
Lest God himself should seem too absolute;
Pulpits their sacred satire learned to spare, 550

9. Accursed. The phrase imitates Virgil's *"auri sacra fames,"* "accursed hunger for gold" (*Aeneid* III.57).
1. Scandalously wicked.
2. Charles II. The concluding lines of Part II discuss the corruption of wit and poetry under this monarch.

3. A woman wearing a mask.
4. The "foreign reign" refers to William III, a Dutchman. Socinus was the name of two Italian theologians of the 16th century who denied the divinity of Jesus.

And Vice admired to find a flatterer there!
Encouraged thus, wit's Titans braved the skies,
And the press groaned with licensed blasphemies.
These monsters, critics! with your darts engage,
Here point your thunder, and exhaust your rage!
Yet shun their fault, who, scandalously nice,
Will needs mistake an author into vice;
All seems infected that the infected spy,
As all looks yellow to the jaundiced eye.

1709   1711

The Rape of the Lock[1]

AN HEROI-COMICAL POEM

Nolueram, Belinda, tuos violare capillos;
sed juvat hoc precibus me tribuisse tuis.
—MARTIAL

TO MRS. ARABELLA FERMOR

MADAM,

It will be in vain to deny that I have some regard for this piece,
since I dedicate it to you. Yet you may bear me witness, it was intended only to divert a few young ladies, who have good sense and

1. *The Rape of the Lock* is based upon
an actual episode that provoked a
quarrel between two prominent Catholic
families. Pope's friend John Caryll, to
whom the poem is addressed (line 3),
suggested that Pope write it, in the
hope that a little laughter might serve
to soothe ruffled tempers. Lord Petre had
cut off a lock of hair from the head of
the lovely Arabella Fermor (often
spelled "Farmer" and doubtless so pronounced), much to the indignation of
the lady and her relatives. In its
original version of two cantos and 334
lines, published in 1712, *The Rape of
the Lock* was a great success. In 1713
a new version was undertaken against
the advice of Addison, who considered
the poem perfect as it was first written.
Pope greatly expanded the earlier version, adding the delightful "machinery"
(i.e., the supernatural agents in epic
action) of the Sylphs, Belinda's toilet,
the card game, and the visit to the Cave
of Spleen in Canto IV. In 1717, with
the addition of Clarissa's speech on
good humor, the poem assumed its final
form.

With supreme tact, delicate fancy,
playful wit, and the gentlest satire, Pope
elaborated the trivial episode which occasioned the poem into the semblance of
an epic in miniature, the most nearly
perfect "heroi-comical poem" in English. The poem abounds in parodies
and echoes of the *Iliad*, the *Aeneid*, and
Paradise Lost, thus constantly forcing
the reader to compare small things with
great. The familiar devices of epic are
observed, but the incidents or characters are beautifully proportioned to
the scale of mock epic. The *Rape* tells

of war, but it is the drawing-room war
between the sexes; it has its heroes and
heroines, but they are beaux and belles;
it has its supernatural characters
("machinery") but they are Sylphs
(borrowed, as Pope tells us in his engaging dedicatory letter, from Rosicrucian lore)—creatures of the air, the
souls of dead coquettes, with tasks appropriate to their nature—or the Gnome
Umbriel, once a prude on earth; it has
its epic game, played on the "velvet
plain" of the card table, its feasting
heroes, who sip coffee and gossip, its
battle, fought with the clichés of compliment and conceits, with frowns and
angry glances, with snuff and a bodkin;
it has the traditional epic journey to
the underworld—here the Cave of Spleen,
emblematic of the peevish ill nature
of spoiled and hypochondriacal women.
And Pope creates a world in which these
actions take place, a world that is
dense with beautiful objects: brocades,
ivory and tortoise shell, cosmetics and
diamonds, lacquered furniture, silver
teapot, delicate chinaware. It is a world
that is constantly in motion and that
sparkles and glitters with light, whether
the light of the sun, or of Belinda's eyes,
or that light into which the "fluid"
bodies of the Sylphs seem to dissolve as
they flutter in the shrouds and around
the mast of Belinda's ship. Though Pope
laughs at this world and its creatures—
and remembers that a grimmer, darker
world surrounds it (III.19–24 and V.
145–48)—he makes us very much aware
of its beauty and its charm.

The epigraph may be translated, "I
was unwilling, Belinda, to ravish your
locks; but I rejoice to have conceded

good humor enough to laugh not only at their sex's little unguarded follies, but at their own. But it was communicated with the air of a secret, it soon found its way into the world. An imperfect copy having been offered to a bookseller, you had the good nature for my sake to consent to the publication of one more correct; this I was forced to, before I had executed half my design, for the machinery was entirely wanting to complete it.

The machinery, Madam, is a term invented by the critics, to signify that part which the deities, angels, or demons are made to act in a poem; for the ancient poets are in one respect like many modern ladies: let an action be never so trivial in itself, they always make it appear of the utmost importance. These machines I determined to raise on a very new and odd foundation, the Rosicrucian [1a] doctrine of spirits.

I know how disagreeable it is to make use of hard words before a lady; but 'tis so much the concern of a poet to have his works understood, and particularly by your sex, that you must give me leave to explain two or three difficult terms.

The Rosicrucians are a people I must bring you acquainted with. The best account I know of them is in a French book called *Le Comte de Gabalis*,[1b] which both in its title and size is so like a novel, that many of the fair sex have read it for one by mistake. According to these gentlemen, the four elements are inhabited by spirits, which they call Sylphs, Gnomes, Nymphs, and Salamanders. The Gnomes or Demons of earth delight in mischief; but the Sylphs, whose habitation is in the air, are the best-conditioned creatures imaginable. For they say, any mortals may enjoy the most intimate familiarities with these gentle spirits, upon a condition very easy to all true adepts, an inviolate preservation of chastity.

As to the following cantos, all the passages of them are as fabulous as the vision at the beginning, or the transformation at the end; (except the loss of your hair, which I always mention with reverence). The human persons are as fictitious as the airy ones; and the character of Belinda, as it is now managed, resembles you in nothing but in beauty.

If this poem had as many graces as there are in your person, or in your mind, yet I could never hope it should pass through the world half so uncensured as you have done. But let its fortune be what it will, mine is happy enough, to have given me this occasion of assuring you that I am, with the truest esteem,

MADAM,

Your most obedient, humble servant,

A. POPE

this to your prayers" (Martial, *Epigrams* XII.lxxxiv.1–2). Pope substituted his heroine for Martial's Polytimus. The epigraph is intended to suggest that the poem was published at Miss Fermor's request.

1a. A system of arcane philosophy introduced into England from Germany in the 17th century.
1b. By the Abbé de Montfaucon de Villars, published in 1670.

Canto I

What dire offense from amorous causes springs,
What mighty contests rise from trivial things,
I sing—This verse to Caryll, Muse! is due:
This, even Belinda may vouchsafe to view:
Slight is the subject, but not so the praise,   5
If she inspire, and he approve my lays.
    Say what strange motive, Goddess! could compel
A well-bred lord to assault a gentle belle?
Oh, say what stranger cause, yet unexplored,
Could make a gentle belle reject a lord?   10
In tasks so bold can little men engage,
And in soft bosoms dwells such mighty rage?
    Sol through white curtains shot a timorous ray,
And oped those eyes that must eclipse the day.
Now lapdogs give themselves the rousing shake,   15
And sleepless lovers just at twelve awake:
Thrice rung the bell, the slipper knocked the ground,[2]
And the pressed watch returned a silver sound.
Belinda still her downy pillow pressed,
Her guardian Sylph prolonged the balmy rest: 20
'Twas he had summoned to her silent bed
The morning dream that hovered o'er her head.
A youth more glittering than a birthnight beau[3]
(That even in slumber caused her cheek to glow)
Seemed to her ear his winning lips to lay,   25
And thus in whispers said, or seemed to say:
    "Fairest of mortals, thou distinguished care
Of thousand bright inhabitants of air!
If e'er one vision touched thy infant thought,
Of all the nurse and all the priest have taught,   30
Of airy elves by moonlight shadows seen,
The silver token, and the circled green,[4]
Or virgins visited by angel powers,
With golden crowns and wreaths of heavenly flowers,
Hear and believe! thy own importance know,   35
Nor bound thy narrow views to things below.
Some secret truths, from learned pride concealed,
To maids alone and children are revealed:
What though no credit doubting wits may give?
The fair and innocent shall still believe.   40
Know, then, unnumbered spirits round thee fly,
The light militia of the lower sky:

---

2. Belinda thus summons her maid. A "pressed watch" chimes the hour and the quarter-hour when the stem is pressed down.
3. Courtiers wore especially fine clothes on the sovereign's birthday.
4. According to popular belief fairies skim off the cream from jugs of milk left standing overnight and leave a coin ("silver token") in payment. Rings of bright green grass, which are common in England even in winter, were held to be due to the round dances of fairies.

These, though unseen, are ever on the wing,
Hang o'er the box, and hover round the Ring.[5]
Think what an equipage thou hast in air,⁣   45
And view with scorn two pages and a chair.[6]
As now your own, our beings were of old,
And once enclosed in woman's beauteous mold;
Thence, by a soft transition, we repair
From earthly vehicles to these of air.   50
Think not, when woman's transient breath is fled,
That all her vanities at once are dead:
Succeeding vanities she still regards,
And though she plays no more, o'erlooks the cards.
Her joy in gilded chariots, when alive,   55
And love of ombre,[7] after death survive.
For when the Fair in all their pride expire,
To their first elements[8] their souls retire:
The sprites of fiery termagants in flame
Mount up, and take a Salamander's name.[9]   60
Soft yielding minds to water glide away,
And sip, with Nymphs, their elemental tea.[1]
The graver prude sinks downward to a Gnome,
In search of mischief still on earth to roam.
The light coquettes in Sylphs aloft repair,   65
And sport and flutter in the fields of air.
    "Know further yet; whoever fair and chaste
Rejects mankind, is by some Sylph embraced:
For spirits, freed from mortal laws, with ease
Assume what sexes and what shapes they please.[2]   70
What guards the purity of melting maids,
In courtly balls, and midnight masquerades,
Safe from the treacherous friend, the daring spark,
The glance by day, the whisper in the dark,
When kind occasion prompts their warm desires,   75
When music softens, and when dancing fires?
'Tis but their Sylph, the wise Celestials know,
Though Honor is the word with men below.
    "Some nymphs there are, too conscious of their face,
For life predestined to the Gnomes' embrace.   80
These swell their prospects and exalt their pride,
When offers are disdained, and love denied:
Then gay ideas[3] crowd the vacant brain,

5. The "box" in the theater and the fashionable circular drive ("Ring") in Hyde Park.
6. Sedan chair.
7. The popular card game. See III.27 ff. and note.
8. The four elements out of which all things were believed to have been made were fire, water, earth, and air. One or another of these elements was supposed to be predominant in both the physical and psychological make-up of each human being. In this context they are spoken of as "humors."
9. Pope borrowed his supernatural beings from Rosicrucian mythology. Each element was inhabited by a spirit, as the following lines explain. The salamander is a lizardlike animal, in antiquity believed to live in fire.
1. Pronounce *tay*.
2. Cf. *Paradise Lost* I.427–31; this is one of many allusions to that poem in the *Rape*.
3. Images.

While peers, and dukes, and all their sweeping train,
And garters, stars, and coronets appear,   85
And in soft sounds, 'your Grace' salutes their ear.
'Tis these that early taint the female soul,
Instruct the eyes of young coquettes to roll,
Teach infant cheeks a bidden blush to know,
And little hearts to flutter at a beau.   90
    "Oft, when the world imagine women stray,
The Sylphs through mystic mazes guide their way,
Through all the giddy circle they pursue,
And old impertinence expel by new.
What tender maid but must a victim fall   95
To one man's treat, but for another's ball?
When Florio speaks what virgin could withstand,
If gentle Damon did not squeeze her hand?
With varying vanities, from every part,
They shift the moving toyshop[4] of their heart;   100
Where wigs with wigs, with sword-knots sword-knots strive,
Beaux banish beaux, and coaches coaches drive.
This erring mortals levity may call;
Oh, blind to truth! the Sylphs contrive it all.
    "Of these am I, who thy protection claim,   105
A watchful sprite, and Ariel is my name.
Late, as I ranged the crystal wilds of air,
In the clear mirror of thy ruling star
I saw, alas! some dread event impend,
Ere to the main this morning sun descend,   110
But Heaven reveals not what, or how, or where:
Warned by the Sylph, O pious maid, beware!
This to disclose is all thy guardian can:
Beware of all, but most beware of Man!"
    He said; when Shock,[5] who thought she slept too long,   115
Leaped up, and waked his mistress with his tongue.
'Twas then, Belinda, if report say true,
Thy eyes first opened on a billet-doux;
Wounds, charms, and ardors were no sooner read,
But all the vision vanished from thy head.   120
    And now, unveiled, the toilet stands displayed,
Each silver vase in mystic order laid.
First, robed in white, the nymph intent adores,
With head uncovered, the cosmetic powers.
A heavenly image in the glass appears;   125
To that she bends, to that her eyes she rears.
The inferior priestess, at her altar's side,
Trembling begins the sacred rites of Pride.
Unnumbered treasures ope at once, and here
The various offerings of the world appear;   130
From each she nicely culls with curious toil,

4. A shop stocked with baubles and   5. Belinda's lapdog.
trifles.

And decks the goddess with the glittering spoil.
This casket India's glowing gems unlocks,
And all Arabia breathes from yonder box.
The tortoise here and elephant unite,   135
Transformed to combs, the speckled and the white.
Here files of pins extend their shining rows,
Puffs, powders, patches, Bibles,⁶ billet-doux.
Now awful Beauty puts on all its arms;
The fair each moment rises in her charms,   140
Repairs her smiles, awakens every grace,
And calls forth all the wonders of her face;
Sees by degrees a purer blush arise,
And keener lightnings quicken in her eyes.
The busy Sylphs surround their darling care,   145
These set the head, and those divide the hair,
Some fold the sleeve, whilst others plait the gown;
And Betty's⁷ praised for labors not her own.

Canto II

Not with more glories, in the ethereal plain,
The sun first rises o'er the purpled main,
Than, issuing forth, the rival of his beams
Launched on the bosom of the silver Thames.
Fair nymphs and well-dressed youths around her shone,   5
But every eye was fixed on her alone.
On her white breast a sparkling cross she wore,
Which Jews might kiss, and infidels adore.
Her lively looks a sprightly mind disclose,
Quick as her eyes, and as unfixed as those: 10
Favors to none, to all she smiles extends;
Oft she rejects, but never once offends.
Bright as the sun, her eyes the gazers strike,
And, like the sun, they shine on all alike.
Yet graceful ease, and sweetness void of pride,   15
Might hide her faults, if belles had faults to hide:
If to her share some female errors fall,
Look on her face, and you'll forget 'em all.
This nymph, to the destruction of mankind,
Nourished two locks which graceful hung behind   20
In equal curls, and well conspired to deck
With shining ringlets the smooth ivory neck.
Love in these labyrinths his slaves detains,
And mighty hearts are held in slender chains.
With hairy springes⁸ we the birds betray,   25
Slight lines of hair surprise the finny prey,
Fair tresses man's imperial race ensnare,
And beauty draws us with a single hair.
   The adventurous Baron the bright locks admired,

6. It has been suggested that Pope intended here not "Bibles," but "bibelots," (trinkets), but this interpetation has not gained wide acceptance.

7. Belinda's maid, the "inferior priestess" mentioned in line 127.

8. Snares; pronounced *sprín-jez.*

He saw, he wished, and to the prize aspired. 30
Resolved to win, he meditates the way,
By force to ravish, or by fraud betray;
For when success a lover's toil attends,
Few ask if fraud or force attained his ends.
 For this, ere Phoebus rose, he had implored 35
Propitious Heaven, and every power adored,
But chiefly Love—to Love an altar built,
Of twelve vast French romances, neatly gilt.
There lay three garters, half a pair of gloves,
And all the trophies of his former loves. 40
With tender billet-doux he lights the pyre,
And breathes three amorous sighs to raise the fire.
Then prostrate falls, and begs with ardent eyes
Soon to obtain, and long possess the prize:
The powers gave ear, and granted half his prayer, 45
The rest the winds dispersed in empty air.
 But now secure the painted vessel glides,
The sunbeams trembling on the floating tides,
While melting music steals upon the sky,
And softened sounds along the waters die. 50
Smooth flow the waves, the zephyrs gently play,
Belinda smiled, and all the world was gay.
All but the Sylph—with careful thoughts oppressed,
The impending woe sat heavy on his breast.
He summons straight his denizens of air; 55
The lucid squadrons round the sails repair:
Soft o'er the shrouds aërial whispers breathe
That seemed but zephyrs to the train beneath.
Some to the sun their insect-wings unfold,
Waft on the breeze, or sink in clouds of gold. 60
Transparent forms too fine for mortal sight,
Their fluid bodies half dissolved in light,
Loose to the wind their airy garments flew,
Thin glittering textures of the filmy dew,
Dipped in the richest tincture of the skies, 65
Where light disports in ever-mingling dyes,
While every beam new transient colors flings,
Colors that change whene'er they wave their wings.
Amid the circle, on the gilded mast,
Superior by the head was Ariel placed; 70
His purple[9] pinions opening to the sun,
He raised his azure wand, and thus begun:
 "Ye Sylphs and Sylphids, to your chief give ear!
Fays, Fairies, Genii, Elves, and Daemons, hear!
Ye know the spheres and various tasks assigned 75
By laws eternal to the aërial kind.
Some in the fields of purest ether play,

9. In 18th-century poetic diction the word might mean "blood-red," "purple," or simply (as is likely here) "brightly colored." The word derives from Virgil, *Eclogue* IX, 40, *purpureus*. An example of the Latinate nature of some poetic diction of the period.

And bask and whiten in the blaze of day.
Some guide the course of wandering orbs on high,
Or roll the planets through the boundless sky. 80
Some less refined, beneath the moon's pale light
Pursue the stars that shoot athwart the night,
Or suck the mists in grosser air below,
Or dip their pinions in the painted bow,
Or brew fierce tempests on the wintry main, 85
Or o'er the glebe[1] distill the kindly rain.
Others on earth o'er human race preside,
Watch all their ways, and all their actions guide:
Of these the chief the care of nations own,
And guard with arms divine the British Throne. 90
    "Our humbler province is to tend the Fair,
Not a less pleasing, though less glorious care:
To save the powder from too rude a gale,
Nor let the imprisoned essences exhale;
To draw fresh colors from the vernal flowers; 95
To steal from rainbows e'er they drop in showers
A brighter wash;[2] to curl their waving hairs,
Assist their blushes, and inspire their airs;
Nay oft, in dreams invention we bestow,
To change a flounce, or add a furbelow. 100
    "This day black omens threat the brightest fair,
That e'er deserved a watchful spirit's care;
Some dire disaster, or by force or slight,
But what, or where, the Fates have wrapped in night:
Whether the nymph shall break Diana's law,[3] 105
Or some frail china jar receive a flaw,
Or stain her honor or her new brocade,
Forget her prayers, or miss a masquerade,
Or lose her heart, or necklace, at a ball;
Or whether Heaven has doomed that Shock must fall. 110
Haste, then, ye spirits! to your charge repair:
The fluttering fan be Zephyretta's care;
The drops[4] to thee, Brillante, we consign;
And, Momentilla, let the watch be thine;
Do thou, Crispissa,[5] tend her favorite Lock; 115
Ariel himself shall be the guard of Shock.
    "To fifty chosen Sylphs, of special note,
We trust the important charge, the petticoat;
Oft have we known that sevenfold fence to fail,
Though stiff with hoops, and armed with ribs of whale. 120
Form a strong line about the silver bound,
And guard the wide circumference around.
    "Whatever spirit, careless of his charge,
His post neglects, or leaves the fair at large,
Shall feel sharp vengeance soon o'ertake his sins, 125

1. Cultiviated field.
2. Cosmetic lotion.
3. Diana was the goddess of chastity.
4. Diamond earrings. Observe the ap-
propriateness of the names of the Sylphs
to their assigned functions.
5. From Latin *crispere*, to curl.

Be stopped in vials, or transfixed with pins,
Or plunged in lakes of bitter washes lie,
Or wedged whole ages in a bodkin's eye;[6]
Gums and pomatums shall his flight restrain,
While clogged he beats his silken wings in vain,   130
Or alum styptics with contracting power
Shrink his thin essence like a riveled[7] flower:
Or, as Ixion[8] fixed, the wretch shall feel
The giddy motion of the whirling mill,
In fumes of burning chocolate shall glow,   135
And tremble at the sea that froths below!"
  He spoke; the spirits from the sails descend;
Some, orb in orb, around the nymph extend;
Some thread the mazy ringlets of her hair;
Some hang upon the pendants of her ear: 140
With beating hearts the dire event they wait,
Anxious, and trembling for the birth of Fate.

Canto III

  Close by those meads, forever crowned with flowers,
Where Thames with pride surveys his rising towers,
There stands a structure of majestic frame,
Which from the neighboring Hampton takes its name.[9]
Here Britain's statesmen oft the fall foredoom   5
Of foreign tyrants and of nymphs at home;
Here thou, great Anna! whom three realms obey,
Dost sometimes counsel take—and sometimes tea.
  Hither the heroes and the nymphs resort,
To taste awhile the pleasures of a court;   10
In various talk the instructive hours they passed,
Who gave the ball, or paid the visit last;
One speaks the glory of the British Queen,
And one describes a charming Indian screen;
A third interprets motions, looks, and eyes;   15
At every word a reputation dies.
Snuff, or the fan, supply each pause of chat,
With singing, laughing, ogling, and all that.
  Meanwhile, declining from the noon of day,
The sun obliquely shoots his burning ray;   20
The hungry judges soon the sentence sign,
And wretches hang that jurymen may dine;
The merchant from the Exchange returns in peace,
And the long labors of the toilet cease.
  Belinda now, whom thirst of fame invites,   25
Burns to encounter two adventurous knights,

6. A "bodkin" is a blunt needle with a large eye, used for drawing ribbon through eyelets in the edging of women's garments.
7. To "rivel" is to "contract into wrinkles and corrugations" (Johnson's *Dictionary*).
8. In the Greek myth Ixion was punished in the underworld by being bound on an everturning wheel.
9. Hampton Court, the royal palace, about fifteen miles up the Thames from London.

At ombre[1] singly to decide their doom,
And swells her breast with conquests yet to come.
Straight the three bands prepare in arms to join,
Each band the number of the sacred nine.   30
Soon as she spreads her hand, the aërial guard
Descend, and sit on each important card:
First Ariel perched upon a Matadore,
Then each according to the rank they bore;
For Sylphs, yet mindful of their ancient race,   35
Are, as when women, wondrous fond of place.
     Behold, four Kings in majesty revered,
With hoary whiskers and a forky beard;
And four fair Queens whose hands sustain a flower,
The expressive emblem of their softer power;   40
Four Knaves in garbs succinct,[2] a trusty band,
Caps on their heads, and halberts in their hand;
And parti-colored troops, a shining train,
Draw forth to combat on the velvet plain.
     The skillful nymph reviews her force with care;   45
"Let Spades be trumps!" she said, and trumps they were.
     Now move to war her sable Matadores,
In show like leaders of the swarthy Moors.
Spadillio first, unconquerable lord!
Led off two captive trumps, and swept the board.   50
As many more Manillio forced to yield,
And marched a victor from the verdant field.
Him Basto followed, but his fate more hard
Gained but one trump and one plebeian card.
With his broad saber next, a chief in years,   55
The hoary Majesty of Spades appears,
Puts forth one manly leg, to sight revealed,
The rest his many-colored robe concealed.
The rebel Knave, who dares his prince engage,
Proves the just victim of his royal rage.   60
Even mighty Pam,[3] that kings and queens o'erthrew
And mowed down armies in the fights of loo,
Sad chance of war! now destitute of aid,
Falls undistinguished by the victor Spade.
     Thus far both armies to Belinda yield;   65
Now to the Baron fate inclines the field.
His warlike amazon her host invades,

1. The game of ombre which Belinda plays against the Baron and another young man is too complicated for complete explication here. Pope has carefully arranged the cards so that Belinda wins. The Baron's hand is strong enough to be a threat, but the third player's is of little account. The hand is played exactly according to the rules of ombre, and Pope's description of the cards is equally accurate. Each player holds nine cards (line 30). The "Matadores" (line 33), when spades are trumps, are "Spadillio" (line 49), the ace of spades; "Manillio" (line 51), the two of spades; "Basto" (line 53), the ace of clubs; Belinda holds all three of these. (For a more complete description of ombre, see Appendix C, *The Rape of the Lock and Other Poems*, ed. Geoffrey Tillotson, in the Twickenham Edition of Pope's poems, Vol. II.)
2. Girded up.
3. The knave of clubs, the highest trump in the game of loo.

The imperial consort of the crown of Spades.
The Club's black tyrant first her victim died,
Spite of his haughty mien and barbarous pride. 70
What boots the regal circle on his head,
His giant limbs, in state unwieldy spread?
That long behind he trails his pompous robe,
And of all monarchs only grasps the globe?

    The Baron now his Diamonds pours apace; 75
The embroidered King who shows but half his face,
And his refulgent Queen, with powers combined
Of broken troops an easy conquest find.
Clubs, Diamonds, Hearts, in wild disorder seen,
With throngs promiscuous strew the level green. 80
Thus when dispersed a routed army runs,
Of Asia's troops, and Afric's sable sons,
With like confusion different nations fly,
Of various habit, and of various dye,
The pierced battalions disunited fall 85
In heaps on heaps; one fate o'erwhelms them all.

    The Knave of Diamonds tries his wily arts,
And wins (oh, shameful chance!) the Queen of Hearts.
At this, the blood the virgin's cheek forsook,
A livid paleness spreads o'er all her look; 90
She sees, and trembles at the approaching ill,
Just in the jaws of ruin, and Codille,[4]
And now (as oft in some distempered state)
On one nice trick depends the general fate.
An Ace of Hearts steps forth: the King unseen 95
Lurked in her hand, and mourned his captive Queen.
He springs to vengeance with an eager pace,
And falls like thunder on the prostrate Ace.
The nymph exulting fills with shouts the sky,
The walls, the woods, and long canals reply. 100

    O thoughtless mortals! ever blind to fate,
Too soon dejected, and too soon elate:
Sudden these honors shall be snatched away,
And cursed forever this victorious day.

    For lo! the board with cups and spoons is crowned, 105
The berries crackle, and the mill turns round;[5]
On shining altars of Japan[6] they raise
The silver lamp; the fiery spirits blaze:
From silver spouts the grateful liquors glide,
While China's earth receives the smoking tide. 110
At once they gratify their scent and taste,
And frequent cups prolong the rich repast.
Straight hover round the fair her airy band;
Some, as she sipped, the fuming liquor fanned,

---

4. The term applied to losing a hand
at cards.
5. I.e., coffee is roasted and ground.
6. I.e., small, lacquered tables. The word
"altars" suggests the ritualistic character of coffee-drinking in Belinda's
world.

Some o'er her lap their careful plumes displayed,   115
Trembling, and conscious of the rich brocade.
Coffee (which makes the politician wise,
And see through all things with his half-shut eyes)
Sent up in vapors to the Baron's brain
New stratagems, the radiant Lock to gain.   120
Ah, cease, rash youth! desist ere 'tis too late,
Fear the just Gods, and think of Scylla's fate![7]
Changed to a bird, and sent to flit in air,
She dearly pays for Nisus' injured hair!
     But when to mischief mortals bend their will,   125
How soon they find fit instruments of ill!
Just then, Clarissa drew with tempting grace
A two-edged weapon from her shining case:
So ladies in romance assist their knight,
Present the spear, and arm him for the fight.   130
He takes the gift with reverence, and extends
The little engine on his fingers' ends;
This just behind Belinda's neck he spread,
As o'er the fragrant steams she bends her head.
Swift to the Lock a thousand sprites repair,   135
A thousand wings, by turns, blow back the hair,
And thrice they twitched the diamond in her ear,
Thrice she looked back, and thrice the foe drew near.
Just in that instant, anxious Ariel sought
The close recesses of the virgin's thought;   140
As on the nosegay in her breast reclined,
He watched the ideas rising in her mind,
Sudden he viewed, in spite of all her art,
An earthly lover lurking at her heart.
Amazed, confused, he found his power expired,   145
Resigned to fate, and with a sigh retired.
     The Peer now spreads the glittering forfex[8] wide,
To enclose the Lock; now joins it, to divide.
Even then, before the fatal engine closed,
A wretched Sylph too fondly interposed;   150
Fate urged the shears, and cut the Sylph in twain
(But airy substance soon unites again):
The meeting points the sacred hair dissever
From the fair head, forever, and forever!
     Then flashed the living lightning from her eyes,   155
And screams of horror rend the affrighted skies.
Not louder shrieks to pitying heaven are cast,
When husbands, or when lapdogs breathe their last;
Or when rich china vessels fallen from high,
In glittering dust and painted fragments lie!   160

7. Scylla, daughter of Nisus, was turned into a sea bird because, for the sake of her love for Minos of Crete, who was besieging her father's city of Megara, she cut from her father's head the pur-ple lock on which his safety depended. She is not the Scylla of "Scylla and Charybdis."
8. Scissors.

"Let wreaths of triumph now my temples twine,"
The victor cried, "the glorious prize is mine!
While fish in streams, or birds delight in air,
Or in a coach and six the British Fair,
As long as *Atalantis*[9] shall be read,   165
Or the small pillow grace a lady's bed,
While visits shall be paid on solemn days,
When numerous wax-lights in bright order blaze,
While nymphs take treats, or assignations give,
So long my honor, name, and praise shall live!   170
What Time would spare, from Steel receives its date,
And monuments, like men, submit to fate!
Steel could the labor of the Gods destroy,
And strike to dust the imperial towers of Troy;
Steel could the works of mortal pride confound,   175
And hew triumphal arches to the ground.
What wonder then, fair nymph! thy hairs should feel,
The conquering force of unresisted Steel?"

Canto IV

But anxious cares the pensive nymph oppressed,
And secret passions labored in her breast.
Not youthful kings in battle seized alive,
Not scornful virgins who their charms survive,
Not ardent lovers robbed of all their bliss,   5
Not ancient ladies when refused a kiss,
Not tyrants fierce that unrepenting die,
Not Cynthia when her manteau's[1] pinned awry,
E'er felt such rage, resentment, and despair,
As thou, sad virgin! for thy ravished hair.   10
    For, that sad moment, when the Sylphs withdrew
And Ariel weeping from Belinda flew,
Umbriel,[2] a dusky, melancholy sprite
As ever sullied the fair face of light,
Down to the central earth, his proper scene,   15
Repaired to search the gloomy Cave of Spleen.[3]
    Swift on his sooty pinions flits the Gnome,
And in a vapor reached the dismal dome.
No cheerful breeze this sullen region knows,
The dreaded east is all the wind that blows.   20
Here in a grotto, sheltered close from air,
And screened in shades from day's detested glare,
She sighs forever on her pensive bed,
Pain at her side, and Megrim[4] at her head.
    Two handmaids wait the throne: alike in place   25
But differing far in figure and in face.
Here stood Ill-Nature like an ancient maid,

9. Mrs. Manley's *New Atalantis* (1709) was notorious for its thinly concealed allusions to contemporary scandals.
1. Negligee or loose robe.
2. The name suggests shade and darkness.
3. Ill humor.
4. Headache.

Her wrinkled form in black and white arrayed;
With store of prayers for mornings, nights, and noons,
Her hand is filled; her bosom with lampoons.   30
    There Affectation, with a sickly mien,
Shows in her cheek the roses of eighteen,
Practiced to lisp, and hang the head aside,
Faints into airs, and languishes with pride,
On the rich quilt sinks with becoming woe,   35
Wrapped in a gown, for sickness and for show.
The fair ones feel such maladies as these,
When each new nightdress gives a new disease.
    A constant vapor[5] o'er the palace flies,
Strange phantoms rising as the mists arise;   40
Dreadful as hermit's dreams in haunted shades,
Or bright as visions of expiring maids.
Now glaring fiends, and snakes on rolling spires,[6]
Pale specters, gaping tombs, and purple fires;
Now lakes of liquid gold, Elysian scenes,   45
And crystal domes, and angels in machines.[7]
    Unnumbered throngs on every side are seen
Of bodies changed to various forms by Spleen.
Here living teapots stand, one arm held out,
One bent; the handle this, and that the spout: 50
A pipkin[8] there, like Homer's tripod, walks;
Here sighs a jar, and there a goose pie talks;
Men prove with child, as powerful fancy works,
And maids, turned bottles, call aloud for corks.
    Safe passed the Gnome through this fantastic band,   55
A branch of healing spleenwort[9] in his hand.
Then thus addressed the Power: "Hail, wayward Queen!
Who rule the sex to fifty from fifteen:
Parent of vapors and of female wit,
Who give the hysteric or poetic fit,   60
On various tempers act by various ways,
Make some take physic, others scribble plays;
Who cause the proud their visits to delay,
And send the godly in a pet to pray.
A nymph there is that all your power disdains,   65
And thousands more in equal mirth maintains.
But oh! if e'er thy Gnome could spoil a grace,
Or raise a pimple on a beauteous face,
Like citron-waters[1] matrons' cheeks inflame,
Or change complexions at a losing game;   70

---

5. Emblematic of "the vapors," i.e., hypochondria, melancholy, peevishness, often affected by fashionable women.
6. Coils.
7. Mechanical devices used in the theaters for spectacular effects. The fantasies of neurotic women here merge with the sensational stage effects popular with contemporary audiences.
8. An earthen pot. In *Iliad* XVIII.373–

77, Vulcan furnishes the gods with self-propelling "tripods" (three-legged stools).
9. An herb, efficacious against the spleen. Pope alludes to the golden bough that Aeneas and the Cumaean sybil carry with them for protection into the underworld in *Aeneid* VI.
1. Brandy flavored with orange or lemon peel.

If e'er with airy horns[2] I planted heads,
Or rumpled petticoats, or tumbled beds,
Or caused suspicion when no soul was rude,
Or discomposed the headdress of a prude,
Or e'er to costive lapdog gave disease,   75
Which not the tears of brightest eyes could ease,
Hear me, and touch Belinda with chagrin:[3]
That single act gives half the world the spleen."
    The Goddess with a discontented air
Seems to reject him though she grants his prayer.   80
A wondrous bag with both her hands she binds,
Like that where once Ulysses held the winds;[4]
There she collects the force of female lungs,
Sighs, sobs, and passions, and the war of tongues.
A vial next she fills with fainting fears,   85
Soft sorrows, melting griefs, and flowing tears.
The Gnome rejoicing bears her gifts away,
Spreads his black wings, and slowly mounts to day.
    Sunk in Thalestris'[5] arms the nymph he found,
Her eyes dejected and her hair unbound.   90
Full o'er their heads the swelling bag he rent,
And all the Furies issued at the vent.
Belinda burns with more than mortal ire,
And fierce Thalestris fans the rising fire.
"O wretched maid!" she spread her hands, and cried   95
(While Hampton's echoes, "Wretched maid!" replied),
"Was it for this you took such constant care
The bodkin, comb, and essence to prepare?
For this your locks in paper durance bound,
For this with torturing irons wreathed around?   100
For this with fillets strained your tender head,
And bravely bore the double loads of lead?[6]
Gods! shall the ravisher display your hair,
While the fops envy, and the ladies stare!
Honor forbid! at whose unrivaled shrine   105
Ease, pleasure, virtue, all, our sex resign.
Methinks already I your tears survey,
Already hear the horrid things they say,
Already see you a degraded toast,
And all your honor in a whisper lost!   110
How shall I, then, your helpless fame defend?
'Twill then be infamy to seem your friend!

2. Horns, the symbol of the cuckold, the man whose wife has been unfaithful to him; here "airy," because they exist only in the jealous suspicions of the husband, the victim of the mischievous Umbriel.
3. Ill humor.
4. Aeolus (later conceived of as god of the winds) gave Ulysses a bag containing all the winds adverse to his voyage home. When his ship was in sight of Ithaca, his companions opened the bag and the storms that ensued drove Ulysses far away (*Odyssey* X.19 ff.).
5. The name is borrowed from a queen of the Amazons, hence a fierce and warlike woman. Thalestris, according to legend, traveled 30 days in order to have a child by Alexander the Great. Plutarch denies the story.
6. The frame on which the elaborate coiffures of the day were arranged.

And shall this prize, the inestimable prize,
Exposed through crystal to the gazing eyes,
And heightened by the diamond's circling rays,   115
On that rapacious hand forever blaze?
Sooner shall grass in Hyde Park Circus grow,
And wits take lodgings in the sound of Bow;[7]
Sooner let earth, air, sea, to chaos fall,
Men, monkeys, lapdogs, parrots, perish all!"   120
    She said; then raging to Sir Plume repairs,
And bids her beau demand the precious hairs
(Sir Plume of amber snuffbox justly vain,
And the nice conduct of a clouded cane),
With earnest eyes, and round unthinking face,   125
He first the snuffbox opened, then the case,
And thus broke out—"My Lord, why, what the devil!
Z——ds! damn the lock! 'fore Gad, you must be civil!
Plague on't! 'tis past a jest—nay prithee, pox!
Give her the hair"—he spoke, and rapped his box.   130
    "It grieves me much," replied the Peer again,
"Who speaks so well should ever speak in vain.
But by this Lock, this sacred Lock I swear
(Which never more shall join its parted hair;
Which never more its honors shall renew,   135
Clipped from the lovely head where late it grew),
That while my nostrils draw the vital air,
This hand, which won it, shall forever wear."
He spoke, and speaking, in proud triumph spread
The long-contended honors[8] of her head.   140
    But Umbriel, hateful Gnome, forbears not so;
He breaks the vial whence the sorrows flow.
Then see! the nymph in beauteous grief appears,
Her eyes half languishing, half drowned in tears;
On her heaved bosom hung her drooping head,   145
Which with a sigh she raised, and thus she said:
    "Forever cursed be this detested day,
Which snatched my best, my favorite curl away!
Happy! ah, ten times happy had I been,
If Hampton Court these eyes had never seen!   150
Yet am not I the first mistaken maid,
By love of courts to numerous ills betrayed.
Oh, had I rather unadmired remained
In some lone isle, or distant northern land;
Where the gilt chariot never marks the way,   155
Where none learn ombre, none e'er taste bohea![9]
There kept my charms concealed from mortal eye,
Like roses that in deserts bloom and die.
What moved my mind with youthful lords to roam?
Oh, had I stayed, and said my prayers at home!   160

7. A person born within sound of the bells of St. Mary-le-Bow in Cheapside is said to be a cockney. No fashionable wit would have so vulgar an address.
8. Ornaments, hence locks; a Latinism.
9. A costly sort of tea.

'Twas this the morning omens seemed to tell,
Thrice from my trembling hand the patch box[1] fell;
The tottering china shook without a wind,
Nay, Poll sat mute, and Shock was most unkind!
A Sylph too warned me of the threats of fate,   165
In mystic visions, now believed too late!
See the poor remnants of these slighted hairs!
My hands shall rend what e'en thy rapine spares.
These in two sable ringlets taught to break,
Once gave new beauties to the snowy neck;   170
The sister lock now sits uncouth, alone,
And in its fellow's fate foresees its own;
Uncurled it hangs, the fatal shears demands,
And tempts once more thy sacrilegious hands.
Oh, hadst thou, cruel! been content to seize   175
Hairs less in sight, or any hairs but these!"

Canto V

She said: the pitying audience melt in tears.
But Fate and Jove had stopped the Baron's ears.
In vain Thalestris with reproach assails,
For who can move when fair Belinda fails?
Not half so fixed the Trojan[2] could remain,   5
While Anna begged and Dido raged in vain.
Then grave Clarissa graceful waved her fan;
Silence ensued, and thus the nymph began:
   "Say why are beauties praised and honored most,
The wise man's passion, and the vain man's toast?   10
Why decked with all that land and sea afford,
Why angels called, and angel-like adored?
Why round our coaches crowd the white-gloved beaux,
Why bows the side box from its inmost rows?
How vain are all these glories, all our pains,   15
Unless good sense preserve what beauty gains;
That men may say when we the front box grace,
'Behold the first in virtue as in face!'
Oh! if to dance all night, and dress all day,
Charmed the smallpox, or chased old age away,   20
Who would not scorn what housewife's cares produce,
Or who would learn one earthly thing of use?
To patch, nay ogle, might become a saint,
Nor could it sure be such a sin to paint.
But since, alas! frail beauty must decay,   25
Curled or uncurled, since locks will turn to gray;
Since painted, or not painted, all shall fade,
And she who scorns a man must die a maid;

1. A box to hold the ornamental patches
of court plaster worn on the face by
both sexes. Cf. *Spectator* 81.
2. Aeneas, who forsook Dido at the
bidding of the gods, despite her reproaches and the supplications of her
sister Anna. Virgil compares him to a
steadfast oak that withstands a storm
(*Aeneid* IV.437–43).

What then remains but well our power to use,
And keep good humor still whate'er we lose?   30
And trust me, dear, good humor can prevail
When airs, and flights, and screams, and scolding fail.
Beauties in vain their pretty eyes may roll;
Charms strike the sight, but merit wins the soul."[3]
    So spoke the dame, but no applause ensued;   35
Belinda frowned, Thalestris called her prude.
"To arms, to arms!" the fierce virago cries,
And swift as lightning to the combat flies.
All side in parties, and begin the attack;
Fans clap, silks rustle, and tough whalebones crack;   40
Heroes' and heroines' shouts confusedly rise,
And bass and treble voices strike the skies.
No common weapons in their hands are found,
Like Gods they fight, nor dread a mortal wound.
    So when bold Homer makes the Gods engage,   45
And heavenly breasts with human passions rage;
'Gainst Pallas, Mars; Latona, Hermes arms;
And all Olympus rings with loud alarms:
Jove's thunder roars, heaven trembles all around,
Blue Neptune storms, the bellowing deeps resound: 50
Earth shakes her nodding towers, the ground gives way,
And the pale ghosts start at the flash of day!
    Triumphant Umbriel on a sconce's height
Clapped his glad wings, and sat to view the fight:
Propped on the bodkin spears, the sprites survey   55
The growing combat, or assist the fray.
    While through the press enraged Thalestris flies,
And scatters death around from both her eyes,
A beau and witling perished in the throng,
One died in metaphor, and one in song.   60
"O cruel nymph! a living death I bear,"
Cried Dapperwit, and sunk beside his chair.
A mournful glance Sir Fopling upwards cast,
"Those eyes are made so killing"—was his last.
Thus on Maeander's flowery margin lies   65
The expiring swan, and as he sings he dies.
    When bold Sir Plume had drawn Clarissa down,
Chloe stepped in, and killed him with a frown;
She smiled to see the doughty hero slain,
But, at her smile, the beau revived again.   70
    Now Jove suspends his golden scales in air,
Weighs the men's wits against the lady's hair;
The doubtful beam long nods from side to side;
At length the wits mount up, the hairs subside.
    See, fierce Belinda on the Baron flies,   75

---

3. The speech is a close parody of Pope's own translation of the speech of Sarpedon to Glaucus, first published in 1709 and slightly revised in his version of the *Iliad* (XII.371–96).

With more than usual lightning in her eyes;
Nor feared the chief the unequal fight to try,
Who sought no more than on his foe to die.
　　But this bold lord with manly strength endued,
She with one finger and a thumb subdued: 　　　　　　　　80
Just where the breath of life his nostrils drew,
A charge of snuff the wily virgin threw;
The Gnomes direct, to every atom just,
The pungent grains of titillating dust.
Sudden, with starting tears each eye o'erflows, 　　　　　85
And the high dome re-echoes to his nose.
　　"Now meet thy fate," incensed Belinda cried,
And drew a deadly bodkin[4] from her side.
(The same, his ancient personage to deck,
Her great-great-grandsire wore about his neck, 　　　　　90
In three seal rings; which after, melted down,
Formed a vast buckle for his widow's gown:
Her infant grandame's whistle next it grew,
The bells she jingled, and the whistle blew;
Then in a bodkin graced her mother's hairs, 　　　　　　95
Which long she wore, and now Belinda wears.)
　　"Boast not my fall," he cried, "insulting foe!
Thou by some other shalt be laid as low.
Nor think to die dejects my lofty mind:
All that I dread is leaving you behind! 　　　　　　　　　100
Rather than so, ah, let me still survive,
And burn in Cupid's flames—but burn alive."
　　"Restore the Lock!" she cries; and all around
"Restore the Lock!" the vaulted roofs rebound.
Not fierce Othello in so loud a strain 　　　　　　　　　105
Roared for the handkerchief that caused his pain.[5]
But see how oft ambitious aims are crossed,
And chiefs contend till all the prize is lost!
The lock, obtained with guilt, and kept with pain,
In every place is sought, but sought in vain: 　　　　　　110
With such a prize no mortal must be blessed,
So Heaven decrees! with Heaven who can contest?
　　　Some thought it mounted to the lunar sphere,
Since all things lost on earth are treasured there.
There heroes' wits are kept in ponderous vases, 　　　　　115
And beaux' in snuffboxes and tweezer cases.
There broken vows and deathbed alms are found,
And lovers' hearts with ends of riband bound,
The courtier's promises, and sick man's prayers,
The smiles of harlots, and the tears of heirs, 　　　　　　120
Cages for gnats, and chains to yoke a flea,
Dried butterflies, and tomes of casuistry.
　　　But trust the Muse—she saw it upward rise,

---

4. An ornamental pin shaped like a
dagger, to be worn in the hair.

5. *Othello* III.iv.

Though marked by none but quick, poetic eyes
  (So Rome's great founder to the heavens withdrew,[6]   125
To Proculus alone confessed in view);
A sudden star, it shot through liquid air,
And drew behind a radiant trail of hair.
Not Berenice's locks first rose so bright,[7]
The heavens bespangling with disheveled light.   130
The Sylphs behold it kindling as it flies,
And pleased pursue its progress through the skies.
    This the beau monde shall from the Mall[8] survey,
And hail with music its propitious ray.
This the blest lover shall for Venus take,   135
And send up vows from Rosamonda's Lake.[9]
This Partridge[1] soon shall view in cloudless skies,
When next he looks through Galileo's eyes;
And hence the egregious wizard shall foredoom
The fate of Louis, and the fall of Rome.   140
    Then cease, bright nymph! to mourn thy ravished hair,
Which adds new glory to the shining sphere!
Not all the tresses that fair head can boast,
Shall draw such envy as the Lock you lost.
For, after all the murders of your eye,   145
When, after millions slain, yourself shall die:
When those fair suns shall set, as set they must,
And all those tresses shall be laid in dust,
This Lock the Muse shall consecrate to fame,
And 'midst the stars inscribe Belinda's name.   150
1712   1714

Ode on Solitude[2]

Happy the man whose wish and care
    A few paternal acres bound,
Content to breathe his native air,
        In his own ground.

Whose herds with milk, whose fields with bread,   5
    Whose flocks supply him with attire,
Whose trees in summer yield him shade,
        In winter fire.

6. Romulus, the "founder" and first king of Rome, was snatched to heaven in a storm cloud while reviewing his army in the Campus Martius (Livy I. xvi).

7. Berenice, the wife of Ptolemy III, dedicated a lock of her hair to the gods to ensure her husband's safe return from war. It was turned into a constellation.

8. A walk laid out by Charles II in St. James's Park, a resort for strollers of all sorts.

9. In St. James's Park; associated with unhappy lovers.

1. John Partridge, the astrologer whose annually published predictions had been amusingly satirized by Swift and other wits in 1708. "Galileo's eyes": i.e., a telescope.

2. The hint for this poem was taken from Horace's well-known *Epode II*, which praises the simplicity and innocence of country life, a favorite literary theme in Pope's time.

Blest, who can unconcernedly find
    Hours, days, and years slide soft away,   10
In health of body, peace of mind,
          Quiet by day,

Sound sleep by night; study and ease,
    Together mixed; sweet recreation;
And innocence, which most does please   15
          With meditation.

Thus let me live, unseen, unknown;
    Thus unlamented let me die;
Steal from the world, and not a stone
          Tell where I lie.   20

ca. 1700–1709   1717, 1736

Epistle to Miss Blount[1]

ON HER LEAVING THE TOWN, AFTER THE CORONATION

As some fond virgin, whom her mother's care
Drags from the town to wholesome country air,
Just when she learns to roll a melting eye,
And hear a spark,[2] yet think no danger nigh;
From the dear man unwilling she must sever,   5
Yet takes one kiss before she parts forever:
Thus from the world fair Zephalinda[3] flew,
Saw others happy, and with sighs withdrew;
Not that their pleasures caused her discontent;
She sighed not that they stayed, but that she went.   10
    She went to plain-work,[4] and to purling brooks,
Old-fashioned halls, dull aunts, and croaking rooks:
She went from opera, park, assembly, play,
To morning walks, and prayers three hours a day;
To part her time 'twixt reading and bohea,[5]   15
To muse, and spill her solitary tea,
Or o'er cold coffee trifle with the spoon,
Count the slow clock, and dine exact at noon;[6]
Divert her eyes with pictures in the fire,
Hum half a tune, tell stories to the squire;   20
Up to her godly garret after seven,
There starve and pray, for that's the way to heaven.
    Some squire, perhaps, you take delight to rack,
Whose game is whist, whose treat a toast in sack;
Who visits with a gun, presents you birds,   25

1. Teresa Blount, sister of Pope's life-long friend Martha Blount. The "coronation" was that of George I (1714).
2. A fop, a beau.
3. A fanciful name adopted by Miss Blount.
4. "Needlework, as distinguished from embroidery" (Johnson's *Dictionary*).
5. A costly sort of tea.
6. The fashionable hour for dining in London was three or four o'clock. A noon dinner is a sign of old-fashioned rusticity.

Then gives a smacking buss, and cries—"No words!"
Or with his hounds comes hollowing from the stable,
Makes love with nods and knees beneath a table;
Whose laughs are hearty, though his jests are coarse,
And loves you best of all things—but his horse.   30
   In some fair evening, on your elbow laid,
You dream of triumphs in the rural shade;
In pensive thought recall the fancied scene,
See coronations rise on every green:
Before you pass the imaginary sights   35
Of lords and earls and dukes and gartered knights,
While the spread fan o'ershades your closing eyes;
Then gives one flirt,[7] and all the vision flies.
Thus vanish scepters, coronets, and balls,
And leave you in lone woods, or empty walls!   40
   So when your slave,[8] at some dear idle time
(Not plagued with headaches or the want of rhyme)
Stands in the streets, abstracted from the crew,
And while he seems to study, thinks of you;
Just when his fancy points[9] your sprightly eyes,   45
Or sees the blush of soft Parthenia[1] rise,
Gay[2] pats my shoulder, and you vanish quite;
Streets, chairs, and coxcombs rush upon my sight;
Vexed to be still in town, I knit my brow,
Look sour, and hum a tune—as you may now.   50

1717

Eloisa to Abelard[1]

The Argument

Abelard and Eloisa flourished in the twelfth century; they were
two of the most distinguished persons of their age in learning and

---

7. I.e., opens and closes her fan with a jerk.
8. I.e., Pope.
9. Notices
1. Martha Blount.
2. John Gay, the poet.
1. Like Ovid's *Sappho to Phaon*, which Pope had translated in his teens, *Eloisa to Abelard* is an heroic epistle: strictly defined, a versified love letter, involving historical persons, which dramatizes the feelings of a woman who has been forsaken. Pope took his subject from one of the most famous affairs of history. Peter Abelard (1079–1142), a brilliant scholastic theologian, seduced a young girl, his pupil Heloise; eventually she bore him a child, and they were secretly married. Enraged at the betrayal of trust, and what he regarded as the casting off of Heloise, her uncle Fulbert revenged himself by having Abelard cas-

trated. The lovers separated; each of them entered a monastery, and went on to a distinguished career in the Church. Yet their greatest fame derives from the letters they are supposed to have exchanged late in their lives (modern scholars have cast doubt on the authenticity of Heloise's letters). It is this correspondence, made newly popular by French and English translations of the original Latin, that inspired Pope's poem.
   The heroic epistle challenges an author in two ways: he must exert his historical imagination, projecting himself into another time and place; and he must enter the mind and passions of a woman, acting her part, and showing everything through her point of view. Historically, Pope draws on his knowledge of Roman Catholic ritual to envelop Eloisa in a rich medieval atmosphere. The dark

beauty, but for nothing more famous than for their unfortunate passion. After a long course of calamities, they retired each to a several[2] convent, and consecrated the remainder of their days to religion. It was many years after this separation, that a letter of Abelard's to a friend which contained the history of his misfortune, fell into the hands of Eloisa. This awakening all her tenderness, occasioned those celebrated letters (out of which the following is partly extracted)[3] which give so lively a picture of the struggles of grace and nature, virtue and passion.

In these deep solitudes and awful cells,
Where heavenly-pensive contemplation dwells,
And ever-musing melancholy reigns;
What means this tumult in a vestal's[4] veins?
Why rove my thoughts beyond this last retreat?   5
Why feels my heart its long-forgotten heat?
Yet, yet I love!—From Abelard it[5] came,
And Eloisa yet must kiss the name.
　　Dear fatal name! rest ever unrevealed,
Nor pass these lips in holy silence sealed.   10
Hide it, my heart, within that close disguise,
Where mixed with God's, his loved idea[6] lies.
O write it not, my hand—the name appears
Already written—wash it out, my tears!
In vain lost Eloisa weeps and prays,   15
Her heart still dictates, and her hand obeys.
　　Relentless walls! whose darksome round contains
Repentant sighs, and voluntary pains:
Ye rugged rocks! which holy knees have worn;
Ye grots and caverns shagged with horrid[7] thorn!   20
Shrines! where their vigils pale-eyed virgins keep,
And pitying saints, whose statues learn to weep![8]

Gothic convent, situated in an imaginary landscape of grottos, mountains, and pine forests, embodies the 18th-century sense of the "romantic": fantastic, legendary, extravagant. Here Eloisa is cloistered, not only physically but mentally, by religious mysticism that surrounds her with a melancholy as palpable as the image of her lover. The greatest triumph of the poem, however, is psychological. In *Eloisa*, for the only time in his career, Pope tells a story wholly through another's voice. Confused and tormented, the heroine tosses between two kinds of love: an erotic passion for the earthly lover whose memory she cannot quell; and the divine, chaste love that must content a nun. Abelard and God, within her fantasy, compete for her soul. Pope brings these internal struggles to the surface by externalizing them in bold dramatic rhetoric, formal and intense as an aria in an opera (the poem was long a favorite for reading aloud). Eloisa views herself theatrically, if only because, in the letter, she is trying to make Abelard visualize the pathos of her situation. There is literally no way out for her; and at the end of the poem, she can break the static circle of desire and loneliness only by picturing herself in the peace of death. Yet the high reputation of the work, well into the Romantic era, owes less to its theatrics than to its convincing image of a mind in pain. "If you search for passion," Byron wrote more than a century later, "where is it to be found stronger than in the Epistle from Eloisa to Abelard?"
2. Separate.
3. Pope's source was a highly romanticized English version of the letters by John Hughes, published in 1713.
4. Nun's. Here, as elsewhere, Eloisa substitutes a pagan form for a Christian; nor is she in fact a virgin (vestal).
5. The letter to which Eloisa is replying.
6. Mental image or shape.
7. Bristling.
8. In damp places, stone "weeps" through condensation.

Tho' cold like you, unmoved, and silent grown,
I have not yet forgot myself to stone.
All is not Heaven's while Abelard has part,   25
Still rebel nature holds out half my heart;
Nor prayers nor fasts its stubborn pulse restrain,
Nor tears, for ages taught to flow in vain.
   Soon as thy letters trembling I unclose,
That well-known name awakens all my woes.   30
Oh name for ever sad! for ever dear!
Still breathed in sighs, still ushered with a tear.
I tremble too, where'er my own I find,
Some dire misfortune follows close behind.
Line after line my gushing eyes o'erflow,   35
Led through a sad variety of woe:
Now warm in love, now withering in my bloom,
Lost in a convent's solitary gloom!
There stern religion quenched the unwilling flame,
There died the best of passions, love and fame.   40
   Yet write, oh write me all, that I may join
Griefs to thy griefs, and echo sighs to thine.
Nor foes nor fortune take this power away.
And is my Abelard less kind than they?
Tears still are mine, and those I need not spare,   45
Love but demands what else were shed in prayer;
No happier task these faded eyes pursue,
To read and weep is all they now can do.
   Then share thy pain, allow that sad relief;
Ah, more than share it! give me all thy grief.   50
Heaven first taught letters for some wretch's aid,
Some banished lover, or some captive maid;
They live, they speak, they breathe what love inspires,
Warm from the soul, and faithful to its fires,
The virgin's wish without her fears impart,   55
Excuse the blush, and pour out all the heart,
Speed the soft intercourse from soul to soul,
And waft a sigh from Indus[9] to the Pole.
   Thou knowest how guiltless first I met thy flame,
When love approached me under friendship's name;   60
My fancy formed thee of angelic kind,
Some emanation of the all-beauteous Mind.[1]
Those smiling eyes, attempering[2] every ray,
Shone sweetly lambent with celestial day:
Guiltless I gazed; heaven listened while you sung;   65
And truths divine came mended from that tongue.[3]
From lips like those what precept failed to move?
Too soon they taught me 'twas no sin to love.
Back through the paths of pleasing sense I ran,
Nor wished an angel whom I loved a man.   70

---

9. A southern constellation.
1. God, conceived (as is proper to a student of philosophy) in Platonic terms.

2. Moderating, assuaging.
3. "He was her preceptor in philosophy and divinity" [Pope's note].

Dim and remote the joys of saints I see,
Nor envy them, that heaven I lose for thee.
　　How oft, when pressed to marriage, have I said,
Curse on all laws but those which love has made!
Love, free as air, at sight of human ties, 75
Spreads his light wings, and in a moment flies.
Let wealth, let honor, wait the wedded dame,
August her deed, and sacred be her fame;
Before true passion all those views remove,[4]
Fame, wealth, and honor! what are you to love? 80
The jealous god, when we profane his fires,
Those restless passions in revenge inspires,
And bids them make mistaken mortals groan,
Who seek in love for aught but love alone.
Should at my feet the world's great master fall, 85
Himself, his throne, his world, I'd scorn 'em all:
Not Caesar's empress would I deign to prove;[5]
No, make me mistress to the man I love;
If there be yet another name more free,
More fond than mistress, make me that to thee! 90
Oh happy state! when souls each other draw,
When love is liberty, and nature, law:
All then is full, possessing, and possessed,
No craving void left aching in the breast:
Even thought meets thought ere from the lips it part, 95
And each warm wish springs mutual from the heart.
This sure is bliss (if bliss on earth there be)
And once the lot of Abelard and me.
　　Alas how changed! what sudden horrors rise!
A naked lover bound and bleeding lies! 100
Where, where was Eloise? her voice, her hand,
Her poniard, had opposed the dire command.
Barbarian, stay! that bloody stroke restrain;
The crime was common,[6] common be the pain.
I can no more; by shame, by rage suppressed, 105
Let tears, and burning blushes speak the rest.
　　Canst thou forget that sad, that solemn day,
When victims at yon altar's foot we lay?
Canst thou forget what tears that moment fell,
When, warm in youth, I bade the world farewell? 110
As with cold lips I kissed the sacred veil,
The shrines all trembled, and the lamps grew pale:
Heaven scarce believed the conquest it surveyed,
And saints with wonder heard the vows I made.
Yet then, to those dread altars as I drew, 115
Not on the Cross my eyes were fixed, but you;
Not grace, or zeal, love only was my call,
And if I lose thy love, I lose my all.

---

4. Depart.
5. Try.

6. Shared; "pain": punishment.

Come! with thy looks, thy words, relieve my woe;
Those still at least are left thee to bestow.   120
Still on that breast enamored let me lie,
Still drink delicious poison from thy eye,
Pant on thy lip, and to thy heart be pressed;
Give all thou canst—and let me dream the rest.
Ah no! instruct me other joys to prize,   125
With other beauties charm my partial[7] eyes,
Full in my view set all the bright abode,
And make my soul quit Abelard for God.
   Ah think at least thy flock deserves thy care,
Plants of thy hand, and child'ren of thy prayer.   130
From the false world in early youth they fled,
By thee to mountains, wilds, and deserts led.
You raised these hallowed walls;[8] the desert smiled,
And paradise was opened in the wild.
No weeping orphan saw his father's stores   135
Our shrines irradiate,[9] or emblaze the floors;
No silver saints, by dying misers given,
Here bribed the rage of ill-requited heaven:
But such plain roofs as piety could raise,
And only vocal with the Maker's[1] praise.   140
In these lone walls (their day's eternal bound)
These moss-grown domes with spiry turrets crowned,
Where awful arches make a noon-day night,
And the dim windows shed a solemn light,
Thy eyes diffused a reconciling ray,   145
And gleams of glory brightened all the day.
But now no face divine contentment wears,
'Tis all blank sadness, or continual tears.
See how the force of others' prayers I try,
(O pious fraud of amorous charity!)   150
But why should I on others' prayers depend?
Come thou, my father, brother, husband, friend!
Ah let thy handmaid, sister, daughter move,
And all those tender names in one, thy love!
The darksome pines that o'er yon rocks reclined   155
Wave high, and murmur to the hollow wind,
The wandering streams that shine between the hills,
The grots that echo to the tinkling rills,
The dying gales that pant upon the trees,
The lakes that quiver to the curling breeze;   160
No more these scenes my meditation aid,
Or lull to rest the visionary[2] maid.
But o'er the twilight groves and dusky caves,

7. Fond; seeing only a part.
8. "He founded the monastery" [Pope's note]. Abelard erected the "Paraclete," a modest oratory near Troyes, in 1122; seven years later, when the nunnery of which Heloise was prioress was evicted from its property, he ceded the lands of the Paraclete to her.
9. Adorn with splendor.
1. God's or Abelard's.
2. Given to visions.

Long-sounding isles,[3] and intermingled graves,
Black Melancholy sits, and round her throws   165
A death-like silence, and a dread repose:
Her gloomy presence saddens all the scene,
Shades every flower, and darkens every green,
Deepens the murmur of the falling floods,
And breathes a browner horror on the woods.[4]   170
    Yet here for ever, ever must I stay;
Sad proof how well a lover can obey!
Death, only death, can break the lasting chain;
And here, even then, shall my cold dust remain,
Here all its frailties, all its flames resign,   175
And wait, till 'tis no sin to mix with thine.
    Ah wretch! believed the spouse of God in vain,
Confessed within the slave of love and man.
Assist me, heaven! but whence arose that prayer?
Sprung it from piety, or from despair?   180
Even here, where frozen chastity retires,
Love finds an altar for forbidden fires.
I ought to grieve, but cannot what I ought;
I mourn the lover, not lament the fault;
I view my crime, but kindle at the view,   185
Repent old pleasures, and solicit new;
Now turned to heaven, I weep my past offense,
Now think of thee, and curse my innocence.
Of all affliction taught a lover yet,
'Tis sure the hardest science[5] to forget!   190
How shall I lose the sin, yet keep the sense,[6]
And love the offender, yet detest the offense?
How the dear object from the crime remove,
Or how distinguish penitence from love?
Unequal task! a passion to resign,   195
For hearts so touched, so pierced, so lost as mine.
Ere such a soul regains its peaceful state,
How often must it love, how often hate!
How often hope, despair, resent, regret,
Conceal, disdain—do all things but forget.   200
But let heaven seize it, all at once 'tis fired,
Not touched, but rapt; not wakened, but inspired![7]
Oh come! oh teach me nature to subdue,
Renounce my love, my life, my self—and you.
Fill my fond heart with God alone, for he   205
Alone can rival, can succeed to thee.
    How happy is the blameless vestal's lot!

---

3. Sounds reverberate over water as in the *aisles* of a church.
4. "The image of the Goddess Melancholy sitting over the convent, and, as it were, expanding her dreadful wings over its whole circuit, and diffusing her gloom all around it, is truly sublime, and strongly conceived" [Joseph Warton].
5. Knowledge.
6. Both perception and sensation.
7. I.e., when touched, at once rapt; when wakened, at once inspired.

The world forgetting, by the world forgot.
Eternal sun-shine of the spotless mind!
Each prayer accepted, and each wish resigned; 210
Labor and rest, that equal periods keep;
"Obedient slumbers that can wake and weep;"[8]
Desires composed, affections ever even;
Tears that delight, and sighs that waft to heaven.
Grace shines around her with serenest beams, 215
And whispering angels prompt her golden dreams.
For her the unfading rose of Eden blooms,
And wings of seraphs shed divine perfumes,
For her the Spouse prepares the bridal ring,
For her white virgins hymenaeals[9] sing, 220
To sounds of heavenly harps she dies away,
And melts in visions of eternal day.
   Far other dreams my erring soul employ,
Far other raptures, of unholy joy:
When at the close of each sad, sorrowing day, 225
Fancy restores what vengeance snatched away,
Then conscience sleeps, and leaving nature free,
All my loose soul unbounded springs to thee.
O curst, dear horrors of all-conscious night![1]
How glowing guilt exalts the keen delight! 230
Provoking daemons all restraint remove,
And stir within me every source of love.
I hear thee, view thee, gaze o'er all thy charms,
And round thy phantom glue my clasping arms.
I wake—no more I hear, no more I view, 235
The phantom flies me, as unkind as you.
I call aloud; it hears not what I say;
I stretch my empty arms; it glides away:
To dream once more I close my willing eyes;
Ye soft illusions, dear deceits, arise! 240
Alas, no more!—methinks we wandering go
Through dreary wastes, and weep each other's woe;
Where round some moldering tower pale ivy creeps,
And low-browed rocks hang nodding o'er the deeps.
Sudden you mount! you beckon from the skies; 245
Clouds interpose, waves roar, and winds arise.
I shriek, start up, the same sad prospect find,
And wake to all the griefs I left behind.[2]
   For thee the fates, severely kind, ordain
A cool suspense[3] from pleasure and from pain; 250
Thy life a long dead calm of fixed repose;

8. A quotation from *Description of a
Religious House*, by Richard Crashaw.
9. Wedding hymns. Every nun is the
bride of Christ, her spouse.
1. The night knows everything; and
Eloisa is conscious (guiltily aware) all
through the night.
2. Cf. the conclusion to the *Epistle to
Miss Blount*, a comic companion-piece to
this poem.
3. Suspension.

No pulse that riots, and no blood that glows.
Still as the sea, ere winds were taught to blow,
Or moving spirit bade the waters flow;
Soft as the slumbers of a saint forgiven,   255
And mild as opening gleams of promised heaven.
    Come, Abelard! for what hast thou to dread?
The torch of Venus burns not for the dead.
Nature stands checked; religion disapproves;
Even thou art cold—yet Eloisa loves.   260
Ah hopeless, lasting flames! like those that burn
To light the dead, and warm the unfruitful urn.[4]
    What scenes appear where'er I turn my view?
The dear ideas, where I fly, pursue,
Rise in the grove, before the altar rise,   265
Stain all my soul, and wanton in my eyes!
I waste the matin lamp in sighs for thee,
Thy image steals between my God and me,
Thy voice I seem in every hymn to hear,
With every bead I drop too soft a tear.   270
When from the censer clouds of fragrance roll,
And swelling organs lift the rising soul,
One thought of thee puts all the pomp to flight,
Priests, tapers, temples, swim before my sight:
In seas of flame[5] my plunging soul is drowned,   275
While altars blaze, and angels tremble round.
    While prostrate here in humble grief I lie,
Kind, virtuous drops just gathering in my eye,
While praying, trembling, in the dust I roll,
And dawning grace is opening on my soul: 280
Come, if thou dar'st, all charming as thou art!
Oppose thyself to heaven; dispute[6] my heart;
Come, with one glance of those deluding eyes
Blot out each bright idea of the skies.
Take back that grace, those sorrows, and those tears,   285
Take back my fruitless penitence and prayers,
Snatch me, just mounting, from the blest abode,
Assist the fiends and tear me from my God!
    No, fly me, fly me! far as pole from pole;
Rise Alps between us! and whole oceans roll!   290
Ah come not, write not, think not once of me,
Nor share one pang of all I felt for thee.
Thy oaths I quit,[7] thy memory resign,
Forget, renounce me, hate whate'er was mine.
Fair eyes, and tempting looks (which yet I view!)   295
Long loved, adored ideas! all adieu!
O grace serene! oh virtue heavenly fair!

---

4. Perpetual fires were placed in Roman   6. Contend for.
tombs.   7. Absolve.
5. Love, or Hell.

Divine oblivion of low-thoughted care!
Fresh blooming hope, gay daughter of the sky!
And faith, our early immortality!   300
Enter, each mild, each amicable guest;
Receive, and wrap me in eternal rest!
    See in her cell sad Eloisa spread,
Propped on some tomb, a neighbor of the dead!
In each low wind methinks a spirit calls,   305
And more than echoes talk along the walls.
Here, as I watched the dying lamps around,
From yonder shrine I heard a hollow sound.
"Come, sister, come! (it said, or seemed to say)
Thy place is here, sad sister, come away!   310
Once like thyself, I trembled, wept, and prayed,
Love's victim then, tho' now a sainted maid:
But all is calm in this eternal sleep;
Here grief forgets to groan, and love to weep,
Even superstition loses every fear: 315
For God, not man, absolves our frailties here."
    I come, I come! prepare your roseate bowers,
Celestial palms, and ever-blooming flowers.
Thither, where sinners may have rest, I go,
Where flames refined in breasts seraphic glow.   320
Thou, Abelard! the last sad office pay,
And smooth my passage to the realms of day:
See my lips tremble, and my eyeballs roll,
Suck my last breath, and catch my flying soul!
Ah no—in sacred vestments may'st thou stand,   325
The hallowed taper trembling in thy hand,
Present the Cross before my lifted eye,
Teach me at once, and learn of[8] me to die.
Ah then, thy once-loved Eloisa see!
It will be then no crime to gaze on me.   330
See from my cheek the transient roses fly!
See the last sparkle languish in my eye!
Till every motion, pulse, and breath be o'er;
And even my Abelard be loved no more.
O death all-eloquent! you only prove   335
What dust we doat on, when 'tis man we love.
    Then too, when fate shall thy fair frame destroy,
(That cause of all my guilt, and all my joy)
In trance ecstatic may thy pangs be drowned,
Bright clouds descend, and angels watch thee round,   340
From opening skies may streaming glories shine,
And saints embrace thee with a love like mine.
    May one kind grave unite each hapless name,[9]

8. Learn from.
9. "Abelard and Eloisa were interred in the same grave, or in monuments adjoining, in the monastery of Paraclete" [Pope's note].

And graft my love immortal on thy fame!
Then, ages hence, when all my woes are o'er, 345
When this rebellious heart shall beat no more;
If ever chance two wandering lovers brings
To Paraclete's white walls, and silver springs,
O'er the pale marble shall they join their heads,
And drink the falling tears each other sheds, 350
Then sadly say, with mutual pity moved,
"Oh may we never love as these have loved!"
From the full choir when loud Hosannas rise,
And swell the pomp of dreadful sacrifice,[1]
Amid that scene if some relenting eye 355
Glance on the stone where our cold relics lie,
Devotion's self shall steal a thought from heaven,
One human tear shall drop, and be forgiven.
And sure if fate some future bard shall join
In sad similitude of griefs to mine, 360
Condemned whole years in absence to deplore,[2]
And image charms he must behold no more,
Such if there be, who loves so long, so well,
Let him our sad, our tender story tell;
The well-sung woes will sooth my pensive ghost; 365
He best can paint 'em, who shall feel 'em most.

1717

1. The celebration of the Eucharist (Mass).
2. Lament. Pope, imagining himself imagined by Eloisa, hints that he too is separated from a loved one; probably Lady Mary Wortley Montagu, who was in Turkey. Pope and Lady Mary later quarreled, and she appears as Sappho in Epistle II, *To a Lady*.

An Essay on Man

Pope's philosophical poem, *An Essay on Man*, is a fragment of an ambitious but never completed scheme for what the poet referred to as his "ethic work," which was to have been a large survey of man and of the society which he has created. The work is dedicated to Henry St. John (pronounced *Sín-jun*), Viscount Bolingbroke (1678–1751), the brilliant, though erratic, Secretary of State in the Tory ministry of 1710–14, whom Pope had come to know through Swift. After the accession of George I he fled to France, attainted of treason, but was pardoned and allowed to return in 1723. He settled near Pope at Dawley Farm and a close friendship developed between the two men. In their conversations Bolingbroke, who fancied himself a philosopher, helped Pope to formulate the optimistic system that is expounded in this poem, though the notion that Pope merely versified ideas that Bolingbroke furnished him in prose is no longer considered valid.

It is clear that the poem would have been pretty much what it is had the two men never met, for it expresses doctrines widely circulated and generally accepted at the time by enlightened minds throughout Europe.

The *Essay* gives memorable expression to ideas about the nature of the universe and man's place in it, ideas upon which 18th-century optimism rested. The evolutionary theories of the 19th century and the history of the first half of the 20th century have made such optimism untenable today; but this does not mean that the *Essay* is either trivial or cheap.

Pope's purpose is to "vindicate the ways of God to man," a phrase that consciously echoes *Paradise Lost* I.26. Like Milton, Pope faces the problem of the existence of evil in a world presumed to be the creation of a good God (a philosophical work that deals with this problem is called a "theodicy"). *Paradise Lost* is Biblical in content, Christian in doctrine; the *Essay on Man* avoids all specifically Christian doctrines, not because Pope disbelieved them, but because "man," the subject of the poem, includes millions who never heard of Christianity, and Pope is concerned with the universal. Milton tells a mythological story. Pope writes in abstract terms.

The *Essay* is divided into four Epistles. In the first Pope asserts the essential order and goodness of the universe and the rightness of man's place in it. The other Epistles deal with how man may emulate in his nature and in society the cosmic harmony revealed in the first Epistle. The second seeks to show how he may attain a psychological harmony which can become the basis of a virtuous life through the co-operation of self-love and the passions (both necessary to our complete humanity) with reason, the controller and director. The third is concerned with man in society, which, it teaches, was created through the co-operation of self-love (the egoistic drives that motivate us) and social love (our dependence on others, our inborn benevolence). The fourth is concerned with happiness, which lies within the reach of all, for it is dependent upon virtue, which becomes possible when—though only when—self-love is transmuted into love of man and love of God. Such, in brief summary, are Pope's main ideas in the poem. He has given them expression in splendid language, unforgettable phrases (many have detached themselves from the poem and have become a part of our daily speech), and astonishing metrical virtuosity; and though the poem is didactic, it is richly musical and is distinguished by subtly beautiful visual imagery.

From An Essay on Man

TO HENRY ST. JOHN, LORD BOLINGBROKE

Epistle I. Of the Nature and State of Man,
With Respect to the Universe

Awake, my St. John! leave all meaner things
To low ambition, and the pride of kings.
Let us (since life can little more supply
Than just to look about us and to die)
Expatiate free[1] o'er all this scene of man;   5

1. Range freely.

A mighty maze! but not without a plan;
A wild, where weeds and flowers promiscuous shoot,
Or garden, tempting with forbidden fruit.
Together let us beat this ample field,
Try what the open, what the covert yield;   10
The latent tracts, the giddy heights, explore
Of all who blindly creep, or sightless soar;
Eye Nature's walks, shoot folly as it flies,
And catch the manners living as they rise;
Laugh where we must, be candid[2] where we can;   15
But vindicate the ways of God to man.[3]

    1. Say first, of God above, or man below,
What can we reason, but from what we know?
Of man, what see we but his station here,
From which to reason, or to which refer?   20
Through worlds unnumbered though the God be known,
'Tis ours to trace him only in our own.
He, who through vast immensity can pierce,
See worlds on worlds compose one universe,
Observe how system into system runs,   25
What other planets circle other suns,
What varied Being peoples every star,
May tell why Heaven has made us as we are.
But of this frame the bearings, and the ties,
The strong connections, nice dependencies,   30
Gradations just, has thy pervading soul
Looked through? or can a part contain the whole?
    Is the great chain, that draws all to agree,
And drawn supports, upheld by God, or thee?

    2. Presumptuous man! the reason wouldst thou find,   35
Why formed so weak, so little, and so blind?
First, if thou canst, the harder reason guess,
Why formed no weaker, blinder, and no less!
Ask of thy mother earth, why oaks are made
Taller or stronger than the weeds they shade?   40
Or ask of yonder argent fields above,
Why Jove's satellites[4] are less than Jove?
    Of systems possible, if 'tis confessed
That Wisdom Infinite must form the best,
Where all must full or not coherent be,   45
And all that rises, rise in due degree;
Then, in the scale of reasoning life, 'tis plain,
There must be, somewhere, such a rank as man:
And all the question (wrangle e'er so long)
Is only this, if God has placed him wrong?   50
    Respecting man, whatever wrong we call,
May, must be right, as relative to all.

2. Kindly.
3. Pope deliberately echoes *Paradise Lost* I.26.
4. In his *Dictionary* Johnson notes and condemns Pope's giving his word four syllables, as in Latin.

In human works, though labored on with pain,
A thousand movements scarce one purpose gain;
In God's, one single can its end produce; 55
Yet serves to second too some other use.
So man, who here seems principal alone,
Perhaps acts second to some sphere unknown,
Touches some wheel, or verges to some goal;
'Tis but a part we see, and not a whole. 60
    When the proud steed shall know why man restrains
His fiery course, or drives him o'er the plains;
When the dull ox, why now he breaks the clod,
Is now a victim, and now Egypt's god:
Then shall man's pride and dullness comprehend 65
His actions', passions', being's use and end;
Why doing, suffering, checked, impelled; and why
This hour a slave, the next a deity.
    Then say not man's imperfect, Heaven in fault;
Say rather, man's as perfect as he ought: 70
His knowledge measured to his state and place,
His time a moment, and a point his space.
If to be perfect in a certain sphere,[5]
What matter, soon or late, or here or there?
The blest today is as completely so, 75
As who began a thousand years ago.

    3. Heaven from all creatures hides the book of Fate,
All but the page prescribed, their present state:
From brutes what men, from men what spirits know:
Or who could suffer Being here below? 80
The lamb thy riot dooms to bleed today,
Had he thy reason, would he skip and play?
Pleased to the last, he crops the flowery food,
And licks the hand just raised to shed his blood.
O blindness to the future! kindly given, 85
That each may fill the circle marked by Heaven:
Who sees with equal eye, as God of all,
A hero perish, or a sparrow fall,
Atoms or systems[6] into ruin hurled,
And now a bubble burst, and now a world. 90
    Hope humbly then; with trembling pinions soar;
Wait the great teacher Death, and God adore!
What future bliss, he gives not thee to know,
But gives that hope to be thy blessing now.
Hope springs eternal in the human breast: 95
Man never is, but always to be blest:
The soul, uneasy and confined from home,
Rests and expatiates in a life to come.
    Lo! the poor Indian, whose untutored mind
Sees God in clouds, or hears him in the wind; 100
His soul proud Science never taught to stray

5. I.e., in one's "state and place."   6. Solar systems.

Far as the solar walk, or milky way;
Yet simple Nature to his hope has given,
Behind the cloud-topped hill, an humbler heaven;
Some safer world in depth of woods embraced,   105
Some happier island in the watery waste,
Where slaves once more their native land behold,
No fiends torment, no Christians thirst for gold!
To be, contents his natural desire,
He asks no angel's wing, no seraph's fire;   110
But thinks, admitted to that equal sky,
His faithful dog shall bear him company.

4. Go, wiser thou! and, in thy scale of sense,
Weigh thy opinion against Providence;
Call imperfection what thou fancy'st such,   115
Say, here he gives too little, there too much;
Destroy all creatures for thy sport or gust,[7]
Yet cry, if man's unhappy, God's unjust;
If man alone engross not Heaven's high care,
Alone made perfect here, immortal there: 120
Snatch from his hand the balance and the rod,
Rejudge his justice, be the God of God!
In pride, in reasoning pride, our error lies;
All quit their sphere, and rush into the skies.
Pride still is aiming at the blest abodes,   125
Men would be angels, angels would be gods.
Aspiring to be gods, if angels fell,
Aspiring to be angels, men rebel:
And who but wishes to invert the laws
Of order, sins against the Eternal Cause.   130

5. Ask for what end the heavenly bodies shine,
Earth for whose use? Pride answers, " 'Tis for mine:
For me kind Nature wakes her genial power,
Suckles each herb, and spreads out every flower;
Annual for me, the grape, the rose renew   135
The juice nectareous, and the balmy dew;
For me, the mine a thousand treasures brings;
For me, health gushes from a thousand springs;
Seas roll to waft me, suns to light me rise;
My footstool earth, my canopy the skies."   140
    But errs not Nature from this gracious end,
From burning suns when livid deaths descend,
When earthquakes swallow, or when tempests sweep
Towns to one grave, whole nations to the deep?
"No," 'tis replied, "the first Almighty Cause   145
Acts not by partial, but by general laws;
The exceptions few; some change since all began,
And what created perfect?"—Why then man?
If the great end be human happiness,

7. "Sense of tasting" (Johnson's *Dictionary*).

Then Nature deviates; and can man do less?   150
As much that end a constant course requires
Of showers and sunshine, as of man's desires;
As much eternal springs and cloudless skies,
As men forever temperate, calm, and wise.
If plagues or earthquakes break not Heaven's design,   155
Why then a Borgia, or a Catiline?[8]
Who knows but he whose hand the lightning forms,
Who heaves old ocean, and who wings the storms,
Pours fierce ambition in a Caesar's mind,
Or turns young Ammon[9] loose to scourge mankind?   160
From pride, from pride, our very reasoning springs;
Account for moral, as for natural things:
Why charge we Heaven in those, in these acquit?
In both, to reason right is to submit.
    Better for us, perhaps, it might appear,   165
Were there all harmony, all virtue here;
That never air or ocean felt the wind;
That never passion discomposed the mind:
But ALL subsists by elemental strife;
And passions are the elements of life.   170
The general ORDER, since the whole began,
Is kept in Nature, and is kept in man.

    6. What would this man? Now upward will he soar,
And little less than angel, would be more;
Now looking downwards, just as grieved appears   175
To want the strength of bulls, the fur of bears.
Made for his use all creatures if he call,
Say what their use, had he the powers of all?
Nature to these, without profusion, kind,
The proper organs, proper powers assigned;   180
Each seeming want compénsated of course,
Here with degrees of swiftness, there of force;
All in exact proportion to the state;
Nothing to add, and nothing to abate.
Each beast, each insect, happy in its own;   185
Is Heaven unkind to man, and man alone?
Shall he alone, whom rational we call,
Be pleased with nothing, if not blessed with all?
    The bliss of man (could pride that blessing find)
Is not to act or think beyond mankind;   190
No powers of body or of soul to share,
But what his nature and his state can bear.
Why has not man a microscopic eye?

---

8. The Renaissance Italian family of the Borgias were notorious for their crimes: ruthless lust for power, cruelty, rapaciousness, treachery, and murder (especially by poisoning); Cesare Borgia (1476–1507), son of Pope Alexander VI, is here referred to. Lucius Sergius Catiline (ca. 108–62 B.C.), an ambitious, greedy, and cruel conspirator against the Roman state, was denounced in Cicero's famous orations before the senate and in the Forum.
9. Alexander the Great.

For this plain reason, man is not a fly.
Say what the use, were finer optics given,   195
To inspect a mite, not comprehend the heaven?
Or touch, if tremblingly alive all o'er,
To smart and agonize at every pore?
Or quick effluvia[1] darting through the brain,
Die of a rose in aromatic pain?   200
If nature thundered in his opening ears,
And stunned him with the music of the spheres,
How would he wish that Heaven had left him still
The whispering zephyr, and the purling rill?
Who finds not Providence all good and wise,   205
Alike in what it gives, and what denies?

7. Far as creation's ample range extends,
The scale of sensual,[2] mental powers ascends:
Mark how it mounts, to man's imperial race,
From the green myriads in the peopled grass: 210
What modes of sight betwixt each wide extreme,
The mole's dim curtain, and the lynx's beam:[3]
Of smell, the headlong lioness between,
And hound sagacious[4] on the tainted green:
Of hearing, from the life that fills the flood,   215
To that which warbles through the vernal wood:
The spider's touch, how exquisitely fine!
Feels at each thread, and lives along the line:
In the nice[5] bee, what sense so subtly true
From poisonous herbs extracts the healing dew: 220
How instinct varies in the groveling swine,
Compared, half-reasoning elephant, with thine!
'Twixt that, and reason, what a nice barrier;[6]
Forever separate, yet forever near!
Remembrance and reflection how allied;   225
What thin partitions sense from thought divide: ·
And middle natures, how they long to join,
Yet never pass the insuperable line!
Without this just gradation, could they be
Subjected, these to those, or all to thee?   230
The powers of all subdued by thee alone,
Is not thy reason all these powers in one?

8. See, through this air, this ocean, and this earth,
All matter quick, and bursting into birth.
Above, how high progressive life may go!   235
Around, how wide! how deep extend below!

---

1. According to the philosophy of Epicurus (adopted by Robert Boyle, the chemist, and other 17th-century scientists), the senses are stirred to perception by being bombarded through the pores by steady streams of "effluvia," incredibly thin and tiny—but material—images of the objects which surround us.
2. Sensory.
3. One of several early theories of vision held that the eye casts a beam of light which makes objects visible.
4. Quick of scent.
5. Exact, accurate.
6. Pronounced *ba-réer*.

Vast Chain of Being! which from God began,
Natures ethereal, human, angel, man,
Beast, bird, fish, insect, what no eye can see,
No glass can reach! from Infinite to thee,   240
From thee to nothing.—On superior powers
Were we to press, inferior might on ours:
Or in the full creation leave a void,
Where, one step broken, the great scale's destroyed:
From Nature's chain whatever link you strike,   245
Tenth or ten thousandth, breaks the chain alike.
   And, if each system in gradation roll
Alike essential to the amazing Whole,
The least confusion but in one, not all
That system only, but the Whole must fall.   250
Let earth unbalanced from her orbit fly,
Planets and suns run lawless through the sky,
Let ruling angels from their spheres be hurled,
Being on being wrecked, and world on world,
Heaven's whole foundations to their center nod,   255
And Nature tremble to the throne of God:
All this dread ORDER break—for whom? for thee?
Vile worm!—oh, madness, pride, impiety!

   9. What if the foot, ordained the dust to tread,
Or hand, to toil, aspired to be the head?   260
What if the head, the eye, or ear repined
To serve mere engines to the ruling Mind?[7]
Just as absurd for any part to claim
To be another, in this general frame:
Just as absurd, to mourn the tasks or pains,   265
The great directing MIND of ALL ordains.
   All are but parts of one stupendous whole,
Whose body Nature is, and God the soul;
That, changed through all, and yet in all the same,
Great in the earth, as in the ethereal frame,   270
Warms in the sun, refreshes in the breeze,
Glows in the stars, and blossoms in the trees,
Lives through all life, extends through all extent,
Spreads undivided, operates unspent,
Breathes in our soul, informs our mortal part,   275
As full, as perfect, in a hair as heart;
As full, as perfect, in vile man that mourns,
As the rapt seraph that adores and burns;
To him no high, no low, no great, no small;
He fills, he bounds, connects, and equals all.   280

   10. Cease then, nor ORDER imperfection name:
Our proper bliss depends on what we blame.
Know thy own point: this kind, this due degree
Of blindness, weakness, Heaven bestows on thee.

7. Cf. I Corinthians xii.14–26.

Submit—In this, or any other sphere,   285
Secure to be as blest as thou canst bear:
Safe in the hand of one disposing Power,
Or in the natal, or the mortal hour.
All Nature is but art, unknown to thee;
All chance, direction, which thou canst not see;   290
All discord, harmony not understood;
All partial evil, universal good:
And, spite of pride, in erring reason's spite,
One truth is clear: Whatever IS, is RIGHT.

From *Epistle II. Of the Nature and State of Man With Respect to Himself, as an Individual*

1. Know then thyself, presume not God to scan;
The proper study of mankind is Man.
Placed on this isthmus of a middle state,
A being darkly wise, and rudely great:
With too much knowledge for the skeptic side,   5
With too much weakness for the Stoic's pride,
He hangs between; in doubt to act, or rest,
In doubt to deem himself a god, or beast;
In doubt his mind or body to prefer,
Born but to die, and reasoning but to err;   10
Alike in ignorance, his reason such,
Whether he thinks too little, or too much:
Chaos of thought and passion, all confused;
Still by himself abused, or disabused;
Created half to rise, and half to fall;   15
Great lord of all things, yet a prey to all;
Sole judge of truth, in endless error hurled:
The glory, jest, and riddle of the world!

* * *

1733

The Universal Prayer

Father of all! in every age,
    In every clime adored,
By saint, by savage, and by sage,
    Jehovah, Jove, or Lord!

Thou Great First Cause, least understood: 5
    Who all my sense confined
To know but this—that thou art good,
    And that myself am blind:

Yet gave me, in this dark estate,
    To see the good from ill;   10

And binding Nature fast in fate,
   Left free the human will.

What conscience dictates to be done,
   Or warns me not to do,
This, teach me more than Hell to shun,   15
   That, more than Heaven pursue.

What blessings thy free bounty gives,
   Let me not cast away;
For God is paid when man receives,
   To enjoy is to obey.   20

Yet not to earth's contracted span,
   Thy goodness let me bound,
Or think thee Lord alone of man,
   When thousand worlds are round:

Let not this weak, unknowing hand   25
   Presume thy bolts to throw,
And deal damnation round the land,
   On each I judge thy foe.

If I am right, thy grace impart,
   Still in the right to stay;   30
If I am wrong, oh teach my heart
   To find that better way.

Save me alike from foolish pride,
   Or impious discontent,
At aught thy wisdom has denied,   35
   Or aught thy goodness lent.

Teach me to feel another's woe,
   To hide the fault I see;
That mercy I to others show,
   That mercy show to me.   40

Mean though I am, not wholly so
   Since quickened by thy breath;
Oh lead me wheresoe'er I go,
   Through this day's life or death.

This day, be bread and peace my lot: 45
   All else beneath the sun,
Thou know'st if best bestowed or not,
   And let thy will be done.

To thee, whose temple is all space,
   Whose altar, earth, sea, skies!   50
One chorus let all being raise!
   All Nature's incense rise!

ca. 1715   1738

Epistle II. To a Lady[1]

OF THE CHARACTERS OF WOMEN

Nothing so true as what you once let fall,
"Most women have no characters at all."
Matter too soft a lasting mark to bear,
And best distinguished by black, brown, or fair.
    How many pictures[2] of one nymph we view,   5
All how unlike each other, all how true!
Arcadia's countess, here, in ermined pride,
Is, there, Pastora by a fountain side.
Here Fannia, leering on her own good man,
And there, a naked Leda with a swan.[3]   10
Let then the fair one beautifully cry,
In Magdalen's loose hair and lifted eye,
Or dressed in smiles of sweet Cecilia shine,[4]
With simpering angels, palms, and harps divine;
Whether the charmer sinner it, or saint it,   15
If folly grow romantic,[5] I must paint it.
    Come then, the colors and the ground[6] prepare!

1. This is one of four poems that Pope grouped together under the title *Epistles to Several Persons*, but that have usually been known by the less appropriate title *Moral Essays*. They were conceived as parts of Pope's ambitious "ethic work," of which only the first part, the *Essay on Man*, was completed. *Epistle I* treats the characters of men, *Epistle II* the characters of women. The other two epistles are concerned with the use of riches, a subject that engaged Pope's attention during the 1730's, since he distrusted the influence on private morals and public life of the rapidly growing wealth of England under the first Hanoverians.
    Epistle II contains a series of brilliantly executed portraits (the metaphor of portrait painting dominates the poem) which among them illustrate the thesis that women are consistent only in being inconsistent. As we move from portrait to portrait, we not only observe ladies who are changeable and fickle in their own nature, but we also meet a variety of female characters—the affected, the slatternly, the soft-natured, the silly, the lewd, for instance—which remind us that ladies are as variegated as tulips (line 41).
    Are the portraits imaginary or do they represent women whom Pope knew and whom his readers could recognize? This question exercised the gossips of Pope's own time and after; and it has occupied the attention of Pope's editors and commentators ever since his death. Many of the portraits indubitably allude to actual women (Sappho); some doubtless are composite (Atossa); others are mere types. Questions of identity, however, pertain rather to Pope's biography and character than to his art. It should matter little if at all to the reader first approaching Pope's satire whether in fact Atossa is Sarah, Duchess of Marlborough, or, as is much more likely, Katherine, Duchess of Buckinghamshire, or, most likely of all, Katherine combined with a few traits of Sarah. Occasionally, perhaps, a lady's name might have hinted to some of Pope's contemporaries that a real person was intended. Today the reader who is not a specialist will do well to neglect particular applications of Pope's satire and to concern himself with the generally, the permanently human, which is always the center of Pope's works.
    The "lady" of the title is Martha Blount (1690–1763), Pope's best-loved female friend, to whom he left the bulk of his property.
2. Ladies of the 17th and 18th centuries liked to have themselves painted in the costumes and attitudes of fanciful, mythological, or historical characters.
3. Leda was seduced by Zeus, who approached her in the form of a swan.
4. St. Mary Magdalen was often painted during the 17th century in the attitude described in line 12. St. Cecilia, the reputed inventor of the organ, was traditionally painted in the manner which Pope satirically glances at here.
5. Extravagant.
6. The first coatings of paint on the canvas before the figures in the picture are sketched in.

Dip in the rainbow, trick her off in air;
Choose a firm cloud, before it fall, and in it
Catch, ere she change, the Cynthia[7] of this minute.   20
    Rufa, whose eye quick-glancing o'er the park,
Attracts each light gay meteor of a spark,
Agrees as ill with Rufa studying Locke,[8]
As Sappho's diamonds with her dirty smock,
Or Sappho at her toilet's greasy task,[9]   25
With Sappho fragrant at an evening masque:
So morning insects that in muck begun,
Shine, buzz, and flyblow in the setting sun.
    How soft is Silia! fearful to offend,
The frail one's advocate, the weak one's friend: 30
To her, Calista proved her conduct nice,
And good Simplicius asks of her advice.
Sudden, she storms! she raves! You tip the wink,
But spare your censure; Silia does not drink.
All eyes may see from what the change arose,   35
All eyes may see—a pimple on her nose.
    Papillia,[1] wedded to her amorous spark,
Sighs for the shades—"How charming is a park!"
A park is purchased, but the fair he sees
All bathed in tears—"Oh, odious, odious trees!"   40
    Ladies, like variegated tulips, show;
'Tis to their changes half their charms we owe;
Fine by defect, and delicately weak,
Their happy spots the nice admirer take,
'Twas thus Calypso[2] once each heart alarmed,   45
Awed without virtue, without beauty charmed;
Her tongue bewitched as oddly as her eyes,
Less wit than mimic, more a wit than wise;
Strange graces still, and stranger flights she had,
Was just not ugly, and was just not mad;   50
Yet ne'er so sure our passion to create,
As when she touched the brink of all we hate.
    Narcissa's[3] nature, tolerably mild,
To make a wash,[4] would hardly stew a child;
Has even been proved to grant a lover's prayer,   55
And paid a tradesman once to make him stare,
Gave alms at Easter, in a Christian trim,
And made a widow happy, for a whim.
Why then declare good nature is her scorn,
When 'tis by that alone she can be borne?   60

7. One of the names of Diana, goddess of the moon, a notoriously changeable heavenly body.
8. John Locke, author of *An Essay Concerning Human Understanding* (1690).
9. Lady Mary Wortley Montagu, though beautiful as a young woman, became notorious for her slatternly appearance and personal uncleanliness. Both Sappho and Lady Mary were female poets.
1. The name comes from Latin for "butterfly."
2. The name is borrowed from the fascinating goddess who detained Odysseus on her island for seven years after the fall of Troy, thus preventing his return to his kingdom, Ithaca.
3. Type of extreme self-love. Narcissus, a beautiful youth, fell in love with his own image when he saw it reflected in a fountain.
4. Cosmetic lotion.

Why pique all mortals, yet affect a name?
A fool to pleasure, yet a slave to fame:
Now deep in Taylor and the *Book of Martyrs*,[5]
Now drinking citron[6] with his Grace and Chartres.
Now conscience chills her, and now passion burns;   65
And atheism and religion take their turns;
A very heathen in the carnal part,
Yet still a sad, good Christian at her heart.
    See Sin in state, majestically drunk;
Proud as a peeress, prouder as a punk;   70
Chaste to her husband, frank[6a] to all beside,
A teeming mistress, but a barren bride.
What then? let blood and body bear the fault,
Her head's untouched, that noble seat of thought:
Such this day's doctrine—in another fit   75
She sins with poets through pure love of wit.
What has not fired her bosom or her brain?
Caesar and Tallboy,[7] Charles and Charlemagne.
As Helluo,[8] late dictator of the feast,
The nose of hautgout,[9] and the tip of taste,   80
Criticked your wine, and analyzed your meat,
Yet on plain pudding deigned at home to eat;
So Philomedé,[1] lecturing all mankind
On the soft passion, and the taste refined,
The address, the delicacy—stoops at once,   85
And makes her hearty meal upon a dunce.
    Flavia's a wit, has too much sense to pray;
To toast our wants and wishes, is her way;
Nor asks of God, but of her stars, to give
The mighty blessing, "while we live, to live."   90
Then all for death, that opiate of the soul!
Lucretia's dagger,[2] Rosamonda's bowl.
Say, what can cause such impotence of mind?
A spark too fickle, or a spouse too kind.
Wise wretch! with pleasures too refined to please,   95
With too much spirit to be e'er at ease,
With too much quickness ever to be taught,

5. Jeremy Taylor, 17th-century Anglican divine, whose *Holy Living and Holy Dying* was often reprinted in the 18th century. John Foxe's *Acts and Monuments* (usually referred to as Foxe's *Book of Martyrs*), 1563, was a household book in most Protestant families in the 17th and 18th centuries; a record of the Protestants who perished for their faith under the persecution of Mary Tudor (1553–58), it was instrumental in keeping anti-Catholic sentiments alive.
6. I.e., citron-water, brandy flavored with lemon or orange peel. "His Grace" is usually said to be the Duke of Wharton, an old enemy of Swift's and a notorious libertine; Francis Chartres: a debauchee often mentioned by Pope.
6a. "Liberal; generous" (Johnson's *Dictionary*).

7. A crude young man in Richard Brome's comedy *The Jovial Crew* (1641) or the opera adapted from the play (1731); "Charles," as F. W. Bateson points out, was a generic name for a footman in the period.
8. Latin for "glutton."
9. "Anything with a strong relish or strong scent, as overkept venison" (Johnson's *Dictionary*).
1. The name is Pope's adaptation of a Greek epithet meaning "laughter-loving," frequently applied to Aphrodite, the goddess of love.
2. Lucretia, violated by Tarquin, committed suicide; according to tradition, the "fair Rosamonda," mistress of Henry II, was forced by Queen Eleanor to drink poison.

With too much thinking to have common thought:
You purchase pain with all that joy can give,
And die of nothing but a rage to live.   100
   Turn then from wits; and look on Simo's mate,
No ass so meek, no ass so obstinate.
Or her, that owns her faults, but never mends,
Because she's honest, and the best of friends:
Or her, whose life the Church and scandal share,   105
Forever in a passion, or a prayer:
Or her, who laughs at hell, but (like her Grace)
Cries, "Ah! how charming, if there's no such place!"
Or who in sweet vicissitude appears
Of mirth and opium, ratafie[3] and tears,   110
The daily anodyne, and nightly draught,
To kill those foes to fair ones, time and thought.
Woman and fool are two hard things to hit,
For true no-meaning puzzles more than wit.
   But what are these to great Atossa's mind?[4]   115
Scarce once herself, by turns all womankind!
Who, with herself, or others, from her birth
Finds all her life one warfare upon earth:
Shines in exposing knaves, and painting fools,
Yet is whate'er she hates and ridicules.   120
No thought advances, but her eddy brain
Whisks it about, and down it goes again.
Full sixty years the world has been her trade,
The wisest fool much time has ever made.
From loveless youth to unrespected age,   125
No passion gratified except her rage.
So much the fury still outran the wit,
The pleasure missed her, and the scandal hit.
Who breaks with her, provokes revenge from hell,
But he's a bolder man who dares be well:[5]   130
Her every turn with violence pursued,
Nor more a storm her hate than gratitude:
To that each passion turns, or soon or late;
Love, if it makes her yield, must make her hate:
Superiors? death! and equals? what a curse!   135
But an inferior not dependent? worse.
Offend her, and she knows not to forgive;
Oblige her, and she'll hate you while you live:
But die, and she'll adore you—Then the bust
And temple rise—then fall again to dust.   140
Last night, her lord was all that's good and great;
A knave this morning, and his will a cheat.
Strange! by the means defeated of the ends,
By spirit robbed of power, by warmth of friends,
By wealth of followers! without one distress   145

3. "A fine liquor, prepared from the kernels of apricots and spirits" (Johnson's *Dictionary*).
4. Atossa, daughter of Cyrus, Emperor of Persia (d. 529 B.C.). If the Duchess of Buckinghamshire is alluded to, the name is appropriate, for she was the natural daughter of James II.
5. Be in her favor.

Sick of herself through very selfishness!
Atossa, cursed with every granted prayer,
Childless with all her children, wants an heir.
To heirs unknown descends the unguarded store,
Or wanders, Heaven-directed, to the poor.   150
    Pictures like these, dear Madam, to design,
Asks no firm hand, and no unerring line;
Some wandering touches, some reflected light,
Some flying stroke alone can hit 'em right:
For how should equal colors do the knack?[6]   155
Chameleons who can paint in white and black?
    "Yet Chloe sure was formed without a spot—"
Nature in her then erred not, but forgot.
"With every pleasing, every prudent part,
Say, what can Chloe want?"—She wants a heart.   160
She speaks, behaves, and acts just as she ought;
But never, never, reached one generous thought.
Virtue she finds too painful an endeavor,
Content to dwell in decencies forever.
So very reasonable, so unmoved,   165
As never yet to love, or to be loved.
She, while her lover pants upon her breast,
Can mark[6a] the figures on an Indian chest;
And when she sees her friend in deep despair,
Observes how much a chintz exceeds mohair.   170
Forbid it Heaven, a favor or a debt
She e'er should cancel—but she may forget.
Safe is your secret still in Chloe's ear;
But none of Chloe's shall you ever hear.
Of all her dears she never slandered one,   175
But cares not if a thousand are undone.
Would Chloe know if you're alive or dead?
She bids her footman put it in her head.
Chloe is prudent—Would you too be wise?
Then never break your heart when Chloe dies.   180
    One certain portrait may (I grant) be seen,
Which Heaven has varnished out, and made a *Queen*:[7]
The same forever! and described by all
With Truth and Goodness, as with crown and ball.
Poets heap virtues, painters gems at will,   185
And show their zeal, and hide their want of skill.
'Tis well—but, artists! who can paint or write,
To draw the naked is your true delight.
That robe of quality so struts and swells,
None see what parts of Nature it conceals: 190
The exactest traits of body or of mind,
We owe to models of an humble kind.
If Queensberry[8] to strip there's no compelling,

6. Do the trick.
6a. Pay attention to.
7. Pope refers as usual to Queen Caroline with disapprobation.

8. The Duchess of Queensberry, whom Pope valued because of her kindness to his friend John Gay, had been a famous beauty.

'Tis from a handmaid we must take a Helen.
From peer or bishop 'tis no easy thing   195
To draw the man who loves his God, or king:
Alas! I copy (or my draft would fail)
From honest Mah'met[9] or plain Parson Hale.
    But grant, in public men sometimes are shown,
A woman's seen in private life alone: 200
Our bolder talents in full light displayed;
Your virtues open fairest in the shade.
Bred to disguise, in public 'tis you hide;
There, none distinguish 'twixt your shame or pride,
Weakness or delicacy; all so nice,   205
That each may seem a virtue, or a vice.
    In men, we various ruling passions find;
In women, two almost divide the kind;
Those, only fixed, they first or last obey,
The love of pleasure, and the love of sway.   210
    That, Nature gives; and where the lesson taught
Is but to please, can pleasure seem a fault?
Experience, this; by man's oppression cursed,
They seek the second not to lose the first.
    Men, some to business, some to pleasure take;   215
But every woman is at heart a rake;
Men, some to quiet, some to public strife;
But every lady would be queen for life.
    Yet mark the fate of a whole sex of queens!
Power all their end, but beauty all the means: 220
In youth they conquer, with so wild a rage,
As leaves them scarce a subject in their age:
For foreign glory, foreign joy, they roam;
No thought of peace or happiness at home.
But wisdom's triumph is well-timed retreat,   225
As hard a science to the fair as great!
Beauties, like tyrants, old and friendless grown,
Yet hate repose, and dread to be alone,
Worn out in public, weary every eye,
Nor leave one sigh behind them when they die.   230
    Pleasures the sex, as children birds, pursue,
Still out of reach, yet never out of view,
Sure, if they catch, to spoil the toy at most,
To covet flying, and regret when lost:
At last, to follies youth could scarce defend,   235
It grows their age's prudence to pretend;
Ashamed to own they gave delight before,
Reduced to feign it, when they give no more:
As hags hold sabbaths,[1] less for joy than spite,
So these their merry, miserable night;   240
Still round and round the ghosts of beauty glide,

---

9. Mahomet, a Turkish servant of
George I; Dr. Stephen Hales was an
Anglican clergyman and friend of Pope.
1. Obscene rites popularly supposed
to be held by witches ("hags"); "night,"
in the next line, refers to evenings on
which ladies entertained guests.

And haunt the places where their honor died.
   See how the world its veterans rewards!
A youth of frolics, an old age of cards;
Fair to no purpose, artful to no end,   245
Young without lovers, old without a friend;
A fop their passion, but their prize a sot;
Alive, ridiculous, and dead, forgot!
   Ah friend! to dazzle let the vain design;
To raise the thought, and touch the heart be thine!   250
That charm shall grow, while what fatigues the Ring[2]
Flaunts and goes down, an unregarded thing:
So when the sun's broad beam has tired the sight,
All mild ascends the moon's more sober light,
Serene in virgin modesty she shines,   255
And unobserved the glaring orb declines.
   Oh! blest with temper, whose unclouded ray
Can make tomorrow cheerful as today;
She, who can love a sister's charms, or hear
Sighs for a daughter with unwounded ear;   260
She, who ne'er answers till a husband cools,
Or, if she rules him, never shows she rules;
Charms by accepting, by submitting sways,
Yet has her humor most, when she obeys;
Let fops or fortune fly which way they will;   265
Disdains all loss of tickets[3] or Codille;
Spleen, vapors, or smallpox, above them all,
And mistress of herself, though China[4] fall.
   And yet, believe me, good as well as ill,
Woman's at best a contradiction still.   270
Heaven, when it strives to polish all it can
Its last best work, but forms a softer man;
Picks from each sex, to make the favorite blest,
Your love of pleasure, our desire of rest:
Blends, in exception to all general rules,   275
Your taste of follies, with our scorn of fools:
Reserve with frankness, art with truth allied,
Courage with softness, modesty with pride;
Fixed principles, with fancy ever new;
Shakes all together, and produces—you.   280
   Be this a woman's fame: with this unblest,
Toasts live a scorn, and queens may die a jest.
This Poebus promised (I forget the year)
When those blue eyes first opened on the sphere;
Ascendant Phoebus watched that hour with care,   285
Averted half your parents' simple prayer;
And gave you beauty, but denied the pelf
That buys your sex a tyrant o'er itself.
The generous god, who wit and gold refines,

---

2. The fashionable drive in Hyde Park.
3. I.e., lottery tickets; "Codille": the
loss of a hand at the card games of
ombre or quadrille.

4. Pope refers punningly to the chinaware which fashionable women collected
enthusiastically.

And ripens spirits as he ripens mines,[5] 290
Kept dross for duchesses, the world shall know it,
To you gave sense, good humor, and a poet.

1735, 1744

Epistle to Dr. Arbuthnot[1]

Advertisement

TO THE FIRST PUBLICATION OF THIS *Epistle*

This paper is a sort of bill of complaint, begun many years since, and drawn up by snatches, as the several occasions offered. I had no thoughts of publishing it, till it pleased some persons of rank and fortune (the authors of *Verses to the Imitator of Horace*, and of an *Epistle to a Doctor of Divinity from a Nobleman at Hampton Court*) to attack, in a very extraordinary manner, not only my writings (of which, being public, the public is judge) but my person, morals, and family, whereof, to those who know me

5. Phoebus Apollo, as god of poetry "ripens wit"; as god of the sun, he "ripens mines," for respectable scientific theory held that the sun's rays mature precious metals in the earth.

1. Dr. John Arbuthnot (1667–1735), to whom Pope addressed his best-known verse epistle, was distinguished both as a physician and as a man of wit. He had been one of the liveliest members of the Martinus Scriblerus Club, helping his friends to create the character and shape the career of the learned pedant whose *Memoirs* the Club had undertaken to write.

Pope had long been meditating such a poem, which was to be both an attack on his detractors and a defense of his own character and career. In his usual way he had jotted down hints, lines, couplets, fragments over a period of two decades, but the poem might never have been completed had it not been for two events: Arbuthnot, from his deathbed, wrote to urge Pope to continue his abhorrence of vice and to express it in his writings; and, during 1733, Pope was the victim of two bitter attacks by "persons of rank and fortune," as the "Advertisement" has it. The *Verses Addressed to the Imitator of Horace* was the work of Lady Mary Wortley Montagu, helped by her friend Lord Hervey (pronounced "Harvey"), a close friend and confidant of Queen Caroline; *An Epistle to a Doctor of Divinity from a Nobleman at Hampton Court* was the work of Lord Hervey alone. Lady Mary, it must be admitted, had provocation enough, especially in Pope's recent reference to her in *The First Satire of the Second Book of Horace*, lines 83–84; but Hervey had little to complain of beyond occasional covert references to

him as "Lord Fanny." At any rate, the two scurrilous attacks goaded Pope into action, and the poem was completed by the end of the summer of 1734.

The *Epistle* is a masterpiece of poetic rhetoric. The very fact that it is addressed to Dr. Arbuthnot, a man who had the general approbation of the world because of his kindliness and probity, in some degree seems to guarantee the integrity of the "I" of the poem and to diminish the moral stature of his enemies. This acquisition of virtue through association, an effective stroke, is supported by every device of persuasive rhetoric: reasonable argument and emotional appeals, subtly suggestive imagery, and superbly controlled shifts in tone and style which help to sway the reader's judgment to the side of the speaker. The poem opens in the flat language of commonplace prose discourse, tinged with a wry humor and a tone of exasperation: "Shut, shut the door, good John! (fatigued, I said)" and as it progresses it rises or falls in language and style according to the emotions which the speaker expresses— anger, contempt, amusement, sarcasm, mock self-pity, indignation, hatred, affection, gratitude, tenderness—to return at the end to the homely tone of the opening.

It is not clear that Pope intended the poem to be thought of as a dialogue, as it has usually been printed since Warburton's edition of 1751. The original edition, while suggesting interruptions in the flow of the monologue, kept entirely to the form of a letter. The introduction of the friend, who speaks from time to time, of course converts the original letter into a dramatic dialogue.

not, a truer information may be requisite. Being divided between the necessity to say something of myself, and my own laziness to undertake so awkward a task, I thought it the shortest way to put the last hand to this epistle. If it have anything pleasing, it will be that by which I am most desirous to please, the truth and the sentiment; and if anything offensive, it will be only to those I am least sorry to offend, the vicious or the ungenerous.

Many will know their own pictures in it, there being not a circumstance but what is true; but I have, for the most part, spared their names, and they may escape being laughed at, if they please.

I would have some of them know, it was owing to the request of the learned and candid friend to whom it is inscribed, that I make not as free use of theirs as they have done of mine. However, I shall have this advantage, and honor, on my side, that whereas, by their proceeding, any abuse may be directed at any man, no injury can possibly be done by mine, since a nameless character can never be found out, but by its truth and likeness. P.

P. Shut, shut the door, good John![2] (fatigued, I said),
Tie up the knocker, say I'm sick, I'm dead.
The Dog Star[3] rages! nay 'tis past a doubt
All Bedlam,[4] or Parnassus, is let out:
Fire in each eye, and papers in each hand,　　　　　　　　　5
They rave, recite, and madden round the land.
　　What walls can guard me, or what shades can hide?
They pierce my thickets, through my grot[5] they glide,
By land, by water, they renew the charge,
They stop the chariot, and they board the barge.　　　　10
No place is sacred, not the church is free;
Even Sunday shines no Sabbath day to me:
Then from the Mint[6] walks forth the man of rhyme,
Happy to catch me just at dinner time.
　　Is there a parson, much bemused in beer,　　　　　　15
A maudlin poetess, a rhyming peer,
A clerk foredoomed his father's soul to cross,
Who pens a stanza when he should engross?[7]
Is there who,[7a] locked from ink and paper, scrawls
With desperate charcoal round his darkened walls?　　20
All fly to Twit'nam,[8] and in humble strain
Apply to me to keep them mad or vain.
Arthur,[9] whose giddy son neglects the laws,

2. John Serle, Pope's gardener.
3. Sirius, associated with the period of greatest heat (and hence of madness) because it sets with the sun in late summer. August, in ancient Rome, was the season for reciting poetry.
4. Bethlehem Hospital for the insane in London.
5. See *First Satire of the Second Book of Horace,* line 124 and note.
6. A place in Southwark where debtors were free from arrest (they could not

be arrested anywhere on Sundays).
7. Write out legal documents.
7a. Is there some madman who, locked up without ink or paper* * * ?
8. I.e., Twickenham, Pope's villa on the bank of the Thames, a few miles above Hampton Court.
9. Arthur Moore, whose son, James Moore Smythe, dabbled in literature. Moore Smythe had earned Pope's enmity by using in one of his plays some unpublished lines from Pope's *Epistle*

Imputes to me and my damned works the cause:
Poor Cornus[1] sees his frantic wife elope,   25
And curses wit, and poetry, and Pope.
    Friend to my life (which did not you prolong,
The world had wanted many an idle song)
What drop or nostrum[2] can this plague remove?
Or which must end me, a fool's wrath or love?   30
A dire dilemma! either way I'm sped,[2a]
If foes, they write, if friends, they read me dead.
Seized and tied down to judge, how wretched I!
Who can't be silent, and who will not lie.
To laugh were want of goodness and of grace,   35
And to be grave exceeds all power of face.
I sit with sad civility, I read
With honest anguish and an aching head,
And drop at last, but in unwilling ears,
This saving counsel, "Keep your piece nine years."[3]   40
    "Nine years!" cries he, who high in Drury Lane,[4]
Lulled by soft zephyrs through the broken pane,
Rhymes ere he wakes, and prints before term[5] ends,
Obliged by hunger and request of friends:
"The piece, you think, is incorrect? why, take it,   45
I'm all submission, what you'd have it, make it."
    Three things another's modest wishes bound,
My friendship, and a prologue, and ten pound.
    Pitholeon[6] sends to me: "You know his Grace,
I want a patron; ask him for a place."   50
Pitholeon libeled me—"but here's a letter
Informs you, sir, 'twas when he knew no better.
Dare you refuse him? Curll[7] invites to dine,
He'll write a *Journal*, or he'll turn divine."[8]
Bless me! a packet.—" 'Tis a stranger sues,   55
A virgin tragedy, an orphan Muse."
If I dislike it, "Furies, death, and rage!"
If I approve, "Commend it to the stage."
There (thank my stars) my whole commission ends,
The players and I are, luckily, no friends.   60
Fired that the house reject him, " 'Sdeath, I'll print it,
And shame the fools—Your interest, sir, with Lintot!"[9]
Lintot, dull rogue, will think your price too much.
"Not, sir, if you revise it, and retouch."

---

to a Lady in spite of Pope's objections.
1. Latin for "horn," the traditional emblem of the cuckold.
2. Medicine.
2a. Destroyed; killed (Johnson's *Dictionary*).
3. The advice of Horace in *Ars Poetica* (line 388).
4. I.e., living in a garret in Drury Lane, site of one of the theaters and the haunt of the profligate.
5. One of the four annual periods in which the law courts are in session and with which the publishing season coincided.
6. "A foolish poet of Rhodes, who pre-

tended much to Greek" [Pope's note]; he is Leonard Welsted, who translated Longinus and had attacked and slandered Pope. See line 375.
7. Edmund Curll, shrewd and disreputable bookseller, published pirated works, works falsely ascribed to reputable writers, scandalous biographies, and other ephemera. Pope had often attacked him and had assigned to him a low role in the *Dunciad*.
8. I.e., he will attack Pope in the *London Journal* or write a treatise on theology, as Welsted in fact did.
9. Bernard Lintot, publisher of Pope's Homer and other early works.

All my demurs but double his attacks;   65
At last he whispers, "Do; and we go snacks."[1]
Glad of a quarrel, straight I clap the door,
"Sir, let me see your works and you no more."
    'Tis sung, when Midas' ears began to spring
(Midas, a sacred person and a king),   70
His very minister who spied them first,
(Some say his queen) was forced to speak, or burst.[2]
And is not mine, my friend, a sorer case,
When every coxcomb perks them in my face?
    A. Good friend, forbear! you deal in dangerous things.   75
I'd never name queens, ministers, or kings;
Keep close to ears, and those let asses prick;
'Tis nothing—— P. Nothing? if they bite and kick?
Out with it, *Dunciad!* let the secret pass,
That secret to each fool, that he's an ass: 80
The truth once told (and wherefore should we lie?)
The queen of Midas slept, and so may I.
    You think this cruel? take it for a rule,
No creature smarts so little as a fool.
Let peals of laughter, Codrus! round thee break,   85
Thou unconcerned canst hear the mighty crack.
Pit, box, and gallery in convulsions hurled,
Thou stand'st unshook amidst a bursting world.
Who shames a scribbler? break one cobweb through,
He spins the slight, self-pleasing thread anew: 90
Destroy his fib or sophistry, in vain;
The creature's at his dirty work again,
Throned in the center of his thin designs,
Proud of a vast extent of flimsy lines.
Whom have I hurt? has poet yet or peer   95
Lost the arched eyebrow or Parnassian sneer?
And has not Colley[3] still his lord and whore?
His butchers Henley? his freemasons Moore?
Does not one table Bavius[4] still admit?
Still to one bishop Philips seem a wit?   100
Still Sappho[5]—— A. Hold! for God's sake—you'll offend.
No names—be calm—learn prudence of a friend.
I too could write, and I am twice as tall;
But foes like these!—— P. One flatterer's worse than all.

---

1. Go shares.
2. Midas, king of ancient Lydia, had the bad taste to prefer the flute-playing of Pan to that of Apollo, whereupon the god endowed him with ass's ears. It was his barber (not his wife or his minister) who discovered the secret and whispered it into a hole in the earth. The reference to "queen" and "minister" makes it plain that Pope is alluding to George II, Queen Caroline, and Walpole.
3. Colley Cibber, the laureate John Henley, known as "Orator" Henley, an independent preacher of marked eccentricity, was popular among the lower orders, especially for his elocution.
4. The bad poet alluded to in Virgil's *Eclogues* III. The "Bishop" is Hugh Boulter, Bishop of Armagh; he had employed as his secretary Ambrose Philips (1674–1749), whose insipid and babbling simplicity of manner in poetry earned him the nickname of "Namby-Pamby."
5. Lady Mary Wortley Montagu.

Of all mad creatures, if the learn'd are right,   105
It is the slaver kills, and not the bite.
A fool quite angry is quite innocent:
Alas! 'tis ten times worse when they repent.
      One dedicates in high heroic prose,
And ridicules beyond a hundred foes;   110
One from all Grub Street[6] will my fame defend,
And, more abusive, calls himself my friend.
This prints my letters,[7] that expects a bribe,
And others roar aloud, "Subscribe, subscribe!"[8]
      There are, who to my person pay their court: 115
I cough like Horace, and, though lean, am short;
Ammon's great son[9] one shoulder had too high,
Such Ovid's nose, and "Sir! you have an eye—"
Go on, obliging creatures, make me see
All that disgraced my betters met in me.   120
Say for my comfort, languishing in bed,
"Just so immortal Maro[1] held his head":
And when I die, be sure you let me know
Great Homer died three thousand years ago.
      Why did I write? what sin to me unknown   125
Dipped me in ink, my parents', or my own?
As yet a child, nor yet a fool to fame,
I lisped in numbers, for the numbers came.
I left no calling for this idle trade,
No duty broke, no father disobeyed.   130
The Muse but served to ease some friend, not wife,
To help me through this long disease, my life,
To second, Arbuthnot! thy art and care,
And teach the being you preserved, to bear.[2]
      A. But why then publish? P. Granville the polite,   135
And knowing Walsh, would tell me I could write;
Well-natured Garth inflamed with early praise,
And Congreve loved, and Swift endured my lays;
The courtly Talbot, Somers, Sheffield, read;
Even mitered Rochester would nod the head,   140
And St. John's self (great Dryden's friends before)
With open arms received one poet more.[3]

6. A term denoting the whole society of literary, political, and journalistic hack writers.
7. In 1726 Curll had surreptitiously acquired and published without permission some of Pope's letters to Henry Cromwell.
8. To ensure the financial success of a work, the public was often asked to "subscribe" to it by taking a certain number of copies before printing was undertaken. Pope's Homer was published thus.
9. Alexander the Great. "Ovid's nose": Ovid's family name Naso suggests the Latin word *nasus* ("nose"), hence the pun.

1. Virgil.
2. Endure.
3. The purpose of this list is to establish Pope as the successor of Dryden and thus to place him far above his Grub-Street persecutors. George Granville, Lord Lansdowne, poet and statesman; William Walsh, poet and critic; Sir Samuel Garth, physician and mock-epic poet; William Congreve, the playwright; the statesmen Charles Talbot, Duke of Shrewsbury; Lord Sommers; John Sheffield, Duke of Buckinghamshire; and Francis Atterbury, Bishop of Rochester, had all been associated with Dryden in his later years and had all encouraged the young Pope.

Happy my studies, when by these approved!
Happier their author, when by these beloved!
From these the world will judge of men and books,   145
Not from the Burnets, Oldmixons, and Cookes.[4]
    Soft were my numbers; who could take offense
While pure description held the place of sense?
Like gentle Fanny's[5] was my flowery theme,
A painted mistress, or a purling stream.   150
Yet then did Gildon[6] draw his venal quill;
I wished the man a dinner, and sat still.
Yet then did Dennis[7] rave in furious fret;
I never answered, I was not in debt.
If want provoked, or madness made them print,   155
I waged no war with Bedlam or the Mint.
    Did some more sober critic come abroad?
If wrong, I smiled; if right, I kissed the rod.
Pains, reading, study are their just pretense,
And all they want is spirit, taste, and sense.   160
Commas and points they set exactly right,
And 'twere a sin to rob them of their mite.
Yet ne'er one sprig of laurel graced these ribalds,
From slashing Bentley down to piddling Tibbalds.[8]
Each wight who reads not, and but scans and spells,   165
Each word-catcher that lives on syllables,
Even such small critics some regard may claim,
Preserved in Milton's or in Shakespeare's name.
Pretty! in amber to observe the forms
Of hairs, or straws, or dirt, or grubs, or worms!   170
The things, we know, are neither rich nor rare,
But wonder how the devil they got there.
    Were others angry? I excused them too;
Well might they rage; I gave them but their due.
A man's true merit 'tis not hard to find;   175
But each man's secret standard in his mind,
That casting weight[9] pride adds to emptiness,
This, who can gratify? for who can guess?
The bard[1] whom pilfered pastorals renown,

4. Thomas Burnet, John Oldmixon,
and Thomas Cooke; Pope identifies
them in a note as "authors of secret
and scandalous history."
5. John, Lord Hervey, whom Pope
satirizes in the character of Sporus,
lines 305–33 below.
6. Charles Gildon, minor critic and
scribbler, who, Pope believed, early
attacked him at the instigation of Addison; hence "venal quill."
7. John Dennis (see *Essay on Criticism*, line 270 and its note).
8. Richard Bentley (1662–1742), the
eminent classical scholar, seemed to
both Pope and Swift the perfect type
of the pedant: he is called "slashing"
because, in his edition of *Paradise Lost*

(1732), he had set in square brackets
all passages which he disliked on the
grounds they had been slipped into the
poem without the blind poet's knowledge. Lewis Theobald (1688–1744),
whose minute learning in Elizabethan
literature had enabled him to expose
Pope's defects as an editor of Shakespeare in 1726. Pope made him King
of the Dunces in the *Dunciad* (1728).
9. The weight that turns the scale;
here, the "deciding factor."
1. Ambrose Philips, Pope's rival in
pastoral poetry in 1709, when their
pastorals were published in Tonson's
sixth *Miscellany*. Philips had also
translated some Persian tales. Cf. line
100.

Who turns a Persian tale for half a crown,   180
Just writes to make his barrenness appear,
And strains from hard-bound brains eight lines a year:
He, who still wanting, though he lives on theft,
Steals much, spends little, yet has nothing left;
And he who now to sense, now nonsense leaning,   185
Means not, but blunders round about a meaning:
And he whose fustian's so sublimely bad,
It is not poetry, but prose run mad:
All these, my modest satire bade translate,
And owned that nine such poets made a Tate.[2]   190
How did they fume, and stamp, and roar, and chafe!
And swear, not Addison himself was safe.

    Peace to all such! but were there one whose fires
True Genius kindles, and fair Fame inspires;
Blessed with each talent and each art to please,   195
And born to write, converse, and live with ease:
Should such a man, too fond to rule alone,
Bear, like the Turk, no brother near the throne;
View him with scornful, yet with jealous eyes,
And hate for arts that caused himself to rise;   200
Damn with faint praise, assent with civil leer,
And without sneering, teach the rest to sneer;
Willing to wound, and yet afraid to strike,
Just hint a fault, and hesitate dislike;
Alike reserved to blame or to commend,   205
A timorous foe, and a suspicious friend;
Dreading even fools; by flatterers besieged,
And so obliging that he ne'er obliged;
Like Cato, give his little senate[3] laws,
And sit attentive to his own applause;   210
While wits and Templars[4] every sentence raise,
And wonder with a foolish face of praise—
Who but must laugh, if such a man there be?
Who would not weep, if Atticus[5] were he?

    What though my name stood rubric[6] on the walls   215
Or plastered posts, with claps, in capitals?
Or smoking forth, a hundred hawkers' load,
On wings of winds came flying all abroad?
I sought no homage from the race that write;
I kept, like Asian monarchs, from their sight: 220

2. Nahum Tate (1652–1715), poet laureate (1692–1715). His popular re-writing of Shakespeare's *King Lear* provided a happy ending; he wrote most of Part II of *Absalom and Achitophel.* The line refers to the old adage that it takes nine tailors to make one man.
3. Addison's tragedy *Cato* had been a sensational success in 1713. Pope had written the prologue, in which occurs the line, "While Cato gives his little senate laws." The satirical reference here is to Addison in the role of ar-

biter of taste among his friends and admirers, mostly Whigs, at Button's Coffee House. It was these people who had worked against the success of Pope's Homer.
4. Law students.
5. Pope's satiric pseudonym for Addison; Atticus (109–32 B.C.) was a wealthy man of letters and a friend of Cicero, known as a wise and disinterested man.
6. In red letters. "Claps": posters.

Poems I heeded (now berhymed so long)
No more than thou, great George! a birthday song.
I ne'er with wits or witlings passed my days
To spread about the itch of verse and praise;
Nor like a puppy daggled through the town   225
To fetch and carry sing-song up and down;
Nor at rehearsals sweat, and mouthed, and cried,
With handkerchief and orange at my side;
But sick of fops, and poetry, and prate,
To Bufo[7] left the whole Castalian state.   230

  Proud as Apollo on his forkéd hill,[8]
Sat full-blown Bufo, puffed by every quill;
Fed with soft dedication all day long,
Horace and he went hand in hand in song.
His library (where busts of poets dead   235
And a true Pindar stood without a head)
Received of wits an undistinguished race,
Who first his judgment asked, and then a place:
Much they extolled his pictures, much his seat,[9]
And flattered every day, and some days eat: 240
Till grown more frugal in his riper days,
He paid some bards with port, and some with praise;
To some a dry rehearsal was assigned,
And others (harder still) he paid in kind.
Dryden alone (what wonder?) came not nigh;   245
Dryden alone escaped this judging eye:
But still the great have kindness in reserve:
He helped to bury whom he helped to starve.

  May some choice patron bless each gray goose quill!
May every Bavius have his Bufo still!   250
So when a statesman wants a day's defense,
Or Envy holds a whole week's war with Sense,
Or simple Pride for flattery makes demands,
May dunce by dunce be whistled off my hands!
Blessed be the great! for those they take away,   255
And those they left me—for they left me Gay;[1]
Left me to see neglected genius bloom,
Neglected die, and tell it on his tomb;
Of all thy blameless life the sole return
My verse, and Queensberry weeping o'er thy urn!   260
Oh, let me live my own, and die so too!
("To live and die is all I have to do")
Maintain a poet's dignity and ease,

7. A type of tasteless patron of the arts. The Castalian spring on Mt. Parnassus was sacred to Apollo and the Muses.
8. Mt. Parnassus had two peaks, one sacred to Apollo, one to Bacchus.
9. Pronounced *sate*, and rhymed in next line with "eat" (*ate*). *Seat* means "estate."
1. John Gay (1685–1732), author of

the *Beggar's Opera* (1728) and other delightful works, dear friend of Swift and Pope. His failure to obtain patronage from the court intensified Pope's hostility to the Whig administration and the queen. Gay spent the last years of his life under the protection of the Duke and Duchess of Queensberry.

And see what friends, and read what books I please;
Above a patron, though I condescend   265
Sometimes to call a minister my friend.
I was not born for courts or great affairs;
I pay my debts, believe, and say my prayers,
Can sleep without a poem in my head,
Nor know if Dennis be alive or dead.   270
    Why am I asked what next shall see the light?
Heavens! was I born for nothing but to write?
Has life no joys for me? or (to be grave)
Have I no friend to serve, no soul to save?
"I found him close with Swift"—"Indeed? no doubt"   275
Cries prating Balbus, "something will come out."
'Tis all in vain, deny it as I will.
"No, such a genius never can lie still,"
And then for mine obligingly mistakes
The first lampoon Sir Will or Bubo makes.[2]   280
Poor guiltless I! and can I choose but smile,
When every coxcomb knows me by my style?
    Cursed be the verse, how well soe'er it flow,
That tends to make one worthy man my foe,
Give Virtue scandal, Innocence a fear,   285
Or from the soft-eyed virgin steal a tear!
But he who hurts a harmless neighbor's peace,
Insults fallen worth, or Beauty in distress,
Who loves a lie, lame Slander helps about,
Who writes a libel, or who copies out: 290
That fop whose pride affects a patron's name,
Yet absent, wounds an author's honest fame;
Who can your merit selfishly approve,
And show the sense of it without the love;
Who has the vanity to call you friend,   295
Yet wants the honor, injured, to defend;
Who tells whate'er you think, whate'er you say,
And, if he lie not, must at least betray:
Who to the dean and silver bell can swear,
And sees at Cannons what was never there:[3]   300
Who reads but with a lust to misapply,
Make satire a lampoon, and fiction, lie:
A lash like mine no honest man shall dread,
But all such babbling blockheads in his stead.
    Let Sporus[4] tremble—— A. What? that thing of silk,   305
Sporus, that mere white curd of ass's milk?[5]
Satire or sense, alas! can Sporus feel?

2. Sir William Yonge, Whig politician and poetaster; George Bubb ("Bubo") Dodington was a Whig patron of letters.

3. Pope's enemies had accused him of satirizing Cannons, the ostentatious estate of the Duke of Chandos, in his description of Timon's villa in the *Epistle to Burlington*. This Pope quite justly denied. The bell of Timon's chapel was of silver, and there preached a dean who "never mentions Hell to ears polite."

4. John, Lord Hervey, effeminate courtier and confidant of Queen Caroline; see title footnote. The original Sporus was a boy, whom the Emperor Nero publicly married (see Suetonius' life of Nero in *The Twelve Caesars*).

5. Ass's milk was drunk by invalids.

Who breaks a butterfly upon a wheel?
   P. Yet let me flap this bug with gilded wings,
This painted child of dirt, that stinks and stings;   310
Whose buzz the witty and the fair annoys,
Yet wit ne'er tastes, and beauty ne'er enjoys;
So well-bred spaniels civilly delight
In mumbling of the game they dare not bite.
Eternal smiles his emptiness betray,   315
As shallow streams run dimpling all the way.
Whether in florid impotence he speaks,
And, as the prompter breathes, the puppet squeaks;
Or at the ear of Eve,[6] familiar toad,
Half froth, half venom, spits himself abroad,   320
In puns, or politics, or tales, or lies,
Or spite, or smut, or rhymes, or blasphemies.
His wit all seesaw between *that* and *this*,
Now high, now low, now master up, now miss,
And he himself one vile antithesis.   325
Amphibious thing! that acting either part,
The trifling head or the corrupted heart,
Fop at the toilet, flatterer at the board,
Now trips a lady, and now struts a lord.
Eve's tempter thus the rabbins[7] have expressed,   330
A cherub's face, a reptile all the rest;
Beauty that shocks you, parts that none will trust,
Wit that can creep, and pride that licks the dust.
   Not Fortune's worshiper, nor Fashion's fool,
Not Lucre's madman, nor Ambition's tool,   335
Not proud, nor servile, be one poet's praise,
That if he pleased, he pleased by manly ways:
That flattery, even to kings, he held a shame,
And thought a lie in verse or prose the same:
That not in fancy's maze he wandered long,   340
But stooped[8] to truth, and moralized his song:
That not for fame, but Virtue's better end,
He stood the furious foe, the timid friend,
The damning critic, half approving wit,
The coxcomb hit, or fearing to be hit;   345
Laughed at the loss of friends he never had,
The dull, the proud, the wicked, and the mad;
The distant threats of vengeance on his head,
The blow unfelt, the tear he never shed;
The tale revived, the lie so oft o'erthrown,   350
The imputed trash, and dullness not his own;
The morals blackened when the writings 'scape,
The libeled person, and the pictured shape;[9]

6. "Eve" is the queen. The allusion is
to *Paradise Lost* IV.799–809.
7. Scholars of and authorities on Jewish law and doctrine.
8. The falcon is said to "stoop" to its

prey when it swoops down and seizes
it in flight.
9. Pope's deformity was frequently
ridiculed and occasionally caricatured.

Abuse on all he loved, or loved him, spread,
A friend in exile, or a father dead;   355
The whisper, that to greatness still too near,
Perhaps yet vibrates on his Sovereign's ear—
Welcome for thee, fair Virtue! all the past!
For thee, fair Virtue! welcome even the last!
  A. But why insult the poor, affront the great?   360
P. A knave's a knave to me in every state:
Alike my scorn, if he succeed or fail,
Sporus at court, or Japhet[1] in a jail,
A hireling scribbler, or a hireling peer,
Knight of the post[2] corrupt, or of the shire,   365
If on a pillory, or near a throne,
He gain his prince's ear, or lose his own.
  Yet soft by nature, more a dupe than wit,
Sappho[3] can tell you how this man was bit:
This dreaded satirist Dennis will confess   370
Foe to his pride, but friend to his distress:[4]
So humble, he has knocked at Tibbald's door,
Has drunk with Cibber, nay, has rhymed for Moore.
Full ten years slandered, did he once reply?
Three thousand suns went down on Welsted's lie.   375
To please a mistress one aspersed his life;
He lashed him not, but let her be his wife.
Let Budgell charge low Grub Street on his quill,
And write whate'er he pleased, except his will;[5]
Let the two Curlls of town and court,[6] abuse   380
His father, mother, body, soul, and muse.
Yet why? that father held it for a rule,
It was a sin to call our neighbor fool;
That harmless mother thought no wife a whore:
Hear this, and spare his family, James Moore!   385
Unspotted names, and memorable long,
If there be force in virtue, or in song.
  Of gentle blood (part shed in honor's cause,
While yet in Britain honor had applause)
Each parent sprung—— A. What fortune, pray?—— P. Their own,
And better got than Bestia's[7] from the throne.   391
Born to no pride, inheriting no strife,
Nor marrying discord in a noble wife,
Stranger to civil and religious rage,
The good man walked innoxious through his age.   395
No courts he saw, no suits would ever try,

1. Japhet Crook, a notorious forger.
2. One who lives by selling false evidence.
3. Lady Mary Wortley Montagu. "Bit": taken in; deceived.
4. Pope wrote the prologue to Cibber's *Provoked Husband* when that play was performed for Dennis's benefit, shortly before the old critic died.
5. Eustace Budgell attacked the *Grub Street Journal* for publishing what he took to be a squib by Pope charging him with having forged the will of Dr. Matthew Tindal.
6. I.e., the publisher and Lord Hervey.
7. Probably the Duke of Marlborough, whose vast fortune was made through the favor of Queen Anne. The actual Bestia was a corrupt Roman consul.

Nor dared an oath,[8] nor hazarded a lie.
Unlearn'd, he knew no schoolman's subtle art,
No language but the language of the heart.
By nature honest, by experience wise,   400
Healthy by temperance, and by exercise;
His life, though long, to sickness passed unknown,
His death was instant, and without a groan.
Oh, grant me thus to live, and thus to die!
Who sprung from kings shall know less joy than I.   405
    O friend! may each domestic bliss be thine!
Be no unpleasing melancholy mine:
Me, let the tender office long engage,
To rock the cradle of reposing Age,
With lenient arts extend a mother's breath,   410
Make Languor smile, and smooth the bed of Death,
Explore the thought, explain the asking eye,
And keep a while one parent from the sky![9]
On cares like these if length of days attend,
May Heaven, to bless those days, preserve my friend,   415
Preserve him social, cheerful, and serene,
And just as rich as when he served a Queen![1]
A. Whether that blessing be denied or given,
Thus far was right—the rest belong to Heaven.

                                                          1735

8. As a Catholic, Pope's father refused to take the Oaths of Allegiance and Supremacy, and the oath against the Pope. He thus rendered himself vulnerable to the many repressive anti-Catholic laws then in force.
9. Pope was a tender and devoted son. His mother had died in 1733, and the earliest version of these lines dates from 1731, when the poet was nursing her through a serious illness.
1. Pope alludes to the fact that Arbuthnot, a man of strict probity, left the queen's service no wealthier than when he entered it.

The Dunciad: Book the Fourth

The Fourth Book of *The Dunciad*, Pope's last major work, was originally intended as a continuation of *An Essay on Man*. To Swift, the spiritual ancestor of the poem, Pope confided in 1736 that he was at work on a series of epistles on the uses of human reason and learning, to conclude with "a satire against the misapplication of all these, exemplified by pictures, characters, and examples." But the epistles never appeared; instead, the satire grew until it took their place. As Pope surveyed England in his last years, the complex literary and social order that had sustained him seemed to be crumbling. It was a time for desperate measures, for satire. And the means of retribution was at hand, in the structure of Pope's own *Dunciad*, the long work that had already impaled so many enemies.

The first *Dunciad*, published in three books in 1728, is a mock-epic reply to Pope's critics and other petty authors. Its hero and victim, Lewis Theobald, had attacked Pope's edition of Shakespeare (1725); other victims had offended Pope either by personal abuse or simply by ineptitude. Inspired by

Dryden's *Mac Flecknoe*, the *Dunciad* celebrates the triumph of the hordes
of Grub Street. Indeed, so many obscure hacks were mentioned that a *Dunciad Variorum* (1729) was soon required, in which mock-scholarly notes
identify the victims, "since it is only in this monument that they must
expect to survive." But a modern reader need not catch every reference to
enjoy the dazzling wit of the poem, or the sheer sense of fun with which
Pope remakes the London literary world into a tiny insane fair-ground of
his own.

  The New Dunciad (1742), however, plays a far more serious game: here
Pope takes aim at the rot of the whole social fabric. The satire goes deep,
and works at many levels. For convenience, these may be divided into four.
1) Politics: From 1721 to 1742 England had been ruled by the Whig
supremacy of Robert Walpole, First Minister. To Pope and his circle, the
immensely powerful Walpole (no friend of poets) seemed a crass and
greedy vulgarian, like his monarch George II. It is no accident, in the kingdom of the *Dunciad*, that Dulness personified sits on a throne. 2) Society:
Just as the action of the *Aeneid* had been the removal of the empire of
Troy to Latium, the action of the *Dunciad*, according to Pope, is "the
removal of the empire of Dulness from the City of London to the polite
world, Westminster"; that is, the abdication of civility in favor of commerce and financial interests. In modern England authors write for money,
and ministers govern for profit; conspicuous consumption (especially the
consumption of paper by scribblers) has replaced the old values of the
yeoman and the aristocrat. In 1743 Pope revised the original *Dunciad*, sub-
stituting the actor and poet laureate Colley Cibber for Theobald as the
hero, and incorporating *The New Dunciad* as Book Four (the version
printed here). Dulness, he implies, has achieved her final triumph; Cibber
is laureate in England. 3) Education: The word "dunce" is derived from
the scholastic philosopher John Duns Scotus (ca. 1265–1308), whose name
had come to stand for silly and useless subtlety, logical hair-splitting. Pope,
as an heir of the Renaissance, believes that the central subject of education
must always be its relevance for human behavior: "The proper study of
mankind is Man," and moral philosophy, the relation of men to each other
and to the world, should be the teacher's first and last concern. By contrast,
Dunces waste their time on grammar (words alone) or the "science" of the
collector (things alone); they never comprehend that word and thing, like
spirit and matter, are essentially dead unless they join. 4) Religion: At its
deepest level, the subject of the *Dunciad* is the undoing of God's creation.
Many passages from Book Four echo *Paradise Lost*, and one of Pope's starting places seems to be Satan's threat (*Paradise Lost* II. 968–87) to return
the world to its original darkness, chaos, and ancient night. The *Dunciad*
ends in a great apocalypse, with a yawn that signals the death of *Logos*; as
words have become meaningless, so has the whole creation, which the Lord
called forth with words. Here Pope invokes, with terrifying intensity, the
old idea that God was the first poet, whose poem was the world, and suggests that the sickness of the world has infected all nature. But there is one
consolation: out of non-art itself, out of matter without spirit and substance without essence, the poet creates his own final artistic triumph, and
makes a poem.

From The Dunciad

From *Book the Fourth*

Yet, yet a moment, one dim ray of light
Indulge, dread Chaos, and eternal Night!
Of darkness visible[1] so much be lent,
As half to show, half veil the deep intent.
Ye Powers![2] whose mysteries restored I sing,   5
To whom Time bears me on his rapid wing,
Suspend a while your force inertly strong,
Then take at once the poet and the song.

    Now flamed the Dog-star's[3] unpropitious ray,
Smote every brain, and withered every bay,[4]   10
Sick was the sun, the owl forsook his bower,
The moon-struck prophet felt the madding hour:
Then rose the seed[5] of Chaos, and of Night,
To blot out Order, and extinguish Light,
Of dull and venal a new world to mold,   15
And bring Saturnian[6] days of lead and gold.

    She mounts the throne: her head a cloud concealed,
In broad effulgence all below revealed,
('Tis thus aspiring Dulness ever shines)
Soft on her lap her Laureate son[7] reclines.   20

    Beneath her foot-stool, *Science* groans in chains,
And *Wit* dreads exile, penalties and pains.
There foamed rebellious *Logic*, gagged and bound,
There, stripped, fair *Rhetoric* languished on the ground;
His blunted arms by *Sophistry* are born,   25
And shameless *Billingsgate*[8] her robes adorn.
Morality, by her false guardians drawn,
Chicane in furs, and *Casuistry* in lawn,[9]
Gasps, as they straighten at each end the cord,
And dies, when Dulness gives her Page[1] the word.   30

[THE EDUCATOR]

    Now crowds on crowds around the Goddess press,   135
Each eager to present the first Address.[2]
Dunce scorning dunce beholds the next advance,
But fop shows fop superior complaisance.

1. Cf. *Paradise Lost* I. 63.
2. Chaos and Night, invoked in place of the Muse, since "the restoration of their empire is the action of the poem" [Pope].
3. Sirius, associated with the heat of summer and the madness of poets (see *Epistle to Dr. Arbuthnot*, line 3).
4. The laurel, whose garlands are bestowed on poets.
5. The Goddess Dulness.
6. Saturn ruled during the golden age; the new age of "gold" will be re-established by the dull and venal.
7. Colley Cibber, the poet laureate.
8. Fishmarket slang, which now covers the noble science of rhetoric.
9. Chicanery (legal trickery) wears the ermine robe of a judge; casuistry wears the linen sleeves of a bishop.
1. Sir Francis Page, a notorious "hanging judge"; court page, used to strangle criminals in Turkey; page of writing on which a dull author "kills" moral sentiments.
2. The Goddess, newly enthroned, is receiving petitions and congratulations.

When lo! a Specter[3] rose, whose index-hand
Held forth the virtue of the dreadful wand;   140
His beavered brow a birchen garland wears,[4]
Dropping with infant's blood, and mother's tears.
O'er every vein a shuddering horror runs;
Eton and Winton shake through all their sons.
All flesh is humbled, Westminster's bold race[5]   145
Shrink, and confess the Genius[6] of the place:
The pale boy-Senator yet tingling stands,
And holds his breeches close with both his hands.
   Then thus. "Since Man from beast by words is known,
Words are Man's province, words we teach alone.   150
When reason doubtful, like the Samian letter,[7]
Points him two ways, the narrower is the better.
Placed at the door of learning, youth to guide,
We never suffer it to stand too wide.
To ask, to guess, to know, as they commence,   155
As fancy opens the quick springs of sense,
We ply the memory, we load the brain,
Bind rebel wit, and double chain on chain,
Confine the thought, to exercise the breath;[8]
And keep them in the pale of words till death.   160
Whate'er the talents, or howe'er designed,
We hang one jingling padlock on the mind:
A poet the first day, he dips his quill;
And what the last? a very poet still.
Pity! the charm works only in our wall,   165
Lost, lost too soon in yonder House or Hall."[9]

[THE CARNATION AND THE BUTTERFLY]

   Then thick as locusts blackening all the ground,
A tribe,[1] with weeds and shells fantastic crowned,
Each with some wondrous gift approached the Power,
A nest, a toad, a fungus, or a flower.   400
But far the foremost, two, with earnest zeal,
And aspect ardent to the throne appeal.
   The first thus opened: "Hear thy suppliant's call,
Great Queen, and common Mother of us all!
Fair from its humble bed I reared this flower,   405
Suckled, and cheer'd, with air, and sun, and shower,
Soft on the paper ruff its leaves I spread,
Bright with the gilded button tipped its head,

3. The ghost of Dr. Busby, stern head-master of Westminster School.
4. He wears a hat (beaver) and a gar-land of birch twigs, used for flogging. "Wand": cane used for beating.
5. Alumni of Westminster School, with a play on the justices and members of Parliament who meet at Westminster Hall.
6. I.e., admit that Dr. Busby is the pre-siding deity (Genius).
7. The letter *Y*, which Pythagoras (a na-tive of Samos) used as an emblem of the different roads of virtue and vice.
8. Students are taught only to recite the classic poets by heart.
9. The House of Commons and West-minster Hall, where law cases were heard. The eloquence learned by rote disappears on occasions for public speak-ing.
1. The Virtuosi, or amateur scientists and collectors.

Then throned in glass, and named it C A R O L I N E:[2]
Each maid cried, charming! and each youth, divine!   410
Did Nature's pencil ever blend such rays,
Such varied light in one promiscuous blaze?
Now prostrate! dead! behold that Caroline:
No maid cries, charming! and no youth, divine!
And lo the wretch! whose vile, whose insect lust   415
Laid this gay daughter of the Spring in dust.
Oh punish him, or to th' Elysian shades
Dismiss my soul, where no carnation fades."
    He ceased, and wept. With innocence of mien,
The accused stood forth, and thus addressed the Queen.   420
    "Of all th' enameled race,[3] whose silvery wing
Waves to the tepid zephyrs of the spring,
Or swims along the fluid atmosphere,
Once brightest shined this child of heat and air.
I saw, and started from its vernal bower   425
The rising game, and chased from flower to flower.
It fled, I followed; now in hope, now pain;
It stopped, I stopped; it moved, I moved again.
At last it fixed, 'twas on what plant it pleased,
And where it fixed, the beauteous bird[4] I seized: 430
Rose or carnation was below my care;
I meddle, Goddess! only in my sphere.
I tell the naked fact without disguise,
And, to excuse it, need but show the prize;
Whose spoils this paper offers to your eye,   435
Fair even in death! this peerless *Butterfly*."
    "My sons!" (she answered) "both have done your parts:
Live happy both, and long promote our arts.
But hear a mother, when she recommends
To your fraternal care, our sleeping friends.   440
The common soul, of heaven's more frugal make,
Serves but to keep fools pert, and knaves awake:
A drowsy watchman, that just gives a knock,
And breaks our rest, to tell us what's a clock.[5]
Yet by some object every brain is stirred;   445
The dull may waken to a hummingbird;
The most recluse, discreetly opened, find
Congenial matter in the cockle-kind:[6]
The mind, in metaphysics at a loss,
May wander in a wilderness of moss;   450
The head that turns at super-lunar things,
Poised with a tail, may steer on Wilkins' wings.[7]

2. Queen Caroline, an enthusiastic gardener, is an appropriate choice to lend her name to the perfect carnation.
3. Colored insects.
4. Insect.
5. Eighteenth-century watchmen kept guard in the streets and announced the hours.
6. Cockle-shells, popular with collectors, as were hummingbirds and varieties of moss.
7. John Wilkins (1614–72), one of the founders of the Royal Society, had speculated "that a man may be able to fly, by the application of wings to his own body."

"O! would the Sons of Men once think their eyes
And reason given them but to study *flies!*[8]
See Nature in some partial narrow shape,   455
And let the Author of the whole escape:
Learn but to trifle; or, who most observe,
To wonder at their Maker, not to serve."

[THE TRIUMPH OF DULNESS]

Then blessing all,[9] "Go children of my care!
To practice now from theory repair.   580
All my commands are easy, short, and full:
My sons! be proud, be selfish, and be dull.
Guard my prerogative, assert my throne:
This nod confirms each privilege your own.
The cap and switch be sacred to his Grace;[1]   585
With staff and pumps[2] the Marquis lead the race;
From stage to stage the licensed[3] Earl may run,
Paired with his fellow-charioteer the Sun;
The learned Baron butterflies design,
Or draw to silk Arachne's subtle line;[4]   590
The Judge to dance his brother Sergeant[5] call;
The Senator at cricket urge the ball;
The Bishop stow (pontific luxury!)
An hundred souls of turkeys in a pie;[6]
The sturdy squire to Gallic masters[7] stoop,   595
And drown his lands and manors in a Soup.
Others import yet nobler arts from France,
Teach kings to fiddle, and make senates dance.
Perhaps more high some daring son may soar,[8]
Proud to my list to add one monarch more;   600
And nobly conscious, Princes are but things
Born for First Ministers, as slaves for kings,
Tyrant supreme! shall three estates command,
And MAKE ONE MIGHTY DUNCIAD OF THE LAND!"
      More she had spoke, but yawned—All Nature nods: 605
What mortal can resist the Yawn of Gods?
Churches and chapels instantly it reached;
(St. James's first, for leaden Gilbert[9] preached)
Then catched the schools; the Hall scarce kept awake;
The Convocation gaped,[1] but could not speak: 610
Lost was the Nation's Sense,[2] nor could be found,
While the long solemn unison went round:
Wide, and more wide, it spread o'er all the realm;
Even Palinurus[3] nodded at the helm:

8. C.f. *An Essay on Man* I.189–96: "Say what the use, were finer optics given / T' inspect a mite, not comprehend the heaven?"

9. Having conferred her titles, Dulness bids each of the rulers of England to indulge in the triviality closest to his heart.

1. His Grace, a duke who loves horse-racing, is to use the cap and switch of a jockey.

2. Footmen, who wore pumps (low-cut shoes for running), were matched in races.

3. The license required by the owner of a stagecoach; also, privileged or licentious.

The vapor mild o'er each committee crept; 615
Unfinished treaties in each office slept;
And chiefless armies dozed out the campaign;
And navies yawned for orders on the main.
    O Muse! relate (for you can tell alone,
Wits have short memories, and dunces none) 620
Relate, who first, who last resigned to rest;
Whose heads she partly, whose completely blessed;
What charms could faction, what ambition lull,
The venal quiet, and entrance the dull;
'Till drowned was sense, and shame, and right, and wrong— 625
O sing, and hush the nations with thy song!

                *   *   *   *   *   *

    In vain, in vain,—the all-composing Hour
Resistless falls: The Muse obeys the Power.
She comes! she comes![4] the sable throne behold
Of *Night* primeval, and of *Chaos* old! 630
Before her, *Fancy's* gilded clouds decay,
And all its varying rainbows die away.
Wit shoots in vain its momentary fires,
The meteor drops, and in a flash expires.
As one by one, at dread Medea's strain, 635
The sickening stars fade off the ethereal plain;[5]
As Argus' eyes by Hermes' wand oppressed,
Closed one by one to everlasting rest;[6]
Thus at her felt approach, and secret might,
Art after *Art* goes out, and all is Night. 640
See skulking *Truth* to her old cavern fled,[7]
Mountains of casuistry heaped o'er her head!
Philosophy, that leaned on Heaven before,
Shrinks to her second cause,[8] and is no more.
Physic[9] of *Metaphysic* begs defense, 645
And *Metaphysic* calls for aid on *Sense!*
See *Mystery*[1] to *Mathematics* fly!
In vain! they gaze, turn giddy, rave, and die.
Religion blushing veils her sacred fires,
And unawares *Morality* expires. 650

4. A spiderweb.
5. A lawyer or legislative officer; formal
ceremonies at the Inns of Court are said
to have resembled a country dance, "a
call of sergeants."
6. According to Pope, a hundred turkeys
had been "not unfrequently deposited in
one Pye in the Bishopric of Durham."
7. French chefs.
8. A bold, direct attack on Walpole.
9. Dr. John Gilbert, Dean of Exeter.
1. The Convocation, an assembly of
clergy consulting on ecclesiastical affairs,
had been adjourned since 1717.
2. A term for Parliament.
3. The pilot of Aeneas' ship; here Walpole.
4. Having triumphed in the contemporary world of affairs, Dulness (like her
antitype Christ) has a Second Coming, a

prophetic vision in which she extin-
guishes the light of the arts and sciences.
5. In Seneca's *Medea*, the stars obey the
curse of Medea, a magician and avenger.
6. Argus, Hera's hundred-eyed watchman, was charmed to sleep and slain by
Hermes.
7 ."Alluding to the saying of Democritus, that Truth lay at the bottom of a
deep well" [Pope's note].
8. Science (philosophy) no longer accepts God as the first cause, or final explanation of how all things came to be;
instead, it accepts only the second or
material cause, and tries to account for
all things by physical principles alone.
9. Natural science in general.
1. A religious truth known only through
divine revelation.

Nor *public* flame, nor *private*, dares to shine;
Nor *human* spark is left, nor glimpse *divine!*
Lo! thy dread Empire, C H A O S is restored;
Light dies before thy uncreating word:[2]
Thy hand, great Anarch! lets the curtain fall;   **655**
And Universal Darkness buries All.

        1743

2. Cf. God's first creating words in Genesis, "Let there be light."

SAMUEL JOHNSON
(1709–1784)

1737:	Settles in London.
1747–55:	At work on the *Dictionary*.
1762:	Pensioned by the Crown.
1765:	Edition of Shakespeare.
1779, 1781:	*Lives of the Poets*.

Throughout the 19th century it was generally agreed that although John-son himself was interesting, especially as a conversationalist, most of his works were unreadable. His poems were condemned as prosaic, his essays as tritely moralistic, his criticism as wrongheaded and tasteless. The case is altered today: a few of the poems, it is agreed, belong with the best of the century; the grave *Rambler* essays, which in his own time established his reputation as a stylist and a moralist, prove not so forbidding as we have been told they are; and the criticism is ranked with that of Dryden and Samuel Taylor Coleridge as the best in English. Boswell's Johnson is chiefly a conversationalist whose talk came hot from a mind that was wise, humane, honest, truthful, and well stored with knowledge drawn from books and experience. The talk is that of a wit and a poet who was quick to seize and to use the unexpected but appropriate image to illumi-nate truth as it was apprehended by a deeply moral imagination. Any fair examination of Johnson's best writings will demonstrate that for all its studied formality, Johnson's prose possesses most of the virtues of his con-versation. The object of the talker and of the moral essayist or critic proves in general to be the same—the search for truth in the wide field of human experience; and the wit and wisdom and energy of Johnson's spontaneous talk are also present in his prose.

     Two examples must suffice here. When Mrs. Anna Williams wondered why a man should make a beast of himself through drunkenness, John-son answered that "he who makes a beast of himself gets rid of the pain of being a man." In this reply Mrs. Williams' tired metaphor is so charged with an awareness of the dark aspects of human life that it comes almost unbearably alive. Such moments characterize Johnson's writings as well. For instance, in reviewing the book of a fatuous would-be philosopher who blandly explained away the pains of poverty by declaring that a kindly providence compensates the poor by making them more hopeful, more healthy, more capable of relishing small pleasures and less sensitive to small annoyances than the rich, Johnson, who had known extreme poverty, retorted: "The poor indeed are insensible of many little vexations which sometimes embitter the possessions and pollute the enjoyment of the rich. They are not pained by casual incivility, or mortified by the mutilation of a compliment; but this happiness is like that of the malefactor who ceases to feel the cords that bind him when the pincers are tearing his flesh."

Johnson had himself known the pains of poverty. During his boyhood and youth, his father's financial circumstances steadily worsened, so that he was forced to leave Oxford before he had taken a degree. An imprudent marriage drove him to open a school which was unsuccessful; and the failure of the school prompted him to attempt to make his way as a writer in London. The years between 1737, when he first arrived there with his pupil David Garrick (later to become the leading actor of his generation), and 1755, when the publication of the *Dictionary* established his reputation, were very difficult. He supported himself at first as best he could by doing hack work for the *Gentleman's Magazine*, but gradually his own original writings began to attract attention, though hardly to support his wife and himself.

In 1746 Johnson published the *Plan* of his *Dictionary*, and the next seven years were occupied in compiling it—although he had been sanguine enough to count on finishing it in three years. Boswell remarks that "the world contemplated with wonder" a work "achieved by one man, while other countries had thought such undertakings fit only for whole academies." When in 1748 Dr. Adams, a friend from Oxford days, questioned his ability to carry out such a work alone in so short a time, and reminded him that the *Dictionary* of the French Academy had been compiled by forty academicians working for forty years, Johnson replied with humorous jingoism: "Sir, thus it is. This is the proportion. Let me see; forty times forty is sixteen hundred. As three to sixteen hundred, so is the proportion of an Englishman to a Frenchman."

Johnson's achievement in compiling the *Dictionary* becomes even greater when it is realized that he was writing some of his best essays and poems during the same period, for although the booksellers who published the *Dictionary* paid him what was then the large sum of £1575, it was not enough to enable him to support his household, buy materials, and pay the wages of the six amanuenses whom he employed year by year until the task was accomplished. He therefore had to exert himself to earn more money by writing. Thus, in 1749, his early tragedy *Irene* (pronounced I-re-nĕ) was produced at long last by his old friend Garrick, by then not only a successful actor but also the manager of Drury Lane. The play, deservedly, was not a success, though Johnson made some profit from it. In the same year appeared his finest poem, *The Vanity of Human Wishes*. The *Rambler* (1750–52) and the later *Idler* (1758–60), Johnson's very un-Addisonian imitations of the *Spectator*, found admiring readers and spread his reputation as a moralist throughout the island.

Boswell said of the *Rambler* essays that "in no writings whatever can be found more bark and steel [i.e., quinine and iron] for the mind." Moral strength and health; the importance of applying reason to experience; the testing of a man by what he does, not by what he says or merely "feels"; faith in God: these are the centers to which Johnson's moral writings always return. As such critics as Walter Jackson Bate remind us, what Johnson uniquely offers us is the quality of his understanding of the human condition, based on wide reading but always ultimately referred to his own passionate and often anguished experience. Such understanding had to be fought for again and again, as our two selections from the *Prayers and Meditations* show.

Johnson is thought of as the great generalizer, but what gives his generalizations strength is that they are rooted in the particulars of his self-knowledge. He had constantly to fight against what he called "filling the mind" with illusions, in order to avoid the call of duty, his own black melancholy, and the realties of life. The portrait (largely a self-portrait) of Sober in *Idler* 31 is revealing: he occupies his idle hours with crafts and hobbies, and has now taken up chemistry—he "sits and counts the drops as they come from his retort, and forgets that, whilst a drop is falling, a moment flies away." So clear a vision is some distance away from the secure ease of the Addisonian essay.

His theme of themes is expressed in the title of his poem, *The Vanity of Human Wishes*, by which Johnson means the dangerous but all-pervasive illusion of what we now call wishful thinking, the feverish intrusion of our desires and hopes which distorts reality and interferes with the possibility of sensibly relying on what we have reason to expect. Almost all of Johnson's major writings—verse satire, moral essay, or the prose fable *Rasselas* (1759)—bear this theme. In *Rasselas* it is called "the hunger of imagination, which preys upon life," the seeing of things as one would like them to be, rather than as they are. The travelers who are the fable's protagonists pursue supposed guarantees of happiness; they reflect our naïve hopefulness, against the accumulation of contrary experience, that such a guarantee exists.

During this time of great activity, in which he produced the bulk of his moral writings, Johnson developed his characteristic style: the rotund periods, proceeding through balanced or parallel words; phrases or clauses moving to carefully controlled rhythms, in language that is characteristically general, often Latinate, and frequently polysyllabic. It is a style which is at the opposite extreme from Swift's simplicity or Addison's neatness. In Johnson's writings this style never becomes obscure or turgid, for even a very complex sentence reveals—as it should—the structure of the thought, and the learned words are always precisely used. "Sesquipedalian" words are not so frequent in Johnson's writings as his reputation for using them would imply. He learned many of them when he was reading early scientists to collect words for the *Dictionary*—such words as *obtund, exuberate, fugacity, frigorific*, which most people have been willing to forget. But he used many of these strange words in conversation as well as in his writings, often with a peculiarly Johnsonian felicity, although everyone is familiar with the notoriously infelicitous definition of *network* in the *Dictionary*: "Anything reticulated or decussated, at equal distances, with interstices between the intersections."

After Johnson received his pension in 1762, he no longer had to write for a living, and since he held that "no man but a blockhead" ever wrote for any other reason, he produced as little as he decently could during the last twenty years of his life. His edition of Shakespeare, long delayed, was published in 1765, with its fine preface and its fascinating notes, both textual and explicatory. Johnson's praise of Shakespeare and his discussion and destruction of the doctrine of the three unities are printed below. His last important work is the *Lives of the Poets*, which came out in two parts in 1779 and 1781. These biographical and critical prefaces were written at the instigation of a group of booksellers who had joined together to publish a large collection of the English poets and who wished to give their venture the prestige that it would acquire if Johnson took part in it. The poets to be included (except for four insisted on by Johnson) were selected by the booksellers, and their choice was determined by the current fashions. We have, therefore, a collection that begins with Cowley and Milton and ends with Gray and the poetaster Lord Lyttleton, and that omits poets whom we regard as "standard," such as Chaucer, Spenser, Sidney, or the metaphysicals.

In the *Lives of the Poets* and in the earlier *Life of Richard Savage* (1744), Johnson did much to advance the art of biography in England. The public had long been familiar with biography as panegyric or as scandalous memoir, and therefore Johnson's insistence on truth, even about the subject's defects, and on concrete, often minute, details was a new departure, disliked by many readers, as Boswell was to find when he followed his master's principles both in the *Journal of a Tour to the Hebrides* and in the *Life* itself. "The biographical part of literature is what I love most," Johnson said, for he found every biography useful in revealing human nature and the way men live. His insistence on truth in biography (and knowing that Boswell intended to write his life, he insisted that he should write it truthfully) was due to his conviction that the more truthful such a work is the more useful it will be to all of us who are concerned with the business of living. The value of the lives of the poets varies, for Johnson wrote some more casually than he did others. He is at his best as a critic when he draws up a general character of a writer's genius and when he discusses individual works.

Johnson's taste was conservative, and he therefore liked little in contemporary literature. He valued Richardson for his knowledge of the human heart, but he considered Fielding "low" and immoral, and Sterne merely perversely odd and trivial. Though he loved Collins, he regretted his fanciful subjects and "harsh" diction, and he offended many by his strictures on what he considered Gray's affectations. He poked gentle fun at his friend Thomas Warton's revival of antique words and "Ode, and elegy, and sonnet." But if he was conservative, he was no worshiper of authority, and least of all was he prone to follow mere theory. As a critic Johnson is always the empiricist, testing theory, as he tested all notions, by experience. His attitude toward the rules is perfectly expressed in these words from *Rambler* 156: "It ought to be the first endeavor of a writer to distinguish nature from custom; or that which is established because it is right, from that which is right only because it is established; that he may neither violate essential principles by a desire of novelty, nor debar himself from the attainment of beauties within his view, by a needless fear of breaking rules which no literary dictator has authority to enact." And the perfect illustration of this attitude is his treatment of the long-revered principle of the three dramatic unities in the Preface to Shakespeare.

That there were "essential principles" which any writer must follow seemed to him self-evident. He must adhere to universal truth and experience, i.e., to "Nature"; he must please, but he must also instruct; he must not offend against religion or promote immorality; he must avoid cold and slavish imitation of others, and he must not cultivate "singularity," the eccentrically original. In the passages from the *Lives of the Poets* below, some of his principles are illustrated. The well-known and influential discussion of metaphysical poetry, with its brilliant definition of "wit" as "a kind of *discordia concors*," at once illustrates Johnson's genius for formulating broad philosophical principles and reveals clearly why he equated the general with the natural. The notorious attack on Milton's *Lycidas*, which damaged Johnson's reputation as a critic for over a century, puzzles us until we recall that Johnson himself had his critical singularities, which in this case stood between him and a liking for a very great poem: he was justly contemptuous of 18th-century pastoral poetry, which was always conventional, artificial, and bookish, and which could be produced by mere imitation; and he had a great dislike on religious grounds for the Renaissance habit of mingling pagan and Christian materials in a poem. The praise of Dryden, Pope, and Shakespeare, on the other hand, is admirable because those poets, as was not the case with Donne or Milton, nobly illustrated the literary standards that Johnson respected throughout his career.

The Vanity of Human Wishes[1]

IN IMITATION OF THE TENTH SATIRE OF JUVENAL

Let Observation, with extensive view,
Survey mankind, from China to Peru;
Remark each anxious toil, each eager strife,
And watch the busy scenes of crowded life;
Then say how hope and fear, desire and hate   5
O'erspread with snares the clouded maze of fate,
Where wavering man, betrayed by venturous pride
To tread the dreary paths without a guide,
As treacherous phantoms in the mist delude,
Shuns fancied ills, or chases airy good;   10

1. *The Vanity of Human Wishes* is an imitation of Juvenal's *Satire X.* Although it closely follows the order and the ideas of the Latin poem, it remains a very personal work, for Johnson has used the Roman Stoic's satire as a means of expressing his own Christian stoicism and his sense of the tragic in human life. He has tried to reproduce in English verse the qualities he thought especially Juvenalian: stateliness, pointed sentences, declamatory grandeur. The poem is difficult because of the extreme compactness of the style: every verse is forced to convey the greatest possible amount of meaning, and as a result the syntax is occasionally obscure. At first the language may seem too general, the frequent personifications mere abstractions. But although Johnson's poetic theory demanded that the poet should deal in the general rather than the particular (cf. his phrase "the grandeur of generality") he certainly did not intend that the general should become the merely abstract: observe, for example, how he makes abstract nouns concrete, active, and dramatic by using them as subjects of active and dramatic verbs: "Hate *dogs* their flight, and Insult *mocks* their end" (line 78). And when the more usual 18th-century combination of general adjective modifying general noun is used, the adjectives are carefully chosen for foreseen effects, as in lines 113–16 (in the first three lines they are used to create a cumulative effect of regal splendor, and in the last line a witty and intellectual impression of Cardinal Wolsey's pride and power): "At once is lost the pride of *awful* state, / The *golden* canopy, the *glittering* plate, / The *regal* palace, the *luxurious* board, / The *liveried* army, and the *menial* lord." The personified abstractions of Collins and Gray, however, are essentially pictorial, grouped in expressive attitudes as they would be in an allegorical painting. A comparison of their method of personification with Johnson's can be readily made by studying Gray's *Eton* ode, stanzas 5–8, along with lines 135–164 of the *Vanity*.

How rarely Reason guides the stubborn choice,
Rules the bold hand, or prompts the suppliant voice;
How nations sink, by darling schemes oppressed,
When Vengeance listens to the fool's request.
Fate wings with every wish the afflictive dart,   15
Each gift of nature, and each grace of art;
With fatal heat impetuous courage glows,
With fatal sweetness elocution flows,
Impeachment stops the speaker's powerful breath,
And restless fire precipitates on death.   20

But scarce observed, the knowing and the bold
Fall in the general massacre of gold;
Wide-wasting pest! that rages unconfined,
And crowds with crimes the records of mankind;
For gold his sword the hireling ruffian draws,   25
For gold the hireling judge distorts the laws;
Wealth heaped on wealth, nor truth nor safety buys,
The dangers gather as the treasures rise.

Let History tell where rival kings command,
And dubious title shakes the madded land,   30
When statutes glean the refuse of the sword,
How much more safe the vassal than the lord,
Low skulks the hind beneath the rage of power,
And leaves the wealthy traitor[2] in the Tower,
Untouched his cottage, and his slumbers sound,   35
Though Confiscation's vultures hover round.

The needy traveler, serene and gay,
Walks the wild heath, and sings his toil away.
Does envy seize thee? crush the upbraiding joy,
Increase his riches and his peace destroy;   40
New fears in dire vicissitude invade,
The rustling brake[3] alarms, and quivering shade,
Nor light nor darkness bring his pain relief,
One shows the plunder, and one hides the thief.

Yet still one general cry the skies assails,   45
And gain and grandeur load the tainted gales;
Few know the toiling statesman's fear or care,
The insidious rival and the gaping heir.

Once more, Democritus,[4] arise on earth,
With cheerful wisdom and instructive mirth,   50
See motley life in modern trappings dressed,
And feed with varied fools the eternal jest:
Thou who couldst laugh where Want enchained Caprice,
Toil crushed Conceit, and man was of a piece;
Where Wealth unloved without a mourner died;   55
And scarce a sycophant was fed by Pride;
Where ne'er was known the form of mock debate,

2. Johnson first wrote "bonny traitor,"
recalling the Jacobite uprising of 1745
and the execution of four of its Scot
leaders.
3. Thicket.

4. A Greek philosopher of the late 5th
century B.C., remembered as the "laughing philosopher" because men's follies
only moved him to mirth.

Or seen a new-made mayor's unwieldy state;
Where change of favorites made no change of laws,
And senates heard before they judged a cause; 60
How wouldst thou shake at Britain's modish tribe,
Dart the quick taunt, and edge the piercing gibe?
Attentive truth and nature to descry,
And pierce each scene with philosophic eye,
To thee were solemn toys or empty show 65
The robes of pleasures and the veils of woe:
All aid the farce, and all thy mirth maintain,
Whose joys are causeless, or whose griefs are vain.

    Such was the scorn that filled the sage's mind,
Renewed at every glance on human kind; 70
How just that scorn ere yet thy voice declare,
Search every state, and canvass every prayer.

    Unnumbered suppliants crowd Preferment's gate,
Athirst for wealth, and burning to be great;
Delusive Fortune hears the incessant call, 75
They mount, they shine, evaporate, and fall.
On every stage the foes of peace attend,
Hate dogs their flight, and Insult mocks their end.
Love ends with hope, the sinking statesman's door
Pours in the morning worshiper no more;[5] 80
For growing names the weekly scribbler lies,
To growing wealth the dedicator flies;
From every room descends the painted face,
That hung the bright palladium[6] of the place;
And smoked in kitchens, or in auctions sold, 85
To better features yields the frame of gold;
For now no more we trace in every line
Heroic worth, benevolence divine:
The form distorted justifies the fall,
And Detestation rids the indignant wall. 90

    But will not Britain hear the last appeal,
Sign her foes' doom, or guard her favorites' zeal?
Through Freedom's sons no more remonstrance rings,
Degrading nobles and controlling kings;
Our supple tribes repress their patriot throats, 95
And ask no questions but the price of votes,
With weekly libels and septennial ale.[7]
Their wish is full to riot and to rail.

    In full-blown dignity, see Wolsey[8] stand,
Law in his voice, and fortune in his hand: 100
To him the church, the realm, their powers consign,

---

5. Statesmen gave interviews and received friends and petitioners at levees, or morning receptions.
6. An image of Pallas Athena, which fell from heaven and was preserved at Troy. Not until it was stolen by Diomedes could the city fall to the Greeks.
7. Ministers and even the king freely bought support by bribing members of Parliament, who in turn won elections by buying votes. "Weekly libels": politically motivated lampoons published in the weekly newspapers; "septennial ale": the ale given away by candidates at parliamentary elections, held at least every seven years.
8. Thomas Cardinal Wolsey (ca. 1475–1530), Lord Chancellor and favorite of Henry VIII. Shakespeare dramatized his fall in *Henry VIII.*

Through him the rays of regal bounty shine;
Turned by his nod the stream of honor flows,
His smile alone security bestows:
Still to new heights his restless wishes tower, 105
Claim leads to claim, and power advances power;
Till conquest unresisted ceased to please,
And rights submitted, left him none to seize.
At length his sovereign frowns—the train of state
Mark the keen glance, and watch the sign to hate. 110
Where'er he turns, he meets a stranger's eye,
His suppliants scorn him, and his followers fly;
At once is lost the pride of awful state,
The golden canopy, the glittering plate,
The regal palace, the luxurious board, 115
The liveried army, and the menial lord.
With age, with cares, with maladies oppressed,
He seeks the refuge of monastic rest.
Grief aids disease, remembered folly stings,
And his last sighs reproach the faith of kings. 120
  Speak thou, whose thoughts at humble peace repine,
Shall Wolsey's wealth, with Wolsey's end be thine?
Or liv'st thou now, with safer pride content,
The wisest justice on the banks of Trent?
For why did Wolsey, near the steeps of fate, 125
On weak foundations raise the enormous weight?
Why but to sink beneath misfortune's blow,
With louder ruin to the gulfs below?
  What gave great Villiers[9] to the assassin's knife,
And fixed disease on Harley's closing life? 130
What murdered Wentworth, and what exiled Hyde,
By kings protected and to kings allied?
What but their wish indulged in courts to shine,
And power too great to keep or to resign?
  When first the college rolls receive his name, 135
The young enthusiast quits his ease for fame;
Resistless burns the fever of renown
Caught from the strong contagion of the gown:
O'er Bodley's dome his future labors spread,
And Bacon's mansion trembles o'er his head.[1] 140
Are these thy views? proceed, illustrious youth,
And Virtue guard thee to the throne of Truth!
Yet should thy soul indulge the generous heat,

9. George Villiers, 1st Duke of Buckingham, favorite of James I and Charles
I, was assassinated in 1628. Mentioned
in the following lines are: Robert Harley, Earl of Oxford, Chancellor of the
Exchequer and later Lord Treasurer
under Queen Anne (1710–14), impeached and imprisoned by the Whigs
in 1715; Thomas Wentworth, Earl of
Strafford, intimate and adviser of
Charles I, impeached by the Long
Parliament and executed 1641; Edward Hyde, Earl of Clarendon ("to
kings allied" because his daughter
married James, Duke of York), Lord
Chancellor under Charles II; impeached
in 1667, he fled to the Continent.
1. "Bodley's dome" is the Bodleian Library, Oxford. Roger Bacon (ca. 1214–
94), scientist and philosopher, taught
at Oxford, where his study, according to
tradition, would collapse when a man
greater than he should appear at Oxford.

Till captive Science yields her last retreat;
Should Reason guide thee with her brightest ray,   145
And pour on misty Doubt resistless day;
Should no false kindness lure to loose delight,
Nor praise relax, nor difficulty fright;
Should tempting Novelty thy cell refrain,
And Sloth effuse her opiate fumes in vain;   150
Should Beauty blunt on fops her fatal dart,
Nor claim the triumph of a lettered heart;
Should no disease thy torpid veins invade,
Nor Melancholy's phantoms haunt thy shade;
Yet hope not life from grief or danger free,   155
Nor think the doom of man reversed for thee:
Deign on the passing world to turn thine eyes,
And pause a while from letters, to be wise;
There mark what ills the scholar's life assail,
Toil, envy, want, the patron,[2] and the jail.   160
See nations slowly wise, and meanly just,
To buried merit raise the tardy bust.
If dreams yet flatter, once again attend,
Hear Lydiat's life, and Galileo's end.[3]
    Nor deem, when Learning her last prize bestows,   165
The glittering eminence exempt from foes;
See when the vulgar 'scapes, despised or awed,
Rebellion's vengeful talons seize on Laud.[4]
From meaner minds though smaller fines content,
The plundered palace, or sequestered rent;[5]   170
Marked out by dangerous parts he meets the shock,
And fatal Learning leads him to the block:
Around his tomb let Art and Genius weep,
But hear his death, ye blockheads, hear and sleep.
    The festal blazes, the triumphal show,   175
The ravished standard, and the captive foe,
The senate's thanks, the gazette's pompous tale,
With force resistless o'er the brave prevail.
Such bribes the rapid Greek[6] o'er Asia whirled,
For such the steady Romans shook the world;   180
For such in distant lands the Britons shine,
And stain with blood the Danube or the Rhine;
This power has praise that virtue scarce can warm,
Till fame supplies the universal charm.
Yet Reason frowns on War's unequal game,   185
Where wasted nations raise a single name,
And mortgaged states their grandsires' wreaths regret

2. In the first edition, "garret." For the reason of the change see Boswell's *Life of Johnson*.
3. Thomas Lydiat (1572–1646), Oxford scholar, died impoverished because of his Royalist sympathies. Galileo (1564–1642), the famous astronomer, was imprisoned as a heretic by the Inquisition in 1633; he died blind.
4. Appointed Archbishop of Canterbury by Charles I, William Laud followed rigorously high-church policies and was executed by order of the Long Parliament in 1645.
5. During the Commonwealth, the estates of many Royalists were pillaged and their incomes confiscated ("sequestered") by the state.
6. Alexander the Great.

From age to age in everlasting debt;
Wreaths which at last the dear-bought right convey
To rust on medals, or on stones decay.   190
    On what foundation stands the warrior's pride,
How just his hopes, let Swedish Charles[7] decide;
A frame of adamant, a soul of fire,
No dangers fright him, and no labors tire;
O'er love, o'er fear, extends his wide domain,   195
Unconquered lord of pleasure and of pain;
No joys to him pacific scepters yield,
War sounds the trump, he rushes to the field;
Behold surrounding kings their powers combine,
And one capitulate, and one resign;[8]   200
Peace courts his hand, but spreads her charms in vain;
"Think nothing gained," he cries, "till naught remain,
On Moscow's walls till Gothic standards fly,
And all be mine beneath the polar sky."
The march begins in military state,   205
And nations on his eye suspended wait;
Stern Famine guards the solitary coast,
And Winter barricades the realms of Frost;
He comes, nor want nor cold his course delay—
Hide, blushing Glory, hide Pultowa's day: 210
The vanquished hero leaves his broken bands,
And shows his miseries in distant lands;
Condemned a needy supplicant to wait,
While ladies interpose, and slaves debate.
But did not Chance at length her error mend?   215
Did no subverted empire mark his end?
Did rival monarchs give the fatal wound?
Or hostile millions press him to the ground?
His fall was destined to a barren strand,
A petty fortress, and a dubious hand;   220
He left the name at which the world grew pale,
To point a moral, or adorn a tale.
    All times their scenes of pompous woes afford,
From Persia's tyrant to Bavaria's lord.[9]
In gay hostility, and barbarous pride,   225
With half mankind embattled at his side,
Great Xerxes comes to seize the certain prey,
And starves exhausted regions in his way;
Attendant Flattery counts his myriads o'er,
Till counted myriads soothe his pride no more;   230

7. Charles XII of Sweden (1682–1718). Defeated by the Russians at Pultowa (1709), he escaped to Turkey and tried to form an alliance against Russia with the sultan. Returning to Sweden, he attacked Norway and was killed in the attack on Fredrikshald.

8. Frederick IV of Denmark capitulated to Charles in 1700; Augustus II of Poland resigned his throne to Charles in 1704.

9. Xerxes ("Persia's tyrant") invaded Greece and was totally defeated in the sea battle off Salamis, 480 B.C.; the Elector Charles Albert ("Bavaria's Lord") caused the War of the Austrian Succession (1740–48) when he contested the crown of the Empire with Maria Theresa ("Fair Austria" in line 245).

Fresh praise is tried till madness fires his mind,
The waves he lashes, and enchains the wind;
New powers are claimed, new powers are still bestowed,
Till rude resistance lops the spreading god;
The daring Greeks deride the martial show,   235
And heap their valleys with the gaudy foe;
The insulted sea with humbler thought he gains,
A single skiff to speed his flight remains;
The encumbered oar scarce leaves the dreaded coast
Through purple billows and a floating host.   240
    The bold Bavarian, in a luckless hour,
Tries the dread summits of Caesarean power,
With unexpected legions bursts away,
And sees defenseless realms receive his sway;
Short sway! fair Austria spreads her mournful charms, 245
The queen, the beauty, sets the world in arms;
From hill to hill the beacon's rousing blaze
Spreads wide the hope of plunder and of praise;
The fierce Croatian, and the wild Hussar,[1]
With all the sons of ravage crowd the war;   250
The baffled prince, in honor's flattering bloom
Of hasty greatness finds the fatal doom;
His foes' derision, and his subjects' blame,
And steals to death from anguish and from shame.
    Enlarge my life with multitude of days!   255
In health, in sickness, thus the suppliant prays;
Hides from himself his state, and shuns to know,
That life protracted is protracted woe.
Time hovers o'er, impatient to destroy,
And shuts up all the passages of joy;   260
In vain their gifts the bounteous seasons pour,
The fruit autumnal, and the vernal flower;
With listless eyes the dotard views the store,
He views, and wonders that they please no more;
Now pall the tasteless meats, and joyless wines,   265
And Luxury with sighs her slave resigns.
Approach, ye minstrels, try the soothing strain,
Diffuse the tuneful lenitives[2] of pain:
No sounds, alas! would touch the impervious ear,
Though dancing mountains witnessed Orpheus[2a] near;   270
Nor lute nor lyre his feeble powers attend,
Nor sweeter music of a virtuous friend,
But everlasting dictates crowd his tongue,
Perversely grave, or positively wrong.
The still returning tale, and lingering jest,   275
Perplex the fawning niece and pampered guest,
While growing hopes scarce awe the gathering sneer,
And scarce a legacy can bribe to hear;

1. Hungarian light cavalry.
2 Medicines that relieve pain.
2a. A legendary poet who played on the lyre so beautifully that wild beasts were spellbound.

The watchful guests still hint the last offense;
The daughter's petulance, the son's expense,   280
Improve his heady rage with treacherous skill,
And mold his passions till they make his will.
    Unnumbered maladies his joints invade,
Lay siege to life and press the dire blockade;
But unextinguished avarice still remains,   285
And dreaded losses aggravate his pains;
He turns, with anxious heart and crippled hands,
His bonds of debt, and mortgages of lands;
Or views his coffers with suspicious eyes,
Unlocks his gold, and counts it till he dies.   290
But grant, the virtues of a temperate prime
Bless with an age exempt from scorn or crime;
An age that melts with unperceived decay,
And glides in modest innocence away;
Whose peaceful day Benevolence endears,   295
Whose night congratulating Conscience cheers;
The general favorite as the general friend:
Such age there is, and who shall wish its end?
    Yet even on this her load Misfortune flings,
To press the weary minutes' flagging wings;   300
New sorrow rises as the day returns,
A sister sickens, or a daughter mourns.
Now kindred Merit fills the sable bier,
Now lacerated Friendship claims a tear;
Year chases year, decay pursues decay,   305
Still drops some joy from withering life away;
New forms arise, and different views engage,
Superfluous lags the veteran[3] on the stage,
Till pitying Nature signs the last release,
And bids afflicted Worth retire to peace.   310
    But few there are whom hours like these await,
Who set unclouded in the gulfs of Fate.
From Lydia's monarch[4] should the search descend,
By Solon cautioned to regard his end,
In life's last scene what prodigies surprise,   315
Fears of the brave, and follies of the wise!
From Marlborough's eyes the streams of dotage flow,
And Swift expires a driveler and a show.[5]
    The teeming mother, anxious for her race,
Begs for each birth the fortune of a face: 320
Yet Vane could tell what ills from beauty spring;[6]

---

3. A veteran of life, not of war.
4. Croesus, the wealthy and fortunate king, was warned by Solon not to count himself happy till he ceased to live. He lost his crown to Cyrus the Great of Persia.
5. John Churchill, Duke of Marlborough, England's brilliant general during most of the War of the Spanish Succession (1702–13); Jonathan Swift, who passed the last four years of his life in utter senility.
6. Anne Vane, mistress of Frederick, Prince of Wales (son of George II). Catherine Sedley, mistress of James II.

And Sedley cursed the form that pleased a king.
Ye nymphs of rosy lips and radiant eyes,
Whom Pleasure keeps too busy to be wise,
Whom Joys with soft varieties invite,   325
By day the frolic, and the dance by night;
Who frown with vanity, who smile with art,
And ask the latest fashion of the heart;
What care, what rules your heedless charms shall save,
Each nymph your rival, and each youth your slave?   330
Against your fame with Fondness Hate combines,
The rival batters, and the lover mines.
With distant voice neglected Virtue calls,
Less heard and less, the faint remonstrance falls;
Tired with contempt, she quits the slippery reign,   335
And Pride and Prudence take her seat in vain.
In crowd at once, where none the pass defend,
The harmless freedom, and the private friend.
The guardians yield, by force superior plied:
To Interest, Prudence; and to Flattery, Pride.   340
Now Beauty falls betrayed, despised, distressed,
And hissing Infamy proclaims the rest.
    Where then shall Hope and Fear their objects find?
Must dull Suspense corrupt the stagnant mind?
Must helpless man, in ignorance sedate,   345
Roll darkling down the torrent of his fate?
Must no dislike alarm, no wishes rise,
No cries invoke the mercies of the skies?
Inquirer, cease; petitions yet remain,
Which Heaven may hear, nor deem religion vain.   350
Still raise for good the supplicating voice,
But leave to Heaven the measure and the choice.
Safe in His power, whose eyes discern afar
The secret ambush of a specious prayer.
Implore His aid, in His decisions rest,   355
Secure, whate'er He gives, He gives the best.
Yet when the sense of sacred presence fires,
And strong devotion to the skies aspires,
Pour forth thy fervors for a healthful mind,
Obedient passions, and a will resigned;   360
For love, which scarce collective man can fill;
For patience sovereign o'er transmuted ill;
For faith, that panting for a happier seat,
Counts death kind Nature's signal of retreat:
These goods for man the laws of Heaven ordain,   365
These goods He grants, who grants the power to gain;
With these celestial Wisdom calms the mind,
And makes the happiness she does not find.

1749

Prologue Spoken by Mr. Garrick[1]

AT THE OPENING OF THE THEATRE ROYAL, DRURY LANE, 1747

When Learning's triumph o'er her barbarous foes
First reared the stage, immortal Shakespeare rose;
Each change of many-colored life he drew,
Exhausted worlds, and then imagined new:
Existence saw him spurn her bounded reign,   5
And panting Time toiled after him in vain.
His powerful strokes presiding Truth impressed,
And unresisted Passion stormed the breast.
    Then Jonson came, instructed from the school
To please in method and invent by rule;   10
His studious patience and laborious art
By regular approach essayed the heart;
Cold Approbation gave the lingering bays,
For those who durst not censure, scarce could praise.[2]
A mortal born, he met the general doom,   15
But left, like Egypt's kings, a lasting tomb.
    The wits of Charles[3] found easier ways to fame,
Nor wished for Jonson's art, or Shakespeare's flame;
Themselves they studied; as they felt, they writ;
Intrigue was plot, obscenity was wit.   20
Vice always found a sympathetic friend;
They pleased their age, and did not aim to mend.
Yet bards like these aspired to lasting praise,
And proudly hoped to pimp in future days.
Their cause was general, their supports were strong,   25
Their slaves were willing, and their reign was long:
Till Shame regained the post that Sense betrayed,
And Virtue called Oblivion to her aid.
    Then, crushed by rules,[4] and weakened as refined,
For years the power of Tragedy declined;   30
From bard to bard the frigid caution crept,
Till Declamation roared while Passion slept;
Yet still did Virtue deign the stage to tread;
Philosophy remained though Nature fled;
But forced at length her ancient reign to quit,   35
She saw great Faustus[5] lay the ghost of Wit;
Exulting Folly hailed the joyous day,
And Pantomime and Song confirmed her sway.
    But who the coming changes can presage,
And mark the future periods of the stage?   40
Perhaps if skill could distant times explore,

1. David Garrick, the famous actor, had become joint patentee and manager of Drury Lane Theatre. Boswell says that this Prologue is unrivaled "for just and manly dramatic criticism."

2. Cf. Dryden's contrast of Shakespeare and Ben Jonson in his *Essay of Dramatic Poesy*.

3. The comic poets of the Restoration period.

4. Cf. Johnson's remarks on the dramatic unities in his preface to Shakespeare.

5. Dr. Faustus at that time was a popular subject for both farce and pantomime.

New Behns,[6] new Durfeys, yet remain in store;
Perhaps where Lear has raved, and Hamlet died,
On flying cars new sorcerers may ride;[7]
Perhaps (for who can guess the effects of chance?)   45
Here Hunt may box, or Mahomet may dance.[8]
   Hard is his lot that, here by fortune placed,
Must watch the wild vicissitudes of taste;
With every meteor of caprice must play,
And chase the new-blown bubbles of the day.   50
Ah! let not censure term our fate our choice,
The stage but echoes back the public voice;
The drama's laws, the drama's patrons give,
For we that live to please, must please to live.
   Then prompt no more the follies you decry,   55
As tyrants doom their tools of guilt to die;
'Tis yours this night to bid the reign commence
Of rescued Nature and reviving Sense;
To chase the charms of Sound, the pomp of Show,
For useful Mirth and salutary Woe;   60
Bid scenic Virtue form the rising age,
And Truth diffuse her radiance from the stage.

                           1747

On the Death of Dr. Robert Levet[1]

Condemned to Hope's delusive mine,
   As on we toil from day to day,
By sudden blasts, or slow decline,
   Our social comforts drop away.

Well tried through many a varying year,   5
   See Levet to the grave descend;
Officious,[2] innocent, sincere,
   Of every friendless name the friend.

Yet still he fills Affection's eye,
   Obscurely wise, and coarsely kind;   10
Nor, lettered Arrogance, deny
   Thy praise to merit unrefined.

When fainting Nature called for aid,
   And hovering Death prepared the blow,

---

6. Aphra Behn (1640–89), first English-woman to earn her living by writing. Thomas Durfey (1653–1723), satirist and writer of songs and plays.
7. It was a common complaint that the use of increasingly elaborate stage machinery was subordinating drama to mere spectacle.
8. Edward Hunt, a popular pugilist; Mahomet, a tightrope dancer.

1. An unlicensed physician, who lived in Johnson's house for many years and who died in 1782. His practice was among the very poor. Boswell wrote: "He was of a strange grotesque appearance, stiff and formal in his manner, and seldom said a word while any company was present."
2. "Kind, doing good offices" (Johnson's *Dictionary*).

His vigorous remedy displayed 15
    The power of art without the show.

In Misery's darkest cavern known,
    His useful care was ever nigh,
Where hopeless Anguish poured his groan,
    And lonely Want retired to die. 20

No summons mocked by chill delay,
    No petty gain disdained by pride,
The modest wants of every day
    The toil of every day supplied.

His virtues walked their narrow round, 25
    Nor made a pause, nor left a void;
And sure the Eternal Master found
    The single talent well employed.

The busy day, the peaceful night,
    Unfelt, uncounted, glided by;
His frame was firm, his powers were bright, 30
    Though now his eightieth year was nigh.

Then with no throbbing fiery pain,
    No cold gradations of decay,
Death broke at once the vital chain, 35
    And freed his soul the nearest way.

1783

A Short Song of Congratulation

Long-expected one and twenty
    Lingering year at last is flown,
Pomp and Pleasure, Pride and Plenty,
    Great Sir John,[1] are all your own.

Loosened from the minor's tether, 5
    Free to mortgage or to sell,
Wild as wind, and light as feather
    Bid the slaves of thrift farewell.

Call the Bettys, Kates, and Jennys
    Every name that laughs at Care,
Lavish of your grandsire's guineas, 10
    Show the spirit of an heir.

All that prey on vice and folly
    Joy to see their quarry fly,
Here the gamester light and jolly 15
    There the lender grave and sly.

1. Sir John Lade, nephew of Johnson's friend Henry Thrale. He came into his property in 1780, and, as Johnson fore- told, he had squandered it all by his death.

Wealth, Sir John, was made to wander,
    Let it wander as it will;
See the jockey, see the pander,
    Bid them come, and take their fill.   20

When the bonny blade carouses,
    Pockets full, and spirits high,
What are acres? What are houses?
    Only dirt, or wet or dry.

If the guardian or the mother   25
    Tell the woes of willful waste,
Scorn their counsel and their pother,
    You can hang or drown at last.

1780
                                      1794

Translation of Horace, *Odes,* Book IV.vii[1]

The snow dissolved no more is seen,
The fields, and woods, behold, are green,
The changing year renews the plain,
The rivers know their banks again,
The spritely nymph and naked grace[2]   5
The mazy dance together trace.
The changing year's successive plan
Proclaims mortality to man.
Rough winter's blasts to spring give way,
Spring yields to summer's sovereign ray,   10
Then summer sinks in autumn's reign,
And winter chills the world again.
Her losses soon the moon supplies,
But wretched man, when once he lies
Where Priam[3] and his sons are laid,   15
Is naught but ashes and a shade.
Who knows if Jove who counts our score
Will toss us in a morning more?
What with your friend you nobly share
At least you rescue from your heir.   20
Not you, Torquatus, boast of Rome,
When Minos once has fixed your doom,[4]
Or eloquence, or splendid birth,
Or virtue shall replace on earth.
Hippolytus[5] unjustly slain   25

1. Johnson composed this translation the month before his death.
2. One of the Three Graces, emblematic of beauty.
3. Last king of Troy, slain with his sons at the end of the Trojan War.
4. Sentence. L. Manlius Torquatus, a friend of Horace and an advocate, is represented as pleading his case before Minos, judge of the dead.
5. Phaedra, wife of Theseus, falsely accused his chaste son Hippolytus of rape; Theseus brought about the death of his son, and even Diana, goddess of chastity, could not restore him.

Diana calls to life in vain,
Nor can the might of Theseus rend
The chains of hell that hold his friend.[6]

1784

Rambler No. 5[1]

[*On Spring*]

TUESDAY, *April 3, 1750*

Et nunc omnis ager, nunc omnis parturit arbos,
Nunc frondent silvae, nunc formosissimus annus.
VIRGIL, *Eclogues* III. v. 56
Now ev'ry field, now ev'ry tree is green;
Now genial nature's fairest face is seen.
ELPHINSTON

Every man is sufficiently discontented with some circumstances of his present state, to suffer his imagination to range more or less in quest of future happiness, and to fix upon some point of time, in which, by the removal of the inconvenience which now perplexes him, or acquisition of the advantage which he at present wants, he shall find the condition of his life very much improved.

When this time, which is too often expected with great impatience, at last arrives, it generally comes without the blessing for which it was desired; but we solace ourselves with some new prospect, and press forward again with equal eagerness.

It is lucky for a man, in whom this temper prevails, when he turns his hopes upon things wholly out of his own power; since he forbears then to precipitate [2] his affairs, for the sake of the great event that is to complete his felicity, and waits for the blissful hour, with less neglect of the measures necessary to be taken in the mean time.

I have long known a person of this temper, who indulged his dream of happiness with less hurt to himself than such chimerical wishes commonly produce, and adjusted his scheme with such address, that his hopes were in full bloom three parts of the year, and in the other part never wholly blasted. Many, perhaps, would be desirous of learning by what means he procured to himself such a cheap and lasting satisfaction. It was gained by a constant practice of referring the removal of all his

6. Pirithous, held prisoner with Theseus in Hell.
1. The *Rambler*, almost wholly written by Johnson himself, appeared every Tuesday and Saturday from March 20, 1750, to March 14, 1752—years in which Johnson was writing the *Dictionary*. It is a successor of the *Tatler* and the *Spectator*, but it is much more serious in tone than the earlier periodicals. Johnson's reputation as a moralist and a stylist was established by these essays; because of them Boswell first conceived the ambition to seek Johnson's acquaintance.
2. "To hurry blindly or rashly" (Johnson's *Dictionary*).

uneasiness to the coming of the next spring; if his health was impaired, the spring would restore it; if what he wanted was at a high price, it would fall in value in the spring.

The spring, indeed, did often come without any of these effects, but he was always certain that the next would be more propitious; nor was ever convinced that the present spring would fail him before the middle of summer; for he always talked of the spring as coming till it was past, and when it was once past, everyone agreed with him that it was coming.

By long converse with this man, I am, perhaps, brought to feel immoderate pleasure in the contemplation of this delightful season; but I have the satisfaction of finding many, whom it can be no shame to resemble, infected with the same enthusiasm; for there is, I believe, scarce any poet of eminence, who has not left some testimony of his fondness for the flowers, the zephyrs, and the warblers of the spring. Nor has the most luxuriant imagination been able to describe the serenity and happiness of the golden age, otherwise than by giving a perpetual spring, as the highest reward of uncorrupted innocence.

There is, indeed, something inexpressibly pleasing, in the annual renovation of the world, and the new display of the treasures of nature. The cold and darkness of winter, with the naked deformity of every object on which we turn our eyes, make us rejoice at the succeeding season, as well for what we have escaped, as for what we may enjoy; and every budding flower, which a warm situation brings early to our view, is considered by us as a messenger to notify the approach of more joyous days.

The spring affords to a mind, so free from the disturbance of cares or passions as to be vacant[3] to calm amusements, almost every thing that our present state makes us capable of enjoying. The variegated verdure of the fields and woods, the succession of grateful odors, the voice of pleasure pouring out its notes on every side, with the gladness apparently conceived by every animal, from the growth of his food, and the clemency of the weather, throw over the whole earth an air of gaiety, significantly expressed by the smile of nature.

Yet there are men to whom these scenes are able to give no delight, and who hurry away from all the varieties of rural beauty, to lose their hours, and divert their thoughts by cards, or assemblies, a tavern dinner, or the prattle of the day.

It may be laid down as a position which will seldom deceive, that when a man cannot bear his own company there is something wrong. He must fly from himself, either because he feels a tediousness in life from the equipoise of an empty mind, which, having no tendency to one motion more than another but as it is impelled

---

3. "At leisure" (Johnson's *Dictionary*).

by some external power, must always have recourse to foreign objects; or he must be afraid of the intrusion of some unpleasing ideas, and, perhaps, is struggling to escape from the remembrance of a loss, the fear of a calamity, or some other thought of greater horror.

Those whom sorrow incapacitates to enjoy the pleasures of contemplation, may properly apply to such diversions, provided they are innocent, as lay strong hold on the attention; and those, whom fear of any future affliction chains down to misery, must endeavor to obviate the danger.

My considerations shall, on this occasion, be turned on such as are burthensome to themselves merely because they want subjects for reflection, and to whom the volume of nature is thrown open, without affording them pleasure or instruction, because they never learned to read the characters.

A French author has advanced this seeming paradox, that *very few men know how to take a walk*; and, indeed, it is true, that few know how to take a walk with a prospect of any other pleasure, than the same company would have afforded them at home.

There are animals that borrow their color from the neighboring body, and, consequently, vary their hue as they happen to change their place. In like manner it ought to be the endeavor of every man to derive his reflections from the objects about him; for it is to no purpose that he alters his position, if his attention continues fixed to the same point. The mind should be kept open to the access of every new idea, and so far disengaged from the predominance of particular thoughts, as easily to accommodate itself to occasional entertainment.

A man that has formed this habit of turning every new object to his entertainment, finds in the productions of nature an inexhaustible stock of materials upon which he can employ himself, without any temptations to envy or malevolence; faults, perhaps, seldom totally avoided by those, whose judgment is much exercised upon the works of art. He has always a certain prospect of discovering new reasons for adoring the sovereign author of the universe, and probable hopes of making some discovery of benefit to others, or of profit to himself. There is no doubt but many vegetables and animals have qualities that might be of great use, to the knowledge of which there is not required much force of penetration, or fatigue of study, but only frequent experiments, and close attention. What is said by the chemists of their darling mercury, is, perhaps, true of everybody through the whole creation, that if a thousand lives should be spent upon it, all its properties would not be found out.

Mankind must necessarily be diversified by various tastes, since life affords and requires such multiplicity of employments, and a nation of naturalists is neither to be hoped, or desired; but it is surely not improper to point out a fresh amusement to those who languish in health, and repine in plenty, for want of some source of diversion that may be less easily exhausted, and to inform the multitudes of both sexes, who are burthened with every new day, that there are many shows which they have not seen.

He that enlarges his curiosity after the works of nature, demonstrably multiplies the inlets to happiness; and, therefore, the younger part of my readers, to whom I dedicate this vernal speculation, must excuse me for calling upon them, to make use at once of the spring of the year, and the spring of life; to acquire, while their minds may be yet impressed with new images, a love of innocent pleasures, and an ardor for useful knowledge; and to remember, that a blighted spring makes a barren year, and that the vernal flowers, however beautiful and gay, are only intended by nature as preparatives to autumnal fruits.

Rambler No. 203

[Futurity]

Tuesday, February 25, 1752

Cum volet illa dies, quae nil nisi corporis hujus
Jus habet, incerti spatium mihi finiat aevi.
—OVID, *Metamorphoses*, xv. 873–74

Come, soon or late, death's undetermined day,
This mortal being only can decay.
—WELSTED

It seems to be the fate of man to seek all his consolations in futurity. The time present is seldom able to fill desire or imagination with immediate enjoyment, and we are forced to supply its deficiencies by recollection or anticipation.

Everyone has so often detected the fallaciousness of hope, and the inconvenience of teaching himself to expect what a thousand accidents may preclude, that, when time has abated the confidence with which youth rushes out to take possession of the world, we endeavor, or wish, to find entertainment in the review of life, and to repose upon real facts, and certain experience. This is perhaps one reason, among many, why age delights in narratives.

But so full is the world of calamity, that every source of pleasure is polluted, and every retirement of tranquillity disturbed. When time has supplied us with events sufficient to employ our thoughts, it has mingled them with so many disasters, that we shrink from their remembrance, dread their intrusion upon our minds, and fly from them as from enemies that pursue us with torture.

No man past the middle point of life can sit down to feast upon the pleasures of youth without finding the banquet embittered by the cup of sorrow; he may revive lucky accidents, and pleasing extravagancies; many days of harmless frolic, or nights of honest festivity, will perhaps recur; or, if he has been engaged in scenes of action, and acquainted with affairs of difficulty and vicissitudes of fortune, he may enjoy the nobler pleasure of looking back upon distress firmly supported, dangers resolutely encountered, and opposition artfully defeated. Aeneas properly comforts his companions, when, after the horrors of a storm, they have landed on an unknown and desolate country, with the hope that their miseries will be at some distant time recounted with delight.[1] There are few higher gratifications than that of reflection on surmounted evils, when they were not incurred nor protracted by our fault, and neither reproach us with cowardice, nor guilt.

But this felicity is almost always abated by the reflection that they with whom we should be most pleased to share it are now in the grave. A few years make such havoc in human generations, that we soon see ourselves deprived of those with whom we entered the world, and whom the participation of pleasures or fatigues had endeared to our remembrance. The man of enterprise recounts his adventures and expedients, but is forced at the close of the relation to pay a sigh to the names of those that contributed to his success; he that passes his life among the gayer part of mankind, has his remembrance stored with remarks and repartees of wits, whose sprightliness and merriment are now lost in perpetual silence; the trader whose industry has supplied the want of inheritance, repines in solitary plenty at the absence of companions, with whom he had planned out amusements for his latter years; and the scholar, whose merit, after a long series of efforts, raises him from obscurity, looks round in vain from his exaltation for his old friends or enemies, whose applause or mortification would heighten his triumph.

Among Martial's requisites to happiness is, *res non parta labore, sed relicta,* an estate not gained by industry, but left by inheritance. It is necessary to the completion of every good, that it be timely obtained; for whatever comes at the close of life will come too late to give much delight; yet all human happiness has its defects. Of what we do not gain for ourselves we have only a faint and imperfect fruition, because we cannot compare the difference between want and possession, or at least can derive from it no conviction of our own abilities, nor any increase of self-esteem; what we acquire

1. *Aeneid,* I. 203.

by bravery or science, by mental or corporal diligence, comes at last when we cannot communicate, and therefore cannot enjoy it.[2]

Thus every period of life is obliged to borrow its happiness from the time to come. In youth we have nothing past to entertain us, and in age we derive little from retrospect but hopeless sorrow. Yet the future likewise has its limits, which the imagination dreads to approach, but which we see to be not far distant. The loss of our friends and companions impresses hourly upon us the necessity of our own departure; we know that the schemes of man are quickly at an end, that we must soon lie down in the grave with the forgotten multitudes of former ages, and yield our place to others, who, like us, shall be driven a while by hope or fear about the surface of the earth, and then like us be lost in the shades of death.

Beyond this termination of our material existence, we are therefore obliged to extend our hopes; and almost every man indulges his imagination with something, which is not to happen till he has changed his manner of being. Some amuse themselves with entails and settlements, provide for the perpetuation of families and honors, or contrive to obviate the dissipation of the fortunes, which it has been their business to accumulate; others, more refined or exalted, congratulate their own hearts upon the future extent of their reputation, the reverence of distant nations, and the gratitude of unprejudiced posterity.

They whose souls are so chained down to coffers and tenements, that they cannot conceive a state in which they shall look upon them with less solicitude, are seldom attentive or flexible to arguments; but the votaries of fame are capable of reflection, and therefore may be called to reconsider the probability of their expectations.

Whether to be remembered in remote times be worthy of a wise man's wish, has not yet been satisfactorily decided; and, indeed, to be long remembered, can happen to so small a number, that the bulk of mankind has very little interest in the question. There is never room in the world for more than a certain quantity or measure of renown. The necessary business of life, the immediate pleasures or pains of every condition, leave us not leisure beyond a fixed proportion for contemplations which do not forcibly influence our present welfare. When this vacuity is filled, no characters can be admitted into the circulation of fame, but by occupying the place of some that must be thrust into oblivion. The eye of the mind, like that of the body, can only extend its view to new objects, by losing sight of those which are now before it.

2. When Johnson wrote this, his wife Elizabeth ("Tetty") was near death. She died a few weeks later, on the day that the last *Rambler* essay was published. Both the Johnsons thought that the *Rambler* series was the crown of all his work.

Reputation is therefore a meteor which blazes a while and disappears forever; and if we except a few transcendent and invincible names, which no revolutions of opinion or length of time is able to suppress; all those that engage our thoughts, or diversify our conversation, are every moment hasting to obscurity, as new favorites are adopted by fashion.

It is not therefore from this world, that any ray of comfort can proceed, to cheer the gloom of the last hour. But futurity has still its prospects; there is yet happiness in reserve, which, if we transfer our attention to it, will support us in the pains of disease, and the languor of decay. This happiness we may expect with confidence, because it is out of the power of chance, and may be attained by all that sincerely desire and earnestly pursue it. On this therefore every mind ought finally to rest. Hope is the chief blessing of man, and that hope only is rational, of which we are certain that it cannot deceive us.

Idler No. 31 [1]

[On Idleness]

SATURDAY, *November* 18, 1758

Many moralists have remarked, that Pride has of all human vices the widest dominion, appears in the greatest multiplicity of forms, and lies hid under the greatest variety of disguises; of disguises, which, like the moon's *veil of brightness*, are both *its luster and its shade*, and betray it to others, though they hide it from ourselves.

It is not my intention to degrade Pride from this pre-eminence of mischief, yet I know not whether Idleness may not maintain a very doubtful and obstinate competition.

There are some that profess Idleness in its full dignity, who call themselves the Idle, as Busiris in the play "calls himself the Proud"; [2] who boast that they do nothing, and thank their stars that they have nothing to do; who sleep every night till they can sleep no longer, and rise only that exercise may enable them to sleep again; who prolong the reign of darkness by double curtains, and never see the sun but to "tell him how they hate his beams"; [3] whose whole labor is to vary the postures of indulgence, and whose day differs from their night but as a couch or chair differs from a bed.

1. Johnson wrote and published the *Idler*, a periodical similar to the *Rambler*, from 1758 until 1760.

2. Edward Young, *Busiris* (1719), I.13.
3. *Paradise Lost* IV.37.

These are the true and open votaries of Idleness, for whom she weaves the garlands of poppies, and into whose cup she pours the waters of oblivion; who exist in a state of unruffled stupidity, forgetting and forgotten; who have long ceased to live, and at whose death the survivors can only say, that they have ceased to breathe.

But Idleness predominates in many lives where it is not suspected; for being a vice which terminates in itself, it may be enjoyed without injury to others; and is therefore not watched like Fraud, which endangers property, or like Pride, which naturally seeks its gratifications in another's inferiority. Idleness is a silent and peaceful quality, that neither raises envy by ostentation, nor hatred by opposition; and therefore nobody is busy to censure or detect it.

As Pride sometimes is hid under humility, Idleness is often covered by turbulence and hurry. He that neglects his known duty and real employment, naturally endeavors to crowd his mind with something that may bar out the remembrance of his own folly, and does any thing but what he ought to do with eager diligence, that he may keep himself in his own favor.

Some are always in a state of preparation, occupied in previous measures, forming plans, accumulating materials, and providing for the main affair. These are certainly under the secret power of Idleness. Nothing is to be expected from the workman whose tools are forever to be sought. I was once told by a great master, that no man ever excelled in painting, who was eminently curious about pencils and colors.

There are others to whom Idleness dictates another expedient, by which life may be passed unprofitably away without the tediousness of many vacant hours. The art is, to fill the day with petty business, to have always something in hand which may raise curiosity, but not solicitude, and keep the mind in a state of action, but not of labor.

This art has for many years been practiced by my old friend Sober, with wonderful success. Sober is a man of strong desires and quick imagination, so exactly balanced by the love of ease, that they can seldom stimulate him to any difficult undertaking; they have, however, so much power, that they will not suffer him to lie quite at rest, and though they do not make him sufficiently useful to others, they make him at least weary of himself.

Mr. Sober's chief pleasure is conversation; there is no end of his talk or his attention; to speak or to hear is equally pleasing; for he still fancies that he is teaching or learning something, and is free for the time from his own reproaches.

But there is one time at night when he must go home, that his friends may sleep; and another time in the morning, when all the world agrees to shut out interruption. These are the moments of which poor Sober trembles at the thought. But the misery of these tiresome intervals, he has many means of alleviating. He has persuaded himself that the manual arts are undeservedly overlooked; he has observed in many trades the effects of close thought, and just ratiocination. From speculation he proceeded to practice, and supplied himself with the tools of a carpenter, with which he mended his coalbox very successfully, and which he still continues to employ, as he finds occasion.

He has attempted at other times the crafts of the shoemaker, tinman, plumber, and potter; in all these arts he has failed, and resolves to qualify himself for them by better information. But his daily amusement is chemistry. He has a small furnace, which he employs in distillation, and which has long been the solace of his life. He draws oils and waters, and essences and spirits, which he knows to be of no use; sits and counts the drops as they come from his retort, and forgets that, whilst a drop is falling, a moment flies away.

Poor Sober![4] I have often teased him with reproof, and he has often promised reformation; for no man is so much open to conviction as the Idler, but there is none on whom it operates so little. What will be the effect of this paper I know not; perhaps he will read it and laugh, and light the fire in his furnace; but my hope is that he will quit his trifles, and betake himself to rational and useful diligence.

Idler No. 58

[*Expectations of Pleasure*]

Saturday, May 26, 1759

Pleasure is very seldom found where it is sought. Our brightest blazes of gladness are commonly kindled by unexpected sparks. The flowers which scatter their odors from time to time in the paths of life, grow up without culture from seeds scattered by chance.

Nothing is more hopeless than a scheme of merriment. Wits and humorists are brought together from distant quarters by preconcerted invitations; they come attended by their admirers prepared to laugh and to applaud: they gaze a while on each other, ashamed to be silent, and afraid to speak; every man is discontented with himself, grows angry with those that give him pain, and resolves that he

---

4. Sober represents aspects of Johnson's own character. He was much given to indolence, and he performed chemical experiments in a small laboratory in his garret.

will contribute nothing to the merriment of such worthless company. Wine inflames the general malignity, and changes sullenness to petulance, till at last none can bear any longer the presence of the rest. They retire to vent their indignation in safer places, where they are heard with attention; their importance is restored, they recover their good humor, and gladden the night with wit and jocularity.

Merriment is always the effect of a sudden impression. The jest which is expected is already destroyed. The most active imagination will be sometimes torpid, under the frigid influence of melancholy, and sometimes occasions will be wanting to tempt the mind, however volatile, to sallies and excursions. Nothing was ever said with uncommon felicity, but by the cooperation of chance; and therefore, wit as well as valor must be content to share its honors with fortune.

All other pleasures are equally uncertain; the general remedy of uneasiness is change of place; almost everyone has some journey of pleasure in his mind, with which he flatters his expectation. He that travels in theory has no inconveniences; he has shade and sunshine at his disposal, and wherever he alights finds tables of plenty and looks of gaiety. These ideas are indulged till the day of departure arrives, the chaise is called, and the progress of happiness begins.

A few miles teach him the fallacies of imagination. The road is dusty, the air is sultry, the horses are sluggish, and the postilion brutal. He longs for the time of dinner that he may eat and rest. The inn is crowded, his orders are neglected, and nothing remains but that he devour in haste what the cook has spoiled, and drive on in quest of better entertainment. He finds at night a more commodious house, but the best is always worse than he expected.

He at last enters his native province, and resolves to feast his mind with the conversation of his old friends, and the recollection of juvenile frolics. He stops at the house of his friend whom he designs to overpower with pleasure by the unexpected interview. He is not known till he tells his name, and revives the memory of himself by a gradual explanation. He is then coldly received, and ceremoniously feasted. He hastes away to another whom his affairs have called to a distant place, and having seen the empty house, goes away disgusted by a disappointment which could not be intended because it could not be foreseen. At the next house he finds every face clouded with misfortune, and is regarded with malevolence as an unreasonable intruder, who comes not to visit but to insult them.[1]

---

1. Johnson had not been able to bring himself to revisit his own native town, Lichfield, for many years, even though his mother had lived there until her death the previous January. Three years later, when he did return, he found "the streets much narrower and shorter than I thought I had left them, inhabited by a new race of people, to whom I was very little known."

It is seldom that we find either men or places such as we expect them. He that has pictured a prospect upon his fancy, will receive little pleasure from his eyes; he that has anticipated the conversation of a wit, will wonder to what prejudice he owes his reputation. Yet it is necessary to hope, though hope should always be deluded, for hope itself is happiness, and its frustrations, however frequent, are yet less dreadful than its extinction.

From The History of Rasselas, Prince of Abyssinia[1]

Chapter I. Description of a Palace in a Valley

Ye who listen with credulity to the whispers of fancy, and pursue with eagerness the phantoms of hope; who expect that age will perform the promises of youth, and that the deficiencies of the present day will be supplied by the morrow—attend to the history of Rasselas, prince of Abyssinia.

Rasselas was the fourth son of the mighty emperor in whose dominions the Father of Waters[2] begins his course; whose bounty

1. Johnson wrote *Rasselas* in January, 1759, during the evenings of one week, a remarkable instance of his ability to write rapidly and brilliantly under the pressure of necessity. His mother lay dying in Lichfield. Her son, famous for his *Dictionary*, was nonetheless oppressed by poverty and in great need of ready money with which to make her last days comfortable, pay her funeral expenses, and settle her small debts. He was paid £100 for the first edition of *Rasselas*, but not in time to attend her deathbed or her funeral. Because of these circumstances, the tale has often been read as an expression of the gloom of the moment; but acquaintance with Johnson's other writings and his conversation makes it plain that the book expresses his settled view of life and what human beings may reasonably expect from it.

Rasselas is a philosophical fable cast in the popular form of an Oriental tale, a type of fiction that owed its popularity to the vogue of the *Arabian Nights*, first translated into English in the early 18th century. Since the work is a fable, we should not approach it as a novel: psychologically credible characters and a series of intricately involved actions that lead to a necessary resolution and conclusion are not to be found in

Rasselas. The action, the characters, the majestic prose rhythms, and the melancholy resonance of much of the language serve to articulate the theme, which is very similar to that of *The Vanity of Human Wishes*. Johnson formulated it in a magnificent phrase: the "hunger of imagination which preys incessantly upon life" (Chapter XXXII) and which lures us to "listen with credulity to the whispers of fancy and pursue with eagerness the phantoms of hope" (Chapter I). The tale is a gentle satire on one of the perennial topics of satirists, the folly of all of us who stubbornly cling to our illusions despite the evidence of experience. *Rasselas* is not all darkness and gloom, for Johnson's theme invites comic as well as tragic treatment, and some of the episodes evoke that laughter of the mind which is the effect of high comedy. In its main theme, however— the folly of cherishing the dream of ever attaining unalloyed happiness in a world which can never wholly satisfy our desires, however disinterested—and in many of the sayings of its characters, especially of the sage Imlac, *Rasselas* expresses some of Johnson's own deepest convictions.
2. The Nile.

pours down the streams of plenty, and scatters over half the world the harvests of Egypt.

According to the custom which has descended from age to age among the monarchs of the torrid zone, Rasselas was confined in a private palace, with the other sons and daughters of Abyssinian royalty, till the order of succession should call him to the throne.

The place which the wisdom or policy of antiquity had destined for the residence of the Abyssinian princes was a spacious valley[3] in the kingdom of Amhara, surrounded on every side by mountains, of which the summits overhang the middle part. The only passage by which it could be entered was a cavern that passed under a rock, of which it has long been disputed whether it was the work of nature or of human industry. The outlet of the cavern was concealed by a thick wood, and the mouth which opened into the valley was closed with gates of iron, forged by the artificers of ancient days, so massy that no man could, without the help of engines, open or shut them.

From the mountains on every side rivulets descended that filled all the valley with verdure and fertility, and formed a lake in the middle, inhabited by fish of every species, and frequented by every fowl whom nature has taught to dip the wing in water. This lake discharged its superfluities by a stream, which entered a dark cleft of the mountain on the northern side, and fell with dreadful noise from precipice to precipice till it was heard no more.

The sides of the mountains were covered with trees, the banks of the brooks were diversified with flowers; every blast shook spices from the rocks, and every month dropped fruits upon the ground. All animals that bite the grass, or browse the shrub, whether wild or tame, wandered in this extensive circuit, secured from beasts of prey by the mountains which confined them. On one part were flocks and herds feeding in the pastures, on another all the beasts of chase frisking in the lawns; the sprightly kid was bounding on the rocks, the subtle monkey frolicking in the trees, and the solemn elephant reposing in the shade. All the diversities of the world were brought together, the blessings of nature were collected, and its evils extracted and excluded.

The valley, wide and fruitful, supplied its inhabitants with the necessaries of life, and all delights and superfluities were added at the annual visit which the emperor paid his children, when the iron gate was opened to the sound of music, and during eight days everyone that resided in the valley was required to propose whatever might contribute to make seclusion pleasant, to fill up the

3. Johnson had read of the Happy Valley in the Portuguese Jesuit Father Lobo's book on Abyssinia, which he translated in 1735. The description in this and the immediately following paragraphs illustrates well enough Johnson's preference for the "general" over the "particular" (see Chapter X, below). It owes something to the description of the Garden in *Paradise Lost* IV, and Coleridge's *Kubla Khan* owes something to it.

vacancies of attention, and lessen the tediousness of time. Every desire was immediately granted. All the artificers of pleasure were called to gladden the festivity; the musicians exerted the power of harmony, and the dancers showed their activity before the princes, in hope that they should pass their lives in this blissful captivity, to which those only were admitted whose performance was thought able to add novelty to luxury. Such was the appearance of security and delight which this retirement afforded, that they to whom it was new always desired that it might be perpetual; and as those on whom the iron gate had once closed were never suffered to return, the effect of longer experience could not be known. Thus every year produced new schemes of delight and new competitors for imprisonment.

The palace stood on an eminence, raised about thirty paces above the surface of the lake. It was divided into many squares or courts, built with greater or less magnificence according to the rank of those for whom they were designed. The roofs were turned into arches of massy stone, joined with a cement that grew harder by time, and the building stood from century to century, deriding the solstitial rains and equinoctial hurricanes, without need of reparation.

This house, which was so large as to be fully known to none but some ancient officers, who successively inherited the secrets of the place, was built as if suspicion herself had dictated the plan. To every room there was an open and secret passage; every square had a communication with the rest, either from the upper stories by private galleries, or by subterranean passages from the lower apartments. Many of the columns had unsuspected cavities, in which a long race of monarchs had reposited their treasures. They then closed up the opening with marble, which was never to be removed but in the utmost exigencies of the kingdom, and recorded their accumulations in a book, which was itself concealed in a tower, not entered but by the emperor, attended by the prince who stood next in succession.

Chapter II. The Discontent of Rasselas in the Happy Valley

Here the sons and daughters of Abyssinia lived only to know the soft vicissitudes of pleasure and repose, attended by all that were skillful to delight, and gratified with whatever the senses can enjoy. They wandered in gardens of fragrance, and slept in the fortresses of security. Every art was practiced to make them pleased with their own condition. The sages who instructed them told them of nothing but the miseries of public life, and described all beyond the mountains as regions of calamity, where discord was always raging, and where man preyed upon man.

To heighten their opinion of their own felicity, they were daily entertained with songs, the subject of which was the *happy valley*.

Their appetites were excited by frequent enumerations of different enjoyments, and revelry and merriment was the business of every hour, from the dawn of morning to the close of even.

These methods were generally successful; few of the princes had ever wished to enlarge their bounds, but passed their lives in full conviction that they had all within their reach that art or nature could bestow, and pitied those whom fate had excluded from this seat of tranquility, as the sport of chance and the slaves of misery.

Thus they rose in the morning and lay down at night, pleased with each other and with themselves; all but Rasselas, who, in the twenty-sixth year of his age, began to withdraw himself from their pastimes and assemblies, and to delight in solitary walks and silent meditation. He often sat before tables covered with luxury, and forgot to taste the dainties that were placed before him; he rose abruptly in the midst of the song, and hastily retired beyond the sound of music. His attendants observed the change, and endeavored to renew his love of pleasure. He neglected their officiousness, repulsed their invitations, and spent day after day on the banks of rivulets sheltered with trees, where he sometimes listened to the birds in the branches, sometimes observed the fish playing in the stream, and anon cast his eyes upon the pastures and mountains filled with animals, of which some were biting the herbage, and some sleeping among the bushes.

This singularity of his humor made him much observed. One of the sages, in whose conversation he had formerly delighted, followed him secretly, in hope of discovering the cause of his disquiet. Rasselas, who knew not that anyone was near him, having for some time fixed his eyes upon the goats that were browsing among the rocks, began to compare their condition with his own.

"What," said he, "makes the difference between man and all the rest of the animal creation? Every beast that strays beside me has the same corporal necessities with myself; he is hungry, and crops the grass, he is thirsty, and drinks the stream, his thirst and hunger are appeased, he is satisfied, and sleeps; he rises again, and he is hungry, he is again fed, and is at rest. I am hungry and thirsty like him, but when thirst and hunger cease, I am not at rest; I am, like him, pained with want, but am not, like him, satisfied with fullness. The intermediate hours are tedious and gloomy; I long again to be hungry that I may again quicken my attention. The birds peck the berries or the corn, and fly away to the groves, where they sit in seeming happiness on the branches, and waste their lives in tuning one unvaried series of sounds. I likewise can call the lutanist and the singer, but the sounds that pleased me yesterday weary me today, and will grow yet more wearisome tomorrow. I can discover within me no power of perception which is not glutted with its proper pleasure, yet I do not feel myself delighted. Man has surely some latent sense for which this place affords no gratification, or he has some desires distinct from sense, which must be satisfied before he can be happy."

After this he lifted up his head, and seeing the moon rising, walked towards the palace. As he passed through the fields, and saw the animals around him, "Ye," said he, "are happy, and need not envy me that walk thus among you, burthened with myself; nor do I, ye gentle beings, envy your felicity, for it is not the felicity of man. I have many distresses from which ye are free; I fear pain when I do not feel it; I sometimes shrink at evils recollected, and sometimes start at evils anticipated. Surely the equity of Providence has balanced peculiar sufferings with peculiar enjoyments."

With observations like these the prince amused himself as he returned, uttering them with a plaintive voice, yet with a look that discovered him to feel some complacence in his own perspicacity, and to receive some solace of the miseries of life from consciousness of the delicacy with which he felt, and the eloquence with which he bewailed them. He mingled cheerfully in the diversions of the evening, and all rejoiced to find that his heart was lightened.

Chapter III. The Wants of Him That Wants Nothing

On the next day his old instructor, imagining that he had now made himself acquainted with his disease of mind, was in the hope of curing it by counsel, and officiously sought an opportunity of conference, which the prince, having long considered him as one whose intellects were exhausted, was not very willing to afford. "Why," said he, "does this man thus intrude upon me; shall I be never suffered to forget those lectures which pleased only while they were new, and to become new again must be forgotten?" He then walked into the wood, and composed himself to his usual meditations; when, before his thoughts had taken any settled form, he perceived his pursuer at his side, and was at first prompted by his impatience to go hastily away; but, being unwilling to offend a man whom he had once reverenced and still loved, he invited him to sit down with him on the bank.

The old man, thus encouraged, began to lament the change which had been lately observed in the prince, and to inquire why he so often retired from the pleasures of the palace, to loneliness and silence. "I fly from pleasure," said the prince, "because pleasure has ceased to please; I am lonely because I am miserable, and am unwilling to cloud with my presence the happiness of others." "You, sir," said the sage, "are the first who has complained of misery in the *happy valley*. I hope to convince you that your complaints have no real cause. You are here in full possession of all that the emperor of Abyssinia can bestow; here is neither labor to be endured nor danger to be dreaded, yet here is all that labor or danger can procure or purchase. Look round and tell me which of your wants is without supply; if you want nothing, how are you unhappy?"

"That I want nothing," said the prince, "or that I know not what I want, is the cause of my complaint; if I had any known want, I should have a certain wish; that wish would excite endeavor, and I should not then repine to see the sun move so slowly towards the western mountain, or lament when the day breaks, and sleep will no longer hide me from myself. When I see the kids and the lambs chasing one another, I fancy that I should be happy if I had something to pursue. But, possessing all that I can want, I find one day and one hour exactly like another, except that the latter is still more tedious than the former. Let your experience inform me how the day may now seem as short as in my childhood, while nature was yet fresh and every moment showed me what I never had observed before. I have already enjoyed too much; give me something to desire."

The old man was surprised at this new species of affliction and knew not what to reply, yet was unwilling to be silent. "Sir," said he, "if you had seen the miseries of the world you would know how to value your present state." "Now," said the prince, "you have given me something to desire. I shall long to see the miseries of the world, since the sight of them is necessary to happiness."[4]

Chapter X. Imlac's History Continued. A Dissertation upon Poetry

"Wherever I went, I found that poetry was considered as the highest learning, and regarded with a veneration somewhat approaching to that which man would pay to the angelic nature. And yet it fills me with wonder that, in almost all countries, the most ancient poets are considered as the best: whether it be that every other kind of knowledge is an acquisition gradually attained, and poetry is a gift conferred at once; or that the first poetry of every nation surprised them as a novelty, and retained the credit by consent which it received by accident at first; or whether, as the province of poetry is to describe nature and passion, which are always the same, the first writers took possession of the most striking objects for description and the most probable occurrences for fiction, and left nothing to those that followed them, but transcription of the same events, and new combinations of the same images—whatever be the reason, it is commonly observed that the early writers are in possession of nature, and their followers of art; that the first excel in strength and invention, and the latter in elegance and refinement.

4. In the chapters here omitted Rasselas, meditating escape, comes to know Imlac, a poet and "man of learning" who has experienced life in all its phases, and who, finally despairing of happiness, has willingly retired to the Happy Valley. Imlac's account of his experiences whets the prince's desire to see the world and make a "choice of life."

"I was desirous to add my name to this illustrious fraternity. I read all the poets of Persia and Arabia, and was able to repeat by memory the volumes that are suspended in the mosque of Mecca. But I soon found that no man was ever great by imitation. My desire of excellence impelled me to transfer my attention to nature and to life. Nature was to be my subject, and men to be my auditors: I could never describe what I had not seen; I could not hope to move those with delight or terror, whose interests and opinions I did not understand.

"Being now resolved to be a poet, I saw everything with a new purpose; my sphere of attention was suddenly magnified; no kind of knowledge was to be overlooked. I ranged mountains and deserts for images and resemblances, and pictured upon my mind every tree of the forest and flower of the valley. I observed with equal care the crags of the rock and the pinnacles of the palace. Sometimes I wandered along the mazes of the rivulet, and sometimes watched the changes of the summer clouds. To a poet nothing can be useless. Whatever is beautiful, and whatever is dreadful, must be familiar to his imagination; he must be conversant with all that is awfully vast or elegantly little. The plants of the garden, the animals of the wood, the minerals of the earth, and meteors of the sky, must all concur to store his mind with inexhaustible variety: for every idea[5] is useful for the enforcement or decoration of moral or religious truth; and he who knows most will have most power of diversifying his scenes, and of gratifying his reader with remote allusions and unexpected instruction.

"All the appearances of nature I was therefore careful to study, and every country which I have surveyed has contributed something to my poetical powers."

"In so wide a survey," said the prince, "you must surely have left much unobserved. I have lived till now within the circuit of these mountains, and yet cannot walk abroad without the sight of something which I have never beheld before, or never heeded."

"The business of a poet," said Imlac, "is to examine, not the individual, but the species; to remark general properties and large appearances; he does not number the streaks of the tulip, or describe the different shades in the verdure of the forest. He is to exhibit in his portraits of nature such prominent and striking features as recall the original to every mind, and must neglect the minuter discriminations, which one may have remarked and another have neglected, for those characteristics which are alike obvious to vigilance and carelessness.

"But the knowledge of nature is only half the task of a poet; he must be acquainted likewise with all the modes of life. His character requires that he estimate the happiness and misery of every condition; observe the power of all the passions in all their com-

5. Mental image.

binations, and trace the changes of the human mind, as they are modified by various institutions and accidental influences of climate or custom, from the sprightliness of infancy to the despondence of decrepitude. He must divest himself of the prejudices of his age or country; he must consider right and wrong in their abstracted and invariable state; he must disregard present laws and opinions, and rise to general and transcendental[6] truths, which will always be the same. He must, therefore, content himself with the slow progress of his name, contemn the applause of his own time, and commit his claims to the justice of posterity. He must write as the interpreter of nature and the legislator of mankind, and consider himself as presiding over the thoughts and manner of future generations, as a being superior to time and place.

"His labor is not yet at an end; he must know many languages and many sciences; and, that his style may be worthy of his thoughts, must by incessant practice familiarize to himself every delicacy of speech and grace of harmony."

Chapter XI. Imlac's Narrative Continued. A Hint on Pilgrimage

Imlac now felt the enthusiastic fit, and was proceeding to aggrandize his own profession, when the prince cried out: "Enough! thou hast convinced me that no human being can ever be a poet. Proceed with thy narration."

"To be a poet," said Imlac, "is indeed very difficult." "So difficult," returned the prince, "that I will at present hear no more of his labors. Tell me whither you went when you had seen Persia."

"From Persia," said the poet, "I traveled through Syria, and for three years resided in Palestine, where I conversed with great numbers of the northern and western nations of Europe, the nations which are now in possession of all power and all knowledge, whose armies are irresistible, and whose fleets command the remotest parts of the globe. When I compared these men with the natives of our own kingdom, and those that surround us, they appeared almost another order of beings. In their countries it is difficult to wish for anything that may not be obtained; a thousand arts, of which we never heard, are continually laboring for their convenience and pleasure; and whatever their own climate has denied them is supplied by their commerce."

"By what means," said the prince, "are the Europeans thus powerful, or why, since they can so easily visit Asia and Africa for trade or conquest, cannot the Asiatics and Africans invade their coasts, plant colonies in their ports, and give laws to their natural princes? The same wind that carries them back would bring us thither."

"They are more powerful, sir, than we," answered Imlac, "be-

6. "General; pervading many particulars" (Johnson's *Dictionary*).

cause they are wiser; knowledge will always predominate over ignorance, as man governs the other animals. But why their knowledge is more than ours, I know not what reason can be given, but the unsearchable will of the Supreme Being."

"When," said the prince with a sigh, "shall I be able to visit Palestine, and mingle with this mighty confluence of nations? Till that happy moment shall arrive, let me fill up the time with such representations as thou canst give me. I am not ignorant of the motive that assembles such numbers in that place, and cannot but consider it as the center of wisdom and piety, to which the best and wisest men of every land must be continually resorting."

"There are some nations," said Imlac, "that send few visitants to Palestine; for many numerous and learned sects in Europe concur to censure pilgrimage as superstitious, or deride it as ridiculous."

"You know," said the prince, "how little my life has made me acquainted with diversity of opinions. It will be too long to hear the arguments on both sides; you, that have considered them, tell me the result."

"Pilgrimage," said Imlac, "like many other acts of piety, may be reasonable or superstitious, according to the principles upon which it is performed. Long journeys in search of truth are not commanded. Truth, such as is necessary to the regulation of life, is always found where it is honestly sought. Change of place is no natural cause of the increase of piety, for it inevitably produces dissipation of mind. Yet, since men go every day to view the fields where great actions have been performed, and return with stronger impressions of the event, curiosity of the same kind may naturally dispose us to view that country whence our religion had its beginning; and I believe no man surveys those awful scenes without some confirmation of holy resolutions. That the Supreme Being may be more easily propitiated in one place than in another is the dream of idle superstition, but that some places may operate upon our own minds in an uncommon manner is an opinion which hourly experience will justify. He who supposes that his vices may be more successfully combated in Palestine, will, perhaps, find himself mistaken, yet he may go thither without folly; he who thinks they will be more freely pardoned, dishonors at once his reason and religion."

"These," said the prince, "are European distinctions. I will consider them another time. What have you found to be the effect of knowledge? Are those nations happier than we?"

"There is so much infelicity," said the poet, "in the world that scarce any man has leisure from his own distresses to estimate the comparative happiness of others. Knowledge is certainly one of the means of pleasure, as is confessed by the natural desire which every mind feels of increasing its ideas. Ignorance is mere privation, by which nothing can be produced; it is a vacuity in which the soul sits motionless and torpid for want of attraction; and, without knowing why, we always rejoice when we learn, and grieve when we forget. I am therefore inclined to conclude that if nothing counteracts the natural consequence of learning, we grow more happy as our minds take a wider range.

"In enumerating the particular comforts of life, we shall find many advantages on the side of the Europeans. They cure wounds and diseases with which we languish and perish. We suffer inclemencies of weather which they can obviate. They have engines for the despatch of many laborious works, which we must perform by manual industry. There is such communication between distant places that one friend can hardly be said to be absent from another. Their policy removes all public inconveniences; they have roads cut through their mountains, and bridges laid upon their rivers. And, if we descend to the privacies of life, their habitations are more commodious, and their possessions are more secure."

"They are surely happy," said the prince, "who have all these conveniencies, of which I envy none so much as the facility with which separated friends interchange their thoughts."

"The Europeans," answered Imlac, "are less unhappy than we, but they are not happy. Human life is everywhere a state in which much is to be endured, and little to be enjoyed."[7]

Chapter XVI. *They Enter Cairo, and Find Every Man Happy*

As they approached the city, which filled the strangers with astonishment, "This," said Imlac to the prince, "is the place where travelers and merchants assemble from all the corners of the earth. You will here find men of every character and every occupation. Commerce is here honorable. I will act as a merchant, and you shall live as strangers, who have no other end of travel than curiosity. It will soon be observed that we are rich; our reputation will procure us access to all whom we shall desire to know; you will see all the conditions of humanity, and enable yourself at leisure to make your *choice of life*."

They now entered the town, stunned by the noise, and offended by the crowds. Instruction had not yet so prevailed over habit, but that they wondered to see themselves pass undistinguished along the street, and met by the lowest of the people without reverence or notice. The princess could not at first bear the thought of being leveled with the vulgar, and for some days continued in her chamber, where she was served by her favorite, Pekuah, as in the palace of the valley.

7. In the omitted chapters Rasselas and Imlac tunnel through the mountain, starting from a cavern earlier discovered by Rasselas. Laden with wealth and guided by Imlac, Rasselas, his sister Nekayah, and her maid Pekuah escape from the Happy Valley and make their way to Cairo.

Imlac, who understood traffic,[8] sold part of the jewels the next day, and hired a house, which he adorned with such magnificence that he was immediately considered as a merchant of great wealth. His politeness attracted many acquaintance, and his generosity made him courted by many dependents. His table was crowded by men of every nation, who all admired his knowledge, and solicited his favor. His companions, not being able to mix in the conversation, could make no discovery of their ignorance or surprise, and were gradually initiated in the world as they gained knowledge of the language.

The prince had, by frequent lectures, been taught the use and nature of money; but the ladies could not for a long time comprehend what the merchants did with small pieces of gold and silver, or why things of so little use should be received as equivalent to the necessaries of life.

They studied the language two years, while Imlac was preparing to set before them the various ranks and conditions of mankind. He grew acquainted with all who had anything uncommon in their fortune or conduct. He frequented the voluptuous and the frugal, the idle and the busy, the merchants and the men of learning.

The prince being now able to converse with fluency, and having learned the caution necessary to be observed in his intercourse with strangers, began to accompany Imlac to places of resort, and to enter into all assemblies, that he might make his *choice of life*.

For some time he thought choice needless, because all appeared to him equally happy. Wherever he went he met gaiety and kindness, and heard the song of joy or the laugh of carelessness. He began to believe that the world overflowed with universal plenty, and that nothing was withheld either from want or merit; that every hand showered liberality, and every heart melted with benevolence: "And who then," says he, "will be suffered to be wretched?"

Imlac permitted the pleasing delusion, and was unwilling to crush the hope of inexperience, till one day, having sat awhile silent, "I know not," said the prince, "what can be the reason that I am more unhappy than any of our friends. I see them perpetually and unalterably cheerful, but feel my own mind restless and uneasy. I am unsatisfied with those pleasures which I seem most to court; I live in the crowds of jollity, not so much to enjoy company as to shun myself, and am only loud and merry to conceal my sadness."

"Every man," said Imlac, "may, by examining his own mind, guess what passes in the minds of others; when you feel that your own gaiety is counterfeit, it may justly lead you to suspect that of your companions not to be sincere. Envy is commonly reciprocal. We are long before we are convinced that happiness is never to be found, and each believes it possessed by others, to keep alive the

8. Commerce.

hope of obtaining it for himself. In the assembly where you passed the last night, there appeared such sprightliness of air, and volatility of fancy, as might have suited beings of an higher order, formed to inhabit serener regions, inaccessible to care or sorrow; yet, believe me, prince, there was not one who did not dread the moment when solitude should deliver him to the tyranny of reflection."

"This," said the prince, "may be true of others, since it is true of me; yet, whatever be the general infelicity of man, one condition is more happy than another, and wisdom surely directs us to take the least evil in the *choice of life*."

"The causes of good and evil," answered Imlac, "are so various and uncertain, so often entangled with each other, so diversified by various relations, and so much subject to accidents which cannot be foreseen, that he who would fix his condition upon incontestable reasons of preference must live and die inquiring and deliberating."

"But, surely," said Rasselas, "the wise men, to whom we listen with reverence and wonder, chose that mode of life for themselves which they thought most likely to make them happy."

"Very few," said the poet, "live by choice. Every man is placed in his present condition by causes which acted without his foresight, and with which he did not always willingly co-operate; and therefore you will rarely meet one who does not think the lot of his neighbor better than his own."

"I am pleased to think," said the prince, "that my birth has given me at least one advantage over others, by enabling me to determine for myself. I have here the world before me. I will review it at leisure; surely happiness is somewhere to be found."[9]

Chapter XVIII. The Prince Finds a Wise and Happy Man

As he was one day walking in the street, he saw a spacious building which all were, by the open doors, invited to enter: he followed the stream of people, and found it a hall or school of declamation, in which professors read lectures to their auditory. He fixed his eye upon a sage raised above the rest, who discoursed with great energy on the government of the passions. His look was venerable, his action graceful, his pronunciation clear, and his diction elegant. He showed with great strength of sentiment and variety of illustration that human nature is degraded and debased, when the lower faculties predominate over the higher; that when fancy, the parent of passion, usurps the dominion of the mind, nothing ensues but the natural effect of unlawful government, perturbation, and confusion; that she betrays the fortresses of the intellect to rebels, and excites her children to sedition against reason, their lawful sovereign. He compared reason to the sun, of which the light is constant, uniform and lasting; and fancy to a meteor, of bright but transitory luster,

9. In Chapter XVII, here omitted, Rasselas fails to find happiness among the gay and dissipated young men of Cairo.

irregular in its motion, and delusive in its direction.

He then communicated the various precepts given from time to time for the conquest of passion, and displayed the happiness of those who had obtained the important victory, after which man is no longer the slave of fear, nor the fool of hope; is no more emaciated by envy, inflamed by anger, emasculated by tenderness, or depressed by grief; but walks on calmly through the tumults or the privacies of life, as the sun pursues alike his course through the calm or the stormy sky.

He enumerated many examples of heroes immovable by pain or pleasure, who looked with indifference on those modes or accidents to which the vulgar give the names of good and evil. He exhorted his hearers to lay aside their prejudices, and arm themselves against the shafts of malice or misfortune, by invulnerable patience; concluding that this state only was happiness, and that his happiness was in everyone's power.

Rasselas listened to him with the veneration due to the instructions of a superior being, and, waiting for him at the door, humbly implored the liberty of visiting so great a master of true wisdom. The lecturer hesitated a moment, when Rasselas put a purse of gold into his hand, which he received with a mixture of joy and wonder.

"I have found," said the prince at his return to Imlac, "a man who can teach all that is necessary to be known; who, from the unshaken throne of rational fortitude, looks down on the scenes of life changing beneath him. He speaks, and attention watches his lips. He reasons, and conviction closes his periods. This man shall be my future guide; I will learn his doctrines, and imitate his life."

"Be not too hasty," said Imlac, "to trust or to admire the teachers of morality: they discourse like angels, but they live like men."

Rasselas, who could not conceive how any man could reason so forcibly without feeling the cogency of his own arguments, paid his visit in a few days, and was denied admission. He had now learned the power of money, and made his way by a piece of gold to the inner apartment, where he found the philosopher in a room half darkened, with his eyes misty and his face pale. "Sir," said he, "you are come at a time when all human friendship is useless; what I suffer cannot be remedied, what I have lost cannot be supplied. My daughter, my only daughter, from whose tenderness I expected all the comforts of my age, died last night of a fever. My views, my purposes, my hopes are at an end; I am now a lonely being, disunited from society."

"Sir," said the prince, "mortality is an event by which a wise man can never be surprised; we know that death is always near, and it should therefore always be expected." "Young man," answered the philosopher, "you speak like one that has never felt the pangs of separation." "Have you then forgot the precepts," said Rasselas, "which you so powerfully enforced? Has wisdom no strength to arm the heart against calamity? Consider that external things are naturally variable, but truth and reason are always the same." "What comfort," said the mourner, "can truth and reason afford me? Of what effect are they now, but to tell me that my daughter will not be restored?"

The prince, whose humanity would not suffer him to insult misery with reproof, went away, convinced of the emptiness of rhetorical sound, and the inefficacy of polished periods and studied sentences.

Chapter XIX. A Glimpse of Pastoral Life

He was still eager upon the same inquiry; and having heard of a hermit that lived near the lowest cataract of the Nile, and filled the whole country with the fame of his sanctity, resolved to visit his retreat, and inquire whether that felicity which public life could not afford was to be found in solitude; and whether a man whose age and virtue made him venerable could teach any peculiar art of shunning evils, or enduring them.

Imlac and the princess agreed to accompany him, and, after the necessary preparations, they began their journey. Their way lay through fields, where shepherds tended their flocks and the lambs were playing upon the pasture. "This," said the poet, "is the life which has been often celebrated for its innocence and quiet; let us pass the heat of the day among the shepherds' tents, and know whether all our searches are not to terminate in pastoral simplicity."

The proposal pleased them, and they induced the shepherds, by small presents and familiar questions, to tell their opinion of their own state. They were so rude and ignorant, so little able to compare the good with the evil of the occupation, and so indistinct in their narratives and descriptions, that very little could be learned from them. But it was evident that their hearts were cankered with discontent; that they considered themselves as condemned to labor for the luxury of the rich, and looked up with stupid malevolence toward those that were placed above them.

The princess pronounced with vehemence that she would never suffer these envious savages to be her companions, and that she should not soon be desirous of seeing any more specimens of rustic happiness; but could not believe that all the accounts of primeval pleasures were fabulous, and was yet in doubt whether life had anything that could be justly preferred to the placid gratifications of fields and woods. She hoped that the time would come, when, with a few virtuous and elegant companions, she could gather flowers planted by her own hand, fondle the lambs of her own ewe, and listen without care, among brooks and breezes, to one of her maidens reading in the shade.[1]

Chapter XXII. The Happiness of a Life
Led According to Nature

Rasselas went often to an assembly of learned men, who met at stated times to unbend their minds and compare their opinions. Their manners were somewhat coarse, but their conversation was instructive, and their disputations acute, though sometimes too violent, and often continued till neither controvertist remembered upon what question they began. Some faults were almost general among them; everyone was desirous to dictate to the rest, and everyone was pleased to hear the genius or knowledge of another depreciated.

In this assembly Rasselas was relating his interview with the hermit, and the wonder with which he heard him censure a course of life which he had so deliberately chosen, and so laudably followed. The sentiments of the hearers were various. Some were of opinion that the folly of his choice had been justly punished by condemnation to perpetual perseverance. One of the youngest among them, with great vehemence, pronounced him an hypocrite. Some talked of the right of society to the labor of individuals, and considered retirement as a desertion of duty. Others readily allowed that there was a time when the claims of the public were satisfied, and when a man might properly sequester himself, to review his life and purify his heart.

One, who appeared more affected with the narrative than the rest, thought it likely that the hermit would in a few years go back to his retreat, and perhaps, if shame did not restrain, or death intercept him, return once more from his retreat into the world. "For the hope of happiness," said he, "is so strongly impressed that the longest experience is not able to efface it. Of the present state, whatever it be, we feel and are forced to confess the misery; yet when the same state is again at a distance, imagination paints it as desirable. But the time will surely come when desire will be no longer our torment, and no man shall be wretched but by his own fault."

"This," said a philosopher who had heard him with tokens of great impatience, "is the present condition of a wise man. The time is already come when none are wretched but by their own fault. Nothing is more idle than to inquire after happiness, which nature has kindly placed within our reach. The way to be happy is to live according to nature, in obedience to that universal and

1. In the omitted chapters the travelers discover the unease and danger of being wealthy, and then find the hermit, who, far from being piously content, is on the point of abandoning his hermitage and returning to society.

unalterable law with which every heart is originally impressed; which is not written on it by precept, but engraven by destiny, not instilled by education, but infused at our nativity. He that lives according to nature will suffer nothing from the delusions of hope, or importunities of desire; he will receive and reject with equability of temper, and act or suffer as the reason of things shall alternately prescribe. Other men may amuse themselves with subtle definitions, or intricate ratiocination. Let them learn to be wise by easier means; let them observe the hind of the forest, and the linnet of the grove; let them consider the life of animals, whose motions are regulated by instinct; they obey their guide, and are happy. Let us therefore, at length, cease to dispute, and learn to live; throw away the encumbrance of precepts, which they who utter them with so much pride and pomp do not understand, and carry with us this simple and intelligible maxim, that deviation from nature is deviation from happiness."

When he had spoken, he looked round him with a placid air, and enjoyed the consciousness of his own beneficence. "Sir," said the prince with great modesty, "as I, like all the rest of mankind, am desirous of felicity, my closest attention has been fixed upon your discourse. I doubt not the truth of a position which a man so learned has so confidently advanced. Let me only know what it is to live according to nature."

"When I find young men so humble and so docile," said the philosopher, "I can deny them no information which my studies have enabled me to afford. To live according to nature, is to act always with due regard to the fitness arising from the relations and qualities of causes and effects; to concur with the great and unchangeable scheme of universal felicity; to co-operate with the general disposition and tendency of the present system of things."

The prince soon found that this was one of the sages whom he should understand less as he heard him longer. He therefore bowed and was silent; and the philosopher, supposing him satisfied, and the rest vanquished, rose up and departed with the air of a man that had co-operated with the present system.[2]

From *Chapter XXVI. The Princess Continues Her Remarks upon Private Life*

Nekayah, perceiving her brother's attention fixed, proceeded in her narrative.

"In families where there is or is not poverty, there is commonly discord. If a kingdom be, as Imlac tells us, a great family, a family likewise is a little kingdom, torn with factions and exposed to revolutions. An unpracticed observer expects the love of parents and

2. In the omitted chapters Rasselas resolves to observe the happiness of men of high position, leaving the study of domestic life to his sister; they report their findings to each other.

children to be constant and equal; but this kindness seldom continues beyond the years of infancy: in a short time the children become rivals to their parents. Benefits are allayed[3] by reproaches, and gratitude debased by envy.

"Parents and children seldom act in concert; each child endeavors to appropriate the esteem or fondness of the parents, and the parents, with yet less temptation, betray each other to their children. Thus, some place their confidence in the father, and some in the mother, and by degrees the house is filled with artifices and feuds.

"The opinions of children and parents, of the young and the old, are naturally opposite, by the contrary effects of hope and despondence, of expectation and experience, without crime or folly on either side. The colors of life in youth and age appear different, as the face of nature in spring and winter. And how can children credit the assertions of parents, which their own eyes show them to be false?

"Few parents act in such a manner as much to enforce their maxims by the credit of their lives. The old man trusts wholly to slow contrivance and gradual progression; the youth expects to force his way by genius, vigor, and precipitance. The old man pays regard to riches, and the youth reverences virtue. The old man deifies prudence; the youth commits himself to magnanimity and chance. The young man, who intends no ill, believes that none is intended, and therefore acts with openness and candor; but his father, having suffered the injuries of fraud, is impelled to suspect, and too often allured to practice it. Age looks with anger on the temerity of youth, and youth with contempt on the scrupulosity[4] of age. Thus parents and children, for the greatest part, live on to love less and less; and, if those whom nature has thus closely united are the torments of each other, where shall we look for tenderness and consolation?"

"Surely," said the prince, "you must have been unfortunate in your choice of acquaintance: I am unwilling to believe that the most tender of all relations is thus impeded in its effects by natural necessity."

"Domestic discord," answered she, "is not inevitably and fatally necessary, but yet is not easily avoided. We seldom see that a whole family is virtuous; the good and evil cannot well agree, and the evil can yet less agree with one another. Even the virtuous fall sometimes to variance, when their virtues are of different kinds, and tending to extremes. In general, those parents have most reverence who most deserve it; for he that lives well cannot be despised.

"Many other evils infest private life. Some are the slaves of servants whom they have trusted with their affairs. Some are kept in continual anxiety to the caprice of rich relations, whom they cannot

---

3. To allay is "to join anything to another, so as to abate its predominant qualities" (Johnson's *Dictionary*).

4. "Fear of acting in any manner" (Johnson's *Dictionary*).

please, and dare not offend. Some husbands are imperious, and some wives perverse; and, as it is always more easy to do evil than good, though the wisdom or virtue of one can very rarely make many happy, the folly or vice of one may often make many miserable."

"If such be the general effect of marriage," said the prince, "I shall for the future think it dangerous to connect my interest with that of another, lest I should be unhappy by my partner's fault."

"I have met," said the princess, "with many who live single for that reason; but I never found that their prudence ought to raise envy. They dream away their time without friendship, without fondness, and are driven to rid themselves of the day, for which they have no use, by childish amusements, or vicious delights. They act as beings under the constant sense of some known inferiority that fills their minds with rancor, and their tongues with censure. They are peevish at home, and malevolent abroad; and, as the outlaws of human nature, make it their business and their pleasure to disturb that society which debars them from its privileges. To live without feeling or exciting sympathy, to be fortunate without adding to the felicity of others, or afflicted without tasting the balm of pity, is a state more gloomy than solitude; it is not retreat but exclusion from mankind. Marriage has many pains, but celibacy has no pleasures."[5] * * *

Chapter XXIX. *The Debate on Marriage Continued*

"The good of the whole," says Rasselas, "is the same with the good of all its parts. If marriage be best for mankind it must be evidently best for individuals, or a permanent and necessary duty must be the cause of evil, and some must be inevitably sacrificed to the convenience of others. In the estimate which you have made of the two states, it appears that the incommodities of a single life are, in a great measure, necessary and certain, but those of the conjugal state accidental and avoidable.

"I cannot forbear to flatter myself that prudence and benevolence will make marriage happy. The general folly of mankind is the cause of general complaint. What can be expected but disappointment and repentance from a choice made in the immaturity of youth, in the ardor of desire, without judgment, without foresight, without inquiry after conformity of opinions, similarity of manners, rectitude of judgment, or purity of sentiment.

"Such is the common process of marriage. A youth and maiden meeting by chance, or brought together by artifice, exchange glances, reciprocate civilities, go home, and dream of one another. Having little to divert attention, or diversify thought, they find

---

5. In the omitted chapters Rasselas reports that even the highest stations afford no happiness, and the conversation continues.

themselves uneasy when they are apart, and therefore conclude that they shall be happy together. They marry, and discover what nothing but voluntary blindness had before concealed; they wear out life in altercations, and charge nature with cruelty.

"From those early marriages proceeds likewise the rivalry of parents and children: the son is eager to enjoy the world before the father is willing to forsake it, and there is hardly room at once for two generations. The daughter begins to bloom before the mother can be content to fade, and neither can forbear to wish for the absence of the other.

"Surely all these evils may be avoided by that deliberation and delay which prudence prescribes to irrevocable choice. In the variety and jollity of youthful pleasures life may be well enough supported without the help of a partner. Longer time will increase experience, and wider views will allow better opportunities of inquiry and selection: one advantage, as least, will be certain; the parents will be visibly older than their children."

"What reason cannot collect," said Nekayah, "and what experiment has not yet taught, can be known only from the report of others. I have been told that late marriages are not eminently happy. This is a question too important to be neglected, and I have often proposed it to those, whose accuracy of remark, and comprehensiveness of knowledge, made their suffrages worthy of regard. They have generally determined that it is dangerous for a man and woman to suspend their fate upon each other, at a time when opinions are fixed, and habits are established; when friendships have been contracted on both sides, when life has been planned into method, and the mind has long enjoyed the contemplation of its own prospects.

"It is scarcely possible that two traveling through the world under the conduct of chance should have been both directed to the same path, and it will not often happen that either will quit the track which custom has made pleasing. When the desultory levity of youth has settled into regularity, it is soon succeeded by pride ashamed to yield, or obstinacy delighting to contend. And even though mutual esteem produces mutual desire to please, time itself, as it modifies unchangeably the external mien, determines likewise the direction of the passions, and gives an inflexible rigidity to the manners. Long customs are not easily broken: he that attempts to change the course of his own life very often labors in vain; and how shall we do that for others which we are seldom able to do for ourselves?"

"But surely," interposed the prince, "you suppose the chief motive of choice forgotten or neglected. Whenever I shall seek a wife, it shall be my first question, whether she be willing to be led by reason?"

"Thus it is," said Nekayah, "that philosophers are deceived. There are a thousand familiar disputes which reason never can decide; questions that elude investigation, and make logic ridiculous; cases where something must be done, and where little can be said. Consider the state of mankind, and inquire how few can be supposed to act upon any occasions, whether small or great, with all the reasons of action present to their minds. Wretched would be the pair above all names of wretchedness, who should be doomed to adjust by reason every morning all the minute detail of a domestic day.

"Those who marry at an advanced age will probably escape the encroachments of their children; but, in diminution of this advantage, they will be likely to leave them, ignorant and helpless, to a guardian's mercy: or, if that should not happen, they must at least go out of the world before they see those whom they love best either wise or great.

"From their children, if they have less to fear, they have less also to hope, and they lose, without equivalent, the joys of early love, and the convenience of uniting with manners pliant and minds susceptible of new impressions, which might wear away their dissimilitudes by long cohabitation, as soft bodies, by continual attrition, conform their surfaces to each other.

"I believe it will be found that those who marry late are best pleased with their children, and those who marry early with their partners."

"The union of these two affections," said Rasselas, "would produce all that could be wished. Perhaps there is a time when marriage might unite them, a time neither too early for the father, nor too late for the husband."

"Every hour," answered the princess, "confirms my prejudice in favor of the position so often uttered by the mouth of Imlac, 'That nature sets her gifts on the right hand and on the left.' Those conditions, which flatter hope and attract desire, are so constituted that, as we approach one, we recede from another. There are goods so opposed that we cannot seize both, but, by too much prudence, may pass between them at too great a distance to reach either. This is often the fate of long consideration; he does nothing who endeavors to do more than is allowed to humanity. Flatter not yourself with contrarieties of pleasure. Of the blessings set before you make your choice, and be content. No man can taste the fruits of autumn, while he is delighting his scent with the flowers of the spring: no man can, at the same time, fill his cup from the source and from the mouth of the Nile."[6]

6. In Chapter XXX, here omitted, Imlac proposes a visit to the Pyramids.

Chapter XXXI. They Visit the Pyramids

The resolution being thus taken, they set out the next day. They laid tents upon their camels, being resolved to stay among the pyramids till their curiosity was fully satisfied. They traveled gently, turned aside to everything remarkable, stopped from time to time and conversed with the inhabitants, and observed the various appearances of towns ruined and inhabited, of wild and cultivated nature.

When they came to the great pyramid, they were astonished at the extent of the base, and the height of the top. Imlac explained to them the principles upon which the pyramidal form was chosen for a fabric intended to coextend its duration with that of the world; he showed that its gradual diminution gave it such stability as defeated all the common attacks of the elements, and could scarcely be overthrown by earthquakes themselves, the least resistible of natural violence. A concussion that should shatter the pyramid would threaten the dissolution of the continent.

They measured all its dimensions, and pitched their tents at its foot. Next day they prepared to enter its interior apartments, and having hired the common guides, climbed up to the first passage, when the favorite of the princess, looking into the cavity, stepped back and trembled. "Pekuah," said the princess, "of what art thou afraid?" "Of the narrow entrance," answered the lady, "and of the dreadful gloom. I dare not enter a place which must surely be inhabited by unquiet souls. The original possessors of these dreadful vaults will start up before us, and perhaps shut us in forever." She spoke, and threw her arms round the neck of her mistress.

"If all your fear be of apparitions," said the prince, "I will promise you safety. There is no danger from the dead; he that is once buried will be seen no more."

"That the dead are seen no more," said Imlac, "I will not undertake to maintain, against the concurrent and unvaried testimony of all ages, and of all nations. There is no people, rude or learned, among whom apparitions of the dead are not related and believed. This opinion, which perhaps prevails as far as human nature is diffused, could become universal only by its truth; those that never heard of one another would not have agreed in a tale which nothing but experience can make credible. That it is doubted by single cavilers can very little weaken the general evidence; and some who deny it with their tongues confess it by their fears.

"Yet I do not mean to add new terrors to those which have already seized upon Pekuah. There can be no reason why specters should haunt the pyramid more than other places, or why they should have power or will to hurt innocence and purity. Our entrance is no violation of their privileges; we can take nothing from them, how then can we offend them?"

"My dear Pekuah," said the princess, "I will always go before you, and Imlac shall follow you. Remember that you are the companion of the princess of Abyssinia."

"If the princess is pleased that her servant should die," returned the lady, "let her command some death less dreadful than enclosure in this horrid cavern. You know I dare not disobey you; I must go if you command me, but if I once enter, I never shall come back."

The princess saw that her fear was too strong for expostulation or reproof, and, embracing her, told her that she should stay in the tent till their return. Pekuah was yet not satisfied, but entreated the princess not to pursue so dreadful a purpose as that of entering the recesses of the pyramid. "Though I cannot teach courage," said Nekayah, "I must not learn cowardice, nor leave at last undone what I came hither only to do."

Chapter XXXII. They Enter the Pyramid

Pekuah descended to the tents, and the rest entered the pyramid. They passed through the galleries, surveyed the vaults of marble, and examined the chest in which the body of the founder is supposed to have been reposited. They then sat down in one of the most spacious chambers to rest a while before they attempted to return.

"We have now," said Imlac, "gratified our minds with an exact view of the greatest work of man, except the wall of China.

"Of the wall it is very easy to assign the motive. It secured a wealthy and timorous nation from the incursions of barbarians, whose unskillfulness in arts made it easier for them to supply their wants by rapine than by industry, and who from time to time poured in upon the habitations of peaceful commerce, as vultures descend upon domestic fowl. Their celerity and fierceness made the wall necessary, and their ignorance made it efficacious.

"But for the pyramids, no reason has ever been given adequate to the cost and labor of the work. The narrowness of the chambers proves that it could afford no retreat from enemies, and treasures might have been reposited at far less expense with equal security. It seems to have been erected only in compliance with that hunger of imagination which preys incessantly upon life, and must be always appeased by some employment. Those who have already all that they can enjoy must enlarge their desires. He that has built for use till use is supplied, must begin to build for vanity, and extend his plan to the utmost power of human performance, that he may not be soon reduced to form another wish.

"I consider this mighty structure as a monument of the insufficiency of human enjoyments. A king, whose power is unlimited, and whose treasures surmount all real and imaginary wants, is compelled to solace, by the erection of a pyramid, the satiety of dominion and tastelessness of pleasures, and to amuse the tediousness of declining life by seeing thousands laboring without end, and one stone, for no purpose, laid upon another. Whoever thou art, that, not content with a moderate condition, imaginest happiness in royal magnificence, and dreamest that command or riches can feed the appetite of novelty with perpetual gratifications, survey the pyramids, and confess thy folly!"[7]

Chapter XLIV. The Dangerous Prevalence[8] of Imagination

"Disorders of intellect," answered Imlac, "happen much more often than superficial observers will easily believe. Perhaps, if we speak with rigorous exactness, no human mind is in its right state. There is no man whose imagination does not sometimes predominate over his reason, who can regulate his attention wholly by his will, and whose ideas will come and go at his command. No man will be found in whose mind airy notions do not sometimes tyrannize, and force him to hope or fear beyond the limits of sober probability. All power of fancy over reason is a degree of insanity; but while this power is such as we can control and repress, it is not visible to others, nor considered as any depravation of the mental faculties; it is not pronounced madness but when it comes ungovernable, and apparently influences speech or action.

"To indulge the power of fiction, and send imagination out upon the wing, is often the sport of those who delight too much in silent speculation. When we are alone we are not always busy; the labor of excogitation is too violent to last long; the ardor of inquiry will sometimes give way to idleness or satiety. He who has nothing external that can divert him must find pleasure in his own thoughts, and must conceive himself what he is not; for who is pleased with what he is? He then expatiates in boundless futurity, and culls from all imaginable conditions that which for the present moment he should most desire, amuses his desires with impossible enjoyments, and confers upon his pride unattainable dominion. The mind dances from scene to scene, unites all pleasures in all combinations, and riots in delights which nature and fortune, with all their bounty, cannot bestow.

"In time, some particular train of ideas fixes the attention; all other intellectual gratifications are rejected; the mind, in weariness

7. Chapters XXXIII-XLIII are here omitted. While the travelers are in the Pyramid, Pekuah is abducted by an Arab chieftain, from whom she is eventually ransomed. The travelers return to Cairo, and Imlac makes the acquaintance of an astronomer, who proves to be mad, having yielded to the delusion that he has learned to control the weather. Chapter XLIII concludes: "Rasselas * * * inquired of Imlac whether he thought such maladies of the mind frequent, and how they were contracted."
8. Predominance.

or leisure, recurs constantly to the favorite conception, and feasts on the luscious falsehood, whenever she is offended with the bitterness of truth. By degrees the reign of fancy is confirmed; she grows first imperious, and in time despotic. Then fictions begin to operate as realities, false opinions fasten upon the mind, and life passes in dreams of rapture or of anguish.

"This, sir, is one of the dangers of solitude, which the hermit has confessed not always to promote goodness, and the astronomer's misery has proved to be not always propitious to wisdom."

"I will no more," said the favorite, "imagine myself the queen of Abyssinia. I have often spent the hours which the princess gave to my own disposal, in adjusting ceremonies and regulating the court; I have repressed the pride of the powerful, and granted the petitions of the poor; I have built new palaces in more happy situations, planted groves upon the tops of mountains, and have exulted in the beneficence of royalty, till, when the princess entered, I had almost forgotten to bow down before her."

"And I," said the princess, "will not allow myself any more to play the shepherdess in my waking dreams. I have often soothed my thoughts with the quiet and innocence of pastoral employments, till I have in my chamber heard the winds whistle, and the sheep bleat; sometimes freed the lamb entangled in the thicket, and sometimes with my crook encountered the wolf. I have a dress like that of the village maids, which I put on to help my imagination, and a pipe on which I play softly, and suppose myself followed by my flocks."

"I will confess," said the prince, "an indulgence of fantastic delight more dangerous than yours. I have frequently endeavored to image the possibility of a perfect government, by which all wrong should be restrained, all vice reformed, and all the subjects preserved in tranquility and innocence. This thought produced innumerable schemes of reformation, and dictated many useful regulations and salutary edicts. This has been the sport, and sometimes the labor, of my solitude; and I start, when I think with how little anguish I once supposed the death of my father and my brothers."

"Such," says Imlac, "are the effects of visionary schemes; when we first form them, we know them to be absurd, but familiarize them by degrees, and in time lose sight of their folly."

Chapter XLV. They Discourse with an Old Man

The evening was now far past, and they rose to return home. As they walked along the bank of the Nile, delighted with the beams of the moon quivering on the water, they saw at a small distance an old man, whom the prince had often heard in the assembly of the sages. "Yonder," said he, "is one whose years have calmed his passions, but not clouded his reason. Let us close the disquisitions of the night by inquiring what are his sentiments of his own state, that we may know whether youth alone is to struggle with vexation, and whether any better hope remains for the latter part of life."

Here the sage approached and saluted them. They invited him to join their walk, and prattled a while, as acquaintance that had unexpectedly met one another. The old man was cheerful and talkative, and the way seemed short in his company. He was pleased to find himself not disregarded, accompanied them to their house, and, at the prince's request, entered with them. They placed him in the seat of honor, and set wine and conserves before him.

"Sir," said the princess, "an evening walk must give to a man of learning like you pleasures which ignorance and youth can hardly conceive. You know the qualities and the causes of all that you behold, the laws by which the river flows, the periods in which the planets perform their revolutions. Everything must supply you with contemplation, and renew the consciousness of your own dignity."

"Lady," answered he, "let the gay and the vigorous expect pleasure in their excursions; it is enough that age can obtain ease. To me the world has lost its novelty; I look round, and see what I remember to have seen in happier days. I rest against a tree, and consider that in the same shade I once disputed upon the annual overflow of the Nile with a friend who is now silent in the grave. I cast my eyes upward, fix them on the changing moon, and think with pain on the vicissitudes of life. I have ceased to take much delight in physical truth; for what have I to do with those things which I am soon to leave?"

"You may at least recreate yourself," said Imlac, "with the recollection of an honorable and useful life, and enjoy the praise which all agree to give you."

"Praise," said the sage with a sigh, "is to an old man an empty sound. I have neither mother to be delighted with the reputation of her son, nor wife to partake the honors of her husband. I have outlived my friends and my rivals. Nothing is now of much importance; for I cannot extend my interest beyond myself. Youth is delighted with applause, because it is considered as the earnest of some future good, and because the prospect of life is far extended; but to me, who am now declining to decrepitude, there is little to be feared from the malevolence of men, and yet less to be hoped from their affection or esteem. Something they may yet take away, but they can give me nothing. Riches would now be useless, and high employment would be pain. My retrospect of life recalls to my view many opportunities of good neglected, much time squandered upon trifles, and more lost in idleness and vacancy. I leave many great designs unattempted, and many great attempts unfinished. My mind is burthened with no heavy crime, and therefore I compose myself to tranquility; endeavor to abstract my thoughts from hopes and cares which, though reason knows them to be vain, still try to keep their old possession of the heart; expect,[9] with serene humility, that hour which nature cannot long delay; and hope to possess, in a better state, that happiness which here I could not find, and that virtue which here I have not attained."

He arose and went away, leaving his audience not much elated with the hope of long life. The prince consoled himself with remarking that it was not reasonable to be disappointed by this account; for age had never been considered as the season of felicity, and if it was possible to be easy in decline and weakness, it was likely that the days of vigor and alacrity might be happy; that the noon of life might be bright, if the evening could be calm.

The princess suspected that age was querulous and malignant, and delighted to repress the expectations of those who had newly entered the world. She had seen the possessors of estates look with envy on their heirs, and known many who enjoy pleasure no longer than they can confine it to themselves.

Pekuah conjectured that the man was older than he appeared, and was willing to impute his complaints to delirious dejection; or else supposed that he had been unfortunate, and was therefore discontented. "For nothing," said she, "is more common than to call our own condition the condition of life."

Imlac, who had no desire to see them depressed, smiled at the comforts which they could so readily procure to themselves, and remembered that, at the same age, he was equally confident of unmingled prosperity, and equally fertile of consolatory expedients. He forebore to force upon them unwelcome knowledge, which time itself would too soon impress. The princess and her lady retired; the madness of the astronomer hung upon their minds, and they desired Imlac to enter upon his office, and delay next morning the rising of the sun.[1]

Chapter XLIX. *The Conclusion, in Which Nothing Is Concluded*

It was now the time of the inundation of the Nile: a few days after their visit to the catacombs, the river began to rise.

They were confined to their house. The whole region being under water gave them no invitation to any excursions, and being well supplied with materials for talk, they diverted themselves with comparisons of the different forms of life which they had observed, and with various schemes of happiness which each of them had formed.

9. Await.
1. Chapters XLVI-XLVIII are here omitted. The travelers converse with the astronomer and learn that he too regrets his choice of life. A discourse on the nature of the soul (in the penultimate chapter) raises the hope of happiness in a future state.

Pekuah was never so much charmed with any place as the convent of St. Anthony, where the Arab restored her to the princess, and wished only to fill it with pious maidens, and to be made prioress of the order; she was weary of expectation and disgust,[2] and would gladly be fixed in some unvariable state.

The princess thought that, of all sublunary things, knowledge was the best: she desired first to learn all sciences, and then purposed to found a college of learned women, in which she would preside, that, by conversing with the old and educating the young, she might divide her time between the acquisition and communication of wisdom, and raise up for the next age models of prudence, and patterns of piety.

The prince desired a little kingdom, in which he might administer justice in his own person, and see all the parts of government with his own eyes; but he could never fix the limits of his dominion, and was always adding to the number of his subjects.

Imlac and the astronomer were contented to be driven along the stream of life, without directing their course to any particular port.

Of these wishes that they had formed, they well knew that none could be obtained. They deliberated a while what was to be done, and resolved, when the inundation should cease, to return to Abyssinia.[3]

1759

From Prayers and Meditations[1]

Easter Eve, 1761

Since the communion of last Easter, I have led a life so dissipated and useless, and my terrors and perplexities have so much increased, that I am under great depression and discouragement; yet I purpose to present myself before God tomorrow, with humble hope that he will not break the bruised reed.

Come unto me all ye that travail.[2]

I have resolved, I hope not presumptuously, till I am afraid to resolve again. Yet hoping in God, I steadfastly purpose to lead a new life. O God, enable me, for Jesus Christ's sake.

2. Aversion.
3. Probably not, as is often suggested, to the Happy Valley (in Chapter I we were told that none who leave the valley can ever return). Presumably the travelers return, with whatever wisdom they have gained, but also with their cherished illusions, to share the common destiny of mankind. But Johnson, hurrying to his conclusion, may have left the place to which they returned vague.

1. During much of his life Johnson observed with prayer and meditation certain seasons: his own birthday, the anniversary of the death of his wife, Good Friday, and Easter. He was accustomed to writing down his prayers and thoughts. This document gives a moving insight into his spiritual struggles and his sense of sin.
2. Matthew xi.28.

Good Friday, 1779, 11 P.M.

I am now to review the last year, and find little but dismal vacuity, neither business nor pleasure; much intended, and little done. My health is much broken; my nights afford me little rest. I have tried opium, but its help is counterbalanced with great disturbance; it prevents the spasms, but it hinders sleep. O God, have mercy on me.

Last week I published the *Lives of the Poets*, written, I hope, in such a manner as may tend to the promotion of piety.

In this last year I have made little acquisition; I have scarcely read anything. I maintain Mrs. [Desmoulins] and her daughter. Other good of myself I know not where to find, except a little charity.

But I am now in my seventieth year; what can be done, ought not to be delayed.

Rambler No. 4

[On Fiction]

Saturday, March 31, 1750

Simul et jucunda et idonea dicere vitae.
—HORACE, *Art of Poetry,* 334
And join both profit and delight in one.
—CREECH

The works of fiction with which the present generation seems more particularly delighted are such as exhibit life in its true state, diversified only by accidents that daily happen in the world, and influenced by passions and qualities which are really to be found in conversing with mankind.

This kind of writing may be termed, not improperly, the comedy of romance, and is to be conducted nearly by the rules of comic poetry. Its province is to bring about natural events by easy means, and to keep up curiosity without the help of wonder: it is therefore precluded from the machines[1] and expedients of the heroic romance, and can neither employ giants to snatch away a lady from the nuptial rites, nor knights to bring her back from captivity; it can neither bewilder its personages in deserts, nor lodge them in imaginary castles.

I remember a remark made by Scaliger upon Pontanus,[2] that all his writings are filled with the same images; and that if you take from him his lilies and his roses, his satyrs and his dryads, he will have nothing left that can be called poetry. In like manner, almost

1. The technical term in neoclassical critical theory for the supernatural agents who intervene in human affairs in epic and tragedy.

2. Julius Caesar Scaliger (1484–1558) criticized the Latin poems of the Italian poet Jovianus Pontanus (1426–1503).

all the fictions of the last age will vanish if you deprive them of a hermit and a wood, a battle and a shipwreck.

Why this wild strain of imagination found reception so long in polite and learned ages, it is not easy to conceive; but we cannot wonder that while readers could be procured, the authors were willing to continue it; for when a man had by practice gained some fluency of language, he had no further care than to retire to his closet, let loose his invention, and heat his mind with incredibilities; a book was thus produced without fear of criticism, without the toil of study, without knowledge of nature, or acquaintance with life.

The task of our present writers is very different; it requires, together with that learning which is to be gained from books, that experience which can never be attained by solitary diligence, but must arise from general converse and accurate observation of the living world. Their performances have, as Horace expresses it, *plus oneris quanto veniae minus*,[3] little indulgence, and therefore more difficulty. They are engaged in portraits of which everyone knows the original, and can detect any deviation from exactness of resemblance. Other writings are safe, except from the malice of learning, but these are in danger from every common reader; as the slipper ill executed was censured by a shoemaker who happened to stop in his way at the Venus of Appeles.[4]

But the fear of not being approved as just copiers of human manners is not the most important concern that an author of this sort ought to have before him. These books are written chiefly to the young, the ignorant, and the idle, to whom they serve as lectures of conduct, and introductions into life. They are the entertainment of minds unfurnished with ideas, and therefore easily susceptible of impressions; not fixed by principles, and therefore easily following the current of fancy; not informed by experience, and consequently open to every false suggestion and partial account.

That the highest degree of reverence should be paid to youth, and that nothing indecent should be suffered to approach their eyes or ears, are precepts extorted by sense and virtue from an ancient writer by no means eminent for chastity of thought. The same kind, though not the same degree, of caution, is required in everything which is laid before them, to secure them from hearing unjust prejudices, perverse opinions, and incongruous combinations of images.

In the romances formerly written, every transaction and sentiment was so remote from all that passes among men that the reader was in very little danger of making any applications to himself; the virtues and crimes were equally beyond his sphere of activity; and

3. *Epistles* II.i.170.
4. According to Pliny the Younger (*Naturalis Historia* XXXV.85), the Greek painter Apelles of Kos (4th century B.C.) corrected the drawing of a sandal after hearing a shoemaker criticize it as faulty, but when the flattered artisan dared to find fault with the drawing of a leg, the artist bade him "stick to his last."

he amused himself with heroes and with traitors, deliverers and persecutors, as with beings of another species, whose actions were regulated upon motives of their own, and who had neither faults nor excellencies in common with himself.

But when an adventurer is leveled with the rest of the world, and acts in such scenes of the universal drama as may be the lot of any other man, young spectators fix their eyes upon him with closer attention, and hope, by observing his behavior and success, to regulate their own practices when they shall be engaged in the like part.

For this reason these familiar histories may perhaps be made of greater use than the solemnities of professed morality, and convey the knowledge of vice and virtue with more efficacy than axioms and definitions. But if the power of example is so great as to take possession of the memory by a kind of violence, and produce effects almost without the intervention of the will, care ought to be taken that when the choice is unrestrained, the best examples only should be exhibited; and that which is likely to operate so strongly should not be mischievous or uncertain in its effects.

The chief advantage which these fictions have over real life is that their authors are at liberty, though not to invent, yet to select objects, and to cull from the mass of mankind those individuals upon which the attention ought most to be employed; as a diamond, though it cannot be made, may be polished by art, and placed in such situation as to display that luster which before was buried among common stones.

It is justly considered as the greatest excellency of art to imitate nature; but it is necessary to distinguish those parts of nature which are most proper for imitation: greater care is still required in representing life, which is so often discolored by passion or deformed by wickedness. If the world be promiscuously described, I cannot see of what use it can be to read the account; or why it may not be as safe to turn the eye immediately upon mankind as upon a mirror which shows all that presents itself without discrimination.

It is therefore not a sufficient vindication of a character that it is drawn as it appears; for many characters ought never to be drawn: nor of a narrative that the train of events is agreeable to observation and experience; for that observation which is called knowledge of the world will be found much more frequently to make men cunning than good. The purpose of these writings is surely not only to show mankind, but to provide that they may be seen hereafter with less hazard; to teach the means of avoiding the snares which are laid by Treachery for Innocence, without infusing any wish for that superiority with which the betrayer flatters his vanity; to give the power of counteracting fraud without the temptation to practice it; to initiate youth by mock encounters in the art of necessary defense, and to increase prudence without impairing virtue.

Many writers, for the sake of following nature, so mingle good and bad qualities in their principal personages that they are both equally conspicuous; and as we accompany them through their adventures with delight, and are led by degrees to interest ourselves in their favor, we lose the abhorrence of their faults because they do not hinder our pleasure, or perhaps regard them with some kindness for being united with so much merit.

There have been men indeed splendidly wicked, whose endowments threw a brightness on their crimes, and whom scarce any villainy made perfectly detestable because they never could be wholly divested of their excellencies; but such have been in all ages the great corrupters of the world, and their resemblance ought no more to be preserved than the art of murdering without pain.

Some have advanced, without due attention to the consequence of this notion, that certain virtues have their correspondent faults, and therefore that to exhibit either apart is to deviate from probability. Thus men are observed by Swift to be "grateful in the same degree as they are resentful." This principle, with others of the same kind, supposes man to act from a brute impulse, and pursue a certain degree of inclination without any choice of the object; for, otherwise, though it should be allowed that gratitude and resentment arise from the same constitution of the passions, it follows not that they will be equally indulged when reason is consulted; yet, unless that consequence be admitted, this sagacious maxim becomes an empty sound, without any relation to practice or to life.

Nor is it evident that even the first motions to these effects are always in the same proportion. For pride, which produces quickness of resentment, will obstruct gratitude by unwillingness to admit that inferiority which obligation implies; and it is very unlikely that he who cannot think he receives a favor will acknowledge or repay it.

It is of the utmost importance to mankind that positions of this tendency should be laid open and confuted; for while men consider good and evil as springing from the same root, they will spare the one for the sake of the other, and in judging, if not of others at least of themselves, will be apt to estimate their virtues by their vices. To this fatal error all those will contribute who confound the colors of right and wrong, and, instead of helping to settle their boundaries, mix them with so much art that no common mind is able to disunite them.

In narratives where historical veracity has no place, I cannot discover why there should not be exhibited the most perfect idea of virtue; of virtue not angelical, nor above probability (for what we cannot credit, we shall never imitate), but the highest and purest that humanity can reach, which, exercised in such trials as the various revolutions of things shall bring upon it, may, by conquering some calamities and enduring others, teach us what we may hope, and what we can perform. Vice (for vice is necessary to be shown) should always disgust; nor should the graces of gaiety, nor the dignity of courage, be so united with it as to reconcile it to the mind. Wherever it appears, it should raise hatred by the malignity of its practices, and contempt by the meanness of its stratagems: for while it is supported by either parts or spirit, it will be seldom heartily abhorred. The Roman tyrant was content to be hated if he was but feared;[5] and there are thousands of the readers of romances willing to be thought wicked if they may be allowed to be wits. It is therefore to be steadily inculcated that virtue is the highest proof of understanding, and the only solid basis of greatness; and that vice is the natural consequence of narrow thoughts; that it begins in mistake, and ends in ignominy.

Rambler No. 60

[Biography]

Saturday, October 13, 1750

—Quid sit pulchrum, quid turpe, quid utile, quid non,
Plenius ac melius Chrysippo et Crantore dicit.
—HORACE, *Epistles*, I.ii. 3–4

Whose works the beautiful and base contain,
Of vice and virtue more instructive rules,
Than all the sober sages of the schools.
—FRANCIS

All joy or sorrow for the happiness or calamities of others is produced by an act of the imagination, that realizes the event, however fictitious, or approximates it, however remote, by placing us, for a time, in the condition of him whose fortune we contemplate; so that we feel, while the deception lasts, whatever motions would be excited by the same good or evil happening to ourselves.

Our passions are therefore more strongly moved, in proportion as we can more readily adopt the pains or pleasure proposed to our minds, by recognizing them as once our own, or considering them as naturally incident to our state of life. It is not easy for the most artful writer to give us an interest in happiness or misery, which we think ourselves never likely to feel, and with which we have never yet been made acquainted. Histories of the downfall of kingdoms, and revolutions of empires, are read with great tranquility; the

imperial tragedy pleases common auditors only by its pomp of ornament, and grandeur of ideas; and the man whose faculties have
been engrossed by business, and whose heart never fluttered but at
the rise or fall of stocks, wonders how the attention can be seized,
or the affections agitated, by a tale of love.

Those parallel circumstances, and kindred images to which we
readily conform our minds, are, above all other writings, to be
found in narratives of the lives of particular persons; and therefore
no species of writing seems more worthy of cultivation than biography, since none can be more delightful or more useful, none can
more certainly enchain the heart by irresistible interest, or more
widely diffuse instruction to every diversity of condition.

The general and rapid narratives of history, which involve a thousand fortunes in the business of a day, and complicate innumerable
incidents in one great transaction, afford few lessons applicable to
private life, which derives its comforts and its wretchedness from
the right or wrong management of things, which nothing but their
frequency makes considerable, *Parva si non fiunt quotidie*, says
Pliny,[1] and which can have no place in those relations which never
descend below the consultation of senates, the motions of armies,
and the schemes of conspirators.

I have often thought that there has rarely passed a life of which a
judicious and faithful narrative would not be useful. For, not only
every man has in the mighty mass of the world great numbers in
the same condition with himself, to whom his mistakes and miscar-
riages, escapes and expedients, would be of immediate and apparent
use; but there is such an uniformity in the state of man, considered
apart from adventitious and separable decorations and disguises,
that there is scarce any possibility of good or ill, but is common to
humankind. A great part of the time of those who are placed at the
greatest distance by fortune, or by temper, must unavoidably pass in
the same manner; and though, when the claims of nature are satisfied, caprice, and vanity, and accident, begin to produce discriminations and peculiarities, yet the eye is not very heedful or quick,
which cannot discover the same causes still[2] terminating their influence in the same effects, though sometimes accelerated, sometimes
retarded, or perplexed by multiplied combinations. We are all
prompted by the same motives, all deceived by the same fallacies,
all animated by hope, obstructed by danger, entangled by desire,
and seduced by pleasure.

It is frequently objected to relations of particular lives, that they
are not distinguished by any striking or wonderful vicissitudes. The
scholar who passed his life among his books, the merchant who conducted only his own affairs, the priest whose sphere of action was

---

1. Pliny the Younger, *Epistles*, III, i.
Johnson translates the phrase in the preceding clause.
2. Always.

not extended beyond that of his duty, are considered as no proper objects of public regard, however they might have excelled in their several stations, whatever might have been their learning, integrity, and piety. But this notion arises from false measures of excellence and dignity, and must be eradicated by considering, that in the esteem of uncorrupted reason, what is of most use is of most value.

It is, indeed, not improper to take honest advantages of prejudice, and to gain attention by a celebrated name; but the business of the biographer is often to pass slightly over those performances and incidents, which produce vulgar greatness, to lead the thoughts into domestic privacies, and display the minute details of daily life, where exterior appendages are cast aside, and men excel each other only by prudence and by virtue. The account of Thuanus[3] is, with great propriety, said by its author to have been written, that it might lay open to posterity the private and familiar character of that man, *cujus ingenium et candorem ex ipsius scriptis sunt olim semper miraturi*, whose candor and genius will to the end of time be by his writings preserved in admiration.

There are many invisible circumstances which, whether we read as inquirers after natural or moral knowledge, whether we intend to enlarge our science, or increase our virtue, are more important than public occurrences. Thus Sallust, the great master of nature, has not forgot, in his account of Catiline,[4] to remark that *his walk was now quick, and again slow*, as an indication of a mind revolving something with violent commotion. Thus the story of Melancthon[5] affords a striking lecture on the value of time, by informing us that when he made an appointment, he expected not only the hour, but the minute to be fixed, that the day might not run out in the idleness of suspense; and all the plans and enterprises of De Witt are now of less importance to the world, than that part of his personal character, which represents him as careful of his health, and negligent of his life.[6]

But biography has often been allotted to writers who seem very little acquainted with the nature of their task, or very negligent about the performance. They rarely afford any other account than might be collected from public papers, but imagine themselves writing a life when they exhibit a chronological series of actions or preferments; and so little regard the manners or behavior of their heroes, that more knowledge may be gained of a man's real character, by a short conversation with one of his servants, than from a

3. Jacques-Auguste de Thou (1553–1617), an important French historian, of whom Nicholas Rigault wrote a brief biography, a sentence of which Johnson quotes and translates below.
4. Sallust, a Roman historian of the first century B.C., wrote an account of Catiline's conspiracy against the Roman state.
5. Camerarius wrote a life of Melancthon, a German theologian of the 16th century.
6. Sir William Temple, characterizing the Dutch statesman John De Witt.

formal and studied narrative, begun with his pedigree, and ended
with his funeral.

If now and then they condescend to inform the world of particular facts, they are not always so happy as to select the most important. I know not well what advantage posterity can receive from the
only circumstance by which Tickell has distinguished Addison from
the rest of mankind, the irregularity of his pulse:[7] nor can I think
myself overpaid for the time spent in reading the life of Malherbe,
by being enabled to relate, after the learned biographer,[8] that Malherbe had two predominant opinions; one, that the looseness of a
single woman might destroy all her boast of ancient descent; the
other, that the French beggars made use very improperly and barba-
rously of the phrase *noble gentleman,* because either word included
the sense of both.

There are, indeed, some natural reasons why these narratives are
often written by such as were not likely to give much instruction or
delight, and why most accounts of particular persons are barren and
useless. If a life be delayed till interest and envy are at an end, we
may hope for impartiality, but must expect little intelligence; for
the incidents which give excellence to biography are of a volatile
and evanescent kind, such as soon escape the memory, and are
rarely transmitted by tradition. We know how few can portray a
living acquaintance, except by his most prominent and observable
particularities, and the grosser features of his mind; and it may be
easily imagined how much of this little knowledge may be lost in
imparting it, and how soon a succession of copies will lose all
resemblance of the original.

If the biographer writes from personal knowledge, and makes
haste to gratify the public curiosity, there is danger lest his interest,
his fear, his gratitude, or his tenderness, overpower his fidelity, and
tempt him to conceal, if not to invent. There are many who think
it an act of piety to hide the faults or failings of their friends, even
when they can no longer suffer by their detection; we therefore see
whole ranks of characters adorned with uniform panegyric, and not
to be known from one another, but by extrinsic and casual circumstances. "Let me remember," says Hale, "when I find myself inclined
to pity a criminal, that there is likewise a pity due to the country."[9]
If we owe regard to the memory of the dead, there is yet more
respect to be paid to knowledge, to virtue, and to truth.

7. From Thomas Tickell's preface to Addison's *Works* (1721).
8. The life of the French poet François
de Malherbe (1555–1628) was written by
Honorat de Racan.
9. From Gilbert Burnet's *Life and Death
of Sir Matthew Hale* (1682).

From The Preface to Shakespeare[1]

[Shakespeare and General Nature]

The poet of whose works I have undertaken the revision may now begin to assume the dignity of an ancient and claim the privilege of established fame and prescriptive veneration. He has long outlived his century, the term commonly fixed as the test of literary merit.[1a] Whatever advantages he might once derive from personal allusions, local customs, or temporary opinions, have for many years been lost; and every topic of merriment or motive of sorrow which the modes of artificial life afforded him now only obscure the scenes which they once illuminated. The effects of favor and competition are at an end; the tradition of his friendships and his enmities has perished; his works support no opinion with arguments nor supply any faction with invectives; they can neither indulge vanity nor gratify malignity; but are read without any other reason than the desire of pleasure, and are therefore praised only as pleasure is obtained; yet, thus unassisted by interest or passion, they have passed through variations of taste and changes of manners, and, as they devolved from one generation to another, have received new honors at every transmission.

But because human judgment, though it be gradually gaining upon certainty, never becomes infallible, and approbation, though long continued, may yet be only the approbation of prejudice or fashion, it is proper to inquire by what peculiarities of excellence Shakespeare has gained and kept the favor of his countrymen.

Nothing can please many, and please long, but just representa-

---

5. The Emperor Tiberius. See Suetonius' *Lives of the Caesars.*

1. This, the finest piece of Shakespeare criticism in the 18th century, is the culmination of a critical tradition that began with Nicholas Rowe's edition of the plays in 1709 (indeed with Dryden's critical remarks on Shakespeare) and that was continued by subsequent editors, notably Pope, Lewis Theobald, and William Warburton. Johnson's topics are in the main the conventional ones of 18th-century Shakespeare criticism: Shakespeare as the poet of nature, not of learning; as the creator of memorable characters; as a poet who supremely expresses and evokes the passions. Johnson follows his tradition in weighing Shakespeare's poetic virtues against his faults and finding that the virtues out-

weigh the faults. No one has praised Shakespeare more nobly and generously. The *Preface* is most original when Johnson attacks and dismisses the long-standing reverence in critical theory for the unities of time and place. By appealing to the experience of the play-goer, he demonstrates that, thanks to the imagination of the spectator, the playwright need not contain his action within a period of twenty-four hours or restrict it to one place throughout the drama.

Johnson's edition of Shakespeare also contained footnotes and brief introductions to each of the plays. We reprint here the introductory headnote to the two Henry IV plays.

1a. Horace, *Epistles* II.1.39.

tions of general nature. Particular manners can be known to few, and therefore few only can judge how nearly they are copied. The irregular combinations of fanciful invention may delight awhile by that novelty of which the common satiety of life sends us all in quest; but the pleasures of sudden wonder are soon exhausted, and the mind can only repose on the stability of truth.

Shakespeare is, above all writers, at least above all modern writers, the poet of nature, the poet that holds up to his readers a faithful mirror of manners and of life. His characters are not modified by the customs of particular places, unpracticed by the rest of the world; by the peculiarities of studies or professions, which can operate but upon small numbers; or by the accidents of transient fashions or temporary opinions: they are the genuine progeny of common humanity, such as the world will always supply and observation will always find. His persons act and speak by the influence of those general passions and principles by which all minds are agitated and the whole system of life is continued in motion. In the writings of other poets a character is too often an individual: in those of Shakespeare it is commonly a species.

It is from this wide extension of design that so much instruction is derived. It is this which fills the plays of Shakespeare with practical axioms and domestic wisdom. It was said of Euripides[2] that every verse was a precept; and it may be said of Shakespeare that from his works may be collected a system of civil and economical prudence. Yet his real power is not shown in the splendor of particular passages, but by the progress of his fable and the tenor of his dialogue; and he that tries to recommend him by select quotations will succeed like the pedant in Hierocles[3] who, when he offered his house to sale, carried a brick in his pocket as a specimen.

It will not easily be imagined how much Shakespeare excels in accommodating his sentiments to real life but by comparing him with other authors. It was observed of the ancient schools of declamation that the more diligently they were frequented, the more was the student disqualified for the world, because he found nothing there which he should ever meet in any other place. The same remark may be applied to every stage but that of Shakespeare. The theater, when it is under any other direction, is peopled by such characters as were never seen, conversing in a language which was never heard, upon topics which will never arise in the commerce of mankind. But the dialogue of this author is often so evidently determined by the incident which produces it, and is pursued with so much ease and simplicity, that it seems scarcely to claim the

---

2. The Greek tragic poet (ca. 480–406 B.C.). The observation is Cicero's.

3. Hierocles of Alexandria, a Greek philosopher of the 5th century A.D.

merit of fiction, but to have been gleaned by diligent selection out of common conversation and common occurrences.

Upon every other stage the universal agent is love, by whose power all good and evil is distributed and every action quickened or retarded. To bring a lover, a lady, and a rival into the fable; to entangle them in contradictory obligations, perplex them with oppositions of interest, and harass them with violence of desires inconsistent with each other; to make them meet in rapture, and part in agony; to fill their mouths with hyperbolical joy and outrageous sorrow; to distress them as nothing human ever was distressed; to deliver them as nothing human ever was delivered, is the business of a modern dramatist. For this, probability is violated, life is misrepresented, and language is depraved. But love is only one of many passions; and as it has no great influence upon the sum of life, it has little operation in the dramas of a poet who caught his ideas from the living world and exhibited only what he saw before him. He knew that any other passion, as it was regular or exorbitant, was a cause of happiness or calamity.

Characters thus ample and general were not easily discriminated and preserved; yet perhaps no poet ever kept his personages more distinct from each other. I will not say with Pope that every speech may be assigned to the proper speaker,[4] because many speeches there are which have nothing characteristical; but perhaps though some may be equally adapted to every person, it will be difficult to find that any can be properly transferred from the present possessor to another claimant. The choice is right when there is reason for choice.

Other dramatists can only gain attention by hyperbolical or aggravated characters, by fabulous and unexampled excellence or depravity, as the writers of barbarous romances invigorated the reader by a giant and a dwarf; and he that should form his expectations of human affairs from the play or from the tale would be equally deceived. Shakespeare has no heroes; his scenes are occupied only by men, who act and speak as the reader thinks that he should himself have spoken or acted on the same occasion; even where the agency is supernatural, the dialogue is level with life. Other writers disguise the most natural passions and most frequent incidents so that he who contemplates them in the book will not know them in the world: Shakespeare approximates[5] the remote, and familiarizes the wonderful; the event which he represents will not happen, but, if it were possible, its effects would probably be such as he has assigned; and it may be said that he has not only shown human na-

---

4. In the preface to his edition of Shakespeare's plays (1725).

5. Brings near.

ture as it acts in real exigencies, but as it would be found in trials to which it cannot be exposed.

This therefore is the praise of Shakespeare, that his drama is the mirror of life; that he who has mazed his imagination in following the phantoms which other writers raise up before him, may here be cured of his delirious ecstasies by reading human sentiments in human language, by scenes from which a hermit may estimate the transactions of the world, and a confessor predict the progress of the passions.

[Shakespeare's Faults. The Three Dramatic Unities]

Shakespeare with his excellencies has likewise faults, and faults sufficient to obscure and overwhelm any other merit. I shall show them in the proportion in which they appear to me, without envious malignity or superstitious veneration. No question can be more innocently discussed than a dead poet's pretensions to renown; and little regard is due to that bigotry which sets candor[6] higher than truth.

His first defect is that to which may be imputed most of the evil in books or in men. He sacrifices virtue to convenience, and is so much more careful to please than to instruct that he seems to write without any moral purpose. From his writings indeed a system of social duty may be selected, for he that thinks reasonably must think morally, but his precepts and axioms drop casually from him; he makes no just distribution of good or evil, nor is always careful to show in the virtuous a disapprobation of the wicked; he carries his persons indifferently through right and wrong, and at the close dismisses them without further care, and leaves their examples to operate by chance. This fault the barbarity of his age cannot extenuate; for it is always a writer's duty to make the world better, and justice is a virtue independent on time or place.

The plots are often so loosely formed that a very slight consideration may improve them, and so carelessly pursued that he seems not always fully to comprehend his own design. He omits opportunities of instructing or delighting which the train of his story seems to force upon him, and apparently rejects those exhibitions which would be more affecting for the sake of those which are more easy.

It may be observed that in many of his plays the latter part is evidently neglected. When he found himself near the end of his work, and in view of his reward, he shortened the labor to snatch the profit. He therefore remits his efforts where he should most

6. Kindness.

vigorously exert them, and his catastrophe is improbably produced or imperfectly represented.

He had no regard to distinction of time or place, but gives to one age or nation, without scruple, the customs, institutions, and opinions of another, at the expense not only of likelihood but of possibility. These faults Pope has endeavored, with more zeal than judgment, to transfer to his imagined interpolators. We need not wonder to find Hector quoting Aristotle, when we see the loves of Theseus and Hippolyta combined with the Gothic mythology of fairies.[7] Shakespeare, indeed, was not the only violator of chronology, for in the same age Sidney, who wanted not the advantages of learning, has, in his *Arcadia*, confounded the pastoral with the feudal times, the days of innocence, quiet, and security with those of turbulence, violence, and adventure.

In his comic scenes he is seldom very successful when he engages his characters in reciprocations of smartness and contests of sarcasm; their jests are commonly gross, and their pleasantry licentious; neither his gentlemen nor his ladies have much delicacy, nor are sufficiently distinguished from his clowns by any appearance of refined manners. Whether he represented the real conversation of his time is not easy to determine: the reign of Elizabeth is commonly supposed to have been a time of stateliness, formality, and reserve; yet perhaps the relaxations of that severity were not very elegant. There must, however, have been always some modes of gaiety preferable to others, and a writer ought to choose the best.

In tragedy his performance seems constantly to be worse as his labor is more. The effusions of passion, which exigence forces out, are for the most part striking and energetic; but whenever he solicits his invention, or strains his faculties, the offspring of his throes is tumor,[8] meanness, tediousness, and obscurity.

In narration he affects a disproportionate pomp of diction and a wearisome train of circumlocution, and tells the incident imperfectly in many words which might have been more plainly delivered in few. Narration in dramatic poetry is naturally tedious, as it is unanimated and inactive, and obstructs the progress of the action; it should therefore always be rapid and enlivened by frequent interruption. Shakespeare found it an encumbrance, and instead of lightening it by brevity, endeavored to recommend it by dignity and splendor.

His declamations or set speeches are commonly cold and weak, for his power was the power of nature; when he endeavored, like other tragic writers, to catch opportunities of amplification and,

7. In *Troilus and Cressida*, II.2.166, and in *Midsummer Night's Dream*, re-

spectively.
8. Inflated grandeur, false magnificence.

instead of inquiring what the occasion demanded, to show how much his stores of knowledge could supply, he seldom escapes without the pity or resentment of his reader.

It is incident to him to be now and then entangled with an unwieldy sentiment which he cannot well express, and will not reject; he struggles with it awhile, and, if it continues stubborn, comprises it in words such as occur, and leaves it to be disentangled and evolved by those who have more leisure to bestow upon it.

Not that always where the language is intricate the thought is subtle, or the image always great where the line is bulky; the equality of words to things is very often neglected, and trivial sentiments and vulgar[9] ideas disappoint the attention, to which they are recommended by sonorous epithets and swelling figures.

But the admirers of this great poet have most reason to complain when he approaches nearest to his highest excellence, and seems fully resolved to sink them in dejection and mollify them with tender emotions by the fall of greatness, the danger of innocence, or the crosses of love. What he does best, he soon ceases to do. He is not long soft and pathetic without some idle conceit or contemptible equivocation. He no sooner begins to move than he counteracts himself; and terror and pity, as they are rising in the mind, are checked and blasted by sudden frigidity.

A quibble[1] is to Shakespeare what luminous vapors are to the traveler: he follows it at all adventures; it is sure to lead him out of his way, and sure to engulf him in the mire. It has some malignant power over his mind, and its fascinations are irresistible. Whatever be the dignity or profundity of his disquisitions, whether he be enlarging knowledge or exalting affection, whether he be amusing[2] attention with incidents, or enchaining it in suspense, let but a quibble spring up before him, and he leaves his work unfinished. A quibble is the golden apple for which he will always turn aside from his career[3] or stoop from his elevation. A quibble, poor and barren as it is, gave him such delight that he was content to purchase it by the sacrifice of reason, propriety, and truth. A quibble was to him the fatal Cleopatra for which he lost the world, and was content to lose it.

It will be thought strange that in enumerating the defects of this writer, I have not yet mentioned his neglect of the unities; his

9. "Mean; low; being of the common rate" (Johnson's *Dictionary*).
1. Pun.
2. "To entertain with tranquility; to fill with thoughts that engage the mind, without distracting it" (Johnson's *Dictionary*).

3. In Greek legend Atalanta refused to marry any man who could not defeat her in a foot race. Hippomenes won her by dropping, as he ran, three of the golden apples of the Hesperides, which she paused to pick up.

violation of those laws which have been instituted and established by the joint authority of poets and critics.

For his other deviations from the art of writing, I resign him to critical justice without making any other demand in his favor than that which must be indulged to all human excellence: that his virtues be rated with his failings. But from the censure which this irregularity may bring upon him I shall, with due reverence to that learning which I must oppose, adventure to try how I can defend him.

His histories, being neither tragedies nor comedies, are not subject to any of their laws; nothing more is necessary to all the praise which they expect than that the changes of action be so prepared as to be understood; that the incidents be various and affecting, and the characters consistent, natural, and distinct. No other unity is intended, and therefore none is to be sought.

In his other works he has well enough preserved the unity of action. He has not, indeed, an intrigue regularly perplexed and regularly unraveled: he does not endeavor to hide his design only to discover it, for this is seldom the order of real events, and Shakespeare is the poet of nature: but his plan has commonly what Aristotle requires,[4] a beginning, a middle, and an end; one event is concatenated with another, and the conclusion follows by easy consequence. There are, perhaps, some incidents that might be spared, as in other poets there is much talk that only fills up time upon the stage; but the general system makes gradual advances, and the end of the play is the end of expectation.

To the unities of time and place he has shown no regard; and perhaps a nearer view of the principles on which they stand will diminish their value and withdraw from them the veneration which, from the time of Corneille,[5] they have very generally received, by discovering that they have given more trouble to the poet than pleasure to the auditor.

The necessity of observing the unities of time and place arises from the supposed necessity of making the drama credible. The critics hold it impossible that an action of months or years can be possibly believed to pass in three hours; or that the spectator can suppose himself to sit in the theater while ambassadors go and return between distant kings, while armies are levied and towns besieged, while an exile wanders and returns, or till he whom they saw courting his mistress shall lament the untimely fall of his son. The mind revolts from evident falsehood, and fiction loses its force when it

---

4. *Poetics* VII.
5. Pierre Corneille (1606–84), the

French playwright, discussed the unities in his *Discours des trois unités* (1660).

departs from the resemblance of reality.

From the narrow limitation of time necessarily arises the contraction of place. The spectator who knows that he saw the first act at Alexandria cannot suppose that he sees the next at Rome, at a distance to which not the dragons of Medea could, in so short a time, have transported him; he knows with certainty that he has not changed his place; and he knows that place cannot change itself, that what was a house cannot become a plain, that what was Thebes can never be Persepolis.

Such is the triumphant language with which a critic exults over the misery of an irregular poet, and exults commonly without resistance or reply. It is time, therefore, to tell him by the authority of Shakespeare that he assumes, as an unquestionable principle, a position which, while his breath is forming it into words, his understanding pronounces to be false. It is false that any representation is mistaken for reality; that any dramatic fable in its materiality was ever credible or, for a single moment, was ever credited.

The objection arising from the impossibility of passing the first hour at Alexandria and the next at Rome supposes that when the play opens the spectator really imagines himself at Alexandria, and believes that his walk to the theater has been a voyage to Egypt, and that he lives in the days of Antony and Cleopatra. Surely he that imagines this may imagine more. He that can take the stage at one time for the palace of the Ptolemies may take it in half an hour for the promontory of Actium. Delusion, if delusion be admitted, has no certain limitation; if the spectator can be once persuaded that his old acquaintances are Alexander and Caesar, that a room illuminated with candles is the plain of Pharsalia or the bank of Granicus, he is in a state of elevation above the reach of reason or of truth, and from the heights of empyrean poetry may despise the circumscriptions of terrestrial nature. There is no reason why a mind thus wandering in ecstasy should count the clock, or why an hour should not be a century in that calenture[6] of the brain that can make the stage a field.

The truth is that the spectators are always in their senses, and know, from the first act to the last, that the stage is only a stage, and that the players are only players. They came to hear a certain number of lines recited with just gesture and elegant modulation. The lines relate to some action, and an action must be in some place; but the different actions that complete a story may be in places very remote from each other; and where is the absurdity of allowing that space to represent first Athens, and then Sicily, which

6. A delirium produced by tropical heat, which causes sailors to leap into the sea under the delusion that it is a green field.

was always known to be neither Sicily nor Athens but a modern theater?

By supposition, as place is introduced, time may be extended; the time required by the fable elapses, for the most part, between the acts; for, of so much of the action as is represented, the real and poetical duration is the same. If, in the first act, preparations for war against Mithridates are represented to be made in Rome, the event of the war may, without absurdity, be represented, in the catastrophe, as happening in Pontus; we know that there is neither war nor preparation for war; we know that we are neither in Rome nor Pontus, that neither Mithridates nor Lucullus are before us. The drama exhibits successive imitations of successive actions; and why may not the second imitation represent an action that happened years after the first, if it be so connected with it that nothing but time can be supposed to intervene? Time is, of all modes of existence, most obsequious[7] to the imagination; a lapse of years is as easily conceived as a passage of hours. In contemplation we easily contract the time of real actions, and therefore willingly permit it to be contracted when we only see their imitation.

It will be asked how the drama moves if it is not credited. It is credited with all the credit due to a drama. It is credited, whenever it moves, as a just picture of a real original; as representing to the auditor what he would himself feel if he were to do or suffer what is there feigned to be suffered or to be done. The reflection that strikes the heart is not that the evils before us are real evils, but that they are evils to which we ourselves may be exposed. If there be any fallacy, it is not that we fancy the players, but that we fancy ourselves, unhappy for a moment; but we rather lament the possibility than suppose the presence of misery, as a mother weeps over her babe when she remembers that death may take it from her. The delight of tragedy proceeds from our consciousness of fiction; if we thought murders and treasons real, they would please no more.

Imitations produce pain or pleasure, not because they are mistaken for realities, but because they bring realities to mind. When the imagination is recreated by a painted landscape, the trees are not supposed capable to give us shade or the fountains coolness; but we consider how we should be pleased with such fountains playing beside us and such woods waving over us. We are agitated in reading the history of *Henry the Fifth*; yet no man takes his book for the field of Agincourt. A dramatic exhibition is a book recited with concomitants that increase or diminish its effect. Familiar comedy is often more powerful on the theater than in the page; imperial tragedy is always less. The humor of Petruchio may be heightened by grimace; but what voice or what gesture can hope to

7. "Obedient; compliant" (Johnson's *Dictionary*).

add dignity or force to the soliloquy of Cato?[8]

A play read affects the mind like a play acted. It is therefore evident that the action is not supposed to be real; and it follows that between the acts a longer or shorter time may be allowed to pass, and that no more account of space or duration is to be taken by the auditor of a drama than by the reader of a narrative, before whom may pass in an hour the life of a hero or the revolutions of an empire.

Whether Shakespeare knew the unities and rejected them by design or deviated from them by happy ignorance, it is, I think, impossible to decide and useless to inquire. We may reasonably suppose that, when he rose to notice, he did not want[9] the counsels and admonitions of scholars and critics, and that he at last deliberately persisted in a practice which he might have begun by chance. As nothing is essential to the fable but unity of action, and as the unities of time and place arise evidently from false assumptions, and, by circumscribing the extent of the drama, lessen its variety, I cannot think it much to be lamented that they were not known by him, or not observed: nor, if such another poet could arise, should I very vehemently reproach him that his first act passed at Venice and his next in Cyprus.[1] Such violations of rules merely positive become the comprehensive genius of Shakespeare, and such censures are suitable to the minute and slender criticism of Voltaire.

> *Non usque adeo permiscuit imis*
> *Longus summa dies, ut non, si voce Metelli*
> *Serventur leges, malint a Caesare tolli.*[2]

Yet when I speak thus slightly of dramatic rules, I cannot but recollect how much wit and learning may be produced against me; before such authorities I am afraid to stand: not that I think the present question one of those that are to be decided by mere authority, but because it is to be suspected that these precepts have not been so easily received but for better reasons than I have yet been able to find. The result of my inquiries, in which it would be ludicrous to boast of impartiality, is that the unities of time and place are not essential to a just drama, that though they may sometimes conduce to pleasure, they are always to be sacrificed to the nobler beauties of variety and instruction; and that a play written with nice observation of critical rules is to be contemplated as an elaborate curiosity, as the product of superfluous and ostentatious art, by which is shown rather what is possible than what is necessary.

---

8. Petruchio is the hero of Shakespeare's comedy *The Taming of the Shrew*. In Addison's tragedy *Cato* (V.i), the hero soliloquizes on immortality shortly before committing suicide.
9. Lack.

1. As is the case in *Othello*.
2. Lucan, *Pharsalia* III.138–40: "The course of time has not wrought such confusion that the laws would not rather be trampled on by Caesar than saved by Metellus."

He that without diminution of any other excellence shall preserve all the unities unbroken deserves the like applause with the architect who shall display all the orders of architecture in a citadel without any deduction for its strength; but the principal beauty of a citadel is to exclude the enemy, and the greatest graces of a play are to copy nature and instruct life. * * *

[*Henry IV*]

None of Shakespeare's plays are more read than the first and second parts of *Henry the fourth*. Perhaps no author has ever in two plays afforded so much delight. The great events are interesting, for the fate of kingdoms depends upon them; the slighter occurrences are diverting, and, except one or two, sufficiently probable; the incidents are multiplied with wonderful fertility of invention, and the characters diversified with the utmost nicety of discernment, and the profoundest skill in the nature of man.

The prince, who is the hero both of the comic and tragic part, is a young man of great abilities and violent passions, whose sentiments are right, though his actions are wrong; whose virtues are obscured by negligence, and whose understanding is dissipated by levity. In his idle hours he is rather loose than wicked, and when the occasion forces out his latent qualities, he is great without effort, and brave without tumult. The trifler is roused into a hero, and the hero again reposes in the trifler. This character is great, original, and just.[3]

Percy is a rugged soldier, choleric, and quarrelsome, and has only the soldier's virtues, generosity and courage.

But Falstaff, unimitated, unimitable Falstaff, how shall I describe thee? Thou compound of sense and vice; of sense which may be admired but not esteemed, of vice which may be despised, but hardly detested. Falstaff is a character loaded with faults, and with those faults which naturally produce contempt. He is a thief, and a glutton, a coward, and a boaster, always ready to cheat the weak, and prey upon the poor; to terrify the timorous and insult the defenseless. At once obsequious and malignant, he satirizes in their absence those whom he lives by flattering. He is familiar with the prince only as an agent of vice, but of this familiarity he is so proud as not only to be supercilious and haughty with common men, but to think his interest of importance to the duke of Lancaster. Yet the man thus corrupt, thus despicable, makes himself necessary to the prince that despises him, by the most pleasing of all qualities, perpetual gaiety, by an unfailing power of exciting laughter, which is the more freely indulged, as his wit is not of the splendid or ambitious kind, but consists in easy escapes and sallies of levity, which make sport but raise no envy. It must be

3. **Exact.**

observed that he is stained with no enormous or sanguinary crimes, so that his licentiousness is not so offensive but that it may be borne for his mirth.

The moral to be drawn from this representation is that no man is more dangerous than he that with a will to corrupt, hath the power to please; and that neither wit nor honesty ought to think themselves safe with such a companion when they see Henry seduced by Falstaff.

1765

[King Lear]

The tragedy of *Lear* is deservedly celebrated among the dramas of Shakespeare. There is perhaps no play which keeps the attention so strongly fixed; which so much agitates our passions and interests our curiosity. The artful involutions[1] of distinct interests, the striking opposition of contrary characters, the sudden changes of fortune, and the quick succession of events, fill the mind with a perpetual tumult of indignation, pity, and hope. There is no scene which does not contribute to the aggravation of the distress or conduct of the action, and scarce a line which does not conduce to the progress of the scene. So powerful is the current of the poet's imagination, that the mind, which once ventures within it, is hurried irresistibly along.

On the seeming improbability of Lear's conduct it may be observed, that he is represented according to histories at that time vulgarly[2] received as true. And perhaps if we turn our thoughts upon the barbarity and ignorance of the age to which this story is referred, it will appear not so unlikely as while we estimate Lear's manners by our own. Such preference of one daughter to another, or resignation of dominion on such conditions, would be yet credible, if told of a petty prince of Guinea or Madagascar. Shakespeare, indeed, by the mention of his Earls and Dukes, has given us the idea of times more civilized, and of life regulated by softer manners; and the truth is, that though he so nicely discriminates, and so minutely describes the characters of men, he commonly neglects and confounds the characters of ages, by mingling customs ancient and modern, English and foreign.

My learned friend Mr. Warton, who has in the *Adventurer* very minutely criticized this play,[3] remarks, that the instances of cruelty

1. Entanglements.
2. Popularly.
3. Joseph Warton (1722–1800) contrib- uted several papers to Johnson's periodi- cal *The Adventurer*; numbers 113, 116, and 122 discuss *King Lear*.

If by a more noble and more adequate conception that be considered as wit which is at once natural and new, that which though not obvious is, upon its first production, acknowledged to be just; if it be that which he that never found it, wonders how he missed; to wit of this kind the metaphysical poets have seldom risen. Their thoughts are often new, but seldom natural; they are not obvious, but neither are they just;[6] and the reader, far from wondering that he missed them, wonders more frequently by what perverseness of industry they were ever found.

But wit, abstracted from its effects upon the hearer, may be more rigorously and philosophically considered as a kind of *discordia concors;*[7] a combination of dissimilar images, or discovery of occult resemblances in things apparently unlike. Of wit, thus defined, they have more than enough. The most heterogeneous ideas are yoked by violence together; nature and art are ransacked for illustrations, comparisons, and allusions; their learning instructs, and their subtlety surprises; but the reader commonly thinks his improvement dearly bought, and, though he sometimes admires, is seldom pleased.

From this account of their compositions it will be readily inferred that they were not successful in representing or moving the affections. As they were wholly employed on something unexpected and surprising, they had no regard to that uniformity of sentiment which enables us to conceive and to excite the pains and the pleasure of other minds: they never inquired what on any occasion they should have said or done, but wrote rather as beholders than partakers of human nature; as beings looking upon good and evil, impassive and at leisure; as Epicurean deities making remarks on the actions of men and the vicissitudes of life, without interest and without emotion. Their courtship was void of fondness and their lamentation of sorrow. Their wish was only to say what they hoped had been never said before.

Nor was the sublime more within their reach than the pathetic; for they never attempted that comprehension and expanse of thought which at once fills the whole mind, and of which the first effect is sudden astonishment, and the second rational admiration. Sublimity is produced by aggregation, and littleness by dispersion. Great thoughts are always general, and consist in positions not limited by exceptions, and in descriptions not descending to minuteness. It is with great propriety that subtlety, which in its original

6. Exact, proper.
7. Literally, "a harmonious discord." Johnson is himself being witty in using this phrase, a familiar philosophical concept denoting the general harmony of God's creation despite its manifold and often contradictory particulars.

import means exility[8] of particles, is taken in its metaphorical meaning for nicety of distinction. Those writers who lay on the watch for novelty could have little hope of greatness; for great things cannot have escaped former observation. Their attempts were always analytic: they broke every image into fragments, and could no more represent by their slender conceits and labored particularities the prospects of nature or the scenes of life, than he who dissects a sunbeam with a prism can exhibit the wide effulgence of a summer noon.

What they wanted however of the sublime they endeavored to supply by hyperbole;[9] their amplification had no limits: they left not only reason but fancy behind them, and produced combinations of confused magnificence that not only could not be credited, but could not be imagined.

Yet great labor directed by great abilities is never wholly lost: if they frequently threw away their wit upon false conceits, they likewise sometimes struck out unexpected truth: if their conceits were farfetched, they were often worth the carriage.[10] To write on their plan it was at least necessary to read and think. No man could be born a metaphysical poet, nor assume the dignity of a writer by descriptions copied from descriptions, by imitations borrowed from imitations, by traditional imagery and hereditary similes, by readiness of rhyme and volubility of syllables.

1779

From Milton[1]

[Lycidas]

One of the poems on which much praise has been bestowed is *Lycidas*; of which the diction is harsh,[2] the rhymes uncertain, and the numbers unpleasing. What beauty there is, we must therefore seek in the sentiments and images. It is not to be considered as the effusion of real passion; for passion runs not after remote allusions and obscure opinions. Passion plucks no berries from the

8. Thinness.
9. An image heightened beyond reality (see Johnson's *Dictionary*).
10. In the *Life of Addison*, Johnson wrote: "A simile may be compared to lines converging at a point, and is more excellent as the lines approach from greater distance * * * "
1. Johnson's treatment of Milton as man and poet gave great offense to many ardent Miltonians in his own day and damaged his reputation as a critic in the following century. He did not ad-

mire Milton's character, and he detested his politics and religion. But no one has praised *Paradise Lost* more handsomely. Especially offensive in the 19th century was his attack on *Lycidas*. Johnson disliked modern pastorals, recognizing that the tradition had been worn threadbare. His views on the genre may be read in *Ramblers* 36 and 37.
2. This notorious word does not mean "unmelodious," but "strained, forced, affected, or labored."

myrtle and ivy, nor calls upon Arethuse and Mincius, nor tells of "rough satyrs and fauns with cloven heel." Where there is leisure for fiction there is little grief.

In this poem there is no nature, for there is no truth; there is no art, for there is nothing new. Its form is that of a pastoral, easy, vulgar, and therefore disgusting:[3] whatever images it can supply are long ago exhausted; and its inherent improbability always forces dissatisfaction on the mind. When Cowley tells of Hervey that they studied together, it is easy to suppose how much he must miss the companion of his labors and the partner of his discoveries;[4] but what image of tenderness can be excited by these lines!

> We drove afield, and both together heard
> What time the grayfly winds her sultry horn,
> Battening our flocks with the fresh dews of night.

We know that they never drove afield, and that they had no flocks to batten; and though it be allowed that the representation may be allegorical, the true meaning is so uncertain and remote that it is never sought because it cannot be known when it is found.

Among the flocks and copses and flowers appear the heathen deities, Jove and Phoebus, Neptune and Aeolus, with a long train of mythological imagery, such as a college easily supplies. Nothing can less display knowledge or less exercise invention than to tell how a shepherd has lost his companion and must now feed his flocks alone, without any judge of his skill in piping; and how one god asks another god what is become of Lycidas, and how neither god can tell. He who thus grieves will excite no sympathy; he who thus praises will confer no honor.

This poem has yet a grosser fault. With these trifling fictions are mingled the most awful and sacred truths, such as ought never to be polluted with such irreverent combinations. The shepherd likewise is now a feeder of sheep, and afterwards an ecclesiastical pastor, a superintendent of a Christian flock. Such equivocations are always unskillful; but here they are indecent,[5] and at least approach to impiety, of which, however, I believe the writer not to have been conscious.

Such is the power of reputation justly acquired that its blaze drives away the eye from nice examination. Surely no man could have fancied that he read *Lycidas* with pleasure had he not known its author.

---

3. I.e., displeasing ("disgusting") because its stale conventionality made it "vulgar" by putting it within the reach of the many.

4. Cowley's *On the Death of Mr. William Hervey* (1656).
5. Unbecoming, lacking in decorum.

[L'Allegro. Il Penseroso]

Of the two pieces, L'Allegro and Il Penseroso, I believe opinion is uniform; every man that reads them, reads them with pleasure. The author's design is not, what Theobald [1] has remarked, merely to show how objects derived their colors from the mind, by representing the operation of the same things upon the gay and the melancholy temper, or upon the same man as he is differently disposed; but rather how, among the successive variety of appearances, every disposition of mind takes hold on those by which it may be gratified.

The cheerful man hears the lark in the morning; the pensive man hears the nightingale in the evening. The cheerful man sees the cock strut, and hears the horn and hounds echo in the wood; then walks "not unseen" to observe the glory of the rising sun or listen to the singing milkmaid, and view the labors of the plowman and the mower; then casts his eyes about him over scenes of smiling plenty, and looks up to the distant tower, the residence of some fair inhabitant: thus he pursues rural gaiety through a day of labor or of play, and delights himself at night with the fanciful narratives of superstitious ignorance.

The pensive man at one time walks "unseen" to muse at midnight, and at another hears the sullen curfew. If the weather drives him home he sits in a room lighted only by "glowing embers"; or by a lonely lamp outwatches the North Star to discover the habitation of separate souls, and varies the shades of meditation by contemplating the magnificent or pathetic scenes of tragic and epic poetry. When the morning comes, a morning gloomy with rain and wind, he walks into the dark trackless woods, falls asleep by some murmuring water, and with melancholy enthusiasm expects some dream of prognostication or some music played by aerial performers.

Both Mirth and Melancholy are solitary, silent inhabitants of the breast that neither receive nor transmit communication: no mention is therefore made of a philosophical friend or a pleasant companion. The seriousness does not arise from any participation of calamity, nor the gaiety from the pleasures of the bottle.

The man of cheerfulness having exhausted the country tries what "towered cities" will afford, and mingles with scenes of splendor, gay assemblies, and nuptial festivities; but he mingles a mere spectator as, when the learned comedies of Jonson or the wild dramas of Shakespeare are exhibited, he attends the theater.

The pensive man never loses himself in crowds, but walks the cloister or frequents the cathedral. Milton probably had not yet forsaken the Church.

Both his characters delight in music; but he seems to think that

1. Lewis Theobald (1688–1744), the editor of Shakespeare and the enemy of Pope.

cheerful notes would have obtained from Pluto a complete dismission of Eurydice, of whom solemn sounds only procured a conditional release.

For the old age of Cheerfulness he makes no provision; but Melancholy he conducts with great dignity to the close of life. His Cheerfulness is without levity, and his Pensiveness without asperity.

Through these two poems the images are properly selected and nicely distinguished, but the colors of the diction seem not sufficiently discriminated. I know not whether the characters are kept sufficiently apart. No mirth can, indeed, be found in his melancholy; but I am afraid that I always meet some melancholy in his mirth. They are two noble efforts of imagination.

[Paradise Lost]

Those little pieces may be dispatched without much anxiety; a greater work calls for greater care. I am now to examine *Paradise Lost*, a poem which, considered with respect to design, may claim the first place, and with respect to performance the second, among the productions of the human mind.

By the general consent of critics the first praise of genius is due to the writer of an epic poem, as it requires an assemblage of all the powers which are singly sufficient for other compositions. Poetry is the art of uniting pleasure with truth, by calling imagination to the help of reason. Epic poetry undertakes to teach the most important truths by the most pleasing precepts, and therefore relates some great event in the most affecting manner. History must supply the writer with the rudiments of narration, which he must improve and exalt by a nobler art, must animate by dramatic energy, and diversify by retrospection and anticipation; morality must teach him the exact bounds and different shades of vice and virtue; from policy and the practice of life he has to learn the discriminations of character and the tendency of the passions, either single or combined; and physiology must supply him with illustrations and images. To put these materials to poetical use is required an imagination capable of painting nature and realizing fiction. Nor is he yet a poet till he has attained the whole extension of his language, distinguished all the delicacies of phrase, and all the colors of words, and learned to adjust their different sounds to all the varieties of metrical modulation.

Bossu is of opinion that the poet's first work is to find a *moral*, which his fable is afterwards to illustrate and establish.[1] This seems to have been the process only of Milton: the moral of other poems is incidental and consequent; in Milton's only it is essential and intrinsic. His purpose was the most useful and the most arduous: "to vindicate the ways of God to man"; to show the reasonableness

---

1. Père le Bossu wrote a treatise on the epic poem, *Traité du Poëme Épique*, 1675, much admired during the late 17th and early 18th centuries.

of religion, and the necessity of obedience to the Divine Law.

To convey this moral there must be a *fable*, a narration artfully constructed, so as to excite curiosity and surprise expectation. In this part of his work Milton must be confessed to have equaled every other poet. He has involved in his account of the Fall of Man the events which preceded, and those that were to follow it: he has interwoven the whole system of theology with such propriety that every part appears to be necessary, and scarcely any recital is wished shorter for the sake of quickening the progress of the main action.

The subject of an epic poem is naturally an event of great importance. That of Milton is not the destruction of a city, the conduct of a colony, or the foundation of an empire. His subject is the fate of worlds, the revolutions of heaven and of earth; rebellion against the Supreme King raised by the highest order of created beings; the overthrow of their host and the punishment of their crime; the creation of a new race of reasonable creatures; their original happiness and innocence, their forfeiture of immortality, and their restoration to hope and peace.

Great events can be hastened or retarded only by persons of elevated dignity. Before the greatness displayed in Milton's poem all other greatness shrinks away. The weakest of his agents are the highest and noblest of human beings, the original parents of mankind; with whose actions the elements consented; on whose rectitude or deviation of will depended the state of terrestrial nature and the condition of all the future inhabitants of the globe.

Of the other agents in the poem, the chief are such as it is irreverence to name on slight occasions. The rest were lower powers;

> of which the least could wield
> Those elements, and arm him with the force
> Of all their regions; [2]

powers which only the control of Omnipotence restrains from laying creation waste, and filling the vast expanse of space with ruin and confusion. To display the motives and actions of beings thus superior, so far as human reason can examine them or human imagination represent them, is the task which this mighty poet has undertaken and performed.

In the examination of epic poems much speculation is commonly employed upon the *characters*. The characters in the *Paradise Lost* which admit of examination are those of angels and of man; of angels good and evil, of man in his innocent and sinful state.

Among the angels the virtue of Raphael is mild and placid, of easy condescension and free communication; that of Michael is regal and lofty, and, as may seem, attentive to the dignity of his own nature. Abdiel and Gabriel appear occasionally, and act as every

2. *Paradise Lost* VI.221.

incident requires; the solitary fidelity of Abdiel is very amiably painted.[3]

Of the evil angels the characters are more diversified. To Satan, as Addison observes, such sentiments are given as suit "the most exalted and most depraved being." [4] Milton has been censured by Clarke for the impiety which sometimes breaks from Satan's mouth. For there are thoughts, as he justly remarks, which no observation of character can justify, because no good man would willingly permit them to pass, however transiently, through his own mind.[5] To make Satan speak as a rebel, without any such expressions as might taint the reader's imagination, was indeed one of the great difficulties in Milton's undertaking, and I cannot but think that he has extricated himself with great happiness. There is in Satan's speeches little that can give pain to a pious ear. The language of rebellion cannot be the same with that of obedience. The malignity of Satan foams in haughtiness and obstinacy; but his expressions are commonly general, and no otherwise offensive than as they are wicked.

The other chiefs of the celestial rebellion are very judiciously discriminated in the first and second books; and the ferocious character of Moloch appears, both in the battle and the council, with exact consistency.

To Adam and to Eve are given during their innocence such sentiments as innocence can generate and utter. Their love is pure benevolence and mutual veneration; their repasts are without luxury and their diligence without toil. Their addresses to their Maker have little more than the voice of admiration and gratitude. Fruition left them nothing to ask, and Innocence left them nothing to fear.

But with guilt enter distrust and discord, mutual accusation, and stubborn self-defense; they regard each other with alienated minds, and dread their Creator as the avenger of their transgression. At last they seek shelter in his mercy, soften to repentance, and melt in supplication. Both before and after the Fall the superiority of Adam is diligently sustained.

Of the *probable* and the *marvelous*,[6] two parts of a vulgar epic poem which immerge the critic in deep consideration, the *Paradise Lost* requires little to be said. It contains the history of a miracle, of Creation and Redemption; it displays the power and the mercy of the Supreme Being: the probable therefore is marvelous, and the marvelous is probable. The substance of the narrative is truth; and as truth allows no choice, it is, like necessity, superior to rule. To the accidental or adventitious parts, as to every thing human, some slight exceptions may be made. But the main fabric is immovably supported.

3. *Paradise Lost* V.803 ff.
4. *Spectator* 303.
5. John Clarke, *Essay upon Study*, 1731.

6. Actions in an epic poem which are wonderful because they exceed the probable.

It is justly remarked by Addison [7] that this poem has, by the nature of its subject, the advantage above all others, that it is universally and perpetually interesting. All mankind will, through all ages, bear the same relation to Adam and to Eve, and must partake of that good and evil which extend to themselves.

Of the *machinery*, so called from θεὸς ἀπὸ μηχανῆς [8] by which is meant the occasional interposition of supernatural power, another fertile topic of critical remarks, here is no room to speak, because every thing is done under the immediate and visible direction of Heaven; but the rule is so far observed that no part of the action could have been accomplished by any other means.

Of *episodes* [9] I think there are only two, contained in Raphael's relation of the war in heaven and Michael's prophetic account of the changes to happen in this world. Both are closely connected with the great action; one was necessary to Adam as a warning, the other as a consolation.

To the completeness or *integrity* of the design nothing can be objected; it has distinctly and clearly what Aristotle requires, a beginning, a middle, and an end. There is perhaps no poem of the same length from which so little can be taken without apparent mutilation. Here are no funeral games, nor is there any long description of a shield. The short digressions at the beginning of the third, seventh, and ninth books might doubtless be spared; but superfluities so beautiful who would take away? or who does not wish that the author of the *Iliad* had gratified succeeding ages with a little knowledge of himself? Perhaps no passages are more frequently or more attentively read than those extrinsic paragraphs; and since the end of poetry is pleasure, that cannot be unpoetical with which all are pleased.

The questions, whether the action of the poem be strictly *one*,[1] whether the poem can be properly termed *heroic*, and who is the hero, are raised by such readers as draw their principles of judgment rather from books than from reason. Milton, though he entitled *Paradise Lost* only a "poem," yet calls it himself "heroic song." [2] Dryden, petulantly and indecently, denies the heroism of Adam because he was overcome; but there is no reason why the hero should not be unfortunate except established practice, since success and virtue do not go necessarily together. Cato is the hero of Lucan, but Lucan's authority will not be suffered by Quintilian to decide. However, if success be necessary, Adam's deceiver was at last crushed; Adam was restored to his Maker's favor, and therefore may securely resume his human rank.

After the scheme and fabric of the poem must be considered its

7. *Spectator* 273.
8. Aristotle, *Poetics* XV.10. "Deus ex machina," the intervention of supernatural powers into the affairs of men.
9. Incidental but related narratives within an epic poem. Johnson is citing *Paradise Lost* V.577 ff. and XI.334 ff.
1. I.e., a single action dealing with a single character.
2. *Paradise Lost* IX.25.

ever wished it longer than it is. Its perusal is a duty rather than a pleasure. We read Milton for instruction, retire harassed and over-burdened, and look elsewhere for recreation; we desert our master, and seek for companions.

* * *

Dryden remarks that Milton has some flats among his eleva-tions.[4] This is only to say that all the parts are not equal. In every work one part must be for the sake of others; a palace must have passages, a poem must have transitions. It is no more to be required that wit should always be blazing than that the sun should always stand at noon. In a great work there is a vicissitude [5] of luminous and opaque parts, as there is in the world a succession of day and night. Milton, when he has expatiated in the sky, may be allowed some-times to revisit earth; for what other author ever soared so high or sustained his flight so long?

* * *

The highest praise of genius is original invention. Milton cannot be said to have contrived the structure of an epic poem, and there-fore owes reverence to that vigor and amplitude of mind to which all generations must be indebted for the art of poetical narration, for the texture of the fable, the variation of incidents, the interposi-tion of dialogue, and all the stratagems that surprise and enchain attention. But of all the borrowers from Homer Milton is perhaps the least indebted. He was naturally a thinker for himself, confident of his own abilities and disdainful of help or hindrance; he did not refuse admission to the thoughts or images of his predecessors, but he did not seek them. From his contemporaries he neither courted nor received support; there is in his writings nothing by which the pride of other authors might be gratified or favor gained, no ex-change of praise or solicitation of support. His great works were performed under discountenance and in blindness, but difficulties vanished at his touch; he was born for whatever is arduous; and his work is not the greatest of heroic poems, only because it is not the first.

1779

From Pope

[*Pope's Intellectual Character. Pope and Dryden Compared*]

Of his intellectual character, the constituent and fundamental principle was good sense, a prompt and intuitive perception of consonance and propriety. He saw immediately, of his own con-ceptions, what was to be chosen, and what was to be rejected; and, in

4. Preface to *Sylvae;* see Essays (ed. W. P. Ker), I.268.
5. Change.

the works of others, what was to be shunned, and what was to be copied.

But good sense alone is a sedate and quiescent quality, which manages its possessions well, but does not increase them; it collects few materials for its own operations, and preserves safety, but never gains supremacy. Pope had likewise genius; a mind active, ambitious, and adventurous, always investigating, always aspiring; in its widest searches still longing to go forward, in its highest flights still wishing to be higher; always imagining something greater than it knows, always endeavoring more than it can do.

To assist these powers, he is said to have had great strength and exactness of memory. That which he had heard or read was not easily lost; and he had before him not only what his own meditation suggested, but what he had found in other writers that might be accommodated to his present purpose.

These benefits of nature he improved by incessant and unwearied diligence; he had recourse to every source of intelligence, and lost no opportunity of information; he consulted the living as well as the dead; he read his compositions to his friends, and was never content with mediocrity when excellence could be attained. He considered poetry as the business of his life, and however he might seem to lament his occupation, he followed it with constancy: to make verses was his first labor, and to mend them was his last.

From his attention to poetry he was never diverted. If conversation offered anything that could be improved, he committed it to paper; if a thought, or perhaps an expression more happy than was common, rose to his mind, he was careful to write it; an independent distich was preserved for an opportunity of insertion, and some little fragments have been found containing lines, or parts of lines, to be wrought upon at some other time.

He was one of those few whose labor is their pleasure; he was never elevated to negligence, nor wearied to impatience; he never passed a fault unamended by indifference, nor quitted it by despair. He labored his works first to gain reputation, and afterwards to keep it.

Of composition there are different methods. Some employ at once memory and invention, and, with little intermediate use of the pen, form and polish large masses by continued meditation, and write their productions only when, in their own opinion, they have completed them. It is related of Virgil[1] that his custom was to pour out a great number of verses in the morning, and pass the day in retrenching exuberances and correcting inaccuracies. The method of Pope, as may be collected from his translation, was to write his first thoughts in his first words, and gradually to amplify, decorate, rectify, and refine them.

1. By Suetonius in his brief life of the poet.

With such faculties and such dispositions, he excelled every other writer in *poetical prudence;* he wrote in such a manner as might expose him to few hazards. He used almost always the same fabric of verse; and, indeed, by those few essays which he made of any other, he did not enlarge his reputation. Of this uniformity the certain consequence was readiness and dexterity. By perpetual practice, language had in his mind a systematical arrangement; having always the same use for words, he had words so selected and combined as to be ready at his call. This increase of facility he confessed himself to have perceived in the progress of his translation.

But what was yet of more importance, his effusions were always voluntary, and his subjects chosen by himself. His independence secured him from drudging at a task, and laboring upon a barren topic: he never exchanged praise for money, nor opened a shop of condolence or congratulation. His poems, therefore, were scarce ever temporary. He suffered coronations and royal marriages to pass without a song, and derived no opportunities from recent events, nor any popularity from the accidental disposition of his readers. He was never reduced to the necessity of soliciting the sun to shine upon a birthday, of calling the Graces and Virtues to a wedding, or of saying what multitudes have said before him. When he could produce nothing new, he was at liberty to be silent.

His publications were for the same reason never hasty. He is said to have sent nothing to the press till it had lain two years under his inspection: it is at least certain that he ventured nothing without nice examination. He suffered the tumult of imagination to subside, and the novelties of invention to grow familiar. He knew that the mind is always enamored of its own productions, and did not trust his first fondness. He consulted his friends, and listened with great willingness to criticism; and, what was of more importance, he consulted himself, and let nothing pass against his own judgment.

He professed to have learned his poetry from Dryden, whom, whenever an opportunity was presented, he praised through his whole life with unvaried liberality; and perhaps his character may receive some illustration, if he be compared with his master.

Integrity of understanding and nicety of discernment were not allotted in a less proportion to Dryden than to Pope. The rectitude of Dryden's mind was sufficiently shown by the dismission of his poetical prejudices, and the rejection of unnatural thoughts and rugged numbers. But Dryden never desired to apply all the judgment that he had. He wrote, and professed to write, merely for the people; and when he pleased others, he contented himself. He spent no time in struggles to rouse latent powers; he never attempted to make that better which was already good, nor often to mend what he must have known to be faulty. He wrote, as he tells us, with very little consideration; when occasion or necessity called upon him, he poured out what the present moment happened to supply, and, when once it had passed the press, ejected it from his mind; for when he had no pecuniary interest, he had no further solicitude.

Pope was not content to satisfy; he desired to excel, and therefore always endeavored to do his best: he did not court the candor, but dared the judgment of his reader, and, expecting no indulgence from others, he showed none to himself. He examined lines and words with minute and punctilious observation, and retouched every part with indefatigable diligence, till he had left nothing to be forgiven.

For this reason he kept his pieces very long in his hands, while he considered and reconsidered them. The only poems which can be supposed to have been written with such regard to the times as might hasten their publication were the two satires of *Thirty-Eight*; of which Dodsley[2] told me that they were brought to him by the author, that they might be fairly copied. "Almost every line," he said, "was then written twice over; I gave him a clean transcript, which he sent some time afterwards to me for the press, with almost every line written twice over a second time."

His declaration, that his care for his works ceased at their publication, was not strictly true. His parental attention never abandoned them; what he found amiss in the first edition, he silently corrected in those that followed. He appears to have revised the *Iliad*, and freed it from some of its imperfections; and the *Essay on Criticism* received many improvements after its first appearance. It will seldom be found that he altered without adding clearness, elegance, or vigor. Pope had perhaps the judgment of Dryden; but Dryden certainly wanted the diligence of Pope.

In acquired knowledge, the superiority must be allowed to Dryden, whose education was more scholastic, and who before he became an author had been allowed more time for study, with better means of information. His mind has a larger range, and he collects his images and illustrations from a more extensive circumference of science. Dryden knew more of man in his general nature, and Pope in his local manners. The notions of Dryden were formed by comprehensive speculation, and those of Pope by minute attention. There is more dignity in the knowledge of Dryden, and more certainty in that of Pope.

Poetry was not the sole praise of either; for both excelled likewise in prose; but Pope did not borrow his prose from his predecessor. The style of Dryden is capricious and varied, that of Pope is cautious and uniform; Dryden obeys the motions of his own mind, Pope constrains his mind to his own rules of composition. Dryden

2. Robert Dodsley, the publisher.

many years he had half-jestingly, half-seriously, made the Scots as a nation the butt of his satiric wit. But such were Boswell's social tact and
Johnson's vigor and curiosity that the tour was a great success. "There
have been many people," wrote Boswell of himself, "who built castles in
the air, but I believe I am the first that ever attempted to move into
them." The trip to the Hebrides is a fine example of this eminently Bos-
wellian trait. Johnson's sober and unflattering account of the trip in his
Journey to the Western Isles of Scotland (1775) gave some offense to
Scottish national pride. Boswell's *Journal of a Tour to the Hebrides*
(1785), a preliminary study for the *Life*, is a lively and entertaining diary,
kept throughout the journey and approved, at least in part, by Johnson
himself.

In 1788, four years after Johnson's death, Boswell abandoned his Scotch
practice, removed with his family to London, was admitted to the English
bar (but never actually practiced), and, amidst domestic difficulties not
made less perplexing by his own frailties, began the *Life*. Fortunately he
had the help and encouragement of the distinguished literary scholar
Edmond Malone, without whose guidance he might never have finished his
task.

The *Life* is the work of an impressive literary artist who was dominated
by a Johnsonian regard for accuracy and truth. A lesser craftsman might
have been overwhelmed by the very abundance of material that Boswell
had to deal with: his own journals, all of Johnson's letters that he could
find, his voluminous writings, and every scrap of information that his
friends would furnish—all of which had to be collected, verified, and
somehow reduced to unity. The *Life* is a record not of Johnson alone
but of literary England during the last half of the century. Its pages are
populated by men as eminent in their way as was Johnson, most of whom
Boswell knew, all of whom are interesting to the reader. But Boswell
wrote with his eye on the object, and that object was Samuel Johnson,
to whom every detail in the book is relevant, toward whom such eminent
persons as Sir Joshua Reynolds, Edmund Burke, Oliver Goldsmith, Lord
Chesterfield—even the king himself—always face. Boswell's sense of unity
and of proportion is perfect. Although his book is dense with details, they
never impede the flow of the narrative. The movement is always forward,
individual episodes are designed to reveal the great protagonist in a variety
of aspects, and the world that Boswell created and populated is sustained
both by the animation of his own imagination and by the vitality of his
hero.

Boswell's gift is not only narrative: it is also dramatic. He himself was
a good deal of an actor and a superb mimic, with a flair for detecting the
characteristic gesture, word, tone, or trait. In reading the journals and
the *Life* one often feels that their author is a gifted theatrical improviser,
creating dramatic "scenes" (the word is a favorite of his) with living people, and playing simultaneously and with incredible sureness the several
roles of contriver of the dialogue, director of the plot, actor in the scene,
and applauding audience—for Boswell never failed to watch and applaud
or condemn his own curious conduct. The quintessence of Boswell as both
a social genius and a literary artist (the two complemented each other)
is to be found in his description of his visit to Voltaire: "I placed myself
by him. I touched the keys in unison with his imagination. I wish you had

heard the music." Boswell's art, as an interviewer, a conversationalist, and a biographer is, like all great art, the product of a deep and humane interpretative imagination. The scene with Voltaire, like all the famous scenes in the *Life*, is contrived with such apparent ease and by seemingly such simple means, that the genius responsible for them may go undetected by the casual reader.

Although the Johnson who has become a part of our heritage is largely Boswell's Johnson, there was much in his life about which Boswell had no first-hand knowledge, and there were aspects of his nature which he did not have much opportunity to observe. When Boswell met him, Johnson was 54, a widower, already established as "Dictionary" Johnson and the author of the *Rambler*, pensioned by the Crown and consequently no longer compelled to earn his living. Boswell knew nothing at first hand of Johnson's boyhood and youth in Lichfield, of his brief stay at Oxford, of his marriage, and of the long, difficult, and heroic years (more than a quarter of a century), during which Johnson made his way up from obscurity to eminence through difficulties that it is painful to imagine. Boswell knew him as the sage, the moralist, the scholar, the critic, and as a man moving in a largely male society in tavern, coffeehouse, and club. The chief glory of the *Life* is the conversation, always dominated by Johnson but not at all a monologue. It is the talk of a man, or rather of men, who have experienced broadly, read widely, observed and reflected on their observations, whose ideas are constantly brought to the test of experience, and whose experience is habitually transmuted into ideas. The book is as large as life and as human as its central character.

From Boswell on the Grand Tour

[*Boswell Interviews Voltaire*[1]]

And whence do I now write to you, my friend?[2] From the château of Monsieur de Voltaire. I had a letter for him from a Swiss colonel at The Hague. I came hither Monday and was presented to him. He received me with dignity and that air of a man who has been much in the world which a Frenchman acquires in perfection. I saw him for about half an hour before dinner. He was not in spirits. Yet he gave me some brilliant sallies. He did not dine with us, and I was obliged to post away immediately after dinner, because the gates of Geneva shut before five and Ferney is a good hour from town. I was by no means satisfied to have been so little time with the monarch of French literature. A happy scheme sprung up in my adventurous mind. Madame Denis, the niece of Monsieur de

1. Voltaire was the name assumed by François Marie Arouet (1694–1778), the most famous French writer of his generation. Playwright, poet, satirist, philosopher, enemy of the church, and irrepressible ironist, after a stormy career he was living in splendor at his chateau at Ferney near the border of Switzerland and France, just outside Geneva. His housekeeper and mistress was his niece Marie-Louise Denis. He and Jean-Jacques Rousseau, whom Boswell had just visited and whose avowed disciple he had become, were deadly enemies.

2. This passage is taken from a letter, dated 28 December, 1764, written to Boswell's closest friend, a young clergyman named William Temple.

Voltaire, had been extremely good to me. She is fond of our language. I wrote her a letter in English begging her interest to obtain for me the privilege of lodging a night under the roof of Monsieur de Voltaire, who, in opposition to our sun, rises in the evening. I was in the finest humor and my letter was full of wit. I told her, "I am a hardy and a vigorous Scot. You may mount me to the highest and coldest garret. I shall not even refuse to sleep upon two chairs in the bedchamber of your maid. I saw her pass through the room where we sat before dinner." I sent my letter on Tuesday by an express. It was shown to Monsieur de Voltaire, who with his own hand wrote this answer in the character of Madame Denis: "You will do us much honor and pleasure. We have few beds. But you will (*shall*) not sleep on two chairs. My uncle, though very sick, hath guessed at your merit. I know it better; for I have seen you longer." * * *

I returned yesterday to this enchanted castle. The magician appeared a very little before dinner. But in the evening he came into the drawing room in great spirits. I placed myself by him. I touched the keys in unison with his imagination. I wish you had heard the music. He was all brilliance. He gave me continued flashes of wit. I got him to speak English, which he does in a degree that made me now and then start up and cry. "Upon my soul this is astonishing!" When he talked our language he was animated with the soul of a Briton. He had bold flights. He had humor. He had an extravagance; he had a forcible oddity of style that the most comical of our *dramatis personae* could not have exceeded. He swore bloodily, as was the fashion when he was in England.[3] He hummed a ballad; he repeated nonsense. Then he talked of our Constitution with a noble enthusiasm. I was proud to hear this from the mouth of an illustrious Frenchman. At last we came upon religion. Then did he rage. The company went to supper. Monsieur de Voltaire and I remained in the drawing room with a great Bible before us; and if ever two mortal men disputed with vehemence, we did. Yes, upon that occasion he was one individual and I another. For a certain portion of time there was a fair opposition between Voltaire and Boswell. The daring bursts of his ridicule confounded my understanding. He stood like an orator of ancient Rome. Tully[4] was never more agitated than he was. He went too far. His aged frame trembled beneath him. He cried, "Oh, I am very sick; my head turns round," and he let himself gently fall upon an easy chair. He recovered. I resumed our conversation, but changed the tone. I talked to him serious and earnest. I demanded of him an honest confession of

3. In 1726, in order to avoid imprisonment because of a quarrel with a nobleman, Voltaire had gone into exile in England, where he remained for three years, meeting many distinguished English writers and statesmen and learning to admire the British Constitution and the English principle of religious toleration. His *Lettres philosophiques sur les Anglais* (1734) expressed his admiration of English institutions and is an indirect criticism of France.
4. Marcus Tullius Cicero.

his real sentiments. He gave it me with candor and with a mild eloquence which touched my heart. I did not believe him capable of thinking in the manner that he declared to me was "from the bottom of his heart." He expressed his veneration—his love—of the Supreme Being, and his entire resignation to the will of Him who is All-wise. He expressed his desire to resemble the Author of Goodness by being good himself. His sentiments go no farther. He does not inflame his mind with grand hopes of the immortality of the soul. He says, it may be, but he knows nothing of it. And his mind is in perfect tranquility. I was moved; I was sorry. I doubted his sincerity. I called to him with emotion, "Are you sincere? are you really sincere?" He answered "Before God, I am." Then with the fire of him whose tragedies have so often shone on the theater of Paris, he said, "I suffer much. But I suffer with patience and resignation; not as a Christian—but as a man."

Temple, was not this an interesting scene? Would a journey from Scotland to Ferney have been too much to obtain such a remarkable interview? * * *

1764   1928

From The Life of Samuel Johnson, LL.D.

[Plan of the Life]

* * * Had Dr. Johnson written his own life, in conformity with the opinion which he has given, that every man's life may be best written by himself;[1] had he employed in the preservation of his own history, that clearness of narration and elegance of language in which he has embalmed so many eminent persons, the world would probably have had the most perfect example of biography that was ever exhibited. But although he at different times, in a desultory manner, committed to writing many particulars of the progress of his mind and fortunes, he never had persevering diligence enough to form them into a regular composition. Of these memorials a few have been preserved; but the greater part was consigned by him to the flames, a few days before his death.

As I had the honor and happiness of enjoying his friendship for upwards of twenty years; as I had the scheme of writing his life constantly in view; as he was well apprised of this circumstance, and from time to time obligingly satisfied my inquiries, by communicating to me the incidents of his early years; as I acquired a facility in recollecting, and was very assiduous in recording, his conversation, of which the extraordinary vigor and vivacity constituted one of the first features of his character; and as I have spared no pains in obtaining materials concerning him, from every quarter where I could discover that they were to be found, and have been favored

1. *Idler* 84.

with the most liberal communications by his friends; I flatter myself that few biographers have entered upon such a work as this with more advantages; independent of literary abilities, in which I am not vain enough to compare myself with some great names who have gone before me in this kind of writing. * * *

Instead of melting down my materials into one mass, and constantly speaking in my own person, by which I might have appeared to have more merit in the execution of the work, I have resolved to adopt and enlarge upon the excellent plan of Mr. Mason, in his *Memoirs of Gray*.[2] Wherever narrative is necessary to explain, connect, and supply, I furnish it to the best of my abilities; but in the chronological series of Johnson's life, which I trace as distinctly as I can, year by year, I produce, wherever it is in my power, his own minutes, letters, or conversation, being convinced that this mode is more lively, and will make my readers better acquainted with him than even most of those were who actually knew him, but could know him only partially; whereas there is here an accumulation of intelligence from various points, by which his character is more fully understood and illustrated.

Indeed I cannot conceive a more perfect mode of writing any man's life than not only relating all the most important events of it in their order, but interweaving what he privately wrote, and said, and thought; by which mankind are enabled as it were to see him live, and to "live o'er each scene"[3] with him, as he actually advanced through the several stages of his life. Had his other friends been as diligent and ardent as I was, he might have been almost entirely preserved. As it is, I will venture to say that he will be seen in this work more completely than any man who has ever yet lived.

And he will be seen as he really was; for I profess to write, not his panegyric, which must be all praise, but his Life; which, great and good as he was, must not be supposed to be entirely perfect. To be as he was, is indeed subject of panegyric enough to any man in this state of being; but in every picture there should be shade as well as light, and when I delineate him without reserve, I do what he himself recommended, both by his precept and his example. * * *

I am fully aware of the objections which may be made to the minuteness on some occasions of my detail of Johnson's conversation, and how happily it is adapted for the petty exercise of ridicule, by men of superficial understanding and ludicrous fancy; but I remain firm and confident in my opinion, that minute particulars are frequently characteristic, and always amusing, when they relate to a distinguished man. I am therefore exceedingly unwilling that

2. William Mason, poet and dramatist, published his life of Thomas Gray in 1774.   3. Pope's Prologue to Addison's *Cato*, line 4.

anything, however slight, which my illustrious friend thought it worth his while to express, with any degree of point, should perish. * * *

Of one thing I am certain, that considering how highly the small portion which we have of the table-talk and other anecdotes of our celebrated writers is valued, and how earnestly it is regretted that we have not more, I am justified in preserving rather too many of Johnson's sayings, than too few; especially as from the diversity of dispositions it cannot be known with certainty beforehand, whether what may seem trifling to some, and perhaps to the collector himself, may not be most agreeable to many; and the greater number that an author can please in any degree, the more pleasure does there arise to a benevolent mind. * * *

[Johnson's Early Years. Marriage and London]

[1709] Samuel Johnson was born at Lichfield, in Staffordshire, on the 18th of September, N.S.,[4] 1709; and his initiation into the Christian Church was not delayed; for his baptism is recorded, in the register of St. Mary's parish in that city, to have been performed on the day of his birth. His father is there styled *Gentleman*, a circumstance of which an ignorant panegyrist has praised him for not being proud; when the truth is, that the appellation of Gentleman, though now lost in the indiscriminate assumption of *Esquire*, was commonly taken by those who could not boast of gentility. His father was Michael Johnson, a native of Derbyshire, of obscure extraction, who settled in Lichfield as a bookseller and stationer. His mother was Sarah Ford, descended of an ancient race of substantial yeomanry in Warwickshire. They were well advanced in years when they married, and never had more than two children, both sons; Samuel, their first-born, who lived to be the illustrious character whose various excellence I am to endeavor to record, and Nathanael, who died in his twenty-fifth year.

Mr. Michael Johnson was a man of a large and robust body, and of a strong and active mind; yet, as in the most solid rocks veins of unsound substance are often discovered, there was in him a mixture of that disease, the nature of which eludes the most minute inquiry, though the effects are well known to be a weariness of life, an unconcern about those things which agitate the greater part of mankind, and a general sensation of gloomy wretchedness. From him then his son inherited, with some other qualities, "a vile melancholy," which in his too strong expression of any disturbance of the mind, "made him mad all his life, at least not sober." Michael

4. New Style. In 1752 Great Britain adopted the Gregorian Calendar, introduced in 1582 by Pope Gregory XIII, to correct the accumulated inaccuracies of Julius Caesar's calendar, which had been in use since 46 B.C. By 1752 the error amounted to eleven days. Dates before September 2, 1752, must therefore be corrected by adding eleven days or by using the Julian date, followed by "O.S." (Old Style).

was, however, forced by the narrowness of his circumstances to be very diligent in business, not only in his shop, but by occasionally resorting to several towns in the neighborhood, some of which were at a considerable distance from Lichfield. At that time booksellers' shops in the provincial towns of England were very rare, so that there was not one even in Birmingham, in which town old Mr. Johnson used to open a shop every market day. He was a pretty good Latin scholar, and a citizen so creditable as to be made one of the magistrates of Lichfield; and, being a man of good sense, and skill in his trade, he acquired a reasonable share of wealth, of which however he afterwards lost the greatest part, by engaging unsuccessfully in a manufacture of parchment. He was a zealous high-church man and royalist, and retained his attachment to the unfortunate house of Stuart, though he reconciled himself, by casuistical arguments of expediency and necessity, to take the oaths imposed by the prevailing power. * * *

Johnson's mother was a woman of distinguished understanding. I asked his old schoolfellow, Mr. Hector,[5] surgeon of Birmingham, if she was not vain of her son. He said, "She had too much good sense to be vain, but she knew her son's value." Her piety was not inferior to her understanding; and to her must be ascribed those early impressions of religion upon the mind of her son, from which the world afterwards derived so much benefit. He told me that he remembered distinctly having had the first notice of Heaven, "a place to which good people went," and hell, "a place to which bad people went," communicated to him by her, when a little child in bed with her; and that it might be the better fixed in his memory, she sent him to repeat it to Thomas Jackson, their manservant; he not being in the way, this was not done; but there was no occasion for any artificial aid for its preservation. * * *

[1728] That a man in Mr. Michael Johnson's circumstances should think of sending his son to the expensive University of Oxford, at his own charge, seems very improbable. The subject was too delicate to question Johnson upon. But I have been assured by Dr. Taylor[6] that the scheme never would have taken place had not a gentleman of Shropshire, one of his schoolfellows, spontaneously undertaken to support him at Oxford, in the character of his companion; though, in fact, he never received any assistance whatever from that gentleman.

He, however, went to Oxford, and was entered a Commoner of Pembroke College on the 31st of October, 1728, being then in his nineteenth year.

The Reverend Dr. Adams,[7] who afterwards presided over Pembroke College with universal esteem, told me he was present, and

5. Edmund Hector, a lifelong friend of Johnson's.
6. A well-to-do clergyman, who had been Johnson's school fellow in Lich-

field.
7. The Rev William Adams, D.D., elected Master of Pembroke in 1775.

gave me some account of what passed on the night of Johnson's arrival at Oxford. On that evening, his father, who had anxiously accompanied him, found means to have him introduced to Mr. Jorden, who was to be his tutor. * * *

His father seemed very full of the merits of his son, and told the company he was a good scholar, and a poet, and wrote Latin verses. His figure and manner appeared strange to them; but he behaved modestly and sat silent, till upon something which occurred in the course of conversation, he suddenly struck in and quoted Macrobius; and thus he gave the first impression of that more extensive reading in which he had indulged himself.

His tutor, Mr. Jorden, fellow of Pembroke, was not, it seems, a man of such abilities as we should conceive requisite for the instructor of Samuel Johnson, who gave me the following account of him. "He was a very worthy man, but a heavy man, and I did not profit much by his instructions. Indeed, I did not attend him much. The first day after I came to college I waited upon him, and then stayed away four. On the sixth, Mr. Jorden asked me why I had not attended. I answered I had been sliding in Christ Church meadow. And this I said with as much *nonchalance* as I am now talking to you. I had no notion that I was wrong or irreverent to my tutor." Boswell: "That, Sir, was great fortitude of mind." Johnson: "No, Sir; stark insensibility." * * *

[1729] The "morbid melancholy," which was lurking in his constitution, and to which we may ascribe those particularities and that aversion to regular life, which, at a very early period, marked his character, gathered such strength in his twentieth year as to afflict him in a dreadful manner. While he was at Lichfield, in the college vacation of the year 1729, he felt himself overwhelmed with an horrible hypochondria, with perpetual irritation, fretfulness, and impatience; and with a dejection, gloom, and despair, which made existence misery. From this dismal malady he never afterwards was perfectly relieved; and all his labors, and all his enjoyments, were but temporary interruptions of its baleful influence. He told Mr. Paradise[8] that he was sometimes so languid and inefficient that he could not distinguish the hour upon the town-clock. * * *

To Johnson, whose supreme enjoyment was the exercise of his reason, the disturbance or obscuration of that faculty was the evil most to be dreaded. Insanity, therefore, was the object of his most dismal apprehension; and he fancied himself seized by it, or approaching to it, at the very time when he was giving proofs of a more than ordinary soundness and vigor of judgment. That his own diseased imagination should have so far deceived him, is strange; but it is stranger still that some of his friends should have given credit to his groundless opinion, when they had such undoubted

8. John Paradise, a member of the Essex Head Club, which Johnson founded in 1783.

proofs that it was totally fallacious; though it is by no means surprising that those who wish to depreciate him should, since his death, have laid hold of this circumstance, and insisted upon it with very unfair aggravation. * * *

Dr. Adams told me that Johnson, while he was at Pembroke College, "was caressed and loved by all about him, was a gay and frolicsome fellow, and passed there the happiest part of his life." But this is a striking proof of the fallacy of appearances, and how little any of us know of the real internal state even of those whom we see most frequently; for the truth is, that he was then depressed by poverty, and irritated by disease. When I mentioned to him this account as given me by Dr. Adams, he said, "Ah, Sir, I was mad and violent. It was bitterness which they mistook for frolic. I was miserably poor, and I thought to fight my way by my literature and my wit; so I disregarded all power and all authority." * * *

[1734] In a man whom religious education has secured from licentious indulgences, the passion of love, when once it has seized him, is exceedingly strong; being unimpaired by dissipation, and totally concentrated in one object. This was experienced by Johnson, when he became the fervent admirer of Mrs. Porter, after her first husband's death. Miss Porter told me that when he was first introduced to her mother, his appearance was very forbidding: he was then lean and lank, so that his immense structure of bones was hideously striking to the eye, and the scars of the scrofula were deeply visible. He also wore his hair,[9] which was straight and stiff, and separated behind: and he often had, seemingly, convulsive starts and odd gesticulations, which tended to excite at once surprise and ridicule. Mrs. Porter was so much engaged by his conversation that she overlooked all these external disadvantages, and said to her daughter, "This is the most sensible man that I ever saw in my life."

[1735] Though Mrs. Porter was double the age of Johnson, and her person and manner, as described to me by the late Mr. Garrick,[1] were by no means pleasing to others, she must have had a superiority of understanding and talents, as she certainly inspired him with a more than ordinary passion; and she having signified her willingness to accept of his hand, he went to Lichfield to ask his mother's consent to the marriage, which he could not but be conscious was a very imprudent scheme, both on account of their disparity of years and her want of fortune. But Mrs. Johnson knew too well the ardor of her son's temper, and was too tender a parent to oppose his inclinations.

I know not for what reason the marriage ceremony was not performed at Birmingham; but a resolution was taken that it should be at Derby, for which place the bride and bridegroom set out on horseback, I suppose in very good humor. But though Mr. Topham

9. I.e., he wore no wig.
1. David Garrick (1717–79), the most famous actor of his day. In 1736 he was one of Johnson's three pupils in an unsuccessful school at Edial.

Beauclerk[2] used archly to mention Johnson's having told him, with much gravity, "Sir, it was a love marriage on both sides," I have had from my illustrious friend the following curious account of their journey to church upon the nuptial morn:

9th July: "Sir, she had read the old romances, and had got into her head the fantastical notion that a woman of spirit should use her lover like a dog. So, Sir, at first she told me that I rode too fast, and she could not keep up with me; and, when I rode a little slower, she passed me, and complained that I lagged behind. I was not to be made the slave of caprice; and I resolved to begin as I meant to end. I therefore pushed on briskly, till I was fairly out of her sight. The road lay between two hedges, so I was sure she could not miss it; and I contrived that she should soon come up with me. When she did, I observed her to be in tears." * * *

[1737] Johnson now thought of trying his fortune in London, the great field of genius and exertion, where talents of every kind have the fullest scope and the highest encouragement. It is a memorable circumstance that his pupil David Garrick went thither at the same time, with intention to complete his education, and follow the profession of the law, from which he was soon diverted by his decided preference for the stage.[3] * * *

[1744] * * * He produced one work this year, fully sufficient to maintain the high reputation which he had acquired. This was *The Life of Richard Savage;*[4] a man of whom it is difficult to speak impartially without wondering that he was for some time the intimate companion of Johnson; for his character was marked by profligacy, insolence, and ingratitude: yet, as he undoubtedly had a warm and vigorous, though unregulated mind, had seen life in all its varieties, and been much in the company of the statesmen and wits of his time, he could communicate to Johnson an abundant supply of such materials as his philosophical curiosity most eagerly desired; and as Savage's misfortunes and misconduct had reduced him to the lowest state of wretchedness as a writer for bread, his visits to St. John's Gate[5] naturally brought Johnson and him together.

It is melancholy to reflect that Johnson and Savage were some-

---

2. Topham Beauclerk, a descendant of Charles II and the actress Nell Gwynn. He was brilliant and dissolute.

3. Johnson had hoped to complete his tragedy *Irene* and to get it produced, but this was not accomplished until Garrick staged it in 1749. Meanwhile Johnson struggled against poverty, at first as a writer and translator for Edward Cave's *Gentleman's Magazine*. He gradually won recognition, but was never financially secure until he was pensioned in 1762. Garrick succeeded in the theater much more rapidly than did Johnson in literature.

4. Richard Savage, poet, courted and gained notoriety by claiming to be the illegitimate son of Earl Rivers and the Countess of Macclesfield, whose husband had divorced her because of her unfaithfulness with Rivers. Savage publicized his claim and persecuted his alleged mother. Johnson and many others believed Savage's story and resented what they considered the lady's inhumanity. Savage was a gifted man, but he lived in poverty as a hack writer, though he was long assisted by Pope and others. He died in a debtor's prison in Bristol in 1743.

5. Where Cave published the *Gentleman's Magazine*.

times in such extreme indigence that they could not pay for a lodging; so that they have wandered together whole nights in the streets. Yet in these almost incredible scenes of distress, we may suppose that Savage mentioned many of the anecdotes with which Johnson afterwards enriched the life of his unhappy companion, and those of other poets.

He told Sir Joshua Reynolds that one night in particular, when Savage and he walked round St. James's Square for want of a lodging, they were not at all depressed by their situation; but in high spirits and brimful of patriotism, traversed the square for several hours, inveighed against the minister, and "resolved they would *stand by their country.*" * * *

[1752] That there should be a suspension of his literary labors during a part of the year 1752[6] will not seem strange when it is considered that soon after closing his *Rambler*, he suffered a loss which, there can be no doubt, affected him with the deepest distress. For on the 17th of March, O.S., his wife died. * * *

The following very solemn and affecting prayer was found, after Dr. Johnson's decease, by his servant, Mr. Francis Barber, who delivered it to my worthy friend the Reverend Mr. Strahan, Vicar of Islington, who at my earnest request has obligingly favored me with a copy of it, which he and I compared with the original:

"April 26, 1752, being after 12 at night of the 25th.

"O Lord! Governor of heaven and earth, in whose hands are embodied and departed spirits, if thou hast ordained the souls of the dead to minister to the living, and appointed my departed wife to have care of me, grant that I may enjoy the good effects of her attention and ministration, whether exercised by appearance, impulses, dreams or in any other manner agreeable to thy government. Forgive my presumption, enlighten my ignorance, and however meaner agents are employed, grant me the blessed influences of thy holy Spirit, through Jesus Christ our Lord. Amen." * * *

One night when Beauclerk and Langton[7] had supped at a tavern in London, and sat till about three in the morning, it came into their heads to go and knock up Johnson, and see if they could prevail on him to join them in a ramble. They rapped violently at the door of his chambers in the Temple,[8] till at last he appeared in his shirt, with his little black wig on the top of his head, instead of a nightcap, and a poker in his hand, imagining, probably, that some ruffians were coming to attack him. When he discovered who they were, and was told their errand, he smiled, and with great good

6. Johnson's important works written before the publication of the *Dictionary* are the poems *London* (1738) and *The Vanity of Human Wishes* (1749), the *Life of Savage* (1744), and the essays which made up his periodical *The Rambler* (1750–52).
7. Bennet Langton. As a boy he so much admired the *Rambler* that he

sought Johnson's acquaintance. They became lifelong friends.
8. Since Johnson lived in Inner Temple Lane between 1760 and 1765, the "frisk" could not have taken place in the year of his wife's death, where Boswell, for his own convenience, placed it.

humor agreed to their proposal: "What, is it you, you dogs! I'll have a frisk with you." He was soon dressed, and they sallied forth together into Covent Garden, where the greengrocers and fruiterers were beginning to arrange their hampers, just come in from the country. Johnson made some attempts to help them; but the honest gardeners stared so at his figure and manner and odd interference, that he soon saw his services were not relished. They then repaired to one of the neighboring taverns, and made a bowl of that liquor called *Bishop*,[9] which Johnson had always liked; while in joyous contempt of sleep, from which he had been roused, he repeated the festive lines,

> Short, O short then be thy reign,
> And give us to the world again![1]

They did not stay long, but walked down to the Thames, took a boat, and rowed to Billingsgate. Beauclerk and Johnson were so well pleased with their amusement that they resolved to persevere in dissipation for the rest of the day: but Langton deserted them, being engaged to breakfast with some young ladies. Johnson scolded him for "leaving his social friends, to go and sit with a set of wretched *un-idea'd* girls." Garrick being told of this ramble, said to him smartly, "I heard of your frolic t'other night. You'll be in the *Chronicle*." Upon which Johnson afterwards observed, "*He* durst not do such a thing. His *wife* would not *let* him!" * * *

[The Letter to Chesterfield]

[1754] Lord Chesterfield,[2] to whom Johnson had paid the high compliment of addressing to his Lordship the *Plan* of his *Dictionary*, had behaved to him in such a manner as to excite his contempt and indignation. The world has been for many years amused with a story confidently told, and as confidently repeated with additional circumstances, that a sudden disgust was taken by Johnson upon occasion of his having been one day kept long in waiting in his Lordship's antechamber, for which the reason assigned was that he had company with him; and that at last, when the door opened, out walked Colley Cibber;[3] and that Johnson was so violently provoked when he found for whom he had been so long excluded, that he went away in a passion, and never would return. I remember having mentioned this story to George Lord Lyttelton, who told me he was very intimate with Lord Chesterfield; and holding it as a well-known truth, defended Lord Chesterfield, by saying, that Cibber, who had been introduced familiarly by the back stairs, had

9. A drink made of wine, sugar, and either lemon or orange.
1. Misquoted from Lansdowne's *Drinking Song to Sleep*.
2. Philip Dormer Stanhope, Earl of Chesterfield (1694–1773), statesman, wit, man of fashion. His *Letters*, written for the guidance of his natural son, are famous for their worldly good

sense and for their expression of the ideal of an 18th-century gentleman.
3. Colley Cibber (1671–1757), playwright, comic actor, and (after 1730) poet laureate. A fine actor but a very bad poet, Cibber was a constant object of ridicule by the wits of the town. Pope made him King of the Dunces in the *Dunciad* of 1743.

probably not been there above ten minutes. It may seem strange even to entertain a doubt concerning a story so long and so widely current, and thus implicitly adopted, if not sanctioned, by the authority which I have mentioned; but Johnson himself assured me that there was not the least foundation for it. He told me that there never was any particular incident which produced a quarrel between Lord Chesterfield and him; but that his Lordship's continued neglect was the reason why he resolved to have no connection with him. When the *Dictionary* was upon the eve of publication, Lord Chesterfield, who, it is said, had flattered himself with expectations that Johnson would dedicate the work to him, attempted, in a courtly manner, to soothe, and insinuate himself with the sage, conscious, as it should seem, of the cold indifference with which he had treated its learned author; and further attempted to conciliate him, by writing two papers in *The World*, in recommendation of the work; and it must be confessed that they contain some studied compliments, so finely turned, that if there had been no previous offense, it is probable that Johnson would have been highly delighted. Praise, in general, was pleasing to him; but by praise from a man of rank and elegant accomplishments, he was peculiarly gratified. * * *

This courtly device failed of its effect. Johnson, who thought that "all was false and hollow,"[4] despised the honeyed words, and was even indignant that Lord Chesterfield should, for a moment, imagine that he could be dupe of such an artifice. His expression to me concerning Lord Chesterfield, upon this occasion, was, "Sir, after making great professions, he had, for many years, taken no notice of me; but when my *Dictionary* was coming out, he fell a-scribbling in *The World* about it. Upon which, I wrote him a letter expressed in civil terms, but such as might show him that I did not mind what he said or wrote, and that I had done with him."

This is that celebrated letter of which so much has been said, and about which curiosity has been so long excited, without being gratified. I for many years solicited Johnson to favor me with a copy of it, that so excellent a composition might not be lost to posterity. He delayed from time to time to give it me; till at last in 1781, when we were on a visit at Mr. Dilly's,[5] at Southill in Bedfordshire, he was pleased to dictate it to me from memory. He afterwards found among his papers a copy of it, which he had dictated to Mr. Baretti,[6] with its title and corrections, in his own handwriting. This he gave to Mr. Langton; adding that if it were to come into print, he wished it to be from that copy. By Mr. Langton's kindness, I am enabled to enrich my work with a perfect transcript of what the world has so eagerly desired to see.

4. *Paradise Lost* II.112.
5. Southill was the country home of Charles and Edward Dilly, publishers. The firm published all of Boswell's serious works and shared in the publica-tion of Johnson's *Lives of the Poets* (1779–81).
6. Giuseppe Baretti, an Italian writer and lexicographer whom Johnson introduced into his circle.

To the Right Honorable the Earl of Chesterfield

February 7, 1755.

My Lord,

I have been lately informed, by the proprietor of *The World*, that two papers, in which my Dictionary is recommended to the public, were written by your Lordship. To be so distinguished, is an honor, which, being very little accustomed to favors from the great, I know not well how to receive, or in what terms to acknowledge.

When, upon some slight encouragement, I first visited your Lordship, I was overpowered, like the rest of mankind, by the enchantment of your address; and could not forbear to wish that I might boast myself *Le vainqueur du vainqueur de la terre*[7]—that I might obtain that regard for which I saw the world contending; but I found my attendance so little encouraged that neither pride nor modesty would suffer me to continue it. When I had once addressed your Lordship in public, I had exhausted all the art of pleasing which a retired and uncourtly scholar can possess. I had done all that I could; and no man is well pleased to have his all neglected, be it ever so little.

Seven years, my Lord, have now passed since I waited in your outward rooms, or was repulsed from your door; during which time I have been pushing on my work through difficulties of which it is useless to complain, and have brought it, at last, to the verge of publication, without one act of assistance, one word of encouragement, or one smile of favor. Such treatment I did not expect, for I never had a patron before.

The shepherd in Virgil grew at last acquainted with Love, and found him a native of the rocks.[8]

Is not a patron, my Lord, one who looks with unconcern on a man struggling for life in the water, and, when he has reached ground, encumbers him with help? The notice which you have been pleased to take of my labors, had it been early, had been kind; but it has been delayed till I am indifferent, and cannot enjoy it; till I am solitary, and cannot impart it; till I am known, and do not want it. I hope it is no very cynical asperity not to confess obligations where no benefit has been received, or to be unwilling that the public should consider me as owing that to a patron which Providence has enabled me to do for myself.

Having carried on my work thus far with so little obligation to any favorer of learning, I shall not be disappointed though I should conclude it, if less be possible, with less; for I have been long wakened from that dream of hope in which I once boasted myself with so much exultation, my Lord, your Lordship's most humble, most obedient servant,

Sam. Johnson.

"While this was the talk of the town," says Dr. Adams, in a letter to me, "I happened to visit Dr. Warburton,[9] who finding that

7. "The conqueror of the conqueror of the earth." From the first line of Scudéry's epic *Alaric* (1654).
8. *Eclogues* VIII.44.

9. William Warburton, Bishop of Gloucester, friend and literary executor of Pope, editor of Pope and Shakespeare, theological controversialist.

I was acquainted with Johnson, desired me earnestly to carry his compliments to him, and to tell him that he honored him for his manly behavior in rejecting these condescensions of Lord Chesterfield, and for resenting the treatment he had received from him, with a proper spirit. Johnson was visibly pleased with this compliment, for he had always a high opinion of Warburton. Indeed, the force of mind which appeared in this letter was congenial with that which Warburton himself amply possessed."

There is a curious minute circumstance which struck me, in comparing the various editions of Johnson's imitations of Juvenal. In the tenth satire, one of the couplets upon the vanity of wishes even for literary distinction stood thus:

> Yet think what ills the scholar's life assail,
> Pride, envy, want, the *garret*, and the jail.

But after experiencing the uneasiness which Lord Chesterfield's fallacious patronage made him feel, he dismissed the word *garret* from the sad group, and in all the subsequent editions the line stands

> Pride, envy, want, the *patron*, and the jail.

[1762] The accession of George the Third to the throne of these kingdoms[1] opened a new and brighter prospect to men of literary merit, who had been honored with no mark of royal favor in the preceding reign. His present Majesty's education in this country, as well as his taste and beneficence, prompted him to be the patron of science and the arts; and early this year Johnson, having been represented to him as a very learned and good man, without any certain provision, his Majesty was pleased to grant him a pension of three hundred pounds a year. The Earl of Bute,[2] who was then Prime Minister, had the honor to announce this instance of his Sovereign's bounty, concerning which many and various stories, all equally erroneous, have been propagated: maliciously representing it as a political bribe to Johnson, to desert his avowed principles, and become the tool of a government which he held to be founded in usurpation. I have taken care to have it in my power to refute them from the most authentic information. Lord Bute told me that Mr. Wedderburne, now Lord Loughborough, was the person who first mentioned this subject to him. Lord Loughborough told me that the pension was granted to Johnson solely as the reward of his literary merit, without any stipulation whatever, or even tacit understanding that he should write for administration. His Lordship added that he was confident the political tracts which Johnson afterwards did write, as they were entirely consonant with his

1. In 1760.
2. An intimate friend of George III's mother, he early gained an ascendancy over the young prince and was largely responsible for the king's autocratic views. He was hated in England both as a favorite and as a Scot.

own opinions, would have been written by him though no pension had been granted to him.[3] * * *

[A Memorable Year: Boswell Meets Johnson]

[1763] This is to me a memorable year; for in it I had the happiness to obtain the acquaintance of that extraordinary man whose memoirs I am now writing; an acquaintance which I shall ever esteem as one of the most fortunate circumstances in my life. * * *

Mr. Thomas Davies the actor, who then kept a bookseller's shop in Russel Street, Covent Garden, told me that Johnson was very much his friend, and came frequently to his house, where he more than once invited me to meet him; but by some unlucky accident or other he was prevented from coming to us. * * *

At last, on Monday the 16th of May, when I was sitting in Mr. Davies's back parlor, after having drunk tea with him and Mrs. Davies, Johnson unexpectedly came into the shop; and Mr. Davies having perceived him through the glass door in the room in which we were sitting, advancing towards us—he announced his awful approach to me, somewhat in the manner of an actor in the part of Horatio, when he addresses Hamlet on the appearance of his father's ghost, "Look, my Lord, it comes." I found that I had a very perfect idea of Johnson's figure, from the portrait of him painted by Sir Joshua Reynolds soon after he had published his *Dictionary*, in the attitude of sitting in his easy chair in deep meditation, which was the first picture his friend did for him, which Sir Joshua very kindly presented to me, and from which an engraving has been made for this work. Mr. Davies mentioned my name, and respectfully introduced me to him. I was much agitated; and recollecting his prejudice against the Scotch, of which I had heard much, I said to Davies, "Don't tell where I come from."—"From Scotland," cried Davies roguishly. "Mr. Johnson," said I, "I do indeed come from Scotland, but I cannot help it." I am willing to flatter myself that I meant this as light pleasantry to soothe and conciliate him, and not as an humiliating abasement at the expense of my country. But however that might be, this speech was somewhat unlucky; for with that quickness of wit for which he was so remarkable, he seized the expression "come from Scotland," which I used in the sense of being of that country; and, as if I had said that I had come away from it, or left it, retorted, "That, Sir, I find, is what a very great many of your countrymen cannot help." This stroke stunned me a good deal; and when we had sat down, I felt myself not a little embarrassed, and apprehensive of what might come next. He then addressed himself to Davies: "What do

---

3. Johnson's few political pamphlets in the 1770's invariably supported the policies of the Crown. The best-known is his answer to the American colonies, *Taxation No Tyranny* (1775). His dislike of the Americans was in large part due to the fact they owned slaves.

you think of Garrick? He has refused me an order for the play for Miss Williams,[4] because he knows the house will be full, and that an order would be worth three shillings." Eager to take any opening to get into conversation with him, I ventured to say, "O Sir, I cannot think Mr. Garrick would grudge such a trifle to you." "Sir," said he, with a stern look, "I have known David Garrick longer than you have done: and I know no right you have to talk to me on the subject." Perhaps I deserved this check; for it was rather presumptuous in me, an entire stranger, to express any doubt of the justice of his animadversion upon his old acquaintance and pupil. I now felt myself much mortified, and began to think that the hope which I had long indulged of obtaining his acquaintance was blasted. And, in truth, had not my ardor been uncommonly strong, and my resolution uncommonly persevering, so rough a reception might have deterred me forever from making any further attempts. Fortunately, however, I remained upon the field not wholly discomfited. * * *

I was highly pleased with the extraordinary vigor of his conversation, and regretted that I was drawn away from it by an engagement at another place. I had, for a part of the evening, been left alone with him, and had ventured to make an observation now and then, which he received very civilly; so that I was satisfied that though there was a roughness in his manner, there was no ill nature in his disposition. Davies followed me to the door, and when I complained to him a little of the hard blows which the great man had given me, he kindly took upon him to console me by saying, "Don't be uneasy. I can see he likes you very well."

A few days afterwards I called on Davies, and asked him if he thought I might take the liberty of waiting on Mr. Johnson at his chambers in the Temple. He said I certainly might, and that Mr. Johnson would take it as a compliment. So upon Tuesday the 24th of May, after having been enlivened by the witty sallies of Messieurs Thornton, Wilkes, Churchill, and Lloyd,[5] with whom I had passed the morning, I boldly repaired to Johnson. His chambers were on the first floor of No. 1, Inner Temple Lane, and I entered them with an impression given me by the Reverend Dr. Blair,[6] of Edinburgh, who had been introduced to him not long before, and described his having "found the giant in his den"; an expression, which, when I came to be pretty well acquainted with Johnson, I repeated to him, and he was diverted at this picturesque account

4. Mrs. Anna Williams (1706–83), a blind poet and friend of Mrs. Johnson. She continued to live in Johnson's house after his wife's death, and habitually sat up to make tea for him whenever he came home.
5. Bonnell Thornton, journalist; Charles Churchill, satirist; Robert Lloyd, poet and essayist. For Wilkes see a later episode. The four were bound together by a common love of wit and dissipation. Boswell enjoyed their company in 1763.
6. The Rev. Hugh Blair (1718–1800), Scottish divine and Professor of Rhetoric and Belles Lettres at the University of Edinburgh.

of himself. Dr. Blair had been presented to him by Dr. James
Fordyce.[7] At this time the controversy concerning the pieces published by Mr. James Macpherson, as translations of *Ossian*, was at
its height.[8] Johnson had all along denied their authenticity; and,
what was still more provoking to their admirers, maintained that
they had no merit. The subject having been introduced by Dr.
Fordyce, Dr. Blair, relying on the internal evidence of their antiquity, asked Dr. Johnson whether he thought any man of a
modern age could have written such poems? Johnson replied, "Yes,
Sir, many men, many women, and many children." Johnson, at
this time, did not know that Dr. Blair had just published a dissertation, not only defending their authenticity, but seriously ranking
them with the poems of Homer and Virgil; and when he was afterwards informed of this circumstance, he expressed some displeasure
at Dr. Fordyce's having suggested the topic, and said, "I am not
sorry that they got thus much for their pains. Sir, it was like leading
one to talk of a book when the author is concealed behind the
door."

He received me very courteously; but, it must be confessed that
his apartment, and furniture, and morning dress, were sufficiently
uncouth. His brown suit of clothes looked very rusty; he had on a
little old shriveled unpowdered wig, which was too small for his
head; his shirt neck and knees of his breeches were loose; his black
worsted stockings ill drawn up; and he had a pair of unbuckled
shoes by way of slippers. But all these slovenly particularities were
forgotten the moment that he began to talk. Some gentlemen,
whom I do not recollect, were sitting with him; and when they
went away, I also rose; but he said to me, "Nay, don't go." "Sir,"
said I, "I am afraid that I intrude upon you. It is benevolent to
allow me to sit and hear you." He seemed pleased with this compliment, which I sincerely paid him, and answered, "Sir, I am
obliged to any man who visits me." I have preserved the following
short minute of what passed this day:

"Madness frequently discovers itself merely by unnecessary
deviation from the usual modes of the world. My poor friend
Smart showed the disturbance of his mind by falling upon his
knees, and saying his prayers in the street, or in any other unusual
place. Now although, rationally speaking, it is greater madness not
to pray at all than to pray as Smart did, I am afraid there are so
many who do not pray, that their understanding is not called in
question."

Concerning this unfortunate poet, Christopher Smart, who was
confined in a madhouse, he had, at another time, the following

7. A Scottish preacher.
8. Macpherson had imposed on most
of his contemporaries, Scottish and
English, by convincing them of the
genuineness of prose poems which he
had concocted but which he claimed to
have translated from the original Gaelic
of Ossian, a blind epic poet of the 3rd
century. The vogue of the poems both
in Europe and in America was enormous.

conversation with Dr. Burney:[9] BURNEY. "How does poor Smart do, Sir; is he likely to recover?" JOHNSON. "It seems as if his mind had ceased to struggle with the disease; for he grows fat upon it." BURNEY. "Perhaps, Sir, that may be from want of exercise." JOHNSON. "No, Sir; he has partly as much exercise as he used to have, for he digs in the garden. Indeed, before his confinement, he used for exercise to walk to the ale house; but he was *carried* back again. I did not think he ought to be shut up. His infirmities were not noxious to society. He insisted on people praying with him; and I'd as lief pray with Kit Smart as anyone else. Another charge was that he did not love clean linen; and I have no passion for it." —Johnson continued. "Mankind have a great aversion to intellectual labor; but even supposing knowledge to be easily attainable, more people would be content to be ignorant than would take even a little trouble to acquire it."

Talking of Garrick, he said, "He is the first man in the world for sprightly conversation."

When I rose a second time he again pressed me to stay, which I did. * * *

[Goldsmith. Sundry Opinions. Johnson Meets His King]

As Dr. Oliver Goldsmith will frequently appear in this narrative, I shall endeavor to make my readers in some degree acquainted with his singular character. He was a native of Ireland, and a contemporary with Mr. Burke[1] at Trinity College, Dublin, but did not then give much promise of future celebrity. He, however, observed to Mr. Malone,[2] that "though he made no great figure in mathematics, which was a study in much repute there, he could turn an ode of Horace into English better than any of them." He afterwards studied physic at Edinburgh, and upon the Continent; and I have been informed, was enabled to pursue his travels on foot, partly by demanding at universities to enter the lists as a disputant, by which, according to the custom of many of them, he was entitled to the premium of a crown, when luckily for him his challenge was not accepted; so that, as I once observed to Dr. Johnson, he *disputed* his passage through Europe. He then came to England, and was employed successively in the capacities of an usher[3] to an academy, a corrector of the press, a reviewer, and a writer for a newspaper. He had sagacity enough to cultivate assiduously the acquaintance of Johnson, and his faculties were gradually enlarged by the contemplation of such a model. To me and many others it

9. Dr. Charles Burney (1726–1814), historian of music and father of the novelist and diarist Fanny Burney, whom Johnson knew and loved in his old age.
1. Edmund Burke (1729–97), statesman, orator, and political philosopher.

2. Edmond Malone (1741–1812), distinguished editor and literary scholar. He helped Boswell in the writing and publication of the *Life*.
3. An assistant teacher; then a disagreeable and ill-paid job.

appeared that he studiously copied the manner of Johnson, though, indeed, upon a smaller scale.

At this time I think he had published nothing with his name, though it was pretty generally known that *one Dr. Goldsmith* was the author of *An Enquiry into the Present State of Polite Learning in Europe,* and of *The Citizen of the World,* a series of letters supposed to be written from London by a Chinese. No man had the art of displaying, with more advantage as a writer, whatever literary acquisitions he made. "*Nihil quod tetigit non ornavit.*"[4] His mind resembled a fertile, but thin soil. There was a quick, but not a strong vegetation, of whatever chanced to be thrown upon it. No deep root could be struck. The oak of the forest did not grow there; but the elegant shrubbery and the fragrant parterre[5] appeared in gay succession. It has been generally circulated and believed that he was a mere fool in conversation; but, in truth, this has been greatly exaggerated. He had, no doubt, a more than common share of that hurry of ideas which we often find in his countrymen, and which sometimes produces a laughable confusion in expressing them. He was very much what the French call *un étourdi,*[6] and from vanity and an eager desire of being conspicuous wherever he was, he frequently talked carelessly without knowledge of the subject, or even without thought. His person was short, his countenance coarse and vulgar, his deportment that of a scholar awkwardly affecting the easy gentleman. Those who were in any way distinguished, excited envy in him to so ridiculous an excess that the instances of it are hardly credible. When accompanying two beautiful young ladies with their mother on a tour in France, he was seriously angry that more attention was paid to them than to him; and once at the exhibition of the *Fantoccini* in London, when those who sat next him observed with what dexterity a puppet was made to toss a pike, he could not bear that it should have such praise, and exclaimed with some warmth, "Pshaw! I can do it better myself."[7] * * *

I had as my guests this evening at the Mitre Tavern, Dr. Johnson, Dr. Goldsmith, Mr. Thomas Davies, Mr. Eccles, an Irish gentleman, for whose agreeable company I was obliged to Mr. Davies, and the Reverend Mr. John Ogilvie,[8] who was desirous of being in company with my illustrious friend, while I, in my turn, was proud to have the honor of showing one of my countrymen upon what easy terms Johnson permitted me to live with him. * * *

Mr. Ogilvie was unlucky enough to choose for the topic of his

4. "He touched nothing that he did not adorn." From Johnson's epitaph for Goldsmith's monument in Westminster Abbey.
5. A flower garden with beds laid out in patterns.
6. One who acts without thought.

7. It is difficult to believe that Boswell did not recognize that Goldsmith was joking. Indeed, his entire characterization of Goldsmith is not without malice and distortion.
8. An eminent Scottish divine.

conversation the praises of his native country. He began with saying that there was very rich land round Edinburgh. Goldsmith, who had studied physic there, contradicted this, very untruly, with a sneering laugh. Disconcerted a little by this, Mr. Ogilvie then took new ground, where, I suppose, he thought himself perfectly safe; for he observed that Scotland had a great many noble wild prospects. JOHNSON. "I believe, Sir, you have a great many. Norway, too, has noble wild prospects; and Lapland is remarkable for prodigious noble wild prospects. But, Sir, let me tell you, the noblest prospect which a Scotchman ever sees, is the highroad that leads him to England!" This unexpected and pointed sally produced a roar of applause. After all, however, those who admire the rude grandeur of nature cannot deny it to Caledonia. * * *

At night Mr. Johnson and I supped in a private room at the Turk's Head Coffeehouse, in the Strand. "I encourage this house," said he, "for the mistress of it is a good civil woman, and has not much business.

"Sir, I love the acquaintance of young people; because, in the first place, I don't like to think myself growing old. In the next place, young acquaintances must last longest, if they do last; and then, Sir, young men have more virtue than old men: they have more generous sentiments in every respect. I love the young dogs of this age: they have more wit and humor and knowledge of life than we had; but then the dogs are not so good scholars. Sir, in my early years I read very hard. It is a sad reflection, but a true one, that I knew almost as much at eighteen as I do now. My judgment, to be sure, was not so good; but I had all the facts. I remember very well, when I was at Oxford, an old gentleman said to me, 'Young man, ply your book diligently now, and acquire a stock of knowledge; for when years come upon you, you will find that poring upon books will be but an irksome task.' " * * *

He again insisted on the duty of maintaining subordination of rank. "Sir, I would no more deprive a nobleman of his respect than of his money. I consider myself as acting a part in the great system of society, and I do to others as I would have them to do to me. I would behave to a nobleman as I should expect he would behave to me, were I a nobleman and he Sam. Johnson. Sir, there is one Mrs. Macaulay[9] in this town, a great republican. One day when I was at her house, I put on a very grave countenance, and said to her, 'Madam, I am now become a convert to your way of thinking. I am convinced that all mankind are upon an equal footing; and to give you an unquestionable proof, Madam, that I am in earnest, here is a very sensible, civil, well-behaved fellow citizen, your footman; I desire that he may be allowed to sit down and dine with us.' I thus, Sir, showed her the absurdity of the leveling doctrine.

9. Mrs. Catharine Macaulay, at this time much in the public eye as a female historian and a propounder of libertarian and egalitarian ideas.

She has never liked me since. Sir, your levelers wish to level *down* as far as themselves; but they cannot bear leveling *up* to themselves. They would all have some people under them; why not then have some people above them?" * * *

At supper this night he talked of good eating with uncommon satisfaction. "Some people," said he, "have a foolish way of not minding, or pretending not to mind, what they eat. For my part, I mind my belly very studiously, and very carefully; for I look upon it that he who does not mind his belly will hardly mind anything else." He now appeared to me *Jean Bull philosophe*,[1] and he was, for the moment, not only serious but vehement. Yet I have heard him, upon other occasions, talk with great contempt of people who were anxious to gratify their palates; and the 206th number of his *Rambler* is a masterly essay against gulosity.[2] His practice, indeed, I must acknowledge, may be considered as casting the balance of his different opinions upon this subject; for I never knew any man who relished good eating more than he did. When at table, he was totally absorbed in the business of the moment; his looks seemed riveted to his plate; nor would he, unless when in very high company, say one word, or even pay the least attention to what was said by others, till he had satisfied his appetite, which was so fierce, and indulged with such intenseness, that while in the act of eating, the veins of his forehead swelled, and generally a strong perspiration was visible. To those whose sensations were delicate, this could not but be disgusting; and it was doubtless not very suitable to the character of a philosopher, who should be distinguished by self-command. But it must be owned that Johnson, though he could be rigidly *abstemious*, was not a *temperate* man either in eating or drinking. He could refrain, but he could not use moderately. He told me that he had fasted two days without inconvenience, and that he had never been hungry but once. They who beheld with wonder how much he eat upon all occasions when his dinner was to his taste, could not easily conceive what he must have meant by hunger; and not only was he remarkable for the extraordinary quantity which he eat, but he was, or affected to be, a man of very nice discernment in the science of cookery. * * *

[1767] In February, 1767, there happened one of the most remarkable incidents of Johnson's life, which gratified his monarchical enthusiasm, and which he loved to relate with all its circumstances, when requested by his friends. This was his being honored by a private conversation with his Majesty, in the library at the Queen's house. He had frequently visited those splendid rooms and noble collection of books, which he used to say was more numerous and curious than he supposed any person could have made in the time which the King had employed. Mr. Barnard,

1. I.e., John Bull (the typical hard-headed Englishman) in the role of philosopher.
2. Greediness.

the librarian, took care that he should have every accommodation that could contribute to his ease and convenience, while indulging his literary taste in that place; so that he had here a very agreeable resource at leisure hours.

His Majesty having been informed of his occasional visits, was pleased to signify a desire that he should be told when Dr. Johnson came next to the library. Accordingly, the next time that Johnson did come, as soon as he was fairly engaged with a book, on which, while he sat by the fire, he seemed quite intent, Mr Barnard stole round to the apartment where the King was, and, in obedience to his Majesty's commands, mentioned that Dr. Johnson was then in the library. His Majesty said he was at leisure, and would go to him; upon which Mr. Barnard took one of the candles that stood on the King's table, and lighted his Majesty through a suite of rooms, till they came to a private door into the library, of which his Majesty had the key. Being entered, Mr. Barnard stepped forward hastily to Dr. Johnson, who was still in a profound study, and whispered him, "Sir, here is the King." Johnson started up, and stood still. His Majesty approached him, and at once was courteously easy.

His Majesty began by observing that he understood he came sometimes to the library; and then mentioning his having heard that the Doctor had been lately at Oxford, asked him if he was not fond of going thither. To which Johnson answered that he was indeed fond of going to Oxford sometimes, but was likewise glad to come back again. The King then asked him what they were doing at Oxford. Johnson answered, he could not much commend their diligence, but that in some respects they were mended, for they had put their press under better regulations, and were at that time printing Polybius. He was then asked whether there were better libraries at Oxford or Cambridge. He answered, he believed the Bodleian was larger than any they had at Cambridge; at the same time adding, "I hope, whether we have more books or not than they have at Cambridge, we shall make as good use of them as they do." Being asked whether All Souls or Christ Church library was the largest, he answered, "All Souls library is the largest we have, except the Bodleian." "Aye," said the King, "that is the public library."

His Majesty inquired if he was then writing anything. He answered, he was not, for he had pretty well told the world what he knew, and must now read to acquire more knowledge. The King, as it should seem with a view to urge him to rely on his own stores as an original writer, and to continue his labors, then said "I do not think you borrow much from anybody." Johnson said he thought he had already done his part as a writer. "I should have thought so too," said the King, "if you had not written so well."—

Johnson observed to me, upon this, that "No man could have paid a handsomer compliment; and it was fit for a king to pay. It was decisive." When asked by another friend, at Sir Joshua Reynolds's, whether he made any reply to this high compliment, he answered, "No, Sir. When the King had said it, it was to be so. It was not for me to bandy civilities with my sovereign." Perhaps no man who had spent his whole life in courts could have shown a more nice and dignified sense of true politeness than Johnson did in this instance. * * *

[Fear of Death]

[1769] When we were alone, I introduced the subject of death, and endeavored to maintain that the fear of it might be got over. I told him that David Hume said to me, he was no more uneasy to think he should *not be* after this life, than that he *had not been* before he began to exist. JOHNSON. "Sir, if he really thinks so, his perceptions are disturbed; he is mad: if he does not think so, he lies. He may tell you, he holds his finger in the flame of a candle, without feeling pain; would you believe him? When he dies, he at least gives up all he has." BOSWELL. "Foote,[3] Sir, told me, that when he was very ill he was not afraid to die." JOHNSON. "It is not true, Sir. Hold a pistol to Foote's breast, or to Hume's breast, and threaten to kill them, and you'll see how they behave." BOSWELL. "But may we not fortify our minds for the approach of death?" Here I am sensible I was in the wrong, to bring before his view what he ever looked upon with horror; for although when in a celestial frame, in his *Vanity of Human Wishes,* he has supposed death to be "kind Nature's signal for retreat," from this state of being to "a happier seat," his thoughts upon this awful change were in general full of dismal apprehensions. His mind resembled the vast amphitheater, the Colosseum at Rome. In the center stood his judgment, which, like a mighty gladiator, combated those apprehensions that, like the wild beasts of the arena, were all around in cells, ready to be let out upon him. After a conflict, he drives them back into their dens; but not killing them, they were still assailing him. To my question, whether we might not fortify our minds for the approach of death, he answered, in a passion, "No, Sir, let it alone. It matters not how a man dies, but how he lives. The act of dying is not of importance, it lasts so short a time." He added (with an earnest look), "A man knows it must be so, and submits. It will do him no good to whine."

I attempted to continue the conversation. He was so provoked that he said, "Give us no more of this"; and was thrown into such a state of agitation that he expressed himself in a way that alarmed

3. Samuel Foote, actor and dramatist, famous for his wit and his skill in mimicry.

and distressed me; showed an impatience that I should leave him, and when I was going away, called to me sternly, "Don't let us meet tomorrow." * * *

[*Ossian. "Talking for Victory"*]

MR. BOSWELL TO DR. JOHNSON

Edinburgh, Feb. 2, 1775.

* * * As to Macpherson, I am anxious to have from yourself a full and pointed account of what has passed between you and him. It is confidently told here that before your book[4] came out he sent to you, to let you know that he understood you meant to deny the authenticity of Ossian's poems; that the originals were in his possession; that you might have inspection of them, and might take the evidence of people skilled in the Erse language; and that he hoped, after this fair offer, you would not be so uncandid as to assert that he had refused reasonable proof. That you paid no regard to his message, but published your strong attack upon him; and then he wrote a letter to you, in such terms as he thought suited to one who had not acted as a man of veracity. * * *

What words were used by Mr. Macpherson in his letter to the venerable sage, I have never heard; but they are generally said to have been of a nature very different from the language of literary contest. Dr. Johnson's answer appeared in the newspapers of the day, and has since been frequently republished; but not with perfect accuracy. I give it as dictated to me by himself, written down in his presence, and authenticated by a note in his own handwriting, "*This, I think, is a true copy.*"

MR. JAMES MACPHERSON,

I received your foolish and impudent letter. Any violence offered me I shall do my best to repel; and what I cannot do for myself, the law shall do for me. I hope I shall never be deterred from detecting what I think a cheat, by the menaces of a ruffian.

What would you have me retract? I thought your book an imposture; I think it an imposture still. For this opinion I have given my reasons to the public, which I here dare you to refute. Your rage I defy. Your abilities, since your Homer, are not so formidable; and what I hear of your morals inclines me to pay regard not to what you shall say, but to what you shall prove. You may print this if you will.

SAM. JOHNSON.

Mr. Macpherson little knew the character of Dr. Johnson if he supposed that he could be easily intimidated; for no man was ever more remarkable for personal courage. He had, indeed, an awful dread of death, or rather, "of something after death"; and what rational man, who seriously thinks of quitting all that he has ever

4. Johnson's *Journey to the Western Islands* (1775), in which he had pub- licly expressed his views on the Os- sianic poems.

known, and going into a new and unknown state of being, can be without that dread? But his fear was from reflection; his courage natural. His fear, in that one instance, was the result of philosophical and religious consideration. He feared death, but he feared nothing else, not even what might occasion death. Many instances of his resolution may be mentioned. One day, at Mr. Beauclerk's house in the country, when two large dogs were fighting, he went up to them, and beat them till they separated; and at another time, when told of the danger there was that a gun might burst if charged with many balls, he put in six or seven, and fired it off against a wall. Mr. Langton told me that when they were swimming together near Oxford, he cautioned Dr. Johnson against a pool which was reckoned particularly dangerous; upon which Johnson directly swam into it. He told me himself that one night he was attacked in the street by four men, to whom he would not yield, but kept them all at bay, till the watch came up, and carried both him and them to the roundhouse. In the playhouse at Lichfield, as Mr. Garrick informed me, Johnson having for a moment quitted a chair which was placed for him between the side-scenes, a gentleman took possession of it, and when Johnson on his return civilly demanded his seat, rudely refused to give it up; upon which Johnson laid hold of it, and tossed him and the chair into the pit. Foote, who so successfully revived the old comedy, by exhibiting living characters, had resolved to imitate Johnson on the stage, expecting great profits from his ridicule of so celebrated a man. Johnson being informed of his intention, and being at dinner at Mr. Thomas Davies's the bookseller, from whom I had the story, he asked Mr. Davies what was the common price of an oak stick; and being answered sixpence, "Why then, Sir," said he, "give me leave to send your servant to purchase me a shilling one. I'll have a double quantity; for I am told Foote means to *take me off*, as he calls it, and I am determined the fellow shall not do it with impunity." Davies took care to acquaint Foote of this, which effectually checked the wantonness of the mimic. Mr. Macpherson's menaces made Johnson provide himself with the same implement of defense; and had he been attacked, I have no doubt that, old as he was, he would have made his corporal prowess be felt as much as his intellectual. * * *

[1776] I mentioned a new gaming club, of which Mr. Beauclerk had given me an account, where the members played to a desperate extent. JOHNSON. "Depend upon it, Sir, this is mere talk. Who is ruined by gaming? You will not find six instances in an age. There is a strange rout made about deep play: whereas you have many more people ruined by adventurous trade, and yet we do not hear such an outcry against it." THRALE.[5] "There may be few people

---

5. Johnson met Henry Thrale, the wealthy brewer, and his charming wife   Hester in 1765. Thereafter he was domesticated as much as he wished to be

absolutely ruined by deep play; but very many are much hurt in their circumstances by it." JOHNSON. "Yes, Sir, and so are very many by other kinds of expense." I had heard him talk once before in the same manner; and at Oxford he said, he wished he had learnt to play at cards. The truth, however, is that he loved to display his ingenuity in argument; and therefore would sometimes in conversation maintain opinions which he was sensible were wrong, but in supporting which, his reasoning and wit would be most conspicuous. He would begin thus: "Why, Sir, as to the good or evil of card playing——" "Now, said Garrick, "he is thinking which side he shall take." He appeared to have a pleasure in contradiction, especially when any opinion whatever was delivered with an air of confidence; so that there was hardly any topic, if not one of the great truths of religion and morality, that he might not have been incited to argue, either for or against. Lord Elibank[6] had the highest admiration of his powers. He once observed to me, "Whatever opinion Johnson maintains, I will not say that he convinces me; but he never fails to show me that he has good reasons for it." I have heard Johnson pay his Lordship this high compliment: "I never was in Lord Elibank's company without learning something." * * *

[Dinner with Wilkes]

My worthy booksellers and friends, Messieurs Dilly in the Poultry, at whose hospitable and well-covered table I have seen a greater number of literary men than at any other, except that of Sir Joshua Reynolds, had invited me to meet Mr. Wilkes[7] and some more gentlemen on Wednesday, May 15. "Pray," said I, "let us have Dr. Johnson."—"What, with Mr. Wilkes? not for the world," said Mr. Edward Dilly, "Dr. Johnson would never forgive me."—"Come," said I, "if you'll let me negotiate for you, I will be answerable that all shall go well." DILLY. "Nay, if you will take it upon you, I am sure I shall be very happy to see them both here."

Notwithstanding the high veneration which I entertained for Dr. Johnson, I was sensible that he was sometimes a little actuated by the spirit of contradiction, and by means of that I hoped I

at their house at Streatham near London. There he enjoyed the good things of life, as well as the companionship of Mrs. Thrale and her children. Thrale died in 1781. His widow's marriage to Gabriel Piozzi, an Italian musician, in 1784, caused Johnson to quarrel with her and darkened the last months of his life.

6. Prominent in Scottish literary circles. Johnson, who admired him, had visited him on his tour of Scotland with Boswell in 1773.

7. John Wilkes (1727–97) was obnoxious to the Christian and Tory Johnson in every way. He was profane and dissolute, and his personal life was a public scandal; for over a decade he had been notorious as a courageous, resourceful, and finally victorious opponent of the arbitrary and tyrannical policies of the king and his ministers, and had been the envenomed critic of Lord Bute, to whom Johnson owed his pension. When Johnson met him he had totally defeated his enemies, had served as Lord Mayor, and was again a Member of Parliament, a post from which he had been expelled and driven into exile as an outlaw in 1764. Boswell had found Wilkes a gay and congenial companion in Italy in 1764.

should gain my point. I was persuaded that if I had come upon him with a direct proposal, "Sir, will you dine in company with Jack Wilkes?" he would have flown into a passion, and would probably have answered, "Dine with Jack Wilkes, Sir! I'd as soon dine with Jack Ketch."[8] I therefore, while we were sitting quietly by ourselves at his house in an evening, took occasion to open my plan thus: "Mr. Dilly, Sir, sends his respectful compliments to you, and would be happy if you would do him the honor to dine with him on Wednesday next along with me, as I must soon go to Scotland." JOHNSON. "Sir, I am obliged to Mr. Dilly. I will wait upon him—" BOSWELL. "Provided, Sir, I suppose, that the company which he is to have, is agreeable to you." JOHNSON. "What do you mean, Sir? What do you take me for? Do you think I am so ignorant of the world as to imagine that I am to prescribe to a gentleman what company he is to have at his table?" BOSWELL. "I beg your pardon, Sir, for wishing to prevent you from meeting people whom you might not like. Perhaps he may have some of what he calls his patriotic[9] friends with him." JOHNSON. "Well, Sir, and what then? What care *I* for his *patriotic friends?* Poh!" BOSWELL. "I should not be surprised to find Jack Wilkes there." JOHNSON. "And if Jack Wilkes *should* be there, what is that to *me*, Sir? My dear friend, let us have no more of this. I am sorry to be angry with you; but really it is treating me strangely to talk to me as if I could not meet any company whatever, occasionally." BOSWELL. "Pray forgive me, Sir: I meant well. But you shall meet whoever comes, for me." Thus I secured him, and told Dilly that he would find him very well pleased to be one of his guests on the day appointed.

Upon the much-expected Wednesday, I called on him about half an hour before dinner, as I often did when we were to dine out together, to see that he was ready in time, and to accompany him. I found him buffeting his books, as upon a former occasion, covered with dust, and making no preparation for going abroad. "How is this, Sir?" said I. "Don't you recollect that you are to dine at Mr. Dilly's?" JOHNSON. "Sir, I did not think of going to Dilly's: it went out of my head. I have ordered dinner at home with Mrs. Williams." BOSWELL. "But, my dear Sir, you know you were engaged to Mr. Dilly, and I told him so. He will expect you, and will be much disappointed if you don't come." JOHNSON. "You must talk to Mrs. Williams about this."

Here was a sad dilemma. I feared that what I was so confident I had secured would yet be frustrated. He had accustomed himself

---

8. After the public hangman, Jack Ketch, died in 1686, his name became the common designation of all those who filled that office.
9. In Tory circles the word had come to be used ironically of those who op-posed the government. The "patriots" considered themselves the defenders of the ancient liberties of the English. They included the partisans of both Wilkes and of the American colonists.

to show Mrs. Williams such a degree of humane attention as frequently imposed some restraint upon him; and I knew that if she should be obstinate, he would not stir. I hastened downstairs to the blind lady's room, and told her I was in great uneasiness, for Dr. Johnson had engaged to me to dine this day at Mr. Dilly's, but that he had told me he had forgotten his engagement, and had ordered dinner at home. "Yes, Sir," said she, pretty peevishly, "Dr. Johnson is to dine at home."—"Madam," said I, "his respect for you is such that I know he will not leave you unless you absolutely desire it. But as you have so much of his company, I hope you will be good enough to forego it for a day; as Mr. Dilly is a very worthy man, has frequently had agreeable parties at his house for Dr. Johnson, and will be vexed if the Doctor neglects him today. And then, Madam, be pleased to consider my situation; I carried the message, and I assured Mr. Dilly that Dr. Johnson was to come, and no doubt he has made a dinner, and invited a company, and boasted of the honor he expected to have. I shall be quite disgraced if the Doctor is not there." She gradually softened to my solicitations, which were certainly as earnest as most entreaties to ladies upon any occasion, and was graciously pleased to empower me to tell Dr. Johnson that all things considered, she thought he should certainly go. I flew back to him, still in dust, and careless of what should be the event, "indifferent in his choice to go or stay";[1] but as soon as I had announced to him Mrs. Williams' consent, he roared, "Frank, a clean shirt," and was very soon dressed. When I had him fairly seated in a hackney coach with me, I exulted as much as a fortune hunter who has got an heiress into a post chaise with him to set out for Gretna Green.[2]

When we entered Mr. Dilly's drawing room, he found himself in the midst of a company he did not know. I kept myself snug and silent, watching how he would conduct himself. I observed him whispering to Mr. Dilly, "Who is that gentleman, Sir?"— "Mr. Arthur Lee."—JOHNSON. "Too, too, too" (under his breath), which was one of his habitual mutterings. Mr. Arthur Lee could not but be very obnoxious to Johnson, for he was not only a *patriot* but an *American*.[3] He was afterwards minister from the United States at the court of Madrid. "And who is the gentleman in lace?" —"Mr. Wilkes, Sir." This information confounded him still more; he had some difficulty to restrain himself, and taking up a book, sat down upon a window seat and read, or at least kept his eye upon it intently for some time, till he composed himself. His feel-

1. Addison's *Cato* V.i.40. Boswell cleverly adapts to his own purpose Cato's words, "Indifferent in his choice to sleep or die."
2. A village just across the Scottish border where runaway couples were married by the local innkeeper or the blacksmith.

3. Johnson was extremely hostile to the rebelling American colonists. On one occasion he said: "I am willing to love all mankind, except an American." Lee had been educated in England and Scotland, and had recently been admitted to the English bar. He had been a loyal supporter of Wilkes.

ings, I dare say, were awkward enough. But he no doubt recollected
his having rated me for supposing that he could be at all disconcerted by any company, and he, therefore, resolutely set himself
to behave quite as an easy man of the world, who could adapt himself at once to the disposition and manners of those whom he
might chance to meet.

The cheering sound of "Dinner is upon the table," dissolved
his reverie, and we *all* sat down without any symptom of ill humor.
There were present, beside Mr. Wilkes, and Mr. Arthur Lee, who
was an old companion of mine when he studied physic at Edinburgh, Mr. (now Sir John) Miller, Dr. Lettsom, and Mr. Slater
the druggist. Mr. Wilkes placed himself next to Dr. Johnson, and
behaved to him with so much attention and politeness that he
gained upon him insensibly. No man eat more heartily than Johnson, or loved better what was nice and delicate. Mr. Wilkes was
very assiduous in helping him to some fine veal. "Pray give me
leave, Sir—It is better here—A little of the brown—Some fat,
Sir—A little of the stuffing—Some gravy—Let me have the pleasure of giving you some butter—Allow me to recommend a squeeze
of this orange—or the lemon, perhaps, may have more zest."—
"Sir, Sir, I am obliged to you, Sir," cried Johnson, bowing, and
turning his head to him with a look for some time of "surly virtue,"
but, in a short while, of complacency.

Foote being mentioned, Johnson said, "He is not a good mimic."
One of the company added, "A merry Andrew, a buffoon." JOHN-
SON. "But he has wit too, and is not deficient in ideas, or in fertility and variety of imagery, and not empty of reading; he has knowledge enough to fill up his part. One species of wit he has in an
eminent degree, that of escape. You drive him into a corner with
both hands; but he's gone, Sir, when you think you have got him
—like an animal that jumps over your head. Then he has a great
range for wit; he never lets truth stand between him and a jest,
and he is sometimes mighty coarse. Garrick is under many restraints
from which Foote is free." WILKES. "Garrick's wit is more like
Lord Chesterfield's." JOHNSON. "The first time I was in company
with Foote was at Fitzherbert's. Having no good opinion of the
fellow, I was resolved not to be pleased; and it is very difficult to
please a man against his will. I went on eating my dinner pretty
sullenly, affecting not to mind him. But the dog was so very comical, that I was obliged to lay down my knife and fork, throw myself back upon my chair, and fairly laugh it out. No, Sir, he was
irresistible. He upon one occasion experienced, in an extraordinary
degree, the efficacy of his powers of entertaining. Amongst the many
and various modes which he tried of getting money, he became a
partner with a small-beer[4] brewer, and he was to have a share of

4. Weak beer, served in the servants' hall.

the profits for procuring customers amongst his numerous acquaintance. Fitzherbert was one who took his small beer; but it was so bad that the servants resolved not to drink it. They were at some loss how to notify their resolution, being afraid of offending their master, who they knew liked Foote much as a companion. At last they fixed upon a little black boy, who was rather a favorite, to be their deputy, and deliver their remonstrance; and having invested him with the whole authority of the kitchen, he was to inform Mr. Fitzherbert, in all their names, upon a certain day, that they would drink Foote's small beer no longer. On that day Foote happened to dine at Fitzherbert's, and this boy served at table; he was so delighted with Foote's stories, and merriment, and grimace, that when he went downstairs, he told them, 'This is the finest man I have ever seen. I will not deliver your message. I will drink his small beer.' "

Somebody observed that Garrick could not have done this. WILKES. "Garrick would have made the small beer still smaller. He is now leaving the stage; but he will play *Scrub*[5] all his life." I knew that Johnson would let nobody attack Garrick but himself, as Garrick once said to me, and I had heard him praise his liberality; so to bring out his commendation of his celebrated pupil, I said, loudly, "I have heard Garrick is liberal." JOHNSON. "Yes, Sir, I know that Garrick has given away more money than any man in England that I am acquainted with, and that not from ostentatious views. Garrick was very poor when he began life; so when he came to have money, he probably was very unskillful in giving away, and saved when he should not. But Garrick began to be liberal as soon as he could; and I am of opinion, the reputation of avarice which he has had, has been very lucky for him, and prevented his having many enemies. You despise a man for avarice, but do not hate him. Garrick might have been much better attacked for living with more splendor than is suitable to a player: if they had had the wit to have assaulted him in that quarter, they might have galled him more. But they have kept clamoring about his avarice, which has rescued him from much obloquy and envy."

Talking of the great difficulty of obtaining authentic information for biography, Johnson told us, "When I was a young fellow I wanted to write the *Life of Dryden*, and in order to get materials, I applied to the only two persons then alive who had seen him; these were old Swinney,[6] and old Cibber. Swinney's information was no more than this, that at Will's Coffeehouse Dryden had a particular chair for himself, which was set by the fire in winter, and was then called his winter chair; and that it was carried out for him to the balcony in summer, and was then called his summer

5. The servant of Squire Sullen in George Farquhar's *Beaux' Stratagem*: a favorite role of Garrick's.
6. Owen Mac Swinney, a playwright.

chair. Cibber could tell no more but that he remembered him a decent old man, arbiter of critical disputes at Will's. You are to consider that Cibber was then at a great distance from Dryden, had perhaps one leg only in the room, and durst not draw in the other." BOSWELL. "Yet Cibber was a man of observation?" JOHNSON. "I think not." BOSWELL. "You will allow his *Apology* to be well done." JOHNSON. "Very well done, to be sure, Sir. That book is a striking proof of the justice of Pope's remark:

> Each might his several province well command,
> Would all but stoop to what they understand."[7]

BOSWELL. "And his plays are good." JOHNSON. "Yes; but that was his trade; *l'esprit du corps:* he had been all his life among players and play writers. I wondered that he had so little to say in conversation, for he had kept the best company, and learnt all that can be got by the ear. He abused Pindar to me, and then showed me an ode of his own, with an absurd couplet, making a linnet soar on an eagle's wing. I told him that when the ancients made a simile, they always made it like something real."

Mr. Wilkes remarked that "among all the bold flights of Shakespeare's imagination, the boldest was making Birnam Wood march to Dunsinane;[8] creating a wood where there never was a shrub; a wood in Scotland! ha! ha! ha!" And he also observed, that "the clannish slavery of the Highlands of Scotland was the single exception to Milton's remark of 'The mountain nymph, sweet Liberty,'[9] being worshiped in all hilly countries."—"When I was at Inverary," said he, "on a visit to my old friend, Archibald, Duke of Argyle, his dependents congratulated me on being such a favorite of his Grace. I said, 'It is then, gentlemen, truly lucky for me; for if I had displeased the Duke, and he had wished it, there is not a Campbell among you but would have been ready to bring John Wilkes's head to him in a charger. It would have been only

Off with his head! So much for Aylesbury.'[1]

I was then member for Aylesbury." * * *

Mr. Arthur Lee mentioned some Scotch who had taken possession of a barren part of America, and wondered why they should choose it. JOHNSON. "Why, Sir, all barrenness is comparative. The *Scotch* would not know it to be barren." BOSWELL. "Come, come, he is flattering the English. You have now been in Scotland, Sir, and say if you did not see meat and drink enough there." JOHNSON. "Why yes, Sir; meat and drink enough to give the inhabitants sufficient strength to run away from home." All these quick and lively sallies were said sportively, quite in jest, and with a smile, which

7. *Essay on Criticism* I.66–67.
8. *Macbeth* V.v.30–52.
9. *L'Allegro,* line 36.

1. "Off with his head! So much for Buckingham." A line in Cibber's version of Shakespeare's *Richard III.*

showed that he meant only wit. Upon this topic he and Mr. Wilkes could perfectly assimilate; here was a bond of union between them, and I was conscious that as both of them had visited Caledonia, both were fully satisfied of the strange narrow ignorance of those who imagine that it is a land of famine. But they amused themselves with persevering in the old jokes. When I claimed a superiority for Scotland over England in one respect, that no man can be arrested there for a debt merely because another swears it against him; but there must first be the judgment of a court of law ascertaining its justice; and that a seizure of the person, before judgment is obtained, can take place only if his creditor should swear that he is about to fly from the country, or, as it is technically expressed, is *in meditatione fugae:* WILKES. "That, I should think, may be safely sworn of all the Scotch nation." JOHNSON (to Mr. Wilkes). "You must know, Sir, I lately took my friend Boswell and showed him genuine civilized life in an English provincial town. I turned him loose at Lichfield, my native city, that he might see for once real civility: for you know he lives among savages in Scotland, and among rakes in London." WILKES. "Except when he is with grave, sober, decent people like you and me." JOHNSON (smiling). "And we ashamed of him."

They were quite frank and easy. Johnson told the story of his asking Mrs. Macaulay to allow her footman to sit down with them, to prove the ridiculousness of the argument for the equality of mankind; and he said to me afterwards, with a nod of satisfaction, "You saw Mr. Wilkes acquiesced." * * *

This record, though by no means so perfect as I could wish, will serve to give a notion of a very curious interview, which was not only pleasing at the time, but had the agreeable and benignant effect of reconciling any animosity and sweetening any acidity, which in the various bustle of political contest, had been produced in the minds of two men, who, though widely different, had so many things in common—classical learning, modern literature, wit, and humor, and ready repartee—that it would have been much to be regretted if they had been forever at a distance from each other.

Mr. Burke gave me much credit for this successful "negotiation"; and pleasantly said that there was nothing to equal it in the whole history of the *Corps Diplomatique.* * * *

[Dread of Solitude]

[1777] I talked to him of misery being "the doom of man" in this life, as displayed in his *Vanity of Human Wishes.* Yet I observed that things were done upon the supposition of happiness; grand houses were built, fine gardens were made, splendid places of public amusement were contrived, and crowded with company. JOHNSON. "Alas, Sir, these are all only struggles for happiness. When

I first entered Ranelagh,[2] it gave an expansion and gay sensation to my mind, such as I never experienced anywhere else. But, as Xerxes wept when he viewed his immense army, and considered that not one of that great multitude would be alive a hundred years afterwards, so it went to my heart to consider that there was not one in all that brilliant circle that was not afraid to go home and think; but that the thoughts of each individual there, would be distressing when alone." * * *

["A Bottom of Good Sense." Bet Flint.
"Clear Your Mind of Cant"]

[1781] Talking of a very respectable author, he told us a curious circumstance in his life, which was that he had married a printer's devil.[3] REYNOLDS. "A printer's devil, Sir! Why, I thought a printer's devil was a creature with a black face and in rags." JOHNSON. "Yes, Sir. But I suppose, he had her face washed, and put clean clothes on her." Then looking very serious, and very earnest: "And she did not disgrace him; the woman had a bottom of good sense." The word *bottom* thus introduced was so ludicrous when contrasted with his gravity, that most of us could not forbear tittering and laughing; though I recollect that the Bishop of Killaloe kept his countenance with perfect steadiness, while Miss Hannah More[4] slyly hid her face behind a lady's back who sat on the same settee with her. His pride could not bear that any expression of his should excite ridicule, when he did not intend it; he therefore resolved to assume and exercise despotic power, glanced sternly around, and called out in a strong tone, "Where's the merriment?" Then collecting himself, and looking awful, to make us feel how he could impose restraint, and as it were searching his mind for a still more ludicrous word, he slowly pronounced, "I say the *woman* was *fundamentally* sensible"; as if he had said, "hear this now, and laugh if you dare." We all sat composed as at a funeral. * * *

He gave us an entertaining account of Bet Flint, a woman of the town, who, with some eccentric talents and much effrontery, forced herself upon his acquaintance. "Bet," said he, "wrote her own Life in verse, which she brought to me, wishing that I would furnish her with a Preface to it" (laughing). "I used to say of her that she was generally slut and drunkard; occasionally, whore and thief. She had, however, genteel lodgings, a spinnet on which she played, and a boy that walked before her chair. Poor Bet was taken up on a charge of stealing a counterpane, and tried at the Old Bailey. Chief Justice ———, who loved a wench, summed up favorably, and she was acquitted. After which Bet said, with a gay and

2. Pleasure gardens in Chelsea, where concerts were held, fireworks displayed, food and drink sold.
3. Apprentice in a print shop.

4. Hannah More (1745–1833), blue-stocking and religious writer, one of the promoters of the Sunday School movement.

satisfied air, 'Now that the counterpane is *my own*, I shall make a petticoat of it.' " * * *

[1783] I have no minute of any interview with Johnson till Thursday, May 15, when I find what follows: BOSWELL. "I wish much to be in Parliament, Sir." JOHNSON. "Why, Sir, unless you come resolved to support any administration, you would be the worse for being in Parliament, because you would be obliged to live more expensively." BOSWELL. "Perhaps, Sir, I should be the less happy for being in Parliament. I never would sell my vote, and I should be vexed if things went wrong." JOHNSON. "That's cant,[5] Sir. It would not vex you more in the house than in the gallery: public affairs vex no man." BOSWELL. "Have not they vexed yourself a little, Sir? Have not you been vexed by all the turbulence of this reign, and by that absurd vote of the House of Commons, 'That the influence of the Crown has increased, is increasing, and ought to be diminished?' " JOHNSON. "Sir, I have never slept an hour less, nor eat an ounce less meat. I would have knocked the factious dogs on the head, to be sure; but I was not *vexed*." BOSWELL. "I declare, Sir, upon my honor, I did imagine I was vexed, and took a pride in it; but it *was*, perhaps, cant; for I own I neither ate less, nor slept less." JOHNSON. "My dear friend, clear your *mind* of cant. You may *talk* as other people do: you may say to a man, 'Sir, I am your most humble servant.' You are *not* his most humble servant. You may say, 'These are bad times; it is a melancholy thing to be reserved to such times.' You don't mind the times. You tell a man, 'I am sorry you had such bad weather the last day of your journey, and were so much wet.' You don't care sixpence whether he is wet or dry. You may *talk* in this manner; it is a mode of talking in society: but don't *think* foolishly." * * *

[Johnson Prepares for Death]

My anxious apprehensions at parting with him this year proved to be but too well founded; for not long afterwards he had a dreadful stroke of the palsy, of which there are very full and accurate accounts in letters written by himself, to show with what composure of mind, and resignation to the Divine Will, his steady piety enabled him to behave. * * *

Two days after he wrote thus to Mrs. Thrale:

"On Monday, the 16th, I sat for my picture, and walked a considerable way with little inconvenience. In the afternoon and evening I felt myself light and easy, and began to plan schemes of life. Thus I went to bed, and in a short time waked and sat up, as has been long my custom, when I felt a confusion and indistinctness in my head, which lasted, I suppose, about half a minute. I was alarmed,

5. "A whining pretension to goodness in formal and affected terms" (Johnson's *Dictionary*).

and prayed God that however he might afflict my body, he would spare my understanding. This prayer, that I might try the integrity of my faculties, I made in Latin verse. The lines were not very good, but I knew them not to be very good: I made them easily, and concluded myself to be unimpaired in my faculties.

"Soon after I perceived that I had suffered a paralytic stroke, and that my speech was taken from me. I had no pain, and so little dejection in this dreadful state, that I wondered at my own apathy, and considered that perhaps death itself, when it should come, would excite less horror than seems now to attend it.

"In order to rouse the vocal organs, I took two drams. Wine has been celebrated for the production of eloquence. I put myself into violent motion, and I think repeated it; but all was vain. I then went to bed and strange as it may seem, I think slept. When I saw light, it was time to contrive what I should do. Though God stopped my speech, he left me my hand; I enjoyed a mercy which was not granted to my dear friend Lawrence,[6] who now perhaps overlooks me as I am writing, and rejoices that I have what he wanted. My first note was necessarily to my servant, who came in talking, and could not immediately comprehend why he should read what I put into his hands.

"I then wrote a card to Mr. Allen,[7] that I might have a discreet friend at hand, to act as occasion should require. In penning this note, I had some difficulty; my hand, I knew not how nor why, made wrong letters. I then wrote to Dr. Taylor to come to me, and bring Dr. Heberden; and I sent to Dr. Brocklesby, who is my neighbor.[8] My physicians are very friendly, and give me great hopes; but you may imagine my situation. I have so far recovered my vocal powers as to repeat the Lord's Prayer with no very imperfect articulation. My memory, I hope, yet remains as it was; but such an attack produces solicitude for the safety of every faculty." * * *

[1784] To Mr. Henry White, a young clergyman, with whom he now formed an intimacy, so as to talk to him with great freedom, he mentioned that he could not in general accuse himself of having been an undutiful son. "Once, indeed," said he, "I was disobedient; I refused to attend my father to Uttoxeter market. Pride was the source of that refusal, and the remembrance of it was painful. A few years ago, I desired to atone for this fault; I went to Uttoxeter in very bad weather, and stood for a considerable time bareheaded in the rain, on the spot where my father's stall used to stand. In contrition I stood, and I hope the penance was expiatory."

"I told him," says Miss Seward,[9] "in one of my latest visits to him, of a wonderful learned pig, which I had seen at Nottingham; and which did all that we have observed exhibited by dogs

6. Dr. Thomas Lawrence, president of the Royal College of Physicians and Johnson's own doctor, had died paralyzed shortly before this was written.
7. Edmund Allen, a printer, Johnson's landlord and neighbor.
8. These two physicians attended Johnson on his deathbed.
9. Anna Seward, "the Swan of Lichfield," a poet.

and horses. The subject amused him. 'Then,' said he, 'the pigs are a race unjustly calumniated. *Pig* has, it seems, not been wanting to *man*, but *man* to *pig*. We do not allow *time* for his education, we kill him at a year old.' Mr. Henry White, who was present, observed that if this instance had happened in or before Pope's time, he would not have been justified in instancing the swine as the lowest degree of groveling instinct.[1] Dr. Johnson seemed pleased with the observation, while the person who made it proceeded to remark that great torture must have been employed, ere the indocility of the animal could have been subdued. 'Certainly,' said the Doctor; 'but,' turning to me, 'how old is your pig?' I told him, three years old. 'Then,' said he, 'the pig has no cause to complain; he would have been killed the first year if he had not been *educated*, and protracted existence is a good recompense for very considerable degrees of torture.' "

[Johnson Faces Death]

As Johnson had now very faint hopes of recovery, and as Mrs. Thrale was no longer devoted to him, it might have been supposed that he would naturally have chosen to remain in the comfortable house of his beloved wife's daughter,[2] and end his life where he began it. But there was in him an animated and lofty spirit, and however complicated diseases might depress ordinary mortals, all who saw him, beheld and acknowledged the *invictum animum Catonis*.[3] Such was his intellectual ardor even at this time that he said to one friend, "Sir, I look upon every day to be lost, in which I do not make a new acquaintance"; and to another, when talking of his illness, "I will be conquered; I will not capitulate." And such was his love of London, so high a relish had he of its magnificent extent, and variety of intellectual entertainment, that he languished when absent from it, his mind having become quite luxurious from the long habit of enjoying the metropolis; and, therefore, although at Lichfield, surrounded with friends, who loved and revered him, and for whom he had a very sincere affection, he still found that such conversation as London affords, could be found nowhere else. These feelings, joined, probably, to some flattering hopes of aid from the eminent physicians and surgeons in London, who kindly and generously attended him without accepting fees, made him resolve to return to the capital. * * * Death had always been to him an object of terror; so that, though by no means happy, he still clung to life with an eagerness at which many have wondered. At any time when he was ill, he was very much pleased to be told that he looked better. An ingenious mem-

1. *Essay on Man* I.221.
2. Lucy Porter.
3. "The unconquered soul of Cato."

An adaptation of a phrase in Horace's *Odes* II.i.24.

ber of the Eumelian Club[4] informs me that upon one occasion when he said to him that he saw health returning to his cheek, Johnson seized him by the hand and exclaimed, "Sir, you are one of the kindest friends I ever had." * * *

Dr. Heberden, Dr. Brocklesby, Dr. Warren, and Dr. Butter, physicians, generously attended him, without accepting any fees, as did Mr. Cruikshank, surgeon; and all that could be done from professional skill and ability was tried, to prolong a life so truly valuable. He himself, indeed, having, on account of his very bad constitution, been perpetually applying himself to medical inquiries, united his own efforts with those of the gentlemen who attended him; and imagining that the dropsical collection of water which oppressed him might be drawn off by making incisions in his body, he, with his usual resolute defiance of pain, cut deep, when he thought that his surgeon had done it too tenderly.

About eight or ten days before his death, when Dr. Brocklesby paid him his morning visit, he seemed very low and desponding, and said, "I have been as a dying man all night." He then emphatically broke out in the words of Shakespeare:

> "Canst thou not minister to a mind diseased;
> Pluck from the memory a rooted sorrow,
> Raze out the written troubles of the brain,
> And with some sweet oblivious antidote
> Cleanse the stuffed bosom of that perilous stuff
> Which weighs upon the heart?"

To which Dr. Brocklesby readily answered, from the same great poet:

> "Therein the patient
> Must minister to himself."[5]

Johnson expressed himself much satisfied with the application. * * *

Amidst the melancholy clouds which hung over the dying Johnson, his characteristical manner showed itself on different occasions.

When Dr. Warren, in the usual style, hoped that he was better; his answer was, "No, Sir; you cannot conceive with what acceleration I advance towards death."

A man whom he had never seen before was employed one night to sit up with him. Being asked next morning how he liked his attendant, his answer was, "Not at all, Sir: the fellow's an idiot; he is as awkward as a turnspit[6] when first put into the wheel, and as sleepy as a dormouse."

Mr. Windham[7] having placed a pillow conveniently to support

---

4. A club to which Boswell and Reynolds belonged.
5. *Macbeth* V.iii.40–46.
6. A dog kept to turn the roasting-spit by running within a tread-wheel con-

nected to it (*NED*).
7. William Windham, one of Johnson's younger friends, later a Member of Parliament.

him, he thanked him for his kindness, and said, "That will do—all that a pillow can do." * * *

Johnson, with that native fortitude, which, amidst all his bodily distress and mental sufferings, never forsook him, asked Dr. Brocklesby, as a man in whom he had confidence, to tell him plainly whether he could recover. "Give me," said he, "a direct answer." The Doctor having first asked him if he could bear the whole truth, which way soever it might lead, and being answered that he could, declared that, in his opinion, he could not recover without a miracle. "Then," said Johnson, "I will take no more physic, not even my opiates; for I have prayed that I may render up my soul to God unclouded." In this resolution he persevered, and, at the same time, used only the weakest kinds of sustenance. Being pressed by Mr. Windham to take somewhat more generous nourishment, lest too low a diet should have the very effect which he dreaded, by debilitating his mind, he said, "I will take anything but inebriating sustenance."

The Reverend Mr. Strahan,[8] who was the son of his friend, and had been always one of his great favorites, had, during his last illness, the satisfaction of contributing to soothe and comfort him. That gentleman's house, at Islington, of which he is Vicar, afforded Johnson, occasionally and easily, an agreeable change of place and fresh air; and he attended also upon him in town in the discharge of the sacred offices of his profession.

Mr. Strahan has given me the agreeable assurance that, after being in much agitation, Johnson became quite composed, and continued so till his death.

Dr. Brocklesby, who will not be suspected of fanaticism, obliged me with the following account:

"For some time before his death, all his fears were calmed and absorbed by the prevalence of his faith, and his trust in the merits and *propitiation* of Jesus Christ." * * *

Johnson having thus in his mind the true Christian scheme, at once rational and consolatory, uniting justice and mercy in the Divinity, with the improvement of human nature, previous to his receiving the Holy Sacrament in his apartment, composed and fervently uttered this prayer:

"Almighty and most merciful Father, I am now as to human eyes, it seems, about to commemorate, for the last time, the death of thy Son Jesus Christ, our Saviour and Redeemer. Grant, O Lord, that my whole hope and confidence may be in his merits, and thy mercy; enforce and accept my imperfect repentance; make this commemoration available to the confirmation of my faith, the establishment

8. The Rev. George Strahan (pronounced *Strawn*), who later published Johnson's *Prayers and Meditations*.

of my hope, and the enlargement of my charity; and make the death of thy Son Jesus Christ effectual to my redemption. Have mercy upon me, and pardon the multitude of my offenses. Bless my friends; have mercy upon all men. Support me, by thy Holy Spirit, in the days of weakness, and at the hour of death; and receive me, at my death, to everlasting happiness, for the sake of Jesus Christ. Amen."

Having * * * made his will on the 8th and 9th of December, and settled all his worldly affairs, he languished till Monday, the 13th of that month, when he expired, about seven o'clock in the evening, with so little apparent pain that his attendants hardly perceived when his dissolution took place. * * *

1791

EDMUND BURKE

(1729–1797)

1757:	*Enquiry into the Sublime and Beautiful*
1766:	Elected to Parliament.
1774–77:	Speeches on America.
1782–83:	Serves as Paymaster General.
1786:	Moves for the impeachment of Warren Hastings.
1790:	*Reflections on the Revolution in France*

Burke was born and educated in Dublin, the son of an Anglican father and Catholic mother, and came to London in 1750 to study law at the Middle Temple and make his fortune. But he was never admitted to the bar; instead he gained a reputation as a philosopher and a man of letters. A *Philosophical Enquiry into the Origin of our Ideas of the Sublime and Beautiful* (1757) is an important attempt to explain aesthetic ideas in terms of natural human responses; the sublime, for instance, is that which arouses feelings of terror in the mind and body. When Burke became a founding member of Johnson's famous Club in 1764, he was known as "the first man everywhere," a man who could succeed at any work he chose. Yet already he had begun to devote himself to politics, as secretary to William Hamilton in Ireland, and in 1765 he took a post as secretary to the premier, the Marquis of Rockingham. Shortly afterward he entered Parliament as a "Rockingham Whig," a liberal faction unpopular with the King. Here, for the next twenty-nine years, he served in the opposition—a perpetual opposition interrupted only for eight months, in 1782–83, when he was appointed Paymaster General. Aside from this interlude, Burke spent his talents in a career of politics without power, as a voice of protest and conscience directed not only against the Tory government but against his fellow Whigs.

What is unique about Burke's career, however, is not so much his combination of talents—the philosopher, the literary man, the politician—as his full use of them upon the great issues of his time. The events he witnessed have helped to shape our world: American independence and the birth of the United States, the French Revolution, the founding of Britain's vast colonial empire in the East. No one defined the meaning of these events more profoundly than Burke, or spoke more eloquently about them; the history of the man is a history of his age. But Burke also stands *against* his age; for most of the time he espoused the losing side. In his great speeches on *American Taxation* (1774) and *Conciliation with the Colonies* (1775), as well as his *Letter to the Sheriffs of Bristol* (1777), he spoke for understanding and reconciliation between Britain and America, but could not persuade others to avert the war. In tracts on the Irish question and Catholicism, he argued against the persecution of Irish Catholics that has poisoned relations between England and Ireland to the present day, but he encountered such prejudice that the voters of Bristol cast him out (in 1781 he was re-elected to Parliament from Malton). In a series of speeches on India, most notably the four-day speech opening the trial of Warren Hastings (1788), he pleaded for justice and responsibility in the administration of Britain's colonies, but after a trial of seven years Hastings was acquitted. Most bitter of all was Burke's resistance to the French Revolution, in a stream of impassioned works that includes *Reflections on the Revolution in France* (1790), *An Appeal from the New to the Old Whigs* (1791), *Thoughts on French Affairs* (1791), *Letter to a Noble Lord* (1795), and *Letters on a Regicide Peace* (1796). Despite his hatred of the revolutionaries, Burke sensed that the tide of history was running against him; and when he died, he arranged to keep his burial place secret, lest his corpse be desecrated. "I believe, in any body of men in England, I should have been in the Minority," he once said. "I have always been in the Minority." Yet many later generations have taken his side.

As a political thinker, Burke suggests that every statesman must be partly a visionary, partly a practical man of affairs. Tireless in research, he probably knew more about America and India than did any other man in England. But at the same time, like a poet, he tries to project his imagination beyond the particulars of things as they are, to envision the world as it once was, or as it might be. Thus he is known as a "conservative," who sees the essential continuity between the past and present, and as a "reformer," who preserves institutions by adapting them to meet changing circumstances. Yet such principles are never merely abstract for Burke; they are founded on a sense of history and a respect for concrete reality. Again and again he describes nations as living organisms, like an old oak tree or a family, that grow according to their own nature, not according to a program or theory. A wise statesman will accommodate himself to this nature. He will not, like the "metaphysicians" who inspired the French Revolution, destroy life in the hope of remaking men to his abstract ideal. But, of course, to understand things as they are does not mean to acquiesce in the *status quo*. It requires an active and penetrating intelligence, an intelligence that can confront complexity without oversimplification, and eternal change without despair. Such, for Burke, is the art of politics.

None of Burke's writings illustrates his grasp of fact and his imaginative scope better than his *Speech on Conciliation with the Colonies*. He had studied America in depth—his early *Account of European Settlements in America* (1757) is a standard authority—and his arguments draw on a full sense of the land itself, "Such as she was, such as she would become." The issue, he keeps insisting, is not some mythical America, an idea in the minds of Englishmen, but a country already existing, inhabited by real people with real interests. No solution will work unless it takes account of those realities. American strength, American liberty cannot be blotted out with the stroke of a pen; rather, they can be used to keep England strong and free. In the light of history, Burke's vision of America and his warning against war seem prophetic. Even more impressive than his specific analysis, however, is the example his speech provides of a political mind in action: a mind at once practical, generous, and creative.

From Speech on Conciliation with the Colonies[1]

The proposition is peace. Not peace through the medium of war; not peace to be hunted through the labyrinth of intricate and endless negotiations; not peace to arise out of universal discord, fomented from principle, in all parts of the empire; not peace to depend on the juridical determination of perplexing questions, or the precise marking the shadowy boundaries of a complex government. It is simple peace, sought in its natural course and in its ordinary haunts. It is peace sought in the spirit of peace, and laid in principles purely pacific. I propose, by removing the ground of the difference, and by restoring the *former unsuspecting confidence of the colonies in the mother country,*[2] to give permanent satisfaction to your people—and (far from a scheme of ruling by discord) to reconcile them to each other in the same act and by the bond of the very same interest which reconciles them to British government. * * * I mean to give peace. Peace implies reconciliation; and where there has been a material dispute, reconciliation does in a manner always imply concession on the one part or on the other. In this state of things I make no difficulty in affirming that the proposal ought to originate from us. Great and acknowledged force is not impaired, either in effect or in opinion, by an unwillingness to exert itself. The superior power may offer peace with honor and

---

1. By the spring of 1775, American resentment of taxation and restraints on trade threatened to erupt into war. In Britain the ruling party of Lord North tried to mollify the colonies without compromising its right to tax them or govern them individually. Burke was convinced, both from his own knowledge of America and from conversation with Benjamin Franklin, that such policies would fail. Moreover, he represented two constituencies which opposed them: the colony of New York, which he served as agent, and the voters of Bristol, a commercial city suffering from the drop in colonial trade. On March 22, 1775, Burke rose in Parliament to present a series of his own resolutions, intended to grant the Americans their right to representation, and thus to enlist them more strongly in the British empire. He spoke for three hours, and even political enemies found him "very reasonable, and very eloquent." The speech immediately became famous; two months later it was published.

2. A quotation from the American Congress at Philadelphia, 1774.

with safety. Such an offer from such a power will be attributed to magnanimity. But the concessions of the weak are the concessions of fear. When such a one is disarmed, he is wholly at the mercy of his superior; and he loses forever that time and those chances which, as they happen to all men, are the strength and resources of all inferior power.

The capital leading questions on which you must this day decide are these two: First, whether you ought to concede; and secondly, what your concession ought to be. On the first of these questions we have gained (as I have just taken the liberty of observing to you) some ground. But I am sensible that a good deal more is still to be done. Indeed, Sir, to enable us to determine both on the one and the other of these great questions with a firm and precise judgment, I think it may be necessary to consider distinctly the true nature and the peculiar circumstances of the object which we have before us: because, after all our struggle, whether we will or not, we must govern America according to that nature and to those circumstances, and not according to our own imaginations, not according to abstract ideas of right, by no means according to mere general theories of government, the resort to which appears to me, in our present situation, no better than arrant trifling. I shall therefore endeavor, with your leave, to lay before you some of the most material of these circumstances in as full and as clear a manner as I am able to state them.

The first thing that we have to consider with regard to the nature of the object is the number of people in the colonies. I have taken for some years a good deal of pains on that point. I can by no calculation justify myself in placing the number below two millions of inhabitants of our own European blood and color—besides at least 500,000 others, who form no inconsiderable part of the strength and opulence of the whole.[3] This, Sir, is, I believe, about the true number. There is no occasion to exaggerate, where plain truth is of so much weight and importance. But whether I put the present numbers too high or too low is a matter of little moment. Such is the strength with which population shoots in that part of the world, that, state the numbers as high as we will, whilst the dispute continues, the exaggeration ends. Whilst we are discussing any given magnitude, they are grown to it. Whilst we spend our time in deliberating on the mode of governing two millions, we shall find we have millions more to manage. Your children do not grow faster from infancy to manhood than they spread from families to communities, and from villages to nations.

I put this consideration of the present and the growing numbers in the front of our deliberation, because, Sir, this consideration will

3. Burke's calculations are correct. Between 1750 and 1775 the population of the colonies had doubled.

make it evident to a blunter discernment than yours, that no partial, narrow, contracted, pinched, occasional system will be at all suitable to such an object. It will show you that it is not to be considered as one of those *minima*[4] which are out of the eye and consideration of the law—not a paltry excrescence of the state—not a mean dependant, who may be neglected with little damage and provoked with little danger. It will prove that some degree of care and caution is required in the handling such an object; it will show that you ought not, in reason, to trifle with so large a mass of the interests and feelings of the human race. You could at no time do so without guilt; and be assured you will not be able to do it long with impunity.

But the population of this country, the great and growing population, though a very important consideration, will lose much of its weight, if not combined with other circumstances. The commerce of your colonies is out of all proportion beyond the numbers of the people. * * *

* * * At the beginning of the century some of these colonies imported corn[5] from the mother country. For some time past the Old World has been fed from the New. The scarcity which you have felt would have been a desolating famine, if this child of your old age, with a true filial piety, with a Roman charity,[6] had not put the full breast of its youthful exuberance to the mouth of its exhausted parent.

As to the wealth which the colonies have drawn from the sea by their fisheries, you had all that matter fully opened at your bar.[7] You surely thought those acquisitions of value, for they seemed even to excite your envy; and yet the spirit by which that enterprising employment has been exercised ought rather, in my opinion, to have raised your esteem and admiration. And pray, Sir, what in the world is equal to it? Pass by the other parts, and look at the manner in which the people of New England have of late carried on the whale-fishery. Whilst we follow them among the tumbling mountains of ice, and behold them penetrating into the deepest frozen recesses of Hudson's Bay and Davis's Straits, whilst we are looking for them beneath the arctic circle, we hear that they have pierced into the opposite region of polar cold, that they are at the antipodes, and engaged under the frozen serpent of the South.[8] Falkland Island, which seemed too remote and romantic an object

---

4. Matters too small for legal consideration.
5. Grain.
6. The ancient story of Xanthippe, who fed her father Cimon from her own breast, was conventionally called the Roman Charity.
7. Before Parliament. A rail, or bar, separated the part of the House where Members met from the part non-members could visit.
8. The Hydrus, a constellation visible from Antarctica.

for the grasp of national ambition,[9] is but a stage and resting-place in the progress of their victorious industry. Nor is the equinoctial heat more discouraging to them than the accumulated winter of both the poles. We know, that, whilst some of them draw the line and strike the harpoon on the coast of Africa, others run the longitude,[1] and pursue their gigantic game along the coast of Brazil. No sea but what is vexed by their fisheries. No climate that is not witness to their toils. Neither the perseverance of Holland, nor the activity of France, nor the dexterous and firm sagacity of English enterprise, ever carried this most perilous mode of hardy industry to the extent to which it has been pushed by this recent people—a people who are still, as it were, but in the gristle, and not yet hardened into the bone of manhood. When I contemplate these things —when I know that the colonies in general owe little or nothing to any care of ours, and that they are not squeezed into this happy form by the constraints of watchful and suspicious government, but that, through a wise and salutary neglect, a generous nature has been suffered to take her own way to perfection—when I reflect upon these effects, when I see how profitable they have been to us, I feel all the pride of power sink, and all presumption in the wisdom of human contrivances melt and die away within me—my rigor relents—I pardon something to the spirit of liberty.

I am sensible, Sir, that all which I have asserted in my detail is admitted in the gross, but that quite a different conclusion is drawn from it. America, gentlemen say, is a noble object—it is an object well worth fighting for. Certainly it is, if fighting a people be the best way of gaining them. Gentlemen in this respect will be led to their choice of means by their complexions[2] and their habits. Those who understand the military art will of course have some predilection for it. Those who wield the thunder of the state may have more confidence in the efficacy of arms. But I confess, possibly for want of this knowledge, my opinion is much more in favor of prudent management than of force—considering force not as an odious, but a feeble instrument, for preserving a people so numerous, so active, so growing, so spirited as this, in a profitable and subordinate connection with us.

First, Sir, permit me to observe, that the use of force alone is but *temporary*. It may subdue for a moment; but it does not remove the necessity of subduing again: and a nation is not governed which is perpetually to be conquered.

My next objection is its *uncertainty*. Terror is not always the effect of force, and an armament is not a victory. If you do not suc-

9. In 1771, war with Spain had been narrowly averted over the issue of England's right to the Falkland Islands (off the coast of Argentina).
1. Sail south.
2. Temperaments or modes of life.

ceed, you are without resource: for, conciliation failing, force remains; but, force failing, no further hope of reconciliation is left. Power and authority are sometimes bought by kindness; but they can never be begged as alms by an impoverished and defeated violence.

A further objection to force is, that you *impair the object* by your very endeavors to preserve it. The thing you fought for is not the thing which you recover, but depreciated, sunk, wasted, and consumed in the contest. Nothing less will content me than *whole America*. I do not choose to consume its strength along with our own; because in all parts it is the British strength that I consume. I do not choose to be caught by a foreign enemy at the end of this exhausting conflict, and still less in the midst of it. I may escape, but I can make no insurance against such an event. Let me add, that I do not choose wholly to break the American spirit; because it is the spirit that has made the country.

Lastly, we have no sort of *experience* in favor of force as an instrument in the rule of our colonies. Their growth and their utility has been owing to methods altogether different. Our ancient indulgence has been said to be pursued to a fault. It may be so; but we know, if feeling is evidence, that our fault was more tolerable than our attempt to mend it, and our sin far more salutary than our penitence.

These, Sir, are my reasons for not entertaining that high opinion of untried force by which many gentlemen, for whose sentiments in other particulars I have great respect, seem to be so greatly captivated. But there is still behind a third consideration concerning this object, which serves to determine my opinion on the sort of policy which ought to be pursued in the management of America, even more than its population and its commerce: I mean its *temper and character*.

In this character of the Americans a love of freedom is the predominating feature which marks and distinguishes the whole: and as an ardent is always a jealous affection, your colonies become suspicious, restive, and untractable, whenever they see the least attempt to wrest from them by force, or shuffle from them by chicane, what they think the only advantage worth living for. This fierce spirit of liberty is stronger in the English colonies, probably, than in any other people of the earth, and this from a great variety of powerful causes; which, to understand the true temper of their minds, and the direction which this spirit takes, it will not be amiss to lay open somewhat more largely.

First, the people of the colonies are descendants of Englishmen. England, Sir, is a nation which still, I hope, respects, and formerly adored, her freedom. The colonists emigrated from you when this part of your character was most predominant; and they took this bias and direction the moment they parted from your hands. They are therefore not only devoted to liberty, but to liberty according to English ideas and on English principles. Abstract liberty, like other mere abstractions, is not to be found. Liberty inheres in some sensible object;[3] and every nation has formed to itself some favorite point, which by way of eminence becomes the criterion of their happiness. It happened, you know, Sir, that the great contests for freedom in this country were from the earliest times chiefly upon the question of taxing. Most of the contests in the ancient commonwealths turned primarily on the right of election of magistrates, or on the balance among the several orders of the state. The question of money was not with them so immediate. But in England it was otherwise. On this point of taxes the ablest pens and most eloquent tongues have been exercised, the greatest spirits have acted and suffered. In order to give the fullest satisfaction concerning the importance of this point, it was not only necessary for those who in argument defended the excellence of the English Constitution to insist on this privilege of granting money as a dry point of fact, and to prove that the right had been acknowledged in ancient parchments and blind usages to reside in a certain body called a House of Commons: they went much further: they attempted to prove, and they succeeded, that in theory it ought to be so, from the particular nature of a House of Commons, as an immediate representative of the people, whether the old records had delivered this oracle or not. They took infinite pains to inculcate, as a fundamental principle, that in all monarchies the people must in effect themselves, mediately or immediately, possess the power of granting their own money, or no shadow of liberty could subsist. The colonies draw from you, as with their life-blood, these ideas and principles. Their love of liberty, as with you, fixed and attached on this specific point of taxing. Liberty might be safe or might be endangered in twenty other particulars without their being much pleased or alarmed. Here they felt its pulse; and as they found that beat, they thought themselves sick or sound. I do not say whether they were right or wrong in applying your general arguments to their own case. It is not easy, indeed, to make a monopoly of theorems and corollaries. The fact is, that they did thus apply those general arguments; and your mode of governing them, whether through lenity or indolence, through wisdom or mistake, confirmed them in the imagination, that they, as well as you, had an interest in these common principles.

They were further confirmed in this pleasing error by the form of their provincial legislative assemblies. Their governments are popular[4] in an high degree: some are merely[5] popular; in all, the

---

3. Object perceived by the senses.
4. Elected by the people. In 18th-century

England the masses could not vote.
5. Entirely.

popular representative is the most weighty; and this share of the people in their ordinary government never fails to inspire them with lofty sentiments, and with a strong aversion from whatever tends to deprive them of their chief importance.

If anything were wanting to this necessary operation of the form of government, religion would have given it a complete effect. Religion, always a principle of energy, in this new people is no way worn out or impaired; and their mode of professing it is also one main cause of this free spirit. The people are Protestants, and of that kind which is the most adverse to all implicit submission of mind and opinion. This is a persuasion not only favorable to liberty, but built upon it. I do not think, Sir, that the reason of this averseness in the dissenting churches from all that looks like absolute government is so much to be sought in their religious tenets as in their history. Every one knows that the Roman Catholic religion is at least coeval with most of the governments where it prevails, that it has generally gone hand in hand with them, and received a great favor and every kind of support from authority. The Church of England, too, was formed from her cradle under the nursing care of regular government. But the dissenting interests have sprung up in direct opposition to all the ordinary powers of the world, and could justify that opposition only on a strong claim to natural liberty. Their very existence depended on the powerful and unremitted assertion of that claim. All Protestantism, even the most cold and passive, is a sort of dissent. But the religion most prevalent in our northern colonies is a refinement on the principle of resistance: it is the dissidence of dissent, and the protestantism of the Protestant religion. This religion, under a variety of denominations agreeing in nothing but in the communion of the spirit of liberty, is predominant in most of the northern provinces, where the Church of England, notwithstanding its legal rights, is in reality no more than a sort of private sect, not composing, most probably, the tenth of the people. The colonists left England when this spirit was high, and in the emigrants was the highest of all; and even that stream of foreigners which has been constantly flowing into these colonies has, for the greatest part, been composed of dissenters from the establishments of their several countries, and have brought with them a temper and character far from alien to that of the people with whom they mixed.

Sir, I can perceive, by their manner, that some gentlemen object to the latitude of this description, because in the southern colonies the Church of England forms a large body, and has a regular establishment. It is certainly true. There is, however, a circumstance attending these colonies, which, in my opinion, fully counterbalances this difference, and makes the spirit of liberty still more high and haughty than in those to the northward. It is, that in Virginia and the Carolinas they have a vast multitude of slaves. Where this is the case in any part of the world, those who are free are by far the most proud and jealous of their freedom. Freedom is to them not only an enjoyment, but a kind of rank and privilege. Not seeing there, that freedom, as in countries where it is a common blessing, and as broad and general as the air, may be united with much abject toil, with great misery, with all the exterior of servitude, liberty looks, amongst them, like something that is more noble and liberal. I do not mean, Sir, to commend the superior morality of this sentiment, which has at least as much pride as virtue in it,[6] but I cannot alter the nature of man. The fact is so; and these people of the southern colonies are much more strongly, and with an higher and more stubborn spirit, attached to liberty, than those to the northward. Such were all the ancient commonwealths; such were our Gothic ancestors; such in our days were the Poles;[7] and such will be all masters of slaves, who are not slaves themselves. In such a people, the haughtiness of domination combines with the spirit of freedom, fortifies it, and renders it invincible.

Permit me, Sir, to add another circumstance in our colonies, which contributes no mean part towards the growth and effect of this untractable spirit: I mean their education. In no country, perhaps, in the world is the law so general a study. * * * This study renders men acute, inquisitive, dexterous, prompt in attack, ready in defense, full of resources. In other countries, the people, more simple, and of a less mercurial cast, judge of an ill principle in government only by an actual grievance; here they anticipate the evil, and judge the pressure of the grievance by the badness of the principle. They augur misgovernment at a distance, and snuff the approach of tyranny in every tainted breeze.

The last cause of this disobedient spirit in the colonies is hardly less powerful than the rest, as it is not merely moral, but laid deep in the natural constitution of things. Three thousand miles of ocean lie between you and them. No contrivance can prevent the effect of this distance in weakening government. Seas roll, and months pass, between the order and the execution; and the want of a speedy explanation of a single point is enough to defeat an whole system. You have, indeed, winged ministers of vengeance, who carry your bolts in their pounces[8] to the remotest verge of the sea: but there a power steps in, that limits the arrogance of raging passions and furious elements, and says, "So far shalt thou go, and no farther."[9] Who are you, that should fret and rage, and bite the chains of Nature? Nothing worse happens to you than does to all nations

---

6. Burke himself passionately opposed slavery. In 1765 he had argued against American representation in Parliament on the ground that slave-owners had no right to make laws for free men.
7. Slavery was abolished in Poland in 1772.

8. 1) Talons; 2) gunpowder. Burke compares the ships of the British navy to Milton's avenging angels. Cf. Blake's *America*.
9. A reference to King Canute, who could not command the sea.

who have extensive empire; and it happens in all the forms into which empire can be thrown. In large bodies, the circulation of power must be less vigorous at the extremities. Nature has said it. The Turk cannot govern Egypt, and Arabia, and Kurdistan, as he governs Thrace; nor has he the same dominion in Crimea and Algiers which he has at Brusa and Smyrna. Despotism itself is obliged to truck and huckster. The Sultan gets such obedience as he can. He governs with a loose rein, that he may govern at all; and the whole of the force and vigor of his authority in his center is derived from a prudent relaxation in all his borders. Spain, in her provinces, is perhaps not so well obeyed as you are in yours. She complies, too; she submits; she watches times. This is the immutable condition, the eternal law, of extensive and detached empire.

Then, Sir, from these six capital sources, of descent, of form of government, of religion in the northern provinces, of manners in the southern, of education, of the remoteness of situation from the first mover of government—from all these causes a fierce spirit of liberty has grown up. It has grown with the growth of the people in your colonies, and increased with the increase of their wealth: a spirit, that, unhappily meeting with an exercise of power in England, which, however lawful, is not reconcilable to any ideas of liberty, much less with theirs, has kindled this flame that is ready to consume us.

I do not mean to commend either the spirit in this excess, or the moral causes which produce it. Perhaps a more smooth and accommodating spirit of freedom in them would be more acceptable to us. Perhaps ideas of liberty might be desired more reconcilable with an arbitrary and boundless authority. Perhaps we might wish the colonists to be persuaded that their liberty is more secure when held in trust for them by us (as their guardians during a perpetual minority) than with any part of it in their own hands. But the question is not, whether their spirit deserves praise or blame—what, in the name of God, shall we do with it? You have before you the object, such as it is—with all its glories, with all its imperfections on its head. You see the magnitude, the importance, the temper, the habits, the disorders. By all these considerations we are strongly urged to determine something concerning it. We are called upon to fix some rule and line for our future conduct, which may give a little stability to our politics, and prevent the return of such unhappy deliberations as the present. Every such return will bring the matter before us in a still more untractable form. For what astonishing and incredible things have we not seen already! What monsters have not been generated from this unnatural contention! Whilst every principle of authority and resistance has been pushed, upon both sides, as far as it would go, there is nothing so solid and certain, either in reasoning or in practice, that has not been shaken.

Until very lately, all authority in America seemed to be nothing but an emanation from yours. Even the popular part of the colony constitution derived all its activity, and its first vital movement, from the pleasure of the crown. We thought, Sir, that the utmost which the discontented colonists could do was to disturb authority; we never dreamt they could of themselves supply it, knowing in general what an operose business it is to establish a government absolutely new. But having, for our purposes in this contention, resolved that none but an obedient assembly should sit, the humors[1] of the people there, finding all passage through the legal channel stopped, with great violence broke out another way. Some provinces have tried their experiment, as we have tried ours; and theirs has succeeded. They have formed a government sufficient for its purposes, without the bustle of a revolution, or the troublesome formality of an election. Evident necessity and tacit consent have done the business in an instant. So well they have done it, that Lord Dunmore (the account is among the fragments on your table) tells you that the new institution is infinitely better obeyed than the ancient government ever was in its most fortunate periods. Obedience is what makes government, and not the names by which it is called: not the name of Governor, as formerly, or Committee, as at present. This new government has originated directly from the people, and was not transmitted through any of the ordinary artificial media[2] of a positive constitution. It was not a manufacture ready formed, and transmitted to them in that condition from England. The evil arising from hence is this: that the colonists having once found the possibility of enjoying the advantages of order in the midst of a struggle for liberty, such struggles will not henceforward seem so terrible to the settled and sober part of mankind as they had appeared before the trial.

Pursuing the same plan of punishing by the denial of the exercise of government to still greater lengths, we wholly abrogated the ancient government of Massachusetts. We were confident that the first feeling, if not the very prospect of anarchy, would instantly enforce a complete submission. The experiment was tried. A new, strange, unexpected face of things appeared. Anarchy is found tolerable. A vast province has now subsisted, and subsisted in a considerable degree of health and vigor, for near a twelvemonth, without governor, without public council, without judges, without executive magistrates. How long it will continue in this state, or what may arise out of this unheard-of situation, how can the wisest of us conjecture? Our late experience has taught us that many of those fundamental principles formerly believed infallible are either not of the importance they were imagined to be, or that we have not at all adverted to some other far more important and far more powerful

1. Dispositions.   2. Means.

principles which entirely overrule those we had considered as omnipotent. I am much against any further experiments which tend to
put to the proof any more of these allowed opinions which contribute so much to the public tranquillity. In effect, we suffer as much
at home by this loosening of all ties, and this concussion[3] of all
established opinions, as we do abroad. For, in order to prove that
the Americans have no right to their liberties, we are every day
endeavoring to subvert the maxims which preserve the whole spirit
of our own. To prove that the Americans ought not to be free, we
are obliged to depreciate the value of freedom itself; and we never
seem to gain a paltry advantage over them in debate, without
attacking some of those principles, or deriding some of those feelings, for which our ancestors have shed their blood.

* * *

  Sir, I think you must perceive that I am resolved this day to have
nothing at all to do with the question of the right of taxation.
Some gentlemen startle,[4]—but it is true: I put it totally out of the
question. It is less than nothing in my consideration. I do not
indeed wonder, nor will you, Sir, that gentlemen of profound learning are fond of displaying it on this profound subject. But my consideration is narrow, confined, and wholly limited to the policy of
the question. I do not examine whether the giving away a man's
money be a power excepted and reserved out of the general trust of
government, and how far all mankind, in all forms of polity, are
entitled to an exercise of that right by the charter of Nature,—or
whether, on the contrary, a right of taxation is necessarily involved
in the general principle of legislation, and inseparable from the ordinary supreme power. These are deep questions, where great names
militate against each other, where reason is perplexed, and an
appeal to authorities only thickens the confusion: for high and reverend authorities lift up their heads on both sides, and there is no
sure footing in the middle. This point is the *great Serbonian bog,*
betwixt Damiata and Mount Casius old, where armies whole have
sunk.[5] I do not intend to be overwhelmed in that bog, though in
such respectable company. The question with me is, not whether
you have a right to render your people miserable, but whether it is
not your interest to make them happy. It is not what a lawyer tells
me I *may* do, but what humanity, reason, and justice tell me I
ought to do. Is a politic act the worse for being a generous one? Is
no concession proper, but that which is made from your want of
right to keep what you grant? Or does it lessen the grace or dignity
of relaxing in the exercise of an odious claim, because you have your
evidence-room full of titles, and your magazines stuffed with arms

3. Violent shaking.   5. *Paradise Lost* II. 592–94.
4. Are startled.

to enforce them? What signify all those titles and all those arms? Of what avail are they, when the reason of the thing tells me that the assertion of my title is the loss of my suit, and that I could do nothing but wound myself by the use of my own weapons?

Such is steadfastly my opinion of the absolute necessity of keeping up the concord of this empire by a unity of spirit, though in a diversity of operations, that, if I were sure the colonists had, at their leaving this country, sealed a regular compact of servitude, that they had solemnly abjured all the rights of citizens, that they had made a vow to renounce all ideas of liberty for them and their posterity to all generations, yet I should hold myself obliged to conform to the temper I found universally prevalent in my own day, and to govern two million of men, impatient of servitude, on the principles of freedom. I am not determining a point of law; I am restoring tranquillity; and the general character and situation of a people must determine what sort of government is fitted for them. That point nothing else can or ought to determine.

My idea, therefore, without considering whether we yield as matter of right or grant as matter of favor, is, *to admit the people of our colonies into an interest in the Constitution,* and, by recording that admission in the journals of Parliament, to give them as strong an assurance as the nature of the thing will admit that we mean forever to adhere to that solemn declaration of systematic indulgence.

* * *

I do not know that the colonies have, in any general way, or in any cool hour, gone much beyond the demand of immunity in relation to taxes. It is not fair to judge of the temper or dispositions of any man or any set of men, when they are composed and at rest, from their conduct or their expressions in a state of disturbance and irritation. It is, besides, a very great mistake to imagine that mankind follow up practically any speculative principle, either of government or of freedom, as far as it will go in argument and logical illation. We Englishmen stop very short of the principles upon which we support any given part of our Constitution, or even the whole of it together. I could easily, if I had not already tired you, give you very striking and convincing instances of it. This is nothing but what is natural and proper. All government, indeed every human benefit and enjoyment, every virtue and every prudent act, is founded on compromise and barter. We balance inconveniences; we give and take; we remit some rights, that we may enjoy others; and we choose rather to be happy citizens than subtle disputants. As we must give away some natural liberty, to enjoy civil advantages, so we must sacrifice some civil liberties, for the advantages to be derived from the communion and fellowship of a great empire. But, in all fair dealings, the thing bought must bear some proportion to the purchase paid.[6] None will barter away the immediate jewel of his soul. Though a great house is apt to make slaves haughty, yet it is purchasing a part of the artificial importance of a great empire too dear, to pay for it all essential rights, and all the intrinsic dignity of human nature. None of us who would not risk his life rather than fall under a government purely arbitrary. But although there are some amongst us who think our Constitution wants many improvements to make it a complete system of liberty, perhaps none who are of that opinion would think it right to aim at such improvement by disturbing his country and risking everything that is dear to him. In every arduous enterprise, we consider what we are to lose, as well as what we are to gain; and the more and better stake of liberty every people possess, the less they will hazard in a vain attempt to make it more. These are *the cords of man*. Man acts from adequate motives relative to his interest, and not on metaphysical speculations. Aristotle, the great master of reasoning, cautions us, and with great weight and propriety, against this species of delusive geometrical accuracy in moral arguments, as the most fallacious of all sophistry.[7]

The Americans will have no interest contrary to the grandeur and glory of England, when they are not oppressed by the weight of it; and they will rather be inclined to respect the acts of a superintending legislature, when they see them from the acts of that power which is itself the security, not the rival, of their secondary importance. In this assurance my mind most perfectly acquiesces, and I confess I feel not the least alarm from the discontents which are to arise from putting people at their ease; nor do I apprehend the destruction of this empire from giving, by an act of free grace and indulgence, to two millions of my fellow-citizens some share of those rights upon which I have always been taught to value myself.

* * * My hold of the colonies is in the close affection which grows from common names, from kindred blood, from similar privileges, and equal protection. These are ties which, though light as air, are as strong as links of iron. Let the colonies always keep the idea of their civil rights associated with your government,—they will cling and grapple to you, and no force under heaven will be of power to tear them from their allegiance. But let it be once understood that your government may be one thing and their privileges another, that these two things may exist without any mutual relation—the cement is gone, the cohesion is loosened, and everything hastens to decay and dissolution. As long as you have the wisdom to keep the sovereign authority of this country as the sanctuary of liberty, the sacred temple consecrated to our common faith, wherever the chosen race and sons of England worship freedom, they will

---

6. The money paid for purchase.   7. See the *Ethics*, Book I.

turn their faces towards you. The more they multiply, the more friends you will have; the more ardently they love liberty, the more perfect will be their obedience. Slavery they can have anywhere. It is a weed that grows in every soil. They may have it from Spain, they may have it from Prussia. But, until you become lost to all feeling of your true interest and your natural dignity, freedom they can have from none but you. This is the commodity of price, of which you have the monopoly. This is the true Act of Navigation, which binds to you the commerce of the colonies, and through them secures to you the wealth of the world. Deny them this partic- ipation of freedom, and you break that sole bond which originally made, and must still preserve, the unity of the empire. Do not entertain so weak an imagination as that your registers and your bonds, your affidavits and your sufferances, your cockets[8] and your clearances, are what form the great securities of your commerce. Do not dream that your letters of office, and your instructions, and your suspending clauses are the things that hold together the great con- texture of this mysterious whole. These things do not make your government. Dead instruments, passive tools as they are, it is the spirit of the English communion that gives all their life and efficacy to them. It is the spirit of the English Constitution, which, infused through the mighty mass, pervades, feeds, unites, invigorates, vivi- fies every part of the empire, even down to the minutest member.

Is it not the same virtue which does everything for us here in England? Do you imagine, then, that it is the Land-Tax Act which raises your revenue? that it is the annual vote in the Committee of Supply which gives you your army? or that it is the Mutiny Bill which inspires it with bravery and discipline? No! surely, no! It is the love of the people; it is their attachment to their government, from the sense of the deep stake they have in such a glorious insti- tution, which gives you your army and your navy, and infuses into both that liberal obedience without which your army would be a base rabble and your navy nothing but rotten timber.

All this, I know well enough, will sound wild and chimerical to the profane herd of those vulgar and mechanical politicians who have no place among us: a sort of people who think that nothing exists but what is gross and material—and who, therefore, far from being qualified to be directors of the great movement of empire, are not fit to turn a wheel in the machine. But to men truly initiated and rightly taught, these ruling and master principles, which in the opinion of such men as I have mentioned have no substantial exist- ence, are in truth everything, and all in all. Magnanimity in politics is not seldom the truest wisdom; and a great empire and little minds go ill together. If we are conscious of our situation, and glow

---

8. A custom-house seal or sealed docu- ment. All the nouns of this clause are drawn from bureaucratic routine.

with zeal to fill our place as becomes our station and ourselves, we ought to auspicate all our public proceedings on America with the old warning of the Church, *Sursum corda!*[9] We ought to elevate our minds to the greatness of that trust to which the order of Providence has called us. By adverting to the dignity of this high calling our ancestors have turned a savage wilderness into a glorious empire, and have made the most extensive and the only honorable conquests, not by destroying, but by promoting the wealth, the number, the happiness of the human race. Let us get an American revenue as we have got an American empire. English privileges have made it all that it is; English privileges alone will make it all it can be.[1]

1775

9. Lift up your hearts.
1. Burke's resolutions were defeated by a vote of 270 to 78. A month later fighting broke out at Concord and Lexington.

The Poetry of Sensibility

JAMES THOMSON
(1700–1748)

Perhaps it is significant that Thomson, the first and most popular nature
poet of the century, did not see London until he was 25 years old. He
grew up in the picturesque border country of Roxboroughshire in Scotland
and came to London in 1725, bringing with him, in addition to a memory
well stored with images of the external world, the earliest version of his
descriptive poem *Winter* in 405 lines of blank verse. Published in 1726,
it soon became popular. Thomson went on to publish *Summer* (1727),
Spring (1728), and *Autumn* in the first collected edition of *The Seasons*
(1730), to which he added the *Hymn to the Seasons*. During the next
sixteen years, because of constant revisions and additions, the poem grew
in length to 5,541 lines. The continued popularity of *The Seasons* is easily
demonstrated: between 1730 and 1800 it was printed fifty times; and it
continued in favor with readers well into the Romantic period.

Thomson is sometimes said to have been a premature "Romantic," but
this is hardly the case, for if he was, then so were all his numerous readers
in the second quarter of the century. The success that *Winter* enjoyed
shows plainly that the poem was not ahead of its time. It should not be
hard to believe that 18th-century readers had as catholic tastes as modern
readers have: readers who liked *Winter*, also, in that very year (1726),
liked Pope's *Odyssey* and Swift's *Gulliver's Travels*. Thomson's blank verse
pleased those who were pleased by Pope's couplets; Swift's simple colloquial
language charmed those who were also charmed by Thomson's Latinized
diction and not infrequent Miltonic tricks of style. The readers who thrilled
to the heroic world of Homer and admired the wit of Swift could also
enjoy Thomson's poetry of sentiment and visual imagery. In short, it is
plain that when in the Preface to the second edition of *Winter* (1726),
Thomson called for a poetry dealing with subjects "such as are fair, useful,
and magnificent, [executed] so as at once to please, instruct, surprise, and
astonish," he spoke not so much *to* as *for* the common reader.

The Seasons set the fashion for the poetry of natural description. Generations of readers learned to look at the external world through Thomson's eyes and with the emotions which he had taught them to feel. The
eye dominates the literature of external nature during the 18th century
as the *imagination* was to do in the poetry of Wordsworth. And Thomson

amazed his readers by his capacity to see: the general effects of light and cloud and foliage or the particular image of a leaf tossed in the gale or the slender feet of a robin or the delicate film of ice at the edge of a brook. As the poem grew, it became an *omnium gatherum* of contemporary ideas and interests: natural history; ideas about the nature of man and society, primitive and civilized; the conception of created nature as a source of religious experience, as an object of religious veneration, as a continuing revelation of the Deity himself.

From The Seasons
From *Summer*

[DAWN]

         Young day pours in apace,
And opens all the lawny prospect wide.
The dripping rock, the mountain's misty top
Swell on the sight and brighten with the dawn.   55
Blue through the dusk the smoking currents shine;
And from the bladed field the fearful hare
Limps awkward; while along the forest glade
The wild deer trip, and often turning gaze
At early passenger. Music awakens,   60
The native voice of undissembled joy;
And thick around the woodland hymns arise.
Roused by the cock, the soon-clad shepherd leaves
His mossy cottage, where with peace he dwells,
And from the crowded fold in order drives   65
His flock to taste the verdure of the morn.

[SWIMMING]

    Cheered by the milder beam, the sprightly youth
Speeds to the well-known pool, whose crystal depth   1245
A sandy bottom shows. Awhile he stands
Gazing the inverted landscape, half afraid
To meditate the blue profound below;
Then plunges headlong down the circling flood.
His ebon tresses and his rosy cheek   1250
Instant emerge; and through the obedient wave,
At each short breathing by his lip repelled,
With arms and legs according well, he makes,
As humor leads, an easy-winding path;
While from his polished sides a dewy light   1255
Effuses on the pleased spectators round.

[EVENING]

    Confessed from yonder slow-extinguished clouds,
All ether softening, sober Evening takes

Her wonted station in the middle air,
A thousand shadows at her beck. First this   1650
She sends on earth; then that of deeper dye
Steals soft behind; and then a deeper still,
In circle following circle, gathers round
To close the face of things. A fresher gale
Begins to wave the wood and stir the stream,   1655
Sweeping with shadowy gust the fields of corn,
While the quail clamors for his running mate.
Wide o'er the thistly lawn, as swells the breeze,
A whitening shower of vegetable down
Amusive[1] floats. The kind impartial care   1660
Of Nature naught disdains: thoughtful to feed
Her lowest sons, and clothe the coming year,
From field to field the feathered seeds she wings.
    His folded flock[2] secure, the shepherd home
Hies, merry-hearted; and by turns relieves   1665
The ruddy milkmaid of her brimming pail—
The beauty whom perhaps his witless heart,
Unknowing what the joy-mixed anguish means,
Sincerely loves, by that best language shown
Of cordial glances and obliging deeds.   1670
Onward they pass, o'er many a panting height
And valley sunk and unfrequented; where
At fall of eve the fairy people throng,
In various game and revelry to pass
The summer night, as village stories tell.   1675
But far about they wander from the grave
Of him whom his ungentle fortune urged
Against his own sad breast to lift the hand
Of impious violence. The lonely tower
Is also shunned; whose mournful chambers hold,   1680
So night-struck fancy dreams, the yelling ghost.
    Among the crooked lanes, on every hedge,
The glowworm lights his gem; and, through the dark,
A moving radiance twinkles. Evening yields
The world to Night; not in her winter robe   1685
Of massy Stygian woof, but loose arrayed
In mantle dun. A faint erroneous[3] ray,
Glanced from the imperfect surfaces of things,
Flings half an image on the straining eye;
While wavering woods, and villages, and streams,   1690
And rocks, and mountain-tops that long retained
The ascending gleam are all one swimming scene,
Uncertain if beheld. Sudden to heaven
Thence weary vision turns; where, leading soft
The silent hours of love, with purest ray   1695

---

1. Amusing—i.e. (according to John- 2. Flocks secured for the night within
son's *Dictionary*), "entertaining with the sheepfold.
tranquility."   3. Wandering, irregular.

Sweet Venus shines; and, from her genial rise,
When daylight sickens, till it springs afresh,
Unrivaled reigns the fairest lamp of night.

1727

From *Winter*
[A SNOWSTORM]

The keener tempests come: and, fuming dun
From all the livid east or piercing north,
Thick clouds ascend, in whose capacious womb   225
A vapory deluge lies, to snow congealed.
Heavy they roll their fleecy world along,
And the sky saddens with the gathered storm.
Through the hushed air the whitening shower descends,
At first thin-wavering; till at last the flakes   230
Fall broad and wide and fast, dimming the day
With a continual flow. The cherished fields
Put on their winter robe of purest white.
'Tis brightness all; save where the new snow melts
Along the mazy current. Low the woods   235
Bow their hoar head; and, ere the languid sun
Faint from the west emits his evening ray,
Earth's universal face, deep-hid and chill,
Is one wild dazzling waste that buries wide
The works of man. Drooping, the laborer-ox   240
Stands covered o'er with snow, and then demands
The fruit of all his toil. The fowls of heaven,
Tamed by the cruel season, crowd around
The winnowing store, and claim the little boon
Which Providence assigns them. One alone,   245
The redbreast, sacred to the household gods,
Wisely regardful of the embroiling sky,
In joyless fields and thorny thickets leaves
His shivering mates, and pays to trusted man
His annual visit. Half afraid, he first   250
Against the window beats; then brisk alights
On the warm hearth; then, hopping o'er the floor,
Eyes all the smiling family askance,
And pecks, and starts, and wonders where he is—
Till, more familiar grown, the table crumbs   255
Attract his slender feet. The foodless wilds
Pour forth their brown inhabitants. The hare,
Though timorous of heart, and hard beset
By death in various forms, dark snares, and dogs,
And more unpitying men, the garden seeks,   260

---

4. Genus, class.

Urged on by fearless want. The bleating kind[4]
Eye the bleak heaven, and next the glistening earth,
With looks of dumb despair; then, sad-dispersed,
Dig for the withered herb through heaps of snow.

1726

THOMAS GRAY
(1716–1771)

The man who wrote the English poem best known and most loved by
unsophisticated readers was oddly enough a scholarly recluse who lived
the quiet life of a university professor in the stagnant atmosphere of mid-
18th-century Cambridge, where toward the end of his life he held the
Professorship of Modern History without feeling called upon to give a
single lecture. He was educated at Eton College, where he made his first
intimate friends—Richard West, Thomas Ashton, and Horace Walpole,
the son of the Prime Minister. After a little over four years at Cambridge
he left without a degree in order to make the grand tour of France and
Italy as the guest of his friend Walpole. Their different interests caused
a quarrel, and after two years of traveling Gray returned to England
alone. Fortunately, a few years later the quarrel was made up, and Walpole, who was Gray's ardent admirer, was able to play an important role
in making his friend's poems public. The death of West in 1742 was a
depressing event for Gray, who, still alienated from Walpole, felt keenly
the loss of this gifted and congenial friend. The Eton *Ode* and possibly
some of the stanzas of the *Elegy Written in a Country Churchyard* are associated with this melancholy event.

After 1742 Gray returned to Cambridge, pursuing his studies and indulging his tastes. He was learned in the classics and modern literatures
as well as history, and his curiosity led him to explore the then little-
known fields of pre-Elizabethan poetry and old Welsh and Norse literature. He was a connoisseur of painting and music, a careful and scientific
observer of nature, and an enthusiastic admirer of wild and picturesque landscape. He seldom left Cambridge except to read in the newly
opened British Museum or to go in the summer to the Lake District or
to Scotland in search of the sublime and beautiful in nature. He wrote
little, for he worked slowly and carefully, fastidiously seeking perfection
of form and phrase. His early poetry is a carefully impersonal expression
of his own somewhat melancholy temperament: the solitary, brooding
speaker of the Eton *Ode* and the *Elegy* is a dramatic projection of Gray
and of his personal dilemma: though colored by his own feeling, the
poems are not confessions, but public reflections on death, the sorrows
of life, and the mysteries of human destiny. The later poems—the two
grandiloquent Pindaric odes, *The Progress of Poesy* and *The Bard* (1757),
and the translations from Welsh and Norse poetry—are accomplished
literary exercises. The living Gray is to be sought in his correspondence,

where his genial humor, shy affection, and wide intellectual interests are revealed in some of the most delightful letters of the age that made letter writing an art.

Though Gray never knew Collins and had no association with the Wartons in the 1740's, he shared their interests and many of their tastes. The melancholy of Collins' *Ode to Evening* is that of the opening stanzas of the *Elegy*, and in both poems mood and landscape mutually sustain each other. Like Collins Gray wrote both greater and lesser odes (see title note to Dryden's *Ode to * * * Mistress Anne Killigrew*, above), creating a body of lyric poetry entirely characteristic of the midcentury. Without laying aside his veneration for Dryden, whom he considered his master in versification, he could share his contemporaries' enthusiasm for Spenser and Milton—especially the Milton of the minor poems, whom he often echoes. His evocation of the image of the bard, in the second of the Pindaric odes, is very much in the manner of the period. Gray wrote often in a highly artificial diction and a distorted word order (see the first four stanzas of the Eton *Ode*, for example), for he held that "the language of the age is never the language of poetry," a heresy that earned him the harsh criticism of Wordsworth in his Preface to *Lyrical Ballads*.

The *Elegy* stands alone in Gray's work: it is his one poem that belongs to mankind and that is known in many translations. It speaks to our common humanity through an art so subtle that one can know the poem for many years before becoming aware of its scores of echoes from other poems, its author's sure control of language, imagery, cadence, and his subtle modulation of style and tone. If to express the universal is to be classic, then the *Elegy* is one of our true classics. Dr. Johnson, no friend of Gray's poetry in general, long ago said the final word on this aspect of the poem:

The Churchyard abounds with images which find a mirror in every mind, and with sentiments to which every bosom returns an echo. The four stanzas beginning "Yet even these bones" are to me original: I have never seen the notions in any other place; yet he that reads them here, persuades himself that he has always felt them. Had Gray written often thus, it had been in vain to blame, and useless to praise him.

Ode on a Distant Prospect of Eton College

Ἄνθρωπος· ἱκανὴ πρόφασις εἰς τὸ δυστυχεῖν.[1]
MENANDER

Ye distant spires, ye antique towers,
    That crown the watery glade,
Where grateful Science[2] still adores
    Her Henry's holy shade;[3]
And ye, that from the stately brow   5

1. "I am a man: sufficient reason for being miserable."
2. Learning.
3. Henry VI founded Eton in 1440.

Of Windsor's heights the expanse below
   Of grove, of lawn, of mead survey,
Whose turf, whose shade, whose flowers among
Wanders the hoary Thames along
   His silver-winding way.   10

Ah happy hills, ah pleasing shade,
   Ah fields beloved in vain,
Where once my careless childhood strayed,
   A stranger yet to pain!
I feel the gales, that from ye blow,   15
A momentary bliss bestow,
   As waving fresh their gladsome wing,
My weary soul they seem to soothe,
And, redolent of joy and youth,
   To breathe a second spring.   20

Say, Father Thames, for thou hast seen
   Full many a sprightly race
Disporting on thy margent green
   The paths of pleasure trace,
Who foremost now delight to cleave   25
With pliant arm thy glassy wave?
   The captive linnet which enthrall?[4]
What idle progeny succeed[5]
To chase the rolling circle's speed,
   Or urge the flying ball?   30

While some on earnest business bent
   Their murmuring labors ply
'Gainst graver hours, that bring constraint
   To sweeten liberty:
Some bold adventurers disdain   35
The limits of their little reign,
   And unknown regions dare descry:
Still as they run they look behind,
They hear a voice in every wind,
   And snatch a fearful joy.   40

Gay hope is theirs by fancy fed,
   Less pleasing when possessed;
The tear forgot as soon as shed,
   The sunshine of the breast:
Theirs buxom health of rosy hue,   45
Wild wit, invention ever new,
   And lively cheer of vigor born;
The thoughtless day, the easy night,

4. Make prisoner.
5. I.e., follow in succession Gray's generation; "rolling circle": a hoop.

The spirits pure, the slumbers light,
    That fly the approach of morn.'   50

Alas, regardless of their doom,
    The little victims play!
No sense have they of ills to come,
    Nor care beyond today.
Yet see how all around 'em wait   55
The ministers of human fate,
    And black Misfortune's baleful train!
Ah, show them where in ambush stand
To seize their prey the murderous band!
    Ah, tell them they are men!   60

These shall the fury Passions tear,
    The vultures of the mind,
Disdainful Anger, pallid Fear,
    And Shame that skulks behind;
Or pining Love shall waste their youth, 65
Or Jealousy with rankling tooth,
    That inly gnaws the secret heart,
And Envy wan, and faded Care,
Grim-visaged comfortless Despair,
    And Sorrow's piercing dart.   70

Ambition this shall tempt to rise,
    Then whirl the wretch from high,
To bitter Scorn a sacrifice,
    And grinning Infamy.
The stings of Falsehood those shall try, 75
And hard Unkindness' altered eye,
    That mocks the tear it forced to flow;
And keen Remorse with blood defiled,
And moody Madness laughing wild
    Amid severest woe.   80

Lo, in the vale of years beneath
    A grisly troop are seen,
The painful family of Death,
    More hideous than their queen:
This racks the joints, this fires the veins, 85
That every laboring sinew strains,
    Those in the deeper vitals rage:
Lo, Poverty, to fill the band,
That numbs the soul with icy hand,
    And slow-consuming Age.   90

To each his sufferings: all are men,
    Condemned alike to groan;
The tender for another's pain,
    The unfeeling for his own.

Yet ah! why should they know their fate?   95
Since sorrow never comes too late,
        And happiness too swiftly flies.
Thought would destroy their paradise.
No more; where ignorance is bliss,
        'Tis folly to be wise.

1742   100

                                          1747

Hymn to Adversity

Ζῆνα . . .
τὸν φρονεῖν βροτοὺς ὁδώ—
σαντα, τῷ πάθει μάθος
θεντα κυρίως ἔχειν.
AESCHYLUS, *Agamemnon* 174–78[1]

Daughter of Jove, relentless power,
Thou tamer of the human breast,
Whose iron scourge and torturing hour
The bad affright, afflict the best!
Bound in thy adamantine chain,   5
The proud are taught to taste of pain,
And purple tyrants vainly groan
With pangs unfelt before, unpitied and alone.

When first thy sire to send on earth
Virtue, his darling child, designed,   10
To thee he gave the heavenly birth,
And bade to form her infant mind.
Stern rugged nurse! thy rigid lore
With patience many a year she bore:
What sorrow was, thou bad'st her know,   15
And from her own she learned to melt at others' woe.

Scared at thy frown terrific, fly
Self-pleasing Folly's idle brood,
Wild Laughter, Noise, and thoughtless Joy,
And leave us leisure to be good.   20
Light they disperse, and with them go
The summer friend, the flattering foe;
By vain Prosperity received,
To her they vow their truth, and are again believed.

Wisdom, in sable garb arrayed,   25
Immersed in rapturous thought profound,
And Melancholy, silent maid
With leaden eye, that loves the ground,

---

1. "Zeus, who leads mortals to understanding, who has established as a fixed ordinance that wisdom comes by suffering."

Still on thy solemn steps attend:
Warm Charity, the general friend,   30
With Justice, to herself severe,
And Pity, dropping soft the sadly-pleasing tear.

Oh, gently on thy suppliant's head,
Dread Goddess, lay thy chastening hand!
Not in thy Gorgon[2] terrors clad,   35
Nor circled with the vengeful band
(As by the impious thou art seen)
With thundering voice, and threatening mien,
With screaming Horror's funeral cry,
Despair, and fell Disease, and ghastly Poverty.   40

Thy form benign, O Goddess, wear,
Thy milder influence impart,
Thy philosophic train be there
To soften, not to wound, my heart,
The generous spark extinct revive,   45
Teach me to love and to forgive,
Exact my own defects to scan,
What others are, to feel, and know myself a man.

1742   1753

Elegy Written in a Country Churchyard

The curfew tolls the knell of parting day,
   The lowing herd wind slowly o'er the lea,
The plowman homeward plods his weary way,
   And leaves the world to darkness and to me.

Now fades the glimmering landscape on the sight,   5
   And all the air a solemn stillness holds,
Save where the beetle wheels his droning flight,
   And drowsy tinklings lull the distant folds;

Save that from yonder ivy-mantled tower
   The moping owl does to the moon complain   10
Of such, as wandering near her secret bower,
   Molest her ancient solitary reign.

Beneath those rugged elms, that yew tree's shade,
   Where heaves the turf in many a moldering heap,

2. Goodwin Sands is a dangerous shoal
off Ramsgate. Legend has it that it was
once a fertile estate owned by Earl
Goodwin.
3. Unscrupulous politicians who had
been allied with and had deserted Fox,
as Fox himself had been allied with
and deserted Pitt and Bute.
4. Westminster Abbey, dedicated to
St. Peter; St. Paul's is the cathedral
church of the City of London.

Each in his narrow cell forever laid,
  The rude[1] forefathers of the hamlet sleep.

The breezy call of incense-breathing Morn,
  The swallow twittering from the straw-built shed,
The cock's shrill clarion, or the echoing horn,[2]
  No more shall rouse them from their lowly bed.

For them no more the blazing hearth shall burn,
  Or busy housewife ply her evening care;
No children run to lisp their sire's return,
  Or climb his knees the envied kiss to share.

Oft did the harvest to their sickle yield,
  Their furrow oft the stubborn glebe[3] has broke;
How jocund did they drive their team afield!
  How bowed the woods beneath their sturdy stroke!

Let not Ambition mock their useful toil,
  Their homely joys, and destiny obscure;
Nor Grandeur hear with a disdainful smile
  The short and simple annals of the poor.

The boast of heraldry,[4] the pomp of power,
  And all that beauty, all that wealth e'er gave,
Awaits alike the inevitable hour.
  The paths of glory lead but to the grave.

Nor you, ye proud, impute to these the fault,
  If Memory o'er their tomb no trophies[5] raise,
Where through the long-drawn aisle and fretted[6] vault
  The pealing anthem swells the note of praise.

Can storied urn[7] or animated bust
  Back to its mansion call the fleeting breath?
Can Honor's voice provoke[8] the silent dust,
  Or Flattery soothe the dull cold ear of Death?

Perhaps in this neglected spot is laid
  Some heart once pregnant with celestial fire;
Hands that the rod of empire might have swayed,
  Or waked to ecstasy the living lyre.

But Knowledge to their eyes her ample page
  Rich with the spoils of time did ne'er unroll;
Chill Penury repressed their noble rage,
  And froze the genial current of the soul.

Full many a gem of purest ray serene,
  The dark unfathomed caves of ocean bear:

15

20

25

30

35

40

45

50

1. Untaught.
2. The hunter's horn.
3. Soil, turf.
4. Noble birth.
5. An ornamental or symbolic group of figures depicting the achievements of the dead man.
6. Decorated with intersecting lines in relief.
7. A funeral urn with an epitaph inscribed on it; "animated": lifelike.
8. Call forth.

Full many a flower is born to blush unseen,   55
    And waste its sweetness on the desert air.

Some village Hampden,[9] that with dauntless breast
    The little tyrant of his fields withstood;
Some mute inglorious Milton here may rest,
    Some Cromwell guiltless of his country's blood.   60

The applause of listening senates to command,
    The threats of pain and ruin to despise,
To scatter plenty o'er a smiling land,
    And read their history in a nation's eyes,

Their lot forbade: nor circumscribed alone   65
    Their growing virtues, but their crimes confined;
Forbade to wade through slaughter to a throne,
    And shut the gates of mercy on mankind,

The struggling pangs of conscious truth to hide,
    To quench the blushes of ingenuous shame,   70
Or heap the shrine of Luxury and Pride
    With incense kindled at the Muse's flame.

Far from the madding crowd's ignoble strife,
    Their sober wishes never learned to stray;
Along the cool sequestered vale of life   75
    They kept the noiseless tenor of their way.

Yet even these bones from insult to protect
    Some frail memorial still erected nigh,
With uncouth rhymes and shapeless sculpture decked,[1]
    Implores the passing tribute of a sigh.   80

Their name, their years, spelt by the unlettered Muse,
    The place of fame and elegy supply:
And many a holy text around she strews,
    That teach the rustic moralist to die.

For who to dumb Forgetfulness a prey,   85
    This pleasing anxious being e'er resigned,
Left the warm precincts of the cheerful day,
    Nor cast one longing lingering look behind?

On some fond breast the parting soul relies,
    Some pious drops the closing eye requires;   90
Even from the tomb the voice of Nature cries,
    Even in our ashes live their wonted fires.

For thee, who mindful of the unhonored dead
    Dost in these lines their artless tale relate;
If chance, by lonely contemplation led,   95
    Some kindred spirit shall inquire thy fate,

9. John Hampden (1594–1643), who, both as a private citizen and as a Member of Parliament, zealously defended the rights of the people against the autocratic policies of Charles I. A gallant soldier, he was mortally wounded in a skirmish near Oxford.
1. Cf. "the storied urn or animated bust" dedicated inside the church to "the proud" (line 41).

Haply some hoary-headed swain may say,
  "Oft have we seen him at the peep of dawn
Brushing with hasty steps the dews away
  To meet the sun upon the upland lawn.   100

"There at the foot of yonder nodding beech
  That wreathes its old fantastic roots so high,
His listless length at noontide would he stretch,
  And pore upon the brook that babbles by.

"Hard by yon wood, now smiling as in scorn,   105
  Muttering his wayward fancies he would rove,
Now drooping, woeful wan, like one forlorn,
  Or crazed with care, or crossed in hopeless love.

"One morn I missed him on the customed hill,
  Along the heath and near his favorite tree;   110
Another came; nor yet beside the rill,
  Nor up the lawn, nor at the wood was he;

"The next with dirges due in sad array
  Slow through the churchway path we saw him borne.
Approach and read (for thou canst read) the lay,   115
  Graved on the stone beneath yon aged thorn."

THE EPITAPH

Here rests his head upon the lap of Earth
  A youth to Fortune and to Fame unknown.
Fair Science[2] frowned not on his humble birth,
  And Melancholy marked him for her own.   120

Large was his bounty, and his soul sincere,
  Heaven did a recompense as largely send:
He gave to Misery all he had, a tear,
  He gained from Heaven ('twas all he wished) a friend.

No farther seek his merits to disclose,   125
  Or draw his frailties from their dread abode
(There they alike in trembling hope repose),
  The bosom of his Father and his God.

ca. 1742–50   1751

2. Learning.

WILLIAM COLLINS
(1721–1759)

William Collins was born at Chichester and was educated at Winchester
and Oxford. Coming up to London from the university, he tried to establish himself as an author, but he was given rather to planning than to

writing books. He came to know Dr. Johnson, who recorded in the *Lives of the Poets* that he had once "delighted to converse with him." In 1746 Collins published his *Odes on Several Descriptive and Allegorical Subjects*, his part in an undertaking, with his friend Joseph Warton, to create a "new," more lyrical and imaginative poetry than the generation of Dryden and Pope had done. Collins' *Odes*, as their title suggests, are addressed to personified abstractions (Fear, Pity, the Passions) which are rendered vividly and pictorially, in expressive attitudes and allegorical groups. The volume was not much liked; Gray, however, commented favorably on it in private; and the enterprising publisher Robert Dodsley included three of the simpler odes in the first volume of his *Miscellany* (1748). The more ambitious odes were thought to be obscure and too "visionary." In form they represent a new version of the "great" or Cowleian ode (see title note to Dryden's *Anne Killigrew*, above), for Collins gave them at least an approximate regularity of structure, since in several of them strophe and antistrophe are more or less symmetrical. Curiously, however, he departed from the normal Pindaric order of parts by placing epodes between strophes and antistrophes.

Inheriting some money, the poet traveled for a while, but fits of depression gradually deepened into insanity. He spent his last years in Chichester, forgotten by all but a small circle of loyal friends. As the century progressed he gained in reputation, although the tendency to find signs of incipient madness in his vividly realized imaginary figures is regrettable. The Romantics admired his poems and felt akin to him as they did to Thomas Chatterton and Robert Burns. The *Ode to Evening*, which combines a chaste and cool classicism with a delicate feeling for landscape and mood, is one of the delightful poems of the century.

Ode Written in the Beginning of the Year 1746

> How sleep the brave[1] who sink to rest
> By all their country's wishes blest!
> When Spring, with dewy fingers cold,
> Returns to deck their hallowed mold,
> She there shall dress a sweeter sod   5
> Than Fancy's feet have ever trod.
>
> By fairy hands their knell is rung,
> By forms unseen their dirge is sung;
> There Honor comes, a pilgrim gray,
> To bless the turf that wraps their clay,   10
> And Freedom shall awhile repair,
> To dwell a weeping hermit there!

1746

1. Collins is presumably thinking of those who lost their lives defending England in 1745, when the Scotch Jacobites, led by Bonnie Prince Charlie, penetrated to within 127 miles of London.

Ode on the Poetical Character[1]

STROPHE

As once, if not with light regard,
I read aright that gifted bard
(Him whose school above the rest
His loveliest Elfin Queen has blest),[2]
One, only one, unrivaled fair,   5
Might hope the magic girdle wear,
At solemn tourney hung on high,
The wish of each love-darting eye;[3]
Lo! to each other nymph in turn applied,
    As if, in air unseen, some hovering hand,   10
Some chaste and angel-friend to virgin-fame,
    With whispered spell had burst the starting band,
It left unblest her loathed dishonored side;
    Happier, hopeless fair, if never
    Her baffled hand with vain endeavor   15
Had touched that fatal zone to her denied!
Young Fancy thus, to me divinest name,
    To whom, prepared and bathed in Heaven
    The cest of amplest power is given:
    To few the godlike gift assigns,   20
    To gird their blest, prophetic loins,
And gaze her visions wild, and feel unmixed her flame!

EPODE

The band, as fairy legends say,
Was wove on that creating day,
When He,[4] who called with thought to birth   25
Yon tented sky, this laughing earth,

---

1. This ode, long held in comparative disregard, has more recently been elevated in critical estimation, for it is now seen as an early, dramatic engagement with one of the central concerns of the Romantic Age—the origin and role of the creative imagination and, indeed, of the poet himself. "It is an allegory," A. S. P. Woodhouse tells us, "whose subject is the *creative imagination* and the poet's passionate desire for its power."

In the strophe an analogy is drawn between the *cestus* or girdle of Venus, which only the chaste can wear, and the cest of Fancy, or the creative imagination. In the epode the act of the creation of the world is presented as an act of the divine imagination.

What is especially new, such critics as Harold Bloom and Northrop Frye suggest, is Collins' implication, in the epode, that "a poet is born from the quasi-sexual union of God and imagination," or Fancy (lines 30–40). Such a reading animates the personifications in a way that we do not encounter again until the work of William Blake. The poet's creative act is divine, analogous to the creation of the world, and he is born of the divine act.

In the antistrophe, Milton is regarded as the type of poet true enough to wear the girdle of Fancy. Collins pictures himself pursuing the "guiding steps" (line 71) of Milton, as of Spenser (in the epode)—both poet-prophets. He retreats from the elegant school of Waller (and, by implication, that of Pope, as well)—"In vain" (line 72), however, for he lives in an age of sensibility.
2. Edmund Spenser.
3. *Faerie Queene* IV.v tells of the contest of many beautiful ladies for the girdle of Venus.
4. God, on the day of creation.

And dressed with springs, and forests tall,
And poured the main engirting all,
Long by the loved Enthusiast [5] wooed,
Himself in some diviner mood,   30
Retiring, sate with her alone,
And placed her on his sapphire throne;
The whiles, the vaulted shrine around,
Seraphic wires were heard to sound,
Now sublimest triumph swelling,   35
Now on love and mercy dwelling;
And she, from out the veiling cloud,
Breathed her magic notes aloud:
And thou, thou rich-haired Youth of Morn,[6]
And all thy subject life was born!   40
The dangerous Passions kept aloof,
Far from the sainted growing woof:
But near it sate ecstatic Wonder,
Listening the deep applauding thunder:
And Truth, in sunny vest arrayed,   45
By whose the tarsel's [7] eyes were made;
All the shadowy tribes of Mind,
In braided dance their murmurs joined,
And all the bright uncounted Powers
Who feed on Heaven's ambrosial flowers.   50
Where is the bard, whose soul can now
Its high presuming hopes avow?
Where he who thinks, with rapture blind,
This hallow'd work [8] for him designed?

ANTISTROPHE

High on some cliff, to Heaven up-piled,   55
Of rude access, of prospect wild,
Where, tangled round the jealous steep,
Strange shades o'erbrow the valleys deep,
And holy Genii guard the rock,
Its glooms embrown, its springs unlock,   60
While on its rich ambitious head,
An Eden, like his [9] own, lies spread:
I view that oak, the fancied glades among,
By which as Milton lay, his evening ear,
From many a cloud that dropped ethereal dew,   65
Nigh sphered in Heaven its native strains could hear:
On which that ancient trump he reached was hung;
    Thither oft, his glory greeting,
    From Waller's [1] myrtle shades retreating,
With many a vow from Hope's aspiring tongue,   70
My trembling feet his guiding steps pursue;
    In vain—such bliss to one alone,[2]

---

5. I.e., Fancy.
6. Apollo, god of the sun and of poetry, associated with the poet himself.
7. The falcon's.
8. The girdle of Fancy.
9. Milton's.

1. Edmund Waller (1606–87). The myrtle is the symbol of love poetry, Waller's poetry is thought of as trivial compared to Milton's grandeur.
2. Milton.

Of all the sons of soul was known,
And Heaven, and Fancy, kindred powers,
Have now o'erturned the inspiring bowers,   75
Or curtained close such scene from every future view.

1746

Ode to Evening[1]

If aught of oaten stop, or pastoral song,
May hope, chaste Eve, to soothe thy modest ear,
  Like thy own solemn springs,
  Thy springs and dying gales,
O nymph reserved, while now the bright-haired sun   5
Sits in yon western tent, whose cloudy skirts,
  With brede[2] ethereal wove,
  O'erhang his wavy bed:
Now air is hushed, save where the weak-eyed bat,
With short shrill shrieks flits by on leathern wing,   10
  Or where the beetle winds
  His small but sullen horn,
As oft he rises 'midst the twilight path,
Against the pilgrim borne in heedless hum:
  Now teach me, maid composed,   15
  To breathe some softened strain,
Whose numbers, stealing through thy darkening vale,
May not unseemly with its stillness suit,
  As, musing slow, I hail
  Thy genial loved return!   20
For when thy folding-star[3] arising shows
His paly circlet, at his warning lamp
  The fragrant Hours, and elves
  Who slept in flowers the day,
And many a nymph who wreaths her brows with sedge,   25
And sheds the freshening dew, and, lovelier still,
  The pensive Pleasures sweet,
  Prepare thy shadowy car.
Then lead, calm vot'ress, where some sheety lake
Cheers the lone heath, or some time-hallowed pile   30
  Or upland fallows gray
  Reflect its last cool gleam.
But when chill blustering winds, or driving rain,
Forbid my willing feet, be mine the hut
  That from the mountain's side   35
  Views wilds, and swelling floods,

---

1. Collins borrowed the metrical structure and the rhymeless lines of this ode
from Milton's translation of Horace,
Odes I.5 (1673). The text printed here
is based on the revised version, published in Dodsley's *Miscellany* (1748).
2. Embroidery.
3. The evening star, which signals the
hour for herding the sheep into the
sheepfold.

And hamlets brown, and dim-discovered spires,
And hears their simple bell, and marks o'er all
    Thy dewy fingers draw
    The gradual dusky veil.   40
While Spring shall pour his showers, as oft he wont,
And bathe thy breathing tresses, meekest Eve;
    While Summer loves to sport
    Beneath thy lingering light;
While sallow Autumn fills thy lap with leaves;   45
Or Winter, yelling through the troublous air,
    Affrights thy shrinking train,
    And rudely rends thy robes;
So long, sure-found beneath the sylvan shed,
Shall Fancy, Friendship, Science, rose-lipped Health,   50
    Thy gentlest influence own,
    And hymn thy favorite name!

                            1746, 1748

CHRISTOPHER SMART

(1722–1771)

In 1756 Christopher Smart, who had won prizes at Pembroke College, Cambridge, as a scholar and poet, and was known in London as a wit and *bon vivant*, was seized by religious mania: "a preternatural excitement to prayer," according to Mrs. Thrale, "which he held it as a duty not to control or repress." If Smart had been content to pray in private, his life might have ended as happily as it began; but unfortunately for him, he insisted on kneeling down in the streets, in parks, in assembly rooms. He became a public nuisance, and the public took its revenge. For most of the next seven years Smart was confined, first in St. Luke's hospital, then in a private madhouse. Here, severed from his wife, his children, and his friends, he began to write a bold new sort of poetry: vivid, concise, abrupt, syntactically daring. Few of his contemporaries noticed it. After Smart's release from the madhouse (1763) he fell into debt—he had always been profligate—and his *Translation of the Psalms of David* (1765) *and Hymns for the Amusement of Children* (1770) were almost completely ignored. He died, forgotten, in a debtor's prison. But in the 19th century his reputation revived, and since the publication of *Jubilate Agno* in 1939 his poems have become newly famous.

The work of Smart's great period (1759–1765) resembles nothing else in English. Its sources lie partly in the classics, especially Horace (whom Smart translated both in verse and prose), but far more in the Old Testament. Above all, the spirit that informs the poetry is praise and celebration, an intense vision of the divine presence shining through ordinary life. Smart believed that the world had been called into being solely to pay homage to its Maker; the function of man, and the poet most of all, was to be "minister of praise at large," to provide a voice of prayer for the whole creation. Thus the hero of his masterpiece, *A Song to David* (1763), is not only King but Psalmist of Israel, the inspired man and poet, possessed by the spirit of the Lord, who orders and blesses everything that exists. Such poets, like the first Creator, strive to construct a microcosm in which every element—word, image, and number—fits into one grand design. The stanzas of *A Song to David* are organized in groups of three and seven (divine numbers), and separate stanzas are devoted to each of David's twelve virtues, the seven days of creation, the ten commandments, the four seasons, the five senses, and finally, in a mighty climax, the five degrees in which David excelled. To critics who accused the poem of incoherence, Smart properly replied that its chief fault, if any, was "the *exact* REGULARITY and METHOD with which it is conducted." At its best, however, the poem transports its reader into that state of adoration "Where ask is have, where seek is find, / Where knock is open wide," a state of true prayer that acknowledges no division between desire and its fulfillment or God and his worshipper.

From Jubilate Agno[1]

[*My Cat Jeoffry*]

For I will consider my Cat Jeoffry.
For he is the servant of the Living God duly and daily serving him.
For at the first glance of the glory of God in the East[2] he worships in his way.
For is this done by wreathing his body seven times round with elegant quickness.
For then he leaps up to catch the musk, wch is the blessing of God upon his prayer.   5
For he rolls upon prank[3] to work it in.
For having done duty and received blessing he begins to consider himself.
For this he performs in ten degrees.
For first he looks upon his fore-paws to see if they are clean.
For secondly he kicks up behind to clear away there.   10
For thirdly he works it upon stretch with the fore-paws extended.

1. *Jubilate Agno* (*Rejoice in the Lamb*), written a few lines at a time during Smart's confinement in a madhouse from 1759 to 1763, is (1) a record of his daily life and thoughts; (2) the note-book of a scholar, crammed with puns and obscure learning, which sets out elaborate correspondences between the world of the Bible and modern England; (3) a personal Testament or book of worship, antiphonally arranged in lines beginning alternately with *Let* and *For*, which seeks to join the material and spiritual universes in one unending prayer. It has also come to be recognized, since first published in 1939 by

W. F. Stead, as a poem—a poem unique in English for its ecstatic sense of the presence of the Divine Spirit. The most famous passage describes Smart's cat Jeoffry, his only companion during the years of confinement: "For I am possessed of a cat, surpassing in beauty, from whom I take occasion to bless Almighty God." At once a real cat, lovingly observed in all its frisks, and visible evidence of the providential plan, Jeoffry celebrates the Maker, as all things do, in his very being.
2. The sunrise.
3. Prankishly.

For fourthly he sharpens his paws by wood.

For fifthly he washes himself.

For Sixthly he rolls upon wash.

For Seventhly he fleas himself, that he may not be interrupted upon the beat.   15

For Eighthly he rubs himself against a post.

For Ninthly he looks up for his instructions.

For Tenthly he goes in quest of food.

For having consider'd God and himself he will consider his neighbor.

For if he meets another cat he will kiss her in kindness.   20

For when he takes his prey he plays with it to give it a chance.

For one mouse in seven escapes by his dallying.

For when his day's work is done his business more properly begins.

For he keeps the Lord's watch in the night against the adversary.

For he counteracts the powers of darkness by his electrical skin & glaring eyes.   25

For he counteracts the Devil, who is death, by brisking about the life.

For in his morning orisons he loves the sun and the sun loves him.

For he is of the tribe of Tiger.

For the Cherub Cat is a term of the Angel Tiger.[4]

For he has the subtlety and hissing of a serpent, which in goodness he suppresses.   30

For he will not do destruction if he is well-fed, neither will he spit without provocation.

For he purrs in thankfulness, when God tells him he's a good Cat.

For he is an instrument for the children to learn benevolence upon.

For every house is incomplete without him & a blessing is lacking in the spirit.

For the Lord commanded Moses concerning the cats at the departure of the Children of Israel from Egypt.[5]   35

For every family had one cat at least in the bag.

For the English Cats are the best in Europe.

For he is the cleanest in the use of his fore-paws of any quadrupede.

For the dexterity of his defence is an instance of the love of God to him exceedingly.

For he is the quickest to his mark of any creature.   40

For he is tenacious of his point.

For he is a mixture of gravity and waggery.

For he knows that God is his Saviour.

For there is nothing sweeter than his peace when at rest.

For there is nothing brisker than his life when in motion.   45

For he is of the Lord's poor and so indeed is he called by benevolence perpetually—Poor Jeoffry! poor Jeoffry! the rat has bit thy throat.

For I bless the name of the Lord Jesus that Jeoffry is better.

For the divine spirit comes about his body to sustain it in complete cat.

---

4. As a cherub is a small angel, so a cat is a small tiger.   5. No cats are mentioned in the Bible.

For his tongue is exceeding pure so that it has in purity what it
    wants in music.
For he is docile and can learn certain things.   50
For he can set up with gravity which is patience upon approbation.
For he can fetch and carry, which is patience in employment.
For he can jump over a stick which is patience upon proof positive.
For he can spraggle upon waggle[6] at the word of command.
For he can jump from an eminence into his master's bosom.   55
For he can catch the cork and toss it again.
For he is hated by the hypocrite and miser.
For the former is afraid of detection.
For the latter refuses the charge.
For he camels his back to bear the first notion of business.   60
For he is good to think on, if a man would express himself neatly.
For he made a great figure in Egypt for his signal services.
For he killed the Icneumon-rat very pernicious by land.[7]
For his ears are so acute that they sting again.
For from this proceeds the passing quickness of his attention.   65
For by stroking of him I have found out electricity.
For I perceived God's light about him both wax and fire.
For the Electrical fire is the spiritual substance, which God sends
    from heaven to sustain the bodies both of man and beast.
For God has blessed him in the variety of his movements.   70
For, though he cannot fly, he is an excellent clamberer.
For his motions upon the face of the earth are more than any other
    quadrupede.
For he can tread to all the measures upon the music.
For he can swim for life.
For he can creep.   75
1759–63   1939

A Song to David[1]

David the son of Jesse said, and the man who was raised up on
high, the anointed of the God of Jacob, and the sweet psalmist of
Israel, said, "The Spirit of the Lord spake by me, and His Word
was in my tongue."

—II SAMUEL xxiii.1,2

I

O Thou, that sit'st upon a throne,
With harp of high majestic tone,   *[Invocation]*
    To praise the King of kings;

6. He can sprawl when his master wag-
gles a finger or stick.
7. The Ichneumon, which resembles a
weasel, was venerated and domesticated
by the ancient Egyptians.

1. For the first edition of the poem,
Smart supplied a summary of the argument, here reprinted as a running series
of marginal glosses.

And voice of heaven-ascending swell,
Which, while its deeper notes excel,
    Clear, as a clarion, rings: 5

II

To bless each valley, grove and coast,
And charm the cherubs to the post
    Of gratitude in throngs;
To keep the days on Zion's mount,   10
And send the year to his account,
    With dances and with songs:

III

O Servant of God's holiest charge,
The minister of praise at large,
    Which thou may'st now receive;   15
From thy blessed mansion hail and hear,
From topmost eminence appear
    To this the wreath I weave.[1a]

IV

Great, valiant, pious, good, and clean,   *[The excellence and luster*
Sublime, contemplative, serene,   *of David's character in* 20
    Strong, constant, pleasant, wise!   *twelve points of view;]*
Bright effluence of exceeding grace;
Best man!—the swiftness and the race,
    The peril, and the prize!

V

Great—from the luster of his crown,   *[proved from the* 25
From Samuel's horn[2] and God's renown,   *history of his life]*
    Which is the people's voice;
For all the host from rear to van,
Applauded and embraced the man—
    The man of God's own choice.   30

VI

Valiant—the word, and up he rose—
The fight—he triumphed o'er the foes,
    Whom God's just laws abhor;

1a. David, a king among men, and now an angel in heaven, serves the King of kings by praising him with music, which keeps the world below in tune; Smart, in turn, sings the praises of David, the poet's intermediary with God.

2. "Then Samuel took the horn of oil, and anointed him in the midst of his brethren: and the spirit of the Lord came upon David from that day forward" (I Samuel xvi.13).

And armed in gallant faith he took
Against the boaster,[3] from the brook,   35
    The weapons of the war.

VII

Pious—magnificent and grand;
'Twas he the famous temple planned:
    (The seraph in his soul)[4]
Foremost to give the Lord his dues,   40
Foremost to bless the welcome news,
    And foremost to condole.

VIII

Good—from Jehudah's genuine vein,
From God's best nature good in grain,[5]
    His aspect and his heart;   45
To pity, to forgive, to save,
Witness En-gedi's conscious cave,
    And Shimei's blunted dart.[6]

IX

Clean—if perpetual prayer be pure,
And love, which could itself inure   50
    To fasting and to fear—
Clean in his gestures, hands, and feet,
To smite the lyre, the dance complete,
    To play the sword and spear.

X

Sublime—invention ever young,   55
Of vast conception, towering tongue
    To God the eternal theme;
Notes from yon exaltations caught,
Unrivaled royalty of thought,
    O'er meaner strains supreme.   60

XI

Contemplative—on God to fix
His musings, and above the six
    The sabbath-day he blessed;

3. Goliath, whom David slew with a stone from the brook.
4. According to I Chronicles xxviii, David's plan for the Temple in Jerusalem was directly inspired by the Lord's "seraph" within him.
5. In background and substance; Judah, David's tribe, was the tribe of kings.
6. In a cave in En-gedi, David spared Saul, who had wanted to kill him (I Samuel xxiv); though Shimei threw stones and curses at him, David later refused to take his life (II Samuel xvi, xix).

'Twas then his thoughts self-conquest pruned,
And heavenly melancholy tuned,   65
     To bless and bear the rest.

XII

Serene—to sow the seeds of peace,
Remembering, when he watched the fleece,
     How sweetly Kidron purled[7]—
To further knowledge, silence vice,   70
And plant perpetual paradise
     When God had calmed the world.

XIII

Strong—in the Lord, who could defy
Satan, and all his powers that lie
     In sempiternal night;   75
And hell, and horror, and despair
Were as the lion and the bear[8]
     To his undaunted might.

XIV

Constant—in love to God The Truth,
Age, manhood, infancy, and youth—   80
     To Jonathan his friend
Constant, beyond the verge of death;
And Ziba, and Mephibosheth,
     His endless fame attend.[9]

XV

Pleasant—and various as the year;   85
Man, soul, and angel, without peer,
     Priest, champion, sage and boy;
In armor, or in ephod[1] clad,
His pomp, his piety was glad;
     Majestic was his joy.   90

XVI

Wise—in recovery from his fall,
Whence rose his eminence o'er all,
     Of all the most reviled;
The light of Israel in his ways,
Wise are his precepts, prayer and praise,   95
     And counsel to his child.[2]

7. As a young man, David kept his father's sheep near Kidron, a brook that borders the district of Jerusalem; later, fleeing his own son Absalom, he crossed Kidron into the wilderness.
8. As a shepherd, David slew a lion and a bear with the help of the Lord, as later he slew Goliath (I Samuel xvii).
9. Jonathan's son Mephibosheth was restored to Saul's land by David, and was attended by Saul's servant Ziba.
1. Vestment of a Hebrew priest.

XVII

His muse, bright angel of his verse,
Gives balm for all the thorns that pierce,
 For all the pangs that rage;
Blessed light, still gaining on the gloom,
The more than Michal of his bloom,
 The Abishag of his age.[3]

*[He consecrates his genius
for consolation and
edification]*
100

XVIII

He sung of God—the mighty source
Of all things—the stupendous force
 On which all strength depends;
From whose right arm, beneath whose eyes,
All period, power, and enterprise
 Commences, reigns, and ends.

*[The subjects he made
choice of—the Supreme
Being;]* 105

XIX

Angels—their ministry and meed,
Which to and fro with blessings speed,
 Or with their citterns[4] wait;
Where Michael with his millions[5] bows,
Where dwells the seraph and his spouse,
 The cherub and her mate.

[angels;] 110

XX

Of man—the semblance and effect
Of God and Love—the Saint elect
 For infinite applause—
To rule the land, and briny broad,
To be laborious in his laud,
 And heroes in his cause.

[men of renown;] 115

120

XXI

The world—the clustering spheres he made,
The glorious light, the soothing shade,
 Dale, champaign, grove, and hill;
The multitudinous abyss,
Where secrecy remains in bliss,
 And wisdom hides her skill.

*[the works of
nature in all directions,
either particularly or
collectively considered]*

125

XXII

Trees, plants, and flowers—of virtuous[6] root;
Gem yielding blossom, yielding fruit,

2. The Proverbs and Psalms were supposed to be intended by David for his son Solomon.
3. More than Michal, his first wife, or Abishag, who ministered to him in old age, David's consolation is his muse, which gives balm for his sorrow as the Holy Spirit for Christ's.
4. Zither or lute.
5. God's legions, commanded by the archangel Michael.
6. Potent, medicinal; "Gem": bud.

Choice gums and precious balm;
Bless ye the nosegay in the vale,   130
And with the sweeteners of the gale
    Enrich the thankful psalm.

XXIII

Of fowl—e'en every beak and wing
Which cheer the winter, hail the spring,
    That live in peace or prey;   135
They that make music, or that mock,
The quail, the brave domestic cock,
    The raven, swan, and jay.

XXIV

Of fishes—every size and shape,
Which nature frames of light escape,   140
    Devouring man to shun:
The shells are in the wealthy deep,
The shoals[7] upon the surface leap,
    And love the glancing sun.

XXV

Of beasts—the beaver plods his task;   145
While the sleek tigers roll and bask,
    Nor yet the shades arouse;
Her cave the mining coney[8] scoops;
Where o'er the mead the mountain stoops,
    The kids exult and browse.   150

XXVI

Of gems—their virtue and their price,
Which hid in earth from man's device,
    Their darts of luster sheathe;
The jasper of the master's stamp,[9]
The topaz blazing like a lamp   155
    Among the mines beneath.

XXVII

Blessed was the tenderness he felt   *[He obtains power*
When to his graceful harp he knelt,   *over infernal spirits,]*
    And did for audience call;
When Satan with his hand he quelled,   160
And in serene suspense he held
    The frantic throes of Saul.[1]

7. Schools of fish.
8. Rabbit.
9. Jasper is used to make seals or sig-
nets of authority; hid in earth, it signi-

fies no authority but God's.
1. When Saul was oppressed by an evil
spirit, David cured him by playing on
the harp (I Samuel xvi).

XXVIII

His furious foes no more maligned
As he such melody divined,
⠀⠀⠀And sense and soul detained; ⠀⠀⠀⠀⠀*[and the malignity*
Now striking strong, now soothing soft, ⠀⠀⠀⠀⠀*of his enemies;]* 165
He sent the godly sounds aloft,
⠀⠀⠀Or in delight refrained.

XXIX

When up to heaven his thoughts he piled, ⠀⠀⠀*[wins the heart*
From fervent lips fair Michal smiled, ⠀⠀⠀⠀⠀*of Michal]* 170
⠀⠀⠀As blush to blush she stood;
And chose herself the queen, and gave
Her utmost from her heart, "so brave,
⠀⠀⠀And plays his hymns so good."[2]

XXX

The pillars of the Lord are seven, ⠀⠀⠀⠀*[Shows that the* 175
Which stand from earth to topmost heaven; ⠀⠀*pillars of knowledge*
⠀⠀⠀His wisdom drew the plan; ⠀⠀⠀⠀⠀⠀*are the monuments of*
His Word accomplished the design, ⠀⠀⠀⠀⠀*God's works in the*
From brightest gem to deepest mine, ⠀⠀⠀⠀⠀*first week]*
⠀⠀⠀From Christ enthroned to man.[3] ⠀⠀⠀⠀⠀⠀⠀180

XXXI

Alpha, the cause of causes, first
In station, fountain, whence the burst
⠀⠀⠀Of light, and blaze of day;
Whence bold attempt, and brave advance,
Have motion, life, and ordinance, ⠀⠀⠀⠀⠀⠀185
⠀⠀⠀And heaven itself its stay.[4]

XXXII

Gamma supports the glorious arch
On which angelic legions march,
⠀⠀⠀And is with sapphires paved;
Thence the fleet clouds are sent adrift, ⠀⠀⠀⠀⠀190

2. Though intended by her father Saul to be a "snare" to David, Michal fell in love with him, as her speech (invented by Smart) indicates.
3. The seven pillars of the house of wisdom, referred to in Proverbs, are associated by the Masons with the building of the first Temple, erected by Solomon in Jerusalem according to divine order. Smart believed that both Proverbs and the Temple had been planned by David.

In the following seven stanzas, each pillar is conflated with one of the days of Creation and with a Greek letter that represents one of the names of God. The implicit suggestion is that David, the greatest of poets and leaders, resembles the Creator, who called the universe into being with a Word.
4. Support. On the first day God called forth light.

And thence the painted folds, that lift
    The crimson veil, are waved.[5]

XXXIII

Eta with living sculpture breathes,
With verdant carvings, flowery wreathes
    Of never-wasting bloom:
In strong relief his goodly base
All instruments of labor grace,
    The trowel, spade, and loom.   195

XXXIV

Next Theta stands to the Supreme—
Who formed, in number, sign,[6] and scheme,
    The illustrious lights that are;   200
And one addressed[7] his saffron robe,
And one, clad in a silver globe,
    Held rule with every star.

XXXV

Iota's tuned to choral hymns   205
Of those that fly, while he that swims
    In thankful safety lurks;
And foot, and chapitre,[8] and niche,
The various histories enrich
    Of God's recorded works.   210

XXXVI

Sigma presents the social droves,
With him that solitary roves,
    And man of all the chief;
Fair on whose face, and stately frame,
Did God impress his hallowed name,   215
    For ocular belief.

XXXVII

OMEGA! GREATEST and the BEST,
Stands sacred to the day of rest,
    For gratitude and thought;
Which blessed the world upon his pole,   220
And gave the universe his goal,
    And closed the infernal draught.[9]

---

5. The firmament, created on the second day, is compared to the oracle of the Temple, which holds the ark of the covenant.

6. Constellation.

7. Put on. The sun, with the moon and stars, was created on the fourth day.

8. Capital of a pillar. The abundance of fish and fowl, created on the fifth day, is compared to the rich decorations of the Temple (I Kings vii).

9. The completed structure of the house of God (the world) shuts out the currents of Hell.

XXXVIII

O DAVID, scholar of the Lord!
Such is thy science, whence reward
    And infinite degree;[1]
O strength, O sweetness, lasting ripe!
God's harp thy symbol, and thy type[2]
    The lion and the bee!

225

XXXIX

There is but one who ne'er rebelled,
But One by passion unimpelled,
    By pleasure unenticed;
He from himself his semblance sent,
Grand object of his own content,
And saw the God in CHRIST.

230

XL

"Tell them, I am," JEHOVA said
To Moses; while earth heard in dread,
    And smitten to the heart,
At once above, beneath, around,
All Nature, without voice or sound,
    Replied, "O Lord, THOU ART."

[An exercise upon 235
the decalogue]

240

XLI

Thou art—to give and to confirm,
For each his talent and his term;
    All flesh thy bounties share:
Thou shalt not call thy brother fool;
The porches[3] of the Christian school
    Are meekness, peace, and prayer.

245

XLII

Open, and naked of offense,
Man's made of mercy, soul, and sense;
    God armed the snail and wilk;[4]
Be good to him that pulls thy plough;
Due food and care, due rest, allow
    For her that yields thee milk.

250

1. Elevation, rank.
2. Emblem. Theologically, a type is something in the Old Testament that prefigures some Christian truth. The lion and the bee, emblemizing the union of strength with sweetness (Judges xiv), prefigure David; and David himself pre- figures Christ, though, as the next stanza explains, no man can equal Him, since God is His own type.
3. Porticos where ancient philosophers debated.
4. Shellfish (the whelk).

XLIII

Rise up before the hoary head,
And God's benign commandment dread,
    Which says thou shalt not die;   255
"Not as I will, but as thou wilt,"[5]
Prayed He whose conscience knew no guilt;
    With whose blessed pattern vie.

XLIV

Use all thy passions!—love is thine,
And joy, and jealousy[6] divine,   260
    Thine hope's eternal fort,
And care thy leisure to disturb,
With fear concupiscence to curb,
    And rapture to transport.

XLV

Act simply, as occasion asks;   265
Put mellow wine in seasoned casks;
    Till not with ass and bull:
Remember thy baptismal bond;
Keep from commixtures foul and fond,
    Nor work thy flax with wool.   270

XLVI

Distribute: pay the Lord his tithe,
And make the widow's heart-strings blithe;
    Resort with those that weep:
As you from all and each expect,
For all and each thy love direct,   275
    And render as you reap.

XLVII

The slander and its bearer spurn,
And propagating praise sojourn
    To make thy welcome last;
Turn from old Adam to the New;[7]   280
By hope futurity pursue;
    Look upwards to the past.

XLVIII

Control thine eye, salute success,
Honor the wiser, happier bless,

5. Matthew xxvi.39. Christ exemplifies the fifth commandment by submitting to his Father's will.
6. Devotion.
7. Christ. As elsewhere in this section, Smart interprets the commandment positively, less as a warning against bearing false witness than as encouragement to bear witness to truth.

And for thy neighbor feel;   285
Grutch not of mammon and his leaven,[8]
Work emulation up to heaven
    By knowledge and by zeal.

XLIX

O DAVID, highest in the list
Of worthies, on God's ways insist,   290
    The genuine word repeat.[9]
Vain are the documents of men,
And vain the flourish of the pen
    That keeps the fool's conceit.

L

Praise above all—for praise prevails;   *[The transcendent virtue* 295
Heap up the measure, load the scales,   *of praise and adoration]*
    And good to goodness add:
The generous soul her Saviour aids,
But peevish obloquy degrades;
    The Lord is great and glad.   300

LI

For ADORATION all the ranks
Of angels yield eternal thanks,
    And DAVID in the midst;
With God's good poor, which, last and least
In man's esteem, thou to thy feast,   305
    O blessed bride-groom, bidst.

LII

For ADORATION seasons change,   *[An exercise upon the*
And order, truth, and beauty range,   *seasons, and the right*
    Adjust, attract, and fill: *use of them]*
The grass the polyanthus checks;[1]   310
And polished porphyry reflects,
    By the descending rill.

LIII

Rich almonds color to the prime
For ADORATION; tendrils climb,
    And fruit-trees pledge their gems;   315
And Ivis[2] with her gorgeous vest
Builds for her eggs her cunning nest,
    And bell-flowers bow their stems.

---

8. Do not begrudge the wealthy man his rise.
9. "Psalm 119" [Smart's note].

1. Checkers.
2. "Humming-bird" [Smart's note].

LIV

With vinous syrup cedars spout;
From rocks pure honey gushing out,
    For ADORATION springs: 320
All scenes of painting crowd the map
Of nature; to the mermaid's pap
    The scaléd infant clings.

LV

The spotted ounce and playsome cubs   325
Run rustling 'mongst the flowering shrubs,
    And lizards feed[3] the moss;
For ADORATION beasts embark,[4]
While waves upholding halcyon's ark
    No longer roar and toss.   330

LVI

While Israel sits beneath his fig,[5]
With coral root and amber sprig
    The weaned adventurer sports;
Where to the palm the jasmin cleaves,
For ADORATION 'mong the leaves   335
    The gale his peace reports.

LVII

Increasing days their reign exalt,
Nor in the pink and mottled vault
    The opposing spirits tilt;[6]
And, by the coasting reader spied,   340
The silverlings and crusions[7] glide
    For ADORATION gilt.

LVIII

For ADORATION ripening canes
And cocoa's purest milk detains
    The western pilgrim's staff;   345
Where rain in clasping boughs inclosed,
And vines with oranges disposed,
    Embower the social laugh.

---

3. Eat; "ounce": lynx.
4. "There is a large quadruped that preys upon fish, and provides himself with a piece of timber for that purpose, with which he is very handy" [Smart's note]. "Halcyon's ark": the kingfisher's nest was supposed to calm the sea by floating on it.
5. According to Micah iv.4, "they shall sit every man under his vine and his fig tree; and none shall make them afraid"; "weaned adventurer": a child. As spring turns into summer, so mankind shall mature into peace.
6. Clouds clash together.
7. Tarpon and carp; "coasting": floating in a boat.

LIX

Now labor his reward receives,
For ADORATION counts his sheaves   350
    To peace, her bounteous prince;
The nectarine his strong tint imbibes,
And apples of ten thousand tribes,
    And quick[8] peculiar quince.

LX

The wealthy crops of whitening rice,
'Mongst thyine[9] woods and groves of spice,   355
    For ADORATION grow;
And, marshalled in the fencèd land,
The peaches and pomegranates stand,
    Where wild carnations blow.   360

LXI

The laurels with the winter strive;
The crocus burnishes alive
    Upon the snow-clad earth:
For ADORATION myrtles stay
To keep the garden from dismay,   365
    And bless the sight from dearth.

LXII

The pheasant shows his pompous neck;
And ermine, jealous of a speck[1]
    With fear eludes offense:
The sable, with his glossy pride,   370
For ADORATION is descried,
    Where frosts the wave condense.

LXIII

The cheerful holly, pensive yew,
And holy thorn,[2] their trim renew;
    The squirrel hoards his nuts: 375
All creatures batten o'er their stores,
And careful nature all her doors
    For ADORATION shuts.

LXIV

For ADORATION, DAVID's psalms
Lift up the heart to deeds of alms;   380
    And he, who kneels and chants,

8. Pungent.   1. Suspicious of distant things.
9. Sweet.   2. Hawthorn.

Prevails his passions to control,
Finds meat and medicine to the soul,
    Which for translation[3] pants.

LXV

For ADORATION, beyond match,   *[An exercise upon the senses,* 385
The scholar[4] bulfinch aims to catch   *and how to subdue them]*
    The soft flute's ivory touch;
And careless on the hazel spray,
The daring redbreast keeps at bay
    The damsel's greedy clutch.   390

LXVI

For ADORATION, in the skies,
The Lord's philosopher espies
    The Dog, the Ram, and Rose;
The planets' ring, Orion's sword;
Nor is his greatness less adored   395
    In the vile worm that glows.

LXVII

For ADORATION on the strings[5]
The western breezes work their wings,
    The captive ear to sooth—
Hark! 'tis a voice—how still, and small—[6]   400
That makes the cataracts to fall,
    Or bids the sea be smooth.

LXVIII

For ADORATION, incense comes
From bezoar,[7] and Arabian gums;
    And from the civet's fur.   405
But as for prayer, or ere it faints,
Far better is the breath of saints
    Than galbanum and myrrh.[8]

LXIX

For ADORATION from the down
Of damasins[9] to the anana's crown,   410
    God sends to tempt the taste;
And while the luscious zest invites

---

3. Transference to heaven.
4. Imitative (the bullfinch can learn a tune).
5. "Aeolian harp" [Smart's note], played by the wind.
6. In I Kings xix.11–12, the Lord does not speak in the wind but in "a still small voice."
7. A medicinal lump that forms in the stomachs of some animals; "civet": civet cat.
8. Gum resins used in incense.
9. Damson plums; "anana's crown": pineapple's tuft.

The sense, that in the scene delights,
    Commands desire be chaste.

LXX

For ADORATION, all the paths   415
Of grace are open, all the baths
    Of purity refresh;
And all the rays of glory beam
To deck the man of God's esteem,
    Who triumphs o'er the flesh.   420

LXXI

For ADORATION, in the dome
Of Christ the sparrows find an home,
    And on his olives perch:
The swallow also dwells with thee,
O man of God's humility,   425
    Within his Saviour CHURCH.

LXXII

Sweet is the dew that falls betimes,   *[An amplification*
And drops upon the leafy limes;   *in five degrees,]*
    Sweet Hermon's fragrant air:[1]
Sweet is the lily's silver bell,   430
And sweet the wakeful tapers smell
    That watch for early prayer.

LXXIII

Sweet the young nurse with love intense,
Which smiles o'er sleeping innocence;
    Sweet when the lost arrive: 435
Sweet the musician's ardor beats,
While his vague mind's in quest of sweets,
    The choicest flowers to hive.

LXXIV

Sweeter in all the strains of love,
The language of thy turtle dove,   440
    Paired to thy swelling chord;
Sweeter with every grace endued,
The glory of thy gratitude,
    Respired unto the Lord.

1. The dew of Hermon, a mountain in   Psalm 133.
Syria, is associated with Zion's dew in

LXXV

Strong is the horse upon his speed; 445
Strong in pursuit the rapid glede,[2]
    Which makes at once his game:
Strong the tall ostrich on the ground;
Strong through the turbulent profound
    Shoots xiphias[3] to his aim. 450

LXXVI

Strong is the lion—like a coal
His eyeball—like a bastion's mole[4]
    His chest against the foes:
Strong the gier-eagle[5] on his sail,
Strong against tide, the enormous whale 455
    Emerges, as he goes.

LXXVII

But stronger still, in earth and air,
And in the sea, the man of prayer;
    And far beneath the tide;
And in the seat to faith assigned,
Where ask is have, where seek is find, 460
    Where knock is open wide.

LXXVIII

Beauteous the fleet before the gale;
Beauteous the multitudes in mail,
    Ranked arms and crested heads:
Beauteous the garden's umbrage mild, 465
Walk, water, meditated wild,[6]
    And all the bloomy beds.

LXXIX

Beauteous the moon full on the lawn;
And beauteous, when the veil's withdrawn, 470
    The virgin to her spouse:
Beauteous the temple decked and filled,
When to the heaven of heavens they build
    Their heart-directed vows.

LXXX

Beauteous, yea beauteous more than these, 475
The shepherd king upon his knees,

---

2. Hawk.
3. "The sword-fish" [Smart's note].
4. Fortified wall.

5. Vulture.
6. Artificial wild place within a garden or park.

For his momentous trust;
With wish of infinite conceit,[7]
For man, beast, mute, the small and great,
    And prostrate dust to dust.   480

LXXXI

Precious the bounteous widow's mite;
And precious, for extreme delight,
    The largess from the churl:[8]
Precious the ruby's blushing blaze,
And alba's[9] blest imperial rays,   485
    And pure cerulean pearl.

LXXXII

Precious the penitential tear;
And precious is the sigh sincere,
    Acceptable to God:
And precious are the winning flowers,   490
In gladsome Israel's feast of bowers,[1]
    Bound on the hallowed sod.

LXXXIII

More precious that diviner part
Of David, even the Lord's own heart,
    Great, beautiful, and new: 495
In all things where it was intent,
In all extremes, in each event,
    Proof[2]—answering true to true.

LXXXIV

Glorious the sun in mid career;
Glorious the assembled fires appear;   500
    Glorious the comet's train:
Glorious the trumpet and alarm;
Glorious the almighty stretched-out arm;
    Glorious the enraptured main:

LXXXV

Glorious the northern lights astream;   505
Glorious the song, when God's the theme;
    Glorious the thunder's roar:

---

7. Conception; "mute": fish.
8. "Samuel 25:18" [Smart's note]. Against the will of Nabal, a churlish rich man, his wife Abigail gave largess to David.
9. "Revelation 2:17" [Smart's note]; a white stone, given to the church trium-phant.
1. The Feast of Tabernacles, or Succoth, ordained five days after the day of atonement, in thanksgiving for deliverance from Egypt.
2. Meeting the test.

Glorious hosanna from the den;
Glorious the catholic amen;
   Glorious the martyr's gore:

LXXXVI

Glorious—more glorious is the crown
Of Him, that brought salvation down
   By meekness, called thy Son;
Thou at stupendous truth believed,
And now the matchless deed's achieved,
   DETERMINED, DARED, and DONE.

[which is wrought up
to this conclusion, That
the best poet which 510
ever lived was thought
worthy of the highest
honor which possibly can
be conceived, as
*the Saviour of the
World was ascribed
to his house, and
called his son in the* 515
body.]

1763

OLIVER GOLDSMITH
(ca. 1730–1774)

It is difficult to distinguish fact from fiction in the accounts that we have of Goldsmith's first thirty years. Unlike the works of most 18th-century authors, his writings contain much that is personal, but it is of little use to biographers, for it has been heightened and romanticized until it belongs at least as much to fiction as to autobiography. The Goldsmith legend, which has served as the poet's biography, is to some degree the creation of Goldmith himself.

He was born in Ireland, the son of an Anglican clergyman whose geniality he inherited and whose improvidence he imitated. He was early disfigured by smallpox and grew up ugly of face, ungraceful of figure, and in his early years apparently stupid and certainly idle. Nonetheless, he was sent to Trinity College, Dublin, as a sizar—i.e., a student who did menial jobs for well-to-do undergraduates—and there he took his A.B. in 1749. After several false starts in choosing a career, he was sent by a generous uncle to study medicine at the University of Edinburgh. Instead of taking a degree, he wandered for a while on the Continent, visiting Holland, France, Italy, and Switzerland. A much romanticized account of this journey can be read in the story of George Primrose in Goldsmith's novel, *The Vicar of Wakefield* (1766). He returned to England in 1756 with a mysteriously acquired M.D. and tried in vain to support himself as a physician among the poor in the Borough of Southwark. After serving for a while as an usher in a school, he drifted into the profession of hack writer for Ralph Griffiths, the proprietor of the *Monthly Review*, and later worked for and with the benevolent publisher Edward Newbery. He first attracted attention by a short book, *An Inquiry into the Present State of Polite Learning in Europe* (1759), in which he traced what he considered to be the decline of the fine arts in mid-18th-century Europe to the lack of enlightened patronage and to the malign influence of criticism and scholarship. From then until his death he earned by his writings very large sums indeed, but his habitual extravagance and generosity kept him always in debt, no matter how ample his income. When he was in funds he lived richly; when he was without money, he borrowed. He died owing the then prodigious sum (for a man whose only source of income was writing) of £2,000.

The variety and excellence of Goldsmith's work is astonishing. His easy and pleasant prose style, his abundant humor, his shrewd observations of character and scene have made his essays constantly popular. His great gift for the comedy of character and situation enabled him to achieve in his two plays, *The Good-Natured Man* (1768) and *She Stoops to Conquer* (1773), a sort of pure and mirthful comedy—uncomplicated by ethical or social criticism and unspoiled by the fashionable sentimentality of the moment—that is unique in the century. His two important poems, *The Traveler, or A Prospect of Society* (1764) and *The Deserted Village*, are distinguished for the purity and harmony of their language. The couplets of *The Deserted Village* lack the rhetoric and formality of Pope's or Johnson's couplets and become almost lyrical in sound and movement.

Goldsmith was an intimate of the circle of brilliant men of whom Johnson was the center. Boswell's description of him in famous scenes in the *Life* is certainly ill-natured and unfair. He was not the inspired idiot, the blundering Irishman with a dash of genius, that Boswell and other members of the group insisted he was. His sly humor, often directed against himself, seems not to have been understood by most of his friends, who took pains to repeat solemnly as examples of Irish "bulls" (verbal blunders) what Goldsmith certainly meant in jest. He was not a profound thinker and his learning was not extensive; but even such hack-work compilations as the *History of Rome*, the *History of Greece*, and the *History of Animated Nature*, which he put together carelessly and rapidly, were ensured a certain life by the charm of his manner and style.

The Deserted Village[1]

Sweet Auburn! loveliest village of the plain,
Where health and plenty cheered the laboring swain,
Where smiling spring its earliest visit paid,

1. *The Deserted Village* is an idealization of English rural life, mingled with poignant memories of the poet's own youth in Lissoy, Ireland. Goldsmith was seriously concerned about the effects of the agricultural revolution then in progress which was being hastened by Enclosure Acts. Either for the sake of more profitable farming or to create vast private parks and landscape gardens, arable land was being taken out of the hands of small proprietors (i.e., "enclosed"), thus displacing yeoman farmers who, like their ancestors, had lived for generations in small villages, grazing their cattle on common land and raising food on small holdings. The only alternative available to many such people was to seek employment in the city or to migrate to America. Goldsmith certainly exaggerates the effects of the enclosures, nor are his diatribes against the debilitating influence of luxury borne out by history; Waterloo and the glories of the 19th century lay ahead for England. In the poem Goldsmith opposes "luxury" (the increase of wealth, the growth of cities, the costly country estates of great noblemen and wealthy merchants) to "rural virtue" (the old agrarian economy which supported a sturdy population of independent peas-

· *Oliver Goldsmith*

And parting summer's lingering blooms delayed:
Dear lovely bowers of innocence and ease, 5
Seats of my youth, when every sport could please,
How often have I loitered o'er thy green,
Where humble happiness endeared each scene;
How often have I paused on every charm,
The sheltered cot, the cultivated farm, 10
The never-failing brook, the busy mill,
The decent church that topped the neighboring hill,
The hawthorn bush, with seats beneath the shade,
For talking age and whispering lovers made;
How often have I blessed the coming day, 15
When toil remitting lent its turn to play,
And all the village train, from labor free,
Led up their sports beneath the spreading tree,
While many a pastime circled in the shade,
The young contending as the old surveyed; 20
And many a gambol frolicked o'er the ground,
And sleights of art and feats of strength went round;
And still as each repeated pleasure tired,
Succeeding sports the mirthful band inspired;
The dancing pair that simply sought renown, 25
By holding out to tire each other down;
The swain mistrustless of his smutted face,
While secret laughter tittered round the place;
The bashful virgin's sidelong looks of love,
The matron's glance that would those looks reprove: 30
These were thy charms, sweet village! sports like these,
With sweet succession, taught even toil to please;
These round thy bowers their cheerful influence shed,
These were thy charms—But all these charms are fled.
    Sweet smiling village, loveliest of the lawn, 35
Thy sports are fled, and all thy charms withdrawn;
Amidst thy bowers the tyrant's hand is seen,
And desolation saddens all thy green:
One only master grasps the whole domain,
And half a tillage stints thy smiling plain; 40
No more thy glassy brook reflects the day,
But choked with sedges, works its weedy way;
Along thy glades, a solitary guest,
The hollow-sounding bittern guards its nest;
Amidst thy desert walks the lapwing flies, 45
And tires their echoes with unvaried cries.
Sunk are thy bowers, in shapeless ruin all,
And the long grass o'ertops the moldering wall,
And, trembling, shrinking from the spoiler's hand,
Far, far away thy children leave the land. 50
    Ill fares the land, to hastening ills a prey,

---

ants). His poem is thus at once a nostalgic lament for a doomed way of life and a denunciation of what he regarded as the corrupting, destructive force of new wealth.

Where wealth accumulates, and men decay;
Princes and lords may flourish, or may fade;
A breath can make them, as a breath has made;
But a bold peasantry, their country's pride,   55
When once destroyed, can never be supplied.
    A time there was, ere England's griefs began,
When every rood of ground maintained its man;
For him light labor spread her wholesome store,
Just gave what life required, but gave no more: 60
His best companions, innocence and health;
And his best riches, ignorance of wealth.
    But times are altered; Trade's unfeeling train
Usurp the land and dispossess the swain;
Along the lawn, where scattered hamlets rose,   65
Unwieldy wealth, and cumbrous pomp repose;
And every want to opulence allied,
And every pang that folly pays to pride.
These gentle hours that plenty bade to bloom,
Those calm desires that asked but little room,   70
Those healthful sports that graced the peaceful scene,
Lived in each look, and brightened all the green;
These far departing seek a kinder shore,
And rural mirth and manners are no more.
    Sweet Auburn! parent of the blissful hour,   75
Thy glades forlorn confess the tyrant's power.
Here, as I take my solitary rounds,
Amidst thy tangling walks, and ruined grounds,
And, many a year elapsed, return to view
Where once the cottage stood, the hawthorn grew,   80
Remembrance wakes with all her busy train,
Swells at my breast, and turns the past to pain.
    In all my wanderings round this world of care,
In all my griefs—and God has given my share—
I still had hopes my latest hours to crown,   85
Amidst these humble bowers to lay me down;
To husband out life's taper at the close,
And keep the flame from wasting by repose.
I still had hopes, for pride attends us still,
Amidst the swains to show my book-learned skill,   90
Around my fire an evening group to draw,
And tell of all I felt, and all I saw;
And, as an hare whom hounds and horns pursue,
Pants to the place from whence at first she flew,
I still had hopes, my long vexations past,   95
Here to return—and die at home at last.
    O blest retirement, friend to life's decline,
Retreats from care that never must be mine,
How happy he who crowns in shades like these,
A youth of labor with an age of ease;   100
Who quits a world where strong temptations try,
And, since 'tis hard to combat, learns to fly!

For him no wretches, born to work and weep,
Explore the mine, or tempt the dangerous deep;
No surly porter stands in guilty state   105
To spurn imploring famine from the gate;
But on he moves to meet his latter end,
Angels around befriending virtue's friend;
Bends to the grave with unperceived decay,
While Resignation gently slopes the way;   110
And, all his prospects brightening to the last,
His Heaven commences ere the world be passed!
    Sweet was the sound when oft at evening's close,
Up yonder hill the village murmur rose;
There, as I passed with careless steps and slow,   115
The mingling notes came softened from below;
The swain responsive as the milkmaid sung,
The sober herd that lowed to meet their young,
The noisy geese that gabbled o'er the pool,
The playful children just let loose from school;   120
The watchdog's voice that bayed the whispering wind,
And the loud laugh that spoke the vacant[2] mind;
These all in sweet confusion sought the shade,
And filled each pause the nightingale had made.
But now the sounds of population fail,   125
No cheerful murmurs fluctuate in the gale,
No busy steps the grass-grown footway tread,
For all the bloomy flush of life is fled.
All but yon widowed, solitary thing
That feebly bends beside the plashy spring;   130
She, wretched matron, forced, in age, for bread,
To strip the brook with mantling cresses spread,
To pick her wintry faggot from the thorn,
To seek her nightly shed, and weep till morn;
She only left of all the harmless train,   135
The sad historian of the pensive plain.
    Near yonder copse, where once the garden smiled,
And still where many a garden flower grows wild,
There, where a few torn shrubs the place disclose,
The village preacher's modest mansion rose.   140
A man he was, to all the country dear,
And passing rich with forty pounds a year;
Remote from towns he ran his godly race,
Nor e'er had changed, nor wished to change his place;
Unpracticed he to fawn, or seek for power,   145
By doctrines fashioned to the varying hour;
Far other aims his heart had learned to prize,
More skilled to raise the wretched than to rise.
His house was known to all the vagrant train,
He chid their wanderings, but relieved their pain;   150
The long-remembered beggar was his guest,

2. Idle.

Whose beard descending swept his aged breast;
The ruined spendthrift, now no longer proud,
Claimed kindred there, and had his claims allowed;
The broken soldier, kindly bade to stay,   155
Sate by his fire, and talked the night away;
Wept o'er his wounds, or tales of sorrow done,
Shouldered his crutch, and showed how fields were won.
Pleased with his guests, the good man learned to glow,
And quite forgot their vices in their woe;   160
Careless their merits, or their faults to scan,
His pity gave ere charity began.
  Thus to relieve the wretched was his pride,
And even his failings leaned to Virtue's side;
But in his duty prompt at every call,   165
He watched and wept, he prayed and felt, for all.
And, as a bird each fond endearment tries,
To tempt its new-fledged offspring to the skies,
He tried each art, reproved each dull delay,
Allured to brighter worlds, and led the way.   170
  Beside the bed where parting life was laid,
And sorrow, guilt, and pain, by turns dismayed,
The reverend champion stood. At his control,
Despair and anguish fled the struggling soul;
Comfort came down the trembling wretch to raise,   175
And his last faltering accents whispered praise.
  At church, with meek and unaffected grace,
His looks adorned the venerable place;
Truth from his lips prevailed with double sway,
And fools, who came to scoff, remained to pray.   180
The service past, around the pious man,
With steady zeal each honest rustic ran;
Even children followed with endearing wile,
And plucked his gown, to share the good man's smile.
His ready smile a parent's warmth expressed,   185
Their welfare pleased him, and their cares distressed;
To them his heart, his love, his griefs were given,
But all his serious thoughts had rest in Heaven.
As some tall cliff that lifts its awful form,
Swells from the vale, and midway leaves the storm,   190
Though round its breast the rolling clouds are spread,
Eternal sunshine settles on its head.
  Beside yon straggling fence that skirts the way,
With blossomed furze unprofitably gay,
There, in his noisy mansion, skilled to rule,   195
The village master taught his little school;
A man severe he was, and stern to view,
I knew him well, and every truant knew;
Well had the boding tremblers learned to trace
The day's disasters in his morning face;   200
Full well they laughed with counterfeited glee,

At all his jokes, for many a joke had he;
Full well the busy whisper circling round,
Conveyed the dismal tidings when he frowned;
Yet he was kind, or if severe in aught,   205
The love he bore to learning was in fault;[3]
The village all declared how much he knew;
'Twas certain he could write, and cipher too;
Lands he could measure, terms[4] and tides presage,
And even the story ran that he could gauge.[5]   210
In arguing too, the parson owned his skill,
For even though vanquished, he could argue still;
While words of learned length, and thundering sound,
Amazed the gazing rustics ranged around;
And still they gazed, and still the wonder grew,   215
That one small head could carry all he knew.
    But past is all his fame. The very spot
Where many a time he triumphed, is forgot.
Near yonder thorn, that lifts its head on high,
Where once the signpost caught the passing eye,   220
Low lies that house where nut-brown draughts inspired,
Where graybeard Mirth and smiling Toil retired,
Where village statesmen talked with looks profound,
And news much older than their ale went round.
Imagination fondly stoops to trace   225
The parlor splendors of that festive place:
The whitewashed wall, the nicely sanded floor,
The varnished clock that clicked behind the door;
The chest contrived a double debt to pay,
A bed by night, a chest of drawers by day;   230
The pictures placed for ornament and use,
The twelve good rules,[6] the royal game of goose;
The hearth, except when winter chilled the day,
With aspen boughs, and flowers, and fennel gay,
While broken teacups, wisely kept for show,   235
Ranged o'er the chimney, glistened in a row.
    Vain transitory splendors! Could not all
Reprieve the tottering mansion from its fall!
Obscure it sinks, nor shall it more impart
An hour's importance to the poor man's heart;   240
Thither no more the peasant shall repair
To sweet oblivion of his daily care;
No more the farmer's news, the barber's tale,
No more the woodman's ballad shall prevail;
No more the smith his dusky brow shall clear,   245
Relax his ponderous strength, and lean to hear;

3. Since the *l* was silent, "fault" and
"aught" rhymed perfectly.
4. Dates on which rent, wages, etc.,
were due and tenancy began or ended;
"tides": feasts and seasons in the church
year.
5. Measure the content of casks and
other vessels.

6. "The twelve good rules" of conduct,
attributed to Charles I, were printed
in a broadside that was often seen on
the walls of taverns; "goose" was a
game in which counters were moved
on a board according to the throw of
the dice.

The host himself no longer shall be found
Careful to see the mantling bliss[7] go round;
Nor the coy maid, half willing to be pressed,
Shall kiss the cup to pass it to the rest.   250
    Yes! let the rich deride, the proud disdain,
These simple blessings of the lowly train,
To me more dear, congenial to my heart,
One native charm, than all the gloss of art;
Spontaneous joys, where nature has its play,   255
The soul adopts, and owns their first-born sway;
Lightly they frolic o'er the vacant mind,
Unenvied, unmolested, unconfined.
But the long pomp, the midnight masquerade,
With all the freaks of wanton wealth arrayed,   260
In these, ere triflers half their wish obtain,
The toiling pleasure sickens into pain;
And, even while fashion's brightest arts decoy,
The heart distrusting asks if this be joy.
    Ye friends to truth, ye statesmen, who survey   265
The rich man's joys increase, the poor's decay,
'Tis yours to judge how wide the limits stand
Between a splendid and an happy land.
Proud swells the tide with loads of freighted ore,
And shouting Folly hails them from her shore;   270
Hoards, even beyond the miser's wish abound,
And rich men flock from all the world around.
Yet count our gains. This wealth is but a name
That leaves our useful products still the same.
Not so the loss. The man of wealth and pride,   275
Takes up a space that many poor supplied;
Space for his lake, his park's extended bounds,
Space for his horses, equipage, and hounds;
The robe that wraps his limbs in silken sloth
Has robbed the neighboring fields of half their growth;   280
His seat, where solitary sports are seen,
Indignant spurns the cottage from the green;
Around the world each needful product flies,
For all the luxuries the world supplies.
While thus the land adorned for pleasure, all   285
In barren splendor feebly waits the fall.
    As some fair female unadorned and plain,
Secure to please while youth confirms her reign,
Slights every borrowed charm that dress supplies,
Nor shares with art the triumph of her eyes: 290
But when those charms are past, for charms are frail,
When time advances, and when lovers fail,
She then shines forth, solicitous to bless,
In all the glaring impotence of dress.
Thus fares the land, by luxury betrayed;   295
In nature's simplest charms at first arrayed;

7. Foaming bliss, i.e., foaming ale.

But verging to decline, its splendors rise,
Its vistas strike, its palaces surprise;
While scourged by famine from the smiling land,
The mournful peasant leads his humble band; 300
And while he sinks without one arm to save,
The country blooms—a garden, and a grave.
　　Where then, ah where, shall Poverty reside,
To 'scape the pressure of contiguous Pride?
If to some common's fenceless limits strayed, 305
He drives his flock to pick the scanty blade,
Those fenceless fields the sons of wealth divide,
And even the bare-worn common is denied.
　　If to the city sped—What waits him there?
To see profusion that he must not share; 310
To see ten thousand baneful arts combined
To pamper luxury, and thin mankind;
To see those joys the sons of pleasure know,
Extorted from his fellow creature's woe.
Here, while the courtier glitters in brocade, 315
There the pale artist[8] plies the sickly trade;
Here, while the proud their long-drawn pomps display,
There the black gibbet glooms beside the way.
The dome where Pleasure holds her midnight reign,
Here, richly decked, admits the gorgeous train; 320
Tumultuous grandeur crowds the blazing square,
The rattling chariots clash, the torches glare.
Sure scenes like these no troubles e'er annoy!
Sure these denote one universal joy!
Are these thy serious thoughts?—Ah, turn thine eyes 325
Where the poor houseless shivering female lies.
She once, perhaps, in village plenty blest,
Has wept at tales of innocence distressed;
Her modest looks the cottage might adorn,
Sweet as the primrose peeps beneath the thorn; 330
Now lost to all; her friends, her virtue fled,
Near her betrayer's door she lays her head,
And pinched with cold, and shrinking from the shower,
With heavy heart deplores that luckless hour,
When idly first, ambitious of the town, 335
She left her wheel and robes of country brown.
　　Do thine, sweet Auburn, thine, the loveliest train,
Do thy fair tribes participate her pain?
Even now, perhaps, by cold and hunger led,
At proud men's doors they ask a little bread! 340
　　Ah, no. To distant climes, a dreary scene,
Where half the convex world intrudes between,
Through torrid tracts with fainting steps they go,
Where wild Altama[9] murmurs to their woe.
Far different there from all that charmed before, 345
The various terrors of that horrid shore;

8. Artisan. 　　　　　　　　　　　9. The Altamaha River in Georgia.

Those blazing suns that dart a downward ray,
And fiercely shed intolerable day;
Those matted woods where birds forget to sing,
But silent bats in drowsy clusters cling,
Those poisonous fields with rank luxuriance crowned,   350
Where the dark scorpion gathers death around;
Where at each step the stranger fears to wake
The rattling terrors of the vengeful snake;
Where crouching tigers wait their hapless prey,[1]   355
And savage men, more murderous still than they;
While oft in whirls the mad tornado flies,
Mingling the ravaged landscape with the skies.
Far different these from every former scene,
The cooling brook, the grassy vested green,   360
The breezy covert of the warbling grove,
That only sheltered thefts of harmless love.
      Good Heaven! what sorrows gloomed that parting day,
That called them from their native walks away;
When the poor exiles, every pleasure past,   365
Hung round their bowers, and fondly looked their last,
And took a long farewell, and wished in vain
For seats like these beyond the western main;
And shuddering still to face the distant deep,
Returned and wept, and still returned to weep.   370
The good old sire, the first prepared to go
To new-found worlds, and wept for other's woe.
But for himself, in conscious virtue brave,
He only wished for worlds beyond the grave.
His lovely daughter, lovelier in her tears,   375
The fond companion of his helpless years,
Silent went next, neglectful of her charms,
And left a lover's for a father's arms.
With louder plaints the mother spoke her woes,
And blessed the cot where every pleasure rose;   380
And kissed her thoughtless babes with many a tear,
And clasped them close in sorrow doubly dear;
Whilst her fond husband strove to lend relief
In all the silent manliness of grief.
      O luxury! Thou cursed by Heaven's decree,   385
How ill exchanged are things like these for thee!
How do thy potions, with insidious joy,
Diffuse their pleasures only to destroy!
Kingdoms, by thee, to sickly greatness grown,
Boast of a florid vigor not their own.   390
At every draught more large and large they grow,
A bloated mass of rank unwieldy woe;
Till sapped their strength, and every part unsound,
Down, down they sink, and spread a ruin round.
      Even now the devastation is begun,   395
And half the business of destruction done;

1. Not the Asiatic tiger, but the puma.

Even now, methinks, as pondering here I stand,
I see the rural Virtues leave the land.
Down where yon anchoring vessel spreads the sail,
That idly waiting flaps with every gale,   460
Downward they move, a melancholy band,
Pass from the shore, and darken all the strand.
Contented Toil, and hospitable Care,
And kind connubial Tenderness are there;
And Piety, with wishes placed above,   405
And steady Loyalty, and faithful Love:
And thou, sweet Poetry, thou loveliest maid,
Still first to fly where sensual joys invade;
Unfit in these degenerate times of shame,
To catch the heart, or strike for honest fame;   410
Dear charming Nymph, neglected and decried,
My shame in crowds, my solitary pride;
Thou source of all my bliss, and all my woe,
That found'st me poor at first, and keep'st me so;
Thou guide by which the nobler arts excel,   415
Thou nurse of every virtue, fare thee well.
Farewell, and O! where'er thy voice be tried
On Torno's cliffs, or Pambamarca's side,[2]
Whether where equinoctial fervors glow,
Or winter wraps the polar world in snow,   420
Still let thy voice, prevailing over time,
Redress the rigors of the inclement clime;
Aid slighted truth, with thy persuasive strain
Teach erring man to spurn the rage of gain;
Teach him that states of native strength possessed,   425
Though very poor, may still be very blest;
That Trade's proud empire hastes to swift decay,
As ocean sweeps the labored mole[3] away;
While self-dependent power can time defy,
As rocks resist the billows and the sky.[4]   430

1770

2. The river Torne in Sweden falls into   3. The laboriously built breakwater.
the Gulf of Bothnia; Pambamarca is a   4. Johnson composed the last four lines
mountain in Ecuador.   of the poem.

GEORGE CRABBE

(1754–1832)

Crabbe belongs to the early 19th rather than to the 18th century, but his
first successful poem is very much a part of the literature of our period.
Born to poverty in a small, decayed Suffolk seaport, Aldeburgh, he was
apprenticed to a surgeon, but found it impossible to earn a living by
practicing in his native village. In 1780 he went to London, and succeeded

neither in finding a patron nor in securing literary employment, until, reduced to desperate straits, he sent an appeal to Edmund Burke, who recognized his merit and gave him timely help. Through Burke's influence *The Library* was published; Dr. Johnson agreed to correct *The Village*; and Crabbe was ordained a minister in the Anglican Church. His appointment as chaplain to the Duke of Rutland enabled him to marry the woman to whom he had long been engaged.

After 1785 he published nothing until 1807, when *The Parish Register* appeared. It was followed by *The Borough* (1810), *Tales* (1812), and *Tales of the Hall* (1819). In these poems, which won the admiration of Wordsworth, Scott, and Byron, Crabbe continued the vein of realism which had distinguished *The Village*, and developed his great gift for narrative and characterization. He was well aware of the difference between his poetry, written in rather prosaic language and heroic couplets, abounding in realistic details and concerned with ordinary people, and that of his two great Romantic contemporaries, Sir Walter Scott and Lord Byron. Scott's medieval and Byron's Oriental tales possessed the charm of the remote and exotic. Crabbe described his own poetry as "poetry without an atmosphere." It is, however, almost always interesting and often dramatic and moving.

The Village was widely read and admired despite the fact that it is not free from faults that Crabbe never overcame: slipshod rhymes, and sometimes flat and often stilted language. But its unrelieved realism and its gloomy darkness of tone set it sharply apart from conventional poems on rural life during the century. Indeed it is an angry, a scornful reply to the sentimental cult of rural simplicity, innocence, and happiness. It glances at the unrealities of the pastoral convention and, somewhat more systematically, it answers Goldsmith's charming idealization of villagers and their life in *The Deserted Village*. Crabbe knew the degrading effect of hopeless poverty, he had observed rural vice, he knew the gulf that sometimes separated the landed gentry from their laboring tenants. Out of recollections of Aldeburgh and the neighboring seacoast he fashioned a setting for his poem in which the penury of a niggardly nature seems the only proper background for the penury of the men who inhabit it. The accuracy and vividness of the details created a poetry of the ugly which is at variance with the long tradition of natural description from Thomson to Cowper.

From The Village

Book I

The village life, and every care that reigns
O'er youthful peasants and declining swains;
What labor yields, and what, that labor past,
Age, in its hour of languor, finds at last;
What form the real picture of the poor,   5
Demand a song—the Muse can give no more.
Fled are those times when, in harmonious strains,

The rustic poet praised his native plains.
No shepherds now, in smooth altérnate verse,
Their country's beauty or their nymphs' rehearse;   10
Yet still for these we frame the tender strain,
Still in our lays fond Corydons[1] complain,
And shepherds' boys their amorous pains reveal,
The only pains, alas! they never feel.
    On Mincio's[2] banks, in Caesar's bounteous reign,   15
If Tityrus found the Golden Age again,
Must sleepy bards the flattering dream prolong,
Mechanic echoes of the Mantuan song?
From Truth and Nature shall we widely stray,
Where Virgil, not where Fancy, leads the way?   20
    Yes, thus the Muses sing of happy swains,
Because the Muses never knew their pains.
They boast their peasants' pipes; but peasants now
Resign their pipes and plod behind the plow;
And few, amid the rural tribe, have time   25
To number syllables, and play with rhyme;
Save honest Duck,[3] what son of verse could share
The poet's rapture, and the peasant's care?
Or the great labors of the field degrade,
With the new peril of a poorer trade?   30
    From this chief cause these idle praises spring,
That themes so easy few forbear to sing;
For no deep thought the trifling subjects ask:
To sing of shepherds is an easy task.
The happy youth assumes the common strain,   35
A nymph his mistress, and himself a swain;
With no sad scenes he clouds his tuneful prayer,
But all, to look like her, is painted fair.
    I grant indeed that fields and flocks have charms
For him that grazes or for him that farms;   40
But when amid such pleasing scenes I trace
The poor laborious natives of the place,
And see the midday sun, with fervid ray,
On their bare heads and dewy temples play;
While some, with feebler heads and fainter hearts,   45
Deplore their fortune, yet sustain their parts:
Then shall I dare these real ills to hide
In tinsel trappings of poetic pride?
    No; cast by Fortune on a frowning coast,
Which neither groves nor happy valleys boast;   50
Where other cares than those the Muse relates,
And other shepherds dwell with other mates;
By such examples taught, I paint the cot,

1. "Corydon" is a stock name for a
shepherd in pastorals, used by both
Theocritus and Virgil.
2. Virgil was born near Mantua, in
Italy, not far from the river Mincius.
Tityrus is one of the speakers in Vir-

gil's *Eclogues* I.
3. Stephen Duck (1705–56), the
"Thresher Poet," was a self-educated
agricultural laborer whose verses attracted attention and finally won him
the patronage of Queen Caroline.

As Truth will paint it, and as bards will not:
Nor you, ye poor, of lettered scorn complain,　　　　55
To you the smoothest song is smooth in vain;
O'ercome by labor, and bowed down by time,
Feel you the barren flattery of a rhyme?
Can poets soothe you, when you pine for bread,
By winding myrtles round your ruined shed?　　　　60
Can their light tales your weighty griefs o'erpower,
Or glad with airy mirth the toilsome hour?
　　Lo! where the heath, with withering brake grown o'er,
Lends the light turf that warms the neighboring poor;
From thence a length of burning sand appears,　　　65
Where the thin harvest waves its withered ears;
Rank weeds, that every art and care defy,
Reign o'er the land, and rob the blighted rye:
There thistles stretch their prickly arms afar,
And to the ragged infant threaten war;　　　　70
There poppies, nodding, mock the hope of toil;
There the blue bugloss paints the sterile soil;
Hardy and high, above the slender sheaf,
The slimy mallow waves her silky leaf;
O'er the young shoot the charlock throws a shade,　　75
And clasping tares cling round the sickly blade;
With mingled tints the rocky coasts abound,
And a sad splendor vainly shines around.
So looks the nymph whom wretched arts adorn,
Betrayed by man, then left for man to scorn;　　　80
Whose cheek in vain assumes the mimic rose,
While her sad eyes the troubled breast disclose;
Whose outward splendor is but folly's dress,
Exposing most, when most it gilds distress.
　　Here joyless roam a wild amphibious race,　　　85
With sullen woe displayed in every face;
Who far from civil arts and social fly,
And scowl at strangers with suspicious eye.
　　Here too the lawless merchant of the main
Draws from his plow the intoxicated swain;　　　90
Want only claimed the labor of the day,
But vice now steals his nightly rest away.
　　Where are the swains, who, daily labor done,
With rural games played down the setting sun;
　　Who struck with matchless force the bounding ball,　95
Or made the ponderous quoit obliquely fall;
While some huge Ajax, terrible and strong,
Engaged some artful stripling of the throng,
And fell beneath him, foiled, while far around
Hoarse triumph rose, and rocks returned the sound?　100
Where now are these?—Beneath yon cliff they stand,
To show the freighted pinnace where to land;[4]

4. Crabbe refers to smuggling.

To load the ready steed with guilty haste;
To fly in terror o'er the pathless waste;
Or, when detected in their straggling course,   105
To foil their foes by cunning or by force;
Or, yielding part (which equal knaves demand),
To gain a lawless passport through the land.
   Here, wandering long amid these frowning fields,
I sought the simple life that Nature yields;   110
Rapine and Wrong and Fear usurped her place,
And a bold, artful, surly, savage race;
Who, only skilled to take the finny tribe,
The yearly dinner, or septennial bribe,[5]
Wait on the shore, and, as the waves run high,   115
On the tossed vessel bend their eager eye,
Which to their coast directs its venturous way;
Theirs, or the ocean's, miserable prey.
   As on their neighboring beach yon swallows stand,
And wait for favoring winds to leave the land,   120
While still for flight the ready wing is spread:
So waited I the favoring hour, and fled;
Fled from these shores where guilt and famine reign,
And cried, "Ah! hapless they who still remain;
Who still remain to hear the ocean roar,   125
Whose greedy waves devour the lessening shore;
Till some fierce tide, with more imperious sway,
Sweeps the low hut and all it holds away;
When the sad tenant weeps from door to door,
And begs a poor protection from the poor!"   130
   But these are scenes where Nature's niggard hand
Gave a spare portion to the famished land;
Hers is the fault, if here mankind complain
Of fruitless toil and labor spent in vain.
But yet in other scenes, more fair in view,   135
Where Plenty smiles—alas! she smiles for few—
And those who taste not, yet behold her store,
Are as the slaves that dig the golden ore,
The wealth around them makes them doubly poor.
   Or will you deem them amply paid in health,   140
Labor's fair child, that languishes with wealth?
Go, then! and see them rising with the sun,
Through a long course of daily toil to run;
See them beneath the dog star's raging heat,
When the knees tremble and the temples beat;   145
Behold them, leaning on their scythes, look o'er
The labor past, and toils to come explore;
See them alternate suns and showers engage,
And hoard up aches and anguish for their age;
Through fens and marshy moors their steps pursue,   150
When their warm pores imbibe the evening dew;

---

5. Paid to electors by candidates for election to Parliament. Since Parlia- ments must be elected at least every seven years, the bribes are "septennial."

Then own that labor may as fatal be
To these thy slaves, as thine excess to thee.
　　Amid this tribe too oft a manly pride
Strives in strong toil the fainting heart to hide;　　155
There may you see the youth of slender frame
Contend, with weakness, weariness, and shame;
Yet, urged along, and proudly loath to yield,
He strives to join his fellows of the field;
Till long-contending nature droops at last,　　160
Declining health rejects his poor repast,
His cheerless spouse the coming danger sees,
And mutual murmurs urge the slow disease.
　　Yet grant them health, 'tis not for us to tell,
Though the head droops not, that the heart is well;　　165
Or will you praise that homely, healthy fare,
Plenteous and plain, that happy peasants share?
Oh! trifle not with wants you cannot feel,
Nor mock the misery of a stinted meal,
Homely, not wholesome; plain, not plenteous; such　　170
As you who praise would never deign to touch.
　　Ye gentle souls, whom dream of rural ease,
Whom the smooth stream and smoother sonnet please;
Go! if the peaceful cot your praises share,
Go, look within, and ask if peace be there:　　175
If peace be his—that drooping weary sire,
Or theirs, that offspring round their feeble fire;
Or hers, that matron pale, whose trembling hand
Turns on the wretched hearth the expiring brand!
　　Nor yet can Time itself obtain for these　　180
Life's latest comforts, due respect and ease:
For yonder see that hoary swain, whose age
Can with no cares except his own engage;
Who, propped on that rude staff, looks up to see
The bare arms broken from the withering tree,　　185
On which, a boy, he climbed the loftiest bough,
Then his first joy, but his sad emblem now.
　　He once was chief in all the rustic trade;
His steady hand the straightest furrow made;
Full many a prize he won, and still is proud　　190
To find the triumphs of his youth allowed.
A transient pleasure sparkles in his eyes;
He hears and smiles, then thinks again and sighs;
For now he journeys to his grave in pain;
The rich disdain him, nay, the poor disdain;　　195
Alternate masters now their slave command,
Urge the weak efforts of his feeble hand;
And, when his age attempts its task in vain,
With ruthless taunts, of lazy poor complain.
　　Oft may you see him, when he tends the sheep,　　200
His winter charge, beneath the hillock weep;

Oft hear him murmur to the winds that blow
O'er his white locks and bury them in snow,
When, roused by rage and muttering in the morn
He mends the broken hedge with icy thorn: 205
  "Why do I live, when I desire to be
At once from life and life's long labor free?
Like leaves in spring, the young are blown away,
Without the sorrows of a slow decay;
I, like yon withered leaf, remain behind,   210
Nipped by the frost, and shivering in the wind;
There it abides till younger buds come on,
As I, now all my fellow swains are gone;
Then, from the rising generation thrust,
It falls, like me, unnoticed to the dust.   215
  "These fruitful fields, these numerous flocks I see,
Are others' gain, but killing cares to me:
To me the children of my youth are lords,
Cool in their looks, but hasty in their words:
Wants of their own demand their care; and who   220
Feels his own want and succors others too?
A lonely, wretched man, in pain I go,
None need my help, and none relieve my woe;
Then let my bones beneath the turf be laid,
And men forget the wretch they would not aid!"   225
  Thus groan the old, till, by disease oppressed,
They taste a final woe, and then they rest.
  Theirs is yon house that holds the parish poor,
Whose walls of mud scarce bear the broken door;
There, where the putrid vapors, flagging, play,   230
And the dull wheel hums doleful through the day—
There children dwell who know no parents' care;
Parents, who know no children's love, dwell there!
Heartbroken matrons on their joyless bed,
Forsaken wives, and mothers never wed;   235
Dejected widows with unheeded tears,
And crippled age with more than childhood fears;
The lame, the blind, and, far the happiest they!
The moping idiot and the madman gay.
Here too the sick their final doom receive,   240
Here brought, amid the scenes of grief, to grieve,
Where the loud groans from some sad chamber flow,
Mixed with the clamors of the crowd below;
Here, sorrowing, they each kindred sorrow scan,
And the cold charities of man to man: 245
Whose laws indeed for ruined age provide,
And strong compulsion plucks the scrap from pride;
But still that scrap is bought with many a sigh,
And pride embitters what it can't deny.
  Say ye, oppressed by some fantastic woes,   250
Some jarring nerve that baffles your repose;

Who press the downy couch, while slaves advance
With timid eye to read the distant glance;
Who with sad prayers the weary doctor tease,
To name the nameless ever-new disease;   255
Who with mock patience dire complaints endure,
Which real pain, and that alone, can cure—
How would ye bear in real pain to lie,
Despised, neglected, left alone to die?
How would ye bear to draw your latest breath,   260
Where all that's wretched paves the way for death?
    Such is that room which one rude beam divides,
And naked rafters form the sloping sides;
Where the vile bands that bind the thatch are seen,
And lath and mud are all that lie between,   265
Save one dull pane, that, coarsely patched, gives way
To the rude tempest, yet excludes the day.
Here, on a matted flock, with dust o'erspread,
The drooping wretch reclines his languid head;
For him no hand the cordial cup applies,   270
Or wipes the tear that stagnates in his eyes;
No friends with soft discourse his pain beguile,
Or promise hope till sickness wears a smile.
    But soon a loud and hasty summons calls,
Shakes the thin roof, and echoes round the walls.   275
Anon, a figure enters, quaintly neat,
All pride and business, bustle and conceit;
With looks unaltered by these scenes of woe,
With speed that, entering, speaks his haste to go,
He bids the gazing throng around him fly,   280
And carries fate and physic in his eye:
A potent quack, long versed in human ills,
Who first insults the victim whom he kills;
Whose murderous hand a drowsy Bench protect,[6]
And whose most tender mercy is neglect.   285
    Paid by the parish for attendance here,
He wears contempt upon his sapient sneer;
In haste he seeks the bed where Misery lies,
Impatience marked in his averted eyes;
And, some habitual queries hurried o'er,   290
Without reply, he rushes on the door.
His drooping patient, long inured to pain,
And long unheeded, knows remonstrance vain;
He ceases now the feeble help to crave
Of man; and silent sinks into the grave.   295
    But ere his death some pious doubts arise,
Some simple fears, which "bold bad" men despise:
Fain would he ask the parish priest to prove

6. Crabbe, who had practiced medicine among the poor of Aldeborough, well knew the indifference of the local magistrates ("the drowsy Bench") to the incompetence and callousness of the physician hired by the parish to attend its paupers.

His title certain to the joys above;
For this he sends the murmuring nurse, who calls   300
The holy stranger to these dismal walls;
And doth not he, the pious man, appear,
He, "passing rich with forty pounds a year"?[7]
Ah! no; a shepherd of a different stock:
And far unlike him, feeds this little flock: 305
A jovial youth, who thinks his Sunday's task
As much as God or man can fairly ask;
The rest he gives to loves and labors light,
To fields the morning, and to feasts the night;
None better skilled the noisy pack to guide,   310
To urge their chase, to cheer them or to chide;
A sportsman keen, he shoots through half the day,
And, skilled at whist, devotes the night to play.
Then, while such honors bloom around his head,
Shall he sit sadly by the sick man's bed,   315
To raise the hope he feels not, or with zeal
To combat fears that e'en the pious feel?
    Now once again the gloomy scene explore,
Less gloomy now; the bitter hour is o'er,
The man of many sorrows sighs no more.—   320
Up yonder hill, behold how sadly slow
The bier moves winding from the vale below;
There lie the happy dead, from trouble free,
And the glad parish pays the frugal fee.
No more, O Death! thy victim starts to hear   325
Churchwarden stern, or kingly overseer;
No more the farmer claims his humble bow,
Thou art his lord, the best of tyrants thou!
    Now to the church behold the mourners come,
Sedately torpid and devoutly dumb;   330
The village children now their games suspend,
To see the bier that bears their ancient friend:
For he was one in all their idle sport,
And like a monarch ruled their little court;
The pliant bow he formed, the flying ball,   335
The bat, the wicket, were his labors all;
Him now they follow to his grave, and stand
Silent and sad, and gazing, hand in hand;
While bending low, their eager eyes explore
The mingled relics of the parish poor.   340
The bell tolls late, the moping owl flies round,
Fear marks the flight and magnifies the sound;
The busy priest, detained by weightier care,
Defers his duty till the day of prayer;
And, waiting long, the crowd retire distressed,   345
To think a poor man's bones should lie unblessed.

1780–83   1783

7. Cf. Goldsmith's *Deserted Village*, line 142.

WILLIAM COWPER
(1731–1800)

There are no saner poems in the language than Cowper's, yet they were written by a man who was periodically insane and who, for forty years, lived with the possibility of madness in full view. One form that his madness took was a conviction that he was damned for having committed the unforgivable sin, the "sin against the Holy Ghost." When he recovered from his first attack, in which he had attempted suicide, he was persuaded by his physician that this conviction was a delusion, and he embraced the doctor's own hopeful Evangelical creed. Relieved of his guilts, he felt inwardly assured of salvation and of the healing and sustaining power of divine grace freely extended to him.

From then on, a refugee from life, he found shelter first, in 1765, in the pious family of the Evangelical clergyman, Morley Unwin, and after Unwin's death, with Mrs. Unwin, who gave him exactly the sort of loving shelter that he needed. They were never separated until her death in 1796, by which time Cowper had experienced his final attack of madness. The removal of Mary Unwin and Cowper from Huntington to Olney (pronounced *Own-y*) in 1765 brought the couple under the influence of the strenuous and fervent Evangelical clergyman John Newton. With him Cowper wrote the famous *Olney Hymns*, still familiar to Methodists and other Nonconformists. But here a second attack of madness, in 1773, not only frustrated his planned marriage to Mary, but left him for the rest of his life with the assurance that he had been cast out by God and was inevitably damned. He never again attended divine service, and the main purpose of his life thereafter was to divert his mind by every possible innocent device from the numb despair that was his lot in life. He gardened, he kept pets, he walked, he wrote letters (some of the best of the century), he conversed, he read—and he wrote poetry. When it was published, it brought him a measure of fame that his modest nature could never have hoped for.

Despair could suppress neither his humor and gentle wit nor the religious side of his nature, which finds expression in the poems of the next decade—not only in their ethical point of view, but in the tone of gentle, if wistful, piety that pervades them. The first volume, *Poems* (didactic and gently satiric verse in heroic couplets), won the praise of Johnson and the approval of the public. But his major work is *The Task*, undertaken at the bidding—hence the title—of the lively and charming Lady Austen, who, when he complained that he had no subject, directed him to write about the sofa in his parlor. It began with a mock-heroic account of the development of the sofa from a simple stool, but it grew into a long meditative poem of over five thousand lines in delicately modulated blank verse. The poet describes in his murmuring voice his small world of country, village, garden, and parlor, and from time to time he glances toward the great world to condemn cities and worldliness, war and slavery, luxury and corruption. The tone is muted, the sensibility delicate, the language on the whole pure and simple. The truthfulness of Cowper's description of landscape and of the human figures that animate it, his moralizing, his generous spirit of humanitarianism, all appealed to the Englishmen of the late 18th century. His religious piety, domestic sentiment, and humanitarianism made his poems especially acceptable to Methodists and their Anglican counterparts, the Evangelicals, who between them were transforming the religious life of England and establishing the values and manners which came to characterize the Victorian age. No poet of the century expressed more completely the interests and taste of the new enlightened and religious middle class.

Many of Cowper's themes are identical with Wordsworth's. No doubt a taste for Cowper's poetry made it easier for some people to accept Wordsworth when he appeared. But the similarity is superficial and deceptive. Cowper may seem a Wordsworth who never beheld the visionary gleam— but such a Wordsworth is inconceivable. We may agree today that Cowper was too highly valued by his contemporaries, but it is agreeable to take up his poems from time to time, and to allow his gentle talk to re-create for us the serenity and simplicity of life in an English village just before the French Revolution announced a new era.

From The Task

From *Book I*

[A LANDSCAPE DESCRIBED. RURAL SOUNDS]

Thou[1] knowest my praise of nature most sincere,   150
And that my raptures are not conjured up
To serve occasions of poetic pomp,
But genuine, and art partner of them all.
How oft upon yon eminence our pace
Has slackened to a pause, and we have borne   155
The ruffling wind, scarce conscious that it blew,
While admiration, feeding at the eye,
And still unsated, dwelt upon the scene.
Thence with what pleasure have we just discerned
The distant plow slow moving, and beside   160
His laboring team, that swerved not from the track,
The sturdy swain diminished to a boy!
Here Ouse,[2] slow winding through a level plain
Of spacious meads with cattle sprinkled o'er,
Conducts the eye along its sinuous course   165
Delighted. There, fast rooted in their bank,
Stand, never overlooked, our favorite elms,
That screen the herdsman's solitary hut;

1. Mary Unwin.
2. The village of Olney, where Cowper

and Mary Unwin were living, is situated
on the river Ouse.

While far beyond, and overthwart the stream
That, as with molten glass, inlays the vale,   170
The sloping land recedes into the clouds;
Displaying on its varied side the grace
Of hedgerow beauties numberless, square tower,
Tall spire, from which the sound of cheerful bells
Just undulates upon the listening ear,   175
Groves, heaths, and smoking villages, remote.
Scenes must be beautiful, which, daily viewed,
Please daily, and whose novelty survives
Long knowledge and the scrutiny of years—
Praise justly due to those that I describe.   180
    Nor rural sights alone, but rural sounds,
Exhilarate the spirit, and restore
The tone of languid Nature. Mighty winds,
That sweep the skirt of some far-spreading wood
Of ancient growth, make music not unlike   185
The dash of ocean on his winding shore,
And lull the spirit while they fill the mind;
Unnumbered branches waving in the blast,
And all their leaves fast fluttering, all at once.
Nor less composure waits upon the roar   190
Of distant floods, or on the softer voice
Of neighboring fountain, or of rills that slip
Through the cleft rock, and, chiming as they fall
Upon loose pebbles, lose themselves at length
In matted grass, that with a livelier green   195
Betrays the secret of their silent course.
Nature inanimate employs sweet sounds,
But animated nature sweeter still,
To soothe and satisfy the human ear.
Ten thousand warblers cheer the day, and one   200
The livelong night: nor these alone, whose notes
Nice-fingered art must emulate in vain,
But cawing rooks, and kites that swim sublime
In still repeated circles, screaming loud,
The jay, the pie, and even the boding owl   205
That hails the rising moon, have charms for me.
Sounds inharmonious in themselves and harsh,
Yet heard in scenes where peace forever reigns,
And only there, please highly for their sake.

[CRAZY KATE. GYPSIES]

    There often wanders one, whom better days
Saw better clad, in cloak of satin trimmed   535
With lace, and hat with splendid ribband bound.
A servingmaid was she, and fell in love

With one who left her, went to sea, and died.
Her fancy followed him through foaming waves
To distant shores; and she would sit and weep   540
At what a sailor suffers; fancy, too,
Delusive most where warmest wishes are,
Would oft anticipate his glad return,
And dream of transports she was not to know.
She heard the doleful tidings of his death—   545
And never smiled again! And now she roams
The dreary waste; there spends the livelong day,
And there, unless when charity forbids,
The livelong night. A tattered apron hides,
Worn as a cloak, and hardly hides, a gown   550
More tattered still; and both but ill conceal
A bosom heaved with never-ceasing sighs.
She begs an idle pin of all she meets,
And hoards them in her sleeve; but needful food,
Though pressed with hunger oft, or comelier clothes,   555
Though pinched with cold, asks never.—Kate is crazed!
   I see a column of slow rising smoke
O'ertop the lofty wood that skirts the wild.
A vagabond and useless tribe there eat
Their miserable meal. A kettle, slung   560
Between two poles upon a stick transverse,
Receives the morsel—flesh obscene of dog,
Or vermin,[3] or, at best, of cock purloined
From his accustomed perch. Hard faring race!
They pick their fuel out of every hedge,   565
Which, kindled with dry leaves, just saves unquenched
The spark of life. The sportive wind blows wide
Their fluttering rags, and shows a tawny skin,
The vellum of the pedigree they claim.
Great skill have they in palmistry, and more   570
To conjure clean away the gold they touch,
Conveying worthless dross into its place;
Loud when they beg, dumb only when they steal.
Strange! that a creature rational, and cast
In human mold, should brutalize by choice   575
His nature; and, though capable of arts
By which the world might profit, and himself,
Self-banished from society, prefer
Such squalid sloth to honorable toil!
Yet even these, though, feigning sickness oft,   580
They swathe the forehead, drag the limping limb,
And vex their flesh with artificial sores,
Can change their whine into a mirthful note
When safe occasion offers; and, with dance,

---

3. Any small, noxious animal, such as a rat or weasel.

And music of the bladder and the bag, 585
Beguile their woes, and make the woods resound.
Such health and gaiety of heart enjoy
The houseless rovers of the sylvan world;
And, breathing wholesome air, and wandering much,
Need other physic none to heal the effects 590
Of loathsome diet, penury, and cold.

From *Book III*

[THE STRICKEN DEER]

I was a stricken deer, that left the herd
Long since; with many an arrow deep infixed
My panting side was charged, when I withdrew 110
To seek a tranquil death in distant shades.
There was I found by one who had himself
Been hurt by the archers. In his side he bore,
And in his hands and feet, the cruel scars.
With gentle force soliciting[4] the darts, 115
He drew them forth, and healed, and bade me live.
Since then, with few associates, in remote
And silent woods I wander, far from those
My former partners of the peopled scene;
With few associates, and not wishing more. 120
Here much I ruminate, as much I may,
With other views of men and manners now
Than once, and others of a life to come.
I see that all are wanderers, gone astray
Each in his own delusions; they are lost 125
In chase of fancied happiness, still wooed
And never won. Dream after dream ensues;
And still they dream that they shall still succeed.
And still are disappointed. Rings the world
With the vain stir. I sum up half mankind 130
And add two-thirds of the remaining half,
And find the total of their hopes and fears
Dreams, empty dreams.

From *Book IV*

[THE WINTER EVENING]

Hark! 'tis the twanging horn[5] o'er yonder bridge,
That with its wearisome but needful length
Bestrides the wintry flood, in which the moon
Sees her unwrinkled face reflected bright—
He comes, the herald of a noisy world, 5

---

4. "To endeavor to draw out by the use of gentle force" (*NED*).

5. The post-horn, announcing the arrival of the mail coach.

With spattered boots, strapped waist, and frozen locks;
News from all nations lumbering at his back.
True to his charge, the close-packed load behind,
Yet careless what he brings, his one concern
Is to conduct it to the destined inn: 10
And, having dropped the expected bag, pass on.
He whistles as he goes, light-hearted wretch,
Cold and yet cheerful: messenger of grief
Perhaps to thousands, and of joy to some;
To him indifferent whether grief or joy.   15
Houses in ashes, and the fall of stocks,
Births, deaths, and marriages, epistles wet
With tears that trickled down the writer's cheeks
Fast as the periods from his fluent quill,
Or charged with amorous sighs of absent swains   20
Or nymphs responsive, equally affect
His horse and him, unconscious of them all.
But oh, the important budget![6] ushered in
With such heart-shaking music, who can say
What are its tidings? Have our troops awaked?   25
Or do they still, as if with opium drugged,
Snore to the murmurs of the Atlantic wave?[7]
Is India free, and does she wear her plumed
And jeweled turban with a smile of peace,
Or do we grind her still? The grand debate,[8]   30
The popular harangue, the tart reply,
The logic, and the wisdom, and the wit,
And the loud laugh—I long to know them all;
I burn to set the imprisoned wranglers free,
And give them voice and utterance once again.   35

* * *

O Winter, ruler of the inverted year,   120
Thy scattered hair with sleet like ashes filled,
Thy breath congealed upon thy lips, thy cheeks
Fringed with a beard made white with other snows
Than those of age, thy forehead wrapped in clouds,
A leafless branch thy scepter, and thy throne   125
A sliding car, indebted to no wheels,
But urged by storms along its slippery way,
I love thee, all unlovely as thou seem'st,

---

6. Newspaper.
7. Though a recluse, Cowper followed public affairs with interest. Here he expresses concern for what he considers the inactivity of British arms since the surrender at Yorktown, despite the hostility of France. He was much disturbed by the revelations of the cruelty and rapacity of the British in India (where his old schoolfellow Warren Hastings, Governor of Bengal, had been under attack for his brutal, if efficient, rule), and he longed to see India freed from the tyranny of the East India Company, as Pitt's India Bill of 1784 proposed that it should be.
8. In Parliament, as reported in the newspaper.

And dreaded as thou art! Thou hold'st the sun
A prisoner in the yet undawning east,   130
Shortening his journey between morn and noon,
And hurrying him, impatient of his stay,
Down to the rosy west; but kindly still
Compensating his loss with added hours
Of social converse and instructive ease,   135
And gathering, at short notice, in one group
The family dispersed, and fixing thought,
Not less dispersed by daylight and its cares.
I crown thee king of intimate delights,
Fireside enjoyments, home-born happiness,   140
And all the comforts that the lowly roof
Of undisturbed retirement and the hours
Of long uninterrupted evening know.
No rattling wheels stop short before these gates;
No powdered pert,[9] proficient in the art   145
Of sounding an alarm, assaults these doors
Till the street rings; no stationary steeds
Cough their own knell, while, heedless of the sound,
The silent circle[1] fan themselves, and quake:
But here the needle plies its busy task,   150
The pattern grows, the well-depicted flower,
Wrought patiently into the snowy lawn,[2]
Unfolds its bosom; buds, and leaves, and sprigs,
And curling tendrils, gracefully disposed,
Follow the nimble finger of the fair—   155
A wreath that cannot fade, of flowers that blow
With most success when all besides decay.
The poet's or historian's page, by one
Made vocal for the amusement of the rest;
The sprightly lyre, whose treasure of sweet sounds   160
The touch from many a trembling chord shakes out;
And the clear voice symphonious, yet distinct,
And in the charming strife triumphant still,
Beguile the night, and set a keener edge
On female industry: the threaded steel   165
Flies swiftly, and unfelt the task proceeds.
The volume closed, the customary rites
Of the last meal commence. A Roman meal,
Such as the mistress of the world once found
Delicious, when her patriots of high note,   170
Perhaps by moonlight, at their humble doors,
And under an old oak's domestic shade,
Enjoyed—spare feast!—a radish and an egg!

                                                               1785

---

9. Footmen wore powdered hair.   2. A fine sheer fabric.
1. The audience in the theater.

The Castaway

Obscurest night involved the sky,
   The Atlantic billows roared,
When such a destined wretch as I,
   Washed headlong from on board,
Of friends, of hope, of all bereft,   5
His floating home forever left.

No braver chief[1] could Albion boast
   Than he with whom he went,
Nor ever ship left Albion's coast,
   With warmer wishes sent.   10
He loved them both, but both in vain,
Nor him beheld, nor her again.

Not long beneath the whelming brine,
   Expert to swim, he lay;
Nor soon he felt his strength decline,   15
   Or courage die away;
But waged with death a lasting strife,
Supported by despair of life.

He shouted; nor his friends had failed
   To check the vessel's course,
But so the furious blast prevailed,   20
   That, pitiless perforce,
They left their outcast mate behind,
And scudded still before the wind.

Some succor yet they could afford;   25
   And, such as storms allow,
The cask, the coop, the floated cord,
   Delayed not to bestow.
But he (they knew) nor ship, nor shore,
Whate'er they gave, should visit more.   30

Nor, cruel as it seemed, could he
   Their haste himself condemn,
Aware that flight, in such a sea,
   Alone could rescue them;
Yet bitter felt it still to die   35
Deserted, and his friends so nigh.

He·long survives, who lives an hour
   In ocean, self-upheld;

1. George, Lord Anson (1697–1762), in whose *Voyage* (1748), Cowper, years before writing this poem, had read the story of the sailor washed overboard in a storm.

And so long he, with unspent power,
  His destiny repelled;   40
And ever, as the minutes flew,
Entreated help, or cried, "Adieu!"

At length, his transient respite past,
  His comrades, who before
Had heard his voice in every blast,   45
  Could catch the sound no more.
For then, by toil subdued, he drank
The stifling wave, and then he sank.

No poet wept him; but the page
  Of narrative sincere,
That tells his name, his worth, his age,   50
  Is wet with Anson's tear.
And tears by bards or heroes shed
Alike immortalize the dead.

I therefore purpose not, or dream,   55
  Descanting on his fate,
To give the melancholy theme
  A more enduring date:
But misery still delights to trace
Its semblance in another's case.   60

No voice divine the storm allayed,
  No light propitious shone,
When, snatched from all effectual aid,
  We perished, each alone;
But I beneath a rougher sea,   65
And whelmed in deeper gulfs than he.

1799   1803

Topic in Restoration and Eighteenth-Century Literature

GENIUS

Few arts were so fully developed, in the Restoration and 18th century, as the art of conversation. Many of the famous authors of the period were also famous talkers; and after the death of Samuel Johnson, memorialists and publishers seemed intent on recording every word that had ever fallen from his lips. But the most remarkable conversations of the time were not those spoken aloud, but those that developed between authors through more than a century of continuing argument and rebuttal, point and counterpoint. Writers of the 18th century seldom compose their thoughts in isolation, or without paying attention to each other. Like any good conversationalist, they know how to listen; they respond to each other's ideas and try progressively to improve them. Thus many of the intellectual issues of the period —the nature of the mind, the reality of a standard of taste, the basis of morals, the proper function of wit—seem to be defined in a great debate, lasting over a century, to which each new speaker contributes his own modifications of a single line of thought. Below we present some fragments from one of those debates, a conversation on genius.

Like most such conversations, this one had begun in ancient times, with famous remarks by Plato and Longinus. But its revival in the late 17th century responds to a particular need, the desire for a theoretical justification for poets who break the "rules." Unlike French critics, who tended to insist that poetry must be "correct"—i.e., follow the doctrine of the unities of time, place, and action, the conventional structure and language of each literary kind, etc.—English critics tend to extol native poets like Chaucer, Spenser, and Shakespeare, who catch "a grace beyond the reach of art": that ultimate, inexpressible charm which converts the merely formal and regular into vital and animated beauty. In the face of such genius, Dryden and Addison argue, the rules of art seem to fade.

But where does such genius come from? Does it not obey rules of its own? During the 18th century the conversation entered a new phase, as philosophers sought answers to such questions. Genius now became opposed less to the rules than to imitation: imitation of earlier authors as well as of nature. If genius depends wholly on inspiration, some writers suggested, then a great artist will owe nothing to anyone but himself and his own powers; he will not be in thrall to the world. The religious implications of this argument, which suggests that a poet may be a kind of god, above mere ordinary mortals, alarmed orthodox Christians like Samuel Johnson; a true genius, he argued, is no special divinity but a man among men: "a mind of large general powers, accidentally determined to some particular direction." Sir Joshua Reynolds, in his sixth Discourse, suggested that genius and imitation, like nature and art, may be one. But the prophets of Romanticism, convinced that the spirit of a poet stands above rules and imitation, had no patience with such arguments; and eventually Reynolds' most faithful disciple, James Northcote, grown old in a Romantic world, was forced to acknowledge that Reynolds himself had been not a teacher of rules but a genius. In his annotations to Reynolds' *Discourses*, however, William Blake had already struck to the crowning blow, when he cast scorn upon all efforts to reduce genius to reasons—and broke the conversation.

SAMUEL JOHNSON: [Definitions of Genius][1]

GE'NIUS [Latin; *génie*, French]

1. The protecting or ruling power of men, places, or things.

There is none but he
Whose bearing I do fear: and, under him,
My *genius* is rebuked; as it is said
Antony's was by Caesar. *Shakespeare's Macbeth*

The *genius* and the mortal instruments
Are then in council; and the state of man,
Like to a little kingdom, suffers then. *Shakes. Jul. Caesar*

And as I awake, sweet music breathe,
Sent by some spirit to mortals good,
Or the unseen *genius* of the wood. *Milton*

And the tame demon that should guard my throne,
Shrinks at a *genius* greater than his own. *Dryden*

To your glad *genius* sacrifice this day;
Let common meats respectfully give way. *Dryden*

2. A man endowed with superior faculties.

There is no little writer of Pindaric who is not mentioned as a prodigious *genius*. *Addison*

3. Mental power or faculties.

The state and order does proclaim
The *genius* of that royal dame. *Waller*

4. Disposition of nature by which anyone is qualified for some particular employment.

A happy *genius* is the gift of nature. *Dryden's Dufresnoy*

Your majesty's sagacity, and happy *genius* for natural history, is a better preparation for enquiries of this kind than all the dead learning of the schools. *Burnet's Theory of the Earth, Preface*

1. Johnson's *Dictionary* illustrates its definitions, as here, with examples from the usage of the best English authors. Note that the Latin root of the word ("a tutelary divinity") casts some influence on all the 18th-century definitions of genius.

One science only will one *genius* fit;
So vast is art, so narrow human wit.   *Pope on Criticism*

The Romans, though they had no great *genius* for trade, yet were not entirely neglectful of it.   *Arbuthnot on Coins*

5. Nature; disposition.
Studious to please the *genius* of the times,
With periods, points and tropes he slurs his crimes.   *Dryden*

Another *genius* and disposition improper for philosophical contemplations is not so much from the narrowness of their spirit and understanding, as because they will not take time to extend them.   *Burnet's Theory, Preface*

He tames the *genius* of the stubborn plain.   *Pope*

[*English Dictionary*, 1755]

JOHN DRYDEN: [Genius Is above Correctness]

* * * I must take leave to tell them that they wholly mistake the nature of criticism who think its business is principally to find fault. Criticism, as it was first instituted by Aristotle, was meant a standard of judging well, the chiefest part of which is to observe those excellencies which should delight a reasonable reader. If the design, the conduct, the thought, and the expressions of a poem be generally such as proceed from a true genius of poetry, the critic ought to pass his judgment in favor of the author. 'Tis malicious and unmanly to snarl at the little lapses of a pen from which Virgil himself stands not exempted. Horace acknowledges that honest Homer nods sometimes:[2] he is not equally awake in every line; * * * And Longinus, who was undoubtedly, after Aristotle, the greatest critic amongst the Greeks, in his twenty-seventh chapter of περὶ Ὕψους,[3] has judiciously preferred the sublime genius that sometimes errs, to the middling, or indifferent one, which makes few faults but seldom or never rises to any excellence. He compares the first to a man of large possessions, who has not leisure to consider of every slight expense, will not debase himself to the management of every trifle: particular sums are not laid out, or spared, to the greatest advantage in his economy, but are sometimes suffered to run to waste, while he is only careful of the main. On the other side, he likens a mediocrity of wit to one of a mean fortune, who manages his store with extreme frugality, or rather parsimony; but who, with fear of running into profuseness, never arrives to the magnificence of living. This kind of genius writes indeed correctly. A wary man he is in grammar, very nice as to solecism or barbarism,

2. *Ars Poetica*, line 359.
3. The title of this Greek rhetorical treatise of the 1st century A.D. (tradi-

tionally but erroneously attributed to Longinus) is usually translated "On the Sublime."

judges to a hair of little decencies, knows better than any man what
is not to be written, and never hazards himself so far as to fall, but
plods on deliberately, and as a grave man ought, is sure to put his
staff before him * * *

[From *The Author's Apology for Heroic Poetry and
Heroic License*, 1677]

JOSEPH ADDISON: [The Beauties of Great Geniuses Independent of Rules]

They [ignorant critics] are often led into those numerous absurdities in which they daily instruct the people by not considering that,
first, there is sometimes a greater judgment shown in deviating from
the rules of art than in adhering to them; and, secondly, that there
is more beauty in the works of a great genius who is ignorant of all
the rules of art than in the works of a little genius who not only
knows, but scrupulously observes them.

First, we may often take notice of men who are perfectly
acquainted with all the rules of good writing, and notwithstanding
choose to depart from them on extraordinary occasions. I could give
instances out of all the tragic writers of antiquity who have shown
their judgment in this particular, and purposely receded from an
established rule of the drama when it has made way for a much
higher beauty than the observation of such a rule would have been.
Those who have surveyed the noblest pieces of architecture and
statuary, both ancient and modern, know very well that there are
frequent deviations from art in the works of the greatest masters,
which have produced a much nobler effect than a more accurate
and exact way of proceeding could have done. This often arises
from what the Italians call the *gusto grande* in these arts, which is
what we call the sublime in writing.

In the next place, our critics do not seem sensible that there is
more beauty in the works of a great genius who is ignorant of the
rules of art than in those of a little genius who knows and observes
them. * * * Our inimitable Shakespeare is a stumbling-block to
the whole tribe of these rigid critics. Who would not rather read
one of his plays, where there is not a single rule of the stage
observed, than any production of a modern critic where there is not
one of them violated! * * *

[From *Spectator* 592, September 10, 1714]

SAMUEL JOHNSON: [Genius Requires Invention]

The man whose genius qualifies him for great undertakings, must
at least be content to learn from books the present state of human

knowledge; that he may not ascribe to himself the invention of arts generally known; weary his attention with experiments of which the event has been long registered; and waste, in attempts which have already succeeded or miscarried, that time which might have been spent with usefulness and honor upon new undertakings.

But, though the study of books is necessary, it is not sufficient to constitute literary eminence. He that wishes to be counted among the benefactors of posterity, must add by his own toil to the acquisitions of his ancestors, and secure his money from neglect by some valuable improvement. This can only be effected by looking out upon the wastes of the intellectual world, and extending the power of learning over regions yet undisciplined and barbarous; or by surveying more exactly our ancient dominions, and driving ignorance from the fortresses and retreats where she skulks undetected and undisturbed. Every science has its difficulties, which yet call for solution before we attempt new systems of knowledge; as every country has its forests and marshes, which it would be wise to cultivate and drain, before distant colonies are projected as a necessary discharge of the exuberance of inhabitants.

No man ever yet became great by imitation. Whatever hopes for the veneration of mankind must have invention in the design or the execution; either the effect must itself be new, or by the means by which it is produced. Either truths hitherto unknown must be discovered, or those which are already known enforced by stronger evidence, facilitated by clearer method, or elucidated by brighter illustrations.

Fame cannot spread wide or endure long that is not rooted in nature, and manured by art. That which hopes to resist the blast of malignity, and stand firm against the attacks of time, must contain in itself some original principle of growth. The reputation which arises from the detail or transposition of borrowed sentiments, may spread for awhile, like ivy on the rind of antiquity, but will be torn away by accident or contempt, and suffered to rot unheeded on the ground.

[From *Rambler* 154, 1751]

EDWARD YOUNG: [Imitation and Genius]

Must we then, you say, not imitate ancient authors? Imitate them, by all means, but imitate aright. He that imitates the divine *Iliad*, does not imitate Homer; but he who takes the same method, which Homer took, for arriving at a capacity of accomplishing a work so great. Tread in his steps to the sole fountain of immortality; drink where he drank, at the true Helicon, that is, at the breast of nature. Imitate, but imitate not the composition, but the man.

* * * What, for the most part, mean we by genius, but the power of accomplishing great things without the means generally reputed necessary to that end? A genius differs from a good understanding, as a magician from a good architect: *that* raises his structure by means invisible; *this* by the skillful use of common tools. Hence genius has ever been supposed to partake of something divine.

[From *Conjectures on Original Composition*, 1759]

SAMUEL JOHNSON: [Genius and Knowledge]

"* * * There is nothing so little comprehended among mankind as what is genius. They give to it all, when it can be but a part. Genius is nothing more than knowing the use of tools; but there must be tools for it to use: a man who has spent all his life in this room will give a very poor account of what is contained in the next."

[Miss Burney:] "Certainly, sir; yet there is such a thing as invention? Shakespeare could never have seen a Caliban."[4]

[Johnson:] "No; but he had seen a man, and knew, therefore, how to vary him to a monster. A man who would draw a monstrous cow, must first know what a cow commonly is; or how can he tell that to give her an ass's head or an elephant's tusk will make her monstrous? Suppose you show me a man who is a very expert carpenter; another will say he was born to be a carpenter—but what if he had never seen any wood? Let two men, one with genius, the other with none, look at an overturned wagon:—he who has no genius, will think of the wagon only as he sees it, overturned, and walk on; he who has genius, will paint it to himself before it was overturned,—standing still, and moving on, and heavy loaded, and empty; but both must see the wagon, to think of it at all."

[From *Diaries and Letters of Madame d'Arblay*, 1784]

ALEXANDER GERARD: [The Origins of Genius]

Genius implies such *comprehensiveness* of imagination as enables a man on every occasion to call in the conceptions that are necessary for executing the designs or completing the works in which he engages. This takes place when the associating principles are strong and fit for acting in an extensive sphere. If they be weak, they will call in memory to their aid. Unable to guide our steps in an unknown country, they keep in the roads to which we have been accustomed, and are directed in suggesting ideas by the connections

---

4. The man-monster in Shakespeare's *The Tempest*.

which we remember. Every production of a man who labors under this debility of mind bears evident marks of barrenness, a quality more opposite to true genius than any other. Nothing appears in it uncommon or new; everything is trite and unoriginal. Or, if he attempts to quit the beaten path and start new game, he can find out but a few ideas; he is exhausted by a short excursion and must either make a stop or return to the tracks of memory. Industry, endeavoring in this manner to supply the want of a copious imagination by accurate remembrance or diligent observation, will produce instead of a philosopher a devoted follower or a dull laborious commentator; instead of a poet, a servile imitator or a painful translator. But when the associating principles are vigorous, imagination, conscious as it were of its own strength, sallies forth, without needing support or asking assistance, into regions hitherto unexplored, and penetrates into their remotest corners, unfatigued with the length of the way. In a man of genius, the power of association is so great that when any idea is present to his mind, it immediately leads him to the conception of those that are connected with it. No sooner almost is a design formed, or the hint of a subject started, than all the ideas which are requisite for completing it rush into his view as if they were conjured up by the force of magic. His daring imagination traverses all nature and collects materials fit for his purpose from all the most distant corners of the universe and presents them at the very instant when they become useful or necessary. In consequence of this, he takes in a comprehensive view of every subject to which his genius is adapted.

Thus, when the associating principles are strong and have an extensive influence, they naturally form, in proportion to the degree of their strength, that boundless fertility, that inexhaustible copiousness of invention, which is not only one necessary ingredient in true genius but the first and most essential constituent of it. The smallest production will in some measure discover in what extent this power is possessed. A work of real genius always proclaims in the clearest manner that immense quantities of materials have been collected by fancy and subjected to the author's choice. * * *

[From *An Essay on Genius*, 1774]

JOHN MOIR: [The Unique Vision of Original Genius]

What is it a truly original genius will not improve? Everything is prolific of novelty in the hand of a master. His ideas are not the crude conceptions of dullness; nor his sentiments either the vapid yawning of a listless, or the insignificant prattle of an empty, heart. He generally plans entirely for himself, and always executes in a manner preceded by nothing similar. The light he strikes out is so singular, and withal so true, that we are equally pleased with what we never saw before, and surprised that we now only see it for the first time. Who, for example, before Virgil, expected to find the fable of the *Iliad* capable of being so beautifull[y] diversified with new elegance and truth, as we find it in the *Aeneid?*

In descriptive poetry, as in landscape painting, fancy has the full-est scope. Here, however, fiction does not consist in feigning objects unknown to the senses, but in embellishing them with colors, endowing them with qualities, connecting them by relations, and disposing them in attitudes and groups of which we have little or no acquaintance. In truth, ideal arrangements are endless. While our affections retain their usual aversion to uniformity, the multifar-ious objects of our respective senses and faculties must unavoidably admit of new combinations.

This, like every other art, is improved by practice: for the more a fertile imagination creates or fabricates the exercise becomes the easier, new veins of verisimilitude are disclosed, and we may give over for want of patience or strength, but not of materials. The human genius is so versatile, and the original sources of beauty so inexhaustible, that every new inspection of the most common and familiar phenomena of nature discovers a thousand new variations, distinctions, and resemblances, at the same time that it opens up a multiplicity of avenues, where novelty wantons in all her charms, where science displays her happiest attractions, where the fancy is feasted, and the heart at once entertained and made better. * * *

Want of real discrimination is one of the greatest defects in thinking, acting, or writing. It infallibly degrades every species of composition; and indeed is a decisive criterion by which the most genuine offspring of dullness is everywhere known and distin-guished. Ordinary minds are seldom struck with anything, because they never particularize or examine the objects of their respective senses. All their literary efforts, whatever departments they may fill, or consequence they may effect, are but an echo, which dies with the sound that begets, or the situation that occasions it. Original genius never rests in generals, never runs in a circle, but gives, in vivid, glowing, and permanent characters, the identical impression it receives.

Perhaps no better account can be given of a quality which, from the beginning of the world, has continued in full possession of uni-versal homage, than that individual minds are distinguished by nature in the formation and structure of the organs by which they respectively operate; that we have all our own way of thinking whenever we do think; and that our sentiments and ideas are never destitute of novelty or justness but when we cease to think.

[From "Originality," *Gleanings or Fugitive Pieces*, 1785]

SIR JOSHUA REYNOLDS: [Genius the Child of Imitation]

Genius is supposed to be a power of producing excellencies, which are out of the reach of the rules of art; a power which no precepts can teach, and which no industry can acquire.

This opinion of the impossibility of acquiring those beauties, which stamp the work with the character of genius, supposes, that it is something more fixed than in reality it is; and that we always do, and ever did agree in opinion, with respect to what should be considered as the characteristic of genius. But the truth is, that the *degree* of excellence which proclaims *Genius* is different, in different times and different places; and what shews it to be so is, that mankind have often changed their opinion upon this matter.

When the arts were in their infancy, the power of merely drawing the likeness of any object, was considered as one of its greatest efforts. The common people, ignorant of the principles of art, talk the same language, even to this day. But when it was found that every man could be taught to do this, and a great deal more, merely by the observance of certain precepts; the name of Genius then shifted its application, and was given only to him who added the peculiar character of the object he represented; to him who had invention, expression, grace, or dignity; in short, those qualities, or excellencies, the power of producing which, could not *then* be taught by any known and promulgated rules.

* * *

What we now call Genius, begins, not where rules, abstractedly taken, end; but where known vulgar and trite rules have no longer any place. It must of necessity be, that even works of Genius, like every other effect, as they must have their cause, must likewise have their rules; it cannot be by chance, that excellencies are produced with any constancy or any certainty, for this is not the nature of chance; but the rules by which men of extraordinary parts, and such as are called men of Genius work, are either such as they discover by their own peculiar observations, or of such a nice texture as not easily to admit being expressed in words; especially as artists are not very frequently skillful in that mode of communicating ideas. Unsubstantial, however, as these rules may seem, and difficult as it may be to convey them in writing, they are still seen and felt in the mind of the artist; and he works from them with as much certainty, as if they were embodied, as I may say, upon paper. It is true, these refined principles cannot be always made palpable, like the more gross rules of art; yet it does not follow, but that the mind may be put in such a train, that it shall perceive, by a kind of scientific sense, that propriety, which words, particularly words of unpracticed writers, such as we are, can but very feebly suggest.

Invention is one of the great marks of genius; but if we consult experience, we shall find, that it is by being conversant with the inventions of others, that we learn to invent; as by reading the thoughts of other we learn to think.

* * *

To find excellencies, however dispersed, to discover beauties, however concealed by the multitude of defects with which they are surrounded, can be the work only of him, who having a mind always alive to his art, has extended his views to all ages and to all schools; and has acquired from that comprehensive mass which he has thus gathered to himself, a well-digested and perfect idea of his art, to which every thing is referred. Like a sovereign judge and arbiter of art, he is possessed of that presiding power which separates and attracts every excellence from every school; selects both from what is great, and what is little; brings home knowledge from the East and from the West; making the universe tributary toward furnishing his mind and enriching his works with originality and variety of inventions.

[From *Discourse* VI, 1774]

WILLIAM BLAKE: [Genius Unbound]

When a man talks of acquiring invention & of learning how to produce original conception he must expect to be called a fool by men of understanding; but such a hired knave cares not for the few. His eye is on the many, or rather on the money.

The man who says that the genius is not born, but taught—is a knave.

How ridiculous it would be to see the sheep endeavoring to walk like the dog, or the ox striving to trot like the horse; just as ridiculous it is to see one man striving to imitate another. Man varies from man more than animal from animal of different species.

Reynolds thinks that man learns all that he knows. I say on the contrary that man brings all that he has or can have into the world with him. Man is like a garden ready planted & sown. This world is too poor to produce one seed.

He who can be bound down is no genius. Genius cannot be bound; it may be rendered indignant & outrageous.

"Oppression makes the wise man mad."   Solomon

[From his marginalia to Reynolds'
Discourse VI, *ca.* 1808]

WILLIAM HAZLITT: [Reynolds' Genius][5]

Northcote began by saying, "You don't much like Sir Joshua, I know; but I think that is one of your prejudices. If I was to compare him with Vandyke and Titian, I should say that Vandyke's portraits are like pictures (very perfect ones, no doubt), Sir Joshua's like the reflection in a looking-glass, and Titian's like the real people. There is an atmosphere of light and shade about Sir Joshua's, which neither of the others have in the same degree, together with a vagueness that gives them a visionary and romantic character, and makes them seem like dreams or vivid recollections of persons we have seen. * * *" I mentioned that I thought Sir Joshua more like Rembrandt than like either Titian or Vandyke: he enveloped objects in the same brilliant haze of a previous mental conception.—"Yes," he said; "but though Sir Joshua borrowed a great deal, he drew largely from himself: or rather, it was a strong and peculiar feeling of nature working in him and forcing its way out in spite of all impediments, and that made whatever he touched his own. In spite of his deficiency in drawing, and his want of academic rules and a proper education, you see this breaking out like a devil in all his works. It is this that has stamped him. There is a charm in his portraits, a mingled softness and force, a grasping at the end with nothing harsh or unpleasant in the means, that you will find nowhere else. He may go out of fashion for a time: but you must come back to him again, while a thousand imitators and academic triflers are forgotten. This proves him to have been a real genius.

[From *Third Conversation with Northcote*, 1826]

5. Between 1826 and 1830 William Hazlitt, the Romantic critic, published a series of conversations with James Northcote (1746–1831), a painter who had been Reynolds' best student and remained his staunchest defender. Northcote defended Reynolds against Hazlitt's attacks, but only by insisting, against all Reynolds' teachings, that nothing counts but genius.

Selected Bibliographies

SUGGESTED GENERAL READINGS

Histories of England and of English Literature

George Macaulay Trevelyan's *History of England*,‡ rev., 1945, is an excellent survey in one volume; for detailed studies of single periods, see *The Oxford History of England*, 15 vols., 1934 ff., by a variety of historians. The projected 12-volume *Oxford History of English Literature*, edited by F. P. Wilson and Bonamy Dobrée, 1945–, is nearing completion; see the listings below. *A Guide to English Literature*, ed. Boris Ford (1954–61), is available in 6 paperback volumes. Up-to-date one-volume histories are Albert C. Baugh and others, *A Literary History of England*,‡ rev., 1967; Hardin Craig and others, *A History of English Literature*, 1950; and (less densely factual, and more a running literary appreciation) David Daiches, *A Critical History of English Literature*, 2 vols., 1961.

Drama

Allardyce Nicoll, *British Drama*, rev., 1962, and *A History of English Drama, 1660–1900*, 6 vols., rev., 1952–59.

The Novel

The most detailed, although somewhat pedestrian, history is Ernest A. Baker's *History of the English Novel*, 10 vols., 1924–39. Among the short histories are Walter A. Raleigh, *The English Novel*, rev., 1911, which stops at Walter Scott; and, more up-to-date, Arnold Kettle, *An Introduction to the English Novel*,‡ 2 vols., 1951–53; Walter Allen, *The English Novel*,‡ 1954; Ian Watt, *The Rise of the Novel*,‡ 1957; and Lionel Stevenson, *The English Novel*,‡ 1960.

Poetry

W. J. Courthope, *A History of English Poetry*, 6 vols., 1895–1910, and H. J. C. Grierson and J. C. Smith, *A Critical History of English Poetry*, rev., 1947. In addition, Douglas Bush's two books, *Mythology and the Renaissance Tradition in English Poetry*,‡ 1932, 1957, and *Mythology and the Romantic Tradition in English Poetry*,‡ 1937, 1957, constitute an excellent running account, from their special perspective, of English poetry from the 16th century through T. S. Eliot. Another book which ranges widely in English poetry from the Middle Ages through the 18th century is E. M. W. Tillyard, *The English Epic and Its Background*,‡ 1954.

Literary Criticism

George Saintsbury, *A History of English Criticism*, 1911, is still referred to. More recent histories of English criticism are M. H. Abrams, *The Mirror and the Lamp: Romantic Theory and the Critical Tradition*,‡ 1953; W. K. Wimsatt, Jr., and Cleanth Brooks, *Literary Criticism: A Short History*,‡ 1957; George Watson, *The Literary Critics*, 1962; and René Wellek, *A History of Modern Criticism: 1750–1950*, 1955–, of which four of the projected five volumes have been published.

Reference Works

The Cambridge Bibliography of English Literature, edited by F. W. Bateson, 4 vols., 1941, with a supplementary vol. 5, edited by George Watson, 1957, lists all the books of the major and many minor British authors, together with a large selection from biographical, scholarly, and critical works written about these authors. A revision, *The New Cambridge Bibliography*, is nearing completion. Literary biographies and critical books published since that time can be found in the "Annual Bibliography" *PMLA*; for separate periods, see the listings below. *Poetry Explication,*‡ rev. by Joseph M. Kuntz, 1962, lists close analyses of English poems, old and recent, and I. F. Bell and Donald Baird, *The English Novel, 1578–1956,*‡ 1958, provides a useful list of 20th-century criticisms of fiction. Further bibliographical aids are described in Richard D. Altick and Andrew Wright, *Selective Bibliography for the Study of English and American Literature,*‡ 1971, and Arthur G. Kennedy, *A Concise Bibliography for Students of English,* rev., 1972.

For compact biographies of English authors see the multi-volumed *Dictionary of National Biography,* edited by Leslie Stephen and Sidney Lee in 1885–1900, with supplements that carry the work to persons who died up to 1950; condensed biographies will be found in the *Concise Dictionary of National Biography,* Part I (1953) and Part II (1961). Handy reference books on authors, works, and various literary terms and allusions are *The Oxford Companion to English Literature,* edited by Paul Harvey, rev., 1967; *The Oxford Companion to the Theater,* edited by Phyllis Hartnoll, rev., 1967; *Dictionary of World Literature,*‡ edited by Joseph T. Shipley, rev., 1953; and *Encyclopedia of Poetry and Poetics,* ed. Alex Preminger and others, 1965. Low-priced handbooks which define and illustrate literary concepts and terms are: M. H. Abrams, *A Glossary of Literary Terms,* rev., 1971; W. F. Thrall and Addison Hibbard, *A Handbook to Literature,*‡ revised by G. Hugh Holman, 1960; and Lee T. Lemon, *A Glossary for the Study of English,*‡ 1971.

Albert C. Baugh, *A History of the English Language,* rev., 1957, will be found helpful, as will various treatments of English meters and stanza forms, such as: R. M. Alden, *English Verse,* 1903; Karl Shapiro and Robert Beum, *A Prosody Handbook,* 1965; Paul Fussell, Jr., *Poetic Meter and Poetic Form,*‡ 1966; and *The Structure of Verse: Modern Essays in Prosody,*‡ ed. Harvey Gross, 1966.

Intellectual History and Criticism

Students interested in intellectual history as a background for reading

English literature will profit from Arthur T. Lovejoy, *The Great Chain of Being,*‡ 1936, and *Essays in the History of Ideas,*‡ 1948; Marjorie Nicolson, *The Breaking of the Circle,*‡ 1950, *Science and Imagination,*‡ 1956, and *Mountain Gloom and Mountain Glory,*‡ 1959; John Herman Randall, Jr., *The Making of the Modern Mind,* rev., 1940; Basil Willey, *The Seventeenth Century Background,* 1934, *The Eighteenth Century Background,* 1940, and *Nineteenth Century Studies,* 1949; and M. H. Abrams, *Natural Supernaturalism: Tradition and Revolution in Romantic Literature,*‡ 1971. In addition, the following is a selection from those books in literary history and criticism which have been notably influential in shaping modern approaches to English literature and literary forms: Erich Auerbach, *Mimesis: The Representation of Reality in Western Literature,*‡ 1953; Maud Bodkin, *Archetypal Patterns in Poetry,*‡ 1934; Cleanth Brooks, *The Well Wrought Urn,*‡ 1947; Ronald Crane, *The Languages of Criticism and the Structure of Poetry,*‡ 1953, *The Idea of the Humanities,* 2 vols., 1967; and, as editor, *Critics and Criticism, Ancient and Modern,*‡ 1952; T. S. Eliot, *Selected Essays,*‡ 3rd edition, 1951, and *On Poetry and Poets,*‡ 1957; William Empson, *Seven Types of Ambiguity,*‡ 3rd edition, 1953; Francis Fergusson, *The Idea of a Theater,*‡ 1949; Northrop Frye, *Anatomy of Criticism,* 1957; Henry James, *The Art of the Novel: Critical Prefaces,*‡ 1934; F. R. Leavis, *Revaluation,*‡ 1936, and *The Great Tradition*‡ (i.e., in the novel), 1948; C. S. Lewis, *The Allegory of Love,*‡ rev., 1938; John Livingston Lowes, *The Road to Xanadu,*‡ rev., 1930; Percy Lubbock, *The Craft of Fiction,*‡ 1926; I. A. Richards, *Principles of Literary Criticism,*‡ 5th edition, 1934, and *Practical Criticism,*‡ 1930; Caroline Spurgeon, *Shakespeare's Imagery,*‡ 1935; Lionel Trilling. *The Liberal Imagination,*‡ 1950, and *The Opposing Self,*‡ 1955; Edmund Wilson, *Axel's Castle: A Study in the Imaginaitve Literature of 1870–1930,*‡ 1936, and *The Wound and the Bow,*‡ 1941; and Wayne C. Booth, *The Rhetoric of Fiction,*‡ 1961.

THE MIDDLE AGES

The Old English Period

The reader who wishes to acquire historical background for the literature of the period will profit greatly from Dorothy Whitelock's concise study, *The Beginnings of English So-* *ciety,*‡ Penguin (Pelican), 1952. The most detailed history is F. M. Stenton's authoritative *Anglo-Saxon England,* 3rd edition, 1971. Also highly informative are P. Hunter Blair's *An Introduction to Anglo-Saxon Eng-*

land,‡ 1956, and *Roman Britain and Early England, 55 B.C.-A.D. 871*,‡ 1963. The classic study of the culture of the primitive Germanic peoples is H. M. Chadwick's *The Heroic Age*, 1912. For those who wish to sample basic historical documents of the period, there are available the translations by G. N. Garmonsway of *The Anglo-Saxon Chronicle*, 1953, and by L. Sherley-Price of Bede's *Ecclesiastical History*, published under the title *A History of the English Church and People*,‡ Penguin, 1955.

All the surviving poetry in Old English is contained in the six volumes edited by G. P. Krapp and E. V. K. Dobbie, *The Anglo-Saxon Poetic Records*, 1931–53, but the absence of glossaries makes this edition difficult for nonspecialists. Excellent texts of the shorter poems translated in this anthology are contained in J. C. Pope's *Seven Old English Poems*,‡ 1966. The standard text of *Beowulf and the Fight of Finnsburg* is F. Klaeber's 3rd edition, 1950; C. L. Wrenn's edition, *Beowulf, with the Finnesburg Fragment*, rev. 1958, is very useful. Modern English translations of many of the Old English poems have been published by C. W. Kennedy under various titles.

Good critical discussion of Old English literature will be found in Volume I of the *Cambridge History of English Literature*; in Kemp Malone's section of *A Literary History of England*,‡ edited by A. C. Baugh, rev. 1967; in S. B. Greenfield's *A Critical History of Old English Literature*,‡ 1965; and in C. L. Wrenn, *A Study of Old English Literature*,‡ 1966. Important critical articles have been collected by J. B. Bessinger and S. J. Kahrl, *Essential Articles for the Study of Old English Poetry*, 1968. The best critical essay on *Beowulf* remains J. R. R. Tolkien's Gollancz lecture, *Beowulf, the Monsters, and the Critics*, 1937. The most exhaustive scholarly discussion is R. W. Chambers' *Beowulf: An Introduction to the Study of the Poem*, 3rd edition, with a supplement by C. L. Wrenn, 1959. W. W. Lawrence's *Beowulf and the Epic Tradition*, 1928, is still of value. Recent works by Dorothy Whitelock, *The Audience of Beowulf*, 1958, A. C. Brodeur, *The Art of Beowulf*, 1959, Kenneth Sisam, *The Structure of Beowulf*, 1965, and E. B. Irving, *A Reading of Beowulf*,‡ 1968, and *Introduction to Beowulf*, 1969, mingle fine general criticism with some highly specialized discussion. Donald K. Fry has made a useful collection of essays on *Beowulf*, including Tolkien's lecture, in *The Beowulf Poet*,‡ 1968.

The Middle English Period

Good and fairly compact accounts of the history of England between the Norman Conquest and the end of the Middle Ages are contained in the two volumes by Christopher Brooke, *From Alfred to Henry III, 871–1272*,‡ 1961, and George Holmes, *The Later Middle Ages, 1272–1485*,‡ 1962; see also in the Pelican series D. M. Stenton, *English Society in the Early Middle Ages (1066–1307)*,‡ Penguin, 1951, and A. R. Myers, *England in the Late Middle Ages*,‡ Penguin, 1952. Interesting illustrations of life in the Middle Ages, especially in the later centuries, will be found in three books by G. G. Coulton: *Chaucer and His England*,‡ 1908, *The Medieval Scene*,‡ 1930, *Medieval Panorama*,‡ 1938; in Eileen Power's *Medieval People*,‡ 1924; in Edith Rickert's *Chaucer's World*,‡ 1948; in Volume I of G. M. Trevelyan's *Illustrated English Social History, Chaucer's England and the Early Tudors*, 1949; and in R. S. Loomis' *A Mirror of Chaucer's World*, 1965. The spirit of the 15th and late 14th century is brilliantly discussed by J. Huizinga, *The Waning of the Middle Ages*,‡ 1924, 1954.

For general discussions of Middle English literature including Chaucer, see Volume II of the *Cambridge History of English Literature* and A. C. Baugh's section of *A Literary History of England*,‡ edited by Baugh, 1948. W. P. Ker's *English Literature: Medieval*, 1912, is still provocative. D. M. Zesmer's *Guide to English Literature from Beowulf through Chaucer and Medieval Drama*,‡ 1961, is a most useful survey; C. S. Lewis, *The Discarded Image*,‡ 1964, is very popular; W. L. Renwick and H. Orton, *The Beginnings of English Literature to Skelton*, 3rd edition, 1966, is a good survey with bibliographical notes; also useful is H. S. Bennett, *Chaucer and the Fifteenth Century*, 1947. Edward Vasta's collection of essays by various scholars, *Middle English Survey: Critical Essays*,‡ 1965, will offer stimulation to students of *Piers Plowman*, *Sir Gawain and the Green Knight*, the drama, and the ballads. J. A. Burrow, *Ricardian Poetry: Chaucer, Gower, Langland and the Gawain Poet*, 1971, is extremely interesting on the authors in his title and their period. Chapters 6–10 of Erich Auerbach's *Mimesis: The Representation of Reality in Western Literature*,‡ translated by W. R. Trask, 1953, while dealing with none of the works included in this anthology, shed much light on the spirit of medieval literature. For the Middle English language, see Helge Kökeritz's *A Guide to Chaucer's Pronunciation*,‡ 1954; Samuel Moore's *Historical Outlines of English Sounds and Inflections*, revised by A. H. Marckwardt, 1951; and John W. Clark's *Early English*,‡ 1957.

For general discussion of non-Chaucerian Middle English literature, see R. M. Wilson, *Early Middle English Literature*, 1939, and E. K. Chambers, *English Literature at the Close of the Middle Ages*, 1954, which between them thoroughly cover the beginning and the end of the period. The only recent work attempting to survey the whole non-Chaucerian field is John Speirs's erratic but stimulating *Medieval English Poetry: The Non-Chaucerian Tradition*, 1957. George Kane's *Middle English Literature*, 1951, has good chapters on the romances, the religious lyrics, and *Piers Plowman*, and A. L. Kellogg, *Chaucer, Langland, Arthur*, 1972, treats his selected topics provocatively. A broad sampling of non-Chaucerian literature in translation is offered by *Medieval English Verse and Poetry*, edited by R. S. Loomis and R. Willard, 1948.

The standard bibliography is J. E. Wells, *A Manual of the Writings in Middle English, 1050–1400*, 1916; nine supplements extend coverage through 1945. Two volumes of a revised edition of Wells edited by J. B. Severs and containing chapters on the Middle English romances and the Gawain-poet have appeared, 1967 and 1970, as well as a third edited by Albert E. Hartung with a chapter on Malory, 1972.

Geoffrey Chaucer

The standard edition of Chaucer's writing is F. N. Robinson's *The Complete Works of Chaucer*, 2nd edition, 1957. The present editor's anthology of Chaucer's poetry, from which are taken the selections printed here, is helpful to the nonspecialist, as is A. C. Baugh's *Chaucer's Major Poetry*, 1963. Vivid presentations of Chaucer in the background of 14th-century England are found in Marchette Chute's *Geoffrey Chaucer of England*,‡ 1946, and D. S. Brewer's *Chaucer and His Time*, 1963. The raw material for Chaucer's biography is contained in *Chaucer Life-Records*, edited by M. M. Crow and C. C. Olson, 1966. For a succinct account of the sources and literary background of Chaucer's works, see R. D. French's *A Chaucer Handbook*, 2nd edition, 1947; a complete reproduction of the known sources of the *Canterbury Tales* is contained in the scholarly compendium *Sources and*

Analogues of Chaucer's Canterbury Tales, edited by W. F. Bryan and Germaine Dempster, 1941, 1958. Muriel Bowden, *A Commentary on the General Prologue to the Canterbury Tales*, 1948, provides a wealth of background information on the individual Canterbury pilgrims. Various scholars deal with a number of aspects of Chaucer's work in *Chaucer and Chaucerians*, edited by D. S. Brewer, 1966; *Companion to Chaucer Studies*,‡ edited by Beryl Rowland, 1968; and *Chaucer's Mind and Art*, edited by A. C. Cawley, 1969. For literary criticism, all the following works contain stimulating material: P. F. Baum, *Chaucer: A Critical Appreciation*, 1958; H. S. Bennett, *Chaucer and the Fifteenth Century*, 1947; D. S. Brewer, *Chaucer*, 1953; B. H. Bronson, *In Search of Chaucer*,‡ 1960; G. K. Chesterton, *Chaucer*, 1932; Nevill Coghill, *The Poet Chaucer*, 1949, and *Geoffrey Chaucer*, 1956; H. S. Corsa, *Chaucer, Poet of Mirth and Morality*, 1964; T. W. Craik, *The Comic Tales of Chaucer*, 1964; W. C. Curry, *Chaucer and the Medieval Sciences*,‡ rev. 1960; Germaine Dempster, *Dramatic Irony in Chaucer*, 1932; E. T. Donaldson, *Speaking of Chaucer*,‡ 1970; Maurice Hussey, A. C. Spearing, and James Winny, *An Introduction to Chaucer*,‡ 1965; S. S. Hussey, *Chaucer: An Introduction*, 1971; P. M. Kean, *Chaucer and the Making of English Poetry*, 2 vols., 1972; G. L. Kittredge, *Chaucer and His Poetry*, 1915; W. W. Lawrence, *Chaucer and the Canterbury Tales*, 1950; Emile Legouis, *Geoffrey Chaucer*, 1913; J. L. Lowes, *Geoffrey Chaucer and the Development of His Genius*, 1934; R. M. Lumiansky, *Of Sondry Folk*, 1955; Kemp Malone, *Chapters on Chaucer*, 1951; J. M. Manly, *Some New Light on Chaucer*, 1926; Charles Muscatine, *Chaucer and the French Tradition*,‡ 1957; H. R. Patch, *On Rereading Chaucer*, 1939; R. O. Payne, *The Key of Remembrance*, 1963; Raymond Preston, *Chaucer*, 1952; R. K. Root, *The Poetry of Chaucer*, 2nd edition, 1922; T. W. Ross, *Chaucer's Bawdy*,‡ 1972; P. V. D. Shelley, *The Living Chaucer*, 1940; John Speirs, *Chaucer the Maker*, 1951; and J. S. P. Tatlock, *The Mind and Art of Chaucer*, 1950. D. W. Robertson's *A Preface to Chaucer*, 1962, is a most learned, stimulating, doctrinaire, and controversial introduction to the reading of Chaucer. The following are collections of critical essays by various writers: *Discussions of the Canterbury Tales*,‡ edited by C. J. Owen, 1961; *Chaucer Criticism: The Canterbury Tales*,‡ edited by R. J. Schoeck and J. Taylor, 1960; *Chaucer: Modern Essays in Criticism,*‡ edited by E. C. Wagenknecht, 1959; and *Geoffrey Chaucer: A Critical Anthology,*‡ Penguin, 1969, edited by J. A. Burrow. See the prefatory remarks to Chaucer's poems in Robinson's edition and the editor's commentary in his anthology.

The standard bibliographies are E. P. Hammond, *Chaucer: A Bibliographical Manual,* 1908; D. D. Griffith, *Bibliography of Chaucer,* 1955; W. R. Crawford, *Bibliography of Chaucer 1954–63,* 1967; and A. C. Baugh‡ *Chaucer,* 1968. See also Caroline Spurgeon's *Five Hundred Years of Chaucer Criticism and Allusion, 1357–1900,* 1925.

Sir Gawain and the Green Knight

The standard Middle English text of the poem is that of J. R. R. Tolkien and E. V. Gordon, 1925 (revised by Norman Davis, 1967). Perhaps easier to use are the editions by R. A. Waldron,‡ 1970, and J. A. Burrow, 1972. Good discussion of various aspects of the poem appear in Marie Borroff's *Sir Gawain and the Green Knight: A Stylistic and Metrical Study,* 1962; L. D. Benson, *Art and Tradition in Sir Gawain and the Green Knight,* 1965 (especially good on the sources); and J. A. Burrow, *A Reading of Sir Gawain and the Green Knight,* 1965. Interesting chapters on the poem are contributed by A. C. Spearing in *Criticism and Medieval Poetry,* 2nd edition, 1972, and *The Gawain Poet,* 1971, and D. R. Howard in *The Three Temptations: Medieval Man in Search of the World,* 1966. There are three collections of critical essays on the poet: R. J. Blanch's *Sir Gawain and Pearl,* 1966; Denton Fox's *Twentieth-Century Interpretations of Sir Gawain and the Green Knight,*‡ 1968; and D. R. Howard and C. K. Zacher's *Critical Studies of Sir Gawain and the Green Knight.*

Piers Plowman

The most handy edition of *Piers Plowman* is W. W. Skeat's *The Vision of William Concerning Piers the Plowman * * *,* 2 vols., 1886, which gives all three versions. J. A. W. Bennett's edition of the first eight sections of the B text,‡ 1972, is very useful, as is Elizabeth Salter and D. A. Pearsall's selections from C,‡ 1967. There are modern translations by H. W. Wells, *The Vision of Piers Plowman,* 1935, and by Nevill Coghill (selections only), *Visions from Piers Plowman,* 1949. A literal prose translation is J. F. Goodridge's *Langland: Piers the Ploughman,*‡ revised 1966.

The best general account of the poem is in Chapters IV–V of R. W. Chambers' *Man's Unconquerable Mind,* 1939; see also Kane's chapter in *Middle English Literature.* Recent studies by Elizabeth Salter, *Piers Plowman: An Introduction,* 1962, and John Lawlor, *Piers Plowman: An Essay in Criticism,* 1962, are most useful to the beginner, as are chapters on the poem in the works by Howard and Spearing mentioned above under *Sir Gawain and the Green Knight.* Collections of critical essays have been made by Edward Vasta, *Interpretations of Piers Plowman,* 1968; R. J. Blanch, *Style and Symbolism in Piers Plowman,* 1969; and S. S. Hussey, *Piers Plowman: Critical Approaches,* 1969.

Middle English Lyrics

The best selection of Middle English lyrics are *Early English Lyrics,*‡ edited by E. K. Chambers and F. Sidgwick, 1921; *Medieval English Lyrics: A Critical Anthology,* edited by R. T. Davies, 1963; *The Oxford Book of Medieval English Verse,* edited by Celia and Kenneth Sisam, 1970; *English Lyrics before 1500,* edited by Theodore Silverstein, 1971; modernized and semi-modernized selections appear in M. R. Adamson's *A Treasury of Middle English Verse,* 1930, and in R. D. Stevick's *One Hundred Middle English Poems,*‡ 1964. For criticism see A. K. Moore, *The Secular Lyric in Middle English,* 1951, and Kane's chapter.

The Second Shepherds' Play; The Brome Play of Abraham and Isaac; Everyman

The classic work on the medieval drama is E. K. Chambers' *The Medieval Stage,* 1905. More recent are Hardin Craig's exhaustive *English Religious Drama of the Middle Ages,* 1955, and O. B. Hardison's fine study, *Christian Rite and Christian Drama in the Middle Ages,*‡ 1965. For a good discussion of the Middle English mystery cycle, see V.A. Kolve's *The Play Called Corpus Christi,* 1966. Good selections of Middle English plays are presented by J. Q. Adams, *Chief Pre-Shakespearean Dramas,* 1924, and by A. C. Cawley, *Everyman and Medieval Miracle Plays,*‡ 1960. Cawley's *The Wakefield Pageants in the Towneley Cycle,* 1958, has a discussion of the work of the "Wakefield Masters" whose hand is seen in the *Second Shepherds' Play.*

Popular Ballads

The great ballad collection is that of F. J. Child, *The English and Scottish Popular Ballads,*‡ 1882, more available in the somewhat abridged edition by H. C. Sargent and G. L. Kittredge, 1904. Selections will be found in *The Faber Book of Ballads*,‡ edited by M. J. C. Hodgart, 1965, and *The Oxford Book of Ballads*, edited by James Kinsley, 1969. For general discussion, see F. B. Gummere, *The Popular Ballads*,‡ 1907; G. H. Gerould, *The Ballad of Tradition*, 1932; W. J. Entwistle, *European Balladry*, 1939; and M. J. C. Hodgart, *The Ballads*,‡ 1950.

Sir Thomas Malory

The Winchester manuscript of Malory's *Morte Darthur*, with full commentary and valuable discussion, is given in Eugène Vinaver's *The Works of Sir Thomas Malory*, 3 vols., 2nd edition, 1967; the one-volume edition, 2nd edition, Oxford, 1970, contains the text only. The Caxton version is most readily available in *Le Morte D'Arthur*, edited by E. Rhys, 1906. Vinaver's *Malory*, 1929, surveys Malory's life and career. A number of critical problems in Malory's work, especially its unity, are discussed in two collections of essays by various scholars: *Essays on Malory*, edited by J. A. W. Bennett, 1963, and *Malory's Originality*, edited by R. M. Lumiansky, 1964. In *The Ill-Framed Knight*, 1966, William Matthews challenges the traditional identification of the author of the *Morte Darthur* with that knight-prisoner, the details of whose stormy career have been unearthed by scholars interested in the book.

A most valuable summary of the Arthurian literary background is R. S. Loomis' *The Development of Arthurian Romance*,‡ 1963.

THE SIXTEENTH CENTURY

General books on the political, social, and economic history of the period are: A. L. Rowse, *The England of Elizabeth*, 1950; J. B. Black, *The Reign of Elizabeth*, 1936; A. F. Pollard, *The History of England, 1547–1603*; J. E. Neale, *Queen Elizabeth I*, ‡ 1934; Conyers Read, *Mr. Secretary Walsingham*, 1925; J. D. Mackie, *The Earlier Tudors*, 1952; Katharine Garvin, ed., *The Great Tudors*, 1935; J. E. Neale, *Elizabeth I and Her Parliaments 1559–1581, 1584–1601*,‡ 1953, 1957; D. L. Keir, *The Constitutional History of Modern Britain Since 1484*,‡ 5th ed., 1953; *R. H. Tawney, Religion and the Rise of Capitalism*,‡ 1926; R. H. Tawney and E. Power, *Tudor Economic Documents*, 1924; W. H. Dunham and S. Pargellis, eds., *Complaint and Reform in England*, 1938. H. D. Traill, *Social England*, 1897 and 1901–4; *Shakespeare's England*, 1916.

Discussions of church history include W. H. Frere, *The English Church in the Reigns of Elizabeth and James*, 1911; R. W. Dixon, *History of the Church of England*, 1878–1902; J. H. Pollen, *The English Catholics in the Reign of Elizabeth*, 1920; A. F. Scott Pearson, *Thomas Cartwright and Elizabethan Puritanism*, 1925; W. Haller, *The Rise of Puritanism*,‡ 1938; A. C. Southern, *Elizabethan Recusant Prose*, 1950; H. C. White, *The Tudor Books of Private Devotion*, 1951.

The important topics of geography and exploration are treated in E. G. R. Taylor, *Tudor Geography, 1485–1583*, 1930, and *Late Tudor and Early Stuart Geography, 1583–1658*, 1934; A. L. Rowse, *Sir Richard Grenville of the Revenge*, 1937; J. A. Williamson, *The Age of Drake*,‡ 1938, 2nd edition, 1946, and *Hawkins of Plymouth*, 1949.

Intellectual history is discussed in E. M. W. Tillyard, *The Elizabethan World Picture*,‡ 1943, 1956; Theodore Spencer, *Shakespeare and the Nature of Man*,‡ 1942; L. B. Wright, *Middle-Class Culture in Elizabethan England*, 1935; F. R. Johnson, *Astronomical Thought in Renaissance England*, 1937; P. Kocher, *Science and Religion in Elizabethan England*, 1953.

Books on the fine arts in Elizabethan England include: John Stevens, *Music and Poetry in the Early Tudor Court*, 1961; Bruce Pattison, *Music and Poetry of the English Renaissance*, 1948; E. H. Fellowes, *The English Madrigal Composers*, 1921; M. C. Boyd, *Elizabethan Music and Music Criticism*, 1940; W. Chappell, *Popular Music of the Olden Time*, 1855; R. Blomfield, *History of Renaissance Architecture in England*, 1897; J. A. Gotch and W. T. Brown, *Architecture of the Renaissance in England*, 1891–94; T. Garner and A. Stratton, *The Domestic Architecture of England during the Tudor Period*, 1911, 1929; R. Blomfield, *The Formal Garden in England*, 1901; C. H. C. Baker and W. G. Constable, *English Painting of the Sixteenth and Seventeenth Centuries*, 1930; S. Colvin, *Early Engraving and Engravers in England, 1545–1695*, 1905; F. B. Williams, Jr., *Elizabethan England*, 1939.

The standard reference work on Elizabethan drama is E. K. Chambers, *The Elizabethan Stage*, 4 vols., 1923. An introduction is Tucker Brooke's *The Tudor Drama*. See also C. Walter Hodges, *The Globe Restored*, 1954.

The new professions of writing, printing, and publishing are discussed in H. S. Bennett, *English Books and Readers, 1475–1557*, 1952, and *English Books and Readers, 1558–1603*, 1965; J. W. Saunders, "The Stigma of Print," *Essays in Criticism I* (1951) 139–164; E. H. Miller, *The Professional Writer in Elizabethan England*, 1959; D. N. Smith, "Authors and Patrons" in *Shakespeare's England*, Vol. II, 1916; R. B .McKerrow, *An Introduction to Bibliography for Literary Students*, 1928; A. W. Pollard, *Shakespeare's Fight with the Pirates*, 1917; W. W. Greg, *English Literary Autographs*, 1925–32, and (ed.) *Records of the Court of the Stationers' Company*, 1930; Percy Simpson, *Proofreading in the Sixteenth, Seventeenth and Eighteenth Centuries*, 1935.

Useful histories and criticism of literature are: V. de Sola Pinto, *The English Renaissance*, 1938; Helen Morris, *Elizabethan Literature*, 1958; Douglas L. Peterson, *The English Lyric from Wyatt to Donne*, 1966; Maurice Evans, *English Poetry in the Sixteenth Century*,‡ 1955; Douglas Bush, *Prefaces to Renaissance Literature*,‡ 1965; J. M. Berdan, *Early Tudor Poetry*, 1920; Louis B. Wright, *Middle-Class Culture in Elizabethan England*, 1935; Douglas Bush, *Mythology and the Renaissance Tradition in English Poetry*,‡ 1932; Sidney Lee, *The French Renaissance in England*, 1910; Geoffrey Tillotson, *Essays in Criticism and Research*, 1942; E. A. Baker, *The History of the English Novel*, Vol. II, 1929; F. P. Wilson, *Elizabethan and Jacobean*, 1945; Hallett Smith, *Elizabethan Poetry*, 1952; C. S. Lewis, *English Literature in the Sixteenth Century*, 1954.

The general bibliographies are F. W. Bateson, ed., *Cambridge Bibliography of English Literature*, Vol. I, 1940; Conyers Read, ed., *Bibliography of British Hisotry, Tudor Period*, 1933; A. W. Pollard and G. R. Redgrave, eds., *A Short-Title Catalogue of books * * * 1475–1640*, 1927; E. Arber, ed., *A Transcript of the Registers of the Company of Stationers*, 1875–94.

Sir Thomas Wyatt

The best edition of Wyatt's poetry is the *Collected Poems*,‡ edited by Kenneth Muir and Patricia Thomson, 1969. *Tottel's Miscellany* is edited by Hyder E. Rollins, rev. 1965. Recent biographical and critical works are Kenneth Muir, *Life and Letters of* Sir Thomas Wyatt, 1963; Patricia Thomson, *Sir Thomas Wyatt and His Background*, 1965; Raymond Southall, *The Courtly Maker*, 1964; and Donald M. Friedman, "The Mind in the Poem: Wyatt's *They Flee from Me*," *Studies in English Literature* VII (1967 1–13. Earlier studies are Hallett Smith, "The Art of Sir Thomas Wyatt," *Huntington Library Quarterly* IX (1946) 323–55; E. K. Chambers, *Sir Thomas Wyatt and Some Collected Studies*, 1933; and E. M. W. Tillyard, *The Poetry of Sir Thomas Wyatt*, 1929.

Henry Howard, Earl of Surrey

A recent edition of Surrey's poems is by Emrys Jones, 1964; an older one is by F. M. Padelford, rev. 1928. *Tottel's Miscellany* is edited by Hyder E. Rollins, rev. 1965. The most recent biography is by E. Casaday, *Henry Howard, Earl of Surrey*, 1938.

Sir Philip Sidney

The definitive edition of Sidney's poetry is edited by William Ringler, 1962. The complete works are available in the edition of A. Feuillarat, 1912–26. The *Apology* has been edited separately by E. S. Shuckburgh, 1891, and by G. Gregory Smith in *Elizabethan Critical Essays*, 1904.

Recent books on Sidney are Walter R. Davis, *Sidney's Arcadia*, 1965; R. B. Young, *English Petrarke*, 1958; David Kalstone, *Sidney's Poetry*, 1965; R. L. Montgomery, *Symmetry and Sense; the Poetry of Sir Philip Sidney*, 1961, and James M. Osborn, *Young Philip Sidney*, 1972.

An important critical article on the poetry is Theodore Spencer, "The Poetry of Sir Philip Sidney," *English Literary History*, XII (1945), 251–78. The biography of Mona Wilson, *Sir Philip Sidney*, 1931, is still the best. Also useful are: J. E. Spingarn, *A History of Literary Criticism in the Renaissance*,‡ 1899; K. T. Myrick, *Sir Philip Sidney as a Literary Craftsman*,‡ 1935; J. W. H. Atkins, *English Literary Criticism: the Renascence*, 1947; John Buxton, *Sir Philip Sidney and the English Renaissance*,‡ 1954; and Frederick S. Boas, *Sir Philip Sidney, Representative Elizabethan, His Life and Writings*, 1955.

Edmund Spenser

The most useful selection of Spenser's poetry and criticism of it is *Edmund Spenser's Poetry*,‡ selected and edited by Hugh Maclean, 1968. Modern critical works of value are Graham Hough, *A Preface to The Faerie Queene*, 1962; William Nelson, *The Poetry of Edmund Spenser*, 1963;

Thomas P. Roche, *The Kindly Flame*, 1964; Donald Cheney, *Spenser's Image of Nature*, 1966; Kathleen Williams, *Spenser's World of Glass*, 1966; Paul J. Alpers, *The Poetry of The Faerie Queene*, 1967; J. E. Hankins, *Source and Meaning in Spenser's Allegory*, 1971; and John B. Bender, *Spenser and Literary Pictorialism*, 1972. Older scholarship is summarized in *The Works of Edmund Spenser: A Variorum Edition*, edited by Edwin Greenlaw and others, 10 volumes, 1932–49.

Sir Walter Ralegh

The standard edition of the poems is by A. M. C. Latham, rev. 1950. An important study of Ralegh's ideas is Ernest A. Strathmann, *Sir Walter Ralegh, A Study in Elizabethan Skepticism*, 1951. Recent books include Philip Edwards, *Sir Walter Ralegh*, 1953; Margaret Irwin, *The Great Lucifer*, 1960; W. F. Oakeshott, *The Queen and the Poet*, 1960; A. L. Rowse, *Ralegh and the Throckmortons*, 1962; and Willard M. Wallace, *Sir Walter Raleigh*, 1959.

Christopher Marlowe

The standard edition of Marlowe's works is in six volumes, under the general editorship of R. H. Case, 1930. *Dr. Faustus* has been edited by Sir W. W. Greg, in a large parallel-text edition with elaborate commentary, 1950, and a smaller reconstruction of the original text, also 1950. General studies of Marlowe are by Paul Kocher, 1946, by F. S. Boas, 1940, and by John Bakeless, 1937. Most interesting and valuable recent treatments are those by Harry Levin, *The Overreacher*,‡ 1952, and F. P. Wilson, *Marlowe and the Early Shakespeare*, 1953. The circumstances of Marlowe's death are told by their discoverer, Leslie Hotson, in *The Death of Christopher Marlowe*, 1925, and Marlowe's involvement in another fatal quarrel is the subject of Mark Eccles, *Christopher Marlowe in London*, 1934.

Recent critical studies are: Douglas Cole, *Suffering and Evil in the Plays of Christopher Marlowe*, 1962; and J. B. Steane, *Marlowe: A Critical Study*, 1964.

William Shakespeare

On *1 Henry IV* see *The Variorum Shakespeare, Henry the Fourth Part One*, ed. S. B. Hemmingway, 1936; G. B. Evans, "Supplement to Henry IV. Part I" *Shakespeare Quarterly*, VII (1956), 3; John Dover Wilson, *The Fortunes of Falstaff*,‡ 1944; F. P. Wilson, *Marlowe and the Early Shakespeare*, 1953; Irving Ribner, *The English History Play in the Age of Shakespeare*, 1957; L. B. Campbell, *Shakespeare's "Histories,"* 1947; H. Levin, "Falstaff Uncolted," *Modern Language Notes*, LXI (1946), 305–10; E. M. W. Tillyard, *Shakespeare's History Plays*,‡ 1946.

On *King Lear* see *Shakespeare, King Lear: A Casebook*, ed. Frank Kermode, 1969; Maynard Mack, *King Lear in Our Time*, 1965; William R. Elton, *King Lear and the Pagan Gods*, 1966; Paul A. Jorgensen, *Lear's Self-Discovery*, 1967.

There are many editions of the sonnets, ranging from the convenient paperback Signet edition, 1964, with an introduction by W. H. Auden, to the two-volume *New Variorum* edited by Hyder E. Rollins, 1944. Commentary is extensive and much of it worthless, but sensible guidance may be found in Tucker Brooke's edition, 1936, which attempts a rearrangement; Edward Hubler, *The Sense of Shakespeare's Sonnets*,‡ 1952; J. B. Leishman, *Themes and Variations in Shakespeare's Sonnets*,‡ 1961; *The Riddle of Shakespeare's Sonnets: Essays by Edward Hubler, Northrop Frye, Leslie Fiedler, Stephen Spender and R. P. Blackmur*, 1962; Hilton Landry, *Interpretations in Shakespeare's Sonnets*, 1963; Brents Stirling, *The Shakespeare Sonnet Order*, 1968; Stephen Booth, *An Essay on Shakespeare's Sonnets*, 1969.

The poems have been edited by Hyder E. Rollins in the *New Variorum* edition, 1938. More manageable are the recent editions by F. T. Prince, 1960, and J. C. Maxwell, 1966. William H. Matchett has published *The Phoenix and the Turtle*, 1965. G. Wilson Knight's *The Mutual Flame*, 1955, discusses the sonnets and *The Phoenix and the Turtle*.

The standard scholarly authority on the life and works is E. K. Chambers, *William Shakespeare, A Study of Facts and Problems*, 1930. A well-written and dependable biography for the student and general reader is Marchette Chute, *Shakespeare of London*,‡ 1949. A scrupulously objective account is G. E. Bentley's *Shakespeare: A Biographical Handbook*, 1961. Bibliographies of Shakespearean studies appear in the periodical *Shakespeare Quarterly*.

John Skelton

Stanley E. Fish, *Skelton's Poetry*, 1965; Arthur R. Heiserman, *Skelton and Satire*, 1961; H. L. R. Edwards, *Skelton*, 1949; Ian A. Gordon, *John Skelton*, 1943; L. J. Lloyd, *John Skelton*, 1938; William Nelson, *John Skelton, Laureate*, 1939.

Fulke Greville, Lord Brooke

The recently published *Life of Fulke Greville* by R. A. Rebholz, 1971, and a critical work by Joan Rees, *Fulke Greville, Lord Brooke*, 1971, as well as Richard Waswo, *The Fatal Mirror: Themes and Techniques in the Poetry of Fulke Greville*, 1972, show the current interest in this heretofore neglected poet. Earlier short studies are the first chapter in Yvor Winters, *Forms of Discovery*, 1967, and Hugh Maclean, "Greville's Poetic," *Studies in Philology* LXI (1964) 170–91. The standard edition of the *Poems and Dramas* is by Geoffrey Bullough, 1939, in two volumes. Thom Gunn edited *Selected Poems* with an introduction in 1968.

Robert Southwell

Two studies are Pierre Janelle, *Robert Southwell the Writer*, London, 1935, and Christopher Devlin, *The Life of Robert Southwell, Poet and Martyr*, 1956.

Samuel Daniel

A. C. Sprague has edited *Poems and a Defence of Ryme,‡* 1930. See also G. K. Brady, *Samuel Daniel*, 1923.

Michael Drayton

The *Works of Michael Drayton*, edited by J. W. Hebel, 5 vols., 1931–41, is the standard edition. B. H. Newdigate, *Michael Drayton and His Circle*, 1941, is a biography.

Thomas Nashe

R. B. McKerrow's edition of *The Works*, 5 vols., 1904–10, is a great work of scholarship. Volume V contains the best account yet written of Nashe's life, the Martin Marprelate controversy, and the Nashe-Harvey quarrel. This edition was reprinted in 1958 with corrections and additions by F. P. Wilson.

Thomas Campion

The best edition of Campion's English works, with a selection from his Latin poetry, is by Walter R. Davis, 1967. A critical biography is Miles Kastendieck, *England's Musical Poet, Thomas Campion*, 1938; a more recent study is by Edward Lowbury, Timothy Salter, and Alison Young, *Thomas Campion, Poet, Composer, Physician*, 1970. Campion's musical settings are reprinted in *The English School of Lutenist Song-Writers*, edited by E. H. Fellowes, 1926.

Hugh Latimer

Recent studies of Latimer include A. G. Chester, *Hugh Latimer, Apostle to the English*, 1954; C. M. Gray, *Hugh Latimer and the Sixteenth Century*, 1950; and D. M. Loades, *The Oxford Martyrs*, 1970.

John Foxe

An indispensable work for the understanding of John Foxe is William Haller, *The Elect Nation: The Meaning and Relevance of Foxe's Book of Martyrs*, 1963; J. F. Mozley, *John Foxe and His Book*, 1940.

"Martin Marprelate"

The best account of the Marprelate controversy is in Volume V of R. B. McKerrow's edition of Nashe, reprinted and corrected by F. P. Wilson, 1958. The tracts were printed in an edition by William Pierce in 1911, who had published *An Historical Introduction* to them in 1908. The authorship of individual tracts is still a matter of controversy.

Richard Hooker

The Laws were edited by J. Keble, 3 vols., 1936, revised by R. W. Church and F. Paget, 1888. There are various editions of individual Books; R. Bayne edited Books I–V in 1907. Izaak Walton wrote the first biography of Hooker; C. J. Sisson's *The Judicious Marriage of Mr. Hooker*, 1940, corrects Walton in many respects. See also E. N. S. Thompson, "Richard Hooker among the Controversialists," *Philological Quarterly*, XX (1941), 454–64; Peter Munz, *The Place of Hooker in the History of Thought*, 1952; and F. J. Shirley, *Richard Hooker and Contemporary Political Ideas*, 1949.

Sir Thomas More

More's life is told in several early biographies, one by his son-in-law William Roper, edited by E. V. Hitchcock, 1935, and another by Nicholas Harpsfield, also edited by Hitchcock, 1932. The standard modern life is *Thomas More,‡* by R. W. Chambers, 1935. *Utopia* was early translated into English by Ralph Robinson (1551); there are many editions of this translation. Others are by Gilbert Burnet in the 17th century, and the modern translation, by H. V. S. Ogden, 1949. A great edition of the complete works is now in progress at the Yale University Press, edited by Richard S. Sylvester and others (1963–).

Important modern commentaries are J. H. Hexter, *More's Utopia: The Biography of an Idea,‡* 1952; Russell Ames, *Citizen Thomas More and His Utopia*, 1949, Edward L. Surtz, *The Praise of Pleasure: Philosophy, Edu-*

cation and Communism in More's Utopia, 1957; and the same author's The Praise of Wisdom: Religious and Moral Problems and Backgrounds of St. Thomas More's Utopia, 1957.

Richard Hakluyt

Sir Walter Alexander Raleigh's introduction to an edition of Hakluyt

and published separately as The English Voyages of the Sixteenth Century is still excellent reading. More recent works include George B. Parks, Richard Hakluyt and the English Voyages, 1928; Richard Hakluyt and His Successors, ed. Edward Lynam, 1946; and David B. Quinn, Richard Hakluyt, Editor, 1967.

THE SEVENTEENTH CENTURY

Two standard general histories of England during the 17th century are Godfrey Davies, The Early Stuarts, 2nd edition, 1959, and G. M. Trevelyan, England Under the Stuarts, London, 1949. Clarendon's History, dealing with the Civil War and Protectorate, is a fascinating contemporary document, and Samuel Rawson Gardiner's History of England from 1603 to 1656, 10 vols., rev., 1894–96, is rich in facts. Over the past decade or so, a prodigious series of books by Christopher Hill, the Master of Balliol (books fundamentally Marxist in their approach), have done much to transfigure our understanding of the 17th-century revolution, seen under its political, economic, and social aspects. One of these The Century of Revolution, 1603–1714,‡ 1966, forms part of the Norton Library History of England. For a less tendentious view the two volumes of C. V. Wedgwood, The Great Rebellion, may be consulted: they are The King's Peace,‡ 1955, and The King's War, 1958. Carl J. Friedrich, The Age of the Baroque, 1952, is European in its purview, and cultural as well as political in emphasis.

On the intellectual background of the age, one would do well to consult E. M. W. Tillyard's fascinating little study The Elizabethan World Picture,‡ 1943, 1956, modifying its perhaps excessive simplicities by reference to C. S. Lewis's brilliantly forensic The Discarded Image,‡ 1964, and to the collection of original documents reproduced in James Winny's The Frame of Order, 1957. Sir Herbert J. C. Grierson's Cross Currents in English Literature of the 17th Century,‡ 1929, and Sir Basil Willey's The 17th Century Background,‡ 1934, should be supplemented by more recent studies, like John R. Mulder's The Temple of the Mind,‡ 1969, and Frances Yates' extraordinary series of books on Giordano Bruno, 1964,‡ The Art of Memory, 1966, and The Theater of the World,‡ 1968. Among collections of essays, which are many, one might specify those of Joseph Mazzeo, Renaissance and 17th-century Studies,

1964, and of Rosemond Tuve, Essays in Spenser, Herbert, Milton, 1970, as particularly likely to stimulate thought.

General literary histories of the age include Douglas Bush, English Literature in the Earlier Seventeenth Century, 1945, and a shorter, less bibliographical introduction, C. V. Wedgwood's Seventeenth Century English Literature, 1950.

Special studies of social and economic problems in relation to the intellectual life of the day are Max Weber's The Protestant Ethic and the Spirit of Capitalism,‡ translated by Talcott Parsons, 1948, 1958, and R. H. Tawney, Religion and the Rise of Capitalism,‡ 1937; also, the various criticisms to which this theory has been subjected by H. R. Trevor-Roper and others should not be overlooked. They are mostly to be found in the Economic History Review. William Haller's The Rise of Puritanism,‡ 1938, is a classic account of the Puritans viewed through their propaganda; M. M. Knappen also offers a fine historical introduction in his Tudor Puritanism: A Chapter in the History of Idealism,‡ 1939. L. C. Knight's Drama and Society in the Age of Jonson, 1937, is a shrewd analytic study of a special problem with wide implications.

The growth of science in the 17th century may be studied in Abraham Wolf's History of Science, Technology, and Philosophy in the 16th and 17th Centuries, 2nd edition, prep. by D. McKie, 1950; its impact on the daily thought of men is traced by E. A. Burtt, Metaphysical Foundations of Modern Science,‡ rev., 1950. A. O. Lovejoy's The Great Chain of Being: A Study of the History of an Idea,‡ 1936, is a classic reconstruction of an important Renaissance idea, and an account of how it decayed in the 17th century and after.

The literary criticism of the age is best studied in the documents collected by G. Gregory Smith, Elizabethan Critical Essays, 1904, and by J. E. Spingarn, Critical Essays of the 17th Century, 1908–9. Donald L. Clark, in Rhetoric and Poetry in the

Renaissance, 1922; Rosemond Tuve, in *Elizabethan and Metaphysical Imagery*,‡ 1947; and Ruth Wallerstein, in *Studies in 17th Century Poetic*,‡ 1950, have probed into the relation between critical theory and poetic practice. Finally, Wylie Sypher, *Four Stages of Renaissance Style*,‡ 1955, offers some very interesting and provocative analogies between poetic styles and styles in the graphic arts during the 17th century. Other books in this area, where classifications are indefinite and terminologies luxuriant, include Odette de Mourgues, *Metaphysical, Baroque, and Précieux Poetry*, 1953, and Frank Warnke, *Versions of Baroque*, 1972.

In addition to the references given below for individual poets, the following titles may prove useful for the student of 17th-century poetry: George Saintsbury edited, in three volumes, the texts of the *Minor Poets of the Caroline Period*, 1905–21, and Norman Ault collected some interesting lyrics of the age, *Seventeenth-Century Lyrics*, 1928. Edward Dowden's *Puritan and Anglican*, 1900, and Edmund Gosse's *The Jacobean Poets*, 1894, are older studies which retain a good deal of vitality. They may be supplemented by more recent collections of essays, such as L. C. Knights' *Explorations*, 1946, and, in a more limited context, George Williamson's *Six Metaphysical Poets*, 1967. A spate of books on the metaphysical poets appeared during the 1930's, of which the best are Joan Bennett's *Four Metaphysical Poets*,‡ 1934, 2nd edition, 1953 (Donne, Herbert, Crashaw, and Vaughan); Helen C. White's *The Metaphysical Poets*,‡ 1936; and J. B. Leishman's book, of the same title, 1934. Louis L. Martz, in *The Poetry of Meditation*,‡ discusses a traditional mode of thought as it influenced the metaphysicals; the same line of investigation is continued in *The Paradise Within*, 1964. Mario Praz has several important *Studies in 17th Century Imagery*, 1939. Other studies involving several different poets are those of Odette de Mourgues, *Metaphysical, Baroque, and Précieux Poetry*, 1953; Marjorie Nicolson, *The Breaking of the Circle*, 1960; and Don C. Allen, *Image and Meaning*, 1960. Allen's *Mysteriously Meant*, 1970, is a broad study of allegory and symbolism; Harry Levin, *The Myth of the Golden Age in the Renaissance*, 1969, and A. B. Giammati, *The Earthly Paradise and the Renaissance Epic*, 1966, though specialized studies, have many general implications as well. Of particular interest to students of classic myth in 17th-century poetry is Douglas Bush's erudite *Mythology and the Renaissance Tradition in English Poetry*,‡ 1932, 1963. Until 1969 *Studies in Philology* published an annual bibliography of Renaissance and 17th-century studies; after that date, the appropriate section of the MLA bibliography should be consulted.

John Webster

The reputation of Webster, and particularly of "The Duchess of Malfi," became a subject of active dispute in the late 19th century, with Swinburne taking a very high position, William Archer a relatively low one. These essays with many others have been reprinted by G. K. and S. K. Hunter, eds., *John Webster, a Critical Anthology*, 1969. Other studies directly and indirectly related to Webster are those of Rupert Brooke, *John Webster and the Elizabethan Drama*, 1917; Fredson Bowers, *Elizabethan Revenge Tragedy*, 1940; Robert Dent, *John Webster's Borrowings*, 1960; and Gunnar Boklund, *The Duchess of Malfi: Sources, Themes, Characters*, 1962. Frank L. Lucas edited the *Complete Works of John Webster*, 1927. Samuel Tannenbaum's *John Webster, a Concise Bibliography*, 1962, updates an earlier bibliography by the same author.

John Donne

For nearly fifty years the standard edition of Donne's poems was that in two volumes edited by Sir Herbert J. C. Grierson, 1912. In 1952 Dame Helen Gardner re-edited the *Divine Poems* and in 1965 a volume of *Elegies and the Songs and Sonnets*. In this same series, W. Milgate added the *Satires, Epigrams, and Verse Letters*, 1967. These new editions alter the text of some poems in some particulars on the basis of new manuscript evidence and offer to redate many of them. It is by no means clear that the text is always improved by the new readings or that the new dating will hold up; William Empson has been a particularly vigorous and outspoken critic. One can only say that many questions remain open. Under the editorship of G. R. Potter and Evelyn Simpson, a new edition of Donne's *Sermons*‡ has been issued in ten volumes, 1953–59. A *Complete Poetry and Selected Prose*, ed. John Hayward, 1929, is one of several handy, handsome popular editions.

For many years after its publication in 1899, Sir Edmund Gosse's *Life and Letters of John Donne* was the best biography available, though recognized as inadequate in many ways. R. C. Bald's *John Donne, a life*, 1970, though the author most regrettably did not live to give it the finishing touches, adds immensely to our detailed knowledge of Donne's career. Izaak Walton's contemporary "biography" is charming and artistic.

T. S. Eliot's several essays on Donne and the metaphysical poets generally have been most influential; some are to be found in his *Selected Essays*, 1932, others must be sought through his bibliography (by Donald Gallup). Collections of critical essays by several hands have been assembled by Helen Gardner‡ and Frank Kermode (both 1962). Hardly any of Donne's poems have not been the subject of several articles at least; but Cleanth Brooks's *The Well Wrought Urn*, 1947, contains in its discussion of "The Canonization" one of the most influential poetic explications of modern criticism.

Pierre Legouis' *Donne the Craftsman*, 1928, was an interesting early study; more recently, Clay Hunt, 1954, Arnold Stein, 1962, and Wilbur Sanders, 1971, have offered close scrutinies of the poetry. Many specialized studies in different aspects of Donne's thought and technique have appeared, for instance, Mary Ramsay's *Les doctrines mediévales chez Donne*, rev. ed., 1924, Marjorie Nicolson's *The Breaking of the Circle*,‡ 1960 (on Donne and science), and D. L. Guss's *John Donne, Petrarchist*, 1966. Two major studies which dedicate long sections to the poetry of Donne are Rosemond Tuve's influential *Elizabethan and Metaphysical Imagery*,‡ 1947, and Robert Ellrodt's three-volume *L'inspiration personnelle et l'esprit du temps chez les poètes métaphysiques anglais*, 1960. Leonard Unger, in *Donne's Poetry and Modern Criticism*, 1950, undertook to survey a troubled field, which has since become even more troubled and less surveyable. The standard bibliography of Donne, first published by Geoffrey Keynes in 1914, was revised in 1932 and again in 1958.

Ben Jonson

The standard edition of Jonson's works is that of C. H. Herford and Percy and Evelyn Simpson, published by the Clarendon Press in eleven volumes, 1925–52. This edition is meticulous in reproducing the old spellings, and typographically it is very elegant; but to find one's way around in it takes some practice. Of earlier editions, the handiest and most correct (though the text has been modernized) is that of W. Gifford, 9 vols., 1875. A handy edition of the verse is that of William B. Hunter, ed., *The Complete Poetry of Ben Jonson*, 1963; Stephen Orgel has edited the *Complete Masques*, 1969.

Because Jonson's work falls into several different categories, general introductory accounts of the whole man are few. G. Gregory Smith did a biography for the English Men of Letters series, 1919, and a more recent popular introduction, graceful, dexterous, and perceptive, is that of J. B. Bamborough, *Ben Jonson*, 1970. A. C. Swinburne wrote a characteristically acute and enthusiastic *Study of Ben Jonson*, 1889, and Maurice Castelain a weighty *Ben Jonson, l'homme et l'oeuvre*, 1907; both these books, though long out of date, retain the power to instruct and interest.

Special studies of the masques generally, and of Jonson's masques in particular, have been written by Enid Welsford, *The Court Masque*, 1927, Allardyce Nicoll, *Stuart Masques and the Renaissance Stage*, 1937, and Stephen Orgel, *The Jonsonian Masque*, 1965. Angus Fletcher's *The Transcendental Masque*, 1971, though mainly about Milton's "Comus," contains many brilliant speculative insights about masques in general, and an extended discussion of the issues involved in Jonson's quarrel with Inigo Jones. Wesley Trimpi has written a good account of *Ben Jonson's Poems*, 1962; and C. F. Wheeler has studied *Classical Mythology in the Plays, Masques, and Poems of Ben Jonson*, 1938. There are of course many studies of Jonson as a dramatist, the comedies and satires having received particular attention. Jonas Barish has edited *Ben Jonson*,‡ 1963, a collection of critical essays. In 1938 S. A. Tannenbaum published a *Concise Bibliography* of Jonson, and in 1947 added a Supplement to it.

Robert Herrick

The standard edition is the *Poetical Works*, edited by L. C. Martin, Oxford Standard Authors, 1956. F. W. Moorman produced a full-length study, *Robert Herrick*, 1910; and Marchette Chute, joining Herrick with George Herbert, has described their lives, *Two Gentle Men*, 1959. There is an interesting novel about Herrick by Rose Macaulay, *The Shadow Flies*, 1932.

George Herbert

The standard edition of *The Temple* is that edited by F. E. Hutchinson, 1941. Margaret Bottrall has written an introductory appreciation, *George Herbert*, 1954, and Rosemond Tuve's *A Reading of George Herbert*, 1952, is, like all her work, erudite and acute. As part of the same revival of interest in Herbert appeared J. H. Summers, *George Herbert, His Religion and His Art*, 1954. Special studies have been made of Herbert's technical ingenuities by A. Hayes in *Studies in Philology* XXXV (1938) and M. E. Rickey, *Utmost Art*, 1966. A recent study is Arnold Stein, *George Herbert's Lyrics*, 1968.

Richard Crashaw

The standard edition is that prepared by L. C. Martin, 1927, 2nd edition, 1957. Two interesting books are those of Ruth Wallerstein, *Richard Crashaw: A Study in Style and Poetic Development*,‡ 1935, and of Austin Warren, *Richard Crashaw: A Study in Baroque Sensibility*,‡ 1939, 1957. Influential ideas about Crashaw are found in William Empson, *Seven Types of Ambiguity*,‡ 1935, 1947, 1953; in Wylie Sypher, *Four Stages of Renaissance Style*, 1955; and in Mario Praz, *The Flaming Heart*, 1958. Also to be consulted are George W. Williams, *Image and Symbol in the Sacred Poetry of Richard Crashaw*, 1963, and Robert Peterson, *The Art of Ecstasy: Teresa, Bernini, and Crashaw*, 1970.

Henry Vaughan

The works of Henry Vaughan were edited by L. C. Martin, 1914, 1957; F. E. Hutchinson wrote the standard life, *Henry Vaughan, a Life and an Interpretation*, 1947. Elizabeth Holmes opened up the interesting topic of *Henry Vaughan and the Hermetic Philosophy*, 1932, and there have been a number of studies in this area since; see, for instance, E. C. Pettet, *Of Paradise and Light*, 1960, and R. A. Durr, *On the Mystical Poetry of Henry Vaughan*, 1962. Louis Martz's *The Paradise Within*,‡ 1964, gives much careful attention to Vaughan.

Andrew Marvell

The standard edition is the *Poems and Letters*, edited by H. M. Margoliouth, 1927, 1952. Pierre Legouis' *André Marvell, poète, puritain, patriote*, 1928, was translated and abridged in 1968. Another good introduction is that of M. C. Bradbrook and Lloyd Thomas, *Andrew Marvell*, 1940. Ruth Wallerstein's *Studies in 17th Century Poetic*,‡ 1950, are knotty and hard to read, but they illuminate the medieval backgrounds of Marvell's thought. H. E. Toliver, *Marvell's Ironic Vision*, 1965, and J. B. Leishman, *The Art of Marvell's Poetry*, 1966, were but the precursors of a flood of recent books on Marvell. John Wallace, in *Destiny His*

Choice, 1968, carefully studied Marvell's intricate political attitudes; Andrew Cullen, in *Spenser, Marvell, and Renaissance Pastoral*, and Donald Friedman, in *Marvell's Pastoral Art*, both 1970, concentrated on Marvell's pastoral poetry. Two general studies appearing in the same year dealt with his poetic art as a whole: Rosalie Colie, *My Echoing Song*, and Anne Berthoff, *The Resolved Soul*. In 1968 George de F. Lord edited a collection of critical essays on Marvell.

John Milton

Despite occasional textual eccentricities, the opulent Columbia Milton, a complete edition of poetry and prose, 18 vols., 1931–38, is widely accepted as standard; controversy continues over details, however, and anyone interested may consult Harris Fletcher's 4-volume facsimile edition of the *Poetical Works*, 1943–48, Miss Helen Darbishire's radical re-editing of the poetry, 1952–55, and the currently appearing Yale edition of the *Prose Works*, for a spectrum of editorial procedures and principles. Of the annotated editions of *Paradise Lost*, A. W. Verity's text, 1910, is probably still the least cumbersome and the most sensible. But it is long out of print, and for most purposes the student will want to use M. Y. Hughes, ed., *Complete Poems and Major Prose*, 1957, or John Carey and Alistair Fowler, eds., *Poems*, 1968. The notes of both editions are weighty, penetrating, and perhaps a bit depressing for the beginner; used with discretion, they may help but not overwhelm.

The old grand-scale biography of David Masson in eight volumes, 1881–1896, has been replaced by that of W. R. Parker in two volumes, 1968. Sir Walter Raleigh's *Milton*, 1900, is still relevant, though much disputed. Harris Fletcher's *Intellectual Development of John Milton* (two vols., 1956 and 1961) has so far covered 24 years of Milton's development (to 1632). While it takes no account at all of Milton the rebel (in fact, denies his existence), C. S. Lewis's *Preface to Paradise Lost*,‡ 1942, rev., 1960, is bright, persuasive, and enormously useful as a first approach. It may be corrected by A. J. A. Waldock's *Paradise Lost and Its Critics*,‡ 1947; B. Rajan's *Paradise Lost and the 17-Century Reader*, 1947; Joseph Summers, *The Muse's Method*, 1962; Anne Ferry, *Milton's Epic Voice*, 1963, and Helen Gardner, *A Reading of Paradise Lost*, 1965. E. M. W. Tillyard's handbook, *Milton*, 1930, 1949, is in some ways more acute in setting forth the outstanding problems than J. H. Hanford's *Milton Hand-book*, 4th edition, 1946. David Daiches, under the short, sufficient title of *Milton,*‡ 1961, offers a general introductory survey of the poet's accomplishment; and the beginning student is likely to profit as well by Marjorie H. Nicolson's *John Milton, a Reader's Guide to his Poetry,*‡ 1963. Collections of critical essays have been edited by A. E. Barker, 1965, and Louis L. Martz, 1966; the latter has also done an informative thematic study of *The Paradise Within,*‡ 1964, which includes discussions of Vaughan and Traherne as well as of Milton.

As might have been anticipated, the 300th anniversary of the publication of *Paradise Lost* (1967) brought forth many books on the epic, including Stanley Fish's provocative *Surprised by Sin*, Wayne Shumaker's *Unpremeditated Verse*, John Steadman's *Milton and the Renaissance Hero*, and collections of essays edited by A. P. Fiore. *The Upright Heart and Pure*, and R. D. Emma and J. T. Shawcross, *Language and Style in Milton*. Among more recent studies still one should mention W. G. Madsen, *From Shadowy Types to Truth*, 1968, B. Rajan, *The Lofty Rhyme*, 1970, and J. R. Knott, *Milton's Pastoral Vision*, 1971. In 1970 appeared the first volume of a *Variorum Commentary*, ed. M. Y. Hughes.

Specialized studies are beyond enumeration; only a scattering of the most useful can be named here. Robert Bridges has written the best account of *Milton's Prosody*, 2nd edition, 1921; Maurice Kelley has shown the intimate relation of Milton's theology, as expressed in the treatise *On Christian Doctrine* with his views in *Paradise Lost*, in *This Great Argument*, 1941; Malcolm M. Ross, *Poetry and Dogma*, 1954, suggests some of the theological complexities behind Milton's problems with incarnation; F. T. Prince has traced *The Italian Element in Milton's Verse*, 1954; Theodore Banks has studied *Milton's Imagery*, 1950; and Christopher Ricks has written persuasively on Milton's *Grand Style*, 1963. Characteristically incisive is Rosemond Tuve's *Images and Themes in Five Poems by Milton*, 1957. Among studies of "Comus," John Arthos, *On a Masque Presented at Ludlow Castle* (1954) contrasts with the more free-wheeling approach of Angus Fletcher, *The Transcendental Masque*, 1972. There are several collections of studies bearing on "Lycidas," including those of C. A. Patrides, 1961, and Scott Elledge, 1966. Douglas Bush, in a series

of lectures published as *Paradise Lost in Our Time*, 1945, defended Milton against his New Critical enemies, and sometimes against his friends. D. H. Stevens did the basic bibliography, a *Reference Guide to Milton from 1800 to the Present Day*, 1930; it was supplemented by Harris Fletcher in *Contributions to a Milton Bibliography*, 1931, and by Calvin Huckabay, *Milton Bibliography 1929–1968*, 1969. But the bibliographers seem to have been falling far behind the current terrifying spate of books and articles on Milton.

Seventeenth-Century Lyrics

Geoffrey Walton in *Metaphysical to Augustan*, 1955, and Jerome Mazzaro in *Transformations in the English Renaissance Lyric*, 1970, provide perspective on the transitions of lyric style. Lowry Nelson, Jr., in *Baroque Lyric Poetry*, 1961, focuses chiefly on Milton but puts him in a Continental context.

The always admirable Oxford English poets series includes the poems of Carew, ed. Rhodes Dunlap, 1949, and of Lovelace, ed. C. H. Wilkinson, 1930; there has been no edition of Waller since that of G. Thorn-Drury in 1905. Important work has been done recently on Carew's masque *Coelum Britannicum* by Stephen Orgel and Roy C. Strong in the course of their giant joint study of the work of Inigo Jones, 1973. Waller's contribution to English versification has been described by A. W. Allison, *Towards an Augustan Poetic*, 1962. Cleveland and Suckling are too slight to have attracted commentators in number, but the student interested in literary curiosities may be amused to track down the former's very bad poem on the death of Edward King (it appeared in the same volume as Milton's "Lycidas") and the latter's little treatise on natural religion. *Poems* of Cleveland, ed. Morris and Withington, 1967; *Works* of Suckling, ed. A. H. Thompson, 1910.

Cowley's *English Writings* were edited in two volumes by A. R. Waller, 1905–6, and his biography written by A. H. Nethercot, *The Muse's Hannibal*, 1931; Robert Hinman did a critical study, *Cowley's World of Order*, 1960. The work of Thomas Traherne, after its discovery and first publication by Bertram Dobell, 1903, was edited by H. M. Margoliouth for the Oxford English Poets in two volumes, 1958. There have been recent studies by A. J. Sherrington, *Mystical Symbolism in the Poetry of Thomas Traherne*, and A. L. Clements, *Mystical Poetry of Thomas Traherne*, both 1969.

Seventeenth-Century Prose

Several recent histories and collections have started to fill out our picture of the development of 17th-century prose. Used in combination with Stanley Fish's anthology of essays, *17th-Century Prose*, 1970, Robert Adolph's *The Rise of Modern Prose Style*, 1968, provides access to a still-much-controverted area. The basic work in the field was that done by Morris Croll in a series of articles on Ciceronian and anti-Ciceronian styles in the 16th and 17th centuries: these were collected posthumously in a volume titled *Style, Rhetoric, and Rhythm*, 1966. R. F. Jones, in *Ancients and Moderns*, 1946, 1961, urged the importance of the new science and the Royal Society, thus making the turning point to modern prose somewhat later than Croll had placed it. Most discussion since has taken place within that framework. George Williamson's *The Senecan Amble,*‡ 1951, deals with an influential variety of jog trot. Other specialized studies are those of W. F. Mitchell, *English Pulpit Oratory*, 1932, and W. G. Crane, *Wit and Rhetoric in the Renaissance*, 1937. D. J. Milburn, *The Age of Wit*, 1966, concerns himself with the century 1650–1750, but is useful for students of the earlier period as well. In a similar series of articles, R. F. Jones discussed the influence of the Royal Society on prose style in the later 17th century; these are collected in R. F. Jones, *The Seventeenth Century*, 1951. William Haller's fascinating account of Puritan propaganda techniques in *The Rise of Puritanism,*‡ 1938, is balanced by an account of late-century developments in G. R. Cragg, *From Puritanism to the Age of Reason,*‡ 1950. And the greatest book written in the 17th, or any other century, is discussed by David Daiches, *The King James Version of the English Bible*, 1941, by C. C. Butterworth, *The Literary Lineage of the King James Bible*, 1941, and by a host of others.

Francis Bacon

The big edition of Bacon is *The Works*, 15 vols., edited by Spedding, Ellis, and Heath, 1860–64. Among the biographical introductions may be recommended that done for the English Men of Letters series by R. W. Church, 1884, and two more recent ones, *Francis Bacon: A Biography*, by Mary Sturt, 1932, and *Bacon*, by Charles Williams, 1933. Christopher Hill's *Intellectual Origins of the English Revolution*, 1965, demonstrates most tellingly the existence of a popular scientific tradition, in the vernacular, which lent body and popular support to Bacon's magisterial scientific dicta. An old-fashioned but still interesting book is *Francis Bacon of Verulaam* by Kuno Fischer, translated from the German and published in 1857. Two specialized studies of particular interest are F. H. Anderson's *The Philosophy of Francis Bacon*, 1948, and Brian Vickers, *Francis Bacon and Renaissance Prose*, 1968.

Especially in the late 19th century, an immense amount of nonsense was written setting forth alleged cryptographic evidence for Bacon's authorship of Shakespeare's plays, Spenser's poetry, and various other literary works, real or imaginary. William F. and Elizabeth S. Friedman, in *The Shakespearean Ciphers Examined*, 1957, subject all these theories to scrupulous technical examination and dismiss them all as worthless. It would be pleasant if this closed the matter, but that is doubtless too much to hope.

Robert Burton

The handiest edition of *The Anatomy* for a modern reader is that of Floyd Dell and P. Jordan-Smith, 1927, in which the Latin quotations and tags are translated. Bergen Evans has written, with professional assistance, an interesting study in *The Psychiatry of Robert Burton*, 1944, and W. R. Mueller an analysis of Burton's background called *The Anatomy of Robert Burton's England*, 1952.

Sir Thomas Browne

The standard complete edition of Browne is *The Works of Sir Thomas Browne*, edited in 6 volumes by Geoffrey L. Keynes, 1928–31. Recent studies are those of Joan Bennett, *Sir Thomas Browne*, 1962, and Leonard Nathanson, *The Strategy of Truth*, 1967. There is a classic account of the backgrounds of skepticism and fideism in Louis Bredvold, *The Intellectual Milieu of John Dryden,*‡ 1934; this makes frequent reference to Browne.

Joseph Hall;
Sir Thomas Overbury;
John Earle

A general account of the vogue of the character in England may be found in Benjamin Boyce, *The Theophrastan Character in England to 1642*, 1947. Gwendolyn Murphy has collected many of the best essays in the genre into *A Cabinet of Characters*, 1925, and W. J. Payor has edited

The Overburian Characters, Percy Reprints XIII, 1936. D. Nichol Smith's *Characters from the Histories & Memoirs of the 17th Century*, 1918, contains, not characters in the strict Theophrastan sense, but verbal portraits of actual 17th-century figures—which in many ways are more interesting. Bibliographies of the genre have been done by Miss Murphy, 1925, and by Chester N. Greenough with the aid of J. Milton French, 1947.

Edward Hyde, Earl of Clarendon

As befits the man who founded the Clarendon Press, Clarendon has always been well printed; the 1888 edition of the *History*, edited by W. Dunn Macray, includes fresh readings and previously suppressed passages. The *Autobiography* was first printed in 1759; and a *Life* in two volumes by Sir Henry Craik supplemented it, 1911. Brian Wormald's *Clarendon: Politics, History, and Religion*, 1951, is the most recent study.

Izaak Walton

A major study of Walton the biographer is David Novarr's *The Making of Walton's Lives*, 1958. Editions of *The Complete Angler* are too numerous to describe; for many years, the book has been one of the classics for the fine-binding trade. A life of Walton by Nicols for the 1836 edition of the *Angler* is said to be particularly meritorious; but no full-length independent biography has yet been published. Under the elegant title of *Every Man a Phoenix*, 1958, Margaret Bottrall has studied 17th-century autobiography.

John Aubrey

Aubrey has been more appreciated than discussed; this is a way of saying that his own self-portrait is so vivid as to make an outsider's effort at biography appear gratuitous. Still, Anthony Powell, in *John Aubrey and His Friends*, 1963, has made the effort. Andrew Clark's standard edition of the *Brief Lives* has gone through many editions since 1898. Anyone who is taken with Aubrey's crotchety, vagrant, credulous spirit will want to investigate his *Miscellanies upon Various Subjects*, including marvels, apparitions, glances of love and envy, omens, magic, and transportation in the air.

Samuel Pepys

J. R. Tanner, in a series of lectures reprinted as *Samuel Pepys and the Royal Navy*, 1920, was one of the first to call attention to the serious work of Pepys' life. *Samuel Pepys* by Arthur Bryant appeared in three volumes: *The Man in the Making*, *The Years of Peril*, and *The Saviour of the Navy*, 1933, 1935, and 1938.

King James I

The *Political Works* of James the First were edited by C. H. McIlwaine, 1918; a recent biography is that by D. H. Willson, *James VI and I*,‡ 1956.

Thomas Hobbes

The standard edition of Hobbes is that edited by Sir William Molesworth: *The English Works* in 11 volumes, the *Opera Philosophica* in five, 1839–45. G. C. Robertson in *Hobbes*, 1886, provides a good general introduction, and for the student of literature there is a useful study of the philosopher's literary theory, by C. D. Thorpe, *The Aesthetic Theory of Thomas Hobbes*, 1940. The most recent edition of *Leviathan* has a very perceptive introduction by Michael Oakeshott, 1946. S. I. Mintz, *The Hunting of Leviathan*, 1958, describes the interesting 17th-century reactions to Hobbes' thought.

John Lilburne

The activities of John Lilburne may be traced through William Haller's two fine volumes, *Tracts on Liberty in the Puritan Revolution*, 1934, and his spacious *Rise of Puritanism*,‡ 1938. More recently there has been a biography of M. A. Gibb, *John Lilburne the Leveller*, 1947.

Gerrard Winstanley

The scarce pamphlets and relevant documents left by Winstanley were assembled by George Sabine in a collection of his *Works*, 1941. D. W. Petegorsky studied the Diggers in *Left Wing Democracy in the English Civil War*, 1940.

John Locke

A good course in the history of English philosophy is the best preparation for coming to terms with Locke. Short of that, M. W. Cranston has written an account of the man in *John Locke a Biography*; and of the hundreds of specialized studies of his thought one might begin with a veteran, J. W. Gough, *John Locke's Political Philosophy*, 1900, and a relative newcomer, J. W. Yolton, *John Locke and the Way of Ideas*, 1956.

THE RESTORATION AND THE EIGHTEENTH CENTURY

The relevant chapters of George M. Trevelyan's *History of England*,‡ 1926, offer a readable narrative of English history during the 18th century; J. H. Plumb, *England in the Eighteenth Century*,‡ 1950, describes the structure of society. A fuller account is provided by the *Oxford History of England*, in three volumes: Sir George Clark, *The Later Stuarts, 1660–1714*, 1956; Basil Williams and C. H. Stuart, *The Whig Supremacy, 1714–60*, 1962; J. Steven Watson, *The Reign of George III, 1760–1815*, 1960. Studies in the social life of the period abound—among them A. S. Turberville's *English Men and Manners in the Eighteenth Century*,‡ 1926, and as editor, *Johnson's England: An Account of the Life and Manners of His Age*, 2 vols., 1933; M. Dorothy George's *London Life in the Eighteenth Century*,‡ 1925, largely a study of urban poverty; Dorothy Marshall's *English People in the Eighteenth Century*, 1956; and George Rudé's *Hanoverian London, 1714–1808*, 1971. Two useful guides for the literary student are A. R. Humphreys' *The Augustan World: Society, Thought, and Letters in Eighteenth-Century England*,‡ 1954, and Donald Greene's *The Age of Exuberance: Backgrounds to Eighteenth-Century English Literature*,‡ 1970.

Helpful books dealing with the intellectual background of the period are Arthur O. Lovejoy's *The Great Chain of Being*,‡ 1942, and *Essays in the History of Ideas*,‡ 1948; Sir Leslie Stephen's *History of English Thought in the Eighteenth Century*,‡ 2 vols., 1876; Basil Willey's *The Eighteenth-Century Background*,‡ 1940, a study of the idea of nature; and J. W. Johnson's *The Formation of Neo-Classical Thought*, 1967. Paul Hazard's *The European Mind, 1680–1715*,‡ 1953, and *European Thought in the Eighteenth Century*,‡ 1954, are translations from the French by J. L. May, rapid, readable surveys of intellectual movements on the Continent as well as in England. Peter Gay's *The Enlightenment: An Interpretation*,‡ 2 vols., 1969, forcefully defends the philosophers of the "age of reason." Marjorie H. Nicolson's *Newton Demands the Muse: Newton's "Opticks" and the Eighteenth-Century Poets*,‡ 1946, and her many articles, some of which have been republished in *Science and the Imagination*, 1956, are valuable studies of the relation between science and literature in the period; which may be supplemented

by William P. Jones' *The Rhetoric of Science*, 1966. Martin Price's *To the Palace of Wisdom: Studies in Order and Energy from Dryden to Blake*,‡ 1964, Paul Fussell's *The Rhetorical World of Augustan Humanism*, 1965, and W. J. Bate's *The Burden of the Past and the English Poet*,‡ 1970, are all thoughtful and stimulating studies that relate ideas to literary art.

Two volumes of the *Oxford History of English Literature* deal with our period in some detail: James Sutherland's *English Literature of the Late Seventeenth Century*, 1969, and Bonamy Dobrée's *English Literature in the Early Eighteenth Century, 1700–1740*, 1959. Briefer surveys of the literature of the age include George Sherburn's "The Restoration and Eighteenth Century" (the standard work), in A. C. Baugh, ed., *A Literary History of England*,‡ rev. 1967; and Roger Lonsdale, ed., *Dryden to Johnson*,‡ 1971, Vol. 4 of the Sphere History of Literature. Oliver Elton's *A Survey of English Literature 1730–1800*, 2 vols., 1928, is much more detailed.

Among books that deal with a single literary mode, James Sutherland's *A Preface to Eighteenth-Century Poetry*,‡ 1948, skillfully introduces a body of poetry that sometimes seems alien to modern readers; it may be supplemented by Ian Jack's *Augustan Satire: Intention and Idiom in English Poetry 1660–1750*,‡ 1952; Rachel Trickett's *The Honest Muse: A Study in Augustan Verse*, 1967; Patricia Spacks' *The Poetry of Vision*, 1967; and P. W. K. Stone's *Art of Poetry, 1750–1820*, 1967. Allardyce Nicoll's *A History of Restoration Drama, 1660–1700*, *A History of Early Eighteenth-Century Drama, 1700–1750*, and *A History of Late Eighteenth-Century Drama, 1750–1800*, rev. 1952, are standard sources of information; supplemented by Bonamy Dobrée's *Restoration Comedy*, 1924, and *Restoration Tragedy*, 1929, as well as by Arthur Sherbo's *English Sentimental Drama*, 1957. Two collections, Earl Miner, ed., *Restoration Dramatists*,‡ 1966, and John Loftis, ed., *Restoration Drama, Modern Essays in Criticism*,‡ 1966, provide studies by various writers; Loftis has also analyzed *Comedy and Society from Congreve to Fielding*, 1959. Walter Graham has surveyed *English Literary Periodicals*, 1930; and Donald A. Stauffer, *English Biography before 1700*, 1930, and *The Art of Biography in Eighteenth-Century England*, 2 vols., 1941. John N.

Morris, *Versions of the Self: Studies in English Autobiography from John Bunyan to John Stuart Mill*, 1966, and Howard Anderson, Philip B. Daghlian, and Irvin Ehrenpreis, eds., *The Familiar Letter in the Eighteenth Century*, 1966, provide introductions to two influential but neglected genres. The novel is treated in detail in E. A. Baker's *The History of the English Novel*, Vol. III (1930), Vol. IV (1930), Vol. V (1934). This work should be supplemented by two excellent modern studies, Ian Watt's *The Rise of the Novel: Studies in Defoe, Richardson and Fielding*,‡ 1957, and Alan D. McKillop's *The Early Masters of English Fiction*, 1956, which deals with Defoe, Richardson, Fielding, Smollett, and Sterne. Sheridan Baker, "The Idea of Romance in the Eighteenth-Century Novel," *Papers of the Michigan Academy of Science, Arts, and Letters*, XLIX, discusses an important aspect of the background of the novel, as does Ronald Paulson, *Satire and the Novel in Eighteenth Century England*, 1967.

Studies of critical movements in this period are numerous and tend to be rather specialized. The two standard collections of neoclassical criticisms are Joel E. Spingarn's *Critical Essays of the Seventeenth Century*, Vols. II and III, 1908 (the preface is not yet outdated), and Scott Elledge's *Eighteenth-Century Critical Essays*, 2 vols., 1961. The best statement of the critical canons of the age is Ronald S. Crane's "Neo-Classical Criticism," in J. T. Shipley, ed., *A Dictionary of World Literature*,‡ 1943. The student may also consult Francis Gallaway's *Reason, Rule, and Revolt in English Classicism*,‡ 1940; René Wellek, *A History of Modern Criticism 1750–1950*, 1955, Vol. I, and William K. Wimsatt, Jr., and Cleanth Brooks, *Literary Criticism: A Short History*,‡ 1957. M. H. Abrams, *The Mirror and the Lamp*,‡ 1953, though primarily concerned with romantic theory, has much to say that is valuable about the 18th century.

Studies that discuss the treatment of external nature in the literature of the period (a theme as important for the 18th as it was for the 19th century) include Samuel Holt Monk's *The Sublime: A Study of Critical Theories in Eighteenth-Century England*,‡ 1935, John Arthos' *The Language of Natural Description in Eighteenth-Century Poetry*, 1949, and Edward Malins, *English Landscaping and Literature, 1660–1840*, 1966. B. Sprague Allen's *Tides of English Taste 1619–1800*, 2 vols., 1937, on architecture, gardening, and decoration, and Sir Kenneth Clark's *The Gothic Revival*, 2nd edition,‡ 1950, on architecture, are not irrelevant to literature. Jean Hagstrum has studied *The Sister Arts*, 1958, and Lawrence Lipking, *The Ordering of the Arts in Eighteenth-Century England*, 1970. In addition, many of the best essays on 18th-century topics have appeared in collections dedicated to a single scholar: for instance, for Frederick A. Pottle, *From Sensibility to Romanticism*, eds. F. W. Hilles and Harold Bloom, 1965; and for Samuel H. Monk, *Studies in Criticism and Aesthetics, 1660–1800*, eds. Howard Anderson and John S. Shea, 1967. James L. Clifford has collected a number of essays of various writers on the period in *Eighteenth-Century English Literature: Modern Essays in Criticism*,‡ 1959. *Studies in English Literature* devotes its summer issue to the Restoration and Eighteenth Century and includes an article reviewing important work on the period published in the preceding year.

Finally, for further and elaborate bibliographies of 18th-century studies, the student may be referred to the bibliography of English literature, 1600–1800, that has appeared annually since 1926 in *Philological Quarterly*.

John Dryden

Charles E. Ward's *Life of John Dryden*, 1961, the standard biography, may be supplemented by the excellent sketch in George R. Noyes' edition of the *Poetical Works*, 2nd edition, 1950. Until recently, the only edition of the *Works* has been the unsatisfactory one in 18 volumes by Sir Walter Scott and George Saintsbury, 1882–93. A new edition of the *Works*, begun under the general editorship of the late Edward N. Hooker and carried on under H. T. Swedenberg, has been appearing at intervals since 1956. The poems have been edited by James Kinsley, 4 vols., 1958; W. P. Ker, 1900, 1926, and George Watson, 2 vols., 1962, have edited the *Essays*.

Mark Van Doren's *John Dryden: A Study of His Poetry*,‡ 1920, remains valuable for its fresh critical responses, as do T. S. Eliot's brief studies, *Homage to John Dryden*, 1924, and *John Dryden the Poet, the Dramatist, the Critic*, 1932. Important modern criticism includes Arthur Hoffman's *John Dryden's Imagery*, 1962, Alan Roper's *Dryden's Poetic Kingdom*s, 1965, and Earl Miner's *Dryden's Poetry*, 1967. Louis Bredvold's *The Intellectual Milieu of John Dryden*, 1934, an influential study of Dryden's philosophical, political, and religious ideas, has been superseded, especially with regard to religion, by Philip Harth's fine *Contexts of Dryden's Thought*, 1968. Robert Hume analyzes *Dryden's Criticism*, 1970, and John C. Aden, in *The Critical Opinions of John Dryden, A Dictionary*, 1963, brings together Dryden's critical ideas under convenient headings.

John Bunyan

Bunyan was a prolific writer: Part II of *The Pilgrim's Progress*, dealing with the journey of Christian's wife and children, appeared in 1684; *The Life and Death of Mr. Badman* in 1680; *The Holy War* in 1682. But these major works form only a small part of all his writings.

The standard life is John Brown's *John Bunyan: His Life, Times, and Work*, 1885, revised by Frank M. Harrison, 1928. The critical edition of *The Pilgrim's Progress* is by J. B. Wharey, 1928, revised by Roger Sharrock,‡ 1960; Sharrock has also edited *Grace Abounding to the Chief of Sinners*, 1962. Among interesting modern studies are George B. Harrison, *John Bunyan: A Study in Personality*, 1928; William Y. Tindall, *John Bunyan, Mechanick, Preacher*, 1934; Henri A. Talon, *John Bunyan, The Man and His Work*, 1951, a translation from the French; and U. Milo Kaufmann, *The Pilgrim's Progress and Traditions in Puritan Meditation*, 1966.

William Congreve

Congreve's *Complete Works* have been edited by Montague Summers, 4 vols., 1923; and the *Plays* by Herbert Davis in 1967. Bonamy Dobrée edited the *Comedies*, 1925, and *The Mourning Bride*, etc., 1928. The best biography is John C. Hodges' *William Congreve the Man*, 1941. Kathleen Lynch's *A Congreve Gallery*, 1951, contains studies of some members of Congreve's circle, including one of Henrietta, Duchess of Marlborough. Criticism of Congreve is abundant in books on Restoration comedy. See, for example, Thomas H. Fujimura's *The Restoration Comedy of Wit*, 1952, Dale Underwood's *Etherege and the Seventeenth-Century Comedy*, 1957, Norman N. Holland's *The First Modern Comedies*,‡ 1959, and Ian Donaldson's *The World Upside-Down: Comedy from Jonson to Fielding*, 1970. An interesting special study is Paul and Miriam Mueschke's *A New View of Congreve's Way of the World*, 1958.

Daniel Defoe

The best biography of Defoe is James Sutherland's *Defoe*, 1937, rev., 1950; Sutherland has also written a fine critical study, *Daniel Defoe*, 1971. The *Letters* were edited by George H. Healey, 1955. Ian Watt's *The Rise of the Novel*,‡ 1957, contains an interesting study of Defoe's novels in relation to social and economic history. Recent full-length studies include John R. Moore's *Daniel Defoe: Citizen of the Modern World*, 1958; Maximilian E. Novak, *Economics and the Fiction of Daniel Defoe*, 1962, and *Defoe and the Nature of Man*, 1963; G. A. Starr, *Defoe and Spiritual Autobiography*, 1965, and *Defoe and Casuistry*, 1971. J. R. Moore has also provided a useful *Checklist of the Writings of Daniel Defoe*, 1960.

Samuel Butler

Materials for a full-length biography of Butler do not exist. Of editions of *Hudibras*, Zacharay Grey's, 2 vols., 1744, is still useful for its illustrative notes. The best modern edition is John Wilders', 1967. *Characters*, ed. Charles W. Daves, 1970, is invaluable for studying Butler's opinions; René Lamar has edited *Satires and Miscellaneous Poetry and Prose*, 1928. E. A. Richards' *Hudibras in the Burlesque Tradition*, 1937, is useful. An excellent essay on Butler is included in Ian Jack's *Augustan Satire 1660–1750*,‡ 1952.

John Wilmot, Earl of Rochester

David M. Vieth's fine edition of Rochester's *Complete Poems*, 1968, supersedes the useful earlier edition by Vivian de Sola Pinto, 1964. Pinto's biography, *Enthusiast in Wit*, 1962, may be supplemented by John Harold Wilson's edition of *The Rochester-Savile Letters, 1671–1680*, 1941.

Anne Finch, Countess of Winchilsea

Myra Reynolds added a long biographical introduction to her standard edition of the *Poems*, 1903. Reuben Brower's "Lady Winchilsea and the Poetic Tradition of the Seventeenth Century," *Studies in Philology*, XLII (1945), 61–80, and a chapter of John Buxton's *A Tradition of Poetry*, 1967, correct the notion that she was a "romantic."

Matthew Prior

The complete critical edition of Prior is *Literary Works*, edited by H. B. Wright and M. K. Spears, 2 vols., 1959. The older and less complete edition in 2 volumes by A. R. Waller, 1905, 1907, is useful. The best biography is Charles K. Eves' *Matthew Prior, Poet and Diplomatist*, 1939.

John Gay

The standard life is W. H. Irving's *John Gay: Favorite of the Wits*, 1940. G. C. Farber has edited the *Poetical Works*, 1926, and C. F. Burgess the *Letters*, 1966. Critical studies include Sven Armens, *John Gay, Social Critic*, 1954, Patricia Spacks' *John Gay*, 1965, and Adina Forsgren's *Gay: Poet "of a Lower Order,"* 2 vols., 1964, 1971.

Jonathan Swift

Biographers have found it difficult to write of Swift without advancing some special and private thesis about his character and personal life. Louis A. Landa's *Swift and the Church of Ireland*, 1954, is reliable, and Irvin Ehrenpreis's *The Personality of Jonathan Swift*, 1958, is full of good things as well as of a certain amount of ingenious and not wholly convincing theorizing. Ehrenpreis has so far published two excellent volumes of a three-volume biography: *Mr. Swift and His Contemporaries*, 1962, and *Dr. Swift*, 1967.

The standard edition of the poems is by Sir Harold Williams, 3 vols., 1937, rev., 1958. Joseph Horrell's edition of the *Collected Poems*, 2 vols., The Muses' Library, 1958, is less expensive than Williams' and almost, but not entirely, relies on the canon and text established by Williams in his edition. Herbert Davis's edition of the prose works in 14 volumes, published over a period of years, is now complete, Swift's *Correspondence* has been edited by Sir Harold Williams, 5 vols., 1963–65. Distinguished editions of other works are Herbert Davis's *The Drapier's Letters*, 1935; Harold Williams' *Journal to Stella*, 1948; A. C. Guthkelch and D. Nichol Smith, *A Tale of a Tub*, 2nd edition, 1958; and Frank H. Ellis, *A Discourse of the Contests and Dissentions Between the Nobles and the Commons in Athens and Rome*, 1967. Useful bibliographies have been provided by Arthur H. Scouten in his edition of H. Teerink's *A Bibliography of the Writings of Jonathan Swift*, 1963, Louis A. Landa and James E. Tobin, *Jonathan Swift: A List of Critical Studies Published from 1895 to 1945*, 1945, and James J. Stathis, *A Bibliography of Swift Studies, 1945–65*, 1967.

Critical studies long and short abound. The student should find especially helpful Ricardo Quintana's *The Mind and Art of Jonathan Swift*, 1936, and *Swift: an Introduction*,‡ 1955; and Kathleen Williams' *Jonathan Swift and the Age of Compromise*, 1958. Arthur E. Case's *Four Essays on Gulliver's Travels*, 1945, and Maurice Johnson's *The Sin of Wit: Jonathan Swift as a Poet*, 1950, are useful special studies. Most of Herbert Davis's excellent critical pieces on Swift have been brought together in *Jonathan Swift, Essays on his Satire and Other Studies*,‡ 1964; in recent years there have appeared a number of paperbound collections of important essays, particularly those on *Gulliver's Travels*. Milton Voight has summarized the movements in Swift studies in *Swift and the Twentieth Century*, 1964.

Joseph Addison and Sir Richard Steele

There is no scholarly edition of the collected works; the Bohn edition of Addison, 6 vols., 1854–56, rev. and enl., 1869–73, is available in libraries. *Letters* were edited by Walter Graham, 1941. *The Spectator* in five volumes was published by Donald F. Bond, 1965. This is the definitive edition. The authoritative biography of Addison is by Peter Smithers, 1968. Edward and Lillian Bloom survey Addison's ideas of society in *Joseph Addison's Sociable Animal*, 1971. Of lives of Steele, George A. Aitken's, 2 vols., 1889, Willard Connely's, 1934, and Calhoun Winton's *Captain Steele: The Early Career of Richard Steele*, 1964, and *Sir Richard Steele, M.P.: The Later Career*, 1970, are the best. Rae Blanchard has edited Steele's *Correspondence*, 1941; *Tracts and Pamphlets*, 1944; *Occasional Verse*, 1952; and also other lesser works. Walter Graham's *English Literary Periodicals*, 1930, may be consulted on both the *Tatler* and the *Spectator*. *The Tatler*, ed. G. A. Aitken, 4 vols., 1898–1899, is the best modern edition of that work. Richmond P. Bond has analyzed *The Tatler: The Making of a Literary Journal*, 1971.

Alexander Pope

There is no reliable complete edition of all of Pope's works. Defective though it is in many respects, the Victorian edition in 10 volumes by Elwin and Courthope, 1871–89, must still be consulted, though with caution. The excellent Twickenham Edition of the poems, a co-operative undertaking by several scholars (the general editor is John Butt), is now complete in 11 volumes, with valuable introductory and critical materials and notes. A convenient selection in a single volume, with selected notes,‡ omits the translations of Homer. Only one volume of Norman Ault's edition of *The Prose Works*, 1936, was published before the editor's death.

No sound biography of Pope exists. George Sherburn's *Early Career* of *Alexander Pope*, 1934, is authoritative, but unfortunately it does not study the poet's life beyond about 1726. It is an essential book, for it corrects many misinterpretations and distortions of Pope's character and motives that mar earlier biographies. Maynard Mack's elegant study, *The Garden and the City: Retirement and Politics in the Later Poetry of Pope, 1731–1743*, 1969, is the first installment of a biography that should set new standards. Ault's *New Light on Pope*, 1949, makes important miscellaneous contributions to Pope's biography. Sherburn's edition of the *Correspondence*, 1956, 5 vols., is standard, though it should be supplemented by his publication of some further letters in the *Review of English studies*, new ser., IX (1958), 388–406. R. H. Griffith, *Alexander Pope: A Bibliography*, 1962, is a 2-volume listing of Pope's writings.

The best detailed critical study of the poems is Geoffrey Tillotson's *On the Poetry of Pope*, 2nd edition, 1950; and the same author's *Pope and Human Nature*, 1958, throws light on a difficult subject. Austen Warren's *Alexander Pope as Critic and Humanist*, 1929, though somewhat dated, is still useful. Much information is gathered up in Robert W. Rogers' *The Major Satires of Alexander Pope*, 1955. Reuben A. Brower's *Alexander Pope: The Poetry of Allusion*, 1959, is an enlightening study of Pope's lifelong habit of felicitous quotation from and adaptation of phrases, images, and ideas from earlier European poets, especially, though not exclusively, from the poets of classical antiquity. Aubrey Williams incisively analyzes *Pope's Dunciad*, 1955, and may be supplemented by John F. Sitter's *The Poetry of Pope's Dunciad*, 1971. Maynard Mack, ed., *Essential Articles for the Study of Alexander Pope*, 1964, conveniently brings together a number of short studies.

Samuel Johnson

Others among Johnson's friends besides Boswell wrote of him: notably, Mrs. Hester Lynch Thrale Piozzi, whose *Anecdotes* appeared in 1786; Sir John Hawkins, whose *Life* was published in 1787 and reissued in 1961, edited and abridged by Bertram H. Davis; and Fanny Burney (Mme D'Arblay), from whose diary the Johnsonian passages are found most conveniently in C. B. Tinker's *Dr. Johnson and Fanny Burney*, 1911. James L. Clifford's *Young Sam Johnson*,‡ 1955, is a thorough study of Johnson's early life and a necessary supplement to Boswell's rather

sketchy account of Johnson's life before their meeting in 1763. The poems were admirably edited by David Nichol Smith and E. L. McAdam, 1941. The best collected edition of Johnson's *Works* appeared as long ago as 1825. A new Yale edition, which has been coming out irregularly since 1958, has now reached 9 vols. G. B. Hill's editions of *Johnsonian Miscellanies*, 2 vols., 1897, and *The Lives of the Poets*, 3 vols., 1905, both with superb notes, have recently been reprinted. R. W. Chapman's edition of the letters, 3 vols., 1952, is authoritative. There is a valuable survey and bibliography of critical studies, rev. ed. 1970, by J. L. Clifford and D. J. Greene.

Some interesting modern studies of Johnson are J. W. Krutch's *Samuel Johnson*,‡ 1944; B. H. Bronson's "Johnson Agonistes," 1944 (reissued in *Johnson Agonistes and Other Essays*, 1965); W. J. Bate's *The Achievement of Samuel Johnson*, 1955; W. K. Wimsatt, Jr., *The Prose Style of Samuel Johnson*,‡ 1941; Donald J. Greene's *The Politics of Samuel Johnson*, 1960; Arieh Sachs' *Passionate Intelligence: Imagination and Reason in the Work of Samuel Johnson*, 1967; and Paul Fussell's *Samuel Johnson and the Life of Writing*, 1971. *Johnson, Boswell, and Their Circle*, 1965, and Donald J. Greene, ed., *Samuel Johnson, A Collection of Critical Essays*,‡ 1965, bring together short studies by various hands. Aspects of Johnson's criticism are treated in Joseph E. Brown's *The Critical Opinions of Samuel Johnson*, 1926; and Jean Hagstrum's *Samuel Johnson's Literary Criticism*, 1952. E. L. McAdam's *Johnson and Boswell: A Survey of their Writings*,‡ 1969, and D. J. Greene's *Samuel Johnson*, 1970, are brief, useful guides.

James Boswell

A vast amount has been written about Boswell, much now outmoded by the discovery within the last half century of Boswell's private papers. Most of this outdated material is now simply ill informed, prejudiced, and worthless. Frederick A. Pottle's *James Boswell, The Earlier Years, 1740–1769*, 1966, makes good use of the private papers. C. B. Tinker's lively and percipient *Young Boswell*, 1922, is useful. Pottle's *The Literary Career of James Boswell*, 1929, was the first attempt to establish the canon of Boswell's writings. The *Letters*, edited by C. B. Tinker, 2 vols., 1924, will have to be supplemented by the recently recovered correspondence, of which two volumes have been published: Ralph S. Walker, ed. *The Correspondence of James Boswell and John Johnston of Grange*, 1966; *Correspondence and Other Papers of James Boswell Relating to the Making of the Life of Johnson*, 1969. The *Private Papers of James Boswell from Malahide Castle*, edited by Geoffrey Scott and F. A. Pottle, 18 vols., 1928–34, made available the first of Boswell's papers to be discovered. Volumes of the trade edition of the *Journals*, under the general editorship of F. A. Pottle, appear regularly. The *Journal of a Tour to the Hebrides* has been edited, as first published, by R. W. Chapman, 1924; and, as originally written, by Frederick A. Pottle, 1936. The introductory material and illustrative notes in these volumes and the Malahide papers are of great value.

A wise and sympathetic brief study of Boswell is B. H. Bronson's "Boswell's Boswell," in *Johnson and Boswell,‡ 1944. Johnson, Boswell, and Their Circle: Essays Presented to L. F. Powell*, 1965, is a valuable collection. The best edition of the *Life* is L. F. Powell's revised and enlarged edition of the earlier edition by G. B. Hill, 6 vols., 1934–50. A helpful guide through the *Life* is J. L. Smith-Dampier's *Who's Who in Boswell?*, 1935. Mention should perhaps be made of Thomas Babington Macaulay's brilliantly paradoxical, highly prejudiced account of Boswell in his review in 1831 of Croker's edition of the *Life of Johnson*. It blackened Boswell's reputation for nearly a century and its influence is still alive. It is easily available in any of the numerous printings of Macaulay's *Critical and Historical Essays*.

Edmund Burke

There is no definitive edition of Burke; E. J. Payne's *Select Works*, 3 vols., 1874–78, has useful notes. *The Sublime and Beautiful* is edited by J. T. Boulton, 1958; the *Correspondence* has now reached 9 vols., edited by Thomas Copeland and others, 1958–. For biography, see the life of Philip Magnus, 1939, and the essays by T. W. Copeland, *Our Eminent Friend Edmund Burke*, 1949. Most studies of Burke, like Charles Parkins' *The Moral Basis of Burke's Political Thought*, 1956, concentrate on his politics; for the literary student, D. C. Bryant's *Edmund Burke and His Literary Friends*, 1939, and Gerald W. Chapman's *Edmund Burke: The Practical Imagination*, 1967, are especially useful.

James Thomson

The most recent biographical study of Thomson is Douglas Grant's *James Thomson, Poet of "The Seasons,"* 1951. A. D. McKillop has edited *James Thomson (1700–1748): Letters and Documents*, 1958, which contains much about Thomson's friends and the interests of his literary circle, and *James Thomson: The Castle of Indolence and Other Poems*, 1961. The most valuable study of the content of *The Seasons* is McKillop's *The Background of Thomson's Seasons*, 1942. Ralph Cohen, *The Art of Discrimination: Thomson's The Seasons and the Language of Criticism*, 1964, is a valuable work which uses responses to the poem to illustrate the development of critical theory; and Cohen has added a critical study, *The Unfolding of the Seasons*, 1970. Patricia Meyer Spacks, *The Poetry of Vision: Five Eighteenth-Century Poets*, 1966, contains a chapter on Thomson, as well as others on Collins, Gray, Smart, and Cowper.

Thomas Gray

The poems of Gray, Collins, and Goldsmith have been edited, with authoritative notes, by Roger Lonsdale, 1969. The standard edition of Gray's *Works* is that of Edmund Gosse, 4 vols., rev., 1902–6; of the *Correspondence*, that of Paget Toynbee and Leonard Whibley, 3 vols., 1935; of the poems that of H. W. Starr and J. R. Hendrickson, 1966. R. W. Ketton-Cremer's *Thomas Gray*, 1955, is the most recent and the best biography. The best extended critical study is unfortunately in French: Roger Martin's *Essai sur Gray*, 1934. A more specialized study is William P. Jones's *Thomas Gray, Scholar*, 1937. Frederick W. Hilles and Harold Bloom, eds., *From Sensibility to Romanticism*, 1965, contains studies of the *Elegy* by F. Brady, B. H. Bronson, and I. Jack; as well as an important essay on Collins by A. S. P. Woodhouse.

William Collins

Lonsdale's edition (see Gray above) incorporates an interesting recent discovery, a group of Collins's hitherto unpublished verse, edited by J. S. Cunningham in *Drafts & Fragments of Verse*, 1956. E. G. Ainsworth's *Poor Collins*, 1937, is the most detailed biographical and critical study of the poet. A valuable general work, important for understanding Collins and other 18th-century poets, is Chester F. Chapin's *Personification in Eighteenth-Century English Poetry*, 1955.

Christopher Smart

Norman Callan edited Smart's *Collected Poems*, 2 vols., 1949; and there is a good selection by R. E. Brittain, 1950. *Jubilate Agno* was first edited, as *Rejoice in the Lamb*, by W. F. Stead, 1939; W. H. Bond's edition, 1954, is better. On the life, Christopher Devlin's *Poor Kit Smart*, 1961, should be supplemented by Arthur Sherbo's *Christopher Smart, Scholar of the University*, 1967; Moira Dearnley surveys *The Poetry of Christopher Smart*, 1968.

Oliver Goldsmith

The Collected Works of Goldsmith was published by Arthur Friedman in 1966. The most recent biography of Goldsmith is Ralph M. Wardle's *Oliver Goldsmith*, 1957. Sir James Prior's *Life of Oliver Goldsmith*, 2 vols., 1837, is the important biography of the last century. Kathleen C. Balderston has edited the *Collected Letters*, 1928; Austin Dobson edited the *Plays*, 1901. An important addition to the canon of Goldsmith's works was made by Ronald S. Crane in his edition of *New Essays*, 1927. The notes in Lonsdale's edition of the *Poems* (see Gray above) are valuable; Ricardo Quintana's *Oliver Goldsmith*, 1967, is a useful critical survey.

George Crabbe

Crabbe's biography was written by his son, George, in 1834. It has been re-edited by E. M. Forster, 1932, and by Edmund Blunden, 1947. The *Poetical Works*, well edited by A. J. and R. M. Carlyle, were published in 1914. *New Poems*, edited by Arthur Pollard, 1960, contains hitherto unpublished poems. Howard Mills has edited *George Crabbe: Tales (1812) and Other Selected Poems*, 1967. Lilian Haddakin's *Poetry of Crabbe*, 1955, and Oliver Sigworth's *Nature's Sternest Painter*, 1965, are essays in criticism.

William Cowper

The poems have been reprinted many times. A convenient modern edition in one volume is H. S. Milford's, 4th edition, 1934. Thomas Wright has edited the *Correspondence*, 4 vols., 1904, and *Unpublished and Uncollected Letters*, 1925. Maurice J. Quinlan's *William Cowper*, 1953, is the most recent scholarly biography. See also his useful edition of Cowper's *Memoir* (first published 1816), in *Proceedings of the American Philosophical Society* XCVII (1953), 359–82. Charles Ryskamp's *William Cowper*, 1959, concentrates on the poet's early life. Useful critical studies include Norman Nicholson's *William Cowper*,‡ 1951, and Morris Golden's *In Search of Stability: The Poetry of William Cowper*, 1960.‡

Poetic Forms and Literary Terminology

Verse is generally distinguished from prose as a more compressed and more regularly rhythmic form of statement. This approximate truth underlines the importance of **meter** in poetry, as the means by which rhythm is measured and described.

In the classical languages, meter was established on a **quantitative** basis, by the regular alternation of long and short syllables (that is, syllables classified according to the time taken to pronounce them). Outside of a few experiments (and the songs of Thomas Campion), this system has never proved congenial to English, which distinguishes, instead, between **stressed** and **unstressed,** or accented and unaccented syllables. Two varieties of accented stress may be distinguished. On the one hand, there is the natural stress pattern of words themselves; *sýllable* is accented on the first syllable, *deplórable* on the second, and so on. Then there is the sort of stress which indicates rhetorical emphasis. If the sentence "You went to Greece?" is given a pronounced accent on the last word, it implies "Greece (of all places)?" If the accent falls on the first word, it implies "you (of all people)?" The meter of poetry—that is, its rhythm—is ordinarily built up out of a regular recurrence of accents, whether established as **word accents** or **rhetorical accents;** once started in the reader's mind, it has (like all rhythm) a persistent effect of its own.

The unit which is repeated to give steady rhythm to a poem is called a **poetic foot;** in English it usually consists of accented and unaccented syllables in one of five fairly simple patterns:

The **iambic foot** (or **iamb**) consists of an unstressed followed by a stressed syllable, as in *uníte, repeát,* or *insíst.* Most English verse falls naturally into the iambic pattern.

The **trochaic foot** (**trochee**) inverts this order; it is a stressed followed by an unstressed syllable—for example, *únit, réaper,* or *ínstant.*

The **anapestic foot** (**anapest**) consists of two unstressed syllables followed by a stressed syllable, as in *intercéde, disarránge,* or *Cameróon.*

The **dactylic foot** (**dactyl**) consists of a stressed syllable followed by two unstressed syllables, as in *Wáshington, Écuador,* or *ápplejack.*

The **spondaic foot** (**spondee**) consists of two successive stressed syllables, as in *heartbreak, headline,* or *Kashmir.*

In all the examples above, word accent and the quality of the metrical foot coincide exactly. But the metrical foot may well consist of several words, or, on the other hand, one word may well consist of several metrical feet. *Phótolithógraphy* consists of two excellent dactyls in a single word; *dárk and with spóts on it*, though it consists of six words rather than one, is also two dactyls—not quite such good ones. When we read a piece of poetry with the intention of discovering its underlying metrical pattern, we are said to **scan** it—that is, we go through it line by line, indicating by conventional signs which are the accented and which the unaccented syllables within the feet (the ictus ′ generally designates accented, the mora �‿ unaccented syllables). We also count the number of feet in each line, or, more properly, **verse**—since a single poetic line is generally called a "verse." Verse lengths are conventionally described in terms derived from the Greek:

Monometer: one foot (of rare occurrence)
Dimeter: two feet (also rare)
Trimeter: three feet
Tetrameter: four feet
Pentameter: five feet
Hexameter: six feet (six iambic feet make an **Alexandrine**)
Heptameter: seven feet (also rare)

Doctor Johnson's little parody of simpleminded poets would thus be scanned this way:

> Í pŭt my̆ hát ŭpón my̆ héad
> Ånd wálked ĭnto thĕ Stránd,
> Ånd thére Ĭ mét ănóthĕr mán
> Whŏse hát wăs ĭn hĭs hánd.

The poem is iambic in rhythm, alternating tetrameter and trimeter in verse length. The fact that it scans so nicely is, however, no proof that it is good poetry. Quite the contrary. Many of poetry's most subtle effects are achieved by establishing an underlying rhythm and then varying it by means of a whole series of devices, some dramatic and expressive, others designed simply to lend variety and interest to the verse. A well-known sonnet of Shakespeare's (CXVI) begins,

> Let me not to the marriage of true minds
> Admit impediments. Love is not love
> Which alters when it alteration finds,
> Or bends with the remover to remove.

It is perfectly possible, if one crushes all one's sensitivities, to read the first line of this poem as mechanical iambic pentameter:

> Lĕt mé nŏt tó thĕ márriăge óf trúe mínds.

But of course nobody ever reads it that way, except to make a point; read with normal English accent and some sense of what it is saying, the line would probably form a pattern something like this:

> Lét mĕ nŏt tŏ thĕ márriăge ŏf trúe mínds,

which is neither pentameter nor in any way iambic. The second line is a little more iambic, but, read for expression, falls just as far short of penta-meter:

Ădmĭt ĭmpédĭmĕnts. Lóve ĭs nŏt lóve.

Only in the third and fourth lines of the sonnet do we get verses which read as well as scan like five iambic feet.

The fact is that perfectly regular metrical verse is easy to write and dull to read. Among the devices in common use for varying too regular a pattern are, for instance, the insertion of a trochaic foot among iambics, especially at the opening of a line, where the soft first syllable of the iambic foot often needs stiffening (see line 1 above); the more or less free addition of extra unaccented syllables; and the use of **caesura,** or strong grammatical pause within a line (conventionally indicated, in scan-ning, by the sign ||). The second line of the sonnet above is a good example of caesura:

Admit impediments. || Love is not love.

The strength of the caesura, and its placing in the line, may be varied to produce striking variations of effect. More broadly, the whole relation between the poem's sound- and rhythm-patterns and its pattern as a se-quence of assertions (phrases, clauses, sentences) may be manipulated by the poet. Sometimes his statements fit neatly within the lines, so that each line ends with a strong mark of punctuation; they are then known as **end-stopped lines.** Sometimes the sense flows over the ends of the lines, creating **run-on lines;** this process is also known, from the French, as **enjambment** (literally, "straddling").

End-stopped lines (Marlowe, *Hero and Leander*, First Sestiad, lines 45–48):

> So lovely fair was Hero, Venus' nun,
> As Nature wept, thinking she was undone,
> Because she took more from her than she left,
> And of such wondrous beauty her bereft.

Run-on lines (Keats, *Endymion* I.89–93):

> Full in the middle of this pleasantness
> There stood a marble altar, with a tress
> Of flowers budded newly; and the dew
> Had taken fairy fantasies to strew
> Daisies upon the sacred sward, * * *

Following the example of such poets as Blake, Rimbaud, and Whitman, many poets of the 20th century have undertaken to write what is called **free verse**—that is, verse which has neither a fixed metrical foot, nor (con-sequently) a fixed number of feet in its lines, but which depends for its rhythm on a pattern of cadences, or the rise and fall of the voice in utter-ance. All freedom in art is of course relative; free verse, with its special aptitude for metrical variety and nervous, colloquial phrasing—its total responsiveness, in other words, to its subject matter—has so successfully established itself that it is now widely recognized as a new and rather demanding form of artistic discipline.

SENSE AND SOUND

The very words of which poetic lines—whether free or traditional—are composed cause them to have different sounds and produce different effects. Polysyllables, being pronounced fast, often cause a line to move swiftly; monosyllables, especially when heavy and requiring distinct accents, may cause it to move heavily, as in Milton's famous line (*Paradise Lost* II.621):

> Rocks, caves, lakes, fens, bogs, dens, and shades of death.

Poetic assertions are often dramatized and reinforced by means of **alliteration**—that is, the use of several nearby words or stressed syllables beginning with the same consonant. When Shakespeare writes (*Sonnet LXIV*),

> Ruin hath taught me thus to ruminate
> That Time will come and take my love away,

the rich, round, vague echoes of the first line contrast most effectively with the sharp anxiety and directness of the alliterative *t*'s in the second. When Dryden starts *Absalom and Achitophel* with that wicked couplet,

> In pious times, ere priestcraft did begin,
> Before polygamy was made a sin,

the satiric undercutting is strongly reinforced by the triple alliteration which links "*p*ious" with "*p*riestcraft" and "*p*olygamy."

Assonance, or repetition of the same or similar vowel sounds within a passage (usually in accented syllables), also serves to enrich it, as in two lines from Keats's *Ode on Melancholy:*

> For shade to shade will come too drowsily,
> And drown the wakeful anguish of the soul.

It is clear that the round, hollow tones of "drowsily," repeated in "drown" and darkening to the full o-sound of "soul," have much to do with the effect of the passage. A related device is **consonance,** or the repetition of a pattern of consonants with changes in the intervening vowels—for example: *linger, longer, languor; rider, reader, raider, ruder.*

Direct verbal imitation of natural sounds (known as **onomatopoeia**) has has been much attempted, from Virgil's galloping horse—

> *Quadrupedante putrem sonitu quatit ungula campum*—

to Tennyson's account, in *The Princess,* of

> The moan of doves in immemorial elms
> And murmuring of innumerable bees.

Often ingeniously exploited as a side effect, onomatopoeia is essentially a trick, with about the same value in poetry as it has in music.

RHYME AND STANZA

Rhyme consists of a repetition of accented sounds in words, usually those falling at the end of verse lines. If the rhyme sound is the very last syllable of the line (*rebound, sound*), the rhyme is called **masculine;** if the accented syllable is followed by an unaccented syllable (*hounding, bounding*), the rhyme is called **feminine.** Rhymes amounting to three or more syllables, like forced rhymes, generally have a comic effect in English, and have been freely used for this purpose, e.g., by Ogden Nash (*opportunity, impunity; failure, azalea*). Rhymes occurring within a single line are called **internal**; for instance, the Mother-Goose rhyme, "Mary, Mary, quite contrary," or Coleridge's *Ancient Mariner* ("We were the first that ever burst / Into that silent sea"). **Eye rhymes** are words used as rhymes which look alike but actually sound different (for example, *alone, done; remove, love*); **off rhymes** (sometimes called **partial, imperfect,** or **slant rhymes**) are occasionally the result of pressing exigencies or lack of skill, but are also, at times, used deliberately by modern poets for special effects. For instance, a sonnet by Dylan Thomas contains such "rhymes" as *knees, toes; Eve, grave; van, bone;* and *winter, ladder* (*Holy Sonnet* 3). Pairings like the last two are sometimes loosely described as consonance, rather than rhyme.

Blank verse is unrhymed iambic pentameter; until the recent advent of free verse, it was the only unrhymed measure to achieve general popularity in English. First used by the Earl of Surrey, blank verse was during the 16th century largely dramatic in character. *Paradise Lost* was one of the first nondramatic poems in English to use blank verse. But Milton's authority and his success were so great that during the 18th and 19th centuries blank verse came to be used for a great variety of discursive, descriptive, and philosophical poems—besides remaining the standard metrical form for epics. Thomson's *Seasons,* Cowper's *Task,* Wordsworth's *Prelude,* and Tennyson's *Idylls of the King* were all written in blank verse.

A **stanza** is a recurring unit of a poem, consisting of a number of verses. Certain poetic forms (as a notable example, Pindaric odes) have stanzas comprising a variable number of verses, of varying lengths. Others are more regular, hence easier to describe.

The simplest form of stanza is the **couplet**; it is simply two lines rhyming together. When a single couplet is considered in isolation, it is sometimes called a **distich;** when it includes a complete unified thought, ending with a terminal mark of punctuation, it is called a **closed couplet.** The iambic pentameter couplet seems to work best when it is strict and regular, but to regularize it was a work of considerable time and practice. Even as skillful a versifier as Ben Jonson, though he writes iambic pentameter couplets in a poem like *To Penshurst,* has not yet mastered what we call the **heroic couplet.** This is a strictly iambic pentameter couplet, strongly end-stopped, and with the couplets prevailingly closed. Heroic couplets generally are varied by means of a decided caesura, and limited to precisely ten syllables per line. The heroic couplet is the principal form of English neoclassical style. A model of its swift, keen, yet weighty wit is the opening of Dryden's *Absalom and Achitophel.* Occasionally, as in this poem, heroic couplets are varied by the introduction of a third rhyme, to make a **tercet** (usually enclosed by a marginal brace); and a striking terminal effect is sometimes achieved by the introduction of an Alexandrine (a line of iambic hexameter) as the third line of the tercet.

Another customary and challenging form of couplet is the **tetrameter,** or **four-beat couplet.** The more closely rhymes recur, the harder couplets are to manage; in addition, a four-beat line is hard to divide by caesura without splitting it into two tick-tock .dimeters. For this reason, tetrameter couplets have posed a perpetual challenge to poets, and still provide an admirable finger-exercise for aspiring versifiers. A model of tetrameter couplets managed with marvelous variety, complexity, and expressiveness is Marvell's *To His Coy Mistress:*

> Thou by the Indian Ganges' side
> Shouldst rubies find; I by the tide
> Of Humber would complain. I would
> Love you ten years before the flood,
> And you should, if you please, refuse
> Till the conversion of the Jews.

English has not done much with rhymes grouped in threes, but has borrowed from Italian the form known as **terza rima,** in which Dante composed his *Divine Comedy.* This form consists of linked groups of three rhymes according to the following pattern: *aba bcb cdc ded,* etc. Shelley's *Ode to the West Wind* is composed in stanzas of *terza rima,* the poem as a whole ending with a couplet.

Quatrains are stanzas of four lines; the lines usually rhyme alternately, *abab,* or in the second and fourth lines, *abcb.* When they alternate tetrameter and trimeter lines, as in Johnson's little poem about men in hats (above), or as in *Sir Patrick Spens,* they are called **ballad stanza.** Dryden's *Annus Mirabilis* and Gray's *Elegy Written in a Country Churchyard* are in heroic quatrains; these rhyme alternately, and employ five-stress iambic verse throughout. Tennyson used for *In Memoriam* a tetrameter quatrain rhymed *abba,* and FitzGerald translated *The Rubáiyát of Omar Khayyám* into a pentameter rhymed *aaba;* but these forms have not been very generally adopted.

Chaucer's *Troilus and Criseyde* is an early example in English of **rime royal,** a seven-line iambic pentameter stanza consisting essentially of a quatrain dovetailed onto two couplets, according to the rhyme scheme *ababbcc* (the fourth line serves both as the final line of the quatrain and the first line of the first couplet). Closely akin to rime royal, but differentiated by an extra *a*-rhyme between the two *b*-rhymes, is **ottava rima,** that is, an eight-line stanza rhyming *abababcc.* As its name suggests, ottava rima is of Italian origin; it was first used in English by Wyatt. Its final couplet, being less prepared for than in rime royal, and usually set off as a separate verbal unit, has a special witty snap to it, for which Byron found good use in *Don Juan.*

The longest and most intricate stanza generally used for narrative purposes in English is that devised by Edmund Spenser for *The Faerie Queene.* The **Spenserian stanza** has nine lines rhyming *ababbcbcc;* the first eight lines are pentameter, the last line an Alexandrine. Slow-moving, intricate of pattern, and demanding in its rhyme scheme (the *b*-sound recurs four times, the *c*-sound three), the Spenserian stanza has nonetheless appealed widely to poets seeking a rich and complicated metrical form. Keats's *Eve of St. Agnes* and Shelley's *Adonais* are brilliantly successful 19th-century examples of its use.

The **sonnet,** originally a stanza of Italian origin which has developed into an independent lyric form, is usually defined as fourteen lines of iambic pentameter. None of the elements in this definition is absolute. The first sonnet of Sidney's *Astrophel and Stella* is in hexameters, and Milton has one sonnet of twenty lines (*On the New Forcers of Conscience*), while Meredith wrote a whole series of sixteen-line sonnets (*Modern Love*). Most sonnets, however, conform to the definition. Sonnets generally follow one of two conventional rhyme schemes. The **Petrarchan** or **Italian sonnet** is divided into sections of eight lines (**octave**) and six lines (**sestet**), rhyming *abba abba* and *cdecde*. (There are many variations of the rhyme scheme in the sestet; that described is the most frequent.) Under this arrangement, the poet tends to use his octave to state the problem and his sestet to resolve it. The **English** or **Shakespearean** sonnet takes the form of three quatrains and a final couplet, rhyming *abab cdcd efef gg*. The couplet is ideally suited for producing a summary statement or witty twist after the problem has been turned about in the three quatrains. Both these forms represent ideal models, not absolute prescriptions. Many sonnets approximate these patterns without following them precisely; indeed, the term "sonnet" was slow in acquiring any meaning more specific than that of "short lyric poem." Among Donne's *Songs and Sonnets* there is just one sonnet in the more modern sense, *The Token*, and it has eighteen lines.

In the Elizabethan period, the sonnet underwent its most intensive cultivation in connection with themes of courtly love. Perhaps in revulsion, Donne used the sonnet mostly to express religious devotion (*Holy Sonnets, La Corona*), while Milton employed it on satiric, social, or political themes. In Wordsworth, it expanded in the direction of moral reflection and commentary, while G. M. Hopkins loaded it with a rich philosophical and rhetorical complexity which sometimes threatened to swamp the form altogether. But the applications of the sonnet are truly limitless, for it is a form just long and complex enough to provide compressed yet dignified statement of almost any major theme.

In blank verse or irregularly rhymed verse, where stanzaic divisions do not exist or are indistinct, the poetry sometimes falls into **verse paragraphs,** which are in effect divisions of sense like prose paragraphs. This division can be clearly seen in Milton's *Lycidas* or Spenser's *Epithalamion*. In the latter poem, it is reinforced by a **refrain,** which is simply a line repeated at the end of each stanza. Ballads also customarily have refrains; for example, the refrain of *Lord Randall* is

> mother, make my bed soon,
> For I'm weary wi' hunting, and fain wad lie down.

FIGURATIVE LANGUAGE

The act of bringing words together into rich and vigorous poetic lines is complex and demanding, chiefly because so many variables require control. There is the "thought" of the lines, their verbal texture, their emotional resonance, the developing perspective of the reader—all these to be managed at once. One of the poet's chief resources toward this end is figurative language. Here, as in matters of meter, one may distinguish a great variety of devices, some of which we use in everyday speech without special awareness of their names and natures. When we say someone eats "like a horse" or "like a bird," we are using a **simile**, that is, a comparison marked out by a specific word of likening—"like" or "as." When we omit the word of comparison but imply a likeness—as in the sentence, "That hog has guzzled all the champagne"—we are making use of **metaphor**. The **epic simile**, frequent in epic poetry, is an extended simile in which the thing compared is described as an object in its own right, beyond its point of likeness with the main subject. Milton starts to compare Satan to Leviathan, but concludes his simile with the story of a sailor who moored his ship by mistake, one night, to a whale (*Paradise Lost* I.200–208). Metaphors and similes have been complexly but usefully distinguished according to their special effects; they may be, for instance, violent, comic, degrading, decorative.

When we speak of "forty head of cattle" or ask someone to "lend a hand" with a job, we are using **synecdoche**, a figure which substitutes the part for the whole. When we speak of a statement "coming from the White House," or a man much interested in "the turf," we are using **metonymy**, or the substitution of one term for another with which it is closely associated. **Antithesis** is a device for placing opposing ideas in grammatical parallel, as, for example, in the following passage from Pope's *Rape of the Lock* (V.25–30), where there are more examples of antithesis than there are lines:

> But since, alas! frail beauty must decay,
> Curled or uncurled, since locks will turn to gray;
> Since painted, or not painted, all shall fade,
> And she who scorns a man, must die a maid;
> What then remains but well our power to use,
> And keep good humor still whate'er we lose?

Irony is a verbal device which implies an attitude quite different from (and often opposite to) that which is literally expressed. When Job answers his comforters, saying "No doubt but ye are the people, and wisdom shall die with you" (Job xii.2), he is using irony thick to the point of sarcasm. When Eliot writes, in *Whispers of Immortality*, that "Grishkin is nice," the adjective is carefully chosen to let an ironic grimace of distaste appear. And when Donne "proves," in *The Canonization*, that he and his mistress are going to found a new religion of love, he seems to be inviting us to take a subtly ironic attitude toward religion as well as love.

Because it is easy to see through, **hyperbole**, or willful exaggeration, is a favorite device of irony—which is not to say that it may not be "serious" as well. When she hears that a young man is "dying for love" of her, a sensible girl does not accept this statement literally, but it may convey a serious meaning to her nonetheless. The **pun**, or play on words (known to the learned, sometimes, as **paronomasia**), may also be serious or comic in intent; witness, for example, the famous series of puns in Donne's *Hymn to God the Father*. **Oxymoron** is a figure of flat contradiction—for instance, Milton's famous description of hell as containing "darkness visible" (*Paradise Lost* I.63). A **paradox** is a statement which seems absurd but turns out to have rational meaning after all, usually in some unexpected sense; Donne speaks of fear being great courage and high valor (*Satire III*, line 16), and turns out to mean that fear of God is greater courage than any earthly bravery. The **Petrarchan conceit** was an ingenious, complimentary comparison or turn of thought; Wyatt compares the state of a lover to a ship tossed in a storm, and a hundred different sonneteers explored the possibility of describing their ladies' anatomy in conventional Petrarchan conceits—her teeth like pearls, lips like rubies, hair like finespun gold, etc. On the other hand, the **metaphysical conceit** was a more ingenious many-leveled comparison, worked out in some detail and giving a strong sense of the poet's ingenuity in overcoming obstacles—for instance, Donne's comparison of separated lovers to the legs of a compass (*A Valediction: Forbidding Mourning*) or Herbert's comparison of devotion to a pulley (*The Pulley*).

Images are often described as "mental pictures"; it is more accurate to say that they are verbal representations of something capable of being visualized: some readers have such mental pictures, some do not. Images not only convey what things look like, but direct us, by their pattern of associated and involved feelings, in our reactions to what is being represented. Indeed, there may be such a weight of meaning or feeling behind the image that the verbal picture itself becomes transparent and its "meaning" becomes primary. Abstract ideas can get attached to specific images—water, snake, bird, sun, worm, lion, whatever—in a multitude of ways, of which the reader need sometimes only be reminded. Of course the poet can also be arbitrary about it, letting his reader know simply that Red Cross "stands for" Holiness and Archimago "stands for" Hypocrisy. If that's as far as it goes, we have a primitive variety of **allegory.** But the relation between the tenor of the image (its abstract meaning) and the vehicle (the concrete picture) can be much more indefinite and insubstantial. If the poet mentions a peacock, he may or may not intend his reader to think of immortality, because the unfolding of the peacock's tail and the opening of its "eyes" has traditionally suggested the rebirth of the soul after death. If that is the way the image works, then it is a **symbol.** Or again, if the poet mentions a fish, he may well intend the reader to think of Christ. This isn't because of any similarity between the fish and Christ; the identification depends on a mildly esoteric bit of information, that the Greek word for fish, *ichthys*, forms an anagram of the Greek words for "Jesus Christ, Son of God, Savior." When the connection between tenor and vehicle is arbitrary, or involves the elements of a puzzle, the image may be referred to as an **emblem.** In the 16th and 17th centuries, emblems often took the form of puzzling little drawings, the meaning of which was explained in appended verses: for an example see the emblem prefixed to Crashaw's poem *To the Countess of Denbigh.*

Personification is the attribution of human qualities to an inanimate object (for example, the Sea) or an abstract concept (Freedom); a special variety of it is called (in a term of John Ruskin's invention) the **pathetic fallacy.** When we speak of leaves "dancing" or a lake "smiling," we attribute human traits to nonhuman objects. Ruskin thought this was false and therefore "morbid"; modern criticism tends to view the practice as artistically and morally neutral. A more formal and abstract variety of personification is **allegory,** in which a narrative (such as *Pilgrim's Progress*) is constructed by representing general concepts (Faithfulness, Sin, Despair) as persons. A **fable** (like the Nun's Priest's Tale) represents beasts behaving like humans; a **parable** is a brief story, or simply an observation, with strong moral application; and an **exemplum** is a story told to illustrate a point in a sermon. A special series of devices, nearly obsolete today, used to be available to poets who could count on readers trained in the classics. These were the devices of **classical epithet** and **allusion**. In their simplest form, the classic myths used to provide a repertoire of agreeable stage properties, and a convenient shorthand for expressing emotional attitudes. Picturesque creatures like centaurs, satyrs, and sphinxes, heroes and heroines like Hector and Helen, and the whole pantheon of Olympic deities could be used to make ready reference to a great many aspects of human nature. One does not have to explain the problems of a man who is "cleaning the Augean stables"; if he is afflicted with an "Achilles' heel," or is assailing "Hydra-headed difficulties," his state is clear. These epithets, or descriptive phrases, making reference to mythological stories, suggest in a phrase situations which would normally require cumbersome explanations. Conceivably other mythologies might have served the same end in analogous ways. But because they could be taken for granted as the common possession of all educated readers, the classic myths entered into English literature as early as Chaucer, and are only now passing away as a viable system of allusions. In poets like Spenser and Milton, classical allusion becomes a kind of enormously learned game, in which the poet seeks to make his points as indirectly as possible. For instance, Spenser writes in the *Epithalamion*, lines 328–29:

> Lyke as when Jove with fayre Alcmena lay,
> When he begot the great Tirynthian groom.

The mere mention of Alcmena in the first line suggests, to the knowing reader, Hercules; Spenser's problem in the second line is to find a way of referring to him which is neither redundant nor heavy-handed. "Tirynthian" reminds us of his long connection with the city of Tiryns, stretching our minds (as it were) across his whole career; and "groom" compresses references to a man-child, a servant, and a bridegroom, all of which apply to different aspects of Hercules' history. Thus, far from simply avoiding redundancy, Spencer has enriched the whole texture of his verse, thought, and feeling by his gift for precise classical epithet.

PERIODS

Dividing English literature into manageable, more or less homogeneous periods is bound to be an arbitrary, an inexact, and in the end an inconsistent procedure. But a few handy dates are worth memorizing as a frame on which to hang details. Chaucer died in 1400; he was the literary high point of the English **Middle Ages,** a millennium reaching from 500 to 1500. Though no thousand-year period of existence can be compressed to a phrase, we may say that the Christian church structured and came close to dominating the imaginative life of this period. The first flowering of the English **Renaissance** took place around 1500; it has often been called the **Age of Humanism.** Less a formal philosophy than an attitude of interest in the full potentialities of the human mind, Humanism took on many colorings; most English writers, as **Christian Humanists,** tried to reconcile or combine the values of Greece and Rome with those of Christianity, while granting the former an independent authenticity that the Middle Ages had never conceded. The precise end of the Renaissance, with its tumultuous sense of human potential and delight in verbal invention, is hard to fix; but the death of Dryden in 1700 is a handy date for marking the onset of the **Age of Reason,** also called the **Enlightenment** or the **Neo-Classical Age.** Frequently, this age is expanded to include also the **Restoration** (1660–1700). The new era, emphasizing correctness, sought to discipline the individual consciousness to a generalized definition of rational human nature, one pattern for which was sought in the classics. To this vision of general human nature the age tended to subordinate any particular religious dispensation or creed, any social custom peculiar to a single time or place. The publication of *Lyrical Ballads* in 1798 opens the English **Age of Romanticism,** in which many writers undertook to explore the individual human mind independent of Christian dogma, and also as transcending experience—as an agent with active characteristics and initiatives of its own.

After 1798, the periods of English literature get shorter and less distinct. (From a longer perspective than we can easily assume, the whole era from 1798 to the present may someday be known as the age of Romanticism.) For the last half of the 19th century we have no real name but that of the ruling monarch: it is the **Age of Victorianism.** Some writers have tried to follow through with **Edwardian** for the period 1901–1910, and **Georgian** for the period after 1910. But George V ruled till 1936, and the postwar generation did not at all think of themselves as Georgians. Besides, somewhere in here we have to find room to start the **Modern Period,** whatever that is—if only so that we will have space to inaugurate our own time, for which there exist as yet only makeshift titles like the **Post-Modern Age.** Concerning all these periods, it is idle to dispute exact boundaries and precise characteristics. They don't have or need any, for the simple reason that their only function is to help the memory make a few gross distinctions and groupings within an otherwise uncontrollable sea of particulars.

SCHOOLS

Within the broad periods it is customary to group in **schools** writers who show common stylistic traits or thematic concerns. Whether they considered themselves a group doesn't much matter. None of the **Romantic poets** knew they were being romantic, although Hazlitt, Shelley, and other writers of the time recognized shared features that they called "the spirit of the age." The followers of Spenser are known as **Spenserians;** they knew they liked Spenser, but didn't realize that made them a group. **Cavalier** poets are set decisively apart from **metaphysical** poets, though pretty surely none of the two dozen men involved knew that was what they were. And so with the **Gothic novelists,** and the so-called **Graveyard School** at the end of the 18th century, so with the modern surrealists. These schools are generally grouped, defined, and named by scholars and critics after the event. Use of a common form or subject matter constitutes a more superficial similarity than use of a common style, common techniques, or common philosophical backgrounds. But literary history, being nothing if not pragmatic, makes use of all sorts of common denominators.

Intellectual affinities have led some writers to be classified under the names of the philosophical schools of Greece and Rome. These are chiefly the **Epicureans,** who specify that the aim of life and the source of value is pleasure; the **Stoics,** who emphasize the avoidance of pain and the dignified endurance of what cannot be avoided; and the **Skeptics,** who doubt that anything can be known for sure. These categories are useful as capsule descriptions, but they aren't very tidy, as they overlap one another and cut across other categories. Dryden is an author strongly tinged with **skepticism,** but many of his poems suggest an unabashed **epicureanism.** *The Vanity of Human Wishes,* by Doctor Johnson, is the classic poem in English of **stoic** philosophy, but it also expresses a particularly strong coloring of **Christian humanism.**

Plato and **Aristotle,** as they summarized contrasting attitudes toward existence, are often used to define the outlook of writers. Both were prolific writers of enormous range and complexity, but in literary contexts their names most often define attitudes toward reality. Aristotle tended to find reality, not exclusively but primarily, in concrete and particular substances, which he brilliantly categorized and generalized. Plato tended to place reality in abstract ideal forms, of which the concrete things we experience in daily life are but partial and shadowy manifestations. During the Middle Ages, the Dominican friars (St. Thomas Aquinas was one) were **Aristotelians;** the Franciscans (St. Bonaventura was one) were **Platonists.** During the Renaissance Spenser, and during the Romantic period Shelley, were **Platonists** or **Neo-Platonists.** (A neo-Platonist is a Platonist diluted with other world-views—perhaps Pythagorean mysticism, perhaps Christian theology, perhaps Aristotelian thought itself. In a narrower sense, the term is applied to philosophers writing in the tradition of Plotinus (3rd century A.D.), who held that all things in the world, spiritual and material, "emanate," or flow out, from the "Absolute," or the "One"—the single source of all truth, goodness, and beauty. **Aristotelianism,** as it is more commonsensical, had faded by Spenser's time to the common teaching of the schools, and by Shelley's time to the practical, pragmatic materialism of everyday life.

SECTS

Religious distinctions and denominations are important in British social history, hence deeply woven into the nation's literature. The numerous (over 300) British churches and sects divide along a scale from high to low, depending on the amount of authority they give to the church or the amount of liberty they concede to the individual conscience. At one end of the scale is the **Roman Catholic Church,** asserting papal infallibility, universal jurisdiction, and the supreme importance of hierarchy as guide and intercessor. For political and social reasons, Catholicism struck deep roots in Ireland but was the object of prolonged, bitter hatred on the part of Protestants from the Reformation through the 19th century. The **Established English (Anglican) Episcopal Church** has been the official national church since the 16th century; it enjoys the support (once direct and exclusive, now indirect and peripheral) of the national government. Its creed is defined by Thirty-Nine Articles, but these are intentionally vague, so there are numerous ways of adhering to the Church of England. Roughly and intermittently, the chief classes of Anglicans have been known as **High Church** (with its highest portion calling itself **Anglo-Catholic**); **Broad Church** or **Latitudinarian** (when they get so broad that they admit anyone believing in God, they may be known as **Deists,** or some may leave the church altogether and be known as **Unitarians**); and **Low Church,** whose adherents may stay in the English church and yet come close to shaking hands with **Presbyterians** or **Methodists.** These various groups may be arranged, from the High down to the Low Church, in direct relation to the amount of ritual each prefers and in the degree of authority conceded to the upper clergy—and in inverse relation to the importance ascribed to a saving faith directly infused by God into an individual conscience.

All Protestants who decline to subscribe to the English established church are classed as **Dissenters** or **Nonconformists;** for a time in the 16th and 17th centuries, they were also known as **Puritans.** The **Presbyterians** model their church government on that established by John Calvin in the Swiss city of Geneva. It has no bishops, and therefore is more democratic for the clergy; but it gains energy by associating lay elders with clergymen in matters of social discipline, and tends to be strict with the ungodly. From its first reformation the Scottish Kirk was fixed on the Presbyterian model. During the civil wars of the 17th century, a great many sects sprang up on the left wing of the Presbyterians, most of them touched by Calvinism but some rebelling against it; a few of these still survive. The **Independents** became our modern **Congregationalists;** the **Quakers** are still Quakers, as **Baptists** are still Baptists, though multiply divided. But many of the sects flourished and perished within the space of a few years. Among these now-vanished groups were the Shakers (though a few groups still exist in America), the Seekers, the Ranters, the Anabaptists, the Muggletonians, the Fifth Monarchy Men, the Family of Love, the Sweet Singers of Israel, and many others, forgotten by all except scholars. During the 18th and 19th centuries, new sects arose, supplanting old ones; the **Methodists,** under John and Charles Wesley, became numerous and important, taking root particularly in Wales. (The three "subject" nationalities, Ireland, Scotland, and Wales, thus turned three different ways to avoid the Anglican church.) With the passage of time a small number of Swedenborgians sprang up, followers of the Swedish mystic Emmanuel Swedenborg—to be followed by the Plymouth Brethren, Christian Scientists, Jehovah's Witnesses, and countless other 19th-century groups. All these sects constantly grow, shrink, split, and occasionally disappear as they succeed or fail in attracting new converts.

Within the various churches and sects, independent of them all but amazingly persistent, there has always survived a stream of **esoteric** or **hermetic** thought—a belief in occult powers, and sometimes in magic as well, exemplified by the pseudo-sciences of astrology and alchemy but taking many other forms. From the mythical Egyptian seer Hermes Trismegistus through Paracelsus, Cornelius Agrippa, Giordano Bruno, Jakob Boehme, the society of Rosicrucians, and a hundred other shadowy figures, the line can be traced to William Blake and William Butler Yeats, who both in their different ways brought hermetic protestantism close to its ultimate goal, a mystic church of one single man, poised within his own mind-elaborated cosmos.

TERMS OF ART

The following section groups together various sets of frequently used and closely related literary terms in an effort to discriminate and define them.

Allegory, Symbolism. They are both extended metaphors, distinguished chiefly by the fact that the figures in an **allegory** are more tightly and unequivocally related to their underlying meanings than in a work of symbolism. Though he has other significances as well, Spenser's Red-Cross Knight stands squarely for Holiness. In a work of **symbolism,** the meaning of the individual symbol grows out of its configuration with other symbols—it is an indirect and multiplex, not a one-for-one relation, as in Blake's poem *The Sick Rose.*

Baroque and **Mannerist** are terms imported into literary study from the history of art, and applied by analogy. Michelangelo is a **baroque** artist; he holds great masses in powerful dynamic tension, his style is heavily ornamented and restless. In these respects he is sometimes compared to Milton. El Greco is a **mannerist,** whose gaunt and distorted figures often seem to be laboring under great spiritual stress, whose light seems to be focused in spots against a dark background. He has been compared to Donne. Analogies of this sort are occasionally suggestive, but they must be carefully handled to avoid degenerating into parallels which are forced and nominal rather than substantial.

Burlesque and **Mock Heroic** differ in that the former makes its subject ludicrous by inflating it. In Pope's mock-heroic **Dunciad,** the figure of Dulness (Colley Cibber) is given inappropriately heroic dimensions; in Butler's burlesque **Hudibras,** the knightly hero is characterized by low and vulgar attributes, and persistently engages in inappropriately low adventures.

Genre, Decorum. A **genre** is an established literary form, such as a stage comedy, the picaresque novel, the epic, the sonnet. Being of a certain genre predisposes a work to represent certain characters and events and to seek certain effects. Its success in achieving these effects and avoiding incongruous ones can thus be judged; and this is one sort of **decorum** (fittingness), the decorum of genre. Satire was once considered a low, popular form, for which only low, popular speech was decorous (fitting). There are also decorums of character, of occasion, of rhetorical mode, etc.

Gothic and **Classic** distinguish styles and tendencies in art and literature. **Gothic** implies vital, primitive, and deeply energetic work, with the qualities of Northern barbarism. **Classic** implies lucid, rational, and idealized work, as in the Southern sunlit civilizations of Greece and Rome. For the 18th century, the classics, which had proved their universality by maintaining their popularity for so many centuries, were the school of all civilized thinking; "Gothic" was a term connoting barbarity, wild and disorganized details, and a lack of artistic decorum and control. For a man like Ruskin, deeply imbued with the ideal of organic unity, "Gothic" was a term of ultimate approval; partly under his influence, Victorian Gothic (often called the "Gothic Revival") became a widely popular style. Currently, the term "Gothic" refers mainly to the artistic (and primarily architectural) style prevalent in Western Europe from the 12th to about the end of the 15th century.

Humors and **Temperaments** are psychological terms used by Renaissance writers. The four basic humors of every constitution were the **choleric** (bile), the **sanguine** (blood), the **phlegmatic** (phlegm), and the **melancholy** (black bile). A man's **temperament** was determined by the mixture of these humors, the way in which they were "tempered." When a particular humor predominated, it pushed the character in that direction: choler = anger; sanguine = geniality; phlegm = cold torpor; and melancholy = gloomy self-absorption.

Imitation and **Parody** are devices by which a literary work assumes an attitude toward its own predecessor. **Imitation** involves not simply copying, but transposing the different features of the earlier work into modern particulars, while retaining the same pattern and the same approximate tonal level. **Parody** generally lowers the level of its original; it is a device of ridicule, though sometimes of self-ridicule. When Joyce parodies ancient Irish legend (as in the "Cyclops" chapter of *Ulysses*), there is no separating ridicule of the past from contempt for the present.

Irony, Sarcasm, Satire. Irony and **Sarcasm** are distinct, though both are ways of saying one thing and meaning another. Sarcasm is broader and more deliberate in its reversal of meanings; irony may be, and in literature generally is, very fine. It often conveys an attitude of detachment. In **dramatic irony,** a character says something which has one meaning for him but quite another for the privileged audience. **Satire** includes all of the many literary ways for diminishing a subject by making it ridiculous.

Myth and **Legend** are stories which incorporate themselves into men's instinctual thinking. **Myths** are narratives which purport to account, in supernatural terms, for why the world is as it is, why men act as they do. Myths often spring up to explain rituals, the original meanings of which have been forgotten; or they may be folk tales based on popular nightmares or fantasies. An ordinary or even inferior tale may take on mythic dimensions—witness Mrs. Shelley's *Frankenstein* or the wooden volumes of Horatio Alger, Jr. A **legend** is any old and popularly repeated story; the word usually implies, in addition, that the story is false. But a proper myth hardly pretends to be historically true—it is a flowering of the mind into narrative. Three great bodies of mythical material are the Celtic, the Norse or Germanic, and the classical fables. A body of associated myths is a **mythology;** a student and collector of myths is a **mythographer.**

Ode, Elegy, Lyric. Lyric poetry gets its name from once having been set to music and chanted to the accompaniment of a lyre; but that's ancient history. Now any short poem directly expressing the poet's thought or feeling will be classed as a lyric; and within this general class, **odes** and **elegies** are two specific varieties. The former implies a dignified occasion and a formal effort to praise or judge its subject. **Pindaric odes,** following the example of the Theban Pindar, are enthusiastic, irregular, and sublime; **Horatian odes,** after the Roman Horace, are cool, judicious, and regular. **Elegies** were originally poems written in elegiac meter, alternating hexameters and pentameters. This limping meter, which has never done as well in English as in the classical tongues, was thought appropriate to the expression of serious, even mournful sentiments. In the narrow sense, then, an elegy is a poem of mourning for the dead. But it can also be any pensive poem on a meditative theme; and a man like Donne, who enjoyed overstepping boundaries, wrote some elegies which are jocose, even bawdy.

Realism and **Naturalism** are both terms used to describe fiction which aims at minute fidelity to actual existence. **Realism** connotes an attempt to give the illusion of ordinary life, in which unexceptional people undergo everyday experiences. **Naturalism** is associated with the example of Emile Zola and the thesis that a novel should present a "slice of life," a cross-section of actual existence; the emphasis is usually on man's instinctual nature, especially the sexual and acquisitive instincts. This type flourished during the late 19th and early 20th centuries. Harold Biffen, a character in George Gissing's novel *New Grub Street*, is devoting his life to a work of "absolute realism in the sphere of the ignobly decent"—and this can epitomize realism. A work of naturalism, on the other hand, might be said to devote itself to the ignobly indecent.

Romance, Novel. Medieval romances are narratives of adventure, following a hero through the successive episodes of a quest toward his chosen or appointed goal. Novels are more or less realistic studies of social relationships, more tightly structured than romances, less given to the fabulous, and dealing generally with the middle strata of society. But these distinctions were far from airtight to begin with, and with the years have grown steadily vaguer. Is Kafka's *The Castle* a novel or a romance? It is always called the former, it looks much more like the latter, and it is actually more like an extended parable.

Style in a minimal sense is the way anyone uses language; thus each of us possesses (for better or worse) his own style. In the better sense, of language endowed with point and force, language of special distinction which accomplishes its ends swiftly and clearly, it has been described by Swift as "proper words in proper places"—a definition on which there is no improving.

Wit is one of those words which are too useful ever to be defined. As employed during the 17th and 18th centuries, it may mean general intelligence or the ability to say something funny, wisdom or ability, prudence, fancy, vivacity of speech, quickness of repartee, spiritual insight, and a plethora of other qualities.

Contents of Volume 2

The Victorian Age (1832–1901)   875

Contents of Volume 2 · 2493

The Twentieth Century
(1890 to the Present)

Index